College Edition

HARPER COLLINS
FRENCH
DICTIONARY

College Edition

HARPER COLLINS
FRENCH
DICTIONARY

FRENCH•ENGLISH   ENGLISH•FRENCH

COLLINS
London and Glasgow
HARPER & ROW
New York

by/par
Pierre-Henri Cousin, Lorna Sinclair,
Jean-François Allain, Catherine E. Love

contributors/avec la collaboration de
Claude Nimmo, Vivian Marr

American language consultant/anglais américain
Dr. Donald Windham

editorial staff/secrétariat de rédaction
Elspeth Anderson, Angela Campbell,
Barbara Christie

The Collins French Dictionary. Copyright © 1990 by
William Collins Sons & Co. Ltd. All rights reserved. Printed in
Great Britain. No part of this book may be used or reproduced in
any manner whatsoever without written permission except in the
case of brief quotations embodied in critical articles and reviews.
For information address William Collins Sons & Co. Ltd,
8 Grafton Street, London W1X 3LA, Great Britain.

First Edition 1990

ISBN 0-06-055250-6 (casebound)
ISBN 0-06-091954-X (paperback)

TABLE DES MATIÈRES

CONTENTS

Les marques déposées

Les termes qui constituent à notre connaissance une marque déposée ont été désignés comme tels. La présence ou l'absence de cette désignation ne peut toutefois être considérée comme ayant valeur juridique.

Note on trademarks

Words which we have reason to believe constitute trademarks have been designated as such. However, neither the presence nor the absence of such designation should be regarded as affecting the legal status of any trademark.

INTRODUCTION

Pour comprendre l'anglais

Ce dictionnaire nouveau, résolument tourné vers le monde moderne, rend compte de l'usage actuel de la langue anglaise, y compris dans les domaines du commerce et de la micro-informatique, et contient un choix étendu d'abréviations, sigles et noms géographiques fréquemment rencontrés dans la presse. Pour faciliter les recherches, les formes irrégulières des verbes et substantifs anglais font l'objet d'une entrée séparée qui renvoie à la forme de base suivie de sa traduction.

Pour vous exprimer en anglais

Pour vous aider à vous exprimer dans un anglais correct et idiomatique, de nombreuses indications précisant le sens ou le domaine d'emploi sont là pour vous guider et vous orienter vers la traduction la mieux adaptée à votre contexte. Tous les termes courants sont traités en détail et illustrés d'exemples.

Un compagnon de travail

Par le soin apporté à sa confection, ce nouveau dictionnaire Collins constitue un outil fiable et facile d'emploi qui saura répondre à vos besoins linguistiques et se montrer un fidèle compagnon de route dans vos études ou votre travail.

Understanding French

This new and thoroughly up-to-date dictionary provides the user with wide-ranging, practical coverage of current usage, including terminology relevant to business and office automation, and a comprehensive selection of abbreviations, acronyms and geographical names commonly found in the press. You will also find, for ease of consultation, irregular forms of French verbs and nouns with a cross-reference to the basic form where a translation is given.

Self-expression in French

To help you express yourself correctly and idiomatically in French, numerous indications – think of them as signposts – guide you to the most appropriate translation for your context. All the most commonly used words are given detailed treatment, with many examples of typical usage.

A working companion

Much care has been taken to make this new Collins dictionary thoroughly reliable, easy to use and relevant to your work and study. We hope it will become a long-serving companion for all your foreign language needs.

ABRÉVIATIONS

ABBREVIATIONS

adjectif, locution adjective	**a**	adjective, adjectival phrase
abréviation	**ab(b)r**	abbreviation
adverbe, locution adverbiale	**ad**	adverb, adverbial phrase
administration	**ADMIN**	administration
agriculture	**AGR**	agriculture
anatomie	**ANAT**	anatomy
architecture	**ARCHIT**	architecture
l'automobile	**AUT(O)**	automobiles
aviation, voyages aériens	**AVIAT**	flying, air travel
biologie	**BIO(L)**	biology
botanique	**BOT**	botany
anglais de Grande-Bretagne	**Brit**	British English
conjonction	**cj**	conjunction
langue familière (! emploi vulgaire)	**col (!)**	colloquial usage (! particularly offensive)
commerce, finance, banque	**COMM**	commerce, finance, banking
informatique	**COMPUT**	computing
construction	**CONSTR**	building
nom utilisé comme adjectif, ne peut s'employer ni comme attribut, ni après le nom qualifié	**cpd**	compound element: noun used as an adjective and which cannot follow the noun it qualifies
cuisine, art culinaire	**CULIN**	cookery
déterminant: article, adjectif démonstratif ou indéfini etc	**dét, det**	determiner: article, demonstrative etc
économie	**ECON**	economics
électricité, électronique	**ELEC**	electricity, electronics
exclamation, interjection	**excl**	exclamation, interjection
féminin	**f**	feminine
langue familière (! emploi vulgaire)	**fam (!)**	colloquial usage (! particularly offensive)
emploi figuré	**fig**	figurative use
(verbe anglais) dont la particule est inséparable du verbe	**fus**	(phrasal verb) where the particle cannot be separated from main verb
dans la plupart des sens; généralement	**gén, gen**	in most or all senses; generally
géographie, géologie	**GEO**	geography, geology
géométrie	**GEOM**	geometry
histoire	**HIST**	history
informatique	**INFORM**	computing
invariable	**inv**	invariable
irrégulier	**irg**	irregular
domaine juridique	**JUR**	law
grammaire, linguistique	**LING**	grammar, linguistics
masculin	**m**	masculine
mathématiques, algèbre	**MATH**	mathematics, calculus
médecine	**MED**	medical term, medicine
masculin ou féminin, suivant le sexe	**m/f**	either masculine or feminine depending on sex
domaine militaire, armée	**MIL**	military matters
musique	**MUS**	music
nom	**n**	noun

ABRÉVIATIONS

ABBREVIATIONS

navigation, nautisme	**NAVIG, NAUT**	sailing, navigation
adjectif ou nom numérique	**num**	numeral adjective or noun
	o.s.	oneself
péjoratif	**péj, pej**	derogatory, pejorative
photographie	**PHOT(O)**	photography
physiologie	**PHYSIOL**	physiology
pluriel	**pl**	plural
politique	**POL**	politics
participe passé	**pp**	past participle
préposition	**prép, prep**	preposition
psychologie, psychiatrie	**PSYCH**	psychology, psychiatry
temps du passé	**pt**	past tense
nom non comptable: ne peut s'utiliser au pluriel	**q**	collective (uncountable) noun: is not used in the plural
quelque chose	**qch**	
quelqu'un	**qn**	
religions, domaine ecclésiastique	**REL**	religions, church service
	sb	somebody
enseignement, système scolaire et universitaire	**SCOL**	education, schools and universities
singulier	**sg**	singular
	sth	something
subjonctif	**sub**	subjunctive
sujet (grammatical)	**su(b)j**	(grammatical) subject
techniques, technologie	**TECH**	technical term, technology
télécommunications	**TEL**	telecommunications
télévision	**TV**	television
typographie	**TYP(O)**	typography, printing
anglais des USA	**US**	American English
verbe	**vb**	verb
verbe ou groupe verbal à fonction intransitive	**vi**	verb or phrasal verb used intransitively
verbe ou groupe verbal à fonction transitive	**vt**	verb or phrasal verb used transitively
zoologie	**ZOOL**	zoology
marque déposée	**®**	registered trademark
indique une équivalence culturelle	**≈**	introduces a cultural equivalent

TRANSCRIPTION PHONÉTIQUE

CONSONNES

CONSONANTS

NB. **p, b, t, d, k, g** sont suivis d'une aspiration en anglais.

NB. **p, b, t, d, k, g** are not aspirated in French.

*pou*pée	p	*pu*ppy
*b*om*b*e	b	*b*a*b*y
*t*en*t*e *th*ermal	t	*t*en*t*
*d*in*d*e	d	*d*og ro*d*
*c*oq *qu*i *k*épi	k	*c*ork *k*iss *ch*ord
*g*a*g* ba*gu*e	g	*g*a*g* *gu*ess
*s*ale *c*e na*t*ion	s	*s*o ri*c*e ki*ss*
*z*éro ro*s*e	z	cou*s*in bu*zz*
ta*ch*e *ch*at	sh	*sh*eep *s*ugar
gilet *j*uge	zh	plea*s*ure vi*s*ion
	ch	*ch*ur*ch*
	j	*j*udge *g*eneral
*f*er *ph*are	f	*f*arm hal*f*
*v*al*v*e	v	*v*ery e*v*e
	th	*th*in bo*th*
	th	*th*at o*th*er
*l*ent sa*ll*e	l	*l*itt*l*e ba*ll*
*r*are *r*ent*r*er	r	*r*at ra*r*e
*m*a*m*an fe*mm*e	m	*m*ove co*mb*
*n*on *n*o*nn*e	n	*n*o ra*n*
a*gn*eau vi*gn*e	ny	
campi*ng*	ng	si*ng*ing ba*n*k
	h	*h*at re*h*earse
*y*eux pa*ill*e p*i*ed	y	*y*et
no*u*er o*u*i	w	*w*all a*w*ay

DIVERS

MISCELLANEOUS

pour l'anglais: suit la syllabe accentuée	'	in French transcription: no liaison
indique que les deux consonnes se prononcent séparément	·	shows where two consonants should be pronounced separately

PHONETIC TRANSCRIPTION

VOYELLES

NB. La mise en équivalence de certains sons n'indique qu'une ressemblance approximative.

VOWELS

NB. The pairing of some vowel sounds only indicates approximate equivalence.

	a	*a*dd m*a*p l*au*gh
pl*a*t *a*mour	å	
b*a*s p*â*te	â	p*a*lm f*a*ther *o*dd
jou*er* *é*té	ā	*a*ce r*a*te g*au*ge
	är	c*a*re *ai*r
l*ai*t jou*et* m*e*rci	e	s*e*t t*e*nt
i*ç*i v*ie* l*y*re	ē	h*ee*l b*ea*d
l*e* pr*e*mier	ə	d*a*rk*e*n *a*bove
	i	h*i*t p*i*ty
	ī	*i*ce d*i*me *ai*sle
*o*r h*o*mme	o	
	ô	l*aw* d*o*g *o*rder
m*o*t *eau* g*au*che	ō	*o*pen s*o*
gen*ou* r*ou*e	o͞o	p*oo*l f*oo*d
	o͝o	t*oo*k f*u*ll
	yo͞o	*u*se f*ew*
b*eu*rre p*eu*r	oe	
p*eu* d*eu*x	o͞e	
	u	f*u*n d*o*ne *u*p
*u*rne h*ui*le r*ue*	ü	
	ûr	*u*rn t*e*rm

DIPHTONGUES

DIPHTHONGS

	oi	*oi*l b*oy*
	ou	*ou*t n*ow*

NASALES

NASAL VOWELS

mat*in* pl*ein*	aṅ
br*un*	œṅ
s*ang* *an* d*ans*	âṅ
n*on* p*ont*	ôṅ

FRENCH VERB FORMS

1 Participe présent *2* Participe passé *3* Présent *4* Imparfait *5* Futur *6* Conditionnel *7* Subjonctif présent

acquérir *1* acquérant *2* acquis *3* acquiers, acquérons, acquièrent *4* acquérais *5* acquerrai *7* acquière

ALLER *1* allant *2* allé *3* vais, vas, va, allons, allez, vont *4* allais *5* irai *6* irais *7* aille

asseoir *1* asseyant *2* assis *3* assieds, asseyons, asseyez, asseyent *4* asseyais *5* assiérai *7* asseye

atteindre *1* atteignant *2* atteint *3* atteins, atteignons *4* atteignais *7* atteigne

AVOIR *1* ayant *2* eu *3* ai, as, a, avons, avez, ont *4* avais *5* aurai *6* aurais *7* aie, aies, ait, ayons, ayez, aient

battre *1* battant *2* battu *3* bats, bat, battons *4* battais *7* batte

boire *1* buvant *2* bu *3* bois, buvons, boivent *4* buvais *7* boive

bouillir *1* bouillant *2* bouilli *3* bous, bouillons *4* bouillais *7* bouille

conclure *1* concluant *2* conclu *3* conclus, concluons *4* concluais *7* conclue

conduire *1* conduisant *2* conduit *3* conduis, conduisons *4* conduisais *7* conduise

connaître *1* connaissant *2* connu *3* connais, connaît, connaissons *4* connaissais *7* connaisse

coudre *1* cousant *2* cousu *3* couds, cousons, cousez, cousent *4* cousais *7* couse

courir *1* courant *2* couru *3* cours, courons *4* courais *5* courrai *7* coure

couvrir *1* couvrant *2* couvert *3* couvre, couvrons *4* couvrais *7* couvre

craindre *1* craignant *2* craint *3* crains, craignons *4* craignais *7* craigne

croire *1* croyant *2* cru *3* crois, croyons, croient *4* croyais *7* croie

croître *1* croissant *2* crû, crue, crus, crues *3* croîs, croissons *4* croissais *7* croisse

cueillir *1* cueillant *2* cueilli *3* cueille, cueillons *4* cueillais *5* cueillerai *7* cueille

devoir *1* devant *2* dû, due, dus, dues *3* dois, devons, doivent *4* devais *5* devrai *7* doive

dire *1* disant *2* dit *3* dis, disons, dites, disent *4* disais *7* dise

dormir *1* dormant *2* dormi *3* dors, dormons *4* dormais *7* dorme

écrire *1* écrivant *2* écrit *3* écris, écrivons *4* écrivais *7* écrive

ÊTRE *1* étant *2* été *3* suis, es, est, sommes, êtes, sont *4* étais *5* serai *6* serais *7* sois, sois, soit, soyons, soyez, soient

FAIRE *1* faisant *2* fait *3* fais, fais, fait, faisons, faites, font *4* faisais *5* ferai *6* ferais *7* fasse

falloir *2* fallu *3* faut *4* fallait *5* faudra *7* faille

FINIR *1* finissant *2* fini *3* finis, finis, finit, finissons, finissez, finissent *4* finissais *5* finirai *6* finirais *7* finisse

fuir *1* fuyant *2* fui *3* fuis, fuyons, fuient *4* fuyais *7* fuie

joindre *1* joignant *2* joint *3* joins, joignons *4* joignais *7* joigne

lire *1* lisant *2* lu *3* lis, lisons *4* lisais *7* lise

luire *1* luisant *2* lui *3* luis, luisons *4* luisais *7* luise

maudire *1* maudissant *2* maudit *3* maudis, maudissons *4* maudissait *7* maudisse

mentir *1* mentant *2* menti *3* mens, mentons *4* mentais *7* mente

mettre *1* mettant *2* mis *3* mets, mettons *4* mettais *7* mette

mourir *1* mourant *2* mort *3* meurs, mourons, meurent *4* mourais *5* mourrai *7* meure

naître *1* naissant *2* né *3* nais, naît, naissons *4* naissais *7* naisse

offrir *1* offrant *2* offert *3* offre, offrons *4* offrais *7* offre

PARLER *1* parlant *2* parlé *3* parle, parles, parle, parlons, parlez, parlent *4* parlais, parlais, parlait, parlions, parliez, parlaient *5* parlerai, parleras, parlera, parlerons, parlerez, parleront *6* parlerais, parlerais, parlerait, parlerions, parleriez, parleraient *7* parle, parles, parle, parlions, parliez, parlent *impératif* parle! parlez!

partir *1* partant *2* parti *3* pars, partons *4* partais *7* parte

plaire *1* plaisant *2* plu *3* plais, plaît, plaisons *4* plaisais *7* plaise

pleuvoir *1* pleuvant *2* plu *3* pleut, pleuvent *4* pleuvait *5* pleuvra *7* pleuve

pourvoir *1* pourvoyant *2* pourvu *3* pourvois, pourvoyons, pourvoient *4* pourvoyais *7* pourvoie

pouvoir *1* pouvant *2* pu *3* peux, peut, pouvons, peuvent *4* pouvais *5* pourrai *7* puisse

prendre *1* prenant *2* pris *3* prends, prenons, prennent *4* prenais *7* prenne

prévoir *like voir* *5* prévoirai

RECEVOIR *1* recevant *2* reçu *3* reçois, reçois, reçoit, recevons, recevez, reçoivent *4* recevais *5* recevrai *6* recevrais *7* reçoive

RENDRE *1* rendant *2* rendu *3* rends, rends, rend, rendons, rendez, rendent *4* rendais *5* rendrai *6* rendrais *7* rende

résoudre *1* résolvant *2* résolu *3* résous, résout, résolvons *4* résolvais *7* résolve

rire *1* riant *2* ri *3* ris, rions *4* riais *7* rie

savoir *1* sachant *2* su *3* sais, savons, savent *4* savais *5* saurai *7* sache *impératif* sache, sachons, sachez

servir *1* servant *2* servi *3* sers, servons *4* servais *7* serve

sortir *1* sortant *2* sorti *3* sors, sortons *4* sortais *7* sorte

souffrir *1* souffrant *2* souffert *3* souffre, souffrons *4* souffrais *7* souffre

suffire *1* suffisant *2* suffi *3* suffis, suffisons *4* suffisais *7* suffise

suivre *1* suivant *2* suivi *3* suis, suivons *4* suivais *7* suive

taire *1* taisant *2* tu *3* tais, taisons *4* taisais *7* taise

tenir *1* tenant *2* tenu *3* tiens, tenons, tiennent *4* tenais *5* tiendrai *7* tienne

vaincre *1* vainquant *2* vaincu *3* vaincs, vainc, vainquons *4* vainquais *7* vainque

valoir *1* valant *2* valu *3* vaux, vaut, valons *4* valais *5* vaudrai *7* vaille

venir *1* venant *2* venu *3* viens, venons, viennent *4* venais *5* viendrai *7* vienne

vivre *1* vivant *2* vécu *3* vis, vivons *4* vivais *7* vive

voir *1* voyant *2* vu *3* vois, voyons, voient *4* voyais *5* verrai *7* voie

vouloir *1* voulant *2* voulu *3* veux, veut, voulons, veulent *4* voulais *5* voudrai *7* veuille *impératif* veuillez

LE VERBE ANGLAIS

present	pt	pp	present	pt	pp
arise (arising)	arose	arisen	eat	ate	eaten
awake (awaking)	awoke	awaked	fall	fell	fallen
be (am, is, are, being)	was, were	been	feed	fed	fed
			feel	felt	felt
bear	bore	born(e)	fight	fought	fought
beat	beat	beaten	find	found	found
become (becoming)	became	become	flee	fled	fled
			fling	flung	flung
befall	befell	befallen	fly (flies)	flew	flown
begin (beginning)	began	begun	forbid (forbidding)	forbade	forbidden
behold	beheld	beheld	forecast	forecast	forecast
bend	bent	bent	forego	forewent	foregone
beseech	besought	besought	foresee	foresaw	foreseen
beset (besetting)	beset	beset	foretell	foretold	foretold
			forget (forgetting)	forgot	forgotten
bet (betting)	bet (also betted)	bet (also betted)	forgive (forgiving)	forgave	forgiven
bid (bidding)	bid (also bade)	bid (also bidden)	forsake (forsaking)	forsook	forsaken
bind	bound	bound	freeze (freezing)	froze	frozen
bite (biting)	bit	bitten	get (getting)	got	got, (US) gotten
bleed	bled	bled			
blow	blew	blown	give (giving)	gave	given
break	broke	broken	go (goes)	went	gone
breed	bred	bred	grind	ground	ground
bring	brought	brought	grow	grew	grown
build	built	built	hang	hung (also hanged)	hung (also hanged)
burn	burned (also burnt)	burned (also burnt)	have (has; having)	had	had
burst	burst	burst	hear	heard	heard
buy	bought	bought	hide (hiding)	hid	hidden
can	could	(been able)	hit (hitting)	hit	hit
cast	cast	cast	hold	held	held
catch	caught	caught	hurt	hurt	hurt
choose (choosing)	chose	chosen	keep	kept	kept
cling	clung	clung	kneel	knelt (also kneeled)	knelt (also kneeled)
come (coming)	came	come	know	knew	known
cost	cost	cost	lay	laid	laid
creep	crept	crept	lead	led	led
cut (cutting)	cut	cut	lean	leaned (also leant)	leaned (also leant)
deal	dealt	dealt			
dig (digging)	dug	dug	leap	leaped (also leapt)	leaped (also leapt)
do (3rd person: he/she/it/does)	did	done	learn	learned (also learnt)	learned (also learnt)
draw	drew	drawn	leave (leaving)	left	left
dream	dreamed (also dreamt)	dreamed also dreamt)	lend	lent	lent
			let (letting)	let	let
drink	drank	drunk	lie (lying)	lay	lain
drive (driving)	drove	driven	light	lighted (also lit)	lighted (also lit)
dwell	dwelt	dwelt	lose (losing)	lost	lost

present	pt	pp	present	pt	pp
make (making)	made	made	spell	spelled (*also* spelt)	spelled (*also* spelt)
may	might	—	spend	spent	spent
mean	meant	meant	spill	spilled (*also* spilt)	spilled (*also* spilt)
meet	met	met	spin (spinning)	spun	spun
mistake (mistaking)	mistook	mistaken	spit (spitting)	spat	spat
mow	mowed	mowed (*also* mown)	split (splitting)	split	split
must	(had to)	(had to)	spoil	spoiled (*also* spoilt)	spoiled (*also* spoilt)
pay	paid	paid	spread	spread	spread
put (putting)	put	put	spring	sprang	sprung
quit (quitting)	quit (*also* quitted)	quit (*also* quitted)	stand	stood	stood
read	read	read	steal	stole	stolen
rend	rent	rent	stick	stuck	stuck
rid (ridding)	rid	rid	sting	stung	stung
ride (riding)	rode	ridden	stink	stank	stunk
ring	rang	rung	stride (striding)	strode	stridden
rise (rising)	rose	risen	strike (striking)	struck	struck (*also* stricken)
run (running)	ran	run	strive (striving)	strove	striven
saw	sawed	sawn	swear	swore	sworn
say	said	said	sweep	swept	swept
see	saw	seen	swell	swelled	swelled (*also* swollen)
seek	sought	sought			
sell	sold	sold	swim (swimming)	swam	swum
send	sent	sent			
set (setting)	set	set	swing	swung	swung
shake (shaking)	shook	shaken	take (taking)	took	taken
			teach	taught	taught
shall	should	—	tear	tore	torn
shear	sheared	sheared (*also* shorn)	tell	told	told
			think	thought	thought
shed (shedding)	shed	shed	throw	threw	thrown
			thrust	thrust	thrust
shine (shining)	shone	shone	tread	trod	trodden
shoot	shot	shot	wake (waking)	woke (*also* waked)	waked (*also* woken)
show	showed	shown			
shrink	shrank	shrunk	waylay	waylaid	waylaid
shut (shutting)	shut	shut	wear	wore	worn
sing	sang	sung	weave (weaving)	wove (*also* weaved)	woven (*also* weaved)
sink	sank	sunk	wed (wedding)	wedded	wedded (*also* wed)
sit (sitting)	sat	sat			
slay	slew	slain	weep	wept	wept
sleep	slept	slept	win (winning)	won	won
slide (sliding)	slid	slid	wind	wound	wound
sling	slung	slung	withdraw	withdrew	withdrawn
slit (slitting)	slit	slit	withhold	withheld	withheld
smell	smelled (*Brit* smelt)	smelled (*Brit* smelt)	withstand	withstood	withstood
sow	sowed	sown (*also* sowed)	wring	wrung	wrung
			write (writing)	wrote	written
speak	spoke	spoken			
speed	sped (*also* speeded)	sped (*also* speeded)			

LES NOMBRES

NUMBERS

un(une)	1	one
deux	2	two
trois	3	three
quatre	4	four
cinq	5	five
six	6	six
sept	7	seven
huit	8	eight
neuf	9	nine
dix	10	ten
onze	11	eleven
douze	12	twelve
treize	13	thirteen
quatorze	14	fourteen
quinze	15	fifteen
seize	16	sixteen
dix-sept	17	seventeen
dix-huit	18	eighteen
dix-neuf	19	nineteen
vingt	20	twenty
vingt et un(une)	21	twenty-one
vingt-deux	22	twenty-two
trente	30	thirty
quarante	40	forty
cinquante	50	fifty
soixante	60	sixty
soixante-dix	70	seventy
soixante et onze	71	seventy-one
soixante-douze	72	seventy-two
quatre-vingts	80	eighty
quatre-vingt-un(-une)	81	eighty-one
quatre-vingt-dix	90	ninety
quatre-vingt-onze	91	ninety-one
cent	100	a hundred
cent un(une)	101	a hundred and one
trois cents	300	three hundred
trois cent un(une)	301	three hundred and one
mille	1 000	a thousand
un million	1 000 000	a million

premier(première), 1er	first, 1st
deuxième, 2e or 2ème	second, 2nd
troisième, 3e or 3ème	third, 3rd
quatrième	fourth, 4th
dixième	tenth
onzième	eleventh
douzième	twelfth
treizième	thirteenth
dix-septième	seventeenth
dix-huitième	eighteenth
dix-neuvième	nineteenth
vingtième	twentieth
vingt-et-unième	twenty-first
vingt-deuxième	twenty-second
trentième	thirtieth
centième	hundredth
cent-unième	hundred-and-first
millième	thousandth

A

A, a [â] *nm inv* A, a ♦ *abr* = **anticyclone, are**; (= *ampère*) amp; (= *autoroute*) ≈ I (*US*), ≈ M (*Brit*); **A comme Anatole** A for Able; **de a à z** from a to z; **prouver qch par a + b** to prove sth conclusively.

a [â] *vb voir* **avoir**.

à [â] (*à + le* = **au**, *à + les* = **aux**) [à, ō] *prép* (*situation*) at, in; (*direction, attribution*) to; (*provenance*) from; (*moyen*) with, by; **donner qch à qn** to give sb sth, give sth to sb; **prendre de l'eau à la fontaine** to take some water from the fountain; **payé au mois** paid by the month; **100 km/unités à l'heure** 100 km/units per hour; **à 3 heures/minuit** at 3 o'clock/midnight; **il habite à 5 minutes de la gare** he lives 5 minutes (away) from the station; **ils vivent à deux heures de Paris, par la route** they live two hours' drive (away) from Paris; **au mois de juin** in the month of June; **au départ** at the start, at the outset; **se chauffer au gaz/à l'électricité** to heat one's house with gas/electricity, to have gas/electric heating; **à la main/machine** by hand/machine; **à bicyclette** by bicycle *ou* on a bicycle; **à pied** by *ou* on foot; **être/aller à la campagne** to be in/go to the country; **l'homme aux yeux bleus/à la veste rouge** the man with the blue eyes/with *ou* in the red jacket; **un ami à moi** a friend of mine; **cinq à six heures** five to six hours; **à demain/la semaine prochaine!** see you tomorrow/next week!; **à la russe** the Russian way, in the Russian fashion; **à bien réfléchir** if you think about it; **maison à vendre** house for sale; **à sa grande surprise** to his great surprise; **à ce qu'il prétend** according to him, from what he says; **tasse à café** coffee cup.

Å *abr* (= *Angstrom*) A *ou* Å.

A2 *abr* (= *Antenne 2*) French TV channel.

abaissement [àbesmáṅ] *nm* lowering; pulling down.

abaisser [àbāsā] *vt* to lower, bring down; (*manette*) to pull down; (*fig*) to debase; to humiliate; **s'~** *vi* to go down; (*fig*) to demean o.s.; **s'~ à faire/à qch** to stoop *ou* descend to doing/to sth.

abandon [àbáṅdôṅ] *nm* abandoning; deserting; giving up; withdrawal; surrender, relinquishing; (*fig*) lack of constraint; relaxed pose *ou* mood; **être à l'~** to be in a state of neglect; **laisser à l'~** to abandon.

abandonné, e [àbáṅdonā] *a* (*solitaire*) deserted; (*route, usine*) disused; (*jardin*) abandoned.

abandonner [àbáṅdonā] *vt* to leave, abandon, desert; (*projet, activité*) to abandon, give up; (*SPORT*) to retire *ou* withdraw from; (*céder*) to surrender, relinquish; **s'~** *vi* to let o.s. go;

s'~ à (*paresse, plaisirs*) to give o.s. up to; **~ qch à qn** to give sth up to sb.

abasourdir [àbàzōōrdēr] *vt* to stun, stagger.

abat [àbá] *etc vb voir* **abattre**.

abat-jour [àbázhōōr] *nm inv* lampshade.

abats [àbá] *vb voir* **abattre** ♦ *nmpl* (*de bœuf, porc*) entrails (*US*), offal *sg* (*Brit*); (*de volaille*) giblets.

abattage [àbátázh] *nm* cutting down, felling.

abattant [àbátáṅ] *vb voir* **abattre** ♦ *nm* leaf, flap.

abattement [àbátmáṅ] *nm* (*physique*) enfeeblement; (*moral*) dejection, despondency; (*déduction*) reduction; **~ fiscal** ≈ tax allowance.

abattis [àbátē] *vb voir* **abattre** ♦ *nmpl* giblets.

abattoir [àbátwár] *nm* abattoir (*Brit*), slaughterhouse.

abattre [àbátr(ə)] *vt* (*arbre*) to cut down, fell; (*mur, maison*) to pull down; (*avion, personne*) to shoot down; (*animal*) to shoot, kill; (*fig: physiquement*) to wear out, tire out; (*: moralement*) to demoralize; **s'~** *vi* to crash down; **s'~ sur** (*suj: pluie*) to beat down on; (*: coups, injures*) to rain down on; **~ ses cartes** (*aussi fig*) to lay one's cards on the table; **~ du travail** *ou* **de la besogne** to get through a lot of work.

abattu, e [àbátü] *pp de* **abattre** ♦ *a* (*déprimé*) downcast.

abbaye [àbāē] *nf* abbey.

abbé [àbā] *nm* priest; (*d'une abbaye*) abbot; **M l'~** Father.

abbesse [àbes] *nf* abbess.

abc, ABC [àbāsā] *nm* alphabet primer; (*fig*) rudiments *pl*.

abcès [àpse] *nm* abscess.

abdication [àbdēkásyôṅ] *nf* abdication.

abdiquer [àbdēkā] *vi* to abdicate ♦ *vt* to renounce, give up.

abdomen [àbdomen] *nm* abdomen.

abdominal, e, aux [àbdomēnàl, -ō] *a* abdominal ♦ *nmpl*: **faire des abdominaux** to do exercises for the stomach muscles.

abécédaire [àbāsāder] *nm* alphabet primer.

abeille [àbey] *nf* bee.

aberrant, e [àberáṅ, -áṅt] *a* absurd.

aberration [àberásyôṅ] *nf* aberration.

abêtir [àbātēr] *vt* to make morons (*ou* a moron) of.

abhorrer [àborā] *vt* to abhor, loathe.

abîme [àbēm] *nm* abyss, gulf.

abîmer [àbēmā] *vt* to spoil, damage; **s'~** *vi* to get spoilt *ou* damaged; (*fruits*) to spoil; (*tomber*) to sink, founder; **s'~ les yeux** to ruin one's eyes *ou* eyesight.

abject, e [àbzhekt] *a* abject, despicable.

abjurer [àbzhürā] *vt* to abjure, renounce.

ablation [áblâsyôṅ] *nf* removal.

ablutions [áblüsyôṅ] *nfpl*: **faire ses** ~ to perform one's ablutions.

abnégation [ábnāgâsyôṅ] *nf* (self-)abnegation.

aboie [ábwá] *etc vb voir* **aboyer.**

aboiement [ábwámâṅ] *nm* bark, barking *q.*

aboierai [ábwáyərā] *etc vb voir* **aboyer.**

abois [ábwá] *nmpl*: **aux** ~ at bay.

abolir [ábolēr] *vt* to abolish.

abolition [ábolēsyôṅ] *nf* abolition.

abolitionniste [ábolēsyonēst(ə)] *a*, *nm/f* abolitionist.

abominable [ábomēnábl(ə)] *a* abominable.

abomination [ábomēnâsyôṅ] *nf* abomination.

abondamment [ábôṅdámâṅ] *ad* abundantly.

abondance [ábôṅdâṅs] *nf* abundance; (*richesse*) affluence; **en** ~ in abundance.

abondant, e [ábôṅdâṅ, -âṅt] *a* plentiful, abundant, copious.

abonder [ábôṅdā] *vi* to abound, be plentiful; ~ **en** to be full of, abound in; ~ **dans le sens de qn** to concur with sb.

abonné, e [ábonā] *nm/f* subscriber; season ticket holder ♦ *a*: **être** ~ **à un journal** to subscribe to *ou* have a subscription to a periodical; **être** ~ **au téléphone** to have a (tele)phone.

abonnement [ábonmâṅ] *nm* subscription; (*pour transports en commun, concerts*) season ticket.

abonner [ábonā] *vt*: **s'**~ **à** to subscribe to, take out a subscription to.

abord [ábor] *nm*: **être d'un** ~ **facile** to be approachable; **être d'un** ~ **difficile** (*personne*) to be unapproachable; (*lieu*) to be hard to reach *ou* difficult to get to; **de prime** ~, **au premier** ~ at first sight; **d'**~ *ad* first; **tout d'**~ first of all.

abordable [ábordábl(ə)] *a* (*personne*) approachable; (*marchandise*) reasonably priced; (*prix*) affordable, reasonable.

abordage [ábordázh] *nm* boarding.

aborder [ábordā] *vi* to land ♦ *vt* (*sujet, difficulté*) to tackle; (*personne*) to approach; (*rivage etc*) to reach; (*NAVIG: attaquer*) to board; (: *heurter*) to collide with.

abords [ábor] *nmpl* surroundings.

aborigène [áborēzhen] *nm* aborigine, native.

Abou Dhabî, Abu Dhabî [ábōōdábē] *nm* Abu Dhabi.

aboulique [ábōōlēk] *a* totally lacking in willpower.

aboutir [ábōōtēr] *vi* (*négociations etc*) to succeed; (*abcès*) to come to a head; ~ **à/dans/sur** to end up at/in/on.

aboutissants [ábōōtēsâṅ] *nmpl voir* **tenants.**

aboutissement [ábōōtēsmâṅ] *nm* success; (*de concept, projet*) successful realization; (*d'années de travail*) successful conclusion.

aboyer [ábwáyā] *vi* to bark.

abracadabrant, e [ábrákádábrâṅ, -âṅt] *a* incredible, preposterous.

abrasif, ive [ábrázēf, -ēv] *a, nm* abrasive.

abrégé [ábrāzhā] *nm* summary; **en** ~ in a shortened *ou* abbreviated form.

abréger [ábrāzhā] *vt* (*texte*) to shorten, abridge; (*mot*) to shorten, abbreviate; (*réunion, voyage*) to cut short, shorten.

abreuver [ábrœvā] *vt* to water; (*fig*): ~ **qn de**

to shower *ou* swamp sb with; (*injures etc*) to shower sb with; **s'**~ *vi* to drink.

abreuvoir [ábrœvwár] *nm* watering place.

abréviation [ábrāvyâsyôṅ] *nf* abbreviation.

abri [ábrē] *nm* shelter; **à l'**~ under cover; **être/se mettre à l'**~ to be/get under cover *ou* shelter; **à l'**~ **de** sheltered from; (*fig*) safe from.

abricot [ábrēkō] *nm* apricot.

abricotier [ábrēkotyā] *nm* apricot tree.

abrité, e [ábrētā] *a* sheltered.

abriter [ábrētā] *vt* to shelter; (*loger*) to accommodate; **s'**~ to shelter, take cover.

abrogation [ábrogâsyôṅ] *nf* (*JUR*) repeal, abrogation.

abroger [ábrozhā] *vt* to repeal, abrogate.

abrupt, e [ábrüpt] *a* sheer, steep; (*ton*) abrupt.

abruti, e [ábrütē] *nm/f* (*fam*) idiot, moron.

abrutir [ábrütēr] *vt* to daze; (*fatiguer*) to exhaust; (*abêtir*) to stupefy.

abrutissant, e [ábrütēsâṅ, -âṅt] *a* (*bruit, travail*) stupefying.

abscisse [ápsēs] *nf* X axis, abscissa.

absence [ápsâṅs] *nf* absence; (*MÉD*) blackout; (*distraction*) mental blank; **en l'**~ **de** in the absence of.

absent, e [ápsâṅ, -âṅt] *a* absent; (*chose*) missing, lacking; (*distrait: air*) vacant, faraway ♦ *nm/f* absentee.

absentéisme [ápsâṅtāēsm(ə)] *nm* absenteeism.

absenter [ápsâṅtā]: **s'**~ *vi* to take time off work; (*sortir*) to leave, go out.

abside [ápsēd] *nf* (*ARCHIT*) apse.

absinthe [ápsâṅt] *nf* (*boisson*) absinth(e); (*BOT*) wormwood, absinth(e).

absolu, e [ápsolü] *a* absolute; (*caractère*) rigid, uncompromising ♦ *nm* (*PHILOSOPHIE*): **l'**~ the Absolute; **dans l'**~ in the absolute, in a vacuum.

absolument [ápsolümâṅ] *ad* absolutely.

absolution [ápsolusyôṅ] *nf* absolution; (*JUR*) dismissal (*of case*).

absolutisme [ápsolütēsm(ə)] *nm* absolutism.

absolvais [ápsolve] *etc vb voir* **absoudre.**

absorbant, e [ápsorbâṅ, -âṅt] *a* absorbent; (*tâche*) absorbing, engrossing.

absorbé, e [ápsorbā] *a* absorbed, engrossed.

absorber [ápsorbā] *vt* to absorb; (*gén MÉD: manger, boire*) to take; (*ÉCON: firme*) to take over, absorb.

absorption [ápsorpsyôṅ] *nf* absorption.

absoudre [ápsōōdr(ə)] *vt* to absolve; (*JUR*) to dismiss.

absous, oute [ápsōō, -ōōt] *pp de* **absoudre.**

abstenir [ápstənēr]: **s'**~ *vi* (*POL*) to abstain; **s'**~ **de qch/de faire** to refrain from sth/from doing.

abstention [ápstâṅsyôṅ] *nf* abstention.

abstentionniste [ápstâṅsyonēst(ə)] *nm* abstentionist.

abstenu, e [ápstənü] *pp de* **abstenir.**

abstiendrai [ápstyaṅdrā], **abstiens** [ápstyaṅ] *etc voir* **abstenir.**

abstinence [ápstēnâṅs] *nf* abstinence; **faire** ~ to abstain (*from meat on Fridays*).

abstint [ápstaṅ] *etc vb voir* **abstenir.**

abstraction [ápstráksyôṅ] *nf* abstraction; **faire** ~ **de** to set *ou* leave aside; ~ **faite de** ...

leaving aside ....

abstraire [ápstrer] *vt* to abstract; **s'~** *vi*: **s'~ (de)** (*s'isoler*) to cut o.s. off (from).

abstrait, e [ápstre, -et] *pp de* **abstraire** ♦ *a* abstract ♦ *nm*: **dans l'~** in the abstract.

abstraitement [ápstretmâń] *ad* abstractly.

abstrayais [ápstreye] *etc vb voir* **abstraire**.

absurde [ápsürd(ə)] *a* absurd ♦ *nm* absurdity; (*PHILOSOPHIE*): **l'~** absurd; **par l'~** ad absurdum.

absurdité [ápsürdētá] *nf* absurdity.

abus [ábü] *nm* (*excès*) abuse, misuse; (*injustice*) abuse; **~ de confiance** breach of trust; (*détournement de fonds*) embezzlement; **~ de pouvoir** abuse of power.

abuser [ábüzá] *vi* to go too far, overstep the mark ♦ *vt* to deceive, mislead; **s'~** *vi* (*se méprendre*) to be mistaken; **~ de** *vt* (*force, droit*) to misuse; (*alcool*) to take to excess; (*violer, duper*) to take advantage of.

abusif, ive [ábüzēf, -ēv] *a* exorbitant; (*punition*) excessive; (*pratique*) improper.

abusivement [ábüzēvmâń] *ad* exorbitantly; excessively; improperly.

AC *sigle f* (= *appellation contrôlée*) *guarantee of quality of wine*.

acabit [ákábē] *nm*: **du même ~** of the same type.

acacia [ákàsyá] *nm* (*BOT*) acacia.

académicien, ne [ákádāmēsyań, -en] *nm/f* academician.

académie [ákádāmē] *nf* (*société*) learned society; (*école: d'art, de danse*) academy; (*ART: nu*) nude; (*SCOL: circonscription*) ≈ regional education authority; **l'A~ (française)** the French Academy.

académique [ákádāmēk] *a* academic.

Acadie [ákádē] *nf*: **l'~** the Maritime Provinces.

acadien, ne [ákádyań, -cn] *a* Acadian, of *ou* from the Maritime Provinces.

acajou [ákázhōō] *nm* mahogany.

acariâtre [ákáryâtr(ə)] *a* cantankerous.

accablant, e [ákáblâń, -âńt] *a* (*témoignage, preuve*) overwhelming.

accablement [ákábləmâń] *nm* deep despondency.

accabler [ákáblá] *vt* to overwhelm, overcome; (*suj: témoignage*) to condemn, damn; **~ qn d'injures** to heap *ou* shower abuse on sb; **~ qn de travail** to overburden sb with work; **accablé de dettes/soucis** weighed down with debts/cares.

accalmie [ákálmē] *nf* lull.

accaparant, e [ákápárâń, -âńt] *a* that takes up all one's time *ou* attention.

accaparer [ákápárá] *vt* to monopolize; (*suj: travail etc*) to take up (all) the time *ou* attention of.

accéder [áksādā]: **~ à** *vt* (*lieu*) to reach; (*fig: pouvoir*) to accede to; (*: poste*) to attain; (*accorder: requête*) to grant, accede to.

accélérateur [áksālārátœr] *nm* accelerator.

accélération [áksālārâsyôń] *nf* speeding up; acceleration.

accéléré [áksālārā] *nm*: **en ~** (*CINÉMA*) speeded up.

accélérer [áksālārā] *vt* (*mouvement, travaux*) to speed up ♦ *vi* (*AUTO*) to accelerate.

accent [áksâń] *nm* accent; (*inflexions expressives*) tone (of voice); (*PHONÉTIQUE, fig*) stress; **aux ~s de** (*musique*) to the strains of; **mettre l'~ sur** (*fig*) to stress; **~ aigu/grave/circonflexe** acute/grave/circumflex accent.

accentuation [áksâńtüâsyôń] *nf* accenting; stressing.

accentué, e [áksâńtüā] *a* marked, pronounced.

accentuer [áksâńtüā] *vt* (*LING: orthographe*) to accent; (*: phonétique*) to stress, accent; (*fig*) to accentuate, emphasize; (*: effort, pression*) to increase; **s'~** *vi* to become more marked *ou* pronounced.

acceptable [ákseptábl(ə)] *a* satisfactory, acceptable.

acceptation [ákseptâsyôń] *nf* acceptance.

accepter [ákseptā] *vt* to accept; (*tolérer*): **~ que qn fasse** to agree to sb doing; **~ de faire** to agree to do.

acception [áksepsyôń] *nf* meaning, sense; **dans toute l'~ du terme** in the full sense *ou* meaning of the word.

accès [ákse] *nm* (*à un lieu, INFORM*) access, (*MÉD*) attack; (*: de toux*) fit, bout ♦ *nmpl* (*routes etc*) means of access, approaches; **d'~ facile/malaisé** easily/not easily accessible; **donner ~ à** (*lieu*) to give access to; (*carrière*) to open the door to; **avoir ~ auprès de qn** to have access to sb; **l'~ aux quais est interdit aux personnes non munies d'un billet** ticket-holders only on platforms, no access to platforms without a ticket; **~ de colère** fit of anger; **~ de joie** burst of joy.

accessible [áksāsēbl(ə)] *a* accessible; (*personne*) approachable; (*livre, sujet*): **~ à qn** within the reach of sb; (*sensible*): **~ à la pitié/l'amour** open to pity/love.

accession [áksesyôń] *nf*: **~ à** accession to; (*à un poste*) attainment of; **~ à la propriété** home-ownership.

accessit [áksāsēt] *nm* (*SCOL*) ≈ certificate of merit.

accessoire [áksāswár] *a* secondary, of secondary importance; (*frais*) incidental ♦ *nm* accessory; (*THÉÂTRE*) prop.

accessoirement [áksāswármâń] *ad* secondarily; incidentally.

accessoiriste [áksāswárēst(ə)] *nm/f* (*TV, CINÉMA*) property man/woman.

accident [áksēdâń] *nm* accident; **par ~** by chance; **~ de parcours** mishap; **~ de la route** road accident; **~ du travail** accident at work; industrial injury *ou* accident; **~s de terrain** unevenness of the ground.

accidenté, e [áksēdâńtā] *a* damaged *ou* injured (in an accident); (*relief, terrain*) uneven; hilly.

accidentel, le [áksēdâńtel] *a* accidental.

accidentellement [áksēdâńtelmâń] *ad* (*par hasard*) accidentally; (*mourir*) in an accident.

accidenter [áksēdâńtā] *vt* (*personne*) to injure; (*véhicule*) to damage.

accise [áksēz] *nf*: **droit d'~(s)** excise duty.

acclamation [áklámásyôń] *nf*: **par ~** (*vote*) by acclamation; **~s** *nfpl* cheers, cheering *sg*.

acclamer [áklámā] *vt* to cheer, acclaim.

acclimatation [àklēmátâsyôǹ] *nf* acclimatization.

acclimater [àklēmátā] *vt* to acclimatize; **s'~** *vi* to become acclimatized.

accointances [àkwaǹtâǹs] *nfpl*: **avoir des ~ avec** to have contacts with.

accolade [àkolád] *nf* (*amicale*) embrace; (*signe*) brace; **donner l'~ à qn** to embrace sb.

accoler [àkolā] *vt* to place side by side.

accommodant, e [àkomodáǹ, -âǹt] *a* accommodating, easy-going.

accommodement [àkomodmáǹ] *nm* compromise.

accommoder [àkomodā] *vt* (*CULIN*) to prepare; (*points de vue*) to reconcile; **~ qch à** (*adapter*) to adapt sth to; **s'~ de** to put up with; (*se contenter de*) to make do with; **s'~ à** (*s'adapter*) to adapt to.

accompagnateur, trice [àkòǹpányátœr, -trēs] *nm/f* (*MUS*) accompanist; (*de voyage*) guide; (: *de voyage organisé*) courier; (*d'enfants*) accompanying adult.

accompagnement [àkòǹpánymáǹ] *nm* (*MUS*) accompaniment; (*MIL*) support.

accompagner [àkòǹpányā] *vt* to accompany, be *ou* go *ou* come with; (*MUS*) to accompany; **s'~ de** to bring, be accompanied by.

accompli, e [àkòǹplē] *a* accomplished.

accomplir [àkòǹplēr] *vt* (*tâche, projet*) to carry out; (*souhait*) to fulfill (*US*), fulfil (*Brit*); **s'~** *vi* to be fulfilled.

accomplissement [àkòǹplēsmáǹ] *nm* carrying out; fulfillment (*US*), fulfilment (*Brit*).

accord [àkor] *nm* (*entente, convention, LING*) agreement; (*entre des styles, tons etc*) harmony; (*consentement*) agreement, consent; (*MUS*) chord; **donner son ~** to give one's agreement; **mettre 2 personnes d'~** to make 2 people come to an agreement, reconcile 2 people; **se mettre d'~** to come to an agreement (with each other); **être d'~** to agree; **être d'~ avec qn** to agree with sb; **d'~!** OK!, right!; **d'un commun ~** of one accord; **~ parfait** (*MUS*) tonic chord.

accord-cadre, *pl* **accords-cadres** [àkorkâdr(ə)] *nm* framework *ou* outline agreement.

accordéon [àkordāôǹ] *nm* (*MUS*) accordion.

accordéoniste [àkordāonēst(ə)] *nm/f* accordionist.

accorder [àkordā] *vt* (*faveur, délai*) to grant; (*attribuer*): **~ de l'importance/de la valeur à qch** to attach importance/value to sth; (*harmoniser*) to match; (*MUS*) to tune; **s'~** to get on together; (*être d'accord*) to agree; (*couleurs, caractères*) to go together, match; (*LING*) to agree; **je vous accorde que ...** I grant you that ....

accordeur [àkordœr] *nm* (*MUS*) tuner.

accoster [àkostā] *vt* (*NAVIG*) to draw alongside; (*personne*) to accost ♦ *vi* (*NAVIG*) to berth.

accotement [àkotmáǹ] *nm* (*de route*) shoulder; **~ stabilisé/non stabilisé** hard shoulder/soft shoulder.

accoter [àkotā] *vt*: **~ qch contre/à** to lean *ou* rest sth against/on; **s'~ contre/à** to lean against/on.

accouchement [àkōōshmáǹ] *nm* delivery,

(child)birth; (*travail*) labor (*US*), labour (*Brit*); **~ à terme** delivery at (full) term; **~ sans douleur** natural childbirth.

accoucher [àkōōshā] *vi* to give birth, have a baby; (*être en travail*) to be in labor (*US*) *ou* labour (*Brit*) ♦ *vt* to deliver; **~ d'un garçon** to give birth to a boy.

accoucheur [àkōōshœr] *nm*: (**médecin**) **~** obstetrician.

accoucheuse [àkōōshœz] *nf* midwife.

accouder [àkōōdā]: **s'~** *vi*: **s'~ à/contre/sur** to rest one's elbows on/against/on; **accoudé à la fenêtre** leaning on the windowsill.

accoudoir [àkōōdwàr] *nm* armrest.

accouplement [àkōōpləmáǹ] *nm* coupling; mating.

accoupler [àkōōplā] *vt* to couple; (*pour la reproduction*) to mate; **s'~** to mate.

accourir [àkōōrēr] *vi* to rush *ou* run up.

accoutrement [àkōōtrəmáǹ] *nm* (*péj*) outfit.

accoutrer [àkōōtrā] (*péj*) *vt* to do *ou* get up; **s'~** to do *ou* get o.s. up.

accoutumance [àkōōtümáǹs] *nf* (*gén*) adaptation; (*MÉD*) addiction.

accoutumé, e [àkōōtümā] *a* (*habituel*) customary, usual; **comme à l'~e** as is customary *ou* usual.

accoutumer [àkōōtümā] *vt*: **~ qn à qch/faire** to accustom sb to sth/to doing; **s'~ à** to get accustomed *ou* used to.

accréditer [àkrādētā] *vt* (*nouvelle*) to substantiate; **~ qn (auprès de)** to accredit sb (to).

accro [àkrō] *nm/f* (*fam*: = *accroché(e)*) addict.

accroc [àkrō] *nm* (*déchirure*) tear; (*fig*) hitch, snag; **sans ~** without a hitch; **faire un ~ à** (*vêtement*) to make a tear in, tear; (*fig: règle etc*) to infringe.

accrochage [àkrosházh] *nm* hanging (up); hitching (up); (*AUTO*) (minor) collision; (*MIL*) encounter, engagement; (*dispute*) clash, brush.

accroche-cœur [àkroshkœr] *nm* spit curl (*US*), kiss-curl (*Brit*).

accrocher [àkroshā] *vt* (*suspendre*): **~ qch à** to hang sth (up) on; (*attacher: remorque*): **~ qch à** to hitch sth (up) to; (*heurter*) to catch; to hit; (*déchirer*): **~ qch (à)** to catch sth (on); (*MIL*) to engage; (*fig*) to catch, attract ♦ *vi* to stick, get stuck; (*fig: pourparlers etc*) to hit a snag; (*plaire: disque etc*) to catch on; **s'~** (*se disputer*) to have a clash *ou* brush; (*ne pas céder*) to hold one's own, hang on in (*fam*); **s'~ à** (*rester pris à*) to catch on; (*agripper, fig*) to hang on *ou* cling to.

accrocheur, euse [àkroshœr, -œz] *a* (*vendeur, concurrent*) tenacious; (*publicité*) eye-catching; (*titre*) catchy, eye-catching.

accroire [àkrwàr] *vt*: **faire** *ou* **laisser ~ à qn qch/que** to give sb to believe sth/that.

accroîs [àkrwà], **accroissais** [àkrwàsc] *etc vb voir* **accroître**.

accroissement [àkrwàsmáǹ] *nm* increase.

accroître [àkrwàtr(ə)] *vt*, **s'~** *vi* to increase.

accroupi, e [àkrōōpē] *a* squatting, crouching (down).

accroupir [àkrōōpēr]: **s'~** *vi* to squat, crouch

(down).

accru, e [ákrü] *pp de* **accroître**.

accu [ákü] *nm* (*fam*: = *accumulateur*) battery.

accueil [ákœy] *nm* welcome; (*endroit*) reception (desk); (*: dans une gare*) information kiosk; **comité/centre d'~** reception committee/center.

accueillant, e [ákœyáṅ, -áṅt] *a* welcoming, friendly.

accueillir [ákœyēr] *vt* to welcome; (*loger*) to accommodate.

acculer [ákülā] *vt*: **~ qn à** *ou* **contre** to drive sb back against; **~ qn dans** to corner sb in; **~ qn à** (*faillite*) to drive sb to the brink of.

accumulateur [ákümülátœr] *nm* battery.

accumulation [ákümülâsyôṅ] *nf* accumulation; **chauffage/radiateur à ~** (night-)storage heating/heater.

accumuler [ákümülā] *vt* to accumulate, amass; **s'~** *vi* to accumulate; to pile up.

accusateur, trice [áküzátœr, -trēs] *nm/f* accuser ♦ *a* accusing; (*document, preuve*) incriminating.

accusatif [áküzátēf] *nm* (*LING*) accusative.

accusation [áküzásyôṅ] *nf* (*gén*) accusation; (*JUR*) charge; (*partie*): **l'~** the prosecution; **mettre en ~** to indict; **acte d'~** bill of indictment.

accusé, e [áküzā] *nm/f* accused; (*prévenu(e)*) defendant ♦ *nm*: **~ de réception** acknowledgement of receipt.

accuser [áküzā] *vt* to accuse; (*fig*) to emphasize, bring out; (*: montrer*) to show; **s'~** *vi* (*s'accentuer*) to become more marked; **~ qn de** to accuse sb of; (*JUR*) to charge sb with; **~ qn/qch de qch** (*rendre responsable*) to blame sb/sth for sth; **s'~ de qch/d'avoir fait qch** to admit sth/having done sth; to blame o.s. for sth/for having done sth; **~ réception de** to acknowledge receipt of; **~ le coup** (*aussi fig*) to be visibly affected.

acerbe [áserb(ə)] *a* caustic, acid.

acéré, e [ásārā] *a* sharp.

acétate [ásátát] *nm* acetate.

acétique [ásátēk] *a*: **acide ~** acetic acid.

acétone [ásáton] *nf* acetone.

acétylène [ásátēlen] *nm* acetylene.

ACF *sigle m* (= *Automobile Club de France*) ≈ AAA (*US*), ≈ AA (*Brit*).

ach. *abr* = **achète**.

achalandé, e [áshàlándā] *a*: **bien/mal ~** well-/poorly stocked.

acharné, e [ásharnā] *a* (*lutte, adversaire*) fierce, bitter; (*travail*) relentless, unremitting.

acharnement [áshàrnəmáṅ] *nm* fierceness; relentlessness.

acharner [ásharnā]: **s'~** *vi*: **s'~ sur** to go at fiercely, hound; **s'~ contre** to set o.s. against; to dog, pursue; (*suj: malchance*) to hound; **s'~ à faire** to try doggedly to do; to persist in doing.

achat [áshá] *nm* buying *q*; (*article acheté*) purchase; **faire l'~ de** to buy, purchase; **faire des ~s** to do some shopping, buy a few things.

acheminement [áshmēnmáṅ] *nm* conveyance.

acheminer [áshmēnā] *vt* (*courrier*) to forward, dispatch; (*troupes*) to convey, transport;

(*train*) to route; **s'~ vers** to head for.

acheter [áshtā] *vt* to buy, purchase; (*soudoyer*) to buy, bribe; **~ qch à** (*marchand*) to buy *ou* purchase sth from; (*ami etc: offrir*) to buy sth for; **~ à crédit** to buy on credit.

acheteur, euse [áshtœr, -ēz] *nm/f* buyer; shopper; (*COMM*) buyer; (*JUR*) vendee, purchaser.

achevé, e [áshvā] *a*: **d'un ridicule ~** thoroughly *ou* absolutely ridiculous; **d'un comique ~** absolutely hilarious.

achèvement [áshevmáṅ] *nm* completion, finishing.

achever [áshvā] *vt* to complete; (*blessé*) to finish off; **s'~** *vi* to end.

achoppement [áshopmáṅ] *nm*: **pierre d'~** stumbling block.

acide [ásēd] *a* sour, sharp; (*ton*) acid, biting; (*CHIMIE*) acid(ic) ♦ *nm* acid.

acidifier [ásēdēfyā] *vt* to acidify.

acidité [ásēdētā] *nf* sharpness; acidity.

acidulé, e [ásēdülā] *a* slightly acid; **bonbons ~s ~** lemon drops (*US*), acid drops (*Brit*).

acier [ásyā] *nm* steel; **~ inoxydable** stainless steel.

aciérie [ásyārē] *nf* steelworks *sg*.

acné [áknā] *nf* acne.

acolyte [ákolēt] *nm* (*péj*) associate.

acompte [ákôṅt] *nm* deposit; (*versement régulier*) installment (*US*), instalment (*Brit*); (*sur somme due*) payment on account; (*sur salaire*) advance; **un ~ de 100 F** 100 F on account.

acoquiner [ákokēnā]: **s'~ avec** *vt* (*péj*) to team up with.

Açores [ásor] *nfpl*: **les ~** the Azores.

à-côté [ákōtā] *nm* side-issue; (*argent*) extra.

à-coup [ákōō] *nm* (*du moteur*) (hic)cough; (*fig*) jolt; **sans ~s** smoothly; **par ~s** by fits and starts.

acoustique [ákōōstēk] *nf* (*d'une salle*) acoustics *pl*; (*science*) acoustics *sg* ♦ *a* acoustic.

acquéreur [ákārœr] *nm* buyer, purchaser; **se porter/se rendre ~ de qch** to announce one's intention to purchase/to purchase sth.

acquérir [ákārēr] *vt* to acquire; (*par achat*) to purchase, acquire; (*valeur*) to gain; (*résultats*) to achieve; **ce que ses efforts lui ont acquis** what his efforts have won *ou* gained (for) him.

acquiers [ákyer] *etc vb voir* **acquérir**.

acquiescement [ákyesmáṅ] *nm* acquiescence; agreement.

acquiescer [ákyásā] *vi* (*opiner*) to agree; (*consentir*): **~ (à qch)** to acquiesce *ou* assent (to sth).

acquis, e [ákē, -ēz] *pp de* **acquérir** ♦ *nm* (accumulated) experience; (*avantage*) gain ♦ *a* (*voir acquérir*) acquired; gained; achieved; **être ~ à** (*plan, idée*) to be in full agreement with; **son aide nous est ~e** we can count on *ou* be sure of his help; **tenir qch pour ~** to take sth for granted.

acquisition [ákēzēsyôṅ] *nf* acquisition; (*achat*) purchase; **faire l'~ de** to acquire; to purchase.

acquit [ákē] *vb voir* **acquérir** ♦ *nm* (*quittance*) receipt; **pour ~** received; **par ~ de**

conscience to set one's mind at rest.

acquittement [àkẽtmâṅ] *nm* acquittal; payment, settlement.

acquitter [àkẽtā] *vt* (*JUR*) to acquit; (*facture*) to pay, settle; **s'~ de** to discharge; (*promesse, tâche*) to fulfill (*US*), fulfil (*Brit*), carry out.

âcre [àkr(ə)] *a* acrid, pungent.

âcreté [àkrətā] *nf* acridness, pungency.

acrobate [àkrobát] *nm/f* acrobat.

acrobatie [àkrobásẽ] *nf* (*art*) acrobatics *sg*; (*exercice*) acrobatic feat; ~ **aérienne** aerobatics *sg*.

acrobatique [àkrobátẽk] *a* acrobatic.

acronyme [àkronẽm] *nm* acronym.

Acropole [àkropol] *nf*: **l'~** the Acropolis.

acrylique [àkrēlẽk] *a, nm* acrylic.

acte [àkt(ə)] *nm* act, action; (*THÉÂTRE*) act; ~**s** *nmpl* (*compte-rendu*) proceedings; **prendre ~ de** to note, take note of; **faire ~ de présence** to put in an appearance; **faire ~ de candidature** to submit an application; ~ **d'accusation** bill of indictment; ~ **de baptême** baptismal certificate; ~ **de mariage/naissance** marriage/birth certificate; ~ **de vente** bill of sale.

acteur [àktœr] *nm* actor.

actif, ive [àktẽf, -ẽv] *a* active ♦ *nm* (*COMM*) assets *pl*; (*LING*) active (voice); (*fig*): **avoir à son ~** to have to one's credit; ~**s** *nmpl* people in employment; **mettre à son ~** to add to one's list of achievements; **l'~ et le passif** assets and liabilities; **prendre une part active à qch** to take an active part in sth; **population active** working population.

action [àksyôṅ] *nf* (*gén*) action; (*COMM*) share; **une bonne/mauvaise ~** a good/an unkind deed; **mettre en ~** to put into action; **passer à l'~** to take action; **sous l'~ de** under the effect of; **l'~ syndicale** (the) union action; **un film d'~** an action film *ou* movie; ~ **en diffamation** libel suit; ~ **de grâce(s)** (*REL*) thanksgiving.

actionnaire [àksyoner] *nm/f* shareholder.

actionner [àksyonā] *vt* to work; to activate; to operate.

active [àktẽv] *af voir* **actif**.

activement [àktẽvmâṅ] *ad* actively.

activer [àktẽvā] *vt* to speed up; (*CHIMIE*) to activate; **s'~** *vi* (*s'affairer*) to bustle about; (*se hâter*) to hurry up.

activisme [àktẽvẽsm(ə)] *nm* activism.

activiste [àktẽvẽst(ə)] *nm/f* activist.

activité [àktẽvētā] *nf* activity; **en ~** (*volcan*) active; (*fonctionnaire*) in active life; (*militaire*) on active service.

actrice [àktrẽs] *nf* actress.

actualiser [àktüälẽzā] *vt* to actualize; (*mettre à jour*) to bring up to date.

actualité [àktüälētā] *nf* (*d'un problème*) topicality; (*événements*): **l'~** current events; **les ~s** (*CINÉMA, TV*) the news; **l'~ politique/sportive** the political/sports news; **les ~s télévisées** the television news; **d'~** topical.

actuel, le [àktüel] *a* (*présent*) present; (*d'actualité*) topical; (*non virtuel*) actual; **à l'heure ~le** at this moment in time, at the moment.

actuellement [àktüelmâṅ] *ad* at present, at the present time.

acuité [àküētā] *nf* acuteness.

acuponcteur, acupuncteur [àküpôṅktœr] *nm* acupuncturist.

acuponcture, acupuncture [àküpôṅktür] *nf* acupuncture.

adage [ádàzh] *nm* adage.

adaptable [àdáptábl(ə)] *a* adaptable.

adaptateur, trice [àdáptátœr, -trẽs] *nm/f* adapter.

adaptation [àdáptàsyôṅ] *nf* adaptation.

adapter [àdáptā] *vt* to adapt; **s'~ (à)** (*suj: personne*) to adapt (to); (*: objet, prise etc*) to apply (to); ~ **qch à** (*approprier*) to adapt sth to (fit); ~ **qch sur/dans/à** (*fixer*) to fit sth on/into/to.

addenda [àdàṅdà] *nm inv* addenda.

Addis-Ababa [àdēsábábá], **Addis-Abeba** [àdēsábəbá] *n* Addis Ababa.

additif [àdētēf] *nm* additional clause; (*substance*) additive; ~ **alimentaire** food additive.

addition [àdēsyôṅ] *nf* addition; (*au café*) bill.

additionnel, le [àdēsyonel] *a* additional.

additionner [àdēsyonā] *vt* to add (up); **s'~** *vi* to add up; ~ **un produit d'eau** to add water to a product.

adduction [àdüksyôṅ] *nf* (*de gaz, d'eau*) conveyance.

ADEP *sigle f* (= *Agence nationale pour le développement de l'éducation permanente*) national body which promotes adult education.

adepte [àdept(ə)] *nm/f* follower.

adéquat, e [àdākwá, -àt] *a* appropriate, suitable.

adéquation [àdākwâsyôṅ] *nf* appropriateness; (*LING*) adequacy.

adhérence [àdárâṅs] *nf* adhesion.

adhérent, e [àdárâṅ, -âṅt] *nm/f* (*de club*) member.

adhérer [àdárā] *vi* (*coller*) to adhere, stick; ~ **à** (*coller*) to adhere *ou* stick to; (*se rallier à: parti, club*) to join; to be a member of; (*: opinion, mouvement*) to support.

adhésif, ive [àdāzēf, -ēv] *a* adhesive, sticky ♦ *nm* adhesive.

adhésion [àdāzyôṅ] *nf* (*à un club*) joining; membership; (*à une opinion*) support.

ad hoc [àd ok] *a* ad hoc.

adieu, x [àdyœ̃] *excl* goodbye ♦ *nm* farewell; **dire ~ à qn** to say goodbye *ou* farewell to sb; **dire ~ à qch** (*renoncer*) to say *ou* wave goodbye to sth.

adipeux, euse [àdēpœ̃, -œ̃z] *a* bloated, fat; (*ANAT*) adipose.

adjacent, e [àdzhàsâṅ, -âṅt] *a*: ~ **(à)** adjacent (to).

adjectif [àdzhektēf] *nm* adjective; ~ **attribut** adjectival complement; ~ **épithète** attributive adjective.

adjoignais [àdzhwànye] *etc vb voir* **adjoindre**.

adjoindre [àdzhwàṅdr(ə)] *vt*: ~ **qch à** to attach sth to; (*ajouter*) to add sth to; ~ **qn à** (*personne*) to appoint sb as an assistant to; (*comité*) to appoint sb to, attach sb to; **s'~** *vt* (*collaborateur etc*) to take on, appoint.

adjoint, e [àdzhwàṅ, -wàṅt] *pp de* **adjoindre** ♦

nm/f assistant; **directeur** ~ assistant manager.

adjonction [àdzhôṅksyôṅ] *nf* (*voir adjoindre*) attaching; addition; appointment.

adjudant [àdzhüdàṅ] *nm* (*MIL*) warrant officer; ~**-chef** ≈ chief warrant officer (*US*), ≈ warrant officer 1st class (*Brit*).

adjudicataire [àdzhüdēkáter] *nm/f* successful bidder, purchaser; (*pour travaux*) successful bidder.

adjudicateur, trice [àdzhüdēkátœr, -trēs] *nm/f* (*aux enchères*) seller.

adjudication [àdzhüdēkâsyôṅ] *nf* sale by auction; (*pour travaux*) invitation to bid.

adjuger [àdzhüzhā] *vt* (*prix, récompense*) to award; (*lors d'une vente*) to auction (off); **s'**~ *vt* to take for o.s; **adjugé!** (*vendu*) gone!, sold!

adjurer [àdzhürā] *vt*: ~ **qn de faire** to implore *ou* beg sb to do.

adjuvant [àdzhüvàṅ] *nm* (*médicament*) adjuvant; (*additif*) additive; (*stimulant*) stimulant.

admettre [àdmɛtr(ə)] *vt* (*visiteur, nouveau-venu*) to admit, let in; (*candidat*: *SCOL*) to pass; (*TECH*: *gaz, eau, air*) to admit; (*tolérer*) to allow, accept; (*reconnaître*) to admit, acknowledge; (*supposer*) to suppose; **j'admets que** ... I admit that ...; **je n'admets pas que tu fasses cela** I won't allow you to do that; **admettons que** ... let's suppose that ...; **admettons** let's suppose so.

administrateur, trice [àdmēnēstrátœr, -trēs] *nm/f* (*COMM*) director; (*ADMIN*) administrator; ~ **délégué** managing director; ~ **judiciaire** receiver.

administratif, ive [àdmēnéstratēf, -ev] *a* administrative ♦ *nm* person in administration.

administration [àdmēnēstrâsyôṅ] *nf* administration; **l'A**~ ≈ the Civil Service.

administré, e [àdmēnēstrā] *nm/f* ≈ citizen.

administrer [àdmēnēstrā] *vt* (*firme*) to manage, run; (*biens, remède, sacrement etc*) to administer.

admirable [àdmērábl(ə)] *a* admirable, wonderful.

admirablement [àdmēráblǝmàṅ] *ad* admirably.

admirateur, trice [àdmērátœr, -trēs] *nm/f* admirer.

admiratif, ive [àdmērátēf, -ēv] *a* admiring.

admiration [àdmērâsyôṅ] *nf* admiration; **être en** ~ **devant** to be lost in admiration before.

admirativement [àdmērátēvmàṅ] *ad* admiringly.

admirer [àdmērā] *vt* to admire.

admis, e [àdmē, -ēz] *pp de* **admettre**.

admissibilité [àdmēsēbēlētā] *nf* eligibility; admissibility, acceptability.

admissible [àdmēsēbl(ə)] *a* (*candidat*) eligible; (*comportement*) admissible, acceptable; (*JUR*) receivable.

admission [àdmēsyôṅ] *nf* admission; **tuyau d'**~ intake pipe; **demande d'**~ application for membership; **service des** ~**s** admissions.

admonester [àdmonestā] *vt* to admonish.

ADN *sigle m* (= *acide désoxyribonucléique*) DNA.

ado [àdō] *nm/f* (*fam*: = *adolescent(e)*) adolescent, teenager.

adolescence [àdolāsàṅs] *nf* adolescence.

adolescent, e [àdolāsàṅ, -àṅt] *nm/f* adolescent, teenager.

adonner [àdonā]: **s'**~ **à** *vt* (*sport*) to devote o.s. to; (*boisson*) to give o.s. over to.

adopter [àdoptā] *vt* to adopt; (*projet de loi etc*) to pass.

adoptif, ive [àdoptēf, -ēv] *a* (*parents*) adoptive; (*fils, patrie*) adopted.

adoption [àdopsyôṅ] *nf* adoption; **son pays/sa ville d'**~ his adopted country/town.

adorable [àdorábl(ə)] *a* adorable.

adoration [àdorâsyôṅ] *nf* adoration; (*REL*) worship; **être en** ~ **devant** to be lost in adoration before.

adorer [àdorā] *vt* to adore; (*REL*) to worship.

adosser [àdōsā] *vt*: ~ **qch à** *ou* **contre** to stand sth against; **s'**~ **à** *ou* **contre** to lean with one's back against; **être adossé à** *ou* **contre** to be leaning with one's back against.

adoucir [àdōosēr] *vt* (*goût, température*) to make milder; (*avec du sucre*) to sweeten; (*peau, voix, eau*) to soften; (*caractère, personne*) to mellow; (*peine*) to soothe, allay; **s'**~ *vi* to become milder; to soften; to mellow.

adoucissement [àdōosēsmàṅ] *nm* becoming milder; sweetening; softening; mellowing; soothing.

adoucisseur [àdōosēsœr] *nm*: ~ (**d'eau**) water softener.

adr. *abr* = **adresse, adresser**.

adrénaline [àdrānálēn] *nf* adrenaline.

adresse [àdrɛs] *nf* (*voir adroit*) skill, dexterity; (*domicile, INFORM*) address; **à l'**~ **de** (*pour*) for the benefit of.

adresser [àdrāsā] *vt* (*lettre*: *expédier*) to send; (: *écrire l'adresse sur*) to address; (*injure, compliments*) to address; ~ **qn à un docteur/bureau** to refer *ou* send sb to a doctor/an office; ~ **la parole à qn** to speak to *ou* address sb; **s'**~ **à** (*parler à*) to speak to, address; (*s'informer auprès de*) to go and see, go and speak to; (: *bureau*) to enquire at; (*suj: livre, conseil*) to be aimed at.

Adriatique [àdrēyàtēk] *nf*: **l'**~ the Adriatic.

adroit, e [àdrwà, -wàt] *a* (*joueur, mécanicien*) skillful (*US*), skilful (*Brit*), dext(e)rous; (*politicien etc*) shrewd, skilled.

adroitement [àdrwàtmàṅ] *ad* skillfully (*US*), skilfully (*Brit*), dext(e)rously; shrewdly.

AdS *sigle f* = *Académie des Sciences*.

aduler [àdülā] *vt* to adulate.

adulte [àdült(ə)] *nm/f* adult, grown-up ♦ *a* (*personne, attitude*) adult, grown-up; (*chien, arbre*) fully-grown, mature; **l'âge** ~ adulthood; **formation/film pour** ~**s** adult training/film.

adultère [àdülter] *a* adulterous ♦ *nm/f* adulterer/adulteress ♦ *nm* (*acte*) adultery.

adultérin, e [àdültāraṅ, -ēn] *a* born of adultery.

advenir [àdvǝnēr] *vi* to happen; **qu'est-il advenu de?** what has become of?; **quoi qu'il advienne** whatever befalls *ou* happens.

adventiste [àdvàṅtēst(ə)] *nm/f* (*REL*) Adventist.

adverbe [ȧdverb(ə)] *nm* adverb; ~ **de manière** adverb of manner.

adverbial, e, aux [ȧdvcrbyȧl, -ō] *a* adverbial.

adversaire [ȧdverser] *nm/f* (*SPORT*, *gén*) opponent, adversary; (*MIL*) adversary, enemy.

adverse [ȧdvers(ə)] *a* opposing.

adversité [ȧdversētā] *nf* adversity.

AE *sigle m* (= *adjoint d'enseignement*) *non-certificated teacher.*

AELE *sigle f* (= *Association européenne de libre échange*) EFTA (= *European Free Trade Association*).

AEN *sigle f* (= *Agence pour l'énergie nucléaire*) ≈ AEC (= *Atomic Energy Commission*).

aérateur [āārátœr] *nm* ventilator.

aération [āārȧsyôṅ] *nf* airing; (*circulation de l'air*) ventilation; **conduit d'~** ventilation shaft; **bouche d'~** air vent.

aéré, e [āārā] *a* (*pièce*, *local*) airy, well-ventilated; (*tissu*) loose-woven; **centre ~** outdoor (recreation) center.

aérer [āārā] *vt* to air; (*fig*) to lighten; **s'~** *vi* to get some (fresh) air.

aérien, ne [āāryaṅ, -en] *a* (*AVIAT*) air *cpd*, aerial; (*câble*, *métro*) overhead; (*fig*) light; **compagnie ~ne** airline (company); **ligne ~ne** airline.

aérobic [āārobēk] *nm* aerobics *sg*.

aérobie [āārobē] *a* aerobic.

aéro-club [āāroklœb] *nm* flying club.

aérodrome [āārodrom] *nm* airfield, airdrome (*US*), aerodrome (*Brit*).

aérodynamique [āārodēnȧmēk] *a* aerodynamic, streamlined ♦ *nf* aerodynamics *sg*.

aérogare [āāroɡȧr] *nf* airport (buildings); (*en ville*) air terminal.

aéroglisseur [āāroglēsœr] *nm* hovercraft.

aérogramme [āārogrȧm] *nm* air letter, aerogram(me).

aéromodélisme [āāromodālēsm(ə)] *nm* model aircraft making.

aéronaute [āāronōt] *nm/f* aeronaut.

aéronautique [āāronōtēk] *a* aeronautical ♦ *nf* aeronautics *sg*.

aéronaval, e [āāronȧvȧl] *a* air and sea *cpd* ♦ *nf*: **l'A~e** ≈ the Naval Air Force (*US*), ≈ the Fleet Air Arm (*Brit*).

aéronef [āāronef] *nm* aircraft.

aérophagie [āārofȧzhē] *nf* aerophagy.

aéroport [āāropor] *nm* airport; ~ **d'embarquement** departure airport.

aéroporté, e [āāroportā] *a* airborne, airlifted.

aéroportuaire [āāroportüer] *a* of an *ou* the airport, airport *cpd*.

aéropostal, e, aux [āāropostȧl, -ō] *a* airmail *cpd*.

aérosol [āārosol] *nm* aerosol.

aérospatial, e, aux [āārospȧsyȧl, -ō] *a* aerospace ♦ *nf* the aerospace industry.

aérostat [āārostȧ] *nm* aerostat.

aérotrain [āārotraṅ] *nm* hovertrain.

AF *sigle fpl* = **allocations familiales** ♦ *sigle f* (*Suisse*) = **Assemblée fédérale.**

AFAT [ȧfȧt] *sigle m* (= *Auxiliaire féminin de l'armée de terre*) member of the women's army.

affable [ȧfȧbl(ə)] *a* affable.

affabulateur, trice [ȧfȧbülátœr, -trēs] *nm/f* storyteller.

affabuler [ȧfȧbülā] *vi* to make up stories.

affacturage [ȧfȧktürȧzh] *nm* factoring.

affadir [ȧfȧdēr] *vt* to make insipid *ou* tasteless.

affaiblir [ȧfȧblēr] *vt* to weaken; **s'~** *vi* to weaken, grow weaker; (*vue*) to grow dim.

affaiblissement [ȧfȧblēsmáṅ] *nm* weakening.

affaire [ȧfer] *nf* (*problème*, *question*) matter; (*criminelle*, *judiciaire*) case; (*scandaleuse etc*) affair; (*entreprise*) business; (*marché*, *transaction*) (business) deal, (piece of) business *q*; (*occasion intéressante*) good deal, bargain; ~**s** *nfpl* affairs; (*activité commerciale*) business · *sg*; (*effets personnels*) things, belongings; **tirer qn/se tirer d'~** to get sb/o.s. out of trouble; **ceci fera l'~** this will do (nicely); **avoir ~ à** (*comme adversaire*) to be faced with; (*en contact*) to be dealing with; **tu auras ~ à moi!** (*menace*) you'll have me to contend with!; **c'est une ~ de goût/d'argent** it's a question *ou* matter of taste/money; **c'est l'~ d'une minute/heure** it'll only take a minute/ an hour; **ce sont mes ~s** (*cela me concerne*) that's my business; **toutes ~s cessantes** forthwith; **les ~s étrangères** (*POL*) foreign affairs.

affairé, e [ȧfārā] *a* busy.

affairer [ȧfārā]: **s'~** *vi* to busy o.s., bustle about.

affairisme [ȧfārēsm(ə)] *nm* (political) racketeering.

affaissement [ȧfesmáṅ] *nm* subsidence; collapse.

affaisser [ȧfāsā]: **s'~** *vi* (*terrain*, *immeuble*) to subside, sink; (*personne*) to collapse.

affaler [ȧfȧlā]: **s'~** *vi*: **s'~ dans/sur** to collapse *ou* slump into/onto.

affamé, e [ȧfȧmā] *a* starving, famished.

affamer [ȧfȧmā] *vt* to starve.

affectation [ȧfektȧsyôṅ] *nf* (*voir affecter*) allotment; appointment; posting; (*voir affecté*) affectedness.

affecté, e [ȧfektā] *a* affected.

affecter [ȧfektā] *vt* (*émouvoir*) to affect, move; (*feindre*) to affect, feign; (*telle ou telle forme etc*) to take on, assume; ~ **qch à** to allocate *ou* allot sth to; ~ **qn à** to appoint sb to; (*diplomate*) to post sb to; ~ **qch de** (*de coefficient*) to modify sth by.

affectif, ive [ȧfektēf, -ēv] *a* emotional, affective.

affection [ȧfeksyôṅ] *nf* affection; (*mal*) ailment; **avoir de l'~ pour** to feel affection for; **prendre en ~** to become fond of.

affectionner [ȧfeksyonā] *vt* to be fond of.

affectueusement [ȧfektüœzmáṅ] *ad* affectionately.

affectueux, euse [ȧfektüœ̄, -œ̄z] *a* affectionate.

afférent, e [ȧfāráṅ, -áṅt] *a*: ~ **à** pertaining *ou* relating to.

affermir [ȧfermēr] *vt* to consolidate, strengthen.

affichage [ȧfēshȧzh] *nm* billposting, billsticking; (*électronique*) display; "~ **interdit**" "post no bills"; ~ **à cristaux liquides** liquid crystal display, LCD; ~ **numérique** *ou* **digital** digital display.

affiche [áfēsh] *nf* poster; (*officielle*) (public) notice; (*THÉÂTRE*) bill; **être à l'~** (*THÉÂTRE*) to be on; **tenir l'~** to run.

afficher [áfēshā] *vt* (*affiche*) to put up, post up; (*réunion*) to put up a notice about; (*électroniquement*) to display; (*fig*) to exhibit, display; **s'~** (*péj*) to flaunt o.s.; **"défense d'~"** "post no bills".

affichette [áfēshet] *nf* small poster *ou* notice.

affilé, e [áfēlā] *a* sharp.

affilée [áfēlā]: **d'~** *ad* at a stretch.

affiler [áfēlā] *vt* to sharpen.

affiliation [áfēlyâsyôn] *nf* affiliation.

affilié, e [áfēlyā] *a*: **être ~ à** to be affiliated with ♦ *nm/f* affiliated party *ou* member.

affilier [áfēlyā] *vt*: **s'~ à** to become affiliated with.

affiner [áfēnā] *vt* to refine; **s'~** *vi* to become (more) refined.

affinité [áfēnētā] *nf* affinity.

affirmatif, ive [áfērmátēf, -ēv] *a* affirmative ♦ *nf*: **répondre par l'affirmative** to reply in the affirmative; **dans l'affirmative** (*si oui*) if (the answer is) yes, if he does (*ou* you do *etc*)

affirmation [áfērmásyôn] *nf* assertion.

affirmativement [áfērmátēvmán] *ad* affirmatively, in the affirmative.

affirmer [áfērmā] *vt* (*prétendre*) to maintain, assert; (*autorité etc*) to assert; **s'~** to assert o.s.; to assert itself.

affleurer [áflœrā] *vi* to show on the surface.

affliction [áflēksyôn] *nf* affliction.

affligé, c [áflēzhā] *a* distressed, grieved; **~ de** (*maladie, tare*) afflicted with.

affligeant, e [áflezhàn, -ánt] *a* distressing.

affliger [áflēzhā] *vt* (*peiner*) to distress, grieve.

affluence [áfluans] *nf* crowds *pl*; **heures d'~** rush hour *sy*; **jours d'~** busiest days.

affluent [áflüán] *nm* tributary.

affluer [áflüā] *vi* (*secours, biens*) to flood in, pour in; (*sang*) to rush, flow.

afflux [áflü] *nm* flood, influx; rush.

affolant, e [áfolàn, -ánt] *a* terrifying.

affolé, e [áfolā] *a* panic-stricken, panicky.

affolement [áfolmán] *nm* panic.

affoler [áfolā] *vt* to throw into a panic; **s'~** *vi* to panic.

affranchir [áfrānshēr] *vt* to put a stamp *ou* stamps on; (*à la machine*) to meter (*US*), frank (*Brit*); (*esclave*) to enfranchise, emancipate; (*fig*) to free, liberate; **s'~ de** to free o.s. from; **machine à ~** franking machine, postage meter.

affranchissement [áfrânshēsmán] *nm* metering (*US*), franking (*Brit*); freeing; (*POSTES*: *prix payé*) postage; **tarifs d'~** postage rates.

affres [áfr(ə)] *nfpl*: **dans les ~ de** in the throes of.

affréter [áfrātā] *vt* to charter.

affreusement [áfrœzmán] *ad* dreadfully, awfully.

affreux, euse [áfrœ͞, -œ͞z] *a* dreadful, awful.

affriolant, e [áfrēyolán, -ánt] *a* tempting, enticing.

affront [áfrôn] *nm* affront.

affrontement [áfrôntmán] *nm* (*MIL, POL*) clash, confrontation.

affronter [áfrôntā] *vt* to confront, face; **s'~** to confront each other.

affubler [áfüblā] *vt* (*péj*): **~ qn de** to rig *ou* deck sb out in; (*surnom*) to attach to sb.

affût [áfü] *nm* (*de canon*) gun carriage; **à l'~ (de)** (*gibier*) lying in wait (for); (*fig*) on the look-out (for).

affûter [áfütā] *vt* to sharpen, grind.

afghan, e [áfgán, -án] *a* Afghan.

Afghanistan [áfgánēstán] *nm*: **l'~** Afghanistan.

afin [áfán]: **~ que** *cj* so that, in order that; **~ de faire** in order to do, so as to do.

AFNOR [áfnor] *sigle f* (= *Association française de normalisation*) *industrial standards authority*.

a fortiori [áforsyorē] *ad* all the more, a fortiori.

AFP *sigle f* = *Agence France-Presse*.

AFPA *sigle f* = *Association pour la formation professionnelle des adultes*.

africain, e [áfrēkán, -en] *a* African ♦ *nm/f*: **A~,** **e** African.

afrikaans [áfrēkán] *nm, a inv* Afrikaans.

Afrikaner [áfrēkáner], **Afrikander** [áfrēkánder] *nm/f* Afrikaner.

Afrique [áfrēk] *nf*: **l'~** Africa; **l'~ australe/du Nord/du Sud** southern/North/South Africa.

afro [áfrō] *a inv*: **coupe ~** Afro hairstyle ♦ *nm/f*: **A~** Afro.

afro-américain, e [áfrōámārēkán, -en] *a* Afro-American.

afro-asiatique [áfroàzyàtēk] *a* Afro-Asian.

AG *sigle f* = *assemblée générale*.

ag. *abr* = **agence**.

agaçant, e [àgàsán, -ánt] *a* irritating, aggravating.

agacement [àgàsmán] *nm* irritation, aggravation.

agacer [àgàsā] *vt* to pester, tease; (*involontairement*) to irritate, aggravate; (*aguicher*) to excite, lead on.

agapes [àgáp] *nfpl* (*humoristique*: *festin*) feast.

agate [àgát] *nf* agate.

AGE *sigle f* = *assemblée générale extraordinaire*.

âge [àzh] *nm* age; **quel ~ as-tu?** how old are you?; **une femme d'un certain ~** a middle-aged woman, a woman who is getting on (in years); **bien porter son ~** to wear well; **prendre de l'~** to be getting on (in years), grow older; **limite d'~** age limit; **dispense d'~** special exemption from age limit; **troisième ~** (*période*) retirement; (*personnes âgées*) senior citizens; **l'~ ingrat** the awkward *ou* difficult age; **~ légal** legal age; **~ mental** mental age; **l'~ mûr** maturity, middle age; **~ de raison** age of reason.

âgé, e [àzhā] *a* old, elderly; **~ de 10 ans** 10 years old.

agence [àzhâns] *nf* agency, office; (*succursale*) branch; **~ immobilière** real estate agency (*US*), estate agent's (office) (*Brit*); **~ matrimoniale** marriage bureau; **~ de placement** employment agency; **~ de publicité** advertising agency; **~ de voyages** travel agency.

agencé, e [àzhânsā] *a*: **bien/mal ~** well/badly put together; well/badly laid out *ou* arranged.

agencement [àzhânsmán] *nm* putting

together; arrangement, laying out.
agencer |àzhàńsā| *vt* to put together; (*local*) to arrange, lay out.
agenda |àzhańdà| *nm* appointment book, diary (*Brit*).
agenouiller |àzhnōōyā|: **s'~** *vi* to kneel (down).
agent |àzhàń| *nm* (*aussi*: **~ de police**) policeman; (*ADMIN*) official, officer; (*fig: élément, facteur*) agent; **~ d'assurances** insurance agent (*US*) *ou* broker (*Brit*); **~ de change** stockbroker; **~ commercial** sales representative; **~ immobilier** realtor (*US*), estate agent (*Brit*); **~ (secret)** (secret) agent.
agglomérat |àglomàrā| *nm* (*GÉO*) agglomerate.
agglomération |àglomārâsyôń| *nf* town; (*AUTO*) built-up area; **l'~ parisienne** the urban area of Paris.
aggloméré |àglomārā| *nm* (*bois*) particleboard (*US*), chipboard (*Brit*); (*pierre*) conglomerate.
agglomérer |àglomàrā| *vt* to pile up; (*TECH: bois, pierre*) to compress; **s'~** *vi* to pile up.
agglutiner |àglütēnā| *vt* to stick together; **s'~** *vi* to congregate.
aggravant, e |àgràvàń, -àńt| *a*: **circonstances ~es** aggravating circumstances.
aggravation |àgràvâsyôń| *nf* worsening, aggravation; increase.
aggraver |àgràvā| *vt* to worsen, aggravate; (*JUR: peine*) to increase; **s'~** *vi* to worsen; **~ son cas** to make one's case worse.
agile |àzhēl| *a* agile, nimble.
agilité |àzhēlētā| *nf* agility, nimbleness.
agio |àzhyō| *nm* (bank) charges *pl*.
agir |àzhēr| *vi* (*se comporter*) to behave, act; (*faire quelque chose*) to act, take action; (*avoir de l'effet*) to act; **il s'agit de** it's a matter *ou* question of; it is about; (*il importe que*): **il s'agit de faire** we (*ou* you *etc*) must do; **de quoi s'agit-il?** what is it about?
agissements |àzhēsmàń| *nmpl* (*gén péj*) schemes, intrigues.
agitateur, trice |àzhētàtœr, -trēs| *nm/f* agitator.
agitation |àzhētàsyôń| *nf* (hustle and) bustle; (*trouble*) agitation, excitement; (*politique*) unrest, agitation.
agité, e |àzhētā| *a* (*remuant*) fidgety, restless; (*troublé*) agitated, perturbed; (*journée*) hectic; (*mer*) rough; (*sommeil*) disturbed, broken.
agiter |àzhētā| *vt* (*bouteille, chiffon*) to shake; (*bras, mains*) to wave; (*préoccuper, exciter*) to trouble, perturb; **s'~** *vi* to bustle about; (*dormeur*) to toss and turn; (*enfant*) to fidget; (*POL*) to grow restless; **"~ avant l'emploi"** "shake before use".
agneau, x |àŋyō| *nm* lamb; (*toison*) lambswool.
agnelet |àŋyle| *nm* little lamb.
agnostique |àgnostēk| *a, nm/f* agnostic.
agonie |àgonē| *nf* mortal agony, death pangs *pl*; (*fig*) death throes *pl*.
agonir |àgonēr| *vt*: **~ qn d'injures** to hurl abuse at sb.
agoniser |àgonēzā| *vi* to be dying; (*fig*) to be in its death throes.

agrafe |àgràf| *nf* (*de vêtement*) hook, fastener; (*de bureau*) staple; (*MÉD*) clip.
agrafer |àgràfā| *vt* to fasten; to staple.
agrafeuse |àgràtœz| *nf* stapler.
agraire |àgrer| *a* agrarian; (*mesure, surface*) land *cpd*.
agrandir |àgràńdēr| *vt* (*magasin, domaine*) to extend, enlarge; (*trou*) to enlarge, make bigger; (*PHOTO*) to enlarge, blow up; **s'~** *vi* to be extended; to be enlarged.
agrandissement |àgràńdēsmàń| *nm* extension; enlargement; (*photographie*) enlargement.
agrandisseur |àgràńdēscer| *nm* (*PHOTO*) enlarger.
agréable |àgrāàbl(ə)| *a* pleasant, nice.
agréablement |àgrāàbləmàń| *ad* pleasantly.
agréé, e |àgrāā| *a*: **concessionnaire ~** registered dealer; **magasin ~** registered dealer('s).
agréer |àgrāā| *vt* (*requête*) to accept; **~ à** *vt* to please, suit; **veuillez ~ ...** (*formule épistolaire*) sincerely yours (*US*), yours faithfully (*Brit*).
agrég |àgreg| *nf* (*fam*) = **agrégation**.
agrégat |àgrāgà| *nm* aggregate.
agrégation |àgrāgàsyôń| *nf* highest teaching diploma in France (*competitive examination*).
agrégé, e |àgrāzhā| *nm/f* holder of the *agrégation*.
agréger |àgrāzhā|: **s'~** *vi* to aggregate.
agrément |àgrāmàń| *nm* (*accord*) consent, approval; (*attraits*) charm, attractiveness; (*plaisir*) pleasure; **voyage/jardin d'~** pleasure trip/garden.
agrémenter |àgrāmàńtā| *vt*: **~ (de)** to embellish (with), adorn (with).
agrès |àgre| *nmpl* (gymnastics) apparatus *sg*.
agresser |àgràsā| *vt* to attack.
agresseur |àgrescer| *nm* aggressor.
agressif, ive |àgrescf, -ēv| *a* aggressive.
agression |àgresyôń| *nf* attack; (*POL, MIL, PSYCH*) aggression.
agressivement |àgresēvmàń| *ad* aggressively.
agressivité |àgresēvētā| *nf* aggressiveness.
agreste |àgrest(ə)| *a* rustic.
agricole |àgrēkol| *a* agricultural, farm *cpd*.
agriculteur, trice |àgrēkültœr, -trēs| *nm/f* farmer.
agriculture |àgrēkültür| *nf* agriculture; farming.
agripper |àgrēpā| *vt* to grab, clutch; (*pour arracher*) to snatch, grab; **s'~ à** to cling (on) to, clutch, grip.
agro-alimentaire |àgroàlēmàńter| *a* farming *cpd* ♦ *nm*: **l'~** agribusiness.
agronomique |àgronomēk| *a* agronomic(al).
agrumes |àgrüm| *nmpl* citrus fruit(s).
aguerrir |àgārēr| *vt* to harden; **s'~ (contre)** to become hardened (to).
aguets |àge|: **aux ~** *ad*: **être aux ~** to be on the look-out.
aguichant, e |àgēshàń, -àńt| *a* enticing.
aguicher |àgēshā| *vt* to entice.
aguicheur, euse |àgēshœr, -œz| *a* enticing.
ah |â| *excl* ah!; **~ bon?** really?, is that so?; **~ mais ...** yes, but ...; **~ non!** oh no!
ahuri, e |àürē| *a* (*stupéfait*) flabbergasted;

(idiot) dim-witted.

ahurir [äürēr] *vt* to stupefy, stagger.

ahurissant, e [áürēsáṅ, -áṅt] *a* stupefying, staggering.

ai [ā] *vb voir* **avoir.**

aide [ed] *nm/f* assistant ♦ *nf* assistance, help; *(secours financier)* aid; **à l'~** de with the help *ou* aid of; **aller à l'~ de qn** to go to sb's aid, go to help sb; **venir en ~ à qn** to help sb, come to sb's assistance; **appeler (qn) à l'~** to call for help (from sb); **à l'~!** help!; ~ **de camp** *nm* aide-de-camp; ~ **comptable** *nm* accountant's assistant; ~ **électricien** *nm* electrician's helper *(US)* ou mate *(Brit)*; ~ **familiale** *nf* mother's helper *(US)* ou help *(Brit)*, ≈ home help; ~ **judiciaire** *nf* legal aid; ~ **de laboratoire** *nm/f* laboratory assistant; ~ **ménagère** *nf* ≈ home help; ~ **sociale** *nf (assistance)* welfare *(US)*, social security *(Brit)*; ~ **soignant, e** *nm/f* nurse's aide *(US)*, auxiliary nurse *(Brit)*; ~ **technique** *nf* ≈ Peace Corps *(US)*, ≈ VSO *(Brit)*.

aide-mémoire [edmāmwàr] *nm inv* (key facts) handbook.

aider [ādā] *vt* to help; ~ **à qch** to help (towards) sth; ~ **qn à faire qch** to help sb to do sth; **s'~ de** *(se servir de)* to use, make use of.

aie [ɛ] *etc vb voir* **avoir.**

aïe [áy] *excl* ouch!

AIEA *sigle f* (= *Agence internationale de l'énergie nucléaire*) IAEA (= *International Atomic Energy Agency*).

aïeul, e [áycœl] *nm/f* grandparent, grandfather/grandmother; *(ancêtre)* forebear.

aïeux [áyœ] *nmpl* grandparents; forebears, forefathers.

aigle [ɛgl(ǝ)] *nm* eagle.

aiglefin [ɛglǝfáṅ] *nm* = **églefin.**

aigre [ɛgr(ǝ)] *a* sour, sharp; *(fig)* sharp, cutting; **tourner à l'~** to turn sour.

aigre-doux, -douce [ɛgrǝdoō, -dōōs] *a (fruit)* bitter-sweet; *(sauce)* sweet and sour.

aigrefin [ɛgrǝfáṅ] *nm* swindler.

aigrelet, te [ɛgrǝlɛ, -et] *a (taste)* sourish; *(voix, son)* sharpish.

aigrette [ɛgret] *nf (plume)* feather.

aigreur [ɛgrœr] *nf* sourness; sharpness; **~s d'estomac** heartburn *sg.*

aigri, e [ɛgrē] *a* embittered.

aigrir [ɛgrēr] *vt (personne)* to embitter; *(caractère)* to sour; **s'~** *vi* to become embittered; to sour; *(lait etc)* to turn sour.

aigu, ë [āgü] *a (objet, arête)* sharp, pointed; *(son, voix)* high-pitched, shrill; *(note)* high(-pitched); *(douleur, intelligence)* acute, sharp.

aigue-marine, *pl* **aigues-marines** [ɛgmárēn] *nf* aquamarine.

aiguillage [āgüēyàzh] *nm (RAIL)* switch *(US)*, points *pl (Brit)*.

aiguille [āgüēy] *nf* needle; *(de montre)* hand; ~ **à tricoter** knitting needle.

aiguiller [āgüēyā] *vt (orienter)* to direct; *(RAIL)* to switch *(US)*, shunt *(Brit)*.

aiguillette [āgüēyet] *nf (CULIN)* aiguillette.

aiguilleur [āgüēyœr] *nm (RAIL)* switchman *(US)*, pointsman *(Brit)*; ~ **du ciel** air traffic controller.

aiguillon [āgüēyôṅ] *nm (d'abeille)* sting; *(fig)* spur, stimulus.

aiguillonner [āgüēyonā] *vt* to spur *ou* goad on.

aiguiser [āgēzā] *vt* to sharpen, grind; *(fig)* to stimulate; *(: esprit)* to sharpen; *(: sens)* to excite.

aïkido [áykēdō] *nm* aikido.

ail [áy] *nm* garlic.

aile [ɛl] *nf* wing; *(de voiture)* fender *(US)*, wing *(Brit)*; **battre de l'~** *(fig)* to be in a sorry state; **voler de ses propres ~s** to stand on one's own two feet; ~ **libre** hang-glider.

ailé, e [ālā] *a* winged.

aileron [ɛlrôṅ] *nm (de requin)* fin; *(d'avion)* aileron.

ailette [ɛlet] *nf (TECH)* fin; *(: de turbine)* blade.

ailier [ālyā] *nm (SPORT)* wing *(US)*, winger *(Brit)*.

aille [áy] *etc vb voir* **aller.**

ailleurs [áycœr] *ad* elsewhere, somewhere else; **partout/nulle part ~** everywhere/nowhere else; **d'~** *ad (du reste)* moreover, besides; **par ~** *ad (d'autre part)* moreover, furthermore.

ailloli [áyolē] *nm* garlic mayonnaise.

aimable [ɛmábl(ǝ)] *a* kind, nice; **vous êtes bien ~** that's very nice *ou* kind of you, how kind (of you)!

aimablement [ɛmáblǝmáṅ] *ad* kindly.

aimant [ɛmáṅ] *nm* magnet.

aimant, e [ɛman, -ant] *a* loving, affectionate.

aimanté, e [ɛmáṅtā] *a* magnetic.

aimanter [ɛmáṅtā] *vt* to magnetize.

aimer [ɛmā] *vt* to love; *(d'amitié, affection, par goût)* to like; *(souhait)*: **j'aimerais ... I** would like ...; **s'~** to love each other; to like each other; **je n'aime pas beaucoup Paul I** don't like Paul much, I don't care much for Paul; ~ **faire qch** to like doing sth, like to do sth; **aimeriez-vous je je vous accompagne?** would you like me to come with you?; **j'aimerais (bien) m'en aller I** should (really) like to go; **bien ~ qn/qch** to like sb/sth; **j'aime mieux Paul (que Pierre) I** prefer Paul (to Pierre); **j'aime mieux** *ou* **autant vous dire que I** may as well tell you that; **j'aimerais autant** *ou* **mieux y aller maintenant I'd** sooner *ou* rather go now; **j'aime assez aller au cinéma I** quite like going to the cinema.

aine [ɛn] *nf* groin.

aîné, e [ānā] *a* elder, older; *(le plus âgé)* eldest, oldest ♦ *nm/f* oldest child *ou* one, oldest boy *ou* son/girl *ou* daughter; **~s** *nmpl (fig: anciens)* elders; **il est mon ~ (de 2 ans)** he's (2 years) older than me, he's 2 years my senior.

aînesse [ɛnes] *nf*: **droit d'~** birthright.

ainsi [áṅsē] *ad (de cette façon)* like this, in this way, thus; *(ce faisant)* thus ♦ *cj* thus, so; ~ **que** *(comme)* (just) as; *(et aussi)* as well as; **pour ~ dire** so to speak, as it were; ~ **donc** and so; ~ **soit-il** *(REL)* so be it; **et ~ de suite** and so on (and so forth).

aïoli [áyolē] *nm* = **ailloli.**

air [ɛr] *nm* air; *(mélodie)* tune; *(expression)* look, air; *(atmosphère, ambiance)*: **dans l'~**

in the air (*fig*); **prendre de grands** ~s **(avec qn)** to give o.s. airs (with sb); **en l'**~ (up) into the air; **tirer en l'**~ to fire shots in the air; **paroles/menaces en l'**~ idle words/ threats; **prendre l'**~ to get some (fresh) air; (*avion*) to take off; **avoir l'**~ **triste** to look *ou* seem sad; **avoir l'**~ **de qch** to look like sth; **avoir l'**~ **de faire** to look as though one is doing, appear to be doing; **courant d'**~ draft (*US*), draught (*Brit*); **le grand** ~ the open air; **mal de l'**~ air-sickness; **tête en l'**~ scatterbrain; ~ **comprimé** compressed air; ~ **conditionné** air-conditioning.

aire [er] *nf* (*zone, fig,* MATH) area; (*nid*) eyrie, aerie (*US*); ~ **d'atterrissage** landing strip; landing patch; ~ **de jeu** play area; ~ **de lancement** launching site; ~ **de stationnement** parking area.

airelle [erel] *nf* bilberry.

aisance [ezãs] *nf* ease; (COUTURE) easing, freedom of movement; (*richesse*) affluence; **être dans l'**~ to be well-off *ou* affluent.

aise [ez] *nf* comfort ♦ *a*: **être bien** ~ **de/que** to be delighted to/that; ~s *nfpl*: **aimer ses** ~s to like one's (creature) comforts; **prendre ses** ~s to make o.s. comfortable; **frémir d'**~ to shudder with pleasure; **être à l'**~ *ou* **à son** ~ to be comfortable; (*pas embarrassé*) to be at ease; (*financièrement*) to be comfortably off; **se mettre à l'**~ to make o.s. comfortable; **être mal à l'**~ *ou* **à son** ~ to be uncomfortable; (*gêné*) to be ill at ease; **mettre qn à l'**~ to put sb at his (*ou* her) ease; **mettre qn mal à l'**~ to make sb feel ill at ease; **à votre** ~ please yourself, just as you like; **en faire à son** ~ to do as one likes; **en prendre à son** ~ **avec qch** to be free and easy with sth, do as one likes with sth.

aisé, e [eze] *a* easy; (*assez riche*) well-to-do, well-off.

aisément [ezemã] *ad* easily.

aisselle [esel] *nf* armpit.

ait [e] *vb voir* **avoir**.

ajonc [aʒõ] *nm* gorse *q*.

ajouré, e [aʒure] *a* openwork *cpd*.

ajournement [aʒurnəmã] *nm* adjournment; deferment, postponement.

ajourner [aʒurne] *vt* (*réunion*) to adjourn; (*décision*) to defer, postpone; (*candidat*) to fail; (*conscrit*) to defer.

ajout [aʒu] *nm* addition.

ajouter [aʒute] *vt* to add; (INFORM) to append; ~ **à** *vt* (*accroître*) to add to; **s'**~ **à** to add to; ~ **que** to add that; ~ **foi à** to lend *ou* give credence to.

ajustage [aʒüstaʒ] *nm* fitting.

ajusté, e [aʒüsta] *a*: **bien** ~ (*robe etc*) close-fitting.

ajustement [aʒüstəmã] *nm* adjustment.

ajuster [aʒüsta] *vt* (*régler*) to adjust; (*vêtement*) to alter; (*arranger*): ~ **sa cravate** to adjust one's tie; (*coup de fusil*) to aim; (*cible*) to aim at; (*adapter*): ~ **qch à** to fit sth to.

ajusteur [aʒüstœr] *nm* metal worker.

al *abr* = **année-lumière**.

alaise [alez] *nf* = **alèse**.

alambic [alãbek] *nm* still.

alambiqué, e [alãbeka] *a* convoluted, over-

complicated.

alangui, e [alãge] *a* languid.

alanguir [alãger]: **s'**~ *vi* to grow languid.

alarme [alarm(ə)] *nf* alarm; **donner l'**~ to give *ou* raise the alarm; **jeter l'**~ to cause alarm.

alarmer [alarma] *vt* to alarm; **s'**~ *vi* to become alarmed.

alarmiste [alarmēst(ə)] *a* alarmist.

Alaska [alaska] *nm*: **l'**~ Alaska.

albanais, e [albanε, -ez] *a* Albanian ♦ *nm* (LING) Albanian ♦ *nm/f*: **A**~, **e** Albanian.

Albanie [albanē] *nf*: **l'**~ Albania.

albâtre [albatr(ə)] *nm* alabaster.

albatros [albatrōs] *nm* albatross.

albigeois, e [albēzhwa, -waz] *a* of *ou* from Albi.

albinos [albēnōs] *nm/f* albino.

album [albom] *nm* album; ~ **à colorier** coloring book; ~ **de timbres** stamp album.

albumen [albümen] *nm* albumen.

albumine [albümēn] *nf* albumin; **avoir** *ou* **faire de l'**~ to suffer from albuminuria.

alcalin, e [alkalã, -ēn] *a* alkaline.

alchimiste [alshēmēst(ə)] *nm* alchemist.

alcool [alkol] *nm*: **l'**~ alcohol; **un** ~ a spirit, a brandy; ~ **à brûler** wood alcohol (*US*), methylated spirit(s) (*Brit*); ~ **à 90°** rubbing alcohol (*US*), surgical spirit (*Brit*); ~ **camphré** camphorated alcohol; ~ **de prune** *etc* plum *etc* brandy.

alcoolémie [alkolāmē] *nf* blood alcohol level.

alcoolique [alkolēk] *a, nm/f* alcoholic.

alcoolisé, e [alkolēza] *a* alcoholic.

alcoolisme [alkolēsm(ə)] *nm* alcoholism.

alco(o)test [alkotest] *nm* ® (*objet*) Breathalyzer ®; (*test*) breath-test; **faire subir l'**~ **à qn** to Breathalyze ® sb.

alcôve [alkōv] *nf* alcove, recess.

aléas [aláā] *nmpl* hazards.

aléatoire [aláātwár] *a* uncertain; (INFORM, STATISTIQUE) random.

alentour [alãtōōr] *ad* around (about); ~s *nmpl* surroundings; **aux** ~s **de** in the vicinity *ou* neighborhood of, around about; (*temps*) around about.

Aléoutiennes [aláōōsyen] *nfpl*: **les (îles)** ~ the Aleutian Islands.

alerte [alert(ə)] *a* agile, nimble; (*style*) brisk, lively ♦ *nf* alert; warning; **donner l'**~ to give the alert; **à la première** ~ at the first sign of trouble *ou* danger.

alerter [alerta] *vt* to alert.

alèse [alez] *nf* (*drap*) undersheet, drawsheet.

aléser [aláza] *vt* to ream.

alevin [alvañ] *nm* alevin, young fish.

alevinage [alvēnazh] *nm* fish farming.

Alexandrie [aleksãdrē] *n* Alexandria.

alexandrin [aleksãdrañ] *nm* alexandrine.

alezan, e [alzãn, -ãn] *a* chestnut.

algarade [algarad] *nf* row, dispute.

algèbre [alzhebr(ə)] *nf* algebra.

Alger [alzha] *n* Algiers.

Algérie [alzharē] *nf*: **l'**~ Algeria.

algérien, ne [alzharyañ, -en] *a* Algerian ♦ *nm/f*: **A**~, **ne** Algerian.

algérois, e [alzharwa, -waz] *a* of *ou* from Algiers ♦ *nm*: **l'A**~ (*région*) the Algiers region.

algorithme [algoretm(ə)] *nm* algorithm.

algue [álg(ə)] *nf* (*gén*) seaweed *q*; (*BOT*) alga (*pl* -ae).

alias [ályàs] *ad* alias.

alibi [álēbē] *nm* alibi.

aliénation [ályānâsyóṅ] *nf* alienation.

aliéné, e [ályānā] *nm/f* insane person, lunatic (*péj*).

aliéner [ályānā] *vt* to alienate; (*bien, liberté*) to give up; **s'~** *vt* to alienate.

alignement [álēnymáṅ] *nm* alignment, lining up; **à l'~** in line.

aligner [álēnyā] *vt* to align, line up; (*idées, chiffres*) to string together; (*adapter*): **~ qch sur** to bring sth into alignment with; **s'~** (*soldats etc*) to line up; **s'~ sur** (*POL*) to align o.s. with.

aliment [álēmáṅ] *nm* food; **~ complet** natural (*US*) *ou* whole (*Brit*) food.

alimentaire [álēmáṅter] *a* food *cpd*; (*péj: besogne*) done merely to earn a living; **produits ~s** foodstuffs, foods.

alimentation [álēmáṅtâsyóṅ] *nf* feeding; supplying, supply; (*commerce*) food trade; (*produits*) groceries *pl*; (*régime*) diet; (*IN-FORM*) feed; **~ (générale)** (general) grocer's; **~ de base** staple diet; **~ en feuilles/en continu/en papier** form/continuous/sheet feed.

alimenter [álēmáṅtā] *vt* to feed; (*TECH*): **~ (en)** to supply (with), feed (with); (*fig*) to sustain, keep going.

alinéa [álēnáá] *nm* paragraph; **"nouvel ~"** "new paragraph".

aliter [álētā]: **s'~** *vi* to take to one's bed; **infirme alité** bedridden person *ou* invalid.

alizé [álēzā] *a, nm*: **(vent) ~** trade wind.

allaitement [áletmáṅ] *nm* feeding; **~ maternel/au biberon** breast-/bottle-feeding; **~ mixte** mixed feeding.

allaiter [álátā] *vt* (*suj: femme*) to (breast-) feed, nurse; (*suj: animal*) to suckle; **~ au biberon** to bottle-feed.

allant [áláṅ] *nm* drive, go.

alléchant, e [álāsháṅ, -áṅt] *a* tempting, enticing.

allécher [álāshā] *vt*: **~ qn** to make sb's mouth water; to tempt sb, entice sb.

allée [álā] *nf* (*de jardin*) path; (*en ville*) avenue, drive; **~s et venues** comings and goings.

allégation [álāgâsyóṅ] *nf* allegation.

alléger [álāzhā] *vt* (*voiture*) to make lighter; (*chargement*) to lighten; (*souffrance*) to alleviate, soothe.

allégorie [álāgorē] *nf* allegory.

allégorique [álāgorēk] *a* allegorical.

allègre [álegr(ə)] *a* lively, jaunty (*Brit*); (*personne*) cheerful.

allégresse [álāgres] *nf* elation, gaiety.

alléguer [álāgā] *vt* to offer (as proof *ou* an excuse).

Allemagne [áləmány] *nf*: **l'~** Germany; **l'~ de l'Est/Ouest** East/West Germany; **l'~ fédérale (RFA)** the Federal Republic of Germany (FRG).

allemand, e [álmáṅ, -áṅd] *a* German ♦ *nm* (*LING*) German ♦ *nm/f*: **A~,** e German; **A~ de l'Est/l'Ouest** East/West German.

aller [álā] *nm* (*trajet*) outward journey;

(*billet*): **~ (simple)** one-way ticket *ou* single (*Brit*); **~ (et) retour (AR)** (*trajet*) round trip (*US*), return trip *ou* journey (*Brit*); (*billet*) round-trip (*US*) *ou* return (*Brit*) ticket ♦ *vi* (*gén*) to go; **~ à** (*convenir*) to suit; (*suj: forme, pointure etc*) to fit; **cela me va** (*couleur*) that suits me; (*vêtement*) that suits me; that fits me; (*projet, disposition*) that suits me, that's fine *ou* OK by me; **~ à la chasse/pêche** to go hunting/fishing; **~ avec** (*couleurs, style etc*) to go (well) with; **je vais le faire/me fâcher** I'm going to do it/to get angry; **~ voir/chercher qn** to go and see/look for sb; **comment allez-vous?** how are you?; **comment ça va?** how are you?; (*affaires etc*) how are things?; **ça va?** — **oui** (**ça va**)**!** how are things? — fine!; **ça va (comme ça)** that's fine (as it is); **il va bien/mal** he's well/ not well, he's fine/ill; **ça va bien/mal** (*affaires etc*) it's going well/not going well; **tout va bien** everything's fine; **ça ne va pas!** (*mauvaise humeur etc*) that won't do!, hey, come on!; **ça ne va pas sans difficultés** it's not without difficulties; **~ mieux** to be better; **il y va de leur vie** their lives are at stake; **se laisser ~** to let o.s. go; **s'en ~** *vi* (*partir*) to be off, go, leave; (*disparaître*) to go away; **~ jusqu'à** to go as far as; **ça va de soi, ça va sans dire** that goes without saying; **tu y vas un peu fort** you're going a bit (too) far; **allez!** go on!; come on!; **allons-y!** let's go!; **allez, au revoir** right *ou* OK then, bye-bye!

allergie [álerzhē] *nf* allergy.

allergique [álerzhēk] *a* allergic; **~ à** allergic to.

allez [álā] *vb voir* **aller**.

alliage [ályázh] *nm* alloy.

alliance [ályáṅs] *nf* (*MIL, POL*) alliance; (*mariage*) marriage; (*bague*) wedding ring; **neveu par ~** nephew by marriage.

allié, e [ályā] *nm/f* ally; **parents et ~s** relatives and relatives by marriage.

allier [ályā] *vt* (*métaux*) to alloy; (*POL, gén*) to ally; (*fig*) to combine; **s'~** to become allies; (*éléments, caractéristiques*) to combine; **s'~ à** to become allied to *ou* with.

alligator [álēgátor] *nm* alligator.

allitération [álētārâsyóṅ] *nf* alliteration.

allô [álō] *excl* hello, hallo.

allocataire [álokáter] *nm/f* beneficiary.

allocation [álokásyóṅ] *nf* allowance; **~ (de) chômage** unemployment benefit; **~ (de) logement** rent allowance; **~s familiales** ≈ family allowance *ou* subsidy; **~s de maternité** maternity allowance.

allocution [áloküsyóṅ] *nf* short speech.

allongé, e [álóṅzhā] *a* (*étendu*): **être ~** to be stretched out *ou* lying down; (*long*) long; (*étiré*) elongated; (*oblong*) oblong; **rester ~** to be lying down; **mine ~e** long face.

allonger [álóṅzhā] *vt* to lengthen, make longer; (*étendre: bras, jambe*) to stretch (out); (*sauce*) to spin out, make go further; **s'~** *vi* to get longer; (*se coucher*) to lie down, stretch out; **~ le pas** to hasten one's step(s).

allouer [álwā] *vt*: **~ qch à** to allocate sth to, allot sth to.

allumage [álümázh] *nm* (*AUTO*) ignition.

allume-cigare [álümsēgár] *nm inv* cigar lighter.

allume-gaz [álümgâz] *nm inv* gas lighter.

allumer [álümā] *vt* (*lampe, phare, radio*) to turn *ou* switch on; (*pièce*) to turn *ou* switch the light(s) on in; (*feu, bougie, cigare, pipe, gaz*) to light; (*chauffage*) to turn on; **s'~** *vi* (*lumière, lampe*) to come *ou* go on; **~ (la lumière** *ou* **l'électricité)** to turn on the light.

allumette [álümet] *nf* match; (*morceau de bois*) matchstick; (*CULIN*): **~ au fromage** cheese straw; **~ de sûreté** safety match.

allumeuse [álümœz] *nf* (*péj*) tease (*woman*).

allure [álür] *nf* (*vitesse*) speed; (*: à pied*) pace; (*démarche*) walk; (*maintien*) bearing; (*aspect, air*) look; **avoir de l'~** to have style *ou* a certain elegance; **à toute ~** at top *ou* full speed.

allusion [álüzyôň] *nf* allusion; (*sous-entendu*) hint; **faire ~ à** to allude *ou* refer to; to hint at.

alluvions [álüvyôň] *nfpl* alluvial deposits, alluvium *sg*.

almanach [álmáná] *nm* almanac.

aloès [áloes] *nm* (*BOT*) aloe.

aloi [álwá] *nm*: **de bon/mauvais ~** of genuine/doubtful worth *ou* quality.

alors [álor] *ad* then, at that time ♦ *cj* then, so; **~, Paul?** well, Paul?; **~? quoi de neuf?** well *ou* so? what's new?; **et ~?** and then (what)?; (*indifférence*) so?; **jusqu'~** up till *ou* until then; **ça ~!** well really!; **~ que** *cj* (*au moment où*) when, as; (*pendant que*) while, when; (*opposition*) whereas, while.

alouette [álwet] *nf* (sky)lark.

alourdir [áloordēr] *vt* to weigh down, make heavy; **s'~** *vi* to grow heavy *ou* heavier.

aloyau [álwàyō] *nm* sirloin.

alpaga [álpágá] *nm* (*tissu*) alpaca.

alpage [álpázh] *nm* high mountain pasture.

Alpes [álp(ə)] *nfpl*: **les ~** the Alps.

alpestre [álpestr(ə)] *a* alpine.

alphabet [álfábe] *nm* alphabet; (*livre*) ABC (book), primer.

alphabétique [álfábātēk] *a* alphabetic(al); **par ordre ~** in alphabetical order.

alphabétisation [álfábātēzâsyôň] *nf* literacy teaching.

alphabétiser [álfábátēzá] *vt* to teach to read and write; (*pays*) to eliminate illiteracy in.

alphanumérique [álfánümārēk] *a* alphanumeric.

alpin, e [álpaň, -ēn] *a* (*plante etc*) alpine; (*club*) climbing.

alpinisme [álpēnēsm(ə)] *nm* mountaineering, climbing.

alpiniste [álpēnēst(ə)] *nm/f* mountaineer, climber.

Alsace [álzás] *nf*: **l'~** Alsace.

alsacien, ne [álzásyaň, -en] *a* Alsatian.

altercation [álterkásyôň] *nf* altercation.

alter ego [álterāgō] *nm* alter ego.

altérer [áltārā] *vt* (*faits, vérité*) to falsify, distort; (*qualité*) to debase, impair; (*données*) to corrupt; (*donner soif à*) to make thirsty; **s'~** *vi* to deteriorate; to spoil.

alternance [álternâňs] *nf* alternation; **en ~** alternately; **formation en ~** work-study program (*US*), sandwich course (*Brit*).

alternateur [álternátœr] *nm* alternator.

alternatif, ive [álternátēf, -ēv] *a* alternating ♦ *nf* alternative.

alternativement [álternátēvmáň] *ad* alternately.

alterner [álternā] *vt* to alternate ♦ *vi*: **~ (avec)** to alternate (with); **(faire) ~ qch avec qch** to alternate sth with sth.

Altesse [áltes] *nf* Highness.

altier, ière [áltyā, -yer] *a* haughty.

altimètre [áltēmetr(ə)] *nm* altimeter.

altiport [áltēpor] *nm* mountain airfield.

altiste [áltēst(ə)] *nm/f* viola player, violist.

altitude [áltētüd] *nf* altitude, height; **à 1000 m d'~** at a height *ou* an altitude of 1000 m; **en ~** at high altitudes; **perdre/prendre de l'~** to lose/gain height; **voler à haute/basse ~** to fly at a high/low altitude.

alto [áltō] *nm* (*instrument*) viola ♦ *nf* (*contr*)alto.

altruisme [áltrüēsm(ə)] *nm* altruism.

altruiste [áltrüēst(ə)] *a* altruistic.

aluminium [álümēnyom] *nm* aluminum (*US*), aluminium (*Brit*).

alun [álœň] *nm* alum.

alunir [álünēr] *vi* to land on the moon.

alvéole [álváol] *nf* (*de ruche*) alveolus; **alvéolé, e** [álvâolā] *a* honeycombed.

AM *sigle f* = **assurance maladie**.

amabilité [ámábēlētā] *nf* kindness; **il a eu l'~ de** he was kind *ou* good enough to.

amadou [ámádōō] *nm* touchwood, amadou.

amadouer [ámádwā] *vt* to coax, cajole; (*adoucir*) to mollify, soothe.

amaigrir [ámāgrēr] *vt* to make thin *ou* thinner.

amaigrissant, e [ámāgrēsâň, -âňt] *a*: **régime ~** weight-reduction (*US*) *ou* slimming (*Brit*) diet.

amalgame [ámálgám] *nm* amalgam; (*fig: de gens, d'idées*) hotch-potch, mixture.

amalgamer [ámálgámā] *vt* to amalgamate.

amande [ámâňd] *nf* (*de l'amandier*) almond; (*de noyau de fruit*) kernel; **en ~** (*yeux*) almond *cpd*, almond-shaped.

amandier [ámâňdyā] *nm* almond (tree).

amant [ámâň] *nm* lover.

amarre [ámár] *nf* (*NAVIG*) (mooring) rope *ou* line; **~s** *nfpl* moorings.

amarrer [ámárā] *vt* (*NAVIG*) to moor; (*gén*) to make fast.

amaryllis [ámárēlēs] *nf* amaryllis.

amas [ámá] *nm* heap, pile.

amasser [ámâsā] *vt* to amass; **s'~** *vi* to pile up, accumulate; (*foule*) to gather.

amateur [ámátœr] *nm* amateur; **en ~** (*péj*) amateurishly; **musicien/sportif ~** amateur musician/sportsman; **~ de musique/sport** *etc* music/sports *etc* lover.

amateurisme [ámátœrēsm(ə)] *nm* amateurism; (*péj*) amateurishness.

Amazone [ámázon] *nf*: **l'~** the Amazon; **en a~** sidesaddle.

Amazonie [ámázonē] *nf*: **l'~** Amazonia.

ambages [âňbázh]: **sans ~** *ad* without beating about the bush, plainly.

ambassade [âňbásád] *nf* embassy; (*mission*): **en ~** on a mission.

ambassadeur, drice [âňbásádœr, -drēs] *nm/f* ambassador/ambassadress.

ambiance [âňbyâňs] *nf* atmosphere; **il y a de**

l'~ everyone's having a good time.
ambiant, e [ãṅbyãṅ, -ãṅt] *a* (*air, milieu*) surrounding; (*température*) ambient.
ambidextre [ãṅbēdɛkstr(ə)] *a* ambidextrous.
ambigu, ë [ãṅbēgü] *a* ambiguous.
ambiguïté [ãṅbēgüētã] *nf* ambiguousness *q*, ambiguity.
ambitieux, euse [ãṅbēsyœ̃, -œ̃z] *a* ambitious.
ambition [ãṅbēsyôṅ] *nf* ambition.
ambitionner [ãṅbēsyonã] *vt* to have as one's aim *ou* ambition.
ambivalent, e [ãṅbēvãlãṅ, -ãṅt] *a* ambivalent.
amble [ãṅbl(ə)] *nm*: **aller l'~** to amble.
ambre [ãṅbr(ə)] *nm*: **~ (jaune)** amber; **~ gris** ambergris.
ambré, e [ãṅbrã] *a* (*couleur*) amber; (*parfum*) ambergris-scented.
ambulance [ãṅbülãṅs] *nf* ambulance.
ambulancier, ière [ãṅbülãṅsyã, -yɛr] paramedic (*US*), ambulanceman/woman (*Brit*).
ambulant, e [ãṅbülãṅ, -ãṅt] *a* traveling (*US*), travelling (*Brit*), itinerant.
âme [ãm] *nf* soul; **rendre l'~** to give up the ghost; **bonne ~** (*aussi ironique*) kind soul; **un joueur/tricheur dans l'~** a gambler/cheat through and through; **~ sœur** kindred spirit.
amélioration [ãmãlyorãsyôṅ] *nf* improvement.
améliorer [ãmãlyorã] *vt* to improve; **s'~** *vi* to improve, get better.
aménagement [ãmãnãzhmãṅ] *nm* fitting out; laying out; development; **~s** *nmpl* developments; **l'~ du territoire** ≈ town and country planning; **~s fiscaux** tax adjustments.
aménager [ãmãnãzhã] *vt* (*agencer: espace, local*) to fit out; (: *terrain*) to lay out; (: *quartier, territoire*) to develop; (*installer*) to fix up, put in; **ferme aménagée** converted farmhouse.
amende [ãmãṅd] *nf* fine; **mettre à l'~** to penalize; **faire ~ honorable** to make amends.
amendement [ãmãṅdmãṅ] *nm* (*JUR*) amendment.
amender [ãmãṅdã] *vt* (*loi*) to amend; (*terre*) to enrich; **s'~** *vi* to mend one's ways.
amène [ãmɛn] *a* affable; **peu ~** unkind.
amener [ãmnã] *vt* to bring; (*causer*) to bring about; (*baisser: drapeau, voiles*) to strike; **s'~** *vi* (*fam*) to show up, turn up; **~ qn à qch/à faire** to lead sb to sth/to do.
amenuiser [ãmənüczã]: **s'~** *vi* to dwindle; (*chances*) to grow slimmer, lessen.
amer, amère [ãmɛr] *a* bitter.
amèrement [ãmɛrmãṅ] *ad* bitterly.
américain, e [ãmãrēkãṅ, -ɛn] *a* American ♦ *nm* (*LING*) American (English) ♦ *nm/f*: **A~, e** American; **en vedette ~e** as a special guest (star).
américaniser [ãmãrēkãnēzã] *vt* to Americanize.
américanisme [ãmãrēkãnēsm(ə)] *nm* Americanism.
amérindien, ne [ãmãrãṅdyãṅ, -ɛn] *a* Amerindian, American Indian.
Amérique [ãmãrēk] *nf* America; **l'~ centrale** Central America; **l'~ latine** Latin America; **l'~ du Nord** North America; **l'~ du Sud** South America.
amerloque [ãmɛrlok] *n* (*péj*) Yank, Yankee.
amerrir [ãmãrēr] *vi* to land (on the sea);

(*capsule spatiale*) to splash down.
amerrissage [ãmãrēsãzh] *nm* landing (on the sea); splash-down.
amertume [ãmɛrtüm] *nf* bitterness.
améthyste [ãmãtɛst(ə)] *nf* amethyst.
ameublement [ãmœblэmãṅ] *nm* furnishing; (*meubles*) furniture; **articles d'~** furnishings; **tissus d'~** home furnishings, upholstery fabrics.
ameuter [ãmœtã] *vt* (*badauds*) to draw a crowd of; (*peuple*) to rouse, stir up.
ami, e [ãmē] *nm/f* friend; (*amant/maitresse*) boyfriend/girlfriend ♦ *a*: **pays/groupe ~** friendly country/group; **être (très) ~ avec qn** to be (very) friendly with sb; **être ~ de l'ordre** to be a lover of order; **un ~ des arts** a patron of the arts; **un ~ des chiens** a dog lover; **petit ~/petite ~e** (*fam*) boyfriend/girlfriend.
amiable [ãmyãbl(ə)]: **à l'~** *ad* (*JUR*) out of court; (*gén*) amicably.
amiante [ãmyãṅt] *nm* asbestos.
amibe [ãmēb] *nf* amoeba (*pl* -ae).
amical, e, aux [ãmēkãl, -ō] *a* friendly ♦ *nf* (*club*) association.
amicalement [ãmēkãlmãṅ] *ad* in a friendly way; (*formule épistolaire*) regards.
amidon [ãmēdôṅ] *nm* starch.
amidonner [ãmēdonã] *vt* to starch.
amincir [ãmãṅsēr] *vt* (*objet*) to thin (down); **s'~** *vi* to get thinner *ou* slimmer; **~ qn** to make sb thinner *ou* slimmer.
aminé, e [ãmēnã] *a*: **acide ~** amino acid.
amiral, aux [ãmērãl, -ō] *nm* admiral.
amirauté [ãmērōtã] *nf* admiralty.
amitié [ãmētyã] *nf* friendship; **prendre en ~** to take a liking to; **faire ou présenter ses ~s à qn** to send sb one's best wishes; **~s** (*formule épistolaire*) (with) best wishes.
ammoniac [ãmonyãk] *nm*: **(gaz) ~** ammonia.
ammoniaque [ãmonyãk] *nf* ammonia (water).
amnésie [ãmnãzē] *nf* amnesia.
amniocentèse [ãmnyōsãntez] *nf* amniocentesis.
amnistie [ãmnēstē] *nf* amnesty.
amnistier [ãmnēstyã] *vt* to amnesty.
amoindrir [ãmwãṅdrēr] *vt* to reduce.
amollir [ãmolēr] *vt* to soften.
amonceler [ãmôṅslã] *vt*, **s'~** *vi* to pile *ou* heap up; (*fig*) to accumulate.
amoncellement [ãmôṅsɛlmãṅ] *nm* piling *ou* heaping up; accumulation; (*tas*) pile, heap; accumulation.
amont [ãmôṅ]: **en ~** *ad* upstream; (*sur une pente*) uphill; **en ~ de** *prép* upstream from; uphill from, above.
amoral, e, aux [ãmorãl, -ō] *a* amoral.
amorce [ãmors(ə)] *nf* (*sur un hameçon*) bait; (*explosif*) cap; (*tube*) primer; (: *contenu*) priming; (*fig: début*) beginning(s), start.
amorcer [ãmorsã] *vt* to bait; to prime; (*commencer*) to begin, start.
amorphe [ãmorf(ə)] *a* passive, lifeless.
amortir [ãmortēr] *vt* (*atténuer: choc*) to absorb, cushion; (*bruit, douleur*) to deaden; (*COMM: dette*) to pay off, amortize; (: *mise de fonds, matériel*) to write off; **~ un abonnement** to make a season ticket pay (for itself).

amortissable [àmortēsábl(ə)] *a* (*COMM*) that can be paid off.

amortissement [àmortēsmáñ] *nm* (*de matériel*) writing off; (*d'une dette*) paying off.

amortisseur [àmortēscœr] *nm* shock absorber.

amour [àmoor] *nm* love; (*liaison*) love affair, love; (*statuette etc*) cupid; **un ~ de** a lovely little; **faire l'~** to make love.

amouracher [àmooráshā]: **s'~ de** *vt* (*péj*) to become infatuated with.

amourette [àmooret] *nf* passing fancy.

amoureusement [àmoorœzmáñ] *ad* lovingly.

amoureux, euse [àmoorœ̄, -œ̄z] *a* (*regard, tempérament*) amorous; (*vie, problèmes*) love *cpd*; (*personne*): **~ (de qn)** in love (with sb) ♦ *nm/f* lover ♦ *nmpl* courting couple(s); **tomber ~ de qn** to fall in love with sb; **être ~ de qch** to be passionately fond of sth; **un ~ de la nature** a nature lover.

amour-propre, *pl* **amours-propres** [àmoorpropr(ə)] *nm* self-esteem.

amovible [àmovēbl(ə)] *a* removable, detachable.

ampère [àñper] *nm* amp(ere).

ampèremètre [àñpermetr(ə)] *nm* ammeter.

amphétamine [àñfàtàmēn] *nf* amphetamine.

amphi [àñfē] *nm* (*SCOL fam*: = *amphithéâtre*) lecture hall *ou* theater.

amphibie [àñfēbē] *a* amphibious.

amphibien [àñfēbyañ] *nm* (*ZOOL*) amphibian.

amphithéâtre [àñfētàâtr(ə)] *nm* amphitheater (*US*), amphitheatre (*Brit*); (*d'université*) lecture hall, auditorium.

amphore [àñfor] *nf* amphora.

ample [àñpl(ə)] *a* (*vêtement*) roomy, ample; (*gestes, mouvement*) broad; (*ressources*) ample; **jusqu'à plus ~ informé** (*ADMIN*) until further details are available.

amplement [àñpləmáñ] *ad* amply; **~ suffisant** ample, more than enough.

ampleur [àñplœr] *nf* scale, size; extent, magnitude.

ampli [àñplē] *nm* (*fam*: = *amplificateur*) amplifier, amp.

amplificateur [àñplēfēkàtœr] *nm* amplifier.

amplification [àñplēfēkàsyóñ] *nf* amplification; expansion, increase.

amplifier [àñplēfyá] *vt* (*son, oscillation*) to amplify; (*fig*) to expand, increase.

amplitude [àñplētūd] *nf* amplitude; (*des températures*) range.

ampoule [àñpool] *nf* (*électrique*) bulb; (*de médicament*) phial; (*aux mains, pieds*) blister.

ampoulé, e [àñpoolā] *a* (*péj*) pompous, bombastic.

amputation [àñpütàsyóñ] *nf* amputation.

amputer [àñpütá] *vt* (*MÉD*) to amputate; (*fig*) to cut *ou* reduce drastically; **~ qn d'un bras/pied** to amputate sb's arm/foot.

Amsterdam [àmsterdàm] *n* Amsterdam.

amulette [àmület] *nf* amulet.

amusant, e [àmüzáñ, -áñt] *a* (*divertissant, spirituel*) entertaining, amusing; (*comique*) funny, amusing.

amusé, e [àmüzá] *a* amused.

amuse-gueule [àmüzgœl] *nm inv* appetizer, snack.

amusement [àmüzmáñ] *nm* (*voir amusé*)

amusement; (*voir amuser*) entertaining, amusing; (*jeu etc*) pastime, diversion.

amuser [àmüzá] *vt* (*divertir*) to entertain, amuse; (*égayer, faire rire*) to amuse; (*détourner l'attention de*) to distract; **s'~** *vi* (*jouer*) to amuse o.s., play; (*se divertir*) to enjoy o.s., have fun; (*fig*) to mess around; **s'~ de qch** (*trouver comique*) to find sth amusing; **s'~ avec** *ou* **de qn** (*duper*) to make a fool of sb.

amusette [àmüzet] *nf* idle pleasure, trivial pastime.

amuseur [àmüzœr] *nm* entertainer; (*péj*) clown.

amygdale [àmēdál] *nf* tonsil; **opérer qn des ~s** to take sb's tonsils out.

amygdalite [àmēdálēt] *nf* tonsillitis.

AN *sigle f* = **Assemblée nationale.**

an [áñ] *nm* year; **être âgé de** *ou* **avoir 3 ~s** to be 3 (years old); **en l'~ 1980** in the year 1980; **le jour de l'~, le premier de l'~, le nouvel ~** New Year's Day.

anabolisant [ànábolēzáñ] *nm* anabolic steroid.

anachronique [ànákronēk] *a* anachronistic.

anachronisme [ànákronēsm(ə)] *nm* anachronism.

anaconda [ànákóñdà] *nm* (*ZOOL*) anaconda.

anagramme [ànàgràm] *nf* anagram.

ANAH *sigle f* = *Agence nationale pour l'amélioration de l'habitat.*

anal, e, aux [ànál, -ō] *a* anal.

analgésique [ànálzhàzēk] *nm* analgesic.

anallergique [ànálerzhēk] *a* hypoallergenic.

analogie [ànàlozhē] *nf* analogy.

analogique [ànàlozhēk] *a* (*LOGIQUE*: *raisonnement*) analogical; (*calculateur, montre etc*) analog (*US*), analogue (*Brit*); (*INFORM*) analog.

analogue [ànàlog] *a*: **~ (à)** analogous (to), similar (to).

analphabète [ànálfàbet] *nm/f* illiterate.

analphabétisme [ànálfàbàtēsm(ə)] *nm* illiteracy.

analyse [ànàlēz] *nf* analysis; (*MÉD*) test; **faire l'~ de** to analyze (*US*), analyse (*Brit*); **une ~ approfondie** an in-depth analysis; **en dernière ~** in the last analysis; **avoir l'esprit d'~** to have an analytical turn of mind; **~ grammaticale** grammatical analysis, parsing (*SCOL*).

analyser [ànàlēzá] *vt* to analyze (*US*), analyse (*Brit*); (*MÉD*) to test.

analyste [ànàlēst(ə)] *nm/f* analyst; (*psychanalyste*) (psycho)analyst.

analyste-programmeur, euse, *pl* **analystes-programmeurs, euses** [ànàlēstprográmœr, -œ̄z] *nm/f* systems analyst.

analytique [ànàlētēk] *a* analytical.

analytiquement [ànàlētēkmáñ] *ad* analytically.

ananas [ànàná] *nm* pineapple.

anarchie [ànàrshē] *nf* anarchy.

anarchique [ànàrshēk] *a* anarchic.

anarchisme [ànàrshēsm(ə)] *nm* anarchism.

anarchiste [ànàrshēst(ə)] *a* anarchistic ♦ *nm/f* anarchist.

anathème [ànàtem] *nm*: **jeter l'~ sur, lancer l'~ contre** to anathematize, curse.

anatomie [ànàtomē] *nf* anatomy.

anatomique [ánátomēk] *a* anatomical.

ancestral, e, aux [áṅsestrál, -ō] *a* ancestral.

ancêtre [áṅsetr(ə)] *nm/f* ancestor; (*fig*): **l'~ de** the forerunner of.

anche [áṅsh] *nf* reed.

anchois [áṅshwá] *nm* anchovy.

ancien, ne [áṅsyaṅ, -en] *a* old; (*de jadis, de l'antiquité*) ancient; (*précédent, ex-*) former, old ♦ *nm* (*mobilier ancien*): **l'~** antiques *pl* ♦ *nm/f* (*dans une tribu etc*) elder; **un ~ ministre** a former minister; **mon ~ne voiture** my previous car; **être plus ~ que qn dans une maison** to have been in a firm longer than sb; (*dans l'hiérarchie*) to be senior to sb in a firm; **~ combattant** ex-serviceman; **~ (élève)** (*SCOL*) alumnus (*US*), ex-pupil (*Brit*).

anciennement [áṅsyenmáṅ] *ad* formerly.

ancienneté [áṅsyentá] *nf* oldness; antiquity; (*ADMIN*) (length of) service; seniority.

ancrage [áṅkrázh] *nm* anchoring; (*NAVIG*) anchorage; (*CONSTR*) anchor.

ancre [áṅkr(ə)] *nf* anchor; **jeter/lever l'~** to cast/weigh anchor; **à l'~** at anchor.

ancrer [áṅkɪá] *vt* (*CONSTR*) to anchor; (*fig*) to fix firmly; **s'~** *vi* (*NAVIG*) to (cast) anchor.

andalou, ouse [áṅdálōō, -ōōz] *a* Andalusian.

Andalousie [áṅdálōōzē] *nf*: **l'~** Andalusia.

andante [áṅdáṅt] *ad, nm* andante.

Andes [áṅd] *nfpl*: **les ~** the Andes.

Andorre [áṅdor] *n* Andorra.

andouille [áṅdōōy] *nf* (*CULIN*) sausage made of chitterlings; (*fam*) dope, knucklehead (*US*).

andouillette [áṅdōōyet] *nf* small andouille.

âne [ân] *nm* donkey, ass; (*péj*) dunce, fool.

anéantir [ánááṅtēr] *vt* to annihilate, wipe out; (*fig*) to obliterate, destroy; (*déprimer*) to overwhelm.

anecdote [ánekdot] *nf* anecdote.

anecdotique [ánekdotēk] *a* anecdotal.

anémie [ánámē] *nf* anemia (*US*), anaemia (*Brit*).

anémié, e [ánámyá] *a* anemic (*US*), anaemic (*Brit*); (*fig*) enfeebled.

anémique [ánámēk] *a* anemic (*US*), anaemic (*Brit*).

anémone [ánámon] *nf* anemone; **~ de mer** sea anemone.

ânerie [ânrē] *nf* stupidity; (*parole etc*) stupid *ou* idiotic comment *etc*.

anéroïde [ánároēd] *a voir* **baromètre**.

ânesse [ânes] *nf* she-ass.

anesthésie [ánestázē] *nf* anesthesia (*US*), anaesthesia (*Brit*); **sous ~** under anesthetic; **~ générale/locale** general/local anesthetic; **faire une ~ locale à qn** to give sb a local anesthetic.

anesthésier [ánestázyá] *vt* to anesthetize (*US*), anaesthetize (*Brit*).

anesthésique [ánestázēk] *a* anesthetic (*US*), anaesthetic (*Brit*).

anesthésiste [ánestázēst(ə)] *nm/f* anesthesiologist (*US*), anaesthetist (*Brit*).

anfractuosité [áṅfráktüōzētá] *nf* crevice.

ange [áṅzh] *nm* angel; **être aux ~s** to be in seventh heaven; **~ gardien** guardian angel.

angélique [áṅzhālēk] *a* angelic(al) ♦ *nf* angelica.

angelot [áṅzhlō] *nm* cherub.

angélus [áṅzhālüs] *nm* angelus; (*cloches*) evening bells *pl*.

angevin, e [áṅzhvaṅ, -ēn] *a* of *ou* from Anjou; of *ou* from Angers.

angine [áṅzhēn] *nf* sore throat, throat infection; **~ de poitrine** angina (pectoris).

angiome [áṅzhyōm] *nm* angioma.

anglais, e [áṅgle, -ez] *a* English ♦ *nm* (*LING*) English ♦ *nm/f*: **A~, e** Englishman/woman; **les A~** the English; **filer à l'~e** to take French leave; **à l'~e** (*CULIN*) boiled.

anglaises [áṅglez] *nfpl* (*cheveux*) ringlets.

angle [áṅgl(ə)] *nm* angle; (*coin*) corner; **~ droit/obtus/aigu/mort** right/obtuse/acute/dead angle.

Angleterre [áṅglətɛr] *nf*: **l'~** England.

anglican, e [áṅglēkáṅ, -áṅ] *a, nm/f* Anglican.

anglicisme [áṅglēsēsm(ə)] *nm* anglicism.

angliciste [áṅglēsēst(ə)] *nm/f* English scholar; (*étudiant*) student of English.

anglo... [áṅglo] *préfixe* Anglo-, anglo(-).

anglo-américain, e [áṅgloámārēkaṅ, -en] *a* Anglo-American ♦ *nm* (*LING*) American English.

anglo-arabe [áṅgloáráb] *a* Anglo-Arab.

anglo-canadien, ne [áṅglokánádyaṅ, -en] *a* Anglo-Canadian ♦ *nm* (*LING*) Canadian English.

anglo-normand, e [áṅglonormáṅ, -áṅd] *a* Anglo-Norman; **les îles ~es** the Channel Islands.

anglophile [áṅglofēl] *a* anglophilic.

anglophobe [áṅglofob] *a* anglophobic.

anglophone [áṅglofon] *a* English-speaking.

anglo-saxon, ne [áṅglosáksóṅ, -on] *a* Anglo-Saxon.

angoissant, e [áṅgwásáṅ, -áṅt] *a* harrowing.

angoisse [áṅgwás] *nf*: **l'~** anguish *q*.

angoissé, e [áṅgwásá] *a* anguished; (*personne*) full of anxieties *ou* hang-ups (*fam*).

angoisser [áṅgwásá] *vt* to harrow, cause anguish to ♦ *vi* to worry, fret.

Angola [áṅgolá] *nm*: **l'~** Angola.

angolais, e [áṅgole, -ez] *a* Angolan.

angora [áṅgorá] *a, nm* angora.

anguille [áṅgēy] *nf* eel; **~ de mer** conger (eel); **il y a ~ sous roche** (*fig*) there's something going on, there's something beneath all this.

angulaire [áṅgüler] *a* angular.

anguleux, euse [áṅgülœ, -œz] *a* angular.

anicroche [ánēkrosh] *nf* hitch, snag.

animal, e, aux [ánēmál, -ō] *a, nm* animal; **~ domestique/sauvage** domestic/wild animal.

animalier [ánēmályá] *a*: **peintre ~** animal painter.

animateur, trice [ánēmátœr, -trēs] *nm/f* (*de télévision*) host; (*de music-hall*) MC, emcee (*US*), compère (*Brit*); (*de groupe*) leader, organizer; (*CINÉMA*: *technicien*) animator.

animation [ánēmásyóṅ] *nf* (*voir animé*) busyness; liveliness; (*CINÉMA*: *technique*) animation; (*activité*): **~s** activities; **centre d'~** ≈ community center.

animé, e [ánēmá] *a* (*rue, lieu*) busy, lively; (*conversation, réunion*) lively, animated; (*opposé à inanimé, aussi LING*) animate.

animer [ánēmá] *vt* (*ville, soirée*) to liven up,

enliven; (mettre en mouvement) to drive; (stimuler) to drive, impel; **s'~** vi to liven up, come to life.

animosité [ánēmōzētā] nf animosity.

anis [ánē] nm (CULIN) aniseed; (BOT) anise.

anisette [ánēzet] nf anisette.

Ankara [áṅkárá] n Ankara.

ankyloser [áṅkēlōzā]: **s'~** vi to get stiff, ankylose.

annales [ánál] nfpl annals.

anneau, x [ánō] nm ring; (de chaîne) link; (SPORT): **exercices aux ~x** ring exercises.

année [ánā] nf year; **souhaiter la bonne ~ à qn** to wish sb a Happy New Year; **tout au long de l'~** all year long; **d'une ~ à l'autre** from one year to the next; **d'~ en ~** from year to year; **l'~ scolaire/fiscale** the school/tax year.

année-lumière, pl **années-lumières** [ánālümyer] nf light year.

annexe [áneks(ə)] a (problème) related; (document) appended; (salle) adjoining ♦ nf (bâtiment) annex(e); (de document, ouvrage) annex, appendix; (jointe à une lettre, un dossier) enclosure.

annexer [áneksā] vt to annex; **s'~** (pays) to annex; **~ qch à** (joindre) to append sth to.

annexion [áneksyōṅ] nf annexation.

annihiler [ánēēlā] vt to annihilate.

anniversaire [ánēverser] nm birthday; (d'un événement, bâtiment) anniversary ♦ a: **jour ~** anniversary.

annonce [ánōṅs] nf announcement; (signe, indice) sign; (aussi: **~ publicitaire**) advertisement; (CARTES) declaration; **~ personnelle** personal message; **les petites ~s** the want (US) ou classified ads.

annoncer [ánōṅsā] vt to announce; (être le signe de) to herald; (CARTES) to declare; **je vous annonce que ...** I wish to tell you that ...; **s'~ bien/difficile** to look promising/difficult; **~ la couleur** (fig) to lay one's cards on the table.

annonceur, euse [ánōṅscœr, -œz] nm/f (TV, RADIO: speaker) announcer; (publicitaire) advertiser.

annonciateur, trice [ánōṅsyátœr, -trēs] a: **~ d'un événement** presaging an event.

Annonciation [ánōṅsyâsyōṅ] nf: **l'~** (REL) the Annunciation; (jour) Annunciation Day.

annotation [ánotâsyōṅ] nf annotation.

annoter [ánotā] vt to annotate.

annuaire [ánüer] nm yearbook, annual; **~ téléphonique** (telephone) directory, phone book.

annuel, le [ánüel] a annual, yearly.

annuellement [ánüelmáṅ] ad annually, yearly.

annuité [ánüētā] nf annual installment.

annulaire [ánüler] nm ring finger, fourth (US) ou third (Brit) finger.

annulation [ánülâsyōṅ] nf cancellation; annulment; repeal (US), quashing (Brit).

annuler [ánülā] vt (rendez-vous, voyage) to cancel, call off; (mariage) to annul; (jugement) to repeal (US), quash (Brit); (résultats) to declare void; (MATH, PHYSIQUE) to cancel out; **s'~** to cancel each other out.

anoblir [ánoblēr] vt to ennoble.

anode [ánod] nf anode.

anodin, e [ánodaṅ, -ēn] a harmless; (sans importance) insignificant, trivial.

anomalie [ánomálē] nf anomaly.

ânon [ánôṅ] nm baby donkey; (petit âne) little donkey.

ânonner [ánonā] vi, vt to read in a drone; (hésiter) to read in a fumbling manner.

anonymat [ánonēmā] nm anonymity; **garder l'~** to remain anonymous.

anonyme [ánonēm] a anonymous; (fig) impersonal.

anonymement [ánonēmmáṅ] ad anonymously.

anorak [ánorák] nm anorak.

anorexie [ánoreksē] nf anorexia.

anormal, e, aux [ánormál, -ō] a abnormal; (insolite) unusual, abnormal.

anormalement [ánormálmáṅ] ad abnormally; unusually.

ANPE sigle f (= Agence nationale pour l'emploi) national employment agency (functions include job creation).

anse [áṅs] nf handle; (GÉO) cove.

antagonisme [áṅtágonēsm(ə)] nm antagonism.

antagoniste [áṅtágonēst(ə)] a antagonistic ♦ nm antagonist.

antan [áṅtáṅ] nm: **d'~** a of yesteryear, of long ago.

antarctique [áṅtárktēk] a Antarctic ♦ nm: **l'A~** the Antarctic; **le cercle A~** the Antarctic Circle; **l'océan A~** the Antarctic Ocean.

antécédent [áṅtāsādáṅ] nm (LING) antecedent; **~s** nmpl (MÉD etc) past history sg; **~s professionnels** record, career to date.

antédiluvien, ne [áṅtādēlüvyáṅ, -en] a (fig) ancient, antediluvian.

antenne [áṅten] nf (de radio, télévision) aerial; (d'insecte) antenna (pl -ae), feeler; (poste avancé) outpost; (petite succursale) sub-branch; **sur l'~** on the air; **passer à/avoir l'~** to go/be on the air; **2 heures d'~** 2 hours' broadcasting time; **hors ~** off the air; **~ chirurgicale** (MIL) advance surgical unit.

antépénultième [áṅtāpānültyem] a antepenultimate.

antérieur, e [áṅtāryœr] a (d'avant) previous, earlier; (de devant) front; **~ à** prior ou previous to; **passé/futur ~** (LING) past/future anterior.

antérieurement [áṅtāryœrmáṅ] ad earlier; (précédemment) previously; **~ à** prior ou previous to.

antériorité [áṅtāryorētā] nf precedence (in time).

anthologie [áṅtolozhē] nf anthology.

anthracite [áṅtrásēt] nm anthracite ♦ a: **(gris) ~ charcoal** (gray).

anthropologie [áṅtropolozhē] nf anthropology.

anthropologue [áṅtropolog] nm/f anthropologist.

anthropomorphisme [áṅtropomorfēsm(ə)] nm anthropomorphism.

anthropophagie [áṅtropofázhē] nf cannibalism, anthropophagy.

anti... [áṅtē] préfixe anti....

antiaérien, ne [áṅtēāáryáṅ, -en] a antiaircraft; **abri ~** air-raid shelter.

antialcoolique [àṅtēálkolēk] *a* anti-alcohol; **ligue** ~ temperance league.

antiatomique [àṅtēátomēk] *a*: **abri** ~ fallout shelter.

antibiotique [àṅtēbyotēk] *nm* antibiotic.

antibrouillard [àṅtēbrōōyár] *a*: **phare** ~ fog light.

antibruit [àṅtēbrüē] *a inv*: **mur** ~ (*sur autoroute*) sound-muffling wall.

antibuée [àṅtēbüā] *a inv*: **dispositif** ~ defogger (*US*), demister (*Brit*); **bombe** ~ antifog (*US*) ou demister (*Brit*) spray.

anticancéreux, euse [àṅtēkáṅsārōē, -ōēz] *a* cancer *cpd*.

anticasseur(s) [àṅtēkásœr] *a*: **loi/mesure** ~ law/measure against damage done by demonstrators.

antichambre [àṅtēshàṅbr(ə)] *nf* antechamber, anteroom; **faire** ~ to wait (for an audience).

antichar [àṅtēshár] *a* anti-tank.

antichoc [àṅtēshok] *a* shockproof.

anticipation [àṅtēsēpâsyôṅ] *nf* anticipation; (*COMM*) payment in advance; **par** ~ in anticipation, in advance; **livre/film d'**~ science fiction book/film.

anticipé, e [àṅtēsēpā] *a* (*règlement, paiement*) early, in advance; (*joie etc*) anticipated, early; **avec mes remerciements** ~**s** thanking you in advance ou anticipation.

anticiper [àṅtēsēpā] *vt* to anticipate, foresee; (*paiement*) to pay ou make in advance ♦ *vi* to look ou think ahead; (*en racontant*) to jump ahead; (*prévoir*) to anticipate; ~ **sur** to anticipate.

anticlérical, e, aux [àṅtēklārēkál, -ō] *a* anticlerical.

anticoagulant, e [àṅtēkoágülàṅ, -àṅt] *a*, *nm* anticoagulant.

anticonceptionnel, le [àṅtēkôṅsepsyonel] *a* contraceptive.

anticonformisme [àṅtēkôṅformēsm(ə)] *nm* nonconformism.

anticonstitutionnel, le [àṅtēkôṅstētüsyonel] *a* unconstitutional.

anticorps [àṅtēkor] *nm* antibody.

anticyclone [àṅtēsēklôn] *nm* anticyclone.

antidater [àṅtēdátá] *vt* to backdate, predate.

antidémocratique [àṅtēdāmokrátēk] *a* antidemocratic; (*peu démocratique*) undemocratic.

antidérapant, e [àṅtēdárápàṅ, -àṅt] *a* nonskid.

antidopage [àṅtēdopázh], **antidoping** [àṅtēdopēng] *a* (*lutte*) against drugs; (*contrôle*) drug *cpd*.

antidote [àṅtēdot] *nm* antidote.

antienne [àṅtyen] *nf* (*fig*) chant, refrain.

antigang [àṅtēgàṅg] *a inv*: **brigade** ~ commando unit.

antigel [àṅtēzhel] *nm* antifreeze.

antigène [àṅtēzhen] *nm* antigen.

antigouvernemental, e, aux [àṅtēgōōvernəmàṅtál, -ō] *a* anti-government.

Antigua et Barbude [àṅtēgáábàrbüd] *nf* Antigua and Barbuda.

antihistaminique [àṅtēēstámēnēk] *nm* antihistamine.

anti-inflammatoire [àṅtēàṅflàmàtwár] *a* anti-inflammatory.

anti-inflationniste [àṅtēàṅflâsyonēst(ə)] *a* anti-inflationary.

antillais, e [àṅtēyē, -ez] *a* West Indian.

Antilles [àṅtēy] *nfpl*: **les** ~ the West Indies; **les Grandes/Petites** ~ the Greater/Lesser Antilles.

antilope [àṅtēlop] *nf* antelope.

antimilitariste [àṅtēmēlētárēst(ə)] *a* antimilitarist.

antimissile [àṅtēmēsēl] *a* antimissile.

antimite(s) [àṅtēmēt] *a*, *nm*: (**produit**) ~ mothproofer, moth repellent.

antinucléaire [àṅtēnüklāer] *a* antinuclear.

antioxydant [àṅtēoksēdàṅ] *nm* antioxidant.

antiparasite [àṅtēpárázēt] *a* (*RADIO, TV*) anti-interference; **dispositif** ~ suppressor.

antipathie [àṅtēpátē] *nf* antipathy.

antipathique [àṅtēpátēk] *a* unpleasant, disagreeable.

antipelliculaire [àṅtēpālēküler] *a* antidandruff.

antiphrase [àṅtēfráz] *nf*: **par** ~ ironically.

antipodes [àṅtēpod] *nmpl* (*GÉO*): **les** ~ the antipodes; (*fig*): **être aux** ~ **de** to be the opposite extreme of.

antipoison [àṅtēpwázôṅ] *a inv*: **centre** ~ poison control center.

antipoliomyélitique [àṅtēpolyomyālētēk] *a* polio *cpd*.

antiprotectionniste [àṅtēproteksyonēst(ə)] *a* free-trade.

antiquaire [àṅtēker] *nm/f* antique dealer.

antique [àṅtēk] *a* antique; (*très vieux*) ancient, antiquated.

antiquité [àṅtēkētā] *nf* (*objet*) antique; **l'A**~ Antiquity; **magasin/marchand d'**~**s** antique shop/dealer.

antirabique [àṅtērábēk] *a* rabies *cpd*.

antiraciste [àṅtērásēst(ə)] *a* antiracist, anti-racialist.

antirépublicain, e [àṅtērāpüblēkaṅ, -en] *a* antirepublican.

antirides [àṅtērēd] *a* (*crème*) anti-wrinkle.

antirouille [àṅtērōōy] *a inv*: **peinture** ~ antirust paint; **traitement** ~ rustproofing.

antisémite [àṅtēsāmēt] *a* anti-semitic.

antisémitisme [àṅtēsāmētēsm(ə)] *nm* anti-semitism.

antiseptique [àṅtēseptēk] *a*, *nm* antiseptic.

antisocial, e, aux [àṅtēsosyál, -ō] *a* antisocial.

antisportif, ive [àṅtēsportēf, -ēv] *a* unsporting; (*hostile au sport*) against sport, anti-sport.

antitétanique [àṅtētātánēk] *a* tetanus *cpd*.

antithèse [àṅtētez] *nf* antithesis.

antitrust [àṅtētrœst] *a inv* (*loi, mesures*) anti-trust (*US*), anti-monopoly (*Brit*).

antituberculeux, euse [àṅtētüberkülōē, -ōēz] *a* tuberculosis *cpd*.

antitussif, ive [àṅtētüsēf, -ēv] *a* antitussive, cough *cpd*.

antivariolique [àṅtēváryolēk] *a* smallpox *cpd*.

antivol [àṅtēvol] *a*, *nm*: (**dispositif**) ~ antitheft device; (*pour vélo*) padlock.

antonyme [àṅtonēm] *nm* antonym.

antre [àṅtr(ə)] *nm* den, lair.

anus [ánüs] *nm* anus.

Anvers [àṅver] *n* Antwerp.

anxiété [áṅksyátā] *nf* anxiety.

anxieusement [áṅksyēēzmáṅ] *ad* anxiously)

anxieux, euse [ăŋksyœ̃, -œ̃z] a anxious, worried; **être ~ de faire** to be anxious to do.

AOC sigle f (= Appellation d'origine contrôlée) guarantee of quality of wine.

aorte [ăort(ə)] nf aorta.

août [oo] nm August; voir aussi **juillet**.

aoûtien, ne [ăoosyaŋ, -en] nm/f August vacationer (US) ou holiday-maker (Brit).

AP sigle f = **Assistance publique**.

apaisement [ăpezmăŋ] nm calming; soothing; (aussi POL) appeasement; **~s** nmpl soothing reassurances; (pour calmer) pacifying words.

apaiser [ăpāzā] vt (colère) to calm, quell, soothe; (faim) to appease, assuage; (douleur) to soothe; (personne) to calm (down), pacify; **s'~** vi (tempête, bruit) to die down, subside.

apanage [ăpánázh] nm: **être l'~ de** to be the privilege ou prerogative of.

aparté [ăpártā] nm (THÉÂTRE) aside; (entretien) private conversation; **en ~** ad in an aside; (entretien) in private.

apartheid [ăpárted] nm apartheid.

apathie [ăpătē] nf apathy.

apathique [ăpátēk] a apathetic.

apatride [ăpátrēd] nm/f stateless person.

Apennins [ăpenaŋ] nmpl: **les ~** the Apennines.

apercevoir [ăpersəvwár] vt to see; **s'~ de** vt to notice; **s'~ que** to notice that; **sans s'en ~** without realizing ou noticing.

aperçu, e [ăpersü] pp de **apercevoir** ♦ nm (vue d'ensemble) general survey; (intuition) insight.

apéritif, ive [ăpārētēf, -ēv] a which stimulates the appetite ♦ nm (boisson) aperitif; (réunion) (pre-lunch ou -dinner) drinks pl; **prendre l'~** to have drinks (before lunch ou dinner) ou an aperitif.

apesanteur [ăpozăntœr] nf weightlessness.

à-peu-près [ăpœpre] nm inv (péj) vague approximation.

apeuré, e [ăpœrā] a frightened, scared.

aphone [ăfon] a voiceless.

aphorisme [ăforēsm(ə)] nm aphorism.

aphrodisiaque [ăfrodēzyák] a, nm aphrodisiac.

aphte [ăft(ə)] nm mouth ulcer.

aphteuse [ăftœz] af: **fièvre ~** foot-and-mouth disease.

apicole [ăpēkol] a beekeeping cpd.

apiculture [ăpēkültür] nf beekeeping, apiculture.

apitoiement [ăpētwámăŋ] nm pity, compassion.

apitoyer [ăpētwáyā] vt to move to pity; **~ qn sur qn/qch** to move sb to pity for sb/over sth; **s'~ (sur qn/qch)** to feel pity ou compassion (for sb/over sth).

ap. J.-C. abr (= après Jésus-Christ) AD.

APL sigle f (= aide personnalisée au logement) type of loan for house purchase.

aplanir [ăplănēr] vt to level; (fig) to smooth away, iron out.

aplati, e [ăplátē] a flat, flattened.

aplatir [ăplátēr] vt to flatten; **s'~** vi to become flatter; (écrasé) to be flattened; (fig) to lie flat on the ground; (: fam) to fall flat on one's face; (: péj) to grovel.

aplomb [ăplôŋ] nm (équilibre) balance, equilibrium; (fig) self-assurance; (: péj) nerve; **d'~** ad steady; (CONSTR) plumb.

apocalypse [ăpokálēps(ə)] nf apocalypse.

apocalyptique [ăpokálēptēk] a (fig) apocalyptic.

apocryphe [ăpokrēf] a apocryphal.

apogée [ăpozhā] nm (fig) peak, apogee.

apolitique [ăpolētēk] a (indifférent) apolitical; (indépendant) unpolitical, non-political.

apologie [ăpolozhē] nf praise; (JUR) vindication.

apoplexie [ăpopleksē] nf apoplexy.

a posteriori [ăpostáryorē] ad after the event, with hindsight, a posteriori.

apostolat [ăpostolá] nm (REL) apostolate, discipleship; (gén) evangelism.

apostolique [ăpostolēk] a apostolic.

apostrophe [ăpostrof] nf (signe) apostrophe; (appel) interpellation.

apostropher [ăpostrofā] vt (interpeller) to shout at, address sharply.

apothéose [ăpotāōz] nf pinnacle (of achievement); (MUS etc) grand finale.

apothicaire [ăpotēker] nm apothecary.

apôtre [ăpōtr(ə)] nm apostle, disciple.

Appalaches [ăpálásh] nmpl: **les ~** the Appalachian Mountains.

appalachien, ne [ăpálăshyaŋ, -en] a Appalachian.

apparaître [ăpáretr(ə)] vi to appear ♦ vb avec attribut to appear, seem.

apparat [ăpárá] nm: **tenue/dîner d'~** ceremonial dress/dinner.

appareil [ăpárey] nm (outil, machine) piece of apparatus, device; (électrique etc) appliance; (politique, syndical) machinery; (avion) (air)plane (US), (aero)plane (Brit), aircraft inv; (téléphonique) telephone; (dentier) braces (US), brace (Brit); **~ digestif/reproducteur** digestive/reproductive system ou apparatus; **l'~ productif** the means of production; **qui est à l'~?** who's speaking?; **dans le plus simple ~** in one's birthday suit; **~ (photographique)** camera; **~ 24 x 36** ou **petit format** 35 mm camera.

appareillage [ăpáreyázh] nm (appareils) equipment; (NAVIG) casting off, getting under way.

appareiller [ăpáráyā] vi (NAVIG) to cast off, get under way ♦ vt (assortir) to match up.

appareil-photo, pl **appareils-photos** [ăpáreyfoto] nm camera.

apparemment [ăpárámáŋ] ad apparently.

apparence [ăpáráŋs] nf appearance; **malgré les ~s** despite appearances; **en ~** apparently, seemingly.

apparent, e [ăpáráŋ, -áŋt] a visible; (évident) obvious; (superficiel) apparent; **coutures ~es** topstitched seams; **poutres ~es** exposed beams.

apparenté, e [ăpárăntā] a: **~ à** related to; (fig) similar to.

apparenter [ăpárăntā]: **s'~ à** vt to be similar to.

apparier [ăpáryā] vt (gants) to pair, match.

appariteur [ăpárētœr] nm attendant, porter (in French universities), ≈ campus policeman (US).

apparition [àpárēsÿôń] *nf* appearance; (*surnaturelle*) apparition; **faire son** ~ to appear.

appartement [àpártəmâń] *nm* apartment (*US*), flat (*Brit*).

appartenance [àpártənâńs] *nf*: ~ **à** belonging to, membership in (*US*) *ou* of (*Brit*).

appartenir [àpártənēr]: ~ **à** *vt* to belong to; (*faire partie de*) to belong to, be a member of; **il lui appartient de** it is up to him to.

appartiendrai [àpártyańdrā], **appartiens** [àpártyań] *etc voir* **appartenir**.

apparu, e [àpárü] *pp de* **apparaître**.

appas [àpâ] *nmpl* (*d'une femme*) charms.

appât [àpâ] *nm* (*PÊCHE*) bait; (*fig*) lure, bait.

appâter [àpâtā] *vt* (*hameçon*) to bait; (*poisson, fig*) to lure, entice.

appauvrir [àpōvrēr] *vt* to impoverish; **s'**~ *vi* to grow poorer, become impoverished.

appauvrissement [àpōvrēsmâń] *nm* impoverishment.

appel [àpel] *nm* call; (*nominal*) roll call; (*SCOL*) roll, register (*Brit*); (*MIL: recrutement*) call-up; (*JUR*) appeal; **faire** ~ **à** (*in voquer*) to appeal to; (*avoir recours à*) to call on; (*nécessiter*) to call for, require; **faire ou interjeter** ~ (*JUR*) to appeal, file (*US*) *ou* lodge (*Brit*) an appeal; **faire l'**~ to call the roll; to call the register; **indicatif d'**~ call sign; **numéro d'**~ (*TÉL*) number; **produit d'**~ (*COMM*) loss leader; **sans** ~ (*fig*) final, irrevocable; ~ **d'air** in-draft (*US*), in-draught (*Brit*); ~ **d'offres** (*COMM*) invitation to bid; **faire un** ~ **de phares** to flash one's headlights; ~ **(téléphonique)** (tele)phone call.

appelé [àplā] *nm* (*MIL*) draftee.

appeler [àpla] *vt* to call; (*TÉL*) to call, ring; (*faire venir: médecin etc*) to call, send for; (*fig: nécessiter*) to call for, demand; ~ **au secours** to call for help; ~ **qn à l'aide** *ou* **au secours** to call to sb to help; ~ **qn à un poste/des fonctions** to appoint sb to a post/ assign duties to sb; **être appelé à** (*fig*) to be destined to; ~ **qn à comparaître** (*JUR*) to summon sb to appear; **en** ~ **à** to appeal to; **s'**~: **elle s'appelle Gabrielle** her name is Gabrielle, she's called Gabrielle; **comment ça s'appelle?** what is it *ou* that called?

appellation [àpālâsÿôń] *nf* designation, appellation; **vin d'**~ **contrôlée** 'appellation contrôlée' wine, *wine guaranteed of a certain quality*.

appelle [àpel] *etc vb voir* **appeler**.

appendice [àpańdēs] *nm* appendix.

appendicite [àpańdēsēt] *nf* appendicitis.

appentis [àpâńtē] *nm* lean-to.

appert [àper] *vb*: **il** ~ **que** it appears that, it is evident that.

appesantir [àpzâńtēr]: **s'**~ *vi* to grow heavier; **s'**~ **sur** (*fig*) to dwell at length on.

appétissant, e [àpātēsâń, -âńt] *a* appetizing, mouth-watering.

appétit [àpātē] *nm* appetite; **couper l'**~ **à qn** to take away sb's appetite; **bon** ~! enjoy your meal!

applaudimètre [àplōdēmetr(ə)] *nm* applause meter.

applaudir [àplōdēr] *vt* to applaud ♦ *vi* to applaud, clap; ~ **à** *vt* (*décision*) to applaud, commend.

applaudissements [àplōdēsmâń] *nmpl* applause *sg*, clapping *sg*.

applicable [àplēkábl(ə)] *a* applicable.

applicateur [àplēkátœr] *nm* applicator.

application [àplēkásyôń] *nf* application; (*d'une loi*) enforcement; **mettre en** ~ to implement.

applique [àplēk] *nf* wall lamp.

appliqué, e [àplēkā] *a* (*élève etc*) industrious, assiduous; (*science*) applied.

appliquer [àplēkā] *vt* to apply; (*loi*) to enforce; (*donner: gifle, châtiment*) to give; **s'**~ *vi* (*élève etc*) to apply to o.s.; **s'**~ **à** (*loi, remarque*) to apply to; **s'**~ **à faire qch** to apply o.s. to doing sth, take pains to do sth; **s'**~ **sur** (*coïncider avec*) to fit over.

appoint [àpwań] *nm* (*extra*) contribution *ou* help; **avoir/faire l'**~ (*en payant*) to have/give the exact change; **chauffage d'**~ extra heating.

appointements [àpwańtmâń] *nmpl* salary *sg*, stipend (*surtout REL*).

appointer [àpwańtā] *vt*: **être appointé à l'année/au mois** to be paid yearly/monthly.

appontement [àpôńtmâń] *nm* landing stage, wharf.

apponter [àpôńtā] *vi* (*avion, hélicoptère*) to land.

apport [àpor] *nm* supply; (*argent, biens etc*) contribution.

apporter [àportā] *vt* to bring; (*preuve*) to give, provide; (*modification*) to make; (*suj: remarque*) to contribute, add.

apposer [àpōzā] *vt* to append; (*sceau etc*) to affix.

apposition [àpōzēsÿôń] *nf* appending; affixing; (*LING*): **en** ~ in apposition.

appréciable [àprāsyábl(ə)] *a* (*important*) appreciable, significant.

appréciation [àprāsyásÿôń] *nf* appreciation; estimation, assessment; ~**s** *nfpl* (*avis*) assessment *sg*, appraisal *sg*.

apprécier [àprāsyā] *vt* to appreciate; (*évaluer*) to estimate, assess; **j'apprécierais que tu** ... I should appreciate (it) if you ....

appréhender [àprāâńdā] *vt* (*craindre*) to dread; (*arrêter*) to apprehend; ~ **que** to fear that; ~ **de faire** to dread doing.

appréhensif, ive [àprāâńsēf, -ēv] *a* apprehensive.

appréhension [àprāâńsÿôń] *nf* apprehension.

apprendre [àprâńdr(ə)] *vt* to learn; (*événement, résultats*) to learn of, hear of; ~ **qch à qn** (*informer*) to tell sb (of) sth; (*enseigner*) to teach sb sth; **tu me l'apprends!** that's news to me!; ~ **à faire qch** to learn to do sth; ~ **à qn à faire qch** to teach sb to do sth.

apprenti, e [àprâńtē] *nm/f* apprentice; (*fig*) novice, beginner.

apprentissage [àprâńtēsázh] *nm* learning; (*COMM, SCOL: période*) apprenticeship; **école ou centre d'**~ training school *ou* centre; **faire l'**~ **de qch** (*fig*) to be initiated into sth.

apprêt [àpre] *nm* (*sur un cuir, une étoffe*) dressing; (*sur un mur*) size; (*sur un papier*) finish; **sans** ~ (*fig*) without artifice, unaffectedly.

apprêté, e [àprātā] *a* (*fig*) affected.

apprêter [áprātā] *vt* to dress, finish; **s'~** *vi*: **s'~ à qch/à faire qch** to prepare for sth/for doing sth.
appris, e [áprē, -ēz] *pp de* **apprendre**.
apprivoisé, e [áprēvwázā] *a* tame, tamed.
apprivoiser [áprēvwázā] *vt* to tame.
approbateur, trice [áprobátœr, -trēs] *a* approving.
approbatif, ive [áprobátēf, -ēv] *a* approving.
approbation [áprobásyóń] *nf* approval; **digne d'~** (*conduite, travail*) praiseworthy, commendable.
approchant, e [áprosháń, -áńt] *a* similar, close; **quelque chose d'~** something similar.
approche [áprosh] *nf* approaching; (*arrivée, attitude*) approach; **~s** *nfpl* (*abords*) surroundings; **à l'~ du bateau/de l'ennemi** as the ship/enemy approached *ou* drew near; **l'~ d'un problème** the approach to a problem; **travaux d'~** (*fig*) maneuvers.
approché, e [áproshā] *a* approximate.
approcher [áproshā] *vi* to approach, come near ♦ *vt* (*vedette, artiste*) to come close to, approach; (*rapprocher*): **~ qch (de qch)** to bring *ou* put *ou* move sth near (to sth); **~ de** *vt* to draw near to; (*quantité, moment*) to approach; **s'~ de** *vt* to approach, go *ou* come *ou* move near to; **approchez-vous** come *ou* go nearer.
approfondi, e [áprofóńdē] *a* thorough, detailed.
approfondir [áprofóńdēr] *vt* to deepen; (*question*) to go further into; **sans ~** without going too deeply into it.
appropriation [áproprēyásyóń] *nf* appropriation.
approprié, e [áproprēyā] *a*: **~ (à)** appropriate (to), suited to.
approprier [áproprēyā] *vt* (*adapter*) adapter; **s'~** *vt* to appropriate, take over.
approuver [áproōvā] *vt* to agree with; (*autoriser: loi, projet*) to approve, pass; (*trouver louable*) to approve of; **je vous approuve entièrement/ne vous approuve pas** I agree with you entirely/don't agree with you; **lu et approuvé** (read and) approved.
approvisionnement [áprovēzyonmáń] *nm* supplying; (*provisions*) supply, stock.
approvisionner [áprovēzyonā] *vt* to supply; (*compte bancaire*) to pay funds into; **~ qn en** to supply sb with; **s'~** *vi*: **s'~ dans un certain magasin/au marché** to shop in a certain shop/at the market; **s'~ en** to stock up with.
approximatif, ive [áproksēmátēf, -ēv] *a* approximate, rough; (*imprécis*) vague.
approximation [áproksēmásyóń] *nf* approximation.
approximativement [áproksēmátēvmáń] *ad* approximately, roughly; vaguely.
appt *abr* = **appartement**.
appui [ápüē] *nm* support; **prendre ~ sur** to lean on; (*objet*) to rest on; **point d'~** fulcrum; (*fig*) something to lean on; **à l'~ de** (*pour prouver*) in support of; **à l'~** *ad* to support one's argument; **l'~ de la fenêtre** the windowsill, the window ledge.
appuie [ápüē] *etc vb voir* **appuyer**.
appui-tête, appuie-tête [ápüētet] *nm inv* head-

rest.
appuyé, e [ápüēyā] *a* (*regard*) meaningful; (*: insistant*) intent, insistent; (*excessif: politesse, compliment*) exaggerated, overdone.
appuyer [ápüēyā] *vt* (*poser*): **~ qch sur/contre/à** to lean *ou* rest sth on/against/on; (*soutenir: personne, demande*) to support, back (up) ♦ *vi*: **~ sur** (*bouton, frein*) to press, push; (*mot, détail*) to stress, emphasize; (*suj: chose: peser sur*) to rest (heavily) on, press against; **s'~ sur** *vt* to lean on; (*compter sur*) to rely on; **s'~ sur qn** to lean on sb; **~ contre** (*toucher: mur, porte*) to lean *ou* rest against; **~ à droite** *ou* **sur sa droite** to bear (to the) right; **~ sur le champignon** to put one's foot down.
apr. *abr* = **après**.
âpre [ápr(ə)] *a* acrid, pungent; (*fig*) harsh; (*lutte*) bitter; **~ au gain** grasping, greedy.
après [ápre] *prép* after ♦ *ad* afterwards; **2 heures ~** 2 hours later; **~ qu'il est** *ou* **soit parti/avoir fait** after he left/having done; **courir ~ qn** to run after sb; **crier ~ qn** to shout at sb; **être toujours ~ qn** (*critiquer etc*) to be always nagging (at) sb; **~ quoi** after which; **d'~ prép** (*selon*) according to; **d'~ lui** according to him; **d'~ moi** in my opinion; **~ coup** *ad* after the event, afterwards; **~ tout** *ad* (*au fond*) after all; **et (puis) ~?** so what?
après-demain [ápredmań] *ad* the day after tomorrow.
après-guerre [ápreger] *nm* post-war years *pl*; **d'~** *a* post-war.
après-midi [ápremēdē] *nm ou nf inv* afternoon.
après-rasage [áprerázazh] *nm inv*: **(lotion) ~** after-shave (lotion).
après-ski [ápreskē] *nm inv* (*chaussure*) snow boot; (*moment*) après-ski.
après-vente [áprevảnt] *a inv* after-sales *cpd*.
âpreté [áprətā] *nf* (*voir âpre*) pungency; harshness; bitterness.
à-propos [ápropō] *nm* (*d'une remarque*) aptness; **faire preuve d'~** to show presence of mind, do the right thing; **avec ~** suitably, aptly.
apte [ápt(ə)] *a*: **~ à qch/faire qch** capable of sth/doing sth; **~ (au service)** (*MIL*) fit (for service).
aptitude [áptētüd] *nf* ability, aptitude.
apurer [ápürā] *vt* to balance.
aquaplanage [ákwáplánázh] *nm* (*AUTO*) aquaplaning.
aquaplane [ákwáplán] *nm* (*planche*) aquaplane; (*sport*) aquaplaning.
aquarelle [ákwárel] *nf* (*tableau*) watercolor (*US*), watercolour (*Brit*); (*genre*) watercolo(u)rs *pl*, aquarelle.
aquarium [ákwáryom] *nm* aquarium.
aquatique [ákwátēk] *a* aquatic, water *cpd*.
aqueduc [ákdük] *nm* aqueduct.
aqueux, euse [ákœ, -œz] *a* aqueous.
aquilin [ákēlań] *am*: **nez ~** aquiline nose.
AR *sigle m* (= *accusé de réception*): **lettre/paquet avec ~** ≈ certified letter/parcel (*US*), ≈ recorded delivery letter/parcel (*Brit*); (*AVIAT, RAIL etc*) = **aller (et) retour** ♦ *abr*

(*AUTO*) = **arrière**.

arabe [àràb] *a* Arabic; (*désert, cheval*) Arabian; (*nation, peuple*) Arab ♦ *nm* (*LING*) Arabic ♦ *nm/f*: **A∼** Arab.

arabesque [àràbesk(ə)] *nf* arabesque.

Arabie [àràbē] *nf*: **l'∼** Arabia; **l'∼ Saoudite** *ou* **Séoudite** Saudi Arabia.

arable [àràbl(ə)] *a* arable.

arachide [àràshēd] *nf* groundnut (plant); (*graine*) peanut, groundnut.

araignée [àrànyā] *nf* spider; **∼ de mer** spider crab.

araser [àràzā] *vt* to level; (*en rabotant*) to plane (down).

aratoire [àràtwàr] *a*: **instrument ∼** plowing (*US*) *ou* ploughing (*Brit*) implement.

arbalète [àrbàlet] *nf* crossbow.

arbitrage [àrbētràzh] *nm* refereeing; umpiring; arbitration.

arbitraire [àrbētrer] *a* arbitrary.

arbitrairement [àrbētrermàń] *ad* arbitrarily.

arbitre [àrbētr(ə)] *nm* (*SPORT*) referee; (*TENNIS, CRICKET*) umpire; (*fig*) arbiter, judge; (*JUR*) arbitrator.

arbitrer [àrbētrā] *vt* to referee; to umpire; to arbitrate.

arborer [àrborā] *vt* to bear, display; (*avec ostentation*) to sport.

arborescence [àrborāsàńs] *nf* tree structure.

arboriculture [àrborēkültür] *nf* arboriculture; **∼ fruitière** fruit (tree) growing.

arbre [àrbr(ə)] *nm* tree; (*TECH*) shaft; **∼ à cames** (*AUTO*) camshaft; **∼ fruitier** fruit tree; **∼ généalogique** family tree; **∼ de Noël** Christmas tree; **∼ de transmission** (*AUTO*) driveshaft.

arbrisseau, x [àrbrēsō] *nm* shrub.

arbuste [àrbüst(ə)] *nm* small shrub, bush.

arc [àrk] *nm* (*arme*) bow; (*GÉOM*) arc; (*ARCHIT*) arch; **∼ de cercle** arc of a circle; **en ∼ de cercle** *a* semi-circular.

arcade [àrkàd] *nf* arch(way); **∼s** *nfpl* arcade *sg*, arches; **∼ sourcilière** arch of the eyebrows.

arcanes [àrkàn] *nmpl* mysteries.

arc-boutant, pl arcs-boutants [àrkbōōtàń] *nm* flying buttress.

arc-bouter [àrkbōōtā]: **s'∼** *vi*: **s'∼ contre** to lean *ou* press against.

arceau, x [àrsō] *nm* (*métallique etc*) hoop.

arc-en-ciel, pl arcs-en-ciel [àrkàńsyel] *nm* rainbow.

archaïque [àrkàēk] *a* archaic.

archaïsme [àrkàēsm(ə)] *nm* archaism.

archange [àrkàńzh] *nm* archangel.

arche [àrsh(ə)] *nf* arch; **∼ de Noé** Noah's Ark.

archéologie [àrkāolozhē] *nf* arch(a)eology.

archéologique [àrkāolozhēk] *a* arch(a)eological.

archéologue [àrkāolog] *nm/f* arch(a)eologist.

archer [àrshā] *nm* archer.

archet [àrshe] *nm* bow.

archétype [àrkātēp] *nm* archetype.

archevêché [àrshəvāshā] *nm* archbishopric; (*palais*) archbishop's palace.

archevêque [àrshəvek] *nm* archbishop.

archi... [àrshē] *préfixe* (*très*) dead, extra.

archibondé, e [àrshēbóńdā] *a* chock-a-block (*Brit*), packed solid.

archiduc [àrshēdük] *nm* archduke.

archiduchesse [àrshēdüshes] *nf* archduchess.

archipel [àrshēpel] *nm* archipelago.

archisimple [àrshēsàńpl(ə)] *a* dead easy *ou* simple.

architecte [àrshētekt(ə)] *nm* architect.

architectural, e, aux [àrshētektüràl, -ō] *a* architectural.

architecture [àrshētektür] *nf* architecture.

archive [àrshēv] *nf* file; **∼s** *nfpl* archives.

archiver [àrshēvā] *vt* to file.

archiviste [àrshēvēst(ə)] *nm/f* archivist.

arçon [àrsóń] *nm voir* **cheval**.

arctique [àrktēk] *a* Arctic ♦ *nm*: **l'A∼** the Arctic; **le cercle A∼** the Arctic Circle; **l'océan A∼** the Arctic Ocean.

ardemment [àrdàmàń] *ad* ardently, fervently.

ardent, e [àrdàń, -àńt] *a* (*soleil*) blazing; (*fièvre*) raging; (*amour*) ardent, passionate; (*prière*) fervent.

ardeur [àrdœr] *nf* blazing heat; (*fig*) fervor (*US*), fervour (*Brit*), ardor (*US*), ardour (*Brit*).

ardoise [àrdwàz] *nf* slate.

ardu, e [àrdü] *a* arduous, difficult; (*pente*) steep, abrupt.

are [àr] *nm* are, 100 square meters.

arène [àren] *nf* arena; (*fig*): **l'∼ politique/ littéraire** the political/literary arena; **∼s** *nfpl* bull-ring *sg*.

arête [àret] *nf* (*de poisson*) bone; (*d'une montagne*) ridge; (*GÉOM etc*) edge (*where two faces meet*).

arg. *abr* = **argus**.

argent [àrzhàń] *nm* (*métal*) silver; (*monnaie*) money; (*couleur*) silver; **en avoir pour son ∼** to get one's money's worth; **gagner beaucoup d'∼** to earn a lot of money; **∼ comptant** (hard) cash; **∼ liquide** ready money, (ready) cash; **∼ de poche** pocket money.

argenté, e [àrzhàńtā] *a* silver(y); (*métal*) silver-plated.

argenter [àrzhàńtā] *vt* to silver(-plate).

argenterie [àrzhàńtrē] *nf* silverware; (*en métal argenté*) silver plate.

argentin, e [àrzhàńtàń, -ēn] *a* (*son*) silvery; (*d'Argentine*) Argentinian, Argentine ♦ *nm/f*: **A∼, e** Argentinian, Argentine.

Argentine [àrzhàńtēn] *nf*: **l'∼** Argentina, the Argentine.

argile [àrzhēl] *nf* clay.

argileux, euse [àrzhēlœ, -œz] *a* clayey.

argot [àrgō] *nm* slang.

argotique [àrgotēk] *a* slang *cpd*; (*très familier*) slangy.

arguer [àrgüà]: **∼ de** *vt* to put forward as a pretext *ou* reason; **∼ que** to argue that.

argument [àrgümàń] *nm* argument.

argumentaire [àrgümàńter] *nm* list of selling points; (*brochure*) sales brochure.

argumenter [àrgümàńtā] *vi* to argue.

argus [àrgüs] *nm* guide to second-hand car etc prices.

arguties [àrgüsē] *nfpl* quibbles.

aride [àrēd] *a* arid.

aridité [àrēdētā] *nf* aridity.

arien, ne [àryàń, -en] *a* Arian.

aristocrate [àrēstokràt] *nm/f* aristocrat.

aristocratie [àrēstokràsē] *nf* aristocracy.
aristocratique [àrēstokràtēk] *a* aristocratic.
arithmétique [àrētmàtēk] *a* arithmetic(al) ◆ *nf* arithmetic.
armagnac [àrmànyàk] *nm* armagnac.
armateur [àrmàtœr] *nm* shipowner.
armature [àrmàtür] *nf* framework; (*de tente etc*) frame; (*de corset*) bone; (*de soutien-gorge*) underwiring.
arme [àrm(ə)] *nf* weapon; (*section de l'armée*) arm; ~**s** *nfpl* weapons, arms; (*blason*) (coat of) arms; **les** ~**s** (*profession*) soldiering *sg*; **à** ~**s égales** on equal terms; **en** ~**s** up in arms; **passer par les** ~**s** to execute (by firing squad); **prendre/présenter les** ~**s** to take up/present arms; **se battre à l'**~ **blanche** to fight with blades; ~ **à feu** firearm.
armé, e [àrmā] *a* armed; ~ **de** armed with.
armée [àrmā] *nf* army; ~ **de l'air** Air Force; **l'**~ **du Salut** the Salvation Army; ~ **de terre** Army.
armement [àrmərmàṅ] *nm* (*matériel*) arms *pl*, weapons *pl*; (*: d'un pays*) arms *pl*, armament; (*action d'équiper: d'un navire*) fitting out; ~**s nucléaires** nuclear armaments; **course aux** ~**s** arms race.
Arménie [àrmānē] *nf*: **l'**~ Armenia.
arménien, ne [àrmānyaṅ, -en] *a* Armenian ◆ *nm* (*LING*) Armenian ◆ *nm/f*: **A**~, **ne** Armenian.
armer [àrmā] *vt* to arm; (*arme à feu*) to cock; (*appareil-photo*) to wind on; ~ **qch de** to fit sth with; (*renforcer*) to reinforce sth with; ~ **qn de** to arm *ou* equip sb with; **s'**~ **de** to arm o.s. with.
armistice [àrmēstēs] *nm* armistice; **l'A**~ ≈ Veterans (*US*) *ou* Remembrance (*Brit*) Day.
armoire [àrmwár] *nf* (tall) cupboard; (*penderie*) closet (*US*), wardrobe (*Brit*); ~ **à pharmacie** medicine chest.
armoiries [àrmwárē] *nfpl* coat of arms *sg*.
armure [àrmür] *nf* armor *q* (*US*), armour *q* (*Brit*), suit of armor.
armurerie [àrmürrē] *nf* arms factory; (*magasin*) gunsmith's (shop).
armurier [àrmüryā] *nm* gunsmith; (*MIL*, *d'armes blanches*) armorer (*US*), armourer (*Brit*).
ARN *sigle m* (= *acide ribonucléique*) RNA.
arnaque [àrnàk] *nf*: **de l'**~ highway (*US*) *ou* daylight (*Brit*) robbery.
arnaquer [àrnàkā] *vt* to do (*fam*), swindle; **se faire** ~ to be had (*fam*) *ou* done.
arnaqueur [àrnàkœr] *nm* swindler.
arnica [àrnēkà] *nm*: (**teinture d'**)~ arnica.
aromates [àromàt] *nmpl* seasoning *sg*, herbs (and spices).
aromatique [àromàtēk] *a* aromatic.
aromatiser [àromàtēzā] *vt* to flavor (*US*) *ou* flavour (*Brit*).
arôme [àrōm] *nm* aroma; (*d'une fleur etc*) fragrance.
arpège [àrpezh] *nm* arpeggio.
arpentage [àrpàṅtàzh] *nm* (land) surveying.
arpenter [àrpàṅtā] *vt* to pace up and down.
arpenteur [àrpàṅtœr] *nm* land surveyor.
arqué, e [àrkā] *a* arched; (*jambes*) bow *cpd*, bandy.
arr. *abr* = **arrondissement**.

arrachage [àràshàzh] *nm*: ~ **des mauvaises herbes** weeding.
arraché [àràshā] *nm* (*SPORT*) snatch; **obtenir à l'**~ (*fig*) to snatch.
arrache-pied [àràshpyā]: **d'**~ *ad* relentlessly.
arracher [àràshā] *vt* to pull out; (*page etc*) to tear off, tear out; (*déplanter: légume*) to lift; (*: herbe, souche*) to pull up; (*bras etc: par explosion*) to blow off; (*: par accident*) to tear off; **s'**~ *vt* (*article très recherché*) to fight over; ~ **qch à qn** to snatch sth from sb; (*fig*) to wring sth out of sb, wrest sth from sb; ~ **qn à** (*solitude, rêverie*) to drag sb out of; (*famille etc*) to tear *ou* wrench sb away from; **se faire** ~ **une dent** to have a tooth out *ou* pulled (*US*); **s'**~ **de** (*lieu*) to tear o.s. away from; (*habitude*) to force o.s. out of.
arraisonner [àrezonā] *vt* to board and search.
arrangeant, e [àràṅzhàṅ, -àṅt] *a* accommodating, obliging.
arrangement [àràṅzhmàṅ] *nm* arrangement.
arranger [àràṅzhā] *vt* to arrange; (*réparer*) to fix, put right; (*régler*) to settle, sort out; (*convenir à*) to suit, be convenient for; **s'**~ (*se mettre d'accord*) to come to an agreement *ou* arrangement; (*s'améliorer: querelle, situation*) to be sorted out; (*se débrouiller*) : **s'**~ **pour que ...** to arrange things so that ...; **je vais m'**~ I'll manage; **ça va s'**~ it'll sort itself out; **s'**~ **pour faire** to make sure that *ou* see to it that one can do.
arrangeur [àràṅzhœr] *nm* (*MUS*) arranger.
arrestation [àrestàsyôṅ] *nf* arrest.
arrêt [àre] *nm* stopping; (*de bus etc*) stop; (*JUR*) judgment, decision; (*FOOTBALL*) save; ~**s** *nmpl* (*MIL*) arrest *sg*; **être à l'**~ to be stopped, have come to a halt; **rester** *ou* **tomber en** ~ **devant** to stop short in front of; **sans** ~ without stopping, non-stop; (*fréquemment*) continually; ~ **d'autobus** bus stop; ~ **facultatif** request stop; ~ **de mort** death sentence; ~ **de travail** stoppage (of work).
arrêté, e [àrētā] *a* (*idées*) firm, fixed ◆ *nm* order, decree; ~ **municipal** ≈ bylaw, byelaw.
arrêter [àrātā] *vt* to stop; (*chauffage etc*) to turn off, switch off; (*COMM: compte*) to settle; (*COUTURE: point*) to fasten off; (*fixer: date etc*) to appoint, decide on; (*criminel, suspect*) to arrest; **s'**~ *vi* to stop; (*s'interrompre*) to stop o.s.; ~ **de faire** to stop doing; **arrête de te plaindre** stop complaining; **ne pas** ~ **de faire** to keep on doing; **s'**~ **de faire** to stop doing; **s'**~ **sur** (*suj: choix, regard*) to fall on.
arrhes [àr] *nfpl* deposit *sg*.
arrière [àryer] *nm* back; (*SPORT*) fullback ◆ *a inv*: **siège/roue** ~ back *ou* rear seat/wheel; ~**s** *nmpl* (*fig*): **protéger ses** ~**s** to protect the rear; **à l'**~ *ad* behind, at the back; **en** ~ *ad* behind; (*regarder*) back, behind; (*tomber, aller*) backwards; **en** ~ **de** *prép* behind.
arriéré, e [àryārā] *a* (*péj*) backward ◆ *nm* (*d'argent*) arrears *pl*.
arrière-boutique [àryerbōōtēk] *nf* back shop.
arrière-cour [àryerkōōr] *nf* backyard.
arrière-cuisine [àryerküēzēn] *nf* scullery.
arrière-garde [àryergàrd(ə)] *nf* rearguard.
arrière-goût [àryergōō] *nm* aftertaste.

arrière-grand-mère, *pl* **arrière-grand-mères** [àryergrânmer] *nf* great-grandmother.

arrière-grand-père, *pl* **arrière-grands-pères** [àryergrânper] *nm* great-grandfather.

arrière-grands-parents [àryergrânpárân] *nmpl* great-grandparents.

arrière-pays [àryerpāē] *nm inv* hinterland.

arrière-pensée [àryerpânsā] *nf* ulterior motive; (*doute*) mental reservation.

arrière-petite-fille, *pl* **arrière-petites-filles** [àryerpətētfēy] *nf* great-granddaughter.

arrière-petit-fils, *pl* **arrière-petits-fils** [àryerpətēfēs] *nm* great-grandson.

arrière-petits-enfants [àryerpətēzânfân] *nmpl* great-grandchildren.

arrière-plan [àryerplân] *nm* background; **d'~** *a* (*INFORM*) background *cpd*.

arriérer [àryārā]: **s'~** *vi* (*COMM*) to fall into arrears.

arrière-saison [àryersezôn] *nf* late fall (*US*) or autumn.

arrière-salle [àryersàl] *nf* back room.

arrière-train [àryertrân] *nm* hindquarters *pl*.

arrimer [àrēmā] *vt* to stow; (*fixer*) to secure, fasten securely.

arrivage [àrēvàzh] *nm* arrival.

arrivant, e [àrēvân, -ânt] *nm/f* newcomer.

arrivée [àrēvā] *nf* arrival; (*ligne d'arrivée*) finish; **~ d'air/de gaz** air/gas inlet; **courrier à l'~** incoming mail; **à mon ~** when I arrived.

arriver [àrēvā] *vi* to arrive; (*survenir*) to happen, occur; **j'arrive!** (I'm) just coming!; **il arrive à Paris à 8h** he gets to *ou* arrives in Paris at 8; **~ à destination** to arrive at one's destination; **~ à** (*atteindre*) to reach; **~ à** (*faire*) **qch** (*réussir*) to manage (to do) sth; **~ à échéance** to fall due; **en ~ à faire** to end up doing, get to the point of doing; **il lui arrive de faire** he sometimes does.

arrivisme [àrēvēsm(ə)] *nm* ambition, ambitiousness.

arriviste [àrēvēst(ə)] *nm/f* go-getter.

arrogance [àrogâns] *nf* arrogance.

arrogant, e [àrogân, -ânt] *a* arrogant.

arroger [àrozhā]: **s'~** *vt* to assume (without right); **s'~ le droit de ...** to assume the right to ....

arrondi, e [àrôndē] *a* round ♦ *nm* roundness.

arrondir [àrôndēr] *vt* (*forme, objet*) to round; (*somme*) to round off; **s'~** *vi* to become round(ed); **~ ses fins de mois** to supplement one's pay.

arrondissement [àrôndēsmân] *nm* (*ADMIN*) ≈ district.

arrosage [àrōzàzh] *nm* watering; **tuyau d'~** hose(pipe).

arroser [àrōzā] *vt* to water; (*victoire etc*) to celebrate (over a drink); (*CULIN*) to baste.

arroseur [àrōzœr] *nm* (*tourniquet*) sprinkler.

arroseuse [àrōzœz] *nf* street cleaning truck.

arrosoir [àrōzwàr] *nm* watering can.

arrt *abr* = **arrondissement.**

arsenal, aux [àrsənàl, -ō] *nm* (*NAVIG*) naval dockyard; (*MIL*) arsenal; (*fig*) gear, paraphernalia.

arsenic [àrsənēk] *nm* arsenic.

art [àr] *nm* art; **avoir l'~ de faire** (*fig:*

personne) to have a talent for doing; **les ~s** the arts; **livre/critique d'~** art book/critic; **objet d'~** objet d'art; **~ dramatique** dramatic art; **~s et métiers** industrial (*US*) *ou* applied (*Brit*) arts and crafts; **~s ménagers** home economics *sg*; **~s plastiques** plastic arts.

art. *abr* = **article.**

artère [àrter] *nf* (*ANAT*) artery; (*rue*) main road.

artériel, le [àrtāryel] *a* arterial.

artériosclérose [àrtāryosklārōz] *nf* arteriosclerosis.

arthrite [àrtrēt] *nf* arthritis.

arthrose [àrtrōz] *nf* (degenerative) osteoarthritis.

artichaut [àrtēshō] *nm* artichoke.

article [àrtēkl(ə)] *nm* article; (*COMM*) item, article; (*INFORM*) record, item; **faire l'~** (*COMM*) to give one's sales pitch; **faire l'~ de** (*fig*) to sing the praises of; **à l'~ de la mort** at the point of death; **~ défini/indéfini** definite/indefinite article; **~ de fond** (*PRESSE*) feature article; **~s de bureau** office equipment; **~s de voyage** travel goods *ou* items.

articulaire [àrtēkùler] *a* of the joints, articular.

articulation [àrtēkùlàsyôn] *nf* articulation; (*ANAT*) joint.

articulé, e [àrtēkùlā] *a* (*membre*) jointed; (*poupée*) with moving joints.

articuler [àrtēkùlā] *vt* to articulate; **s'~** (**sur**) (*ANAT, TECH*) to articulate (with); **s'~ autour de** (*fig*) to center around *ou* on, turn on.

artifice [àrtēfes] *nm* device, trick.

artificiel, le [àrtēfēsyel] *a* artificial.

artificiellement [artetesyelmân] *ad* artificially.

artificier [àrtēfēsyā] *nm* pyrotechnist.

artificieux, euse [àrtēfēsyœ, -œz] *a* guileful, deceitful.

artillerie [àrtēyrē] *nf* artillery, ordnance.

artilleur [àrtēyœr] *nm* artilleryman, gunner.

artisan [àrtēzân] *nm* artisan, (self-employed) craftsman; **l'~ de la victoire/du malheur** the architect of victory/of the disaster.

artisanal, e, aux [àrtēzànàl, -ō] *a* of *ou* made by craftsmen; (*péj*) cottage industry *cpd*, unsophisticated.

artisanat [àrtēzànà] *nm* arts and crafts *pl*.

artiste [àrtēst(ə)] *nm/f* artist; (*THÉÂTRE, MUS*) artist, performer; (*: de variétés*) entertainer.

artistique [àrtēstēk] *a* artistic.

artistiquement [àrtēstēkmân] *ad* artistically.

aryen, ne [àryan, -en] *a* Aryan.

AS *sigle fpl* (*ADMIN*) = **assurances sociales** ♦ *sigle f* (*SPORT*) = Association sportive.

as *vb* [à] *voir* avoir ♦ *nm* [às] ace.

a/s *abr* (= *aux soins de*) c/o.

ASBL *sigle f* (= *association sans but lucratif*) non-profit-making organization.

asc. *abr* = **ascenseur.**

ascendance [àsândâns] *nf* (*origine*) ancestry; (*ASTROLOGIE*) ascendant.

ascendant, e [àsândân, -ânt] *a* upward ♦ *nm* influence; **~s** *nmpl* ascendants.

ascenseur [àsânsœr] *nm* elevator (*US*), lift (*Brit*).

ascension [àsânsyôn] *nf* ascent; climb; **l'A~** (*REL*) the Ascension; **(île de) l'A~** Ascension

Island.

ascète [ásɛt] *nm/f* ascetic.

ascétisme [àsàtɛ́sm(ə)] *nm* asceticism.

ascorbique [àskorbɛ́k] *a*: **acide** ~ ascorbic acid.

ASE *sigle f* (= *Agence spatiale européenne*) ESA (= *European Space Agency*).

asepsie [àsɛpsɛ́] *nf* asepsis.

aseptique [àsɛptɛ́k] *a* aseptic.

aseptiser [àsɛptɛ́zà] *vt* to sterilize; (*plaie*) to disinfect.

Asiate [àzyàt] *nm/f* Asian.

asiatique [àzyátɛ́k] *a* Asian, Asiatic ♦ *nm/f*: A~ Asian.

Asie [àzɛ́] *nf*: l'~ Asia.

asile [àzɛ́l] *nm* (*refuge*) refuge, sanctuary; (*POL*): **droit d'~** (political) asylum; (*pour malades, vieillards etc*) home; **accorder l'~ politique à qn** to grant *ou* give sb political asylum; **chercher/trouver** ~ **quelque part** to seek/find refuge somewhere.

asocial, e, aux [àsosyál, -ō] *a* antisocial.

aspect [àspɛ] *nm* appearance, look; (*fig*) aspect, side; (*LING*) aspect; **à l'~ de** at the sight of.

asperge [àspɛrzh(ə)] *nf* asparagus *q*.

asperger [àspɛrzhā] *vt* to spray, sprinkle.

aspérité [àspārɛ́tā] *nf* excrescence, protruding bit (of rock *etc*).

aspersion [àspɛrsyôn] *nf* spraying, sprinkling.

asphalte [àsfált(ə)] *nm* asphalt.

asphyxie [àsfɛ́ksɛ́] *nf* suffocation, asphyxia, asphyxiation.

asphyxier [àsfɛ́ksyā] *vt* to suffocate, asphyxiate; (*fig*) to stifle; **mourir asphyxié** to die of suffocation *ou* asphyxiation.

aspic [àspɛ́k] *nm* (*ZOOL*) asp; (*CULIN*) aspic.

aspirant, e [àspɛ́rân, -ânt] *a*: **pompe** ~**e** suction pump ♦ *nm* (*NAVIG*) midshipman.

aspirateur [àspɛ́rátœr] *nm* vacuum cleaner.

aspiration [àspɛ́râsyôn] *nf* inhalation; sucking (up); drawing up; ~**s** *nfpl* (*ambitions*) aspirations.

aspirer [àspɛ́rā] *vt* (*air*) to inhale; (*liquide*) to suck (up); (*suj: appareil*) to suck *ou* draw up; ~ **à** *vt* to aspire to.

aspirine [àspɛ́rɛn] *nf* aspirin.

assagir [àsázhɛr] *vt*, **s'~** *vi* to quieten down, sober down.

assaillant, e [àsáyân, -ânt] *nm/f* assailant, attacker.

assaillir [àsáyɛr] *vt* to assail, attack; ~ **qn de** (*questions*) to assail *ou* bombard sb with.

assainir [àsánɛr] *vt* to clean up; (*eau, air*) to purify.

assainissement [àsánɛsmân] *nm* cleaning up; purifying.

assaisonnement [àsɛzonmân] *nm* seasoning.

assaisonner [àsɛzonā] *vt* to season; **bien assaisonné** highly seasoned.

assassin [àsàsan] *nm* murderer; assassin.

assassinat [àsàsɛ́nā] *nm* murder; assassination.

assassiner [àsàsɛ́nā] *vt* to murder; (*surtout POL*) to assassinate.

assaut [àsō] *nm* assault, attack; **prendre d'~** to (take by) storm, assault; **donner l'~ (à)** to attack; **faire** ~ **de** (*rivaliser*) to vie with *ou* rival each other in.

assèchement [àsɛshmân] *nm* draining, drainage.

assécher [àsāshā] *vt* to drain.

ASSEDIC [àsādɛ́k] *sigle f* (= *Association pour l'emploi dans l'industrie et le commerce*) unemployment insurance plan.

assemblage [àsânblázh] *nm* assembling; (*MENUISERIE*) joint; **un** ~ **de** (*fig*) a collection of; **langage d'~** (*INFORM*) assembly language.

assemblée [àsânblā] *nf* (*réunion*) meeting; (*public, assistance*) gathering; assembled people; (*POL*) assembly; (*REL*): **l'~ des fidèles** the congregation; **l'A~ nationale (AN)** the (French) National Assembly.

assembler [àsânblā] *vt* (*joindre, monter*) to assemble, put together; (*amasser*) to gather (together), collect (together); **s'~** *vi* to gather, collect.

assembleur [àsânblœr] *nm* assembler, fitter; (*INFORM*) assembler.

assener, asséner [àsɛnā] *vt*: ~ **un coup à qn** to deal sb a blow.

assentiment [àsântɛmân] *nm* assent, consent; (*approbation*) approval.

asseoir [àswàr] *vt* (*malade, bébé*) to sit up; (*personne debout*) to sit down; (*autorité, réputation*) to establish; **s'~** *vi* to sit up; to sit (o.s.) down; **faire** ~ **qn** to ask sb to sit down; ~ **qch sur** to build sth on; (*appuyer*) to base sth on.

assermenté, e [àsɛrmântā] *a* sworn, on oath.

assertion [àsɛrsyôn] *nf* assertion.

asservir [àsɛrvɛr] *vt* to subjugate, enslave.

assesseur [àsɛ̀sœr] *nm* (*JUR*) assessor.

asseyais [àsɛye] *etc vb voir* **asseoir**.

assez [àsā] *ad* (*suffisamment*) enough, sufficiently; (*passablement*) rather, quite, fairly; ~**!** enough!, that'll do!; ~**/pas** ~ **cuit** well enough done/underdone; **est-il** ~ **fort/rapide?** is he strong/fast enough *ou* sufficiently strong/fast?; **il est passé** ~ **vite** he went past rather *ou* quite *ou* fairly fast; ~ **de pain/livres** enough *ou* sufficient bread/books; **vous en avez** ~**?** have you got enough?; **en avoir** ~ **de qch** (*en être fatigué*) to have had enough of sth; **travailler** ~ to work sufficiently (hard), work (hard) enough.

assidu, e [àsɛ́dü] *a* assiduous, painstaking; (*régulier*) regular; ~ **auprès de qn** attentive towards sb.

assiduité [àsɛ́düɛtā] *nf* assiduousness, painstaking; regularity; attentiveness; ~**s** *nfpl* assiduous attentions.

assidûment [àsɛ́dümân] *ad* assiduously, painstakingly; attentively.

assied [àsyā] *etc vb voir* **asseoir**.

assiéger [àsyāzhā] *vt* to besiege, lay siege to; (*suj: foule, touristes*) to mob, besiege.

assiérai [àsyārā] *etc vb voir* **asseoir**.

assiette [àsyɛt] *nf* plate; (*contenu*) plate(ful); (*équilibre*) seat; (*de colonne*) seating; (*de navire*) trim; ~ **anglaise** assorted cold meats; ~ **creuse** (soup) dish, soup plate; ~ **à dessert** dessert *ou* side plate; ~ **de l'impôt** basis of (tax) assessment; ~ **plate** (dinner) plate.

assiettée [àsyātā] *nf* plateful.

assignation [àsɛ́nyâsyôn] *nf* assignation; (*JUR*)

summons; (: *de témoin*) subpoena.

assigner [àsēnyā] *vt*: ~ **qch à** to assign *ou* allot sth to; (*valeur, importance*) to attach sth to; (*somme*) to allocate sth to; (*limites*) to set *ou* fix sth to; (*cause, effet*) to ascribe *ou* attribute sth to; ~ **qn à** (*affecter*) to assign sb to; ~ **qn à résidence** (*JUR*) to place sb under house arrest.

assimilable [àsēmēlàbl(ə)] *a* easily assimilated *ou* absorbed.

assimilation [àsēmēlàsyóñ] *nf* assimilation, absorption.

assimiler [àsēmēlā] *vt* to assimilate, absorb; (*comparer*): ~ **qch/qn à** to liken *ou* compare sth/sb to; **s'~** *vi* (*s'intégrer*) to be assimilated *ou* absorbed; **ils sont assimilés aux infirmières** (*ADMIN*) they are classed as nurses.

assis, e [àsē, -ēz] *pp de* **asseoir** ♦ *a* sitting (down), seated ♦ *nf* (*CONSTR*) course; (*GÉO*) stratum (*pl* -a); (*fig*) basis (*pl* bases), foundation; ~ **en tailleur** sitting cross-legged.

assises [àsēz] *nfpl* (*JUR*) assizes; (*congrès*) (annual) conference.

assistanat [àsēstáná] *nm* assistantship; (*à l'université*) instructorship (*US*), lectureship (*Brit*).

assistance [àsēstáñs] *nf* (*public*) audience; (*aide*) assistance; **porter** *ou* **prêter** ~ **à qn** to give sb assistance; **A~ publique** (**AP**) *public health service*; **enfant de l'A~ (publique)** ward of the state; ~ **technique** technical aid.

assistant, e [àsēstáñ, -áñt] *nm/f* assistant; (*d'université*) instructor (*US*), lecturer (*Brit*); **les ~s** *nmpl* (*auditeurs etc*) those present; **~e sociale** social worker.

assisté, e [àsēstā] *a* (*AUTO*) power assisted ♦ *nm/f* person receiving aid from the State.

assister [àsēstā] *vt* to assist; ~ **à** *vt* (*scène, événement*) to witness; (*conférence, séminaire*) to attend, be (present) at; (*spectacle, match*) to be at, see.

association [àsosyásyóñ] *nf* association; (*COMM*) partnership; ~ **d'idées/images** association of ideas/images.

associé, e [àsosyā] *nm/f* associate; (*COMM*) partner.

associer [àsosyā] *vt* to associate; ~ **qn à** (*profits*) to give sb a share of; (*affaire*) to make sb a partner in; (*joie, triomphe*) to include sb in; ~ **qch à** (*joindre, allier*) to combine sth with; **s'~** *vi* to join together; (*COMM*) to form a partnership ♦ *vt* (*collaborateur*) to take on (as a partner); **s'~ à** to be combined with; (*opinions, joie de qn*) to share in; **s'~ à** *ou* **avec qn pour faire** to join (forces) *ou* join together with sb to do.

assoie [àswà] *etc vb voir* **asseoir**.

assoiffé, e [àswàfā] *a* thirsty; (*fig*): ~ **de** (*sang*) thirsting for; (*gloire*) thirsting after.

assoirai [àswàrā], **assois** [àswà] *etc vb voir* **asseoir**.

assolement [àsolmáñ] *nm* (systematic) rotation of crops.

assombrir [àsóñbrēr] *vt* to darken; (*fig*) to fill with gloom; **s'~** *vi* to darken; (*devenir nuageux, fig: visage*) to cloud over; (*fig*) to become gloomy.

assommer [àsomā] *vt* (*étourdir, abrutir*) to knock out, stun; (*fam: ennuyer*) to bore stiff.

Assomption [àsóñpsyóñ] *nf*: **l'~** the Assumption.

assorti, e [àsortē] *a* matched, matching; **fromages/légumes ~s** assorted cheeses/vegetables; ~ **à** matching; ~ **de** accompanied with; (*conditions, conseils*) coupled with; **bien/mal** ~ well/ill-matched.

assortiment [àsortēmáñ] *nm* (*choix*) assortment, selection; (*harmonie de couleurs, formes*) arrangement; (*COMM: lot, stock*) selection.

assortir [àsortēr] *vt* to match; **s'~** to go well together, match; ~ **qch à** to match sth with; ~ **qch de** to accompany sth with; **s'~ de** to be accompanied by.

assoupi, e [àsōōpē] *a* dozing, sleeping; (*fig*) (be)numbed; (*sens*) dulled.

assoupir [àsōōpēr]: **s'~** *vi* (*personne*) to doze off; (*sens*) to go numb.

assoupissement [àsōōpēsmáñ] *nm* (*sommeil*) dozing; (*fig: somnolence*) drowsiness.

assouplir [àsōōplēr] *vt* to make supple, soften; (*membres, corps*) to limber up, make supple; (*fig*) to relax; (: *caractère*) to soften, make more flexible; **s'~** *vi* to soften; to limber up; to relax; to become more flexible.

assouplissement [àsōōplēsmáñ] *nm* softening; limbering up; relaxation; **exercices d'~** limbering up exercises.

assourdir [àsōōrdēr] *vt* (*bruit*) to deaden, muffle; (*suj: bruit*) to deafen.

assourdissant, e [àsōōrdēsáñ, -áñt] *a* (*bruit*) deafening.

assouvir [àsōōvēr] *vt* to satisfy, appease.

assoyais [àswàye] *etc vb voir* **asseoir**.

ASSU [àsü] *sigle f* = *Association du sport scolaire et universitaire*.

assujetti, e [àsüzhātē] *a*: ~ **(à)** subject (to); (*ADMIN*): ~ **à l'impôt** subject to tax(ation).

assujettir [àsüzhātēr] *vt* to subject, subjugate; (*fixer: planches, tableau*) to secure, fix securely; ~ **qn à** (*règle, impôt*) to subject sb to.

assujettissement [àsüzhātēsmáñ] *nm* subjection, subjugation.

assumer [àsümā] *vt* (*fonction, emploi*) to assume, take on; (*accepter: conséquence, situation*) to accept.

assurance [àsüráñs] *nf* (*certitude*) assurance; (*confiance en soi*) (self-)confidence; (*contrat*) insurance (policy); (*secteur commercial*) insurance; **prendre une** ~ **contre** to take out insurance *ou* an insurance policy against; ~ **contre l'incendie** fire insurance; ~ **contre le vol** insurance against theft; **société d'~, compagnie d'~s** insurance company; ~ **maladie** (**AM**) health insurance; ~ **au tiers** third party insurance; ~ **tous risques** (*AUTO*) comprehensive insurance; **~s sociales** (**AS**) ≈ Social Security (*US*), ≈ National Insurance (*Brit*).

assurance-vie, *pl* assurances-vie [àsüráñsvē] *nf* life insurance *ou* assurance (*Brit*).

assurance-vol, *pl* assurances-vol [àsüráñsvol] *nf* insurance against theft.

assuré, e [àsürā] *a* (*victoire etc*) certain, sure; (*démarche, voix*) assured, (self-)confident; (*certain*): ~ **de** confident of; (*ASSURANCES*) insured ♦ *nm/f* insured (person); ~ **social** ≈ member of the Social Security plan (*US*) *ou* National Insurance scheme (*Brit*).

assurément [àsürámáṅ] *ad* assuredly, most certainly.

assurer [àsürā] *vt* (*COMM*) to insure; (*stabiliser*) to steady, stabilize; (*victoire etc*) to ensure, make certain; (*frontières, pouvoir*) to make secure; (*service, garde*) to provide, operate; ~ **qch à qn** (*garantir*) to secure *ou* guarantee sth for sb; (*certifier*) to assure sb of sth; ~ **à qn que** to assure sb that; **je vous assure que non/si** I assure you that that is not the case/is the case; ~ **qn de** to assure sb of; ~ **ses arrières** (*fig*) to be sure one has something to fall back on; **s'~ (contre)** (*COMM*) to insure o.s. (against); **s'~ de/que** (*vérifier*) to make sure of/that: **s'~ (de)** (*aide de qn*) to secure; **s'~ sur la vie** to take out a life insurance; **s'~ le concours/la collaboration de qn** to secure sb's aid/ collaboration.

assureur [àsürœr] *nm* insurance agent; (*société*) insurers *pl*.

Assyrie [àsērē] *nf*: **l'~** Assyria.

assyrien, ne [àsēryaṅ, -en] *a* Assyrian.

astérisque [àstārēsk(ə)] *nm* asterisk.

asthmatique [àsmátēk] *a* asthmatic.

asthme [àsm(ə)] *nm* asthma.

asticot [àstēkō] *nm* maggot.

astigmate [àstēgmát] *a* (*MÉD*: *personne*) astigmatic, having an astigmatism.

astiquer [àstēkā] *vt* to polish, shine.

astrakan [àstrákáṅ] *nm* astrakhan.

astral, e, aux [àstrál, -ō] *a* astral.

astre [àstr(ə)] *nm* star.

astreignant, e [àstrenyáṅ, -áṅt] *a* demanding.

astreindre [àstraṅdr(ə)] *vt*: ~ **qn à qch** to force sth upon sb; ~ **qn à faire** to compel *ou* force sb to do; **s'~ à** to compel *ou* force o.s. to.

astringent, e [àstraṅzháṅ, -áṅt] *a* astringent.

astrologie [àstrolozhē] *nf* astrology.

astrologique [àstrolozhēk] *a* astrological.

astrologue [àstrolog] *nm/f* astrologer.

astronaute [àstronōt] *nm/f* astronaut.

astronome [àstronom] *nm/f* astronomer.

astronomie [àstronomē] *nf* astronomy.

astronomique [àstronomēk] *a* astronomic(al).

astrophysicien, ne [àstrofēzēsyaṅ, -en] *nm/f* astrophysicist.

astuce [àstüs] *nf* shrewdness, astuteness; (*truc*) trick, clever way; (*plaisanterie*) wisecrack.

astucieusement [àstüsyœzmáṅ] *ad* shrewdly, cleverly, astutely.

astucieux, euse [àstüsyœ, -œz] *a* shrewd, clever, astute.

asymétrique [àsēmátrēk] *a* asymmetric(al).

AT *sigle m* (= *Ancien Testament*) OT.

atavisme [àtávēsm(ə)] *nm* atavism, heredity.

atelier [àtəlyā] *nm* workshop; (*de peintre*) studio.

atermoiements [àtermwámáṅ] *nmpl* procrastination *sg*.

atermoyer [àtermwáyā] *vi* to temporize, procrastinate.

athée [àtā] *a* atheistic ♦ *nm/f* atheist.

athéisme [àtāēsm(ə)] *nm* atheism.

Athènes [àten] *n* Athens.

athénien, ne [àtānyaṅ, -en] *a* Athenian.

athlète [àtlet] *nm/f* (*SPORT*) athlete; (*costaud*) muscleman.

athlétique [àtlātēk] *a* athletic.

athlétisme [àtlātēsm(ə)] *nm* athletics *sg*; **faire de l'~** to do athletics; **tournoi d'~** athletics meet (*US*) *ou* meeting (*Brit*).

Atlantide [àtláṅtēd] *nf*: **l'~** Atlantis.

atlantique [àtláṅtēk] *a* Atlantic ♦ *nm*: **l'(océan) A~** the Atlantic (Ocean).

atlantiste [àtláṅtēst(ə)] *a, nm/f* Atlanticist.

Atlas [àtlâs] *nm*: **l'~** the Atlas Mountains.

atlas [àtlâs] *nm* atlas.

atmosphère [àtmosfer] *nf* atmosphere.

atmosphérique [àtmosfārēk] *a* atmospheric.

atoll [àtol] *nm* atoll.

atome [àtōm] *nm* atom.

atomique [àtomēk] *a* atomic, nuclear; (*usine*) nuclear; (*nombre, masse*) atomic.

atomiseur [àtomēzœr] *nm* atomizer.

atomiste [àtomēst(ə)] *nm/f* (*aussi*: **savant, ingénieur** *etc* ~) atomic scientist.

atone [àton] *a* lifeless; (*LING*) unstressed, un-accented.

atours [àtōōr] *nmpl* attire *sg*, finery *sg*.

atout [àtōō] *nm* trump; (*fig*) asset; (: *plus fort*) trump card; "~ **pique/trèfle**" "spades/ clubs are trumps".

ATP *sigle f* (= *Association des tennismen professionnels*) ATP (= *Association of Tennis Professionals*) ♦ *sigle mpl* (= *arts et traditions populaires*): **musée des** ~ ≈ folk museum.

âtre [âtr(ə)] *nm* hearth.

atroce [àtros] *a* atrocious, horrible.

atrocement [àtrosmáṅ] *ad* atrociously, horribly.

atrocité [àtrosētā] *nf* atrocity.

atrophie [àtrofē] *nf* atrophy.

atrophier [àtrofyā]: **s'~** *vi* to atrophy.

atropine [àtropēn] *nf* (*CHIMIE*) atropine.

attabler [àtáblā]: **s'~** *vi* to sit down at (the) table; **s'~ à la terrasse** to sit down (at a table) on the terrace.

attachant, e [àtásháṅ, -áṅt] *a* engaging, like-able.

attache [àtásh] *nf* clip, fastener; (*fig*) tie; **~s** *nfpl* (*relations*) connections; **à l'~** (*chien*) tied up.

attaché, e [àtáshā] *a*: **être ~ à** (*aimer*) to be attached to ♦ *nm* (*ADMIN*) attaché; **~ de presse/d'ambassade** press/embassy attaché; **~ commercial** commercial attaché.

attaché-case [àtáshākez] *nm inv* attaché case, briefcase.

attachement [àtáshmáṅ] *nm* attachment.

attacher [àtáshā] *vt* to tie up; (*étiquette*) to attach, tie on; (*souliers*) to tie ♦ *vi* (*poêle, riz*) to stick; **s'~** (*robe etc*) to button up; **s'~ à** (*par affection*) to become attached to; **s'~ à faire qch** to endeavor to do sth; ~ **qch à** to tie *ou* fasten *ou* attach sth to; ~ **qn à** (*fig*: *lier*) to attach sb to; ~ **du prix/de l'importance à** to attach great value/attach importance to.

attaquant [àtákáṅ] *nm* (*MIL*) attacker; (*SPORT*) striker, forward.

attaque [àták] *nf* attack; (*cérébrale*) stroke;

(*d'épilepsie*) fit; **être/se sentir d'**~ to be/feel in top form; ~ **à main armée** armed attack.

attaquer [átákā] *vt* to attack; (*en justice*) to bring an action against, sue; (*travail*) to tackle, set about ♦ *vi* to attack; **s'**~ **à** to attack; (*épidémie, misère*) to tackle, attack.

attardé, e [átárdā] *a* (*passants*) late; (*enfant*) backward; (*conceptions*) old-fashioned.

attarder [átárdā]: **s'**~ *vi* (*sur qch, en chemin*) to linger; (*chez qn*) to stay on.

atteignais [átānye] *etc vb voir* **atteindre**.

atteindre [átaŋdr(ə)] *vt* to reach; (*blesser*) to hit; (*contacter*) to reach, contact, get in touch with; (*émouvoir*) to affect.

atteint, e [átaŋ, -aŋt] *pp de* **atteindre** ♦ *a* (*MÉD*): **être** ~ **de** to be suffering from ♦ *nf* attack; **hors d'**~**e** out of reach; **porter** ~**e à** to strike a blow at, undermine.

attelage [átlázh] *nm* (*de remorque etc*) (*trailer*) hitch (*US*), coupling (*Brit*); (*animaux*) team; (*harnachement*) harness; (*: de bœufs*) yoke.

atteler [átlā] *vt* (*cheval, bœufs*) to hitch up; (*wagons*) to couple; **s'**~ **à** (*travail*) to buckle down to.

attelle [átɛl] *nf* splint.

attenant, e [átnaŋ, -aŋt] *a*: ~ (**à**) adjoining.

attendant [átaŋdaŋ]: **en** ~ *ad* (*dans l'intervalle*) meanwhile, in the meantime.

attendre [átaŋdr(ə)] *vt* to wait for; (*être destiné ou réservé à*) to await, be in store for ♦ *vi* to wait; **je n'attends plus rien (de la vie)** I expect nothing more (from life); **attendez que je réfléchisse** wait while I think; **s'**~ **à** (**cc que**) (*escompter*) to expect (that); **je ne m'y attendais pas** I didn't expect that; **ce n'est pas ce à quoi je m'attendais** that's not what I expected; ~ **un enfant** to be expecting a baby; ~ **de pied ferme** to wait determinedly; ~ **de faire/d'être** to wait until one does/is; ~ **que** to wait until; ~ **qch de** to expect sth of; **faire** ~ **qn** to keep sb waiting; **se faire** ~ to keep people (*ou* us *etc*) waiting; **en attendant** *ad voir* **attendant**.

attendri, e [átaŋdrē] *a* tender.

attendrir [átaŋdrēr] *vt* to move (to pity); (*viande*) to tenderize; **s'**~ (**sur**) to be moved *ou* touched (by).

attendrissant, e [átaŋdrēsaŋ, -aŋt] *a* moving, touching.

attendrissement [átaŋdrēsmaŋ] *nm* (*tendre*) emotion; (*apitoyé*) pity.

attendrisseur [átaŋdrēsœr] *nm* tenderizer.

attendu, e [átaŋdü] *pp de* **attendre** ♦ *a* long-awaited; (*prévu*) expected ♦ *nm*: ~**s** *reasons adduced for a judgment*; ~ **que** *cj* considering that, since.

attentat [átaŋtá] *nm* (*contre une personne*) assassination attempt; (*contre un bâtiment*) attack; ~ **à la bombe** bomb attack; ~ **à la pudeur** (*exhibitionnisme*) indecent exposure *q*; (*agression*) indecent assault *q*.

attente [átaŋt] *nf* wait; (*espérance*) expectation; **contre toute** ~ contrary to (all) expectations.

attenter [átaŋtā]: ~ **à** *vt* (*liberté*) to violate; ~ **à la vie de qn** to make an attempt on sb's life; ~ **à ses jours** to make an attempt on one's life.

attentif, ive [átaŋtēf, -ēv] *a* (*auditeur*) attentive; (*soin*) scrupulous; (*travail*) careful; ~ **à paying** attention to; (*devoir*) mindful of; ~ **à faire** careful to do.

attention [átaŋsyôŋ] *nf* attention; (*prévenance*) attention, thoughtfulness *q*; **mériter** ~ to be worthy of attention; **à l'**~ **de** for the attention of; **porter qch à l'**~ **de qn** to bring sth to sb's attention; **attirer l'**~ **de qn sur qch** to draw sb's attention to sth; **faire** ~ (**à**) to be careful (of); **faire** ~ (**à ce**) **que** to be *ou* make sure that; ~**!** careful!, watch!, watch out!; ~, **si vous ouvrez cette lettre** (*sanction*) just watch out, if you open that letter; ~, **respectez les consignes de sécurité** be sure to observe the safety instructions.

attentionné, e [átaŋsyonā] *a* thoughtful, considerate.

attentisme [átaŋtēsm(ə)] *nm* wait-and-see policy.

attentiste [átaŋtēst(ə)] *a* (*politique*) wait-and-see ♦ *nm/f* believer in a wait-and-see policy.

attentivement [átaŋtēvmáŋ] *ad* attentively.

atténuant, e [átaŋüaŋ, -aŋt] *a*: **circonstances** ~**es** extenuating circumstances.

atténuer [átaŋüā] *vt* to alleviate, ease; (*diminuer*) to lessen; (*amoindrir*) to mitigate the effects of; **s'**~ *vi* to ease; (*violence etc*) to abate.

atterrer [átárā] *vt* to dismay, appal (l).

atterrir [átárēr] *vi* to land.

atterrissage [átárēsázh] *nm* landing; ~ **sur le ventre/sans visibilité/forcé** belly/blind/forced landing.

attestation [átɛstásyôŋ] *nf* certificate, testimonial; ~ **médicale** doctor's certificate

attester [átɛstā] *vt* to testify to, vouch for; (*démontrer*) to attest, testify to; ~ **que** to testify that.

attiédir [átyādēr]: **s'**~ *vi* to become lukewarm; (*fig*) to cool down.

attifé, e [átēfā] *a* (*fam*) decked out.

attifer [átēfā] *vt* to deck out.

attique [átēk] *nm*: **appartement en** ~ penthouse (apartment (*US*) *ou* flat (*Brit*)).

attirail [átēráy] *nm* gear; (*péj*) paraphernalia.

attirance [átēráŋs] *nf* attraction; (*séduction*) lure.

attirant, e [átēráŋ, -aŋt] *a* attractive, appealing.

attirer [átērā] *vt* to attract; (*appâter*) to lure, entice; ~ **qn dans un coin/vers soi** to draw sb into a corner/towards one; ~ **l'attention de qn** to attract sb's attention; ~ **l'attention de qn sur qch** to draw sb's attention to sth; ~ **des ennuis à qn** to make trouble for sb; **s'**~ **des ennuis** to bring trouble upon o.s., get into trouble.

attiser [átēzā] *vt* (*feu*) to poke (up), stir up; (*fig*) to fan the flame of, stir up.

attitré, e [átētrā] *a* qualified; (*agréé*) accredited, appointed.

attitude [átētüd] *nf* attitude; (*position du corps*) bearing.

attouchements [átōōshmáŋ] *nmpl* touching *sg*; (*sexuels*) fondling *sg*, stroking *sg*.

attraction [átráksyôŋ] *nf* attraction; (*de cabaret, cirque*) number.

attrait [átrɛ] *nm* appeal, attraction; (*plus fort*)

lure; **~s** *nmpl* attractions; **éprouver de l'~ pour** to be attracted to.

attrape |àtràp| *nf voir* farce.

attrape-nigaud |àtràpnēgō| *nm* con.

attraper |àtràpā| *vt* to catch; (*habitude, amende*) to get, pick up; (*fam: duper*) to con.

attrayant, e |àtreyàn̄, -àn̄t| *a* attractive.

attribuer |àtrēbüā| *vt* (*prix*) to award; (*rôle, tâche*) to allocate, assign; (*imputer*): **~ qch à** to attribute sth to, ascribe sth to, put sth down to; **s'~** *vt* (*s'approprier*) to claim for o.s.

attribut |àtrēbü| *nm* attribute; (*LING*) complement.

attribution |àtrēbüsyón̄| *nf* (*voir* attribuer) awarding; allocation, assignment; attribution; **~s** *nfpl* (*compétence*) attributions; **complément d'~** (*LING*) indirect object.

attrister |àtrēstā| *vt* to sadden; **s'~ de qch** to be saddened by sth.

attroupement |àtr͞o͞opmàn̄| *nm* crowd, mob.

attrouper |àtr͞o͞opā|: **s'~** *vi* to gather.

au |ō| *prép* + *dét voir* à.

aubade |ōbàd| *nf* dawn serenade.

aubaine |ōbɛn| *nf* godsend; (*financière*) windfall; (*COMM*) bonanza.

aube |ōb| *nf* dawn, daybreak; (*REL*) alb; **à l'~** at dawn *ou* daybreak; **à l'~ de** (*fig*) at the dawn of.

aubépine |ōbāpēn| *nf* hawthorn.

auberge |ōberzh(ə)| *nf* inn; **~ de jeunesse** youth hostel.

aubergine |ōbàrzhēn| *nf* eggplant, aubergine.

aubergiste |ōberzhēst(ə)| *nm/f* inn-keeper, hotel-keeper.

auburn |ōbɛrn| *a inv* auburn.

aucun, e |ōkœn̄, -ün| *dét* no, *tournure négative* + any; (*positif*) any ♦ *pronom* none, *tournure négative* + any; (*positif*) any(one); **il n'y a ~ livre** there isn't any book, there is no book; **je n'en vois ~ qui** I can't see any which, I (can) see none which; **~ homme** no man; **sans ~ doute** without any doubt; **sans ~e hésitation** without hesitation; **plus qu'~ autre** more than any other; **plus qu'~ de ceux qui ...** more than any of those who ...; **en ~e façon** in no way at all; **~ des deux** neither of the two; **~ d'entre eux** none of them; **d'~s** (*certains*) some.

aucunement |ōkünmàn̄| *ad* in no way, not in the least.

audace |ōdàs| *nf* daring, boldness; (*péj*) audacity; **il a eu l'~ de ...** he had the audacity to ...; **vous ne manquez pas d'~!** you're not lacking in nerve *ou* cheek!

audacieux, euse |ōdàsyœ̄, -œ̄z| *a* daring, bold.

au-dedans |ōdədàn̄| *ad, prép* inside.

au-dehors |ōdəor| *ad, prép* outside.

au-delà |ōdlà| *ad* beyond ♦ *nm*: **l'~** the hereafter; **~ de** *prép* beyond.

au-dessous |ōds͞o͞o| *ad* underneath; below; **~ de** *prép* under(neath), below; (*limite, somme etc*) below, under; (*dignité, condition*) below.

au-dessus |ōdsü| *ad* above; **~ de** *prép* above.

au-devant |ōdvàn̄|: **~ de** *prép*: **aller ~ de** to go (out) and meet; (*souhaits de qn*) to anticipate.

audible |ōdēbl(ə)| *a* audible.

audience |ōdyàn̄s| *nf* audience; (*JUR: séance*) hearing; **trouver ~ auprès de** to arouse much interest among, get the (interested) attention of.

audiogramme |ōdyogràm| *nm* audiogram (*US*), audiogramme (*Brit*).

audio-visuel, le |ōdyovēzüel| *a* audio-visual ♦ *nm* (*équipement*) audio-visual aids *pl*; (*méthodes*) audio-visual methods *pl*; **l'~** radio and television.

auditeur, trice |ōdētœr, -trēs| *nm/f* (*à la radio*) listener; (*à une conférence*) member of the audience, listener; **~ libre** auditor (*US*), unregistered student (*attending lectures*).

auditif, ive |ōdētēf, -ēv| (*mémoire*) auditory; **appareil ~** hearing aid.

audition |ōdēsyón̄| *nf* (*ouïe, écoute*) hearing; (*JUR: de témoins*) examination; (*MUS, THÉÂTRE: épreuve*) audition.

auditionner |ōdēsyonā| *vt, vi* to audition.

auditoire |ōdētwàr| *nm* audience.

auditorium |ōdētoryom| *nm* (public) studio.

auge |ōzh| *nf* trough.

augmentation |ogmàn̄tàsyón̄| *nf* (*action*) increasing; raising; (*résultat*) increase; **~ (de salaire)** (pay) raise (*US*), rise (in salary) (*Brit*).

augmenter |ogmàn̄tā| *vt* to increase; (*salaire, prix*) to increase, raise, put up; (*employé*) to increase the salary of, give a (pay) raise (*US*) *ou* (salary) rise (*Brit*) to ♦ *vi* to increase; **~ de poids/volume** to gain (in) weight/volume.

augure |ogür| *nm* soothsayer, oracle; **de bon/mauvais ~** of good/ill omen.

augurer |ogürā| *vt*: **~ qch de** to foresee sth (coming) from *ou* out of; **~ bien de** to augur well for.

auguste |ogüst(ə)| *a* august, noble, majestic.

aujourd'hui |ōzh͞o͞ordüē| *ad* today; **~ en huit/quinze** a week/two weeks from now *ou* today; **à dater** *ou* **partir d'~** from today('s date).

aumône |omōn| *nf* alms *sg* (*pl inv*); **faire l'~ (à qn)** to give alms (to sb); **faire l'~ de qch à qn** (*fig*) to favor sb with sth.

aumônerie |omōnrē| *nf* chaplaincy.

aumônier |omōnyā| *nm* chaplain.

auparavant |ōpàràvàn̄| *ad* before(hand).

auprès |ōpre|: **~ de** *prép* next to, close to; (*recourir, s'adresser*) to; (*en comparaison de*) compared with, next to; (*dans l'opinion de*) in the opinion of.

auquel |ōkel| *prép* + *pronom voir* lequel.

aurai |orā| *etc vb voir* avoir.

auréole |oràol| *nf* halo; (*tache*) ring.

auréolé, e |oràolā| *a* (*fig*): **~ de gloire** crowned with *ou* in glory.

auriculaire |orēküler| *nm* little finger.

aurore |oror| *nf* dawn, daybreak; **~ boréale** northern lights *pl*.

ausculter |oskültā| *vt* to sound.

auspices |ospēs| *nmpl*: **sous les ~ de** under the patronage *ou* auspices of; **sous de bons/mauvais ~** under favorable/unfavorable auspices.

aussi |ōsē| *ad* (*également*) also, too; (*de comparaison*) as ♦ *cj* therefore, consequently; **~ fort que** as strong as; **lui ~** (*sujet*) he too;

(*objet*) him too; ~ **bien que** (*de même que*) as well as.

aussitôt [ōsētō] *ad* straight away, immediately; ~ **que** as soon as; ~ **envoyé** as soon as it is (*ou* was) sent; ~ **fait** no sooner done.

austère [oster] *a* austere; (*sévère*) stern.

austérité [ostārētā] *nf* austerity; . **plan/budget d'**~ austerity plan/budget.

austral, e [ostrál] *a* southern; **l'océan A**~ the Antarctic Ocean; **les Terres A**~**es** Antarctica.

Australie [ostrálē] *nf*: **l'**~ Australia.

australien, ne [ostrályań, -en] *a* Australian ♦ *nm/f*: **A**~, **ne** Australian.

autant [ōtáń] *ad* so much; (*comparatif*): ~ **(que)** as much (as); (*nombre*) as many (as); ~ **(de)** so much (*ou* many); as much (*ou* many); **n'importe qui aurait pu en faire** ~ anyone could have done the same *ou* as much; ~ **partir** we (*ou* you *etc*) may as well leave; ~ **ne rien dire** best not say anything; ~ **dire que** ... one might as well say that ...; **fort** ~ **que courageux** as strong as he is brave; **il n'est pas découragé pour** ~ he isn't discouraged for all that; **pour** ~ **que** *cj* assuming, as long as; **d'**~ *ad* accordingly, in proportion; **d'**~ **plus/mieux (que)** all the more/the better (since).

autarcie [ōtársē] *nf* autarky, self-sufficiency.

autel [otel] *nm* altar.

auteur [ōtœr] *nm* author; **l'**~ **de cette remarque** the person who said that, droit **d'**~ copyright.

authenticité [ōtäntēsētá] *nf* authenticity.

authentifier [ōtáńtēfyā] *vt* to authenticate.

authentique [otántek] *a* authentic, genuine.

auto [otō] *nf* car; ~**s tamponneuses** bumper cars, dodgems.

auto... [otō] *préfixe* auto..., self-.

autobiographie [otobyográfē] *nf* autobiography.

autobiographique [otobyográfēk] *a* autobiographical.

autobus [otobüs] *nm* bus.

autocar [otokár] *nm* bus, coach (*Brit*).

autochtone [otokton] *nm/f* native.

autocollant, e [otokolâń, -âńt] *a* self-adhesive; (*enveloppe*) self-seal ♦ *nm* sticker.

auto-couchettes [otokōōshet] *a inv*: **train** ~ car sleeper train, motorail ® train (*Brit*).

autocratique [otokrátēk] *a* autocratic.

autocritique [otokrētēk] *nf* self-criticism.

autocuiseur [otokwēzœr] *nm* (*CULIN*) pressure cooker.

autodéfense [otodāfâńs] *nf* self-defence; **groupe d'**~ vigilante committee.

autodétermination [otodātermēnâsyôń] *nf* self-determination.

autodidacte [otodēdákt(ə)] *nm/f* self-taught person.

autodiscipline [otodēsēplēn] *nf* self-discipline.

autodrome [otodrōm] *nm* motor-racing stadium.

auto-école [otoákol] *nf* driving school.

autofinancement [otofēnâńsmâń] *nm* self-financing.

autogéré, e [otozhārá] *a* self-managed, managed internally.

autographe [otográf] *nm* autograph.

autoguidé, e [otogēdā] *a* self-guided.

automate [otomát] *nm* (*robot*) automaton; (*machine*) (automatic) machine.

automatique [otomátēk] *a, nm* automatic; **l'**~ (*TÉL*) ≈ direct dialling.

automatiquement [otomátēkmâń] *ad* automatically.

automatiser [otomátēzá] *vt* to automate.

automatisme [otomátēsm(ə)] *nm* automatism.

automédication [otomādēkâsyôń] *nf* self-medication.

automitrailleuse [otomētrâyœz] *nf* armored (*US*) *ou* armoured (*Brit*) car.

automnal, e, aux [otonál, -ō] *a* autumnal.

automne [oton] *nm* fall (*US*), autumn.

automobile [otomobēl] *a* motor *cpd* ♦ *nf* (*motor*) car; **l'**~ motoring; (*industrie*) the car *ou* automobile (*US*) industry.

automobiliste [otomobēlēst(ə)] *nm/f* motorist.

autonettoyant, e [otonetwàyâń, -âńt] *a*: **four** ~ self-cleaning oven.

autonome [otonom] *a* autonomous; (*INFORM*) stand alonc; **(en mode)** ~ off line.

autonomie [otonomē] *nf* autonomy; (*POL*) self-government, autonomy; ~ **de vol** range.

autoportrait [otoportre] *nm* self-portrait.

autopsie [otopsē] *nf* post-mortem (examination), autopsy.

autopsier [otopsyā] *vt* to carry out a post-mortem *ou* an autopsy on.

autoradio [otorádyō] *nf* car radio.

autorail [otoráy] *nm* railcar.

autorisation [otorēzâsyôń] *nf* permission, authorization; (*papiers*) permit; **donner à qn l'**~ **de** to give sb permission to, authorize sb to; **avoir l'**~ **de faire** to be allowed *ou* have permission to do, be authorized to do.

autorisé, e [otorēzá] *a* (*opinion, sources*) authoritative; (*permis*): ~ **à faire** authorized *ou* permitted to do; **dans les milieux** ~**s** in official circles.

autoriser [otorēzá] *vt* to give permission for, authorize; (*fig*) to allow (of), sanction; ~ **qn à faire** to give permission to sb to do, authorize sb to do.

autoritaire [otoréter] *a* authoritarian.

autoritarisme [otorētárēsm(ə)] *nm* authoritarianism.

autorité [otorētá] *nf* authority; **faire** ~ to be authoritative; ~**s constituées** constitutional authorities.

autoroute [otorōōt] *nf* expressway (*US*), motorway (*Brit*).

autoroutier, ière [otorōōtyā, -yer] *a* expressway *cpd* (*US*), motorway *cpd* (*Brit*).

autosatisfaction [otosátēsfáksyôń] *nf* self-satisfaction.

auto-stop [otostop] *nm*: **l'**~ hitch-hiking; **faire de l'**~ to hitch-hike; **prendre qn en** ~ to give sb a lift.

auto-stoppeur, euse [otostopœr, -œz] *nm/f* hitch-hiker.

autosuffisant, e [otosüfēzâń, -âńt] *a* self-sufficient.

autosuggestion [otosügzhestyôń] *nf* auto-suggestion.

autour [ōtōōr] *ad* around; ~ **de** *prép* around; (*environ*) around, about; **tout** ~ *ad* all

around.
autre [ōtr(ə)] *a* other; **un ~ verre** (*supplémentaire*) one more glass, another glass; (*différent*) another glass, a different glass; **un ~** another (one); **l'~** the other (one); **les ~s** (*autrui*) others; **l'un et l'~** both (of them); **se détester** *etc* **l'un l'~/les uns les ~s** to hate *etc* each other/one another; **ni l'un ni l'~** neither (one) of them; **d'une semaine à l'~** from one week to the next; (*incessamment*) any week now; **de temps à ~** from time to time; **d'~s** others; **d'~s verres** other glasses; **j'en ai vu d'~s** I've seen worse; **à d'~s!** tell that to the marines!; **se sentir ~** to feel different; **la difficulté est ~** the difficulty is not there, that's not the difficulty; **~ chose** something else; **~ part** *ad* somewhere else; **d'~ part** *ad* on the other hand; **entre ~s** (*gens*) among others; (*choses*) among other things; **nous/vous ~s** us/you.
autrefois [ōtrəfwå] *ad* in the past.
autrement [ōtrəmåń] *ad* differently; (*d'une manière différente*) in another way; (*sinon*) otherwise; **je n'ai pas pu faire ~** I couldn't do anything else, I couldn't do otherwise; **~ dit** in other words; (*c'est-à-dire*) that is to say.
Autriche [ōtrēsh] *nf:* **l'~** Austria.
autrichien, ne [ōtrēshyåń, -en] *a* Austrian ♦ *nm/f:* **A~, ne** Austrian.
autruche [ōtrüsh] *nf* ostrich; **faire l'~** (*fig*) to bury one's head in the sand.
autrui [ōtrüē] *pronom* others.
auvent [ōvåń] *nm* canopy.
auvergnat, e [overnyå, -åt] *a* of *ou* from the Auvergne.
Auvergne [overny(ə)] *nf:* **l'~** the Auvergne.
aux [ō] *prép* + *dét* voir **à**.
auxiliaire [oksēlyer] *a, nm/f* auxiliary.
auxquels, auxquelles [ōkel] *prép* + *pronom* voir **lequel**.
AV *sigle m* (*BANQUE:* = *avis de virement*) advice of bank transfer ♦ *abr* (*AUTO*) = **avant**.
av. *abr* (= *avenue*) Av(e).
avachi, e [åvåshē] *a* limp, flabby; (*chaussure, vêtement*) out-of-shape; (*personne*): **~ sur qch** slumped on *ou* across sth.
avais [åve] *etc vb voir* **avoir**.
aval [åvål] *nm* (*accord*) endorsement, backing; (*GÉO*): **en ~** downstream, downriver; (*sur une pente*) downhill; **en ~ de** downstream *ou* downriver from; downhill from.
avalanche [åvålåńsh] *nf* avalanche; **~ poudreuse** powder snow avalanche.
avaler [åvålā] *vt* to swallow.
avaliser [åvålēzā] *vt* (*plan, entreprise*) to back, support; (*COMM, JUR*) to guarantee.
avance [åvåńs] *nf* (*de troupes etc*) advance; (*progrès*) progress; (*d'argent*) advance; (*opposé à retard*) lead; being ahead of schedule; **~s** *nfpl* overtures; (*amoureuses*) advances; **une ~ de 300 m/4 h** (*SPORT*) a 300 m/4 hour lead; (**être**) **en ~** (to be) early; (*sur un programme*) (to be) ahead of schedule; **on n'est pas en ~!** we're kind of late!; **être en ~ sur qn** to be ahead of sb; **d'~, à l'~, par ~** in advance; **~ (du) papier** (*INFORM*) paper advance.
avancé, e [åvåńsā] *a* advanced; (*travail etc*) well on, well under way; (*fruit, fromage*) overripe ♦ *nf* projection; overhang; **il est ~ pour son âge** he is advanced for his age.
avancement [åvåńsmåń] *nm* (*professionnel*) promotion; (*de travaux*) progress.
avancer [åvåńsā] *vi* to move forward, advance; (*projet, travail*) to make progress; (*être en saillie*) to overhang; to project; (*montre, réveil*) to be fast; (: *d'habitude*) to gain ♦ *vt* to move forward, advance; (*argent*) to advance; (*montre, pendule*) to put forward; (*faire progresser: travail etc*) to advance, move on; **s'~** *vi* to move forward, advance; (*fig*) to commit o.s.; (*faire saillie*) to overhang; to project; **j'avance (d'une heure)** I'm (an hour) fast.
avanies [åvånē] *nfpl* insults.
avant [åvåń] *prép* before ♦ *ad:* **trop/plus ~** too far/further forward ♦ *a inv:* **siège/roue ~** front seat/wheel ♦ *nm* front; (*SPORT: joueur*) forward; **~ qu'il parte/de partir** before he leaves/leaving; **~ qu'il (ne) pleuve** before it rains (*ou* rained); **~ tout** (*surtout*) above all; **à l'~** (*dans un véhicule*) in (the) front; **en ~** *ad* forward(s); **en ~ de** *prép* in front of; **aller de l'~** to steam ahead (*fig*), make good progress.
avantage [åvåńtåzh] *nm* advantage; (*TENNIS*): **~ service/dehors** advantage *ou* ad (*US*) *ou* van (*Brit*) in/out; **tirer ~ de** to take advantage of; **vous auriez ~ à faire** you would be well-advised to do, it would be to your advantage to do; **à l'~ de qn** to sb's advantage; **être à son ~** to be at one's best; **~s en nature** benefits in kind; **~s sociaux** fringe benefits.
avantager [åvåńtåzhā] *vt* (*favoriser*) to favor (*US*) *ou* favour (*Brit*); (*embellir*) to flatter.
avantageux, euse [åvåńtåzhœ̄, -œ̄z] *a* attractive; (*intéressant*) attractively priced; (*portrait, coiffure*) flattering; **conditions avantageuses** favorable terms.
avant-bras [åvåńbrå] *nm inv* forearm.
avant-centre [åvåńsåńtr(ə)] *nm* center forward (*US*), centre-forward (*Brit*).
avant-coureur [åvåńkōōrœr] *a inv* (*bruit etc*) precursory; **signe ~** advance indication *ou* sign.
avant-dernier, ière [åvåńdernyå, -yer] *a, nm/f* next to last, last but one.
avant-garde [åvåńgård(ə)] *nf* (*MIL*) vanguard; (*fig*) avant-garde; **d'~** avant-garde.
avant-goût [åvåńgōō] *nm* foretaste.
avant-hier [åvåńtyer] *ad* the day before yesterday.
avant-poste [åvåńpost(ə)] *nm* outpost.
avant-première [åvåńprəmyer] *nf* (*de film*) preview; **en ~** as a preview, in a preview showing.
avant-projet [åvåńprozhe] *nm* preliminary draft.
avant-propos [åvåńpropō] *nm* foreword.
avant-veille [åvåńvey] *nf:* **l'~** two days before.
avare [åvår] *a* miserly, avaricious ♦ *nm/f* miser; **~ de compliments** stingy *ou* sparing with one's compliments.
avarice [åvårēs] *nf* avarice, miserliness.

avaricieux, euse [àvàrēsyœ̄, -œ̄z] *a* miserly, niggardly.

avarié, e [àvàryā] *a* (*viande, fruits*) rotting; (*NAVIG*: *navire*) damaged.

avaries [àvàrē] *nfpl* (*NAVIG*) damage *sg*.

avatar [àvàtár] *nm* misadventure; (*transformation*) metamorphosis (*pl* -phoses).

avec [àvek] *prép* with; (*à l'égard de*) to(wards), with ♦ *ad* (*fam*) with it (*ou* him *etc*); ~ **habileté/lenteur** skilfully/slowly; ~ **eux/ces diseases** with them/these diseases; ~ **ça** (*malgré ça*) for all that; **et** ~ **ça?** (*dans un magasin*) anything *ou* something else?

avenant, e [àvnáǹ, -áǹt] *a* pleasant ♦ *nm* (*ASSURANCES*) additional clause; **à l'**~ *ad* in keeping.

avènement [àvenmáǹ] *nm* (*d'un roi*) accession, succession; (*d'un changement*) advent; (*d'une politique, idée*) coming.

avenir [àvnēr] *nm*: **l'**~ the future; **à l'**~ in future; **sans** ~ with no future, without a future; **carrière/politicien d'**~ career/ politician with prospects *ou* a future.

Avent [àváǹ] *nm*: **l'**~ Advent.

aventure [àvâǹtür] *nf*: **l'**~ adventure; **une** ~ an adventure; (*amoureuse*) an affair; **partir à l'**~ to go off in search of adventure; (*au hasard*) to go where one's fancy takes one; **roman/film d'**~ adventure story/film.

aventurer [àvâǹtürā] *vt* (*somme, réputation, vie*) to stake; (*remarque, opinion*) to venture; **s'**~ *vi* to venture, **s'**~ **à faire qch** to venture into sth.

aventureux, euse [àvâǹtürœ̄, œ̄z] *a* adventurous, venturesome; (*projet*) risky, chancy.

aventurier, ière [àvâǹtüryā, -yer] *nm/f* adventurer ♦ *nf* (*péj*) adventuress.

avenu, e [àvnü] *a*: **nul et non** ~ null and void.

avenue [àvnü] *nf* avenue.

avéré, e [àvàrā] *a* recognized, acknowledged.

avérer [àvàrā]: **s'**~ *vb avec attribut*: **s'**~ **faux/coûteux** to prove (to be) wrong/ expensive.

averse [àvers(ə)] *nf* shower.

aversion [àversyôǹ] *nf* aversion, loathing.

averti, e [àvertē] *a* (well-)informed.

avertir [àvertēr] *vt*: ~ **qn (de qch/que)** to warn sb (of sth/that); (*renseigner*) to inform sb (of sth/that); ~ **qn de ne pas faire qch** to warn sb not to do sth.

avertissement [àvertēsmáǹ] *nm* warning.

avertisseur [àvertēscœr] *nm* horn, siren; ~ **(d'incendie)** (fire) alarm.

aveu, x [àvœ̄] *nm* confession; **passer aux** ~**x** to make a confession; **de l'**~ **de** according to.

aveuglant, e [àvœglàǹ, -áǹt] *a* blinding.

aveugle [àvœgl(ə)] *a* blind ♦ *n* blind person; **les** ~**s** the blind; **test en (double)** ~ **(double)** blind test.

aveuglement [àvœglǝmáǹ] *nm* blindness.

aveuglément [àvœglāmáǹ] *ad* blindly.

aveugler [àvœglā] *vt* to blind.

aveuglette [àvœglet]: **à l'**~ groping one's way along; (*fig*) in the dark, blindly.

avez [àvā] *vb voir* **avoir**.

aviateur, trice [àvyátœr, -trēs] *nm/f* aviator, pilot.

aviation [àvyàsyôǹ] *nf* (*secteur commercial*) aviation; (*sport, métier de pilote*) flying; (*MIL*) air force; **terrain d'**~ airfield; ~ **de chasse** fighter force.

aviculteur, trice [àvēkültœr, -trēs] *nm/f* poultry farmer; bird breeder.

avide [àvēd] *a* eager; (*péj*) greedy, grasping; ~ **de** (*sang etc*) thirsting for; ~ **d'honneurs/d'argent** greedy for honors/ money; ~ **de connaître/d'apprendre** eager to know/learn.

avidité [àvēdētā] *nf* eagerness; greed.

avilir [àvēlēr] *vt* to debase.

avilissant, e [àvēlēsáǹ, -áǹt] *a* degrading.

aviné, e [àvēnā] *a* drunken.

avion [àvyôǹ] *nm* (air)plane (*US*), (aero)plane (*Brit*); **aller (quelque part) en** ~ to go (somewhere) by plane, fly (somewhere); **par** ~ by airmail; ~ **de chasse** fighter; ~ **de ligne** airliner; ~ **à réaction** jet (plane).

avion-cargo [àvyôǹkàrgō] *nm* air freighter.

avion-citerne [àvyôǹsētern(ə)] *nm* air tanker.

aviron [àvērôǹ] *nm* oar; (*sport*): **l'**~ rowing.

avis [àvē] *nm* opinion; (*notification*) notice; (*COMM*): ~ **de crédit/débit** credit/debit advice; **à mon** ~ in my opinion; **je suis de votre** ~ I share your opinion, I am of your opinion; **être d'**~ **que** to be of the opinion that; **changer d'**~ to change one's mind; **sauf** ~ **contraire** unless you hear to the contrary; **sans** ~ **préalable** without notice; **jusqu'à nouvel** ~ until further notice; ~ **de décès** death announcement.

avisé, e [àvēzā] *a* sensible, wise, **être bien/mal** ~ **de faire** to be well-/ill-advised to do.

aviser [àvēzā] *vt* (*voir*) to notice, catch sight of; (*informer*): ~ **qn de/que** to advise *ou* inform *ou* notify sb of/that ♦ *vi* to think about things, assess the situation; **s'**~ **de qch/que** to become suddenly aware of sth/that; **s'**~ **de faire** to take it into one's head to do.

aviver [àvēvā] *vt* (*douleur, chagrin*) to intensify; (*intérêt, désir*) to sharpen; (*colère, querelle*) to stir up; (*couleur*) to brighten up.

av. J.-C. *abr* (= *avant Jésus-Christ*) BC.

avocat [àvòkà, -át] *nm/f* (*JUR*) lawyer, ≈ barrister (*Brit*); (*fig*) advocate, champion ♦ *nm* (*CULIN*) avocado (pear); **se faire l'**~ **du diable** to be the devil's advocate; **l'**~ **de la défense/partie civile** the counsel for the defense/plaintiff; ~ **d'affaires** business lawyer; ~ **général** prosecuting attorney (*US*), assistant public prosecutor (*Brit*).

avocat-conseil, *pl* **avocats-conseils** [àvòkàkôǹsey] *nm* ≈ attorney (*US*), ≈ barrister (*Brit*).

avoine [àvwán] *nf* oats *pl*.

avoir [àvwár] *nm* assets *pl*, resources *pl*; (*COMM*): ~ **(fiscal)** (tax) credit ♦ *vt* (*gén*) to have; (*fam*: *duper*) to do, have ♦ *vb auxiliaire* to have; **vous avez du sel?** do you have any salt?, have you got any salt?; ~ **à faire qch** to have to do sth; **tu n'as pas à me poser de questions** it's not for you to ask me questions; **il a 3 ans** he is 3 (years old); *voir* **faim, peur** *etc*; ~ **3 mètres de haut** to be 3 metres high; ~ **les cheveux blancs/un chapeau rouge** to have white hair/a red hat; ~ **mangé/dormi** to have eaten/slept; **il y a** there is + *sg*, there are + *pl*; (*temporel*): **il y**

a 10 ans 10 years ago; **il y a 10 ans/ longtemps que je le sais** I've known (it) for 10 years/a long time; **il y a 10 ans qu'il est arrivé** it's 10 years since he arrived; **qu'y-a-t-il?, qu'est-ce qu'il y a?** what is it?, what's the matter?; **il doit y ~** there must be; **il ne peut y en ~ qu'un** there can only be one; **il n'y a qu'à ...** we (ou you etc) will just have to ...; **en ~ à** ou **contre qn** to have a grudge against sb; **en ~ assez** to be fed up; **j'en ai pour une demi-heure** it'll take me half an hour; **n'~ que faire de qch** to have no use for sth.

avoisinant, e [ávwázēnâń, -âńt] a neighboring (US), neighbouring (Brit).

avoisiner [ávwázēnā] vt to be near ou close to; (fig) to border ou verge on.

avons [ávôń] vb voir **avoir**.

avortement [ávortəmâń] nm abortion.

avorter [ávortā] vi (MÉD) to have an abortion; (fig) to fail; **faire ~** to abort; **se faire ~** to have an abortion.

avorton [ávortôń] nm (péj) little runt.

avoué, e [ávwā] a avowed ♦ nm (JUR) lawyer.

avouer [ávwā] vt (crime, défaut) to confess (to) ♦ vi (se confesser) to confess; (admettre) to admit; **~ avoir fait/que** to admit ou confess to having done/that; **~ que oui/non** to admit that that is so/not so; **s'~ vaincu** to admit defeat.

avril [ávrēl] nm April; voir aussi **juillet**.

avt abr = **avant**.

axe [áks(ə)] nm axis (pl axes); (de roue etc) axle; (prolongement): **dans l'~ de** directly in line with; (fig) main line; **~ routier** main road.

axer [áksā] vt: **~ qch sur** to center sth on.

axial, e, aux [áksyál, -ō] a axial.

axiome [áksyōm] nm axiom.

ayant [eyâń] vb voir **avoir** ♦ nm: **~ droit** assignee; **~ droit à** (pension etc) person eligible for ou entitled to.

ayons [eyôń] etc vb voir **avoir**.

azalée [ázálā] nf azalea.

azimut [ázēmüt] nm azimuth; **tous ~s** a (fig) omnidirectional.

azote [ázot] nm nitrogen.

azoté, e [ázotā] a nitrogenous.

aztèque [áztek] a Aztec.

azur [ázür] nm (couleur) azure, sky blue; (ciel) sky, skies pl.

azyme [ázēm] a: **pain ~** unleavened bread.

B

B, b [bā] nm inv B, b ♦ abr (= bien) g (= good); **B comme Bertha** B for Baker.

BA sigle f (= bonne action) good deed.

baba [bábá] a inv: **en être ~** (fam) to be flabbergasted ♦ nm: **~ au rhum** rum baba.

babil [bábē] nm prattle.

babillage [bábēyázh] nm chatter.

babiller [bábēyā] vi to prattle, chatter; (bébé) to babble.

babines [bábēn] nfpl chops.

babiole [bábyol] nf (bibelot) trinket; (vétille) trifle.

bâbord [bábor] nm: **à** ou **par ~** to port, on the port side.

babouin [bábwań] nm baboon.

baby-foot [bábēfōōt] nm inv table football.

Babylone [bábēlon] n Babylon.

babylonien, ne [bábēlonyań, -en] a Babylonian.

baby-sitter [bábēsētœr] nm/f baby-sitter.

baby-sitting [bábēsētēng] nm baby-sitting.

bac [bák] nm (SCOL) = **baccalauréat** (bateau) ferry; (récipient) tub; (: PHOTO etc) tray; (: INDUSTRIE) tank; **~ à glace** ice-tray; **~ à légumes** vegetable compartment ou rack.

baccalauréat [bákálorāá] nm ≈ high school diploma (US), ≈ GCE A-levels pl (Brit).

bâche [básh] nf tarpaulin, canvas sheet.

bachelier, ière [báshəlyā, -yer] nm/f holder of the baccalauréat.

bâcher [báshā] vt to cover (with a canvas sheet ou a tarpaulin).

bachot [báshō] nm = **baccalauréat**.

bachotage [báshotázh] nm (SCOL) cramming.

bachoter [báshotā] vi (SCOL) to cram (for an exam).

bacille [básēl] nm bacillus (pl -i).

bâcler [báklā] vt to botch (up).

bactéricide [báktārēsēd] nm (MÉD) bactericide.

bactérie [báktārē] nf bacterium (pl -ia).

bactériologie [báktāryolozhē] nf bacteriology.

bactériologique [báktāryolozhēk] a bacteriological.

bactériologiste [báktāryolozhēst(ə)] nm/f bacteriologist.

badaud, e [bádō, -ōd] nm/f idle onlooker, stroller.

baderne [bádern(ə)] nf (péj): **(vieille) ~** old fossil.

badge [bádzh(ə)] nm badge.

badigeon [bádēzhôń] nm distemper; whitewash.

badigeonner [bádēzhonā] vt to distemper; to whitewash; (péj: barbouiller) to daub; (MÉD) to paint.

badin, e [bádań, -ēn] a light-hearted, playful.

badinage [bádēnázh] nm banter.

badine [bádēn] nf switch (stick).

badiner [bádēnā] vi: **~ avec qch** to treat sth lightly; **ne pas ~ avec qch** not to trifle with sth.

badminton [bádmēnton] nm badminton.

BAFA [báfá] sigle m (= Brevet d'aptitude aux fonctions d'animation) diploma for youth leaders and workers.

baffe [báf] nf (fam) slap, clout.

Baffin [báfēn] nf: **terre de ~** Baffin Island.

baffle [báfl(ə)] nm baffle (board).

bafouer [báfwā] vt to deride, ridicule.

bafouillage [báfōōyázh] nm (fam: propos incohérents) jumble of words.

bafouiller [báfōōyā] vi, vt to stammer.

bâfrer [báfrā] vi, vt (fam) to guzzle, gobble.

bagage [bágázh] nm: **~s** luggage sg, baggage sg; **~ littéraire** (stock of) literary knowledge;

~s à main hand-luggage.

bagarre [bágár] *nf* fight, brawl; **il aime la** ~ he loves a fight, he likes fighting.

bagarrer [bágárā]: **se** ~ *vi* to (have a) fight.

bagarreur, euse [bágárœr, -œ̄z] *a* pugnacious ♦ *nm/f*: **il est** ~ he loves a fight.

bagatelle [bágátel] *nf* trifle, trifling sum (*ou* matter).

Bagdad, Baghdâd [bágdád] *n* Baghdad.

bagnard [bányár] *nm* convict.

bagne [bány] *nm* penal colony; **c'est le** ~ (*fig*) it's forced labor.

bagnole [bányol] *nf* (*fam*) car, wheels *pl*.

bagout [bágōō] *nm* glibness; **avoir du** ~ to have the gift of the gab.

bague [bág] *nf* ring; ~ **de fiançailles** engagement ring; ~ **de serrage** clip.

baguenauder [bágnōdā]: **se** ~ *vi* to trail around, loaf around.

baguer [bágā] *vt* to ring.

baguette [báget] *nf* stick; (*cuisine chinoise*) chopstick; (*de chef d'orchestre*) baton; (*pain*) stick of (French) bread; (*CONSTR: moulure*) beading; **mener qn à la** ~ to rule sb with a rod of iron; ~ **magique** magic wand; ~ **de sourcier** divining rod; ~ **de tambour** drumstick.

Bahamas [báámás] *nfpl*: **les (îles)** ~ the Bahamas.

Bahrein [báren] *nm* Bahrain *ou* Bahrein.

bahut [báü] *nm* chest.

bai, e [be] *a* (*cheval*) bay.

baie [be] *nf* (*GÉO*) bay; (*fruit*) berry; ~ **(vitrée)** picture window.

baignade [benyad] *nf* (*action*) bathing; (*bain*) bathe; (*endroit*) bathing place.

baigné, e [banya] *a*: ~ **de** bathed in; (*trempé*) soaked with; (*inondé*) flooded with.

baigner [bānyā] *vt* (*bébé*) to bath ♦ *vi*: ~ **dans son sang** to lie in a pool of blood; ~ **dans la brume** to be shrouded in mist; **se** ~ *vi* to go swimming *ou* bathing; (*dans une baignoire*) to have a bath; **ça baigne!** (*fam*) everything's great!

baigneur, euse [benyœr, -œ̄z] *nm/f* bather ♦ *nm* (*poupée*) baby doll.

baignoire [benywár] *nf* bath(tub); (*THÉÂTRE*) ground-floor box.

bail, baux [báy, bō] *nm* lease; **donner** *ou* **prendre qch à** ~ to lease sth.

bâillement [báymáń] *nm* yawn.

bâiller [báyā] *vi* to yawn; (*être ouvert*) to gape.

bailleur [báyœr] *nm*: ~ **de fonds** sponsor, backer; (*COMM*) silent *ou* sleeping (*Brit*) partner.

bâillon [báyôń] *nm* gag.

bâillonner [báyonā] *vt* to gag.

bain [bań] *nm* (*dans une baignoire, PHOTO, TECH*) bath; (*dans la mer, une piscine*) swim; **costume de** ~ bathing suit, swimsuit; **prendre un** ~ to have a bath; **se mettre dans le** ~ (*fig*) to get into the swing of it *ou* things; ~ **de bouche** mouthwash; ~ **de foule** walkabout; ~ **de pieds** footbath; (*au bord de la mer*) wade; ~ **de siège** hip bath; ~ **de soleil** sunbathing *q*; **prendre un** ~ **de soleil** to sunbathe; ~**s de mer** sea bathing *sg*; ~**s(- douches) municipaux** public baths.

bain-marie, *pl* **bains-marie** [bańmárē] *nm* double boiler; **faire chauffer au** ~ (*boîte etc*) to immerse in boiling water.

baïonnette [báyonet] *nf* bayonet; (*ÉLEC*): **douille à** ~ snap-up (*US*) *ou* bayonet (*Brit*) socket; **ampoule à** ~ bulb with a bayonet fitting.

baisemain [bezmań] *nm* kissing a lady's hand.

baiser [bāzā] *nm* kiss ♦ *vt* (*main, front*) to kiss; (*fam!*) to screw (*!*).

baisse [bes] *nf* fall, drop; (*COMM*): "~ **sur la viande**" "meat prices down"; **en** ~ (*cours, action*) falling; **à la** ~ downwards.

baisser [bāsā] *vt* to lower; (*radio, chauffage*) to turn down; (*AUTO: phares*) to dim (*US*), lower (*US*), dip (*Brit*) ♦ *vi* to fall, drop, go down; **se** ~ *vi* to bend down.

bajoues [bázhōō] *nfpl* chaps, chops.

bal [bál] *nm* dance; (*grande soirée*) ball; ~ **costumé/masqué** fancy-dress/masked ball; ~ **musette** dance (*with accordion accompaniment*).

balade [bálád] *nf* walk, stroll; (*en voiture*) drive; **faire une** ~ to go for a walk *ou* stroll; to go for a drive.

balader [báládā] *vt* (*traîner*) to carry around; **se** ~ *vi* to go for a walk *ou* stroll; to go for a drive.

baladeur [báládœr] *nm* personal stereo.

baladeuse [báládœ̄z] *nf* trouble light (*US*), inspection lamp (*Brit*).

baladin [báládań] *nm* wandering entertainer.

balafre [báláfr(ə)] *nf* gash, slash; (*cicatrice*) scar.

balafrer [báláfrā] *vt* to gash, slash.

balai [bále] *nm* broom, brush; (*AUTO: d'essuie-glace*) blade; (*MUS: de batterie etc*) brush; **donner un coup de** ~ to give the floor a sweep; ~ **mécanique** carpet sweeper.

balai-brosse, *pl* **balais-brosses** [bálcbros] *nm* (long-handled) scrubbing brush.

balance [bálâńs] *nf* (*à plateaux*) scales *pl*; (*de précision*) balance; (*COMM, POL*): ~ **des comptes** *ou* **paiements** balance of payments; (*signe*): **la B**~ Libra, the Scales; **être de la B**~ to be Libra; ~ **commerciale** balance of trade; ~ **des forces** balance of power; ~ **romaine** steelyard.

balancelle [bálâńsel] *nf* glider (*US*), garden hammock-seat (*Brit*).

balancer [bálâńsā] *vt* to swing; (*lancer*) to fling, chuck; (*renvoyer, jeter*) to chuck out ♦ *vi* to swing; **se** ~ *vi* to swing; (*bateau*) to rock; (*branche*) to sway; **se** ~ **de qch** (*fam*) not to give a darn about sth.

balancier [bálâńsyā] *nm* (*de pendule*) pendulum; (*de montre*) balance wheel; (*perche*) (balancing) pole.

balançoire [bálâńswár] *nf* swing; (*sur pivot*) seesaw.

balayage [báleyázh] *nm* sweeping; scanning.

balayer [báleyā] *vt* (*feuilles etc*) to sweep up, brush up; (*pièce, cour*) to sweep; (*chasser*) to sweep away *ou* aside; (*suj: radar*) to scan; (*: phares*) to sweep across.

balayette [báleyet] *nf* small brush.

balayeur, euse [báleyœr, -œ̄z] *nm/f* streetsweeper ♦ *nf* (*engin*) streetsweeper.

balayures [báleyür] *nfpl* sweepings.

balbutiement [bálbüsēmáṅ] *nm* (*paroles*) stammering *q*; ~**s** *nmpl* (*fig: débuts*) first faltering steps.

balbutier [bálbüsyā] *vi*, *vt* to stammer.

balcon [bálkôṅ] *nm* balcony; (*THÉÂTRE*) dress circle.

baldaquin [báldákaṅ] *nm* canopy.

Bâle [bál] *n* Basle *ou* Basel.

Baléares [bálāár] *nfpl*: **les** ~ the Balearic Islands.

baleine [bálen] *nf* whale; (*de parapluie*) rib; (*de corset*) bone.

baleinier [bálānyā] *nm* (*NAVIG*) whaler.

baleinière [bálenyer] *nf* whaleboat.

balisage [bálēzázh] *nm* (*signaux*) beacons *pl*; buoys *pl*; runway lights *pl*; signs *pl*, markers *pl*.

balise [bálēz] *nf* (*NAVIG*) beacon, (marker) buoy; (*AVIAT*) runway light, beacon; (*AUTO*, *SKI*) sign, marker.

baliser [bálēzā] *vt* to mark out (with beacons *ou* lights *etc*).

balistique [bálēstēk] *a* (*engin*) ballistic ♦ *nf* ballistics.

balivernes [bálēvern(ə)] *nfpl* twaddle *sg*, nonsense *sg*.

balkanique [bálkánēk] *a* Balkan.

Balkans [bálkáṅ] *nmpl*: **les** ~ the Balkans.

ballade [bálád] *nf* ballad.

ballant, e [báláṅ, -áṅt] *a* dangling.

ballast [bálást] *nm* ballast.

balle [bál] *nf* (*de fusil*) bullet; (*de sport*) ball; (*du blé*) chaff; (*paquet*) bale; (*fam: franc*) franc; ~ **perdue** stray bullet.

ballerine [bálrēn] *nf* ballet dancer; (*chaussure*) pump, ballerina.

ballet [bále] *nm* ballet; (*fig*): ~ **diplomatique** diplomatic to-ings and fro-ings.

ballon [bálôṅ] *nm* (*de sport*) ball; (*jouet*, *AVIAT*, *de bande dessinée*) balloon; (*de vin*) glass; ~ **d'essai** (*météorologique*) trial (*US*) *ou* pilot balloon; (*fig*) feeler(s); ~ **de football** football; ~ **d'oxygène** oxygen bottle.

ballonner [bálonā] *vt*: **j'ai le ventre ballonné** I feel bloated.

ballon-sonde, *pl* **ballons-sondes** [bálôṅsôṅd] *nm* sounding balloon.

ballot [bálo] *nm* bundle; (*péj*) nitwit.

ballottage [bálotázh] *nm* (*POL*) second ballot.

ballotter [bálotā] *vi* to roll around; (*bateau etc*) to toss ♦ *vt* to shake *ou* throw about; to toss; **être ballotté entre** (*fig*) to be shunted between; (*: indécis*) to be torn between.

ballottine [báloten] *nf* (*CULIN*): ~ **de volaille** meat loaf made with poultry.

ball-trap [báltráp] *nm* (*appareil*) trap; (*tir*) clay pigeon shooting.

balluchon [bálüshôṅ] *nm* bundle (of clothes).

balnéaire [bálnāer] *a* seaside *cpd*.

balnéothérapie [bálnāotárápē] *nf* spa bath therapy.

BALO *sigle m* (= *Bulletin des annonces légales obligatoires*) ≈ Legal (*US*) *ou* Public (*Brit*) Notices (*in newspapers etc*).

balourd, e [bálōōr, -ōōrd(ə)] *a* clumsy ♦ *nm/f* clodhopper.

balourdise [bálōōrdēz] *nf* clumsiness; (*gaffe*) blunder.

balte [bált] *a* Baltic ♦ *nm/f*: **B**~ native of the Baltic States.

baltique [báltēk] *a* Baltic ♦ *nf*: **la** (**mer**) **B**~ the Baltic (Sea).

baluchon [bálüshôṅ] *nm* = **balluchon**.

balustrade [bálüstrád] *nf* railings *pl*, handrail.

bambin [báṅbaṅ] *nm* little child.

bambou [báṅbōō] *nm* bamboo.

ban [báṅ] *nm* round of applause, cheer; **être/mettre au** ~ **de** to be outlawed/to outlaw from; **le** ~ **et l'arrière-**~ **de sa famille** every last one of his relatives; ~**s** (**de mariage**) banns, bans.

banal, e [bánál] *a* banal, commonplace; (*péj*) trite; **four/moulin** ~ village oven/mill.

banalisé, e [bánálēzā] *a* (*voiture de police*) unmarked.

banalité [bánálētā] *nf* banality; (*remarque*) truism, trite remark.

banane [bánán] *nf* banana.

bananeraie [bánánre] *nf* banana plantation.

bananier [bánányā] *nm* banana tree; (*bateau*) banana boat.

banc [báṅ] *nm* seat, bench; (*de poissons*) school (*US*), shoal (*Brit*); ~ **des accusés** dock; ~ **d'essai** (*fig*) testing ground; ~ **de sable** sandbank; ~ **des témoins** witness stand.

bancaire [báṅker] *a* banking, bank *cpd*.

bancal, e [báṅkál] *a* wobbly; (*personne*) bow-legged; (*fig: projet*) shaky.

bandage [báṅdázh] *nm* bandaging; (*pansement*) bandage; ~ **herniaire** truss.

bande [báṅd] *nf* (*de tissu etc*) strip; (*MÉD*) bandage; (*motif, dessin*) stripe; (*CINÉMA*) film; (*INFORM*) tape; (*RADIO, groupe*) band; (*péj*): **une** ~ **de** a bunch *ou* crowd of; **par la** ~ in a roundabout way; **donner de la** ~ to list; **faire** ~ **à part** to keep to o.s.; ~ **dessinée** (**BD**) comic strip, strip cartoon (*Brit*); ~ **magnétique** magnetic tape; ~ **perforée** punched tape; ~ **de roulement** (*de pneu*) tread; ~ **sonore** sound track; ~ **de terre** strip of land; ~ **Velpeau** ® (*MÉD*) Ace ® (*US*) *ou* crêpe (*Brit*) bandage.

bandé, e [báṅdā] *a* bandaged; **les yeux** ~**s** blindfold.

bande-annonce, *pl* **bandes-annonces** [báṅdánôṅs] *nf* (*CINÉMA*) trailer.

bandeau, x [báṅdō] *nm* headband; (*sur les yeux*) blindfold; (*MÉD*) head bandage.

bandelette [báṅdlet] *nf* strip of cloth, bandage.

bander [báṅdā] *vt* to bandage; (*muscle*) to tense; (*arc*) to bend ♦ *vi* (*fam!*) to have a hard on (*!*); ~ **les yeux à qn** to blindfold sb.

banderole [báṅdrol] *nf* banderole; (*dans un défilé etc*) streamer.

bande-son, *pl* **bandes-son** [báṅdsôṅ] *nf* (*CINÉMA*) soundtrack.

bande-vidéo, *pl* **bandes-vidéo** [báṅdvēdāō] *nf* video tape.

bandit [báṅdē] *nm* bandit.

banditisme [báṅdētēsm(ə)] *nm* violent crime, armed robberies *pl*.

bandoulière [báṅdōōlyer] *nf*: **en** ~ (slung *ou* worn) across the shoulder.

Bangkok [báṅgkok] *n* Bangkok.

Bangla Desh [báṅglàdesh] *nm*: **le** ~ Bangladesh.

banjo [bán(d)zhō] *nm* banjo.

banlieue [bánlyōē] *nf* suburbs *pl*; **lignes/ quartiers de** ~ suburban lines/areas; **trains de** ~ commuter trains.

banlieusard, e [bánlyōēzár, -árd(ə)] *nm/f* suburbanite.

bannière [bányer] *nf* banner.

bannir [bánēr] *vt* to banish.

banque [bánk] *nf* bank; (*activités*) banking; ~ **des yeux/du sang** eye/blood bank; ~ **d'affaires** commercial (*US*) *ou* merchant (*Brit*) bank; ~ **de dépôt** deposit bank; ~ **de données** (*INFORM*) data bank; ~ **d'émission** bank of issue.

banqueroute [bánkrōōt] *nf* bankruptcy.

banquet [bánke] *nm* (*de club*) dinner; (*de noces*) reception; (*d'apparat*) banquet.

banquette [bánket] *nf* seat.

banquier [bánkyā] *nm* banker.

banquise [bánkēz] *nf* ice field.

bantou, e [bántōō] *a* Bantu.

baptême [bátem] *nm* (*sacrement*) baptism; (*cérémonie*) christening, baptism; (*d'un navire*) launching; (*d'une cloche*) consecration, dedication; ~ **de l'air** first flight.

baptiser [bátēzā] *vt* to christen; to baptize; to launch; to consecrate, dedicate.

baptismal, e, aux [bátēsmál, -ō] *a*: **eau** ~**e** baptismal water.

baptiste [bátēst(ə)] *a*, *nm/f* Baptist.

baquet [báke] *nm* tub, bucket.

bar [bár] *nm* bar; (*poisson*) bass.

baragouin [bárágwań] *nm* gibberish.

baragouiner [bárágwēnā] *vi* to gibber, jabber.

baraque [bárák] *nf* shed; (*fam*) house; ~ **foraine** fairground stand.

baraque, e [báráká] *a* well-built, hefty.

baraquements [barakmán] *nmpl* huts (*for refugees, workers etc*).

baratin [bárátań] *nm* (*fam*) smooth talk, patter.

baratiner [bárátēnā] *vt* to sweet-talk.

baratte [bárát] *nf* churn.

Barbade [bárbád] *nf*: **la** ~ Barbados.

barbant, e [bárbáń, -áńt] *a* (*fam*) deadly (boring).

barbare [bárbár] *a* barbaric ♦ *nm/f* barbarian.

Barbarie [bárbárē] *nf*: **la** ~ the Barbary Coast.

barbarie [bárbárē] *nf* barbarism; (*cruauté*) barbarity.

barbarisme [bárbárēsm(ə)] *nm* (*LING*) barbarism.

barbe [bárb(ə)] *nf* beard; **(au nez et) à la** ~ **de qn** (*fig*) under sb's very nose; **quelle** ~! (*fam*) what a drag *ou* bore!; ~ **à papa** cotton candy (*US*), candy-floss (*Brit*).

barbecue [bárbəkyōō] *nm* barbecue.

barbelé [bárbəlā] *nm* barbed wire *q*.

barber [bárbā] *vt* (*fam*) to bore stiff.

barbiche [bárbēsh] *nf* goatee.

barbichette [bárbēshet] *nf* small goatee.

barbiturique [bárbētürēk] *nm* barbiturate.

barboter [bárbotā] *vi* to paddle, dabble ♦ *vt* (*fam*) to filch.

barboteuse [bárbotēz] *nf* rompers *pl*.

barbouiller [bárbōōyā] *vt* to daub; (*péj: écrire, dessiner*) to scribble; **avoir l'estomac barbouillé** to feel queasy *ou* sick.

barbu, e [bárbü] *a* bearded.

barbue [bárbü] *nf* (*poisson*) brill.

Barcelone [bársəlon] *n* Barcelona.

barda [bárdá] *nm* (*fam*) kit, gear.

barde [bárd(ə)] *nf* (*CULIN*) piece of fat bacon ♦ *nm* (*poète*) bard.

bardé, e [bárdā] *a*: ~ **de médailles** *etc* bedecked with medals *etc*.

bardeaux [bárdō] *nmpl* shingle *q*.

barder [bárdā] *vt* (*CULIN: rôti, volaille*) to bard ♦ *vi* (*fam*): **ça va** ~ sparks will fly, things are going to get hot.

barème [bárem] *nm* scale; (*liste*) table; ~ **des salaires** salary scale.

barguigner [bárgēnyā] *vi*: **sans** ~ without (any) hemming and hawing *ou* shilly-shallying.

baril [bárēl] *nm* (*tonneau*) barrel; (*de poudre*) keg.

barillet [bárēye] *nm* (*de revolver*) cylinder.

bariolé, e [báryolā] *a* many-colored, rainbow-colored.

barman [bármáń] *nm* bartender (*US*), barman.

baromètre [bárometr(ə)] *nm* barometer; ~ **anéroïde** aneroid barometer.

baron [bárōń] *nm* baron.

baronne [báron] *nf* baroness.

baroque [bárok] *a* (*ART*) baroque; (*fig*) weird.

baroud [bárōōd] *nm*: ~ **d'honneur** gallant last stand.

baroudeur [bárōōdœr] *nm* (*fam*) fighter.

barque [bárk(ə)] *nf* small boat.

barquette [bárket] *nf* small boat-shaped tart; (*récipient: en aluminium*) tub; (: *en bois*) basket.

barracuda [báráküdá] *nm* barracuda.

barrage [bárázh] *nm* dam; (*sur route*) roadblock, barricade; ~ **de police** police roadblock.

barre [bár] *nf* (*de fer etc*) rod, bar; (*NAVIG*) helm; (*écrite*) line, stroke; (*DANSE*) barre; (*JUR*): **comparaître à la** ~ to appear as a witness; **être à** *ou* **tenir la** ~ (*NAVIG*) to be at the helm; **coup de** ~ (*fig*): **c'est le coup de** ~! it's highway (*US*) *ou* daylight (*Brit*) robbery!; **j'ai le coup de** ~! I'm exhausted!; ~ **fixe** (*GYM*) horizontal bar; ~ **de mesure** (*MUS*) bar line; ~ **à mine** crowbar; ~**s parallèles/asymétriques** (*GYM*) parallel/asymmetric bars.

barreau, x [bárō] *nm* bar; (*JUR*): **le** ~ the Bar.

barrer [bárā] *vt* (*route etc*) to block; (*mot*) to cross out; (*chèque*) to mark "for deposit only" (*US*), cross (*Brit*); (*NAVIG*) to steer; **se** ~ *vi* (*fam*) to clear out.

barrette [báret] *nf* (*pour cheveux*) (hair) clip (*US*) *ou* slide (*Brit*); (*REL: bonnet*) biretta; (*broche*) brooch.

barreur [bárœr] *nm* helmsman; (*aviron*) coxswain.

barricade [bárēkád] *nf* barricade.

barricader [bárēkádā] *vt* to barricade; **se** ~ **chez soi** (*fig*) to lock o.s. in.

barrière [báryer] *nf* fence; (*obstacle*) barrier; (*porte*) gate; **la Grande B**~ the Great Barrier Reef; ~ **de dégel** (*ADMIN: on road-signs*) no heavy vehicles - road liable to subsidence due to thaw; ~**s douanières** trade barriers.

barrique [bárĕk] *nf* barrel, cask.
barrir [bárēr] *vi* to trumpet.
baryton [bárētôn] *nm* baritone.
BAS *sigle m* (= *bureau d'aide sociale*) ≈ Welfare office (*US*), ≈ social security office (*Brit*).
bas, basse [bâ, bâs] *a* low; (*action*) low, ignoble ♦ *nm* (*vêtement*) stocking; (*partie inférieure*): **le ~ de** the lower part *ou* foot *ou* bottom of ♦ *nf* (*MUS*) bass ♦ *ad* low; (*parler*) softly; **plus ~** lower down; more softly; (*dans un texte*) further on, below; **la tête basse** with lowered head; (*fig*) with head hung low; **avoir la vue basse** to be short-sighted; **au ~ mot** at the lowest estimate; **enfant en ~ âge** infant, young child; **en ~** down below; at (*ou* to) the bottom; (*dans une maison*) downstairs; **en ~ de** at the bottom of; **de ~ en haut** upwards; from the bottom to the top; **des hauts et des ~** ups and downs; **un ~ de laine** (*fam*: *économies*) money under the mattress (*fig*); **mettre ~** *vi* to give birth; **à ~ la dictature!** down with dictatorship!; **~ morceaux** (*viande*) cheap cuts.
basalte [bázált(ə)] *nm* basalt.
basané, e [bázáná] *a* tanned, bronzed; (*immigré etc*) swarthy.
bas-côté [bákōtá] *nm* (*de route*) shoulder; (*d'église*) (side) aisle.
bascule [báskül] *nf*: (**jeu de**) **~** seesaw; (**balance à**) **~** scales *pl*; **fauteuil à ~** rocking chair; **système à ~** tip-over device; rocker device.
basculer [báskülá] *vi* to fall over, topple (over); (*benne*) to tip up ♦ *vt* (*aussi*: **faire ~**) to topple over; to tip out, tip up.
base [báz] *nf* base; (*POL*): **la ~** the rank and file, the grass roots; (*fondement, principe*) basis (*pl* bases); **jeter les ~s de** to lay the foundations of; **à la ~ de** (*fig*) at the root of; **sur la ~ de** (*fig*) on the basis of; **de ~** basic; **à ~ de café** *etc* coffee *etc* -based; **~ de données** (*INFORM*) database; **~ de lancement** launching site.
base-ball [bezbōl] *nm* baseball.
baser [bázá] *vt*: **~ qch sur** to base sth on; **se ~ sur** (*données, preuves*) to base one's argument on; **être basé à/dans** (*MIL*) to be based at/in.
bas-fond [báfôn] *nm* (*NAVIG*) shallow; **~s** *nmpl* (*fig*) dregs.
BASIC [bázĕk] *nm* BASIC.
basilic [bázĕlĕk] *nm* (*CULIN*) basil.
basilique [bázĕlĕk] *nf* basilica.
basket(-ball) [básket(bōl)] *nm* basketball.
baskets [básket] *nmpl* (*chaussures*) sneakers (*US*), trainers (*Brit*).
basketteur, euse [básketœr, -œz] *nm/f* basketball player.
basquaise [báskez] *af* Basque ♦ *nf*: **B~** Basque.
basque [básk(ə)] *a, nm* (*LING*) Basque ♦ *nm/f*: **B~** Basque; **le Pays ~** the Basque country.
basques [básk(ə)] *nfpl* skirts; **pendu aux ~ de qn** constantly pestering sb; (*mère etc*) hanging on sb's apron strings.
bas-relief [bárəlyef] *nm* bas-relief.
basse [bás] *af, nf voir* **bas**.

basse-cour, pl basses-cours [báskōōr] *nf* farmyard; (*animaux*) farmyard animals.
bassement [bâsmân] *ad* basely.
bassesse [báses] *nf* baseness; (*acte*) base act.
basset [báse] *nm* (*ZOOL*) basset (hound).
bassin [básań] *nm* (*cuvette*) bowl; (*pièce d'eau*) pond, pool; (*de fontaine, GÉO*) basin; (*ANAT*) pelvis; (*portuaire*) dock; **~ houiller** coalfield.
bassine [básēn] *nf* basin; (*contenu*) bowl, bowlful.
bassiner [básēná] *vt* (*plaie*) to bathe; (*lit*) to warm with a warming pan; (*fam: ennuyer*) to bore; (*: importuner*) to bug, pester.
bassiste [básēst(ə)] *nm/f* (double) bass player.
basson [básôn] *nm* bassoon.
bastide [bástēd] *nf* (*maison*) country house (*in Provence*); (*ville*) walled town (*in SW France*).
bastingage [bástańgázh] *nm* (*ship's*) rail.
bastion [bástyôn] *nm* (*aussi fig, POL*) bastion.
bas-ventre [bávântr(ə)] *nm* (lower part of the) stomach.
bât [bâ] *nm* packsaddle.
bataille [bátáy] *nf* battle; **en ~** (*en travers*) at an angle; (*en désordre*) awry; **~ rangée** pitched battle.
bataillon [bátáyôn] *nm* battalion.
bâtard, e [bâtár, -árd(ə)] *a* (*enfant*) illegitimate; (*fig*) hybrid ♦ *nm/f* illegitimate child, bastard (*péj*) ♦ *nm* (*BOULANGERIE*) ≈ Vienna loaf; **chien ~** mongrel.
batavia [bátávyá] *nf* ≈ Webb lettuce.
bateau, x [bátō] *nm* boat; (*grand*) ship ♦ *a inv* (*banal, rebattu*) hackneyed; **~ de pêche/à moteur** fishing/motor boat.
bateau-citerne [bátōsētern(ə)] *nm* tanker.
bateau-mouche [bátōmōōsh] *nm* (passenger) pleasure boat (*on the Seine*).
bateau-pilote [bátōpēlot] *nm* pilot ship.
bateleur, euse [bátlœr, -œz] *nm/f* street performer.
batelier, ière [bátəlyá, -yer] *nm/f* ferryman/woman.
bat-flanc [báflân] *nm inv* raised boards for sleeping, in cells, army huts etc.
bâti, e [bâtē] *a* (*terrain*) developed ♦ *nm* (*armature*) frame; (*COUTURE*) tacking; **bien ~** (*personne*) well-built.
batifoler [bátēfolá] *vi* to frolic *ou* lark about.
batik [bátĕk] *nm* batik.
bâtiment [bâtēmân] *nm* building; (*NAVIG*) ship, vessel; (*industrie*): **le ~** the building trade.
bâtir [bâtēr] *vt* to build; (*COUTURE: jupe, ourlet*) to tack; **fil à ~** (*COUTURE*) tacking thread.
bâtisse [bâtēs] *nf* building.
bâtisseur, euse [bâtēsœr, -œz] *nm/f* builder.
batiste [bátēst(ə)] *nf* (*COUTURE*) batiste, cambric.
bâton [bâtôn] *nm* stick; **mettre des ~s dans les roues à qn** to throw a monkey wrench (*US*) *ou* a spanner (*Brit*) into the works for sb; **à ~s rompus** informally; **~ de rouge (à lèvres)** lipstick; **~ de ski** ski pole.
bâtonnet [bátone] *nm* short stick *ou* rod.
bâtonnier [bâtonyá] *nm* (*JUR*) ≈ President of the Bar.

batraciens [bátrásyań] *nmpl* amphibians.

battage [bátázh] *nm* (*publicité*) (hard) plugging.

battant, e [bátáń, -áńt] *vb voir* **battre** ♦ *a*: **pluie** ~**e** pelting rain ♦ *nm* (*de cloche*) clapper; (*de volets*) shutter, flap; (*de porte*) side; (*fig: personne*) fighter; **porte à double** ~ double door; **tambour** ~ briskly.

batte [bát] *nf* (*SPORT*) bat.

battement [bátmáń] *nm* (*de cœur*) beat; (*intervalle*) interval (*between classes, trains etc*); ~ **de paupières** blinking *q* (of eyelids); **un** ~ **de 10 minutes, 10 minutes de** ~ 10 minutes to spare.

batterie [bátrē] *nf* (*MIL, ÉLEC*) battery; (*MUS*) drums *pl*, drum set (*US*) *ou* kit (*Brit*); ~ **de cuisine** kitchen utensils *pl*; (*casseroles etc*) pots and pans *pl*; **une** ~ **de tests** a string of tests.

batteur [bátœr] *nm* (*MUS*) drummer; (*appareil*) whisk.

batteuse [bátœz] *nf* (*AGR*) threshing machine.

battoir [bátwár] *nm* (*à linge*) beetle (*for laundry*); (*à tapis*) (carpet) beater.

battre [bátr(ə)] *vt* to beat; (*suj: pluie, vagues*) to beat *ou* lash against; (*œufs etc*) to beat up, whisk; (*blé*) to thresh; (*cartes*) to shuffle; (*passer au peigne fin*) to scour ♦ *vi* (*cœur*) to beat; (*volets etc*) to bang, rattle; **se** ~ *vi* to fight; ~ **la mesure** to beat time; ~ **en brèche** (*MIL: mur*) to batter; (*fig: théorie*) to demolish; (: *institution etc*) to attack; ~ **son plein** to be at its height, be going full swing; ~ **pavillon britannique** to fly the British flag; ~ **des mains** to clap one's hands; ~ **des ailes** to flap its wings; ~ **de l'aile** (*fig*) to be in a bad way *ou* in bad shape; ~ **la semelle** to stamp one's feet; ~ **en retraite** to beat a retreat.

battu, e [bátü] *pp de* **battre** ♦ *nf* (*chasse*) beat; (*policière etc*) search, hunt.

baud [bō(d)] *nm* baud.

baudruche [bōdrüsh] *nf*: **ballon en** ~ (toy) balloon; (*fig*) windbag.

baume [bōm] *nm* balm.

bauxite [bōksět] *nf* bauxite.

bavard, e [bávár, -árd(ə)] *a* (very) talkative; gossipy.

bavardage [bávárdázh] *nm* chatter *q*; gossip *q*.

bavarder [bávárdá] *vi* to chatter; (*indiscrètement*) to gossip; (: *révéler un secret*) to blab.

bavarois, e [bávárwá, -wáz] *a* Bavarian ♦ *nm ou nf* (*CULIN*) Bavarian cream (*US*), bavarois (*Brit*).

bave [báv] *nf* dribble; (*de chien etc*) slobber, drool (*US*), slaver (*Brit*); (*d'escargot*) slime.

baver [bává] *vi* to dribble; to slobber, drool (*US*), slaver (*Brit*); (*encre, couleur*) to run; **en** ~ (*fam*) to have a hard time (of it).

bavette [bávet] *nf* bib.

baveux, euse [bávœ̃, -œ̃z] *a* dribbling; (*omelette*) runny.

Bavière [bávyer] *nf*: **la** ~ Bavaria.

bavoir [bávwár] *nm* (*de bébé*) bib.

bavure [bávür] *nf* smudge; (*fig*) hitch; blunder.

bayer [báyá] *vi*: ~ **aux corneilles** to stand gap-

ing.

bazar [bázár] *nm* general store; (*fam*) jumble.

bazarder [bázárdá] *vt* (*fam*) to chuck out.

BCBG *sigle a* (= *bon chic bon genre*) ≈ preppy.

BCG *sigle m* (= *bacille Calmette-Guérin*) BCG.

bcp *abr* = **beaucoup.**

BD *sigle f* = **bande dessinée**; (= *base de données*) DB.

bd *abr* = **boulevard.**

b.d.c. *abr* (*TYPO*: = *bas de casse*) l.c.

béant, e [bááń, -áńt] *a* gaping.

béarnais, e [báárne, -ez] *a* of *ou* from the Béarn.

béat, e [báá, -át] *a* showing open-eyed wonder; (*sourire etc*) blissful.

béatitude [báátētüd] *nf* bliss.

beau (bel), belle, beaux [bō, bel] *a* beautiful, lovely; (*homme*) handsome ♦ *nf* (*SPORT*) deciding game ♦ *ad*: **il fait** ~ the weather's fine ♦ *nm*: **avoir le sens du** ~ to have an aesthetic sense; **le temps est au** ~ the weather is set fair; **un** ~ **geste** (*fig*) a fine gesture; **un** ~ **salaire** a good salary; **un** ~ **gâchis/rhume** a fine mess/nasty cold; **en faire/dire de belles** to do/say (some) stupid things; **le** ~ **monde** high society; ~ **parleur** smooth talker; **un** ~ **jour** one (fine) day; **de plus belle** more than ever, even more; **bel et bien** well and truly; (*vraiment*) really (and truly); **le plus** ~ **c'est que ...** the best of it is that ...; **c'est du** ~! that's great, that is!; **on a** ~ **essayer** however hard *ou* no matter how hard we try; **il a** ~ **jeu de protester** *etc* it's easy for him to protest *etc*; **faire le** ~ (*chien*) to sit up and beg.

beauceron, ne [bōsrố, -on] *a* of *ou* from the Beauce.

beaucoup [bōkōō] *ad* a lot; much (*gén en tournure négative*); **il ne boit pas** ~ he doesn't drink much *ou* a lot; ~ **de** (*nombre*) many, a lot of; (*quantité*) a lot of, much; **pas** ~ **de** not much *ou* not a lot of; ~ **plus/trop** far *ou* much more/too much; **de** ~ *ad* by far.

beau-fils, *pl* **beaux-fils** [bōfes] *nm* son-in-law; (*remariage*) stepson.

beau-frère, *pl* **beaux-frères** [bōfrer] *nm* brother-in-law.

beau-père, *pl* **beaux-pères** [bōper] *nm* father-in-law; (*remariage*) stepfather.

beauté [bōtá] *nf* beauty; **de toute** ~ beautiful; **en** ~ *ad* with a flourish, brilliantly.

beaux-arts [bōzár] *nmpl* fine arts.

beaux-parents [bōpáráń] *nmpl* wife's/husband's family *sg ou pl*, in-laws.

bébé [bábá] *nm* baby.

bébé-éprouvette, *pl* **bébés-éprouvette** [bábááprōōvet] *nm* test-tube baby.

bec [bek] *nm* beak, bill; (*de plume*) nib; (*de cafetière etc*) spout; (*de casserole etc*) lip; (*d'une clarinette etc*) mouthpiece; (*fam*) mouth; **clouer le** ~ **à qn** (*fam*) to shut sb up; **ouvrir le** ~ (*fam*) to open one's mouth; ~ **de gaz** (street) gaslamp; ~ **verseur** pouring lip.

bécane [bákán] *nf* (*fam*) bike.

bécarre [bákár] *nm* (*MUS*) natural.

bécasse [bákás] *nf* (*ZOOL*) woodcock; (*fam*)

silly goose.

bec-de-cane, *pl* **becs-de-cane** [bɛkdəkán] *nm* (*poignée*) door handle.

bec-de-lièvre, *pl* **becs-de-lièvre** [bɛkdəlyɛvr(ə)] *nm* harelip.

béchamel [bāshámɛl] *nf*: (**sauce**) ~ white sauce, bechamel sauce.

bêche [bɛsh] *nf* spade.

bêcher [bɛshā] *vt* (*terre*) to dig; (*personne: critiquer*) to criticize severely; (: *snober*) to look down on.

bêcheur, euse [bɛshœr, -œ̄z] *a* (*fam*) stuck-up ♦ *nm/f* fault-finder; (*snob*) stuck-up person.

bécoter [bākotā]: **se** ~ *vi* to smooch.

becquée [bākā] *nf*: **donner la** ~ **à** to feed.

becqueter [bɛktā] *vt* (*fam*) to eat.

bedaine [bədɛn] *nf* paunch.

bédé [bādā] *nf* (*fam*: = *bande dessinée*) comic strip.

bedeau, x [bədō] *nm* beadle.

bedonnant, e [bədonáṅ, -áṅt] *a* paunchy, potbellied.

bée [bā] *a*: **bouche** ~ gaping.

beffroi [bāfrwá] *nm* belfry.

begaiement [bāgemáṅ] *nm* stammering.

bégayer [bāgāyā] *vt, vi* to stammer.

bégonia [bāgonyá] *nm* (*BOT*) begonia.

bègue [bɛg] *nm/f*: **être** ~ to have a stammer.

bégueule [bāgœl] *a* prudish.

béguin [bāgáṅ] *nm*: **avoir le** ~ **de** *ou* **pour** to have a crush on.

beige [bɛzh] *a* beige.

beignet [bɛnyɛ] *nm* fritter.

bel [bɛl] *am voir* beau.

bêler [bālā] *vi* to bleat.

belette [bəlɛt] *nf* weasel.

belge [bɛlzh(ə)] *a* Belgian ♦ *nm/f*: **B~** Belgian.

Belgique [bɛlzhēk] *nf*: **la** ~ Belgium.

Belgrade [bɛlgrád] *n* Belgrade.

bélier [bālyā] *nm* ram; (*engin*) (battering) ram; (*signe*): **le B~** Aries, the Ram; **être du B~** to be Aries.

Bélize [bālēz] *nm*: **le** ~ Belize.

bellâtre [bɛlâtr(ə)] *nm* dandy.

belle [bɛl] *af, nf voir* beau.

belle-famille, *pl* **belles-familles** [bɛlfámēy] *nf* (*fam*) in-laws *pl*.

belle-fille, *pl* **belles-filles** [bɛlfēy] *nf* daughter-in-law; (*remariage*) stepdaughter.

belle-mère, *pl* **belles-mères** [bɛlmɛr] *nf* mother-in-law; (*remariage*) stepmother.

belle-sœur, *pl* **belles-sœurs** [bɛlsœr] *nf* sister-in-law.

belliciste [bālēsēst(ə)] *a* warmongering.

belligérance [bālēzhāráṅs] *nf* belligerence.

belligérant, e [bālēzhāráṅ, -áṅt] *a* belligerent.

belliqueux, euse [bālēkœ̄, -œ̄z] *a* aggressive, warlike.

belote [bəlot] *nf* belote (*card game*).

belvédère [bɛlvādɛr] *nm* panoramic viewpoint (*or small building there*).

bémol [bāmol] *nm* (*MUS*) flat.

ben [bãṅ] *excl* (*fam*) well.

bénédiction [bānādēksyôṅ] *nf* blessing.

bénéfice [bānāfēs] *nm* (*COMM*) profit; (*avantage*) benefit; **au** ~ **de** in aid of.

bénéficiaire [bānāfēsyɛr] *nm/f* beneficiary.

bénéficier [bānāfēsyā] *vi*: ~ **de** to enjoy; (*profiter*) to benefit by *ou* from; (*obtenir*) to

get, be given.

bénéfique [bānāfēk] *a* beneficial.

Bénélux [bānālüks] *nm*: **le** ~ Benelux, the Benelux countries.

benêt [bənɛ] *nm* simpleton.

bénévolat [bānāvolá] *nm* voluntary service *ou* work.

bénévole [bānāvol] *a* voluntary, unpaid.

bénévolement [bānāvolmáṅ] *ad* voluntarily.

Bengale [bãṅgál] *nm*: **le** ~ Bengal; **le golfe du** ~ the Bay of Bengal.

bengali [bãṅgálē] *a* Bengali, Bengalese ♦ *nm* (*LING*) Bengali.

Bénin [bānáṅ] *nm*: **le** ~ Benin.

bénin, igne [bānáṅ, -ēny] *a* minor, mild; (*tumeur*) benign.

bénir [bānēr] *vt* to bless.

bénit, e [bānē, -ēt] *a* consecrated; **eau** ~**e** holy water.

bénitier [bānētyā] *nm* stoup, font (*for holy water*).

benjamin, e [bãṅzhámáṅ, -ēn] *nm/f* youngest child; (*SPORT*) under-13.

benne [bɛn] *nf* tub (*US*), skip (*Brit*); (*de téléphérique*) (cable) car; ~ **basculante** dump *ou* dumper truck.

benzine [bãṅzēn] *nf* benzine.

béotien, ne [bāosyaṅ, -ɛn] *nm/f* philistine.

BEP *sigle m* (= *Brevet d'études professionnelles*) *school-leaving diploma, taken at approx. 18 years*.

BEPA [bāpá] *sigle m* (= *Brevet d'études professionnelles agricoles*) *school-leaving diploma in agriculture, taken at approx. 18 years*.

BEPC *sigle m* (= *Brevet d'études du premier cycle*) *former school certificate (taken at approx. 16 years)*.

béquille [bākēy] *nf* crutch; (*de bicyclette*) stand.

berbère [bɛrber] *a* Berber ♦ *nm* (*LING*) Berber ♦ *nm/f*: **B~** Berber.

bercail [bɛrkáy] *nm* fold.

berceau, x [bɛrsō] *nm* cradle, crib.

bercer [bɛrsā] *vt* to rock, cradle; (*suj: musique etc*) to lull; ~ **qn de** (*promesses etc*) to delude sb with.

berceur, euse [bɛrsœr, -œ̄z] *a* soothing ♦ *nf* (*chanson*) lullaby.

béret (basque) [bāre(básk(ə))] *nm* beret.

bergamote [bɛrgámot] *nf* (*BOT*) bergamot.

berge [bɛrzh(ə)] *nf* bank.

berger, ère [bɛrzhā, -er] *nm/f* shepherd/ shepherdess; ~ **allemand** (*chien*) German shepherd (dog) (*US*), alsatian (dog) (*Brit*).

bergerie [bɛrzhərē] *nf* sheep pen.

béribéri [bārēbārē] *nm* beriberi.

Berlin [bɛrláṅ] *n* Berlin; ~**-Est/-Ouest** East/ West Berlin.

berline [bɛrlēn] *nf* (*AUTO*) sedan (*US*), saloon (car) (*Brit*).

berlingot [bɛrlãṅgō] *nm* (*emballage*) carton (*pyramid shaped*); (*bonbon*) lozenge.

berlinois, e [bɛrlēnwá, -wáz] *a* of *ou* from Berlin ♦ *nm/f*: **B~**, **e** Berliner.

berlue [bɛrlü] *nf*: **j'ai la** ~ I must be seeing things.

bermuda [bɛrmüdá] *nm* (*short*) Bermuda shorts.

Bermudes [bermüd] *nfpl*: **les (îles)** ~ Bermuda.

Berne [bern(ǝ)] *n* Bern.

berne [bern(ǝ)] *nf*: **en** ~ at half-mast; **mettre en** ~ to fly at half-mast.

berner [bernā] *vt* to fool.

bernois, e [bernwà, -wàz] *a* Bernese.

berrichon, ne [bereshóń, -on] *a* of *ou* from the Berry.

besace [bǝzás] *nf* beggar's bag.

besogne [bǝzony] *nf* work *q*, job.

besogneux, euse [bǝzonyœ̈, -œ̈z] *a* hard-working.

besoin [bǝzwań] *nm* need; (*pauvreté*): **le** ~ need, want; **le** ~ **d'argent/de gloire** the need for money/glory; ~**s (naturels)** nature's needs; **faire ses** ~**s** to relieve o.s.; **avoir** ~ **de qch/faire qch** to need sth/to do sth; **il n'y a pas** ~ **de (faire)** there is no need to (do); **au** ~, **si** ~ **est** if need be; **pour les** ~**s de la cause** for the purpose in hand.

bestial, e, aux [bestyàl, -ō] *a* bestial, brutish ♦ *nmpl* cattle.

bestiole [bestyol] *nf* (tiny) creature.

bétail [bātáy] *nm* livestock, cattle *pl*.

bétaillère [bātáyer] *nf* livestock truck.

bête [bet] *nf* animal; (*bestiole*) insect, creature ♦ *a* stupid, silly; **les** ~**s** (the) animals; **chercher la petite** ~ to nit-pick; ~ **noire** pet peeve (*US*) *ou* hate (*Brit*); ~ **sauvage** wild beast; ~ **de somme** beast of burden.

bêtement [betmâń] *ad* stupidly; **tout** ~ quite simply.

Bethléem [betlàem] *n* Bethlehem.

bêtifier [bātēfyā] *vi* to talk nonsense.

bêtise [batez] *nf* stupidity; (*action, remarque*) stupid thing (to say *ou* do); (*bonbon*) type of mint candy (*US*) *ou* sweet (*Brit*); **faire/dire une** ~ to do/say something stupid.

béton [bātóń] *nm* concrete; **(en)** ~ (*fig: alibi, argument*) cast iron; ~ **armé** reinforced concrete; ~ **précontraint** prestressed concrete.

bétonner [bātonā] *vt* to concrete (over).

bétonnière [bātonyer] *nf* cement mixer.

bette [bet] *nf* (*BOT*) Chinese cabbage.

betterave [betràv] *nf* (*rouge*) beet (*US*), beetroot (*Brit*); ~ **fourragère** mangel-wurzel; ~ **sucrière** sugar beet.

beugler [bœ̄glā] *vi* to low; (*péj: radio etc*) to blare ♦ *vt* (*péj: chanson etc*) to belt out.

Beur [bœr] *a*, *nm/f* second-generation Arab immigrant.

beurre [bœr] *nm* butter; **mettre du** ~ **dans les épinards** (*fig*) to add a little to the kitty; ~ **de cacao** cocoa butter; ~ **noir** brown butter (sauce).

beurrer [bœrā] *vt* to butter.

beurrier [bœryā] *nm* butter dish.

beuverie [bœvrē] *nf* drinking session.

bévue [bāvü] *nf* blunder.

Beyrouth [bārōōt] *n* Beirut.

Bhoutan [bōōtáń] *nm*: **le** ~ Bhutan.

bi... [bē] *préfixe* bi..., two-.

biais [bye] *nm* (*moyen*) device, expedient; (*aspect*) angle; (*bande de tissu*) piece of cloth cut on the bias; **en** ~, **de** ~ (*obliquement*) at an angle; (*fig*) indirectly.

biaiser [byāzā] *vi* (*fig*) to sidestep the issue.

bibelot [bēblō] *nm* trinket, curio.

biberon [bēbróń] *nm* (feeding) bottle; **nourrir au** ~ to bottle-feed.

bible [bēbl(ǝ)] *nf* bible.

bibliobus [bēblēyobüs] *nm* bookmobile (*US*), mobile library van (*Brit*).

bibliographie [bēblēyográfē] *nf* bibliography.

bibliophile [bēblēyofēl] *nm/f* book-lover.

bibliothécaire [bēblēyotāker] *nm/f* librarian.

bibliothèque [bēblēyotek] *nf* library; (*meuble*) bookcase; ~ **municipale** public library.

biblique [bēblēk] *a* biblical.

bicarbonate [bēkárbonát] *nm*: ~ **(de soude)** bicarbonate of soda.

bicentenaire [bēsáńtner] *nm* bicentenary.

biceps [bēseps] *nm* biceps.

biche [bēsh] *nf* doe.

bichonner [bēshonā] *vt* to groom.

bicolore [bēkolor] *a* two-colored (*US*), two-coloured (*Brit*).

bicoque [bēkok] *nf* (*péj*) shack, dump.

bicorne [bēkorn(ǝ)] *nm* cocked hat.

bicyclette [bēsēklet] *nf* bicycle.

bide [bēd] *nm* (*fam: ventre*) belly; (*THÉÂTRE*) flop.

bidet [bēde] *nm* bidet.

bidirectionnel, le [bēdēreksyonel] *a* bidirectional.

bidon [bēdóń] *nm* can ♦ *a inv* (*fam*) phoney.

bidonville [bēdóńvēl] *nm* shanty town.

bidule [bēdül] *nm* (*fam*) thingamajig.

bielle [byel] *nf* connecting rod; (*AUTO*) tie (*US*) *ou* track (*Brit*) rod.

bien [byań] *nm* good; (*patrimoine*) property *q*; **le** ~ **public** the public good; **faire du** ~ **à qn** to do sb good; **dire/penser du** ~ **de** to speak/think well of; **changer en** ~ to turn to the good; ~**s de consommation/ d'équipement** consumer/capital goods; ~**s durables** durables ♦ *ad* (*travailler*) well; (*approximativement*): **il y a** ~ **2 ans** at least 2 years ago; (*intensif*): ~ **jeune** rather young; ~ **assez** quite enough; ~ **mieux** very much better; ~ **du temps/des gens** quite a time/a number of people; **j'espère** ~ **y aller** I do hope to go; **il semble** ~ **que** it really seems that; **je veux** ~ **le faire** I'm (quite) willing *ou* happy to do it; **il faut** ~ **le faire** it has to be done; **tu as eu** ~ **raison de faire ça** you were quite right to do that; ~ **sûr**, ~ **entendu** certainly, of course; **c'est** ~ **fait** (*mérité*) it serves him (*ou* her *etc*) right; **croyant** ~ **faire** thinking he *etc* was doing the right thing; **faire** ~ **de ...** to be right to ...; **peut-être** ~ it could well be; **aimer** ~ to like; **aller** ~ to be well; **eh** ~! well!; **si** ~ **que** with the result that ♦ *excl* right!, OK!, fine! ♦ *a inv* good; (*joli*) good-looking; (*à l'aise*): **être** ~ to be fine; **ce n'est pas** ~ **de** it's not right to; **c'est (très)** ~ **(comme ça)** it's fine (like that); **ce n'est pas si** ~ **que ça** it's not as good *ou* great as all that; **c'est** ~? is that all right?; **des gens** ~ respectable people; **être** ~ **avec qn** to be on good terms with sb.

bien-aimé, e [byańnāmā] *a*, *nm/f* beloved.

bien-être [byańnetr(ǝ)] *nm* well-being.

bienfaisance [byańfǝzáńs] *nf* charity.

bienfaisant, e [byańfəzáń, -áńt] a (chose) beneficial.

bienfait [byańfe] nm act of generosity, benefaction; (de la science etc) benefit.

bienfaiteur, trice [byańfetœr, -trēs] nm/f benefactor/benefactress.

bien-fondé [byańfóńdā] nm soundness.

bien-fonds [byańfóń] nm property.

bienheureux, euse [byańnœrœ, -œz] a happy; (REL) blessed, blest.

biennal, e, aux [byānàl, -ō] a biennial.

bien-pensant, e [byańpáńsáń, -áńt] a rightthinking ♦ nm/f: **les** ~**s** right-minded people.

bien que [byańk(ə)] cj although.

bienséance [byańsááńs] nf propriety, decorum q; **les** ~**s** (convenances) the proprieties.

bienséant, e [byańsááń, -áńt] a proper, seemly.

bientôt [byańtō] ad soon; **à** ~ see you soon.

bienveillance [byańveyáńs] nf kindness.

bienveillant, e [byańveyáń, -áńt] a kindly.

bienvenu, e [byańvnü] a welcome ♦ nm/f: **être le** ~**/la** ~**e** to be welcome ♦ nf: **souhaiter la** ~**e à** to welcome; ~**e à** welcome to.

bière [byer] nf (boisson) beer; (cercueil) bier; ~ **blonde** light beer, lager (Brit); ~ **brune** dark beer, brown ale (Brit); ~ **(à la) pression** draft (US) ou draught (Brit) beer.

biffer [bēfā] vt to cross out.

bifteck [bēftek] nm steak.

bifurcation [bēfürkásyóń] nf fork (in road); (fig) new direction.

bifurquer [bēfürkā] vi (route) to fork; (véhicule) to turn off.

bigame [bēgàm] a bigamous.

bigamie [bēgàmē] nf bigamy.

bigarré, e [bēgàrā] a multicolored (US), multicoloured (Brit); (disparate) motley.

bigarreau, x [bēgàrō] nm type of cherry.

bigorneau, x [bēgornō] nm winkle.

bigot, e [bēgō, -ot] (péj) a bigoted ♦ nm/f bigot.

bigoterie [bēgotrē] nf bigotry.

bigoudi [bēgōōdē] nm curler.

bigrement [bēgrəmáń] ad (fam) fantastically.

bijou, x [bēzhōō] nm jewel.

bijouterie [bēzhōōtrē] nf (magasin) jewelry store (US), jeweller's (shop) (Brit); (bijoux) jewelry (US), jewellery (Brit).

bijoutier, ière [bēzhōōtyā, -yer] nm/f jeweler (US), jeweller (Brit).

bikini [bēkēnē] nm bikini.

bilan [bēláń] nm (COMM) balance sheet(s); (annuel) end of year statement; (fig) (net) outcome; (: de victimes) toll; **faire le** ~ **de** to assess; to review; **déposer son** ~ to file a bankruptcy statement; ~ **de santé** (MÉD) check-up; ~ **social** statement of a firm's policies towards its employees.

bilatéral, e, aux [bēlátārál, -ō] a bilateral.

bilboquet [bēlboke] nm (jouet) cup-and-ball game.

bile [bēl] nf bile; **se faire de la** ~ (fam) to worry o.s. sick.

biliaire [bēlyer] a biliary.

bilieux, euse [bēlyœ, -œz] a bilious; (fig: colérique) testy.

bilingue [bēlańg] a bilingual.

bilinguisme [bēlańgüēsm(ə)] nm bilingualism.

billard [bēyàr] nm billiards sg; (table) billiard table; **c'est du** ~ (fam) it's a cinch; **passer sur le** ~ (fam) to have an (ou one's) operation; ~ **électrique** pinball.

bille [bēy] nf ball; (du jeu de billes) marble; (de bois) log; **jouer aux** ~**s** to play marbles.

billet [bēye] nm (aussi: ~ **de banque**) (bank)note; (de cinéma, de bus etc) ticket; (courte lettre) note; ~ **à ordre** ou **de commerce** (COMM) promissory note, IOU; ~ **d'avion/de train** plane/train ticket; ~ **circulaire** round-trip ticket; ~ **doux** love letter; ~ **de faveur** complimentary ticket; ~ **de loterie** lottery ticket; ~ **de quai** platform ticket.

billetterie [bēyetrē] nf ticket office; (distributeur) ticket dispenser; (BANQUE) cash dispenser.

billion [bēlyóń] nm trillion (US), billion (Brit).

billot [bēyō] nm block.

BIMA sigle m = Bulletin d'information du ministère de l'agriculture.

bimbeloterie [bańblotrē] nf (objets) knickknacks pl.

bimensuel, le [bēmáńsüel] a bimonthly, twice-monthly.

bimestriel, le [bēmestrēyel] a bimonthly, two-monthly.

bimoteur [bēmotœr] a twin-engined.

binaire [bēner] a binary.

biner [bēnā] vt to hoe.

binette [bēnet] nf (outil) hoe.

binoclard [bēnoklàr, -àrd(ə)] (fam) nm/f four-eyes.

binocle [bēnokl(ə)] nm pince-nez.

binoculaire [bēnoküler] a binocular.

binôme [bēnōm] nm binomial.

bio... [byo] préfixe bio....

biochimie [byoshēmē] nf biochemistry.

biochimique [byoshēmēk] a biochemical.

biochimiste [byoshēmēst(ə)] nm/f biochemist.

biodégradable [byodāgràdábl(ə)] a biodegradable.

biographe [byogràf] nm/f biographer.

biographie [byogràfē] nf biography.

biographique [byogràfēk] a biographical.

biologie [byolōzhē] nf biology.

biologique [byolōzhēk] a biological.

biologiste [byolozhēst(ə)] nm/f biologist.

biopsie [byopsē] nf (MÉD) biopsy.

biosphère [byosfer] nf biosphere.

bipartisme [bēpàrtēsm(ə)] nm bipartisanship.

bipède [bēped] nm biped, two-footed creature.

biphasé, e [bēfàzā] a (ÉLEC) two-phase.

biplace [bēplàs] a, nm (avion) two-seater.

biplan [bēpláń] nm biplane.

bique [bēk] nf nanny goat; (péj) old hag.

biquet, te [bēke, -et] nm/f: **mon** ~ (fam) my lamb.

biréacteur [bērāàktœr] nm twin-engined jet.

birman, e [bērmáń, -àn] a Burmese.

Birmanie [bērmánē] nf: **la** ~ Burma.

bis, e [bē, bēz] a (couleur) grayish (US) ou greyish (Brit) brown ♦ ad [bēs]: **12** ~ 12a ou A ♦ excl, nm [bēs] encore ♦ nf (baiser) kiss; (vent) North wind.

bisaïeul, e [bēsàyœl] nm/f great-grandfather/great-grandmother.

bisannuel, le [bēzánüel] a biennial.

bisbille [bēsbēy] *nf*: être en ~ avec qn to be at loggerheads with sb.

Biscaye [bēskā] *nf*: le golfe de ~ the Bay of Biscay.

biscornu, e [bēskornü] *a* crooked; *(bizarre)* weird(-looking).

biscotte [bēskot] *nf* ≈ melba toast.

biscuit [bēsküē] *nm* cookie *(US)*, biscuit *(Brit)*; *(gateau)* sponge cake; ~ à la cuiller ladyfinger *(US)*, sponge finger *(Brit)*.

biscuiterie [bēsküētrē] *nf* cookie *(US)* ou biscuit *(Brit)* manufacturing.

bise [bēz] *af, nf voir* **bis**.

biseau, x [bēzō] *nm* bevelled edge; en ~ bevelled.

biseauter [bēzōtā] *vt* to bevel.

bisexué, e [bēseksüā] *a* bisexual.

bismuth [bēsmüt] *nm* bismuth.

bison [bēzôň] *nm* bison.

bisou [bēzōō] *nm (fam)* kiss.

bisque [bēsk(ə)] *nf*: ~ d'écrevisses shrimp bisque.

bissectrice [bēsektrēs] *nf* bisector.

bisser [bēsā] *vt (faire rejouer: artiste, chanson)* to encore; *(rejouer: morceau)* to give an encore of.

bissextile [bēsekstēl] *a*: année ~ leap year.

bistouri [bēstōōrē] *nm* lancet.

bistre [bēstr(ə)] *a (couleur)* bistre; *(peau, teint)* tanned.

bistro(t) [bēstrō] *nm* bistro, café.

BIT *sigle m* (= *Bureau international du travail*) ILO.

bit [bēt] *nm (INFORM)* bit.

biterrois, e [bētcrwā, -wàz] *a* of ou from Béziers.

bitte [bēt] *nf*: ~ d'amarrage bollard *(NAUT)*.

bitume [bētüm] *nm* asphalt.

bitumer [bētümā] *vt* to asphalt.

bivalent, e [bēválâň, âňt] *a* bivalent.

bivouac [bēvwàk] *nm* bivouac.

bivouaquer [bēvwàkā] *vi* to bivouac.

bizarre [bēzár] *a* strange, odd.

bizarrement [bēzàrmáň] *ad* strangely, oddly.

bizarrerie [bēzàrrē] *nf* strangeness, oddness.

blackbouler [blàkbōōlā] *vt (à une élection)* to blackball.

blafard, e [blàfàr, -àrd(ə)] *a* wan.

blague [blàg] *nf (propos)* joke; *(farce)* trick; sans ~! no kidding!; ~ à tabac tobacco pouch.

blaguer [blàgā] *vi* to joke ♦ *vt* to tease.

blagueur, euse [blàgœr, -œz] *a* teasing ♦ *nm/f* joker.

blair [blēr] *nm (fam)* beak.

blaireau, x [blerō] *nm (ZOOL)* badger; *(brosse)* shaving brush.

blairer [blārā] *vt*: je ne peux pas le ~ I can't bear ou stand him.

blâmable [blâmábl(ə)] *a* blameworthy.

blâme [blâm] *nm* blame; *(sanction)* reprimand.

blâmer [blâmā] *vt (réprouver)* to blame; *(réprimander)* to reprimand.

blanc, blanche [blâň, blâňsh] *a* white; *(non imprimé)* blank; *(innocent)* pure ♦ *nm (couleur)* white, white man/woman ♦ *nm (couleur)* white; *(linge)*: le ~ whites *pl*; *(espace non écrit)* blank; *(aussi:* ~ d'œuf) (egg-)white;

(aussi: ~ de poulet) breast, white meat; *(aussi:* vin ~) white wine ♦ *nf (MUS)* half note *(US)*, minim *(Brit)*; d'une voix blanche in a toneless voice; aux cheveux ~s white-haired; le ~ de l'œil the white of the eye; laisser en ~ to leave blank; chèque en ~ blank check; à ~ *ad (chauffer)* white-hot; *(tirer, charger)* with blanks; saigner à ~ to bleed white; ~ cassé off-white.

blanc-bec, *pl* **blancs-becs** [blâňbek] *nm* greenhorn.

blanchâtre [blâňshâtr(ə)] *a (teint, lumière)* whitish.

blancheur [blâňshœr] *nf* whiteness.

blanchir [blâňshēr] *vt (gén)* to whiten; *(linge, fig: argent)* to launder; *(CULIN)* to blanch; *(fig: disculper)* to clear ♦ *vi* to grow white; *(cheveux)* to go white; blanchi à la chaux whitewashed.

blanchissage [blâňshēsàzh] *nm (du linge)* laundering.

blanchisserie [blâňshēsrē] *nf* laundry.

blanchisseur, euse [blâňshēsœr, -œz] *nm/f* launderer.

blanc-seing, *pl* **blancs-seings** [blâňsaň] *nm* signed blank paper.

blanquette [blâňket] *nf (CULIN)*: ~ de veau veal in a white sauce, blanquette de veau.

blasé, e [blàzā] *a* blasé.

blaser [blàzā] *vt* to make blasé.

blason [blàzôň] *nm* coat of arms.

blasphémateur, trice [blàsfāmàtœr, -trēs] *nm/f* blasphemer.

blasphématoire [blàsfāmàtwàr] *a* blasphemous.

blasphème [blàsfem] *nm* blasphemy.

blasphémer [blàsfāmā] *vi* to blaspheme ♦ *vt* to blaspheme against.

blatte [blàt] *nf* cockroach.

blazer [blàzer] *nm* blazer.

blé [blā] *nm* wheat; ~ en herbe wheat on the ear; ~ noir buckwheat.

bled [bled] *nm (péj)* hole; *(en Afrique du Nord)*: le ~ the interior.

blême [blem] *a* pale.

blêmir [blāmēr] *vi (personne)* to (turn) pale; *(lueur)* to grow pale.

blennorragie [blānorázhē] *nf* gonorrhoea.

blessant, e [blesàň, -àňt] *a* hurtful.

blessé, e [blāsā] *a* injured ♦ *nm/f* injured person, casualty; un ~ grave, un grand ~ a seriously injured ou wounded person.

blesser [blāsā] *vt* to injure; *(délibérément: MIL etc)* to wound; *(suj: souliers etc, offenser)* to hurt; se ~ to injure o.s.; se ~ au pied *etc* to injure one's foot *etc*.

blessure [blāsür] *nf* injury; wound.

blet, te [blc, blct] *a* overripe.

blette [blet] *nf* = **bette**.

bleu, e [blœ̄] *a* blue; *(bifteck)* very rare ♦ *nm (couleur)* blue; *(novice)* greenhorn; *(contusion)* bruise; *(vêtement: aussi:* ~s) coveralls *pl (US)*, overalls *pl (Brit)*; avoir une peur ~e to be scared stiff; zone ~e ≈ restricted parking area; fromage ~ blue cheese; au ~ *(CULIN)* au bleu; ~ (de lessive) ≈ bluing *(US)*, ≈ blue bag *(Brit)*; ~ de méthylène *(MÉD)* methylene blue; ~ marine/nuit/roi navy/midnight/royal blue.

bleuâtre [blœ̄âtr(ə)] *a* (*fumée etc*) bluish, blue-ish.

bleuet [blœ̄c] *nm* cornflower.

bleuir [blœ̄ēr] *vt*, *vi* to turn blue.

bleuté, e [blœ̄tā] *a* blue-shaded.

blindage [blaṅdâzh] *nm* armor-plating (*US*), armour-plating (*Brit*).

blindé, e [blaṅdā] *a* armored (*US*), armoured (*Brit*); (*fig*) hardened ♦ *nm* armored *ou* armoured car; (*char*) tank.

blinder [blaṅdā] *vt* to armor (*US*), armour (*Brit*); (*fig*) to harden.

blizzard [blēzàr] *nm* blizzard.

bloc [blok] *nm* (*de pierre etc*, *INFORM*) block; (*de papier à lettres*) pad; (*ensemble*) group, block; **serré à ~** tightened right down; **en ~** as a whole; wholesale; **faire ~** to unite; **~ opératoire** operating rooms (*US*), theatre block (*Brit*); **~ sanitaire** toilet block; **~ sténo** shorthand notebook.

blocage [blokâzh] *nm* (*voir bloquer*) blocking; jamming; freezing; (*PSYCH*) hang-up.

bloc-cuisine, *pl* **blocs-cuisines** [blokkǖēzēn] *nm* kitchen unit.

bloc-cylindres, *pl* **blocs-cylindres** [bloksēlaṅdr(ə)] *nm* cylinder block.

bloc-évier, *pl* **blocs-éviers** [blokāvyā] *nm* sink unit.

bloc-moteur, *pl* **blocs-moteurs** [blokmotœr] *nm* engine block.

bloc-notes, *pl* **blocs-notes** [bloknot] *nm* note pad.

blocus [blokǖs] *nm* blockade.

blond, e [blóṅ, -óṅd] *a* fair; (*plus clair*) blond; (*sable, blés*) golden ♦ *nm/f* fair-haired *ou* blond man/woman; **~ cendré** ash blond.

blondeur [blóṅdœr] *nf* fairness; blondness.

blondin, e [blóṅdań, -ēn] *nm/f* fair-haired *ou* blond child *ou* young person.

blondinet, te [blóṅdēnc, -et] *nm/f* blondy.

blondir [blóṅdēr] *vi* (*personne, cheveux*) to go fair *ou* blond.

bloquer [blokā] *vt* (*passage*) to block; (*pièce mobile*) to jam; (*crédits, compte*) to freeze; (*personne, négociations etc*) to hold up; (*regrouper*) to group; **~ les freins** to jam on the brakes.

blottir [blotēr]: **se ~** *vi* to huddle up.

blousant, e [blōōzáṅ, áṅt] *a* blousing out.

blouse [blōōz] *nf* smock.

blouser [blōōzā] *vi* to blouse out.

blouson [blōōzóṅ] *nm* blouson (jacket); **~ noir** (*fig*) ≈ hell's angel.

blue-jean(s) [blōōdzhēn(s)] *nm* jeans.

blues [blōōz] *nm* blues *pl*.

bluet [blüe] *nm* = **bleuet**.

bluff [blœf] *nm* bluff.

bluffer [blœfā] *vi, vt* to bluff.

BN *sigle f* = *Bibliothèque nationale*.

BNP *sigle f* = *Banque nationale de Paris*.

boa [boá] *nm* (*ZOOL*): **~ (constricteur)** boa (constrictor); (*tour de cou*) (feather *ou* fur) boa.

bobard [bobàr] *nm* (*fam*) tall story.

bobèche [bobcsh] *nf* bobeche (*US*), candle-ring (*Brit*).

bobine [bobēn] *nf* (*de fil*) reel; (*de machine à coudre*) spool; (*de machine à écrire*) ribbon; (*ÉLEC*) coil; **~ (d'allumage)** (*AUTO*) coil; **~**

de pellicule (*PHOTO*) roll of film.

bobo [bōbō] *nm* (*aussi fig*) sore spot.

bob(sleigh) [bob(slcg)] *nm* bobsled (*US*), bob(sleigh) (*Brit*).

bocage [bokázh] *nm* (*GÉO*) bocage, *farmland criss-crossed by hedges and trees*; (*bois*) grove, copse.

bocal, aux [bokàl, -ō] *nm* jar.

bock [bok] *nm* (*beer*) glass; (*contenu*) glass of beer.

bœuf [bœf, *pl* bœ̄] *nm* ox (*pl* oxen), steer; (*CULIN*) beef.

bof [bof] *excl* (*fam*: *indifférence*) don't care!; (: *pas terrible*) nothing special.

Bogotá [bogotá] *n* Bogotá.

Bohême [boem] *nf*: **la ~** Bohemia.

bohème [boem] *a* happy-go-lucky, unconventional.

bohémien, ne [boāmyań, -en] *a* Bohemian ♦ *nm/f* gipsy.

boire [bwàr] *vt* to drink; (*s'imprégner de*) to soak up; **~ un coup** to have a drink.

bois [bwà] *vb voir* **boire** ♦ *nm* wood; (*ZOOL*) antler; (*MUS*): **les ~** the woodwinds (*US*), the woodwind (*Brit*); **de ~**, **en ~** wooden; **~ vert** green wood; **~ mort** deadwood; **~ de lit** bedstead.

boisé, e [bwàzā] *a* woody, wooded.

boiser [bwàzā] *vt* (*galerie de mine*) to timber; (*chambre*) to panel; (*terrain*) to plant with trees.

boiseries [bwàzrē] *nfpl* panelling *sg*.

boisson [bwàsóṅ] *nf* drink; **pris de ~** drunk, intoxicated; **~s alcoolisées** alcoholic beverages *ou* drinks; **~s non alcoolisées** soft drinks.

boit [bwà] *vb voir* **boire**.

boîte [bwàt] *nf* box; (*fam*: *entreprise*) firm, company; **aliments en ~** canned *ou* tinned (*Brit*) foods; **~ de sardines/petits pois** can *ou* tin (*Brit*) of sardines/peas; **mettre qn en ~** (*fam*) to have a laugh at sb's expense; **~ d'allumettes** box of matches; (*vide*) matchbox; **~ de conserves** can *ou* tin (*Brit*) (of food); **~ crânienne** cranium; **~ à gants** glove compartment; **~ aux lettres** letter box, mailbox (*US*); (*INFORM*) mailbox; **~ à musique** music box; **~ noire** (*AVIAT*) black box; **~ de nuit** night club; **~ à ordures** trash can (*US*), dustbin (*Brit*); **~ postale (BP)** PO box; **~ de vitesses** transmission (*US*), gear box (*Brit*).

boiter [bwàtā] *vi* to limp; (*fig*) to wobble; (*raisonnement*) to be shaky.

boiteux, euse [bwàtœ̄, -ēz] *a* lame; wobbly; shaky.

boîtier [bwàtyā] *nm* case; (*d'appareil-photo*) body; **~ de montre** watch case.

boitiller [bwàtēyā] *vi* to limp slightly, have a slight limp.

boive [bwàv] *etc vb voir* **boire**.

bol [bol] *nm* bowl; (*contenu*): **un ~ de café** *etc* a bowl of coffee *etc*; **un ~ d'air** a breath of fresh air; **en avoir ras le ~** (*fam*) to have had a bellyful.

bolée [bolā] *nf* bowlful.

bolet [bole] *nm* boletus (mushroom).

bolide [bolēd] *nm* racing car; **comme un ~** like a rocket.

Bolivie [bolēvē] *nf*: **la** ~ Bolivia.

bolivien, ne [bolēvyań, -en] *a* Bolivian ♦ *nm/f*: **B~, ne** Bolivian.

bolognais, e [bolonye, -ez] *a* Bolognese.

Bologne [bolony] *n* Bologna.

bombance [bôṅbâṅs] *nf*: **faire** ~ to have a feast, revel.

bombardement [bôṅbárdəmâṅ] *nm* bombing.

bombarder [bôṅbárdā] *vt* to bomb; ~ **qn de** (*cailloux, lettres*) to bombard sb with; ~ **qn directeur** to thrust sb into the director's seat.

bombardier [bôṅbárdyā] *nm* (*avion*) bomber; (*aviateur*) bombardier.

bombe [bôṅb] *nf* bomb; (*atomiseur*) (aerosol) spray; (*ÉQUITATION*) riding cap; **faire la** ~ (*fam*) to go on a binge; ~ **atomique** atomic bomb; ~ **à retardement** time bomb.

bombé, e [bôṅbā] *a* rounded; (*mur*) bulging; (*front*) domed; (*route*) steeply cambered.

bomber [bôṅbā] *vi* to bulge; (*route*) to camber ♦ *vt*: ~ **le torse** to swell out one's chest.

bon, bonne [bôṅ, bon] *a* good; (*charitable*): ~ (**envers**) good (to), kind (to); (*juste*): **le** ~ **numéro/moment** the right number/moment; (*intensif*): **un** ~ **nombre** a good number; (*approprié*): ~ **à/pour** fit to/for ♦ *nm* (*billet*) voucher; (*aussi*): ~ **cadeau**) gift certificate (*US*), gift voucher (*Brit*) ♦ *nf* (*domestique*) maid ♦ *ad*: **il fait** ~ it's *ou* the weather's fine ♦ *excl* right!, good!; **vous êtes trop** ~ you are too kind; **avoir** ~ **goût** to taste nice *ou* good; (*fig*) to have good taste; **avoir** ~ **dos** to be always willing to shoulder responsibility; (*chose*) to be a good excuse; **de bonne heure** early; **sentir** ~ to smell good; **tenir** ~ to stand firm, hold out; **pour de** ~ for good; **à quoi** ~ (...)? what's the good *ou* use (of ...)?; **juger** ~ **de faire** ... to think fit to do ...; **ah** ~? (oh) really?; **il y a du** ~ **dans cela** there are some advantages in it; **il y a du** ~ **dans ce qu'il dit** there is some sense in what he says; ~ **anniversaire!** happy birthday!; ~ **voyage!** have a good journey!, enjoy your trip!; **bonne chance!** good luck!; **bonne année!** happy New Year!; **bonne nuit!** good night!; ~ **de caisse** cash voucher; ~ **enfant** *a inv* accommodating, easy-going; ~ **d'essence** gas (*US*) *ou* petrol (*Brit*) coupon; ~ **marché** *a inv, ad* cheap; ~ **mot** witticism; ~ **sens** common sense; ~ **à tirer** ready (*US*) *ou* pass (*Brit*) for press; ~ **du Trésor** Treasury bond; ~ **vivant** jovial chap; **bonne d'enfant** nanny; **bonne femme** (*péj*) woman; female (*péj*); **bonne sœur** nun; **bonne à tout faire** general help; **bonnes œuvres** charitable works; charities.

bonasse [bonås] *a* soft, meek.

bonbon [bôṅbôṅ] *nm* (boiled) candy (*US*) *ou* sweet (*Brit*).

bonbonne [bôṅbon] *nf* demijohn; carboy.

bonbonnière [bôṅbonycr] *nf* candy (*US*) *ou* sweet (*Brit*) box.

bond [bôṅ] *nm* leap; (*d'une balle*) rebound, ricochet; **faire un** ~ to leap in the air; **d'un seul** ~ in one bound, with one leap; ~ **en avant** (*fig: progrès*) leap forward.

bonde [bôṅd] *nf* (*d'évier etc*) plug; (: *trou*) plughole; (*de tonneau*) bung; bunghole.

bondé, e [bôṅdā] *a* packed (full).

bondieuserie [bôṅdyēzrē] *nf* (*péj: objet*) religious knick-knack.

bondir [bôṅdēr] *vi* to leap; ~ **de joie** (*fig*) to jump for joy; ~ **de colère** (*fig*) to be hopping mad.

bonheur [boncer] *nm* happiness; **avoir le** ~ **de** to have the good fortune to; **porter** ~ (**à qn**) to bring (sb) luck; **au petit** ~ haphazardly; **par** ~ fortunately.

bonhomie [bonomē] *nf* goodnaturedness.

bonhomme [bonom], *pl* **bonshommes** [bôṅzom] *nm* fellow ♦ *a* good-natured; **un vieux** ~ an old chap; **aller son** ~ **de chemin** to carry on in one's own sweet way; ~ **de neige** snowman.

boni [bonē] *nm* profit.

bonification [bonēfēkâsyôṅ] *nf* bonus.

bonifier [bonēfyā] *vt*, **se** ~ *vi* to improve.

boniment [bonēmâṅ] *nm* patter *q*.

bonjour [bôṅzhōōr] *excl, nm* hello; (*selon l'heure*) good morning (*ou* afternoon); **donner** *ou* **souhaiter le** ~ **à qn** to bid sb good morning *ou* afternoon.

Bonn [bon] *n* Bonn.

bonne [bon] *af*, *nf voir* **bon**.

bonne-maman, *pl* **bonnes-mamans** [bonmámâṅ] granny, grandma, gran.

bonnement [bonmâṅ] *ad*: **tout** ~ quite simply.

bonnet [bone] *nm* bonnet, hat; (*de soutien-gorge*) cup; ~ **d'âne** dunce's cap; ~ **de bain** bathing cap; ~ **de nuit** nightcap.

bonneterie [bonetrē] *nf* hosiery.

bon-papa, *pl* **bons-papas** [bôṅpápá] *nm* grandpa, grandad.

bonsoir [bôṅswar] *excl* good evening.

bonté [bôṅtā] *nf* kindness *q*; **avoir la** ~ **de** to be kind *ou* good enough to.

bonus [bonüs] *nm* (*assurances*) no-claims discount (*US*) *ou* bonus (*Brit*).

bonze [bôṅz] *nm* (*REL*) bonze.

boomerang [bōōmráṅg] *nm* boomerang.

borborygme [borborēgm(ə)] *nm* rumbling noise.

bord [bor] *nm* (*de table, verre, falaise*) edge; (*de rivière, lac*) bank; (*de route*) side; (*de vêtement*) edge, border; (*de chapeau*) brim; (**monter**) **à** ~ (to go) on board; **jeter pardessus** ~ to throw overboard; **le commandant/les hommes du** ~ the ship's captain/crew; **du même** ~ (*fig*) of the same opinion; **au** ~ **de la mer/route** at the seaside/roadside; **être au** ~ **des larmes** to be on the verge of tears; **virer de** ~ (*NAVIG*) to tack; **sur les** ~s (*fig*) slightly; **de tous** ~s on all sides; ~ **du trottoir** curb (*US*), kerb (*Brit*).

bordage [bordázh] *nm* (*NAVIG*) planking *q*; plating *q*.

bordeaux [bordō] *nm* Bordeaux ♦ *a inv* maroon.

bordée [bordā] *nf* broadside; **une** ~ **d'injures** a volley of abuse; **tirer une** ~ to go on the town.

bordel [bordel] *nm* brothel; (*fam!*) goddamn (*US*) *ou* bloody (*Brit*) mess (!) ♦ *excl* hell!

bordelais, e [bordəle, -ez] *a* of *ou* from Bordeaux.

border [bordā] *vt* (*être le long de*) to border, line; (*garnir*): ~ **qch de** to line sth with; to trim sth with; (*qn dans son lit*) to tuck in.
bordereau, x [bordərō] *nm* docket, slip.
bordure [bordür] *nf* border; (*sur un vêtement*) trim(ming), border; **en ~ de** on the edge of.
boréal, e, aux [borāál, -ō] *a* boreal, northern.
borgne [borny(ə)] *a* one-eyed; **hôtel ~** shady hotel; **fenêtre ~** obstructed window.
bornage [bornázh] *nm* (*d'un terrain*) demarcation.
borne [born(ə)] *nf* boundary stone; (*aussi:* ~ **kilométrique**) kilometer-marker, ≈ milestone; **~s** *nfpl* (*fig*) limits; **dépasser les ~s** to go too far; **sans ~(s)** boundless.
borné, e [bornā] *a* narrow; (*obtus*) narrow-minded.
Bornéo [bornāō] *nm*: **le ~** Borneo.
borner [bornā] *vt* (*délimiter*) to limit; (*limiter*) to confine; **se ~ à faire** to content o.s. with doing; to limit o.s. to doing.
bosniaque [boznyák] *a* Bosnian.
bosnien, ne [boznyań, -en] *a* Bosnian.
Bosphore [bosfor] *nm*: **le ~** the Bosphorus.
bosquet [boske] *nm* copse, grove.
bosse [bos] *nf* (*de terrain etc*) bump; (*enflure*) lump; (*du bossu, du chameau*) hump; **avoir la ~ de l'anglais** *etc* to have a gift for English *etc*; **il a roulé sa ~** he's been around.
bosseler [boslā] *vt* (*ouvrer*) to emboss; (*abîmer*) to dent.
bosser [bosā] *vi* (*fam*) to work; (: *dur*) to slave (away).
bosseur, euse [bosœr, -œz] *nm/f* (hard) worker.
bossu, e [bosü] *nm/f* hunchback.
bot [bō] *am*: **pied ~** club foot.
botanique [botánēk] *nf* botany ♦ *a* botanic(al).
botaniste [botánēst(ə)] *nm/f* botanist.
Botswana [botswáná] *nm*: **le ~** Botswana.
botte [bot] *nf* (*soulier*) (high) boot; (*ESCRIME*) thrust; (*gerbe*): ~ **de paille** bundle of straw; ~ **de radis/d'asperges** bundle of radishes/asparagus; **~s de caoutchouc** wellington boots.
botter [botā] *vt* to put boots on; (*donner un coup de pied à*) to kick; (*fam*): **ça me botte** I like that.
bottier [botyā] *nm* bootmaker.
bottillon [botēyóń] *nm* bootee.
bottin [botań] *nm* ® directory.
bottine [botēn] *nf* ankle boot.
botulisme [botülēsm(ə)] *nm* botulism.
bouc [bōōk] *nm* goat; (*barbe*) goatee; ~ **émissaire** scapegoat.
boucan [bōōkáń] *nm* din, racket.
bouche [bōōsh] *nf* mouth; **une ~ à nourrir** a mouth to feed; **les ~s inutiles** the non-productive members of the population; **faire le ~ à ~ à qn** to give sb mouth-to-mouth resuscitation; **de ~ à oreille** confidentially; **pour la bonne ~** (*pour la fin*) till last; **faire venir l'eau à la ~** to make one's mouth water; ~ **cousue!** mum's the word!; ~ **d'aération** air vent; ~ **de chaleur** hot air vent; ~ **d'égout** manhole; ~ **d'incendie** fire hydrant; ~ **de métro** métro entrance.

bouché, e [bōōshā] *a* (*flacon etc*) stoppered; (*temps, ciel*) overcast; (*carrière*) blocked; (*péj: personne*) thick; (*trompette*) muted; **avoir le nez ~** to have a stuffy (*US*) *ou* blocked(-up) (*Brit*) nose.
bouchée [bōōshā] *nf* mouthful; **ne faire qu'une ~ de** (*fig*) to make short work of; **pour une ~ de pain** (*fig*) for next to nothing; **~s à la reine** chicken vol-au-vents.
boucher [bōōshā] *nm* butcher ♦ *vt* (*pour colmater*) to stop up; to fill up; (*obstruer*) to block (up); **se ~** (*tuyau etc*) to block up, get blocked up; **se ~ le nez** to hold one's nose.
bouchère [bōōsher] *nf* butcher; (*femme du boucher*) butcher's wife.
boucherie [bōōshrē] *nf* butcher's (shop); (*métier*) butchery; (*fig*) slaughter, butchery.
bouche-trou [bōōshtrōō] *nm* (*fig*) stop-gap.
bouchon [bōōshóń] *nm* (*en liège*) cork; (*autre matière*) stopper; (*fig: embouteillage*) hold-up; (*PÊCHE*) float; ~ **doseur** measuring cap.
bouchonner [bōōshonā] *vt* to rub down ♦ *vi* to form a traffic jam.
bouchot [bōōsho] *nm* mussel bed.
bouclage [bōōklázh] *nm* sealing off.
boucle [bōōkl(ə)] *nf* (*forme, figure, aussi IN-FORM*) loop; (*objet*) buckle; ~ **(de cheveux)** curl; ~ **d'oreilles** earring.
bouclé, e [bōōklā] *a* curly; (*tapis*) uncut.
boucler [bōōklā] *vt* (*fermer: ceinture etc*) to fasten; (: *magasin*) to shut; (*terminer*) to finish off; (: *circuit*) to complete; (*budget*) to balance; (*enfermer*) to shut away; (: *condamné*) to lock up; (: *quartier*) to seal off ♦ *vi* to curl; **faire ~** (*cheveux*) to curl; ~ **la boucle** (*AVIAT*) to loop the loop.
bouclette [bōōklet] *nf* small curl.
bouclier [bōōklēyā] *nm* shield.
bouddha [bōōdá] *nm* Buddha.
bouddhisme [bōōdēsm(ə)] *nm* Buddhism.
bouddhiste [bōōdēst(ə)] *nm/f* Buddhist.
bouder [bōōdá] *vi* to sulk ♦ *vt* (*chose*) to turn one's nose up at; (*personne*) to refuse to have anything to do with.
bouderie [bōōdrē] *nf* sulking *q*.
boudeur, euse [bōōdœr, -œz] *a* sullen, sulky.
boudin [bōōdań] *nm* (*CULIN*) blood sausage (*US*), black pudding (*Brit*); (*TECH*) roll; ~ **blanc** sausage (*US*), white pudding (*Brit*).
boudiné, e [bōōdēnā] *a* (*doigt*) podgy; (*serré*): ~ **dans** (*vêtement*) bulging out of.
boudoir [bōōdwár] *nm* boudoir; (*biscuit*) ladyfinger (*US*), sponge finger (*Brit*).
boue [bōō] *nf* mud.
bouée [bwā] *nf* buoy; (*de baigneur*) rubber ring; ~ **(de sauvetage)** lifebuoy; (*fig*) life-line.
boueux, euse [bwœ, -œz] *a* muddy ♦ *nm* garbage (*US*) *ou* refuse (*Brit*) collector.
bouffant, e [bōōfáń, -áńt] *a* puffed out.
bouffe [bōōf] *nf* (*fam*) grub, food.
bouffée [bōōfā] *nf* puff; ~ **de chaleur** blast of hot air; ~ **de fièvre/de honte** flush of fever/shame; ~ **d'orgueil** fit of pride.
bouffer [bōōfā] *vi* (*fam*) to eat; (*COUTURE*) to puff out ♦ *vt* (*fam*) to eat.
bouffi, e [bōōfē] *a* swollen.
bouffon, ne [bōōfóń, -on] *a* farcical, comical ♦ *nm* jester.

bouge [boozh] *nm* (*bar louche*) (low) dive; (*taudis*) hovel.

bougeoir [boozhwàr] *nm* candlestick.

bougeotte [boozhot] *nf*: **avoir la** ~ to have the fidgets.

bouger [boozhā] *vi* to move; (*dent etc*) to be loose; (*changer*) to alter; (*agir*) to stir ♦ *vt* to move; **se** ~ (*fam*) to move (o.s.).

bougie [boozhē] *nf* candle; (*AUTO*) spark plug.

bougon, ne [boogón, -on] *a* grumpy.

bougonner [boogonā] *vi*, *vt* to grumble.

bougre [boogr(ə)] *nm* chap; (*fam*): **ce** ~ **de** ... that confounded ....

bouillabaisse [booyàbes] *nf type of fish soup*.

bouillant, e [booyàn, -ànt] *a* (*qui bout*) boiling; (*très chaud*) boiling (hot); (*fig: ardent*) hot-headed; ~ **de colère** *etc* seething with anger *etc*.

bouilleur [booycer] *nm*: ~ **de cru** (home) distiller.

bouillie [booyē] *nf* gruel; (*de bébé*) cereal; **en** ~ (*fig*) crushed.

bouillir [booyēr] *vi* to boil ♦ *vt* (*aussi*: **faire** ~; *CULIN*) to boil; ~ **de colère** *etc* to seethe with anger *etc*.

bouilloire [booywàr] *nf* kettle.

bouillon [booyón] *nm* (*CULIN*) stock *q*; (*bulles, écume*) bubble; ~ **de culture** culture medium.

bouillonnement [booyonmàn] *nm* (*d'un liquide*) bubbling; (*des idées*) ferment.

bouillonner [booyonā] *vi* to bubble; (*fig*) to bubble up; (*torrent*) to foam.

bouillotte [booyot] *nf* hot-water bottle.

boulanger, ère [boolànzhā, -er] *nm/f* baker ♦ *nf* (*femme du boulanger*) baker's wife.

boulangerie [boolànzhrē] *nf* bakery, baker's (shop); (*commerce*) bakery; ~ **industrielle** bakery.

boulangerie-pâtisserie, *pl* **boulangeries-pâtisseries** [boolànzhrēpàtēsrē] *nf* baker's and confectioner's (shop).

boule [bool] *nf* (*gén*) ball; (*pour jouer*) bowl; (*de machine à écrire*) typing element (*US*), golf ball (*Brit*); **roulé en** ~ curled up in a ball; **se mettre en** ~ (*fig*) to fly off the handle, blow one's top; **perdre la** ~ (*fig: fam*) to go off one's rocker; ~ **de gomme** (*bonbon*) gum(drop), pastille; ~ **de neige** snowball; **faire** ~ **de neige** (*fig*) to snowball.

bouleau, x [boolō] *nm* (silver) birch.

bouledogue [booldog] *nm* bulldog.

boulet [boole] *nm* (*aussi*: ~ **de canon**) cannonball; (*de bagnard*) ball and chain; (*charbon*) briquette.

boulette [boolet] *nf* ball.

boulevard [boolvàr] *nm* boulevard.

bouleversant, e [boolversàn, -ànt] *a* (*récit*) deeply distressing; (*nouvelle*) shattering.

bouleversé, e [boolversā] *a* (*ému*) deeply distressed; shattered.

bouleversement [boolversəmàn] *nm* (*politique, social*) upheaval.

bouleverser [boolversā] *vt* (*émouvoir*) to overwhelm; (*causer du chagrin à*) to distress; (*pays, vie*) to disrupt; (*papiers, objets*) to turn upside down, upset.

boulier [boolyā] *nm* abacus; (*de jeu*) scoring board.

boulimie [boolēmē] *nf* compulsive eating.

boulingrin [boolàngrań] *nm* lawn.

bouliste [boolēst(ə)] *nm/f* bowler.

boulocher [booloshā] *vi* (*laine etc*) to develop little snarls.

boulodrome [boolodrom] *nm* bowling ground.

boulon [boolón] *nm* bolt.

boulonner [boolonā] *vt* to bolt.

boulot [boolō] *nm* (*fam: travail*) work.

boulot, te [boolō, -ot] *a* plump, tubby.

boum [boom] *nm* bang ♦ *nf* party.

bouquet [booke] *nm* (*de fleurs*) bunch (of flowers), bouquet; (*de persil etc*) bunch; (*parfum*) bouquet; (*fig*) crowning piece; **c'est le** ~! that's the last straw!; ~ **garni** (*CULIN*) bouquet garni.

bouquetin [booktan] *nm* ibex.

bouquin [bookań] *nm* (*fam*) book.

bouquiner [bookēnā] *vi* (*fam*) to read.

bouquiniste [bookēnēst(ə)] *nm/f* bookseller.

bourbeux, euse [boorbœ, -œz] *a* muddy.

bourbier [boorbyā] *nm* (*quag*)mire.

bourde [boord(ə)] *nf* (*erreur*) howler; (*gaffe*) blunder.

bourdon [boordón] *nm* bumblebee.

bourdonnement [boordonmàn] *nm* buzzing *q*, buzz; **avoir des** ~**s d'oreilles** to have a buzzing (noise) in one's ears.

bourdonner [boordonā] *vi* to buzz; (*moteur*) to hum.

bourg [boor] *nm* small market town (*ou* village).

bourgade [boorgàd] *nf* township.

bourgeois, e [boorzhwà, -wàz] *a* (*péj*) ≈ (upper) middle class; bourgeois; (*maison etc*) very comfortable ♦ *nm/f* (*autrefois*) burgher.

bourgeoisie [boorzhwàzē] *nf* ≈ upper middle classes *pl*; bourgeoisie; **petite** ~ middle classes.

bourgeon [boorzhón] *nm* bud.

bourgeonner [boorzhonā] *vi* to bud.

Bourgogne [boorgony] *nf*: **la** ~ Burgundy ♦ *nm*: **b**~ burgundy (wine).

bourguignon, ne [boorgēnyón, -on] *a* of *ou* from Burgundy, Burgundian; **bœuf** ~ **bœuf** bourguignon.

Bourkina [boorkēnā] *nm*: **le** ~ Burkina Faso.

bourlinguer [boorlàngā] *vi* to knock about a lot, get around a lot.

bourrade [booràd] *nf* shove, thump.

bourrage [booràzh] *nm* (*papier*) jamming; ~ **de crâne** brainwashing; (*SCOL*) cramming.

bourrasque [booràsk(ə)] *nf* squall.

bourratif, ive [booràtēf, -ēv] *a* filling, stodgy.

bourre [boor] *nf* (*de coussin, matelas etc*) stuffing.

bourré, e [boorā] *a* (*rempli*): ~ **de** crammed full of; (*fam: ivre*) pickled, plastered.

bourreau, x [boorō] *nm* executioner; (*fig*) torturer; ~ **de travail** workaholic, glutton for work.

bourrelé, e [boorlā] *a*: **être** ~ **de remords** to be racked by remorse.

bourrelet [boorle] *nm* weather strip(ping); (*de peau*) fold *ou* roll (of flesh).

bourrer [boorā] *vt* (*pipe*) to fill; (*poêle*) to pack; (*valise*) to cram (full); ~ **de** to cram (full) with, stuff with; ~ **de coups** to hammer blows on, pummel; ~ **le crâne à qn** to pull the wool over sb's eyes; *(endoctriner)* to brainwash sb.

bourricot [bo͞orēkō] *nm* small donkey.

bourrique [bo͞orēk] *nf (âne)* ass.

bourru, e [bo͞orü] *a* surly, gruff.

bourse [bo͞ors(ə)] *nf (subvention)* scholarship; *(porte-monnaie)* purse; **sans** ~ **délier** without spending a penny; **la B**~ the Stock Exchange; ~ **du travail** ≈ labor *(US)* ou trades *(Brit)* union council (regional headquarters).

boursicoter [bo͞orsēkotā] *vi (COMM)* to dabble on the Stock Market.

boursier, ière [bo͞orsyā, -yer] *a (COMM)* Stock Market *cpd* ♦ *nm/f (SCOL)* scholarship holder.

boursouflé, e [bo͞orso͞oflā] *a* swollen, puffy; *(fig)* bombastic, turgid.

boursoufler [bo͞orso͞oflā] *vt* to puff up, bloat; **se** ~ *vi (visage)* to swell ou puff up; *(peinture)* to blister.

boursouflure [bo͞orso͞oflür] *nf (du visage)* swelling, puffiness; *(de la peinture)* blister; *(fig: du style)* pomposity.

bous [bo͞o] *vb voir* **bouillir**.

bousculade [bo͞oskülād] *nf (hâte)* rush; *(poussée)* crush.

bousculer [bo͞oskülā] *vt* to knock over; to knock into; *(fig)* to push, rush.

bouse [bo͞oz] *nf*: ~ **(de vache)** (cow) dung *q*, manure *q*.

bousiller [bo͞ozēyā] *vt (fam)* to wreck.

boussole [bo͞osol] *nf* compass.

bout [bo͞o] *vb voir* **bouillir** ♦ *nm* bit; *(extrémité: d'un bâton etc)* tip; *(: d'une ficelle, table, rue, période)* end; **au** ~ **de** at the end of, after; **au** ~ **du compte** at the end of the day; **pousser qn à** ~ to push sb to the limit (of his patience); **venir à** ~ **de** to manage to finish (off) ou overcome; ~ **à** ~ end to end; **à tout** ~ **de champ** at every turn; **d'un** ~ **à l'autre, de** ~ **en** ~ from one end to the other; **à** ~ **portant** at point-blank range; **un** ~ **de chou** *(enfant)* a little tot; ~ **d'essai** *(CINÉMA etc)* screen test; ~ **filtre** filter tip.

boutade [bo͞otād] *nf* quip, sally.

boute-en-train [bo͞otâṅtraṅ] *nm inv* live wire *(fig)*.

bouteille [bo͞otey] *nf* bottle; *(de gaz butane)* cylinder.

boutiquaire [bo͞otēker] *a*: **niveau** ~ shopping level.

boutique [bo͞otēk] *nf* store *(US)*, shop; *(de grand couturier, de mode)* boutique.

boutiquier, ière [bo͞otēkyā, -yer] *nm/f* storekeeper *(US)*, shopkeeper.

boutoir [bo͞otwär] *nm*: **coup de** ~ *(choc)* thrust; *(fig: propos)* barb.

bouton [bo͞otôṅ] *nm (de vêtement, électrique etc)* button; *(BOT)* bud; *(sur la peau)* spot; *(de porte)* knob; ~ **de manchette** cuff-link; ~ **d'or** buttercup.

boutonner [bo͞otonā] *vt* to button up; **se** ~ to button one's clothes up.

boutonneux, euse [bo͞otonœ̄, -œ̄z] *a* pimply.

boutonnière [bo͞otonyer] *nf* buttonhole.

bouton-poussoir, *pl* **boutons-poussoirs** [bo͞otôṅpo͞oswär] *nm* push button.

bouton-pression, *pl* **boutons-pression** [bo͞otôṅprāsyóṅ] *nm* snap fastener.

bouture [bo͞otür] *nf* cutting; **faire des** ~**s** to take cuttings.

bouvreuil [bo͞ovrœy] *nm* bullfinch.

bovidé [bovēdā] *nm* bovine.

bovin, e [bovaṅ, -ēn] *a* bovine ♦ *nm*: ~**s** cattle.

bowling [bolēng] *nm* (tenpin) bowling; *(salle)* bowling alley.

box [boks] *nm* lock-up stall *(US)*, lock-up (garage) *(Brit)*; *(de salle, dortoir)* cubicle; *(d'écurie)* box stall *(US)*, loose-box *(Brit)*; **le** ~ **des accusés** the dock.

box(-calf) [boks(kálf)] *nm inv* box calf.

boxe [boks(ə)] *nf* boxing.

boxer [boksā] *vi* to box ♦ *nm* [bokser] *(chien)* boxer.

boxeur [boksœr] *nm* boxer.

boyau, x [bwáyō] *nm (corde de raquette etc)* (cat) gut; *(galerie)* passage(way); *(narrow)* gallery; *(pneu de bicyclette)* tubeless tire *(US)* ou tyre *(Brit)* ♦ *nmpl (viscères)* entrails, guts.

boycottage [boēkotázh] *nm (d'un produit)* boycotting.

boycotter [boykotā] *vt* to boycott.

BP *sigle f =* **boîte postale**.

BPAL *sigle f (= base de plein air et de loisir)* open-air leisure center.

BPF *sigle (= bon pour francs) printed on checks before space for amount to be inserted*.

brabançon, ne [brábâṅsôṅ, -on] *a* of ou from Brabant.

Brabant [brábâṅ] *nm*: **le** ~ Brabant.

bracelet [brásle] *nm* bracelet.

bracelet-montre [bráslemôṅtr(ə)] *nm* wristwatch.

braconnage [brákonázh] *nm* poaching.

braconner [brákonā] *vi* to poach.

braconnier [brákonyā] *nm* poacher.

brader [brádā] *vt* to sell off, sell cheaply.

braderie [brádrē] *nf* clearance sale; *(par des particuliers)* ≈ garage sale *(US)*, ≈ car boot sale *(Brit)*; *(magasin)* discount store; *(sur marché)* cut-rate *(US)* ou cut-price *(Brit)* stall.

braguette [bráget] *nf* zipper *(US)*, fly, flies *pl (Brit)*.

braille [brây] *nm* Braille.

braillement [brâymáṅ] *nm (cri)* bawling *q*, yelling *q*.

brailler [brâyā] *vi* to bawl, yell ♦ *vt* to bawl out, yell out.

braire [brer] *vi* to bray.

braise [brez] *nf* embers *pl*.

braiser [brāzā] *vt* to braise; **bœuf braisé** braised steak.

bramer [brâmā] *vi* to bell; *(fig)* to wail.

brancard [brâṅkár] *nm (civière)* stretcher; *(bras, perche)* shaft.

brancardier [brâṅkárdyā] *nm* stretcher-bearer.

branchages [brâṅsházh] *nmpl* branches, boughs.

branche [brâṅsh] *nf* branch; *(de lunettes)* side(-piece).

branché, e [brâṅshā] *a (fam)* switched-on, trendy ♦ *nm/f (fam)* trendy.

branchement [brȧ̇nshmȧ̇n] *nm* connection.
brancher [brȧ̇nshā] *vt* to connect (up); *(en mettant la prise)* to plug in; ~ **qn/qch sur** *(fig)* to get sb/sth launched onto.
branchies [brȧ̇nshē] *nfpl* gills.
brandade [brȧ̇ndȧ̇d] *nf* brandade *(cod dish)*.
brandebourgeois, e [brȧ̇ndbōōrzhwȧ̇, -wȧ̇z] *a* of *ou* from Brandenburg.
brandir [brȧ̇ndēr] *vt (arme)* to brandish, wield; *(document)* to flourish, wave.
brandon [brȧ̇ndôn̈] *nm* firebrand.
branlant, e [brȧ̇nlȧ̇n̈, -ȧ̇n̈t] *a (mur, meuble)* shaky.
branle [brȧ̇nl] *nm*: **mettre en** ~ to set swinging; **donner le** ~ **à** to set in motion.
branle-bas [brȧ̇nlbȧ̇] *nm inv* commotion.
branler [brȧ̇nlā] *vi* to be shaky, be loose ♦ *vt*: ~ **la tête** to shake one's head.
braquage [brȧ̇kȧ̇zh] *nm (fam)* stick-up, hold-up; *(AUTO)*: **rayon de** ~ turning radius *(US) ou* circle *(Brit)*.
braque [brȧ̇k] *nm (ZOOL)* pointer.
braquer [brȧ̇kā] *vi (AUTO)* to turn (the wheel) ♦ *vt (revolver etc)*: ~ **qch sur** to aim sth at, point sth at; *(mettre en colère)*: ~ **qn** to antagonize sb, put sb's back up; ~ **son regard sur** to fix one's gaze on; **se** ~ *vi*: **se** ~ **(contre)** to take a stand (against).
bras [brȧ̇] *nm* arm; *(de fleuve)* branch ♦ *nmpl (fig: travailleurs)* labor *sg (US)*, labour *sg (Brit)*, hands; ~ **dessus** ~ **dessous** arm in arm; **à** ~ **raccourcis** with fists flying; **à tour de** ~ with all one's might; **baisser les** ~ to give up; ~ **droit** *(fig)* right hand man; ~ **de fer** arm-wrestling; **une partie de** ~ **de fer** *(fig)* a trial of strength; ~ **de levier** lever arm; ~ **de mer** arm of the sea, sound.
brasero [brȧ̇zȧ̇rō] *nm* brazier.
brasier [brȧ̇zyā] *nm* blaze, (blazing) inferno; *(fig)* inferno.
Brasilia [brȧ̇zēlyȧ̇] *n* Brasilia.
bras-le-corps [brȧ̇lkor]: **à** ~ *ad* (a)round the waist.
brassage [brȧ̇sȧ̇zh] *nm (de la bière)* brewing; *(fig)* mixing.
brassard [brȧ̇sȧ̇r] *nm* armband.
brasse [brȧ̇s] *nf (nage)* breast-stroke; *(mesure)* fathom; ~ **papillon** butterfly(-stroke).
brassée [brȧ̇sā] *nf* armful; **une** ~ **de** *(fig)* a number of.
brasser [brȧ̇sā] *vt (bière)* to brew; *(remuer: salade)* to toss; *(: cartes)* to shuffle; *(fig)* to mix; ~ **l'argent/les affaires** to handle a lot of money/business.
brasserie [brȧ̇srē] *nf (restaurant)* bar *(selling food)*, brasserie; *(usine)* brewery.
brasseur [brȧ̇sœr] *nm (de bière)* brewer; ~ **d'affaires** big businessman.
brassière [brȧ̇syer] *nf (baby's)* undershirt *(US) ou* vest *(Brit)*; *(de sauvetage)* life jacket.
bravache [brȧ̇vȧ̇sh] *nm* blusterer, braggart.
bravade [brȧ̇vȧ̇d] *nf*: **par** ~ out of bravado.
brave [brȧ̇v] *a (courageux)* brave; *(bon, gentil)* good, kind.
bravement [brȧ̇vmȧ̇n] *ad* bravely; *(résolument)* boldly.
braver [brȧ̇vā] *vt* to defy.

bravo [brȧ̇vō] *excl* bravo! ♦ *nm* cheer.
bravoure [brȧ̇vōōr] *nf* bravery.
BRB *sigle f (POLICE)* = *Brigade de répression du banditisme)* ≈ serious crime squad.
break [brek] *nm (AUTO)* station wagon *(US)*, estate car *(Brit)*.
brebis [brəbē] *nf* ewe; ~ **galeuse** black sheep.
brèche [bresh] *nf* breach, gap; **être sur la** ~ *(fig)* to be on the go.
bredouille [brədōōy] *a* empty-handed.
bredouiller [brədōōyā] *vi, vt* to mumble, stammer.
bref, brève [bref, brev] *a* short, brief ♦ *ad* in short ♦ *nf (voyelle)* short vowel; *(information)* brief news item; **d'un ton** ~ sharply, curtly; **en** ~ in short, in brief; **à** ~ **délai** shortly.
brelan [brəlȧ̇n̈] *nm*: **un** ~ three of a kind; **un** ~ **d'as** three aces.
breloque [brəlok] *nf* charm.
brème [brem] *nf* bream.
Brésil [brāzēl] *nm*: **le** ~ Brazil.
brésilien, ne [brāzēlyȧ̇n̈, -en] *a* Brazilian ♦ *nm/f*: **B~, ne** Brazilian.
bressan [bresȧ̇n̈, -ȧ̇n] *a of ou* from Bresse.
Bretagne [brətȧ̇ny] *nf*: **la** ~ Brittany.
bretelle [brətel] *nf (de fusil etc)* sling; *(de vêtement)* strap; *(d'autoroute)* on *ou* off ramp *(US)*, slip road *(Brit)*; ~**s** *nfpl (pour pantalon)* suspenders *(US)*, braces *(Brit)*; ~ **de contournement** *(AUTO)* bypass; ~ **de raccordement** *(AUTO)* access road.
breton, ne [brətôn̈, -on] *a* Dreton ♦ *nm (LING)* Breton ♦ *nm/f*: **B~, ne** Breton.
breuvage [brœvȧ̇zh] *nm* beverage, drink.
brève [brev] *af, nf voir* **bref**.
brevet [brəve] *nm* diploma, certificate; ~ **(d'invention)** patent; ~ **d'apprentissage** certificate of apprenticeship; ~ **(des collèges)** *school certificate, taken at approx. 16 years.*
breveté, e [brəvtā] *a* patented; *(diplômé)* qualified.
breveter [brəvtā] *vt* to patent.
bréviaire [brāvyer] *nm* breviary.
BRGM *sigle m* = *Bureau de recherches géologiques et minières.*
briard, e [brēyȧ̇r, -ȧ̇rd(ə)] *a of ou* from Brie ♦ *nm (chien)* briard.
bribes [brēb] *nfpl* bits, scraps; *(d'une conversation)* snatches; **par** ~ piecemeal.
bric [brēk]: **de** ~ **et de broc** *ad* with any old thing.
bric-à-brac [brēkȧ̇brȧ̇k] *nm inv* bric-a-brac, jumble.
bricolage [brēkolȧ̇zh] *nm*: **le** ~ do-it-yourself (jobs); *(péj)* patched-up job.
bricole [brēkol] *nf (babiole, chose insignifiante)* trifle; *(petit travail)* small job.
bricoler [brēkolā] *vi* to do odd jobs; *(en amateur)* to do do-it-yourself jobs; *(passe-temps)* to putter around *(US)*, potter about *(Brit)* ♦ *vt (réparer)* to fix up; *(mal réparer)* to tinker with; *(trafiquer: voiture etc)* to doctor, fix.
bricoleur, euse [brēkolœr, -œz] *nm/f* handyman/woman, do-it-yourselfer.
bride [brēd] *nf* bridle; *(d'un bonnet)* string, tie; **à** ~ **abattue** flat out, hell for leather;

tenir en ~ to keep in check; **lâcher la** ~ **à, laisser la** ~ **sur le cou à** to give free rein to.
bridé, e [brĕdā] *a:* **yeux ~s** slit eyes.
brider [brĕdā] *vt* (*réprimer*) to keep in check; (*cheval*) to bridle; (*CULIN*: *volaille*) to truss.
bridge [brĕdzh(ə)] *nm* bridge.
brie [brē] *nm* Brie (*cheese*).
brièvement [brēyevmáṅ] *ad* briefly.
brièveté [brēyevtā] *nf* brevity.
brigade [brēgàd] *nf* squad; (*MIL*) brigade.
brigadier [brēgàdyā] *nm* (*POLICE*) ≈ sergeant; (*MIL*) bombardier; corporal.
brigadier-chef, *pl* **brigadiers-chefs** [brēgàdyāshef] *nm corporal acting temporarily as a sergeant.*
brigand [brēgáṅ] *nm* brigand.
brigandage [brēgáṅdàzh] *nm* robbery.
briguer [brēgà] *vt* to aspire to; (*suffrages*) to canvass.
brillamment [brēyámáṅ] *ad* brilliantly.
brillant, e [brēyáṅ, -áṅt] *a* brilliant; bright; (*luisant*) shiny, shining ♦ *nm* (*diamant*) brilliant.
briller [brēyā] *vi* to shine.
brimade [brēmàd] *nf* vexation, harassment *q*; bullying *q*.
brimbaler [braṅbálā] *vb* = **bringuebaler**.
brimer [brēmā] *vt* to harass; to bully.
brin [braṅ] *nm* (*de laine, ficelle etc*) strand; (*fig*): **un** ~ **de** a bit of; **un** ~ **mystérieux** *etc* (*fam*) a weeny bit mysterious *etc*; ~ **d'herbe** blade of grass; ~ **de muguet** sprig of lily of the valley; ~ **de paille** wisp of straw.
brindille [braṅdēy] *nf* twig.
bringue [braṅg] *nf* (*fam*): **faire la** ~ to go on a binge.
bringuebaler [braṅgbálā] *vi* to shake (about) ♦ *vt* to cart about.
brio [brēyō] *nm* brilliance; (*MUS*) brio; **avec** ~ brilliantly, with panache.
brioche [brēyosh] *nf* brioche (bun); (*fam*: *ventre*) paunch.
brioché, e [brēyoshā] *a* brioche-style.
brique [brēk] *nf* brick; (*fam*) 10,000 francs ♦ *a inv* brick red.
briquer [brēkā] *vt* (*fam*) to polish up.
briquet [brēke] *nm* (cigarette) lighter.
briqueterie [brēktrē] *nf* brickyard.
bris [brē] *nm:* ~ **de clôture** (*JUR*) breaking in; ~ **de glaces** (*AUTO*) breaking of windows.
brisant [brēzáṅ] *nm* reef; (*vague*) breaker.
brise [brēz] *nf* breeze.
brisé, e [brēzā] *a* broken; ~ **(de fatigue)** exhausted; **d'une voix** ~ in a voice broken with emotion; **pâte** ~**e** pie crust (*US*) *ou* shortcrust (*Brit*) pastry.
brisées [brēzā] *nfpl:* **aller** *ou* **marcher sur les** ~ **de qn** to compete with sb in his own province.
brise-glace [brēzglás] *nm inv* icebreaker.
brise-jet [brēzzhe] *nm inv* spray filter.
brise-lames [brēzlám] *nm inv* breakwater.
briser [brēzā] *vt* to break; **se** ~ *vi* to break.
brise-tout [brēztōō] *nm inv* wrecker.
briseur, euse [brēzœr, -œz] *nm/f:* ~ **de grève** strike-breaker.
brise-vent [brēzváṅ] *nm inv* windbreak.
bristol [brēstol] *nm* (*carte de visite*) visiting card.

britannique [brētánĕk] *a* British ♦ *nm/f:* **B**~ Briton, British person; **les B**~**s** the British.
broc [brō] *nm* pitcher.
brocante [brokáṅt] *nf* (*objets*) secondhand goods *pl*, junk; (*commerce*) secondhand trade; junk dealing.
brocanteur, euse [brokáṅtœr, -œz] *nm/f* junkshop owner; junk dealer.
brocart [brokár] *nm* brocade.
broche [brosh] *nf* brooch; (*CULIN*) spit; (*fiche*) spike, peg; (*MÉD*) pin; **à la** ~ spit-roasted, roasted on a spit.
broché, e [broshā] *a* (*livre*) paper-backed; (*tissu*) brocaded.
brochet [broshe] *nm* pike *inv*.
brochette [broshet] *nf* skewer; ~ **de décorations** row of medals.
brochure [broshür] *nf* pamphlet, brochure, booklet.
brocoli [brokolē] *nm* broccoli.
brodequins [brodkaṅ] *nmpl* (*de marche*) (lace-up) boots.
broder [brodā] *vt* to embroider ♦ *vi:* ~ **(sur des faits** *ou* **une histoire)** to embroider the facts.
broderie [brodrē] *nf* embroidery.
bromure [bromür] *nm* bromide.
broncher [brōṅshā] *vi:* **sans** ~ without flinching, without turning a hair.
bronches [brōṅsh] *nfpl* bronchial tubes.
bronchite [brōṅshĕt] *nf* bronchitis.
broncho-pneumonie [brōṅkopnœmonē] *nf* broncho-pneumonia.
bronzage [brōṅzázh] *nm* (*hâle*) (sun)tan.
bronze [brōṅz] *nm* bronze.
bronzé, e [brōṅzā] *a* tanned.
bronzer [brōṅzā] *vt* to tan ♦ *vi* to get a tan; **se** ~ to sunbathe.
brosse [bros] *nf* brush; **donner un coup de** ~ **à qch** to give sth a brush; **coiffé en** ~ with a crewcut; ~ **à cheveux** hairbrush; ~ **à dents** toothbrush; ~ **à habits** clothesbrush.
brosser [brosā] *vt* (*nettoyer*) to brush; (*fig:* *tableau etc*) to paint; to draw; **se** ~ to brush one's clothes; **se** ~ **les dents** to brush one's teeth; **tu peux te** ~! (*fam*) you can whistle for it!
brou [brōō] *nm:* ~ **de noix** (*pour bois*) walnut stain; (*liqueur*) walnut liqueur.
brouette [brōōet] *nf* wheelbarrow.
brouhaha [brōōáá] *nm* hubbub.
brouillage [brōōyázh] *nm* (*d'une émission*) jamming.
brouillard [brōōyár] *nm* fog; **être dans le** ~ (*fig*) to be all at sea.
brouille [brōōy] *nf* quarrel.
brouillé, e [brōōyā] *a* (*fâché*): **il est** ~ **avec ses parents** he has fallen out with his parents; (*teint*) muddy.
brouiller [brōōyā] *vt* to mix up; to confuse; (*RADIO*) to cause interference to; (*: délibérément*) to jam; (*rendre trouble*) to cloud; (*désunir: amis*) to set at odds; **se** ~ *vi* (*ciel, vue*) to cloud over; (*détails*) to become confused; **se** ~ **(avec)** to fall out (with); ~ **les pistes** to cover one's tracks; (*fig*) to confuse the issue.
brouillon, ne [brōōyóṅ, -on] *a* disorganized, unmethodical ♦ *nm* (first) draft; **cahier de** ~

notebook for rough drafts.
broussailles [broosáy] *nfpl* undergrowth *sg*.
broussailleux, euse [broosáyœ̃, -œ̃z] *a* bushy.
brousse [broos] *nf*: **la** ~ the bush.
brouter [brootá] *vt* to graze on ♦ *vi* to graze; (*AUTO*) to chatter (*US*), judder (*Brit*).
broutille [brootéy] *nf* trifle.
broyer [brwáyá] *vt* to crush; ~ **du noir** to be down in the dumps.
bru [brü] *nf* daughter-in-law.
brucelles [brüsel] *nfpl*: (**pinces**) ~ tweezers.
brugnon [brünyôñ] *nm* nectarine.
bruine [brüen] *nf* drizzle.
bruiner [brüená] *vb impersonnel*: **il bruine** it's drizzling, there's a drizzle.
bruire [brüer] *vi* (*eau*) to murmur; (*feuilles, étoffe*) to rustle.
bruissement [brüesmáñ] *nm* murmuring; rustling.
bruit [brüe] *nm*: **un** ~ a noise, a sound; (*fig: rumeur*) a rumor (*US*), a rumour (*Brit*); **le** ~ noise; **pas/trop de** ~ no/too much noise; **sans** ~ without a sound, noiselessly; **faire du** ~ to make a noise; ~ **de fond** background noise.
bruitage [brüetázh] *nm* sound effects *pl*.
bruiteur, euse [brüetœr, -œ̃z] *nm/f* sound-effects engineer.
brûlant, e [brülâñ, -âñt] *a* burning (hot); (*liquide*) boiling (hot); (*regard*) fiery; (*sujet*) red-hot.
brûlé, e [brülá] *a* (*fig: démasqué*) blown; (: *homme politique etc*) discredited ♦ *nm*: **odeur de** ~ smell of burning.
brûle-pourpoint [brülpoorpwañ]: **à** ~ *ad* point-blank.
brûler [brülá] *vt* to burn; (*suj: eau bouillante*) to scald; (*consommer: électricité, essence*) to use; (*feu rouge, signal*) to run ♦ *vi* to burn; (*jeu*): **tu brûles** you're getting warm *ou* hot; **se** ~ to burn o.s.; to scald o.s.; **se** ~ **la cervelle** to blow one's brains out; ~ **les étapes** to make rapid progress; (*aller trop vite*) to cut corners; ~ (**d'impatience**) **de faire qch** to burn with impatience to do sth, be dying to do sth.
brûleur [brülœr] *nm* burner.
brûlot [brülő] *nm* (*CULIN*) flaming brandy; **un** ~ **de contestation** (*fig*) a hotbed of dissent.
brûlure [brülür] *nf* (*lésion*) burn; (*sensation*) burning *q*, burning sensation; ~**s d'estomac** heartburn *sg*.
brume [brüm] *nf* mist.
brumeux, euse [brümœ̃, -œ̃z] *a* misty; (*fig*) hazy.
brun, e [brœñ, -üñ] *a* brown; (*cheveux, personne*) dark ♦ *nm* (*couleur*) brown.
brunâtre [brünâtr(ǝ)] *a* brownish.
Brunei [brünáé] *nm*: **le** ~ Brunei.
brunir [brünér] *vi* (*aussi*: **se** ~) to get a tan ♦ *vt* to tan.
brushing [brœshéng] *nm* blow-dry.
brusque [brüsk(ǝ)] *a* (*soudain*) abrupt, sudden; (*rude*) abrupt, brusque.
brusquement [brüskǝmáñ] *ad* (*soudainement*) abruptly, suddenly.
brusquer [brüská] *vt* to rush.
brusquerie [brüskǝré] *nf* abruptness, brusqueness.

brut, e [brüt] *a* raw, crude, rough; (*diamant*) uncut; (*soie, minéral*, *INFORM*: *données*) raw; (*COMM*) gross ♦ *nf* brute; (**champagne**) ~ **brut champagne**; (**pétrole**) ~ crude (oil).
brutal, e, aux [brütál, -ő] *a* brutal.
brutalement [brütálmáñ] *ad* brutally.
brutaliser [brütálézá] *vt* to handle roughly, manhandle.
brutalité [brütálétá] *nf* brutality *q*.
brute [brüt] *af, nf voir* **brut**.
Bruxelles [brüsel] *n* Brussels.
bruxellois, e [brüselwà, -wàz] *a* of *ou* from Brussels ♦ *nm/f*: **B~, e** inhabitant *ou* native of Brussels.
bruyamment [brüeyámáñ] *ad* noisily.
bruyant, e [brüeyáñ, -áñt] *a* noisy.
bruyère [brüeyer] *nf* heather.
BT *sigle m* (= *Brevet de technicien*) *vocational training certificate, taken at approx. 18 years*.
BTA *sigle m* (= *Brevet de technicien agricole*) *agricultural training certificate, taken at approx. 18 years*.
BTP *sigle mpl* (= *Bâtiments et travaux publics*) *public buildings and works sector*.
BTS *sigle m* (= *Brevet de technicien supérieur*) *vocational training certificate taken at end of 2-year higher education course*.
BU *sigle f* = *Bibliothèque universitaire*.
bu, e [bü] *pp de* **boire**.
buanderie [büáñdré] *nf* laundry.
Bucarest [bükárest] *n* Bucharest.
buccal, e, aux [bükál, -ő] *a*: **par voie** ~**e** orally.
bûche [büsh] *nf* log; **prendre une** ~ (*fig*) to fall flat on one's face; ~ **de Noël** Yule log.
bûcher [büshá] *nm* pyre; bonfire ♦ *vi* (*fam: étudier*) to grind (*US*), swot (*Brit*) ♦ *vt* to cram.
bûcheron [büshrôñ] *nm* woodcutter.
bûchette [büshet] *nf* (*de bois*) stick, twig; (*pour compter*) rod.
bûcheur, euse [büshœr, -œ̃z] *nm/f* (*fam: étudiant*) grind (*US*), swot (*Brit*).
bucolique [bükolék] *a* bucolic, pastoral.
Budapest [büdápest] *n* Budapest.
budget [büdzhe] *nm* budget.
budgétaire [büdzhäter] *a* budgetary, budget *cpd*.
budgétiser [büdzhätézá] *vt* to budget (for).
buée [büá] *nf* (*sur une vitre*) mist; (*de l'haleine*) steam.
Buenos Aires [bwănozer] *n* Buenos Aires.
buffet [büfe] *nm* (*meuble*) sideboard; (*de réception*) buffet; ~ (**de gare**) (station) buffet, snack bar.
buffle [büfl(ǝ)] *nm* buffalo.
buis [büe] *nm* box tree; (*bois*) box(wood).
buisson [büesôñ] *nm* bush.
buissonnière [büesonyer] *af*: **faire l'école** ~ to play hooky, skip school.
bulbe [bülb(ǝ)] *nm* (*BOT, ANAT*) bulb; (*coupole*) onion-shaped dome.
bulgare [bülgár] *a* Bulgarian ♦ *nm* (*LING*) Bulgarian ♦ *nm/f*: **B~** Bulgarian, Bulgar.
Bulgarie [bülgárẽ] *nf*: **la** ~ Bulgaria.
bulldozer [boolddozœr] *nm* bulldozer.
bulle [bül] *a, nm*: (**papier**) ~ manil(l)a paper ♦ *nf* bubble; (*de bande dessinée*) balloon; (*papale*) bull; ~ **de savon** soap bubble.

bulletin [bültañ] *nm* (*communiqué, journal*) bulletin; (*papier*) form; (: *de bagages*) baggage check (*US*) *ou* ticket (*Brit*); (*SCOL*) report card (*US*), report (*Brit*); ~ **d'informations** news bulletin; ~ **météorologique** weather report; ~ **de naissance** birth certificate; ~ **de salaire** check stub (*US*), pay slip (*Brit*); ~ **de santé** medical bulletin; ~ **(de vote)** ballot paper.

buraliste [büràlēst(ə)] *nm/f* (*de bureau de tabac*) tobacconist; (*de poste*) clerk.

bure [bür] *nf* homespun; (*de moine*) frock.

bureau, x [bürō] *nm* (*meuble*) desk; (*pièce, service*) office; ~ **de change** (foreign) exchange office *ou* bureau; ~ **d'embauche** employment office; ~ **d'études** research department; ~ **de location** box office; ~ **de placement** employment agency; ~ **de poste** post office; ~ **de tabac** cigar store (*US*), tobacco shop (*US*), tobacconist's (shop) (*Brit*); ~ **de vote** polling station.

bureaucrate [bürōkrát] *nm* bureaucrat.

bureaucratie [bürōkràsē] *nf* bureaucracy.

bureaucratique [bürōkrátēk] *a* bureaucratic.

bureautique [bürotēk] *nf* office automation.

burette [büret] *nf* (*de mécanicien*) oilcan; (*de chimiste*) burette.

burin [bürañ] *nm* cold chisel; (*ART*) burin.

buriné, e [bürēnā] *a* (*fig: visage*) craggy, seamed.

burlesque [bürlesk(ə)] *a* ridiculous; (*LITTÉRATURE*) burlesque.

burnous [bürnōō(s)] *nm* burnous.

Burundi [bōōrōōndē] *nm*: **le** ~ Burundi.

BUS *sigle m* = *Bureau universitaire de statistiques.*

bus *vb* [bü] *voir* **boire** ♦ *nm* [büs] (*véhicule, aussi INFORM*) bus.

busard [büzár] *nm* harrier.

buse [büz] *nf* buzzard.

busqué, e [büskā] *a*: **nez** ~ hook(ed) nose.

buste [büst(ə)] *nm* (*ANAT*) chest; (: *de femme*) bust; (*sculpture*) bust.

bustier [büstyā] *nm* (*soutien-gorge*) long-line bra.

but [bü] *vb voir* **boire** ♦ *nm* (*cible*) target; (*fig*) goal, aim; (*FOOTBALL etc*) goal; **de** ~ **en blanc** point-blank; **avoir pour** ~ **de faire** to aim to do; **dans le** ~ **de** with the intention of.

butane [bütán] *nm* butane; (*domestique*) butane, calor gas ® (*Brit*).

buté, e [bütā] *a* stubborn, obstinate ♦ *nf* (*TECH*) stop; (*ARCHIT*) abutment.

buter [bütā] *vi*: ~ **contre** *ou* **sur** to bump into; (*trébucher*) to stumble against ♦ *vt* to antagonize; **se** ~ *vi* to get obstinate, dig in one's heels.

buteur [bütœr] *nm* goal-scorer.

butin [bütañ] *nm* booty, spoils *pl*; (*d'un vol*) loot.

butiner [bütēnā] *vi* to gather nectar.

butor [bütor] *nm* (*fig*) lout.

butte [büt] *nf* mound, hillock; **être en** ~ **à** to be exposed to.

buvable [büvábl(ə)] *a* (*eau, vin*) drinkable; (*MÉD: ampoule etc*) to be taken orally; (*fig: roman etc*) reasonable.

buvais [büve] *etc vb voir* **boire**.

buvard [büvár] *nm* blotter.

buvette [büvet] *nf* refreshment stand; (*comptoir*) bar.

buveur, euse [büvœr, -ēz] *nm/f* drinker.

buvons [büvôñ] *etc vb voir* **boire**.

BVP *sigle m* (= *Bureau de vérification de la publicité*) *advertising standards authority*.

Byzance [bēzáñs] *n* Byzantium.

byzantin, e [bēzáñtañ, -ēn] *a* Byzantine.

BZH *abr* (= *Breizh*) Brittany.

C

C, c [sā] *nm inv* C, c ♦ *abr* (= *centime*) c; (= *Celsius*) C; **C comme Célestin** C for Charlie.

c' [s] *dét voir* **ce**.

CA *sigle m* = **chiffre d'affaires, conseil d'administration, corps d'armée** ♦ *sigle f* = **chambre d'agriculture.**

ca *abr* (= *centiare*) *1 m².*

ça [sà] *pronom* (*pour désigner*) this; (: *plus loin*) that; (*comme sujet indéfini*) it; ~ **m'étonne que** it surprises me that; ~ **va?** how are you?; how are things?; (*d'accord?*) OK?, all right?; ~ **alors!** (*désapprobation*) well!, really!; (*étonnement*) heavens!; **c'est** ~ that's right.

çà [sà] *ad*: ~ **et là** here and there.

cabale [kábál] *nf* (*THÉÂTRE, POL*) cabal, clique.

caban [kábáñ] *nm* reefer jacket.

cabane [kábán] *nf* hut, cabin.

cabanon [kábánôñ] *nm* chalet; (*country*) cottage.

cabaret [kábáre] *nm* night club.

cabas [kábá] *nm* shopping bag.

cabestan [kábestáñ] *nm* capstan.

cabillaud [kábēyō] *nm* cod *inv*.

cabine [kábēn] *nf* (*de bateau*) cabin; (*de plage*) (beach) hut; (*de piscine etc*) cubicle; (*de camion, train*) cab; (*d'avion*) cockpit; ~ **(d'ascenseur)** elevator car (*US*), lift cage (*Brit*); ~ **d'essayage** fitting room; ~ **de projection** projection room; ~ **spatiale** space capsule; ~ **(téléphonique)** (tele)phone booth, call *ou* (tele)phone box (*Brit*).

cabinet [kábēne] *nm* (*petite pièce*) closet; (*de médecin*) office (*US*), surgery (*Brit*); (*de notaire etc*) office; (: *clientèle*) practice; (*POL*) cabinet; (*d'un ministre*) advisers *pl*; ~**s** *nmpl* (*w.-c.*) toilet *sg*; ~ **d'affaires** business consultants' (bureau), business partnership; ~ **de toilette** washroom; ~ **de travail** study.

câble [kábl(ə)] *nm* cable.

câblé, e [káblā] *a* (*fam*) switched on; (*TECH*) linked to cable television.

câbler [káblā] *vt* to cable.

câblogramme [káblográm] *nm* cablegram.

cabosser [kábosā] *vt* to dent.

cabot [kábō] *nm* (*péj: chien*) mutt.

cabotage [kábotázh] *nm* coastal navigation.

caboteur [kábotœr] *nm* coaster.

cabotin, e [kábotań, -ēn] *nm/f* (*péj: personne maniérée*) poseur; (*: acteur*) ham ♦ *a* dramatic, theatrical.

cabotinage [kábotēnázh] *nm* playacting; third-rate acting, ham acting.

cabrer [kábrā]: **se** ~ *vi* (*cheval*) to rear up; (*avion*) to nose up; (*fig*) to revolt, rebel; to jib.

cabri [kábrē] *nm* kid.

cabriole [kábrēyol] *nf* caper; (*gymnastique etc*) somersault.

cabriolet [kábrēyole] *nm* convertible.

CAC [kàk] *sigle f* (= *Compagnie des agents de change*): **indice** ~ ≈ Dow Jones average (*US*); ≈ FT index (*Brit*).

caca [káká] *nm* (*langage enfantin*) pooh; (*couleur*): ~ **d'oie** greenish-yellow; **faire** ~ (*fam*) to go pooh-pooh (*US*), do a pooh (*Brit*).

cacahuète [kákáüet] *nf* peanut.

cacao [kákáō] *nm* cocoa (powder); (*boisson*) cocoa.

cachalot [káshálō] *nm* sperm whale.

cache [kásh] *nm* mask, card (*for masking*) ♦ *nf* hiding place.

cache-cache [káshkásh] *nm*: **jouer à** ~ to play hide-and-seek.

cache-col [káshkol] *nm* scarf (*pl* scarves).

cachemire [káshmēr] *nm* cashmere ♦ *a*: **dessin** ~ paisley pattern; **le C**~ Kashmir.

cache-nez [káshnā] *nm inv* scarf (*pl* scarves), muffler.

cache-pot [káshpō] *nm inv* flower-pot holder.

cache-prise [káshprēz] *nm inv* socket cover.

cacher [káshā] *vt* to hide, conceal; ~ **qch à qn** to hide *ou* conceal sth from sb; **se** ~ to hide; to be hidden *ou* concealed; **il ne s'en cache pas** he makes no secret of it.

cache-sexe [káshseks] *nm inv* G-string.

cachet [káshe] *nm* (*comprimé*) tablet; (*sceau: du roi*) seal; (*: de la poste*) postmark; (*rétribution*) fee; (*fig*) style, character.

cacheter [káshtā] *vt* to seal; **vin cacheté** vintage wine.

cachette [káshet] *nf* hiding place; **en** ~ on the sly, secretly.

cachot [káshō] *nm* dungeon.

cachotterie [káshotrē] *nf* mystery; **faire des** ~s to be secretive.

cachottier, ière [káshotyā, -yer] *a* secretive.

cachou [káshōō] *nm*: (**pastille de**) ~ cachou (*candy*).

cacophonie [kákofonē] *nf* cacophony, din.

cactus [káktüs] *nm* cactus.

c-à-d *abr* (= *c'est-à-dire*) i.e.

cadastre [kádástr(ə)] *nm* land register.

cadavéreux, euse [kádávārœ̃, -œ̃z] *a* (*teint, visage*) deathly pale.

cadavérique [kádávārēk] *a* deathly (pale), deadly pale.

cadavre [kádávr(ə)] *nm* corpse, (dead) body.

caddie [kádē] *nm* shopping cart (*US*), (supermarket) trolley (*Brit*).

cadeau, x [kádō] *nm* present, gift; **faire un** ~ **à qn** to give sb a present *ou* gift; **faire** ~ **de qch à qn** to make a present of sth to sb, give sb sth as a present.

cadenas [kádná] *nm* padlock.

cadenasser [kádnásā] *vt* to padlock.

cadence [kádáńs] *nf* (*MUS*) cadence; (*: rythme*) rhythm; (*de travail etc*) rate; ~s *nfpl* (*en usine*) production rate *sg*; **en** ~ rhythmically; in time.

cadencé, e [kádáńsā] *a* rhythmic(al); **au pas** ~ (*MIL*) in quick time.

cadet, te [kàde, -et] *a* younger; (*le plus jeune*) youngest ♦ *nm/f* youngest child *ou* one, youngest boy *ou* son/girl *ou* daughter; **il est mon** ~ **de deux ans** he's 2 years younger than me, he's 2 years my junior; **les** ~s (*SPORT*) the juniors (*15 - 17 years*); **le** ~ **de mes soucis** the least of my worries.

cadran [kádráń] *nm* dial; ~ **solaire** sundial.

cadre [kàdr(ə)] *nm* frame; (*environnement*) surroundings *pl*; (*limites*) scope ♦ *nm/f* (*ADMIN*) managerial employee, executive ♦ *a*: **loi** ~ outline *ou* framework law; ~ **moyen/supérieur** (*ADMIN*) middle/senior management employee, junior/senior executive; **rayer qn des** ~s to discharge sb; to dismiss sb; **dans le** ~ **de** (*fig*) within the framework *ou* context of.

cadrer [kádrā] *vi*: ~ **avec** to tally *ou* correspond with ♦ *vt* (*CINÉMA*) to center (*US*) *ou* centre (*Brit*).

cadreur, euse [kádrœr, -œ̃z] *nm/f* (*CINÉMA*) cameraman/woman.

caduc, uque [kádük] *a* obsolete; (*BOT*) deciduous.

CAF *sigle f* (= *Caisse d'allocations familiales*) *family allowance office*.

caf *abr* (= *coût, assurance, fret*) cif.

cafard [káfár] *nm* cockroach; **avoir le** ~ to be down in the dumps, be feeling low.

cafardeux, euse [káfárdœ̃, -œ̃z] *a* (*personne, ambiance*) depressing, melancholy.

café [kátā] *nm* coffee; (*bistro*) café ♦ *a inv* coffee *cpd*; ~ **crème** coffee with cream; ~ **au lait** coffee with milk (*US*), white coffee (*Brit*); ~ **noir** black coffee; ~ **en grains** coffee beans; ~ **en poudre** instant coffee; ~ **tabac** *tobacconist's or newsagent's also serving coffee and spirits*; ~ **liégeois** *coffee ice cream with whipped cream*.

café-concert, *pl* **cafés-concerts** [káfākôńser] *nm* (*aussi:* **caf'conc'**) *café with a cabaret*.

caféine [káfāēn] *nf* caffeine.

cafétéria [káfātáryá] *nf* cafeteria.

café-théâtre, *pl* **cafés-théâtres** [káfātáâtr(ə)] *nm café used as a venue by (experimental) theatre groups.*

cafetier, ière [káftyā, -yer] *nm/f* café-owner ♦ *nf* (*pot*) coffee-pot.

cafouillage [káfōōyázh] *nm* shambles *sg*.

cafouiller [káfōōyā] *vi* to get into a shambles; (*machine etc*) to work in fits and starts.

cage [kázh] *nf* cage; ~ (**des buts**) goal; **en** ~ in a cage, caged up *ou* in; ~ **d'ascenseur** elevator (*US*) *ou* lift shaft (*Brit*); ~ **d'escalier** (stair)well; ~ **thoracique** rib cage.

cageot [kázhō] *nm* crate.

cagibi [kázhēbē] *nm* shed.

cagneux, euse [kányœ̃, -œ̃z] *a* knock-kneed.

cagnotte [kányot] *nf* kitty.

cagoule [kágōōl] *nf* cowl; hood.

cahier [káyá] *nm* notebook; (*TYPO*) signature; (*revue*): ~s *journal*; ~ **de revendications/doléances** *list of claims/grievances*; ~ **de**

brouillon notebook for rough drafts; ~ **des charges** specifications *pl* (*US*), specification (*Brit*); ~ **d'exercices** workbook.

cahin-caha [káaṅkáá] *ad*: **aller** ~ to jog along; (*fig*) to be so-so.

cahot [káõ] *nm* jolt, bump.

cahoter [káotā] *vi* to bump along, jog along.

cahoteux, euse [káotœ̄, -œ̄z] *a* bumpy.

cahute [káüt] *nf* shack, hut.

caïd [káēd] *nm* big chief, boss.

caillasse [káyás] *nf* (*pierraille*) loose stones *pl*.

caille [káy] *nf* quail.

caillé, e [káyā] *a*: **lait** ~ curdled milk, curds *pl*.

caillebotis [káybotē] *nm* duckboard.

cailler [káyā] *vi* (*lait*) to curdle; (*sang*) to clot; (*fam*) to be cold.

caillot [káyõ] *nm* (blood) clot.

caillou, x [káyōō] *nm* (little) stone.

caillouter [káyōōtā] *vt* (*chemin*) to metal.

caillouteux, euse [káyōōtœ̄, -œ̄z] *a* stony; pebbly.

cailloutis [káyōōtē] *nm* (*petits graviers*) gravel.

caïman [káēmáṅ] *nm* cayman.

Caïmans [káēmáṅ] *nfpl*: **les** ~ the Cayman Islands.

Caire [ker] *nm*: **le** ~ Cairo.

caisse [kes] *nf* box; (*où l'on met la recette*) cashbox; (: *machine*) till; (*où l'on paye*) checkout counter; (: *au supermarché*) checkout; (*de banque*) cashier's desk; (*TECH*) case, casing; **faire sa** ~ (*COMM*) to count the takings; ~ **claire** (*MUS*) side *ou* snare drum; ~ **éclair** express checkout; ~ **enregistreuse** cash register; ~ **d'épargne (CE)** savings bank; ~ **noire** slush fund; ~ **de retraite** pension fund; ~ **de sortie** checkout; *voir* **grosse**.

caissier, ière [kāsyá, -yer] *nm/f* cashier.

caisson [kesóṅ] *nm* box, case.

cajoler [kázholā] *vt* to wheedle, coax; to surround with love and care, make a fuss of.

cajoleries [kázholrē] *nfpl* coaxing *sg*, flattery *sg*.

cajou [kázhōō] *nm* cashew nut.

cake [kek] *nm* fruit cake.

CAL *sigle m* (= *Comité d'action lycéen*) *pupils' action group seeking to reform school system.*

cal [kál] *nm* callus.

cal. *abr* = **calorie**.

calamar [kálámár] *nm* = **calmar**.

calaminé, e [kálámēnā] *a* (*AUTO*) caked with soot.

calamité [kálámētā] *nf* calamity, disaster.

calandre [káláṅdr(ə)] *nf* radiator grill; (*machine*) calender, mangle.

calanque [káláṅk] *nf* rocky inlet.

calcaire [kálker] *nm* limestone ♦ *a* (*eau*) hard; (*GÉO*) limestone *cpd*.

calciné, e [kálsēnā] *a* burnt to ashes.

calcium [kálsyom] *nm* calcium.

calcul [kálkül] *nm* calculation; **le** ~ (*SCOL*) arithmetic; ~ **différentiel/intégral** differential/integral calculus; ~ **mental** mental arithmetic; ~ **(biliaire)** (gall)stone; ~ **(rénal)** (kidney) stone; **d'après mes** ~**s** by my reckoning.

calculateur [kálkülàtœr] *nm*, **calculatrice** [kálkülàtrēs] *nf* calculator.

calculé, e [kálkülā] *a*: **risque** ~ calculated risk.

calculer [kálkülā] *vt* to calculate, work out, reckon; (*combiner*) to calculate; ~ **qch de tête** to work sth out in one's head.

calculette [kálkület] *nf* (pocket) calculator.

cale [kál] *nf* (*de bateau*) hold; (*en bois*) wedge, chock; ~ **sèche** *ou* **de radoub** dry dock.

calé, e [kálā] *a* (*fam*) clever, bright.

calebasse [kálbás] *nf* calabash, gourd.

calèche [kálesh] *nf* horse-drawn carriage.

caleçon [kálsóṅ] *nm* pair of underpants, trunks *pl*; ~ **de bain** bathing trunks *pl*.

calembour [káláṅbōōr] *nm* pun.

calendes [káláṅd] *nfpl*: **renvoyer aux** ~ **grecques** to postpone indefinitely.

calendrier [káláṅdrēyā] *nm* calendar; (*fig*) timetable.

cale-pied [kálpyā] *nm inv* toe clip.

calepin [kálpaṅ] *nm* notebook.

caler [kálā] *vt* to wedge, chock up; ~ **(son moteur/véhicule)** to stall (one's engine/vehicle); **se** ~ **dans un fauteuil** to make o.s. comfortable in an armchair.

calfater [kálfátā] *vt* to caulk.

calfeutrer [kálfœtrā] *vt* to (make) draftproof (*US*) *ou* draughtproof (*Brit*); **se** ~ to make o.s. snug and comfortable.

calibre [kálēbr(ə)] *nm* (*d'un fruit*) grade; (*d'une arme*) bore, caliber (*US*), calibre (*Brit*); (*fig*) caliber, calibre.

calibrer [kálēbrā] *vt* to grade.

calice [kálēs] *nm* (*REL*) chalice; (*BOT*) calyx.

calicot [kálēkō] *nm* (*tissu*) calico.

Californie [kálēfornē] *nf*: **la** ~ California.

californien, ne [kálēfornyaṅ, -en] *a* Californian.

califourchon [kálēfōōrshóṅ]: **à** ~ *ad* astride; **à** ~ **sur** astride, straddling.

câlin, e [kálaṅ, -ēn] *a* cuddly, cuddlesome; tender.

câliner [kálēnā] *vt* to fondle, cuddle.

câlineries [kálēnrē] *nfpl* cuddles.

calisson [kálēsóṅ] *nm diamond-shaped candy made with ground almonds.*

calleux, euse [kálœ̄, -œ̄z] *a* horny, callous.

calligraphie [kálēgráfē] *nf* calligraphy.

callosité [kálōzētā] *nf* callus.

calmant [kálmáṅ] *nm* tranquillizer, sedative; (*contre la douleur*) painkiller.

calmar [kálmár] *nm* squid.

calme [kálm(ə)] *a* calm, quiet ♦ *nm* calm(ness), quietness; **sans perdre son** ~ without losing one's cool *ou* calmness; ~ **plat** (*NAVIG*) dead calm.

calmer [kálmā] *vt* to calm (down); (*douleur, inquiétude*) to ease, soothe; **se** ~ to calm down.

calomniateur, trice [kálomnyátœr, -trēs] *nm/f* slanderer; libeller.

calomnie [kálomnē] *nf* slander; (*écrite*) libel.

calomnier [kálomnyā] *vt* to slander; to libel.

calomnieux, euse [kálomnyœ̄, -œ̄z] *a* slanderous; libel(l)ous.

calorie [kálorē] *nf* calorie.

calorifère [kálorēfer] *nm* stove.

calorifique [kálorēfēk] *a* calorific.

calorifuge [kálorēfüzh] *a* (heat-)insulating, heat-retaining.

calot [kálō] *nm* overseas *ou* garrison cap (*US*), forage cap (*Brit*).

calotte [kálot] *nf* (*coiffure*) skullcap; (*gifle*) slap; **la ~** (*péj: clergé*) the cloth, the clergy; **~ glaciaire** icecap.

calque [kálk(ə)] *nm* (*aussi:* **papier ~**) tracing paper; (*dessin*) tracing; (*fig*) carbon copy.

calquer [kálkā] *vt* to trace; (*fig*) to copy exactly.

calvados [kálvádōs] *nm* Calvados (*apple brandy*).

calvaire [kálver] *nm* (*croix*) wayside cross, calvary; (*souffrances*) suffering, martyrdom.

calvitie [kálvēsē] *nf* baldness.

camaïeu [kámáyœ̄] *nm*: (**motif en**) **~** monochrome motif.

camarade [kámárád] *nm/f* friend, pal; (*POL*) comrade.

camaraderie [kámárádrē] *nf* friendship.

camarguais, e [kámárge, ez] *a* of *ou* from the Camargue.

Camargue [kámárg] *nf*: **la ~** the Camargue.

cambiste [kánbēst(ə)] *nm* (*COMM*) foreign exchange dealer, exchange agent.

Cambodge [kánbodzh] *nm*: **le ~** Cambodia.

cambodgien, ne [kánbodzhyan, -en] *a* Cambodian ♦ *nm/f*: **C~, ne** Cambodian.

cambouis [kánbwē] *nm* dirty oil *ou* grease.

cambré, e [kánbrā] *a*: **avoir les reins ~s** to have an arched back; **avoir le pied très ~** to have very high arches *ou* insteps.

cambrer [kánbrā] *vt* to arch; **se ~** to arch one's back; **~ la taille** *ou* **les reins** to arch one's back.

cambriolage [kánbrēyolázh] *nm* burglary.

cambrioler [kánbrēyolā] *vt* to burglarize (*US*), burgle (*Brit*).

cambrioleur, euse [kánbrēyolœr, -œz] *nm/f* burglar.

cambrure [kánbrür] *nf* (*du pied*) arch; (*de la route*) camber; **~ des reins** small of the back.

cambuse [kánbüz] *nf* storeroom.

came [kám] *nf*: **arbre à ~s** camshaft; **arbre à ~s en tête** overhead camshaft.

camée [kámā] *nm* cameo.

caméléon [kámālāōn] *nm* chameleon.

camélia [kámālyá] *nm* camellia.

camelot [kámlō] *nm* street pedlar.

camelote [kámlot] *nf* rubbish, trash, junk.

camembert [kámánber] *nm* Camembert (*cheese*).

caméra [kámárá] *nf* (*CINÉMA, TV*) camera; (*d'amateur*) cine-camera.

Cameroun [kámrōōn] *nm*: **le ~** Cameroon.

camerounais, e [kámrōōne, -ez] *a* Cameroonian.

camescope [kámskop] *nm* camcorder.

camion [kámyón] *nm* truck; (*plus petit, fermé*) van; (*charge*): **~ de sable/cailloux** truck-load of sand/stones; **~ de dépannage** tow (*US*) *ou* breakdown (*Brit*) truck.

camion-citerne, *pl* **camions-citernes** [kámyónsētern(ə)] *nm* tanker.

camionnage [kámyonázh] *nm* trucking (*US*), haulage (*Brit*); **frais/entreprise de ~** haulage costs/business.

camionnette [kámyonet] *nf* (small) truck.

camionneur [kámyonœr] *nm* (*entrepreneur*)

trucker (*US*), haulage contractor (*Brit*); (*chauffeur*) truck driver; van driver.

camisole [kámēzol] *nf*: **~ (de force)** straitjacket.

camomille [kámoméy] *nf* camomile; (*boisson*) camomile tea.

camouflage [kámōōflázh] *nm* camouflage.

camoufler [kámōōflā] *vt* to camouflage; (*fig*) to conceal, cover up.

camouflet [kámōōfle] *nm* (*fam*) snub.

camp [kán] *nm* camp; (*fig*) side; **~ de nudistes/vacances** nudist/vacation (*US*) *ou* holiday (*Brit*) camp; **~ de concentration** concentration camp.

campagnard, e [kánpányár, -árd(ə)] *a* country *cpd* ♦ *nm/f* countryman/woman.

campagne [kánpány] *nf* country, countryside; (*MIL, POL, COMM*) campaign; **en ~** (*MIL*) in the field; **à la ~** in/to the country; **faire ~ pour** to campaign for; **~ électorale** election campaign; **~ de publicité** advertising campaign.

campé, e [kánpā] *a*: **bien ~** (*personnage, tableau*) well drawn.

campement [kánpmán] *nm* camp, encampment.

camper [kánpā] *vi* to camp ♦ *vt* (*chapeau etc*) to pull *ou* put on firmly; (*dessin*) to sketch; **se ~ devant** to plant o.s. in front of.

campeur, euse [kánpœr, -œz] *nm/f* camper.

camphre [kánfr(ə)] *nm* camphor.

camphré, e [kánfrā] *a* camphorated.

camping [kánpēng] *nm* camping; (**terrain de**) **~** campsite, camping site; **faire du ~** to go camping; **faire du ~ sauvage** to camp in the wild.

camping-car [kánpēngkár] *nm* camper.

campus [kánpüs] *nm* campus.

camus, e [kámü, -üz] *a*: **nez ~** pug nose.

Canada [kánádá] *nm*: **le ~** Canada.

canadair [kánáder] *nm* ® fire-fighting plane.

canadien, ne [kánádyan, -en] *a* Canadian ♦ *nm/f*: **C~, ne** Canadian ♦ *nf* (*veste*) fur-lined jacket.

canaille [kánáy] *nf* (*péj*) scoundrel; (*populace*) riff-raff ♦ *a* raffish, rakish.

canal, aux [kánál, -ō] *nm* canal; (*naturel*) channel; (*ADMIN*): **par le ~ de** through (the medium of), via; **~ de distribution/télévision** distribution/television channel; **~ de Panama/Suez** Panama/Suez Canal.

canalisation [kánálēzâsyôn] *nf* (*tuyau*) pipe.

canaliser [kánálēzā] *vt* to canalize; (*fig*) to channel.

canapé [kánápā] *nm* settee, sofa; (*CULIN*) canapé, open sandwich.

canapé-lit, *pl* **canapés-lits** [kánápālē] *nm* sofa bed.

canaque [kánák] *a* of *ou* from New Caledonia ♦ *nm/f*: **C~** native of New Caledonia.

canard [kánár] *nm* duck.

canari [kánárē] *nm* canary.

Canaries [kánárē] *nfpl*: **les (îles) ~** the Canary Islands, the Canaries.

cancaner [kánkánā] *vi* to gossip (maliciously); (*canard*) to quack.

cancanier, ière [kánkányā, -yer] *a* gossiping.

cancans [kánkán] *nmpl* (malicious) gossip *sg*.

cancer [kánser] *nm* cancer; (*signe*): **le C~**

Cancer, the Crab; **être du C~** to be Cancer; **il a un ~** he has cancer.
cancéreux, euse [kȧ́sȧrœ̄, -œ̄z] a cancerous; (*personne*) suffering from cancer.
cancérigène [kȧ́sȧrēzhen] a carcinogenic.
cancérologue [kȧ́sȧrolog] nm/f cancer specialist.
cancre [kȧ́kr(ə)] nm dunce.
cancrelat [kȧ́krəlȧ] nm cockroach.
candélabre [kȧ́dȧlȧbr(ə)] nm candelabrum; (*lampadaire*) street lamp, lamppost.
candeur [kȧ́dœr] nf ingenuousness, guilelessness.
candi [kȧ́dē] a inv: **sucre ~** (sugar-)candy.
candidat, e [kȧ́dēdȧ, -ȧt] nm/f candidate; (à un poste) applicant, candidate.
candidature [kȧ́dēdȧtür] nf candidacy; application; **poser sa ~** to submit an application, apply.
candide [kȧ́dēd] a ingenuous, guileless, naïve.
cane [kȧn] nf (female) duck.
caneton [kȧntṓ] nm duckling.
canette [kȧnet] nf (de bière) (flip-top) bottle; (de machine à coudre) spool.
canevas [kȧnvȧ] nm (*COUTURE*) canvas (for tapestry work); (fig) framework, structure.
caniche [kȧnēsh] nm poodle.
caniculaire [kȧnēküler] a (chaleur, jour) scorching.
canicule [kȧnēkül] nf scorching heat; midsummer heat, dog days pl.
canif [kȧnēf] nm penknife, pocket knife.
canin, e [kȧnań, -ēn] a canine ♦ nf canine (tooth), eye tooth; **exposition ~e** dog show.
caniveau, x [kȧnēvō] nm gutter.
cannabis [kȧnȧbēs] nm cannabis.
canne [kȧn] nf (walking) stick; **~ à pêche** fishing rod; **~ à sucre** sugar cane; **les ~s blanches** (les aveugles) the blind.
canné, e [kȧnȧ] a (chaise) cane cpd.
cannelé, e [kȧnlȧ] a fluted.
cannelle [kȧnel] nf cinnamon.
cannelure [kȧnlür] nf fluting q.
canner [kȧnȧ] vt (chaise) to make ou repair with cane.
cannibale [kȧnēbȧl] nm/f cannibal.
canoë [kȧnoȧ] nm canoe; (sport) canoeing; **~ (kayak)** kayak.
canon [kȧnṓ] nm (arme) gun; (*HIST*) cannon; (d'une arme: tube) barrel; (fig) model; (*MUS*) canon ♦ a: **droit ~** canon law; **~ rayé** rifled barrel.
cañon [kȧnyṓ] nm canyon.
canonique [kȧnonēk] a: **âge ~** respectable age.
canoniser [kȧnonēzȧ] vt to canonize.
canonnade [kȧnonȧd] nf cannonade.
canonnier [kȧnonyȧ] nm gunner.
canonnière [kȧnonyer] nf gunboat.
canot [kȧnō] nm boat, ding(h)y; **~ pneumatique** rubber ou inflatable ding(h)y; **~ de sauvetage** lifeboat.
canotage [kȧnotȧzh] nm rowing.
canoter [kȧnotȧ] vi to go rowing.
canoteur, euse [kȧnotœr, -œ̄z] nm/f rower.
canotier [kȧnotyȧ] nm boater.
Cantal [kȧ́tȧl] nm: **le ~** Cantal.
cantate [kȧ́tȧt] nf cantata.
cantatrice [kȧ́tȧtrēs] nf (opera) singer.

cantilène [kȧ́tēlen] nf (*MUS*) cantilena.
cantine [kȧ́tēn] nf canteen; (réfectoire d'école) dining hall.
cantique [kȧ́tek] nm hymn.
canton [kȧ́tṓ] nm district consisting of several communes; (en Suisse) canton.
cantonade [kȧ́tonȧd]: **à la ~** ad to everyone in general; (crier) from the rooftops.
cantonais, e [kȧ́tone, -ez] a Cantonese ♦ nm (*LING*) Cantonese.
cantonner [kȧ́tonȧ] vt (*MIL*) to billet, quarter; to station; **se ~ dans** to confine o.s. to.
cantonnier [kȧ́tonyȧ] nm roadmender.
canular [kȧnülȧr] nm hoax.
CAO sigle f (= conception assistée par ordinateur) CAD.
caoutchouc [kȧōōtshōō] nm rubber; **~ mousse** foam rubber; **en ~** rubber cpd.
caoutchouté, e [kȧōōtshōōtȧ] a rubberized.
caoutchouteux, euse [kȧōōtshōōtœ̄, -œ̄z] a rubbery.
CAP sigle m (= Certificat d'aptitude professionnelle) vocational training certificate taken at high school.
cap [kȧp] nm (*GÉO*) cape; headland; (fig) hurdle; watershed; (*NAVIG*): **changer de ~** to change course; **mettre le ~ sur** to head ou steer for; **doubler ou passer le ~** (fig) to get over the worst; **Le C~** Cape Town; **le ~ de Bonne Espérance** the Cape of Good Hope; **le ~ Horn** Cape Horn; **les îles du C~ Vert** (aussi: **le C~-Vert**) the Cape Verde Islands.
capable [kȧpȧbl(ə)] a able, capable; **~ de qch/faire** capable of sth/doing; **il est ~ d'oublier** he could easily forget; **spectacle/livre ~ d'intéresser** show/book liable ou likely to be of interest.
capacité [kȧpȧsētȧ] nf (compétence) ability; (*JUR, INFORM*, d'un récipient) capacity; **~ (en droit)** basic legal qualification.
caparaçonner [kȧpȧrȧsonȧ] vt (fig) to clad.
cape [kȧp] nf cape, cloak; **rire sous ~** to laugh up one's sleeve.
capeline [kȧplen] nf wide-brimmed hat.
CAPES [kȧpes] sigle m (= Certificat d'aptitude au professorat de l'enseignement du second degré) secondary teaching diploma.
capésien, ne [kȧpȧsyań, -en] nm/f person who holds the CAPES.
CAPET [kȧpet] sigle m (= Certificat d'aptitude au professorat de l'enseignement technique) technical teaching diploma.
capharnaüm [kȧfȧrnȧom] nm shambles sg.
capillaire [kȧpēler] a (soins, lotion) hair cpd; (vaisseau etc) capillary; **artiste ~** hair artist ou designer.
capillarité [kȧpēlȧrētȧ] nf capillary action.
capilliculteur [kȧpēlēkültœr] nm hair-care specialist.
capilotade [kȧpēlotȧd]: **en ~** ad crushed to a pulp; smashed to pieces.
capitaine [kȧpēten] nm captain; **~ des pompiers** fire marshal (*US*), fire chief (*Brit*); **~ au long cours** master mariner.
capitainerie [kȧpētenrȧ] nf (du port) harbor (*US*) ou harbour (*Brit*) master's (office).
capital, e, aux [kȧpētȧl, -ō] a major; of paramount importance; fundamental; (*JUR*)

capital ♦ *nm* capital; (*fig*) stock; asset ♦ *nf* (*ville*) capital; (*lettre*) capital (letter); ♦ *nmpl* (*fonds*) capital *sg*, money *sg*; **les sept péchés capitaux** the seven deadly sins; **peine ~e** capital punishment; **~** **(social)** capital stock (*US*), authorized capital (*Brit*); **~ d'exploitation** working capital.
capitaliser [kápētálēzā] *vt* to amass, build up; (*COMM*) to capitalize ♦ *vi* to save.
capitalisme [kápētálēsm(ə)] *nm* capitalism.
capitaliste [kápētálēst(ə)] *a*, *nm/f* capitalist.
capiteux, euse [kápētœ̄, -œ̄z] *a* (*vin*, *parfum*) heady; (*sensuel*) sensuous, alluring.
capitonné, e [kápētonā] *a* padded.
capitulation [kápētülásyôn] *nf* capitulation.
capituler [kápētülā] *vi* to capitulate.
caporal, aux [káporál, -ō] *nm* ≈ corporal (*US*), ≈ lance corporal (*Brit*).
caporal-chef, *pl* **caporaux-chefs** [káporálshef, kåporō-] *nm* corporal.
capot [kápō] *nm* (*AUTO*) hood (*US*), bonnet (*Brit*) ♦ *a inv* (*CARTES*): **être ~** to lose without taking a single trick.
capote [kápot] *nf* (*de voiture*) top (*US*), hood (*Brit*); (*de soldat*) greatcoat; **~ (anglaise)** (*fam*) rubber, condom.
capoter [kápotā] *vi* to overturn; (*négociations*) to founder.
câpre [kâpr(ə)] *nf* caper.
caprice [káprēs] *nm* whim, caprice; passing fancy; **~s** *nmpl* (*de la mode etc*) vagaries; **faire un ~** to throw a tantrum; **faire des ~s** to be temperamental.
capricieux, euse [káprēsyœ̄, -œ̄z] *a* capricious; whimsical; temperamental.
Capricorne [káprēkorn] *nm*: **le ~** Capricorn, the Goat; **être du ~** to be Capricorn.
capsule [kápsul] *nf* (*de bouteille*) cap; (*amorce*) primer; cap; (*BOT etc*, *spatiale*) capsule.
capter [káptā] *vt* (*ondes radio*) to pick up; (*eau*) to harness; (*fig*) to win, capture.
capteur [káptœr] *nm*: **~ solaire** solar collector.
captieux, euse [kápsyœ̄, -œ̄z] *a* specious.
captif, ive [káptēf, -ēv] *a*, *nm/f* captive.
captiver [káptēvā] *vt* to captivate.
captivité [káptēvētā] *nf* captivity; **en ~** in captivity.
capture [káptür] *nf* capture, catching *q*; catch.
capturer [káptürā] *vt* to capture, catch.
capuche [kápüsh] *nf* hood.
capuchon [kápüshôn] *nm* hood; (*de stylo*) cap, top.
capucin [kápüsan] *nm* Capuchin monk.
capucine [kápüsēn] *nf* (*BOT*) nasturtium.
caquelon [káklôn] *nm* (*ustensile de cuisson*) fondue pot.
caquet [kákє] *nm*: **rabattre le ~ à qn** to bring sb down a peg or two.
caqueter [káktā] *vi* (*poule*) to cackle; (*fig*) to prattle.
car [kár] *nm* bus, coach (*Brit*) ♦ *cj* because, for; **~ de police** police van; **~ de reportage** broadcasting *ou* radio van.
carabine [kárábēn] *nf* carbine, rifle; **~ à air comprimé** airgun.
carabiné, e [kárábēnā] *a* violent; (*cocktail*, *amende*) stiff.

Caracas [kárákás] *n* Caracas.
caracoler [kárákolā] *vi* to caracole, prance.
caractère [kárákter] *nm* (*gén*) character; **en ~s gras** in bold type; **en petits ~s** in small print; **en ~s d'imprimerie** in block letters; **avoir du ~** to have character; **avoir bon/mauvais ~** to be good-/ill-natured *ou* tempered; **~ de remplacement** wild card (*INFORM*); **~s/seconde (cps)** characters per second (cps).
caractériel, le [káráktāryєl] *a* (*enfant*) (emotionally) disturbed ♦ *nm/f* problem child; **troubles ~s** emotional problems.
caractérisé, e [káráktārēzā] *a*: **c'est une grippe/de l'insubordination ~e** it is a clear(-cut) case of flu/insubordination.
caractériser [káráktārēzā] *vt* to characterize; **se ~ par** to be characterized *ou* distinguished by.
caractéristique [káráktārēstēk] *a*, *nf* characteristic.
carafe [kárāf] *nf* decanter; carafe.
carafon [kárāfôn] *nm* small carafe.
caraïbe [kárāēb] *a* Caribbean; **les C~s** *nfpl* the Caribbean (Islands); **la mer des C~s** the Caribbean Sea.
carambolage [kárânbolázh] *nm* multiple crash, pileup.
caramel [kárámєl] *nm* (*bonbon*) caramel, toffee; (*substance*) caramel.
caraméliser [kárámālēzā] *vt* to caramelize.
carapace [kárápás] *nf* shell.
carapater [kárápátā]: **se ~** *vi* to take to one's heels, scram.
carat [kárá] *nm* carat; **or à 18 ~s** 18-carat gold.
caravane [kárāván] *nf* (*véhicule*) trailer (*US*), caravan (*Brit*).
caravanier [kárāványā] *nm* camper (*using a trailer/caravan (Brit)*).
caravaning [kárāvánēng] *nm* camping with a trailer (*US*), caravanning (*Brit*); (*emplacement*) campground (*US*), caravan site (*Brit*).
caravelle [kárávєl] *nf* caravel.
carbonate [kárbonát] *nm* (*CHIMIE*): **~ de soude** sodium carbonate.
carbone [kárbon] *nm* carbon; (*feuille*) carbon, sheet of carbon paper; (*double*) carbon (copy).
carbonique [kárbonēk] *a*: **gaz ~** carbon dioxide; **neige ~** dry ice.
carbonisé, e [kárbonēzā] *a* charred; **mourir ~** to be burned to death.
carboniser [kárbonēzā] *vt* to carbonize; (*brûler complètement*) to burn down, reduce to ashes.
carburant [kárbürán] *nm* (motor) fuel.
carburateur [kárbürátœr] *nm* carburetor (*US*), carburettor (*Brit*).
carburation [kárbürásyôn] *nf* carburetion (*US*), carburation (*Brit*).
carburer [kárbürā] *vi* (*moteur*): **bien/mal ~** to be well/badly tuned.
carcan [kárkán] *nm* (*fig*) yoke, shackles *pl*.
carcasse [kárkás] *nf* carcass; (*de véhicule etc*) frame.
carcéral, e, aux [kársārál, -ō] *a* prison *cpd*.
carcinogène [kársēnozhen] *a* carcinogenic.
cardan [kárdán] *nm* universal joint.

carder [kárdã] *vt* to card.
cardiaque [kárdyák] *a* cardiac, heart *cpd* ♦ *nm/f* heart patient; **être ~** to have a heart condition.
cardigan [kárdēgáṅ] *nm* cardigan.
cardinal, e, aux [kárdēnál, -ō] *a* cardinal ♦ *nm* (*REL*) cardinal.
cardiologie [kárdyolozhē] *nf* cardiology.
cardiologue [kárdyolog] *nm/f* cardiologist, heart specialist.
cardio-vasculaire [kárdyováskülcr] *a* cardiovascular.
cardon [kárdôṅ] *nm* cardoon.
carême [kárem] *nm*: **le C~** Lent.
carence [káráṅs] *nf* incompetence, inadequacy; (*manque*) deficiency; **~ vitaminique** vitamin deficiency.
carène [káren] *nf* hull.
caréner [kárānā] *vt* (*NAVIG*) to career; (*carrosserie*) to streamline.
caressant, e [kárcsãṅ, -âṅt] *a* affectionate; caressing, tender.
caresse [kárcs] *nf* caress.
caresser [kárãsā] *vt* to caress, stroke, fondle; (*fig: projet, espoir*) to toy with.
cargaison [kárgezôṅ] *nf* cargo, freight.
cargo [kárgō] *nm* cargo boat, freighter; **~ mixte** cargo and passenger ship.
cari [kárē] *nm* = **curry**.
caricatural, e, aux [kárēkátürál, -ō] *a* caricatural, caricature-like.
caricature [kárēkátür] *nf* caricature; (*politique etc*) (satirical) cartoon.
caricaturer [kárēkátürā] *vt* (*personne*) to caricature; (*politique etc*) to satirize.
caricaturiste [kárēkátürēst(ə)] *nm/f* caricaturist; (satirical) cartoonist.
carie [kárē] *nf*: **la ~ (dentaire)** tooth decay; **une ~** a bad tooth.
carié, e [káryā] *a*: **dent ~e** bad *ou* decayed tooth.
carillon [kárēyôṅ] *nm* (*d'église*) bells *pl*; (*de pendule*) chimes *pl*; (*de porte*): **~ (électrique)** (electric) door chime *ou* bell.
carillonner [kárēyonā] *vi* to ring, chime, peal.
carlingue [kárlaṅg] *nf* cabin.
carmin [kármaṅ] *a inv* crimson.
carnage [kárnázh] *nm* carnage, massacre, slaughter.
carnassier, ière [kárnásyã, -yer] *a* carnivorous ♦ *nm* carnivore.
carnation [kárnâsyôṅ] *nf* complexion; **~s** *nfpl* (*PEINTURE*) flesh tones.
carnaval [kárnávál] *nm* carnival.
carné, e [kárnã] *a* meat *cpd*, meat-based.
carnet [kárne] *nm* (*calepin*) notebook; (*de tickets, timbres etc*) book; (*d'école*) report card (*US*), school report (*Brit*); (*journal intime*) diary; **~ d'adresses** address book; **~ de chèques** check (*US*) *ou* cheque (*Brit*) book; **~ de commandes** order book; **~ de notes** (*SCOL*) report card (*US*), (school) report (*Brit*); **~ à souches** stub (*US*) *ou* counterfoil (*Brit*) book.
carnier [kárnyã] *nm* gamebag.
carnivore [kárnēvor] *a* carnivorous ♦ *nm* carnivore.
Carolines [károlēn] *nfpl*: **les ~** the Caroline Islands.
carotide [károtēd] *nf* carotid (artery).

carotte [károt] *nf* (*aussi fig*) carrot.
Carpates [kárpát] *nfpl*: **les ~** the Carpathians, the Carpathian Mountains.
carpe [kárp(ə)] *nf* carp.
carpette [kárpet] *nf* rug.
carquois [kárkwá] *nm* quiver.
carre [kár] *nf* (*de ski*) edge.
carré, e [kárã] *a* square; (*fig: franc*) straightforward ♦ *nm* (*de terrain, jardin*) patch, plot; (*NAVIG: salle*) wardroom; (*MATH*) square; (*CARTES*): **~ d'as/de rois** four aces/kings; **élever un nombre au ~** to square a number; **mètre/kilomètre ~** square meter/kilometer; **~ de soie** silk headscarf; **~ d'agneau** loin of lamb.
carreau, x [kárō] *nm* (*en faïence etc*) (floor) tile; (*wall*) tile; (*de fenêtre*) (window) pane; (*motif*) check, square; (*CARTES: couleur*) diamonds *pl*; (: *carte*) diamond; **tissu à ~x** checked fabric; **papier à ~x** squared paper.
carrefour [kárfōōr] *nm* crossroads *sg*.
carrelage [kárlázh] *nm* tiling; (tiled) floor.
carreler [kárlã] *vt* to tile.
carrelet [kárlc] *nm* (*poisson*) plaice.
carreleur [kárlcr] *nm* (floor) tiler.
carrément [kárāmáṅ] *ad* (*franchement*) straight out, bluntly; (*sans détours, sans hésiter*) straight; (*nettement*) definitely; **il l'a ~ mis à la porte** he threw him straight out.
carrer [kárã]: **se ~** *vi*: **se ~ dans un fauteuil** to settle o.s. comfortably *ou* ensconce o.s. in an armchair.
carrier [káryā] *nm*: **(ouvrier) ~** quarryman, quarrier.
carrière [káryer] *nf* (*de roches*) quarry; (*métier*) career; **militaire de ~** professional soldier; **faire ~ dans** to make one's career in.
carriole [káryol] *nf* (*péj*) old cart.
carrossable [károsábl(ə)] *a* suitable for (motor) vehicles.
carrosse [káros] *nm* (horse-drawn) coach.
carrosserie [károsrē] *nf* body; (*activité, commerce*) (car) body manufacturing; **atelier de ~** (*pour réparations*) body shop.
carrossier [károsyã] *nm* (car) body repairer; (*dessinateur*) car designer.
carrousel [károōzel] *nm* (*ÉQUITATION*) carousel; (*fig*) merry-go-round.
carrure [kárur] *nf* build; (*fig*) stature.
cartable [kártábl(ə)] *nm* (*d'écolier*) satchel, (school)bag.
carte [kárt(ə)] *nf* (*de géographie*) map; (*marine, du ciel*) chart; (*de fichier, d'abonnement etc, à jouer*) card; (*au restaurant*) menu; (*aussi*: **~ postale**) (post)card; (*aussi*: **~ de visite**) (visiting) card; **avoir/donner ~ blanche** to have/give carte blanche *ou* a free hand; **tirer les ~s à qn** to read sb's cards; **jouer aux ~s** to play cards; **jouer ~s sur table** (*fig*) to put one's cards on the table; **à la ~** (*au restaurant*) à la carte; **~ bancaire** banking (*US*) *ou* cash (*Brit*) card; **~ à circuit imprimé** printed circuit; **~ de crédit** credit card; **~ d'état-major** ≈ Geological (*US*) *ou* Ordnance (*Brit*) Survey map; **la ~ grise** (*AUTO*) ≈ the (car) registration document; **~ d'identité** identity card; **~ perforée** punch(ed) card; **~ de séjour**

residence permit; ~ **routière** road map; ~
verte (*AUTO*) *international insurance
certificate;* la ~ **des vins** the wine list.
cartel [kártel] *nm* cartel.
carte-lettre, *pl* **cartes-lettres** [kàrtəletr(ə)] *nf*
letter-card.
carte-mère, *pl* **cartes-mères** [kàrtəmer] *nf* (*IN-
FORM*) mother board.
carter [kárter] *nm* (*AUTO*: *d'huile*) oil pan
(*US*), sump (*Brit*); (: *de la boîte de vitesses*)
housing (*US*), casing (*Brit*); (*de bicyclette*)
chain guard.
carte-réponse, *pl* **cartes-réponses**
[kárt(ə)rāpôńs] *nf* reply card.
Carthage [kàrtàzh] *n* Carthage.
carthaginois, e [kàrtázhčnwá, -wàz] *a*
Carthaginian.
cartilage [kàrtēlázh] *nm* (*ANAT*) cartilage.
cartilagineux, euse [kàrtēlázhēnœ̄, -œ̄z] *a*
(*viande*) gristly.
cartographe [kártográf] *nm/f* cartographer.
cartographie [kártográfē] *nf* cartography,
map-making.
cartomancie [kàrtomáńsē] *nf* fortune-telling,
card-reading.
cartomancien, ne [kártomáńsyań, -eń] *nm/f*
fortune-teller (*with cards*).
carton [kártôń] *nm* (*matériau*) cardboard;
(*boîte*) (cardboard) box; (*d'invitation*) invitation card; (*ART*) sketch; cartoon; **en** ~ cardboard *cpd*; **faire un** ~ (*au tir*) to have a go
at the rifle range; to score a hit; ~ (**à dessin**)
portfolio.
cartonnage [kártonázh] *nm* cardboard (packing).
cartonné, e [kártonā] *a* (*livre*) hardback,
cased.
carton-pâte [kártôńpát] *nm* pasteboard; **de** ~
(*fig*) cardboard *cpd*.
cartouche [kártōōsh] *nf* cartridge; (*de cigarettes*) carton.
cartouchière [kártōōshyer] *nf* cartridge belt.
cas [ká] *nm* case; **faire peu de** ~/**grand** ~ **de**
to attach little/great importance to; **le** ~
échéant if need be; **en aucun** ~ on no
account, under no circumstances (whatsoever); **au** ~ **où** in case; **dans ce** ~ in that
case; **en** ~ **de** in case of, in the event of; **en**
~ **de besoin** if need be; **en** ~ **d'urgence** in
an emergency; **en ce** ~ in that case; **en tout**
~ in any case, at any rate; ~ **de conscience**
matter of conscience; ~ **de force majeure**
case of absolute necessity; (*ASSURANCES*) act
of God; ~ **limite** borderline case; ~ **social**
social problem.
Casablanca [kázáblàńká] *n* Casablanca.
casanier, ière [kázányá, -yer] *a* stay-at-home.
casaque [kázák] *nf* (*de jockey*) blouse.
cascade [káskád] *nf* waterfall, cascade; (*fig*)
stream, torrent.
cascadeur, euse [káskádœr, -œ̄z] *nm/f*
stuntman/girl.
case [káz] *nf* (*hutte*) hut; (*compartiment*)
compartment; (*pour le courrier*) pigeonhole;
(*de mots croisés, d'échiquier*) square; (*sur
un formulaire*) box.
casemate [kázmát] *nf* blockhouse.
caser [kázā] *vt* (*mettre*) to put; (*loger*) to put
up; (*péj*) to find a job for; to marry off; **se**

~ (*personne*) to settle down.
caserne [kázern(ə)] *nf* barracks.
casernement [kázernəmàń] *nm* barrack buildings *pl*.
cash [kásh] *ad*: **payer** ~ to pay cash.
casier [kázyā] *nm* (*à journaux etc*) rack; (*de
bureau*) filing cabinet; (: *à cases*) set of
pigeonholes; (*case*) compartment; pigeonhole; (: *à clef*) locker; (*PÊCHE*) lobster pot;
~ **à bouteilles** bottle rack; ~ **judiciaire**
police record.
casino [kázēnō] *nm* casino.
casque [kásk(ə)] *nm* helmet; (*chez le coiffeur*)
(hair-)drier; (*pour audition*) (head-)phones
pl, headset; **les C~s bleus** the UN peace-
keeping force.
casquer [káskā] *vi* (*fam*) to cough up.
casquette [kásket] *nf* cap.
cassable [kásàbl(ə)] *a* (*fragile*) breakable.
cassant, e [kásáń, -áńt] *a* brittle; (*fig*)
brusque, abrupt.
cassate [kását] *nf*: (**glace**) ~ cassata.
cassation [kásásyóń] *nf*: **se pourvoir en** ~ to
lodge an appeal; **recours en** ~ appeal to the
Supreme Court.
casse [kás] *nf* (*pour voitures*): **mettre à la** ~
to scrap; (*dégâts*): **il y a eu de la** ~ there
were a lot of breakages; (*TYPO*): **haut/bas
de** ~ upper/lower case.
cassé, e [kásā] *a* (*voix*) cracked; (*vieillard*)
bent.
casse-cou [káskōō] *a inv* daredevil, reckless;
crier ~ **à qn** to warn sb (*against a risky
undertaking*).
casse-croûte [káskrōōt] *nm inv* snack.
casse-noisette(s) [kásnwázet], **casse-noix**
[kásnwá] *nm inv* nutcracker (*US*), nutcrack-
ers *pl* (*Brit*).
casse-pieds [káspyá] *a, nm/f inv* (*fam*): **il est**
~, **c'est un** ~ he's a pain (in the neck).
casser [kásā] *vt* to break; (*ADMIN: gradé*) to
demote; (*JUR*) to quash; (*COMM*): ~ **les prix**
to slash prices; **se** ~ *vi* to break; (*fam*) to
go, leave ♦ *vt*: **se** ~ **la jambe/une jambe** to
break one's leg/a leg; **à tout** ~ fantastic,
brilliant; **se** ~ **net** to break clean off.
casserole [kásrol] *nf* saucepan; **à la** ~
(*CULIN*) braised.
casse-tête [kástet] *nm inv* (*fig*) brain teaser;
(*difficultés*) headache (*fig*).
cassette [káset] *nf* (*bande magnétique*) cassette; (*coffret*) casket.
casseur [kásœr] *nm* hooligan; rioter.
cassis [kásēs] *nm* blackcurrant; (*de la route*)
dip, bump.
cassonade [kásonád] *nf* brown sugar.
cassoulet [kásōōle] *nm* sausage and bean hotpot.
cassure [kásür] *nf* break, crack.
castagnettes [kástányet] *nfpl* castanets.
caste [kást(ə)] *nf* caste.
castillan, e [kástēyáń, -áń] *a* Castilian ♦ *nm*
(*LING*) Castilian.
Castille [kástēy] *nf*: **la** ~ Castile.
castor [kástor] *nm* beaver.
castrer [kástrā] *vt* (*mâle*) to castrate;
(*femelle*) to spay; (*cheval*) to geld; (*chat,
chien*) to fix (*US*), doctor (*Brit*).
cataclysme [kátáklēsm(ə)] *nm* cataclysm.

catacombes [kàtákôṅb] *nfpl* catacombs.
catadioptre [kàtàdyoptr(ə)] *nm* = **cataphote**.
catafalque [kàtáfálk(ə)] *nm* catafalque.
catalan, e [kàtálàṅ, -àn] *a* Catalan, Catalonian ♦ *nm (LING)* Catalan.
Catalogne [kàtálony] *nf:* **la ~** Catalonia.
catalogue [kàtálog] *nm* catalogue.
cataloguer [kàtálogā] *vt* to catalogue, list; *(péj)* to put a label on.
catalyse [kàtálēz] *nf* catalysis.
catalyseur [kàtálēzœr] *nm* catalyst.
catamaran [kàtámáráṅ] *nm (voilier)* catamaran.
cataphote [kàtáfot] *nm* reflector.
cataplasme [kàtáplàsm(ə)] *nm* poultice.
catapulte [kàtápült(ə)] *nf* catapult.
catapulter [kàtápültā] *vt* to catapult.
cataracte [kàtárákt(ə)] *nf* cataract; **opérer qn de la ~** to operate on sb for a cataract.
catarrhe [kàtár] *nm* catarrh.
catarrheux, euse [kàtárœ̄, -œ̄z] *a* catarrhal.
catastrophe [kàtástrof] *nf* catastrophe, disaster; **atterrir en ~** to make an emergency landing; **partir en ~** to rush away.
catastropher [kàtástrofā] *vt (personne)* to shatter.
catastrophique [kàtástrofēk] *a* catastrophic, disastrous.
catch [kàtsh] *nm* freestyle *(US) ou* all-in *(Brit)* wrestling.
catcheur, euse [kàtshœr, -œ̄z] *nm/f* freestyle *(US) ou* (all-in) *(Brit)* wrestler.
catéchiser [kàtáshēzā] *vt* to indoctrinate; to lecture.
catéchisme [kàtáshēsm(ə)] *nm* catechism.
catéchumène [kàtākümen] *nm/f* catechumen, *person attending religious instruction prior to baptism.*
catégorie [kàtágorē] *nf* category; *(BOUCHE-RIE):* **morceaux de première/deuxième ~** prime/second cuts.
catégorique [kàtágorēk] *a* categorical.
catégoriquement [kàtágorēkmàṅ] *ad* categorically.
catégoriser [kàtágorēzā] *vt* to categorize.
caténaire [kàtāner] *nf (RAIL)* overhead line.
cathédrale [kàtádrál] *nf* cathedral.
cathéter [kàtāter] *nm (MÉD)* catheter.
cathode [kàtod] *nf* cathode.
cathodique [kàtodēk] *a:* **rayons ~s** cathode rays; **tube/écran ~** cathode-ray tube/screen.
catholicisme [kàtolēsēsm(ə)] *nm* (Roman) Catholicism.
catholique [kàtolēk] *a, nm/f* (Roman) Catholic; **pas très ~** a bit shady *ou* fishy.
catimini [kàtēmēnē]: **en ~** *ad* on the sly, on the quiet.
catogan [kàtogáṅ] *nm* bow *(tying hair on neck)*.
Caucase [kokâz] *nm:* **le ~** the Caucasus (Mountains).
caucasien, ne [kokâzyaṅ, -en] *a* Caucasian.
cauchemar [koshmár] *nm* nightmare.
cauchemardesque [koshmárdesk(ə)] *a* nightmarish.
caudal, e, aux [kōdál, -ō] *a* caudal, tail *cpd.*
causal, e [kōzál] *a* causal.
causalité [kōzálētā] *nf* causality.
cause [kōz] *nf* cause; *(JUR)* lawsuit, case;

brief; **faire ~ commune avec qn** to take sides with sb; **être ~ de** to be the cause of; **à ~ de** because of, owing to; **pour ~ de** on account of; owing to; **(et) pour ~** and for (a very) good reason; **être en ~** *(intérêts)* to be at stake; *(personne)* to be involved; *(qualité)* to be in question; **mettre en ~** to implicate; to call into question; **remettre en ~** to challenge, call into question; **c'est hors de ~** it's out of the question; **en tout état de ~** in any case.
causer [kōzā] *vt* to cause ♦ *vi* to chat, talk.
causerie [kōzrē] *nf* talk.
causette [kōzet] *nf:* **faire la** *ou* **un brin de ~** to have a chat.
caustique [kōstēk] *a* caustic.
cauteleux, euse [kōtlœ̄, -œ̄z] *a* wily.
cautériser [kōtārēzā] *vt* to cauterize.
caution [kōsyóṅ] *nf* guarantee, security; deposit; *(JUR)* bail (bond); *(fig)* backing, support; **payer la ~ de qn** to go *(US) ou* stand *(Brit)* bail for sb; **se porter ~ pour qn** to stand surety for sb; **libéré sous ~** released on bail; **sujet à ~** unconfirmed.
cautionnement [kōsyonmáṅ] *nm (somme)* guarantee, surety.
cautionner [kōsyonā] *vt* to guarantee; *(soutenir)* to support.
cavalcade [kàválkád] *nf (fig)* stampede.
cavale [kávál] *nf:* **en ~** on the run.
cavalerie [káválrē] *nf* cavalry.
cavalier, ière [kàvályà, -yer] *a (désinvolte)* offhand ♦ *nm/f* rider; *(au bal)* partner ♦ *nm (ÉCHECS)* knight; **faire ~ seul** to go it alone; **allée** *ou* **piste cavalière** riding path.
cave [káv] *nf* cellar; *(cabaret)* (cellar) nightclub ♦ *a:* **yeux ~s** sunken eyes; **joues ~s** hollow cheeks.
caveau, x [kávō] *nm* vault.
caverne [kávern(ə)] *nf* cave.
caverneux, euse [kávernœ̄, -œ̄z] *a* cavernous.
caviar [kávyár] *nm* caviar(e).
cavité [kávētā] *nf* cavity.
Cayenne [kàyen] *n* Cayenne.
CB [sēbē] *sigle f (= citizens' band, canaux banalisés)* CB.
CC *sigle m* = **corps consulaire, compte courant.**
CCI *sigle f* = **Chambre de commerce et d'industrie.**
CCP *sigle m* = **compte chèque postal.**
CD *sigle m (= chemin départemental)* secondary road; *(= compact disc)* CD; *(= comité directeur)* steering committee; *(POL)* = **corps diplomatique.**
CDF, CdF *sigle mpl (= Charbonnages de France)* national coal board.
CDI *sigle m (= Centre de documentation et d'information)* school library.
CDS *sigle m (= Centre des démocrates sociaux)* political party.
CE *sigle f (= Communauté européenne)* EEC, EC *(Brit)*; *(COMM)* = **caisse d'épargne** ♦ *sigle m (INDUSTRIE)* = **comité d'entreprise;** *(SCOL)* = **cours élémentaire.**
ce (c'), cet, cette, ces [sə, set, sā] *dét (gén)* this; these *pl; (non-proximité)* that; those *pl;* **cette nuit** *(qui vient)* tonight; *(passée)* last night ♦ *pronom:* **~ qui, ~ que** what; *(chose*

qui ...): **il est bête, ~ qui me chagrine** he's stupid, which saddens me; **tout ~ qui bouge** everything that *ou* which moves; **tout ~ que je sais** all I know; **~ dont j'ai parlé** what I talked about; **~ que c'est grand!** how big it is!, **what a size it is!**; **c'est: c'est petit/ grand/un livre** it's *ou* it is small/big/a book; **c'est un peintre** he's *ou* he is a painter; **~ sont des livres/ peintres** they're *ou* they are books/painters; **c'est le facteur** *etc* (*à la porte*) it's the mailman *etc*; **qui est-~?** who is it?; (*en désignant*) who is he/she?; **qu'est-~?** what is it?; **c'est ça** (*correct*) that's it, that's right; **c'est qu'il n'a pas faim** the fact is he's not hungry; **ce n'est pas à moi de faire** it's not up to me to do; *voir aussi* **-ci, est-ce que, n'est-ce pas, c'est- à-dire.**

CEA *sigle m* (= *Commissariat à l'énergie atomique*) ≈ AEC (= *Atomic Energy Commission*) (*US*), ≈ AEA (= *Atomic Energy Authority*) (*Brit*).

CECA [sāká] *sigle f* (= *Communauté européenne du charbon et de l'acier*) ECSC (= *European Coal and Steel Community*).

ceci [səsē] *pronom* this.

cécité [sāsētā] *nf* blindness.

céder [sādā] *vt* to give up ♦ *vi* (*pont, barrage*) to give way; (*personne*) to give in; **~ à** to yield to, give in to.

CEDEX [sādcks] *sigle m* (= *courrier d'entreprise à distribution exceptionnelle*) *accelerated postal service for bulk users.*

cédille [sādēy] *nf* cedilla.

cèdre [sedr(ə)] *nm* cedar.

CEE *sigle f* (= *Communauté économique européenne*) EEC.

CEG *sigle m* (= *Collège d'enseignement général*) ≈ junior high school.

ceindre [saṅdr(ə)] *vt* (*mettre*) to put on, don; (*entourer*): **~ qch de qch** to put sth around sth.

ceinture [saṅtür] *nf* belt; (*taille*) waist; (*fig*) ring; belt; circle; **~ de sauvetage** lifebelt; **~ de sécurité** safety *ou* seat belt; **~ (de sécurité) à enrouleur** inertia reel seat belt; **~ verte** green belt.

ceinturer [saṅtürā] *vt* (*saisir*) to grasp (around the waist); (*entourer*) to surround.

ceinturon [saṅtüróṅ] *nm* belt.

cela [səlá] *pronom* that; (*comme sujet indéfini*) it; **~ m'étonne que** it surprises me that; **quand/où ~?** when/where (was that)?

célébrant [sālābráṅ] *nm* (*REL*) celebrant.

célébration [sālābrásyóṅ] *nf* celebration.

célèbre [sālebr(ə)] *a* famous.

célébrer [sālābrā] *vt* to celebrate; (*louer*) to extol.

célébrité [sālābrētā] *nf* fame; (*star*) celebrity.

céleri [sālrē] *nm*: **~(-rave)** celeriac; **~ (en branche)** celery.

célérité [sālārētā] *nf* speed, swiftness.

céleste [sālest(ə)] *a* celestial; heavenly.

célibat [sālēbá] *nm* celibacy; bachelor/ spinsterhood.

célibataire [sālēbáter] *a* single, unmarried ♦ *nm/f* bachelor/unmarried *ou* single woman; **mère ~** single *ou* unmarried mother.

celle, celles [sel] *pronom voir* **celui.**

cellier [sālyā] *nm* storeroom.

cellophane [sālofán] *nf* ® cellophane.

cellulaire [sālüler] *a* (*BIO*) cell *cpd*, cellular; **voiture** *ou* **fourgon ~** prison *ou* police van; **régime ~** confinement.

cellule [sālül] *nf* (*gén*) cell; **~ (photo- électrique)** electronic eye.

cellulite [sālülēt] *nf* cellulite.

celluloïd [sālüloēd] *nm* ® Celluloid.

cellulose [sālülōz] *nf* cellulose.

celte [selt(ə)], **celtique** [seltēk] *a* Celt, Celtic.

celui, celle, ceux, celles [səlüē, sel, sœ] *pronom* the one; **~ qui bouge** the one which *ou* that moves; (*personne*) the one who moves; **~ que je vois** the one (which *ou* that) I see; the one (whom) I see; **~ dont je parle** the one I'm talking about; **~ qui veut** (*valeur indéfinie*) whoever wants, the one *ou* person who wants; **~ du salon/du dessous** the one in (*ou* from) the lounge/below; **~ de mon frère** my brother's; **celui-ci/-là, celle-ci/-là** this/that one; the latter/former; **ceux- ci, celles-ci** these ones; the latter; **ceux-là, celles-là** those (ones); the former.

cénacle [sānákl(ə)] *nm* (*literary*) coterie *ou* set.

cendre [sáṅdr(ə)] *nf* ash; **~s** (*d'un foyer*) ash(es), cinders; (*volcaniques*) ash *sg*; (*d'un défunt*) ashes; **sous la ~** (*CULIN*) in (the) embers.

cendré, e [sáṅdrā] *a* (*couleur*) ashen; (*piste*) **~e** cinder track.

cendreux, euse [sáṅdrœ, -œz] *a* (*terrain, substance*) cindery; (*teint*) ashen.

cendrier [sáṅdrēyā] *nm* ashtray.

cène [sen] *nf*: **la ~** (Holy) Communion; (*ART*) **the Last Supper.**

censé, e [sáṅsā] *a*: **être ~ faire** to be supposed to do.

censément [sáṅsāmáṅ] *ad* supposedly.

censeur [sáṅscr] *nm* (*SCOL*) assistant- *ou* vice-principal; (*CINÉMA, POL*) censor.

censure [sáṅsür] *nf* censorship.

censurer [sáṅsürā] *vt* (*CINÉMA, PRESSE*) to censor; (*POL*) to censure.

cent [sáṅ] *num* a hundred, one hundred; **pour ~ (%)** per cent (%); **faire les ~ pas** to pace up and down.

centaine [sáṅten] *nf*: **une ~ (de)** about a hundred, a hundred or so; (*COMM*) a hundred; **plusieurs ~s (de)** several hundred; **des ~s (de)** hundreds (of).

centenaire [sáṅtner] *a* hundred-year-old ♦ *nm/f* centenarian ♦ *nm* (*anniversaire*) centenary.

centième [sáṅtyem] *num* hundredth.

centigrade [sáṅtēgrád] *nm* centigrade.

centigramme [sáṅtēgràm] *nm* centigramme.

centilitre [sáṅtēlētr(ə)] *nm* centiliter (*US*), centilitre (*Brit*).

centime [sáṅtēm] *nm* centime.

centimètre [sáṅtēmetr(ə)] *nm* centimeter (*US*), centimetre (*Brit*); (*ruban*) tape measure, measuring tape.

centrafricain, e [sáṅtráfrēkáṅ, -en] *a* of *ou* from the Central African Republic.

central, e, aux [sáṅtrál, -ō] *a* central ♦ *nm*: **~ (téléphonique)** (telephone) exchange ♦ *nf*: **~e d'achat** (*COMM*) central buying service; **~e électrique/nucléaire** electric/nuclear power station; **~e syndicale** group of affiliated trade unions.

centralisation [sȧ̊ntrȧ́lēzȧ̂syôṅ] *nf* centralization.

centraliser [sȧ̊ntrȧ́lēzǡ] *vt* to centralize.

centraméricain, e [sȧ̊ntrȧ́mȧrēkȧṅ, -en] *a* Central American.

centre [sȧ̊ntr(ə)] *nm* center (US), centre (Brit); ~ **commercial/sportif/culturel** shopping/sports/arts center; ~ **aéré** outdoor (recreation) center; ~ **d'apprentissage** training college; ~ **d'attraction** center of attraction; ~ **de gravité** center of gravity; ~ **hospitalier** hospital complex; ~ **de tri** (POSTES) sorting office; ~**s nerveux** (ANAT) nerve centers.

centrer [sȧ̊ntrǡ] *vt* to center (US), centre (Brit) ♦ *vi* (FOOTBALL) to center (US) ou centre (Brit) the ball.

centre-ville, *pl* **centres-villes** [sȧ̊ntrəvēl] *nm* town center (US) ou centre (Brit), downtown (area) (US).

centrifuge [sȧ̊ntrēfüzh] *a*: **force** ~ centrifugal force.

centrifuger [sȧ̊ntrēfüzhǡ] *vt* to centrifuge.

centrifugeuse [sȧ̊ntrēfüzhȫz] *nf* (pour fruits) juice extractor.

centripète [sȧ̊ntrēpet] *a*: **force** ~ centripetal force.

centriste [sȧ̊ntrēst(ə)] *a, nm/f* centrist.

centuple [sȧ̊ntüpl(ə)] *nm*: **le** ~ **de qch** a hundred times sth; **au** ~ a hundredfold.

centupler [sȧ̊ntüplǡ] *vi, vt* to increase a hundredfold.

CEP *sigle m* = **Certificat d'études (primaires).**

cep [sep] *nm* (vine) stock.

cépage [sāpȧzh] *nm* (type of) vine.

cèpe [sep] *nm* (edible) boletus.

cependant [səpȧ̊ndȧṅ] *ad* however, nevertheless.

céramique [sārȧmēk] *a* ceramic ♦ *nf* ceramic; (art) ceramics *sg*.

céramiste [sārȧmēst(ə)] *nm/f* ceramist.

cerbère [serber] *nm* (fig: péj) bad-tempered doorkeeper.

cerceau, x [sersō] *nm* (d'enfant, de tonnelle) hoop.

cercle [serkl(ə)] *nm* circle; (objet) band, hoop; **décrire un** ~ (avion) to circle; (projectile) to describe a circle; ~ **d'amis** circle of friends; ~ **de famille** family circle; ~ **vicieux** vicious circle.

cercler [serklǡ] *vt*: **lunettes cerclées d'or** gold-rimmed glasses.

cercueil [serkœy] *nm* coffin.

céréale [sārāȧl] *nf* cereal.

céréalier, ière [sārāȧlyǡ, -yer] *a* (production, cultures) cereal *cpd*.

cérébral, e, aux [sārābrȧl, -ō] *a* (ANAT) cerebral, brain *cpd*; (fig) mental, cerebral.

cérémonial [sārāmonyȧl] *nm* ceremonial.

cérémonie [sārāmonē] *nf* ceremony; ~**s** *nfpl* (péj) fuss *sg*, to-do *sg*.

cérémonieux, euse [sārāmonyȫ, -ȫz] *a* ceremonious, formal.

CERES [sāres] *sigle m* (= Centre d'études, de recherches et d'éducation socialiste) (formerly) intellectual section of the French Socialist party.

cerf [ser] *nm* stag.

cerfeuil [serfœy] *nm* chervil.

cerf-volant [servolȧṅ] *nm* kite; **jouer au** ~ to fly a kite.

cerisaie [sərēze] *nf* cherry orchard.

cerise [sərēz] *nf* cherry.

cerisier [sərēzyȧ] *nm* cherry (tree).

CERN [sern] *sigle m* (= Conseil européen pour la recherche nucléaire) CERN.

cerné, e [sernȧ] *a*: **les yeux** ~**s** with dark rings ou shadows under the eyes.

cerner [sernȧ] *vt* (MIL etc) to surround; (fig: problème) to delimit, define.

cernes [sern(ə)] *nfpl* (dark) rings, shadows (under the eyes).

certain, e [sertȧṅ, -en] *a* certain; (sûr): ~ **(de/que)** certain ou sure (of/ that) ♦ *dét* certain; **d'un** ~ **âge** past one's prime, not so young; **un** ~ **temps** (quite) some time; **sûr et** ~ absolutely certain; ~**s** *pronom* some.

certainement [sertenmȧ̊ṅ] *ad* (probablement) most probably ou likely; (bien sûr) certainly, of course.

certes [sert(ə)] *ad* admittedly; of course; indeed (yes).

certificat [sertēfēkȧ] *nm* certificate; **C**~ **d'études (primaires) (CEP)** former school leaving certificate (taken at the end of primary education); **C**~ **de fin d'études secondaires (CFES)** school leaving certificate.

certifié, e [sertēfyȧ] *a*: **professeur** ~ qualified teacher; (ADMIN): **copie** ~**e conforme (à l'original)** certified copy (of the original).

certifier [sertēfyȧ] *vt* to certify, guarantee; ~ **à qn que** to assure sb that, guarantee to sb that; ~ **qch à qn** to guarantee sth to sb.

certitude [sertētüd] *nf* certainty.

cérumen [sārümen] *nm* (ear)wax.

cerveau, x [servō] *nm* brain; ~ **électronique** electronic brain.

cervelas [servəlȧ] *nm* saveloy.

cervelle [servel] *nf* (ANAT) brain; (CULIN) brain(s); **se creuser la** ~ to rack one's brains.

cervical, e, aux [servēkȧl, -ō] *a* cervical.

cervidés [servēdȧ] *nmpl* cervidae.

CES *sigle m* (= Collège d'enseignement secondaire) junior high school.

ces [se] *dét voir* **ce.**

césarienne [sāzȧryen] *nf* caesarean (section).

cessantes [sesȧṅt] *afpl*: **toutes affaires** ~ forthwith.

cessation [sesȧsyôṅ] *nf*: ~ **des hostilités** suspension of hostilities; ~ **de paiements/commerce** suspension of payments/trading.

cesse [ses]: **sans** ~ *ad* continually, constantly; continuously; **il n'avait de** ~ **que** he would not rest until.

cesser [sȧsȧ] *vt* to stop ♦ *vi* to stop, cease; ~ **de faire** to stop doing; **faire** ~ (bruit, scandale) to put a stop to.

cessez-le-feu [sȧsȧlfœ] *nm inv* ceasefire.

cession [sesyôṅ] *nf* transfer.

c'est [se] *pronom + vb voir* **ce.**

c'est-à-dire [setȧdēr] *ad* that is (to say); (demander de préciser): ~**?** what does that mean?; ~ **que ...** (en conséquence) which means that ...; (manière d'excuse) well, in fact ....

CET *sigle m* (= Collège d'enseignement

technique) formerly technical school.
cet [sɛt] *dét voir* **ce.**
cétacé [sātāsā] *nm* cetacean.
cette [sɛt] *dét voir* **ce.**
ceux [sœ̃] *pronom voir* **celui.**
cévenol, e [sāvnɔl] *a* of *ou* from the Cévennes region.
cf. *abr* (= *confer*) cf, cp.
CFAO *sigle f* (= *conception de fabrication assistée par ordinateur*) CAM.
CFDT *sigle f* (= *Confédération française et démocratique du travail*) trade union.
CFES *sigle m* = **Certificat de fin d'études secondaires.**
CFF *sigle m* (= *Chemin de fer fédéral*) Swiss railroad.
CFL *sigle m* (= *Chemin de fer luxembourgeois*) Luxembourg railroad.
CFP *sigle m* = *Centre de formation professionnelle* ♦ *sigle f* – *Compagnie française des pétroles.*
CFTC *sigle f* (= *Confédération française des travailleurs chrétiens*) trade union.
CGC *sigle f* (= *Confédération générale des cadres*) management union.
CGPME *sigle f* = *Confédération générale des petites et moyennes entreprises.*
CGT *sigle f* (= *Confédération générale du travail*) trade union.
CH *abr* (= *Confédération helvétique*) CH.
ch. *abr* = **charges, chauffage, cherche.**
chacal [ʃakal] *nm* jackal.
chacun, e [ʃakœ̃, -ün] *pronom* each; (*indéfini*) everyone, everybody.
chagrin, e [ʃagraɲ, -ɛn] *a* morose ♦ *nm* grief, sorrow; **avoir du ~** to be grieved *ou* sorrowful.
chagriner [ʃagrɛnā] *vt* to grieve, distress; (*contrarier*) to bother, worry.
chahut [ʃaü] *nm* uproar.
chahuter [ʃaütā] *vt* to rag, bait ♦ *vi* to make an uproar.
chahuteur, euse [ʃaütœr, -ɛz] *nm/f* rowdy.
chai [ʃe] *nm* wine and spirit store (house).
chaîne [ʃen] *nf* chain; (*RADIO, TV*) channel; (*INFORM*) string; **~s** *nfpl* (*liens, asservissement*) fetters, bonds; **travail à la ~** production line work; **réactions en ~** chain reactions; **faire la ~** to form a (human) chain; **~ d'entraide** mutual aid association; **~ (haute-fidélité** *ou* **hi-fi)** hi-fi system; **~ (de montage** *ou* **de fabrication)** production *ou* assembly line; **~ (de montagnes)** (mountain) range; **~ de solidarité** solidarity network; **~ (stéréo** *ou* **audio)** stereo (system).
chaînette [ʃenet] *nf* (small) chain.
chaînon [ʃenɔ̃] *nm* link.
chair [ʃer] *nf* flesh ♦ *a:* (*couleur*) **~** flesh-colored; **avoir la ~ de poule** to have goosepimples *ou* gooseflesh; **bien en ~** plump, well-padded; **en ~ et en os** in the flesh; **~ à saucisses** sausage meat.
chaire [ʃer] *nf* (*d'église*) pulpit; (*d'université*) chair.
chaise [ʃez] *nf* chair; **~ de bébé** high chair; **~ électrique** electric chair; **~ longue** deck-chair.
chaland [ʃalāɲ] *nm* (*bateau*) barge.
châle [ʃal] *nm* shawl.

chalet [ʃale] *nm* chalet.
chaleur [ʃalœr] *nf* heat; (*fig*) warmth; fire, fervor (*US*), fervour (*Brit*); heat; **en ~** (*ZOOL*) on heat.
chaleureusement [ʃalœrœ̃zmāɲ] *ad* warmly.
chaleureux, euse [ʃalœrœ̃, -ɛz] *a* warm.
challenge [ʃalāɲzh] *nm* contest, tournament.
challenger [ʃalāɲzher] *nm* (*SPORT*) challenger.
chaloupe [ʃalōōp] *nf* launch; (*de sauvetage*) lifeboat.
chalumeau, x [ʃalümō] *nm* blowtorch.
chalut [ʃalü] *nm* trawl (net); **pêcher au ~** to trawl.
chalutier [ʃalütyā] *nm* trawler; (*pêcheur*) trawlerman.
chamade [ʃamad] *nf:* **battre la ~** to beat wildly.
chamailler [ʃamāyā]: **se ~** *vi* to squabble, bicker.
chamarré, e [ʃamārā] *a* richly brocaded.
chambard [ʃāɲbár] *nm* rumpus.
chambardement [ʃāɲbárdəmāɲ] *nm:* **c'est le grand ~** everything has been (*ou* is being) turned upside down.
chambarder [ʃāɲbárdā] *vt* to turn upside down.
chamboulement [ʃāɲbōōlmāɲ] *nm* disruption.
chambouler [ʃāɲbōōlā] *vt* to disrupt, turn upside down.
chambranle [ʃāɲbrāɲl] *nm* (door) frame.
chambre [ʃāɲbr(ə)] *nf* bedroom; (*TECH*) chamber; (*POL*) chamber, house; (*JUR*) court; (*COMM*) chamber; federation; **faire ~ à part** to sleep in separate rooms; **stratège/alpiniste en ~** armchair strategist/mountaineer; **~ à un lit/deux lits** single/twin-bedded room; **~ pour une/deux personne(s)** single/double room; **~ d'accusation** court of criminal appeal; **~ d'agriculture** *body responsible for the agricultural interests of a département;* **~ à air** (*de pneu*) (inner) tube; **~ d'amis** spare *ou* guest room; **~ de combustion** combustion chamber; **~ de commerce et d'industrie (CCI)** chamber of commerce and industry; **~ à coucher** bedroom; **la C~ des députés** the Chamber of Deputies, ≈ the House of Representatives (*US*), ≈ the House (of Commons) (*Brit*); **~ forte** strongroom; **~ froide** *ou* **frigorifique** cold room; **~ à gaz** gas chamber; **~ d'hôte** ≈ bed and breakfast (*in private home*); **~ des machines** engine-room; **~ des métiers (CM)** *chamber of commerce for trades;* **~ meublée** furnished room; **~ noire** (*PHOTO*) dark room.
chambrée [ʃāɲbrā] *nf* room.
chambrer [ʃāɲbrā] *vt* (*vin*) to bring to room temperature.
chameau, x [ʃamō] *nm* camel.
chamois [ʃamwā] *nm* chamois ♦ *a:* (*couleur*) **~** fawn, buff.
champ [ʃāɲ] *nm* (*aussi INFORM*) field; (*PHOTO*): **dans le ~** in the picture; **prendre du ~** to draw back; **laisser le ~ libre à qn** to leave sb a clear field; **~ d'action** sphere of operation(s); **~ de bataille** battlefield; **~ de courses** racecourse; **~ d'honneur** field of

honor; ~ **de manœvre** (*MIL*) parade ground; ~ **de mines** minefield; ~ **de tir** shooting *ou* rifle range; ~ **visuel** field of vision.

Champagne [shânpány] *nf*: **la** ~ Champagne, the Champagne region.

champagne [shânpány] *nm* champagne.

champenois, e [shânpɔnwâ, -wáz] *a* of *ou* from Champagne; (*vin*): **méthode** ~**e** champagne-type.

champêtre [shânpεtr(ɔ)] *a* country *cpd*, rural.

champignon [shânpēnyôn] *nm* mushroom; (*terme générique*) fungus (*pl* -i); (*fam*: *accélérateur*) accelerator, gas pedal (*US*); ~ **de couche** *ou* **de Paris** button mushroom; ~ **vénéneux** toadstool, poisonous mushroom.

champion, ne [shânpyôn, -on] *a*, *nm/f* champion.

championnat [shânpyoná] *nm* championship.

chance [shâns] *nf*: **la** ~ luck; **une** ~ a stroke *ou* piece of luck *ou* good fortune; (*occasion*) a lucky break; ~**s** *nfpl* (*probabilités*) chances; **avoir de la** ~ to be lucky; **il a des** ~**s de gagner** he has a chance of winning; **il y a de fortes** ~**s pour que Paul soit malade** it's highly probable that Paul is ill; **bonne** ~! good luck!; **encore une** ~ **que tu viennes!** it's lucky you're coming; **je n'ai pas de** ~ I'm out of luck; (*toujours*) I never have any luck; **donner sa** ~ **à qn** to give sb a chance.

chancelant, e [shânslân, -ânt] *a* (*personne*) tottering; (*santé*) failing.

chanceler [shânslâ] *vi* to totter.

chancelier [shânsɔlyâ] *nm* (*allemand*) chancellor; (*d'ambassade*) secretary.

chancellerie [shânselrē] *nf* (*en France*) ministry of justice; (*en Allemagne*) chancellery; (*d'ambassade*) chancery.

chanceux, euse [shânsœ̄, -ēz] *a* lucky, fortunate.

chancre [shânkr(ɔ)] *nm* canker.

chandail [shândáy] *nm* (thick) sweater.

Chandeleur [shândlœr] *nf*: **la** ~ Candlemas.

chandelier [shândɔlyâ] *nm* candlestick; (*à plusieurs branches*) candelabra.

chandelle [shândel] *nf* (tallow) candle; (*TENNIS*): **faire une** ~ to lob; (*AVIAT*): **monter en** ~ to climb vertically; **tenir la** ~ to be the odd one out in a threesome, play gooseberry (*Brit*); **dîner aux** ~**s** candlelight dinner.

change [shânzh] *nm* (*COMM*) exchange; **opérations de** ~ (foreign) exchange transactions; **contrôle des** ~**s** exchange control; **gagner/perdre au** ~ to be better/worse off (for it); **donner le** ~ **à qn** (*fig*) to lead sb down (*US*) *ou* up (*Brit*) the garden path.

changeant, e [shânzhân, -ânt] *a* changeable, fickle.

changement [shânzhmân] *nm* change; ~ **de vitesse** (*dispositif*) gears *pl*; (*action*) gear change.

changer [shânzhâ] *vt* (*modifier*) to change, alter; (*remplacer*, *COMM*, *rhabiller*) to change ♦ *vi* to change, alter; **se** ~ to change (o.s.); ~ **de** (*remplacer: adresse, nom etc*) to change one's; (*échanger, alterner: côté, place, train etc*) to change + *npl*; ~ **d'air** to have a change of scenery *ou* air (*Brit*); ~ **de couleur/direction** to change color/direction;

~ **d'idée** to change one's mind; ~ **de place avec qn** to change places with sb; ~ **de vitesse** (*AUTO*) to change gear; ~ **qn/qch de place** to move sb/sth to another place; ~ **(de train** *etc*) to change (trains *etc*); ~ **qch en** to change sth into.

changeur [shânzhœr] *nm* (*personne*) money-changer; ~ **automatique** change machine; ~ **de disques** record changer.

chanoine [shânwán] *nm* canon.

chanson [shânsôn] *nf* song.

chansonnette [shânsonet] *nf* ditty.

chansonnier [shânsonyâ] *nm* cabaret artist (*specializing in political satire*); (*recueil*) song book.

chant [shân] *nm* song; (*art vocal*) singing; (*d'église*) hymn; (*de poème*) canto; (*TECH*): **posé de** *ou* **sur** ~ placed edgeways; ~ **de Noël** Christmas carol.

chantage [shântázh] *nm* blackmail; **faire du** ~ to use blackmail; **soumettre qn à un** ~ to blackmail sb.

chantant, e [shântân, -ânt] *a* (*accent, voix*) sing-song.

chanter [shântâ] *vt, vi* to sing; ~ **juste/faux** to sing in tune/out of tune; **si cela lui chante** (*fam*) if he feels like it *ou* fancies it (*Brit*).

chanterelle [shântrel] *nf* chanterelle (*edible mushroom*).

chanteur, euse [shântœr, -ēz] *nm/f* singer; ~ **de charme** crooner.

chantier [shântyâ] *nm* (building) site; (*sur une route*) (road) construction (*US*), roadworks *pl* (*Brit*); **mettre en** ~ to start work on; ~ **naval** shipyard.

chantilly [shântēyâ] *nf voir* **crème**.

chantonner [shântonâ] *vi, vt* to sing to oneself, hum.

chantre [shântr(ɔ)] *nm* (*fig*) eulogist.

chanvre [shânvr(ɔ)] *nm* hemp.

chaos [kâô] *nm* chaos.

chaotique [káotēk] *a* chaotic.

chap. *abr* (= *chapitre*) ch.

chapardage [shápárdázh] *nm* pilfering.

chaparder [shápárdâ] *vt* to swipe.

chapeau, x [shápō] *nm* hat; (*PRESSE*) introductory paragraph; ~! well done!; ~ **melon** derby (*US*) *ou* bowler (*Brit*) hat; ~ **mou** fedora (*US*), trilby (*Brit*); ~**x de roues** hub caps.

chapeauter [shápōtâ] *vt* (*ADMIN*) to head, oversee.

chapelain [sháplan] *nm* (*REL*) chaplain.

chapelet [sháplɛ] *nm* (*REL*) rosary; (*fig*): **un** ~ **de** a string of; **dire son** ~ to tell one's beads.

chapelier, ière [shápɔlyâ, -yer] *nm/f* hatter; milliner.

chapelle [shápel] *nf* chapel; ~ **ardente** mortuary chapel.

chapelure [sháplür] *nf* (dried) bread-crumbs *pl*.

chaperon [sháprôn] *nm* chaperon.

chaperonner [shápronâ] *vt* to chaperon.

chapiteau, x [shápētō] *nm* (*ARCHIT*) capital; (*de cirque*) big top.

chapitre [shápɛtr(ɔ)] *nm* chapter; (*fig*) subject, matter; **avoir voix au** ~ to have a say in the matter.

chapitrer [shàpētrā] *vt* to lecture, reprimand.

chapon [shàpôń] *nm* capon.

chaque [shàk] *dét* each, every; (*indéfini*) every.

char [shàr] *nm* (*à foin etc*) cart, wagon; (*de carnaval*) float; ~ **(d'assaut)** tank.

charabia [shàràbyá] *nm* (*péj*) gibberish, gobbledygook.

charade [shàràd] *nf* riddle; (*mimée*) charade.

charbon [shàrbôń] *nm* coal; ~ **de bois** charcoal.

charbonnage [shàrbonàzh] *nm*: **les ~s de France** the (French) Coal Board *sg*.

charbonnier [shàrbonyá] *nm* coalman.

charcuterie [shàrkütrē] *nf* (*magasin*) pork butcher's shop and delicatessen; (*produits*) cooked pork meats *pl*.

charcutier, ière [shàrkütyā, -ycr] *nm/f* pork butcher.

chardon [shàrdôń] *nm* thistle.

chardonneret [shàrdonre] *nm* goldfinch.

charentais, e [shàrâńtc, -ez] *a* of *ou* from Charente ♦ *nf* (*pantoufle*) slipper.

charge [shàrzh(ə)] *nf* (*fardeau*) load; (*explosif*, ÉLEC, MIL, JUR) charge; (*rôle*, *mission*) responsibility; ~s *nfpl* (*du loyer*) service charges; **à la ~ de** (*dépendant de*) dependent upon, supported by; (*aux frais de*) chargeable to, payable by; **j'accepte, à ~ de revanche** I accept, provided I can do the same for you (in return) one day; **prendre en ~** to take charge of; (*suj: véhicule*) to take on; (*dépenses*) to take care of; ~ **utile** (*AUTO*) live load; (*COMM*) payload; ~s **sociales** social security contributions.

chargé [shàrzhā] *a* (*voiture, animal, personne*) laden; (*fusil, caméra*) loaded; (*batterie*) charged; (*occupé: emploi du temps, journée*) busy, full; (*estomac*) heavy, full; (*langue*) coated (*US*), furred (*Brit*); (*décoration, style*) heavy, ornate ♦ *nm*: ~ **d'affaires** chargé d'affaires; ~ **de cours** ≈ assistant professor (*US*), ≈ lecturer (*Brit*); ~ **de** (*responsable de*) responsible for.

chargement [shàrzhəmàń] *nm* (*action*) loading; charging; (*objets*) load.

charger [shàrzhā] *vt* (*voiture, fusil, caméra, INFORM*) to load; (*batterie*) to charge ♦ *vi* (*MIL etc*) to charge; **se ~ de** *vt* to see to, take care of; ~ **qn de qch/faire qch** to give sb the responsibility for sth/of doing sth; to put sb in charge of sth/doing sth; **se ~ de faire qch** to take it upon o.s. to do sth.

chargeur [shàrzhœr] *nm* (*dispositif: d'arme à feu*) magazine; (: *PHOTO*) cartridge; ~ **de batterie** (*ÉLEC*) battery charger.

chariot [shàryō] *nm* cart (*US*), trolley (*Brit*); (*charrette*) wagon; (*de machine à écrire*) carriage; ~ **élévateur** fork-lift truck.

charisme [kàrēsm(ə)] *nm* charisma.

charitable [shàrētàbl(ə)] *a* charitable; kind.

charité [shàrētā] *nf* charity; **faire la ~** to give to charity; to do charitable works; **faire la ~ à** to give (something) to; **fête/vente de ~** fête/sale in aid of charity.

charivari [shàrēvàrē] *nm* hullabaloo.

charlatan [shàrlàtàń] *nm* charlatan.

charmant, e [shàrmàń, -àńt] *a* charming.

charme [shàrm(ə)] *nm* charm; ~s *nmpl*

(*appas*) charms; **c'est ce qui en fait le ~** that is its attraction; **faire du ~** to be charming, turn on the charm; **aller** *ou* **se porter comme un ~** to be in the pink.

charmer [shàrmā] *vt* to charm; **je suis charmé de** I'm delighted to.

charmeur, euse [shàrmœr, -ēz] *nm/f* charmer; ~ **de serpents** snake charmer.

charnel, le [shàrnel] *a* carnal.

charnier [shàrnyā] *nm* mass grave.

charnière [shàrnyer] *nf* hinge; (*fig*) turning-point.

charnu, e [shàrnü] *a* fleshy.

charogne [shàrony] *nf* carrion *q*; (*fam!*) bastard (*!*).

charolais, e [shàrole, -ez] *a* of *ou* from the Charolais.

charpente [shàrpâńt] *nf* frame(work); (*fig*) structure, framework; (*carrure*) build, frame.

charpenté, e [shàrpâńtā] *a*: **bien** *ou* **solidement ~** (*personne*) well-built; (*texte*) well-constructed.

charpenterie [shàrpâńtrē] *nf* carpentry.

charpentier [shàrpâńtyā] *nm* carpenter.

charpie [shàrpē] *nf*: **en ~** (*fig*) in shreds *ou* ribbons.

charretier [shàrtyā] *nm* carter; **de ~** (*péj*: *langage, manières*) uncouth.

charrette [shàrct] *nf* cart.

charrier [shàryā] *vt* to carry (along); to cart, carry ♦ *vi* (*fam*) to exaggerate.

charrue [shàrü] *nf* plow (*US*), plough (*Brit*).

charte [shàrt(ə)] *nf* charter.

charter [tshàrtœr] *nm* (*vol*) charter flight; (*avion*) charter plane.

chasse [shàs] *nf* hunting; (*au fusil*) shooting; (*poursuite*) chase; (*aussi*: ~ **d'eau**) flush; **la ~ est ouverte** the hunting season is open; **la ~ est fermée** it is the closed (*US*) *ou* close (*Brit*) season; **aller à la ~** to go hunting; **prendre en ~, donner la ~ à** to give chase to; **tirer la ~ (d'eau)** to flush the toilet; ~ **aérienne** aerial pursuit; ~ **à courre** hunting; ~ **à l'homme** manhunt; ~ **gardée** private hunting grounds *pl*; ~ **sous-marine** underwater fishing.

châsse [shàs] *nf* reliquary, shrine.

chassé-croisé, *pl* **chassés-croisés** [shàsākrwàzā] *nm* (*DANSE*) chassé-croisé; (*fig*) mix-up (*where people miss each other in turn*).

chasse-neige [shàsnezh] *nm inv* snowplow (*US*), snowplough (*Brit*).

chasser [shàsā] *vt* to hunt; (*expulser*) to chase away *ou* out, drive away *ou* out; (*dissiper*) to chase *ou* sweep away; to dispel, drive away.

chasseur, euse [shàscr, -ēz] *nm/f* hunter ♦ *nm* (*avion*) fighter; (*domestique*) messenger (boy); ~ **d'images** roving photographer; ~ **de têtes** (*fig*) headhunter; ~s **alpins** mountain infantry.

chassieux, euse [shàsyœ, -ēz] *a* sticky, gummy.

châssis [shàsē] *nm* (*AUTO*) chassis; (*cadre*) frame; (*de jardin*) cold frame.

chaste [shàst(ə)] *a* chaste.

chasteté [shàstətā] *nf* chastity.

chasuble [shazubl(ə)] *nf* chasuble; **robe ~**

jumper (*US*), pinafore dress (*Brit*).

chat [shà] *nm* cat; ~ **sauvage** wildcat.

châtaigne [shàteny] *nf* chestnut.

châtaignier [shàtãnyā] *nm* chestnut (tree).

châtain [shàtań] *a inv* chestnut (brown); (*personne*) chestnut-haired.

château, x [shàtō] *nm* castle; ~ **d'eau** water tower; ~ **fort** stronghold, fortified castle; ~ **de sable** sandcastle.

châtelain, e [shàtlań, -en] *nm/f* lord/lady of the manor ♦ *nf* (*ceinture*) chatelaine.

châtier [shàtyā] *vt* to punish, castigate; (*fig: style*) to polish, refine.

chatière [shàtyer] *nf* (*porte*) cat door (*US*) ou flap (*Brit*).

châtiment [shàtēmàń] *nm* punishment, castigation; ~ **corporel** corporal punishment.

chatoiement [shàtwàmàń] *nm* shimmer(ing).

chaton [shàtôń] *nm* (*ZOOL*) kitten; (*BOT*) catkin; (*de bague*) bezel; stone.

chatouiller [shàtōōyā] *vt* to tickle; (*l'odorat, le palais*) to titillate.

chatouilleux, euse [shàtōōyœ, -œz] *a* ticklish; (*fig*) touchy, over-sensitive.

chatoyant, e [shàtwàyàń, -àńt] *a* (*reflet, étoffe*) shimmering; (*couleurs*) sparkling.

chatoyer [shàtwàyā] *vi* to shimmer.

châtrer [shàtrā] *vt* (*mâle*) to castrate; (*femelle*) to spay; (*cheval*) to geld; (*chat, chien*) to fix (*US*), doctor (*Brit*); (*fig*) to mutilate.

chatte [shàt] *nf* (she-)cat.

chatterton [shàtertoń] *nm* (*ruban isolant*: *ÉLEC*) (adhesive) insulating tape.

chaud, e [shō, -ōd] *a* (*gén*) warm; (*très chaud*) hot; (*fig: félicitations*) hearty; (*discussion*) heated; **il fait ~** it's warm; it's hot; **manger ~** to have something hot to eat; **avoir ~** to be warm; to be hot; **tenir ~** to keep hot; **ça me tient ~** it keeps me warm; **tenir au ~** to keep in a warm place; **rester au ~** to stay where it's warm.

chaudement [shōdmàń] *ad* warmly; (*fig*) hotly.

chaudière [shōdyer] *nf* boiler.

chaudron [shōdróń] *nm* cauldron.

chaudronnerie [shōdronrē] *nf* (*usine*) boiler-works; (*activité*) boilermaking; (*boutique*) coppersmith's workshop.

chauffage [shōfàzh] *nm* heating; ~ **au gaz/à l'électricité** gas/electric heating; ~ **au charbon** heating with coal (*US*), solid fuel heating (*Brit*); ~ **central** central heating; ~ **par le sol** underfloor heating.

chauffagiste [shōfàzhēst(ə)] *nm* (*installateur*) heating specialist (*US*) ou engineer (*Brit*).

chauffant, e [shōfàń, -àńt] *a*: **couverture ~e** electric blanket; **plaque ~e** hotplate.

chauffard [shōfàr] *nm* (*péj*) reckless driver; roadhog; (*après un accident*) hit-and-run driver.

chauffe-bain [shōfbàń] *nm* = **chauffe-eau**.

chauffe-biberon [shōfbēbrôń] *nm* (baby's) bottle warmer.

chauffe-eau [shōfō] *nm inv* water heater.

chauffe-plats [shōfplà] *nm inv* dish warmer.

chauffer [shōfā] *vt* to heat ♦ *vi* to heat up, warm up; (*trop chauffer: moteur*) to overheat; **se ~** (*se mettre en train*) to warm up;

(*au soleil*) to warm o.s.

chaufferie [shōfrē] *nf* boiler room.

chauffeur [shōfœr] *nm* driver; (*privé*) chauffeur; **voiture avec/sans ~** chauffeur-driven/self-drive car.

chauffeuse [shōfœz] *nf* fireside chair.

chauler [shōlā] *vt* (*mur*) to whitewash.

chaume [shōm] *nm* (*du toit*) thatch; (*tiges*) stubble.

chaumière [shōmyer] *nf* (thatched) cottage.

chaussée [shōsā] *nf* road(way); (*digue*) causeway.

chausse-pied [shōspyā] *nm* shoe-horn.

chausser [shōsā] *vt* (*bottes, skis*) to put on; (*enfant*) to put shoes on; (*suj: soulier*) to fit; ~ **du 38/42** to take size 38/42; ~ **grand** to be too big; ~ **bien** to fit well; **se ~** to put one's shoes on.

chausse-trappe [shōstràp] *nf* trap.

chaussette [shōset] *nf* sock.

chausseur [shōsœr] *nm* (*marchand*) footwear specialist, shoemaker.

chausson [shōsôń] *nm* slipper; (*de bébé*) bootee; ~ **(aux pommes)** (apple) turnover.

chaussure [shōsür] *nf* shoe; (*commerce*): **la** ~ the shoe industry ou trade; **~s basses** flat shoes; **~s montantes** ankle boots; **~s de ski** ski boots.

chaut [shō] *vb*: **peu me ~** it matters little to me.

chauve [shōv] *a* bald.

chauve-souris, *pl* **chauves-souris** [shōvsōōrē] *nf* bat.

chauvin, e [shōvań, -ēn] *a* chauvinistic; jingoistic.

chauvinisme [shōvēnēsm(ə)] *nm* chauvinism; jingoism.

chaux [shō] *nf* lime; **blanchi à la ~** whitewashed.

chavirer [shàvērā] *vi* to capsize, overturn.

chef [shef] *nm* head, leader; (*patron*) boss; (*de cuisine*) chef; **au premier ~** extremely, to the nth degree; **de son propre ~** on his ou her own initiative; **général en ~** general (*US*), general-in-chief (*Brit*); **commandant en ~** commander-in-chief; ~ **d'accusation** (*JUR*) charge, count (of indictment); ~ **d'atelier** (*shop*) foreman; ~ **de bureau** head of department; ~ **d'entreprise** company manager (*US*) ou head (*Brit*); ~ **d'équipe** team leader; ~ **d'état** head of state; ~ **de famille** head of the family; ~ **de file** (*de parti etc*) leader; ~ **de gare** station master; ~ **d'orchestre** conductor; ~ **de rayon** department(al) supervisor; ~ **de service** departmental head.

chef-d'œuvre, *pl* **chefs-d'œuvre** [shedœvr(ə)] *nm* masterpiece.

chef-lieu, *pl* **chefs-lieux** [sheflyœ] *nm* county seat.

cheftaine [sheften] *nf* girl scout troop leader (*US*), (*guide*) captain (*Brit*).

cheik [shek] *nm* sheik.

chemin [shəmań] *nm* path; (*itinéraire, direction, trajet*) way; **en ~, ~ faisant** on the way; ~ **de fer** railroad (*US*), railway (*Brit*); **par ~ de fer** by rail; **les ~s de fer** the railroad (*US*), the railways (*Brit*); ~ **de terre** dirt road.

cheminée [shəmēnā] *nf* chimney; (*à l'intérieur*) chimney piece, fireplace; (*de bateau*) funnel.
cheminement [shəmēnmáṅ] *nm* progress; course.
cheminer [shəmēnā] *vi* to walk (along).
cheminot [shəmēnō] *nm* railroad worker (*US*), railwayman (*Brit*).
chemise [shəmēz] *nf* shirt; (*dossier*) folder; ~ **de nuit** nightgown (*US*), nightdress (*Brit*).
chemiserie [shəmēzrē] *nf* men's shop, (gentlemen's) outfitters' (*Brit*).
chemisette [shəmēzet] *nf* short-sleeved shirt.
chemisier [shəmēzyā] *nm* blouse.
chenal, aux [shənál, -ō] *nm* channel.
chenapan [shənápáṅ] *nm* (*garnement*) rascal; (*péj: vaurien*) rogue.
chêne [shen] *nm* oak (tree); (*bois*) oak.
chenet [shəne] *nm* fire-dog, andiron.
chenil [shənēl] *nm* kennels *pl*.
chenille [shənēy] *nf* (*ZOOL*) caterpillar; (*AUTO*) caterpillar track; **véhicule à ~s** caterpillar (*vehicle*).
chenillette [shənēyet] *nf* caterpillar (*vehicle*).
cheptel [sheptel] *nm* livestock.
chèque [shek] *nm* check (*US*), cheque (*Brit*); **faire/toucher un ~** to write/cash a check; **par ~** by check; ~ **barré** check marked "for deposit only" (*US*), crossed cheque (*Brit*); ~ **sans provision** bad check; ~ **en blanc** blank check; ~ **au porteur** bearer check; ~ **postal** post office check, ~ **de voyage** traveler's check.
chèque-cadeau, *pl* **chèques-cadeaux** [shekkàdō] *nm* gift certificate (*US*) *ou* token (*Brit*).
chèque-repas, *pl* **chèques-repas** [shekrəpâ], **chèque-restaurant,** *pl* **chèques-restaurant** [shekrestoráṅ] *nm* ≈ luncheon voucher.
chéquier [shākyā] *nm* check book (*US*), cheque book (*Brit*).
cher, ère *a* (*aimé*) dear; (*coûteux*) expensive, dear ♦ *ad*: **coûter/payer ~** to cost/pay a lot; **cela coûte ~** it's expensive, it costs a lot of money ♦ *nf*: **la bonne chère** good food; **mon ~, ma chère** my dear.
chercher [shershā] *vt* to look for; (*gloire etc*) to seek; (*INFORM*) to search; ~ **des ennuis/la bagarre** to be looking for trouble/a fight; **aller ~** to go for, go and get; ~ **à faire** to try to do.
chercheur, euse [shershœr, -œz] *nm/f* researcher, research worker; ~ **de** seeker of; hunter of; ~ **d'or** gold digger.
chère [sher] *af*, *nf voir* **cher**.
chèrement [shermáṅ] *ad* dearly.
chéri, e [shārē] *a* beloved, dear; (**mon**) ~ darling.
chérir [shārēr] *vt* to cherish.
cherté [shertā] *nf*: **la ~ de la vie** the high cost of living.
chérubin [shārūbaṅ] *nm* cherub.
chétif, ive [shātēf, -ēv] *a* puny, stunted.
cheval, aux [shəvál, -ō] *nm* horse; (*AUTO*): ~ **(vapeur) (CV)** horsepower *q*; **50 chevaux (au frein)** 50 brake horsepower, 50 b.h.p.; **10 chevaux (fiscaux)** 10 horsepower (*for tax purposes*); **faire du ~** to go (horseback) riding; **à ~** on horseback; **à ~ sur** astride,

straddling; (*fig*) overlapping; ~ **d'arçons** pommel (*US*) *ou* vaulting (*Brit*) horse; ~ **à bascule** rocking horse; ~ **de bataille** charger; (*fig*) hobby-horse; ~ **de course** race horse; **chevaux de bois** (*des manèges*) wooden (fairground) horses; (*manège*) merry-go-round.
chevaleresque [shəválrɛsk(ə)] *a* chivalrous.
chevalerie [shəválrē] *nf* chivalry; knighthood.
chevalet [shəvále] *nm* easel.
chevalier [shəvályā] *nm* knight; ~ **servant** escort.
chevalière [shəvályer] *nf* signet ring.
chevalin, e [shəválaṅ, -ēn] *a* of horses, equine; (*péj*) horsy; **boucherie ~e** horse-meat butcher's.
cheval-vapeur, *pl* **chevaux-vapeur** [shəválvápœr, shəvō-] *nm voir* **cheval**.
chevauchée [shəvōshā] *nf* ride; cavalcade.
chevauchement [shəvōshmáṅ] *nm* overlap.
chevaucher [shəvōshā] *vi* (*aussi*: **se ~**) to overlap (each other) ♦ *vt* to be astride, straddle.
chevaux [shəvō] *nmpl voir* **cheval**.
chevelu, e [shəvlü] *a* with a good head of hair, hairy (*péj*).
chevelure [shəvlür] *nf* hair *q*.
chevet [shəve] *nm*: **au ~ de qn** at sb's bedside; **lampe de ~** bedside lamp.
cheveu, x [shəvœ] *nm* hair ♦ *nmpl* (*chevelure*) hair *sg*; **avoir les ~x courts/en brosse** to have short hair/a crew cut; **se faire couper les ~x** to get *ou* have one's hair cut; **tiré par les ~x** (*histoire*) far-fetched.
cheville [shəvēy] *nf* (*ANAT*) ankle; (*de bois*) peg; (*pour enfoncer une vis*) plug; **être en ~ avec qn** to be in cahoots with sb; ~ **ouvrière** (*fig*) kingpin.
chèvre [shevr(ə)] *nf* (she-)goat; **ménager la ~ et le chou** to try to please everyone.
chevreau, x [shəvrō] *nm* kid.
chèvrefeuille [shəvrəfœy] *nm* honeysuckle.
chevreuil [shəvrœy] *nm* roe deer *inv*; (*CULIN*) venison.
chevron [shəvróṅ] *nm* (*poutre*) rafter; (*motif*) chevron, v(-shape); **à ~s** chevron-patterned; (*petits*) herringbone.
chevronné, e [shəvronā] *a* seasoned, experienced.
chevrotant, e [shəvrotáṅ, -áṅt] *a* quavering.
chevroter [shəvrotā] *vi* (*personne, voix*) to quaver.
chevrotine [shəvrotēn] *nf* buckshot *q*.
chewing-gum [shwēṅgom] *nm* chewing gum.
chez [shā] *prép* (*à la demeure de*): ~ **qn** at (*ou* to) sb's house *ou* place; (*parmi*) among; ~ **moi** at home; (*avec direction*) home; ~ **le boulanger** (*à la boulangerie*) at the baker's; ~ **les Français** (*dans leur caractère*) among the French; ~ **ce musicien/poète** (*dans ses œuvres*) in this musician/poet.
chez-soi [shāswá] *nm inv* home.
Chf. cent. *abr* (= *chauffage central*) c.h.
chic [shēk] *a inv* chic, smart; (*généreux*) nice, decent ♦ *nm* stylishness; **avoir le ~ de** *ou* **pour** to have the knack of *ou* for; **de ~** *ad* off the cuff; ~**!** great!, terrific!
chicane [shēkán] *nf* (*obstacle*) zigzag; (*querelle*) squabble.

chicaner [shēkánā] *vi* (*ergoter*): ~ **sur** to quibble about.

chiche [shēsh] *a* (*mesquin*) niggardly, mean; (*pauvre*) meager (*US*), meagre (*Brit*) ♦ *excl* (*en réponse à un défi*) you're on!; **tu n'es pas ~ de lui parler!** you wouldn't (dare) speak to her!

chichement [shēshmáṅ] *ad* (*pauvrement*) meagerly (*US*), meagrely (*Brit*); (*mesquinement*) meanly.

chichi [shēshē] *nm* (*fam*) fuss; **faire des ~s** to make a fuss.

chicorée [shēkorā] *nf* (*café*) chicory; (*salade*) endive; ~ **frisée** curly endive.

chicot [shēkō] *nm* stump.

chien [shyaṅ] *nm* dog; (*de pistolet*) hammer; **temps de ~** rotten weather; **vie de ~** dog's life; **couché en ~ de fusil** curled up; ~ **d'aveugle** guide dog; ~ **de chasse** gun dog; ~ **de garde** guard dog; ~ **policier** police dog; ~ **de race** pedigree dog; ~ **de traîneau** husky.

chiendent [shyaṅdáṅ] *nm* couch grass.

chien-loup, *pl* **chiens-loups** [shyaṅlōō] *nm* wolfhound.

chienne [shyen] *nf* (she-)dog, bitch.

chier [shyā] *vi* (*fam!*) to crap (!), shit (!); **faire ~ qn** (*importuner*) to bug sb; (*causer des ennuis à*) to piss sb off (*US!*) *ou* around (*Brit!*); **se faire ~** (*s'ennuyer*) to be bored stiff.

chiffe [shēf] *nf*: **il est mou comme une ~, c'est une ~ molle** he's spineless.

chiffon [shēfóṅ] *nm* (piece of) rag.

chiffonné, e [shēfonā] *a* (*fatigué: visage*) worn-looking.

chiffonner [shēfonā] *vt* to crumple, crease; (*tracasser*) to concern.

chiffonnier [shēfonyā] *nm* ragman; (*meuble*) chiffonier.

chiffrable [shēfrábl(ə)] *a* numerable.

chiffre [shētr(ə)] *nm* (*représentant un nombre*) figure; numeral; (*montant, total*) total, sum; (*d'un code*) code, cipher; **~s romains/arabes** roman/arabic numerals; **en ~s ronds** in round figures; **écrire un nombre en ~s** to write a number in figures; **~ d'affaires (CA)** turnover; **~ de ventes** sales figures.

chiffrer [shēfrā] *vt* (*dépense*) to put a figure to, assess; (*message*) to (en)code, cipher ♦ *vi*: **~ à, se ~ à** to add up to.

chignole [shēnyol] *nf* drill.

chignon [shēnyóṅ] *nm* chignon, bun.

Chili [shēlē] *nm*: **le ~** Chile.

chilien, ne [shēlyaṅ, -en] *a* Chilean ♦ *nm/f*: **C~, ne** Chilean.

chimère [shēmer] *nf* (wild) dream; pipe dream, idle fancy.

chimérique [shēmārēk] *a* (*utopique*) fanciful.

chimie [shēmē] *nf* chemistry.

chimio [shēmyo], **chimiothérapie** [shēmyotárápē] *nf* chemotherapy.

chimique [shēmēk] *a* chemical; **produits ~s** chemicals.

chimiste [shēmēst(ə)] *nm/f* chemist.

chinchilla [shaṅshēlá] *nm* chinchilla.

Chine [shēn] *nf*: **la ~** China; **la ~ libre, la république de ~** the Republic of China, Nationalist China (*Taiwan*).

chine [shēn] *nm* rice paper; (*porcelaine*) china (vase).

chiné, e [shēnā] *a* flecked.

chinois, e [shēnwá, -wáz] *a* Chinese; (*fig: péj*) persnickety, fussy ♦ *nm* (*LING*) Chinese ♦ *nm/f*: **C~, e** Chinese.

chinoiserie(s) [shēnwázrē] *nf(pl)* (*péj*) red tape, fuss.

chiot [shyō] *nm* pup(py).

chiper [shēpā] *vt* (*fam*) to swipe.

chipie [shēpē] *nf* shrew.

chipolata [shēpolátá] *nf* chipolata.

chipoter [shēpotā] *vi* (*manger*) to nibble; (*ergoter*) to quibble, haggle.

chips [shēps] *nfpl* (*aussi*: **pommes ~**) (potato) chips (*US*), crisps (*Brit*).

chique [shēk] *nf* quid, chew.

chiquenaude [shēknōd] *nf* flick, flip.

chiquer [shēkā] *vi* to chew tobacco.

chiromancie [kēromáṅsē] *nf* palmistry.

chiromancien, ne [kēromáṅsyaṅ, -en] *nm/f* palmist.

chiropracteur [kēropráktœr] *nm*, **chiropracticien, ne** [kēropráktēsyaṅ, -en] *nm/f* chiropractor.

chirurgical, e, aux [shērürzhēkál, -ō] *a* surgical.

chirurgie [shērürzhē] *nf* surgery; **~ esthétique** cosmetic *ou* plastic surgery.

chirurgien [shērürzhyaṅ] *nm* surgeon; **~ dentiste** dental surgeon.

chiure [shyür] *nf*: **~s de mouche** fly specks.

ch.-l. *abr* = **chef-lieu**.

chlore [klor] *nm* chlorine.

chloroforme [kloroform(ə)] *nm* chloroform.

chlorophylle [klorofēl] *nf* chlorophyll.

chlorure [kloṙür] *nm* chloride.

choc [shok] *nm* impact; shock; crash; (*moral*) shock; (*affrontement*) clash ♦ *a*: **prix ~** amazing *ou* incredible price/prices; **de ~** (*troupe, traitement*) shock *cpd*; (*patron etc*) high-powered; **~ opératoire/nerveux** post-operative/nervous shock; **~ en retour** return shock; (*fig*) backlash.

chocolat [shokolá] *nm* chocolate; (*boisson*) (hot) chocolate; **~ à cuire** cooking chocolate; **~ au lait** milk chocolate; **~ en poudre** drrrinking chocolate.

chocolaté, e [shokolátā] *a* chocolate *cpd*, chocolate-flavoured.

chocolaterie [shokolátrē] *nf* (*fabrique*) chocolate factory.

chocolatier, ière [shokolátyā, -yer] *nm/f* chocolate maker.

chœur [kœr] *nm* (*chorale*) choir; (*OPÉRA, THÉÂTRE*) chorus; (*ARCHIT*) choir, chancel; **en ~** in chorus.

choir [shwár] *vi* to fall.

choisi, e [shwázē] *a* (*de premier choix*) carefully chosen; select; **textes ~s** selected writings.

choisir [shwázēr] *vt* to choose, select; **~ de faire qch** to choose *ou* opt to do sth.

choix [shwá] *nm* choice; selection; **avoir le ~** to have the choice; **je n'avais pas le ~** I had no choice; **de premier ~** (*COMM*) class *ou* grade one; **de ~** choice *cpd*, selected; **au ~** as you wish *ou* prefer; **de mon/son ~** of my/his *ou* her choosing.

choléra [kolãrá] *nm* cholera.

cholestérol [kolestãrol] *nm* cholesterol.

chômage [shōmázh] *nm* unemployment; **mettre au** ~ to make redundant, put out of work; **être au** ~ to be unemployed *ou* out of work; ~ **partiel** short-time working; ~ **structurel** structural unemployment; ~ **technique** lay-offs *pl.*

chômer [shōmã] *vi* to be unemployed, be idle; **jour chômé** public holiday.

chômeur, euse [shōmœr, -œz] *nm/f* unemployed person, person out of work.

chope [shop] *nf* tankard.

choquant, e [shokáň, -áňt] *a* shocking.

choquer [shokã] *vt (offenser)* to shock; *(commotionner)* to shake (up).

choral, e [korál] *a* choral ♦ *nf* choral society, choir.

chorégraphe [korãgráf] *nm/f* choreographer.

chorégraphie [korãgráfē] *nf* choreography.

choriste [korēst(ə)] *nm/f* choir member; *(OPÉRA)* chorus member.

chorus [korüs] *nm*: **faire** ~ **(avec)** to voice one's agreement (with).

chose [shōz] *nf* thing ♦ *nm (fam: machin)* thingamajig ♦ *a inv:* **être/se sentir tout** ~ *(bizarre)* to be/feel a bit odd; *(malade)* to be/feel out of sorts; **dire bien des** ~**s à qn** to give sb's regards to sb; **parler de** ~**(s) et d'autre(s)** to talk about one thing and another; **c'est peu de** ~ it's nothing much.

chou, x [shoō] *nm* cabbage ♦ *a inv* cute; **mon petit** ~ (my) sweetheart; **faire** ~ **blanc** to draw a blank; **feuille de** ~ *(fig: journal)* rag; ~ **à la crème** cream puff *(made of choux pastry)*; ~ **de Bruxelles** Brussels sprout.

choucas [shoōká] *nm* jackdaw.

chouchou, te [shoōshoō, -oōt] *nm/f (SCOL)* teacher's pet.

chouchouter [shoōshoōtã] *vt* to pet.

choucroute [shoōkroōt] *nf* sauerkraut; ~ **garnie** sauerkraut with cooked meats and potatoes.

chouette [shwet] *nf* owl ♦ *a (fam)* great, neat *(US)*.

chou-fleur, *pl* choux-fleurs [shoōflœr] *nm* cauliflower.

chou-rave, *pl* choux-raves [shoōráv] *nm* kohlrabi.

choyer [shwáyã] *vt* to cherish; to pamper.

CHR *sigle m* = *Centre hospitalier régional.*

chrétien, ne [krãtyaň, -en] *a, nm/f* Christian.

chrétiennement [krãtyenmáň] *ad* in a Christian way *ou* spirit.

chrétienté [krãtyaňtã] *nf* Christendom.

Christ [krēst] *nm*: **le** ~ Christ; **c~** *(crucifix etc)* figure of Christ; **Jésus** ~ Jesus Christ.

christianiser [krēstyánězã] *vt* to convert to Christianity.

christianisme [krēstyáněsm(ə)] *nm* Christianity.

Christmas [krēstmás] *nf*: **(l'île)** ~ Christmas Island.

chromatique [kromátēk] *a* chromatic.

chrome [krōm] *nm* chromium; *(revêtement)* chrome, chromium.

chromé, e [krōmã] *a* chrome-plated,

chromium-plated.

chromosome [kromōzōm] *nm* chromosome.

chronique [kronēk] *a* chronic ♦ *nf (de journal)* column, page; *(historique)* chronicle; *(RADIO, TV)*: **la** ~ **sportive/ théâtrale** the sports/theater review; **la** ~ **locale** local news and gossip.

chroniqueur [kronēkœr] *nm* columnist; chronicler.

chronologie [kronolozhē] *nf* chronology.

chronologique [kronolozhēk] *a* chronological.

chronomètre [kronometr(ə)] *nm* stopwatch.

chronométrer [kronomãtrã] *vt* to time.

chronométreur [kronomãtrœr] *nm* time-keeper.

chrysalide [krēzálēd] *nf* chrysalis.

chrysanthème [krēzáňtem] *nm* chrysan-themum.

CHU *sigle m* (= *Centre hospitalo-universitaire)* ≃ *(teaching)* hospital.

chu, e [shü] *pp de* **choir.**

chuchotement [shüshotmáň] *nm* whisper.

chuchoter [shüshotã] *vt, vi* to whisper.

chuintement [shüáňtmáň] *nm* hiss.

chuinter [shüáňtã] *vi* to hiss.

chut *excl* [shüt] ♦ *vb* [shü] *voir* **choir.**

chute [shüt] *nf* fall; *(de bois, papier: déchet)* scrap; **la** ~ **des cheveux** hair loss; **faire une** ~ **(de 10 m)** to fall (10 m); ~**s de pluie/ neige** rain/snowfalls; ~ **(d'eau)** waterfall; ~ **du jour** nightfall; ~ **libre** free fall; ~ **des reins** small of the back.

Chypre [shēpr] *nm.* **le** ~ Cyprus.

chypriote [shēprēot] *a, nm/f* = **cypriote.**

CIA *sigle f* CIA.

cial *abr* = **commercial.**

ciao [tshãō] *excl (fam)* (bye-)bye.

ci-après [sēapre] *ad* hereafter.

cibiste [sēbēst(ə)] *nm* CB enthusiast.

cible [sēbl(ə)] *nf* target.

cibler [sēblã] *vt* to target.

ciboire [sēbwár] *nm* ciborium *(vessel).*

ciboule [sēboōl] *nf* (large) chive.

ciboulette [sēboōlet] *nf* (small) chive.

cicatrice [sēkátrēs] *nf* scar.

cicatriser [sēkátrēzã] *vt* to heal; **se** ~ to heal (up), form a scar.

ci-contre [sēkôntr(ə)] *ad* opposite.

ci-dessous [sēdəsoō] *ad* below.

ci-dessus [sēdəsü] *ad* above.

ci-devant [sēdəváň] *nm/f inv* aristocrat who lost his/her title in the French Revolution.

CIDEX *sigle m* (= *Courrier individuel à distribution exceptionnelle)* system which groups mailboxes in country areas, rather than each house having its mailbox at its front door.

CIDJ *sigle m* (= *Centre d'information et de documentation de la jeunesse)* careers advisory service.

cidre [sēdr(ə)] *nm* cider.

CIDUNATI [sēdünátā] *sigle m* (= *Comité inter-professionnel de défense de l'union nationale des artisans et travailleurs indépendants)* union of self-employed craftsmen.

Cie *abr* (= *compagnie)* Co.

ciel [syel] *nm* sky; *(REL)* heaven; ~**s** *nmpl (PEINTURE etc)* skies; **cieux** *nmpl* sky *sg*, skies; *(REL)* heaven *sg*; **à** ~ **ouvert** open-air;

(*mine*) opencut (*US*), opencast (*Brit*); **tomber du** ~ (*arriver à l'improviste*) to appear out of the blue; (*être stupéfait*) to be unable to believe one's eyes; **C~!** good heavens!; ~ **de lit** canopy.

cierge [syɛrzh(ə)] *nm* candle; ~ **pascal** Easter candle.

cieux [syœ] *nmpl voir* ciel.

cigale [sɛgál] *nf* cicada.

cigare [sɛgár] *nm* cigar.

cigarette [sɛgáret] *nf* cigarette; ~ **(à) bout filtre** filter cigarette.

ci-git [sɛzhɛ] *ad* here lies.

cigogne [sɛgony] *nf* stork.

ciguë [sɛgü] *nf* hemlock.

ci-inclus, e [sɛánklü, -üz] *a, ad* enclosed.

ci-joint, e [sɛzhwaṅ, -áṅt] *a, ad* enclosed; **veuillez trouver** ~ please find enclosed.

cil [sɛl] *nm* (eye)lash.

ciller [sɛyá] *vi* to blink.

cimaise [sɛmez] *nf* picture rail.

cime [sɛm] *nf* top; (*montagne*) peak.

ciment [sɛmáṅ] *nm* cement; ~ **armé** reinforced concrete.

cimenter [sɛmáṅtá] *vt* to cement.

cimenterie [sɛmáṅtrɛ] *nf* cement works *sg*.

cimetière [sɛmtyer] *nm* cemetery; (*d'église*) churchyard; ~ **de voitures** junkyard.

cinéaste [sɛnáást(ə)] *nm/f* film-maker.

ciné-club [sɛnáklœb] *nm* film club; film society.

cinéma [sɛnámá] *nm* cinema; **aller au** ~ to go to the cinema *ou* movies; ~ **d'animation** cartoon (film).

cinémascope [sɛnámáskop] *nm* ® Cinemascope ®.

cinémathèque [sɛnámátek] *nf* film archives *pl ou* library.

cinématographie [sɛnámátográfɛ] *nf* cinematography.

cinématographique [sɛnámátográfɛk] *a* film *cpd*, cinema *cpd*.

cinéphile [sɛnáfɛl] *nm/f* film buff.

cinérama [sɛnárámá] *nm* ®: **en** ~ in Cinerama ®.

cinétique [sɛnátɛk] *a* kinetic.

cing(h)alais, e [sáṅgálc, -ez] *a* Sin(g)halese.

cinglant, e [sáṅgláṅ, -áṅt] *a* (*propos, ironie*) scathing, biting; (*échec*) crushing.

cinglé, e [sáṅglá] *a* (*fam*) crazy.

cingler [sáṅglá] *vt* to lash; (*fig*) to sting ♦ *vi* (*NAVIG*): ~ **vers** to make *ou* head for.

cinq [sáṅk] *num* five.

cinquantaine [sáṅkáṅten] *nf*: **une** ~ **(de)** about fifty; **avoir la** ~ (*âge*) to be around fifty.

cinquante [sáṅkáṅt] *num* fifty.

cinquantenaire [sáṅkáṅtner] *a, nm/f* fifty-year-old.

cinquantième [sáṅkáṅtyem] *num* fiftieth.

cinquième [sáṅkyem] *num* fifth.

cinquièmement [sáṅkyemmáṅ] *ad* fifthly.

cintre [sáṅtr(ə)] *nm* coat-hanger; (*ARCHIT*) arch; **plein** ~ semicircular arch.

cintré, e [sáṅtrá] *a* curved; (*chemise*) fitted, slim-fitting.

CIO *sigle m* (= *Comité international olympique*) IOC (= *International Olympic Committee*).

cirage [sɛrázh] *nm* (shoe) polish.

circoncis, e [sɛrkóṅsɛ, -ɛz] *a* circumcised.

circoncision [sɛrkóṅsɛzyóṅ] *nf* circumcision.

circonférence [sɛrkóṅfáráṅs] *nf* circumference.

circonflexe [sɛrkóṅfleks(ə)] *a*: **accent** ~ circumflex accent.

circonscription [sɛrkóṅskrɛpsyóṅ] *nf* district; ~ **électorale** (*d'un député*) constituency; ~ **militaire** military area.

circonscrire [sɛrkóṅskrɛr] *vt* to define, delimit; (*incendie*) to contain; (*propriété*) to mark out; (*sujet*) to define.

circonspect, e [sɛrkóṅspekt] *a* circumspect, cautious.

circonspection [sɛrkóṅspeksyóṅ] *nf* circumspection, caution.

circonstance [sɛrkóṅstáṅs] *nf* circumstance; (*occasion*) occasion; **œuvre de** ~ occasional work; **air de** ~ fitting air; **tête de** ~ appropriate demeanor (*US*) *ou* demeanour (*Brit*); **~s atténuantes** mitigating circumstances.

circonstancié, e [sɛrkóṅstáṅsyá] *a* detailed.

circonstanciel, le [sɛrkóṅstáṅsyel] *a*: **complément/proposition** ~(**le**) adverbial phrase/clause.

circonvenir [sɛrkóṅvnɛr] *vt* to circumvent.

circonvolutions [sɛrkóṅvolüsyóṅ] *nfpl* twists, convolutions.

circuit [sɛrküɛ] *nm* (*trajet*) tour, (round) trip; (*ÉLEC, TECH*) circuit; ~ **automobile** motor circuit; ~ **de distribution** distribution network; ~ **fermé** closed circuit; ~ **intégré** integrated circuit.

circulaire [sɛrküler] *a, nf* circular.

circulation [sɛrkulásyóṅ] *nf* circulation; (*AUTO*): **la** ~ (the) traffic; **bonne/mauvaise** ~ good/bad circulation; **mettre en** ~ to put into circulation.

circulatoire [sɛrkülátwár] *a*: **avoir des troubles ~s** to have problems with one's circulation.

circuler [sɛrkülá] *vi* to drive (along); to walk along; (*train etc*) to run; (*sang, devises*) to circulate; **faire** ~ (*nouvelle*) to spread (around), circulate; (*badauds*) to move on.

cire [sɛr] *nf* wax; ~ **à cacheter** sealing wax.

ciré [sɛrá] *nm* oilskin.

cirer [sɛrá] *vt* to wax, polish.

cireur [sɛrœr] *nm* shoeshine-boy.

cireuse [sɛrœz] *nf* floor polisher.

cireux, euse [sɛrœ, -œz] *a* (*fig: teint*) sallow, waxen.

cirque [sɛrk(ə)] *nm* circus; (*arène*) amphitheater (*US*), amphitheatre (*Brit*); (*GÉO*) cirque; (*fig: désordre*) chaos, bedlam; (*: chichis*) fuss.

cirrhose [sɛróz] *nf*: ~ **du foie** cirrhosis of the liver.

cisailler [sɛzâyá] *vt* to clip.

cisaille(s) [sɛzây] *nf(pl)* (gardening) shears *pl*.

ciseau, x [sɛzó] *nm*: ~ **(à bois)** chisel ♦ *nmpl* (pair of) scissors; **sauter en ~x** to do a scissors jump; ~ **à froid** cold chisel.

ciseler [sɛzlá] *vt* to chisel, carve.

ciselure [sɛzlür] *nf* engraving; (*bois*) carving.

Cisjordanie [sɛszhordánɛ] *nf*: **la** ~ the West Bank (of Jordan).

citadelle [sētádel] *nf* citadel.

citadin, e [sētádaṅ, -ēn] *nm/f* city dweller ♦ *a* town *cpd*, city *cpd*, urban.

citation [sētâsyóṅ] *nf* (*d'auteur*) quotation; (*JUR*) summons *sg*; (*MIL*: *récompense*) citation (*US*), mention (*Brit*).

cité [sētā] *nf* town; (*plus grande*) city; ~ **ouvrière** (*workers'*) housing development; ~ **universitaire** students' residences *pl*.

cité-dortoir, *pl* **cités-dortoirs** [sētādortwár] *nf* bedroom community (*US*), dormitory town (*Brit*).

cité-jardin, *pl* **cités-jardins** [sētāzhárdaṅ] *nf* garden city.

citer [sētā] *vt* (*un auteur*) to quote (from); (*nommer*) to name; (*JUR*) to summon; ~ **(en exemple)** (*personne*) to hold up (as an example); **je ne veux** ~ **personne** I don't want to name names.

citerne [sētcrn(ə)] *nf* tank.

cithare [sētár] *nf* zither.

citoyen, ne [sētwáyaṅ, -en] *nm/f* citizen.

citoyenneté [sētwáyentā] *nf* citizenship.

citrique [sētrēk] *a*: **acide** ~ citric acid.

citron [sētróṅ] *nm* lemon; ~ **pressé** (fresh) lemon juice; ~ **vert** lime.

citronnade [sētronád] *nf* lemonade.

citronné, e [sētronā] *a* (*boisson*) lemon-flavored (*US*) *ou* -flavoured (*Brit*); (*eau de toilette*) lemon-scented.

citronnier [sētronyā] *nm* lemon tree.

citrouille [sētrōōy] *nf* pumpkin.

cive(s) [sēv] *nf(pl)* (*BOT*) chive(s), (*CULIN*) chives.

civet [sēvc] *nm* stew; ~ **de lièvre** ≈ rabbit stew, jugged hare (*Brit*).

civette [sēvet] *nf* (*BOT*) chives *pl*; (*ZOOL*) civet (cat).

civière [sēvyer] *nf* stretcher.

civil, e [sēvēl] *a* (*JUR, ADMIN, poli*) civil; (*non militaire*) civilian ♦ *nm* civilian; **en** ~ in civilian clothes; **dans le** ~ in civilian life.

civilement [sēvēlmáṅ] *ad* (*poliment*) civilly; **se marier** ~ to have a civil wedding.

civilisation [sēvēlēzásyóṅ] *nf* civilization.

civilisé, e [sēvēlēzā] *a* civilized.

civiliser [sēvēlēzā] *vt* to civilize.

civilité [sēvēlētā] *nf* civility; **présenter ses ~s** to present one's compliments.

civique [sēvēk] *a* civic; **instruction** ~ (*SCOL*) civics *sg*.

civisme [sēvēsm(ə)] *nm* public-spiritedness.

cl. *abr* (= *centilitre*) cl.

clafoutis [kláfōōtē] *nm* batter pudding (*containing fruit*).

claie [kle] *nf* grid, riddle.

clair, e [kler] *a* light; (*chambre*) light, bright; (*eau, son, fig*) clear ♦ *ad*: **voir** ~ to see clearly ♦ *nm*: **mettre au** ~ (*notes etc*) to tidy up; **tirer qch au** ~ to clear sth up, clarify sth; **bleu** ~ light blue; **pour être** ~ so as to make it plain; **y voir** ~ (*comprendre*) to understand, see; **le plus** ~ **de son temps/argent** the better part of his time/money; ~ **de lune** moonlight.

claire [kler] *nf*: **(huître de)** ~ fattened oyster.

clairement [klermáṅ] *ad* clearly.

claire-voie [klervwá]: **à** ~ *a* letting the light through; openwork *cpd*.

clairière [kleryer] *nf* clearing.

clair-obscur, *pl* **clairs-obscurs** [kleropskür] *nm* half-light; (*fig*) uncertainty.

clairon [kleróṅ] *nm* bugle.

claironner [kleronā] *vt* (*fig*) to trumpet, shout from the rooftops.

clairsemé, e [klersəmā] *a* sparse.

clairvoyant, e [klervwáyáṅ, -áṅt] *a* perceptive, clear-sighted.

clam [klám] *nm* (*ZOOL*) clam.

clamer [klámā] *vt* to proclaim.

clameur [klámœr] *nf* clamor (*US*), clamour (*Brit*).

clandestin, e [kláṅdestaṅ, -ēn] *a* clandestine; covert; (*POL*) underground, clandestine; **passager** ~ stowaway.

clandestinité [kláṅdestēnētā] *nf*: **dans la** ~ (*en secret*) under cover; (*en se cachant*: *vivre*) underground; **entrer dans la** ~ to go underground.

clapet [klápe] *nm* (*TECH*) valve.

clapier [klápyā] *nm* (rabbit) hutch.

clapotement [klápotmáṅ] *nm* lap(ping).

clapoter [klápotā] *vi* to lap.

clapotis [klápotē] *nm* lap(ping).

claquage [klákázh] *nm* pulled *ou* strained muscle.

claque [klák] *nf* (*gifle*) slap; (*THÉÂTRE*) claque ♦ *nm* (*chapeau*) opera hat.

claquement [klákmáṅ] *nm* (*de porte: bruit répété*) banging; (: *bruit isolé*) slam.

claquemurer [klákmürā]: **se** ~ *vi* to shut o.s. away, closet o.s.

claquer [klákā] *vi* (*drapeau*) to flap; (*porte*) to bang, slam; (*coup de feu*) to ring out ♦ *vt* (*porte*) to slam, bang; (*doigts*) to snap; **elle claquait des dents** her teeth were chattering; **se** ~ **un muscle** to pull *ou* strain a muscle.

claquettes [kláket] *nfpl* tap-dancing *sg*.

clarification [klárēfēkásyóṅ] *nf* (*fig*) clarification.

clarifier [klárēfyā] *vt* (*fig*) to clarify.

clarinette [klárēnet] *nf* clarinet.

clarinettiste [klárēnātēst(ə)] *nm/f* clarinettist.

clarté [klártā] *nf* lightness; brightness; (*d'un son, de l'eau*) clearness; (*d'une explication*) clarity.

classe [klâs] *nf* class; (*SCOL: local*) class(room); (: *leçon*) class; (: *élèves*) class, grade (*US*), form (*Brit*); **1ère/2ème** ~ 1st/2nd class; **un (soldat de) deuxième** ~ (*MIL*: *armée de terre*) ≈ private (soldier); (: *armée de l'air*) ≈ airman basic (*US*), ≈ aircraftman (*Brit*); **de** ~ luxury *cpd*; **faire ses ~s** (*MIL*) to go through basic training; **faire la** ~ (*SCOL*) to be a *ou* the teacher; to teach; **aller en** ~ to go to school; **aller en** ~ **verte/de neige/de mer** to go to the countryside/skiing/to the seaside with the school; ~ **ouvrière** working class; ~ **sociale** social class; ~ **touriste** economy class.

classement [klâsmáṅ] *nm* classifying; filing; grading; closing; (*rang*: *SCOL*) rank (*US*), place (*Brit*); (: *SPORT*) ranking (*US*), placing (*Brit*); (*liste*: *SCOL*) class list (in order of merit); (: *SPORT*) rankings *pl* (*US*), placings *pl* (*Brit*); **premier au** ~ **général** (*SPORT*) first overall.

classer [klâsā] *vt* (*idées, livres*) to classify;

(*papiers*) to file; (*candidat, concurrent*) to grade; (*personne: juger: péj*) to rate; (*JUR: affaire*) to close; **se ~ premier/dernier** to come first/last; (*SPORT*) to finish first/last.

classeur [klàsœr] *nm* (*cahier*) file; (*meuble*) filing cabinet; **~ à feuillets mobiles** ring binder.

classification [klàsēfēkàsyôṅ] *nf* classification.

classifier [klàsēfyà] *vt* to classify.

classique [klàsēk] *a* classical; (*sobre: coupe etc*) classic(al); (*habituel*) standard, classic ♦ *nm* classic; classical author; **études ~s** classical studies, classics.

claudication [klōdēkàsyôṅ] *nf* limp.

clause [klōz] *nf* clause.

claustrer [klōstrà] *vt* to confine.

claustrophobie [klōstrofobē] *nf* claustrophobia.

clavecin [klàvsaṅ] *nm* harpsichord.

claveciniste [klàvsēnēst(ə)] *nm/f* harpsichordist.

clavicule [klàvēkül] *nf* clavicle, collarbone.

clavier [klàvyà] *nm* keyboard.

clé *ou* **clef** [klà] *nf* key; (*MUS*) clef; (*de mécanicien*) wrench (*US*), spanner (*Brit*) ♦ *a*: **problème/position ~** key problem/position; **mettre sous ~** to place under lock and key; **prendre la ~ des champs** to run away, make off; **prix ~s en main** (*d'une voiture*) sticker (*US*) *ou* on-the-road (*Brit*) price; (*d'un appartement*) ready-for-occupancy price (*US*), price with immediate entry (*Brit*); **~ de sol/de fa/d'ut** treble/bass/alto clef; **livre/film** *etc* **à ~** *book/film etc* in which real people are depicted under fictitious names; **à la ~** (*à la fin*) at the end of it all; **~ anglaise** – **~ à molette**; **~ de contact** ignition key; **~ à molette** adjustable wrench, monkey wrench; **~ de voûte** keystone.

clématite [klàmàtēt] *nf* clematis.

clémence [klàmàṅs] *nf* mildness; leniency.

clément, e [klàmàṅ, -àṅt] *a* (*temps*) mild; (*indulgent*) lenient.

clémentine [klàmàṅtēn] *nf* (*BOT*) tangerine (*US*), clementine (*Brit*).

clenche [klàṅsh] *nf* latch.

cleptomane [kleptomàn] *nm/f* = **kleptomane**.

clerc [kler] *nm*: **~ de notaire** *ou* **d'avoué** lawyer's clerk.

clergé [klerzhà] *nm* clergy.

clérical, e, aux [klàrēkàl, -ō] *a* clerical.

cliché [klēshà] *nm* (*PHOTO*) negative; print; (*TYPO*) (printing) plate; (*LING*) cliché.

client, e [klēyàṅ, -àṅt] *nm/f* (*acheteur*) customer, client; (*d'hôtel*) guest, patron; (*du docteur*) patient; (*de l'avocat*) client.

clientèle [klēyàṅtel] *nf* (*du magasin*) customers *pl*, clientèle; (*du docteur, de l'avocat*) practice; **accorder sa ~ à** to give one's business to; **retirer sa ~ à** to take one's business away from.

cligner [klēnyà] *vi*: **~ des yeux** to blink (one's eyes); **~ de l'œil** to wink.

clignotant [klēnyotàṅ] *nm* (*AUTO*) turn signal (*US*), indicator (*Brit*).

clignoter [klēnyotà] *vi* (*étoiles etc*) to twinkle; (*lumière: à intervalles réguliers*) to flash; (*: vaciller*) to flicker; (*yeux*) to blink.

climat [klēmà] *nm* climate.

climatique [klēmàtēk] *a* climatic.

climatisation [klēmàtēzàsyôṅ] *nf* air conditioning.

climatisé, e [klēmàtēzà] *a* air-conditioned.

climatiseur [klēmàtēzœr] *nm* air conditioner.

clin d'œil [klaṅdœy] *nm* wink; **en un ~** in a flash.

clinique [klēnēk] *a* clinical ♦ *nf* nursing home, (*private*) clinic.

clinquant, e [klaṅkàṅ, -àṅt] *a* flashy.

clip [klēp] *nm* (*pince*) clip; (*vidéo*) pop (*ou* promotional) video.

clique [klēk] *nf* (*péj: bande*) clique, set; **prendre ses ~s et ses claques** to pack one's bags.

cliqueter [klēktà] *vi* to clash; (*ferraille, clefs, monnaie*) to jangle, jingle; (*verres*) to clink.

cliquetis [klēktē] *nm* jangle, jingle; clink.

clitoris [klētorēs] *nm* clitoris.

clivage [klēvàzh] *nm* cleavage; (*fig*) rift, split.

cloaque [kloàk] *nm* (*fig*) cesspool.

clochard, e [kloshár, -àrd(ə)] *nm/f* tramp.

cloche [klosh] *nf* (*d'église*) bell; (*fam*) idiot, dope; (*chapeau*) cloche (hat); **~ à fromage** cheese-cover.

cloche-pied [kloshpyà]: **à ~** *ad* on one leg, hopping (along).

clocher [kloshà] *nm* church tower; (*en pointe*) steeple ♦ *vi* (*fam*) to be *ou* go wrong; **de ~** (*péj*) parochial.

clocheton [kloshtôṅ] *nm* pinnacle.

clochette [kloshet] *nf* bell.

clodo [klodō] *nm* (*fam*: = *clochard*) tramp.

cloison [klwàzôṅ] *nf* partition (wall); **~ étanche** (*fig*) impenetrable barrier, brick wall (*fig*).

cloisonner [klwàzonà] *vt* to partition (off); to divide up; (*fig*) to compartmentalize.

cloître [klwàtr(ə)] *nm* cloister.

cloîtrer [klwàtrà] *vt*: **se ~** to shut o.s. up *ou* away; (*REL*) to enter a convent *ou* monastery.

clone [klon] *nm* clone.

clope [klop] *nm* (*fam*) cigarette.

clopin-clopant [klopàṅklopàṅ] *ad* hobbling along; (*fig*) so-so.

clopiner [klopēnà] *vi* to hobble along.

cloporte [kloport(ə)] *nm* pill *ou* sow bug (*US*), woodlouse (*pl -lice*) (*Brit*).

cloque [klok] *nf* blister.

cloqué, e [klokà] *a*: **étoffe ~e** seersucker.

cloquer [klokà] *vi* (*peau, peinture*) to blister.

clore [klor] *vt* to close; **~ une session** (*INFORM*) to log out.

clos, e [klō, -ōz] *pp de* **clore** ♦ *a voir* **maison, huis, vase** ♦ *nm* (enclosed) field.

clôt [klō] *vb voir* **clore**.

clôture [klōtür] *nf* closure, closing; (*barrière*) enclosure, fence.

clôturer [klōtürà] *vt* (*terrain*) to enclose, close off; (*festival, débats*) to close.

clou [klōō] *nm* nail; (*MÉD*) boil; **~s** *nmpl* = **passage clouté**; **pneus à ~s** studded tires; **le ~ du spectacle** the highlight of the show; **~ de girofle** clove.

clouer [klōōà] *vt* to nail down (*ou* up); (*fig*): **~ sur/contre** to pin to/against.

clouté, e [klōōtà] *a* studded.

clown [klŏōn] *nm* clown; **faire le** ~ *(fig)* to clown (around), play the fool.

CLT *sigle f* = *Compagnie Luxembourgeoise de Télévision.*

club [klœb] *nm* club.

CM *sigle f* = **chambre des métiers ♦** *sigle m* = **conseil municipal;** *(SCOL)* = **cours moyen.**

cm. *abr* (= *centimètre*) cm.

CNAT *sigle f* (= *Commission nationale d'aménagement du territoire*) *national development agency.*

CNC *sigle m* (= *Conseil national de la consommation*) *national consumers' council.*

CNCL *sigle f* (= *Commission nationale de la communication et des libertés*) *independent broadcasting authority.*

CNDP *sigle m* = *Centre national de documentation pédagogique.*

CNE *sigle f* (= *Caisse nationale d'épargne*) *national savings bank.*

CNEC *sigle m* = *Centre national de l'enseignement par correspondance.*

CNIL *sigle f* (= *Commission nationale de l'informatique et des libertés*) *board which enforces law on data protection.*

CNIT *sigle m* (= *Centre national des industries et des techniques*) *exhibition center in Paris.*

CNJA *sigle m* (= *Centre national des jeunes agriculteurs*) *farmers' union.*

CNL *sigle f* (= *Confédération nationale du logement*) *consumer group for housing.*

CNP *sigle f* (= *Caisse nationale de prévoyance*) *savings bank.*

CNPF *sigle m* (= *Conseil national du patronat français*) *national council of French employers.*

CNRS *sigle m* = *Centre national de la recherche scientifique.*

c/o *abr* (= *care of*) c/o.

coagulant [kɔágülâ̂] *nm* (*MÉD*) coagulant.

coaguler [kɔágülã] *vi, vt,* **se** ~ *vi* to coagulate.

coaliser [kɔálēzã]: **se** ~ *vi* to unite, join forces.

coalition [kɔálēsyôń] *nf* coalition.

coasser [kɔásâ] *vi* to croak.

coauteur [kɔ̄ōtœr] *nm* co-author.

cobalt [kɔbált] *nm* cobalt.

cobaye [kɔbáy] *nm* guinea-pig.

COBOL *ou* **Cobol** [kɔbɔl] *nm* COBOL.

cobra [kɔbrá] *nm* cobra.

coca [kɔká] *nm* ® Coke ®.

cocagne [kɔkány] *nf*: **pays de** ~ land of plenty; **mât de** ~ greasy pole (*fig*).

cocaïne [kɔkáēn] *nf* cocaine.

cocarde [kɔkárd(ə)] *nf* rosette.

cocardier, ière [kɔkárdyã, -yer] *a* jingoistic, chauvinistic; militaristic.

cocasse [kɔkás] *a* comical, funny.

coccinelle [kɔksēnel] *nf* ladybug (*US*), ladybird (*Brit*).

coccyx [kɔksēs] *nm* coccyx.

cocher [kɔshã] *nm* coachman ♦ *vt* to check off; (*entailler*) to notch.

cochère [kɔsher] *af*: **porte** ~ carriage entrance.

cochon, ne [kɔshôń, -on] *nm* pig ♦ *nm/f* (*péj: sale*) (filthy) pig; (*: méchant*) swine ♦ *a*

(*fam*) dirty, smutty; ~ **d'Inde** guinea-pig; ~ **de lait** (*CULIN*) suckling (*US*) *ou* sucking (*Brit*) pig.

cochonnaille [kɔshonáy] *nf* (*péj: charcuterie*) (cold) pork.

cochonnerie [kɔshonrē] *nf* (*fam: saleté*) filth; (*: marchandises*) rubbish, trash.

cochonnet [kɔshone] *nm* (*BOULES*) jack.

cocker [kɔker] *nm* cocker spaniel.

cocktail [kɔktel] *nm* cocktail; (*réception*) cocktail party.

coco [kɔkō] *nm voir* **noix**; (*fam*) dude (*US*), bloke (*Brit*).

cocon [kɔkôń] *nm* cocoon.

cocorico [kɔkorēkō] *excl, nm* cock-a-doodle-do.

cocotier [kɔkotyã] *nm* coconut palm.

cocotte [kɔkot] *nf* (*en fonte*) casserole; **ma** ~ (*fam*) sweetie (pie); ~ **(minute)** ® pressure cooker; ~ **en papier** paper shape.

cocu [kɔkü] *nm* cuckold.

code [kɔd] *nm* code; **se mettre en** ~**(s)** to dim (*US*) *ou* dip (*Brit*) one's (head)lights; ~ **à barres** bar code; ~ **de caractère** (*INFORM*) character code; ~ **civil** Civil Code (*US*), Common Law (*Brit*); ~ **machine** machine code; ~ **pénal** penal code; ~ **postal** (*numéro*) zip code (*US*), postcode (*Brit*); ~ **de la route** rules of the road; ~ **secret** secret code, cipher (*Brit*).

codéine [kɔdāēn] *nf* codeine.

coder [kɔdã] *vt* to (en)code.

codétenu, e [kɔdetnü] *nm/f* fellow prisoner *ou* inmate.

codicille [kɔdēsēl] *nm* codicil.

codifier [kɔdētyã] *vt* to codify.

codirecteur, trice [kɔdērektœr, -trēs] *nm/f* co-director.

coéditeur, trice [kɔādētœr, -trēs] *nm/f* co-publisher; (*rédacteur*) co-editor.

coefficient [kɔāfēsyâ̂] *nm* coefficient; ~ **d'erreur** margin of error.

coéquipier, ière [kɔākēpyã, -yer] *nm/f* team-mate, partner.

coercition [kɔersēsyôń] *nf* coercion.

cœur [kœr] *nm* heart; (*CARTES: couleur*) hearts *pl*; (*: carte*) heart; (*CULIN*): ~ **de laitue/d'artichaut** lettuce/artichoke heart; (*fig*): ~ **du débat** heart of the debate; ~ **de l'été** height of summer; ~ **de la forêt** depths *pl* of the forest; **affaire de** ~ love affair; **avoir bon** ~ to be kind-hearted; **avoir mal au** ~ to feel sick to one's stomach; **contre** *ou* **sur son** ~ to one's breast; **opérer qn à** ~ **ouvert** to perform open-heart surgery on sb; **recevoir qn à** ~ **ouvert** to welcome sb with open arms; **parler à** ~ **ouvert** to open one's heart; **de tout son** ~ with all one's heart; **avoir le** ~ **gros** *ou* **serré** to have a heavy heart; **en avoir le** ~ **net** to be clear in one's own mind (about it); **par** ~ by heart; **de bon** ~ willingly; **avoir à** ~ **de faire** to be very eager to do; **cela lui tient à** ~ that's (very) close to his heart; **prendre les choses à** ~ to take things to heart; **à** ~ **joie** to one's heart's content; **être de tout** ~ **avec qn** to be (completely) in accord with sb.

coexistence [kɔegzēstâ̂s] *nf* coexistence.

coexister [kɔāgzēstã] *vi* to coexist.

coffrage [kɔfrázh] *nm* (*CONSTR: dispositif*)

form.
coffre [kofr(ə)] *nm* (*meuble*) chest; (*coffre-fort*) safe; (*d'auto*) trunk (*US*), boot (*Brit*); **avoir du ~** (*fam*) to have a lot of breath.
coffre-fort, pl coffres-fortes [kofrəfor] *nm* safe.
coffrer [kofrā] *vt* (*fam*) to put inside, lock up.
coffret [kofre] *nm* casket; **~ à bijoux** jewel box.
cogérant, e [kozhārāṅ, -āṅt] *nm/f* joint manager/manageress.
cogestion [kozhāstyôṅ] *nf* joint management.
cogiter [kozhētā] *vi* to cogitate.
cognac [konyàk] *nm* brandy, cognac.
cognement [konymāṅ] *nm* knocking.
cogner [konyā] *vi* to knock, bang; **se ~** to bump o.s.
cohabitation [koàbētâsyôṅ] *nf* living together; (*POL, JUR*) cohabitation.
cohabiter [koàbētā] *vi* to live together.
cohérence [koārāṅs] *nf* coherence.
cohérent, e [koārāṅ, -āṅt] *a* coherent.
cohésion [koāzyôṅ] *nf* cohesion.
cohorte [koort(ə)] *nf* troop.
cohue [koü] *nf* crowd.
coi, coite [kwá, kwát] *a*: **rester ~** to remain silent.
coiffe [kwáf] *nf* headdress.
coiffé, e [kwáfā] *a*: **bien/mal ~** with tidy/untidy hair; **~ d'un béret** wearing a beret; **~ en arrière** with one's hair brushed *ou* combed back; **~ en brosse** with a crew cut.
coiffer [kwáfā] *vt* (*fig*) to cover, top; **~ qn** to do sb's hair; **~ qn d'un béret** to put a beret on sb; **se ~** to do one's hair; to put on a *ou* one's hat.
coiffeur, euse [kwáfœr, -œz] *nm/f* hairdresser ♦ *nf* (*table*) dressing table.
coiffure [kwáfür] *nf* (*cheveux*) hairstyle, hairdo; (*chapeau*) hat, headgear *q*; (*art*): **la ~** hairdressing.
coin [kwan] *nm* corner; (*pour graver*) die; (*pour coincer*) wedge; (*poinçon*) hallmark; **l'épicerie du ~** the local grocer; **dans le ~** (*aux alentours*) in the area, around about; locally; **au ~ du feu** by the fireside; **du ~ de l'œil** out of the corner of one's eye; **regard en ~** side(ways) glance; **sourire en ~** half-smile.
coincé, e [kwaṅsā] *a* stuck, jammed; (*fig: inhibé*) inhibited, with hang-ups.
coincer [kwaṅsā] *vt* to jam; (*fam*) to catch; to nab; **se ~** to get stuck *ou* jammed.
coïncidence [koaṅsēdāṅs] *nf* coincidence.
coïncider [koaṅsēdā] *vi*: **~ (avec)** to coincide (with); (*correspondre: témoignage etc*) to correspond *ou* tally (with).
coin-coin [kwaṅkwaṅ] *nm inv* quack.
coing [kwaṅ] *nm* quince.
coït [koēt] *nm* coitus.
coite [kwát] *af voir* **coi.**
coke [kok] *nm* coke.
col [kol] *nm* (*de chemise*) collar; (*encolure, cou*) neck; (*de montagne*) pass; **~ du fémur** neck of the thighbone; **~ roulé** polo-neck; **~ de l'utérus** cervix.
coléoptère [kolāopter] *nm* beetle.
colère [koler] *nf* anger; **une ~** a fit of anger; **être en ~ (contre qn)** to be angry (with sb);

mettre qn en ~ to make sb angry; **se mettre en ~** to get angry.
coléreux, euse [kolārœ̄, -œz] *a*, **colérique** [kolārēk] *a* quick-tempered, irascible.
colibacillose [kolēbásēlōz] *nf* colibacillosis.
colifichet [kolēfēshe] *nm* trinket.
colimaçon [kolēmásôṅ] *nm*: **escalier en ~** spiral staircase.
colin [kolaṅ] *nm* hake.
colin-maillard [kolaṅmáyár] *nm* (*jeu*) blind man's buff.
colique [kolēk] *nf* diarrhea (*US*), diarrhoea (*Brit*); (*douleurs*) colic (pains *pl*); (*fam: personne ou chose ennuyeuse*) pain.
colis [kolē] *nm* parcel; **par ~ postal** by parcel post.
colistier, ière [kolēstyā, -yer] *nm/f* fellow candidate.
colite [kolēt] *nf* colitis.
coll. *abr* = **collection**; (= *collaborateurs*): **et ~ et al.**
collaborateur, trice [koláborátœr, -trēs] *nm/f* (*aussi POL*) collaborator; (*d'une revue*) contributor.
collaboration [koláborâsyôṅ] *nf* collaboration.
collaborer [koláborā] *vi* to collaborate; **~ à** to collaborate on; (*revue*) to contribute to.
collage [kolázh] *nm* (*ART*) collage.
collant, e [kolâṅ, -âṅt] *a* sticky; (*robe etc*) clinging, skintight; (*péj*) clinging ♦ *nm* (*bas*) pantyhose *pl* (*US*), tights *pl* (*Brit*).
collatéral, e, aux [kolátārál, -ō] *nm/f* collateral.
collation [kolâsyôṅ] *nf* light meal.
colle [kol] *nf* glue; (*à papiers peints*) (wall-paper) paste; (*devinette*) teaser, riddle; (*SCOL fam*) detention; **~ forte** superglue ®.
collecte [kolekt(ə)] *nf* collection; **faire une ~** to take up a collection.
collecter [kolektā] *vt* to collect.
collecteur [kolektœr] *nm* (*égout*) main sewer.
collectif, ive [kolektēf, -ēv] *a* collective; (*visite, billet etc*) group *cpd* ♦ *nm*: **~ budgétaire** mid-term budget; **immeuble ~** apartment building (*US*), block of flats (*Brit*).
collection [koleksyôṅ] *nf* collection; (*ÉDITION*) series; **pièce de ~** collector's item; **faire (la) ~ de** to collect; **(toute) une ~ de ...** (*fig*) a (complete) set of ....
collectionner [koleksyonā] *vt* (*tableaux, timbres*) to collect.
collectionneur, euse [koleksyonœr, -œz] *nm/f* collector.
collectivement [kolektēvmāṅ] *ad* collectively.
collectiviste [kolektēvēst(ə)] *a* collectivist.
collectivité [kolektēvētā] *nf* group; **la ~** the community, the collectivity; **les ~s locales** local governments.
collège [kolezh] *nm* (*école*) (high) school; (*assemblée*) body; **~ électoral** electoral college; **~ d'enseignement secondaire (CES)** ≈ junior high school.
collégial, e, aux [kolāzhyál, -ō] *a* collegiate.
collégien, ne [kolāzhyaṅ, -en] *nm/f* high school student (*US*), secondary school pupil (*Brit*).
collègue [koleg] *nm/f* colleague.
coller [kolā] *vt* (*papier, timbre*) to stick (on); (*affiche*) to stick up; (*appuyer, placer contre*): **~ son front à la vitre** to press one's

face to the window; (*enveloppe*) to seal; (*morceaux*) to stick *ou* glue together; (*fam: mettre, fourrer*) to stick, shove; (*SCOL fam*) to keep in, give detention to ♦ *vi* (*être collant*) to be sticky; (*adhérer*) to stick; ~ **qch sur** to stick (*ou* paste *ou* glue) sth on(to); ~ **à** to stick to; (*fig*) to cling to.

collerette [kolrεt] *nf* ruff; (*TECH*) flange.

collet [kolε] *nm* (*piège*) snare, noose; (*cou*): **prendre qn au** ~ to grab sb by the throat; ~ **monté** *a inv* straight-laced.

colleter [koltā] *vt* (*adversaire*) to collar, grab by the throat; **se** ~ **avec** to wrestle with.

colleur [kolœr] *nm*: ~ **d'affiches** bill-poster.

collier [kolyā] *nm* (*bijou*) necklace; (*de chien, TECH*) collar; ~ (**de barbe**), **barbe en** ~ narrow beard along the line of the jaw; ~ **de serrage** choke collar.

collimateur [kolēmátœr] *nm*: **être dans le** ~ (*fig*) to be in the firing line; **avoir qn/qch dans le** ~ (*fig*) to have sb/sth in one's sights.

colline [kolēn] *nf* hill.

collision [kolēzyôn] *nf* collision, crash; **entrer en** ~ (**avec**) to collide (with).

colloque [kolok] *nm* colloquium, symposium.

collusion [kolüzyôn] *nf* collusion.

collutoire [kolütwár] *nm* (*MÉD*) oral medication; (*en bombe*) throat spray.

collyre [kolēr] *nm* (*MÉD*) eye lotion.

colmater [kolmátā] *vt* (*fuite*) to seal off; (*brèche*) to plug, fill in.

Cologne [kolony] *n* Cologne.

colombe [kolônb] *nf* dove.

Colombie [kolônbē] *nf*: **la** ~ Colombia.

colombien, ne [kolónbyan, -en] *a* Colombian ♦ *nm/f*: **C~, ne** Colombian.

colon [kolôn] *nm* settler; (*enfant*) boarder (*in children's summer camp*).

côlon [kôlôn] *nm* colon (*MÉD*).

colonel [kolonεl] *nm* colonel; (*armée de l'air*) colonel (*US*), group captain (*Brit*).

colonial, e, aux [kolonyál, -ō] *a* colonial.

colonialisme [kolonyálēsm(ə)] *nm* colonialism.

colonie [kolonē] *nf* colony; ~ (**de vacances**) summer camp (*for children*).

colonisation [kolonēzâsyôn] *nf* colonization.

coloniser [kolonēzā] *vt* to colonize.

colonnade [kolonád] *nf* colonnade.

colonne [kolon] *nf* column; **se mettre en** ~ **par deux/quatre** to line up two/four abreast; **en** ~ **par deux** in double file; ~ **de secours** rescue party; ~ (**vertébrale**) spine, spinal column.

colonnette [kolonεt] *nf* small column.

colophane [kolofán] *nf* rosin.

colorant [kolorân] *nm* coloring (*US*), colouring (*Brit*).

coloration [kolorâsyôn] *nf* color(ing) (*US*), colour(ing) (*Brit*); **se faire faire une** ~ (*chez le coiffeur*) to have one's hair dyed.

coloré, e [kolorā] *a* (*fig*) colorful (*US*), colourful (*Brit*).

colorer [kolorā] *vt* to color (*US*), colour (*Brit*); **se** ~ *vi* to turn red; to blush.

coloriage [koloryàzh] *nm* coloring (*US*), colouring (*Brit*).

colorier [koloryā] *vt* to color (*US*) *ou* colour (*Brit*) (in); **album à** ~ coloring book.

coloris [kolorē] *nm* color (*US*), colour (*Brit*),

shade.

coloriste [kolorēst(ə)] *nm/f* colorist (*US*), colourist (*Brit*).

colossal, e, aux [kolosál, -ō] *a* colossal, huge.

colosse [kolos] *nm* giant.

colostrum [kolostrom] *nm* colostrum.

colporter [kolportā] *vt* to hawk, peddle.

colporteur, euse [kolportœr, -ēz] *nm/f* hawker, pedlar.

colt [kolt] *nm* revolver, Colt ®.

coltiner [koltēnā] *vt* to lug around.

colza [kolzá] *nm* rape(seed).

coma [komá] *nm* coma; **être dans le** ~ to be in a coma.

comateux, euse [komátœ, -ēz] *a* comatose.

combat [kônbá] *vb voir* **combattre** ♦ *nm* fight; fighting *q*; ~ **de boxe** boxing match; ~ **de rues** street fighting *q*; ~ **singulier** single combat.

combatif, ive [kônbátēf, -ēv] *a* with a lot of fight.

combativité [kônbátēvētā] *nf* fighting spirit.

combattant [kônbátân] *vb voir* **combattre** ♦ *nm* combatant; (*d'une rixe*) brawler; **ancien** ~ war veteran.

combattre [kônbátr(ə)] *vi* to fight ♦ *vt* to fight; (*épidémie, ignorance*) to combat, fight (against).

combien [kônbyań] *ad* (*quantité*) how much; (*nombre*) how many; (*exclamatif*) how; ~ **de** how much; how many; ~ **de temps** how long, how much time; ~ **coûte/pèse ceci?** how much does this cost/weigh?; **vous mesurez** ~? what size are you?; **ça fait** ~ **en largeur?** how wide is that?

combinaison [kônbēnezôn] *nf* combination; (*astuce*) device, scheme; (*de femme*) slip; (*d'aviateur*) jump suit; (*d'homme-grenouille*) wetsuit; (*bleu de travail*) coveralls *pl* (*US*); boilersuit (*Brit*).

combine [kônbēn] *nf* trick; (*péj*) scheme.

combiné [kônbēnā] *nm* (*aussi*: ~ **téléphonique**) receiver; (*SKI*) combination (*event*); (*vêtement de femme*) corselet.

combiner [kônbēnā] *vt* to combine; (*plan, horaire*) to work out, devise.

comble [kônbl(ə)] *a* (*salle*) packed (full) ♦ *nm* (*du bonheur, plaisir*) height; ~**s** *nmpl* (*CONSTR*) attic *sg*, loft *sg*; **de fond en** ~ from top to bottom; **pour** ~ **de malchance** to cap it all; **c'est le** ~! that beats everything!; **sous les** ~**s** in the attic.

combler [kônblā] *vt* (*trou*) to fill in; (*besoin, lacune*) to fill; (*déficit*) to make good; (*satisfaire*) to gratify, fulfill (*US*), fulfil (*Brit*); ~ **qn de joie** to fill sb with joy; ~ **qn d'honneurs** to shower sb with honors.

combustible [kônbüstēbl(ə)] *a* combustible ♦ *nm* fuel.

combustion [kônbüstyôn] *nf* combustion.

COMECON [komákon] *sigle m* Comecon.

comédie [komādē] *nf* comedy; (*fig*) playacting *q*; **jouer la** ~ (*fig*) to put on an act; ~ **musicale** musical.

comédien, ne [komādyań, -en] *nm/f* actor/actress; (*comique*) comedy actor/actress, comedian/comedienne; (*fig*) sham.

COMES [komes] *sigle m* = *Commissariat à l'énergie solaire*.

comestible [komɛstēbl(ə)] *a* edible; ~s *nmpl* foods.

comète [komɛt] *nf* comet.

comice [komēs] *nm*: ~ **agricole** agricultural show.

comique [komēk] *a* (*drôle*) comical; (*THÉÂTRE*) comic ♦ *nm* (*artiste*) comic, comedian; **le** ~ **de qch** the funny *ou* comical side of sth.

comité [komētā] *nm* committee; **petit** ~ select group; ~ **directeur** executive (*US*) *ou* management (*Brit*) committee; ~ **d'entreprise (CE)** work council; ~ **des fêtes** festival committee.

commandant [komáńdáń] *nm* (*gén*) commander, commandant; (*MIL*: *grade*) major; (*: armée de l'air*) major (*US*), squadron leader (*Brit*); (*NAVIG*) captain; ~ **(de bord)** (*AVIAT*) captain.

commande [komáńd] *nf* (*COMM*) order; (*INFORM*) command; ~**s** *nfpl* (*AVIAT etc*) controls; **passer une** ~ **(de)** to put in an order (for); **sur** ~ to order; ~ **à distance** remote control; **véhicule à double** ~ vehicle with dual controls.

commandement [komáńdmáń] *nm* command; (*ordre*) command, order; (*REL*) commandment.

commander [komáńdā] *vt* (*COMM*) to order; (*diriger, ordonner*) to command; ~ **à** (*MIL*) to command; (*contrôler, maîtriser*) to have control over; ~ **à qn de faire** to command *ou* order sb to do.

commanditaire [komáńdēter] *nm* silent (*US*) *ou* sleeping (*Brit*) partner.

commandite [komáńdēt] *nf*: **(société en)** ~ limited partnership.

commanditer [komáńdētā] *vt* (*COMM*) to finance, back; to commission.

commando [komáńdō] *nm* commando (squad).

comme [kom] *prép* like; (*en tant que*) as ♦ *cj* as; (*parce que, puisque*) as, since ♦ *ad*: ~ **il est fort/c'est bon!** how strong he is/good it is!; **donner** ~ **prix/heure** to give the price/ time as; ~ **si** as if, as though; ~ **quoi** (*disant que*) with the result that; (*d'où il s'ensuit que*) which shows that; **faites-le** ~ **cela** *ou* **ça** do it like this *ou* this way; ... ~ **ça** *ou* **cela on n'aura pas d'ennuis** that way we won't have any problems; **comment ça va?** — ~ **ça** how are things? — OK; ~ **ci** ~ **ça** so-so, middling; **joli** ~ **tout** ever so pretty; ~ **on dit** as they say; ~ **de juste** needless to say; ~ **il faut** properly.

commémoration [komāmorásyóń] *nf* commemoration.

commémorer [komāmorā] *vt* to com. .emorate.

commencement [komáńsmáń] *nm* beginning, start, commencement; ~**s** *nmpl* (*débuts*) beginnings.

commencer [komáńsā] *vt* to begin, start, commence; (*être placé au début de*) to begin ♦ *vi* to begin, start, commence; ~ **à** *ou* **de faire** to begin *ou* start doing; ~ **par qch** to begin with sth; ~ **par faire qch** to begin by doing sth.

commensal, e, aux [komáńsál, -ō] *nm/f* table

companion.

comment [komáń] *ad* how; ~**?** (*que dites-vous*) (I beg your) pardon?; ~**!** what! ♦ *nm*: **le** ~ **et le pourquoi** the whys and wherefores; **et** ~**!** and how!; ~ **donc!** of course!; ~ **faire?** how will we do it?; ~ **se fait-il que?** how is it that?

commentaire [komáńter] *nm* comment; remark; ~ **(de texte)** (*SCOL*) commentary; ~ **sur image** voice-over.

commentateur, trice [komáńtátœr, -trēs] *nm/f* commentator.

commenter [komáńtā] *vt* (*jugement, événement*) to comment (up)on; (*RADIO, TV*: *match, manifestation*) to cover, give a commentary on.

commérages [komārázh] *nmpl* gossip *sg*.

commerçant, e [komersáń, -áńt] *a* commercial; trading; (*rue*) shopping *cpd*; (*personne*) commercially shrewd ♦ *nm/f* shopkeeper, trader.

commerce [komers(ə)] *nm* (*activité*) trade, commerce; (*boutique*) business; **le petit** ~ small business owners *pl*; **faire** ~ **de** to trade in; (*fig*: *péj*) to trade on; **chambre de** ~ Chamber of Commerce; **livres de** ~ (account) books; **vendu dans le** ~ sold in the stores; **vendu hors-**~ sold directly to the public; ~ **en** *ou* **de gros/détail** wholesale/ retail trade; ~ **intérieur/extérieur** domestic/ foreign market.

commercer [komersā] *vi*: ~ **avec** to trade with.

commercial, e, aux [komersyál, -ō] *a* commercial, trading; (*péj*) commercial ♦ *nm*: **les commerciaux** the commercial people.

commercialisation [komersyálēzásyóń] *nf* marketing.

commercialiser [komersyálēzā] *vt* to market.

commère [komer] *nf* gossip.

commettant [komátáń] *vb voir* **commettre** ♦ *nm* (*JUR*) principal.

commettre [kometr(ə)] *vt* to commit; **se** ~ to compromise one's good name.

commis [komē] *vb voir* **commettre** ♦ *nm* (*de magasin*) sales clerk (*US*), (shop) assistant (*Brit*); (*de banque*) clerk; ~ **voyageur** traveling salesman.

commis, e [komē, -ēz] *pp de* **commettre**.

commisération [komēzārásyóń] *nf* commiseration.

commissaire [komēser] *nm* (*de police*) ≈ (police) captain (*US*), (police) superintendent (*Brit*); (*de rencontre sportive etc*) steward; ~ **du bord** (*NAVIG*) purser; ~ **aux comptes** (*ADMIN*) auditor.

commissaire-priseur, *pl* **commissaires-priseurs** [komēserprēzœr] *nm* (*official*) auctioneer.

commissariat [komēsáryá] *nm* police station; (*ADMIN*) commissionership.

commission [komēsyóń] *nf* (*comité, pourcentage*) commission; (*message*) message; (*course*) errand; ~**s** *nfpl* (*achats*) shopping *sg*; ~ **d'examen** examining board.

commissionnaire [komēsyoner] *nm* delivery boy (*ou* man); messenger; (*TRANSPORTS*) (forwarding) agent.

commissure [komēsür] *nf*: les ~s des lèvres the corners of the mouth.

commode [komod] *a* (*pratique*) convenient, handy; (*facile*) easy; (*air, personne*) easygoing; (*personne*): **pas** ~ awkward (to deal with) ♦ *nf* chest of drawers.

commodité [komodētā] *nf* convenience.

commotion [komōsyôṅ] *nf*: ~ **(cérébrale)** concussion.

commotionné, e [komōsyonā] *a* shocked, shaken.

commuer [komüā] *vt* to commute.

commun, e [komœṅ, -üṅ] *a* common; (*pièce*) communal, shared; (*réunion, effort*) joint ♦ *nf* (*ADMIN*) commune, ≈ district; (*: urbaine*) ≈ borough; ~s *nmpl* (*bâtiments*) outbuildings; **cela sort du** ~ it's out of the ordinary; **le** ~ **des mortels** the common run of people; **sans** ~e **mesure** incomparable; **être** ~ **à** (*suj: chose*) to be shared by; **en** ~ (*faire*) jointly; **mettre en** ~ to pool, share; **peu** ~ unusual; **d'un** ~ **accord** of one accord; with one accord.

communal, e, aux [komünál, -ō] *a* (*ADMIN*) of the commune, ≈ (district *ou* borough) council *cpd*.

communautaire [komünōter] *a* community *cpd*.

communauté [komünōtā] *nf* community; (*JUR*): **régime de la** ~ joint estate settlement.

commune [komün] *af, nf voir* **commun**.

Communes [komün] *nfpl* (*Brit: parlement*) Commons.

communiant, e [komünyáṅ, -áṅt] *nm/f* communicant; **premier** ~ child taking his first communion.

communicant, e [komünēkáṅ, -áṅt] *a* communicating.

communicatif, ive [komünēkátēf, -ēv] *a* (*personne*) communicative; (*rire*) infectious.

communication [komünēkásyôṅ] *nf* communication; ~ **(téléphonique)** (telephone) call; **avoir la** ~ **(avec)** to get through (to); **vous avez la** ~ your party is on the line (*US*), you're through (*Brit*); **donnez-moi la** ~ **avec** put me through to; **mettre qn en** ~ **avec qn** (*en contact*) to put sb in touch with sb; (*au téléphone*) to connect sb with sb; ~ **interurbaine** long-distance call; ~ **en PCV** collect (*US*) *ou* reverse charge (*Brit*) call; ~ **avec préavis** person-to-person call.

communier [komünyā] *vi* (*REL*) to receive communion; (*fig*) to be united.

communion [komünyôṅ] *nf* communion.

communiqué [komünēkā] *nm* communiqué; ~ **de presse** press release.

communiquer [komünēkā] *vt* (*nouvelle, dossier*) to pass on, convey; (*maladie*) to pass on; (*peur etc*) to communicate; (*chaleur, mouvement*) to transmit ♦ *vi* to communicate; ~ **avec** (*suj: salle*) to communicate with; **se** ~ **à** (*se propager*) to spread to.

communisant, e [komünēzáṅ, -áṅt] *a* communistic ♦ *nm/f* communist sympathizer.

communisme [komünēsm(ə)] *nm* communism.

communiste [komünēst(ə)] *a, nm/f* communist.

commutateur [komütátœr] *nm* (*ÉLEC*) (change-over) switch, commutator.

commutation [komütásyôṅ] *nf* (*INFORM*): ~ **de messages** message switching; ~ **de paquets** packet switching.

Comores [komor] *nfpl*: **les (îles)** ~ the Comoros (Islands).

comorien, ne [komoryáṅ, -en] *a* of *ou* from the Comoros.

compact, e [kôṅpákt] *a* dense; compact.

compagne [kôṅpány] *nf* companion.

compagnie [kôṅpányē] *nf* (*firme, MIL*) company; (*groupe*) gathering; (*présence*): **la** ~ **de qn** sb's company; **homme/femme de** ~ escort; **tenir** ~ **à qn** to keep sb company; **fausser** ~ **à qn** to give sb the slip, slip *ou* sneak away from sb; **en** ~ **de** in the company of; **Dupont et** ~, **Dupont et Cie** Dupont and Company, Dupont and Co; ~ **aérienne** airline (company).

compagnon [kôṅpányôṅ] *nm* companion; (*autrefois: ouvrier*) craftsman; journeyman.

comparable [kôṅpárábl(ə)] *a*: ~ **(à)** compa rable (to).

comparais [kôṅpáre] *etc vb voir* **comparaître**.

comparaison [kôṅpárezôṅ] *nf* comparison; (*métaphore*) simile; **en** ~ **(de)** in comparison (with); **par** ~ **(à)** by comparison (with).

comparaître [kôṅpáretr(ə)] *vi*: ~ **(devant)** to appear (before).

comparatif, ive [kôṅpárátēf, -ēv] *a, nm* comparative.

comparativement [kôṅpárátēvmáṅ] *ad* comparatively; ~ **à** by comparison with.

comparé, e [kôṅpárā] *a*: **littérature** *etc* ~**e** comparative literature *etc*.

comparer [kôṅpárā] *vt* to compare; ~ **qch/qn à** *ou* **et** (*pour choisir*) to compare sth/sb with *ou* and; (*pour établir une similitude*) to compare sth/sb *à ou* and.

comparse [kôṅpárs(ə)] *nm/f* (*péj*) associate, stooge.

compartiment [kôṅpártēmáṅ] *nm* compartment.

compartimenté, e [kôṅpártēmáṅtā] *a* partitioned; (*fig*) compartmentalized.

comparu, e [kôṅpárü] *pp de* **comparaître**.

comparution [kôṅpárüsyôṅ] *nf* appearance.

compas [kôṅpá] *nm* (*GÉOM*) (pair of) compasses *pl*; (*NAVIG*) compass.

compassé, e [kôṅpásā] *a* starchy, formal.

compassion [kôṅpásyôṅ] *nf* compassion.

compatibilité [kôṅpátēbēlētā] *nf* compatibility.

compatible [kôṅpátēbl(ə)] *a*: ~ **(avec)** compatible (with).

compatir [kôṅpátēr] *vi*: ~ **(à)** to sympathize (with).

compatissant, e [kôṅpátēsáṅ, -áṅt] *a* sympathetic.

compatriote [kôṅpátrēyot] *nm/f* compatriot, fellow countryman/woman.

compensateur, trice [kôṅpáṅsátœr, -trēs] *a* compensatory.

compensation [kôṅpáṅsásyôṅ] *nf* compensation; (*BANQUE*) clearing; **en** ~ in *ou* as compensation.

compensé, e [kôṅpáṅsā] *a*: **semelle** ~**e** platform sole.

compenser [kôṅpåṅsā] *vt* to compensate for, make up for.

compère [kôṅpɛr] *nm* accomplice; fellow musician *ou* comedian *etc*.

compétence [kôṅpātåṅs] *nf* competence.

compétent, e [kôṅpātåṅ, -åṅt] *a* (*apte*) competent, capable; (*JUR*) competent.

compétitif, ive [kôṅpātētēf, -ēv] *a* competitive.

compétition [kôṅpātēsyôṅ] *nf* (*gén*) competition; (*SPORT*: *épreuve*) event; **la ~** competitive sport; **être en ~ avec** to be competing with; **la ~ automobile** car racing.

compétitivité [kôṅpātētēvētā] *nf* competitiveness.

compilateur [kôṅpēlátœr] *nm* (*INFORM*) compiler.

compiler [kôṅpēlā] *vt* to compile.

complainte [kôṅplåṅt] *nf* lament.

complaire [kôṅplɛr]: **se ~** *vi*: **se ~ dans/parmi** to take pleasure in/in being among.

complaisais [kôṅpleze] *etc vb voir* **complaire**.

complaisamment [kôṅplezámåṅ] *ad* kindly; complacently.

complaisance [kôṅplezåṅs] *nf* kindness; (*péj*) indulgence; (: *fatuité*) complacency; **attestation de ~** *certificate produced to oblige a patient etc*; **pavillon de ~** flag of convenience.

complaisant, e [kôṅplezåṅ, -åṅt] *vb voir* **complaire** ♦ *a* (*aimable*) kind; obliging; (*péj*) accommodating; (: *fat*) complacent.

complaît [kôṅplɛ] *vb voir* **complaire**.

complément [kôṅplāmåṅ] *nm* complement; (*reste*) remainder; (*LING*) complement; **~ d'information** (*ADMIN*) supplementary *ou* further information; **~ d'agent** agent; **~ (d'objet) direct/indirect** direct/indirect object; **~ (circonstanciel) de lieu/temps** adverbial phrase of place/time; **~ de nom** possessive phrase.

complémentaire [kôṅplāmåṅtɛr] *a* complementary; (*additionnel*) supplementary.

complet, ète [kôṅplɛ, -ɛt] *a* complete; (*plein: hôtel etc*) full ♦ *nm* (*aussi*: **~-veston**) suit; **au (grand) ~** all together.

complètement [kôṅpletmåṅ] *ad* (*en entier*) completely; (*absolument: fou, faux etc*) absolutely; (*à fond: étudier etc*) fully, in depth.

compléter [kôṅplātā] *vt* (*porter à la quantité voulue*) to complete; (*augmenter*) to complement, supplement; to add to; **se ~** (*personnes*) to complement one another; (*collection etc*) to become complete.

complexe [kôṅpleks(ə)] *a* complex ♦ *nm* (*PSYCH*) complex, hang-up; (*bâtiments*): **~ hospitalier/industriel** hospital/industrial complex.

complexé, e [kôṅpleksā] *a* mixed-up, hung-up.

complexité [kôṅpleksētā] *nf* complexity.

complication [kôṅplēkásyôṅ] *nf* complexity, intricacy; (*difficulté, ennui*) complication; **~s** *nfpl* (*MÉD*) complications.

complice [kôṅplēs] *nm* accomplice.

complicité [kôṅplēsētā] *nf* complicity.

compliment [kôṅplēmåṅ] *nm* (*louange*) compliment; **~s** *nmpl* (*félicitations*) congratulations.

complimenter [kôṅplēmåṅtā] *vt*: **~ qn (sur** *ou* **de)** to congratulate *ou* compliment sb (on).

compliqué, e [kôṅplēkā] *a* complicated, complex, intricate; (*personne*) complicated.

compliquer [kôṅplēkā] *vt* to complicate; **se ~** *vi* (*situation*) to become complicated; **se ~ la vie** to make life difficult *ou* complicated for o.s.

complot [kôṅplō] *nm* plot.

comploter [kôṅplotā] *vi, vt* to plot.

complu, e [kôṅplü] *pp de* **complaire**.

comportement [kôṅportəmåṅ] *nm* behavior (*US*), behaviour (*Brit*); (*TECH*: *d'une pièce, d'un véhicule*) behavior (*US*), behaviour (*Brit*), performance.

comporter [kôṅportā] *vt* to be composed of, consist of, comprise; (*être équipé de*) to have; (*impliquer*) to entail, involve; **se ~** *vi* to behave; (*TECH*) to behave, perform.

composant [kôṅpōzåṅ] *nm* component, constituent.

composante [kôṅpōzåṅt] *nf* component.

composé, e [kôṅpōzā] *a* (*visage, air*) studied; (*BIO, CHIMIE, LING*) compound ♦ *nm* (*CHIMIE, LING*) compound; **~ de** made up of.

composer [kôṅpōzā] *vt* (*musique, texte*) to compose; (*mélange, équipe*) to make up; (*faire partie de*) to make up, form; (*TYPO*) to (type)set ♦ *vi* (*SCOL*) to take a test; (*transiger*) to come to terms; **se ~ de** to be composed of, be made up of; **~ un numéro** (*au téléphone*) to dial a number.

composite [kôṅpozēt] *a* heterogeneous.

compositeur, trice [kôṅpōzētœr, -trēs] *nm/f* (*MUS*) composer; (*TYPO*) compositor, typesetter.

composition [kôṅpōzēsyôṅ] *nf* composition; (*SCOL*) test; (*TYPO*) (type)setting, composition; **de bonne ~** (*accommodant*) easy to deal with; **amener qn à ~** to get sb to come to terms; **~ française** (*SCOL*) French essay.

compost [kôṅpost] *nm* compost.

composter [kôṅpostā] *vt* to date-stamp; to punch.

composteur [kôṅpostœr] *nm* date stamp; punch; (*TYPO*) composing stick.

compote [kôṅpot] *nf* stewed fruit *q*; **~ de pommes** stewed apples.

compotier [kôṅpotyā] *nm* fruit dish *ou* bowl.

compréhensible [kôṅprāåṅsēbl(ə)] *a* comprehensible; (*attitude*) understandable.

compréhensif, ive [kôṅprāåṅsēf, -ēv] *a* understanding.

compréhension [kôṅprāåṅsyôṅ] *nf* understanding; comprehension.

comprendre [kôṅpråṅdr(ə)] *vt* to understand; (*se composer de*) to comprise, consist of; (*inclure*) to include; **se faire ~** to make o.s. understood; to get one's ideas across; **mal ~** to misunderstand.

compresse [kôṅpres] *nf* compress.

compresser [kôṅprāsā] *vt* to squash in, crush together.

compresseur [kôṅpresœr] *am voir* **rouleau**.

compressible [kôṅprāsēbl(ə)] *a* (*PHYSIQUE*) compressible; (*dépenses*) reducible.

compression [kôṅpresyôṅ] *nf* compression; (*d'un crédit etc*) reduction.

comprimé, e [kôṅprēmā] *a*: **air ~** compressed

air ♦ *nm* tablet.

comprimer [kɔ̃prēmā] *vt* to compress; *(fig: crédit etc)* to reduce, cut down.

compris, e [kɔ̃prē, -ēz] *pp de* **comprendre** ♦ *a (inclus)* included; ~? understood?, is that clear?; ~ **entre** *(situé)* contained between; **la maison** ~e/non ~e, **y/non** ~ **la maison** including/excluding the house; **service** ~ service (charge) included; **100 F tout** ~ 100 F all-inclusive.

compromettre [kɔ̃prɔmetr(ə)] *vt* to compromise.

compromis [kɔ̃prɔmē] *vb voir* **compromettre** ♦ *nm* compromise.

compromission [kɔ̃prɔmēsyɔ̃] *nf* compromise, deal.

comptabiliser [kɔ̃tábēlēzā] *vt (valeur)* to post; *(fig)* to evaluate.

comptabilité [kɔ̃tábēlētā] *nf (activité, technique)* accounting, accountancy; *(d'une société: comptes)* accounts *pl*, books *pl*; *(: service)* accounts office *ou* department; ~ **à partie double** double-entry book-keeping.

comptable [kɔ̃tábl(ə)] *nm/f* accountant ♦ *a* accounts *cpd*, accounting.

comptant [kɔ̃tāñ] *ad:* **payer** ~ to pay cash; **acheter** ~ to buy for cash.

compte [kɔ̃t] *nm* count, counting; *(total, montant)* count, (right) number; *(bancaire, facture)* account; ~**s** *nmpl* accounts, books; *(fig)* explanation *sg*; **ouvrir un** ~ to open an account; **rendre des** ~**s à qn** *(fig)* to be answerable to sb; **faire le** ~ **de** to count up, make a count of; **tout** ~ **fait** on the whole; **à ce** ~**-là** *(dans ce cas)* in that case; *(à ce train-là)* at that rate; **en fin de** ~ *(fig)* all things considered, weighing it all up; **au bout du** ~ in the final analysis; **à bon** ~ at a favorable price; *(fig)* lightly; **avoir son** ~ *(fig: fam)* to have had it; **pour le** ~ **de** on behalf of; **pour son propre** ~ for one's own benefit; **sur le** ~ **de qn** *(à son sujet)* about sb; **travailler à son** ~ to work for oneself; **mettre qch sur le** ~ **de qn** *(le rendre responsable)* to attribute sth to sb; **prendre qch à son** ~ to take responsibility for sth; **trouver son** ~ **à qch** to profit by sth; **régler un** ~ *(s'acquitter de qch)* to settle an account; *(se venger)* to settle a score; **rendre** ~ **(à qn) de qch** to give (sb) an account of sth; **tenir** ~ **de qch** to take sth into account; ~ **tenu de** taking into account; ~ **chèque(s)** checking *(US)* ou current *(Brit)* account; ~ **chèque postal (CCP)** Post Office account; ~ **client** *(sur bilan)* accounts receivable; ~ **courant (CC)** checking *(US)* ou current *(Brit)* account; ~ **de dépôt** deposit account; ~ **d'exploitation** operating account; ~ **fournisseur** *(sur bilan)* accounts payable; ~ **à rebours** countdown; ~ **rendu** account, report; *(de film, livre)* review; *voir aussi* **rendre**.

compte-gouttes [kɔ̃tgōot] *nm inv* dropper.

compter [kɔ̃tā] *vt* to count; *(facturer)* to charge for; *(avoir à son actif, comporter)* to have; *(prévoir)* to allow, reckon; *(tenir compte de, inclure)* to include; *(penser, espérer):* ~ **réussir/revenir** to expect to succeed/return ♦ *vi* to count; *(être économe)* to economize; *(être non négligeable)* to count, matter; *(valoir):* ~ **pour** to count for; *(figurer):* ~ **parmi** to be ou rank among; ~ **sur** to count (up)on; ~ **avec qch/qn** to reckon with ou take account of sth/sb; ~ **sans qch/qn** to reckon without sth/sb; **sans** ~ **que** besides which; **à** ~ **du 10 janvier** *(COMM)* (as) from 10th January.

compte-tours [kɔ̃ttōōr] *nm inv* rev(olution) counter.

compteur [kɔ̃tœr] *nm* meter; ~ **de vitesse** speedometer.

comptine [kɔ̃tēn] *nf* nursery rhyme.

comptoir [kɔ̃twár] *nm (de magasin)* counter; *(de café)* counter, bar; *(colonial)* trading post.

compulser [kɔ̃pülsā] *vt* to consult.

comte, comtesse [kɔ̃t, kɔ̃tes] *nm/f* count/countess.

con, ne [kɔ̃, kɔn] *a (fam!)* damned *ou* bloody *(Brit)* stupid (!).

concasser [kɔ̃kāsā] *vt (pierre, sucre)* to crush; *(poivre)* to grind.

concave [kɔ̃káv] *a* concave.

concéder [kɔ̃sādā] *vt* to grant; *(défaite, point)* to concede; ~ **que** to concede that.

concentration [kɔ̃sāñtrāsyɔ̃] *nf* concentration.

concentrationnaire [kɔ̃sāñtrāsyoner] *a* of ou in concentration camps.

concentré [kɔ̃sāñtrā] *nm* concentrate; ~ **de tomates** tomato purée.

concentrer [kɔ̃sāñtrā] *vt* to concentrate; **se** ~ to concentrate.

concentrique [kɔ̃sāñtrēk] *a* concentric.

concept [kɔ̃sept] *nm* concept.

concepteur, trice [kɔ̃septœr, -trēs] *nm/f* designer.

conception [kɔ̃sepsyɔ̃] *nf* conception; *(d'une machine etc)* design.

concernant [kɔ̃sernāñ] *prép (se rapportant à)* concerning; *(en ce qui concerne)* as regards.

concerner [kɔ̃sernā] *vt* to concern; **en ce qui me concerne** as far as I am concerned; **en ce qui concerne ceci** as far as this is concerned, with regard to this.

concert [kɔ̃ser] *nm* concert; **de** ~ *ad* in unison; together.

concertation [kɔ̃sertāsyɔ̃] *nf (échange de vues)* dialogue; *(rencontre)* meeting.

concerter [kɔ̃sertā] *vt* to devise; **se** ~ *vi (collaborateurs etc)* to put our *(ou their etc)* heads together, consult (each other).

concertiste [kɔ̃sertēst(ə)] *nm/f* concert artist.

concerto [kɔ̃sertō] *nm* concerto.

concession [kɔ̃sāsyɔ̃] *nf* concession.

concessionnaire [kɔ̃sāsyoner] *nm/f* agent, dealer.

concevable [kɔ̃svábl(ə)] *a* conceivable.

concevoir [kɔ̃svwár] *vt (idée, projet)* to conceive (of); *(méthode, plan d'appartement, décoration etc)* to plan, design; *(enfant)* to conceive; **maison bien/mal conçue** well-/badly-designed *ou* -planned house.

concierge [kɔ̃syerzh(ə)] *nm/f* caretaker; *(d'hôtel)* head porter.

conciergerie [kɔ̃syerzhərē] *nf* caretaker's lodge.

concile [kôňsēl] *nm* council, synod.

conciliable [kôňsēlyábl(ə)] *a* (*opinions etc*) reconcilable.

conciliabules [kôňsēlyábül] *nmpl* (private) discussions.

conciliant, e [kôňsēlyáň, -âňt] *a* conciliatory.

conciliateur, trice [kôňsēlyátœr, -trēs] *nm/f* mediator, go-between.

conciliation [kôňsēlyâsyôň] *nf* conciliation.

concilier [kôňsēlyā] *vt* to reconcile; **se ~ qn/l'appui de qn** to win sb over/sb's support.

concis, e [kôňsē, -ēz] *a* concise.

concision [kôňsēzyôň] *nf* concision, conciseness.

concitoyen, ne [kôňsētwáyaň, -en] *nm/f* fellow citizen.

conclave [kôňkláv] *nm* conclave.

concluant, e [kôňklüäň, -âňt] *vb voir* **conclure** ♦ *a* conclusive.

conclure [kôňklür] *vt* to conclude; (*signer: accord, pacte*) to enter into; (*déduire*): **~ qch de qch** to deduce sth from sth; **~ à l'acquittement** to decide in favor of an acquittal; **~ au suicide** to come to the conclusion (*ou* (*JUR*) to pronounce) that it is a case of suicide; **~ un marché** to clinch a deal; **j'en conclus que** from that I conclude that.

conclusion [kôňklüzyôň] *nf* conclusion; **~s** *nfpl* (*JUR*) submissions; findings; **en ~** in conclusion.

concocter [kôňkoktā] *vt* to concoct.

conçois [kôňswá], **conçoive** [kôňswáv] *etc vb voir* **concevoir**.

concombre [kôňkôňbr(ə)] *nm* cucumber.

concomitant, e [kôňkomētáň, -âňt] *a* concomitant.

concordance [kôňkordáňs] *nf* concordance; **la ~ des temps** (*LING*) the sequence of tenses.

concordant, e [kôňkordáň, -âňt] *a* (*témoignages, versions*) corroborating.

concorde [kôňkord(ə)] *nf* concord.

concorder [kôňkordā] *vi* to tally, agree.

concourir [kôňkōōrēr] *vi* (*SPORT*) to compete; **~ à** *vt* (*effet etc*) to work towards.

concours [kôňkōōr] *vb voir* **concourir** ♦ *nm* competition; (*SCOL*) competitive examination; (*assistance*) aid, help; **recrutement par voie de ~** recruitment by (competitive) examination; **apporter son ~ à** to give one's support to; **~ de circonstances** combination of circumstances; **~ hippique** horse show; *voir* **hors**.

concret, ète [kôňkre, -et] *a* concrete.

concrètement [kôňkretmâň] *ad* in concrete terms.

concrétiser [kôňkrātēzā] *vt* to realize; **se ~** *vi* to materialize.

conçu, e [kôňsü] *pp de* **concevoir**.

concubin, e [kôňkübaň, -ēn] *nm/f* (*JUR*) cohabitant.

concubinage [kôňkübēnázh] *nm* (*JUR*) cohabitation.

concupiscence [kôňküpēsáňs] *nf* concupiscence.

concurremment [kôňkürámáň] *ad* concurrently; jointly.

concurrence [kôňküráňs] *nf* competition; **jusqu'à ~ de** up to; **~ déloyale** unfair competition.

concurrent, e [kôňküráň, -âňt] *a* competing ♦ *nm/f* (*SPORT, ECON etc*) competitor; (*SCOL*) competitor (*US*), candidate (*Brit*).

conçus [kôňsü] *vb voir* **concevoir**.

condamnable [kôňdânábl(ə)] *a* (*action, opinion*) reprehensible.

condamnation [kôňdânâsyôň] *nf* (*action*) condemnation; sentencing; (*peine*) sentence; conviction; **~ à mort** death sentence.

condamné, e [kôňdânā] *nm/f* (*JUR*) convict.

condamner [kôňdânā] *vt* (*blâmer*) to condemn; (*JUR*) to sentence; (*porte, ouverture*) to fill in, block up; (*malade*) to give up (hope for); (*obliger*): **~ qn à qch/faire** to condemn sb to sth/to do; **~ qn à 2 ans de prison** to sentence sb to 2 years' imprisonment; **~ qn à une amende** to impose a fine on sb.

condensateur [kôňdâňsátœr] *nm* condenser.

condensation [kôňdâňsâsyôň] *nf* condensation.

condensé [kôňdâňsā] *nm* digest.

condenser [kôňdâňsā] *vt*, **se ~** *vi* to condense.

condescendant, e [kôňdāsâňdâň, -âňt] *a* (*personne, attitude*) condescending.

condescendre [kôňdāsâňdr(ə)] *vi*: **~ à** to condescend to.

condiment [kôňdēmâň] *nm* condiment.

condisciple [kôňdēsēpl(ə)] *nm/f* school fellow, fellow student.

condition [kôňdēsyôň] *nf* condition; **~s** *nfpl* (*tarif, prix*) terms; (*circonstances*) conditions; **sans ~** *a* unconditional ♦ *ad* unconditionally; **sous ~ que** on condition that; **à ~ de ou que** provided that; **en bonne ~** in good condition; **mettre en ~** (*SPORT etc*) to get fit; (*PSYCH*) to condition (mentally); **~s de vie** living conditions.

conditionnel, le [kôňdēsyonel] *a* conditional ♦ *nm* conditional (tense).

conditionnement [kôňdēsyonmâň] *nm* (*emballage*) packaging; (*fig*) conditioning.

conditionner [kôňdēsyonā] *vt* (*déterminer*) to determine; (*COMM: produit*) to package; (*fig: personne*) to condition; **air conditionné** air conditioning; **réflexe conditionné** conditioned reflex.

condoléances [kôňdolāáňs] *nfpl* condolences.

conducteur, trice [kôňdüktœr, -trēs] *a* (*ÉLEC*) conducting ♦ *nm/f* (*AUTO etc*) driver; (*machine*) operator ♦ *nm* (*ÉLEC etc*) conductor.

conduire [kôňdüēr] *vt* (*véhicule, passager*) to drive; (*délégation, troupeau*) to lead; **se ~** *vi* to behave; **~ vers/à** to lead towards/to; **~ qn quelque part** to take sb somewhere; to drive sb somewhere.

conduit, e [kôňdüē, -ēt] *pp de* **conduire** ♦ *nm* (*TECH*) conduit, pipe; (*ANAT*) duct, canal.

conduite [kôňdüēt] *nf* (*en auto*) driving; (*comportement*) behavior (*US*), behaviour (*Brit*); (*d'eau, de gaz*) pipe; **sous la ~ de** led by; **~ forcée** penstock (*US*), pressure pipe (*Brit*); **~ à gauche** left-hand drive; **~ intérieure** sedan (*US*), saloon (car) (*Brit*).

cône [kōn] *nm* cone; **en forme de ~** cone-shaped.

conf. *abr* (= *confort*): **tt ~** all modern conveniences.

confection [kôňfeksyôň] *nf* (*fabrication*) making; (*COUTURE*): **la** ~ the clothing industry, the rag trade (*fam*); **vêtement de** ~ ready-to-wear garment, off-the-rack (*US*) *ou* off-the-peg (*Brit*) garment.

confectionner [kôṅfeksyonā] *vt* to make.

confédération [kôṅfādārâsyôṅ] *nf* confederation.

conférence [kôṅfārâṅs] *nf* (*exposé*) lecture; (*pourparlers*) conference; ~ **de presse** press conference; ~ **au sommet** summit (conference).

conférencier, ière [kôṅfārâṅsyā, -yer] *nm/f* lecturer.

conférer [kôṅfārā] *vt*: ~ **à qn** (*titre, grade*) to confer on sb; ~ **à qch/qn** (*aspect etc*) to endow sth/sb with, give (to) sth/sb.

confesser [kôṅfāsā] *vt* to confess; **se** ~ *vi* (*REL*) to go to confession.

confesseur [kôṅfāsœr] *nm* confessor.

confession [kôṅfesyôṅ] *nf* confession; (*culte: catholique etc*) denomination.

confessionnal, aux [kôṅfāsyonàl, -ō] *nm* confessional.

confessionnel, le [kôṅfāsyonel] *a* denominational.

confetti [kôṅfātē] *nm* confetti *q*.

confiance [kôṅfyâṅs] *nf* confidence, trust; faith; **avoir** ~ **en** to have confidence *ou* faith in, trust; **faire** ~ **à** to trust; **en toute** ~ with complete confidence; **de** ~ trustworthy, reliable; **mettre qn en** ~ to win sb's trust; **vote de** ~ (*POL*) vote of confidence; **inspirer** ~ **à** to inspire confidence in; ~ **en soi** self confidence; *voir* **question**.

confiant, e [kôṅfyâṅ, -âṅt] *a* confident; trusting.

confidence [kôṅfēdâṅs] *nf* confidence.

confident, e [kôṅfēdâṅ, -âṅt] *nm/f* confidant/confidante.

confidentiel, le [kôṅfēdâṅsyel] *a* confidential.

confier [kôṅfyā] *vt*: ~ **à qn** (*objet en dépôt, travail etc*) to entrust to sb; (*secret, pensée*) to confide to sb; **se** ~ **à qn** to confide in sb.

configuration [kôṅfēgūrâsyôṅ] *nf* configuration, layout; (*INFORM*) configuration.

confiné, e [kôṅfēnā] *a* enclosed; (*air*) stale.

confiner [kôṅfēnā] *vt*: ~ **à** to confine to; (*toucher*) to border on; **se** ~ **dans** *ou* **à** to confine o.s. to.

confins [kôṅfaṅ] *nmpl*: **aux** ~ **de** on the borders of.

confirmation [kôṅfērmâsyôṅ] *nf* confirmation.

confirmer [kôṅfērmā] *vt* to confirm; ~ **qn dans une croyance/ses fonctions** to strengthen sb in a belief/his duties.

confiscation [kôṅfēskâsyôṅ] *nf* confiscation.

confiserie [kôṅfēzrē] *nf* (*magasin*) confectioner's *ou* candy store (*US*), sweet shop (*Brit*); ~**s** *nfpl* (*bonbons*) confectionery *sg*, candy *q*, sweets (*Brit*).

confiseur, euse [kôṅfēzœr, -œz] *nm/f* confectioner.

confisquer [kôṅfēskā] *vt* to confiscate.

confit, e [kôṅfē, -ēt] *a*: **fruits** ~**s** candied fruits ♦ *nm*: ~ **d'oie** potted goose.

confiture [kôṅfētūr] *nf* jam; ~ **d'oranges** (orange) marmalade.

conflagration [kôṅflāgrâsyôṅ] *nf* cataclysm.

conflictuel, le [kôṅflēktūel] *a* full of clashes *ou* conflicts.

conflit [kôṅflē] *nm* conflict.

confluent [kôṅflüâṅ] *nm* confluence.

confondre [kôṅfôṅdr(ə)] *vt* (*jumeaux, faits*) to confuse, mix up; (*témoin, menteur*) to confound; **se** ~ *vi* to merge; **se** ~ **en excuses** to offer profuse apologies, apologize profusely; ~ **qch/qn avec qch/qn d'autre** to mistake sth/sb for sth/sb else.

confondu, e [kôṅfôṅdü] *pp de* **confondre** ♦ *a* (*stupéfait*) speechless, overcome; **toutes catégories** ~**es** taking all categories together.

conformation [kôṅformâsyôṅ] *nf* conformation.

conforme [kôṅform(ə)] *a*: ~ **à** (*en accord avec*) in accordance with, in keeping with; (*identique à*) true to; **copie certifiée** ~ (*ADMIN*) certified copy; ~ **à la commande** as per order.

conformé, e [kôṅformā] *a*: **bien** ~ well-formed.

conformément [kôṅformāmâṅ] *ad*: ~ **à** in accordance with.

conformer [kôṅformā] *vt*: ~ **qch à** to model sth on; **se** ~ **à** to conform to.

conformisme [kôṅformēsm(ə)] *nm* conformity.

conformiste [kôṅformēst(ə)] *a, nm/f* conformist.

conformité [kôṅformētā] *nf* conformity; agreement; **en** ~ **avec** in accordance with.

confort [kôṅfor] *nm* comfort; **tout** ~ (*COMM*) with all modern conveniences.

confortable [kôṅfortabl(ə)] *a* comfortable.

confortablement [kôṅfortáblemâṅ] *ad* comfortably.

conforter [kôṅfortā] *vt* to reinforce, strengthen.

confrère [kôṅfrer] *nm* colleague; fellow member.

confrérie [kôṅfrārē] *nf* brotherhood.

confrontation [kôṅfrôṅtâsyôṅ] *nf* confrontation.

confronté, e [kôṅfrôṅtā] *a*: ~ **à** confronted by, facing.

confronter [kôṅfrôṅtā] *vt* to confront; (*textes*) to compare, collate.

confus, e [kôṅfü, -üz] *a* (*vague*) confused; (*embarrassé*) embarrassed.

confusément [kôṅfüzāmâṅ] *ad* (*distinguer, ressentir*) vaguely; (*parler*) confusedly.

confusion [kôṅfüzyôṅ] *nf* (*voir confus*) confusion; embarrassment; (*voir confondre*) confusion; mixing up; (*erreur*) confusion; ~ **des peines** (*JUR*) concurrency of sentences.

congé [kôṅzhā] *nm* (*vacances*) vacation (*US*), holiday (*Brit*); (*arrêt de travail*) time off *q*; leave *q*; (*MIL*) leave *q*; (*avis de départ*) notice; **en** ~ on vacation (*US*) *ou* holiday (*Brit*); off (*work*); on leave; **semaine/jour de** ~ week/day off; **prendre** ~ **de qn** to take one's leave of sb; **donner son** ~ **à** to hand *ou* give one's notice to; ~ **de maladie** sick leave; ~ **de maternité** maternity leave; ~**s payés** paid vacation *ou* leave.

congédier [kôṅzhādyā] *vt* to dismiss.

congélateur [kôṅzhālâtœr] *nm* freezer, deep freeze.

congeler [kɔ̃zhlā] *vt*, **se** ~ *vi* to freeze.
congénère [kɔ̃zhānér] *nm/f* fellow (bear *ou* lion *etc*), fellow creature.
congénital, e, aux [kɔ̃zhānētàl, -ō] *a* congenital.
congère [kɔ̃zher] *nf* snowdrift.
congestion [kɔ̃zhestyɔ̃n] *nf* congestion; ~ **cérébrale** stroke; ~ **pulmonaire** congestion of the lungs.
congestionner [kɔ̃zhestyonā] *vt* to congest; (*MÉD*) to flush.
conglomérat [kɔ̃glomārá] *nm* conglomerate.
Congo [kɔ̃gō] *nm*: **le** ~ (*pays, fleuve*) the Congo.
congolais, e [kɔ̃gole, -ez] *a* Congolese ♦ *nm/f*: **C**~, **e** Congolese.
congratuler [kɔ̃grátülā] *vt* to congratulate.
congre [kɔ̃gr(ə)] *nm* conger (eel).
congrégation [kɔ̃grāgásyɔ̃n] *nf* (*REL*) congregation; (*gén*) assembly; gathering.
congrès [kɔ̃gre] *nm* congress.
congressiste [kɔ̃grāsēst(ə)] *nm/f* delegate, participant (at a congress).
congru, e [kɔ̃grü] *a*: **la portion** ~**e** the smallest *ou* meanest share.
conifère [konēfer] *nm* conifer.
conique [konēk] *a* conical.
conjecture [kɔ̃zhektür] *nf* conjecture, speculation *q*.
conjecturer [kɔ̃zhektürā] *vt, vi* to conjecture.
conjoint, e [kɔ̃zhwañ, -wañt] *a* joint ♦ *nm/f* spouse.
conjointement [kɔ̃zhwañtmâñ] *ad* jointly.
conjonctif, ive [kɔ̃zhɔ̃ktēf, -ēv] *a*: **tissu** ~ connective tissue.
conjonction [kɔ̃zhɔ̃ksyɔ̃n] *nf* (*LING*) conjunction.
conjonctivite [kɔ̃zhɔ̃ktēvēt] *nf* conjunctivitis.
conjoncture [kɔ̃zhɔ̃ktür] *nf* circumstances *pl*; **la** ~ (**économique**) the economic climate *ou* situation.
conjugaison [kɔ̃zhügezɔ̃n] *nf* (*LING*) conjugation.
conjugal, e, aux [kɔ̃zhügàl, -ō] *a* conjugal; married.
conjuguer [kɔ̃zhügā] *vt* (*LING*) to conjugate; (*efforts etc*) to combine.
conjuration [kɔ̃zhürásyɔ̃n] *nf* conspiracy.
conjuré, e [kɔ̃zhürā] *nm/f* conspirator.
conjurer [kɔ̃zhürā] *vt* (*sort, maladie*) to avert; (*implorer*): ~ **qn de faire qch** to beseech *ou* entreat sb to do sth.
connais [kone], **connaissais** [konese] *etc vb voir* **connaître**.
connaissance [konesâñs] *nf* (*savoir*) knowledge *q*; (*personne connue*) acquaintance; (*conscience, perception*) consciousness; ~**s** *nfpl* knowledge *q*; **être sans** ~ to be unconscious; **perdre/reprendre** ~ to lose/regain consciousness; **à ma/sa** ~ to (the best of) my/his knowledge; **faire** ~ **avec qn** *ou* **la** ~ **de qn** (*rencontrer*) to meet sb; (*apprendre à connaître*) to get to know sb; **avoir** ~ **de** to be aware of; **prendre** ~ **de** (*document etc*) to peruse; **en** ~ **de cause** with full knowledge of the facts; **de** ~ (*personne, visage*) familiar.
connaissant [konesâñ] *etc vb voir* **connaître**.

connaissement [konesmâñ] *nm* bill of lading.
connaisseur, euse [konesœr, -œz] *nm/f* connoisseur ♦ *a* expert.
connaître [konetr(ə)] *vt* to know; (*éprouver*) to experience; (*avoir*) to have; to enjoy; ~ **de nom/vue** to know by name/sight; **se** ~ to know each other; (*soi-même*) to know o.s.; **ils se sont connus à Genève** they (first) met in Geneva; **s'y** ~ **en qch** to know about sth.
connecté, e [konektā] *a* (*INFORM*) on line.
connecter [konektā] *vt* to connect.
connerie [konrē] *nf* (*fam*) damn-fool (*US*) *ou* (bloody) stupid (*Brit*) thing to do *ou* say.
connexe [koneks(ə)] *a* closely related.
connexion [koneksyɔ̃n] *nf* connection.
connivence [konēvâñs] *nf* connivance.
connu, e [konü] *pp de* **connaître** ♦ *a* (*célèbre*) well-known.
conquérant, e [kɔ̃kārâñ, -âñt] *nm/f* conqueror.
conquérir [kɔ̃kārēr] *vt* to conquer, win.
conquerrai [kɔ̃kerrā] *etc vb voir* **conquérir**.
conquête [kɔ̃ket] *nf* conquest.
conquière, conquiers [kɔ̃kyer] *etc vb voir* **conquérir**.
conquis, e [kɔ̃kē, -ēz] *pp de* **conquérir**.
consacrer [kɔ̃sàkrā] *vt* (*REL*): ~ **qch (à)** to consecrate sth (to); (*fig: usage etc*) to sanction, establish; (*employer*): ~ **qch à** to devote *ou* dedicate sth to; **se** ~ **à qch/faire** to dedicate *ou* devote o.s. to sth/to doing.
consanguin, e [kɔ̃sáñgàñ, -ēn] *a* between blood relations; **frère** ~ half-brother (*on father's side*); **mariage** ~ intermarriage.
consciemment [kɔ̃syámâñ] *ad* consciously.
conscience [kɔ̃syâñs] *nf* conscience; (*perception*) consciousness; **avoir/prendre** ~ **de** to be/become aware of; **perdre/reprendre** ~ to lose/regain consciousness; **avoir bonne/mauvaise** ~ to have a clear/guilty conscience; **en (toute)** ~ in all conscience; ~ **professionnelle** professional conscience.
consciencieux, euse [kɔ̃syáñsyœ̄, -œ̄z] *a* conscientious.
conscient, e [kɔ̃syáñ, -âñt] *a* conscious; ~ **de** aware *ou* conscious of.
conscription [kɔ̃skrēpsyɔ̃n] *nf* draft.
conscrit [kɔ̃skrē] *nm* draftee.
consécration [kɔ̃sākrásyɔ̃n] *nf* consecration.
consécutif, ive [kɔ̃sākütēf, -ēv] *a* consecutive; ~ **à** following upon.
consécutivement [kɔ̃sākütēvmâñ] *ad* consecutively; ~ **à** following on.
conseil [kɔ̃sey] *nm* (*avis*) piece of advice, advice *q*; (*assemblée*) council; (*expert*): ~ **en recrutement** recruitment consultant ♦ *a*: **ingénieur-**~ consulting engineer, engineering consultant; **tenir** ~ to hold a meeting; to deliberate; **donner un** ~ *ou* **des** ~**s à qn** to give sb (a piece of) advice; **demander** ~ **à qn** to ask sb's advice; **prendre** ~ (**auprès de qn**) to seek advice (from sb); ~ **d'administration (CA)** board (of directors); ~ **de classe** (*SCOL*) meeting of teachers, parents and class representatives to discuss pupils' progress; ~ **de discipline** disciplinary committee; ~ **général** regional council; ~ **de guerre** court-martial; **le** ~ **des ministres** ≈ the Cabinet; ~ **municipal (CM)** town council;

~ régional regional board of elected representatives; **~ de révision** recruitment ou draft (US) board.

conseiller [kôṅsāyā] vt (personne) to advise; (méthode, action) to recommend, advise; **~ qch à qn** to recommend sth to sb; **~ à qn de faire qch** to advise sb to do sth.

conseiller, ère [kôṅsāyā, -er] nm/f adviser; **~ matrimonial** marriage guidance counsellor; **~ municipal** town ou city councilman (US), town councillor (Brit).

consentement [kôṅsâṅtmâṅ] nm consent.

consentir [kôṅsâṅtēr] vt: **~ (à qch/faire)** to agree ou consent (to sth/to doing); **~ qch à qn** to grant sb sth.

conséquence [kôṅsākâṅs] nf consequence, outcome; **~s** nfpl consequences, repercussions; **en ~** (donc) consequently; (de façon appropriée) accordingly; **ne pas tirer à ~** to be unlikely to have any repercussions; **sans ~** unimportant; **de ~** important.

conséquent, e [kôṅsākâṅ, -âṅt] a logical, rational; (fam: important) substantial; **par ~** consequently.

conservateur, trice [kôṅservátœr, -trēs] a conservative ♦ nm/f (POL) conservative; (de musée) curator.

conservation [kôṅservâsyôṅ] nf retention; keeping; preserving; preservation.

conservatoire [kôṅservātwár] nm academy; (ÉCOLOGIE) conservation area.

conserve [kôṅserv(ə)] nf (gén pl) canned food; **~s de poisson** canned fish; **en ~** canned; **de ~** (ensemble) in concert; (naviguer) in convoy.

conservé, e [kôṅservā] a: **bien ~** (personne) well-preserved.

conserver [kôṅservā] vt (faculté) to retain, keep; (habitude) to keep up; (amis, livres) to keep; (préserver, aussi CULIN) to preserve; **se ~** vi (aliments) to keep; **"~ au frais"** "store in a cool place".

conserverie [kôṅservarē] nf canning factory.

considérable [kôṅsēdārábl(ə)] a considerable, significant, extensive.

considération [kôṅsēdārásyôṅ] nf consideration; (estime) esteem, respect; **~s** nfpl (remarques) reflections; **prendre en ~** to take into consideration ou account; **ceci mérite ~** this is worth considering; **en ~ de** given, because of.

considéré, e [kôṅsēdārā] a respected; **tout bien ~** all things considered.

considérer [kôṅsēdārā] vt to consider; (regarder) to consider, study; **~ qch comme** to regard sth as.

consigne [kôṅsēny] nf (COMM) deposit; (de gare) checkroom (US), left luggage (office) (Brit); (punition: SCOL) detention; (: MIL) confinement to barracks; (ordre, instruction) instructions pl; **~ automatique** luggage locker; **~s de sécurité** safety instructions.

consigné, e [kôṅsēnyā] a (COMM: bouteille, emballage) returnable; **non ~** non-returnable.

consigner [kôṅsēnyā] vt (note, pensée) to record; (marchandises) to deposit; (punir: MIL) to confine to barracks; (: élève) to keep in; (COMM) to put a deposit on.

consistance [kôṅsēstâṅs] nf consistency.

consistant, e [kôṅsēstâṅ, -âṅt] a thick; solid.

consister [kôṅsēstā] vi: **~ en/dans/à faire** to consist of/in/in doing.

consœur [kôṅsœr] nf (lady) colleague; fellow member.

consolation [kôṅsolâsyôṅ] nf consolation q, comfort q.

console [kôṅsol] nf console; **~ graphique** ou **de visualisation** (INFORM) visual display unit, VDU.

consoler [kôṅsolā] vt to console; **se ~ (de qch)** to console o.s. (for sth).

consolider [kôṅsolēdā] vt to strengthen, reinforce; (fig) to consolidate; **bilan consolidé** consolidated balance sheet.

consommateur, trice [kôṅsomátœr, -trēs] nm/f (ÉCON) consumer; (dans un café) customer.

consommation [kôṅsomâsyôṅ] nf consumption; (JUR) consummation; (boisson) drink; **~ aux 100 km** (AUTO) (fuel) consumption per 100 km, ≈ miles per gallon (mpg), ≈ gas mileage (US); **de ~** (biens, société) consumer cpd.

consommé, e [kôṅsomā] a consummate ♦ nm consommé.

consommer [kôṅsomā] vt (suj: personne) to eat ou drink, consume; (suj: voiture, usine, poêle) to use, consume; (JUR) to consummate ♦ vi (dans un café) to (have a) drink.

consonance [kôṅsonâṅs] nf consonance; **nom à ~ étrangère** foreign-sounding name.

consonne [kôṅson] nf consonant.

consorts [kôṅsor] nmpl: **et ~** (péj) and company, and his bunch ou like.

conspirateur, trice [kôṅspērátœr, -trēs] nm/f conspirator, plotter.

conspiration [kôṅspērâsyôṅ] nf conspiracy.

conspirer [kôṅspērā] vi to conspire, plot; **~ à** (tendre à) to conspire to.

conspuer [kôṅspüā] vt to boo, shout down.

constamment [kôṅstámâṅ] ad constantly.

constant, e [kôṅstâṅ, -âṅt] a constant; (personne) steadfast ♦ nf constant.

Constantinople [kôṅstâṅtēnopl(ə)] n Constantinople.

constat [kôṅstá] nm (d'huissier) certified report (by bailiff); (de police) report; (observation) (observed) fact, observation; (affirmation) statement; **~ (à l'amiable)** (jointly agreed) statement for insurance purposes.

constatation [kôṅstátâsyôṅ] nf noticing; certifying; (remarque) observation.

constater [kôṅstátā] vt (remarquer) to note, notice; (ADMIN, JUR: attester) to certify; (dégâts) to note; **~ que** (dire) to state that.

constellation [kôṅstālāsyôṅ] nf constellation.

constellé, e [kôṅstālā] a: **~ de** (étoiles) studded ou spangled with; (taches) spotted with.

consternation [kôṅsternâsyôṅ] nf consternation, dismay.

consterner [kôṅsternā] vt to dismay.

constipation [kôṅstēpâsyôṅ] nf constipation.

constipé, e [kôṅstēpā] a constipated; (fig) stiff.

constituant, e [kôṅstētüâṅ, -âṅt] a (élément)

constituent; **assemblée** ~e (POL) constituent assembly.

constitué, e |kôństětüä| a: ~ **de** made up ou composed of; **bien** ~ of sound constitution; well-formed.

constituer [kôństětüä] vt (comité, équipe) to set up, form; (dossier, collection) to put together, build up; (suj: éléments, parties: composer) to make up, constitute; (représenter, être) to constitute; **se** ~ **prisonnier** to give o.s. up; **se** ~ **partie civile** to bring an independent action for damages.

constitution [kôństětüsyôń] nf setting up; building up; (composition) composition, make-up; (santé, POL) constitution.

constitutionnel, le [kôństětüsyonel] a constitutional.

constructeur [kôństrüktœr] nm manufacturer, builder.

constructif, ive [kôństrüktēf, -ēv] a (positif) constructive.

construction [kôństrüksyôń] nf construction, building.

construire [kôństrüēr] vt to build, construct; **se** ~: **l'immeuble s'est construit très vite** the building went up ou was built very quickly.

consul [kôńsül] nm consul.

consulaire [kôńsüler] a consular.

consulat [kôńsülä] nm consulate.

consultatif, ive [kôńsültätēf, -ēv] a advisory.

consultation [kôńsültâsyôń] nf consultation; ~s nfpl (POL) talks; **être en** ~ (délibération) to be in consultation; (médecin) to be consulting; **aller à la** ~ (MÉD) to go to the doctor's office (US) ou surgery (Brit); **heures de** ~ (MÉD) office (US) ou surgery (Brit) hours.

consulter [kôńsültä] vt to consult ♦ vi (médecin) to be in (the office) (US), hold surgery (Brit); **se** ~ to confer.

consumer [kôńsümä] vt to consume; **se** ~ vi to burn; **se** ~ **de chagrin/douleur** to be consumed with sorrow/grief.

consumérisme [kôńsümärēsm(ə)] nm consumerism.

contact [kôńtäkt] nm contact; **au** ~ **de** (air, peau) on contact with; (gens) through contact with; **mettre/couper le** ~ (AUTO) to switch on/off the ignition; **entrer en** ~ (fils, objets) to come into contact, make contact; **se mettre en** ~ **avec** (RADIO) to make contact with; **prendre** ~ **avec** (relation d'affaires, connaissance) to get in touch ou contact with.

contacter [kôńtäktä] vt to contact, get in touch with.

contagieux, euse [kôńtázhyœ̄, -œ̄z] a contagious; infectious.

contagion [kôńtázhyôń] nf contagion.

container [kôńtener] nm container.

contaminer [kôńtämēnä] vt to contaminate.

conte [kôńt] nm tale; ~ **de fées** fairy tale.

contemplation [kôńtâńplásyôń] nf contemplation; (REL, PHILOSOPHIE) meditation.

contempler [kôńtâńplä] vt to contemplate, gaze at.

contemporain, e [kôńtâńporań, -en] a, nm/f contemporary.

contenance [kôńtnâńs] nf (d'un récipient) capacity; (attitude) bearing, attitude; **perdre** ~ to lose one's composure; **se donner une** ~ to give the impression of composure; **faire bonne** ~ **(devant)** to put on a bold front (in the face of).

conteneur [kôńtnœr] nm container.

conteneurisation [kôńtnœrēzâsyôń] nf containerization.

contenir [kôńtnēr] vt to contain; (avoir une capacité de) to hold; **se** ~ (se retenir) to control o.s. ou one's emotions, contain o.s.

content, e [kôńtâń, -âńt] a pleased, glad; ~ **de** pleased with; **je serais** ~ **que tu** ... I would be pleased if you ....

contentement [kôńtâńtmâń] nm contentment, satisfaction.

contenter [kôńtâńtä] vt to satisfy, please; (envie) to satisfy; **se** ~ **de** to content o.s. with.

contentieux [kôńtâńsyœ̄] nm (COMM) litigation; (: service) litigation department; (POL etc) contentious issues pl.

contenu, e [kôńtnü] pp de **contenir** ♦ nm (d'un bol) contents pl; (d'un texte) content.

conter [kôńtä] vt to recount, relate; **en** ~ **de belles à qn** to tell tall stories to sb.

contestable [kôńtestábl(ə)] a questionable.

contestataire [kôńtestáter] a (journal, étudiant) anti-establishment ♦ nm/f (anti-establishment) protester.

contestation [kôńtestâsyôń] nf questioning, contesting; (POL): **la** ~ anti-establishment activity, protest.

conteste [kôńtest(ə)]: **sans** ~ ad unquestionably, indisputably.

contesté, e [kôńtestä] a (roman, écrivain) controversial.

contester [kôńtestä] vt to question, contest ♦ vi (POL, gén) to protest, rebel (against established authority).

conteur, euse [kôńtœr, -œ̄z] nm/f story-teller.

contexte [kôńtekst(ə)] nm context.

contiendrai [kôńtyańdrä], **contiens** [kôńtyań] etc vb voir **contenir**.

contigu, ë [kôńtēgü] a: ~ **(à)** adjacent to.

continent [kôńtēnâń] nm continent.

continental, e, aux [kôńtēnâńtál, -ō] a continental.

contingences [kôńtańzhâńs] nfpl contingencies.

contingent [kôńtańzhâń] nm (MIL) contingent; (COMM) quota.

contingenter [kôńtańzhâńtä] vt (COMM) to fix a quota on.

contins [kôńtań] etc vb voir **contenir**.

continu, e [kôńtēnü] a continuous; **(courant)** ~ direct current, DC.

continuation [kôńtēnüäsyôń] nf continuation.

continuel, le [kôńtēnüel] a (qui se répète) constant, continual; (continu) continuous.

continuellement [kôńtēnüelmâń] ad continually; continuously.

continuer [kôńtēnüä] vt (travail, voyage etc) to continue (with), carry on (with), go on (with); (prolonger: alignement, rue) to continue ♦ vi (pluie, vie, bruit) to continue, go on; (voyageur) to go on; **se** ~ vi to carry on; ~ **à** ou **de faire** to go on ou continue doing.

continuité [kôńtēnüčtä] nf continuity; continuation.

contondant, e [kôntôndâṅ, -âṅt] *a*: **arme** ~**e** blunt instrument.

contorsion [kôntorsyôṅ] *nf* contortion.

contorsionner [kôntorsyonā]: **se** ~ *vi* to contort o.s., writhe about.

contour [kôntōōr] *nm* outline, contour; ~**s** *nmpl* (*d'une rivière etc*) windings.

contourner [kôntōōrnā] *vt* to bypass, walk (*ou* drive) around.

contraceptif, ive [kôntráseptēf, -ēv] *a, nm* contraceptive.

contraception [kôntrásepsyôṅ] *nf* contraception.

contracté, e [kôntráktā] *a* (*muscle*) tense, contracted; (*personne: tendu*) tense, tensed up; **article** ~ (*LING*) contracted article.

contracter [kôntráktā] *vt* (*muscle etc*) to tense, contract; (*maladie, dette, obligation*) to contract; (*assurance*) to take out; **se** ~ *vi* (*métal, muscles*) to contract.

contraction [kôntráksyôṅ] *nf* contraction.

contractuel, le [kôntráktüel] *a* contractual ♦ *nm/f* (*agent*) traffic policeman (*US*)/meter maid (*US*), traffic warden (*Brit*); (*employé*) contract employee.

contradiction [kôntrádēksyôṅ] *nf* contradiction.

contradictoire [kôntrádēktwâr] *a* contradictory, conflicting; **débat** ~ (open) debate.

contraignant, e [kôntrenyâṅ, -âṅt] *vb voir* **contraindre** ♦ *a* restricting.

contraindre [kôntraṅdr(ə)] *vt*: ~ **qn à faire** to force *ou* compel sb to do.

contraint, e [kôntraṅ, -âṅt] *pp de* **contraindre** ♦ *a* (*mine, air*) constrained, forced ♦ *nf* constraint; **sans** ~**e** unrestrainedly, unconstrainedly.

contraire [kôntrɛr] *a, nm* opposite; ~ **à** contrary to; **au** ~ *ad* on the contrary.

contrairement [kôntrermâṅ] *ad*: ~ **à** contrary to, unlike.

contralto [kôntráltō] *nm* contralto.

contrariant, e [kôntráryâṅ, -âṅt] *a* (*personne*) contrary, perverse; (*incident*) annoying.

contrarier [kôntráryā] *vt* (*personne*) to annoy, bother; (*fig*) to impede; to thwart, frustrate.

contrariété [kôntráryātā] *nf* annoyance.

contraste [kôntrást(ə)] *nm* contrast.

contraster [kôntrástā] *vt, vi* to contrast.

contrat [kôntrá] *nm* contract; (*fig: accord, pacte*) agreement; ~ **de travail** employment contract.

contravention [kôntrávâṅsyôṅ] *nf* (*infraction*): ~ **à** infraction (*US*) *ou* contravention (*Brit*) of; (*amende*) fine; (*PV pour stationnement interdit*) parking ticket; **dresser** ~ **à** (*automobiliste*) to write out a parking ticket for.

contre [kôntr(ə)] *prép* against; (*en échange*) (in exchange) for; **par** ~ on the other hand.

contre-amiral, aux [kôntrámērál, -ō] *nm* rear admiral.

contre-attaque [kôntráták] *nf* counter-attack.

contre-attaquer [kôntrátákā] *vi* to counter-attack.

contre-balancer [kôntrəbálâṅsā] *vt* to counter-balance; (*fig*) to offset.

contrebande [kôntrəbâṅd] *nf* (*trafic*) contraband, smuggling; (*marchandise*) contraband, smuggled goods *pl*; **faire la** ~ **de** to smuggle.

contrebandier, ière [kôntrəbâṅdyā, -yer] *nm/f* smuggler.

contrebas [kôntrəbâ]: **en** ~ *ad* (down) below.

contrebasse [kôntrəbâs] *nf* (double) bass.

contrebassiste [kôntrəbâsēst(ə)] *nm/f* (double) bass player.

contre-braquer [kôntrəbrákā] *vi* to steer into a skid.

contrecarrer [kôntrəkárā] *vt* to thwart.

contrechamp [kôntrəshâṅ] *nm* (*CINÉMA*) reverse shot.

contrecœur [kôntrəkœr]: **à** ~ *ad* (be)grudgingly, reluctantly.

contrecoup [kôntrəkōō] *nm* repercussions *pl*; **par** ~ as an indirect consequence.

contre-courant [kôntrəkōōrâṅ]: **à** ~ *ad* against the current.

contredire [kôntrədēr] *vt* (*personne*) to contradict; (*témoignage, assertion, faits*) to refute; **se** ~ to contradict o.s.

contredit, e [kôntrədē, -ēt] *pp de* **contredire** ♦ *nm*: **sans** ~ without question.

contrée [kôntrā] *nf* region; land.

contre-écrou [kôntrākrōō] *nm* lock nut.

contre-espionnage [kôntrespyonázh] *nm* counter-espionage.

contre-expertise [kôntrekspertēz] *nf* second (expert) assessment.

contrefaçon [kôntrəfásôṅ] *nf* forgery; ~ **de brevet** patent infringement.

contrefaire [kôntrəfer] *vt* (*document, signature*) to forge, counterfeit; (*personne, démarche*) to mimic; (*dénaturer: sa voix etc*) to disguise.

contrefait, e [kôntrəfe, -et] *pp de* **contrefaire** ♦ *a* misshapen, deformed.

contrefasse [kôntrətás], **contreferai** [kôntrətrā] *etc vb voir* **contrefaire**.

contre-filet [kôntrəfēle] *nm* (*CULIN*) sirloin.

contreforts [kôntrəfor] *nmpl* foothills.

contre-haut [kôntrəō]: **en** ~ *ad* (up) above.

contre-indication [kôntraṅdēkâsyôṅ] *nf* contra-indication.

contre-interrogatoire [kôntraṅtārogâtwâr] *nm*: **faire subir un** ~ **à qn** to cross-examine sb.

contre-jour [kôntrəzhōōr]: **à** ~ *ad* against the light.

contremaître [kôntrəmetr(ə)] *nm* foreman.

contre-manifestation [kôntrəmánēfestásyôṅ] *nf* counter-demonstration.

contremarque [kôntrəmárk(ə)] *nf* (*ticket*) pass-out check (*US*) *ou* ticket (*Brit*).

contre-offensive [kôntrofâṅsēv] *nf* counter-offensive.

contre-ordre [kôntrordr(ə)] *nm* = **contrordre**.

contrepartie [kôntrəpártē] *nf* compensation; **en** ~ in compensation; in return.

contre-performance [kôntrəperformâṅs] *nf* below-average performance.

contrepèterie [kôntrəpātrē] *nf* spoonerism.

contre-pied [kôntrəpyā] *nm* (*inverse, opposé*): **le** ~ **de** ... the exact opposite of ...; **prendre le** ~ **de** to take the opposing view of; to take the opposite course to; **prendre qn à** ~ (*SPORT*) to throw sb off balance.

contre-plaqué |kòntrəplákā| *nm* plywood.
contre-plongée |kòntrəplónzhā| *nf* low-angle shot.
contrepoids |kòntrəpwá| *nm* counterweight, counterbalance; **faire** ~ to act as a counterbalance.
contrepoil |kòntrəpwál|: **à** ~ *ad* the wrong way.
contrepoint |kòntrəpwaň| *nm* counterpoint.
contrepoison |kòntrəpwázóň| *nm* antidote.
contrer |kòntrā| *vt* to counter.
contre-révolution |kòntrərāvolüsyóň| *nf* counter-revolution.
contresens |kòntrəsáňs| *nm* misinterpretation; *(mauvaise traduction)* mistranslation; *(absurdité)* nonsense *q*; **à** ~ *ad* the wrong way.
contresigner |kòntrəsēnyā| *vt* to countersign.
contretemps |kòntrətáň| *nm* hitch, contretemps; **à** ~ *ad* (*MUS*) out of time; (*fig*) at an inopportune moment.
contre-terrorisme |kòntrəterorēsm(ə)| *nm* counter-terrorism.
contre-torpilleur |kòntrətorpēyœr| *nm* destroyer.
contrevenant, e |kòntrəvnáň, -áňt| *vb voir* **contrevenir ♦** *nm/f* offender.
contrevenir |kòntrəvnēr|: ~ **à** *vt* to contravene.
contrevoie |kòntrəvwá|: **à** ~ *ad* (*en sens inverse*) on the wrong track; (*du mauvais côté*) on the wrong side.
contribuable |kòntrēbüábl(ə)| *nm/f* taxpayer.
contribuer |kòntrēbüā|: ~ **à** *vt* to contribute towards.
contribution |kòntrēbüsyóň| *nf* contribution; **les** ~**s** (*bureaux*) the tax office; **mettre à** ~ to call upon; ~**s directes/indirectes** direct/indirect taxation.
contrit, e |kòntrē, -ēt| *a* contrite.
contrôle |kòntrōl| *nm* checking *q*, check; supervision; monitoring; (*test*) test, examination; **perdre le** ~ **de son véhicule** to lose control of one's vehicle; ~ **des changes** (*COMM*) exchange controls; ~ **continu** (*SCOL*) continuous assessment; ~ **d'identité** identity check; ~ **des naissances** birth control; ~ **des prix** price control.
contrôler |kòntrōlā| *vt* (*vérifier*) to check; (*surveiller*) to supervise; to monitor, control; (*maîtriser, COMM: firme*) to control; **se** ~ to control o.s.
contrôleur, euse |kòntrōlœr, -ēz| *nm/f* (*de train*) (ticket) inspector; (*de bus*) (bus) conductor/tress; ~ **de la navigation aérienne** air traffic controller; ~ **financier** financial controller.
contrordre |kòntrordr(ə)| *nm* counter-order, countermand; **sauf** ~ unless otherwise directed.
controverse |kòntrovers(ə)| *nf* controversy.
controversé, e |kòntroversā| *a* (*personnage, question*) controversial.
contumace |kòntümás|: **par** ~ *ad* in absentia.
contusion |kòntüzyóň| *nf* bruise, contusion.
contusionné, e |kòntüzyonā| *a* bruised.
conurbation |konürbásyóň| *nf* conurbation.
convaincant, e |kòňvaňkáň, -áňt| *vb voir* **convaincre ♦** *a* convincing.

convaincre |kòňvaňkr(ə)| *vt*: ~ **qn (de qch)** to convince sb (of sth); ~ **qn (de faire)** to persuade sb (to do); ~ **qn de** (*JUR*: *délit*) to convict sb of.
convaincu, e |kòňvaňkü| *pp de* **convaincre ♦** *a*: **d'un ton** ~ with conviction.
convainquais |kòňvaňkc| *etc vb voir* **convaincre.**
convalescence |kòňválāsáňs| *nf* convalescence; **maison de** ~ convalescent home.
convalescent, e |kòňválāsáň, -áňt| *a*, *nm/f* convalescent.
convenable |kòňvnábl(ə)| *a* suitable; (*décent*) acceptable, proper; (*assez bon*) decent, acceptable; adequate, passable.
convenablement |kòňvnábləmáň| *ad* (*placé, choisi*) suitably; (*s'habiller, s'exprimer*) properly; (*payé, logé*) decently.
convenance |kòňvnáňs| *nf*: **à ma/votre** ~ to my/your liking; ~**s** *nfpl* proprieties.
convenir |kòňvnēr| *vt* to be suitable; ~ **à** to suit; **il convient de** it is advisable to; (*bienséant*) it is right *ou* proper to; ~ **de** (*bien-fondé de qch*) to admit (to), acknowledge; (*date, somme etc*) to agree upon; ~ **que** (*admettre*) to admit that, acknowledge the fact that; ~ **de faire qch** to agree to do sth; **il a été convenu que** it has been agreed that; **comme convenu** as agreed.
convention |kòňváňsyóň| *nf* convention; ~**s** *nfpl* (*convenances*) convention *sg*, social conventions; **de** ~ conventional; ~ **collective** (*ÉCON*) collective agreement.
conventionné, e |kòňváňsyonā| *a* (*ADMIN*) applying charges laid down by the state.
conventionnel, le |kòňváňsyonel| *a* conventional.
conventuel, le |kòňváňtüel| *a* monastic; monastery *cpd*; conventual, convent *cpd*.
convenu, e |kòňvnoo| *pp de* **convenir ♦** *a* agreed.
convergent, e |kòňverzháň, -áňt| *a* convergent.
converger |kòňverzhā| *vi* to converge; ~ **vers** *ou* **sur** to converge on.
conversation |kòňversásyóň| *nf* conversation; **avoir de la** ~ to be a good conversationalist.
converser |kòňversā| *vi* to converse.
conversion |kòňversyóň| *nf* conversion; (*SKI*) kick turn.
convertible |kòňvertēbl(ə)| *a* (*ÉCON*) convertible; (**canapé**) ~ sofa bed.
convertir |kòňvertēr| *vt*: ~ **qn (à)** to convert sb (to); ~ **qch en** to convert sth into; **se** ~ (**à**) to be converted (to).
convertisseur |kòňvertēsœr| *nm* (*ÉLEC*) converter.
convexe |kòňveks(ə)| *a* convex.
conviction |kòňvēksyóň| *nf* conviction.
conviendrai |kòňvyaňdrā|, **conviens** |kòňvyaň| *etc vb voir* **convenir.**
convier |kòňvyā| *vt*: ~ **qn à** (*dîner etc*) to (cordially) invite sb to; ~ **qn à faire** to urge sb to do.
convint |kòňvaň| *etc vb voir* **convenir.**
convive |kòňvēv| *nm/f* guest (*at table*).
convivial, e |kòňvēvyál| *a* (*INFORM*) user-friendly.

convocation [kôṅvokâsyôṅ] *nf* (*voir con-voquer*) convening, convoking; summoning; invitation; (*document*) notification to attend; summons *sg*.

convoi [kôṅvwá] *nm* (*de voitures, prisonniers*) convoy; (*train*) train; ~ **(funèbre)** funeral procession.

convoiter [kôṅvwátā] *vt* to covet.

convoitise [kôṅvwátēz] *nf* covetousness; (*sexuelle*) lust, desire.

convoler [kôṅvolá] *vi:* ~ **(en justes noces)** to be wed.

convoquer [kôṅvokā] *vt* (*assemblée*) to convene, convoke; (*subordonné, témoin*) to summon; (*candidat*) to ask to attend; ~ **qn (à)** (*réunion*) to invite sb (to attend).

convoyer [kôṅvwáyā] *vt* to escort.

convoyeur [kôṅvwáyœr] *nm* (*NAVIG*) escort ship; ~ **de fonds** security guard.

convulsé, e [kôṅvülsā] *a* (*visage*) distorted.

convulsions [kôṅvülsyôṅ] *nfpl* convulsions.

coopérant [koopārâṅ] *nm* ≈ member of the Peace Corps (*US*), ≈ person doing Voluntary Service Overseas (*Brit*).

coopératif, ive [koopārátēf, -ēv] *a, nf* cooperative.

coopération [koopārâsyôṅ] *nf* co-operation; (*ADMIN*): **la C**~ ≈ the Peace Corps (*US*), done as alternative to military service, ≈ Voluntary Service Overseas (*Brit*).

coopérer [koopārā] *vi:* ~ **(à)** to co-operate (in).

coordination [koordēnâsyôṅ] *nf* coordination.

coordonné, e [koordonā] *a* coordinated ♦ *nf* (*LING*) coordinate clause; ~**s** *nmpl* (*vêtements*) coordinates; ~**es** *nfpl* (*MATH*) co-ordinates; (*détails personnels*) address, phone number, schedule *etc*; whereabouts.

coordonner [koordonā] *vt* to coordinate.

copain, copine [kopaṅ, kopēn] *nm/f* pal, chum ♦ *a:* **être** ~ **avec** to be chummy with.

copeau, x [kopō] *nm* shaving; (*de métal*) turning.

Copenhague [kopənág] *n* Copenhagen.

copie [kopē] *nf* copy; (*SCOL*) paper; exercise; ~ **certifiée conforme** certified copy; ~ **papier** (*INFORM*) hard copy.

copier [kopyā] *vt, vi* to copy; ~ **sur** to copy from.

copieur [kopyœr] *nm* (photo)copier.

copieusement [kopyœzmâṅ] *ad* copiously.

copieux, euse [kopyœ, -œz] *a* copious, hearty.

copilote [kopēlot] *nm* (*AVIAT*) co-pilot; (*AUTO*) co-driver, navigator.

copine [kopēn] *nf voir* **copain**.

copiste [kopēst(ə)] *nm/f* copyist, transcriber.

coproduction [koprodüksyôṅ] *nf* coproduction, joint production.

copropriété [koproprēyātā] *nf* co-ownership, joint ownership; **acheter en** ~ to buy on a co-ownership basis.

copulation [kopülâsyôṅ] *nf* copulation.

coq [kok] *nm* cock, rooster ♦ *a inv* (*BOXE*): **poids** ~ bantamweight; ~ **de bruyère** grouse; ~ **du village** (*fig: péj*) ladykiller.

coq-à-l'âne [kokálân] *nm inv* abrupt change of subject.

coque [kok] *nf* (*de noix, mollusque*) shell; (*de bateau*) hull; **à la** ~ (*CULIN*) (soft-)boiled.

coquelet [kokle] *nm* (*CULIN*) cockerel.

coquelicot [koklēkō] *nm* poppy.

coqueluche [koklüsh] *nf* whooping-cough; (*fig*): **être la** ~ **de qn** to be sb's flavor of the month.

coquet, te [koke, -et] *a* appearance-conscious; (*joli*) pretty.

coquetier [koktyā] *nm* egg-cup.

coquettement [koketmâṅ] *ad* (*s'habiller*) attractively; (*meubler*) prettily.

coquetterie [koketrē] *nf* appearance-conciousness.

coquillage [kokēyázh] *nm* (*mollusque*) shellfish *inv*; (*coquille*) shell.

coquille [kokēy] *nf* shell; (*TYPO*) misprint; ~ **de beurre** shell of butter; ~ **d'œuf** *a* (*couleur*) eggshell; ~ **de noix** nutshell; ~ **St Jacques** scallop.

coquillettes [kokēyet] *nfpl* pasta shells.

coquin, e [kokaṅ, -ēn] *a* mischievous, roguish; (*polisson*) naughty ♦ *nm/f* (*péj*) rascal.

cor [kor] *nm* (*MUS*) horn; (*MÉD*): ~ **(au pied)** corn; **réclamer à** ~ **et à cri** to clamor for; ~ **anglais** English horn, cor anglais; ~ **de chasse** hunting horn.

corail, aux [koráy, -ō] *nm* coral *q*.

Coran [koráṅ] *nm:* **le** ~ the Koran.

coraux [korō] *pl de* **corail**.

corbeau, x [korbō] *nm* crow.

corbeille [korbey] *nf* basket; (*BOURSE*): **la** ~ ≈ the floor (of the Stock Exchange); ~ **de mariage** (*fig*) wedding presents *pl*; ~ **à ouvrage** work-basket; ~ **a pain** bread-basket; ~ **à papier** waste paper basket *ou* bin.

corbillard [korbēyàr] *nm* hearse.

cordage [kordázh] *nm* rope; ~**s** *nmpl* (*de voilure*) rigging *sg*.

corde [kord(ə)] *nf* rope; (*de violon, raquette, d'arc*) string; (*trame*): **la** ~ the thread; (*ATHLÉTISME, AUTO*): **la** ~ the rails *pl*; **les** ~**s** (*BOXE*) the ropes; **les (instruments à)** ~**s** (*MUS*) the strings, the stringed instruments; **semelles de** ~ rope soles; **tenir la** ~ (*ATHLÉTISME, AUTO*) to be in the inside lane; **tomber des** ~**s** to rain cats and dogs; **tirer sur la** ~ to go too far; **la** ~ **sensible** the right chord; **usé jusqu'à la** ~ threadbare; ~ **à linge** clothes line; ~ **lisse** (climbing) rope; ~ **à nœuds** knotted climbing rope; ~ **raide** tight-rope; ~ **à sauter** jump (*US*) *ou* skipping (*Brit*) rope; ~**s vocales** vocal cords.

cordeau, x [kordō] *nm* string, line; **tracé au** ~ as straight as an arrow.

cordée [kordā] *nf* (*d'alpinistes*) rope, roped party.

cordelière [kordəlyer] *nf* cord (belt).

cordial, e, aux [kordyál, -ō] *a* warm, cordial ♦ *nm* cordial, pick-me-up.

cordialement [kordyálmâṅ] *ad* cordially, heartily; (*formule épistolaire*) (kind) regards.

cordialité [kordyálētā] *nf* warmth, cordiality.

cordillère [kordēyer] *nf:* **la** ~ **des Andes** the Andes cordillera *ou* range.

cordon [kordôṅ] *nm* cord, string; ~ **sanitaire/de police** sanitary/police cordon; ~ **littoral** sandbank, sandbar; ~ **ombilical** umbilical cord.

cordon-bleu [kordôṅblœ] *a, nm/f* cordon bleu.

cordonnerie [kordonrē] *nf* shoe repairer's *ou* mender's (shop).

cordonnier [kordonyā] *nm* shoe repairer *ou* mender, cobbler.

cordouan, e [kordōōáń, -án] *a* Cordovan.

Cordoue [kordōō] *n* Cordoba.

Corée [korā] *nf*: **la ~** Korea; **la ~ du Sud/du Nord** South/North Korea; **la République (démocratique populaire) de ~** the (Democratic People's) Republic of Korea.

coréen, ne [korāań, -en] *a* Korean ♦ *nm* (*LING*) Korean ♦ *nm/f*: **C~, ne** Korean.

coreligionnaire [korəlēzhyoner] *nm/f* fellow Christian/Muslim/Jew *etc*.

Corfou [korfōō] *n* Corfu.

coriace [koryás] *a* tough.

Corinthe [korańt] *n* Corinth.

cormoran [kormoráń] *nm* cormorant.

cornac [kornák] *nm* elephant driver.

corne [korn(ə)] *nf* horn; (*de cerf*) antler; (*de la peau*) callus; **~ d'abondance** horn of plenty; **~ de brume** (*NAVIG*) foghorn.

cornée [kornā] *nf* cornea.

corneille [korney] *nf* crow.

cornélien, ne [kornālyań, -en] *a* (*débat etc*) where love and duty conflict.

cornemuse [kornəmüz] *nf* bagpipes *pl*; **joueur de ~** piper.

corner *nm* [korner] (*FOOTBALL*) corner (kick) ♦ *vb* [kornā] *vt* (*pages*) to make dog-eared ♦ *vi* (*klaxonner*) to blare out.

cornet [korne] *nm* (*paper*) cone; (*de glace*) cornet, cone; **~ à piston** cornet.

cornette [kornet] *nf* cornet (*headgear*).

corniaud [kornyō] *nm* (*chien*) mongrel; (*péj*) dope, idiot.

corniche [kornēsh] *nf* (*de meuble, neigeuse*) cornice; (*route*) coast road.

cornichon [kornēshóń] *nm* gherkin.

Cornouailles [kornwáy] *nf(pl)* Cornwall.

cornue [kornü] *nf* retort.

corollaire [korolɛr] *nm* corollary.

corolle [korol] *nf* corolla.

coron [koróń] *nm* mining cottage; mining village.

coronaire [koroner] *a* coronary.

corporation [korporásyóń] *nf* corporate body; (*au moyen-âge*) guild.

corporel, le [korporel] *a* bodily; (*punition*) corporal; **soins ~s** care *sg* of the body.

corps [kor] *nm* (*gén*) body; (*cadavre*) (dead) body; **à son ~ défendant** against one's will; **à ~ perdu** headlong; **perdu ~ et biens** lost with all hands; **prendre ~** to take shape; **faire ~ avec** to be joined to; to form one body with; **~ d'armée (CA)** army corps; **~ de ballet** corps de ballet; **~ constitués** (*POL*) constitutional bodies; **le ~ consulaire (CC)** the consular corps; **~ à ~** *ad* hand-to-hand ♦ *nm* clinch; **le ~ du délit** (*JUR*) corpus delicti; **le ~ diplomatique (CD)** the diplomatic corps; **le ~ électoral** the electorate; **le ~ enseignant** the teaching profession; **~ étranger** (*MÉD*) foreign body; **~ expéditionnaire** task force; **~ de garde** guardroom; **~ législatif** legislative body; **le ~ médical** the medical profession.

corpulence [korpüláńs] *nf* build; (*embonpoint*) stoutness, corpulence; **de forte ~** of large build.

corpulent, e [korpüláń, -áńt] *a* stout, corpulent.

correct, e [korekt] *a* (*exact*) accurate, correct; (*bienséant, honnête*) correct; (*passable*) adequate.

correctement [korektəmáń] *ad* accurately; correctly; adequately.

correcteur, trice [korektœr, -trēs] *nm/f* (*SCOL*) examiner, grader (*US*), marker (*Brit*); (*TYPO*) proofreader.

correctif, ive [korektēf, -ēv] *a* corrective ♦ *nm* (*mise au point*) rider, qualification.

correction [koreksyóń] *nf* (*voir corriger*) correction; grading (*US*), marking (*Brit*); (*voir correct*) correctness; (*rature, surcharge*) correction, emendation; (*coups*) thrashing; **~ sur écran** (*INFORM*) screen editing; **~ (des épreuves)** proofreading.

correctionnel, le [koreksyonel] *a* (*JUR*): **tribunal ~** ≈ criminal court.

corrélation [korālásyóń] *nf* correlation.

correspondance [korespóńdáńs] *nf* correspondence; (*de train, d'avion*) connection; **ce train assure la ~ avec l'avion de 10 heures** this train connects with the 10 o'clock plane; **cours par ~** correspondence course; **vente par ~** mail-order business.

correspondancier, ière [korespóńdáńsyā, -yer] *nm/f* correspondence clerk.

correspondant, e [korespóńdáń, -áńt] *nm/f* correspondent; (*TÉL*) person phoning (*ou* being phoned).

correspondre [korespóńdr(ə)] *vi* (*données, témoignages*) to correspond, tally; (*chambres*) to communicate; **~ à** to correspond to; **~ avec qn** to correspond with sb.

corrida [korēdà] *nf* bullfight.

corridor [korēdor] *nm* corridor, passage.

corrigé [korēzhā] *nm* (*SCOL*) correct version; fair copy.

corriger [korēzhā] *vt* (*devoir*) to correct, grade (*US*), mark (*Brit*); (*texte*) to correct, emend; (*erreur, défaut*) to correct, put right; (*punir*) to thrash; **~ qn de** (*défaut*) to cure sb of; **se ~ de** to cure o.s. of.

corroborer [korobora] *vt* to corroborate.

corroder [korodā] *vt* to corrode.

corrompre [koróńpr(ə)] *vt* (*dépraver*) to corrupt; (*acheter: témoin etc*) to bribe.

corrompu, e [koróńpü] *a* corrupt.

corrosif, ive [korōzēf, -ēv] *a* corrosive.

corrosion [korōzyóń] *nf* corrosion.

corruption [korüpsyóń] *nf* corruption; bribery.

corsage [korsázh] *nm* (*d'une robe*) bodice; (*chemisier*) blouse.

corsaire [korser] *nm* pirate, corsair; privateer.

corse [kors(ə)] *a* Corsica ♦ *nm/f*: **C~** Corsican ♦ *nf*: **la C~** Corsica.

corsé, e [korsā] *a* vigorous; (*café etc*) full-flavored (*US*) *ou* -flavoured (*Brit*); (*goût*) full; (*fig*) spicy; tricky.

corselet [korsəle] *nm* corselet.

corser [korsā] *vt* (*difficulté*) to aggravate; (*intrigue*) to liven up; (*sauce*) to add spice to.

corset [korse] *nm* corset; (*d'une robe*) bodice; **~ orthopédique** surgical corset.

corso [korsō] *nm*: **~ fleuri** procession of floral

floats.

cortège [kortezh] *nm* procession.

cortisone [kortēzon] *nf* (*MÉD*) cortisone.

corvée [korvā] *nf* chore, drudgery *q*; (*MIL*) fatigue (duty).

cosignataire [kosēnyáter] *a*, *nm/f* co-signatory.

cosinus [kosēnüs] *nm* (*MATH*) cosine.

cosmétique [kosmātēk] *nm* (*pour les cheveux*) hair-oil; (*produit de beauté*) beauty care product.

cosmique [kosmēk] *a* cosmic.

cosmonaute [kosmonōt] *nm/f* cosmonaut, astronaut.

cosmopolite [kosmopolēt] *a* cosmopolitan.

cosmos [kosmos] *nm* outer space; cosmos.

cosse [kos] *nf* (*BOT*) pod, hull.

cossu, e [kosü] *a* opulent-looking, well-to-do.

Costa Rica [kostárēkā] *nm*: **le** ~ Costa Rica.

costaricien, ne [kostárēsyań, -en] *a* Costa Rican ♦ *nm/f*: **C~, ne** Costa Rican.

costaud, e [kostō, -ōd] *a* strong, sturdy.

costume [kostüm] *nm* (*d'homme*) suit; (*de théâtre*) costume.

costumé, e [kostümā] *a* dressed up.

costumier, ière [kostümyā, -yer] *nm/f* (*fabricant, loueur*) costumier; (*THÉÂTRE*) wardrobe master/mistress.

cotangente [kotáñzhâñt] *nf* (*MATH*) cotangent.

cotation [kotásyóñ] *nf* quoted value.

cote [kot] *nf* (*en Bourse etc*) quotation; quoted value; (*d'un cheval*): **la** ~ **de** the odds *pl* on; (*d'un candidat etc*) rating; (*mesure: sur une carte*) elevation point (*US*), spot height (*Brit*); (: *sur un croquis*) dimension; (*de classement*) reference number; **avoir la** ~ to be very popular; **inscrit à la** ~ listed on the Stock Exchange; ~ **d'alerte** danger *ou* flood level; ~ **mal taillée** (*fig*) compromise; ~ **de popularité** popularity rating.

coté, e [kotā] *a*: **être** ~ to be listed *ou* quoted; **être** ~ **en Bourse** to be listed on the Stock Exchange; **être bien/mal** ~ to be highly/poorly rated.

côte [kōt] *nf* (*rivage*) coast(line); (*pente*) slope; (: *sur une route*) hill; (*ANAT*) rib; (*d'un tricot, tissu*) rib, ribbing *q*; ~ **à** ~ *ad* side by side; **la C~** (**d'Azur**) the (French) Riviera; **la C~ d'Ivoire** the Ivory Coast.

côté [kōtā] *nm* (*gén*) side; (*direction*) way, direction; **de chaque** ~ (**de**) on each side of; **de tous les** ~**s** from all directions; **de quel** ~ **est-il parti?** which way *ou* in which direction did he go?; **de ce/de l'autre** ~ this/the other way; **d'un** ~ ... **de l'autre** (*alternative*) on (the) one hand ... on the other (hand); **du** ~ **de** (*provenance*) from; (*direction*) towards; **du** ~ **de Lyon** (*proximité*) near Lyons; **du** ~ **gauche** on the left-hand side; **de** ~ *ad* sideways; on one side; to one side; aside; **laisser de** ~ to leave aside; **mettre de** ~ to put aside; **de mon** ~ (*quant à moi*) for my part; **à** ~ *ad* (right) nearby; beside; next door; (*d'autre part*) besides; **à** ~ **de** beside; next to; (*fig*) in comparison to; **à** ~ (**de la cible**) off target, wide (of the mark); **être aux** ~**s de** to be by the side of.

coteau, x [kotō] *nm* hill.

côtelé, e [kōtlā] *a* ribbed; **pantalon en velours**

~ corduroy pants *pl.*

côtelette [kōtlet] *nf* chop.

coter [kotā] *vt* (*BOURSE*) to quote.

coterie [kotrē] *nf* set.

côtier, ière [kōtyā, -yer] *a* coastal.

cotisation [kotēzásyóñ] *nf* subscription, dues *pl*; (*pour une pension*) contributions *pl.*

cotiser [kotēzā] *vi*: ~ (**à**) to pay contributions (to); (*à une association*) to subscribe (to); **se** ~ to club together.

coton [kotóñ] *nm* cotton; ~ **hydrophile** absorbent cotton (*US*), cotton wool (*Brit*).

cotonnade [kotonád] *nf* cotton (fabric).

coton-tige [kotóñtēzh] *nm* ® Q-tip ® (*US*), cotton bud ® (*Brit*).

côtoyer [kōtwáyā] *vt* to be close to; (*rencontrer*) to rub shoulders with; (*longer*) to run alongside; (*fig: friser*) to be bordering *ou* verging on.

cotte [kot] *nf*: ~ **de mailles** coat of mail.

cou [kōō] *nm* neck.

couac [kwák] *nm* (*fam*) squawk.

couard, e [kwàr, -àrd(ə)] *a* cowardly.

couchage [kōōsházh] *nm voir* **sac.**

couchant [kōōshàñ] *a*: **soleil** ~ setting sun.

couche [kōōsh] *nf* (*strate: gén, GÉO*) layer, stratum (*pl* -a); (*de peinture, vernis*) coat; (*de poussière, crème*) layer; (*de bébé*) diaper (*US*), nappy (*Brit*); ~**s** *nfpl* (*MÉD*) childbirth; ~**s sociales** social levels *ou* strata.

couché, e [kōōshā] *a* (*étendu*) lying down; (*au lit*) in bed.

couche-culotte, *pl* **couches-culottes** [kōōshkülot] *nf* (plastic-coated) disposable diaper (*US*) *ou* nappy (*Brit*).

coucher [kōōshā] *nm* (*du soleil*) setting ♦ *vt* (*personne*) to put to bed; (: *loger*) to put up; (*objet*) to lay on its side; (*écrire*) to inscribe, couch ♦ *vi* (*dormir*) to sleep, spend the night; ~ **avec qn** to sleep with sb, go to bed with sb; **se** ~ *vi* (*pour dormir*) to go to bed; (*pour se reposer*) to lie down; (*soleil*) to set, go down; **à prendre avant le** ~ (*MÉD*) take at night *ou* before going to bed; ~ **de soleil** sunset.

couchette [kōōshet] *nf* berth, couchette; (*de marin*) bunk.

coucheur [kōōshœr] *nm*: **mauvais** ~ tough customer.

couci-couça [kōōsēkōōsá] *ad* (*fam*) so-so.

coucou [kōōkōō] *nm* cuckoo ♦ *excl* peek-a-boo.

coude [kōōd] *nm* (*ANAT*) elbow; (*de tuyau, de la route*) bend; ~ **à** ~ *ad* shoulder to shoulder, side by side.

coudée [kōōdā] *nf*: **avoir ses** ~**s franches** (*fig*) to have a free rein.

cou-de-pied, *pl* **cous-de-pied** [kōōdpyā] *nm* instep.

coudoyer [kōōdwáyā] *vt* to brush past *ou* against; (*fig*) to rub shoulders with.

coudre [kōōdr(ə)] *vt* (*bouton*) to sew on; (*robe*) to sew (up) ♦ *vi* to sew.

couenne [kwán] *nf* (*de lard*) rind.

couette [kwet] *nf* duvet, (continental) quilt; ~**s** *nfpl* (*cheveux*) bunches.

couffin [kōōfañ] *nm* wicker cradle.

couilles [kōōy] *nfpl* (*fam!*) balls (*!*).

couiner [kwēnā] *vi* to squeal.

coulage [kōōlázh] *nm* (*COMM*) loss of stock

(*due to theft or negligence*).

coulant, e [kōōláń, -áńt] *a* (*indulgent*) easy-going; (*fromage etc*) runny.

coulée [kōōlā] *nf* (*de lave, métal en fusion*) flow; ~ **de neige** snowslide.

couler [kōōlā] *vi* to flow, run; (*fuir: stylo, récipient*) to leak; (*sombrer: bateau*) to sink ♦ *vt* (*cloche, sculpture*) to cast; (*bateau*) to sink; (*fig*) to ruin, bring down; (: *passer*): ~ **une vie heureuse** to enjoy a happy life; **se** ~ **dans** (*interstice etc*) to slip into; **faire** ~ (*eau*) to run; **faire** ~ **un bain** to run a bath; **il a coulé une bielle** (*AUTO*) his crankshaft broke; ~ **de source** to follow on naturally; ~ **à pic** to sink *ou* go straight to the bottom.

couleur [kōōlœr] *nf* color (*US*), colour (*Brit*); (*CARTES*) suit; ~**s** *nfpl* (*du teint*) color *sg*; **les** ~**s** (*MIL*) the colors; **en** ~**s** (*film*) in color; **télévision en** ~**s** color television; **de** ~ (*homme, femme*) colored; **sous** ~ **de** on the pretext of.

couleuvre [kōōlœvr(ə)] *nf* grass snake.

coulisse [kōōlēs] *nf* (*TECH*) runner; ~**s** *nfpl* (*THÉÂTRE*) wings; (*fig*): **dans les** ~**s** behind the scenes; **porte à** ~ sliding door.

coulisser [kōōlēsā] *vi* to slide, run.

couloir [kōōlwàr] *nm* corridor, passage; (*de bus*) aisle; (: *sur la route*) bus lane; (*SPORT: de piste*) lane; (*GÉO*) gully; ~ **aérien** air corridor *ou* lane; ~ **de navigation** shipping lane.

coulpe [kōōlp(ə)] *nf*: **battre sa** ~ to repent openly.

coup [kōō] *nm* (*heurt, choc*) knock; (*affectif*) blow, shock; (*agressif*) blow; (*avec arme à feu*) shot; (*de l'horloge*) chime; stroke; (*SPORT*) stroke; shot; blow; (*fam: fois*) time; (*ÉCHECS*) move; ~ **de coude/genou** nudge (with the elbow)/with the knee; **à** ~**s de hache/marteau** (hitting) with an axe/a hammer; ~ **de tonnerre** clap of thunder; ~ **de sonnette** ring of the bell; ~ **de crayon/pinceau** stroke of the pencil/brush; **donner un** ~ **de balai** to sweep up, give the floor a sweep; **donner un** ~ **de chiffon** to dust; **avoir le** ~ (*fig*) to have the knack; **être dans le/hors du** ~ to be/not to be in on it; **boire un** ~ to have a drink; **d'un seul** ~ (*subitement*) suddenly; (*à la fois*) at one try; in one blow; **du** ~ so (you see); **du premier** ~ first time, at the first attempt; **du même** ~ at the same time; **à** ~ **sûr** definitely, without fail; **après** ~ afterwards; ~ **sur** ~ in quick succession; **être sur un** ~ to be on to something; **sur le** ~ outright; **sous le** ~ **de** (*surprise etc*) under the influence of; **tomber sous le** ~ **de la loi** to constitute a statutory offense; **à tous les** ~**s** every time; **il a raté son** ~ he didn't pull it off; **pour le** ~ for once; ~ **bas** (*fig*): **donner un** ~ **bas à qn** to hit sb below the belt; ~ **de chance** stroke of luck; ~ **de chapeau** (*fig*) pat on the back; ~ **de couteau** stab (of a knife); ~ **dur** hard blow; ~ **d'éclat** (great) feat; ~ **d'envoi** kick-off; ~ **d'essai** first attempt; ~ **d'état** coup d'état; ~ **de feu** shot; ~ **de filet** (*POLICE*) haul; ~ **de foudre** (*fig*) love at first sight; ~ **fourré** stab in the back; ~ **franc** free kick; ~ **de frein** (sharp) braking *q*; ~

de fusil rifle shot; ~ **de grâce** coup de grâce; ~ **du lapin** (*AUTO*) whiplash; ~ **de main**: **donner un** ~ **de main à qn** to give sb a (helping) hand; ~ **de maître** master stroke; ~ **d'œil** glance; ~ **de pied** kick; ~ **de poing** punch; ~ **de soleil** sunburn *q*; ~ **de téléphone** phone call; ~ **de tête** (*fig*) (sudden) impulse; ~ **de théâtre** (*fig*) dramatic turn of events; ~ **de vent** gust of wind; **en** ~ **de vent** (*rapidement*) in a great hurry.

coupable [kōōpábl(ə)] *a* guilty; (*pensée*) guilty, culpable ♦ *nm/f* (*gén*) culprit; (*JUR*) guilty party; ~ **de** guilty of.

coupant, e [kōōpáń, -áńt] *a* (*lame*) sharp; (*fig: voix, ton*) cutting.

coupe [kōōp] *nf* (*verre*) goblet; (*à fruits*) dish; (*SPORT*) cup; (*de cheveux, de vêtement*) cut; (*graphique, plan*) (cross) section; **être sous la** ~ **de** to be under the control of; **faire des** ~**s sombres dans** to make drastic cuts in.

coupé, e [kōōpā] *a* (*communications, route*) cut, blocked; (*vêtement*): **bien/mal** ~ well/badly cut ♦ *nm* (*AUTO*) coupé.

coupe-circuit [kōōpsērküē] *nm inv* cutout, circuit breaker.

coupée [kōōpā] *nf* (*NAVIG*) gangway.

coupe-feu [kōōpfœ] *nm inv* firebreak.

coupe-gorge [kōōpgorzh(ə)] *nm inv* cut-throats' den.

coupe-ongles [kōōpóńgl(ə)] *nm inv* (*pince*) nail clippers; (*ciseaux*) nail scissors.

coupe-papier [kōōppápyā] *nm inv* paper knife.

couper [kōōpā] *vt* to cut; (*retrancher*) to cut (out), take out; (*route, courant*) to cut off; (*appétit*) to take away; (*fièvre*) to take down, reduce; (*vin, cidre*) to blend; (: *à table*) to dilute (with water) ♦ *vi* to cut; (*prendre un raccourci*) to take a short-cut; (*CARTES: diviser le paquet*) to cut; (: *avec l'atout*) to trump; **se** ~ (*se blesser*) to cut o.s.; (*en témoignant etc*) to give o.s. away; ~ **l'appétit à qn** to spoil sb's appetite; ~ **la parole à qn** to cut sb short; ~ **les vivres à qn** to cut off sb's vital supplies; ~ **le contact** *ou* **l'allumage** (*AUTO*) to turn off the ignition; ~ **les ponts avec qn** to break with sb; **se faire** ~ **les cheveux** to have *ou* get one's hair cut.

couperet [kōōpre] *nm* cleaver, chopper.

couperosé, e [kōōprōzā] *a* blotchy.

couple [kōōpl(ə)] *nm* couple; ~ **de torsion** torque.

coupler [kōōplā] *vt* to couple (together).

couplet [kōōple] *nm* verse.

coupleur [kōōplœr] *nm*: ~ **acoustique** acoustic coupler.

coupole [kōōpol] *nf* dome; cupola.

coupon [kōōpóń] *nm* (*ticket*) coupon; (*de tissu*) remnant; roll.

coupon-réponse, *pl* **coupons-réponses** [kōōpóńrāpóńs] *nm* reply coupon.

coupure [kōōpür] *nf* cut; (*billet de banque*) note; (*de journal*) cutting; ~ **de courant** power cut.

cour [kōōr] *nf* (*de ferme, jardin*) (court)yard; (*d'immeuble*) back yard; (*JUR, royale*) court; **faire la** ~ **à qn** to court sb; ~ **d'appel**

appellate court (*US*), appeal court (*Brit*); ~ **d'assises** court of assizes; ~ **de cassation** final court of appeal; ~ **des comptes** (*ADMIN*) ≈ General Accounting Office (*US*), revenue court (*Brit*); ~ **martiale** court-martial; ~ **de récréation** (*SCOL*) schoolyard, playground.

courage [kōōrázh] *nm* courage, bravery.
courageux, euse [kōōrázhœ̄, -œ̄z] *a* brave, courageous.
couramment [kōōrámáń] *ad* commonly; (*parler*) fluently.
courant, e [kōōráń, -áńt] *a* (*fréquent*) common; (*COMM, gén: normal*) standard; (*en cours*) current ♦ *nm* current; (*fig*) movement; trend; **être au** ~ **(de)** (*fait, nouvelle*) to know (about); **mettre qn au** ~ **(de)** (*fait, nouvelle*) to tell sb (about); (*nouveau travail etc*) to teach sb the basics (of), brief sb (about); **se tenir au** ~ **(de)** (*techniques etc*) to keep o.s. up-to-date (on); **dans le** ~ **de** (*pendant*) in the course of; ~ **octobre** *etc* in the course of October *etc*; **le 10** ~ (*COMM*) the 10th of this month; ~ **d'air** draft (*US*), draught (*Brit*); ~ **électrique** (electric) current, power.
courbature [kōōrbátūr] *nf* ache.
courbaturé, e [kōōrbátūrá] *a* aching.
courbe [kōōrb(ə)] *a* curved ♦ *nf* curve; ~ **de niveau** contour line.
courber [kōōrbá] *vt* to bend; ~ **la tête** to bow one's head; **se** ~ *vi* (*branche etc*) to bend, curve; (*personne*) to bend (down).
courbette [kōōrbet] *nf* low bow.
coure [kōōr] *etc vb voir* **courir**.
coureur, euse [kōōrœ̄r, -œ̄z] *nm/f* (*SPORT*) runner (*ou* driver); (*péj*) womanizer/manhunter; ~ **cycliste/automobile** racing cyclist/driver.
courge [kōōrzh(ə)] *nf* (*BOT*) gourd; (*CULIN*) marrow.
courgette [kōōrzhet] *nf* zucchini (*US*), courgette (*Brit*).
courir [kōōrēr] *vi* (*gén*) to run; (*se dépêcher*) to rush; (*fig: rumeurs*) to go around; (*COMM: intérêt*) to accrue ♦ *vt* (*SPORT: épreuve*) to compete in; (*risque*) to run; (*danger*) to face; ~ **les cafés/bals** to make the rounds of the cafés/dances; **le bruit court que** ... the rumor is going around that ..., rumor has it that ...; **par les temps qui courent** at the present time; ~ **après qn** to run after sb, chase (after) sb; **laisser** ~ to let things alone; **faire** ~ **qn** to make sb run around (all over the place); **tu peux (toujours)** ~! you can always try!
couronne [kōōron] *nf* crown; (*de fleurs*) wreath, circlet; (*funéraire ou mortuaire*) (funeral) wreath.
couronnement [kōōronmáń] *nm* coronation, crowning; (*fig*) crowning achievement.
couronner [kōōroná] *vt* to crown.
courons [kōōróń], **courrai** [kōōrá] *etc vb voir* **courir**.
courre [kōōr] *vb voir* **chasse**.
courrier [kōōryá] *nm* mail, post; (*lettres à écrire*) letters *pl*; (*rubrique*) column; **qualité** ~ letter quality; **long/moyen** ~ *a* (*AVIAT*) long-/medium-haul; ~ **du cœur** advice column; ~ **électronique** electronic mail.
courroie [kōōrwâ] *nf* strap; (*TECH*) belt; ~ **de transmission/de ventilateur** driving/fan belt.
courrons [kōōróń] *etc vb voir* **courir**.
courroucé, e [kōōrōōsá] *a* wrathful.
cours [kōōr] *vb voir* **courir** ♦ *nm* (*leçon*) lesson; class; (*série de leçons*) course; (*cheminement*) course; (*écoulement*) flow; (*avenue*) walk; (*COMM*) rate; price; (*BOURSE*) quotation; **donner libre** ~ **à** to give free expression to; **avoir** ~ (*monnaie*) to be legal tender; (*fig*) to be current; (*SCOL*) to have a class *ou* lecture; **en** ~ (*année*) current; (*travaux*) in progress; **en** ~ **de route** on the way; **au** ~ **de** in the course of, during; **le** ~ **du change** the exchange rate; ~ **d'eau** waterway; ~ **élémentaire (CE)** *2nd and 3rd years of grade school*; ~ **moyen (CM)** *4th and 5th years of grade school*; ~ **préparatoire** ≈ 1st grade (*US*), ≈ infants' class (*Brit*); ~ **du soir** night school.
course [kōōrs(ə)] *nf* running; (*SPORT*) épreuve) race; (*trajet: du soleil*) course; (: *d'un projectile*) flight; (: *d'une pièce mécanique*) travel; (*excursion*) outing; climb; (*d'un taxi, autocar*) journey, trip; (*petite mission*) errand; ~s *nfpl* (*achats*) shopping *sg*; (*HIPPISME*) races; **faire les** *ou* **ses** ~s to go shopping; **jouer aux** ~s to bet on the races; **à bout de** ~ (*épuisé*) exhausted; ~ **automobile** motor race; ~ **de côte** (*AUTO*) hill climb; ~ **par étapes** *ou* **d'étapes** race in stages; ~ **d'obstacles** obstacle race; ~ **à pied** walking race; ~ **de vitesse** sprint; ~s **de chevaux** horse racing.
court, e [kōōr, kōōrt(ə)] *a* short ♦ *ad* short ♦ *nm* (: **de tennis**) (tennis) court; **tourner** ~ to come to a sudden end; **couper** ~ **à** to cut short; **à** ~ **de** short of; **prendre qn de** ~ to catch sb unawares; **pour faire** ~ briefly, to cut a long story short; **ça fait** ~ that's not very long; **tirer à la** ~**e paille** to draw lots; **faire la** ~**e échelle à qn** to give sb a boost (*US*) *ou* leg up (*Brit*); ~ **métrage** (*CINÉMA*) short (film).
court-bouillon, *pl* **courts-bouillons** [kōōrbōōyóń] *nm* court-bouillon.
court-circuit, *pl* **courts-circuits** [kōōrsērküē] *nm* short circuit.
court-circuiter [kōōrsērküētá] *vt* (*fig*) to by-pass.
courtier, ière [kōōrtyá, -yer] *nm/f* broker.
courtisan [kōōrtēzáń] *nm* courtier.
courtisane [kōōrtēzáń] *nf* courtesan.
courtiser [kōōrtēzá] *vt* to court, woo.
courtois, e [kōōrtwá, -wáz] *a* courteous.
courtoisie [kōōrtwázē] *nf* courtesy.
couru, e [kōōrü] *pp de* **courir** ♦ *a* (*spectacle etc*) popular; **c'est** ~ **(d'avance)**! (*fam*) it's a safe bet!
cousais [kōōze] *etc vb voir* **coudre**.
couscous [kōōskōōs] *nm* couscous.
cousin, e [kōōzáń, -ēn] *nm/f* cousin ♦ *nm* (*ZOOL*) mosquito; ~ **germain** first cousin.
cousons [kōōzóń] *etc vb voir* **coudre**.
coussin [kōōsáń] *nm* cushion; ~ **d'air** (*TECH*) air cushion.
cousu, e [kōōzü] *pp de* **coudre** ♦ *a*: ~ **d'or** rolling in riches.

coût [kōō] *nm* cost; **le ~ de la vie** the cost of living.

coûtant [kōōtáṅ] *am*: **au prix ~** at cost price.

couteau, x [kōōtō] *nm* knife; **~ à cran d'arrêt** switchblade (knife); **~ de cuisine** kitchen knife; **~ à pain** bread knife; **~ de poche** pocket knife.

couteau-scie, *pl* **couteaux-scies** [kōōtōsē] *nm* serrated(-edged) knife.

coutellerie [kōōtɛlrē] *nf* cutlery shop; cutlery.

coûter [kōōtā] *vt* to cost ♦ *vi*: **~ à qn** to cost sb a lot; **~ cher** to be expensive; **~ cher à qn** (*fig*) to cost sb dear *ou* dearly; **combien ça coûte?** how much is it?, what does it cost?; **coûte que coûte** at all costs.

coûteux, euse [kōōtœ̄, -ēz] *a* costly, expensive.

coutume [kōōtüm] *nf* custom; **de ~** usual, customary.

coutumier, ière [kōōtümyā, -ycr] *a* customary: **elle est coutumière du fait** that's her usual trick.

couture [kōōtür] *nf* sewing; dress-making; (*points*) seam.

couturier [kōōtüryā] *nm* fashion designer, couturier.

couturière [kōōtüryɛr] *nf* dressmaker.

couvée [kōōvā] *nf* brood, clutch.

couvent [kōōváṅ] *nm* (*de sœurs*) convent; (*de frères*) monastery; (*établissement scolaire*) convent (school).

couver [kōōvā] *vt* to hatch; (*maladie*) to be coming down with ♦ *vi* (*feu*) to smolder (*US*), smoulder (*Brit*); (*révolte*) to be brewing; **~ qn/qch des yeux** to look lovingly at sb/sth; (*convoiter*) to look longingly at sb/sth.

couvercle [kōōvɛrkl(ə)] *nm* lid; (*de bombe aérosol etc, qui se visse*) cap, top.

couvert, e [kōōvɛr, -ert(ə)] *pp de* **couvrir** ♦ *a* (*ciel*) overcast; (*coiffé d'un chapeau*) wearing a hat ♦ *nm* place setting; (*place à table*) place; (*au restaurant*) cover charge; **~s** *nmpl* place settings; cutlery *sg*; **~ de** covered with *ou* in; **bien ~** (*habillé*) well wrapped up; **mettre le ~** to set the table; **à ~ under cover; **sous le ~ de** under the shelter of; (*fig*) under cover of.

couverture [kōōvertür] *nf* (*de lit*) blanket; (*de bâtiment*) roofing; (*de livre, fig: d'un espion etc*) cover; (*ASSURANCES*) coverage (*US*), cover (*Brit*); (*PRESSE*) coverage; **de ~** (*lettre etc*) covering; **~ chauffante** electric blanket.

couveuse [kōōvēz] *nf* (*à poules*) sitter, brooder; (*de maternité*) incubator.

couvre [kōōvr(ə)] *etc vb voir* **couvrir**.

couvre-chef [kōōvrəshef] *nm* hat.

couvre-feu, x [kōōvrəfœ̄] *nm* curfew.

couvre-lit [kōōvrəlē] *nm* bedspread.

couvre-pieds [kōōvrəpyā] *nm inv* quilt.

couvreur [kōōvrœr] *nm* roofer.

couvrir [kōōvrēr] *vt* to cover; (*dominer, étouffer: voix, pas*) to drown out; (*erreur*) to cover up; (*ZOOL*: *s'accoupler à*) to cover; **se ~** (*ciel*) to cloud over; (*s'habiller*) to cover up, wrap up; (*se coiffer*) to put on one's hat; (*par une assurance*) to cover o.s.; **se ~ de** (*fleurs, boutons*) to become covered in.

coyote [koyot] *nm* coyote.

CP *sigle m* = **cours préparatoire.**

CPAM *sigle f* (= *Caisse primaire d'assurances maladie*) *health insurance office.*

cps *abr* (= *caractères par seconde*) cps.

cpt *abr* = **comptant.**

CQFD *abr* (= *ce qu'il fallait démontrer*) QED (= *quod erat demonstrandum*).

CR *sigle m* = **compte rendu.**

crabe [kráb] *nm* crab.

crachat [kráshá] *nm* spittle *q*, spit *q*.

craché, e [kráshā] *a*: **son père tout ~** the spitting image of his (*ou* her) father.

cracher [kráshā] *vi* to spit ♦ *vt* to spit out; (*fig: lave etc*) to belch (out); **~ du sang** to spit blood.

crachin [kráshaṅ] *nm* drizzle.

crachiner [kráshēnā] *vi* to drizzle.

crachoir [kráshwár] *nm* spittoon; (*de dentiste*) basin.

crachoter [kráshotā] *vi* (*haut-parleur, radio*) to crackle.

crack [krák] *nm* (*intellectuel*) whizzkid; (*sportif*) ace; (*poulain*) hot favorite (*US*) *ou* favourite (*Brit*).

Cracovie [krákovē] *n* Kraków (*US*), Cracow (*Brit*).

cradingue [krádaṅg] *a* (*fam*) disgustingly dirty, filthy-dirty.

craie [kre] *nf* chalk.

craignais [krenye] *etc vb voir* **craindre.**

craindre [kraṅdr(ə)] *vt* to fear, be afraid of; (*être sensible à: chaleur, froid*) to be easily damaged by; **~ de/que** to be afraid of/that; **je crains qu'il (ne) vienne** I am afraid he may come.

crainte [kraṅt] *nf* fear; **de ~ de/que** for fear of/that.

craintif, ive [kraṅtēf, -ēv] *a* timid.

cramoisi, e [krámwázē] *a* crimson.

crampe [kráṅp] *nf* cramp; **~ d'estomac** stomach cramp.

crampon [kráṅpóṅ] *nm* (*de semelle*) cleat (*US*), stud (*Brit*); (*ALPINISME*) crampon.

cramponner [kráṅponā]: **se ~** *vi*: **se ~ (à)** to hang *ou* cling on (to).

cran [kráṅ] *nm* (*entaille*) notch; (*de courroie*) hole; (*courage*) guts *pl*; **~ d'arrêt** safety catch; **~ de mire** bead; **~ de sûreté** safety catch.

crâne [krán] *nm* skull.

crâner [kránā] *vi* (*fam*) to swank, show off.

crânien, ne [krányaṅ, -en] *a* cranial, skull *cpd*, brain *cpd*.

crapaud [krápō] *nm* toad.

crapule [krápül] *nf* villain.

crapuleux, euse [krápülœ̄, -ēz] *a*: **crime ~** villainous crime.

craquelure [kráklür] *nf* crack; crackle *q*.

craquement [krákmáṅ] *nm* crack, snap; (*du plancher*) creak, creaking *q*.

craquer [krákā] *vi* (*bois, plancher*) to creak; (*fil, branche*) to snap; (*couture*) to come apart, burst; (*fig*) to break down, fall apart; (: *être enthousiasmé*) to go wild ♦ *vt*: **~ une allumette** to strike a match.

crasse [krás] *nf* grime, filth ♦ *a* (*fig: ignorance*) crass.

crassier [krásyā] *nm* slag heap.

cratère [krátɛr] *nm* crater.

cravache [kråvåsh] *nf* (riding) crop.
cravacher [kråvåshā] *vt* to use the crop on.
cravate [kråvåt] *nf* tie.
cravater [kråvåtā] *vt* to put a tie on; (*fig*) to grab around the neck.
crawl [krōl] *nm* crawl.
crawlé, e [krōlā] *a*: **dos** ~ backstroke.
crayeux, euse [kreyœ̄, -œ̄z] *a* chalky.
crayon [kreyõn] *nm* pencil; (*de rouge à lèvres etc*) stick, pencil; **écrire au** ~ to write in pencil; ~ **à bille** ball-point pen; ~ **de couleur** crayon; ~ **optique** light pen.
crayon-feutre, *pl* **crayons-feutres** [kreyõnfœ̄tr(ə)] *nm* felt(-tip) pen.
crayonner [kreyonā] *vt* to scribble, sketch.
CRDP *sigle m* (= *Centre régional de documentation pédagogique*) *teachers' resource center.*
créance [krāāńs] *nf* (*COMM*) (financial) claim, (recoverable) debt; **donner** ~ **à qch** to lend credence to sth.
créancier, ière [krāāńsyā, -yer] *nm/f* creditor.
créateur, trice [krāātœr, -trēs] *a* creative ♦ *nm/f* creator; **le C**~ (*REL*) the Creator.
créatif, ive [krāātēf, -ēv] *a* creative.
création [krāāsyõn] *nf* creation.
créativité [krāātēvētā] *nf* creativity.
créature [krāātür] *nf* creature.
crécelle [krāsel] *nf* rattle.
crèche [kresh] *nf* (*de Noël*) manger; (*garderie*) day-care center (*US*), day nursery (*Brit*).
crédence [krādāńs] *nf* (small) sideboard.
crédibilité [krādēbēlētā] *nf* credibility.
crédible [krādēbl(ə)] *a* credible.
CREDIF [krādēf] *sigle m* (= *Centre de recherche et d'étude pour la diffusion du français*) *official body promoting use of the French language.*
crédit [krådē] *nm* (*gén*) credit; ~**s** *nmpl* funds; **payer/acheter à** ~ to pay/buy on credit *ou* on easy terms; **faire** ~ **à qn** to give sb credit; ~ **municipal** pawnshop; ~ **relais** bridge (*US*) *ou* bridging (*Brit*) loan.
crédit-bail, *pl* **crédits-bails** [krādēbây] *nm* (*ÉCON*) leasing.
créditer [krādētā] *vt*: ~ **un compte (de)** to credit an account (with).
créditeur, trice [krādētœr, -trēs] *a* in credit, credit *cpd* ♦ *nm/f* customer in credit.
credo [krādō] *nm* credo, creed.
crédule [krādül] *a* credulous, gullible.
crédulité [krādülētā] *nf* credulity, gullibility.
créer [krāā] *vt* to create; (*THÉÂTRE: pièce*) to produce (for the first time); (: *rôle*) to create.
crémaillère [krāmåyer] *nf* (*RAIL*) rack; (*tige crantée*) trammel; **direction à** ~ (*AUTO*) rack and pinion steering; **pendre la** ~ to have a house-warming party.
crémation [krāmåsyõn] *nf* cremation.
crématoire [krāmātwár] *a*: **four** ~ crematorium.
crème [krem] *nf* cream; (*entremets*) cream dessert ♦ *a inv* cream; **un (café)** ~ ≈ coffee with cream (*US*), ≈ a white coffee (*Brit*); ~ **chantilly** whipped cream, crème Chantilly; ~ **fouettée** whipped cream; ~ **glacée** ice cream; ~ **à raser** shaving cream.

crémerie [kremrē] *nf* dairy; (*restaurant*) tearoom.
crémeux, euse [krāmœ̄, -œ̄z] *a* creamy.
crémier, ière [krāmyā, -yer] *nm/f* dairyman/woman.
créneau, x [krānō] *nm* (*de fortification*) crenel(le); (*fig, aussi COMM*) gap, slot; (*AUTO*): **faire un** ~ to reverse into a parking space (*between cars alongside the curb*).
créole [krāol] *a, nm/f* Creole.
créosote [krāōzot] *nf* creosote.
crêpe [krep] *nf* (*galette*) pancake ♦ *nm* (*tissu*) crêpe; (*de deuil*) black mourning crêpe; (*ruban*) black armband (*ou* hatband *ou* ribbon); **semelle (de)** ~ crêpe sole; ~ **de Chine** crêpe de Chine.
crêpé, e [krāpā] *a* (*cheveux*) backcombed.
crêperie [krcprē] *nf* pancake shop *ou* restaurant.
crépi [krāpē] *nm* roughcast.
crépir [krāpēr] *vt* to roughcast.
crépiter [krāpētā] *vi* to sputter, splutter, crackle.
crépon [krāpõn] *nm* seersucker.
CREPS [kreps] *sigle m* (= *Centre régional d'éducation physique et sportive*) ≈ sports *ou* recreation center (*US*) *ou* centre (*Brit*).
crépu, e [krāpü] *a* frizzy, fuzzy.
crépuscule [krāpüskül] *nm* twilight, dusk.
crescendo [krāshendō] *nm, ad* (*MUS*) crescendo; **aller** ~ (*fig*) to rise higher and higher, grow ever greater.
cresson [krāsõn] *nm* watercress.
Crète [kret] *nf*: **la** ~ Crete.
crête [kret] *nf* (*de coq*) comb; (*de vague, montagne*) crest.
crétin, e [krātań, -ēn] *nm/f* cretin.
crétois, e [krātwá, -wáz] *a* Cretan.
cretonne [krəton] *nf* cretonne.
creuser [krœzā] *vt* (*trou, tunnel*) to dig; (*sol*) to dig a hole in; (*bois*) to hollow out; (*fig*) to go (deeply) into; **ça creuse** that gives you a real appetite; **se** ~ **(la cervelle)** to rack one's brains.
creuset [krœze] *nm* crucible; (*fig*) melting pot; (*severe*) test.
creux, euse [krœ̄, -œ̄z] *a* hollow ♦ *nm* hollow; (*fig: sur graphique etc*) trough; **heures creuses** slack periods; off-peak periods; **le** ~ **de l'estomac** the pit of the stomach.
crevaison [krœvezõn] *nf* puncture, flat.
crevasse [krœvás] *nf* (*dans le sol*) crack, fissure; (*de glacier*) crevasse; (*de la peau*) crack.
crevé, e [krœvā] *a* (*fam: fatigué*) worn out, dead beat.
crève-cœur [krevkœr] *nm inv* heartbreak.
crever [krœvā] *vt* (*papier*) to tear, break; (*tambour, ballon*) to burst ♦ *vi* (*pneu*) to burst; (*automobiliste*) to have a flat (tire) (*US*) *ou* a puncture (*Brit*); (*abcès, outre, nuage*) to burst (open); (*fam*) to die; **cela lui a crevé un œil** it blinded him in one eye; ~ **l'écran** to have real screen presence.
crevette [krœvet] *nf*: ~ **(rose)** prawn; ~ **grise** shrimp.
cri [krē] *nm* cry, shout; (*d'animal: spécifique*) cry, call; **à grands** ~**s** at the top of one's voice; **c'est le dernier** ~ (*fig*) it's the latest

fashion.

criant, e [krēyåṅ, -åṅt] *a* (*injustice*) glaring.

criard, e [krēyàr, -àrd(ə)] *a* (*couleur*) garish, loud; (*voix*) yelling.

crible [krēbl(ə)] *nm* riddle; (*mécanique*) screen, jig; **passer qch au** ~ to put sth through a riddle; (*fig*) to go over sth with a fine-tooth comb.

criblé, e [krēblā] *a*: ~ **de** riddled with.

cric [krēk] *nm* (*AUTO*) jack.

cricket [krēket] *nm* cricket.

criée [krēyā] *nf*: (**vente à la**) ~ (sale by) auction.

crier [krēyā] *vi* (*pour appeler*) to shout, cry (out); (*de peur, de douleur etc*) to scream, yell; (*fig: grincer*) to squeal, screech ♦ *vt* (*ordre, injure*) to shout (out), yell (out); **sans** ~ **gare** without warning; ~ **grâce** to cry for mercy; ~ **au secours** to shout for help.

crieur, euse [krēyœr, -œz] *nm/f*: ~ **de journaux** newspaper seller.

crime [krēm] *nm* crime; (*meurtre*) murder.

Crimée [krēmā] *nf*: **la** ~ the Crimea.

criminaliste [krēmēnálēst(ə)] *nm/f* specialist in criminal law.

criminalité [krēmēnálētā] *nf* criminality, crime.

criminel, le [krēmēnel] *a* criminal ♦ *nm/f* criminal; murderer; ~ **de guerre** war criminal.

criminologiste [krēmēnolozhēst(ə)] *nm/f* criminologist.

crin [kraṅ] *nm* hair *q*; (*fibre*) horsehair; **à tous** ~**s, à tout** ~ diehard, out-and-out.

crinière [krēnyer] *nf* mane.

crique [krēk] *nf* creek, inlet.

criquet [krēke] *nm* grasshopper.

crise [krēz] *nf* crisis (*pl* crises); (*MÉD*) attack; fit; ~ **cardiaque** heart attack; ~ **de foi** crisis of belief; ~ **de foie** bilious attack; ~ **de nerfs** attack of nerves.

crispant, e [krēspåṅ, -åṅt] *a* annoying, irritating.

crispation [krēspásyóṅ] *nf* (*spasme*) twitch; (*contraction*) contraction; tenseness.

crispé, e [krēspā] *a* tense, nervous.

crisper [krēspā] *vt vi* to tense; (*poings*) to clench; **se** ~ to tense; to clench; (*personne*) to get tense.

crissement [krēsmåṅ] *nm* crunch; rustle; screech.

crisser [krēsā] *vi* (*neige*) to crunch; (*tissu*) to rustle; (*pneu*) to screech.

cristal, aux [krēstál, -ō] *nm* crystal ♦ *nmpl* (*objets*) crystal(ware) *sg*; ~ **de plomb** (lead) crystal; ~ **de roche** rock-crystal; **cristaux de soude** washing soda *sg*.

cristallin, e [krēstálåṅ, -ēn] *a* crystal-clear ♦ *nm* (*ANAT*) crystalline lens.

cristalliser [krēstálēzā] *vi, vt, se* ~ *vi* to crystallize.

critère [krēter] *nm* criterion (*pl* -ia).

critiquable [krētēkáhbl(ə)] *a* open to criticism.

critique [krētēk] *a* critical ♦ *nm/f* (*de théâtre, musique*) critic ♦ *nf* criticism; (*THÉÂTRE etc*: *article*) review; **la** ~ (*activité*) criticism; (*personnes*) the critics *pl*.

critiquer [krētēkā] *vt* (*dénigrer*) to criticize;

(*évaluer, juger*) to assess, examine (critically).

croasser [kroàsā] *vi* to caw.

croate [kroàt] *a* Croatian ♦ *nm* (*LING*) Croat, Croatian.

Croatie [kroàsē] *nf*: **la** ~ Croatia.

croc [krō] *nm* (*dent*) fang; (*de boucher*) hook.

croc-en-jambe, *pl* **crocs-en-jambe** [krokåṅyåṅb] *nm*: **faire un** ~ **à qn** to trip sb up.

croche [krosh] *nf* (*MUS*) eighth note (*US*), quaver (*Brit*); **double** ~ sixteenth note (*US*), semiquaver (*Brit*).

croche-pied [kroshpyā] *nm* = **croc-en-jambe**.

crochet [kroshe] *nm* hook; (*clef*) picklock; (*détour*) detour; (*BOXE*): ~ **du gauche** left hook; (*TRICOT*: *aiguille*) crochet hook; (: *technique*) crochet; ~**s** *nmpl* (*TYPO*) square brackets; **vivre aux** ~**s de qn** to live *ou* sponge off sb.

crocheter [kroshtā] *vt* (*serrure*) to pick.

crochu, e [kroshü] *a* hooked; claw-like.

crocodile [krokodēl] *nm* crocodile.

crocus [kroküs] *nm* crocus.

croire [krwár] *vt* to believe; ~ **qn honnête** to believe sb (to be) honest; **se** ~ **fort** to think one is strong; ~ **que** to believe *ou* think that; **vous croyez?** do you think so?; ~ **être/faire** to think one is/does; ~ **à,** ~ **en** to believe in.

crois [krwà] *etc vb voir* **croître**.

croisade [krwázàd] *nf* crusade.

croisé, e [krwázā] *a* (*veston*) double-breasted ♦ *nm* (*guerrier*) crusader ♦ *nf* (*fenêtre*) window, casement; ~**e d'ogives** intersecting ribs; **à la** ~**e des chemins** at the crossroads.

croisement [krwázmåṅ] *nm* (*carrefour*) crossroads *sg*; (*BIO*) crossing; crossbreed.

croiser [krwázā] *vt* (*personne, voiture*) to pass; (*route*) to cross, cut across; (*BIO*) to cross ♦ *vi* (*NAVIG*) to cruise; ~ **les jambes/bras** to cross one's legs/fold one's arms; **se** ~ (*personnes, véhicules*) to pass each other; (*routes*) to cross, intersect; (*lettres*) to cross (in the mail); (*regards*) to meet; **se** ~ **les bras** (*fig*) to twiddle one's thumbs.

croiseur [krwázœr] *nm* cruiser (*warship*).

croisière [krwázyer] *nf* cruise; **vitesse de** ~ (*AUTO etc*) cruising speed.

croisillon [krwázēyóṅ] *nm*: **motif/fenêtre à** ~**s** lattice pattern/window.

croissais [krwàse] *etc vb voir* **croître**.

croissance [krwásåṅs] *nf* growing, growth; **troubles de la** ~ growing pains; **maladie de** ~ growth disease; ~ **économique** economic growth.

croissant, e [krwásåṅ, -åṅt] *vb voir* **croître** ♦ *a* growing; rising ♦ *nm* (*à manger*) croissant; (*motif*) crescent; ~ **de lune** crescent moon.

croître [krwàtr(ə)] *vi* to grow; (*lune*) to wax.

croix [krwà] *nf* cross; **en** ~ *a, ad* in the form of a cross; **la C**~ **Rouge** the Red Cross.

croquant, e [krokåṅ, -åṅt] *a* crisp, crunchy ♦ *nm/f* (*péj*) yokel, (country) bumpkin.

croque-madame [krokmàdàm] *nm inv* toasted cheese sandwich with a fried egg on top.

croque-mitaine [krokmēten] *nm* bog(e)y-man (*pl* -men).

croque-monsieur [krokməsyœ] *nm inv*

toasted ham and cheese sandwich.

croque-mort [krokmor] *nm* (*péj*) pallbearer.

croquer [krokā] *vt* (*manger*) to crunch; to munch; (*dessiner*) to sketch ♦ *vi* to be crisp *ou* crunchy; **chocolat à** ~ plain dessert chocolate.

croquet [kroke] *nm* croquet.

croquette [kroket] *nf* croquette.

croquis [krokē] *nm* sketch.

cross(-country), *pl* **cross(-countries)** [kros(kōōntrē)] *nm* cross-country race *ou* run; cross-country racing *ou* running.

crosse [kros] *nf* (*de fusil*) butt; (*de revolver*) grip; (*d'évêque*) crook, crosier; (*de hockey*) hockey stick.

crotale [krotàl] *nm* rattlesnake.

crotte [krot] *nf* droppings *pl*; ~! (*fam*) damn!

crotté, e [krotā] *a* muddy, mucky.

crottin [krotàn] *nm*: ~ **(de cheval)** (horse) dung *ou* manure.

croulant, e [krōōlàn, -ànt] *nm/f* (*fam*) old fogey.

crouler [krōōlā] *vi* (*s'effondrer*) to collapse; (*être délabré*) to be crumbling.

croupe [krōōp] *nf* croup, rump; **en** ~ pillion.

croupier [krōōpyā] *nm* croupier.

croupir [krōōpēr] *vi* to stagnate.

CROUS [krōōs] *sigle m* (= *Centre régional des œuvres universitaires et scolaires*) students' representative body.

croustillant, e [krōōstēyàn, -ànt] *a* crisp; (*fig*) spicy.

croustiller [krōōstēyā] *vt* to be crisp *ou* crusty.

croûte [krōōt] *nf* crust; (*du fromage*) rind; (*de vol-au-vent*) shell; (*MÉD*) scab; **en** ~ (*CULIN*) in pastry, in a pie; ~ **aux champignons** mushrooms on toast; ~ **au fromage** cheese on toast *q*; ~ **de pain** (*morceau*) crust (of bread); ~ **terrestre** earth's crust.

croûton [krōōtôn] *nm* (*CULIN*) crouton; (*bout du pain*) crust, heel.

croyable [krwàyàbl(ə)] *a* believable, credible.

croyais [krwàyc] *etc vb voir* **croire.**

croyance [krwàyàns] *nf* belief.

croyant, e [krwàyàn, -ànt] *vb voir* **croire** ♦ *a*: **être/ne pas être** ~ to be/not to be a believer ♦ *nm/f* believer.

Crozet [krōze] *n*: **les îles** ~ the Crozet Islands.

CRS *sigle fpl* (= *Compagnies républicaines de sécurité*) state security police force ♦ *sigle m* member of the CRS.

cru, e [krü] *pp de* **croire** ♦ *a* (*non cuit*) raw; (*lumière, couleur*) harsh; (*description*) crude; (*paroles, langage: franc*) blunt; (*: grossier*) crude ♦ *nm* (*vignoble*) vineyard; (*vin*) wine ♦ *nf* (*d'un cours d'eau*) swelling, rising; **de son (propre)** ~ (*fig*) of his own devising; **monter à** ~ to ride bareback; **du** ~ local; **en** ~e in spate.

crû [krü] *pp de* **croître.**

cruauté [krüōtā] *nf* cruelty.

cruche [krüsh] *nf* pitcher, (earthenware) jug.

crucial, e, aux [krüsyàl, -ō] *a* crucial.

crucifier [krüsēfyā] *vt* to crucify.

crucifix [krüsēfē] *nm* crucifix.

crucifixion [krüsēfēksyôn] *nf* crucifixion.

cruciforme [krüsēform(ə)] *a* cruciform, cross-shaped.

cruciverbiste [krüsēverbēst(ə)] *nm/f* crossword puzzle enthusiast.

crudité [krüdētā] *nf* crudeness *q*; harshness *q*; ~**s** *nfpl* (*CULIN*) mixed salads (*as hors-d'œuvre*).

crue [krü] *nf voir* **cru.**

cruel, le [krüel] *a* cruel.

cruellement [krüelmàn] *ad* cruelly.

crûment [krümàn] *ad* (*voir* **cru**) harshly; bluntly; crudely.

crus, crûs [krü] *etc vb voir* **croire, croître.**

crustacés [krüstàsā] *nmpl* shellfish.

crypte [krēpt(ə)] *nf* crypt.

cse *abr* = **cause.**

CSEN *sigle f* (= *Confédération des syndicats de l'éducation nationale*) group of teachers' unions.

Cte *abr* = **Comtesse.**

CU *sigle f* = *communauté urbaine.*

Cuba [kübà] *nf*: **la** ~ Cuba.

cubage [kübàzh] *nm* cubage, cubic content.

cubain, e [kübàn, -en] *a* Cuban ♦ *nm/f*: **C**~, **e** Cuban.

cube [küb] *nm* cube; (*jouet*) brick, building block; **gros** ~ powerful motorbike; **mètre** ~ cubic meter; **2 au** ~ = **8** 2 cubed is 8; **élever au** ~ to cube.

cubique [kübēk] *a* cubic.

cubisme [kübēsm(ə)] *nm* cubism.

cubitus [kübētüs] *nm* ulna.

cueillette [kœyet] *nf* picking, gathering; harvest *ou* crop (of fruit).

cueillir [kœyēr] *vt* (*fruits, fleurs*) to pick, gather; (*fig*) to catch.

cuiller *ou* **cuillère** [küēyer] *nf* spoon; ~ **à café** coffee spoon; (*CULIN*) ≈ teaspoonful; ~ **à soupe** soup spoon; (*CULIN*) ≈ tablespoonful.

cuillerée [küēyrā] *nf* spoonful; (*CULIN*): ~ **à soupe/café** tablespoonful/teaspoonful.

cuir [küēr] *nm* leather; (*avant tannage*) hide; ~ **chevelu** scalp.

cuirasse [küēràs] *nf* breastplate.

cuirassé [küēràsā] *nm* (*NAVIG*) battleship.

cuire [küēr] *vt* (*aliments*) to cook; (*au four*) to bake; (*poterie*) to fire ♦ *vi* to cook; (*picoter*) to smart, sting, burn; **bien cuit** (*viande*) well done; **trop cuit** overdone; **pas assez cuit** underdone; **cuit à point** medium done; done to a turn.

cuisant, e [küēzàn, -ànt] *vb voir* **cuire** ♦ *a* (*douleur*) smarting, burning; (*fig: souvenir, échec*) bitter.

cuisine [küēzēn] *nf* (*pièce*) kitchen; (*art culinaire*) cookery, cooking; (*nourriture*) cooking, food; **faire la** ~ to cook.

cuisiné, e [küēzēnā] *a*: **plat** ~ ready-made meal *ou* dish.

cuisiner [küēzēnā] *vt* to cook; (*fam*) to grill ♦ *vi* to cook.

cuisinette [küēzēnet] *nf* kitchenette.

cuisinier, ière [küēzēnyā, -yer] *nm/f* cook ♦ *nf* (*poêle*) cooker.

cuisis [küēzē] *etc vb voir* **cuire.**

cuissardes [küēsàrd] *nfpl* (*de pêcheur*) waders; (*de femme*) thigh boots.

cuisse [küēs] *nf* (*ANAT*) thigh; (*CULIN*) leg.

cuisson [küēsôn] *nf* cooking; (*de poterie*) firing.

cuissot [küēsō] *nm* haunch.

cuistre [küēstr(ə)] *nm* prig.

cuit, e [kɥĕ, -ĕt] *pp de* **cuire.**
cuivre [kɥĕvr(ə)] *nm* copper; **les ~s** (*MUS*) the brass; **~ rouge** copper; **~ jaune** brass.
cuivré, e [kɥĕvrā] *a* coppery; (*peau*) bronzed.
cul [kü] *nm* (*fam!*) ass (*US !*), arse (*Brit !*); **~ de bouteille** bottom of a bottle.
culasse [külás] *nf* (*AUTO*) cylinder-head; (*de fusil*) breech.
culbute [külbüt] *nf* somersault; (*accidentelle*) tumble, fall.
culbuter [külbütā] *vi* to (take a) tumble, fall (head over heels).
culbuteur [külbütœr] *nm* (*AUTO*) rocker arm.
cul-de-jatte, *pl* **culs-de-jatte** [küdzhàt] *nm/f* legless cripple.
cul-de-sac, *pl* **culs-de-sac** [küdsák] *nm* cul-de-sac.
culinaire [külēner] *a* culinary.
culminant, e [külmēnàn̄, -àn̄t] *a*: **point ~** highest point; (*fig*) height, climax.
culminer [külmēnā] *vi* to reach its highest point; to tower.
culot [külō] *nm* (*d'ampoule*) base (*US*), cap (*Brit*); (*effronterie*) nerve.
culotte [külot] *nf* (*de femme*) panties *pl*; (*d'homme*) underpants *pl*; (*pantalon*) trousers *pl*, pants *pl* (*US*); **~ de cheval** riding breeches *pl*.
culotté, e [külotā] *a* (*pipe*) seasoned; (*cuir*) mellowed; (*effronté*) sassy (*US*), cheeky (*Brit*).
culpabiliser [külpábēlēzā] *vt*: **~ qn** to make sb feel guilty.
culpabilité [külpábēlētā] *nf* guilt.
culte [kült(ə)] *nm* (*religion*) religion; (*hommage, vénération*) worship; (*protestant*) service.
cultivateur, trice [kültēvàtœr, -trēs] *nm/f* farmer.
cultivé, e [kültēvā] *a* (*personne*) cultured, cultivated.
cultiver [kültēvā] *vt* to cultivate; (*légumes*) to grow, cultivate.
culture [kültür] *nf* cultivation; growing; (*connaissances etc*) culture; (**champs de**) **~s** land(s) under cultivation.
culturel, le [kültürel] *a* cultural.
culturisme [kültürēsm(ə)] *nm* body-building.
culturiste [kültürēst(ə)] *nm/f* body-builder.
cumin [kümàn̄] *nm* (*CULIN*) caraway seeds *pl*; cumin.
cumul [kümül] *nm* (*voir cumuler*) holding (*ou* drawing) concurrently; **~ de peines** sentences to run consecutively.
cumuler [kümülā] *vt* (*emplois, honneurs*) to hold concurrently; (*salaires*) to draw concurrently; (*JUR: droits*) to accumulate.
cupide [küpēd] *a* greedy, grasping.
curable [kürábl(ə)] *a* curable.
Curaçao [kürásō] *n* Curaçao ◊ *nm*: **c~** curaçao.
curatif, ive [kürátēf, -ēv] *a* curative.
cure [kür] *nf* (*MÉD*) course of treatment; (*REL*) cure; presbytery, ≈ vicarage; **faire une ~ de fruits** to go on a fruit cure *ou* diet; **faire une ~ thermale** to visit a spa; **n'avoir ~ de** to pay no attention to; **~ d'amaigrissement** reducing *ou* weight-loss treatment (*US*), slimming course (*Brit*); **~ de repos**

rest cure; **~ de sommeil** sleep therapy *q*.
curé [kürā] *nm* parish priest; **M le ~** ≈ Vicar.
cure-dent [kürdàn̄] *nm* toothpick.
curée [kürā] *nf* (*fig*) scramble for the pickings.
cure-ongles [kürŏn̄gl(ə)] *nm inv* nail cleaner.
cure-pipe [kürpēp] *nm* pipe cleaner.
curer [kürā] *vt* to clean out; **se ~ les dents** to pick one's teeth.
curieusement [küryēzmàn̄] *ad* oddly.
curieux, euse [küryœ̄, -œ̄z] *a* (*étrange*) strange, curious; (*indiscret*) curious, inquisitive; (*intéressé*) inquiring, curious ◊ *nmpl* (*badauds*) onlookers, bystanders.
curiosité [küryōzētā] *nf* curiosity, inquisitiveness; (*objet*) curio(sity); (*site*) unusual feature *ou* sight.
curiste [kürēst(ə)] *nm/f* spa guest.
curriculum vitae (CV) [kürēkülomvētā] *nm inv* curriculum vitae (CV).
curry [kürē] *nm* curry; **poulet au ~** curried chicken, chicken curry.
curseur [kürsœr] *nm* (*INFORM*) cursor; (*de règle*) slide; (*de fermeture-éclair*) slider.
cursif, ive [kürsēf, -ēv] *a*: **écriture cursive** cursive script.
cursus [kürsüs] *nm* degree course.
cutané, e [kütánā] *a* cutaneous, skin *cpd*.
cuti-réaction [kütērāàksyôn̄] *nf* (*MÉD*) skin-test.
cuve [küv] *nf* vat; (*à mazout etc*) tank.
cuvée [küvā] *nf* vintage.
cuvette [küvet] *nf* (*récipient*) bowl, basin; (*du lavabo*) (wash)basin; (*des w.-c.*) bowl; (*GÉO*) basin.
CV *sigle m* (*AUTO*) = **cheval vapeur**; (*ADMIN*) = **curriculum vitae.**
CVS *sigle a* (= *corrigées des variations saisonnières*) seasonally adjusted.
cx *abr* (= *coefficient de pénétration dans l'air*) drag coefficient.
cyanure [syánür] *nm* cyanide.
cybernétique [sēbernátēk] *nf* cybernetics *sg*.
cyclable [sēklábl(ə)] *a*: **piste ~** bike path *ou* lane.
cyclamen [sēklámen] *nm* cyclamen.
cycle [sēkl(ə)] *nm* cycle; (*SCOL*): **premier/second ~** ≈ junior/senior high school (*US*), ≈ middle/upper school (*Brit*).
cyclique [sēklēk] *a* cyclic(al).
cyclisme [sēklēsm(ə)] *nm* cycling.
cycliste [sēklēst(ə)] *nm/f* cyclist ◊ *a* cycle *cpd*; **coureur ~** racing cyclist.
cyclo-crosse [sēklokros] *nm* (*SPORT*) cyclo-cross; (*épreuve*) cyclo-cross race.
cyclomoteur [sēklomotœr] *nm* moped.
cyclomotoriste [sēklomotorēst(ə)] *nm/f* moped rider.
cyclone [sēklōn] *nm* cyclone, hurricane.
cyclotourisme [sēklotŏōrēsm(ə)] *nm* (bi)cycle touring.
cygne [sēny] *nm* swan.
cylindre [sēlàn̄dr(ə)] *nm* cylinder; **moteur à 4 ~s en ligne** straight-4 engine.
cylindrée [sēlàn̄drā] *nf* (*AUTO*) (cubic) capacity; **une (voiture de) grosse ~** a big-engined car.
cylindrique [sēlàn̄drēk] *a* cylindrical.
cymbale [sàn̄bál] *nf* cymbal.
cynique [sēnĕk] *a* cynical.

cynisme [sēnēsm(ə)] *nm* cynicism.
cyprès [sēpre] *nm* cypress.
cypriote [sēprēyot] *a* Cypriot ♦ *nm/f*: **C~** Cypriot.
cyrillique [sērēlēk] *a* Cyrillic.
cystite [sēstēt] *nf* cystitis.
cytise [sētēz] *nm* laburnum.
cytologie [sētolozhē] *nf* cytology.

D

D, d [dā] *nm inv* D, d ♦ *abr*: **D** (*MÉTÉO*: = *dépression*) low, depression; **D comme Désiré** D for Dog; *voir* **système**.
d' *prép*, *dét voir* **de**.
Dacca [dáká] *n* Dacca.
dactylo [dáktēlō] *nf* (*aussi*: **~graphe**) typist; (*aussi*: **~graphie**) typing, typewriting.
dactylographier [dáktēlográfyā] *vt* to type (out).
dada [dádá] *nm* hobby-horse.
dadais [dáde] *nm* ninny, lump.
dague [dág] *nf* dagger.
dahlia [dályá] *nm* dahlia.
dahoméen, ne [dáomáañ, -en] *a* Dahomean.
Dahomey [dáomá] *nm*: **le ~** Dahomey.
daigner [dānyā] *vt* to deign.
daim [dań] *nm* (fallow) deer *inv*; (*peau*) buckskin; (*imitation*) suede.
dais [de] *nm* (*tenture*) canopy.
Dakar [dákár] *n* Dakar.
dal. *abr* (= *décalitre*) dal.
dallage [dálázh] *nm* paving.
dalle [dál] *nf* slab; (*au sol*) paving stone, flag(stone); **que ~** nothing at all, zilch.
daller [dálā] *vt* to pave.
dalmate [dálmát] *a* Dalmatian.
Dalmatie [dálmásē] *nf*: **la ~** Dalmatia.
dalmatien, ne [dálmásyañ, -en] *nm/f* (*chien*) Dalmatian.
daltonien, ne [dáltonyañ, -en] *a* color-blind (*US*), colour-blind (*Brit*).
daltonisme [dáltonēsm(ə)] *nm* color (*US*) *ou* colour (*Brit*) blindness.
dam [dań] *nm*: **au grand ~ de** much to the detriment (*ou* annoyance) of.
Damas [dámá] *n* Damascus.
damas [dámá] *nm* (*étoffe*) damask.
damassé, e [dámásā] *a* damask *cpd*.
dame [dám] *nf* lady; (*CARTES*, *ÉCHECS*) queen; **~s** *nfpl* (*jeu*) checkers *sg* (*US*), draughts *sg* (*Brit*); **les (toilettes des) ~s** the ladies' (toilets); **~ de charité** benefactress; **~ de compagnie** lady's companion.
dame-jeanne, *pl* **dames-jeannes** [dámzhán] *nf* demijohn.
damer [dámā] *vt* to ram *ou* pack down; **~ le pion à** (*fig*) to get the better of.
damier [dámyā] *nm* checkerboard (*US*), draughtboard (*Brit*); (*dessin*) check (pattern); **en ~** check.
damner [dánā] *vt* to damn.

dancing [dáñsēng] *nm* dance hall.
dandiner [dáñdēnā]: **se ~** *vi* to sway about; (*en marchant*) to waddle along.
Danemark [dánmárk] *nm*: **le ~** Denmark.
danger [dáñzhā] *nm* danger; **mettre en ~** to endanger, put in danger; **être en ~ de mort** to be in peril of one's life; **être hors de ~** to be out of danger.
dangereusement [dáñzhrœzmáñ] *ad* dangerously.
dangereux, euse [dáñzhrœ, -œz] *a* dangerous.
danois, e [dánwá, -wáz] *a* Danish ♦ *nm* (*LING*) Danish ♦ *nm/f*: **D~, e** Dane.
dans [dáñ] *prép* in; (*direction*) into, to; (*à l'intérieur de*) in, inside; **je l'ai pris ~ le tiroir/la chambre** I took it out of *ou* from the drawer/the bedroom; **boire ~ un verre** to drink out of *ou* from a glass; **~ 2 mois** in 2 months, in 2 months' time, 2 months from now; **~ quelques instants** in a few minutes; **~ quelques jours** in a few days' time; **il part ~ quinze jours** he's leaving in two weeks' (time); **~ les 20 F** about 20 F.
dansant, e [dáñsáñ, áñt] *a*: **soirée ~e** evening of dancing; (*bal*) dinner dance.
danse [dáñs] *nf*: **la ~** dancing; (*classique*) (ballet) dancing; **une ~** a dance; **~ du ventre** belly dancing.
danser [dáñsā] *vi*, *vt* to dance.
danseur, euse [dáñsœr, -œz] *nm/f* ballet dancer; (*au bal etc*) dancer; (*: cavalier*) partner; **~ de claquettes** tap-dancer; **en danseuse** (*à vélo*) standing on the pedals.
Danube [dánüb] *nm*: **le ~** the Danube.
DAO *sigle m* (= *dessin assisté par ordinateur*) CAD.
dard [dár] *nm* sting (*organ*).
Dardanelles [dárdánel] *nfpl*: **les ~** the Dardanelles.
darder [dárdā] *vt* to shoot, send forth.
dare-dare [dárdár] *ad* in double-quick time.
Dar es Salaam, Dar-es-Salam [dáresálám] *n* Dar es Salaam.
darse [dárs(ə)] *nf* sheltered dock (*in a Mediterranean port*).
datation [dátásyóñ] *nf* dating.
date [dát] *nf* date; **faire ~** to mark a milestone; **de longue ~** a longstanding; **~ de naissance** date of birth; **~ limite** deadline; (*d'un aliment*: *aussi*: **~ limite de vente**) sell-by date.
dater [dátā] *vt*, *vi* to date; **~ de** to date from, go back to; **à ~ de** (as) from.
dateur [dátœr] *nm* (*de montre*) date indicator; **timbre ~** date stamp.
datif [dátēf] *nm* dative.
datte [dát] *nf* date.
dattier [dátyā] *nm* date palm.
daube [dōb] *nf*: **bœuf en ~** beef casserole.
dauphin [dōfañ] *nm* (*ZOOL*) dolphin; (*du roi*) dauphin; (*fig*) heir apparent.
Dauphiné [dōfēnā] *nm*: **le ~** the Dauphiné.
dauphinois, e [dōfēnwá, -wáz] *a* of *ou* from the Dauphiné.
daurade [dorád] *nf* sea bream.
davantage [dáváñtázh] *ad* more; (*plus longtemps*) longer; **~ de** more; **~ que** more than.
DB *sigle f* (*MIL*) = *division blindée*.

DCT *sigle m* (= *diphtérie coqueluche tétanos*) DPT.

DDASS [dás] *sigle f* (= *Direction départementale d'action sanitaire et sociale*) ≈ SSA (= *Social Security Administration*) (*US*), ≈ DHSS (= *Department of Health and Social Security*) (*Brit*).

DDT *sigle m* (= *dichloro-diphénol-trichloréthane*) DDT.

de (*de + le* = **du**, *de + les* = **des**) [də, dü, dā] *prép* of; (*provenance*) from; (*moyen*) with; **la voiture d'Élisabeth/de mes parents** Elizabeth's/my parents' car; **un mur de brique/bureau d'acajou** a brick wall/mahogany desk; **augmenter** *etc* **de 10 F** to increase *etc* by 10 F; **une pièce de 2 m de large** *ou* **large de 2 m** a room 2 m wide *ou* in width, a 2 m wide room; **un bébé de 10 mois** a 10-month-old baby; **un séjour de 2 ans** a 2-year stay; **12 mois de crédit/travail** 12 months' credit/work; **de 14 à 18h** from 2pm till 6pm ♦ *dét*: **du vin, de l'eau, des pommes** (some) wine, (some) water, (some) apples; **des enfants sont venus** some children came; **a-t-il du vin?** has he got any wine?; **il ne veut pas de pommes** he doesn't want any apples; **il n'a pas d'enfants** he has no children, he hasn't (got) any children; **pendant des mois** for months.

dé [dā] *nm* (*à jouer*) die *ou* dice (*pl* dice); (*aussi*) ~ **à coudre**) thimble; ~s *nmpl* (*jeu*) (game of) dice; **un coup de** ~s a throw of the dice; **couper en** ~s (*CULIN*) to dice.

DEA *sigle m* (= *Diplôme d'études approfondies*) post-graduate diploma.

déambuler [dāáñbülā] *vi* to stroll about.

déb. *abr* = **débutant**; (*COMM*) = *à débattre*.

débâcle [dābákl(ə)] *nf* rout.

déballer [dābálā] *vt* to unpack.

débandade [dābáñdád] *nf* scattering; (*déroute*) rout.

débander [dābáñdā] *vt* to unbandage.

débaptiser [dābátēzā] *vt* (*rue*) to rename.

débarbouiller [dābárbōōyā] *vt* to wash; **se** ~ to wash (one's face).

débarcadère [dābárkáder] *nm* wharf, pier.

débardeur [dābárdœr] *nm* docker, stevedore; (*maillot*) slipover, tank top.

débarquement [dābárkəmáñ] *nm* unloading, landing; disembarkation; (*MIL*) landing; **le D~** the Normandy landings.

débarquer [dābárkā] *vt* to unload, land ♦ *vi* to disembark; (*fig*) to turn up.

débarras [dābárá] *nm* junk room; (*placard*) junk closet (*US*) *ou* cupboard (*Brit*); (*remise*) outbuilding, shed; **bon** ~! good riddance!

débarrasser [dābárásā] *vt* to clear ♦ *vi* (*enlever le couvert*) to clear; ~ **qn de** (*vêtements, paquets*) to relieve sb of; (*habitude, ennemi*) to rid sb of; ~ **qch de** (*fouillis etc*) to clear sth of; **se** ~ **de** *vt* to get rid of; to rid o.s. of.

débat [dābá] *vb voir* **débattre** ♦ *nm* discussion, debate; ~s *nmpl* (*POL*) proceedings, debates.

débattre [dābátr(ə)] *vt* to discuss, debate; **se** ~ *vi* to struggle.

débauche [dābōsh] *nf* debauchery; **une** ~ **de** (*fig*) a profusion of; (*: de couleurs*) a riot of.

débauché, e [dābōshā] *a* debauched ♦ *nm/f* profligate.

débaucher [dābōshā] *vt* (*licencier*) to lay off, dismiss; (*entraîner*) to lead astray, debauch; (*inciter à la grève*) to incite.

débile [dābēl] *a* weak, feeble; (*fam: idiot*) dim-witted ♦ *nm/f*: ~ **mental, e** mental defective.

débilitant, e [dābēlētáñ, -áñt] *a* debilitating.

débilité [dābēlētā] *nf* debility; (*fam: idiotie*) stupidity; ~ **mentale** mental debility.

débiner [dābēnā]: **se** ~ *vi* to clear out, do a bunk (*Brit*).

débit [dābē] *nm* (*d'un liquide, fleuve*) (rate of) flow; (*d'un magasin*) turnover (of goods); (*élocution*) delivery; (*bancaire*) debit; **avoir un** ~ **de 10 F** to be 10 F in debit; ~ **de boissons** drinking establishment; ~ **de tabac** tobacco shop (*US*), tobacconist's (shop) (*Brit*).

débiter [dābētā] *vt* (*compte*) to debit; (*liquide, gaz*) to yield, produce, give out; (*couper: bois, viande*) to cut up; (*vendre*) to retail; (*péj: paroles etc*) to come out with, churn out.

débiteur, trice [dābētœr, -trēs] *nm/f* debtor ♦ *a* in debit; (*compte*) debit *cpd*.

déblai [dāble] *nm* earth (*moved*).

déblaiement [dāblemáñ] *nm* clearing; **travaux de** ~ earth moving *sg*.

déblatérer [dāblátārā] *vi*: ~ **contre** to go on about.

déblayer [dāblāyā] *vt* to clear; ~ **le terrain** (*fig*) to clear the ground.

débloquer [dāblokā] *vt* (*frein, fonds*) to release; (*prix*) to free ♦ *vi* (*fam*) to talk nonsense.

débobiner [dābobēnā] *vt* to unwind.

déboires [dābwár] *nmpl* setbacks.

déboisement [dābwázmáñ] *nm* deforestation.

déboiser [dābwázā] *vt* to clear of trees; (*région*) to deforest; **se** ~ *vi* (*colline, montagne*) to become bare of trees.

déboîter [dābwátā] *vt* (*AUTO*) to pull out; **se** ~ **le genou** *etc* to dislocate one's knee *etc*.

débonnaire [dāboner] *a* easy-going, good-natured.

débordant, e [dābordáñ, -áñt] *a* (*joie*) unbounded; (*activité*) exuberant.

débordé, e [dābordā] *a*: **être** ~ **de** (*travail, demandes*) to be snowed under with.

débordement [dābordəmáñ] *nm* overflowing.

déborder [dābordā] *vi* to overflow; (*lait etc*) to boil over ♦ *vt* (*MIL, SPORT*) to outflank; ~ (**de**) **qch** (*dépasser*) to extend beyond sth; ~ **de** (*joie, zèle*) to be brimming over with *ou* bursting with.

débouché [dābōōshā] *nm* (*pour vendre*) outlet; (*perspective d'emploi*) opening; (*sortie*) au ~ **de la vallée** where the valley opens out (onto the plain).

déboucher [dābōōshā] *vt* (*évier, tuyau etc*) to unblock; (*bouteille*) to uncork, open ♦ *vi*: ~ **de** to emerge from, come out of; ~ **sur** to come out onto; to open out onto; (*fig*) to arrive at, lead up to.

débouler [dābōōlā] *vi* to go (*ou* come) tumbling down; (*sans tomber*) to come careering down ♦ *vt*: ~ **l'escalier** to belt down the stairs.

déboulonner [dābōōlonā] *vt* to dismantle; *(fig:* renvoyer) to dismiss; (: *détruire le prestige de*) to discredit.

débours [dābōōr] *nmpl* outlay.

débourser [dābōōrsā] *vt* to pay out, lay out.

déboussoler [dābōōsolā] *vt* to disorientate, disorient.

debout [dəbōō] *ad*: **être** ~ *(personne)* to be standing, stand; (: *levé, éveillé*) to be up (and about); *(chose)* to be upright; **être encore** ~ *(fig: en état)* to be still going; to be still standing; to be still up; **mettre qn** ~ to get sb to his feet; **mettre qch** ~ to stand sth up; **se mettre** ~ to get up (on one's feet); **se tenir** ~ to stand; ~! get up!; **cette histoire ne tient pas** ~ this story doesn't hold water.

débouter [dābōōtā] *vt* (*JUR*) to dismiss; ~ **qn de sa demande** to dismiss sb's petition.

déboutonner [dābōōtonā] *vt* to undo, unbutton; **se** ~ *vi* to come undone *ou* unbuttoned.

débraillé, e [dābrâyā] *a* slovenly, untidy.

débrancher [dābrãnshā] *vt* (*appareil électrique*) to unplug; *(téléphone, courant électrique)* to disconnect, cut off.

débrayage [dābreyazh] *nm* (*AUTO*) clutch; (: *action*) disengaging the clutch: *(grève)* stoppage; **faire un double** ~ to ᴊuble-clutch *(US) ou* double-declutch *(Brit)*.

débrayer [dābrāyā] *vi* (*AUTO*) to declutch, disengage the clutch; *(cesser le travail)* to stop work.

débridé, e [dābrēdā] *a* unbridled, unrestrained.

débrider [dābrēdā] *vt* (*cheval*) to unbridle; (*CULIN: volaille*) to untruss.

débris [dābrē] *nm* (*fragment*) fragment ♦ *nmpl* (*déchets*) pieces, debris *sg*; garbage *sg* (*US*); rubbish *sg* (*Brit*).

débrouillard, e [dābrōōyàr, -àrd(ə)] *a* smart, resourceful.

débrouillardise [dābrōōyárdēz] *nf* smartness, resourcefulness.

débrouiller [dābrōōyā] *vt* to disentangle, untangle; *(fig)* to sort out, unravel; **se** ~ *vi* to manage.

débroussailler [dābrōōsàyā] *vt* to clear (of brushwood).

débusquer [dābüskā] *vt* to drive out (from cover).

début [dābü] *nm* beginning, start; ~**s** *nmpl* beginnings; *(de carrière)* début *sg*; **faire ses** ~**s** to start out; **au** ~ in *ou* at the beginning, at first; **au** ~ **de** at the beginning *ou* start of; **dès le** ~ from the start.

débutant, e [dābütán, -ánt] *nm/f* beginner, novice.

débuter [dābütā] *vi* to begin, start; *(faire ses débuts)* to start out.

deçà [dəsà]: **en** ~ **de** *prép* this side of; **en** ~ *ad* on this side.

décacheter [dākáshtā] *vt* to unseal, open.

décade [dākàd] *nf* (*10 jours*) (period of) ten days; *(10 ans)* decade.

décadence [dākádáns] *nf* decadence; decline.

décadent, e [dākádán, -ánt] *a* decadent.

décaféiné, e [dākáfáēnā] *a* decaffeinated, caffeine free.

décalage [dākálázh] *nm* move forward *ou* back; shift forward *ou* back; *(écart)* gap; *(désaccord)* discrepancy; ~ **horaire** time difference (between time zones), time-lag.

décalaminer [dākálámēnā] *vt* to decarbonize (*US*), decoke *(Brit)*.

décalcomanie [dākálkománē] *nf* decal (*US*), transfer.

décaler [dākálā] *vt* (*dans le temps: avancer*) to move forward; (: *retarder*) to put back; *(changer de position)* to shift forward *ou* back; ~ **de 10 cm** to move forward *ou* back by 10 cm; ~ **de 2 h** to bring *ou* move forward 2 hours; to put back 2 hours.

décalitre [dākálētr(ə)] *nm* decaliter (*US*), decalitre *(Brit)*.

décalquer [dākálkā] *vt* to trace; *(par pression)* to transfer.

décamètre [dākámetr(ə)] *nm* decameter (*US*), decametre *(Brit)*.

décamper [dākánpā] *vi* to clear out *ou* off.

décan [dākán] *nm* (*ASTROLOGIE*) decan.

décanter [dākántā] *vt* to (allow to) settle (and decant); **se** ~ *vi* to settle.

décapage [dākápázh] *nm* stripping; scouring; sanding.

décapant [dākápán] *nm* acid solution; scouring agent; paint stripper.

décaper [dākápā] *vt* to strip; *(avec abrasif)* to scour; *(avec papier de verre)* to sand.

décapiter [dākápētā] *vt* to behead; *(par accident)* to decapitate; *(fig)* to cut the top off; (: *organisation*) to remove the top people from.

décapotable [dākápotábl(ə)] *a* convertible.

décapoter [dākápotā] *vt* to put down the top of.

décapsuler [dākápsülā] *vt* to take the cap *ou* top off.

décapsuleur [dākápsülœr] *nm* bottle-opener.

décathlon [dākátlón] *nm* decathlon.

décati, e [dākátē] *a* faded, aged.

décédé, e [dāsādā] *a* deceased.

décéder [dāsādā] *vi* to die.

déceler [dāslā] *vt* to discover, detect; *(révéler)* to indicate, reveal.

décélération [dāsālārâsyón] *nf* deceleration.

décélérer [dāsālārā] *vi* to decelerate, slow down.

décembre [dāsánbr(ə)] *nm* December; *voir aussi* **juillet**.

décemment [dāsámán] *ad* decently.

décence [dāsáns] *nf* decency.

décennal, e, aux [dāsánàl, -ō] *a* (*qui dure dix ans*) having a term of ten years, ten-year; *(qui revient tous les dix ans)* ten-yearly.

décennie [dāsānē] *nf* decade.

décent, e [dāsán, -ánt] *a* decent.

décentralisation [dāsántrālēzásyón] *nf* decentralization.

décentraliser [dāsántrálēzā] *vt* to decentralize.

décentrer [dāsántrā] *vt* to decenter (*US*) *ou* decentre *(Brit)*; **se** ~ to move off-center (*US*) *ou* off-centre *(Brit)*.

déception [dāsepsyón] *nf* disappointment.

décerner [dāsernā] *vt* to award.

décès [dāse] *nm* death, decease; **acte de** ~ death certificate.

décevant, e [desvắn, -ánt] *a* disappointing.

décevoir [desvwár] *vt* to disappoint.

déchaîné, e |dāshānā| a unbridled, raging.

déchaîner |dāshānā| vt (passions, colère) to unleash; (rires etc) to give rise to, arouse; **se ~** vi to be unleashed; (rires) to burst out; (se mettre en colère) to fly into a rage; **se ~ contre qn** to unleash one's fury on sb.

déchanter |dāshāntā| vi to become disillusioned.

décharge |dāshārzh(ə)| nf (dépôt d'ordures) garbage dump (US), rubbish tip ou dump (Brit); (électrique) electrical discharge; (salve) volley of shots; **à la ~ de** in defense of.

déchargement |dāshārzhəmāń| nm unloading.

décharger |dāshārzhā| vt (marchandise, véhicule) to unload; (ÉLEC) to discharge; (arme: neutraliser) to unload; (: faire feu) to discharge, fire; **~ qn de** (responsabilité) to relieve sb of, release sb from; **~ sa colère (sur)** to vent one's anger (on); **~ sa conscience** to unburden one's conscience; **se ~ dans** (se déverser) to flow into; **se ~ d'une affaire sur qn** to hand a matter over to sb.

décharné, e |dāshārnā| a bony, emaciated, fleshless.

déchaussé, e |dāshōsā| a (dent) loose.

déchausser |dāshōsā| vt (personne) to take the shoes off; (skis) to take off; **se ~** to take off one's shoes; (dent) to come ou work loose.

dèche |dcsh| nf (fam): **être dans la ~** to be flat broke.

déchéance |dāshāāńs| nf (déclin) degeneration, decay, decline; (chute) fall.

déchet |dāshc| nm (de bois, tissu etc) scrap; (perte: gén COMM) wastage, waste; **~s** nmpl (ordures) refuse sg, garbage sg (US), rubbish sg (Brit); **~s radioactifs** radioactive waste.

déchiffrage |dāshēfrázh| nm sight-reading.

déchiffrer |dāshēfrā| vt to decipher.

déchiqueté, e |dāshčktā| a jagged(-edged), ragged.

déchiqueter |dāshčktā| vt to tear ou pull to pieces.

déchirant, e |dāshēráń, -áńt| a heart-breaking, heart-rending.

déchiré, e |dāshčrā| a torn; (fig) heart-broken.

déchirement |dāshčrmáń| nm (chagrin) wrench, heartbreak; (gén pl: conflit) rift, split.

déchirer |dāshčrā| vt to tear, rip; (mettre en morceaux) to tear up; (pour ouvrir) to tear off; (arracher) to tear out; (fig) to tear apart; **se ~** vi to tear, rip; **se ~ un muscle/tendon** to tear a muscle/tendon.

déchirure |dāshčrür| nf (accroc) tear, rip; **~ musculaire** torn muscle.

déchoir |dāshwár| vi (personne) to lower o.s., demean o.s; **~ de** to fall from.

déchu, e |dāshü| pp de **déchoir** ♦ a fallen; (roi) deposed.

décibel |dāsčbcl| nm decibel.

décidé, e |dāsēdā| a (personne, air) determined; **c'est ~** it's decided; **être ~ à faire** to be determined to do.

décidément |dāsēdāmáń| ad undoubtedly; really.

décider |dāsēdā| vt: **~ qch** to decide on sth; **~ de faire/que** to decide to do/that; **~ qn (à**

faire qch) to persuade ou induce sb (to do sth); **~ de qch** to decide upon sth; (suj: chose) to determine sth; **se ~** vi (personne) to decide, make up one's mind; (problème, affaire) to be resolved; **se ~ à qch** to decide on sth; **se ~ à faire** to decide ou make up one's mind to do; **se ~ pour qch** to decide on ou in favor of sth.

décilitre |dāsēlētr(ə)| nm deciliter (US), decilitre (Brit).

décimal, e, aux |dāsēmál, -ō| a, nf decimal.

décimalisation |dāsēmálzásyóń| nf decimalization.

décimaliser |dāsēmálēzā| vt to decimalize.

décimer |dāsēmā| vt to decimate.

décimètre |dāsēmctr(ə)| nm decimeter (US), decimetre (Brit); **double ~** (20 cm) ruler.

décisif, ive |dāsčzčf, -čv| a decisive; (qui l'emporte): **le facteur/l'argument ~** the deciding factor/argument.

décision |dāsčzyóń| nf decision; (fermeté) decisiveness, decision; **prendre une ~** to make a decision; **prendre la ~ de faire** to make the decision to do; **emporter** ou **faire la ~** to be decisive.

déclamation |dāklámásyóń| nf declamation; (péj) ranting, spouting.

déclamatoire |dāklámátwár| a declamatory.

déclamer |dāklámā| vt to declaim; (péj) to spout ♦ vi: **~ contre** to rail against.

déclarable |dāklárábl(ə)| a (marchandise) dutiable; (revenus) declarable.

déclaration |dāklárásyóń| nf declaration; registration; (discours: POL etc) statement; (compte rendu) report; **fausse ~** misrepresentation; **~ (d'amour)** declaration; **~ de décès** registration of death; **~ de guerre** declaration of war; **~ (d'impôts)** statement of income, tax declaration, ≈ tax return; **~ (de sinistre)** (insurance) claim; **~ de revenus** statement of income.

déclaré, e |dāklárā| a (juré) avowed.

déclarer |dāklárā| vt to declare, announce; (revenus, employés, marchandises) to declare; (décès, naissance) to register; (vol etc: à la police) to report; **se ~** vi (feu, maladie) to break out; **~ la guerre** to declare war.

déclassé, e |dāklásā| a relegated, downgraded; (matériel) (to be) sold off.

déclassement |dāklásmáń| nm relegation, downgrading; (RAIL etc) change of class.

déclasser |dāklásā| vt to relegate, downgrade; (déranger: fiches, livres) to get out of order.

déclenchement |dākláńshmáń| nm release; setting off.

déclencher |dākláńshā| vt (mécanisme etc) to release; (sonnerie) to set off, activate; (attaque, grève) to launch; (provoquer) to trigger off; **se ~** vi to release itself; to go off.

déclencheur |dākláńshœr| nm release mechanism.

déclic |dāklčk| nm trigger mechanism; (bruit) click.

déclin |dāklań| nm decline.

déclinaison |dāklēnczóń| nf declension.

décliner |dāklēnā| vi to decline ♦ vt (invitation) to decline, refuse; (responsabilité) to refuse to accept; (*nom, adresse*) to state; (*LING*) to decline; **se ~** (*LING*) to decline.

déclivité [dāklēvētā] *nf* slope, incline; **en ~** sloping, on the incline.

décloisonner [dāklwázonā] *vt* to decompartmentalize.

déclouer [dāklōōā] *vt* to unnail.

décocher [dākoshā] *vt* to hurl; (*flèche, regard*) to shoot.

décoction [dākoksyôn] *nf* decoction.

décodage [dākodàzh] *nm* deciphering, decoding.

décoder [dākodā] *vt* to decipher, decode.

décodeur [dākodœr] *nm* decoder.

décoiffé, e [dākwáfā] *a*: **elle est toute ~e** her hair is in a mess.

décoiffer [dākwáfā] *vt*: **~ qn** to disarrange *ou* mess up sb's hair; to take sb's hat off; **se ~** to take off one's hat.

décoincer [dākwáñsā] *vt* to unjam, loosen.

déçois [dāswà] *etc*, **déçoive** [dāswàv] *etc vb voir* **décevoir**.

décolérer [dākolārā] *vi*: **Il ne décolère pas** he's still angry, he hasn't calmed down.

décollage [dākolàzh] *nm* (*AVIAT, ÉCON*) takeoff.

décollé, e [dākolā] *a*: **oreilles ~es** sticking-out ears.

décollement [dākolmáñ] *nm* (*MÉD*): **~ de la rétine** retinal detachment.

décoller [dākolā] *vt* to unstick ♦ *vi* to take off; (*projet, entreprise*) to take off, get off the ground; **se ~** *vi* to come unstuck.

décolleté, e [dākoltā] *a* low-necked, low-cut; (*femme*) wearing a low-cut dress ♦ *nm* low neck(line); (*épaules*) (bare) neck and shoulders; (*plongeant*) cleavage.

décolleter [dākoltā] *vt* (*vêtement*) to give a low neckline to; (*TECH*) to cut.

décoloniser [dākolonēzā] *vt* to decolonize.

décolorant [dākoloráñ] *nm* decolorant, bleaching agent.

décoloration [dākolorásyôñ] *nf*: **se faire faire une ~** (*chez le coiffeur*) to have one's hair bleached *ou* lightened.

décoloré, e [dākolorā] *a* (*vêtement*) faded; (*cheveux*) bleached.

décolorer [dākolorā] *vt* (*tissu*) to fade; (*cheveux*) to bleach, lighten; **se ~** *vi* to fade.

décombres [dākôñbr(ə)] *nmpl* rubble *sg*, debris *sg*.

décommander [dākomáñdā] *vt* to cancel; (*invités*) to put off; **se ~** to cancel, cry off.

décomposé, e [dākôñpōzā] *a* (*pourri*) decomposed; (*visage*) haggard, distorted.

décomposer [dākôñpōzā] *vt* to break up; (*CHIMIE*) to decompose; (*MATH*) to factor (*US*), factorize (*Brit*); **se ~** *vi* to decompose.

décomposition [dākôñpōzēsyôñ] *nf* breaking up; decomposition; factorization; **en ~** (*organisme*) in a state of decay, decomposing.

décompresseur [dākôñprāsœr] *nm* decompressor.

décompression [dākôñprásyôñ] *nf* decompression.

décomprimer [dākôñprēmā] *vt* to decompress.

décompte [dākôñt] *nm* deduction; (*facture*) breakdown (of an account), detailed account.

décompter [dākôñtā] *vt* to deduct.

déconcentration [dākôñsáñtrâsyôñ] *nf* (*des industries etc*) dispersal; **~ des pouvoirs** devolution.

déconcentré, e [dākôñsáñtrā] *a* (*sportif etc*) who has lost (his/her) concentration.

déconcentrer [dākôñsáñtrā] *vt* (*ADMIN*) to disperse; **se ~** *vi* to lose (one's) concentration.

déconcertant, e [dākôñsertáñ, -áñt] *a* disconcerting.

déconcerter [dākôñsertā] *vt* to disconcert, confound.

déconfit, e [dākôñfē, -ēt] *a* crestfallen, downcast.

déconfiture [dākôñfētür] *nf* collapse, ruin; (*morale*) defeat.

décongélation [dākôñzhālâsyôñ] *nf* defrosting, thawing.

décongeler [dākôñzhlā] *vt* to thaw (out).

décongestionner [dākôñzhestyonā] *vt* (*MÉD*) to decongest; (*rues*) to relieve congestion in.

déconnecter [dākonektā] *vt* to disconnect.

déconner [dākonā] *vi* (*fam!*: *en parlant*) to talk (a load of) garbage (*US*) *ou* rubbish (*Brit*); (*: faire des bêtises*) to mess around; **sans ~** no kidding.

déconseiller [dākôñsāyā] *vt*: **~ qch (à qn)** to advise (sb) against sth; **~ à qn de faire** to advise sb against doing; **c'est déconseillé** it's not advised *ou* advisable.

déconsidérer [dākôñsādārā] *vt* to discredit.

décontaminer [dākôñtámēnā] *vt* to decontaminate.

décontenancer [dākôñtnáñsā] *vt* to disconcert, discountenance.

décontracté, e [dākôñtráktā] *a* relaxed.

décontracter [dākôñtráktā] *vt*, **se ~** *vi* to relax.

décontraction [dākôñtráksyôñ] *nf* relaxation.

déconvenue [dākôñvnü] *nf* disappointment.

décor [dākor] *nm* décor; (*paysage*) scenery; **~s** *nmpl* (*THÉÂTRE*) scenery *sg*, decor *sg*; (*CINÉMA*) set *sg*; **changement de ~** (*fig*) change of scene; **entrer dans le ~** (*fig*) to run off the road; **en ~ naturel** (*CINÉMA*) on location.

décorateur, trice [dākorátœr, -trēs] *nm/f* (interior) decorator; (*CINÉMA*) set designer.

décoratif, ive [dākorátēf, -ēv] *a* decorative.

décoration [dākorásyôñ] *nf* decoration.

décorer [dākorā] *vt* to decorate.

décortiqué, e [dākortēkā] *a* shelled; hulled.

décortiquer [dākortēkā] *vt* to shell; (*riz*) to hull; (*fig*) to dissect.

décorum [dākorom] *nm* decorum; etiquette.

décote [dākot] *nf* tax relief.

découcher [dākōōshā] *vi* to spend the night away.

découdre [dākōōdr(ə)] *vt* (*vêtement, couture*) to unpick, take the stitching out of; (*bouton*) to take off; **se ~** *vi* to come unstitched; (*bouton*) to come off; **en ~** (*fig*) to fight, do battle.

découler [dākōōlā] *vi*: **~ de** to ensue *ou* follow from.

découpage [dākōōpàzh] *nm* cutting up; carving; (*image*) cut-out (figure); **~ électoral** division into constituencies.

découper [dākōōpā] *vt* (*papier, tissu etc*) to cut up; (*volaille, viande*) to carve; (*déta-*

cher: manche, article) to cut out; **se ~ sur** *(ciel, fond)* to stand out against.

découplé, e [dākoōplā] *a*: **bien ~** well-built, well-proportioned.

découpure [dākoōpür] *nf*: **~s** *(morceaux)* cut-out bits; *(d'une côte, arête)* indentations, jagged outline *sg*.

découragement [dākoōrázhmáṅ] *nm* discouragement, despondency.

décourager [dākoōrázhā] *vt* to discourage, dishearten; *(dissuader)* to discourage, put off; **se ~** *vi* to lose heart, become discouraged; **~ qn de faire/de qch** to discourage sb from doing/from sth, put sb off doing/sth.

décousu, e [dākoōzü] *pp de* **découdre ♦** *a* unstitched; *(fig)* disjointed, disconnected.

découvert, e [dākoōver, -ert(ə)] *pp de* **découvrir ♦** *a (tête)* bare, uncovered; *(lieu)* open, exposed **♦** *nm (bancaire)* overdraft **♦** *nf* discovery; **à ~** *ad (MIL)* exposed, without cover; *(fig)* openly **♦** *a (COMM)* overdrawn; **à visage ~** openly; **aller à la ~e de** to go in search of.

découvrir [dākoōvrēr] *vt* to discover; *(apercevoir)* to see; *(enlever ce qui couvre ou protège)* to uncover; *(montrer, dévoiler)* to reveal; **se ~** to take off one's hat; *(se déshabiller)* to take something off; *(au lit)* to uncover o.s.; *(ciel)* to clear; **se ~ des talents** to find hidden talents in o.s.

décrasser [dākrásā] *vt* to clean.

décrêper [dākrāpā] *vt (cheveux)* to straighten.

décrépi, e [dākrāpē] *a* peeling; with roughcast rendering removed.

décrépit, e [dākrāpē, -ēt] *a* decrepit.

décrépitude [dākrāpētüd] *nf* decrepitude, decay.

decrescendo [dākrāshendō] *nm (MUS)* decrescendo; **aller ~** *(fig)* to decline, be on the wane.

décret [dākre] *nm* decree.

décréter [dākrātā] *vt* to decree; *(ordonner)* to order.

décret-loi [dākrelwá] *nm* statutory order.

décrié, e [dākrēyā] *a* disparaged.

décrire [dākrēr] *vt* to describe; *(courbe, cercle)* to follow, describe.

décrisper [dākrēspā] *vt* to defuse.

décrit, e [dākrē, -ēt] *pp de* **décrire**.

décrivais [dākrēve] *etc vb voir* **décrire**.

décrochement [dākroshmáṅ] *nm (d'un mur etc)* recess.

décrocher [dākroshā] *vt (dépendre)* to take down; *(téléphone)* to take off the hook; *(: pour répondre)*: **~ (le téléphone)** to pick up *ou* lift the receiver; *(fig: contrat etc)* to get, land **♦** *vi* to drop out; to switch off; **se ~** *vi (tableau, rideau)* to fall down.

décrois [dākrwá] *etc vb voir* **décroître**.

décroiser [dākrwázā] *vt (bras)* to unfold; *(jambes)* to uncross.

décroissant, e [dākrwásáṅ, -áṅt] *vb voir* **décroître ♦** *a* decreasing, declining, diminishing; **par ordre ~** in descending order.

décroître [dākrwátr(ə)] *vi* to decrease, decline, diminish.

décrotter [dākrotā] *vt (chaussures)* to clean the mud from; **se ~ le nez** to pick one's nose.

décru, e [dākrü] *pp de* **décroître**.

décrue [dākrü] *nf* drop in level (of the waters).

décrypter [dākrēptā] *vt* to decipher.

déçu, e [dāsü] *pp de* **décevoir ♦** *a* disappointed.

déculotter [dākülotā] *vt*: **~ qn** to take off sb's pants *(US) ou* trousers *(Brit)*; **se ~** to take off one's pants *ou* trousers.

déculpabiliser [dākülpábēlēzā] *vt (personne)* to relieve of guilt; *(chose)* to decriminalize.

décuple [dāküpl(ə)] *nm*: **le ~ de** ten times; **au ~** tenfold.

décupler [dāküplā] *vt, vi* to increase tenfold.

déçut [dāsü] *etc vb voir* **décevoir**.

dédaignable [dādenyábl(ə)] *a*: **pas ~** not to be despised.

dédaigner [dādānyā] *vt* to despise, scorn; *(négliger)* to disregard, spurn; **~ de faire** to consider it beneath one to do, not deign to do.

dédaigneusement [dādenyᴂzmáṅ] *ad* scornfully, disdainfully.

dédaigneux, euse [dādenyᴂ, -ᴂz] *a* scornful, disdainful.

dédain [dādaṅ] *nm* scorn, disdain.

dédale [dādál] *nm* maze.

dedans [dədáṅ] *ad* inside; *(pas en plein air)* indoors, inside **♦** *nm* inside; **au ~** on the inside; inside; **en ~** *(vers l'intérieur)* inwards; *voir aussi* **là**.

dédicace [dādēkás] *nf (imprimée)* dedication; *(manuscrite, sur une photo etc)* inscription.

dédicacer [dādēkásā] *vt*: **~ (à qn)** to sign (for sb), autograph (for sb), inscribe (to sb).

dédié, e [dādyā] *a*: **ordinateur ~** dedicated computer.

dédier [dādyā] *vt* to dedicate.

dédire [dādēr]: **se ~** *vi* to go back on one's word; *(se rétracter)* to retract, recant.

dédit, e [dādē, -ēt] *pp de* **dédire ♦** *nm (COMM)* forfeit, penalty.

dédommagement [dādomázhmáṅ] *nm* compensation.

dédommager [dādomázhā] *vt*: **~ qn (de)** to compensate sb (for); *(fig)* to repay sb (for).

dédouaner [dādwánā] *vt* to clear through customs.

dédoublement [dādoōbləmáṅ] *nm* splitting; *(PSYCH)*: **~ de la personnalité** split *ou* dual personality.

dédoubler [dādoōblā] *vt (classe, effectifs)* to split (into two); *(couverture etc)* to unfold; *(manteau)* to remove the lining of; **~ un train/les trains** to run a relief train/additional trains; **se ~** *vi (PSYCH)* to have a split personality.

dédramatiser [dādrámátēzā] *vt (situation)* to defuse; *(événement)* to play down.

déductible [dādüktēbl(ə)] *a* deductible.

déduction [dādüksyóṅ] *nf (d'argent)* deduction; *(raisonnement)* deduction, inference.

déduire [dādüēr] *vt*: **~ qch (de)** *(ôter)* to deduct sth (from); *(conclure)* to deduce *ou* infer sth (from).

déesse [dāes] *nf* goddess.

DEFA *sigle m (= Diplôme d'État relatif aux fonctions d'animation)* diploma for senior youth leaders.

défaillance [dāfáyáṅs] *nf (syncope)* blackout; *(fatigue)* (sudden) weakness *q*; *(technique)* fault, failure; *(morale etc)* weakness; **~**

cardiaque heart failure.

défaillant, e [dāfáyâṅ, -âṅt] *a* defective; (*JUR*: *témoin*) defaulting.

défaillir [dāfáyēr] *vi* to faint; to feel faint; (*mémoire etc*) to fail.

défaire [dāfɛr] *vt* (*installation, échafaudage*) to take down, dismantle; (*paquet etc, nœud, vêtement*) to undo; (*bagages*) to unpack; (*ouvrage*) to undo, unpick; (*cheveux*) to undo, let down; **se** ~ *vi* to come undone; **se** ~ **de** *vt* (*se débarrasser de*) to get rid of; (*se séparer de*) to part with; ~ **le lit** (*pour changer les draps*) to strip the bed; (*pour se coucher*) to turn back the bedclothes.

défait, e [dāfɛ, -et] *pp de* **défaire** ♦ *a* (*visage*) haggard, ravaged ♦ *nf* defeat.

défaites [dāfɛt] *vb voir* **défaire**.

défaitisme [dāfɛtēsm(ə)] *nm* defeatism.

défaitiste [dāfɛtēst(ə)] *a, nm/f* defeatist.

défalcation [dāfálkâsyôṅ] *nf* deduction.

défalquer [dāfálkā] *vt* to deduct.

défasse [dāfás] *etc vb voir* **défaire**.

défausser [dāfōsā] *vt* to get rid of; **se** ~ *vi* (*CARTES*) to discard.

défaut [dāfō] *nm* (*moral*) fault, failing, defect; (*d'étoffe, métal*) fault, flaw, defect; (*manque, carence*): ~ **de** lack of; shortage of; (*IN-FORM*) bug; ~ **de la cuirasse** (*fig*) chink in the armor; **en** ~ at fault; in the wrong; **faire** ~ (*manquer*) to be lacking; **à** ~ *ad* failing that; **à** ~ **de** for lack *ou* want of; **par** ~ (*JUR*) in his (*ou* her *etc*) absence.

défaveur [dāfávœr] *nf* disfavor (*US*), disfavour (*Brit*).

défavorable [dāfávorábl(ə)] *a* unfavorable (*US*), unfavourable (*Brit*).

défavoriser [dátavorēzā] *vt* to put at a disadvantage.

défectif, ive [dāfɛktēf, -ēv] *a*: **verbe** ~ defective verb.

défection [dāfɛksyôṅ] *nf* defection, failure to give support *ou* assistance; failure to appear; **faire** ~ (*d'un parti etc*) to withdraw one's support, leave.

défectueux, euse [dāfɛktüœ̄, -œ̄z] *a* faulty, defective.

défectuosité [dāfɛküōzētā] *nf* defectiveness *q*; (*défaut*) defect, fault.

défendable [dāfâṅdábl(ə)] *a* defensible.

défendeur, eresse [dāfâṅdœr, -drɛs] *nm/f* (*JUR*) defendant.

défendre [dāfâṅdr(ə)] *vt* to defend; (*interdire*) to forbid; ~ **à qn qch/de faire** to forbid sb sth/to do; **il est défendu de cracher** spitting (is) prohibited *ou* is not allowed; **c'est défendu** it is forbidden; **se** ~ to defend o.s.; **il se défend** (*fig*) he can hold his own; **ça se défend** (*fig*) it holds together; **se** ~ **de/contre** (*se protéger*) to protect o.s. from/against; **se** ~ **de** (*se garder de*) to refrain from; (*nier*): **se** ~ **de vouloir** to deny wanting.

défenestrer [dāfənestrā] *vt* to throw out of the window.

défense [dāfâṅs] *nf* defense (*US*), defence (*Brit*); (*d'éléphant etc*) tusk; **ministre de la** ~ Secretary of Defense (*US*), Minister of Defence (*Brit*); **la** ~ **nationale** defense; **la** ~ **contre avions** anti-aircraft defense; "~ **de**

fumer/cracher" "no smoking/spitting", "smoking/spitting prohibited"; **prendre la** ~ **de qn** to stand up for sb; ~ **des consommateurs** consumerism.

défenseur [dāfâṅsœr] *nm* defender; (*JUR*) counsel for the defense (*US*) *ou* defence (*Brit*).

défensif, ive [dāfâṅsēf, -ēv] *a, nf* defensive; **être sur la défensive** to be on the defensive.

déferai [dāfrā] *etc vb voir* **défaire**.

déférence [dāfārâṅs] *nf* deference.

déférent, e [dāfārâṅ, -âṅt] *a* (*poli*) deferential, deferent.

déférer [dāfārā] *vt* (*JUR*) to refer; ~ **à** *vt* (*requête, décision*) to defer to; ~ **qn à la justice** to hand sb over to justice.

déferlant, e [dāfɛrlâṅ, -âṅt] *a*: **vague** ~**e** breaker.

déferlement [dāfɛrləmâṅ] *nm* breaking; surge.

déferler [dāfɛrlā] *vi* (*vagues*) to break; (*fig*) to surge.

défi [dāfē] *nm* (*provocation*) challenge; (*bravade*) defiance; **mettre qn ou** ~ **de faire qch** to challenge sb to do sth; **relever un** ~ to take up *ou* accept a challenge.

défiance [dāfyâṅs] *nf* mistrust, distrust.

déficeler [dāfēslā] *vt* (*paquet*) to undo, untie.

déficience [dāfēsyâṅs] *nf* deficiency.

déficient, e [dāfēsyâṅ, -âṅt] *a* deficient.

déficit [dāfēsēt] *nm* (*COMM*) deficit; (*PSYCH etc: manque*) defect; ~ **budgétaire** budget deficit; **être en** ~ to be in deficit.

déficitaire [dāfēsēter] *a* (*année, récolte*) bad; **entreprise/budget** ~ business/budget in deficit.

défier [dāfyā] *vt* (*provoquer*) to challenge; (*fig*) to defy, brave; **se** ~ **de** (*se méfier de*) to distrust, mistrust; ~ **qn de faire** to challenge *ou* defy sb to do; ~ **qn à** to challenge sb to; ~ **toute comparaison/concurrence** to be incomparable/unbeatable.

défigurer [dāfēgürā] *vt* to disfigure; (*suj: boutons etc*) to mar *ou* spoil (the looks of); (*fig: œuvre*) to mutilate, deface.

défilé [dāfēlā] *nm* (*GÉO*) (narrow) gorge *ou* pass; (*soldats*) parade; (*manifestants*) procession, march; **un** ~ **de** (*voitures, visiteurs etc*) a stream of.

défiler [dāfēlā] *vi* (*troupes*) to march past; (*sportifs*) to parade; (*manifestants*) to march; (*visiteurs*) to pour, stream; **se** ~ *vi* (*se dérober*) to slip away, sneak off; **faire** ~ (*bande, film*) to put on; (*INFORM*) to scroll.

défini, e [dāfēnē] *a* definite.

définir [dāfēnēr] *vt* to define.

définissable [dāfēnēsábl(ə)] *a* definable.

définitif, ive [dāfēnētēf, -ēv] *a* (*final*) final, definitive; (*pour longtemps*) permanent, definitive; (*sans appel*) final, definite ♦ *nf*: **en définitive** eventually; (*somme toute*) when all is said and done.

définition [dāfēnēsyôṅ] *nf* definition; (*de mots croisés*) clue; (*TV*) (picture) resolution.

définitivement [dāfēnētēvmâṅ] *ad* definitively; permanently; definitively.

défit [dāfē] *etc vb voir* **défaire**.

déflagration [dāflágrásyôṅ] *nf* explosion.

déflation [dāflâsyôṅ] *nf* deflation.

déflationniste [dāflăsyonēst(ə)] *a* deflationist, deflationary.

déflecteur [dāflɛktœr] *nm* (*AUTO*) deflector (*US*), quarterlight (*Brit*).

déflorer [dāflorā] *vt* (*jeune fille*) to deflower; (*fig*) to spoil the charm of.

défoncé, e [dāfônsā] *a* smashed in; broken down; (*route*) full of potholes ♦ *nm/f* addict.

défoncer [dāfônsā] *vt* (*caisse*) to stave in; (*porte*) to smash in *ou* down; (*lit, fauteuil*) to burst (the springs of); (*terrain, route*) to rip up, plow (*US*) *ou* plough (*Brit*) up; **se** ~ *vi* (*se donner à fond*) to give it all one's got.

défont [dāfôn] *vb voir* **défaire**.

déformant, e [dāformân, -ânt] *a*: **glace** *ou* **miroir** ~(e) distorting mirror.

déformation [dāformāsyôn] *nf* loss of shape; deformation; distortion; ~ **professionnelle** conditioning by one's job.

déformer [dāformā] *vt* to put out of shape; (*corps*) to deform; (*pensée, fait*) to distort; **se** ~ *vi* to lose its shape.

défoulement [dāfo͞olmân] *nm* release of tension; unwinding.

défouler [dāfo͞olā]: **se** ~ *vi* (*PSYCH*) to work off one's tensions, release one's pent-up feelings; (*gén*) to unwind, let off steam.

défraîchi, e [dāfrāshē] *a* faded; (*article à vendre*) shopworn (*US*), shop-soiled (*Brit*).

défraîchir [dāfrāshēr]: **se** ~ *vi* to fade; to become shopworn (*US*) *ou* shop-soiled (*Brit*).

défrayer [dāfrāyā] *vt*: ~ **qn** to pay sb's expenses; ~ **la chronique** to be in the news; ~ **la conversation** to be the main topic of conversation.

défrichement [dāfrēshmân] *nm* clearance.

défricher [dāfrēshā] *vt* to clear (for cultivation).

défriser [dāfrēzā] *vt* (*cheveux*) to straighten; (*fig*) to annoy.

défroisser [dāfrwàsā] *vt* to smooth out.

défroque [dāfrok] *nf* castoff.

défroqué [dāfrokā] *nm* former monk (*ou* priest).

défroquer [dāfrokā] *vi* (*aussi*: **se** ~) to give up the cloth, renounce one's vows.

défunt, e [dāfœn, -œnt] *a*: **son** ~ **père** his late father ♦ *nm/f* deceased.

dégagé, e [dāgázhā] *a* clear; (*ton, air*) casual, jaunty.

dégagement [dāgàzhmân] *nm* emission; freeing; clearing; (*espace libre*) clearing; passage; clearance; (*FOOTBALL*) clearance; **voie de** ~ on *ou* off ramp (*US*), slip road (*Brit*); **itinéraire de** ~ alternative route (*to relieve traffic congestion*).

dégager [dāgàzhā] *vt* (*exhaler*) to give off, emit; (*délivrer*) to free, extricate; (*MIL*: *troupes*) to relieve; (*désencombrer*) to clear; (*isoler, mettre en valeur*) to bring out; (*crédits*) to release; **se** ~ *vi* (*odeur*) to emanate, be given off; (*passage, ciel*) to clear; ~ **qn de** (*engagement, parole etc*) to release *ou* free sb from; **se** ~ **de** (*fig: engagement etc*) to get out of; (: *promesse*) to go back on.

dégaine [dāgɛn] *nf* awkward way of walking.

dégainer [dāgɛnā] *vt* to draw.

dégarni, e [dāgàrnē] *a* bald.

dégarnir [dāgàrnēr] *vt* (*vider*) to empty, clear; **se** ~ *vi* to empty; to be cleaned out *ou* cleared; (*tempes, crâne*) to go bald.

dégâts [dāgà] *nmpl* damage *sg*; **faire des** ~ to damage.

dégazer [dāgàzā] *vi* (*pétrolier*) to clean its tanks.

dégel [dāzhel] *nm* thaw; (*fig: des prix etc*) unfreezing.

dégeler [dāzhlā] *vt* to thaw (out); (*fig*) to unfreeze ♦ *vi* to thaw (out); **se** ~ *vi* (*fig*) to thaw out.

dégénéré, e [dāzhānārā] *a*, *nm/f* degenerate.

dégénérer [dāzhānārā] *vi* to degenerate; (*empirer*) to go from bad to worse; (*devenir*): ~ **en** to degenerate into.

dégénérescence [dāzhānārāsâns] *nf* degeneration.

dégingandé, e [dāzhàngândā] *a* gangling, lanky.

dégivrage [dāzhēvrázh] *nm* defrosting; de-icing.

dégivrer [dāzhēvrā] *vt* (*frigo*) to defrost; (*vitres*) to de-ice.

dégivreur [dāzhēvrœr] *nm* defroster; de-icer.

déglinguer [dāglângā] *vt* to bust.

déglutir [dāglütēr] *vt, vi* to swallow.

déglutition [dāglütēsyôn] *nf* swallowing.

dégonflé, e [dāgônflā] *a* (*pneu*) flat; (*fam*) chicken ♦ *nm/f* (*fam*) chicken.

dégonfler [dāgônflā] *vt* (*pneu, ballon*) to let down, deflate ♦ *vi* (*désenfler*) to go down; **se** ~ *vi* (*fam*) to chicken out.

dégorger [dāgorzhā] *vi* (*CULIN*): **faire** ~ to (leave to) sweat; (*aussi*: **se** ~: *rivière*): ~ **dans** to flow into ♦ *vt* to disgorge.

dégoter [dāgotā] *vt* (*fam*) to dig up, find.

dégouliner [dāgo͞olēnā] *vi* to trickle, drip; ~ **de** to be dripping with.

dégoupiller [dāgo͞opēyā] *vt* (*grenade*) to take the pin out of.

dégourdi, e [dāgo͞ordē] *a* smart, resourceful.

dégourdir [dāgo͞ordēr] *vt* to warm (up); **se** ~ (**les jambes**) to stretch one's legs.

dégoût [dāgo͞o] *nm* disgust, distaste.

dégoûtant, e [dāgo͞otân, -ânt] *a* disgusting.

dégoûté, e [dāgo͞otā] *a* disgusted; ~ **de** sick of.

dégoûter [dāgo͞otā] *vt* to disgust; **cela me dégoûte** I find this disgusting *ou* revolting; ~ **qn de qch** to put sb off sth; **se** ~ **de** to get *ou* become sick of.

dégoutter [dāgo͞otā] *vi* to drip; ~ **de** to be dripping with.

dégradant, e [dāgrádân, -ânt] *a* degrading.

dégradation [dāgrádàsyôn] *nf* reduction in rank; defacement; degradation, debasement; deterioration; (*aussi*: ~**s**: *dégâts*) damage *q*.

dégradé, e [dāgrádā] *a* (*couleur*) shaded off; (*teintes*) faded; (*cheveux*) layered ♦ *nm* (*PEINTURE*) gradation.

dégrader [dāgrádā] *vt* (*MIL*: *officier*) to degrade; (*abîmer*) to damage, deface; (*avilir*) to degrade, debase; **se** ~ *vi* (*relations, situation*) to deteriorate.

dégrafer [dāgráfā] *vt* to unclip, unhook, unfasten.

dégraissage [dāgrɛsázh] *nm* (*ÉCON*) cutbacks *pl*; ~ **et nettoyage à sec** dry cleaning.

dégraissant [dāgresáṅ] *nm* spot remover.

dégraisser [dāgrāsā] *vt* (*soupe*) to skim; (*vêtement*) to take the grease marks out of; (*ÉCON*) to cut back; (: *entreprise*) to slim down.

degré [dəgrā] *nm* degree; (*d'escalier*) step; **brûlure au 1er/2ème** ~ 1st/2nd degree burn; **équation du 1er/2ème** ~ linear/quadratic equation; **le premier** ~ (*SCOL*) elementary (*US*) *ou* primary (*Brit*) level; **alcool à 90** ~**s** rubbing alcohol (*US*), surgical spirit (*Brit*); **vin de 10** ~**s** 10° wine (*on Gay-Lussac scale*); **par** ~(**s**) *ad* by degrees, gradually.

dégressif, ive [dāgrāsēf, -ēv] *a* on a decreasing scale, degressive; **tarif** ~ decreasing rate of charge.

dégrèvement [dāgrevmáṅ] *nm* tax relief.

dégrever [dāgrəvā] *vt* to grant tax relief to; to reduce the tax burden on.

dégriffé, e [dāgrēfā] *a* (*vêtement*) sold without the designer's label.

dégringolade [dāgraṅgolád] *nf* tumble; (*fig*) collapse.

dégringoler [dāgraṅgolā] *vi* to tumble (down); (*fig: prix, monnaie etc*) to collapse.

dégriser [dāgrēzā] *vt* to sober up.

dégrossir [dāgrōsēr] *vt* (*bois*) to trim; (*fig*) to rough out; (: *personne*) to knock the rough edges off.

déguenillé, e [degnēyā] *a* ragged, tattered.

déguerpir [dāgerpēr] *vi* to clear out.

dégueulasse [dāgœlás] *a* (*fam*) disgusting.

dégueuler [dāgœlā] *vi* (*fam*) to puke, throw up.

déguisé, e [dāgēzā] *a* disguised; dressed up; ~ **en** disguised (*ou* dressed up) as.

déguisement [dāgēzmáṅ] *nm* disguise; (*habits: pour s'amuser*) dressing-up clothes, (: *pour tromper*) disguise.

déguiser [dāgēzā] *vt* to disguise; **se** ~ (**en**) (*se costumer*) to dress up (as); (*pour tromper*) to disguise o.s. (as).

dégustation [dāgüstâsyôṅ] *nf* tasting; sampling; savoring (*US*), savouring (*Brit*); (*séance*): ~ **de vin(s)** wine-tasting.

déguster [dāgüstā] *vt* (*vins*) to taste; (*fromages etc*) to sample; (*savourer*) to enjoy, savor (*US*), savour (*Brit*).

déhancher [dāáṅshā]: **se** ~ *vi* to sway one's hips; to lean (one's weight) on one hip.

dehors [dəor] *ad* outside; (*en plein air*) outdoors, outside ♦ *nm* outside ♦ *nmpl* (*apparences*) appearances, exterior *sg*; **mettre** *ou* **jeter** ~ to throw out; **au** ~ outside; (*en apparence*) outwardly; **au** ~ **de** outside; **de** ~ from outside; **en** ~ outside; outwards; **en** ~ **de** apart from.

déifier [dāēfyā] *vt* to deify.

déjà [dāzhá] *ad* already; (*auparavant*) before, already; **as-tu** ~ **été en France?** have you been to France before?; **c'est** ~ **pas mal** that's not too bad (at all); **c'est** ~ **quelque chose** (at least) it's better than nothing; **quel nom,** ~? what was the name again?

déjanter [dāzhâṅtā]: **se** ~ *vi* (*pneu*) to come off the rim.

déjà-vu [dāzhàvü] *nm*: **c'est du** ~ there's nothing new in that.

déjeté, e [dezhtā] *a* lop-sided, crooked.

déjeuner [dāzhœnā] *vi* to (have) lunch; (*le matin*) to have breakfast ♦ *nm* lunch; (*petit déjeuner*) breakfast; ~ **d'affaires** business lunch.

déjouer [dāzhwā] *vt* to elude; to foil, thwart.

déjuger [dāzhüzhā]: **se** ~ *vi* to reverse one's opinion.

delà [dəlá] *ad*: **par** ~, **en** ~ (**de**), **au** ~ (**de**) beyond.

délabré, e [dālābrā] *a* dilapidated, broken-down.

délabrement [dālâbrəmáṅ] *nm* decay, dilapidation.

délabrer [dālâbrā]: **se** ~ *vi* to fall into decay, become dilapidated.

délacer [dālâsā] *vt* to unlace, untie.

délai [dālē] *nm* (*attente*) waiting period; (*sursis*) extension (of time); (*temps accordé*: *aussi*: ~**s**) time limit; **sans** ~ without delay; **à bref** ~ shortly, very soon; at short notice; **dans les** ~**s** within the time limit; **un** ~ **de 30 jours** a period of 30 days; **comptez un** ~ **de livraison de 10 jours** allow 10 days for delivery.

délaissé, e [dālāsā] *a* abandoned, deserted; neglected.

délaisser [dālāsā] *vt* (*abandonner*) to abandon, desert; (*négliger*) to neglect.

délassant, e [dālāsáṅ, -áṅt] *a* relaxing.

délassement [dālāsmáṅ] *nm* relaxation.

délasser [dālāsā] *vt* (*reposer*) to relax; (*divertir*) to divert, entertain; **se** ~ *vi* to relax.

délateur, trice [dālátœr, -trēs] *nm/f* informer.

délation [dālâsyôṅ] *nf* denouncement, informing.

délavé, e [dālávā] *a* faded.

délayage [dāleyázh] *nm* mixing; thinning down.

délayer [dālāyā] *vt* (*CULIN*) to mix (with water etc); (*peinture*) to thin down; (*fig*) to pad out, spin out.

delco [delkō] *nm* ® (*AUTO*) distributor; **tête de** ~ distributor cap.

délectation [dālēktâsyôṅ] *nf* delight.

délecter [dālēktā]: **se** ~ *vi*: **se** ~ **de** to revel *ou* delight in.

délégation [dālāgâsyôṅ] *nf* delegation; ~ **de pouvoir** delegation of power.

délégué, e [dālāgā] *a* delegated ♦ *nm/f* delegate; representative; **ministre** ~ **à** minister with special responsibility for.

déléguer [dālāgā] *vt* to delegate.

délestage [dālestázh] *nm*: **itinéraire de** ~ alternative route (*to relieve traffic congestion*).

délester [dālestā] *vt* (*navire*) to unballast; ~ **une route** to relieve traffic congestion on a road by diverting traffic.

Delhi [delē] *n* Delhi.

délibérant, e [dālēbāráṅ, -áṅt] *a*: **assemblée** ~**e** deliberative assembly.

délibératif, ive [dālēbārátēf, -ēv] *a*: **avoir voix** ~ **délibérative** to have voting rights.

délibération [dālēbārâsyôṅ] *nf* deliberation.

délibéré, e [dālēbārā] *a* (*conscient*) deliberate; (*déterminé*) determined, resolute; **de propos** ~ (*à dessein, exprès*) intentionally.

délibérément [dālēbārámáṅ] *ad* deliberately;

(*résolument*) resolutely.

délibérer [dālēbārā] *vi* to deliberate.

délicat, e [dālēká. -át] *a* delicate; (*plein de tact*) tactful; (*attentionné*) thoughtful; (*exigeant*) fussy, particular; **procédés peu ~s** unscrupulous methods.

délicatement [dālēkátmáṅ] *ad* delicately; (*avec douceur*) gently.

délicatesse [dālēkátes] *nf* delicacy; tactfulness; thoughtfulness; **~s** *nfpl* attentions, consideration *sg*.

délice [dālēs] *nm* delight.

délicieusement [dālēsyēzmáṅ] *ad* deliciously; delightfully.

délicieux, euse [dālēsyēœ. -ēz] *a* (*au goût*) delicious; (*sensation, impression*) delightful.

délictueux, euse [dālēktūœ. -ēz] *a* criminal.

délié, e [dālyā] *a* nimble, agile; (*mince*) slender, fine ♦ *nm*: **les ~s** the upstrokes (*in handwriting*).

délier [dālyā] *vt* to untie; **~ qn de** (*serment etc*) to free *ou* release sb from.

délimitation [dālēmētásyóṅ] *nf* delimitation.

délimiter [dālēmētā] *vt* to delimit.

délinquance [dālaṅkáṅs] *nf* criminality; **~ juvénile** juvenile delinquency.

délinquant, e [dālaṅkáṅ. -áṅt] *a*, *nm/f* delinquent.

déliquescence [dālēkásáṅs] *nf*: **en ~** in a state of decay.

déliquescent, e [dālēkásáṅ. -áṅt] *a* decaying.

délirant, e [dālēráṅ. -áṅt] *a* (*MÉD*: *fièvre*) delirious; (*imagination*) frenzied; (*fam*: *déraisonnable*) crazy.

délire [dālēr] *nm* (*fièvre*) delirium; (*fig*) frenzy; (: *folie*) lunacy.

délirer [dālērā] *vi* to be delirious; (*fig*) to be raving.

délit [dālē] *nm* (criminal) offense (*US*) *ou* offence (*Brit*); **~ de droit commun** violation of common law; **~ de fuite** failure to stop after an accident; **~ de presse** violation of the press laws.

délivrance [dālēvráṅs] *nf* freeing, release; (*sentiment*) relief.

délivrer [dālēvrā] *vt* (*prisonnier*) to (set) free, release; (*passeport, certificat*) to issue; **~ qn de** (*ennemis*) to set sb free from, deliver *ou* free sb from; (*fig*) to rid sb of.

déloger [dālozhā] *vt* (*locataire*) to evict; (*objet coincé, ennemi*) to dislodge.

déloyal, e, aux [dālwáyál. -ō] *a* (*personne, conduite*) disloyal; (*procédé*) unfair.

Delphes [delf] *n* Delphi.

delta [deltá] *nm* (*GÉO*) delta.

deltaplane [deltáplán] *nm* ® hang glider.

déluge [dālüzh] *nm* (*biblique*) Flood, Deluge; (*grosse pluie*) downpour, deluge; (*grand nombre*): **~ de** flood of.

déluré, e [dālürā] *a* smart, resourceful; (*péj*) forward, pert.

démagogie [dāmágozhē] *nf* demagogy.

démagogique [dāmágozhēk] *a* demagogic, popularity-seeking; (*POL*) vote-catching.

démagogue [dāmágog] *a* demagogic ♦ *nm* demagogue.

démaillé, e [dāmáyā] *a* (*bas*) with a run (*ou* runs), laddered (*Brit*).

demain [dəmaṅ] *ad* tomorrow; **~ matin/soir** tomorrow morning/evening; **~ midi** tomorrow at midday; **à ~!** see you tomorrow!

demande [dəmáṅd] *nf* (*requête*) request; (*revendication*) demand; (*ADMIN, formulaire*) application; (*ÉCON*) **la ~** demand; **"~s d'emploi"** "jobs *ou* work wanted" (*US*), "situations wanted" (*Brit*); **à la ~ générale** by popular request; **~ en mariage** (marriage) proposal; **faire sa ~ (en mariage)** to propose (marriage); **~ de naturalisation** application for naturalization; **~ de poste** job application.

demandé, e [dəmáṅdā] *a* (*article etc*): **très ~** (very) much in demand.

demander [dəmáṅdā] *vt* to ask for; (*question: date, heure, chemin*) to ask; (*requérir, nécessiter*) to require, demand; **~ qch à qn** to ask sb for sth, ask sb sth; **ils demandent 2 secrétaires et un ingénieur** they're looking for 2 secretaries and an engineer; **~ la main de qn** to ask for sb's hand (in marriage); **~ pardon à qn** to apologize to sb; **~ à ou de voir/faire** to ask to see/ask if one can do; **~ à qn de faire** to ask sb to do; **~ que/pourquoi** to ask that/why; **se ~ si/pourquoi** *etc* to wonder if/why *etc*; (*sens purement réfléchi*) to ask o.s. if/why *etc*; **on vous demande au téléphone** you're wanted on the phone, there's someone for you on the phone; **il ne demande que ça** that's all he wants; **je ne demande pas mieux** I'm asking nothing more; **il ne demande qu'à faire** all he wants is to do.

demandeur, euse [dəmáṅdœr. -ēz] *nm/f*: **~ d'emploi** job-seeker.

démangeaison [dāmáṅzhezóṅ] *nf* itching.

démanger [dāmáṅzhā] *vi* to itch; **la main me démange** my hand is itching; **l'envie** *ou* **ça me démange de faire** I'm itching to do.

démanteler [dāmáṅtlā] *vt* to break up; to demolish.

démaquillant [dāmákēyáṅ] *nm* make-up remover.

démaquiller [dāmákēyā] *vt*: **se ~** to remove one's make-up.

démarcage [dāmárkàzh] *nm* = **démarquage**.

démarcation [dāmárkásyóṅ] *nf* demarcation.

démarchage [dāmárshàzh] *nm* (*COMM*) door-to-door selling.

démarche [dāmársh(ə)] *nf* (*allure*) gait, walk; (*intervention*) step; approach; (*fig*: *intellectuelle*) thought processes *pl*; approach; **faire** *ou* **entreprendre des ~s** to take action; **faire des ~s auprès de qn** to approach sb.

démarcheur, euse [dāmárshœr. -ēz] *nm/f* (*COMM*) door-to-door salesman/woman; (*POL etc*) canvasser.

démarquage [dāmárkàzh] *nm* marking down.

démarque [dāmárk(ə)] *nf* (*COMM*: *d'un article*) markdown.

démarqué, e [dāmárkā] *a* (*FOOTBALL*) unmarked; (*COMM*) reduced; **prix ~s** marked-down prices.

démarquer [dāmárkā] *vt* (*prix*) to mark down; (*joueur*) to stop marking; **se ~** *vi* (*SPORT*) to shake off one's marker.

démarrage [dāmárázh] *nm* starting *q*, start; **~ en côte** hill start.

démarrer [dāmárā] *vt* to start up ♦ *vi* (*con-*

ducteur) to start (up); (*véhicule*) to move off; (*travaux, affaire*) to get moving; (*coureur: accélérer*) to pull away.

démarreur [dāmároer] *nm* (*AUTO*) starter.

démasquer [dāmáskā] *vt* to unmask; **se** ~ to unmask; (*fig*) to drop one's mask.

démâter [dāmátā] *vt* to dismast ♦ *vi* to be dismasted.

démêlant, e [dāmālāń, -âńt] *a*: **baume** ~, **crème** ~e (hair) conditioner.

démêler [dāmālā] *vt* to untangle, disentangle.

démêlés [dāmālā] *nmpl* problems.

démembrer [dāmáńbrā] *vt* to slice up, tear apart.

déménagement [dāmānázhmáń] *nm* (*du point de vue du locataire etc*) move; (: *du déménageur*) moving (*US*), removal (*Brit*); **entreprise/camion de** ~ moving (*US*) *ou* removal (*Brit*) firm/van.

déménager [dāmānázhā] *vt* (*meubles*) to (re)move ♦ *vi* to move.

déménageur [dāmānázhœr] *nm* (furniture) mover (*US*), removal man (*Brit*); (*entrepreneur*) furniture mover (*US*) *ou* remover (*Brit*).

démence [dāmáńs] *nf* madness, insanity; (*MÉD*) dementia.

démener [dāmnā]: **se** ~ *vi* to thrash about; (*fig*) to exert o.s.

dément, e [dāmáń, -âńt] *vb voir* **démentir** ♦ *a* (*fou*) crazy; (*fam*) brilliant, fantastic.

démentiel, le [dāmáńsyel] *a* insane.

démentir [dāmáńtēr] *vt* (*nouvelle, témoin*) to refute; (*suj: faits etc*) to belie, refute; ~ **que** to deny that; **ne pas se** ~ not to fail, keep up.

démerder [dāmerdā]: **se** ~ *vi* (*fam!*) to look after o.s., look out for o.s.

démériter [dāmārētā] *vi*: ~ **auprès de qn** to come down in sb's esteem.

démesure [dāməzür] *nf* immoderation, immoderateness.

démesuré, e [dāməzürā] *a* immoderate, disproportionate.

démesurément [dāməzürāmáń] *ad* disproportionately.

démettre [dāmetr(ə)] *vt*: ~ **qn de** (*fonction, poste*) to dismiss sb from; **se** ~ (**de ses fonctions**) to resign (from) one's duties; **se** ~ **l'épaule** *etc* to dislocate one's shoulder *etc*.

demeurant [dəmœráń]: **au** ~ *ad* for all that.

demeure [dəmœr] *nf* residence; **dernière** ~ (*fig*) last resting place; **mettre qn en** ~ **de faire** to enjoin *ou* order sb to do; **à** ~ *ad* permanently.

demeuré, e [dəmœrā] *a* backward ♦ *nm/f* backward person.

demeurer [dəmœrā] *vi* (*habiter*) to live; (*séjourner*) to stay; (*rester*) to remain; **en** ~ **là** (*suj: personne*) to leave it at that; (: *choses*) to be left at that.

demi, e [dəmē] *a*: **et** ~: **trois heures/ bouteilles et** ~**es** three and a half hours/ bottles, three hours/bottles and a half ♦ *nm* (*bière*) ≈ half-pint (*.25 litre*); (*FOOTBALL*) halfback; **il est 2 heures/midi et** ~**e** it's half past 2/12; ~ **de mêlée/d'ouverture** (*RUGBY*) scrum/stand-off half; **à** ~ *ad* half-; **ouvrir à** ~ to half-open; **faire les choses à** ~ to do

things by halves; **à la** ~**e** (*heure*) on the half-hour.

demi... [dəmē] *préfixe* half-, semi-..., demi-.

demi-bas [dəməbá] *nm inv* (*chaussette*) knee-sock.

demi-bouteille [dəməbōōtey] *nf* half-bottle.

demi-cercle [dəmēserkl(ə)] *nm* semicircle; **en** ~ *a* semicircular ♦ *ad* in a semicircle.

demi-douzaine [dəmēdōōzen] *nf* half-dozen, half a dozen.

demi-finale [dəmēfēnál] *nf* semifinal.

demi-finaliste [dəmēfēnálēst(ə)] *nm/f* semifinalist.

demi-fond [dəmēfóń] *nm* (*SPORT*) medium-distance running.

demi-frère [dəmēfrer] *nm* half-brother.

demi-gros [dəməgrō] *nm inv* wholesale trade.

demi-heure [dəmēyœr] *nf*: **une** ~ a half-hour, half an hour.

demi-jour [dəmēzhōōr] *nm* half-light.

demi-journée [dəmēzhōōrnā] *nf* half-day, half a day.

démilitariser [dāmēlētárēzā] *vt* to demilitarize.

demi-litre [dəmēlēt(ə)] *nm* half-liter (*US*), half-litre (*Brit*), half a liter *ou* litre.

demi-livre [dəmēlēvr(ə)] *nf* half-pound, half a pound.

demi-longueur [dəmēlóńgœr] *nf* (*SPORT*) half-length, half a length.

demi-lune [dəmēlün]: **en** ~ *a inv* semicircular.

demi-mal [dəmēmál] *nm*: **il n'y a que** ~ there's not much harm done.

demi-mesure [dəmēmzür] *nf* half-measure.

demi-mot [dəmēmō]: **à** ~ *ad* without having to spell things out.

déminer [dāmēnā] *vt* to clear of mines.

démineur [dāmēnœr] *nm* bomb disposal expert.

demi-pension [dəmēpáńsyóń] *nf* half-board; **être en** ~ (*SCOL*) to buy lunch at school.

demi-pensionnaire [dəmēpáńsyoner] *nm/f* (*SCOL*) day student (*US*) *ou* pupil (*Brit*).

demi-place [dəmēplás] *nf* half-price; (*TRANSPORTS*) half-fare.

démis, e [dāmē, -ēz] *pp de* **démettre** ♦ *a* (*épaule etc*) dislocated.

demi-saison [dəmēsezóń] *nf*: **vêtements de** ~ spring *ou* fall (*US*) *ou* autumn (*Brit*) clothing.

demi-sel [dəmēsel] *a inv* slightly salted.

demi-sœur [dəmēsœr] *nf* half-sister.

demi-sommeil [dəmēsomey] *nm* doze.

demi-soupir [dəmēsōōpēr] *nm* (*MUS*) eighth (*US*) *ou* quaver (*Brit*) rest.

démission [dāmēsyóń] *nf* resignation; **donner sa** ~ to give *ou* hand in one's notice, hand in one's resignation.

démissionnaire [dāmēsyoner] *a* outgoing ♦ *nm/f* person resigning.

démissionner [dāmēsyonā] *vi* (*de son poste*) to resign, give *ou* hand in one's notice.

demi-tarif [dəmētárēf] *nm* half-price; (*TRANSPORTS*) half-fare.

demi-ton [dəmētóń] *nm* (*MUS*) half step (*US*), semitone.

demi-tour [dəmētōōr] *nm* about-face (*US*), about-turn (*Brit*); **faire un** ~ (*MIL etc*) to make an about-face (*US*) *ou* about-turn (*Brit*); **faire** ~ to turn (and go) back;

(AUTO) to make a U-turn.

démobilisation [dāmobēlēzâsyóń] *nf* demobilization; (*fig*) demotivation, demoralization.

démobiliser [dāmobēlēzā] *vt* to demobilize; (*fig*) to demotivate, demoralize.

démocrate [dāmokrát] *a* democratic ♦ *nm/f* democrat.

démocrate-chrétien, ne [dāmokrátkrātyań, -en] *nm/f* Christian Democrat.

démocratie [dāmokrásē] *nf* democracy; ~ **populaire/libérale** people's/liberal democracy.

démocratique [dāmokrátēk] *a* democratic.

démocratiquement [dāmokrátēkmáń] *ad* democratically.

démocratiser [dāmokrátēzā] *vt* to democratize.

démodé, e [dāmodā] *a* old-fashioned.

démoder [dāmodā]: **se** ~ *vi* to go out of fashion.

démographie [dāmográfē] *nf* demography.

démographique [dāmográfēk] *a* demographic; **poussée** ~ increase in population.

demoiselle [dəmwázel] *nf* (*jeune fille*) young lady; (*célibataire*) single lady, maiden lady; ~ **d'honneur** bridesmaid.

démolir [dāmolēr] *vt* to demolish; (*fig: personne*) to do in.

démolisseur [dāmolēscer] *nm* demolition worker.

démolition [dāmolēsyóń] *nf* demolition.

démon [dāmóń] *nm* demon, fiend; evil spirit; (*enfant turbulent*) devil, demon; **le** ~ **du jeu/des femmes** a mania for gambling/ women; **le D**~ the Devil.

démonétiser [dāmonātēzā] *vt* to demonetize.

démoniaque [dāmonyak] *a* fiendish.

démonstrateur, trice [dāmóństrátœr, -trēs] *nm/f* demonstrator.

démonstratif, ive [dāmóństrátēf, -ēv] *a, nm* (*aussi* LING) demonstrative.

démonstration [dāmóństrásyóń] *nf* demonstration; (*aérienne, navale*) display.

démontable [dāmóńtábl(ə)] *a* folding.

démontage [dāmóńtázh] *nm* dismantling.

démonté, e [dāmóńtā] *a* (*fig*) raging, wild.

démonte-pneu [dāmóńtəpnō̄] *nm* tire iron (*US*), tyre lever (*Brit*).

démonter [dāmóńtā] *vt* (*machine etc*) to take down, dismantle; (*pneu, porte*) to take off; (*cavalier*) to throw, unseat; (*fig: personne*) to disconcert; **se** ~ *vi* (*personne*) to lose countenance.

démontrable [dāmóńtrábl(ə)] *a* demonstrable.

démontrer [dāmóńtrā] *vt* to demonstrate, show.

démoralisant, e [dāmorálēzáń, -áńt] *a* demoralizing.

démoralisateur, trice [dāmorálēzátœr, -trēs] *a* demoralizing.

démoraliser [dāmorálēzā] *vt* to demoralize.

démordre [dāmordr(ə)] *vi*: **ne pas** ~ **de** to refuse to give up, stick to.

démouler [dāmō̄olā] *vt* (*gâteau*) to unmold (*US*), turn out (*Brit*).

démoustiquer [dāmō̄ostēkā] *vt* to clear of mosquitoes.

démultiplication [dāmültēplēkâsyóń] *nf* reduction; reduction ratio.

démuni, e [dāmünē] *a* (*sans argent*) impoverished; ~ **de** without, lacking in.

démunir [dāmünēr] *vt*: ~ **qn de** to deprive sb of; **se** ~ **de** to part with, give up.

démuseler [dāmüzlā] *vt* to unmuzzle.

démystifier [dāmēstēfyā] *vt* to demystify.

démythifier [dāmētēfyā] *vt* to demythologize.

dénatalité [dānátálētā] *nf* fall in the birth rate.

dénationalisation [dānásyonálēzâsyóń] *nf* denationalization.

dénationaliser [dānásyonálēzā] *vt* to denationalize.

dénaturé, e [dānátürā] *a* (*alcool*) denatured (*US*), denaturized (*Brit*); (*goûts*) unnatural.

dénaturer [dānátürā] *vt* (*goût*) to alter (completely); (*pensée, fait*) to distort, misrepresent.

dénégations [dānāgásyóń] *nfpl* denials.

déneigement [dānezhmáń] *nm* snow removal.

déneiger [dānāzhā] *vt* to remove *ou* shovel snow from.

déni [dānē] *nm*: ~ **(de justice)** denial of justice.

déniaiser [dānyāzā] *vt*: ~ **qn** to teach sb about life.

dénicher [dānēshā] *vt* to unearth.

dénicotinisé, e [dānēkotēnēzā] *a* nicotine-free.

denier [dənyā] *nm* (*monnaie*) formerly, *a coin of small value*; (*de bas*) denier; ~ **du culte** contribution to parish upkeep; ~**s publics** public money; **de ses (propres)** ~**s** out of one's own pocket.

dénier [dānyā] *vt* to deny; ~ **qch à qn** to deny sb sth.

dénigrer [dānēgrā] *vt* to denigrate, run down.

dénivelé, e [dānēvlā] *a* (*chaussée*) on a lower level ♦ *nm* difference in height.

déniveler [dānēvlā] *vt* to make uneven; to put on a lower level.

dénivellation [dānēvelâsyóń] *nf*, **dénivellement** [dānēvelmáń] *nm* difference in level; (*pente*) ramp; (*creux*) dip.

dénombrer [dānóńbrā] *vt* (*compter*) to count; (*énumérer*) to enumerate, list.

dénominateur [dānomēnátœr] *nm* denominator; ~ **commun** common denominator.

dénomination [dānomēnásyóń] *nf* designation, appellation.

dénommé, e [dānomā] *a*: **le** ~ **Dupont** the man by the name of Dupont.

dénommer [dānomā] *vt* to name.

dénoncer [dānóńsā] *vt* to denounce; **se** ~ to give o.s. up, come forward.

dénonciation [dānóńsyásyóń] *nf* denunciation.

dénoter [dānotā] *vt* to denote.

dénouement [dānō̄omáń] *nm* outcome, conclusion; (*THÉÂTRE*) dénouement.

dénouer [dānwā] *vt* to unknot, undo.

dénoyauter [dānwáyōtā] *vt* to pit (*US*), stone (*Brit*); **appareil à** ~ pitter (*US*), stoner (*Brit*).

dénoyauteur [dānwáyōtœr] *nm* pitter (*US*), stoner (*Brit*).

denrée [dáńrā] *nf* commodity; (*aussi*: ~ **alimentaire**) food(stuff).

dense [dáńs] *a* dense.

densité [dáńsētā] *nf* denseness; (*PHYSIQUE*) density.

dent [dáń] *nf* tooth (*pl* teeth); **avoir/garder**

une ~ contre qn to have/hold a grudge against sb; se mettre qch sous la ~ to eat sth; être sur les ~s to be on one's last legs; faire ses ~s to teethe, cut (one's) teeth; en ~s de scie serrated; (irrégulier) jagged; avoir les ~s longues (fig) to be ruthlessly ambitious; ~ de lait/sagesse milk/wisdom tooth.

dentaire [dánter] a dental; **cabinet** ~ dentist's office (US), dental surgery (Brit); **école** ~ dental school.

denté, e [dántā] a: **roue** ~**e** cog wheel.

dentelé, e [dántlā] a jagged, indented.

dentelle [dántel] nf lace q.

dentelure [dántlür] nf (aussi: ~s) jagged outline.

dentier [dántyā] nm denture.

dentifrice [dántĉfrĉs] a, nm: **(pâte)** ~ toothpaste; **eau** ~ mouthwash.

dentiste [dántēst(ə)] nm/f dentist.

dentition [dántēsyóń] nf teeth pl, dentition.

dénucléariser [dānükláárēzā] vt to make nuclear-free.

dénudé, e [danudā] a bare.

dénuder [dānüdā] vt to bare; **se** ~ (personne) to strip.

dénué, e [dūnüā] a: ~ **de** lacking in; (intérêt) devoid of.

dénuement [dānümáń] nm destitution.

dénutrition [dānütrēsyóń] nf undernourishment.

déodorant [dáodoráń] nm deodorant.

déodoriser [dáodorēzā] vt to deodorize.

déontologie [dáóntolozhē] nf code of ethics; (professionnelle) (professional) code of practice.

dép. abr (ADMIN: = département) dept; (= départ) dep.

dépannage [dāpánázh] nm: **service/camion de** ~ (AUTO) breakdown service/truck.

dépanner [dāpánā] vt (voiture, télévision) to fix, repair; (fig) to bail out, help out.

dépanneur [dāpáncœr] nm (AUTO) breakdown mechanic, (TV) television repairman.

dépanneuse [dāpánœz] nf tow truck (US), breakdown lorry (Brit).

dépareillé, e [dāpáráyā] a (collection, service) incomplete; (gant, volume, objet) odd.

déparer [dāpárā] vt to spoil, mar.

départ [dāpár] nm leaving q, departure; (SPORT) start; (sur un horaire) departure; **à son** ~ when he left; **au** ~ (au début) initially, at the start; **courrier au** ~ outgoing mail.

départager [dāpártázhā] vt to decide between.

département [dāpártəmáń] nm department.

départemental, e, aux [dāpártəmáńtál, -ō] a departmental.

départementaliser [dāpártəmáńtálēzā] vt to devolve authority to.

départir [dāpártēr]: **se** ~ **de** vt to abandon, depart from.

dépassé, e [dāpásā] a superseded, outmoded; (fig) out of one's depth.

dépassement [dāpásmáń] nm (AUTO) passing.

dépasser [dāpásā] vt (véhicule, concurrent) to pass; (endroit) to pass, go past; (somme, limite) to exceed; (fig: en beauté etc) to

surpass, outshine; (être en saillie sur) to jut out above (ou in front of); (dérouter): **cela me dépasse** it's beyond me ♦ vi (AUTO) to pass; (jupon) to show; **se** ~ to outdo o.s.

dépassionner [dāpásyonā] vt (débat etc) to take the heat out of.

dépaver [dāpávā] vt to remove the cobblestones from.

dépaysé, e [dāpáēzā] a disorientated.

dépaysement [dāpáēzmáń] nm disorientation; change of scenery.

dépayser [dāpáēzā] vt (désorienter) to disorientate; (changer agréablement) to provide with a change of scenery.

dépecer [dāpəsā] vt (suj: boucher) to joint, cut up; (suj: animal) to dismember.

dépêche [dāpesh] nf dispatch; ~ **(télégraphique)** telegram, wire.

dépêcher [dāpāshā] vt to dispatch; **se** ~ vi to hurry; **se** ~ **de faire qch** to hasten to do sth, to hurry (in order) to do sth.

dépeindre [dāpańdr(ə)] vt to depict.

dépendance [dāpáńdáńs] nf (interdépendance) dependence q, dependency; (bâtiment) outbuilding.

dépendant, e [dāpáńdáń, -áńt] vb voir **dépendre** ♦ a (financièrement) dependent.

dépendre [dāpáńdr(ə)] vt (tableau) to take down; ~ **de** vt to depend on; (financièrement etc) to be dependent on; (appartenir) to belong to.

dépens [dāpáń] nmpl: **aux** ~ **de** at the expense of.

dépense [dāpáńs] nf spending q, expense, expenditure q; (fig) consumption; (: de temps, de forces) expenditure; **pousser qn à la** ~ to make sb incur an expense; ~ **physique** (physical) exertion; ~ **de temps** investment of time; ~**s de fonctionnement** revenue expenditure; ~**s d'investissement** capital expenditure; ~**s publiques** government spending.

dépenser [dāpáńsā] vt to spend; (gaz, eau) to use; (fig) to expend, use up; **se** ~ (se fatiguer) to exert o.s.

dépensier, ière [dāpáńsyā, -yer] a: **il est** ~ he's a spendthrift.

déperdition [dāperdēsyóń] nf loss.

dépérir [dāpārēr] vi (personne) to waste away; (plante) to wither.

dépersonnaliser [dāpersonálēzā] vt to depersonalize.

dépêtrer [dāpātrā] vt: **se** ~ **de** (situation) to extricate o.s. from.

dépeuplé, e [dāpœplā] a depopulated.

dépeupler [dāpœplā] vt to depopulate; **se** ~ to be depopulated.

déphasage [dāfázázh] nm (fig) being out of touch.

déphasé, e [dāfázā] a (ÉLEC) out of phase; (fig) out of touch.

déphaser [dāfázā] vt (fig) to put out of touch.

dépilation [dāpēlásyóń] nf hair loss; hair removal.

dépilatoire [dāpēlátwár] a depilatory, hair-removing.

dépiler [dāpēlā] vt (épiler) to depilate, remove hair from.

dépistage [dāpēstázh] nm (MÉD) screening.

dépister |dāpēstā| *vt* to detect; (*MÉD*) to screen; (*voleur*) to track down; (*poursuivants*) to throw off the scent.

dépit |dāpē| *nm* vexation, frustration; **en ~ de** *prép* in spite of; **en ~ du bon sens** contrary to all good sense.

dépité, e |dāpētā| *a* vexed, frustrated.

dépiter |dāpētā| *vt* to vex, frustrate.

déplacé, e |dāplásā| *a* (*propos*) out of place, uncalled-for; **personne ~e** displaced person.

déplacement |dāplásmáń| *nm* moving; shifting; transfer; (*voyage*) trip, traveling *q* (*US*), travelling *q* (*Brit*); **en ~** away (on a trip); **~ d'air** displacement of air; **~ de vertèbre** slipped disc.

déplacer |dāplásā| *vt* (*table, voiture*) to move, shift; (*employé*) to transfer, move; **se ~** *vi* (*objet*) to move; (*organe*) to become displaced; (*personne: bouger*) to move, walk; (*: voyager*) to travel ♦ *vt* (*vertèbre etc*) to displace.

déplaire |dāplcr| *vi*: **ceci me déplaît** I don't like this, I dislike this; **il cherche à nous ~** he's trying to displease us *ou* be disagreeable to us; **se ~ quelque part** to dislike it *ou* be unhappy somewhere.

déplaisant, e |dāplczáń, -áńt| *vb voir* **déplaire** ♦ *a* disagreeable, unpleasant.

déplaisir |dāplāzēr| *nm* displeasure, annoyance.

déplaît |dāplc| *vb voir* **déplaire**.

dépliant |dāplēyáń| *nm* leaflet.

déplier |dāplēyā| *vt* to unfold; **se ~** (*parachute*) to open.

déplisser |dāplēsā| *vt* to smooth out.

déploiement |dāplwámáń| *nm* (*voir* **déployer**) deployment; display.

déplomber |dāplóńbā| *vt* (*caisse, compteur*) to break (open) the seal of.

déplorable |dāplorábl(ə)| *a* deplorable; lamentable.

déplorer |dāplorā| *vt* (*regretter*) to deplore; (*pleurer sur*) to lament.

déployer |dāplwáyā| *vt* to open out, spread; (*MIL*) to deploy; (*montrer*) to display, exhibit.

déplu |dāplü| *pp de* **déplaire**.

dépointer |dāpwantā| *vi* to punch (*US*) *ou* clock (*Brit*) out.

dépoli, e |dāpolē| *a*: **verre ~** frosted glass.

dépolitiser |dāpolētēzā| *vt* to depoliticize.

déportation |dāportásyóń| *nf* deportation.

déporté, e |dāportā| *nm/f* deportee; (*1939-45*) concentration camp prisoner.

déporter |dāportā| *vt* (*POL*) to deport; (*dévier*) to carry off course; **se ~** *vi* (*voiture*) to swerve.

déposant, e |dāpōzáń, -áńt| *nm/f* (*épargnant*) depositor.

dépose |dāpōz| *nf* taking out; taking down.

déposé, e |dāpōzā| *a* registered; *voir aussi* **marque**.

déposer |dāpōzā| *vt* (*gén: mettre, poser*) to lay down, put down, set down; (*à la banque, à la consigne*) to deposit; (*caution*) to put down; (*passager*) to drop (off); (*démonter: serrure, moteur*) to take out; (*: rideau*) to take down; (*roi*) to depose; (*ADMIN*: *faire enregistrer*) to file; to register ♦ *vi* to form a

sediment *ou* deposit; (*JUR*): **~ (contre)** to testify *ou* give evidence (against); **se ~** *vi* to settle; **~ son bilan** (*COMM*) to go into (voluntary) liquidation.

dépositaire |dāpozētcr| *nm/f* (*JUR*) depository; (*COMM*) agent; **~ agréé** authorized agent.

déposition |dāpōzēsyóń| *nf* (*JUR*) deposition.

déposséder |dāposādā| *vt* to dispossess.

dépôt |dāpō| *nm* (*à la banque, sédiment*) deposit; (*entrepôt, réserve*) warehouse, store; (*gare*) depot; (*prison*) cells *pl*; **~ d'ordures** garbage (*US*) *ou* rubbish (*Brit*) dump; **~ de bilan** (voluntary) liquidation; **~ légal** registration of copyright.

dépoter |dāpotā| *vt* (*plante*) to take from the pot, transplant.

dépotoir |dāpotwár| *nm* dumping ground, garbage (*US*) *ou* rubbish (*Brit*) dump; **~ nucléaire** nuclear (waste) dump.

dépouille |dāpōōy| *nf* (*d'animal*) skin, hide; (*humaine*): **~ (mortelle)** mortal remains *pl*.

dépouillé, e |dāpōōyā| *a* (*fig*) bare, bald; **~ de** stripped of; lacking in.

dépouillement |dāpōōymáń| *nm* (*de scrutin*) count, counting *q*.

dépouiller |dāpōōyā| *vt* (*animal*) to skin; (*spolier*) to deprive of one's possessions; (*documents*) to go through, peruse; **~ qn/qch de** to strip sb/sth of; **~ le scrutin** to count the votes.

dépourvu, e |dāpōōrvü| *a*: **~ de** lacking in, without; **au ~** *ad*: **prendre qn au ~** to catch sb unawares.

dépoussiérer |dāpōōsyārā| *vt* to remove dust from.

dépravation |dāprávásyóń| *nf* depravity.

dépravé, e |dāprávā| *a* depraved.

dépraver |dāprávā| *vt* to deprave.

dépréciation |dāprāsyásyóń| *nf* depreciation.

déprécier |dāprāsyā| *vt*, **se ~** *vi* to depreciate.

déprédations |dāprādásyóń| *nfpl* damage *sg*.

dépressif, ive |dāprāsēf, -ēv| *a* depressive.

dépression |dāprāsyóń| *nf* depression; **~ (nerveuse)** (nervous) breakdown.

déprimant, e |dāprēmáń, -áńt| *a* depressing.

déprime |dāprēm| *nf* (*fam*): **la ~** depression.

déprimé, e |dāprēmā| *a* (*découragé*) depressed.

déprimer |dāprēmā| *vt* to depress.

déprogrammer |dāprográmā| *vt* (*supprimer*) to cancel.

DEPS *sigle* (*= dernier entré premier sorti*) LIFO (*= last in first out*).

dépt *abr* (*= département*) dept.

dépuceler |dāpüslā| *vt* (*fam*) to take the virginity of.

depuis |dəpüē| *prép* (*temps: date*) since; (*: période*) for; (*lieu*) since, from; (*quantité, rang*) from ♦ *ad* (ever) since; **~ que** (*temps*) (ever) since; **je le connais ~ 3 ans** I've known him for 3 years; **il est parti ~ mardi** he has been gone since Tuesday; **~ quand le connaissez-vous?** how long have you known him?; **elle a téléphoné ~ Valence** she phoned from Valence; **~ lors** since then.

dépuratif, ive |dāpürátēf, -ēv| *a* depurative, purgative.

députation |dāpütásyóń| *nf* deputation; (*fonction*) position of deputy, ≈ seat in Congress

(*US*), ≈ parliamentary seat (*Brit*).

député, e [dāpütā] *nm/f* (*POL*) deputy, ≈ Congressman/woman (*US*), ≈ Member of Parliament (*Brit*).

députer [dāpütā] *vt* to delegate; ~ **qn auprès de** to send sb (as a representative) to.

déraciner [dārásēnā] *vt* to uproot.

déraillement [dārâymáǹ] *nm* derailment.

dérailler [dārâyā] *vi* (*train*) to be derailed, go off *ou* jump the rails; (*fam*) to be completely off the track; **faire** ~ to derail.

dérailleur [dārâyœr] *nm* (*de vélo*) derailleur (*US*), dérailleur gears *pl* (*Brit*).

déraison [dārezóǹ] *nf* unreasonableness.

déraisonnable [dārezonábl(ə)] *a* unreasonable.

déraisonner [dārezonā] *vi* to talk nonsense, rave.

dérangement [dāráǹzhmáǹ] *nm* (*gêne, déplacement*) trouble; (*gastrique etc*) disorder; (*mécanique*) breakdown; **en** ~ (*téléphone*) out of order.

déranger [dāráǹzhā] *vt* (*personne*) to trouble, bother, disturb; (*projets*) to disrupt, upset; (*objets, vêtements*) to disarrange; **se** ~ to put o.s. out; (*se déplacer*) to (take the trouble to) come (*ou* go) out; **est-ce que cela vous dérange si ...?** do you mind if ...?; **ça te dérangerait de faire ...?** would you mind doing ...?; **ne vous dérangez pas** don't go to any trouble; don't disturb yourself.

dérapage [dārápázh] *nm* skid, skidding *q*; going out of control.

déraper [dārápā] *vi* (*voiture*) to skid; (*personne, semelles, couteau*) to slip; (*fig: économie etc*) to go out of control.

dératé, e [dārátā] *nm/f*: **courir comme un** ~ to run like the wind.

dératiser [dārátēzā] *vt* to rid of rats.

déréglé, e [dārāglā] *a* (*mœurs*) dissolute.

dérèglement [dāregləmáǹ] *nm* upsetting *q*, upset.

dérégler [dārāglā] *vt* (*mécanisme*) to put out of order, cause to break down; (*estomac*) to upset; **se** ~ *vi* to break down, go wrong.

dérider [dārēdā] *vt*, **se** ~ *vi* to brighten *ou* cheer up.

dérision [dārēzyóǹ] *nf* derision; **tourner en** ~ to deride; **par** ~ in mockery.

dérisoire [dārēzwár] *a* derisory.

dérivatif [dārēvátēf] *nm* distraction.

dérivation [dārēvásyóǹ] *nf* derivation; diversion.

dérive [dārēv] *nf* (*de dériveur*) centerboard (*US*), centreboard (*Brit*); **aller à la** ~ (*NAVIG, fig*) to drift; ~ **des continents** (*GÉO*) continental drift.

dérivé, e [dārēvā] *a* derived ♦ *nm* (*LING*) derivative; (*TECH*) by-product ♦ *nf* (*MATH*) derivative.

dériver [dārēvā] *vt* (*MATH*) to derive; (*cours d'eau etc*) to divert ♦ *vi* (*bateau*) to drift; ~ **de** to derive from.

dériveur [dārēvœr] *nm* sailing dinghy.

dermatite [dermátēt] *nf* dermatitis.

dermato [dermátō] *nm/f* (*fam*: = *dermatologue*) dermatologist.

dermatologie [dermátolozhē] *nf* dermatology.

dermatologue [dārmátolog] *nm/f* dermatolo-

gist.

dermite [dermēt] *nf* = **dermatite**.

dernier, **ière** [dernyā, -yer] *a* (*dans le temps, l'espace*) last; (*le plus récent: gén avant n*) latest, last; (*final, ultime: effort*) final; (*échelon, grade*) top, highest ♦ *nm* (*étage*) top floor; **lundi/le mois** ~ last Monday/month; **du** ~ **chic** extremely smart; **le** ~ **cri** the last word (in fashion); **les** ~**s honneurs** the last tribute; **le** ~ **soupir: rendre le** ~ **soupir** to breathe one's last; **en** ~ *ad* last; **ce** ~, **cette dernière** the latter.

dernièrement [dernyermáǹ] *ad* recently.

dernier-né, **dernière-née** [dernyānā, dernyernā] *nm/f* (*enfant*) last-born.

dérobade [dārobád] *nf* side-stepping *q*.

dérobé, e [dārobā] *a* (*porte*) secret, hidden; **à la** ~**e** surreptitiously.

dérober [dārobā] *vt* to steal; (*cacher*): ~ **qch à (la vue de) qn** to conceal *ou* hide sth from sb('s view); **se** ~ *vi* (*s'esquiver*) to slip away; (*fig*) to shy away; **se** ~ **sous** (*s'effondrer*) to give way beneath; **se** ~ **à** (*justice, regards*) to hide from; (*obligation*) to shirk.

dérogation [dārogásyóǹ] *nf* (special) dispensation.

déroger [dārozhā]: ~ **à** *vt* to go against, depart from.

dérouiller [dārōōyā] *vt*: **se** ~ **les jambes** to stretch one's legs.

déroulement [dārōōlmáǹ] *nm* (*d'une opération etc*) progress.

dérouler [dārōōlā] *vt* (*ficelle*) to unwind; (*papier*) to unroll; **se** ~ *vi* to unwind; to unroll, come unrolled; (*avoir lieu*) to take place; (*se passer*) to go.

déroutant, e [dārōōtāǹ, -áǹt] *a* disconcerting.

déroute [dārōōt] *nf* (*MIL*) rout; (*fig*) total collapse; **mettre en** ~ to rout; **en** ~ routed.

dérouter [dārōōtā] *vt* (*avion, train*) to reroute, divert; (*étonner*) to disconcert, throw (off).

derrière [deryer] *ad, prép* behind ♦ *nm* (*d'une maison*) back; (*postérieur*) behind, bottom; **les pattes de** ~ the back legs, the hind legs; **par** ~ from behind; (*fig*) in an underhanded (*US*) *ou* underhand way, behind one's back.

des [dā] *dét, prép* + *dét voir* **de**.

dès [de] *prép* from; ~ **que** *cj* as soon as; ~ **à présent** here and now; ~ **son retour** as soon as he was (*ou* is) back; ~ **réception** upon receipt; ~ **lors** *ad* from then on; ~ **lors que** *cj* from the moment (that).

désabusé, e [dāzábüzā] *a* disillusioned.

désaccord [dāzákor] *nm* disagreement.

désaccordé, e [dāzákordā] *a* (*MUS*) out of tune.

désacraliser [dāsákrálēzā] *vt* to deconsecrate; (*fig: profession, institution*) to take the mystique out of.

désaffecté, e [dāzáfektā] *a* disused.

désaffection [dāzáfeksyóǹ] *nf*: ~ **pour** estrangement from.

désagréable [dāzágrāábl(ə)] *a* unpleasant, disagreeable.

désagréablement [dāzágrāábləmáǹ] *ad* disagreeably, unpleasantly.

désagrégation [dāzágrāgásyóǹ] *nf* disintegration.

désagréger [dāzàgrāzhā]: **se** ~ *vi* to disintegrate, break up.

désagrément [dàzagramàn] *nm* annoyance, trouble *q*.

désaltérant, e [dāzáltārán, -ánt] *a* thirst-quenching.

désaltérer [dāzáltārā] *vt*: **se** ~ to quench one's thirst; **ça désaltère** it's thirst-quenching, it quenches your thirst.

désamorcer [dāzámorsā] *vt* to remove the primer from; (*fig*) to defuse; (: *prévenir*) to forestall.

désappointé, e [dāzápwàntā] *a* disappointed.

désapprobateur, trice [dāzáprobátœr, -trēs] *a* disapproving.

désapprobation [dāzáprobàsyón] *nf* disapproval.

désapprouver [dāzáprōōvā] *vt* to disapprove of. ♦

désarçonner [dāzàrsonā] *vt* to unseat, throw; (*fig*) to throw, nonplus, disconcert.

désargenté, e [dāzárzhántā] *a* impoverished.

désarmant, e [dāzàrmán, -ánt] *a* disarming.

désarmé, e [dāzàrmā] *a* (*fig*) disarmed.

désarmement [dāzàrməmán] *nm* disarmament.

désarmer [dāzàrmā] *vt* (*MIL*, *aussi fig*) to disarm; (*NAVIG*) to lay up; (*fusil*) to unload; (: *mettre le cran de sûreté*) to put the safety catch on ♦ *vi* (*pays*) to disarm; (*haine*) to wane; (*personne*) to give up.

désarrimer [dāzàrēmā] *vt* to shift.

désarroi [dāzàrwá] *nm* helplessness, disarray.

désarticulé, e [dāzártēkülā] *a* (*pantin*, *corps*) dislocated.

désarticuler [dāzártēkülā] *vt*: **se** ~ to contort (o.s.).

désassorti, e [dāzásortē] *a* unmatching, unmatched; (*magasin*, *marchand*) sold out.

désastre [dāzàstr(ə)] *nm* disaster.

désastreux, euse [dāzástrœ, -œz] *a* disastrous.

désavantage [dāzàvántázh] *nm* disadvantage; (*inconvénient*) drawback, disadvantage.

désavantager [dāzávántázhā] *vt* to put at a disadvantage.

désavantageux, euse [dāzávántázhœ, -œz] *a* unfavorable (*US*), unfavourable (*Brit*), disadvantageous.

désaveu [dāzávœ] *nm* repudiation; (*déni*) disclaimer.

désavouer [dāzávwā] *vt* to disown, repudiate, disclaim.

désaxé, e [dāzáksā] *a* (*fig*) unbalanced.

désaxer [dāzáksā] *vt* (*roue*) to put out of true; (*personne*) to throw off balance.

desceller [dāsálā] *vt* (*pierre*) to pull free.

descendance [dāsándáns] *nf* (*famille*) descendants *pl*, issue; (*origine*) descent.

descendant, e [dāsándán, -ánt] *vb voir* **descendre** ♦ *nm/f* descendant.

descendeur, euse [dāsándœr, -œz] *nm/f* (*SPORT*) downhiller.

descendre [dāsándr(ə)] *vt* (*escalier*, *montagne*) to go (*ou* come) down; (*valise*, *paquet*) to take *ou* get down; (*étagère etc*) to lower; (*fam*: *abattre*) to shoot down; (: *boire*) to knock back ♦ *vi* to go (*ou* come) down; (*passager*: *s'arrêter*) to get out, alight; (*niveau*, *température*) to go *ou* come down, fall, drop; (*marée*) to go out; ~ **à pied/en voiture** to walk/drive down, go down on foot/by car; ~ **de** (*famille*) to be descended from; ~ **du train** to get out of *ou* off the train; ~ **d'un arbre** to climb down from a tree; ~ **de cheval** to dismount, get off one's horse; ~ **à l'hôtel** to stay at a hotel; ~ **dans la rue** (*manifester*) to take to the streets; ~ **en ville** to go into town, go down town.

descente [dāsánt] *nf* descent, going down; (*chemin*) way down; (*SKI*) downhill (race); **au milieu de la** ~ halfway down; **freinez dans les** ~**s** use the brakes going downhill; ~ **de lit** bedside rug; ~ **(de police)** (police) raid.

descriptif, ive [deskrēptēf, -ēv] *a* descriptive ♦ *nm* explanatory leaflet.

description [deskrēpsyón] *nf* description.

désembourber [dāzánbōōrbā] *vt* to pull out of the mud.

désembourgeoiser [dāzánbōōrzhwàzā] *vt*: ~ **qn** to get sb out of his (*ou* her) middle-class attitudes.

désembuer [dāzánbüā] *vt* to defog (*US*), demist (*Brit*).

désemparé, e [dāzánpárā] *a* bewildered, distraught; (*bateau*, *avion*) crippled.

désemparer [dāzánpárā] *vi*: **sans** ~ without stopping.

désemplir [dāzánplēr] *vi*: **ne pas** ~ to be always full.

désenchanté, e [dāzánshántā] *a* disenchanted, disillusioned.

désenchantement [dāzánshántmán] *nm* disenchantment, disillusion.

désenclaver [dāzánklávā] *vt* to open up.

désencombrer [dāzánkónbrā] *vt* to clear.

désenfler [dāzánflā] *vi* to become less swollen.

désengagement [dāzángázhmán] *nm* (*POL*) disengagement.

désensabler [dāzánsáblā] *vt* to pull out of the sand.

désensibiliser [dāsánsēbēlēzā] *vt* (*MÉD*) to desensitize.

désenvenimer [dāzánvnēmā] *vt* (*plaie*) to remove the poison from; (*fig*) to take the sting out of.

désépaissir [dāzápāsēr] *vt* to thin (out).

déséquilibre [dāzākēlēbr(ə)] *nm* (*position*): **être en** ~ to be unsteady; (*fig*: *des forces*, *du budget*) imbalance; (*PSYCH*) unbalance.

déséquilibré, e [dāzākēlēbrā] *nm/f* (*PSYCH*) unbalanced person.

déséquilibrer [dāzākēlēbrā] *vt* to throw off balance.

désert, e [dāzer, -ert(ə)] *a* deserted ♦ *nm* desert.

déserter [dāzertā] *vi*, *vt* to desert.

déserteur [dāzertœr] *nm* deserter.

désertion [dāzersyón] *nf* desertion.

désertique [dāzertēk] *a* desert *cpd*; (*inculte*) barren, empty.

désescalade [dāzeskálád] *nf* (*MIL*) de-escalation.

désespérant, e [dāzespārán, -ánt] *a* hopeless, despairing.

désespéré, e [dāzespārā] *a* desperate; (*regard*) despairing; **état** ~ (*MÉD*) hopeless condition.

désespérément [dāzespārāmáń] *ad* desperately.

désespérer [dāzespārā] *vt* to drive to despair ♦ *vi*, **se** ~ *vi* to despair; ~ **de** to despair of.

désespoir [dāzespwár] *nm* despair; **être** *ou* **faire le** ~ **de qn** to be the despair of sb; **en** ~ **de cause** in desperation.

déshabillé, e [dāzábēyā] *a* undressed ♦ *nm* negligee.

déshabiller [dāzábēyā] *vt* to undress; **se** ~ to undress (o.s.).

déshabituer [dāzábētüä] *vt*: **se** ~ **de** to get out of the habit of.

désherbant [dāzerbáń] *nm* weed-killer.

désherber [dāzerbā] *vt* to weed.

déshérité, e [dāzārētā] *a* disinherited ♦ *nm/f*: **les** ~**s** (*pauvres*) the underprivileged, the deprived.

déshériter [dāzārētā] *vt* to disinherit.

déshonneur [dāzonœr] *nm* dishonor (*US*), dishonour (*Brit*), disgrace.

déshonorer [dāzonorā] *vt* to dishonor (*US*), dishonour (*Brit*), bring disgrace upon; **se** ~ to bring dishono(u)r on o.s.

déshumaniser [dāzümánēzā] *vt* to dehumanize.

déshydratation [dāzēdrátásyóń] *nf* dehydration.

déshydraté, e [dāzēdrátā] *a* dehydrated.

déshydrater [dāzēdrátā] *vt* to dehydrate.

desiderata [dāzēdárátá] *nmpl* requirements.

design [dēzáyn] *a* (*mobilier*) designer *cpd* ♦ *nm* (industrial) design.

désignation [dāzēnyásyóń] *nf* naming, appointment; (*signe, mot*) name, designation.

designer [dēzáyner] *nm* designer.

désigner [dāzēnyā] *vt* (*montrer*) to point out, indicate; (*dénommer*) to denote, refer to; (*nommer: candidat etc*) to name, appoint.

désillusion [dāzēlüzyóń] *nf* disillusion(ment).

désillusionner [dāzēlüzyonā] *vt* to disillusion.

désincarné, e [dāzańkárnā] *a* disembodied.

désinence [dāzēnáńs] *nf* ending, inflection.

désinfectant, e [dāzańfektáń, -áńt] *a, nm* disinfectant.

désinfecter [dāzańfektā] *vt* to disinfect.

désinformation [dāzańformásyóń] *nf* disinformation.

désintégrer [dāzańtāgrā] *vt*, **se** ~ *vi* to disintegrate.

désintéressé, e [dāzańtārāsā] *a* (*généreux, bénévole*) disinterested, unselfish.

désintéressement [dāzańtāresmáń] *nm* (*générosité*) disinterestedness.

désintéresser [dāzańtārāsā] *vt*: **se** ~ (**de**) to lose interest (in).

désintérêt [dāzańtāre] *nm* (*indifférence*) disinterest.

désintoxication [dāzańtoksēkásyóń] *nf* treatment for alcoholism (*ou* drug addiction); **faire une cure de** ~ to have *ou* undergo treatment for alcoholism (*ou* drug addiction).

désintoxiquer [dāzańtoksēkā] *vt* to treat for alcoholism (*ou* drug addiction).

désinvolte [dāzańvoltä] *a* casual, off-hand.

désinvolture [dāzańvoltür] *nf* casualness.

désir [dāzēr] *nm* wish; (*fort, sensuel*) desire.

désirer [dāzērā] *vt* to want, wish for; (*sexuelle-ment*) to desire; **je désire** ... (*formule de politesse*) I would like ...; **il désire que tu l'aides** he would like *ou* he wants you to help him; ~ **faire** to want *ou* wish to do; **ça laisse à** ~ it leaves something to be desired.

désireux, euse [dāzērœ, -œz] *a*: ~ **de faire** anxious to do.

désistement [dāzēstəmáń] *nm* withdrawal.

désister [dāzēstā]: **se** ~ *vi* to withdraw.

désobéir [dāzobāēr] *vi*: ~ (**à qn/qch**) to disobey (sb/sth).

désobéissance [dāzobāēsáńs] *nf* disobedience.

désobéissant, e [dāzobāēsáń, -áńt] *a* disobedient.

désobligeant, e [dāzoblēzháń, -áńt] *a* disagreeable, unpleasant.

désobliger [dāzoblēzhā] *vt* to offend.

désodorisant [dāzodorēzáń] *nm* air freshener, deodorizer.

désodoriser [dāzodorēzā] *vt* to deodorize.

désœuvré, e [dāzœvrā] *a* idle.

désœuvrement [dāzœvrəmáń] *nm* idleness.

désolant, e [dāzoláń, -áńt] *a* distressing.

désolation [dāzolásyóń] *nf* (*affliction*) distress, grief; (*d'un paysage etc*) desolation, devastation.

désolé, e [dāzolā] *a* (*paysage*) desolate; **je suis** ~ I'm sorry.

désoler [dāzolā] *vt* to distress, grieve; **se** ~ to be upset.

désolidariser [dāsolēdárēzā] *vt*: **se** ~ **de** *ou* **d'avec** to dissociate o.s. from.

désopilant, e [dāzopēláń, -áńt] *a* screamingly funny, hilarious.

désordonné, e [dāzordonā] *a* untidy, disorderly.

désordre [dāzordr(ə)] *nm* disorder(liness), untidiness; (*anarchie*) disorder; ~**s** *nmpl* (*POL*) disturbances, disorder *sg*; **en** ~ in a mess, untidy.

désorganiser [dāzorgánēzā] *vt* to disorganize.

désorienté, e [dāzoryáńtā] *a* disorientated; (*fig*) bewildered.

désormais [dāzorme] *ad* in the future, from now on.

désosser [dāzosā] *vt* to bone.

despote [despot] *nm* despot; (*fig*) tyrant.

despotique [despotēk] *a* despotic.

despotisme [despotēsm(ə)] *nm* despotism.

desquamer [deskwámā]: **se** ~ *vi* to flake off.

desquels, desquelles [dākel] *prép* + *pronom voir* **lequel**.

DESS *sigle m* (= *Diplôme d'études supérieures spécialisées*) *post-graduate diploma*.

dessaisir [dāsāzēr] *vt*: ~ **un tribunal d'une affaire** to remove a case from a court; **se** ~ **de** *vt* to give up, part with.

dessaler [dāsálā] *vt* (*eau de mer*) to desalinate; (*CULIN: morue etc*) to soak; (*fig fam: délurer*): ~ **qn** to teach sb a thing or two ♦ *vi* (*voilier*) to capsize.

Desse *abr* = **duchesse**.

desséché, e [dāsāshā] *a* dried up.

dessèchement [dāseshmáń] *nm* drying out; dryness; hardness.

dessécher [dāsāshā] *vt* (*terre, plante*) to dry out, parch; (*peau*) to dry out; (*volontairement: aliments etc*) to dry, dehydrate; *(fig: cœur)* to harden; **se ~** *vi* to dry out; *(peau, lèvres)* to go dry.

dessein [dāsaṅ] *nm* design; **dans le ~ de** with the intention of; **à ~** intentionally, deliberately.

desserrer [dāsārā] *vt* to loosen; *(frein)* to release; *(poing, dents)* to unclench; *(objets alignés)* to space out; **ne pas ~ les dents** not to open one's mouth.

dessert [dāser] *vb voir* **desservir ♦** *nm* dessert.

desserte [dāsert(ə)] *nf (table)* serving table; *(transport)*: **la ~ du village est assurée par autocar** there is a bus service to the village; **chemin** *ou* **voie de ~** service road.

desservir [dāservēr] *vt (ville, quartier)* to serve; *(: suj: voie de communication)* to lead into; *(suj: vicaire: paroisse)* to serve; *(nuire à: personne)* to do a disservice to; *(débarrasser)*: **~ (la table)** to clear the table.

dessiller [dāsēyā] *vt (fig)*: **~ les yeux à qn** to open sb's eyes.

dessin [dāsaṅ] *nm (œuvre, art)* drawing; *(motif)* pattern, design; *(contour)* (out)line; **le ~ industriel** draftsmanship *(US)*, draughtsmanship *(Brit)*; **~ animé** cartoon (film); **~ humoristique** cartoon.

dessinateur, trice [dāsēnátœr. -trēs] *nm/f* drawer; *(de bandes dessinées)* cartoonist; *(industriel)* draftsman *(US)*, draughtsman *(Brit)*; **dessinatrice de mode** fashion designer.

dessiner [dāsēnā] *vt* to draw; *(concevoir: carrosserie, maison)* to design; *(suj: robe: taille)* to show off; **se ~** *vi (forme)* to be outlined; *(fig: solution)* to emerge.

dessoûler [dāsōōlā] *vt, vi* to sober up.

dessous [dəsōō] *ad* underneath, beneath **♦** *nm* underside; *(étage inférieur)*: **les voisins du ~** the downstairs neighbors **♦** *nmpl (sous-vêtements)* underwear *sg*; *(fig)* hidden aspects; **en ~** underneath; *(fig: en catimini)* slyly, on the sly; **par ~** underneath; below; **de ~ le lit** from under the bed; **au-~** *ad* below; **au-~ de** *prép* below; *(peu digne de)* beneath; **au-~ de tout** the (absolute) limit; **avoir le ~** to get the worst of it.

dessous-de-bouteille [dəsōōdbōōtcy] *nm inv* coaster.

dessous-de-plat [dəsōōdplá] *nm inv* hot pad *(US)*, tablemat *(Brit)*.

dessous-de-table [dəsōōdtábl(ə)] *nm inv (fig)* bribe, under-the-counter payment.

dessus [dəsü] *ad* on top; *(collé, écrit)* on it **♦** *nm* top; *(étage supérieur)*: **les voisins/l'appartement du ~** the upstairs neighbors/apartment; **en ~** above; **par ~** *ad* over it **♦** *prép* over; **au-~** above; **au-~ de** above; **avoir/prendre le ~** to have/get the upper hand; **reprendre le ~** to get over it; **bras ~ bras dessous** arm in arm; **sens ~ dessous** upside down; *voir* **ci-, là-.**

dessus-de-lit [dəsüdlē] *nm inv* bedspread.

déstabiliser [dāstábēlēzā] *vt (POL)* to destabilize.

destin [destaṅ] *nm* fate; *(avenir)* destiny.

destinataire [destēnátēr] *nm/f (POSTES)* addressee; *(d'un colis)* consignee; *(d'un mandat)* payee; **aux risques et périls du ~**

at owner's risk.

destination [destēnásyóṅ] *nf (lieu)* destination; *(usage)* purpose; **à ~ de** *(avion etc)* bound for; *(voyageur)* bound for, traveling to.

destinée [destēnā] *nf* fate; *(existence, avenir)* destiny.

destiner [destēnā] *vt*: **~ qn à** *(poste, sort)* to destine sb for, intend sb to + *verbe*; **~ qn/qch à** *(prédestiner)* to mark sb/sth out for, destine sb/sth to + *verbe*; **~ qch à** *(envisager d'affecter)* to intend to use sth for; **~ qch à qn** *(envisager de donner)* to intend to give sth to sb, intend sb to have sth; *(adresser)* to intend sth for sb; **se ~ à l'enseignement** to intend to become a teacher; **être destiné à** *(sort)* to be destined to + *verbe*; *(usage)* to be intended *ou* meant for; *(suj: sort)* to be in store for.

destituer [destētüā] *vt* to depose; **~ qn de ses fonctions** to relieve sb of his duties.

destitution [destētüsyóṅ] *nf* deposition.

destructeur, trice [destrüktœr. -trēs] *a* destructive.

destructif, ive [destrüktēf. -ēv] *a* destructive.

destruction [destrüksyóṅ] *nf* destruction.

désuet, ète [dāsüc. -et] *a* outdated, outmoded.

désuétude [dāsüātüd] *nf*: **tomber en ~** to fall into disuse, become obsolete.

désuni, e [dāzünē] *a* divided, disunited.

désunion [dāzünyóṅ] *nf* disunity.

désunir [dāzünēr] *vt* to disunite; **se ~** *vi (athlète)* to break one's stride.

détachable [dātáshábl(ə)] *a (coupon etc)* tear-off *cpd*; *(capuche etc)* detachable.

détachant [dātásháṅ] *nm* stain remover.

détaché, e [dātáshā] *a (fig)* detached **♦** *nm/f (représentant)* person on an assignment.

détachement [dātáshmáṅ] *nm* detachment; *(fonctionnaire, employé)*: **être en ~** to be on an assignment.

détacher [dātáshā] *vt (enlever)* to detach, remove; *(délier)* to untie; *(ADMIN)*: **~ qn (auprès de ou à)** to assign sb (to); *(MIL)* to detail; *(vêtement: nettoyer)* to remove the stains from; **se ~** *vi (tomber)* to come off; to come out; *(se défaire)* to come undone; *(SPORT)* to pull *ou* break away; *(se délier: chien, prisonnier)* to break loose; **se ~ sur** to stand out against; **se ~ de** *(se désintéresser)* to grow away from.

détail [dātáy] *nm* detail; *(COMM)*: **le ~** retail; **prix de ~** retail price; **au ~** *ad (COMM)* retail; *(: individuellement)* separately; **donner le ~ de** to give a detailed account of; *(compte)* to give a breakdown of; **en ~** in detail.

détaillant, e [dātáyáṅ, -áṅt] *nm/f* retailer.

détaillé, e [dātáyā] *a (récit)* detailed.

détailler [dātáyā] *vt (COMM)* to sell retail; to sell separately; *(expliquer)* to explain in detail; to detail; *(examiner)* to look over, examine.

détaler [dātálā] *vi (lapin)* to scamper off; *(fam: personne)* to make off, skedaddle

(fam).
détartrant |dātártráň| *nm* scale remover.
détartrer |dātártrā| *vt* to scale *(US)*, descale *(Brit)*; *(dents)* to remove the tartar from.
détaxe |dātáks(ə)| *nf* *(réduction)* reduction in tax; *(suppression)* removal of tax; *(remboursement)* tax refund.
détaxer |dātáksā| *vt* *(réduire)* to reduce the tax on; *(ôter)* to remove the tax on.
détecter |dātektā| *vt* to detect.
détecteur |dātektœr| *nm* detector, sensor; ~ **de mensonges** lie detector; ~ **(de mines)** mine detector.
détection |dāteksyóň| *nf* detection.
détective |dātektēv| *nm* *(Brit:* policier*)* detective; ~ **(privé)** private detective *ou* investigator.
déteindre |dātǎňdɪ(ə)| *vi* to fade; *(fig)*: ~ **sur** to rub off on.
déteint, e |dātǎň, -áňt| *pp de* **déteindre**.
dételer |dɛtlā| *vt* to unharness; *(voiture, wagon)* to unhitch ♦ *vi (fig: s'arrêter)* to stop (working).
détendeur |dātǎňdœr| *nm* *(de bouteille à gaz)* regulator.
détendre |dātǎňdr(ə)| *vt* *(fil)* to slacken, loosen; *(relaxer: personne, atmosphère)* to relax; *(: situation)* to relieve; **se** ~ to lose its tension; to relax.
détendu, e |dātǎňdū| *a* relaxed.
détenir |dātnēr| *vt* *(fortune, objet, secret)* to be in possession of, have (in one's possession); *(prisonnier)* to detain, hold; *(record)* to hold; ~ **le pouvoir** to be in power.
détente |dātǎňt| *nf* relaxation; *(POL)* détente; *(d'une arme)* trigger; *(d'un athlète qui saute)* spring.
détenteur, trice |dātǎňtœr, -trēs| *nm/f* holder.
détention |dātǎňsyóň| *nf* *(voir détenir)* possession; detention; holding; ~ **préventive** (pre-trial) custody.
détenu, e |dātnū| *pp de* **détenir** ♦ *nm/f* prisoner.
détergent |dātɛrzháň| *nm* detergent.
détérioration |dātārɪyorāsyóň| *nf* damaging; deterioration.
détériorer |dātāryorā| *vt* to damage; **se** ~ *vi* to deteriorate.
déterminant, e |dātɛrmēnáň, -áňt| *a*: **un facteur** ~ a determining factor ♦ *nm (LING)* determiner.
détermination |dātɛrmēnāsyóň| *nf* determining; *(résolution)* decision; *(fermeté)* determination.
déterminé, e |dātɛrmēnā| *a* *(résolu)* determined; *(précis)* specific, definite.
déterminer |dātɛrmēnā| *vt* *(fixer)* to determine; *(décider)*: ~ **qn à faire** to decide sb to do; **se** ~ **à faire** to make up one's mind to do.
déterminisme |dātɛrmēnēsm(ə)| *nm* determinism.
déterré, e |dātārā| *nm/f*: **avoir une mine de** ~ to look like death warmed over *(US)* ou up *(Brit)*.
déterrer |dātārā| *vt* to dig up.
détersif, ive |dātɛrsēf, -ēv| *a*, *nm* detergent.
détestable |dātɛstábl(ə)| *a* foul, detestable.
détester |dātɛstā| *vt* to hate, detest.

détiendrai |dātyaňdrā|, **détiens** |dātyaň| *etc vb voir* **détenir**.
détonant, e |dātonáň, -áňt| *a*: **mélange** ~ explosive mixture.
détonateur |dātonātœr| *nm* detonator.
détonation |dātonásyóň| *nf* detonation, bang, report (of a gun).
détoner |dātonā| *vi* to detonate, explode.
détonner |dātonā| *vi* *(MUS)* to go out of tune; *(fig)* to clash.
détordre |dātordr(ə)| *vt* to untwist, unwind.
détour |dātōōr| *nm* detour; *(tournant)* bend, curve; *(fig: subterfuge)* roundabout means; **au** ~ **de chemin** at the bend in the path; **sans** ~ *(fig)* plainly.
détourné, e |dātōōrnā| *a* *(sentier, chemin, moyen)* roundabout.
détournement |dātōōrnəmáň| *nm* diversion, rerouting; ~ **d'avion** hijacking; ~ **(de fonds)** embezzlement *ou* misappropriation (of funds); ~ **de mineur** corruption of a minor.
détourner |dātōōrnā| *vt* to divert; *(avion)* to divert, reroute; *(: par la force)* to hijack; *(yeux, tête)* to turn away; *(de l'argent)* to embezzle, misappropriate; **se** ~ to turn away; ~ **la conversation** to change the subject; ~ **qn de son devoir** to divert sb from his duty; ~ **l'attention (de qn)** to distract *ou* divert (sb's) attention.
détracteur, trice |dātráktœr, -trēs| *nm/f* disparager, critic.
détraqué, e |dātrákā| *a* *(machine, santé)* broken-down ♦ *nm/f (fam)*: **c'est un** ~ he's unhinged.
détraquer |dātrákā| *vt* to put out of order; *(estomac)* to upset; **se** ~ *vi* to go wrong.
détrempe |dātráňp| *vt* *(ART)* tempera.
détrempé, e |dātráňpā| *a* *(sol)* sodden, waterlogged.
détremper |dātráňpā| *vt* *(peinture)* to water down.
détresse |dātrɛs| *nf* distress; **en** ~ *(avion etc)* in distress; **appel/signal de** ~ distress call/signal.
détriment |dātrēmáň| *nm*: **au** ~ **de** to the detriment of.
détritus |dātrētūs| *nmpl* rubbish *sg*, refuse *sg*, garbage *sg (US)*.
détroit |dātrwá| *nm* strait; **le** ~ **de Bering** *ou* **Behring** the Bering Strait; **le** ~ **de Gibraltar** the Strait of Gibraltar; **le** ~ **du Bosphore** the Bosphorus; **le** ~ **de Magellan** the Strait of Magellan, the Magellan Strait.
détromper |dātróňpā| *vt* to disabuse; **se** ~: **détrompez-vous** don't believe it.
détrôner |dātrōnā| *vt* to dethrone, depose; *(fig)* to oust, dethrone.
détrousser |dātrōōsā| *vt* to rob.
détruire |dātrüēr| *vt* to destroy; *(fig: santé, réputation)* to ruin; *(documents)* to shred.
détruit, e |dātrüē, -ēt| *pp de* **détruire**.
dette |dɛt| *nf* debt; ~ **publique** *ou* **de l'État** national debt.
DEUG |dœg| *sigle m* = *Diplôme d'études universitaires générales*.
deuil |dœy| *nm* *(perte)* bereavement; *(période)* mourning; *(chagrin)* grief; **porter le** ~ to wear mourning; **prendre le/être en** ~ to go into/be in mourning.

DEUST [dœst] *sigle m* = *Diplôme d'études universitaires scientifiques et techniques.*

deux [dœ̄] *num* two; **les** ~ both; **ses** ~ **mains** both his hands, his two hands; **à** ~ **pas** a short distance away; **tous les** ~ **mois** every two months, every other month; ~ **points** colon *sg*.

deuxième [dœ̄zyem] *num* second.

deuxièmement [dœ̄zyemmâń] *ad* secondly, in the second place.

deux-pièces [dœ̄pyes] *nm inv* (*tailleur*) two-piece (suit); (*de bain*) two-piece (swimsuit); (*appartement*) two-room apartment.

deux-roues [dœ̄rōō] *nm* two-wheeled vehicle.

deux-temps [dœ̄táń] *a* two-stroke.

devais [dəve] *etc vb voir* **devoir**.

dévaler [dāválā] *vt* to hurtle down.

dévaliser [dāválézā] *vt* to rob, burglarize (*US*), burgle (*Brit*).

dévalorisant, e [dāválorēzáń, -áńt] *a* depreciatory.

dévalorisation [dāválorēzásyôń] *nf* depreciation.

dévaloriser [dāválorēzā] *vt*, **se** ~ *vi* to depreciate.

dévaluation [dāválüâsyôń] *nf* depreciation; (*ÉCON: mesure*) devaluation.

dévaluer [dāválüā] *vt*, **se** ~ *vi* to devalue.

devancer [dəvâńsā] *vt* to be ahead of; (*distancer*) to get ahead of; (*arriver avant*) to arrive before; (*prévenir*) to anticipate; ~ **l'appel** (*MIL*) to enlist before call-up.

devancier, ière [dəvâńsyā, -yer] *nm/f* precursor.

devant [dəvâń] *vb voir* **devoir** ♦ *ad* in front; (*à distance: en avant*) ahead ♦ *prép* in front; ahead of; (*avec mouvement: passer*) past; (*fig*) before, in front of; (*: face à*) faced with, in the face of; (*: vu*) in view of ♦ *nm* front; **prendre les** ~**s** to make the first move; **de** ~ (*roue, porte*) front; **les pattes de** ~ the front legs, the forelegs; **par** ~ (*boutonner*) at the front; (*entrer*) the front way; **par-**~ **notaire** in the presence of a notary; **aller au-**~ **de qn** to go out to meet sb; **aller au-**~ **de** (*désirs de qn*) to anticipate; **aller au-**~ **des ennuis** *ou* **difficultés** to be asking for trouble.

devanture [dəvâńtür] *nf* (*façade*) storefront (*US*), (shop) front (*Brit*); (*étalage*) display; (store (*US*) *ou* shop (*Brit*)) window.

dévastateur, trice [dāvástátœr, -trēs] *a* devastating.

dévastation [dāvástâsyôń] *nf* devastation.

dévaster [dāvástā] *vt* to devastate.

déveine [dāven] *nf* rotten luck *q*.

développement [dāvlopmáń] *nm* development.

développer [dāvlopā] *vt*, **se** ~ *vi* to develop.

devenir [dəvnēr] *vb avec attribut* to become; ~ **instituteur** to become a teacher; **que sont-ils devenus?** what has become of them?

devenu, e [dəvnü] *pp de* **devenir**.

dévergondé, e [dāvergôńdā] *a* wild, shameless.

dévergonder [dāvergôńdā] *vt*, **se** ~ *vi* to run wild.

déverminer [dāvermēnā] *vt* (*INFORM*) to debug.

déverrouiller [dāverōōyā] *vt* to unbolt.

devers [dəver] *ad*: **par** ~ **soi** to oneself.

déverser [dāversā] *vt* (*liquide*) to pour (out); (*ordures*) to dump; **se** ~ **dans** (*fleuve, mer*) to flow into.

déversoir [dāverswár] *nm* overflow.

dévêtir [dāvātēr] *vt*, **se** ~ *vi* to undress.

devez [dəvā] *vb voir* **devoir**.

déviation [dāvyâsyôń] *nf* deviation; (*AUTO*) detour (*US*), diversion (*Brit*); ~ **de la colonne (vertébrale)** curvature of the spine.

dévider [dāvēdā] *vt* to unwind.

dévidoir [dāvēdwár] *nm* reel.

deviendrai [dəvyańdrā], **deviens** [dəvyań] *etc vb voir* **devenir**.

dévier [dāvyā] *vt* (*fleuve, circulation*) to divert; (*coup*) to deflect ♦ *vi* to veer (off course); (**faire**) ~ (*projectile*) to deflect; (*véhicule*) to push off course.

devin [dəvań] *nm* soothsayer, seer.

deviner [dəvēnā] *vt* to guess; (*prévoir*) to foretell, foresee; (*apercevoir*) to distinguish.

devinette [dəvēnet] *nf* riddle.

devint [dəvań] *etc vb voir* **devenir**.

devis [dəvē] *nm* estimate, quote; ~ **descriptif/estimatif** detailed/preliminary estimate.

dévisager [dāvēzázhā] *vt* to stare at.

devise [dəvēz] *nf* (*formule*) motto, watchword; (*ÉCON: monnaie*) currency; ~**s** *nfpl* (*argent*) currency *sg*.

deviser [dəvēzā] *vi* to converse.

dévisser [dāvēsā] *vt* to unscrew, undo; **se** ~ *vi* to come unscrewed.

de visu [dəvēzü] *ad*: **se rendre compte de qch** ~ to see sth for o.s.

dévitaliser [dāvētálēzā] *vt* (*dent*) to kill the nerve of.

dévoiler [dāvwálā] *vt* to unveil.

devoir [dəvwár] *nm* duty; (*SCOL*) homework assignment, homework *q*; (*: en classe*) exercise ♦ *vt* (*argent, respect*): ~ **qch (à qn)** to owe (sb) sth; (*suivi de l'infinitif: obligation*): **il doit le faire** he has to do it, he must do it; (*: fatalité*): **cela devait arriver un jour** it was bound to happen; (*: intention*): **il doit partir demain** he is (due) to leave tomorrow; (*: probabilité*): **il doit être tard** it must be late; **se faire un** ~ **de faire qch** to make it one's duty to do sth; ~**s de vacances** homework assigned for the holidays; **se** ~ **de faire qch** to be duty bound to do sth; **je devrais faire** I ought to *ou* should do; **tu n'aurais pas dû** you ought not to have *ou* shouldn't have; **comme il se doit** (*comme il faut*) as is right and proper.

dévolu, e [dāvolü] *a*: ~ **à** allotted to ♦ *nm*: **jeter son** ~ **sur** to fix one's choice on.

devons [dəvôń] *vb voir* **devoir**.

dévorant, e [dāvoráń, -áńt] *a* (*faim, passion*) raging.

dévorer [dāvorā] *vt* to devour; (*suj: feu, soucis*) to consume; ~ **qn/qch des yeux** *ou* **du regard** (*fig*) to eye sb/sth intently; (*: convoitise*) to eye sb/sth greedily.

dévot, e [dāvō, -ot] *a* devout, pious ♦ *nm/f* devout person; **un faux** ~ a falsely pious person.

dévotion [dāvōsyôń] *nf* devoutness; **être à la** ~ **de qn** to be totally devoted to sb; **avoir**

une ~ **pour qn** to worship sb.

dévoué, e [dāvwā] *a* devoted.

dévouement [dāvōōmáṅ] *nm* devotion, dedication.

dévouer [dāvwā]: **se** ~ *vi* (*se sacrifier*): **se** ~ **(pour)** to sacrifice o.s. (for); (*se consacrer*): **se** ~ **à** to devote *ou* dedicate o.s. to.

dévoyé, e [dāvwáyā] *a* delinquent.

dévoyer [dāvwáyā] *vt* to lead astray; **se** ~ *vi* to go off the rails; ~ **l'opinion publique** to influence public opinion.

devrai [dəvrā] *etc vb voir* **devoir**.

dextérité [dekstārētā] *nf* skill, dexterity.

dfc *abr* (= *désire faire connaissance*) *in personal column of newspaper*.

DG *sigle m* = **directeur général**.

dg. *abr* (= *décigramme*) dg.

DGE *sigle f* (= *Dotation globale d'équipement*) *state contribution to local government budget*.

DGSE *sigle f* (= *Direction générale des services extérieurs*) ≈ CIA (*US*), ≈ MI6 (*Brit*).

DI *sigle f* (*MIL*) = *division d'infanterie*.

dia [dyá] *abr* = **diapositive**.

diabète [dyábet] *nm* diabetes *sg*.

diabétique [dyábātēk] *nm/f* diabetic.

diable [dyábl(ə)] *nm* devil; **une musique du** ~ an unholy racket; **il fait une chaleur du** ~ it's fiendishly hot; **avoir le** ~ **au corps** to be the very devil.

diablement [dyâbləmáṅ] *ad* fiendishly.

diableries [dyâblərc] *nfpl* (*d'enfant*) devilment *sg*, mischief *sg*.

diablesse [dyábles] *nf* (*petite fille*) little devil.

diablotin [dyáblotan] *nm* imp; (*pétard*) cracker.

diabolique [dyábolēk] *a* diabolical.

diabolo [dyábolō] *nm* (*jeu*) diabolo; (*boisson*) lemonade and fruit cordial; ~**(-menthe)** lemonade and mint cordial.

diacre [dyákr(ə)] *nm* deacon.

diadème [dyádem] *nm* diadem.

diagnostic [dyágnostēk] *nm* diagnosis *sg*.

diagnostiquer [dyágnostēkā] *vt* to diagnose.

diagonal, e, aux [dyágonál, -ō] *a*, *nf* diagonal; **en** ~**e** diagonally; **lire en** ~**e** (*fig*) to skim through.

diagramme [dyágrám] *nm* chart, graph.

dialecte [dyálekt(ə)] *nm* dialect.

dialogue [dyálog] *nm* dialogue; ~ **de sourds** dialogue of the deaf.

dialoguer [dyálogā] *vi* to converse; (*POL*) to have a dialogue.

dialoguiste [dyálogēst(ə)] *nm/f* dialogue writer.

diamant [dyámáṅ] *nm* diamond.

diamantaire [dyámáṅter] *nm* diamond dealer.

diamétralement [dyámātrálmáṅ] *ad* diametrically; ~ **opposés** (*opinions*) diametrically opposed.

diamètre [dyámetr(ə)] *nm* diameter.

diapason [dyápázóṅ] *nm* tuning fork; (*fig*): **être/se mettre au** ~ **(de)** to be/get in tune (with).

diaphane [dyáfán] *a* diaphanous.

diaphragme [dyáfrágm(ə)] *nm* (*ANAT*, *PHOTO*) diaphragm; (*contraceptif*) diaphragm; **ouverture du** ~ (*PHOTO*) aperture.

diapo [dyápō], **diapositive** [dyápōzētēv] *nf* transparency, slide.

diaporama [dyáporámá] *nm* slide show.

diapré, e [dyáprā] *a* many-colored (*US*), many-coloured (*Brit*).

diarrhée [dyárā] *nf* diarrhea (*US*), diarrhoea (*Brit*).

diatribe [dyátrēb] *nf* diatribe.

dichotomie [dēkotomē] *nf* dichotomy.

dictaphone [dēktáfon] *nm* Dictaphone ®.

dictateur [dēktátœr] *nm* dictator.

dictatorial, e, aux [dēktátoryál, -ō] *a* dictatorial.

dictature [dēktátür] *nf* dictatorship.

dictée [dēktā] *nf* dictation; **prendre sous** ~ to take down (*sth dictated*).

dicter [dēktā] *vt* to dictate.

diction [dēksyóṅ] *nf* diction, delivery; **cours de** ~ speech production lesson(s).

dictionnaire [dēksyoner] *nm* dictionary; ~ **géographique** gazetteer.

dicton [dēktóṅ] *nm* saying, dictum.

didacticiel [dēdáktēsyel] *nm* educational software.

didactique [dēdáktēk] *a* didactic.

dièse [dyez] *nm* (*MUS*) sharp.

diesel [dyázel] *nm*, *a inv* diesel.

diète [dyct] *nf* diet; **être à la** ~ to be on a diet.

diététicien, ne [dyātātēsyaṅ, -en] *nm/f* dietician.

diététique [dyátātēk] *nf* dietetics *sg* ♦ *a*: **magasin** ~ health food store (*US*) *ou* shop (*Brit*).

dieu, x [dyœ̄] *nm* god; **D**~ God; **le bon D**~ the good Lord; **mon D**~! good heavens!

diffamant, e [dēfámáṅ, -áṅt] *a* slanderous, defamatory; libellous.

diffamation [dēfámásyóṅ] *nf* slander; (*écrite*) libel; **attaquer qn en** ~ to sue sb for slander (*ou* libel).

diffamatoire [dēfámátwár] *a* slanderous, defamatory; libellous.

diffamer [dēfámā] *vt* to slander, defame; to libel.

différé [dēfārā] *a* (*INFORM*): **traitement** ~ batch processing; **crédit** ~ deferred credit ♦ *nm* (*TV*): **en** ~ (pre-)recorded.

différemment [dēfárámáṅ] *ad* differently.

différence [dēfāráṅs] *nf* difference; **à la** ~ unlike.

différencier [dēfāráṅsyā] *vt* to differentiate; **se** ~ *vi* (*organisme*) to become differentiated; **se** ~ **de** to differentiate o.s. from; (*être différent*) to differ from.

différend [dēfāráṅ] *nm* difference (of opinion), disagreement.

différent, e [dēfāráṅ, -áṅt] *a*: ~ **(de)** different (from); ~**es objets** different *ou* various objects; **à** ~**es reprises** on various occasions.

différentiel, le [dēfāráṅsyel] *a*, *nm* differential.

différer [dēfārā] *vt* to postpone, put off ♦ *vi*: ~ **(de)** to differ (from); ~ **de faire** (*tarder*) to delay doing.

difficile [dēfēsēl] *a* difficult; (*exigeant*) hard to please, difficult (to please); **faire le** *ou* **la** ~ to be hard to please, be difficult.

difficilement [dēfēsēlmáṅ] *ad* (*marcher, s'expliquer etc*) with difficulty; ~ **lisible/compréhensible** difficult *ou* hard to read/

understand.

difficulté [dēfēkültā] *nf* difficulty; **en ~** (*bateau, alpiniste*) in trouble *ou* difficulties; **avoir de la ~ à faire** to have difficulty (in) doing.

difforme [dēform(ə)] *a* deformed, misshapen.

difformité [dēformētā] *nf* deformity.

diffracter [dēfráktā] *vt* to diffract.

diffus, e [dēfü, -üz] *a* diffuse.

diffuser [dēfüzā] *vt* (*chaleur, bruit, lumière*) to diffuse; (*émission, musique*) to broadcast; (*nouvelle, idée*) to circulate; (*COMM*: *livres, journaux*) to distribute.

diffuseur [dēfüzœr] *nm* diffuser; distributor.

diffusion [dēfüzyôń] *nf* diffusion; broadcast(ing); circulation; distribution.

digérer [dēzhārā] *vt* (*suj*: *personne*) to digest; (: *machine*) to process; (*fig*: *accepter*) to stomach, put up with.

digeste [dēzhest(ə)] *a* easily digestible.

digestible [dēzhestēbl(ə)] *a* digestible.

digestif, ive [dēzhestēf, -ēv] *a* digestive ♦ *nm* (after-dinner) liqueur.

digestion [dēzhestyôń] *nf* digestion.

digit [dēdzhēt] *nm*: ~ **binaire** binary digit.

digital, e, aux [dēzhētál, -ō] *a* digital.

digitale [dēzhētál] *nf* digitalis, foxglove.

digne [dēny] *a* dignified; ~ **de** worthy of; ~ **de foi** trustworthy.

dignitaire [dēnyēter] *nm* dignitary.

dignité [dēnyētā] *nf* dignity.

digression [dēgrāsyóń] *nf* digression.

digue [dēg] *nf* dike, dyke; (*pour protéger la côte*) sea wall.

dijonnais, e [dēzhone, -ez] *a* of *ou* from Dijon ♦ *nm/f*: **D~, e** inhabitant *ou* native of Dijon.

dilapider [dēlápēdā] *vt* to squander, waste; (*détourner*: *biens, fonds publics*) to embezzle, misappropriate.

dilater [dēlátā] *vt* to dilate; (*gaz, métal*) to cause to expand; (*ballon*) to distend; **se ~** *vi* to expand.

dilemme [dēlem] *nm* dilemma.

dilettante [dēlātáńt] *nm/f* dilettante [dilətant']; **en ~** in a dilettantish way.

diligence [dēlēzháńs] *nf* stagecoach, diligence; (*empressement*) dispatch; **faire ~** to make haste.

diligent, e [dēlēzháń, -áńt] *a* prompt and efficient; diligent.

diluant [dēlüáń] *nm* thinner(s).

diluer [dēlüā] *vt* to dilute.

diluvien, ne [dēlüvyań, -en] *a*: **pluie ~ne** torrential rain.

dimanche [dēmáńsh] *nm* Sunday; **le ~ des Rameaux/de Pâques** Palm/Easter Sunday; *voir aussi* **lundi**.

dîme [dēm] *nf* tithe.

dimension [dēmáńsyóń] *nf* (*grandeur*) size; (*gén pl*: *cotes, MATH*: *de l'espace*) dimension.

diminué, e [dēmēnüā] *a* (*personne*: *physiquement*) run-down; (: *mentalement*) less alert.

diminuer [dēmēnüā] *vt* to reduce, decrease; (*ardeur etc*) to lessen; (*personne*: *physiquement*) to undermine; (*dénigrer*) to belittle ♦ *vi* to decrease, diminish.

diminutif [dēmēnütēf] *nm* (*LING*) diminutive; (*surnom*) pet name.

diminution [dēmēnüsyôń] *nf* decreasing, diminishing.

dinatoire [dēnátwàr] *a*: **apéritif ~** ≈ evening buffet.

dinde [dańd] *nf* turkey; (*femme stupide*) goose.

dindon [dańdôń] *nm* turkey.

dindonneau, x [dańdonō] *nm* turkey poult.

dîner [dēnā] *nm* dinner ♦ *vi* to have dinner; ~ **d'affaires/de famille** business/family dinner.

dînette [dēnet] *nf* (*jeu*): **jouer à la ~** to play at having a tea party.

dingue [dańg] *a* (*fam*) crazy.

dinosaure [dēnōzor] *nm* dinosaur.

diode [dyod] *nf* diode.

diphasé, e [dēfàzā] *a* (*ÉLEC*) two-phase.

diphtérie [dēftārē] *nf* diphtheria.

diphtongue [dēftòńg] *nf* diphthong.

diplomate [dēplomát] *a* diplomatic ♦ *nm* diplomat; (*fig*: *personne habile*) diplomatist; (*CULIN*: *gâteau*) dessert made of sponge cake, candied fruit and custard, ≈ trifle (*Brit*).

diplomatie [dēplomásē] *nf* diplomacy.

diplomatique [dēplomátēk] *a* diplomatic.

diplôme [dēplōm] *nm* diploma; (*examen*) (diploma) examination.

diplômé, e [dēplōmā] *a* qualified.

dire [dēr] *nm*: **au ~ de** according to; **leur ~s** what they say ♦ *vt* to say; (*secret, mensonge*) to tell; ~ **l'heure/la vérité** to tell the time/the truth; **dis pardon/merci** say "I'm sorry"/thank you; ~ **qch à qn** to tell sb sth; ~ **à qn qu'il fasse** *ou* **de faire** to tell sb to do; ~ **que** to say that; **on dit que** they say that; **comme on dit** as they say; **on dirait que** it looks (*ou* sounds *etc*) as though; **on dirait du vin** you'd *ou* one would think it was wine; **que dites-vous de** (*penser*) what do you think of; **si cela lui dit** if he feels like it, if it appeals to him; **cela ne me dit rien** that doesn't appeal to me; **à vrai ~** ... to tell the truth ...; **pour ainsi ~** so to speak; **cela va sans ~** that goes without saying; **dis donc!, dites donc!** (*pour attirer l'attention*) hey!; (*au fait*) by the way; **et ~ que** ... and to think that ...; **ceci** *ou* **cela dit** that being said; (*à ces mots*) whereupon; **c'est dit, voilà qui est dit** so that's settled; **il n'y a pas à ~** there's no getting away from it; **c'est ~ si** ... that just shows that ...; **c'est beaucoup/peu ~** that's saying a lot/not saying much; **se ~** (*à soi-même*) to say to oneself; (*se prétendre*): **se ~ malade** *etc* to say (that) one is ill *etc*; **ça se dit ... en anglais** that is ... in English; **cela ne se dit pas comme ça** you don't say it like that; **se ~ au revoir** to say goodbye (to each other).

direct, e [dērekt] *a* direct ♦ *nm* (*train*) through train; **en ~** (*émission*) live; **train/bus ~** express train/bus.

directement [dērektəmáń] *ad* directly.

directeur, trice [dērektœr, -trēs] *nm/f* (*d'entreprise*) director; (*de service*) manager/eress; (*d'école*) principal; **comité ~** executive (*US*) *ou* management (*Brit*) committee; ~ **général** general manager; ~ **de thèse** ≈ dissertation advisor (*US*), Ph.D. supervisor (*Brit*).

direction [dēreksyóń] *nf* management; conducting; supervision; (*AUTO*) steering; (*sens*) direction; **sous la ~ de** (*MUS*) conducted by; **en ~ de** (*avion, train, bateau*) for; **"toutes ~s"** (*AUTO*) "all routes".

directive [dērektēv] *nf* directive, instruction.

directorial, e, aux [dērektoryàl, -ō] *a* (*bureau*) director's; manager's; principal's.

directrice [dērektrēs] *af, nf voir* **directeur**.

dirent [dēr] *vb voir* **dire**.

dirigeable [dērēzhábl(ə)] *a, nm*: (**ballon**) ~ dirigible.

dirigeant, e [dērēzháń, -áńt] *a* managerial; (*classes*) ruling ♦ *nm/f* (*d'un parti etc*) leader; (*d'entreprise*) manager, member of the management.

diriger [dērēzhā] *vt* (*entreprise*) to manage, run; (*véhicule*) to steer; (*orchestre*) to conduct; (*recherches, travaux*) to supervise, be in charge of; (*braquer: regard, arme*): ~ **sur** to point ou level ou aim at; (*fig: critiques*): ~ **contre** to aim at; **se** ~ (*s'orienter*) to find one's way; **se** ~ **vers** ou **sur** to make ou head for.

dirigisme [dērēzhēsm(ə)] *nm* (*ÉCON*) government intervention, interventionism.

dirigiste [dērēzhēst(ə)] *a* interventionist.

dis [dē], **disais** [dēze] *etc vb voir* **dire**.

discal, e, aux [dēskál, -ō] *a* (*MÉD*): **hernie ~e** slipped disk.

discernement [dēsernəmáń] *nm* discernment, judgment.

discerner [dēsernā] *vt* to discern, make out.

disciple [dēsēpl(ə)] *nm/f* disciple.

disciplinaire [dēsēplēner] *a* disciplinary.

discipline [dēsēplēn] *nf* discipline.

discipline, e [dēsēplēnā] *a* (well-)disciplined.

discipliner [deseplena] *vt* to discipline; (*cheveux*) to control.

discobole [dēskobol] *nm/f* discus thrower.

discontinu, e [dēskóńtēnü] *a* intermittent; (*bande: sur la route*) broken.

discontinuer [dēskóńtēnüā] *vi*: **sans ~** without stopping, without a break.

disconvenir [dēskóńvnēr] *vi*: **ne pas ~ de qch/que** not to deny sth/that.

discophile [dēskofēl] *nm/f* record enthusiast.

discordance [dēskordáńs] *nf* discordance; conflict.

discordant, e [dēskordáń, -áńt] *a* discordant; conflicting.

discorde [dēskord(ə)] *nf* discord, dissension.

discothèque [dēskotek] *nf* (*disques*) record collection; (*: dans une bibliothèque*): ~ **(de prêt)** record library; (*boîte de nuit*) disco(thèque).

discourais [dēskoōre] *etc vb voir* **discourir**.

discourir [dēskoōrēr] *vi* to discourse, hold forth.

discours [dēskoōr] *vb voir* **discourir** ♦ *nm* speech; ~ **direct/indirect** (*LING*) direct/indirect ou reported speech.

discrédit [dēskrādē] *nm*: **jeter le ~ sur** to discredit.

discréditer [dēskrādētā] *vt* to discredit.

discret, ète [dēskre, -et] *a* discreet; (*fig: musique, style*) unobtrusive; (*: endroit*) quiet.

discrètement [dēskretmáń] *ad* discreetly.

discrétion [dēskrāsyóń] *nf* discretion; **à la ~ de qn** at sb's discretion; in sb's hands; **à ~** (*boisson etc*) unlimited, as much as one wants.

discrétionnaire [dēskrāsyoner] *a* discretionary.

discrimination [dēskrēmēnásyóń] *nf* discrimination; **sans ~** indiscriminately.

discriminatoire [dēskrēmēnátwár] *a* discriminatory.

disculper [dēskülpā] *vt* to exonerate.

discussion [dēsküsyóń] *nf* discussion.

discutable [dēskütábl(ə)] *a* (*contestable*) doubtful; (*à débattre*) debatable.

discuté, e [dēskütā] *a* controversial.

discuter [dēskütā] *vt* (*contester*) to question, dispute; (*débattre: prix*) to discuss ♦ *vi* to talk; (*ergoter*) to argue; ~ **de** to discuss.

dise [dēz] *etc vb voir* **dire**.

disert, e [dēzer, -ert(ə)] *a* loquacious.

disette [dēzet] *nf* food shortage.

diseuse [dēzœz] *nf*: ~ **de bonne aventure** fortuneteller.

disgrâce [dēsgrâs] *nf* disgrace; **être en ~** to be in disgrace.

disgracieux, euse [dēsgrásyœ, -œz] *a* ungainly, awkward.

disjoindre [dēszhwàńdr(ə)] *vt* to take apart; **se ~** *vi* to come apart.

disjoint, e [dēszhwàń, -áńt] *pp de* **disjoindre** ♦ *a* loose.

disjoncteur [dēszhóńktœr] *nm* (*ÉLEC*) circuit breaker.

dislocation [dēslokásyóń] *nf* dislocation.

disloquer [dēslokā] *vt* (*membre*) to dislocate; (*chaise*) to dismantle; (*troupe*) to disperse; **se ~** *vi* (*parti, empire*) to break up; **se ~ l'épaule** to dislocate one's shoulder.

disparaître [dēspáretr(ə)] *vi* to disappear; (*à la vue*) to vanish, disappear; to be hidden ou concealed; (*être manquant*) to be missing, disappear; (*se perdre: traditions etc*) to die out; (*personne: mourir*) to die; **faire ~** (*objet, tache, trace*) to remove; (*personne*) to get rid of.

disparate [dēspárát] *a* disparate; (*couleurs*) ill-assorted.

disparité [dēspárētā] *nf* disparity.

disparition [dēspárēsyóń] *nf* disappearance.

disparu, e [dēspárü] *pp de* **disparaître** ♦ *nm/f* missing person; (*défunt*) departed; **être porté ~** to be reported missing.

dispendieux, euse [dēspáńdyœ, -œz] *a* extravagant, expensive.

dispensaire [dēspáńser] *nm* free (*US*) ou community (*Brit*) clinic.

dispense [dēspáńs] *nf* exemption; (*permission*) special permission; ~ **d'âge** special exemption from age limit.

dispenser [dēspáńsā] *vt* (*donner*) to lavish, bestow; (*exempter*): ~ **qn de** to exempt sb from; **se ~ de** *vt* to avoid, get out of.

disperser [dēspersā] *vt* to scatter; (*fig: son attention*) to dissipate; **se ~** *vi* to scatter; (*fig*) to dissipate one's efforts.

disponibilité [dēsponēbēlētā] *nf* availability; (*ADMIN*): **être en ~** to be on leave of absence; ~**s** *nfpl* (*COMM*) liquid assets.

disponible [dēsponēbl(ə)] *a* available.

dispos [dēspō] *am*: **(frais et)** ~ fresh (as a daisy).

disposé, e [dēspōzā] *a* (*d'une certaine manière*) arranged, laid-out; **bien/mal** ~ (*humeur*) in a good/bad mood; **bien/mal** ~ **pour** *ou* **envers qn** well/badly disposed towards sb; ~ **à** (*prêt à*) willing *ou* prepared to.

disposer [dēspōzā] *vt* (*arranger, placer*) to arrange; (*inciter*): ~ **qn à qch/faire qch** to dispose *ou* incline sb towards sth/to do sth ♦ *vi*: **vous pouvez** ~ you may leave; ~ **de** *vt* to have (at one's disposal); **se** ~ **à faire** to prepare to do, be about to do.

dispositif [dēspōzētēf] *nm* device; (*fig*) system, plan of action; set-up; (*d'un texte de loi*) operative part; ~ **de sûreté** safety device.

disposition [dēspōzēsyōn] *nf* (*arrangement*) arrangement, layout; (*humeur*) mood; (*tendance*) tendency; ~**s** *nfpl* (*mesures*) steps, measures; (*préparatifs*) arrangements; (*de loi, testament*) provisions; (*aptitudes*) bent *sg*, aptitude *sg*; **à la** ~ **de qn** at sb's disposal.

disproportion [dēsproporsyōn] *nf* disproportion.

disproportionné, e [dēsproporsyonā] *a* disproportionate, out of all proportion.

dispute [dēspüt] *nf* quarrel, argument.

disputer [dēspütā] *vt* (*match*) to play; (*combat*) to fight; (*course*) to run; **se** ~ *vi* to quarrel, have a quarrel; (*match, combat, course*) to take place; ~ **qch à qn** to fight with sb for *ou* over sth.

disquaire [dēsker] *nm/f* record dealer.

disqualification [dēskálēfēkâsyōn] *nf* disqualification.

disqualifier [dēskálēfyā] *vt* to disqualify; **se** ~ *vi* to bring discredit on o.s.

disque [dēsk(ə)] *nm* (*MUS*) record; (*INFORM*) disk, disc; (*forme, pièce*) disc; (*SPORT*) discus; ~ **compact** compact disc; ~ **dur** hard disk; ~ **d'embrayage** (*AUTO*) clutch plate; ~ **laser** compact disc; ~ **de stationnement** parking disk; ~ **système** system disk.

disquette [dēsket] *nf* diskette, floppy (disk); ~ **(à) simple/double densité** single/double density disk; ~ **une face/double face** single-/double-sided disk.

dissection [dēseksyōn] *nf* dissection.

dissemblable [dēsânblábl(ə)] *a* dissimilar.

dissemblance [dēsânblâns] *nf* dissimilarity, difference.

disséminer [dēsāmēnā] *vt* to scatter; (*chasser*) to disperse.

dissension [dēsânsyōn] *nf* dissension; ~**s** *nfpl* dissension.

disséquer [dēsākā] *vt* to dissect.

dissertation [dēsertâsyōn] *nf* (*SCOL*) essay.

disserter [dēsertā] *vi*: ~ **sur** to discourse upon.

dissident, e [dēsēdân, -ânt] *a*, *nm/f* dissident.

dissimilitude [dēsēmēlētüd] *nf* dissimilarity.

dissimulateur, trice [dēsēmültœr, -trēs] *a* dissembling ♦ *nm/f* dissembler.

dissimulation [dēsēmülâsyōn] *nf* concealing; (*duplicité*) dissimulation; ~ **de bénéfices/de revenus** concealment of profits/income.

dissimulé, e [dēsēmülā] (*personne: secret*) secretive; (*: fourbe, hypocrite*) deceitful.

dissimuler [dēsēmülā] *vt* to conceal; **se** ~ to conceal o.s.; to be concealed.

dissipation [dēsēpâsyōn] *nf* squandering; unruliness; (*débauche*) dissipation.

dissipé, e [dēsēpā] *a* (*indiscipliné*) unruly.

dissiper [dēsēpā] *vt* to dissipate; (*fortune*) to squander, fritter away; **se** ~ *vi* (*brouillard*) to clear, disperse; (*doutes*) to disappear, melt away; (*élève*) to become undisciplined *ou* unruly.

dissociable [dēsosyábl(ə)] *a* separable.

dissocier [dēsosyā] *vt* to dissociate; **se** ~ *vi* (*éléments, groupe*) to break up, split up; **se** ~ **de** (*groupe, point de vue*) to dissociate o.s. from.

dissolu, e [dēsolü] *a* dissolute.

dissoluble [dēsolübl(ə)] *a* (*POL: assemblée*) dissolvable.

dissolution [dēsolüsyōn] *nf* dissolving; (*POL, JUR*) dissolution.

dissolvant, e [dēsolvân, -ânt] *vb voir* **dissoudre** ♦ *nm* (*CHIMIE*) solvent; ~ **(gras)** nail polish remover.

dissonant, e [dēsonân, -ânt] *a* discordant.

dissoudre [dēsōōdr(ə)] *vt*, **se** ~ *vi* to dissolve.

dissous, oute [dēsōō, -ōōt] *pp de* **dissoudre**.

dissuader [dēsüádā] *vt*: ~ **qn de faire/de qch** to dissuade sb from doing/from sth.

dissuasion [dēsüázyōn] *nf* dissuasion; **force de** ~ deterrent power.

distance [dēstâns] *nf* distance; (*fig: écart*) gap; **à** ~ at *ou* from a distance; (*mettre en marche, commander*) by remote control; (*situé*) **à** ~ (*INFORM*) remote; **tenir qn à** ~ to keep sb at a distance; **se tenir à** ~ to keep one's distance; **à une** ~ **de 10 km, à 10 km de** ~ 10 km away, at a distance of 10 km; **à 2 ans de** ~ with a gap of 2 years; **prendre ses** ~**s** to spread out; **garder ses** ~**s** to keep one's distance; **tenir la** ~ (*SPORT*) to cover the distance, last the course; ~ **focale** (*PHOTO*) focal length.

distancer [dēstânsā] *vt* to outdistance, leave behind.

distancier [dēstânsyā]: **se** ~ *vi* to distance o.s.

distant, e [dēstân, -ânt] *a* (*réservé*) distant, aloof; (*éloigné*) distant, far away; ~ **de** (*lieu*) far away *ou* a long way from; ~ **de 5 km** (*d'un lieu*) 5 km away (from a place).

distendre [dēstândr(ə)] *vt*, **se** ~ *vi* to distend.

distillation [dēstēlâsyōn] *nf* distillation, distilling.

distillé, e [dēstēlā] *a*: **eau** ~**e** distilled water.

distiller [dēstēlā] *vt* to distill (*US*) *ou* distil (*Brit*); (*fig*) to exude; to elaborate.

distillerie [dēstēlrē] *nf* distillery.

distinct, e [dēstań(kt), dēstańkt(ə)] *a* distinct.

distinctement [dēstańktəmân] *ad* distinctly.

distinctif, ive [dēstańktēf, -ēv] *a* distinctive.

distinction [dēstańksyōn] *nf* distinction.

distingué, e [dēstańgā] *a* distinguished.

distinguer [dēstańgā] *vt* to distinguish; **se** ~ *vi* (*s'illustrer*) to distinguish o.s.; (*différer*): **se** ~ **(de)** to distinguish o.s. *ou* be distinguished (from).

distinguo [dēstańgō] *nm* distinction.

distraction [dēstráksyōn] *nf* (*manque*

d'attention) absent-mindedness; (oubli) lapse (in concentration ou attention); (détente) diversion, recreation; (passe-temps) distraction, entertainment.

distraire [dēstrer] vt (déranger) to distract; (divertir) to entertain, divert; (détourner: somme d'argent) to divert, misappropriate; **se ~** to amuse ou enjoy o.s.

distrait, e [dēstre, -et] pp de **distraire ♦** a absent-minded.

distraitement [dēstretmáń] ad absent-mindedly.

distrayant, e [dēstreyáń, -áńt] vb voir **distraire ♦** a entertaining.

distribanque [dēstrēbáńk] nm automated teller machine (ATM).

distribuer [dēstrēbüä] vt to distribute; to hand out; (CARTES) to deal (out); (courrier) to deliver.

distributeur [dēstrēbütœr] nm (AUTO, COMM) distributor; (automatique) (vending) machine; **~ de billets** (RAIL) ticket machine; (BANQUE) automated teller machine (ATM).

distribution [dēstrēbüsyôń] nf distribution; (postale) delivery; (choix d'acteurs) casting; **circuits de ~** (COMM) distribution network; **~ des prix** (SCOL) awards ceremony (US), prize giving (Brit).

district [dēstrēk(t)] nm district.

dit, e [dē, dēt] pp de **dire ♦** a (fixé): **le jour ~** the appointed day; (surnommé): **X, ~ Pierrot** X, known as ou called Pierrot.

dites [dēt] vb voir **dire.**

dithyrambique [dētēráńbēk] a eulogistic.

DIU sigle m (= dispositif intra-utérin) IUD.

diurétique [dyuratek] a, nm diuretic.

diurne [dyürn(ə)] a diurnal, daytime cpd.

divagations [dēvágásyôń] nfpl ramblings; ravings.

divaguer [dēvágä] vi to ramble; (malade) to rave.

divan [dēváń] nm divan.

divan-lit [dēváńlē] nm divan (bed).

divergent, e [dēverzháń, -áńt] a divergent.

diverger [dēverzhä] vi to diverge.

divers, e [dēvcr, -crs(ə)] a (varié) diverse, varied; (différent) different, various ♦ dét (plusieurs) various, several; **(frais) ~** (COMM) sundries, miscellaneous (expenses); **"~"** (rubrique) "miscellaneous".

diversement [dēversəmáń] ad in various ou diverse ways.

diversification [dēversēfēkásyôń] nf diversification.

diversifier [dēversēfyä] vt, **se ~** vi to diversify.

diversion [dēversyôń] nf diversion; **faire ~ to** create a diversion.

diversité [dēversētä] nf diversity, variety.

divertir [dēvertēr] vt to amuse, entertain; **se ~** to amuse ou enjoy o.s.

divertissant, e [dēvertēsáń, -áńt] a entertaining.

divertissement [dēvertēsmáń] nm entertainment; (MUS) divertimento, divertissement.

dividende [dēvēdáńd] nm (MATH, COMM) dividend.

divin, e [dēvań, -ēn] a divine; (fig: excellent)

heavenly, divine.

divinateur, trice [dēvēnátœr, -trēs] a perspicacious.

divinatoire [dēvēnátwár] a (art, science) divinatory; **baguette ~** divining rod.

diviniser [dēvēnēzä] vt to deify.

divinité [dēvēnētä] nf divinity.

divisé, e [dēvēzä] a divided.

diviser [dēvēzä] vt (gén, MATH) to divide; (morceler, subdiviser) to divide (up), split (up); **se ~ en** to divide into; **~ par** to divide by.

diviseur [dēvēzœr] nm (MATH) divisor.

divisible [dēvēzēbl(ə)] a divisible.

division [dēvēzyôń] nf (gén) division; **~ du travail** (ÉCON) division of labor.

divisionnaire [dēvēsyoner] a: **commissaire ~** ≈ police chief (US), ≈ chief superintendent (Brit).

divorce [dēvors(ə)] nm divorce.

divorcé, e [dēvorsä] nm/f divorcee.

divorcer [dēvorsä] vi to get a divorce, get divorced; **~ de** ou **d'avec qn** to divorce sb.

divulgation [dēvülgásyôń] nf disclosure.

divulguer [dēvülgä] vt to divulge, disclose.

dix [dē, dēs, dēz] num ten.

dix-huit [dēzüēt] num eighteen.

dix-huitième [dēzüētyem] num eighteenth.

dixième [dēzyem] num tenth.

dix-neuf [dēznœf] num nineteen.

dix-neuvième [dēznœvyem] num nineteenth.

dix-sept [dēset] num seventeen.

dix-septième [dēsetyem] num seventeenth.

dizaine [dēzen] nf (10) ten; (environ 10): **une ~** (de) about ten, ten or so.

Djakarta [dzhákártá] n Djakarta.

Djibouti [dzhēbōōtē] n Djibouti.

DM abr (= Deutschmark) DM.

dm. abr (= décimètre) dm.

do [dō] nm (note) C; (en chantant la gamme) do(h).

docile [dosēl] a docile.

docilité [dosēlētä] nf docility.

dock [dok] nm dock; (hangar, bâtiment) warehouse.

docker [dokcr] nm docker.

docte [dokt(ə)] a (péj) learned.

docteur [doktœr] nm doctor; **~ en médecine** doctor of medicine.

doctoral, e, aux [doktorál, -ō] a pompous, bombastic.

doctorat [doktorä] nm: **~ (d'Université)** ≈ doctorate; **~ d'État** ≈ PhD; **~ de troisième cycle** ≈ doctorate.

doctoresse [doktores] nf lady doctor.

doctrinaire [doktrēner] a doctrinaire; (sentencieux) pompous, sententious.

doctrinal, e, aux [doktrēnál, ō] a doctrinal.

doctrine [doktrēn] nf doctrine.

document [dokümáń] nm document.

documentaire [dokümáńter] a, nm documentary.

documentaliste [dokümáńtálēst(ə)] nm/f archivist; (PRESSE, TV) researcher.

documentation [dokümáńtásyôń] nf documentation, literature; (PRESSE, TV: service) research.

documenté, e [dokümáńtä] a well-informed, well-documented; well-researched.

documenter [dokümâṅtā] *vt*: **se ~ (sur)** to gather information *ou* material (on *ou* about).

Dodécanèse [dodākânez] *nm* Dodecanese (Islands).

dodeliner [dodlēnā] *vi*: **~ de la tête** to nod one's head gently.

dodo [dodō] *nm*: **aller faire ~** to go to beddy-bye.

dodu, e [dodü] *a* plump.

dogmatique [dogmátēk] *a* dogmatic.

dogme [dogm(ə)] *nm* dogma.

dogue [dog] *nm* mastiff.

doigt [dwá] *nm* finger; **à deux ~s de** within an ace *ou* an inch of; **un ~ de lait/whisky** a drop of milk/whiskey; **désigner** *ou* **montrer du ~** to point at; **au ~ et à l'œil** to the letter; **connaître qch sur le bout du ~** to know sth backwards; **mettre le ~ sur la plaie** (*fig*) to find the sensitive spot; **~ de pied** toe.

doigté [dwátā] *nm* (*MUS*) fingering; (*fig: habileté*) diplomacy, tact.

doigtier [dwátyā] *nm* fingerstall.

dois [dwá], **doive** [dwáv] *etc vb voir* **devoir**.

doléances [dolāâṅs] *nfpl* complaints; (*réclamations*) grievances.

dolent, e [dolâṅ, -âṅt] *a* doleful, mournful.

dollar [dolár] *nm* dollar.

dolmen [dolmen] *nm* dolmen.

DOM [dāōem, dom] *sigle m ou mpl* = *Département(s) d'outre-mer*.

domaine [domen] *nm* estate, property; (*fig*) domain, field; **tomber dans le ~ public** (*livre etc*) to be out of copyright; **dans tous les ~s** in all areas.

domanial, e, aux [dományál, -ō] *a* national, state *cpd*.

dôme [dōm] *nm* dome.

domestication [domestēkâsyôṅ] *nf* (*voir domestiquer*) domestication; harnessing.

domesticité [domestēsētā] *nf* (domestic) staff.

domestique [domestēk] *a* domestic ♦ *nm/f* servant, domestic.

domestiquer [domestēkā] *vt* to domesticate; (*vent, marées*) to harness.

domicile [domēsēl] *nm* home, place of residence; **à ~** at home; **élire ~** à to take up residence in; **sans ~ fixe** of no fixed abode; **~ conjugal** marital home; **~ légal** domicile.

domicilié, e [domēsēlyā] *a*: **êtré ~** à to have one's home in *ou* at.

dominant, e [domēnâṅ, -âṅt] *a* dominant; (*plus important*) predominant.

dominateur, trice [domēnátœr, -trēs] *a* dominating; (*qui aime à dominer*) domineering.

domination [domēnâsyôṅ] *nf* domination.

dominer [domēnā] *vt* to dominate; (*passions etc*) to control, master; (*surpasser*) to outclass, surpass; (*surplomber*) to tower above, dominate ♦ *vi* to be in the dominant position; **se ~** to control o.s.

dominicain, e [domēnēkaṅ, -en] *a* Dominican.

dominical, e, aux [domēnēkál, -ō] *a* Sunday *cpd*, dominical.

Dominique [domēnēk] *nf*: **la ~** Dominica.

domino [domēnō] *nm* domino; **~s** *nmpl* (*jeu*) dominoes *sg*.

dommage [domázh] *nm* (*préjudice*) harm, in-

jury; (*dégâts, pertes*) damage *q*; **c'est ~ de faire/que** it's a shame *ou* pity to do/that; **~s corporels** physical injury.

dommages-intérêts [domázh(əz)aṅtāre] *nmpl* damages.

dompter [dôṅtā] *vt* to tame.

dompteur, euse [dôṅtœr, -œz] *nm/f* trainer; (*de lion*) liontamer.

DOM-TOM [domtom] *sigle m ou mpl* = *Département(s) d'outre-mer/Territoire(s) d'outre-mer*.

don [dôṅ] *nm* (*cadeau*) gift; (*charité*) donation; (*aptitude*) gift, talent; **avoir des ~s pour** to have a gift *ou* talent for; **faire ~ de** to make a gift of; **~ en argent** cash donation.

donateur, trice [donátœr, -trēs] *nm/f* donor.

donation [donâsyôṅ] *nf* donation.

donc [dôṅk] *cj* therefore, so; (*après une digression*) so, then; (*intensif*): **voilà ~ la solution** so there's the solution; **je disais ~ que** ... as I was saying, ...; **venez ~ dîner à la maison** do come for dinner; **allons ~!** come now!; **faites ~** go ahead.

donjon [dôṅzhôṅ] *nm* keep.

donnant, e [donáṅ, -âṅt] *a*: **~, ~** fair's fair.

donne [don] *nf* (*CARTES*): **il y a mauvaise** *ou* **fausse ~** there's been a misdeal.

donné, e [donā] *a* (*convenu*) given; (*pas cher*) dirt cheap, very cheap ♦ *nf* (*MATH, INFORM, gén*) datum (*pl* data); **c'est ~** it's a gift; **étant ~** ... given ....

donner [donā] *vt* to give; (*vieux habits etc*) to give away; (*spectacle*) to put on; (*film*) to show; **~ qch à qn** to give sb sth, give sth to sb; **~ sur** (*suj: fenêtre, chambre*) to look (*out*) onto; **~ dans** (*piège etc*) to fall into; **faire ~ l'infanterie** (*MIL*) to send in the infantry; **~ l'heure à qn** to tell sb the time; **~ le ton** (*fig*) to set the tone; **~ à penser/entendre que** ... to make one think/give one to understand that ...; **se ~ à fond (à son travail)** to give one's all (to one's work), devote o.s. heart and soul (to one's work); **se ~ du mal** *ou* **de la peine (pour faire qch)** to go to a lot of trouble (to do sth); **s'en ~ à cœur joie** (*fam*) to have a great time.

donneur, euse [donœr, -œz] *nm/f* (*MÉD*) donor; (*CARTES*) dealer; **~ de sang** blood donor.

dont [dôṅ] *pronom relatif*: **la maison ~ je vois le toit** the house whose roof I can see, the house I can see the roof of; **la maison ~ le toit est rouge** the house whose roof is red *ou* the roof of which is red; **l'homme ~ je connais la sœur** the man whose sister I know; **10 blessés, ~ 2 grièvement** 10 injured, 2 of them seriously; **2 livres, ~ l'un est** ... 2 books, one of which is ...; **il y avait plusieurs personnes, dont Gabrielle** there were several people, among them Gabrielle; **le fils ~ il est si fier** the son he's so proud of; **ce ~ je parle** what I'm talking about; *voir adjectifs et verbes à complément prépositionnel*: **responsable de, souffrir de** etc.

donzelle [dôṅzel] *nf* (*péj*) young madam.

dopage [dopázh] *nm* doping.

dopant [dopáṅ] *nm* dope.

doper [dopā] *vt* to dope; **se** ~ to take dope.

doping [dopĕng] *nm* doping; *(excitant)* dope.

dorade [dorád] *nf* = **daurade**.

doré, e [dorā] *a* golden; *(avec dorure)* gilt, gilded.

dorénavant [dorānávǎń] *ad* from now on, henceforth.

dorer [dorā] *vt* *(cadre)* to gild; **(faire)** ~ *(CULIN)* to brown; *(: gâteau)* to glaze; **se** ~ **au soleil** to sunbathe; ~ **la pilule à qn** to sugarcoat *(US)* ou sugar *(Brit)* the pill for sb.

dorloter [dorlotā] *vt* to pamper, cosset *(Brit)*; **se faire** ~ to be pampered *ou* cosseted.

dormant, e [dormáń, -áńt] *a*: **eau** ~**e** still water.

dorme [dorm(ə)] *etc vb voir* **dormir**.

dormeur, euse [dormœr, -œz] *nm/f* sleeper.

dormir [dormēr] *vi* to sleep; *(être endormi)* to be asleep; ~ **à poings fermés** to sleep very soundly.

dorsal, e, aux [dorsál, -ō] *a* dorsal; *voir* **rouleau**.

dortoir [dortwár] *nm* dormitory.

dorure [dorür] *nf* gilding.

doryphore [dorēfor] *nm* Colorado beetle.

dos [dō] *nm* back; *(de livre)* spine; **"voir au** ~**"** "see other side"; **robe décolletée dans le** ~ low-backed dress; **de** ~ from the back, from behind; ~ **à** ~ back to back; **sur le** ~ on one's back; **à** ~ **de chameau** riding on a camel; **avoir bon** ~ to be a good excuse; **se mettre qn à** ~ to turn sb against one.

dosage [dōzázh] *nm* mixture.

dos-d'âne [dōdán] *nm* humpback; **pont en** ~ humpbacked bridge.

dose [dōz] *nf* (*MÉD*) dose; **forcer la** ~ *(fig)* to overstep the mark.

doser [dōzā] *vt* to measure out; *(mélanger)* to mix in the correct proportions; *(fig)* to expend in the right amounts *ou* proportions; to strike a balance between.

doseur [dōzœr] *nm* measure; **bouchon** ~ measuring cap.

dossard [dōsár] *nm* number *(worn by competitor)*.

dossier [dōsyā] *nm* *(renseignements, fichier)* file; *(enveloppe)* folder, file; *(de chaise)* back; *(PRESSE)* feature; **le** ~ **social/monétaire** *(fig)* the social/financial question; ~ **suspendu** suspension file.

dot [dot] *nf* dowry.

dotation [dotâsyóń] *nf* block grant; endowment.

doté, e [dotā] *a*: ~ **de** equipped with.

doter [dotā] *vt*: ~ **qn/qch de** to equip sb/sth with.

douairière [dweryer] *nf* dowager.

douane [dwán] *nf* *(poste, bureau)* customs *pl*; *(taxes)* (customs) duty; **passer la** ~ to go through customs; **en** ~ *(marchandises, entrepôt)* bonded.

douanier, ière [dwányā, -yer] *a* customs *cpd* ♦ *nm* customs officer.

doublage [dōōblázh] *nm* (*CINÉMA*) dubbing.

double [dōōbl(ə)] *a, ad* double ♦ *nm* (*2 fois plus*): **le** ~ **(de)** twice as much *(ou* many) (as), double the amount *(ou* number) (of); *(autre exemplaire)* duplicate, copy; *(sosie)* double; *(TENNIS)* doubles *sg*; **voir** ~ to see double; **en** ~ **(exemplaire)** in duplicate; **faire** ~ **emploi** to be redundant; **à** ~ **sens** with a double meaning; **à** ~ **tranchant** two-edged; ~ **carburateur** twin carburetor; **à** ~**s commandes** dual-control; ~ **messieurs/mixte** men's/mixed doubles *sg*; ~ **toit** *(de tente)* rainfly *(US)*, fly sheet *(Brit)*; ~ **vue** second sight.

doublé, e [dōōblā] *a* *(vêtement)*: ~ **(de)** lined (with).

doublement [dōōbləmáń] *nm* doubling; two-fold increase ♦ *ad* doubly; *(pour deux raisons)* in two ways, on two counts.

doubler [dōōblā] *vt* *(multiplier par 2)* to double; *(vêtement)* to line; *(dépasser)* to overtake, pass; *(film)* to dub; *(acteur)* to stand in for ♦ *vi* to double, increase twofold; **se** ~ **de** to be coupled with; ~ **(la classe)** *(SCOL)* to repeat a year; ~ **un cap** *(NAVIG)* to round a cape; *(fig)* to get over a hurdle.

doublure [dōōblür] *nf* lining; (*CINÉMA*) stand-in.

douce [dōōs] *af voir* **doux**.

douceâtre [dōōsátr(ə)] *a* sickly sweet.

doucement [dōōsmáń] *ad* gently; *(à voix basse)* softly; *(lentement)* slowly.

doucereux, euse [dōōsrœ, -œz] *a* *(péj)* sugary.

douceur [dōōsœr] *nf* softness; sweetness; mildness; gentleness; ~**s** *nfpl* *(friandises)* candy *sg* *(US)*, sweets *(Brit)*; **en** ~ gently.

douche [dōōsh] *nf* shower; ~**s** *nfpl* shower room *sg*; **prendre une** ~ to have *ou* take a shower; ~ **écossaise** *(fig)*, ~ **froide** *(fig)* letdown.

doucher [dōōshā] *vt*: ~ **qn** to give sb a shower; *(mouiller)* to drench sb; *(fig)* to tell sb off; **se** ~ to have *ou* take a shower.

doudoune [dōōdōōn] *nf* padded jacket; *(fam)* boob.

doué, e [dwā] *a* gifted, talented; ~ **de** endowed with; **être** ~ **pour** to have a gift for.

douille [dōōy] *nf* (*ÉLEC*) socket; *(de projectile)* case.

douillet, te [dōōye, -et] *a* cosy; *(péj)* soft.

douleur [dōōlœr] *nf* pain; *(chagrin)* grief, distress; **ressentir des** ~**s** to feel pain; **il a eu la** ~ **de perdre son père** he suffered the grief of losing his father.

douloureux, euse [dōōlōōrœ, -œz] *a* painful.

doute [dōōt] *nm* doubt; **sans** ~ no doubt; *(probablement)* probably; **sans nul** *ou* **aucun** ~ without (a) doubt; **hors de** ~ beyond doubt; **nul** ~ **que** there's no doubt that; **mettre en** ~ to call into question; **mettre en** ~ **que** to question whether.

douter [dōōtā] *vt* to doubt; ~ **de** *vt* *(allié)* to doubt, have (one's) doubts about; *(résultat)* to be doubtful of; ~ **que** to doubt whether *ou* if; **j'en doute** I have my doubts; **se** ~ **de qch/que** to suspect sth/that; **je m'en doutais** I suspected as much; **il ne se doutait de rien** he didn't suspect a thing.

douteux, euse [dōōtœ, -œz] *a* *(incertain)* doubtful; *(discutable)* dubious, questionable; *(péj)* dubious-looking.

douve [dōōv] *nf* *(de château)* moat; *(de tonneau)* stave.

Douvres [dŌŌvr(ə)] *n* Dover.

doux, douce [dŌŌ, dŌŌs] *a (lisse, moelleux, pas vif: couleur, non calcaire: eau)* soft; *(sucré, agréable)* sweet; *(peu fort: moutarde etc, clément: climat)* mild; *(pas brusque)* gentle; **en douce** *(partir etc)* on the q.t.

douzaine [dŌŌzen] *nf (12)* dozen; *(environ 12)*: **une ~ (de)** a dozen or so, twelve or so.

douze [dŌŌz] *num* twelve; **les D~** *(membres de la CEE)* the Twelve.

douzième [dŌŌzyem] *num* twelfth.

doyen, ne [dwáyań, -en] *nm/f (en âge, ancienneté)* most senior member; *(de faculté)* dean.

DPLG *sigle (= diplômé par le gouvernement) extra certificate for architects, engineers etc.*

Dr *abr (= docteur)* Dr.

dr. *abr (= droit(e))* R, r.

draconien, ne [drákonyań, -en] *a* draconian, stringent.

dragage [drágázh] *nm* dredging.

dragée [drázhā] *nf* sugared almond; *(MÉD)* (sugar-coated) pill.

dragéifié, e [drázhāefyā] *a (MÉD)* sugar-coated.

dragon [drágoń] *nm* dragon.

drague [drág] *nf (filet)* dragnet; *(bateau)* dredger.

draguer [drágā] *vt (rivière: pour nettoyer)* to dredge; *(: pour trouver qch)* to drag; *(fam)* to try and pick up ♦ *vi (fam)* to try and pick sb up.

dragueur [drágœr] *nm (aussi: ~ de mines)* minesweeper; *(fam)*: **quel ~!** he's a great one for picking up girls!

drain [drań] *nm (MÉD)* drain.

drainage [drenázh] *nm* drainage.

drainer [drānā] *vt* to drain; *(fig: visiteurs, région)* to drain off.

dramatique [drámátēk] *a* dramatic; *(tragique)* tragic ♦ *nf (TV)* (television) drama.

dramatiser [drámátēzā] *vt* to dramatize.

dramaturge [drámátürzh(ə)] *nm* dramatist, playwright.

drame [drám] *nm (THÉÂTRE)* drama; *(catastrophe)* drama, tragedy; **~ familial** family drama.

drap [drá] *nm (de lit)* sheet; *(tissu)* woolen *(US) ou* woollen *(Brit)* fabric; **~ de plage** beach towel.

drapé [drápā] *nm (d'un vêtement)* hang.

drapeau, x [drápō] *nm* flag; **sous les ~x** in the army.

draper [drápā] *vt* to drape; *(robe, jupe)* to arrange.

draperies [dráprē] *nfpl* hangings.

drap-housse, *pl* **draps-housses** [dráŌŌs] *nm* fitted sheet.

drapier [drápyā] *nm* (woolen *(US) ou* woollen *(Brit)*) cloth manufacturer; *(marchand)* clothier.

drastique [drástēk] *a* drastic.

dressage [dresázh] *nm* training.

dresser [drāsā] *vt (mettre vertical, monter: tente)* to put up, erect; *(fig: liste, bilan, contrat)* to draw up; *(animal)* to train; **se ~** *vi (falaise, obstacle)* to stand; *(avec grandeur, menace)* to tower (up); *(personne)* to draw

o.s. up; **~ l'oreille** to prick up one's ears; **~ la table** to set the table; **~ qn contre qn d'autre** to set sb against sb else; **~ un procès-verbal** *ou* **une contravention à qn** to book sb, give sb a ticket.

dresseur, euse [dresœr, -œz] *nm/f* trainer.

dressoir [dreswár] *nm* dresser.

dribbler [drēblā] *vt, vi (SPORT)* to dribble.

drille [drēy] *nm*: **joyeux ~** cheerful sort.

drogue [drog] *nf* drug; **la ~** drugs *pl*; **~ dure/douce** hard/soft drugs *pl*.

drogué, e [drogā] *nm/f* drug addict.

droguer [drogā] *vt (victime)* to drug; *(malade)* to give drugs to; **se ~** *(aux stupéfiants)* to take drugs; *(péj: de médicaments)* to dose o.s. up.

droguerie [drogrē] *nf* ≈ hardware store *(US) ou* shop *(Brit)*.

droguiste [drogēst(ə)] *nm* ≈ manager *(ou* owner) of a hardware store.

droit, e [drwá, drwát] *a (non courbe)* straight; *(vertical)* upright, straight; *(fig: loyal, franc)* upright, straight(forward); *(opposé à gauche)* right, right-hand ♦ *ad* straight ♦ *nm (prérogative, BOXE)* right; *(taxe)* duty, tax; *(: d'inscription)* fee; *(lois, branche)*: **le ~** law ♦ *nf (POL)* right (wing); *(ligne)* straight line; **~ au but** *ou* **au fait/cœur** straight to the point/heart; **avoir le ~ de** to be allowed to; **avoir ~ à** to be entitled to; **être en ~ de** to have a *ou* the right to; **faire ~ à** to grant, accede to; **être dans son ~** to be within one's rights; **à bon ~** *(justement)* with good reason; **de quel ~?** by what right?; **à qui de ~** to whom it may concern; **à ~e** on the right; *(direction)* (to the) right; **à ~e de** to the right of; **de ~e** *(POL)* right-wing; **~ d'auteur** copyright; **avoir ~ de cité (dans)** *(fig)* to belong (to); **~ coutumier** common law; **~ de regard** right of access *ou* inspection; **~ de réponse** right to reply; **~ de visite** (right of) access; **~ de vote** (right to) vote; **~s d'auteur** royalties; **~s de douane** customs duties; **~s d'inscription** enrolment *ou* registration fees.

droitement [drwátmań] *ad (agir)* uprightly.

droitier, ière [drwátyā, -yer] *nm/f* right-handed person.

droiture [drwátür] *nf* uprightness, straightness.

drôle [drōl] *a (amusant)* funny, amusing; *(bizarre)* funny, peculiar; **un ~ de ...** *(bizarre)* a strange *ou* funny ...; *(intensif)* an incredible ..., a terrific ....

drôlement [drōlmań] *ad* funnily; peculiarly; *(très)* terribly, awfully; **il fait ~ froid** it's awfully cold.

drôlerie [drōlrē] *nf* funniness; funny thing.

dromadaire [dromáder] *nm* dromedary.

dru, e [drü] *a (cheveux)* thick, bushy; *(pluie)* heavy ♦ *ad (pousser)* thickly; *(tomber)* heavily.

drugstore [drœgstor] *nm* drugstore.

druide [drüēd] *nm* Druid.

ds *abr* = **dans**.

DST *sigle f (= Direction de la surveillance du territoire)* internal security service, ≈ CIA *(US)*, ≈ MI5 *(Brit)*.

DT *sigle m = diphtérie tétanos)* vaccine.

DTCP *sigle m (= diphtérie tétanos coqueluche*

polio) vaccine.
DTP *sigle m* (= *diphtérie tétanos polio) vaccine.*
DTTAB *sigle m* (= *diphtérie tétanos typhoïde A et B) vaccine.*
du |dü| *prép + dét, dét voir* **de.**
dû, due |dü| *pp de* **devoir** ♦ *a (somme)* owing, owed; (: *venant à échéance)* due; (*causé par*): ~ **à** due to ♦ *nm* due; (*somme)* dues *pl.*
Dubaï, Dubay |dübáy| *n* Dubai.
dubitatif, ive |dübētátēf, -ēv| *a* doubtful, dubious.
Dublin |düblaṅ| *n* Dublin.
duc |dük| *nm* duke.
duché |düshā| *nm* dukedom, duchy.
duchesse |düshes| *nf* duchess.
DUEL |düel| *sigle m* = *Diplôme universitaire d'études littéraires.*
duel |düel| *nm* duel.
DUES |dües| *sigle m* = *Diplôme universitaire d'études scientifiques.*
duffel-coat |dœfœlkōt| *nm* duffelcoat.
dûment |dümáṅ| *ad* duly.
dune |dün| *nf* dune.
Dunkerque |dœṅkerk| *n* Dunkirk.
duo |düō| *nm* (*MUS)* duet; (*fig: couple)* duo, pair.
dupe |düp| *nf* dupe ♦ *a*: (**ne pas)** **être** ~ **de** (not) to be taken in by.
duper |düpā| *vt* to dupe, deceive.
duperie |düprē| *nf* deception, dupery.
duplex |düpleks| *nm* (*appartement)* split-level apartment, duplex; (*TV*): **émission en** ~ link-up.
duplicata |düplēkátá| *nm* duplicate.
duplicateur |düplēkátœr| *nm* duplicator; ~ **à alcool** spirit duplicator.
duplicité |düplēsētá| *nf* duplicity.
duquel |dükel| *prép + pronom voir* **lequel.**
dur, e |dür| *a (pierre, siège, travail, problème)* hard; (*lumière, voix, climat)* harsh; (*sévère)* hard, harsh; (*cruel)* hard(-hearted); (*porte, col)* stiff; (*viande)* tough ♦ *ad* hard ♦ *nf*: **à la** ~**e** rough; **mener la vie** ~**e à qn** to give sb a hard time; ~ **d'oreille** hard of hearing.
durabilité |dürábēlētá| *nf* durability.
durable |dürábl(ə)| *a* lasting.
durablement |dürábləmáṅ| *ad* for the long term.
durant |düráṅ| *prép (au cours de)* during; (*pendant)* for; ~ **des mois, des mois** ~ for months.
durcir |dürsēr| *vt, vi,* **se** ~ *vi* to harden.
durcissement |dürsēsmáṅ| *nm* hardening.
durée |dürā| *nf* length; (*d'une pile etc)* life; (*déroulement: des opérations etc)* duration; **pour une** ~ **illimitée** for an unlimited length of time; **de courte** ~ (*séjour, répit)* brief, short-term; **de longue** ~ (*effet)* long-term; **pile de longue** ~ long-life battery.
durement |dürmáṅ| *ad* harshly.
durent |dür| *vb voir* **devoir.**
durer |dürā| *vi* to last.
dureté |dürtā| *nf (voir* **dur)** hardness; harshness; stiffness; toughness.
durillon |dürēyóṅ| *nm* callus.
durit |dürēt| *nf* ® (car radiator) hose.
DUT *sigle m* = *Diplôme universitaire de*

technologie.
dut |dü| *etc vb voir* **devoir.**
duvet |düve| *nm* down; (**sac de couchage en)** ~ down-filled sleeping bag.
duveteux, euse |düvtœ, -œz| *a* downy.
dynamique |dēnámēk| *a* dynamic.
dynamiser |dēnámēzā| *vt* to pep up, enliven; (*équipe, service)* to inject some dynamism into.
dynamisme |dēnámēsm(ə)| *nm* dynamism.
dynamite |dēnámēt| *nf* dynamite.
dynamiter |dēnámētā| *vt* to (blow up with) dynamite.
dynamo |dēnámō| *nf* dynamo.
dynastie |dēnástē| *nf* dynasty.
dysenterie |dēsáṅtrē| *nf* dysentery.
dyslexie |dēsleksē| *nf* dyslexia, word-blindness.
dyslexique |dēsleksēk| *a* dyslexic.
dyspepsie |dēspepsē| *nf* dyspepsia.

E

E, e |ə| *nm inv* E, e ♦ *abr* (= *Est)* E; **E comme Eugène** E for Easy.
EAO *sigle m* (= *enseignement assisté par ordinateur)* CAL (= *computer-aided learning).*
EAU *sigle mpl* (= *Émirats arabes unis)* UAE (= *United Arab Emirates).*
eau, x |ō| *nf* water ♦ *nfpl* waters; **prendre l'**~ (*chaussure etc)* to leak, let in water; **prendre les** ~**x** to visit a spa; **faire** ~ to leak; **tomber à l'**~ (*fig)* to fall through; **à l'**~ **de rose** slushy, sentimental; ~ **bénite** holy water; ~ **de Cologne** eau de Cologne; ~ **courante** running water; ~ **distillée** distilled water; ~ **douce** fresh water; ~ **de Javel** bleach; ~ **lourde** heavy water; ~ **minérale** mineral water; ~ **oxygénée** hydrogen peroxide; ~ **plate** still water; ~ **de pluie** rainwater; ~ **salée** salt water; ~ **de toilette** toilet water; ~**x ménagères** dirty water (*from washing up etc)*; ~**x territoriales** territorial waters; ~**x usées** liquid waste.
eau-de-vie, *pl* **eaux-de-vie** |ōdvē| *nf* brandy.
eau-forte, *pl* **eaux-fortes** |ōfort(ə)| *nf* etching.
ébahi, e |ábáē| *a* dumbfounded, flabbergasted.
ébahir |ábáēr| *vt* to astonish, astound.
ébats |ábá| *vb voir* **ébattre** ♦ *nmpl* frolics, gambols.
ébattre |ábátr(ə)|: **s'**~ *vi* to frolic.
ébauche |ábōsh| *nf* (rough) outline, sketch.
ébaucher |ábōshā| *vt* to sketch out, outline; (*fig)*: ~ **un sourire/geste** to give a hint of a smile/make a slight gesture; **s'**~ *vi* to take shape.
ébène |ábɛn| *nf* ebony.
ébéniste |ábānēst(ə)| *nm* cabinetmaker.
ébénisterie |ábānēstrē| *nf* cabinetmaking; (*bâti)* cabinetwork.
éberlué, e |áberlüā| *a* astounded, flabbergasted.

éblouir [āblōōēr] *vt* to dazzle.
éblouissant, e [āblōōēsáň, -áňt] *a* dazzling.
éblouissement [āblōōēsmáň] *nm* dazzle; (*faiblesse*) dizzy turn.
ébonite [ābonēt] *nf* vulcanite.
éborgner [ābornyā] *vt*: ~ **qn** to blind sb in one eye.
éboueur [ābwœr] *nm* garbageman (*US*), dustman (*Brit*).
ébouillanter [ābōōyáňtā] *vt* to scald; (*CULIN*) to blanch; **s'~** to scald o.s.
éboulement [ābōōlmáň] *nm* falling rocks *pl*, rock fall; (*amas*) heap of boulders *etc*.
ébouler [ābōōlā]: **s'~** *vi* to crumble, collapse.
éboulis [ābōōlē] *nmpl* fallen rocks.
ébouriffé, e [ābōōrēfā] *a* tousled, ruffled.
ébouriffer [ābōōrēfā] *vt* to tousle, ruffle.
ébranlement [ābráňlmáň] *nm* shaking.
ébranler [ābráňlā] *vt* to shake; (*rendre instable: mur, santé*) to weaken; **s'~** *vi* (*partir*) to move off.
ébrécher [ābrāshā] *vt* to chip.
ébriété [ābrēyātā] *nf*: **en état d'~** in a state of intoxication.
ébrouer [ābrōōā]: **s'~** *vi* (*souffler*) to snort; (*s'agiter*) to shake o.s.
ébruiter [ābrüētā] *vt*, **s'~** *vi* to spread.
ébullition [ābülēsyóň] *nf* boiling point; **en ~** boiling; (*fig*) in an uproar.
écaille [ākáy] *nf* (*de poisson*) scale; (*de coquillage*) shell; (*matière*) tortoiseshell; (*de roc etc*) flake.
écaillé, e [ākáyā] *a* (*peinture*) flaking.
écailler [ākáyā] *vt* (*poisson*) to scale; (*huître*) to open; **s'~** *vi* to flake *ou* peel (off).
écarlate [ākárlát] *a* scarlet.
écarquiller [ākárkēyā] *vt*: ~ **les yeux** to stare wide-eyed.
écart [ākár] *nm* gap; (*embardée*) swerve; (*saut*) sideways leap; (*fig*) departure, deviation; **à l'~** *ad* out of the way; **à l'~ de** *prép* away from; (*fig*) out of; **faire le grand ~** (*DANSE, GYM*) to do the splits; **~ de conduite** misdemeanor.
écarté, e [ākártā] *a* (*lieu*) out-of-the-way, remote; (*ouvert*): **les jambes ~es** legs apart; **les bras ~s** arms outstretched.
écarteler [ākártəlā] *vt* to quarter; (*fig*) to tear.
écartement [ākártəmáň] *nm* space, gap; (*RAIL*) gauge.
écarter [ākártā] *vt* (*séparer*) to move apart, separate; (*éloigner*) to push back, move away; (*ouvrir: bras, jambes*) to spread, open; (*: rideau*) to draw (back); (*éliminer: candidat, possibilité*) to dismiss; (*CARTES*) to discard; **s'~** *vi* to part; (*personne*) to move away; **s'~ de** to wander from.
ecchymose [ākēmōz] *nf* bruise.
ecclésiastique [āklāzyástēk] *a* ecclesiastical ♦ *nm* ecclesiastic.
écervelé, e [āservəlā] *a* scatterbrained, featherbrained.
échafaud [āsháfō] *nm* scaffold.
échafaudage [āsháfōdázh] *nm* scaffolding; (*fig*) heap, pile.
échafauder [āsháfōdā] *vt* (*plan*) to construct.
échalas [āshálá] *nm* stake, pole; (*personne*) beanpole.
échalote [āshálot] *nf* shallot.

échancré, e [āsháňkrā] *a* (*robe, corsage*) low-necked; (*côte*) indented.
échancrure [āsháňkrür] *nf* (*de robe*) scoop neckline; (*de côte, arête rocheuse*) indentation.
échange [āsháňzh] *nm* exchange; **en ~** in exchange; **en ~ de** in exchange *ou* return for; **libre ~** free trade; **~ de lettres/politesses/vues** exchange of letters/civilities/views; **~s commerciaux** trade; **~s culturels** cultural exchanges.
échangeable [āsháňzhábl(ə)] *a* exchangeable.
échanger [āsháňzhā] *vt*: ~ **qch (contre)** to exchange sth (for).
échangeur [āsháňzhœr] *nm* (*AUTO*) interchange.
échantillon [āsháňtēyóň] *nm* sample.
échantillonnage [āsháňtēyonázh] *nm* selection of samples.
échappatoire [āshápátwár] *nf* way out.
échappée [āshápā] *nf* (*vue*) vista; (*CYCLISME*) breakaway.
échappement [āshápmáň] *nm* (*AUTO*) exhaust; **~ libre** cutout.
échapper [āshápā]: ~ **à** *vt* (*gardien*) to escape (from); (*punition, péril*) to escape; ~ **à qn** (*détail, sens*) to escape sb; (*objet qu'on tient: aussi*): ~ **des mains de qn**) to slip out of sb's hands; **laisser ~** to let fall; (*cri etc*) to let out; **s'~** *vi* to escape; **l'~ belle** to have a narrow escape.
écharde [āshárd(ə)] *nf* splinter (of wood).
écharpe [āshárp(ə)] *nf* scarf (*pl* scarves); (*de maire*) sash; (*MÉD*) sling; **prendre en ~** (*dans une collision*) to hit sideways on.
écharper [āshárpā] *vt* to tear to pieces.
échasse [āshás] *nf* stilt.
échassier [āshásyā] *nm* wader.
échauder [āshōdā] *vt*: **se faire ~** (*fig*) to get one's fingers burnt.
échauffement [āshōfmáň] *nm* overheating; (*SPORT*) warm-up.
échauffer [āshōfā] *vt* (*métal, moteur*) to overheat; (*fig: exciter*) to fire, excite; **s'~** *vi* (*SPORT*) to warm up; (*discussion*) to become heated.
échauffourée [āshōfōōrā] *nf* clash, brawl; (*MIL*) skirmish.
échéance [āshāáns] *nf* (*d'un paiement: date*) due date; (*: somme due*) financial commitment(s); (*fig*) deadline; **à brève/longue ~** *a* short-/long-term ♦ *ad* in the short/long term.
échéancier [āshāáňsyā] *nm* schedule.
échéant [āshāáň]: **le cas ~** *ad* if the case arises.
échec [āshek] *nm* failure; (*ÉCHECS*): ~ **et mat/au roi** checkmate/check; **~s** *nmpl* (*jeu*) chess *sg*; **mettre en ~** to put in check; **tenir en ~** to hold in check; **faire ~ à** to foil, thwart.
échelle [āshel] *nf* ladder; (*fig, d'une carte*) scale; **à l'~ de** on the scale of; **sur une grande/petite ~** on a large/small scale; **faire la courte ~ à qn** to give sb a boost (*US*) *ou* leg up (*Brit*); **~ de corde** rope ladder.
échelon [āshlóň] *nm* (*d'échelle*) rung; (*ADMIN*) grade.
échelonner [āshlonā] *vt* to space out, spread out; (*versement*) **échelonné** (payment) by in-

stal(l)ments.

écheveau, x |eshvō] *nm* skein, hank.

échevelé, e [āshəvlā] *a* tousled, dishevelled; *(fig)* wild, frenzied.

échine [āshēn] *nf* backbone, spine.

échiner [āshēnā]: **s'~** *vi (se fatiguer)* to work o.s. to the bone.

échiquier [āshēkyā] *nm* chessboard.

écho [ākō] *nm* echo; **~s** *nmpl (potins)* gossip *sg*, rumors *(US)*, rumours *(Brit)*; *(PRESSE: rubrique)* "news in brief"; **rester sans ~** *(suggestion etc)* to come to nothing; **se faire l'~ de** to repeat, spread around.

échographie [ākogrȧfē] *nf* ultrasound (scan).

échoir [āshwȧr] *vi (dette)* to fall due; *(délais)* to expire; **~ à** *vt* to fall to.

échoppe [āshop] *nf* stall, booth.

échouer [āshwā] *vi* to fail; *(débris etc: sur la plage)* to be washed up; *(aboutir: personne dans un café etc)* to arrive ♦ *vt (bateau)* to ground; **s'~** *vi* to run aground.

échu, e [āshü] *pp de* **échoir** ♦ *a* due, mature.

échut [āshü] *etc vb voir* **échoir.**

éclabousser [āklȧbōōsā] *vt* to splash; *(fig)* to tarnish.

éclaboussure [āklȧbōōsür] *nf* splash; *(fig)* stain.

éclair [ākler] *nm (d'orage)* flash of lightning, lightning *q*; *(PHOTO: de flash)* flash; *(fig)* flash, spark; *(gâteau)* éclair.

éclairage [āklerȧzh] *nm* lighting.

éclairagiste [āklerȧzhēst(ə)] *nm/f* lighting technician.

éclaircie [āklersē] *nf* bright *ou* sunny interval.

éclaircir [āklɛrsēr] *vt* to lighten; *(fig)* to clear up, clarify; *(CULIN)* to thin (down); **s'~** *vi (ciel)* to brighten up, clear; *(cheveux)* to go thin; *(situation etc)* to become clearer; **s'~ la voix** to clear one's throat.

éclaircissement [āklɛrsēsmȧn] *nm* clearing up, clarification.

éclairer [āklārā] *vt (lieu)* to light (up); *(personne: avec une lampe de poche etc)* to light the way for; *(fig: instruire)* to enlighten; *(: rendre comprehensible)* to shed light on ♦ *vi:* **~ mal/bien** to give a poor/good light; **s'~** *vi (phare, rue)* to light up; *(situation etc)* to become clearer; **s'~ à la bougie/l'électricité** to use candlelight/have electric lighting.

éclaireur, euse [āklerœr, -œz] *nm/f (scout)* (boy) scout/girl scout *(US) ou* (girl) guide *(Brit)* ♦ *nm (MIL)* scout; **partir en ~** to go off to reconnoiter.

éclat [āklȧ] *nm (de bombe, de verre)* fragment; *(du soleil, d'une couleur etc)* brightness, brilliance; *(d'une cérémonie)* splendor *(US)*, splendour *(Brit)*; *(scandale)*: **faire un ~** to cause a commotion; **action d'~** outstanding action; **voler en ~s** to shatter; **des ~s de verre** broken glass; flying glass; **~ de rire** burst *ou* roar of laughter; **~ de voix** shout.

éclatant, e [āklȧtȧn, -ȧnt] *a* brilliant, bright; *(succès)* resounding; *(revanche)* devastating.

éclater [āklȧtā] *vi (pneu)* to blow out; *(bombe)* to explode; *(guerre, épidémie)* to break out; *(groupe, parti)* to break up; **~ de rire/en sanglots** to burst out laughing/sobbing.

éclectique [āklektēk] *a* eclectic.

éclipse [āklēps(ə)] *nf* eclipse.

éclipser [āklēpsā] *vt* to eclipse; **s'~** *vi* to slip away.

éclopé, e [āklopā] *a* lame.

éclore [āklor] *vi (œuf)* to hatch; *(fleur)* to open (out).

éclosion [āklōzyȯn] *nf* blossoming.

écluse [āklüz] *nf* lock.

éclusier [āklüzyā] *nm* lock keeper.

écœurant, e [ākœrȧn, -ȧnt] *a* sickening; *(gâteau etc)* sickly.

écœurement [ākœrmȧn] *nm* disgust.

écœurer [ākœrā] *vt:* **~ qn** to make sb feel sick; *(fig: démoraliser)* to disgust sb.

école [ākol] *nf* school; **aller à l'~** to go to school; **faire ~** to collect a following; **les grandes ~s** *prestige university-level colleges with competitive entrance examinations;* **~ maternelle** nursery school; **~ primaire** grade *(US) ou* primary *(Brit)* school; **~ secondaire** high *(US) ou* secondary *(Brit)* school; **~ privée/publique/élémentaire** private/public *(US) ou* state *(Brit)/* elementary school; **~ de dessin/danse/musique** art/dancing/music school; **~ hôtelière** hotel management school; **~ normale (d'instituteurs) (ENI)** *elementary school teachers' training college;* **~ normale supérieure (ENS)** *grande école for training high school teachers;* **~ de secrétariat** secretarial school.

écolier, ière [ākolya, -yer] *nm/f* schoolboy/girl.

écolo [ākolō] *nm/f (fam)* ecologist ♦ *a* ecological.

écologie [ākolozhē] *nf* ecology; *(sujet scolaire)* environmental studies *pl.*

écologique [ākolozhēk] *a* ecological; environmental.

écologiste [ākolozhēst(ə)] *nm/f* ecologist; environmentalist.

éconduire [ākȯndüēr] *vt* to dismiss.

économat [ākonomȧ] *nm (fonction)* treasurership *(US)*, bursarship *(Brit)*; *(bureau)* bursar's office.

économe [ākonom] *a* thrifty ♦ *nm/f (de lycée etc)* bursar.

économétrie [ākonomātrē] *nf* econometrics *sg.*

économie [ākonomē] *nf (vertu)* economy, thrift; *(gain: d'argent, de temps etc)* saving; *(science)* economics *sg*; *(situation économique)* economy; **~s** *nfpl (pécule)* savings; **une ~ de temps/d'argent** a saving in time/of money; **~ dirigée** planned economy.

économique [ākonomēk] *a (avantageux)* economical; *(ÉCON)* economic.

économiquement [ākonomēkmȧn] *ad* economically; **les ~ faibles** *(ADMIN)* the low-paid, people on low incomes.

économiser [ākonomēzā] *vt, vi* to save.

économiste [ākonomēst(ə)] *nm/f* economist.

écoper [ākopā] *vi* to bail out; *(fig)* to catch it; **~ (de)** *vt* to get.

écorce [ākors(ə)] *nf* bark; *(de fruit)* peel.

écorcer [ākorsā] *vt* to bark.

écorché, e [ākorshā] *a:* **~ vif** flayed alive ♦ *nm* cut-away drawing.

écorcher [ākorshā] *vt (animal)* to skin;

(*égratigner*) to graze; ~ **une langue** to speak a language brokenly; **s'~ le genou** *etc* to scrape *ou* graze one's knee *etc*.

écorchure [ākorshür] *nf* graze.

écorner [ākornā] *vt* (*taureau*) to dehorn; (*livre*) to dog-ear.

écossais, e [ākose, -ez] *a* (*lacs, tempérament*) Scottish, Scots; (*whisky, confiture*) Scotch; (*écharpe, tissu*) tartan ♦ *nm* (*LING*) Scots; (: *gaélique*) Gaelic; (*tissu*) tartan (cloth); **É~** Scot, Scotsman; **les É~** the Scots ♦ *nf*: **É~e** Scot, Scotswoman.

Écosse [ākos] *nf*: **l'~** Scotland.

écosser [ākosā] *vt* to shell.

écosystème [ākosēstem] *nm* ecosystem.

écot [ākō] *nm*: **payer son** ~ to pay one's share.

écoulement [ākōōlmáṅ] *nm* (*de faux billets*) circulation; (*de stock*) selling.

écouler [ākōōlā] *vt* to dispose of; **s'~** *vi* (*eau*) to flow (out); (*foule*) to drift away; (*jours, temps*) to pass (by).

écourter [ākōōrtā] *vt* to curtail, cut short.

écoute [ākōōt] *nf* (*NAVIG*: *cordage*) sheet; (*RADIO, TV*): **temps/heure d'~** listening (*ou* viewing) time/hour; **heure de grande** ~ prime time; **prendre l'~** to tune in; **rester à l'~ (de)** to keep listening (to), stay tuned in (to); **~s téléphoniques** phone tapping *sg*.

écouter [ākōōtā] *vt* to listen to.

écouteur [ākōōtœr] *nm* (*TÉL*) (additional) earphone; **~s** *nmpl* (*RADIO*) headphones, headset *sg*.

écoutille [ākōōtēy] *nf* hatch.

écr. *abr* = **écrire**.

écrabouiller [ākrábōōyā] *vt* to squash, crush.

écran [ākráṅ] *nm* screen; (*INFORM*) VDU, screen; ~ **de fumée/d'eau** curtain of smoke/water; **porter à l'~** (*CINÉMA*) to adapt for the screen; **le petit** ~ television, the small screen.

écrasant, e [ākrázáṅ, -áṅt] *a* overwhelming.

écraser [ākrāzā] *vt* to crush; (*piéton*) to run over; (*INFORM*) to overwrite; **se faire** ~ to be run over; **écrase-toi)!** shut up!; **s'~ (au sol)** to crash; **s'~ contre** to crash into.

écrémer [ākrāmā] *vt* to skim.

écrevisse [ākrəvēs] *nf* crayfish *inv*.

écrier [ākrēyā]: **s'~** *vi* to exclaim.

écrin [ākráṅ] *nm* case, box.

écrire [ākrēr] *vt, vi* to write; ~ **à qn que** to write and tell sb that; **s'~** to write to one another ♦ *vi*: **ça s'écrit comment?** how is it spelled?

écrit, e [ākrē, -ēt] *pp de* **écrire** ♦ *a*: **bien/mal** ~ well/badly written ♦ *nm* document; (*examen*) written exam; **par** ~ in writing.

écriteau, x [ākrētō] *nm* notice, sign.

écritoire [ākrētwár] *nf* desk folder (*US*), writing case (*Brit*).

écriture [ākrētür] *nf* writing; (*COMM*) entry; **~s** *nfpl* (*COMM*) accounts, books; **l'É~ (sainte), les É~s** the Scriptures.

écrivain [ākrevaṅ] *nm* writer.

écrivais [ākrēve] *etc vb voir* **écrire**.

écrou [ākrōō] *nm* nut.

écrouer [ākrōōā] *vt* to imprison; (*provisoirement*) to remand in custody.

écroulé, e [ākrōōlā] *a* (*de fatigue*) exhausted; (*par un malheur*) overwhelmed; ~ **(de rire)** in stitches.

écroulement [ākrōōlmáṅ] *nm* collapse.

écrouler [ākrōōlā]: **s'~** *vi* to collapse.

écru, e [ākrü] *a* (*toile*) raw, unbleached; (*couleur*) off-white, écru.

écu [ākü] *nm* (*bouclier*) shield; (*monnaie: ancienne*) crown; (: *de la CEE*) ECU.

écueil [ākœy] *nm* reef; (*fig*) pitfall; stumbling block.

écuelle [āküel] *nf* bowl.

éculé, e [ākülā] *a* (*chaussure*) down at the heel(s) (*US*), down-at-heel (*Brit*); (*fig*: *péj*) hackneyed.

écume [āküm] *nf* foam; (*CULIN*) scum; ~ **de mer** meerschaum.

écumer [ākümā] *vt* (*CULIN*) to skim; (*fig*) to plunder ♦ *vi* (*mer*) to foam; (*fig*) to boil with rage.

écumoire [ākümwár] *nf* skimmer.

écureuil [āküræy] *nm* squirrel.

écurie [ākürē] *nf* stable.

écusson [āküsôṅ] *nm* badge.

écuyer, ère [āküēyā, -er] *nm/f* rider.

eczéma [egzāmá] *nm* eczema.

éd. *abr* = **édition**.

édam [ādám] *nm* (*fromage*) Edam.

édelweiss [ādelvás] *nm inv* edelweiss.

éden [āden] *nm* Eden.

édenté, e [ādáṅtā] *a* toothless.

EDF *sigle f* (= *Électricité de France*) national electricity company.

édifiant, e [ādēfyáṅ, -áṅt] *a* edifying.

édifice [ādēfēs] *nm* building, edifice.

édifier [ādēfyā] *vt* to build, erect; (*fig*) to edify.

édiles [ādēl] *nmpl* city fathers.

Édimbourg [ādáṅbōōr] *n* Edinburgh.

édit [ādē] *nm* edict.

édit. *abr* = **éditeur**.

éditer [ādētā] *vt* (*publier*) to publish; (: *disque*) to produce; (*préparer: texte, INFORM*) to edit.

éditeur, trice [ādētœr, -trēs] *nm/f* publisher; editor.

édition [ādēsyôṅ] *nf* editing *q*; (*série d'exemplaires*) edition; (*industrie du livre*): **l'~** publishing; ~ **sur écran** (*INFORM*) screen editing.

édito [ādētō] *nm* (*fam* = *éditorial*) editorial.

éditorial, aux [ādētoryál, -ō] *nm* editorial.

éditorialiste [ādētoryálēst(ə)] *nm/f* editorial writer.

édredon [ādrədôṅ] *nm* eiderdown, comforter (*US*).

éducateur, trice [ādükátœr, -trēs] *nm/f* teacher; ~ **spécialisé** specialist teacher.

éducatif, ive [ādükátēf, -ēv] *a* educational.

éducation [ādükásyôṅ] *nf* education; (*familiale*) upbringing; (*manières*) (good) manners *pl*; **bonne/mauvaise** ~ good/bad upbringing; **sans** ~ bad-mannered, ill-bred; **l'É~ (nationale)** the education department; ~ **permanente** continuing education; ~ **physique** physical education.

édulcorer [ādülkorā] *vt* to sweeten; (*fig*) to tone down.

éduquer [ādükā] *vt* to educate; (*élever*) to

bring up; (*faculté*) to train; **bien/mal éduqué** well/badly brought up.

effacé, e [āfásā] *a* (*fig*) retiring, unassuming.

effacer [āfásā] *vt* to erase, rub out; (*bande magnétique*) to erase; (*INFORM*: *fichier, fiche*) to delete, erase; **s'~** *vi* (*inscription etc*) to wear off; (*pour laisser passer*) to step aside; **~ le ventre** to pull one's stomach in.

effarant, e [āfárān, -ānt] *a* alarming.

effaré, e [āfárā] *a* alarmed.

effarement [āfármān] *nm* alarm.

effarer [āfárā] *vt* to alarm.

effarouchement [āfárōōshmān] *nm* alarm.

effaroucher [āfárōōshā] *vt* to frighten *ou* scare away; (*personne*) to alarm.

effectif, ive [āfektēf, -ēv] *a* real; effective ♦ *nm* (*MIL*) strength; (*SCOL*) total number of pupils, size; **~s** numbers, strength *sg*; (*COMM*) manpower *sg*.

effectivement [āfektēvmān] *ad* effectively; (*réellement*) actually, really; (*en effet*) indeed.

effectuer [āfektüā] *vt* (*opération, mission*) to carry out; (*déplacement, trajet*) to make, complete; (*mouvement*) to execute, make; **s'~** to be carried out.

efféminé, e [āfāmēnā] *a* effeminate.

effervescence [āfervāsāns] *nf* (*fig*): **en ~** in a turmoil.

effervescent, e [āfervāsān, -ānt] *a* (*cachet, boisson*) effervescent; (*fig*) agitated, in a turmoil.

effet [āfe] *nm* (*résultat, artifice*) effect; (*impression*) impression; (*COMM*) bill; (*JUR*: *d'une loi, d'un jugement*): **avec ~ rétroactif** applied retroactively; **~s** *nmpl* (*vêtements etc*) things; **~ de style/couleur/lumière** stylistic/color/lighting effect; **~s de voix** dramatic effects with one's voice; **faire de l'~** (*médicament, menace*) to have an effect, be effective; **sous l'~ de** under the effect of; **donner de l'~ à une balle** (*TENNIS*) to put some spin on a ball; **à cet ~** to that end; **en ~** *ad* indeed; **~ (de commerce)** bill of exchange; **~s spéciaux** (*CINÉMA*) special effects.

effeuiller [āfœyā] *vt* to remove the leaves (*ou* petals) from.

efficace [āfēkás] *a* (*personne*) efficient; (*action, médicament*) effective.

efficacité [āfēkásētā] *nf* efficiency; effectiveness.

effigie [āfēzhē] *nf* effigy; **brûler qn en ~** to burn sb in effigy.

effilé, e [āfēlā] *a* slender; (*pointe*) sharp; (*carrosserie*) streamlined.

effiler [āfēlā] *vt* (*cheveux*) to thin (out); (*tissu*) to fray.

effilocher [āfēloshā]: **s'~** *vi* to fray.

efflanqué, e [āflānkā] *a* emaciated.

effleurement [āflœrmān] *nm*: **touche à ~** touch-sensitive control *ou* key.

effleurer [āflœrā] *vt* to brush (against); (*sujet*) to touch upon; (*suj: idée, pensée*): **~ qn** to cross sb's mind.

effluves [āflüv] *nmpl* exhalation(s).

effondré, e [āfōndrā] *a* (*abattu: par un malheur, échec*) overwhelmed.

effondrement [āfōndrəmān] *nm* collapse.

effondrer [āfōndrā]: **s'~** *vi* to collapse.

efforcer [āforsā]: **s'~ de** *vt*: **s'~ de faire** to try hard to do.

effort [āfor] *nm* effort; **faire un ~** to make an effort; **faire tous ses ~s** to try one's hardest; **faire l'~ de ...** to make the effort to ...; **sans ~** *a* effortless ♦ *ad* effortlessly; **~ de mémoire** attempt to remember; **~ de volonté** effort of will.

effraction [āfráksyōn] *nf* breaking-in; **s'introduire par ~ dans** to break into.

effrangé, e [āfrānzhā] *a* fringed; (*effiloché*) frayed.

effrayant, e [āfreyān, -ānt] *a* frightening, fearsome; (*sens affaibli*) dreadful.

effrayer [āfrāyā] *vt* to frighten, scare; (*rebuter*) to put off; **s'~ (de)** to be frightened *ou* scared (by).

effréné, e [āfrānā] *a* wild.

effritement [āfrētmān] *nm* crumbling; erosion; slackening off.

effriter [āfrētā]: **s'~** *vi* to crumble; (*monnaie*) to be eroded; (*valeurs*) to slacken off.

effroi [āfrwâ] *nm* terror, dread *q*.

effronté, e [āfrōntā] *a* insolent.

effrontément [āfrōntāmān] *ad* insolently.

effronterie [āfrōntrē] *nf* insolence.

effroyable [āfrwáyábl(ə)] *a* horrifying, appalling.

effusion [āfüzyōn] *nf* effusion; **sans ~ de sang** without bloodshed.

égailler [āgáyā]: **s'~** *vi* to scatter, disperse.

égal, e, aux [āgál, -ō] *a* (*identique, ayant les mêmes droits*) equal; (*plan: surface*) even, level; (*constant: vitesse*) steady; (*équitable*) even ♦ *nm/f* equal; **être ~ à** (*prix, nombre*) to be equal to; **ça lui est ~** it's all the same to him, it doesn't matter to him, he doesn't mind; **c'est ~, ...** all the same, ...; **sans ~** matchless, unequalled; **à l'~ de** (*comme*) just like; **d'~ à ~** as equals.

également [āgálmān] *ad* equally; evenly; steadily; (*aussi*) too, as well.

égaler [āgálā] *vt* to equal.

égalisateur, trice [āgálēzátœr, -trēs] *a* (*SPORT*): **but ~** tying goal *ou* score (*US*), equalizer (*Brit*).

égalisation [āgálēzásyōn] *nf* (*SPORT*) tying (*US*), equalization (*Brit*).

égaliser [āgálēzā] *vt* (*sol, salaires*) to level (out); (*chances*) to equalize ♦ *vi* (*SPORT*) to tie (*US*), equalize (*Brit*).

égalitaire [āgálētɛr] *a* egalitarian.

égalitarisme [āgálētárēsm(ə)] *nm* egalitarianism.

égalité [āgálētā] *nf* equality; evenness; steadiness; (*MATH*) equality; **être à ~ (de points)** to be even; **~ de droits** equality of rights; **~ d'humeur** evenness of temper.

égard [āgár] *nm*: **~s** *nmpl* consideration *sg*; **à cet ~** in this respect; **à certains ~s/tous ~s** in certain respects/all respects; **eu ~ à** in view of; **par ~ pour** out of consideration for; **sans ~ pour** without regard for; **à l'~ de** *prép* towards; (*en ce qui concerne*) concerning, as regards.

égaré, e [āgárā] *a* lost.

égarement [āgármān] *nm* distraction; aberration.

égarer [āgárā] *vt* (*objet*) to mislay; (*morale-ment*) to lead astray; **s'~** *vi* to get lost, lose one's way; (*objet*) to go astray; (*fig: dans une discussion*) to wander.

égayer [āgāyā] *vt* (*personne*) to amuse; (*: remonter*) to cheer up; (*récit, endroit*) to brighten up, liven up.

Égée [āzhā] *a*: **la mer ~** the Aegean (Sea).

égéen, ne [āzhāań, -en] *a* Aegean.

égérie [āzhārē] *nf*: **l'~ de qn/qch** the brains behind sb/sth.

égide [āzhēd] *nf*: **sous l'~ de** under the aegis of.

églantier [āglántyā] *nm* wild *ou* dog rose(-bush).

églantine [āglántēn] *nf* wild *ou* dog rose.

églefin [āgləfań] *nm* haddock.

église [āglēz] *nf* church.

égocentrique [āgosántrēk] *a* egocentric, self-centered (*US*), self-centred (*Brit*).

égocentrisme [āgosántrēsm(ə)] *nm* egocentricity.

égoïne [āgoēn] *nf* handsaw.

égoïsme [āgoēsm(ə)] *nm* selfishness, egoism.

égoïste [āgoēst(ə)] *a* selfish, egoistic ♦ *nm/f* egoist.

égoïstement [āgoēstəmáń] *ad* selfishly.

égorger [āgorzhā] *vt* to cut the throat of.

égosiller [āgōzēyā]: **s'~** *vi* to shout o.s. hoarse.

égotisme [āgotēsm(ə)] *nm* egotism, egoism.

égout [āgōō] *nm* sewer; **eaux d'~** sewage.

égoutier [āgōōtyā] *nm* sewer worker.

égoutter [āgōōtā] *vt* (*linge*) to wring out; (*vaisselle, fromage*) to drain ♦ *vi*, **s'~** *vi* to drip.

égouttoir [āgōōtwár] *nm* drainboard (*US*), draining board (*Brit*); (*mobile*) (dish) drainer.

égratigner [āgrátēnyā] *vt* to scratch; **s'~** to scratch o.s.

égratignure [āgrátēnyür] *nf* scratch.

égrener [āgrənā] *vt*: **~ une grappe, ~ des raisins** to pick grapes off a bunch; **s'~** *vi* (*fig: heures etc*) to pass by; (*: notes*) to chime out.

égrillard, e [āgrēyár, -árd(ə)] *a* ribald, bawdy.

Égypte [āzhēpt] *nf*: **l'~** Egypt.

égyptien, ne [āzhēpsyań, -en] *a* Egyptian ♦ *nm/f*: **É~, ne** Egyptian.

égyptologue [āzhēptolog] *nm/f* Egyptologist.

eh [ā] *excl* hey!; **~ bien** well.

éhonté, e [āóńtā] *a* shameless, brazen.

éjaculation [āzhákülāsyóń] *nf* ejaculation.

éjaculer [āzhákülā] *vi* to ejaculate.

éjectable [āzhektábl(ə)] *a*: **siège ~** ejector seat.

éjecter [āzhektā] *vt* (*TECH*) to eject; (*fam*) to kick *ou* chuck out.

éjection [āzheksyóń] *nf* ejection.

élaboration [ālábôrâsyóń] *nf* elaboration.

élaboré, e [āláborā] *a* (*complexe*) elaborate.

élaborer [āláborā] *vt* to elaborate; (*projet, stratégie*) to work out; (*rapport*) to draft.

élagage [ālágazh] *nm* pruning.

élaguer [ālágā] *vt* to prune.

élan [āláń] *nm* (*ZOOL*) elk, moose; (*SPORT*: *avant le saut*) run-up; (*de véhicule ou objet en mouvement*) momentum; (*fig: de ten-*

dresse etc) surge; **prendre son ~/de l'~** to make (*US*) *ou* take (*Brit*) a run-up/gather speed; **perdre son ~** to lose one's momentum.

élancé, e [āláńsā] *a* slender.

élancement [āláńsmáń] *nm* shooting pain.

élancer [āláńsā]: **s'~** *vi* to dash, hurl o.s.; (*fig: arbre, clocher*) to soar (upwards).

élargir [ālárzhēr] *vt* to widen; (*vêtement*) to let out; (*JUR*) to release; **s'~** *vi* to widen; (*vêtement*) to stretch.

élargissement [ālárzhēsmáń] *nm* widening; letting out.

élasticité [ālástēsētā] *nf* (*aussi ÉCON*) elasticity; **~ de l'offre/de la demande** flexibility of supply/demand.

élastique [ālástēk] *a* elastic ♦ *nm* (*de bureau*) rubber band; (*pour la couture*) elastic *q*.

élastomère [ālástomer] *nm* elastomer.

Elbe [elb] *nf*: **l'île d'~** (the Island of) Elba; (*fleuve*): **l'~** the Elbe.

eldorado [eldorádō] *nm* Eldorado.

électeur, trice [ālektœr, -trēs] *nm/f* elector, voter.

électif, ive [ālektēf, -ēv] *a* elective.

élection [āleksyóń] *nf* election; **~s** *nfpl* (*POL*) election(s); **sa terre/patrie d'~** one's chosen land/country, the land/country of one's choice; **~ partielle** ≈ by-election; **~s législatives** general election *sg*.

électoral, e, aux [ālektorál, -ō] *a* electoral, election *cpd*.

électoralisme [ālektorálēsm(ə)] *nm* electioneering.

électorat [ālektorá] *nm* electorate.

électricien, ne [ālektrēsyań, -en] *nm/f* electrician.

électricité [ālektrēsētā] *nf* electricity; **allumer/éteindre l'~** to turn on/off the light; **~ statique** static electricity.

électrification [ālektrēfēkásyóń] *nf* (*RAIL*) electrification; **l'~ d'un village** bringing electric power to a village.

électrifier [ālektrēfyā] *vt* (*RAIL*) to electrify.

électrique [ālektrēk] *a* electric(al).

électriser [ālektrēzā] *vt* to electrify.

électro... [ālektro] *préfixe* electro....

électro-aimant [ālektroemáń] *nm* electromagnet.

électrocardiogramme [ālektrokárdyográm] *nm* electrocardiogram.

électrocardiographe [ālektrokárdyográf] *nm* electrocardiograph.

électrochoc [ālektroshok] *nm* electroshock therapy.

électrocuter [ālektrokütā] *vt* to electrocute.

électrocution [ālektrokütüsyóń] *nf* electrocution.

électrode [ālektrod] *nf* electrode.

électro-encéphalogramme [ālektroáńsáfálográm] *nm* electroencephalogram.

électrogène [ālektrozhen] *a*: **groupe ~** electrical power unit, generator.

électrolyse [ālektrolēz] *nf* electrolysis *sg*.

électromagnétique [ālektrománnyātēk] *a* electromagnetic.

électroménager [ālektrománázhā] *a*: **appareils ~s** household (electrical) appliances ♦ *nm*: **l'~** household appliances.

électron [ālektróń] *nm* electron.

électronicien, ne [ālektronēsyań, -en] *nm/f* electrical (*US*) *ou* electronics (*Brit*) engineer.

électronique [ālektronēk] *a* electronic ♦ *nf* (*science*) electronics *sg*.

électronucléaire [ālektronüklāer] *a* nuclear power *cpd* ♦ *nm*: **l'~** nuclear power.

électrophone [ālektrofon] *nm* record player.

élégamment [ālāgàmàń] *ad* elegantly.

élégance [ālāgàńs] *nf* elegance.

élégant, e [ālāgàń, -àńt] *a* elegant; (*solution*) neat, elegant; (*attitude, procédé*) courteous, civilized.

élément [ālāmàń] *nm* element; (*pièce*) component, part; **~s** *nmpl* (*aussi: rudiments*) elements.

élémentaire [ālāmàńter] *a* elementary; (*CHIMIE*) elemental.

éléphant [ālāfàń] *nm* elephant; **~ de mer** elephant seal.

éléphanteau, x [ālāfàńtō] *nm* baby elephant.

éléphantesque [ālāfàńtesk(ə)] *a* elephantine.

élevage [elvàzh] *nm* breeding; (*de bovins*) cattle breeding *ou* rearing; (*ferme*) cattle farm.

élévateur [ālāvàtœr] *nm* elevator.

élévation [ālāvàsyóń] *nf* (*gén*) elevation; (*voir élever*) raising; (*voir s'élever*) rise.

élevé, e [elvā] *a* (*prix, sommet*) high; (*fig: noble*) elevated; **bien/mal ~** well-/ill-mannered.

élève [ālev] *nm/f* pupil; **~ infirmière** student nurse.

élever [elvā] *vt* (*enfant*) to bring up, raise; (*bétail, volaille*) to breed; (*abeilles*) to keep; (*hausser: taux, niveau*) to raise; (*fig: âme, esprit*) to elevate; (*édifier: monument*) to put up, erect; **s'~** *vi* (*avion, alpiniste*) to go up; (*niveau, température, aussi: cri etc*) to rise; (*survenir: difficultés*) to arise; **s'~ à** (*suj: frais, dégâts*) to amount to, add up to; **s'~ contre** to rise up against; **~ une protestation/critique** to raise a protest/make a criticism; **~ la voix** to raise one's voice; **~ qn au rang de** to raise *ou* elevate sb to the rank of; **~ un nombre au carré/au cube** to square/cube a number.

éleveur, euse [àlvœr, -œz] *nm/f* stock breeder.

elfe [elf(ə)] *nm* elf.

élidé, e [ālēdā] *a* elided.

élider [ālēdā] *vt* to elide.

éligibilité [ālēzhēbēlētā] *nf* eligibility.

éligible [ālēzhēbl(ə)] *a* eligible.

élimé, e [ālēmā] *a* worn (thin), threadbare.

élimination [ālēmēnàsyóń] *nf* elimination.

éliminatoire [ālēmēnàtwár] *a* eliminatory; (*SPORT*) disqualifying ♦ *nf* (*SPORT*) heat.

éliminer [ālēmēnā] *vt* to eliminate.

élire [ālēr] *vt* to elect; **~ domicile à** to take up residence in *ou* at.

élision [ālēzyóń] *nf* elision.

élite [ālēt] *nf* elite; **tireur d'~** crack rifleman; **chercheur d'~** top-notch researcher.

élitiste [ālētēst(ə)] *a* elitist.

élixir [ālēksēr] *nm* elixir.

elle [el] *pronom* (*sujet*) she; (: *chose*) it; (*complément*) her; it; **~s** (*sujet*) they; (*complément*) them; **~-même** herself; itself; **~s-mêmes** themselves; *voir* **il.**

ellipse [ālēps(ə)] *nf* ellipse; (*LING*) ellipsis *sg*.

elliptique [ālēptēk] *a* elliptical.

élocution [āloküsyóń] *nf* delivery; **défaut d'~** speech impediment.

éloge [ālozh] *nm* praise (*gén q*); **faire l'~ de** to praise.

élogieusement [ālozhyœzmàń] *ad* very favorably (*US*) *ou* favourably (*Brit*).

élogieux, euse [ālozhyœ, -œz] *a* laudatory, full of praise.

éloigné, e [ālwànyā] *a* distant, far-off.

éloignement [ālwànymàń] *nm* removal; putting off; estrangement; (*fig: distance*) distance.

éloigner [ālwànyā] *vt* (*objet*): **~ qoh (de)** to move *ou* take sth away (from); (*personne*): **~ qn (de)** to take sb away *ou* remove sb (from); (*échéance*) to put off, postpone; (*soupçons, danger*) to ward off; **s'~ (de)** (*personne*) to go away (from); (*véhicule*) to move away (from); (*affectivement*) to become estranged (from).

élongation [ālóńgàsyóń] *nf* strained muscle.

éloquence [ālokàńs] *nf* eloquence.

éloquent, e [ālokàń, -àńt] *a* eloquent.

élu, e [ālü] *pp de* **élire** ♦ *nm/f* (*POL*) elected representative.

élucider [ālüsēdā] *vt* to elucidate.

élucubrations [ālükübràsyóń] *nfpl* wild imaginings.

éluder [ālüdā] *vt* to evade.

élus [ālü] *etc vb voir* **élire.**

éluslf, lve [āluzēf, -ēv] *a* elusive.

Élysée [ālēzā] *nm*: **(le palais de) l'~** the Élysée palace (*the French president's residence and offices*); **les Champs ~s** the Champs Élysées.

émacié, e [āmàsyā] *a* emaciated.

émail, aux [āmày, -ō] *nm* enamel.

émaillé, e [āmáyā] *a* enameled (*US*), enamelled (*Brit*); (*fig*): **~ de** dotted with.

émailler [āmáyā] *vt* to enamel.

émanation. [āmànàsyóń] *nf* emanation; **être l'~ de** to emanate from; to proceed from.

émancipation [āmàńsēpàsyóń] *nf* emancipation.

émancipé, e [āmàńsēpā] *a* emancipated.

émanciper [āmàńsēpā] *vt* to emancipate; **s'~** (*fig*) to become emancipated *ou* liberated.

émaner [āmànā]: **~ de** *vt* to emanate from; (*ADMIN*) to proceed from.

émarger [āmàrzhā] *vt* to sign; **~ de 1000 F à un budget** to receive 1000 F out of a budget.

émasculer [āmàskülā] *vt* to emasculate.

emballage [àńbàlàzh] *nm* wrapping; packing; (*papier*) wrapping; (*carton*) packaging.

emballer [àńbàlā] *vt* to wrap (up); (*dans un carton*) to pack (up); (*fig: fam*) to thrill (to pieces); **s'~** *vi* (*moteur*) to race; (*cheval*) to bolt; (*fig: personne*) to get carried away.

emballeur, euse [àńbàlœr, -œz] *nm/f* packer.

embarcadère [àńbàrkàder] *nm* wharf, pier.

embarcation [àńbàrkàsyóń] *nf* (small) boat, (small) craft *inv*.

embardée [àńbàrdā] *nf* swerve; **faire une ~** to swerve.

embargo [àńbàrgō] *nm* embargo; **mettre l'~ sur** to put an embargo on, embargo.

embarquement [àńbarkəmàń] *nm* embarkation; loading; boarding.

embarquer [ãṅbárkā] *vt* (*personne*) to embark; (*marchandise*) to load; (*fam*) to cart off; (: *arrêter*) to nab ♦ *vi* (*passager*) to board; (*NAVIG*) to ship water; **s'~** *vi* to board; **s'~ dans** (*affaire, aventure*) to embark upon.

embarras [ãṅbárá] *nm* (*obstacle*) hindrance; (*confusion*) embarrassment; (*ennuis*): **être dans l'~** to be in a predicament *ou* an awkward position; (*gêne financière*) to be having financial difficulties; **~ gastrique** stomach upset.

embarrassant, e [ãṅbárásãṅ, -ãṅt] *a* cumbersome; embarrassing; awkward.

embarrassé, e [ãṅbárásā] *a* (*encombré*) encumbered; (*gêné*) embarrassed; (*explications etc*) awkward.

embarrasser [ãṅbárásā] *vt* (*encombrer*) to clutter (up); (*gêner*) to hinder, hamper; (*fig*) to cause embarrassment to; to put in an awkward position; **s'~ de** to burden o.s. with.

embauche [ãṅbōsh] *nf* hiring; **bureau d'~** employment *ou* hiring (*US*) office.

embaucher [ãṅbōshā] *vt* to take on, hire; **s'~ comme** to get (o.s.) a job as.

embauchoir [ãṅbōshwàr] *nm* shoetree.

embaumer [ãṅbōmā] *vt* to embalm; (*parfumer*) to fill with its fragrance; **~ la lavande** to be fragrant with (the scent of) lavender.

embellie [ãṅbālē] *nf* bright spell, brighter period.

embellir [ãṅbālēr] *vt* to make more attractive; (*une histoire*) to embellish ♦ *vi* to grow lovelier *ou* more attractive.

embellissement [ãṅbālēsmãṅ] *nm* embellishment.

embêtant, e [ãṅbātãṅ, -ãṅt] *a* annoying.

embêtement [ãṅbetmãṅ] *nm* problem, difficulty; **~s** *nmpl* trouble *sg*.

embêter [ãṅbātā] *vt* to bother; **s'~** *vi* (*s'ennuyer*) to be bored; **il ne s'embête pas!** (*ironique*) he does all right for himself!

emblée [ãṅblā]: **d'~** *ad* right away.

emblème [ãṅblcm] *nm* emblem.

embobiner [ãṅbobēnā] *vt* (*enjôler*): **~ qn** to get around sb.

emboîtable [ãṅbwàtàbl(ə)] *a* interlocking.

emboîter [ãṅbwàtā] *vt* to fit together; **s'~ dans** to fit into; **s'~ (l'un dans l'autre)** to fit together; **~ le pas à qn** to follow in sb's footsteps.

embolie [ãṅbolē] *nf* embolism.

embonpoint [ãṅbõṅpwaṅ] *nm* stoutness, corpulence; **prendre de l'~** to grow stout *ou* corpulent.

embouché, e [ãṅbōōshā] *a*: **mal ~** foulmouthed.

embouchure [ãṅbōōshür] *nf* (*GÉO*) mouth; (*MUS*) mouthpiece.

embourber [ãṅbōōrbā]: **s'~** *vi* to get stuck in the mud; (*fig*): **s'~ dans** to sink into.

embourgeoiser [ãṅbōōrzhwázā]: **s'~** *vi* to adopt a middle-class outlook.

embout [ãṅbōō] *nm* (*de canne*) tip; (*de tuyau*) nozzle.

embouteillage [ãṅbōōteyàzh] *nm* traffic jam.

embouteiller [ãṅbōōtāyā] *vt* (*suj: véhicules etc*) to block.

emboutir [ãṅbōōtēr] *vt* (*TECH*) to stamp; (*heurter*) to crash into, ram.

embranchement [ãṅbrãṅshmãṅ] *nm* (*routier*) junction; (*classification*) branch.

embrancher [ãṅbrãṅshā] *vt* (*tuyaux*) to join; **~ qch sur** to join sth to.

embraser [ãṅbrázā]: **s'~** *vi* to flare up.

embrassades [ãṅbrásàd] *nfpl* hugging and kissing *sg*.

embrasse [ãṅbrás] *nf* (*de rideau*) tie-back, loop.

embrasser [ãṅbrásā] *vt* to kiss; (*sujet, période*) to embrace, encompass; (*carrière*) to embark on; (*métier*) to go in for, take up; **~ du regard** to take in (*with eyes*); **s'~** to kiss (each other).

embrasure [ãṅbrázür] *nf*: **dans l'~ de la porte** in the door(way).

embrayage [ãṅbreyázh] *nm* clutch.

embrayer [ãṅbrāyā] *vi* (*AUTO*) to let in the clutch ♦ *vt* (*fig: affaire*) to set in motion; **~ sur qch** to begin on sth.

embrigader [ãṅbrēgàdā] *vt* to recruit.

embrocher [ãṅbroshā] *vt* to (put on a) spit (*ou* skewer).

embrouillamini [ãṅbrōōyámēnē] *nm* (*fam*) muddle.

embrouillé, e [ãṅbrōōyā] *a* (*affaire*) confused, muddled.

embrouiller [ãṅbrōōyā] *vt* (*fils*) to tangle (up); (*fiches, idées, personne*) to muddle up; **s'~** *vi* to get in a muddle.

embroussaillé, e [ãṅbrōōsáyā] *a* overgrown, scrubby; (*cheveux*) bushy, shaggy.

embruns [ãṅbrœṅ] *nmpl* sea spray *sg*.

embryologie [ãṅbrēyolozhē] *nf* embryology.

embryon [ãṅbrēyõṅ] *nm* embryo.

embryonnaire [ãṅbrēyoner] *a* embryonic.

embûches [ãṅbüsh] *nfpl* pitfalls, traps.

embué, e [ãṅbüā] *a* misted up; **yeux ~s de larmes** eyes misty with tears.

embuscade [ãṅbüskàd] *nf* ambush; **tendre une ~ à** to lay an ambush for.

embusqué, e [ãṅbüskā] *a* in ambush ♦ *nm* (*péj*) shirker.

embusquer [ãṅbüskā] *vt*: **s'~** *vi* to take up position (for an ambush).

éméché, e [āmāshā] *a* tipsy.

émeraude [emrōd] *nf* emerald ♦ *a inv* emerald-green.

émergence [āmerzhãṅs] *nf* (*fig*) emergence.

émerger [āmerzhā] *vi* to emerge; (*faire saillie, aussi fig*) to stand out.

émeri [emrē] *nm*: **toile** *ou* **papier ~** emery paper.

émérite [āmārēt] *a* highly skilled.

émerveillement [āmerveymãṅ] *nm* wonderment.

émerveiller [āmervāyā] *vt* to fill with wonder; **s'~ de** to marvel at.

émet [āme] *etc vb voir* **émettre**.

émétique [āmātēk] *nm* emetic.

émetteur, trice [āmetœr, -trēs] *a* transmitting; (*poste*) ~ transmitter.

émettre [āmetr(ə)] *vt* (*son, lumière*) to give out, emit; (*message etc: RADIO*) to transmit; (*billet, timbre, emprunt, chèque*) to issue;

(hypothèse, avis) to voice, put forward; *(vœu)* to express ♦ *vi:* ~ **sur ondes courtes** to broadcast on short wave.

émeus [āmœ̄] *etc vb voir* **émouvoir**.

émeute [āmœ̄t] *nf* riot.

émeutier, ière [āmœ̄tyā, -yer] *nm/f* rioter.

émeuve [āmœv] *etc vb voir* **émouvoir**.

émietter [āmyātā] *vt (pain, terre)* to crumble; *(fig)* to split up, disperse; **s'~** *vi (pain, terre)* to crumble.

émigrant, e [āmēgrāṅ, -āṅt] *nm/f* emigrant.

émigration [āmēgrāsyóṅ] *nf* emigration.

émigré, e [āmēgrā] *nm/f* expatriate.

émigrer [āmēgrā] *vi* to emigrate.

émincer [āmaṅsā] *vt (CULIN)* to slice thinly.

éminemment [āmēnámáṅ] *ad* eminently.

éminence [āmēnáṅs] *nf* distinction; *(colline)* knoll, hill; **Son É~** His Eminence; ~ **grise** éminence grise.

éminent, e [āmēnáṅ, -áṅt] *a* distinguished.

émir [āmēr] *nm* emir.

émirat [āmērá] *nm* emirate; **les É~s arabes unis (EAU)** the United Arab Emirates (UAE).

émis, e [āmē, -ēz] *pp de* **émettre**.

émissaire [āmēser] *nm* emissary.

émission [āmēsyóṅ] *nf (voir émettre)* emission; transmission; issue; *(RADIO, TV)* program *(US)*, programme *(Brit)*, broadcast.

émit [āmē] *etc vb voir* **émettre**.

emmagasinage [àṅmágázēnázh] *nm* storage; storing away.

emmagasiner [àṅmágázēnā] *vt* to (put into) store; *(fig)* to store up.

emmailloter [àṅmáyotā] *vt* to wrap up.

emmanchure [àṅmáṅshür] *nf* armhole.

emmêlement [àṅmelmáṅ] *nm (état)* tangle.

emmêler [àṅmālā] *vt* to tangle (up); *(fig)* to muddle up; **s'~** to get into a tangle.

emménagement [àṅmānázhmáṅ] *nm* settling in.

emménager [àṅmānázhā] *vi* to move in; ~ **dans** to move into.

emmener [àṅmnā] *vt* to take (with one); *(comme otage, capture)* to take away; ~ **qn au concert** to take sb to a concert.

emment(h)al [āmaṅtàl] *nm (fromage)* Emmenthal.

emmerder [àṅmerdā] *(fam!)* vt to bug, bother; **s'~** *vi (s'ennuyer)* to be bored stiff; **je t'emmerde!** to hell with you!

emmitoufler [àṅmētōōflā] *vt* to wrap up (warmly); **s'~** to wrap (o.s.) up (warmly).

emmurer [àṅmürā] *vt* to wall up, immure.

émoi [āmwá] *nm (agitation, effervescence)* commotion; *(trouble)* agitation; **en** ~ *(sens)* excited, stirred.

émollient, e [āmolyáṅ, -áṅt] *a (MÉD)* emollient.

émoluments [āmolümáṅ] *nmpl* remuneration *sg*, fee *sg*.

émonder [āmóṅdā] *vt (arbre etc)* to prune; *(amande etc)* to blanch.

émotif, ive [āmotēf, -ēv] *a* emotional.

émotion [āmōsyóṅ] *nf* emotion; **avoir des ~s** *(fig)* to have a fright; **donner des ~s à** to give a fright to; **sans** ~ without emotion, coldly.

émotionnant, e [āmōsyonáṅ, -áṅt] *a* upsetting.

émotionnel, le [āmōsyonel] *a* emotional.

émotionner [āmōsyonā] *vt* to upset.

émoulu, e [āmōōlü] *a:* **frais** ~ **de** fresh from, just out of.

émoussé, e [āmōōsā] *a* blunt.

émousser [āmōōsā] *vt* to blunt; *(fig)* to dull.

émoustiller [āmōōstēyā] *vt* to titillate, arouse.

émouvant, e [āmōōváṅ, -áṅt] *a* moving.

émouvoir [āmōōvwár] *vt (troubler)* to stir, affect; *(toucher, attendrir)* to move; *(indigner)* to rouse; *(effrayer)* to disturb, worry; **s'~** *vi* to be affected; to be moved; to be roused; to be disturbed *ou* worried.

empailler [àṅpâyā] *vt* to stuff.

empailleur, euse [àṅpâyœr, -ēz] *nm/f (d'animaux)* taxidermist.

empaler [àṅpálā] *vt* to impale.

empaquetage [àṅpàktázh] *nm* packing, packaging.

empaqueter [àṅpàktā] *vt* to pack up.

emparer [àṅpárā]: **s'~ de** *vt (objet)* to seize, grab; *(comme otage, MIL)* to seize; *(suj: peur etc)* to take hold of.

empâter [àṅpâtā]: **s'~** *vi* to thicken out.

empattement [àṅpátmáṅ] *nm (AUTO)* wheelbase; *(TYPO)* serif.

empêché, e [àṅpāshā] *a* detained.

empêchement [àṅpeshmáṅ] *nm (unexpected)* obstacle, hitch.

empêcher [àṅpāshā] *vt* to prevent; ~ **qn de faire** to prevent *ou* stop sb (from) doing; ~ **que qch (n')arrive/qn (ne) fasse** to prevent sth from happening/sb from doing; **il n'empêche que** nevertheless, he that as it may; **il n'a pas pu s'~ de rire** he couldn't help laughing.

empêcheur [àṅpeshœr] *nm:* ~ **de danser en rond** spoilsport, killjoy.

empeigne [àṅpeny] *nf* upper *(of shoe)*.

empennage [àṅpenázh] *nm (AVIAT)* tail assembly *(US)*, tailplane *(Brit)*.

empereur [àṅprœr] *nm* emperor.

empesé, e [àṅpəzā] *a (fig)* stiff, starchy.

empeser [àṅpəzā] *vt* to starch.

empester [àṅpestā] *vt (lieu)* to stink up *(US)* *ou* out *(Brit)* ♦ *vi* to stink, reek; ~ **le tabac/ le vin** to stink *ou* reek of tobacco/wine.

empêtrer [àṅpātrā] *vt:* **s'~ dans** *(fils etc, aussi fig)* to get tangled up in.

emphase [àṅfáz] *nf* pomposity, bombast; **avec** ~ pompously.

emphatique [àṅfátēk] *a* emphatic.

empiècement [àṅpyesmáṅ] *nm (COUTURE)* yoke.

empierrer [àṅpyārā] *vt (route)* to gravel *(US)*, metal *(Brit)*.

empiéter [àṅpyātā]: ~ **sur** *vt* to encroach upon.

empiffrer [àṅpēfrā]: **s'~** *vi (péj)* to stuff o.s.

empiler [àṅpēlā] *vt* to pile (up), stack (up); **s'~** *vi* to pile up.

empire [àṅpēr] *nm* empire; *(fig)* influence; **style E~** Empire style; **sous l'~ de** in the grip of.

empirer [àṅpērā] *vi* to worsen, deteriorate.

empirique [àṅpērēk] *a* empirical.

empirisme [àṅpērēsm(ə)] *nm* empiricism.

emplacement [àṅplásmáṅ] *nm* site; **sur l'~ de** on the site of.

emplâtre [ãᵖlâtr(ə)] *nm* plaster; *(fam)* clod.

emplette [ãᵖlɛt] *nf*: **faire l'~ de** to purchase; **~s** shopping *sg*; **faire des ~s** to go shopping

emplir [ãᵖlēr] *vt* to fill; **s'~ (de)** to fill (with).

emploi [ãᵖlwá] *nm* use; *(COMM, ÉCON)*: **l'~** employment; *(poste)* job, situation; **d'~ facile** easy to use; **le plein ~** full employment; **~ du temps** timetable, schedule.

emploie [ãᵖlwá] *etc vb voir* **employer**.

employé, e [ãᵖlwáyã] *nm/f* employee; **~ de bureau/banque** office/bank employee *ou* clerk; **~ de maison** domestic (servant).

employer [ãᵖlwáyã] *vt (outil, moyen, méthode, mot)* to use; *(ouvrier, main-d'œuvre)* to employ; **s'~ à qch/à faire** to apply *ou* devote o.s. to sth/to doing.

employeur, euse [ãᵖlwáycœr, -ēz] *nm/f* employer.

empocher [ãᵖoshã] *vt* to pocket.

empoignade [ãᵖwányàd] *nf* row, set-to.

empoigne [ãᵖwány] *nf*: **foire d'~** free-for-all.

empoigner [ãᵖwányã] *vt* to grab; **s'~** *(fig)* to have a row *ou* set-to.

empois [ãᵖwá] *nm* starch.

empoisonnement [ãᵖwázonmãᵑ] *nm* poisoning; *(fam: ennui)* annoyance, irritation.

empoisonner [ãᵖwázonã] *vt* to poison; *(empester: air, pièce)* to stink up *(US)* ou out *(Brit)*; *(fam)*: **~ qn** to drive sb mad; **s'~** to poison o.s.; **~ l'atmosphère** *(aussi fig)* to poison the atmosphere; **il nous empoisonne l'existence** he's the bane of our life.

empoissonner [ãᵖwásonã] *vt (étang, rivière)* to stock with fish.

emporté, e [ãᵖortã] *a (personne, caractère)* fiery.

emportement [ãᵖortəmãᵑ] *nm* fit of rage, anger *q*.

emporte-pièce [ãᵖortəpyes] *nm inv (TECH)* punch; **à l'~** *a (fig)* incisive.

emporter [ãᵖortã] *vt* to take (with one); *(en dérobant ou enlevant, emmener: blessés, voyageurs)* to take away; *(entraîner)* to carry away *ou* along; *(arracher)* to tear off; *(suj: rivière, vent)* to carry away; *(MIL: position)* to take; *(avantage, approbation)* to win; **s'~** *vi (de colère)* to fly into a rage, lose one's temper; **la maladie qui l'a emporté** the illness which caused his death; **l'~** to win; **l'~ (sur)** to get the upper hand (of); *(méthode etc)* to prevail (over); **boissons à ~** drinks to go *(US)*, take-away drinks *(Brit)*.

empoté, e [ãᵖotã] *a (maladroit)* clumsy.

empourpré, e [ãᵖōōrprã] *a* crimson.

empreint, e [ãᵖrań, -ańt] *a*: **~ de** marked with; tinged with ♦ *nf (de pied, main)* print; *(fig)* stamp, mark; **~e (digitale)** fingerprint.

empressé, e [ãᵖrãsã] *a* attentive; *(péj)* overanxious to please, overattentive.

empressement [ãᵖresmãᵑ] *nm* eagerness.

empresser [ãᵖrãsã]: **s'~** *vi*: **s'~ auprès de qn** to surround sb with attentions; **s'~ de faire** to hasten to do.

emprise [ãᵖrēz] *nf* hold, ascendancy; **sous l'~ de** under the influence of.

emprisonnement [ãᵖrēzonmãᵑ] *nm* imprisonment.

emprisonner [ãᵖrēzonã] *vt* to imprison, jail.

emprunt [ãᵖrœń] *nm* borrowing *q*, loan

(from debtor's point of view); *(LING etc)* borrowing; **nom d'~** assumed name; **~ d'État** government *ou* state loan; **~ public à 5%** 5% public loan.

emprunté, e [ãᵖrœńtã] *a (fig)* ill-at-ease, awkward.

emprunter [ãᵖrœńtã] *vt* to borrow; *(itinéraire)* to take, follow; *(style, manière)* to adopt, assume.

emprunteur, euse [ãᵖrœńtœr, -ēz] *nm/f* borrower.

empuantir [ãᵖüãńtēr] *vt* to stink up *(US)* ou out *(Brit)*.

EMT *sigle f* (= *éducation manuelle et technique*) *handwork as a school subject*.

ému, e [ãmü] *pp de* **émouvoir** ♦ *a* excited; touched; moved.

émulation [ãmülãsyóń] *nf* emulation.

émule [ãmül] *nm/f* imitator.

émulsion [ãmülsyóń] *nf* emulsion; *(cosmétique)* (water-based) lotion.

émut [ãmü] *etc vb voir* **émouvoir**.

en [ãń] *prép* in; *(avec direction)* to; *(temps: durée)*: **~ 3 jours/20 ans** in 3 days/20 years; *(: moment)*: **~ mars/hiver** in March/winter; *(moyen)*: **~ avion/taxi** by plane/taxi; *(composition)*: **~ verre** made of glass, glass *cpd*; **~ deux volumes/une pièce** in two volumes/one piece; **se casser ~ deux/plusieurs morceaux** to break in two/into several pieces; **~ dormant** while sleeping, as one sleeps; **~ sortant** on going out, as he *etc* went out; **fort ~ maths** good at math; **~ bonne santé** in good *ou* sound health; **~ réparation** being repaired, under repair; **~ T/étoile** T-/star-shaped; **~ chemise/chaussettes** in one's shirt/socks; **partir ~ vacances/voyage** to go (off) on vacation/on a trip; **peindre qch ~ rouge** to paint sth red; **~ soldat** as a soldier; **~ bon diplomate, il n'a rien dit** tactful as he is, he said nothing; **le même ~ plus grand** the same only *ou* but bigger ♦ *pronom (provenance)*: **j'~ viens** I've come from there; *(cause)*: **il ~ est malade** he's ill because of it; *(agent)*: **il ~ est aimé** he's loved by her; *(complément de nom)*: **j'~ connais les dangers** I know its dangers; *(indéfini)*: **j'~ ai/veux** I have/want some; **~ as-tu?** have you got any?; **je n'~ veux pas** I don't want any; **j'~ ai assez** I've got enough (of it *ou* them); *(fig)* I've had enough; **j'~ ai 2** I've got 2 (of them); **combien y ~ a-t-il?** how many (of them) are there?; **j'~ suis fier/ai besoin** I am proud of it/need it; **où ~ étais-je?** where was I?, where had I got to? *: voir le verbe ou l'adjectif lorsque 'en' correspond à 'de' introduisant un complément prépositionnel*.

ENA [ãnã] *sigle f* (= *École nationale d'administration) grande école for training civil servants*.

énarque [ãnárk(ə)] *nm/f* former ENA student.

encablure [ãᵑkáblür] *nf (NAVIG)* cable's length.

encadrement [ãᵑkádrəmãᵑ] *nm* framing; training; *(de porte)* frame; **~ du crédit** credit regulation.

encadrer [ãᵑkádrã] *vt (tableau, image)* to frame; *(fig: entourer)* to surround;

(*personnel, soldats etc*) to train; (*COMM: crédit*) to regulate.
encadreur [ãṅkãdrœr] *nm* (picture) framer.
encaisse [ãṅkɛs] *nf* cash in hand; ~ **or/ métallique** gold/gold and silver reserves.
encaissé, e [ãṅkãsã] *a* (*vallée*) steep-sided; (*rivière*) with steep banks.
encaisser [ãṅkãsã] *vt* (*chèque*) to cash; (*argent*) to collect; (*fig: coup, défaite*) to take.
encaisseur [ãṅkɛsœr] *nm* collector (*of debts etc*).
encan [ãṅkãṅ]: **à l'~** *ad* by auction.
encanailler [ãṅkãnãyã]: **s'~** *vi* to become vulgar *ou* common; to mix with the riff-raff.
encart [ãṅkár] *nm* insert; ~ **publicitaire** advertising insert.
encarter [ãṅkártã] *vt* to insert.
en-cas [ãṅkã] *nm inv* snack.
encastrable [ãṅkãstráblə] *a* (*four, élément*) that can be built in.
encastré, e [ãṅkãstrã] *a* (*four, baignoire*) built-in.
encastrer [ãṅkãstrã] *vt*: ~ **qch dans** (*mur*) to embed sth in(to); (*boîtier*) to fit sth into; **s'~ dans** to fit into; (*heurter*) to crash into.
encaustiquage [ãṅkostēkãzh] *nm* polishing, waxing.
encaustique [ãṅkostēk] *nf* polish, wax.
encaustiquer [ãṅkostēkã] *vt* to polish, wax.
enceinte [ãṅsãṅt] *af*: ~ **(de 6 mois)** (6 months) pregnant ♦ *nf* (*mur*) wall; (*espace*) enclosure; ~ **(acoustique)** speaker.
encens [ãṅsãṅ] *nm* incense.
encenser [ãṅsãṅsã] *vt* to (in)cense; (*fig*) to praise to the skies.
encensoir [ãṅsãṅswár] *nm* thurible (*Brit*), censer.
encercler [ãṅsɛrklã] *vt* to surround.
enchaîné [ãṅshãnã] *nm* (*CINÉMA*) lap dissolve.
enchaînement [ãṅshenmãṅ] *nm* (*fig*) linking.
enchaîner [ãṅshãnã] *vt* to chain up; (*mouvements, séquences*) to link (together) ♦ *vi* to carry on.
enchanté, e [ãṅshãṅtã] *a* (*ravi*) delighted; (*ensorcelé*) enchanted; ~ **(de faire votre connaissance)** pleased to meet you, how do you do?
enchantement [ãṅshãṅtmãṅ] *nm* delight; (*magie*) enchantment; **comme par** ~ as if by magic.
enchanter [ãṅshãṅtã] *vt* to delight.
enchanteur, teresse [ãṅshãṅtœr, -trɛs] *a* enchanting.
enchâsser [ãṅshãsã] *vt*: ~ **qch (dans)** to set sth (in).
enchère [ãṅshɛr] *nf* bid; **faire une** ~ to (make a) bid; **mettre/vendre aux ~s** to put up for (sale by)/sell by auction; **les ~s montent** the bids are rising; **faire monter les ~s** (*fig*) to raise the bidding.
enchérir [ãṅshãrēr] *vi*: ~ **sur qn** (*aux enchères, aussi fig*) to outbid sb.
enchérisseur, euse [ãṅshãrēsœr, -œz] *nm/f* bidder.
enchevêtrement [ãṅshvɛtrəmãṅ] *nm* tangle.
enchevêtrer [ãṅshvãtrã] *vt* to tangle (up).
enclave [ãṅklãv] *nf* enclave.
enclaver [ãṅklãvã] *vt* to enclose, hem in.

enclencher [ãṅklãṅshã] *vt* (*mécanisme*) to engage; (*fig: affaire*) to set in motion; **s'~** *vi* to engage.
enclin, e [ãṅklãṅ, -ēn] *a*: ~ **à qch/à faire** inclined *ou* prone to sth/to do.
enclore [ãṅklor] *vt* to enclose.
enclos [ãṅklō] *nm* enclosure; (*clôture*) fence.
enclume [ãṅklüm] *nf* anvil.
encoche [ãṅkosh] *nf* notch.
encoder [ãṅkodã] *vt* to encode.
encodeur [ãṅkodœr] *nm* encoder.
encoignure [ãṅkonyür] *nf* corner.
encoller [ãṅkolã] *vt* to paste.
encolure [ãṅkolür] *nf* (*tour de cou*) collar size; (*col, cou*) neck.
encombrant, e [ãṅkõṅbrãṅ, -ãṅt] *a* cumbersome, bulky.
encombre [ãṅkõṅbr(ə)]: **sans** ~ *ad* without mishap *ou* incident.
encombré, e [ãṅkõṅbrã] *a* (*pièce, passage*) cluttered; (*lignes téléphoniques*) busy; (*marché*) saturated.
encombrement [ãṅkõṅbrəmãṅ] *nm* (*d'un lieu*) cluttering (up); (*d'un objet: dimensions*) bulk.
encombrer [ãṅkõṅbrã] *vt* to clutter (up); (*gêner*) to hamper; **s'~ de** (*bagages etc*) to load *ou* burden o.s. with; ~ **le passage** to block *ou* obstruct the way.
encontre [ãṅkõṅtr(ə)]: **à l'~ de** *prép* against, counter to.
encorbellement [ãṅkorbelmãṅ] *nm*: **fenêtre en** ~ oriel window.
encorder [ãṅkordã] *vt*: **s'~** (*ALPINISME*) to rope up.
encore [ãṅkor] *ad* (*continuation*) still; (*de nouveau*) again; (*restriction*) even then *ou* so; (*intensif*): ~ **plus fort/mieux** even louder/better; ~**!** (*insatisfaction*) not again!; **pas** ~ not yet; ~ **que** even though; ~ **une fois** (once) again; ~ **deux jours** still two days, two more days; ~ **un effort** just a little more effort; **hier** ~ ... even yesterday ...; **non seulement** ... **mais** ~ not only ... but also; **(et puis) quoi** ~**?** what else?; **si** ~ if only.
encourageant, e [ãṅkōōrãzhãṅ, -ãṅt] *a* encouraging.
encouragement [ãṅkōōrãzhmãṅ] *nm* encouragement; (*récompense*) incentive.
encourager [ãṅkōōrãzhã] *vt* to encourage; ~ **qn à faire qch** to encourage sb to do sth.
encourir [ãṅkōōrēr] *vt* to incur.
encrasser [ãṅkrãsã] *vt* to dirty; (*AUTO etc*) to soot up.
encre [ãṅkr(ə)] *nf* ink; ~ **de Chine** India (*US*) *ou* Indian (*Brit*) ink; ~ **indélébile** indelible ink; ~ **sympathique** invisible ink.
encrer [ãṅkrã] *vt* to ink.
encreur [ãṅkrœr] *am*: **rouleau** ~ inking roller.
encrier [ãṅkrēyã] *nm* inkwell.
encroûter [ãṅkrōōtã]: **s'~** *vi* (*fig*) to get into a rut, get set in one's ways.
encyclique [ãṅsēklēk] *nf* encyclical.
encyclopédie [ãṅsēklopãdē] *nf* encyclopedia (*US*), encyclopaedia (*Brit*).
encyclopédique [ãṅsēklopãdēk] *a* encyclopedic (*US*), encyclopaedic (*Brit*).
endémique [ãṅdãmēk] *a* endemic.

endetté, e [ȧṅdātā] *a* in debt; (*fig*): **très ~ envers qn** deeply indebted to sb.

endettement [ȧṅdctmȧṅ] *nm* debts *pl*.

endetter [ȧṅdātā] *vt*, **s'~** *vi* to get into debt.

endeuiller [ȧṅdœyā] *vt* to plunge into mourning; **manifestation endeuillée par** event over which a tragic shadow was cast by.

endiablé, e [ȧṅdyȧblā] *a* furious; (*enfant*) boisterous.

endiguer [ȧṅdēgā] *vt* to dike (up); (*fig*) to check, hold back.

endimancher [ȧṅdēmȧṅshā] *vt*: **s'~** to put on one's Sunday best; **avoir l'air endimanché** to be all dressed up to the nines (*fam*).

endive [ȧṅdēv] *nf* chicory *q*.

endocrine [ȧṅdokrēn] *af*: **glande ~** endocrine (gland).

endoctrinement [ȧṅdoktrēnmȧṅ] *nm* indoctrination.

endoctriner [ȧṅdoktrēnā] *vt* to indoctrinate.

endolori, e [ȧṅdolorē] *a* painful.

endommager [ȧṅdomȧzhā] *vt* to damage.

endormant, e [ȧṅdormȧṅ, -ȧṅt] *a* dull, boring.

endormi, e [ȧṅdormē] *pp de* **endormir** ♦ *a* (*personne*) asleep; (*fig: indolent, lent*) sluggish; (*engourdi: main, pied*) numb.

endormir [ȧṅdormēr] *vt* to put to sleep; (*MÉD: dent, nerf*) to anesthetize (*US*), anaesthetize (*Brit*); (*fig: soupçons*) to allay; **s'~** *vi* to fall asleep, go to sleep.

endoscope [ȧṅdoskop] *nm* (*MÉD*) endoscope.

endoscopie [ȧṅdoskopē] *nf* endoscopy.

endosser [ȧṅdōsā] *vt* (*responsabilité*) to take, shoulder; (*chèque*) to endorse; (*uniforme, tenue*) to put on, don.

endroit [ȧṅdrwȧ] *nm* place; (*localité*): **les gens de l'~** the local people; (*opposé à l'envers*) right side; **à cet ~** in this place; **à l'~** right side out; the right way up; (*vêtement*) the right side out; **à l'~ de** *prép* regarding, with regard to; **par ~s** in places.

enduire [ȧṅdüēr] *vt* to coat; **~ qch de** to coat sth with.

enduit, e [ȧṅdüē, -ēt] *pp de* **enduire** ♦ *nm* coating.

endurance [ȧṅdürȧṅs] *nf* endurance.

endurant, e [ȧṅdürȧṅ, -ȧṅt] *a* tough, hardy.

endurcir [ȧṅdürsēr] *vt* (*physiquement*) to toughen; (*moralement*) to harden; **s'~** *vi* to become tougher; to become hardened.

endurer [ȧṅdürā] *vt* to endure, bear.

énergétique [ānerzhātēk] *a* (*ressources etc*) energy *cpd*; (*aliment*) energizing.

énergie [ānerzhē] *nf* (*PHYSIQUE*) energy; (*TECH*) power; (*fig: physique*) energy; (: *morale*) vigor (*US*), vigour (*Brit*), spirit.

énergique [ānerzhēk] *a* energetic, vigorous; (*mesures*) drastic, stringent.

énergiquement [ānerzhēkmȧṅ] *ad* energetically; drastically.

énergisant, e [ānerzhēzȧṅ, -ȧṅt] *a* energizing.

énergumène [ānergümen] *nm* rowdy character *ou* customer.

énervant, e [ānervȧṅ, -ȧṅt] *a* irritating.

énervé, e [ānervā] *a* on edge; (*agacé*) irritated.

énervement [ānervəmȧṅ] *nm* edginess; irritation.

énerver [ānervā] *vt* to irritate, annoy; **s'~** *vi* to get excited, get worked up.

enfance [ȧṅfȧṅs] *nf* (*âge*) childhood; (*fig*) infancy; (*enfants*) children *pl*; **c'est l'~ de l'art** it's child's play; **petite ~** infancy; **souvenir/ami d'~** childhood memory/friend; **retomber en ~** to lapse into one's second childhood.

enfant [ȧṅfȧṅ] *nm/f* child (*pl* children); **~ adoptif/naturel** adopted/natural child; **bon ~** *a* good-natured, easy-going; **~ de chœur** *nm* (*REL*) altar boy; **~ prodige** child prodigy; **~ unique** only child.

enfanter [ȧṅfȧṅtā] *vi* to give birth ♦ *vt* to give birth to.

enfantillage [ȧṅfȧṅtēyȧzh] *nm* (*péj*) childish behavior *q* (*US*) *ou* behaviour *q* (*Brit*).

enfantin, e [ȧṅfȧṅtȧṅ, -ēn] *a* childlike; (*péj*) childish; (*langage*) child *cpd*.

enfer [ȧṅfer] *nm* hell; **allure/bruit d'~** horrendous speed/noise.

enfermer [ȧṅfermā] *vt* to shut up; (*à clef, interner*) to lock up; **s'~** to shut o.s. away; **s'~ à clé** to lock o.s. in; **s'~ dans la solitude/le mutisme** to retreat into solitude/silence.

enferrer [ȧṅfārā]: **s'~** *vi*: **s'~ dans** to tangle o.s. up in.

enfiévré, e [ȧṅfyȧvrā] *a* (*fig*) feverish.

enfilade [ȧṅfēlȧd] *nf*: **une ~ de** a series *ou* line of; **prendre des rues en ~** to cross directly from one street into the next.

enfiler [ȧṅfēlā] *vt* (*vêtement*): **~ qch** to slip sth on, slip into sth; (*insérer*): **~ qch dans** to stick sth into; (*rue, couloir*) to take; (*perles*) to string; (*aiguille*) to thread; **s'~ dans** to disappear into.

enfin [ȧṅfȧṅ] *ad* at last; (*en énumérant*) lastly; (*de restriction, résignation*) still; (*eh bien*) well; (*pour conclure*) in a word.

enflammé, e [ȧṅflȧmā] *a* (*torche, allumette*) burning; (*MÉD: plaie*) inflamed; (*fig: nature, discours, déclaration*) fiery.

enflammer [ȧṅflȧmā] *vt* to set fire to; (*MÉD*) to inflame; **s'~** *vi* to catch fire; to become inflamed.

enflé, e [ȧṅflā] *a* swollen; (*péj: style*) bombastic, turgid.

enfler [ȧṅflā] *vi* to swell (up); **s'~** *vi* to swell.

enflure [ȧṅflür] *nf* swelling.

enfoncé, e [ȧṅfōṅsā] *a* staved-in, smashed-in; (*yeux*) deep-set.

enfoncement [ȧṅfōṅsmȧṅ] *nm* (*recoin*) nook.

enfoncer [ȧṅfōṅsā] *vt* (*clou*) to drive in; (*faire pénétrer*): **~ qch dans** to push (*ou* drive) sth into; (*forcer: porte*) to break open; (: *plancher*) to cause to cave in; (*défoncer: côtes etc*) to smash; (*fam: surpasser*) to lick, beat (hollow) ♦ *vi* (*dans la vase etc*) to sink in; (*sol, surface porteuse*) to give way; **s'~** *vi* to sink; **s'~ dans** to sink into; (*forêt, ville*) to disappear into; **~ un chapeau sur la tête** to ram a hat on one's head; **~ qn dans la dette** to drag sb into debt.

enfouir [ȧṅfwēr] *vt* (*dans le sol*) to bury; (*dans un tiroir etc*) to tuck away; **s'~ dans/sous** to bury o.s. in/under.

enfourcher [ȧṅfōōrshā] *vt* to mount; **~ son dada** (*fig*) to get on one's hobby-horse.

enfourner [ȧṅfōōrnā] *vt* to put in the oven;

(*poterie*) to put in the kiln; ~ **qch dans** to shove *ou* stuff sth into; **s'~ dans** (*suj: personne*) to dive into.

enfreignais [ãnfrenye] *etc vb voir* **enfreindre**.

enfreindre [ãnfrãndr(ə)] *vt* to infringe, break.

enfuir [ãnfüēr]: **s'~** *vi* to run away *ou* off.

enfumer [ãnfümã] *vt* to smoke out.

enfuyais [ãnfüēye] *etc vb voir* **enfuir**.

engagé, e [ãngázhã] *a* (*littérature etc*) engagé, committed.

engageant, e [ãngázhãn, -ãnt] *a* attractive, appealing.

engagement [ãngázhmãn] *nm* taking on, engaging; starting; investing; (*promesse*) commitment; (*MIL: combat*) engagement; (*: recrutement*) enlistment; (*SPORT*) entry; **prendre l'~ de faire** to undertake to do; **sans ~** (*COMM*) without obligation.

engager [ãngázhã] *vt* (*embaucher*) to take on, engage; (*commencer*) to start; (*lier*) to bind, commit; (*impliquer, entraîner*) to involve; (*investir*) to invest, lay out; (*faire intervenir*) to engage; (*SPORT: concurrents, chevaux*) to enter; (*inciter*): ~ **qn à faire** to urge sb to do; (*faire pénétrer*): ~ **qch dans** to insert sth into; ~ **qn à qch** to urge sth on sb; **s'~** to take a job; (*MIL*) to enlist; (*promettre, politiquement*) to commit o.s.; (*débuter*) to start (up); **s'~ à faire** to undertake to do; **s'~ dans** (*rue, passage*) to enter, turn into; (*s'emboîter*) to engage *ou* fit into; (*fig: affaire, discussion*) to enter into, embark on.

engazonner [ãngázonã] *vt* to turf.

engeance [ãnzhãns] *nf* mob.

engelure [ãnzhlür] *nf* chilblain.

engendrer [ãnzhãndrã] *vt* to father; (*fig*) to create, breed.

engin [ãnzhãn] *nm* machine; instrument; vehicle; (*péj*) gadget; (*AVIAT: avion*) aircraft *inv*; (*: missile*) missile; ~ **blindé** armored vehicle; ~ (**explosif**) (explosive) device; **~s** (**spéciaux**) missiles.

englober [ãnglobã] *vt* to include.

engloutir [ãnglōōtēr] *vt* to swallow up; (*fig: dépenses*) to devour; **s'~** to be engulfed.

engoncé, e [ãngõnsã] *a*: ~ **dans** cramped in.

engorgement [ãngorzhəmãn] *nm* blocking; (*MÉD*) engorgement.

engorger [ãngorzhã] *vt* to obstruct, block; **s'~** *vi* to become blocked.

engouement [ãngōōmãn] *nm* (sudden) passion.

engouffrer [ãngōōfrã] *vt* to swallow up, devour; **s'~ dans** to rush into.

engourdi, e [ãngōōrdē] *a* numb.

engourdir [ãngōōrdēr] *vt* to numb; (*fig*) to dull, blunt; **s'~** *vi* to go numb.

engrais [ãngre] *nm* manure; ~ (**chimique**) (chemical) fertilizer; ~ **organique/inorganique** organic/inorganic fertilizer.

engraisser [ãngrãsã] *vt* to fatten (up); (*terre: fertiliser*) to fertilize ♦ *vi* (*péj*) to get fat(ter).

engranger [ãngrãnzhã] *vt* (*foin*) to bring in; (*fig*) to store away.

engrenage [ãngrənázh] *nm* gears *pl*, gearing; (*fig*) chain.

engueuler [ãngœlã] *vt* (*fam*) to bawl out.

enguirlander [ãngērlãndã] *vt* (*fam*) to give sb

a bawling out.

enhardir [ãnárdēr]: **s'~** *vi* to grow bolder.

ENI [ãnē] *sigle f* = **école normale** (**d'instituteurs**).

énième [ãnyem] *a* = **nième**.

énigmatique [ãnēgmátēk] *a* enigmatic.

énigmatiquement [ãnēgmátēkmãn] *ad* enigmatically.

énigme [ãnēgm(ə)] *nf* riddle.

enivrant, e [ãnēvrãn, -ãnt] *a* intoxicating.

enivrer [ãnēvrã] *vt*: **s'~** to get drunk; **s'~ de** (*fig*) to become intoxicated with.

enjambée [ãnzhãnbã] *nf* stride; **d'une** ~ with one stride.

enjamber [ãnzhãnbã] *vt* to stride over; (*suj: pont etc*) to span, straddle.

enjeu, x [ãnzhœ] *nm* stakes *pl*.

enjoindre [ãnzhwãndr(ə)] *vt*: ~ **à qn de faire** to enjoin *ou* order sb to do.

enjôler [ãnzhōlã] *vt* to coax, wheedle.

enjôleur, euse [ãnzhōlœr, -œz] *a* (*sourire, paroles*) winning.

enjolivement [ãnzholēvmãn] *nm* embellishment.

enjoliver [ãnzholēvã] *vt* to embellish.

enjoliveur [ãnzholēvœr] *nm* (*AUTO*) hub cap.

enjoué, e [ãnzhwã] *a* playful.

enlacer [ãnlásã] *vt* (*étreindre*) to embrace, hug; (*suj: lianes*) to wind around, entwine.

enlaidir [ãnlãdēr] *vt* to make ugly ♦ *vi* to become ugly.

enlevé, e [ãnlvã] *a* (*morceau de musique*) played brightly.

enlèvement [ãnlevmãn] *nm* removal; (*rapt*) abduction, kidnapping; **l'~ des ordures ménagères** garbage (*US*) *ou* refuse (*Brit*) collection.

enlever [ãnlvã] *vt* (*ôter: gén*) to remove; (*: vêtement, lunettes*) to take off; (*: MÉD: organe*) to remove; (*emporter: ordures etc*) to collect, take away; (*prendre*): ~ **qch à qn** to take sth (away) from sb; (*kidnapper*) to abduct, kidnap; (*obtenir: prix, contrat*) to win; (*MIL: position*) to take; (*morceau de piano etc*) to execute with spirit *ou* brio; **s'~** *vi* (*tache*) to come out *ou* off; **la maladie qui nous l'a enlevé** (*euphémisme*) the illness which took him from us.

enliser [ãnlēzã]: **s'~** *vi* to sink, get stuck; (*dialogue etc*) to get bogged down.

enluminure [ãnlümēnür] *nf* illumination.

ENM *sigle f* (= *École nationale de la magistrature*) grande école for law students.

enneigé, e [ãnnãzhã] *a* snowy; (*col*) snowbound; (*maison*) snowed-in.

enneigement [ãnnezhmãn] *nm* depth of snow, snowfall; **bulletin d'~** snow report.

ennemi, e [enmē] *a* hostile; (*MIL*) enemy *cpd* ♦ *nm/f* enemy; **être ~ de** to be strongly averse *ou* opposed to.

ennième [enyem] *a* = **nième**.

ennoblir [ãnnoblēr] *vt* to ennoble.

ennui [ãnnüē] *nm* (*lassitude*) boredom; (*difficulté*) trouble *q*; **avoir des ~s** to have problems; **s'attirer des ~s** to cause problems for o.s.

ennuie [ãnnüē] *etc vb voir* **ennuyer**.

ennuyé, e [ãnnüēyã] *a* (*air, personne*) preoccupied, worried.

ennuyer [ánnüēyā] *vt* to bother; *(lasser)* to bore; **s'~** *vi* to be bored; **s'~ de** *(regretter)* to miss; **si cela ne vous ennuie pas** if it's no trouble to you.

ennuyeux, euse [ánnüēyœ̄, -ēz] *a* boring, tedious; *(agaçant)* annoying.

énoncé [ānóńsā] *nm* terms *pl*; wording; *(LING)* utterance.

énoncer [ānóńsā] *vt* to say, express; *(conditions)* to set out, lay down, state.

énonciation [ānóńsyásyôń] *nf* statement.

enorgueillir [ánnorgœyēr]: **s'~ de** *vt* to pride o.s. on; to boast.

énorme [ānorm(ə)] *a* enormous, huge.

énormément [ānormāmáń] *ad* enormously, tremendously; **~ de neige/gens** an enormous amount of snow/number of people.

énormité [ānormētā] *nf* enormity, hugeness; *(propos)* outrageous remark.

enquérir [áńkārēr]: **s'~ de** *vt* to inquire about.

enquête [áńket] *nf* *(de journaliste, de police)* investigation; *(judiciaire, administrative)* inquiry; *(sondage d'opinion)* survey.

enquêter [áńkātā] *vi* to investigate; to hold an inquiry; *(faire un sondage)*: **~ (sur)** to do a survey (on), carry out an opinion poll (on).

enquêteur, euse *ou* **trice** [áńkɛtœr, -ēz, -trēs] *nm/f* officer in charge of an investigation; person conducting a survey; pollster.

enquiers, enquière [áńkyer] *etc vb voir* **enquérir**.

enquiquiner [áńkēkēnā] *vt* to rile, irritate.

enquis, e [áńkē, -ēz] *pp de* **enquérir**.

enraciné, e [áńrásēnā] *a* deep-rooted.

enragé, e [áńrázhā] *a* *(MÉD)* rabid, with rabies; *(furieux)* furiously angry; *(fig)* fanatical; **~ de** wild about.

enrageant, e [áńrázháń, -áńt] *a* infuriating.

enrager [áńrázhā] *vi* to be furious, be in a rage; **faire ~ qn** to make sb wild with anger.

enrayer [áńrāyā] *vt* to check, stop; **s'~** *vi* *(arme à feu)* to jam.

enrégimenter [áńrāzhēmáńtā] *vt* *(péj)* to enlist.

enregistrement [áńrzhēstrəmáń] *nm* recording; *(ADMIN)* registration; **~ des bagages** *(à l'aéroport)* baggage check-in; **~ magnétique** tape-recording.

enregistrer [áńrzhēstrā] *vt* *(MUS, INFORM etc)* to record; *(remarquer, noter)* to note, record; *(COMM: commande)* to note, enter; *(fig: mémoriser)* to make a mental note of; *(ADMIN)* to register; *(aussi:* **faire ~***: bagages: par train)* to register; *(: à l'aéroport)* to check in.

enregistreur, euse [áńrzhēstrœr, -ēz] *a* *(machine)* recording *cpd* ♦ *nm* *(appareil)*: **~ de vol** *(AVIAT)* flight recorder.

enrhumé, e [áńrümā] *a*: **il est ~** he has a cold.

enrhumer [áńrümā]: **s'~** *vi* to catch a cold.

enrichir [áńrēshēr] *vt* to make rich(er); *(fig)* to enrich; **s'~** to get rich(er).

enrichissement [áńrēshēsmáń] *nm* enrichment.

enrober [áńrobā] *vt*: **~ qch de** to coat sth with; *(fig)* to wrap sth up in.

enrôlement [áńrôlmáń] *nm* enlistment.

enrôler [áńrōlā] *vt* to enlist; **s'~ (dans)** to enlist (in).

enroué, e [áńrwā] *a* hoarse.

enrouer [áńrwā]: **s'~** *vi* to go hoarse.

enrouler [áńrōōlā] *vt* *(fil, corde)* to wind (up); **s'~** to coil up; **~ qch autour de** to wind sth (a)round.

enrouleur, euse [áńrōōlœr, -ēz] *a* *(TECH)* winding ♦ *nm voir* **ceinture**.

enrubanné, e [áńrübánā] *a* trimmed with ribbon.

ENS *sigle f* = **école normale supérieure**.

ensabler [áńsáblā] *vt* *(port, canal)* to silt up, sand up; *(embarcation)* to strand (on a sandbank); **s'~** *vi* to silt up; to get stranded.

ensacher [áńsáshā] *vt* to pack into bags.

ENSAM *sigle f* (= *École nationale supérieure des arts et métiers)* *grande école for engineering students.*

ensanglanté, e [áńsáńgláńtā] *a* covered with blood.

enseignant, e [áńsenyáń, -áńt] *a* teaching ♦ *nm/f* teacher.

enseigne [áńseny] *nf* sign ♦ *nm*: **~ de vaisseau** ensign *(US)*, lieutenant *(Brit)*; **à telle ~ que** so much so that; **être logés à la même ~** *(fig)* to be in the same boat; **~ lumineuse** neon sign.

enseignement [áńsenymáń] *nm* teaching; **~ ménager** home economics; **~ primaire** grade school *(US) ou* primary *(Brit)* education; **~ secondaire** high school *(US) ou* secondary *(Brit)* education.

enseigner [áńsānyā] *vt, vi* to teach; **~ qch à qn/à qn que** to teach sb sth/sb that.

ensemble [áńsáńbl(ə)] *ad* together ♦ *nm* *(assemblage, MATH)* set; *(totalité)*: **l'~ du/ de la** the whole *ou* entire; *(vêtement féminin)* ensemble, suit; *(unité, harmonie)* unity; *(résidentiel)* housing development; **aller ~** to go together; **impression/idée d'~** overall *ou* general impression/idea; **dans l'~** *(en gros)* on the whole; **dans son ~** overall, in general; **~ vocal/musical** vocal/musical ensemble.

ensemblier [áńsáńblēyā] *nm* interior designer.

ensemencer [áńsmáńsā] *vt* to sow.

enserrer [áńsárā] *vt* to hug (tightly).

ENSET [enset] *sigle f* (= *École normale supérieure de l'enseignement technique)* *grande école for training technical teachers.*

ensevelir [áńsəvlēr] *vt* to bury.

ensilage [áńsēlázh] *nm* *(aliment)* silage.

ensoleillé, e [áńsolāyā] *a* sunny.

ensoleillement [áńsoleymáń] *nm* period *ou* hours *pl* of sunshine.

ensommeillé, e [áńsomāyā] *a* sleepy, drowsy.

ensorceler [áńsorsəlā] *vt* to enchant, bewitch.

ensuite [áńsüēt] *ad* then, next; *(plus tard)* afterwards, later; **~ de quoi** after which.

ensuivre [áńsüēvr(ə)]: **s'~** *vi* to follow, ensue; **il s'ensuit que ...** it follows that ...; **et tout ce qui s'ensuit** and all that goes with it.

entaché, e [áńtáshā] *a*: **~ de** marred by; **~ de nullité** null and void.

entacher [áńtáshā] *vt* to soil.

entaille [áńtây] *nf* *(encoche)* notch; *(blessure)* cut; **se faire une ~** to cut o.s.

entailler [áńtáyā] *vt* to notch; to cut; **s'~ le doigt** to cut one's finger.

entamer [ãntámã] *vt* to start; (*hostilités, pourparlers*) to open; (*fig: altérer*) to make a dent in; to damage.

entartrer [ãntártrã]: **s'~** *vi* to fur up; (*dents*) to become covered with plaque.

entassement [ãntásmãn] *nm* (*tas*) pile, heap.

entasser [ãntásã] *vt* (*empiler*) to pile up, heap up; (*tenir à l'étroit*) to cram together; **s'~** *vi* to pile up; to cram; **s'~ dans** to cram into.

entendement [ãntãndmãn] *nm* understanding.

entendre [ãntãndr(ə)] *vt* to hear; (*comprendre*) to understand; (*vouloir dire*) to mean; (*vouloir*): **~ être obéi/que** to intend *ou* mean to be obeyed/that; **j'ai entendu dire que** I've heard (it said) that; **je suis heureux de vous l'~ dire** I'm pleased to hear you say it; **~ parler de** to hear of; **laisser ~ que**, **donner à ~ que** to let it be understood that; **~ raison** to listen to reason; **qu'est-ce qu'il ne faut pas ~!** what next!; **j'ai mal entendu** I didn't catch what was said; **je vous entends très mal** I can hardly hear you; **s'~** *vi* (*sympathiser*) to get along; (*se mettre d'accord*) to agree; **s'~ a qch/a faire** (*être compétent*) to be good at sth/doing; **ça s'entend** (*est audible*) it's audible; **je m'entends** I mean; **entendons-nous!** let's be clear what we mean.

entendu, e [ãntãndü] *pp de* **entendre ♦** *a* (*réglé*) agreed; (*au courant: air*) knowing; **étant ~ que** since (it's understood *ou* agreed that); **(c'est) ~** all right, agreed; **c'est ~** (*concession*) all right, granted; **bien ~** of course.

entente [ãntãnt] *nf* (*entre amis, pays*) understanding, harmony; (*accord, traité*) agreement, understanding; **à double ~** (*sens*) with a double meaning.

entériner [ãntãrénã] *vt* to ratify, confirm.

entérite [ãntãret] *nf* enteritis *q*.

enterrement [ãntermãn] *nm* burying; (*cérémonie*) funeral, burial; (*cortège funèbre*) funeral procession.

enterrer [ãntãrã] *vt* to bury.

entêtant, e [ãntetãn, ãnt] *a* heady.

entêté, e [ãntãtã] *a* stubborn.

en-tête [ãntet] *nm* heading; (*de papier à lettres*) letterhead; **papier à ~** letterhead (*US*), headed notepaper (*Brit*).

entêtement [ãntetmãn] *nm* stubbornness.

entêter [ãntãtã]: **s'~** *vi*: **s'~ (à faire)** to persist (in doing).

enthousiasmant, e [ãntōōzyásmãn, -ãnt] *a* exciting.

enthousiasme [ãntōōzyásm(ə)] *nm* enthusiasm; **avec ~** enthusiastically.

enthousiasmé, e [ãntōōzyásmã] *a* filled with enthusiasm.

enthousiasmer [ãntōōzyásmã] *vt* to fill with enthusiasm; **s'~ (pour qch)** to get enthusiastic (about sth).

enthousiaste [ãntōōzyást(ə)] *a* enthusiastic.

enticher [ãntēshã]: **s'~ de** *vt* to become infatuated with.

entier, ière [ãntyã, -yer] *a* (*non entamé, en totalité*) whole; (*total, complet*) complete; (*fig: caractère*) unbending, averse to compromise **♦** *nm* (*MATH*) whole; **en ~** totally; in its entirety; **se donner tout ~ à qch**

to devote o.s. completely to sth; **lait ~** whole (*US*) *ou* full-cream (*Brit*) milk; **pain ~** whole wheat (*US*) *ou* wholemeal (*Brit*) bread; **nombre ~** whole number.

entièrement [ãntyermãn] *ad* entirely, completely, wholly.

entité [ãntētã] *nf* entity.

entomologie [ãntomolozhē] *nf* entomology.

entonner [ãntonã] *vt* (*chanson*) to strike up.

entonnoir [ãntonwár] *nm* (*ustensile*) funnel; (*trou*) shell-hole, crater.

entorse [ãntors(ə)] *nf* (*MÉD*) sprain; (*fig*): **~ à la loi/au règlement** infringement of the law/rule; **se faire une ~ à la cheville/au poignet** to sprain one's ankle/wrist.

entortiller [ãntortēyã] *vt* (*envelopper*): **~ qch dans/avec** to wrap sth in/with; (*enrouler*): **~ qch autour de** to twist *ou* wind sth (a)round; (*fam*): **~ qn** to get (a)round sb; (*: duper*) to hoodwink *ou* trick sb; **s'~ dans** (*draps*) to roll o.s. up in; (*fig: réponses*) to get tangled up in.

entourage [ãntōōrázh] *nm* circle; family (circle); (*d'une vedette etc*) entourage; (*ce qui enclôt*) border, frame.

entouré, e [ãntōōrã] *a* (*recherché, admiré*) popular; **~ de** surrounded by.

entourer [ãntōōrã] *vt* to surround; (*apporter son soutien à*) to rally round; **~ de** to surround with; (*trait*) to encircle with; **s'~ de** to surround o.s. with; **s'~ de précautions** to take all possible precautions.

entourloupette [ãntōōrlōōpet] *nf* mean trick.

entournures [ãntōōrnür] *nfpl*: **gêné aux ~** in financial difficulties; (*fig*) a bit awkward.

entracte [ãntrákt(ə)] *nm* interval.

entraide [ãntred] *nf* mutual aid *ou* assistance.

entraider [ãntrãdã]: **s'~** *vi* to help each other.

entrailles [ãntráy] *nfpl* entrails; (*humaines*) bowels.

entrain [ãntrãn] *nm* spirit; **avec ~** (*répondre, travailler*) energetically; **faire qch sans ~** to do sth half-heartedly *ou* without enthusiasm.

entraînant, e [ãntrenãn, -ãnt] *a* (*musique*) stirring, rousing.

entraînement [ãntrenmãn] *nm* training; (*TECH*): **~ à chaîne/galet** chain/wheel drive; **manquer d'~** to be unfit; **~ par ergots/friction** (*INFORM*) tractor/friction feed.

entraîner [ãntrãnã] *vt* (*tirer: wagons*) to pull; (*charrier*) to carry *ou* drag along; (*TECH*) to drive; (*emmener: personne*) to take (off); (*mener à l'assaut, influencer*) to lead; (*SPORT*) to train; (*impliquer*) to entail; (*causer*) to lead to, bring about; **~ qn à faire** (*inciter*) to lead sb to do; **s'~** (*SPORT*) to train; **s'~ à qch/à faire** to train o.s. for sth/to do.

entraîneur [ãntrenœr] *nm* (*SPORT*) coach, trainer; (*HIPPISME*) trainer.

entraîneuse [ãntrenēz] *nf* (*de bar*) B-girl (*US*), hostess (*Brit*).

entrapercevoir [ãntrápersəvwár] *vt* to catch a glimpse of.

entrave [ãntráv] *nf* hindrance.

entraver [ãntrãvã] *vt* (*circulation*) to hold up; (*action, progrès*) to hinder, hamper.

entre [ãntr(ə)] *prép* between; (*parmi*) among(st); **l'un d'~ eux/nous** one of them/

us; **le meilleur d'~ eux/nous** the best of them/us; **ils préfèrent rester ~ eux** they prefer to keep to themselves; **~ autres (choses)** among other things; **~ nous, ...** between ourselves ..., between you and me ...; **ils se battent ~ eux** they are fighting among(st) themselves.

entrebâillé, e |aṅtrəbáyā| *a* half-open, ajar.

entrebâillement |aṅtrəbáymáṅ| *nm*: **dans l'~ (de la porte)** in the half-open door.

entrebâiller |aṅtrəbáyā| *vt* to half open.

entrechat |aṅtrəshá| *nm* leap.

entrechoquer |aṅtrəshokā|: **s'~** *vi* to knock *ou* bang together.

entrecôte |aṅtrəkōt| *nf* entrecôte *ou* rib steak.

entrecoupé, e |aṅtrəkōopā| *a* (*paroles, voix*) broken.

entrecouper |aṅtrəkōopā| *vt*: **~ qch de** to intersperse sth with; **~ un récit/voyage de** to interrupt a story/journey with; **s'~** (*traits, lignes*) to cut across each other.

entrecroiser |aṅtrəkrwázā| *vt*, **s'~** *vi* to intertwine.

entrée |aṅtrā| *nf* entrance; (*accès: au cinéma etc*) admission; (*billet*) (admission) ticket; (*CULIN*) first course; (*COMM*: *de marchandises*) entry; (*INFORM*) entry, input; **~s** *nfpl*: **avoir ses ~s chez** *ou* **auprès de** to be a welcome visitor to; **d'~** *ad* from the outset; **erreur d'~** input error; **"~ interdite"** "no admittance *ou* entry"; **~ des artistes** stage door; **~ en matière** introduction; **~ en scène** entrance; **~ de service** service entrance.

entrefaites |aṅtrəfet|: **sur ces ~** *ad* at this juncture.

entrefilet |aṅtrəfēlε| *nm* (*article*) paragraph, short report.

entregent |aṅtrəzháṅ| *nm*: **avoir de l'~** to have an easy manner.

entre-jambes |aṅtrəzháṅb| *nm inv* crotch.

entrelacement |aṅtrəlásmáṅ| *nm*: **un ~ de ...** a network of ....

entrelacer |aṅtrəlásā| *vt*, **s'~** *vi* to intertwine.

entrelarder |aṅtrəlárdā| *vt* to lard; (*fig*): **entrelardé de** interspersed with.

entremêler |aṅtrəmālā| *vt*: **~ qch de** to (inter)mingle sth with.

entremets |aṅtrəmε| *nm* (cream) dessert.

entremetteur, euse |aṅtrəmεtœr, -ēz| *nm/f* go-between.

entremettre |aṅtrəmεtr(ə)|: **s'~** *vi* to intervene.

entremise |aṅtrəmēz| *nf* intervention; **par l'~ de** through.

entrepont |aṅtrəpóṅ| *nm* steerage; **dans l'~** in steerage.

entreposer |aṅtrəpōzā| *vt* to store, put into storage.

entrepôt |aṅtrəpō| *nm* warehouse.

entreprenant, e |aṅtrəprənáṅ, -áṅt| *vb voir* **entreprendre ♦** *a* (*actif*) enterprising; (*trop galant*) forward.

entreprendre |aṅtrəpráṅdr(ə)| *vt* (*se lancer dans*) to undertake; (*commencer*) to begin *ou* start (upon); (*personne*) to buttonhole; **~ qn sur un sujet** to tackle sb on a subject; **~ de faire** to undertake to do.

entrepreneur |aṅtrəprənœr| *nm*: **~ (en**

bâtiment) (building) contractor; **~ de pompes funèbres** funeral director, undertaker.

entreprenne |aṅtrəprεn| *etc vb voir* **entreprendre.**

entrepris, e |aṅtrəprē, -ēz| *pp de* **entreprendre ♦** *nf* (*société*) firm, business; (*action*) undertaking, venture.

entrer |aṅtrā| *vi* to go (*ou* come) in, enter **♦** *vt* (*INFORM*) to input, enter; (**faire**) **~ qch dans** to get sth into; **~ dans** (*gén*) to enter; (*pièce*) to go (*ou* come) into, enter; (*club*) to join; (*heurter*) to run into; (*partager: vues, craintes de qn*) to share; (*être une composante de*) to go into; (*faire partie de*) to form part of; **~ au couvent** to enter a convent; **~ à l'hôpital** to go into the hospital; **~ dans le système** (*INFORM*) to log in; **~ en fureur** to become angry; **~ en ébullition** to start to boil; **~ en scène** to come on stage; **laisser ~ qn/qch** to let sb/sth in; **faire ~** (*visiteur*) to show in.

entresol |aṅtrəsol| *nm* entresol, mezzanine.

entre-temps |aṅtrətáṅ| *ad* meanwhile, (in the) meantime.

entretenir |aṅtrətnēr| *vt* to maintain; (*amitié*) to keep alive; (*famille, maîtresse*) to support, keep; **~ qn (de)** to speak to sb (about); **s'~ (de)** to converse (about); **~ qn dans l'erreur** to let sb remain in ignorance.

entretenu, e |aṅtrətnü| *pp de* **entretenir ♦** *a* (*femme*) kept; **bien/mal ~** (*maison, jardin*) well/badly kept.

entretien |aṅtrətyaṅ| *nm* maintenance; (*discussion*) discussion, talk; (*audience*) interview; **frais d'~** maintenance charges.

entretiendrai |aṅtrətyaṅdrā|, **entretiens** |aṅtrətyaṅ| *etc vb voir* **entretenir.**

entre-tuer |aṅtrətüā|: **s'~** *vi* to kill one another.

entreverrai |aṅtrəvεrā|, **entrevit** |aṅtrəvē| *etc vb voir* **entrevoir.**

entrevoir |aṅtrəvwár| *vt* (*à peine*) to make out; (*brièvement*) to catch a glimpse of.

entrevu, e |aṅtrəvü| *pp de* **entrevoir ♦** *nf* meeting; (*audience*) interview.

entrouvert, e |aṅtrōōver, -ert(ə)| *pp de* **entrouvrir ♦** *a* half-open.

entrouvrir |aṅtrōōvrēr| *vt*, **s'~** *vi* to half open.

énumération |ānümārásyóṅ| *nf* enumeration.

énumérer |ānümārā| *vt* to list, enumerate.

énurésie |ānürāzē| *nf* enuresis.

envahir |aṅváēr| *vt* to invade; (*suj: inquiétude, peur*) to come over.

envahissant, e |aṅváēsáṅ, -áṅt| *a* (*péj: personne*) interfering, intrusive.

envahissement |aṅváēsmáṅ| *nm* invasion.

envahisseur |aṅváēsœr| *nm* (*MIL*) invader.

envasement |aṅnvázmáṅ| *nm* silting up.

envaser |aṅnvázā|: **s'~** *vi* to get bogged down (in the mud).

enveloppe |aṅvlop| *nf* (*de lettre*) envelope; (*TECH*) casing; outer layer; **mettre sous ~** to put in an envelope; **~ autocollante** self-seal envelope; **~ budgétaire** budget; **~ à fenêtre** window envelope.

envelopper |aṅvlopā| *vt* to wrap; (*fig*) to envelop, shroud; **s'~ dans un châle/une couverture** to wrap o.s. in a shawl/blanket.

envenimer [ãṅvnēmā] *vt* to aggravate; **s'~** *vi* (*plaie*) to fester; (*situation, relations*) to worsen.

envergure [ãṅvergür] *nf* (*d'un oiseau, avion*) wingspan; (*fig: étendue*) scope; (: *valeur*) calibre.

enverrai [ãṅverā] *etc vb voir* **envoyer**.

envers [ãṅver] *prép* towards, to ♦ *nm* other side; (*d'une étoffe*) wrong side; **à l'~** upside down; back to front; (*vêtement*) inside out; **~ et contre tous** *ou* **tout** against all opposition.

enviable [ãṅvyábl(ə)] *a* enviable; **peu ~** unenviable.

envie [ãṅvē] *nf* (*sentiment*) envy; (*souhait*) desire, wish; (*tache sur la peau*) birthmark; (*filet de peau*) hangnail; **avoir ~ de** to feel like; (*désir plus fort*) to want; **avoir ~ de faire** to feel like doing; to want to do; **avoir ~ que** to wish that; **donner à qn l'~ de faire** to make sb want to do; **ça lui fait ~** he would like that.

envier [ãṅvyā] *vt* to envy; **~ qch à qn** to envy sb sth; **n'avoir rien à ~ à** to have no cause to be envious of.

envieux, euse [ãṅvyœ̄, -œ̄z] *a* envious.

environ [ãṅvēróṅ] *ad*: **~ 3 h/2 km, 3 h/2 km ~** (around) about 3 o'clock/2 km, 3 o'clock/2 km or so.

environnant, e [ãṅvēronãṅ, -ãṅt] *a* surrounding.

environnement [ãṅvēronmãṅ] *nm* environment.

environnementaliste [ãṅvēronmãṅtálēst(ə)] *nm/f* environmentalist.

environner [ãṅvēronā] *vt* to surround.

environs [ãṅvēróṅ] *nmpl* surroundings; **aux ~ de** around.

envisageable [ãṅvēzàzhábl(ə)] *a* conceivable.

envisager [ãṅvēzàzhā] *vt* (*examiner, considérer*) to view, contemplate; (*avoir en vue*) to envisage; **~ de faire** to consider *ou* contemplate doing.

envoi [ãṅvwá] *nm* sending; (*paquet*) parcel, consignment; **~ contre remboursement** (*COMM*) cash on delivery.

envoie [ãṅvwá] *etc vb voir* **envoyer**.

envol [ãṅvol] *nm* takeoff.

envolée [ãṅvolā] *nf* (*fig*) flight.

envoler [ãṅvolā]: **s'~** *vi* (*oiseau*) to fly away *ou* off; (*avion*) to take off; (*papier, feuille*) to blow away; (*fig*) to vanish (into thin air).

envoûtement [ãṅvo͞otmãṅ] *nm* bewitchment.

envoûter [ãṅvo͞otā] *vt* to bewitch.

envoyé, e [ãṅvwáyā] *nm/f* (*POL*) envoy; (*PRESSE*) correspondent ♦ *a*: **bien ~** (*remarque, réponse*) well-aimed.

envoyer [ãṅvwáyā] *vt* to send; (*lancer*) to hurl, throw; **~ une gifle/un sourire à qn** to aim a blow/flash a smile at sb; **~ les couleurs** to run up the colors; **~ chercher** to send for; **~ par le fond** (*bateau*) to send to the bottom.

envoyeur, euse [ãṅvwáyœr, -œ̄z] *nm/f* sender.

enzyme [ãṅzēm] *nm* enzyme.

éolien, ne [āolyaṅ, -en] *a* wind *cpd*; **pompe ~ne** windmill.

EOR *sigle m* (= *élève officier de réserve*) ≈ military cadet.

éosine [āozēn] *nf* eosin (*antiseptic used in France to treat skin ailments*).

épagneul, e [āpányœl] *nm/f* spaniel.

épais, se [āpe, -es] *a* thick.

épaisseur [āpescœr] *nf* thickness.

épaissir [āpāsēr] *vt*, **s'~** *vi* to thicken.

épaississement [āpāsēsmãṅ] *nm* thickening.

épanchement [āpãṅshmãṅ] *nm*: **un ~ de sinovie** water on the knee; **~s** *nmpl* (*fig*) (sentimental) outpourings.

épancher [āpãṅshā] *vt* to give vent to; **s'~** *vi* to open one's heart; (*liquide*) to pour out.

épandage [āpãṅdázh] *nm* manure spreading.

épanoui, e [āpãṅwē] *a* (*éclos, ouvert, développé*) blooming; (*radieux*) radiant.

épanouir [āpãṅwēr]: **s'~** *vi* (*fleur*) to bloom, open out; (*visage*) to light up; (*fig: se développer*) to blossom (out); (: *mentalement*) to open up.

épanouissement [āpãṅwēsmãṅ] *nm* blossoming; opening up.

épargnant, e [āpárnyãṅ, -ãṅt] *nm/f* saver, investor.

épargne [āpárny(ə)] *nf* saving; **l'~-logement** property investment.

épargner [āpárnyā] *vt* to save; (*ne pas tuer ou endommager*) to spare ♦ *vi* to save; **~ qch à qn** to spare sb sth.

éparpiller [āpárpēyā] *vt* to scatter; (*pour répartir*) to disperse; (*fig: efforts*) to dissipate; **s'~** *vi* to scatter; (*fig*) to dissipate one's efforts.

épars, e [āpár, -árs(ə)] *a* (*maisons*) scattered; (*cheveux*) sparse.

épatant, e [āpátáṅ, -áṅt] *a* (*fam*) super, splendid.

épaté, e [āpátā] *a*: **nez ~** flat nose (with wide nostrils).

épater [āpátā] *vt* to amaze; (*impressionner*) to impress.

épaule [āpōl] *nf* shoulder.

épaulé-jeté, pl épaulés-jetés [āpōlázhətā] *nm* (*SPORT*) clean-and-jerk.

épaulement [āpōlmáṅ] *nm* escarpment; (*mur*) retaining wall.

épauler [āpōlā] *vt* (*aider*) to back up, support; (*arme*) to raise (to one's shoulder) ♦ *vi* to (take) aim.

épaulette [āpōlet] *nf* (*MIL, d'un veston*) epaulette; (*de combinaison*) shoulder strap.

épave [āpáv] *nf* wreck.

épée [āpā] *nf* sword.

épeler [āplā] *vt* to spell.

éperdu, e [āperdü] *a* (*personne*) overcome; (*sentiment*) passionate; (*fuite*) frantic.

éperdument [āperdümáṅ] *ad* (*aimer*) wildly; (*espérer*) fervently.

éperlan [āperláṅ] *nm* (*ZOOL*) smelt.

éperon [āpəróṅ] *nm* spur.

éperonner [āpəronā] *vt* to spur (on); (*navire*) to ram.

épervier [āpervyā] *nm* (*ZOOL*) sparrowhawk; (*PÊCHE*) casting net.

éphèbe [āfeb] *nm* beautiful young man.

éphémère [āfāmer] *a* ephemeral, fleeting.

éphéméride [āfāmārēd] *nf* block *ou* tear-off calendar.

épi [āpē] *nm* (*de blé, d'orge*) ear; **~ de cheveux** tuft of hair; **stationnement/se garer**

en ~ parking/to park at an angle to the curb.
épice [āpēs] *nf* spice.
épicé, e [āpēsā] *a* highly spiced, spicy; *(fig)* spicy.
épicéa [āpēsāà] *nm* spruce.
épicentre [āpēsáńtr(ə)] *nm* epicenter *(US)*, epicentre *(Brit)*.
épicer [āpēsā] *vt* to spice; *(fig)* to add spice to.
épicerie [āpēsrē] *nf* *(magasin)* grocery, grocer's store *(US)* ou shop *(Brit)*; *(denrées)* groceries *pl*; ~ **fine** delicatessen (shop).
épicier, ière [āpēsyā, -yer] *nm/f* grocer.
épidémie [āpēdāmē] *nf* epidemic.
épidémique [āpēdāmēk] *a* epidemic.
épiderme [āpēderm(ə)] *nm* skin, epidermis.
épidermique [āpēdermēk] *a* skin *cpd*, epidermic.
épier [āpyā] *vt* to spy on, watch closely; *(occasion)* to look out for.
épieu, x [āpyœ] *nm* (hunting-)spear.
épigramme [āpēgrám] *nf* epigram.
épilation [āpēlásyóń] *nf* removal of unwanted hair.
épilatoire [āpēlátwár] *a* depilatory, hair-removing.
épilepsie [āpēlepsē] *nf* epilepsy.
épileptique [āpēleptēk] *a*, *nm/f* epileptic.
épiler [āpēlā] *vt* *(jambes)* to remove the hair from; *(sourcils)* to pluck; **s'~ les jambes** to remove the hair from one's legs; **s'~ les sourcils** to pluck one's eyebrows; **se faire ~** to get unwanted hair removed; **crème à ~** hair-removing ou depilatory cream; **pince à ~** eyebrow tweezers.
épilogue [āpēlog] *nm* *(fig)* conclusion, dénouement.
épiloguer [āpēlogā] *vi*: ~ **sur** to hold forth on.
épinard [āpēnár] *nm* *(aussi: ~s)* spinach *sg*.
épine [āpēn] *nf* thorn, prickle; *(d'oursin etc)* spine, prickle; ~ **dorsale** backbone.
épineux, euse [āpēnœ̄, -œ̄z] *a* thorny, prickly.
épinglage [āpáńglázh] *nm* pinning.
épingle [āpáńgl(ə)] *nf* pin; **tirer son ~ du jeu** to play one's game well; **tiré à quatre ~s** well turned-out; **monter qch en ~** to build sth up, make a thing of sth *(fam)*; ~ **à chapeau** hatpin; ~ **à cheveux** hairpin; **virage en ~ à cheveux** hairpin curve *(US)* ou bend *(Brit)*; ~ **de cravate** stickpin *(US)*, tiepin; ~ **de nourrice** ou **de sûreté** ou **double** safety pin, diaper *(US)* ou nappy *(Brit)* pin.
épingler [āpáńglā] *vt* *(badge, décoration)*: ~ **qch sur** to pin sth on(to); *(COUTURE: tissu, robe)* to pin together; *(fam)* to catch, nab.
épinière [āpēnyer] *af voir* **moelle**.
Épiphanie [āpēfánē] *nf* Epiphany.
épique [āpēk] *a* epic.
épiscopal, e, aux [āpēskopál, -ō] *a* episcopal.
épiscopat [āpēskopá] *nm* bishopric, episcopate.
épisiotomie [āpēzyotōmē] *nf* *(MÉD)* episiotomy.
épisode [āpēzod] *nm* episode; **film/roman à ~s** serialized film/novel, serial.
épisodique [āpēzodēk] *a* occasional.
épissure [āpēsür] *nf* splice.
épistémologie [āpēstāmolozhē] *nf* epistemology.
épistolaire [āpēstoler] *a* epistolary; **être en**

relations ~s avec qn to correspond with sb.
épitaphe [āpētáf] *nf* epitaph.
épithète [āpētet] *nf* *(nom, surnom)* epithet; **adjectif ~** attributive adjective.
épître [āpētr(ə)] *nf* epistle.
éploré, e [āplorā] *a* in tears, tearful.
épluchage [āplüsházh] *nm* peeling; *(de dossier etc)* careful reading ou analysis.
épluche-légumes [āplüshlāgüm] *nm inv* potato peeler.
éplucher [āplüshā] *vt* *(fruit, légumes)* to peel; *(comptes, dossier)* to go over with a fine-tooth comb.
éplucheur [āplüshœr] *nm* (automatic) peeler.
épluchures [āplüshür] *nfpl* peelings.
épointer [āpwańtā] *vt* to blunt.
éponge [āpóńzh] *nf* sponge; **passer l'~ (sur)** *(fig)* to let bygones be bygones (with regard to); **jeter l'~** *(fig)* to throw in the towel; ~ **métallique** scouring pad.
éponger [āpóńzhā] *vt* *(liquide)* to mop ou sponge up; *(surface)* to sponge; *(fig: déficit)* to soak up, absorb; **s'~ le front** to mop one's brow.
épopée [āpopā] *nf* epic.
époque [āpok] *nf* *(de l'histoire)* age, era; *(de l'année, la vie)* time; **d'~** *a* *(meuble)* period *cpd*; **à cette ~** at this *(ou* that) time *ou* period; **faire ~** to make history.
épouiller [āpōōyā] *vt* to pick lice off; *(avec un produit)* to delouse.
époumoner [āpōōmonā]: **s'~** *vi* to shout *(ou* sing) o.s. hoarse.
épouse [āpōōz] *nf* wife *(pl* wives).
épouser [āpōōzā] *vt* to marry; *(fig: idées)* to espouse; *(: forme)* to fit.
époussetage [āpōōstázh] *nm* dusting.
épousseter [āpōōstā] *vt* to dust.
époustouflant, e [āpōōstōōflań, -áńt] *a* staggering, mind-boggling.
époustoufler [āpōōstōōflā] *vt* to flabbergast, astound.
épouvantable [āpōōváńtábl(ə)] *a* appalling, dreadful.
épouvantail [āpōōváńtáy] *nm* *(à moineaux)* scarecrow; *(fig)* bog(e)y; bugbear.
épouvante [āpōōváńt] *nf* terror; **film d'~** horror film.
épouvanter [āpōōváńtā] *vt* to terrify.
époux [āpōō] *nm* husband ♦ *nmpl*: **les ~** the (married) couple, the husband and wife.
éprendre [āpráńdr(ə)]: **s'~ de** *vt* to fall in love with.
épreuve [āprœv] *nf* *(d'examen)* test; *(malheur, difficulté)* trial, ordeal; *(PHOTO)* print; *(TYPO)* proof; *(SPORT)* event; **à l'~ des balles/du feu** *(vêtement)* bulletproof/fireproof; **à toute ~** unfailing; **mettre à l'~** to put to the test; ~ **de force** test of strength; *(fig)* showdown; ~ **de résistance** test of resistance; ~ **de sélection** *(SPORT)* heat.
épris, e [āprē, -ēz] *vb voir* **éprendre** ♦ *a*: ~ **de** in love with.
éprouvant, e [āprōōváń, -áńt] *a* trying.
éprouvé, e [āprōōvā] *a* tested, proven.
éprouver [āprōōvā] *vt* *(tester)* to test; *(mettre à l'épreuve)* to put to the test; *(marquer, faire souffrir)* to afflict, distress; *(ressentir)*

to experience.
éprouvette [āprōōvet] *nf* test tube.
EPS *sigle f* (= *Éducation physique et sportive*) ≈ PE.
épuisant, e [āpüēzȧṅ, -ȧṅt] *a* exhausting.
épuisé, e [āpüēzā] *a* exhausted; (*livre*) out of print.
épuisement [āpüēzmȧṅ] *nm* exhaustion; **jusqu'à ~ des stocks** while stocks last.
épuiser [āpüēzā] *vt* (*fatiguer*) to exhaust, wear *ou* tire out; (*stock, sujet*) to exhaust; **s'~** *vi* to wear *ou* tire o.s. out, exhaust o.s.; (*stock*) to run out.
épuisette [āpüēzet] *nf* landing net; shrimp(ing) net.
épuration [āpürȧsyôṅ] *nf* purification; purging; refinement.
épurer [āpürā] *vt* (*liquide*) to purify; (*parti, administration*) to purge; (*langue, texte*) to refine.
équarrir [ākȧrēr] *vt* (*pierre, arbre*) to square (off); (*animal*) to quarter.
équateur [ākwȧtœr] *nm* equator; **(la république de) l'É~** Ecuador.
équation [ākwȧsyôṅ] *nf* equation; **mettre en ~** to equate; **~ du premier/second degré** linear/quadratic equation.
équatorial, e, aux [ākwȧtoryȧl, -ō] *a* equatorial.
équatorien, ne [ākwȧtoryaṅ, -en] *a* Ecuadorian ♦ *nm/f:* **É~, ne** Ecuadorian.
équerre [āker] *nf* (*à dessin*) (set) square; (*pour fixer*) brace; **en ~** at right angles; **à l'~, d'~** straight; **double ~** T-square.
équestre [ākestr(ə)] *a* equestrian.
équeuter [ākētā] *vt* (*CULIN*) to remove the stalk(s) from.
équidé [ākēdā] *nm* (*ZOOL*) member of the horse family.
équidistance [āküēdēstȧṅs] *nf:* **à ~ (de)** equidistant (from).
équidistant, e [āküēdēstȧṅ, -ȧṅt] *a:* **~ (de)** equidistant (from).
équilatéral, e, aux [āküēlȧtārȧl, -ō] *a* equilateral.
équilibrage [ākēlēbrȧzh] *nm* (*AUTO*): **~ des roues** wheel balancing.
équilibre [ākēlēbr(ə)] *nm* balance; (*d'une balance*) equilibrium; **~ budgétaire** balanced budget; **garder/perdre l'~** to keep/lose one's balance; **être en ~** to be balanced; **mettre en ~** to make steady; **avoir le sens de l'~** to be well-balanced.
équilibré, e [ākēlēbrā] *a* (*fig*) well-balanced, stable.
équilibrer [ākēlēbrā] *vt* to balance; **s'~** (*poids*) to balance; (*fig: défauts etc*) to balance each other out.
équilibriste [ākēlēbrēst(ə)] *nm/f* tightrope walker.
équinoxe [ākēnoks] *nm* equinox.
équipage [ākēpȧzh] *nm* crew; **en grand ~** in great array.
équipe [ākēp] *nf* team; (*bande:* *parfois péj*) bunch; **travailler par ~s** to work in shifts; **travailler en ~** to work as a team; **faire ~ avec** to team up with; **~ de chercheurs** research team; **~ de secours** *ou* **de sauvetage** rescue team.

équipé, e [ākēpā] *a* (*cuisine etc*) equipped, fitted(-out) ♦ *nf* escapade.
équipement [ākēpmȧṅ] *nm* equipment; **~s** *nmpl* amenities, facilities; installations; **biens/dépenses d'~** capital goods/ expenditure; **ministère de l'É~** department of public works; **~s sportifs/collectifs** sports/community facilities *ou* resources.
équiper [ākēpā] *vt* to equip; (*voiture, cuisine*) to equip, fit out; **~ qn/qch de** to equip sb/sth with; **s'~** (*sportif*) to equip o.s.
équipier, ière [ākēpyā, -yer] *nm/f* team member.
équitable [ākētȧbl(ə)] *a* fair.
équitation [ākētȧsyôṅ] *nf* (horse-)riding; **faire de l'~** to go (horse-)riding.
équité [ākētā] *nf* equity.
équivalence [ākēvȧlȧṅs] *nf* equivalence.
équivalent, e [ākēvȧlȧṅ, -ȧṅt] *a, nm* equivalent.
équivaloir [ākēvȧlwȧr]: **~ à** *vt* to be equivalent to; (*représenter*) to amount to.
équivaut [ākēvō] *etc vb voir* **équivaloir**.
équivoque [ākēvok] *a* equivocal, ambiguous; (*louche*) dubious ♦ *nf* ambiguity.
érable [ārȧbl(ə)] *nm* maple.
éradiquer [ārȧdēkā] *vt* to eradicate.
érafler [ārȧflā] *vt* to scratch; **s'~ la main/les jambes** to scrape *ou* scratch one's hand/legs.
éraflure [ārȧflür] *nf* scratch.
éraillé, e [ārȧyā] *a* (*voix*) rasping, hoarse.
ère [er] *nf* era; **en l'an 1050 de notre ~** in the year 1050 A.D.
érection [ārcksyôṅ] *nf* erection.
éreintant, e [āraṅtȧṅ, -ȧṅt] *a* exhausting.
éreinté, e [āraṅtā] *a* exhausted.
éreintement [āraṅtmȧṅ] *nm* exhaustion.
éreinter [āraṅtā] *vt* to exhaust, wear out; (*fig: critiquer*) to pan; **s'~ (à faire qch/à qch)** to wear o.s. out (doing sth/with sth).
ergonomie [ergonomē] *nf* ergonomics *sg*.
ergonomique [ergonomēk] *a* ergonomic.
ergot [ergō] *nm* (*de coq*) spur; (*TECH*) lug.
ergoter [ergotā] *vi* to split hairs, argue over details.
ergoteur, euse [ergotœr, -œz] *nm/f* hair-splitter.
ériger [ārēzhā] *vt* (*monument*) to erect; **~ qch en principe/loi** to make sth a principle/law; **s'~ en critique (de)** to set o.s. up as a critic (of).
ermitage [ermētȧzh] *nm* retreat.
ermite [ermēt] *nm* hermit.
éroder [ārodā] *vt* to erode.
érogène [ārozhen] *a* erogenous.
érosion [ārōzyôṅ] *nf* erosion.
érotique [ārotēk] *a* erotic.
érotiquement [ārotēkmȧṅ] *ad* erotically.
érotisme [ārotēsm(ə)] *nm* eroticism.
errance [erȧṅs] *nf* wandering.
errant, e [erȧṅ, -ȧṅt] *a:* **un chien ~** a stray dog.
erratum, a [erȧtom, -ȧ] *nm* erratum (*pl* -a).
errements [ermȧṅ] *nmpl* misguided ways.
errer [erā] *vi* to wander.
erreur [erœr] *nf* mistake, error; (*INFORM:* *de programme*) bug; (*morale*): **~s** *nfpl* errors; **être dans l'~** to be wrong; **induire qn en ~**

to mislead sb; **par** ~ by mistake; **sauf** ~ unless I'm mistaken; **faire** ~ to be mistaken; ~ **de date** mistake in the date; ~ **de fait** error of fact; ~ **d'impression** (*TYPO*) misprint; ~ **judiciaire** miscarriage of justice; ~ **de jugement** error of judgment; ~ **matérielle** *ou* **d'écriture** clerical error; ~ **tactique** tactical error.

erroné, e [erɔnā] *a* wrong, erroneous.

éructer [ārüktā] *vi* to belch.

érudit, e [ārüdē, -ēt] *a* erudite, learned ♦ *nm/f* scholar.

érudition [ārüdēsyôň] *nf* erudition, scholarship.

éruptif, ive [ārüptēf, -ēv] *a* eruptive.

éruption [ārüpsyôň] *nf* eruption; (*cutanée*) outbreak; (*: boutons*) rash; (*fig: de joie, colère, folie*) outburst.

es [e] *vb voir* **être**.

ès [es] *prép:* **licencié** ~ **lettres/sciences** ≈ Bachelor of Arts/Science; **docteur** ~ **lettres** ≈ doctor of philosophy, PhD.

E/S *abr* (= *entrée/sortie*) I/O (= *in/out*).

esbroufe [esbrōōf] *nf:* **faire de l'**~ to put (*US*) *ou* have (*Brit*) people on.

escabeau, x [eskábō] *nm* (*tabouret*) stool; (*échelle*) stepladder.

escadre [eskádr(ə)] *nf* (*NAVIG*) squadron; (*AVIAT*) wing.

escadrille [eskádrēy] *nf* (*AVIAT*) flight.

escadron [eskádrôň] *nm* squadron.

escalade [eskálád] *nf* climbing *q*; (*POL etc*) escalation.

escalader [eskáládá] *vt* to climb, scale.

escale [eskál] *nf* (*NAVIG*) call; (*: port*) port of call; (*AVIAT*) stop(over); **faire** ~ **à** to put in at, call in at; to stop over at; ~ **technique** (*AVIAT*) refuelling stop.

escalier [eskályā] *nm* stairs *pl*; **dans l'**~ *ou* **les** ~**s** on the stairs; **descendre l'**~ *ou* **les** ~**s** to go downstairs; ~ **mécanique** *ou* **roulant** escalator; ~ **de secours** fire escape; ~ **de service** backstairs; ~ **à vis** *ou* **en colimaçon** spiral staircase.

escalope [eskálop] *nf* cutlet (*US*), escalope (*Brit*).

escamotable [eskámotábl(ə)] *a* (*train d'atterrissage, antenne*) retractable; (*table, lit*) fold-away.

escamoter [eskámotá] *vt* (*esquiver*) to get around, evade; (*faire disparaître*) to conjure away; (*dérober: portefeuille etc*) to snatch; (*train d'atterrissage*) to retract; (*mots*) to leave out, skip.

escapade [eskápád] *nf:* **faire une** ~ to go on a jaunt; (*s'enfuir*) to run away *ou* off.

escarbille [eskárbēy] *nf* cinder.

escarcelle [eskársel] *nf:* **faire tomber dans l'**~ (*argent*) to bring in.

escargot [eskárgō] *nm* snail.

escarmouche [eskármōōsh] *nf* (*MIL*) skirmish; (*fig: propos hostiles*) angry exchange.

escarpé, e [eskárpā] *a* steep.

escarpement [eskárpəmáň] *nm* steep slope.

escarpin [eskárpaň] *nm* flat(-heeled) shoe.

escarre [eskár] *nf* bedsore.

Escaut [eskō] *nm:* **l'**~ the Scheldt.

escient [āsyáň] *nm:* **à bon** ~ advisedly.

esclaffer [eskláfá]: **s'**~ *vi* to guffaw.

esclandre [eskláňdr(ə)] *nm* scene, fracas.

esclavage [esklávázh] *nm* slavery.

esclave [esklávʼ] *nm/f* slave; **être** ~ **de** (*fig*) to be a slave of.

escogriffe [eskogrēf] *nm* (*péj*) beanpole.

escompte [eskôňt] *nm* discount.

escompter [eskôňtá] *vt* (*COMM*) to discount; (*espérer*) to expect, anticipate; ~ **que** to reckon *ou* expect that.

escorte [eskort(ə)] *nf* escort; **faire** ~ **à** to escort.

escorter [eskortá] *vt* to escort.

escorteur [eskortœr] *nm* (*NAVIG*) escort (ship).

escouade [eskwád] *nf* squad; (*fig: groupe de personnes*) group.

escrime [eskrēm] *nf* fencing; **faire de l'**~ to fence.

escrimer [eskrēmá]: **s'**~ *vi:* **s'**~ **à faire** to wear o.s. out doing.

escrimeur, euse [eskrēmœr, -œz] *nm/f* fencer.

escroc [eskrō] *nm* swindler, con-man.

escroquer [eskroká] *vt:* ~ **qn (de qch)/qch à qn** to swindle sb (out of sth)/sth out of sb.

escroquerie [eskrokrē] *nf* swindle.

ésotérique [āzotārēk] *a* esoteric.

espace [espás] *nm* space; ~ **publicitaire** advertising space; ~ **vital** living space.

espacé, e [espásā] *a* spaced out.

espacement [espásmáň] *nm:* ~ **proportionnel** proportional spacing (*on printer*).

espacer [espásá] *vt* to space out; **s'**~ *vi* (*visites etc*) to become less frequent.

espadon [espádôň] *nm* swordfish *inv*.

espadrille [espádrēy] *nf* rope-soled sandal.

Espagne [espány(ə)] *nf:* **l'**~ Spain.

espagnol, e [espányol] *a* Spanish ♦ *nm* (*LING*) Spanish ♦ *nm/f:* **E**~, **e** Spaniard.

espagnolette [espányolet] *nf* (*window*) catch; **fermé à l'**~ half-shut (resting on the catch).

espalier [espályā] *nm* (*arbre fruitier*) espalier.

espèce [espes] *nf* (*BIO, BOT, ZOOL*) species *inv*; (*gén: sorte*) sort, kind, type; (*péj*): ~ **de maladroit/de brute!** you clumsy oaf/you brute!; ~**s** *nfpl* (*COMM*) cash *sg*; (*REL*) species; **de toute** ~ of all kinds *ou* sorts; **en l'**~ *ad* in the case in point; **payer en** ~**s** to pay (in) cash; **cas d'**~ individual case; **l'**~ **humaine** humankind.

espérance [espāráňs] *nf* hope; ~ **de vie** life expectancy.

espéranto [espāráňtō] *nm* Esperanto.

espérer [espārā] *vt* to hope for; **j'espère (bien)** I hope so; ~ **que/faire** to hope that/to do; ~ **en** to trust in.

espiègle [espyegl(ə)] *a* mischievous.

espièglerie [espyeglərē] *nf* mischievousness; (*tour, farce*) piece of mischief, prank.

espion, ne [espyôň, -on] *nm/f* spy; **avion** ~ spy plane.

espionnage [espyonázh] *nm* espionage, spying; **film/roman d'**~ spy film/novel.

espionner [espyoná] *vt* to spy (up)on.

esplanade [esplánád] *nf* esplanade.

espoir [espwár] *nm* hope; **l'**~ **de qch/de faire qch** the hope of sth/of doing sth; **avoir bon** ~ **que ...** to have high hopes that ...; **garder l'**~ **que ...** to remain hopeful that ...; **un** ~ **de la boxe/du ski** one of boxing's/skiing's hopefuls, one of the hopes of boxing/skiing;

sans ~ *a* hopeless.

esprit [esprē] *nm* (*pensée, intellect*) mind; (*humour, ironie*) wit; (*mentalité, d'une loi etc, fantôme etc*) spirit; **l'~ d'équipe/de compétition** team/competitive spirit; **faire de l'~** to try to be witty; **reprendre ses ~s** to come to; **perdre l'~** to lose one's mind; **avoir bon/mauvais ~** to be of a good/bad disposition; **avoir l'~ à faire qch** to have a mind to do sth; **avoir l'~ critique** to be critical; **~ de contradiction** contrariness; **~ de corps** esprit de corps; **~ de famille** family loyalty; **l'~ malin** (*le diable*) the Evil One; **~s chagrins** faultfinders.

esquif [eskēf] *nm* skiff.

esquimau, de, x [eskēmō, -ōd] *a* Eskimo ♦ *nm* (*LING*) Eskimo; (*glace*): **E~** ® Popsicle ® (*US*), ice lolly (*Brit*) ♦ *nm/f*: **E~, de** Eskimo; **chien ~** husky.

esquinter [eskaṅtā] *vt* (*fam*) to mess up; **s'~** *vi*: **s'~ à faire qch** to knock o.s. out doing sth.

esquisse [eskēs] *nf* sketch; **l'~ d'un sourire/ changement** a hint of a smile/of change.

esquisser [eskēsā] *vt* to sketch; **s'~** *vi* (*amélioration*) to begin to be detectable; **~ un sourire** to give a hint of a smile.

esquive [eskēv] *nf* (*BOXE*) dodging; (*fig*) side-stepping.

esquiver [eskēvā] *vt* to dodge; **s'~** *vi* to slip away.

essai [āse] *nm* trying; (*tentative*) attempt, try; (*RUGBY*) try; (*LITTERATURE*) essay; **~s** *nmpl* (*AUTO*) trials; **à l'~** on a trial basis; **~ gratuit** (*COMM*) free trial.

essaim [āsaṅ] *nm* swarm.

essaimer [āsāmā] *vi* to swarm; (*fig*) to spread, expand.

essayage [āseyàzh] *nm* (*d'un vêtement*) trying on, fitting; **salon d'~** fitting room; **cabine d'~** fitting room (*cubicle*).

essayer [āsāyā] *vt* (*gén*) to try; (*vêtement, chaussures*) to try (on); (*restaurant, méthode, voiture*) to try (out) ♦ *vi* to try; **~ de faire** to try ou attempt to do; **s'~ à faire** to try one's hand at doing; **essayez un peu!** (*menace*) just you try!

essayeur, euse [āseyœr, -œz] *nm/f* (*chez un tailleur etc*) fitter.

ESSEC [esek] *sigle f* (= *École supérieure des sciences économiques et sociales*) *grande école for management and business studies.*

essence [āsâṅs] *nf* (*de voiture*) gas(oline) (*US*), petrol (*Brit*); (*extrait de plante, PHILOSOPHIE*) essence; (*espèce: d'arbre*) species *inv*; **prendre de l'~** to get (some) gas; **par ~** (*essentiellement*) essentially; **~ de citron/rose** lemon/rose oil; **~ de térébenthine** turpentine.

essentiel, le [āsâṅsyel] *a* essential ♦ *nm*: **l'~ d'un discours/d'une œuvre** the essence of a speech/work of art; **emporter l'~** to take the essentials; **c'est l'~** (*ce qui importe*) that's the main thing; **l'~ de** (*la majeure partie*) the main part of.

essentiellement [āsâṅsyelmáṅ] *ad* essentially.

esseulé, e [āsœlā] *a* forlorn.

essieu, x [āsyœ] *nm* axle.

essor [āsor] *nm* (*de l'économie etc*) rapid

expansion; **prendre son ~** (*oiseau*) to fly off.

essorage [āsorázh] *nm* wringing out; spin-drying; spinning; shaking.

essorer [āsorā] *vt* (*en tordant*) to wring (out); (*par la force centrifuge*) to spin-dry; (*salade*) to spin; (*: en secouant*) to shake dry.

essoreuse [āsorœz] *nf* mangle, wringer; (*à tambour*) spin-dryer.

essouffler [āsōōflā] *vt* to make breathless; **s'~** *vi* to get out of breath; (*fig: économie*) to run out of steam.

essuie [āsüē] *etc vb voir* **essuyer.**

essuie-glace [āsüēglás] *nm* windshield (*US*) *ou* windscreen (*Brit*) wiper.

essuie-mains [āsüēmaṅ] *nm inv* hand towel.

essuierai [āsüērā] *etc vb voir* **essuyer.**

essuie-tout [āsüētōō] *nm inv* paper towel.

essuyer [āsüēyā] *vt* to wipe; (*fig: subir*) to suffer; **s'~** (*après le bain*) to dry o.s.; **~ la vaisselle** to dry the dishes.

est [e] *vb voir* **être** ♦ *nm* [est]: **l'~** the east ♦ *a inv* east; (*région*) east(ern); **à l'~** in the east; (*direction*) to the east, east(wards); **à l'~ de** (to the) east of, **les pays de l'E~** the eastern countries.

estafette [estáfet] *nf* (*MIL*) courier (*US*), dispatch rider (*Brit*).

estafilade [estáfēlàd] *nf* gash, slash.

est-allemand, e [estàlmáṅ, -áṅd] *a* East German.

estaminet [estámēne] *nm* tavern.

estampe [estâṅp] *nf* print, engraving.

estamper [estâṅpā] *vt* (*monnaies etc*) to stamp; (*fam: escroquer*) to swindle.

estampille [estâṅpēy] *nf* stamp.

est-ce que [eska] *ad*: **~ c'est cher/c'était bon?** is it expensive/was it good?; **quand est-ce qu'il part?** when does he leave?, when is he leaving?; **où est-ce qu'il va?** where's he going?; **qui est-ce qui le connaît/a fait ça?** who knows him/did that?; *voir aussi* **que.**

este [est(ə)] *a* Estonian ♦ *nm/f*: **E~** Estonian.

esthète [estet] *nm/f* aesthete.

esthéticienne [estātēsyen] *nf* beautician.

esthétique [estātēk] *a* (*sens, jugement*) aesthetic; (*beau*) attractive, aesthetically pleasing ♦ *nf* aesthetics *sg*; **l'~ industrielle** industrial design.

esthétiquement [estātēkmáṅ] *ad* aesthetically. •

estimable [estēmábl(ə)] *a* respected.

estimatif, ive [estēmátēf, -ēv] *a* estimated.

estimation [estēmâsyôṅ] *nf* valuation; assessment; **d'après mes ~s** according to my calculations.

estime [estēm] *nf* esteem, regard; **avoir de l'~ pour qn** to think highly of sb.

estimer [estēmā] *vt* (*respecter*) to esteem, hold in high regard; (*expertiser*) to value; (*évaluer*) to assess, estimate; (*penser*): **~ que/être** to consider that/o.s. to be; **s'~ satisfait/heureux** to feel satisfied/happy; **j'estime la distance à 10 km** I reckon the distance to be 10 km.

estival, e, aux [estēvál, -ō] *a* summer *cpd*; **station ~e** (summer) vacation (*US*) *ou* holiday (*Brit*) resort.

estivant, e [estēváṅ, -áṅt] *nm/f* (summer) vacationer (*US*) *ou* holiday-maker (*Brit*).

estoc [estɔk] *nm*: **frapper d'~ et de taille** to cut and thrust.

estocade [estɔkâd] *nf* death-blow.

estomac [estɔmá] *nm* stomach; **avoir mal à l'~** to have stomach ache; **avoir l'~ creux** to have an empty stomach.

estomaqué, e [estɔmákā] *a* flabbergasted.

estompe [estôɲp] *nf* stump; (*dessin*) stump-drawing.

estompé, e [estôɲpâ] *a* blurred.

estomper [estôɲpâ] *vt* (ART) to shade off; (*fig*) to blur, dim; **s'~** *vi* (*sentiments*) to soften; (*contour*) to become blurred.

Estonie [estɔnē] *nf*: **l'~** Estonia.

estonien, ne [estɔnyań, -en] *a* Estonian.

estrade [estrâd] *nf* platform, rostrum.

estragon [estrágôń] *nm* tarragon.

estropié, e [estrɔpyâ] *nm/f* cripple.

estropier [estrɔpyâ] *vt* to cripple, maim; (*fig*) to twist, distort.

estuaire [estüer] *nm* estuary.

estudiantin, e [estüdyáńtań, -ēn] *a* student *cpd*.

esturgeon [estürzhôń] *nm* sturgeon.

et [â] *cj* and; **~ lui?** what about him?; **~ alors?, ~ (puis) après?** so what?; (*ensuite*) and then?

ét. *abr* = **étage.**

ETA [âtá] *sigle m* (POL: = *Euzkadi ta Askatsuna*) ETA (*Basque separatist movement*).

étable [âtâbl(ə)] *nf* cowshed.

établi, e [âtâblē] *a* established ♦ *nm* (work)bench.

établir [âtâblēr] *vt* (*papiers d'identité, facture*) to make out; (*liste, programme*) to draw up; (*gouvernement, artisan etc*: *aider à s'installer*) to set up, establish; (*entreprise, atelier, camp*) to set up; (*réputation, usage, fait, culpabilité, relations*) to establish; (SPORT: *record*) to set; **s'~** *vi* (*se faire: entente etc*) to be established; **s'~ (à son compte)** to set up in business; **s'~ à/près de** to settle in/near.

établissement [âtâblēsmâń] *nm* making out; drawing up; setting up, establishing; (*entreprise, institution*) establishment; **~ de crédit** credit institution; **~ hospitalier** hospital complex; **~ industriel** industrial plant, factory; **~ scolaire** school, educational establishment.

étage [âtázh] *nm* (*d'immeuble*) story (US), storey (Brit), floor; (*de fusée*) stage; (GÉO: *de culture, végétation*) level; **au 2ème ~** on the 3rd (US) *ou* 2nd (Brit) floor; **à l'~** upstairs; **maison à deux ~s** two-story house; **de bas ~** *a* low-born; (*médiocre*) inferior.

étager [âtázhâ] *vt* (*cultures*) to lay out in tiers; **s'~** *vi* (*prix*) to range; (*zones, cultures*) to lie on different levels.

étagère [âtázher] *nf* (*rayon*) shelf; (*meuble*) shelves *pl*, set of shelves.

étai [âte] *nm* stay, prop.

étain [âtań] *nm* tin; (ORFÈVRERIE) pewter *q*.

étais [âte] *etc vb voir* **être.**

étal [âtál] *nm* stall.

étalage [âtálázh] *nm* display; (*vitrine*) display window; **faire ~ de** to show off, parade.

étalagiste [âtálázhēst(ə)] *nm/f* window-dresser.

étale [âtál] *a* (*mer*) slack.

étalement [âtálmâń] *nm* spreading; (*échelonnement*) staggering.

étaler [âtálâ] *vt* (*carte, nappe*) to spread (out); (*peinture, liquide*) to spread; (*échelonner: paiements, dates, vacances*) to spread, stagger; (*exposer: marchandises*) to display; (*richesses, connaissances*) to parade; **s'~** *vi* (*liquide*) to spread out; (*fam*) to fall flat on one's face; **s'~ sur** (*suj: paiements etc*) to be spread over.

étalon [âtálôń] *nm* (*mesure*) standard; (*cheval*) stallion; **l'~-or** the gold standard.

étalonner [âtálonâ] *vt* to calibrate.

étamer [âtámâ] *vt* (*casserole*) to tin(plate); (*glace*) to silver.

étamine [âtámēn] *nf* (BOT) stamen; (*tissu*) cheesecloth.

étanche [âtáńsh] *a* (*récipient; aussi fig*) watertight; (*montre, vêtement*) waterproof; **~ à l'air** airtight.

étanchéité [âtáńshâetâ] *nf* watertightness; airtightness.

étancher [âtáńshâ] *vt* (*liquide*) to stop (flowing); **~ sa soif** to quench *ou* slake one's thirst.

étançon [âtáńsôń] *nm* (TECH) prop.

étançonner [âtáńsonâ] *vt* to prop up.

étang [âtáń] *nm* pond.

étant [âtáń] *vb voir* **être, donné.**

étape [âtáp] *nf* stage; (*lieu d'arrivée*) stopping place; (: CYCLISME) staging point; **faire ~ à** to stop off at; **brûler les ~s** (*fig*) to cut corners.

état [âtá] *nm* (POL, *condition*) state; (*d'un article d'occasion etc*) condition, state; (*liste*) inventory, statement; (*condition professionnelle*) profession, trade; (: *sociale*) status; **en mauvais ~** in poor condition; **en ~ (de marche)** in (working) order; **remettre en ~** to repair; **hors d'~** out of order; **être en ~/hors d'~ de faire** to be in a state/in no fit state to do; **en tout ~ de cause** in any event; **être dans tous ses ~s** to be in a state; **faire ~ de** (*alléguer*) to put forward; **en ~ d'arrestation** under arrest; **~ de grâce** (REL) state of grace; (*fig*) honeymoon period; **en ~ de grâce** (*fig*) inspired; **en ~ d'ivresse** under the influence of drink; **~ de choses** (*situation*) state of affairs; **~ civil** civil status; (*bureau*) registry office; **~ d'esprit** frame of mind; **~ des lieux** inventory of fixtures; **~ de santé** state of health; **~ de siège/d'urgence** state of siege/emergency; **~ de veille** (PSYCH) waking state; **~s d'âme** moods; **les É~s barbaresques** the Barbary States; **les É~s du Golfe** the Gulf States; **~s de service** service record *sg*.

étatique [âtátēk] *a* state *cpd*, State *cpd*.

étatiser [âtátēzâ] *vt* to bring under state control.

étatisme [âtátēsm(ə)] *nm* state control.

étatiste [âtátēst(ə)] *a* (*doctrine etc*) of state control ♦ *nm/f* partisan of state control.

état-major, pl états-majors [âtámázhor] *nm* (MIL) staff; (*d'un parti etc*) top advisers *pl*; (*d'une entreprise*) top management.

État-providence [âtáprovēdâńs] *nm* welfare state.

États-Unis [ātázünē] *nmpl*: **les ~ (d'Amérique)** the United States (of America).

étau, x [ātō] *nm* vise (*US*), vice (*Brit*).

étayer [ātāyā] *vt* to prop *ou* shore up; (*fig*) to back up.

et c(a)etera [etsātārá], **etc.** *ad* et cetera, and so on, etc.

été [ātā] *pp de* **être** ♦ *nm* summer; **en ~** in summer.

éteignais [ātenye] *etc vb voir* **éteindre**.

éteignoir [ātenywár] *nm* (candle) snuffer; (*péj*) killjoy, wet blanket.

éteindre [ātáńdr(ə)] *vt* (*lampe, lumière, radio, chauffage*) to turn *ou* switch off; (*cigarette, incendie, bougie*) to put out, extinguish; (*JUR: dette*) to extinguish; **s'~** *vi* to go off; to go out; (*mourir*) to pass away.

éteint, e [ātań, -ańt] *pp de* **éteindre** ♦ *a* (*fig*) lackluster (*US*), lacklustre (*Brit*), dull; (*volcan*) extinct; **tous feux ~s** (*AUTO*: *rouler*) without lights.

étendard [ātáńdár] *nm* standard.

étendre [ātáńdr(ə)] *vt* (*appliquer: pâte, liquide*) to spread; (*déployer: carte etc*) to spread out; (*sur un fil: lessive, linge*) to hang up *ou* out; (*bras, jambes, par terre: blessé*) to stretch out; (*diluer*) to dilute, thin; (*fig: agrandir*) to extend; (*fam: adversaire*) to floor; **s'~** *vi* (*augmenter, se propager*) to spread; (*terrain, forêt etc*): **s'~ jusqu'à/de ... à** to stretch as far as/from ... to; **s'~ (sur)** (*s'allonger*) to stretch out (upon); (*se coucher*) to lie down (on); (*fig: expliquer*) to elaborate *ou* enlarge (upon).

étendu, e [ātáńdü] *a* extensive ♦ *nf* (*d'eau, de sable*) stretch, expanse; (*importance*) extent.

éternel, le [āternel] *a* eternal; **les neiges ~les** perpetual snow.

éternellement [āternelmáń] *ad* eternally.

éterniser [āternēzā]: **s'~** *vi* to last for ages; (*personne*) to stay for ages.

éternité [āternētā] *nf* eternity; **il y a** *ou* **ça fait une ~ que** it's ages since; **de toute ~** from time immemorial.

éternuement [āternümáń] *nm* sneeze.

éternuer [āternüā] *vi* to sneeze.

êtes [et] *vb voir* **être**.

étêter [ātātā] *vt* (*arbre*) to poll(ard); (*clou, poisson*) to cut the head off.

éther [āter] *nm* ether.

éthéré, e [ātārā] *a* ethereal.

Éthiopie [ātyopē] *nf*: **l'~** Ethiopia.

éthiopien, ne [ātyopyań, -en] *a* Ethiopian.

éthique [ātēk] *a* ethical ♦ *nf* ethics *sg*.

ethnie [etnē] *nf* ethnic group.

ethnique [etnēk] *a* ethnic.

ethnographe [etnográf] *nm/f* ethnographer.

ethnographique [etnográfēk] *a* ethnographic(al).

ethnologique [etnolozhēk] *a* ethnological.

ethnologue [etnolog] *nm/f* ethnologist.

éthylique [ātēlēk] *a* alcoholic.

éthylisme [ātēlēsm(ə)] *nm* alcoholism.

étiage [ātyázh] *nm* low water.

étiez [ātyā] *vb voir* **être**.

étincelant, e [ātańslań, -ańt] *a* sparkling.

étinceler [ātańslā] *vi* to sparkle.

étincelle [ātańsel] *nf* spark.

étioler [ātyolā]: **s'~** *vi* to wilt.

étions [ātyôń] *vb voir* **être**.

étique [ātēk] *a* skinny, bony.

étiqueter [ātēktā] *vt* to label.

étiquette [ātēket] *vb voir* **étiqueter** ♦ *nf* label; (*protocole*): **l'~** etiquette.

étirer [ātērā] *vt* to stretch; (*ressort*) to stretch out; **s'~** *vi* (*personne*) to stretch; (*convoi, route*): **s'~ sur** to stretch out over.

étoffe [ātof] *nf* material, fabric; **avoir l'~ d'un chef** *etc* to be cut out to be a leader *etc*; **avoir de l'~** to be a forceful personality.

étoffer [ātofā] *vt, s'~ vi* to fill out.

étoile [ātwál] *nf* star ♦ *a*: **danseuse** *ou* **danceur ~** leading dancer; **la bonne/mauvaise ~ de qn** sb's lucky/unlucky star; **à la belle ~** (out) in the open; **~ filante** shooting star; **~ de mer** starfish; **~ polaire** pole star.

étoilé, e [ātwálā] *a* starry.

étole [ātol] *nf* stole.

étonnant, e [ātonáń, -áńt] *a* surprising.

étonné, e [ātonā] *a* surprised.

étonnement [ātonmáń] *nm* surprise; **à mon grand ~ ...** to my great surprise *ou* amazement ....

étonner [ātonā] *vt* to surprise; **s'~ que/de** to be surprised that/at; **cela m'étonnerait (que)** (*j'en doute*) I'd be (very) surprised (if).

étouffant, e [ātōōfáń, -áńt] *a* stifling.

étouffée [ātōōfā] *a* (*asphyxié*) suffocated; (*assourdi: cris, rires*) smothered ♦ *nf*: **à l'~e** (*CULIN: poisson, légumes*) steamed; (: *viande*) braised.

étouffement [ātōōfmáń] *nm* suffocation.

étouffer [ātōōfā] *vt* to suffocate; (*bruit*) to muffle; (*scandale*) to hush up ♦ *vi* to suffocate; (*avoir trop chaud; aussi fig*) to feel stifled; **s'~** *vi* (*en mangeant etc*) to choke.

étouffoir [ātōōfwár] *nm* (*MUS*) damper.

étourderie [ātōōrdərē] *nf* heedlessness *q*; thoughtless blunder; **faute d'~** careless mistake.

étourdi, e [ātōōrdē] *a* (*distrait*) scatterbrained, heedless.

étourdir [ātōōrdēr] *vt* (*assommer*) to stun, daze; (*griser*) to make dizzy *ou* giddy.

étourdissant, e [ātōōrdēsáń, -áńt] *a* staggering.

étourdissement [ātōōrdēsmáń] *nm* dizzy spell.

étourneau, x [ātōōrnō] *nm* starling.

étrange [ātráńzh] *a* strange.

étrangement [ātráńzhmáń] *ad* strangely.

étranger, ère [ātráńzhā, -er] *a* foreign; (*pas de la famille, non familier*) strange ♦ *nm/f* foreigner; stranger ♦ *nm*: **l'~** foreign countries; **à l'~** abroad; **de l'~** from abroad; **~ à** (*mal connu*) unfamiliar to; (*sans rapport*) irrelevant to.

étrangeté [ātráńzhtā] *nf* strangeness.

étranglé, e [ātráńglā] *a*: **d'une voix ~e** in a strangled voice.

étranglement [ātráńgləmáń] *nm* (*d'une vallée etc*) constriction, narrow passage.

étrangler [ātráńglā] *vt* to strangle; (*fig: presse, libertés*) to stifle; **s'~** *vi* (*en mangeant etc*) to choke; (*se resserrer*) to make a bottleneck.

étrave [ātráv] *nf* stem.

être [ɛtr(ə)] *nm* being ♦ *vb avec attribut*, *vi* to be ♦ *vb auxiliaire* to have *(ou parfois* be*)*; **il est instituteur** he is a teacher; ~ **à qn** *(appartenir)* to be sb's, to belong to sb; **c'est à moi/eux** it is *ou* it's mine/theirs; **c'est à lui de le faire** it's up to him to do it; **il est à Paris/au salon** he is *ou* he's in Paris/the sitting room; ~ **de** *(provenance, origine)* to be from; *(appartenance)* to belong to; ~ **de Genève/de la même famille** to come from Geneva/belong to the same family; **nous sommes le 10 janvier** it's the 10th of January *(today)*; **il est 10 heures, c'est 10 heures** it is *ou* it's 10 o'clock; **c'est à réparer** it needs repairing; **c'est à essayer** it should be tried; **il est à espérer que** it is to be hoped that; ~ **fait par** to be made by; **il a été promu** he has been promoted; ~ **humain** human being; *voir aussi* **est-ce que, n'est-ce pas, c'est-à-dire, ce.**

étreindre [ātrādr(ə)] *vt* to clutch, grip; *(amoureusement, amicalement)* to embrace; **s'~** to embrace.

étreinte [ātrãt] *nf* clutch, grip; embrace; **resserrer son ~ autour de** *(fig)* to tighten one's grip on *ou* around.

étrenner [ātrānā] *vt* to use *(ou* wear*)* for the first time.

étrennes [ātren] *nfpl (cadeaux)* New Year's present; *(gratifications)* ≈ Christmas bonus.

étrier [ātrēyā] *nm* stirrup.

étriller [ātrēyā] *vt (cheval)* to curry; *(fam: battre)* to slaughter *(fig)*.

étriper [ātrēpā] *vt* to gut; *(fam)*: ~ **qn** to tear sb's guts out.

étriqué, e [ātrēkā] *a* skimpy.

étroit, e [ātrwà, -wàt] *a* narrow; *(vêtement)* tight; *(fig: serré)* close, tight; **à l'~** cramped; ~ **d'esprit** narrow-minded.

étroitement [ātrwàtmán] *ad* closely.

étroitesse [ātrwàtes] *nf* narrowness; ~ **d'esprit** narrow-mindedness.

Étrurie [ātrürē] *nf*: **l'~** Etruria.

étrusque [ātrüsk(ə)] *a* Etruscan.

étude [ātüd] *nf* studying; *(ouvrage, rapport, MUS)* study; *(de notaire: bureau)* office; *(: charge)* practice; *(SCOL: salle de travail)* study hall *(US)* *ou* room *(Brit)*; ~**s** *nfpl (SCOL)* studies; **être à l'~** *(projet etc)* to be under consideration; **faire des ~s (de droit/médecine)** to study (law/medicine); ~**s secondaires/supérieures** secondary/higher education; ~ **de cas** case study; ~ **de faisabilité** feasibility study; ~ **de marché** *(ÉCON)* market research.

étudiant, e [ātüdyáń, -áńt] *a, nm/f* student.

étudié, e [ātüdyā] *a (démarche)* studied; *(système)* carefully designed; *(prix)* competitive.

étudier [ātüdyā] *vt, vi* to study.

étui [ātüē] *nm* case.

étuve [ātüv] *nf* steamroom; *(appareil)* sterilizer.

étuvée [ātüvā]: **à l'~** *ad* braised.

étymologie [ātēmolozhē] *nf* etymology.

étymologique [ātēmolozhēk] *a* etymological.

eu, eue [ü] *pp de* **avoir.**

EU(A) *sigle mpl* (= *États-Unis (d'Amérique)*) US(A).

eucalyptus [ōekálēptüs] *nm* eucalyptus.

Eucharistie [ōekárēstē] *nf*: **l'~** the Eucharist, the Lord's Supper.

eugénique [ōezhānēk] *a* eugenic ♦ *nf* eugenics *sg*.

eugénisme [ōezhānēsm(ə)] *nm* eugenics *sg*.

euh [ōe] *excl* er.

eunuque [ōenük] *nm* eunuch.

euphémique [ōefāmēk] *a* euphemistic.

euphémisme [ōefāmēsm(ə)] *nm* euphemism.

euphonie [ōefonē] *nf* euphony.

euphorbe [ōeforb(ə)] *nf (BOT)* spurge.

euphorie [ōeforē] *nf* euphoria.

euphorique [ōeforēk] *a* euphoric.

euphorisant, e [ōeforēzáń, -áńt] *a* exhilarating.

Euphrate [ōefrát] *nm*: **l'~** the Euphrates *sg*.

eurafricain, e [ōeráfrēkań, -en] *a* Eurafrican.

eurasiatique [ōerázyátēk] *a* Eurasiatic.

Eurasie [ōerázē] *nf*: **l'~** Eurasia.

eurasien, ne [ōerázyań, -en] *a* Eurasian.

EURATOM [ōerátom] *sigle f* Euratom.

eurent [ür(ə)] *vb voir* **avoir.**

eurocrate [ōerokrát] *nm/f (péj)* Eurocrat.

eurodevise [ōerodəvēz] *nf* Eurocurrency.

euromonnaie [ōeromone] *nf* Eurocurrency.

Europe [ōerop] *nf*: **l'~** Europe; **l'~ centrale** Central Europe; **l'~ verte** European agriculture.

européaniser [ōeropáánēzā] *vt* to Europeanize.

européen, ne [ōeropáń, -en] *a* European ♦ *nm/f*: **E~, ne** European.

eus [ü] *etc vb voir* **avoir.**

euthanasie [ōetánázē] *nf* euthanasia.

eux [ōe] *pronom (sujet)* they; *(objet)* them; ~, **ils ont fait** ... THEY did ....

EV *abr* (= *en ville*) *used on mail to be delivered by hand, courier etc within the same town.*

évacuation [āváküásyóń] *nf* evacuation.

évacuer [āváküā] *vt (salle, région)* to evacuate, clear; *(occupants, population)* to evacuate; *(toxine etc)* to evacuate, discharge.

évadé, e [āvádā] *a* escaped ♦ *nm/f* escapee.

évader [āvádā]: **s'~** *vi* to escape.

évaluation [āválüásyóń] *nf* assessment, evaluation.

évaluer [āválüā] *vt* to assess, evaluate.

évanescent, e [āvánāsáń, -áńt] *a* evanescent.

évangélique [āváńzhālēk] *a* evangelical.

évangéliser [āváńzhālēzā] *vt* to evangelize.

évangéliste [āváńzhālēst(ə)] *nm* evangelist.

évangile [āváńzhēl] *nm* gospel; *(texte de la Bible)*: **É~** Gospel; **ce n'est pas l'É~** *(fig)* it's not gospel.

évanoui, e [āvánwē] *a* in a faint; **tomber ~** to faint.

évanouir [āvánwēr]: **s'~** *vi* to faint, pass out; *(disparaître)* to vanish, disappear.

évanouissement [āvánwēsmáń] *nm (syncope)* fainting spell; *(MÉD)* loss of consciousness.

évaporation [āváporâsyóń] *nf* evaporation.

évaporé, e [āváporā] *a* giddy, scatterbrained.

évaporer [āváporā]: **s'~** *vi* to evaporate.

évasé, e [āvázā] *a (jupe etc)* flared.

évaser [āvázā] *vt (tuyau)* to widen, open out; *(jupe, pantalon)* to flare; **s'~** *vi* to widen, open out.

évasif, ive [āvázēf, -ēv] *a* evasive.

évasion [āvázyóń] *nf* escape; **littérature d'~**

escapist literature; ~ **des capitaux** (ÉCON) flight of capital; ~ **fiscale** tax avoidance.

évasivement [āvázĕvmáṅ] ad evasively.

évêché [āvāshā] nm (fonction) bishopric; (palais) bishop's palace.

éveil [āvey] nm awakening; **être en** ~ to be alert; **mettre qn en** ~, **donner l'**~ **à qn** to arouse sb's suspicions; **activités d'**~ early-learning activities.

éveillé, e [āvāyā] a awake; (vif) alert, sharp.

éveiller [āvāyā] vt to (a)waken; **s'**~ vi to (a)waken; (fig) to be aroused.

événement [āvɛnmáṅ] nm event.

éventail [āvâṅtáy] nm fan; (choix) range; **en** ~ fanned out; fan-shaped.

éventaire [āvâṅter] nm stall, stand.

éventé, e [avánta] a (parfum, vin) stale.

éventer [āvâṅtā] vt (secret, complot) to uncover; (avec un éventail) to fan; **s'**~ vi (parfum, vin) to go stale.

éventrer [āvâṅtrā] vt to disembowel; (fig) to tear ou rip open.

éventualité [āvâṅtüälĕtā] nf eventuality; possibility; **dans l'**~ **de** in the event of; **parer à toute** ~ to guard against all eventualities.

éventuel, le [āvâṅtüel] a possible.

éventuellement [āvâṅtüelmáṅ] ad possibly.

évêque [āvek] nm bishop.

Everest [evrest] nm: **(mont)** ~ (Mount) Everest.

évertuer [āvertüā]: **s'**~ vi: **s'**~ **à faire** to try very hard to do.

éviction [āvĕksyóṅ] nf ousting, supplanting; (de locataire) eviction.

évidemment [āvēdamáṅ] ad obviously.

évidence [āvēdâṅs] nf obviousness; (fait) obvious fact; **se rendre à l'**~ to bow before the evidence; **nier l'**~ to deny the evidence; **à l'**~ evidently; **en** ~ conspicuous; **mettre en** ~ to bring to the fore.

évident, e [āvēdâṅ, -âṅt] a obvious, evident; **ce n'est pas** ~ (cela pose des problèmes) it's not (all that) straightforward, it's not as simple as all that.

évider [āvēdā] vt to scoop out.

évier [āvyā] nm (kitchen) sink.

évincement [āvaṅsmáṅ] nm ousting.

évincer [āvaṅsā] vt to oust, supplant.

évitable [āvētábl(ə)] a avoidable.

évitement [āvētmáṅ] nm: **place d'**~ (AUTO) passing place.

éviter [āvētā] vt to avoid; ~ **de faire/que qch ne se passe** to avoid doing/sth happening; ~ **qch à qn** to spare sb sth.

évocateur, trice [āvokátœr, -trēs] a evocative, suggestive.

évocation [āvokâsyóṅ] nf evocation.

évolué, e [āvolüā] a advanced; (personne) broad-minded.

évoluer [āvolüā] vi (enfant, maladie) to develop; (situation, moralement) to evolve, develop; (aller et venir: danseur etc) to move about, circle.

évolutif, ive [āvolütēf, -ēv] a evolving.

évolution [āvolüsyóṅ] nf development; evolution; ~**s** nfpl movements.

évoquer [āvokā] vt to call to mind, evoke; (mentionner) to mention.

ex. abr (= exemple) ex.

ex- [eks] préfixe ex-.

exacerber [egzàserbā] vt to exacerbate.

exact, e [egzákt] a (précis) exact, accurate, precise; (correct) correct; (ponctuel) punctual; **l'heure** ~**e** the right ou exact time.

exactement [egzáktəmáṅ] ad exactly, accurately, precisely; correctly; (c'est cela même) exactly.

exactions [egzáksyóṅ] nfpl exactions.

exactitude [egzáktētüd] nf exactitude, accurateness, precision.

ex aequo [egzākō] a tied; **classé 1er** ~ tied for first place.

exagération [egzázhārâsyóṅ] nf exaggeration.

exagéré, e [egzázhārā] a (prix etc) excessive.

exagérément [egzázhāramán] ad excessively.

exagérer [egzázhārā] vt to exaggerate ♦ vi (abuser) to go too far; (dépasser les bornes) to overstep the mark; (déformer les faits) to exaggerate; **s'**~ **qch** to exaggerate sth.

exaltation [egzáltásyóṅ] nf exaltation.

exalté, e [egzáltā] a (over)excited ♦ nm/f (péj) fanatic.

exalter [egzáltā] vt (enthousiasmer) to excite, elate; (glorifier) to exalt.

examen [egzámaṅ] nm examination; (SCOL) exam, examination; **à l'**~ (dossier, projet) under consideration; (COMM) on approval; ~ **blanc** practice test; ~ **de la vue** eye test.

examinateur, trice [egzámēnátœr, -trēs] nm/f examiner.

examiner [egzámēnā] vt to examine.

exaspération [egzáspárâsyóṅ] nf exasperation.

exaspéré, e [egzáspārā] a exasperated.

exaspérer [egzáspārā] vt to exasperate; (aggraver) to exacerbate.

exaucer [egzōsā] vt (vœu) to grant, fulfil; ~ **qn** to grant sb's wishes.

excavateur [ekskávátœr] nm excavator, steam shovel.

excavation [ekskávâsyóṅ] nf excavation.

excavatrice [ekskávátrēs] nf = **excavateur**.

excédent [eksádáṅ] nm surplus; **en** ~ surplus; **payer 600 F d'**~ (de bagages) to pay 600 F excess luggage; ~ **de bagages** excess luggage; ~ **commercial** trade surplus.

excédentaire [eksādâṅter] a surplus, excess.

excéder [eksādā] vt (dépasser) to exceed; (agacer) to exasperate; **excédé de fatigue** exhausted; **excédé de travail** worn out with work.

excellence [ekselâṅs] nf excellence; (titre) Excellency; **par** ~ par excellence.

excellent, e [ekselâṅ, -âṅt] a excellent.

exceller [eksālā] vi: ~ **(dans)** to excel (in).

excentricité [eksâṅtrēsētā] nf eccentricity.

excentrique [eksâṅtrēk] a eccentric; (quartier) outlying ♦ nm/f eccentric.

excepté, e [eksɛptā] a, prép: **les élèves** ~**s**, ~ **les élèves** except for ou apart from the pupils; ~ **si/quand** except if/when; ~ **que** except that.

excepter [eksɛptā] vt to except.

exception [eksɛpsyóṅ] nf exception; **faire** ~ to be an exception; **faire une** ~ to make an exception; **sans** ~ without exception; **à l'**~ **de** except for, with the exception of; **d'**~ (mesure, loi) special, exceptional.

exceptionnel, le |eksepsyonel| *a* exceptional; (*prix*) special.

exceptionnellement |eksepsyonelmän| *ad* exceptionally; (*par exception*) by way of exception, on this occasion.

excès |ekse| *nm* surplus ♦ *nmpl* excesses; **à l'~** (*méticuleux, généreux*) to excess; **avec ~** to excess; **sans ~** in moderation; **tomber dans l'~** **inverse** to go to the opposite extreme; **~ de langage** immoderate language; **~ de pouvoir** abuse of power; **~ de vitesse** speeding *q*, exceeding the speed limit; **~ de zèle** overzealousness *q*.

excessif, ive |eksäsēf, -ēv| *a* excessive.

exciper |eksēpā|: **~ de** *vt* to plead.

excipient |eksēpyäṅ| *nm* (*MÉD*) inert base, excipient.

exciser |eksēzā| *vt* (*MÉD*) to excise.

excitant, e |eksētäṅ, -äṅt| *a* exciting ♦ *nm* stimulant.

excitation |eksētásyóṅ| *nf* (*état*) excitement.

excité, e |eksētā| *a* excited.

exciter |eksētā| *vt* to excite; (*suj: café etc*) to stimulate; **s'~** *vi* to get excited; **~ qn à** (*révolte etc*) to incite sb to.

exclamation |eksklàmásyóṅ| *nf* exclamation.

exclamer |eksklámā|: **s'~** *vi* to exclaim.

exclu, e |eksklü| *pp de* **exclure** ♦ *a*: **il est/n'est pas ~ que** ... it's out of the question/not impossible that ...; **ce n'est pas exclu** it's not impossible, I don't rule that out.

exclure |eksklür| *vt* (*faire sortir*) to expel; (*ne pas compter*) to exclude, leave out; (*rendre impossible*) to exclude, rule out.

exclusif, ive |eksklüzēf, -ēv| *a* exclusive; **avec la mission exclusive/ dans le but ~ de** ... with the sole mission/aim of ...; **agent ~** sole agent.

exclusion |eksklüzyóṅ| *nf* expulsion; **à l'~ de** with the exclusion *ou* exception of.

exclusivement |eksklüzēvmäṅ| *ad* exclusively.

exclusivité |eksklüzēvētā| *nf* exclusiveness; (*COMM*) exclusive rights *pl*; **film passant en ~ à** film showing only at.

excommunier |ekskomünyā| *vt* to excommunicate.

excréments |ekskrämäṅ| *nmpl* excrement *sg*, feces (*US*), faeces (*Brit*).

excroissance |ekskrwásàṅs| *nf* excrescence, outgrowth.

excursion |ekskürsyóṅ| *nf* (*en autocar*) excursion, trip; (*à pied*) walk, hike; **faire une ~** to go on an excursion *ou* a trip; to go on a walk *ou* hike.

excursionniste |ekskürsyonēst(ǝ)| *nm/f* traveler (*US*), tripper, tourist; hiker.

excuse |eksküz| *nf* excuse; **~s** *nfpl* apology *sg*, apologies; **faire des ~s** to apologize; **faire ses ~s** to offer one's apologies; **mot d'~** (*SCOL*) note from one's parent(s) (*to explain absence etc*); **lettre d'~s** letter of apology.

excuser |eksküzä| *vt* to excuse; **~ qn de qch** (*dispenser*) to excuse sb from sth; **s'~ (de)** to apologize (for); **"excusez-moi"** "I'm sorry"; (*pour attirer l'attention*) "excuse me"; **se faire ~** to ask to be excused.

exécrable |egzäkrábl(ǝ)| *a* atrocious.

exécrer |egzäkrā| *vt* to loathe, abhor.

exécutant, e |egzäkütäṅ, -äṅt| *nm/f* performer.

exécuter |egzäkütä| *vt* (*prisonnier*) to execute; (*tâche etc*) to execute, carry out; (*MUS*: *jouer*) to perform, execute; (*INFORM*) to run; **s'~** *vi* to comply.

exécuteur, trice |egzäkütœr, -trēs| *nm/f* (*testamentaire*) executor ♦ *nm* (*bourreau*) executioner.

exécutif, ive |egzäkütēf, -ēv| *a, nm* (*POL*) executive.

exécution |egzäküsyóṅ| *nf* execution; carrying out; **mettre à ~** to carry out.

exécutoire |egzäkütwár| *a* (*JUR*) (legally) binding.

exégèse |egzäzhez| *nf* exegesis.

exemplaire |egzáṅpler| *a* exemplary ♦ *nm* copy.

exemple |egzáṅpl(ǝ)| *nm* example; **par ~** for instance, for example; (*valeur intensive*) really!; **sans ~** (*bêtise, gourmandise etc*) unparalleled; **donner l'~** to set an example; **prendre ~ sur** to take as a model; **à l'~ de** just like; **pour l'~** (*punir*) as an example.

exempt, e |egzäṅ, -äṅt| *a*: **~ de** (*dispensé de*) exempt from; (*sans*) free from; **~ de taxes** tax-free.

exempter |egzäṅtä| *vt*: **~ de** to exempt from.

exercé, e |egzersä| *a* trained.

exercer |egzersä| *vt* (*pratiquer*) to exercise, practice (*US*), practise (*Brit*); (*faire usage de: prérogative*) to exercise; (*effectuer: influence, contrôle, pression*) to exert; (*former*) to exercise, train ♦ *vi* (*médecin*) to be in practice; **s'~** (*sportif, musicien*) to practice (*US*), practise (*Brit*); (*se faire sentir: pression etc*): **s'~ (sur ou contre)** to be exerted (on); **s'~ à faire qch** to train o.s. to do sth.

exercice |egzersēs| *nm* practice; exercising; (*tâche, travail*) exercise; (*COMM, ADMIN*: *période*) accounting period; **l'~** (*sportive etc*) exercise; (*MIL*) drill; **en ~** (*juge*) in office; (*médecin*) practising (*US*), practising (*Brit*); **dans l'~ de ses fonctions** in the discharge of his duties; **~s d'assouplissement** limbering-up (exercises).

exergue |egzerg(ǝ)| *nm*: **mettre en ~** (*inscription*) to inscribe; **porter en ~** to be inscribed with.

exhalaison |egzálezóṅ| *nf* exhalation.

exhaler |egzälä| *vt* (*parfum*) to exhale; (*souffle, son, soupir*) to utter, breathe; **s'~** *vi* to rise (up).

exhausser |egzōsä| *vt* to raise (up).

exhaustif, ive |egzōstēf, -ēv| *a* exhaustive.

exhiber |egzēbä| *vt* (*montrer: papiers, certificat*) to present, produce; (*péj*) to display, flaunt; **s'~** (*personne*) to parade; (*suj: exhibitionniste*) to expose o.s.

exhibitionnisme |egzēbēsyonēsm(ǝ)| *nm* exhibitionism.

exhibitionniste |egzēbēsyonēst(ǝ)| *nm/f* exhibitionist.

exhorter |egzortä| *vt*: **~ qn à faire** to urge sb to do.

exhumer |egzümä| *vt* to exhume.

exigeant, e |egzēzhäṅ, -äṅt| *a* demanding; (*péj*) hard to please.

exigence |egzēzháṅs| *nf* demand, requirement.

exiger |egzēzhä| *vt* to demand, require.

exigible [egzēzhēbl(ə)] *a* (*COMM*, *JUR*) payable.

exigu, ë [egzēgü] *a* cramped, tiny.

exil [egzēl] *nm* exile; **en ~** in exile.

exilé, e [egzēlā] *nm/f* exile.

exiler [egzēlā] *vt* to exile; **s'~** to go into exile.

existant, e [egzēstāṅ, -āṅt] *a* (*actuel*, *présent*) existing.

existence [egzēstāṅs] *nf* existence; **dans l'~** in life.

existentialisme [egzēstāṅsyálēsm(ə)] *nm* existentialism.

existentiel, le [egzēstāṅsyel] *a* existential.

exister [egzēstā] *vi* to exist; **il existe un/des** there is a/are (some).

exode [egzod] *nm* exodus.

exonération [egzonārāsyóṅ] *nf* exemption.

exonéré, e [egzonārā] *a*: **~ de TVA** exempt from value-added tax.

exonérer [egzonārā] *vt*: **~ de** to exempt from.

exorbitant, e [egzorbētāṅ, -āṅt] *a* exorbitant.

exorbité, e [egzorbētā] *a*: **yeux ~s** bulging eyes.

exorciser [egzorsēzā] *vt* to exorcize.

exorde [egzord(ə)] *nm* introduction.

exotique [egzotēk] *a* exotic.

exotisme [egzotēsm(ə)] *nm* exoticism.

expansif, ive [ekspáṅsēf, -ēv] *a* expansive, communicative.

expansion [ekspáṅsyóṅ] *nf* expansion.

expansionniste [ekspáṅsyonēst(ə)] *a* expansionist.

expatrié, e [ekspátrēyā] *nm/f* expatriate.

expatrier [ekspátrēyā] *vt* (*argent*) to take *ou* send out of the country; **s'~** to leave one's country.

expectative [ekspektátēv] *nf*: **être dans l'~** to be waiting to see.

expectorant, e [ekspektoráṅ, -áṅt] *a*: **sirop ~** expectorant (syrup).

expédient [ekspādyáṅ] *nm* (*parfois péj*) expedient; **vivre d'~s** to live by one's wits.

expédier [ekspādyā] *vt* (*lettre*, *paquet*) to send; (*troupes*, *renfort*) to dispatch; (*péj*: *travail etc*) to dispose of, dispatch.

expéditeur, trice [ekspādētœr, -trēs] *nm/f* (*POSTES*) sender.

expéditif, ive [ekspādētēf, -ēv] *a* quick, expeditious.

expédition [ekspādēsyóṅ] *nf* sending; (*scientifique*, *sportive*, *MIL*) expedition; **~ punitive** punitive raid.

expéditionnaire [ekspādēsyoner] *a*: **corps ~** (*MIL*) task force.

expérience [ekspāryáṅs] *nf* (*de la vie*, *des choses*) experience; (*scientifique*) experiment; **avoir de l'~** to have experience, be experienced; **avoir l'~ de** to have experience of; **faire l'~ de qch** to experience sth; **~ de chimie/d'électricité** chemical/electrical experiment.

expérimental, e, aux [ekspārēmáṅtál, -ō] *a* experimental.

expérimenté, e [ekspārēmáṅtā] *a* experienced.

expérimenter [ekspārēmáṅtā] *vt* (*machine*, *technique*) to test out, experiment with.

expert, e [eksper, -ert(ə)] *a*: **~ en** expert in ♦ *nm* (*spécialiste*) expert; **~ en assurances** insurance appraiser.

expert-comptable, pl experts-comptables [eksperkóṅtábl(ə)] *nm* ≈ certified public (*US*) *ou* chartered (*Brit*) accountant.

expertise [ekspertēz] *nf* valuation; assessment; valuer's (*ou* assessor's) report; (*JUR*) (forensic) examination.

expertiser [ekspertēzā] *vt* (*objet de valeur*) to value; (*voiture accidentée etc*) to assess damage to.

expier [ekspyā] *vt* to expiate, atone for.

expiration [ekspērāsyóṅ] *nf* expiration; breathing out *q*.

expirer [ekspērā] *vi* (*prendre fin*, *littéraire*: *mourir*) to expire; (*respirer*) to breathe out.

explétif, ive [eksplātēf, -ēv] *a* (*LING*) expletive.

explicable [eksplēkábl(ə)] *a*: **pas ~** inexplicable.

explicatif, ive [eksplēkátēf, -ēv] *a* (*mot*, *texte*, *note*) explanatory.

explication [eksplēkāsyóṅ] *nf* explanation; (*discussion*) discussion; **~ de texte** (*SCOL*) critical analysis (of a text).

explicite [eksplēsēt] *a* explicit.

explicitement [eksplēsētmáṅ] *ad* explicitly.

expliciter [eksplēsētā] *vt* to make explicit.

expliquer [eksplēkā] *vt* to explain; **~ (à qn) comment/que** to point out *ou* explain (to sb) how/that; **s'~** (*se faire comprendre*: *personne*) to explain o.s.; (*discuter*) to discuss things; (*se disputer*) to have it out; (*comprendre*): **je m'explique son retard/absence** I understand his lateness/absence; **son erreur s'explique** one can understand his mistake.

exploit [eksplwá] *nm* exploit, feat.

exploitable [eksplwátábl(ə)] *a* (*gisement etc*) that can be exploited; **~ par une machine** machine-readable.

exploitant [eksplwátáṅ] *nm* farmer.

exploitation [eksplwátásyóṅ] *nf* exploitation; running; (*entreprise*): **~ agricole** farming concern.

exploiter [eksplwátā] *vt* to exploit; (*entreprise*, *ferme*) to fun, operate.

exploiteur, euse [eksplwátœr, -ēz] *nm/f* (*péj*) exploiter.

explorateur, trice [eksplorátœr, -trēs] *nm/f* explorer.

exploration [eksplorásyóṅ] *nf* exploration.

explorer [eksplorā] *vt* to explore.

exploser [eksplōzā] *vi* to explode, blow up; (*engin explosif*) to go off; (*fig*: *joie*, *colère*) to burst out, explode; (: *personne*: *de colère*) to explode, flare up; **faire ~** (*bombe*) to explode, detonate; (*bâtiment*, *véhicule*) to blow up.

explosif, ive [eksplōzēf, -ēv] *a*, *nm* explosive.

explosion [eksplōzyóṅ] *nf* explosion; **~ de joie/colère** outburst of joy/rage; **~ démographique** population explosion.

exponentiel, le [ekspónáṅsyel] *a* exponential.

exportateur, trice [eksportátœr, -trēs] *a* exporting ♦ *nm* exporter.

exportation [eksportásyóṅ] *nf* export.

exporter [eksportā] *vt* to export.

exposant [ekspōzáṅ] *nm* exhibitor; (*MATH*) exponent.

exposé, e [ekspōzā] *nm* (*écrit*) exposé; (*oral*) talk ♦ *a*: **~ au sud** facing south, with a southern exposure; **bien** ~ well situated; **très** ~ very exposed.

exposer [ekspōzã] *vt* (*montrer: marchandise*) to display; (*: peinture*) to exhibit, show; (*parler de: problème, situation*) to explain, expose, set out; (*mettre en danger, orienter: maison etc*) to expose; ~ **qn/qch à** to expose sb/sth to; ~ **sa vie** to risk one's life; **s'**~ **à** (*soleil, danger*) to expose o.s. to; (*critiques, punition*) to lay o.s. open to.

exposition [ekspōzēsyôñ] *nf* (*voir exposer*) displaying; exhibiting; explanation, exposition; exposure; (*voir exposé*) exposure, situation; (*manifestation*) exhibition; (*PHOTO*) exposure; (*introduction*) exposition.

exprès [ekspre] *ad* (*délibérément*) on purpose; (*spécialement*) specially; **faire** ~ **de faire qch** to do sth on purpose.

exprès, esse [ekspres] *a* (*ordre, défense*) express, formal ♦ *a inv, ad* (*POSTES*) special delivery (*US*), express (*Brit*); **envoyer qch en** ~ to send sth special delivery (*US*) *ou* express (*Brit*).

express [ekspres] *a, nm:* (**café**) ~ espresso; (**train**) ~ express (train).

expressément [ekspresāmâñ] *ad* expressly, specifically.

expressif, ive [eksprāsēf, -ēv] *a* expressive.

expression [ekspresyôñ] *nf* expression; **réduit à sa plus simple** ~ reduced to its simplest terms; **liberté/moyens d'**~ freedom/means of expression; ~ **toute faite** set phrase.

exprimer [eksprēmã] *vt* (*sentiment, idée*) to express; (*faire sortir: jus, liquide*) to press out; **s'**~ *vi* (*personne*) to express o.s.

expropriation [eksproprēyásyôñ] *nf* expropriation; **frapper d'**~ to expropriate.

exproprier [eksprōprēyã] *vt* to expropriate.

expulser [ekspülsã] *vt* (*d'une salle, d'un groupe*) to expel; (*locataire*) to evict; (*FOOTBALL*) to send off.

expulsion [ekspülsyôñ] *nf* expulsion; eviction; sending off.

expurger [ekspürzhã] *vt* to expurgate, bowdlerize.

exquis, e [ekskē, -ēz] *a* (*gâteau, parfum, élégance*) exquisite; (*personne, temps*) delightful.

exsangue [eksâñg] *a* bloodless, drained of blood.

exsuder [eksüdã] *vt* to exude.

extase [ekstáz] *nf* ecstasy; **être en** ~ to be in raptures.

extasier [ekstázyã]: **s'**~ *vi:* **s'**~ **sur** to go into raptures over.

extatique [ekstátēk] *a* ecstatic.

extenseur [ekstâñsœr] *nm* (*SPORT*) chest expander.

extensible [ekstâñsēbl(ə)] *a* extensible.

extensif, ive [ekstâñsēf, -ēv] *a* extensive.

extension [ekstâñsyôñ] *nf* (*d'un muscle, ressort*) stretching; (*MÉD*): **à l'**~ in traction; (*fig*) extension; expansion.

exténuant [ekstānüâñ, -âñt] *a* exhausting.

exténuer [ekstānüã] *vt* to exhaust.

extérieur, e [ekstāryœr] *a* (*de dehors: porte, mur etc*) outer, outside; (*: commerce, politique*) foreign; (*: influences, pressions*) external; (*au dehors: escalier, w.-c.*) outside;

(*apparent: calme, gaieté etc*) outer ♦ *nm* (*d'une maison, d'un récipient etc*) outside, exterior; (*d'une personne: apparence*) exterior; (*d'un pays, d'un groupe social*): **l'**~ the outside world; **à l'**~ (*dehors*) outside; (*fig: à l'étranger*) abroad.

extérieurement [ekstāryœrmâñ] *ad* (*de dehors*) on the outside; (*en apparence*) on the surface.

extérioriser [ekstāryorēzã] *vt* to exteriorize.

exterminer [ekstermēnã] *vt* to exterminate, wipe out.

externat [eksternã] *nm* day school.

externe [ekstern(ə)] *a* external, outer ♦ *nm/f* (*MÉD*) non-resident medical student, extern (*US*); (*SCOL*) day pupil.

extincteur [ekstâñktœr] *nm* (*fire*) extinguisher.

extinction [ekstâñksyôñ] *nf* extinction; (*JUR: d'une dette*) extinguishment; ~ **de voix** (*MÉD*) loss of voice.

extirper [ekstērpã] *vt* (*tumeur*) to extirpate; (*plante*) to root out, pull up; (*préjugés*) to eradicate.

extorquer [ekstorkã] *vt* (*de l'argent, un renseignement*): ~ **qch à qn** to extort sth from sb.

extorsion [ekstorsyôñ] *nf:* ~ **de fonds** extortion of money.

extra [ekstrá] *a inv* first-rate; (*marchandises*) top-quality ♦ *nm inv* extra help ♦ *préfixe* extra(-).

extraction [ekstráksyôñ] *nf* extraction.

extrader [ekstrádã] *vt* to extradite.

extradition [ekstrádēsyôñ] *nf* extradition.

extra-fin, e [ekstráfañ, -ēn] *a* extra-fine.

extra-fort, e [ekstráfor, -fort(ə)] *a* extra strong.

extraire [ekstrer] *vt* to extract.

extrait, e [ekstre, -et] *pp de* **extraire** ♦ *nm* (*de plante*) extract; (*de film, livre*) extract, excerpt; ~ **de naissance** birth certificate.

extra-lucide [ekstrálüsēd] *a:* **voyante** ~ clairvoyant.

extraordinaire [ekstráordēner] *a* extraordinary; (*POL, ADMIN*) special; **ambassadeur** ~ ambassador extraordinary; **assemblée** ~ special meeting; **par** ~ by some unlikely chance.

extraordinairement [ekstráordēnermâñ] *ad* extraordinarily.

extrapoler [ekstrápolã] *vt, vi* to extrapolate.

extra-sensoriel, le [ekstrásâñsoryel] *a* extrasensory.

extra-terrestre [ekstráterestr(ə)] *nm/f* extraterrestrial.

extra-utérin, e [ekstráütãrañ, -ēn] *a* extrauterine.

extravagance [ekstrávágâñs] *nf* extravagance *q*; extravagant behavior *q* (*US*) *ou* behaviour *q* (*Brit*).

extravagant, e [ekstrávágâñ, -âñt] *a* (*personne, attitude*) extravagant; (*idée*) wild.

extraverti, e [ekstrávertē] *a* extrovert.

extrayais [ekstreye] *etc vb voir* **extraire**.

extrême [ekstrem] *a, nm* extreme; (*intensif*): **d'une** ~ **simplicité/brutalité** extremely simple/brutal; **d'un** ~ **à l'autre** from one extreme to another; **à l'**~ in the extreme; **à l'**~ **rigueur** in the absolute extreme.

extrêmement [ekstremmâñ] *ad* extremely.

extrême-onction, *pl* **extrêmes-onctions** [ekstremônksyôn] *nf* (*REL*) last rites *pl*, Extreme Unction.

Extrême-Orient [ekstremoryáń] *nm*: **l'~** the Far East.

extrême-oriental, e, aux [ekstremoryáńtàl, -ô] *a* Far Eastern.

extrémiste [ekstrāmēst(ə)] *a, nm/f* extremist.

extrémité [ekstrāmētā] *nf* (*bout*) end; (*situation*) straits *pl*, plight; (*geste désespéré*) extreme action; **~s** *nfpl* (*pieds et mains*) extremities; **à la dernière ~** (*à l'agonie*) on the point of death.

extroverti, e [ekstrovertē] *a* = **extraverti.**

exubérant, e [egzübāráń, -áńt] *a* exuberant.

exulter [egzültā] *vi* to exult.

exutoire [egzütwár] *nm* outlet, release.

ex-voto [eksvotō] *nm inv* ex-voto.

eye-liner [áyláynœr] *nm* eyeliner.

F

F, f [ef] *nm inv* F, f ♦ *abr* = **féminin; femme;** (= *franc*) fr.; (= *Fahrenheit*) F; (= *frère*) Br(o).; (*appartement*): **un F2/F3** a 2-/3-roomed apartment; **F comme François** F for Fox.

fa [fâ] *nm inv* (*MUS*) F; (*en chantant la gamme*) fa.

table [fâbl(ə)] *nf* fable; (*mensonge*) story, tale.

fabricant [fabrēkáń] *nm* manufacturer, maker.

fabrication [fâbrēkâsyôń] *nf* manufacture, making.

fabrique [fábrēk] *nf* factory.

fabriquer [fâbrēkā] *vt* to make; (*industriellement*) to manufacture, make; (*construire: voiture*) to manufacture, build; (*: maison*) to build; (*fig: inventer: histoire, alibi*) to make up; (*fam*): **qu'est-ce qu'il fabrique?** what is he up to?; **~ en série** to mass-produce.

fabulateur, trice [fábülátœr, -trēs] *nm/f*: **c'est un ~** he fantasizes, he makes up stories.

fabulation [fâbülâsyôń] *nf* (*PSYCH*) fantasizing.

fabuleusement [fâbülēzmáń] *ad* fabulously, fantastically.

fabuleux, euse [fâbülœ̄, -ēz] *a* fabulous, fantastic.

fac [fâk] *abr f* (*fam*: = *faculté*) ≈ college (*US*), Uni (*Brit fam*).

façade [fásád] *nf* front, façade; (*fig*) façade.

face [fás] *nf* face; (*fig: aspect*) side ♦ *a*: **le côté ~** heads; **perdre/sauver la ~** to lose/save face; **regarder qn en ~** to look sb in the face; **la maison/le trottoir d'en ~** the house/sidewalk opposite; **en ~ de** *prép* opposite; (*fig*) in front of; **de ~** *ad* from the front; head-on; **~ à** *prép* facing; (*fig*) faced with, in the face of; **faire ~ à** to face face; **faire ~ à la demande** (*COMM*) to meet the demand; **~ à ~** *ad* facing each other ♦ *nm inv* encounter.

face-à-main, *pl* **faces-à-main** [fásámáń] *nm* lorgnette.

facéties [fásāsē] *nfpl* jokes, pranks.

facétieux, euse [fásāsyœ̄, -ēz] *a* mischievous.

facette [fáset] *nf* facet.

fâché, e [fâshā] *a* angry; (*désolé*) sorry.

fâcher [fâshā] *vt* to anger; **se ~** *vi* to get angry; **se ~ avec** (*se brouiller*) to fall out with.

fâcherie [fâshrē] *nf* quarrel.

fâcheusement [fâshœ̄zmáń] *ad* unpleasantly; (*impressionné etc*) badly; **avoir ~ tendance à** to have an irritating tendency to.

fâcheux, euse [fâshœ̄, -ēz] *a* unfortunate, regrettable.

facho [fáshō] *a, nm/f* (*fam*: = *fasciste*) fascist.

facial, e, aux [fásyál, -ô] *a* facial.

faciès [fásyes] *nm* (*visage*) features *pl*.

facile [fásēl] *a* easy; (*accommodant*) easygoing; **~ d'emploi** (*INFORM*) user-friendly.

facilement [fásēlmáń] *ad* easily.

facilité [fásēlētā] *nf* easiness; (*disposition, don*) aptitude; (*moyen, occasion, possibilité*): **il a la ~ de rencontrer les gens** he has every opportunity to meet people; **~s** *nfpl* facilities; (*COMM*) terms; **~s de crédit** credit terms; **~s de paiement** easy terms.

faciliter [fásēlētā] *vt* to make easier.

façon [fásôń] *nf* (*manière*) way; (*d'une robe etc*) tailoring; cut; (*: main-d'œuvre*) labor (*US*), labour (*Brit*); (*imitation*): **châle ~ cachemire** cashmere-style shawl; **~s** *nfpl* (*péj*) fuss *sg*; **faire des ~s** (*péj: être affecté*) to be affected; (*: faire des histoires*) to make a fuss; **de quelle ~?** (in) what way?; **sans ~** *ad* without fuss ♦ *a* unaffected; **d'une autre ~** in another way; **en aucune ~** in no way; **de ~ à so as to; de ~ à ce que, de (telle) ~ que** so that; **de toute ~** anyway, in any case; **(c'est une) ~ de parler** it's a way of putting it; **travail à ~** tailoring.

façonner [fásonā] *vt* (*fabriquer*) to manufacture; (*travailler: matière*) to shape, fashion; (*fig*) to mold (*US*), mould (*Brit*), shape.

fac-similé [fáksēmēlā] *nm* facsimile.

facteur, trice [fáktœr, -trēs] *nm/f* mailman/woman (*US*), postman/woman (*Brit*) ♦ *nm* (*MATH, gén*) factor; **~ d'orgues** organ builder; **~ de pianos** piano maker; **~ rhésus** Rh *ou* rhesus factor.

factice [fáktēs] *a* artificial.

faction [fáksyôń] *nf* (*groupe*) faction; (*MIL*) guard *ou* sentry (duty); watch; **en ~** on guard; standing watch.

factionnaire [fáksyoner] *nm* guard, sentry.

factoriel, le [fáktoryel] *a, nf* factorial.

factotum [fáktotom] *nm* odd-job man, gofer.

factuel, le [fáktüel] *a* factual.

facturation [fáktürásyôń] *nf* invoicing; (*bureau*) invoicing (office).

facture [fáktür] *nf* (*à payer: gén*) bill; (*: COMM*) invoice; (*d'un artisan, artiste*) technique, workmanship.

facturer [fáktürā] *vt* to invoice.

facturier, ière [fáktüryē, -yer] *nm/f* invoice clerk.

facultatif, ive [fákültátēf, -ēv] *a* optional; (*arrêt de bus*) request *cpd*.

faculté [fákültā] *nf* (*intellectuelle, d'université*) faculty; (*pouvoir, possibilité*) power.

fadaises [fádez] *nfpl* twaddle *sg*.

fade [fàd] *a* insipid.
fading [fàdēng] *nm* (*RADIO*) fading.
fagot [fágō] *nm* (*de bois*) bundle of sticks.
fagoté, e [fágotā] *a* (*fam*): **drôlement** ~ oddly dressed.
faible [febl(ə)] *a* weak; (*voix, lumière, vent*) faint; (*élève, copie*) poor; (*rendement, intensité, revenu etc*) low ♦ *nm* weak point; (*pour quelqu'un*) weakness, soft spot; ~ **d'esprit** feeble-minded.
faiblement [febləmâṅ] *ad* weakly; (*peu: éclairer etc*) faintly.
faiblesse [febles] *nf* weakness.
faiblir [fàblēr] *vi* to weaken; (*lumière*) to dim; (*vent*) to drop.
faïence [fáyâṅs] *nf* earthenware *q*; (*objet*) piece of earthenware.
faignant, e [fenyâṅ, -âṅt] *nm/f* = **fainéant, e**.
faille [fày] *vb voir* **falloir** ♦ *nf* (*GÉO*) fault; (*fig*) flaw, weakness.
failli, e [fàyē] *a, nm/f* bankrupt.
faillible [fàyēbl(ə)] *a* fallible.
faillir [fàyēr] *vi*: **j'ai failli tomber/lui dire** I almost *ou* nearly fell/told him; ~ **à une promesse/un engagement** to break a promise/an agreement.
faillite [fàyēt] *nf* bankruptcy; (*échec: d'une politique etc*) collapse; **être en** ~ to be bankrupt; **faire** ~ to go bankrupt.
faim [faṅ] *nf* hunger; (*fig*): ~ **d'amour/de richesse** hunger *ou* yearning for love/wealth; **avoir** ~ to be hungry; **rester sur sa** ~ (*aussi fig*) to be left wanting more.
fainéant, e [fenāāṅ, -âṅt] *nm/f* idler, loafer.
fainéantise [fānāâṅtēz] *nf* idleness, laziness.
faire [fer] *vt* to do; (*fabriquer, préparer*) to make; (*maison*) to build; (*produire*) to produce; "**vraiment?**" **fit-il** "really?" he said; **je n'ai pas pu** ~ **autrement** I couldn't do otherwise; **fait à la main/machine** hand-/machine-made; ~ **du bruit/des taches** to make a noise/marks; ~ **du droit/du français** to study law/French; ~ **du rugby/du piano** to play rugby/play the piano; ~ **le malade/l'ignorant** to act the invalid/the fool; ~ **du diabète** to suffer from *ou* have diabetes; ~ **de la tension** to have high blood pressure; ~ **de la fièvre** to run a temperature; ~ **les magasins** to make the rounds of the stores; ~ **de qn un frustré/avocat** to make sb frustrated/a lawyer; **ça ne me fait rien** (*m'est égal*) I don't care *ou* mind; (*me laisse froid*) it has no effect on me; **ça ne fait rien** it doesn't matter; **qu'est-ce que ça peut** ~**?** what does it matter?; **je vous le fais 10 F** I'll let you have it for 10 F; **que faites-vous?** (*quel métier etc*) what do you do?; (*quelle activité: au moment de la question*) what are you doing?; **que** ~**?** what are we going to do?, what can be done (about it)?; **tu as bien fait de me le dire** you did well *ou* right to tell me; **comment a-t-il fait pour ...?** how did he manage to ...?; **qu'a-t-il fait de sa valise?** what has he done with his suitcase?; **n'avoir que** ~ **de qch** to have no need of sth; **2 et 2 font 4** 2 and 2 are *ou* make 4; **9 divisé par 3 fait 3** 9 divided by 3 makes *ou* gives *ou* is 3; ~ **que** (*impliquer*) to mean that ♦ *vi* (*agir,*

s'y prendre) to act; (*faire ses besoins*) to go (to the bathroom); **faites comme chez vous** make yourself at home ♦ *vb avec attribut*: **ça fait 10 m/15 F** it's 10 m/15 F; ~ **vieux/démodé** to look old/old-fashioned ♦ *vb substitut*: **remets-le en place** — **je viens de le** ~ put it back in its place — I've just done so *ou* I just did; **faites!** please do!; **il ne fait que critiquer** (*sans cesse*) all he (ever) does is criticize; (*seulement*) he's only criticizing ♦ *vb impersonnel*: **il fait beau** *etc* the weather is fine *etc*; *voir* **jour, froid** *etc*; **ça fait 2 ans qu'il est parti** it's 2 years since he left; **ça fait 2 ans qu'il y est** he's been there for 2 years ♦ ~ **faire**: ~ **réparer qch** to get *ou* have sth repaired; ~ **tomber/bouger qch** to make sth fall/move; **cela fait dormir** it makes you sleep; ~ **travailler les enfants** to make the children work, get the children to work; ~ **punir les enfants** to have the children punished; **il m'a fait traverser la rue** (*aidé*) he helped me (to) cross the road, he helped me across the road; ~ **démarrer un moteur/chauffer de l'eau** to start up an engine/heat some water; **se** ~ **couper les cheveux** to get *ou* have one's hair cut; **se** ~ **examiner la vue/opérer** to have one's eyes tested/have an operation; **il s'est fait aider (par qn)** he got sb to help him; **il va se** ~ **tuer/punir** he's going to get himself killed/get (himself) punished; **elle s'est fait expliquer le problème** she had the problem explained to her; **se** ~ **faire un vêtement** to get a garment made for o.s. ♦ **se** ~ *vi* (*fromage, vin*) to mature; **se** ~ **à** (*s'habituer*) to get used to; **cela se fait beaucoup/ne se fait pas** it's done a lot/not done; **comment se fait-il que ...?** how is it that ...?; **il peut se** ~ **que ...** it can happen that ...; **se** ~ **vieux** to be getting old; **se** ~ **beau** to make o.s. beautiful; **se** ~ **les yeux/ongles** to do one's eyes/nails; **se** ~ **une jupe** to make o.s. a skirt; **se** ~ **des amis** to make friends; **se** ~ **du souci** to worry; **il ne s'en fait pas** he doesn't worry; **sans s'en** ~ without worrying.
faire-part [ferpàr] *nm inv* announcement (*of birth, marriage etc*).
fair-play [ferple] *a inv* fair.
fais [fe] *vb voir* **faire**.
faisable [fəzàbl(ə)] *a* feasible.
faisais [fəze] *etc vb voir* **faire**.
faisan [fəzâṅ, -âṅ] *nm/f* pheasant.
faisandé, e [fəzâṅdā] *a* high (*bad*); (*fig péj*) corrupt, decadent.
faisceau, x [fesō] *nm* (*de lumière etc*) beam; (*de branches etc*) bundle.
faiseur, euse [fəzœr, -ẽz] *nm/f* (*gén: péj*): ~ **de** maker of ♦ *nm* (*custom (US) ou* bespoke (*Brit*)) tailor; ~ **d'embarras** fusspot; ~ **de projets** schemer.
fait [fe] *vb voir* **faire** ♦ *nm* (*événement*) event, occurrence; (*réalité, donnée*) fact; **le** ~ **que/de manger** the fact that/of eating; **être le** ~ **de** (*causé par*) to be the work of; **être au** ~ **(de)** to be informed (of); **mettre qn au** ~ to inform sb; **au** ~ (*à propos*) by the way; **en venir au** ~ to get to the point; **de** ~ *a* (*opposé à: de droit*) de facto ♦ *ad* in fact; **du** ~ **de ceci/qu'il a menti** because of *ou* on

account of this/his having lied; **de ce ~** therefore, for this reason; **en ~** in fact; **en ~ de repas** by way of a meal; **prendre ~ et cause pour qn** to support sb, side with sb; **prendre qn sur le ~** to catch sb in the act; **dire à qn son ~** to give sb a piece of one's mind; **hauts ~s** (*exploits*) exploits; **~ d'armes** feat of arms; **~ divers** (short) news item; **les ~s et gestes de qn** sb's actions *ou* doings.

fait, e [fε, fεt] *pp de* **faire** ♦ *a* (*mûr: fromage, melon*) ripe; (*maquillé: yeux*) made-up; (*vernis: ongles*) painted, polished; **un homme ~** a grown man; **tout(e) ~(e)** (*préparé à l'avance*) ready-made; **c'en est ~ de notre tranquillité** that's the end of our peace; **c'est bien ~ (pour lui** *ou* **eux** *etc*) it serves him (*ou* them *etc*) right.

faîte [fεt] *nm* top; (*fig*) pinnacle, height.

faites [fεt] *vb voir* **faire.**

faîtière [fεtyεr] *nf* (*de tente*) ridge pole.

fait-tout *nm inv*, **faitout** *nm* [fεtoo] stewpan (*US*), stewpot (*Brit*).

fakir [fakεr] *nm* (*THÉÂTRE*) wizard.

falaise [falεz] *nf* cliff.

falbalas [falbálá] *nmpl* fripperies, frills.

fallacieux, euse [fálásyœ, -œz] *a* (*raisonnement*) fallacious; (*apparences*) deceptive; (*espoir*) illusory.

falloir [tálwár] *vb impersonnel*: **il faut faire les lits** we (*ou* you *etc*) have to *ou* must make the beds; **il faut que je fasse les lits** I have to *ou* must make the beds; **il a fallu qu'il parte** he had to leave; **il faudrait qu'elle rentre** she ought to go home; **il va ~ 100 F** we'll (*ou* I'll *etc*) need 100 F; **il doit ~ du temps** that must take time; **il vous faut tourner à gauche après l'église** you have to turn left past the church; **nous avons ce qu'il (nous) faut** we have what we need; **il faut qu'il ait oublié** he must have forgotten; **il a fallu qu'il l'apprenne** he would have to hear about it; **il ne fallait pas** (*pour remercier*) you shouldn't have (done it); **faut le faire!** (it) takes some doing! ♦ **s'en ~:** **il s'en est fallu de 100 F/5 minutes** we (*ou* they *etc*) were 100 F short/5 minutes late (*ou* early); **il s'en faut de beaucoup qu'il soit** ... he is far from being ...; **il s'en est fallu de peu que cela n'arrive** it very nearly happened; **ou peu s'en faut** or just about, or as good as; **comme il faut** *a* proper ♦ *ad* properly.

fallu [fálü] *pp de* **falloir.**

falot, e [fálõ, -ɔt] *a* dreary, colorless (*US*), colourless (*Brit*) ♦ *nm* lantern.

falsifier [fálsifyá] *vt* to falsify; to doctor.

famé, e [fámá] *a*: **mal ~** disreputable, of ill repute.

famélique [fámálék] *a* half-starved.

fameux, euse [fámœ, -œz] *a* (*illustre: parfois péj*) famous; (*bon: repas, plat etc*) first-rate, first-class; (*intensif*): **un ~ problème** *etc* a real problem *etc*; **pas ~** not great, not much good.

familial, e, aux [fámĕlyál, -ō] *a* family *cpd* ♦ *nf* (*AUTO*) station wagon (*US*), estate car (*Brit*).

familiariser [fámĕlyárĕzá] *vt*: **~ qn avec** to familiarize sb with; **se ~ avec** to familiarize

o.s. with.

familiarité [fámĕlyárĕtá] *nf* familiarity; informality; **~s** *nfpl* familiarities; **~ avec** (*sujet, science*) familiarity with.

familier, ière [fámĕlyá, -yεr] *a* (*connu, impertinent*) familiar; (*dénotant une certaine intimité*) informal, friendly; (*LING*) informal, colloquial ♦ *nm* regular (visitor).

famille [fámĕy] *nf* family; **il a de la ~ à Paris** he has relatives in Paris.

famine [fámĕn] *nf* famine.

fan [fán] *nm/f* fan.

fana [fáná] *a, nm/f* (*fam*) = **fanatique.**

fanal, aux [fánál, -ō] *nm* beacon; lantern.

fanatique [fánátĕk] *a*: **~ (de)** fanatical (about) ♦ *nm/f* fanatic.

fanatisme [fánátĕsm(ə)] *nm* fanaticism.

fane [fán] *nf* top.

fané, e [fáná] *a* faded.

faner [fáná]: **se ~** *vi* to fade.

faneur, euse [fánœr, -œz] *nm/f* haymaker ♦ *nf* (*TECH*) tedder.

fanfare [fáɴfár] *nf* (*orchestre*) brass band; (*musique*) fanfare; **en ~** (*avec bruit*) noisily.

fanfaron, ne [fáɴfárõɴ, -on] *nm/f* braggart.

fanfaronnades [fáɴfáronád] *nfpl* bragging *q.*

fanfreluches [fáɴfrəlüsh] *nfpl* trimming *q.*

fange [fáɴzh] *nf* mire.

fanion [fányõɴ] *nm* pennant.

fanon [fánõɴ] *nm* (*de baleine*) plate of baleen; (*repli de peau*) dewlap, wattle.

fantaisie [fáɴtázĕ] *nf* (*spontanéité*) fancy, imagination; (*caprice*) whim; extravagance; (*MUS*) fantasia ♦ *a*: **bijou (de) ~** (piece of) costume jewelry (*US*) *ou* jewellery (*Brit*); **pain (de) ~** fancy bread.

fantaisiste [fáɴtázĕst(ə)] *a* (*péj*) unorthodox, eccentric ♦ *nm/f* (*de music-hall*) variety artist *ou* entertainer.

fantasme [fáɴtásm(ə)] *nm* fantasy.

fantasmer [fáɴtásmá] *vi* to fantasize.

fantasque [fáɴtásk(ə)] *a* whimsical, capricious; fantastic.

fantassin [fáɴtásáɴ] *nm* infantryman.

fantastique [fáɴtástĕk] *a* fantastic.

fantoche [fáɴtosh] *nm* (*péj*) puppet.

fantomatique [fáɴtomátĕk] *a* ghostly.

fantôme [fáɴtõm] *nm* ghost, phantom.

FAO *sigle f* (= *Food and Agricultural Organization*) FAO.

faon [fáɴ] *nm* fawn (*deer*).

faramineux, euse [fárámĕnœ, -œz] *a* (*fam*) fantastic.

farce [fárs(ə)] *nf* (*viande*) stuffing; (*blague*) (practical) joke; (*THÉÂTRE*) farce; **faire une ~ à qn** to play a (practical) joke on sb; **~s et attrapes** jokes and novelties.

farceur, euse [fársœr, -œz] *nm/f* practical joker; (*fumiste*) clown.

farci, e [fársĕ] *a* (*CULIN*) stuffed.

farcir [fársĕr] *vt* (*viande*) to stuff; (*fig*): **~ qch de** to stuff sth with; **se ~** (*fam*): **je me suis farci la vaisselle** I've been stuck with (doing) the dishes.

fard [fár] *nm* make-up; **~ à joues** blusher.

fardeau, x [fárdō] *nm* burden.

farder [fárdá] *vt* to make up; (*vérité*) to disguise; **se ~** to make o.s. up.

farfelu, e [fárfəlü] *a* wacky (*fam*), hare-

brained.
farfouiller [fárfōōyā] *vi* (*péj*) to rummage around.
fariboles [fárēbol] *nfpl* nonsense *q*.
farine [fárēn] *nf* flour; ~ **de blé** wheat flour; ~ **de maïs** cornstarch (*US*), cornflour (*Brit*); ~ **lactée** (*pour bouillie*) gruel.
fariner [fárēnā] *vt* to flour.
farineux, euse [fárēnœ̄, -œ̄z] *a* (*sauce, pomme*) floury ♦ *nmpl* (*aliments*) starchy foods.
farniente [fárnyentā] *nm* idleness.
farouche [fárōōsh] *a* shy, timid; (*sauvage*) savage, wild; (*violent*) fierce.
farouchement [fárōōshmáń] *ad* fiercely.
fart [fár(t)] *nm* (ski) wax.
farter [fártā] *vt* to wax.
fascicule [fásēkül] *nm* volume.
fascinant, e [fásēnáń, -áńt] *a* fascinating.
fascination [fásēnâsyôń] *nf* fascination.
fasciner [fásēnā] *vt* to fascinate.
fascisant, e [fáshēzáń, -áńt] *a* fascistic.
fascisme [fáshēsm(ə)] *nm* fascism.
fasciste [fáshēst(ə)] *a, nm/f* fascist.
fasse [fás] *etc vb voir* **faire.**
faste [fást(ə)] *nm* splendor (*US*), splendour (*Brit*) ♦ *a*: **c'est un jour** ~ it's his (*ou* our *etc*) lucky day.
fastidieux, euse [fástēdyœ̄, -œ̄z] *a* tedious, tiresome.
fastueux, euse [fástüœ̄, -œ̄z] *a* sumptuous, luxurious.
fat [fá] *am* conceited, smug.
fatal, e [fátál] *a* fatal; (*inévitable*) inevitable.
fatalement [fátálmáń] *ad* inevitably.
fatalisme [fátálēsm(ə)] *nm* fatalism.
fataliste [fátálēst(ə)] *a* fatalistic.
fatalité [fátálētā] *nf* (*destin*) fate; (*coïncidence*) fateful coincidence; (*caractère inévitable*) inevitability.
fatidique [fátēdēk] *a* fateful.
fatigant, e [fátēgáń, -áńt] *a* tiring; (*agaçant*) tiresome.
fatigue [fátēg] *nf* tiredness, fatigue; (*détérioration*) fatigue; **les** ~**s du voyage** the wear and tear of the journey.
fatigué, e [fátēgā] *a* tired.
fatiguer [fátēgā] *vt* to tire, make tired; (*TECH*) to put a strain on, strain; (*fig: importuner*) to wear out ♦ *vi* (*moteur*) to labor (*US*), labour (*Brit*), strain; **se** ~ *vi* to get tired; to tire o.s. (out); **se** ~ **à faire qch** to tire o.s. out doing sth.
fatras [fátrá] *nm* jumble, hodgepodge.
fatuité [fátüētā] *nf* conceitedness, smugness.
faubourg [fōbōōr] *nm* suburb.
faubourien, ne [fōbōōryań, -en] *a* (*accent*) working-class.
fauché, e [fōshā] *a* (*fam*) broke.
faucher [fōshā] *vt* (*herbe*) to cut; (*champs, blés*) to reap; (*fig*) to cut down; to mow down; (*fam: voler*) to swipe.
faucheur, euse [fōshœr, -œ̄z] *nm/f* reaper, mower.
faucille [fōsēy] *nf* sickle.
faucon [fōkóń] *nm* falcon, hawk.
faudra [fōdrá] *etc vb voir* **falloir.**
faufil [fōfēl] *nm* (*COUTURE*) basting thread.
faufilage [fōfēlázh] *nm* (*COUTURE*) basting.

faufiler [fōfēlā] *vt* to tack, baste; **se** ~ *vi*: **se** ~ **dans** to edge one's way into; **se** ~ **parmi/entre** to thread one's way among/between.
faune [fōn] *nf* (*ZOOL*) wildlife, fauna; (*fig péj*) set, crowd ♦ *nm* faun; ~ **marine** marine (animal) life.
faussaire [fōser] *nm/f* forger.
fausse [fōs] *af voir* **faux.**
faussement [fōsmáń] *ad* (*accuser*) wrongly, wrongfully; (*croire*) falsely, erroneously.
fausser [fōsā] *vt* (*objet*) to bend, buckle; (*fig*) to distort; ~ **compagnie à qn** to give sb the slip.
fausset [fōse] *nm*: **voix de** ~ falsetto voice.
fausseté [fōstā] *nf* wrongness; falseness.
faut [fō] *vb voir* **falloir.**
faute [fōt] *nf* (*erreur*) mistake, error; (*péché, manquement*) misdemeanor (*US*), misdemeanour (*Brit*); (*FOOTBALL etc*) foul, infraction (*US*); (*TENNIS*) fault; (*responsabilité*): **par la** ~ **de** through the fault of, because of; **c'est de sa/ma** ~ it's his/my fault; **être en** ~ to be in the wrong; **prendre qn en** ~ to catch *ou* trap sb; ~ **de** (*temps, argent*) for *ou* through lack of; ~ **de mieux** for want of anything *ou* something better; **sans** ~ *ad* without fail; ~ **de frappe** typing error; ~ **d'inattention** careless mistake; ~ **d'orthographe** spelling mistake; ~ **professionnelle** professional misconduct *q*.
fauteuil [fōtœy] *nm* armchair; ~ **à bascule** rocking chair; ~ **club** (big) easy chair; ~ **d'orchestre** seat in the orchestra (*US*) *ou* the front stalls (*Brit*); ~ **roulant** wheelchair.
fauteur [fōtœr] *nm*: ~ **de troubles** troublemaker.
fautif, ive [fōtēf, -ēv] *a* (*incorrect*) incorrect, inaccurate; (*responsable*) at fault, in the wrong; (*coupable*) guilty ♦ *nm/f* culprit.
fauve [fōv] *nm* wildcat; (*peintre*) Fauve ♦ *a* (*couleur*) fawn.
fauvette [fōvet] *nf* warbler.
faux [fō] *nf* scythe.
faux, fausse [fō, fōs] *a* (*inexact*) wrong; (*piano, voix*) out of tune; (*falsifié*) fake, forged; (*sournois, postiche*) false ♦ *ad* (*MUS*) out of tune ♦ *nm* (*copie*) fake, forgery; (*opposé au vrai*): **le** ~ falsehood; **le** ~ **numéro/la fausse clé** the wrong number/key; **faire fausse route** to go the wrong way; **faire** ~ **bond à qn** to let sb down; ~ **ami** (*LING*) deceptive cognate; ~ **col** detachable collar; ~ **départ** (*SPORT, fig*) false start; ~ **frais** *nmpl* extras, incidental expenses; ~ **frère** (*fig péj*) false friend; ~ **mouvement** awkward movement; ~ **nez** false nose; ~ **nom** assumed name; ~ **pas** tripping *q*; (*fig*) faux pas; ~ **témoignage** (*délit*) perjury; **fausse alerte** false alarm; **fausse clé** skeleton key; **fausse couche** (*MÉD*) miscarriage; **fausse joie** vain joy; **fausse note** wrong note.
faux-filet [fōfēle] *nm* sirloin.
faux-fuyant [fōfüēyáń] *nm* equivocation.
faux-monnayeur [fōmoneyœr] *nm* counterfeiter, forger.
faux-semblant [fōsáńbláń] *nm* pretense (*US*), pretence (*Brit*).
faux-sens [fōsáńs] *nm* mistranslation.
faveur [fávœr] *nf* favor (*US*), favour (*Brit*);

traitement de ~ preferential treatment; **à la** ~ **de** under cover of; (*grâce à*) thanks to; **en** ~ **de** in favor of.

favorable [fávoràbl(ə)] *a* favorable (*US*), favourable (*Brit*).

favori, te [fávorē, -ēt] *a, nm/f* favorite (*US*), favourite (*Brit*).

favoris [fávorē] *nmpl* (*barbe*) sideburns.

favoriser [fávorēzā] *vt* to favor (*US*), favour (*Brit*).

favoritisme [fávorētēsm(ə)] *nm* (*péj*) favoritism (*US*), favouritism (*Brit*).

fayot [fáyō] *nm* (*fam*) bootlicker.

FB *abr* (= *franc belge*) BF, FB.

FBI *sigle m* FBI.

FC *sigle m* = *Football Club*.

fébrile [tābrēl] *a* feverish, febrile; **capitaux** ~**s** (*ÉCON*) hot money.

fébrilement [fābrēlmáǹ] *ad* feverishly.

fécal, e, aux [fākál, -ō] *a voir* **matière**.

fécond, e [fākóǹ, -óǹd] *a* fertile.

fécondation [fākóǹdâsyóǹ] *nf* fertilization.

féconder [fākóǹdā] *vt* to fertilize.

fécondité [fākóndeta] *nf* fertility.

fécule [fākül] *nf* potato flour.

féculent [fākülâǹ] *nm* starchy food.

fédéral, e, aux [fādārál, -ō] *a* federal.

fédéralisme [fādārálēsm(ə)] *nm* federalism.

fédération [fādārásyóǹ] *nf* federation.

fée [fā] *nf* fairy.

féerie [fārē] *nf* enchantment.

féerique [fārēk] *a* magical, fairytale *cpd*.

feignant, e [fenyáǹ, -áǹt] *nm/f* = **fainéant, e**.

feindre [faǹdr(ə)] *vt* to feign ♦ *vi* to dissemble; ~ **de faire** to pretend to do.

feint, e [faǹ, faǹt] *pp de* **feindre** ♦ *a* feigned ♦ *nf* (*SPORT*) dummy.

fêler [fālā] *vt* to crack.

félicitations [fālēsētâsyóǹ] *nfpl* congratulations.

félicité [fālēsētā] *nf* bliss.

féliciter [fālēsētā] *vt*: ~ **qn (de)** to congratulate sb (on).

félin, e [fālaǹ, -ēn] *a* feline ♦ *nm* (big) cat.

félon, ne [fālóǹ, on] *a* perfidious, treacherous.

félonie [fālonē] *nf* treachery.

fêlure [fālür] *nf* crack.

femelle [fəmel] *a* (*aussi* ÉLEC, TECH) female ♦ *nf* female.

féminin, e [fāmēnaǹ, -ēn] *a* feminine; (*sexe*) female; (*équipe, vêtements etc*) women's; (*parfois péj: homme*) effeminate ♦ *nm* (LING) feminine.

féminiser [fāmēnēzā] *vt* to feminize; (*rendre efféminé*) to make effeminate; **se** ~ *vi*: **cette profession se féminise** this profession is attracting more women.

féminisme [fāmēnēsm(ə)] *nm* feminism.

féministe [fāmēnēst(ə)] *a, nf* feminist.

féminité [fāmēnētā] *nf* femininity.

femme [fám] *nf* woman; (*épouse*) wife (*pl* wives); **être très** ~ to be very much a woman; **devenir** ~ to attain womanhood; ~ **d'affaires** businesswoman; ~ **de chambre** chambermaid; ~ **fatale** femme fatale; ~ **au foyer** housewife; ~ **d'intérieur** (real) homemaker; ~ **de ménage** domestic help, cleaning lady; ~ **du monde** society woman; ~ **de tête** determined, intellectual woman.

fémur [fāmür] *nm* femur, thighbone.

FEN [fen] *sigle f* (= *Fédération de l'éducation nationale*) *teachers' union*.

fenaison [fənezóǹ] *nf* haymaking.

fendillé, e [fáǹdēyā] *a* (*terre etc*) crazed.

fendre [fáǹdr(ə)] *vt* (*couper en deux*) to split; (*fissurer*) to crack; (*fig: traverser*) to cut through; **to push one's way through; se** ~ *vi* to crack.

fendu, e [fáǹdü] *a* (*sol, mur*) cracked; (*jupe*) slit.

fenêtre [fənetr(ə)] *nf* window; ~ **à guillotine** sash window.

fenouil [fənōōy] *nm* fennel.

fente [fáǹt] *nf* slit; (*fissure*) crack.

féodal, e, aux [fāodál, -ō] *a* feudal.

féodalisme [fāodalēsm(ə)] *nm* feudalism.

fer [fer] *nm* iron; (*de cheval*) shoe; ~**s** *pl* (MÉD) forceps; **mettre aux** ~**s** (*enchaîner*) to put in chains; **au** ~ **rouge** with a red-hot iron; **santé/main de** ~ iron constitution/ hand; ~ **à cheval** horseshoe; **en** ~ **à cheval** (*fig*) horseshoe-shaped; ~ **forgé** wrought iron; ~ **à friser** curling iron (*US*) ou tongs *pl* (*Brit*); ~ **de lance** spearhead; ~ **(à repasser)** iron; ~ **à souder** soldering iron.

ferai [fərā] *etc vb voir* **faire**.

fer-blanc [ferbláǹ] *nm* tin(plate).

ferblanterie [ferblâǹtrē] *nf* tinplate making; (*produit*) tinware.

ferblantier [ferblâǹtyā] *nm* tinsmith.

férié, c [fūryā] *a*: **jour** ~ public holiday.

férir [fārēr]: **sans coup** ~ *ad* without meeting any opposition.

fermage [fermázh] *nm* tenant farming.

ferme [ferm(ə)] *a* firm ♦ *ad* (*travailler etc*) hard; (*discuter*) ardently ♦ *nf* (*exploitation*) farm; (*maison*) farmhouse; **tenir** ~ to stand firm.

fermé, e [fermā] *a* closed, shut; (*gaz, eau etc*) off; (*fig: personne*) uncommunicative; (: *milieu*) exclusive.

fermement [fermǝmáǹ] *ad* firmly.

ferment [fermáǹ] *nm* ferment.

fermentation [fermâǹtásyóǹ] *nf* fermentation.

fermenter [fermáǹtā] *vi* to ferment.

fermer [fermā] *vt* to close, shut; (*cesser l'exploitation de*) to close down, shut down; (*eau, lumière, électricité, robinet*) to turn off; (*aéroport, route*) to close ♦ *vi* to close, shut; to close down, shut down; **se** ~ *vi* (*yeux*) to close, shut; (*fleur, blessure*) to close up; ~ **à clef** to lock; ~ **au verrou** to bolt; ~ **les yeux (sur qch)** (*fig*) to close one's eyes (to sth); **se** ~ **à** (*pitié, amour*) to close one's heart ou mind to.

fermeté [fermǝtā] *nf* firmness.

fermette [fermet] *nf* farmhouse.

fermeture [fermǝtür] *nf* (*voir fermer*) closing; shutting; closing ou shutting down; turning off; (*dispositif*) catch; fastening, fastener; **heure de** ~ (COMM) closing time; **jour de** ~ (COMM) day on which the shop (*etc*) is closed; ~ **éclair** ® ou **à glissière** zipper.

fermier, ière [fermyā, -yer] *nm/f* farmer ♦ *nf* (*femme de fermier*) farmer's wife ♦ *a*: **beurre/cidre** ~ farm butter/cider.

fermoir [fermwár] *nm* clasp.

féroce [fāros] *a* ferocious, fierce.

férocement [fărosmáɴ] *ad* ferociously.
férocité [fărosētā] *nf* ferocity, ferociousness.
ferons [fərôɴ] *etc vb voir* **faire**.
ferraille [ferây] *nf* scrap iron; **mettre à la ~** to scrap; **bruit de ~** clanking.
ferrailler [ferâyā] *vi* to clank.
ferrailleur [ferâyœr] *nm* scrap iron dealer.
ferrant [feráɴ] *am voir* **maréchal-ferrant**.
ferré, e [ferā] *a* (*chaussure*) hobnailed; (*canne*) steel-tipped; **~ sur** (*fam: savant*) well up on.
ferrer [ferā] *vt* (*cheval*) to shoe; (*chaussure*) to nail; (*canne*) to tip; (*poisson*) to strike.
ferreux, euse [ferœ̄, -œ̄z] *a* ferrous.
ferronnerie [feronrē] *nf* ironwork; **~ d'art** wrought iron work.
ferronnier [feronyā] *nm* craftsman in wrought iron; (*marchand*) ironware merchant.
ferroviaire [ferovyer] *a* rail *cpd*, railroad *cpd* (*US*), railway *cpd* (*Brit*).
ferrure [ferür] *nf* (*ornamental*) hinge.
ferry(-boat) [ferā(bōt)] *nm* ferry.
fertile [fertēl] *a* fertile; **~ en incidents** eventful, packed with incidents.
fertilisant [fertēlēzāɴ] *nm* fertilizer.
fertiliser [fertēlēzā] *vt* to fertilize.
fertilité [fertēlētā] *nf* fertility.
féru, e [fărü] *a*: **~ de** with a keen interest in.
férule [fărül] *nf*: **être sous la ~ de qn** to be under sb's (iron) rule.
fervent, e [fervâɴ, -âɴt] *a* fervent.
ferveur [fervœr] *nf* fervor (*US*), fervour (*Brit*).
fesse [fes] *nf* buttock; **les ~s** the bottom *sg*, the buttocks.
fessée [fāsā] *nf* spanking.
fessier [fāsyā] *nm* (*fam*) behind.
festin [festáɴ] *nm* feast.
festival [festēvál] *nm* festival.
festivalier [festēvályā] *nm* festival-goer.
festivités [festēvētā] *nfpl* festivities, merrymaking *sg*.
feston [festôɴ] *nm* (*ARCHIT*) festoon; (*COUTURE*) scallop.
festoyer [festwáyā] *vi* to feast.
fêtard [fetár] *nm* (*péj*) high liver, merrymaker.
fête [fet] *nf* (*religieuse*) feast; (*publique*) holiday; (*en famille etc*) celebration; (*kermesse*) fête, fair, festival; (*du nom*) feast day, name day; **faire la ~** to live it up; **faire ~ à qn** to give sb a warm welcome; **se faire une ~ de** to look forward to; to enjoy; **ça va être sa ~!** (*fam*) he's going to get it!; **jour de ~** holiday; **les ~s (de fin d'année)** the holiday (*US*) *ou* festive (*Brit*) season; **la salle/le comité des ~s** the (village) hall/festival committee; **la ~ des Mères/Pères** Mother's/Father's Day; **~ de charité** charity bazaar; **~ foraine** carnival (*US*), (fun)fair (*Brit*); **~ mobile** movable holiday; **la F~ Nationale** the national holiday.
Fête-Dieu [fetdyœ̄] *nf*: **la ~** Corpus Christi.
fêter [fātā] *vt* to celebrate; (*personne*) to have a celebration for.
fétiche [fātēsh] *nm* fetish; **animal ~**, **objet ~** mascot.
fétichisme [fātēshēsm(ə)] *nm* fetishism.
fétide [fātēd] *a* fetid.
fétu [fātü] *nm*: **~ de paille** wisp of straw.

feu [fœ̄] *a inv*: **~ son père** his late father.
feu, x [fœ̄] *nm* (*gén*) fire; (*signal lumineux*) light; (*de cuisinière*) burner (*US*), ring (*Brit*); (*sensation de brûlure*) burning (sensation); **~x** *nmpl* fire *sg*; (*AUTO*) (traffic) lights; **tous ~x éteints** (*NAVIG, AUTO*) without lights; **au ~!** (*incendie*) fire!; **à ~ doux/vif** over a slow/brisk heat; **à petit ~** (*CULIN*) over a gentle heat; (*fig*) slowly; **faire ~** to fire; **ne pas faire long ~** (*fig*) not to last long; **commander le ~** (*MIL*) to give the order to (open) fire; **tué au ~** (*MIL*) killed in action; **mettre à ~** (*fusée*) to fire; **pris entre deux ~x** caught in the crossfire; **en ~** on fire; **être tout ~ tout flammes (pour)** (*passion*) to be aflame with passion (for); (*enthousiasme*) to be fired with enthusiasm (for); **prendre ~** to catch fire; **mettre le ~ à** to set fire to, set on fire; **faire du ~** to make a fire; **avez-vous du ~?** (*pour cigarette*) have you (got) a light?; **~ rouge/vert/orange** (*AUTO*) red/green/yellow (*US*) *ou* amber (*Brit*) light; **donner le ~ vert à qch/qn** (*fig*) to give sth/sb the go-ahead *ou* green light; **~ arrière** (*AUTO*) taillight; **~ d'artifice** firework; (*spectacle*) fireworks *pl*; **~ de camp** campfire; **~ de cheminée** chimney fire; **~ de joie** bonfire; **~ de paille** (*fig*) flash in the pan; **~x de brouillard** (*AUTO*) fog lights *ou* lamps; **~x de croisement** (*AUTO*) dimmed (*US*) *ou* dipped (*Brit*) headlights; **~x de position** (*AUTO*) parking lights (*US*), sidelights (*Brit*); **~x de route** (*AUTO*) headlights (on high (*US*) *ou* full (*Brit*) beam); **~x de stationnement** parking lights.
feuillage [fœy̆ázh] *nm* foliage, leaves *pl*.
feuille [fœy̆] *nf* (*d'arbre*) leaf (*pl* leaves); **~ (de papier)** sheet (of paper); **rendre ~ blanche** (*SCOL*) to hand *ou* turn in a blank paper; **~ d'or/de métal** gold/metal leaf; **~ de chou** (*péj: journal*) rag; **~ d'impôts** tax form; **~ de maladie** medical expenses claim form; **~ morte** dead leaf; **~ de paye** check stub (*US*), pay slip (*Brit*); **~ de présence** attendance sheet; **~ de température** temperature chart; **~ de vigne** (*BOT*) vine leaf; (*sur statue*) fig leaf; **~ volante** loose sheet.
feuillet [fœy̆e] *nm* leaf (*pl* leaves), page.
feuilletage [fœy̆ázh] *nm* (*aspect feuilleté*) flakiness.
feuilleté, e [fœy̆tā] *a* (*CULIN*) flaky; (*verre*) laminated.
feuilleter [fœy̆tā] *vt* (*livre*) to leaf through.
feuilleton [fœy̆tôɴ] *nm* serial.
feuillette [fœy̆et] *etc vb voir* **feuilleter**.
feuillu, e [fœy̆ü] *a* leafy ♦ *nm* broad-leaved tree.
feulement [fœ̄lmáɴ] *nm* growl.
feutre [fœ̄tr(ə)] *nm* felt; (*chapeau*) felt hat; (*stylo*) felt-tip(ped pen).
feutré, e [fœ̄trā] *a* feltlike; (*pas, voix*) muffled.
feutrer [fœ̄trā] *vt* to felt; (*fig: bruits*) to muffle ♦ *vi*, **se ~** *vi* (*tissu*) to felt.
feutrine [fœ̄trēn] *nf* (lightweight) felt.
fève [fev] *nf* broad bean; (*dans la galette des Rois*) charm (*hidden in cake eaten on Twelfth Night*).
février [făvrēyā] *nm* February; *voir aussi*

juillet.

fez [fĕz] *nm* fez.

FF *abr* (= *franc français*) FF.

FFA *sigle fpl* (= *Forces françaises en Allemagne*) French forces in Germany.

FFI *sigle fpl* = *Forces françaises de l'intérieur* (1942-45) ♦ *sigle m* member of the FFI.

FFL *sigle fpl* (= *Forces françaises libres*) Free French Army.

Fg *abr* = **faubourg**.

FGA *sigle m* (= *Fonds de garantie automobile*) *fund financed through insurance premiums, to compensate victims of uninsured losses.*

FGEN *sigle f* (= *Fédération générale de l'éducation nationale*) *teachers' union.*

fi [fi] *excl:* **faire ~ de** to snap one's fingers at.

fiabilité [fyåbēlētā] *nf* reliability.

fiable [fyåbl(ə)] *a* reliable.

fiacre [fyàkr(ə)] *nm* (hackney) cab *ou* carriage.

fiançailles [fyáñsáy] *nfpl* engagement *sg*.

fiancé, e [fyáñsā] *nm/f* fiancé/fiancée ♦ *a*: **être ~ (à)** to be engaged (to).

fiancer [fyáñsā]. **se ~** *vi.* **se ~ (avec)** to become engaged (to).

fiasco [fyàskō] *nm* fiasco.

fibranne [fēbrán] *nf* bonded fibre (*US*) *ou* fibre.

fibre [fēbr(ə)] *nf* fiber (*US*), fibre; **avoir la ~ paternelle/militaire** to be a born father/soldier; **~ optique** optical fiber *ou* fibre; **~ de verre** fiberglass (*US*), fibreglass (*Brit*), glass fiber *ou* fibre.

fibreux, euse [fēbrœ̄, -œz] *a* fibrous; (*viande*) stringy.

fibrome [fēbrōm] *nm* (*MÉD*) fibroma.

ficelage [fēslázh] *nm* tying (up).

ficeler [fēslā] *vt* to tie up.

ficelle [fēsel] *nf* string *q*; (*morceau*) piece *ou* length of string; (*pain*) stick of French bread; **~s** *pl* (*fig*) strings; **tirer sur la ~** (*fig*) to go too far.

fiche [fēsh] *nf* (*carte*) (index) card; (*INFORM*) record; (*formulaire*) form; (*ÉLEC*) plug; **~ de paye** check stub (*US*), pay slip (*Brit*); **~ signalétique** (*POLICE*) description sheet; **~ technique** data sheet, specification *ou* spec sheet.

ficher [fēshā] *vt* (*dans un fichier*) to file; (*: POLICE*) to put on file; (*planter*): **~ qch dans** to stick *ou* drive sth into; (*fam*) to do; (*: donner*) to give; (*: mettre*) to stick *ou* shove; **~ qn à la porte** (*fam*) to kick *ou* throw sb out; **fiche(-moi) le camp** (*fam*) clear out, beat it; **fiche-moi la paix** (*fam*) leave me alone; **se ~ dans** (*s'enfoncer*) to get stuck in, embed itself in; **se ~ de** (*fam*) to make fun of; not to care about.

fichier [fēshyā] *nm* (*gén*, *INFORM*) file; (*à cartes*) card index; **~ actif** *ou* **en cours d'utilisation** (*INFORM*) active file; **~ d'adresses** mailing list; **~ d'archives** (*INFORM*) archive file.

fichu, e [fēshü] *pp de* **ficher** (*fam*) ♦ *a* (*fam: fini, inutilisable*) done for; (*: intensif*) wretched, darned ♦ *nm* (*foulard*) (head)scarf (*pl* -scarves); **être ~ de** to be capable of; **mal ~** feeling lousy; useless; **bien ~** great.

fictif, ive [fēktēf, -ēv] *a* fictitious.

fiction [fēksyôn] *nf* fiction; (*fait imaginé*) invention.

fictivement [fēktēvmán] *ad* fictitiously.

fidèle [fēdel] *a:* **~ (à)** faithful (to) ♦ *nm/f* (*REL*): **les ~s** the faithful; (*à l'église*) the congregation.

fidèlement [fēdelmán] *ad* faithfully.

fidélité [fēdālētā] *nf* faithfulness.

Fidji [fēdzhē] *nfpl:* (**les îles**) **~** Fiji.

fief [fyef] *nm* fief; (*fig*) preserve; stronghold.

fieffé, e [fyāfā] *a* (*ivrogne, menteur*) arrant, out-and-out.

fiel [fyel] *nm* gall.

fiente [fyáñt] *nf* (bird) droppings *pl*.

fier [fyā]: **se ~ à** *vt* to trust.

fier, fière [fyer] *a* proud; **~ de** proud of; **avoir fière allure** to cut a fine figure.

fièrement [fyermán] *ad* proudly.

fierté [fyertā] *nf* pride.

fièvre [fyevr(ə)] *nf* fever; **avoir de la ~/39 de ~** to have a high temperature/a temperature of 39°C; **~ typhoïde** typhoid fever.

fiévreusement [fyāvrœ̄zmán] *ad* (*fig*) feverishly.

fiévreux, euse [fyāvrœ̄, -œz] *a* feverish.

FIFA [fēfá] *sigle f* (= *Fédération internationale de Football Association*) FIFA.

fifre [fēfr(ə)] *nm* fife; (*personne*) fife-player.

figer [fēzhā] *vt* to congeal; (*fig: personne*) to freeze, root to the spot; **se ~** *vi* to congeal; to freeze; (*institutions etc*) to become set, stop evolving.

fignoler [fēnyolā] *vt* to put the finishing touches to.

figue [fēg] *nf* fig.

figuier [fēgyā] *nm* fig tree.

figurant, e [fēgürán, -áñt] *nm/f* (*THÉÂTRE*) walk-on actor; (*CINÉMA*) extra.

figuratif, ive [fēgürátēf, -ēv] *a* representational, figurative.

figuration [fēgürásyôn] *nf* walk-on parts *pl*; extras *pl*.

figure [fēgür] *nf* (*visage*) face; (*image, tracé, forme, personnage*) figure; (*illustration*) picture, diagram; **faire ~ de** to look like; **faire bonne ~** to put up a good show; **faire triste ~** to be a sorry sight; **~ de rhétorique** figure of speech.

figuré, e [fēgürā] *a* (*sens*) figurative.

figurer [fēgürā] *vi* to appear ♦ *vt* to represent; **se ~ que** to imagine that; **figurez-vous que** ... would you believe that ...?

figurine [fēgürēn] *nf* figurine.

fil [fēl] *nm* (*brin, fig: d'une histoire*) thread; (*du téléphone*) cable, wire; (*textile de lin*) linen; (*d'un couteau: tranchant*) edge; **au ~ des années** with the passing of the years; **au ~ de l'eau** with the stream *ou* current; **de ~ en aiguille** one thing leading to another; **ne tenir qu'à un ~** (*vie, réussite etc*) to hang by a thread; **donner du ~ à retordre à qn** to make life difficult for sb; **donner/recevoir un coup de ~** to make/get a phone call; **~ à coudre** (sewing) thread *ou* yarn; **~ électrique** electric wire; **~ de fer** wire; **~ de fer barbelé** barbed wire; **~ à pêche** fishing line; **~ à plomb** plumbline; **~ à souder** soldering wire.

filament [fēlámán] *nm* (*ÉLEC*) filament; (*de*

liquide) trickle, thread.

filandreux, euse |filândrœ̄, -œ̄z| *a* stringy.

filant, e |filān, -ānt| *a*: **étoile** ~**e** shooting star.

filasse |filàs| *a inv* white blond.

filature |filátür| *nf* (*fabrique*) mill; (*policière*) shadowing *q*, tailing *q*; **prendre qn en** ~ to shadow *ou* tail sb.

fildefériste |fēldəfārēst(ə)| *nm/f* high-wire artist.

file |fēl| *nf* line; ~ (**d'attente**) line (*US*), queue (*Brit*); **prendre la** ~ to join the (end of the) line; **prendre la** ~ **de droite** (*AUTO*) to move into the right-hand lane; **se mettre en** ~ to form a line; (*AUTO*) to get into the correct lane; **stationner en double** ~ (*AUTO*) to double-park; **à la** ~ *ad* (*d'affilée*) in succession; (*à la suite*) one after another; **à la** *ou* **en** ~ **indienne** in single file.

filer |fēlā| *vt* (*tissu, toile, verre*) to spin; (*dérouler: câble etc*) to pay *ou* let out; (*prendre en filature*) to shadow, tail; (*fam: donner*): ~ **qch à qn** to slip sb sth ♦ *vi* (*bas, maille, liquide, pâte*) to run; (*aller vite*) to fly past *ou* by; (*fam: partir*) to make off; ~ **à l'anglaise** to take French leave; ~ **doux** to behave o.s., toe the line; ~ **un mauvais coton** to be in a bad way.

filet |fēlc| *nm* net; (*CULIN*) fillet; (*d'eau, de sang*) trickle; **tendre un** ~ (*suj: police*) to set a trap; ~ (**à bagages**) (*RAIL*) luggage rack; ~ (**à provisions**) string bag.

filetage |fēltázh| *nm* threading; thread.

fileter |fēltā| *vt* to thread.

filial, e, aux |fēlyàl, -ō| *a* filial ♦ *nf* (*COMM*) subsidiary; affiliate.

filiation |fēlyàsyόṅ| *nf* filiation.

filière |fēlyer| *nf*: **passer par la** ~ to go through the (administrative) channels; **suivre la** ~ to work one's way up (through the hierarchy).

filiforme |fēlēform(ə)| *a* spindly; threadlike.

filigrane |fēlēgrán| *nm* (*d'un billet, timbre*) watermark; **en** ~ (*fig*) showing just beneath the surface.

filin |fēlaṅ| *nm* (*NAVIG*) rope.

fille |fēy| *nf* girl; (*opposé à fils*) daughter; **vieille** ~ old maid; ~ **de joie** prostitute; ~ **de salle** waitress.

fille-mère, *pl* **filles-mères** |fēymcr| *nf* unmarried mother.

fillette |fēyet| *nf* (little) girl.

filleul, e |fēyœl| *nm/f* godchild, godson/ daughter.

film |fēlm| *nm* (*pour photo*) (roll of) film; (*œuvre*) film, picture, movie; (*couche*) film; ~ **muet/parlant** silent/talking picture *ou* movie; ~ **d'animation** animated film; ~ **policier** thriller.

filmer |fēlmā| *vt* to film.

filon |fēlόṅ| *nm* vein, lode; (*fig*) lucrative line, moneymaker.

filou |fēlōō| *nm* (*escroc*) swindler.

fils |fēs| *nm* son; ~ **de famille** moneyed young man; ~ **à papa** (*péj*) daddy's boy.

filtrage |fēltrázh| *nm* filtering.

filtrant, e |fēltráṅ, -áṅt| *a* (*huile solaire etc*) filtering.

filtre |fēltr(ə)| *nm* filter; "~ **ou sans** ~?"

(*cigarettes*) "filter-tipped or plain?"; ~ **à air** air filter.

filtrer |fēltrā| *vt* to filter; (*fig: candidats, visiteurs*) to screen ♦ *vi* to filter (through).

fin |faṅ| *nf* end; ~**s** *nfpl* (*but*) ends; **à** (**la**) ~ **mai**, ~ **mai** at the end of May; **en** ~ **de semaine** at the end of the week; **prendre** ~ to come to an end; **toucher à sa** ~ to be drawing to a close; **mettre** ~ **à** to put an end to; **mener à bonne** ~ to bring to a successful conclusion; **à cette** ~ to this end; **à toutes** ~**s utiles** for your information; **à la** ~ in the end, eventually; **sans** ~ *a* endless ♦ *ad* endlessly; ~ **de non-recevoir** (*JUR, ADMIN*) objection; ~ **de section** (*de ligne d'autobus*) (fare) stage.

fin, e |faṅ, fēn| *a* (*papier, couche, fil*) thin; (*cheveux, poudre, pointe, visage*) fine; (*taille*) neat, slim; (*esprit, remarque*) subtle; shrewd ♦ *ad* (*moudre, couper*) finely ♦ *nm*: **vouloir jouer au plus** ~ (**avec qn**) to try to outsmart sb ♦ *nf* (*alcool*) liqueur brandy; **c'est** ~! (*ironique*) how clever!; ~ **prêt/soûl** quite ready/drunk; **un** ~ **gourmet** a gourmet; **un** ~ **tireur** a crack shot; **avoir la vue/l'ouïe** ~**e** to have sharp eyes/ears, have keen eyesight/hearing; **or/linge/vin** ~ fine gold/linen/wine; **le** ~ **fond de** the very depths of; **le** ~ **mot de** the real story behind; **la** ~**e fleur de** the flower of; **une** ~ **mouche** (*fig*) a sharp customer; ~**es herbes** mixed herbs.

final, e |fēnàl| *a, nf* final ♦ *nm* (*MUS*) finale; **quarts de** ~**e** quarter finals; **8èmes/16èmes de** ~**e** 2nd/1st round (*in 5 round knock-out competition*).

finalement |fēnàlmáṅ| *ad* finally, in the end; (*après tout*) after all.

finaliste |fēnàlēst(ə)| *nm/f* finalist.

finance |fēnáṅs| *nf* finance; ~**s** *nfpl* (*situation financière*) finances; (*activités financières*) finance *sg*; **moyennant** ~ for a fee *ou* consideration.

financement |fēnáṅsmáṅ| *nm* financing.

financer |fēnáṅsā| *vt* to finance.

financier, ière |fēnáṅsyā, -yer| *a* financial ♦ *nm* financier.

financièrement |fēnáṅsycrmáṅ| *ad* financially.

finasser |fēnàsā| *vi* (*péj*) to wheel and deal.

finaud, e |fēnō, -ōd| *a* wily.

fine |fēn| *af*, *nf voir* **fin, e**.

finement |fēnmáṅ| *ad* thinly; finely; neatly, slimly; subtly; shrewdly.

finesse |fēncs| *nf* thinness; fineness; neatness, slimness; subtlety; shrewdness; ~**s** *nfpl* (*subtilités*) niceties; finer points.

fini, e |fēnē| *a* finished; (*MATH*) finite; (*intensif*): **un menteur** ~ a liar through and through ♦ *nm* (*d'un objet manufacturé*) finish.

finir |fēnēr| *vt* to finish ♦ *vi* to finish, end; ~ **quelque part** to end *ou* finish up somewhere; ~ **de faire** to finish doing; (*cesser*) to stop doing; ~ **par faire** to end *ou* finish up doing; **il finit par m'agacer** he's beginning to get on my nerves; ~ **en pointe/tragédie** to end in a point/in tragedy; **en** ~ **avec** to be *ou* have done with; **à n'en plus** ~ (*route, discussions*) never-ending; **il va mal** ~ he will come to a bad end; **c'est bientôt fini?** (*reproche*) have

you quite finished?
finish [fĕnĕsh] *nm* (*SPORT*) finish.
finissage [fēnēsázh] *nm* finishing.
finisseur, euse [fēnēsœr, -ēz] *nm/f* (*SPORT*) strong finisher.
finition [fēnēsyôṅ] *nf* finishing; finish.
finlandais, e [fańlâṅde, -ez] *a* Finnish ♦ *nm/f*: F~, e Finn.
Finlande [fańlâṅd] *nf*: **la** ~ Finland.
finnois, e [fēnwá, -wáz] *a* Finnish ♦ *nm* (*LING*) Finnish.
fiole [fyol] *nf* phial.
fiord [fyor(d)] *nm* = **fjord**.
fioriture [fyorētür] *nf* embellishment, flourish.
fioul [fyōōl] *nm* fuel oil.
firent [fēr] *vb voir* **faire**.
firmament [fērmámâṅ] *nm* firmament, skies *pl*.
firme [fērm(ə)] *nf* firm.
fis [fē] *vb voir* **faire**.
fisc [fēsk] *nm* tax authorities *pl*, ≈ Internal Revenue Service (*US*), ≈ Inland Revenue (*Brit*).
fiscal, e, aux [fēskál, ō] *a* tax *cpd*, fiscal.
fiscaliser [fēskálēzá] *vt* to subject to tax.
fiscaliste [fēskálēst(ə)] *nm/f* tax specialist.
fiscalité [fēskálētá] *nf* tax system; (*charges*) taxation.
fission [fēsyôṅ] *nf* fission.
fissure [fēsür] *nf* crack.
fissurer [fēsürá] *vt*, **se** ~ *vi* to crack.
fiston [fēstôṅ] *nm* (*fam*) son, lad.
fit [fē] *vb voir* **faire**.
fixage [fēksázh] *nm* (*PHOTO*) fixing.
fixateur [fēksátœr] *nm* (*PHOTO*) fixer; (*pour cheveux*) hair cream.
fixatif [fēksátēf] *nm* fixative.
fixation [fēksásyôṅ] *nf* fixing; fastening; setting; (*de ski*) binding; (*PSYCH*) fixation.
fixe [fēks(ə)] *a* fixed; (*emploi*) steady, regular ♦ *nm* (*salaire*) basic salary; **à heure** ~ at a set time; **menu à prix** ~ table d'hôte.
fixé, e [fēksá] *a* (*heure, jour*) appointed; **être** ~ **(sur)** to have made up one's mind (about); to know for certain (about).
fixement [fēksəmâṅ] *ad* fixedly, steadily.
fixer [fēksá] *vt* (*attacher*): ~ **qch (à/sur)** to fix *ou* fasten sth (to/onto); (*déterminer*) to fix, set; (*CHIMIE, PHOTO*) to fix; (*poser son regard sur*) to look hard at, stare at; **se** ~ (*s'établir*) to settle down; ~ **son choix sur qch** to decide on sth; **se** ~ **sur** (*suj: attention*) to focus on.
fixité [fēksētá] *nf* fixedness.
fjord [fyor(d)] *nm* fjord, fiord.
fl. *abr* (= *fleuve*) r, R; (= *florin*) fl.
flacon [fláköṅ] *nm* bottle.
flagellation [flázhelásyôṅ] *nf* flogging.
flageller [fláyhālá] *vt* to flog, scourge.
flageoler [fláyholá] *vi* to have knees like jelly.
flageolet [fláyhole] *nm* (*MUS*) flageolet; (*CULIN*) dwarf kidney bean.
flagornerie [flágornərē] *nf* toadying, fawning.
flagorneur, euse [flágornœr, -ēz] *nm/f* toady, fawner.
flagrant, e [flágráṅ, -âṅt] *a* flagrant, blatant; **en** ~ **délit** in the act, in flagrante delicto.
flair [flɛr] *nm* sense of smell; (*fig*) intuition.
flairer [flɛrá] *vt* (*humer*) to sniff (at);

(*détecter*) to scent.
flamand, e [flámâṅ, -âṅd] *a* Flemish ♦ *nm* (*LING*) Flemish ♦ *nm/f*: F~, e Fleming; **les** F~s the Flemish.
flamant [flámâṅ] *nm* flamingo.
flambant [flâṅbâṅ] *ad*: ~ **neuf** brand new.
flambé, e [flâṅbá] *a* (*CULIN*) flambé ♦ *nf* blaze; (*fig*) flaring-up, explosion.
flambeau, x [flâṅbō] *nm* (flaming) torch; **se passer le** ~ (*fig*) to hand down the (*ou* a) tradition.
flambée [flâṅbá] *nf* (*feu*) blaze; (*COMM*): ~ **des prix** (sudden) shooting up of prices.
flamber [flâṅbá] *vi* to blaze (up) ♦ *vt* (*poulet*) to singe; (*aiguille*) to sterilize.
flamboyant, e [flâṅbwáyâṅ, -âṅt] *a* blazing; flaming.
flamboyer [flâṅbwáyá] *vi* to blaze (up); (*fig*) to flame.
flamingant, e [flámaṅgâṅ, -âṅt] *a* Flemish-speaking ♦ *nm/f*: F~, e Flemish speaker; (*POL*) Flemish nationalist.
flamme [flám] *nf* flame; (*fig*) fire, fervor (*US*), fervour (*Brit*); **en** ~**s** on fire, ablaze.
flammèche [flámesh] *nf* (flying) spark.
flammerole [flámrol] *nf* will-o'-the-wisp.
flan [flâṅ] *nm* (*CULIN*) baked custard (*US*), custard tart *ou* pie (*Brit*).
flanc [flâṅ] *nm* side; (*MIL*) flank; **à** ~ **de colline** on the hillside; **prêter le** ~ **à** (*fig*) to lay o.s. open to.
flancher [flâṅshá] *vi* (*cesser de fonctionner*) to fail, pack up; (*armée*) to quit.
Flandre [flâṅdr(ə)] *nf*: **la** ~ (*aussi*: **les** ~**s**) Flanders.
flanelle [flánel] *nf* flannel.
flâner [flânâ] *vi* to stroll.
flânerie [flânrē] *nf* stroll.
flâneur, euse [flânœr, -ēz] *a* idle ♦ *nm/f* stroller.
flanquer [flâṅká] *vt* to flank; (*fam: jeter*): ~ **par terre/à la porte** to fling to the ground/throw *ou* kick out; (: *donner*): ~ **la frousse à qn** to give sb an awful fright.
flapi, e [flápē] *a* dog-tired.
flaque [flák] *nf* (*d'eau*) puddle; (*d'huile, de sang etc*) pool.
flash, pl flashes [flásh] *nm* (*PHOTO*) flash; ~ **(d'information)** newsflash.
flasque [flásk(ə)] *a* flabby ♦ *nf* (*flacon*) flask.
flatter [flátá] *vt* to flatter; (*caresser*) to stroke; **se** ~ **de qch** to pride o.s. on sth.
flatterie [flátrē] *nf* flattery.
flatteur, euse [flátœr, -ēz] *a* flattering ♦ *nm/f* flatterer.
flatulence [flátülâṅs], **flatuosité** [flátüōzētá] *nf* (*MÉD*) flatulence, wind.
FLB *abr* (= *franco long du bord*) FAS ♦ *sigle m* (*POL*) = *Front de libération de la Bretagne*.
FLC *sigle m* = *Front de libération de la Corse*.
fléau, x [flāō] *nm* scourge, curse; (*de balance*) beam; (*pour le blé*) flail.
fléchage [flāsházh] *nm* (*d'un itinéraire*) sign-posting.
flèche [flesh] *nf* arrow; (*de clocher*) spire; (*de grue*) jib; (*trait d'esprit, critique*) shaft; **monter en** ~ (*fig*) to soar, rocket; **partir en** ~ (*fig*) to be off like a shot; **à** ~ **variable**

(*avion*) variable geometry wing *cpd* (*US*), swing-wing *cpd* (*Brit*).

flécher [flāshā] *vt* to mark with arrows.

fléchette [flāshet] *nf* dart; ~s *nfpl* (*jeu*) darts *sg*.

fléchir [flāshēr] *vt* (*corps, genou*) to bend; (*fig*) to sway, weaken ♦ *vi* (*poutre*) to sag, bend; (*fig*) to weaken, flag; (: *baisser: prix*) to fall off.

fléchissement [flāshēsmān] *nm* bending; sagging; flagging; (*de l'économie*) dullness.

flegmatique [flegmàtēk] *a* phlegmatic.

flegme [flegm(ə)] *nm* composure.

flemmard, e [flāmár, -àrd(ə)] *nm/f* lazybones *sg*, loafer.

flemme [flem] *nf* (*fam*): **j'ai la ~ de faire** I can't be bothered to do.

flétan [flātàn] *nm* (*ZOOL*) halibut.

flétrir [flātrēr] *vt* to wither; (*stigmatiser*) to condemn (in the most severe terms); **se ~** *vi* to wither.

fleur [flœr] *nf* flower; (*d'un arbre*) blossom; **être en ~** (*arbre*) to be in blossom; **tissu à ~s** flowered *ou* flowery fabric; **la (fine) ~ de** (*fig*) the flower of; **être ~ bleue** to be soppy *ou* sentimental; **à ~ de terre** just above the ground; **faire une ~ à qn** to do sb a favor; **~ de lis** fleur-de-lis.

fleurer [flœrā] *vt*: **~ la lavande** to have the scent of lavender.

fleuret [flœre] *nm* (*arme*) foil; (*sport*) fencing.

fleurette [flœret] *nf*: **conter ~ à qn** to whisper sweet nothings to sb.

fleuri, e [flœrē] *a* in flower *ou* bloom; surrounded by flowers; (*fig: style*) flowery; (: *teint*) glowing.

fleurir [flœrēr] *vi* (*rose*) to flower; (*arbre*) to blossom; (*fig*) to flourish ♦ *vt* (*tombe*) to put flowers on; (*chambre*) to decorate with flowers.

fleuriste [flœrēst(ə)] *nm/f* florist.

fleuron [flœrôn] *nm* jewel (*fig*).

fleuve [flœv] *nm* river; **roman-~** saga; **discours-~** interminable speech.

flexibilité [fleksēbēlētā] *nf* flexibility.

flexible [fleksēbl(ə)] *a* flexible.

flexion [fleksyôn] *nf* flexing, bending; (*LING*) inflection.

flibustier [flēbüstyā] *nm* buccaneer.

flic [flēk] *nm* (*fam: péj*) cop.

flipper *nm* [flēpœr] pinball (machine) ♦ *vi* [flēpā] (*fam: être déprimé*) to feel down, be on a downer; (: *être exalté*) to freak out.

flirt [flœrt] *nm* flirting; (*personne*) boyfriend, girlfriend.

flirter [flœrtā] *vi* to flirt.

FLN *sigle m* = *Front de libération nationale* (*during the Algerian war*).

FLNKS *sigle m* (= *Front de libération nationale kanak et socialiste*) *political movement in New Caledonia*.

flocon [flokôn] *nm* flake; (*de laine etc: boulette*) flock; **~s d'avoine** oatflakes.

floconneux, euse [flokonœ, -œz] *a* fluffy, fleecy.

flonflons [flônflôn] *nmpl* blare *sg*.

flopée [flopā] *nf*: **une ~ de** loads of.

floraison [florezôn] *nf* (*voir fleurir*) flowering; blossoming; flourishing.

floral, e, aux [florál, -ō] *a* floral, flower *cpd*.

floralies [florálē] *nfpl* flower show *sg*.

flore [flor] *nf* flora.

Florence [florâns] *n* (*ville*) Florence.

florentin, e [florântàn, -ēn] *a* Florentine.

floriculture [florēkültür] *nf* flower-growing.

florissant, e [florēsàn, -ânt] *vb voir* **fleurir** ♦ *a* flourishing; (*santé, teint, mine*) blooming.

flot [flō] *nm* flood, stream; (*marée*) flood tide; **~s** *nmpl* (*de la mer*) waves; **être à ~** (*NAVIG*) to be afloat; (*fig*) to be on an even keel; **à ~s** (*couler*) in torrents; **entrer à ~s** to stream *ou* pour in.

flottage [flotâzh] *nm* (*du bois*) floating.

flottaison [flotezôn] *nf*: **ligne de ~** waterline.

flottant, e [flotàn, -ânt] *a* (*vêtement*) loose(-fitting); (*cours, barème*) floating.

flotte [flot] *nf* (*NAVIG*) fleet; (*fam*) water; rain.

flottement [flotmân] *nm* (*fig*) wavering, hesitation; (*ÉCON*) floating.

flotter [flotā] *vi* to float; (*nuage, odeur*) to drift; (*drapeau*) to fly; (*vêtements*) to hang loose ♦ *vb impersonnel* (*fam: pleuvoir*): **il flotte** it's raining ♦ *vt* to float; **faire ~** to float.

flotteur [flotœr] *nm* float.

flottille [flotēy] *nf* flotilla.

flou, e [flōō] *a* fuzzy, blurred; (*fig*) vague; (*non ajusté: robe*) loose(-fitting).

flouer [flōōā] *vt* to swindle.

FLQ *abr* (= *franco too du quai*) FAQ.

fluctuation [flüktüàsyôn] *nf* fluctuation.

fluctuer [flüktüā] *vi* to fluctuate.

fluet, te [flüe, -et] *a* thin, slight; (*voix*) thin.

fluide [flüēd] *a* fluid; (*circulation etc*) flowing freely ♦ *nm* fluid; (*force*) (mysterious) power.

fluidifier [flüēdēfyā] *vt* to make fluid.

fluidité [flüēdētā] *nf* fluidity; free flow.

fluor [flüor] *nm* fluorine.

fluoré, e [flüorā] *a* fluoridated.

fluorescent, e [flüoresàn, -ânt] *a* fluorescent.

flûte [flüt] *nf* (*aussi*: **~ traversière**) flute; (*verre*) flute glass; (*pain*) long loaf (*pl* loaves); **petite ~** piccolo (*pl* -s); **~!** drat it!; **~ (à bec)** recorder; **~ de Pan** panpipes *pl*.

flûtiste [flütēst(ə)] *nm/f* flautist, flute player.

fluvial, e, aux [flüvyál, -ō] *a* river *cpd*, fluvial.

flux [flü] *nm* incoming tide; (*écoulement*) flow; **le ~ et le reflux** the ebb and flow.

fluxion [flüksyôn] *nf*: **~ de poitrine** pneumonia.

FM *sigle f* (= *frequency modulation*) FM.

Fme *abr* = **femme**.

FMI *sigle m* (= *Fonds monétaire international*) IMF.

FN *sigle m* (= *Front national*) political party.

FNAC [fnàk] *sigle f* (= *Fédération nationale des achats des cadres*) chain of discount shops (*hi-fi, photo etc*).

FNAH *sigle m* (= *Fonds national d'amélioration de l'habitat*).

FNEF [fnef] *sigle f* (= *Fédération nationale des étudiants de France*) student union.

FNSEA *sigle f* (= *Fédération nationale des syndicats d'exploitants agricoles*) farmers' union.

FO *sigle f* (= *Force ouvrière*) labor union.

foc [fɔk] *nm* jib.

focal, e, aux [fɔkál, -ō] *a* focal ♦ *nf* focal length.

focaliser [fɔkálēzā] *vt* to focus.

foehn [fœn] *nm* foehn, föhn.

fœtal, e, aux [fātál, -ō] *a* fetal, foetal (*Brit*).

fœtus [fātüs] *nm* fetus, foetus (*Brit*).

foi [fwá] *nf* faith; **sous la ~ du serment** under *ou* on oath; **ajouter ~ à** to lend credence to; **faire ~** (*prouver*) to be evidence; **digne de ~** reliable; **sur la ~ de** on the word *ou* strength of; **être de bonne/mauvaise ~** to be in good faith/not to be in good faith; **ma ~!** well!

foie [fwá] *nm* liver; **~ gras** foie gras.

foin [fwań] *nm* hay; **faire les ~s** to make hay; **faire du ~** (*fam*) to kick up a row.

foire [fwár] *nf* fair; (*fête foraine*) carnival (*US*), (fun)fair (*Brit*); (*fig: désordre, confusion*) bear garden; **faire la ~** to whoop it up; **~ (exposition)** trade fair.

fois [fwá] *nf* time; **une/deux ~** once/twice; **trois/vingt ~** three/twenty times; **2 ~ 2** 2 times 2; **deux/quatre ~ plus grand (que)** twice/four times as big (as); **une ~** (*passé*) once; (*futur*) sometime; **une (bonne) ~ pour toutes** once and for all; **encore une ~** again, once more; **il était une ~** once upon a time; **une ~ que c'est fait** once it's done; **une ~ parti** once he (*ou* I *etc*) had left; **des ~** (*parfois*) sometimes; **si des ~ ...** ... (*fam*) if ever ...; **non mais des ~!** (*fam*) (now) look here!; **à la ~** (*ensemble*) (all) at once; **à la ~ grand et beau** both tall and handsome.

foison [fwázóń] *nf*: **une ~ de** an abundance of; **à ~** *ad* in plenty.

foisonnant, e [fwázonáń, -áńt] *a* teeming.

foisonnement [fwázonmáń] *nm* profusion, abundance.

foisonner [fwázonā] *vi* to abound; **~ en** *ou* **de** to abound in.

fol [fɔl] *am voir* **fou.**

folâtre [fɔlátr(ə)] *a* playful.

folâtrer [fɔlátrā] *vi* to frolic (around).

folichon, ne [fɔlēshóń, -on] *a*: **ça n'a rien de ~** it's not a lot of fun.

folie [fɔlē] *nf* (*d'une décision, d'un acte*) madness, folly; (*état*) madness, insanity; (*acte*) folly; **la ~ des grandeurs** delusions of grandeur; **faire des ~s** (*en dépenses*) to be in extravagant.

folklore [fɔlklɔr] *nm* folklore.

folklorique [fɔlklɔrēk] *a* folk *cpd*; (*fam*) weird.

folle [fɔl] *af*, *nf voir* **fou.**

follement [fɔlmáń] *ad* (*très*) madly, wildly.

follet [fɔlē] *am*: **feu ~** will-o'-the-wisp.

fomentateur, trice [fɔmáńtátœr, -trēs] *nm/f* agitator.

fomenter [fɔmáńtā] *vt* to stir up, foment.

foncé, e [fóńsā] *a* dark; **bleu ~** dark blue.

foncer [fóńsā] *vt* to make darker; (*CULIN: moule etc*) to line ♦ *vi* to go darker; (*fam: aller vite*) to tear *ou* belt along; **~ sur** to charge at.

fonceur, euse [fóńsœr, -ēz] *nm/f* whizz kid.

foncier, ière [fóńsyā, -yer] *a* (*honnêteté etc*) basic, fundamental; (*malhonnêteté*) deep-rooted; (*COMM*) real estate *cpd*.

foncièrement [fóńsyermáń] *ad* basically; (*absolument*) thoroughly.

fonction [fóńksyóń] *nf* (*rôle*, MATH, LING) function; (*emploi*, *poste*) post, position; **~s** (*professionnelles*) duties; **entrer en ~s** to take up one's post *ou* duties; to take up office; **voiture de ~** company car; **être ~ de** (*dépendre de*) to depend on; **en ~ de** (*par rapport à*) according to; **faire ~ de** to serve as; **la ~ publique** the civil service.

fonctionnaire [fóńksyoner] *nm/f* state employee *ou* official; (*dans l'administration*) ≈ civil servant.

fonctionnariser [fóńksyonárēzā] *vt* (ADMIN: *personne*) to give the status of a state employee to.

fonctionnel, le [fóńksyonel] *a* functional.

fonctionnellement [fóńksyonelmáń] *ad* functionally.

fonctionnement [fóńksyonmáń] *nm* working; functioning; operation.

fonctionner [fóńksyonā] *vi* to work, function; (*entreprise*) to operate, function; **faire ~** to work, operate.

fond [fóń] *nm voir aussi* **fonds**; (*d'un récipient, trou*) bottom; (*d'une salle, scène*) back; (*d'un tableau, décor*) background; (*opposé à la forme*) content; (*petite quantité*): **un ~ de verre** a drop; (SPORT): **le ~** long distance (running); **course/épreuve de ~** long-distance race/trial; **au ~ de** at the bottom of; at the back of; **aller au ~ des choses** to get to the root of things; **le ~ de sa pensée** his (*ou* her) true thoughts *ou* feelings; **sans ~** a bottomless; **envoyer par le ~** (NAVIG: *couler*) to sink, scuttle; **à ~** *ad* (*connaître, soutenir*) thoroughly; (*appuyer, visser*) right down *ou* home; **à ~ (de train)** *ad* (*fam*) full tilt; **dans le ~, au ~ de** (*en somme*) basically, really; **de ~ en comble** *ad* from top to bottom; **~ sonore** background noise; background music; **~ de teint** (makeup) foundation.

fondamental, e, aux [fóńdámáńtál, -ō] *a* fundamental.

fondamentalement [fóńdámáńtálmáń] *ad* fundamentally.

fondamentalisme [fóńdámáńtálēsm(ə)] *nm* fundamentalism.

fondant, e [fóńdáń, -áńt] *a* (*neige*) melting; (*poire*) that melts in the mouth; (*chocolat*) fondant.

fondateur, trice [fóńdátœr, -trēs] *nm/f* founder; **membre ~** founding (*US*) *ou* founder (*Brit*) member.

fondation [fóńdásyóń] *nf* founding; (*établissement*) foundation; **~s** *nfpl* (*d'une maison*) foundations; **travail de ~** foundation works *pl*.

fondé, e [fóńdā] *a* (*accusation etc*) well-founded; **mal ~** unfounded; **être ~ à croire** to have grounds for believing *ou* good reason to believe ♦ *nm*: **~ de pouvoir** authorized representative.

fondement [fóńdmáń] *nm* (*derrière*) behind; **~s** *nmpl* foundations; **sans ~** a (*rumeur etc*) groundless, unfounded.

fonder [fóńdā] *vt* to found; (*fig*): **~ qch sur** to base sth on; **se ~ sur** (*suj: personne*) to base o.s. on; **~ un foyer** (*se marier*) to set up house.

fonderie [fôṅdrē] *nf* smelting works *sg*.

fondeur, euse [fôṅdœr, -ēz] *nm/f* (*skieur*) long-distance skier ♦ *nm*: (*ouvrier*) ~ caster.

fondre [fôṅdr(ə)] *vt* to melt; (*dans l'eau: sucre, sel*) to dissolve; (*fig: mélanger*) to merge, blend ♦ *vi* to melt; to dissolve; (*fig*) to melt away; (*se précipiter*): ~ **sur** to swoop down on; **se** ~ *vi* (*se combiner, se confondre*) to merge into each other; to dissolve; ~ **en larmes** to dissolve into tears.

fondrière [fôṅdrēyer] *nf* rut.

fonds [fôṅ] *nm* (*de bibliothèque*) collection; (*COMM*): ~ **(de commerce)** business; (*fig*): ~ **de probité** *etc* fund of integrity *etc* ♦ *nmpl* (*argent*) funds; **à** ~ **perdus** *ad* with little or no hope of getting the money back; **être en** ~ to be in funds; **mise de** ~ investment, (capital) outlay; **F~ Monétaire International (FMI)** International Monetary Fund (IMF); ~ **de roulement** *nm* working capital.

fondu, e [fôṅdü] *a* (*beurre, neige*) melted; (*métal*) molten ♦ *nm* (*CINÉMA*): ~ **(enchaîné)** dissolve ♦ *nf* (*CULIN*) fondue.

fongicide [fôṅzhēsēd] *nm* fungicide.

font [fôṅ] *vb voir* **faire**.

fontaine [fôṅten] *nf* fountain; (*source*) spring.

fonte [fôṅt] *nf* melting; (*métal*) cast iron; ~ **des neiges** the (spring) thaw.

fonts baptismaux [fôṅbàtēsmō] *nmpl* (baptismal) font *sg*.

foot(ball) [foot(bōl)] *nm* football, soccer.

footballeur, euse [footbōlœr, -ēz] *nm/f* football *ou* soccer player.

footing [footēng] *nm* jogging; **faire du** ~ to go jogging.

for [for] *nm*: **dans** *ou* **en son** ~ **intérieur** in one's heart of hearts.

forage [foràzh] *nm* drilling, boring.

forain, e [foraṅ, -en] *a* fairground *cpd* ♦ *nm* (*marchand*) boothkeeper (*US*), stallkeeper (*US*), stallholder (*Brit*); (*acteur etc*) fairground entertainer.

forban [forbàṅ] *nm* (*pirate*) pirate; (*escroc*) crook.

forçat [forsà] *nm* convict.

force [fors(ə)] *nf* strength; (*puissance: surnaturelle etc*) power; (*PHYSIQUE, MÉCANIQUE*) force; ~**s** *nfpl* (*physiques*) strength *sg*; (*MIL*) forces; (*effectifs*): **d'importantes** ~**s de police** big contingents of police; **avoir de la** ~ to be strong; **être à bout de** ~ to have no strength left; **à la** ~ **du poignet** (*fig*) by the sweat of one's brow; **à** ~ **de faire** by dint of doing; **arriver en** ~ (*nombreux*) to arrive in force; **cas de** ~ **majeure** case of absolute necessity; (*ASSURANCES*) act of God; ~ **de la nature** natural force; **de** ~ *ad* forcibly, by force; **de toutes mes/ses** ~**s** with all my/his strength; **par la** ~ using force; **par la** ~ **des choses/d'habitude** by force of circumstances/habit; **à toute** ~ (*absolument*) at all costs; **faire** ~ **de rames/voiles** to ply the oars/crowd on sail; **être de** ~ **à faire** to be up to doing; **de première** ~ first class; **la** ~ **armée** (*les troupes*) the army; ~ **d'âme** fortitude; ~ **de frappe** strike force; ~ **d'inertie** force of inertia; **la** ~ **publique** the authorities respon-

sible for public order; ~**s d'intervention** (*MIL, POLICE*) peace-keeping force *sg*; **les** ~**s de l'ordre** the police.

forcé, e [forsā] *a* forced; (*bain*) unintended; (*inevitable*): **c'est** ~! it's inevitable!, it HAS to be!

forcément [forsāmâṅ] *ad* necessarily; inevitably; (*bien sûr*) of course.

forcené, e [forsənā] *a* frenzied ♦ *nm/f* maniac.

forceps [forseps] *nm* forceps *pl*.

forcer [forsā] *vt* (*contraindre*): ~ **qn à faire** to force sb to do; (*porte, serrure, plante*) to force; (*moteur, voix*) to strain ♦ *vi* (*SPORT*) to overtax o.s.; **se** ~ **à faire qch** to force o.s. to do sth; ~ **la dose/l'allure** to overdo it/increase the pace; ~ **l'attention/le respect** to command attention/respect; ~ **la consigne** to bypass orders.

forcing [forsēng] *nm* (*SPORT*): **faire le** ~ to pile on the pressure.

forcir [forsēr] *vi* (*grossir*) to broaden out; (*vent*) to freshen.

forclore [forklor] *vt* (*JUR: personne*) to debar.

forclusion [forklüzyôṅ] *nf* (*JUR*) debarment.

forer [forā] *vt* to drill, bore.

forestier, ière [forestyā, -yer] *a* forest *cpd*.

foret [fore] *nm* drill.

forêt [fore] *nf* forest; **Office National des F~s** (*ADMIN*) ≈ National Forest Service (*US*), ≈ Forestry Commission (*Brit*); **la F~ Noire** the Black Forest.

foreuse [forēz] *nf* (electric) drill.

forfait [forfe] *nm* (*COMM*) fixed *ou* set price; package deal, all-inclusive price; (*crime*) infamy; **déclarer** ~ to withdraw; **gagner par** ~ to win by default; **travailler à** ~ to work for a lump sum.

forfaitaire [forfeter] *a* set; inclusive.

forfait-vacances, *pl* **forfaits-vacances** [forfevàkâṅs] *nm* package tour.

forfanterie [forfàṅtrē] *nf* boastfulness *q*.

forge [forzh(ə)] *nf* forge, smithy.

forger [forzhā] *vt* to forge; (*fig: personnalité*) to form; (*: prétexte*) to contrive, make up; **être forgé de toutes pièces** to be a complete fabrication.

forgeron [forzhərôṅ] *nm* (black)smith.

formaliser [formálēzā]: **se** ~ *vi*: **se** ~ **(de)** to take offense (*US*) *ou* offence (*Brit*) (at).

formalisme [formálēsm(ə)] *nm* formality.

formalité [formálētā] *nf* formality.

format [formá] *nm* size; **petit** ~ small size; (*PHOTO*) 35 mm (film).

formater [formàtā] *vt* (*disque*) to format; **non formaté** unformatted.

formateur, trice [formàtœr, -trēs] *a* formative.

formation [formàsyôṅ] *nf* forming; (*éducation*) training; (*MUS*) group; (*MIL, AVIAT, GÉO*) formation; **la** ~ **permanente** *ou* **continue** continuing education; **la** ~ **professionnelle** vocational training.

forme [form(ə)] *nf* (*gén*) form; (*d'un objet*) shape, form; ~**s** *nfpl* (*bonnes manières*) proprieties; (*d'une femme*) figure *sg*; **en** ~ **de poire** pear-shaped, in the shape of a pear; **sous** ~ **de** in the form of; in the guise of; **sous** ~ **de cachets** in the form of tablets; **être en (bonne** *ou* **pleine)** ~, **avoir la** ~ (*SPORT etc*) to be in good shape; **en bonne et**

due ~ in due form; **pour la** ~ for the sake of form; **sans autre** ~ **de procès** (*fig*) without further ado; **prendre** ~ to take shape.

formel, le [formel] *a* (*preuve, décision*) definite, positive; (*logique*) formal.

formellement [formelmáñ] *ad* (*interdit*) strictly.

former [formã] *vt* (*gén*) to form; (*éduquer: soldat, ingénieur etc*) to train; **se** ~ to form; to train.

formidable [formēdàbl(ə)] *a* tremendous.

formidablement [formēdábləmáñ] *ad* tremendously.

formol [formol] *nm* formalin, formol.

formosan, e [formōzáň, -àn] *a* Formosan.

Formose [formōz] *nm* Formosa.

formulaire [formüler] *nm* form.

formule [formül] *nf* (*gén*) formula; (*formulaire*) form; **selon la** ~ **consacrée** as one says; ~ **de politesse** polite phrase; (*en fin de lettre*) letter ending.

formuler [formülã] *vt* (*émettre: réponse, vœux*) to formulate; (*expliciter: sa pensée*) to express.

forniquer [fornēkã] *vi* to fornicate.

fort, e [for, fort(ə)] *a* strong; (*intensité, rendement*) high, great; (*corpulent*) large; (*doué*) **être** ~ **(en)** to be good (at) ♦ *ad* (*serrer, frapper*) hard; (*sonner*) loud(ly); (*beaucoup*) greatly, very much; (*très*) very ♦ *nm* (*édifice*) fort; (*point fort*) strong point, forte; (*gén pl: personne, pays*): **le** ~, **les** ~**s** the strong; **c'est un peu** ~! it's a bit much!; **à plus** ~**e raison** even more so, all the more reason; **avoir** ~ **à faire avec qn** to have one's work cut out with sb; **se faire** ~ **de faire** to claim one can do; ~ **bien/peu** very well/few; **au plus** ~ **de** (*au milieu de*) in the thick of, at the height of; ~**e tête** rebel.

fortement [fortəmáñ] *ad* strongly; (*s'intéresser*) deeply.

forteresse [fortəres] *nf* fortress.

fortifiant [fortēfyáñ] *nm* tonic.

fortifications [fortēfēkàsyòn] *nfpl* fortifications.

fortifier [fortēfyã] *vt* to strengthen, fortify; (*MIL*) to fortify; **se** ~ *vi* (*personne, santé*) to grow stronger.

fortin [fortań] *nm* (small) fort.

fortiori [forsyorē]: **à** ~ *ad* all the more so.

FORTRAN [fortráň] *nm* FORTRAN.

fortuit, e [fortüē, -ēt] *a* fortuitous, chance *cpd*.

fortuitement [fortüētmáñ] *ad* fortuitously.

fortune [fortün] *nf* fortune; **faire** ~ to make one's fortune; **de** ~ *a* makeshift; (*compagnon*) chance *cpd*.

fortuné, e [fortünã] *a* wealthy, well-off.

forum [forom] *nm* forum.

fosse [fōs] *nf* (*grand trou*) pit; (*tombe*) grave; **la** ~ **aux lions/ours** the lions' den/bear pit; ~ **commune** common *ou* communal grave; ~ **(d'orchestre)** (orchestra) pit; ~ **à purin** cesspit; ~ **septique** septic tank; ~**s nasales** nasal fossae.

fossé [fōsã] *nm* ditch; (*fig*) gulf, gap.

fossette [fōset] *nf* dimple.

fossile [fōsēl] *nm* fossil ♦ *a* fossilized, fossil *cpd*.

fossoyeur [tōswàyœr] *nm* gravedigger.

fou (fol), folle [fōō, fol] *a* mad, crazy; (*déréglé etc*) wild, erratic; (*mèche*) stray; (*herbe*) wild; (*fam: extrême, très grand*) terrific, tremendous ♦ *nm/f* madman/woman ♦ *nm* (*du roi*) jester, fool; (*ÉCHECS*) bishop; ~ **à lier**, ~ **furieux (folle furieuse)** raving mad; **être** ~ **de** to be mad *ou* crazy about; (*chagrin, joie, colère*) to be wild with; **faire le** ~ to play *ou* act the fool; **avoir le** ~ **rire** to have the giggles.

foucade [fōōkàd] *nf* caprice.

foudre [fōōdr(ə)] *nf* lightning; ~**s** *nfpl* (*fig: colère*) wrath *sg*.

foudroyant, e [fōōdrwàyáñ, -áñt] *a* devastating; (*maladie, poison*) violent.

foudroyer [fōōdrwàyã] *vt* to strike down; ~ **qn du regard** to look daggers at sb; **il a été foudroyé** he was struck by lightning.

fouet [fwe] *nm* whip; (*CULIN*) whisk; **de plein** ~ *ad* head on.

fouettement [fwetmáñ] *nm* lashing *q*.

fouetter [fwãtã] *vt* to whip; to whisk.

fougasse [fōōgàs] *nf* type of flat pastry.

fougère [fōōzher] *nf* fern.

fougue [fōōg] *nf* ardor (*US*), ardour (*Brit*).

fougueusement [fōōgœzmáñ] *ad* ardently.

fougueux, euse [fōōgœ, -œz] *a* fiery, ardent.

fouille [fōōy] *nf* search; ~**s** *nfpl* (*archéologiques*) excavations; **passer à la** ~ to be searched.

fouillé, e [fōōyã] *a* detailed.

fouiller [fōōyã] *vt* to search; (*creuser*) to dig; (: *suj: archéologue*) to excavate; (*approfondir: étude etc*) to go into ♦ *vi* (*archéologue*) to excavate; ~ **dans/parmi** to rummage in/among.

fouillis [fōōyē] *nm* jumble, muddle.

fouine [fwēn] *nf* stone marten.

fouiner [fwēnã] *vi* (*péj*): ~ **dans** to nose around *ou* about in.

fouineur, euse [fwēnœr, -œz] *a* nosey ♦ *nm/f* nosey parker, snooper.

fouir [fwēr] *vt* to dig.

fouisseur, euse [fwēsœr, -œz] *a* burrowing.

foulage [fōōlàzh] *nm* pressing.

foulante [fōōláñt] *af*: **pompe** ~ force pump.

foulard [fōōlàr] *nm* scarf (*pl* scarves).

foule [fōōl] *nf* crowd; **une** ~ **de** masses of; **venir en** ~**s** to come in droves.

foulée [fōōlã] *nf* stride; **dans la** ~ **de** on the heels of.

fouler [fōōlã] *vt* to press; (*sol*) to tread upon; **se** ~ *vi* (*fam*) to overexert o.s.; **se** ~ **la cheville** to sprain one's ankle; ~ **aux pieds** to trample underfoot.

foulure [fōōlür] *nf* sprain.

four [fōōr] *nm* oven; (*de potier*) kiln; (*THÉÂTRE: échec*) flop; **allant au** ~ ovenproof.

fourbe [fōōrb(ə)] *a* deceitful.

fourberie [fōōrbərē] *nf* deceit.

fourbi [fōōrbē] *nm* (*fam*) gear, junk.

fourbir [fōōrbēr] *vt*: ~ **ses armes** (*fig*) to get ready for the fray.

fourbu, e [fōōrbü] *a* exhausted.

fourche [fōōrsh(ə)] *nf* pitchfork; (*de bicyclette*) fork.

fourcher [fōōrshã] *vi*: **ma langue a fourché** it was a slip of the tongue.

fourchette [fŏŏrshet] *nf* fork; (*STATISTIQUE*) bracket, margin.

fourchu, e [fŏŏrshü] *a* split; (*arbre etc*) forked.

fourgon [fŏŏrgôn] *nm* truck, van; (*RAIL*) wag(g)on; ~ **mortuaire** hearse.

fourgonnette [fŏŏrgonet] *nf* (delivery) truck.

fourmi [fŏŏrmē] *nf* ant; **avoir des ~s** (*fig*) to have pins and needles.

fourmilière [fŏŏrmēlyer] *nf* anthill; (*fig*) hive of activity.

fourmillement [fŏŏrmēymân] *nm* (*démangeaison*) pins and needles *pl*; (*grouillement*) swarming *q*.

fourmiller [fŏŏrmēyā] *vi* to swarm; ~ **de** to be teeming with, be swarming with.

fournaise [fŏŏrnez] *nf* blaze; (*fig*) furnace, oven.

fourneau, x [fŏŏrnō] *nm* stove.

fournée [fŏŏrnā] *nf* batch.

fourni, e [fŏŏrnē] *a* (*barbe, cheveux*) thick; (*magasin*): **bien ~ (en)** well stocked (with).

fournil [fŏŏrnē] *nm* bakery.

fournir [fŏŏrnēr] *vt* to supply; (*preuve, exemple*) to provide, supply; (*effort*) to put in; ~ **qch à qn** to supply sth to sb, supply *ou* provide sb with sth; ~ **qn en** (*COMM*) to supply sb with; **se ~ chez** to shop at.

fournisseur, euse [fŏŏrnēsœr, -ēz] *nm/f* supplier.

fourniture [fŏŏrnētür] *nf* supply(ing); **~s** *nfpl* supplies; **~s de bureau** office supplies, stationery; **~s scolaires** school supplies.

fourrage [fŏŏrázh] *nm* fodder.

fourrager [fŏŏrázhā] *vi*: ~ **dans/parmi** to rummage through/among.

fourrager, ère [fŏŏrázhā, -er] *a* fodder *cpd* ♦ *nf* (*MIL*) fourragère.

fourré, e [fŏŏrā] *a* (*bonbon, chocolat*) filled; (*manteau, botte*) fur-lined ♦ *nm* thicket.

fourreau, x [fŏŏrō] *nm* sheath; (*de parapluie*) cover; **robe/jupe ~** figure-hugging dress/skirt.

fourrer [fŏŏrā] *vt* (*fam*): ~ **qch dans** to stick *ou* shove sth into; **se ~ dans/sous** to get into/under; **se ~ dans** (*une mauvaise situation*) to land o.s. in.

fourre-tout [fŏŏrtŏŏ] *nm inv* (*sac*) tote bag, carryall (*US*); (*péj*) junk room (*ou* closet); (*fig*) rag-bag.

fourreur [fŏŏrœr] *nm* furrier.

fourrière [fŏŏryer] *nf* pound.

fourrure [fŏŏrür] *nf* fur; (*sur l'animal*) coat; **manteau/col de ~** fur coat/collar.

fourvoyer [fŏŏrvwáyā]: **se ~** *vi* to go astray, stray; **se ~ dans** to stray into.

foutre [fŏŏtr(ə)] *vt* (*fam!*) = **ficher** (*fam*).

foutu, e [fŏŏtü] *a* (*fam!*) = **fichu**.

foyer [fwáyā] *nm* (*de cheminée*) hearth; (*fig*) seat, center (*US*), centre (*Brit*); (*famille*) family; (*domicile*) home; (*local de réunion*) (social) club; (*résidence*) hostel; (*salon*) foyer; (*OPTIQUE, PHOTO*) focus; **lunettes à double ~** bifocal glasses.

FP *sigle f* (= *franchise postale*) exemption from postage.

FPA *sigle f* (= *Formation professionnelle pour adultes*) adult education.

FPLP *sigle m* = *Front populaire de la libération de la Palestine*.

FR3 [efertrwá] *sigle f* (= *France Régions 3*) TV channel.

fracas [fráká] *nm* din; crash.

fracassant, e [frákásân, -ânt] *a* sensational, staggering.

fracasser [frákásā] *vt* to smash; **se ~ contre** *ou* **sur** to crash against.

fraction [fráksyôn] *nf* fraction.

fractionnement [fráksyonmân] *nm* division.

fractionner [fráksyonā] *vt* to divide (up), split (up).

fracture [fráktür] *nf* fracture; ~ **du crâne** fractured skull; ~ **de la jambe** broken leg.

fracturer [fráktürā] *vt* (*coffre, serrure*) to break open; (*os, membre*) to fracture.

fragile [frázhēl] *a* fragile, delicate; (*fig*) frail.

fragiliser [frázhēlēzā] *vt* to weaken, make fragile.

fragilité [frázhēlētā] *nf* fragility.

fragment [frágmân] *nm* (*d'un objet*) fragment, piece; (*d'un texte*) passage, extract.

fragmentaire [frágmânter] *a* sketchy.

fragmenter [frágmântā] *vt* to split up.

frai [fre] *nm* spawn; (*ponte*) spawning.

fraîche [fresh] *af voir* **frais**.

fraîchement [freshmân] *ad* (*sans enthousiasme*) coolly; (*récemment*) freshly, newly.

fraîcheur [freshœr] *nf* (*voir frais*) coolness; freshness.

fraîchir [freshēr] *vi* to get cooler; (*vent*) to freshen.

frais, fraîche [fre, fresh] *a* (*air, eau, accueil*) cool; (*petit pois, œufs, nouvelles, couleur, troupes*) fresh; **le voilà ~!** he's in a (real) mess! ♦ *ad* (*récemment*) newly, fresh(ly); **il fait ~** it's cool; **servir ~** chill before serving, serve chilled ♦ *nm*: **mettre au ~** to put in a cool place; **prendre le ~** to take a breath of cool air ♦ *nmpl* (*débours*) expenses; (*COMM*) costs; charges; **faire des ~** to spend; to go to a lot of expense; **faire les ~ de** to bear the brunt of; **faire les ~ de la conversation** (*parler*) to do most of the talking; (*en être le sujet*) to be the topic of conversation; **il en a été pour ses ~** he could have spared himself the trouble; **rentrer dans ses ~** to recover one's expenses; ~ **de déplacement** travel(ing) expenses; ~ **d'entretien** upkeep; ~ **généraux** overhead charges *ou* costs; ~ **de scolarité** school fees, tuition (*US*).

fraise [frez] *nf* strawberry; (*TECH*) countersink (bit); (*de dentiste*) drill; ~ **des bois** wild strawberry.

fraiser [frāzā] *vt* to countersink; (*CULIN: pâte*) to knead.

fraiseuse [frezœz] *nf* (*TECH*) milling machine.

fraisier [frāzyā] *nm* strawberry plant.

framboise [frânbwáz] *nf* raspberry.

framboisier [frânbwázyā] *nm* raspberry bush.

franc, franche [frân, frânsh] *a* (*personne*) frank, straightforward; (*visage*) open; (*net: refus, couleur*) clear; (*: coupure*) clean; (*intensif*) downright; (*exempt*): ~ **de port** post free, postage paid; (*zone, port*) free; (*boutique*) duty-free ♦ *ad*: **parler ~** to be frank *ou* candid ♦ *nm* franc.

français, e [frânse, -ez] *a* French ♦ *nm* (*LING*)

French ♦ *nm/f*: F~, e Frenchman/woman; **les F~** the French.

franc-comtois, e, *mpl* **francs-comtois** [fråṅkóṅtwá, -wáz] *a* of *ou* from (the) Franche-Comté.

France [fråṅs] *nf*: **la** ~ France; **en** ~ in France.

Francfort [fråṅkfor] *n* Frankfurt.

franche [fråṅsh] *af voir* **franc.**

franchement [fråṅshmáṅ] *ad* (*voir franc*) frankly; clearly; (*tout à fait*) downright ♦ *excl* well, really!

franchir [fråṅshēr] *vt* (*obstacle*) to clear, get over; (*seuil, ligne, rivière*) to cross; (*distance*) to cover.

franchisage [fråṅshēzázh] *nm* (*COMM*) franchising.

franchise [fråṅshēz] *nf* frankness; (*douanière, d'impôt*) exemption; (*ASSURANCES*) deductible (*US*), excess (*Brit*); (*COMM*) franchise; ~ **de bagages** baggage allowance.

franchissable [fråṅshēsábl(ə)] *a* (*obstacle*) surmountable.

franciscain, e [fråṅsēskaṅ, -en] *a* Franciscan.

franciser [fråṅsēzā] *vt* to gallicize, Frenchify.

franc-jeu [fråṅzhœ̄] *nm*: **jouer** ~ to play fair.

franc-maçon, *pl* **francs-maçons** [fråṅmásôṅ] *nm* Freemason.

franc-maçonnerie [fråṅmásonrē] *nf* Freemasonry.

franco [fråṅkō] *ad* (*COMM*): ~ **(de port)** postage paid.

franco... [fråṅkō] *préfixe* franco-.

franco-canadien [fråṅkokánádyaṅ] *nm* (*LING*) Canadian French.

francophile [fråṅkofēl] *a* francophile.

francophone [fråṅkofon] *a* French-speaking ♦ *nm/f* French speaker.

francophonie [fråṅkofonē] *nf* French-speaking communities *pl.*

franco-québécois [fråṅkokābākwá] *nm* (*LING*) Quebec French.

franc-parler [fråṅpárlā] *nm inv* outspokenness.

franc-tireur [fråṅtērœr] *nm* (*MIL*) irregular; (*fig*) freelance.

frange [fråṅzh] *nf* fringe; (*cheveux*) bangs (*US*), fringe (*Brit*).

frangipane [fråṅzhēpán] *nf* almond paste.

franglais [fråṅgle] *nm* Franglais.

franquette [fråṅkāt] *nf*: **à la bonne** ~ *ad* without any fuss.

frappant, e [frápáṅ, -áṅt] *a* striking.

frappe [fráp] *nf* (*d'une dactylo, pianiste, machine à écrire*) touch; (*BOXE*) punch; (*péj*) hood, thug.

frappé, e [frápā] *a* (*CULIN*) chilled; ~ **de panique** panic-stricken; ~ **de stupeur** thunderstruck, dumbfounded.

frapper [frápā] *vt* to hit, strike; (*étonner*) to strike; (*monnaie*) to strike, stamp; **se** ~ *vi* (*s'inquiéter*) to get worked up; ~ **à la porte** to knock at the door; ~ **dans ses mains** to clap one's hands; ~ **du poing sur** to bang one's fist on; ~ **un grand coup** (*fig*) to strike a blow.

frasques [frásk(ə)] *nfpl* escapades; **faire des** ~**s** to get up to mischief.

fraternel, le [fráternel] *a* brotherly, fraternal.

fraternellement [fráternelmáṅ] *ad* in a brotherly way.

fraterniser [fráternēzā] *vi* to fraternize.

fraternité [fráternētā] *nf* brotherhood.

fratricide [frátrēsēd] *a* fratricidal.

fraude [frōd] *nf* fraud; (*SCOL*) cheating; **passer qch en** ~ to smuggle sth in (*ou* out); ~ **fiscale** tax evasion.

frauder [frōdā] *vi, vt* to cheat; ~ **le fisc** to evade paying tax(es).

fraudeur, euse [frōdœr, -œz] *nm/f* person guilty of fraud; (*candidat*) examinee who cheats; (*au fisc*) tax evader.

frauduleux, euse [frōdülœ̄, -œz] *a* fraudulent.

frayer [frāyā] *vt* to open up, clear ♦ *vi* to spawn; (*fréquenter*): ~ **avec** to mix *ou* associate with; **se** ~ **un passage dans** to clear o.s. a path through, force one's way through.

frayeur [freyœr] *nf* fright.

fredaines [frədcn] *nfpl* mischief *sg*, escapades.

fredonner [frədonā] *vt* to hum.

freezer [frēzœr] *nm* freezer compartment.

frégate [frāgát] *nf* frigate.

frein [fraṅ] *nm* brake; **mettre un** ~ **à** (*fig*) to put a brake on, check; **sans** ~ (*sans limites*) unchecked; ~ **à main** handbrake; ~ **moteur** engine braking; ~**s à disques** disc brakes; ~**s à tambour** drum brakes.

freinage [frcnázh] *nm* braking; **distance de** ~ braking distance; **traces de** ~ tire (*US*) *ou* tyre (*Brit*) marks.

freiner [frānā] *vi* to brake ♦ *vt* (*progrès etc*) to check.

frelaté, e [frəlátā] *a* adulterated; (*fig*) tainted.

frêle [frel] *a* frail, fragile.

frelon [frəlôṅ] *nm* hornet.

freluquet [frəlüke] *nm* (*péj*) whippersnapper.

frémir [framer] *vi* (*de froid, de peur*) to tremble, shiver; (*de joie*) to quiver; (*eau*) to (begin to) bubble.

frémissement [frāmēsmáṅ] *nm* shiver; quiver; bubbling *q*.

frêne [fren] *nm* ash (tree).

frénésie [frānāzē] *nf* frenzy.

frénétique [frānātēk] *a* frenzied, frenetic.

fréquemment [frākámáṅ] *ad* frequently.

fréquence [frākáṅs] *nf* frequency.

fréquent, e [frākáṅ, -áṅt] *a* frequent.

fréquentable [frākáṅtábl(ə)] *a*: **il est peu** ~ he's not the type one can associate oneself with.

fréquentation [frākáṅtásyôṅ] *nf* frequenting; seeing; ~**s** *nfpl* company *sg*.

fréquenté, e [frākáṅtā] *a*: **très** ~ (very) busy; **mal** ~ patronized by disreputable elements.

fréquenter [frākáṅtā] *vt* (*lieu*) to frequent; (*personne*) to see; **se** ~ to see a lot of each other.

frère [frer] *nm* brother ♦ *a*: **partis/pays** ~**s** sister parties/countries.

fresque [fresk(ə)] *nf* (*ART*) fresco.

fret [fre] *nm* freight.

fréter [frātā] *vt* to charter.

frétiller [frātēyā] *vi* to wriggle; to quiver; ~ **de la queue** to wag its tail.

fretin [frətaṅ] *nm*: **le menu** ~ the small fry.

freux [frœ̄] *nm* (*ZOOL*) rook.

friable [frēyábl(ə)] *a* crumbly.

friand, e [frēyáṅ, -áṅd] *a*: ~ **de** very fond of ♦

nm (*CULIN*) small ground-meat (*US*) *ou* minced-meat (*Brit*) pie; (: *sucré*) small almond cake.

friandise [frĕyáńdēz] *nf* sweet.

fric [frĕk] *nm* (*fam*) cash, bread.

fricassée [frĕkásā] *nf* fricassee.

fric-frac [frĕkfrák] *nm* break-in.

friche [frēsh]: **en** ~ *a*, *ad* (lying) fallow.

friction [frĕksyóń] *nf* (*massage*) rub, rub-down; (*chez le coiffeur*) scalp massage; (*TECH*, *fig*) friction.

frictionner [frĕksyonā] *vt* to rub (down); to massage.

frigidaire [frēzhēder] *nm* ® refrigerator.

frigide [frēzhēd] *a* frigid.

frigidité [frēzhēdētā] *nf* frigidity.

frigo [frēgō] *nm* (= *frigidaire*) fridge.

frigorifier [frēgorēfyā] *vt* to refrigerate; (*fig: personne*) to freeze.

frigorifique [frēgorēfēk] *a* refrigerating.

frileusement [frēlœzmáń] *ad* with a shiver.

frileux, euse [frēlœ̄, -œ̄z] *a* sensitive to (the) cold; (*fig*) overcautious.

frimas [frēmá] *nmpl* wintry weather *sg*.

frime [frēm] *nf* (*fam*): **c'est de la** ~ it's all put on; **pour la** ~ just for show.

frimer [frēmá] *vi* to put on an act.

frimeur, euse [frēmœr, -œ̄z] *nm/f* poser.

frimousse [frēmoōs] *nf* (sweet) little face.

fringale [frańgál] *nf*: **avoir la** ~ to be ravenous.

fringant, e [frańgáń, -áńt] *a* dashing.

fringues [frańg] *nfpl* (*fam*) clothes, gear *q*.

fripé, e [frēpā] *a* crumpled.

friperie [frēprē] *nf* (*commerce*) secondhand clothes shop; (*vêtements*) secondhand clothes.

fripes [frēp] *nfpl* secondhand clothes.

fripier, ière [frēpyā, -yer] *nm/f* secondhand clothes dealer.

fripon, ne [frēpóń, -on] *a* roguish, mischievous ♦ *nm/f* rascal, rogue.

fripouille [frēpoōy] *nf* scoundrel.

frire [frēr] *vt* (*aussi*: **faire** ~), *vi* to fry.

frise [frēz] *nf* frieze.

frisé, e [frēzā] *a* curly, curly-haired ♦ *nf*: **(chicorée)** ~**e** curly endive.

friser [frēzā] *vt* to curl; (*fig: surface*) to skim, graze; (: *mort*) to come within a hair's breadth of; (: *hérésie*) to verge on ♦ *vi* (*cheveux*) to curl; (*personne*) to have curly hair; **se faire** ~ to have one's hair curled.

frisette [frēzet] *nf* little curl.

frisotter [frēzotā] *vi* (*cheveux*) to curl tightly.

frisquet [frēske] *am* chilly.

frisson [frēsóń], **frissonnement** [frēsonmáń] *nm* shudder, shiver; quiver.

frissonner [frēsonā] *vi* (*personne*) to shudder, shiver; (*feuilles*) to quiver.

frit, e [frē, frēt] *pp de* **frire** ♦ *a* fried ♦ *nf*: **(pommes)** ~**es** French fries, chips (*Brit*).

friterie [frētrē] *nf* ≈ hamburger stand (*US*), ≈ chip shop (*Brit*).

friteuse [frētœ̄z] *nf* deep (fat) fryer.

friture [frētür] *nf* (*huile*) (deep) fat; (*plat*): ~ **(de poissons)** fried fish; (*RADIO*) crackle, crackling *q*; ~**s** *nfpl* (*aliments frits*) fried food *sg*.

frivole [frēvol] *a* frivolous.

frivolité [frēvolētā] *nf* frivolity.

froc [frok] *nm* (*REL*) habit; (*fam: pantalon*) pants *pl* (*US*), trousers *pl* (*Brit*).

froid, e [frwá, frwád] *a* cold ♦ *nm* cold; (*absence de sympathie*) coolness *q*; **il fait** ~ it's cold; **avoir** ~ to be cold; **prendre** ~ to catch a chill *ou* cold; **à** ~ *ad* (*démarrer*) (from) cold; **(pendant) les grands** ~**s** (in) the depths of winter, (during) the cold season; **jeter un** ~ (*fig*) to cast a chill; **être en** ~ **avec** to be on bad terms with; **battre** ~ **à qn** to give sb the cold shoulder.

froidement [frwádmáń] *ad* (*accueillir*) coldly; (*décider*) coolly.

froideur [frwádœr] *nf* coolness *q*.

froisser [frwásā] *vt* to crumple (up), crease; (*fig*) to hurt, offend; **se** ~ *vi* to crumple, crease; to take offense (*US*) *ou* offence (*Brit*); **se** ~ **un muscle** to strain a muscle.

frôlement [frōlmáń] *nm* (*contact*) light touch.

frôler [frōlā] *vt* to brush against; (*suj: projectile*) to skim past; (*fig*) to come within a hair's breadth of, come very close to.

fromage [fromázh] *nm* cheese; ~ **blanc** soft white cheese; ~ **de tête** headcheese (*US*), pork brawn (*Brit*).

fromager, ère [fromázhā, -er] *nm/f* cheese merchant ♦ *a* (*industrie*) cheese *cpd*.

fromagerie [fromázhrē] *nf* cheese dairy.

froment [fromáń] *nm* wheat.

fronce [fróńs] *nf* (*de tissu*) gather.

froncement [fróńsmáń] *nm*: ~ **de sourcils** frown.

froncer [fróńsā] *vt* to gather; ~ **les sourcils** to frown.

frondaison [fróńdezóń] *nf* foliage.

fronde [fróńd] *nf* sling; (*fig*) rebellion, rebelliousness.

frondeur, euse [fróńdœr, -œ̄z] *a* rebellious.

front [fróń] *nm* forehead, brow; (*MIL*, *MÉTÉOROLOGIE*, *POL*) front; **avoir le** ~ **de faire** to have the effrontery *ou* front to do; **de** ~ *ad* (*se heurter*) head-on; (*rouler*) together (*i.e. 2 or 3 abreast*); (*simultanément*) at once; **faire** ~ **à** to face up to; ~ **de mer** (sea) front.

frontal, e, aux [fróńtál, -ō] *a* frontal.

frontalier, ière [fróńtályā, -yer] *a* border *cpd*, frontier *cpd* ♦ *nm/f*: **(travailleurs)** ~**s** workers who cross the border to go to work, commuters from across the border.

frontière [fróńtyer] *nf* (*GÉO*, *POL*) frontier, border; (*fig*) frontier, boundary.

frontispice [fróńtēspēs] *nm* frontispiece.

fronton [fróńtóń] *nm* pediment; (*de pelote basque*) (front) wall.

frottement [frotmáń] *nm* rubbing, scraping; ~**s** *nmpl* (*fig: difficultés*) friction *sg*.

frotter [frotā] *vi* to rub, scrape ♦ *vt* to rub; (*pour nettoyer*) to polish; (: *avec une brosse*) to scrub; ~ **une allumette** to strike a match; **se** ~ **à qn** to cross swords with sb; **se** ~ **à qch** to come up against sth; **se** ~ **les mains** (*fig*) to rub one's hands (gleefully).

frottis [frotē] *nm* (*MÉD*) smear.

frottoir [frotwár] *nm* (*d'allumettes*) friction strip; (*pour encaustiquer*) (long-handled) brush.

frou-frou, *pl* frous-frous [froōfroō] *nm* rustle.

frousse [froōs] *nf* (*fam: peur*): **avoir la** ~ to

be in a blue funk.

fructifier [früktĉfyā] *vi* to yield a profit; **faire** ~ to turn to good account.

fructueux, euse [früktüœ̄, -œ̄z] *a* fruitful; profitable.

frugal, e, aux [frügál, -ō] *a* frugal.

fruit [früē] *nm* fruit *gén q*; ~**s de mer** (*CULIN*) seafood(s); ~**s secs** dried fruit *sg*.

fruité, e [früĉtā] *a* (*vin*) fruity.

fruiterie [früĉtrē] *nf* (*boutique*) fruit (and vegetable) store (*US*), greengrocer's (*Brit*).

fruitier, ière [früĉtyā, -yer] *a*: **arbre** ~ fruit tree ♦ *nm/f* fruit merchant (*US*), fruiterer (*Brit*).

fruste [früst(ə)] *a* unpolished, uncultivated.

frustrant, e [früstrâñ, -âñt] *a* frustrating.

frustration [früstrâsyôñ] *nf* frustration.

frustré, e [früstrā] *a* frustrated.

frustrer [früstrā] *vt* to frustrate; (*priver*): ~ **qn de qch** to deprive sb of sth.

FS *abr* (= *franc suisse*) FS, SF.

FSE *sigle m* (= *foyer socio-éducatif*) community home.

FTP *sigle mpl* (= *Francs-tireurs et partisans*) *Communist Resistance in 1940-45.*

fuel(-oil) [fyōōl(oyl)] *nm* fuel oil; (*pour chauffer*) heating oil.

fugace [fügás] *a* fleeting.

fugitif, ive [füzhĉtĉf, -ēv] *a* (*lueur, amour*) fleeting; (*prisonnier etc*) runaway ♦ *nm/f* fugitive, runaway.

fugue [füg] *nf* (*d'un enfant*) running away *q*; (*MUS*) fugue; **faire une** ~ to run away, abscond.

fuir [tüēr] *vt* to flee from; (*éviter*) to shun ♦ *vi* to run away; (*gaz, robinet*) to leak.

fuite [tüĉt] *nf* flight; (*écoulement*) leak, leakage; (*divulgation*) leak; **être en** ~ to be on the run; **mettre en** ~ to put to flight; **prendre la** ~ to take flight.

fulgurant, e [fülgürâñ, -âñt] *a* lightning *cpd*, dazzling.

fulminant, e [fülmēnâñ, -âñt] *a* (*lettre, regard*) furious; ~ **de colère** raging with anger.

fulminer [fülmĉnā] *vi*: ~ (**contre**) to thunder forth (against).

fumant, e [fümâñ, -âñt] *a* smoking; (*liquide*) steaming; **un coup** ~ (*fam*) a master stroke.

fumé, e [fümā] *a* (*CULIN*) smoked; (*verre*) tinted ♦ *nf* smoke; **partir en** ~e to go up in smoke.

fume-cigarette [fümsēgáret] *nm inv* cigarette holder.

fumer [fümā] *vi* to smoke; (*liquide*) to steam ♦ *vt* to smoke; (*terre, champ*) to manure.

fumerie [fümrē] *nf*: ~ **d'opium** opium den.

fumerolles [fümrol] *nfpl* gas and smoke (*from volcano*).

fûmes [füm] *vb voir* **être**.

fumet [füme] *nm* aroma.

fumeur, euse [fümœr, -œ̄z] *nm/f* smoker; (**compartiment**) ~**s** smoking compartment.

fumeux, euse [fümœ̄, -œ̄z] *a* (*péj*) hazy.

fumier [fümyā] *nm* manure.

fumigation [fümēgásyôñ] *nf* fumigation.

fumigène [fümēzhen] *a* smoke *cpd*.

fumiste [fümēst(ə)] *nm* (*ramoneur*) chimney sweep ♦ *nm/f* (*péj: paresseux*) shirker;

(*charlatan*) phoney.

fumisterie [fümēstərē] *nf* (*péj*) fraud, con.

fumoir [fümwár] *nm* smoking room.

funambule [fünâñbül] *nm* tightrope walker.

funèbre [fünebr(ə)] *a* funeral *cpd*; (*fig*) doleful; funereal.

funérailles [fünārây] *nfpl* funeral *sg*.

funéraire [fünārer] *a* funeral *cpd*, funerary.

funeste [fünest(ə)] *a* disastrous; deathly.

funiculaire [fünĉküler] *nm* funicular (railway).

FUNU [fünü] *sigle f* (= *Force d'urgence des Nations Unies*) UNEF (= *United Nations Emergency Forces*).

fur [für]: **au** ~ **et à mesure** *ad* as one goes along; **au** ~ **et à mesure que** as; **au** ~ **et à mesure de leur progression** as they advance (*ou* advanced).

furax [füráks] *a inv* (*fam*) livid.

furent [für] *vb voir* **être**.

furet [füre] *nm* ferret.

fureter [fürtā] *vi* (*péj*) to nose about.

fureur [fürœr] *nf* fury; (*passion*): ~ **de** passion for; **faire** ~ to be all the rage.

furibard, c [fürĉbár, -ärd(ə)] *a* (*fam*) livid, absolutely furious.

furibond, e [fürēbôñ, -ôñd] *a* livid, absolutely furious.

furie [fürē] *nf* fury; (*femme*) shrew, vixen; **en** ~ (*mer*) raging.

furieusement [füryœzmâñ] *ad* furiously.

furieux, euse [füryœ̄, -œ̄z] *a* furious.

furoncle [fürôñkl(ə)] *nm* boil.

furtif, ive [fürtēf, -ev] *a* furtive.

fus [fü] *vb voir* **être**.

fusain [füzañ] *nm* (*BOT*) spindle-tree; (*ART*) charcoal.

fuseau, x [füzō] *nm* (*pantalon*) (ski-)pants *pl*; (*pour filer*) spindle; **en** ~ (*jambes*) tapering; (*colonne*) bulging; ~ **horaire** time zone.

fusée [füzā] *nf* rocket; ~ **éclairante** flare.

fuselage [füzlázh] *nm* fuselage.

fuselé, e [füzlā] *a* slender; (*galbé*) tapering.

fuser [füzā] *vi* (*rires etc*) to burst forth.

fusible [füzēbl(ə)] *nm* (*ÉLEC: fil*) fuse wire; (: *fiche*) fuse.

fusil [füzĉ] *nm* (*de guerre, à canon rayé*) rifle, gun; (*de chasse, à canon lisse*) shotgun, gun; ~ **à deux coups** double-barreled rifle *ou* shotgun; ~ **sous-marin** spear-gun.

fusilier [füzēlyā] *nm* (*MIL*) rifleman.

fusillade [füzēyád] *nf* gunfire *q*, shooting *q*; (*combat*) gun battle.

fusiller [füzēyā] *vt* to shoot; ~ **qn du regard** to look daggers at sb.

fusil-mitrailleur, *pl* **fusils-mitrailleurs** [füzēmētrâyœr] *nm* machine gun.

fusion [füzyôñ] *nf* fusion, melting; (*fig*) merging; (*COMM*) merger; **en** ~ (*métal, roches*) molten.

fusionnement [füzyonmâñ] *nm* merger.

fusionner [füzyonā] *vi* to merge.

fustiger [füstēzhā] *vt* to denounce.

fut [fü] *vb voir* **être**.

fût [fü] *vb voir* **être** ♦ *nm* (*tonneau*) barrel, cask; (*de canon*) stock; (*d'arbre*) bole, trunk; (*de colonne*) shaft.

futaie [fütε] *nf* forest, plantation.

futé, e [fütā] *a* crafty.

fûtes [fut] *vb voir* **être**.

futile |fütēl| *a* (*inutile*) futile; (*frivole*) frivolous.

futilité |fütēlētā| *nf* futility; frivolousness; (*chose futile*) futile pursuit (*ou* thing *etc*).

futur, e |fütür| *a, nm* future; **son ~ époux** her husband-to-be; **au ~** (*LING*) in the future.

futuriste |fütürēst(ə)| *a* futuristic.

fuyant, e |füēyâṅ, -âṅt| *vb voir* **fuir** ♦ *a* (*regard etc*) evasive; (*lignes etc*) receding; (*perspective*) vanishing.

fuyard, e |füēyàr, -àrd(ə)| *nm/f* runaway.

fuyons |füēyôṅ| *etc vb voir* **fuir**.

G

G, g |zhā| *nm inv* G, g ♦ *abr* (= *gramme*) g; (= *gauche*) L, l; **G comme Gaston** G for George.

gabardine |gàbárdēn| *nf* gabardine.

gabarit |gàbárē| *nm* (*fig: dimension, taille*) size; (*: valeur*) calibre; (*TECH*) template; **du même ~** (*fig*) of the same type, of that ilk.

gabegie |gàbzhē| *nf* (*péj*) chaos.

Gabon |gàbôṅ| *nm*: **le ~** Gabon.

gabonais, e |gàbonc, -ez| *a* Gabonese.

gâcher |gàshā| *vt* (*gâter*) to spoil, ruin; (*gaspiller*) to waste; (*plâtre*) to temper; (*mortier*) to mix.

gâchette |gàshet| *nf* trigger.

gâchis |gàshē| *nm* (*désordre*) mess; (*gaspillage*) waste *q*.

gadget |gàdzhet| *nm* thingumajig; (*nouveauté*) gimmick.

gadoue |gàdoō| *nf* sludge.

gaélique |gáàlēk| *a* Gaelic ♦ *nm* (*LING*) Gaelic.

gaffe |gàf| *nf* (*instrument*) boat hook; (*fam: erreur*) blunder; **faire ~** (*fam*) to watch out.

gaffer |gàfā| *vi* to blunder.

gaffeur, euse |gàfœr, -ēz| *nm/f* blunderer.

gag |gàg| *nm* gag.

gaga |gàgà| *a* (*fam*) gaga.

gage |gàzh| *nm* (*dans un jeu*) forfeit; (*fig: de fidélité*) token; **~s** *nmpl* (*salaire*) wages; (*garantie*) guarantee *sg*; **mettre en ~** to pawn; **laisser en ~** to leave as security.

gager |gàzhā| *vt*: **~ que** to bet *ou* wager that.

gageure |gàzhür| *nf*: **c'est une ~** it's attempting the impossible.

gagnant, e |gàṅyâṅ, -âṅt| *a*: **billet/numéro ~** winning ticket/number ♦ *ad*: **jouer ~** (*aux courses*) to be bound to win ♦ *nm/f* winner.

gagne-pain |gàṅypaṅ| *nm inv* job.

gagne-petit |gàṅypətē| *nm inv* low wage earner.

gagner |gàṅyā| *vt* (*concours, procès, pari*) to win; (*somme d'argent, revenu*) to earn; (*aller vers, atteindre*) to reach; (*s'emparer de*) to overcome; (*envahir*) to spread to; (*se concilier*): **~ qn** to win sb over ♦ *vi* to win; (*fig*) to gain; **~ du temps/de la place** to gain time/save space; **~ sa vie** to earn one's liv-

ing; **~ du terrain** (*aussi fig*) to gain ground; **~ qn de vitesse** (*aussi fig*) to outstrip sb; **~ à faire** (*s'en trouver bien*) to be better off doing; **il y gagne** it's in his interest, it's to his advantage.

gagneur |gàṅyœr| *nm* winner.

gai, e |gā| *a* cheerful; (*livre, pièce de théâtre*) light-hearted; (*un peu ivre*) tipsy.

gaieté |gātā| *nf* cheerfulness; **~s** *nfpl* (*souvent ironique*) delights; **de ~ de cœur** with a light heart.

gaillard, e |gàyàr, -àrd(ə)| *a* (*robuste*) sprightly; (*grivois*) bawdy, ribald ♦ *nm/f* (*strapping*) fellow/wench.

gaillardement |gàyàrdəmâṅ| *ad* cheerfully.

gain |gaṅ| *nm* (*revenu*) earnings *pl*; (*bénéfice: gén pl*) profits *pl*; (*au jeu: gén pl*) winnings *pl*; (*fig: de temps, place*) saving; (*: avantage*) benefit; (*: lucre*) gain; **avoir ~ de cause** to win the case; (*fig*) to be proved right; **obtenir ~ de cause** (*fig*) to win out.

gaine |gen| *nf* (*corset*) girdle; (*fourreau*) sheath; (*de fil électrique etc*) outer covering.

gaine-culotte, *pl* **gaines-culottes** |genkülot| *nf* panty girdle.

gainer |genā| *vt* to cover.

gala |gàlà| *nm* official reception; **soirée de ~** gala evening.

galant, e |gàlâṅ, -âṅt| *a* (*courtois*) courteous, gentlemanly; (*entreprenant*) flirtatious, gallant; (*aventure, poésie*) amorous; **en ~e compagnie** (*homme*) with a lady friend; (*femme*) with a gentleman friend.

Galapagos |gàlàpàgos| *nfpl*: **les (îles) ~** the Galapagos Islands.

galaxie |gàlàksē| *nf* galaxy.

galbe |gàlb(ə)| *nm* curve(s); shapeliness.

gale |gàl| *nf* (*MÉD*) scabies *sg*; (*de chien*) mange.

galéjade |gàlāzhàd| *nf* tall story.

galère |gàler| *nf* galley.

galérer |gàlārā| *vi* to work hard, slave (away).

galerie |gàlrē| *nf* gallery; (*THÉÂTRE*) circle; (*de voiture*) roof rack; (*fig: spectateurs*) audience; **~ marchande** shopping mall; **~ de peinture** (*private*) art gallery.

galérien |gàlāryaṅ| *nm* galley slave.

galet |gàle| *nm* pebble; (*TECH*) wheel; **~s** *nmpl* pebbles, shingle *sg*.

galette |gàlet| *nf* (*gâteau*) flat pastry cake; (*crêpe*) savory (*US*) *ou* savoury (*Brit*) pancake; **la ~ des Rois** cake traditionally eaten on Twelfth Night.

galeux, euse |gàlœ, -ēz| *a*: **un chien ~** a mangy dog.

Galice |gàlēs| *nf*: **la ~** Galicia (*in Spain*).

Galicie |gàlēsē| *nf*: **la ~** Galicia (*in Central Europe*).

galiléen, ne |gàlēlāàṅ, -en| *a* Galilean.

galimatias |gàlēmàtyà| *nm* (*péj*) gibberish.

galipette |gàlēpet| *nf*: **faire des ~s** to turn somersaults.

Galles |gàl| *nfpl*: **le pays de ~** Wales.

gallicisme |gàlēsēsm(ə)| *nm* French idiom; (*tournure fautive*) gallicism.

gallois, e |gàlwà, -wàz| *a* Welsh ♦ *nm* (*LING*) Welsh ♦ *nm/f*: **G~, e** Welshman/woman.

galoche |gàlosh| *nf* clog.

galon [gàlôṅ] *nm* (*MIL*) stripe; (*décoratif*) piece of braid; **prendre du ~** to be promoted.
galop [gàlō] *nm* gallop; **au ~** at a gallop; **~ d'essai** (*fig*) trial run.
galopade [gàlopàd] *nf* stampede.
galopant, e [gàlopàṅ, -àṅt] *a*: **inflation ~e** galloping inflation; **démographie ~e** exploding population.
galoper [gàlopā] *vi* to gallop.
galopin [gàlopaṅ] *nm* urchin, ragamuffin.
galvaniser [gàlvánēzā] *vt* to galvanize.
galvauder [gàlvōdā] *vt* to debase.
gambade [gàṅbàd] *nf*: **faire des ~s** to skip *ou* frisk around.
gambader [gàṅbàdā] *vi* to skip *ou* frisk around.
gamberger [gàṅberzhā] (*fam*) *vi* to (have a) think ♦ *vt* to dream up.
Gambie [gàṅbē] *nf*: **la ~** (*pays*) Gambia; (*fleuve*) the Gambia.
gamelle [gàmel] *nf* mess tin; billy can; (*fam*): **ramasser une ~** to fall flat on one's face.
gamin, e [gàmaṅ, -ēn] *nm/f* kid ♦ *a* mischievous, playful.
gaminerie [gàmēnrē] *nf* mischievousness, playfulness.
gamme [gàm] *nf* (*MUS*) scale; (*fig*) range.
gammé, e [gàmā] *a*: **croix ~e** swastika.
Gand [gàṅ] *n* Ghent.
gang [gàṅg] *nm* gang.
Gange [gàṅzh] *nm*: **le ~** the Ganges.
ganglion [gàṅglēyôṅ] *nm* ganglion; (*lymphatique*) gland; **avoir des ~s** to have swollen glands.
gangrène [gàṅgren] *nf* gangrene; (*fig*) corruption; corrupting influence.
gangster [gàṅgster] *nm* gangster.
gangue [gàṅg] *nf* coating.
ganse [gàṅs] *nf* braid.
gant [gàṅ] *nm* glove; **prendre des ~s** (*fig*) to handle the situation with kid gloves; **relever le ~** (*fig*) to take up the gauntlet; **~ de crin** massage glove; **~ de toilette** face cloth; **~s de boxe** boxing gloves; **~ de caoutchouc** rubber gloves.
ganté, e [gàṅtā] *a*: **~ de blanc** wearing white gloves.
ganterie [gàṅtrē] *nf* glove trade; (*magasin*) glove shop.
garage [gàràzh] *nm* garage; **~ à vélos** bicycle shed.
garagiste [gàràzhēst(ə)] *nm/f* (*propriétaire*) garage owner; (*mécanicien*) garage mechanic.
garant, e [gàràṅ, -àṅt] *nm/f* guarantor ♦ *nm* guarantee; **se porter ~ de** to vouch for; to be answerable for.
garantie [gàràṅtē] *nf* guarantee, warranty; (*gage*) security, surety; (**bon de**) **~** guarantee *ou* warranty slip; **~ de bonne exécution** performance bond.
garantir [gàràṅtēr] *vt* to guarantee; (*protéger*): **~ de** to protect from; **je vous garantis que** I can assure you that; **garanti pure laine/2 ans** guaranteed pure wool/for 2 years.
garce [gàrs(ə)] *nf* (*péj*) bitch.
garçon [gàrsôṅ] *nm* boy; (*célibataire*) bachelor; (*jeune homme*) boy, lad; (*aussi*: **~ de café**) waiter; **~ boucher/coiffeur** butcher's/hairdresser's assistant; **~ de courses** messenger; **~ d'écurie** stableboy; **~ manqué** tomboy.
garçonnet [gàrsone] *nm* small boy.
garçonnière [gàrsonyer] *nf* bachelor apartment.
garde [gàrd(ə)] *nm* (*de prisonnier*) guard; (*de domaine etc*) warden; (*soldat, sentinelle*) guardsman ♦ *nf* guarding; looking after; (*soldats, BOXE, ESCRIME*) guard; (*faction*) watch; (*d'une arme*) hilt; (*TYPO: aussi*: **page** *ou* **feuille de ~**) flyleaf; (: *collée*) endpaper; **de ~** *a, ad* on duty; **monter la ~** to stand guard; **être sur ses ~s** to be on one's guard; **mettre en ~** to warn; **mise en ~** warning; **prendre ~ (à)** to be careful (of); **avoir la ~ des enfants** (*après divorce*) to have custody of the children; **~ champêtre** *nm* rural policeman; **~ du corps** *nm* bodyguard; **~ d'enfants** *nf* child tender (*US*) *ou* minder (*Brit*); **~ forestier** *nm* forest ranger (*US*) *ou* warden (*Brit*); **~ mobile** *nm, nf* mobile guard; **~ des Sceaux** *nm* ≈ Attorney General (*US*), ≈ Lord Chancellor (*Brit*); **~ à vue** *nf* (*JUR*) ≈ police custody.
garde-à-vous [gàrdàvōō] *nm inv*: **être/se mettre au ~** to be at/stand to attention; **~ (fixe)!** (*MIL*) attention!
garde-barrière, *pl* **gardes-barrière(s)** [gàrdəbáryer] *nm/f* gatekeeper (*at a grade crossing*) (*US*), level-crossing keeper (*Brit*).
garde-boue [gàrdəbōō] *nm inv* mudguard, fender (*US*).
garde-chasse, *pl* **gardes-chasse(s)** [gàrdəshás] *nm* gamekeeper.
garde-côte [gàrdəkōt] *nm* (*vaisseau*) coastguard boat.
garde-feu [gàrdəfœ] *nm inv* fire screen, fireguard.
garde-fou [gàrdəfōō] *nm* railing, parapet.
garde-malade, *pl* **gardes-malade(s)** [gàrdəmàlàd] *nf* home nurse.
garde-manger [gàrdmàṅzhā] *nm inv* (*boîte*) cooler (*US*), meat safe (*Brit*); (*placard*) pantry, larder.
garde-meuble [gàrdəmœbl(ə)] *nm* furniture storehouse.
garde-pêche [gàrdəpesh] *nm inv* (*personne*) fish warden (*US*), water bailiff (*Brit*); (*navire*) fisheries protection ship.
garder [gàrdā] *vt* (*conserver*) to keep; (: *sur soi: vêtement, chapeau*) to keep on; (*surveiller: enfants*) to look after; (: *immeuble, lieu, prisonnier*) to guard; **se ~** *vi* (*aliment: se conserver*) to keep; **se ~ de faire** to be careful not to do; **~ le lit/la chambre** to stay in bed/indoors; **~ le silence** to keep silent *ou* quiet; **~ la ligne** to keep one's figure; **~ à vue** to keep in custody; **pêche/chasse gardée** private fishing/hunting (ground).
garderie [gàrdərē] *nf* day-care center (*US*), day nursery (*Brit*).
garde-robe [gàrdərob] *nf* wardrobe.
gardeur, euse [gàrdœr, -œz] *nm/f* (*de vaches*) cowherd; (*de chèvres*) goatherd.
gardian [gàrdyàṅ] *nm* cowboy (*in the Camargue*).
gardien, ne [gàrdyaṅ, -en] *nm/f* (*garde*) guard;

(*de prison*) guard, warder (*Brit*); (*de domaine, réserve*) warden; (*de musée etc*) attendant; (*de phare, cimetière*) keeper; (*d'immeuble*) caretaker; (*fig*) guardian; ~ **de but** goalkeeper; ~ **de nuit** night watchman; ~ **de la paix** policeman.

gare [gár] *nf* (railway) station, train station (*US*) ◊ *excl*: ~ **à** ... watch out for ...!; ~ **à ne pas** ... make sure you don't ...; ~ **à toi!** watch out!; **sans crier** ~ without warning; ~ **maritime** harbor (*US*) *ou* harbour (*Brit*) station; ~ **routière** bus station; (*camions*) trucking (*US*) *ou* haulage (*Brit*) depot; ~ **de triage** marshal(l)ing yard.

garenne [gáren] *nf voir* **lapin**.

garer [gárá] *vt* to park; **se** ~ to park; (*pour laisser passer*) to pull over.

gargantuesque [gárgántüesk(ə)] *a* gargantuan.

gargariser [gárgárēzá]: **se** ~ *vi* to gargle; **se** ~ **de** (*fig*) to revel in.

gargarisme [gárgárēsm(ə)] *nm* gargling *q*; (*produit*) gargle.

gargote [gárgot] *nf* cheap restaurant, greasy spoon (*fam*).

gargouille [gárgōōy] *nf* gargoyle.

gargouiller [gárgōōyá] *vi* (*estomac*) to rumble; (*eau*) to gurgle.

garnement [gárnəmáñ] *nm* rascal, scallywag.

garni, e [gárnē] *a* (*plat*) served with vegetables (*and French fries or pasta or rice*) ◊ *nm* (*appartement*) furnished accommodations *pl* (*US*) *ou* accommodation *q* (*Brit*).

garnir [gárnēr] *vt* to decorate; (*remplir*) to fill; (*recouvrir*) to cover; **se** ~ *vi* (*pièce, salle*) to fill up; ~ **qch de** (*orner*) to decorate sth with; to trim sth with; (*approvisionner*) to fill *ou* stock sth with; (*protéger*) to fit sth with; (*CULIN*) to garnish sth with.

garnison [gárnēzóñ] *nf* garrison.

garniture [gárnētür] *nf* (*CULIN*: *légumes*) vegetables *pl*; (*: persil etc*) garnish; (*: farce*) filling; (*décoration*) trimming; (*protection*) fittings *pl*; ~ **de cheminée** mantelpiece ornaments *pl*; ~ **de frein** (*AUTO*) brake lining; ~ **intérieure** (*AUTO*) interior trim; ~ **périodique** sanitary napkin (*US*) *ou* towel (*Brit*).

garrigue [gárēg] *nf* scrubland.

garrot [gárō] *nm* (*MÉD*) tourniquet; (*torture*) garrotte.

garrotter [gárotá] *vt* to tie up; (*fig*) to muzzle.

gars [gá] *nm* lad; (*type*) guy.

Gascogne [gáskony] *nf*: **la** ~ Gascony.

gascon, ne [gáskóñ, -on] *a* Gascon ◊ *nm*: **G~** (*hâbleur*) braggart.

gas-oil [gázoyl] *nm* diesel oil.

gaspillage [gáspēyázh] *nm* waste.

gaspiller [gáspēyá] *vt* to waste.

gaspilleur, euse [gáspēyœr, -œz] *a* wasteful.

gastrique [gástrēk] *a* gastric, stomach *cpd*.

gastro-entérite [gástroáñtárēt] *nf* (*MÉD*) gastro-enteritis.

gastronome [gástronom] *nm/f* gourmet.

gastronomie [gástronomē] *nf* gastronomy.

gastronomique [gástronomēk] *a*: **menu** ~ gourmet menu.

gâteau, x [gátō] *nm* cake ◊ *a inv* (*fam*: *trop indulgent*): **papa-/maman-~** doting father/

mother; ~ **d'anniversaire** birthday cake; ~ **de riz** ≈ rice pudding; ~ **sec** cookie (*US*), biscuit (*Brit*).

gâter [gátá] *vt* to spoil; **se** ~ *vi* (*dent, fruit*) to go bad; (*temps, situation*) to change for the worse.

gâterie [gátrē] *nf* little treat.

gâteux, euse [gátœ, -œz] *a* senile.

gâtisme [gátēsm(ə)] *nm* senility.

GATT [gát] *sigle m* (= *General Agreement on Tariffs and Trade*) GATT.

gauche [gōsh] *a* left, left-hand; (*maladroit*) awkward, clumsy ◊ *nf* (*POL*) left (wing); (*BOXE*) left; **à** ~ on the left; (*direction*) (to the) left; **à** ~ **de** (on *ou* to the) left of; **à la** ~ **de** to the left of; **de** ~ (*POL*) left-wing.

gauchement [gōshmáñ] *ad* awkwardly, clumsily.

gaucher, ère [gōshá, -er] *a* left-handed.

gaucherie [gōshrē] *nf* awkwardness, clumsiness.

gauchir [gōshēr] *vt* (*planche, objet*) to warp; (*fig*: *fait, idée*) to distort.

gauchisant, e [gōshēzáñ, -áñt] *a* with left-wing tendencies.

gauchisme [gōshēsm(ə)] *nm* leftism.

gauchiste [gōshēst(ə)] *a, nm/f* leftist.

gaufre [gōfr(ə)] *nf* (*pâtisserie*) waffle; (*de cire*) honeycomb.

gaufrer [gōfrá] *vt* (*papier*) to emboss; (*tissu*) to goffer.

gaufrette [gōfret] *nf* wafer.

gaufrier [gōfrēyá] *nm* (*moule*) waffle iron.

Gaule [gōl] *nf*: **la** ~ Gaul.

gaule [gōl] *nf* (*perche*) (long) pole; (*canne à pêche*) fishing rod.

gaulliste [gōlēst(ə)] *a, nm/f* Gaullist.

gaulois, e [gōlwá, -wáz] *a* Gallic; (*grivois*) bawdy ◊ *nm/f*: **G~, e** Gaul.

gauloiserie [gōlwázrē] *nf* bawdiness.

gausser [gōsá]: **se** ~ **de** *vt* to deride.

gaver [gává] *vt* to force-feed; (*fig*): ~ **de** to cram with, fill up with; (*personne*): **se** ~ **de** to stuff o.s. with.

gaz [gáz] *nm inv* gas; **mettre les** ~ (*AUTO*) to step on the gas (*US*), put one's foot down (*Brit*); **chambre/masque à** ~ gas chamber/mask; ~ **en bouteilles** bottled gas; ~ **butane** butane; ~ **carbonique** carbon dioxide; ~ **hilarant** laughing gas; ~ **lacrymogène** tear gas; ~ **naturel** natural gas; ~ **de ville** manufactured domestic gas.

gaze [gáz] *nf* gauze.

gazéifié, e [gázáēfyá] *a* carbonated, aerated.

gazelle [gázel] *nf* gazelle.

gazer [gázá] *vt* to gas ◊ *vi* (*fam*) to be going *ou* working well.

gazette [gázet] *nf* newsletter.

gazeux, euse [gázœ, -œz] *a* gaseous; (*eau*) sparkling; (*boisson*) fizzy.

gazoduc [gázodük] *nm* gas pipeline.

gazole [gázol] *nm* = **gas-oil**.

gazomètre [gázometr(ə)] *nm* gasometer.

gazon [gázóñ] *nm* (*herbe*) turf, grass; (*pelouse*) lawn.

gazonner [gázoná] *vt* (*terrain*) to grass over.

gazouiller [gázōōyá] *vi* (*oiseau*) to chirp; (*enfant*) to babble.

gazouillis [gázōōyē] *nmpl* chirp *sg*.

GB *sigle f* (= *Grande Bretagne*) GB.
gd *abr* (= *grand*) L.
GDF *sigle m* (= *Gaz de France*) *national gas company.*
geai [zhε] *nm* jay.
géant, e [zhāāṅ, -āṅt] *a* gigantic, giant; (*COMM*) giant-size ♦ *nm/f* giant.
geignement [zhεnymāṅ] *nm* groaning, moaning.
geindre [zhaṅdr(ə)] *vi* to groan, moan.
gel [zhεl] *nm* frost; (*de l'eau*) freezing; (*fig: des salaires, prix*) freeze; freezing; (*produit de beauté*) gel.
gélatine [zhālātēn] *nf* gelatine.
gélatineux, euse [zhālátēnœ̄, -ø̄z] *a* jelly-like, gelatinous.
gelé, e [zhəlā] *a* frozen ♦ *nf* jelly; (*gel*) frost; ~ **blanche** hoarfrost, white frost.
geler [zhəlā] *vt, vi* to freeze; **il gèle** it's freezing.
gélule [zhālül] *nf* capsule.
gelures [zhəlür] *nfpl* frostbite *sg.*
Gémeaux [zhāmō] *nmpl:* **les** ~ Gemini, the Twins; **être des** ~ to be Gemini.
gémir [zhāmēr] *vi* to groan, moan.
gémissement [zhāmēsmāṅ] *nm* groan, moan.
gemme [zhεm] *nf* gem(stone).
gémonies [zhāmonē] *nfpl:* **vouer qn aux** ~ to subject sb to public scorn.
gênant, e [zhenāṅ, -āṅt] *a* (*objet*) awkward, in the way; (*histoire, personne*) embarrassing.
gencive [zháṅsēv] *nf* gum.
gendarme [zhaṅdárm(ə)] *nm* gendarme.
gendarmer [zháṅdármā]: **se** ~ *vi* to kick up a fuss.
gendarmerie [zháṅdármərē] *nf military police force in countryside and small towns; their police station or barracks.*
gendre [zháṅdr(ə)] *nm* son-in-law.
gène [zhεn] *nm* (*BIO*) gene.
gêne [zhεn] *nf* (*à respirer, bouger*) discomfort, difficulty; (*dérangement*) bother, trouble; (*manque d'argent*) financial difficulties *pl ou* straits *pl;* (*confusion*) embarrassment; **sans** ~ *a* inconsiderate.
gêné, e [zhānā] *a* embarrassed; (*dépourvu d'argent*) short (of money).
généalogie [zhānāàlozhē] *nf* genealogy.
généalogique [zhānāàlozhēk] *a* genealogical.
gêner [zhānā] *vt* (*incommoder*) to bother; (*encombrer*) to hamper; (*bloquer le passage*) to be in the way of; (*déranger*) to bother; (*embarrasser*): ~ **qn** to make sb feel ill-at-ease; **se** ~ to put o.s. out; **ne vous gênez pas!** (*ironique*) go right ahead!, don't mind me!; **je vais me** ~! (*ironique*) why should I care?
général, e, aux [zhānārál, -ō] *a, nm* general ♦ *nf:* (*répétition*) ~**e** final dress rehearsal; **en** ~ usually, in general; **à la satisfaction** ~**e** to everyone's satisfaction.
généralement [zhānārálmāṅ] *ad* generally.
généralisable [zhānārálēzábl(ə)] *a* generally applicable.
généralisation [zhānārálēzásyóṅ] *nf* generalization.
généraliser [zhānārálēzā] *vt, vi* to generalize; **se** ~ *vi* to become widespread.
généraliste [zhānārálēst(ə)] *nm/f* (*MÉD*) gen-

eral practitioner, GP.
généralité [zhānārálētā] *nf:* **la** ~ **des** ... the majority of ...; ~**s** *nfpl* generalities; (*introduction*) general points.
générateur, trice [zhānārátœr, -trēs] *a:* ~ **de** which causes *ou* brings about ♦ *nf* (*ÉLEC*) generator.
génération [zhānārāsyóṅ] *nf* (*aussi INFORM*) generation.
généreusement [zhānārœ̄zmāṅ] *ad* generously.
généreux, euse [zhānārœ̄, -œ̄z] *a* generous.
générique [zhānārēk] *a* generic ♦ *nm* (*CINÉMA, TV*) credits *pl*, credit titles *pl.*
générosité [zhānārōzētā] *nf* generosity.
Gênes [zhεn] *n* Genoa.
genèse [zhənεz] *nf* genesis.
genêt [zhənε] *nm* (*BOT*) broom *q.*
généticien, ne [zhānātēsyaṅ, -εn] *nm/f* geneticist.
génétique [zhānātēk] *a* genetic ♦ *nf* genetics *sg.*
gêneur, euse [zhεnœr, -œ̄z] *nm/f* (*personne qui gêne*) obstacle; (*importun*) intruder.
Genève [zhənεv] Geneva.
genevois, e [zhənəvwà, -wàz] *a* Genevan.
genévrier [zhānāvrēyá] *nm* juniper.
génial, e, aux [zhānyál, -ō] *a* of genius; (*fam*) fantastic, brilliant.
génie [zhānē] *nm* genius; (*MIL*): **le** ~ ≈ the Corps of Engineers; **avoir du** ~ to have genius; ~ **civil** civil engineering.
genievre [zhənyevr(ə)] *nm* (*BOT*) juniper (tree); (*boisson*) ≈ gin; **grain de** ~ juniper berry.
génisse [zhānēs] *nf* heifer; **foie de** ~ ox liver.
génital, e, aux [zhānētál, -ō] *a* genital.
génitif [zhānētēf] *nm* genitive.
génocide [zhānōsēd] *nm* genocide.
génois, e [zhānwà, -wàz] *a* Genoese ♦ *nf* (*gâteau*) ≈ sponge cake.
genou, x [zhnōō] *nm* knee; **à** ~**x** on one's knees; **se mettre à** ~**x** to kneel down.
genouillère [zhənōōyεr] *nf* (*SPORT*) kneepad.
genre [zháṅr] *nm* (*espèce, sorte*) kind, type, sort; (*allure*) manner; (*LING*) gender; (*ART*) genre; (*ZOOL etc*) genus; **se donner du** ~ to put on airs; **avoir bon** ~ to have style; **avoir mauvais** ~ to be ill-mannered.
gens [zháṅ] *nmpl (f in some phrases)* people *pl;* **les** ~ **d'Église** the clergy; **les** ~ **du monde** society people; ~ **de maison** domestics.
gentiane [zháṅsyán] *nf* gentian.
gentil, le [zháṅtē, -ēy] *a* kind; (*enfant: sage*) good; (*sympa: endroit etc*) nice; **c'est très** ~ **à vous** it's very kind *ou* good *ou* nice of you.
gentilhommière [zháṅtēyomyεr] *nf* (*small*) manor house.
gentillesse [zháṅtēyεs] *nf* kindness.
gentillet, te [zháṅtēye, -εt] *a* a nice little.
gentiment [zháṅtēmāṅ] *ad* kindly.
génuflection [zhānüfleksyóṅ] *nf* genuflexion.
géodésique [zhāodāzēk] *a* geodesic.
géographe [zhāográf] *nm/f* geographer.
géographie [zhāográfē] *nf* geography.
géographique [zhāográfēk] *a* geographical.
geôlier [zhōlyā] *nm* jailer.
géologie [zhāolozhē] *nf* geology.

géologique [zhāolozhēk] *a* geological.

géologue [zhāolog] *nm/f* geologist.

géomètre [zhāometr(ə)] *nm/f*: **(arpenteur-)**~ (land) surveyor.

géométrie [zhāomātrē] *nf* geometry; **à** ~ **variable** (*AVIAT*) variable geometry (*US*), swing-wing (*Brit*).

géométrique [zhāomātrēk] *a* geometric.

géophysique [zhāofēzēk] *nf* geophysics *sg*.

géopolitique [zhāopolētēk] *nf* geopolitics *sg*.

Géorgie [gāorzhē] *nf*: **la** ~ (*URSS, USA*) Georgia; **la** ~ **du Sud** South Georgia.

géorgien, ne [gāorzhyań, -en] *a* Georgian.

géothermique [zhāotermēk] *a*: **énergie** ~ geothermal energy.

gérance [zhārâńs] *nf* management; **mettre en** ~ to appoint a manager for; **prendre en** ~ to take over (the management of).

géranium [zhārányom] *nm* geranium.

gérant, e [zhārâń, -âńt] *nm/f* manager/ manageress; ~ **d'immeuble** managing agent.

gerbe [zherb(ə)] *nf* (*de fleurs, d'eau*) spray; (*de blé*) sheaf (*pl* sheaves); (*fig*) shower, burst.

gercé, e [zhersā] *a* chapped.

gercer [zhersā] *vi*, **se** ~ *vi* to chap.

gerçure [zhersür] *nf* crack.

gérer [zhārā] *vt* to manage.

gériatrie [zhāryātrē] *nf* geriatrics *sg*.

gériatrique [zhāryātrēk] *a* geriatric.

germain, e [zhermań, -en] *a*: **cousin** ~ first cousin.

germanique [zhermánēk] *a* Germanic.

germaniste [zhermánēst(ə)] *nm/f* German scholar.

germe [zherm(ə)] *nm* germ.

germer [zhermā] *vi* to sprout; (*semence, aussi fig*) to germinate.

gérondif [zhārôńdēf] *nm* gerund; (*en latin*) gerundive.

gérontologie [zherôńtolozhē] *nf* gerontology.

gésier [zhāzyā] *nm* gizzard.

gésir [zhāzēr] *vi* to be lying (down); *voir aussi* **ci-gît**.

gestation [zhestâsyôń] *nf* gestation.

geste [zhest(ə)] *nm* gesture; move; motion; **il fit un** ~ **de la main pour m'appeler** he signed to me to come over, he waved me over; **ne faites pas un** ~ (*ne bouger pas*) don't move.

gesticuler [zhestēkülā] *vi* to gesticulate.

gestion [zhestyôń] *nf* management; ~ **des disques** (*INFORM*) housekeeping; ~ **de fichier(s)** (*INFORM*) file management.

gestionnaire [zhestyoner] *nm/f* administrator; ~ **de fichier** (*INFORM*) file manager.

geyser [zhezer] *nm* geyser.

Ghana [gánà] *nm*: **le** ~ Ghana.

ghanéen, ne [gánàeń, -en] *a* Ghanaian.

ghetto [getō] *nm* ghetto.

gibecière [zhēbsyer] *nf* (*de chasseur*) gamebag; (*sac en bandoulière*) shoulder bag.

gibet [zhēbe] *nm* gallows *pl*.

gibier [zhēbyā] *nm* (*animaux*) game; (*fig*) prey.

giboulée [zhēbōōlā] *nf* sudden shower.

giboyeux, euse [zhēbwáyœ̄, -ēz] *a* well-stocked with game.

Gibraltar [zhēbráltár] *nm* Gibraltar.

gibus [zhēbüs] *nm* opera hat.

giclée [zhēklā] *nf* spurt, squirt.

gicler [zhēklā] *vi* to spurt, squirt.

gicleur [zhēklœr] *nm* (*AUTO*) spray nozzle.

GIE *sigle m* = **groupement d'intérêt économique**.

gifle [zhēfl(ə)] *nf* slap (in the face).

gifler [zhēflā] *vt* to slap (in the face).

gigantesque [zhēgâńtesk(ə)] *a* gigantic.

GIGN *sigle m* (= *Groupe d'intervention de la gendarmerie nationale*) special crack force of the gendarmerie.

gigogne [zhēgony] *a*: **lits** ~**s** trundle (*US*) *ou* truckle (*Brit*) beds; **tables/poupées** ~**s** nest of tables/dolls.

gigot [zhēgō] *nm* leg (of mutton *ou* lamb).

gigoter [zhēgotā] *vi* to wriggle (about).

gilet [zhēle] *nm* vest (*US*), waistcoat (*Brit*); (*pull*) cardigan; (*de corps*) undershirt (*US*), vest (*Brit*); ~ **pare-balles** bulletproof vest (*US*) *ou* jacket (*Brit*); ~ **de sauvetage** life jacket.

gin [dzhēn] *nm* gin.

gingembre [zhańzhâńbr(ə)] *nm* ginger.

girafe [zhēráf] *nf* giraffe.

giratoire [zhērátwár] *a*: **sens** ~ traffic circle (*US*), roundabout (*Brit*).

girofle [zhērofl(ə)] *nm*: **clou de** ~ clove.

giroflée [zhēroflā] *nf* wallflower.

girolle [zhērol] *nf* chanterelle.

giron [zhērôń] *nm* (*genoux*) lap; (*fig: sein*) bosom.

Gironde [zhērôńd] *nf*: **la** ~ the Gironde.

girophare [zhērofár] *nm* revolving (flashing) light.

girouette [zhērwet] *nf* weather vane *ou* cock.

gis [zhē], **gisais** [zhēze] *etc vb voir* **gésir**.

gisement [zhēzmâń] *nm* deposit.

gît [zhē] *vb voir* **gésir**.

gitan, e [zhētâń, -án] *nm/f* gipsy.

gîte [zhēt] *nm* home; shelter; (*du lièvre*) form; ~ (**rural**) (country) vacation cottage *ou* apartment.

gîter [zhētā] *vi* (*NAVIG*) to list.

givrage [zhēvrázh] *nm* icing.

givrant, e [zhēvrâń, -âńt] *a*: **brouillard** ~ freezing fog.

givre [zhēvr(ə)] *nm* (hoar) frost.

givré, e [zhēvrā] *a*: **citron** ~/**orange** ~**e** lemon/orange sorbet (*served in fruit skin*).

glabre [glâbr(ə)] *a* hairless; (*menton*) clean-shaven.

glace [glàs] *nf* ice; (*crème glacée*) ice cream; (*verre*) sheet of glass; (*miroir*) mirror; (*de voiture*) window; ~**s** *nfpl* (*GÉO*) ice sheets, ice *sg*; **de** ~ (*fig: accueil, visage*) frosty, icy; **rester de** ~ to remain unmoved.

glacé, e [glásā] *a* icy; (*boisson*) iced.

glacer [glásā] *vt* to freeze; (*boisson*) to chill, ice; (*gâteau*) to ice, frost (*US*); (*papier, tissu*) to glaze; (*fig*): ~ **qn** to chill sb; (*fig*) to make sb's blood run cold.

glaciaire [glásyer] *a* (*période*) ice *cpd*; (*relief*) glacial.

glacial, e [glásyàl] *a* icy.

glacier [glásyā] *nm* (*GÉO*) glacier; (*marchand*) ice-cream maker.

glacière [glásyer] *nf* icebox.

glaçon [glásôń] *nm* icicle; (*pour boisson*) ice

cube.

gladiateur [glådyåtœr] *nm* gladiator.

glaïeul [glåyœl] *nm* gladiola.

glaire [gler] *nf* (*MÉD*) phlegm *q*.

glaise [glez] *nf* clay.

glaive [glev] *nm* two-edged sword.

gland [glåṅ] *nm* (*de chêne*) acorn; (*décoration*) tassel; (*ANAT*) glans.

glande [glåṅd] *nf* gland.

glaner [glånå] *vt*, *vi* to glean.

glapir [glåpēr] *vi* to yelp.

glas [glå] *nm* knell, toll.

glauque [glōk] *a* dull blue-green.

glissade [glēsåd] *nf* (*par jeu*) slide; (*chute*) slip; (*dérapage*) skid; **faire des ~s** to slide.

glissant, e [glēsåṅ, -åṅt] *a* slippery.

glissement [glēsmåṅ] *nm* sliding; (*fig*) shift; **~ de terrain** landslide.

glisser [glēså] *vi* (*avancer*) to glide *ou* slide along; (*coulisser, tomber*) to slide; (*déraper*) to slip; (*être glissant*) to be slippery ♦ *vt*: **~ qch sous/dans/à** to slip sth under/into/to; **~ sur** (*fig: détail etc*) to skate over; **se ~ dans/entre** to slip into/between.

glissière [glēsyer] *nf* slide channel; **à ~** (*porte, fenêtre*) sliding; **~ de sécurité** (*AUTO*) crash barrier.

glissoire [glēswår] *nf* slide.

global, e, aux [globål, -ō] *a* overall.

globalement [globålmåṅ] *ad* taken as a whole.

globe [glob] *nm* globe; **sous ~** under glass; **~ oculaire** eyeball; **le ~ terrestre** the globe.

globule [globül] *nm* (*du sang*): **~ blanc/rouge** white/red corpuscle.

globuleux, euse [globülœ, -œz] *a*: **yeux ~** protruding eyes.

gloire [glwår] *nf* glory; (*mérite*) distinction, credit; (*personne*) celebrity.

glorieux, euse [gloryœ, -œz] *a* glorious.

glorifier [glorēfyå] *vt* to glorify; extol; **se ~ de** to glory in.

gloriole [gloryol] *nf* vainglory.

glose [glōz] *nf* gloss.

glossaire [gloser] *nm* glossary.

glotte [glot] *nf* (*ANAT*) glottis.

glouglouter [glooglootå] *vi* to gurgle.

glousser [glooså] *vi* to cluck; (*rire*) to chuckle.

glouton, ne [glootóṅ, -on] *a* gluttonous, greedy.

gloutonnerie [glootonrē] *nf* gluttony.

glu [glü] *nf* birdlime.

gluant, e [glüåṅ, -åṅt] *a* sticky, gummy.

glucose [glükōz] *nm* glucose.

gluten [glüten] *nm* gluten.

glycérine [glēsårēn] *nf* glycerine.

glycine [glēsēn] *nf* wisteria.

GMT *sigle a* (= *Greenwich Mean Time*) GMT.

GNL *sigle m* (= *gaz naturel liquéfié*) LNG (= *liquefied natural gas*).

gnôle [nyōl] *nf* (*fam*) booze *q*; **un petit verre de ~** a drop of the hard stuff.

gnome [gnōm] *nm* gnome.

GO *sigle fpl* (= *grandes ondes*) LW ♦ *sigle m* (= *gentil organisateur*) title given to leaders on Club Méditerranée vacations; *extended to* refer to easy-going leader of any group.

go [gō]: **tout de ~** *ad* straight out.

goal [gōl] *nm* goalkeeper.

gobelet [goble] *nm* (*en métal*) tumbler; (*en plastique*) beaker; (*à dés*) cup.

gober [gobå] *vt* to swallow.

goberger [goberzhå]: **se ~** *vi* to pamper o.s.

Gobi [gobē] *n*: **désert de ~** Gobi Desert.

godasse [godås] *nf* (*fam*) shoe.

godet [gode] *nm* pot; (*COUTURE*) unpressed pleat.

godiller [godēyå] *vi* (*NAVIG*) to scull; (*SKI*) to wedeln.

goéland [goålåṅ] *nm* (sea)gull.

goélette [goålet] *nf* schooner.

goémon [goåmóṅ] *nm* wrack.

gogo [gogō] *nm* (*péj*) sucker; **à ~** *ad* galore.

goguenard [gognår, -ård(ə)] *a* mocking.

goguette [goget] *nf*: **en ~** on the binge.

goinfre [gwaṅfr(ə)] *nm* glutton.

goinfrer [gwaṅfrå]: **se ~** *vi* to make a pig of o.s.; **se ~ de** to guzzle.

goitre [gwåtr(ə)] *nm* goiter (*US*), goitre (*Brit*).

golf [golf] *nm* (*jeu*) golf; (*terrain*) golf course; **~ miniature** crazy *ou* miniature golf.

golfe [golf(ə)] *nm* gulf; bay; **le ~ d'Aden** the Gulf of Aden; **le ~ de Gascogne** the Bay of Biscay; **le ~ du Lion** the Gulf of Lions; **le ~ Persique** the Persian Gulf.

gominé, e [gominå] *a* slicked down.

gomme [gom] *nf* (*à effacer*) eraser; (*résine*) gum; **boule** *ou* **pastille de ~** throat pastille.

gommé, e [gomå] *a*: **papier ~** gummed paper.

gommer [gomå] *vt* (*effacer*) to erase; (*enduire de gomme*) to gum.

gond [góṅ] *nm* hinge; **sortir de ses ~s** (*fig*) to fly off the handle.

gondole [góṅdol] *nf* gondola; (*pour l'étalage*) shelves *pl*, gondola.

gondoler [góṅdolå]: **se ~** *vi* to warp, buckle; (*fam: rire*) to hoot with laughter; to be in stitches.

gondolier [góṅdolyå] *nm* gondolier.

gonflable [góṅflåbl(ə)] *a* inflatable.

gonflage [góṅflåzh] *nm* inflating, blowing up.

gonflé, e [góṅflå] *a* swollen; (*ventre*) bloated; (*fam: culotté*): **être ~** to have a nerve.

gonfler [góṅflå] *vt* (*pneu, ballon*) to inflate, blow up; (*nombre, importance*) to inflate ♦ *vi* (*pied etc*) to swell (up); (*CULIN: pâte*) to rise.

gonfleur [góṅflœr] *nm* air pump.

gong [góṅg] *nm* gong.

gonzesse [góṅzes] *nf* (*fam*) chick.

goret [gore] *nm* piglet.

gorge [gorzh(ə)] *nf* (*ANAT*) throat; (*poitrine*) breast; (*GÉO*) gorge; (*rainure*) groove; **avoir mal à la ~** to have a sore throat; **avoir la ~ serrée** to have a lump in one's throat.

gorgé, e [gorzhå] *a*: **~ de** filled with; (*eau*) saturated with ♦ *nf* mouthful; sip; gulp; **boire à petites/grandes ~es** to take little sips/big gulps.

gorille [gorēy] *nm* gorilla; (*fam*) bodyguard.

gosier [gōzyå] *nm* throat.

gosse [gos] *nm/f* kid.

gothique [gotēk] *a* gothic.

gouaille [gwåy] *nf* street wit, cocky humor (*US*) *ou* humour (*Brit*).

goudron [goodróṅ] *nm* (*asphalte*) asphalt; (*du tabac*) tar.

goudronner [gōōdronā] *vt* to asphalt.

gouffre [gōōfr(ə)] *nm* abyss, gulf.

goujat [gōōzhá] *nm* boor.

goujon [gōōzhôṅ] *nm* gudgeon.

goulée [gōōlā] *nf* gulp.

goulet [gōōle] *nm* bottleneck.

goulot [gōōlō] *nm* neck; **boire au** ~ to drink from the bottle.

goulu, e [gōōlü] *a* greedy.

goupille [gōōpēy] *nf* (metal) pin.

goupiller [gōōpēyā] *vt* to pin (together).

goupillon [gōōpēyôṅ] *nm* (*REL*) sprinkler; (*brosse*) bottle brush; **le** ~ (*fig*) the cloth, the clergy.

gourd, e [gōōr, gōōrd(ə)] *a* numb (with cold); (*fam*) oafish.

gourde [gōōrd(ə)] *nf* (*récipient*) flask; (*fam*) dumbbell, (clumsy) oaf.

gourdin [gōōrdaṅ] *nm* club, bludgeon.

gourmand, e [gōōrmáṅ, -âṅd] *a* greedy.

gourmandise [gōōrmáṅdēz] *nf* greed; (*bonbon*) piece of candy (*US*), sweet (*Brit*).

gourmet [gōōrme] *nm* epicure.

gourmette [gōōrmet] *nf* chain bracelet.

gourou [gōōrōō] *nm* guru.

gousse [gōōs] *nf* (*de vanille etc*) pod; ~ **d'ail** clove of garlic.

gousset [gōōse] *nm* (*de gilet*) fob.

goût [gōō] *nm* taste; (*fig: appréciation*) taste, liking; **le (bon)** ~ good taste; **de bon** ~ in good taste, tasteful; **de mauvais** ~ in bad taste, tasteless; **avoir bon/mauvais** ~ (*aliment*) to taste good/bad; (*personne*) to have good/bad taste; **avoir du/manquer de** ~ to have/lack taste; **avoir du** ~ **pour** to have a liking for; **prendre** ~ **à** to develop a taste *ou* a liking for.

goûter [gōōtā] *vt* (*essayer*) to taste; (*apprécier*) to enjoy ♦ *vi* to have an afternoon snack ♦ *nm* afternoon snack; ~ **à** to taste, sample; ~ **de** to have a taste of; ~ **d'enfants/d'anniversaire** children's tea/birthday party.

goutte [gōōt] *nf* drop; (*MÉD*) gout; (*alcool*) drop (*US*), nip (*Brit*); ~**s** *nfpl* (*MÉD*) drops; ~ **à** ~ *ad* a drop at a time; **tomber** ~ **à** ~ to drip.

goutte-à-goutte [gōōtágōōt] *nm inv* (*MÉD*) I.V. (*US*), drip (*Brit*); **alimenter au** ~ to put on an I.V. (*US*), drip-feed (*Brit*).

gouttelette [gōōtlet] *nf* droplet.

goutter [gōōtā] *vi* to drip.

gouttière [gōōtyer] *nf* gutter.

gouvernail [gōōvernáy] *nm* rudder; (*barre*) helm, tiller.

gouvernant, e [gōōvernáṅ, -áṅt] *a* ruling *cpd* ♦ *nf* housekeeper; (*d'un enfant*) governess.

gouverne [gōōvern(ə)] *nf*: **pour sa** ~ for his guidance.

gouvernement [gōōvernəmáṅ] *nm* government.

gouvernemental, e, aux [gōōvernəmáṅtál, -ō] *a* (*politique*) government *cpd*; (*journal, parti*) pro-government.

gouverner [gōōvernā] *vt* to govern; (*diriger*) to steer; (*fig*) to control.

gouverneur [gōōvernœr] *nm* governor; (*MIL*) commanding officer.

goyave [goyáv] *nf* guava.

GPL *sigle m* (= *gaz de pétrole liquéfié*) LPG (= *liquefied petroleum gas*).

GQG *sigle m* (= *grand quartier général*) GHQ.

grabataire [grábáter] *a* bedridden ♦ *nm/f* bedridden invalid.

grâce [grâs] *nf* grace; (*faveur*) favor (*US*), favour (*Brit*); (*JUR*) pardon; ~**s** *nfpl* (*REL*) grace *sg*; **de bonne/mauvaise** ~ with (a) good/bad grace; **dans les bonnes** ~**s de qn** in favor with sb; **faire** ~ **à qn de qch** to spare sb sth; **rendre** ~**(s) à** to give thanks to; **demander** ~ to beg for mercy; **droit de** ~ right of reprieve; **recours en** ~ plea for pardon; ~ **à** *prép* thanks to.

gracier [grásyā] *vt* to pardon.

gracieusement [grásyœzmáṅ] *ad* graciously, kindly; (*gratuitement*) freely; (*avec grâce*) gracefully.

gracieux, euse [grásyœ, -œz] *a* (*charmant, élégant*) graceful; (*aimable*) gracious, kind; **à titre** ~ free of charge.

gracile [grásēl] *a* slender.

gradation [grádâsyôṅ] *nf* gradation.

grade [grád] *nm* (*MIL*) rank; (*SCOL*) degree; **monter en** ~ to be promoted.

gradé [grádā] *nm* (*MIL*) (noncommissioned) officer.

gradin [grádaṅ] *nm* (*dans un théâtre*) tier; (*de stade*) step; ~**s** *nmpl* (*de stade*) stands (*US*), terracing *q* (*Brit*); **en** ~**s** terraced.

graduation [grádüâsyôṅ] *nf* graduation.

gradué, e [grádüā] *a* (*exercices*) graded (for difficulty); (*thermomètre, verre*) graduated.

graduel, le [grádüel] *a* gradual; progressive.

graduer [grádüā] *vt* (*effort etc*) to increase gradually; (*règle, verre*) to graduate; (*exercices*) to increase in difficulty.

graffiti [gráfētē] *nmpl* graffiti.

grain [graṅ] *nm* (*gén*) grain; (*de chapelet*) bead; (*NAVIG*) squall; (*averse*) heavy shower; (*fig: petite quantité*): **un** ~ **de** a touch of; ~ **de beauté** beauty spot; ~ **de café** coffee bean; ~ **de poivre** peppercorn; ~ **de poussière** speck of dust; ~ **de raisin** grape.

graine [gren] *nf* seed; **mauvaise** ~ (*mauvais sujet*) bad lot; **une** ~ **de voyou** a hooligan in the making.

grainetier, -ière [grentyā, -yer] seed merchant.

graissage [gresázh] *nm* lubrication, greasing.

graisse [gres] *nf* fat; (*lubrifiant*) grease.

graisser [grásā] *vt* to lubricate, grease; (*tacher*) to make greasy.

graisseux, euse [gresœ, -œz] *a* greasy; (*ANAT*) fatty.

grammaire [grámer] *nf* grammar.

grammatical, e, aux [grámátēkál, -ō] *a* grammatical.

gramme [grám] *nm* gram (*US*), gramme (*Brit*).

grand, e [graṅ, grâṅd] *a* (*haut*) tall; (*gros, vaste, large*) big, large; (*long*) long; (*sens abstraits*) great ♦ *ad*: **ouvert** wide open; **un** ~ **buveur** a heavy drinker; **un** ~ **homme** a great man; **son** ~ **frère** his big *ou* older brother; **avoir** ~ **besoin de** to be in dire *ou* desperate need of; **il est** ~ **temps de** it's high time to; **il est assez** ~ **pour** he's big *ou* old enough to; **voir** ~ to think big; **en** ~ on a large scale; **au ~ air** in the open (air); **les ~s blessés/brûlés** the severely injured/burned; **de ~ matin** at the crack of dawn; **~ écart** splits *pl*; **~ ensemble** housing project (*US*) *ou* scheme (*Brit*); **~ jour** broad daylight; **~ livre** (*COMM*) ledger; **~ magasin** department store; **~ malade** very sick person; **~ public** general public; **~e personne** grown-up; **~e surface** superstore; **~es écoles** *prestige university-level colleges with competitive entrance examinations*; **~es lignes** (*RAIL*) main lines; **~es vacances** summer vacation *sg* (*US*) *ou* holidays (*Brit*).

grand-angle, *pl* **grands-angles** [grâṅtâṅgl(ə)] *nm* (*PHOTO*) wide-angle lens.

grand-angulaire, *pl* **grands-angulaires** [grâṅtâṅgüler] *nm* (*PHOTO*) wide-angle lens.

grand-chose [grâṅshōz] *nm/f inv*: **pas ~** not much.

Grande-Bretagne [grâṅdbrətàny] *nf*: **la ~** (Great) Britain; **en ~** in (Great) Britain.

grandement [grâṅdmâṅ] *ad* (*tout à fait*) greatly; (*largement*) easily; (*généreusement*) lavishly.

grandeur [grâṅdœr] *nf* (*dimension*) size; (*fig: ampleur, importance*) magnitude; (*: gloire, puissance*) greatness; **~ nature** a life-size.

grand-guignolesque [grâṅgēnyolesk(ə)] *a* gruesome.

grandiloquent, **e** [grâṅdēlokâṅ, -âṅt] *a* bombastic, grandiloquent.

grandir [grâṅdēr] *vi* (*enfant, arbre*) to grow; (*bruit, hostilité*) to increase, grow ♦ *vt*: **~ qn** (*suj: vêtement, chaussure*) to make sb look taller; (*fig*) to make sb grow in stature.

grandissant, **e** [grâṅdēsâṅ, -âṅt] growing.

grand-mère [grâṅmer] *nf* grandmother.

grand-messe [grâṅmes] *nf* high mass.

grand-peine [grâṅpen]: **à ~** *ad* with (great) difficulty.

grand-père, *pl* **grands-pères** [grâṅper] *nm* grandfather.

grand-route [grâṅrōōt] *nf* main road.

grand-rue [grâṅrü] *nf* main street.

grands-parents [grâṅpàrâṅ] *nmpl* grandparents.

grand-voile [grâṅvwàl] *nf* mainsail.

grange [grâṅzh] *nf* barn.

granit(e) [grànēt] *nm* granite.

granule [grànül] *nm* small pill.

granulé [grànülā] *nm* granule.

granuleux, **euse** [grànülœ̄, -œ̄z] *a* granular.

graphe [gràf] *nm* graph.

graphie [gràfē] *nf* written form.

graphique [gràfēk] *a* graphic ♦ *nm* graph.

graphisme [gràfēsm(ə)] *nm* graphic arts *pl*; graphics *sg*; (*écriture*) handwriting.

graphiste [gràfēst(ə)] *nm/f* graphic designer.

graphologue [gràfolog] *nm/f* graphologist.

grappe [gràp] *nf* cluster; **~ de raisin** bunch of grapes.

grappiller [gràpēyā] *vt* to glean.

grappin [gràpàṅ] *nm* grapnel; **mettre le ~ sur** (*fig*) to get one's claws on.

gras, **se** [grâ, grâs] *a* (*viande, soupe*) fatty; (*personne*) fat; (*surface, main, cheveux*) greasy; (*terre*) sticky; (*toux*) loose, phlegmy; (*rire*) throaty; (*plaisanterie*) coarse; (*crayon*) soft-lead; (*TYPO*) bold ♦ *nm*

(*CULIN*) fat; **faire la ~se matinée** to sleep late; **matière ~se** fat (content).

gras-double [grâdōōbl(ə)] *nm* (*CULIN*) tripe.

grassement [grâsmâṅ] *ad* (*généreusement*): **~ payé** handsomely paid; (*grossièrement: rire*) coarsely.

grassouillet, **te** [grâsōōye, -et] *a* pudgy, plump.

gratifiant, **e** [gràtēfyâṅ, -âṅt] *a* gratifying, rewarding.

gratification [gràtēfēkàsyôṅ] *nf* bonus.

gratifier [gràtēfyā] *vt*: **~ qn de** to favor (*US*) *ou* favour (*Brit*) sb with; to reward sb with; (*sourire etc*) to favor sb with.

gratin [gràtàṅ] *nm* (*CULIN*) cheese- (*ou* crumb-)topped dish; (*: croûte*) topping; **au ~ au gratin**; **tout le ~ parisien** all the best people of Paris.

gratiné, **e** [gràtēnā] *a* (*CULIN*) au gratin; (*fam*) hellish ♦ *nf* (*soupe*) onion soup au gratin.

gratis [gràtēs] *ad, a* free.

gratitude [gràtētüd] *nf* gratitude.

gratte-ciel [gràtsyel] *nm inv* skyscraper.

grattement [gràtmâṅ] *nm* (*bruit*) scratching (noise).

gratte-papier [gràtpàpyā] *nm inv* (*péj*) pencil pusher (*US*), penpusher (*Brit*).

gratter [gràtā] *vt* (*frotter*) to scrape; (*enlever*) to scrape off; (*bras, bouton*) to scratch; **se ~** to scratch o.s.

grattoir [gràtwàr] *nm* scraper.

gratuit, **e** [gràtüē, -üēt] *a* (*entrée*) free; (*billet*) free, complimentary; (*fig*) gratuitous.

gratuité [gràtüētā] *nf* being free (of charge); gratuitousness.

gratuitement [gràtüētmâṅ] *ad* (*sans payer*) free; (*sans preuve, motif*) gratuitously.

gravats [gràvà] *nmpl* rubble *sg*.

grave [gràv] *a* (*dangereux: maladie, accident*) serious, bad; (*sérieux: sujet, problème*) serious, grave; (*personne, air*) grave, solemn; (*voix, son*) deep, low-pitched ♦ *nm* (*MUS*) low register; **ce n'est pas ~!** it's all right, don't worry; **blessé ~** seriously injured person.

graveleux, **euse** [gràvlœ̄, -œ̄z] *a* (*terre*) gravelly; (*fruit*) gritty; (*contes, propos*) smutty.

gravement [gràvmâṅ] *ad* seriously; badly; gravely.

graver [gràvā] *vt* (*plaque, nom*) to engrave; (*fig*): **~ qch dans son esprit/sa mémoire** to etch sth in one's mind/memory.

graveur [gràvœr] *nm* engraver.

gravier [gràvyà] *nm* (loose) gravel *q*.

gravillons [gràvēyôṅ] *nmpl* gravel *sg*.

gravir [gràvēr] *vt* to climb (up).

gravité [gràvētā] *nf* (*voir grave*) seriousness; gravity; (*PHYSIQUE*) gravity.

graviter [gràvētā] *vi*: **~ autour de** to revolve around.

gravure [gràvür] *nf* engraving; (*reproduction*) print; plate.

GRE *sigle f* = *garantie contre les risques à l'exportation*.

gré [grā] *nm*: **à son ~** *a* to his liking ♦ *ad* as he pleases; **au ~ de** according to, following; **contre le ~ de qn** against sb's will; **de son (plein) ~** of one's own free will; **de ~ ou de**

force whether one likes it or not; **de bon** ~ willingly; **bon** ~ **mal** ~ like it or not; willy-nilly; **de** ~ **à** ~ (*COMM*) by mutual agreement; **savoir (bien)** ~ **à qn de qch** to be (most) grateful to sb for sth.

grec, grecque [grɛk] *a* Greek; (*classique: vase etc*) Grecian ♦ *nm* (*LING*) Greek ♦ *nm/f:* **G~**, **Grecque** Greek.

Grèce [grɛs] *nf:* **la** ~ Greece.

gredin, e [grədã, -ɛn] *nm/f* rogue, rascal.

gréement [grãmã] *nm* rigging.

greffe [grɛf] *nf* graft; transplant ♦ *nm* (*JUR*) office.

greffer [grɛfã] *vt* (*BOT, MÉD: tissu*) to graft; (*MÉD: organe*) to transplant.

greffier [grɛfyã] *nm* clerk of the court.

grégaire [grɛgɛr] *a* gregarious.

grège [grɛʒ] *a:* **soie** ~ raw silk.

grêle [grɛl] *a* (very) thin ♦ *nf* hail.

grêlé, e [grɛlã] *a* pockmarked.

grêler [grɛlã] *vb impersonnel:* **il grêle** it's hailing ♦ *vt:* **la région a été grêlée** the region was damaged by hail.

grêlon [grɛlõ] *nm* hailstone.

grelot [grəlo] *nm* little bell.

grelotter [grəlotã] *vi* (*trembler*) to shiver.

Grenade [grənad] *n* Granada ♦ *nf* (*île*) Grenada.

grenade [grənad] *nf* (*explosive*) grenade; (*BOT*) pomegranate; ~ **lacrymogène** teargas grenade.

grenadier [grənadyã] *nm* (*MIL*) grenadier; (*BOT*) pomegranate tree.

grenadine [grənadɛn] *nf* grenadine.

grenat [grəna] *a inv* dark red.

grenier [grənyã] *nm* (*de maison*) attic; (*de ferme*) loft.

grenouille [grənooy] *nf* frog.

grenouillère [grənooyɛr] *nf* (*de bébé*) leggings; (*: combinaison*) sleeper (*US*), sleepsuit (*Brit*).

grenu, e [grənü] *a* grainy, grained.

grès [grɛ] *nm* (*roche*) sandstone; (*poterie*) stoneware.

grésil [grãzɛl] *nm* (fine) hail.

grésillement [grãzɛymã] *nm* sizzling; crackling.

grésiller [grãzɛyã] *vi* to sizzle; (*RADIO*) to crackle.

grève [grɛv] *nf* (*d'ouvriers*) strike; (*plage*) shore; **se mettre en/faire** ~ to go on/be on strike; ~ **bouchon** partial strike (*in key areas of a company*); ~ **de la faim** hunger strike; ~ **perlée** slowdown (*US*), go-slow (*Brit*); ~ **sauvage** wildcat strike; ~ **de solidarité** sympathy strike; ~ **sur le tas** sit-down strike; ~ **tournante** strike staggered; ~ **du zèle** slowdown (*US*), work-to-rule (*Brit*).

grever [grəvã] *vt* (*budget, économie*) to put a strain on; **grevé d'impôts** crippled by taxes; **grevé d'hypothèques** heavily mortgaged.

gréviste [grãvɛst(ə)] *nm/f* striker.

gribouillage [gribooyãzh] *nm* scribble, scrawl.

gribouiller [gribooyã] *vt* to scribble, scrawl ♦ *vi* to doodle.

grief [grɛyɛf] *nm* grievance; **faire** ~ **à qn de** to reproach sb for.

grièvement [grɛyɛvmã] *ad* seriously.

griffe [grɛf] *nf* claw; (*fig*) signature; (*: d'un couturier, parfumeur*) label, signature.

griffé, e [grɛtã] *a* designer(-label) *cpd*.

griffer [grɛfã] *vt* to scratch.

griffonnage [grɛfonãzh] *nm* scribble.

griffonner [grɛfonã] *vt* to scribble.

griffure [grɛfür] *nf* scratch.

grignoter [grɛnyotã] *vt, vi* to nibble.

gril [grɛl] *nm* steak *ou* grill pan.

grillade [grɛyãd] *nf* grill.

grillage [grɛyãzh] *nm* (*treillis*) wire netting; (*clôture*) wire fencing.

grille [grɛy] *nf* (*portail*) (metal) gate; (*clôture*) railings *pl*; (*d'égout*) (metal) grate; (*fig*) grid.

grille-pain [grɛypã] *nm inv* toaster.

griller [grɛyã] *vt* (*aussi:* **faire** ~: *pain*) to toast; (*: viande*) to broil (*US*), grill (*Brit*); (*: café*) to roast; (*fig: ampoule etc*) to burn out, blow ♦ *vi* (*brûler*) to be roasting; ~ **un feu rouge** to run a stoplight (*US*), jump the lights (*Brit*).

grillon [grɛyõ] *nm* (*ZOOL*) cricket.

grimace [grɛmãs] *nf* grimace; (*pour faire rire*) **faire des** ~**s** to pull *ou* make faces.

grimacer [grɛmãsã] *vi* to grimace.

grimer [grɛmã] *vt* to make up.

grimpant, e [grãpã, -ãt] *a:* **plante** ~**e** climbing plant, climber.

grimper [grãpã] *vi, vt* to climb ♦ *nm:* **le** ~ (*SPORT*) rope-climbing; ~ **à/sur** to climb (up)/climb onto.

grimpeur, euse [grãpœr, -ɶz] *nm/f* climber.

grinçant, e [grãsã, -ãt] *a* grating.

grincement [grãsmã] *nm* grating (noise); creaking (noise).

grincer [grãsã] *vi* (*porte, roue*) to grate; (*plancher*) to creak; ~ **des dents** to grind one's teeth.

grincheux, euse [grãshɶ, -ɶz] *a* grumpy.

gringalet [grãgãlɛ] *am* puny ♦ *nm* weakling.

griotte [grãyot] *nf* Morello cherry.

grippe [grɛp] *nf* flu, influenza; **avoir la** ~ to have (the) flu; **prendre qn/qch en** ~ (*fig*) to take a sudden dislike to sb/sth.

grippé, e [grɛpã] *a:* **être** ~ to have (the) flu; (*moteur*) to have jammed.

gripper [grɛpã] *vt, vi* to jam.

gris, e [grɛ, grɛz] *a* gray (*US*), grey (*Brit*); (*ivre*) tipsy ♦ *nm* (*couleur*) gray (*US*), grey (*Brit*); **il fait** ~ it's a dull *ou* gray day; **faire** ~**e mine** to look miserable *ou* morose; **faire** ~**e mine à qn** to give sb a cool reception.

grisaille [grɛzãy] *nf* grayness (*US*), greyness (*Brit*), dullness.

grisant, e [grɛzã, -ãt] *a* intoxicating, exhilarating.

grisâtre [grɛzãtr(ə)] *a* grayish (*US*), greyish (*Brit*).

griser [grɛzã] *vt* to intoxicate; **se** ~ **de** (*fig*) to become intoxicated with.

grisonnant, e [grɛzonã, -ãt] *a* graying (*US*), greying (*Brit*).

grisonner [grɛzonã] *vi* to be going gray (*US*) *ou* grey (*Brit*).

grisou [grɛzoo] *nm* firedamp.

grive [grɛv] *nf* (*ZOOL*) thrush.

grivois, e [grɛvwã, -wãz] *a* saucy.

Groenland [groɛnlãd] *nm:* **le** ~ Greenland.

groenlandais, e [grœnlầnde, -ez] *a* of *ou* from Greenland ♦ *nm/f*: **G~, e** Greenlander.
grog [grog] *nm* grog.
grogne [grony] *nf* grumble.
grogner [gronyā] *vi* to growl; *(fig)* to grumble.
grognon, ne [grôṅnyôṅ, -on] *a* grumpy, grouchy.
groin [grwaṅ] *nm* snout.
grommeler [gromlā] *vi* to mutter to o.s.
grondement [grôṅdmâṅ] *nm* rumble; growl.
gronder [grôṅdā] *vi* (*canon, moteur, tonnerre*) to rumble; (*animal*) to growl; (*fig: révolte*) to be brewing ♦ *vt* to scold.
groom [grōōm] *nm* page, bellhop (*US*).
gros, se [grō, grōs] *a* big, large; (*obèse*) fat; (*problème, quantité*) great; (*travaux, dégâts*) extensive; (*large: trait, fil*) thick, heavy ♦ *ad*: **risquer/gagner ~** to risk/win a lot ♦ *nm* (*COMM*): **le ~** the wholesale business; **écrire ~** to write in big letters; **prix de ~** wholesale price; **par ~ temps/~se mer** in rough weather/heavy seas; **le ~ de** the main body of; (*du travail etc*) the bulk of; **en avoir ~ sur le cœur** to be upset; **en ~** roughly; (*COMM*) wholesale; **~ intestin** large intestine; **~ lot** jackpot; **~ mot** coarse word, vulgarity; **~ œuvre** shell (of building); **~ plan** (*PHOTO*) close-up; **~ porteur** wide-bodied aircraft, jumbo (jet); **~ sel** cooking salt; **~ titre** headline; **~se caisse** bass drum.
groseille [grōzey] *nf*: **~ (rouge)/(blanche)** red/white currant; **~ à maquereau** gooseberry.
groseillier [grōzāyā] *nm* red *ou* white currant bush; gooseberry bush.
grosse [grōs] *af voir* **gros** ♦ *nf* (*COMM*) gross.
grossesse [grōses] *nf* pregnancy; **~ nerveuse** phantom pregnancy.
grosseur [grōsœr] *nf* size; fatness; (*tumeur*) lump.
grossier, ière [grōsyā, -yer] *a* coarse; (*travail*) rough; crude; (*évident: erreur*) gross.
grossièrement [grōsyermâṅ] *ad* coarsely; roughly; crudely; (*en gros*) roughly.
grossièreté [grōsyertā] *nf* coarseness; rudeness.
grossir [grōsēr] *vi* (*personne*) to put on weight; (*fig*) to grow, get bigger; (*rivière*) to swell ♦ *vt* to increase; (*exagérer*) to exaggerate; (*au microscope*) to magnify, enlarge; (*suj: vêtement*): **~ qn** to make sb look fatter.
grossissant, e [grōsēsâṅ, -âṅt] *a* magnifying, enlarging.
grossissement [grōsēsmâṅ] *nm* (*optique*) magnification.
grossiste [grōsēst(ə)] *nm/f* wholesaler.
grosso modo [grōsōmodō] *ad* roughly.
grotesque [grotesk(ə)] *a* grotesque.
grotte [grot] *nf* cave.
grouiller [grōōyā] *vi* (*foule*) to mill about; (*fourmis*) to swarm about; **~ de** to be swarming with.
groupe [grōōp] *nm* group; **cabinet de ~** group practice; **médecine de ~** group practice; **~ électrogène** generator; **~ de pression** pressure group; **~ sanguin** blood group; **~ scolaire** school complex.
groupement [grōōpmâṅ] *nm* grouping;

(*groupe*) group; **~ d'intérêt économique (GIE)** ≈ trade association.
grouper [grōōpā] *vt* to group; (*ressources, moyens*) to pool; **se ~** to get together.
groupuscule [grōōpüskül] *nm* clique.
gruau [grüō] *nm*: **pain de ~** wheaten bread.
grue [grü] *nf* crane; **faire le pied de ~** (*fam*) to hang around (waiting), cool one's heels.
gruger [grüzhā] *vt* to cheat, dupe.
grumeaux [grümō] *nmpl* (*CULIN*) lumps.
grumeleux, euse [grümlœ, -œz] *a* (*sauce etc*) lumpy; (*peau etc*) bumpy.
grutier [grütyā] *nm* crane driver.
gruyère [grüyer] *nm* Swiss cheese.
Guadeloupe [gwàdlōōp] *nf*: **la ~** Guadeloupe.
guadeloupéen, ne [gwàdlōōpāāṅ, -en] *a* Guadelupian.
Guatémala [gwàtāmàlà] *nm*: **le ~** Guatemala.
guatémalien, ne [gwàtāmàlyaṅ, -en] *a* Guatemalan.
guatémaltèque [gwàtāmàltek] *a* Guatemalan.
GUD [güd] *sigle m* (= *Groupe Union Défense*) student union.
gué [gā] *nm* ford; **passer à ~** to ford.
guenilles [gənēy] *nfpl* rags.
guenon [gənôṅ] *nf* female monkey.
guépard [gāpàr] *nm* cheetah.
guêpe [gep] *nf* wasp.
guêpier [gāpyā] *nm* (*fig*) trap.
guère [ger] *ad* (*avec adjectif, adverbe*): **ne ... ~** hardly; (*avec verbe*): **ne ... ~ tournure négative** + much; hardly ever; **tournure négative** + (very) long; **il n'y a ~ que/de** there's hardly anybody (*ou* anything) but/ hardly any.
guéridon [gārēdôṅ] *nm* pedestal table.
guérilla [gārēyà] *nf* guerrilla warfare.
guérillero [gārēyārō] *nm* guerrilla.
guérir [gārēr] *vt* (*personne, maladie*) to cure; (*membre, plaie*) to heal ♦ *vi* (*personne*) to recover, be cured; (*plaie, chagrin*) to heal; **~ de** to be cured of, recover from; **~ qn de** to cure sb of.
guérison [gārēzôṅ] *nf* curing; healing; recovery.
guérissable [gārēsàbl(ə)] *a* curable.
guérisseur, euse [gārēsœr, -œz] *nm/f* healer.
guérite [gārēt] *nf* (*MIL*) sentry box; (*sur un chantier*) (workman's) hut.
Guernesey [gernəze] *nf* Guernsey.
guernesiais, e [gernəzye, -ez] *a* of *ou* from Guernsey.
guerre [ger] *nf* war; (*méthode*): **~ atomique/ de tranchées** atomic/trench warfare *q*; **en ~** at war; **faire la ~ à** to wage war against; **de ~ lasse** (*fig*) tired of fighting *ou* resisting; **de bonne ~** fair and square; **~ civile/mondiale** civil/world war; **~ froide/sainte** cold/holy war; **~ d'usure** war of attrition.
guerrier, ière [geryā, -yer] *a* warlike ♦ *nm/f* warrior.
guerroyer [gerwàyā] *vi* to wage war.
guet [ge] *nm*: **faire le ~** to be on the watch *ou* look-out.
guet-apens, *pl* **guets-apens** [getàpâṅ] *nm* ambush.
guêtre [getr(ə)] *nf* gaiter.
guetter [gātā] *vt* (*épier*) to watch (intently); (*attendre*) to watch (out) for; (: *pour*

surprendre) to be lying in wait for.

guetteur [getœr] *nm* look-out.

gueule [gœl] *nf* mouth; (*fam: visage*) mug; (*: bouche*) trap (*!*), mouth; **ta ~!** (*fam*) shut up!; **~ de bois** (*fam*) hangover.

gueule-de-loup, *pl* **gueules-de-loup** [gœldəlōō] *nf* snapdragon.

gueuler [gœlā] *vi* (*fam*) to bawl.

gueux [gœ̄] *nm* beggar; (*coquin*) rogue.

gui [gē] *nm* mistletoe.

guichet [gēshe] *nm* (*de bureau, banque*) counter, window; (*d'une porte*) wicket, hatch; **les ~s** (*à la gare, au théâtre*) the ticket office; **jouer à ~s fermés** to play to a full house.

guichetier, ière [gēshtyā, -yer] *nm/f* counter clerk.

guide [gēd] *nm* guide; (*livre*) guide(book) ♦ *nf* (*fille scout*) girl scout (*US*), (girl) guide (*Brit*); **~s** *nfpl* (*d'un cheval*) reins.

guider [gēdā] *vt* to guide.

guidon [gēdóṅ] *nm* handlebars *pl*.

guignol [gēnyol] *nm* ≈ Punch and Judy show; (*fig*) clown.

guillemets [gēyme] *nmpl*: **entre ~** in quotation marks; **~ de répétition** ditto marks.

guilleret, te [gēyre, -et] *a* perky, bright.

guillotine [gēyotēn] *nf* guillotine.

guillotiner [gēyotēnā] *vt* to guillotine.

guimauve [gēmōv] *nf* (*BOT*) marshmallow; (*fig*) sentimentality, sloppiness.

guimbarde [gaṅbárd(ə)] *nf* jalopy, clunker (*US*).

guindé, e [gaṅdā] *a* stiff, starchy.

Guinée [gēnā] *nf*: **la (République de) ~** (the Republic of) Guinea; **la ~ équatoriale** Equatorial Guinea.

Guinée-Bissau [gēnābēsō] *nf*: **la ~** Guinea-Bissau.

guinéen, ne [gēnāaṅ, -en] *a* Guinean.

guingette [gaṅget] *nf* open-air café or dance-hall.

guingois [gaṅgwá] **de ~** *ad* askew.

guirlande [gērláṅd] *nf* garland; (*de papier*) paper chain; **~ lumineuse** string of Christmas tree lights; **~ de Noël** tinsel *q*.

guise [gēz] *nf*: **à votre ~** as you wish *ou* please; **en ~ de** by way of.

guitare [gētár] *nf* guitar.

guitariste [gētárēst(ə)] *nm/f* guitarist, guitar player.

gustatif, ive [güstátēf, -ēv] *a* gustatory; *voir* **papille.**

guttural, e, aux [gütürál, -ō] *a* guttural.

guyanais, e [güēyáne, -ez] *a* Guyanese, Guyanan; (*français*) Guianese, Guianan.

Guyane [güēyán] *nf*: **la ~** Guyana; **la ~ (française)** (French) Guiana.

gvt *abr* (= *gouvernement*) govt.

gym [zhēm] *abr f* = **gymnastique.**

gymkhana [zhēmkáná] *nm* rally; **~ motocycliste** motocross.

gymnase [zhēmnáz] *nm* gym(nasium).

gymnaste [zhēmnást(ə)] *nm/f* gymnast.

gymnastique [zhēmnástēk] *nf* gymnastics *sg*; (*au réveil etc*) stay-fit (*US*) *ou* keep-fit (*Brit*) exercises *pl*; **~ corrective** remedial gymnastics.

gynécologie [zhēnākolozhē] *nf* gynecology

(*US*), gynaecology (*Brit*).

gynécologue [zhēnākolog] *nm/f* gynecologist (*US*), gynaecologist (*Brit*).

gypse [zhēps(ə)] *nm* gypsum.

gyrophare [zhērofár] *nm* (*sur une voiture*) revolving (flashing) light.

H

H, h [ásh] *nm inv* H, h ♦ *abr* (= *homme*) M; (= *hydrogène*) H; **bombe ~** H bomb; (= *heure*): **à l'heure ~** at zero hour; **H comme Henri** H for How.

ha. *abr* (= *hectare*) ha.

hab. *abr* = **habitant.**

habile [ábēl] *a* skillful (*US*), skilful (*Brit*); (*malin*) clever.

habilement [ábēlmáṅ] *ad* skillfully (*US*), skilfully (*Brit*); cleverly.

habileté [ábēltā] *nf* skill, skillfulness (*US*), skilfulness (*Brit*); cleverness.

habilité, e [ábēlētā] *a*: **~ à faire** entitled to do, empowered to do.

habiliter [ábēlētā] *vt* empower, entitle.

habillage [ábēyázh] *nm* dressing.

habillé, e [ábēyā] *a* dressed; (*chic*) dressy; (*TECH*): **~ de** covered with; encased in.

habillement [ábēymáṅ] *nm* clothes *pl*; (*profession*) clothing industry.

habiller [ábēyā] *vt* to dress; (*fournir en vêtements*) to clothe; **s'~** to dress (o.s.); (*se déguiser, mettre des vêtements chic*) to dress up; **s'~ de/en** to dress in/dress up as; **s'~ chez/à** to buy one's clothes from/at.

habilleuse [ábēyœ̄z] *nf* (*CINÉMA, THÉÂTRE*) dresser.

habit [ábē] *nm* outfit; **~s** *nmpl* (*vêtements*) clothes; **~ (de soirée)** tails *pl*; evening dress; **prendre l'~** (*REL: entrer en religion*) to enter (holy) orders.

habitable [ábētábl(ə)] *a* (in)habitable.

habitacle [ábētákl(ə)] *nm* cockpit; (*AUTO*) passenger cell.

habitant, e [ábētáṅ, -áṅt] *nm/f* inhabitant; (*d'une maison*) occupant, occupier; **loger chez l'~** to stay with local residents.

habitat [ábētá] *nm* housing conditions *pl*; (*BOT, ZOOL*) habitat.

habitation [ábētâsyóṅ] *nf* living; (*demeure*) residence, home; (*maison*) house; **~s à loyer modéré (HLM)** low-rent, state-owned housing, ≈ public housing units (*US*), ≈ council housing *sg* (*Brit*).

habité, e [ábētā] *a* inhabited; lived in.

habiter [ábētā] *vt* to live in; (*suj: sentiment*) to dwell in ♦ *vi*: **~ à/dans** to live in *ou* at/in; **~ chez** *ou* **avec qn** to live with sb; **~ 16 rue Montmartre** to live at number 16 rue Montmartre; **~ rue Montmartre** to live on rue Montmartre.

habitude [ábētüd] *nf* habit; **avoir l'~ de faire** to be in the habit of doing; **avoir l'~ des**

enfants to be used to children; **prendre l'~ de faire qch** to get into the habit of doing sth; **perdre une ~** to get out of a habit; **d'~** usually; **comme d'~** as usual; **par ~** out of habit.

habitué, e [ábētüã] *a*: **être ~ à** to be used *ou* accustomed to ♦ *nm/f* regular visitor; *(client)* regular (customer).

habituel, le [ábētüel] *a* usual.

habituellement [ábētüelmáṅ] *ad* usually.

habituer [ábētüã] *vt*: **~ qn à** to get sb used to; **s'~ à** to get used to.

'hâbleur, euse ['âblœr, -œz] *a* boastful.

'hache ['ásh] *nf* axe.

'haché, e ['áshā] *a* ground *(US)*, minced *(Brit)*; *(persil)* chopped; *(fig)* jerky.

'hache-légumes ['áshlāgüm] *nm inv* vegetable chopper.

'hacher ['áshā] *vt (viande)* to grind *(US)*, mince *(Brit)*; *(persil)* to chop; **~ menu** to grind finely; to chop finely.

'hachette ['áshet] *nf* hatchet.

'hache-viande ['áshvyáṅd] *nm inv* (meat) grinder *(US)* ou mincer *(Brit)*; *(couteau)* (meat) cleaver.

'hachis ['áshē] *nm* hamburger meat *(US)*, mince *q (Brit)*; **~ de viande** ground *(US)* ou minced *(Brit)* meat.

'hachisch ['áshēsh] *nm* hashish.

'hachoir ['áshwár] *nm* chopper; (meat) grinder *(US)* ou mincer *(Brit)*; *(planche)* chopping board.

'hachurer ['áshürā] *vt* to hatch.

'hachures ['áshür] *nfpl* hatching *sg*.

'hagard, e ['agar, -ard(ə)] *a* wild, distraught.

'haie ['c] *nf* hedge; *(SPORT)* hurdle; *(fig: rang)* line, row; **200 m ~s** 200 m hurdles; **~ d'honneur** guard of honor.

'haillons ['áyóṅ] *nmpl* rags.

'haine ['en] *nf* hatred.

'haineux, euse ['enœ, -œz] *a* full of hatred.

'haïr ['áẽr] *vt* to detest, hate; **se ~** to hate each other.

'hais ['e], **'haïs** ['áē] *etc vb voir* haïr.

'haïssable ['áēsábl(ə)] *a* detestable.

Haïti [áētē] *n* Haiti.

haïtien, ne [áēsyaṅ, -en] *a* Haitian.

'halage ['álázh] *nm*: **chemin de ~** towpath.

'hâle ['ál] *nm* (sun)tan.

'hâlé, e ['álā] *a* (sun)tanned, sunburned.

haleine [álen] *nf* breath; **perdre ~** to get out of breath; **à perdre ~** until one is gasping for breath; **avoir mauvaise ~** to have bad breath; **reprendre ~** to get one's breath back; **hors d'~** out of breath; **tenir en ~** to hold spellbound; *(en attente)* to keep in suspense; **de longue ~** *a* long-term.

'haler ['álā] *vt* to haul in; *(remorquer)* to tow.

'haleter ['áltā] *vi* to pant.

'hall ['ōl] *nm* hall.

hallali [álálē] *nm* kill.

'halle ['ál] *nf* (covered) market; **~s** *nfpl* central food market *sg*.

hallucinant, e [álüsēnáṅ, -áṅt] *a* staggering.

hallucination [álüsēnásyóṅ] *nf* hallucination.

hallucinatoire [álüsēnátwár] *a* hallucinatory.

halluciné, e [álüsēnā] *nm/f* person suffering from hallucinations; *(fou)* (raving) lunatic.

'halo ['álō] *nm* halo.

halogène [álozhen] *nm*: **lampe (à) ~** halogen lamp.

'halte ['ált(ə)] *nf* stop, break; *(escale)* stopping place; *(RAIL)* halt ♦ *excl* stop!; **faire ~** to stop.

'halte-garderie, *pl* **'haltes-garderies** ['áltgárdərē] *nf* child-care facility.

haltère [álter] *nm (à boules, disques)* dumb-bell, barbell; **(poids et) ~s** weightlifting.

haltérophile [áltārofēl] *nm/f* weightlifter.

haltérophilie [áltārofēlē] *nf* weightlifting.

'hamac ['ámák] *nm* hammock.

'Hambourg ['áṅbōōr] *n* Hamburg.

'hameau, x ['ámō] *nm* hamlet.

hameçon [ámsóṅ] *nm* (fish) hook.

'hampe ['áṅp] *nf (de drapeau etc)* pole; *(de lance)* shaft.

'hamster ['ámstcr] *nm* hamster.

'hanche ['áṅsh] *nf* hip.

'hand-ball ['áṅdbál] *nm* handball.

'handicap ['áṅdēkáp] *nm* handicap.

'handicapé, e ['áṅdēkápā] *a* handicapped ♦ *nm/f* physically *(ou* mentally) handicapped person; **~ moteur** spastic.

'handicaper ['áṅdēkápā] *vt* to handicap.

'hangar ['áṅgár] *nm* shed; *(AVIAT)* hangar.

'hanneton ['áṅtóṅ] *nm* cockchafer.

'Hanovre ['ánovr(ə)] *n* Hanover.

'hanovrien, ne ['ánovryaṅ, -en] *a* Hanoverian.

'hanter ['áṅtā] *vt* to haunt.

'hantise ['áṅtēz] *nf* obsessive fear.

'happer ['ápā] *vt* to snatch; *(suj: train etc)* to hit.

'haranguer ['áráṅgā] *vt* to harangue.

'haras ['árá] *nm* stud farm.

'harassant, e ['árásáṅ, -áṅt] *a* exhausting.

'harceler ['ársəlā] *vt (MIL, CHASSE)* to harass, harry; *(importuner)* to plague.

'hardes ['árd(ə)] *nfpl* rags.

'hardi, e ['árdē] *a* bold, daring.

'hareng ['áráṅ] *nm* herring.

'hargne ['árny(ə)] *nf* aggressivity, aggressiveness.

'haricot ['árēkō] *nm* bean; **~ blanc/rouge** haricot/kidney bean; **~ vert** green bean.

harmonica [ármonēkā] *nm* harmonica.

harmonie [ármonē] *nf* harmony.

harmonieux, euse [ármonyœ, -œz] *a* harmonious.

harmonique [ármonēk] *a, nm ou nf* harmonic.

harmoniser [ármonēzā] *vt* to harmonize; **s'~** *(couleurs, teintes)* to go well together.

harmonium [ármonyom] *nm* harmonium.

'harnaché, e ['árnáshā] *a (fig)* rigged out.

'harnachement ['árnáshmáṅ] *nm (habillement)* rig-out; *(équipement)* harness, equipment.

'harnacher ['árnáshā] *vt* to harness.

'harnais ['árne] *nm* harness.

'haro ['árō] *nm*: **crier ~ sur qn/qch** to inveigh against sb/sth.

'harpe ['árp(ə)] *nf* harp.

'harpiste ['árpēst(ə)] *nm/f* harpist.

'harpon ['árpóṅ] *nm* harpoon.

'harponner ['árponā] *vt* to harpoon; *(fam)* to collar.

'hasard ['ázár] *nm*: **le ~** chance, fate; **un ~** a coincidence; *(aubaine, chance)* a stroke of luck; **au ~** *(sans but)* aimlessly; *(à* '*l'aveuglette*) at random, haphazardly; **par ~** by chance; **comme par ~** as if by chance; **à tout ~** on the off chance; (*en cas de besoin*) just in case.

'**hasarder** ['àzárdā] *vt* (*mot*) to venture; (*fortune*) to risk; **se ~ à faire** to risk doing, venture to do.

'**hasardeux, euse** ['àzárdœ̄, -œ̄z] *a* hazardous, risky; (*hypothèse*) rash.

'**haschisch** ['àshēsh] *nm* hashish.

'**hâte** ['àt] *nf* haste; **à la ~** hurriedly, hastily; **en ~** posthaste, with all possible speed; **avoir ~ de** to be eager *ou* anxious to.

'**hâter** ['àtā] *vt* to hasten; **se ~** to hurry; **se ~ de** to hurry *ou* hasten to.

'**hâtif, ive** ['àtēf, -ēv] *a* (*travail*) hurried; (*décision*) hasty; (*légume*) early.

'**hâtivement** ['àtēvmȧṅ] *ad* hurriedly; hastily.

'**hauban** ['ōbȧṅ] *nm* (*NAVIG*) shroud.

'**hausse** ['ōs] *nf* rise, increase; (*de fusil*) backsight adjuster; **à la ~** upwards; **en ~** rising.

'**hausser** ['ōsā] *vt* to raise; **~ les épaules** to shrug (one's shoulders); **se ~ sur la pointe des pieds** to stand (up) on tiptoe *ou* tippy-toe (*US*).

'**haut, e** ['ō, 'ōt] *a* high; (*grand*) tall; (*son, voix*) high(-pitched) ♦ *ad* high ♦ *nm* top (part); **de 3m de ~, ~ de 3m** 3m high, 3m in height; **en ~e montagne** high up in the mountains; **en ~ lieu** in high places; **à ~e voix, (tout) ~** aloud, out loud; **des ~s et des bas** ups and downs; **du ~ de** from the top of; **tomber de ~** to fall from a height; (*fig*) to have one's hopes dashed; **dire qch bien ~** to say sth plainly; **prendre qch de (très) ~** to react haughtily to sth; **traiter qn de ~** to treat sb with disdain; **de ~ en bas** from top to bottom; downwards; **~ en couleur** (*chose*) highly colored; (*personne*): **un personnage ~ en couleur** a colorful character; **plus ~** higher up, further up; (*dans un texte*) above; (*parler*) louder; **en ~** up above; at (*ou* to) the top; (*dans une maison*) upstairs; **en ~ de** at the top of; **~ les mains!** hands up!, stick 'em up!; **la ~e couture/ coiffure** haute couture/coiffure; **~e fidélité** hi-fi, high fidelity; **la ~e finance** high finance; **~e trahison** high treason.

'**hautain, e** ['ōtȧṅ, -en] *a* (*personne, regard*) haughty.

'**hautbois** ['ōbwâ] *nm* oboe.

'**hautboïste** ['ōboēst(ə)] *nm/f* oboist.

'**haut-de-forme**, *pl* '**hauts-de-forme** ['ōdform(ə)] *nm* top hat.

'**haute-contre**, *pl* '**hautes-contre** ['ōtkȯṅtr(ə)] *nf* counter-tenor.

'**hauteur** ['ōtœr] *nf* height; (*GÉO*) height, hill; (*fig*) loftiness; haughtiness; **à ~ de** up to (the level of); **à ~ des yeux** at eye level; **à la ~ de** (*sur la même ligne*) level with; by; (*fig*) equal to; **à la ~** (*fig*) up to it, equal to the task.

'**Haute-Volta** ['ōtvoltà] *nf*: **la ~** Upper Volta.

'**haut-fond**, *pl* '**hauts-fonds** ['ōfȯṅ] *nm* shallow.

'**haut-fourneau**, *pl* '**hauts-fourneaux** ['ōfōōrnō] *nm* blast *ou* smelting furnace.

'**haut-le-cœur** ['ōlkœr] *nm inv* retch, heave.

'**haut-le-corps** ['ōlkor] *nm inv* start, jump.

'**haut-parleur**, *pl* '**haut-parleurs** ['ōpárlœr] *nm* (loud)speaker.

'**hauturier, ière** ['ōtüryā, -yer] *a* (*NAVIG*) deep-sea.

'**havanais, e** ['àvânc, -cz] *a* of *ou* from Havana.

'**Havane** ['àvàn] *nf*: **la ~** Havana ♦ *nm*: '**h~** (*cigare*) Havana.

'**hâve** ['àv] *a* gaunt.

'**havrais, e** ['àvre, -ez] *a* of *ou* from Le Havre.

'**havre** ['àvr(ə)] *nm* haven.

'**havresac** ['àvrəsàk] *nm* haversack.

Hawaï *ou* **Hawaii** [àwàē] *n* Hawaii; **les îles ~** the Hawaiian Islands.

hawaïen, ne [àwàyaṅ, -en] *a* Hawaiian ♦ *nm* (*LING*) Hawaiian.

'**Haye** ['e] *n*: **la ~** the Hague.

'**hayon** ['eyȯṅ] *nm* tailgate.

hdb. *abr* (= *heures de bureau*) o.h. (= *office hours*).

'**hé** ['ā] *excl* hey!

hebdo [ebdō] *nm* (*fam*) weekly.

hebdomadaire [ebdomáder] *a*, *nm* weekly.

hébergement [àberzhəmȧṅ] *nm* accommodations *pl* (*US*), accommodation (*Brit*), lodging; taking in.

héberger [àberzhā] *vt* to accommodate, lodge; (*réfugiés*) to take in.

hébété, e [àbātā] *a* dazed.

hébétude [àbātüd] *nf* stupor.

hébraïque [àbràēk] *a* Hebrew, Hebraic.

hébreu, x [àbrœ̄] *am*, *nm* Hebrew.

Hébrides [àbrēd] *nf*: **les ~** the Hebrides.

HEC *sigle fpl* (= *École des hautes études commerciales*) *grande école for management and business studies*.

hécatombe [àkàtȯṅb] *nf* slaughter.

hectare [ektàr] *nm* hectare, 10,000 square meters.

hecto... [ektō] *préfixe* hecto....

hectolitre [ektolētr(ə)] *nm* hectoliter (*US*), hectolitre (*Brit*).

hédoniste [àdonēst(ə)] *a* hedonistic.

hégémonie [àzhāmonē] *nf* hegemony.

'**hein** ['aṅ] *excl* eh?; (*sollicitant l'approbation*): **tu m'approuves, ~?** so I did the right thing then?; **Paul est venu, ~?** Paul came, did he?; **que fais-tu, ~?** hey! what are you doing?

'**hélas** ['àlás] *excl* alas! ♦ *ad* unfortunately.

'**héler** ['àlā] *vt* to hail.

hélice [àlēs] *nf* propeller.

hélicoïdal, e, aux [àlēkoēdàl, -ō] *a* helical; helicoid.

hélicoptère [àlēkopter] *nm* helicopter.

hélio(gravure) [àlyo(grávür)] *nf* heliogravure.

héliomarin, e [àlyomáraṅ, -ēn] *a*: **centre ~** center offering sea and sun therapy.

héliotrope [àlyotrop] *nm* (*BOT*) heliotrope.

héliport [àlēpor] *nm* heliport.

héliporté, e [àlēportā] *a* transported by helicopter.

hélium [àlyom] *nm* helium.

hellénique [àlānēk] *a* Hellenic.

hellénisant, e [àlānēzáṅ, -áṅt], **helléniste** [àlānēst(ə)] *nm/f* Hellenist.

Helsinki [elzēnkē] *n* Helsinki.

helvète [elvet] *a* Helvetian ♦ *nm/f*: **H~** Helvetian.

Helvétie [elvāsē] *nf*: **la ~** Helvetia.

helvétique [elvātēk] *a* Swiss.

hématologie [āmátolozhē] *nf* (*MÉD*) hematology (*US*), haematology (*Brit*).

hématome [āmátōm] *nm* hematoma (*US*), haematoma (*Brit*).

hémicycle [āmēsēkl(ə)] *nm* semicircle; (*POL*): **l'~** the benches (*in French parliament*).

hémiplégie [āmēplāzhē] *nf* paralysis of one side, hemiplegia.

hémisphère [āmēsfer] *nf*: **~ nord/sud** northern/southern hemisphere.

hémisphérique [āmēsfārēk] *a* hemispherical.

hémoglobine [āmoglobēn] *nf* hemoglobin (*US*), haemoglobin (*Brit*).

hémophile [āmofēl] *a* hemophiliac (*US*), haemophiliac (*Brit*).

hémophilie [āmofēlē] *nf* hemophilia (*US*), haemophilia (*Brit*).

hémorragie [āmorázhē] *nf* bleeding *q*, hemorrhage (*US*), haemorrhage (*Brit*); **~ cérébrale** cerebral hemorrhage; **~ interne** internal bleeding *ou* hemorrhage.

hémorroïdes [āmoroēd] *nfpl* piles, hemorrhoids (*US*), haemorrhoids (*Brit*).

hémostatique [āmostátēk] *a* hemostatic (*US*), haemostatic (*Brit*).

'henné ['ānā] *nm* henna.

'hennir ['ānēr] *vi* to neigh, whinny.

'hennissement ['ānēsmāń] *nm* neighing, whinnying.

'hep ['ep] *excl* hey!

hépatite [āpátēt] *nf* hepatitis, liver infection.

héraldique [āráldēk] *a* heraldry.

herbacé, e [erbásā] *a* herbaceous.

herbage [erbázh] *nm* pasture.

herbe [erb(ə)] *nf* grass; (*CULIN, MÉD*) herb; **en ~** unripe; (*fig*) budding; **touffe/brin d'~** clump/blade of grass.

herbeux, euse [erbœ̄, -œ̄z] *a* grassy.

herbicide [erbēsēd] *nm* weed-killer.

herbier [erbyā] *nm* herbarium.

herbivore [erbēvor] *nm* herbivore.

herboriser [erborēzā] *vi* to collect plants.

herboriste [erborēst(ə)] *nm/f* herbalist.

herboristerie [erborēstrē] *nf* (*magasin*) herbalist's shop; (*commerce*) herb trade.

herculéen, ne [erkülāań, -en] *a* (*fig*) herculean.

'hère ['er] *nm*: **pauvre ~** poor wretch.

héréditaire [ārādēter] *a* hereditary.

hérédité [ārādētā] *nf* heredity.

hérésie [ārāzē] *nf* heresy.

hérétique [ārātēk] *nm/f* heretic.

'hérissé, e ['ārēsā] *a* bristling; **~ de** spiked with; (*fig*) bristling with.

'hérisser ['ārēsā] *vt*: **~ qn** (*fig*) to ruffle sb; **se ~** *vi* to bristle, bristle up.

'hérisson ['ārēsóń] *nm* hedgehog.

héritage [ārētázh] *nm* inheritance; (*fig*) heritage; (*: legs*) legacy; **faire un (petit) ~** to come into (a little) money.

hériter [ārētā] *vi*: **~ de qch (de qn)** to inherit sth (from sb); **~ de qn** to inherit sb's property.

héritier, ière [ārētyā, -yer] *nm/f* heir/heiress.

hermaphrodite [ermáfrodēt] *a* (*BOT, ZOOL*) hermaphrodite.

hermétique [ermātēk] *a* (à l'air) airtight; (à

l'eau) watertight; (*fig: écrivain, style*) abstruse; (*: visage*) impenetrable.

hermétiquement [ermātēkmáń] *ad* hermetically.

hermine [ermēn] *nf* ermine.

'hernie ['ernē] *nf* hernia.

héroïne [āroēn] *nf* heroine; (*drogue*) heroin.

héroïnomane [āroēnomán] *nm/f* heroin addict.

héroïque [āroēk] *a* heroic.

héroïquement [āroēkmáń] *ad* heroically.

héroïsme [āroēsm(ə)] *nm* heroism.

'héron ['āróń] *nm* heron.

'héros ['ārō] *nm* hero.

herpès [erpes] *nm* herpes.

'herse ['ers(ə)] *nf* harrow; (*de château*) portcullis.

hertz [erts] *nm* (*ÉLEC*) hertz.

hertzien, ne [ertsyań, -en] *a* (*ÉLEC*) Hertzian.

hésitant, e [āzētáń, -áńt] *a* hesitant.

hésitation [āzētásyóń] *nf* hesitation.

hésiter [āzētā] *vi*: **~ (à faire)** to hesitate (to do); **~ sur qch** to hesitate over sth.

hétéro [ātārō] *a inv* (= *hétérosexuel(le)*) hetero.

hétéroclite [ātāroklēt] *a* heterogeneous; (*objets*) sundry.

hétérogène [ātārozhen] *a* heterogeneous.

hétérosexuel, le [ātārosekücl] *a* heterosexual.

'hêtre ['ctr(ə)] *nm* beech.

heure [œr] *nf* hour; (*SCOL*) period; (*moment, moment fixé*) time; **c'est l'~** it's time; **pourriez-vous me donner l'~, s'il vous plaît?** could you tell me the time, please?; **quelle ~ est-il?** what time is it?; **2 ~s (du matin)** 2 o'clock (in the morning); **à la bonne ~!** (*parfois ironique*) splendid!; **être à l'~** to be on time; (*montre*) to be right; **le bus passe à l'~** the bus runs on the hour; **mettre a l'~** to set right; **100km à l'~** = 60 miles an *ou* per hour; **à toute ~** at any time; **24 ~s sur 24** around the clock, 24 hours a day; **à l'~ qu'il est** at this time (of day); (*fig*) now; **à l'~ actuelle** at the present time; **sur l'~** at once; **pour l'~** for the time being; **d'~ en ~** from one hour to the next; (*régulièrement*) hourly; **d'une ~ à l'autre** from hour to hour; **de bonne ~** early; **2 ~s de marche/travail** 2 hours' walking/work; **une ~ d'arrêt** an hour's break *ou* stop; **~ d'été** daylight saving time; **~ de pointe** rush hour; **~s de bureau** office hours; **~s supplémentaires** overtime *sg*.

heureusement [œrēzmáń] *ad* (*par bonheur*) fortunately, luckily; **~ que ...** it's a good thing that ..., fortunately .....

heureux, euse [œrœ̄, -œ̄z] *a* happy; (*chanceux*) lucky, fortunate; (*judicieux*) felicitous, fortunate; **être ~ de qch** to be pleased *ou* happy about sth; **être ~ de faire/que** to be pleased *ou* happy to do/that; **s'estimer ~ de qch/que** to consider o.s. fortunate with/that; **encore ~ que ...** just as well that .....

'heurt ['œr] *nm* (*choc*) collision; **~s** *nmpl* (*fig*) clashes.

'heurté, e ['œrtā] *a* (*fig*) jerky, uneven; (*: couleurs*) clashing.

'heurter ['œrtā] *vt* (*mur*) to strike, hit; (*personne*) to collide with; (*fig*) to go against, upset; **se ~** (*couleurs, tons*) to clash; **se ~ à**

to collide with; (*fig*) to come up against; ~ **qn de front** to clash head-on with sb.

'heurtoir ['œrtwâr] *nm* door knocker.

hévéa [āvāā] *nm* rubber tree.

hexagonal, e, aux [egzāgonál, -ō] *a* hexagonal; (*français*) French (*see note at hexagone*).

hexagone [egzāgon] *nm* hexagon; (*la France*) France (*because of its roughly hexagonal shape*).

HF *sigle f* (= *haute fréquence*) HF.

hiatus [yàtüs] *nm* hiatus.

hibernation [ēbernâsyóń] *nf* hibernation.

hiberner [ēbernā] *vi* to hibernate.

hibiscus [ēbēsküs] *nm* hibiscus.

'hibou, x ['ēbōō] *nm* owl.

'hic ['ēk] *nm* (*fam*) snag.

'hideusement ['ēdēzmâń] *ad* hideously.

'hideux, euse ['ēdœ̄, -œ̄z] *a* hideous.

hier [yer] *ad* yesterday; ~ **matin/soir/midi** yesterday morning/evening/at midday; **toute la journée d'~** all day yesterday; **toute la matinée d'~** all yesterday morning.

'hiérarchie ['yārârshē] *nf* hierarchy.

'hiérarchique ['yārârshēk] *a* hierarchic.

'hiérarchiquement ['yārârshēkmâń] *ad* hierarchically.

'hiérarchiser ['yārârshēzā] *vt* to organize into a hierarchy.

'hiéroglyphe ['yāroglēf] *nm* hieroglyphic.

'hiéroglyphique ['yāroglēfēk] *a* hieroglyphic.

hilarant, e [ēlárâ, -âńt] *a* hilarious.

hilare [ēlár] *a* mirthful.

hilarité [ēlárētā] *nf* hilarity, mirth.

Himalaya [ēmáláyá] *nm*: **l'~** the Himalayas *pl*.

himalayen, ne [ēmáláyań, -en] *a* Himalayan.

hindou, e [ańdōō] *a*, *nm/f* Hindu; (*Indien*) Indian.

hindouisme [ańdōōēsm(ə)] *nm* Hinduism.

Hindoustan [ańdōōstâń] *nm*: **l'~** Hindustan.

hippique [ēpēk] *a* equestrian, horse *cpd*.

hippisme [ēpēsm(ə)] *nm* (horse) riding.

hippocampe [ēpokâńp] *nm* sea horse.

hippodrome [ēpodrōm] *nm* racecourse.

hippophagique [ēpofázhēk] *a*: **boucherie** ~ horse butcher's.

hippopotame [ēpopotám] *nm* hippopotamus.

hirondelle [ērôńdel] *nf* swallow.

hirsute [ērsüt] *a* (*personne*) hairy; (*barbe*) shaggy; (*tête*) tousled.

hispanique [ēspánēk] *a* Hispanic.

hispanisant, e [ēspánēzâń, -âńt], **hispaniste** [ēspánēst(ə)] *nm/f* Hispanist.

hispano-américain, e [ēspánoámārēkań, -en] *a* Spanish-American.

hispano-arabe [ēspánoáráb] *a* Hispano-Moresque.

'hisser ['ēsā] *vt* to hoist, haul up; **se** ~ **sur** to haul o.s. up onto.

histoire [ēstwár] *nf* (*science, événements*) history; (*anecdote, récit, mensonge*) story; (*affaire*) business *q*; (*chichis: gén pl*) fuss *q*; **~s** *nfpl* (*ennuis*) trouble *sg*; **l'~ de France** French history, the history of France; **l'~ sainte** biblical history; **une** ~ **de** (*fig*) a question of.

histologie [ēstolozhē] *nf* histology.

historien, ne [ēstoryań, -en] *nm/f* historian.

historique [ēstorēk] *a* historical; (*important*)

historic ♦ *nm* (*exposé, récit*): **faire l'~ de** to give the background to.

historiquement [ēstorēkmâń] *ad* historically.

hiver [ēver] *nm* winter; **en** ~ in winter.

hivernal, e, aux [ēvernál, -ō] *a* (*de l'hiver*) winter *cpd*; (*comme en hiver*) wintry.

hivernant, e [ēvernâ, -âńt] *n* winter vacationer (*US*) *ou* holidaymaker (*Brit*).

hiverner [ēvernā] *vi* to winter.

HLM *sigle m ou f* (= *habitations à loyer modéré*) low-rent, state-owned housing; **un(e)** ~ ≈ a public housing unit (*US*), ≈ a council flat (*ou* house) (*Brit*).

Hme *abr* (= *homme*) M.

HO *abr* (= *hors œuvre*) labor (*US*) *ou* labour (*Brit*) not included (*on invoices*).

'hobby ['obē] *nm* hobby.

'hochement ['oshmâń] *nm*: ~ **de tête** nod; shake of the head.

'hocher ['oshā] *vt*: ~ **la tête** to nod; (*signe négatif ou dubitatif*) to shake one's head.

'hochet ['oshe] *nm* rattle.

'hockey ['oke] *nm*: ~ **(sur glace/gazon)** (ice/field) hockey.

'hockeyeur, euse ['okeyœr, -œ̄z] *nm/f* hockey player.

'hola ['olá] *nm*: **mettre le** ~ **à qch** to put a stop to sth.

'holding ['oldēng] *nm* holding company.

'hold-up ['oldœp] *nm inv* hold-up.

'hollandais, e ['olâńde, -ez] *a* Dutch ♦ *nm* (*LING*) Dutch ♦ *nm/f*: **H~, e** Dutchman/woman; **les H~** the Dutch.

'Hollande ['olâńd] *nf*: **la** ~ Holland ♦ *nm*: **h~** (*fromage*) Dutch cheese.

holocauste [olokōst(ə)] *nm* holocaust.

hologramme [olográm] *nm* hologram.

homard ['omár] *nm* lobster.

homéopathe [omāopát] *n* homeopath, homoeopath (*Brit*).

homéopathie [omāopātē] *nf* homeopathy, homoeopathy (*Brit*).

homéopathique [omāopátēk] *a* homeopathic, homoeopathic (*Brit*).

homérique [omārēk] *a* Homeric.

homicide [omēsēd] *nm* murder ♦ *nm/f* murderer/eress; ~ **involontaire** manslaughter.

hommage [omázh] *nm* tribute; **~s** *nmpl*: **présenter ses** ~**s** to pay one's respects; **rendre** ~ **à** to pay tribute *ou* homage to; **en** ~ **de** as a token of; **faire** ~ **de qch à qn** to present sb with sth.

homme [om] *nm* man; (*espèce humaine*): **l'~** man, mankind; ~ **d'affaires** businessman; ~ **des cavernes** caveman; ~ **d'Église** churchman, clergyman; ~ **d'État** statesman; ~ **de loi** lawyer; ~ **de main** hired man; ~ **de paille** stooge; **l'~ de la rue** the man in the street; ~ **à tout faire** odd-job man.

homme-grenouille, *pl* **hommes-grenouilles** [omgrənōōy] *nm* frogman.

homme-orchestre, *pl* **hommes-orchestres** [omorkestr(ə)] *nm* one-man band.

homme-sandwich, *pl* **hommes-sandwichs** [omsâńdwētsh] *nm* sandwich (board) man.

homogène [omozhen] *a* homogeneous.

homogénéisé, e [omozhānāēzā] *a*: **lait** ~ homogenized milk.

homogénéité [ɔmozhānāētā] *nf* homogeneity.
homologation [ɔmologásyôn] *nf* ratification; official recognition.
homologue [ɔmolog] *nm/f* counterpart, opposite number.
homologué, e [ɔmologā] *a* (*SPORT*) officially recognized, ratified; (*tarif*) authorized.
homologuer [ɔmologā] *vt* (*JUR*) to ratify; (*SPORT*) to recognize officially, ratify.
homonyme [ɔmonēm] *nm* (*LING*) homonym; (*d'une personne*) namesake.
homosexualité [ɔmoseksüálētā] *nf* homosexuality.
homosexuel, le [ɔmoseksüel] *a* homosexual.
'Honduras ['ôňdürás] *nm*: **le** ~ Honduras.
'hondurien, ne ['ôňdüryaň, -en] *a* Honduran.
'Hong-Kong ['ôňgkôňg] *n* Hong Kong.
'hongre ['ôňgr(ǝ)] *a* (*cheval*) gelded ♦ *nm* gelding.
'Hongrie ['ôňgrē] *nf*: **la** ~ Hungary.
'hongrois, e ['ôňgrwá, -wáz] *a* Hungarian ♦ *nm* (*LING*) Hungarian ♦ *nm/f*: **'H**~, **e** Hungarian.
honnête [onet] *a* (*intègre*) honest; (*juste, satisfaisant*) fair.
honnêtement [onetmáň] *ad* honestly.
honnêteté [onettā] *nf* honesty.
honneur [onœr] *nm* honor (*US*), honour (*Brit*); (*mérite*): **l'**~ **lui revient** the credit is his; **à qui ai-je l'**~? to whom have I the pleasure of speaking?; **"j'ai l'**~ **de ..."** "I have the honor of ..."; **en l'**~ **de** (*personne*) in honor of; (*événement*) on the occasion of; **faire** ~ **à** (*engagements*) to honor; (*famille, professeur*) to be a credit to; (*fig: repas etc*) to do justice to; **être à l'**~ to be in the place of honor; **être en** ~ to be in favor; **membre d'**~ honorary member; **table d'**~ top table.
Honolulu [onolülü] *n* Honolulu.
honorable [onorábl(ǝ)] *a* worthy, honorable (*US*), honourable (*Brit*); (*suffisant*) decent.
honorablement [onoráblǝmáň] *ad* honorably (*US*), honourably (*Brit*); decently.
honoraire [onorer] *a* honorary; ~**s** *nmpl* fees; **professeur** ~ professor emeritus.
honorer [onorā] *vt* to honor (*US*), honour (*Brit*); (*estimer*) to hold in high regard; (*faire honneur à*) to do credit to; ~ **qn de** to honor sb with; **s'**~ **de** to pride o.s. upon.
honorifique [onorēfēk] *a* honorary.
'honte ['ôňt] *nf* shame; **avoir** ~ **de** to be ashamed of; **faire** ~ **à qn** to make sb (feel) ashamed.
'honteusement ['ôňtœzmáň] *ad* ashamedly; shamefully.
'honteux, euse ['ôňtœ, -œz] *a* ashamed; (*conduite, acte*) shameful, disgraceful.
hôpital, aux [opētál, -ō] *nm* hospital.
'hoquet ['oke] *nm* hiccough; **avoir le** ~ to have (the) hiccoughs.
'hoqueter ['oktā] *vi* to hiccough.
horaire [orer] *a* hourly ♦ *nm* timetable, schedule; ~**s** *nmpl* (*heures de travail*) hours; ~ **flexible** *ou* **mobile** *ou* **à la carte** *ou* **souple** flex(i)time.
'horde ['ord(ǝ)] *nf* horde.
'horions [oryôň] *nmpl* blows.
horizon [orēzôň] *nm* horizon; (*paysage*) landscape, view; **sur l'**~ on the skyline *ou* horizon.

horizontal, e, aux [orēzôňtál, -ō] *a* horizontal ♦ *nf*: **à l'**~**e** on the horizontal.
horizontalement [orēzôňtálmáň] *ad* horizontally.
horloge [orlozh] *nf* clock; **l'**~ **parlante** Time (*US*), the speaking clock (*Brit*); ~ **normande** grandfather clock.
horloger, ère [orlozhā, -er] *nm/f* watchmaker; clockmaker.
horlogerie [orlozhrē] *nf* watch-making; watch-maker's (shop); clockmaker's (shop); **pièces d'**~ watch parts *ou* components.
'hormis ['ormē] *prép* save.
hormonal, e, aux [ormonál, -ō] *a* hormonal.
hormone [ormon] *nf* hormone.
horodaté, e [orodátā] *a* (*ticket*) time- and date-stamped; (*stationnement*) automatically timed.
horodateur, trice [orodátœr, -trēs] *a* (*appareil*) for stamping the time and date ♦ *nm/f* (*parking*) ticket machine.
horoscope [oroskop] *nm* horoscope.
horreur [orœr] *nf* horror; **avoir** ~ **de** to loathe, detest; **quelle** ~! how awful!; **cela me fait** ~ I find that awful.
horrible [orēbl(ǝ)] *a* horrible.
horriblement [orēblǝmáň] *ad* horribly.
horrifiant, e [orēfyáň, -áňt] *a* horrifying.
horrifier [orēfyā] *vt* to horrify.
horrifique [orēfēk] *a* horrific.
horripiler [orēpēlā] *vt* to exasperate.
'hors ['or] *prép* except (for); ~ **de** out of; ~ **ligne**, ~ **pair** outstanding; ~ **de propos** inopportune; ~ **série** (*sur mesure*) made-to-order; (*exceptionnel*) exceptional; ~ **service (HS)**, ~ **d'usage** out of use; ~ **taxe (HT)** (*article, boutique*) duty-free; (*prix*) before tax; **être** ~ **de soi** to be beside o.s.
'hors-bord ['orbor] *nm inv* outboard motor; (*canot*) speedboat (with outboard motor).
'hors-concours ['orkôňkōor] *a inv* ineligible to compete; (*fig*) in a class of one's own.
'hors-d'œuvre ['ordœvr(ǝ)] *nm inv* hors d'œuvre.
'hors-jeu ['orzhœ] *nm inv* being offside *q*.
'hors-la-loi ['orlálwá] *nm inv* outlaw.
'hors-piste(s) ['orpēst] *nm inv* (*SKI*) cross-country.
'hors-texte ['ortekst(ǝ)] *nm inv* plate.
hortensia [ortáňsyá] *nm* hydrangea.
horticole [ortēkol] *a* horticultural.
horticulteur, trice [ortēkültœr, -trēs] *nm/f* horticulturist (*US*), horticulturalist (*Brit*).
horticulture [ortēkültür] *nf* horticulture.
hospice [ospēs] *nm* (*de vieillards*) home; (*asile*) hospice.
hospitalier, ière [ospētályā, -yer] *a* (*accueillant*) hospitable; (*MÉD: service, centre*) hospital *cpd*.
hospitalisation [ospētálēzásyôň] *nf* hospitalization.
hospitaliser [ospētálēzā] *vt* to take (*ou* send) to the hospital, hospitalize.
hospitalité [ospētálētā] *nf* hospitality.
hospitalo-universitaire [ospētálouňēvērsēter] *a*: **centre** ~ **(CHU)** ≈ (teaching) hospital.
hostie [ostē] *nf* host (*REL*).
hostile [ostēl] *a* hostile.

hostilité [ostēlētā] *nf* hostility; ~**s** *nfpl* hostilities.

hôte [ōt] *nm* (*maître de maison*) host; (*invité*) guest; (*client*) patron; (*fig*) inhabitant, occupant; ~ **payant** paying guest.

hôtel [ōtel] *nm* hotel; **aller à l'~** to stay in a hotel; ~ (**particulier**) (private) mansion; ~ **de ville** town hall.

hôtelier, ière [ōtəlyā, -yer] *a* hotel *cpd* ♦ *nm/f* hotelier, hotel-keeper.

hôtellerie [ōtelrē] *nf* (*profession*) hotel business; (*auberge*) inn.

hôtesse [ōtes] *nf* hostess; ~ **de l'air** stewardess; ~ (**d'accueil**) receptionist.

'**hotte** ['ot] *nf* (*panier*) basket (*carried on the back*); (*de cheminée*) hood; ~ **aspirante** range (*US*) *ou* exhaust (*US*) *ou* cooker (*Brit*) hood.

'**houblon** ['ōōblôn] *nm* (*BOT*) hop; (*pour la bière*) hops *pl*.

'**houe** ['ōō] *nf* hoe.

'**houille** ['ōōy] *nf* coal; ~ **blanche** hydroelectric power.

'**houiller, ère** ['ōōyā, -er] *a* coal *cpd*; (*terrain*) coal-bearing ♦ *nf* coal mine.

'**houle** ['ōōl] *nf* swell.

'**houlette** ['ōōlet] *nf*: **sous la** ~ **de** under the guidance of.

'**houleux, euse** ['ōōlœ, -œz] *a* heavy, swelling; (*fig*) stormy, turbulent.

'**houppe** ['ōōp] *nf*, '**houppette** ['ōōpet] *nf* powder puff; (*cheveux*) tuft.

'**hourra** ['ōōrà] *nm* cheer ♦ *excl* hurrah!

'**houspiller** ['ōōspēyā] *vt* to scold.

'**housse** ['ōōs] *nf* cover; (*pour protégér provisoirement*) dust cover; (*pour recouvrir à neuf*) loose *ou* stretch cover; ~ (**penderie**) garment bag (*US*), hanging wardrobe (*Brit*).

'**houx** ['ōō] *nm* holly.

HS *abr* = **hors service**.

HT *abr* = **hors taxe**.

'**hublot** ['ūblō] *nm* porthole.

'**huche** ['üsh] *nf*: ~ **à pain** bread box (*US*) *ou* bin (*Brit*).

'**huées** ['üä] *nfpl* boos.

'**huer** ['üä] *vt* to boo; (*hibou, chouette*) to hoot.

huile [üēl] *nf* oil; (*ART*) oil painting; (*fam*) bigwig; **mer d'~** (*très calme*) glassy sea, sea of glass; **faire tache d'~** (*fig*) to spread; ~ **d'arachide** peanut oil; ~ **essentielle** essential oil; ~ **de foie de morue** cod-liver oil; ~ **de ricin** castor oil; ~ **solaire** suntan oil; ~ **de table** salad oil.

huiler [üēlā] *vt* to oil.

huilerie [üēlrē] *nf* (*usine*) oil-works.

huileux, euse [üēlœ, -œz] *a* oily.

huilier [üēlyā] *nm* (oil and vinegar) cruet.

huis [üē] *nm*: **à** ~ **clos** in camera.

huissier [üēsyā] *nm* usher; (*JUR*) ≈ bailiff.

'**huit** ['üē(t)] *num* eight; **samedi en** ~ a week from Saturday; **dans** ~ **jours** in a week('s time).

'**huitaine** ['üēten] *nf*: **une** ~ **de** about eight, eight or so; **une** ~ **de jours** a week or so.

'**huitante** ['üētànt] *num* (*Suisse*) eighty.

'**huitième** ['üētyem] *num* eighth.

huître [üētr(ə)] *nf* oyster.

'**hululer** ['ülülā] *vi* to hoot.

humain, e [ümań, -en] *a* human;

(*compatissant*) humane ♦ *nm* human (being).

humainement [ümenmáń] *ad* humanly; humanely.

humaniser [umaneza] *vt* to humanize.

humaniste [ümánēst(ə)] *nm/f* (*LING*) classicist; humanist.

humanitaire [ümánēter] *a* humanitarian.

humanitarisme [ümánētárēsm(ə)] *nm* humanitarianism.

humanité [ümánētā] *nf* humanity.

humanoïde [ümánoēd] *nm/f* humanoid.

humble [œńbl(ə)] *a* humble.

humblement [œńbləmáń] *ad* humbly.

humecter [ümektā] *vt* to dampen; **s'~ les lèvres** to moisten one's lips.

'**humer** ['ümā] *vt* to inhale; (*pour sentir*) to smell.

humérus [ümārüs] *nf* (*ANAT*) humerus.

humeur [ümœr] *nf* mood; (*tempérament*) temper; (*irritation*) bad temper; **de bonne/mauvaise** ~ in a good/bad mood; **être d'~ à faire qch** to be in the mood for doing sth.

humide [ümēd] *a* (*linge*) damp; (*main, yeux*) moist; (*climat, chaleur*) humid; (*saison, route*) wet.

humidificateur [ümēdēfēkátœr] *nm* humidifier.

humidifier [ümēdēfyā] *vt* to humidify.

humidité [ümēdētā] *nf* humidity; dampness; **traces d'~** traces of moisture *ou* damp.

humiliant, e [ümēlyáń, -áńt] humiliating.

humiliation [ümēlyàsyôń] *nf* humiliation.

humilier [ümēlyā] *vt* to humiliate; **s'~ devant qn** to humble o.s. before sb.

humilité [ümēlētā] *nf* humility.

humoriste [ümorēst(ə)] *nm/f* humorist.

humoristique [ümorēstēk] *a* humorous; humoristic.

humour [ümōōr] *nm* humor (*US*), humour (*Brit*); **avoir de l'~** to have a sense of humor; ~ **noir** sick humor.

humus [ümüs] *nm* humus.

'**huppé, e** ['üpā] *a* crested; (*fam*) posh.

'**hurlement** ['ürləmáń] *nm* howling *q*, howl; yelling *q*, yell.

'**hurler** ['ürlā] *vi* to howl, yell; (*fig: vent*) to howl; (*: couleurs etc*) to clash; ~ **à la mort** (*suj: chien*) to bay at the moon.

hurluberlu [ürlüberlü] *nm* (*péj*) crank ♦ *a* cranky.

'**hutte** ['üt] *nf* hut.

hybride [ēbrēd] *a* hybrid.

hydratant, e [ēdrátáń, -áńt] *a* (*crème*) moisturizing.

hydrate [ēdrát] *nm*: ~**s de carbone** carbohydrates.

hydrater [ēdrátā] *vt* to hydrate.

hydraulique [ēdrōlēk] *a* hydraulic.

hydravion [ēdrávyôń] *nm* seaplane, hydroplane.

hydro... [ēdro] *préfixe* hydro....

hydrocarbure [ēdrokárbür] *nm* hydrocarbon.

hydrocution [ēdroküsyôń] *nf* immersion syncope.

hydro-électrique [ēdroālektrēk] *a* hydro-electric.

hydrogène [ēdrozhen] *nm* hydrogen.

hydroglisseur [ēdroglēsœr] *nm* hydroplane.

hydrographie [ēdrográfē] *nf* (*fleuves*) hydrography.

hydrophile [ēdrofēl] *a voir* **coton.**

hyène [yen] *nf* hyena.

hygiène [ēzhyen] *nf* hygiene; ~ **intime** personal hygiene.

hygiénique [ēzhānēk] *a* hygienic.

hymne [ēmn(ə)] *nm* hymn; ~ **national** national anthem.

hyper... [ēper] *préfixe* hyper....

hypermarché [ēpermárshā] *nm* superstore.

hypermétrope [ēpermātrop] *a* farsighted, longsighted.

hypernerveux, euse [ēpernervœ̃, -œz] *a* high-strung (*US*), highly-strung (*Brit*).

hypersensible [ēpersáṅsēbl(ə)] *a* hypersensitive.

hypertendu, e [ēpertáṅdü] *a* having high blood pressure, hypertensive.

hypertension [ēpertáṅsyóṅ] *nf* high blood pressure, hypertension.

hypertrophié, e [ēpertrofyā] *a* hypertrophic.

hypnose [ēpnōz] *nf* hypnosis.

hypnotique [ēpnotēk] *a* hypnotic.

hypnotiser [ēpnotēzā] *vt* to hypnotize.

hypnotiseur [ēpnotēzœr] *nm* hypnotist.

hypnotisme [ēpnotēsm(ə)] *nm* hypnotism.

hypocondriaque [ēpokóṅdrēyák] *a* hypochondriac.

hypocrisie [ēpokrēzē] *nf* hypocrisy.

hypocrite [ēpokrēt] *a* hypocritical ♦ *nm/f* hypocrite.

hypocritement [ēpokrētmáṅ] *ad* hypocritically.

hypotendu, e [ēpotáṅdü] *a* having low blood pressure, hypotensive.

hypotension [ēpotáṅsyóṅ] *nf* low blood pressure, hypotension.

hypoténuse [ēpotānüz] *nf* hypotenuse.

hypothécaire [ēpotāker] *a* hypothecary; **garantie/prêt** ~ mortgage security/loan.

hypothèque [ēpotek] *nf* mortgage.

hypothéquer [ēpotākā] *vt* to mortgage.

hypothermie [ēpotermē] *nf* hypothermia.

hypothèse [ēpotez] *nf* hypothesis; **dans l'~ où** assuming that.

hypothétique [ēpotātēk] *a* hypothetical.

hystérectomie [ēstārektomē] *nf* hysterectomy.

hystérie [ēstārē] *nf* hysteria; ~ **collective** mass hysteria.

hystérique [ēstārēk] *a* hysterical.

Hz *abr* (= *Hertz*) Hz.

I

I, i [ē] *nm inv* I, i; **I comme Irma** I for Item.

IAC *sigle f* (= *insémination artificielle entre conjoints*) AIH.

IAD *sigle f* (= *insémination artificielle par donneur extérieur*) AID.

ibère [ēber] *a* Iberian ♦ *nm/f*: **I~** Iberian.

ibérique [ēbārēk] *a*: **la péninsule** ~ the Iberian peninsula.

iceberg [ēsberg] *nm* iceberg.

ici [ēsē] *ad* here; **jusqu'~** as far as this; (*temporel*) until now; **d'~ là** by then; (*en attendant*) in the meantime; **d'~ peu** before long.

icône [ēkōn] *nf* (*aussi INFORM*) icon.

iconoclaste [ēkonoklást(ə)] *nm/f* iconoclast.

iconographie [ēkonográfē] *nf* iconography; (*illustrations*) (collection of) illustrations.

idéal, e, aux [ēdáál, -ō] *a* ideal ♦ *nm* ideal; (*système de valeurs*) ideals *pl*.

idéalement [ēdáálmáṅ] *ad* ideally.

idéalisation [ēdáálēzásyóṅ] *nf* idealization.

idéaliser [ēdáálēzā] *vt* to idealize.

idéalisme [ēdáálēsm(ə)] *nm* idealism.

idéaliste [ēdáálēst(ə)] *a* idealistic ♦ *nm/f* idealist.

idée [ēdā] *nf* idea; (*illusion*): **se faire des ~s** to imagine things, get ideas into one's head; **avoir dans l'~ que** to have an idea that; **mon ~, c'est que ...** I suggest that ..., I think that ...; **à l'~ de/que** at the idea of/that, at the thought of/that; **je n'ai pas la moindre ~** I haven't the faintest idea; **avoir ~ que** to have an idea that; **avoir des ~s larges/étroites** to be broad-/narrow-minded; **venir à l'~ de qn** to occur to sb; **en voilà des ~s!** the very idea!; ~ **fixe** idée fixe, obsession; **~s noires** black *ou* dark thoughts; **~s reçues** accepted ideas *ou* wisdom.

identification [ēdáṅtēfēkásyóṅ] *nf* identification.

identifier [ēdáṅtēfyā] *vt* to identify; ~ **qch/qn à** to identify sth/sb with; **s'~ avec** *ou* **à qn/qch** (*héros etc*) to identify with sb/sth.

identique [ēdáṅtēk] *a*: ~ (**à**) identical (to).

identité [ēdáṅtētā] *nf* identity; ~ **judiciaire** (*POLICE*) ≈ Criminal Records Office.

idéologie [ēdāolozhē] *nf* ideology.

idéologique [ēdāolozhēk] *a* ideological.

idiomatique [ēdyomátēk] *a*: **expression** ~ idiom, idiomatic expression.

idiome [ēdyōm] *nm* (*LING*) idiom.

idiot, e [ēdyō, ēdyot] *a* idiotic ♦ *nm/f* idiot.

idiotie [ēdyosē] *nf* idiocy; (*propos*) idiotic remark *etc*.

idiotisme [ēdyotēsm(ə)] *nm* idiom, idiomatic phrase.

idoine [ēdwán] *a* fitting.

idolâtrer [ēdolátrā] *vt* to idolize.

idolâtrie [ēdolâtrē] *nf* idolatry.

idole [ēdol] *nf* idol.

IDS *sigle f* (= *Initiative de défense stratégique*) SDI.

idylle [ēdēl] *nf* idyll.

idyllique [ēdēlēk] *a* idyllic.

if [ēf] *nm* yew.

IFOP [ēfop] *sigle m* (= *Institut français d'opinion publique*) French market research institute.

IGF *sigle m* (= *Impôt sur les grandes fortunes*) wealth tax.

IGH *sigle m* (= *immeuble de grande hauteur*).

igloo [ēglōō] *nm* igloo.

IGN *sigle m* = *Institut géographique national*.

ignare [ēnyár] *a* ignorant.

ignifuge [ēgnēfüzh] *a* fireproofing ♦ *nm* fireproofing (substance).

ignifuger [ēgnēfüzhā] *vt* to fireproof.

ignoble [ēnyobl(ə)] *a* vile.
ignominie [ēnyomēnē] *nf* ignominy; (*acte*) ignominious *ou* base act.
ignominieux, euse [ēnyomēnyœ̄, œ̄z] *a* ignominious.
ignorance [ēnyorâns] *nf* ignorance; **dans l'~ de** in ignorance of, ignorant of.
ignorant, e [ēnyorâṅ, -âṅt] *a* ignorant ♦ *nm/f*: **faire l'~** to pretend one doesn't know; **~ de** ignorant of, not aware of; **~ en** ignorant of, knowing nothing of.
ignoré, e [ēnyorā] *a* unknown.
ignorer [ēnyorā] *vt* (*ne pas connaître*) not to know, be unaware *ou* ignorant of; (*être sans expérience de: plaisir, guerre etc*) not to know about, have no experience of; (*bouder: personne*) to ignore; **j'ignore comment/si** I do not know how/if; **~ que** to be unaware that, not to know that; **je n'ignore pas que ...** I'm not forgetting that ..., I'm not unaware that ...; **je l'ignore** I don't know.
IGPN *sigle f* (= *Inspection générale de la police nationale*) police disciplinary body.
IGS *sigle f* (= *Inspection générale des services*) police disciplinary body for Paris.
iguane [ēgwàn] *nm* iguana.
il [ēl] *pronom* he; (*animal, chose, en tournure impersonnelle*) it; *NB: en anglais les navires et les pays sont en général assimilés aux femelles, et les bébés aux choses, si le sexe n'est pas spécifié;* **~s** they; **~ neige** it's snowing; *voir aussi* **avoir.**
iliaque [ēlyák] *a* (*ANAT*): **os/artère ~** iliac bone/artery.
illégal, e, aux [ēlāgál, -ō] *a* illegal, unlawful (*ADMIN*).
illégalement [ēlāgálmâṅ] *ad* illegally.
illégalité [ēlāgálētā] *nf* illegality; unlawfulness; **être dans l'~** to be outside the law.
illégitime [ēlāzhētēm] *a* illegitimate; (*optimisme, sévérité*) unjustified, unwarranted.
illégitimement [ēlāzhētēmmâṅ] *ad* illegitimately.
illégitimité [ēlāzhētēmētā] *nf* illegitimacy; **gouverner dans l'~** to rule illegally.
illettré, e [ēlātrā] *a*, *nm/f* illiterate.
illicite [ēlēsēt] *a* illicit.
illicitement [ēlēsētmâṅ] *ad* illicitly.
illico [ēlēkō] *ad* (*fam*) pronto.
illimité, e [ēlēmētā] *a* (*immense*) boundless, unlimited; (*congé, durée*) indefinite, unlimited.
illisible [ēlēzēbl(ə)] *a* illegible; (*roman*) unreadable.
illisiblement [ēlēzēbləmâṅ] *ad* illegibly.
illogique [ēlozhēk] *a* illogical.
illogisme [ēlozhēsm(ə)] *nm* illogicality.
illumination [ēlümēnâsyôṅ] *nf* illumination, floodlighting; (*inspiration*) flash of inspiration; **~s** *nfpl* illuminations, lights.
illuminé, e [ēlümēnā] *a* lit up; illuminated, floodlit ♦ *nm/f* (*fig: péj*) crank.
illuminer [ēlümēnā] *vt* to light up; (*monument, rue: pour une fête*) to illuminate, floodlight; **s'~** *vi* to light up.
illusion [ēlüzyôṅ] *nf* illusion; **se faire des ~s** to delude o.s.; **faire ~** to delude *ou* fool people; **~ d'optique** optical illusion.

illusionner [ēlüzyonā] *vt* to delude; **s'~ (sur qn/qch)** to delude o.s. (about sb/sth).
illusionnisme [ēlüzyonēsm(ə)] *nm* conjuring.
illusionniste [ēlüzyonēst(ə)] *nm/f* conjuror.
illusoire [ēlüzwár] *a* illusory, illusive.
illustrateur [ēlüstrátœr] *nm* illustrator.
illustratif, ive [ēlüstrátēf, -ēv] *a* illustrative.
illustration [ēlüstrâsyôṅ] *nf* illustration; (*d'un ouvrage: photos*) illustrations *pl*.
illustre [ēlüstr(ə)] *a* illustrious, renowned.
illustré, e [ēlüstrā] *a* illustrated ♦ *nm* illustrated magazine; (*pour enfants*) comic.
illustrer [ēlüstrā] *vt* to illustrate; **s'~** to become famous, win fame.
ils [ēl] *pronom voir* **il.**
image [ēmázh] *nf* (*gén*) picture; (*comparaison, ressemblance, OPTIQUE*) image; **~ de** picture *ou* image of; **~ d'Épinal** (*social*) stereotype; **~ de marque** brand image; (*d'une personne*) (public) image; (*d'une entreprise*) corporate image; **~ pieuse** holy picture.
imagé, e [ēmázhā] *a* full of imagery.
imaginable [ēmázhēnábl(ə)] *a* imaginable; **difficilement ~** hard to imagine.
imaginaire [ēmázhēner] *a* imaginary.
imaginatif, ive [ēmázhēnátēf, -ēv] *a* imaginative.
imagination [ēmázhēnâsyôṅ] *nf* imagination; (*chimère*) fancy, imagining; **avoir de l'~** to be imaginative, have a good imagination.
imaginer [ēmázhēnā] *vt* to imagine; (*croire*): **qu'allez-vous ~ là?** what on earth are you thinking of?; (*inventer: expédient, mesure*) to devise, think up; **s'~** *vt* (*se figurer: scène etc*) to imagine, picture; **s'~ à 60 ans** to picture *ou* imagine o.s. at 60; **s'~ que** to imagine that; **s'~ pouvoir faire qch** to think one can do sth; **j'imagine qu'il a voulu plaisanter** I suppose he was joking; **~ de faire** (*se mettre dans l'idée de*) to dream up the idea of doing.
imbattable [aṅbátábl(ə)] *a* unbeatable.
imbécile [aṅbāsēl] *a* idiotic ♦ *nm/f* idiot; (*MÉD*) imbecile.
imbécillité [aṅbāsēlētā] *nf* idiocy; imbecility; idiotic action (*ou* remark *etc*).
imberbe [aṅberb(ə)] *a* beardless.
imbiber [aṅbēbā] *vt*: **~ qch de** to moisten *ou* wet sth with; **s'~ de** to become saturated with; **imbibé(e) d'eau** (*chaussures, étoffe*) saturated; (*terre*) waterlogged.
imbriqué, e [aṅbrēkā] *a* overlapping.
imbriquer [aṅbrēkā] **s'~** *vi* to overlap (each other); (*fig*) to become interlinked *ou* interwoven.
imbu, e [aṅbü] *a*: **~ de** full of; **~ de soi-même/sa supériorité** full of oneself/one's superiority.
imbuvable [aṅbüvábl(ə)] *a* undrinkable.
imitable [ēmētábl(ə)] *a* imitable; **facilement ~** easily imitated.
imitateur, trice [ēmētátœr, -trēs] *nm/f* (*gén*) imitator; (*MUSIC-HALL*): **d'une personnalité** impersonator.
imitation [ēmētâsyôṅ] *nf* imitation; impersonation; **sac ~ cuir** bag in imitation *ou* simulated leather; **à l'~ de** in imitation of.
imiter [ēmētā] *vt* to imitate; (*personne*) to

imitate, impersonate; (*contrefaire: signature, document*) to forge, copy; (*ressembler à*) to look like; **il se leva et je l'imitai** he got up and I did likewise.

imm. *abr* = **immeuble**.

immaculé, e [ēmȧkülā] *a* spotless, immaculate; **l'I~e Conception** (*REL*) the Immaculate Conception.

immanent, e [ēmȧnȧn̄, -ȧn̄t] *a* immanent.

immangeable [ȧn̄mȧn̄zhȧbl(ə)] *a* inedible, uneatable.

immanquable [ȧn̄mȧn̄kȧbl(ə)] *a* (*cible*) impossible to miss; (*fatal, inévitable*) bound to happen, inevitable.

immanquablement [ȧn̄mȧn̄kȧbləmȧn̄] *ad* inevitably.

immatériel, le [ēmȧtāryel] *a* ethereal; (*PHILOSOPHIE*) immaterial.

immatriculation [ēmȧtrēkülȧsyôn̄] *nf* registration.

immatriculer [ēmȧtrēkülā] *vt* to register; **faire/se faire** ~ to register; **voiture immatriculée dans la Seine** car with a Seine registration (number).

immature [ēmȧtür] *a* immature.

immaturité [ēmȧtürētā] *nf* immaturity.

immédiat, e [ēmādyȧ, -ȧt] *a* immediate ♦ *nm*: **dans l'~** for the time being; **dans le voisinage** ~ **de** in the immediate vicinity of.

immédiatement [ēmādyȧtmȧn̄] *ad* immediately.

immémorial, e, aux [ēmāmoryȧl, -ō] *a* ancient, age-old.

immense [ēmȧn̄s] *a* immense.

immensément [ēmȧn̄sāmȧn̄] *ad* immensely.

immensité [ēmȧn̄sētā] *nf* immensity.

immerger [ēmerzhā] *vt* to immerse, submerge; (*câble etc*) to lay under water; (*déchets*) to dump at sea; **s'~** *vi* (*sous-marin*) to dive, submerge.

immérité, e [ēmārētā] *a* undeserved.

immersion [ēmersyôn̄] *nf* immersion.

immettable [ȧn̄metȧbl(ə)] *a* unwearable.

immeuble [ēmœbl(ə)] *nm* building ♦ *a* (*JUR*) immovable, real; ~ **locatif** rental building (*US*), block of rented flats (*Brit*); ~ **de rapport** investment property.

immigrant, e [ēmēgrȧn̄, -ȧn̄t] *nm/f* immigrant.

immigration [ēmēgrȧsyôn̄] *nf* immigration.

immigré, e [ēmēgrā] *nm/f* immigrant.

immigrer [ēmēgrā] *vi* to immigrate.

imminence [ēmēnȧn̄s] *nf* imminence.

imminent, e [ēmēnȧn̄, -ȧn̄t] *a* imminent, impending.

immiscer [ēmēsā]: **s'~** *vi*: **s'~ dans** to interfere in *ou* with.

immixtion [ēmēksyôn̄] *nf* interference.

immobile [ēmobēl] *a* still, motionless; (*pièce de machine*) fixed; (*fig*) unchanging; **rester/se tenir** ~ to stay/keep still.

immobilier, ière [ēmobēlyȧ, -yer] *a* property *cpd*, in real property ♦ *nm*: **l'~** the property *ou* the real estate business.

immobilisation [ēmobēlēzȧsyôn̄] *nf* immobilization; **~s** *nfpl* (*JUR*) fixed assets.

immobiliser [ēmobēlēzā] *vt* (*gén*) to immobilize; (*circulation, véhicule, affaires*) to bring to a standstill; **s'~** (*personne*) to stand still; (*machine, véhicule*) to come to a

halt *ou* a standstill.

immobilisme [ēmobēlēsm(ə)] *nm* strong resistance *ou* opposition to change.

immobilité [ēmobēlētā] *nf* immobility.

immodéré, e [ēmodārā] *a* immoderate, inordinate.

immodérément [ēmodārāmȧn̄] *ad* immoderately.

immoler [ēmolā] *vt* to sacrifice.

immonde [ēmôn̄d] *a* foul; (*sale: ruelle, taudis*) squalid.

immondices [ēmôn̄dēs] *nmpl* (*ordures*) refuse *sg*; (*saletés*) filth *sg*.

immoral, e, aux [ēmorȧl, -ō] *a* immoral.

immoralité [ēmorȧlētā] *nf* immorality.

immortaliser [ēmortȧlēzā] *vt* to immortalize.

immortel, le [ēmortel] *a* immortal ♦ *nf* (*BOT*) everlasting (flower).

immuable [ēmüȧbl(ə)] *a* (*inébranlable*) immutable; (*qui ne change pas*) unchanging; (*personne*): ~ **dans ses convictions** immovable (in one's convictions).

immunisation [ēmünēzȧsyôn̄] *nf* immunization.

immuniser [ēmünēzā] *vt* (*MÉD*) to immunize; ~ **qn contre** to immunize sb against; (*fig*) to make sb immune to.

immunité [ēmünētā] *nf* immunity; ~ **diplomatique** diplomatic immunity; ~ **parlementaire** parliamentary privilege.

immunologie [ēmünolozhē] *nf* immunology.

impact [ȧn̄pȧkt] *nm* impact; **point d'~** point of impact.

impair, e [ȧn̄per] *a* odd ♦ *nm* faux pas, blunder; **numéros ~s** odd numbers.

impaludation [ȧn̄pȧlüdȧsyôn̄] *nf* inoculation against malaria.

imparable [ȧn̄pȧrȧbl(ə)] *a* unstoppable.

impardonnable [ȧn̄pȧrdonȧbl(ə)] *a* unpardonable, unforgivable; **vous êtes ~ d'avoir fait cela** it's unforgivable of you to have done that.

imparfait, e [ȧn̄pȧrfe, -et] *a* imperfect ♦ *nm* (*LING*) imperfect (tense).

imparfaitement [ȧn̄pȧrfetmȧn̄] *ad* imperfectly.

impartial, e, aux [ȧn̄pȧrsyȧl, -ō] *a* impartial, unbiased.

impartialité [ȧn̄pȧrsyȧlētā] *nf* impartiality.

impartir [ȧn̄pȧrtēr] *vt*: ~ **qch à qn** to assign sth to sb; (*dons*) to bestow sth upon sb; **dans les délais impartis** in the time allowed.

impasse [ȧn̄pȧs] *nf* dead end, cul-de-sac; (*fig*) deadlock; **être dans l'~** (*négociations*) to have reached deadlock; ~ **budgétaire** budget deficit.

impassibilité [ȧn̄pȧsēbēlētā] *nf* impassiveness.

impassible [ȧn̄pȧsēbl(ə)] *a* impassive.

impatiemment [ȧn̄pȧsyȧmȧn̄] *ad* impatiently.

impatience [ȧn̄pȧsyȧn̄s] *nf* impatience.

impatient, e [ȧn̄pȧsyȧn̄, -ȧn̄t] *a* impatient; ~ **de faire qch** impatient to do sth.

impatienter [ȧn̄pȧsyȧn̄tā] *vt* to irritate, annoy; **s'~** *vi* to get impatient; **s'~ de/contre** to lose patience at/with, grow impatient at/with.

impayable [ȧn̄peyȧbl(ə)] *a* (*drôle*) priceless.

impayé, e [ȧn̄pāyā] *a* unpaid, outstanding.

impeccable [ȧn̄pȧkȧbl(ə)] *a* faultless, impeccable; (*propre*) spotlessly clean; (*chic*) impeccably dressed; (*fam*) great, neat.

impeccablement [aṅpākábləmáṅ] *ad* impeccably.

impénétrable [aṅpānātrábl(ə)] *a* impenetrable.

impénitent, e [aṅpānētáṅ, -áṅt] *a* unrepentant.

impensable [aṅpáṅsábl(ə)] *a* unthinkable, unbelievable.

imper [aṅper] *nm* (= *imperméable*) raincoat.

impératif, ive [aṅpārátēf, -ēv] *a* imperative; (*JUR*) mandatory ♦ *nm* (*LING*) imperative; ~s *nmpl* requirements; demands.

impérativement [aṅpārátēvmáṅ] *ad* imperatively.

impératrice [aṅpārátrēs] *nf* empress.

imperceptible [aṅperseptēbl(ə)] *a* imperceptible.

imperceptiblement [aṅperseptēbləmáṅ] *ad* imperceptibly.

imperdable [aṅperdábl(ə)] *a* that cannot be lost.

imperfectible [aṅperfektēbl(ə)] *a* which cannot be perfected.

imperfection [aṅperfeksyóṅ] *nf* imperfection.

impérial, e, aux [aṅpāryál, -ō] *a* imperial ♦ *nf* upper deck; **autobus à ~e** double-decker bus.

impérialisme [aṅpāryálēsm(ə)] *nm* imperialism.

impérialiste [aṅpāryálēst(ə)] *a* imperialist.

impérieusement [aṅpāryœ̄zmáṅ] *ad*: **avoir ~ besoin de qch** to have urgent need of sth.

impérieux, euse [aṅpāryœ̄, -œ̄z] *a* (*caractère, ton*) imperious; (*obligation, besoin*) pressing, urgent.

impérissable [aṅpārēsábl(ə)] *a* undying, imperishable.

imperméabilisation [aṅpermāábēlēzásyóṅ] *nf* waterproofing.

imperméabiliser [aṅpermāábēlēzá] *vt* to waterproof.

imperméable [aṅpermāábl(ə)] *a* waterproof; (*GÉO*) impermeable; (*fig*): ~ **à** impervious to ♦ *nm* raincoat; ~ **à l'air** airtight.

impersonnel, le [aṅpersonel] *a* impersonal.

impertinemment [aṅpertēnámáṅ] *ad* impertinently.

impertinence [aṅpertēnáṅs] *nf* impertinence.

impertinent, e [aṅpertēnáṅ, -áṅt] *a* impertinent.

imperturbable [aṅpertürbábl(ə)] *a* (*personne*) imperturbable; (*sang-froid*) unshakeable; **rester ~** to remain unruffled.

imperturbablement [aṅpertürbábləmáṅ] *ad* imperturbably; unshakeably.

impétrant, e [aṅpātráṅ, -áṅt] *nm/f* (*JUR*) applicant.

impétueux, euse [aṅpātüœ̄, -œ̄z] *a* fiery.

impétuosité [aṅpātüōzētá] *nf* fieriness.

impie [aṅpē] *a* impious, ungodly.

impiété [aṅpyātá] *nf* impiety.

impitoyable [aṅpētwáyábl(ə)] *a* pitiless, merciless.

impitoyablement [aṅpētwáyábləmáṅ] *ad* mercilessly.

implacable [aṅplákábl(ə)] *a* implacable.

implacablement [aṅplákábləmáṅ] *ad* implacably.

implant [aṅpláṅ] *nm* (*MÉD*) implant.

implantation [aṅpláṅtásyóṅ] *nf* establishment;

settling; implantation.

implanter [aṅpláṅtá] *vt* (*usine, industrie, usage*) to establish; (*colons etc*) to settle; (*idée, préjugé*) to implant; **s'~ dans** to be established in; to settle in; to become implanted in.

implication [aṅplēkásyóṅ] *nf* implication.

implicite [aṅplēsēt] *a* implicit.

implicitement [aṅplēsētmáṅ] *ad* implicitly.

impliquer [aṅplēká] *vt* to imply; ~ **qn (dans)** to implicate sb (in).

implorer [aṅplorá] *vt* to implore.

imploser [aṅplōzá] *vi* to implode.

implosion [aṅplōzyóṅ] *nf* implosion.

impoli, e [aṅpolē] *a* impolite, rude.

impoliment [aṅpolēmáṅ] *ad* impolitely.

impolitesse [aṅpolētes] *nf* impoliteness, rudeness; (*propos*) impolite *ou* rude remark.

impondérable [aṅpóṅdārábl(ə)] *nm* imponderable.

impopulaire [aṅpopüler] *a* unpopular.

impopularité [aṅpopülárētá] *nf* unpopularity.

importable [aṅportábl(ə)] *a* (*COMM*: *marchandise*) importable; (*vêtement*: *immettable*) unwearable.

importance [aṅportáṅs] *nf* importance; **avoir de l'~** to be important; **sans ~** unimportant; **d'~** important, considerable; **quelle ~?** what does it matter?

important, e [aṅportáṅ, -áṅt] *a* important; (*en quantité*) considerable, sizeable; (: *gamme, dégâts*) extensive; (*péj*: *airs, ton*) self-important ♦ *nm*: **l'~** the important thing.

importateur, trice [aṅportátœr, -trēs] *a* importing ♦ *nm/f* importer; **pays ~ de blé** wheat-importing country.

importation [aṅportásyóṅ] *nf* import; introduction; (*produit*) import.

importer [aṅportá] *vt* (*COMM*) to import; (*maladies, plantes*) to introduce ♦ *vi* (*être important*) to matter; ~ **à qn** to matter to sb; **il importe de** it is important to; **il importe qu'il fasse** he must do, it is important that he should do; **peu m'importe** I don't mind, I don't care; **peu importe** it doesn't matter; **peu importe (que)** it doesn't matter (if); **peu importe le prix** never mind the price; *voir aussi* **n'importe**.

import-export [aṅporekspor] *nm* import-export business.

importun, e [aṅportœ̄, -ün] *a* irksome, importunate; (*arrivée, visite*) inopportune, ill-timed ♦ *nm* intruder.

importuner [aṅportüná] *vt* to bother.

imposable [aṅpōzábl(ə)] *a* taxable.

imposant, e [aṅpōzáṅ, -áṅt] *a* imposing.

imposé, e [aṅpōzá] *a* (*soumis à l'impôt*) taxed; (*GYM etc*: *figures*) set.

imposer [aṅpōzá] *vt* (*taxer*) to tax; (*REL*): **les mains** to lay on hands; ~ **qch à qn** to impose sth on sb; **s'~** (*être nécessaire*) to be imperative; (*montrer sa proéminence*) to stand out, emerge; (*artiste: se faire connaître*) to win recognition, come to the fore; **en ~** to be imposing; **en ~ à** to impress; **ça s'impose** it's essential, it's a must.

imposition [aṅpōzēsyóṅ] *nf* (*ADMIN*) taxation.

impossibilité [aṅposēbēlētá] *nf* impossibility; **être dans l'~ de faire** to be unable to do, find it impossible to do.

impossible [aṅposēbl(ə)] *a* impossible ♦ *nm*: **l'~** the impossible; **~ à faire** impossible to do; **il m'est ~ de le faire** it is impossible for me to do it, I can't possibly do it; **faire l'~ (pour que)** to do one's utmost (so that); **si, par ~ ...** if, by some miracle ....

imposteur [aṅpostœr] *nm* impostor.

imposture [aṅpostür] *nf* imposture, deception.

impôt [aṅpō] *nm* tax; *(taxes)* taxation, taxes *pl*; **~s** *nmpl* *(contributions)* (income) tax *sg*; **payer 1.000 F d'~s** to pay 1,000 F in tax; **~ direct/indirect** direct/indirect tax; **~ sur le chiffre d'affaires** tax on turnover; **~ foncier** property tax; **~ sur la fortune** wealth tax; **~ sur les plus-values** capital gains tax; **~ sur le revenu** income tax; **~ sur le RPP** personal income tax; **~ sur les sociétés** corporate tax; **~s locaux** rates.

impotence [aṅpotāṅs] *nf* disability.

impotent, e [aṅpotāṅ, -āṅt] *a* disabled.

impraticable [aṅprátēkábl(ə)] *a* *(projet)* impracticable, unworkable; *(piste)* impassable.

imprécation [aṅprākásyóṅ] *nf* imprecation.

imprécis, e [aṅprāsē, -ēz] *a* *(contours, souvenir)* imprecise, vague; *(tir)* inaccurate, imprecise.

imprécision [aṅprāsēzyóṅ] *nf* imprecision.

imprégner [aṅprānyā] *vt* *(tissu, tampon)*: **~ (de)** to soak *ou* impregnate (with); *(lieu, air)*: **~ (de)** to fill (with); *(suj: amertume, ironie)* to pervade; **s'~ de** to become impregnated with; to be filled with; *(fig)* to absorb.

imprenable [aṅprənábl(ə)] *a* *(forteresse)* impregnable; **vue ~** unrestricted view.

impresario [aṅprəsáryō] *nm* manager, impresario.

impression [aṅprāsyóṅ] *nf* impression; *(d'un ouvrage, tissu)* printing; *(PHOTO)* exposure; **faire bonne ~** to make a good impression; **donner une ~ de/l'~ que** to give the impression of/that; **avoir l'~ de/que** to have the impression of/that; **faire ~** to make an impression; **~s de voyage** impressions of one's journey.

impressionnable [aṅprāsyonábl(ə)] *a* impressionable.

impressionnant, e [aṅprāsyonāṅ, -āṅt] *a* impressive; upsetting.

impressionner [aṅprāsyonā] *vt* *(frapper)* to impress; *(troubler)* to upset; *(PHOTO)* to expose.

impressionnisme [aṅprāsyonēsm(ə)] *nm* impressionism.

impressionniste [aṅprāsyonēst(ə)] *a, nm/f* impressionist.

imprévisible [aṅprāvēzēbl(ə)] *a* unforeseeable; *(réaction, personne)* unpredictable.

imprévoyance [aṅprāvwáyáṅs] *nf* lack of foresight.

imprévoyant, e [aṅprāvwàyàṅ, -āṅt] *a* lacking in foresight; *(en matière d'argent)* improvident.

imprévu, e [aṅprāvü] *a* unforeseen, unexpected ♦ *nm* unexpected incident; **l'~** the unexpected; **en cas d'~** if anything unexpected happens; **sauf ~** barring anything un-

expected.

imprimante [aṅprēmāṅt] *nf* *(INFORM)* printer; **~ à jet d'encre** ink-jet printer; **~ à laser** laser printer; **~ (ligne par) ligne** line printer; **~ à marguerite** daisy-wheel printer; **~ matricielle** dot-matrix printer; **~ thermique** thermal printer.

imprimé [aṅprēmā] *nm* *(formulaire)* printed form; *(POSTES)* printed matter *q*; *(tissu)* printed fabric; **un ~ à fleurs/pois** *(tissu)* a floral/polka-dot print.

imprimer [aṅprēmā] *vt* to print; *(INFORM)* to print (out); *(apposer: visa, cachet)* to stamp; *(empreinte etc)* to imprint; *(publier)* to publish; *(communiquer: mouvement, impulsion)* to impart, transmit.

imprimerie [aṅprēmrē] *nf* printing; *(établissement)* printing works *sg*; *(atelier)* print shop, printery.

imprimeur [aṅprēmœr] *nm* printer; **imprimeur-éditeur/-libraire** printer and publisher/bookseller.

improbable [aṅprobábl(ə)] *a* unlikely, improbable.

improductif, ive [aṅprodüktēf, -ēv] *a* unproductive.

impromptu, e [aṅpróṅptü] *a* impromptu; *(départ)* sudden.

imprononçable [aṅpronóṅsábl(ə)] *a* unpronounceable.

impropre [aṅpropr(ə)] *a* inappropriate; **~ à** unsuitable for.

improprement [aṅpropramāṅ] *ad* improperly.

impropriété [aṅproprēyātā] *nf*: **~ (de langage)** incorrect usage *q*.

improvisation [aṅprovēzásyóṅ] *nf* improvisation.

improvisé, e [aṅprovēzā] *a* makeshift, improvised; *(jeu etc)* scratch, improvised; **avec des moyens ~s** using whatever is on *ou* at hand.

improviser [aṅprovēzā] *vt, vi* to improvise; **s'~** *(secours, réunion)* to be improvised; **s'~ cuisinier** to (decide to) act as cook; **~ qn cuisinier** to get sb to act as cook.

improviste [aṅprovēst(ə)]: **à l'~** *ad* unexpectedly, without warning.

imprudemment [aṅprüdámáṅ] *ad* carelessly; unwisely, imprudently.

imprudence [aṅprüdáṅs] *nf* carelessness *q*; imprudence *q*; act of carelessness; foolish *ou* unwise action.

imprudent, e [aṅprüdáṅ, -āṅt] *a* *(conducteur, geste, action)* careless; *(remarque)* unwise, imprudent; *(projet)* foolhardy.

impubère [aṅpuber] *a* below the age of puberty.

impudemment [aṅpüdámáṅ] *ad* impudently.

impudence [aṅpüdáṅs] *nf* impudence.

impudent, e [aṅpüdáṅ, -āṅt] *a* impudent.

impudeur [aṅpüdœr] *nf* shamelessness.

impudique [aṅpüdēk] *a* shameless.

impuissance [aṅpüēsáṅs] *nf* helplessness; ineffectualness; impotence.

impuissant, e [aṅpüēsáṅ, -āṅt] *a* helpless; *(sans effet)* ineffectual; *(sexuellement)* impotent ♦ *nm* impotent man; **~ à faire qch** powerless to do sth.

impulsif, ive [aṅpülsēf, -ēv] *a* impulsive.

impulsion [aṅpülsyôṅ] *nf* (*ÉLEC*, *instinct*) impulse; (*élan*, *influence*) impetus.

impulsivement [aṅpülsēvmâṅ] *ad* impulsively.

impulsivité [aṅpülsēvētā] *nf* impulsiveness.

impunément [aṅpünāmâṅ] *ad* with impunity.

impuni, e [aṅpünē] *a* unpunished.

impunité [aṅpünētā] *nf* impunity.

impur, e [aṅpür] *a* impure.

impureté [aṅpürtā] *nf* impurity.

imputable [aṅpütábl(ə)] *a* (*attribuable*): ~ à imputable to, ascribable to; (*COMM*: *somme*): ~ **sur** chargeable to.

imputation [aṅpütâsyôṅ] *nf* imputation, charge.

imputer [aṅpütā] *vt* (*attribuer*): ~ **qch à** to ascribe *ou* impute sth to; (*COMM*): ~ **qch à** *ou* **sur** to charge sth to.

imputrescible [aṅpütrāsēbl(ə)] *a* rotproof.

in [ēn] *a inv* in, trendy.

INA [ēnà] *sigle m* (= *Institut national de l'audio-visuel*) *library of television archives*.

inabordable [ēnábordábl(ə)] *a* (*lieu*) inaccessible; (*cher*) prohibitive.

inaccentué, e [ēnáksâṅtüä] *a* (*LING*) unstressed.

inacceptable [ēnákseptábl(ə)] *a* unacceptable.

inaccessible [ēnáksāsēbl(ə)] *a* inaccessible; (*objectif*) unattainable; (*insensible*): ~ à impervious to.

inaccoutumé, e [ēnákōōtümā] *a* unaccustomed.

inachevé, e [ēnáshvā] *a* unfinished.

inactif, ive [ēnáktēf, -ēv] *a* inactive, idle.

inaction [ēnáksyôṅ] *nf* inactivity.

inactivité [ēnáktēvētā] *nf* (*ADMIN*): **en** ~ out of active service.

inadaptation [ēnádáptâsyôṅ] *nf* (*PSYCH*) maladjustment.

inadapté, e [ēnádáptā] *a* (*PSYCH*: *adulte, enfant*) maladjusted ♦ *nm/f* (*péj*: *adulte: asocial*) misfit; ~ à not adapted to, unsuited to.

inadéquat, e [ēnádākwá, wát] *a* inadequate.

inadéquation [ēnádākwâsyôṅ] *nf* inadequacy.

inadmissible [ēnádmēsēbl(ə)] *a* inadmissible.

inadvertance [ēnádvertâṅs]: **par** ~ *ad* inadvertently.

inaliénable [ēnályānábl(ɔ)] *a* inalienable.

inaltérable [ēnáltárábl(ə)] *a* (*matière*) stable; (*fig*) unchanging; ~ à unaffected by; **couleur** ~ (**au lavage/à la lumière**) fast color/fade-resistant color.

inamovible [ēnámovēbl(ə)] *a* fixed; (*JUR*) irremovable.

inanimé, e [ēnánēmā] *a* (*matière*) inanimate; (*évanoui*) unconscious; (*sans vie*) lifeless.

inanité [ēnánētā] *nf* futility.

inanition [ēnánēsyôṅ] *nf*: **tomber d'**~ to faint with hunger (and exhaustion).

inaperçu, e [ēnápersü] *a*: **passer** ~ to go unnoticed.

inappétence [ēnápātâṅs] *nf* lack of appetite.

inapplicable [ēnáplēkábl(ə)] *a* inapplicable.

inapplication [ēnáplēkâsyôṅ] *nf* lack of application.

inappliqué, e [ēnáplēkā] *a* lacking in application.

inappréciable [ēnáprāsyábl(ə)] *a* (*service*) invaluable; (*différence, nuance*) inappreciable.

inapte [ēnápt(ə)] *a*: ~ à incapable of; (*MIL*) unfit for.

inaptitude [ēnáptētüd] *nf* inaptitude; unfitness.

inarticulé, e [ēnártēkülā] *a* inarticulate.

inassimilable [ēnásēmēlábl(ɔ)] *a* that cannot be assimilated.

inassouvi, e [ēnásōōvē] *a* unsatisfied, unfulfilled.

inattaquable [ēnátákábl(ɔ)] *a* (*MIL*) unassailable; (*texte, preuve*) irrefutable.

inattendu, e [ēnátâṅdü] *a* unexpected ♦ *nm*: **l'**~ the unexpected.

inattentif, ive [ēnátâṅtēf, -ēv] *a* inattentive; ~ à (*dangers, détails*) heedless of.

inattention [ēnátâṅsyôṅ] *nf* inattention; (*inadvertance*): **une minute d'**~ a minute of inattention, a minute's carelessness; **par** ~ inadvertently; **faute d'**~ careless mistake.

inaudible [ēnōdēbl(ɔ)] *a* inaudible.

inaugural, e, aux [ēnogürál, -ō] *a* (*cérémonie*) inaugural, opening; (*vol, voyage*) maiden.

inauguration [ēnogürâsyôṅ] *nf* unveiling; opening; **discours/cérémonie d'**~ inaugural speech/ceremony.

inaugurer [ēnogürā] *vt* (*monument*) to unveil; (*exposition, usine*) to open; (*fig*) to inaugurate.

inauthenticité [ēnotâṅtēsētā] *nf* inauthenticity.

inavouable [ēnávwábl(ɔ)] *a* undisclosable; (*honteux*) shameful.

inavoué, e [ēnávwā] *a* unavowed.

INC *sigle m* (= *Institut national de la consommation*) *consumer research organization*.

inca [aṅkà] *a inv* Inca ♦ *nm/f*: **l'**~ Inca.

incalculable [aṅkálkülábl(ɔ)] *a* incalculable; **un nombre** ~ **de** countless numbers of.

incandescence [aṅkâṅdāsâṅs] *nf* incandescence; **en** ~ incandescent, white-hot; **porter à** ~ to heat white-hot; **lampe/manchon à** ~ incandescent lamp/(gas) mantle.

incandescent, e [aṅkâṅdāsâṅ, -âṅt] *a* incandescent, white-hot.

incantation [aṅkâṅtâsyôṅ] *nf* incantation.

incapable [aṅkápábl(ɔ)] *a* incapable; ~ **de faire** incapable of doing; (*empêché*) unable to do.

incapacitant, e [aṅkápásētâṅ, -âṅt] *a* (*MIL*) incapacitating.

incapacité [aṅkápásētā] *nf* incapability; (*JUR*) incapacity; **être dans l'**~ **de faire** to be unable to do; ~ **permanente/de travail** permanent/industrial disablement; ~ **électorale** ineligibility to vote.

incarcération [aṅkársārâsyôṅ] *nf* incarceration.

incarcérer [aṅkársārā] *vt* to incarcerate.

incarnat, e [aṅkárná, -át] *a* (rosy) pink.

incarnation [aṅkárnâsyôṅ] *nf* incarnation.

incarné, e [aṅkárnā] *a* incarnate; (*ongle*) ingrown.

incarner [aṅkárnā] *vt* to embody, personify; (*THÉÂTRE*) to play; (*REL*) to incarnate; **s'**~ **dans** (*REL*) to be incarnate in.

incartade [aṅkártád] *nf* prank, escapade.

incassable [aṅkásábl(ə)] *a* unbreakable.

incendiaire [aṅsâṅdyer] *a* incendiary; (*fig: discours*) inflammatory ♦ *nm/f* arsonist.

incendie [aṅsâṅdē] *nm* fire; ~ **criminel** arson

q; ~ **de forêt** forest fire.
incendier [aṅsåṅdyā] *vt (mettre le feu à)* to set fire to; *(brûler complètement)* to burn down.
incertain, e [aṅsertaṅ, -en] *a* uncertain; *(temps)* uncertain, unsettled; *(imprécis: contours)* indistinct, blurred.
incertitude [aṅsertētüd] *nf* uncertainty.
incessamment [aṅsesámáṅ] *ad* very shortly.
incessant, e [aṅsesáṅ, -åṅt] *a* incessant, unceasing.
incessible [aṅsāsēbl(ə)] *a (JUR)* nontransferable.
inceste [aṅsest(ə)] *nm* incest.
incestueux, euse [aṅsestüœ̄, -ēz] *a* incestuous.
inchangé, e [aṅshåṅzhā] *a* unchanged, unaltered.
inchauffable [aṅshōfábl(ə)] *a* impossible to heat.
incidemment [aṅsēdámáṅ] *ad* in passing.
incidence [aṅsēdáṅs] *nf (effet, influence)* effect; *(PHYSIQUE)* incidence.
incident [aṅsēdáṅ] *nm* incident; ~ **de frontière** border incident; ~ **de parcours** minor hitch *ou* setback; ~ **technique** technical difficulties *pl,* technical hitch.
incinérateur [aṅsēnárátœr] *nm* incinerator.
incinération [aṅsēnārásyóṅ] *nf (d'ordures)* incineration; *(crémation)* cremation.
incinérer [aṅsēnārā] *vt (ordures)* to incinerate; *(mort)* to cremate.
incise [aṅsēz] *nf (LING)* interpolated clause.
inciser [aṅsezá] *vt* to make an incision in; *(abcès)* to lance.
incisif, ive [aṅsēzēf, -ēv] *a* incisive, cutting ♦ *nf* incisor.
incision [aṅsēzyóṅ] *nf* incision; *(d'un abcès)* lancing.
incitation [aṅsētâsyóṅ] *nf (encouragement)* incentive; *(provocation)* incitement.
inciter [aṅsētā] *vt:* ~ **qn à (faire) qch** to prompt *ou* encourage sb to do sth; *(à la révolte etc)* to incite sb to do sth.
incivil, e [aṅsēvēl] *a* uncivil.
incivilité [aṅsēvēlētā] *nf* incivility.
inclinable [aṅklēnábl(ə)] *a (dossier etc)* tilting; **siège à dossier** ~ reclining seat.
inclinaison [aṅklēnezóṅ] *nf (déclivité: d'une route etc)* incline; *(: d'un toit)* slope; *(état penché: d'un mur)* lean; *(: de la tête)* tilt; *(: d'un navire)* list.
inclination [aṅklēnâsyóṅ] *nf (penchant)* inclination, tendency; **montrer de l'**~ **pour les sciences** *etc* to show an inclination for the sciences *etc*; ~**s égoïstes/altruistes** egoistic/altruistic tendencies; ~ **de (la) tête** nod (of the head); ~ **(de buste)** bow.
incliner [aṅklēnā] *vt (bouteille)* to tilt; *(tête)* to incline; *(inciter):* ~ **qn à qch/à faire** to encourage sb towards sth/to do ♦ *vi:* ~ **à qch/à faire** *(tendre à, pencher pour)* to incline towards sth/doing, tend towards sth/to do; **s'**~ *(route)* to slope; *(toit)* to be sloping; **s'**~ **(devant)** to bow (before).
inclure [aṅklür] *vt* to include; *(joindre à un envoi)* to enclose; **jusqu'au 10 mars inclus** until March 10(th) inclusive.
inclus, e [aṅklü, -üz] *pp de* **inclure** ♦ *a (joint à un envoi)* enclosed; *(compris: frais, dépense)*

included; *(MATH: ensemble):* ~ **dans** included in; **jusqu'au troisième chapitre** ~ up to and including the third chapter.
inclusion [aṅklüzyóṅ] *nf (voir inclure)* inclusion; enclosing.
inclusivement [aṅklüzēvmáṅ] *ad* inclusively.
inclut [aṅklü] *vb voir* **inclure.**
incoercible [aṅkoersēbl(ə)] *a* uncontrollable.
incognito [aṅkonyētō] *ad* incognito ♦ *nm:* **garder l'**~ to remain incognito.
incohérence [aṅkoáráṅs] *nf* inconsistency; incoherence.
incohérent, e [aṅkoāráṅ, -áṅt] *a* inconsistent; incoherent.
incollable [aṅkolábl(ə)] *a (riz)* that does not stick; *(fam: personne):* **il est** ~ he's got all the answers.
incolore [aṅkolor] *a* colorless *(US),* colourless *(Brit)*.
incomber [aṅkóṅbā]: ~ **à** *vt (suj: devoirs, responsabilité)* to rest *ou* be incumbent upon; *(: frais, travail)* to be the responsibility of.
incombustible [aṅkóṅbüstēbl(ə)] *a* incombustible.
incommensurable [aṅkomáṅsürábl(ə)] *a* immeasurable.
incommodant, e [aṅkomodáṅ, -áṅt] *a (bruit)* annoying; *(chaleur)* uncomfortable.
incommode [aṅkomod] *a* inconvenient; *(posture, siège)* uncomfortable.
incommodément [aṅkomodámáṅ] *ad (installé, assis)* uncomfortably; *(logé, situé)* inconveniently.
incommoder [aṅkomodā] *vt:* ~ **qn** to bother *ou* inconvenience sb; *(embarrasser)* to make sb feel uncomfortable *ou* ill at ease.
incommodité [aṅkomodētā] *nf* inconvenience.
incomparable [aṅkóṅpárábl(ə)] *a* not comparable; *(inégalable)* incomparable, matchless.
incomparablement [aṅkóṅpárâblamáṅ] *ad* incomparably.
incompatibilité [aṅkóṅpátēbēlētā] *nf* incompatibility; ~ **d'humeur** (mutual) incompatibility.
incompatible [aṅkóṅpátēbl(ə)] *a* incompatible.
incompétence [aṅkóṅpátáṅs] *nf* lack of expertise; incompetence.
incompétent, e [aṅkóṅpátáṅ, -áṅt] *a (ignorant)* inexpert; *(incapable)* incompetent, not competent.
incomplet, ète [aṅkóṅplè, -et] *a* incomplete.
incomplètement [aṅkóṅpletmáṅ] *ad* not completely, incompletely.
incompréhensible [aṅkóṅprāáṅsēbl(ə)] *a* incomprehensible.
incompréhensif, ive [aṅkóṅprāáṅsēf, -ēv] *a* lacking in understanding, unsympathetic.
incompréhension [aṅkóṅpráásyóṅ] *nf* lack of understanding.
incompressible [aṅkóṅprāsēbl(ə)] *a (PHYSIQUE)* incompressible; *(fig: dépenses)* that cannot be reduced; *(JUR: peine)* irreducible.
incompris, e [aṅkóṅprē, -ēz] *a* misunderstood.
inconcevable [aṅkóṅsvábl(ə)] *a (conduite etc)* inconceivable; *(mystère)* incredible.
inconciliable [aṅkóṅsēlyábl(ə)] *a* irreconcilable.
inconditionnel, le [aṅkóṅdēsyonel] *a* uncondi-

tional; (*partisan*) unquestioning ♦ *nm/f* (*partisan*) unquestioning supporter.

inconditionnellement [aṅkôṅdēsyonelmâṅ] *ad* unconditionally.

inconduite [aṅkôṅdüēt] *nf* bad *ou* unsuitable behavior *q* (*US*) *ou* behaviour *q* (*Brit*).

inconfort [aṅkôṅfor] *nm* lack of comfort, discomfort.

inconfortable [aṅkôṅfortábl(ə)] *a* uncomfortable.

inconfortablement [aṅkôṅfortáblə mâṅ] *ad* uncomfortably.

incongru, e [aṅkôṅgrü] *a* unseemly; (*remarque*) ill-chosen, incongruous.

incongruité [aṅkôṅgrüētā] *nf* unseemliness; incongruity; (*parole incongrue*) ill-chosen remark.

inconnu, e [aṅkonü] *a* unknown; (*sentiment, plaisir*) new, strange ♦ *nm/f* stranger; unknown person (*ou* artist *etc*) ♦ *nm*: **l'~** the unknown ♦ *nf* (*MATH*) unknown; (*fig*) unknown factor.

inconsciemment [aṅkôṅsyàmâṅ] *ad* unconsciously.

inconscience [aṅkôṅsyâṅs] *nf* unconsciousness; recklessness.

inconscient, e [aṅkôṅsyâṅ, -âṅt] *a* unconscious; (*irréfléchi*) reckless ♦ *nm* (*PSYCH*): **l'~** the subconscious, the unconscious; **~ de** unaware of.

inconséquence [aṅkôṅsākâṅs] *nf* inconsistency; thoughtlessness; (*action, parole*) thoughtless thing to do (*ou* say).

inconséquent, e [aṅkôṅsākâṅ, -âṅt] *a* (*illogique*) inconsistent; (*irréfléchi*) thoughtless.

inconsidéré, e [aṅkôṅsēdārā] *a* ill-considered.

inconsidérément [aṅkôṅsēdārāmâṅ] *ad* thoughtlessly.

inconsistant, e [aṅkôṅsēstâṅ, -âṅt] *a* flimsy, weak; (*crème etc*) runny.

inconsolable [aṅkôṅsolábl(ə)] *a* inconsolable.

inconstance [aṅkôṅstâṅs] *nf* inconstancy, fickleness.

inconstant, e [aṅkôṅstâṅ, -âṅt] *a* inconstant, fickle.

inconstitutionnel, le [aṅkôṅstētüsyonel] *a* unconstitutional.

incontestable [aṅkôṅtestábl(ə)] *a* unquestionable, indisputable.

incontestablement [aṅkôṅtestáblə mâṅ] *ad* unquestionably, indisputably.

incontesté, e [aṅkôṅtestā] *a* undisputed.

incontinence [aṅkôṅtēnâṅs] *nf* (*MÉD*) incontinence.

incontinent, e [aṅkôṅtēnâṅ, -âṅt] *a* (*MÉD*) incontinent ♦ *ad* (*tout de suite*) forthwith.

incontournable [aṅkôṅtōōrnábl(ə)] *a* unavoidable.

incontrôlable [aṅkôṅtrōlábl(ə)] *a* unverifiable.

incontrôlé, e [aṅkôṅtrōlā] *a* uncontrolled.

inconvenance [aṅkôṅvnâṅs] *nf* (*parole, action*) impropriety.

inconvenant, e [aṅkôṅvnâṅ, -âṅt] *a* unseemly, improper.

inconvénient [aṅkôṅványâṅ] *nm* (*d'une situation, d'un projet*) disadvantage, drawback; (*d'un remède, changement etc*) risk, inconvenience; **si vous n'y voyez pas d'~** if

you have no objections; **y a-t-il un ~ à ...?** (*risque*) isn't there a risk in ...?; (*objection*) is there any objection to ...?

inconvertible [aṅkôṅvertēbl(ə)] *a* inconvertible.

incorporation [aṅkorporâsyôṅ] *nf* (*MIL*) induction (*US*), call-up (*Brit*).

incorporé, e [aṅkorporā] *a* (*micro etc*) built-in.

incorporel, le [aṅkorporel] *a* (*JUR*): **biens ~s** intangible property.

incorporer [aṅkorporā] *vt*: **~ (à)** to mix in (with); (*paragraphe etc*): **~ (dans)** to incorporate (in); (*territoire, immigrants*): **~ (dans)** to incorporate (into); (*MIL*: *appeler*) to induct (*US*), call up (*Brit*); (: *affecter*): **~ qn dans** to enlist sb into.

incorrect, e [aṅkorekt] *a* (*impropre, inconvenant*) improper; (*défectueux*) faulty; (*inexact*) incorrect; (*impoli*) impolite; (*déloyal*) underhand.

incorrectement [aṅkorektəmâṅ] *ad* improperly; faultily; incorrectly; impolitely; in an underhand way.

incorrection [aṅkoreksyôṅ] *nf* impropriety; incorrectness; underhand nature; (*terme impropre*) impropriety; (*action, remarque*) improper behavior (*US*) *ou* behaviour (*Brit*) (*ou* remark).

incorrigible [aṅkorēzhēbl(ə)] *a* incorrigible.

incorruptible [aṅkorüptēbl(ə)] *a* incorruptible.

incrédibilité [aṅkrādēbēlētā] *nf* incredibility.

incrédule [aṅkrādül] *a* incredulous; (*REL*) unbelieving.

incrédulité [aṅkrādülētā] *nf* incredulity; **avec ~** incredulously.

increvable [aṅkrəvábl(ə)] *a* (*pneu*) punctureproof; (*fam*) tireless.

incriminer [aṅkrēmēnā] *vt* (*personne*) to incriminate; (*action, conduite*) to bring under attack; (*bonne foi, honnêteté*) to call into question; **livre/article incriminé** offending book/article.

incrochetable [aṅkroshtábl(ə)] *a* (*serrure*) that can't be picked, burglarproof.

incroyable [aṅkrwàyábl(ə)] *a* incredible, unbelievable.

incroyablement [aṅkrwàyábləmâṅ] *ad* incredibly, unbelievably.

incroyant, e [aṅkrwàyâṅ, -âṅt] *nm/f* nonbeliever.

incrustation [aṅkrüstásyôṅ] *nf* inlaying *q*; inlay; (*dans une chaudière etc*) fur *q*, scale *q*.

incruster [aṅkrüstā] *vt* (*ART*): **~ qch dans/qch de** to inlay sth into/sth with; (*radiateur etc*) to coat with scale *ou* fur; **s'~** *vi* (*invité*) to take root; (*radiateur etc*) to become coated with fur *ou* scale; **s'~ dans** (*suj*: *corps étranger, caillou*) to become embedded in.

incubateur [aṅkübatœr] *nm* incubator.

incubation [aṅkübâsyôṅ] *nf* incubation.

inculpation [aṅkülpâsyôṅ] *nf* charging *q*; charge; **sous l'~ de** on a charge of.

inculpé, e [aṅkülpā] *nm/f* accused.

inculper [aṅkülpā] *vt*: **~ (de)** to charge (with).

inculquer [aṅkülkā] *vt*: **~ qch à** to inculcate sth in, instill (*US*) *ou* instil (*Brit*) sth into.

inculte [aṅkült(ə)] *a* uncultivated; (*esprit,*

peuple) uncultured; (*barbe*) unkempt.
incultivable [aṅkültēvábl(ə)] *a* (*terrain*) unworkable.
inculture [aṅkültür] *nf* lack of education.
incurable [aṅkürábl(ə)] *a* incurable.
incurie [aṅkürē] *nf* carelessness.
incursion [aṅkürsyôṅ] *nf* incursion, foray.
incurvé, e [aṅkürvā] *a* curved.
incurver [aṅkürvā] *vt* (*barre de fer*) to bend into a curve; **s'~** *vi* (*planche, route*) to bend.
Inde [aṅd] *nf*: **l'~** India.
indécemment [aṅdāsámáṅ] *ad* indecently.
indécence [aṅdāsáṅs] *nf* indecency; (*propos, acte*) indecent remark (*ou* act *etc*).
indécent, e [aṅdāsáṅ, -áṅt] *a* indecent.
indéchiffrable [aṅdāshēfrábl(ə)] *a* indecipherable.
indéchirable [aṅdāshērábl(ə)] *a* tearproof.
indécis, e [aṅdāsē, -ēz] *a* indecisive; (*perplexe*) undecided.
indécision [aṅdāsēzyôṅ] *nf* indecision, indecisiveness.
indéclinable [aṅdāklēnábl(ə)] *a* (*LING*: *mot*) indeclinable.
indécomposable [aṅdākôṅpōzábl(ə)] *a* that cannot be broken down.
indéfectible [aṅdāfektēbl(ə)] *a* (*attachement*) indestructible.
indéfendable [aṅdāfáṅdábl(ə)] *a* indefensible.
indéfini, e [aṅdāfēnē] *a* (*imprécis, incertain*) undefined; (*illimité, LING*) indefinite.
indéfiniment [aṅdāfēnēmáṅ] *ad* indefinitely.
indéfinissable [aṅdāfēnēsábl(ə)] *a* indefinable.
indéformable [aṅdāformábl(ə)] *a* that keeps its shape.
indélébile [aṅdālābēl] *a* indelible.
indélicat, e [aṅdālēká, -át] *a* tactless; (*malhonnête*) dishonest.
indélicatesse [aṅdālēkátes] *nf* tactlessness; dishonesty.
indémaillable [aṅdāmáyábl(ə)] *a* run resistant, runproof.
indemne [aṅdemn(ə)] *a* unharmed.
indemnisable [aṅdemnēzábl(ə)] *a* entitled to compensation.
indemnisation [aṅdemnēzásyôṅ] *nf* (*somme*) indemnity, compensation.
indemniser [aṅdemnēzā] *vt*: **~ qn (de)** to compensate sb (for); **se faire ~** to get compensation.
indemnité [aṅdemnētā] *nf* (*dédommagement*) compensation *q*; (*allocation*) allowance; **~ de licenciement** severance pay; **~ de logement** housing allowance; **~ parlementaire** ≈ Congressman's (*US*) *ou* M.P.'s (*Brit*) salary.
indémontable [aṅdāmôṅtábl(ə)] *a* (*meuble etc*) that cannot be dismantled, in one piece.
indéniable [aṅdānyábl(ə)] *a* undeniable, indisputable.
indéniablement [aṅdānyáblǝmáṅ] *ad* undeniably.
indépendamment [aṅdāpáṅdámáṅ] *ad* independently; **~ de** independently of; (*abstraction faite de*) irrespective of; (*en plus de*) over and above.
indépendance [aṅdāpáṅdáṅs] *nf* independence; **~ matérielle** financial independence.

indépendant, e [aṅdāpáṅdáṅ, -áṅt] *a* independent; **~ de** independent of; **chambre ~e** room with private entrance; **travailleur ~** self-employed worker.
indépendantiste [aṅdāpáṅdáṅtēst(ə)] *a, nm/f* separatist.
indéracinable [aṅdārásēnábl(ə)] *a* (*fig*: *croyance etc*) ineradicable.
indéréglable [aṅdārāglábl(ə)] *a* which will not break down.
indescriptible [aṅdeskrēptēbl(ə)] *a* indescribable.
indésirable [aṅdāzērábl(ə)] *a* undesirable.
indestructible [aṅdestrüktēbl(ə)] *a* indestructible; (*marque, impression*) indelible.
indéterminable [aṅdātērmēnábl(ə)] *a* indeterminable.
indétermination [aṅdātērmēnásyôṅ] *nf* indecision, indecisiveness.
indéterminé, e [aṅdātērmēnā] *a* unspecified; indeterminate; indeterminable.
index [aṅdeks] *nm* (*doigt*) index finger; (*d'un livre etc*) index; **mettre à l'~** to blacklist.
indexation [aṅdeksásyôṅ] *nf* indexing.
indexé, e [aṅdeksā] *a* (*ÉCON*): **~ (sur)** index-linked (to).
indexer [aṅdeksā] *vt* (*salaire, emprunt*): **~ (sur)** to index (on).
indicateur [aṅdēkátœr] *nm* (*POLICE*) informer; (*livre*) guide; (: *liste*) directory; (*TECH*) gauge; indicator; (*ÉCON*) indicator ♦ *a*: **poteau ~** signpost; **tableau ~** indicator (board); **~ des chemins de fer** railroad (*US*) *ou* railway (*Brit*) timetable; **~ de direction** (*AUTO*) indicator; **~ immobilier** real estate directory (*US*), property gazette (*Brit*); **~ de niveau** level, gauge; **~ de pression** pressure gauge; **~ de rues** street directory; **~ de vitesse** speedometer.
indicatif, ive [aṅdēkátēf, -ēv] *a*: **à titre ~** for (your) information ♦ *nm* (*LING*) indicative; (*d'une émission*) theme song, signature (tune (*Brit*)); (*TÉL*) area code; **~ d'appel** (*RADIO*) call letters *pl* (*US*) *ou* sign (*Brit*).
indication [aṅdēkásyôṅ] *nf* indication; (*renseignement*) information *q*; **~s** *nfpl* (*directives*) instructions; **~ d'origine** (*COMM*) place of origin.
indice [aṅdēs] *nm* (*marque, signe*) indication, sign; (*POLICE*: *lors d'une enquête*) clue; (*JUR*: *présomption*) piece of evidence; (*SCIENCE, ÉCON, TECH*) index; (*ADMIN*) grading; rating; **~ du coût de la vie** cost-of-living index; **~ inférieur** subscript; **~ d'octane** octane rating; **~ des prix** price index; **~ de traitement** salary scale.
indicible [aṅdēsēbl(ə)] *a* inexpressible.
indien, ne [aṅdyaṅ, -en] *a* Indian ♦ *nm/f*: **I~, ne** (*d'Amérique*) (American *ou* Red) Indian; (*d'Inde*) Indian.
indifféremment [aṅdēfārámáṅ] *ad* (*sans distinction*) equally; indiscriminately.
indifférence [aṅdēfāráṅs] *nf* indifference.
indifférencié, e [aṅdēfāráṅsyā] *a* undifferentiated.
indifférent, e [aṅdēfāráṅ, -áṅt] *a* (*peu intéressé*) indifferent; **~ à** (*insensible à*) indifferent to, unconcerned about; (*peu intéressant pour*) indifferent to; immaterial to; **ça m'est**

~ **(que ...)** it doesn't matter to me (whether ...).

indifférer [ȧdēfārā] *vt*: **cela m'indiffère** I'm indifferent about it.

indigence [ȧdēzhȧńs] *nf* poverty; **être dans l'**~ to be destitute.

indigène [ȧdēzhen] *a* native, indigenous; *(de la région)* local ♦ *nm/f* native.

indigent, e [ȧdēzhȧń, -ȧ̇nt] *a* destitute, poverty-stricken; *(fig)* poor.

indigeste [ȧdēzhest(ə)] *a* indigestible.

indigestion [ȧdēzhestyȯń] *nf* indigestion *q*; **avoir une** ~ to have indigestion.

indignation [ȧdēnyȧsyȯń] *nf* indignation; **avec** ~ indignantly.

indigne [ȧdēny] *a*: ~ **(de)** unworthy (of).

indigné, e [ȧdēnyā] *a* indignant.

indignement [ȧdēnymȧ̇ń] *ad* shamefully.

indigner [ȧdēnyā] *vt* to make indignant; **s'**~ **(de/contre)** to be *(ou* become) indignant (at).

indignité [ȧdēnyētā] *nf* unworthiness *q*; *(acte)* shameful act.

indigo [ȧdēgō] *nm* indigo.

indiqué, e [ȧdēkā] *a* *(date, lieu)* given, appointed; *(adéquat)* appropriate, suitable; *(conseillé)* advisable; *(remède, traitement)* appropriate.

indiquer [ȧdēkā] *vt* *(désigner)*: ~ **qch/qn à qn** to point sth/sb out to sb; *(suj: pendule, aiguille)* to show; *(suj: étiquette, plan)* to show, indicate; *(faire connaître: médecin, restaurant)*: ~ **qch/qn à qn** to tell sb of sth/ sb; *(renseigner sur)* to point out, tell; *(déterminer: date, lieu)* to give, state; *(dénoter)* to indicate, point to; ~ **du doigt** to point out; ~ **de la main** to indicate with one's hand; ~ **du regard** to glance towards *ou* in the direction of; **pourriez-vous m'**~ **les toilettes/l'heure?** could you direct me to the toilets/tell me the time?

indirect, e [ȧdērekt] *a* indirect.

indirectement [ȧdērektəmȧ̇ń] *ad* indirectly; *(apprendre)* in a roundabout way.

indiscernable [ȧdēsernȧbl(ə)] *a* indiscernible.

indiscipline [ȧdēsēplēn] *nf* lack of discipline.

indiscipliné, e [ȧdēsēplēnā] *a* undisciplined; *(fig)* unmanageable.

indiscret, ète [ȧdēskre, -et] *a* indiscreet.

indiscrétion [ȧdēskrāsyȯń] *nf* indiscretion; **sans** ~, ... without wishing to be indiscreet, ...

indiscutable [ȧdēskütȧbl(ə)] *a* indisputable.

indiscutablement [ȧdēskütȧbləmȧ̇ń] *ad* indisputably.

indiscuté, e [ȧdēstütā] *a* *(incontesté: droit, chef)* undisputed.

indispensable [ȧdēspȧ̇nsȧbl(ə)] *a* indispensable, essential; ~ **à qn/pour faire qch** essential for sb/to do sth.

indisponibilité [ȧdēsponēbēlētā] *nf* unavailability.

indisponible [ȧdēsponēbl(ə)] *a* unavailable.

indisposé, e [ȧdēspōzā] *a* indisposed, unwell.

indisposer [ȧdēspōzā] *vt* *(incommoder)* to upset; *(déplaire à)* to antagonize.

indisposition [ȧdēspōzēsyȯń] *nf* (slight) illness, indisposition.

indistinct, e [ȧdēstȧń, -ȧ̇nkt(ə)] *a* indistinct.

indistinctement [ȧdēstȧnktəmȧ̇ń] *ad* *(voir,*

prononcer) indistinctly; *(sans distinction)* without distinction, indiscriminately.

individu [ȧdēvēdü] *nm* individual.

individualiser [ȧdēvēdüȧlēzā] *vt* to individualize; *(personnaliser)* to tailor to individual requirements; **s'**~ to develop one's own identity.

individualisme [ȧdēvēdüȧlēsm(ə)] *nm* individualism.

individualiste [ȧdēvēdüȧlēst(ə)] *nm/f* individualist.

individualité [ȧdēvēdüȧlētā] *nf* individuality.

individuel, le [ȧdēvēdüel] *a* *(gén)* individual; *(opinion, livret, contrôle, avantages)* personal; **chambre** ~**le** single room; **maison** ~**le** detached house; **propriété** ~**le** personal *ou* private property.

individuellement [ȧdēvēdüelmȧ̇ń] *ad* individually.

indivis, e [ȧdēvē, -ēz] *a* *(JUR: bien, propriété, succession)* indivisible; *(: cohéritiers, propriétaires)* joint.

indivisible [ȧdēvēzēbl(ə)] *a* indivisible.

Indochine [ȧdoshen] *nf:* **l'**~ Indochina.

indochinois, e [ȧdoshēnwȧ, -wȧz] *a* Indochinese.

indocile [ȧdosēl] *a* unruly.

indo-européen, ne [ȧdoœ̄ropȧȧń, -en] *a* Indo-European ♦ *nm* *(LING)* Indo-European.

indolence [ȧdolȧ̇ńs] *nf* indolence.

indolent, e [ȧdolȧ̇ń, -ȧ̇nt] *a* indolent.

indolore [ȧdolor] *a* painless.

indomptable [ȧdȯńtȧbl(ə)] *a* untameable; *(fig)* invincible, indomitable.

indompté, e [ȧdȯńtā] *a* *(cheval)* unbroken.

Indonésie [ȧdonȧzē] *nf:* **l'**~ Indonesia.

indonésien, ne [ȧdonȧzyȧ̇ń, -en] *a* Indonesian ♦ *nm/f:* **I**~, **ne** Indonesian.

indu, e [ȧdü] *a:* **à des heures** ~**es** at an ungodly hour.

indubitable [ȧdübētȧbl(ə)] *a* indubitable.

indubitablement [ȧdübētȧbləmȧ̇ń] *ad* indubitably.

induire [ȧdüēr] *vt*: ~ **qch de** to induce sth from; ~ **qn en erreur** to lead sb astray, mislead sb.

indulgence [ȧdülzhȧ̇ńs] *nf* indulgence; leniency; **avec** ~ indulgently; leniently.

indulgent, e [ȧdülzhȧ̇ń, -ȧ̇nt] *a* *(parent, regard)* indulgent; *(juge, examinateur)* lenient.

indûment [ȧdümȧ̇ń] *ad* without due cause; *(illégitimement)* wrongfully.

industrialisation [ȧdüstrēyȧlēzȧsyȯń] *nf* industrialization.

industrialiser [ȧdüstrēyȧlēzā] *vt* to industrialize; **s'**~ to become industrialized.

industrie [ȧdüstrē] *nf* industry; ~ **automobile/textile** car/textile industry; ~ **du spectacle** entertainment business.

industriel, le [ȧdüstrēyel] *a* industrial; *(produit industriellement: pain etc)* massproduced, factory-produced ♦ *nm* industrialist; *(fabricant)* manufacturer.

industriellement [ȧdüstrēyelmȧ̇ń] *ad* industrially.

industrieux, euse [ȧdüstrēyœ̄, -œ̄z] *a* industrious.

inébranlable [ēnābrȧ̇nlȧbl(ə)] *a* *(masse, colonne)* solid; *(personne, certitude, foi)* steadfast, unwavering.

inédit, e [ēnādē, -ēt] *a* (*correspondance etc*) (hitherto) unpublished; (*spectacle, moyen*) novel, original.

ineffable [ēnāfábl(ə)] *a* inexpressible, ineffable.

ineffaçable [ēnāfásábl(ə)] *a* indelible.

inefficace [ēnāfēkás] *a* (*remède, moyen*) ineffective; (*machine, employé*) inefficient.

inefficacité [ēnāfēkásētā] *nf* ineffectiveness; inefficiency.

inégal, e, aux [ēnāgàl, -ō] *a* unequal; (*irrégulier*) uneven.

inégalable [ēnāgálábl(ə)] *a* matchless.

inégalé, e [ēnāgálā] *a* unmatched, unequalled.

inégalement [ēnāgálmáṅ] *ad* unequally.

inégalité [ēnāgálētā] *nf* inequality; unevenness *q*; **~ de 2 hauteurs** difference *ou* disparity between 2 heights; **~s de terrain** uneven ground.

inélégance [ēnālāgáṅs] *nf* inelegance.

inélégant, e [ēnālāgáṅ, -áṅt] *a* inelegant; (*indélicat*) discourteous.

inéligible [ēnālezhēbl(ə)] *a* ineligible.

inéluctable [ēnālüktábl(ə)] *a* inescapable.

inéluctablement [ēnālüktábləmáṅ] *ad* inescapably.

inemployable [ēnáṅplwáyábl(ə)] *a* unusable.

inemployé, e [ēnáṅplwáyā] *a* unused.

inénarrable [ēnānárábl(ə)] *a* hilarious.

inepte [ēnept(ə)] *a* inept.

ineptie [ēnepsē] *nf* ineptitude; (*propos*) nonsense *q*.

inépuisable [ēnāpüēzábl(ə)] *a* inexhaustible.

inéquitable [ēnākētábl(ə)] *a* inequitable.

inerte [ēnert(ə)] *a* lifeless; (*apathique*) passive, inert; (*PHYSIQUE, CHIMIE*) inert.

inertie [ēnersē] *nf* inertia.

inescompté, e [ēneskôṅtā] *a* unexpected, unhoped-for.

inespéré, e [ēnespārā] *a* unhoped-for, unexpected.

inesthétique [ēnestātēk] *a* unsightly.

inestimable [ēnestēmábl(ə)] *a* priceless; (*fig: bienfait*) invaluable.

inévitable [ēnāvētábl(ə)] *a* unavoidable; (*fatal, habituel*) inevitable.

inévitablement [ēnāvētábləmáṅ] *ad* inevitably.

inexact, e [ēnegzákt] *a* inaccurate, inexact; (*non ponctuel*) unpunctual.

inexactement [ēnegzáktəmáṅ] *ad* inaccurately.

inexactitude [ēnegzáktētüd] *nf* inaccuracy.

inexcusable [ēneksküzábl(ə)] *a* inexcusable, unforgivable.

inexécutable [ēnegzākütábl(ə)] *a* impracticable, unworkable; (*MUS*) unplayable.

inexistant, e [ēnegzēstáṅ, -áṅt] *a* non-existent.

inexorable [ēnegzorábl(ə)] *a* inexorable; (*personne: dur*): **~ (à)** unmoved (by).

inexorablement [ēnegzorábləmáṅ] *ad* inexorably.

inexpérience [ēnekspāryáṅs] *nf* inexperience, lack of experience.

inexpérimenté, e [ēnekspārēmáṅtā] *a* inexperienced; (*arme, procédé*) untested.

inexplicable [ēneksplēkábl(ə)] *a* inexplicable.

inexpliqué, e [ēneksplēkā] *a* unexplained.

inexploité, e [ēneksplwátā] *a* unexploited, untapped.

inexploré, e [ēneksplorā] *a* unexplored.

inexpressif, ive [ēnekspräsēf, -ēv] *a* inexpressive; (*regard etc*) expressionless.

inexpressivité [ēnekspräsēvētā] *nf* expressionlessness.

inexprimable [ēneksprēmábl(ə)] *a* inexpressible.

inexprimé, e [ēneksprēmā] *a* unspoken, unexpressed.

inexpugnable [ēnekspügnábl(ə)] *a* impregnable.

inextensible [ēnekstáṅsēbl(ə)] *a* (*tissu*) nonstretch.

in extenso [ēnekstaṅsō] *ad* in full.

inextinguible [ēnekstaṅgēbl(ə)] *a* (*soif*) unquenchable; (*rire*) uncontrollable.

in extremis [ēnekstrāmēs] *ad* at the last minute ♦ *a* last-minute; (*testament*) death bed *cpd*.

inextricable [ēnekstrēkábl(ə)] *a* inextricable.

inextricablement [ēnekstrēkábləmáṅ] *ad* inextricably.

infaillible [aṅfáyēbl(ə)] *a* infallible; (*instinct*) infallible, unerring.

infailliblement [aṅfáyēbləmáṅ] *ad* (*certainement*) without fail.

infaisable [aṅfəzábl(ə)] *a* (*travail etc*) impossible, impractical.

infamant, e [aṅfámáṅ, -áṅt] *a* libel(l)ous (*US*), libellous (*Brit*), defamatory.

infâme [aṅfám] *a* vile.

infamie [aṅfámē] *nf* infamy.

infanterie [aṅfáṅtrē] *nf* infantry.

infanticide [aṅfáṅtēsēd] *nm/f* child-murderer/ eress ♦ *nm* (*meurtre*) infanticide.

infantile [aṅfáṅtēl] *a* (*MÉD*) infantile, child *cpd*; (*péj: ton, réaction*) infantile, childish.

infantilisme [aṅfáṅtēlēsm(ə)] *nm* infantilism.

infarctus [aṅfárktüs] *nm*: **~ (du myocarde)** coronary (thrombosis).

infatigable [aṅfátēgábl(ə)] *a* tireless, indefatigable.

infatué, e [aṅfátüā] *a* conceited; **~ de** full of.

infécond, e [aṅfākóṅ, -óṅd] *a* infertile, barren.

infect, e [aṅfekt] *a* vile, foul; (*repas, vin*) revolting, foul.

infecter [aṅfektā] *vt* (*atmosphère, eau*) to contaminate; (*MÉD*) to infect; **s'~** to become infected *ou* septic.

infectieux, euse [aṅfeksyœ, -œz] *a* infectious.

infection [aṅfeksyóṅ] *nf* infection.

inféoder [aṅfáodā] *vt*: **s'~ à** to pledge allegiance to.

inférer [aṅfārā] *vt*: **~ qch de** to infer sth from.

inférieur, e [aṅfāryœr] *a* lower; (*en qualité, intelligence*) inferior ♦ *nm/f* inferior; **~ à** (*somme, quantité*) less *ou* smaller than; (*moins bon que*) inferior to; (*tâche: pas à la hauteur de*) unequal to.

infériorité [aṅfāryorētā] *nf* inferiority; **~ en nombre** inferiority in numbers.

infernal, e, aux [aṅfernál, -ō] *a* (*chaleur, rythme*) infernal; (*méchanceté, complot*) diabolical.

infester [aṅfestā] *vt* to infest; **infesté de moustiques** infested with mosquitoes, mosquito-ridden.

infidèle [aṅfēdel] *a* unfaithful; (*REL*) infidel.

infidélité [aṅfēdālētā] *nf* unfaithfulness *q*.

infiltration [aṅfēltrásyôṅ] *nf* infiltration.

infiltrer [aṅfēltrā]: **s'~** *vi:* **s'~ dans** to penetrate into; (*liquide*) to seep into; (*fig: noyauter*) to infiltrate.

infime [aṅfēm] *a* minute, tiny; (*inférieur*) lowly.

infini, e [aṅfēnē] *a* infinite ♦ *nm* infinity; **à l'~** (*MATH*) to infinity; (*discourir*) ad infinitum, endlessly; (*agrandir, varier*) infinitely; (*à perte de vue*) endlessly (into the distance).

infiniment [aṅfēnēmáṅ] *ad* infinitely; **~ grand/petit** (*MATH*) infinitely great/ infinitesimal.

infinité [aṅfēnētā] *nf:* **une ~ de** an infinite number of.

infinitésimal, e, aux [aṅfēnētāzēmál, -ō] *a* infinitesimal.

infinitif, ive [aṅfēnētēf, -ēv] *a, nm* infinitive.

infirme [aṅfērm(ə)] *a* disabled ♦ *nm/f* disabled person; **~ mental** mentally handicapped person; **~ moteur** spastic; **~ de guerre** handicapped veteran (*US*), war cripple (*Brit*); **~ du travail** industrially disabled person.

infirmer [aṅfērmā] *vt* to invalidate.

infirmerie [aṅfērmərē] *nf* sick bay.

infirmier, ière [aṅfērmyā, -yer] *nm/f* nurse ♦ *a:* **élève ~** student nurse; **infirmière chef** head nurse (*US*), sister (*Brit*); **infirmière diplômée** registered nurse; **infirmière visiteuse** visiting nurse (*US*), ≈ district nurse (*Brit*).

infirmité [aṅfērmētā] *nf* disability.

inflammable [aṅflámábl(ə)] *a* (in)flammable.

inflammation [aṅflámásyôṅ] *nf* inflammation.

inflammatoire [aṅflámátwár] *a* (*MÉD*) inflammatory.

inflation [aṅflâsyôṅ] *nf* inflation; **~ rampante/ galopante** creeping/galloping inflation.

inflationniste [aṅflâsyonēst(ə)] *a* inflationist.

infléchir [aṅflāshēr] *vt* (*fig: politique*) to reorientate, redirect; **s'~** *vi* (*poutre, tringle*) to bend, sag.

inflexibilité [aṅfleksēbēlētā] *nf* inflexibility.

inflexible [aṅfleksēbl(ə)] *a* inflexible.

inflexion [aṅfleksyôṅ] *nf* inflection; **~ de la tête** slight nod (of the head).

infliger [aṅflēzhā] *vt:* **~ qch (à qn)** to inflict sth (on sb); (*amende, sanction*) to impose sth (on sb).

influençable [aṅflüáṅsábl(ə)] *a* easily influenced.

influence [aṅflüáṅs] *nf* influence; (*d'un médicament*) effect.

influencer [aṅflüáṅsā] *vt* to influence.

influent, e [aṅflüáṅ, -áṅt] *a* influential.

influer [aṅflüā]: **~ sur** *vt* to have an influence upon.

influx [aṅflü] *nm:* **~ nerveux** (nervous) impulse.

infographie [aṅfográfē] *nf* computer graphics *sg*.

informateur, trice [aṅformátœr, -trēs] *nm/f* informant.

informaticien, ne [aṅformátēsyaṅ, -en] *nm/f* computer scientist.

informatif, ive [aṅformátēf, -ēv] *a* informative.

information [aṅformâsyôṅ] *nf* (*renseignement*) piece of information; (*PRESSE, TV: nouvelle*) item of news; (*diffusion de renseignements, INFORM*) information; (*JUR*) inquiry, investigation; **~s** *nfpl* (*TV*) news *sg*; **voyage d'~** fact-finding trip; **agence d'~** news agency; **journal d'~** serious newspaper.

informatique [aṅformátēk] *nf* (*technique*) data processing; (*science*) computer science ♦ *a* computer *cpd*.

informatisation [aṅformátēzâsyôṅ] *nf* computerization.

informatiser [aṅformátēzā] *vt* to computerize.

informe [aṅform(ə)] *a* shapeless.

informé, e [aṅformā] *a:* **jusqu'à plus ample ~** until further information is available.

informer [aṅformā] *vt:* **~ qn (de)** to inform sb (of) ♦ *vi* (*JUR*): **~ contre qn/sur qch** to initiate inquiries about sb/sth; **s'~ (sur)** to inform o.s. (about); **s'~ (de qch/si)** to inquire *ou* find out (about sth/whether *ou* if).

informulé, e [aṅformülā] *a* unformulated.

infortune [aṅfortün] *nf* misfortune.

infos [aṅfō] *nfpl* (= *informations*) news.

infraction [aṅfráksyôṅ] *nf* offence; **~ à** violation *ou* breach of; **être en ~** to be in breach of the law.

infranchissable [aṅfrâṅshēsábl(ə)] *a* impassable; (*fig*) insuperable.

infrarouge [aṅfrárōōzh] *a, nm* infrared.

infrason [aṅfrásôṅ] *nm* infrasonic vibration.

infrastructure [aṅfrástrüktür] *nf* (*d'une route etc*) substructure; (*AVIAT, MIL*) ground installations *pl*; (*touristique etc*) facilities.

infréquentable [aṅfrākáṅtábl(ə)] *a* not to be associated with.

infroissable [aṅfrwásábl(ə)] *a* crease-resistant.

infructueux, euse [aṅfrüktüœ, -ēz] *a* fruitless, unfruitful.

infus, e [aṅfü, -üz] *a:* **avoir la science ~e** to have innate knowledge.

infuser [aṅfüzā] *vt* (*aussi:* **faire ~**: *thé*) to brew; (: *tisane*) to infuse ♦ *vi* to brew; to infuse; **laisser ~** (to leave) to brew.

infusion [aṅfüzyôṅ] *nf* (*tisane*) infusion, herb tea.

ingambe [aṅgáṅb] *a* spry, nimble.

ingénier [aṅzhānyā]: **s'~** *vi:* **s'~ à faire** to strive to do.

ingénierie [aṅzhānērē] *nf* engineering.

ingénieur [aṅzhānyœr] *nm* engineer; **~ agronome/chimiste** agricultural/chemical engineer; **~ conseil** consulting engineer; **~ du son** sound engineer.

ingénieusement [aṅzhānyœzmáṅ] *ad* ingeniously.

ingénieux, euse [aṅzhānyœ, -ēz] *a* ingenious, clever.

ingéniosité [aṅzhānyōzētā] *nf* ingenuity.

ingénu, e [aṅzhānü] *a* ingenuous, artless ♦ *nf* (*THÉÂTRE*) ingénue.

ingénuité [aṅzhānüētā] *nf* ingenuousness.

ingénument [aṅzhānümáṅ] *ad* ingenuously.

ingérence [aṅzhāráṅs] *nf* interference.

ingérer [aṅzhārā]: **s'~** *vi:* **s'~ dans** to interfere in.

ingouvernable [aṅgōōvernábl(ə)] *a* ungovernable.

ingrat, e [aṅgrá, -át] *a* (*personne*) ungrateful; (*sol*) poor; (*travail, sujet*) arid, thankless; (*visage*) unprepossessing.

ingratitude [aṅgrátētüd] *nf* ingratitude.
ingrédient [aṅgrādyâṅ] *nm* ingredient.
inguérissable [aṅgārēsábl(ə)] *a* incurable.
ingurgiter [aṅgürzhētā] *vt* to swallow; **faire ~ qch à qn** to make sb swallow sth; (*fig: connaissances*) to force sth into sb.
inhabile [ēnábēl] *a* clumsy; (*fig*) inept.
inhabitable [ēnábētábl(ə)] *a* uninhabitable.
inhabité, e [ēnábētā] *a* (*régions*) uninhabited; (*maison*) unoccupied.
inhabituel, le [ēnábētüel] *a* unusual.
inhalateur [ēnálátœr] *nm* inhaler; **~ d'oxygène** oxygen mask.
inhalation [ēnálâsyôṅ] *nf* (*MÉD*) inhalation; **faire des ~s** to use an inhalation bath.
inhaler [ēnálā] *vt* to inhale.
inhérent, e [ēnārâṅ, -âṅt] *a*: **~ à** inherent in.
inhiber [ēnēbā] *vt* to inhibit.
inhibition [ēnēbēsyôṅ] *nf* inhibition.
inhospitalier, ière [ēnospētályā, -yer] *a* inhospitable.
inhumain, e [ēnüman, -en] *a* inhuman.
inhumation [ēnümâsyôṅ] *nf* interment, burial.
inhumer [ēnümā] *vt* to inter, bury.
inimaginable [ēnēmázhēnábl(ə)] *a* unimaginable.
inimitable [ēnēmētábl(ə)] *a* inimitable.
inimitié [ēnēmētyā] *nf* enmity.
ininflammable [ēnaṅflámábl(ə)] *a* non-flammable.
inintelligent, e [ēnaṅtālēzhâṅ, -âṅt] *a* unintelligent.
inintelligible [ēnaṅtālēzhēbl(ə)] *a* unintelligible.
inintéressant, e [ēnaṅtāresâṅ, -âṅt] *a* uninteresting.
ininterrompu, e [ēnaṅterôṅpü] *a* (*file, série*) unbroken; (*flot, vacarme*) uninterrupted, non-stop; (*effort*) unremitting, continuous.
iniquité [ēnēkētā] *nf* iniquity.
initial, e, aux [ēnēsyál, -ō] *a*, *nf* initial; **~es** *nfpl* initials.
initialement [ēnēsyálmâṅ] *ad* initially.
initialiser [ēnēsyálēzā] *vt* to initialize.
initiateur, trice [ēnēsyátœr, -trēs] *nm/f* initiator; (*d'une mode, technique*) innovator, pioneer.
initiation [ēnēsyâsyôṅ] *nf* initiation.
initiatique [ēnēsyátēk] *a* (*rites, épreuves*) initiatory.
initiative [ēnēsyátēv] *nf* initiative; **prendre l'~ de qch/de faire** to take the initiative for sth/of doing; **avoir de l'~** to have initiative, show enterprise; **esprit/qualités d'~** spirit/qualities of initiative; **à** *ou* **sur l'~ de qn** on sb's initiative; **de sa propre ~** on one's own initiative.
initié, e [ēnēsyā] *a* initiated ♦ *nm/f* initiate.
initier [ēnēsyā] *vt* to initiate; **~ qn à** to initiate sb into; (*faire découvrir: art, jeu*) to introduce sb to; **s'~ à** (*métier, profession, technique*) to become initiated into.
injecté, e [aṅzhektā] *a*: **yeux ~s de sang** bloodshot eyes.
injecter [aṅzhektā] *vt* to inject.
injection [aṅzheksyôṅ] *nf* injection; **à ~** (*AUTO*) fuel injection *cpd*.
injonction [aṅzhôṅksyôṅ] *nf* injunction, order; **~ de payer** (*JUR*) order to pay.

injouable [aṅywábl(ə)] *a* unplayable.
injure [aṅzhür] *nf* insult, abuse *q*.
injurier [aṅzhüryā] *vt* to insult, abuse.
injurieux, euse [aṅzhüryœ̄, -œ̄z] *a* abusive, insulting.
injuste [aṅzhüst(ə)] *a* unjust, unfair.
injustement [aṅyüstəmâṅ] *ad* unjustly, unfairly.
injustice [aṅzhüstēs] *nf* injustice.
injustifiable [aṅyüstēfyábl(ə)] *a* unjustifiable.
injustifié, e [aṅyüstēfyā] *a* unjustified, unwarranted.
inlassable [aṅlâsábl(ə)] *a* tireless, indefatigable.
inné, e [ēnā] *a* innate, inborn.
innocemment [ēnosámâṅ] *ad* innocently.
innocence [ēnosáṅs] *nf* innocence.
innocent, c [ēnosâṅ, -âṅt] *a* innocent ♦ *nm/f* innocent person; **faire l'~** to play *ou* come the innocent.
innocenter [ēnosâṅtā] *vt* to clear, prove innocent.
innocuité [ēnoküētā] *nf* innocuousness.
innombrable [ēnôṅbrábl(ə)] *a* innumerable.
innommable [ēnomábl(ə)] *a* unspeakable.
innovateur, trice [ēnovátœr, -trēs] *a* innovatory.
innovation [ēnovásyôṅ] *nf* innovation.
innover [ēnovā] *vi*: **~ en matière d'art** to break new ground in the field of art.
inobservance [ēnopservâṅs] *nf* non-observance.
inobservation [ēnopservásyôṅ] *nf* non-observation, inobservance.
inoccupé, e [ēnoküpā] *a* unoccupied.
inoculer [ēnokülā] *vt*: **~ qch à qn** (*volontairement*) to inoculate sb with sth; (*accidentellement*) to infect sb with sth; **~ qn contre** to inoculate sb against.
inodore [ēnodor] *a* (*gaz*) odorless (*US*), odourless (*Brit*); (*fleur*) scentless.
inoffensif, ive [ēnofâṅsēf, -ēv] *a* harmless, innocuous.
inondable [ēnôṅdábl(ə)] *a* (*zone etc*) liable to flooding.
inondation [ēnôṅdâsyôṅ] *nf* flooding *q*; (*torrent, eau*) flood.
inonder [ēnôṅdā] *vt* to flood; (*fig*) to inundate, overrun; **~ de** (*fig*) to flood *ou* swamp with.
inopérable [ēnopārábl(ə)] *a* inoperable.
inopérant, e [ēnopārâṅ, -âṅt] *a* inoperative, ineffective.
inopiné, e [ēnopēnā] *a* unexpected, sudden.
inopinément [ēnopēnámâṅ] *ad* unexpectedly.
inopportun, e [ēnoportœ̄n, -ün] *a* ill-timed, untimely; inappropriate; (*moment*) inopportune.
inorganisation [ēnorgánēzásyôṅ] *nf* lack of organization.
inorganisé, e [ēnorgánēzā] *a* (*travailleurs*) unorganized.
inoubliable [ēnōōblēyábl(ə)] *a* unforgettable.
inouï, e [ēnwē] *a* unheard-of, extraordinary.
inox [ēnoks] *a*, *nm* (= *inoxydable*) stainless (steel).
inoxydable [ēnoksēdábl(ə)] *a* stainless; (*couverts*) stainless steel *cpd*.
inqualifiable [aṅkálēfyábl(ə)] *a* unspeakable.
inquiet, ète [aṅkyc, -et] *a* (*par nature*)

anxious; (*momentanément*) worried; ~ **de qch/au sujet de qn** worried about sth/sb.

inquiétant, e [aṅkyātâṅ, -âṅt] *a* worrying, disturbing.

inquiéter [aṅkyātā] *vt* to worry, disturb; (*harceler*) to harass; **s'~** to worry, become anxious; **s'~ de** to worry about; (*s'enquérir de*) to inquire about.

inquiétude [aṅkyātüd] *nf* anxiety; **donner de l'~** *ou* **des ~s à** to worry; **avoir de l'~** *ou* **des ~s au sujet de** to feel anxious *ou* worried about.

inquisiteur, trice [aṅkēzētœr, -trēs] *a* (*regards, questions*) inquisitive, prying.

inquisition [aṅkēzēsyôṅ] *nf* inquisition.

INR *sigle m* = *Institut national (belge) de radiodiffusion.*

INRA [ēnrá] *sigle m* = *Institut national de la recherche agronomique.*

insaisissable [aṅsāzēsábl(ə)] *a* elusive.

insalubre [aṅsálübr(ə)] *a* insalubrious, unhealthy.

insanité [aṅsánētā] *nf* madness *q*, insanity *q*.

insatiable [aṅsásyábl(ə)] *a* insatiable.

insatisfaction [aṅsátēsfáksyôṅ] *nf* dissatisfaction.

insatisfait, e [aṅsátēsfe, -et] *a* (*non comblé*) unsatisfied; (: *passion, envie*) unfulfilled; (*mécontent*) dissatisfied.

inscription [aṅskrēpsyôṅ] *nf* (*sur un mur, écriteau etc*) inscription; (*à une institution: voir s'inscrire*) enrollment (*US*), enrolment (*Brit*); registration.

inscrire [aṅskrēr] *vt* (*marquer: sur son calepin etc*) to note *ou* write down; (: *sur un mur, une affiche etc*) to write; (: *dans la pierre, le métal*) to inscribe; (*mettre: sur une liste, un budget etc*) to put down; (*enrôler: soldat*) to enlist; **~ qn à** (*club, école etc*) to enroll (*US*) *ou* enrol (*Brit*) sb at; **s'~** (*pour une excursion etc*) to put one's name down; **s'~** (**à**) (*club, parti*) to join; (*université*) to register *ou* enroll (at); (*examen, concours*) to register *ou* enter (for); **s'~ dans** (*se situer: négociations etc*) to come within the scope of; **s'~ en faux contre** to deny (strongly); (*JUR*) to challenge.

inscrit, e [aṅskrē, ēt] *pp de* **inscrire** ♦ *a* (*étudiant, électeur etc*) registered.

insecte [aṅsekt(ə)] *nm* insect.

insecticide [aṅsektēsēd] *nm* insecticide.

insécurité [aṅsākürētā] *nf* insecurity, lack of security.

INSEE [ēnsā] *sigle m* (= *Institut national de la statistique et des études économiques*) national institute of statistical and economic information.

insémination [aṅsāmēnâsyôṅ] *nf* insemination.

insensé, e [aṅsâṅsā] *a* insane, mad.

insensibiliser [aṅsâṅsēbēlēzā] *vt* to anesthetize (*US*), anaesthetize (*Brit*); (*à une allergie*) to desensitize; **~ à qch** (*fig*) to cause to become insensitive to sth.

insensibilité [aṅsâṅsēbēlētā] *nf* insensitivity.

insensible [aṅsâṅsēbl(ə)] *a* (*nerf, membre*) numb; (*dur, indifférent*) insensitive; (*imperceptible*) imperceptible.

insensiblement [aṅsâṅsēbləmâṅ] *ad* (*doucement, peu à peu*) imperceptibly.

inséparable [aṅsāpárábl(ə)] *a:* ~ (**de**) inseparable (from) ♦ *nmpl:* **~s** (*oiseaux*) lovebirds.

insérer [aṅsārā] *vt* to insert; **s'~ dans** to fit into; (*fig*) to come within.

INSERM [aṅserm] *sigle m* (= *Institut national de la santé et de la recherche médicale*) national institute for medical research.

insert [aṅser] *nm* enclosed fireplace burning solid fuel.

insertion [aṅsersyôṅ] *nf* (*d'une personne*) integration.

insidieusement [aṅsēdyœzmâṅ] *ad* insidiously.

insidieux, euse [aṅsēdyœ, -œz] *a* insidious.

insigne [aṅsēny] *nm* (*d'un parti, club*) badge ♦ *a* distinguished; **~s** *nmpl* (*d'une fonction*) insignia *pl*.

insignifiant, e [aṅsēnyēfyâṅ, -âṅt] *a* insignificant; (*somme, affaire, détail*) trivial, insignificant.

insinuant, e [aṅsēnüâṅ, -âṅt] *a* ingratiating.

insinuation [aṅsēnüâsyôṅ] *nf* innuendo, insinuation.

insinuer [aṅsēnüā] *vt* to insinuate, imply; **s'~ dans** to seep into; (*fig*) to worm one's way into, creep into.

insipide [aṅsēpēd] *a* insipid.

insistance [aṅsēstâṅs] *nf* insistence; **avec ~** insistently.

insistant, e [aṅsēstâṅ, -âṅt] *a* insistent.

insister [aṅsēstā] *vi* to insist; (*s'obstiner*) to keep on; **~ sur** (*détail, note*) to stress; **~ pour qch/pour faire qch** to be insistent about sth/about doing sth.

insociable [aṅsosyábl(ə)] *a* unsociable.

insolation [aṅsolâsyôṅ] *nf* (*MÉD*) sunstroke *q*; (*ensoleillement*) period of sunshine.

insolence [aṅsolâṅs] *nf* insolence *q*; **avec ~** insolently.

insolent, e [aṅsolâṅ, -âṅt] *a* insolent.

insolite [aṅsolēt] *a* strange, unusual.

insoluble [aṅsolübl(ə)] *a* insoluble.

insolvable [aṅsolvábl(ə)] *a* insolvent.

insomniaque [aṅsomnyák] *a, nm/f* insomniac.

insomnie [aṅsomnē] *nf* insomnia *q*, sleeplessness *q*; **avoir des ~s** to suffer from insomnia.

insondable [aṅsôṅdábl(ə)] *a* unfathomable.

insonore [aṅsonor] *a* soundproof.

insonorisation [aṅsonorēzâsyôṅ] *nf* soundproofing.

insonoriser [aṅsonorēzā] *vt* to soundproof.

insouciance [aṅsōōsyâṅs] *nf* carefree attitude; heedless attitude.

insouciant, e [aṅsōōsyâṅ, -âṅt] *a* carefree; (*imprévoyant*) heedless.

insoumis, e [aṅsōōmē, -ēz] *a* (*caractère, enfant*) rebellious, refractory; (*contrée, tribu*) unsubdued; (*MIL: soldat*) AWOL, absent without leave ♦ *nm* (*MIL: soldat*) AWOL (*US*), absentee (*Brit*).

insoumission [aṅsōōmēsyôṅ] *nf* rebelliousness; (*MIL*) absence without leave.

insoupçonnable [aṅsōōpsonábl(ə)] *a* above suspicion.

insoupçonné, e [aṅsōōpsonā] *a* unsuspected.

insoutenable [aṅsōōtnábl(ə)] *a* (*argument*) untenable; (*chaleur*) unbearable.

inspecter [aṅspektā] *vt* to inspect.

inspecteur, trice [aṅspektœr, -trɛs] *nm/f* inspector; *(des assurances)* assessor; ~ **d'Académie** ≈ accreditation officer *(US)*, (regional) director of education; ~ **des finances** ≈ Internal Revenue Service agent *(US)*, ≈ tax inspector *(Brit)*; ~ **(de police)** (police) inspector.

inspection [aṅspeksyôṅ] *nf* inspection.

inspirateur, trice [aṅspēratœr, -trɛs] *nm/f (instigateur)* instigator; *(animateur)* inspirer.

inspiration [aṅspērâsyôṅ] *nf* inspiration; breathing in *q*; *(idée)* flash of inspiration, brain wave; **sous l'~ de** prompted by.

inspiré, e [aṅspērā] *a*: **être bien/mal ~ de faire qch** to be well-advised/ill-advised to do sth.

inspirer [aṅspērā] *vt (gén)* to inspire ♦ *vi (aspirer)* to breathe in; **s'~ de** *(suj: artiste)* to draw one's inspiration from; *(suj: tableau)* to be inspired by; ~ **qch à qn** *(œuvre, project, action)* to inspire sb with sth; *(dégoût, crainte, honneur)* to fill sb with sth; **ça ne m'inspire pas** I'm not crazy about the idea.

instabilité [aṅstábēlētā] *nf* instability.

instable [aṅstábl(ǝ)] *a (meuble, équilibre)* unsteady; *(population, temps)* unsettled; *(paix, régime, caractère)* unstable.

installateur [aṅstálátœr] *nm* fitter.

installation [aṅstálásyôṅ] *nf* installation; putting in *ou* up; fitting out; settling in; *(appareils etc)* fittings *pl*, installations *pl*; ~**s** *nfpl* installations; *(industrielles)* plant *sg*; *(de loisirs)* facilities.

installé, e [aṅstálā] *a*: **bien/mal ~** well/poorly equipped; *(personne)* well/not very well set up *ou* organized.

installer [aṅstálā] *vt (loger)*: ~ **qn** to get sb settled, install sb; *(asseoir, coucher)* to settle (down); *(placer)* to put, place; *(meuble)* to put in; *(rideau, étagère, tente)* to put up; *(gaz, électricité etc)* to put in, install; *(aménager: appartement, pièce)* to fit out; **s'~** *(s'établir: artisan, dentiste etc)* to set o.s. up; *(se loger)*: **s'~ à l'hôtel/chez qn** to move into a hotel/in with sb; *(emménager)* to settle in; *(sur un siège, à un emplacement)* to settle (down); *(fig: maladie, grève)* to take a firm hold *ou* grip.

instamment [aṅstámáṅ] *ad* urgently.

instance [aṅstáṅs] *nf (JUR: procédure)* (legal) proceedings *pl*; *(ADMIN: autorité)* authority; ~**s** *nfpl (prières)* entreaties; **affaire en ~** matter pending; **courrier en ~** mail ready for mailing *(US) ou* posting *(Brit)*; **être en ~ de divorce** to be awaiting a divorce; **train en ~ de départ** train on the point of departure; **tribunal de première ~** court of first instance; **en seconde ~** on appeal.

instant [aṅstáṅ] *nm* moment, instant; **dans un ~** in a moment; **à l'~** this instant; **je l'ai vu à l'~** I've just this minute seen him, I saw him a moment ago; **à l'~ (même) où** at the (very) moment that *ou* when, (just) as; **à chaque ~, à tout ~** at any moment; constantly; **pour l'~** for the moment, for the time being; **par ~s** at times; **de tous les ~s** perpetual; **dès l'~ où *ou* que ...** from the moment when ..., since that moment when ....

instantané, e [aṅstâṅtánā] *a (lait, café)* instant; *(explosion, mort)* instantaneous ♦ *nm* snapshot.

instantanément [aṅstâṅtánámâṅ] *ad* instantaneously.

instar [aṅstár]: **à l'~ de** *prép* following the example of, like.

instaurer [aṅstorā] *vt* to institute; **s'~** *vi* to set o.s. up; *(collaboration etc)* to be established.

instigateur, trice [aṅstēgátœr, -trɛs] *nm/f* instigator.

instigation [aṅstēgásyôṅ] *nf*: **à l'~ de qn** at sb's instigation.

instiller [aṅstēlā] *vt* to instill *(US)*, instil *(Brit)*, apply.

instinct [aṅstaṅ] *nm* instinct; **d'~** *(spontanément)* instinctively; ~ **grégaire** herd instinct; ~ **de conservation** instinct of self-preservation.

instinctif, ive [aṅstaṅktēf, -ēv] *a* instinctive.

instinctivement [aṅstaṅktēvmâṅ] *ad* instinctively.

instituer [aṅstētüā] *vt* to institute, set up; **s'~ défenseur d'une cause** to set o.s up as defender of a cause.

institut [aṅstētü] *nm* institute; ~ **de beauté** beauty salon; ~ **médico-légal** mortuary; **l~ universitaire de technologie (IUT)** technical college.

instituteur, trice [aṅstētütœr, -trɛs] *nm/f* (grade *(US)) ou* primary *(Brit)* school) teacher.

institution [aṅstētüsyôṅ] *nf* institution; *(collège)* private school.

institutionnaliser [aṅstētüsyonálēzā] *vt* to institutionalize.

instructeur, trice [aṅstrüktœr, -trɛs] *a (MIL)*: **sergent ~** drill sergeant; *(JUR)*: **juge ~** committing *(US) ou* examining *(Brit)* magistrate ♦ *nm/f* instructor.

instructif, ive [aṅstrüktēf, -ēv] *a* instructive.

instruction [aṅstrüksyôṅ] *nf (enseignement, savoir)* education; *(JUR)* (preliminary) investigation and hearing; *(directive)* instruction; *(ADMIN: document)* directive; ~**s** *nfpl* instructions; *(mode d'emploi)* directions, instructions; ~ **civique** civics *sg*; ~ **primaire/publique** elementary/public education; ~ **religieuse** religious instruction; ~ **professionnelle** vocational training.

instruire [aṅstrüēr] *vt (élèves)* to teach; *(recrues)* to train; *(JUR: affaire)* to conduct the investigation for; **s'~** to educate o.s.; **s'~ auprès de qn de qch** *(s'informer)* to find sth out from sb; ~ **qn de qch** *(informer)* to inform *ou* advise sb of sth; ~ **contre qn** *(JUR)* to investigate sb.

instruit, e [aṅstrüē, -ēt] *pp de* **instruire** ♦ *a* educated.

instrument [aṅstrümâṅ] *nm* instrument; ~ **à cordes/vent** stringed/wind instrument; ~ **de mesure** measuring instrument; ~ **de musique** musical instrument; ~ **de travail** (working) tool.

instrumental, e, aux [aṅstrümâṅtál, -ō] *a* instrumental.

instrumentation [aṅstrümâṅtâsyôṅ] *nf* instrumentation.

instrumentiste [aṅstrümâṅtēst(ǝ)] *nm/f* instrumentalist.

insu [ansü] *nm*: **à l'~ de qn** without sb knowing.

insubmersible [ansübmersēbl(ə)] *a* unsinkable.

insubordination [ansübordēnåsyóń] *nf* rebelliousness; (*MIL*) insubordination.

insubordonné, e [ansübordonā] *a* insubordinate.

insuccès [ansükse] *nm* failure.

insuffisamment [ansüfēzåmåń] *ad* insufficiently.

insuffisance [ansüfēzåńs] *nf* insufficiency; inadequacy; **~s** *nfpl* (*lacunes*) inadequacies; **~ cardiaque** cardiac insufficiency *q*; **~ hépatique** liver deficiency.

insuffisant, e [ansüfēzåń, -åńt] *a* insufficient; (*élève, travail*) inadequate.

insuffler [ansüflā] *vt*: **~ qch dans** to blow sth into; **~ qch à qn** to inspire sb with sth.

insulaire [ansüler] *a* island *cpd*; (*attitude*) insular.

insularité [ansülårētā] *nf* insularity.

insuline [ansülēn] *nf* insulin.

insultant, e [ansültåń, -åńt] *a* insulting.

insulte [ansült(ə)] *nf* insult.

insulter [ansültā] *vt* to insult.

insupportable [ansüportåbl(ə)] *a* unbearable.

insurgé, e [ansürzhā] *a*, *nm/f* insurgent, rebel.

insurger [ansürzhā]: **s'~** *vi*: **s'~ (contre)** to rise up *ou* rebel (against).

insurmontable [ansürmôntåbl(ə)] *a* (*difficulté*) insuperable; (*aversion*) unconquerable.

insurpassable [ansürpåsåbl(ə)] *a* unsurpassable, unsurpassed.

insurrection [ansüreksyóń] *nf* insurrection, revolt.

insurrectionnel, le [ansüreksyonel] *a* insurrectionary.

intact, e [antåkt] *a* intact.

intangible [antåńzhēbl(ə)] *a* intangible; (*principe*) inviolable.

intarissable [antårēsåbl(ə)] *a* inexhaustible.

intégral, e, aux [antågrål, -ō] *a* complete ♦ *nf* (*MATH*) integral; (*œuvres complètes*) complete works.

intégralement [antågrålmåń] *ad* in full, fully.

intégralité [antågrålētā] *nf* (*d'une somme, d'un revenu*) whole (*ou* full) amount; **dans son ~** in its entirety.

intégrant, e [antågråń, -åńt] *a*: **faire partie ~e de** to be an integral part of, be part and parcel of.

intégration [antågråsyóń] *nf* integration.

intégrationniste [antågråsyonēst(ə)] *a*, *nm/f* integrationist.

intègre [antegr(ə)] *a* perfectly honest, upright.

intégré, e [antågrā] *a*: **circuit ~** integrated circuit.

intégrer [antågrā] *vt*: **~ qch à** *ou* **dans** to integrate sth into; **s'~ à** *ou* **dans** to become integrated into.

intégrisme [antågrēsm(ə)] *nm* fundamentalism.

intégriste [antågrēst(ə)] *a*, *nm/f* fundamentalist.

intégrité [antågrētā] *nf* integrity.

intellect [antålekt] *nm* intellect.

intellectualisme [antåleküålēsm(ə)] *nm* in-

tellectualism.

intellectuel, le [antålektüel] *a*, *nm/f* intellectual; (*péj*) highbrow.

intellectuellement [antålektüelmåń] *ad* intellectually.

intelligemment [antålēzhåmåń] *ad* intelligently.

intelligence [antålēzhåńs] *nf* intelligence; (*compréhension*): **l'~ de** the understanding of; (*complicité*): **regard d'~** glance of complicity, meaningful *ou* knowing look; (*accord*): **vivre en bonne ~ avec qn** to be on good terms with sb; **~s** *nfpl* (*MIL*, *fig*) secret contacts; **être d'~** to have an understanding; **~ artificielle** artificial intelligence (A.I.).

intelligent, e [antålēzhåń, -åńt] *a* intelligent; (*capable*): **~ en affaires** competent in business.

intelligentsia [antålēdzhensyå] *nf* intelligentsia.

intelligible [antålēzhēbl(ə)] *a* intelligible.

intello [antålō] *a*, *nm/f* (*fam*) highbrow.

intempérance [antåńpåråńs] *nf* overindulgence *q*; intemperance *q*.

intempérant, e [antåńpåråń, -åńt] *a* overindulgent; (*moralement*) intemperate.

intempéries [antåńpårē] *nfpl* bad weather *sg*.

intempestif, ive [antåńpestēf, -ēv] *a* untimely.

intenable [antnåbl(ə)] *a* unbearable.

intendance [antåńdåńs] *nf* (*MIL*) army materiel command (*US*), supply corps (*Brit*); (: *bureau*) supplies office; (*SCOL*) bursar's office.

intendant, e [antåńdåń, -åńt] *nm/f* (*MIL*) quartermaster; (*SCOL*) bursar; (*d'une propriété*) steward.

intense [antåńs] *a* intense.

intensément [antåńsåmåń] *ad* intensely.

intensif, ive [antåńsēf, -ēv] *a* intensive; **cours ~** crash course; **~ en main-d'œuvre** labor-intensive; **~ en capital** capital-intensive.

intensifier [antåńsēfyå] *vt*, **s'~** *vi* to intensify.

intensité [antåńsētā] *nf* intensity.

intensivement [antåńsēvmåń] *ad* intensively.

intenter [antåńtā] *vt*: **~ un procès contre** *ou* **à qn** to start proceedings against sb.

intention [antåńsyóń] *nf* intention; (*JUR*) intent; **avoir l'~ de faire** to intend to do, have the intention of doing; **dans l'~ de faire qch** with a view to doing sth; **à l'~ de** *prép* for; (*renseignement*) for the benefit *ou* information of; (*film, ouvrage*) aimed at; **à cette ~** with this aim in view; **sans ~** unintentionally; **faire qch sans mauvaise ~** to do sth without ill intent; **agir dans une bonne ~** to act with good intentions.

intentionné, e [antåńsyonā] *a*: **bien ~** well-meaning *ou* -intentioned; **mal ~** ill-intentioned.

intentionnel, le [antåńsyonel] *a* intentional, deliberate.

intentionnellement [antåńsyonelmåń] *ad* intentionally, deliberately.

inter [anter] *nm* (*TÉL*: = *interurbain*) long-distance call service; (*SPORT*): **~ gauche/droit** inside-left/-right.

interactif, ive [anteråktēf, -ēv] *a* (*aussi IN-FORM*) interactive.

interaction [anteråksyóń] *nf* interaction.

interarmées [aṅterármā] *a inv* inter-army, combined.

interbancaire [aṅterbáṅker] *a* interbank.

intercalaire [aṅterkáler] *a, nm*: **(feuillet)** ~ insert; **(fiche)** ~ divider.

intercaler [aṅterkálā] *vt* to insert; **s'~ entre** to come in between; to slip in between.

intercéder [aṅtersādā] *vi*: ~ **(pour qn)** to intercede (on behalf of sb).

intercepter [aṅterseptā] *vt* to intercept; *(lumière, chaleur)* to cut off.

intercepteur [aṅterseptœr] *nm* (*AVIAT*) interceptor.

interception [aṅtersepsyóṅ] *nf* interception; **avion d'~** interceptor.

intercession [aṅtersāsyóṅ] *nf* intercession.

interchangeable [aṅtersháṅzhábl(ə)] *a* interchangeable.

interclasse [aṅterklâs] *nm* (*SCOL*) break (between classes).

interclubs [aṅterklœb] *a inv* interclub.

intercommunal, e, aux [aṅterkomünál, -ō] *a* intervillage, intercommunity.

intercommunautaire [aṅterkomünōter] *a* intercommunity.

interconnexion [aṅterkoneksyóṅ] *nf* (*INFORM*) networking.

intercontinental, e, aux [aṅterkóṅtēnáṅtál, -ō] *a* intercontinental.

intercostal, e, aux [aṅterkostál, -ō] *a* intercostal, between the ribs.

interdépartemental, e, aux [aṅterdāpártəmáṅtál, -ō] interdepartmental.

interdépendance [aṅterdāpáṅdáṅs] *nf* interdependence.

interdépendant, e [aṅterdāpáṅdáṅ, -áṅt] *a* interdependent.

interdiction [aṅterdēksyóṅ] *nf* ban; ~ **de faire qch** ban on doing sth; ~ **de séjour** (*JUR*) *order banning ex-prisoner from frequenting specified places.*

interdire [aṅterdēr] *vt* to forbid; (*ADMIN*: *stationnement, meeting, passage*) to ban, prohibit; (: *journal, livre*) to ban; ~ **qch à qn** to forbid sb sth; ~ **à qn de faire** to forbid sb to do, prohibit sb from doing; (*suj: empêchement*) to prevent *ou* preclude sb from doing; **s'~ qch** (*éviter*) to refrain *ou* abstain from sth; (*se refuser*): **il s'interdit d'y penser** he doesn't allow himself to think about it.

interdisciplinaire [aṅterdēsēplēner] *a* interdisciplinary.

interdit, e [aṅterdē, -ēt] *pp de* **interdire** ♦ *a* (*stupéfait*) taken aback; (*défendu*) forbidden, prohibited ♦ *nm* interdict, prohibition; **film ~ aux moins de 18/13 ans** ≈ X-/R-rated (*US*) *ou* 18-/PG-rated (*Brit*) film; **sens ~** one way; **stationnement ~** no parking; ~ **de chéquier** having checking account (*US*) *ou* cheque book facilities (*Brit*) suspended; ~ **de séjour** subject to an *interdiction de séjour.*

intéressant, e [aṅtārésáṅ, -áṅt] *a* interesting; **faire l'~** to draw attention to o.s.

intéressé, e [aṅtārāsā] *a* (*parties*) involved, concerned; (*amitié, motifs*) self-interested ♦ *nm*: **l'~** the interested party; **les ~s** those concerned *ou* involved.

intéressement [aṅtāresmáṅ] *nm* (*COMM*) profit-sharing.

intéresser [aṅtārāsā] *vt* to interest; (*toucher*) to be of interest *ou* concern to; (*ADMIN*: *concerner*) to affect, concern; (*COMM*: *travailleur*) to give a share in the profits to; (: *partenaire*) to interest (in the business); **s'~ à** to take an interest in, be interested in; ~ **qn à qch** to get sb interested in sth.

intérêt [aṅtāre] *nm* (*aussi COMM*) interest; (*égoïsme*) self-interest; **porter de l'~ à qn** to take an interest in sb; **agir par** ~ to act out of self-interest; **avoir des ~s dans** (*COMM*) to have a financial interest *ou* a stake in; **avoir** ~ **à faire** to do well to do; **il y a** ~ **à ...** it would be a good thing to ...; ~ **composé** compound interest.

interface [aṅterfâs] *nf* (*INFORM*) interface.

interférence [aṅterfāráṅs] *nf* interference.

interférer [aṅterfārā] *vi*: ~ **(avec)** to interfere (with).

intergouvernemental, e, aux [aṅtergōōvernə-máṅtál, -ō] *a* intergovernmental.

intérieur, e [aṅtāryœr] *a* (*mur, escalier, poche*) inside; (*commerce, politique*) domestic; (*cour, calme, vie*) inner; (*navigation*) inland ♦ *nm* (*d'une maison, d'un récipient etc*) inside; (*d'un pays, aussi: décor, mobilier*) interior; (*POL*): **l'l~** (the Department of) the Interior; **à l'~ (de)** inside; (*fig*) within; **de l'~** (*fig*) from the inside; **en** ~ (*CINÉMA*) in the studio; **vêtement d'~** indoor garment.

intérieurement [aṅtāryœrmáṅ] *ad* inwardly.

intérim [aṅtārēm] *nm* interim period; **assurer l'~ (de)** to deputize (for); **par** ~ *a* interim ♦ *ad* in a temporary capacity.

intérimaire [aṅtārēmer] *a* temporary, interim ♦ *nm/f* (*secrétaire etc*) temporary; (*suppléant*) deputy.

intérioriser [aṅtāryorēzā] *vt* to internalize.

interjection [aṅterzheksyóṅ] *nf* interjection.

interjeter [aṅterzhətā] *vt* (*JUR*): ~ **appel** to file (*US*) *ou* lodge (*Brit*) an appeal.

interligne [aṅterlēny] *nm* interline space ♦ *nf* (*TYPO*) lead, leading; **simple/double** ~ single/double spacing.

interlocuteur, trice [aṅterlokütœr, -trēs] *nm/f* speaker; (*POL*): ~ **valable** valid representative; **son** ~ the person he *ou* she was speaking to.

interlope [aṅterlop] *a* illicit; (*milieu, bar*) shady.

interloquer [aṅterlokā] *vt* to take aback.

interlude [aṅterlüd] *nm* interlude.

intermède [aṅtermed] *nm* interlude.

intermédiaire [aṅtermādyer] *a* intermediate; middle; half-way ♦ *nm/f* intermediary; (*COMM*) middleman; **sans** ~ directly; **par l'~ de** through.

interminable [aṅtermēnábl(ə)] *a* never-ending.

interminablement [aṅtermēnábləmáṅ] *ad* interminably.

interministériel, le [aṅtermēnēstáryel] *a*: **comité** ~ interdepartmental committee.

intermittence [aṅtermētáṅs] *nf*: **par** ~ intermittently, sporadically.

intermittent, e [aṅtermētáṅ, -áṅt] *a* intermittent, sporadic.

internat [aṅternâ] *nm* (*SCOL*) boarding school.

international, e, aux [aṅternásyonál, -ō] *a*,

nm/f international.
internationaliser [aṅternâsyonâlēzā] *vt* to internationalize.
internationalisme [aṅternâsyonâlēsm(ə)] *nm* internationalism.
interne [aṅtern(ə)] *a* internal ♦ *nm/f* (*SCOL*) boarder; (*MÉD*) intern (*US*), houseman (*Brit*).
internement [aṅternəmâṅ] *nm* (*POL*) internment; (*MÉD*) confinement.
interner [aṅternā] *vt* (*POL*) to intern; (*MÉD*) to confine to a mental institution.
interparlementaire [aṅterpârləmâṅter] *a* interparliamentary.
interpellation [aṅterpālâsyôṅ] *nf* interpellation; (*POL*) question.
interpeller [aṅterpālā] *vt* (*appeler*) to call out to; (*apostropher*) to shout at; (*POLICE*) to take in for questioning; (*POL*) to question; **s'~** to exchange insults.
interphone [aṅterfon] *nm* intercom.
interplanétaire [aṅterplánāter] *a* interplanetary.
INTERPOL [aṅterpol] *sigle m* Interpol.
interpoler [aṅterpolā] *vt* to interpolate.
interposer [aṅterpōzā] *vt* to interpose; **s'~** *vi* to intervene; **par personnes interposées** through a third party.
interprétariat [aṅterprātâryâ] *nm* interpreting.
interprétation [aṅterprātâsyôṅ] *nf* interpretation.
interprète [aṅterpret] *nm/f* interpreter; (*porte-parole*) spokesman.
interpréter [aṅterprātā] *vt* to interpret.
interprofessionnel, le [aṅterprofāsyonel] *a* interprofessional.
interrogateur, trice [aṅtārogátœr, -tres] *a* questioning, inquiring ♦ *nm/f* (*SCOL*) (oral) examiner.
interrogatif, ive [aṅtārogâtēf, -ēv] *a* (*LING*) interrogative.
interrogation [aṅtārogâsyôṅ] *nf* question; (*SCOL*) (written *ou* oral) test.
interrogatoire [aṅtārogâtwâr] *nm* (*POLICE*) questioning *q*; (*JUR*) cross-examination, interrogation.
interroger [aṅtārozhā] *vt* to question; (*INFORM*) to interrogate; (*SCOL*: *candidat*) to test; **~ qn (sur qch)** to question sb (about sth); **~ qn du regard** to look questioningly at sb, give sb a questioning look; **s'~ sur qch** to ask o.s. about sth, ponder (about) sth.
interrompre [aṅtārôṅpr(ə)] *vt* (*gén*) to interrupt; (*travail, voyage*) to break off, interrupt; **s'~** to break off.
interrupteur [aṅtārüptœr] *nm* switch; **~ à bascule** (*INFORM*) toggle switch.
interruption [aṅtārüpsyôṅ] *nf* interruption; **sans ~** without a break; **~ de grossesse** termination of pregnancy; **~ volontaire de grossesse** voluntary termination of pregnancy, abortion.
interscolaire [aṅterskoler] *a* interschool(s).
intersection [aṅterseksyôṅ] *nf* intersection.
intersidéral, e, aux [aṅtersēdârâl, -ō] *a* intersidereal, interstellar.
interstice [aṅterstēs] *nm* crack, slit.
intersyndical, e, aux [aṅtersaṅdēkâl, -ō] *a* interunion.

interurbain [aṅterürbaṅ] (*TÉL*) *nm* long-distance call service ♦ *a* long-distance.
intervalle [aṅtervâl] *nm* (*espace*) space; (*de temps*) interval; **dans l'~** in the meantime; **à 2 mois d'~** after a space of 2 months; **à ~s rapprochés** at close intervals; **par ~s** at intervals.
intervenant, e [aṅtervənâṅ, -âṅt] *vb voir* **intervenir** ♦ *nm/f* speaker (*at conference*).
intervenir [aṅtervənēr] *vi* (*gén*) to intervene; (*survenir*) to take place; (*faire une conférence*) to give a talk *ou* lecture; **~ auprès de/en faveur de qn** to intervene with/on behalf of sb; **la police a dû ~** police had to step in *ou* intervene; **les médecins ont dû ~** the doctors had to operate.
intervention [aṅtervâṅsyôṅ] *nf* intervention; (*conférence*) talk, paper; **~ (chirurgicale)** operation.
interventionnisme [aṅtervâṅsyonēsm(ə)] *nm* interventionism.
intervenu, e [aṅterv(ə)nü] *pp de* **intervenir**.
intervertible [aṅtervertēbl(ə)] *a* interchangeable.
intervertir [aṅtervertēr] *vt* to invert (the order of), reverse.
interviendrai [aṅtervyaṅdrā], **interviens** [aṅtervyaṅ] *etc vb voir* **intervenir**.
interview [aṅtervyōō] *nf* interview.
interviewer [aṅtervyōōvā] *vt* to interview ♦ *nm* [aṅtervyōōvœr] (*journaliste*) interviewer.
intervins [aṅtervaṅ] *etc vb voir* **intervenir**.
intestat [aṅtestâ] *a* (*JUR*): **décéder ~** to die intestate.
intestin, e [aṅtestaṅ, -ēn] *a* internal ♦ *nm* intestine; **~ grêle** small intestine.
intestinal, e, aux [aṅtestēnâl, -ō] *a* intestinal.
intime [aṅtēm] *a* intimate; (*vie, journal*) private; (*convictions*) inmost; (*dîner, cérémonie*) held among friends, quiet ♦ *nm/f* close friend.
intimement [aṅtēmmâṅ] *ad* (*profondément*) deeply, firmly; (*étroitement*) intimately.
intimer [aṅtēmā] *vt* (*JUR*) to notify; **~ à qn l'ordre de faire** to order sb to do.
intimider [aṅtēmēdā] *vt* to intimidate.
intimité [aṅtēmētā] *nf* intimacy; (*vie privée*) privacy; private life; **dans l'~** in private; (*sans formalités*) with only a few friends, quietly.
intitulé [aṅtētülā] *nm* title.
intituler [aṅtētülā] *vt*: **comment a-t-il intitulé son livre?** what title did he give his book?; **s'~** to be entitled; (*personne*) to call o.s.
intolérable [aṅtolārâbl(ə)] *a* intolerable.
intolérant, e [aṅtolârâṅ, -âṅt] *a* intolerant.
intonation [aṅtonâsyôṅ] *nf* intonation.
intouchable [aṅtōōshâbl(ə)] *a* (*fig*) above the law, sacrosanct; (*REL*) untouchable.
intoxication [aṅtoksēkâsyôṅ] *nf* poisoning *q*; (*toxicomanie*) drug addiction; (*fig*) brainwashing; **~ alimentaire** food poisoning.
intoxiqué, e [aṅtoksēkā] *nm/f* addict.
intoxiquer [aṅtoksēkā] *vt* to poison; (*fig*) to brainwash; **s'~** to poison o.s.
intraduisible [aṅtrâdüēzēbl(ə)] *a* untranslatable; (*fig*) inexpressible.
intraitable [aṅtretâbl(ə)] *a* inflexible, uncompromising.

intransigeance [aṅtrǡnzēzhǡńs] *nf* intransigence.

intransigeant, e [aṅtrǡnzēzhǡń, -ǡńt] *a* intransigent; (*morale, passion*) uncompromising.

intransitif, ive [aṅtrǡnzētēf, -ēv] *a* (*LING*) intransitive.

intransportable [aṅtrǡnsportȧ́bl(ə)] *a* (*blessé*) unable to travel.

intraveineux, euse [aṅtrȧ́venꝏ̄, -ꝏ̄z] *a* intravenous.

intrépide [aṅtrāpēd] *a* dauntless, intrepid.

intrigant, e [aṅtrēgȧ́ń, -ǡńt] *nm/f* schemer.

intrigue [aṅtrēg] *nf* intrigue; (*scénario*) plot.

intriguer [aṅtrēgā] *vi* to scheme ♦ *vt* to puzzle, intrigue.

intrinsèque [aṅtraṅsek] *a* intrinsic.

introductif, ive [aṅtrodüktēf, -ēv] *a* introductory.

introduction [aṅtrodüksyȯ́ń] *nf* introduction; **paroles/chapitre d'~** introductory words/chapter; **lettre/mot d'~** letter/note of introduction.

introduire [aṅtrodüēr] *vt* to introduce; (*visiteur*) to show in; (*aiguille, clef*): **~ qch dans** to insert *ou* introduce sth into; (*personne*): **~ à qch** to introduce to sth; (*: présenter*): **~ qn à qn/dans un club** to introduce sb to sb/to a club; (*INFORM*) to input, enter; **s'~** (*techniques, usages*) to be introduced; **s'~ dans** to gain entry into; to get o.s. accepted into; (*eau, fumée*) to get into; **~ au clavier** to key in.

introduit, e [aṅtrodüē, -ēt] *pp de* **introduire** ♦ *a*: **bien ~** (*personne*) well-received.

introniser [aṅtrȯnēzā] *vt* to enthrone.

introspection [aṅtrospeksyȯ́ń] *nf* introspection.

introuvable [aṅtrꝏ̄ōvȧ́bl(ə)] *a* which cannot be found; (*COMM*) unobtainable.

introverti, e [aṅtrovertē] *nm/f* introvert.

intrus, e [aṅtrü, -üz] *nm/f* intruder.

intrusion [aṅtrüzyȯ́ń] *nf* intrusion; (*ingérence*) interference.

intuitif, ive [aṅtüētēf, ēv] *a* intuitive.

intuition [aṅtüēsyȯ́ń] *nf* intuition; **avoir une ~** to have a feeling; **avoir l'~ de qch** to have an intuition of sth; **avoir de l'~** to have intuition.

intuitivement [aṅtüētēvmȧ́ń] *ad* intuitively.

inusable [ēnüzȧ́bl(ə)] *a* wear-resistant.

inusité, e [ēnüzētā] *a* rarely used.

inutile [ēnütēl] *a* useless; (*superflu*) unnecessary.

inutilement [ēnütēlmȧ́ń] *ad* needlessly.

inutilisable [ēnütēlēzȧ́bl(ə)] *a* unusable.

inutilisé, e [ēnütēlēzā] *a* unused.

inutilité [ēnütēlētā] *nf* uselessness.

invaincu, e [aṅvaṅkü] *a* unbeaten; (*armée, peuple*) unconquered.

invalide [aṅvȧ́lēd] *a* disabled ♦ *nm/f*: **~ de guerre** disabled veteran (*US*) *ou* ex-serviceman (*Brit*); **~ du travail** industrially disabled person.

invalider [aṅvȧ́lēdā] *vt* to invalidate.

invalidité [aṅvȧ́lēdētā] *nf* disability.

invariable [aṅvȧ́ryȧ́bl(ə)] *a* invariable.

invariablement [aṅvȧ́ryȧ́blǝmȧ́ń] *ad* invariably.

invasion [aṅvȧ́zyȯ́ń] *nf* invasion.

invective [aṅvektēv] *nf* invective.

invectiver [aṅvektēvā] *vt* to hurl abuse at ♦ *vi*: **~ contre** to rail against.

invendable [aṅvǡndȧ́bl(ə)] *a* unsaleable, unmarketable.

invendu, e [aṅvǡndü] *a* unsold ♦ *nm* return; **~s** *nmpl* unsold goods.

inventaire [aṅvǡnter] *nm* inventory; (*COMM*: *liste*) stocklist; (*: opération*) stocktaking *q*; (*fig*) survey; **faire un ~** to make an inventory; (*COMM*) to take stock; **faire** *ou* **procéder à l'~** to take stock.

inventer [aṅvǡntā] *vt* to invent; (*subterfuge*) to devise, invent; (*histoire, excuse*) to make up, invent; **~ de faire** to hit on the idea of doing.

inventeur, trice [aṅvǡntœr, -trēs] inventor.

inventif, ive [aṅvǡntēf, -ēv] *a* inventive.

invention [aṅvǡnsyȯ́ń] *nf* invention; (*imagination, inspiration*) inventiveness.

inventivité [aṅvǡntēvētā] *nf* inventiveness.

inventorier [aṅvǡntoryā] *vt* to make an inventory of.

invérifiable [aṅvārēfyȧ́bl(ə)] *a* unverifiable.

inverse [aṅvers(ə)] *a* (*ordre*) reverse; (*sens*) opposite; (*rapport*) inverse ♦ *nm* reverse; inverse; **en proportion ~** in inverse proportion; **dans le sens ~ des aiguilles d'une montre** counterclockwise (*US*), anticlockwise (*Brit*); **en sens ~** in (*ou* from) the opposite direction; **à l'~** conversely.

inversement [aṅversǝmȧ́ń] *ad* conversely.

inverser [aṅversā] *vt* to reverse, invert; (*ÉLEC*) to reverse.

inversion [aṅversyȯ́ń] *nf* reversal; inversion.

invertébré, e [aṅvertābrā] *a, nm* invertebrate.

inverti, e [aṅvertē] *nm/f* homosexual.

investigation [aṅvestēgȧ́syȯ́ń] *nf* investigation, inquiry.

investir [aṅvestēr] *vt* to invest; **s'~** *vi* (*PSYCH*) to involve o.s.; **~ qn de** to vest *ou* invest sb with.

investissement [aṅvestēsmȧ́ń] *nm* investment; (*PSYCH*) involvement.

investiture [aṅvestētür] *nf* investiture; (*à une élection*) nomination.

invétéré, e [aṅvātārā] *a* (*habitude*) ingrained; (*bavard, buveur*) inveterate.

invincible [aṅvaṅsēbl(ə)] *a* invincible, unconquerable.

invinciblement [aṅvaṅsēblǝmȧ́ń] *ad* (*fig*) invincibly.

inviolabilité [aṅvyolȧ́bēlētā] *nf*: **~ parlementaire** parliamentary immunity.

inviolable [aṅvyolȧ́bl(ə)] *a* inviolable.

invisible [aṅvēzēbl(ə)] *a* invisible; (*fig: personne*) not available.

invitation [aṅvētȧ́syȯ́ń] *nf* invitation; **à/sur l'~ de qn** at/on sb's invitation; **carte/lettre d'~** invitation card/letter.

invite [aṅvēt] *nf* invitation.

invité, e [aṅvētā] *nm/f* guest.

inviter [aṅvētā] *vt* to invite; **~ qn à faire qch** to invite sb to do sth; (*suj: chose*) to induce *ou* tempt sb to do sth.

invivable [aṅvēvȧ́bl(ə)] *a* unbearable, impossible.

involontaire [aṅvolȯ́nter] *a* (*mouvement*) involuntary; (*insulte*) unintentional; (*complice*) unwitting.

involontairement [aṅvolôṅtermâṅ] *ad* involuntarily.

invoquer [aṅvokā] *vt* (*Dieu, muse*) to call upon, invoke; (*prétexte*) to put forward (as an excuse); (*témoignage*) to call upon; (*loi, texte*) to refer to; ~ **la clémence de qn** to beg sb *ou* appeal to sb for clemency.

invraisemblable [aṅvresâṅblábl(ə)] *a* unlikely, improbable; (*bizarre*) incredible.

invraisemblance [aṅvresâṅblâṅs] *nf* unlikelihood *q*, improbability.

invulnérable [aṅvülnārábl(ə)] *a* invulnerable.

iode [yod] *nm* iodine.

iodé, e [yodā] *a* iodized.

ion [yôṅ] *nm* ion.

ionique [yonēk] *a* (*ARCHIT*) Ionic; (*SCIENCE*) ionic.

IPC *sigle m* (= *Indice des prix à la consommation*) CPI.

IR. *abr* = **infrarouge**.

IRA *sigle f* (= *Irish Republican Army*) IRA.

irai [ērā] *etc vb voir* **aller**.

Irak [ērák] *nm*: **l'**~ Iraq *ou* Irak.

irakien, ne [ērákyaṅ, -cn] *a* Iraqi ♦ *nm* (*LING*) Iraqi ♦ *nm/f*: **l**~, **ne** Iraqi.

Iran [ērâṅ] *nm*: **l'**~ Iran.

iranien, ne [ērányaṅ, -en] *a* Iranian ♦ *nm* (*LING*) Iranian ♦ *nm/f*: **l**~, **ne** Iranian.

Iraq [ērák] = **Irak**.

iraquien, ne [ērákyaṅ, -en] = **irakien, ne**.

irascible [ērásēbl(ə)] *a* short-tempered, irascible.

irions [ēryôṅ] *etc vb voir* **aller**.

iris [ērēs] *nm* iris.

irisé, e [ērēzā] *a* iridescent.

irlandais, e [ērlâṅde, -ez] *a, nm* (*LING*) Irish ♦ *nm/f*: **l**~, **e** Irishman/woman; **les l**~ the Irish.

Irlande [ērlâṅd] *nf*: **l'**~ (*pays*) Ireland; (*état*) the Irish Republic, the Republic of Ireland, Eire; ~ **du Nord** Northern Ireland, Ulster; ~ **du Sud** Southern Ireland, Irish Republic, Eire; **la mer d'**~ the Irish Sea.

ironie [ēronē] *nf* irony.

ironique [ēronēk] *a* ironical.

ironiquement [ēronēkmâṅ] *ad* ironically.

ironiser [ēronēzā] *vi* to be ironical.

irons [ērôṅ] *etc vb voir* **aller**.

IRPP *sigle m* (= *impôt sur le revenu des personnes physiques*) income tax.

irradiation [ērádyâsyôṅ] *nf* irradiation.

irradier [ērádyā] *vi* to radiate ♦ *vt* to irradiate.

irraisonné, e [ērezonā] *a* irrational, unreasoned.

irrationnel, le [ērásyonel] *a* irrational.

irrattrapable [ērátrápábl(ə)] *a* (*retard*) that cannot be made up; (*bévue*) that cannot be made good.

irréalisable [ērāálēzábl(ə)] *a* unrealizable; (*projet*) impracticable.

irréalisme [ērāálēsm(ə)] *nm* lack of realism.

irréaliste [ērāálēst(ə)] *a* unrealistic.

irréalité [ērāálētā] *nf* unreality.

irrecevable [ērsəvábl(ə)] *a* unacceptable.

irréconciliable [ērākôṅsēlyábl(ə)] *a* irreconcilable.

irrécouvrable [ērákōōvrábl(ə)] *a* irrecover-

able.

irrécupérable [ērāküpārábl(ə)] *a* unreclaimable, beyond repair; (*personne*) beyond redemption *ou* recall.

irrécusable [ērāküzábl(ə)] *a* (*témoignage*) unimpeachable; (*preuve*) incontestable, indisputable.

irréductible [ērādüktēbl(ə)] *a* indomitable, implacable; (*MATH*: *fraction, équation*) irreducible.

irréductiblement [ērādüktēbləmâṅ] *ad* implacably.

irréel, le [ērāel] *a* unreal.

irréfléchi, e [ērāflāshē] *a* thoughtless.

irréfutable [ērāfütábl(ə)] *a* irrefutable.

irréfutablement [ērāfütábləmâṅ] *ad* irrefutably.

irrégularité [ērāgülárētā] *nf* irregularity; unevenness *q*.

irrégulier, ière [ērāgülyā, -yer] *a* irregular; (*surface, rythme, écriture*) uneven, irregular; (*élève, athlète*) erratic.

irrégulièrement [ērāgülyermâṅ] *ad* irregularly.

irrémédiable [ērāmādyábl(ə)] *a* irreparable.

irrémédiablement [ērāmādyábləmâṅ] *ad* irreparably.

irremplaçable [ērâṅplásábl(ə)] *a* irreplaceable.

irréparable [ērāpárábl(ə)] *a* beyond repair, irreparable; (*fig*) irreparable.

irrépréhensible [ērāprāâṅsēbl(ə)] *a* irreprehensible.

irrépressible [ērāprāsēbl(ə)] *a* irrepressible.

irréprochable [ērāproshábl(ə)] *a* irreproachable, beyond reproach; (*tenue, toilette*) impeccable.

irrésistible [ērāzēstēbl(ə)] *a* irresistible; (*preuve, logique*) compelling.

irrésistiblement [ērāzēstēbləmâṅ] *ad* irresistibly.

irrésolu, e [ērāzolü] *a* irresolute.

irrésolution [ērāzolüsyôṅ] *nf* irresoluteness.

irrespectueux, euse [ērespektüœ̄, -œz] *a* disrespectful.

irrespirable [ērespērábl(ə)] *a* unbreathable; (*fig*) oppressive, stifling.

irresponsabilité [ērespôṅsábēlētā] *nf* irresponsibility.

irresponsable [ērespôṅsábl(ə)] *a* irresponsible.

irrévérencieux, euse [ērāvārâṅsyœ̄, -œz] *a* irreverent.

irréversible [ērāversēbl(ə)] *a* irreversible.

irréversiblement [ērāversēbləmâṅ] *ad* irreversibly.

irrévocable [ērāvokábl(ə)] *a* irrevocable.

irrévocablement [ērāvokábləmâṅ] *ad* irrevocably.

irrigation [ērēgásyôṅ] *nf* irrigation.

irriguer [ērēgā] *vt* to irrigate.

irritabilité [ērētábēlētā] *nf* irritability.

irritable [ērētábl(ə)] *a* irritable.

irritant, e [ērētâṅ, -âṅt] *a* irritating; (*MÉD*) irritant.

irritation [ērētásyôṅ] *nf* irritation.

irrité, e [ērētā] *a* irritated.

irriter [ērētā] *vt* (*agacer*) to irritate, annoy; (*MÉD*: *enflammer*) to irritate; **s'**~ **contre qn/de qch** to get annoyed *ou* irritated with sb/at sth.

irruption [ērüpsyôñ] *nf* irruption *q*; **faire ~ dans** to burst into.
ISBN *sigle m* (= *International Standard Book Number*) ISBN.
Islam [ēslám] *nm* Islam.
islamique [ēslámēk] *a* Islamic.
islandais, e [ēslâñde, -ez] *a* Icelandic ♦ *nm* (*LING*) Icelandic ♦ *nm/f*: **I~, e** Icelander.
Islande [ēslâñd] *nf*: **I'~** Iceland.
ISMH *sigle m* (= *Inventaire supplémentaire des monuments historiques*): **monument inscrit à l'~** ≈ historical monument.
isocèle [ēzosel] *a* isoceles.
isolant, e [ēzolâñ, -âñt] *a* insulating; (*insonorisant*) soundproofing ♦ *nm* insulator.
isolateur [ēzolátœr] *nm* (*ÉLEC*) insulator.
isolation [ēzolâsyôñ] *nf* insulation; **~ acoustique/thermique** sound/thermal insulation.
isolationnisme [ēzolâsyonèsm(ə)] *nm* isolationism.
isolé, e [ēzolā] *a* isolated; (*ÉLEC*) insulated.
isolement [ēzolmâñ] *nm* isolation; solitary confinement.
isolément [ēzolāmâñ] *ad* in isolation.
isoler [ēzolā] *vt* to isolate; (*prisonnier*) to put in solitary confinement; (*ville*) to cut off, isolate; (*ÉLEC*) to insulate.
isoloir [ēzolwár] *nm* polling *ou* voting (*US*) booth.
isorel [ēzorel] *nm* ® hardboard.
isotherme [ēzotèrm(ə)] *a* (*camion*) refrigerated.
Israël [ēsràel] *nm*: **l'~** Israel.
israélien, ne [ēsràālyañ, -en] *a* Israeli ♦ *nm/f*: **I~, ne** Israeli.
israélite [ēsràālēt] *a* Jewish; (*dans l'Ancien Testament*) Israelite ♦ *nm/f*: **I~** Jew/Jewess; Israelite.
issu, e [ēsü] *a*: **~ de** descended from; (*fig*) stemming from ♦ *nf* (*ouverture, sortie*) exit; (*solution*) way out, solution; (*dénouement*) outcome; **à l'~e de** at the conclusion *ou* close of; **rue sans ~e** dead end, no through road; **~e de secours** emergency exit.
Istamboul *ou* **Istanbul** [ēstâñbōōl] *n* Istanbul.
isthme [ēsm(ə)] *nm* isthmus.
Italie [ētálē] *nf*: **l'~** Italy.
italien, ne [ētályañ, -en] *a* Italian ♦ *nm* (*LING*) Italian ♦ *nm/f*: **I~, ne** Italian.
italique [ētálēk] *nm*: **en ~(s)** in italics.
item [ētem] *nm* item; (*question*) question, test.
itinéraire [ētēnārer] *nm* itinerary, route.
itinérant, e [ētēnārâñ, -âñt] *a* itinerant, travelling (*US*), travelling (*Brit*).
ITP *sigle m* (= *ingénieur des travaux publics*) civil engineer.
IUT *sigle m* = **Institut universitaire de technologie.**
IVG *sigle f* (= *interruption volontaire de grossesse*) abortion.
ivoire [ēvwár] *nm* ivory.
ivoirien, ne [ēvwáryañ, -en] *a* of *ou* from the Ivory Coast.
ivraie [ēvre] *nf*: **séparer l'~ du bon grain** (*fig*) to separate the wheat from the chaff.
ivre [ēvr(ə)] *a* drunk; **~ de** (*colère*) wild with; (*bonheur*) drunk *ou* intoxicated with; **~ mort** dead drunk.

ivresse [ēvres] *nf* drunkenness; (*euphorie*) intoxication.
ivrogne [ēvrony] *nm/f* drunkard.

J

J, j [zhē] *nm inv* J, j ♦ *abr* (= *jour*): **jour ~** D-day; (= *Joule*) J; **J comme Joseph** J for Jig.
j' [zh] *pronom voir* **je.**
jabot [zhábō] *nm* (*ZOOL*) crop; (*de vêtement*) jabot.
JAC [zhak] *sigle f* (= *Jeunesse agricole catholique*) youth organization.
jacasser [zhákásá] *vi* to chatter.
jachère [zhásher] *nf*: **(être) en ~** (to lie) fallow.
jacinthe [zhásañt] *nf* hyacinth; **~ des bois** bluebell.
jack [dzhák] *nm* jack plug.
jacquerie [zhákrē] *nf* riot.
jade [zhád] *nm* jade.
jadis [zhádēs] *ad* in times past, formerly.
jaguar [zhágwár] *nm* (*ZOOL*) jaguar.
jaillir [zháyēr] *vi* (*liquide*) to spurt out, gush out; (*lumière*) to flood out; (*fig*) to rear up; to burst out.
jaillissement [zháyēsmâñ] *nm* spurt, gush.
jais [zhe] *nm* jet; (**d'un noir) de ~** jet-black.
jalon [zhálôñ] *nm* range pole; (*fig*) milestone; **poser des ~s** (*fig*) to pave the way.
jalonner [zhálonā] *vt* to mark out; (*fig*) to mark, punctuate.
jalousement [zhálōōzmâñ] *ad* jealously.
jalouser [zhálōōzā] *vt* to be jealous of.
jalousie [zhálōōzē] *nf* jealousy; (*store*) (venetian) blind.
jaloux, ouse [zhálōō, -ōōz] *a* jealous; **être ~ de qn/qch** to be jealous of sb/sth.
jamaïquain, e [zhámáékañ, -en] *a* Jamaican.
Jamaïque [zhámáēk] *nf*: **la ~** Jamaica.
jamais [zháme] *ad* never; (*sans négation*) ever; **ne ... ~** never; **~ de la vie!** never!; **si ~ ...** if ever ...; **à (tout) ~, pour ~** for ever, for ever and ever.
jambage [zhâñbázh] *nm* (*de lettre*) downstroke; (*de porte*) jamb.
jambe [zhâñb] *nf* leg; **à toutes ~s** as fast as one's legs can carry one.
jambières [zhâñbyer] *nfpl* legwarmers; (*SPORT*) shin pads.
jambon [zhâñbôñ] *nm* ham.
jambonneau, x [zhâñbonō] *nm* knuckle of ham.
jante [zhâñt] *nf* (wheel) rim.
janvier [zhâñvyā] *nm* January; *voir aussi* **juillet.**
Japon [zhápôñ] *nm*: **le ~** Japan.
japonais, e [zhápone, -ez] *a* Japanese ♦ *nm* (*LING*) Japanese ♦ *nm/f*: **J~, e** Japanese.
japonaiserie [zháponezrē] *nf* (*bibelot*) Japanese curio.

jappement [zhápmáñ] *nm* yap, yelp.

japper [zhápā] *vi* to yap, yelp.

jaquette [zháket] *nf* (*de cérémonie*) morning coat; (*de femme*) jacket; (*de livre*) dust cover, (dust) jacket.

jardin [zhárdañ] *nm* garden; ~ **d'acclimatation** zoological gardens *pl*; ~ **botanique** botanical gardens *pl*; ~ **d'enfants** nursery school; ~ **potager** vegetable garden; ~ **public** (public) park, public gardens *pl*; ~s **suspendus** hanging gardens.

jardinage [zhárdēnázh] *nm* gardening.

jardiner [zhárdēnā] *vi* to garden, do some gardening.

jardinet [zhárdēne] *nm* little garden.

jardinier, ière [zhárdēnyā, -yer] *nm/f* gardener ♦ *nf* (*de fenêtre*) window box; **jardinière d'enfants** nursery school teacher; **jardinière (de légumes)** (*CULIN*) mixed vegetables.

jargon [zhárgôñ] *nm* (*charabia*) gibberish; (*publicitaire, scientifique etc*) jargon.

jarre [zhár] *nf* (earthenware) jar.

jarret [zháre] *nm* back of knee; (*CULIN*) knuckle, shin.

jarretelle [zhártel] *nf* garter (*US*), suspender (*Brit*).

jarretière [zhártyer] *nf* garter.

jars [zhár] *nm* (*ZOOL*) gander.

jaser [zházā] *vi* to chatter, prattle; (*indiscrètement*) to gossip.

jasmin [zhásmañ] *nm* jasmin.

jaspe [zhásp(ə)] *nm* jasper.

jaspé, e [zháspā] *a* marbled, mottled.

jatte [zhát] *nf* basin, bowl.

jauge [zhōzh] *nf* (*capacité*) capacity, tonnage; (*instrument*) gauge; ~ **(de niveau) d'huile** dipstick.

jauger [zhōzhā] *vt* to gauge the capacity of; (*fig*) to size up; ~ **3000 tonneaux** to measure 3,000 tons.

jaunâtre [zhōnātr(ə)] *a* (*couleur, teint*) yellowish.

jaune [zhōn] *a, nm* yellow ♦ *nm/f* Asiatic; (*briseur de grève*) scab ♦ *ad* (*fam*): **rire ~** to laugh out of the other side of one's mouth (*US*), laugh on the other side of one's face; ~ **d'œuf** (egg) yolk.

jaunir [zhōnēr] *vi, vt* to turn yellow.

jaunisse [zhōnēs] *nf* jaundice.

Java [zhává] *nf* Java.

javanais, e [zhávàne, -ez] *a* Javanese.

Javel [zhável] *nf voir* **eau**.

javelliser [zhávēlēsā] *vt* (*eau*) to chlorinate.

javelot [zhávlō] *nm* javelin; (*SPORT*): **faire du ~** to throw the javelin.

jazz [dzház] *nm* jazz.

J.-C. *abr* = **Jésus-Christ**.

JCR *sigle f* (= *Jeunesse communiste révolutionnaire*) communist youth movement.

je, j' [zh(ə)] *pronom* I.

jean [dzhēn] *nm* jeans *pl*.

jeannette [zhánet] *nf* (*planchette*) sleeveboard; (*petite fille scout*) Brownie.

JEC [zhek] *sigle f* (= *Jeunesse étudiante chrétienne*) youth organization.

jérémiades [zhārāmyád] *nfpl* moaning *sg*.

jerrycan [zhārēkán] *nm* jerrycan.

Jersey [zherze] *nf* Jersey.

jersey [zherze] *nm* jersey; (*TRICOT*): **pointe de ~** stocking stitch.

jersiais, e [zherzye, -ez] *a* Jersey *cpd*, of *ou* from Jersey.

Jérusalem [zhārüzálem] *n* Jerusalem.

jésuite [zhāzüēt] *nm* Jesuit.

Jésus-Christ [zhāzükrē(st)] *n* Jesus Christ; **600 avant/après ~** *ou* J.-C. 600 B.C./A.D.

jet [zhe] *nm* (*lancer*) throwing *q*, throw; (*jaillissement*) jet; spurt; (*de tuyau*) nozzle; (*avion*) [dzhet] jet; (*fig*): **premier ~** (*ébauche*) rough outline; **arroser au ~** to hose; **d'un (seul) ~** (*d'un seul coup*) at (*ou* in) one try; **du premier ~** at the first attempt *or* shot; ~ **d'eau** spray; (*fontaine*) fountain.

jetable [zhətábl(ə)] *a* disposable.

jeté [zhətā] *nm*: ~ **de table** (table) runner; ~ **de lit** bedspread.

jetée [zhətā] *nf* jetty; pier.

jeter [zhətā] *vt* (*gén*) to throw; (*se défaire de*) to throw away *ou* out; (*son, lueur etc*) to give out; ~ **qch à qn** to throw sth to sb; (*de façon agressive*) to throw sth at sb; (*NAVIG*): ~ **l'ancre** to drop anchor; ~ **un coup d'œil (à)** to take a look (at); ~ **les bras en avant/la tête en arrière** to throw one's arms forward/ one's head back(ward); ~ **l'effroi parmi** to spread fear among; ~ **un sort à qn** to cast a spell on sb; ~ **qn dans la misère** to reduce sb to poverty; ~ **qn dehors/en prison** to throw sb out/into prison; ~ **l'éponge** (*fig*) to throw in the towel; ~ **des fleurs à qn** (*fig*) to say lovely things to sb; ~ **la pierre à qn** (*accuser, blâmer*) to accuse sb; **se ~ sur** to throw o.s. onto; **se ~ dans** (*suj: fleuve*) to flow into; **se ~ par la fenêtre** to jump out of the window; **se ~ à l'eau** (*fig*) to take the plunge.

jeton [zhətôñ] *nm* (*au jeu*) counter; (*de téléphone*) token; ~s **de présence** (director's) fees.

jette [zhet] *etc vb voir* **jeter**.

jeu, x [zhœ] *nm* (*divertissement*, *TECH*: *d'une pièce*) play; (*défini par des règles*, *TENNIS*: *partie*, *FOOTBALL*: *façon de jouer*) game; (*THÉÂTRE etc*) acting; (*au casino*): **le ~** gambling; (*fonctionnement*) working, interplay; (*série d'objets, jouet*) set; (*CARTES*) hand; **cacher son ~** (*fig*) to keep one's cards hidden, conceal one's hand; **c'est un ~ d'enfant!** (*fig*) it's child's play!; **en ~** at stake; at work; (*FOOTBALL*) in play; **remettre en ~** to throw in; **entrer/mettre en ~** to come/bring into play; **par ~** (*pour s'amuser*) for fun; **d'entrée de ~** (*tout de suite, dès le début*) from the outset; **entrer dans le ~/le ~ de qn** (*fig*) to play the game/sb's game; **jouer gros ~** to play for high stakes; **se piquer/se prendre au ~** to get excited over/ get caught up in *ou* involved in the game; ~ **de boules** game of bowls; (*endroit*) bowling ground; (*boules*) set of bowls; ~ **de cartes** card game; (*paquet*) deck of cards; ~ **de construction** building set; ~ **d'échecs** chess set; ~ **d'écritures** (*COMM*) paper transaction; ~ **de hasard** game of chance; ~ **de mots** pun; ~ **d'orgue(s)** organ stop; ~ **de patience** puzzle; ~ **de physionomie** facial expressions *pl*; ~ **de société** parlor (*US*) *ou* parlour (*Brit*) game; ~**x de lumière** lighting effects; **J~x olympiques (JO)** Olympic Games.

jeu-concours, *pl* **jeux-concours** [yœ̄kóṅkōōr] *nm* competition.

jeudi [zhœ̄dē] *nm* Thursday; ~ **saint** Maundy Thursday; *voir aussi* **lundi.**

jeun [zhœṅ]: **à ~** *ad* on an empty stomach.

jeune [zhœn] *a* young ♦ *ad*: **faire/s'habiller ~** to look/dress young; **les ~s** young people, the young; ~ **fille** *nf* girl; ~ **homme** *nm* young man; ~ **loup** *nm* (*POL*, *ÉCON*) young go-getter; ~ **premier** leading man; ~**s gens** *nmpl* young people; ~**s mariés** *nmpl* newlyweds.

jeûne [zhēn] *nm* fast.

jeûner [zhēnā] *vt* to fast, go without food.

jeunesse [zhœnes] *nf* youth; (*aspect*) youthfulness; (*jeunes*) young people *pl*, youth.

JF *sigle f* = **jeune fille.**

JH *sigle m* = **jeune homme.**

JI *sigle m* = **juge d'instruction.**

jiu-jitsu [zhüzhētsü] *nm inv* (*SPORT*) jujitsu.

JMF *sigle f* (= *Jeunesses musicales de France*) association to promote music among the young.

JO *sigle m* = **Journal officiel** ♦ *sigle mpl* = **Jeux Olympiques.**

joaillerie [zhoâyrē] *nf* jewel trade; jewelry (*US*), jewellery (*Brit*).

joaillier, ière [zhoâyā, -yer] *nm/f* jeweler (*US*), jeweller (*Brit*).

job [dzhob] *nm* job.

jobard [zhobár] *nm* (*péj*) sucker.

JOC [zhok] *sigle f* (= *Jeunesse ouvrière chrétienne*) youth organization.

jockey [zhoke] *nm* jockey.

jodler [zhodlā] *vi* to yodel.

jogging [dzhogĕng] *nm* sweatsuit (*US*), tracksuit (*Brit*); **faire du ~** to jog, go jogging.

joie [zhwá] *nf* joy.

joignais [zhwáṅye] *etc vb voir* **joindre.**

joindre [zhwaṅdr(ə)] *vt* to join; (*à une lettre*): ~ **qch à** to enclose sth with; (*contacter*) to contact, get in touch with; ~ **les mains/talons** to put one's hands/heels together; ~ **les deux bouts** (*fig*: *du mois*) to make ends meet; **se ~** (*mains etc*) to come together; **se ~ à qn** to join sb; **se ~ à qch** to join in sth.

joint, e [zhwaṅ, -aṅt] *pp de* **joindre** ♦ *a*: ~ **(à)** (*lettre*, *paquet*) attached (to), enclosed (with); **pièce ~e** enclosure ♦ *nm* joint; (*ligne*) join; (*de ciment etc*) pointing *q*; **chercher/trouver le ~** (*fig*) to look for/come up with the answer; ~ **de cardan** cardan joint; ~ **de culasse** cylinder head gasket; ~ **de robinet** washer; ~ **universel** universal joint.

jointure [zhwaṅtür] *nf* (*ANAT*: *articulation*) joint; (*TECH*: *assemblage*) joint; (: *ligne*) join.

joker [zhoker] *nm* (*CARTES*) joker.

joli, e [zholē] *a* pretty, attractive; **une ~e somme/situation** a nice little sum/situation; **un ~ gâchis** *etc* a nice mess *etc*; **c'est du ~!** that's very nice!; **tout ça, c'est bien ~ mais** ... that's all very well but ...

joliment [zholēmaṅ] *ad* prettily, attractively; (*fam*: *très*) pretty.

jonc [zhóṅ] *nm* (bul)rush; (*bague, bracelet*) band.

joncher [zhóṅshā] *vt* (*suj: choses*) to be strewed on; **jonché de** strewn with.

jonction [zhóṅksyóṅ] *nf* joining; **(point de)** ~ (*de routes*) junction; (*de fleuves*) confluence; **opérer une ~** (*MIL etc*) to rendezvous.

jongler [zhóṅglā] *vi* to juggle; (*fig*): ~ **avec** to juggle with, play with.

jongleur, euse [zhóṅglœr, -œz] *nm/f* juggler.

jonquille [zhóṅkēy] *nf* daffodil.

Jordanie [zhordánē] *nf*: **la ~** Jordan.

jordanien, ne [zhordányaṅ, -en] *a* Jordanian ♦ *nm/f*: **J~, ne** Jordanian.

jouable [zhwábl(ə)] *a* playable.

joue [zhōō] *nf* cheek; **mettre en ~** to take aim at.

jouer [zhwā] *vt* (*partie*, *carte*, *coup*, *MUS*: *morceau*) to play; (*somme d'argent*, *réputation*) to stake, wager; (*pièce*, *rôle*) to perform; (*film*) to show; (*simuler*: *sentiment*) to affect, feign ♦ *vi* to play; (*THÉÂTRE*, *CINÉMA*) to act, perform; (*bois*, *porte*: *se voiler*) to warp; (*clef*, *pièce*: *avoir du jeu*) to be loose; (*entrer ou être en jeu*) to come into play, come into it; ~ **sur** (*miser*) to gamble on; ~ **de** (*MUS*) to play; ~ **du couteau/des coudes** to use knives/one's elbows; ~ **à** (*jeu*, *sport*, *roulette*) to play; ~ **au héros** to act *ou* play the hero; ~ **avec** (*risquer*) to gamble with; **se ~ de** (*difficultés*) to make light of; **se ~ de qn** to deceive *ou* dupe sb; ~ **un tour à qn** to play a trick on sb; ~ **la comédie** (*fig*) to put on an act, put it on; ~ **aux courses** to back horses, bet on horses; ~ **à la baisse/hausse** (*BOURSE*) to bear/bull the market (*US*), play for a fall/rise (*Brit*); ~ **serré** to play a close game; ~ **de malchance** to be dogged with ill-luck; ~ **sur les mots** to play with words; **à toi/nous de ~** it's your/our *ou* turn.

jouet [zhwe] *nm* toy; **être le ~ de** (*illusion etc*) to be the victim of.

joueur, euse [zhwœr, -œz] *nm/f* player ♦ *a* (*enfant*, *chat*) playful; **être beau/mauvais ~** to be a good/bad loser.

joufflu, e [zhōōflü] *a* chubby(-cheeked).

joug [zhōō] *nm* yoke.

jouir [zhwēr]: ~ **de** *vt* to enjoy.

jouissance [zhwēsáṅs] *nf* pleasure; (*JUR*) use.

jouisseur, euse [zhwēsœr, -œz] *nm/f* sensualist.

joujou [zhōōzhōō] *nm* (*fam*) toy.

jour [zhōōr] *nm* day; (*opposé à la nuit*) day, daytime; (*clarté*) daylight; (*fig*: *aspect*): **sous un ~ favorable/nouveau** in a favorable/new light; (*ouverture*) opening; (*COUTURE*) openwork *q*; **au ~ le ~** from day to day; **de nos ~s** these days, nowadays; **tous les ~s** every day; **de ~ en ~** day by day; **d'un ~ à l'autre** from one day to the next; **du ~ au lendemain** overnight; **il fait ~** it's daylight; **en plein ~** in broad daylight; **au ~** in daylight; **au petit ~** at daybreak; **au grand ~** (*fig*) in the open; **mettre au ~** to uncover, disclose; **être à ~** to be up to date; **mettre à ~** to bring up to date, update; **mise à ~** updating; **donner le ~ à** to give birth to; **voir le ~** to be born; **se faire ~** (*fig*) to become clear; ~ **férié** legal (*US*) *ou* public (*Brit*) holiday; **le ~ J** D-day.

Jourdain [zhŏŏrdàn] *nm*: **le ~** the (River) Jordan.

journal, aux [zhŏŏrnàl, -ŏ] *nm* (news)paper; (*personnel*) journal, diary; ~ **de bord** log; ~ **de mode** fashion magazine; **le J~ officiel (de la République française) (JO)** *bulletin giving details of laws and official announcements*; ~ **parlé/télévisé** radio/television news *sg*.

journalier, ière [zhŏŏrnàlyà, -yer] *a* daily; (*banal*) everyday ♦ *nm* day laborer (*US*) *ou* labourer (*Brit*).

journalisme [zhŏŏrnàlēsm(ə)] *nm* journalism.

journaliste [zhŏŏrnàlēst(ə)] *nm/f* journalist.

journalistique [zhŏŏrnàlēstēk] *a* journalistic.

journée [zhŏŏrnā] *nf* day; **la ~ continue** the 9 to 5 working day (*with short lunch break*).

journellement [zhŏŏrnelmàn] *ad* (*tous les jours*) daily; (*souvent*) every day.

joute [zhŏŏt] *nf* (*tournoi*) duel; (*verbale*) duel, battle of words.

jouvence [zhŏŏvàns] *nf*: **bain de ~** rejuvenating experience.

jouxter [zhŏŏkstā] *vt* to adjoin.

jovial [zhovyàl] *a* jovial, jolly.

jovialité [zhovyàlētā] *nf* joviality.

joyau, x [zhwàyŏ] *nm* gem, jewel.

joyeusement [zhwàyœzmàn] *ad* joyfully, gladly.

joyeux, euse [zhwàyœ, -œz] *a* joyful, merry; ~ **Noël!** merry *ou* happy Christmas!; ~ **anniversaire!** many happy returns!

JT *sigle m* = **journal télévisé**.

jubilation [zhübēlàsyôn] *nf* jubilation.

jubilé [zhübēlā] *nm* jubilee.

jubiler [zhübēlā] *vi* to be jubilant, exult.

jucher [zhüshā] *vt*: ~ **qch sur** to perch sth (up)on ♦ *vi* (*oiseau*): ~ **sur** to perch (up)on; **se ~ sur** to perch o.s. (up)on.

judaïque [zhüdàēk] *a* (*loi*) Judaic; (*religion*) Jewish.

judaïsme [zhüdàēsm(ə)] *nm* Judaism.

judas [zhüdà] *nm* (*trou*) judas hole, peephole.

Judée [zhüdā] *nf*: **la ~** Jud(a)ea.

judéo- [zhüdāo] *préfixe* Judeo-.

judéo-allemand, e [zhüdāoàlmàn, -ànd] *a, nm* Yiddish.

judiciaire [zhüdēsyer] *a* judicial.

judicieusement [zhüdēsyœzmàn] *ad* judiciously.

judicieux, euse [zhüdēsyœ, -œz] *a* judicious.

judo [zhüdŏ] *nm* judo.

judoka [zhüdokà] *nm/f* judoka.

juge [zhüzh] *nm* judge; ~ **des enfants** children's judge, ≈ juvenile magistrate; ~ **d'instruction** committing (*US*) *ou* examining (*Brit*) magistrate; ~ **de paix** justice of the peace; ~ **de touche** linesman.

jugé [zhüzhā]: **au ~** *ad* by guesswork.

jugement [zhüzhmàn] *nm* judgment; (*JUR*: *au pénal*) sentence; (: *au civil*) decision; ~ **de valeur** value judgment.

jugeote [zhüzhot] *nf* (*fam*) gumption.

juger [zhüzhā] *vt* to judge ♦ *nm*: **au ~** by guesswork; ~ **qn/qch satisfaisant** to consider sb/sth (to be) satisfactory; ~ **que** to think *ou* consider that; ~ **bon de faire** to consider it a

good idea to do, see fit to do; ~ **de** *vt* to judge; **jugez de ma surprise** imagine my surprise.

jugulaire [zhügüler] *a* jugular ♦ *nf* (*MIL*) chinstrap.

juguler [zhügülā] *vt* (*maladie*) to halt; (*révolte*) to suppress, put down; (*inflation etc*) to control, curb.

juif, ive [zhüēf, -ēv] *a* Jewish ♦ *nm/f*: **J~, ive** Jew/Jewess *ou* Jewish woman.

juillet [zhüēye] *nm* July; **le premier ~** July first (*US*), the first of July (*Brit*); **le deux/ onze ~** the second/eleventh of July, July second/eleventh; **il est venu le 5 ~** he came on 5th July *ou* July 5th; **en ~** in July; **début/fin ~** at the beginning/end of July.

juin [zhüàn] *nm* June; *voir aussi* **juillet**.

juive [zhwēv] *voir* **juif**.

jumeau, elle, x [zhümŏ, -el] *a, nm/f* twin; **maisons jumelles** duplexes (*US*), semidetached houses (*Brit*).

jumelage [zhümlàzh] *nm* twinning.

jumeler [zhümlā] *vt* to twin; **roues jumelées** double wheels; **billets de loterie jumelés** double series lottery tickets; **pari jumelé** double bet.

jumelle [zhümel] *af, nf voir* **jumeau** ♦ *vb voir* **jumeler**.

jumelles [zhümel] *nfpl* binoculars.

jument [zhümàn] *nf* mare.

jungle [zhôngl(ə)] *nf* jungle.

junior [zhünyor] *a* junior.

junte [zhœnt] *nf* junta.

jupe [zhüp] *nf* skirt.

jupe-culotte, *pl* **jupes-culottes** [zhüpkülot] *nf* divided skirt, culotte(s).

jupette [zhüpct] *nf* short skirt.

jupon [zhüpôn] *nm* waist slip *ou* petticoat.

Jura [zhürà] *nm*: **le ~** the Jura (Mountains).

jurassien, ne [zhüràsyàn, -en] *a* of *ou* from the Jura Mountains.

juré, e [zhürà] *nm/f* juror ♦ *a*: **ennemi ~** sworn *ou* avowed enemy.

jurer [zhürā] *vt* (*obéissance etc*) to swear, vow ♦ *vi* (*dire des jurons*) to swear, curse; (*dissoner*): ~ (**avec**) to clash (with); (*s'engager*): ~ **de faire/que** to swear *ou* vow to do/that; (*affirmer*): ~ **que** to swear *ou* vouch that; ~ **de qch** (*s'en porter garant*) to swear to sth; **ils ne jurent que par lui** they swear by him; **je vous jure!** honestly!

juridiction [zhürēdēksyôn] *nf* jurisdiction; (*tribunal, tribunaux*) court(s) of law.

juridique [zhürēdēk] *a* legal.

juridiquement [zhürēdēkmàn] *ad* (*devant la justice*) juridically; (*du point de vue du droit*) legally.

jurisconsulte [zhürēskônsült(ə)] *nm* jurisconsult.

jurisprudence [zhürēsprüdàns] *nf* (*JUR*: *décisions*) (legal) precedents; (*principes juridiques*) jurisprudence; **faire ~** (*faire autorité*) to set a precedent.

juriste [zhürēst(ə)] *nm/f* jurist; lawyer.

juron [zhürôn] *nm* curse, swearword.

jury [zhürē] *nm* (*JUR*) jury; (*SCOL*) board (of examiners), jury.

jus [zhü] *nm* juice; (*de viande*) gravy, (meat) juice; ~ **de fruits** fruit juice; ~ **de raisin/**

tomates grape/tomato juice.

jusant [zhüzáɴ] *nm* ebb (tide).

jusqu'au-boutiste [zhüskōbōōtēst(ə)] *nm/f* extremist, hardliner.

jusque [zhüsk(ə)]: **jusqu'à** *prép* (*endroit*) as far as, (up) to; (*moment*) until, till; (*limite*) up to; ~ **sur/dans** up to, as far as; (*y compris*) even on/in; **jusque vers** until about; **jusqu'à ce que** *cj* until; **jusque-là** (*temps*) until then; (*espace*) up to there; **jusqu'ici** (*temps*) until now; (*espace*) up to here; **jusqu'à présent** until now, so far.

justaucorps [zhüstōkor] *nm inv* (*DANSE, SPORT*) leotard.

juste [zhüst(ə)] *a* (*équitable*) just, fair; (*légitime*) just, justified; (*exact, vrai*) right; (*étroit, insuffisant*) tight ♦ *ad* right; tight; (*chanter*) in tune; (*seulement*) just; ~ **assez/au-dessus** just enough/above; **pouvoir tout** ~ **faire** to be only just able to do; **au** ~ exactly, actually; **comme de** ~ of course, naturally; **le** ~ **milieu** the happy medium; **à** ~ **titre** rightfully.

justement [zhüstəmáɴ] *ad* rightly; justly; (*précisément*): **c'est** ~ **ce qu'il fallait faire** that's just *ou* precisely what needed doing.

justesse [zhüstes] *nf* (*précision*) accuracy; (*d'une remarque*) aptness; (*d'une opinion*) soundness; **de** ~ just, by a narrow margin.

justice [zhüstēs] *nf* (*équité*) fairness, justice; (*ADMIN*) justice; **rendre la** ~ to dispense justice; **traduire en** ~ to bring before the courts; **obtenir** ~ to obtain justice; **rendre** ~ **à qn** to do sb justice; **se faire** ~ to take the law into one's own hands; (*se suicider*) to take one's life.

justiciable [zhüstēsyábl(ə)] *a*: ~ **de** (*JUR*) answerable to.

justicier, ière [zhüstēsyā, -yer] *nm/f* judge, righter of wrongs.

justifiable [zhüstēfyábl(ə)] *a* justifiable.

justificatif, ive [zhüstēfēkátēf, -ēv] *a* (*document etc*) supporting ♦ *nm* supporting proof.

justification [zhüstēfēkásyóɴ] *nf* justification.

justifier [zhüstēfyā] *vt* to justify; ~ **de** *vt* to prove; **non justifié** unjustified; **justifié à droite/gauche** justified right/left.

jute [zhüt] *nm* jute.

juteux, euse [zhütœ̄, -œ̄z] *a* juicy.

juvénile [zhüvānēl] *a* young, youthful.

juxtaposer [zhükstápōzā] *vt* to juxtapose.

juxtaposition [zhükstàpōzēsyóɴ] *nf* juxtaposition.

K

K, k [ká] *nm inv* K, k ♦ *abr* (= *kilo*) kg; (= *kilooctet*) K; **K comme Kléber** K for King.

Kaboul *ou* **Kabul** [kábōōl] *n* Kabul.

kabyle [kábēl] *a* Kabyle ♦ *nm* (*LING*) Kabyle ♦ *nm/f*: **K~** Kabyle.

Kabylie [kábēlē] *nf*: **la** ~ Kabylia.

kaki [kákē] *a inv* khaki.

Kalahari [kàláárē] *n*: **désert de** ~ Kalahari Desert.

kaléidoscope [kálāēdoskop] *nm* kaleidoscope.

Kampala [káɴpálá] *n* Kampala.

Kampuchéa [káɴpōōtshāá] *nm*: **le** ~ **(démocratique)** (the People's Republic of) Kampuchea.

kangourou [káɴgōōrōō] *nm* kangaroo.

kaolin [káolaɴ] *nm* kaolin.

kapok [kápok] *nm* kapok.

karaté [kárátā] *nm* karate.

kart [kárt] *nm* go-cart.

karting [kártēng] *nm* go-carting, karting.

kascher [kásher] *a inv* kosher.

kayac, kayak [káyák] *nm* kayak.

Kenya [kānyá] *nm*: **le** ~ Kenya.

kenyan, e [kānyáɴ, -áɴ] *a* Kenyan ♦ *nm/f*: **K~, ne** Kenyan.

képi [kāpē] *nm* kepi.

Kerguelen [kergálen] *n*: **les (îles)** ~ Kerguelen.

kermesse [kermes] *nf* charity bazaar; village fair.

kérosène [kārōzen] *nm* jet fuel; rocket fuel.

kg *abr* (= *kilogramme*) kg.

KGB *sigle m* KGB.

khmer, ère [kmer] *a* Khmer ♦ *nm* (*LING*) Khmer.

khôl [kōl] *nm* kohl.

kibboutz [kēbōōts] *nm* kibbutz.

kidnapper [kēdnápā] *vt* to kidnap.

kidnappeur, euse [kēdnápœr, -œ̄z] *nm/f* kidnapper.

Kilimandjaro [kēlēmáɴdzhàrō] *nm*: **le** ~ Mount Kilimanjaro.

kilo [kēlō] *nm* kilo.

kilogramme [kēlográm] *nm* kilogram (*US*), kilogramme (*Brit*).

kilométrage [kēlōmātrázh] *nm* number of kilometers traveled, ≈ mileage.

kilomètre [kēlometr(ə)] *nm* kilometer (*US*), kilometre (*Brit*); ~**s-heure** kilometers per hour.

kilométrique [kēlomātrēk] *a* (*distance*) in kilometers; **compteur** ~ odometer (*US*), ≈ mileage indicator (*Brit*).

kilooctet [kēlooktē] *nm* kilobyte.

kilowatt [kēlowát] *nm* kilowatt.

kinésithérapeute [kēnāzētārápēēt] *nm/f* physical therapist (*US*), physiotherapist (*Brit*).

kiosque [kyosk(ə)] *nm* kiosk, stall; (*TÉL etc*) telephone and/or videotext information service.

kirsch [kērsh] *nm* kirsch.

kiwi [kēwē] *nm* (*ZOOL*) kiwi; (*BOT*) kiwi fruit.

klaxon [klákson] *nm* horn.

klaxonner [kláksoná] *vi, vt* to honk (one's horn) (*US*), hoot (*Brit*).

kleptomane [kleptomán] *nm/f* kleptomaniac.

km *abr* (= *kilomètre*) km.

km/h *abr* (= *kilomètres/heure*) km/h.

knock-out [nokáwt] *nm* knockout.

Ko *abr* (*INFORM*: = *kilooctet*) K.

K.-O. [káō] *a inv* (knocked) out, out for the count.

kolkhoze [kolkōz] *nm* kolkhoz.

Koweit *ou* **Kuweit** [kowet] *nm*: **le ~** Kuwait.
koweïtien, ne [kowetyaṅ, en] *a* Kuwaiti ♦ *nm/f*: **K~**, **ne** Kuwaiti.
krach [kråk] *nm* (*ÉCON*) crash.
kraft [kråft] *nm* brown *ou* kraft paper.
Kremlin [kremlaṅ] *nm*: **le ~** the Kremlin.
Kuala Lumpur [kwålålümpōōr] *n* Kuala Lumpur.
kurde [kürd(ǝ)] *a* Kurdish ♦ *nm* (*LING*) Kurdish ♦ *nm/f*: **K~** Kurd.
Kurdistan [kürdēståṅ] *nm*: **le ~** Kurdistan.
Kuweit [kowet] = **Koweit**.
kW *abr* (= *kilowatt*) kW.
kW/h *abr* (= *kilowatt/heure*) kW/h.
kyrielle [kēryel] *nf*: **une ~** de a stream of.
kyste [kēst(ǝ)] *nm* cyst.

L

L, I [el] *nm inv* L, l ♦ *abr* (= *litre*) l; (*SCOL*): **L ès L** = Licence ès Lettres; **L en D** = Licence en Droit; **L comme Louis** L for Love.
l' [l] *dét voir* **le**.
la [lå] *dét, pronon voir* **le** ♦ *nm* (*MUS*) A; (*en chantant la gamme*) la.
là [lå] *ad* (*voir aussi* **-ci, celui**) there; (*ici*) here; (*dans le temps*) then; **est-ce que Catherine est ~?** is Catherine there (*ou* here)?; **c'est ~ que** this is where; **~ où** where; **de ~** (*fig*) hence; **par ~** (*fig*) by that; **tout est ~** (*fig*) that's what it's all about.
là-bas [låbå] *ad* there.
label [låbel] *nm* stamp, seal.
labeur [låbœr] *nm* toil *q*, toiling *q*.
labo [låbō] *nm* (= *laboratoire*) lab.
laborantin, e [låboråṅtaṅ, -ēn] *nm/f* laboratory assistant.
laboratoire [låborātwår] *nm* laboratory; **~ de langues/d'analyses** language/(medical) analysis laboratory.
laborieux, euse [låboɾyȳē, -ēz] *a* (*tâche*) laborious; **classes ~euses** working classes.
labour [låbōōr] *nm* plowing *q* (*US*), ploughing *q* (*Brit*); **~s** *nmpl* (*champs*) plowed fields; **cheval de ~** plow- *ou* cart-horse; **bœuf de ~** ox (*pl* oxen).
labourage [låbōōråzh] *nm* plowing (*US*), ploughing (*Brit*).
labourer [låbōōrā] *vt* to plow (*US*), plough (*Brit*); (*fig*) to make deep gashes *ou* furrows in.
laboureur [låbōōrœr] *nm* plowman (*US*), ploughman (*Brit*).
labrador [låbrådor] *nm* (*chien*) labrador; (*GÉO*): **le L~** Labrador.
labyrinthe [låbēraṅt] *nm* labyrinth, maze.
lac [låk] *nm* lake; **le ~ Léman** Lake Geneva; **les Grands L~s** the Great Lakes; *voir aussi* **lacs**.
lacer [låså] *vt* to lace *ou* do up.
lacérer [låsārā] *vt* to tear to shreds.
lacet [låse] *nm* (*de chaussure*) lace; (*de route*)

sharp curve (*US*) *ou* bend (*Brit*); (*piège*) snare; **chaussures à ~s** lace-up *ou* lacing shoes.
lâche [låsh] *a* (*poltron*) cowardly; (*desserré*) loose, slack; (*morale, mœurs*) lax ♦ *nm/f* coward.
lâcher [låshā] *nm* (*de ballons, oiseaux*) release ♦ *vt* to let go of; (*ce qui tombe, abandonner*) to drop; (*oiseau, animal: libérer*) to release, set free; (*fig: mot, remarque*) to let slip, come out with; (*SPORT: distancer*) to leave behind ♦ *vi* (*fil, amarres*) to break, give way; (*freins*) to fail; **~ les amarres** (*NAVIG*) to cast off (the moorings); **~ prise** to let go.
lâcheté [låshtā] *nf* cowardice; (*bassesse*) baseness.
lacis [låsē] *nm* (*de ruelles*) maze.
laconique [låkonēk] *a* laconic.
lacrymal, e, aux [låkrēmål, -ō] *a* (*canal, glande*) tear *cpd*.
lacrymogène [låkrēmozhen] *a*: **grenade/gaz ~** tear gas grenade/tear gas.
lacs [lå] *nm* (*piège*) snare.
lactation [låktåsyôṅ] *nf* lactation.
lacté, e [låktā] *a* milk *cpd*.
lactose [låktōz] *nm* lactose, milk sugar.
lacune [låkün] *nf* gap.
lacustre [låküstr(ǝ)] *a* lake *cpd*, lakeside *cpd*.
lad [låd] *nm* stableboy.
là-dedans [lådǝdåṅ] *ad* inside (there), in it; (*fig*) in that.
là-dehors [lådǝor] *ad* out there.
là-derrière [låderyer] *ad* behind there; (*fig*) behind that.
là-dessous [lådsōō] *ad* underneath, under there; (*fig*) behind that.
là-dessus [lådsu] *ad* on there; (*fig*) at that point; (*: à ce sujet*) about that.
là-devant [lådvåṅ] *ad* there (in front).
ladite [lådēt] *dét voir* **ledit**.
ladre [lådr(ǝ)] *a* miserly.
lagon [lågôṅ] *nm* lagoon.
Lagos [lågos] *n* Lagos.
lagune [lågün] *nf* lagoon.
là-haut [låō] *ad* up there.
laïc [låēk] *a*, *nm/f* = **laïque**.
laïcité [låēsētā] *nf* secularity, secularism.
laid, e [lc, lcd] *a* ugly; (*fig: acte*) mean, cheap.
laideron [ledrôṅ] *nm* ugly girl.
laideur [ledœr] *nf* ugliness *q*; meanness *q*.
laie [le] *nf* wild sow.
lainage [lenåzh] *nm* woolen (*US*) *ou* woollen (*Brit*) garment; (*étoffe*) woolen *ou* woollen material.
laine [len] *nf* wool; **~ peignée** worsted (wool); **~ à tricoter** knitting wool; **~ de verre** glass wool; **~ vierge** virgin (*US*) *ou* new (*Brit*) wool.
laineux, euse [lenȳē, -ēz] *a* woolly.
lainier, ière [lānyā, -yer] *a* (*industrie etc*) woolen (*US*), woollen (*Brit*).
laïque [låēk] *a* lay, civil; (*SCOL*) public *cpd* (*US*), state *cpd* (*Brit*) (*as opposed to private and Roman Catholic*) ♦ *nm/f* layman/woman.
laisse [les] *nf* (*de chien*) lead, leash; **tenir en ~** to keep on a lead *ou* leash.
laissé-pour-compte, laissée-, laissés- [lāsāpōōrkôṅt] *a* (*COMM*) unsold; (*: refusé*)

returned ♦ *nm/f* (*fig*) reject; **les laissés-pour-compte de la reprise économique** those who are left out of the economic upturn.

laisser [lesā] *vt* to leave ♦ *vb auxiliaire*: ~ **qn faire** to let sb do; **se ~ exploiter** to let o.s. be exploited; **se ~ aller** to let o.s. go; ~ **qn tranquille** to let *ou* leave sb alone; **laisse-toi faire** let me (*ou* him) do it; **rien ne laisse penser que** ... there is no reason to think that ...; **cela ne laisse pas de surprendre** nonetheless it is surprising.

laisser-aller [lāsāālā] *nm* carelessness, slovenliness.

laisser-faire [lāsāfer] *nm* laissez-faire.

laissez-passer [lāsāpāsā] *nm inv* pass.

lait [le] *nm* milk; **frère/sœur de** ~ foster brother/sister; ~ **écrémé/concentré/ condensé** skimmed/condensed/evaporated milk; ~ **en poudre** powdered milk, milk powder; ~ **de chèvre/vache** goat's/cow's milk; ~ **maternel** mother's milk; ~ **démaquillant/de beauté** cleansing/beauty lotion.

laitage [lctàzh] *nm* milk product.

laiterie [letrē] *nf* dairy.

laiteux, euse [letœ̃, -œ̃z] *a* milky.

laitier, ière [lātyā, -yer] *a* dairy ♦ *nm/f* milkman/dairywoman.

laiton [letôn] *nm* brass.

laitue [lātü] *nf* lettuce.

laïus [lȧyüs] *nm* (*péj*) spiel.

lama [lámá] *nm* llama.

lambeau, x [lȧnbō] *nm* scrap; **en ~x** in tatters, tattered.

lambin, e [lȧnbȧn, -ēn] *a* (*péj*) slow.

lambiner [lȧnbēnā] *vi* (*péj*) to dawdle.

lambris [lȧnbrē] *nm* paneling *q* (*US*), panelling *q* (*Brit*).

lambrissé, e [lȧnbrēsā] *a* paneled (*US*), panelled (*Brit*).

lame [làm] *nf* blade; (*vague*) wave; (*lamelle*) strip; ~ **de fond** ground swell *q*; ~ **de rasoir** razor blade.

lamé [làmā] *nm* lamé.

lamelle [làmcl] *nf* (*lame*) small blade; (*morceau*) sliver; (*de champignon*) gill; **couper en ~s** to slice thinly.

lamentable [làmântȧbl(ə)] *a* (*déplorable*) appalling; (*pitoyable*) pitiful.

lamentation [làmântȧsyôn] *nf* wailing *q*, lamentation; moaning *q*.

lamenter [làmântā]: **se ~** *vi*: **se ~ (sur)** to moan (over).

laminage [làmēnazh] *nm* lamination.

laminer [làmēnā] *vt* to laminate; (*fig: écraser*) to wipe out.

laminoir [làmēnwàr] *nm* rolling mill; **passer au ~** (*fig*) to go (*ou* put) through the mill.

lampadaire [lȧnpáder] *nm* (*de salon*) floor (*US*) *ou* standard (*Brit*) lamp; (*dans la rue*) streetlight.

lampe [lȧnp(ə)] *nf* lamp; (*TECH*) valve; ~ **à alcool** spirit lamp; ~ **à bronzer** sunlamp; ~ **de poche** flashlight, torch (*Brit*); ~ **à souder** blowtorch; ~ **témoin** warning light.

lampée [lànpā] *nf* gulp, swig.

lampe-tempête, *pl* **lampes-tempête** [lȧnptȧnpct] *nf* storm lantern.

lampion [lȧnpyôn] *nm* Chinese lantern.

lampiste [lȧnpēst(ə)] *nm* light (maintenance) man; (*fig*) underling.

lamproie [lȧnprwȧ] *nf* lamprey.

lance [làns] *nf* spear; ~ **d'arrosage** garden hose; ~ **à eau** water hose; ~ **d'incendie** fire hose.

lancée [lȧnsā] *nf*: **être/continuer sur sa ~** to be under way/keep going.

lance-flammes [lȧnsflám] *nm inv* flamethrower.

lance-fusées [lȧnsfüzā] *nm inv* rocket launcher.

lance-grenades [lȧnsgrənád] *nm inv* grenade launcher.

lancement [lȧnsmȧn] *nm* launching *q*, launch; **offre de ~** introductory offer.

lance-missiles [lȧnsmēsēl] *nm inv* missile launcher.

lance-pierres [lȧnspyer] *nm inv* slingshot.

lancer [lȧnsā] *nm* (*SPORT*) throwing *q*, throw; (*PÊCHE*) rod and reel fishing ♦ *vt* to throw; (*émettre, projeter*) to throw out, send out; (*produit, fusée, bateau, artiste*) to launch; (*injure*) to hurl, fling; (*proclamation, mandat d'arrêt*) to issue; (*emprunt*) to float; (*moteur*) to send roaring away; ~ **qch à qn** to throw sth to sb; (*de façon agressive*) to throw sth at sb; ~ **un cri** *ou* **un appel** to shout *ou* call out; **se ~** *vi* (*prendre de l'élan*) to build up speed; (*se précipiter*): **se ~ sur** *ou* **contre** to rush at; **se ~ dans** (*discussion*) to launch into; (*aventure*) to embark on; (*les affaires, la politique*) to go into; ~ **du poids** *nm* putting the shot.

lance-roquettes [lȧnsroket] *nm inv* rocket launcher.

lance-torpilles [lȧnstorpēy] *nm inv* torpedo tube.

lanceur, euse [lȧnscer, -œ̃z] *nm/f* bowler; (*BASEBALL*) pitcher ♦ *nm* (*ESPACE*) launcher.

lancinant, e [lȧnsēnȧn, -ȧnt] *a* (*regrets etc*) haunting; (*douleur*) shooting.

lanciner [lȧnsēnā] *vi* to throb; (*fig*) to nag.

landais, e [lȧnde, -ez] *a* of *ou* from the Landes.

landau [lȧndō] *nm* baby carriage (*US*), pram (*Brit*).

lande [lȧnd] *nf* moor.

Landes [lȧnd] *nfpl*: **les** ~ the Landes.

langage [lȧngȧzh] *nm* language; ~ **d'assemblage** (*INFORM*) assembly language; ~ **évolué/machine** (*INFORM*) high-level/machine language; ~ **de programmation** (*INFORM*) programming language.

lange [lȧnzh] *nm* flannel blanket; ~**s** *nmpl* swaddling clothes.

langer [lȧnzhā] *vt* to change (the diaper (*US*) *ou* nappy (*Brit*) of); **table à ~** changing table.

langoureux, euse [lȧngōōrœ̃, -œ̃z] *a* languorous.

langouste [lȧngōōst(ə)] *nf* crayfish *inv*.

langoustine [lȧngōōstēn] *nf* prawn (*US*), Dublin Bay prawn (*Brit*).

langue [lȧng] *nf* (*ANAT, CULIN*) tongue; (*LING*) language; (*bande*): ~ **de terre** spit of land; **tirer la** ~ (**à**) to stick out one's tongue (at); **donner sa** ~ **au chat** to give up; **de** ~ **française** French-speaking; ~ **de bois** officialese; ~ **maternelle** native language, mother tongue; ~ **verte** slang; ~ **vivante** modern language.

langue-de-chat [lăṅgdəshá] *nf* ladyfinger (*US*), finger biscuit (*Brit*).

languedocien, ne [lăṅgdosyań, -en] *a* of *ou* from the Languedoc.

languette [lăṅget] *nf* tongue.

langueur [lăṅgœr] *nf* languidness.

languir [lăṅgēr] *vi* to languish; (*conversation*) to flag; **se** ~ *vi* to be languishing; **faire** ~ **qn** to keep sb waiting.

languissant, e [lăṅgēsáṅ, -áṅt] *a* languid.

lanière [lányer] *nf* (*de fouet*) lash; (*de valise, bretelle*) strap.

lanoline [lánolēn] *nf* lanolin.

lanterne [lăṅtern(ə)] *nf* (*portable*) lantern; (*électrique*) light, lamp; (*de voiture*) (side)light; ~ **rouge** (*fig*) tail-ender; ~ **vénitienne** Chinese lantern.

lanterneau, x [lăṅternō] *nm* skylight.

lanterner [lăṅternā] *vi*: **faire** ~ **qn** to keep sb hanging around.

Laos [lăos] *nm*: **le** ~ Laos.

laotien, ne [lăosyań, -en] *a* Laotian.

lapalissade [lápálēsád] *nf* statement of the obvious.

La Paz [lăpáz] *n* La Paz.

laper [lápā] *vt* to lap up.

lapereau, x [láprō] *nm* young rabbit.

lapidaire [lápēder] *a* stone *cpd*; (*fig*) terse.

lapider [lápēdā] *vt* to stone.

lapin [lápaṅ] *nm* rabbit; (*fourrure*) cony; **coup du** ~ rabbit punch; **poser un** ~ **à qn** to stand sb up; ~ **de garenne** wild rabbit.

lapon, e [lápōṅ, -on] *a* Lapp, Lappish ♦ *nm* (*LING*) Lapp, Lappish ♦ *nm/f*: **L~, e** Lapp, Laplander.

Laponie [láponē] *nf*: **la** ~ Lapland.

laps [láps] *nm*: ~ **de temps** space of time, time *q*.

lapsus [lápsüs] *nm* slip.

laquais [láke] *nm* lackey.

laque [lák] *nf* lacquer; (*brute*) shellac; (*pour cheveux*) hair spray ♦ *nm* lacquer; piece of lacquer ware.

laqué, e [lákā] *a* lacquered.

laquelle [lákel] *pronom voir* **lequel**.

larbin [larban] *nm* (*péj*) flunkey.

larcin [lársań] *nm* theft.

lard [lár] *nm* (*graisse*) fat; (*bacon*) (streaky) bacon.

larder [lárdā] *vt* (*CULIN*) to lard.

lardon [lárdôṅ] *nm* (*CULIN*) piece of chopped bacon; (*fam: enfant*) kid.

large [lárzh(ə)] *a* wide; broad; (*fig*) generous ♦ *ad*: **calculer/voir** ~ to allow extra/think big ♦ *nm* (*largeur*): **5 m de** ~ 5 m wide *ou* in width; (*mer*): **le** ~ the open sea; **en** ~ *ad* sideways; **au** ~ **de** off; ~ **d'esprit** broad-minded; **ne pas en mener** ~ to have one's heart in one's boots.

largement [lárzhəmáṅ] *ad* widely; (*de loin*) greatly; (*amplement, au minimum*) easily; (*sans compter: donner etc*) generously.

largesse [lárzhes] *nf* generosity; ~**s** *nfpl* liberalities.

largeur [lárzhœr] *nf* (*qu'on mesure*) width; (*impression visuelle*) wideness, width; breadth; broadness.

larguer [lárgā] *vt* to drop; (*fam: se débarrasser de*) to get rid of; ~ **les amarres** to cast off (the moorings).

larme [lárm(ə)] *nf* tear; (*fig*): **une** ~ **de** a drop of; **en** ~**s** in tears; **pleurer à chaudes** ~**s** to cry one's eyes out, cry bitterly.

larmoyant, e [lármwáyáṅ, -áṅt] *a* tearful.

larmoyer [lármwáyā] *vi* (*yeux*) to water; (*se plaindre*) to whimper.

larron [lárôṅ] *nm* thief (*pl* thieves).

larve [lárv(ə)] *nf* (*ZOOL*) larva (*pl* -ae); (*fig*) worm.

larvé, e [lárvā] *a* (*fig*) latent.

laryngite [lárańzhēt] *nf* laryngitis.

laryngologiste [lárańgolozhēst(ə)] *nm/f* throat specialist.

larynx [lárańks] *nm* larynx.

las, lasse [lá, lás] *a* weary.

lasagne [lázány] *nf* lasagne.

lascar [láskár] *nm* character; (*malin*) rogue.

lascif, ive [lásēf, -ēv] *a* lascivious.

laser [lázer] *nm*: (**rayon**) ~ laser (beam); **chaîne** *ou* **platine** ~ compact disc (player); **disque** ~ compact disc.

lassant, e [lásáṅ, -áṅt] *a* tiresome, wearisome.

lasse [lás] *af voir* **las**.

lasser [lásā] *vt* to weary, tire; **se** ~ **de** to grow weary *ou* tired of.

lassitude [lásētüd] *nf* lassitude, weariness.

lasso [lásō] *nm* lasso; **prendre au** ~ to lasso.

latent, e [látáṅ, -áṅt] *a* latent.

latéral, e, aux [látárál, -ō] *a* side *cpd*, lateral.

latéralement [látárálmáṅ] *ad* edgeways; (*arriver, souffler*) from the side.

latex [láteks] *nm inv* latex.

latin, e [látáṅ, -ēn] *a* Latin ♦ *nm* (*LING*) Latin ♦ *nm/f*: **L~, e** Latin; **j'y perds mon** ~ it's all Greek to me.

latiniste [látēnēst(ə)] *nm/f* Latin scholar (*ou* student).

latino-américain, e [látēnoàmārēkań, -en] *a* Latin-American.

latitude [látētüd] *nf* latitude; (*fig*): **avoir la** ~ **de faire** to be left free *ou* be at liberty to do; **à 48° de** ~ **Nord** at latitude 48° North; **sous toutes les** ~**s** (*fig*) worldwide, throughout the world.

latrines [látrēn] *nfpl* latrines.

latte [lát] *nf* lath, slat; (*de plancher*) board.

lattis [látē] *nm* lathwork.

laudatif, ive [lōdátēf, -ēv] *a* laudatory.

lauréat, e [lorāá, -át] *nm/f* winner.

laurier [loryā] *nm* (*BOT*) laurel; (*CULIN*) bay leaves *pl*; ~**s** *nmpl* (*fig*) laurels.

laurier-rose, *pl* **lauriers-rose** [loryārōz] *nm* oleander.

lavable [lávábl(ə)] *a* washable.

lavabo [lávábō] *nm* washbasin; ~**s** *nmpl* toilet *sg*.

lavage [lávázh] *nm* washing *q*, wash; ~ **d'estomac/d'intestin** stomach/intestinal wash; ~ **de cerveau** brainwashing *q*.

lavande [láváṅd] *nf* lavender.

lavandière [láváṅdyer] *nf* washerwoman.

lave [láv] *nf* lava *q*.

lave-glace [lávglás] *nm* (*AUTO*) windshield (*US*) *ou* windscreen (*Brit*) washer.

lave-linge [lávlańzh] *nm inv* washing machine.

lavement [lávmáṅ] *nm* (*MÉD*) enema.

laver [làvà] *vt* to wash; (*tache*) to wash off; (*fig: affront*) to avenge; **se ~** to have a wash, wash; **se ~ les mains/dents** to wash one's hands/brush one's teeth; **~ la vaisselle/le linge** to wash the dishes/clothes; **~ qn de** (*accusation*) to clear sb of.

laverie [làvrē] *nf*: **~ (automatique)** laundromat (*US*), launderette (*Brit*).

lavette [làvet] *nf* (*chiffon*) dishcloth; (*brosse*) dish mop; (*fam: homme*) wimp, drip.

laveur, euse [làvœr, -œz] *nm/f* cleaner.

lave-vaisselle [làvvesel] *nm inv* dishwasher.

lavis [làvē] *nm* (*technique*) washing; (*dessin*) wash drawing.

lavoir [làvwàr] *nm* wash house; (*bac*) washtub.

laxatif, ive [làksàtēf, -ēv] *a, nm* laxative.

laxisme [làksesm(ə)] *nm* laxity.

laxiste [làksēst(ə)] *a* lax.

layette [leyet] *nf* layette.

layon [leyôn] *nm* trail.

lazaret [làzàre] *nm* quarantine area.

lazzi [làdzē] *nm* gibe.

LCR *sigle f* (= *Ligue communiste révolutionnaire*) *political party*.

le (**l'**), **la** (**l'**), **les** [l(ə), là, lā] *dét* the ♦ *pronom* (*personne: mâle*) him; (: *femelle*) her; (*animal, chose*) it; (*remplaçant une phrase*) it *ou non traduit*; (*indique la possession*): **se casser la jambe** *etc* to break one's leg *etc*; *voir note sous* **il**; **les** them; **je ne le savais pas** I didn't know (about it); **il était riche et ne l'est plus** he was once rich but no longer is; **levez la main** put your hand up; **avoir les yeux gris/le nez rouge** to have gray eyes/a red nose; **le jeudi** *etc ad* (*d'habitude*) on Thursdays *etc*; (*ce jeudi-là*) on the Thursday *etc*; **le matin/soir** *ad* in the morning/evening; mornings/evenings; **nous venons le 3 décembre** (*parlé*) we're coming (on) December 3 *ou* 3 December; (*écrit*) we're coming (on) 3rd *ou* 3 December; **10 F le mètre/kilo** 10 F a *ou* per meter/kilo; **le tiers/ quart de** a third/quarter of.

lé [lā] *nm* (*de tissu*) width; (*de papier peint*) strip, length.

leader [lēdœr] *nm* leader.

lèche-bottes [leshbot] *nm inv* bootlicker.

lèchefrite [leshfrēt] *nf* dripping pan *ou* tray.

lécher [làshā] *vt* to lick; (*laper: lait, eau*) to lick *ou* lap up; (*finir, polir*) to over-refine; **~ les vitrines** to go window-shopping; **se ~ les doigts/lèvres** to lick one's fingers/lips.

leçon [ləsôn] *nf* lesson; **faire la ~** to teach; **faire la ~ à** (*fig*) to give a lecture to; **~s de conduite** driving lessons; **~s particulières** private lessons *ou* tuition *sg* (*Brit*).

lecteur, trice [lektœr, -trēs] *nm/f* reader; (*d'université*) (foreign) teaching assistant (*US*), (foreign language) assistant (*Brit*) ♦ *nm* (*TECH*): **~ de cassettes** cassette player; (*INFORM*): **~ de disquette(s)** *ou* **de disque** disk drive; **~ compact-disc** *ou* **CD** compact disc (player).

lectorat [lektorà] *nm* (foreign language *ou* teaching) assistantship.

lecture [lektür] *nf* reading.

LED [led] *sigle f* (= *light emitting diode*) LED; **affichage ~** LED display.

ledit [lədē], **ladite** [làdēt], *mpl* **lesdits** [lādē], *fpl*

lesdites [lādēt] *dét* the aforesaid.

légal, e, aux [lāgàl, -ō] *a* legal.

légalement [lāgàlmân] *ad* legally.

légaliser [lāgàlēzà] *vt* to legalize.

légalité [lāgàlētà] *nf* legality, lawfulness; **être dans/sortir de la ~** to be within/step outside the law.

légat [lāgà] *nm* (*REL*) legate.

légataire [lāgàter] *nm* legatee.

légendaire [lāzhânder] *a* legendary.

légende [lāzhând] *nf* (*mythe*) legend; (*de carte, plan*) key, legend; (*de dessin*) caption, legend.

léger, ère [lāzhā, -er] *a* light; (*bruit, retard*) slight; (*boisson, parfum*) weak; (*couche, étoffe*) thin; (*superficiel*) thoughtless; (*volage*) free and easy; (*peu sérieux*) lightweight; **blessé ~** slightly injured person; **à la légère** *ad* (*parler, agir*) rashly, thoughtlessly.

légèrement [lāzhermân] *ad* lightly; thoughtlessly, rashly; **~ plus grand** slightly bigger.

légèreté [lāzhertà] *nf* lightness; thoughtlessness.

légiférer [lāzhēfārā] *vi* to legislate.

légion [lāzhyôn] *nf* legion; **la L~ étrangère** the Foreign Legion; **la L~ d'honneur** the Legion of Honor.

légionnaire [lāzhyoner] *nm* (*MIL*) legionnaire; (*de la Légion d'honneur*) holder of the Legion of Honor.

législateur [lāzhēslàtœr] *nm* legislator, lawmaker.

législatif, ive [lāzhēslàtēf, -ēv] *a* legislative; **législatives** *nfpl* general election *sg*.

législation [lāzhēslàsyôn] *nf* legislation.

législature [lāzhēslàtür] *nf* legislature; (*période*) term (of office).

légiste [lāzhēst(ə)] *nm* jurist ♦ *a*: **médecin ~** medical examiner (*US*), forensic scientist (*Brit*).

légitime [lāzhētēm] *a* (*JUR*) lawful, legitimate; (*enfant*) legitimate; (*fig*) rightful, legitimate; **en état de ~ défense** in self-defense.

légitimement [lāzhētēmmân] *ad* lawfully; legitimately; rightfully.

légitimer [lāzhētēmà] *vt* (*enfant*) to legitimize; (*justifier: conduite etc*) to justify.

légitimité [lāzhētēmētà] *nf* (*JUR*) legitimacy.

legs [leg] *nm* legacy.

léguer [lāgà] *vt*: **~ qch à qn** (*JUR*) to bequeath sth to sb; (*fig*) to hand sth down *ou* pass sth on to sb.

légume [lāgüm] *nm* vegetable; **~s verts** green vegetables; **~s secs** pulses.

légumier [lāgümyà] *nm* vegetable dish.

Léman [lāmân] *nm voir* **lac**.

lendemain [lândmân] *nm*: **le ~** the next *ou* following day; **le ~ matin/soir** the next *ou* following morning/evening; **le ~ de** the day after; **au ~ de** in the days following; in the wake of; **penser au ~** to think of the future; **sans ~** short-lived; **de beaux ~s** bright prospects; **des ~s qui chantent** a rosy future.

lénifiant, e [lānēfyân, -ânt] *a* soothing.

léniniste [lānēnēst(ə)] *a, nm/f* Leninist.

lent, e [lân, lânt] *a* slow.

lente [lânt] *nf* nit.

lentement [lãntmãn] *ad* slowly.

lenteur [lãntœr] *nf* slowness *q*; **~s** *nfpl* (*actions, décisions lentes*) slowness *sg*.

lentille [lãntēy] *nf* (*OPTIQUE*) lens *sg*; (*BOT*) lentil; **~ d'eau** duckweed; **~s de contact** contact lenses.

léonin, e [lāonañ, -ēn] *a* (*fig: contrat etc*) one-sided.

léopard [lāopár] *nm* leopard.

LEP [lep] *sigle m* (= *lycée d'enseignement professionnel*) *secondary school for vocational training, pre-1986*.

lèpre [lepr(ə)] *nf* leprosy.

lépreux, euse [lāprœ̄, -œ̄z] *nm/f* leper ♦ *a* (*fig*) flaking, peeling.

lequel [ləkel], **laquelle** [làkel], *mpl* **lesquels**, *fpl* **lesquelles** [lākel] (*avec à, de*: **auquel, duquel** *etc*) *pronom* (*interrogatif*) which, which one; (*relatif: personne: sujet*) who; (*: objet, après préposition*) whom; (*: chose*) which ♦ *a*: **auquel cas** in which case.

les [lā] *dét voir* **le**.

lesbienne [lesbyen] *nf* lesbian.

lesdits [lādē], **lesdites** [lādēt] *dét voir* **ledit**.

léser [lāzā] *vt* to wrong; (*MÉD*) to injure.

lésiner [lāzēnā] *vt*: **~ (sur)** to skimp (on).

lésion [lāzyôñ] *nf* lesion, damage *q*; **~s cérébrales** brain damage.

Lesotho [lāzotō] *nm*: **le ~** Lesotho.

lesquels, lesquelles [lākel] *pronom voir* **lequel**.

lessivable [lāsēvábl(ə)] *a* washable.

lessive [lāsēv] *nf* (*poudre*) washing powder; (*linge*) washing *q*, wash; (*opération*) washing *q*; **faire la ~** to do the washing.

lessivé, e [lāsēvā] *a* (*fam*) washed out.

lessiver [lāsēvā] *vt* to wash.

lessiveuse [lāsēvœ̄z] *nf* (*récipient*) (laundry) boiler.

lessiviel [lāsēvyel] *a* detergent.

lest [lest] *nm* ballast; **jeter** *ou* **lâcher du ~** (*fig*) to make concessions.

leste [lest(ə)] *a* (*personne, mouvement*) sprightly, nimble; (*désinvolte: manières*) off-hand; (*osé: plaisanterie*) risqué.

lestement [lestəmãn] *ad* nimbly.

lester [lestā] *vt* to ballast.

letchi [letshē] *nm* = **litchi**.

léthargie [lātárzhē] *nf* lethargy.

léthargique [lātárzhēk] *a* lethargic.

letton, ne [letôñ, -on] *a* Latvian, Lett.

Lettonie [letonē] *nf*: **la ~** Latvia.

lettre [letr(ə)] *nf* letter; **~s** *nfpl* (*étude, culture*) literature *sg*; (*SCOL*) arts (subjects); **à la ~** (*au sens propre*) literally; (*ponctuellement*) to the letter; **en ~s majuscules** *ou* **capitales** in capital letters, in capitals; **en toutes ~s** in words, in full; **~ de change** bill of exchange; **~ piégée** letter bomb; **~ de voiture (aérienne)** (air) waybill, (air) bill of lading; **~s de noblesse** pedigree.

lettré, e [lātrā] *a* well-read, scholarly.

lettre-transfert, *pl* **lettres-transferts** [letrətrânsfer] *nf* (*pressure*) transfer.

leu [lœ̄] *voir* **queue**.

leucémie [lœ̄sāmē] *nf* leukemia (*US*), leukaemia (*Brit*).

leur [lœr] *dét* their ♦ *pronom* them; **le (la) ~**, **les ~s** theirs; **à ~ approche** as they came

near; **à ~ vue** at the sight of them.

leurre [lœr] *nm* (*appât*) lure; (*fig*) delusion; (*: piège*) snare.

leurrer [lœrā] *vt* to delude, deceive.

levain [ləvañ] *nm* leaven; **sans ~** unleavened.

levant, e [ləvãñ, -ãnt] *a*: **soleil ~** rising sun ♦ *nm*: **le L~** the Levant; **au soleil ~** at sunrise.

levantin, e [ləvãntañ, -ēn] *a* Levantine ♦ *nm/f*: **L~, e** Levantine.

levé, e [ləvā] *a*: **être ~** to be up ♦ *nm*: **~ de terrain** land survey; **à mains ~es** (*vote*) by a show of hands; **au pied ~** at a moment's notice.

levée [ləvā] *nf* (*POSTES*) collection; (*CARTES*) trick; **~ de boucliers** general outcry; **~ du corps** *collection of the body from house of the deceased, before funeral*; **~ d'écrou** release from custody; **~ de terre** levee; **~ de troupes** levy.

lever [ləvā] *vt* (*vitre, bras etc*) to raise; (*soulever de terre, supprimer: interdiction, siège*) to lift; (*: difficulté*) to remove; (*séance*) to close; (*impôts, armée*) to levy; (*CHASSE: lièvre*) to start; (*: perdrix*) to flush; (*fam: fille*) to pick up ♦ *vi* (*CULIN*) to rise ♦ *nm*: **au ~** on getting up; **se ~** *vi* to get up; (*soleil*) to rise; (*jour*) to break; (*brouillard*) to lift; **ça va se ~** the weather will clear; **~ du jour** daybreak; **~ du rideau** (*THÉÂTRE*) curtain; **~ de rideau** (*pièce*) curtain raiser; **~ de soleil** sunrise.

lève-tard [levtár] *nm/f inv* late riser.

lève-tôt [levtō] *nm/f inv* early riser, early bird.

levier [ləvyā] *nm* lever; **faire ~ sur** to lever up (*ou* off); **~ de changement de vitesse** gearshift.

levraut [ləvrō] *nm* (*ZOOL*) leveret.

lèvre [levr(ə)] *nf* lip; **~s** *nfpl* (*d'une plaie*) edges; **petites/grandes ~s** labia minora/majora; **du bout des ~s** half-heartedly.

lévrier [lāvrēyā] *nm* greyhound.

levure [ləvür] *nf* yeast; **~ chimique** baking powder.

lexicographe [leksēkográf] *nm/f* lexicographer.

lexicographie [lcksēkográfē] *nf* lexicography, dictionary writing.

lexique [leksēk] *nm* vocabulary, lexicon; (*glossaire*) vocabulary.

lézard [lāzár] *nm* lizard; (*peau*) lizard skin.

lézarde [lāzárd(ə)] *nf* crack.

lézarder [lāzárdā]: **se ~** *vi* to crack.

liaison [lyezôñ] *nf* (*rapport*) connection, link; (*RAIL, AVIAT etc*) link; (*relation: d'amitié*) friendship; (*: d'affaires*) relationship; (*: amoureuse*) affair; (*CULIN, PHONÉTIQUE*) liaison; **entrer/être en ~ avec** to get/be in contact with; **~ radio** radio contact; **~ (de transmission de données)** (*INFORM*) data link.

liane [lyàn] *nf* creeper.

liant, e [lyãñ, -ãnt] *a* sociable.

liasse [lyàs] *nf* wad, bundle.

Liban [lēbáñ] *nm*: **le ~** (the) Lebanon.

libanais, e [lēbáne, -ez] *a* Lebanese ♦ *nm/f*: **L~, e** Lebanese.

libations [lēbâsyôñ] *nfpl* libations.

libelle [lĕbel] *nm* lampoon.

libellé [lĕbālā] *nm* wording.

libeller [lĕbālā] *vt* (*chèque, mandat*): ~ **(au nom de)** to make out (to); (*lettre*) to word.

libellule [lĕbālül] *nf* dragonfly.

libéral, e, aux [lĕbārál, -ō] *a*, *nm/f* liberal; **les professions** ~**es** the professions.

libéralement [lĕberálmáṅ] *ad* liberally.

libéralisation [lĕbārálĕzásyóṅ] *nf* liberalization; ~ **du commerce** easing of trade restrictions.

libéraliser [lĕbārálĕzā] *vt* to liberalize.

libéralisme [lĕbārálĕsm(ə)] *nm* liberalism.

libéralité [lĕbārálĕtā] *nf* liberality *q*, generosity *q*.

libérateur, trice [lĕbārátœr, -trĕs] *a* liberating ♦ *nm/f* liberator.

libération [lĕbārásyóṅ] *nf* liberation, freeing; release; discharge; ~ **conditionnelle** release on parole.

libéré, e [lĕbārā] *a* liberated; ~ **de** freed from; **être** ~ **sous caution/sur parole** to be released on bail/on parole.

libérer [lĕbārā] *vt* (*délivrer*) to free, liberate; (: *moralement, PSYCH*) to liberate; (*relâcher: prisonnier*) to release; (: *soldat*) to discharge; (*dégager: gaz, cran d'arrêt*) to release; (*ÉCON: échanges commerciaux*) to ease restrictions on; **se** ~ (*de rendez-vous*) to try and be free, get out of previous engagements; ~ **qn de** (*liens, dette*) to free sb from; (*promesse*) to release sb from.

Libéria [lĕbāryá] *nm*: **le** ~ Liberia.

libérien, ne [lĕbāryaṅ, -en] *a* Liberian ♦ *nm/f*: **L**~, **ne** Liberian.

libertaire [lĕberter] *a* libertarian.

liberté [lĕbertā] *nf* freedom; (*loisir*) free time; ~**s** *nfpl* (*privautés*) liberties; **mettre/être en** ~ to set/be free; **en** ~ **provisoire/surveillée/conditionnelle** on bail/probation/parole; ~ **d'association** right of association; ~ **de conscience** freedom of conscience; ~ **du culte** freedom of worship; ~ **d'esprit** independence of mind; ~ **d'opinion** freedom of thought; ~ **de la presse** freedom of the press; ~ **de réunion** right of assembly; ~ **syndicale** union rights *pl*; ~**s individuelles** personal freedom *sg*; ~**s publiques** civil rights.

libertin, e [lĕbertaṅ, -ēn] *a* libertine, licentious.

libertinage [lĕbertĕnázh] *nm* licentiousness.

libidineux, euse [lĕbēdēnœ̄, -ēz] *a* libidinous, lustful.

libido [lĕbēdō] *nf* libido.

libraire [lĕbrer] *nm/f* bookseller.

libraire-éditeur, *pl* **libraires-éditeurs** [lĕbrerādētœr] *nm* publisher and bookseller.

librairie [lĕbrārĕ] *nf* bookstore (*US*), bookshop (*Brit*).

librairie-papeterie, *pl* **librairies-papeteries** [lĕbrārĕpápātrĕ] bookseller's and stationer's.

libre [lĕbr(ə)] *a* free; (*route*) clear; (*place etc*) vacant, free; (*fig: propos, manières*) open; (*SCOL*) private and Roman Catholic (*as opposed to "laïque"*); **de** ~ (*place*) free; ~ **de qch/de faire** free from sth/to do; **vente** ~ (*COMM*) unrestricted sale; ~ **arbitre** free will; ~ **concurrence** free-market economy; ~ **entreprise** free enterprise.

libre-échange [lĕbrāsháṅzh] *nm* free trade.

librement [lĕbrəmáṅ] *ad* freely.

libre-penseur, euse [lĕbrəpáṅscer, -ēz] *nm/f* freethinker.

libre-service [lĕbrəservĕs] *nm inv* (*magasin*) self-service store; (*restaurant*) self-service restaurant.

librettiste [lĕbrātĕst(ə)] *nm/f* librettist.

Libye [lĕbē] *nf*: **la** ~ Libya.

libyen, ne [lĕbyaṅ, -en] *a* Libyan ♦ *nm/f*: **L**~, **ne** Libyan.

lice [lĕs] *nf*: **entrer en** ~ (*fig*) to enter the lists.

licence [lĕsáṅs] *nf* (*permis*) permit; (*diplôme*) (first) degree; (*liberté*) liberty; (*poétique, orthographique*) license (*US*), licence (*Brit*); (*des mœurs*) licentiousness; ~ **ès lettres/en droit** arts/law degree.

licencié, e [lĕsáṅsyā] *nm/f* (*SCOL*): ~ **ès lettres/en droit** ≈ Master (*US*) *ou* Bachelor (*Brit*) of Arts/Law, arts/law graduate; (*SPORT*) permit holder.

licenciement [lĕsáṅsēmáṅ] *nm* dismissal; laying off *q*.

licencier [lĕsáṅsyā] *vt* (*renvoyer*) to dismiss; to lay off.

licencieux, euse [lĕsáṅsyœ̄, -ēz] *a* licentious.

lichen [lĕken] *nm* lichen.

licite [lĕsĕt] *a* lawful.

licorne [lĕkórn(ə)] *nf* unicorn.

licou [lĕkōō] *nm* halter.

lie [lē] *nf* dregs *pl*, sediment.

lié, e [lyā] *a*. **très** ~ **avec** (*fig*) very friendly with *ou* close to; ~ **par** (*serment, promesse*) bound by; **avoir partie** ~**e** (**avec qn**) to be involved (with sb).

Liechtenstein [lĕshtenshtáyn] *nm*: **le** ~ Liechtenstein.

lie-de-vin [lĕdvaṅ] *a inv* wine(-colored).

liège [lyezh] *nm* cork.

liégeois, e [lyāzhwá, -wáz] *a ou* from Liège ♦ *nm/f*: **L**~, **e** inhabitant *ou* native of Liège; **café/chocolat** ~ *coffee/chocolate ice cream topped with whipped cream.*

lien [lyaṅ] *nm* (*corde, fig: affectif, culturel*) bond; (*rapport*) link, connection; (*analogie*) link; ~ **de parenté** family tie.

lier [lyā] *vt* (*attacher*) to tie up; (*joindre*) to link up; (*fig: unir, engager*) to bind; (*CULIN*) to thicken; ~ **qch à** (*attacher*) to tie sth to; (*associer*) to link with to; ~ **amitié/conversation** (**avec**) to strike up a friendship/conversation (with); **se** ~ **avec** to make friends with.

lierre [lyer] *nm* ivy.

liesse [lyes] *nf*: **être en** ~ to be jubilant.

lieu, x [lyœ̄] *nm* place; ~**x** *nmpl* (*locaux*) premises; (*endroit: d'un accident etc*) scene *sg*; **en** ~ **sûr** in a safe place; **en haut** ~ in high places; **vider** *ou* **quitter les** ~**x** to leave the premises; **arriver/être sur les** ~**x** to arrive/be on the scene; **en premier** ~ in the first place; **en dernier** ~ lastly; **avoir** ~ to take place; **avoir** ~ **de faire** to have grounds *ou* good reason for doing; **tenir** ~ **de** to take the place of; (*servir de*) to serve as; **donner** ~ **à** to give rise to, give cause for; **au** ~ **de** instead of; **au** ~ **qu'il y aille** instead of him going; ~ **commun** commonplace; ~ **géomé-**

trique locus; ~ **de naissance** place of birth; ~ **de rendez-vous** venue, meeting place.
lieu-dit, *pl* **lieux-dits** |lyœdē| *nm* locality.
lieue [lyœ̄] *nf* league.
lieutenant [lyœ̄tnáṅ] *nm* lieutenant; ~ **de vaisseau** (*NAVIG*) lieutenant.
lièvre [lyevr(ə)] *nm* hare; (*coureur*) pacemaker; **lever un** ~ (*fig*) to bring up a touchy subject.
liftier, ière [lēftyā, -yer] elevator (*US*) *ou* lift (*Brit*) attendant.
lifting [lēftēng] *nm* face lift.
ligament [lēgámáṅ] *nm* ligament.
ligature [lēgátür] *nf* ligature.
lige [lēzh] *a*: **homme** ~ (*péj*) henchman.
ligne [lēny] *nf* (*gén*) line; (*TRANSPORTS*: *liaison*) service; (: *trajet*) route; (*silhouette*): **garder la** ~ to keep one's figure; **en** ~ (*INFORM*) on line; **en** ~ **droite** as the crow flies; **"à la** ~" "new paragraph"; **entrer en** ~ **de compte** to be taken into account; to come into it; ~ **de but/médiane** goal/halfway line; ~ **d'arrivée/de départ** finish (*US*) *ou* finishing (*Brit*)/starting line; ~ **de conduite** course of action; ~ **directrice** guiding line; ~ **d'horizon** skyline; ~ **de mire** line of sight; ~ **de touche** touchline.
ligné, e [lēnyā] *a*: **papier** ~ ruled paper ♦ *nf* (*race, famille*) line, lineage; (*postérité*) descendants *pl*.
ligneux, euse [lēnyœ̄, -œ̄z] *a* ligneous, woody.
lignite [lēnyēt] *nm* lignite.
ligoter [lēgotā] *vt* to tie up.
ligue [lēg] *nf* league.
liguer [lēgā]: **se** ~ *vi* to form a league; **se** ~ **contre** (*fig*) to combine against.
lilas [lēlá] *nm* lilac.
lillois, e [lēlwá, -wáz] *a of ou* from Lille.
Lima [lēmá] *n* Lima.
limace [lēmás] *nf* slug.
limaille [lēmáy] *nf*: ~ **de fer** iron filings *pl*.
limande [lēmáṅd] *nf* dab.
limande-sole [lēmáṅdsōl] *nf* lemon sole.
limbes [laṅb] *nmpl* limbo *sg*; **être dans les** ~ (*fig: projet etc*) to be up in the air.
lime [lēm] *nf* (*TECH*) file; (*BOT*) lime; ~ **à ongles** nail file.
limer [lēmā] *vt* (*bois, métal*) to file (down); (*ongles*) to file; (*fig: prix*) to pare down.
limier [lēmyā] *nm* (*ZOOL*) bloodhound; (*détective*) sleuth.
liminaire [lēmēner] *a* (*propos*) introductory.
limitatif, ive [lēmētátēf, -ēv] *a* restrictive.
limitation [lēmētásyóṅ] *nf* limitation, restriction; **sans** ~ **de temps** with no time limit; ~ **des naissances** birth control; ~ **de vitesse** speed limit.
limite [lēmēt] *nf* (*de terrain*) boundary; (*partie ou point extrême*) limit; **dans la** ~ **de** within the limits of; **à la** ~ (*au pire*) if the worst comes (*ou* came) to the worst; **sans** ~**s** (*bêtise, richesse, pouvoir*) limitless, boundless; **vitesse/charge** ~ maximum speed/load; **cas** ~ borderline case; **date** ~ deadline; **date** ~ **de vente/consommation** sell-by/best-before date; **prix** ~ upper price limit; ~ **d'âge** maximum age, age limit.
limiter [lēmētā] *vt* (*restreindre*) to limit, restrict; (*délimiter*) to border, form the

boundary of; **se** ~ (**à qch/à faire**) (*personne*) to limit *ou* confine o.s. (to sth/to doing sth); **se** ~ **à** (*chose*) to be limited to.
limitrophe [lēmētrof] *a* border *cpd*; ~ **de** bordering on.
limogeage [lēmozházh] *nm* dismissal.
limoger [lēmozhā] *vt* to dismiss.
limon [lēmóṅ] *nm* silt.
limonade [lēmonád] *nf* lemonade.
limonadier, ière [lēmonádyā, -yer] *nm/f* (*commerçant*) café owner; (*fabricant de limonade*) soft drinks manufacturer.
limoneux, euse [lēmonœ̄, -œ̄z] *a* muddy.
limousin, e [lēmōōzaṅ, -ēn] *a of ou* from Limousin ♦ *nm* (*région*): **le L**~ the Limousin.
limpide [laṅpēd] *a* limpid.
lin [laṅ] *nm* (*BOT*) flax; (*tissu, toile*) linen.
linceul [laṅsœl] *nm* shroud.
linéaire [lēnáer] *a* linear ♦ *nm*: ~ (**de vente**) shelves *pl*.
linéament [lēnáámáṅ] *nm* outline.
linge [laṅzh] *nm* (*serviettes etc*) linen; (*pièce de tissu*) cloth; (*aussi*: ~ **de corps**) underwear; (*aussi*: ~ **de toilette**) towel; (*lessive*) washing; ~ **sale** dirty linen.
lingerie [laṅzhrē] *nf* lingerie, underwear.
lingot [laṅgō] *nm* ingot.
linguiste [laṅgǖēst(ə)] *nm/f* linguist.
linguistique [laṅgǖēstēk] *a* linguistic ♦ *nf* linguistics *sg*.
lino(léum) [lēno(lāom)] *nm* linoleum.
linotte [lēnot] *nf*: **tête de** ~ bird brain.
linteau, x [laṅtō] *nm* lintel.
lion, ne [lyóṅ, lyon] *nm/f* lion/lioness; (*signe*): **le L**~ Leo, the Lion; **être du L**~ to be Leo; ~ **de mer** sea lion.
lionceau, x [lyóṅsō] *nm* lion cub.
lippu, e [lēpǖ] *a* thick-lipped.
liquéfier [lēkāfyā] *vt* to liquefy; **se** ~ *vi* (*gaz etc*) to liquefy; (*fig: personne*) to succumb.
liqueur [lēkœr] *nf* liqueur.
liquidateur, trice [lēkēdátœr, -trēs] *nm/f* (*JUR*) receiver; ~ **judiciaire** official liquidator.
liquidation [lēkēdásyóṅ] *nf* liquidation; (*COMM*) clearance (sale); ~ **judiciaire** compulsory liquidation.
liquide [lēkēd] *a* liquid ♦ *nm* liquid; (*COMM*): **en** ~ in ready money *ou* cash.
liquider [lēkēdā] *vt* (*société, biens, témoin gênant*) to liquidate; (*compte, problème*) to settle; (*COMM: articles*) to clear, sell off.
liquidités [lēkēdētā] *nfpl* (*COMM*) liquid assets.
liquoreux, euse [lēkorœ̄, -œ̄z] *a* syrupy.
lire [lēr] *nf* (*monnaie*) lira ♦ *vt, vi* to read; ~ **qch à qn** to read sth (out) to sb.
lis *vb* [lē] *voir* **lire** ♦ *nm* [lēs] = **lys**.
lisais [lēze] *etc vb voir* **lire**.
Lisbonne [lēzbon] *n* Lisbon.
lise [lēz] *etc vb voir* **lire**.
liseré [lēzrā] *nm* border, edging.
liseron [lēzróṅ] *nm* bindweed.
liseuse [lēzœ̄z] *nf* book cover; (*veste*) bed jacket.
lisible [lēzēbl(ə)] *a* legible; (*digne d'être lu*) readable.
lisiblement [lēzēbləmáṅ] *ad* legibly.
lisière [lēzyer] *nf* (*de forêt*) edge; (*de tissu*) selvage.

lisons [lēzôṅ] *vb voir* **lire**.
lisse [lēs] *a* smooth.
lisser [lēsā] *vt* to smooth.
listage [lēstázh] *nm* (*INFORM*) listing.
liste [lēst(ə)] *nf* list; (*INFORM*) listing; **faire la ~ de** to list, make out a list of; **~ d'attente** waiting list; **~ civile** civil list; **~ électorale** electoral roll; **~ de mariage** wedding (present) list.
lister [lēstā] *vt* (*aussi INFORM*) to list; **~ la mémoire** to dump.
listing [lēstēng] *nm* (*INFORM*) listing; **qualité ~** draft quality.
lit [lē] *nm* (*gén*) bed; **faire son ~** to make one's bed; **aller/se mettre au ~** to go to/get into bed; **prendre le ~** to take to one's bed; **d'un premier ~** (*JUR*) of a first marriage; **~ de camp** cot (*US*), campbed (*Brit*); **~ d'enfant** crib (*US*), cot (*Brit*).
litanie [lētánē] *nf* litany.
lit-cage, *pl* **lits-cages** [lēkázh] *nm* folding bed.
litchi [lētshē] *nm* litchi (*US*), lychee (*Brit*).
literie [lētrē] *nf* bedding; (*linge*) bedding, bedclothes *pl*.
litho [lētō], **lithographie** [lētográfē] *nf* litho(graphy); (*épreuve*) litho(graph).
litière [lētyɛr] *nf* litter.
litige [lētēzh] *nm* dispute; **en ~** in contention.
litigieux, euse [lētēzhyœ̄, -œ̄z] *a* litigious, contentious.
litote [lētot] *nf* understatement.
litre [lētr(ə)] *nm* liter (*US*), litre (*Brit*); (*récipient*) liter *ou* litre measure.
littéraire [lētārɛr] *a* literary.
littéral, e, aux [lētárál, -ō] *a* literal.
littérature [lētarutur] *nf* literature.
littoral, e, aux [lētorál, -ō] *a* coastal ♦ *nm* coast.
Lituanie [lētüänē] *nf*: **la ~** Lithuania.
lituanien, ne [lētüányaṅ, -en] *a* Lithuanian.
liturgie [lētürzhē] *nf* liturgy.
liturgique [lētürzhēk] *a* liturgical.
livide [lēvēd] *a* livid, pallid.
living(-room) [lēvēng(rōōm)] *nm* living room.
livrable [lēvrábl(ə)] *a* (*COMM*) that can be delivered.
livraison [lēvrezôṅ] *nf* delivery; **~ à domicile** home delivery (service).
livre [lēvr(ə)] *nm* book; (*imprimerie etc*): **le ~** the book industry ♦ *nf* (*poids, monnaie*) pound; **traduire qch à ~ ouvert** to translate sth off the cuff *ou* at sight; **~ blanc** official report (*prepared by independent body, following war, natural disaster etc*); **~ de bord** (*NAVIG*) logbook; **~ de comptes** account(s) book; **~ de cuisine** cookbook; **~ de messe** mass *ou* prayer book; **~ d'or** guest book; **~ de poche** paperback (*cheap and pocket size*); **~ verte** *unit of account used in calculating contributions to and payments from the Community Agricultural Fund of the ECM*, green pound (*Brit*).
livré, e [lēvrā] *nf* livery ♦ *a*: **~ à** (*l'anarchie etc*) given over to; **~ à soi-même** left to oneself *ou* one's own devices.
livrer [lēvrā] *vt* (*COMM*) to deliver; (*otage, coupable*) to hand over; (*secret, information*) to give away; **se ~ à** (*se confier*) to confide in; (*se rendre*) to give o.s. up to;

(*s'abandonner à: débauche etc*) to give o.s. up *ou* over to; (*faire: pratiques, actes*) to indulge in; (*travail*) to be engaged in, engage in; (: *sport*) to practice (*US*), practise (*Brit*); (: *enquête*) to carry out; **~ bataille** to give battle.
livresque [lēvresk(ə)] *a* (*péj*) bookish.
livret [lēvre] *nm* booklet; (*d'opéra*) libretto (*pl* -s); **~ de caisse d'épargne** (*savings*) bankbook; **~ de famille** (*official*) family record book; **~ scolaire** ≈ (*school*) record (*US*), report book (*Brit*).
livreur, euse [lēvrœr, -œ̄z] *nm/f* delivery boy *ou* man/girl *ou* woman.
LO *sigle f* (= *Lutte ouvrière*) *political party*.
lobe [lob] *nm*: **~ de l'oreille** ear lobe.
lobé, e [lobā] *a* (*ARCHIT*) foiled.
lober [lobā] *vt* to lob.
local, e, aux [lokál, -ō] *a* local ♦ *nm* (*salle*) premises *pl* ♦ *nmpl* premises.
localement [lokálmáṅ] *ad* locally.
localisé, c [lokálēzā] *a* localized.
localiser [lokálēzā] *vt* (*repérer*) to locate, place; (*limiter*) to localize, confine.
localité [lokálētā] *nf* locality.
locataire [lokáter] *nm/f* tenant; (*de chambre*) lodger.
locatif, ive [lokátēf, -ēv] *a* (*charges, réparations*) incumbent upon the tenant; (*valeur*) rental; (*immeuble*) with rented apartments, used as a letting *ou* rental (*US*) concern.
location [lokásyôṅ] *nf* (*par le locataire*) renting; (*par l'usager: de voiture etc*) renting (*US*), hiring (*Brit*); (*par le propriétaire*) renting out, letting; (*de billets, places*) booking; (*bureau*) box *ou* ticket office; "**~ de voitures**" "car rental (*US*) *ou* hire (*Brit*)".
location-vente [lokásyôṅvâṅt] *nf* form of installment plan (*US*) *ou* hire purchase (*Brit*).
lock-out [lokáwt] *nm inv* lockout.
locomoteur, trice [lokomotœr, -trēs] *a, nf* locomotive.
locomotion [lokomōsyôṅ] *nf* locomotion.
locomotive [lokomotēv] *nf* locomotive, engine; (*fig*) pacesetter, pacemaker.
locuteur, trice [lokütœr, -trēs] *nm/f* (*LING*) speaker.
locution [loküsyôṅ] *nf* phrase.
loden [loden] *nm* loden.
lofer [lofā] *vi* (*NAVIG*) to luff.
logarithme [logárētm(ə)] *nm* logarithm.
loge [lozh] *nf* (*THÉÂTRE: d'artiste*) dressing room; (: *de spectateurs*) box; (*de concierge, franc-maçon*) lodge.
logeable [lozhábl(ə)] *a* habitable; (*spacieux*) roomy.
logement [lozhmáṅ] *nm* apartment (*US*), flat (*Brit*); accommodations *q* (*US*), accommodation *q* (*Brit*); **le ~** housing; **chercher un ~** to look for an apartment, look for accommodation(s); **construire des ~s bon marché** to build cheap housing *sg*; **crise du ~** housing shortage; **~ de fonction** (*ADMIN*) company flat *ou* apartment, accommodation(s) provided with one's job.
loger [lozhā] *vt* to accommodate ♦ *vi* to live; **se ~**: **trouver à se ~** to find accommodations (*US*) *ou* accommodation (*Brit*); **se ~**

dans (*suj: balle, flèche*) to lodge itself in.
logeur, euse [lozhœr, -œz] *nm/f* landlord/landlady.
loggia [lodzhyá] *nf* loggia.
logiciel [lozhēsyel] *nm* software.
logique [lozhēk] *a* logical ♦ *nf* logic; **c'est** ~ it stands to reason.
logiquement [lozhēkmáń] *ad* logically.
logis [lozhē] *nm* home; abode, dwelling.
logistique [lozhēstēk] *nf* logistics *sg* ♦ *a* logistic.
logo [logō], **logotype** [logotēp] *nm* logo.
loi [lwá] *nf* law; **faire la** ~ to lay down the law; **les** ~**s de la mode** (*fig*) the dictates of fashion; **proposition de** ~ (private member's) bill; **projet de** ~ (government) bill.
loin [lwań] *ad* far; (*dans le temps: futur*) a long way off; (*: passé*) a long time ago; **plus** ~ further; **moins** ~ (**que**) not as far (as); ~ **de** far from; **pas** ~ **de 1000 F** not far off 1000 F; **au** ~ far off; **de** ~ *ad* from a distance; (*fig: de beaucoup*) by far; **il vient de** ~ he's come a long way; he comes from a long way away; **de** ~ **en** ~ here and there; (*de temps en temps*) (every) now and then; ~ **de là** (*au contraire*) far from it.
lointain, e [lwańtań, -en] *a* faraway, distant; (*dans le futur, passé*) distant, far-off; (*cause, parent*) remote, distant ♦ *nm*: **dans le** ~ in the distance.
loi-programme, *pl* **lois-programmes** [lwáprográm] *nf* (*POL*) act providing framework for government program.
loir [lwár] *nm* dormouse (*pl* -mice).
Loire [lwár] *nf*: **la** ~ the Loire.
loisible [lwàzēbl(ə)] *a*: **il vous est** ~ **de ...** you are free to ....
loisir [lwàzēr] *nm*: **heures de** ~ spare time; ~**s** *nmpl* leisure *sg*; (*activités*) leisure activities; **avoir le** ~ **de faire** to have the time *ou* opportunity to do; (**tout**) **à** ~ (*en prenant son temps*) at leisure; (*autant qu'on le désire*) at one's pleasure.
lombaire [lôńber] *a* lumbar.
lombalgie [lôńbálzhē] *nf* back pain.
lombard, e [lôńbár, -árd(ə)] *a* Lombard.
Lombardie [lôńbárdē] *nf*: **la** ~ Lombardy.
londonien, ne [lôńdonyań, -en] *a* London *cpd*, of London ♦ *nm/f*: **L**~, **ne** Londoner.
Londres [lôńdr(ə)] *n* London.
long, longue [lôń, lôńg] *a* long ♦ *ad*: **en savoir** ~ to know a great deal ♦ *nm*: **de 3 m de** ~ 3 m long, 3 m in length ♦ *nf*: **à la longue** in the end; **faire** ~ **feu** to fizzle out; **ne pas faire** ~ **feu** not to last long; **au** ~ **cours** (*NAVIG*) ocean *cpd*, oceangoing; **de longue date** *a* long-standing; **longue durée** *a* long-term; **de longue haleine** *a* long-term; **être** ~ **à faire** to take a long time to do; **en** ~ *ad* lengthwise, lengthways; (**tout**) **le** ~ **de** (all) along; **tout au** ~ **de** (*année, vie*) throughout; **de** ~ **en large** (*marcher*) to and fro, up and down; **en** ~ **et en large** (*fig*) in every detail.
longanimité [lôńgánēmētā] *nf* forbearance.
long-courrier [lôńkōōryā] *nm* (*AVIAT*) long-haul aircraft.
longe [lôńzh] *nf* (*corde: pour attacher*) tether; (*pour mener*) lead; (*CULIN*) loin.

longer [lôńzhā] *vt* to go (*ou* walk *ou* drive) along(side); (*suj: mur, route*) to border.
longévité [lôńzhāvētā] *nf* longevity.
longiligne [lôńzhēlēny] *a* long-limbed.
longitude [lôńzhētüd] *nf* longitude; **à 45° de** ~ **ouest** at 45° longitude west.
longitudinal, e, aux [lôńzhētüdēnál, -ō] *a* longitudinal, lengthways; (*entaille, vallée*) running lengthways.
longtemps [lôńtáń] *ad* (for) a long time, (for) long; **ça ne va pas durer** ~ it won't last long; **avant** ~ before long; **pour/pendant** ~ for a long time; **je n'en ai pas pour** ~ I shan't be long; **mettre** ~ **à faire** to take a long time to do; **il en a pour** ~ he'll be a long time; **il y a** ~ **que je travaille** I have been working (for) a long time; **il n'y a pas** ~ **que je l'ai rencontré** it's not long since I met him.
longue [lôńg] *af voir* **long**.
longuement [lôńgmáń] *ad* (*longtemps: parler, regarder*) for a long time; (*en détail: expliquer, raconter*) at length.
longueur [lôńgœr] *nf* length; ~**s** *nfpl* (*fig: d'un film etc*) tedious parts; **sur une** ~ **de 10 km** for *ou* over 10 km; **en** ~ *ad* lengthwise, lengthways; **tirer en** ~ to drag on; **à** ~ **de journée** all day long; **d'une** ~ (*gagner*) by a length; ~ **d'onde** wavelength.
longue-vue [lôńgvü] *nf* telescope.
looping [lōōpēng] *nm* (*AVIAT*): **faire des** ~**s** to loop the loop.
lopin [lopań] *nm*: ~ **de terre** patch of land.
loquace [lokás] *a* talkative, loquacious.
loque [lok] *nf* (*personne*) wreck; ~**s** *nfpl* (*habits*) rags; **être** *ou* **tomber en** ~**s** to be in rags.
loquet [loke] *nm* latch.
lorgner [lornyā] *vt* to eye; (*convoiter*) to have one's eye on.
lorgnette [lornyet] *nf* opera glasses *pl*.
lorgnon [lornyôń] *nm* (*face-à-main*) lorgnette; (*pince-nez*) pince-nez.
loriot [loryō] *nm* (golden) oriole.
lorrain, e [lorań, -en] *a* of *ou* from Lorraine; **quiche** ~**e** quiche lorraine.
lors [lor]: ~ **de** *prép* (*au moment de*) at the time of; (*pendant*) during; ~ **même que** even though.
lorsque [lorsk(ə)] *cj* when, as.
losange [lozáńzh] *nm* diamond; (*GÉOM*) lozenge; **en** ~ diamond-shaped.
lot [lō] *nm* (*part*) share; (*de loterie*) prize; (*fig: destin*) fate, lot; (*COMM, INFORM*) batch; ~ **de consolation** consolation prize.
loterie [lotrē] *nf* lottery; (*tombola*) raffle; **L**~ **nationale** French national lottery.
loti, e [lotē] *a*: **bien/mal** ~ well-/badly off, lucky/unlucky.
lotion [lōsyôń] *nf* lotion; ~ **après rasage** after-shave (lotion); ~ **capillaire** hair tonic.
lotir [lotēr] *vt* (*terrain: diviser*) to divide into plots; (*: vendre*) to sell by lots.
lotissement [lotēsmáń] *nm* (*groupe de maisons, d'immeubles*) housing development; (*parcelle*) (building) plot, lot.
loto [lotō] *nm* lotto.
lotte [lot] *nf* (*ZOOL: de rivière*) burbot; (*: de mer*) monkfish.

louable [lwȧbl(ə)] a (appartement, garage) rentable; (action, personne) praiseworthy, commendable.

louage [lwȧzh] nm: **voiture de** ~ rented (US) ou hired (Brit) car; (à louer) rental (US) ou hire (Brit) car.

louange [lwȧn̂zh] nf: **à la** ~ **de** in praise of; **~s** nfpl praise sg.

loubar(d) [lōōbȧr] nm (fam) hoodlum.

louche [lōōsh] a shady, fishy, dubious ♦ nf ladle.

loucher [lōōshā] vi to squint; (fig): ~ **sur** to have one's (beady) eye on.

louer [lwā] vt (maison: suj: propriétaire) to let, rent (out); (: locataire) to rent; (voiture etc) to rent (out); to rent; (réserver) to book; (faire l'éloge de) to praise; **"à** ~**"** "for rent" (US), "to let" (Brit); ~ **qn de** to praise sb for; **se** ~ **de** to congratulate o.s. on.

loufoque [lōōfok] a (fam) crazy, zany.

loukoum [lōōkōōm] nm Turkish delight.

loulou [lōōlōō] nm (chien) spitz; ~ **de Poméranie** Pomeranian (dog).

loup [lōō] nm wolf (pl wolves); (poisson) bass; (masque) (eye) mask; **jeune** ~ young go-getter; ~ **de mer** (marin) old sea dog.

loupe [lōōp] nf magnifying glass; ~ **de noyer** burr walnut; **à la** ~ (fig) in minute detail.

louper [lōōpā] vt (fam: manquer) to miss; (: gâcher) to mess up, bungle.

lourd, e [lōōr, lōōrd(ə)] a heavy; (chaleur, temps) sultry; (fig: personne, style) heavy-handed ♦ ad: **peser** ~ to be heavy; ~ **de** (menaces) charged with; (conséquences) fraught with; **artillerie/industrie** ~**e** heavy artillery/industry.

lourdaud, e [lōōrdō, -ōd] a oafish.

lourdement [lōōrdəmân̂] ad heavily; **se tromper** ~ to make a big mistake.

lourdeur [lōōrdœr] nf heaviness; ~ **d'estomac** indigestion q.

loustic [lōōstēk] nm (fam péj) joker.

loutre [lōōtr(ə)] nf otter; (fourrure) otter skin.

louve [lōōv] nf she-wolf.

louveteau, x [lōōvtō] nm (ZOOL) wolf cub; (scout) cub (scout).

louvoyer [lōōvwȧyā] vi (NAVIG) to tack; (fig) to hedge, evade the issue.

lover [lovā]: **se** ~ vi to coil up.

loyal, e, aux [lwȧyȧl, -ō] a (fidèle) loyal, faithful; (fair-play) fair.

loyalement [lwȧyȧlmân̂] ad loyally, faithfully; fairly.

loyalisme [lwȧyȧlēsm(ə)] nm loyalty.

loyauté [lwȧyōtā] nf loyalty, faithfulness; fairness.

loyer [lwȧyā] nm rent; ~ **de l'argent** interest rate.

LP sigle m (= lycée professionnel) secondary school for vocational training.

LPO sigle f (= Ligue pour la protection des oiseaux) bird protection society.

LSD sigle m (= Lyserg Säure Diäthylamid) LSD.

lu, e [lü] pp de **lire.**

lubie [lübē] nf whim, craze.

lubricité [lübrēsētā] nf lust.

lubrifiant [lübrēfyân̂] nm lubricant.

lubrifier [lübrēfyā] vt to lubricate.

lubrique [lübrēk] a lecherous.

lucarne [lükȧrn(ə)] nf skylight.

lucide [lüsēd] a (conscient) lucid, conscious; (perspicace) clear-headed.

lucidité [lüsēdētā] nf lucidity.

luciole [lüsyol] nf firefly.

lucratif, ive [lükrȧtēf, -ēv] a lucrative; profitable; **à but non** ~ non profit-making.

ludique [lüdēk] a play cpd, playing.

ludothèque [lüdotek] nf toy library.

luette [lüet] nf uvula.

lueur [lüœr] nf (chatoyante) glimmer q; (métallique, mouillée) gleam q; (rougeoyante, chaude) glow q; (pâle) (faint) light; (fig) spark; (: d'espérance) glimmer, gleam.

luge [lüzh] nf sled (US), sledge (Brit); **faire de la** ~ to sled (US), sledge (Brit), toboggan.

lugubre [lügübr(ə)] a gloomy; dismal.

lui [lüē] pp de **luire** ♦ pronom (chose, animal) it; (personne: mâle) him; (: en sujet) he; (: femelle) her; voir note sous **il**; ~, **il** ... HE ... (emphatic); **je la connais mieux que** ~ (que je ne le connais) I know her better than (I know) him; (qu'il ne la connaît) I know her better than he does.

lui-même [lüēmem] pronom (personne) himself; (chose) itself.

luire [lüēr] vi (gén) to shine, gleam; (surface mouillée) to glisten; (reflets chauds, cuivrés) to glow.

luisant, e [lüēzân̂, -ân̂t] vb voir **luire** ♦ a shining, gleaming.

lumbago [lôn̂bȧgō] nm lumbago.

lumière [lümyer] nf light; ~**s** nfpl (d'une personne) knowledge sg, wisdom sg; **à la** ~ **de** by the light of; (fig: événements) in the light of; **fais de la** ~ let's have some light, give us some light; **faire (toute) la** ~ **sur** (fig) to clarify (completely); **mettre en** ~ (fig) to highlight; ~ **du jour/soleil** day/sunlight.

luminaire [lümēner] nm lamp, light.

lumineux, euse [lümēnœ̈, -œ̈z] a (émettant de la lumière) luminous; (éclairé) illuminated; (ciel, journée, couleur) bright; (relatif à la lumière: rayon etc) of light, light cpd; (fig: regard) radiant.

luminosité [lümēnozētā] nf (TECH) luminosity.

lump [lœn̂p] nm: **œufs de** ~ lumpfish roe.

lunaire [lüner] a lunar, moon cpd.

lunatique [lünȧtēk] a whimsical, temperamental.

lunch [lœntsh] nm (réception) buffet lunch.

lundi [lœn̂dē] nm Monday; **on est** ~ it's Monday; **le** ~ **20 août** Monday 20th August; **il est venu** ~ he came on Monday; **le(s)** ~**(s)** on Mondays; **à** ~! see you (on) Monday!; ~ **de Pâques** Easter Monday; ~ **de Pentecôte** Whitmonday.

lune [lün] nf moon; **pleine/nouvelle** ~ full/new moon; **être dans la** ~ (distrait) to have one's head in the clouds; ~ **de miel** honeymoon.

luné, e [lünā] a: **bien/mal** ~ in a good/bad mood.

lunette [lünet] nf: ~**s** nfpl glasses, spectacles; (protectrices) goggles; ~ **d'approche** telescope; ~ **arrière** (AUTO) rear window; ~**s**

noires dark glasses; ~s de soleil sunglasses.
lurent [lür] *vb voir* lire.
lurette [lüret] *nf:* il y a belle ~ ages ago.
luron, ne [lüröñ, -on] *nm/f* lad/lass; joyeux *ou* gai ~ gay dog.
lus [lü] *etc vb voir* lire.
lustre [lüstr(ə)] *nm (de plafond)* chandelier; *(fig: éclat)* luster *(US)*, lustre *(Brit)*.
lustrer [lüstrā] *vt:* ~ qch *(faire briller)* to make sth shine; *(user)* to make sth shiny.
lut [lü] *vb voir* lire.
luth [lüt] *nm* lute.
luthier [lütyā] *nm* (stringed-)instrument maker.
lutin [lütañ] *nm* imp, goblin.
lutrin [lütrañ] *nm* lectern.
lutte [lüt] *nf (conflit)* struggle; *(SPORT)*: la ~ wrestling; de haute ~ after a hard-fought struggle; ~ des classes class struggle; ~ libre *(SPORT)* freestyle *(US) ou* all-in *(Brit)* wrestling.
lutter [lütā] *vi* to fight, struggle; *(SPORT)* to wrestle.
lutteur, euse [lütœr, -ēz] *nm/f (SPORT)* wrestler; *(fig)* battler, fighter.
luxation [lüksâsyöñ] *nf* dislocation.
luxe [lüks(ə)] *nm* luxury; un ~ de *(détails, précautions)* a wealth of; de ~ *a* luxury *cpd.*
Luxembourg [lüksâñbōōr] *nm:* le ~ Luxembourg.
luxembourgeois, e [lüksâñbōōrzhwà, -wáz] *a* of *ou* from Luxembourg ♦ *nm/f:* L~, e inhabitant *ou* native of Luxembourg.
luxer [lüksā] *vt:* se ~ l'épaule to dislocate one's shoulder.
luxueux, euse [lüksüȫ, -ēz] *a* luxurious.
luxure [lüksür] *nf* lust.
luxuriant, e [lüksüryâñ, -âñt] *a* luxuriant, lush.
luzerne [lüzern(ə)] *nf* alfalfa.
lycée [lēsā] *nm* (public *(US) ou* state *(Brit)*) high school; ~ technique technical high school.
lycéen, ne [lēsâañ, -en] *nm/f* high school pupil.
lymphatique [lañfâtēk] *a (fig)* lethargic, sluggish.
lymphe [lañf] *nf* lymph.
lyncher [lañshā] *vt* to lynch.
lynx [lañks] *nm* lynx.
Lyon [lyöñ] *n* Lyons.
lyonnais, e [lyone, -ez] *a* of *ou* from Lyons; *(CULIN)* Lyonnaise.
lyophilisé, e [lyofēlēzā] *a* freeze-dried.
lyre [lēr] *nf* lyre.
lyrique [lērēk] *a* lyrical; *(OPÉRA)* lyric; artiste ~ opera singer; comédie ~ comic opera; théâtre ~ opera house *(for light opera)*.
lyrisme [lērēsm(ə)] *nm* lyricism.
lys [lēs] *nm* lily.

M

M, m [em] *nm inv* M, m ♦ *abr* = majeur, masculin, mètre, Monsieur; (= *million*) M;

M comme **Marcel** M for Mike.
m' [m] *pronom voir* me.
MA *sigle m* = maître auxiliaire.
ma [mà] *dét voir* mon.
maboul, e [màbōōl] *a (fam)* loony.
macabre [màkâbr(ə)] *a* macabre, gruesome.
macadam [màkádâm] *nm* tarmac *(Brit)*, asphalt.
Macao [màkáō] *nf* Macao.
macaron [màkáróñ] *nm (gâteau)* macaroon; *(insigne)* (round) badge.
macaroni(s) [màkáronē] *nm(pl)* macaroni *sg*; ~ au fromage *ou* au gratin macaroni and cheese *(US)*, macaroni cheese *(Brit)*.
macédoine [màsādwàn] *nf:* ~ de fruits fruit salad; ~ de légumes mixed vegetables *pl*.
macérer [màsārā] *vi, vt* to macerate; *(dans du vinaigre)* to pickle.
mâchefer [mâshfer] *nm* clinker, cinders *pl*.
mâcher [mâshā] *vt* to chew; ne pas ~ ses mots not to mince one's words; ~ le travail à qn *(fig)* to spoonfeed sb, do half sb's work for him.
machiavélique [màkyàvālēk] *a* Machiavellian.
machin [màshañ] *nm (fam)* thingamajig, thing; *(personne)*: M~ what's-his(*ou*-her)-name.
machinal, e, aux [màshēnál, -ō] *a* mechanical, automatic.
machination [màshēnàsyöñ] *nf* scheming, frame-up.
machine [màshēn] *nf* machine; *(locomotive; de navire etc)* engine; *(fig: rouages)* machinery; *(fam: personne)*: M~ what's-her-name; faire ~ arrière *(NAVIG)* to go astern; *(fig)* to back-pedal; ~ à laver/coudre/tricoter washing/sewing/knitting machine; ~ à écrire typewriter; ~ à sous slot machine; ~ à vapeur steam engine.
machine-outil, *pl* machines-outils [màshēnōōtē] *nf* machine tool.
machinerie [màshēnrē] *nf* machinery, plant; *(d'un navire)* engine room.
machinisme [màshēnēsm(ə)] *nm* mechanization.
machiniste [màshēnēst(ə)] *nm (THÉÂTRE)* stage hand; *(de bus, métro)* driver.
mâchoire [mâshwàr] *nf* jaw; ~ de frein brake shoe.
mâchonner [mâshonā] *vt* to chew (at).
mâcon [mâköñ] *nm* Mâcon wine.
maçon [màsöñ] *nm* bricklayer; *(constructeur)* builder.
maçonner [màsonā] *vt (revêtir)* to face, render (with cement); *(boucher)* to brick up.
maçonnerie [màsonrē] *nf (murs: de brique)* brickwork; *(: de pierre)* masonry, stonework; *(activité)* bricklaying; building; ~ de béton concrete.
maçonnique [màsonēk] *a* masonic.
macramé [màkràmā] *nm* macramé.
macrobiotique [màkrobyotēk] *a* macrobiotic.
macro-économie [màkroãkonomē] *nf* macroeconomics *sg*.
maculer [màkülā] *vt* to stain; *(TYPO)* to mackle.
Madagascar [màdàgàskár] *nf* Madagascar.

Madame [mádâm], *pl* **Mesdames** [mādâm] *nf*:
~ **X** Mrs X ['mɪsɪz]; **occupez-vous de** ~/
Monsieur/Mademoiselle please help this
lady/gentleman/(young) lady; **bonjour** ~/
Monsieur/Mademoiselle good morning; *(ton
déférent)* good morning Madam/Sir/Madam;
(le nom est connu) good morning Mrs X/Mr
X/Miss X; ~/**Monsieur/Mademoiselle!** *(pour
appeler)* excuse me!; *(ton déférent)* Madam/
Sir/Miss!; ~/**Monsieur/Mademoiselle** *(sur
lettre)* Dear Madam/Sir/Madam; **chère** ~/
cher Monsieur/chère Mademoiselle Dear
Mrs X/Mr X/Miss X; ~ **la Directrice** the director; the manageress; the principal;
Mesdames Ladies.

Madeleine [mádlen]: **îles de la** ~ *nfpl*
Magdalen Islands.

madeleine [mádlen] *nf* madeleine, ~ sponge
finger cake.

Madelinot, e [mádlēnō, -ot] *nm/f* inhabitant *ou*
native of the Magdalen Islands.

Mademoiselle [mádmwázel], *pl*
Mesdemoiselles [mādmwázel] *nf* Miss; *voir
aussi* **Madame**.

Madère [máder] *nf* Madeira ♦ *nm*: **m**~
Madeira (wine).

madone [mádon] *nf* madonna.

madré, e [mádrā] *a* crafty, wily.

Madrid [mádrēd] *n* Madrid.

madrier [mádrēyá] *nm* beam.

madrilène [mádrēlen] *a* of *ou* from Madrid.

maestria [máestrēyá] *nf* (masterly) skill.

maf(f)ia [máfyá] *nf* Maf(f)ia.

magasin [mágázań] *nm* *(boutique)* shop; *(entrepôt)* warehouse; *(d'arme, appareil-photo)*
magazine; **en** ~ *(COMM)* in stock; **faire les**
~**s** to make the rounds of the stores; ~
d'alimentation grocery store *(US)*, grocer's
shop *(Brit)*.

magasinier [mágázēnyá] *nm* warehouseman.

magazine [mágázēn] *nm* magazine.

mage [mázh] *nm*: **les Rois M**~**s** the Magi, the
(Three) Wise Men.

Maghreb [mágreb] *nm*: **le** ~ the Maghreb,
North-(West) Africa.

maghrébin, e [mágrábań, -ēn] *a* of *ou* from
the Maghreb ♦ *nm/f*: **M**~, **e** North African,
Maghrebi.

magicien, ne [mázhēsyań, -en] *nm/f* magician.

magie [mázhē] *nf* magic; ~ **noire** black
magic.

magique [mázhēk] *a* *(occulte)* magic; *(fig)*
magical.

magistral, e, aux [mázhēstrál, -ō] *a* *(œuvre,
adresse)* masterly; *(ton)* authoritative;
(gifle etc) sound, resounding; *(ex cathedra)*:
enseignement ~ lecturing, lectures *pl*; **cours**
~ lecture.

magistrat [mázhēstrá] *nm* magistrate.

magistrature [mázhēstrátür] *nf* magistracy,
magistrature; ~ **assise** judges *pl*, bench; ~
debout state prosecutors *pl*.

magma [mágmá] *nm* *(GÉO)* magma; *(fig)*
jumble.

magnanerie [mányánrē] *nf* silk farm.

magnanime [mányánēm] *a* magnanimous.

magnat [mágná] *nm* tycoon, magnate; ~ **de la
presse** press baron.

magner [mányā]: **se** ~ *vi* *(fam)* to get a move
on.

magnésie [mányāzē] *nf* magnesia.

magnésium [mányāzyom] *nm* magnesium.

magnétique [mányātēk] *a* magnetic.

magnétiser [mányātēzá] *vt* to magnetize; *(fig)*
to mesmerize, hypnotize.

magnétisme [mányātēsm(ə)] *nm* magnetism.

magnéto [mányātō] *nm* (= *magnétocassette*)
cassette deck; (= *magnétophone*) tape recorder.

magnétocassette [mányātokáset] *nm* cassette
deck.

magnétophone [mányātofon] *nm* tape recorder; ~ **à cassettes** cassette recorder.

magnétoscope [mányātoskop] *nm*: ~ **(à
cassette)** video (recorder).

magnificence [mányēfēsâns] *nf* *(faste)*
magnificence, splendor *(US)*, splendour
(Brit); *(générosité, prodigalité)* munificence,
lavishness.

magnifier [mányēfyá] *vt* *(glorifier)* to glorify;
(idéaliser) to idealize.

magnifique [mányēfēk] *a* magnificent.

magnolia [mányolyá] *nm* magnolia.

magnum [mágnom] *nm* magnum.

magot [mágō] *nm* *(argent)* pile (of money);
(économies) nest egg.

magouille [mágōōy] *nf* *(fam)* scheming.

mahométan, e [máomātáń, -áń] *a*
Mohammedan, Mahometan.

mai [me] *nm* May; *voir aussi* **juillet**.

maigre [megr(ə)] *a* *(very)* thin, skinny;
(viande) lean; *(fromage)* low-fat; *(végétation)* thin, sparse; *(fig)* poor, meager *(US)*,
meagre *(Brit)*, skimpy ♦ *ad*: **faire** ~ not to
eat meat; **jours** ~**s** days of abstinence, fish
days.

maigrelet, te [megrəle, -et] *a* skinny, scrawny.

maigreur [megrœr] *nf* thinness.

maigrichon, ne [megreshón, -on] *a* = **maigrelet, te.**

maigrir [māgrēr] *vi* to get thinner, lose weight
♦ *vt*: ~ **qn** *(suj: vêtement)* to make sb look
slim(mer).

mailing [meleng] *nm* direct mail *q*; **un** ~ a
mailing.

maille [mây] *nf* *(boucle)* stitch; *(ouverture)*
hole (in the mesh); **avoir** ~ **à partir avec qn**
to have a bone to pick with sb; ~ **à
l'endroit/à l'envers** knit one/purl one;
(boucle) plain/purl stitch.

maillechort [máyshor] *nm* nickel silver.

maillet [máye] *nm* mallet.

maillon [máyoń] *nm* link.

maillot [máyō] *nm* *(aussi*: ~ **de corps)** undershirt *(US)*, vest *(Brit)*; *(de danseur)* leotard;
(de sportif) jersey; ~ **de bain** bathing suit,
swimsuit; *(d'homme)* bathing trunks *pl*; ~
une pièce one-piece swimsuit; ~ **deux pièces**
two-piece swimsuit, bikini.

main [mań] *nf* hand; **la** ~ **dans la** ~ hand in
hand; **à deux** ~**s** with both hands; **à une** ~
with one hand; **à la** ~ *(tenir, avoir)* in one's
hand; *(faire, tricoter etc)* by hand; **se
donner la** ~ to hold hands; **donner** *ou* **tendre
la** ~ **à qn** to hold out one's hand to sb; **se
serrer la** ~ to shake hands; **serrer la** ~ **à qn**
to shake hands with sb; **sous la** ~ to *ou* at
hand; **haut les** ~**s!** hands up!; **à** ~ **levée**

(*ART*) freehand; **à ~s levées** (*voter*) with a show of hands; **attaque à ~ armée** armed attack; **à ~ droite/gauche** to the right/left; **à remettre en ~s propres** to be delivered personally; **de première ~** (*renseignement*) first-hand; (*COMM: voiture etc*) with only one previous owner; **faire ~ basse sur** to help o.s. to; **mettre la dernière ~ à** to put the finishing touches to; **mettre la ~ à la pâte** (*fig*) to lend a hand; **prendre qch en ~** (*fig*) to take sth in hand; **avoir/passer la ~** (*CARTES*) to lead/hand over the lead; **s'en laver les ~s** (*fig*) to wash one's hands of it; **se faire/perdre la ~** to get one's hand in/lose one's touch; **avoir qch bien en ~** to have got the hang of sth; **en un tour de ~** (*fig*) in the twinkling of an eye; **~ courante** handrail.

mainate [menȧt] *nm* myna(h) bird.

main-d'œuvre [mȧṅdœvr(ə)] *nf* manpower, labor (*US*), labour (*Brit*).

main-forte [maṅfort(ə)] *nf*: **prêter ~ à qn** to come to sb's assistance.

mainmise [maṅmēz] *nf* seizure; (*fig*): **avoir la ~ sur** to have a complete hold on.

maint, e [maṅ, maṅt] *a* many a; **~s** many; **à ~es reprises** time and (time) again.

maintenance [maṅtnȧṅs] *nf* maintenance.

maintenant [maṅtnȧṅ] *ad* now; (*actuellement*) nowadays.

maintenir [maṅtnēr] *vt* (*retenir, soutenir*) to support; (*contenir: foule etc*) to keep in check, hold back; (*conserver*) to maintain, uphold; (*affirmer*) to maintain; **se ~** *vi* (*paix, temps*) to hold; (*préjugé*) to persist; (*malade*) to remain stable.

maintien [maṅtyaṅ] *nm* maintaining, upholding; (*attitude*) bearing; **~ de l'ordre** maintenance of law and order.

maintiendrai [maṅtyaṅdrȧ], **maintiens** [maṅtyaṅ] *etc vb voir* **maintenir**.

maire [mer] *nm* mayor.

mairie [mȧrē] *nf* (*endroit*) town hall; (*administration*) town council.

mais [me] *cj* but; **~ non!** of course not!; **~ enfin** but after all; (*indignation*) look here!; **~ encore?** is that all?

maïs [mȧēs] *nm* corn (*US*), maize (*Brit*).

maison [mezóṅ] *nf* (*bâtiment*) house; (*chezsoi*) home; (*COMM*) firm; (*famille*): **ami de la ~** friend of the family ♦ *a inv* (*CULIN*) home-made; (*: au restaurant*) made by the chef; (*COMM*) in-house, own; (*fam*) firstrate; **à la ~** at home; (*direction*) home; **~ d'arrêt** (short-stay) prison; **~ de campagne** country cottage; **~ centrale** prison; **~ close** *ou* **de passe** brothel; **~ de correction** ≈ reformatory (*US*), ≈ remand home (*Brit*); **~ de la culture** ≈ arts center; **~ des jeunes** ≈ youth club; **~ mère** parent company; **~ de passe** = **~ close**; **~ de repos** convalescent home; **~ de retraite** old people's home; **~ de santé** mental home.

Maison-Blanche [mezóṅblȧṅsh] *nf*: **la ~** the White House.

maisonnée [mezonȧ] *nf* household, family.

maisonnette [mezonet] *nf* small house, cottage.

maître, esse [metr(ə), metres] *nm/f* master/ mistress; (*SCOL*) teacher, schoolmaster/

mistress ♦ *nm* (*peintre etc*) master; (*titre*): **M~ (M^e)** Maître, *term of address for lawyers etc* ♦ *nf* (*amante*) mistress ♦ *a* (*principal, essentiel*) main; **maison de ~** family seat; **être ~ de** (*soi-même, situation*) to be in control of; **se rendre ~ de** (*pays, ville*) to gain control of; (*situation, incendie*) to bring under control; **être passé ~ dans l'art de** to be a (past) master in the art of; **une maîtresse femme** a forceful woman; **~ d'armes** fencing master; **~ auxiliaire (MA)** (*SCOL*) substitute (*US*) *ou* temporary (*Brit*) teacher; **~ chanteur** blackmailer; **~ de chapelle** choirmaster; **~ de conférences** ≈ associate professor (*US*), ≈ senior lecturer (*Brit*); **~/ maîtresse d'école** teacher, schoolmaster/ mistress; **~ d'hôtel** (*domestique*) butler; (*d'hôtel*) headwaiter, maitre d'; **~ de maison** host; **~ nageur** lifeguard; **~ d'œuvre** (*CONSTR*) project manager; **~ d'ouvrage** (*CONSTR*) client; **~ à penser** intellectual leader; **~ queux** chef; **maîtresse de maison** hostess; (*ménagère*) housewife (*pl* -wives).

maître-assistant, e, *pl* **maîtres-assistants, es** [metrȧsēstȧṅ, -ȧṅt] *nm/f* ≈ assistant professor (*US*), ≈ lecturer (*Brit*).

maître-autel, *pl* **maîtres-autels** [metrōtel] *nm* high altar.

maîtrise [mȧtrēz] *nf* (*aussi*: **~ de soi**) selfcontrol, self-possession; (*habileté*) skill, mastery; (*suprématie*) mastery, command; (*diplôme*) ≈ master's degree; (*chefs d'équipe*) supervisory staff.

maîtriser [mȧtrēzȧ] *vt* (*cheval, incendie*) to (bring under) control; (*sujet*) to master; (*émotion*) to control; **se ~** to control o.s.

majesté [mȧzhestȧ] *nf* majesty.

majestueux, euse [mȧzhestüœ̄, -œ̄z] *a* majestic.

majeur, e [mȧzhœr] *a* (*important*) major; (*JUR*) of age; (*fig*) adult ♦ *nm/f* (*JUR*) person who has come of age *ou* attained his (*ou* her) majority ♦ *nm* (*doigt*) middle finger; **en ~e partie** for the most part; **la ~e partie de** the major part of.

major [mȧzhor] *nm* adjutant; (*SCOL*): **~ de la promotion** first in one's *ou* at the head of one's class.

majoration [mȧzhorȧsyóṅ] *nf* increase.

majorer [mȧzhorȧ] *vt* to increase.

majorette [mȧzhoret] *nf* majorette.

majoritaire [mȧzhorēter] *a* majority *cpd*; **système/scrutin ~** majority system/ballot.

majorité [mȧzhoretȧ] *nf* (*gén*) majority; (*parti*) party in power; **en ~** (*composé etc*) mainly.

Majorque [mȧzhork(ə)] *nf* Majorca.

majorquin, e [mȧzhorkȧṅ, -ēn] *a* Majorcan ♦ *nm/f*: **M~, e** Majorcan.

majuscule [mȧzhüskül] *a, nf*: **(lettre) ~** capital (letter).

MAL [mȧl] *sigle f* (= *Maison d'animation et des loisirs*) cultural center.

mal, maux [mȧl, mō] *nm* (*opposé au bien*) evil; (*tort, dommage*) harm; (*douleur physique*) pain, ache; (*maladie*) illness, sickness *q*; (*difficulté, peine*) trouble; (*souffrance morale*) pain ♦ *ad* badly ♦ *a*: **c'est ~ (de faire)** it's bad *ou* wrong (to do); **être ~ to** be uncomfortable; **être ~ avec qn** to be on bad terms with sb; **être au plus ~** (*malade*) to be very bad; (*brouillé*) to be at sword's points (*US*) *ou* daggers drawn (*Brit*); **il comprend ~** he has difficulty in understanding; **il a ~ compris** he misunderstood; **~ tourner** to go wrong; **dire/penser du ~ de** to speak/think ill of; **ne vouloir de ~ à personne** to wish nobody any ill; **il n'a rien fait de ~** he has done nothing wrong; **avoir du ~ à faire qch** to have trouble doing sth; **se donner du ~ pour faire qch** to go to a lot of trouble to do sth; **ne voir aucun ~ à** to see no harm in, see nothing wrong in; **craignant ~ faire** fearing he *etc* was doing the wrong thing; **sans penser** *ou* **songer à ~** without meaning any harm; **faire du ~ à qn** to hurt sb; to harm sb; **se faire ~** to hurt o.s.; **se faire ~ au pied** to hurt one's foot; **ça fait ~** it hurts; **j'ai ~ (ici)** it hurts (here); **j'ai ~ au dos** my back aches, I've got a pain in my back; **avoir ~ à la tête/à la gorge/aux dents** to have a headache/a sore throat/ toothache; **avoir le ~ de l'air** to be airsick; **avoir le ~ du pays** to be homesick; **~ de mer** seasickness; **~ de la route** carsickness; **~ en point** *a imp* in a bad state; **maux de ventre** stomach ache *sg*; *voir* **cœur.**

Malabar [málábár] *nm*: **le ~, la côte de ~** the Malabar (Coast).

malade [málád] *a* ill, sick; (*poitrine, jambe*) bad; (*plante*) diseased; (*fig: entreprise, monde*) ailing ♦ *nm/f* invalid, sick person; (*à l'hôpital etc*) patient; **tomber ~** to fall ill; **être ~ du cœur** to have heart trouble *ou* a bad heart; **grand ~** seriously ill person; **~ mental** mentally sick *ou* ill person.

maladie [máládē] *nf* (*spécifique*) disease, illness; (*mauvaise santé*) illness, sickness; (*fig: manie*) mania; **être rongé par la ~** to be wasting away (through illness); **~ de peau** skin disease.

maladif, ive [máládēf, -ēv] *a* sickly; (*curiosité, besoin*) pathological.

maladresse [máládrɛs] *nf* clumsiness *q*; (*gaffe*) blunder.

maladroit, e [máládrwá, -wát] *a* clumsy.

maladroitement [máládrwátmân] *ad* clumsily.

malais, e [málɛ, -ez] *a* Malay, Malayan ♦ *nm* (*LING*) Malay ♦ *nm/f*: **M~, e** Malay, Malayan.

malaise [mález] *nm* (*MÉD*) feeling of faintness; feeling of discomfort; (*fig*) uneasiness, malaise; **avoir un ~** to feel faint *ou* dizzy.

malaisé, e [málázā] *a* difficult.

Malaisie [málczē] *nf*: **la ~** Malaya, West Malaysia; **la péninsule de ~** the Malay Peninsula.

malappris, e [máláprē, -ēz] *nm/f* ill-mannered *ou* boorish person.

malaria [máláryá] *nf* malaria.

malavisé, e [málávázā] *a* ill-advised, unwise.

Malawi [máláwē] *nm*: **le ~** Malawi.

malaxer [máláksā] *vt* (*pétrir*) to knead; (*mêler*) to mix.

Malaysia [máleʒyá] *nf*: **la ~** Malaysia.

malchance [málshâns] *nf* misfortune, bad luck *q*; **par ~** unfortunately; **quelle ~!** what bad luck!

malchanceux, euse [málshânsœ, -œz] *a* unlucky.

malcommode [málkomod] *a* impractical, inconvenient.

Maldives [máldēv] *nfpl*: **les ~** the Maldive Islands.

maldonne [máldon] *nf* (*CARTES*) misdeal; **il y a ~** (*fig*) there's been a misunderstanding.

mâle [mâl] *a* (*aussi ÉLEC, TECH*) male; (*viril: voix, traits*) manly ♦ *nm* male.

malédiction [máládēksyôn] *nf* curse.

maléfice [málāfēs] *nm* evil spell.

maléfique [málāfēk] *a* evil, baleful.

malencontreux, euse [málânkôntrœ, -œz] *a* unfortunate, untoward.

malentendant, e [málântândân, -ânt] *nm/f*: **les ~s** the hard of hearing.

malentendu [málântândü] *nm* misunderstanding.

malfaçon [málfásòn] *nf* fault.

malfaisant, e [málfəzân, -ânt] *a* evil, harmful.

malfaiteur [málfɛtœr] *nm* lawbreaker, criminal; (*voleur*) thief (*pl* thieves).

malfamé, e [málfámā] *a* disreputable, of ill repute.

malfrat [málfrá] *nm* villain, crook.

malgache [málgásh] *a* Malagasy, Madagascan ♦ *nm* (*LING*) Malagasy ♦ *nm/f*: **M~** Malagasy, Madagascan.

malgré [málgrā] *prép* in spite of, despite; **~ tout** *ad* in spite of everything.

malhabile [málábēl] *a* clumsy.

malheur [málœr] *nm* (*situation*) adversity, misfortune; (*événement*) misfortune; (*: plus fort*) disaster, tragedy; **par ~** unfortunately; **quel ~!** what a shame *ou* pity!; **faire un ~** (*fam: un éclat*) to do something desperate; (*: avoir du succès*) to be a smash hit.

malheureusement [málœrœzmân] *ad* unfortunately.

malheureux, euse [málœrœ, -œz] *a* (*triste*) unhappy, miserable; (*infortuné, regrettable*) unfortunate; (*malchanceux*) unlucky; (*insignifiant*) wretched ♦ *nm/f* (*infortuné, misérable*) poor soul; (*indigent, miséreux*) unfortunate creature; **les ~** the destitute; **avoir la main malheureuse** (*au jeu*) to be unlucky; (*tout casser*) to be ham-handed.

malhonnête [málonet] *a* dishonest; (*impoli*) rude.

malhonnêteté [málonettā] *nf* dishonesty; rudeness *q*.

Mali [málē] *nm*: **le ~** Mali.

malice [málēs] *nf* mischievousness; (*méchanceté*) spite; **par ~** out of malice *ou* spite; **sans ~** guileless.

malicieux, euse [málēsyœ, -œz] *a* mischievous.

malien, ne [mályan, -ɛn] *a* Malian.

malignité [málēnyētā] *nf* (*d'une tumeur, d'un mal*) malignancy.

malin, igne [málan, -ēny] *a* (*futé: f gén*: **maline**) smart, shrewd; (*: sourire*) knowing; (*MÉD, influence*) malignant; **faire le ~** to show off; **éprouver un ~ plaisir à** to take malicious pleasure in.

malingre [málângr(ə)] *a* puny.

malintentionné, e [málântânsyonā] *a* ill-intentioned, malicious.

malle [mál] *nf* trunk; (*AUTO*): **~ (arrière)**

trunk *(US)*, boot *(Brit)*.
malléable [málāābl(ə)] *a* malleable.
malle-poste, *pl* **malles-poste** [málpost(ə)] *nf* mail car *(US)* *ou* coach *(Brit)*.
mallette [málct] *nf* *(valise)* (small) suitcase; *(aussi*: ~ **de voyage**) overnight case; *(pour documents)* attaché case.
malmener [málmənā] *vt* to manhandle; *(fig)* to give a rough ride to.
malodorant, e [málodorāṅ, -āṅt] *a* foul- *ou* bad-smelling.
malotru [málotrü] *nm* lout, boor.
malouin, e [málwaṅ, -ēn] *a* of *ou* from Saint Malo.
Malouines [málwēn] *nfpl*: **les** ~ the Falklands, the Falkland Islands.
malpoli, e [málpolē] *nm/f* rude individual.
malpropre [málpropr(ə)] *a* *(personne, vêtement)* dirty; *(travail)* slovenly; *(histoire, plaisanterie)* unsavory *(US)*, unsavoury *(Brit)*, smutty; *(malhonnête)* dishonest.
malpropreté [málproprətā] *nf* dirtiness.
malsain, e [málsaṅ, -ɛn] *a* unhealthy.
malséant, e [málsāāṅ, -āṅt] *a* unseemly, unbecoming.
malsonnant, e [málsonāṅ, -āṅt] *a* offensive.
malt [mált] *nm* malt; **pur** ~ *(whisky)* malt (whisky).
maltais, e [málte, -ez] *a* Maltese.
Malte [mált(ə)] *nf* Malta.
malté, e [máltā] *a* *(lait etc)* malted.
maltraiter [máltrātā] *vt* *(brutaliser)* to manhandle, ill-treat; *(critiquer, éreinter)* to pan, roast.
malus [málüs] *nm* *(ASSURANCES)* car insurance surcharge, penalty.
malveillance [málveyāṅs] *nf* *(animosité)* ill will; *(intention de nuire)* malevolence; *(JUR)* malicious intent *q*.
malveillant, e [málveyāṅ, -āṅt] *a* malevolent, malicious.
malvenu, e [málvənü] *a*: **être** ~ **de** *ou* **à faire qch** not to be in a position to do sth.
malversation [málversâsyóṅ] *nf* embezzlement, misappropriation (of funds).
maman [mámāṅ] *nf* mom *(US)*, mum(my) *(Brit)*.
mamelle [mámel] *nf* teat.
mamelon [mámlóṅ] *nm* *(ANAT)* nipple; *(colline)* knoll, hillock.
mamie [mámē] *nf* *(fam)* granny.
mammifère [mámēfer] *nm* mammal.
mammouth [mámōōt] *nm* mammoth.
manager [mánádzher] *nm* *(SPORT)* manager; *(COMM)*: ~ **commercial** commercial director.
manceau, elle, x [mánsō, -el] *a* of *ou* from Le Mans.
manche [máṅsh] *nf* *(de vêtement)* sleeve; *(d'un jeu, tournoi)* round; *(GÉO)*: **la M**~ the (English) Channel ♦ *nm* *(d'outil, casserole)* handle; *(de pelle, pioche etc)* shaft; *(de violon, guitare)* neck; *(fam)* clumsy oaf; **faire la** ~ to pass the hat; ~ **à air** *nf* *(AVIAT)* windsock; ~ **à balai** *nm* broomstick; *(AVIAT, INFORM)* joystick.
manchette [máṅshet] *nf* *(de chemise)* cuff; *(coup)* forearm blow; *(titre)* headline.
manchon [máṅshóṅ] *nm* *(de fourrure)* muff;

~ **à incandescence** incandescent (gas) mantle.
manchot [máṅshō] *nm* one-armed man; armless man; *(ZOOL)* penguin.
mandarine [máṅdárēn] *nf* mandarin (orange), tangerine.
mandat [máṅdá] *nm* *(postal)* postal *ou* money order; *(d'un député etc)* mandate; *(procuration)* power of attorney, proxy; *(POLICE)* warrant; ~ **d'amener** summons *sg*; ~ **d'arrêt** warrant for arrest; ~ **de dépôt** committal order; ~ **de perquisition** *(POLICE)* search warrant.
mandataire [máṅdáter] *nm/f* *(représentant, délégué)* representative; *(JUR)* proxy.
mandat-carte, *pl* **mandats-cartes** [máṅdákárt(ə)] *nm* money order *(in postcard form)*.
mandater [máṅdátā] *vt* *(personne)* to appoint; *(POL: député)* to elect.
mandat-lettre, *pl* **mandats-lettres** [máṅdáletr(ə)] *nm* money order *(with space for correspondence)*.
mandchou, e [máṅtshōō] *a* Manchu, Manchurian ♦ *nm* *(LING)* Manchu ♦ *nm/f*: **M**~, **e** Manchu.
Mandchourie [máṅtshōōrē] *nf*: **la** ~ Manchuria.
mander [máṅdā] *vt* to summon.
mandibule [máṅdēbül] *nf* mandible.
mandoline [máṅdolēn] *nf* mandolin(e).
manège [mánezh] *nm* riding school; *(à la foire)* merry-go-round; *(fig)* game, ploy; **faire un tour de** ~ to go for a ride on a *ou* the roundabout *etc*; ~ **(de chevaux de bois)** merry-go-round.
manette [mánet] *nf* lever, tap; ~ **de jeu** *(INFORM)* joystick.
manganèse [máṅgánez] *nm* manganese.
mangeable [máṅzhábl(ə)] *a* edible, eatable.
mangeaille [máṅzhåy] *nf* *(péj)* grub.
mangeoire [máṅzhwár] *nf* trough, manger.
manger [máṅzhā] *vt* to eat; *(ronger: suj: rouille etc)* to eat into *ou* away; *(utiliser, consommer)* to eat up ♦ *vi* to eat.
mange-tout [máṅzhtōō] *nm* *inv* sugar pea *(US)*, mange-tout *(Brit)*.
mangeur, euse [máṅzhœr, -œz] *nm/f* eater.
mangouste [máṅgōōst(ə)] *nf* mongoose.
mangue [máṅg] *nf* mango.
maniable [mányábl(ə)] *a* *(outil)* handy; *(voiture, voilier)* easy to handle, maneuverable *(US)*, manœuvrable *(Brit)*; *(fig: personne)* easily influenced, manipulable.
maniaque [mányák] *a* *(pointilleux, méticuleux)* finicky, fussy; *(atteint de manie)* suffering from a mania ♦ *nm/f* maniac.
manie [mánē] *nf* mania; *(tic)* odd habit.
maniement [mánēmāṅ] *nm* handling; ~ **d'armes** arms drill.
manier [mányā] *vt* to handle; **se** ~ *vi* *(fam)* to get a move on.
manière [mányer] *nf* *(façon)* way, manner; *(genre, style)* style; ~**s** *nfpl* *(attitude)* manners; *(chichis)* fuss *sg*; **de** ~ **à** so as to; **de telle** ~ **que** in such a way that; **de cette** ~ in this way *ou* manner; **d'une** ~ **générale** generally speaking, as a general rule; **de toute** ~ in any case; **d'une certaine** ~ in a

(certain) way; **faire des ~s** to put on airs; **employer la ~ forte** to use strong-arm tactics; **adverbe de ~** adverb of manner.
maniéré, e [mányārā] *a* affected.
manif [mánēf] *nf* (= *manifestation*) demo (*pl* -s).
manifestant, e [mánēfestáñ, -áñt] *nm/f* demonstrator.
manifestation [mánēfestásyôñ] *nf* (*de joie, mécontentement*) expression, demonstration; (*symptôme*) outward sign; (*fête etc*) event; (*POL*) demonstration.
manifeste [mánēfest(ə)] *a* obvious, evident ♦ *nm* manifesto (*pl* -s).
manifester [mánēfestā] *vt* (*volonté, intentions*) to show, indicate; (*joie, peur*) to express, show ♦ *vi* (*POL*) to demonstrate; **se ~** *vi* (*émotion*) to show *ou* express itself; (*difficultés*) to arise; (*symptômes*) to appear; (*témoin etc*) to come forward.
manigance [mánēgáñs] *nf* scheme.
manigancer [mánēgáñsā] *vt* to plot, devise.
Manille [mánēy] *n* Manila.
manioc [mányok] *nm* cassava, manioc.
manipulateur, trice [mánēpülátœr, -trēs] *a* (*technicien*) technician, operator; (*prestidigitateur*) conjurer; (*péj*) manipulator.
manipulation [mánēpülásyôñ] *nf* handling; manipulation.
manipuler [mánēpülā] *vt* to handle; (*fig*) to manipulate.
manivelle [mánēvel] *nf* crank.
manne [mán] *nf* (*REL*) manna; (*fig*) godsend.
mannequin [mánkáñ] *nm* (*COUTURE*) dummy; (*MODE*) model.
manœuvrable [mánœvrábl(ə)] *a* (*bateau, véhicule*) maneuverable (*US*), manœuvrable (*Brit*).
manœuvre [mánœvr(ə)] *nf* (*gén*) maneuver (*US*), manœuvre (*Brit*) ♦ *nm* (*ouvrier*) laborer (*US*), labourer (*Brit*).
manœuvrer [mánœvrā] *vt* to maneuver (*US*), manœuvre (*Brit*); (*levier, machine*) to operate; (*personne*) to manipulate ♦ *vi* to maneuvre *ou* manœuver.
manoir [mánwár] *nm* manor *ou* country house.
manomètre [mánometr(ə)] *nm* gauge, manometer.
manquant, e [mánkáñ, -áñt] *a* missing.
manque [mánk] *nm* (*insuffisance*): **~ de** lack of; (*vide*) emptiness, gap; (*MÉD*) withdrawal; **~s** *nmpl* (*lacunes*) faults, defects; **par ~ de** for want of; **~ à gagner** loss of profit *ou* earnings.
manqué, e [mánkā] *a* failed; **garçon ~** tomboy.
manquement [mánkmáñ] *nm*: **~ à** (*discipline, règle*) breach of.
manquer [mánkā] *vi* (*faire défaut*) to be lacking; (*être absent*) to be missing; (*échouer*) to fail ♦ *vt* to miss ♦ *vb impersonnel*: **il (nous) manque encore 100 F** we are still 100 F short; **il manque des pages (au livre)** there are some pages missing *ou* some pages are missing (from the book); **l'argent qui leur manque** the money they need *ou* are short of; **le pied/la voix lui manqua** he missed his footing/his voice failed him; **~ à qn** (*absent*

etc): **il/cela me manque** I miss him/that; **~ à** *vt* (*règles etc*) to be in breach of, fail to observe; **~ de** *vt* to lack; (*COMM*) to be out of (stock of); **ne pas ~ de faire: il n'a pas manqué de le dire** he certainly said it; **~ (de) faire: il a manqué (de) se tuer** he very nearly got killed; **il ne manquerait plus qu'il fasse** all we need now is for him to do; **je n'y manquerai pas** leave it to me, I'll definitely do it.
mansarde [mánsárd(ə)] *nf* attic.
mansardé, e [mánsárdā] *a* attic *cpd*.
mansuétude [mánsüätüd] *nf* leniency.
mante [mánt] *nf*: **~ religieuse** praying mantis.
manteau, x [mántō] *nm* coat; **~ de cheminée** mantelpiece; **sous le ~** (*fig*) under cover.
mantille [mántēy] *nf* mantilla.
Mantoue [mántōō] *n* Mantua.
manucure [mánükür] *nf* manicurist.
manuel, le [mánüel] *a* manual ♦ *nm/f* manually gifted pupil *etc* (*as opposed to intellectually gifted*) ♦ *nm* (*ouvrage*) manual, handbook.
manuellement [manuelmáñ] *ad* manually.
manufacture [mànüfáktür] *nf* (*établissement*) factory; (*fabrication*) manufacture.
manufacturé, e [mánüfáktürā] *a* manufactured.
manufacturier, ière [mánüfáktüryā, -yer] *nm/f* factory owner.
manuscrit, e [mánüskrē, -ēt] *a* handwritten ♦ *nm* manuscript.
manutention [mánütáñsyôñ] *nf* (*COMM*) handling; (*local*) storehouse.
manutentionnaire [mánütáñsyoner] *nm/f* warehouseman/woman, packer.
manutentionner [mánütáñsyonā] *vt* to handle.
MAP *sigle f* (*PHOTO*: = *mise au point*) focusing.
mappemonde [mápmôñd] *nf* (*plane*) map of the world; (*sphère*) globe.
maquereau, x [mákrō] *nm* mackerel *inv*; (*fam: proxénète*) pimp.
maquerelle [mákrel] *nf* (*fam*) madam.
maquette [máket] *nf* (*d'un décor, bâtiment, véhicule*) (scale) model; (*TYPO*) paste-up; (: *d'une page illustrée, affiche*) paste-up; (: *prêt à la réproduction*) artwork.
maquignon [mákēnyoñ] *nm* horse dealer.
maquillage [mákēyàzh] *nm* making up; faking; (*produits*) make-up.
maquiller, x [mákēyā] *vt* (*personne, visage*) to make up; (*truquer: passeport, statistique*) to fake; (: *voiture volée*) to do over (*respray etc*); **se ~** to make o.s. up.
maquilleur, euse [mákēyœr, -ēz] *nm/f* make-up artist.
maquis [mákē] *nm* (*GÉO*) scrub; (*fig*) tangle; (*MIL*) maquis, underground fighting *q*.
maquisard, e [mákēzár, -árd(ə)] *nm/f* maquis, member of the Resistance.
marabout [márábōō] *nm* (*ZOOL*) marabou(t).
maraîcher, ère [márāshā, máresher] *a*: **cultures maraîchères** truck farming *sg* (*US*), market gardening *sg* (*Brit*) ♦ *nm/f* truck farmer (*US*), market gardener (*Brit*).
marais [máre] *nm* marsh, swamp; **~ salant** saltworks.
marasme [márásm(ə)] *nm* (*POL, ÉCON*)

stagnation, sluggishness; (*accablement*) dejection, depression.

marathon [màrátôn] *nm* marathon.

marâtre [màrátr(ə)] *nf* cruel mother.

maraude [màrōd] *nf* pilfering, thieving (*of poultry, crops*); (*dans un verger*) fruit-stealing; (*vagabondage*) prowling; **en ~** on the prowl; (*taxi*) cruising.

maraudeur, euse [màrōdœr, -ēz] *nm/f* marauder; prowler.

marbre [màrbr(ə)] *nm* (*pierre, statue*) marble; (*d'une table, commode*) marble top; (*TYPO*) stone, bed; **rester de ~** to remain stonily indifferent.

marbrer [màrbrā] *vt* to mottle, blotch; (*TECH: papier*) to marble.

marbrier [màrbrēyā] *nm* monumental mason.

marbrière [màrbrēyer] *nf* marble quarry.

marbrures [màrbrür] *nfpl* blotches *pl*; (*TECH*) marbling *sg*.

marc [màr] *nm* (*de raisin, pommes*) marc; **~ de café** coffee grounds *pl ou* dregs *pl*.

marcassin [màrkàsaṅ] *nm* young wild boar.

marchand, e [màrshâṅ, -âṅd] *nm/f* shopkeeper, tradesman/woman; (*au marché*) stallholder; (*spécifique*): **~ de cycles/tapis** bicycle/carpet dealer; **~ de charbon/vins** coal/wine merchant ♦ *a*: **prix/valeur ~(e)** market price/value; **qualité ~e** standard quality; **~ en gros/au détail** wholesaler/retailer; **~ de biens** real estate agent; **~ de canons** (*péj*) arms dealer; **~ de couleurs** hardware dealer (*US*), ironmonger (*Brit*); **~/e de fruits** fruit seller (*US*), fruiterer (*Brit*); **~/e de journaux** newsagent; **~/e de légumes** produce dealer (*US*), greengrocer (*Brit*); **~/e de poisson** fish seller (*US*), fishmonger (*Brit*); **~e de quatre saisons** street vendor (selling fresh fruit and vegetables); **~ de sable** (*fig*) sandman; **~ de tableaux** art dealer.

marchander [màrshâṅdā] *vt* (*article*) to bargain *ou* haggle over; (*éloges*) to be sparing with ♦ *vi* to bargain, haggle.

marchandise [màrshâṅdēz] *nf* goods *pl*, merchandise *q*.

marche [màrsh(ə)] *nf* (*d'escalier*) step; (*activité*) walking; (*promenade, trajet, allure*) walk; (*démarche*) walk, gait; (*MIL etc, MUS*) march; (*fonctionnement*) running; (*progression*) progress; course; **à une heure de ~** an hour's walk (away); **ouvrir/fermer la ~** to lead the way/bring up the rear; **dans le sens de la ~** (*RAIL*) facing the engine; **en ~** (*monter etc*) while the vehicle is moving *ou* in motion; **mettre en ~** to start; **remettre qch en ~** to set *ou* start sth going again; **se mettre en ~** (*personne*) to get moving; (*machine*) to start; **~ arrière** (*AUTO*) reverse (gear); **faire ~ arrière** (*AUTO*) to reverse; (*fig*) to backtrack, back-pedal; **~ à suivre** (correct) procedure; (*sur notice*) (step by step) instructions *pl*.

marché [màrshā] *nm* (*lieu, COMM, ÉCON*) market; (*ville*) trading center (*US*) *ou* centre (*Brit*); (*transaction*) bargain, deal; **par-dessus le ~** into the bargain; **faire son ~** to do one's shopping; **mettre le ~ en main à qn** to tell sb to take it or leave it; **~ au comptant** (*BOURSE*) spot market; **M~**

commun Common Market; **~ aux fleurs** flower market; **~ noir** black market; **faire du ~ noir** to buy and sell on the black market; **~ aux puces** flea market; **~ à terme** (*BOURSE*) forward market; **~ du travail** labor (*US*) *ou* labour (*Brit*) market.

marchepied [màrshəpyā] *nm* (*RAIL*) step; (*AUTO*) running board; (*fig*) stepping stone.

marcher [màrshā] *vi* to walk; (*MIL*) to march; (*aller: voiture, train, affaires*) to go; (*prospérer*) to go well; (*fonctionner*) to work, run; (*fam*) to go along, agree; (: *croire naïvement*) to be taken in; **~ sur** to walk on; (*mettre le pied sur*) to step on *ou* in; (*MIL*) to march upon; **~ dans** (*herbe etc*) to walk in *ou* on; (*flaque*) to step in; **faire ~ qn** (*pour rire*) to pull sb's leg; (*pour tromper*) to lead sb up the garden path.

marcheur, euse [màrshœr, -ēz] *nm/f* walker.

marcotter [màrkotā] *vt* to layer.

mardi [màrdē] *nm* Tuesday; **M~ gras** Shrove Tuesday; *voir aussi* **lundi**.

mare [màr] *nf* pond; **~ de sang** pool of blood.

marécage [màrākázh] *nm* marsh, swamp.

marécageux, euse [màrākázhœ, -ēz] *a* marshy, swampy.

maréchal, aux [màrāshàl, -ō] *nm* marshal; **~ des logis** (*MIL*) sergeant.

maréchal-ferrant, *pl* **maréchaux-ferrants** [màrāshàlferàṅ, màrāshō-] *nm* blacksmith.

maréchaussée [màrāshōsā] *nf* (*humoristique*: *gendarmes*) police.

marée [màrā] *nf* tide; (*poissons*) fresh (sea) fish; **~ haute/basse** high/low tide; **~ montante/descendante** rising/ebb tide; **~ noire** oil slick.

marelle [màrel] *nf*: **(jouer à) la ~** (to play) hopscotch.

marémotrice [màrāmotrēs] *af* tidal.

mareyeur, euse [màreyœr, -ēz] *nm/f* wholesale (sea) fish merchant.

margarine [màrgàrēn] *nf* margarine.

marge [màrzh(ə)] *nf* margin; **en ~** in the margin; **en ~ de** (*fig*) on the fringe of; (*en dehors de*) cut off from; (*qui se rapporte à*) connected with; **~ bénéficiaire** profit margin, markup; **~ de sécurité** safety margin.

margelle [màrzhel] *nf* coping.

margeur [màrzhœr] *nm* margin stop.

marginal, e, aux [màrzhēnàl, -ō] *a* marginal ♦ *nm/f* dropout.

marguerite [màrgərēt] *nf* marguerite, (oxeye) daisy; (*INFORM*) daisy wheel.

marguillier [màrgēyā] *nm* churchwarden.

mari [màrē] *nm* husband.

mariage [màryàzh] *nm* (*union, état, fig*) marriage; (*noce*) wedding; **~ civil/religieux** civil/church wedding; **un ~ de raison/d'amour** a marriage of convenience/a love match; **~ blanc** unconsummated marriage; **~ en blanc** white wedding.

marié, e [màryā] *a* married ♦ *nm/f* (bride)groom/bride; **les ~s** the bride and groom; **les (jeunes) ~s** the newlyweds.

marier [màryā] *vt* to marry; (*fig*) to blend; **se ~ (avec)** to marry, get married (to); (*fig*) to blend (with).

marijuana [màrēzhwànà] *nf* marijuana.

marin, e [màraṅ, -ēn] *a* sea *cpd*, marine ♦ *nm*

sailor ♦ *nf* navy; (*ART*) seascape; (*couleur*) navy (blue); **avoir le pied** ~ to be a good sailor; (*garder son équilibre*) to have one's sea legs; ~**e de guerre** navy; ~**e marchande** merchant marine (*US*) *ou* navy (*Brit*); ~**e à voiles** sailing ships *pl*.
marinade [màrēnàd] *nf* marinade.
marine [màrēn] *af*, *nf voir* **marin** ♦ *a inv* navy (blue) ♦ *nm* (*MIL*) marine.
mariner [màrēnā] *vi*, *vt* to marinate, marinade.
marinier [màrēnyā] *nm* bargeman (*US*), bargee (*Brit*).
marinière [màrēnyer] *nf* (*blouse*) smock ♦ *a inv*: **moules** ~ (*CULIN*) mussels in white wine.
marionnette [màryonet] *nf* puppet.
marital, e, aux [màrčtàl, -ō] *a*: **autorisation** ~**e** husband's permission.
maritalement [màrčtàlmàǹ] *ad*: **vivre** ~ to live together (as husband and wife).
maritime [màrčtēm] *a* sea *cpd*, maritime; (*ville*) coastal, seaside; (*droit*) shipping, maritime.
marjolaine [màrzholen] *nf* marjoram.
mark [màrk] *nm* (*monnaie*) mark.
marketing [màrkətēng] *nm* (*COMM*) marketing.
marmaille [màrmáy] *nf* (*péj*) (gang of) brats *pl*.
marmelade [màrmǝlàd] *nf* (*compote*) stewed fruit, compote; ~ **d'oranges** (orange) marmalade; **en** ~ (*fig*) crushed (to a pulp).
marmite [màrmēt] *nf* (cooking-)pot.
marmiton [màrmētóǹ] *nm* kitchen boy.
marmonner [màrmonā] *vt*, *vi* to mumble, mutter.
marmot [màrmō] *nm* (*fam*) brat.
marmotte [màrmot] *nf* marmot.
marmotter [màrmotā] *vt* (*prière*) to mumble, mutter.
marne [màrn(ǝ)] *nf* (*GÉO*) marl.
Maroc [màrok] *nm*: **le** ~ Morocco.
marocain, e [màrokàǹ, -en] *a* Moroccan ♦ *nm/f*: **M**~, **e** Moroccan.
maroquin [màrokàǹ] *nm* (*peau*) morocco (leather); (*fig*) (minister's) portfolio.
maroquinerie [màrokēnrē] *nf* (*industrie*) leather craft; (*commerce*) leather shop; (*articles*) fine leather goods *pl*.
marotte [màrot] *nf* fad.
marquant, e [màrkàǹ, -àǹt] *a* outstanding.
marque [màrk(ǝ)] *nf* mark; (*SPORT*, *JEU*: *décompte des points*) score; (*COMM*: *de produits*) brand, make; (*: de disques*) label; (*insigne: d'une fonction*) badge; (*fig*): ~ **d'affection** token of affection; ~ **de joie** sign of joy; **à vos** ~**s!** (*SPORT*) on your marks!; **de** ~ *a* (*COMM*) brand-name *cpd*; proprietary; (*fig*) high-class; (*: personnage, hôte*) distinguished; **produit de** ~ (*COMM*) quality product; ~ **déposée** registered trademark; ~ **de fabrique** trademark.
marqué, e [màrkā] *a* marked.
marquer [màrkā] *vt* to mark; (*inscrire*) to write down; (*bétail*) to brand; (*SPORT*: *but etc*) to score; (*: joueur*) to mark; (*accentuer: taille etc*) to emphasize; (*manifester: refus, intérêt*) to show ♦ *vi*

(*événement, personnalité*) to stand out, be outstanding; (*SPORT*) to score; ~ **qn de son influence/empreinte** to have an influence/ leave its impression on sb; ~ **un temps d'arrêt** to pause momentarily; ~ **le pas** (*fig*) to mark time; **il a marqué ce jour-là d'une pierre blanche** that was a red-letter day for him; ~ **les points** (*tenir la marque*) to keep the score.
marqueté, e [màrkǝtā] *a* inlaid.
marqueterie [màrkǝtrē] *nf* inlaid work, marquetry.
marqueur, euse [màrkœr, -ēz] *nm/f* (*SPORT*: *de but*) scorer ♦ *nm* (*crayon feutre*) marker pen.
marquis, e [màrkē, -ēz] *nm/f* marquis *ou* marquess/marchioness ♦ *nf* (*auvent*) glass canopy *ou* awning.
Marquises [màrkēz] *nfpl*: **les (îles)** ~ the Marquesas Islands.
marraine [màren] *nf* godmother; (*d'un navire, d'une rose etc*) namer.
Marrakech [màràkesh] *n* Marrakech *ou* Marrakesh.
marrant, e [màràǹ, -àǹt] *a* (*fam*) funny.
marre [màr] *ad* (*fam*): **en avoir** ~ **de** to be fed up with.
marrer [màrā]: **se** ~ *vi* (*fam*) to have a (good) laugh.
marron, ne [màróǹ, -on] *nm* (*fruit*) chestnut ♦ *a inv* brown ♦ *a* (*péj*) crooked; (*: faux*) bogus; ~**s glacés** marrons glacés.
marronnier [màronyā] *nm* chestnut (tree).
Mars [màrs] *nm ou nf* Mars.
mars [màrs] *nm* March; *voir aussi* **juillet**.
marseillais, e [màrseye, -ez] *a* of *ou* from Marseilles ♦ *nf*: **la M**~**e** the French national anthem.
Marseille [màrsey] *n* Marseilles.
marsouin [màrswǎǹ] *nm* porpoise.
marsupiaux [màrsüpyō] *nmpl* marsupials.
marteau, x [màrtō] *nm* hammer; (*de porte*) knocker; ~ **pneumatique** pneumatic drill.
marteau-pilon, *pl* **marteaux-pilons** [màrtōpēlóǹ] *nm* drop (*US*) *ou* power (*Brit*) hammer.
marteau-piqueur, *pl* **marteaux-piqueurs** [màrtōpēkœr] *nm* pneumatic drill.
martel [màrtel] *nm*: **se mettre** ~ **en tête** to worry o.s.
martèlement [màrtelmàǹ] *nm* hammering.
marteler [màrtǝlā] *vt* to hammer; (*mots, phrases*) to rap out.
martial, e, aux [màrsyàl, -ō] *a* martial; **cour** ~**e** court-martial.
martien, ne [màrsyàǹ, -en] *a* Martian, of *ou* from Mars.
martinet [màrtēne] *nm* (*fouet*) small whip; (*ZOOL*) swift.
martingale [màrtàǹgàl] *nf* (*COUTURE*) half-belt; (*JEU*) winning formula.
martiniquais, e [màrtēnēke, -ez] *a* of *ou* from Martinique.
Martinique [màrtēnēk] *nf*: **la** ~ Martinique.
martin-pêcheur, *pl* **martins-pêcheurs** [màrtàǹpeshœr] *nm* kingfisher.
martre [màrtr(ǝ)] *nf* marten; ~ **zibeline** sable.
martyr, e [màrtēr] *nm/f* martyr ♦ *a* martyred; **enfants** ~**s** battered children.

martyre [mártēr] *nm* martyrdom; *(fig: sens affaibli)* agony, torture; **souffrir le** ~ to suffer agonies.

martyriser [mártērēzā] *vt (REL)* to martyr; *(fig)* to bully; *(: enfant)* to batter.

marxisme [márksēsm(ə)] *nm* Marxism.

marxiste [márksēst(ə)] *a, nm/f* Marxist.

mas [mâ(s)] *nm traditional house or farm in Provence.*

mascarade [máskárád] *nf* masquerade.

mascotte [máskot] *nf* mascot.

masculin, e [máskülañ, -ēn] *a* masculine; *(sexe, population)* male; *(équipe, vêtements)* men's; *(viril)* manly ♦ *nm* masculine.

masochisme [mázoshēsm(ə)] *nm* masochism.

masque [másk(ə)] *nm* mask; ~ **de beauté** face pack; ~ **à gaz** gas mask; ~ **de plongée** diving mask.

masqué, e [máskā] *a* masked.

masquer [máskā] *vt (cacher: porte, goût)* to hide, conceal; *(dissimuler: vérité, projet)* to mask, obscure.

massacrant, e [másákrâñ, âñt] *a*: **humeur** ~**e** foul temper.

massacre [másàkr(ə)] *nm* massacre, slaughter; *jeu de* ~ *(fig)* wholesale slaughter.

massacrer [másákrā] *vt* to massacre, slaughter; *(fig: adversaire)* to slaughter; *(: texte etc)* to murder.

massage [másázh] *nm* massage.

masse [más] *nf* mass; *(péj):* **la** ~ the masses *pl; (ÉLEC)* earth; *(maillet)* sledgehammer; ~**s** *nfpl* m̄asses; **une** ~ **de, des** ~**s de** *(fam)* masses *ou* loads of; **en** ~ *ad (en bloc)* in bulk; *(en foule)* en masse ♦ *a (exécutions, production)* mass *cpd;* ~ **monétaire** *(ÉCON)* money supply; ~ **salariale** *(COMM)* wage(s) bill.

massepain [máspañ] *nm* marzipan.

masser [másā] *vt (assembler)* to gather; *(pétrir)* to massage; **se** ~ *vi* to gather.

masseur, euse [másœr, -œz] *nm/f (personne)* masseur/masseuse ♦ *nm (appareil)* massager.

massicot [másēkō] *nm (TYPO)* guillotine.

massif, ive [másēf, -ēv] *a (porte)* solid, massive; *(visage)* heavy, large; *(bois, or)* solid; *(dose)* massive; *(déportations etc)* mass *cpd* ♦ *nm (montagneux)* massif; *(de fleurs)* clump, bank.

massue [mású] *nf* club, bludgeon ♦ *a inv:* **argument** ~ sledgehammer argument.

mastic [mástēk] *nm (pour vitres)* putty; *(pour fentes)* filler.

mastication [mástēkásyόñ] *nf* chewing, mastication.

mastiquer [mástēkā] *vt (aliment)* to chew, masticate; *(fente)* to fill; *(vitre)* to putty.

mastoc [mástok] *a inv* hefty.

mastodonte [mástodóñt] *nm* monster *(fig).*

masturbation [mástürbásyόñ] *nf* masturbation.

masturber [mástürbā] *vt:* **se** ~ to masturbate.

m'as-tu-vu [mátüvü] *nm/f inv* show-off.

masure [mázür] *nf* tumbledown cottage.

mat, e [mát] *a (couleur, métal)* mat(t); *(bruit, son)* dull ♦ *a inv (ÉCHECS):* **être** ~ to be checkmated.

mât [mâ] *nm (NAVIG)* mast; *(poteau)* pole, post.

matamore [mátámor] *nm* braggart, blusterer.

match [mátsh] *nm* match; ~ **nul** draw, tie *(US);* **faire** ~ **nul** to tie *(US),* draw *(Brit);* ~ **aller** first leg; ~ **retour** second leg, return match.

matelas [mátlá] *nm* mattress; ~ **pneumatique** air bed *ou* mattress; ~ **à ressorts** innerspring *(US) ou* interior-sprung *(Brit)* mattress.

matelasser [mátlásā] *vt* to pad.

matelot [mátlō] *nm* sailor, seaman.

mater [mátā] *vt (personne)* to bring to heel, subdue; *(révolte)* to put down; *(fam)* to watch, look at.

matérialiser [mátāryálēzā]: **se** ~ *vi* to materialize.

matérialisme [mátāryálēsm(ə)] *nm* materialism.

matérialiste [mátāryálēst(ə)] *a* materialistic ♦ *nm/f* materialist.

matériau, x [mátāryō] *nm* material; ~**x** *nmpl* material(s); ~**x de construction** building materials.

matériel, le [mátāryel] *a* material; *(organisation, aide, obstacle)* practical; *(fig: péj: personne)* materialistic ♦ *nm* equipment *q; (de camping etc)* gear *q;* **il n'a pas le temps** ~ **de le faire** he doesn't have the time (needed) to do it; ~ **d'exploitation** *(COMM)* plant; ~ **roulant** rolling stock.

maternel, le [mátérnel] *a (amour, geste)* motherly, maternal; *(grand-père, oncle)* maternal ♦ *nf (aussi:* **école** ~**le)** (state) nursery school.

materner [máternā] *vt (personne)* to mother.

maternité [máterneta] *nf (établissement)* maternity hospital; *(état de mère)* motherhood, maternity; *(grossesse)* pregnancy.

math [mát] *nfpl* math *(US),* maths *(Brit).*

mathématicien, ne [mátāmátēsyañ, -en] *nm/f* mathematician.

mathématique [mátámátēk] *a* mathematical.

mathématiques [mátámátēk] *nfpl* mathematics *sg.*

matheux, euse [mátœ, -œz] *nm/f (fam)* math *(US) ou* maths *(Brit)* student; *(fort en math)* mathematical genius.

maths [mát] *nfpl* math *(US),* maths *(Brit).*

matière [mátyer] *nf (PHYSIQUE)* matter; *(COMM, TECH)* material, matter *q; (fig: d'un livre etc)* subject matter; *(SCOL)* subject; **en** ~ **de** as regards; **donner** ~ **à** to give cause to; ~ **grise** gray *(US) ou* grey *(Brit)* matter; ~ **plastique** plastic; ~**s fécales** feces *(US),* faeces *(Brit);* ~**s grasses** fat (content) *sg;* ~**s premières** raw materials.

MATIF [mátēf] *sigle m* (= *Marché à terme des instruments financiers*) *body which regulates the activities of the French Stock Exchange.*

Matignon [mátēnyόñ] *n French prime minister's offices.*

matin [mátañ] *nm, ad* morning; **le** ~ *(pendant le* ~) in the morning; **demain** ~ tomorrow morning; **le lendemain** ~ (the) next morning; **du** ~ **au soir** from morning till night; **une heure du** ~ one o'clock in the morning; **de grand** *ou* **bon** ~ early in the morning.

matinal, e, aux [mátēnál, -ō] *a (toilette,*

gymnastique) morning *cpd*; (*de bonne heure*) early; **être** ~ (*personne*) to be up early; (*: habituellement*) to be an early riser.

mâtiné, e [mátēnā] *a* crossbred, mixed race *cpd*.

matinée [mátēnā] *nf* morning; (*spectacle*) matinée, afternoon performance.

matois, e [mátwá, -wáz] *a* wily.

matou [mátōō] *nm* tom(cat).

matraquage [mátrákázh] *nm* beating up; ~ **publicitaire** plug, plugging.

matraque [mátrák] *nf* (*de malfaiteur*) club; (*de policier*) billy (*US*), truncheon (*Brit*).

matraquer [mátrákā] *vt* to beat up (with a truncheon *ou* billy); to club; (*fig: touristes etc*) to rip off; (*: disque*) to plug.

matriarcal, e, aux [mátrēyárkál, -ō] *a* matriarchal.

matrice [mátrēs] *nf* (*ANAT*) womb; (*TECH*) mold (*US*), mould (*Brit*); (*MATH etc*) matrix.

matricule [mátrēkül] *nf* (*aussi:* **registre** ~) roll, register ♦ *nm* (*aussi:* **numéro** ~: *MIL*) regimental number; (*: ADMIN*) reference number.

matrimonial, e, aux [mátrēmonyál, -ō] *a* marital, marriage *cpd*.

matrone [mátron] *nf* matron.

mâture [mátür] *nf* masts *pl*.

maturité [mátürētā] *nf* maturity; (*d'un fruit*) ripeness, maturity.

maudire [mōdēr] *vt* to curse.

maudit, e [mōdē, ēt] *a* (*fam: satané*) blasted, confounded.

maugréer [mōgrāā] *vi* to grumble.

mauresque [moresk(ə)] *a* Moorish.

Maurice [morēs] *nf*: (**l'île**) ~ Mauritius.

mauricien, ne [morēsyaṅ, -en] *a* Mauritian.

Mauritanie [morētánē] *nf*: **la** ~ Mauritania.

mauritanien, ne [morētányaṅ, -en] *a* Mauritanian.

mausolée [mōzolā] *nm* mausoleum.

maussade [mōsád] *a* (*air, personne*) sullen; (*ciel, temps*) dismal.

mauvais, e [move, -ez] *a* bad; (*faux*): **le** ~ **numéro/moment** the wrong number/moment; (*méchant, malveillant*) malicious, spiteful ♦ *nm*: **le** ~ the bad side ♦ *ad*: **il fait** ~ the weather is bad; **sentir** ~ to have a nasty smell, smell bad *ou* nasty; **la mer est** ~**e** the sea is rough; ~ **coucheur** tough customer; ~ **coup** (*fig*) criminal venture; ~ **garçon** tough; ~ **pas** tight spot; ~ **plaisant** hoaxer; ~ **traitements** ill treatment *sg*; ~**e herbe** weed; ~**e langue** gossip, scandalmonger; ~**e passe** difficult situation; (*période*) rough time; ~**e tête** rebellious *ou* headstrong customer.

mauve [mōv] *a* (*couleur*) mauve ♦ *nf* (*BOT*) mallow.

mauviette [mōvyet] *nf* (*péj*) weakling.

maux [mō] *nmpl voir* **mal**.

max. *abr* (= *maximum*) max.

maximal, e, aux [máksēmál, -ō] *a* maximal.

maxime [máksēm] *nf* maxim.

maximum [máksēmom] *a, nm* maximum; **atteindre un/son** ~ to reach a/his peak; **au** ~ *ad* (*le plus possible*) to the full; as much as one can; (*tout au plus*) at the (very) most *ou* maximum.

Mayence [máyâṅs] *n* Mainz.

mayonnaise [máyonez] *nf* mayonnaise.

Mayotte [máyot] *nf* Mayotte.

mazout [mázōōt] *nm* (fuel) oil; **chaudière/poêle à** ~ oil-fired boiler/stove.

mazouté, e [mázōōtā] *a* oil-polluted.

MDM *sigle mpl* (= *Médecins du Monde*) medical association for aid to Third World countries.

M⁰ *abr* = **Maître**.

me, m' [m(ə)] *pronom* me; (*réfléchi*) myself.

méandres [māâṅdr(ə)] *nmpl* meanderings.

mec [mek] *nm* (*fam*) guy.

mécanicien, ne [mākánēsyaṅ, -en] *nm/f* mechanic; (*RAIL*) engineer (*US*), (train *ou* engine) driver (*Brit*); ~ **navigant** *ou* **de bord** (*AVIAT*) flight engineer.

mécanicien-dentiste [mākánēsyaṅdâṅtēst(ə)], **mécanicienne-dentiste** [mākánēsyen-] (*pl* ~**s**-~**s**) *nm/f* dental technician.

mécanique [mākánēk] *a* mechanical ♦ *nf* (*science*) mechanics *sg*; (*technologie*) mechanical engineering; (*mécanisme*) mechanism; engineering; works *pl*; **ennui** ~ engine trouble *q*; **s'y connaître en** ~ to be mechanically inclined; ~ **hydraulique** hydraulics *sg*; ~ **ondulataire** wave mechanics *sg*.

mécaniquement [mākánēkmâṅ] *ad* mechanically.

mécanisation [mākánēzásyóṅ] *nf* mechanization.

mécaniser [mākánēzā] *vt* to mechanize.

mécanisme [makanesm(ə)] *nm* mechanism.

mécano [mākánō] *nm* (*fam*) mechanic.

mécanographie [mākánográfē] *nf* (mechanical) data processing.

mécène [māsen] *nm* patron.

méchamment [māshámâṅ] *ad* nastily, maliciously, spitefully; viciously.

méchanceté [māshâṅstā] *nf* (*d'une personne, d'une parole*) nastiness, maliciousness; spitefulness; (*parole, action*) nasty *ou* spiteful *ou* malicious remark (*ou* action).

méchant, e [māshâṅ, -âṅt] *a* nasty, malicious, spiteful; (*enfant: pas sage*) naughty; (*animal*) vicious; (*avant le nom: valeur péjorative*) nasty; miserable; (*: intensive*) terrific.

mèche [mesh] *nf* (*de lampe, bougie*) wick; (*d'un explosif*) fuze (*US*), fuse (*Brit*); (*MÉD*) pack, dressing; (*de vilebrequin, perceuse*) bit; (*de dentiste*) drill; (*de fouet*) lash; (*de cheveux*) lock; **se faire faire des** ~**s** (*chez le coiffeur*) to have one's hair streaked, have highlights put in one's hair; **vendre la** ~ to give the game away; **de** ~ **avec** in league with.

méchoui [māshwē] *nm* whole sheep barbecue.

mécompte [mākóṅt] *nm* (*erreur*) miscalculation; (*déception*) disappointment.

méconnais [mākone] *etc vb voir* **méconnaître**.

méconnaissable [mākonesábl(ə)] *a* unrecognizable.

méconnaissais [mākonese] *etc vb voir* **méconnaître**.

méconnaissance [mākonesâṅs] *nf* ignorance.

méconnaître [mākonetr(ə)] *vt* (*ignorer*) to be unaware of; (*mésestimer*) to misjudge.

méconnu, e [mākonü] *pp de* **méconnaître** ♦ *a* (*génie etc*) unrecognized.

mécontent, e [mākôṅtáṅ, -áṅt] *a*: ~ **(de)** (*insatisfait*) discontented *ou* dissatisfied *ou* displeased (with); (*contrarié*) annoyed (at) ♦ *nm/f* malcontent, dissatisfied person.

mécontentement [mākôṅtáṅtmáṅ] *nm* dissatisfaction, discontent, displeasure; annoyance.

mécontenter [mākôṅtáṅtā] *vt* to displease.

Mecque [mek] *nf*: **la** ~ Mecca.

mécréant, e [mākrāáṅ, -áṅt] *a* (*peuple*) infidel; (*personne*) atheistic.

méd. *abr* = **médecin**.

médaille [mādáy] *nf* medal.

médaillé, e [mādáyā] *nm/f* (*SPORT*) medalholder.

médaillon [mādáyôṅ] *nm* (*portrait*) medallion; (*bijou*) locket; (*CULIN*) thin, round slice (*of meat etc*), médaillon (*Brit*); **en** ~ *a* (*carte etc*) inset.

médecin [medsaṅ] *nm* doctor; ~ **du bord** (*NAVIG*) ship's doctor; ~ **généraliste** general practitioner, GP; ~ **légiste** medical examiner (*US*), forensic scientist (*Brit*); ~ **traitant** family doctor, GP.

médecine [medsēn] *nf* medicine; ~ **générale** general medicine; ~ **infantile** pediatrics *sg* (*US*), paediatrics *sg* (*Brit*); ~ **légale** forensic medicine; ~ **préventive** preventive medicine; ~ **du travail** occupational *ou* industrial medicine.

médian, e [mādyáṅ, -àn] *a* median.

médias [mādyá] *nmpl*: **les** ~ the media.

médiateur, trice [mādyàtœr, -trēs] *nm/f* (*voir médiation*) mediator; arbitrator.

médiathèque [mādyátek] *nf* media library.

médiation [mādyâsyôṅ] *nf* mediation; (*dans conflit social etc*) arbitration.

médiatique [mādyátēk] *a* media *cpd*.

médiator [mādyátor] *nm* plectrum.

médical, e, aux [mādēkál, -ō] *a* medical; **visiteur** *ou* **délégué** ~ medical rep *ou* representative.

médicament [mādēkámáṅ] *nm* medicine, drug.

médicamenteux, euse [mādēkámáṅtœ̄, -œ̄z] *a* medicinal.

médication [mādēkásyôṅ] *nf* medication.

médicinal, e, aux [mādēsēnál, -ō] *a* medicinal.

médico-légal, e, aux [mādēkolágál, -ō] *a* forensic.

médiéval, e, aux [mādyávál, -ō] *a* medieval.

médiocre [mādyokr(ə)] *a* mediocre, poor.

médiocrité [mādyokrētā] *nf* mediocrity.

médire [mādēr] *vi*: ~ **de** to speak ill of.

médisance [mādēzáṅs] *nf* scandalmongering *q*, mudslinging *q*; (*propos*) piece of scandal *ou* malicious gossip.

médisant, e [mādēzáṅ, -áṅt] *vb voir* **médire** ♦ *a* slanderous, malicious.

médit, e [mādē, -ēt] *pp de* **médire**.

méditatif, ive [mādētátēf, -ēv] *a* thoughtful.

méditation [mādētásyôṅ] *nf* meditation.

méditer [mādētā] *vt* (*approfondir*) to meditate on, ponder (over); (*combiner*) to meditate ♦ *vi* to meditate; ~ **de faire** to contemplate doing, plan to do.

Méditerranée [mādēteránā] *nf*: **la (mer)** ~ the Mediterranean (Sea).

méditerranéen, ne [mādēteránāáṅ, -en] *a*

Mediterranean ♦ *nm/f*: **M**~, **ne** Mediterranean.

médium [mādyom] *nm* medium (*spiritualist*).

médius [mādyüs] *nm* middle finger.

méduse [mādüz] *nf* jellyfish.

méduser [mādüzā] *vt* to dumbfound.

meeting [mētēng] *nm* (*POL*) rally, meeting; (*SPORT*) meet (*US*), meeting (*Brit*); ~ **d'aviation** air show.

méfait [māfe] *nm* (*faute*) misdemeanor (*US*), misdemeanour (*Brit*), wrongdoing; ~**s** *nmpl* (*ravages*) ravages.

méfiance [māfyáṅs] *nf* mistrust, distrust.

méfiant, e [māfyáṅ, -áṅt] *a* mistrustful, distrustful.

méfier [māfyā]: **se** ~ *vi* to be wary; (*faire attention*) to be careful; **se** ~ **de** *vt* to mistrust, distrust, be wary of; to be careful about.

mégalomane [māgálomán] *a* megalomaniac.

mégalomanie [māgálománē] *nf* megalomania.

méga-octet [māgáokte] *nm* megabyte.

mégarde [māgárd(ə)] *nf*: **par** ~ accidentally; (*par erreur*) by mistake.

mégatonne [māgáton] *nf* megaton.

mégère [māzher] *nf* (*péj: femme*) shrew.

mégot [māgō] *nm* cigarette end *ou* butt.

mégoter [māgotā] *vi* to nitpick.

meilleur, e [meyœr] *a, ad* better; (*valeur superlative*) best ♦ *nm*: **le** ~ (*celui qui ...*) the best (one); (*ce qui ...*) the best ♦ *nf*: **la** ~**e** the best (one); **le** ~ **des deux** the better of the two; **de** ~**e heure** earlier; ~ **marché** cheaper.

méjuger [māzhüzhā] *vt* to misjudge.

mélancolie [māláṅkolē] *nf* melancholy, gloom.

mélancolique [māláṅkolēk] *a* melancholy, gloomy.

mélange [māláṅzh] *nm* (*opération*) mixing; blending; (*résultat*) mixture; blend; **sans** ~ unadulterated.

mélanger [māláṅzhā] *vt* (*substances*) to mix; (*vins, couleurs*) to blend; (*mettre en désordre, confondre*) to mix up, muddle (up); **se** ~ (*liquides, couleurs*) to blend, mix.

mélanine [mālánēn] *nf* melanin.

mélasse [mālás] *nf* treacle, molasses *sg*.

mêlée [mālā] *nf* (*bataille, cohue*) mêlée, scramble; (*lutte, conflit*) tussle, scuffle; (*RUGBY*) scrum(mage).

mêler [mālā] *vt* (*substances, odeurs, races*) to mix; (*embrouiller*) to muddle (up), mix up; **se** ~ to mix; (*se joindre, s'allier*) to mingle; **se** ~ **à** (*suj: personne*) to join; to mix with; (*: odeurs etc*) to mingle with; **se** ~ **de** (*suj: personne*) to meddle with, interfere in; **mêle-toi de tes affaires!** mind your own business!; ~ **à** *ou* **avec** *ou* **de** to mix with; to mingle with; ~ **qn à** (*affaire*) to get sb mixed up *ou* involved in.

mélo [mālō] *nm, a* = **mélodrame**, **mélodramatique**.

mélodie [mālodē] *nf* melody.

mélodieux, euse [mālodyœ̄, -œ̄z] *a* melodious, tuneful.

mélodique [mālodēk] *a* melodic.

mélodramatique [mālodrámátēk] *a* melodramatic.

mélodrame [mālodrám] *nm* melodrama.

mélomane [mālomán] *nm/f* music lover.

melon [məlôň] *nm* (*BOT*) (honeydew) melon; (*aussi*: chapeau ~) derby (*US*) *ou* bowler (*Brit*) (hat); ~ **d'eau** watermelon.

mélopée [mālopā] *nf* monotonous chant.

membrane [mãňbrán] *nf* membrane.

membre [mãňbr(ə)] *nm* (*ANAT*) limb; (*personne, pays, élément*) member ♦ *a* member; **être ~ de** to be a member of; ~ (**viril**) (male) organ.

mémé [māmā] *nf* (*fam*) granny; (: *vieille femme*) old dear.

même [mɛm] *a* same ♦ *pronom*: **le (la)** ~ the same (one) ♦ *ad* even; **en ~ temps** at the same time; **ils ont les ~s goûts** they have the same tastes; **ce sont ses paroles/celles-là** ~**s** they are his very words/the very ones; **il est la loyauté** ~ he is loyalty itself, he is loyalty personified; **il n'a ~ pas pleuré** he didn't even cry; **ici** ~ at this very place; ~ **lui a ... even he has ...; à ~ la bouteille** straight from the bottle; **à ~ la peau** next to the skin; **être à ~ de faire** to be in a position *ou* be able to do, **mettre qn à ~ de faire** to enable sb to do; **faire de ~** to do likewise; **lui de ~** so does (*ou* did *ou* is) he; **de lui-~** on his own initiative; **de ~ que** just as; **il en va/est allé de ~ pour** the same goes/happened for; ~ **si** even if.

mémento [māmãňtō] *nm* (*agenda*) appointment book; (*ouvrage*) summary.

mémoire [māmwár] *nf* memory ♦ *nm* (*ADMIN, JUR*) memorandum (*pl* -a); (*SCOL*) dissertation, paper; **avoir la ~ des visages/chiffres** to have a (good) memory for faces/figures; **n'avoir aucune ~** to have a terrible memory; **avoir de la ~** to have a good memory; **à la ~ de** to the *ou* in memory of; **pour ~** *ad* for the record; **de ~** *ad* from memory; **de ~ d'homme** in living memory; **mettre en ~** (*INFORM*) to store; ~ **morte** ROM; ~ **rémanente** *ou* **non volatile** non-volatile memory; ~ **vive** RAM.

mémoires [māmwár] *nmpl* memoirs.

mémorable [māmorábl(ə)] *a* memorable.

mémorandum [māmorándom] *nm* memorandum (*pl* -a); (*carnet*) notebook.

mémorial, aux [māmoryál, -ō] *nm* memorial.

mémoriser [māmorēzā] *vt* to memorize; (*INFORM*) to store.

menaçant, e [mənásãň, -áňt] *a* threatening, menacing.

menace [mənás] *nf* threat; ~ **en l'air** empty threat.

menacer [mənásā] *vt* to threaten; ~ **qn de qch/de faire qch** to threaten sb with sth/to do sth.

ménage [mānázh] *nm* (*travail*) housekeeping, housework; (*couple*) (married) couple; (*famille, ADMIN*) household; **faire le ~** to do the housework; **faire des ~s** to work as a housekeeper (*US*) *ou* cleaner (*Brit*) (*in people's homes*); **monter son ~** to set up house; **se mettre en ~ (avec)** to set up house (with); **heureux en ~** happily married; **faire bon ~ avec** to get along well with; ~ **de poupée** doll's kitchen set; ~ **à trois** love triangle.

ménagement [mānázhmãň] *nm* care and

attention; ~**s** *nmpl* (*égards*) consideration *sg*, attention *sg*.

ménager [mānázhā] *vt* (*traiter avec mesure*) to handle with tact; to treat considerately; (*utiliser*) to use with care; (: *avec économie*) to use sparingly; (*prendre soin de*) to take (great) care of, look after; (*organiser*) to arrange; (*installer*) to put in; to make; **se ~** to look after o.s.; ~ **qch à qn** (*réserver*) to have sth in store for sb.

ménager, ère [mānázhā, -er] *a* household *cpd*, domestic ♦ *nf* (*femme*) housewife (*pl* -wives); (*couverts*) silverware tray (*US*), canteen (of cutlery) (*Brit*).

ménagerie [mānázhrē] *nf* menagerie.

mendiant, e [mãňdyãň, -ãňt] *nm/f* beggar.

mendicité [mãňdēsētā] *nf* begging.

mendier [mãňdyā] *vi* to beg ♦ *vt* to beg (for); (*fig: éloges, compliments*) to fish for.

menées [mənā] *nfpl* intrigues, maneuvers (*US*), manœuvres (*Brit*); (*COMM*) activities.

mener [mənā] *vt* to lead; (*enquête*) to conduct; (*affaires*) to manage, conduct, run ♦ *vi*: ~ (**à la marque**) to lead, be in the lead; ~ **à/dans** (*emmener*) to take to/into; ~ **qch à bonne fin** *ou* **à terme** *ou* **à bien** to see sth through (to a successful conclusion), complete sth successfully.

meneur, euse [mənœr, -ēz] *nm/f* leader; (*péj: agitateur*) ringleader; ~ **d'hommes** born leader; ~ **de jeu** host, quizmaster.

menhir [mānēr] *nm* standing stone.

méningite [mānãňzhēt] *nf* meningitis *q*.

ménopause [mānopōz] *nf* menopause.

menotte [mənot] *nf* (*langage enfantin*) little hand; ~**s** *nfpl* handcuffs; **passer les ~s à** to handcuff.

mens [mãň] *vb voir* **mentir**.

mensonge [mãňsôňzh] *nm*: **le ~** lying *q*; **un ~** a lie.

mensonger, ère [mãňsôňzhā, -er] *a* false.

menstruation [mãňstrüásyôň] *nf* menstruation.

menstruel, le [mãňstrüel] *a* menstrual.

mensualiser [mãňsüálzhēt] *vt* to pay monthly.

mensualité [mãňsüálētā] *nf* (*somme payée*) monthly payment; (*somme perçue*) monthly salary.

mensuel, le [mãňsüel] *a* monthly ♦ *nm/f* (*employé*) employee paid monthly ♦ *nm* (*PRESSE*) monthly.

mensuellement [mãňsüelmãň] *ad* monthly.

mensurations [mãňsürásyôň] *nfpl* measurements.

mentais [mãňte] *etc vb voir* **mentir**.

mental, e, aux [mãňtál, -ō] *a* mental.

mentalement [mãňtálmãň] *ad* in one's head, mentally.

mentalité [mãňtálētā] *nf* mentality.

menteur, euse [mãňtœr, -ēz] *nm/f* liar.

menthe [mãňt] *nf* mint; ~ (**à l'eau**) mint-flavored water (*drink*).

mentholé, e [mãňtolā] *a* menthol *cpd*, mentholated.

mention [mãňsyôň] *nf* (*note*) note, comment; (*SCOL*): ~ (**très**) **bien/passable** (*very*) *good/* satisfactory passmark; **faire ~ de** to mention; "**rayer la ~ inutile**" "delete as appropriate".

mentionner [mâṅsyonā] *vt* to mention.

mentir [mâṅtēr] *vi* to lie.

menton [mâṅtóṅ] *nm* chin.

mentonnière [mâṅtonyer] *nf* chin strap.

menu, e [mǝnü] *a* (*mince*) thin; (*petit*) tiny; (*frais, difficulté*) minor ♦ *ad* (*couper, hacher*) very fine ♦ *nm* menu; **par le ~** (*raconter*) in minute detail; **~ touristique** popular *ou* tourist menu; **~e monnaie** small change.

menuet [mǝnüe] *nm* minuet.

menuiserie [mǝnüēzrē] *nf* (*travail*) joinery, carpentry; (*d'amateur*) woodwork; (*local*) joiner's workshop; (*ouvrages*) woodwork *q*.

menuisier [mǝnüēzyā] *nm* joiner, carpenter.

méprendre [māprâṅdr(ǝ)]: **se ~** *vi*: **se ~ sur** to be mistaken about.

mépris, e [māprē, -ēz] *pp de* **méprendre** ♦ *nm* (*dédain*) contempt, scorn; (*indifférence*): **le ~ de** contempt *ou* disregard for; **au ~ de** regardless of, in defiance of.

méprisable [māprēzábl(ǝ)] *a* contemptible, despicable.

méprisant, e [māprēzâṅ, -âṅt] *a* contemptuous, scornful.

méprise [māprēz] *nf* mistake, error; (*malentendu*) misunderstanding.

mépriser [māprēzā] *vt* to scorn, despise; (*gloire, danger*) to scorn, spurn.

mer [mer] *nf* sea; (*marée*) tide; **~ fermée** inland sea; **en ~** at sea; **prendre la ~** to put out to sea; **en haute** *ou* **pleine ~** off shore, on the open sea; **la ~ Adriatique** the Adriatic (Sea); **la ~ des Antilles** *ou* **des Caraïbes** the Caribbean (Sea); **la ~ Baltique** the Baltic (Sea); **la ~ Caspienne** the Caspian Sea; **la ~ de Corail** the Coral Sea; **la ~ Égée** the Aegean (Sea); **la ~ Ionienne** the Ionian Sea; **la ~ Morte** the Dead Sea; **la ~ Noire** the Black Sea; **la ~ du Nord** the North Sea; **la ~ Rouge** the Red Sea; **la ~ des Sargasses** the Sargasso Sea; **les ~s du Sud** the South Seas; **la ~ Tyrrhénienne** the Tyrrhenian Sea.

mercantile [merkâṅtēl] *a* (*péj*) mercenary.

mercenaire [mersǝner] *nm* mercenary.

mercerie [mersǝrē] *nf* (*COUTURE*) notions *pl* (*US*), haberdashery (*Brit*); (*boutique*) notions store (*US*), haberdasher's shop (*Brit*).

merci [mersē] *excl* thank you ♦ *nf*: **à la ~ de qn/qch** at sb's mercy/the mercy of sth; **~ beaucoup** thank you very much; **~ de** *ou* **pour** thank you for; **sans ~** *a* merciless ♦ *ad* mercilessly.

mercier, ière [mersyā, -yer] *nm/f* notions dealer (*US*), haberdasher (*Brit*).

mercredi [merkrǝdē] *nm* Wednesday; **~ des Cendres** Ash Wednesday; *voir aussi* **lundi**.

mercure [merkür] *nm* mercury.

merde [merd(ǝ)] (*fam!*) *nf* shit (*!*) ♦ *excl* hell (*!*).

merdeux, euse [merdœ, -œz] *nm/f* (*fam!*) little devil.

mère [mer] *nf* mother ♦ *a inv* mother *cpd*; **~ célibataire** single parent, unmarried mother.

merguez [mergez] *nf* spicy North African sausage.

méridien [mārēdyaṅ] *nm* meridian.

méridional, e, aux [mārēdyonál, -ō] *a* southern; (*du midi de la France*) Southern (French) ♦ *nm/f* Southerner.

meringue [mǝraṅg] *nf* meringue.

mérinos [mārēnōs] *nm* merino.

merisier [mǝrēzyā] *nm* wild cherry (tree).

méritant, e [mārētâṅ, -âṅt] *a* deserving.

mérite [mārēt] *nm* merit; **le ~ (de ceci) lui revient** the credit (for this) is his.

mériter [mārētā] *vt* to deserve; **~ de réussir** to deserve to succeed; **il mérite qu'on fasse** ... he deserves people to do ....

méritocratie [mārētokrásē] *nf* meritocracy.

méritoire [mārētwár] *a* praiseworthy, commendable.

merlan [merlâṅ] *nm* whiting.

merle [merl(ǝ)] *nm* blackbird.

mérou [mārōō] *nm* grouper (*fish*).

merveille [mervey] *nf* marvel, wonder; **faire ~** *ou* **des ~s** to work wonders; **à ~** perfectly, wonderfully.

merveilleux, euse [merveyœ, -œz] *a* marvellous, wonderful.

mes [mā] *dét voir* **mon**.

mésalliance [māzályâṅs] *nf* misalliance, mismatch.

mésallier [māzályā]: **se ~** *vi* to marry beneath (*ou* above) o.s.

mésange [māzâṅzh] *nf* tit(mouse) (*pl* -mice); **~ bleue** bluetit.

mésaventure [māzávâṅtür] *nf* misadventure, misfortune.

Mesdames [mādâm] *nfpl voir* **Madame**.

Mesdemoiselles [mādmwázel] *nfpl voir* **Mademoiselle**.

mésentente [māzâṅtâṅt] *nf* dissension, disagreement.

mésestimer [māzestēmā] *vt* to underestimate, underrate.

Mésopotamie [māzopotámē] *nf*: **la ~** Mesopotamia.

mésopotamien, ne [māzopotámyaṅ, -en] *a* Mesopotamian.

mesquin, e [meskaṅ, -ēn] *a* mean, petty.

mesquinerie [meskēnrē] *nf* meanness *q*, pettiness *q*.

mess [mes] *nm* mess.

message [māsázh] *nm* message; **~ d'erreur** (*INFORM*) error message; **~ (de guidage)** (*INFORM*) prompt; **~ publicitaire** ad, advertisement; **~ téléphoné** telegram dictated by telephone.

messager, ère [māsázhā, -er] *nm/f* messenger.

messagerie [māsázhrē] *nf*: **~ (électronique)** (electronic) bulletin board; **~ rose** *lonely hearts and contact service on videotext*; **~s aériennes/ maritimes** air freight/shipping service *sg*; **~s de presse** press distribution service.

messe [mes] *nf* mass; **aller à la ~** to go to mass; **~ de minuit** midnight mass; **faire des ~s basses** (*fig, péj*) to mutter.

messie [māsē] *nm*: **le M~** the Messiah.

Messieurs [māsyœ] *nmpl voir* **Monsieur**.

mesure [mǝzür] *nf* (*évaluation, dimension*) measurement; (*étalon, récipient, contenu*) measure; (*MUS: cadence*) time, tempo; (*: division*) bar; (*retenue*) moderation; (*disposition*) measure, step; **unité/système de ~** unit/system of measurement; **sur ~** (*costume*) made-to-order (*US*), made-to-measure (*Brit*); (*fig*) personally adapted; **à**

la ~ **de** (*fig: personne*) worthy of; (*chambre etc*) on the same scale as; **dans la** ~ **où** insofar as, inasmuch as; **dans une certaine** ~ to some *ou* a certain extent; **à** ~ **que** as; **en** ~ (*MUS*) in time *ou* tempo; **être en** ~ **de** to be in a position to; **dépasser la** ~ (*fig*) to overstep the bounds (*US*) *ou* mark (*Brit*).

mesuré, e [məzürā] *a* (*ton, effort*) measured; (*personne*) restrained.

mesurer [məzürā] *vt* to measure; (*juger*) to weigh, assess; (*limiter*) to limit, ration; (*modérer*) to moderate; (*proportionner*): ~ **qch à** to match sth to, gear sth to; **se** ~ **avec** to have a confrontation with; to tackle; **il mesure 1 m 80** he's 1 m 80 tall.

met [mc] *vb voir* **mettre**.

métabolisme [mātàbolēsm(ə)] *nm* metabolism.

métairie [mātārē] *nf* small farm.

métal, aux [mātál, -ō] *nm* metal.

métalangage [mātálàṅgázh] *nm* metalanguage.

métallique [mātálēk] *a* metallic.

métallisé, e [mātálēzā] *a* metallic.

métallurgie [mātálürzhē] *nf* metallurgy.

métallurgiste [mātálürzhēst(ə)] *nm/f* (*ouvrier*) steel *ou* metal worker; (*industriel*) metallurgist.

métamorphose [mātàmorfōz] *nf* metamorphosis (*pl* -oses).

métaphore [mātáfor] *nf* metaphor.

métaphorique [mātáforēk] *a* metaphorical, figurative.

métaphysique [mātáfēzēk] *nf* metaphysics *sg* ♦ *a* metaphysical.

métapsychique [mātàpsēshēk] *a* psychic, parapsychological.

métayer, ère [mātāyā, mātcyer] *nm/f* sharecropper (*US*), (tenant) farmer (*Brit*).

météo [mātāō] *nf* (*bulletin*) (weather) forecast; (*service*) ≈ National Weather Service (*US*), ≈ Met Office (*Brit*).

météore [mātāor] *nm* meteor.

météorite [mātāorēt] *nf* meteorite.

météorologie [mātāorolozhē] *nf* (*étude*) meteorology; (*service*) ≈ National Weather Service (*US*), ≈ Meteorological Office (*Brit*).

météorologique [mātāorolozhēk] *a* meteorological, weather *cpd*.

météorologue [mātāorolog] *nm/f*, **météorologiste** [mātāorolozhēst(ə)] *nm/f* meteorologist, weather forecaster.

métèque [mātek] *nm* (*péj*) wop.

méthane [mātán] *nm* methane.

méthanier [mātànyā] *nm* (*bateau*) (liquefied) gas carrier *ou* tanker.

méthode [mātod] *nf* method; (*livre, ouvrage*) manual, primer.

méthodique [mātodēk] *a* methodical.

méthodiste [mātodēst(ə)] *a*, *nm/f* (*REL*) Methodist.

méthylène [mātēlen] *nm*: **bleu de** ~ *nm* methylene blue.

méticuleux, euse [mātēkülœ̄, -œ̄z] *a* meticulous.

métier [mātyā] *nm* (*profession: gén*) job; (*: manuel*) trade; (*: artisanal*) craft; (*technique, expérience*) (acquired) skill *ou* technique; (*aussi:* ~ **à tisser**) (weaving)

loom; **être du** ~ to be in the trade *ou* profession.

métis, se [mātēs] *a, nm/f* half-caste, half-breed.

métisser [mātēsā] *vt* to cross(breed).

métrage [mātrázh] *nm* (*de tissu*) length; (*CINÉMA*) footage, length; **long/moyen** ~ feature *ou* full-length/medium-length film; **court** ~ short (film (*Brit*)).

mètre [metr(ə)] *nm* meter (*US*), metre (*Brit*); (*règle*) (meter *ou* metre) rule; (*ruban*) tape measure; ~ **carré/cube** square/cubic meter *ou* metre.

métrer [mātrā] *vt* (*TECH*) to measure (in meters *ou* metres); (*CONSTR*) to survey.

métreur, euse [mātrœr, -œ̄z] *nm/f*: ~ (**vérificateur**), **métreuse** (**vérificatrice**) (quantity) surveyor.

métrique [mātrēk] *a* metric ♦ *nf* metrics *sg*.

métro [mātrō] *nm* subway (*US*), underground (*Brit*).

métronome [mātronom] *nm* metronome.

métropole [mātropol] *nf* (*capitale*) metropolis; (*pays*) mother country.

métropolitain, e [matropoletan, -en] *a* metropolitan.

mets [me] *nm* dish ♦ *vb voir* **mettre**.

mettable [metábl(ə)] *a* fit to be worn, decent.

metteur [metœr] *nm*: ~ **en scène** (*THÉÂTRE*) producer; (*CINÉMA*) director; ~ **en ondes** (*RADIO*) producer.

mettre [metr(ə)] *vt* (*placer*) to put; (*vêtement: revêtir*) to turn on; (*: porter*) to wear; (*installer: gaz, électricité*) to put in; (*faire fonctionner: chauffage, électricité*) to turn on; (*: réveil*) to set; (*noter, écrire*) to say, put down; (*dépenser*) to lay out, give; (*supposer*): **mettons que** let's suppose *ou* say that; ~ **en bouteille/en sac** to bottle/put in bags *ou* sacks; ~ **qn/qch en terre** to bury sb/plant sth; ~ **à la poste** to mail; ~ **une note gaie/amusante** to inject a cheerful/an amusing note; **y** ~ **du sien** to pull one's weight; ~ **du temps/2 heures à faire** to take time/2 hours to do; ~ **qn debout** to stand sb up; **se** ~: **n'avoir rien à se** ~ to have nothing to wear; **se** ~ **de l'encre sur les doigts** to get ink on one's fingers; **se** ~ **au lit** to get into bed; **se** ~ **au piano** (*s'asseoir*) to sit down at the piano; (*apprendre*) to start learning the piano; **se** ~ **à l'eau** to get into the water; **se** ~ **bien/mal avec qn** to get on sb's good/bad side; **se** ~ **qn à dos** to alienate sb, turn sb against one; **se** ~ **avec qn** (*prendre parti*) to side with *ou* go along with sb; (*en ménage*) to move in with sb; **se** ~ **à faire** to begin *ou* start doing *ou* to do; **se** ~ **au travail/à l'étude** to get down to work/one's studies.

meublant, e [mœblàṅ, -áṅt] *a* (*tissus etc*) effective (in the room).

meuble [mœbl(ə)] *nm* (*objet*) piece of furniture; (*ameublement*) furniture *q* ♦ *a* (*terre*) loose, friable; (*JUR*): **biens** ~**s** movables.

meublé [mœblā] *nm* (*pièce*) furnished room; (*appartement*) furnished apartment.

meubler [mœblā] *vt* to furnish; (*fig*): ~ **qch (de)** to fill sth (with); **se** ~ to furnish one's house.

meugler [mœglā] *vi* to low, moo.

meule [mœl] *nf* (*à broyer*) millstone; (*à aiguiser*) grindstone; (*à polir*) buffwheel; (*de foin, blé*) stack; (*de fromage*) round.

meunerie [mœnrē] *nf* (*industrie*) flour trade; (*métier*) milling.

meunier, ière [mœnyā, -yer] *nm* miller ♦ *nf* miller's wife ♦ *af* (*CULIN*) meunière.

meurs [mœr] *etc vb voir* **mourir**.

meurtre [mœrtr(ə)] *nm* murder.

meurtrier, ière [mœrtrēyā, -yer] *a* (*arme, épidémie, combat*) deadly; (*accident*) fatal; (*carrefour, route*) lethal; (*fureur, instincts*) murderous ♦ *nm/f* murderer/murderess ♦ *nf* (*ouverture*) loophole.

meurtrir [mœrtrēr] *vt* to bruise; (*fig*) to wound.

meurtrissure [mœrtrēsür] *nf* bruise; (*fig*) scar.

meus [mœ] *etc vb voir* **mouvoir**.

Meuse [mœz] *nf*: **la** ~ the Meuse.

meute [mœt] *nf* pack.

meuve [mœv] *etc vb voir* **mouvoir**.

mévente [māvánt] *nf* slump (in sales).

mexicain, e [meksēkań, -en] *a* Mexican ♦ *nm/ f*: **M~, e** Mexican.

Mexico [meksēkō] *n* Mexico City.

Mexique [meksēk] *nm*: **le** ~ Mexico.

mezzanine [medzánēn] *nf* mezzanine (floor).

MF *sigle mpl* = *millions de francs* ♦ *sigle f* (*RADIO*: = *modulation de fréquence*) FM.

Mgr *abr* = **Monseigneur**.

mi [mē] *nm* (*MUS*) E; (*en chantant la gamme*) mi.

mi... [mē] *préfixe* half(-); mid-; **à la** ~**-janvier** in mid-January; ~**-bureau,** ~**-chambre** half office, half bedroom; **à** ~**-jambes/-corps** (up *ou* down) to the knees/waist; **à** ~**-hauteur/- pente** halfway up (*ou* down)/up (*ou* down) the hill.

miaou [myáōō] *nm* miaow.

miauler [mēyōlā] *vi* to mew.

mi-bas [mēbâ] *nm inv* knee-length sock.

mica [mēká] *nm* mica.

mi-carême [mēkárem] *nf*: **la** ~ the third Thursday in Lent.

miche [mēsh] *nf* round loaf.

mi-chemin [mēshmań]: **à** ~ *ad* halfway, mid-way.

mi-clos, e [mēklō, -klōz] *a* half-closed.

micmac [mēkmák] *nm* (*péj*) fuss.

mi-côte [mēkōt]: **à** ~ *ad* halfway up (*ou* down) the hill.

mi-course [mēkōōrs]: **à** ~ *ad* halfway through the race.

micro [mēkrō] *nm* mike, microphone; (*IN-FORM*) micro; ~ **cravate** lapel mike.

microbe [mēkrob] *nm* germ, microbe.

microbiologie [mēkrobyolozhē] *nf* microbi-ology.

microchirurgie [mēkroshērürzhē] *nf* micro-surgery.

microcosme [mēkrokosm(ə)] *nm* microcosm.

micro-édition [mēkroādēsyóń] *nf* desktop pub-lishing.

micro-électronique [mēkroālektronēk] *nf* microelectronics *sg*.

microfiche [mēkrofēsh] *nf* microfiche.

microfilm [mēkrofēlm] *nm* microfilm.

micro-onde [mēkroôńd] *nf*: **four à** ~**s** micro-wave oven.

micro-ordinateur [mēkroordēnátœr] *nm* microcomputer.

microphone [mēkrofon] *nm* microphone.

microplaquette [mēkropláket] *nf* microchip.

microprocesseur [mēkroprosesœr] *nm* micro-processor.

microscope [mēkroskop] *nm* microscope; **au** ~ under *ou* through the microscope.

microsillon [mēkrosēyóń] *nm* long-playing rec-ord.

MIDEM [mēdem] *sigle m* (= *Marché international du disque et de l'édition musicale*) *music industry trade fair*.

midi [mēdē] *nm* (*milieu du jour*) midday, noon; (*moment du déjeuner*) lunchtime; (*sud*) south; (*: de la France*): **le M**~ the South (of France), the Midi; **à** ~ at 12 (o'clock) *ou* midday *ou* noon; **tous les** ~**s** every lunchtime; **le repas de** ~ lunch; **en plein** ~ (right) in the middle of the day; (*sud*) facing south.

midinette [mēdēnet] *nf* silly young townie.

mie [mē] *nf* inside (of the loaf).

miel [myel] *nm* honey; **être tout** ~ (*fig*) to be all sweetness and light.

mielleux, euse [myelœ, -œz] *a* (*péj*) sugary, honeyed.

mien, ne [myań, myen] *a, pronom*: **le (la)** ~**(ne), les** ~**s** mine; **les** ~**s** (*ma famille*) my family.

miette [myet] *nf* (*de pain, gâteau*) crumb; (*fig: de la conversation etc*) scrap; **en** ~**s** (*fig*) in pieces *ou* bits.

mieux [myœ] *ad better* ♦ *a* better; (*plus joli*) better-looking ♦ *nm* (*progrès*) improvement; **le** ~ the best (thing); **le (la)** ~, **les** ~ the best; **le** ~ **des deux** the better of the two; **les livres les** ~ **faits** the best made books; **de mon/ton** ~ as best I/you can (*ou* could); **faire de son** ~ to do one's best; **vous feriez** ~ **de faire ...** you would be better to do ...; **aimer** ~ to prefer; **de** ~ **en** ~ better and better; **pour le** ~ for the best; **crier à qui** ~ ~ to try to shout each other down *ou* outshout each other; **du** ~ **qu'il peut** the best he can; **au** ~ at best; **au** ~ **avec** on the best of terms with; **qui** ~ **est** even better, better still; **faute de** ~ for lack of anything better.

mieux-être [myœzetr(ə)] *nm* greater well-being; (*financier*) improved standard of liv-ing.

mièvre [myevr(ə)] *a* sickly sentimental.

mignon, ne [mēnyóń, -on] *a* sweet, cute.

migraine [mēgren] *nf* headache; migraine.

migrant, e [mēgráń, -áńt] *a*, *nm/f* migrant.

migrateur, trice [mēgrátœr, -trēs] *a* migratory.

migration [mēgrásyóń] *nf* migration.

mijaurée [mēzhorā] *nf* pretentious (young) madam.

mijoter [mēzhotā] *vt* to simmer; (*préparer avec soin*) to cook lovingly; (*affaire, projet*) to plot, cook up ♦ *vi* to simmer.

mil [mēl] *num* = **mille**.

Milan [mēláń] *n* Milan.

milanais, e [mēláne, -ez] *a* Milanese.

mildiou [mēldyōō] *nm* mildew.

milice [mēlēs] *nf* militia.

milicien, ne [mēlēsyań, -en] *nm/f* militiaman/woman.

milieu, x [mēlyœ̄] *nm* (*centre*) middle; (*fig*) middle course *ou* way; (*aussi*: **juste ~**) happy medium; (*BIO*, *GÉO*) environment; (*entourage social*) milieu; (*familial*) background; circle; (*pègre*): **le ~** the underworld; **au ~ de** in the middle of; **au beau** *ou* **en plein ~ (de)** in the middle (of); **~ de terrain** (*FOOTBALL*: *joueur*) midfield player; (*: joueurs*) midfield.

militaire [mēlēter] *a* military ♦ *nm* serviceman; **service ~** military service.

militant, e [mēlētāń, -āńt] *a*, *nm/f* militant.

militantisme [mēlētāńtēsm(ə)] *nm* militancy.

militariser [mēlētárēzā] *vt* to militarize.

militer [mēlētā] *vi* to be a militant; **~ pour/contre** to militate in favor of/against.

mille [mēl] *num* a *ou* one thousand ♦ *nm* (*mesure*): **~ (marin)** nautical mile; **mettre dans le ~** to hit the bull's-eye; (*fig*) to be right on (target).

millefeuille [mēlfœy] *nm* napoleon (*US*), cream *ou* vanilla slice (*Brit*).

millénaire [mēlāner] *nm* millennium ♦ *a* thousand-year-old; (*fig*) ancient.

mille-pattes [mēlpát] *nm inv* centipede.

millésime [mēlāzēm] *nm* year.

millésimé, e [mēlāzēmā] *a* vintage *cpd*.

millet [mēye] *nm* millet.

milliard [mēlyár] *nm* milliard, billion (*US*), thousand million (*Brit*).

milliardaire [mēlyárder] *nm/f* billionaire (*US*), multimillionaire (*Brit*).

millième [mēlyem] *num* thousandth.

millier [mēlyū] *nm* thousand; **un ~ (de)** a thousand or so, about a thousand; **par ~s** in (their) thousands, by the thousand.

milligramme [mēlēgrám] *nm* milligram (*US*), milligramme (*Brit*).

millimètre [mēlēmetr(ə)] *nm* millimeter (*US*), millimetre (*Brit*).

millimétré, e [mēlēmātrā] *a*: **papier ~** graph paper.

million [mēlyôń] *nm* million; **deux ~s de** two million; **riche à ~s** worth millions.

millionième [mēlyonyem] *num* millionth.

millionnaire [mēlyoner] *nm/f* millionaire.

mi-lourd [mēloōr] *am*, *nm* light heavyweight.

mime [mēm] *nm/f* (*acteur*) mime(r); (*imitateur*) mimic ♦ *nm* (*art*) mime, miming.

mimer [mēmā] *vt* to mime; (*singer*) to mimic, take off.

mimétisme [mēmātēsm(ə)] *nm* (*BIO*) mimicry.

mimique [mēmēk] *nf* (funny) face; (*signes*) gesticulations *pl*, sign language *q*.

mimosa [mēmōzà] *nm* mimosa.

mi-moyen [mēmwàyań] *am*, *nm* welterweight.

MIN *sigle m* (= *Marché d'intérêt national*) wholesale market for fruit, vegetables and agricultural produce.

min. *abr* (= *minimum*) min.

minable [mēnábl(ə)] *a* (*personne*) shabby(-looking); (*travail*) pathetic.

minaret [mēnáre] *nm* minaret.

minauder [mēnōdā] *vi* to mince, simper.

minauderies [mēnōdrē] *nfpl* simperings.

mince [mańs] *a* thin; (*personne*, *taille*) slim, slender; (*fig*: *profit*, *connaissances*) slight, small; (*: prétexte*) weak ♦ *excl*: **~ (alors)!** darn it!

minceur [mańsœr] *nf* thinness; slimness, slenderness.

mincir [mańsēr] *vi* to get slimmer *ou* thinner.

mine [mēn] *nf* (*physionomie*) expression, look; (*extérieur*) exterior, appearance; (*de crayon*) lead; (*gisement*, *exploitation*, *explosif*) mine; **~s** *nfpl* (*péj*) simpering airs; **les M~s** (*ADMIN*) the national mining and geological service; the government vehicle testing department; **avoir bonne ~** (*personne*) to look well; (*ironique*) to look like an utter idiot; **avoir mauvaise ~** to look unwell *ou* poorly; **faire ~ de faire** to make a pretense (*US*) *ou* pretence (*Brit*) of doing; to make as if to do; **ne pas payer de ~** to be not much to look at; **~ de rien** *ad* with a casual air; although you wouldn't think so; **~ de charbon** coal mine; **~ à ciel ouvert** opencut (*US*) *ou* opencast (*Brit*) mine.

miner [mēnā] *vt* (*saper*) to undermine, erode; (*MIL*) to mine.

minerai [mēnre] *nm* ore.

minéral, e, aux [mēnárál, -ō] *a* mineral; (*CHIMIE*) inorganic ♦ *nm* mineral.

minéralier [mēnárályā] *nm* (*bateau*) ore tanker.

minéralisé, e [mēnárálēzā] *a* mineralized.

minéralogie [mēnárálozhē] *nf* mineralogy.

minéralogique [mēnárálozhēk] *a* mineralogical; **plaque ~** license (*US*) *ou* number (*Brit*) plate; **numéro ~** license (*US*) *ou* registration (*Brit*) number.

minet, te [mēne, et] *nm/f* (*chat*) pussycat; (*péj*) young trendy.

mineur, e [mēnœr] *a* minor ♦ *nm/f* (*JUR*) minor ♦ *nm* (*travailleur*) miner; (*MIL*) sapper; **~ de fond** underground (*US*) *ou* face (*Brit*) worker.

miniature [mēnyátür] *a*, *nf* miniature.

miniaturiser [mēnyátürēzā] *vt* to miniaturize.

minibus [mēnēbüs] *nm* minibus.

mini-cassette [mēnēkáset] *nf* cassette (recorder).

minier, ière [mēnyā, -yer] *a* mining.

mini-jupe [mēnēzhüp] *nf* miniskirt.

minimal, e, aux [mēnēmál, -ō] *a* minimum.

minime [mēnēm] *a* minor, minimal ♦ *nm/f* (*SPORT*) junior.

minimiser [mēnēmēzā] *vt* to minimize; (*fig*) to play down.

minimum [mēnēmom] *a*, *nm* minimum; **au ~** at the very least; **~ vital** (*salaire*) living wage; (*niveau de vie*) subsistence level.

mini-ordinateur [mēnēordēnátœr] *nm* minicomputer.

ministère [mēnēster] *nm* (*cabinet*) government; (*département*) department; (*REL*) ministry; **~ public** (*JUR*) Prosecution, State Prosecutor.

ministériel, le [mēnēstáryel] *a* government *cpd*; ministerial, departmental; (*partisan*) pro-government.

ministre [mēnēstr(ə)] *nm* secretary; (*REL*) minister; **~ d'État** senior secretary.

Minitel [mēnētel] *nm* ® *videotext terminal and service*.

minium [mēnyom] *nm* red lead paint.
minois [mēnwá] *nm* little face.
minorer [mēnorā] *vt* to cut, reduce.
minoritaire [mēnorēter] *a* minority *cpd*.
minorité [mēnorētá] *nf* minority; **être en** ~ to be in the *ou* a minority; **mettre en** ~ (*POL*) to defeat.
Minorque [mēnork] *nf* Minorca.
minorquin, e [mēnorkań, -ēn] *a* Minorcan.
minoterie [mēnotrē] *nf* flour mill.
minuit [mēnüē] *nm* midnight.
minuscule [mēnüskül] *a* minute, tiny ♦ *nf*: (**lettre**) ~ small letter.
minutage [mēnütázh] *nm* timing.
minute [mēnüt] *nf* minute; (*JUR*: *original*) minute, draft ♦ *excl* just a minute!, hang on!; **à la** ~ (*présent*) (just) this instant; (*passé*) there and then; **entrecôte** *ou* **steak** ~ minute steak.
minuter [mēnütá] *vt* to time.
minuterie [mēnütrē] *nf* time switch.
minuteur [mēnütœr] *nm* timer.
minutie [mēnüsē] *nf* meticulousness; minute detail; **avec** ~ meticulously; in minute detail.
minutieux, euse [mēnüsyœ̄, -œ̄z] *a* (*personne*) meticulous; (*inspection*) minutely detailed; (*travail*) requiring painstaking attention to detail.
mioche [myosh] *nm* (*fam*) brat.
mirabelle [mērábel] *nf* (*fruit*) (cherry) plum; (*eau-de-vie*) plum brandy.
miracle [mērákl(ǝ)] *nm* miracle.
miraculé, e [mērákülá] *a* who has been miraculously cured (*ou* rescued).
miraculeux, euse [mērákülœ̄, -œ̄z] *a* miraculous.
mirador [mērádor] *nm* (*MIL*) watchtower.
mirage [mērázh] *nm* mirage.
mire [mēr] *nf* (*d'un fusil*) sight; (*TV*) test pattern (*US*) *ou* card (*Brit*); **point de** ~ target; (*fig*) focal point; **ligne de** ~ line of sight.
mirent [mēr] *vb voir* **mettre**.
mirer [mērá] *vt* (*œufs*) to candle; **se** ~ *vi*: **se** ~ **dans** (*suj: personne*) to gaze at one's reflection in; (: *chose*) to be mirrored in.
mirifique [mērēfēk] *a* wonderful.
mirobolant, e [mērobolâń, -âńt] *a* fantastic.
miroir [mērwár] *nm* mirror.
miroiter [mērwátá] *vi* to sparkle, shimmer; **faire** ~ **qch à qn** to paint sth in glowing colors for sb, dangle sth in front of sb's eyes.
miroiterie [mērwátrē] *nf* (*usine*) mirror factory; (*magasin*) mirror dealer's (shop).
mis, e [mē, mēz] *pp de* **mettre** ♦ *a* (*couvert, table*) set, laid; (*personne*): **bien** ~ well dressed ♦ *nf* (*argent: au jeu*) stake; (*tenue*) clothing; attire; **être de** ~**e** to be acceptable *ou* in season; ~**e en bouteilles** bottling; ~**e à feu** blast-off; ~**e de fonds** capital outlay; ~**e à jour** updating; ~**e à mort** kill; ~**e à pied** (*d'un employé*) suspension; layoff; ~**e sur pied** (*d'une affaire, entreprise*) setting up; ~**e en plis** set; ~**e au point** (*PHOTO*) focusing; (*fig*) clarification; ~**e à prix** upset *ou* reserve (*Brit*) price; ~**e en scène** production.
misaine [mēzen] *nf*: **mât de** ~ foremast.
misanthrope [mēzáńtrop] *nm/f* misanthropist.
Mis(e) *abr* = **marquis(e)**.

mise [mēz] *af*, *nf voir* **mis**.
miser [mēzā] *vt* (*enjeu*) to stake, bet; ~ **sur** *vt* (*cheval, numéro*) to bet on; (*fig*) to bank *ou* count on.
misérable [mēzárábl(ǝ)] *a* (*lamentable, malheureux*) pitiful, wretched; (*pauvre*) poverty-stricken; (*insignifiant, mesquin*) miserable ♦ *nm/f* wretch; (*miséreux*) poor wretch.
misère [mēzer] *nf* (*pauvreté*) (extreme) poverty, destitution; ~**s** *nfpl* (*malheurs*) woes, miseries; (*ennuis*) little troubles; **être dans la** ~ to be destitute *ou* poverty-stricken; **salaire de** ~ starvation wage; **faire des** ~**s à qn** to torment sb; ~ **noire** utter destitution, abject poverty.
miséreux, euse [mēzárœ̄, -œ̄z] *a* poverty-stricken ♦ *nm/f* down-and-out.
miséricorde [mēzárēkord(ǝ)] *nf* mercy, forgiveness.
miséricordieux, euse [mēzárēkordyœ̄, -œ̄z] *a* merciful, forgiving.
misogyne [mēzozhēn] *a* misogynous ♦ *nm/f* misogynist.
missel [mēsel] *nm* missal.
missile [mēsēl] *nm* missile.
mission [mēsyóń] *nf* mission; **partir en** ~ (*ADMIN, POL*) to go on an assignment.
missionnaire [mēsyoner] *nm/f* missionary.
missive [mēsēv] *nf* missive.
mistral [mēstrál] *nm* mistral (wind).
mit [mē] *vb voir* **mettre**.
mitaine [mēten] *nf* mitt(en).
mite [mēt] *nf* clothes moth.
mité, e [mētá] *a* moth-eaten.
mi-temps [mētáń] *nf inv* (*SPORT: période*) half (*pl* halves); (: *pause*) half-time; **à** ~ *a*, *ad* part-time.
miteux, euse [mētœ̄, -œ̄z] *a* seedy, shabby.
mitigé, e [mētēzhá] *a* (*conviction, ardeur*) lukewarm; (*sentiments*) mixed.
mitonner [mētoná] *vt* (*préparer*) to cook with loving care; (*fig*) to cook up quietly.
mitoyen, ne [mētwáyań, -en] *a* common, party *cpd*; **maisons** ~**nes** duplex (*US*) *ou* semi-detached (*Brit*) houses; (*plus de deux*) town (*US*) *ou* terraced (*Brit*) houses.
mitraille [mētráy] *nf* (*balles de fonte*) grapeshot; (*décharge d'obus*) shellfire.
mitrailler [mētráyá] *vt* to machine-gun; (*fig: photographier*) to snap away at; ~ **qn de** to pelt *ou* bombard sb with.
mitraillette [mētráyet] *nf* submachine gun.
mitrailleur [mētráyœr] *nm* machine gunner ♦ *am*: **fusil** ~ machine gun.
mitrailleuse [mētráyœ̄z] *nf* machine gun.
mitre [mētr(ǝ)] *nf* miter (*US*), mitre (*Brit*).
mitron [mētróń] *nm* baker's boy.
mi-voix [mēvwá]: **à** ~ *ad* in a low *ou* hushed voice.
mixage [mēksázh] *nm* (*CINÉMA*) (sound) mixing.
mixer, mixeur [mēksœr] *nm* (*CULIN*) (food) mixer.
mixité [mēksētá] *nf* (*SCOL*) coeducation.
mixte [mēkst(ǝ)] *a* (*gén*) mixed; (*SCOL*) mixed, coeducational; **à usage** ~ dualpurpose; **cuisinière** ~ combined gas and electric cooker; **équipe** ~ combined team.

mixture [mēkstür] *nf* mixture; *(fig)* concoction.

MLF *sigle m* (= *Mouvement de libération de la femme*) Women's Lib(eration) Movement.

Mlle, *pl* **Mlles** *abr* = **Mademoiselle.**

MM *abr* = **Messieurs;** *voir* **Monsieur.**

Mme, *pl* **Mmes** *abr* = **Madame.**

mn. *abr* (= *minute*) min.

mnémotechnique [mnāmoteknēk] *a* mnemonic.

MNS *sigle m* (= *maître nageur sauveteur*) ≈ lifeguard.

MO *sigle f* (= *main-d'œuvre*) labor costs *(on invoices)*.

Mo *abr* = **métro, méga-octet.**

mobile [mobēl] *a* mobile; *(amovible)* loose, removable; *(pièce de machine)* moving; *(élément de meuble etc)* movable ♦ *nm (motif)* motive; *(œuvre d'art)* mobile; *(PHYSIQUE)* moving object *ou* body.

mobilier, ière [mobēlyā, -yer] *a* *(JUR)* personal ♦ *nm (meubles)* furniture; **valeurs mobilières** transferable securities; **vente mobilière** sale of personal property *ou* chattels.

mobilisation [mobēlēzâsyôn] *nf* mobilization.

mobiliser [mobēlēzā] *vt* *(MIL, gén)* to mobilize.

mobilité [mobēlētā] *nf* mobility.

mobylette [mobēlet] *nf* ® moped.

mocassin [mokâsan] *nm* moccasin.

moche [mosh] *a* *(fam: laid)* ugly; *(: mauvais, méprisable)* rotten.

modalité [modálētā] *nf* form, mode; **~s** *nfpl* *(d'un accord etc)* clauses, terms; **~s de paiement** methods of payment.

mode [mod] *nf* fashion; *(commerce)* fashion trade *ou* industry ♦ *nm (manière)* form, mode, method; *(LING)* mood; *(INFORM, MUS)* mode; **travailler dans la ~** to be in the fashion business; **à la ~** fashionable, in fashion; **~ dialogué** *(INFORM)* interactive *ou* conversational mode; **~ d'emploi** directions *pl* (for use); **~ de vie** way of life.

modelage [modlázh] *nm* modeling *(US)*, modelling *(Brit)*.

modelé [modlā] *nm* *(GÉO)* relief; *(du corps etc)* contours *pl*.

modèle [model] *a* model ♦ *nm* model; *(qui pose: de peintre)* sitter; *(type)* type; *(gabarit, patron)* pattern; **~ courant** *ou* **de série** *(COMM)* production model; **~ déposé** registered design; **~ réduit** small-scale model.

modeler [modlā] *vt* *(ART)* to model, mold *(US)*, mould *(Brit)*; *(suj: vêtement, érosion)* to mold *ou* mould, shape; **~ qch sur/d'après** to model sth on.

modélisation [modālēzâsyôn] *nf* *(MATH)* modeling *(US)*, modelling *(Brit)*.

modéliste [modālēst(ə)] *nm/f* *(COUTURE)* designer; *(de modèles réduits)* model maker.

modem [modem] *nm* modem.

Modène [moden] *n* Modena.

modérateur, trice [modārātœr, -trēs] *a* moderating ♦ *nm/f* moderator.

modération [modārâsyôn] *nf* moderation; **~ de peine** reduction of sentence.

modéré, e [modārā] *a*, *nm/f* moderate.

modérément [modārāmân] *ad* moderately, in moderation.

modérer [modārā] *vt* to moderate; **se ~** *vi* to restrain o.s.

moderne [modern(ə)] *a* modern ♦ *nm* *(ART)* modern style; *(ameublement)* modern furniture.

moderniser [modernēzā] *vt* to modernize.

modeste [modest(ə)] *a* modest; *(origine)* humble, lowly.

modestie [modestē] *nf* modesty; **fausse ~** false modesty.

modicité [modēsētā] *nf:* **la ~ des prix** *etc* the low prices *etc*.

modificatif, ive [modēfēkátēf, -ēv] *a* modifying.

modification [modēfēkâsyôn] *nf* modification.

modifier [modēfyā] *vt* to modify, alter; *(LING)* to modify; **se ~** *vi* to alter.

modique [modēk] *a* *(salaire, somme)* modest.

modiste [modēst(ə)] *nf* milliner.

modulaire [modüler] *a* modular.

modulation [modülâsyôn] *nf* modulation; **~ de fréquence (FM** *ou* **MF)** frequency modulation **(FM).**

module [modül] *nm* module.

moduler [modülā] *vt* to modulate; *(air)* to warble.

moelle [mwàl] *nf* marrow; *(fig)* pith, core; **~ épinière** spinal chord.

moelleux, euse [mwàlœ, œz] *a* soft; *(au goût, à l'ouïe)* mellow; *(gracieux, souple)* smooth.

moellon [mwàlôn] *nm* rubble stone.

mœurs [mœr] *nfpl* *(conduite)* morals; *(manières)* manners; *(pratiques sociales)* habits; *(mode de vie)* life style *sg*; *(d'une espèce animale)* behavior *sg* *(US)*, behaviour *sg* *(Brit)*; **femme de mauvaises ~** loose woman; **passer dans les ~** to become the custom; **contraire aux bonnes ~** contrary to proprieties.

mohair [moɛr] *nm* mohair.

moi [mwà] *pronom* me; *(emphatique)*: **~, je** ... for my part, I ..., I myself ... ♦ *nm inv* *(PSYCH)* ego, self; **à ~!** *(à l'aide)* help (me)!

moignon [mwànyôn] *nm* stump.

moi-même [mwàmem] *pronom* myself; *(emphatique)* myself.

moindre [mwàndr(ə)] *a* lesser; lower; **le(la) ~, les ~s** the least; the slightest; **le(la) ~ de** the least of; **c'est la ~ des choses** it's nothing at all.

moindrement [mwàndrəmân] *ad:* **pas le ~** not in the least.

moine [mwàn] *nm* monk, friar.

moineau, x [mwànō] *nm* sparrow.

moins [mwàn] *ad* less ♦ *cj:* **~ 2 minus 2** ♦ *prép:* **dix heures ~ cinq** five to ten ♦ *nm:* **(le signe) ~** the minus sign; **~ je travaille, mieux je me porte** the less I work, the better I feel; **~ grand que** not as tall as, less tall than; **le (la) ~ doué(e)** the least gifted; **le ~** the least; **~ de** *(sable, eau)* less; *(livres, gens)* fewer; **~ de 2 ans/100 F** less than 2 years/100 F; **~ de midi** not yet midday; **100 F/3 jours de ~** 100 F/3 days less; **3 livres en ~** 3 books fewer; 3 books too few; **de l'argent en ~** less money; **le soleil en ~** but for the sun, minus the sun; **à ~ que** *cj* unless; **à ~**

de faire unless we do (*ou* he does); **à ~ de** (*imprévu, accident*) barring any; **au ~** at least; **il a 3 ans de ~ que moi** he is 3 years younger than I; **de ~ en ~** less and less; **pour le ~** at the very least; **du ~** at least; **il fait ~ cinq** it's five below (freezing), it's minus five.

moins-value [mwaṅvàlü] *nf* (*ÉCON, COMM*) depreciation.

moire [mwàr] *nf* moiré.

moiré, e [mwàrā] *a* (*tissu, papier*) moiré, watered; (*reflets*) shimmering.

mois [mwà] *nm* month; (*salaire, somme dû*) (monthly) pay *ou* salary; **treizième ~**, **double ~** extra month's salary.

moïse [moēz] *nm* wicker cradle.

moisi, e [mwàzē] *a* moldy (*US*), mouldy (*Brit*), mildewed ♦ *nm* mold (*US*), mould (*Brit*) mildew; **odeur de ~** musty smell.

moisir [mwàzēr] *vi* to go moldy (*US*) *ou* mouldy (*Brit*); (*fig*) to rot; (*personne*) to hang about ♦ *vt* to make moldy *ou* mouldy.

moisissure [mwàzēsür] *nf* mold *q* (*US*), mould *q* (*Brit*).

moisson [mwàsòṅ] *nf* harvest; (*époque*) harvest (time); (*fig*): **faire une ~ de** to gather a wealth of.

moissonner [mwàsonā] *vt* to harvest, reap; (*fig*) to collect.

moissonneur, euse [mwàsoncr, -ēz] *nm/f* harvester, reaper ♦ *nf* (*machine*) harvester.

moissonneuse-batteuse, *pl* **moissonneuses-batteuses** [mwàsonozbátēz] *nf* combine harvester.

moite [mwàt] *a* (*peau, mains*) sweaty, sticky; (*atmosphère*) muggy.

moitié [mwàtyā] *nf* half (*pl* halves); (*épouse*): **sa ~** his better half; **la ~** half; **la ~ de** half (of), half the amount (*ou* number) of; **la ~ du temps/des gens** half the time/the people; **à la ~ de** halfway through; **~ moins grand** half as tall; **~ plus long** half as long again, longer by half; **à ~** half (*avant le verbe*), half- (*avant l'adjectif*); **à ~ prix** (at) half price, half-price; **de ~** by half; **~ ~** half-and-half.

moka [mokà] *nm* (*café*) mocha coffee; (*gâteau*) mocha cake.

mol [mol] *am voir* **mou.**

molaire [moler] *nf* molar.

moldave [moldàv] *a* Moldavian.

Moldavie [moldàvē] *nf:* **la ~** Moldavia.

môle [mōl] *nm* jetty.

moléculaire [molāküler] *a* molecular.

molécule [molākül] *nf* molecule.

moleskine [moleskēn] *nf* imitation leather.

molester [molestā] *vt* to manhandle, maul (about).

molette [molet] *nf* toothed *ou* cutting wheel.

mollasse [molàs] *a* (*péj: sans énergie*) sluggish; (*: flasque*) flabby.

molle [mol] *af voir* **mou.**

mollement [molmàṅ] *ad* softly; (*péj*) sluggishly; (*protester*) feebly.

mollesse [moles] *nf* (*voir* **mou**) softness; flabbiness; limpness; sluggishness; feebleness.

mollet [mole] *nm* calf (*pl* calves) ♦ *am:* **œuf ~** soft-boiled egg.

molletière [moltyer] *af:* **bande ~** puttee.

molleton [moltòṅ] *nm* (*TEXTILES*) felt.

molletonné, e [moltonā] *a* (*gants etc*) fleece-lined.

mollir [molēr] *vi* (*jambes*) to give way; (*NAVIG: vent*) to drop, die down; (*fig: personne*) to relent; (*: courage*) to fail, flag.

mollusque [molüsk(ə)] *nm* (*ZOOL*) mollusk (*US*), mollusc; (*fig: personne*) lazy lump.

molosse [molos] *nm* big ferocious dog.

môme [mōm] *nm/f* (*fam: enfant*) brat; (*: fille*) chick.

moment [momàṅ] *nm* moment; (*occasion*): **profiter du ~** to take (advantage of) the opportunity; **ce n'est pas le ~** this is not the right time; **à un certain ~** at some point; **à un ~ donné** at a certain point; **à quel ~?** when exactly?; **au même ~** at the same time; (*instant*) at the same moment; **pour un bon ~** for a good while; **pour le ~** for the moment, for the time being; **au ~ de** at the time of; **au ~ où** as; at a time when; **à tout ~** at any time *ou* moment; (*continuellement*) constantly, continually; **en ce ~** at the moment; (*aujourd'hui*) at present; **sur le ~** at the time; **par ~s** now and then, at times; **d'un ~ à l'autre** any time (now); **du ~ où** *ou* **que** seeing that, since; **n'avoir pas un ~ à soi** not to have a minute to oneself.

momentané, e [momàṅtānā] *a* temporary, momentary.

momie [momē] *nf* mummy.

mon [mòṅ], ma [mà], *pl* **mes** [mā] *dét* my.

monacal, e, aux [monàkàl, -ō] *a* monastic.

Monaco [monàkō] *nm:* **le ~** Monaco.

monarchie [monàrshē] *nf* monarchy.

monarchiste [monàrshēst(ə)] *a, nm/f* monarchist.

monarque [monàrk(ə)] *nm* monarch.

monastère [monàster] *nm* monastery.

monastique [monàstēk] *a* monastic.

monceau, x [mòṅsō] *nm* heap.

mondain, e [mòṅdaṅ, -en] *a* (*soirée, vie*) society *cpd*; (*obligations*) social; (*peintre, écrivain*) fashionable; (*personne*) society *cpd* ♦ *nm/f* society man/woman, socialite ♦ *nf:* **la M~e, la police ~e** ≈ the vice squad.

mondanités [mòṅdànētā] *nfpl* (*vie mondaine*) society life *sg*; (*paroles*) (society) small talk *sg*; (*PRESSE*) (society) gossip column *sg*.

monde [mòṅd] *nm* world; (*personnes mondaines*): **le ~** (high) society; (*milieu*): **être du même ~** to move in the same circles; (*gens*): **il y a du ~** (*beaucoup de gens*) there are a lot of people; (*quelques personnes*) there are some people; **y a-t-il du ~ dans la cuisine?** is there anybody in the kitchen?; **beaucoup/peu de ~** many/few people; **le meilleur etc du ~** the best etc in the world *ou* on earth; **mettre au ~** to bring into the world; **pas le moins du ~** not in the least; **se faire un ~ de qch** to make a great deal of fuss about sth; **tour du ~** round-the-world trip; **homme/femme du ~** society man/woman.

mondial, e, aux [mòṅdyàl, -ō] *a* (*population*) world *cpd*; (*influence*) worldwide.

mondialement [mòṅdyàlmàṅ] *ad* throughout the world.

mondialisation [mȯndyȧlēzȧsyȯn] *nf* (*d'une technique*) global application; (*d'un conflit*) global spread.

mondovision [mȯndovēzyȯn] *nf* (world coverage by) satellite television.

monégasque [monȧgȧsk(ə)] *a* Monegasque, of *ou* from Monaco ♦ *nm/f*: **M~** Monegasque.

monétaire [monȧter] *a* monetary.

monétarisme [monȧtȧrēsm(ə)] *nm* monetarism.

monétique [monȧtēk] *nf* electronic money.

mongol, e [mȯngol] *a* Mongol, Mongolian ♦ *nm* (*LING*) Mongolian ♦ *nm/f*: **M~, e** (*MÉD*) Mongol, Mongoloid; (*de la Mongolie*) Mongolian.

Mongolie [mȯngolē] *nf*: **la** ~ Mongolia.

mongolien, ne [mȯngolyȧn, -en] *a*, *nm/f* mongol.

mongolisme [mȯngolēsm(ə)] *nm* mongolism, Down's syndrome.

moniteur, trice [monētœr, -trēs] *nm/f* (*SPORT*) instructor/instructress; (*de colonie de vacances*) supervisor ♦ *nm* (*écran*) monitor; ~ **cardiaque** cardiac monitor; ~ **d'auto-école** driving instructor.

monitorat [monētorȧ] *nm* (*formation*) instructor's training (course); (*fonction*) instructorship.

monnaie [mone] *nf* (*pièce*) coin; (*ÉCON, gén: moyen d'échange*) currency; (*petites pièces*): **avoir de la** ~ to have (some) change; **faire de la** ~ to get (some) change; **avoir/faire la** ~ **de 20 F** to have change for/get change for 20 F; **faire** *ou* **donner à qn la** ~ **de 20 F** to give sb change for 20 F, change 20 F for sb; **rendre à qn la** ~ (**sur 20 F**) to give sb the change (from *ou* out of 20 F); **servir de** ~ **d'échange** (*fig*) to be used as a bargaining token *ou* as bargaining tokens; **payer en** ~ **de singe** to fob (sb) off with empty promises; **c'est** ~ **courante** it's a common occurrence; ~ **légale** legal tender.

monnayer [monȧyȧ] *vt* to convert into cash; (*talent*) to capitalize on.

monnayeur [moneyœr] *nm voir* **faux.**

mono [monō] *nf* (= *monophonie*) mono ♦ *nm* (= *monoski*) monoski.

monochrome [monokrōm] *a* monochrome.

monocle [monokl(ə)] *nm* monocle, eyeglass.

monocoque [monokok] *a* (*voiture*) monocoque ♦ *nm* (*voilier*) monohull.

monocorde [monokord(ə)] *a* monotonous.

monoculture [monokültür] *nf* single-crop farming, monoculture.

monogramme [monogrȧm] *nm* monogram.

monokini [monokēnē] *nm* one-piece bikini, bikini pants *pl.*

monolingue [monolȧng] *a* monolingual.

monologue [monolog] *nm* monologue, soliloquy; ~ **intérieur** stream of consciousness.

monologuer [monologȧ] *vi* to soliloquize.

monôme [monōm] *nm* (*MATH*) monomial; (*d'étudiants*) students' procession.

monoparental, e, aux [monopȧrȧntȧl, -ō] *a* one-parent *cpd*, single-parent *cpd*.

monophasé, e [monofȧzȧ] *a* single-phase *cpd*.

monoplace [monoplȧs] *a, nm, nf* single-seater, one-seater.

monoplan [monoplȧn] *nm* monoplane.

monopole [monopol] *nm* monopoly.

monopoliser [monopolēzȧ] *vt* to monopolize.

monorail [monorȧy] *nm* monorail; monorail train.

monoski [monoskē] *nm* monoski.

monosyllabe [monosēlȧb] *nm* monosyllable, word of one syllable.

monotone [monoton] *a* monotonous.

monotonie [monotonē] *nf* monotony.

monseigneur [mȯnsenyœr] *nm* (*archevêque, évêque*) Your (*ou* His) Grace; (*cardinal*) Your (*ou* His) Eminence; **Mgr Thomas** Bishop Thomas; Cardinal Thomas.

Monsieur [məsyœ], *pl* **Messieurs** [māsyœ] *titre* Mr [mis'tûr] ♦ *nm* (*homme quelconque*): **un/le m~** a/the gentleman; *voir aussi* **Madame.**

monstre [mȯnstr(ə)] *nm* monster ♦ *a* (*fam: effet, publicité*) massive; **un travail** ~ a fantastic amount of work; an enormous job; ~ **sacré** superstar.

monstrueux, euse [mȯnstrüœ, -œz] *a* monstrous.

monstruosité [mȯnstruȯzetȧ] *nf* monstrosity.

mont [mȯn] *nm*: **par ~s et par vaux** over hill and dale; **le M~ Blanc** Mont Blanc; ~ **de Vénus** mons veneris.

montage [mȯntȧzh] *nm* putting up; (*d'un bijou*) mounting, setting; (*d'une machine etc*) assembly; (*PHOTO*) photomontage; (*CINÉMA*) editing; ~ **sonore** sound editing.

montagnard, c [mȯntȧnyȧr, -ȧrd(ə)] *a* mountain *cpd* ♦ *nm/f* mountaindweller.

montagne [mȯntȧny] *nf* (*cime*) mountain; (*région*): **la** ~ the mountains *pl*; **la haute** ~ the high mountains; **les ~s Rocheuses** the Rocky Mountains, the Rockies; **~s russes** roller coaster *sg.*

montagneux, euse [mȯntȧnyœ, -œz] *a* mountainous; hilly.

montant, e [mȯntȧn, -ȧnt] *a* (*mouvement, marée*) rising; (*chemin*) uphill; (*robe, corsage*) high-necked ♦ *nm* (*somme, total*) (sum) total, (total) amount; (*de fenêtre*) upright; (*de lit*) post.

mont-de-piété, *pl* **monts-de-piété** [mȯndpyȧtȧ] *nm* pawnshop.

monte [mȯnt] *nf* (*accouplement*): **la** ~ stud; (*d'un jockey*) seat.

monté, e [mȯntȧ] *a*: **être** ~ **contre qn** to be angry with sb; (*fourni, équipé*): ~ **en** equipped with.

monte-charge [mȯntshȧrzh(ə)] *nm inv* freight elevator (*US*), goods lift (*Brit*), hoist.

montée [mȯntȧ] *nf* rising; rise; (*escalade*) ascent, climb; (*chemin*) way up; (*côte*) hill; **au milieu de la** ~ halfway up; **le moteur chauffe dans les ~s** the engine overheats going uphill.

monte-plats [mȯntplȧ] *nm inv* dumb waiter.

monter [mȯntȧ] *vt* (*escalier, côte*) to go (*ou* come) up; (*valise, paquet*) to take (*ou* bring) up; (*cheval*) to mount; (*femelle*) to cover, serve; (*tente, échafaudage*) to put up; (*machine*) to assemble; (*bijou*) to mount, set; (*COUTURE*) to sew on; (: *manche*) to set in; (*CINÉMA*) to edit; (*THÉÂTRE*) to put on, stage; (*société, coup etc*) to set up; (*fournir, équiper*) to equip ♦ *vi* to go (*ou* come) up;

(avion, voiture) to climb, go up; (chemin, niveau, température, voix, prix) to go up, rise; (brouillard, bruit) to rise, come up; (passager) to get on; (à cheval): ~ **bien/mal** to ride well/badly; ~ **à cheval/bicyclette** to get on ou mount a horse/bicycle; (faire du cheval etc) to ride (a horse); to (ride a) bicycle; ~ **à pied/en voiture** to walk/drive up, go up on foot/by car; ~ **dans le train/ l'avion** to get into the train/plane, board the train/plane; ~ **sur** to climb up onto; ~ **sur** ou **à un arbre/une échelle** to climb (up) a tree/ ladder; ~ **à bord** to (get on) board; ~ **à la tête de qn** to go to sb's head; ~ **sur les planches** to go on the stage; ~ **en grade** to be promoted; **se** ~ (s'équiper) to equip o.s.; **se** ~ **à** (frais etc) to add up to, come to; ~ **qn contre qn** to set sb against sb; ~ **la tête à qn** to give sb ideas.

monteur, euse [mɔ̂tœr, -œz] nm/f (TECH) fitter; (CINÉMA) editor.

monticule [mɔ̂tēkül] nm mound.

montmartrois, e [mɔ̂mártrwà, -wàz] a of ou from Montmartre.

montre [mɔ̂tr(ə)] nf watch; (ostentation): **pour la** ~ for show; ~ **en main** exactly, to the minute; **faire** ~ **de** to show, display; **contre la** ~ (SPORT) against the clock; ~ **de plongée** diver's watch.

Montréal [mɔ̂rãál] n Montreal.

montréalais, e [mɔ̂rãále, -ez] a of ou from Montreal ♦ nm/f: **M~**, **e** Montrealer.

montre-bracelet, pl **montres-bracelets** [mɔ̂trəbrásle] nf wristwatch.

montrer [mɔ̂trã] vt to show; **se** ~ to appear; ~ **qch à qn** to show sb sth; ~ **qch du doigt** to point to sth, point one's finger at sth; **se** ~ **intelligent** to prove (to be) intelligent.

montreur, euse [mɔ̂trœr, -œz] nm/f: ~ **de marionnettes** puppeteer.

monture [mɔ̂tür] nf (bête) mount; (d'une bague) setting; (de lunettes) frame.

monument [monümâ̂] nm monument; ~ **aux morts** war memorial.

monumental, e, aux [monümâ̂tál, -ō] a monumental.

moquer [mokā]: **se** ~ **de** vt to make fun of, laugh at; (fam: se désintéresser de) not to care about; (tromper): **se** ~ **de qn** to take sb for a ride.

moquerie [mokrē] nf mockery q.

moquette [moket] nf fitted carpet, wall-to-wall carpeting q.

moqueter [mokātā] vt to carpet.

moqueur, euse [mokœr, -œz] a mocking.

moral, e, aux [morál, -ō] a moral ♦ nm morale ♦ nf (conduite) morals pl; (règles) moral code, ethic; (valeurs) moral standards pl, morality; (science) ethics sg, moral philosophy; (conclusion: d'une fable etc) moral; **au** ~, **sur le plan** ~ morally; **avoir le** ~ **à zéro** to be really down; **faire la** ~**e à** to lecture, preach at.

moralement [morálmâ̂] ad morally.

moralisateur, trice [morálēzátœr, -trēs] a moralizing, sanctimonious ♦ nm/f moralizer.

moraliser [morálēzā] vt (sermonner) to lecture, preach at.

moraliste [morálēst(ə)] nm/f moralist ♦ a mor-

alistic.

moralité [morálētā] nf (d'une action, attitude) morality; (conduite) morals pl; (conclusion, enseignement) moral.

moratoire [morátwár] am: **intérêts** ~**s** (ÉCON) interest on arrears.

morave [morávɔ] a Moravian.

Moravie [morávē] nf: **la** ~ Moravia.

morbide [morbēd] a morbid.

morceau, x [morsō] nm piece, bit; (d'une œuvre) passage, extract; (MUS) piece; (CULIN: de viande) cut; **mettre en** ~**x** to pull to pieces ou bits.

morceler [morsəlā] vt to break up, divide up.

mordant, e [mordâ̂, -â̂t] a scathing, cutting; (froid) biting ♦ nm (dynamisme, énergie) spirit; (fougue) bite, punch.

mordicus [mordēküs] ad (fam) obstinately, stubbornly.

mordiller [mordēyā] vt to nibble at, chew at.

mordoré, e [mordorā] a lustrous bronze.

mordre [mordr(ə)] vt to bite; (suj: lime, vis) to bite into ♦ vi (poisson) to bite; ~ **dans** to bite into; ~ **sur** (fig) to go over into, overlap into; ~ **à qch** (comprendre, aimer) to take to; ~ **à l'hameçon** to bite, rise to the bait.

mordu, e [mordü] pp de **mordre** ♦ a (amoureux) smitten ♦ nm/f: **un** ~ **du jazz/de la voile** a jazz/sailing fanatic ou buff.

morfondre [morfɔ̂dr(ə)]: **se** ~ vi to mope.

morgue [morg(ə)] nf (arrogance) haughtiness; (lieu: de la police) morgue; (: à l'hôpital) mortuary.

moribond, e [morēbɔ̂, -ɔ̂d] a dying, moribund.

morille [morēy] nf morel (mushroom).

mormon, e [mormɔ̂, -on] a, nm/f Mormon.

morne [morn(ə)] a (personne, visage) glum, gloomy; (temps, vie) dismal, dreary.

morose [morōz] a sullen, morose; (marché) sluggish.

morphine [morfēn] nf morphine.

morphinomane [morfēnomán] nm/f morphine addict.

morphologie [morfolozhē] nf morphology.

mors [mor] nm bit.

morse [mors(ə)] nm (ZOOL) walrus; (TÉL) Morse (code).

morsure [morsür] nf bite.

mort [mor] nf death; **se donner la** ~ to take one's own life; **de** ~ (silence, pâleur) deathly; **blessé à** ~ fatally wounded ou injured; **à la vie, à la** ~ for better, for worse; ~ **clinique** brain death.

mort, e [mor, mort(ə)] pp de **mourir** ♦ a dead ♦ nm/f (défunt) dead man/woman; (victime): **il y a eu plusieurs** ~**s** several people were killed, there were several killed ♦ nm (CARTES) dummy; ~ **ou vif** dead or alive; ~ **de peur/fatigue** frightened to death/dead tired; ~**s et blessés** casualties; **faire le** ~ to play dead; (fig) to lie low.

mortadelle [mortádel] nf mortadella (type of luncheon meat).

mortalité [mortálētā] nf mortality, death rate.

mort-aux-rats [mortōrà] nf inv rat poison.

mortel, le [mortel] a (poison etc) deadly, lethal; (accident, blessure) fatal; (REL, danger, frayeur) mortal; (fig: froid) deathly;

(*: ennui, soirée*) deadly (boring) ♦ *nm/f* mortal.

mortellement [mortelmáň] *ad* (*blessé etc*) fatally, mortally; (*pâle etc*) deathly; (*fig: ennuyeux etc*) deadly.

morte-saison, *pl* **mortes-saisons** [mortəsezóň] *nf* slack *ou* off season.

mortier [mortyā] *nm* (*gén*) mortar.

mortifier [mortēfyā] *vt* to mortify.

mort-né, e [mornā] *a* (*enfant*) stillborn; (*fig*) abortive.

mortuaire [mortüer] *a* funeral *cpd*; **avis** ~**s** death announcements, intimations; **chapelle** ~ mortuary chapel; **couronne** ~ (funeral) wreath; **domicile** ~ house of the deceased; **drap** ~ pall.

morue [morü] *nf* (*ZOOL*) cod *inv*; (*CULIN: salée*) salt-cod.

morutier [morütyā] *nm* (*pêcheur*) cod fisherman; (*bateau*) cod fishing boat.

morvandeau, elle, x [morváňdō, -el] *a* of *ou* from the Morvan region.

morveux, euse [morvœ̄, -œ̄z] *a* (*fam*) snottynosed.

mosaïque [mozáēk] *nf* (*ART*) mosaic; (*fig*) patchwork.

Moscou [moskōō] *n* Moscow.

moscovite [moskovēt] *a* of *ou* from Moscow, Moscow *cpd* ♦ *nm/f*: **M**~ Muscovite.

mosquée [moskā] *nf* mosque.

mot [mō] *nm* word; (*message*) line, note; (*bon mot etc*) saying; **le ~ de la fin** the last word; ~ **à** ~ *a, ad* word for word; ~ **pour** ~ word for word, verbatim; **sur** *ou* **à ces** ~**s** with these words; **en un** ~ in a word; **à** ~**s couverts** in veiled terms; **prendre qn au** ~ to take sb at his word; **se donner le** ~ to send the word around; **avoir son** ~ **à dire** to have a say; ~ **d'ordre** watchword; ~ **de passe** password; ~**s croisés** crossword (puzzle) *sg*.

motard [motár] *nm* biker; (*policier*) motorcycle cop.

motel [motel] *nm* motel.

moteur, trice [motœr, -trēs] *a* (*ANAT, PHYSIOL*) motor; (*TECH*) driving; (*AUTO*): **à 4 roues motrices** 4-wheel drive ♦ *nm* engine, motor; (*fig*) mover, mainspring; **à** ~ powerdriven, motor *cpd*; ~ **à deux temps** twostroke engine; ~ **à explosion** internal combustion engine; ~ **à réaction** jet engine; ~ **thermique** heat engine.

motif [motēf] *nm* (*cause*) motive; (*décoratif*) design, pattern, motif; (*d'un tableau*) subject, motif; (*MUS*) figure, motif; ~**s** *nmpl* (*JUR*) grounds *pl*; **sans** ~ *a* groundless.

motion [mōsyóň] *nf* motion; ~ **de censure** motion of censure, vote of no confidence.

motivation [motēvásyóň] *nf* motivation.

motivé, e [motēvā] *a* (*acte*) justified; (*personne*) motivated.

motiver [motēvā] *vt* (*justifier*) to justify, account for; (*ADMIN, JUR, PSYCH*) to motivate.

moto [motō] *nf* (*motor*)bike; ~ **verte** *ou* **de trial** dirt (*US*) *ou* trail (*Brit*) bike.

moto-cross [motokros] *nm* motocross.

motoculteur [motokültœr] *nm* (*motorized*) cultivator.

motocyclette [motosēklet] *nf* motorbike, motorcycle.

motocyclisme [motosēklēsm(ə)] *nm* motorcycle racing.

motocycliste [motosēklēst(ə)] *nm/f* motorcyclist.

motoneige [motonezh] *nf* snowmobile.

motorisé, e [motorēzā] *a* (*troupe*) motorized; (*personne*) having one's own transport.

motrice [motrēs] *af voir* **moteur.**

motte [mot] *nf:* ~ **de terre** lump of earth, clod (of earth); ~ **de gazon** turf, sod; ~ **de beurre** lump of butter.

motus [motüs] *excl:* ~ **(et bouche cousue)!** mum's the word!

mou (mol), molle [mōō, mol] *a* soft; (*péj: visage, traits*) flabby; (*: geste*) limp; (*: personne*) sluggish; (*: résistance, protestations*) feeble ♦ *nm* (*homme mou*) wimp; (*abats*) lights *pl*, lungs *pl*; (*de la corde*): **avoir du** ~ to be slack; **donner du** ~ to slacken, loosen; **avoir les jambes molles** to be weak at the knees.

mouchard, e [mōōshàr, -àrd(ə)] *nm/f* (*péj: SCOL*) snitch (*US*), squealer; (*: POLICE*) stool pigeon ♦ *nm* (*appareil*) control device; (*: de camion*) tachograph.

mouche [mōōsh] *nf* fly; (*ESCRIME*) button; (*de taffetas*) patch; **prendre la** ~ to go into a huff; **faire** ~ to score a bull's-eye.

moucher [mōōshā] *vt* (*enfant*) to blow the nose of; (*chandelle*) to snuff (out); **se** ~ to blow one's nose.

moucheron [mōōshróň] *nm* midge.

moucheté, e [mōōshtā] *a* (*cheval*) dappled; (*laine*) flecked; (*ESCRIME*) buttoned.

mouchoir [mōōshwár] *nm* handkerchief, hanky; ~ **en papier** tissue, paper hanky.

moudre [mōōdr(ə)] *vt* to grind.

moue [mōō] *nf* pout; **faire la** ~ to pout; (*fig*) to make a face.

mouette [mwet] *nf* (sea)gull.

mouf(f)ette [mōōfet] *nf* skunk.

moufle [mōōfl(ə)] *nf* (*gant*) mitt(en); (*TECH*) pulley block.

mouflon [mōōflóň] *nm* mouf(f)lon.

mouillage [mōōyàzh] *nm* (*NAVIG: lieu*) anchorage, moorings *pl*.

mouillé, e [mōōyā] *a* wet.

mouiller [mōōyā] *vt* (*humecter*) to wet, moisten; (*tremper*): ~ **qn/qch** to make sb/ sth wet; (*CULIN: ragoût*) to add stock *ou* wine to; (*couper, diluer*) to water down; (*mine etc*) to lay ♦ *vi* (*NAVIG*) to lie *ou* be at anchor; **se** ~ to get wet; (*fam*) to commit o.s.; to get (o.s.) involved; ~ **l'ancre** to drop *ou* cast anchor.

mouillette [mōōyet] *nf* sippet (*US*), (bread) finger (*Brit*).

mouillure [mōōyür] *nf* wet *q*; (*tache*) wet spot.

moulage [mōōlàzh] *nm* molding (*US*), moulding (*Brit*); casting; (*objet*) cast.

moulais [mōōle] *etc vb voir* **moudre.**

moulant, e [mōōlàń, -àńt] *a* snug-fitting.

moule [mōōl] *vb voir* **moudre** ♦ *nf* (*mollusque*) mussel ♦ *nm* (*creux, CULIN*) mold (*US*), mould (*Brit*); (*modèle plein*) cast; ~ **à gâteau** *nm* cake pan (*US*) *ou* tin

(*Brit*); ~ **à gaufre** *nm* waffle iron; ~ **à tarte** *nm* pie *ou* flan plate (*US*) *ou* dish (*Brit*).

moulent [mōōl] *vb voir* **moudre, mouler.**

mouler [mōōlā] *vt* (*brique*) to mold (*US*), mould (*Brit*); (*statue*) to cast; (*visage, bas-relief*) to make a cast of; (*lettre*) to shape with care; (*suj: vêtement*) to hug, fit closely round; ~ **qch sur** (*fig*) to model sth on.

moulin [mōōlań] *nm* mill; (*fam*) engine; ~ **à café** coffee mill; ~ **à eau** watermill; ~ **à légumes** (vegetable) shredder; ~ **à paroles** (*fig*) chatterbox; ~ **à poivre** pepper mill; ~ **à prières** prayer wheel; ~ **à vent** windmill.

mouliner [mōōlēnā] *vt* to shred.

moulinet [mōōlēne] *nm* (*de treuil*) winch; (*de canne à pêche*) reel; (*mouvement*): **faire des** ~**s avec qch** to whirl sth around.

moulinette [mōōlēnet] *nf* ® (vegetable) shredder.

moulons [mōōlōń] *etc vb voir* **moudre.**

moulu, e [mōōlü] *pp de* **moudre ♦** *a* (*café*) ground.

moulure [mōōlür] *nf* (*ornement*) molding (*US*), moulding (*Brit*).

mourant, e [mōōrāń, -âńt] *vb voir* **mourir ♦** *a* dying ♦ *nm/f* dying man/woman.

mourir [mōōrēr] *vi* to die; (*civilisation*) to die out; ~ **assassiné** to be murdered; ~ **de froid/faim/vieillesse** to die of exposure/hunger/old age; ~ **de faim/d'ennui** (*fig*) to be starving/be bored to death; ~ **d'envie de faire** to be dying to do; **s'ennuyer à** ~ to be bored to death.

mousquetaire [mōōskətər] *nm* musketeer.

mousqueton [mōōskətōń] *nm* (*fusil*) carbine; (*anneau*) snap-link, karabiner.

moussant, e [mōōsāń, -âńt] *a* foaming; **bain** ~ foam *ou* bubble bath, bath foam.

mousse [mōōs] *nf* (*BOT*) moss; (*écume: sur eau, bière*) froth, foam; (: *shampooing*) lather; (*de champagne*) bubbles *pl*; (*CULIN*) mousse; (*en caoutchouc etc*) foam ♦ *nm* (*NAVIG*) ship's boy; **bain de** ~ bubble bath; **bas** ~ stretch stockings; **balle** ~ rubber ball; ~ **carbonique** (fire-fighting) foam; ~ **de nylon** nylon foam; (*tissu*) stretch nylon; ~ **à raser** shaving foam.

mousseline [mōōslēn] *nf* (*TEXTILES*) muslin; chiffon; **pommes** ~ (*CULIN*) creamed potatoes.

mousser [mōōsā] *vi* to foam; to lather.

mousseux, euse [mōōsœ, -œz] *a* (*chocolat*) frothy; (*eau*) foamy, frothy; (*vin*) sparkling ♦ *nm*: (**vin**) ~ sparkling wine.

mousson [mōōsōń] *nf* monsoon.

moussu, e [mōōsü] *a* mossy.

moustache [mōōstásh] *nf* moustache; ~**s** *nfpl* (*d'animal*) whiskers *pl*.

moustachu, e [mōōstáshü] *a* wearing a moustache.

moustiquaire [mōōstēker] *nf* (*rideau*) mosquito net; (*chassis*) mosquito screen.

moustique [mōōstēk] *nm* mosquito.

moutarde [mōōtárd(ə)] *nf* mustard ♦ *a inv* mustard(-colored).

moutardier [mōōtárdyā] *nm* mustard jar.

mouton [mōōtōń] *nm* (*ZOOL, péj*) sheep *inv*; (*peau*) sheepskin; (*CULIN*) mutton.

mouture [mōōtür] *nf* grinding; (*péj*) rehash.

mouvant, e [mōōvâń, -âńt] *a* unsettled; changing; shifting.

mouvement [mōōvmâń] *nm* (*gén, aussi: mécanisme*) movement; (*ligne courbe*) contours *pl*; (*fig: tumulte, agitation*) activity, bustle; (: *impulsion*) impulse; reaction; (*geste*) gesture; (*MUS: rythme*) tempo (*pl* -s *ou* tempi); **en** ~ in motion; on the move; **mettre qch en** ~ to set sth in motion, set sth going; ~ **d'humeur** fit *ou* burst of temper; ~ **d'opinion** trend of (public) opinion; **le** ~ **perpétuel** perpetual motion.

mouvementé, e [mōōvmâńtā] *a* (*vie, poursuite*) eventful; (*réunion*) turbulent.

mouvoir [mōōvwâr] *vt* (*levier, membre*) to move; (*machine*) to drive; **se** ~ to move.

moyen, ne [mwáyań, -en] *a* average; (*tailles, prix*) medium; (*de grandeur moyenne*) medium-sized ♦ *nm* (*façon*) means *sg*, way ♦ *nf* average; (*STATISTIQUE*) mean; (*SCOL: à l'examen*) pass mark; (*AUTO*) average speed; ~**s** *nmpl* (*capacités*) means; **au** ~ **de** by means of; **y a-t-il** ~ **de ...?** is it possible to ...?, can one ...?; **par quel** ~? how?, which way?, by which means?; **par tous les** ~**s** by every possible means, every possible way; **avec les** ~**s du bord** (*fig*) with what's available *ou* what comes to hand; **employer les grands** ~**s** to resort to drastic measures; **par ses propres** ~**s** all by oneself; **en** ~**ne** on (an) average; **faire la** ~**ne** to work out the average; ~ **de locomotion/d'expression** means of transport/expression; ~ **âge** Middle Ages; ~ **de transport** means of transport; ~**ne d'âge** average age; ~**ne entreprise** (*COMM*) medium-sized firm.

moyen-courrier [mwáyańkōōryā] *nm* (*AVIAT*) medium-haul aircraft.

moyennant [mwáyenâń] *prép* (*somme*) for; (*service, conditions*) in return for; (*travail, effort*) with.

moyennement [mwáyenmâń] *ad* fairly, moderately; (*faire qch*) fairly *ou* moderately well.

Moyen-Orient [mwáyenoryáń] *nm*: **le** ~ the Middle East.

moyeu, x [mwáyœ] *nm* hub.

mozambicain, e [mozáńbēkań, -en] *a* Mozambican.

Mozambique [mozáńbēk] *nm*: **le** ~ Mozambique.

MRAP *sigle m* = *Mouvement contre le racisme, l'antisémitisme et pour la paix.*

MRG *sigle m* (= *Mouvement des radicaux de gauche*) *political party.*

MRP *sigle m* (= *Mouvement républicain populaire*) *political party.*

ms *abr* (= *manuscrit*) MS., ms.

MST *sigle f* (= *maladie sexuellement transmissible*) STD (= *sexually transmitted disease*).

mû, mue [mü] *pp de* **mouvoir.**

mucosité [mükōzētā] *nf* mucus *q.*

mucus [müküs] *nm* mucus *q.*

mue [mü] *pp de* **mouvoir ♦** *nf* molting (*US*), moulting (*Brit*); sloughing; breaking of the voice.

muer [müä] *vi* (*oiseau, mammifère*) to molt (*US*), moult (*Brit*); (*serpent*) to slough;

(*jeune garçon*): **il mue** his voice is breaking; **se ~ en** to transform into.

muet, te [müe, -et] *a* dumb; (*fig*): **~ d'admiration** *etc* speechless with admiration *etc*; (*joie, douleur, CINÉMA*) silent; (*LING*: *lettre*) silent, mute; (*carte*) blank ♦ *nm/f* mute ♦ *nm*: **le ~** (*CINÉMA*) the silent cinema *ou* movies.

mufle [müfl(ə)] *nm* muzzle; (*goujat*) boor ♦ *a* boorish.

mugir [müzhēr] *vi* (*bœuf*) to bellow; (*vache*) to low, moo; (*fig*) to howl.

mugissement [müzhēsmâň] *nm* (*voir mugir*) bellowing; lowing, mooing; howling.

muguet [müge] *nm* (*BOT*) lily of the valley; (*MÉD*) thrush.

mulâtre, tresse [mülâtr(ə), -tres] *nm/f* mulatto.

mule [mül] *nf* (*ZOOL*) (she-)mule.

mules [mül] *nfpl* (*pantoufles*) mules.

mulet [müle] *nm* (*ZOOL*) (he-)mule; (*poisson*) mullet.

muletier, ière [mültyā, -yer] *a*: **sentier** *ou* **chemin ~** mule track.

mulot [mülō] *nm* fieldmouse (*pl* -mice).

multicolore [mültēkolor] *a* multicolored (*US*), multicoloured (*Brit*).

multicoque [mültēkok] *nm* multihull.

multidisplinaire [mültēdēsēplēner] *a* multidisciplinary.

multiforme [mültēform(ə)] *a* many-sided.

multilatéral, e, aux [mültēlátárál, -ō] *a* multilateral.

multimilliardaire [mültēmēlyárder], **multimillionnaire** [mültēmēlyoner] *a, nm/f* multimillionaire.

multinational, e, aux [mültēnáṣyonál, ō] *a, nf* multinational.

multiple [mültēpl(ə)] *a* multiple, numerous; (*varié*) many, manifold ♦ *nm* (*MATH*) multiple.

multiplicateur [mültēplēkátœr] *nm* multiplier.

multiplication [mültēplēkáṣyôň] *nf* multiplication.

multiplicité [mültēplēsētā] *nf* multiplicity.

multiplier [mültēplcyā] *vt* to multiply; **se ~** *vi* to multiply; (*fig: personne*) to be everywhere at once.

multiprogrammation [mültēprográmâsyóň] *nf* (*INFORM*) multiprogramming.

multipropriété [mültēproprēyátā] *nf* timesharing *q*.

multitraitement [mültētretmâň] *nm* (*INFORM*) multiprocessing.

multitude [mültētüd] *nf* multitude; mass; **une ~ de** a vast number of, a multitude of.

Munich [müněk] *n* Munich.

munichois, e [müněkwá, -wáz] *a of ou* from Munich.

municipal, e, aux [müněsēpál, -ō] *a* municipal; town *cpd*.

municipalité [müněsēpálētā] *nf* (*corps municipal*) town council, corporation; (*commune*) town, municipality.

munir [müněr] *vt*: **~ qn/qch de** to equip sb/sth with; **se ~ de** to provide o.s. with.

munitions [müněṣyóň] *nfpl* ammunition *sg*.

muqueuse [mükœz] *nf* mucous membrane.

mur [mür] *nm* wall; (*fig*) stone *ou* brick wall; **faire le ~** (*interne, soldat*) to sneak out (over

the wall); **~ du son** sound barrier.

mûr, e [mür] *a* ripe; (*personne*) mature ♦ *nf* (*de la ronce*) blackberry; (*du mûrier*) mulberry.

muraille [mürây] *nf* (high) wall.

mural, e, aux [mürál, -ō] *a* wall *cpd* ♦ *nm* (*ART*) mural.

mûre [mür] *nf voir* **mûr.**

mûrement [mürmâň] *ad*: **ayant ~ réfléchi** having given the matter much thought.

murène [müren] *nf* moray (eel).

murer [mürā] *vt* (*enclos*) to wall (in); (*porte, issue*) to wall up; (*personne*) to wall up *ou* in.

muret [müre] *nm* low wall.

mûrier [müryā] *nm* mulberry tree; (*ronce*) blackberry bush.

mûrir [mürēr] *vi* (*fruit, blé*) to ripen; (*abcès, furoncle*) to come to a head; (*fig: idée, personne*) to mature; (*projet*) to develop ♦ *vt* (*fruit, blé*) to ripen; (*personne*) to (make) mature; (*pensée, projet*) to nurture.

murmure [mürmür] *nm* murmur; **~s** *nmpl* (*plaintes*) murmurings, mutterings.

murmurer [mürmürā] *vi* to murmur; (*se plaindre*) to mutter, grumble.

mus [mü] *etc vb voir* **mouvoir.**

musaraigne [müzáreny] *nf* shrew.

musarder [müzárdā] *vi* to idle (about); (*en marchant*) to dawdle (along).

musc [müsk] *nm* musk.

muscade [müskád] *nf* (*aussi*: **noix ~**) nutmeg.

muscat [müská] *nm* (*raisin*) muscat grape; (*vin*) muscatel (wine).

muscle [müskl(ə)] *nm* muscle.

musclé, e [müsklā] *a* (*personne, corps*) muscular; (*fig: politique, régime etc*) strong arm *cpd*.

muscler [müsklā] *vt* to develop the muscles of.

musculaire [müsküler] *a* muscular.

musculation [müskülásyóň] *nf*: **exercices de ~** muscle-developing exercises.

musculature [müskülátür] *nf* muscle structure, muscles *pl*, musculature.

muse [müz] *nf* muse.

museau, x [müzō] *nm* muzzle.

musée [müzā] *nm* museum; (*de peinture*) art gallery.

museler [müzlā] *vt* to muzzle.

muselière [müzəlyer] *nf* muzzle.

musette [müzet] *nf* (*sac*) lunchbag ♦ *a inv* (*orchestre etc*) accordion *cpd*.

muséum [müzāom] *nm* museum.

musical, e, aux [müzēkál, -ō] *a* musical.

music-hall [müzēkōl] *nm* variety theater (*US*) *ou* theatre (*Brit*); (*genre*) variety.

musicien, ne [müzēsyeň, -en] *a* musical ♦ *nm/f* musician.

musique [müzēk] *nf* music; (*fanfare*) band; **faire de la ~** to make music; (*jouer d'un instrument*) to play an instrument; **~ de chambre** chamber music; **~ de fond** background music.

musqué, e [müskā] *a* musky.

must [mœst] *nm* must.

musulman, e [müzülmâň, -áň] *a, nm/f* Moslem, Muslim.

mutant, e [mütáň, -âňt] *nm/f* mutant.

mutation [mütásyóň] *nf* (*ADMIN*) transfer; (*BIO*) mutation.

muter [mütā] *vt* (*ADMIN*) to transfer.
mutilation [mütēlâsyôn] *nf* mutilation.
mutilé, e [mütēlā] *nm/f* disabled person (*through loss of limbs*); ~ **de guerre** disabled veteran (*US*) *ou* ex-serviceman (*Brit*); **grand** ~ severely disabled person.
mutiler [mütēlā] *vt* to mutilate, maim; (*fig*) to mutilate, deface.
mutin, e [mütan, -ēn] *a* (*enfant, air, ton*) mischievous, impish ♦ *nm/f* (*MIL*, *NAVIG*) mutineer.
mutiner [mütēnā]: **se** ~ *vi* to mutiny.
mutinerie [mütēnrē] *nf* mutiny.
mutisme [mütēsm(ə)] *nm* silence.
mutualité [mütüālētā] *nf* (*assurance*) mutual (benefit) insurance plan (*US*) *ou* scheme (*Brit*).
mutuel, le [mütüel] *a* mutual ♦ *nf* mutual benefit society.
myocarde [myokård(ə)] *nm voir* **infarctus**.
myope [myop] *a* nearsighted, shortsighted.
myopie [myopē] *nf* nearsightedness, shortsightedness, myopia.
myosotis [myōzotēs] *nm* forget-me-not.
myriade [mēryåd] *nf* myriad.
myrtille [mērtēy] *nf* blueberry (*US*), bilberry (*Brit*), whortleberry.
mystère [mēster] *nm* mystery.
mystérieusement [mēståryœzmån] *ad* mysteriously.
mystérieux, euse [mēståryœ, -œz] *a* mysterious.
mysticisme [mēstēsēsm(ə)] *nm* mysticism.
mystificateur, trice [mēstēfēkátœr, -trēs] *nm/f* hoaxer, practical joker.
mystification [mēstēfēkâsyôn] *nf* (*tromperie, mensonge*) hoax; (*mythe*) mystification.
mystifier [mēstēfyā] *vt* to fool, take in; (*tromper*) to mystify.
mystique [mēstēk] *a* mystic, mystical ♦ *nm/f* mystic.
mythe [mēt] *nm* myth.
mythifier [mētēfyā] *vt* to turn into a myth, mythologize.
mythique [mētēk] *a* mythical.
mythologie [mētolozhē] *nf* mythology.
mythologique [mētolozhēk] *a* mythological.
mythomane [mētomån] *a, nm/f* mythomaniac.

N

N, n [en] *nm inv* N, n ♦ *abr* (= *nord*) N; **N comme Nicolas** N for Nan.
n' [n] *ad voir* **ne**.
nabot [nåbō] *nm* dwarf.
nacelle [nåsel] *nf* (*de ballon*) basket.
nacre [nåkr(ə)] *nf* mother-of-pearl.
nacré, e [nåkrā] *a* pearly.
nage [nåzh] *nf* swimming; (*manière*) style of swimming, stroke; **traverser/s'éloigner à la** ~ to swim across/away; **en** ~ bathed in perspiration; ~ **indienne** sidestroke; ~ **libre**
freestyle; ~ **papillon** butterfly.
nageoire [nåzhwår] *nf* fin.
nager [nåzhā] *vi* to swim; (*fig: ne rien comprendre*) to be all at sea; ~ **dans** to be swimming in; (*vêtements*) to be lost in; ~ **dans le bonheur** to be overjoyed.
nageur, euse [nåzhœr, -œz] *nm/f* swimmer.
naguère [någer] *ad* (*il y a peu de temps*) not long ago; (*autrefois*) formerly.
naïf, ïve [nåēf, nåēv] *a* naïve.
nain, e [nan, nen] *a, nm/f* dwarf.
Nairobi [nåērobē] *n* Nairobi.
nais [ne], **naissais** [nese] *etc vb voir* **naître**.
naissance [nesåns] *nf* birth; **donner** ~ **à** to give birth to; (*fig*) to give rise to; **prendre** ~ to originate; **aveugle de** ~ born blind; **Français de** ~ French by birth; **à la** ~ **des cheveux** at the roots of the hair; **lieu de** ~ place of birth.
naissant, e [nesån, -ånt] *vb voir* **naître** ♦ *a* budding, incipient; (*jour*) dawning.
naît [ne] *vb voir* **naître**.
naître [netr(ə)] *vi* to be born; (*conflit, complications*): ~ **de** to arise from, be born out of; ~ **à** (*amour, poésie*) to awaken to; **il est né en 1960** he was born in 1960; **il naît plus de filles que de garçons** there are more girls born than boys; **faire** ~ (*fig*) to give rise to, arouse.
naïvement [nåēvmån] *ad* naïvely.
naïveté [nåēvtā] *nf* naïvety.
Namibie [nåmēbē] *nf*: **la** ~ Namibia.
nana [nånå] *nf* (*fam: fille*) chick.
nancéien, ne [nånsåyan, -en] *a* of *ou* from Nancy.
nantais, e [nånte, -ez] *a* of *ou* from Nantes.
nantir [nåntēr] *vt*: ~ **qn de** to provide sb with; **les nantis** (*péj*) the well-to-do.
NAP *sigle a* (= *Neuilly Auteuil Passy*) ≈ preppy.
napalm [nåpålm] *nm* napalm.
naphtaline [nåftålēn] *nf*: **boules de** ~ mothballs.
Naples [nåpl(ə)] *n* Naples.
napolitain, e [nåpolētan, -en] *a* Neapolitan; **tranche** ~**e** Neapolitan ice cream.
nappe [nåp] *nf* tablecloth; (*fig*) sheet; layer; ~ **de mazout** oil slick; ~ (**phréatique**) water table.
napper [nåpā] *vt*: ~ **qch de** to coat sth with.
napperon [nåprôn] *nm* table-mat; ~ **individuel** place mat.
naquis [nåkē] *etc vb voir* **naître**.
narcisse [nårsēs] *nm* narcissus.
narcissique [nårsēsēk] *a* narcissistic.
narcotique [nårkotēk] *a, nm* narcotic.
narguer [nårgā] *vt* to taunt.
narine [nårēn] *nf* nostril.
narquois, e [nårkwå, -wåz] *a* derisive, mocking.
narrateur, trice [nårátœr, -trēs] *nm/f* narrator.
narration [nårâsyôn] *nf* narration, narrative; (*SCOL*) essay.
narrer [nårā] *vt* to tell the story of, recount.
NASA [nåså] *sigle f* (= *National Aeronautics and Space Administration*) NASA.
nasal, e, aux [nåzål, -ō] *a* nasal.
naseau, x [nåzō] *nm* nostril.
nasillard, e [nåzēyár, -árd(ə)] *a* nasal.

nasiller [názēyā] *vi* to speak with a (nasal) twang.

Nassau [násō] *n* Nassau.

nasse [nás] *nf* fish trap.

natal, e [nátál] *a* native.

nataliste [nátálēst(ə)] *a* supporting a rising birth rate.

natalité [nátálētā] *nf* birth rate.

natation [nátásyôn] *nf* swimming; **faire de la ~** to go swimming (*regularly*).

natif, ive [nátēf, -ēv] *a* native.

nation [násyôn] *nf* nation; **les N~s Unies (NU)** the United Nations (UN).

national, e, aux [násyonál, -ō] *a* national ♦ *nf*: **(route) ~e** ≈ state highway (*US*), ≈ A road (*Brit*); **obsèques ~es** state funeral.

nationalisation [násyonálēzásyôn] *nf* nationalization.

nationaliser [násyonálēzā] *vt* to nationalize.

nationalisme [násyonálēsm(ə)] *nm* nationalism.

nationaliste [násyonálēst(ə)] *a, nm/f* nationalist.

nationalité [násyonálētā] *nf* nationality; **de ~ française** of French nationality.

natte [nát] *nf* (*tapis*) mat; (*cheveux*) plait.

natter [nátā] *vt* (*cheveux*) to plait.

naturalisation [nátürálēzásyôn] *nf* naturalization.

naturaliser [nátürálēzā] *vt* to naturalize; (*empailler*) to stuff.

naturaliste [nátürálēst(ə)] *nm/f* naturalist; (*empailleur*) taxidermist.

nature [nátür] *nf* nature ♦ *a, ad* (*CULIN*) plain, without seasoning or sweetening; (*café, thé: sans lait*) black; (*: sans sucre*) without sugar; **payer en ~** to pay in kind; **peint d'après ~** painted from life; **être de ~ à faire qch** (*propre à*) to be the sort of thing (*ou* person) to do sth; **~ morte** still life.

naturel, le [nátürel] *a* (*gén, aussi: enfant*) natural ♦ *nm* naturalness; (*caractère*) disposition, nature; (*autochtone*) native; **au ~** (*CULIN*) in water; in its own juices.

naturellement [nátürelmân] *ad* naturally; (*bien sûr*) of course.

naturisme [nátürēsm(ə)] *nm* naturism.

naturiste [nátürēst(ə)] *nm/f* naturist.

naufrage [nōfrázh] *nm* (ship)wreck; (*fig*) wreck; **faire ~** to be shipwrecked.

naufragé, e [nōfrázhā] *nm/f* shipwreck victim, castaway.

Nauru [norü] *nm* Nauru.

nauséabond, e [nōzăábôn, -ônd] *a* foul, nauseous.

nausée [nōzā] *nf* nausea; **avoir la ~** to feel sick; **avoir des ~s** to have waves of nausea, feel nauseous *ou* sick.

nautique [nōtēk] *a* nautical, water *cpd*; **sports ~s** water sports.

nautisme [nōtēsm(ə)] *nm* water sports *pl*.

naval, e [nável] *a* naval.

navarrais, e [návár̄e, -ez] *a* Navarrian.

navet [náve] *nm* turnip; (*péj*) third-rate film.

navette [návet] *nf* shuttle; (*en car etc*) shuttle (service); **faire la ~ (entre)** to go to and fro (between), shuttle (between); **~ spatiale** space shuttle.

navigabilité [návēgábēlētā] *nf* (*d'un navire*) seaworthiness; (*d'un avion*) airworthiness.

navigable [návēgábl(ə)] *a* navigable.

navigant, e [návēgán, -ânt] *a* (*AVIAT: personnel*) flying ♦ *nm/f*: **les ~s** the flying staff *ou* personnel.

navigateur [návēgátœr] *nm* (*NAVIG*) seafarer, sailor; (*AVIAT*) navigator.

navigation [návēgásyôn] *nf* navigation, sailing; (*COMM*) shipping; **compagnie de ~** shipping company; **~ spatiale** space navigation.

naviguer [návēgā] *vi* to navigate, sail.

navire [návēr] *nm* ship; **~ de guerre** warship; **~ marchand** merchantman.

navire-citerne, *pl* **navires-citernes** [návērsētern(ə)] *nm* tanker.

navire-hôpital, *pl* **navires-hôpitaux** [návēropētál, -tō] *nm* hospital ship.

navrant, e [návrân, -ânt] *a* (*affligeant*) upsetting; (*consternant*) annoying.

navrer [návrā] *vt* to upset, distress; **je suis navré (de/de faire/que)** I'm so sorry (for/for doing/that).

nazaréen, ne [názár̄ăn, -en] *a* Nazarene.

Nazareth [názáret] *n* Nazareth.

NB *abr* (= *nota bene*) NB.

nbr. *abr* = **nombreux**.

nbses *abr* = **nombreuses**.

n.c. *abr* = *non communiqué, non coté*.

ND *sigle f* = *Notre Dame*.

n.d. *abr* = *non daté, non disponible*.

NDA *sigle f* = *note de l'auteur*.

NDE *sigle f* = *note de l'éditeur*.

NDLR *sigle f* = *note de la rédaction*.

ne, n' [n(ə)] *ad voir* **pas, plus, jamais** *etc*; (*explétif*) *non traduit*.

né, e [nā] *pp de* **naître; ~ en 1960** born in 1960; **~e Scott** née Scott; **~(e) de ... et de ...** son/daughter of ... and of ...; **~ d'une mère française** having a French mother; **~ pour commander** born to lead ♦ *a*: **un comédien ~** a born comedian.

néanmoins [năânmwaṅ] *ad* nevertheless, yet.

néant [năân] *nm* nothingness; **réduire à ~** to bring to nought; (*espoir*) to dash.

nébuleux, euse [nābülœ̄, -œ̄z] *a* (*ciel*) cloudy; (*fig*) nebulous.

nébuliser [nābülēzā] *vt* (*liquide*) to spray.

nébulosité [nābülōzētā] *nf* cloud cover; **~ variable** cloudy in places.

nécessaire [nāsãer] *a* necessary ♦ *nm* necessary; (*sac*) kit; **faire le ~** to do the necessary; **n'emporter que le strict ~** to take only what is strictly necessary; **~ de couture** sewing kit; **~ de toilette** toilet case (*US*) *ou* bag (*Brit*); **~ de voyage** overnight bag.

nécessairement [nāsãsermân] *ad* necessarily.

nécessité [nāsãsētā] *nf* necessity; **se trouver dans la ~ de faire qch** to find it necessary to do sth; **par ~** out of necessity.

nécessiter [nāsãsētā] *vt* to require.

nécessiteux, euse [nāsãsētœ̄, -œ̄z] *a* needy.

nec plus ultra [nākplüsültrá] *nm*: **le ~ de** the last word in.

nécrologie [nākrolozhē] *nf* obituary.

nécrologique [nākrolozhēk] *a*: **article ~** obituary; **rubrique ~** obituary column.

nécromancie [nākromânsē] *nf* necromancy.

nécromancien, ne [nākromáńsyań, -en] *nm/f* necromancer.

nécrose [nākrōz] *nf* necrosis.

nectar [nektár] *nm* nectar.

nectarine [nektárēn] *nf* nectarine.

néerlandais, e [nāerlấnde, -ez] *a* Dutch, of the Netherlands ♦ *nm* (*LING*) Dutch ♦ *nm/f*: **N~**, **e** Dutchman/woman; **les N~** the Dutch.

nef [nef] *nf* (*d'église*) nave.

néfaste [nāfàst(ə)] *a* baneful; ill-fated.

négatif, ive [nāgátēf, ēv] *a* negative ♦ *nm* (*PHOTO*) negative.

négativement [nāgátēvmáń] *ad*: **répondre ~** to give a negative response.

négligé, e [nāglēzhā] *a* (*en désordre*) slovenly ♦ *nm* (*tenue*) negligee.

négligeable [nāglēzhábl(ə)] *a* insignificant, negligible.

négligemment [nāglēzhámáń] *ad* carelessly.

négligence [nāglēzhấńs] *nf* carelessness *q*; (*faute*) careless omission.

négligent, e [nāglēzhấń, -áńt] *a* careless; (*JUR etc*) negligent.

négliger [nāglēzhā] *vt* (*épouse, jardin*) to neglect; (*tenue*) to be careless about; (*avis, précautions*) to disregard, overlook; **~ de faire** to fail to do, not bother to do; **se ~** to neglect o.s.

négoce [nāgos] *nm* trade.

négociable [nāgosyábl(ə)] *a* negotiable.

négociant [nāgosyáń] *nm* merchant.

négociateur [nāgosyátœr] *nm* negotiator.

négociation [nāgosyásyóń] *nf* negotiation; **~s collectives** collective bargaining *sg*.

négocier [nāgosyā] *vi, vt* to negotiate.

nègre [negr(ə)] *nm* (*péj*) Negro; (*péj*: *écrivain*) ghost writer ♦ *a* Negro.

négresse [nāgres] *nf* (*péj*) Negress.

négrier [nāgrēyā] *nm* (*fig*) slave driver.

négroïde [nāgroēd] *a* negroid.

neige [nezh] *nf* snow; **battre les œufs en ~** (*CULIN*) to whip *ou* beat the egg whites until stiff; **~ carbonique** dry ice; **~ fondue** (*par terre*) slush; (*qui tombe*) sleet; **~ poudreuse** powder snow.

neiger [nāzhā] *vi* to snow.

neigeux, euse [nezhœ̄, -œ̄z] *a* snowy, snow-covered.

nénuphar [nānüfár] *nm* water lily.

néo-calédonien, ne [nāokálādonyań, -en] *a* New Caledonian ♦ *nm/f*: **N~, ne** native of New Caledonia.

néologisme [nāolozhēsm(ə)] *nm* neologism.

néon [nāóń] *nm* neon.

néo-natal, e [nāonátál] *a* neonatal.

néophyte [nāofēt] *nm/f* novice.

néo-zélandais, e [nāozālấnde, -ez] *a* New Zealand *cpd* ♦ *nm/f*: **N~, e** New Zealander.

Népal [nāpál] *nm*: **le ~** Nepal.

népalais, e [nāpále, -ez] *a* Nepalese, Nepali ♦ *nm* (*LING*) Nepalese, Nepali ♦ *nm/f*: **N~, e** Nepalese, Nepali.

néphrétique [nāfrātēk] *a* (*MÉD*: *colique*) nephritic.

néphrite [nāfrēt] *nf* (*MÉD*) nephritis.

nerf [ner] *nm* nerve; (*fig*) spirit; (: *forces*) stamina; **~s** *nmpl* nerves; **être** *ou* **vivre sur les ~s** to be a bundle of nerves; **être à bout de ~s** to be at the end of one's rope; **passer**

ses ~s sur qn to take it out on sb.

nerveusement [nervœ̄zmáń] *ad* nervously.

nerveux, euse [nervœ̄, -œ̄z] *a* nervous; (*cheval*) high-strung (*US*), highly-strung (*Brit*); (*voiture*) responsive; (*tendineux*) sinewy.

nervosité [nervōzētā] *nf* nervousness; (*émotivité*) excitability.

nervure [nervür] *nf* (*de feuille*) vein; (*ARCHIT, TECH*) rib.

n'est-ce pas [nespâ] *ad* isn't it?, won't you? *etc, selon le verbe qui précède*; **c'est bon, ~?** it's good, isn't it?; **il a peur, ~?** he's afraid, isn't he?; **~ que c'est bon?** don't you think it's good?; **lui, ~, il peut se le permettre** he, of course, can afford to do that, can't he?

net, nette [net] *a* (*sans équivoque, distinct*) clear; (*photo*) sharp; (*évident*) definite; (*propre*) neat, clean; (*COMM: prix, salaire, poids*) net ♦ *ad* (*refuser*) flatly ♦ *nm*: **mettre au ~** to copy out; **s'arrêter ~** to stop dead; **la lame a cassé ~** the blade snapped clean through; **faire place nette** to make a clean sweep; **~ d'impôt** tax free.

nettement [netmáń] *ad* (*distinctement*) clearly; (*évidemment*) definitely; (*avec comparatif, superlatif*): **~ mieux** definitely *ou* clearly better.

netteté [nettā] *nf* clearness.

nettoie [netwá] *etc vb voir* **nettoyer**.

nettoiement [nātwámáń] *nm* (*ADMIN*) cleaning; **service du ~** garbage (*US*) *ou* refuse (*Brit*) collection.

nettoierai [netwárā] *etc vb voir* **nettoyer**.

nettoyage [netwàyázh] *nm* cleaning; **~ à sec** dry cleaning.

nettoyant [nātwáyáń] *nm* (*produit*) cleaning agent.

nettoyer [netwáyā] *vt* to clean; (*fig*) to clean out.

neuf [nœf] *num* nine.

neuf, neuve [nœf, nœv] *a* new ♦ *nm*: **repeindre à ~** to redecorate; **remettre à ~** to renovate, refurbish; **n'acheter que du ~** to buy everything new; **quoi de ~?** what's new?

neurasthénique [nœrástānēk] *a* neurasthenic.

neurochirurgien [nœroshērürzhyań] *nm* neurosurgeon.

neuroleptique [nœroleptēk] *a* neuroleptic.

neurologique [nœrolozhēk] *a* neurological.

neurologue [nœrolog] *nm/f* neurologist.

neuropsychiatre [nœropsēkyátr(ə)] *nm/f* neuropsychiatrist.

neutralisation [nœtrálēzásyóń] *nf* neutralization.

neutraliser [nœtrálēzā] *vt* to neutralize.

neutraliste [nœtrálēst(ə)] *a* neutralist.

neutralité [nœtrálētā] *nf* neutrality.

neutre [nœtr(ə)] *a, nm* (*aussi LING*) neutral.

neutron [nœtróń] *nm* neutron.

neuve [nœv] *af voir* **neuf**.

neuvième [nœvyem] *num* ninth.

névé [nāvā] *nm* permanent snowpatch.

neveu, x [nəvœ̄] *nm* nephew.

névralgie [nāvrálzhē] *nf* neuralgia.

névralgique [nāvrálzhēk] *a* (*fig*: *sensible*) sensitive; **centre ~** nerve center (*US*) *ou* centre (*Brit*).

névrite [nāvrēt] *nf* neuritis.

névrose [nāvrōz] *nf* neurosis.
névrosé, e [nāvrōzā] *a, nm/f* neurotic.
névrotique [nāvrotēk] *a* neurotic.
New York [nyōōyork] *n* New York.
new yorkais, e [nyōōyorke, -ez] *a* of *ou* from New York, New York *cpd* ♦ *nm/f*: **New Yorkais, e** New Yorker.
nez [nā] *nm* nose; **rire au ~ de qn** to laugh in sb's face; **avoir du ~** to have flair; **avoir le ~ fin** to have foresight; **~ à ~ avec** face to face with; **à vue de ~** roughly.
NF *sigle mpl = nouveaux francs* ♦ *sigle f (IN-DUSTRIE:* = *norme française) industrial standard.*
ni [nē] *cj*: **~ l'un ~ l'autre ne sont** *ou* **n'est** neither one nor the other is; **il n'a rien dit ~ fait** he hasn't said or done anything.
Niagara [nyágárá] *nm*: **les chutes du ~** the Niagara Falls.
niais, e [nye, -ez] *a* silly, thick.
niaiserie [nyezrē] *nf* gullibility; *(action, propos, futilité)* silliness.
Nicaragua [nēkárágwá] *nm*: **le ~** Nicaragua.
nicaraguayen, ne [nēkárágwáyań, -en] *a* Nicaraguan ♦ *nm/f*: **N~, ne** Nicaraguan.
Nice [nēs] *n* Nice.
niche [nēsh] *nf (du chien)* kennel; *(de mur)* recess, niche; *(farce)* trick.
nichée [nēshā] *nf* brood, nest.
nicher [nēshā] *vi* to nest; **se ~ dans** *(personne: se blottir)* to snuggle into; (: *se cacher)* to hide in; *(objet)* to lodge itself in.
nichon [nēshóń] *nm (fam)* boob, tit.
nickel [nēkel] *nm* nickel.
niçois, e [nēswá, -wáz] *a* of *ou* from Nice; *(CULIN)* Niçoise.
Nicosie [nēkosē] *n* Nicosia.
nicotine [nēkotēn] *nf* nicotine.
nid [nē] *nm* nest; *(fig: repaire etc)* den, lair; **~ d'abeilles** *(COUTURE, TEXTILE)* honeycomb stitch; **~ de poule** pothole.
nièce [nyes] *nf* niece.
nième [enycm] *a*: **la ~ fois** the nth *ou* umpteenth time.
nier [nyā] *vt* to deny.
nigaud, e [nēgō, -ōd] *nm/f* booby, fool.
Niger [nēzher] *nm*: **le ~** Niger; *(fleuve)* the Niger.
Nigéria [nēzhāryá] *nm ou nf* Nigeria.
nigérian, e [nēzhāryań, -án] *a* Nigerian ♦ *nm/f*: **N~, e** Nigerian.
nigérien, ne [nēzhāryań, -en] *a* of *ou* from Niger.
Nil [nēl] *nm*: **le ~** the Nile.
n'importe [nańport(ə)] *ad*: **~!** no matter!; **~ qui/quoi/où** anybody/anything/ anywhere; **~ quoi!** *(fam: désapprobation)* what rubbish!; **~ quand** any time; **~ quel/quelle** any; **~ lequel/laquelle** any (one); **~ comment** *(sans soin)* carelessly; **~ comment, il part ce soir** he's leaving tonight in any case.
nippes [nēp] *nfpl (fam)* duds *(US)*, togs *(Brit)*.
nippon, e *ou* **ne** [nēpóń, -on] *a* Japanese.
nique [nēk] *nf*: **faire la ~ à** to thumb one's nose at *(fig)*.
nitouche [nētōōsh] *nf (péj)*: **c'est une sainte ~** she looks as if butter wouldn't melt in her mouth.

nitrate [nētrát] *nm* nitrate.
nitrique [nētrēk] *a*: **acide ~** nitric acid.
nitroglycérine [nētroglēsārēn] *nf* nitro-glycerin(e).
niveau, x [nēvō] *nm* level; *(des élèves, études)* standard; **au ~ de** at the level of; *(personne)* on a level with; **de ~ (avec)** level (with); **le ~ de la mer** sea level; **~ (à bulle)** spirit level; **~ (d'eau)** water level; **~ de vie** standard of living.
niveler [nēvlā] *vt* to level.
niveleuse [nēvlēz] *nf (TECH)* grader.
nivellement [nēvelmáń] *nm* leveling *(US)*, levelling *(Brit)*.
nivernais, e [nēverne, -ez] *a* of *ou* from Nevers (and region) ♦ *nm/f*: **N~, e** inhabitant *ou* native of Nevers (and region).
NL *sigle f = nouvelle lune.*
NN *abr (= nouvelle norme) revised standard of hotel classification.*
n° *abr (= numéro)* no.
nobiliaire [nobēlyer] *af voir* **particule**.
noble [nobl(ə)] *a* noble; *(de qualité: métal etc)* precious ♦ *nm/f* noble(man/woman).
noblesse [nobles] *nf (classe sociale)* nobility; *(d'une action etc)* nobleness.
noce [nos] *nf* wedding; *(gens)* wedding party *(ou guests pl)*; **il l'a épousée en secondes ~s** she was his second wife; **faire la ~** *(fam)* to go on a binge; **~s d'or/d'argent/de diamant** golden/silver/diamond wedding.
nocif, ive [nosēf, -ēv] *a* harmful, noxious.
noctambule [noktánbül] *nm* night owl.
nocturne [noktürn(ə)] *a* nocturnal ♦ *nf (SPORT)* floodlit fixture; *(d'un magasin)* late opening.
Noël [noel] *nm* Christmas; **la (fête de) ~** Christmas time.
nœud [nē] *nm (de corde, du bois, NAVIG)* knot; *(ruban)* bow; *(fig: liens)* bond, tie; *(fig: d'une question)* crux; *(THÉÂTRE etc)*: **le ~ de l'action** the web of events; **~ coulant** noose; **~ gordien** Gordian knot; **~ papillon** bow tie.
noie [nwá] *etc vb voir* **noyer**.
noir, e [nwár] *a* black; *(obscur, sombre)* dark ♦ *nm/f* black man/woman, Negro/Negro woman ♦ *nm*: **dans le ~** in the dark ♦ *nf (MUS)* quarter note *(US)*, crotchet *(Brit)*; **il fait ~** it is dark; **au ~** *ad (acheter, vendre)* on the black market; **travail au ~** moonlighting.
noirâtre [nwárâtr(ə)] *a (teinte)* blackish.
noirceur [nwársœr] *nf* blackness; darkness.
noircir [nwársēr] *vt, vi* to blacken.
noise [nwáz] *nf*: **chercher ~ à** to try and pick a quarrel with.
noisetier [nwáztyā] *nm* hazel (tree).
noisette [nwázet] *nf* hazelnut; *(morceau: de beurre etc)* small knob ♦ *a (yeux)* hazel.
noix [nwá] *nf* walnut; *(fam)* twit; *(CULIN)*: **une ~ de beurre** a lump of butter; **à la ~ (de coco)** *(fam)* worthless; **~ de cajou** cashew nut; **~ de coco** coconut; **~ muscade** nutmeg; **~ de veau** *(CULIN)* round fillet of veal.
nom [nóń] *nm* name; *(LING)* noun; **connaître qn de ~** to know sb by name; **au ~ de** in the name of; **~ d'une pipe** *ou* **d'un chien!** *(fam)* for goodness' sake!; **~ de Dieu!** *(fam!)* my

God!; ~ **commun/propre** common/proper noun; ~ **composé** (*LING*) compound noun; ~ **déposé** trade name; ~ **d'emprunt** assumed name; ~ **de famille** surname; ~ **de fichier** file name; ~ **de jeune fille** maiden name.

nomade [nomàd] *a* nomadic ♦ *nm/f* nomad.

nombre [nôṅbr(ə)] *nm* number; **venir en ~** to come in large numbers; **depuis ~ d'années** for many years; **ils sont au ~ de 3** there are 3 of them; **au ~ de mes amis** among my friends; **sans ~** countless; **(bon) ~ de** (*beaucoup, plusieurs*) a (large) number of; ~ **premier/entier** prime/whole number.

nombreux, euse [nôṅbrœ, -œz] *a* many, numerous; (*avec nom sg: foule etc*) large; **peu ~** few; small; **de ~ cas** many cases.

nombril [nôṅbrē] *nm* navel.

nomenclature [nomàṅklàtür] *nf* wordlist; list of items.

nominal, e, aux [nomēnàl, -ō] *a* nominal; (*appel, liste*) of names.

nominatif, ive [nomēnàtēf, -ēv] *nm* (*LING*) nominative ♦ *a*: **liste ~ive** list of names; **carte ~ive** calling card; **titre ~** registered name.

nomination [nomēnâsyôṅ] *nf* nomination.

nommément [nomāmàṅ] *ad* (*désigner*) by name.

nommer [nomā] *vt* (*baptiser*) to name, give a name to; (*qualifier*) to call; (*mentionner*) to name, give the name of; (*élire*) to appoint, nominate; **se ~**: **il se nomme Pascal** his name's Pascal, he's called Pascal.

non [nôṅ] *ad* (*réponse*) no; (*suivi d'un adjectif, adverbe*) not; **Paul est venu, ~?** Paul came, didn't he?; **répondre** *ou* **dire que ~** to say no; ~ **pas que** not that; ~ **plus**: **moi ~ plus** neither do I, I don't either; **je préférerais que ~** I would prefer not; **il se trouve que ~** perhaps not; **je pense que ~** I don't think so; ~ **mais!** well really!; ~ **mais des fois!** you must be joking!; ~ **alcoolisé** non-alcoholic; ~ **loin/seulement** not far/only.

nonagénaire [nonázhānɛr] *nm/f* nonagenarian.

non-agression [nonàgrāsyôṅ] *nf*: **pacte de ~** non-aggression pact.

non-aligné, e [nonàlēnyā] *a* nonaligned.

nonante [nonàṅt] *num* (*Belgique, Suisse*) ninety.

nonce [nôṅs] *nm* (*REL*) nuncio.

nonchalance [nôṅshàlàṅs] *nf* nonchalance, casualness.

nonchalant, e [nôṅshàlàṅ, -àṅt] *a* nonchalant, casual.

non-conformiste [nôṅkôṅformēst(ə)] *a*, *nm/f* nonconformist.

non-croyant, e [nôṅkrwàyàṅ, -àṅt] *nm/f* (*REL*) nonbeliever.

non(-)engagé, e [nonàṅgàzhā] *a* nonaligned.

non-fumeur [nôṅfümœr] *nm* nonsmoker.

non-ingérence [nonàṅzhāràṅs] *nf* noninterference.

non-inscrit, e [nonàṅskrē, -ēt] *nm/f* (*POL*: *député*) independent.

non-intervention [nonàṅtervàṅsyôṅ] *nf* nonintervention.

non-lieu [nôṅlyœ] *nm*: **il y a eu ~** the case was dismissed.

nonne [non] *nf* nun.

nonobstant [nonopstàṅ] *prép* notwithstanding.

non-paiement [nôṅpɛmàṅ] *nm* nonpayment.

non-prolifération [nôṅprolēfārâsyôṅ] *nf* nonproliferation.

non-résident [nôṅrāsēdàṅ] *nm* (*ÉCON*) nonresident.

non-retour [nôṅrətōōr] *nm*: **point de ~** point of no return.

non-sens [nôṅsàṅs] *nm* absurdity.

non-syndiqué, e [nôṅsàṅdēkā] *nm/f* nonunion member.

non-violent, e [nôṅvyolàṅ, -àṅt] *a* nonviolent.

nord [nor] *nm* North ♦ *a* northern; north; **au ~** (*situation*) in the north; (*direction*) to the north; **au ~ de** north of, to the north of; **perdre le ~** to lose the place (*fig*).

nord-africain, e [noràfrēkàṅ, -en] *a* North African ♦ *nm/f*: **Nord-Africain, e** North African.

nord-américain, e [noràmārēkàṅ, -en] *a* North American ♦ *nm/f*: **Nord-Américain, e** North American.

nord-coréen, ne [norkorāàṅ, -en] *a* North Korean ♦ *nm/f*: **Nord-Coréen, ne** North Korean.

nord-est [norest] *nm* northeast.

nordique [nordēk] *a* (*pays, race*) Nordic; (*langues*) Scandinavian, Nordic ♦ *nm/f*: **N~** Scandinavian.

nord-ouest [norwest] *nm* northwest.

nord-vietnamien, ne [norvyetnàmyàṅ, -en] *a* North Vietnamese ♦ *nm/f*: **Nord-Vietnamien, ne** North Vietnamese.

normal, e, aux [normàl, -ō] *a* normal ♦ *nf*: **la ~e** the norm, the average.

normalement [normàlmàṅ] *ad* (*en général*) normally; (*comme prévu*): ~, **il le fera demain** he should be doing it tomorrow, he's supposed to do it tomorrow.

normalien, ne [normàlyàṅ, -en] *nm/f* student of École normale supérieure.

normalisation [normàlēzâsyôṅ] *nf* standardization; normalization.

normaliser [normàlēzā] *vt* (*COMM*, *TECH*) to standardize; (*POL*) to normalize.

normand, e [normàṅ, -àṅd] *a* (*de Normandie*) Norman ♦ *nm/f*: **N~, e** (*de Normandie*) Norman.

Normandie [normàṅdē] *nf*: **la ~** Normandy.

norme [norm(ə)] *nf* norm; (*TECH*) standard.

Norvège [norvezh] *nf*: **la ~** Norway.

norvégien, ne [norvāzhyàṅ, -en] *a* Norwegian ♦ *nm* (*LING*) Norwegian ♦ *nm/f*: **N~, ne** Norwegian.

nos [nō] *dét voir* **notre**.

nostalgie [nostàlzhē] *nf* nostalgia.

nostalgique [nostàlzhēk] *a* nostalgic.

notabilité [notàbēlētā] *nf* notability.

notable [notàbl(ə)] *a* notable, noteworthy; (*marqué*) noticeable, marked ♦ *nm* prominent citizen.

notablement [notàbləmàṅ] *ad* notably; (*sensiblement*) noticeably.

notaire [notɛr] *nm* notary; solicitor.

notamment [notàmàṅ] *ad* in particular, among others.

notariat [notàryà] *nm* profession of notary.

notarié, e [notàryā] *a*: **acte ~** deed drawn up by a notary.

notation [notâsyôṅ] *nf* notation.

note [not] *nf* (*écrite*, *MUS*) note; (*SCOL*) grade; (*facture*) bill; **prendre des** ~**s** to take notes; **prendre** ~ **de** to note; (*par écrit*) to note, write down; **dans la** ~ exactly right; **forcer la** ~ to exaggerate; **une** ~ **de tristesse/de gaieté** a sad/happy note; ~ **de service** memorandum.

noté, e [notā] *a*: **être bien/mal** ~ (*employé etc*) to have a good/bad record.

noter [notā] *vt* (*écrire*) to write down, note; (*remarquer*) to note, notice; (*SCOL*, *ADMIN*: *donner une appréciation*) to mark, give a grade to; **notez bien que** ... (please) note that ....

notice [notēs] *nf* summary, short article; (*brochure*): ~ **explicative** explanatory leaflet, instruction booklet.

notification [notēfēkåsyôǹ] *nf* notification.

notifier [notēfyā] *vt*: ~ **qch à qn** to notify sb of sth, notify sth to sb.

notion [nōsyôǹ] *nf* notion, idea; ~**s** *nfpl* (*rudiments*) rudiments.

notoire [notwár] *a* widely known; (*en mal*) notorious; **le fait est** ~ the fact is common knowledge.

notoriété [notoryātā] *nf*: **c'est de** ~ **publique** it's common knowledge.

notre, nos [notr(ə), nō] *dét* our.

nôtre [nôtr(ə)] *pronom*: **le/la** ~ ours; **les** ~**s** ours; (*alliés etc*) our own people; **soyez des** ~**s** join us ♦ *a* ours.

nouer [nwā] *vt* to tie, knot; (*fig: alliance etc*) to strike up; ~ **la conversation** to start a conversation; **se** ~ *vi*: **c'est là où l'intrigue se noue** it's at that point that the strands of the plot come together; **ma gorge se noua** a lump came to my throat.

noueux, euse [nwœ̄, -œ̄z] *a* gnarled.

nougat [nōōgå] *nm* nougat.

nouille [nōōy] *nf* (*pâtes*): ~**s** noodles; pasta *sg*; (*fam*) noodle, fathead.

nounou [nōōnōō] *nf* nanny.

nounours [nōōnōōrs] *nm* teddy (bear).

nourri, e [nōōrē] *a* (*feu etc*) sustained.

nourrice [nōōrēs] *nf* ≈ nanny; (*autrefois*) wet nurse.

nourrir [nōōrēr] *vt* to feed; (*fig: espoir*) to harbor (*US*), harbour (*Brit*); nurse; **logé nourri** with room and board; ~ **au sein** to breast-feed; **se** ~ **de légumes/rêves** to live on vegetables/dreams.

nourrissant, e [nōōrēsåǹ, -åǹt] *a* nourishing, nutritious.

nourrisson [nōōrēsôǹ] *nm* (*unweaned*) infant.

nourriture [nōōrētür] *nf* food.

nous [nōō] *pronom* (*sujet*) we; (*objet*) us.

nous-mêmes [nōōmem] *pronom* ourselves.

nouveau (**nouvel**), **elle, x** [nōōvō, -el] *a* new; (*original*) novel ♦ *nm/f* new pupil (*ou* employee) ♦ *nm*: **il y a du** ~ there's something new ♦ *nf* (piece of) news *sg*; (*LITTÉRATURE*) short story; **nouvelles** *nfpl* (*PRESSE, TV*) news; **de** ~, **à** ~ again; **je suis sans nouvelles de lui** I haven't heard from him; **Nouvel An** New Year; ~ **riche** nouveau riche; ~ **venu**, **nouvelle venue** newcomer; ~**x mariés** newlyweds; **nouvelle vague** new wave.

nouveau-né, e [nōōvōnā] *nm/f* newborn (baby).

nouveauté [nōōvōtā] *nf* novelty; (*chose nouvelle*) innovation, something new; (*COMM*) new film (*ou* book *ou* creation *etc*).

nouvel *am*, **nouvelle** *af*, *nf* [nōōvel] *voir* **nouveau**.

Nouvelle-Angleterre [nōōvelåǹgləter] *nf*: **la** ~ New England.

Nouvelle-Calédonie [nōōvelkålādonē] *nf*: **la** ~ New Caledonia.

Nouvelle-Écosse [nōōvelākos] *nf*: **la** ~ Nova Scotia.

Nouvelle-Galles du Sud [nōōvelgåldüsüd] *nf*: **la** ~ New South Wales.

Nouvelle-Guinée [nōōvelgēnā] *nf*: **la** ~ New Guinea.

nouvellement [nōōvelmâǹ] *ad* (*arrivé etc*) recently, newly.

Nouvelle-Orléans [nōōvelorlââǹ] *nf*: **la** ~ New Orleans.

Nouvelles-Hébrides [nōōvelsābrēd] *nfpl*: **les** ~ the New Hebrides.

Nouvelle-Zélande [nōōvelzālåǹd] *nf*: **la** ~ New Zealand.

nouvelliste [nōōvālēst(ə)] *nm/f* editor *ou* writer of short stories.

novateur, trice [novátœr, -trēs] *a* innovative ♦ *nm/f* innovator.

novembre [novåǹbr(ə)] *nm* November; *voir aussi* **juillet**.

novice [novēs] *a* inexperienced ♦ *nm/f* novice.

noviciat [novēsyá] *nm* (*REL*) novitiate.

noyade [nwåyád] *nf* drowning *q*.

noyau, x [nwåyō] *nm* (*de fruit*) pit (*US*), stone; (*BIO, PHYSIQUE*) nucleus; (*ÉLEC, GÉO, fig: centre*) core; (*fig: d'artistes etc*) group; (: *de résistants etc*) cell.

noyautage [nwåyōtázh] *nm* (*POL*) infiltration.

noyauter [nwåyōtā] *vt* (*POL*) to infiltrate.

noyé, e [nwåyā] *nm/f* drowning (*ou* drowned) man/woman ♦ *a* (*fig: dépassé*) out of one's depth.

noyer [nwåyā] *nm* walnut (tree); (*bois*) walnut ♦ *vt* to drown; (*fig*) to flood; to submerge; (*AUTO: moteur*) to flood; **se** ~ to be drowned, drown; (*suicide*) to drown o.s; ~ **son chagrin** to drown one's sorrows; ~ **le poisson** to duck the issue.

NSP *sigle m* (*REL*) = *Notre Saint Père*; (*dans les sondages*: *ne sais pas*) don't know.

NT *sigle m* (= *Nouveau Testament*) NT.

NU *sigle fpl* (= *Nations Unies*) UN.

nu, e [nü] *a* naked; (*membres*) naked, bare; (*chambre, fil, plaine*) bare ♦ *nm* (*ART*) nude; **le** ~ **intégral** total nudity; **à mains** ~**es** with one's bare hands; **se mettre** ~ to strip; **mettre à** ~ to bare.

nuage [nüázh] *nm* cloud; **être dans les** ~**s** (*distrait*) to have one's head in the clouds; ~ **de lait** drop of milk.

nuageux, euse [nüázhœ̄, -œ̄z] *a* cloudy.

nuance [nüåǹs] *nf* (*de couleur, sens*) shade; **il y a une** ~ (**entre**) there's a slight difference (between); **une** ~ **de tristesse** a tinge of sadness.

nuancé, e [nüåǹsā] *a* (*opinion*) finely-shaded, subtly differing; **être** ~ **dans ses opinions** to have finely-shaded opinions.

nuancer [nüåǹsā] *vt* (*pensée, opinion*) to qualify.

nubile [nübēl] *a* nubile.
nucléaire [nüklāer] *a* nuclear ♦ *nm* nuclear power.
nudisme [nüdēsm(ə)] *nm* nudism.
nudiste [nüdēst(ə)] *a, nm/f* nudist.
nudité [nüdētā] *nf (voir nu)* nudity, nakedness; bareness.
nuée [nüā] *nf*: **une ~ de** a cloud *ou* host *ou* swarm of.
nues [nü] *nfpl*: **tomber des ~** to be taken aback; **porter qn aux ~** to praise sb to the skies.
nui [nüē] *pp de* **nuire.**
nuire [nüēr] *vi* to be harmful; **~ à** to harm, do damage to.
nuisance [nüēzáns] *nf* nuisance; **~s** *nfpl* pollution *sg*.
nuisible [nüēzēbl(ə)] *a* harmful; **(animal) ~** pest.
nuisis [nüēzē] *etc vb voir* **nuire.**
nuit [nüē] *nf* night; **payer sa ~** to pay for one's overnight accommodations (*US*) *ou* accommodation (*Brit*); **il fait ~** it's dark; **cette ~** (*hier*) last night; (*aujourd'hui*) tonight; **de ~** (*vol, service*) night *cpd*; **~ blanche** sleepless night; **~ de noces** wedding night; **~ de Noël** Christmas Eve.
nuitamment [nüētámán] *ad* by night.
nuitées [nüētā] *nfpl* overnight stays, beds occupied (*in statistics*).
nul, nulle [nül] *a* (*aucun*) no; (*minime*) nil, nonexistent; (*non valable*) null; (*péj*) useless, hopeless ♦ *pronom* none, no one; **résultat ~, match ~** draw; **nulle part** *ad* nowhere.
nullement [nülmán] *ad* by no means.
nullité [nülētā] *nf* nullity; (*péj*) hopelessness; (: *personne*) hopeless individual, nonentity.
numéraire [nümārer] *nm* cash; metal currency.
numéral, e, aux [nümārál, -ō] *a* numeral.
numérateur [nümārátœr] *nm* numerator.
numération [nümārásyón] *nf*: **~ décimale/binaire** decimal/binary notation.
numérique [nümārēk] *a* numerical; (*INFORM*) digital.
numériquement [nümārēkmán] *ad* numerically.
numériser [nümārēzā] *vt* (*INFORM*) to digitize.
numéro [nümārō] *nm* number; (*spectacle*) act, turn; **faire** *ou* **composer un ~** to dial a number; **~ d'identification personnel** personal identification number (PIN); **~ d'immatriculation** *ou* **minéralogique** *ou* **de police** license (*US*) *ou* registration (*Brit*) number; **~ de téléphone** (tele)phone number; **~ vert** ≈ toll-free number (*US*), ≈ Freefone ® number (*Brit*).
numérotage [nümārotázh] *nm* numbering.
numérotation [nümārotásyón] *nf* numeration.
numéroter [nümārotā] *vt* to number.
numerus clausus [nümārüsklōzüs] *nm inv* restriction *ou* limitation of numbers.
numismate [nümēsmát] *nm/f* numismatist, coin collector.
nu-pieds [nüpyā] *nm inv* sandal ♦ *a inv* barefoot.
nuptial, e, aux [nüpsyál, -ō] *a* nuptial; wedding *cpd*.
nuptialité [nüpsyálētā] *nf*: **taux de ~** marriage rate.

nuque [nük] *nf* nape of the neck.
nu-tête [nütet] *a inv* bareheaded.
nutritif, ive [nütrētēf, -ēv] *a* nutritional; (*aliment*) nutritious, nourishing.
nutrition [nütrēsyón] *nf* nutrition.
nutritionnel, le [nütrēsyonel] *a* nutritional.
nutritionniste [nütrēsyonēst(ə)] *nm/f* nutritionist.
nylon [nēlón] *nm* nylon.
nymphomane [nánfomán] *a, nf* nymphomaniac.

O

O, o [ō] *nm inv* O, o ♦ *abr* (= *ouest*) W; **O comme Oscar** O for Oboe.
OAS *sigle f* (= *Organisation de l'armée secrète*) organization opposed to Algerian independence (*1961-63*).
oasis [oázēs] *nf* oasis (*pl* oases).
obédience [obādyáns] *nf* allegiance.
obéir [obāēr] *vi* to obey; **~ à** to obey; (*suj: moteur, véhicule*) to respond to.
obéissance [obāēsáns] *nf* obedience.
obéissant, e [obāēsán, -ánt] *a* obedient.
obélisque [obālēsk(ə)] *nm* obelisk.
obèse [obez] *a* obese.
obésité [obāzētā] *nf* obesity.
objecter [obzhektā] *vt* (*prétexter*) to plead, put forward as an excuse; **~ qch à** (*argument*) to put forward sth against; **~ (à qn) que** to object (to sb) that.
objecteur [obzhektœr] *nm*: **~ de conscience** conscientious objector.
objectif, ive [obzhektēf, -ēv] *a* objective ♦ *nm* (*OPTIQUE, PHOTO*) lens *sg*; (*MIL, fig*) objective; **~ grand angulaire/à focale variable** wide-angle/zoom lens.
objection [obzheksyón] *nf* objection; **~ de conscience** conscientious objection.
objectivement [obzhektēvmán] *ad* objectively.
objectivité [obzhektēvētā] *nf* objectivity.
objet [obzhe] *nm* (*chose*) object; (*d'une discussion, recherche*) subject; **être** *ou* **faire l'~ de** (*discussion*) to be the subject of; (*soins*) to be given *ou* shown; **sans ~** *a* purposeless; (*sans fondement*) groundless; **~ d'art** objet d'art; **~s personnels** personal items; **~s de toilette** toiletries; **~s trouvés** lost-and-found *sg* (*US*), lost property *sg* (*Brit*).
objurgations [obzhürgásyón] *nfpl* objurgations; (*prières*) entreaties.
obligataire [oblēgáter] *a* bond *cpd* ♦ *nm/f* bondholder, debenture holder.
obligation [oblēgásyón] *nf* obligation; (*gén pl*: *devoir*) duty; (*COMM*) bond, debenture; **sans ~ d'achat** with no obligation (to buy); **être dans l'~ de faire** to be obliged to do; **avoir l'~ de faire** to be under an obligation to do; **~s familiales** family obligations *ou* re-

sponsibilities; **~s militaires** military obligations *ou* duties.

obligatoire [oblēgátwár] *a* compulsory, obligatory.

obligatoirement [oblēgátwármâṅ] *ad* compulsorily; (*fatalement*) necessarily.

obligé, e [oblēzhā] *a* (*redevable*): **être très ~ à qn** to be most obliged to sb; (*contraint*): **je suis (bien) ~ (de le faire)** I have to (do it); (*nécessaire: conséquence*) necessary; **c'est ~!** it's inevitable.

obligeamment [oblēzhámâṅ] *ad* obligingly.

obligeance [oblēzhâṅs] *nf*: **avoir l'~ de** to be kind *ou* good enough to.

obligeant, e [oblēzhâṅ, -âṅt] *a* obliging; kind.

obliger [oblēzhā] *vt* (*contraindre*): **~ qn à faire** to force *ou* oblige sb to do; (*JUR: engager*) to bind; (*rendre service à*) to oblige.

oblique [oblēk] *a* oblique; **regard ~** sidelong glance; **en ~** *ad* diagonally.

obliquer [oblēkā] *vi*: **~ vers** to turn off towards.

oblitération [oblētārâsyôṅ] *nf* canceling q (*US*), cancelling q (*Brit*), cancellation; obstruction.

oblitérer [oblētārā] *vt* (*timbre-poste*) to cancel; (*MED: canal, vaisseau*) to obstruct.

oblong, oblongue [oblôṅ, oblôṅg] *a* oblong.

obnubiler [obnübēlā] *vt* to obsess.

obole [obol] *nf* offering.

obscène [opsen] *a* obscene.

obscénité [opsēnētā] *nf* obscenity.

obscur, e [opskür] *a* (*sombre*) dark; (*fig: raisons*) obscure; (: *sentiment, malaise*) vague; (: *personne, vie*) humble, lowly.

obscurcir [opskürsēr] *vt* to darken; (*fig*) to obscure; **s'~** *vi* to grow dark.

obscurité [opskürētā] *nf* darkness; **dans l'~** in the dark, in darkness; (*anonymat, médiocrité*) in obscurity.

obsédant, e [opsādâṅ, -âṅt] *a* obsessive.

obsédé, e [opsādā] *nm/f* fanatic; **~(e) sexuel(le)** sex maniac.

obséder [opsādā] *vt* to obsess, haunt.

obsèques [opsek] *nfpl* funeral *sg*.

obséquieux, euse [opsākyē, -ēz] *a* obsequious.

observance [opservâṅs] *nf* observance.

observateur, trice [opservátœr, -trēs] *a* observant, perceptive ♦ *nm/f* observer.

observation [opservâsyôṅ] *nf* observation; (*d'un règlement etc*) observance; (*commentaire*) observation, remark; (*reproche*) reproof; **en ~** (*MÉD*) under observation.

observatoire [opservátwár] *nm* observatory; (*lieu élevé*) observation post, vantage point.

observer [opservā] *vt* (*regarder*) to observe, watch; (*examiner*) to examine; (*scientifiquement, aussi: règlement, jeûne etc*) to observe; (*surveiller*) to watch; (*remarquer*) to observe, notice; **faire ~ qch à qn** (*dire*) to point out sth to sb; **s'~** (*se surveiller*) to keep a check on o.s.

obsession [opsāsyôṅ] *nf* obsession; **avoir l'~ de** to have an obsession with.

obsessionnel, le [opsāsyonel] *a* obsessive.

obsolescent, c [opsolāsâṅ, âṅt] *a* obsolescent.

obstacle [opstákl(ə)] *nm* obstacle; (*ÉQUITA-* *TION*) jump, hurdle; **faire ~ à** (*lumière*) to block out; (*projet*) to hinder, put obstacles in the path of; **~s antichars** tank defenses (*US*) *ou* defences (*Brit*).

obstétricien, ne [obstātrēsyaṅ, -en] *nm/f* obstetrician.

obstétrique [opstātrēk] *nf* obstetrics *sg*.

obstination [opstēnâsyôṅ] *nf* obstinacy.

obstiné, e [opstēnā] *a* obstinate.

obstinément [opstēnāmâṅ] *ad* obstinately.

obstiner [opstēnā]: **s'~** *vi* to insist, dig one's heels in; **s'~ à faire** to persist (obstinately) in doing; **s'~ sur qch** to keep working at sth, labor away at sth.

obstruction [opstrüksyôṅ] *nf* obstruction, blockage; (*SPORT*) obstruction; **faire de l'~** (*fig*) to be obstructive.

obstruer [opstrüā] *vt* to block, obstruct; **s'~** *vi* to become blocked.

obtempérer [optâṅpārā] *vi* to obey; **~ à** to obey, comply with.

obtenir [optənēr] *vt* to obtain, get; (*total*) to arrive at, reach; (*résultat*) to achieve, obtain; **~ de pouvoir faire** to obtain permission to do; **~ qch à qn** to obtain sth for sb; **~ de qn qu'il fasse** to get sb to agree to do(ing).

obtention [optâṅsyôṅ] *nf* obtaining.

obtenu, e [opt(ə)nü] *pp de* obtenir.

obtiendrai [optyaṅdrā], **obtiens** [optyaṅ], **obtint** [optaṅ] *etc vb voir* obtenir.

obturateur [optürátœr] *nm* (*PHOTO*) shutter; **~ à rideau** focal plane shutter.

obturation [optürâsyôṅ] *nf* closing (up); **~ (dentaire)** filling; **vitesse d'~** (*PHOTO*) shutter speed.

obturer [optürā] *vt* to close (up); (*dent*) to fill.

obtus, e [optü, -üz] *a* obtuse.

obus [obü] *nm* shell; **~ explosif** high-explosive shell; **~ incendiaire** incendiary device, fire bomb.

obvier [obvyā]: **~ à** *vt* to obviate.

OC *sigle fpl* (= *ondes courtes*) SW.

occasion [okázyôṅ] *nf* (*aubaine, possibilité*) opportunity; (*circonstance*) occasion; (*COMM: article non neuf*) secondhand buy; (: *acquisition avantageuse*) bargain; **à plusieurs ~s** on several occasions; **à la première ~** at the first *ou* earliest opportunity; **avoir l'~ de faire** to have the opportunity to do; **être l'~ de** to occasion, give rise to; **à l'~** *ad* sometimes, on occasions; (*un jour*) sometime; **à l'~ de** on the occasion of; **d'~** *a, ad* secondhand.

occasionnel, le [okázyonel] *a* (*fortuit*) chance *cpd*; (*non régulier*) occasional; (: *travail*) casual.

occasionner [okázyonā] *vt* to cause, bring about; **~ qch à qn** to cause sb sth.

occident [oksēdâṅ] *nm*: **l'O~** the West.

occidental, e, aux [oksēdâṅtál, -ō] *a* western; (*POL*) Western ♦ *nm/f* Westerner.

occidentaliser [oksēdâṅtálēzā] *vt* (*coutumes, mœurs*) to westernize.

occiput [oksēpüt] *nm* back of the head, occiput.

occire [oksēr] *vt* to slay.

occitan, e [oksētâṅ, -áṅ] *a* of the langue d'oc, of Provençal French.

occlusion [oklüzyôǹ] *nf*: ~ **intestinale** obstruction of the bowel.

occulte [okült(ə)] *a* occult, supernatural.

occulter [okültā] *vt* (*fig*) to overshadow.

occupant, e [oküpáǹ, -áǹt] *a* occupying ♦ *nm/f* (*d'un appartement*) occupier, occupant; (*d'un véhicule*) occupant ♦ *nm* (*MIL*) occupying forces *pl*; (*POL: d'usine etc*) occupier.

occupation [oküpâsyôǹ] *nf* occupation; **l'O~** the Occupation (of France).

occupationnel, le [oküpâsyonel] *a*: **thérapie ~le** occupational therapy.

occupé, e [oküpā] *a* (*MIL, POL*) occupied; (*personne*) *affairé, pris*) busy; (*esprit: absorbé*) occupied; (*place, sièges*) taken; (*toilettes, ligne*) engaged.

occuper [oküpā] *vt* to occupy; (*poste, fonction*) to hold; (*main-d'œuvre*) to employ; **s'~** (*à qch*) to occupy o.s. *ou* keep o.s. busy (with sth); **s'~ de** (*être responsable de*) to be in charge of; (*se charger de: affaire*) to take charge of, deal with; (*: clients etc*) to attend to; (*s'intéresser à, pratiquer: politique etc*) to be involved in; **ça occupe trop de place** it takes up too much room.

occurrence [oküráǹs] *nf*: **en l'~** in this case.

OCDE *sigle f* (= *Organisation de coopération et de développement économique*) OECD.

océan [osāáǹ] *nm* ocean; **l'~ Indien** the Indian Ocean.

Océanie [osāánē] *nf*: **l'~** Oceania, South Sea Islands.

océanique [osāánēk] *a* oceanic.

océanographe [osāánográf] *nm/f* oceanographer.

océanographie [osāánográfē] *nf* oceanography.

océanologie [osāánolozhē] *nf* oceanology.

ocelot [oslō] *nm* (*ZOOL*) ocelot; (*fourrure*) ocelot fur.

ocre [okr(ə)] *a inv* ocher (*US*), ochre (*Brit*).

octane [oktán] *nm* octane.

octante [oktáǹt] *num* (*Belgique, Suisse*) eighty.

octave [oktáv] *nf* octave.

octet [okte] *nm* byte.

octobre [oktobr(ə)] *nm* October; *voir aussi* **juillet**.

octogénaire [oktozhāner] *a, nm/f* octogenarian.

octogonal, e, aux [oktogonál, -ō] *a* octagonal.

octogone [oktogon] *nm* octagon.

octroi [oktrwá] *nm* granting.

octroyer [oktrwáyā] *vt*: ~ **qch à qn** to grant sth to sb, grant sb sth.

oculaire [oküler] *a* ocular, eye *cpd* ♦ *nm* (*de microscope*) eyepiece.

oculiste [okülēst(ə)] *nm/f* eye specialist, oculist.

ode [od] *nf* ode.

odeur [odœr] *nf* smell.

odieusement [odyœzmáǹ] *ad* odiously.

odieux, euse [odyœ̄, -œ̄z] *a* odious, hateful.

odontologie [odôǹtolozhē] *nf* odontology.

odorant, e [odoráǹ, -áǹt] *a* sweet-smelling, fragrant.

odorat [odorá] *nm* (sense of) smell; **avoir l'~ fin** to have a keen sense of smell.

odoriférant, e [odorēfāráǹ, -áǹt] *a* sweet-smelling, fragrant.

odyssée [odēsā] *nf* odyssey.

OEA *sigle f* (= *Organisation des états américains*) OAS.

œcuménique [ākümānēk] *a* ecumenical.

œdème [ādem] *nm* edema (*US*), oedema (*Brit*).

œil [œy], *pl* **yeux** [yœ̄] *nm* eye; **avoir un ~ poché ou au beurre noir** to have a black eye; **à l'~** (*fam*) for free; **à l'~ nu** with the naked eye; **tenir qn à l'~** to keep an eye *ou* a watch on sb; **avoir l'~ à** to keep an eye on; **faire de l'~ à qn** to make eyes at sb; **voir qch d'un bon/mauvais ~** to view sth in a favorable/an unfavorable light; **à l'~ vif** with a lively expression; **à mes/ses yeux** in my/his eyes; **de ses propres yeux** with his own eyes; **fermer les yeux (sur)** (*fig*) to shut one's eyes (to); **les yeux fermés** (*aussi fig*) with one's eyes shut; **fermer l'~** to get a moment's sleep; **~ pour ~, dent pour dent** an eye for an eye, a tooth for a tooth; **pour les beaux yeux de qn** (*fig*) for love of sb; **~ de verre** glass eye.

œil-de-bœuf, *pl* **œils-de-bœuf** [œydəbœf] *nm* bull's-eye (window).

œillade [œyád] *nf*: **lancer une ~ à qn** to wink at sb, give sb a wink; **faire des ~s** to make eyes at.

œillères [œyer] *nfpl* blinders (*US*), blinkers (*Brit*); **avoir des ~** (*fig*) to wear blinders (*US*), be blinkered (*Brit*).

œillet [œye] *nm* (*BOT*) carnation; (*trou*) eyelet.

œnologue [ānolog] *nm/f* wine expert.

œsophage [āzofázh] *nm* esophagus (*US*), oesophagus (*Brit*).

œstrogène [estrozhen] *a* estrogen (*US*), oestrogen (*Brit*).

œuf [œf, *pl* œ̄] *nm* egg; **étouffer dans l'~** to nip in the bud; **~ à la coque/dur/mollet** boiled/hard-boiled/soft-boiled egg; **~ au plat/ poché** fried/poached egg; **~s brouillés** scrambled eggs; **~ de Pâques** Easter egg; **~ à repriser** darning egg.

œuvre [œvr(ə)] *nf* (*tâche*) task, undertaking; (*ouvrage achevé, livre, tableau etc*) work; (*ensemble de la production artistique*) works *pl*; (*organisation charitable*) charity ♦ *nm* (*d'un artiste*) works *pl*; (*CONSTR*): **le gros ~** the shell; **~s** *nfpl* (*actes*) deeds, works; **être/se mettre à l'~** to be at/get (down) to work; **mettre en ~** (*moyens*) to make use of; (*plan, loi, projet etc*) to implement; **~ d'art** work of art; **bonnes ~s** good works *ou* deeds; **~s de bienfaisance** charitable works.

OFCE *sigle m* (= *Observatoire français des conjonctures économiques*) *economic research institute*.

offensant, e [ofáǹsáǹ, -áǹt] *a* offensive, insulting.

offense [ofáǹs] *nf* (*affront*) insult; (*REL: péché*) transgression, trespass.

offenser [ofáǹsā] *vt* to offend, hurt; (*principes, Dieu*) to offend against; **s'~ de** to take offense (*US*) *ou* offence (*Brit*) at.

offensif, ive [ofáǹsēf, -ēv] *a* (*armes, guerre*) offensive ♦ *nf* offensive; (*fig: du froid, de l'hiver*) onslaught; **passer à l'offensive** to go

into the attack *ou* offensive.
offert, e [ɔfɛr, -ɛrt(ə)] *pp de* **offrir**.
offertoire [ɔfɛrtwár] *nm* offertory.
office [ɔfɛs] *nm* (*charge*) office; (*agence*) bureau, agency; (*REL*) service ♦ *nm ou nf* (*pièce*) pantry; **faire** ~ **de** to act as; to do duty as; **d'**~ *ad* automatically; **bons** ~**s** (*POL*) good offices; ~ **du tourisme** tourist bureau.
officialiser [ɔfɛsyálēzā] *vt* to make official.
officiel, le [ɔfɛsyel] *a*, *nm/f* official.
officiellement [ɔfɛsyclmáɴ] *ad* officially.
officier [ɔfɛsyā] *nm* officer ♦ *vi* (*REL*) to officiate; ~ **de l'état-civil** registrar; ~ **ministériel** member of the legal profession; ~ **de police** ≈ police officer.
officieusement [ɔfɛsyœ̄zmáɴ] *ad* unofficially.
officieux, euse [ɔfɛsyœ̄, -œ̄z] *a* unofficial.
officinal, e, aux [ɔfɛsɛ́nál, -ō] *a*: **plantes** ~**es** medicinal plants.
officine [ɔfɛsɛ̄n] *nf* (*de pharmacie*) dispensary; (*ADMIN*: *pharmacie*) pharmacy; (*gén péj*: *bureau*) agency, office.
offrais [ɔfrɛ] *etc vb voir* **offrir**.
offrande [ɔfráɴd] *nf* offering.
offrant [ɔfráɴ] *nm*: **au plus** ~ to the highest bidder.
offre [ɔfr(ə)] *vb voir* **offrir** ♦ *nf* offer; (*aux enchères*) bid; (*ADMIN*: *soumission*) tender; (*ECON*): **l'**~ supply; ~ **d'emploi** job advertised; "~**s d'emploi**" "help wanted" (*US*), "situations vacant" (*Brit*); ~ **publique d'achat (OPA)** takeover bid; ~**s de service** offer of service.
offrir [ɔfrɛr] *vt*: ~ **(à qn)** to offer (to sb); (*faire cadeau*) to give (to sb); **s'**~ *vi* (*se présenter*: *occasion*, *paysage*) to present itself ♦ *vt* (*se payer*: *vacances*, *voiture*) to treat o.s. to; ~ **(à qn) de faire qch** to offer to do sth (for sb); ~ **à boire à qn** to offer sb a drink; **s'**~ **à faire qch** to offer *ou* volunteer to do sth; **s'**~ **comme guide/en otage** to offer one's services as (a) guide/offer o.s. as (a) hostage; **s'**~ **aux regards** (*suj*: *personne*) to expose o.s. to the public gaze.
offset [ɔfsɛt] *nm* offset (printing).
offusquer [ɔfüskā] *vt* to offend; **s'**~ **de** to take offense (*US*) *ou* offence (*Brit*) at, be offended by.
ogive [ozhɛ̄v] *nf* (*ARCHIT*) diagonal rib; (*d'obus*, *de missile*) nose cone; **voûte en** ~ rib vault; **arc en** ~ lancet arch; ~ **nucléaire** nuclear warhead.
ogre [ɔgr(ə)] *nm* ogre.
oh [ō] *excl* oh!; ~ **la la!** oh (dear)!; **pousser des** ~! **et des ah!** to gasp with admiration.
oie [wá] *nf* (*ZOOL*) goose (*pl* geese); ~ **blanche** (*fig*) young innocent.
oignon [ɔnyóɴ] *nm* (*CULIN*) onion; (*de tulipe etc*: *bulbe*) bulb; (*MÉD*) bunion; **ce ne sont pas tes** ~**s** (*fam*) that's none of your business.
oindre [wáɴdr(ə)] *vt* to anoint.
oiseau, x [wázō] *nm* bird; ~ **de proie** bird of prey.
oiseau-mouche, *pl* **oiseaux-mouches** [wázōmōōsh] *nm* hummingbird.
oiseleur [wázlœr] *nm* bird catcher.
oiselier, ière [wázəlyā, -ycr] *nm/f* bird seller.

oisellerie [wázelrē] *nf* bird shop.
oiseux, euse [wázœ̄, -œ̄z] *a* pointless, idle; (*sans valeur*, *importance*) trivial.
oisif, ive [wázēf, -ēv] *a* idle ♦ *nm/f* (*péj*) man/lady of leisure.
oisillon [wázēyóɴ] *nm* little *ou* baby bird.
oisiveté [wázēvtā] *nf* idleness.
OIT *sigle f* (= *Organisation internationale du travail*) ILO.
OK [ōke] *excl* OK!, all right!
OL *sigle fpl* (= *ondes longues*) LW.
oléagineux, euse [ɔlāázhɛ̄nœ̄, -œ̄z] *a* oleaginous, oil-producing.
oléiculture [ɔlāēkültür] *nf* olive growing.
oléoduc [ɔlāodük] *nm* (oil) pipeline.
olfactif, ive [ɔlfáktɛ̄f, -ēv] *a* olfactory.
olibrius [ɔlēbrēyüs] *nm* oddball.
oligarchie [ɔlēgàrshē] *nf* oligarchy.
oligo-élément [ɔlēgoālāmáɴ] *nm* trace element.
oligopole [ɔlēgopol] *nm* oligopoly.
olivâtre [ɔlēvâtr(ə)] *a* olive-greenish; (*teint*) sallow.
olive [ɔlēv] *nf* (*BOT*) olive ♦ *a inv* olive (-green).
oliveraie [ɔlēvrɛ] *nf* olive grove.
olivier [ɔlēvyā] *nm* olive (tree); (*bois*) olive (wood).
olographe [ɔlográf] *a*: **testament** ~ **will** written, dated and signed by the testator.
OLP *sigle f* (= *Organisation de libération de la Palestine*) PLO.
olympiade [ɔláɴpyàd] *nf* (*période*) Olympiad; **les** ~**s** (*jeux*) the Olympiad *sg*.
olympien, ne [ɔláɴpyaɴ, -en] *a* Olympian, of Olympian aloofness.
olympique [ɔláɴpēk] *a* Olympic.
OM *sigle fpl* (= *ondes moyennes*) MW.
Oman [ɔmáɴ] *nm*: **l'**~, **le sultanat d'**~ (the Sultanate of) Oman.
ombilical, e, aux [ɔ̄ɴbēlēkál, -ō] *a* umbilical.
ombrage [ɔ̄ɴbrázh] *nm* (*ombre*) (leafy) shade; (*fig*): **prendre** ~ **de** to take umbrage at; **faire** *ou* **porter** ~ **à qn** to offend sb.
ombragé, e [ɔ̄ɴbrázhā] *a* shaded, shady.
ombrageux, euse [ɔ̄ɴbrázhœ̄, -œ̄z] *a* (*cheval*) skittish, nervous; (*personne*) touchy, easily offended.
ombre [ɔ̄ɴbr(ə)] *nf* (*espace non ensoleillé*) shade; (*ombre portée*, *tache*) shadow; **à l'**~ in the shade; (*fam*: *en prison*) behind bars; **à l'**~ **de** in the shade of; (*tout près de*, *fig*) in the shadow of; **tu me fais de l'**~ you're in my light; **ça nous donne de l'**~ it gives us (some) shade; **il n'y a pas l'**~ **d'un doute** there's not the shadow of a doubt; **dans l'**~ in the shade; **vivre dans l'**~ (*fig*) to live in obscurity; **laisser dans l'**~ (*fig*) to leave in the dark; ~ **à paupières** eyeshadow; ~ **portée** shadow; ~**s chinoises** (*spectacle*) shadow show *sg*.
ombrelle [ɔ̄ɴbrel] *nf* parasol, sunshade.
ombrer [ɔ̄ɴbrá] *vt* to shade.
omelette [ɔmlɛt] *nf* omelette; ~ **baveuse** runny omelette; ~ **au fromage/au jambon** cheese/ham omelette; ~ **aux herbes** omelette with herbs; ~ **norvégienne** baked Alaska.
omettre [ɔmɛtr(ə)] *vt* to omit, leave out; ~ **de faire** to fail *ou* omit to do.

omis, e [omē, -ēz] *pp de* **omettre**.
omission [omēsyôn] *nf* omission.
omnibus [omnēbüs] *nm* slow *ou* local train.
omnipotent, e [omnēpotán, -ánt] *a* omnipotent.
omnipraticien, ne [omnēprátēsyan, -en] *nm/f* (*MÉD*) general practitioner.
omniprésent, e [omnēprāzán, -ánt] *a* omnipresent.
omniscient, e [omnēsyán, -ánt] *a* omniscient.
omnisports [omnēspor] *a inv* (*club*) general sports *cpd*; (*salle*) multi-purpose *cpd*; (*terrain*) all-purpose *cpd*.
omnium [omnyom] *nm* (*COMM*) corporation; (*CYCLISME*) mixed race (*US*), omnium (*Brit*); (*COURSES*) open handicap.
omnivore [omnēvor] *a* omnivorous.
omoplate [omoplát] *nf* shoulder blade.
OMS *sigle f* (= *Organisation mondiale de la santé*) WHO.
on [ôn] *pronom* (*indéterminé*): ~ **peut le faire ainsi** you *ou* one can do it like this, it can be done like this; (*quelqu'un*): ~ **les a attaqués** they were attacked; (*nous*): ~ **va y aller demain** we're going tomorrow; (*les gens*): **autrefois,** ~ **croyait aux fantômes** they used to believe in ghosts years ago; (*ironiquement, affectueusement*): **alors,** ~ **se promène?** off for a stroll then, are we?; ~ **y va!** let's go!; ~ **y va?** are we going?; ~ **vous demande au téléphone** there's a phone call for you, there's somebody on the phone for you; ~ **ne peut plus** *ad*: ~ **ne peut plus stupide** as stupid as can be.
once [ôns] *nf*: **une** ~ **de** an ounce of.
oncle [ônkl(ə)] *nm* uncle.
onction [ônksyôn] *nf voir* **extrême-onction**.
onctueux, euse [ônktüē, -ēz] *a* creamy, smooth; (*fig*) smooth, unctuous.
onde [ônd] *nf* (*PHYSIQUE*) wave; **sur l'**~ **on the waters; sur les** ~**s** on the radio; **mettre en** ~**s** to produce for the radio; ~ **de choc** shock wave; ~**s courtes (OC)** short wave *sg*; **petites** ~**s (PO),** ~**s moyennes (OM)** medium wave *sg*; **grandes** ~**s (GO),** ~**s longues (OL)** long wave *sg*; ~**s sonores** sound waves.
ondée [ôndā] *nf* shower.
on-dit [ôndē] *nm inv* rumor (*US*), rumour (*Brit*).
ondoyer [ôndwáyā] *vi* to ripple, wave ♦ *vt* (*REL*) to baptize (*in an emergency*).
ondulant, e [ôndülán, -ánt] *a* (*démarche*) swaying; (*ligne*) undulating.
ondulation [ôndülásyôn] *nf* undulation; wave.
ondulé, e [ôndülā] *a* undulating; wavy.
onduler [ôndülā] *vi* to undulate; (*cheveux*) to wave.
onéreux, euse [onárē̄, -ē̄z] *a* costly; **à titre** ~ in return for payment.
ONF *sigle m* (= *Office national des forêts*) ≈ National Forest Service (*US*), ≈ Forestry Commission (*Brit*).
ongle [ôngl(ə)] *nm* (*ANAT*) nail; **manger** *ou* **ronger ses** ~**s** to bite one's nails; **se faire les** ~**s** to do one's nails.
onglet [ôngle] *nm* (*rainure*) (thumbnail) groove; (*bande de papier*) tab.
onguent [ôngán] *nm* ointment.

onirique [onērēk] *a* dreamlike, dream *cpd*.
onirisme [onērēsm(ə)] *nm* dreams *pl*.
onomatopée [onomátopā] *nf* onomatopocia.
ont [ôn] *vb voir* **avoir**.
ontarien, ne [ôntáryan, -en] *a* Ontarian.
ONU [onü] *sigle f* (= *Organisation des Nations Unies*) UN(O).
onusien, ne [onüzyan, -en] *a* of the UN(O), of the United Nations (Organization).
onyx [onēks] *nm* onyx.
onze [ônz] *num* eleven.
onzième [ônzyem] *num* eleventh.
op [op] *nf* (= *opération*): **salle d'**~ operating room (*US*), (operating) theatre (*Brit*).
OPA *sigle f* = **offre publique d'achat**.
opacité [opásētā] *nf* opaqueness.
opale [opál] *nf* opal.
opalescent, e [opálāsán, -ánt] *a* opalescent.
opalin, e [opálán, -ēn] *a, nf* opaline.
opaque [opák] *a* (*vitre, verre*) opaque; (*brouillard, nuit*) impenetrable.
OPE *sigle f* (= *offre publique d'échange*) takeover bid where bidder offers shares in his company in exchange for shares in target company.
OPEP [opep] *sigle f* (= *Organisation des pays exportateurs de pétrole*) OPEC.
opéra [opárá] *nm* opera; (*édifice*) opera house.
opérable [opārábl(ə)] *a* operable.
opéra-comique, *pl* **opéras-comiques** [opārákomēk] *nm* light opera, opéra comique.
opérant, e [opārán, -ánt] *a* (*mesure*) effective.
opérateur, trice [opārátœr, -trēs] *nm/f* operator; ~ **(de prise de vues)** cameraman.
opération [opārásyôn] *nf* operation; (*COMM*) dealing; **salle/table d'**~ operating room (*US*) *ou* theatre (*Brit*)/table; ~ **de sauvetage** rescue operation; ~ **à cœur ouvert** open-heart surgery *q*.
opérationnel, le [opārásyonál] *a* operational.
opératoire [opārátwár] *a* (*manœuvre, méthode*) operating; (*choc etc*) post-operative.
opéré, e [opārā] *nm/f* post-operative patient.
opérer [opārā] *vt* (*MÉD*) to operate on; (*faire, exécuter*) to carry out, make ♦ *vi* (*remède: faire effet*) to act, work; (*procéder*) to proceed; (*MÉD*) to operate; **s'**~ *vi* (*avoir lieu*) to occur, take place; **se faire** ~ to have an operation; **se faire** ~ **des amygdales/du cœur** to have one's tonsils out/have a heart operation.
opérette [opāret] *nf* operetta, light opera.
ophtalmique [oftálmēk] *a* ophthalmic.
ophtalmologie [oftálmolozhē] *nf* ophthalmology.
ophtalmologue [oftálmolog] *nm/f* ophthalmologist.
opiacé, e [opyásā] *a* opiate.
opiner [opēnā] *vi*: ~ **de la tête** to nod assent ♦ *vt*: ~ **à** to consent to.
opiniâtre [opēnyátr(ə)] *a* stubborn.
opiniâtreté [opēnyátrətā] *nf* stubbornness.
opinion [opēnyôn] *nf* opinion; **l'**~ **(publique)** public opinion; **avoir bonne/mauvaise** ~ **de** to have a high/low opinion of.
opiomane [opyomán] *nm/f* opium addict.
opium [opyom] *nm* opium.
OPJ *sigle m* = *officier de police judiciaire*.

opportun, e [ɔpɔrtœ̃, -ün] *a* timely, opportune; **en temps** ~ at the appropriate time.

opportunément [ɔpɔrtünāmã̃] *ad* opportunely.

opportunisme [ɔpɔrtünēsm(ə)] *nm* opportunism.

opportuniste [ɔpɔrtünēst(ə)] *a, nm/f* opportunist.

opportunité [ɔpɔrtünētā] *nf* timeliness, opportuneness.

opposant, e [ɔpōzã̃, -ã̃t] *a* opposing ♦ *nm/f* opponent.

opposé, e [ɔpōzā] *a* (*direction, rive*) opposite; (*faction*) opposing; (*couleurs*) contrasting; (*opinions, intérêts*) conflicting; (*contre*): ~ **à** opposed to, against ♦ *nm*: **l'**~ the other *ou* opposite side (*ou* direction); (*contraire*) the opposite; **être** ~ **à** to be opposed to; **à l'**~ (*fig*) on the other hand; **à l'**~ **de** on the other *ou* opposite side from; (*fig*) contrary to, unlike.

opposer [ɔpōzā] *vt* (*meubles, objets*) to place opposite each other; (*personnes, armées, équipes*) to oppose; (*couleurs, termes, tons*) to contrast; (*comparer: livres, avantages*) to contrast; ~ **qch à** (*comme obstacle, défense*) to set sth against; (*comme objection*) to put sth forward against; (*en contraste*) to set sth opposite; to match sth with; **s'**~ (*sens réciproque*) to conflict; to clash; to face each other; to contrast; **s'**~ **à** (*interdire, empêcher*) to oppose; (*tenir tête à*) to rebel against; **sa religion s'y oppose** it's against his religion; **s'**~ **à ce que qn fasse** to be opposed to sb's doing.

opposition [ɔpōzisyō̃] *nf* opposition; **par** ~ in contrast; **par** ~ **à** as opposed to, in contrast with; **entrer en** ~ **avec** to come into conflict with; **être en** ~ **avec** (*idées, conduite*) to be at variance with; **faire** ~ **à un chèque** to stop a check.

oppressant, e [ɔprāsã̃, -ã̃t] *a* oppressive.

oppresser [ɔprāsā] *vt* to oppress; **se sentir oppressé** to feel breathless.

oppresseur [ɔprāsœr] *nm* oppressor.

oppressif, ive [ɔprāsēf, -ēv] *a* oppressive.

oppression [ɔprāsyō̃] *nf* oppression; (*malaise*) feeling of suffocation.

opprimer [ɔprēmā] *vt* (*asservir: peuple, faibles*) to oppress; (*étouffer: liberté, opinion*) to suppress, stifle; (*suj: chaleur etc*) to suffocate, oppress.

opprobre [ɔprobr(ə)] *nm* disgrace.

opter [ɔptā] *vi*: ~ **pour** to opt for; ~ **entre** to choose between.

opticien, ne [ɔptēsyã̃, -en] *nm/f* optician.

optimal, e, aux [ɔptēmāl, -ō] *a* optimal.

optimisation [ɔptēmēzāsyō̃] *nf* optimization.

optimiser [ɔptēmēzā] *vt* to optimize.

optimisme [ɔptēmēsm(ə)] *nm* optimism.

optimiste [ɔptēmēst(ə)] *a* optimistic ♦ *nm/f* optimist.

optimum [ɔptēmom] *a, nm* optimum.

option [ɔpsyō̃] *nf* option; (*AUTO: supplément*) optional extra; **matière à** ~ (*SCOL*) elective (*US*), optional subject (*Brit*); **prendre une** ~ **sur** to take (out) an option on; ~ **par défaut** (*INFORM*) default (option).

optionnel, le [ɔpsyonel] *a* optional.

optique [ɔptēk] *a* (*nerf*) optic; (*verres*) optical ♦ *nf* (*PHOTO: lentilles etc*) optics *pl*; (*science, industrie*) optics *sg*; (*fig: manière de voir*) perspective.

opulence [ɔpülã̃s] *nf* wealth, opulence.

opulent, e [ɔpülã̃, -ã̃t] *a* wealthy, opulent; (*formes, poitrine*) ample, generous.

or [ɔr] *nm* gold ♦ *cj* now, but; **d'**~ (*fig*) golden; **en** ~ gold *cpd*; (*occasion*) golden; **un mari/enfant en** ~ a treasure; **une affaire en** ~ (*achat*) a real bargain; (*commerce*) a gold mine; **plaqué** ~ gold-plated; ~ **noir** black gold.

oracle [ɔrākl(ə)] *nm* oracle.

orage [ɔrāzh] *nm* (thunder)storm.

orageux, euse [ɔrāzhœ̄, -œ̄z] *a* stormy.

oraison [ɔrezō̃] *nf* orison, prayer; ~ **funèbre** funeral oration.

oral, e, aux [ɔrāl, -ō] *a* (*déposition, promesse*) oral, verbal; (*MÉD*): **par voie** ~**e** by mouth, orally ♦ *nm* (*SCOL*) oral.

oralement [ɔrālmã̃] *ad* orally.

orange [ɔrã̃zh] *a inv, nf* orange; ~ **sanguine** blood orange; ~ **pressée** freshly-squeezed orange juice.

orangé, e [ɔrã̃zhā] *a* orangey, orange-colored (*US*), orange-coloured (*Brit*).

orangeade [ɔrã̃zhād] *nf* orangeade.

oranger [ɔrã̃zhā] *nm* orange tree.

orangeraie [ɔrã̃zhre] *nf* orange grove.

orangerie [ɔrã̃zhrē] *nf* orangery.

orang-outan(g) [ɔrã̃ōōtã̃] *nm* orangutan.

orateur [ɔrātœr] *nm* speaker; orator.

oratoire [ɔrātwār] *nm* (*lieu, chapelle*) oratory; (*au bord du chemin*) wayside shrine ♦ *a* oratorical.

oratorio [ɔrātoryō] *nm* oratorio.

orbital, e, aux [ɔrbētāl, -ō] *a* orbital; **station** ~**e** space station.

orbite [ɔrbēt] *nf* (*ANAT*) (eye-)socket; (*PHYSIQUE*) orbit; **mettre sur** ~ to put into orbit; (*fig*) to launch; **dans l'**~ **de** (*fig*) within the sphere of influence of.

Orcades [ɔrkād] *nfpl*: **les** ~ the Orkneys, the Orkney Islands.

orchestral, e, aux [ɔrkestrāl, -ō] *a* orchestral.

orchestrateur, trice [ɔrkestrātœr, -trēs] *nm/f* orchestrator.

orchestration [ɔrkestrāsyō̃] *nf* orchestration.

orchestre [ɔrkestr(ə)] *nm* orchestra; (*de jazz, danse*) band; (*places*) orchestra (*US*), stalls *pl* (*Brit*).

orchestrer [ɔrkestrā] *vt* (*MUS*) to orchestrate; (*fig*) to mount, stage-manage.

orchidée [ɔrkēdā] *nf* orchid.

ordinaire [ɔrdēner] *a* ordinary; (*coutumier: maladresse etc*) usual; (*de tous les jours*) everyday; (*modèle, qualité*) standard ♦ *nm* ordinary; (*menus*) everyday fare ♦ *nf* (*essence*) ≈ regular (gas) (*US*), ≈ two-star (petrol) (*Brit*); **d'**~ usually, normally; **à l'**~ usually, ordinarily.

ordinairement [ɔrdēnermã̃] *ad* ordinarily, usually.

ordinal, e, aux [ɔrdēnāl, -ō] *a* ordinal.

ordinateur [ɔrdēnātœr] *nm* computer; **mettre sur** ~ to computerize, put on computer; ~ **domestique** home computer; ~ **individuel** *ou*

personnel personal computer.

ordination [ordēnåsyôń] *nf* ordination.

ordonnance [ordonåńs] *nf* organization; (*groupement, disposition*) layout; (*MÉD*) prescription; (*JUR*) order; (*MIL*) orderly; **d'~** (*MIL*) regulation *cpd*; **officier d'~** aide-de-camp.

ordonnateur, trice [ordonåtœr, -trēs] *nm/f* (*d'une cérémonie, fête*) organizer; **~ des pompes funèbres** funeral director.

ordonné, e [ordonā] *a* tidy, orderly; (*MATH*) ordered ♦ *nf* (*MATH*) Y-axis, ordinate.

ordonner [ordonā] *vt* (*agencer*) to organize, arrange; (: *meubles, appartement*) to lay out, arrange; (*donner un ordre*): **~ à qn de faire** to order sb to do; (*MATH*) to (arrange in) order; (*REL*) to ordain; (*MÉD*) to prescribe; (*JUR*) to order; **s'~** (*faits*) to organize themselves.

ordre [ordr(ə)] *nm* (*gén*) order; (*propreté et soin*) orderliness, tidiness; (*association professionnelle, honorifique*) association; (*COMM*): **à l'~ de** payable to; (*nature*): **d'~ pratique** of a practical nature; **~s** *nmpl* (*REL*) holy orders; **avoir de l'~** to be tidy *ou* orderly; **mettre en ~** to tidy (up), put in order; **mettre bon ~ à** to put to rights, sort out; **procéder par ~** to take things one at a time; **être aux ~s de qn/sous les ~s de qn** to be at sb's disposal/under sb's command; **rappeler qn à l'~** to call sb to order; **jusqu'à nouvel ~** until further notice; **dans le même ~ d'idées** in this connection; **par ~ d'entrée en scène** in order of appearance; **un ~ de grandeur** some idea of the size (*ou* amount); **de premier ~** first-rate; **~ de grève** strike call; **~ du jour** (*d'une réunion*) agenda; (*MIL*) order of the day; **à l'~ du jour** on the agenda; (*fig*) topical; (*MIL*: *citer*) in dispatches; **~ de mission** (*MIL*) orders *pl*; **~ public** law and order; **~ de route** marching orders *pl*.

ordure [ordür] *nf* filth *q*; (*propos, écrit*) obscenity, (piece of) filth; **~s** *nfpl* (*balayures, déchets*) garbage *sg* (*US*), trash *sg* (*US*), rubbish *sg* (*Brit*), refuse *sg* (*Brit*); **~s ménagères** household garbage (*US*) *ou* refuse (*Brit*).

ordurier, ière [ordüryā, -yer] *a* lewd, filthy.

oreille [orey] *nf* (*ANAT*) ear; (*de marmite, tasse*) handle; (*TECH*: *d'un écrou*) wing; **avoir de l'~** to have a good ear (for music); **avoir l'~ fine** to have good *ou* sharp ears; **l'~ basse** crestfallen, dejected; **se faire tirer l'~** to take a lot of persuading; **dire qch à l'~ de qn** to have a word in sb's ear (about sth).

oreiller [orāyā] *nm* pillow.

oreillette [oreyet] *nf* (*ANAT*) auricle.

oreillons [oreyôń] *nmpl* mumps *sg*.

ores [or]: **d'~ et déjà** *ad* already.

orfèvre [orfevr(ə)] *nm* goldsmith; silversmith.

orfèvrerie [orfevrərē] *nf* (*art, métier*) goldsmith's (*ou* silversmith's) trade; (*ouvrage*) (silver *ou* gold) plate.

orfraie [orfre] *nm* white-tailed eagle; **pousser des cris d'~** to yell at the top of one's voice.

organe [organ] *nm* organ; (*véhicule, instrument*) instrument; (*voix*) voice; (*porte-parole*) representative, mouthpiece; **~s de**

commande (*TECH*) controls; **~s de transmission** (*TECH*) transmission system *sg*.

organigramme [organēgråm] *nm* (*hiérarchique, structurel*) organization chart; (*des opérations*) flow chart.

organique [organēk] *a* organic.

organisateur, trice [organēzåtœr, -trēs] *nm/f* organizer.

organisation [organēzåsyôń] *nf* organization; **O~ des Nations Unies (ONU)** United Nations (Organization) (UN, UNO); **O~ mondiale de la santé (OMS)** World Health Organization (WHO); **O~ du traité de l'Atlantique Nord (OTAN)** North Atlantic Treaty Organization (NATO).

organisationnel, le [organēzåsyonel] *a* organizational.

organiser [organēzā] *vt* to organize; (*mettre sur pied: service etc*) to set up; **s'~** to get organized.

organisme [organēsm(ə)] *nm* (*BIO*) organism; (*corps humain*) body; (*ADMIN, POL etc*) body, organism.

organiste [organēst(ə)] *nm/f* organist.

orgasme [orgåsm(ə)] *nm* orgasm, climax.

orge [orzh(ə)] *nf* barley.

orgeat [orzhå] *nm*: **sirop d'~** barley water.

orgelet [orzhəle] *nm* sty(e).

orgie [orzhē] *nf* orgy.

orgue [org(ə)] *nm* organ; **~s** *nfpl* organ *sg*; **~ de Barbarie** barrel *ou* street organ.

orgueil [orgœy] *nm* pride.

orgueilleux, euse [orgœyœ̄, -œ̄z] *a* proud.

Orient [oryåń] *nm*: **l'~** the East, the Orient.

orientable [oryåńtåbl(ə)] *a* (*phare, lampe etc*) adjustable.

oriental, e, aux [oryåńtål, -ō] *a* oriental, eastern; (*frontière*) eastern ♦ *nm/f*: **O~, e** O-riental.

orientation [oryåńtåsyôń] *nf* positioning; adjustment; orientation; direction; (*d'une maison etc*) exposure; (*d'un journal*) leanings *pl*; **avoir le sens de l'~** to have a (good) sense of direction; **course d'~** orienteering exercise; **~ professionnelle** careers advice *ou* guidance; (*service*) careers advisory service.

orienté, e [oryåńtā] *a* (*fig: article, journal*) slanted; **bien/mal ~** (*appartement*) well/badly positioned; **~ au sud** facing south, with a southern exposure.

orienter [oryåńtā] *vt* (*situer*) to position; (*placer, disposer: pièce mobile*) to adjust, position; (*tourner*) to direct, turn; (*voyageur, touriste, recherches*) to direct; (*fig: élève*) to orientate; **s'~** (*se repérer*) to find one's bearings; **s'~ vers** (*fig*) to turn towards.

orienteur, euse [oryåńtœr, -œ̄z] *nm/f* (*SCOL*) careers adviser.

orifice [orēfēs] *nm* opening, orifice.

oriflamme [orēflåm] *nf* banner, standard.

origan [orēgåń] *nm* oregano.

originaire [orēzhēner] *a* original; **être ~ de** (*pays, lieu*) to be a native of; (*provenir de*) to originate from; to be native to.

original, e, aux [orēzhēnål, -ō] *a* original; (*bizarre*) eccentric ♦ *nm/f* (*fam: excentrique*) eccentric; (: *fantaisiste*) joker ♦ *nm* (*document etc, ART*) original; (*dactylo-*

graphie) original (*US*), top copy (*Brit*).

originalité [orēzhēnálētā] *nf* (*d'un nouveau modèle*) originality *q*; (*excentricité, bizarrerie*) eccentricity.

origine [orēzhēn] *nf* origin; (*d'un message, appel téléphonique*) source; (*d'une révolution, réussite*) root; ~s *nfpl* (*d'une personne*) origins; **d'~** of origin; (*pneus etc*) original; (*bureau postal*) dispatching; **d'~ française** of French origin; **dès l'~** at *ou* from the outset; **à l'~** originally; **avoir son ~ dans** to have its origins in, originate in.

originel, le [orēzhēnel] *a* original.

originellement [orēzhēnelmâń] *ad* (*à l'origine*) originally; (*dès l'origine*) from the beginning.

oripeaux [orēpō] *nmpl* rags.

ORL *sigle f* (= *oto-rhino-laryngologie*) ENT ♦ *sigle m/f* (= *oto-rhino-laryngologiste*) ENT specialist; **être en ~** (*malade*) to be in the ENT hospital *ou* department.

orme [orm(ə)] *nm* elm.

orné, e [ornā] *a* ornate; **~ de** adorned *ou* decorated with.

ornement [ornəmâń] *nm* ornament; (*fig*) embellishment, adornment; **~s sacerdotaux** vestments.

ornemental, e, aux [ornəmâńtál, -ō] *a* ornamental.

ornementer [ornəmâńtā] *vt* to ornament.

orner [ornā] *vt* to decorate, adorn; **~ qch de** to decorate sth with.

ornière [ornyer] *nf* rut; (*fig*): **sortir de l'~** (*routine*) to get out of the rut; (*impasse*) to get out of a spot.

ornithologie [ornētoloozhē] *nf* ornithology.

ornithologue [ornētolog] *nm/f* ornithologist; **~ amateur** birdwatcher.

orphelin, e [orfəlăń, -ēn] *a* orphan(ed) ♦ *nm/f* orphan; **~ de père/mère** fatherless/ motherless.

orphelinat [orfəlēnā] *nm* orphanage.

ORSEC [orsek] *sigle f* (= *Organisation des secours*): **le plan ~** disaster contingency plan.

ORSECRAD [orsekrád] *sigle m* = *ORSEC en cas d'accident nucléaire*.

orteil [ortey] *nm* toe; **gros ~** big toe.

ORTF *sigle m* (= *Office de radio-diffusion télévision française*) (*formerly*) French broadcasting corporation.

orthodontiste [ortodóńtēst(ə)] *nm/f* orthodontist.

orthodoxe [ortodoks(ə)] *a* orthodox.

orthodoxie [ortodoksē] *nf* orthodoxy.

orthogénie [ortozhānē] *nf* family planning.

orthographe [ortográf] *nf* spelling.

orthographier [ortográfyā] *vt* to spell; **mal orthographié** misspelled.

orthopédie [ortopādē] *nf* orthopedics *sg* (*US*), orthopaedics *sg* (*Brit*).

orthopédique [ortopādēk] *a* orthopedic (*US*), orthopaedic (*Brit*).

orthopédiste [ortopādēst(ə)] *nm/f* orthopedic (*US*) *ou* orthopaedic (*Brit*) specialist.

orthophonie [ortofonē] *nf* (*MÉD*) speech therapy; (*LING*) correct pronunciation.

orthophoniste [ortofonēst(ə)] *nm/f* speech therapist.

ortie [ortē] *nf* (stinging) nettle; **~ blanche** white dead-nettle.

OS *sigle m* = **ouvrier spécialisé**.

os [os, *pl* ō] *nm* bone; **sans ~** (*BOUCHERIE*) off the bone, boned; **~ à moelle** marrowbone.

oscillation [osēlásyóń] *nf* oscillation; **~s** *nfpl* (*fig*) fluctuations.

osciller [osēlā] *vi* (*pendule*) to swing; (*au vent etc*) to rock; (*TECH*) to oscillate; (*fig*): **~ entre** to waver *ou* fluctuate between.

osé, e [ōzā] *a* daring, bold.

oseille [ōzey] *nf* sorrel.

oser [ōzā] *vi, vt* to dare; **~ faire** to dare (to) do.

osier [ōzyā] *nm* (*BOT*) willow; **d'~, en ~** wicker(work) *cpd*.

Oslo [oslō] *n* Oslo.

osmose [osmōz] *nf* osmosis.

ossature [osátür] *nf* (*ANAT: squelette*) frame, skeletal structure; (: *du visage*) bone structure; (*fig*) framework.

osselet [osle] *nm* (*ANAT*) ossicle; **jouer aux ~s** to play jacks.

ossements [osmâń] *nmpl* bones.

osseux, euse [osœ̄, œz] *a* bony; (*tissu, maladie, greffe*) bone *cpd*.

ossifier [osēfyā]: **s'~** *vi* to ossify.

ossuaire [osüer] *nm* ossuary.

Ostende [ostâńd] *n* Ostend.

ostensible [ostáńsēbl(ə)] *a* conspicuous.

ostensiblement [ostáńsēbləmâń] *ad* conspicuously.

ostensoir [ostáńswár] *nm* monstrance.

ostentation [ostáńtásyóń] *nf* ostentation; **faire ~ de** to parade, make a display of.

ostentatoir [ostáńtátwár] *a* ostentatious.

ostracisme [ostrásēsm(ə)] *nm* ostracism; **frapper d'~** to ostracize.

ostréicole [ostrākol] *a* oyster *cpd*.

ostréiculture [ostrākültür] *nf* oyster farming.

otage [otázh] *nm* hostage; **prendre qn comme ~** to take sb hostage.

OTAN [otáń] *sigle f* (= *Organisation du traité de l'Atlantique Nord*) NATO.

otarie [otárē] *nf* sea lion.

OTASE [otáz] *sigle f* (= *Organisation du traité de l'Asie du Sud-Est*) SEATO (= *Southeast Asia Treaty Organization*).

ôter [ōtā] *vt* to remove; (*soustraire*) to take away; **~ qch à qn** to take sth (away) from sb; **~ qch de** to remove sth from; **6 ôté de 10 égale 4** 6 from 10 equals *ou* is 4.

otite [otēt] *nf* ear infection.

oto-rhino(-laryngologiste) [otorēno(láráńgolozhēst(ə))] *nm/f* ear, nose and throat specialist.

ottomane [otomán] *nf* ottoman.

ou [oo] *cj* or; **~ ... ~** either ... or; **~ bien** or (else).

où [oo] *ad, pronom* where; (*dans lequel*) in which, into which; from which, out of which; (*hors duquel, duquel*) from which; (*sur lequel*) on which; (*sens de 'que'*): **au train ~ ça va/prix ~ c'est** at the rate it's going/price it is; **le jour ~ il est parti** the day (that) he left; **par ~ passer?** which way should we go?; **les villes par ~ il est passé** the towns he went through; **le village d'~ je viens** the village I come from; **la chambre ~ il était**

the room he was in; **d'~ vient qu'il est parti?** how is it that he left?, how come he left?

OUA sigle f (= Organisation de l'unité africaine) OAU (= Organization of African Unity).

ouais |we| excl yeah.

ouate |wắt| nf cotton (US), cotton wool (Brit); (bourre) padding, wadding; **~ (hydrophile)** (absorbent) cotton (US), cotton wool (Brit).

ouaté, e |wắtā| a cotton (US), cotton-wool (Brit); (doublé) padded; (fig: atmosphère) cocoon-like; (: pas, bruit) muffled.

oubli |ōōblē| nm (acte): **l'~ de** forgetting; (étourderie) forgetfulness q; (négligence) omission, oversight; (absence de souvenirs) oblivion; **~ de soi** self-effacement, self-negation.

oublier |ōōblēyā| vt (gén) to forget; (ne pas voir: erreurs etc) to miss; (ne pas mettre: virgule, nom) to leave out, forget; (laisser quelque part: chapeau etc) to leave behind; **s'~** to forget o.s; (enfant, animal) to have an accident (euphemism); **~ l'heure** to forget (about) the time.

oubliettes |ōōblēyct| nfpl dungeon sg; **(jeter) aux ~** (fig) (to put) completely out of mind.

oublieux, euse |ōōblēyœ̆, -œ̆z| a forgetful.

oued |wed| nm wadi.

ouest |west| nm west ♦ a inv west; (région) western; **à l'~** in the west; (to the) west, westwards; **à l'~ de** (to the) west of; **vent d'~** westerly wind.

ouest-allemand, e |westálmầ, -ầd| a West German.

ouf |ōōf| excl phew!

Ouganda |ōōgầdá| nm: **l'~** Uganda.

ougandais, e |ōōgầdc, -ez| a Ugandan.

oui |wē| ad yes; **répondre (par) ~** to answer yes; **mais ~, bien sûr** yes, of course; **je pense que ~** I think so; **pour un ~ ou pour un non** for no apparent reason.

ouï-dire |wēdēr|: **par ~** ad by hearsay.

ouïe |wē| nf hearing; **~s** nfpl (de poisson) gills; (de violon) sound hole sg.

ouïr |wēr| vt to hear; **avoir ouï dire que** to have heard it said that.

ouistiti |wēstētē| nm marmoset.

ouragan |ōōrágầ| nm hurricane; (fig) storm.

Oural |ōōrál| nm: **l'~** (fleuve) the Ural; (aussi: **les monts ~**) the Urals, the Ural Mountains.

ouralo-altaïque |ōōráloáltắck| a, nm Ural-Altaic.

ourdir |ōōrdēr| vt (complot) to hatch.

ourdou |ōōrdōō| a inv Urdu ♦ nm (LING) Urdu.

ourlé, e |ōōrlā| a hemmed; (fig) rimmed.

ourler |ōōrlā| vt to hem.

ourlet |ōōrle| nm hem; (de l'oreille) rim; **faire un ~** à to hem.

ours |ōōrs| nm bear; **~ brun/blanc** brown/polar bear; **~ marin** fur seal; **~ mal léché** uncouth fellow; **~ (en peluche)** teddy (bear).

ourse |ōōrs(ə)| nf (ZOOL) she-bear; **la Grande/Petite O~** the Great/Little Bear, Ursa Major/Minor.

oursin |ōōrsắ̀| nm sea urchin.

ourson |ōōrsồ| nm (bear) cub.

ouste |ōōst(ə)| excl hop it!

outil |ōōtē| nm tool.

outillage |ōōtēyázh| nm set of tools; (d'atelier) equipment q.

outiller |ōōtēyā| vt (ouvrier, usine) to equip.

outrage |ōōtrázh| nm insult; **faire subir les derniers ~s à** (femme) to rape; **~ aux bonnes mœurs** (JUR) outrage to public decency; **~ à magistrat** (JUR) contempt of court; **~ à la pudeur** (JUR) indecent behavior q (US) ou behaviour q (Brit).

outragé, e |ōōtrázhā| a offended; outraged.

outrageant, e |ōōtrázhầ, -ầt| a offensive.

outrager |ōōtrázhā| vt to offend gravely; (fig: contrevenir à) to outrage, insult.

outrageusement |ōōtrázhœ̆zmầ| ad outrageously.

outrance |ōōtrầs| nf excessiveness q, excess; **à ~ ad** excessively, to excess.

outrancier, ière |ōōtrầsyā, -yer| a extreme.

outre |ōōtr(ə)| nf goatskin bottle ♦ prép besides ♦ ad: **passer ~** to carry on regardless; **passer ~ à** to disregard, take no notice of; **en ~** besides, moreover; **~ que** apart from the fact that; **~ mesure** immoderately; unduly.

outré, e |ōōtrā| a (flatterie, éloge) excessive, exaggerated; (indigné, scandalisé) outraged.

outre-Atlantique |ōōtrátlầtēk| ad across the Atlantic.

outrecuidance |ōōtrəküēdầs| nf presumptuousness q.

outre-Manche |ōōtrəmầsh| ad across the Channel.

outremer |ōōtrəmer| a inv ultramarine.

outre-mer |ōōtrəmer| ad overseas; **d'~** overseas.

outrepasser |ōōtrəpâsā| vt to go beyond, exceed.

outrer |ōōtrā| vt (pensée, attitude) to exaggerate; (indigner: personne) to outrage.

outre-Rhin |ōōtrərắ̀| ad across the Rhine, in Germany.

outsider |áwtsáydœr| nm outsider.

ouvert, e |ōōver, -ert(ə)| pp de **ouvrir** ♦ a open; (robinet, gaz etc) on; **à bras ~s** with open arms.

ouvertement |ōōvertəmầ| ad openly.

ouverture |ōōvertür| nf opening; (MUS) overture; (POL): **l'~** the widening of the political spectrum; (PHOTO): **~ (du diaphragme)** aperture; **~s** nfpl (propositions) overtures; **~ d'esprit** open-mindedness; **heures d'~** (COMM) opening hours; **jours d'~** (COMM) days of opening.

ouvrable |ōōvrábl(ə)| a: **jour ~** working day, weekday; **heures ~s** business hours.

ouvrage |ōōvrázh| nm (tâche, de tricot etc, MIL) work q; (objet: COUTURE, ART) (piece of) work; (texte, livre) work; **panier** ou **corbeille à ~** work basket; **~ d'art** (GÉNIE CIVIL) bridge or tunnel etc.

ouvragé, e |ōōvrázhā| a finely embroidered (ou worked ou carved).

ouvrant, e |ōōvrầ, -ầt| vb voir **ouvrir** ♦ a: **toit ~** sunroof.

ouvré, e |ōōvrā| a finely-worked; **jour ~** working day.

ouvre-boîte(s) |ōōvrəbwát| nm inv can

opener.

ouvre-bouteille(s) [ōōvrəbōōtey] *nm inv* bottle opener.

ouvreuse [ōōvrœz] *nf* usherette.

ouvrier, ière [ōōvrēyā, -yer] *nm/f* worker ♦ *nf* (*ZOOL*) worker (bee) ♦ *a* working-class; (*problèmes, conflit*) industrial, labor *cpd* (*US*), labour *cpd* (*Brit*); (*revendications*) workers'; **classe ouvrière** working class; ~ **agricole** farmworker; ~ **qualifié** skilled worker; ~ **spécialisé** (**OS**) semiskilled worker; ~ **d'usine** factory worker.

ouvrir [ōōvrēr] *vt* (*gén*) to open; (*brèche, passage*) to open up; (*commencer l'exploitation de, créer*) to open (up); (*eau, électricité, chauffage, robinet*) to turn on; (*MÉD: abcès*) to open up, cut open ♦ *vi* to open; to open up; (*CARTES*): ~ **à trèfle** to open with clubs; **s'~** *vi* to open; **s'~ à** (*art etc*) to open one's mind to; **s'~ à qn** (**de qch**) to open one's heart to sb (about sth); **s'~ les veines** to slash *ou* cut one's wrists; ~ **sur** to open onto; ~ **l'appétit à qn** to whet sb's appetite; ~ **des horizons** to open up new horizons; ~ **l'esprit** to broaden one's horizons; ~ **une session** (*INFORM*) to log in.

ouvroir [ōōvrwár] *nm* workroom, sewing room.

ovaire [over] *nm* ovary.

ovale [ovál] *a* oval.

ovation [ovâsyôň] *nf* ovation.

ovationner [ovâsyonā] *vt*: ~ **qn** to give sb an ovation.

ovin, e [ovaň, -ēn] *a* ovine.

OVNI [ovnē] *sigle m* (– *objet volant non identifié*) UFO.

ovoïde [ovoēd] *a* egg-shaped.

ovulation [ovülâsyôň] *nf* (*PHYSIOL*) ovulation.

ovule [ovül] *nm* (*PHYSIOL*) ovum (*pl* ova); (*MÉD*) pessary.

oxfordien, ne [oksfordyaň, -en] *a* Oxonian ♦ *nm/f*: **O~, ne** Oxonian.

oxydable [oksēdábl(ə)] *a* liable to rust.

oxyde [oksēd] *nm* oxide; ~ **de carbone** carbon monoxide.

oxyder [oksēdā]: **s'~** *vi* to become oxidized.

oxygène [oksēzhen] *nm* oxygen; (*fig*): **cure d'~** fresh air cure.

oxygéné, e [oksēzhānā] *a*: **eau ~e** hydrogen peroxide; **cheveux ~s** bleached hair.

ozone [ōzon] *nm* ozone.

P

P, p [pā] *nm inv* P, p ♦ *abr* (= *Père*) Fr; (= *page*) p; **P comme Pierre** P for Peter.

PA *sigle fpl* = **petites annonces**.

PAC *sigle f* (= *Politique agricole commune*) CAP.

pacage [pákazh] *nm* grazing, pasture.

pace-maker [pesmekœr] *nm* pacemaker.

pachyderme [páshēderm(ə)] *nm* pachyderm; elephant.

pacificateur, trice [pásēfēkátœr, -trēs] *a* pacificatory.

pacifier [pásēfyā] *vt* to pacify.

pacifique [pásēfēk] *a* (*personne*) peaceable; (*intentions, coexistence*) peaceful ♦ *nm*: **le P~, l'océan P~** the Pacific (Ocean).

pacifiquement [pásēfēkmáň] *ad* peaceably; peacefully.

pacifiste [pásēfēst(ə)] *nm/f* pacifist.

pack [pák] *nm* pack.

pacotille [pákotēy] *nf* (*péj*) cheap goods *pl*; **de** ~ cheap.

pacte [pákt(ə)] *nm* pact, treaty.

pactiser [páktēzā] *vi*: ~ **avec** to come to terms with.

pactole [páktol] *nm* gold mine (*fig*).

paddock [pádok] *nm* paddock.

Padoue [pádōō] *n* Padua.

PAF *sigle f* (= *Police de l'air et des frontières*) police authority responsible for civil aviation, border control etc.

pagaie [páge] *nf* paddle.

pagaille [págáy] *nf* mess, shambles *sg*; **il y en a en** ~ there are loads *ou* heaps of them.

paganisme [págánēsm(ə)] *nm* paganism.

pagayer [págáyā] *vi* to paddle.

page [pázh] *nf* page; (*passage: d'un roman*) passage ♦ *nm* page (boy); **mettre en ~s** to make up (into pages); **mise en** ~ layout; **à la** ~ (*fig*) up-to-date; ~ **blanche** blank page; ~ **de garde** endpaper.

page-écran, *pl* **pages-écrans** [pázhākráň] *nf* (*INFORM*) screen page.

pagination [pázhēnásyôň] *nf* pagination.

paginer [pázhēnā] *vt* to paginate.

pagne [pány] *nm* loincloth.

pagode [págod] *nf* pagoda.

paie [pe] *nf* = **paye**.

paiement [pemáň] *nm* = **payement**.

païen, ne [páyaň, -en] *a, nm/f* pagan, heathen.

paillard, e [páyár, -árd(ə)] *a* bawdy.

paillasse [páyás] *nf* (*matelas*) straw mattress; (*d'un évier*) drainboard (*US*), draining board (*Brit*).

paillasson [páyâsôň] *nm* doormat.

paille [páy] *nf* straw; (*défaut*) flaw; **être sur la** ~ to be ruined; ~ **de fer** steel wool.

paillé, e [páyā] *a* with a straw seat.

pailleté, e [páytā] *a* sequined.

paillette [páyet] *nf* speck, flake; ~**s** *nfpl* (*décoratives*) sequins, spangles; **lessive en** ~**s** soapflakes *pl*.

pain [páň] *nm* (*substance*) bread; (*unité*) loaf (*pl* loaves) (of bread); (*morceau*): ~ **de cire** etc bar of wax *etc*; (*CULIN*): ~ **de poisson/légumes** fish/vegetable loaf; **petit** ~ (bread) roll; ~ **bis/complet** brown/wholewheat (*US*) *ou* wholemeal (*Brit*) bread; ~ **de campagne** farmhouse bread; ~ **d'épice** ≈ gingerbread; ~ **grillé** toast; ~ **de mie** sandwich loaf; ~ **perdu** French toast; ~ **de seigle** rye bread; ~ **de sucre** sugar loaf.

pair, e [per] *a* (*nombre*) even ♦ *nm* peer; **aller de** ~ (**avec**) to go hand in hand *ou* together (with); **au** ~ (*FINANCE*) at par; **valeur au** ~ par value; **jeune fille au** ~ au pair.

paire [per] *nf* pair; **une** ~ **de lunettes/tenailles** a pair of glasses/pincers; **faire la** ~: **les deux font la** ~ they are two of a kind.

pais [pe] *vb voir* **paître**.
paisible [pāzēbl(ə)] *a* peaceful, quiet.
paisiblement [pāzēbləmáń] *ad* peacefully, quietly.
paître [petr(ə)] *vi* to graze.
paix [pe] *nf* peace; *(fig)* peacefulness, peace; **faire la ~ avec** to make peace with; **avoir la ~** to have peace (and quiet).
Pakistan [påkēstáń] *nm*: **le ~** Pakistan.
pakistanais, e [påkēstáne, -ez] *a* Pakistani.
PAL *sigle m* (= *Phase Alternation Line*) PAL.
palabrer [pálábrā] *vi* to argue endlessly.
palabres [pálábr(ə)] *nfpl* endless discussions.
palace [pálás] *nm* luxury hotel.
palais [pále] *nm* palace; *(ANAT)* palate; **le P~ Bourbon** *the seat of the French National Assembly*; **le P~ de l'Élysée** the Élysée Palace; **~ des expositions** exhibition center *(US)* ou centre *(Brit)*; **le P~ de Justice** the Law Courts *pl*.
palan [pálán] *nm* hoist.
Palatin [pálátań]: **le (mont)** ~ the Palatine (Hill).
pale [pál] *nf* *(d'hélice, de rame)* blade; *(de roue)* paddle.
pâle [pál] *a* pale; *(fig)*: **une ~ imitation** a pale imitation; **bleu ~** pale blue; **~ de colère** white ou pale with anger.
palefrenier [pálfrənyā] *nm* groom.
paléontologie [pálāóntolozhē] *nf* paleontology.
Palerme [pálerm(ə)] *n* Palermo.
Palestine [pálestēn] *nf*: **la ~** Palestine.
palestinien, e [pálestēnyań, -en] *a* Palestinian ♦ *nm/f*: **P~, ne** Palestinian.
palet [pále] *nm* disc; *(HOCKEY)* puck.
paletot [páltō] *nm* (short) coat.
palette [pálet] *nf* palette; *(produits)* range.
pâleur [pálœr] *nf* paleness.
palier [pályā] *nm* *(d'escalier)* landing; *(fig)* level, plateau; *(: phase stable)* leveling *(US)* ou levelling *(Brit)* off, new level; *(TECH)* bearing; **nos voisins de ~** our neighbors across the hall *(US)* ou the landing *(Brit)*; **en ~** *ad* level; **par ~s** in stages.
palière [pályer] *af* landing *cpd*.
pâlir [pálēr] *vi* to turn ou go pale; *(couleur)* to fade; **faire ~ qn** *(de jalousie)* to make sb green (with envy).
palissade [pálēsád] *nf* fence.
palissandre [pálēsáńdr(ə)] *nm* rosewood.
palliatif [pályátēf] *nm* palliative; *(expédient)* stopgap measure.
pallier [pályā] *vt*, **~ à** *vt* to offset, make up for.
palmarès [pálmáres] *nm* record (of achievements); *(SCOL)* prize list; *(SPORT)* list of winners.
palme [pálm(ə)] *nf* *(BOT)* palm leaf *(pl* leaves)*; *(symbole)* palm; *(de plongeur)* flipper; **~s (académiques)** *decoration for services to education.*
palmé, e [pálmā] *a* *(pattes)* webbed.
palmeraie [pálməre] *nf* palm grove.
palmier [pálmyā] *nm* palm tree.
palmipède [pálmēped] *nm* palmiped, webfooted bird.
palois, e [pálwá, -wáz] *a* of ou from Pau ♦ *nm/f*: **P~, e** inhabitant ou native of Pau.

palombe [pálôńb] *nf* woodpigeon, ringdove.
pâlot, te [pálō, -ot] *a* pale, peaky.
palourde [pálōōrd(ə)] *nf* clam.
palpable [pálpábl(ə)] *a* tangible, palpable.
palper [pálpā] *vt* to feel, finger.
palpitant, e [pálpētáń, -áńt] *a* thrilling, gripping.
palpitation [pálpētâsyôń] *nf* palpitation.
palpiter [pálpētā] *vi* *(cœur, pouls)* to beat; *(: plus fort)* to pound, throb; *(narines, chair)* to quiver.
paludisme [pálüdēsm(ə)] *nm* malaria.
palustre [pálüstr(ə)] *a* *(coquillage etc)* marsh *cpd*; *(fièvre)* malarial.
pâmer [pámā]: **se ~** *vi* to swoon; *(fig)*: **se ~ devant** to go into raptures over.
pâmoison [pámwázôń] *nf*: **tomber en ~** to swoon.
pampa [páńpá] *nf* pampas *pl*.
pamphlet [páńfle] *nm* lampoon, satirical tract.
pamphlétaire [páńflāter] *nm/f* lampoonist.
pamplemousse [páńpləmōōs] *nm* grapefruit.
pan [páń] *nm* section, piece; *(côté: d'un prisme, d'une tour)* side, face ♦ *excl* bang!; **~ de chemise** shirt tail; **~ de mur** section of wall.
panacée [pánásā] *nf* panacea.
panachage [pánásházh] *nm* blend, mix; *(POL) voting for candidates from different parties instead of for the set list of one party.*
panache [pánásh] *nm* plume; *(fig)* spirit, panache.
panaché, e [pánáshā] *a*: **œillet ~** variegated carnation; **glace ~e** mixed ice cream; **salade ~e** mixed salad; **bière ~e** shandy.
panais [páne] *nm* parsnip.
Panama [pánámá] *nm*: **le ~** Panama.
panaméen, ne [pánámáeń, -en] *a* Panamanian ♦ *nm/f*: **P~, ne** Panamanian.
panaris [pánárē] *nm* whitlow.
pancarte [páńkárt(ə)] *nf* sign, notice; *(dans un défilé)* placard.
pancréas [páńkrāás] *nm* pancreas.
panda [páńdá] *nm* panda.
pané, e [pánā] *a* fried in breadcrumbs.
panégyrique [pánāzhērēk] *nm*: **faire le ~ de qn** to extol sb's merits ou virtues.
panier [pányā] *nm* basket; *(à diapositives)* magazine; **mettre au ~** to chuck away; **~ de crabes: c'est un ~ de crabes** *(fig)* they're constantly at one another's throats; **~ percé** *(fig)* spendthrift; **~ à provisions** shopping basket; **~ à salade** *(CULIN)* salad shaker; *(POLICE)* paddy wagon, police van.
panier-repas, *pl* **paniers-repas** [pányār(ə)på] *nm* packed lunch.
panification [pánēfēkâsyôń] *nf* bread-making.
panique [pánēk] *a* panicky ♦ *nf* panic.
paniquer [pánēkā] *vi* to panic.
panne [pán] *nf* *(d'un mécanisme, moteur)* breakdown; **être/tomber en ~** to have broken down/break down; **être en ~ d'essence** ou **en ~ sèche** to have run out of gas *(US)* ou petrol *(Brit)*; **mettre en ~** *(NAVIG)* to bring to; **~ d'électricité** ou **de courant** power ou electrical failure.
panneau, x [pánō] *nm* *(écriteau)* sign, notice; *(de boiserie, de tapisserie etc)* panel; **tomber dans le ~** *(fig)* to walk into the trap; **~**

d'affichage bulletin board; ~ **électoral** board for election poster; ~ **indicateur** signpost; ~ **publicitaire** billboard (*US*), hoarding (*Brit*); ~ **de signalisation** roadsign.

panneau-réclame, *pl* **panneaux-réclame** [pånŏråklám] *nm* billboard (*US*), hoarding (*Brit*).

panonceau, x [pánóŋsō] *nm* (*de magasin etc*) sign; (*de médecin etc*) plaque.

panoplie [pánoplē] *nf* (*jouet*) outfit; (*d'armes*) display; (*fig*) array.

panorama [pánoråmá] *nm* (*vue*) all-round view, panorama; (*peinture*) panorama; (*fig: étude complète*) complete overview.

panoramique [pánoråmēk] *a* panoramic; (*carrosserie*) with panoramic windows ♦ *nm* (*CINÉMA, TV*) panoramic shot.

panse [pȧns] *nf* paunch.

pansement [pȧnsmȧn] *nm* dressing, bandage; ~ **adhésif** bandaid ® (*US*), sticking plaster (*Brit*).

panser [pȧnsā] *vt* (*plaie*) to dress, bandage; (*bras*) to put a dressing on, bandage; (*cheval*) to groom.

pantalon [pȧntålóŋ] *nm* (*aussi:* ~**s, paire de** ~**s**) pants *pl* (*US*), trousers *pl* (*Brit*), pair of trousers *ou* pants; ~ **de ski** ski pants *pl*.

pantalonnade [pȧntålonåd] *nf* slapstick (comedy).

pantelant, e [pȧntlȧn, -ȧnt] *a* gasping for breath, panting.

panthère [pȧnter] *nf* panther.

pantin [pȧntáŋ] *nm* (*jouet*) jumping jack; (*péj: personne*) puppet.

pantois [pȧntwá] *am:* **rester** ~ to be flabbergasted

pantomime [pȧntomēm] *nf* mime; (*pièce*) mime show; (*péj*) fuss, carrying-on (*US*), carry-on (*Brit*).

pantouflard, ❶ [pȧntooflar, -árd(ɔ)] *a* (*péj*) stay-at-home.

pantoufle [pȧntōōfl(ɔ)] *nf* slipper.

panure [pánür] *nf* breadcrumbs *pl*.

PAO *sigle f* (= *publication assistée par ordinateur*) desktop publishing.

paon [pȧŋ] *nm* peacock.

papa [pápá] *nm* dad(dy).

papauté [pápŏtå] *nf* papacy.

papaye [pápáy] *nf* pawpaw.

pape [páp] *nm* pope.

paperasse [páprás] *nf* (*péj*) useless papers *pl*; forms *pl*.

paperasserie [páprásrē] *nf* (*péj*) red tape *q*; paperwork *q*.

papeterie [pápȧtrē] *nf* (*fabrication du papier*) paper-making (industry); (*usine*) paper mill; (*magasin*) stationer's; (*articles*) stationery.

papetier, ière [páptyȧ, -yer] *nm/f* paper-maker; stationer.

papetier-libraire, *pl* **papetiers-libraires** [páptyelēbrer] *nm* bookseller and stationer.

papier [pápyȧ] *nm* paper; (*feuille*) sheet *ou* piece of paper; (*article*) article; (*écrit officiel*) document; ~**s** *nmpl* (*aussi:* ~**s d'identité**) (identity) papers; **sur le** ~ (*théoriquement*) on paper; **noircir du** ~ to write page after page; ~ **couché/glacé** art/glazed paper; ~ **(d')aluminium** aluminum (*US*) *ou* aluminium (*Brit*) foil, tinfoil; ~

d'Arménie incense paper; ~ **bible** India *ou* bible paper; ~ **de brouillon** rough *ou* scrap paper; ~ **bulle** manil(l)a paper; ~ **buvard** blotting paper; ~ **calque** tracing paper; ~ **carbone** carbon paper; ~ **collant** Scotch ® (*US*), Sellotape ® (*Brit*) *ou* sticky tape; ~ **en continu** continuous stationery; ~ **à dessin** drawing paper; ~ **d'emballage** wrapping paper; ~ **gommé** gummed paper; ~ **hygiénique** toilet paper; ~ **journal** newsprint; (*pour emballer*) newspaper; ~ **à lettres** writing paper, notepaper; ~ **mâché** papier-mâché; ~ **machine** typing paper; ~ **peint** wallpaper; ~ **pelure** India paper; ~ **à pliage accordéon** fanfold paper; ~ **de soie** tissue paper; ~ **thermique** thermal paper; ~ **de tournesol** litmus paper; ~ **de verre** sandpaper.

papier-filtre, *pl* **papiers-filtres** [pápyȧfēltr(ɔ)] *nm* filter paper.

papier-monnaie, *pl* **papiers-monnaies** [pápyȧmone] *nm* paper money.

papille [pápȧy] *nf:* ~**s gustatives** taste buds.

papillon [pápȧyóŋ] *nm* butterfly; (*fam: contravention*) (parking) ticket; (*TECH: écrou*) wing *ou* butterfly nut; ~ **de nuit** moth.

papillonner [pápȧyonȧ] *vi* to flit from one thing (*ou* person) to another.

papillote [pápȧyot] *nf* (*pour cheveux*) curlpaper; (*de gigot*) (paper) frill.

papilloter [pápȧyotȧ] *vi* (*yeux*) to blink; (*paupières*) to flutter; (*lumière*) to flicker.

papotage [pápotázh] *nm* chitchat.

papoter [pápotȧ] *vi* to chatter.

papou, e [pápōō] *a* Papuan.

Papouasie-Nouvelle-Guinée [pápwȧzē-nōōvelgēnȧ] *nf:* **la** ~ Papua-New-Guinea.

paprika [páprȧkȧ] *nm* paprika.

papyrus [pápȧrüs] *nm* papyrus.

Pâque [pȧk] *nf:* **la** ~ Passover; *voir aussi* **Pâques.**

paquebot [pákbō] *nm* liner.

pâquerette [pȧkret] *nf* daisy.

Pâques [pȧk] *nm, nfpl* Easter; **faire ses** ~ to do one's Easter duties; **l'île de** ~ Easter Island.

paquet [páke] *nm* packet; (*colis*) parcel; (*ballot*) bundle; (*dans négociations*) package (deal); (*fig: tas*): ~**s de** pile *ou* heap of; ~**s** *nmpl* (*bagages*) bags; **mettre le** ~ (*fam*) to give one's all; ~ **de mer** big wave.

paquetage [páktázh] *nm* (*MIL*) kit, pack.

paquet-cadeau, *pl* **paquets-cadeaux** [pákekȧdō] *nm* gift-wrapped parcel.

par [pȧr] *prép* by; **finir** *etc* ~ to end *etc* with; ~ **amour** out of love; **passer** ~ **Lyon/la côte** to go via *ou* through Lyons/along by the coast; ~ **la fenêtre** (*jeter, regarder*) out of the window; **3** ~ **jour/personne** 3 a *ou* per day/head; **2** ~ **2** two at a time; (*marcher etc*) in twos; ~ **où?** which way?; ~ **ici** this way; (*dans le coin*) around here; ~**-ci**, ~**-là** here and there.

para [párá] *nm* = **parachutiste.**

parabole [párȧbol] *nf* (*REL*) parable; (*GÉOM*) parabola.

parabolique [párȧbolēk] *a* parabolic.

parachever [páráshvȧ] *vt* to perfect.

parachute [párȧshüt] *nm* parachute.

parachuter [pàràshütā] *vt* (*soldat etc*) to parachute; (*fig*) to pitchfork.

parachutisme [pàràshütēsm(ə)] *nm* parachuting.

parachutiste [pàràshütēst(ə)] *nm/f* parachutist; (*MIL*) paratrooper.

parade [pàràd] *nf* (*spectacle*, *défilé*) parade; (*ESCRIME*, *BOXE*) parry; (*ostentation*): **faire ~ de** to display, show off; (*défense*, *riposte*): **trouver la ~ à une attaque** to find the answer to an attack; **de ~** *a* ceremonial; (*superficiel*) superficial, outward.

parader [pàràdā] *vi* to swagger (around), show off.

paradis [pàràdē] *nm* heaven, paradise; **P~ terrestre** (*REL*) Garden of Eden; (*fig*) heaven on earth.

paradisiaque [pàràdēzyàk] *a* heavenly, divine.

paradoxal, e, aux [pàràdoksál, -ō] *a* paradoxical.

paradoxe [pàràdoks(ə)] *nm* paradox.

parafe [pàràf] *nm*, **parafer** [pàràfā] *vt* = **paraphe, parapher.**

paraffine [pàràfēn] *nf* paraffin; paraffin wax.

paraffiné, e [pàràfēnā] *a*: **papier ~** wax(ed) paper.

parafoudre [pàràfoōdr(ə)] *nm* (*ÉLEC*) lightning rod (*US*) *ou* conductor (*Brit*).

parages [pàràzh] *nmpl* (*NAVIG*) waters; **dans les ~ (de)** in the area *ou* vicinity (of).

paragraphe [pàràgráf] *nm* paragraph.

Paraguay [pàràgwe] *nm*: **le ~** Paraguay.

paraguayen, ne [pàràgwàyañ, -en] *a* Paraguayan ♦ *nm/f*: **P~, ne** Paraguayan.

paraître [pàretr(ə)] *vb avec attribut* to seem, look, appear ♦ *vi* to appear; (*être visible*) to show; (*PRESSE*, *ÉDITION*) to be published, come out, appear; (*briller*) to show off; **laisser ~ qch** to let (sth) show ♦ *vb impersonnel*: **il paraît que** it seems *ou* appears that; **il me paraît que** it seems to me that; **il paraît absurde de** it seems absurd to; **il ne paraît pas son âge** he doesn't look his age; **~ en justice** to appear before the court(s); **~ en scène/en public/à l'écran** to appear on stage/in public/on the screen.

parallèle [pàràlel] *a* parallel; (*police*, *marché*) unofficial; (*société*, *énergie*) alternative ♦ *nm* (*comparaison*): **faire un ~ entre** to draw a parallel between; (*GÉO*) parallel ♦ *nf* parallel (line); **en ~** in parallel; **mettre en ~** (*choses opposées*) to compare; (*choses semblables*) to parallel.

parallèlement [pàràlelmáñ] *ad* in parallel; (*fig*: *en même temps*) at the same time.

parallélisme [pàràlālēsm(ə)] *nm* parallelism; (*AUTO*) wheel alignment.

parallélogramme [pàràlālográm] *nm* parallelogram.

paralyser [pàràlēzā] *vt* to paralyze.

paralysie [pàràlēzē] *nf* paralysis.

paralytique [pàràlētēk] *a*, *nm/f* paralytic.

paramédical, e, aux [pàràmádēkál, -ō] *a* paramedical.

paramètre [pàràmetr(ə)] *nm* parameter.

paramilitaire [pàràmēlēter] *a* paramilitary.

paranoïaque [pàrànoyàk] *nm/f* paranoiac.

paranormal, e, aux [pàrànormál, -ō] *a* para-

normal.

parapet [pàràpe] *nm* parapet.

paraphe [pàràf] *nm* (*trait*) flourish; (*signature*) initials *pl*; signature.

parapher [pàràfā] *vt* to initial; to sign.

paraphrase [pàràfráz] *nf* paraphrase.

paraphraser [pàràfrázā] *vt* to paraphrase.

paraplégique [pàràplāzhēk] *a*, *nm/f* paraplegic.

parapluie [pàràplüē] *nm* umbrella; **~ atomique** *ou* **nucléaire** nuclear umbrella; **~ pliant** telescopic umbrella.

parapsychique [pàràpsēshēk] *a* parapsychological.

parapsychologie [pàràpsēkolozhē] *nf* parapsychology.

parapublic, ique [pàràpüblēk] *a partly state-controlled*.

parascolaire [pàràskoler] *a* extracurricular.

parasitaire [pàràzēter] *a* parasitic(al).

parasite [pàràzēt] *nm* parasite ♦ *a* (*BOT*, *BIO*) parasitic(al); **~s** *nmpl* (*TÉL*) interference *sg*.

parasol [pàràsol] *nm* parasol, sunshade.

paratonnerre [pàràtoner] *nm* lightning rod (*US*) *ou* conductor (*Brit*).

paravent [pàràváñ] *nm* folding screen; (*fig*) screen.

parc [pàrk] *nm* (*public*) park, gardens *pl*; (*de château etc*) grounds *pl*; (*pour le bétail*) pen, enclosure; (*d'enfant*) playpen; (*MIL*: *entrepôt*) depot; (*ensemble d'unités*) stock; (*de voitures etc*) fleet; **~ d'attractions** amusement park; **~ automobile** (*d'un pays*) number of cars on the roads; **~ à huîtres** oyster bed; **~ national** national park; **~ naturel** nature reserve; **~ de stationnement** parking lot (*US*), car park (*Brit*); **~ zoologique** zoological gardens *pl*.

parcelle [pàrsel] *nf* fragment, scrap; (*de terrain*) plot, parcel.

parcelliser [pàrsālēzā] *vt* to divide *ou* split up.

parce que [pàrsk(ə)] *cj* because.

parchemin [pàrshəmañ] *nm* parchment.

parcheminé, e [pàrshəmēnā] *a* wrinkled; (*papier*) with a parchment finish.

parcimonie [pàrsēmonē] *nf* parsimony, parsimoniousness.

parcimonieux, euse [pàrsēmonyœ̄, -ēz] *a* parsimonious, miserly.

parc(o)mètre [pàrk(o)metr(ə)] *nm* parking meter.

parcotrain [pàrkotrañ] *nm* station parking lot (*US*) *ou* car park (*Brit*).

parcourir [pàrkoōrēr] *vt* (*trajet*, *distance*) to cover; (*article*, *livre*) to skim *ou* glance through; (*lieu*) to go all over, travel up and down; (*suj*: *frisson*, *vibration*) to run through; **~ des yeux** to run one's eye over.

parcours [pàrkoōr] *vb voir* **parcourir** ♦ *nm* (*trajet*) journey; (*itinéraire*) route; (*SPORT*: *terrain*) course; (*: tour*) round; run; lap; **~ du combattant** assault course.

parcouru, e [pàrkoōrü] *pp de* **parcourir**.

par-delà [pàrdəlà] *prép* beyond.

par-dessous [pàrdəsoō] *prép*, *ad* under(neath).

pardessus [pàrdəsü] *nm* overcoat.

par-dessus [pàrdəsü] *prép* over (the top of) ♦ *ad* over (the top); **~ le marché** on top of it all.

par-devant [párdəvåń] *prép* in the presence of, before ♦ *ad* at the front; around (*US*) *ou* round (*Brit*) the front.

pardon [párdóń] *nm* forgiveness *q* ♦ *excl* (*excuses*) (I'm) sorry; (*pour interpeller etc*) excuse me; (*demander de répéter*) pardon me? (*US*), (I beg your) pardon? (*Brit*).

pardonnable [párdonábl(ə)] *a* forgivable, excusable.

pardonner [párdonā] *vt* to forgive; ~ **qch à qn** to forgive sb for sth; **qui ne pardonne pas** (*maladie, erreur*) fatal.

paré, e [párā] *a* ready, prepared.

pare-balles [párbál] *a inv* bulletproof.

pare-boue [párbōō] *nm inv* mudflap.

pare-brise [párbrēz] *nm inv* windshield (*US*), windscreen (*Brit*).

pare-chocs [párshok] *nm inv* bumper.

pare-étincelles [párātańsel] *nm inv* fireguard.

pare-feu [párfœ̄] *nm inv* firebreak ♦ *a inv*: **portes** ~ fire (resistant) doors.

pareil, le [párcy] *a* (*identique*) the same, alike; (*similaire*) similar; (*tel*) : **un courage/livre** ~ such courage/a book, courage/a book like this; **de** ~**s livres** such books ♦ *ad*: **habillés** ~ dressed the same (way), dressed alike; **faire** ~ to do the same (thing); **j'en veux un** ~ I'd like one just like it; **rien de** ~ no (*ou* any) such thing, nothing (*ou* anything) like it; **ses** ~**s** one's fellow men; one's peers; **ne pas avoir son (sa)** ~**(le)** to be second to none; ~ **à** the same as; similar to; **sans** ~ unparalleled, unequaled (*US*), unequalled (*Brit*); **c'est du** ~ **au même** it comes to the same thing, it's six (of one) and half-a-dozen (of the other); **en** ~ **cas** in such a case; **rendre la** ~**le à qn** to pay sb back in his own coin.

pareillement [párcymåń] *ad* the same, alike; in such a way; (*également*) likewise.

parement [pármåń] *nm* (*CONSTR, revers d'un col, d'une manche*) facing; (*REL*): ~ **d'autel** antependium.

parent, e [páråń, -åńt] *nm/f*: **un/une** ~**/e** *a* relative *ou* relation ♦ *a*: **être** ~ **de** to be related to; ~**s** *nmpl* (*père et mère*) parents; (*famille, proches*) relatives, relations; ~**s par alliance** relatives *ou* relations by marriage; ~**s en ligne directe** blood relations.

parental, e, aux [páråńtál, -ō] *a* parental.

parenté [páråńtā] *nf* (*lien*) relationship; (*personnes*) relatives *pl*, relations *pl*.

parenthèse [páråńtcz] *nf* (*ponctuation*), parenthesis; (*MATH*) parenthesis (*US*), bracket (*Brit*); (*digression*) parenthesis, digression; **ouvrir/fermer la** ~ to open/close the parentheses; **entre** ~**s** in parentheses; (*fig*) incidentally.

parer [párā] *vt* to adorn; (*CULIN*) to dress, trim; (*éviter*) to ward off; ~ **à** (*danger*) to ward off; (*inconvénient*) to deal with; **se** ~ **de** (*fig: qualité, titre*) to assume; ~ **à toute éventualité** to be ready for every eventuality; ~ **au plus pressé** to attend to what's most urgent.

pare-soleil [pársoley] *nm inv* sun visor.

paresse [párcs] *nf* laziness.

paresser [párāsā] *vi* to laze around.

paresseusement [páresœ̄zmåń] *ad* lazily; sluggishly.

paresseux, euse [páresœ̄, -œ̄z] *a* lazy; (*fig*) slow, sluggish ♦ *nm* (*ZOOL*) sloth.

parfaire [párfer] *vt* to perfect, complete.

parfait, e [párfe, -et] *pp de* **parfaire** ♦ *a* perfect ♦ *nm* (*LING*) perfect (tense); (*CULIN*) parfait ♦ *excl* fine, excellent.

parfaitement [párfetmåń] *ad* perfectly ♦ *excl* (*most*) certainly.

parfaites [párfet], **parfasse** [párfás], **parferai** [párfrā] *etc vb voir* **parfaire**.

parfois [párfwá] *ad* sometimes.

parfum [párfœ̄ń] *nm* (*produit*) perfume, scent; (*odeur: de fleur*) scent, fragrance; (*: de tabac, vin*) aroma; (*goût: de glace, milkshake*) flavor (*US*), flavour (*Brit*).

parfumé, e [párfümā] *a* (*fleur, fruit*) fragrant; (*papier à lettres etc*) scented; (*femme*) wearing perfume *ou* scent, perfumed; (*aromatisé*): ~ **au café** coffee-flavored (*US*) *ou* -flavoured (*Brit*).

parfumer [párfümā] *vt* (*suj: odeur, bouquet*) to perfume; (*mouchoir*) to put scent *ou* perfume on; (*crème, gâteau*) to flavor (*US*), flavour (*Brit*); **se** ~ to put on (some) perfume *ou* scent; (*d'habitude*) to use perfume *ou* scent.

parfumerie [párfümrē] *nf* (*commerce*) perfumery; (*produits*) perfumes *pl*; (*boutique*) perfume store (*US*) *ou* shop (*Brit*).

pari [párē] *nm* bet, wager; (*SPORT*) bet; ~ **mutuel urbain (PMU)** *system of betting on horses*.

paria [páryá] *nm* outcast.

parier [páryā] *vt* to bet; **i'aurais parié que si/ non** I'd have said he (*ou* you *etc*) would/ wouldn't.

parieur [páryœr] *nm* (*turfiste etc*) punter.

Paris [párē] *n* Paris.

parisien, ne [párēzyań, -en] *a* Parisian; (*GÉO, ADMIN*) Paris *cpd* ♦ *nm/f*: **P**~, **ne** Parisian.

paritaire [párēter] *a*: **commission** ~ joint commission

parité [párētā] *nf* parity; ~ **de change** (*ÉCON*) exchange parity.

parjure [párzhür] *nm* (*faux serment*) false oath, perjury; (*violation de serment*) breach of oath, perjury ♦ *nm/f* perjurer.

parjurer [párzhürā]: **se** ~ *vi* to perjure o.s.

parka [párká] *nf* parka.

parking [párkēng] *nm* (*lieu*) parking lot (*US*), car park (*Brit*).

parlant, e [párlåń, -åńt] *a* (*fig*) graphic, vivid; (*: comparaison, preuve*) eloquent; (*CINÉMA*) talking ♦ *ad*: **généralement** ~ generally speaking.

parlé, e [párlā] *a*: **langue** ~**e** spoken language.

parlement [párləmåń] *nm* parliament.

parlementaire [párləmåńter] *a* parliamentary ♦ *nm/f* (*député*) ≈ Member of Congress (*US*) *ou* Parliament (*Brit*); parliamentarian; (*négociateur*) negotiator, mediator.

parlementarisme [párləmåńtárēsm(ə)] *nm* parliamentary government.

parlementer [párləmåńtā] *vi* (*ennemis*) to negotiate, parley; (*s'entretenir, discuter*) to argue at length, have lengthy talks.

parler [párlā] *nm* speech; dialect ♦ *vi* to speak, talk; (*avouer*) to talk; ~ **(à qn) de** to talk *ou* speak (to sb) about; ~ **pour qn** (*intercéder*) to speak for sb; ~ **en l'air** to say the first thing that comes into one's head; ~ **le/en français** to speak French/in French; ~ **affaires** to talk business; ~ **en dormant/du nez** to talk in one's sleep/through one's nose; **sans** ~ **de** (*fig*) not to mention, to say nothing of; **tu parles!** you must be joking!; **n'en parlons plus!** let's forget it!

parleur [párlœr] *nm*: **beau** ~ fine talker.

parloir [párlwár] *nm* (*d'une prison, d'un hôpital*) visiting room; (*REL*) parlor (*US*), parlour (*Brit*).

parlote [párlot] *nf* chitchat.

Parme [párm(ə)] *n* Parma.

parme [párm(ə)] *a* violet (blue).

parmesan [párməzáń] *nm* Parmesan (cheese).

parmi [pármē] *prép* among(st).

parodie [párodē] *nf* parody.

parodier [párodyā] *vt* (*œuvre, auteur*) to parody.

paroi [párwá] *nf* wall; (*cloison*) partition; ~ **rocheuse** rock face.

paroisse [párwás] *nf* parish.

paroissial, e, aux [párwásyál, -ō] *a* parish *cpd*.

paroissien, ne [párwásyań, -en] *nm/f* parishioner ♦ *nm* prayer book.

parole [párol] *nf* (*faculté*): **la** ~ speech; (*mot, promesse*) word; (*REL*): **la bonne** ~ the word of God; ~**s** *nfpl* (*MUS*) words, lyrics; **tenir** ~ to keep one's word; **avoir la** ~ to have the floor; **n'avoir qu'une** ~ to be true to one's word; **donner la** ~ **à qn** to hand over to sb; **prendre la** ~ to speak; **demander la** ~ to ask for permission to speak; **perdre la** ~ to lose the power of speech; (*fig*) to lose one's tongue; **je le crois sur** ~ I'll take his word for it, I'll take him at his word; **temps de** ~ (*TV, RADIO etc*) discussion time; **ma** ~**!** my word!, good heavens!; ~ **d'honneur** word of honor.

parolier, ière [párolyā, -yer] *nm/f* lyricist; (*OPÉRA*) librettist.

paroxysme [pároksēsm(ə)] *nm* height, paroxysm.

parpaing [párpań] *nm* bondstone.

parquer [párkā] *vt* (*voiture, matériel*) to park; (*bestiaux*) to pen (in *ou* up); (*prisonniers*) to pack in.

parquet [párke] *nm* (parquet) floor; (*JUR*: *bureau*) public prosecutor's office; **le** ~ **(général)** (*magistrats*) ≈ the Bench.

parqueter [párkətā] *vt* to lay a parquet floor in.

parrain [páraṅ] *nm* godfather; (*d'un navire*) namer; (*d'un nouvel adhérent*) sponsor, proposer.

parrainage [párenázh] *nm* sponsorship.

parrainer [párānā] *vt* (*nouvel adhérent*) to sponsor, propose; (*entreprise*) to promote, sponsor.

parricide [párēsēd] *nm, nf* parricide.

pars [pár] *vb voir* partir.

parsemer [pársəmā] *vt* (*suj: feuilles, papiers*) to be scattered over; ~ **qch de** to scatter sth with.

parsi, e [pársē] *a* Parsee.

part [pár] *vb voir* partir **partir** ♦ *nf* (*qui revient à qn*) share; (*fraction, partie*) part; (*de gâteau, fromage*) portion; (*FINANCE*) (non-voting) share; **prendre** ~ **à** (*débat etc*) to take part in; (*soucis, douleur de qn*) to share in; **faire** ~ **de qch à qn** to announce sth to sb, inform sb of sth; **pour ma** ~ as for me, as far as I'm concerned; **à** ~ **entière** *a* full; **de la** ~ **de** (*au nom de*) on behalf of; (*donné par*) from; **c'est de la** ~ **de qui?** (*au téléphone*) who's calling *ou* speaking (please)?; **de toute(s)** ~**(s)** from all sides *ou* quarters; **de** ~ **et d'autre** on both sides, on either side; **de** ~ **en** ~ right through; **d'une** ~ ... **d'autre** ~ on the one hand ... on the other hand; **nulle/ autre/quelque** ~ nowhere/elsewhere/ somewhere; **à** ~ *ad* separately; (*de côté*) aside ♦ *prép* apart from, except for ♦ *a* exceptional, special; **pour une large** *ou* **bonne** ~ to a great extent; **prendre qch en bonne/mauvaise** ~ to take sth well/badly; **faire la** ~ **des choses** to make allowances; **faire la** ~ **du feu** (*fig*) to cut one's losses; **faire la** ~ **(trop) belle à qn** to give sb more than his (*ou* her) share.

part. *abr* = **particulier**.

partage [pártázh] *nm* (*voir partager*) sharing (out) *q*, share-out (*Brit*); sharing; dividing up; (*POL*: *de suffrages*) share; **recevoir qch en** ~ to receive sth as one's share (*ou* lot); **sans** ~ undivided.

partagé, e [pártázhā] *a* (*opinions etc*) divided; (*amour*) shared; **temps** ~ (*INFORM*) time sharing; **être** ~ **entre** to be shared between; **être** ~ **sur** to be divided about.

partager [pártázhā] *vt* to share; (*distribuer, répartir*) to share (out); (*morceler, diviser*) to divide (up); **se** ~ *vt* (*héritage etc*) to share between themselves (*ou* ourselves *etc*).

partance [pártáńs]: **en** ~ *ad* outbound, due to leave; **en** ~ **pour** (bound) for.

partant, e [pártáń, -áńt] *vb voir* **partir** ♦ *a*: **être** ~ **pour qch** (*d'accord pour*) to be quite ready for sth ♦ *nm* (*SPORT*) starter; (*HIPPISME*) runner.

partenaire [pártəner] *nm/f* partner; ~**s sociaux** management and workforce.

parterre [párter] *nm* (*de fleurs*) (flower) bed, border; (*THÉÂTRE*) orchestra (*US*), stalls *pl* (*Brit*).

parti [pártē] *nm* (*POL*) party; (*décision*) course of action; (*personne à marier*) match; **tirer** ~ **de** to take advantage of, turn to good account; **prendre le** ~ **de faire** to make up one's mind to do, resolve to do; **prendre le** ~ **de qn** to stand up for sb, side with sb; **prendre** (*pour/contre*) to take sides *ou* a stand (for/against); **prendre son** ~ **de** to come to terms with; ~ **pris** bias.

partial, e, aux [pársyál, -ō] *a* biased, partial.

partialement [pársyálmáń] *ad* in a biased way.

partialité [pársyálētā] *nf* bias, partiality.

participant, e [pártēsēpáń, -áńt] *nm/f* participant; (*à un concours*) entrant; (*d'une société*) member.

participation [pártēsēpáyóń] *nf* participation; sharing; (*COMM*) interest; **la** ~ **aux bénéfices** profit-sharing; **la** ~ **ouvrière** worker participation; **"avec la ~ de ..."** "featuring ...".

participe [pàrtēsēp] *nm* participle; **~ passé/présent** past/present participle.

participer [pàrtēsēpà]: **~ à** *vt (course, réunion)* to take part in; *(profits etc)* to share in; *(frais etc)* to contribute to; *(entreprise: financièrement)* to cooperate in; *(chagrin, succès de qn)* to share (in); **~ de** *vt* to partake of.

particulariser [pàrtēkülárēzā] *vt:* **se ~** to mark o.s. *(ou* itself) out.

particularisme [pàrtēkülárēsm(ə)] *nm* sense of identity.

particularité [pàrtēkülárētā] *nf* particularity; *(distinctive)* characteristic, feature.

particule [pàrtēkül] *nf* particle; **~ (nobiliaire)** nobiliary particle.

particulier, ière [pàrtēkülyā, -yer] *a (personnel, privé)* private; *(spécial)* special, particular; *(caractéristique)* characteristic, distinctive; *(spécifique)* particular ♦ *nm (individu: ADMIN)* private individual; **"~ vend ..."** *(COMM)* "for sale privately ...", "for sale by owner ..."* (US)*; **~ à** peculiar to; **en ~** *ad (surtout)* in particular, particularly; *(à part)* separately; *(en privé)* in private.

particulièrement [pàrtēkülyermáṅ] *ad* particularly.

partie [pàrtē] *nf (gén)* part; *(profession, spécialité)* field, subject; *(JUR etc: protagonistes)* party; *(de cartes, tennis etc)* game; *(fig: lutte, combat)* struggle, fight; **une ~ de campagne/de pêche** an outing in the country/a fishing party *ou* trip; **en ~** *ad* partly, in part; **faire ~ de** to belong to; *(suj. chose)* to be part of; **prendre qn à ~** to take sb to task; *(malmener)* to set on sb; **en grande ~** largely, in the main; **ce n'est que ~ remise** it will be for another time *ou* the next time; **avoir ~ liée avec qn** to be in league with sb; **~ civile** *(JUR)* party claiming damages in a criminal case.

partiel, le [pàrsyel] *a* partial ♦ *nm (SCOL)* class exam.

partiellement [pàrsyelmáṅ] *ad* partially, partly.

partir [pàrtēr] *vi (gén)* to go; *(quitter)* to leave; *(s'éloigner)* to go *(ou* drive *etc)* away *ou* off; *(moteur)* to start; *(pétard)* to go off; *(bouchon)* to come out; *(bouton)* to come off; **~ de** *(lieu: quitter)* to leave; *(: commencer à)* to start from; *(date)* to run *ou* start from; **~ pour/à** *(lieu, pays etc)* to leave for/go off to; **à ~ de** from.

partisan, e [pàrtēzáṅ, -àn] *nm/f* partisan; *(d'un parti, régime etc)* supporter ♦ *a (lutte, querelle)* partisan, one-sided; **être ~ de qch/faire** to be in favor of sth/doing.

partitif, ive [pàrtētēf, -ēv] *a:* **article ~** partitive article.

partition [pàrtēsyóṅ] *nf (MUS)* score.

partout [pàrtoō] *ad* everywhere; **~ où il allait** everywhere *ou* wherever he went; **trente ~** *(TENNIS)* thirty all.

paru [pàrü] *pp de* **paraître**.

parure [pàrür] *nf (bijoux etc)* finery *q*; jewelry *q (US)*, jewellery *q (Brit)*; *(assortiment)* set.

parus [pàrü] *etc vb voir* **paraître**.

parution [pàrüsyóṅ] *nf* publication, appearance.

parvenir [pàrvənēr]: **~ à** *vt (atteindre)* to reach; *(obtenir, arriver à)* to attain; *(réussir)*: **~ à faire** to manage to do, succeed in doing; **faire ~ qch à qn** to have sth sent to sb.

parvenu, e [pàrvənü] *pp de* **parvenir** ♦ *nm/f (péj)* parvenu, upstart.

parviendrai [pàrvyaṅdrā], **parviens** [pàrvyaṅ] *etc voir* **parvenir**.

parvis [pàrvē] *nm* square *(in front of a church)*.

pas [pâ] *nm voir le mot suivant* ♦ *ad* not; **~ de** no; **ne ... ~:** **il ne le voit ~/ne l'a ~ vu/ne le verra ~** he doesn't see it/hasn't seen it *ou* didn't see it/won't see it; **ils n'ont ~ de voiture/d'enfants** they haven't got a car/any children, they have no car/children; **~ de sucre, merci** no sugar, thank you; **il m'a dit de ne ~ le faire** he told me not to do it; **il n'est ~ plus grand** he isn't bigger, he's no bigger; **... lui ~ ou ~ lui** he doesn't *(ou* isn't *etc)*; **ceci est à vous ou ~?** is this yours or not?; **non ~ que ...** not that ...; **une pomme ~ mûre** an unripe apple, an apple which isn't ripe; **~ du tout** not at all; **~ encore** not yet; **~ plus tard qu'hier** only yesterday; **~ mal** *a* not bad, quite good *(ou* pretty *ou* nice) ♦ *ad* quite well; *(beaucoup)* quite a lot; **~ mal de** quite a lot of.

pas [pâ] *ad voir le mot précédent* ♦ *nm (allure, mesure)* pace; *(démarche)* tread; *(enjambée, DANSE, fig: étape)* step; *(bruit)* (foot)step; *(trace)* footprint; *(allure)* pace; *(d'un cheval)* walk; *(mesure)* pace, *(TECH. de vis, d'écrou)* thread; **~ à ~** step by step; **au ~** at walking pace; **de ce ~** *(à l'instant même)* straightaway, at once; **marcher à grands ~** to stride along; **mettre qn au ~** to bring sb to heel; **au ~ de gymnastique/de course** at a jog trot/at a run; **à ~ de loup** stealthily; **faire les cent ~** to pace up and down; **faire les premiers ~** to make the first move; **retourner** *ou* **revenir sur ses ~** to retrace one's steps; **se tirer d'un mauvais ~** to get o.s. out of a tight spot; **sur le ~ de la porte** on the doorstep; **le ~ de Calais** *(détroit)* the Straits *pl* of Dover.

pascal, e, aux [pàskàl, -ō] *a* Easter *cpd*.

passable [pàsábl(ə)] *a* passable, tolerable.

passablement [pàsábləmáṅ] *ad (pas trop mal)* reasonably well; *(beaucoup)* quite a lot.

passade [pàsàd] *nf* passing fancy, whim.

passage [pàsáʒ] *nm (fait de passer) voir* **passer**; *(lieu, prix de la traversée, extrait de livre etc)* passage; *(chemin)* way; *(itinéraire)*: **sur le ~ du cortège** along the route of the procession; **"laissez/n'obstruez pas le ~"** "keep clear/do not block"; **au ~** *(en passant)* as I *(ou* he *etc)* went by; **de ~** *(touristes)* passing through; *(amants etc)* casual; **~ clouté** pedestrian crossing; **"~ interdit"** "do not enter", "no thoroughfare"; **~ à niveau** grade *(US) ou* level *(Brit)* crossing; **"~ protégé"** right of way over secondary road(s) on your right; **~ souterrain** underpass, subway *(Brit)*; **~ à tabac** beating; **~ à vide** *(fig)* rough spot.

passager, ère [pâsázhā, -cr] *a* passing; (*hôte*) short-stay *cpd*; (*oiseau*) migratory ♦ *nm/f* passenger; ~ **clandestin** stowaway.

passagèrement [pásázhermáṅ] *ad* temporarily, for a short time.

passant, e [pâsâṅ, -âṅt] *a* (*rue, endroit*) busy ♦ *nm/f* passer-by ♦ *nm* (*pour ceinture etc*) loop; **en** ~: **remarquer qch en** ~ to notice sth in passing.

passation [pásâsyôṅ] *nf* (*JUR*: *d'un acte*) signing; ~ **des pouvoirs** transfer *ou* handover of power.

passe [pâs] *nf* (*SPORT, magnétique*) pass; (*NAVIG*) channel ♦ *nm* (*passe-partout*) master *ou* skeleton key; **être en** ~ **de faire** to be on the way to doing; **être dans une bonne** ~ (*fig*) to be in a healthy situation; **être dans une mauvaise** ~ (*fig*) to be having a rough time; ~ **d'armes** (*fig*) heated exchange.

passé, e [pâsā] *a* (*événement, temps*) past; (*couleur, tapisserie*) faded; (*précédent*): **dimanche** ~ last Sunday ♦ *prép* after ♦ *nm* past; (*LING*) past (tense); **il est** ~ **midi** *ou* **midi** ~ it's past twelve; ~ **de mode** out of fashion; ~ **composé** perfect (tense); ~ **simple** past historic.

passe-droit [pâsdrwà] *nm* special privilege.

passéiste [pâsēst(ə)] *a* backward-looking.

passementerie [pâsmáṅtrē] *nf* trimmings *pl*.

passe-montagne [pâsmóṅtány] *nm* balaclava.

passe-partout [pâspártōō] *nm inv* master *ou* skeleton key ♦ *a inv* all-purpose.

passe-passe [pâspâs] *nm*: **tour de** ~ trick, sleight of hand *q*.

passe-plat [pâsplá] *nm* serving hatch.

passeport [pâspor] *nm* passport.

passer [pâsā] *vi* (*se rendre, aller*) to go; (*voiture, piétons: défiler*) to pass (by), go by; (*faire une halte rapide: facteur, laitier etc*) to come, call; (: *pour rendre visite*) to call *ou* drop in; (*courant, air, lumière, franchir un obstacle etc*) to get through; (*accusé, projet de loi*): ~ **devant** to come before; (*film, émission*) to be on; (*temps, jours*) to pass, go by; (*liquide, café*) to go through; (*être digéré, avalé*) to go down; (*couleur, papier*) to fade; (*mode*) to die out; (*douleur*) to pass, go away; (*CARTES*) to pass; (*SCOL*) to be promoted (to the next grade) (*US*), go up (to the next class) (*Brit*); (*devenir*): ~ **président** to be appointed *ou* become president ♦ *vt* (*frontière, rivière etc*) to cross; (*douane*) to go through; (*examen*) to take; (*visite médicale etc*) to have; (*journée, temps*) to spend; (*donner*): ~ **qch à qn** to pass sth to sb; to give sb sth; (*transmettre*): ~ **qch à qn** to pass sth on to sb; (*enfiler: vêtement*) to slip on; (*faire entrer, mettre*): (**faire**) ~ **qch dans/par** to get sth into/ through; (*café*) to pour the water on; (*thé, soupe*) to strain; (*film, pièce*) to show, put on; (*disque*) to play, put on; (*marché, accord*) to agree on; (*tolérer*): ~ **qch à qn** to let sb get away with sth; **se** ~ *vi* (*avoir lieu: scène, action*) to take place; (*se dérouler: entretien etc*) to go; (*arriver*): **que s'est-il passé?** what happened?; (*s'écouler: semaine etc*) to pass, go by; **se** ~ **de** *vt* to go *ou* do

without; **se** ~ **les mains sous l'eau/de l'eau sur le visage** to put one's hands under the tap/run water over one's face; **en passant** in passing; ~ **par** to go through; **passez devant/par ici** go in front/this way; ~ **sur** *vt* (*faute, détail inutile*) to pass over; ~ **dans les mœurs/l'usage** to become the custom/ normal usage; ~ **avant qch/qn** (*fig*) to come before sth/sb; **laisser** ~ (*air, lumière, personne*) to let through; (*occasion*) to let slip, miss; (*erreur*) to overlook; **faire** ~ (*message*) to get over *ou* across; **faire** ~ à **qn le goût de qch** to cure sb of his (*ou* her) taste for sth; ~ à **la radio/fouille** to be X-rayed/searched; ~ à **la radio/télévision** to be on the radio/on television; ~ à **table** to sit down to eat; ~ **au salon** to go into the living room; ~ à **l'opposition** to go over to the opposition; ~ **aux aveux** to confess, make a confession; ~ à **l'action** to go into action; ~ **pour riche** to be taken for a rich man; **il passait pour avoir** he was said to have; **faire** ~ **qn/qch pour** to make sb/sth out to be; **passe encore de le penser, mais de le dire!** it's one thing to think it, but to say it!; **passons!** let's say no more (about it); **et j'en passe!** and that's not all!; ~ **en seconde,** ~ **la seconde** (*AUTO*) to shift into second; ~ **qch en fraude** to smuggle sth in (*ou* out); ~ **la main par la portière** to stick one's hand out of the door; ~ **le balai/l'aspirateur** to sweep up/vacuum; ~ **commande/la parole à qn** to hand over to sb; **je vous passe M X** (*je vous mets en communication avec lui*) I'm putting you through to Mr X; (*je lui passe l'appareil*) here is Mr X, I'll hand you over to Mr X; ~ **prendre** to (come and) get.

passereau, x [pâsrō] *nm* sparrow.

passerelle [pâsrel] *nf* footbridge; (*de navire, avion*) gangway; (*NAVIG*): ~ (**de commandement**) bridge.

passe-temps [pâstáṅ] *nm inv* pastime.

passette [pâset] *nf* (tea-)strainer.

passeur, euse [pâscr, -ɵz] *nm/f* smuggler.

passible [pâsēbl(ə)] *a*: ~ **de** liable to.

passif, ive [pâsēf, -ēv] *a* passive ♦ *nm* (*LING*) passive; (*COMM*) liabilities *pl*.

passion [pâsyôṅ] *nf* passion; **avoir la** ~ **de** to have a passion for; **fruit de la** ~ passion fruit.

passionnant, e [pâsyonâṅ, -âṅt] *a* fascinating.

passionné, e [pâsyonā] *a* (*personne, tempérament*) passionate; (*description*) impassioned ♦ *nm/f*: **c'est un** ~ **d'échecs** he's a chess fanatic; **être** ~ **de** *ou* **pour qch** to have a passion for sth.

passionnel, le [pâsyonel] *a* of passion.

passionnément [pâsyonāmáṅ] *ad* passionately.

passionner [pâsyonā] *vt* (*personne*) to fascinate, grip; (*débat, discussion*) to inflame; **se** ~ **pour** to take an avid interest in; to have a passion for.

passivement [pâscvmáṅ] *ad* passively.

passivité [pâscvētā] *nf* passivity, passiveness.

passoire [pâswár] *nf* sieve; (à *légumes*) colander; (à *thé*) strainer.

pastel [pâstel] *nm, a inv* (*ART*) pastel.

pastèque [pâstek] *nf* watermelon.

pasteur [pástœr] *nm* (*protestant*) minister, pastor.
pasteuriser [pástœrēzā] *vt* to pasteurize.
pastiche [pástēsh] *nm* pastiche.
pastille [pástēy] *nf* (*à sucer*) lozenge, pastille; (*de papier etc*) (small) disc; ~s **pour la toux** cough drops *ou* lozenges.
pastis [pástēs] *nm* anise-flavored alcoholic drink.
pastoral, e, aux [pástorál, -ō] *a* pastoral.
patagon, ne [pátágóń, -on] *a* Patagonian.
Patagonie [pátágonē] *nf*: **la** ~ Patagonia.
patate [pátát] *nf* spud; ~ **douce** sweet potato.
pataud, e [pátō, -ōd] *a* lumbering.
patauger [pátōzhā] *vi* (*pour s'amuser*) to splash about; (*avec effort*) to wade about; (*fig*) to flounder; ~ **dans** (*en marchant*) to wade through.
pâte [pát] *nf* (*à tarte*) pastry; (*à pain*) dough; (*à frire*) batter; (*substance molle*) paste; cream; ~s *nfpl* (*macaroni etc*) pasta *sg*; **fromage à** ~ **dure/molle** hard/soft cheese; ~ **d'amandes** almond paste; ~ **brisée** pie crust (*US*) *ou* shortcrust (*Brit*) pastry; ~ **à choux/feuilletée** choux/puff pastry; ~ **de fruits** candied fruit *q*; ~ **à modeler** modeling (*US*) *ou* modelling (*Brit*) clay; ~ **à papier** paper pulp.
pâté [pátā] *nm* (*charcuterie: terrine*) pâté; (*tache*) ink blot; (*de sable*) sand pie; ~ **(en croûte)** ≈ meat pie; ~ **de foie** liver pâté; ~ **de maisons** block (of houses).
pâtée [pátā] *nf* mash, feed.
patelin [pátlań] *nm* little place.
patente [pátáńt] *nf* (*COMM*) trading license (*US*) *ou* licence (*Brit*).
patenté, e [pátáńtā] *a* (*COMM*) licensed; (*fig: attitré*) registered, (officially) recognized.
patère [páter] *nf* (coat) peg.
paternaliste [páternálēst(ə)] *a* paternalistic.
paternel, le [pátãrnel] *a* (*amour, soins*) fatherly; (*ligne, autorité*) paternal.
paternité [páternētā] *nf* paternity, fatherhood.
pâteux, euse [pátœ̄, -œ̄z] *a* thick; pasty; **avoir la bouche** *ou* **langue pâteuse** to have a coated tongue.
pathétique [pátātēk] *a* pathetic, moving.
pathologie [pátolozhē] *nf* pathology.
pathologique [pátolozhēk] *a* pathological.
patibulaire [pátēbüler] *a* sinister.
patiemment [pásyámáń] *ad* patiently.
patience [pásyáńs] *nf* patience; **être à bout de** ~ to have run out of patience; **perdre/prendre** ~ to lose (one's)/have patience.
patient, e [pásyáń, -áńt] *a*, *nm/f* patient.
patienter [pásyáńtā] *vi* to wait.
patin [pátáń] *nm* skate; (*sport*) skating; (*de traîneau, luge*) runner; (*pièce de tissu*) cloth pad (*used as slippers to protect polished floor*); ~ **(de frein)** brake shoe; ~s **(à glace)** (ice) skates; ~s **à roulettes** roller skates.
patinage [pátēnázh] *nm* skating; ~ **artistique/de vitesse** figure/speed skating.
patine [pátēn] *nf* sheen.
patiner [pátēnā] *vi* to skate; (*embrayage*) to slip; (*roue, voiture*) to spin; **se** ~ *vi* (*meuble, cuir*) to acquire a sheen, become polished.
patineur, euse [pátēnœr, -œ̄z] *nm/f* skater.

patinoire [pátēnwár] *nf* skating rink, (ice) rink.
patio [pátyō] *nm* patio.
pâtir [pátēr]: ~ **de** *vt* to suffer because of.
pâtisserie [pátēsrē] *nf* (*boutique*) pastry (*US*) *ou* cake (*Brit*) shop; (*métier*) confectionery; (*à la maison*) pastry *ou* cake making, baking; ~s *nfpl* (*gâteaux*) pastries, cakes.
pâtissier, ière [pátēsyā, -yer] *nm/f* pastry cook; confectioner.
patois [pátwá] *nm* dialect, patois.
patriarche [pátrēyársh(ə)] *nm* patriarch.
patrie [pátrē] *nf* homeland.
patrimoine [pátrēmwáń] *nm* inheritance, patrimony; (*culture*) heritage; ~ **génétique** *ou* **héréditaire** genetic inheritance.
patriote [pátrēyot] *a* patriotic ♦ *nm/f* patriot.
patriotique [pátrēyotēk] *a* patriotic.
patron, ne [pátróń, -on] *nm/f* (*chef*) boss, manager/eress; (*propriétaire*) owner, proprietor/tress; (*employeur*) employer; (*MÉD*) ≈ senior consultant; (*REL*) patron saint ♦ *nm* (*COUTURE*) pattern; ~ **de thèse** supervisor (of postgraduate thesis).
patronage [pátronázh] *nm* patronage; (*organisation, club*) (parish) youth club; (parish) children's club.
patronal, e, aux [pátronál, -ō] *a* (*syndicat, intérêts*) employers'.
patronat [pátroná] *nm* employers *pl*.
patronner [pátroná] *vt* to sponsor, support.
patronnesse [pátrones] *af*: **dame** ~ patroness.
patronyme [pátronēm] *nm* name.
patronymique [pátronēmēk] *a*: **nom** ~ patronymic (name).
patrouillo [pátroōy] *nf* patrol.
patrouiller [pátroōyā] *vi* to patrol, be on patrol.
patrouilleur [pátroōyœr] *nm* (*AVIAT*) scout (plane); (*NAVIG*) patrol boat.
patte [pát] *nf* (*jambe*) leg; (*pied: de chien, chat*) paw; (: *d'oiseau*) foot; (*languette*) strap; (: *de poche*) flap; (*favoris*): ~s **(de lapin)** (short) sideburns; **à** ~s **d'éléphant** *a* (*pantalon*) flared; ~s **de mouche** (*fig*) spidery scrawl *sg*; ~s **d'oie** (*fig*) crow's feet.
pattemouille [pátmoōy] *nf* damp cloth (*for ironing*).
pâturage [pátürázh] *nm* pasture.
pâture [pátür] *nf* food.
paume [pōm] *nf* palm.
paumé, e [pōmā] *nm/f* (*fam*) dropout.
paumer [pōmā] *vt* (*fam*) to lose.
paupière [pōpyer] *nf* eyelid.
paupiette [pōpyet] *nf*: ~s **de veau** veal olives.
pause [pōz] *nf* (*arrêt*) break; (*en parlant*) pause; (*MUS*) rest, pause.
pause-café, *pl* **pauses-café** [pōzkáfā] *nf* coffee break.
pauvre [pōvr(ə)] *a* poor ♦ *nm/f* poor man/woman; **les** ~s **the** poor; ~ **en calcium** low in calcium.
pauvrement [pōvrəmáń] *ad* poorly.
pauvreté [pōvrotā] *nf* (*état*) poverty.
pavage [pávázh] *nm* paving; cobblestones *pl*.
pavaner [pávánā]: **se** ~ *vi* to strut about.
pavé, e [pávā] *a* (*cour*) paved; (*rue*) cobbled ♦

nm (*bloc*) paving stone; cobblestone; (*pavage*) paving; (*bifteck*) slab of steak; (*fam: livre*) hefty tome; **être sur le ~** (*sans domicile*) to be on the streets; (*sans emploi*) to be out of a job; **~ numérique** (*INFORM*) keypad.

pavillon [pávēyôn̂] *nm* (*de banlieue*) small (detached) house; (*kiosque*) lodge; pavilion; (*d'hôpital*) ward; (*MUS*: *de cor etc*) bell; (*ANAT*: *de l'oreille*) pavilion, pinna; (*NAVIG*) flag; **~ de complaisance** flag of convenience.

pavoiser [pávwàzá] *vt* to deck with flags ♦ *vi* to put out flags; (*fig*) to rejoice, exult.

pavot [pávō] *nm* poppy.

payable [peyábl(ə)] *a* payable.

payant, e [peyân̂, -ân̂t] *a* (*spectateurs etc*) paying; (*billet*) that you pay for, to be paid for; (*fig: entreprise*) profitable; **c'est ~** you have to pay, there is a charge.

paye [pcy] *nf* pay, wages *pl*.

payement [peymân̂] *nm* payment.

payer [pāyā] *vt* (*créancier, employé, loyer*) to pay; (*achat, réparations, fig: faute*) to pay for ♦ *vi* to pay; (*métier*) to pay, be well-paid; (*effort, tactique etc*) to pay off; **il me l'a fait ~ 10 F** he charged me 10 F for it; **~ qn de** (*ses efforts, peines*) to reward sb for; **~ qch à qn** to buy sth for sb, buy sb sth; **ils nous ont payé le voyage** they paid for our trip; **~ de sa personne** to give of oneself; **~ d'audace** to act with great daring; **~ cher qch** to pay dear(ly) for sth; **cela ne paie pas de mine** it doesn't look like much, it's not much to look at; **se ~ qch** to buy o.s. sth; **se ~ de mots** to shoot one's mouth off; **se ~ la tête de qn** to make a fool of sb; (*duper*) to take sb for a ride.

payeur, euse [peyœr, -œz] *a* (*organisme, bureau*) payments *cpd* ♦ *nm/f* payer.

pays [pāē] *nm* (*territoire, habitants*) country, land; (*région*) region; (*village*) village; **du ~** *a* local; **le ~ de Galles** Wales.

paysage [pāēzázh] *nm* landscape.

paysagiste [pāēzázhēst(ə)] *nm/f* (*de jardin*) landscape gardener; (*ART*) landscapist, landscape painter.

paysan, ne [pāēzân̂, -àn] *nm/f* countryman/woman; farmer; (*péj*) peasant ♦ *a* country *cpd*, farming; farmers'.

paysannat [pāēzáná] *nm* peasantry.

Pays-Bas [pāēbá] *nmpl*: **les ~** the Netherlands.

PC *sigle m* (*POL*) = *Parti communiste*; (*INFORM*: = *personal computer*) PC; (= *prêt conventionné*) *type of loan for house purchase*; (*CONSTR*) = **permis de construire**; (*MIL*) = **poste de commandement**.

pcc *abr* (= *pour copie conforme*) c.c.

Pce *abr* = **prince**.

Pcesse *abr* = **princesse**.

PCV *abr* (= *percevoir*) *voir* **communication**.

p de p *abr* = **pas de porte**.

PDG *sigle m* = **président directeur général**.

p.ê. *abr* = **peut-être**.

péage [pāázh] *nm* toll; (*endroit*) tollgate; **pont à ~** toll bridge.

peau, x [pō] *nf* skin; (*cuir*): **gants de ~** leather gloves; **être bien/mal dans sa ~** to be at ease/odds with oneself; **se mettre dans la ~ de qn** to put o.s. in sb's place *ou* shoes; **faire ~ neuve** (*se renouveler*) to change one's image; **~ de chamois** (*chiffon*) chamois leather, shammy; **~ d'orange** orange peel.

peaufiner [pōfēnā] *vt* to polish (up).

Peau-Rouge [pōrōōzh] *nm/f* Red Indian, redskin.

peccadille [pākàdēy] *nf* trifle, peccadillo.

péché [pāshā] *nm* sin; **~ mignon** weakness.

pêche [pesh] *nf* (*sport, activité*) fishing; (*poissons pêchés*) catch; (*fruit*) peach; **aller à la ~** to go fishing; **avoir la ~** (*fam*) to be in (top) form; **~ à la ligne** (*en rivière*) angling; **~ sous-marine** deep-sea fishing.

pêche-abricot, *pl* **pêches-abricots** [peshábrēkō] *nf* yellow peach.

pécher [pāshā] *vi* (*REL*) to sin; (*fig: personne*) to err; (: *chose*) to be flawed; **~ contre la bienséance** to break the rules of good behavior.

pêcher [pāshā] *nm* peach tree ♦ *vi* to go fishing; (*en rivière*) to go angling ♦ *vt* (*attraper*) to catch, land; (*chercher*) to fish for; **~ au chalut** to trawl.

pécheur, eresse [pāshœr, pāshrcs] *nm/f* sinner.

pêcheur [peshœr] *nm* (*voir pêcher*) fisherman; angler; **~ de perles** pearl diver.

pectine [pcktēn] *nf* pectin.

pectoral, e, aux [pcktorál, -ō] *a* (*ANAT*) pectoral; (*sirop*) throat *cpd*, cough *cpd* ♦ *nmpl* pectoral muscles.

pécule [pākül] *nm* savings *pl*, nest egg; (*d'un détenu*) earnings *pl* (*paid on release*).

pécuniaire [pākünyer] *a* financial.

pédagogie [pādágozhē] *nf* educational methods *pl*, pedagogy.

pédagogique [pādágozhēk] *a* educational; **formation ~** teacher training.

pédagogue [pādágog] *nm/f* teacher; education(al)ist.

pédale [pādál] *nf* pedal; **mettre la ~ douce** to soft-pedal.

pédaler [pādàlá] *vi* to pedal.

pédalier [pādályā] *nm* pedal and gear mechanism.

pédalo [pādálō] *nm* pedalo, pedal boat.

pédant, e [pādân̂, -ân̂t] *a* (*péj*) pedantic ♦ *nm/f* pedant.

pédantisme [pādân̂tēsm(ə)] *nm* pedantry.

pédéraste [pādārást(ə)] *nm* homosexual, pederast.

pédérastie [pādárástē] *nf* homosexuality, pederasty.

pédestre [pādestr(ə)] *a*: **tourisme ~** hiking; **randonnée ~** (*activité*) rambling; (*excursion*) ramble.

pédiatre [pādyàtr(ə)] *nm/f* pediatrician *ou* pediatrist (*US*), paediatrician (*Brit*), child specialist.

pédiatrie [pādyàtrē] *nf* pediatrics *sg* (*US*), paediatrics *sg* (*Brit*).

pédicure [pādikür] *nm/f* chiropodist.

pedigree [pādēgrā] *nm* pedigree.

peeling [pēlēng] *nm* exfoliation treatment.

PEEP *sigle f* = *Fédération des parents d'élèves de l'enseignement public*.

pègre [pegr(ə)] *nf* underworld.

peigne [pcny] *vb voir* **peindre, peigner** ♦ *nm*

comb.

peigné, e [pānyā] *a*: **laine** ~**e** worsted wool; combed wool.

peigner [pānyā] *vt* to comb (the hair of); **se** ~ to comb one's hair.

peignez [penyā] *etc vb voir* **peindre.**

peignoir [penywár] *nm* dressing gown; ~ **de bain** bathrobe; ~ **de plage** beach robe.

peignons [penyóń] *vb voir* **peindre.**

peinard, e [penár, -árd(ə)] *a* (*emploi*) easy; (*personne*): **on est** ~ **ici** we're left in peace here.

peindre [pańdr(ə)] *vt* to paint; (*fig*) to portray, depict.

peine [pen] *nf* (*affliction*) sorrow, sadness *q*; (*mal, effort*) trouble *q*, effort; (*difficulté*) difficulty; (*punition, châtiment*) punishment; (*JUR*) sentence; **faire de la** ~ **à qn** to distress *ou* upset sb; **prendre la** ~ **de faire** to go to the trouble of doing; **se donner de la** ~ to make an effort; **ce n'est pas la** ~ **de faire** there's no point in doing, it's not worth doing; **ce n'est pas la** ~ **que vous fassiez** there's no point (in) you doing; **avoir de la** ~ **à faire** to have difficulty doing; **donnez-vous** *ou* **veuillez vous donner la** ~ **d'entrer** please do come in; **c'est** ~ **perdue** it's a waste of time (and effort); **à** ~ *ad* scarcely, hardly, barely; **à** ~ ... **que** hardly ... than; **c'est à** ~ **si** ... it's (*ou* it was) a job to ...; **sous** ~: **sous** ~ **d'être puni** for fear of being punished; **défense d'afficher sous** ~ **d'amende** billposters will be fined; ~ **capital** capital punishment; ~ **de mort** death sentence *ou* penalty.

peiner [pānā] *vi* to work hard; to struggle; (*moteur, voiture*) to labor (*US*), labour (*Brit*) ♦ *vt* to grieve, sadden.

peint, e [pań, pańt] *pp de* **peindre.**

peintre [pańtr(ə)] *nm* painter; ~ **en bâtiment** house painter, painter and decorator; ~ **d'enseignes** signwriter, sign painter (*US*).

peinture [pańtür] *nf* painting; (*couche de couleur, couleur*) paint; (*surfaces peintes: aussi* ~**s**) paintwork; **je ne peux pas le voir en** ~ I can't stand the sight of him; ~ **mate/brillante** matt/gloss paint; "~ **fraîche**" "wet paint".

péjoratif, ive [pāzhorátēf, -ēv] *a* pejorative, derogatory.

Pékin [pākań] *n* Peking.

pékinois, e [pākēnwá, -wáz] *a* Pekin(g)ese ♦ *nm* (*chien*) peke, pekin(g)ese; (*LING*) Mandarin, Pekin(g)ese ♦ *nm/f*: **P**~, **e** Pekin(g)ese.

PEL *sigle m* (= *Plan d'épargne logement*) savings plan providing lower-interest mortgages.

pelade [pəlád] *nf* alopecia.

pelage [pəlázh] *nm* coat, fur.

pelé, e [pəlā] *a* (*chien*) hairless; (*vêtement*) threadbare; (*terrain*) bare.

pêle-mêle [pelmel] *ad* higgledy-piggledy.

peler [pəlā] *vt, vi* to peel.

pèlerin [pelrań] *nm* pilgrim.

pèlerinage [pelrēnázh] *nm* (*voyage*) pilgrimage; (*lieu*) place of pilgrimage, shrine.

pèlerine [pelrēn] *nf* cape.

pélican [pālēkáń] *nm* pelican.

pelle [pel] *nf* shovel; (*d'enfant, de terrassier*) spade; ~ **à gâteau** cake slice; ~ **mécanique** power shovel (*US*), mechanical digger (*Brit*).

pelletée [peltā] *nf* shovelful; spadeful.

pelleter [peltā] *vt* to shovel (up).

pelleteuse [peltœz] *nf* power shovel (*US*), mechanical digger (*Brit*), excavator.

pelletier [peltyā] *nm* furrier.

pellicule [pālēkül] *nf* film; ~**s** *nfpl* (*MÉD*) dandruff *sg*.

Péloponnèse [pāloponez] *nm*: **le** ~ the Peloponnese.

pelote [pəlot] *nf* (*de fil, laine*) ball; (*d'épingles*) pin cushion; ~ **basque** pelota.

peloter [pəlotā] *vt* (*fam*) to feel (up); **se** ~ to pet.

peloton [pəlotóń] *nm* (*groupe: personnes*) group; (*: pompiers, gendarmes*) squad; (*: SPORT*) pack; (*de laine*) ball; ~ **d'exécution** firing squad.

pelotonner [pəlotonā]: **se** ~ *vi* to curl (o.s.) up.

pelouse [pəlōōz] *nf* lawn; (*HIPPISME*) spectating area inside racetrack.

peluche [pəlüsh] *nf* (bit of) fluff; **animal en** ~ soft toy, stuffed animal.

pelucher [p(ə)lüshā] *vi* to become fluffy, fluff up.

pelucheux, euse [p(ə)lüshœ, -œz] *a* fluffy.

pelure [pəlür] *nf* peeling, peel *q*; ~ **d'oignon** onion skin.

pénal, e, aux [pānál, -ō] *a* penal.

pénaliser [pānálēzā] *vt* to penalize.

pénalité [pānálētā] *nf* penalty.

penalty, ies [pānáltē, -z] *nm* (*SPORT*) penalty (kick).

pénard, e [pānár, -árd(ə)] *a* = **peinard**

pénates [pānát] *nmpl*: **regagner ses** ~ to return to the bosom of one's family.

penaud, e [pənō, -ōd] *a* sheepish, contrite.

penchant [páńsháń] *nm*: **un** ~ **à faire/à qch** a tendency to do/to sth; **un** ~ **pour qch** a liking *ou* fondness for sth.

penché, e [páńshā] *a* slanting.

pencher [páńshā] *vi* to tilt, lean over ♦ *vt* to tilt; **se** ~ *vi* to lean over; (*se baisser*) to bend down; **se** ~ **sur** to bend over; (*fig: problème*) to look into; **se** ~ **au dehors** to lean out; ~ **pour** to be inclined to favor.

pendable [páńdábl(ə)] *a*: **tour** ~ rotten trick; **c'est un cas** ~! he (*ou* she) deserves to be shot!

pendaison [páńdezóń] *nf* hanging.

pendant, e [páńdáń, -áńt] *a* hanging (out); (*ADMIN, JUR*) pending ♦ *nm* counterpart; matching piece ♦ *prép* during; **faire** ~ **à** to match; **to be the counterpart of**; ~ **que** while; ~**s d'oreilles** drop *ou* pendant earrings.

pendeloque [páńdlok] *nf* pendant.

pendentif [páńdáńtēf] *nm* pendant.

penderie [páńdrē] *nf* wardrobe; (*placard*) walk-in closet (*US*) *ou* cupboard (*Brit*).

pendiller [páńdēyā] *vi* to flap (about).

pendre [páńdr(ə)] *vt, vi* to hang; **se** ~ **(à)** (*se suicider*) to hang o.s. (on); **se** ~ **à** (*se suspendre*) to hang from; ~ **à** to hang (down) from; ~ **qch à** (*mur*) to hang sth (up) on; (*plafond*) to hang sth (up) from.

pendu, e [pɑ̃dü] *pp de* **pendre** ♦ *nm/f* hanged man (*ou* woman).
pendulaire [pɑ̃düler] *a* pendular, of a pendulum.
pendule [pɑ̃dül] *nf* clock ♦ *nm* pendulum.
pendulette [pɑ̃dület] *nf* small clock.
pêne [pen] *nm* bolt.
pénétrant, e [pɑ̃nātrɑ̃, -ɑ̃t] *a* (*air, froid*) biting; (*pluie*) that soaks right through you; (*fig: odeur*) noticeable; (*œil, regard*) piercing; (*clairvoyant, perspicace*) perceptive ♦ *nf* (*route*) expressway.
pénétration [pɑ̃nātrɑ̃syɔ̃] *nf* (*fig: d'idées etc*) penetration; (*perspicacité*) perception.
pénétré, e [pɑ̃nātrā] *a* (*air, ton*) earnest; **être ~ de soi-même/son** importance to be full of oneself/one's own importance.
pénétrer [pɑ̃nātrā] *vi* to come *ou* get in ♦ *vt* to penetrate; **~ dans** to enter; (*suj: froid, projectile*) to penetrate; (: *air, eau*) to come into, get into; (*mystère, secret*) to fathom; **se ~ de qch** to get sth firmly set in one's mind.
pénible [pɑ̃nēbl(ə)] *a* (*astreignant*) hard; (*affligeant*) painful; (*personne, caractère*) tiresome; **il m'est ~ de ...** I'm sorry to ....
péniblement [pɑ̃nēbləmɑ̃] *ad* with difficulty.
péniche [pɑ̃nēsh] *nf* barge; **~ de débarquement** landing craft *inv*.
pénicilline [pɑ̃nēsēlēn] *nf* penicillin.
péninsule [pɑ̃nɑ̃sül] *nf* peninsula.
pénis [pɑ̃nēs] *nm* penis.
pénitence [pɑ̃nētɑ̃s] *nf* (*repentir*) penitence; (*peine*) penance; (*punition, châtiment*) punishment; **mettre un enfant en ~ ≈** to make a child stand in the corner; **faire ~** to do a penance.
pénitencier [pɑ̃nētɑ̃syā] *nm* prison, penitentiary (*US*).
pénitent, e [pɑ̃nētɑ̃, -ɑ̃t] *a* penitent.
pénitentiaire [pɑ̃nētɑ̃syer] *a* prison *cpd*, penitentiary (*US*).
pénombre [pɑ̃nɔ̃br(ə)] *nf* half-light.
pensable [pɑ̃sábl(ə)] *a*: **ce n'est pas ~** it's unthinkable.
pensant, e [pɑ̃sɑ̃, -ɑ̃t] *a*: **bien ~** right-thinking.
pense-bête [pɑ̃sbɛt] *nm* aide mémoire, mnemonic device.
pensée [pɑ̃sā] *nf* thought; (*démarche, doctrine*) thinking *q*; (*BOT*) pansy; **se représenter qch par la ~** to conjure up a mental picture of sth; **en ~** in one's mind.
penser [pɑ̃sā] *vi* to think ♦ *vt* to think; (*concevoir: problème, machine*) to think out; **~ à** to think of; (*songer à: ami, vacances*) to think of *ou* about; (*réfléchir à: problème, offre*): **~ à qch** to think about sth, think sth over; **~ à faire qch** to think of doing sth; **~ faire qch** to be thinking of doing sth, intend to do sth; **faire ~ à** to remind one of; **n'y pensons plus** let's forget it; **vous n'y pensez pas!** don't let it bother you!; **sans ~ à mal** without meaning any harm; **je le pense aussi** I think so too; **je pense que oui/non** I think so/don't think so.
penseur [pɑ̃sœr] *nm* thinker; **libre ~** free-thinker.
pensif, ive [pɑ̃sēf, -ēv] *a* pensive, thoughtful.

pension [pɑ̃syɔ̃] *nf* (*allocation*) pension; (*prix du logement*) board and lodging, bed and board; (*maison particulière*) boarding house; (*hôtel*) guesthouse, hotel; (*école*) boarding school; **prendre ~ chez** to take board and lodging at; **prendre qn en ~** to take sb (in) as a lodger; **mettre en ~** to send to boarding school; **~ alimentaire** (*d'étudiant*) living allowance; (*de divorcée*) maintenance allowance; alimony; **~ complète** full board; **~ de famille** boarding house, guesthouse; **~ de guerre/d'invalidité** war/disablement pension.
pensionnaire [pɑ̃syoner] *nm/f* boarder; guest.
pensionnat [pɑ̃syonā] *nm* boarding school.
pensionné, e [pɑ̃syonā] *nm/f* pensioner.
pensivement [pɑ̃sēvmɑ̃] *ad* pensively, thoughtfully.
pensum [pɑ̃som] *nm* (*SCOL*) punishment exercise; (*fig*) chore.
pentagone [pɑ̃tágon] *nm* pentagon; **le P~** the Pentagon.
pentathlon [pɑ̃tátlɔ̃] *nm* pentathlon.
pente [pɑ̃t] *nf* slope; **en ~** *a* sloping.
Pentecôte [pɑ̃tkōt] *nf*: **la ~** Pentecost, Whitsun; (*dimanche*) Whitsunday; **lundi de ~** Whitmonday.
pénurie [pɑ̃nürē] *nf* shortage; **~ de main-d'œuvre** undermanning.
pépé [pāpā] *nm* (*fam*) grandad.
pépère [pāper] *a* (*fam*) cushy (*fam*), quiet ♦ *nm* (*fam*) grandad.
pépier [pāpyā] *vi* to chirp, tweet.
pépin [pāpɑ̃] *nm* (*BOT: graine*) pip; (*fam: ennui*) snag, hitch; (: *parapluie*) umbrella.
pépinière [pāpēnyer] *nf* nursery; (*fig*) nest, breeding ground.
pépiniériste [pāpēnyārēst(ə)] *nm* nurseryman.
pépite [pāpēt] *nf* nugget.
PEPS *abr* (= *premier entré premier sorti*) first in first out.
PER [per] *sigle m* (= *plan d'épargne retraite*) type of personal pension plan.
perçant, e [persɑ̃, -ɑ̃t] *a* (*vue, regard, yeux*) sharp, keen; (*cri, voix*) piercing, shrill.
percée [persā] *nf* (*trouée*) opening; (*MIL, COMM, fig*) breakthrough; (*SPORT*) break.
perce-neige [persənezh] *nm ou f inv* snowdrop.
perce-oreille [persorey] *nm* earwig.
percepteur [perseptœr] *nm* tax collector.
perceptible [perseptēbl(ə)] *a* (*son, différence*) perceptible; (*impôt*) payable, collectable.
perception [persepsyɔ̃] *nf* perception; (*d'impôts etc*) collection; (*bureau*) tax (collector's) office.
percer [persā] *vt* to pierce; (*ouverture etc*) to make; (*mystère, énigme*) to penetrate ♦ *vi* to come through; (*réussir*) to break through; **~ une dent** to cut a tooth.
perceuse [persœz] *nf* drill; **~ à percussion** hammer drill.
percevable [persəvábl(ə)] *a* collectable, payable.
percevoir [persəvwár] *vt* (*distinguer*) to perceive, detect; (*taxe, impôt*) to collect; (*revenu, indemnité*) to receive.
perche [persh(ə)] *nf* (*ZOOL*) perch; (*bâton*)

pole; ~ **à son** (sound) boom.
percher [pershã] *vt*: ~ **qch sur** to perch sth on ♦ *vi*, **se** ~ *vi* (*oiseau*) to perch.
perchiste [pershēst(ə)] *nm/f* (*SPORT*) pole vaulter; (*TV etc*) boom operator.
perchoir [pershwàr] *nm* perch; (*fig*) *presidency of the French National Assembly*.
perclus, e [perklü, -üz] *a*: ~ **de** (*rhumatismes*) crippled with.
perçois [perswà] *etc vb voir* **percevoir**.
percolateur [perkolátœr] *nm* percolator.
perçu, e [persü] *pp de* **percevoir**.
percussion [perküsyôn] *nf* percussion.
percussionniste [perküsyonēst(ə)] *nm/f* percussionist.
percutant, e [perkütän, -änt] *a* (*article etc*) resounding, forceful.
percuter [perkütã] *vt* to strike; (*suj: véhicule*) to crash into ♦ *vi*: ~ **contre** to crash into.
percuteur [perkütœr] *nm* firing pin, hammer.
perdant, e [perdän, -änt] *nm/f* loser ♦ *a* losing.
perdition [perdēsyôn] *nf* (*morale*) ruin; **en** ~ (*NAVIG*) in distress; **lieu de** ~ den of vice.
perdre [perdr(ə)] *vt* to lose; (*gaspiller: temps, argent*) to waste; (: *occasion*) to waste, miss; (*personne: moralement etc*) to ruin ♦ *vi* to lose; (*sur une vente etc*) to lose out; (*récipient*) to leak; **se** ~ *vi* (*s'égarer*) to get lost, lose one's way; (*fig: se gâter*) to go to waste; (*disparaître*) to disappear, vanish; **il ne perd rien pour attendre** it can wait, it'll keep.
perdreau, x [perdrō] *nm* (young) partridge.
perdrix [perdrē] *nf* partridge.
perdu, e [perdü] *pp de* **perdre** ♦ *a* (*enfant, cause, objet*) lost; (*isolé*) out-of-the-way; (*COMM: emballage*) non returnable; (*récolte etc*) ruined; (*malade*): **il est** ~ there's no hope left for him; **à vos moments** ~**s** in your spare time.
père [per] *nm* father; ~**s** *nmpl* (*ancêtres*) forefathers; **de** ~ **en fils** from father to son; ~ **de famille** father; family man; **mon** ~ (*REL*) Father; **le** ~ **Noël** Santa Claus.
pérégrinations [pārēgrēnàsyôn] *nfpl* travels.
péremption [pārânpsyôn] *nf*: **date de** ~ expiry date.
péremptoire [pārânptwàr] *a* peremptory.
pérennité [pārānētā] *nf* durability, lasting quality.
péréquation [pārākwàsyôn] *nf* (*des salaires*) realignment; (*des prix, impôts*) equalization.
perfectible [perfektēbl(ə)] *a* perfectible.
perfection [perfeksyôn] *nf* perfection; **à la** ~ *ad* to perfection.
perfectionné, e [perfeksyonã] *a* sophisticated.
perfectionnement [perfeksyonmãn] *nm* improvement.
perfectionner [perfeksyonã] *vt* to improve, perfect; **se** ~ **en anglais** to improve one's English.
perfectionniste [perfeksyonēst(ə)] *nm/f* perfectionist.
perfide [perfēd] *a* perfidious, treacherous.
perfidie [perfēdē] *nf* treachery.
perforant, e [perforän, -änt] *a* (*balle*) armor-piercing (*US*), armour-piercing (*Brit*).
perforateur, trice [perforátœr, -trēs] *nm/f* punch-card operator ♦ *nm* (*perceuse*) borer;

drill ♦ *nf* (*perceuse*) borer; drill; (*pour cartes*) card punch; (*de bureau*) punch.
perforation [perforàsyôn] *nf* perforation; punching; (*trou*) hole.
perforatrice [perforátrēs] *nf voir* **perforateur**.
perforé, e [perforã] *a*: **bande** ~ punched tape; **carte** ~ punch card.
perforer [perforã] *vt* to perforate, punch a hole (*ou holes*) in; (*ticket, bande, carte*) to punch.
perforeuse [perforœz] *nf* (*machine*) (card) punch; (*personne*) card punch operator.
performance [performãns] *nf* performance.
performant, e [performän, -änt] *a* (*ÉCON*: *produit, entreprise*) high-return *cpd*; (*TECH*: *appareil, machine*) high-performance *cpd*.
perfusion [perfüzyôn] *nf* perfusion; **faire une** ~ **à qn** to put sb on an I.V. (*US*) *ou* on a drip (*Brit*).
péricliter [pārēklētã] *vi* to go downhill.
péridurale [pārēdürál] *nf* epidural.
périgourdin, e [pārēgōōrdañ, -ēn] *a* of *ou* from the Perigord.
péril [pārēl] *nm* peril; **au** ~ **de sa vie** at the risk of his life; **à ses risques et** ~**s** at his (*ou* her) own risk.
périlleux, euse [pārēyœ̄, -œ̄z] *a* perilous.
périmé, e [pārēmã] *a* (*out*)dated; (*ADMIN*) out-of-date, expired.
périmètre [pārēmetr(ə)] *nm* perimeter.
périnatal, e [pārēnátál] *a* perinatal.
période [pāryod] *nf* period.
périodique [pāryodēk] *a* (*phases*) periodic; (*publication*) periodical; (*MATH: fraction*) recurring ♦ *nm* periodical; **garniture** *ou* **serviette** ~ sanitary napkin (*US*) *ou* towel (*Brit*).
périodiquement [pāryodēkmãn] *ad* periodically.
péripéties [pārēpāsē] *nfpl* events, episodes.
périphérie [pārēfārē] *nf* periphery; (*d'une ville*) outskirts *pl*.
périphérique [pārēfārēk] *a* (*quartiers*) outlying; (*ANAT, TECH*) peripheral; (*station de radio*) operating from a neighboring country ♦ *nm* (*INFORM*) peripheral; (*AUTO*): (**boulevard**) ~ beltway (*US*), ring road (*Brit*).
périphrase [pārēfráz] *nf* circumlocution.
périple [pārēpl(ə)] *nm* journey.
périr [pārēr] *vi* to die, perish.
périscolaire [pārēskoler] *a* extracurricular.
périscope [pārēskop] *nm* periscope.
périssable [pārēsábl(ə)] *a* perishable.
péritonite [pārētonēt] *nf* peritonitis.
perle [perl(ə)] *nf* pearl; (*de plastique, métal, sueur*) bead; (*personne, chose*) gem, treasure; (*erreur*) gem, howler.
perlé, e [perlã] *a* (*rire*) rippling, tinkling; (*travail*) exquisite; (*orge*) pearl *cpd*; **grève** ~**e** slowdown (*US*), go-slow (*Brit*), selective strike (action).
perler [perlã] *vi* to form in droplets.
perlier, ière [perlyã, -yer] *a* pearl *cpd*.
permanence [permánáns] *nf* permanence; (*local*) (duty) office; strike headquarters; (*service des urgences*) emergency service; (*SCOL*) study hall (*US*) *ou* room (*Brit*); **assurer une** ~ (*service public, bureaux*) to operate *ou* maintain a basic service; **être de**

~ to be on call *ou* duty; **en** ~ *ad* (*toujours*) permanently; (*continûment*) continuously.

permanent, e [pɛrmánáṅ. -áṅt] *a* permanent; (*spectacle*) continuous; (*armée, comité*) standing ♦ *nf* perm ♦ *nm/f* (*d'un syndicat, parti*) paid official.

perméable [pɛrmääbl(ə)] *a* (*terrain*) permeable; ~ **à** (*fig*) receptive *ou* open to.

permettre [pɛrmɛtr(ə)] *vt* to allow, permit; ~ **à qn de faire/qch** to allow sb to do/sth; **se ~ de faire qch** to take the liberty of doing sth; **permettez!** excuse me!

permis, e [pɛrmē, -ēz] *pp de* **permettre** ♦ *nm* permit, license (*US*), licence (*Brit*); ~ **de chasse** hunting permit; ~ (**de conduire**) (driver's) license (*US*), (driving) licence (*Brit*); ~ **de construire** building permit (*US*), planning permission (*Brit*); ~ **d'inhumer** burial certificate; ~ **poids lourds** ≈ class E (driver's) license (*US*), ≈ HGV (driving) licence (*Brit*); ~ **de séjour** residence permit; ~ **de travail** work permit.

permissif, ive [pɛrmēsēf. -ēv] *a* permissive.

permission [pɛrmēsyóṅ] *nf* permission; (*MIL*) leave; (: *papier*) pass; **en** ~ on leave; **avoir la** ~ **de faire** to have permission to do, be allowed to do.

permissionnaire [pɛrmēsyoner] *nm* soldier on leave.

permutable [pɛrmütábl(ə)] *a* which can be changed *ou* switched around.

permuter [pɛrmütä] *vt* to change around, permutate ♦ *vi* to change, swap.

pernicieux, euse [pɛrnēsyœ̄. -ēz] *a* pernicious.

péroné [pārónä] *nm* fibula.

pérorer [pārorä] *vi* to hold forth.

Pérou [pā͞o͞o] *nm*: **le** ~ Peru.

perpendiculaire [pɛrpáṅdēküler] *a*, *nf* perpendicular.

perpète [pɛrpɛt] *nf* (*fam: loin*): **à** ~ miles away; (: *longtemps*) forever.

perpétrer [pɛrpäträ] *vt* to perpetrate.

perpétuel, le [pɛrpätüel] *a* perpetual; (*ADMIN etc*) permanent; for life.

perpétuellement [pɛrpätüelmáṅ] *ad* perpetually, constantly.

perpétuer [pɛrpätüä] *vt* to perpetuate; **se** ~ (*usage, injustice*) to be perpetuated; (*espèces*) to survive.

perpétuité [pɛrpätüētä] *nf*: **à** ~ *a*, *ad* for life; **être condamné à** ~ to be sentenced to life imprisonment, receive a life sentence.

perplexe [pɛrpleks(ə)] *a* perplexed, puzzled.

perplexité [pɛrpleksētä] *nf* perplexity.

perquisition [pɛrkēzēsyóṅ] *nf* (*police*) search.

perquisitionner [pɛrkēzēsyonä] *vi* to carry out a search.

perron [pɛróṅ] *nm* steps *pl* (*in front of mansion etc*).

perroquet [pɛroke] *nm* parrot.

perruche [pärüsh] *nf* parakeet (*US*), budgerigar (*Brit*), budgie (*Brit*).

perruque [pärük] *nf* wig.

persan, e [pɛrsáṅ, -áṅ] *a* Persian ♦ *nm* (*LING*) Persian.

perse [pɛrs(ə)] *a* Persian ♦ *nm* (*LING*) Persian ♦ *nm/f*: **P~** Persian ♦ *nf*: **la P~** Persia.

persécuter [pɛrsäkütä] *vt* to persecute.

persécution [pɛrsäküsyóṅ] *nf* persecution.

persévérance [pɛrsäváráṅs] *nf* perseverance.

persévérant, e [pɛrsäväráṅ. -áṅt] *a* persevering.

persévérer [pɛrsävärä] *vi* to persevere; ~ **à croire que** to continue to believe that.

persiennes [pɛrsyen] *nfpl* (slatted) shutters.

persiflage [pɛrsēflázh] *nm* mockery *q*.

persifleur, euse [pɛrsēflœr. -ēz] *a* mocking.

persil [pɛrsē] *nm* parsley.

persillé, e [pɛrsēyä] *a* (sprinkled) with parsley; (*fromage*) veined; (*viande*) marbled, with fat running through.

Persique [pɛrsēk] *a*: **le golfe** ~ the (Persian) Gulf.

persistance [pɛrsēstáṅs] *nf* persistence.

persistant, e [pɛrsēstáṅ. -áṅt] *a* persistent; (*feuilles*) evergreen; **à feuillage** ~ evergreen.

persister [pɛrsēstä] *vi* to persist; ~ **à faire qch** to persist in doing sth.

personnage [pɛrsonázh] *nm* (*notable*) personality; figure; (*individu*) character, individual; (*THÉÂTRE*) character; (*PEINTURE*) figure.

personnaliser [pɛrsonálēzä] *vt* to personalize; (*appartement*) to give a personal touch to.

personnalité [pɛrsonálētä] *nf* personality; (*personnage*) prominent figure.

personne [pɛrson] *nf* person ♦ *pronom* nobody, no one; (*quelqu'un*) anybody, anyone; ~**s** *nfpl* people *pl*; **il n'y a** ~ there's nobody in *ou* there, there isn't anybody in *ou* there; **10 F par** ~ 10 F per person, 10 F a head; **en** ~ personally, in person; ~ **âgée** elderly person; ~ **à charge** (*JUR*) dependent; ~ **morale** *ou* **civile** (*JUR*) legal entity.

personnel, le [pɛrsonel] *a* personal; (*égoïste: personne*) selfish, self-centered (*US*), self-centred (*Brit*); (*idée, opinion*): **j'ai des idées** ~**les à ce sujet** I have my own ideas about that ♦ *nm* personnel, staff; **service du** ~ personnel department.

personnellement [pɛrsonelmáṅ] *ad* personally.

personnifier [pɛrsonēfyä] *vt* to personify; to typify; **c'est l'honnêteté personifiée** he (*ou* she *etc*) is honesty personified.

perspective [pɛrspektēv] *nf* (*ART*) perspective; (*vue, coup d'œil*) view; (*point de vue*) viewpoint, angle; (*chose escomptée, envisagée*) prospect; **en** ~ in prospect.

perspicace [pɛrspēkás] *a* clear-sighted, gifted with (*ou* showing) insight.

perspicacité [pɛrspēkásētä] *nf* insight, perspicacity.

persuader [pɛrsüádä] *vt*: ~ **qn (de/de faire)** to persuade sb (of/to do); **j'en suis persuadé** I'm quite sure *ou* convinced (of it).

persuasif, ive [pɛrsüázēf. -ēv] *a* persuasive.

persuasion [pɛrsüázyóṅ] *nf* persuasion.

perte [pɛrt(ə)] *nf* loss; (*de temps*) waste; (*fig: morale*) ruin; ~**s** *nfpl* losses; **à** ~ (*COMM*) at a loss; **à** ~ **de vue** as far as the eye can (*ou* could) see; (*fig*) interminably; **en pure** ~ for absolutely nothing; **courir à sa** ~ to be on the road to ruin; **être en** ~ **de vitesse** (*fig*) to be losing momentum; **avec** ~ **et fracas** forcibly; ~ **de chaleur** heat loss; ~ **sèche** dead loss; ~**s blanches** (vaginal) discharge *sg*.

pertinemment [pɛrtēnámáṅ] *ad* to the point;

(savoir) perfectly well, full well.

pertinence [pɛrtɛ̃nɑ̃s] *nf* pertinence, relevance; discernment.

pertinent, e [pɛrtɛ̃nɑ̃, -ɑ̃t] *a (remarque)* apt, pertinent, relevant; *(analyse)* discerning, judicious.

perturbateur, trice [pɛrtürbátœr, -trɛs] *a* disruptive.

perturbation [pɛrtürbásyɔ̃ɲ] *nf (dans un service public)* disruption; *(agitation, trouble)* perturbation; ~ **(atmosphérique)** atmospheric disturbance.

perturber [pɛrtürbā] *vt* to disrupt; *(PSYCH)* to perturb, disturb.

péruvien, ne [pārüvyaɲ, -en] *a* Peruvian ♦ *nm/f*: **P~, ne** Peruvian.

pervenche [pɛrvɑ̃ʃ] *nf* periwinkle; *(fam)* meter maid *(US)*, traffic warden *(Brit)*.

pervers, e [pɛrver, -ers(ə)] *a* perverted, depraved; *(malfaisant)* perverse.

perversion [pɛrversyɔ̃ɲ] *nf* perversion.

perversité [pɛrversɛtā] *nf* depravity; perversity.

perverti, e [pɛrvertɛ] *nm/f* pervert.

pervertir [pɛrvɛrtɛr] *vt* to pervert.

pesage [pəzázh] *nm* weighing; *(HIPPISME: action)* weigh-in; *(: salle)* weighing room; *(: enceinte)* enclosure.

pesamment [pəzàmɑ̃ɲ] *ad* heavily.

pesant, e [pəzɑ̃ɲ, -ɑ̃t] *a* heavy; *(fig)* burdensome ♦ *nm*: **valoir son ~ de** to be worth one's weight in.

pesanteur [pəzɑ̃ntœr] *nf* gravity.

pèse-bébé [pɛzbābā] *nm* (baby) scales *pl*.

pesée [pəzā] *nf* weighing; *(BOXE)* weigh-in; *(pression)* pressure.

pèse-lettre [pɛzletr(ə)] *nm* letter scales *pl*.

pèse-personne [pɛzperson] *nm* (bathroom) scales *pl*.

peser [pəzā] *vt, vb avec attribut* to weigh; *(considérer, comparer)* to weigh ♦ *vi* to be heavy; *(fig)* to carry weight; ~ **sur** *(levier, bouton)* to press, push; *(fig: accabler)* to lie heavy on; *(: influencer)* to influence; ~ **à qn** to weigh heavy on sb.

pessaire [peser] *nm* pessary.

pessimisme [pāsēmēsm(ə)] *nm* pessimism.

pessimiste [pāsēmēst(ə)] *a* pessimistic ♦ *nm/f* pessimist.

peste [pest(ə)] *nf* plague; *(fig)* pest, nuisance.

pester [pestā] *vi*: ~ **contre** to curse.

pesticide [pestēsēd] *nm* pesticide.

pestiféré, e [pestēfārā] *nm/f* plague victim.

pestilentiel, le [pestēlàɲsyel] *a* foul.

pet [pe] *nm (fam!)* fart *(!)*.

pétale [pātál] *nm* petal.

pétanque [pātáɲk] *nf type of* bowls.

pétarader [pātárádā] *vi* to backfire.

pétard [pātár] *nm (feu d'artifice)* firecracker; *(de cotillon)* cracker; *(RAIL)* detonator.

pet-de-nonne, *pl* **pets-de-nonne** [pednoɲ] *nm* ≈ fritter *(US)*, ≈ choux bun *(Brit)*.

péter [pātā] *vi (fam: casser, sauter)* to burst; to bust; *(fam!)* to fart *(!)*.

pète-sec [petsek] *a inv* abrupt, sharp(-tongued).

pétillant, e [pātēyàɲ, -àɲt] *a* sparkling.

pétiller [pātēyā] *vi (flamme, bois)* to crackle; *(mousse, champagne)* to bubble; *(pierre,*

métal) to glisten; *(yeux)* to sparkle; *(fig)*: ~ **d'esprit** to sparkle with wit.

petit, e [pətē, -ēt] *a (gén)* small; *(main, objet, colline, en âge: enfant)* small, little; *(mince, fin: personne, taille, pluie)* slight; *(voyage)* short, little; *(bruit etc)* faint, slight; *(mesquin)* mean; *(peu important)* minor ♦ *nm/f (petit enfant)* little one, child ♦ *nmpl (d'un animal)* young *pl*; **faire des ~s** to have kittens *(ou* puppies *etc)*; **en ~** in miniature; **mon ~** son; little one; **ma ~e** dear; little one; **pauvre ~** poor little thing; **la classe des ~s** the infant class; **pour ~s et grands** for children and adults; **les tout-~s** the little ones, the tiny tots; ~ **à ~** bit by bit, gradually; ~**(e) ami/e** boyfriend/girlfriend; **les ~es annonces** the classified ads; ~ **déjeuner** breakfast; ~**s doigt** little finger; **le ~ écran** the small screen; ~ **four** petit four; ~ **pain** (bread) roll; ~**e monnaie** small change; ~**e vérole** smallpox; ~**s pois** petit pois *pl*, garden peas; ~**es gens** people of modest means.

petit-beurre, *pl* **petits-beurre** [pətēbœr] *nm* sweet butter cookie *(US) ou* biscuit *(Brit)*.

petit(e)-bourgeois(e), *pl* **petit(e)s-bourgeois(es)** [pətē(t)bōōrzhwá(z)] *a (péj)* petit-bourgeois, middle-class.

petite-fille, *pl* **petites-filles** [pətētfēy] *nf* granddaughter.

petitement [pətētmàɲ] *ad* poorly; meanly; **être logé ~** to be in cramped accommodations *(US) ou* accommodation *(Brit)*.

petitesse [pətētes] *nf* smallness; *(d'un salaire, de revenus)* modestness; *(mesquinerie)* meanness.

petit-fils, *pl* **petits-fils** [pətēfēs] *nm* grandson.

pétition [pātēsyɔ̃ɲ] *nf* petition; **faire signer une ~** to get up a petition.

pétitionner [pātēsyonā] *vt* to petition.

petit-lait, *pl* **petits-laits** [pətēle] *nm* whey *q*.

petit-nègre [pətēnegr(ə)] *nm (péj)* pidgin French.

petits-enfants [pətēzáɲfàɲ] *nmpl* grandchildren.

petit-suisse, *pl* **petits-suisses** [pətēsüēs] *nm* small individual pot of cream cheese.

pétoche [pātosh] *nf (fam)*: **avoir la ~** to be scared out of one's wits.

pétri, e [pātrē] *a*: ~ **d'orgueil** filled with pride.

pétrifier [pātrēfyā] *vt* to petrify; *(fig)* to paralyze, transfix.

pétrin [pātraɲ] *nm* kneading trough; *(fig)*: **dans le ~** in a jam *ou* fix.

pétrir [pātrēr] *vt* to knead.

pétrochimie [pātroshēmē] *nf* petrochemistry.

pétrochimique [pātroshēmēk] *a* petrochemical.

pétrodollar [pātrōdolár] *nm* petrodollar.

pétrole [pātrol] *nm* oil; *(aussi*: ~ **lampant)** kerosene *(US)*, paraffin *(Brit)*.

pétrolier, ière [pātrolyā, -yer] *a* oil *cpd*; *(pays)* oil-producing ♦ *nm (navire)* oil tanker; *(financier)* oilman; *(technicien)* petroleum engineer.

pétrolifère [pātrolēfer] *a* oil(-bearing).

P et T *sigle fpl* = postes et télécommunications.

pétulant, e [pātülåṅ, -åṅt] *a* exuberant.
pétunia [pātünyå] *nm* petunia.
peu [pœ] *ad* little, *tournure négative* + much; (*avec adjectif*) *tournure négative* + very; (*avec adverbe*) a little, slightly ♦ *pronom* few ♦ *nm* little; **le ~ de courage qui nous restait** what little courage we still had; **~ avant/après** shortly before/afterwards; **~ de** (*nombre*) few, *négation* + (very) many; (*quantité*) little, *négation* + (very) much; **pour ~ de temps** for (only) a short while; **le ~ de gens qui** the few people who; **le ~ de sable qui** what little sand, the little sand which; **un (petit) ~** a little (bit); **un ~ de a** little; **un ~ plus/moins de** slightly more/less (*ou* fewer); **pour ~ qu'il fasse** if he should do, if by any chance he does; **pour un ~, il ... he** very nearly ...; **de ~** (only) just; **~ à ~** little by little; **à ~ près** *ad* just about, more or less; **à ~ près 10 kg/10 F** approximately 10 kg/10 F; **sous** *ou* **avant ~** before long, shortly; **depuis ~** for a short *ou* little while; **c'est ~ de chose** it's nothing; **c'est si ~ de chose** it's such a small thing; **essayez un ~!** have a go!, just try it!
peuplade [pœplåd] *nf* (*horde, tribu*) tribe, people.
peuple [pœpl(ə)] *nm* people; (*masse indifférenciée*): **un ~ de vacanciers** a crowd of vacationers (*US*) *ou* holiday-makers (*Brit*); **il y a du ~** there are a lot of people.
peuplé, e [pœplå] *a*: **très/peu ~** densely/sparsely populated.
peupler [pœplå] *vt* (*pays, région*) to populate; (*étang*) to stock; (*suj: hommes, poissons*) to inhabit; (*fig: imagination, rêves*) to fill; **se ~** *vi* (*ville, région*) to become populated; (*fig: s'animer*) to fill (up), be filled.
peuplier [pœplēyå] *nm* poplar (tree).
peur [pœr] *nf* fear; **avoir ~ (de/de faire/que)** to be frightened *ou* afraid (of/of doing/that); **prendre ~** to take fright; **faire ~ à** to frighten; **de ~ de/que** for fear of/that; **j'ai ~ qu'il ne soit trop tard** I'm afraid it might be too late; **j'ai ~ qu'il (ne) vienne (pas)** I'm afraid he may (not) come.
peureux, euse [pœrœ, -œz] *a* fearful, timorous.
peut [pœ] *vb voir* **pouvoir.**
peut-être [pœtetr(ə)] *ad* perhaps, maybe; **~ que** perhaps, maybe; **~ bien qu'il fera/est** he may well do/be.
peuvent [pœv], **peux** [pœ] *etc vb voir* **pouvoir.**
p. ex. *abr* (= *par exemple*) e.g.
phalange [fålåṅzh] *nf* (*ANAT*) phalanx (*pl* phalanges); (*MIL, fig*) phalanx (*pl* -es).
phallique [fålēk] *a* phallic.
phallocrate [fålokråt] *nm* male chauvinist.
phallocratie [fålokråsē] *nf* male chauvinism.
phallus [fålüs] *nm* phallus.
pharaon [fåråóṅ] *nm* Pharaoh.
phare [får] *nm* (*en mer*) lighthouse; (*d'aéroport*) beacon; (*de véhicule*) headlight ♦ *a*: **produit ~** leading product; **se mettre en ~s,** **mettre ses ~s** to put on one's headlights; **~s de recul** back-up (*US*) *ou* reversing (*Brit*) lights.
pharmaceutique [fårmåsœtēk] *a* pharmaceutic(al).

pharmacie [fårmåsē] *nf* (*science*) pharmacology; (*magasin*) pharmacy, chemist's (*Brit*); (*officine*) dispensary; (*produits*) pharmaceuticals *pl*; (*armoire*) medicine chest *ou* cupboard, first-aid cupboard.
pharmacien, ne [fårmåsyaṅ, -en] *nm/f* pharmacist, chemist (*Brit*).
pharmacologie [fårmåkolozhē] *nf* pharmacology.
pharyngite [fåråṅzhēt] *nf* pharyngitis *q*.
pharynx [fåraṅks] *nm* pharynx.
phase [fåz] *nf* phase.
phénoménal, e, aux [fānomānál, -ō] *a* phenomenal.
phénomène [fānomen] *nm* phenomenon (*pl* -a); (*monstre*) freak.
philanthrope [fēlåṅtrop] *nm/f* philanthropist.
philanthropie [fēlåṅtropē] *nf* philanthropy.
philatélie [fēlåtālē] *nf* philately, stamp collecting.
philatéliste [fēlåtālēst(ə)] *nm/f* philatelist, stamp collector.
philharmonique [fēlårmonēk] *a* philharmonic.
philippin, e [fēlēpaṅ, -ēn] *a* Filipino.
Philippines [fēlēpēn] *nfpl*: **les ~** the Philippines.
philistin [fēlēstaṅ] *nm* philistine.
philo [fēlō] *nf* (*fam*: = *philosophie*) philosophy.
philosophe [fēlozof] *nm/f* philosopher ♦ *a* philosophical.
philosopher [fēlozofå] *vi* to philisophize.
philosophie [fēlozofē] *nf* philosophy.
philosophique [fēlozofēk] *a* philosophical.
philtre [fēltr(ə)] *nm* philter (*US*), philtre (*Brit*), love potion.
phlébite [flābēt] *nf* phlebitis.
phlébologue [flåbolog] *nm/f* vein specialist.
phobie [fobē] *nf* phobia.
phonétique [fonåtēk] *a* phonetic ♦ *nf* phonetics *sg*.
phonographe [fonogråf] *nm* (wind-up) phonograph (*US*) *ou* gramophone (*Brit*).
phoque [fok] *nm* seal; (*fourrure*) sealskin.
phosphate [fosfåt] *nm* phosphate.
phosphaté, e [fosfåtå] *a* phosphate-enriched.
phosphore [fosfor] *nm* phosphorus.
phosphoré, e [fosforå] *a* phosphorous.
phosphorescent, e [fosforāsåṅ, -åṅt] *a* luminous.
phosphorique [fosforēk] *a*: **acide ~** phosphoric acid.
photo [fotō] *nf* (= *photographie*) photo ♦ *a*: **appareil/pellicule ~** camera/film; **en ~** in *ou* on a photo; **prendre en ~** to take a photo of; **aimer la/faire de la ~** to like taking/take photos; **~ en couleurs** color photo; **~ d'identité** passport photo.
photo... [foto] *préfixe* photo....
photocopie [fotokopē] *nf* (*procédé*) photocopying; (*document*) photocopy.
photocopier [fotokopyå] *vt* to photocopy.
photocopieur [fotokopyœr] *nm*, **photocopieuse** [fotokopyœz] *nf* (photo)copier.
photo-électrique [fotoålektrēk] *a* photoelectric.
photogénique [fotozhānēk] *a* photogenic.
photographe [fotogråf] *nm/f* photographer.
photographie [fotogråfē] *nf* (*procédé, technique*) photography; (*cliché*) photograph;

faire de la ~ to have photography as a hobby; (*comme métier*) to be a photographer.

photographier [fotográfyā] *vt* to photograph, take.

photographique [fotográfēk] *a* photographic.

photogravure [fotográvür] *nf* photoengraving.

photomaton [fotomátôń] *nm* photo booth, photomat.

photomontage [fotomôńtázh] *nm* photomontage.

photo-robot [fotorobō] *nf* Identikit ® (picture).

photosensible [fotosâńsēbl(ǝ)] *a* photosensitive.

photostat [fotostá] *nm* photostat.

phrase [frāz] *nf* (*LING*) sentence; (*propos, MUS*) phrase; ~s *nfpl* (*péj*) flowery language *sg*.

phraséologie [frázǎolozhē] *nf* phraseology; (*rhétorique*) flowery language.

phraseur, euse [frázœr, -ēz] *nm/f*: **c'est un** ~ he uses such flowery language.

phrygien, ne [frēzhyań, -en] *a*: **bonnet** ~ Phrygian cap.

phtisie [ftēzē] *nf* consumption.

phylloxéra [fēloksārá] *nm* phylloxera.

physicien, ne [fēzēsyań, -en] *nm/f* physicist.

physiologie [fēzyolozhē] *nf* physiology.

physiologique [fēzyolozhēk] *a* physiological.

physiologiquement [fēzyolozhēkmâń] *ad* physiologically.

physionomie [fēzyonomē] *nf* face; (*d'un paysage etc*) physiognomy.

physionomiste [fēzyonomēst(ǝ)] *nm/f* good judge of faces; person who has a good memory for faces.

physiothérapie [fēzyotǎrápē] *nf* natural medicine, alternative medicine.

physique [fēzēk] *a* physical ♦ *nm* physique ♦ *nf* physics *sg*; **au** ~ physically.

physiquement [fēzēkmâń] *ad* physically.

phytothérapie [fētotǎrápē] *nf* herbal medicine.

p.i. *abr* = **par intérim**; *voir* **intérim**.

piaffer [pyáfá] *vi* to stamp.

piailler [pyáyā] *vi* to squawk.

pianiste [pyánēst(ǝ)] *nm/f* pianist.

piano [pyánō] *nm* piano; ~ **à queue** grand piano.

pianoter [pyánotā] *vi* to tinkle away (at the piano); (*tapoter*): ~ **sur** to drum one's fingers on.

piaule [pyōl] *nf* (*fam*) pad.

piauler [pyōlā] *vi* (*enfant*) to whimper; (*oiseau*) to cheep.

PIB *sigle m* (= *produit intérieur brut*) GDP.

pic [pēk] *nm* (*instrument*) pick(ax) (*US*), pick(axe) (*Brit*); (*montagne*) peak; (*ZOOL*) woodpecker; **à** ~ *ad* vertically; (*fig*) just at the right time; **couler à** ~ (*bateau*) to go straight down; ~ **à glace** ice pick.

picard, e [pēkár, -árd(ǝ)] *a* of *ou* from Picardy.

Picardie [pēkárdē] *nf*: **la** ~ Picardy.

piccolo [pēkolō] *nm* piccolo.

pichenette [pēshnet] *nf* flick.

pichet [pēshe] *nm* jug.

pickpocket [pēkpoket] *nm* pickpocket.

pick-up [pēkœp] *nm inv* record player.

picorer [pēkorā] *vt* to peck.

picot [pēkō] *nm* sprocket; **entraînement par roue à** ~s sprocket feed.

picotement [pēkotmâń] *nm* smarting *q*, prickling *q*.

picoter [pēkotā] *vt* (*suj: oiseau*) to peck ♦ *vi* (*irriter*) to smart, prickle.

pictural, e, aux [pēktürál, -ō] *a* pictorial.

pie [pē] *nf* magpie; (*fig*) chatterbox ♦ *a inv*: **cheval** ~ piebald; **vache** ~ black and white cow.

pièce [pyes] *nf* (*d'un logement*) room; (*THÉÂTRE*) play; (*de mécanisme, machine*) part; (*de monnaie*) coin; (*COUTURE*) patch; (*document*) document; (*de drap, fragment, d'une collection*) piece; (*de bétail*) head; **mettre en** ~s to smash to pieces; **dix francs** ~ ten francs each; **vendre à la** ~ to sell separately *ou* individually; **travailler/payer à la** ~ to do piecework/pay piece rate; **de toutes** ~s: **c'est inventé de toutes** ~s it's a complete fabrication; **un maillot une** ~ a one-piece swimsuit; **un deux-**~s **cuisine** a two-room(ed) apartment (*US*) with kitchen; **tout d'une** ~ (*personne: franc*) blunt; (: *sans souplesse*) inflexible; ~ **à conviction** exhibit; ~ **d'eau** ornamental lake *ou* pond; ~ **d'identité: avez-vous une** ~ **d'identité?** have you got any (means of) identification?; ~ **montée** tiered cake; ~ **de rechange** spare (part); ~ **de résistance** pièce de résistance; (*plat*) main dish; ~s **détachées** spares, (spare) parts; **en** ~s **détachées** (*à monter*) in kit form; ~s **justificatives** supporting documents.

pied [pyā] *nm* foot (*pl* feet); (*de verre*) stem; (*de table*) leg; (*de lampe*) base; (*plante*) plant; ~s **nus** barefoot; **à** ~ on foot; **à** ~ **sec** without getting one's feet wet; **à** ~ **d'œuvre** ready to start (work); **au** ~ **de la lettre** literally; **au** ~ **levé** at a moment's notice; **de** ~ **en cap** from head to foot; **en** ~ (*portrait*) full-length; **avoir** ~ to be able to touch the bottom, not to be out of one's depth; **avoir le** ~ **marin** to be a good sailor; **perdre** ~ to lose one's footing; (*fig*) to get out of one's depth; **sur** ~ (*AGR*) on the stalk, uncut; (*debout, rétabli*) up and about; **mettre sur** ~ (*entreprise*) to set up; **mettre à** ~ to suspend; to lay off; **mettre qn au** ~ **du mur** to get sb with his (*ou* her) back to the wall; **sur le** ~ **de guerre** ready for action; **sur un** ~ **d'égalité** on an equal footing; **sur** ~ **d'intervention** on standby; **faire du** ~ **à qn** (*prévenir*) to give sb a (warning) kick; (*galamment*) to play footsy with sb; **mettre les** ~s **quelque part** to set foot somewhere; **faire des** ~s **et des mains** (*fig*) to move heaven and earth, pull out all the stops; **c'est le** ~! (*fam*) it's terrific!; **se lever du bon** ~/**du** ~ **gauche** to get out of bed on the right/wrong side; ~ **de lit** footboard; ~ **de nez: faire un** ~ **de nez à** to thumb one's nose at; ~ **de vigne** vine.

pied-à-terre [pyātáter] *nm inv* pied-à-terre.

pied-bot, *pl* **pieds-bots** [pyābō] *nm* person with a club foot.

pied-de-biche, *pl* **pieds-de-biche** [pyādbēsh] *nm* claw; (*COUTURE*) presser foot.

pied-de-poule [pyẽdpōōl] *a inv* hound's-tooth.
piédestal, aux [pyẽdestàl, -ō] *nm* pedestal.
pied-noir, *pl* **pieds-noirs** [pyãnwár] *nm* Algerian-born Frenchman.
piège [pyezh] *nm* trap; **prendre au ~** to trap.
piéger [pyãzhã] *vt* (*animal, fig*) to trap; (*avec une bombe*) to booby-trap; **lettre/voiture piégée** letter-/car-bomb.
pierraille [pyerãy] *nf* loose stones *pl.*
pierre [pyer] *nf* stone; **première ~** (*d'un édifice*) foundation stone; **mur de ~s sèches** drystone wall; **faire d'une ~ deux coups** to kill two birds with one stone; **~ à briquet** flint; **~ fine** semiprecious stone; **~ ponce** pumice stone; **~ de taille** freestone *q*; **~ tombale** tombstone, gravestone; **~ de touche** touchstone.
pierreries [pyerrē] *nfpl* gems, precious stones.
pierreux, euse [pyerœ̃, -œ̃z] *a* stony.
piété [pyãtã] *nf* piety.
piétinement [pyãtẽnmãṅ] *nm* stamping *q.*
piétiner [pyãtẽnã] *vi* (*trépigner*) to stamp (one's foot); (*marquer le pas*) to stand around; (*fig*) to be at a standstill ♦ *vt* to trample on.
piéton, ne [pyãtôṅ, -on] *nm/f* pedestrian ♦ *a* pedestrian *cpd.*
piétonnier, ière [pyãtonyã, -yer] *a* pedestrian *cpd.*
piètre [pyetr(ə)] *a* poor, mediocre.
pieu, x [pyœ̃] *nm* (*piquet*) post; (*pointu*) stake; (*fam: lit*) bed.
pieusement [pyœ̃zmãṅ] *ad* piously.
pieuvre [pyœvr(ə)] *nf* octopus.
pieux, euse [pyœ̃, -œ̃z] *a* pious.
pif [pēf] *nm* (*fam*) beak; **au ~ = au pifomètre**.
piffer [pēfã] *vt* (*fam*): **je ne peux pas le ~** I can't stand him.
pifomètre [pēfometr(ə)] *nm* (*fam*): **choisir** *etc* **au ~** to follow one's nose when choosing *etc*.
pige [pēzh] *nf* piecework rate.
pigeon [pēzhôṅ] *nm* pigeon; **~ voyageur** homing pigeon.
pigeonnant, e [pēzhonãṅ, -ãṅt] *a* full, well-developed.
pigeonnier [pēzhonyã] *nm* pigeon house, dovecot(e).
piger [pēzhã] *vi* (*fam*) to get it ♦ *vt* (*fam*) to get, understand.
pigiste [pēzhēst(ə)] *nm/f* (*typographe*) typesetter on piecework; (*journaliste*) freelance journalist (*paid by the line*).
pigment [pēgmãṅ] *nm* pigment.
pignon [pēnyôṅ] *nm* (*de mur*) gable; (*d'engrenage*) cog(wheel), gearwheel; (*graine*) pine kernel; **avoir ~ sur rue** (*fig*) to have a prosperous business.
pile [pēl] *nf* (*tas, pilier*) pile; (*ÉLEC*) battery ♦ *a*: **le côté ~** tails ♦ *ad* (*net, brusquement*) dead; (*à temps, à point nommé*) just at the right time; **à deux heures ~** at two on the dot; **jouer à ~ ou face** to toss up (for it); **~ ou face?** heads or tails?
piler [pēlã] *vt* to crush, pound.
pileux, euse [pēlœ̃, -œ̃z] *a*: **système ~** (body) hair.
pilier [pēlyã] *nm* (*colonne, support*) pillar; (*personne*) mainstay; (*RUGBY*) prop (for-

ward).
pillage [pēyàzh] *nm* pillaging, plundering, looting.
pillard, e [pēyár, -àrd(ə)] *nm/f* looter; plunderer.
piller [pēyã] *vt* to pillage, plunder, loot.
pilon [pēlôṅ] *nm* (*instrument*) pestle; (*de volaille*) drumstick; **mettre un livre au ~** to pulp a book.
pilonner [pēlonã] *vt* to pound.
pilori [pēlorē] *nm*: **mettre** *ou* **clouer au ~** to pillory.
pilotage [pēlotàzh] *nm* piloting; flying; **~ automatique** automatic piloting; **~ sans visibilité** blind flying.
pilote [pēlot] *nm* pilot; (*de char, voiture*) driver ♦ *a* pilot *cpd*; **usine/ferme ~** experimental factory/farm; **~ de chasse/d'essai/de ligne** fighter/test/airline pilot; **~ de course** racing driver.
piloter [pēlotã] *vt* (*navire*) to pilot; (*avion*) to fly; (*automobile*) to drive; (*fig*): **~ qn** to guide sb round; **piloté par menu** (*INFORM*) menu-driven.
pilotis [pēlotē] *nm* pile; stilt.
pilule [pēlül] *nf* pill; **prendre la ~** to be on the pill.
pimbêche [paṅbesh] *nf* (*péj*) stuck-up girl.
piment [pēmãṅ] *nm* (*BOT*) pepper, capsicum; (*fig*) spice, piquancy; **~ rouge** (*CULIN*) chilli.
pimenté, e [pēmãṅtã] *a* hot and spicy.
pimenter [pēmãṅtã] *vt* (*plat*) to season (with peppers *ou* chillis); (*fig*) to add *ou* give spice to.
pimpant, e [paṅpãṅ, -ãṅt] *a* spruce.
pin [paṅ] *nm* pine (tree); (*bois*) pine(wood).
pinacle [pēnàkl(ə)] *nm*: **porter qn au ~** (*fig*) to praise sb to the skies.
pinard [pēnár] *nm* (*fam*) (cheap) wine.
pince [paṅs] *nf* (*outil*) pliers *pl*; (*de homard, crabe*) pincer, claw; (*COUTURE: pli*) dart; **~ à sucre/glace** sugar/ice tongs *pl*; **~ à épiler** tweezers *pl*; **~ à linge** clothes pin (*US*) *ou* peg (*Brit*); **~ universelle** (universal) pliers *pl*; **~s de cycliste** bicycle clips.
pincé, e [paṅsã] *a* (*air*) stiff; (*mince: bouche*) pinched ♦ *nf*: **une ~e de** a pinch of.
pinceau, x [paṅsō] *nm* (paint)brush.
pince-monseigneur, *pl* **pinces-monseigneur** [paṅsmôṅsenyœr] *nf* crowbar.
pince-nez [paṅsnã] *nm inv* pince-nez.
pincer [paṅsã] *vt* to pinch; (*MUS: cordes*) to pluck; (*COUTURE*) to dart, put darts in; (*fam*) to nab; **se ~ le doigt** to squeeze *ou* nip one's finger; **se ~ le nez** to hold one's nose.
pince-sans-rire [paṅssãṅrēr] *a inv* deadpan.
pincettes [paṅset] *nfpl* tweezers; (*pour le feu*) (fire) tongs.
pinçon [paṅsôṅ] *nm* pinch mark.
pinède [pēnēd] *nf* pinewood, pine forest.
pingouin [paṅgwaṅ] *nm* penguin.
ping-pong [pēngpôṅg] *nm* table tennis.
pingre [paṅgr(ə)] *a* niggardly.
pinson [paṅsôṅ] *nm* chaffinch.
pintade [paṅtàd] *nf* guinea fowl.
pin up [pēnœp] *nf inv* pinup (girl).
pioche [pyosh] *nf* pickaxe, pickax (*US*).
piocher [pyoshã] *vt* to dig up (with a pickaxe);

(*fam*) to grind (*US*) *ou* swot (*Brit*) at; ~ **dans** to dig into.

piolet [pyolɛ] *nm* ice axe *ou* ax (*US*).

pion, ne [pyɔ̃, pyon] *nm/f* (*SCOL*: *péj*) *student paid to supervise schoolchildren* ♦ *nm* (*ÉCHECS*) pawn; (*DAMES*) piece, checker (*US*), draught (*Brit*).

pionnier [pyonyā] *nm* pioneer.

pipe [pēp] *nf* pipe; **fumer la** *ou* **une** ~ to smoke a pipe; ~ **de bruyère** briar pipe.

pipeau, x [pēpō] *nm* (reed) pipe.

pipe-line [pēplēn] *nm* pipeline.

piper [pēpā] *vt* (*dé*) to load; (*carte*) to mark; **sans** ~ **mot** (*fam*) without a peep; **les dés sont pipés** (*fig*) the dice are loaded.

pipette [pēpet] *nf* pipette.

pipi [pēpē] *nm* (*fam*): **faire** ~ to have a pee.

piquant, e [pēkɑ̃, -ɑ̃t] *a* (*barbe, rosier etc*) prickly; (*saveur, sauce*) hot, pungent; (*fig*: *description, style*) racy; (: *mordant, caustique*) biting ♦ *nm* (*épine*) thorn, prickle; (*de hérisson*) quill, spine; (*fig*) spiciness, spice.

pique [pēk] *nf* (*arme*) pike; (*fig*): **envoyer** *ou* **lancer des** ~**s à qn** to make cutting remarks to sb ♦ *nm* (*CARTES*: *couleur*) spades *pl*; (: *carte*) spade.

piqué, e [pēkā] *a* (*COUTURE*) (machine-) stitched; quilted; (*livre, glace*) mildewed; (*vin*) sour; (*MUS*: *note*) staccato; (*fam*: *personne*) nuts ♦ *nm* (*AVIAT*) dive; (*TEXTILE*) piqué.

pique-assiette [pēkásyet] *nm/f inv* (*péj*) scrounger, sponger.

pique-fleurs [pēkflœr] *nm inv* flower holder.

pique-nique [pēknēk] *nm* picnic.

pique-niquer [pēknēkā] *vi* to (have a) picnic.

pique-niqueur, euse [pēknēkœr, -œz] *nm/f* picnicker.

piquer [pēkā] *vt* (*percer*) to prick; (*planter*): ~ **qch dans** to stick sth into; (*fixer*): ~ **qch à** *ou* **sur** to pin sth onto; (*MÉD*) to give an injection to; (: *animal blessé etc*) to put to sleep; (*suj*: *insecte, fumée, ortie*) to sting; (: *poivre*) to burn; (: *froid*) to bite; (*COUTURE*) to machine (stitch); (*intérêt etc*) to arouse; (*fam*: *prendre*) to pick up; (: *voler*) to pinch; (: *arrêter*) to nab ♦ *vi* (*oiseau, avion*) to go into a dive; (*saveur*) to be pungent; to be sour; **se** ~ (*avec une aiguille*) to prick o.s.; (*se faire une piqûre*) to inject o.s.; (*se vexer*) to get annoyed; **se** ~ **de faire** to pride o.s. on doing; ~ **sur** to swoop down on; to head straight for; ~ **du nez** (*avion*) to go into a nose-dive; ~ **une tête** (*plonger*) to dive headfirst; ~ **un galop/un cent mètres** to break into a gallop/put on a sprint; ~ **une crise** to throw a fit; ~ **au vif** (*fig*) to sting.

piquet [pēke] *nm* (*pieu*) post, stake; (*de tente*) peg; **mettre un élève au** ~ to make a pupil stand in the corner; ~ **de grève** (strike-)picket; ~ **d'incendie** fire-fighting squad.

piqueté, e [pēktā] *a*: ~ **de** dotted with.

piquette [pēket] *nf* (*fam*) cheap wine.

piqûre [pēkür] *nf* (*d'épingle*) prick; (*d'ortie*) sting; (*de moustique*) bite; (*MÉD*) injection, shot (*US*); (*COUTURE*) (straight) stitch; straight stitching; (*de ver*) hole; (*tache*)

(spot of) mildew; **faire une** ~ **à qn** to give sb an injection.

piranha [pēránà] *nm* piranha.

piratage [pērátàzh] *nm* piracy.

pirate [pērát] *a* pirate *cpd* ♦ *nm* pirate; (*fig*: *escroc*) crook, shark; ~ **de l'air** hijacker.

pirater [pērátā] *vt* to pirate.

piraterie [pērátrē] *nf* (act of) piracy; ~ **aérienne** hijacking.

pire [pēr] *a* (*comparatif*) worse; (*superlatif*): **le (la)** ~ ... the worst ... ♦ *nm*: **le** ~ **(de)** the worst (of).

Pirée [pērā] *n* Piraeus.

pirogue [pērog] *nf* dugout (canoe).

pirouette [pērwet] *nf* pirouette; (*fig*: *volte-face*) about-face (*US*), about-turn (*Brit*).

pis [pē] *nm* (*de vache*) udder; (*pire*): **le** ~ the worst ♦ *a, ad* worse; **qui** ~ **est** what is worse; **au** ~ **aller** if the worst comes to the worst, at worst.

pis-aller [pēzàlā] *nm inv* stopgap.

pisciculture [pēsēkültür] *nf* fish farming.

piscine [pēsēn] *nf* (swimming) pool; ~ **couverte** indoor (swimming) pool.

Pise [pēz] *n* Pisa.

pissenlit [pēsɑ̃nlē] *nm* dandelion.

pisser [pēsā] *vi* (*fam!*) to pee.

pissotière [pēsotyer] *nf* (*fam*) public urinal.

pistache [pēstàsh] *nf* pistachio (nut).

pistard [pēstàr] *nm* (*CYCLISME*) track cyclist.

piste [pēst(ə)] *nf* (*d'un animal, sentier*) track, trail; (*indice*) lead; (*de stade, de magnéto-phone, INFORM*) track; (*de cirque*) ring; (*de danse*) floor; (*de patinage*) rink; (*de ski*) run; (*AVIAT*) runway; ~ **cavalière** bridle path; ~ **cyclable** bicycle path, bikeway (*US*); ~ **sonore** sound track.

pister [pesta] *vt* to track, trail.

pisteur [pēstœr] *nm* (*SKI*) member of the ski patrol.

pistil [pēstēl] *nm* pistil.

pistolet [pēstole] *nm* (*arme*) pistol, gun; (*à peinture*) spray gun; ~ **à bouchon/air comprimé** popgun/airgun; ~ **à eau** water pistol.

pistolet-mitrailleur, *pl* **pistolets-mitrailleurs** [pēstolemētràycer] *nm* submachine gun.

piston [pēstɔ̃] *nm* (*TECH*) piston; (*MUS*) valve; (*fig*: *appui*) string-pulling.

pistonner [pēstonā] *vt* (*candidat*) to pull strings for.

pitance [pētɑ̃s] *nf* (*péj*) (means of) sustenance.

piteux, euse [pētœ̄, -œz] *a* pitiful, sorry (*avant le nom*); **en** ~ **état** in a sorry state.

pitié [pētyā] *nf* pity; **sans** ~ *a* pitiless, merciless; **faire** ~ to inspire pity; **il me fait** ~ I pity him, I feel sorry for him; **avoir** ~ **de** (*compassion*) to pity, feel sorry for; (*merci*) to have pity *ou* mercy on; **par** ~! for pity's sake!

piton [pētɔ̃] *nm* (*clou*) peg, bolt; ~ **rocheux** rocky outcrop.

pitoyable [pētwáyàbl(ə)] *a* pitiful.

pitre [pētr(ə)] *nm* clown.

pitrerie [pētrərē] *nf* tomfoolery *q*.

pittoresque [pētoresk(ə)] *a* picturesque; (*expression, détail*) colorful (*US*), colourful (*Brit*).

pivert |pēver| *nm* green woodpecker.
pivoine |pēvwàn| *nf* peony.
pivot |pēvō| *nm* pivot; (*d'une dent*) post.
pivoter |pēvotā| *vi* (*fauteuil*) to swivel; (*porte*) to revolve; ~ **sur ses talons** to swing around.
pixel |pēksel| *nm* pixel.
pizza |pēdzá| *nf* pizza.
PJ *sigle f* = **police judiciaire** ♦ *sigle fpl* (= *pièces jointes*) encl.
PL *sigle m* (*AUTO*) = **poids lourd**.
Pl. *abr* = **place**.
placage |plàkàzh| *nm* (*bois*) veneer.
placard |plàkàr| *nm* (*armoire*) closet (*US*), cupboard (*Brit*); (*affiche*) poster, notice; (*TYPO*) galley; ~ **publicitaire** display advertisement.
placarder |plàkàrdā| *vt* (*affiche*) to put up; (*mur*) to stick posters on.
place |plàs| *nf* (*emplacement, situation, classement*) place; (*de ville, village*) square; (*ÉCON*): ~ **financière/boursière** money/stock market; (*espace libre*) room, space; (*de parking*) space; (*siège: de train, cinéma, voiture*) seat; (*prix: au cinéma etc*) price; (: *dans un bus, taxi*) fare; (*emploi*) job; **en** ~ (*mettre*) in its place; **de** ~ **en** ~, **par** ~**s** here and there, in places; **sur** ~ on the spot; **faire** ~ **à** to give way to; **faire de la** ~ **à** to make room for; **ça prend de la** ~ it takes up a lot of room *ou* space; **prendre** ~ to take one's place; **remettre qn à sa** ~ to put sb in his (*ou* her) place; **ne pas rester** *ou* **tenir en** ~ to be always on the go; **à la** ~ **de** in place of, instead of; **une quatre** ~**s** (*AUTO*) a four-seater; **il y a 20** ~**s assises/debout** there are 20 seats/there is standing room for 20; ~ **forte** fortified town; ~ **d'honneur** place (*ou* seat) of honor.
placé, e |plàsā| *a* (*HIPPISME*) placed; **haut** ~ (*fig*) high-ranking; **être bien/mal** ~ to be well/badly placed; (*spectateur*) to have a good/bad seat; **être bien/mal** ~ **pour faire** to be in/not to be in a position to do.
placebo |plàsābō| *nm* placebo.
placement |plàsmàn̂| *nm* placing; (*FINANCE*) investment; **agence** *ou* **bureau de** ~ employment agency.
placenta |plàsàn̂tà| *nm* placenta.
placer |plàsā| *vt* to place, put; (*convive, spectateur*) to seat; (*capital, argent*) to place, invest; (*dans la conversation*) to put *ou* get in; ~ **qn chez** to get sb a job at (*ou* with); **se** ~ **au premier rang** to go and stand (*ou* sit) in the first row.
placide |plàsēd| *a* placid.
placier, ière |plàsyā, -yer| *nm/f* commercial rep(resentative), salesman/woman.
plafond |plàfón̂| *nm* ceiling.
plafonner |plàfonā| *vt* (*pièce*) to put a ceiling (up) in ♦ *vi* to reach one's (*ou* a) ceiling.
plafonnier |plàfonyā| *nm* ceiling light; (*AUTO*) interior light.
plage |plàzh| *nf* beach; (*station*) (seaside) resort; (*fig*) band, bracket; (*de disque*) track, band; ~ **arrière** (*AUTO*) rear window shelf (*US*), parcel *ou* back shelf (*Brit*).
plagiaire |plàzhyer| *nm/f* plagiarist.
plagiat |plàzhyá| *nm* plagiarism.
plagier |plàzhyā| *vt* to plagiarize.

plagiste |plàzhēst(ə)| *nm/f* beach attendant.
plaid |pled| *nm* (*tartan*) car rug, lap robe (*US*).
plaidant, e |pledàn̂, -àn̂t| *a* litigant.
plaider |plādā| *vi* (*avocat*) to plead; (*plaignant*) to go to court, litigate ♦ *vt* to plead; ~ **pour** (*fig*) to speak for.
plaideur, euse |pledœr, -œz| *nm/f* litigant.
plaidoirie |pledwárē| *nf* (*JUR*) speech for the defense (*US*) *ou* defence (*Brit*).
plaidoyer |pledwáyā| *nm* (*JUR*) speech for the defense (*US*) *ou* defence (*Brit*); (*fig*) plea.
plaie |ple| *nf* wound.
plaignant, e |plenyàn̂, -àn̂t| *vb voir* **plaindre** ♦ *nm/f* plaintiff.
plaindre |plàn̂dr(ə)| *vt* to pity, feel sorry for; **se** ~ *vi* (*gémir*) to moan; (*protester, rouspéter*): **se** ~ (**à qn**) (**de**) to complain (to sb) (about); (*souffrir*): **se** ~ **de** to complain of.
plaine |plen| *nf* plain.
plain-pied |plàn̂pyā|: **de** ~ *ad* at street level; (*fig*) straight; **de** ~ (**avec**) on the same level (as).
plaint, e |plàn̂, -àn̂t| *pp de* **plaindre** ♦ *nf* (*gémissement*) moan, groan; (*doléance*) complaint; **porter** ~**e** to lodge a complaint.
plaintif, ive |plàn̂tēf, -ēv| *a* plaintive.
plaire |pler| *vi* to be a success, be successful; to please; ~ **à:** **cela me plaît** I like it; **essayer de** ~ **à qn** (*en étant serviable etc*) to try and please sb; **elle plaît aux hommes** she's a success with men, men like her; **se** ~ **quelque part** to like being somewhere, like it somewhere; **se** ~ **à faire** to take pleasure in doing; **ce qu'il vous plaira** what(ever) you like *ou* wish; **s'il vous plaît** please.
plaisamment |plezàmàn̂| *ad* pleasantly.
plaisance |plezàn̂s| *nf* (*aussi*: **navigation de** ~) (pleasure) sailing, yachting.
plaisancier |plezàn̂syā| *nm* amateur sailor, yachting enthusiast.
plaisant, e |plezàn̂, -àn̂t| *a* pleasant; (*histoire, anecdote*) amusing.
plaisanter |plezàn̂tā| *vi* to joke ♦ *vt* (*personne*) to tease, make fun of; **pour** ~ for a joke; **on ne plaisante pas avec cela** that's no joking matter; **tu plaisantes!** you're joking *ou* kidding!
plaisanterie |plezàn̂trē| *nf* joke; joking *q*.
plaisantin |plezàn̂tàn̂| *nm* joker; (*fumiste*) fly-by-night.
plaise |plez| *etc vb voir* **plaire**.
plaisir |plāzēr| *nm* pleasure; **faire** ~ **à qn** (*délibérément*) to be nice to sb, please sb; (*suj: cadeau, nouvelle etc*): **ceci me fait** ~ I'm delighted *ou* very pleased with this; **prendre** ~ **à/à faire** to take pleasure in/in doing; **j'ai le** ~ **de** ... it is with great pleasure that I ...; **M. et Mme X ont le** ~ **de vous faire part de** ... M. and Mme X are pleased to announce ...; **se faire un** ~ **de faire qch** to be (only too) pleased to do sth; **faites-moi le** ~ **de** ... would you mind ..., would you be kind enough to ...; **à** ~ freely; for the sake of it; **au** ~ (**de vous revoir**) (I hope to) see you again; **pour le** *ou* **pour son** *ou* **par** ~ for pleasure.
plaît |ple| *vb voir* **plaire**.

plan, e [plåṅ, -àn] *a* flåt ♦ *nm* plan; (*GÉOM*) plane; (*fig*) level, plane; (*CINÉMA*) shot; **au premier/second ~** in the foreground/middle distance; **à l'arrière ~** in the background; **mettre qch au premier ~** (*fig*) to consider sth to be of primary importance; **sur le ~ sexuel** sexually, as far as sex is concerned; **laisser/rester en ~** to abandon/be abandoned; **~ d'action** plan of action; **~ directeur** (*ÉCON*) master plan; **~ d'eau** lake; pond; **~ de travail** work-top, work surface; **~ de vol** (*AVIAT*) flight plan.

planche [plåṅsh] *nf* (*pièce de bois*) plank, (wooden) board; (*illustration*) plate; (*de salades, radis, poireaux*) bed; (*d'un plongeur*) (diving) board; **les ~s** (*THÉÂTRE*) the boards; **en ~s** *a* wooden; **faire la ~** (*dans l'eau*) to float on one's back; **avoir du pain sur la ~** to have one's work cut out; **~ à découper** chopping board; **~ à dessin** drawing board; **~ à pain** breadboard; **~ à repasser** ironing board; **~ (à roulettes)** (*planche*) skateboard; (*sport*) skateboarding; **~ de salut** (*fig*) sheet anchor; **~ à voile** (*planche*) windsurfer, sailboard; (*sport*) windsurfing.

plancher [plåṅshā] *nm* floor; (*planches*) floorboards *pl*; (*fig*) minimum level ♦ *vi* to work hard.

planchiste [plåṅshēst(ə)] *nm/f* windsurfer.

plancton [plåṅktóṅ] *nm* plankton.

planer [plånā] *vi* (*oiseau, avion*) to glide; (*fumée, vapeur*) to float, hover; (*drogué*) to be (on a) high; **~ sur** (*fig*) to hang over; to hover above.

planétaire [plånāter] *a* planetary.

planétarium [plånātáryom] *nm* planetarium.

planète [plånet] *nf* planet.

planeur [plånœr] *nm* glider.

planification [plånēfēkåsyóṅ] *nf* (economic) planning.

planifier [plånēfyā] *vt* to plan.

planning [plåneŋg] *nm* program (*US*), programme (*Brit*), schedule; **~ familial** family planning.

planque [plåṅk] *nf* (*fam: combine, filon*) easy number; (*: cachette*) hideout.

planquer [plåṅkā] *vt* (*fam*) to hide (away), stash away; **se ~** to hide.

plant [plåṅ] *nm* seedling, young plant.

plantaire [plåṅter] *a voir* **voûte**.

plantation [plåṅtåsyóṅ] *nf* planting; (*de fleurs, légumes*) bed; (*exploitation*) plantation.

plante [plåṅt] *nf* plant; **~ d'appartement** house ou pot plant; **~ du pied** sole (of the foot); **~ verte** house plant.

planter [plåṅtā] *vt* (*plante*) to plant; (*enfoncer*) to hammer ou drive in; (*tente*) to put up, pitch; (*drapeau, échelle, décors*) to put up; (*fam: mettre*) to dump; (*: abandonner*): **~ là** to ditch; **se ~** *vi* (*fam: se tromper*) to get it wrong; **~ qch dans** to hammer ou drive sth into; to stick sth into; **se ~ dans** to sink into; to get stuck in; **se ~ devant** to plant o.s. in front of.

planteur [plåṅtœr] *nm* planter.

planton [plåṅtóṅ] *nm* orderly.

plantureux, euse [plåṅtūrœ̈, -œ̈z] *a* (*repas*) copious, lavish; (*femme*) buxom.

plaquage [plákàzh] *nm* (*RUGBY*) tackle.

plaque [plåk] *nf* plate; (*de verre*) sheet; (*de verglas, d'eczéma*) patch; (*dentaire*) plaque; (*avec inscription*) plaque; **~ (minéralogique ou de police ou d'immatriculation)** license (*US*) ou number (*Brit*) plate; **~ de beurre** slab of butter; **~ chauffante** hotplate; **~ de chocolat** bar of chocolate; **~ de cuisson** hob; **~ d'identité** identification tag; **~ tournante** (*fig*) center (*US*), centre (*Brit*).

plaqué, e [plåkā] *a*: **~ or/argent** gold-/silver-plated ♦ *nm*: **~ or/argent** gold/silver plate; **~ acajou** with a mahogany veneer.

plaquer [plåkā] *vt* (*bijou*) to plate; (*bois*) to veneer; (*aplatir*): **~ qch sur/contre** to make sth stick ou cling to; (*RUGBY*) to bring down; (*fam: laisser tomber*) to drop, ditch; **se ~ contre** to flatten o.s. against; **~ qn contre** to pin sb to.

plaquette [plåket] *nf* tablet; (*de chocolat*) bar; (*de beurre*) slab; (*livre*) small volume; (*MÉD: de pilules, gélules*) pack, packet; (*INFORM*) circuit board; **~ de frein** (*AUTO*) brake pad.

plasma [plåsmå] *nm* plasma.

plastic [plåstēk] *nm* plastic explosive.

plastifié, e [plåstēfyā] *a* plastic-coated.

plastiquage [plåstēkàzh] *nm* bombing, bomb attack.

plastique [plåstēk] *a* plastic ♦ *nm* plastic ♦ *nf* plastic arts *pl*; (*d'une statue*) modeling (*US*), modelling (*Brit*).

plastiquer [plåstēkā] *vt* to blow up.

plastiqueur [plåstēkœr] *nm* terrorist (*planting a plastic bomb*).

plastron [plåstróṅ] *nm* shirt front.

plastronner [plåstronā] *vi* to swagger.

plat, e [plå, -àt] *a* flat; (*fade: vin*) flat-tasting, insipid; (*personne, livre*) dull ♦ *nm* (*récipient, CULIN*) dish; (*d'un repas*): **le premier ~** the first course; (*partie plate*): **le ~ de la main** the flat of the hand; (*: d'une route*) flat (part); **à ~ ventre** *ad* face down; (*tomber*) flat on one's face; **à ~** *a* (*pneu*) flat; (*batterie*) dead; (*fam: fatigué*) dead tired, tired out; **~ cuisiné** pre-cooked meal (ou dish); **~ du jour** special (*US*) ou dish (*Brit*) of the day; **~ de résistance** main course; **~s préparés** convenience food(s).

platane [plåtán] *nm* plane tree.

plateau, x [plåtō] *nm* (*support*) tray; (*d'une table*) top; (*d'une balance*) pan; (*GÉO*) plateau; (*de tourne-disques*) turntable; (*CINÉMA*) set; (*TV*): **nous avons 2 journalistes sur le ~ ce soir** we have 2 journalists with us tonight; **~ à fromages** cheeseboard.

plateau-repas, *pl* **plateaux-repas** [plåtōrəpå] *nm* tray meal, TV dinner (*US*).

plate-bande, *pl* **plates-bandes** [plåtbåṅd] *nf* flower bed.

platée [plåtā] *nf* dish(ful).

plate-forme, *pl* **plates-formes** [plåtform(ə)] *nf* platform; **~ de forage/pétrolière** drilling/oil rig.

platine [plåtēn] *nm* platinum ♦ *nf* (*d'une tourne-disque*) turntable; **~ disque/cassette** record/cassette deck; **~ laser** *ou* **compact-disc** compact disc (player).

platitude [plátētüd] *nf* platitude.
platonique [plátonēk] *a* platonic.
plâtras [plâtrá] *nm* rubble *q*.
plâtre [plâtr(ə)] *nm* (*matériau*) plaster; (*statue*) plaster statue; (*MÉD*) (plaster) cast; ~**s** *nmpl* plasterwork *sg*; **avoir un bras dans le** ~ to have an arm in plaster.
plâtrer [plâtrā] *vt* to plaster; (*MÉD*) to set *ou* put in a (plaster) cast.
plâtrier [plâtrēyā] *nm* plasterer.
plausible [plōzēbl(ə)] *a* plausible.
play-back [plebák] *nm* miming.
plébiscite [plābēsēt] *nm* plebiscite.
plébisciter [plābēsētā] *vt* (*approuver*) to give overwhelming support to; (*élire*) to elect by an overwhelming majority.
plectre [plektr(ə)] *nm* plectrum.
plein, e [plań, -en] *a* full; (*porte, roue*) solid; (*chienne, jument*) big (with young) ♦ *nm*: **faire le** ~ (**d'essence**) to fill up (with gas (*US*) *ou* petrol (*Brit*)) ♦ *prép*: **avoir de l'argent** ~ **les poches** to have loads of money; ~ **de** full of; **avoir les mains** ~**es** to have one's hands full; **à** ~**es mains** (*ramasser*) in handfuls; (*empoigner*) firmly; **à** ~ **régime** at maximum revs; (*fig*) at full speed; **à** ~ **temps** full-time; **en** ~ **air** in the open air; **jeux en** ~ **air** outdoor games; **en** ~**e mer** on the open sea; **en** ~ **soleil** in direct sunlight; **en** ~**e nuit/rue** in the middle of the night/street; **en** ~ **milieu** right in the middle; **en** ~ **jour** in broad daylight; **les** ~**s** the downstrokes (*in handwriting*); **faire le** ~ **des voix** to get the maximum number of votes possible; **en** ~ **sur** right on; **en avoir** ~ **le dos** (*fam*) to have had it up to here.
pleinement [plenmán] *ad* fully; to the full.
plein-emploi [plenánplwá] *nm* full employment.
plénière [plānyer] *af*: **assemblée** ~ plenary assembly.
plénipotentiaire [plānēpotánsyer] *nm* plenipotentiary.
plénitude [plānētüd] *nf* fullness.
pléthore [plātor] *nf*: ~ **de** overabundance *ou* plethora of.
pleurer [plœrā] *vi* to cry; (*yeux*) to water ♦ *vt* to mourn (for); ~ **sur** *vt* to lament (over), bemoan; ~ **de rire** to laugh till one cries.
pleurésie [plœrāzē] *nf* pleurisy.
pleureuse [plœrēz] *nf* professional mourner.
pleurnicher [plœrnēshā] *vi* to snivel, whine.
pleurs [plœr] *nmpl*: **en** ~ in tears.
pleut [plœ] *vb voir* **pleuvoir**.
pleutre [plœtr(ə)] *a* cowardly.
pleuvait [plœve] *etc vb voir* **pleuvoir**.
pleuviner [plœvēnā] *vb impersonnel* to drizzle.
pleuvoir [plœvwár] *vb impersonnel* to rain ♦ *vi* (*fig*): ~ (**sur**) to shower down (upon), be showered upon; **il pleut** it's raining; **il pleut des cordes** *ou* **à verse** *ou* **à torrents** it's pouring (down), it's raining cats and dogs.
pleuvra [plœvrá] *etc vb voir* **pleuvoir**.
Plexiglas [pleksēglás] *nm* ® acrylic glass, Plexiglas ® (*US*).
pli [plē] *nm* fold; (*de jupe*) pleat; (*de pantalon*) crease; (*aussi*: **faux** ~) crease; (*enveloppe*) envelope; (*lettre*) letter; (*CARTES*) trick; **prendre le** ~ **de faire** to get

into the habit of doing; **ça ne fait pas un** ~! don't you worry!; ~ **d'aisance** inverted pleat.
pliable [plēyábl(ə)] *a* pliable, flexible.
pliage [plēyázh] *nm* folding; (*ART*) origami.
pliant, e [plēyáń, -áńt] *a* folding ♦ *nm* folding stool, campstool.
plier [plēyā] *vt* to fold; (*pour ranger*) to fold up; (*table pliante*) to fold down; (*genou, bras*) to bend ♦ *vi* to bend; (*fig*) to yield; **se** ~ **à** to submit to; ~ **bagages** (*fig*) to pack up (and go).
plinthe [plańt] *nf* baseboard (*US*), skirting board (*Brit*).
plissé, e [plēsā] *a* (*jupe, robe*) pleated; (*peau*) wrinkled; (*GÉO*) folded ♦ *nm* (*COUTURE*) pleats *pl*.
plissement [plēsmáń] *nm* (*GÉO*) fold.
plisser [plēsā] *vt* (*chiffonner: papier, étoffe*) to crease; (*rider: front*) to furrow, wrinkle; (*: bouche*) to pucker; (*jupe*) to put pleats in; **se** ~ *vi* (*vêtement, étoffe*) to crease.
pliure [plēyür] *nf* (*du bras, genou*) bend; (*d'un ourlet*) fold.
plomb [plóń] *nm* (*métal*) lead; (*d'une cartouche*) (lead) shot; (*PÊCHE*) sinker; (*sceau*) (lead) seal; (*ÉLEC*) fuse; **de** ~ (*soleil*) blazing; **sommeil de** ~ heavy *ou* very deep sleep; **mettre à** ~ to plumb.
plombage [plóńbázh] *nm* (*de dent*) filling.
plomber [plóńbā] *vt* (*canne, ligne*) to weight (with lead); (*colis, wagon*) to put a lead seal on; (*TECH: mur*) to plumb; (*dent*) to fill; (*INFORM*) to protect.
plomberie [plóńbrē] *nf* plumbing.
plombier [plóńbyā] *nm* plumber.
plonge [plóńzh] *nf*: **faire la** ~ to be a dishwasher (*person*).
plongeant, e [plóńzháń, -áńt] *a* (*vue*) from above; (*tir, décolleté*) plunging.
plongée [plóńzhā] *nf* (*SPORT*) diving *q*; (*: sans scaphandre*) skin diving; (*de sousmarin*) submersion, dive; **en** ~ (*sous-marin*) submerged; (*prise de vue*) high angle.
plongeoir [plóńzhwár] *nm* diving board.
plongeon [plóńzhóń] *nm* dive.
plonger [plóńzhā] *vi* to dive ♦ *vt*: ~ **qch dans** to plunge sth into; ~ **dans un sommeil profond** to sink straight into a deep sleep; ~ **qn dans l'embarras** to throw sb into a state of confusion.
plongeur, euse [plóńzhœr, -ēz] *nm/f* diver; (*de café*) dishwasher (*person*).
plot [plō] *nm* (*ÉLEC*) contact.
ploutocratie [plōōtokrásē] *nf* plutocracy.
ployer [plwáyā] *vt* to bend ♦ *vi* to bend; (*plancher*) to sag.
plu [plü] *pp de* **plaire, pleuvoir**.
pluie [plüē] *nf* rain; (*averse, ondée*): **une** ~ **brève** a shower; (*fig*): ~ **de** shower of; **une** ~ **fine** fine rain; **retomber en** ~ to shower down; **sous la** ~ in the rain.
plumage [plümázh] *nm* plumage *q*, feathers *pl*.
plume [plüm] *nf* feather; (*pour écrire*) (pen) nib; (*fig*) pen; **dessin à la** ~ pen and ink drawing.
plumeau, x [plümō] *nm* feather duster.
plumer [plümā] *vt* to pluck.
plumet [plüme] *nm* plume.

plumier [plümyā] *nm* pencil box.

plupart [plüpár]: **la ~** *pronom* the majority, most (of them); **la ~ des** most, the majority of; **la ~ du temps/d'entre nous** most of the time/of us; **pour la ~** *ad* for the most part, mostly.

pluralisme [plürálēsm(ə)] *nm* pluralism.

pluralité [plürálētā] *nf* plurality.

pluridisciplinaire [plürēdēsēplēner] *a* multidisciplinary.

pluriel [plüryel] *nm* plural; **au ~** in the plural.

plus *vb* [plü] *voir* **plaire** ♦ *ad* [plü, plüz + *vowel*] (*comparatif*) more, *adjectif court* + ...er; (*davantage*) [plüs] more; (*négatif*): **ne ... ~** no more, *tournure négative* + any more, no longer ♦ *cj* [plüs]: **~ 2** plus 2; **~ que** more than; **~ grand que** bigger than; **~ de 10 personnes** more than 10 people, over 10 people; **~ de minuit** after *ou* past midnight; **~ de pain** more bread; **~ il travaille, ~ il est heureux** the more he works, the happier he is; **le ~ intelligent/grand** the most intelligent/biggest; **3 heures/kilos de ~ que** 3 hours/kilos more than; **il a 3 ans de ~ que moi** he is 3 years older than I; **de ~** (*en outre*) what's more, moreover; **3 kilos en ~** 3 kilos more, 3 extra kilos; **en ~ de** in addition to; **de ~ en ~** more and more; **d'autant ~ que** all the more so since *ou* because; **(tout) au ~** at the (very) most; **sans ~** (but) no more than that, (but) that's all; **~ ou moins** more or less; **ni ~ ni moins** no more, no less; **qui ~ est** what is more.

plusieurs [plüzyœr] *dét, pronom* several; **ils sont ~** there are several of them.

plus-que-parfait [plüskəpárfe] *nm* pluperfect, past perfect.

plus-value [plüválü] *nf* (*d'un bien*) appreciation; (*bénéfice*) capital gain; (*budgétaire*) surplus.

plut [plü] *vb voir* **plaire, pleuvoir.**

plutonium [plütonyom] *nm* plutonium.

plutôt [plütō] *ad* rather; **je ferais ~ ceci** I'd rather *ou* sooner do this; **fais ~ comme ça** try this way instead, you'd better try this way; **~ que (de) faire** rather than *ou* instead of doing.

pluvial, e, aux [plüvyál, -ō] *a* (*eaux*) rain *cpd.*

pluvieux, euse [plüvyœ̄, -œz] *a* rainy, wet.

pluviosité [plüvyozētā] *nf* rainfall.

PM *sigle f* = *Police militaire.*

p.m. *abr* (= *pour mémoire*) for the record.

PME *sigle fpl* = *petites et moyennes entreprises.*

PMI *sigle fpl* = *petites et moyennes industries* ♦ *sigle f* = **protection maternelle et infantile.**

PMU *sigle m* (= *pari mutuel urbain*) system of betting on horses; (*café*) betting agency.

PNB *sigle m* (= *produit national brut*) GNP.

pneu [pnœ̄] *nm* (*de roue*) tire (*US*), tyre (*Brit*); (*message*) letter sent by pneumatic tube.

pneumatique [pnœ̄mátēk] *a* pneumatic; (*gonflable*) inflatable ♦ *nm* tire (*US*), tyre (*Brit*).

pneumonie [pnœ̄monē] *nf* pneumonia.

PO *sigle fpl* (= *petites ondes*) MW.

Pô [pō] *nm*: **le ~** the Po.

po [pō] *abr voir* **science.**

p.o. *abr* (= *par ordre*) p.p. (*on letters etc*).

poche [posh] *nf* pocket; (*déformation*): **faire une/des ~(s)** to bag; (*sous les yeux*) bag, pouch; (*ZOOL*) pouch ♦ *nm* (= *livre de ~*) (pocket-size) paperback; **de ~** pocket *cpd*; **en être de sa ~** to be out of pocket; **c'est dans la ~** it's in the bag.

poché, e [poshā] *a*: **œuf ~** poached egg; **œil ~** black eye.

pocher [poshā] *vt* (*CULIN*) to poach; (*ART*) to sketch ♦ *vi* (*vêtement*) to bag.

poche-revolver, *pl* **poches-revolver** [poshrəvolver] *nf* hip pocket.

pochette [poshet] *nf* (*de timbres*) folder, envelope; (*d'aiguilles etc*) case; (*sac: de femme*) clutch bag, purse; (: *d'homme*) bag; (*sur veston*) breast pocket; (*mouchoir*) breast pocket handkerchief; **~ d'allumettes** book of matches; **~ de disque** record jacket (*US*) *ou* sleeve (*Brit*); **~ surprise** surprise package.

pochoir [poshwár] *nm* (*ART: cache*) stencil; (: *tampon*) transfer.

podium [podyom] *nm* podium (*pl* -ia).

poêle [pwál] *nm* stove ♦ *nf*: **~ (à frire)** frying pan.

poêlon [pwálōn] *nm* casserole.

poème [poem] *nm* poem.

poésie [poāzē] *nf* (*poème*) poem; (*art*): **la ~** poetry.

poète [poet] *nm* poet; (*fig*) dreamer ♦ *a* poetic.

poétique [poātēk] *a* poetic.

pognon [ponyōn] *nm* (*fam: argent*) dough.

poids [pwá] *nm* weight; (*SPORT*) shot; **vendre au ~** to sell by weight; **de ~** *a* (*argument etc*) weighty; **prendre du ~** to put on weight; **faire le ~** (*fig*) to measure up; **~ plume/mouche/coq/moyen** (*BOXE*) feather/fly/bantam/ middleweight; **~ et haltères** *nmpl* weight lifting *sg*; **~ lourd** (*BOXE*) heavyweight; (*camion: aussi:* **PL**) (big) truck (*US*), lorry (*Brit*); (: *ADMIN*) truck (*US*), heavy goods vehicle (*Brit*); **~ mort** dead weight; **~ utile** net weight.

poignant, e [pwányâñ, -âñt] *a* poignant, harrowing.

poignard [pwányárd] *nm* dagger.

poignarder [pwányárdā] *vt* to stab, knife.

poigne [pwány] *nf* grip; (*fig*) firm-handedness; **à ~** firm-handed.

poignée [pwányā] *nf* (*de sel etc, fig*) handful; (*de couvercle, porte*) handle; **~ de main** handshake.

poignet [pwánye] *nm* (*ANAT*) wrist; (*de chemise*) cuff.

poil [pwál] *nm* (*ANAT*) hair; (*de pinceau, brosse*) bristle; (*de tapis, tissu*) strand; (*pelage*) coat; (*ensemble des poils*): **avoir du ~ sur la poitrine** to have hair(s) on one's chest, have a hairy chest; **à ~** *a* (*fam*) stark naked; **au ~** *a* (*fam*) hunky-dory; **de tout ~** of all kinds; **être de bon/mauvais ~** to be in a good/bad mood; **~ à gratter** itching powder.

poilu, e [pwálü] *a* hairy.

poinçon [pwáñsōñ] *nm* awl; bodkin; (*marque*) hallmark.

poinçonner [pwáñsonā] *vt* (*marchandise*) to stamp; (*bijou etc*) to hallmark; (*billet, tick-*

et) to clip, punch.

poinçonneuse [pwaṅsonœ̄z] *nf* (*outil*) punch.

poindre [pwaṅdr(ə)] *vi* (*fleur*) to come up; (*aube*) to break; (*jour*) to dawn.

poing [pwaṅ] *nm* fist; **dormir à ~s fermés** to sleep soundly.

point [pwaṅ] *vb voir* **poindre** ♦ *nm* (*marque, signe*) dot; (: *de ponctuation*) full stop, period (*US*); (*moment, de score etc, fig: question*) point; (*endroit*) spot; (*COUTURE, TRICOT*) stitch ♦ *ad* = **pas; ne ... ~** not (at all); **faire le ~** (*NAVIG*) to take a bearing; (*fig*) to take stock (of the situation); **faire le ~ sur** to review; **en tout ~** in every respect; **sur le ~ de faire** (just) about to do; **au ~ que, à tel ~ que** so much so that; **mettre au ~** (*mécanisme, procédé*) to develop; (*appareil-photo*) to focus; (*affaire*) to settle; **à ~** (*CULIN*) just right; (: *viande*) medium; **à ~ (nommé)** just at the right time; **~ de croix/tige/chaînette** (*COUTURE*) cross/stem/ chain stitch; **~ mousse/jersey** (*TRICOT*) garter/stocking stitch; **~ de départ/ d'arrivée/d'arrêt** departure/arrival/stopping point; **~ chaud** (*MIL, POL*) hot spot; **~ de chute** landing place; (*fig*) stopping-off point; **~ (de côté)** stitch (*pain*); **~ culminant** summit; (*fig*) height, climax; **~ d'eau** spring; water hole; **~ d'exclamation** exclamation mark; **~ faible** weak spot; **~ final** full stop, period (*US*); **~ d'interrogation** question mark; **~ mort** (*FINANCE*) break-even point; **au ~ mort** (*AUTO*) in neutral; (*affaire, entreprise*) at a standstill; **~ noir** (*sur le visage*) blackhead; (*AUTO*) deathtrap (*US*), accident black spot (*Brit*); **~ de non-retour** point of no return; **~ de repère** landmark; (*dans le temps*) point of reference; **~ de vente** retail outlet; **~ de vue** viewpoint; (*fig: opinion*) point of view; **du ~ de vue de** from the point of view of; **~s cardinaux** points of the compass, cardinal points; **~s de suspension** ellipsis *sg* suspension.

pointage [pwaṅtazh] *nm* ticking off; checking in.

pointe [pwaṅt] *nf* point; (*de la côte*) headland; (*allusion*) dig, sally; (*fig*): **une ~ d'ail/ d'accent** a touch *ou* hint of garlic/of an accent; **~s** *nfpl* (*DANSE*) points, point shoes; **être à la ~ de** (*fig*) to be in the forefront of; **faire** *ou* **pousser une ~ jusqu'à ...** to press on as far as ...; **sur la ~ des pieds** on tiptoe; **en ~** *ad* (*tailler*) into a point ♦ *a* pointed, tapered; **de ~** *a* (*technique etc*) leading; (*vitesse*) maximum, top; **heures/jours de ~** peak hours/days; **faire du 180 en ~** (*AUTO*) to have a top *ou* maximum speed of 180; **faire des ~s** (*DANSE*) to dance on points; **~ d'asperge** asparagus tip; **~ de courant** surge (of current); **~ de tension** (*INFORM*) spike; **~ de vitesse** burst of speed.

pointer [pwaṅtā] *vt* (*cocher*) to tick *ou* check (*US*) off; (*employés etc*) to check in; (*diriger: canon, longue-vue, doigt*): **~ vers qch** to point at sth; (*MUS: note*) to dot ♦ *vi* (*employé*) to clock in; (*pousses*) to come through; (*jour*) to break; **~ les oreilles** (*chien*) to prick up its ears.

pointeur, euse [pwaṅtœr, -œ̄z] *nm/f* time-

keeper ♦ *nf* timeclock.

pointillé [pwaṅtēyā] *nm* (*trait*) dotted line; (*ART*) stippling *q*.

pointilleux, euse [pwaṅtēyœ̄, -œ̄z] *a* particular, pernickety.

pointu, e [pwaṅtü] *a* pointed; (*clou*) sharp; (*voix*) shrill; (*analyse*) precise.

pointure [pwaṅtür] *nf* size.

point-virgule, *pl* **points-virgules** [pwaṅvērgül] *nm* semicolon.

poire [pwȧr] *nf* pear; (*fam: péj*) mug; **~ électrique** (*pear-shaped*) switch; **~ à injections** syringe.

poireau, x [pwȧrō] *nm* leek.

poireauter [pwȧrōtā] *vi* (*fam*) to hang around (waiting).

poirier [pwȧryā] *nm* pear tree; (*GYM*): **faire le ~** to do a headstand.

pois [pwȧ] *nm* (*BOT*) pea; (*sur une étoffe*) dot, spot; **à ~** (*cravate etc*) spotted, polka-dot *cpd*; **~ chiche** chickpea; **~ de senteur** sweet pea; **~ cassés** split peas.

poison [pwȧzóṅ] *nm* poison.

poisse [pwȧs] *nf* rotten luck.

poisser [pwȧsā] *vt* to make sticky.

poisseux, euse [pwȧsœ̄, -œ̄z] *a* sticky.

poisson [pwȧsóṅ] *nm* fish *gén inv*; **les P~s** (*signe*) Pisces, the Fish; **être des P~s** to be Pisces; **pêcher** *ou* **prendre du ~** *ou* **des ~s** to fish; **~ d'avril** April fool; (*blague*) April fool's day trick; **~ rouge** goldfish.

poisson-chat, *pl* **poissons-chats** [pwȧsóṅshȧ] *nm* catfish.

poissonnerie [pwȧsonrē] *nf* fishmonger's, fish market (*US*).

poissonneux, euse [pwȧsonœ̄, -œ̄z] *a* abounding in fish.

poissonnier, ière [pwȧsonyȧ, -ycr] *nm/f* fishmonger, fish merchant (*US*) ♦ *nf* (*ustensile*) fish kettle.

poisson-scie, *pl* **poissons-scies** [pwȧsóṅsē] *nm* sawfish.

poitevin, e [pwȧtvaṅ, -ēn] *a* (*région*) of *ou* from Poitou; (*ville*) of *ou* from Poitiers.

poitrail [pwȧtráy] *nm* (*d'un cheval etc*) breast.

poitrine [pwȧtrēn] *nf* (*ANAT*) chest; (*seins*) bust, bosom; (*CULIN*) breast; **~ de bœuf** brisket.

poivre [pwȧvr(ə)] *nm* pepper; **~ en grains/ moulu** whole/ground pepper; **~ de cayenne** cayenne (pepper); **~ et sel** *a* (*cheveux*) pepper-and-salt.

poivré, e [pwȧvrā] *a* peppery.

poivrer [pwȧvrā] *vt* to pepper.

poivrier [pwȧvrēyā] *nm* (*BOT*) pepper plant.

poivrière [pwȧvrēyer] *nf* pepperpot, pepper shaker (*US*).

poivron [pwȧvróṅ] *nm* pepper, capsicum; **~ vert/rouge** green/red pepper.

poix [pwȧ] *nf* pitch (*tar*).

poker [poker] *nm*: **le ~** poker; **partie de ~** (*fig*) gamble; **~ d'as** four aces.

polaire [poler] *a* polar.

polariser [polȧrēzā] *vt* to polarize; (*fig: attirer*) to attract; (: *réunir, concentrer*) to focus; **être polarisé sur** (*personne*) to be completely bound up with *ou* absorbed by.

pôle [pōl] *nm* (*GÉO, ÉLEC*) pole; **le ~ Nord/ Sud** the North/South Pole; **~ d'attraction**

(*fig*) center of attraction.

polémique [polāmēk] *a* controversial, polemic(al) ♦ *nf* controversy.

polémiquer [polāmēkā] *vi* to be involved in controversy.

polémiste [polāmēst(ə)] *nm/f* polemist, polemicist.

poli, e [polē] *a* polite; (*lisse*) smooth; polished.

police [polēs] *nf* police; (*discipline*): **assurer la ~ de** *ou* **dans** to keep order in; **peine de simple ~** *sentence given by a magistrates' or police court*; **~** (**d'assurance**) (insurance) policy; **~** (**de caractères**) (*TYPO, INFORM*) typeface; **~ judiciaire (PJ)** ≈ Federal Bureau of Investigation (FBI) (*US*), ≈ Criminal Investigation Department (CID) (*Brit*); **~ des mœurs** ≈ vice squad; **~ secours** ≈ emergency services *pl*.

polichinelle [polēshēnel] *nm* Punch; (*péj*) buffoon; **secret de ~** open secret.

policier, ière [polēsyā, -yer] *a* police *cpd* ♦ *nm* policeman; (*aussi*: **roman ~**) detective novel.

policlinique [polēklēnēk] *nf* ≈ outpatients (clinic).

poliment [polēmāṅ] *ad* politely.

polio(myélite) [polyo(myālēt)] *nf* polio(myelitis).

polio(myélitique) [polyo(myālētēk)] *nm/f* polio patient *ou* case.

polir [polēr] *vt* to polish.

polisson, ne [polēsóṅ, -on] *a* naughty.

politesse [polētes] *nf* politeness; **~s** *nfpl* (exchange of) courtesies; **rendre une ~ à qn** to return sb's favor.

politicard [polētēkár] *nm* (*péj*) politico, political schemer.

politicien, ne [polētēsyaṅ, -en] *a* political ♦ *nm/f* politician.

politique [polētēk] *a* political ♦ *nf* (*science, activité*) politics *sg*; (*principes, tactique*) policy, policies *pl* ♦ *nm* (*politicien*) politician; **~ étrangère/intérieure** foreign/domestic policy.

politique-fiction [polētēkfēksyóṅ] *nf* political fiction.

politiquement [polētēkmāṅ] *ad* politically.

politiser [polētēzā] *vt* to politicize; **~ qn** to make sb politically aware.

pollen [polen] *nm* pollen.

polluant, e [polüáṅ, -áṅt] *a* polluting ♦ *nm* polluting agent, pollutant.

polluer [polüā] *vt* to pollute.

pollution [polüsyóṅ] *nf* pollution.

polo [polō] *nm* (*sport*) polo; (*tricot*) polo shirt.

Pologne [polony] *nf*: **la ~** Poland.

polonais, e [polone, -ez] *a* Polish ♦ *nm* (*LING*) Polish ♦ *nm/f*: **P~, e** Pole.

poltron, ne [poltróṅ, -on] *a* cowardly.

poly... [polē] *préfixe* poly....

polyamide [polēámēd] *nf* polyamide.

polychrome [polēkrōm] *a* polychrome, polychromatic.

polyclinique [polēklēnēk] *nf* (private) clinic (*treating different illnesses*).

polycopié, e [polēkopyā] *a* duplicated ♦ *nm* handout, duplicated notes *pl*.

polycopier [polēkopyā] *vt* to duplicate.

polyculture [polēkültür] *nf* mixed farming.

polyester [polēester] *nm* polyester.

polyéthylène [polēātēlen] *nm* polyethylene.

polygame [polēgám] *a* polygamous.

polygamie [polēgámē] *nf* polygamy.

polyglotte [polēglot] *a* polyglot.

polygone [polēgon] *nm* polygon.

Polynésie [polēnāzē] *nf*: **la ~** Polynesia; **la ~ française** French Polynesia.

polynésien, ne [polēnāzyaṅ, -en] *a* Polynesian.

polype [polēp] *nm* polyp.

polystyrène [polēstēren] *nm* polystyrene.

polytechnicien, ne [polēteknēsyaṅ, -en] *nm/f* student or former student of the *École Polytechnique*.

polyvalent, e [polēválâṅ, -âṅt] *a* (*vaccin*) polyvalent; (*personne*) versatile; (*salle*) multipurpose ♦ *nm* ≈ tax inspector.

pomélo [pomālō] *nm* grapefruit.

Poméranie [pomārânē] *nf*: **la ~** Pomerania.

pommade [pomád] *nf* ointment, cream.

pomme [pom] *nf* (*BOT*) apple; (*boule décorative*) knob; (*pomme de terre*): **steak ~s (frites)** steak and (French) fries *ou* chips (*Brit*); **tomber dans les ~s** (*fam*) to pass out; **~ d'Adam** Adam's apple; **~s allumettes** French fries (*thin-cut*); **~ d'arrosoir** (sprinkler) rose; **~ de pin** pine *ou* fir cone; **~ de terre** potato; **~s vapeur** boiled potatoes.

pommé, e [pomā] *a* (*chou etc*) firm, with a firm heart.

pommeau, x [pomō] *nm* (*boule*) knob; (*de selle*) pommel.

pommelé, e [pomlā] *a*: **gris ~** dapple grey.

pommette [pomet] *nf* cheekbone.

pommier [pomyā] *nm* apple tree.

pompe [pôṅp] *nf* pump; (*faste*) pomp (and ceremony); **~ de bicyclette** bicycle pump; **~ à eau/essence** water/gas(oline) (*US*) *ou* petrol (*Brit*) pump; **~ à huile** oil pump; **~ à incendie** fire engine (*apparatus*); **~s funèbres** undertaker's *sg*, mortician's *sg* (*US*), funeral parlour *sg* (*Brit*).

Pompéi [pôṅpāē] *n* Pompeii.

pompéien, ne [pôṅpāyaṅ, -en] *a* Pompeiian.

pomper [pôṅpā] *vt* to pump; (*évacuer*) to pump out; (*aspirer*) to pump up; (*absorber*) to soak up ♦ *vi* to pump.

pompeusement [pôṅpȫzmâṅ] *ad* pompously.

pompeux, euse [pôṅpȫ, -ȫz] *a* pompous.

pompier [pôṅpyā] *nm* fireman ♦ *am* (*style*) pretentious, pompous.

pompiste [pôṅpēst(ə)] *nm/f* gas (*US*) *ou* petrol (*Brit*) pump attendant.

pompon [pôṅpóṅ] *nm* pompom, bobble.

pomponner [pôṅ ponā] *vt* to dress up.

ponce [pôṅs] *nf*: **pierre ~** pumice stone.

poncer [pôṅsā] *vt* to sand (down).

ponceuse [pôṅsȫz] *nf* sander.

poncif [pôṅsēf] *nm* cliché.

ponction [pôṅksyóṅ] *nf* (*d'argent etc*) withdrawal; **~ lombaire** lumbar puncture.

ponctualité [pôṅktüálētā] *nf* punctuality.

ponctuation [pôṅktüâsyóṅ] *nf* punctuation.

ponctuel, le [pôṅktüel] *a* (*à l'heure, aussi TECH*) punctual; (*fig: opération etc*) one-shot (*US*), one-off (*Brit*), single; (*scrupuleux*) punctilious, meticulous.

ponctuellement [pôṅktüelmâṅ] *ad* punctu-

ally; punctiliously, meticulously.
ponctuer [pôṅktüā] *vt* to punctuate; (*MUS*) to phrase.
pondéré, e [pôṅdārā] *a* levelheaded, composed.
pondérer [pôṅdārā] *vt* to balance.
pondeuse [pôṅdœz] *nf* layer, laying hen.
pondre [pôṅdr(ǝ)] *vt* to lay; (*fig*) to produce ♦ *vi* to lay.
poney [pone] *nm* pony.
pongiste [pôṅzhēst(ǝ)] *nm/f* table tennis player.

pont [pôṅ] *nm* bridge; (*AUTO*): ~ **arrière/ avant** rear/front axle; (*NAVIG*) deck; **faire le** ~ to take the extra day off; **faire un ~ d'or à qn** to offer sb a fortune to take a job; ~ **aérien** airlift; ~ **basculant** bascule bridge; ~ **d'envol** flight deck; ~ **élévateur** hydraulic ramp; ~ **de graissage** ramp (*in garage*); ~ **à péage** tollbridge; ~ **roulant** traveling crane; ~ **suspendu** suspension bridge; ~ **tournant** swing bridge; **P~s et Chaussées** highways department.
ponte [pôṅt] *nf* laying; (*œufs pondus*) clutch ♦ *nm* (*fam*) big shot.
pontife [pôṅtēf] *nm* pontiff.
pontifier [pôṅtēfyā] *vi* to pontificate.
pont-levis, *pl* **ponts-levis** [pôṅlvē] *nm* drawbridge.
ponton [pôṅtôṅ] *nm* pontoon (*on water*).
pop [pop] *a inv* pop ♦ *nm*: **le** ~ pop (music).
pop-corn [popkorn] *nm* popcorn.
popeline [poplēn] *nf* poplin.
populace [populäs] *nf* (*péj*) rabble.
populaire [popüler] *a* popular; (*manifestation*) mass *cpd*, of the people; (*milieux, clientèle*) working-class; (*LING: mot etc*) used by the lower classes (of society).
populariser [popülärēzā] *vt* to popularize.
popularité [popülärētā] *nf* popularity.
population [popülâsyôṅ] *nf* population; ~ **active/agricole** working/farming population.
populeux, euse [popülœ̄, -œz] *a* densely populated.
porc [por] *nm* (*ZOOL*) pig; (*CULIN*) pork; (*peau*) pigskin.
porcelaine [porsǝlen] *nf* (*substance*) porcelain, china; (*objet*) piece of china(ware).
porcelet [porsǝle] *nm* piglet.
porc-épic, *pl* **porcs-épics** [porkāpēk] *nm* porcupine.
porche [porsh(ǝ)] *nm* porch.
porcher, ère [porshā, -er] *nm/f* swineherd.
porcherie [porshǝrē] *nf* pigsty.
porcin, e [porsaṅ, -ēn] *a* (*race*) porcine; (*élevage*) pig *cpd*; (*fig*) piglike.
pore [por] *nm* pore.
poreux, euse [porœ̄, -œz] *a* porous.
porno [pornō] *a* porno ♦ *nm* porn.
pornographie [pornográfē] *nf* pornography.
pornographique [pornográfēk] *a* pornographic.
port [por] *nm* (*NAVIG*) harbor (*US*), harbour (*Brit*), port; (*ville, aussi INFORM*) port; (*de l'uniforme etc*) wearing; (*pour lettre*) postage; (*pour colis, aussi: posture*) carriage; ~ **de commerce/de pêche** commercial/fishing port; **arriver à bon** ~ to arrive safe and sound; ~ **d'arme** (*JUR*) carrying of a

firearm; ~ **d'attache** (*NAVIG*) port of registry; (*fig*) home base; ~ **d'escale** port of call; ~ **franc** free port.
portable [portäbl(ǝ)] *a* (*vêtement*) wearable; (*portatif*) transportable.
portail [portäy] *nm* gate; (*de cathédrale*) portal.
portant, e [portäṅ, -äṅt] *a* (*murs*) structural, supporting; (*roues*) running; **bien/mal** ~ in good/poor health.
portatif, ive [portätēf, -ēv] *a* portable.
porte [port(ǝ)] *nf* door; (*de ville, forteresse, SKI*) gate; **mettre à la** ~ to throw out; **prendre la** ~ to leave, go away; **à ma/sa** ~ (*tout près*) on my/his (*ou* her) doorstep; ~ (**d'embarquement**) (*AVIAT*) (departure) gate; ~ **d'entrée** front door; ~ **à** ~ *nm* door-to-door selling; ~ **de secours** emergency exit; ~ **de service** service entrance.
porté, e [portä] *a*: **être** ~ **à faire qch** to be apt to do sth, tend to do sth; **être** ~ **sur qch** to be partial to sth.
porte-à-faux [portäfō] *nm*: **en** ~ cantilevered; (*fig*) in an awkward position.
porte-aiguilles [portägüēy] *nm inv* needle case.
porte-avions [portävyôṅ] *nm inv* aircraft carrier.
porte-bagages [portbägäzh] *nm inv* luggage rack (*ou* basket *etc*).
porte-bébé [portbābā] *nm* baby sling *ou* carrier.
porte-bonheur [portbonœr] *nm inv* lucky charm.
porte-bouteilles [portbōōtey] *nm inv* bottle carrier; (*à casiers*) wine rack.
porte-cartes [portǝkárt(ǝ)] *nm inv* (*de cartes d'identité*) card holder; (*de cartes géographiques*) map holder *ou* case.
porte-cigarettes [portsēgáret] *nm inv* cigarette case.
porte-clefs [portǝklā] *nm inv* key ring.
porte-conteneurs [portǝkôṅtnœr] *nm inv* container ship.
porte-couteau, x [portkōōtō] *nm* knife rest.
porte-crayon [portkreyôṅ] *nm* pencil holder.
porte-documents [portdokümáṅ] *nm inv* attaché *ou* document case.
porte-drapeau, x [portdräpō] *nm* standardbearer.
portée [portä] *nf* (*d'une arme*) range; (*fig: importance*) impact, import; (: *capacités*) scope, capability; (*de chatte etc*) litter; (*MUS*) stave, staff (*pl* staves); **à/hors de** ~ (**de**) within/out of reach (of); **à** ~ **de voix** within earshot; **à la** ~ **de qn** (*fig*) at sb's level, within sb's capabilities; **à la** ~ **de toutes les bourses** to suit every pocket, within everyone's means.
portefaix [portǝfe] *nm inv* porter.
porte-fenêtre, *pl* **portes-fenêtres** [portfǝnetr(ǝ)] *nf* French window.
portefeuille [portǝfœy] *nm* wallet; (*POL, BOURSE*) portfolio; **faire un lit en** ~ to shortsheet a bed (*US*), make an apple-pie bed (*Brit*).
porte-jarretelles [portzhärtel] *nm inv* garter (*US*) *ou* suspender (*Brit*) belt.

porte-jupe [portəzhüp] *nm* skirt hanger.
portemanteau, x [portmântō] *nm* coat rack.
porte-mine [portəmēn] *nm* mechanical (*US*) *ou* propelling (*Brit*) pencil.
porte-monnaie [portmone] *nm inv* coin purse.
porte-parapluies [portpáráplüē] *nm inv* umbrella stand.
porte-parole [portpárol] *nm inv* spokesperson.
porte-plume [portəplüm] *nm inv* penholder.

porter [portā] *vt* (*charge ou sac etc, aussi: fœtus*) to carry; (*sur soi: vêtement, barbe, bague*) to wear; (*fig: responsabilité etc*) to bear, carry; (*inscription, marque, titre, patronyme, suj: arbre: fruits, fleurs*) to bear; (*jugement*) to pass; (*apporter*): ~ **qch quelque part/à qn** to take sth somewhere/to sb; (*inscrire*): ~ **qch sur** to put sth down on; to enter sth in ♦ *vi* (*voix, regard, canon*) to carry; (*coup, argument*) to hit home; **se** ~ *vi* (*se sentir*): **se** ~ **bien/mal** to be well/unwell; (*aller*): **se** ~ **vers** to go towards; ~ **sur** (*peser*) to rest on; (*accent*) to fall on; (*conférence etc*) to concern; (*heurter*) to strike; **être porté à faire** to be apt *ou* inclined to do; **elle portait le nom de Rosalie** she was called Rosalie; ~ **qn au pouvoir** to bring sb to power; ~ **bonheur à qn** to bring sb luck; ~ **qn à croire** to lead sb to believe; ~ **son âge** to look one's age; ~ **un toast** to drink a toast; ~ **de l'argent au crédit d'un compte** to credit an account with some money; **se** ~ **partie civile** to associate in a court action with the public prosecutor; **se** ~ **garant de qch** to guarantee sth, vouch for sth; **se** ~ **candidat à la députation** ≈ to run for Congress (*US*), ≈ stand for Parliament (*Brit*); **se faire** ~ **malade** to report sick; ~ **la main à son chapeau** to raise one's hand to one's hat; ~ **son effort sur** to direct one's efforts towards; ~ **un fait à la connaissance de qn** to bring a fact to sb's attention *ou* notice.
porte-savon [portsávôn] *nm* soap dish.
porte-serviettes [portservyet] *nm inv* towel rack (*US*) *ou* rail (*Brit*).
portes-ouvertes [portōōvert(ə)] *a inv:* **journée** ~ open house, open day (*Brit*).
porteur, euse [portœr, -ēz] *a* (*COMM*) strong, promising; (*nouvelle, chèque etc*): **être** ~ **de** to be the bearer of ♦ *nm/f* (*de messages*) bearer ♦ *nm* (*de bagages*) porter; (*COMM: de chèque*) bearer; (*: d'actions*) holder; (*avion*) **gros** ~ wide-bodied aircraft, jumbo (jet).
porte-voix [portəvwá] *nm inv* megaphone.
portier [portyā] *nm* doorman.
portière [portyer] *nf* door.
portillon [portēyôn] *nm* gate.
portion [porsyôn] *nf* (*part*) portion, share; (*partie*) portion, section.
portique [portēk] *nm* (*GYM*) crossbar; (*ARCHIT*) portico; (*RAIL*) gantry.
porto [portō] *nm* port (wine).
portoricain, e [portorēkáň, -en] *a* Puerto Rican.
Porto Rico [portorēkō] *nf* Puerto Rico.
portrait [portre] *nm* portrait; (*photographie*) photograph; (*fig*): **elle est le** ~ **de sa mère** she's the image of her mother.
portraitiste [portrātēst(ə)] *nm/f* portrait painter.

portrait-robot [portrerobō] *nm* Identikit ® picture.
portuaire [portüer] *a* port *cpd*, harbor *cpd* (*US*), harbour *cpd* (*Brit*).
portugais, e [portüge, -ez] *a* Portuguese ♦ *nm* (*LING*) Portuguese ♦ *nm/f:* **P~, e** Portuguese.
Portugal [portügál] *nm:* **le** ~ Portugal.
pose [pōz] *nf* (*de moquette*) laying; (*de rideaux, papier peint*) hanging; (*attitude, d'un modèle*) pose; (*PHOTO*) exposure.
posé, e [pōzā] *a* calm, unruffled.
posément [pōzāmáň] *ad* calmly.
posemètre [pōzmetr(ə)] *nm* exposure meter.
poser [pōzā] *vt* (*déposer*): ~ **qch (sur)/qn à** to put sth down (on)/drop sb at; (*placer*): ~ **qch sur/quelque part** to put sth on/somewhere; (*installer: moquette, carrelage*) to lay; (*rideaux, papier peint*) to hang; (*MATH: chiffre*) to put (down); (*question*) to ask; (*principe, conditions*) to lay *ou* set down; (*problème*) to formulate; (*difficulté*) to pose; (*personne: mettre en valeur*) to give standing to ♦ *vi* (*modèle*) to pose; to sit; **se** ~ (*oiseau, avion*) to land; (*question*) to arise; **se** ~ **en** to pass o.s. off as, pose as; ~ **son** *ou* **un regard sur qn/qch** to turn one's gaze on sb/sth; ~ **sa candidature** to apply; (*POL*) to put o.s. up for election.
poseur, euse [pōzœr, -ēz] *nm/f* (*péj*) show-off, poseur; ~ **de parquets/ carrelages** floor/tile layer.
positif, ive [pōzētēf, -ēv] *a* positive.
position [pōzēsyôn] *nf* position; **prendre** ~ (*fig*) to take a stand.
positionner [pōzēsyonā] *vt* to position; (*compte en banque*) to calculate the balance of.
positivement [pōzētēvmáň] *ad* positively.
posologie [posolozhē] *nf* directions *pl* for use, dosage.
possédant, e [posādáň, -áňt] *a* (*classe*) wealthy ♦ *nm/f:* **les** ~s the haves, the wealthy.
possédé, e [posādā] *nm/f* person possessed.
posséder [posādā] *vt* to own, possess; (*qualité, talent*) to have, possess; (*bien connaître: métier, langue*) to have mastered, have a thorough knowledge of; (*sexuellement, aussi: suj: colère etc*) to possess; (*fam: duper*) to take in.
possesseur [posāsœr] *nm* owner.
possessif, ive [posāsēf, -ēv] *a, nm* (*aussi LING*) possessive.
possession [posāsyôn] *nf* ownership *q*; possession; **être/entrer en** ~ **de qch** to be in/take possession of sth.
possibilité [posēbēlētā] *nf* possibility; ~s *nfpl* (*moyens*) means; (*potentiel*) potential *sg*; **avoir la** ~ **de faire** to be in a position to do; to have the opportunity to do.
possible [posēbl(ə)] *a* possible; (*projet, entreprise*) feasible ♦ *nm:* **faire son** ~ to do all one can, do one's utmost; (**ce n'est**) **pas** ~! impossible!; **le plus/moins de livres** ~ as many/few books as possible; **dès que** ~ as soon as possible; **gentil** *etc* **au** ~ as nice *etc* as it is possible to be.
postal, e, aux [postál, -ō] *a* postal, post office

cpd; **sac** ~ mailbag.

postdater [postdåtā] *vt* to postdate.

poste [post(ə)] *nf* (*service*) post, postal service; (*administration, bureau*) post office ♦ *nm* (*fonction, MIL*) post; (*TÉL*) extension; (*de radio etc*) set; (*de budget*) item; ~**s** *nfpl* post office *sg*; **P~s télécommunications et télédiffusion (PTT)** *postal and telecommunications service*; **agent** *ou* **employé des** ~**s** post office worker; **mettre à la** ~ **to** mail; ~ **de commandement (PC)** *nm* (*MIL etc*) headquarters; ~ **de contrôle** *nm* checkpoint; ~ **de douane** *nm* customs post; ~ **émetteur** *nm* transmitting set; ~ **d'essence** *nm* filling station; ~ **d'incendie** *nm* fire station (*US*) *ou* point (*Brit*); ~ **de péage** *nm* tollgate; ~ **de pilotage** *nm* cockpit; ~ **(de police)** *nm* police station; ~ **de radio** *nm* radio set; ~ **restante (PR)** *nf* general delivery (*US*), poste restante (*Brit*); ~ **de secours** *nm* first-aid post; ~ **de télévision** *nm* television set; ~ **de travail** *nm* work station.

poster *vt* [postā] to post ♦ *nm* [poster] poster; **se** ~ to position o.s.

postérieur, e [postāryœr] *a* (*date*) later; (*partie*) back ♦ *nm* (*fam*) behind.

postérieurement [postāryœrmåñ] *ad* later, subsequently; ~ **à** after.

posteriori [postāryorē]: **a** ~ *ad* with hindsight, a posteriori.

postérité [postārētā] *nf* posterity.

postface [postfås] *nf* appendix.

posthume [postüm] *a* posthumous.

postiche [postēsh] *a* false ♦ *nm* hairpiece.

postier, ière [postyā, -yer] *nm/f* post office worker.

postillonner [postēyonā] *vi* to sp(l)utter.

post-natal, e [postnátál] *a* postnatal.

postopératoire [postopárátwár] *a* postoperative.

postscolaire [postskoler] *a* further, continuing.

post-scriptum [postskrēptom] *nm inv* post-script.

postsynchroniser [postsañkronēzā] *vt* to dub.

postulant, e [postülåñ, -åñt] *nm/f* (*candidat*) applicant; (*REL*) postulant.

postulat [postülá] *nm* postulate.

postuler [postülā] *vt* (*emploi*) to apply for, put in for.

posture [postür] *nf* posture, position; (*fig*) position.

pot [pō] *nm* jar, pot; (*en plastique, carton*) carton; (*en métal*) tin; (*fam*): **avoir du** ~ to be lucky; **boire** *ou* **prendre un** ~ (*fam*) to have a drink; **découvrir le** ~ **aux roses** to find out what's been going on; ~ **(de chambre)** (*chamber*)pot; ~ **d'échappement** exhaust pipe; ~ **de fleurs** plant pot, flowerpot; (*plante*) pot plant; ~ **à tabac** tobacco jar.

potable [potábl(ə)] *a* (*fig: boisson*) drinkable; (*: travail, devoir*) decent; **eau (non)** ~ (not) drinking water.

potache [potásh] *nm* schoolboy.

potage [potázh] *nm* soup.

potager, ère [potázhā, -er] *a* (*plante*) edible, vegetable *cpd*; **(jardin)** ~ kitchen *ou* vegetable garden.

potasse [potás] *nf* potassium hydroxide; (*engrais*) potash.

potasser [potásā] *vt* (*fam*) to cram.

potassium [potásyom] *nm* potassium.

pot-au-feu [potōfœ] *nm inv* (beef) stew; (*viande*) stewing beef ♦ *a* (*fam: personne*) stay-at-home.

pot-de-vin, *pl* **pots-de-vin** [pōdvañ] *nm* bribe.

pote [pot] *nm* (*fam*) pal.

poteau, x [potō] *nm* post; ~ **de départ/arrivée** starting/finish (*US*) *ou* finishing (*Brit*) post; ~ **(d'exécution)** execution post, stake; ~ **indicateur** signpost; ~ **télégraphique** telegraph pole; ~**x (de but)** goal posts.

potée [potā] *nf* baked stew (*of pork and cabbage*).

potelé, e [potlā] *a* plump, chubby.

potence [potåñs] *nf* gallows *sg*; **en** ~ T-shaped.

potentat [potåñtá] *nm* potentate; (*fig, péj*) despot.

potentiel, le [potåñsyel] *a, nm* potential.

poterie [potrē] *nf* (*fabrication*) pottery; (*objet*) piece of pottery.

potiche [potēsh] *nf* large vase.

potier [potyá] *nm* potter.

potins [potañ] *nmpl* gossip *sg*.

potion [pōsyôñ] *nf* potion.

potiron [potērôñ] *nm* pumpkin.

pot-pourri, *pl* **pots-pourris** [pōpōōrē] *nm* (*MUS*) potpourri, medley.

pou, x [pōō] *nm* louse (*pl* lice).

pouah [pwá] *excl* ugh!, yuk!

poubelle [pōōbel] *nf* trash *ou* garbage can (*US*), (dust)bin (*Brit*).

pouce [pōōs] *nm* thumb; **se tourner** *ou* **se rouler les** ~**s** (*fig*) to twiddle one's thumbs; **manger sur le** ~ to eat on the run, grab something to eat.

poudre [pōōdr(ə)] *nf* powder; (*fard*) (face) powder; (*explosif*) gunpowder; **en** ~: **café en** ~ instant coffee; **savon en** ~ soap powder; **lait en** ~ dried *ou* powdered milk; ~ **à canon** gunpowder; ~ **à éternuer** sneezing powder; ~ **à récurer** scouring powder; ~ **de riz** face powder.

poudrer [pōōdrā] *vt* to powder.

poudrerie [pōōdrərē] *nf* gunpowder factory.

poudreux, euse [pōōdrœ̄, -œ̄z] *a* dusty; (*neige*) powdery, powder *cpd*.

poudrier [pōōdrēyā] *nm* (*powder*) compact.

poudrière [pōōdrēyer] *nf* powder magazine; (*fig*) powder keg.

poudroyer [pōōdrwáyā] *vi* to rise in clouds *ou* a flurry.

pouf [pōōf] *nm* pouffe.

pouffer [pōōfā] *vi*: ~ **(de rire)** to snigger; to giggle.

pouffiasse [pōōfyás] *nf* (*fam*) fat cow; (*prostituée*) tart.

pouilleux, euse [pōōyœ̄, -œ̄z] *a* flea-ridden; (*fig*) seedy.

poulailler [pōōláyā] *nm* henhouse; (*THÉÂTRE*): **le** ~ the peanut gallery (*US*), the gods *sg* (*Brit*).

poulain [pōōlañ] *nm* foal; (*fig*) protégé.

poularde [pōōlárd(ə)] *nf* fatted chicken.

poule [pōōl] *nf* (*ZOOL*) hen; (*CULIN*) (boiling) fowl; (*SPORT*) (round-robin) tournament; (*RUGBY*) group; (*fam*) chick, broad (*US*),

bird (*Brit*); (*prostituée*) tart; ~ **d'eau** moorhen; ~ **mouillée** coward; ~ **pondeuse** laying hen, layer; ~ **au riz** chicken and rice.
poulet [poōle] *nm* chicken; (*fam*) cop.
poulette [poōlet] *nf* (*jeune poule*) pullet.
pouliche [poōlēsh] *nf* filly.
poulie [poōlē] *nf* pulley.
poulpe [poōlp(ə)] *nm* octopus.
pouls [poō] *nm* pulse (*ANAT*); **prendre le ~ de qn** to feel sb's pulse.
poumon [poōmóń] *nm* lung; ~ **d'acier** *ou* **artificiel** iron *ou* artificial lung.
poupe [poōp] *nf* stern; **en ~** astern.
poupée [poōpā] *nf* doll; **jouer à la ~** to play with one's doll (*ou* dolls); **de ~** (*très petit*): **jardin de ~** doll's garden, pocket-handkerchief-sized garden.
poupin, e [poōpań, -ēn] *a* chubby.
poupon [poōpóń] *nm* babe-in-arms.
pouponner [poōponā] *vi* to fuss (around).
pouponnière [poōponyer] *nf* day nursery.
pour [poōr] *prép* for ♦ *nm*: **le ~ et le contre** the pros and cons; ~ **faire** (so as) to do, in order to do; ~ **avoir fait** for having done; ~ **que** so that, in order that; ~ **moi** (*à mon avis, pour ma part*) for my part, personally; ~ **riche qu'il soit** rich though he may be; ~ **100 francs d'essence** 100 francs' worth of gas (*US*) *ou* petrol (*Brit*); ~ **cent** per cent; ~ **ce qui est de** as for; **y être** ~ **quelque chose** to have something to do with it.
pourboire [poōrbwár] *nm* tip.
pourcentage [poorsantazh] *nm* percentage; **travailler au** ~ to work on commission.
pourchasser [poōrshásá] *vt* to pursue.
pourfendeur [poōrfáńdœr] *nm* sworn opponent.
pourfendre [poōrfáńdr(ə)] *vt* to assail.
pourlécher [poōrlāshā]: **se ~** *vi* to smack one's lips.
pourparlers [poōrpárlā] *nmpl* talks, negotiations; **être en ~ avec** to be having talks with.
pourpre [poōrpr(ə)] *a* crimson.
pourquoi [poōrkwá] *ad, cj* why ♦ *nm inv*: **le ~ (de)** the reason (for).
pourrai [poōrā] *etc vb voir* **pouvoir**.
pourri, e [poōrē] *a* rotten; (*roche, pierre*) crumbling; (*temps, climat*) filthy, foul ♦ *nm*: **sentir le** ~ to smell rotten.
pourrir [poōrēr] *vi* to rot; (*fruit*) to go rotten *ou* bad; (*fig: situation*) to deteriorate ♦ *vt* to rot; (*fig: corrompre: personne*) to corrupt; (: *gâter: enfant*) to spoil thoroughly.
pourrissement [poōrēsmáń] *nm* deterioration.
pourriture [poōrētür] *nf* rot.
pourrons [poōróń] *etc vb voir* **pouvoir**.
poursuis [poōrsüē] *etc vb voir* **poursuivre**.
poursuite [poōrsüēt] *nf* pursuit, chase; **~s** *nfpl* (*JUR*) legal proceedings; **(course)** ~ track race; (*fig*) chase.
poursuivant, e [poōrsüēváń, -áńt] *vb voir* **poursuivre** ♦ *nm/f* pursuer; (*JUR*) plaintiff.
poursuivre [poōrsüēvr(ə)] *vt* to pursue, chase (after); (*relancer*) to hound, harry; (*obséder*) to haunt; (*JUR*) to bring proceedings against, prosecute; (: *au civil*) to sue; (*but*) to strive towards; (*voyage, études*) to carry on with, continue ♦ *vi* to carry on, go

on; **se ~** *vi* to go on, continue.
pourtant [poōrtáń] *ad* yet; **mais ~** but nevertheless, but even so; **c'est ~ facile** (and) yet it's easy.
pourtour [poōrtōōr] *nm* perimeter.
pourvoi [poōrvwá] *nm* appeal.
pourvoir [poōrvwár] *nm* (*COMM*) supply ♦ *vt*: ~ **qch/qn de** to equip sth/sb with ♦ *vi*: ~ **à** to provide for; (*emploi*) to fill; **se ~** (*JUR*): **se ~ en cassation** to take one's case to the Court of Appeal.
pourvoyeur, euse [poōrvwáyœr, -œz] *nm/f* supplier.
pourvu, e [poōrvü] *pp de* **pourvoir** ♦ *a*: ~ **de** equipped with; ~ **que** *cj* (*si*) provided that, so long as; (*espérons que*) let's hope (that).
pousse [poōs] *nf* growth; (*bourgeon*) shoot.
poussé, e [poōsā] *a* sophisticated, advanced; (*moteur*) souped-up.
pousse-café [poōskafa] *nm inv* (after-dinner) liqueur.
poussée [poōsā] *nf* thrust; (*coup*) push; (*MÉD*) eruption; (*fig*) upsurge.
pousse-pousse [poōspoōs] *nm inv* rickshaw.
pousser [poōsā] *vt* to push; (*inciter*): ~ **qn à** to urge *ou* press sb to + *infinitif*; (*acculer*): ~ **qn à** to drive sb to; (*moteur, voiture*) to drive hard; (*émettre: cri etc*) to give; (*stimuler*) to urge on; to drive hard; (*poursuivre*) to carry on ♦ *vi* to push; (*croître*) to grow; (*aller*): ~ **plus loin** to push on a bit further; **se ~** *vi* to move over; **faire ~** (*plante*) to grow; ~ **le dévouement** *etc* **jusqu'à ...** to take devotion *etc* as far as ....
poussette [poōset] *nf* (*voiture d'enfant*) stroller (*US*), pushchair (*Brit*).
poussette-canne, *pl* **poussettes-cannes** [poōsetkán] *nf* (folding) stroller (*US*), baby buggy (*Brit*).
poussier [poōsyā] *nm* coal dust.
poussière [poōsyer] *nf* dust; (*grain*) speck of dust; **et des ~s** (*fig*) and a bit; ~ **de charbon** coal dust.
poussiéreux, euse [poōsyárœ, -œz] *a* dusty.
poussif, ive [poōsēf, -ēv] *a* wheezy, wheezing.
poussin [poōsań] *nm* chick.
poussoir [poōswár] *nm* button.
poutre [poōtr(ə)] *nf* beam; (*en fer, ciment armé*) girder; **~s apparentes** exposed beams.
poutrelle [poōtrel] *nf* (*petite poutre*) small beam; (*barre d'acier*) girder.
pouvoir [poōvwár] *nm* power; (*POL: dirigeants*): **le ~** those in power, the government ♦ *vb + infinitif* can; (*suj: personne*) can, to be able to; (*permission*) can, may; (*probabilité, hypothèse*) may; **il peut arriver que** it may happen that; **il pourrait pleuvoir** it might rain; **déçu de ne pas** ~ **le faire** disappointed not to be able to do it *ou* that he *etc* couldn't do it; **il aurait pu le dire!** he could *ou* might have said!; **il se peut que** it may be that; **je n'en peux plus** (*épuisé*) I'm exhausted; (*accablé*) I can't take any more; **tu ne peux pas savoir!** you have no idea!; **tu peux le dire!** you can say that again!; **on ne peut mieux** as well as it is possible to; **donner** ~ **de faire qch** (*JUR*) to give proxy to

do sth; ~ **absolu** absolute power; ~ **d'achat** purchasing power; **les** ~**s publics** the authorities.

PP *sigle f* (= *préventive de la pellagre: vitamine*) niacin ♦ *abr* (= *pages*) pp.

p.p. *abr* (= *par procuration*) p.p.

p.p.c.m. *sigle m* (MATH: = *plus petit commun multiple*) LCM (= *lowest common multiple*).

PR *sigle m* = *Parti républicain* ♦ *sigle f* = **poste restante.**

pr *abr* = **pour.**

pragmatique [pràgmàtēk] *a* pragmatic.

Prague [pràg] *n* Prague.

prairie [prārē] *nf* meadow.

praline [pràlēn] *nf* (*bonbon*) sugared almond; (*au chocolat*) praline.

praliné, e [pràlēnā] *a* (*amande*) sugared; (*chocolat, glace*) praline *cpd*.

praticable [pràtēkábl(ə)] *a* (*route etc*) passable, practicable; (*projet*) practicable.

praticien, ne [pràtēsyañ, -en] *nm/f* practitioner.

pratiquant, e [pràtēkáñ, -áñt] *a* practicing (*US*), practising (*Brit*).

pratique [pràtēk] *nf* practice ♦ *a* practical; (*commode: horaire etc*) convenient; (: *outil*) handy, useful; **dans la** ~ in (actual) practice; **mettre en** ~ to put into practice.

pratiquement [pràtēkmáñ] *ad* (*dans la pratique*) in practice; (*pour ainsi dire*) practically, virtually.

pratiquer [pràtēkā] *vt* to practice (*US*), practise (*Brit*); (SPORT *etc*) to go (in for), play; (*appliquer: méthode, théorie*) to apply; (*intervention, opération*) to carry out; (*ouverture, abri*) to make ♦ *vi* (REL) to be a churchgoer.

pré [prā] *nm* meadow.

préalable [prāàlábl(ə)] *a* preliminary; **condition** ~ **(de)** precondition (for), prerequisite (for); **sans avis** ~ without prior *ou* previous notice; **au** ~ first, beforehand.

préalablement [prāàlábləmáñ] *ad* first, beforehand.

Préalpes [prāàlp(ə)] *nfpl*: **les** ~ the Pre-Alps.

préalpin, e [prāàlpañ, -ēn] *a* of the Pre-Alps.

préambule [prāáñbül] *nm* preamble; (*fig*) prelude; **sans** ~ straight away.

préau, x [prāō] *nm* (*d'une cour d'école*) covered playground; (*d'un monastère, d'une prison*) inner courtyard.

préavis [prāàvē] *nm* notice; ~ **de congé** notice; **communication avec** ~ (TÉL) person-to-person call.

prébende [prābáñd] *nf* (*péj*) remuneration.

précaire [prāker] *a* precarious.

précaution [prākōsyóñ] *nf* precaution; **avec** ~ cautiously; **prendre des** *ou* **ses** ~**s** to take precautions; **par** ~ as a precaution; **pour plus de** ~ to be on the safe side; ~**s oratoires** carefully phrased remarks.

précautionneux, euse [prākōsyonȫ, -ȫz] *a* cautious, careful.

précédemment [prāsādámáñ] *ad* before, previously.

précédent, e [prāsādáñ, -áñt] *a* previous ♦ *nm* precedent; **sans** ~ unprecedented; **le jour** ~ the day before, the previous day.

précéder [prāsādā] *vt* to precede; (*marcher ou*

rouler *devant*) to be in front of; (*arriver avant*) to get ahead of.

précepte [prāsept(ə)] *nm* precept.

précepteur, trice [prāsept̄cer, -trēs] *nm/f* (*private*) tutor.

préchauffer [prāshōfā] *vt* to preheat.

prêcher [prāshā] *vt, vi* to preach.

prêcheur, euse [preshœr, -ȫz] *a* moralizing ♦ *nm/f* (REL) preacher; (*fig*) moralizer.

précieusement [prāsyȫzmáñ] *ad* (*avec soin*) carefully; (*avec préciosité*) preciously.

précieux, euse [prāsyȫ, -ȫz] *a* precious; (*collaborateur, conseils*) invaluable; (*style, écrivain*) précieux, precious.

préciosité [prāsyōzētā] *nf* preciosity, preciousness.

précipice [prāsēpēs] *nm* drop, chasm; (*fig*) abyss; **au bord du** ~ at the edge of the precipice.

précipitamment [prāsēpētámáñ] *ad* hurriedly, hastily.

précipitation [prāsēpētâsyóñ] *nf* (*hâte*) haste; ~**s (atmosphériques)** *nfpl* precipitation *sg*.

précipité, e [prāsēpētā] *a* (*respiration*) fast; (*pas*) hurried; (*départ*) hasty.

précipiter [prāsēpētā] *vt* (*faire tomber*): ~ **qn/qch du haut de** to throw *ou* hurl sb/sth off *ou* from; (*hâter: marche*) to quicken; (: *départ*) to hasten; **se** ~ *vi* (*événements*) to move faster; (*respiration*) to speed up; **se** ~ **sur/vers** to rush at/towards; **se** ~ **au-devant de qn** to throw o.s. before sb.

précis, e [prāsē, -ēz] *a* precise; (*tir, mesures*) accurate, precise ♦ *nm* handbook.

précisément [prāsēzámáñ] *ad* precisely; **ma vie n'est pas** ~ **distrayante** my life is not exactly entertaining.

préciser [prāsēzā] *vt* (*expliquer*) to be more specific about, clarify; (*spécifier*) to state, specify; **se** ~ *vi* to become clear(er).

précision [prāsēzyóñ] *nf* precision; accuracy; (*détail*) point *ou* detail (*made clear or to be clarified*); ~**s** *nfpl* further details.

précoce [prākos] *a* early; (*enfant*) precocious; (*calvitie*) premature.

précocité [prākosētā] *nf* earliness; precociousness.

préconçu, e [prākóñsü] *a* preconceived.

préconiser [prākonēzā] *vt* to advocate.

précontraint, e [prākóñtrañ, -áñt] *a*: **béton** ~ prestressed concrete.

précuit, e [prāküē, -ēt] *a* precooked.

précurseur [prākürsœr] *am* precursory ♦ *nm* forerunner, precursor.

prédateur [prādátœr] *nm* predator.

prédécesseur [prādāsāsœr] *nm* predecessor.

prédestiner [prādestēnā] *vt*: ~ **qn à qch/à faire** to predestine sb for sth/to do.

prédicateur [prādēkátœr] *nm* preacher.

prédiction [prādēksyóñ] *nf* prediction.

prédilection [prādēleksyóñ] *nf*: **avoir une** ~ **pour** to be partial to; **de** ~ favorite (*US*), favourite (*Brit*).

prédire [prādēr] *vt* to predict.

prédisposer [prādēspōzā] *vt*: ~ **qn à qch/à faire** to predispose sb to sth/to do.

prédit, e [prādē, -ēt] *pp de* **prédire.**

prédominant, e [prādomēnáñ, -áñt] *a* predominant, prevailing.

prédominer [prādomēnā] *vi* to predominate; (*avis*) to prevail.

pré-électoral, e, aux [prāālektorál, -ō] *a* pre-election *cpd*.

pré-emballé, e [prāánbálā] *a* pre-packed.

prééminent, e [prāāmēnāń, -áńt] *a* pre-eminent.

préemption [prāáńpsyóń] *nf*: **droit de ~** (*JUR*) pre-emptive right.

pré-encollé, e [prāāńkolā] *a* pre-pasted.

préétabli, e [prāātáblē] *a* pre-established.

préexistant, e [prāegzēstáń, -áńt] *a* pre-existing.

préfabriqué, e [prāfábrēkā] *a* prefabricated; (*péj*: *sourire*) artificial ♦ *nm* prefabricated material.

préface [prāfásā] *nf* preface.

préfacer [prāfásā] *vt* to write a preface for.

préfectoral, e, aux [prāfektorál, -ō] *a* prefectorial.

préfecture [prāfektür] *nf* prefecture; **~ de police** police headquarters.

préférable [prāfārábl(ə)] *a* preferable.

préféré, e [prāfārā] *a*, *nm/f* favorite (*US*), favourite (*Brit*).

préférence [prāfāráńs] *nf* preference; **de ~** preferably; **de** *ou* **par ~ à** in preference to, rather than; **donner la ~ à qn** to give preference to sb; **par ordre de ~** in order of preference; **obtenir la ~ sur** to have preference over.

préférentiel, le [prāfāráńsyel] *a* preferential.

préférer [prāfārā] *vt*: **~ qn/qch (à)** to prefer sb/sth (to), like sb/sth better (than); **~ faire** to prefer to do; **je préférerais du thé** I would rather have tea, I'd prefer tea.

préfet [prāfe] *nm* prefect; **~ de police ~** Police Commissioner (*US*), ≈ Chief Constable (*Brit*).

préfigurer [prāfēgürā] *vt* to prefigure.

préfixe [prāfēks(ə)] *nm* prefix.

préhistoire [prāēstwár] *nf* prehistory.

préhistorique [prāēstorēk] *a* prehistoric.

préjudice [prāzhüdēs] *nm* (*matériel*) loss; (*moral*) harm *q*; **porter ~ à** to harm, be detrimental to; **au ~ de** at the expense of.

préjudiciable [prāzhüdēsyábl(ə)] *a*: **à** préjudicial *ou* harmful to.

préjugé [prāzhüzhā] *nm* prejudice; **avoir un ~ contre** to be prejudiced *ou* biased against; **bénéficier d'un ~ favorable** to be viewed favorably.

préjuger [prāzhüzhā]: **~ de** *vt* to prejudge.

prélasser [prālâsā]: **se ~** *vi* to lounge.

prélat [prālá] *nm* prelate.

prélavage [prālávázh] *nm* pre-wash.

prélèvement [prālevmáń] *nm* deduction; withdrawal; **faire un ~ de sang** to take a blood sample.

prélever [prālvā] *vt* (*échantillon*) to take; (*argent*): **~ (sur)** to deduct (from); (: *sur son compte*): **~ (sur)** to withdraw (from).

préliminaire [prālēmēnēr] *a* preliminary; **~s** *nmpl* preliminaries; (*négociations*) preliminary talks.

prélude [prālüd] *nm* prelude; (*avant le concert*) warm-up.

prématuré, e [prāmátürā] *a* premature; (*retraite*) early ♦ *nm* premature baby.

prématurément [prāmátürāmáń] *ad* prematurely.

préméditation [prāmādētâsyóń] *nf*: **avec ~** *a* premeditated ♦ *ad* with intent.

préméditer [prāmādētā] *vt* to premeditate, plan.

prémices [prāmēs] *nfpl* beginnings.

premier, ière [prəmyā, -yer] *a* first; (*branche, marche, grade*) bottom; (*fig: fondamental*) basic; prime; (*en importance*) first, foremost ♦ *nm* (**~ étage**) second (*US*) *ou* first (*Brit*) floor ♦ *nf* (*AUTO*) first (gear); (*RAIL, AVIAT etc*) first class; (*SCOL: classe*) penultimate school year (*age 16-17*); (*THÉÂTRE*) first night; (*CINÉMA*) première; (*exploit*) first; **au ~ abord** at first sight; **au ou du ~ coup** at the first attempt; **de ~ ordre** first-class, first-rate; **de première qualité, de ~ choix** best *ou* top quality; **de première importance** of the highest importance; **de première nécessité** absolutely essential; **le ~ venu** the first person to come along; **jeune ~** leading man; **le ~ de l'an** New Year's Day; **enfant du ~ lit** child of a first marriage; **en lieu** in the first place; **~ âge** (*d'un enfant*) the first 3 months (of life); **P~ Ministre** Prime Minister.

premièrement [prəmyermáń] *ad* firstly.

première-née, pl premières-nées [prəmyernā] *nf* firstborn.

premier-né, pl premiers-nés [prəmyānā] *nm* firstborn.

prémisse [prāmēs] *nf* premise.

prémolaire [prāmolēr] *nf* premolar.

prémonition [prāmonēsyóń] *nf* premonition.

prémonitoire [prāmonētwár] *a* premonitory.

prémunir [prāmünēr]: **se ~** *vt*: **se ~ contre** to protect o.s. from, guard against.

prenant, e [prənáń, -áńt] *vb voir* **prendre** ♦ *a* absorbing, engrossing.

prénatal, e [prānátál] *a* (*MÉD*) antenatal; (*allocation*) maternity *cpd*.

prendre [prándr(ə)] *vt* to take; (*ôter*): **~ qch à** to take sth from; (*aller chercher*) to get, fetch; (*se procurer*) to get; (*réserver: place*) to reserve; (*acquérir: du poids, de la valeur*) to put on, gain; (*malfaiteur, poisson*) to catch; (*passager*) to pick up; (*personnel, aussi: couleur, goût*) to take on; (*locataire*) to take in; (*traiter: enfant, problème*) to handle; (*voix, ton*) to put on; (*prélever: pourcentage, argent*) to take off; (*coincer*): **se ~ les doigts dans** to get one's fingers caught in ♦ *vi* (*liquide, ciment*) to set; (*greffe, vaccin*) to take; (*mensonge*) to be successful; (*feu: foyer*) to go; (: *incendie*) to start; (*allumette*) to light; (*se diriger*): **~ à gauche** to turn to the left; **~ son origine** *ou* **sa source** (*mot, rivière*) to have its source; **~ qn pour** to take sb for; **se ~ pour** to think one is; **~ sur soi de faire qch** to take it upon o.s. to do sth; **~ qn en sympathie/horreur** to get to like/loathe sb; **à tout ~** all things considered; **se ~ à** (*agresser*) to set about; (*passer sa colère sur*) to take it out on; (*critiquer*) to attack; (*remettre en question*) to challenge; **se ~ d'amitié/d'affection pour** to befriend/become fond of; **s'y ~** (*procéder*) to set about it; **s'y**

~ **à l'avance** to see to it in advance; **s'y** ~ **à deux fois** to try twice, make two attempts.
preneur [prənœr] *nm*: **être** ~ to be willing to buy; **trouver** ~ to find a buyer.
prénom [prānôṅ] *nm* first name.
prénommer [prānomā] *vt*: **elle se prénomme Claude** her (first) name is Claude.
prénuptial, e, aux [prānüpsyál, -ō] *a* premarital.
préoccupant, e [prāoküpāṅ, -âṅt] *a* worrying.
préoccupation [prāoküpâsyôṅ] *nf* (*souci*) concern; (*idée fixe*) preoccupation.
préoccupé, e [prāoküpā] *a* concerned; preoccupied.
préoccuper [prāoküpā] *vt* (*tourmenter, tracasser*) to concern; (*absorber, obséder*) to preoccupy; **se** ~ **de qch** to be concerned about sth; to show concern about sth.
préparateur, trice [prāpárátœr, -trēs] *nm/f* assistant.
préparatifs [prāpárátēf] *nmpl* preparations.
préparation [prāpárâsyôṅ] *nf* preparation; (*SCOL*) homework assignment.
préparatoire [prāpárátwár] *a* preparatory.
préparer [prāpárā] *vt* to prepare; (*café, repas*) to make; (*examen*) to prepare for; (*voyage, entreprise*) to plan; **se** ~ *vi* (*orage, tragédie*) to brew, be in the air; **se** ~ **(à qch/à faire)** to prepare (o.s.) *ou* get ready (for sth/to do); ~ **qch à qn** (*surprise etc*) to have sth in store for sb; ~ **qn à qch** (*nouvelle etc*) to prepare sb for sth.
prépondérant, e [prāpôṅdārâṅ, -âṅt] *a* major, dominating; **voix** ~**e** deciding vote.
préposé, e [prāpōzā] *a*: ~ **à** in charge of ♦ *nm/f* (*gén: employé*) employee; (*ADMIN: facteur*) mailman/woman (*US*), postman/woman (*Brit*); (*de la douane etc*) official; (*de vestiaire*) hatcheck person (*US*), attendant (*Brit*).
préposer [prāpōzā] *vt*: ~ **qn à qch** to appoint sb to sth.
préposition [prāpōzēsyôṅ] *nf* preposition.
préretraite [prārətret] *nf* early retirement.
prérogative [prārogátēv] *nf* prerogative.
près [pre] *ad* near, close; ~ **de** *prép* near (to), close to; (*environ*) nearly, almost; **de** ~ *ad* closely; **à 5 kg** ~ to within about 5 kg; **à cela** ~ **que** apart from the fact that; **je ne suis pas** ~ **de lui pardonner** I'm nowhere near ready to forgive him; **on n'est pas à un jour** ~ one day (either way) won't make any difference, we're not going to quibble over one day.
présage [prāzázh] *nm* omen.
présager [prāzázhā] *vt* (*prévoir*) to foresee; (*annoncer*) to portend.
pré-salé, pl prés-salés [prāsálā] *nm* (*CULIN*) salt-meadow lamb.
presbyte [presbēt] *a* farsighted, longsighted.
presbytère [presbēter] *nm* presbytery.
presbytérien, ne [presbētāryaṅ, -en] *a, nm/f* Presbyterian.
presbytie [presbēsē] *nf* farsightedness, longsightedness.
prescience [prāsyâṅs] *nf* prescience, foresight.
préscolaire [prāskoler] *a* preschool *cpd*.
prescription [preskrēpsyôṅ] *nf* (*instruction*) order, instruction; (*MÉD, JUR*) prescription.

prescrire [preskrēr] *vt* to prescribe; **se** ~ *vi* (*JUR*) to lapse.
prescrit, e [preskrē, -ēt] *pp de* **prescrire** ♦ *a* (*date etc*) stipulated.
préséance [prāsāâṅs] *nf* precedence *q*.
présélectionner [prāsāleksyonā] *vt* to preselect; (*dispositif*) to preset; (*candidats*) to screen (*US*), short-list (*Brit*).
présence [prāzâṅs] *nf* presence; (*au bureau etc*) attendance; **en** ~ face to face; **en** ~ **de** in (the) presence of; (*fig*) in the face of; **faire acte de** ~ to put in a token appearance; ~ **d'esprit** presence of mind.
présent, e [prāzâṅ, -âṅt] *a, nm* present; (*ADMIN, COMM*): **la** ~**e lettre/loi** this letter/law ♦ *nm/f*: **les** ~**s** (*personnes*) those present ♦ *nf* (*COMM: lettre*): **la** ~**e** this letter; **à** ~ now, at present; **dès à** ~ here and now; **jusqu'à** ~ up till now, until now; **à** ~ **que** now that.
présentateur, trice [prāzâṅtátœr, -trēs] *nm/f* (TV) announcer, presenter.
présentation [prāzâṅtâsyôṅ] *nf* presentation; introduction; (*allure*) appearance.
présenter [prāzâṅtā] *vt* to present; (*invité, candidat*) to introduce; (*félicitations, condoléances*) to offer; (*montrer: billet, pièce d'identité*) to show, produce; (*faire inscrire: candidat*) to put forward; (*soumettre*) to submit ♦ *vi*: ~ **mal/bien** to have an unattractive/a pleasing appearance; **se** ~ *vi* (*sur convocation*) to report, come; (*se faire connaître*) to come forward; (*à une élection*) to run (*US*), stand (*Brit*), be a candidate; (*occasion*) to arise; **se** ~ **à un examen** to take an exam; **se** ~ **bien/mal** to look good/not too good.
présentoir [prāsâṅtwár] *nm* (*étagère*) display shelf (*pl* shelves); (*vitrine*) showcase; (*étal*) display stand.
préservatif [prāzərvátēf] *nm* condom, prophylactic (*US*), sheath (*Brit*).
préservation [prāzervásyôṅ] *nf* protection, preservation.
préserver [prāzervā] *vt*: ~ **de** (*protéger*) to protect from; (*sauver*) to save from.
présidence [prāzēdâṅs] *nf* presidency; chairmanship.
président [prāzēdâṅ] *nm* (*POL*) president; (*d'une assemblée, COMM*) chairman; ~ **directeur général (PDG)** chairman and chief executive officer, ~ **du jury** (*JUR*) foreman of the jury; (*d'examen*) chairman (*US*), chief examiner (*Brit*).
présidente [prāzēdâṅt] *nf* president; (*femme du président*) president's wife; (*d'une réunion*) chairwoman.
présidentiable [prāzēdâṅsyábl(ə)] *a, nm/f* potential president.
présidentiel, le [prāzēdâṅsyel] *a* presidential; ~**les** *nfpl* presidential election(s).
présider [prāzēdā] *vt* to preside over; (*dîner*) to be the guest of honor (*US*) *ou* honour (*Brit*) at; ~ **à** *vt* to direct; to govern.
présomption [prāzôṅpsyôṅ] *nf* presumption.
présomptueux, euse [prāzôṅptüœ, -œz] *a* presumptuous.
presque [presk(ə)] *ad* almost, nearly; ~ **rien** hardly anything; ~ **pas** hardly (at all); ~

pas de hardly any; **personne, ou** ~ next to nobody, hardly anyone; **la** ~ **totalité (de)** almost *ou* nearly all.

presqu'île [preskēl] *nf* peninsula.

pressant, e [presáń, -áńt] *a* urgent; *(personne)* insistent; **se faire** ~ to become insistent.

presse [pres] *nf* press; *(affluence)*: **heures de** ~ busy times; **sous** ~ gone to press; **mettre sous** ~ to send to press; **avoir une bonne/ mauvaise** ~ to have a good/bad press; ~ **féminine** women's magazines *pl*; ~ **d'information** quality newspapers *pl*.

pressé, e [prāsā] *a* in a hurry; *(besogne)* urgent ♦ *nm*: **aller au plus** ~ to see to first things first; **être** ~ **de faire qch** to be in a hurry to do sth; **orange** ~**e** freshly squeezed orange juice.

presse-citron [pressētróń] *nm inv* lemon squeezer.

pressentiment [prāsáńtēmáń] *nm* foreboding, premonition.

pressentir [prāsáńtēr] *vt* to sense; *(prendre contact avec)* to approach.

presse-papiers [prespápyā] *nm inv* paperweight.

presse-purée [prespürā] *nm inv* potato masher.

presser [prāsā] *vt* *(fruit, éponge)* to squeeze; *(interrupteur, bouton)* to press, push; *(allure, affaire)* to speed up; *(débiteur etc)* to press; *(inciter)*: ~ **qn de faire** to urge *ou* press sb to do ♦ *vi* to be urgent; **se** ~ *(se hâter)* to hurry (up); *(se grouper)* to crowd; **rien ne presse** there's no hurry; **se** ~ **contre qn** to squeeze up against sb; ~ **le pas** to quicken one's step; ~ **qn entre ses bras** to squeeze sb tight.

pressing [prāsēng] *nm* *(repassage)* steampressing; *(magasin)* dry cleaner's.

pression [presyóń] *nf* pressure; *(bouton)* snap fastener; **faire** ~ **sur** to put pressure on; **sous** ~ pressurized, under pressure; *(fig)* keyed up; ~ **artérielle** blood pressure.

pressoir [preswár] *nm* (wine *ou* oil *etc*) press.

pressurer [prāsürā] *vt* *(fig)* to squeeze.

pressurisé, e [prāsürēzā] *a* pressurized.

prestance [prestáńs] *nf* presence, imposing bearing.

prestataire [prestáter] *nm/f* person receiving benefits; *(COMM)*: ~ **de services** provider of services.

prestation [prestásyóń] *nf* *(allocation)* benefit; *(d'une assurance)* coverage *q* *(US)*, cover *q* *(Brit)*; *(d'une entreprise)* service provided; *(d'un joueur, artiste)* performance; ~ **de serment** taking the oath; ~ **de service** provision of a service; ~**s familiales** ≈ child benefit.

preste [prest(ə)] *a* nimble.

prestement [prestəmáń] *ad* nimbly.

prestidigitateur, trice [prestēdēzhētátœr, -trēs] *nm/f* conjurer.

prestidigitation [prestēdēzhētásyóń] *nf* conjuring.

prestige [prestēzh] *nm* prestige.

prestigieux, euse [prestēzhyœ̄, -œ̄z] *a* prestigious.

présumer [prāzümā] *vt*: ~ **que** to presume *ou* assume that; ~ **de** to overrate; ~ **qn coupa-**

ble to presume sb guilty.

présupposé [prāsüpōzā] *nm* presupposition.

présupposer [prāsüpōzā] *vt* to presuppose.

présure [prāzür] *nf* rennet.

prêt, e [pre, pret] *a* ready ♦ *nm* lending *q*; *(somme prêtée)* loan; ~ **à faire** ready to do; ~ **à tout** ready for anything; ~ **sur gages** pawnbroking *q*.

prêt-à-porter, *pl* **prêts-à-porter** [pretáportā] *nm* ready-to-wear clothes *pl*.

prétendant [prātáńdáń] *nm* pretender; *(d'une femme)* suitor.

prétendre [prātáńdr(ə)] *vt* *(affirmer)*: ~ **que** to claim that; *(avoir l'intention de)*: ~ **faire qch** to mean *ou* intend to do sth; ~ **à** *vt* *(droit, titre)* to lay claim to.

prétendu, e [prātáńdü] *a* *(supposé)* so-called.

prétendument [prātáńdümáń] *ad* allegedly.

prête-nom [pretnóń] *nm* *(péj)* figurehead; *(COMM etc)* dummy.

prétentieux, euse [prātáńsyœ̄, -œ̄z] *a* pretentious.

prétention [prātáńsyóń] *nf* pretentiousness; *(exigence, ambition)* claim; **sans** ~ unpretentious.

prêter [prātā] *vt* *(livres, argent)*: ~ **qch (à)** to lend sth (to); *(supposer)*: ~ **à qn** *(caractère, propos)* to attribute to sb ♦ *vi* *(aussi:* **se** ~: *tissu, cuir)* to give; ~ **à** *(commentaires etc)* to be open to, give rise to; **se** ~ **à** to lend o.s. *(ou* itself) to; *(manigances etc)* to go along with; ~ **assistance à** to give help to; ~ **attention** to pay attention; ~ **serment** to take the oath; ~ **l'oreille** to listen.

prêteur, euse [pretœr, -œ̄z] *nm/f* moneylender; ~ **sur gages** pawnbroker.

prétexte [prātekst(ə)] *nm* pretext, excuse; **sous aucun** ~ on no account; **sous (le)** ~ **que/de** on the pretext that/of.

prétexter [prātekstā] *vt* to give as a pretext *ou* an excuse.

prêtre [pretr(ə)] *nm* priest.

prêtre-ouvrier, *pl* **prêtres-ouvriers** [pretrōōvrēyā] *nm* worker-priest.

prêtrise [pretrēz] *nf* priesthood.

preuve [prœv] *nf* proof; *(indice)* proof, evidence *q*; **jusqu'à** ~ **du contraire** until proved otherwise; **faire** ~ **de** to show; **faire ses** ~**s** to prove o.s. *(ou* itself); ~ **matérielle** material evidence.

prévaloir [prāválwár] *vi* to prevail; **se** ~ **de** *vt* to take advantage of; *(tirer vanité de)* to pride o.s. on.

prévarication [prāvárēkásyóń] *nf* maladministration.

prévaut [prāvō] *etc vb voir* **prévaloir**.

prévenances [prevnáńs] *nfpl* thoughtfulness *sg*, kindness *sg*.

prévenant, e [prevnáń, -áńt] *a* thoughtful, kind.

prévenir [prevnēr] *vt* *(avertir)*: ~ **qn (de)** to warn sb (about); *(informer)*: ~ **qn (de)** to tell *ou* inform sb (about); *(éviter)* to avoid, prevent; *(anticiper)* to anticipate; *(influencer)*: ~ **qn contre** to prejudice sb against.

préventif, ive [prāváńtēf, -ēv] *a* preventive.

prévention [prāváńsyóń] *nf* prevention; *(préjugé)* prejudice; *(JUR)* custody, detention; ~

routière road safety.

prévenu, e [prɛvnü] *nm/f* (*JUR*) defendant, accused.

prévisible [prāvēzēbl(ə)] *a* foreseeable.

prévision [prāvēzyôń] *nf*: ~**s** predictions; (*météorologiques, économiques*) forecast *sg*; **en** ~ **de** in anticipation of; ~**s météorologiques** *ou* **du temps** weather forecast *sg*.

prévisionnel, le [prāvēzyonel] *a* concerned with future requirements.

prévit [prāvē] *etc vb voir* **prévoir**.

prévoir [prāvwár] *vt* (*deviner*) to foresee; (*s'attendre à*) to expect, reckon on; (*prévenir*) to anticipate; (*organiser*) to plan; (*préparer, réserver*) to allow; **prévu pour 4 personnes** designed for 4 people; **prévu pour 10h** scheduled for 10 o'clock.

prévoyance [prāvwáyáńs] *nf* foresight; **société/caisse de** ~ provident society/ contingency fund.

prévoyant, e [prāvwáyáń, -áńt] *vb voir* **prévoir** ♦ *a* gifted with (*ou* showing) foresight, farsighted.

prévu, e [prāvü] *pp de* **prévoir**.

prier [prēyā] *vi* to pray ♦ *vt* (*Dieu*) to pray to; (*implorer*) to beg; (*demander*): ~ **qn de faire** to ask sb to do; (*inviter*): ~ **qn à dîner** to invite sb to dinner; **se faire** ~ to need coaxing *ou* persuading; **je vous en prie** (*allez-y*) please do; (*de rien*) don't mention it; **je vous prie de faire** please (would you) do.

prière [prēyer] *nf* prayer; (*demande instante*) plea, entreaty; "~ **de faire** ..." "please do ...".

primaire [prēmer] *a* primary; (*péj: personne*) simple-minded; (*: idées*) simplistic ♦ *nm* (*SCOL*) elementary (*US*) *ou* primary (*Brit*) education.

primauté [prēmōtā] *nf* (*fig*) primacy.

prime [prēm] *nf* (*bonification*) bonus; (*subside*) allowance; (*COMM: cadeau*) free gift; (*ASSURANCES, BOURSE*) premium ♦ *a*: **de** ~ **abord** at first glance; ~ **de risque** hazard pay *q* (*US*), danger money *q* (*Brit*); ~ **de transport** travel allowance.

primer [prēmā] *vt* (*l'emporter sur*) to prevail over; (*récompenser*) to award a prize to ♦ *vi* to dominate, prevail.

primesautier, ière [prēmsōtyā, -yer] *a* impulsive.

primeur [prēmœr] *nf*: **avoir la** ~ **de** to be the first to hear (*ou* see *etc*); ~**s** *nfpl* (*fruits, légumes*) early fruits and vegetables; **marchand de** ~ produce dealer (*US*), greengrocer (*Brit*).

primevère [prēmver] *nf* primrose.

primitif, ive [prēmētēf, -ēv] *a* primitive; (*original*) original ♦ *nm/f* primitive.

primo [prēmō] *ad* first (of all), firstly.

primordial, e, aux [prēmordyál, -ō] *a* essential, primordial.

prince [prańs] *nm* prince; ~ **charmant** Prince Charming; ~ **de Galles** *nm inv* (*tissu*) check cloth; ~ **héritier** crown prince.

princesse [prańses] *nf* princess.

princier, ière [prańsyā, -yer] *a* princely.

principal, e, aux [prańsēpál, -ō] *a* principal,

main ♦ *nm* (*SCOL*) principal (*US*), head(teacher) (*Brit*); (*essentiel*) main thing ♦ *nf* (*LING*): **(proposition)** ~**e** main clause.

principalement [prańsēpálmáń] *ad* principally, mainly.

principauté [prańsēpōtā] *nf* principality.

principe [prańsēp] *nm* principle; **partir du** ~ **que** to work on the principle *ou* assumption that; **pour le** ~ on principle, for the sake of it; **de** ~ *a* (*hostilité*) automatic; (*accord*) in principle; **par** ~ on principle; **en** ~ (*habituellement*) as a rule; (*théoriquement*) in principle.

printanier, ière [prańtányā, -yer] *a* spring *cpd*; spring-like.

printemps [prańtáń] *nm* spring; **au** ~ in spring.

priori [prēyorē]: **a** ~ *ad* at first glance; initially; a priori.

prioritaire [prēyorēter] *a* having priority; (*AUTO*) having right of way; (*INFORM*) foreground.

priorité [prēyorētā] *nf* (*AUTO*): **avoir la** ~ **(sur)** to have right of way (over); ~ **à droite** right of way to vehicles coming from the right; **en** ~ as a (matter of) priority.

pris, e [prē, prēz] *pp de* **prendre** ♦ *a* (*place*) taken; (*billets*) sold; (*journée, mains*) full; (*personne*) busy; (*crème, ciment*) set; (*MÉD: enflammé*): **avoir le nez/la gorge** ~**e**) to have a stuffy nose/a bad throat; (*saisi*): **être** ~ **de peur/de fatigue** to be stricken with fear/overcome with fatigue.

prise [prēz] *nf* (*d'une ville*) capture; (*PÊCHE, CHASSE*) catch; (*de judo ou catch, point d'appui ou pour empoigner*) hold; (*ÉLEC: fiche*) plug; (*: femelle*) socket; (*: au mur*) (wall) outlet (*US*), point (*Brit*); **en** ~ (*AUTO*) in gear; **être aux** ~**s avec** to be grappling with; to be battling with; **lâcher** ~ to let go; **donner** ~ **à** (*fig*) to give rise to; **avoir** ~ **sur qn** to have a hold over sb; ~ **en charge** (*taxi*) ≈ minimum fare; (*par la sécurité sociale*) undertaking to reimburse costs; ~ **de contact** initial meeting, first contact; ~ **de courant** outlet (*US*), power point (*Brit*); ~ **d'eau** hydrant, water (supply) point; tap; ~ **multiple** adaptor; ~ **d'otages** hostagetaking; ~ **à partie** (*JUR*) action against a judge; ~ **de sang** blood test; ~ **de son** sound recording; ~ **de tabac** pinch of snuff; ~ **de terre** earth; ~ **de vue** (*photo*) shot; (*action*): ~ **de vue(s)** filming, shooting.

priser [prēzā] *vt* (*tabac, héroïne*) to take; (*estimer*) to prize, value ♦ *vi* to take snuff.

prisme [prēsm(ə)] *nm* prism.

prison [prēzôń] *nf* prison; **aller/être en** ~ to go to/be in prison *ou* jail; **faire de la** ~ to serve time; **être condamné à 5 ans de** ~ to be sentenced to 5 years' imprisonment *ou* 5 years in prison.

prisonnier, ière [prēzonyā, -yer] *nm/f* prisoner ♦ *a* captive; **faire qn** ~ to take sb prisoner.

prit [prē] *vb voir* **prendre**.

privatif, ive [prēvátēf, -ēv] *a* (*jardin etc*) private; (*peine*) which deprives one of one's liberties.

privations [prēvâsyôń] *nfpl* privations, hardships.

privatisation [prēvătēzâsyôñ] *nf* privatization.
privatiser [prēvătēzā] *vt* to privatize.
privautés [prēvōtā] *nfpl* liberties.
privé, e [prēvā] *a* private; (*dépourvu*): ~ **de** without, lacking; **en ~, dans le ~** in private.
priver [prēvā] *vt:* ~ **qn de** to deprive sb of; **se ~ de** to go *ou* do without; **ne pas se ~ de faire** not to refrain from doing.
privilège [prēvēlezh] *nm* privilege.
privilégié, e [prēvēlāzhyā] *a* privileged.
privilégier [prēvēlāzhyā] *vt* to favor (*US*), favour (*Brit*).
prix [prē] *nm* (*valeur*) price; (*récompense*, *SCOL*) prize; **mettre à ~** to set an upset (*US*) *ou* a reserve (*Brit*) price on; **au ~ fort** at a very high price; **acheter qch à ~ d'or** to pay a (small) fortune for sth; **hors de ~** exorbitantly priced; **à aucun ~** not at any price; **à tout ~** at all costs; **grand ~** (*SPORT*) Grand Prix; ~ **d'achat/de vente/de revient** purchasing/selling/cost price; ~ **conseillé** manufacturer's recommended price (MRP).
pro [prō] *nm* (= *professionnel*) pro.
probabilité [prŏbăbēlētā] *nf* probability; **selon toute ~** in all probability.
probable [prŏbábl(ɔ)] *a* likely, probable.
probablement [prŏbáblǝmáň] *ad* probably.
probant, e [prŏbáň, -áňt] *a* convincing.
probatoire [prŏbátwár] *a* (*examen*, *test*) preliminary; (*stage*) probationary, trial *cpd*.
probité [prŏbētā] *nf* integrity, probity.
problématique [prŏblămátēk] *a* problematic(al) ♦ *nf* problematics *sg*; (*problème*) problem.
problème [problem] *nm* problem.
procédé [prŏsādā] *nm* (*méthode*) process; (*comportement*) behavior *q* (*US*), behaviour *q* (*Brit*).
procéder [prŏsādā] *vi* to proceed; to behave; ~ **à** *vt* to carry out.
procédure [prŏsādür] *nf* (*ADMIN*, *JUR*) procedure.
procès [prose] *nm* (*JUR*) trial; (*: poursuites*) proceedings *pl*; **être en ~ avec** to be involved in a lawsuit with; **faire le ~ de qn/qch** (*fig*) to put sb/sth on trial; **sans autre forme de ~** without further ado.
processeur [prŏsásœr] *nm* processor.
procession [prŏsásyôñ] *nf* procession.
processus [prŏsásüs] *nm* process.
procès-verbal, aux [prŏseverbál, -ō] *nm* (*constat*) statement; (*aussi*: **PV**): **avoir un ~** to get a parking ticket; (*de réunion*) minutes *pl*.
prochain, e [prŏsháñ, -en] *a* next; (*proche*) impending; near ♦ *nm* fellow man; **la ~e fois/semaine** ~e next time/week; **à la ~e!** (*fam*), **à la ~e fois** see you!, till the next time!; **un ~ jour** (some day) soon.
prochainement [proshenmáñ] *ad* soon, shortly.
proche [prosh] *a* nearby; (*dans le temps*) imminent; close at hand; (*parent, ami*) close; ~**s** *nmpl* (*parents*) close relatives, next of kin; (*amis*): **l'un de ses ~s** one of those close to him (*ou* her); **être ~ (de)** to be near, be close (to); **de ~ en ~** gradually.
Proche-Orient [proshoryáñ] *nm:* **le ~** the Near East.

proclamation [proklámâsyôñ] *nf* proclamation.
proclamer [proklámā] *vt* to proclaim; (*résultat d'un examen*) to announce.
procréer [prokrāā] *vt* to procreate.
procuration [prokürásyôñ] *nf* proxy; power of attorney; **voter par ~** to vote by proxy.
procurer [prokürā] *vt* (*fournir*): ~ **qch à qn** to get *ou* obtain sth for sb; (*causer: plaisir etc*): ~ **qch à qn** to bring *ou* give sb sth; **se ~** *vt* to get.
procureur [prokürœr] *nm* public prosecutor; ~ **général** attorney general (*US*), public prosecutor (*in appeal court*) (*Brit*).
prodigalité [prodēgálētā] *nf* (*générosité*) generosity; (*extravagance*) extravagance, wastefulness.
prodige [prodēzh] *nm* (*miracle, merveille*) marvel, wonder; (*personne*) prodigy.
prodigieux, euse [prodēzhyœ̄, -œ̄z] *a* prodigious; phenomenal.
prodigue [prodēg] *a* (*généreux*) generous; (*dépensier*) extravagant, wasteful; **fils ~** prodigal son.
prodiguer [prodēgā] *vt* (*argent, biens*) to lavish with; (*soins, attentions*): ~ **qch à qn** to lavish sth on sb.
producteur, trice [prodüktœr, -trēs] *a:* ~ **de blé** wheat-producing; (*CINÉMA*): **société productrice** film *ou* movie company ♦ *nm/f* producer.
productif, ive [prodüktēf, ēv] *a* productive.
production [prodüksyôñ] *nf* (*gén*) production; (*rendement*) output; (*produits*) products *pl*, goods *pl*; (*œuvres*): **la ~ dramatique du XVIIe siècle** the plays of the 17th century.
productivité [prodüktēvētā] *nf* productivity.
produire [prodüēr] *vt, vi* to produce; **se ~** *vi* (*acteur*) to perform, appear; (*événement*) to happen, occur.
produit, e [prodüē, -ēt] *pp de* **produire** ♦ *nm* (*gén*) product; ~ **d'entretien** cleaning product; ~ **national brut** (**PNB**) gross national product (GNP); ~ **net** net profit; ~ **pour la vaisselle** dish-washing (*US*) *ou* washing-up (*Brit*) liquid; ~ **des ventes** income from sales; ~**s agricoles** farm produce *sg*; ~**s alimentaires** foodstuffs; ~**s de beauté** beauty products, cosmetics.
proéminent, e [proāmēnáñ, -áñt] *a* prominent.
prof [prof] *nm* (*fam*: = *professeur*) teacher; professor; lecturer.
prof. [prof] *abr* = **professeur, professionnel.**
profane [profán] *a* (*REL*) secular; (*ignorant, non initié*) uninitiated ♦ *nm/f* layman.
profaner [profánā] *vt* to desecrate; (*fig: sentiment*) to defile; (*: talent*) to debase.
proférer [profārā] *vt* to utter.
professer [profāsā] *vt* to profess.
professeur [profāsœr] *nm* teacher; (*titulaire d'une chaire*) professor; ~ **(de faculté)** instructor (*US*), (university) lecturer (*Brit*).
profession [profēsyôñ] *nf* (*libérale*) profession; (*gén*) occupation; **faire ~ de** (*opinion, religion*) to profess; **de ~** by profession; **"sans ~"** "unemployed"; (*femme mariée*) "housewife".
professionnel, le [profesyonel] *a* professional ♦ *nm/f* professional; (*ouvrier qualifié*) skilled

worker.

professoral, e, aux [profɛsɔrál, -ō] *a* professorial; **le corps** ~ the teaching profession.

professorat [profɛsɔrá] *nm*: **le** ~ the teaching profession.

profil [profēl] *nm* profile; (*d'une voiture*) line, contour; **de** ~ in profile.

profilé, e [profēlā] *a* shaped; (*aile etc*) streamlined.

profiler [profēlā] *vt* to streamline; **se** ~ *vi* (*arbre, tour*) to stand out, be silhouetted.

profit [profē] *nm* (*avantage*) benefit, advantage; (*COMM, FINANCE*) profit; **au** ~ **de** in aid of; **tirer** *ou* **retirer** ~ **de** to profit from; **mettre à** ~ to take advantage of; to turn to good account; ~**s et pertes** (*COMM*) profit and loss(es).

profitable [profētábl(ə)] *a* beneficial; profitable.

profiter [profētá] *vi*: ~ **de** to take advantage of; to make the most of; ~ **de ce que** ... to take advantage of the fact that ...; ~ **à** to be of benefit to, benefit; to be profitable to.

profiteur, euse [profētœr, -ēz] *nm/f* (*péj*) profiteer.

profond, e [profōṅ, -ôṅd] *a* deep; (*méditation, mépris*) profound; **au plus** ~ **de** in the depths of, at the (very) bottom of; **la France** ~**e** the heartlands of France.

profondément [profôṅdāmáṅ] *ad* deeply; profoundly.

profondeur [profôṅdœr] *nf* depth.

profusément [profüzāmáṅ] *ad* profusely.

profusion [profüzyôṅ] *nf* profusion; **à** ~ in plenty.

progéniture [prɔzhānētür] *nf* offspring *inv*.

progiciel [prɔzhēsyel] *nm* (*INFORM*) (software) package; ~ **d'application** applications package, applications software *q*.

progouvernemental, e, aux [progōōvernəmáṅtál, -ō] *a* pro-government *cpd*.

programmable [prográmábl(ə)] *a* programmable.

programmateur, trice [prográmátœr, -trēs] *nm/f* (*CINÉMA, TV*) program (*US*) *ou* programme (*Brit*) planner ♦ *nm* (*de machine à laver etc*) timer.

programmation [prográmâsyôṅ] *nf* programming.

programme [prográm] *nm* program (*US*), programme (*Brit*); (*TV, RADIO*) program(me)s *pl*; (*SCOL*) syllabus, curriculum; (*INFORM*) program; **au** ~ **de ce soir** (*TV*) among tonight's program(me)s.

programmé, e [prográmā] *a*: **enseignement** ~ programmed learning.

programmer [prográmā] *vt* (*TV, RADIO*) to put on, show; (*organiser, prévoir*) to schedule; (*INFORM*) to program.

programmeur, euse [prográmœr, -ēz] *nm/f* (computer) programmer.

progrès [progrɛ] *nm* progress *q*; **faire des/être en** ~ to make/be making progress.

progresser [progrāsā] *vi* to progress; (*troupes etc*) to make headway *ou* progress.

progressif, ive [progrāsēf, -ēv] *a* progressive.

progression [progrāsyôṅ] *nf* progression;

(*d'une troupe etc*) advance, progress.

progressiste [progrāsēst(ə)] *a* progressive.

progressivement [progrāsēvmáṅ] *ad* progressively.

prohiber [proēbā] *vt* to prohibit, ban.

proie [prwá] *nf* prey *q*; **être la** ~ **de** to fall prey to; **être en** ~ **à** (*doutes, sentiment*) to be prey to; (*douleur, mal*) to be suffering.

projecteur [prozhektœr] *nm* projector; (*de théâtre, cirque*) spotlight.

projectile [prozhektēl] *nm* missile; (*d'arme*) projectile, bullet (*ou* shell *etc*).

projection [prozheksyôṅ] *nf* projection; showing; **conférence avec** ~**s** lecture with slides (*ou* a film).

projectionniste [prozheksyonēst(ə)] *nm/f* (*CINÉMA*) projectionist.

projet [prozhe] *nm* plan; (*ébauche*) draft; **faire des** ~**s** to make plans; ~ **de loi** bill.

projeter [prozhtā] *vt* (*envisager*) to plan; (*film, photos*) to project; (*passer*) to show; (*ombre, lueur*) to throw, cast, project; (*jeter*) to throw up (*ou* off *ou* out); ~ **de faire qch** to plan to do sth.

prolétaire [prolāter] *a, nm/f* proletarian.

prolétariat [prolātáryá] *nm* proletariat.

proliférer [prolēfārā] *vi* to proliferate.

prolifique [prolēfēk] *a* prolific.

prolixe [prolēks(ə)] *a* verbose.

prolo [prolō] *nm/f* (*fam*) = **prolétaire**.

prologue [prolog] *nm* prologue.

prolongateur [prolôṅgátœr] *nm* (*ÉLEC*) extension cable.

prolongation [prolôṅgásyôṅ] *nf* prolongation; extension; ~**s** *nfpl* (*FOOTBALL*) overtime *sg* (*US*), extra time *sg* (*Brit*).

prolongement [prolôṅzhmáṅ] *nm* extension; ~**s** *nmpl* (*fig*) repercussions, effects; **dans le** ~ **de** running on from.

prolonger [prolôṅzhā] *vt* (*débat, séjour*) to prolong; (*délai, billet, rue*) to extend; (*suj: chose*) to be a continuation *ou* an extension of; **se** ~ *vi* to go on.

promenade [promnád] *nf* walk (*ou* drive *ou* ride); **faire une** ~ to go for a walk; **une** ~ (**à pied)/en voiture/à vélo** a walk/drive/(bicycle) ride.

promener [promnā] *vt* (*personne, chien*) to take out for a walk; (*fig*) to carry around; (*doigts, regard*): ~ **qch sur** to run sth over; **se** ~ *vi* (*à pied*) to go for (*ou* be out for) a walk; (*en voiture*) to go for (*ou* be out for) a drive; (*fig*): **se** ~ **sur** to wander over.

promeneur, euse [promnœr, -ēz] *nm/f* walker, stroller.

promenoir [promənwár] *nm* gallery, (covered) walkway.

promesse [promes] *nf* promise; ~ **d'achat** commitment to buy.

prometteur, euse [prometœr, -ēz] *a* promising.

promettre [prometr(ə)] *vt* to promise ♦ *vi* (*récolte, arbre*) to look promising; (*enfant, musicien*) to be promising; **se** ~ **de faire** to resolve *ou* mean to do; ~ **à qn de faire** to promise sb that one will do.

promeus [promœ] *etc vb voir* **promouvoir**.

promis, e [promē, -ēz] *pp de* **promettre** ♦ *a*: **être** ~ **à qch** (*destiné*) to be destined for sth.

promiscuité [promēsküētā] *nf* crowding; lack of privacy.

promit [promē] *vb voir* **promettre**.

promontoire [promôntwár] *nm* headland.

promoteur, trice [promotœr, -trēs] *nm/f* (*instigateur*) instigator, promoter; ~ (**immobilier**) real estate promoter (*US*), property developer (*Brit*).

promotion [promosyôn] *nf* (*avancement*) promotion; (*SCOL*) class; **en** ~ (*COMM*) on special (offer) (*US*) *ou* (special) offer (*Brit*).

promotionnel, le [promosyonel] *a* (*article*) on special (offer) (*US*) *ou* (special) offer (*Brit*); (*vente*) promotional.

promouvoir [promōōvwár] *vt* to promote.

prompt, e [prôn, prônt] *a* swift, rapid; (*intervention, changement*) sudden; ~ **à faire qch** quick to do sth.

prompteur [prôntœr] *nm* ® teleprompter ®.

promptitude [prôntētüd] *nf* swiftness, rapidity.

promu, e [promü] *pp de* **promouvoir**.

promulguer [promülgā] *vt* to promulgate.

prôner [prōnā] *vt* (*louer*) to laud, extol; (*préconiser*) to advocate, commend.

pronom [pronôn] *nm* pronoun.

pronominal, e, aux [pronomēnál, -ō] *a* pronominal; (*verbe*) reflexive, pronominal.

prononcé, e [pronônsā] *a* pronounced, marked.

prononcer [pronônsā] *vt* (*son, mot, jugement*) to pronounce; (*dire*) to utter; (*allocution*) to deliver ♦ *vi* (*JUR*) to deliver *ou* give a verdict; ~ **bien/mal** to have a good/poor pronunciation; **se** ~ *vi* to reach a decision, give a verdict; **se** ~ **sur** to give an opinion on; **se** ~ **contre** to come down against; **ça se prononce comment?** how do you pronounce this?

prononciation [pronônsyâsyôn] *nf* pronunciation.

pronostic [pronostēk] *nm* (*MÉD*) prognosis (*pl* -oses); (*fig: aussi*: ~**s**) forecast.

pronostiquer [pronostēkā] *vt* (*MÉD*) to prognosticate; (*annoncer, prévoir*) to forecast, foretell.

pronostiqueur, euse [pronostēkœr, -œz] *nm/f* forecaster.

propagande [propágând] *nf* propaganda; **faire de la** ~ **pour qch** to plug *ou* push sth.

propager [propázhā] *vt* to spread; **se** ~ *vi* to spread; (*PHYSIQUE*) to be propagated.

propane [propán] *nm* propane.

propension [propânsyôn] *nf*: ~ **à (faire) qch** propensity to (do) sth.

prophète [profet], **prophétesse** [profātes] *nm/f* prophet(ess).

prophétie [profāsē] *nf* prophecy.

prophétiser [profātēzā] *vt* to prophesy.

prophylactique [profēláktēk] *a* prophylactic.

propice [propēs] *a* favorable (*US*), favourable (*Brit*).

proportion [proporsyôn] *nf* proportion; **il n'y a aucune** ~ **entre le prix demandé et le prix réel** the asking price bears no relation to the real price; **à** ~ **de** proportionally to, in proportion to; **en** ~ **(de)** in proportion (to); **hors de** ~ out of proportion; **toute(s)** ~**(s) gardée(s)** making due allowance(s).

proportionné, e [proporsyonā] *a*: **bien** ~ well-proportioned; ~ **à** proportionate to.

proportionnel, le [proporsyonel] *a* proportional; ~ **à** proportional to.

proportionner [proporsyonā] *vt*: ~ **qch à** to proportion *ou* adjust sth to.

propos [propō] *nm* (*paroles*) talk *q*, remark; (*intention, but*) intention, aim; (*sujet*): **à quel** ~? what about?; **à** ~ **de** about, regarding; **à tout** ~ for no reason at all; **à ce** ~ on that subject, in this connection; **à** ~ *ad* by the way; (*opportunément*) (just) at the right moment; **hors de** ~, **mal à** ~ *ad* at the wrong moment.

proposer [propōzā] *vt* (*suggérer*): ~ **qch (à qn)/de faire** to suggest sth (to sb)/doing, propose sth (to sb)/to do; (*offrir*): ~ **qch à qn/de faire** to offer sb sth/to do; (*candidat*) to nominate, put forward; (*loi, motion*) to propose; **se** ~ **(pour faire)** to offer one's services (to do); **se** ~ **de faire** to intend *ou* propose to do.

proposition [propōzēsyôn] *nf* suggestion; proposal; offer; (*LING*) clause; **sur la** ~ **de** at the suggestion of; ~ **de loi** private bill.

propre [propr(ə)] *a* clean; (*net*) neat, tidy; (*qui ne salit pas: chien, chat*) house-broken; (: *enfant*) toilet-trained; (*fig: honnête*) honest; (*possessif*) own; (*sens*) literal; (*particulier*): ~ **à** peculiar to, characteristic of; (*approprié*): ~ **à** suitable *ou* appropriate for; (*de nature à*): ~ **à faire** likely to do, that will do ♦ *nm*: **recopier au** ~ to make a fair copy of; (*particularité*): **le** ~ **de** the peculiarity of, the distinctive feature of; **au** ~ (*LING*) literally; **appartenir à qn en** ~ to belong to sb (exclusively); ~ **à rien** *nm/f* (*péj*) good-for-nothing.

proprement [propromân] *ad* cleanly; neatly, tidily; **à** ~ **parler** strictly speaking; **le village** ~ **dit** the actual village, the village itself.

propret, te [propre, -et] *a* neat and tidy, spick-and-span.

propreté [proprətā] *nf* cleanliness, cleanness; neatness, tidiness.

propriétaire [proprēyāter] *nm/f* owner; (*d'hôtel etc*) proprietor/tress, owner; (*pour le locataire*) landlord/lady; ~ (**immobilier**) house owner; householder; ~ (**récoltant**) grower; ~ (**terrien**) landowner.

propriété [proprēyātā] *nf* (*droit*) ownership; (*objet, immeuble etc*) property *gén q*; (*villa*) residence, property; (*terres*) property *gén q*, land *gén q*; (*qualité, CHIMIE, MATH*) property; (*correction*) appropriateness, suitability; ~ **artistique et littéraire** artistic and literary copyright; ~ **industrielle** patent rights *pl*.

propulser [propülsā] *vt* (*missile*) to propel; (*projeter*) to hurl, fling.

propulsion [propülsyôn] *nf* propulsion.

prorata [prorátá] *nm inv*: **au** ~ **de** in proportion to, on the basis of.

prorogation [prorogâsyôn] *nf* deferment; extension; adjournment.

proroger [prorozhā] *vt* to postpone, defer; (*prolonger*) to extend; (*assemblée*) to adjourn, prorogue.

prosaïque [prōzáēk] *a* mundane, prosaic.

proscription [proskrēpsyóń] *nf* banishment; (*interdiction*) banning; prohibition.

proscrire [proskrēr] *vt* (*bannir*) to banish; (*interdire*) to ban, prohibit.

prose [prōz] *nf* prose (*style*).

prosélyte [prozālēt] *nm/f* proselyte, convert.

prospecter [prospektā] *vt* to prospect; (*COMM*) to canvass.

prospecteur-placier, *pl* **prospecteurs-placiers** [prospektœrplásyā] *nm* placement officer.

prospectif, ive [prospektēf, -ēv] *a* prospective.

prospectus [prospektüs] *nm* (*feuille*) leaflet; (*dépliant*) brochure, leaflet.

prospère [prosper] *a* prosperous; (*santé, entreprise*) thriving, flourishing.

prospérer [prospārā] *vi* to thrive.

prospérité [prospārētā] *nf* prosperity.

prostate [prostát] *nf* prostate (gland).

prosterner [prosternā]: **se** ~ *vi* to bow low, prostrate o.s.

prostituée [prostētüā] *nf* prostitute.

prostitution [prostētüsyóń] *nf* prostitution.

prostré, e [prostrā] *a* prostrate.

protagoniste [protágonēst(ə)] *nm* protagonist.

protecteur, trice [protektœr, -trēs] *a* protective; (*air, ton: péj*) patronizing ♦ *nm/f* (*défenseur*) protector; (*des arts*) patron.

protection [proteksyóń] *nf* protection; (*d'un personnage influent: aide*) patronage; **écran de** ~ protective screen; ~ **civile** state-financed civilian rescue service; ~ **maternelle et infantile (PMI)** social service concerned with child welfare.

protectionniste [proteksyonēst(ə)] *a* protectionist.

protégé, e [protázhā] *nm/f* protégé/e.

protège-cahier [protezhkáyā] *nm* notebook cover.

protéger [protázhā] *vt* to protect; (*aider, patronner: personne, arts*) to be a patron of; (*: carrière*) to further; **se** ~ **de/contre** to protect o.s. from.

protéine [protáēn] *nf* protein.

protestant, e [protestáń, -áńt] *a, nm/f* Protestant.

protestantisme [protestáńtēsm(ə)] *nm* Protestantism.

protestataire [protestáter] *nm/f* protestor.

protestation [protestásyóń] *nf* (*plainte*) protest; (*déclaration*) protestation, profession.

protester [protestā] *vi*: ~ **(contre)** to protest (against *ou* about); ~ **de** (*son innocence, sa loyauté*) to protest.

prothèse [protez] *nf* artificial limb, prosthesis (*pl* -ses); ~ **dentaire** (*appareil*) denture; (*science*) dental engineering.

protocolaire [protokoler] *a* formal; (*questions, règles*) of protocol.

protocole [protokol] *nm* protocol; (*fig*) etiquette; ~ **d'accord** draft treaty; ~ **opératoire** (*MÉD*) operating procedure.

prototype [prototēp] *nm* prototype.

protubérance [protübāráńs] *nf* bulge, protuberance.

protubérant, e [protübāráń, -áńt] *a* protruding, bulging, protuberant.

proue [prōō] *nf* bow(s *pl*), prow.

prouesse [prōōes] *nf* feat.

prouver [prōōvā] *vt* to prove.

provenance [provnáńs] *nf* origin; (*de mot, coutume*) source; **avion en** ~ **de** plane (arriving) from.

provençal, e, aux [provâńsál, -ō] *a* Provençal ♦ *nm* (*LING*) Provençal.

Provence [provâńs] *nf*: **la** ~ Provence.

provenir [provnēr]: ~ **de** *vt* to come from; (*résulter de*) to be due to, be the result of.

proverbe [proverb(ə)] *nm* proverb.

proverbial, e, aux [proverbyál, -ō] *a* proverbial.

providence [provēdáńs] *nf*: **la** ~ providence.

providentiel, le [provēdáńsyel] *a* providential.

province [provâńs] *nf* province.

provincial, e, aux [provâńsyál, -ō] *a, nm/f* provincial.

proviseur [provēzœr] *nm* ≈ principal (*US*), ≈ head(teacher) (*Brit*).

provision [provēzyóń] *nf* (*réserve*) stock, supply; (*avance: à un avocat, avoué*) retainer, retaining fee; (*COMM*) funds *pl* (in account); reserve; ~**s** *nfpl* (*vivres*) provisions, food *q*; **faire** ~ **de** to stock up with; **placard** *ou* **armoire à** ~**s** food closet (*US*) *ou* cupboard (*Brit*).

provisoire [provēzwár] *a* temporary; (*JUR*) provisional; **mise en liberté** ~ release on bail.

provisoirement [provēzwàrmáń] *ad* temporarily, for the time being.

provocant, e [provokáń, -áńt] *a* provocative.

provocateur, trice [provokátœr, -trēs] *a* provocative ♦ *nm* (*meneur*) agitator.

provocation [provokásyóń] *nf* provocation.

provoquer [provokā] *vt* (*défier*) to provoke; (*causer*) to cause, bring about; (*: curiosité*) to arouse, give rise to; (*: aveux*) to prompt, elicit; (*inciter*): ~ **qn à** to incite sb to.

prox. *abr* = **proximité**.

proxénète [proksánet] *nm* procurer.

proximité [proksēmētā] *nf* nearness, closeness, proximity; (*dans le temps*) imminence, closeness; **à** ~ near *ou* close by; **à** ~ **de** near (to), close to.

prude [prüd] *a* prudish.

prudemment [prüdámáń] *ad* (*voir prudent*) carefully; cautiously; prudently; wisely, sensibly.

prudence [prüdáńs] *nf* carefulness; caution; prudence; **avec** ~ carefully; cautiously; wisely; **par (mesure de)** ~ as a precaution.

prudent, e [prüdáń, -áńt] *a* (*pas téméraire*) careful, cautious, prudent; (*: en général*) safety-conscious; (*sage, conseillé*) wise, sensible; (*réservé*) cautious; **ce n'est pas** ~ it's risky; it's not sensible; **soyez** ~ take care, be careful.

prune [prün] *nf* plum.

pruneau, x [prünō] *nm* prune.

prunelle [prünel] *nf* pupil; (*œil*) eye; (*BOT*) sloe; (*eau de vie*) sloe gin.

prunier [prünyā] *nm* plum tree.

PS *sigle m* = *Parti socialiste*; (= *post-scriptum*) PS.

psalmodier [psàlmodyā] *vt* to chant; (*fig*) to drone out.

psaume [psōm] *nm* psalm.

pseudonyme [psɛ̃donɛ̃m] *nm* (*gén*) fictitious name; (*d'écrivain*) pseudonym, pen name; (*de comédien*) stage name.

PSIG *sigle m* (= *Peloton de surveillance et d'intervention de gendarmerie*) *type of police commando squad.*

PSU *sigle m* = *Parti socialiste unifié.*

psy [psɛ] *nm/f* (*fam, péj:* = *psychiatre, psychologue*) shrink.

psychanalyse [psɛ̃kánálɛz] *nf* psychoanalysis.

psychanalyser [psɛ̃kánálɛzá] *vt* to psychoanalyze; **se faire** ~ to undergo (psycho)analysis.

psychanalyste [psɛ̃kánálɛst(ə)] *nm/f* psychoanalyst.

psychédélique [psɛ̃kádálɛk] *a* psychedelic.

psychiatre [psɛ̃kyátr(ə)] *nm/f* psychiatrist.

psychiatrie [psɛ̃kyátrɛ] *nf* psychiatry.

psychiatrique [psɛ̃kyátrɛk] *a* psychiatric; (*hôpital*) mental, psychiatric.

psychique [psɛ̃shɛk] *a* psychological.

psychisme [psɛ̃shɛsm(ə)] *nm* psyche.

psychologie [psɛ̃kolozhɛ] *nf* psychology.

psychologique [psɛ̃kolozhɛk] *a* psychological.

psychologue [psɛ̃koloɡ] *nm/f* psychologist; **être** ~ (*fig*) to be a good psychologist.

psychopathe [psɛ̃kopát] *nm/f* psychopath.

psychopédagogie [psɛ̃kopádágozhɛ] *nf* educational psychology.

psychose [psɛ̃kōz] *nf* (*MÉD*) psychosis (*pl* -ses); (*obsession, idée fixe*) obsessive fear.

psychosomatique [psɛ̃kosomátɛk] *a* psychosomatic.

psychothérapie [psɛ̃kotárápɛ] *nf* psychotherapy.

psychotique [psɛ̃kotɛk] *a* psychotic.

PTCA *sigle m* = *poids total en charge autorisé.*

Pte *abr* = **Porte**.

pte *abr* (= *pointe*) pt.

PTMA *sigle m* (= *poids total maximum autorisé*) maximum loaded weight.

PTT *sigle fpl voir* **poste**.

pu [pü] *pp de* **pouvoir**.

puanteur [püáṅtœr] *nf* stink, stench.

pub [püb] *nf* (*fam:* - *publicité*): **la** ~ advertising.

pubère [püber] *a* pubescent.

puberté [pübertá] *nf* puberty.

pubis [pübɛs] *nm* (*bas-ventre*) pubes *pl*; (*os*) pubis.

public, ique [püblɛk] *a* public; (*école, instruction*) state *cpd*; (*scrutin*) open ♦ *nm* public; (*assistance*) audience; **en** ~ in public; **le grand** ~ the general public.

publication [püblɛkâsyôṅ] *nf* publication.

publiciste [püblɛsɛst(ə)] *nm/f* adman.

publicitaire [püblɛsɛter] *a* advertising *cpd*; (*film, voiture*) publicity *cpd*; (*vente*) promotional ♦ *nm* adman; **rédacteur** ~ copywriter.

publicité [püblɛsɛtá] *nf* (*méthode, profession*) advertising; (*annonce*) advertisement; (*révélations*) publicity.

publier [püblɛyá] *vt* to publish; (*nouvelle*) to publicize, make public.

publipostage [püblɛpostázh] *nm* mailing.

publique [püblɛk] *af voir* **public**.

publiquement [püblɛkmáṅ] *ad* publicly.

puce [püs] *nf* flea; (*INFORM*) chip; (**marché aux**) ~s flea market *sg*; **mettre la** ~ à

l'oreille de qn to give sb something to think about.

puceau, x [püsō] *am:* **être** ~ to be a virgin.

pucelle [püsɛl] *af:* **être** ~ to be a virgin.

puceron [püsrôṅ] *nm* aphid.

pudeur [püdœr] *nf* modesty.

pudibond, e [püdēbôṅ, -ôṅd] *a* prudish.

pudique [püdɛk] *a* (*chaste*) modest; (*discret*) discreet.

puer [püá] (*péj*) *vi* to stink ♦ *vt* to stink of, reek of.

puéricultrice [püárɛkültrɛs] *nf* ≈ nursery nurse.

puériculture [püárɛkültür] *nf* infant care.

puéril, e [püárɛl] *a* childish.

pugilat [püzhɛla] *nm* (*fist*) fight.

puis [püɛ] *vb voir* **pouvoir** ♦ *ad* (*ensuite*) then; (*dans une énumération*) next; (*en outre*): **et** ~ **and** (then); **et** ~ (**après** *ou* **quoi**)? so (what)?

puisard [püɛzár] *nm* (*égout*) cesspool.

puiser [püɛzá] *vt:* ~ (**dans**) to draw (from); ~ **dans qch** to dip into sth.

puisque [püɛsk(ə)] *cj* since; (*valeur intensive*): ~ **je te le dis!** I'm telling you!

puissamment [püɛsámáṅ] *ad* powerfully.

puissance [püɛsáṅs] *nf* power; **en** ~ *a* potential; **2 (à la)** ~ **5** 2 to the power (of) 5.

puissant, e [püɛsáṅ, -áṅt] *a* powerful.

puisse [püɛs] *etc vb voir* **pouvoir**.

puits [püɛ] *nm* well; ~ **artésien** artesian well; ~ **de mine** mine shaft; ~ **de science** font of knowledge.

pull(-over) [pül(ovœr)] *nm* sweater.

pulluler [pülülá] *vi* to swarm; (*fig: erreurs*) to abound, proliferate.

pulmonaire [pülmonɛr] *a* lung *cpd*; (*artère*) pulmonary.

pulpe [pülp(ə)] *nf* pulp.

pulsation [pülsâsyôṅ] *nf* (*MÉD*) beat.

pulsion [pülsyôṅ] *nf* (*PSYCH*) drive, urge.

pulvérisateur [pülvárɛzátœr] *nm* spray.

pulvérisation [pülvárɛzásyôṅ] *nf* spraying.

pulvériser [pülvárɛzá] *vt* (*solide*) to pulverize; (*liquide*) to spray; (*fig: anéantir: adversaire*) to pulverize; (: *record*) to smash, shatter; (: *argument*) to demolish.

puma [pümá] *nm* puma, cougar.

punaise [pünɛz] *nf* (*ZOOL*) bug; (*clou*) thumbtack (*US*), drawing pin (*Brit*).

punch [pôṅsh] *nm* (*boisson*) punch; [pœnsh] (*BOXE*) punching ability; (*fig*) punch.

punching-ball [pœnshɛ̃ṅgbōl] *nm* punching bag.

punir [pünɛr] *vt* to punish; ~ **qn de qch** to punish sb for sth.

punitif, ive [pünɛtɛf, -ɛv] *a* punitive.

punition [pünɛsyôṅ] *nf* punishment.

pupille [püpɛy] *nf* (*ANAT*) pupil ♦ *nm/f* (*enfant*) ward; ~ **de l'État** ward of the state *ou* court (*US*), child in care (*Brit*); ~ **de la Nation** war orphan.

pupitre [püpɛtr(ə)] *nm* (*SCOL*) desk; (*REL*) lectern; (*de chef d'orchestre*) podium; (*INFORM*) console; ~ **de commande** control panel.

pupitreur, euse [püpɛtrœr, -œz] *nm/f* (*INFORM*) (computer) operator, keyboarder.

pur, e [pür] *a* pure; (*vin*) undiluted; (*whisky*)

neat; (*intentions*) honorable (*US*), honourable (*Brit*) ♦ *nm* (*personne*) hard-liner; **en** ~**e perte** fruitlessly, to no avail.

purée [pürā] *nf*: ~ **(de pommes de terre)** ≈ mashed potatoes *pl*; ~ **de marrons** chestnut purée; ~ **de pois** (*fig*) pea soup.

purement [pürmáṅ] *ad* purely.

pureté [pürtā] *nf* purity.

purgatif [pürgàtēf] *nm* purgative, purge.

purgatoire [pürgàtwár] *nm* purgatory.

purge [pürzh(ə)] *nf* (*POL*) purge; (*MÉD*) purging *q*; purge.

purger [pürzhā] *vt* (*radiateur*) to flush (out), drain; (*circuit hydraulique*) to bleed; (*MÉD*, *POL*) to purge; (*JUR*: *peine*) to serve.

purifier [pürēfyā] *vt* to purify; (*TECH*: *métal*) to refine.

purin [püraṅ] *nm* liquid manure.

puriste [pürēst(ə)] *nm/f* purist.

puritain, e [püritaṅ, -en] *a*, *nm/f* Puritan.

puritanisme [püritánēsm(ə)] *nm* Puritanism.

pur-sang [pürsáṅ] *nm inv* thoroughbred, pure-bred.

purulent, e [pürüláṅ, -áṅt] *a* purulent.

pus [pü] *vb voir* **pouvoir** ♦ *nm* pus.

pusillanime [püzēlánēm] *a* fainthearted.

putain [pütaṅ] *nf* (*fam!*) whore (*!*); **ce/cette** ~ **de ...** this goddamn (*US*) *ou* bloody (*Brit*) ... (*!*).

putois [pütwà] *nm* polecat; **crier comme un** ~ to yell one's head off.

putréfier [pütrāfyā] *vt*, **se** ~ *vi* to putrefy, rot.

putride [pütrēd] *a* putrid.

puzzle [pœzl(ə)] *nm* jigsaw (puzzle).

PV *sigle m* = **procès-verbal**.

PVC *sigle f* (= *polychlorure de vinyle*) PVC.

PVD *sigle mpl* (= *pays en voie de développement*) developing countries.

Px *abr* = **prix**.

pygmée [pēgmā] *nm* pygmy.

pyjama [pēzhàmá] *nm* pajamas *pl* (*US*), pyjamas *pl* (*Brit*), pair of pajamas *ou* pyjamas.

pylône [pēlōn] *nm* pylon.

pyramide [pērámēd] *nf* pyramid.

pyrénéen, ne [pērānáäṅ, -en] *a* Pyrenean.

Pyrénées [pērānā] *nfpl*: **les** ~ the Pyrenees.

pyrex [pēreks] *nm* ® Pyrex ®.

pyrogravure [pērogràvür] *nf* poker-work.

pyromane [pēromán] *nm/f* arsonist.

python [pētóṅ] *nm* python.

Q

Q, q [kü] *nm inv* Q, q ♦ *abr* (= *quintal*) q; **Q comme Quintal** Q for Queen.

Qatar [kàtár] *nm*: **le** ~ Qatar.

QCM *sigle fpl* (= *questions à choix multiples*) multiple choice *sg*.

QG *sigle m* (= *quartier général*) HQ.

QHS *sigle m* (= *quartier de haute sécurité*) high-security wing *ou* prison.

QI *sigle m* (= *quotient intellectuel*) IQ.

qqch. *abr* (= *quelque chose*) sth.

qqe(s) *abr* = **quelque(s)**.

qqn *abr* (= *quelqu'un*) sb., s.o.

quadragénaire [kàdràzhāner] *nm/f* (*de quarante ans*) forty-year-old; (*de quarante à cinquante ans*) man/woman in his/her forties.

quadrangulaire [kwàdráṅgüler] *a* quadrangular.

quadrature [kwàdrátür] *nf*: **c'est la** ~ **du cercle** it's like trying to square the circle.

quadrichromie [kwàdrēkromē] *nf* four-color (*US*) *ou* -colour (*Brit*) printing.

quadrilatère [k(w)àdrēláter] *nm* (*GÉOM*, *MIL*) quadrilateral; (*terrain*) four-sided area.

quadrillage [kàdrēyàzh] *nm* (*lignes etc*) square pattern, crisscross pattern.

quadrillé, e [kàdrēyā] *a* (*papier*) squared.

quadriller [kàdrēyā] *vt* (*papier*) to mark out in squares; (*POLICE*: *ville*, *région etc*) to keep under tight control, be positioned throughout.

quadrimoteur [k(w)àdrēmotœr] *nm* four-engined plane.

quadripartite [kwàdrēpártēt] *a* (*entre pays*) four-power; (*entre partis*) four-party.

quadriphonie [kàdrēfonē] *nf* quadraphony.

quadriréacteur [k(w)àdrērāàktœr] *nm* four-engined jet.

quadrupède [k(w)àdrüped] *nm* quadruped.

quadruple [k(w)àdrüpl(ə)] *nm*: **le** ~ **de** four times as much as.

quadrupler [k(w)àdrüplā] *vt*, *vi* to quadruple, increase fourfold.

quadruplés, ées [k(w)àdrüplā] *nm/fpl* quadruplets, quads.

quai [kā] *nm* (*de port*) quay; (*de gare*) platform; (*de cours d'eau*, *canal*) embankment; **être à** ~ (*navire*) to be alongside; (*train*) to be in the station; **le Q**~ **d'Orsay** offices of the French Ministry for Foreign Affairs; **le Q**~ **des Orfèvres** central police headquarters.

qualifiable [kàlēfyábl(ə)] *a*: **ce n'est pas** ~ it defies description.

qualificatif, ive [kàlēfēkàtēf, -ēv] *a* (*LING*) qualifying ♦ *nm* (*terme*) term; (*LING*) qualifier.

qualification [kàlēfēkàsyóṅ] *nf* qualification.

qualifier [kàlēfyā] *vt* to qualify; (*appeler*): ~ **qch/qn de** to describe sth/sb as; **se** ~ *vi* (*SPORT*) to qualify; **être qualifié pour** to be qualified for.

qualitatif, ive [kàlētàtēf, -ēv] *a* qualitative.

qualité [kàlētā] *nf* quality; (*titre*, *fonction*) position; **en** ~ **de** in one's capacity as; **ès** ~**s** in an official capacity; **avoir** ~ **pour** to have authority to; **de** ~ *a* quality *cpd*; **rapport** ~-**prix** value (for money).

quand [káṅ] *cj*, *ad* when; ~ **je serai riche** when I'm rich; ~ **même** (*cependant*, *pourtant*) nevertheless; (*tout de même*) all the same; really; ~ **bien même** even though.

quant [káṅ]: ~ **à** *prép* (*pour ce qui est de*) as for, as to; (*au sujet de*) regarding.

quant-à-soi [káṅtáswá] *nm*: **rester sur son** ~ to remain aloof.

quantième [káṅtyem] *nm* date, day (of the month).

quantifiable [káṅtēfyábl(ə)] *a* quantifiable.

quantifier [káṅtēfyā] *vt* to quantify.

quantitatif, ive [kântētâtēf, -ēv] *a* quantitative.

quantitativement [kântētâtēvmân] *ad* quantitatively.

quantité [kântētā] *nf* quantity, amount; (*SCIENCE*) quantity; (*grand nombre*): **une** *ou* **des ~(s) de** a great deal of; a lot of; **en grande ~** in large quantities; **en ~s industrielles** in vast amounts; **du travail en ~** a great deal of work; **~ de** many.

quarantaine [kârânten] *nf* (*isolement*) quarantine; (*âge*): **avoir la ~** to be around forty; (*nombre*): **une ~ (de)** forty or so, about forty; **mettre en ~** to put into quarantine; (*fig*) to ostracize.

quarante [kârânt] *num* forty.

quarantième [kârântyem] *num* fortieth.

quart [kâɪ] *nm* (*fraction*) quarter; (*surveillance*) watch; (*partie*): **un ~ de poulet/fromage** a chicken quarter/a quarter of a cheese; **un ~ de beurre** a quarter kilo of butter, ≈ a half pound of butter; **un ~ de vin** a quarter liter of wine; **une livre un ~** *ou* **et ~** one and a quarter pounds; **le ~ de** a quarter of; **~ d'heure** quarter of an hour; **2h et** *ou* **un ~** (a) quarter past two, (a) quarter after two (*US*); **il est le ~** it's (a) quarter past *ou* after (*US*); **1h moins le ~** (a) quarter to one, (a) quarter of one (*US*); **il est moins le ~** it's (a) quarter to; **être de/ prendre le ~** to keep/take the watch; **~ de tour** quarter turn; **au ~ de tour** (*fig*) straight off; **~s de finale** (*SPORT*) quarter finals.

quarté [kârtā] *nm* (*COURSES*) *system of forecast betting giving first four horses.*

quarternaire [kwâterner] *a* (*GÉO*) Quaternary.

quarteron [kârtərôñ] *nm* (*péj*) small bunch, handful.

quartette [kwârtet] *nm* quartet(te).

quartier [kârtyā] *nm* (*de ville*) district, area; (*de bœuf, de la lune*) quarter; (*de fruit, fromage*) piece; **~s** *nmpl* (*MIL, BLASON*) quarters; **cinéma/salle de ~** local cinema/ hall; **avoir ~ libre** to be free; (*MIL*) to have leave from barracks; **ne pas faire de ~** to spare no one, give no quarter; **~ commerçant/résidentiel** shopping/residential area; **~ général (QG)** headquarters (HQ).

quartier-maître [kârtyāmetr(ə)] *nm* ≈ leading seaman.

quartz [kwârts] *nm* quartz.

quasi [kâzē] *ad* almost, nearly ♦ *préfixe*: **~- certitude** near certainty.

quasiment [kâzēmâñ] *ad* almost, very nearly.

quatorze [kâtorz(ə)] *num* fourteen.

quatorzième [kâtorzyem] *num* fourteenth.

quatrain [kâtrañ] *nm* quatrain.

quatre [kâtr(ə)] *num* four; **à ~ pattes** on all fours; **tiré à ~ épingles** dressed up to the nines; **faire les ~ cent coups** to be a bit wild; **se mettre en ~ pour qn** to go out of one's way for sb; **~ à ~** (*monter, descendre*) four at a time; **à ~ mains** (*jouer*) four-handed.

quatre-vingt-dix [kâtrəvañdēs] *num* ninety.

quatre-vingts [kâtrəvañ] *num* eighty.

quatrième [kâtrēyem] *num* fourth.

quatuor [kwâtüor] *nm* quartet(te).

que [kə] *cj* (*gén*) that; (*après comparatif*)

than; as: *voir* **plus, aussi, autant** *etc*; (*seulement*): **ne ... ~** only; **il sait ~ tu es là** he knows (that) you're here; **je veux ~ tu acceptes** I want you to accept; **il a dit ~ oui** he said he would (*ou* it was *etc*, *suivant le contexte*); **si vous y allez ou ~ vous lui téléphoniez** if you go there or (if you) phone him; **quand il rentrera et qu'il aura mangé** when he gets back and (when he) has eaten; **qu'il le veuille ou non** whether he likes it or not; **tenez-le qu'il ne tombe pas** hold it so (that) it doesn't fall; **qu'il fasse ce qu'il voudra** let him do as he pleases; **il ne boit ~ de l'eau** he only drinks water; *voir* **avant, pour, tel, à peine** *etc* ♦ *ad*: **qu'il** *ou* **qu'est-ce qu'il est bête/court vite** he's so silly/he runs so fast; **~ de** what a lot of ♦ *pronom*: **l'homme ~ je vois** the man (whom) I see; **le livre ~ tu vois** the book (that *ou* which) you see; **un jour ~ j'étais** a day when I was; **c'est une erreur ~ de croire** it's a mistake to believe; **qu'est-ce que c'est?** (*ceci*) what is it?; (*cela*) what's that?; **~ fais-tu?, qu'est-ce ~ tu fais?** what are you doing?; **~ préfères-tu, celui-ci ou celui-là?** which do you prefer, this one or that one?; **~ faire?** what can one do?

Québec [kâbek] *n* (*ville*) Quebec ♦ *nm*: **le ~** Quebec (Province).

québécois, e [kâbākwâ, -wáz] *a* Quebec *cpd* ♦ *nm* (*LING*) Quebec French ♦ *nm/f*: **Q~, e** Quebecois, Quebec(k)er.

quel, quelle [kel] *a*: **~ livre/homme?** what book/man?; (*parmi un certain choix*) which book/man?; **~ est cet homme?** who is this man?; **~ est ce livre?** what is this book?; **~ est le plus petit?** which is the smallest?; **~s acteurs préférez-vous?** which actors do you prefer?; **dans ~s pays êtes-vous allé?** which *ou* what countries did you go to?; **~le surprise!** what a surprise!; **~ que soit le coupable** whoever is guilty; **~ que soit votre avis** whatever your opinion; whichever is your opinion.

quelconque [kelkôñk] *a* (*médiocre*) indifferent, poor; (*sans attrait*) ordinary, plain; (*indéfini*): **un ami/prétexte ~** some friend/ pretext or other; **un livre ~ suffira** any book will do; **pour une raison ~** for some reason (or other).

quelque [kelk(ə)] *dét* some; a few, *tournure interrogative* + any ♦ *ad* (*environ*): **~ 100 mètres** some 100 meters; **~ espoir** some hope; **il a ~s amis** he has a few *ou* some friends; **a-t-il ~s amis?** has he any friends?; **les ~s livres qui** the few books which; **~ livre qu'il choisisse** whatever (*ou* whichever) book he chooses; **20 kg et ~(s)** a bit over 20 kg; **~ chose** something, *tournure interrogative* + anything; **~ chose d'autre** something else; anything else; **~ part** somewhere; **~ peu** rather, somewhat; **en ~ sorte** as it were.

quelquefois [kelkəfwâ] *ad* sometimes.

quelques-uns, -unes [kelkəzœñ, -ün] *pronom* some, a few; **~ des lecteurs** some of the readers.

quelqu'un [kelkœñ] *pronom* someone, somebody, *tournure interrogative ou négative* + anyone *ou* anybody; **~ d'autre** someone *ou*

somebody else; anybody else.
quémander [kŭmâṅdâ] *vt* to beg for.
qu'en dira-t-on [kâṅdērâtôṅ] *nm inv*: le ~
gossip, what people say.
quenelle [kǝnel] *nf* quenelle.
quenouille [kǝnōōy] *nf* distaff.
querelle [kǝrel] *nf* quarrel; **chercher ~ à qn**
to pick a quarrel with sb.
quereller [kǝrālā]: **se ~** *vi* to quarrel.
querelleur, euse [kǝrelœr, -œz] *a* quarrelsome.
qu'est-ce que (*ou* qui) [keskǝ(kē)] *voir* que,
qui.
question [kestyôṅ] *nf* (*gén*) question; (*fig*)
matter; issue; **il a été ~ de** we (*ou* they)
spoke about; **il est ~ de les emprisonner**
there's talk of them being jailed; **c'est une ~
de temps** it's a matter *ou* question of time;
de quoi est-il ~? what is it about?; **il n'en
est pas ~** there's no question of it; **en ~** in
question; **hors de ~** out of the question; **je
ne me suis jamais posé la ~** I've never
thought about it; **(re)mettre en ~** (*autorité,
science*) to question; **poser la ~ de
confiance** (*POL*) to ask for a vote of confidence; **~ piège** (*d'apparence facile*) trick
question; (*pour nuire*) loaded question; **~
subsidiaire** tiebreaker.
questionnaire [kestyoner] *nm* questionnaire.
questionner [kestyonā] *vt* to question.
quête [ket] *nf* (*collecte*) collection; (*recherche*) quest, search; **faire la ~** (*à l'église*)
to take the collection; (*artiste*) to pass the
hat around; **se mettre en ~ de qch** to go in
search of sth.
quêter [kātā] *vi* (*à l'église*) to take the collection; (*dans la rue*) to collect money (for
charity) ♦ *vt* to seek.
quetsche [kwetsh(ǝ)] *nf* damson.
queue [kœ] *nf* tail; (*fig: du classement*)
bottom; (*: de poêle*) handle; (*: de fruit,
feuille*) stalk; (*: de train, colonne, file*) rear;
(*file: de personnes*) line (*US*), queue (*Brit*);
en ~ (**de train**) at the rear (of the train);
faire la ~ to line up (*US*), queue (up) (*Brit*);
se mettre à la ~ to join the line (*US*) *ou*
queue (*Brit*); **histoire sans ~ ni tête** cock
and bull story; **à la ~ leu leu** in single file;
(*fig*) one after the other; **~ de cheval** ponytail; **~ de poisson: faire une ~ de poisson
à qn** (*AUTO*) to cut in front of sb; **finir en ~
de poisson** (*film*) to come to an abrupt end.
queue-de-pie, *pl* **queues-de-pie** [kœdpē] *nf*
(*habit*) tails *pl*, tail coat.
queux [kœ] *am voir* **maître**.
qui [kē] *pronom* (*personne*) who, *prép* +
whom; (*chose, animal*) which, that;
(*interrogatif indirect: sujet*): **je me demande
~ est là?** I wonder who is there?; (*: objet*):
elle ne sait à ~ se plaindre she doesn't know
who to complain to *ou* to whom to complain;
qu'est-ce ~ est sur la table? what is on the
table?; **à ~ est ce sac?** whose bag is this?; **à
~ parlais-tu?** who were you talking to?, to
whom were you talking?; **chez ~ allez-vous?**
whose house are you going to?; **amenez ~
vous voulez** bring who(ever) you like; **~
est-ce ~ ...?** who?; **~ est-ce que ...?** who?;
whom?; **~ que ce soit** whoever it may be.
quiche [kēsh] *nf* quiche; **~ lorraine** quiche

Lorraine.
quiconque [kēkôṅk] *pronom* (*celui qui*) whoever, anyone who; (*n'importe qui, personne*)
anyone, anybody.
quidam [kŭēdám] *nm* (*hum*) fellow.
quiétude [kyātüd] *nf* (*d'un lieu*) quiet,
tranquillity; (*d'une personne*) peace (of
mind), serenity; **en toute ~** in complete
peace; (*mentale*) with complete peace of
mind.
quignon [kēnyôṅ] *nm*: **~ de pain** (*croûton*)
crust of bread; (*morceau*) hunk of bread.
quille [kēy] *nf* ninepin; (*NAVIG: d'un bateau*)
keel; (**jeu de**) **~s** ninepins *sg*.
quincaillerie [kaṅkâyrē] *nf* (*ustensiles, métier*)
hardware; (*magasin*) hardware store (*US*) *ou*
shop (*Brit*).
quincaillier, ière [kaṅkâyâ, -yer] *nm/f* hardware dealer, ironmonger (*Brit*).
quinconce [kaṅkôṅs] *nm*: **en ~** in staggered
rows.
quinine [kēnēn] *nf* quinine.
quinquagénaire [kaṅkázhāner] *nm/f* (*de
cinquante ans*) fifty-year old; (*de cinquante à
soixante ans*) man/woman in his/her fifties.
quinquennal, e, aux [kaṅkānál, -ō] *a* five-
year, quinquennial.
quintal, aux [kaṅtál, -ō] *nm* quintal (*100 kg*).
quinte [kaṅt] *nf*: **~ (de toux)** coughing fit.
quintessence [kaṅtāsâṅs] *nf* quintessence,
very essence.
quintette [kaṅtet] *nm* quintet(te).
quintuple [kaṅtüpl(ǝ)] *nm*: **le ~ de** five times
as much as.
quintupler [kaṅtüplā] *vt, vi* to increase five-
fold.
quintuplés, ées [kantüpla] *nm/fpl* quintuplets,
quins.
quinzaine [kaṅzen] *nf*: **une ~ (de)** about
fifteen, fifteen or so; **une ~ (de jours)** (*deux
semaines*) two weeks; **~ publicitaire** *ou*
commerciale (two-week) sale.
quinze [kaṅz] *num* fifteen; **demain en ~** two
weeks tomorrow; **dans ~ jours** in two
weeks(' time).
quinzième [kaṅzyem] *num* fifteenth.
quiproquo [kēprokō] *nm* (*méprise sur une
personne*) mistake; (*malentendu sur un
sujet*) misunderstanding; (*THÉÂTRE*) (case
of) mistaken identity.
Quito [kētō] *n* Quito.
quittance [kētâṅs] *nf* (*reçu*) receipt; (*facture*)
bill.
quitte [kēt] *a*: **être ~ envers qn** to be no longer in sb's debt; (*fig*) to be quits with sb; **être
~ de** (*obligation*) to be clear of; **en être ~ à
bon compte** to have got off lightly; **~ à faire**
even if it means doing; **~ ou double** (*jeu*)
double or nothing (*US*), double or quits
(*Brit*); (*fig*): **c'est du ~ ou double** it's a big
risk.
quitter [kētā] *vt* to leave; (*espoir, illusion*) to
give up; (*vêtement*) to take off; **se ~** (*cou-
ples, interlocuteurs*) to part; **ne quittez pas**
(*au téléphone*) hold the line; **ne pas ~ qn
d'une semelle** to stick to sb like glue.
quitus [kētüs] *nm* final discharge; **donner ~ à**
to discharge.
qui-vive [kēvēv] *nm inv*: **être sur le ~** to be

on the alert.

quoi [kwȧ] *pronom* (*interrogatif*) what; ~ **de neuf** *ou* **de nouveau?** what's new *ou* the news?; **as-tu de** ~ **écrire?** have you anything to write with?; **il n'a pas de** ~ **se l'acheter** he can't afford it, he hasn't got the money to buy it; **il y a de** ~ **être fier** that's something to be proud of; **"il n'y a pas de** ~**"** "(please) don't mention it", "not at all"; ~ **qu'il arrive** whatever happens; ~ **qu'il en soit** be that as it may; ~ **que ce soit** anything at all; **en** ~ **puis-je vous aider?** how can I help you?; **à** ~ **bon?** what's the use *ou* point?; **et puis** ~ **encore!** what(ever) next!; ~ **faire?** what's to be done?; **sans** ~ (*ou sinon*) otherwise.

quoique [kwȧk(ə)] *cj* (al)though.

quolibet [kolēbe] *nm* gibe, jeer.

quorum [korom] *nm* quorum.

quota [kwotȧ] *nm* quota.

quote-part [kotpȧr] *nf* share.

quotidien, ne [kotēdyȧṅ, -en] *a* (*journalier*) daily; (*banal*) ordinary, everyday ♦ *nm* (*journal*) daily (paper); (*vie quotidienne*) daily life, day-to-day existence; **les grands** ~**s** the big (national) dailies.

quotidiennement [kotēdyenmȧṅ] *ad* daily, every day.

quotient [kosyȧṅ] *nm* (*MATH*) quotient; ~ **intellectuel (QI)** intelligence quotient (IQ).

quotité [kotētȧ] *nf* (*FINANCE*) quota.

R

R, r [er] *nm inv* R, r ♦ *abr* = **route, rue**; **R comme Raoul** R for Roger.

rab [rȧb] (*fam*), **rabiot** [rȧbyō] *nm* extra, more.

rabâcher [rȧbȧshȧ] *vi* to harp on ♦ *vt* keep on repeating.

rabais [rȧbe] *nm* reduction, discount; **au** ~ at a reduction *ou* discount.

rabaisser [rȧbāsȧ] *vt* (*rabattre*) to reduce; (*dénigrer*) to belittle.

rabane [rȧbȧn] *nf* raffia (matting).

Rabat [rȧbȧ(t)] *n* Rabat.

rabat [rȧbȧ] *vb voir* **rabattre** ♦ *nm* flap.

rabat-joie [rȧbȧzhwȧ] *nm/f inv* killjoy, spoil-sport.

rabatteur, euse [rȧbȧtœr, -ēz] *nm/f* (*de gibier*) beater; (*péj*) tout.

rabattre [rȧbȧtr(ə)] *vt* (*couvercle, siège*) to pull down; (*col*) to turn down; (*couture*) to stitch down; (*gibier*) to drive; (*somme d'un prix*) to deduct, take off; (*orgueil, prétentions*) to humble; (*TRICOT*) to decrease; **se** ~ *vi* (*bords, couvercle*) to fall shut; (*véhicule, coureur*) to cut in; **se** ~ **sur** (*accepter*) to fall back on.

rabattu, e [rȧbȧtü] *pp de* **rabattre** ♦ *a* turned down.

rabbin [rȧbȧṅ] *nm* rabbi.

rabique [rȧbēk] *a* rabies *cpd*.

râble [rȧbl(ə)] *nm* back; (*CULIN*) saddle.

râblé, e [rȧblā] *a* broad-backed, stocky.

rabot [rȧbō] *nm* plane.

raboter [rȧbotȧ] *vt* to plane (down).

raboteux, euse [rȧbotœ, -ēz] *a* uneven, rough.

rabougri, e [rȧbōōgrē] *a* stunted.

rabrouer [rȧbrōōȧ] *vt* to snub, rebuff.

racaille [rȧkȧy] *nf* (*péj*) rabble, riffraff.

raccommodage [rȧkomodȧzh] *nm* mending *q*, repairing *q*; darning *q*.

raccommoder [rȧkomodȧ] *vt* to mend, repair; (*chaussette etc*) to darn; (*fam: réconcilier: amis, ménage*) to bring together again; **se** ~ (**avec**) (*fam*) to patch it up (with).

raccompagner [rȧkôṅpȧnyȧ] *vt* to take *ou* see back.

raccord [rȧkor] *nm* link; ~ **de maçonnerie** pointing *q*; ~ **de peinture** join; touch-up.

raccordement [rȧkordəmȧṅ] *nm* joining up; connection.

raccorder [rȧkordȧ] *vt* to join (up), link up; (*suj: pont etc*) to connect, link; **se** ~ **à** to join up with; (*fig: se rattacher à*) to tie in with; ~ **au réseau du téléphone** to connect to the telephone service.

raccourci [rȧkōōrsē] *nm* short cut; **en** ~ in brief.

raccourcir [rȧkōōrsēr] *vt* to shorten ♦ *vi* (*vêtement*) to shrink.

raccroc [rȧkrō]: **par** ~ *ad* by chance.

raccrocher [rȧkroshȧ] *vt* (*tableau, vêtement*) to hang back up; (*récepteur*) to put down; (*fig: affaire*) to save ♦ *vi* (*TÉL*) to hang up; **se** ~ **à** *vt* to cling to, hang on to; **ne raccrochez pas** (*TÉL*) hold on, don't hang up.

race [rȧs] *nf* race; (*d'animaux, fig: espèce*) breed; (*ascendance, origine*) stock, race; **de** ~ *a* purebred, pedigree.

racé, e [rȧsȧ] *a* thoroughbred.

rachat [rȧshȧ] *nm* buying; buying back; redemption; atonement.

racheter [rȧshtȧ] *vt* (*article perdu*) to buy another; (*davantage*): ~ **du lait/3 œufs** to buy more milk/another 3 eggs *ou* 3 more eggs; (*après avoir vendu*) to buy back; (*d'occasion*) to buy; (*COMM: part, firme*) to buy up; (*: pension, rente*) to redeem; (*REL: pécheur*) to redeem; (*: péché*) to atone for, expiate; (*mauvaise conduite, oubli, défaut*) to make up for; **se** ~ (*REL*) to redeem o.s.; (*gén*) to make amends, make up for it.

rachidien, ne [rȧshēdyȧṅ, -en] *a* rachidian, of the spine.

rachitique [rȧshētēk] *a* suffering from rickets; (*fig*) scraggy, scrawny.

rachitisme [rȧshētēsm(ə)] *nm* rickets *sg*.

racial, e, aux [rȧsyȧl, -ō] *a* racial.

racine [rȧsēn] *nf* root; (*fig: attache*) roots *pl*; ~ **carrée/cubique** square/cube root; **prendre** ~ (*fig*) to take root; to put down roots.

racisme [rȧsēsm(ə)] *nm* racism, racialism.

raciste [rȧsēst(ə)] *a, nm/f* racist, racialist.

racket [rȧket] *nm* racketeering *q*.

racketteur [rȧketœr] *nm* racketeer.

raclée [rȧklȧ] *nf* (*fam*) hiding, thrashing.

raclement [rȧkləmȧṅ] *nm* (*bruit*) scraping (noise).

racler [rȧklȧ] *vt* (*os, plat*) to scrape; (*tache, boue*) to scrape off; (*fig: instrument*) to scrape on; (*suj: chose: frotter contre*) to

scrape (against).
raclette [ráklet] *nf* (*CULIN*) raclette (*Swiss cheese dish*).
racloir [ráklwár] *nm* (*outil*) scraper.
racolage [rákolázh] *nm* soliciting; touting.
racoler [rákolā] *vt* (*attirer: suj: prostituée*) to solicit; (*: parti, marchand*) to tout for; (*attraper*) to pick up.
racoleur, euse [rákolœr, -œz] *a* (*péj: publicité*) cheap and alluring ♦ *nm* (*péj: de clients etc*) tout ♦ *nf* streetwalker.
racontars [rákôńtár] *nmpl* stories, gossip *sg*.
raconter [rákôńtā] *vt*: ~ (à qn) (*décrire*) to relate (to sb), tell (sb) about; (*dire*) to tell (sb).
racorni, e [rákornē] *a* hard(ened).
racornir [rákornēr] *vt* to harden.
radar [rádár] *nm* radar; **système** ~ radar system; **écran** ~ radar screen.
rade [rád] *nf* (natural) harbor (*US*) *ou* harbour (*Brit*); **en** ~ **de Toulon** in Toulon harbor; **rester en** ~ (*fig*) to be left stranded.
radeau, x [rádō] *nm* raft; ~ **de sauvetage** life raft.
radial, e, aux [rádyál, -ō] *a* radial; **pneu à carcasse** ~e radial tire (*US*) *ou* tyre (*Brit*).
radiant, e [rádyáń, -áńt] *a* radiant.
radiateur [rádyátœr] *nm* radiator, heater (*AUTO*) radiator; ~ **électrique/à gaz** electric/gas heater.
radiation [rádyâsyôń] *nf* (*voir radier*) striking off *q*; (*PHYSIQUE*) radiation.
radical, e, aux [rádikál, -ō] *a* radical ♦ *nm* (*LING*) stem; (*MATH*) root sign; (*POL*) radical.
radicalement [rádēkálmáń] *ad* radically, completely.
radicaliser [rádēkálēzā] *vt* (*durcir: opinions etc*) to harden; **se** ~ *vi* (*mouvement etc*) to become more radical.
radicalisme [rádēkálēsm(ə)] *nm* (*POL*) radicalism.
radier [rádyā] *vt* to strike off.
radiesthésie [rádyestāzē] *nf* divination (by radiation).
radiesthésiste [rádyestāzēst(ə)] *nm/f* diviner.
radieux, euse [rádyœ̄, -œz] *a* (*visage, personne*) radiant; (*journée, soleil*) brilliant, glorious.
radin, e [rádań, -ēn] *a* (*fam*) stingy.
radio [rádyō] *nf* radio; (*MÉD*) X-ray ♦ *nm* (*personne*) radio operator; **à la** ~ on the radio; **avoir la** ~ to have a radio; **passer à la** ~ to be on the radio; **se faire faire une** ~/**une** ~ **des poumons** to have an X-ray/a chest X-ray.
radio... [rádyo] *préfixe* radio....
radioactif, ive [rádyoáktēf, -ēv] *a* radioactive.
radioactivité [rádyoáktēvētā] *nf* radioactivity.
radioamateur [rádyoámátœr] *nm* (radio) ham.
radiobalise [rádyobálēz] *nf* radio beacon.
radiocassette [rádyokáset] *nf* cassette radio.
radiodiffuser [rádyodēfūzā] *vt* to broadcast.
radiodiffusion [rádyodēfūzyóń] *nf* (radio) broadcasting.
radioélectrique [rádyoālektrēk] *a* radio *cpd*.
radiogoniomètre [rádyogonyometr(ə)] *nm* direction finder, radiogoniometer.
radiographie [rádyográfē] *nf* radiography;

(*photo*) X-ray photograph, radiograph.
radiographier [rádyográfyā] *vt* to X-ray; **se faire** ~ to have an X-ray.
radioguidage [rádyogēdázh] *nm* (*NAVIG, AVIAT*) radio control; (*AUTO*) (broadcast of) traffic information.
radioguider [rádyogēdā] *vt* (*NAVIG, AVIAT*) to guide by radio, control by radio.
radiologie [rádyolozhē] *nf* radiology.
radiologique [rádyolozhēk] *a* radiological.
radiologue [rádyolog] *nm/f* radiologist.
radionavigant [rádyonávēgáń] *nm* radio officer.
radiophare [rádyofár] *nm* radio beacon.
radiophonique [rádyofonēk] *a*: **programme/émission/jeu** ~ radio program (*US*) *ou* programme (*Brit*)/broadcast/game.
radioreportage [rádyorəportázh] *nm* radio report.
radio(-)réveil [rádyorāvey] *nm* clock radio.
radioscopie [rádyoskopē] *nf* radioscopy.
radio-taxi [rádyotáksē] *nm* radiotaxi.
radiotélégraphie [rádyotālāgráfē] *nf* radiotelegraphy.
radiotéléphone [rádyotālāfon] *nm* radiotelephone.
radiotélescope [rádyotāleskop] *nm* radiotelescope.
radiotélévisé, e [rádyotālāvēzā] *a* broadcast on radio and television.
radiothérapie [rádyotārápē] *nf* radiotherapy.
radis [rádē] *nm* radish; ~ **noir** horseradish *q*.
radium [rádyom] *nm* radium.
radoter [rádotā] *vi* to ramble on.
radoub [rádōō] *nm*: **bassin** *ou* **cale de** ~ dry dock.
radouber [rádōōbā] *vt* to repair, refit.
radoucir [rádōōsēr]: **se** ~ *vi* (*se réchauffer*) to become milder; (*se calmer*) to calm down; to soften.
radoucissement [rádōōsēsmáń] *nm* milder period, better weather.
rafale [ráfál] *nf* (*vent*) gust (of wind); (*de balles, d'applaudissements*) burst; ~ **de mitrailleuse** burst of machine-gun fire.
raffermir [ráfermēr] *vt*, **se** ~ *vi* (*tissus, muscle*) to firm up; (*fig*) to strengthen.
raffermissement [ráfermēsmáń] *nm* (*fig*) strengthening.
raffinage [ráfēnázh] *nm* refining.
raffiné, e [ráfēnā] *a* refined.
raffinement [ráfēnmáń] *nm* refinement.
raffiner [ráfēnā] *vt* to refine.
raffinerie [ráfēnrē] *nf* refinery.
raffoler [ráfolā]: ~ **de** *vt* to be very fond of.
raffut [ráfü] *nm* (*fam*) row, racket.
rafiot [ráfyō] *nm* (*fam*) boat.
rafistoler [ráfēstolā] *vt* (*fam*) to patch up.
rafle [ráfl(ə)] *nf* (*de police*) roundup, raid.
rafler [ráflā] *vt* (*fam*) to swipe.
rafraîchir [ráfrāshēr] *vt* (*atmosphère, température*) to cool (down); (*aussi*: **mettre à** ~) to chill; (*suj: air, eau*) to freshen up; (*: boisson*) to refresh; (*fig: rénover*) to brighten up ♦ *vi*: **mettre du vin/une boisson à** ~ to chill wine/a drink; **se** ~ *vi* to grow cooler; to freshen up; (*personne: en buvant etc*) to refresh o.s.; ~ **la mémoire** *ou* **les idées à qn** to refresh sb's memory.

rafraîchissant, e [ráfrāshēsáṅ, -áṅt] *a* refreshing.

rafraîchissement [ráfrāshēsmáṅ] *nm* cooling; *(boisson)* cool drink; **~s** *nmpl (boissons, fruits etc)* refreshments.

ragaillardir [rágáyárdēr] *vt (fam)* to perk *ou* buck up.

rage [rázh] *nf (MÉD)*: **la ~** rabies; *(fureur)* rage, fury; **faire ~** to rage; **~ de dents** (raging) toothache.

rager [rázhā] *vi* to fume (with rage); **faire ~ qn** to enrage sb, get sb mad.

rageur, euse [ràzhœr, -œz] *a* snarling; illtempered.

raglan [rágláṅ] *a inv* raglan.

ragot [rágō] *nm (fam)* malicious gossip *q*.

ragoût [rágōō] *nm (plat)* stew.

ragoûtant, e [rágōōtáṅ, -áṅt] *a*: **peu ~** unpalatable.

rai [re] *nm*: **un ~ de soleil/lumière** a shaft of sunshine/light.

raid [red] *nm (MIL)* raid; *(attaque aérienne)* air raid; *(SPORT)* long-distance trek.

raide [red] *a (tendu)* taut, tight; *(escarpé)* steep; *(droit: cheveux)* straight; *(ankylosé, dur, guindé)* stiff; *(fam: cher)* steep, stiff; (: *sans argent)* flat broke; *(osé, licencieux)* daring ♦ *ad (en pente)* steeply; **~ mort** stone dead.

raideur [redœr] *nf* steepness; stiffness.

raidir [rēdēr] *vt (muscles)* to stiffen; *(câble)* to pull taut, tighten; **se ~** *vi* to stiffen; to become taut; *(personne: se crisper)* to tense up; (: *devenir intransigeant)* to harden.

raidissement [rēdēsmáṅ] *nm* stiffening; tightening; hardening.

raie [re] *nf (ZOOL)* skate, ray; *(rayure)* stripe; *(des cheveux)* part *(US)*, parting *(Brit)*.

raifort [refor] *nm* horseradish.

rail [rây] *nm (barre d'acier)* rail; *(chemins de fer)* railroads *pl (US)*, railways *pl (Brit)*; **les ~s** *(la voie ferrée)* the rails, the track *sg*; **par ~** by rail; **~ conducteur** live *ou* conductor rail.

railler [ráyā] *vt* to scoff at, jeer at.

raillerie [ráyre] *nf* mockery.

railleur, euse [ráyœr, -œz] *a* mocking.

rail-route [ráyrōōt] *nm* road-rail.

rainurage [ránürázh] *nm (AUTO)* uneven road surface.

rainure [ránür] *nf* groove; slot.

rais [re] *nm inv* = **rai**.

raisin [rezáṅ] *nm (aussi:* **~s**) grapes *pl; (variété)*: **~ blanc/noir** white *(ou* green)/black grape; **~ muscat** muscat grape; **~s secs** raisins.

raison [rezóṅ] *nf* reason; **avoir ~** to be right; **donner ~ à qn** *(personne)* to agree with sb; *(fait)* to prove sb right; **avoir ~ de qn/qch** to get the better of sb/sth; **se faire une ~** to learn to live with it; **perdre la ~** to become insane; *(fig)* to take leave of one's senses; **recouvrer la ~** to come to one's senses; **ramener qn à la ~** to make sb see sense; **demander ~ à qn de** *(affront etc)* to demand satisfaction from sb for; **entendre ~** to listen to reason, see reason; **plus que de ~** too much, more than is reasonable; **à plus forte ~** all the more so; **en ~ de** *(à cause de)* because of; *(à proportion de)* in proportion to; **à ~ de** at the rate of; **~ d'État** reason of state; **~ d'être** raison d'être; **~ sociale** corporate name.

raisonnable [rezonábl(ə)] *a* reasonable, sensible.

raisonnablement [rezonábləmáṅ] *ad* reasonably.

raisonné, e [rezonā] *a* reasoned.

raisonnement [rezonmáṅ] *nm* reasoning; arguing; argument.

raisonner [rezonā] *vi (penser)* to reason; *(argumenter, discuter)* to argue ♦ *vt (personne)* to reason with; *(attitude: justifier)* to reason out; **se ~** to reason with oneself.

raisonneur, euse [rezonœr, -œz] *a (péj)* quibbling.

rajeunir [ràzhœnēr] *vt (suj: coiffure, robe)*: **~ qn** to make sb look younger; *(suj: cure etc)* to rejuvenate; *(fig: rafraîchir)* to brighten up; (: *moderniser)* to give a new look to; (: *en recrutant)* to inject new blood into ♦ *vi (personne)* to become *(ou* look) younger; *(entreprise, quartier)* to be modernized.

rajout [ràzhōō] *nm* addition.

rajouter [ràzhōōtā] *vt (commentaire)* to add; **~ du sel/un œuf** to add some more salt/another egg; **~ que** to add that; **en ~** to lay it on thick.

rajustement [ràzhüstəmáṅ] *nm* adjustment.

rajuster [ràzhüstā] *vt (vêtement)* to straighten, tidy; *(salaires)* to adjust; *(machine)* to readjust; **se ~** to tidy *ou* straighten o.s. up.

râle [rál] *nm (râle); ~ d'agonie* death rattle.

ralenti [ràláṅtē] *nm*: **au ~** *(AUTO)*: **tourner au ~** to idle; *(CINÉMA)* in slow motion; *(fig)* at a slower pace.

ralentir [ràláṅtēr] *vt, vi*, **se ~** *vi* to slow down.

ralentissement [ràláṅtēsmáṅ] *nm* slowing down.

râler [rálā] *vi* to groan; *(fam)* to grouse, moan (and groan).

ralliement [rálēmáṅ] *nm (rassemblement)* rallying; *(adhésion: à une cause, une opinion)* winning over; **point/signe de ~** rallying point/sign.

rallier [rályā] *vt (rassembler)* to rally; *(rejoindre)* to rejoin; *(gagner à sa cause)* to win over; **se ~ à** *(avis)* to come over *ou* round to.

rallonge [rálôṅzh] *nf (de table)* (extra) leaf *(pl* leaves); *(argent etc)* extra *q; (ÉLEC)* extension (cable); *(fig: de crédit etc)* extension.

rallonger [rálôṅzhā] *vt* to lengthen.

rallumer [rálümā] *vt* to light up again, relight; *(fig)* to revive; **se ~** *vi (lumière)* to come on again.

rallye [rálē] *nm* rally; *(POL)* march.

ramages [rámázh] *nmpl (dessin)* leaf pattern *sg; (chants)* songs.

ramassage [rámásázh] *nm*: **~ scolaire** school bus service.

ramassé, e [rámásā] *a (trapu)* squat, stocky; *(concis: expression etc)* compact.

ramasse-miettes [rámásmyet] *nm inv* silent butler *(US)*, table-tidy *(Brit)*.

ramasse-monnaie [ràmâsmone] *nm inv* change-tray.

ramasser [ràmâsā] *vt (objet tombé ou par terre, fam)* to pick up; *(recueillir)* to collect; *(récolter)* to gather; (: *pommes de terre*) to lift; **se ~** *vi (sur soi-même)* to huddle up; to crouch.

ramasseur, euse [ràmâsœr, -ēz] *nm/f:* **~ de balles** ballboy/girl.

ramassis [ràmâsē] *nm (péj: de gens)* bunch; (: *de choses*) jumble.

rambarde [ràñbárd(ɔ)] *nf* guardrail.

rame [ràm] *nf (aviron)* oar; *(de métro)* train; *(de papier)* ream; **~ de haricots** bean support; **faire force de ~s** to row hard.

rameau, x [ràmō] *nm* (small) branch; *(fig)* branch; **les R~x** *(REL)* Palm Sunday *sg*.

ramener [ràmnā] *vt* to bring back; *(reconduire)* to take back; *(rabattre: couverture, visière)*: **~ qch sur** to pull sth back over; **~ qch à** *(réduire à, aussi MATH)* to reduce sth to; **~ qn à la vie/raison** to bring sb back to life/bring sb to his *(ou her)* senses; **se ~** *vi (fam)* to roll *ou* turn up; **se ~ à** *(se réduire à)* to come *ou* boil down to.

ramequin [ràmkań] *nm* ramekin.

ramer [ràmā] *vi* to row.

rameur, euse [ràmœr, -ēz] *nm/f* rower.

rameuter [ràmœtā] *vt* to gather together.

ramier [ràmyā] *nm*: **(pigeon) ~** woodpigeon.

ramification [ràmēfēkâsyóñ] *nf* ramification.

ramifier [ràmēfyā]: **se ~** *vi (tige, secte, réseau)*: **se ~ (en)** to branch out (into); *(veines, nerfs)* to ramify.

ramolli, e [ràmolē] *a* soft.

ramollir [ràmolēr] *vt* to soften; **se ~** *vi (os, tissus)* to get *(ou* go) soft; *(beurre, asphalte)* to soften.

ramonage [ràmonàzh] *nm* (chimney-) sweeping.

ramoner [ràmonā] *vt (cheminée)* to sweep; *(pipe)* to clean.

ramoneur [ràmonœr] *nm* (chimney) sweep.

rampe [ràñp] *nf (d'escalier)* banister(s *pl)*; *(dans un garage, d'un terrain)* ramp; *(THÉÂTRE)*: **la ~** the footlights *pl*; *(lampes: lumineuse, de balisage)* floodlights *pl*; **passer la ~** *(toucher le public)* to get across to the audience; **~ de lancement** launching pad.

ramper [ràñpā] *vi (reptile, animal)* to crawl; *(plante)* to creep.

rancard [ràñkár] *nm (fam)* date; tip.

rancart [ràñkár] *nm*: **mettre au ~** *(article, projet)* to scrap; *(personne)* to put on the scrapheap.

rance [ràñs] *a* rancid.

rancir [ràñsēr] *vi* to go off, go rancid.

rancœur [ràñkœr] *nf* rancor *(US)*, rancour *(Brit)*, resentment.

rançon [ràñsóñ] *nf* ransom; *(fig)*: **la ~ du succès** *etc* the price of success *etc*.

rançonner [ràñsonā] *vt* to hold for *(US)* ou to ransom *(Brit)*.

rancune [ràñkün] *nf* grudge, rancor *(US)*, rancour *(Brit)*; **garder ~ à qn (de qch)** to bear sb a grudge (for sth); **sans ~!** no hard feelings!

rancunier, ière [ràñkünyā, -yer] *a* vindictive, spiteful.

randonnée [ràñdonā] *nf* ride; *(à pied)* walk; ramble; hike, hiking *q*.

randonneur, euse [ràñdonœr, -ēz] *nm/f* hiker.

rang [ràñ] *nm (rangée)* row; *(de perles)* row, string, rope; *(grade, condition sociale, classement)* rank; **~s** *nmpl (MIL)* ranks; **se mettre en ~s/sur un ~** to get into *ou* form rows/a line; **sur 3 ~s** (lined up) 3 deep; **se mettre en ~s par 4** to form rows of 4; **se mettre sur les ~s** *(fig)* to get into the running; **au premier ~** in the first row; *(fig)* ranking first; **rentrer dans le ~** to get into line; **au ~ de** *(au nombre de)* among (the ranks of); **avoir ~ de** to hold the rank of.

rangé, e [ràñzhā] *a (sérieux)* orderly, steady.

rangée [ràñzhā] *nf* row.

rangement [ràñzhmáñ] *nm* tidying-up, putting-away; **faire des ~s** to tidy up.

ranger [ràñzhā] *vt (classer, grouper)* to order, arrange; *(mettre à sa place)* to put away; *(voiture dans la rue)* to park; *(mettre de l'ordre dans)* to tidy up; *(arranger, disposer: en cercle etc)* to arrange; *(fig: classer)*: **~ qn/qch parmi** to rank sb/sth among; **se ~** *vi (se placer, se disposer: autour d'une table etc)* to take one's place, sit around; *(véhicule, conducteur: s'écarter)* to pull over; (: *s'arrêter)* to pull in; *(piéton)* to step aside; *(s'assagir)* to settle down; **se ~ à** *(avis)* to come around to, fall in with.

ranimer [rànēmā] *vt (personne évanouie)* to bring around *(US)* ou round *(Brit)*; *(revigorer: forces, courage)* to restore; *(réconforter: troupes etc)* to kindle new life in; *(douleur, souvenir)* to revive; *(feu)* to rekindle.

rapace [ràpás] *nm* bird of prey ♦ *a (péj)* rapacious, grasping; **~ diurne/nocturne** diurnal/ nocturnal bird of prey.

rapatrié, e [ràpátrēyā] *nm/f* repatriate *(esp French North African settler)*.

rapatriement [ràpátrēmáñ] *nm* repatriation.

rapatrier [ràpátrēyā] *vt* to repatriate; *(capitaux)* to bring (back) into the country.

râpe [ràp] *nf (CULIN)* grater; *(à bois)* rasp.

râpé, e [ràpā] *a (tissu)* threadbare; *(CULIN)* grated.

râper [ràpā] *vt (CULIN)* to grate; *(gratter, racler)* to rasp.

rapetasser [ràptàsā] *vt (fam)* to patch up.

rapetisser [ràptēsā] *vt*: **~ qch** to shorten sth; to make sth look smaller ♦ *vi*, **se ~** *vi* to shrink.

râpeux, euse [ràpœ̄, -ēz] *a* rough.

raphia [ràfyà] *nm* raffia.

rapide [ràpēd] *a* fast; *(prompt)* quick; *(intelligence)* quick ♦ *nm* express (train); *(de cours d'eau)* rapid.

rapidement [ràpēdmáñ] *ad* fast; quickly.

rapidité [ràpēdētā] *nf* speed; quickness.

rapiécer [ràpyāsā] *vt* to patch.

rappel [ràpel] *nm (d'un ambassadeur, MIL)* recall; *(THÉÂTRE)* curtain call; *(MÉD: vaccination)* booster; *(ADMIN: de salaire)* back pay *q*; *(d'une aventure, d'un nom)* reminder; *(de limitation de vitesse: sur écriteau)* speed limit sign *(reminder)*; *(TECH)* return; *(ALPINISME: aussi:* **~ de corde)** rappelling *q (US)*; rappel *(US)*; abseiling *q (Brit)*; abseil

(Brit); ~ **à l'ordre** call to order.

rappeler [ráplā] *vt (pour faire revenir, retéléphoner)* to call back; *(ambassadeur,* MIL, INFORM) to recall; *(acteur)* to call back (onto the stage); *(faire se souvenir)*: ~ **qch à qn** to remind sb of sth; **se** ~ *vt (se souvenir de)* to remember, recall; ~ **qn à la vie** to bring sb back to life; ~ **qn à la décence** to recall sb to a sense of decency; **ça rappelle la Provence** it's reminiscent of Provence, it reminds you of Provence; **se** ~ **que** ... to remember that ....

rappelle [rápɛl] *etc vb voir* **rappeler.**

rappliquer [ráplēkā] *vi (fam)* to turn up.

rapport [rápor] *nm (compte rendu)* report; *(profit)* yield, return; revenue; *(lien, analogie)* relationship; *(corrélation)* connection; *(proportion:* MATH, TECH) ratio *(pl -s)*; ~**s** *nmpl (entre personnes, pays)* relations; **avoir** ~ **à** to have something to do with, concern; **être en** ~ **avec** *(idée de corrélation)* to be related to; **être/se mettre en** ~ **avec qn** to be/get in touch with sb; **par** ~ **à** *(comparé à)* in relation to; *(à propos de)* with regard to; **sous le** ~ **de** from the point of view of; **sous tous (les)** ~**s** in all respects; ~**s (sexuels)** (sexual) intercourse *sg*; ~ **qualité-prix** value (for money).

rapporté, e [ráportā] *a:* **pièce** ~**e** *(COUTURE)* patch.

rapporter [ráportā] *vt (rendre, ramener)* to bring back; *(apporter davantage)* to bring more; *(COUTURE)* to sew on; *(suj: investissement)* to yield; *(: activité)* to bring in; *(relater)* to report; *(JUR: annuler)* to revoke ♦ *vi (investissement)* to give a good return *ou* yield; *(activité)* to be very profitable; *(péj: moucharder)* to tell; ~ **qch à** *(fig: rattacher)* to relate sth to; **se** ~ **à** *(correspondre à)* to relate to; **s'en** ~ **à** to rely on.

rapporteur, euse [ráportœr, -œz] *nm/f (de procès, commission)* reporter; *(péj)* telltale ♦ *nm (GÉOM)* protractor.

rapproché, e [ráproshā] *a (proche)* near, close at hand; ~**e** *(l'un de l'autre)* at close intervals.

rapprochement [ráproshmâṅ] *nm (réconciliation: de nations, familles)* reconciliation; *(analogie, rapport)* parallel.

rapprocher [ráproshā] *vt (chaise d'une table)*: ~ **qch (de)** to bring sth closer (to); *(deux objets)* to bring closer together; *(réunir)* to bring together; *(comparer)* to establish a parallel between; **se** ~ *vi* to draw closer *ou* nearer; *(fig: familles, pays)* to come together; to come closer together; **se** ~ **de** to come closer to; *(présenter une analogie avec)* to be close to.

rapt [rápt] *nm* abduction.

raquette [ráket] *nf (de tennis)* racket; *(de ping-pong)* paddle (US), racket (US), bat *(Brit)*; *(à neige)* snowshoe.

rare [rár] *a* rare; *(main-d'œuvre, denrées)* scarce; *(cheveux, herbe)* sparse; **il est** ~ **que** it's rare that, it's unusual that; **se faire** ~ to become scarce; *(fig: personne)* to make oneself scarce.

raréfaction [ráráfáksyôṅ] *nf* scarcity; *(de l'air)* rarefaction.

raréfier [ráráfyā]: **se** ~ *vi* to grow scarce; *(air)* to rarefy.

rarement [rármâṅ] *ad* rarely, seldom.

rareté [rártā] *nf (voir rare)* rarity; scarcity.

rarissime [rárēsēm] *a* extremely rare.

RAS *abr = rien à signaler.*

ras, e [râ, râz] *a (tête, cheveux)* close-cropped; *(poil, herbe)* short; *(mesure, cuillère)* level ♦ *ad* short; **faire table** ~**e** to make a clean sweep; **en** ~**e campagne** in open country; **à** ~ **bords** to the brim; **au** ~ **de** level with; **en avoir** ~ **le bol** *(fam)* to be fed up; ~ **du cou** *a (pull, robe)* crew-neck.

rasade [rázád] *nf* glassful.

rascasse [ráskás] *nf (ZOOL)* scorpion fish.

rasé, e [rázā] *a:* ~ **de frais** freshly shaven; ~ **de près** close-shaven.

rase-mottes [rázmot] *nm inv:* **faire du** ~ to hedgehop; **vol en** ~ hedgehopping.

raser [rázā] *vt (barbe, cheveux)* to shave off; *(menton, personne)* to shave; *(fam: ennuyer)* to bore; *(démolir)* to raze (to the ground); *(frôler)* to graze, skim; **se** ~ to shave; *(fam)* to be bored (to tears).

rasoir [rázwár] *nm* razor; ~ **électrique** electric shaver *ou* razor; ~ **mécanique** *ou* **de sûreté** safety razor.

rassasier [rásázyā] *vt* to satisfy; **être rassasié** *(dégoûté)* to be sated; to have had more than enough.

rassemblement [rásâṅbləmâṅ] *nm (groupe)* gathering; *(POL)* union; association; *(MIL):* **le** ~ parade.

rassembler [rásâṅblā] *vt (réunir)* to assemble, gather; *(regrouper, amasser)* to gather together, collect; **se** ~ *vi* to gather; ~ **ses idées/ses esprits/son courage** to collect one's thoughts/gather one's wits/screw up one's courage.

rasseoir [ráswár]: **se** ~ *vi* to sit down again.

rasséréner [rásārānā] *vt:* **se** ~ *vi* to recover one's serenity.

rassir [rásēr] *vi* to go stale.

rassis, e [rásē, -ēz] *a (pain)* stale.

rassurant, e [rásurâṅ, -âṅt] *a (nouvelles etc)* reassuring.

rassuré, e [rásürā] *a:* **ne pas être très** ~ to be rather ill at ease.

rassurer [rásürā] *vt* to reassure; **se** ~ to be reassured; **rassure-toi** don't worry.

rat [rá] *nm* rat; ~ **d'hôtel** hotel thief *(pl* thieves); ~ **musqué** muskrat.

ratatiné, e [rátátēnā] *a* shrivelled (up), wrinkled.

ratatiner [rátátēnā] *vt* to shrivel; *(peau)* to wrinkle; **se** ~ *vi* to shrivel; to become wrinkled.

ratatouille [rátátōōy] *nf (CULIN)* ratatouille.

rate [rát] *nf* female rat; *(ANAT)* spleen.

raté, e [rátā] *a (tentative)* unsuccessful, failed ♦ *nm/f* failure ♦ *nm* misfiring *q*.

râteau, x [rátō] *nm* rake.

râtelier [rátəlyā] *nm* rack; *(fam)* false teeth *pl.*

rater [rátā] *vi (ne pas partir: coup de feu)* to fail to go off; *(affaire, projet etc)* to go wrong, fail ♦ *vt (cible, train, occasion)* to miss; *(démonstration, plat)* to spoil; *(examen)* to fail; ~ **son coup** to fail, not to bring it off.

raticide [rátēsēd] *nm* rat poison.
ratification [rátĉfĉkásyôń] *nf* ratification.
ratifier [rátēfyā] *vt* to ratify.
ratio [rásyō] *nm* ratio (*pl* -s).
ration [rásyôń] *nf* ration; (*fig*) share; ~ **alimentaire** food intake.
rationalisation [rásyonálēzâsyôń] *nf* rationalization.
rationaliser [rásyonálēzā] *vt* to rationalize.
rationellement [rásyonelmâń] *ad* rationally.
rationnel, le [rásyonel] *a* rational.
rationnement [rásyonmâń] *nm* rationing; **ticket de** ~ ration coupon.
rationner [rásyonā] *vt* to ration; (*personne*) to put on rations; **se** ~ to ration o.s.
ratisser [rátēsā] *vt* (*allée*) to rake; (*feuiller*) to rake up; (*suj: armée, police*) to comb; ~ **large** to cast one's nets wide.
raton [rátôń] *nm*: ~ **laveur** raccoon.
RATP *sigle f* (= *Régie autonome des transports parisiens*) Paris transport authority.
rattacher [rátàshā] *vt* (*animal, cheveux*) to tie up again; (*incorporer*: ADMIN *etc*): ~ **qch à** to join sth to, unite sth with; (*fig: relier*): ~ **qch à** to link sth with, relate sth to; (*: lier*): ~ **qn à** to bind *ou* tie sb to; **se** ~ **à** (*fig: avoir un lien avec*) to be linked (*ou* connected) with.
rattrapage [rátràpázh] *nm* (SCOL) remedial classes *pl*; (ÉCON) catching up.
rattraper [rátràpā] *vt* (*fugitif*) to recapture; (*retenir, empêcher de tomber*) to catch (hold of); (*atteindre, rejoindre*) to catch up with; (*réparer: imprudence, erreur*) to make up for; **se** ~ *vi* (*regagner: du temps*) to make up for lost time; (*: de l'argent etc*) to make good one's losses; (*réparer une gaffe etc*) to make up for it; **se** ~ **(à)** (*se raccrocher*) to stop o.s. falling (by catching hold of); ~ **son retard/le temps perdu** to make up (for) lost time.
rature [rátür] *nf* deletion, erasure.
raturer [rátürā] *vt* to cross out, delete, erase.
rauque [rōk] *a* raucous; hoarse.
ravagé, e [rávázhā] *a* (*visage*) harrowed.
ravager [rávázhā] *vt* to devastate, ravage.
ravages [rávàzh] *nmpl* ravages; **faire des** ~ to wreak havoc; (*fig: séducteur*) to break hearts.
ravalement [rávàlmâń] *nm* restoration.
ravaler [rávàlā] *vt* (*mur, façade*) to restore; (*déprécier*) to lower; (*avaler de nouveau*) to swallow again; ~ **sa colère/son dégoût** to stifle one's anger/distaste.
ravaudage [rávōdàzh] *nm* repairing, mending.
ravauder [rávōdā] *vt* to repair, mend.
rave [ráv] *nf* (BOT) rape.
ravi, e [rávē] *a* delighted; **être** ~ **de/que** to be delighted with/that.
ravier [rávyā] *nm* hors d'œuvre dish.
ravigote [rávēgot] *a*: **sauce** ~ *oil and vinegar dressing with shallots*.
ravigoter [rávēgotā] *vt* (*fam*) to buck up.
ravin [rávań] *nm* gully, ravine.
raviner [rávēnā] *vt* to furrow, gully.
ravir [rávēr] *vt* (*enchanter*) to delight; (*enlever*): ~ **qch à qn** to rob sb of sth; **à** ~ *ad* delightfully, beautifully; **être beau à** ~ to be ravishingly beautiful.
raviser [rávēzā]: **se** ~ *vi* to change one's mind.
ravissant, e [rávēsáń, -âńt] *a* delightful.
ravissement [rávēsmâń] *nm* (*enchantement, délice*) rapture.
ravisseur, euse [rávēscœr, -ēz] *nm/f* abductor, kidnapper.
ravitaillement [rávētâymâń] *nm* resupplying; refuelling; (*provisions*) supplies *pl*; **aller au** ~ to go for fresh supplies; ~ **en vol** (AVIAT) in-flight refuelling.
ravitailler [rávētâyā] *vt* to resupply; (*véhicule*) to refuel; **se** ~ *vi* to get fresh supplies.
raviver [rávēvā] *vt* (*feu, douleur*) to revive; (*couleurs*) to brighten up.
ravoir [rávwàr] *vt* to get back.
rayé, e [rāyā] *a* (*à rayures*) striped; (*éraflé*) scratched.
rayer [rāyā] *vt* (*érafler*) to scratch; (*barrer*) to cross *ou* score out; (*d'une liste: radier*) to cross *ou* strike off.
rayon [rcyôń] *nm* (*de soleil etc*) ray; (GÉOM) radius; (*de roue*) spoke; (*étagère*) shelf (*pl* shelves); (*de grand magasin*) department; (*fig: domaine*) responsibility, concern; (*de ruche*) (honey)comb; **dans un** ~ **de** within a radius of; ~**s** *nmpl* (*radiothérapie*) radiation; ~ **d'action** range; ~ **de braquage** (AUTO) turning radius; ~ **laser** laser beam; ~ **de soleil** sunbeam, ray of sunshine; ~**s X** X-rays.
rayonnage [reyonàzh] *nm* set of shelves.
rayonnant, e [reyonáń, -âńt] *a* radiant.
rayonne [reyon] *nf* rayon.
rayonnement [reyonmâń] *nm* radiation; (*fig: éclat*) radiance; (*: influence*) influence.
rayonner [reyona] *vi* (*chaleur, énergie*) to radiate; (*fig: émotion*) to shine forth; (*: visage*) to be radiant; (*avenues, axes etc*) to radiate; (*touriste*) to go touring (*from one base*).
rayure [rāyür] *nf* (*motif*) stripe; (*éraflure*) scratch; (*rainure, d'un fusil*) groove; **à** ~**s** striped.
raz-de-marée [rádmàrā] *nm inv* tidal wave.
razzia [rázyà] *nf* raid, foray.
RBE *sigle m* (= *revenu brut d'exploitation*) gross profit (*of a farm*).
R-D *sigle f* (= *Recherche-Développement*) R & D.
RDA *sigle f* (= *République démocratique allemande*) GDR.
RDB *sigle m* (STATISTIQUES: = *revenu disponible brut*) total income (*of a family etc*).
RdC. *abr* = **rez-de-chaussée**.
ré [rā] *nm* (MUS) D; (*en chantant la gamme*) re.
réabonnement [rāàbonmâń] *nm* renewal of subscription.
réabonner [rāàbonā] *vt*: ~ **qn à** to renew sb's subscription to; **se** ~ **(à)** to renew one's subscription (to).
réac [rāàk] *a, nm/f* (*fam*: = *réactionnaire*) reactionary.
réacteur [rāàktœr] *nm* jet engine; ~ **nucléaire** nuclear reactor.
réactif [rāàktēf] *nm* reagent.
réaction [rāàksyôń] *nf* reaction; **par** ~ jet-propelled; **avion/moteur à** ~ jet (plane)/jet

engine; ~ **en chaîne** chain reaction.

réactionnaire [rãáksyoner] *a, nm/f* reactionary.

réadaptation [rãádáptâsyôṅ] *nf* readjustment, rehabilitation.

réadapter [rãádáptã] *vt* to readjust; (*MÉD*) to rehabilitate; **se ~ (à)** to readjust (to).

réaffirmer [rãáfɛ̃rmã] *vt* to reaffirm, reassert.

réagir [rãázhɛr] *vi* to react.

réajuster [rãázhüstã] *vt* = **rajuster.**

réalisable [rãálɛ̃zábl(ə)] *a* (*projet, plan*) feasible; (*COMM: valeur*) realizable.

réalisateur, trice [rãálɛ̃zàtœr, -trɛs] *nm/f* (*TV, CINÉMA*) director.

réalisation [rãálɛ̃zásyôṅ] *nf* carrying out; realization; fulfillment (*US*), fulfilment (*Brit*); achievement; production; (*œuvre*) production, work; (*création*) creation.

réaliser [rãálɛ̃zã] *vt* (*projet, opération*) to carry out, realize; (*rêve, souhait*) to realize, fulfill (*US*), fulfil (*Brit*); (*exploit*) to achieve; (*achat, vente*) to make; (*film*) to produce; (*se rendre compte de, COMM: bien, capital*) to realize; **se ~** *vi* to be realized.

réalisme [rãálɛ̃sm(ə)] *nm* realism.

realiste [rãálɛ̃st(ə)] *a* realistic; (*peintre, roman*) realist ♦ *nm/f* realist.

réalité [rãálɛ̃tã] *nf* reality; **en ~** in (actual) fact; **dans la ~** in reality.

réanimation [rãánɛ̃másyôṅ] *nf* resuscitation; **service de ~** intensive care unit.

réanimer [rãánɛ̃mã] *vt* (*MÉD*) to resuscitate.

réapparaître [rãápárɛtr(ə)] *vi* to reappear.

réapparition [rãápárɛ̃syôṅ] *nf* reappearance.

réarmer [rãármã] *vt* (*arme*) to reload ♦ *vi* (*état*) to rearm.

réassortiment [rãásortɛ̃mãṅ] *nm* (*COMM*) restocking.

réassortir [rãásortɛr] *vt* to match up.

réassurance [rãásüráṅs] *nf* reinsurance.

rébarbatif, ive [rãbárbátɛ̃f, -ɛ̃v] *a* forbidding; (*style*) crabbed.

rebattre [rəbátr(ə)] *vt*: **~ les oreilles à qn de qch** to keep harping on (about (*Brit*)) sth to sb.

rebattu, e [rəbátü] *pp de* **rebattre** ♦ *a* hackneyed.

rebelle [rəbɛl] *nm/f* rebel ♦ *a* (*troupes*) rebel; (*enfant*) rebellious; (*mèche etc*) unruly; **~ à qch** unamenable to sth; **~ à faire** unwilling to do.

rebeller [rəbãlã]: **se ~** *vi* to rebel.

rébellion [rãbãlyôṅ] *nf* rebellion; (*rebelles*) rebel forces *pl*.

reboiser [rəbwázã] *vt* to replant with trees, reforest.

rebond [rəbôṅ] *nm* (*voir rebondir*) bounce; rebound.

rebondi, e [rəbôṅdã] *a* (*ventre*) rounded; (*joues*) chubby, well-rounded.

rebondir [rəbôṅdɛr] *vi* (*ballon: au sol*) to bounce; (: *contre un mur*) to rebound; (*fig: procès, action, conversation*) to get moving again, be suddenly revived.

rebondissement [rəbôṅdɛ̃smãṅ] *nm* new development.

rebord [rəbor] *nm* edge.

reboucher [rəbōōshã] *vt* (*flacon*) to put the stopper (*ou* top) back on, recork; (*trou*) to stop up.

rebours [rəbōōr]: **à ~** *ad* the wrong way.

rebouteux, euse [rəbōōtœ̃, -œ̃z] *nm/f* (*péj*) bonesetter.

reboutonner [rəbōōtonã] *vt* (*vêtement*) to button up (again).

rebrousse-poil [rəbrōōspwál]: **à ~** *ad* the wrong way.

rebrousser [rəbrōōsã] *vt* (*cheveux, poils*) to brush back, brush up; **~ chemin** to turn back.

rebuffade [rəbüfád] *nf* rebuff.

rébus [rãbüs] *nm inv* (*jeu d'esprit*) rebus; (*fig*) puzzle.

rebut [rəbü] *nm*: **mettre au ~** to scrap, discard.

rebutant, e [rəbütãṅ, -ãṅt] *a* (*travail, démarche*) disagreeable.

rebuter [rəbütã] *vt* to put off.

récalcitrant, e [rãkálsɛ̃trãṅ, -ãṅt] *a* refractory, recalcitrant.

recaler [rəkàlã] *vt* (*SCOL*) to fail.

récapitulatif, ive [rãkápɛ̃tülàtɛ̃f, -ɛ̃v] *a* (*liste, tableau*) summary *cpd*, that sums up.

récapituler [rãkápɛ̃tülã] *vt* to recapitulate; (*résumer*) to sum up.

recel [rəsɛl] *nm* fencing.

receler [rəsəlã] *vt* (*produit d'un vol*) to fence; (*malfaiteur*) to harbor (*US*), harbour (*Brit*); (*fig*) to conceal.

receleur, euse [rəsəlœr, -œ̃z] *nm/f* receiver.

récemment [rãsámáṅ] *ad* recently.

recensement [rəsãṅsmãṅ] *nm* census; inventory.

recenser [rəsãṅsã] *vt* (*population*) to take a census of; (*inventorier*) to make an inventory of; (*dénombrer*) to list.

récent, e [rãsãṅ, -ãṅt] *a* recent.

recentrer [rəsãṅtrã] *vt* (*POL*) to move towards the center (*US*) *ou* centre (*Brit*).

récépissé [rãsãpɛ̃sã] *nm* receipt.

récepteur, trice [rãsɛptœr, -trɛs] *a* receiving ♦ *nm* receiver; **~ (de papier)** (*INFORM*) stacker; **~ (de radio)** radio set *ou* receiver.

réceptif, ive [rãsɛptɛ̃f, -ɛ̃v] *a*: **~ (à)** receptive (to).

réception [rãsɛpsyôṅ] *nf* receiving *q*; (*d'une marchandise, commande*) receipt; (*accueil*) reception, welcome; (*bureau*) reception (desk); (*réunion mondaine*) reception, party; (*pièces*) reception rooms *pl*; (*SPORT: après un saut*) landing; (*du ballon*) catching *q*; **jour/heures de ~** day/hours for receiving visitors (*ou* students *etc*).

réceptionnaire [rãsɛpsyoner] *nm/f* receiving clerk.

réceptionner [rãsɛpsyonã] *vt* (*COMM*) to take delivery of; (*SPORT: ballon*) to catch (and control).

réceptionniste [rãsɛpsyonɛst(ə)] *nm/f* receptionist.

récession [rãsãsyôṅ] *nf* recession.

recette [rəsɛt] *nf* (*CULIN*) recipe; (*fig*) formula, recipe; (*COMM*) takings *pl*; (*ADMIN: bureau*) tax *ou* revenue office; **~s** *nfpl* (*COMM: rentrées*) receipts; **faire ~** (*spectacle, exposition*) to be a winner.

receveur, euse [rəsvœr, -œ̃z] *nm/f* (*des contributions*) tax collector; (*des postes*) postmaster/mistress; (*d'autobus*) conductor/conductress; (*MÉD*: *de sang, organe*) recipient.

recevoir [rəsvwȧr] *vt* to receive; (*lettre, prime*) to receive, get; (*client, patient, représentant*) to see; (*jour, soleil: suj: pièce*) to get; (*SCOL*: *candidat*) to pass ♦ *vi* to receive visitors; to give parties; to see patients *etc*; **se ~ vi** (*athlète*) to land; **~ qn à diner** to invite sb to dinner; **il reçoit de 8 à 10** he's at home from 8 to 10, he will see visitors from 8 to 10; (*docteur, dentiste etc*) he sees patients from 8 to 10; **être reçu** (*à un examen*) to pass; **être bien/mal reçu** to be well/badly received.

rechange [rəshȧnzh]: **de ~** *a* (*pièces, roue*) spare; (*fig: solution*) alternative; **des vêtements de ~** a change of clothes.

rechaper [rəshȧpā] *vt* to remold (*US*), remould (*Brit*), retread.

réchapper [rāshȧpā]: **~ de** *ou* **à** *vt* (*accident, maladie*) to come through; **va-t-il en ~?** is he going to get over it?, is he going to come through (it)?

recharge [rəshȧrzh(ə)] *nf* refill.

rechargeable [rəshȧrzhȧbl(ə)] *a* refillable; rechargeable.

recharger [rəshȧrzhā] *vt* (*camion, fusil, appareil-photo*) to reload; (*briquet, stylo*) to refill; (*batterie*) to recharge.

réchaud [rāshō] *nm* (portable) stove; hotplate.

réchauffé [rāshōfā] *nm* (*nourriture*) reheated food; (*fig*) stale news (*ou* joke *etc*).

réchauffer [rāshōfā] *vt* (*plat*) to reheat; (*mains, personne*) to warm; **se ~ vi** to get warmer; **se ~ les doigts** to warm (up) one's fingers.

rêche [resh] *a* rough.

recherche [rəshersh(ə)] *nf* (*action*): **la ~ de** the search for; (*raffinement*) affectedness, studied elegance; (*scientifique etc*): **la ~** research; **~s** *nfpl* (*de la police*) investigations; (*scientifiques*) research *sg*; **être/se mettre à la ~ de** to be/go in search of.

recherché, e [rəshershā] *a* (*rare, demandé*) much sought-after; (*entouré: acteur, femme*) in demand; (*raffiné*) studied, affected.

rechercher [rəshershā] *vt* (*objet égaré, personne*) to look for, search for; (*témoins, coupable, main-d'œuvre*) to look for; (*causes d'un phénomène, nouveau procédé*) to try to find; (*bonheur etc, l'amitié de qn*) to seek; **"~ et remplacer"** (*INFORM*) "search and replace".

rechigner [rəshēnyā] *vi*: **~ (à)** to balk (at).

rechute [rəshüt] *nf* (*MÉD*) relapse; (*dans le péché, le vice*) lapse; **faire une ~** to have a relapse.

rechuter [rəshütā] *vi* (*MÉD*) to relapse.

récidive [rāsēdēv] *nf* (*JUR*) second (*ou* subsequent) offense (*US*) *ou* offence (*Brit*); (*fig*) repetition; (*MÉD*) recurrence.

récidiver [rāsēdēvā] *vi* to commit a second (*ou* subsequent) offense (*US*) *ou* offence (*Brit*); (*fig*) to do it again.

récidiviste [rāsēdēvēst(ə)] *nm/f* second (*ou* habitual) offender, recidivist.

récif [rāsēf] *nm* reef.

récipiendaire [rāsēpyȧnder] *nm* recipient (*of*

diploma *etc*); (*d'une societé*) newly elected member.

récipient [rāsēpyȧṅ] *nm* container.

réciproque [rāsēprok] *a* reciprocal ♦ *nf*: **la ~** (*l'inverse*) the converse.

réciproquement [rāsēprokmȧṅ] *ad* reciprocally; **et ~** and vice versa.

récit [rāsē] *nm* (*action de narrer*) telling; (*conte, histoire*) story.

récital [rāsētȧl] *nm* recital.

récitant, e [rāsētȧṅ, -ȧṅt] *nm/f* narrator.

récitation [rāsētȧsyôṅ] *nf* recitation.

réciter [rāsētā] *vt* to recite.

réclamation [rāklȧmȧsyôṅ] *nf* complaint; **~s** *nfpl* (*bureau*) complaints department *sg*.

réclame [rāklȧm] *nf*: **la ~** advertising; **une ~** an ad(vertisement); **faire de la ~ (pour qch/qn)** to advertise (sth/sb); **article en ~** special offer.

réclamer [rāklȧmā] *vt* (*aide, nourriture etc*) to ask for; (*revendiquer: dû, part, indemnité*) to claim, demand; (*nécessiter*) to demand, require ♦ *vi* to complain; **se ~ de** to give as one's authority; to claim filiation with.

reclassement [rəklȧsmȧṅ] *nm* reclassifying; regrading; rehabilitation.

reclasser [rəklȧsā] *vt* (*fiches, dossiers*) to reclassify; (*fig: fonctionnaire etc*) to regrade; (*: ouvrier licencié*) to place, rehabilitate.

reclus, e [rəklü, -üz] *nm/f* recluse.

réclusion [rāklüzyôṅ] *nf* imprisonment; **~ à perpétuité** life imprisonment.

recoiffer [rəkwȧfā] *vt*: **~ un enfant** to do a child's hair again; **se ~** to do one's hair again.

recoin [rəkwȧṅ] *nm* nook, corner; (*fig*) hidden recess.

reçois [rəswȧ] *etc vb voir* **recevoir**.

reçoive [rəswȧv] *etc vb voir* **recevoir**.

recoller [rəkolā] *vt* (*enveloppe*) to stick back down.

récolte [rākolt(ə)] *nf* harvesting, gathering; (*produits*) harvest, crop; (*fig*) crop, collection; (*: d'observations*) findings.

récolter [rākoltā] *vt* to harvest, gather (in); (*fig*) to get.

recommandable [rəkomȧṅdȧbl(ə)] *a* commendable; **peu ~** not very commendable.

recommandation [rəkomȧṅdȧsyôṅ] *nf* recommendation.

recommandé [rəkomȧṅdā] *nm* (*méthode etc*) recommended; (*POSTES*): **en ~** by registered mail.

recommander [rəkomȧṅdā] *vt* to recommend; (*suj: qualités etc*) to commend; (*POSTES*) to register; **~ qch à qn** to recommend sth to sb; **~ à qn de faire** to recommend sb to do; **~ qn auprès de qn** *ou* **à qn** to recommend sb to sb; **il est recommandé de faire ...** it is recommended that one do ...; **se ~ à qn** to commend o.s. to sb; **se ~ de qn** to give sb's name as a reference.

recommencer [rəkomȧṅsā] *vt* (*reprendre: lutte, séance*) to resume, start again; (*refaire: travail, explications*) to start afresh, start (over) again; (*récidiver: erreur*) to make again ♦ *vi* to start again; (*récidiver*) to do it again; **~ à faire** to start doing again;

ne recommence pas! don't do that again!

récompense [rākôṅpâṅs] *nf* reward; *(prix)* award; **recevoir qch en ~** to get sth as a reward, be rewarded with sth.

récompenser [rākôṅpâṅsā] *vt*: **~ qn (de** *ou* **pour)** to reward sb (for).

réconciliation [rākôṅsēlyâsyôṅ] *nf* reconciliation.

réconcilier [rākôṅsēlyā] *vt* to reconcile; **~ qn avec qn** to reconcile sb with sb; **~ qn avec qch** to reconcile sb to sth; **se ~ (avec)** to be reconciled (with).

reconductible [rəkôṅdüktēbl(ə)] *a (JUR: contrat, bail)* renewable.

reconduction [rəkôṅdüksyôṅ] *nf* renewal; *(POL: d'une politique)* continuation.

reconduire [rəkôṅdüēr] *vt (raccompagner)* to take *ou* see back; *(: à la porte)* to show out; *(: à son domicile)* to see home, take home; *(JUR, POL: renouveler)* to renew.

réconfort [rākôṅfor] *nm* comfort.

réconfortant, e [rākôṅfortâṅ, -âṅt] *a (idée, paroles)* comforting; *(boisson)* fortifying.

réconforter [rākôṅfortā] *vt (consoler)* to comfort; *(revigorer)* to fortify.

reconnais [r(ə)kone] *etc vb voir* **reconnaître.**

reconnaissable [rəkonesâbl(ə)] *a* recognizable.

reconnaissais [r(ə)konese] *etc vb voir* **reconnaître.**

reconnaissance [rəkonesâṅs] *nf* recognition; acknowledgement; *(gratitude)* gratitude, gratefulness; *(MIL)* reconnaissance, recce; **en ~** *(MIL)* on reconnaissance; **~ de dette** acknowledgement of a debt, IOU.

reconnaissant, e [rəkonesâṅ, -âṅt] *vb voir* **reconnaître** ♦ *a* grateful; **je vous serais ~ de bien vouloir** I should be most grateful if you would (kindly).

reconnaître [rəkonetr(ə)] *vt* to recognize; *(MIL: lieu)* to reconnoiter *(US)*, reconnoitre *(Brit)*; *(JUR: enfant, dette, droit)* to acknowledge; **~ que** to admit *ou* acknowledge that; **~ qn/qch à** *(l'identifier grâce à)* to recognize sb/sth by; **~ à qn: je lui reconnais certaines qualités** I recognize certain qualities in him; **se ~ quelque part** *(s'y retrouver)* to find one's way around (a place).

reconnu, e [r(ə)konü] *pp de* **reconnaître** ♦ *a (indiscuté, connu)* recognized.

reconquérir [rəkôṅkārēr] *vt (aussi fig)* to reconquer, recapture; *(sa dignité etc)* to recover.

reconquête [rəkôṅket] *nf* recapture; recovery.

reconsidérer [rəkôṅsēdārā] *vt* to reconsider.

reconstituant, e [rəkôṅstētüâṅ, -âṅt] *a (régime)* strength-building ♦ *nm* tonic, pick-me-up.

reconstituer [rəkôṅstētüā] *vt (monument ancien)* to recreate, build a replica of; *(fresque, vase brisé)* to piece together, reconstitute; *(événement, accident)* to reconstruct; *(fortune, patrimoine)* to rebuild; *(BIO: tissus etc)* to regenerate.

reconstitution [rəkôṅstētüsyôṅ] *nf (d'un accident etc)* reconstruction.

reconstruction [rəkôṅstrüksyôṅ] *nf* rebuilding, reconstruction.

reconstruire [rəkôṅstrüēr] *vt* to rebuild, reconstruct.

reconversion [rəkôṅversyôṅ] *nf (du personnel)* redeployment.

reconvertir [rəkôṅvertēr] *vt (usine)* to reconvert; *(personnel, troupes etc)* to redeploy; **se ~ dans** *(un métier, une branche)* to move into, be redeployed into.

recopier [rəkopyā] *vt (transcrire)* to copy out again, write out again; *(mettre au propre: devoir)* to make a clean *ou* fair copy of.

record [rəkor] *nm, a* record; **~ du monde** world record.

recoucher [rəkōōshā] *vt (enfant)* to put back to bed.

recoudre [rəkōōdr(ə)] *vt (bouton)* to sew back on; *(plaie, incision)* to sew (back) up, stitch up.

recoupement [rəkōōpmâṅ] *nm*: **faire un ~** *ou* **des ~s** to cross-check; **par ~** by cross-checking.

recouper [rəkōōpā] *vt (tranche)* to cut again; *(vêtement)* to recut ♦ *vi (CARTES)* to cut again; **se ~** *vi (témoignages)* to tie *ou* match up.

recourais [rəkōōre] *etc vb voir* **recourir.**

recourbé, e [rəkōōrbā] *a* curved; hooked; bent.

recourber [rəkōōrbā] *vt (branche, tige de métal)* to bend.

recourir [rəkōōrēr] *vi (courir de nouveau)* to run again; *(refaire une course)* to race again; **~ à** *vt (ami, agence)* to turn *ou* appeal to; *(force, ruse, emprunt)* to resort to, have recourse to.

recours [rəkōōr] *vb voir* **recourir** ♦ *nm (JUR)* appeal; **avoir ~ à = recourir à; en dernier ~** as a last resort; **sans ~** final; with no way out; **~ en grâce** plea for clemency *(ou* pardon).

recouru, e [rəkōōrü] *pp de* **recourir.**

recousu, e [rəkōōzü] *pp de* **recoudre.**

recouvert, e [rəkōōver, -ert(ə)] *pp de* **recouvrir.**

recouvrable [rəkōōvrâbl(ə)] *a (somme)* recoverable.

recouvrais [rəkōōvre] *etc vb voir* **recouvrer, recouvrir.**

recouvrement [rəkōōvrəmâṅ] *nm* recovery.

recouvrer [rəkōōvrā] *vt (vue, santé etc)* to recover, regain; *(impôts)* to collect; *(créance)* to recover.

recouvrir [rəkōōvrēr] *vt (couvrir à nouveau)* to re-cover; *(couvrir entièrement, aussi fig)* to cover; *(cacher, masquer)* to conceal, hide; **se ~** *(se superposer)* to overlap.

recracher [rəkrāshā] *vt* to spit out.

récréatif, ive [rākrāātēf, -ēv] *a* of entertainment; recreational.

récréation [rākrāāsyôṅ] *nf* recreation, entertainment; *(SCOL)* break.

recréer [rəkrāā] *vt* to recreate.

récrier [rākrēyā]: **se ~** *vi* to exclaim.

récriminations [rākrēmēnâsyôṅ] *nfpl* remonstrations, complaints.

récriminer [rākrēmēnā] *vi*: **~ contre qn/qch** to remonstrate against sb/sth.

recroqueviller [rəkrokvēyā]: **se ~** *vi (feuilles)* to curl *ou* shrivel up; *(personne)* to huddle up.

recru, e [rəkrü] *a*: ~ **de fatigue** exhausted ♦ *nf* recruit.

recrudescence [rəkrüdāsáńs] *nf* fresh outbreak.

recrutement [rəkrütmáń] *nm* recruiting, recruitment.

recruter [rəkrütā] *vt* to recruit.

rectal, e, aux [rektál, -ō] *a*: **par voie** ~**e** rectally.

rectangle [rektáńgl(ə)] *nm* rectangle; ~ **blanc** (*TV*) "adults only" symbol.

rectangulaire [rektáńgülɛr] *a* rectangular.

recteur [rektœr] *nm* ≈ state superintendent of education (*US*), ≈ (regional) director of education (*Brit*).

rectificatif, ive [rektēfēkátēf, -ēv] *a* corrected ♦ *nm* correction.

rectification [rektēfēkâsyôń] *nf* correction.

rectifier [rektēfyā] *vt* (*tracé, virage*) to straighten; (*calcul, adresse*) to correct; (*erreur, faute*) to rectify, put right.

rectiligne [rektēlēny] *a* straight; (*GÉOM*) rectilinear.

rectitude [rektētüd] *nf* rectitude, uprightness.

recto [rektō] *nm* front (*of a sheet of paper*).

reçu, e [rəsü] *pp de* **recevoir** ♦ *a* (*admis, consacré*) accepted ♦ *nm* (*COMM*) receipt.

recueil [rəkœy] *nm* collection.

recueillement [rəkœymáń] *nm* meditation, contemplation.

recueilli, e [rəkœyē] *a* contemplative.

recueillir [rəkœyēr] *vt* to collect; (*voix, suffrages*) to win; (*accueillir: réfugiés, chat*) to take in; **se** ~ *vi* to gather one's thoughts; to meditate.

recuire [rəküēr] *vi*: **faire** ~ to recook.

recul [rəkül] *nm* retreat; recession; decline; (*d'arme à feu*) recoil, kick; **avoir un mouvement de** ~ to recoil, start back; **prendre du** ~ to stand back; **avec le** ~ with the passing of time, in retrospect.

reculade [rəküláď] *nf* (*péj*) retreat.

reculé, e [rəkülā] *a* remote.

reculer [rəkülā] *vi* to move back, back away; (*AUTO*) to reverse, back (up); (*fig: civilisation, épidémie*) to (be on the) decline; (*: se dérober*) to shrink back ♦ *vt* to move back; to reverse, back (up); (*fig: possibilités, limites*) to extend; (*: date, décision*) to postpone; ~ **devant** (*danger, difficulté*) to shrink from; ~ **pour mieux sauter** (*fig*) to delay the day of reckoning.

reculons [rəkülôń]: **à** ~ *ad* backwards.

récupérable [rāküpārábl(ə)] *a* (*créance*) recoverable; (*heures*) which can be made up; (*ferraille*) salvageable.

récupération [rāküpārâsyôń] *nf* (*de vieux métaux etc*) salvage, reprocessing; (*POL*) bringing into line.

récupérer [rāküpārā] *vt* (*rentrer en possession de*) to recover, get back; (*: forces*) to recover; (*déchets etc*) to salvage (for reprocessing); (*remplacer: journée, heures de travail*) to make up; (*délinquant etc*) to rehabilitate; (*POL*) to bring into line ♦ *vi* to recover.

récurer [rākürā] *vt* to scour; **poudre à** ~ scouring powder.

reçus [rəsü] *etc vb voir* **recevoir**.

récuser [rāküzā] *vt* to challenge; **se** ~ to decline to give an opinion.

recyclage [rəsēklázh] *nm* reorientation; retraining; recycling; **cours de** ~ retraining course.

recycler [rəsēklā] *vt* (*SCOL*) to reorientate; (*employés*) to retrain; (*matériau*) to recycle; **se** ~ to retrain; to take a retraining course.

rédacteur, trice [rādáktœr, -trēs] *nm/f* (*journaliste*) writer; subeditor; (*d'ouvrage de référence*) editor, compiler; ~ **en chef** editor in chief; ~ **publicitaire** copywriter.

rédaction [rādáksyôń] *nf* writing; (*rédacteurs*) editorial staff; (*bureau*) editorial office(s); (*SCOL: devoir*) essay, composition.

reddition [rādēsyôń] *nf* surrender.

redéfinir [rədāfēnēr] *vt* to redefine.

redemander [rədmáńdā] *vt* (*renseignement*) to ask again for; (*nourriture*): ~ **de** to ask for more (*ou* another); (*objet prêté*): ~ **qch** to ask for sth back.

redémarrer [rədāmárā] *vi* (*véhicule*) to start again, get going again; (*fig: industrie etc*) to get going again.

rédemption [rādáńpsyôń] *nf* redemption.

redéploiement [rədāplwámáń] *nm* redeployment.

redescendre [rədāsáńdr(ə)] *vi* (*à nouveau*) to go back down; (*après la montée*) to go down (again) ♦ *vt* (*pente etc*) to go down.

redevable [rədvábl(ə)] *a*: **être** ~ **de qch à qn** (*somme*) to owe sb sth; (*fig*) to be indebted to sb for sth.

redevance [rədváńs] *nf* (*TÉL*) leasing (*US*) *ou* rental (*Brit*) charge; (*TV*) ≈ cable (*US*) *ou* licence (*Brit*) fee.

redevenir [rədvənēr] *vi* to become again.

rediffuser [rədēfüzā] *vt* (*RADIO, TV*) to rerun, broadcast again.

rediffusion [rədēfüzyôń] *nf* rerun.

rédiger [rādēzhā] *vt* to write; (*contrat*) to draw up.

redire [rədēr] *vt* to repeat; **trouver à** ~ **à** to find fault with.

redistribuer [rədēstrēbüā] *vt* (*cartes etc*) to deal again; (*richesses, tâches, revenus*) to redistribute.

redite [rədēt] *nf* (needless) repetition.

redondance [rədôńdáńs] *nf* redundancy.

redonner [rədonā] *vt* (*restituer*) to give back, return; (*du courage, des forces*) to restore.

redoublé, e [rədōōblā] *a*: **à coups** ~**s** even harder, twice as hard.

redoubler [rədōōblā] *vi* (*tempête, violence*) to intensify, get even stronger *ou* fiercer *etc*; (*SCOL*) to repeat a grade (*US*) *ou* year (*Brit*) ♦ *vt* (*SCOL: classe*) to repeat; (*LING: lettre*) to double; ~ **de** *vt* to be twice as + *adjectif*; **le vent redouble de violence** the wind is blowing twice as hard.

redoutable [rədōōtábl(ə)] *a* formidable, fearsome.

redouter [rədōōtā] *vt* to fear; (*appréhender*) to dread; ~ **de faire** to dread doing.

redoux [rədōō] *nm* milder spell.

redressement [rədresmáń] *nm* (*de l'économie etc*) recovery, upturn; **maison de** ~ reformatory; ~ **fiscal** repayment of back taxes.

redresser [rǝdrāsā] *vt* (*arbre, mât*) to set upright, right; (*pièce tordue*) to straighten out; (*AVIAT, AUTO*) to straighten up; (*situation, économie*) to straighten out; **se ~ vi** (*objet penché*) to right itself; to straighten up; (*personne*) to sit (*ou* stand) up; to sit (*ou* stand) up straight; (*fig: pays, situation*) to recover; **~ (les roues)** (*AUTO*) to straighten up.

redresseur [rǝdresœr] *nm*: **~ de torts** righter of wrongs.

réducteur, trice [rādüktœr, -trēs] *a* simplistic.

réduction [rādüksyôň] *nf* reduction; **en ~ ad** in miniature, scaled-down.

réduire [rādüēr] *vt* (*gén, aussi CULIN, MATH*) to reduce; (*prix, dépenses*) to cut, reduce; (*carte*) to scale down, reduce; (*MÉD: fracture*) to set; **~ qn/qch à** to reduce sb/sth to; **se ~ à** (*revenir à*) to boil down to; **se ~ en** (*se transformer en*) to be reduced to; **en être réduit à** to be reduced to.

réduit, e [rādüē, -ēt] *pp de* **réduire** ♦ *a* (*prix, tarif, échelle*) reduced; (*mécanisme*) scaled-down; (*vitesse*) reduced ♦ *nm* tiny room; recess.

rééchelonner [rāāshlonā] *vt* to reschedule.

rééditer [rāādētā] *vt* to republish.

réédition [rāādēsyôň] *nf* new edition.

rééducation [rāādükāsyôň] *nf* (*d'un membre*) re-education; (*de délinquants, d'un blessé*) rehabilitation; **~ de la parole** speech therapy; **centre de ~** physical therapy center (*US*), physiotherapy centre (*Brit*).

rééduquer [rāādükā] *vt* to reeducate; to rehabilitate.

réel, le [rāel] *a* real ♦ *nm*: **le ~** reality.

réélection [rāāleksyôň] *nf* re-election.

réélire [rāālēr] *vt* to re-elect.

réellement [rāelmā] *ad* really.

réembaucher [rāāňbōshā] *vt* to take on again.

réemploi [rāāňplwā] *nm* = **remploi.**

réemployer [rāāňplwāyā] *vt* (*méthode, produit*) to re-use; (*argent*) to reinvest; (*personnel, employé*) to re-employ.

rééquilibrer [rāākēlēbrā] *vt* (*budget*) to balance (again).

réescompte [rāeskôňt] *nm* rediscount.

réessayer [rāesāyā] *vt* to try on again.

réévaluer [rāāvālüā] *vt* to revalue.

réexaminer [rāegzámēnā] *vt* to re-examine.

réexpédier [rāekspādyā] *vt* (*à l'envoyeur*) to return, send back; (*au destinataire*) to send on, forward.

réexporter [rāeksportā] *vt* to re-export.

réf. *abr* (= *référence(s)*): **V/~** Your ref.

refaire [rǝfer] *vt* (*faire de nouveau, recommencer*) to do again; (*réparer, restaurer*) to renovate, redecorate; **se ~ vi** (*en argent*) to make up one's losses; **se ~ une santé** to recuperate; **se ~ à qch** (*se réhabituer à*) to get used to sth again.

refasse [rǝfás] *etc vb voir* **refaire.**

réfection [rāfeksyôň] *nf* repair; **en ~** under repair.

réfectoire [rāfektwár] *nm* refectory.

referai [r(ǝ)frā] *etc vb voir* **refaire.**

référé [rāfārā] *nm* (*JUR*) emergency interim proceedings *ou* ruling.

référence [rāfāräňs] *nf* reference; **~s** *nfpl* (*recommandations*) reference *sg*; **faire ~ à** to refer to; **ouvrage de ~** reference work; **ce n'est pas une ~** (*fig*) that's no recommendation.

référendum [rāfāraňdom] *nm* referendum.

référer [rāfārā]: **se ~ à** *vt* to refer to; **en ~ à qn** to refer the matter to sb.

refermer [rǝfermā] *vt* to close again, shut again.

refiler [rǝfēlā] *vt* (*fam*): **~ qch à qn** to palm *ou* fob sth off on sb; to pass sth on to sb.

refit [rǝfē] *etc vb voir* **refaire.**

réfléchi, e [rāflāshē] *a* (*caractère*) thoughtful; (*action*) well-thought-out; (*LING*) reflexive.

réfléchir [rāflāshēr] *vt* to reflect ♦ *vi* to think; **~ à** *ou* **sur** to think about; **c'est tout réfléchi** my mind's made up.

réflecteur [rāflektœr] *nm* (*AUTO*) reflector.

reflet [rǝflě] *nm* reflection; (*sur l'eau etc*) sheen *q*, glint; **~s** *nmpl* gleam *sg.*

refléter [rǝflātā] *vt* to reflect; **se ~ vi** to be reflected.

réflex [rāfleks] *a inv* (*PHOTO*) reflex.

réflexe [rāfleks(ǝ)] *a, nm* reflex; **~ conditionné** conditioned reflex.

réflexion [rāfleksyôň] *nf* (*de la lumière etc, pensée*) reflection; (*fait de penser*) thought; (*remarque*) remark; **~s** *nfpl* (*méditations*) thought *sg*, reflection *sg*; **sans ~** without thinking; **~ faite, à la ~, après ~** on reflection; **délai de ~** cooling-off period; **groupe de ~** think tank.

refluer [rǝflüā] *vi* to flow back; (*foule*) to surge back.

reflux [rǝflü] *nm* (*de la mer*) ebb; (*fig*) backward surge.

refondre [rǝfôňdr(ǝ)] *vt* (*texte*) to recast.

refont [r(ǝ)fôň] *vb voir* **refaire.**

reformater [rǝformātā] *vt* to reformat.

réformateur, trice [rāformátœr, -trēs] *nm/f* reformer ♦ *a* (*mesures*) reforming.

Réformation [rāformāsyôň] *nf*: **la ~** the Reformation.

réforme [rāform(ǝ)] *nf* reform; (*MIL*) declaration of unfitness for service; discharge (*on health grounds*); (*REL*): **la R~** the Reformation.

réformé, e [rāformā] *a, nm/f* (*REL*) Protestant.

reformer [rǝformā] *vt, se ~ vi* to reform; **~ les rangs** (*MIL*) to fall in again.

réformer [rāformā] *vt* to reform; (*MIL: recrue*) to declare unfit for service; (*: soldat*) to discharge; (*matériel*) to scrap.

réformisme [rāformēsm(ǝ)] *nm* reformism, policy of reform.

réformiste [rāformēst(ǝ)] *a, nm/f* (*POL*) reformist.

refoulé, e [rǝfōōlā] *a* (*PSYCH*) repressed.

refoulement [rǝfōōlmâň] *nm* (*d'une armée*) driving back; (*PSYCH*) repression.

refouler [rǝfōōlā] *vt* (*envahisseurs*) to drive back, repulse; (*liquide*) to force back; (*fig*) to suppress; (*PSYCH*) to repress.

réfractaire [rāfräktēr] *a* (*minerai*) refractory; (*brique*) fire *cpd*; (*maladie*) which is resistant to treatment; (*prêtre*) non-juring; **soldat ~** draft dodger; **être ~ à** to resist.

réfracter [rāfräktā] *vt* to refract.

réfraction [rāfräksyôň] *nf* refraction.

refrain [rəfrań] *nm* (*MUS*) refrain, chorus; (*air, fig*) tune.

refréner, réfréner [rəfrānā, rāfrānā] *vt* to curb, check.

réfrigérant, e [rāfrēzhārāń, -âńt] *a* refrigerant, cooling.

réfrigérateur [rāfrēzhārátœr] *nm* refrigerator.

réfrigération [rāfrēzhārâsyôń] *nf* refrigeration.

réfrigérer [rāfrēzhārā] *vt* to refrigerate; (*fam: glacer, aussi fig*) to cool.

refroidir [rəfrwādēr] *vt* to cool; (*fig*) to have a cooling effect on ♦ *vi* to cool (down); **se** ~ *vi* (*prendre froid*) to catch a chill; (*temps*) to get cooler *ou* colder; (*fig*) to cool (off).

refroidissement [rəfrwādēsmāń] *nm* cooling; (*grippe etc*) chill.

refuge [rəfüzh] *nm* refuge; (*pour piétons*) (traffic) island; **demander** ~ **à qn** to ask sb for refuge.

réfugié, e [rāfüzhyā] *a, nm/f* refugee.

réfugier [rāfüzhyā]: **se** ~ *vi* to take refuge.

refus [rəfü] *nm* refusal; **ce n'est pas de** ~ I won't say no, it's very welcome.

refuser [rəfüzā] *vt* to refuse; (*SCOL: candidat*) to fail ♦ *vi* to refuse; ~ **qch à qn/de faire** to refuse sb sth/to do; ~ **du monde** to have to turn people away; **se** ~ **à qch** *ou* **à faire qch** to refuse to do sth; **il ne se refuse rien** he doesn't deny himself (anything); **se** ~ **à qn** to refuse sb.

réfuter [rāfütā] *vt* to refute.

regagner [rəgânyā] *vt* (*argent, faveur*) to win back; (*lieu*) to get back to; ~ **le temps perdu** to make up (for) lost time; ~ **du terrain** to regain ground.

regain [rəgań] *nm* (*herbe*) second crop of hay; (*renouveau*): **un** ~ **de** renewed + *nom*.

régal [rāgál] *nm* treat; **un** ~ **pour les yeux** a pleasure *ou* delight to look at.

régalade [rāgálád] *ad*: **à la** ~ from the bottle (held away from the lips).

régaler [rāgálā] *vt*: ~ **qn** to treat sb to a delicious meal; ~ **qn de** to treat sb to; **se** ~ *vi* to have a delicious meal; (*fig*) to enjoy o.s.

regard [rəgár] *nm* (*coup d'œil*) look, glance; (*expression*) look (in one's eye); **parcourir/ menacer du** ~ to cast an eye over/look threateningly at; **au** ~ **de** (*loi, morale*) from the point of view of; **en** ~ (*vis à vis*) opposite; **en** ~ **de** in comparison with.

regardant, e [rəgárdāń, -āńt] *a*: **très/peu** ~ (**sur**) quite fussy/very free (about); (*économe*) very tight-fisted/quite generous (with).

regarder [rəgárdā] *vt* (*examiner, observer, lire*) to look at; (*film, télévision, match*) to watch; (*envisager: situation, avenir*) to view; (*considérer: son intérêt etc*) to be concerned with; (*être orienté vers*): ~ (**vers**) to face; (*concerner*) to concern ♦ *vi* to look; ~ **à** *vt* (*dépense, qualité, détails*) to be fussy with *ou* over; ~ **à faire** to hesitate to do; **dépenser sans** ~ to spend freely; ~ **qn/qch comme** to regard sb/sth as; ~ (**qch**) **dans le dictionnaire/l'annuaire** to look (sth up) in the dictionary/directory; ~ **par la fenêtre** to look out of the window; **cela me regarde** it concerns me, it's my business.

régate(s) [rāgát] *nf(pl)* regatta.

régénérer [rāzhānārā] *vt* to regenerate; (*fig*) to revive.

régent [razhaṅ] *nm* regent.

régenter [rāzhâṅtā] *vt* to rule over; to dictate to.

régie [rāzhē] *nf* (*COMM, INDUSTRIE*) state-owned company; (*THÉÂTRE, CINÉMA*) production; (*RADIO, TV*) control room; **la** ~ **de l'État** state control.

regimber [rəzhańbā] *vi* to balk, jib.

régime [rāzhēm] *nm* (*POL*) régime; (*ADMIN: carcéral, fiscal etc*) system; (*MÉD*) diet; (*GÉO*) régime; (*TECH*) (engine) speed; (*fig*) rate, pace; (*de bananes, dattes*) bunch; **se mettre au/suivre un** ~ to go on/be on a diet; ~ **sans sel** salt-free diet; **à bas/haut** ~ (*AUTO*) at low/high revs; **à plein** ~ flat out, at full speed; ~ **matrimonial** marriage settlement.

régiment [rāzhēmāń] *nm* (*MIL*) regiment; (*fig: fam*): **un** ~ **de** an army of; **un copain de** ~ a pal from military service *ou* (one's) army days.

région [rāzhyôń] *nf* region; **la** ~ **parisienne** the Paris area.

régional, e, aux [rāzhyonál, -ō] *a* regional.

régionalisation [rāzhyonálēzásyôń] *nf* regionalization.

régionalisme [rāzhyonálēsm(ə)] *nm* regionalism.

régir [rāzhēr] *vt* to govern.

régisseur [rāzhēsœr] *nm* (*d'un domaine*) steward; (*CINÉMA, TV*) assistant director; (*THÉÂTRE*) stage manager.

registre [rozhēstr(ə)] *nm* (*livre*) register; log-book; ledger; (*MUS, LING*) register; (*d'orgue*) stop; ~ **de comptabilité** ledger; ~ **de l'état civil** register of births, marriages and deaths.

réglable [rāglábl(ə)] *a* (*siège, flamme etc*) adjustable; (*achat*) payable.

réglage [rāglázh] *nm* (*d'une machine*) adjustment; (*d'un moteur*) tuning.

règle [regl(ə)] *nf* (*instrument*) ruler; (*loi, prescription*) rule; ~**s** *nfpl* (*PHYSIOL*) period *sg*; **avoir pour** ~ **de** to make it a rule that *ou* to; **en** ~ (*papiers d'identité*) in order; **être/se mettre en** ~ to be/put o.s. in order with the authorities; **en** ~ **générale** as a (general) rule; **être la** ~ to be the rule; **être de** ~ to be usual; ~ **à calcul** slide rule; ~ **de trois** (*MATH*) rule of three.

réglé, e [rāglā] *a* well-ordered, stable, steady; (*papier*) ruled; (*arrangé*) settled; (*femme*): **bien** ~**e** whose periods are regular.

règlement [reglomāń] *nm* settling; (*paiement*) settlement; (*arrêté*) regulation; (*règles, statuts*) regulations *pl*, rules *pl*; ~ **à la commande** cash with order; ~ **de compte(s)** settling of scores; ~ **en espèces/par chèque** payment in cash/by check; ~ **intérieur** (*SCOL*) school rules *pl*; (*ADMIN*) by-laws *pl*; ~ **judiciaire** compulsory liquidation.

réglementaire [reglomâńter] *a* conforming to the regulations; (*tenue, uniforme*) regulation *cpd*.

réglementation [reglomâńtâsyôń] *nf* regulation, control; (*règlements*) regulations *pl*.

réglementer [reglomâńtā] *vt* to regulate, control.

régler [rāglā] *vt* (*mécanisme, machine*) to regulate, adjust; (*moteur*) to tune; (*thermostat etc*) to set, adjust; (*emploi du temps etc*) to organize, plan; (*question, conflit, facture, dette*) to settle; (*fournisseur*) to settle up with, pay; (*papier*) to rule; ~ **qch sur** to model sth on; ~ **son compte à qn** to fix sb; ~ **un compte avec qn** to settle a score with sb.

réglisse [rāglēs] *nf* licorice, liquorice (*Brit*); **bâton de** ~ licorice stick.

règne [reny] *nm* (*d'un roi etc, fig*) reign; (*BIO*): **le** ~ **végétal/animal** the vegetable/animal kingdom.

régner [rānyā] *vi* (*roi*) to rule, reign; (*fig*) to reign.

regonfler [r(ə)gônflā] *vt* (*ballon, pneu*) to reinflate, blow up again.

regorger [rəgorzhā] *vi* to overflow; ~ **de** to overflow with, be bursting with.

régresser [rāgrāsā] *vi* (*phénomène*) to decline; (*enfant, malade*) to regress.

régressif, ive [rāgrāsēf, -ēv] *a* regressive.

régression [rāgrāsyôn] *nf* decline; regression; **être en** ~ to be on the decline.

regret [rəgre] *nm* regret; **à** ~ with regret; **avec** ~ regretfully; **être au** ~ **de devoir/ne pas pouvoir faire** to regret to have to/that one is unable to do; **j'ai le** ~ **de vous informer que ...** I regret to inform you that ....

regrettable [rəgretābl(ə)] *a* regrettable.

regretter [rəgrātā] *vt* to regret; (*personne*) to miss; ~ **d'avoir fait** to regret doing; ~ **que** to regret that, be sorry that; **non, je regrette no,** I'm sorry.

regroupement [r(ə)grōōpmân] *nm* grouping together; (*groupe*) group.

regrouper [rəgrōōpā] *vt* (*grouper*) to group together; (*contenir*) to include, comprise; **se** ~ *vi* to gather (together).

régulariser [rāgülārēzā] *vt* (*fonctionnement, trafic*) to regulate; (*passeport, papiers*) to put in order; (*sa situation*) to straighten out, regularize.

régularité [rāgülārētā] *nf* regularity.

régulateur, trice [rāgülátœr, -trēs] *a* regulating ♦ *nm* (*TECH*): ~ **de vitesse/de température** speed/temperature regulator.

régulation [rāgülāsyôn] *nf* (*du trafic*) regulation; ~ **des naissances** birth control.

régulier, ière [rāgülyā, -yer] *a* (*gén*) regular; (*vitesse, qualité*) steady; (*répartition, pression, paysage*) even; (*TRANSPORTS: ligne, service*) scheduled, regular; (*légal, réglementaire*) lawful, in order; (*fam: correct*) straight, on the level.

régulièrement [rāgülyermân] *ad* regularly; steadily; evenly; normally.

réhabiliter [rāābēlētā] *vt* to rehabilitate; (*fig*) to restore to favor.

réhabituer [rāābētüā] *vt*: **se** ~ **à qch/à faire qch** to get used to sth again/to doing sth again.

rehausser [rəōsā] *vt* to heighten, raise; (*fig*) to set off, enhance.

réimporter [rāānportā] *vt* to reimport.

réimposer [rāānpōzā] *vt* (*FINANCE*) to reimpose; to tax again.

réimpression [rāānpresyôn] *nf* reprinting; (*ouvrage*) reprint.

réimprimer [rāānprēmā] *vt* to reprint.

Reims [rans] *n* Rheims.

rein [ran] *nm* kidney; ~**s** *nmpl* (*dos*) back *sg*; **avoir mal aux** ~**s** to have backache; ~ **artificiel** kidney machine.

reine [ren] *nf* queen.

reine-claude [renklōd] *nf* greengage.

reinette [renet] *nf* rennet, pippin.

réinitialisation [rāēnēsyālēzāsyôn] *nf* (*INFORM*) reset.

réinsérer [rāānsārā] *vt* (*délinquant, handicapé etc*) to rehabilitate.

réinsertion [rāānsersyôn] *nf* rehabilitation.

réintégrer [rāāntāgrā] *vt* (*lieu*) to return to; (*fonctionnaire*) to reinstate.

réitérer [rāētārā] *vt* to repeat, reiterate.

rejaillir [rəzháyēr] *vi* to splash up; ~ **sur** to splash up onto; (*fig*) to rebound on; to fall upon.

rejet [rəzhe] *nm* (*action, aussi MÉD*) rejection; (*POÉSIE*) enjambement, rejet; (*BOT*) shoot.

rejeter [rəzhtā] *vt* (*relancer*) to throw back; (*vomir*) to bring *ou* throw up; (*écarter*) to reject; (*déverser*) to throw out, discharge; (*reporter*): ~ **un mot à la fin d'une phrase** to transpose a word to the end of a sentence; **se** ~ **sur qch** (*accepter faute de mieux*) to fall back on sth; ~ **la tête/les épaules en arrière** to throw one's head/pull one's shoulders back; ~ **la responsabilité de qch sur qn** to lay the responsibility for sth at sb's door.

rejeton [rəzhtôn] *nm* offspring.

rejette [r(ə)zhet] *etc vb voir* **rejeter**.

rejoignais [r(ə)zhwányc] *etc vb voir* **rejoindre**.

rejoindre [rəzhwandr(ə)] *vt* (*famille, régiment*) to rejoin, return to; (*lieu*) to get (back) to; (*suj: route etc*) to meet, join; (*rattraper*) to catch up (with); **se** ~ *vi* to meet; **je te rejoins au café** I'll see *ou* meet you at the café.

réjoui, e [rāzhwē] *a* joyous.

réjouir [rāzhwēr] *vt* to delight; **se** ~ *vi* to be delighted; **se** ~ **de qch/de faire** to be delighted about sth/to do; **se** ~ **que** to be delighted that.

réjouissances [rāzhwēsâns] *nfpl* (*joie*) rejoicing *sg*; (*fête*) festivities, merry-making *sg*.

réjouissant, e [rāzhwēsân, -ânt] *a* heartening, delightful.

relâche [rəlâsh]: **faire** ~ *vi* (*navire*) to put into port; (*CINÉMA*) to be closed; **c'est le jour de** ~ (*CINÉMA*) it's closed today; **sans** ~ *ad* without respite *ou* a break.

relâché, e [rəlâshā] *a* loose, lax.

relâcher [rəlâshā] *vt* (*ressort, prisonnier*) to release; (*étreinte, cordes*) to loosen; (*discipline*) to relax ♦ *vi* (*NAVIG*) to put into port; **se** ~ *vi* to loosen; (*discipline*) to become slack *ou* lax; (*élève etc*) to slacken off.

relais [rəle] *nm* (*SPORT*): (**course de**) ~ relay (race); (*RADIO, TV*) relay; (*intermédiaire*) go-between; **équipe de** ~ shift team; (*SPORT*) relay team; **prendre le** ~ (**de**) to take over (from); ~ **de poste** post house; ~ **routier** ≈ truck stop (*US*), ~ transport café (*Brit*).

relance [rəláns̄] *nf* boosting, revival; (*ÉCON*) reflation.

relancer [rəláns̄ā] *vt* (*balle*) to throw back (again); (*moteur*) to restart; (*fig*) to boost, revive; (*personne*): ~ **qn** to pester sb.

relater [rəlátā] *vt* to relate, recount.

relatif, ive [rəlátēf, -ēv] *a* relative.

relation [rəlásyón̄] *nf* (*récit*) account, report; (*rapport*) relation(ship); (*fig*) (*rapports*) relations; relationship; (*connaissances*) connections; **être/entrer en ~(s) avec** to be in contact *ou* be dealing/get in contact with; **mettre qn en ~(s) avec** to put sb in touch with; **~s internationales** international relations; **~s publiques (RP)** public relations (PR); **~s (sexuelles)** sexual relations, (sexual) intercourse *sg*.

relativement [rəlátēvmán̄] *ad* relatively; ~ **à** in relation to.

relativiser [rəlátēvēzā] *vt* to see in relation to; to put into context.

relativité [rəlátēvētā] *nf* relativity.

relax [rəláks] *a inv*, **relaxe** [rəláks(ə)] *a* relaxed, informal, casual; easy-going; **(fauteuil-)~** *nm* reclining chair.

relaxant, e [rəláks̄án̄, -án̄t] *a* (*cure, médicament*) relaxant; (*ambiance*) relaxing.

relaxation [r(ə)láksásyón̄] *nf* relaxation.

relaxer [rəláks̄ā] *vt* to relax; (*JUR*) to discharge; **se ~** *vi* to relax.

relayer [rəláyā] *vt* (*collaborateur, coureur etc*) to relieve, take over from; (*RADIO, TV*) to relay; **se ~** (*dans une activité*) to take it in turns.

relecture [r(ə)lektür] *nf* rereading.

relégation [rəlāgásyón̄] *nf* (*SPORT*) relegation.

reléguer [rəlāgā] *vt* to relegate; ~ **au second plan** to push into the background.

relent(s) [rəlán̄] *nm(pl)* stench *sg*.

relevé, e [rəlvā] *a* (*bord de chapeau*) turned-up; (*manches*) rolled-up; (*fig: style*) elevated; (*: sauce*) highly-seasoned ♦ *nm* (*lecture*) reading; (*de cotes*) plotting; (*liste*) statement; list; (*facture*) account; ~ **de compte** bank statement; ~ **d'identité bancaire (RIB)** (bank) account number.

relève [rəlev] *nf* relief; (*équipe*) relief team (*ou* troops *pl*); **prendre la ~** to take over.

relèvement [rəlevmán̄] *nm* (*d'un taux, niveau*) raising.

relever [rəlvā] *vt* (*statue, meuble*) to stand up again; (*personne tombée*) to help up; (*vitre, plafond, niveau de vie*) to raise; (*pays, économie, entreprise*) to put back on its feet; (*col*) to turn up; (*style, conversation*) to elevate; (*plat, sauce*) to season; (*sentinelle, équipe*) to relieve; (*souligner: fautes, points*) to pick out; (*constater: traces etc*) to find, pick up; (*répliquer à: remarque*) to react to, reply to; (*: défi*) to accept, take up; (*noter: adresse etc*) to take down, note; (*: plan*) to sketch; (*: cotes etc*) to plot; (*compteur*) to read; (*ramasser: cahiers, copies*) to collect, take up ♦ *vi* (*jupe, bord*) to ride up; ~ **de** *vt* (*maladie*) to be recovering from; (*être du ressort de*) to be a matter for; (*ADMIN: dépendre de*) to come under; (*fig*) to pertain to; **se ~** *vi* (*se remettre debout*) to get up; (*fig*): **se ~ (de)** to recover (from); ~ **qn de**

(*vœux*) to release sb from; (*fonctions*) to relieve sb of; ~ **la tête** to look up; to hold up one's head.

relief [rəlyef] *nm* relief; (*de pneu*) tread pattern; **~s** *nmpl* (*restes*) remains; **en ~** in relief; (*photographie*) three-dimensional; **mettre en ~** (*fig*) to bring out, highlight.

relier [rəlyā] *vt* to link up; (*livre*) to bind; ~ **qch à** to link sth to; **livre relié cuir** leather-bound book.

relieur, euse [rəlyœr, -ēz] *nm/f* (book)binder.

religieusement [r(ə)lēzhyēzmán̄] *ad* religiously; (*enterré, mariés*) in church; **vivre ~** to lead a religious life.

religieux, euse [rəlēzhyē̄, -ēz] *a* religious ♦ *nm* monk ♦ *nf* nun; (*gâteau*) cream puff.

religion [rəlēzhyón̄] *nf* religion; (*piété, dévotion*) faith; **entrer en ~** to take one's vows.

reliquaire [rəlēker] *nm* reliquary.

reliquat [rəlēkā] *nm* (*d'une somme*) balance; (*JUR: de succession*) residue.

relique [rəlēk] *nf* relic.

relire [rəlēr] *vt* (*à nouveau*) to reread, read again; (*vérifier*) to read over; **se ~** to read through what one has written.

reliure [rəlyür] *nf* binding; (*art, métier*): **la ~** bookbinding.

reloger [r(ə)lozhā] *vt* (*locataires, sinistrés*) to rehouse.

relu, e [rəlü] *pp de* **relire**.

reluire [rəlüēr] *vi* to gleam.

reluisant, e [rəlüēzán̄, -án̄t] *vb voir* **reluire** ♦ *a* gleaming; **peu ~** (*fig*) unattractive; unsavory (*US*), unsavoury (*Brit*).

reluquer [r(ə)lükā] *vt* (*fam*) to eye, ogle.

remâcher [rəmāshā] *vt* to chew *ou* ruminate over.

remailler [rəmāyā] *vt* (*tricot*) to darn; (*filet*) to mend.

remaniement [rəmánēmán̄] *nm*: ~ **ministériel** Cabinet reshuffle.

remanier [rəmányā] *vt* to reshape, recast; (*POL*) to reshuffle.

remarier [r(ə)máryā]: **se ~** *vi* to remarry, get married again.

remarquable [rəmárkábl(ə)] *a* remarkable.

remarquablement [r(ə)márkáblǝmán̄] *ad* remarkably.

remarque [rəmárk(ə)] *nf* remark; (*écrite*) note.

remarquer [rəmárkā] *vt* (*voir*) to notice; (*dire*): ~ **que** to remark that; **se ~** to be noticeable; **se faire ~** to draw attention to o.s.; **faire ~ (à qn) que** to point out (to sb) that; **faire ~ qch (à qn)** to point sth out (to sb); **remarquez, ...** mind you, ...

remballer [rán̄bálā] *vt* to wrap up (again); (*dans un carton*) to pack up (again).

rembarrer [rán̄bárā] *vt*: ~ **qn** (*repousser*) to rebuff sb; (*remettre à sa place*) to put sb in his (*ou her*) place.

remblai [rán̄ble] *nm* embankment.

remblayer [rán̄blāyā] *vt* to bank up; (*fossé*) to fill in.

rembobiner [rán̄bobēnā] *vt* to rewind.

rembourrage [rán̄boōrázh] *nm* stuffing; padding.

rembourré, e [rán̄boōrā] *a* padded.

rembourrer [rán̄boōrā] *vt* to stuff; (*dossier,*

vêtement, souliers) to pad.
remboursable [rånbōōrsábl(ə)] *a* repayable.
remboursement [rånbōōrsəmåń] *nm* repayment; **envoi contre** ~ cash on delivery.
rembourser [rånbōōrsā] *vt* to pay back, repay.
rembrunir [rånbrünēr]: **se** ~ *vi* to grow somber (*US*) *ou* sombre (*Brit*).
remède [rəmed] *nm* (*médicament*) medicine; (*traitement, fig*) remedy, cure; **trouver un** ~ **à** (*MÉD, fig*) to find a cure for.
remédier [rəmādyā]: ~ **à** *vt* to remedy.
remembrement [rəmåńbrəmåń] *nm* (*AGR*) regrouping of lands.
remémorer [rəmāmorā]: **se** ~ *vt* to recall, recollect.
remerciements [rəmersēmåń] *nmpl* thanks; **(avec) tous mes** ~ (with) grateful *ou* many thanks.
remercier [rəmersyā] *vt* to thank; (*congédier*) to dismiss; ~ **qn de/d'avoir fait** to thank sb for/for having done; **non, je vous remercie** no, thank you.
remettre [rəmetr(ə)] *vt* (*vêtement*): ~ **qch** to put sth back on, put sth on again; (*replacer*): ~ **qch quelque part** to put sth back somewhere; (*ajouter*): ~ **du sel/un sucre** to add more salt/another lump of sugar; (*rétablir: personne*): ~ **qn** to set sb back on his (*ou* her) feet; (*rendre, restituer*): ~ **qch à qn** to give sth back to sb, return sth to sb; (*donner, confier: paquet, argent*): ~ **qch à qn** to hand sth over to sb, deliver sth to sb; (*prix, décoration*): ~ **qch à qn** to present sb with sth; (*ajourner*): ~ **qch (à)** to postpone sth *ou* put sth off (until); **se** ~ *vi* to get better, recover; **se** ~ **de** to recover from, get over; **s'en** ~ **à** to leave it (up) to; **se** ~ **à faire/qch** to start doing/sth again; ~ **une pendule à l'heure** to set a clock right; ~ **un moteur/une machine en marche** to get an engine/a machine going again; ~ **en état/en ordre** to repair/sort out; ~ **en cause/question** to challenge/question again; ~ **sa démission** to hand in one's notice; ~ **qch à neuf** to make sth as good as new; ~ **qn à sa place** (*fig*) to put sb in his (*ou* her) place.
remis, e [rəmē, -ēz] *pp de* **remettre** ♦ *nf* delivery; presentation; (*rabais*) discount; (*local*) shed; ~ **en marche/en ordre** starting up again/sorting out; ~ **en cause/question** calling into question/challenging; ~ **de fonds** remittance; ~ **en jeu** (*FOOTBALL*) throw-in; ~ **à neuf** restoration; ~ **de peine** reduction *ou* commutation (*US*) of sentence.
remiser [rəmēzā] *vt* to put away.
rémission [rāmēsyóń]: **sans** ~ *a* irremediable ♦ *ad* unremittingly.
remodeler [rəmodlā] *vt* to remodel; (*fig: restructurer*) to restructure.
rémois, e [rāmwà, -wáz] *a* of *ou* from Rheims ♦ *nm/f*: **R~, e** inhabitant *ou* native of Rheims.
remontant [rəmóńtåń] *nm* tonic, pick-me-up.
remontée [rəmóńtā] *nf* rising; ascent; ~**s mécaniques** (*SKI*) ski lifts, ski tows.
remonte-pente [rəmóńtpåńt] *nm* ski lift, (ski) tow.
remonter [rəmóńtā] *vi* (*à nouveau*) to go back

up; (*sur un cheval*) to remount; (*après une descente*) to go up (again); (*dans une voiture*) to get back in; (*jupe*) to ride up ♦ *vt* (*pente*) to go up; (*fleuve*) to sail (*ou* swim etc) up; (*manches, pantalon*) to roll up; (*col*) to turn up; (*niveau, limite*) to raise; (*fig: personne*) to buck up; (*moteur, meuble*) to put back together, reassemble; (*garde-robe etc*) to renew, replenish; (*montre, mécanisme*) to wind up; ~ **le moral à qn** to raise sb's spirits; ~ **à** (*dater de*) to date *ou* go back to; ~ **en voiture** to get back into the car.
remontoir [rəmóńtwár] *nm* winding mechanism, winder.
remontrance [rəmóńtråńs] *nf* reproof, reprimand.
remontrer [rəmóńtrā] *vt* (*montrer de nouveau*): ~ **qch (à qn)** to show sth again (to sb); (*fig*): **en** ~ **à** to prove one's superiority over.
remords [rəmor] *nm* remorse *q*; **avoir des** ~ to feel remorse, be conscience-stricken.
remorque [rəmork(ə)] *nf* trailer; **prendre/être en** ~ to tow/be on tow; **être à la** ~ (*fig*) to tag along (behind).
remorquer [rəmorkā] *vt* to tow.
remorqueur [rəmorkœr] *nm* tug(boat).
rémoulade [rāmōōlád] *nf* dressing with mustard and herbs.
rémouleur [rāmōōlœr] *nm* (knife- *ou* scissor-) grinder
remous [rəmōō] *nm* (*d'un navire*) (back)wash *q*; (*de rivière*) swirl, eddy ♦ *nmpl* (*fig*) stir *sg*.
rempailler [rånpāyā] *vt* to reseat (*with straw*).
remparts [rånpár] *nmpl* walls, ramparts.
rempiler [rånpēlā] *vt* (*dossiers, livres etc*) to pile up again ♦ *vi* (*MIL, fam*) to join up again.
remplaçant, e [rånplásåń, -åńt] *nm/f* replacement, substitute, stand-in; (*THÉÂTRE*) understudy; (*SCOL*) substitute (*US*) *ou* supply (*Brit*) teacher.
remplacement [rånplásmåń] *nm* replacement; (*job*) replacement work *q*; (*suppléance: SCOL*) substitute (*US*) *ou* supply (*Brit*) teacher; **assurer le** ~ **de qn** (*suj: remplaçant*) to stand in *ou* substitute for sb; **faire des** ~**s** (*professeur*) to do supply *ou* substitute teaching; (*médecin*) to do locum work.
remplacer [rånplásā] *vt* to replace; (*prendre temporairement la place de*) to stand in for; (*tenir lieu de*) to take the place of, act as a substitute for; ~ **qch/qn par** to replace sth/sb with.
rempli, e [rånplē] *a* (*emploi du temps*) full, busy; ~ **de** full of, filled with.
remplir [rånplēr] *vt* to fill (up); (*questionnaire*) to fill out *ou* in; (*obligations, fonction, condition*) to fulfill (*US*), fulfil (*Brit*); **se** ~ *vi* to fill up; ~ **qch de** to fill sth with.
remplissage [rånplēsázh] *nm* (*fig: péj*) padding.
remploi [rånplwá] *nm* re-use.
rempocher [rånposhā] *vt* to put back into one's pocket.
remporter [rånportā] *vt* (*marchandise*) to take

away; *(fig)* to win, achieve.
rempoter [rɑ̃pɔtā] *vt* to repot.
remuant, e [rəmüɑ̃n̄, -ɑ̃t] *a* restless.
remue-ménage [rəmümānäzh] *nm inv*
commotion.
remuer [rəmüā] *vt* to move; *(café, sauce)* to
stir ♦ *vi* to move; *(fig: opposants)* to show
signs of unrest; **se ~** *vi* to move; *(se
démener)* to stir o.s.; *(fam)* to get a move
on.
rémunérateur, trice [rāmünārätœr, -trēs] *a* re-
munerative, lucrative.
rémunération [rāmünārāsyôn̄] *nf* remuneration.
rémunérer [rāmünārā] *vt* to remunerate, pay.
renâcler [rənäklā] *vi* to snort; *(fig)* to grumble,
balk.
renaissance [rənesɑ̃n̄s] *nf* rebirth, revival; **la
R~** the Renaissance.
renaître [rənetr(ə)] *vi* to be revived; **~ à la
vie** to take on a new lease of life; **~ à
l'espoir** to find fresh hope.
rénal, e, aux [rānäl, -ō] *a* renal, kidney *cpd*.
renard [rənär] *nm* fox.
renardeau [rənärdō] *nm* fox cub.
rencard [rɑ̃kär] *nm* = **rancard**.
rencart [rɑ̃kär] *nm* = **rancart**.
renchérir [rɑ̃shārēr] *vi* to become more
expensive; *(fig)*: **~ (sur)** to add something
(to).
renchérissement [rɑ̃shārēsmɑ̃n̄] *nm* increase
(in the cost *ou* price of).
rencontre [rɑ̃kôn̄tr(ə)] *nf* *(de cours d'eau)*
confluence; *(véhicules)* collision; *(entrevue,
congrès, match etc)* meeting; *(imprévue)* encounter; **faire la ~ de qn** to meet sb; **aller à
la ~ de qn** to go and meet sb; **amours de ~**
casual love affairs.
rencontrer [rɑ̃kôn̄trā] *vt* to meet; *(mot,
expression)* to come across; *(difficultés)* to
meet with; **se ~** to meet; *(véhicules)* to
collide.
rendement [rɑ̃dmɑ̃n̄] *nm* *(d'un travailleur,
d'une machine)* output; *(d'une culture)* yield;
(d'un investissement) return; **à plein ~** at
full capacity.
rendez-vous [rɑ̃dāvōō] *nm* *(rencontre)*
appointment; *(: d'amoureux)* date; *(lieu)*
meeting place; **donner ~ à qn** to arrange to
meet sb; **recevoir sur ~** to have an appointment system; **fixer un ~ à qn** to give sb an
appointment; **avoir/prendre ~ (avec)** to
have/make an appointment (with); **prendre
~ chez le médecin** to make an appointment
with the doctor; **~ spatial** *ou* **orbital** docking
(in space).
rendre [rɑ̃dr(ə)] *vt* *(livre, argent etc)* to give
back, return; *(otages, visite, politesse, JUR:
verdict)* to return; *(honneurs)* to pay; *(sang,
aliments)* to bring up; *(sons: suj: instrument)* to produce, make; *(exprimer,
traduire)* to render; *(jugement)* to pronounce,
render; *(faire devenir)*: **~ qn célèbre/qch
possible** to make sb famous/sth possible; **se
~ vi** *(capituler)* to surrender, give o.s. up;
(aller): **se ~ quelque part** to go somewhere;
se ~ à *(arguments etc)* to bow to; *(ordres)*
to comply with; **se ~ compte de qch** to realize sth; **~ la vue/la santé à qn** to restore

sb's sight/health; **~ la liberté à qn** to set sb
free; **~ la monnaie** to give change; **se ~
insupportable/malade** to become unbear-
able/make o.s. ill.
rendu, e [rɑ̃dü] *pp de* **rendre** ♦ *a (fatigué)*
exhausted.
renégat, e [rənägä, -ät] *nm/f* renegade.
renégocier [rənāgosyā] *vt* to renegociate.
rênes [ren] *nfpl* reins.
renfermé, e [rɑ̃fermā] *a (fig)* withdrawn ♦
nm: **sentir le ~** to smell stuffy.
renfermer [rɑ̃fermā] *vt* to contain; **se ~ (sur
soi-même)** to withdraw into o.s.
renfiler [rɑ̃fēlā] *vt (collier)* to rethread; *(pull)*
to slip on.
renflé, e [rɑ̃flā] *a* bulging, bulbous.
renflement [rɑ̃fləmɑ̃n̄] *nm* bulge.
renflouer [rɑ̃flōōā] *vt* to refloat; *(fig)* to set
back on its *(ou* his/her *etc)* feet (again).
renfoncement [rɑ̃fôn̄smɑ̃n̄] *nm* recess.
renforcer [rɑ̃forsā] *vt* to reinforce; **~ qn
dans ses opinions** to confirm sb's opinion.
renfort [rɑ̃for]: **~s** *nmpl* reinforcements; **en
~** as a back-up; **à grand ~ de** with a great
deal of.
renfrogné, e [rɑ̃fronyā] *a* sullen, scowling.
renfrogner [rɑ̃fronyā]: **se ~** *vi* to scowl.
rengager [rɑ̃gäzhā] *vt (personnel)* to take on
again; **se ~** *(MIL)* to re-enlist.
rengaine [rɑ̃gen] *nf (péj)* old tune.
rengainer [rɑ̃gānā] *vt (revolver)* to put back
in its holster; *(épée)* to sheathe; *(fam:
compliment, discours)* to save, withhold.
rengorger [rɑ̃gorzhā]: **se ~** *vi (fig)* to puff
o.s. up.
renier [rənyā] *vt (parents)* to disown, repudiate; *(engagements)* to go back on; *(foi)*
to renounce.
renifler [rənēflā] *vi* to sniff ♦ *vt (tabac)* to sniff
up; *(odeur)* to sniff.
rennais, e [rene, -ez] *a* of *ou* from Rennes ♦
nm/f: **R~, e** inhabitant *ou* native of Rennes.
renne [ren] *nm* reindeer *inv.*
renom [rənôn̄] *nm* reputation; *(célébrité)* renown; **vin de grand ~** celebrated *ou* highly
renowned wine.
renommé, e [r(ə)nomā] *a* celebrated, renowned ♦ *nf* fame.
renoncement [rənôn̄smɑ̃n̄] *nm* abnegation, renunciation.
renoncer [rənôn̄sā] *vi*: **~ à** *vt* to give up; **~ à
faire** to give up the idea of doing; **j'y
renonce!** I give up!
renouer [rənwā] *vt (cravate etc)* to retie; *(fig:
conversation, liaison)* to renew, resume; **~
avec** *(tradition)* to revive; *(habitude)* to take
up again; **~ avec qn** to take up with sb
again.
renouveau, x [rənōōvō] *nm* revival; **~ de
succès** renewed success.
renouvelable [r(ə)nōōvläbl(ə)] *a (contrat,
bail)* renewable; *(expérience)* which can be
renewed.
renouveler [rənōōvlā] *vt* to renew; *(exploit,
méfait)* to repeat; **se ~** *vi (incident)* to recur, happen again, be repeated; *(cellules etc)*
to be renewed or replaced; *(artiste, écrivain)*
to try something new.
renouvellement [r(ə)nōōvelmɑ̃n̄] *nm* renewal;

recurrence.

rénovation [rānovâsyôn] *nf* renovation; restoration; reform(ing); redevelopment.

rénover [rānovā] *vt* (*immeuble*) to renovate, do up; (*meuble*) to restore; (*enseignement*) to reform; (*quartier*) to redevelop.

renseignement [rânsenymân] *nm* information *q*, piece of information; (*MIL*) intelligence *q*; **prendre des ~s sur** to make inquiries about, ask for information about; **(guichet des) ~s** information desk; **(service des) ~s** (*TÉL*) information (*US*), directory inquiries (*Brit*); **service/agent de ~s** (*MIL*) intelligence service/agent; **les ~s généraux** ≈ the secret police.

renseigner [rânsānyā] *vt*: **~ qn (sur)** to give information to sb (about); **se ~** *vi* to ask for information, make inquiries.

rentabiliser [rântábēlēzā] *vt* (*capitaux, production*) to make profitable.

rentabilité [rântábēlētā] *nf* profitability; cost-effectiveness; (*d'un investissement*) return; **seuil de ~** break-even point.

rentable [rântábl(ə)] *a* profitable; cost-effective.

rente [rânt] *nf* income; (*pension*) pension; (*titre*) government stock *ou* bond; **~ viagère** life annuity.

rentier, ière [rântyā, -yer] *nm/f* person of private *ou* independent means.

rentrée [rântrā] *nf*: **~ (d'argent)** cash *q* coming in; **la ~ (des classes)** the start of the new school year; **la ~ (parlementaire)** the reopening *ou* reassembly of parliament; **faire sa ~** (*artiste, acteur*) to make a comeback.

rentrer [rântrā] *vi* (*entrer de nouveau*) to go (*ou* come) back in; (*entrer*) to go (*ou* come) in; (*revenir chez soi*) to go (*ou* come) (back) home; (*air, clou: pénétrer*) to go in; (*revenu, argent*) to come in ♦ *vt* (*foins*) to bring in; (*véhicule*) to put away; (*chemise dans pantalon etc*) to tuck in; (*griffes*) to draw in; (*train d'atterrissage*) to raise; (*fig: larmes, colère etc*) to hold back; **~ le ventre** to pull in one's stomach; **~ dans** to go (*ou* come) back into; to go (*ou* come) into; (*famille, patrie*) to go back *ou* return to; (*heurter*) to crash into; (*appartenir à*) to be included in; (*: catégorie etc*) to fall into; **~ dans l'ordre** to get back to normal; **~ dans ses frais** to recover one's expenses (*ou* initial outlay).

renverrai [rânverā] *etc vb voir* **renvoyer**.

renversant, e [rânversân, -ânt] *a* amazing, astounding.

renverse [rânvers(ə)]: **à la ~** *ad* backwards.

renversé, e [rânversā] *a* (*écriture*) backhand; (*image*) reversed; (*stupéfait*) staggered.

renversement [rânversəmân] *nm* (*d'un régime, des traditions*) overthrow; **~ de la situation** reversal of the situation.

renverser [rânversā] *vt* (*faire tomber: chaise, verre*) to knock over, overturn; (*piéton*) to knock down; (*liquide, contenu*) to spill, upset; (*retourner: verre, image*) to turn upside down, invert; (*: ordre des mots etc*) to reverse; (*fig: gouvernement etc*) to overthrow; (*stupéfier*) to bowl over, stagger; **se ~** *vi* to fall over; to overturn; to spill; **se ~ (en arrière)** to lean back; **~ la tête/le corps**

(en arrière) to tip one's head back/throw oneself back; **~ la vapeur** (*fig*) to change course.

renvoi [rânvwá] *nm* dismissal; return; reflection; postponement; (*référence*) cross-reference; (*éructation*) belch.

renvoyer [rânvwáyā] *vt* to send back; (*congédier*) to dismiss; (*TENNIS*) to return; (*lumière*) to reflect; (*son*) to echo; (*ajourner*): **~ qch (à)** to put sth off *ou* postpone sth (until); **~ qch à qn** (*rendre*) to return sth to sb; **~ qn à** (*fig*) to refer sb to.

réorganisation [rāorgánēzâsyôn] *nf* reorganization.

réorganiser [rāorgánēzā] *vt* to reorganize.

réorienter [rāoryântā] *vt* to reorient(ate), redirect.

réouverture [rāōōvertür] *nf* reopening.

repaire [rəper] *nm* den.

repaître [rəpetr(ə)] *vt* to feast; to feed; **se ~ de** *vt* (*animal*) to feed on; (*fig*) to wallow *ou* revel in.

répandre [rāpândr(ə)] *vt* (*renverser*) to spill; (*étaler, diffuser*) to spread; (*chaleur, odeur*) to give off; **se ~** *vi* to shed; (*chaleur, odeur*) to give off; **se ~** *vi* to spill; to spread; **se ~ en** (*injures etc*) to pour out.

répandu, e [rāpândü] *pp de* **répandre** ♦ *a* (*opinion, usage*) widespread.

réparable [rāpárábl(ə)] *a* (*montre etc*) repairable; (*perte etc*) which can be made up for.

reparaître [rəparetr(ə)] *vi* to reappear.

réparateur, trice [rāpárátœr, -trēs] *nm/f* repairer.

réparation [rāpárâsyôn] *nf* repairing *q*, repair; **en ~** (*machine etc*) under repair; **demander à qn ~ de** (*offense etc*) to ask sb to make amends for.

réparer [rāpárā] *vt* to repair; (*fig: offense*) to make up for, atone for; (*: oubli, erreur*) to make *ou* set right.

reparler [rəparlā] *vi*: **~ de qn/qch** to talk about sb/sth again; **~ à qn** to speak to sb again.

repars [rəpár] *etc vb voir* **repartir**.

repartie [rəpártē] *nf* retort; **avoir de la ~** to be quick at repartee.

repartir [rəpártēr] *vi* to set off again; to leave again; (*fig*) to get going again, pick up again; **~ à zéro** to start from scratch (again).

répartir [rāpártēr] *vt* (*pour attribuer*) to divide up, share out (*Brit*); (*pour disperser, disposer*) to divide up; (*poids, chaleur*) to distribute; (*étaler: dans le temps*): **~ sur** to spread over; (*classer, diviser*): **~ en** to divide into, split up into; **se ~** *vt* (*travail, rôles*) to divide up between themselves.

répartition [rāpártēsyôn] *nf* dividing up; distribution.

repas [rəpâ] *nm* meal; **à l'heure des ~** at mealtimes.

repassage [rəpâsázh] *nm* ironing.

repasser [rəpâsā] *vi* to come (*ou* go) back ♦ *vt* (*vêtement, tissu*) to iron; (*examen*) to retake; (*film*) to show again; (*lame*) to sharpen; (*leçon, rôle: revoir*) to go over (again); (*plat, pain*): **~ qch à qn** to pass sth back to sb.

repasseuse [rəpâsœz] *nf* (*machine*) ironing machine.

repayer [rəpāyā] *vt* to pay again.

repêchage [rəpeshâzh] *nm* (*SCOL*): **question de ~** question to give students (*ou* examinees) a second chance.

repêcher [rəpāshā] *vt* (*noyé*) to recover the body of, fish out; (*fam: candidat*) to pass (*by inflating grades*); to give a second chance to.

repeindre [rəpañdr(ə)] *vt* to repaint.

repentir [rəpáñtēr] *nm* repentance; **se ~** *vi*: **se ~ (de)** to repent (of).

répercussions [rāperküsyóñ] *nfpl* repercussions.

répercuter [rāperkütā] *vt* (*réfléchir, renvoyer: son, voix*) to reflect; (*faire transmettre: consignes, charges etc*) to pass on; **se ~** *vi* (*bruit*) to reverberate; (*fig*): **se ~ sur** to have repercussions on.

repère [rəper] *nm* mark; (*monument etc*) landmark; **(point de) ~** point of reference.

repérer [rəpārā] *vt* (*erreur, connaissance*) to spot; (*abri, ennemi*) to locate; **se ~** *vi* to get one's bearings; **se faire ~** to be spotted.

répertoire [rāpertwár] *nm* (*liste*) (alphabetical) list; (*carnet*) index notebook; (*INFORM*) directory; (*de carnet*) thumb index; (*indicateur*) directory, index; (*d'un théâtre, artiste*) repertoire.

répertorier [rāpertoryā] *vt* to itemize, list.

répéter [rāpātā] *vt* to repeat; (*préparer: leçon: aussi vi*) to learn, go over; (*THÉÂTRE*) to rehearse; **se ~** (*redire*) to repeat o.s.; (*se reproduire*) to be repeated, recur.

répéteur [rāpātœr] *nm* (*TÉL*) repeater.

répétitif, ive [rāpātētēf, -ēv] *a* repetitive.

répétition [rāpátesyóñ] *nf* repetition; (*THÉÂTRE*) rehearsal; **~s** *nfpl* (*leçons*) private tutoring *sg*; **armes à ~** repeater weapons; **~ générale** final dress rehearsal.

repeupler [rəpœplā] *vt* to repopulate; (*forêt, rivière*) to restock.

repiquage [rəpēkázh] *nm* pricking out, planting out; re-recording.

repiquer [rəpēkā] *vt* (*plants*) to prick out, plant out; (*enregistrement*) to re-record.

répit [rāpē] *nm* respite; **sans ~** without letting up.

replacer [rəplásā] *vt* to replace, put back.

replanter [rəplāñtā] *vt* to replant.

replat [rəplá] *nm* ledge.

replâtrer [rəplātrā] *vt* (*mur*) to replaster; (*fig*) to patch up.

replet, ète [rəple, -et] *a* chubby, fat.

repli [rəplē] *nm* (*d'une étoffe*) fold; (*MIL, fig*) withdrawal.

replier [rəplēyā] *vt* (*rabattre*) to fold down *ou* over; **se ~** *vi* (*troupes, armée*) to withdraw, fall back; **se ~ sur soi-même** to withdraw into oneself.

réplique [rāplēk] *nf* (*repartie, fig*) reply; (*objection*) retort; (*THÉÂTRE*) line; (*copie*) replica; **donner la ~ à** to play opposite; **sans ~** a no-nonsense; irrefutable.

répliquer [rāplēkā] *vi* to reply; (*avec impertinence*) to answer back; (*riposter*) to retaliate.

replonger [rəplôñzhā] *vt*: **~ qch dans** to plunge sth back into; **se ~ dans** (*journal etc*)

to immerse o.s. in again.

répondant, e [rāpóñdáñ, -áñt] *nm/f* (*garant*) guarantor, surety.

répondeur [rāpóñdœr] *nm*: **~ (automatique)** (*TÉL*) (telephone) answering machine.

répondre [rāpôñdr(ə)] *vi* to answer, reply; (*freins, mécanisme*) to respond; **~ à** *vt* to reply to, answer; (*avec impertinence*): **~ à qn** to answer sb back; (*invitation, convocation*) to reply to; (*affection, salut*) to return; (*provocation, suj: mécanisme etc*) to respond to; (*correspondre à: besoin*) to answer; (*: conditions*) to meet; (*: description*) to match; **~ que** to answer *ou* reply that; **~ de** to answer for.

réponse [rāpóñs] *nf* answer, reply; **avec ~ payée** (*POSTES*) reply-paid, post-paid (*US*); **avoir ~ à tout** to have an answer for everything; **en ~ à** in reply to; **carte- /bulletin-~** reply card/slip.

report [rəpor] *nm* postponement; transfer; **~ d'incorporation** (*MIL*) deferment.

reportage [rəportázh] *nm* (*bref*) report; (*écrit: documentaire*) story; article; (*en direct*) commentary; (*genre, activité*): **le ~** reporting.

reporter *nm* [rəporter] reporter ♦ *vt* [rəportā] (*total*): **~ qch sur** to carry sth forward *ou* over to; (*ajourner*): **~ qch (à)** to postpone sth (until); (*transférer*): **~ qch sur** to transfer sth to; **se ~ à** (*époque*) to think back to; (*document*) to refer to.

repos [rəpō] *nm* rest; (*fig*) peace (and quiet); (*mental*) peace of mind; (*MIL*): **~!** (stand) at ease!; **en ~** at rest; **au ~** at rest; (*soldat*) at ease; **de tout ~** safe.

reposant, e [r(ə)pōzáñ, -áñt] *a* restful; (*sommeil*) refreshing.

repose [rəpōz] *nf* refitting.

reposé, e [rəpōzā] *a* fresh, rested; **à tête ~e** in a leisurely way, taking time to think.

repose-pied [rəpōzpyā] *nm inv* footrest.

reposer [rəpōzā] *vt* (*verre, livre*) to put down; (*rideaux, carreaux*) to put back; (*délasser*) to rest; (*problème*) to reformulate ♦ *vi* (*liquide, pâte*) to settle, rest; (*personne*): **ici repose** ... here lies ...; **~ sur** to be built on; (*fig*) to rest on; **se ~** *vi* to rest; **se ~ sur qn** to rely on sb.

repoussant, e [rəpōōsáñ, -áñt] *a* repulsive.

repoussé, e [rəpōōsā] *a* (*cuir*) embossed (by hand).

repousser [rəpōōsā] *vi* to grow again ♦ *vt* to repel, repulse; (*offre*) to turn down, reject; (*tiroir, personne*) to push back; (*différer*) to put off, defer.

répréhensible [rāprāáñsēbl(ə)] *a* reprehensible.

reprendre [rəpráñdr(ə)] *vt* (*prisonnier, ville*) to recapture; (*objet prêté, donné*) to take back; (*chercher*): **je viendrai te ~ à 4h** I'll come back for you at 4; (*se resservir de*): **~ du pain/un œuf** to take (*ou* eat) more bread/another egg; (*COMM: article usagé*) to take back; to take as a trade-in; (*firme, entreprise*) to take over; (*travail, promenade*) to resume; (*emprunter: argument, idée*) to take up, use; (*refaire: article etc*) to go over again; (*jupe etc*) to alter; (*émission, pièce*) to put on again; (*réprimander*) to tell off; (*corriger*) to correct ♦ *vi* (*classes, pluie*) to start (up) again; (*activités, travaux, combats*) to resume, start (up) again; (*affaires, industrie*) to pick up; (*dire*): **reprit-il** he went on; **se ~** (*se ressaisir*) to recover, pull o.s. together; **s'y ~** to make another attempt; **~ des forces** to recover one's strength; **~ courage** to take new courage; **~ ses habitudes/sa liberté** to get back into one's old habits/regain one's freedom; **~ la route** to resume one's journey, set off again; **~ connaissance** to come to, regain consciousness; **~ haleine** *ou* **son souffle** to get one's breath back; **~ la parole** to speak again.

repreneur [rəprənœr] *nm* company fixer *ou* doctor.

reprenne [rəpren] *etc vb voir* **reprendre**.

représailles [rəprāzáy] *nfpl* reprisals, retaliation *sg*.

représentant, e [rəprāzáńtáǹ, -áǹt] *nm/f* representative.

représentatif, ive [rəprāzáńtátĕf, -ēv] *a* representative.

représentation [rəprazäntäsyóǹ] *nf* representation; performing; (*symbole, image*) representation; (*spectacle*) performance; (*COMM*): **la ~** commercial traveling (*US*) *ou* travelling (*Brit*); sales representation; **frais de ~** (*d'un diplomate*) entertainment allowance.

représenter [rəprāzáńtā] *vt* to represent; (*donner: pièce, opéra*) to perform; **se ~** *vt* (*se figurer*) to imagine; to visualize ♦ *vi*: **se ~ à** (*POL*) to run again for; (*SCOL*) to retake.

répressif, ive [rāprăsĕf, -ēv] *a* repressive.

répression [rāprăsyóǹ] *nf* (*voir réprimer*) suppression; repression; (*POL*): **la ~** repression; **mesures de ~** repressive measures.

réprimande [rāprēmáǹd] *nf* reprimand, rebuke.

réprimander [rāprēmáǹdā] *vt* to reprimand, rebuke.

réprimer [rāprēmā] *vt* (*émotions*) to suppress; (*peuple etc*) repress.

repris, e [rəprē, -ēz] *pp de* **reprendre** ♦ *nm*: **~ de justice** ex-prisoner, ex-convict.

reprise [rəprēz] *nf* (*recommencement*) resumption; (*économique*) recovery; (*TV*) rerun; (*CINÉMA*) rerun; (*BOXE etc*) round; (*AUTO*) acceleration *q*; (*COMM*) trade-in; (*de location*) sum asked for any extras or improvements made to the property; (*raccommodage*) darn; mend; **la ~ des hostilités** the resumption of hostilities; **à plusieurs ~s** on several occasions, several times.

repriser [rəprēzā] *vt* to darn; to mend; **aiguille/coton à ~** darning needle/thread.

réprobateur, trice [rāprobátœr, -trēs] *a* reproving.

réprobation [rāprobásyóǹ] *nf* reprobation.

reproche [rəprosh] *nm* (*remontrance*) reproach; **ton/air de ~** reproachful tone/look; **faire des ~s à qn** to reproach sb; **faire ~ à qn de qch** to reproach sb for sth; **sans ~(s)** beyond *ou* above reproach.

reprocher [rəproshā] *vt*: **~ qch à qn** to reproach *ou* blame sb for sth; **~ qch à** (*machine, théorie*) to have sth against; **se ~ qch/d'avoir fait qch** to blame o.s. for sth/for doing sth.

reproducteur, trice [rəprodüktœr, -trēs] *a* reproductive.

reproduction [rəprodüksyóǹ] *nf* reproduction; **~ interdite** all rights (of reproduction) reserved.

reproduire [rəprodüēr] *vt* to reproduce; **se ~** *vi* (*BIO*) to reproduce; (*recommencer*) to recur, re-occur.

réprouvé, e [rāprōōvā] *nm/f* reprobate.

réprouver [rāprōōvā] *vt* to reprove.

reptation [reptásyóǹ] *nf* crawling.

reptile [reptēl] *nm* reptile.

repu, e [rəpü] *pp de* **repaître** ♦ *a* satisfied, sated.

républicain, e [rāpüblēkaǹ, -en] *a, nm/f* republican.

république [rāpüblēk] *nf* republic; **R~ arabe du Yémen** Yemen Arab Republic; **R~ Centrafricaine** Central African Republic; **R~ de Corée** South Korea; **R~ démocratique allemande (RDA)** German Democratic Republic (GDR); **R~ dominicaine** Dominican Republic; **R~ fédérale d'Allemagne (RFA)** Federal Republic of Germany; **R~ d'Irlande** Irish Republic, Eire; **R~ populaire de Chine** People's Republic of China; **R~ populaire démocratique de Corée** Democratic People's Republic of Korea; **R~ populaire du Yémen** People's Democratic Republic of Yemen.

répudier [rāpüdyā] *vt* (*femme*) to repudiate; (*doctrine*) to renounce.

répugnance [rāpünyáǹs] *nf* repugnance, loathing; **avoir** *ou* **éprouver de la ~ pour** (*médicament, comportement, travail etc*) to have an aversion to; **avoir** *ou* **éprouver de la ~ à faire qch** to be reluctant to do sth.

répugnant, e [rāpünyáǹ, -áǹt] *a* repulsive, loathsome.

répugner [rāpünyā]: **~ à** *vt*: **~ à qn** to repel *ou* disgust sb; **~ à faire** to be loath *ou* reluctant to do.

répulsion [rāpülsyóǹ] *nf* repulsion.

réputation [rāpütásyóǹ] *nf* reputation; **avoir la ~ d'être ...** to have a reputation for being ...; **connaître qn/qch de ~** to know sb/sth by repute; **de ~ mondiale** world-renowned.

réputé, e [rāpütā] *a* renowned; **être ~ pour** to have a reputation for, be renowned for.

requérir [rəkărēr] *vt* (*nécessiter*) to require, call for; (*au nom de la loi*) to call upon; (*JUR: peine*) to call for, demand.

requête [rəket] *nf* request, petition; (*JUR*) petition.

requiem [rāküèyem] *nm* requiem.

requiers [rəkyer] *etc vb voir* **requérir**.

requin [rəkaǹ] *nm* shark.

requinquer [rəkaǹkā] *vt* to set up, pep up.

requis, e [rəkē, -ēz] *pp de* **requérir** ♦ *a* required.

réquisition [rākēzēsyóǹ] *nf* requisition.

réquisitionner [rākēzēsyonā] *vt* to requisition.

réquisitoire [rākēzētwár] *nm* (*JUR*) closing speech for the prosecution; (*fig*): **~ contre** indictment of.

RER *sigle m* (= *Réseau express régional*) Greater Paris high speed train service.

rescapé, e [reskápā] *nm/f* survivor.

rescousse [reskōōs] *nf*: **aller à la ~ de qn** to go to sb's aid *ou* rescue; **appeler qn à la ~** to call on sb for help.

réseau, x [rāzō] *nm* network.

réséda [rāzādá] *nm* (BOT) reseda, mignonette.

réservation [rāzervâsyôn] *nf* reservation; booking.

réserve [rāzerv(ə)] *nf* (*retenue*) reserve; (*entrepôt*) storeroom; (*restriction, aussi: d'Indiens*) reservation; (*de pêche, chasse*) preserve; (*restrictions*): **faire des ~s** to have reservations; **officier de ~** reserve officer; **sous toutes ~s** with all reserve; (*dire*) with reservations; **sous ~ de** subject to; **sans ~** *ad* unreservedly; **en ~** in reserve; **de ~** (*provisions etc*) in reserve.

réservé, e [rāzervā] *a* (*discret*) reserved; (*chasse, pêche*) private; **~ à** *ou* **pour** reserved for.

réserver [rāzervā] *vt* (*gén*) to reserve; (*chambre, billet etc*) to book, reserve; (*mettre de côté, garder*): **~ qch pour** *ou* **à** to keep *ou* save sth for; **~ qch à qn** to reserve (*ou* book) sth for sb; (*fig: destiner*) to have sth in store for sb; **se ~ le droit de faire** to reserve the right to do.

réserviste [rāzervēst(ə)] *nm* reservist.

réservoir [rāzervwár] *nm* tank.

résidence [rāzēdáns] *nf* residence; **~ principale/secondaire** main/second home; **~ universitaire** residence hall (*US*), dormitory (*US*), hall of residence (*Brit*); **(en) ~ surveillée** (under) house arrest.

résident, e [iāzēdán, -ánt] *nm/f* (*ressortissant*) foreign resident; (*d'un immeuble*) resident ♦ *a* (*INFORM*) resident.

résidentiel, le [rāzēdánsyel] *a* residential.

résider [rāzēdā] *vi*: **~ à** *ou* **dans** *ou* **en** to reside in; **~ dans** (*fig*) to lie in.

résidu [rāzēdü] *nm* residue *q*.

résiduel, le [rāzēdüel] *a* residual.

résignation [rāzēnyásyôn] *nf* resignation.

résigné, e [rāzēnyā] *a* resigned.

résigner [rāzēnyā] *vt* to relinquish, resign; **se ~** *vi*: **se ~ (à qch/à faire)** to resign o.s. (to sth/to doing).

résilier [rāzēlyā] *vt* to terminate.

résille [rāzēy] *nf* (hair)net.

résine [rāzēn] *nf* resin.

résiné, e [rāzēnā] *a*: **vin ~** retsina.

résineux, euse [rāzēnœ̄, -œ̄z] *a* resinous ♦ *nm* coniferous tree.

résistance [rāzēstáns] *nf* resistance; (*de réchaud, bouilloire: fil*) element.

résistant, e [rāzēstán, -ánt] *a* (*personne*) robust, tough; (*matériau*) strong, hard-wearing ♦ *nm/f* (*patriote*) Resistance worker *ou* fighter.

résister [rāzēstā] *vi* to resist; **~ à** *vt* (*assaut, tentation*) to resist; (*effort, souffrance*) to withstand; (*suj: matériau, plante*) to stand up to, withstand; (*personne: désobéir à*) to stand up to, oppose.

résolu, e [rāzolü] *pp de* **résoudre** ♦ *a* (*ferme*) resolute; **être ~ à qch/faire** to be set upon sth/doing.

résolution [rāzolüsyôn] *nf* solving; (*fermeté, décision,* INFORM) resolution; **prendre la ~ de** to make a resolution to.

résolvais [rāzolve] *etc vb voir* **résoudre**.

résonance [rāzonáns] *nf* resonance.

résonner [rāzonā] *vi* (*cloche, pas*) to reverberate, resound; (*salle*) to be resonant; **~ de** to resound with.

résorber [rāzorbā]: **se ~** *vi* (MÉD) to be resorbed; (*fig*) to be absorbed.

résoudre [rāzōōdr(ə)] *vt* to solve; **~ qn à faire qch** to get sb to make up his (*ou* her) mind to do sth; **~ de faire** to resolve to do; **se ~ à faire** to bring o.s. to do.

respect [respe] *nm* respect; **tenir en ~** to keep at bay.

respectabilité [respektábēlētā] *nf* respectability.

respectable [respektábl(ə)] *a* respectable.

respecter [respektā] *vt* to respect; **faire ~** to enforce; **le lexicographe qui se respecte** (*fig*) any self-respecting lexicographer.

respectif, ive [respektēf, -ēv] *a* respective.

respectivement [respektēvmán] *ad* respectively.

respectueusement [respektüœ̄zmán] *ad* respectfully.

respectueux, euse [respektüœ̄, -œ̄z] *a* respectful; **~ de** respectful of.

respirable [respērábl(ə)] *a*: **peu ~** unbreathable.

respiration [respērásyôn] *nf* breathing *q*; **faire une ~ complète** to breathe in and out; **retenir sa ~** to hold one's breath; **~ artificielle** artificial respiration.

respiratoire [respērátwár] *a* respiratory.

respirer [respērā] *vi* to breathe; (*fig: se reposer*) to get one's breath, have a break; (: *être soulagé*) to breathe again ♦ *vt* to breathe (in), inhale; (*manifester: santé, calme etc*) to exude.

resplendir [resplándēr] *vi* to shine; (*fig*): **~ (de)** to be radiant (with).

resplendissant, e [resplándēsán, -ánt] *a* radiant.

responsabilité [respónsábēlētā] *nf* responsibility; (*légale*) liability; **refuser la ~ de** to deny responsibility (*ou* liability) for; **prendre ses ~s** to assume responsibility for one's actions; **~ civile** civil liability; **~ pénale/morale/collective** criminal/moral/collective responsibility.

responsable [respónsábl(ə)] *a* responsible ♦ *nm/f* (*du ravitaillement etc*) person in charge; (*de parti, syndicat*) official; **~ de** responsible for; (*légalement: de dégâts etc*) liable for; (*chargé de*) in charge of, responsible for.

resquiller [reskēyā] *vi* (*au cinéma, au stade*) to sneak in (without paying); (*dans le train*) to grab a free ride.

resquilleur, euse [reskēyœr. -œ̄z] *nm/f* (*qui n'est pas invité*) gate-crasher; (*qui ne paie pas*) fare dodger.

ressac [rəsák] *nm* backwash.

ressaisir [rəsāzēr]: **se ~** *vi* to regain one's self-control; (*équipe sportive*) to rally.

ressasser [rəsásā] *vt* (*remâcher*) to keep turning over; (*redire*) to keep trotting out.

ressemblance [rəsåṅblåṅs] *nf* (*visuelle*) resemblance, similarity, likeness; (: *ART*) likeness; (*analogie, trait commun*) similarity.

ressemblant, e [rəsåṅblåṅ, -åṅt] *a* (*portrait*) lifelike, true to life.

ressembler [rəsåṅblā]: ~ **à** *vt* to be like, resemble; (*visuellement*) to look like; **se** ~ to be (*ou* look) alike.

ressemeler [rəsəmlā] *vt* to (re)sole.

ressens [r(ə)såṅ] *etc vb voir* **ressentir.**

ressentiment [rəsåṅtēmåṅ] *nm* resentment.

ressentir [rəsåṅtēr] *vt* to feel; **se** ~ **de** to feel (*ou* show) the effects of.

resserre [rəser] *nf* shed.

resserrement [r(ə)sermåṅ] *nm* narrowing; strengthening; (*goulet*) narrow part.

resserrer [rəsārā] *vt* (*pores*) to close; (*nœud, boulon*) to tighten (up); (*fig: liens*) to strengthen; **se** ~ *vi* (*route, vallée*) to narrow; (*liens*) to strengthen; **se** ~ (**autour de**) to draw closer (around); to close in (on).

ressers [r(ə)ser] *etc vb voir* **resservir.**

resservir [rəservēr] *vi* to do *ou* serve again ♦ *vt*: ~ **qch (à qn)** to serve sth up again (to sb); ~ **de qch (à qn)** to give (sb) a second helping of sth; ~ **qn (d'un plat)** to give sb a second helping (of a dish); **se** ~ **de** (*plat*) to take a second helping of; (*outil etc*) to use again.

ressort [rəsor] *vb voir* **ressortir** ♦ *nm* (*pièce*) spring; (*force morale*) spirit; (*recours*): **en dernier** ~ as a last resort; (*compétence*): **être du** ~ **de** to fall within the competence of.

ressortir [rəsortēr] *vi* to go (*ou* come) out (again); (*contraster*) to stand out; ~ **de** (*résulter de*): **il ressort de ceci que** it emerges from this that; ~ **à** (*JUR*) to come under the jurisdiction of; (*ADMIN*) to be the concern of; **faire** ~ (*fig: souligner*) to bring out.

ressortissant, e [rəsortēsåṅ, -åṅt] *nm/f* national.

ressouder [rəsōōdā] *vt* to solder together again.

ressource [rəsōōrs(ə)] *nf*: **avoir la** ~ **de** to have the possibility of; ~**s** *nfpl* resources; (*fig*) possibilities; **leur seule** ~ **était de** the only course open to them was to; ~**s d'énergie** energy resources.

ressusciter [rāsüsētā] *vt* to resuscitate, restore to life; (*fig*) to revive, bring back ♦ *vi* to rise (from the dead); (*fig: pays*) to come back to life.

restant, e [reståṅ, -åṅt] *a* remaining ♦ *nm*: **le** ~ **(de)** the remainder (of); **un** ~ **de** (*de trop*) some leftover; (*fig: vestige*) a remnant *ou* last trace of.

restaurant [restoråṅ] *nm* restaurant; **manger au** ~ to eat out; ~ **d'entreprise** staff canteen *ou* cafeteria (*US*); ~ **universitaire (RU)** university refectory *ou* cafeteria (*US*).

restaurateur, trice [restoråtœr, -trēs] *nm/f* restaurant owner, restaurateur; (*de tableaux*) restorer.

restauration [restoråsyôṅ] *nf* restoration; (*hôtellerie*) catering; ~ **rapide** fast food.

restaurer [restorā] *vt* to restore; **se** ~ *vi* to have something to eat.

restauroute [restorōōt] *nm* = **restoroute.**

reste [rest(ə)] *nm* (*restant*): **le** ~ **(de)** the rest (of); (*de trop*): **un** ~ **(de)** some leftover; (*vestige*): **un** ~ **de** a remnant *ou* last trace of; (*MATH*) remainder; ~**s** *nmpl* leftovers; (*d'une cité etc, dépouille mortelle*) remains; **avoir du temps de** ~ to have time to spare; **ne voulant pas être en** ~ not wishing to be outdone; **partir sans attendre** *ou* **demander son** ~ (*fig*) to leave without waiting to hear more; **du** ~, **au** ~ *ad* besides, moreover; **pour le reste, quant au** ~ *ad* as for the rest.

rester [restā] *vi* (*dans un lieu, un état, une position*) to stay, remain; (*subsister*) to remain, be left; (*durer*) to last, live on ♦ *vb impersonnel*: **il reste du pain/2 œufs** there's some bread/there are 2 eggs left (over); **il reste du temps/10 minutes** there's some time/there are 10 minutes left; **il me reste assez de temps** I have enough time left; **voilà tout ce qui (me) reste** that's all I've got left; **ce qui reste à faire** what remains to be done; **ce qui me reste à faire** what remains for me to do; (**il**) **reste à savoir/établir si** ... it remains to be seen/established if *ou* whether ...; **il n'en reste pas moins que** ... the fact remains that ..., it's nevertheless a fact that ...; **en** ~ **à** (*stade, menaces*) to go no further than, only go as far as; **restons-en là** let's leave it at that; ~ **sur une impression** to retain an impression; **y** ~: **il a failli y** ~ he nearly met his end.

restituer [restētüā] *vt* (*objet, somme*): ~ **qch (à qn)** to return *ou* restore sth (to sb); (*énergie*) to release; (*son*) to reproduce.

restitution [restētüsyôṅ] *nf* restoration.

restoroute [restorōōt] *nm* highway (*US*) *ou* motorway (*Brit*) restaurant.

restreindre [restråṅdr(ə)] *vt* to restrict, limit; **se** ~ (*dans ses dépenses etc*) to cut down; (*champ de recherches*) to narrow.

restreint, e [restråṅ, -åṅt] *pp de* **restreindre** ♦ *a* restricted, limited.

restrictif, ive [restrēktēf, -ēv] *a* restrictive, limiting.

restriction [restrēksyôṅ] *nf* restriction; (*condition*) qualification; ~**s** *nfpl* (*mentales*) reservations; **sans** ~ *ad* unreservedly.

restructuration [rəstrüktürâsyôṅ] *nf* restructuring.

restructurer [rəstrüktürā] *vt* to restructure.

résultante [rāzültåṅt] *nf* (*conséquence*) result, consequence.

résultat [rāzültå] *nm* result; (*conséquence*) outcome *q*, result; (*d'élection etc*) results *pl*; ~**s** *nmpl* (*d'une enquête*) findings; ~**s sportifs** sports results.

résulter [rāzültā]: ~ **de** *vt* to result from, be the result of; **il résulte de ceci que** ... the result of this is that ....

résumé [rāzümā] *nm* summary, résumé; **faire le** ~ **de** to summarize; **en** ~ *ad* in brief; (*pour conclure*) to sum up.

résumer [rāzümā] *vt* (*texte*) to summarize; (*récapituler*) to sum up; (*fig*) to epitomize, typify; **se** ~ *vi* (*personne*) to sum up (one's ideas); **se** ~ **à** to come down to.

resurgir [rəsürzhēr] *vi* to reappear, re-emerge.

résurrection [rāzüreksyôṅ] *nf* resurrection;

(fig) revival.

rétablir [rātáblēr] *vt* to restore, re-establish; *(personne: suj: traitement)*: ~ **qn** to restore sb to health, help sb recover; *(ADMIN)*: ~ **dans son emploi/ses droits** to reinstate sb in his post/restore sb's rights; **se** ~ *vi (guérir)* to recover; *(silence, calme)* to return, be restored; *(GYM etc)*: **se** ~ **(sur)** to pull o.s. up (onto).

rétablissement [rātáblēsmân] *nm* restoring; recovery; pull-up.

rétamer [rātámā] *vt* to re-coat, re-tin.

rétameur [rātámœr] *nm* tinker.

retaper [rətápā] *vt (maison, voiture etc)* to renovate; *(fam: revigorer)* to buck up; *(redactylographier)* to retype.

retard [rətár] *nm (d'une personne attendue)* lateness *q*; *(sur l'horaire, un programme, une échéance)* delay; *(fig: scolaire, mental etc)* backwardness; **être en** ~ *(pays)* to be backward; *(dans paiement, travail)* to be behind; **en** ~ **(de 2 heures)** (2 hours) late; **avoir un** ~ **de 2 km** *(SPORT)* to be 2 km behind; **rattraper son** ~ to catch up; **avoir du** ~ to be late; *(sur un programme)* to be behind (schedule); **prendre du** ~ *(train, avion)* to be delayed; *(montre)* to lose (time); **sans** ~ *ad* without delay; ~ **à l'allumage** *(AUTO)* retarded ignition; ~ **scolaire** backwardness at school.

retardataire [rətárdàter] *a* late; *(enfant, idées)* backward ♦ *nm/f* latecomer; backward child.

retardé, e [rətárdā] *a* backward.

retardement [rətárdəmân]: **à** ~ *a* delayed action *cpd*; **bombe à** ~ time bomb.

retarder [rətárdā] *vt (sur un horaire)*: ~ **qn (d'une heure)** to delay sb (an hour); *(sur un programme)*: ~ **qn (de 3 mois)** to set sb back *ou* delay sb (3 months); *(départ, date)*: ~ **qch (de 2 jours)** to delay sth (for *ou* by 2 days); *(horloge)* to set back ♦ *vi (montre)* to be slow; *(: habituellement)* to lose (time); **je retarde (d'une heure)** I'm (an hour) slow.

retendre [rətândr(ə)] *vt (câble etc)* to stretch again; *(MUS: cordes)* to retighten.

retenir [rətnēr] *vt (garder, retarder)* to keep, detain; *(maintenir: objet qui glisse, fig: colère, larmes, rire)* to hold back; *(: objet suspendu)* to hold; *(: chaleur, odeur)* to retain; *(fig: empêcher d'agir)*: ~ **qn (de faire)** to hold sb back (from doing); *(se rappeler)* to retain; *(réserver)* to reserve; *(accepter)* to accept; *(prélever)*: ~ **qch (sur)** to deduct sth (from); **se** ~ *(euphémisme)* to hold on; *(se raccrocher)*: **se** ~ **à** to hold onto; *(se contenir)*: **se** ~ **de faire** to restrain o.s. from doing; ~ **son souffle** *ou* **haleine** to hold one's breath; ~ **qn à dîner** to ask sb to stay for dinner; **je pose 3 et je retiens 2** put down 3 and carry 2.

rétention [rātânsyôn] *nf*: ~ **d'urine** urine retention.

retentir [rətântēr] *vi* to ring out; *(salle)*: ~ **de** to ring *ou* resound with; ~ **sur** *vt (fig)* to have an effect upon.

retentissant, e [rətântēsân, -ânt] *a* resounding; *(fig)* impact-making.

retentissement [rətântēsmân] *nm (re-*

tombées) repercussions *pl*; effect, impact.

retenu, e [rətnü] *pp de* **retenir** ♦ *a (place)* reserved; *(personne: empêché)* held up; *(propos: contenu, discret)* restrained ♦ *nf (prélèvement)* deduction; *(MATH)* number to carry over; *(SCOL)* detention; *(modération)* (self-)restraint; *(réserve)* reserve, reticence; *(AUTO)* (traffic) backup *(US)*, tailback *(Brit)*.

réticence [rātēsâns] *nf* reticence *q*, reluctance *q*; **sans** ~ without hesitation.

réticent, e [rātēsân, -ânt] *a* reticent, reluctant.

retiendrai [rətyândrā], **retiens** [rətyân] *etc vb voir* **retenir**.

rétif, ive [rātēf, -ēv] *a* restive.

rétine [rātēn] *nf* retina.

retint [rətân] *etc vb voir* **retenir**.

retiré, e [rətērā] *a (solitaire)* secluded; *(éloigné)* remote.

retirer [rətērā] *vt* to withdraw; *(vêtement, lunettes)* to take off, remove; *(enlever)*: ~ **qch à qn** to take sth from sb; *(extraire)*: ~ **qn/qch de** to take sb away from/sth out of, remove sb/sth from; *(reprendre: bagages, billets)* to collect, pick up; ~ **des avantages de** to derive advantages from; **se** ~ *vi (partir, reculer)* to withdraw; *(prendre sa retraite)* to retire; **se** ~ **de** to withdraw from; to retire from.

retombées [rətônbā] *nfpl (radioactives)* fallout *sg*; *(fig)* fallout; spin-offs.

retomber [rətônbā] *vi (à nouveau)* to fall again; *(rechuter)*: ~ **malade/dans l'erreur** to fall ill again/fall back into error; *(atterrir: après un saut etc)* to land; *(tomber, redescendre)* to fall back; *(pendre)* to fall, hang (down); *(échoir)*: ~ **sur qn** to fall on sb.

retordre [rətordr(ə)] *vt*: **donner du fil à** ~ **à qn** to make life difficult for sb.

rétorquer [rātorkā] *vt*: ~ **(à qn) que** to retort (to sb) that.

retors, e [rətor, -ors(ə)] *a* wily.

rétorsion [rātorsyôn] *nf*: **mesures de** ~ reprisals.

retouche [rətŏōsh] *nf* touching up *q*; alteration; **faire une** ~ *ou* **des** ~**s à** to touch up.

retoucher [rətŏōshā] *vt (photographie, tableau)* to touch up; *(texte, vêtement)* to alter.

retour [rətŏōr] *nm* return; **au** ~ *(en arrivant)* when we *(ou* they *etc)* get *(ou* got) back; *(en route)* on the way back; **pendant le** ~ on the way *ou* journey back; **à mon/ton** ~ on my/ your return; **au** ~ **de** on the return of; **être de** ~ **(de)** to be back (from); **de** ~ **à .../chez moi** back at .../back home; **en** ~ *ad* in return; **par** ~ **du courrier** by return mail; **par un juste** ~ **des choses** by a favorable twist of fate; **match** ~ return match; ~ **en arrière** *(CINÉMA)* flashback; *(mesure)* backward step; ~ **de bâton** kickback; ~ **de chariot** carriage return; ~ **à l'envoyeur** *(POSTES)* return to sender; ~ **de flamme** backfire; ~ **(automatique) à la ligne** *(INFORM)* word-wrap; ~ **de manivelle** *(fig)* backfire; ~ **offensif** renewed attack; ~ **aux sources** *(fig)* return to basics.

retournement [rətŏōrnəmân] *nm (d'une personne: revirement)* turning (around); ~

de la situation reversal of the situation.

retourner [rətōōrnā] *vt* (*dans l'autre sens: matelas, crêpe*) to turn (over); (: *caisse*) to turn upside down; (: *sac, vêtement*) to turn inside out; (*fig: argument*) to turn back; (*en remuant: terre, sol, foin*) to turn over; (*émouvoir: personne*) to shake; (*renvoyer, restituer*): ~ **qch à qn** to return sth to sb ♦ *vi* (*aller, revenir*): ~ **quelque part/à** to go back *ou* return somewhere/to; ~ **à** (*état, activité*) to return to, go back to; **se** ~ *vi* to turn over; (*tourner la tête*) to turn around; **s'en** ~ to go back; **se** ~ **contre** (*fig*) to turn against; **savoir de quoi il retourne** to know what it is all about; ~ **sa veste** (*fig*) to be a turncoat; ~ **en arrière** *ou* **sur ses pas** to turn back, retrace one's steps; ~ **aux sources** to go back to basics.

retracer [rətràsā] *vt* to relate, recount.

rétracter [rātràktā] *vt*, **se** ~ *vi* to retract.

retraduire [rətràdüēr] *vt* to translate again; (*dans la langue de départ*) to translate back.

retrait [rətre] *nm* (*voir retirer*) withdrawal; collection; (*voir se retirer*) withdrawal; (*rétrécissement*) shrinkage; **en** ~ *a* set back; **écrire en** ~ to indent; ~ **du permis (de conduire)** revocation of driver's license (*US*), disqualification from driving (*Brit*).

retraite [rətret] *nf* (*d'une armée, REL., refuge*) retreat; (*d'un employé*) retirement; (*revenu*) (retirement) pension; **être/mettre à la** ~ to be retired/pension off *ou* retire; **prendre sa** ~ to retire; **se** ~ **anticipée** early retirement; ~ **aux flambeaux** torchlight procession.

retraité, e [rətrātā] *a* retired ♦ *nm/f* (old age) pensioner.

retraitement [rətretmâṅ] *nm* reprocessing.

retraiter [rətretā] *vt* to reprocess.

retranchement [rətrâṅshmâṅ] *nm* entrenchment; **poursuivre qn dans ses derniers** ~**s** to drive sb into a corner.

retrancher [rətrâṅshā] *vt* (*passage, détails*) to take out, remove; (*nombre, somme*): ~ **qch de** to take *ou* deduct sth from; (*couper*) to cut off; **se** ~ **derrière/dans** to entrench o.s. behind/in; (*fig*) to take refuge behind/in.

retranscrire [rətrâṅskrēr] *vt* to retranscribe.

retransmettre [rətrâṅsmetr(ə)] *vt* (*RADIO*) to broadcast, relay; (*TV*) to show.

retransmission [rətrâṅsmēsyôṅ] *nf* broadcast; showing.

retravailler [rətràvàyā] *vi* to start work again ♦ *vt* to work on again.

retraverser [rətràversā] *vt* (*dans l'autre sens*) to cross back over.

rétréci, e [rātrāsē] *a* (*idées, esprit*) narrow.

rétrécir [rātrāsēr] *vt* (*vêtement*) to take in ♦ *vi* to shrink; **se** ~ *vi* to narrow.

rétrécissement [rātrāsēsmâṅ] *nm* narrowing.

retremper [rətrâṅpā] *vt*: **se** ~ **dans** (*fig*) to reimmerse o.s. in.

rétribuer [rātrēbüā] *vt* (*travail*) to pay for; (*personne*) to pay.

rétribution [rātrēbüsyôṅ] *nf* payment.

rétro [rātrō] *a inv* old-style ♦ *nm* (= *rétroviseur*) (rear-view) mirror; **la mode** ~ the nostalgia vogue.

rétroactif, ive [rātroàktēf, -ēv] *a* retroactive.

rétrocéder [rātrosādā] *vt* to retrocede.

rétrocession [rātrosāsyôṅ] *nf* retrocession.

rétrofusée [rātrofüzā] *nf* retrorocket.

rétrograde [rātrográd] *a* reactionary, backward-looking.

rétrograder [rātrográdā] *vi* (*élève*) to fall back; (*économie*) to regress; (*AUTO*) to shift to a lower gear.

rétroprojecteur [rātroprozhektœr] *nm* overhead projector.

rétrospectif, ive [rātrospektēf, -ēv] *a*, *nf* retrospective.

rétrospectivement [rātrospektēvmâṅ] *ad* in retrospect.

retroussé, e [rətrōōsā] *a*: **nez** ~ turned-up nose.

retrousser [rətrōōsā] *vt* to roll up; (*fig: nez*) to wrinkle; (: *lèvres*) to curl up.

retrouvailles [rətrōōvày] *nfpl* reunion *sg*.

retrouver [rətrōōvā] *vt* (*fugitif, objet perdu*) to find; (*occasion*) to find again; (*calme, santé*) to regain; (*reconnaître: expression, style*) to recognize; (*revoir*) to see again; (*rejoindre*) to meet (again), join; **se** ~ *vi* to meet; (*s'orienter*) to find one's way; **se** ~ **quelque part** to find o.s. somewhere; to end up some where; **se** ~ **seul/sans argent** to find o.s. alone/with no money; **se** ~ **dans** (*calculs, dossiers, désordre*) to make sense of; **s'y** ~ (*rentrer dans ses frais*) to break even.

rétroviseur [rātrovēzœr] *nm* (rear-view) mirror.

Réunion [rāünyôṅ] *nf*: **la** ~, **l'île de la** ~ Réunion.

réunion [rāünyôṅ] *nf* bringing together; joining; (*séance*) meeting.

réunionnais, e [rāünyone, -ez] *a* of *ou* from Réunion.

réunir [rāünēr] *vt* (*convoquer*) to call together; (*rassembler*) to gather together; (*cumuler*) to combine; (*rapprocher*) to bring together (again), reunite; (*rattacher*) to join (together); **se** ~ *vi* (*se rencontrer*) to meet; (*s'allier*) to unite.

réussi, e [rāüsē] *a* successful.

réussir [rāüsēr] *vi* to succeed, be successful; (*à un examen*) to pass; (*plante, culture*) to thrive, do well ♦ *vt* to make a success of; to bring off; ~ **à faire** to succeed in doing; ~ **à qn** to go right for sb; (*aliment*) to agree with sb; **le travail/le mariage lui réussit** work/ married life agrees with him.

réussite [rāüsēt] *nf* success; (*CARTES*) solitaire (*US*), patience (*Brit*).

réutiliser [rāütēlēzā] *vt* to re-use.

revaloir [rəvàlwàr] *vt*: **je vous revaudrai cela** I'll repay you some day; (*en mal*) I'll pay you back for this.

revalorisation [rəvàlorēzàsyôṅ] *nf* revaluation; raising.

revaloriser [rəvàlorēzā] *vt* (*monnaie*) to revalue; (*salaires, pensions*) to raise the level of; (*institution, tradition*) to reassert the value of.

revanche [rəvâṅsh] *nf* revenge; **prendre sa** ~ **(sur)** to take one's revenge (on); **en** ~ (*par contre*) on the other hand; (*en compensation*) in return.

rêvasser [revàsā] *vi* to daydream.

rêve [rev] *nm* dream; (*activité psychique*): **le**

~ dreaming; **paysage/silence de** ~ dreamlike landscape/silence; ~ **éveillé** daydreaming *q*, daydream.

rêvé, e [rāvā] *a* (*endroit, mari etc*) ideal.

revêche [rǝvesh] *a* surly, sour-tempered.

réveil [rāvey] *nm* (*d'un dormeur*) waking up *q*; (*fig*) awakening; (*pendule*) alarm (clock); **au** ~ when I (*ou* you *etc*) wake (*ou* woke) up, on waking (up); **sonner le** ~ (*MIL*) to sound the reveille.

réveille-matin [rāveymátań] *nm inv* alarm clock.

réveiller [rāvāyā] *vt* (*personne*) to wake up; (*fig*) to awaken, revive; **se** ~ *vi* to wake up; (*fig*) to be revived, reawaken.

réveillon [rāveyóń] *nm* Christmas Eve; (*de la Saint-Sylvestre*) New Year's Eve; Christmas Eve (*ou* New Year's Eve) party *ou* dinner.

réveillonner [rāveyonā] *vi* to celebrate Christmas Eve (*ou* New Year's Eve).

révélateur, trice [rāvālátœr, -trēs] *a*: ~ (**de qch**) revealing (sth) ♦ *nm* (*PHOTO*) developer.

révélation [rāvālâsyóń] *nf* revelation.

révéler [rāvālā] *vt* (*gén*) to reveal; (*divulguer*) to disclose, reveal; (*dénoter*) to reveal, show; (*faire connaître au public*): ~ **qn/qch** to make sb/sth widely known, bring sb/sth to the public's notice; **se** ~ *vi* to be revealed, reveal itself ♦ *vb avec attribut*: **se** ~ **facile/faux** to prove (to be) easy/false; **se** ~ **cruel/un allié sûr** to show o.s. to be cruel/a trustworthy ally.

revenant, e [rǝvnâń, -âńt] *nm/f* ghost.

revendeur, euse [rǝvâńdœr, -ēz] *nm/f* (*détaillant*) retailer; (*d'occasions*) second-hand dealer.

revendicatif, ive [rǝvâńdēkátēf, -ēv] *a* (*mouvement*) of protest.

revendication [rǝvâńdēkâsyóń] *nf* claim, demand; **journée de** ~ day of protest (in support of one's claims).

revendiquer [rǝvâńdēkā] *vt* to claim, demand; (*responsabilité*) to claim ♦ *vi* to agitate in favor of one's claims.

revendre [rǝvâńdr(ǝ)] *vt* (*d'occasion*) to resell; (*détailler*) to sell; (*vendre davantage de*): ~ **du sucre/un foulard/deux bagues** to sell more sugar/another scarf/another two rings; **à** ~ *ad* (*en abondance*) to spare.

revenir [rǝvnēr] *vi* to come back; (*CULIN*): **faire** ~ to brown; (*coûter*): ~ **cher/à 100 F (à qn)** to cost (sb) a lot/100 F; ~ **à** (*études, projet*) to return to, go back to; (*équivaloir à*) to amount to; ~ **à qn** (*rumeur, nouvelle*) to get back to sb, reach sb's ears; (*part, honneur*) to go to sb, be sb's; (*souvenir, nom*) to come back to sb; ~ **de** (*fig: maladie, étonnement*) to recover from; ~ **sur** (*question, sujet*) to go back over; (*engagement*) to go back on; ~ **à la charge** to return to the attack; ~ **à soi** to come around (*US*) *ou* round (*Brit*); **n'en pas** ~: **je n'en reviens pas** I can't get over it; ~ **sur ses pas** to retrace one's steps; **cela revient à dire que/au même** it amounts to saying that/to the same thing; ~ **de loin** (*fig*) to have been at death's door.

revente [rǝvâńt] *nf* resale.

revenu, e [rǝvnü] *pp de* **revenir** ♦ *nm* income; (*de l'État*) revenue; (*d'un capital*) yield; ~**s** *nmpl* income *sg*; ~ **national brut** gross national income.

rêver [rāvā] *vi, vt* to dream; (*rêvasser*) to (day)dream; ~ **de** (*voir en rêve*) to dream of *ou* about; ~ **de qch/de faire** to dream of sth/of doing; ~ **à** to dream of.

réverbération [rāverbārâsyóń] *nf* reflection.

réverbère [rāverber] *nm* street lamp *ou* light.

réverbérer [rāverbārā] *vt* to reflect.

reverdir [rǝverdēr] *vi* (*arbre etc*) to turn green again.

révérence [rāvārâńs] *nf* (*vénération*) reverence; (*salut: d'homme*) bow; (: *de femme*) curtsey.

révérencieux, euse [rāvārâńsyœ, -œz] *a* reverent.

révérend, e [rāvārâń, -âńd] *a*: **le** ~ **père** Pascal the Reverend Father Pascal.

révérer [rāvārā] *vt* to revere.

rêverie [revrē] *nf* daydreaming *q*, daydream.

reverrai [rāverā] *etc vb voir* **revoir**.

revers [rǝver] *nm* (*de feuille, main*) back; (*d'étoffe*) wrong side; (*de pièce, médaille*) back, reverse; (*TENNIS, PING-PONG*) backhand; (*de veston*) lapel; (*de pantalon*) cuff (*US*), turn-up (*Brit*); (*fig: échec*) setback; ~ **de fortune** reverse of fortune; **d'un** ~ **de main** with the back of one's hand; **le** ~ **de la médaille** (*fig*) the other side of the coin; **prendre à** ~ (*MIL*) to take from the rear.

reverser [rǝversā] *vt* (*reporter: somme etc*): ~ **sur** to put back into; (*liquide*): ~ (**dans**) to pour some more (into).

réversible [rāversēbl(ǝ)] *a* reversible.

revêtement [rǝvetmâń] *nm* (*de paroi*) facing; (*des sols*) flooring; (*de chaussée*) surface; (*de tuyau etc: enduit*) coating.

revêtir [rǝvetēr] *vt* (*habit*) to don, put on; (*fig*) to take on; ~ **qn de** to dress sb in; (*fig*) to endow *ou* invest sb with; ~ **qch de** to cover sth with; (*fig*) to cloak sth in; ~ **d'un visa** to append a visa to.

rêveur, euse [revœr, -ēz] *a* dreamy ♦ *nm/f* dreamer.

reviendrai [rǝvyańdrā] *etc vb voir* **revenir**.

revienne [rǝvyen] *etc vb voir* **revenir**.

revient [rǝvyań] *vb voir* **revenir** ♦ *nm*: **prix de** ~ cost price.

revigorer [rǝvēgorā] *vt* to invigorate, revive, buck up.

revint [rǝvań] *etc vb voir* **revenir**.

revirement [rǝvērmâń] *nm* change of mind; (*d'une situation*) reversal.

revis [rǝvē] *etc vb voir* **revoir**.

révisable [rāvēzâbl(ǝ)] *a* (*procès, taux etc*) reviewable, subject to review.

réviser [rāvēzā] *vt* (*texte*) to revise; (*SCOL: matière*) to review (*US*), revise (*Brit*); (*comptes*) to audit; (*machine, installation, moteur*) to overhaul, service; (*JUR: procès*) to review.

révision [rāvēzyóń] *nf* revision; auditing *q*; overhaul, servicing *q*; review; **conseil de** ~ (*MIL*) draft (*US*) *ou* recruiting (*Brit*) board; **faire ses** ~**s** (*SCOL*) to review (*US*), revise (*Brit*); **la** ~ **des 10000 km** (*AUTO*) the 10,000 km service.

révisionnisme [rāvēzyonēsm(ə)] *nm* revisionism.

revisser [rəvēsā] *vt* to screw back again.

revit [rəvē] *vb voir* **revoir**.

revitaliser [rəvētálēzā] *vt* to revitalize.

revivifier [rəvēvēfyā] *vt* to revitalize.

revivre [rəvēvr(ə)] *vi* (*reprendre des forces*) to come alive again; (*traditions*) to be revived ♦ *vt* (*épreuve, moment*) to relive; **faire** ~ (*mode, institution, usage*) to bring back to life.

révocable [rāvokábl(ə)] *a* (*délégué*) dismissible; (*contrat*) revocable.

révocation [rāvokásyôn] *nf* dismissal; revocation.

revoir [rəvwár] *vt* to see again; (*réviser*) to review (*US*), revise (*Brit*) ♦ *nm*: **au** ~ goodbye; **dire au** ~ **à qn** to say goodbye to sb; **se** ~ (*amis*) to meet (again), see each other again.

révoltant, e [rāvoltán, -ánt] *a* revolting.

révolte [rāvolt(ə)] *nf* rebellion, revolt.

révolter [rāvoltā] *vt* to revolt, outrage; **se** ~ *vi*: **se** ~ (**contre**) to rebel (against); **se** ~ (**à**) to be outraged (by).

révolu, e [rāvolü] *a* past; (*ADMIN*): **âgé de 18 ans** ~**s** over 18 years of age; **après 3 ans** ~**s** when 3 full years have passed.

révolution [rāvolüsyôn] *nf* revolution; **être en** ~ (*pays etc*) to be in revolt; **la** ~ **industrielle** the industrial revolution.

révolutionnaire [rāvolüsyoner] *a, nm/f* revolutionary.

révolutionner [rāvolüsyonā] *vt* to revolutionize; (*fig*) to stir up.

revolver [rāvolver] *nm* gun; (*à barillet*) revolver.

révoquer [rāvokā] *vt* (*fonctionnaire*) to dismiss, remove from office; (*arrêt, contrat*) to revoke.

revoyais [rəvwáyε] *etc vb voir* **revoir**.

revu, e [rəvü] *pp de* **revoir** ♦ *nf* (*inventaire, examen*) review; (*MIL*): **défilé** review, march-past; (: *inspection*) inspection, review; (*périodique*) review, magazine; (*pièce satirique*) revue; (*de music-hall*) variety show; **passer en** ~ to review, inspect; (*fig*) to review; ~ **de (la) presse** press review.

révulsé, e [rāvülsā] *a* (*yeux*) rolled upwards; (*visage*) contorted.

Reykjavik [rākyávēk] *n* Reykjavik.

rez-de-chaussée [rādshōsā] *nm inv* ground floor.

rez-de-jardin [rādzhárdan] *nm inv* garden level.

RF *sigle f* = *République française*.

RFA *sigle f* (= *République fédérale d'Allemagne*) FRG.

RFO *sigle f* (= *Radio-Télévision Française d'Outre-mer*) French overseas broadcasting service.

RG *sigle mpl* (= *renseignements généraux*) security section of the police force.

rhabiller [rábēyā] *vt*: **se** ~ to get dressed again, put one's clothes on again.

rhapsodie [rápsodē] *nf* rhapsody.

rhénan, e [rānán, -án] *a* Rhine *cpd*, of the Rhine.

Rhénanie [rānánē] *nf*: **la** ~ the Rhineland.

rhésus [rāzüs] *a, nm* rhesus; ~ **positif/négatif** Rh- *ou* rhesus positive/negative.

rhétorique [rātorēk] *nf* rhetoric ♦ *a* rhetorical.

rhéto-roman, e [rātoromán, -án] *a* Rhaeto-Romanic.

Rhin [ran] *nm*: **le** ~ the Rhine.

rhinite [rēnēt] *nf* rhinitis.

rhinocéros [rēnosáros] *nm* rhinoceros.

rhinopharyngite [rēnofáranzhēt] *nf* throat infection.

rhodanien, ne [rodányan, -en] *a* Rhône *cpd*, of the Rhône.

Rhodes [rod] *n*: (**l'île de**) ~ (the island of) Rhodes.

Rhodésie [rodāzē] *nf*: **la** ~ Rhodesia.

rhodésien, ne [rodāzyan, -en] *a* Rhodesian.

rhododendron [rododandrôn] *nm* rhododendron.

Rhône [rōn] *nm*: **le** ~ the Rhone.

rhubarbe [rübárb(ə)] *nf* rhubarb.

rhum [rom] *nm* rum.

rhumatisant, e [rümátēzán, -ánt] *a, nm/f* rheumatic.

rhumatismal, e, aux [rümátēsmál, -ō] *a* rheumatic.

rhumatisme [rümátēsm(ə)] *nm* rheumatism *q*.

rhumatologue [rümátolog] *nm/f* rheumatologist.

rhume [rüm] *nm* cold; ~ **de cerveau** head cold; **le** ~ **des foins** hay fever.

rhumerie [romrē] *nf* (*distillerie*) rum distillery.

RI *sigle m* (*MIL*) = *régiment d'infanterie* ♦ *sigle mpl* (= *Républicains indépendants*) *political party*.

ri [rē] *pp de* **rire**.

riant, e [ryán, -ánt] *vb voir* **rire** ♦ *a* smiling, cheerful; (*campagne, paysage*) pleasant.

RIB *sigle m* = **relevé d'identité bancaire**.

ribambelle [rēbánbel] *nf*: **une** ~ **de** a herd *ou* swarm of.

ricain, e [rēkán, -en] *a* (*fam*) Yank, Yankee.

ricanement [rēkánmán] *nm* snigger; giggle.

ricaner [rēkánā] *vi* (*avec méchanceté*) to snigger; (*bêtement, avec gêne*) to giggle.

riche [rēsh] *a* (*gén*) rich; (*personne, pays*) rich, wealthy; ~ **en** rich in; ~ **de** full of; rich in.

richement [rēshmán] *ad* richly.

richesse [rēshes] *nf* wealth; (*fig*) richness; ~**s** *nfpl* wealth *sg*; treasures; ~ **en vitamines** high vitamin content.

richissime [rēshēsēm] *a* extremely rich *ou* wealthy.

ricin [rēsán] *nm*: **huile de** ~ castor oil.

ricocher [rēkoshā] *vi*: ~ (**sur**) to rebound (off); (*sur l'eau*) to bounce (on *ou* off); **faire** ~ (*galet*) to skim.

ricochet [rēkoshe] *nm* rebound; bounce; **faire** ~ to rebound, bounce; (*fig*) to rebound; **faire des** ~**s** to skip stones; **par** ~ *ad* on the rebound; (*fig*) as an indirect result.

rictus [rēktüs] *nm* grin; (*snarling*) grimace.

ride [rēd] *nf* wrinkle; (*fig*) ripple.

ridé, e [rēdā] *a* wrinkled.

rideau, x [rēdō] *nm* curtain; **tirer/ouvrir les** ~**x** to draw/open the curtains; ~ **de fer** metal shutter; (*POL*): **le** ~ **de fer** the Iron Curtain.

ridelle [rēdel] *nf* slatted side (*of truck*).

rider [rēdā] *vt* to wrinkle; (*fig*) to ripple, ruffle the surface of; **se ~** *vi* to become wrinkled.

ridicule [rēdēkül] *a* ridiculous ♦ *nm* ridiculousness *q*; **le ~** ridicule; (*travers: gén pl*) absurdities *pl*; **tourner en ~** to ridicule.

ridiculement [rēdēkülmâṅ] *ad* ridiculously.

ridiculiser [rēdēkülēzā] *vt* to ridicule; **se ~** to make a fool of o.s.

ridule [rēdül] *nf* (*euph: ride*) little wrinkle.

rie [rē] *etc vb voir* **rire**.

rien [ryaṅ] *pronom* nothing; (*quelque chose*) anything; **ne ... ~** nothing, *tournure négative* + anything; **~ d'autre** nothing else; **~ du tout** nothing at all; **~ que** just, only; nothing but; **~ que cela/qu'à faire cela** just that/just doing that; **a-t-il jamais ~ fait pour nous?** has he ever done anything for us?; **il n'a ~** (*n'est pas blessé*) he's all right; **il n'a ~ d'un champion** he has nothing of the champion about him; **il n'y est pour ~** he's got nothing to do with it; **il n'en est ~!** nothing of the sort!; **ça ne fait ~** it doesn't matter; **~ à faire!** it's no good!; **il n'y ~ à faire** ... whatever I (*ou* you *etc*) do ...; **de ~!** (*formule*) not at all!, don't mention it!; **comme si de ~ n'était** as if nothing had happened; **un petit ~** (*cadeau*) a little something; **un ~ de** a hint of; **des ~s** trivia *pl*; **avoir peur d'un ~** to be frightened of every little thing.

rieur, euse [ryœr, -œz] *a* cheerful.

rigide [rēzhēd] *a* stiff; (*fig*) rigid; (*moralement*) strict.

rigidité [rēzhēdētā] *nf* stiffness; **la ~ cadavérique** rigor mortis.

rigolade [rēgolád] *nf*: **la ~** fun; (*fig*): **c'est de la ~** it's a big farce; (*c'est facile*) it's a cinch.

rigole [rēgol] *nf* (*conduit*) channel; (*filet d'eau*) rivulet.

rigoler [rēgolā] *vi* (*rire*) to laugh; (*s'amuser*) to have (some) fun; (*plaisanter*) to be joking *ou* kidding.

rigolo, ote [rēgolō, -ot] *a* (*fam*) funny ♦ *nm/f* comic; (*péj*) fraud, phoney.

rigoureusement [rēgōōrœzmáṅ] *ad* rigorously; **~ vrai/interdit** strictly true/forbidden.

rigoureux, euse [rēgōōrœ, -œz] *a* (*morale*) rigorous, strict; (*personne*) stern, strict; (*climat, châtiment*) rigorous, harsh, severe; (*interdiction, neutralité*) strict; (*preuves, analyse, méthode*) rigorous.

rigueur [rēgœr] *nf* rigor (*US*), rigour (*Brit*); strictness; harshness; **"tenue de soirée de ~"** "evening dress (to be worn)"; **être de ~** to be the usual thing, be the rule; **à la ~** in (*US*) *ou* at (*Brit*) a pinch; possibly; **tenir ~ à qn de qch** to hold sth against sb.

riions [rēyóṅ] *etc vb voir* **rire**.

rillettes [rēyet] *nfpl* ≈ potted meat *sg*.

rime [rēm] *nf* rhyme; **n'avoir ni ~ ni raison** to have neither rhyme nor reason.

rimer [rēmā] *vi*: **~ (avec)** to rhyme (with); **ne ~ à rien** not to make sense.

Rimmel [rēmel] *nm* ® mascara.

rinçage [raṅsázh] *nm* rinsing (out); (*opération*) rinse.

rince-doigts [raṅsdwá] *nm inv* finger bowl.

rincer [raṅsā] *vt* to rinse; (*récipient*) to rinse

out; **se ~ la bouche** to rinse out one's mouth.

ring [rēng] *nm* (boxing) ring; **monter sur le ~** (*aussi fig*) to enter the ring; (: *faire carrière de boxeur*) to take up boxing.

ringard, e [raṅgàr, -àrd(ə)] *a* (*péj*) old-fashioned.

Rio de Janeiro [rēōdzhàner(ō)] *n* Rio de Janeiro.

rions [rēòṅ] *vb voir* **rire**.

ripaille [rēpây] *nf*: **faire ~** to feast.

riper [rēpā] *vi* to slip, slide.

ripoliné, e [rēpolēnā] *a* enamel-painted.

riposte [rēpost(ə)] *nf* retort, riposte; (*fig*) counter-attack, reprisal.

riposter [rēpostā] *vi* to retaliate ♦ *vt*: **~ que** to retort that; **~ à** *vt* to counter; to reply to.

rire [rēr] *vi* to laugh; (*se divertir*) to have fun; (*plaisanter*) to joke ♦ *nm* laugh; **le ~** laughter; **~ de** *vt* to laugh at; **se ~ de** to make light of; **tu veux ~!** you must be joking!; **~ aux éclats/aux larmes** to roar with laughter/ laugh until one cries; **~ jaune** to force oneself to laugh; **~ sous cape** to laugh up one's sleeve; **~ au nez de qn** to laugh in sb's face; **pour ~** (*pas sérieusement*) for a joke *ou* a laugh.

ris [rē] *vb voir* **rire** ♦ *nm*: **~ de veau** (calf) sweetbread.

risée [rēzā] *nf*: **être la ~ de** to be the laughing stock of.

risette [rēzet] *nf*: **faire ~ (à)** to give a nice little smile (to).

risible [rēzēbl(ə)] *a* laughable, ridiculous.

risque [rēsk(ə)] *nm* risk; **l'attrait du ~** the lure of danger; **prendre des ~s** to take risks; **à ses ~s et périls** at his own risk; **au ~ de** at the risk of; **~ d'incendie** fire risk; **~ calculé** calculated risk.

risqué, e [rēskā] *a* risky; (*plaisanterie*) risqué, daring.

risquer [rēskā] *vt* to risk; (*allusion, question*) to venture, hazard; **tu risques qu'on te renvoie** you risk being dismissed; **ça ne risque rien** it's quite safe; **~ de: il risque de se tuer** he could get *ou* risks getting himself killed; **il a risqué de se tuer** he almost got himself killed; **ce qui risque de se produire** what might *ou* could well happen; **il ne risque pas de recommencer** there's no chance of him doing that again; **se ~ dans** (*s'aventurer*) to venture into; **se ~ à faire** (*tenter*) to venture *ou* dare to do; **~ le tout pour le tout** to risk the lot.

risque-tout [rēskətōō] *nm/f inv* daredevil.

rissoler [rēsolā] *vi, vt*: **(faire) ~** to brown.

ristourne [rēstōōrn(ə)] *nf* rebate; discount.

rit [rē] *etc vb voir* **rire**.

rite [rēt] *nm* rite; (*fig*) ritual; **~s d'initiation** initiation rites.

ritournelle [rētōōrnel] *nf* (*fig*) tune; **c'est toujours la même ~** (*fam*) it's always the same old story.

rituel, le [rētüel] *a, nm* ritual.

rituellement [rētüelmâṅ] *ad* religiously.

riv. *abr* (= *rivière*) R.

rivage [rēvázh] *nm* shore.

rival, e, aux [rēvàl, -ō] *a, nm/f* rival; **sans ~** *a* unrivalled.

rivaliser [rēválēzā] *vi*: **~ avec** to rival, vie

with; *(être comparable)* to hold its own against, compare with; ~ **avec qn de** *(élégance etc)* to vie with *ou* rival sb in.
rivalité [rēvȧlētȧ] *nf* rivalry.
rive [rēv] *nf* shore; *(de fleuve)* bank.
river [rēvȧ] *vt (clou, pointe)* to clinch; *(plaques)* to rivet together; **être rivé sur/à** to be riveted on/to.
riverain, e [rēvraṅ, -en] *a* riverside *cpd*; lakeside *cpd*; roadside *cpd* ♦ *nm/f* riverside *(ou* lakeside) resident; local *ou* roadside resident.
rivet [rēve] *nm* rivet.
riveter [rēvtȧ] *vt* to rivet (together).
Riviera [rēvyerȧ] *nf*: **la ~ (italienne)** the Italian Riviera.
rivière [rēvyer] *nf* river; ~ **de diamants** diamond rivière.
rixe [rēks(ə)] *nf* brawl, scuffle.
Riyad [rēyȧd] *n* Riyadh.
riz [rē] *nm* rice; ~ **au lait** ≈ rice pudding.
rizière [rēzyer] *nf* rice paddy.
RMC *sigle f = Radio Monte Carlo.*
RN *sigle f =* **route nationale.**
robe [rob] *nf* dress; *(de juge, d'ecclésiastique)* robe; *(de professeur)* gown; *(pelage)* coat; ~ **de soirée/de mariée** evening/wedding dress; ~ **de baptême** christening robe; ~ **de chambre** dressing gown; ~ **de grossesse** maternity dress.
robinet [robēne] *nm* tap, faucet *(US)*; ~ **du gaz** gas tap; ~ **mélangeur** mixer tap.
robinetterie [robēnetrē] *nf* plumbing.
roboratif, ive [roborȧtēf, -ēv] *a* bracing, invigorating.
robot [robō] *nm* robot; ~ **de cuisine** food processor.
robotique [robotēk] *nf* robotics *sg.*
robotiser [robotēzȧ] *vt (personne, travailleur)* to turn into a robot; *(monde, vie)* to automate.
robuste [robüst(ə)] *a* robust, sturdy.
robustesse [robüstes] *nf* robustness, sturdiness.
roc [rok] *nm* rock.
rocade [rokȧd] *nf (AUTO)* bypass.
rocaille [rokȧy] *nf (pierres)* loose stones *pl;* *(terrain)* rocky *ou* stony ground; *(jardin)* rockery, rock garden ♦ *a (style)* rocaille.
rocailleux, euse [rokȧyœ̄, -œ̄z] *a* rocky, stony; *(voix)* harsh.
rocambolesque [rokȧṅbolesk(ə)] *a* fantastic, incredible.
roche [rosh] *nf* rock.
rocher [roshȧ] *nm* rock; *(ANAT)* petrosal bone.
rochet [roshe] *nm*: **roue à ~** ratchet wheel.
rocheux, euse [roshœ̄, -œ̄z] *a* rocky; **les (montagnes) Rocheuses** the Rockies, the Rocky Mountains.
rock (and roll) [rok(enrol)] *nm (musique)* rock(-'n'-roll); *(danse)* rock.
rocker [rokœr] *nm (chanteur)* rock musician; *(adepte)* rock fan.
rodage [rodȧzh] *nm* breaking in *(US)*, running in *(Brit)*; **en ~** *(AUTO)* running *ou* breaking in.
rodé, e [rodȧ] *a* broken in *(US)*, run in *(Brit)*; *(personne)*: ~ **à qch** having got the hang of sth.
rodéo [rodȧō] *nm* rodeo *(pl* -s).

roder [rodȧ] *vt (moteur, voiture)* to break in *(US)*, run in *(Brit)*; ~ **un spectacle/service** to iron out the initial problems of a show/service.
rôder [rōdȧ] *vi* to roam *ou* wander about; *(de façon suspecte)* to lurk (about *ou* around).
rôdeur, euse [rōdœr, -œ̄z] *nm/f* prowler.
rodomontades [rodomóṅtȧd] *nfpl* bragging *sg*; saber *(US) ou* sabre *(Brit)* rattling *sg.*
rogatoire [rogȧtwȧr] *a*: **commission ~** letters rogatory.
rogne [rony] *nf*: **être en ~** to be mad *ou* in a temper; **se mettre en ~** to get mad *ou* in a temper.
rogner [ronyȧ] *vt* to trim; *(fig)* to whittle down; ~ **sur** *(fig)* to cut down *ou* back on.
rognons [ronyóṅ] *nmpl* kidneys.
rognures [ronyür] *nfpl* trimmings.
rogue [rog] *a* arrogant.
roi [rwȧ] *nm* king; **les R~s mages** the Three Wise Men, the Magi; **le jour** *ou* **la fête des R~s, les R~s** Twelfth Night.
roitelet [rwȧtle] *nm* wren; *(péj)* kinglet.
rôle [rōl] *nm* role; *(contribution)* part.
rollmops [rolmops] *nm* rollmop.
romain, e [romaṅ, -en] *a* Roman ♦ *nm/f*: **R~,** **e** Roman ♦ *nf (CULIN)* romaine *(US) ou* cos *(Brit)* (lettuce).
roman, e [romȧṅ, -ȧn] *a (ARCHIT)* Romanesque; *(LING)* Romance *cpd*, Romantic ♦ *nm* novel; ~ **policier** detective novel; ~ **d'espionnage** spy novel *ou* story; ~ **noir** thriller.
romance [romȧṅs] *nf* ballad.
romancer [romȧṅsȧ] *vt* to romanticize.
romanche [romȧṅsh] *a, nm* Romansh.
romancier, ière [romȧṅsyȧ, -yer] *nm/f* novelist.
romand, e [romȧṅ, -ȧṅd] *a* of *ou* from French-speaking Switzerland ♦ *nm/f*: **R~, e** French-speaking Swiss.
romanesque [romȧnesk(ə)] *a (fantastique)* fantastic; *(sentimental)* romantic; storybook *cpd*; *(LITTÉRATURE)* novelistic.
roman-feuilleton *pl* **romans-feuilletons** [romȧṅfœytóṅ] *nm* serialized novel.
roman-fleuve *pl* **romans-fleuves** [romȧṅflœv] *nm* saga, roman-fleuve.
romanichel, le [romȧnēshel] *nm/f* gipsy.
roman-photo *pl* **romans-photos** [romȧṅfotō] *nm* photo romance.
romantique [romȧṅtēk] *a* romantic.
romantisme [romȧṅtēsm(ə)] *nm* romanticism.
romarin [romȧraṅ] *nm* rosemary.
rombière [róṅbyer] *nf (péj)* old bag.
Rome [rom] *n* Rome.
rompre [róṅpr(ə)] *vt* to break; *(entretien, fiançailles)* to break off ♦ *vi (fiancés)* to break it off; **se ~** *vi* to break; *(MÉD)* to burst, rupture; **se ~ les os** *ou* **le cou** to break one's neck; ~ **avec** to break with; **à tout ~** *ad* wildly; **applaudir à tout ~** to bring down the house, applaud wildly; ~ **la glace** *(fig)* to break the ice; **rompez (les rangs)!** *(MIL)* dismiss!, fall out!
rompu, e [róṅpü] *pp de* **rompre** ♦ *a (fourbu)* exhausted, worn out; ~ **à** with wide experience in; inured to.
romsteck [róṅmstek] *nm* rump steak *q.*
ronce [róṅs] *nf (BOT)* bramble branch;

(*MENUISERIE*): ~ **de noyer** burr walnut; ~**s** *nfpl* brambles, thorns.

ronchonner [rôṅshonã] *vi* (*fam*) to grouse, grouch.

rond, e [rôṅ, rôṅd] *a* round; (*joues, mollets*) well-rounded; (*fam*: *ivre*) tight; (*sincère, décidé*): **être ~ en affaires** to be on the level in business, do an honest deal ♦ *nm* (*cercle*) ring; (*fam*: *sou*): **je n'ai plus un ~** I haven't a penny left ♦ *nf* (*gén*: *de surveillance*) rounds *pl*, patrol; (*danse*) round (dance); (*MUS*) whole note (*US*), semibreve (*Brit*) ♦ *ad*: **tourner ~** (*moteur*) to run smoothly; **ça ne tourne pas ~** (*fig*) there's something not quite right about it; **pour faire un compte ~** to make (it) a round figure, to round (it) off; **avoir le dos ~** to be round-shouldered; **en ~** (*s'asseoir, danser*) in a ring; **à la ~e** (*alentour*): **à 10 km à la ~e** within a 10 km radius; (*à chacun son tour*): **passer qch à la ~e** to pass sth (a)round; **faire des ~s de jambe** to bow and scrape; **~ de serviette** napkin ring.

rond-de-cuir, *pl* **ronds-de-cuir** [rôṅdküẽr] *nm* (*péj*) pencil pusher (*US*), penpusher (*Brit*).

rondelet, te [rôṅdle, -et] *a* plump; (*fig*: *somme*) tidy; (: *bourse*) well-lined, fat.

rondelle [rôṅdel] *nf* (*TECH*) washer; (*tranche*) slice, round.

rondement [rôṅdmã] *ad* (*avec décision*) briskly; (*loyalement*) frankly.

rondeur [rôṅdœr] *nf* (*d'un bras, des formes*) plumpness; (*bonhomie*) friendly straight-forwardness; ~**s** *nfpl* (*d'une femme*) curves.

rondin [rôṅdaṅ] *nm* log.

rond-point, *pl* **ronds-points** [rôṅpwaṅ] *nm* traffic circle (*US*), roundabout (*Brit*).

ronéotyper [ronãotẽpã] *vt* to duplicate, roneo ®.

ronflant, e [rôṅflãṅ, -ãṅt] *a* (*péj*) high-flown, grand.

ronflement [rôṅfləmãṅ] *nm* snore, snoring *q*.

ronfler [rôṅflã] *vi* to snore; (*moteur, poêle*) to hum; (: *plus fort*) to roar.

ronger [rôṅzhã] *vt* to gnaw (at); (*suj*: *vers, rouille*) to eat into; ~ **son frein** to champ (at) the bit (*fig*); **se ~ de souci, se ~ les sangs** to worry o.s. sick, fret; **se ~ les ongles** to bite one's nails.

rongeur, euse [rôṅzhœr, -œz] *nm/f* rodent.

ronronnement [rôṅronmãṅ] *nm* purring; (*bruit*) purr.

ronronner [rôṅronã] *vi* to purr.

roque [rok] *nm* (*ÉCHECS*) castling.

roquer [rokã] *vi* to castle.

roquet [roke] *nm* nasty little lap-dog.

roquette [roket] *nf* rocket; ~ **antichar** anti-tank rocket.

rosace [rôzás] *nf* (*vitrail*) rose window, rosace; (*motif*: *de plafond etc*) rose.

rosaire [rôzer] *nm* rosary.

rosbif [rosbẽf] *nm*: **du ~** roasting beef; (*cuit*) roast beef; **un ~** a joint of (roasting) beef.

rose [rôz] *nf* rose; (*vitrail*) rose window ♦ *a* pink; ~ **bonbon** *a inv* candy pink; ~ **des vents** compass card.

rosé, e [rôzã] *a* pinkish; (*vin*) ~ rosé (wine).

roseau, x [rôzõ] *nm* reed.

rosée [rôzã] *af voir* **rosé** ♦ *nf*: **goutte de ~**

dewdrop.

roseraie [rôzre] *nf* rose garden; (*plantation*) rose nursery.

rosette [rôzet] *nf* rosette (*gen of the Légion d'honneur*).

rosier [rôzyã] *nm* rosebush, rose tree.

rosir [rôzẽr] *vi* to go pink.

rosse [ros] *nf* (*péj*: *cheval*) nag ♦ *a* nasty, vicious.

rosser [rosã] *vt* (*fam*) to thrash.

rossignol [rosẽnyol] *nm* (*ZOOL*) nightingale; (*crochet*) picklock.

rot [rô] *nm* belch; (*de bébé*) burp.

rotatif, ive [rotátẽf, -ẽv] *a* rotary ♦ *nf* rotary press.

rotation [rotãsyôṅ] *nf* rotation; (*fig*) rotation, swap-around; (*renouvellement*) turnover; **par ~** on a rotation (*US*) *ou* rota (*Brit*) basis; ~ **des cultures** rotation of crops; ~ **des stocks** stock turnover.

rotatoire [rotátwár] *a*: **mouvement ~** rotary movement.

roter [rotã] *vi* (*fam*) to burp, belch.

rôti [rôtẽ] *nm*: **du ~** roasting meat; (*cuit*) roast meat; **un ~ de bœuf/porc** a joint of (roasting) beef/pork.

rotin [rotaṅ] *nm* rattan (cane); **fauteuil en ~** cane (arm)chair.

rôtir [rôtẽr] *vt* (*aussi*: **faire ~**) to roast ♦ *vi* to roast; **se ~ au soleil** to bask in the sun.

rôtisserie [rôtẽsrẽ] *nf* (*restaurant*) steakhouse; (*comptoir, magasin*) roast meat counter (*ou* shop).

rôtissoire [rôtẽswár] *nf* (*roasting*) spit.

rotonde [rotôṅd] *nf* (*ARCHIT*) rotunda; (*RAIL*) engine shed.

rotondité [rotôṅdẽtã] *nf* roundness.

rotor [rotor] *nm* rotor.

Rotterdam [roterdám] *n* Rotterdam.

rotule [rotül] *nf* kneecap, patella.

roturier, ière [rotüryã, -yer] *nm/f* commoner.

rouage [rwázh] *nm* cog(wheel), gearwheel; (*de montre*) part; (*fig*) cog; ~**s** *nmpl* (*fig*) internal structure *sg*.

Rouanda [rwãṅdá] *nm*: **le ~** Rwanda.

roubaisien, ne [rōōbãzyaṅ, -en] *a* of *ou* from Roubaix.

roublard, e [rōōblár, -árd(ə)] *a* (*péj*) crafty, wily.

rouble [rōōbl(ə)] *nm* ruble.

roucouler [rōōkōōlã] *vi* to coo; (*fig*: *péj*) to warble; (: *amoureux*) to bill and coo.

roue [rōō] *nf* wheel; **faire la ~** (*paon*) to spread *ou* fan its tail; (*GYM*) to do a cart-wheel; **descendre en ~ libre** to freewheel *ou* coast down; **pousser à la ~** to put one's shoulder to the wheel; **grande ~** (*à la foire*) Ferris wheel; ~ **à aubes** paddle wheel; ~ **dentée** cogwheel; ~ **de secours** spare wheel.

roué, e [rwã] *a* wily.

rouennais, e [rwáne, -ez] *a* of *ou* from Rouen.

rouer [rwã] *vt*: ~ **qn de coups** to give sb a thrashing.

rouet [rwe] *nm* spinning wheel.

rouge [rōōzh] *a*, *nm/f* red ♦ *nm* red; (*fard*) rouge; (*vin*) ~ red wine; **passer au ~** (*signal*) to turn red; (*automobiliste*) to go through a red light; **porter au ~** (*métal*) to bring to red heat; **sur la liste ~** (*TÉL*) unlisted (*US*), ex-directory (*Brit*); ~ **de honte/colère** red with shame/anger; **se fâcher tout/voir** ~ to blow one's top/see red; ~ **(à lèvres)** lipstick.

rougeâtre [rōōzhâtr(ə)] *a* reddish.

rougeaud, e [rōōzhō, -ōd] *a* (*teint*) red; (*personne*) red-faced.

rouge-gorge [rōōzhgorzh(ə)] *nm* robin (redbreast).

rougeoiement [rōōzhwâmâñ] *nm* reddish glow.

rougeole [rōōzhol] *nf* measles *sg*.

rougeoyer [rōōzhwâyā] *vi* to glow red.

rouget [rōōzhe] *nm* mullet.

rougeur [rōōzhœr] *nf* redness; (*du visage*) red face; ~**s** *nfpl* (*MÉD*) red blotches.

rougir [rōōzhēr] *vi* (*de honte, timidité*) to blush, flush; (*de plaisir, colère*) to flush; (*fraise, tomate*) to go *ou* turn red; (*ciel*) to redden.

rouille [rōōy] *a inv* rust-colored (*US*) *ou* -coloured (*Brit*), rusty ♦ *nf* rust; (*CULIN*) spicy (*Provençal*) sauce served with fish dishes.

rouillé, e [rōōyā] *a* rusty.

rouiller [rōōyā] *vt* to rust ♦ *vi* to rust, get rusty; **se** ~ *vi* to rust; (*fig: mentalement*) to become rusty; (: *physiquement*) to grow stiff.

roulade [rōōlád] *nf* (*GYM*) roll; (*CULIN*) meat roll; (*MUS*) roulade, run.

roulant, e [rōōláñ, -âñt] *a* (*meuble*) on wheels; (*surface, trottoir*) moving; **matériel** ~ (*RAIL*) rolling stock; **personnel** ~ (*RAIL*) train crews *pl*.

roulé, e [rōōlā] *a*: **bien** ~**e** (*fam: femme*) shapely, curvy.

rouleau, x [rōōlō] *nm* (*de papier, tissu, pièces de monnaie, SPORT*) roll; (*de machine à écrire*) roller, platen; (*à mise en plis, à peinture, vague*) roller; **être au bout du** ~ (*fig*) to be at the end of one's rope; ~ **compresseur** steamroller; ~ **à pâtisserie** rolling pin; ~ **de pellicule** roll of film.

roulé-boulé, *pl* **roulés-boulés** [rōōlābōōlā] (*SPORT*) roll.

roulement [rōōlmâñ] *nm* (*bruit*) rumbling *q*, rumble; (*rotation*) rotation; turnover; (: *de capitaux*) circulation; **par** ~ on a rotation (*US*) *ou* rota (*Brit*) basis; ~ **(à billes)** ball bearings *pl*; ~ **de tambour** drum roll; ~ **d'yeux** roll(ing) of the eyes.

rouler [rōōlā] *vt* to roll; (*papier, tapis*) to roll up; (*CULIN: pâte*) to roll out; (*fam*) to con ♦ *vi* (*bille, boule*) to roll; (*voiture, train*) to go, run; (*automobiliste*) to drive; (*cycliste*) to ride; (*bateau*) to roll; (*tonnerre*) to rumble, roll; (*dégringoler*): ~ **en bas de** to roll down; ~ **sur** (*suj: conversation*) to turn on; **se** ~ **dans** (*boue*) to roll in; (*couverture*) to roll o.s. (up) in; ~ **dans la farine** (*fam*) to con; ~ **les épaules/hanches** to sway one's shoulders/wiggle one's hips; ~ **les "r"** to roll one's r's; ~ **sur l'or** to be rolling in money, be rolling in it; ~ **(sa bosse)** to get around.

roulette [rōōlet] *nf* (*de table, fauteuil*) castor; (*de pâtissier*) pastry wheel; (*jeu*): **la** ~ roulette; **à** ~**s** on castors; **la** ~ **russe** Russian roulette.

roulis [rōōlē] *nm* roll(ing).

roulotte [rōōlot] *nf* trailer (*US*), caravan (*Brit*).

roumain, e [rōōmañ, -en] *a* Rumanian, Romanian ♦ *nm* (*LING*) Rumanian, Romanian ♦ *nm/f*: **R~, e** Rumanian, Romanian.

Roumanie [rōōmánē] *nf*: **la** ~ Rumania, Romania.

roupiller [rōōpēyā] *vi* (*fam*) to sleep.

rouquin, e [rōōkañ, -ēn] *nm/f* (*péj*) redhead.

rouspéter [rōōspātā] *vi* (*fam*) to moan, grouse.

rousse [rōōs] *af voir* **roux**.

rousseur [rōōsœr] *nf*: **tache de** ~ freckle.

roussi [rōōsē] *nm*: **ça sent le** ~ there's a smell of burning; (*fig*) I can smell trouble.

roussir [rōōsēr] *vt* to scorch ♦ *vi* (*feuilles*) to go *ou* turn brown; (*CULIN*): **faire** ~ to brown.

routage [rōōtázh] *nm* (collective) mailing.

routard, e [rōōtár, -árd(ə)] *nm/f* travel(l)er.

route [rōōt] *nf* road; (*fig: chemin*) way; (*itinéraire, parcours*) route; (*fig: voie*) road, path; **par (la)** ~ by road; **il y a 3h de** ~ it's a 3-hour ride *ou* journey; **en** ~ *ad* on the way; **en** ~! let's go!; **en cours de** ~ en route; **mettre en** ~ to start up; **se mettre en** ~ to set off; **faire** ~ **vers** to head towards; **faire fausse** ~ (*fig*) to be on the wrong track; ~ **nationale (RN)** ≈ state highway (*US*), ≈ A-road (*Brit*).

routier, ière [rōōtyā, -yer] *a* road *cpd* ♦ *nm* (*camionneur*) (long-distance) truck driver; (*restaurant*) ≈ truck stop (*US*), ≈ transport café (*Brit*); (*scout*) ≈ Explorer (*US*), ≈ rover (*Brit*); (*cycliste*) road racer ♦ *nf* (*voiture*) touring car; **vieux** ~ old hand; **carte routière** road map.

routine [rōōtēn] *nf* routine; **visite/contrôle de** ~ routine visit/check.

routinier, ière [rōōtēnyā, -yer] *a* (*péj: travail*) humdrum, routine; (: *personne*) addicted to routine.

rouvert, e [rōōver, -ert(ə)] *pp de* **rouvrir**.

rouvrir [rōōvrēr] *vt, vi* to reopen, open again; **se** ~ *vi* (*blessure*) to open up again.

roux, rousse [rōō, rōōs] *a* red; (*personne*) red-haired ♦ *nm/f* redhead ♦ *nm* (*CULIN*) roux.

royal, e, aux [rwáyâl, -ō] *a* royal; (*fig*) fit for a king, princely; blissful; thorough.

royalement [rwáyálmâñ] *ad* royally.

royaliste [rwáyálēst(ə)] *a, nm/f* royalist.

royaume [rwáyōm] *nm* kingdom; (*fig*) realm; **le** ~ **des cieux** the kingdom of heaven.

Royaume-Uni [rwáyōmünē] *nm*: **le** ~ the United Kingdom.

royauté [rwáyōtā] *nf* (*dignité*) kingship; (*régime*) monarchy.

RP *sigle f* (= *recette principale*) ≈ main post office; = *région parisienne* ♦ *sigle fpl* (= *relations publiques*) PR.

RPR *sigle m* (= *Rassemblement pour la République*) *political party*.

R.S.V.P. *abr* (= *répondez s'il vous plaît*) R.S.V.P.

RTB *sigle f* = *Radio-Télévision belge*.

Rte *abr* = **route**.

RTL *sigle f* = *Radio-Télévision Luxembourg*.

RTVE *sigle f* = *Radio-Télévision espagnole*.
RU [rü] *sigle m* = **restaurant universitaire**.
ruade [rüåd] *nf* kick.
Ruanda [rwåndå] *nm*: **le** ~ Rwanda.
ruban [rübåṅ] *nm* (*gén*) ribbon; (*pour ourlet, couture*) binding; (*de téléscripteur etc*) tape; (*d'acier*) strip; ~ **adhésif** sticky tape; ~ **carbone** carbon ribbon.
rubéole [rübåol] *nf* German measles *sg*, rubella.
rubicond, e [rübēkòṅ, -òṅd] *a* rubicund, ruddy.
rubis [rübē] *nm* ruby; (*HORLOGERIE*) jewel; **payer** ~ **sur l'ongle** to pay cash on the line.
rubrique [rübrēk] *nf* (*titre, catégorie*) heading, rubric; (*PRESSE*: *article*) column.
ruche [rüsh] *nf* hive.
rucher [rüshā] *nm* apiary.
rude [rüd] *a* (*barbe, toile*) rough; (*métier, tâche*) hard, tough; (*climat*) severe, harsh; (*bourru*) harsh, rough; (*fruste*) rugged, tough; (*fam*) real good; **être mis à** ~ **épreuve** to be put through the mill.
rudement [rüdmåṅ] *ad* (*tomber, frapper*) hard; (*traiter, reprocher*) harshly; (*fam*: *très*) terribly; (*: beaucoup*) terribly hard.
rudesse [rüdes] *nf* roughness; toughness; severity; harshness.
rudimentaire [rüdēmåṅter] *a* rudimentary, basic.
rudiments [rüdēmåṅ] *nmpl* rudiments; basic knowledge *sg*; basic principles.
rudoyer [rüdwàyā] *vt* to treat harshly.
rue [rü] *nf* street; **être/jeter qn à la** ~ to be on the streets/throw sb out onto the street.
ruée [rüā] *nf* rush; **la** ~ **vers l'or** the gold rush.
ruelle [rüel] *nf* alley(-way).
ruer [rüā] *vi* (*cheval*) to kick out; **se** ~ *vi*: **se** ~ **sur** to pounce on; **se** ~ **vers/dans/hors de** to rush *ou* dash towards/into/out of; ~ **dans les brancards** to become rebellious.
rugby [rügbē] *nm* Rugby (football); ~ **à treize/quinze** Rugby League/Union.
rugir [rüzhēr] *vi* to roar.
rugissement [rüzhēsmåṅ] *nm* roar, roaring *q*.
rugosité [rügōzētā] *nf* roughness; (*aspérité*) rough spot.
rugueux, euse [rügœ͞, -œ͞z] *a* rough.
ruine [rüēn] *nf* ruin; ~**s** *nfpl* ruins; **tomber en** ~ to fall into ruin(s).
ruiner [rüēnā] *vt* to ruin.
ruineux, euse [rüēnœ͞, -œ͞z] *a* terribly expensive to buy (*ou* run), ruinous; extravagant.
ruisseau, x [rüēsō] *nm* stream, brook; (*caniveau*) gutter; (*fig*): ~**x de larmes/sang** floods of tears/streams of blood.
ruisselant, e [rüēslåṅ, -åṅt] *a* streaming.
ruisseler [rüēslā] *vi* to stream; ~ (**d'eau**) to be streaming (with water); ~ **de lumière** to stream with light.
ruissellement [rüēselmåṅ] *nm* streaming; ~ **de lumière** stream of light.
rumeur [rümœr] *nf* (*bruit confus*) rumbling; hubbub *q*; (*protestation*) murmur(ing); (*nouvelle*) rumor (*US*), rumour (*Brit*).
ruminer [rümēnā] *vt* (*herbe*) to ruminate; (*fig*) to ruminate on *ou* over, chew over ♦ *vi*

(*vache*) to chew the cud, ruminate.
rumsteck [rònmstek] *nm* = **romsteck**.
rupestre [rüpestr(ə)] *a* (*plante*) rock *cpd*; (*art*) cave *cpd*.
rupture [rüptür] *nf* (*de câble, digue*) breaking; (*de tendon*) rupture, tearing; (*de négociations etc*) breakdown; (*de contrat*) breach; (*séparation, désunion*) break-up, split; **en** ~ **de ban** at odds with authority; **en** ~ **de stock** (*COMM*) out of stock.
rural, e, aux [rürål, -ō] *a* rural, country *cpd* ♦ *nmpl*: **les ruraux** country people.
ruse [rüz] *nf*: **la** ~ cunning, craftiness; trickery; **une** ~ a trick, a ruse; **par** ~ by trickery.
rusé, e [rüzā] *a* cunning, crafty.
russe [rüs] *a* Russian ♦ *nm* (*LING*) Russian ♦ *nm/f*: **R**~ Russian.
Russie [rüsē] *nf*: **la** ~ Russia; **la** ~ **blanche** White Russia; **la** ~ **soviétique** Soviet Russia.
rustine [rüstēn] *nf* repair patch (*for bicycle inner tube*).
rustique [rüstēk] *a* rustic; (*plante*) hardy.
rustre [rüstr(ə)] *nm* boor.
rut [rüt] *nm*: **être en** ~ (*animal domestique*) to be in *ou* on heat; (*animal sauvage*) to be rutting.
rutabaga [rütábàgá] *nm* rutabaga (*US*), swede (*Brit*).
rutilant, e [rütēlåṅ, -åṅt] *a* gleaming.
RV *sigle m* = **rendez-vous**.
Rwanda [rwåndå] *nm*: **le** ~ Rwanda.
rythme [rētm(ə)] *nm* rhythm; (*vitesse*) rate; (*: de la vie*) pace, tempo; **au** ~ **de 10 par jour** at the rate of 10 a day.
rythmé, e [rētmā] *a* rhythmic(al).
rythmer [rētmā] *vt* to give rhythm to.
rythmique [rētmēk] *a* rhythmic(al) ♦ *nf* rhythmics *sg*.

S

S, s [es] *nm inv* S, s ♦ *abr* (= *sud*) S; **S comme Suzanne** S for Sugar.
s' [s] *pronom voir* **se**.
s/ *abr* = **sur**.
SA *sigle f* = **société anonyme**; (= *Son Altesse*) HH.
sa [sà] *dét voir* **son**.
sabbatique [sàbátēk] *a*: **année** ~ sabbatical year.
sable [sàbl(ə)] *nm* sand; ~**s mouvants** quicksand(s).
sablé [sàblā] *a* (*allée*) sandy ♦ *nm* shortbread cookie (*US*) *ou* biscuit (*Brit*); **pâte** ~**e** (*CULIN*) shortbread dough.
sabler [sàblā] *vt* to sand; (*contre le verglas*) to sand; ~ **le champagne** to drink champagne.
sableux, euse [sàblœ͞, -œ͞z] *a* sandy.
sablier [sàblēyā] *nm* hourglass; (*de cuisine*) egg timer.
sablière [sàblēyer] *nf* sand quarry.

sablonneux, euse [sâblonœ̄, -œ̄z] *a* sandy.
saborder [sàbordā] *vt* (*navire*) to scuttle; (*fig*) to wind up, shut down.
sabot [sàbō] *nm* clog; (*de cheval, bœuf*) hoof; ~ **(de Denver)** (wheel) clamp; ~ **de frein** brake shoe.
sabotage [sàbotázh] *nm* sabotage.
saboter [sàbotā] *vt* (*travail, morceau de musique*) to botch, make a mess of; (*machine, installation, négociation etc*) to sabotage.
saboteur, euse [sàbotœr, -œ̄z] *nm/f* saboteur.
sabre [sâbr(ə)] *nm* saber (*US*), sabre (*Brit*); **le** ~ (*fig*) the sword, the army.
sabrer [sàbrā] *vt* to cut down.
SAC [sàk] *sigle m* (= *Service d'action civile*) *former Gaullist parapolice.*
sac [sàk] *nm* bag; (*à charbon etc*) sack; (*pillage*) sack(ing); **mettre à** ~ to sack; ~ **à provisions/de voyage** shopping/overnight bag; ~ **de couchage** sleeping bag; ~ **à dos** backpack; ~ **à main** handbag; ~ **de plage** beach bag.
saccade [sàkàd] *nf* jerk; **par** ~s jerkily; haltingly.
saccadé, e [sàkàdā] *a* jerky.
saccage [sàkàzh] *nm* havoc.
saccager [sàkàzhā] *vt* (*piller*) to sack, lay waste; (*dévaster*) to create havoc in, wreck.
saccharine [sàkárēn] *nf* saccharin(e).
SACEM [sàsem] *sigle f* (= *Société des auteurs, compositeurs et éditeurs de musique*) *body responsible for collecting and distributing royalties.*
sacerdoce [sàserdos] *nm* priesthood; (*fig*) calling, vocation.
sacerdotal, e, aux [sàserdotàl, -ō] *a* priestly, sacerdotal.
sachant [sàshàn] *etc vb voir* **savoir.**
sachet [sàshe] *nm* (small) bag; (*de lavande, poudre, shampooing*) sachet; **thé en** ~s tea bags; ~ **de thé** tea bag.
sacoche [sàkosh] *nf* (*gén*) bag; (*de bicyclette*) saddlebag; (*du facteur*) mailbag; (*d'outils*) toolbag.
sacquer [sàkā] *vt* (*fam: candidat, employé*) to fire; (*: réprimander, mal noter*) to flunk.
sacraliser [sàkràlēzā] *vt* to make sacred.
sacre [sàkr(ə)] *nm* coronation; consecration.
sacré, e [sàkrā] *a* sacred; (*fam: satané*) blasted; (*: fameux*): **un** ~ ... a heck of a ...; (*ANAT*) sacral.
sacrement [sàkrəmàn] *nm* sacrament; **les derniers** ~s the last rites.
sacrer [sàkrā] *vt* (*roi*) to crown; (*évêque*) to consecrate ♦ *vi* to curse, swear.
sacrifice [sàkrēfēs] *nm* sacrifice; **faire le** ~ **de** to sacrifice.
sacrificiel, le [sàkrēfēsyel] *a* sacrificial.
sacrifier [sàkrēfyā] *vt* to sacrifice; ~ **à** *vt* to conform to; **se** ~ to sacrifice o.s.; **articles sacrifiés** (*COMM*) items sold at rock-bottom *ou* give-away prices.
sacrilège [sàkrēlezh] *nm* sacrilege ♦ *a* sacrilegious.
sacristain [sàkrēstàn] *nm* sexton; sacristan.
sacristie [sàkrēstē] *nf* sacristy; (*culte protestant*) vestry.
sacro-saint, e [sàkrosàn, -ànt] *a* sacrosanct.

sadique [sàdēk] *a* sadistic ♦ *nm/f* sadist.
sadisme [sàdēsm(ə)] *nm* sadism.
sadomasochiste [sàdomàzoshēst(ə)] *nm/f* sadomasochist.
safari [sàfàrē] *nm* safari; **faire un** ~ to go on safari.
safari-photo [sàfàrēfotō] *nm* photographic safari.
SAFER [sàfer] *sigle f* (= *société d'aménagement foncier et d'établissement rural*) *organization with the right to buy land in order to retain it for agricultural use.*
safran [sàfràn] *nm* saffron.
sagace [sàgàs] *a* sagacious, shrewd.
sagacité [sàgàsētā] *nf* sagacity, shrewdness.
sagaie [sàge] *nf* assegai.
sage [sàzh] *a* wise; (*enfant*) good ♦ *nm* wise man; sage.
sage-femme [sàzhfàm] *nf* midwife (*pl* -wives).
sagement [sàzhmàn] *ad* (*raisonnablement*) wisely, sensibly; (*tranquillement*) quietly.
sagesse [sàzhes] *nf* wisdom.
Sagittaire [sàzhēter] *nm*: **le** ~ Sagittarius, the Archer; **être du** ~ to be Sagittarius.
Sahara [sààrà] *nm*: **le** ~ the Sahara (Desert); **le** ~ **occidental** (*pays*) Western Sahara.
saharien, ne [sààryàn, -en] *a* Saharan ♦ *nf* safari jacket.
sahélien, ne [sàālyàn, -en] *a* Sahelian.
saignant, e [senyàn, -ànt] *a* (*viande*) rare; (*blessure, plaie*) bleeding.
saignée [sānyā] *nf* (*MÉD*) bleeding *q*, bloodletting *q*; (*ANAT*): **la** ~ **du bras** the bend of the arm; (*fig: MIL*) heavy losses *pl*, (*: prélèvement*) deep cut.
saignement [senymàn] *nm* bleeding; ~ **de nez** nosebleed.
saigner [sānyā] *vi* to bleed ♦ *vt* to bleed; (*animal*) to bleed to death; ~ **qn à blanc** (*fig*) to bleed sb white; ~ **du nez** to have a nosebleed.
Saigon [sàygôn] *n* Saigon.
saillant, e [sàyàn, -ànt] *a* (*pommettes, menton*) prominent; (*corniche etc*) projecting; (*fig*) salient, outstanding.
saillie [sàyē] *nf* (*sur un mur etc*) projection; (*trait d'esprit*) witticism; (*accouplement*) covering, serving; **faire** ~ to project, stick out; **en** ~, **formant** ~ projecting, overhanging.
saillir [sàyēr] *vi* to project, stick out; (*veine, muscle*) to bulge ♦ *vt* (*ÉLEVAGE*) to cover, serve.
sain, e [san, sen] *a* healthy; (*dents, constitution*) healthy, sound; (*lectures*) wholesome; ~ **et sauf** safe and sound, unharmed; ~ **d'esprit** sound in mind, sane.
saindoux [sandōō] *nm* lard.
sainement [senmàn] *ad* (*vivre*) healthily; (*raisonner*) soundly.
saint, e [san, sant] *a* holy; (*fig*) saintly ♦ *nm/f* saint; **le S**~ **Esprit** the Holy Spirit *ou* Ghost; **la S**~**e Vierge** the Blessed Virgin.
saint-bernard [sanbernàr] *nm inv* (*chien*) St Bernard.
Sainte-Hélène [santàlen] *nf* St Helena.
Sainte-Lucie [santlüsē] *nf* Saint Lucia.
sainteté [santtā] *nf* holiness; saintliness.
Saint-Laurent [sanlorân] *nm*: **le** ~ the St

Lawrence.
Saint-Marin [sanmáran] *nm*: **le** ~ San Marino.
Saint-Père [sanper] *nm*: **le** ~ the Holy Father, the Pontiff.
Saint-Pierre [sanpyer] *nm* Saint Peter; (*église*) Saint Peter's.
Saint-Pierre-et-Miquelon [sanpyerãmēklón] *nm* Saint Pierre and Miquelon.
Saint-Siège [sansyezh] *nm*: **le** ~ the Holy See.
Saint-Sylvestre [sansēlvestr(ə)] *nf*: **la** ~ New Year's Eve.
Saint-Thomas [santomá] *nf* Saint Thomas.
Saint-Vincent et les Grenadines [sanvansánālāgrənádēn] *nm* St Vincent and the Grenadines.
sais [se] *etc vb voir* **savoir**.
saisie [sāzē] *nf* seizure; **à la** ~ (*texte*) being keyed; ~ **(de données)** (data) capture.
saisine [sāzēn] *nf* (*JUR*) *submission of a case to the court*.
saisir [sāzēr] *vt* to take hold of, grab; (*fig: occasion*) to seize; (*comprendre*) to grasp; (*entendre*) to get, catch; (*suj: émotions*) to take hold of, come over; (*INFORM*) to capture, keyboard; (*CULIN*) to fry quickly; (*JUR: biens, publication*) to seize; (: *juridiction*): ~ **un tribunal d'une affaire** to submit *ou* refer a case to a court; **se** ~ **de** *vt* to seize; **être saisi** (*frappé de*) to be overcome.
saisissant, e [sāzēsán, -ánt] *a* startling, striking; (*froid*) biting.
saisissement [sāzēsmán] *nm*: **muet/figé de** ~ speechless/frozen with emotion.
saison [sezón] *nf* season; **la belle/mauvaise** ~ the summer/winter months; **être de** ~ to be in season; **en/hors** ~ in/out of season; **haute/basse/morte** ~ high/low/slack season; **la** ~ **des pluies/des amours** the rainy/mating season.
saisonnier, ière [sezonyā, -yer] *a* seasonal ♦ *nm* (*travailleur*) seasonal worker; (*vacancier*) seasonal vacationer (*US*) *ou* holiday-maker (*Brit*).
sait [se] *vb voir* **savoir**.
salace [salás] *a* salacious.
salade [salád] *nf* (*BOT*) lettuce *etc* (*generic term*); (*CULIN*) (green) salad; (*fam*) tangle, muddle; ~**s** *nfpl* (*fam*): **raconter des** ~**s** to tell tales (*fam*); **haricots en** ~ bean salad; ~ **de concombres** cucumber salad; ~ **de fruits** fruit salad; ~ **niçoise** salade niçoise; ~ **russe** Russian salad.
saladier [saládyā] *nm* (salad) bowl.
salaire [saler] *nm* (*annuel, mensuel*) salary; (*hebdomadaire, journalier*) pay, wages *pl*; (*fig*) reward; ~ **de base** base pay (*US*), basic salary (*ou* wage) (*Brit*); ~ **de misère** starvation wage; ~ **minimum interprofessionnel de croissance (SMIC)** index-linked guaranteed minimum wage.
salaison [salezón] *nf* salting; ~**s** *nfpl* salt meat *sg*.
salamandre [salāmándr(ə)] *nf* salamander.
salami [salāmē] *nm* salami *q*, salami sausage.
salant [salán] *am*: **marais** ~ salt pan.
salarial, e, aux [saláryál, -ō] *a* salary *cpd*, wage(s) *cpd*.
salariat [saláryá] *nm* salaried staff.
salarié, e [saláryā] *a* salaried; wage-earning ♦

nm/f salaried employee; wage-earner.
salaud [salō] *nm* (*fam!*) bastard (!).
sale [sál] *a* dirty; (*fig: avant le nom*) nasty.
salé, e [sálā] *a* (*liquide, saveur*) salty; (*CULIN*) salted, salt *cpd*; (*fig*) spicy, juicy; (: *note, facture*) steep, stiff ♦ *nm* (*porc salé*) salt pork; **petit** ~ ≈ pickled pork.
salement [sálmán] *ad* (*manger etc*) dirtily, messily.
saler [sálā] *vt* to salt.
saleté [sáltā] *nf* (*état*) dirtiness; (*crasse*) dirt, filth; (*tache etc*) dirt *q*, something dirty, dirty mark; (*fig: tour*) dirty trick; (: *chose sans valeur*) rubbish *q*; (: *obscénité*) filth *q*; (: *microbe etc*) bug; **vivre dans la** ~ to live in squalor.
salière [sályer] *nf* salt shaker (*US*), saltcellar (*Brit*).
saligaud [sálēgō] *nm* (*fam!*) bastard (!).
salin, e [sálán, -ēn] *a* saline ♦ *nf* saltworks *sg*.
salinité [sálēnētā] *nf* salinity, salt-content.
salir [sálēr] *vt* to (make) dirty; (*fig*) to soil the reputation of; **se** ~ to get dirty.
salissant, e [sálēsán, -ánt] *a* (*tissu*) which shows the dirt; (*métier*) dirty, messy.
salissure [sálēsür] *nf* dirt *q*; (*tache*) dirty mark.
salive [sálēv] *nf* saliva.
saliver [sálēvā] *vi* to salivate.
salle [sál] *nf* room; (*d'hôpital*) ward; (*de restaurant*) dining room; (*d'un cinéma*) auditorium; (: *public*) audience; **faire** ~ **comble** to have a full house; ~ **d'armes** (*pour l'escrime*) fencing room; ~ **d'attente** waiting room; ~ **de bain(s)** bathroom; ~ **de bal** ballroom; ~ **de cinéma** cinema; ~ **de classe** classroom; ~ **commune** (*d'hôpital*) ward; ~ **de concert** concert hall; ~ **de consultation** office (*US*), consulting room (*Brit*); ~ **de danse** dance hall; ~ **de douches** shower-room; ~ **d'eau** shower-room; ~ **d'embarquement** (*à l'aéroport*) departure lounge; ~ **d'exposition** showroom; ~ **de jeux** games room; playroom; ~ **des machines** engine room; ~ **à manger** dining room; (*mobilier*) dining room suite; ~ **obscure** movie theater (*US*), cinema (*Brit*); ~ **d'opération** (*d'hôpital*) operating room (*US*) *ou* theatre (*Brit*); ~ **de projection** movie auditorium (*US*), film theatre (*Brit*); ~ **de séjour** living room; ~ **de spectacle** theater (*US*), theatre (*Brit*); cinema; ~ **des ventes** salesroom.
salmonellose [sálmonālōz] *nf* (*MÉD*) salmonella poisoning.
Salomon [sálomón]: **les îles** ~ the Solomon Islands.
salon [sálón] *nm* lounge, living room; (*mobilier*) living room suite; (*exposition*) exhibition, show; (*mondain, littéraire*) salon; ~ **de coiffure** hairdressing salon; ~ **de thé** tearoom.
salopard [sálopár] *nm* (*fam!*) bastard (!).
salope [sálop] *nf* (*fam!*) bitch (!).
saloper [sálopā] *vt* (*fam!*) to botch, bungle, mess up.
saloperie [sáloprē] *nf* (*fam!*) filth *q*; dirty trick; rubbish *q*.
salopette [sálopet] *nf* dungarees *pl*;

(*d'ouvrier*) overall(s).

salpêtre [sålpetr(ə)] *nm* saltpetre.

salsifis [sålsĕfē] *nm* salsify, oyster-plant.

SALT [sålt] *sigle* (= *Strategic Arms Limitation Talks*) SALT.

saltimbanque [såltåṅbåṅk] *nm/f* (travel(l)ing) acrobat.

salubre [sålübr(ə)] *a* healthy, salubrious.

salubrité [sålübrētā] *nf* healthiness, salubrity; ~ **publique** public health.

saluer [sålüā] *vt* (*pour dire bonjour*, *fig*) to greet; (*pour dire au revoir*) to take one's leave; (*MIL*) to salute.

salut [sålü] *nm* (*sauvegarde*) safety; (*REL*) salvation; (*geste*) wave; (*parole*) greeting; (*MIL*) salute ♦ *excl* (*fam: pour dire bonjour*) hi (there); (: *pour dire au revoir*) see you!, 'bye!; (*style relevé*) (all) hail.

salutaire [sålüter] *a* (*remède*) beneficial; (*conseils*) salutary.

salutations [sålütāsyôṅ] *nfpl* greetings; **recevez mes ~ distinguées** *ou* **respectueuses** yours truly (*US*) *ou* faithfully (*Brit*).

salutiste [sålütēst(ə)] *nm/f* Salvationist.

Salvador [sålvådor] *nm*: **le ~** El Salvador.

salve [sålv(ə)] *nf* salvo; volley of shots; ~ **d'applaudissements** burst of applause.

Samarie [såmårē] *nf*: **la ~** Samaria.

samaritain [såmårētaṅ] *nm*: **le bon S~** the Good Samaritan.

samedi [såmdē] *nm* Saturday; *voir aussi* **lundi**.

Samoa [såmoå] *nfpl*: **les (îles) ~** Samoa, the Samoa Islands.

SAMU [såmü] *sigle m* (= *service d'assistance médicale d'urgence*) ≈ paramedics (*US*), ≈ ambulance (service) (*Brit*).

sanatorium [sånåtoryom] *nm* sanatorium (*pl* -a).

sanctifier [såṅktēfyā] *vt* to sanctify.

sanction [såṅksyôṅ] *nf* sanction; (*fig*) penalty; **prendre des ~s contre** to impose sanctions on.

sanctionner [såṅksyonā] *vt* (*loi*, *usage*) to sanction; (*punir*) to punish.

sanctuaire [såṅktüer] *nm* sanctuary.

sandale [såndål] *nf* sandal.

sandalette [såndålet] *nf* sandal.

sandow [såndō] *nm* ® bungee cord (*US*), luggage elastic (*Brit*).

sandwich [såndwētsh] *nm* sandwich; **pris en ~** sandwiched.

sang [såṅ] *nm* blood; **en ~** covered in blood; **jusqu'au ~** (*mordre*, *pincer*) till the blood comes; **se faire du mauvais ~** to fret, get in a state.

sang-froid [såṅfrwå] *nm* calm, sangfroid; **garder/perdre/reprendre son ~** to keep/lose/regain one's cool; **de ~** in cold blood.

sanglant, e [såṅglåṅ, -åṅt] *a* bloody, covered in blood; (*combat*) bloody; (*fig: reproche*, *affront*) cruel.

sangle [såṅgl(ə)] *nf* strap; **~s** *nfpl* (*pour lit etc*) webbing *sg*.

sangler [såṅglā] *vt* to strap up; (*animal*) to girth.

sanglier [såṅglēyā] *nm* (wild) boar.

sanglot [såṅglō] *nm* sob.

sangloter [såṅglotā] *vi* to sob.

sangsue [såṅsü] *nf* leech.

sanguin, e [såṅgaṅ, -ēn] *a* blood *cpd*; (*fig*) fiery ♦ *nf* blood orange; (*ART*) red pencil drawing.

sanguinaire [såṅgēner] *a* (*animal*, *personne*) bloodthirsty; (*lutte*) bloody.

sanguinolent, e [såṅgēnolåṅ, -åṅt] *a* streaked with blood.

sanisette [sånēzet] *nf* (automatic) public toilet.

sanitaire [sånēter] *a* health *cpd*; **~s** *nmpl* (*salle de bain et w.-c.*) bathroom *sg*; **installation/appareil ~** bathroom plumbing/appliance.

sans [såṅ] *prép* without; **~ qu'il s'en aperçoive** without him *ou* his noticing; **~ scrupules** unscrupulous; **~ manches** sleeveless.

sans-abri [såṅzåbrē] *nmpl* homeless.

sans-emploi [såṅzåṅplwå] *nmpl* jobless.

sans-façon [såṅfåsôṅ] *a inv* fuss-free; free and easy.

sans-gêne [såṅzhen] *a inv* inconsiderate ♦ *nm inv* (*attitude*) lack of consideration.

sans-logis [såṅlozhē] *nmpl* homeless.

sans-souci [såṅsōōsē] *a inv* carefree.

sans-travail [såṅtråvåy] *nmpl* unemployed, jobless.

santal [såntål] *nm* sandal(wood).

santé [såntā] *nf* health; **avoir une ~ de fer** to have an iron constitution; **être en bonne ~** to be in good health, be healthy; **boire à la ~ de qn** to drink (to) sb's health; **"à la ~ de"** "here's to"; **à ta** *ou* **votre ~!** cheers!; **service de ~** (*dans un port etc*) quarantine service; **la ~ publique** public health.

Santiago (du Chili) [såntyågō(düshēlē)] *n* Santiago (de Chile).

santon [såntôṅ] *nm* ornamental figure at a Christmas crib.

saoudien, ne [såōōdyaṅ, -en] *a* Saudi (Arabian) ♦ *nm/f*: **S~, ne** Saudi (Arabian).

saoul, e [sōō, sōōl] *a* = **soûl, e.**

sape [såp] *nf*: **travail de ~** (*MIL*) sap; (*fig*) insidious undermining process *ou* work; **~s** *nfpl* (*fam*) gear *sg*, togs.

saper [såpā] *vt* to undermine, sap; **se ~** *vi* (*fam*) to dress.

sapeur [såpœr] *nm* sapper.

sapeur-pompier [såpœrpôṅpyā] *nm* fireman.

saphir [såfēr] *nm* sapphire; (*d'électrophone*) needle, sapphire needle.

sapin [såpaṅ] *nm* fir (tree); (*bois*) fir; **~ de Noël** Christmas tree.

sapinière [såpēnyer] *nf* fir plantation *ou* forest.

SAR *sigle f* (= *Son Altesse Royale*) HRH.

sarabande [såråbåṅd] *nf* saraband; (*fig*) hullabaloo; whirl.

sarbacane [sårbåkån] *nf* blowpipe, blowgun; (*jouet*) peashooter.

sarcasme [sårkåsm(ə)] *nm* sarcasm *q*; (*propos*) piece of sarcasm.

sarcastique [sårkåstēk] *a* sarcastic.

sarcastiquement [sårkåstēkmåṅ] *ad* sarcastically.

sarclage [sårklåzh] *nm* weeding.

sarcler [sårklā] *vt* to weed.

sarcloir [sårklwår] *nm* (weeding) hoe, spud.

sarcophage [sàrkofázh] *nm* sarcophagus (*pl* -i).

Sardaigne [sárdeny] *nf*: **la** ~ Sardinia.

sarde [sárd(ə)] *a* Sardinian.

sardine [sàrdēn] *nf* sardine; ~**s à l'huile** sardines in oil.

sardinier, ière [sárdēnyā, -yer] *a* (*pêche, industrie*) sardine *cpd* ♦ *nm* (*bateau*) sardine boat.

sardonique [sárdonēk] *a* sardonic.

sari [sàrē] *nm* sari.

SARL [sárl] *sigle f* = **société à responsabilité limitée.**

sarment [sàrmâṅ] *nm*: ~ (**de vigne**) vine shoot.

sarrasin [sàrázaṅ] *nm* buckwheat.

sarrau [sàrō] *nm* smock.

Sarre [sár] *nf*: **la** ~ the Saar.

sarriette [sáryet] *nf* savory.

sarrois, e [sárwà, -wàz] *a* Saar *cpd* ♦ *nm/f*: **S~, e** inhabitant *ou* native of the Saar.

sas [sàs] *nm* (*de sous-marin, d'engin spatial*) airlock; (*d'écluse*) lock.

satané, e [sátánā] *a* confounded.

satanique [sátánēk] *a* satanic, fiendish.

satelliser [sátālēzā] *vt* (*fusée*) to put into orbit; (*fig: pays*) to make into a satellite.

satellite [sátālēt] *nm* satellite; **pays** ~ satellite country.

satellite-espion, *pl* **satellites-espions** [sátālētespyóṅ] *nm* spy satellite.

satellite-observatoire, *pl* **satellites-observatoires** [sátālētopservàtwár] *nm* observation satellite.

satellite-relais, *pl* **satellites-relais** [sátālētrəle] *nm* (*TV*) relay satellite.

satiété [sàsyātā]: **à** ~ *ad* to satiety *ou* satiation; (*répéter*) ad nauseam.

satin [sátaṅ] *nm* satin.

satiné, e [sátēnā] *a* satiny; (*peau*) satin-smooth.

satinette [sátēnet] *nf* satinet, sateen.

satire [sátēr] *nf* satire; **faire la** ~ to satirize.

satirique [sátērēk] *a* satirical.

satiriser [sátērēzā] *vt* to satirize.

satiriste [sátērēst(ə)] *nm/f* satirist.

satisfaction [sátēsfáksyóṅ] *nf* satisfaction; **à ma grande** ~ to my great satisfaction; **obtenir** ~ to obtain *ou* get satisfaction; **donner** ~ (**à**) to give satisfaction (to).

satisfaire [sátēsfer] *vt* to satisfy; **se** ~ **de** to be satisfied *ou* content with; ~ **à** *vt* (*engagement*) to fulfill (*US*), fulfil (*Brit*); (*revendications, conditions*) to satisfy, meet.

satisfaisant, e [sátēsfəzâṅ, -âṅt] *vb voir* **satisfaire** ♦ *a* satisfactory; (*qui fait plaisir*) satisfying.

satisfait, e [sátēsfe, -et] *pp de* **satisfaire** ♦ *a* satisfied; ~ **de** happy *ou* satisfied with.

satisfasse [sátēsfás], **satisferai** [sátēsfrā] *etc vb voir* **satisfaire.**

saturation [sátūrâsyóṅ] *nf* saturation; **arriver à** ~ to reach saturation point.

saturer [sátūrā] *vt* to saturate; ~ **qn/qch de** to saturate sb/sth with.

saturnisme [sátürnēsm(ə)] *nm* (*MÉD*) lead poisoning.

satyre [sátēr] *nm* satyr; (*péj*) lecher.

sauce [sōs] *nf* sauce; (*avec un rôti*) gravy; **en** ~ in a sauce; ~ **blanche** white sauce; ~ **chasseur** sauce chasseur; ~ **tomate** tomato sauce.

saucer [sōsā] *vt* (*assiette*) to soak up the sauce from.

saucière [sōsyer] *nf* gravy boat.

saucisse [sōsēs] *nf* sausage.

saucisson [sōsēsóṅ] *nm* (slicing) sausage; ~ **à l'ail** garlic sausage.

saucissonner [sōsēsonā] *vt* to cut up, slice ♦ *vi* to picnic.

sauf [sōf] *prép* except; ~ **si** (*à moins que*) unless; ~ **avis contraire** unless you hear to the contrary; ~ **empêchement** barring (any) problems; ~ **erreur** if I'm not mistaken; ~ **imprévu** unless anything unforeseen arises, barring accidents.

sauf, sauve [sōf, sōv] *a* unharmed, unhurt; (*fig: honneur*) intact, saved; **laisser la vie sauve à qn** to spare sb's life.

sauf-conduit [sōfkóṅdüē] *nm* safe-conduct.

sauge [sōzh] *nf* sage.

saugrenu, e [sōgrənü] *a* preposterous, ludicrous.

saule [sōl] *nm* willow (tree); ~ **pleureur** weeping willow.

saumâtre [sōmâtr(ə)] *a* briny; (*désagréable: plaisanterie*) unsavory (*US*), unsavoury (*Brit*).

saumon [sōmóṅ] *nm* salmon *inv* ♦ *a inv* salmon (pink).

saumoné, e [sōmonā] *a*: **truite saumonée** salmon trout.

saumure [sōmür] *nf* brine.

sauna [sōnà] *nm* sauna.

saupoudrer [sōpōōdrā] *vt*: ~ **qch de** to sprinkle sth with.

saupoudreuse [sōpōōdrœz] *nf* dredger.

saur [sor] *am*: **hareng** ~ smoked *ou* red herring, kipper.

saurai [sorā] *etc vb voir* **savoir.**

saut [sō] *nm* jump; (*discipline sportive*) jumping; **faire un** ~ to (make a) jump *ou* leap; **faire un** ~ **chez qn** to pop over to sb's (place); **au** ~ **du lit** on getting out of bed; ~ **en hauteur/longueur** high/long jump; ~ **à la corde** jumping rope (*US*), skipping (*Brit*); ~ **de page** (*INFORM*) page break; ~ **en parachute** parachuting *q*; ~ **à la perche** pole vaulting; ~ **périlleux** somersault.

saute [sōt] *nf*: ~ **de vent/température** sudden change of wind direction/in the temperature; **avoir des** ~**s d'humeur** to have sudden changes of mood.

sauté, e [sōtā] *a* (*CULIN*) sauté ♦ *nm*: ~ **de veau** sauté of veal.

saute-mouton [sōtmōōtóṅ] *nm*: **jouer à** ~ to play leapfrog.

sauter [sōtā] *vi* to jump, leap; (*exploser*) to blow up, explode; (: *fusibles*) to blow; (*se rompre*) to snap, burst; (*se détacher*) to pop out (*ou* off) ♦ *vt* to jump (over), leap (over); (*fig: omettre*) to jump rope (*US*), skip (*Brit*), miss (out); **faire** ~ to blow up; to burst open; (*CULIN*) to sauté; ~ **à pieds joints/à cloche-pied** to make a standing jump/to hop; ~ **en parachute** to make a parachute jump; ~ **à la corde** to jump rope (*US*), skip (*Brit*); ~ **de joie** to jump for joy; ~ **de colère** to be hopping with rage *ou* hopping mad; ~ **au cou de qn** to fly into sb's arms; ~ **aux yeux** to be quite obvious; ~ **au plafond** (*fig*) to hit the roof.

sauterelle [sōtrɛl] *nf* grasshopper.

sauterie [sōtrē] *nf* party, hop.

sauteur, euse [sōtœr, -œz] *nm/f* (*athlète*) jumper ♦ *nf* (*casserole*) shallow pan, frying pan; ~ **à la perche** pole vaulter; ~ **à skis** skijumper.

sautiller [sōtēyā] *vi* to hop; to skip.

sautoir [sōtwár] *nm* chain; (*SPORT: emplacement*) jumping pit; ~ **(de perles)** string of pearls.

sauvage [sōvàzh] *a* (*gén*) wild; (*peuplade*) savage; (*farouche*) unsociable; (*barbare*) wild, savage; (*non officiel*) unauthorized, unofficial ♦ *nm/f* savage; (*timide*) unsociable type, recluse.

sauvagement [sōvàzhmâṅ] *ad* savagely.

sauvageon, ne [sōvàzhôṅ, -on] *nm/f* little savage.

sauvagerie [sōvàzhrē] *nf* wildness; savagery; unsociability.

sauve [sōv] *af voir* **sauf.**

sauvegarde [sōvgàrd(ə)] *nf* safeguard; **sous la** ~ **de** under the protection of; **disquette/ fichier de** ~ (*INFORM*) backup disk/file.

sauvegarder [sōvgàrdā] *vt* to safeguard; (*INFORM: enregistrer*) to save; (*: copier*) to back up.

sauve-qui-peut [sōvkēpœ̄] *nm inv* stampede, mad rush ♦ *excl* run for your life!

sauver [sōvā] *vt* to save; (*porter secours à*) to rescue; (*récupérer*) to salvage, rescue; **se** ~ *vi* (*s'enfuir*) to run away; (*fam: partir*) to be off; ~ **qn de** to save sb from; ~ **la vie à qn** to save sb's life; ~ **les apparences** to keep up appearances.

sauvetage [sōvtàzh] *nm* rescue; ~ **en montagne** mountain rescue; **ceinture de** ~ life preserver (*US*), life belt (*Brit*); **brassière** *ou* **gilet de** ~ life jacket, life preserver (*US*).

sauveteur [sōvtœr] *nm* rescuer.

sauvette [sōvet]: **à la** ~ *ad* (*vendre*) without authorization; (*se marier etc*) hastily, hurriedly; **vente à la** ~ (unauthorized) street selling, (street) peddling.

sauveur [sōvœr] *nm* savior (*US*), saviour (*Brit*).

SAV *sigle m* = **service après vente.**

savais [sàvā] *etc vb voir* **savoir.**

savamment [sàvàmâṅ] *ad* (*avec érudition*) learnedly; (*habilement*) skillfully (*US*), skilfully (*Brit*), cleverly.

savane [sàvàn] *nf* savannah.

savant, e [sàváṅ, -âṅt] *a* scholarly, learned; (*calé*) clever ♦ *nm* scientist; **animal** ~ performing animal.

savate [sàvát] *nf* worn-out shoe; (*SPORT*) (*type of*) boxing.

saveur [sàvœr] *nm* flavor (*US*), flavour (*Brit*); (*fig*) savour (*US*), savour (*Brit*).

Savoie [sàvwá] *nf*: **la** ~ Savoy.

savoir [sàvwár] *vt* to know; (*être capable de*): **il sait nager** he knows how to swim, he can swim ♦ *nm* knowledge; **se** ~ (*être connu*) to be known; **se** ~ **malade/incurable** to know that one is ill/incurably ill; **il est petit: tu ne**

peux pas ~! you won't believe how small he is!; **vous n'êtes pas sans** ~ **que** you are not *ou* will not be unaware of the fact that; **je crois** ~ **que** ... I believe that ..., I think I know that ...; **je n'en sais rien** I (really) don't know; **à** ~ **(que)** that is, namely; **faire** ~ **qch à qn** to inform sb about sth, let sb know sth; **pas que je sache** not as far as I know; **sans le** ~ *ad* unknowingly, unwittingly; **en** ~ **long** to know a lot.

savoir-faire [sàvwárfer] *nm inv* savoir-faire, know-how.

savoir-vivre [sàvwárvēvr(ə)] *nm inv*: **le** ~ savoir-faire, good manners *pl*.

savon [sàvôṅ] *nm* (*produit*) soap; (*morceau*) bar *ou* tablet of soap; (*fam*): **passer un** ~ **à qn** to give sb a good dressing-down.

savonner [sàvonā] *vt* to soap.

savonnerie [sàvonrē] *nf* soap factory.

savonnette [sàvonet] *nf* bar *ou* tablet of soap.

savonneux, euse [sàvonœ̄, -œz] *a* soapy.

savons [sàvôṅ] *vb voir* **savoir.**

savourer [sàvōōrā] *vt* to savor (*US*), savour (*Brit*).

savoureux, euse [sàvōōrœ̄, -œz] *a* tasty; (*fig*) spicy, juicy.

savoyard, e [sàvwàyár, -àrd(ə)] *a* Savoyard.

sax [sáks] *nm* sax.

Saxe [sáks(ə)] *nf*: **la** ~ Saxony.

saxo(phone) [sákso(fon)] *nm* sax(ophone).

saxophoniste [sáksofonēst(ə)] *nm/f* saxophonist, sax(ophone) player.

saynète [senet] *nf* playlet.

SBB *sigle f* (= *Schweizerische Bundesbahn*) Swiss federal railways.

sbire [sbēr] *nm* (*péj*) henchman.

sc. *abr* = **scène.**

s/c *abr* (= *sous couvert de*) ≈ c/o.

scabreux, euse [skábrœ̄, -œz] *a* risky; (*indécent*) improper, shocking.

scalpel [skálpel] *nm* scalpel.

scalper [skálpā] *vt* to scalp.

scampi [skáṅpē] *nmpl* scampi.

scandale [skáṅdál] *nm* scandal; (*tapage*): **faire du** ~ to make a scene, create a disturbance; **faire** ~ to scandalize people; **au grand** ~ **de** ... to the great indignation of ....

scandaleusement [skáṅdálœ̄zmâṅ] *ad* scandalously, outrageously.

scandaleux, euse [skáṅdálœ̄, -œz] *a* scandalous, outrageous.

scandaliser [skáṅdálēzā] *vt* to scandalize; **se** ~ **(de)** to be scandalized (by).

scander [skáṅdā] *vt* (*vers*) to scan; (*mots, syllabes*) to stress separately; (*slogans*) to chant.

scandinave [skáṅdēnáv] *a* Scandinavian ♦ *nm/ f*: **S~** Scandinavian.

Scandinavie [skáṅdēnávē] *nf*: **la** ~ Scandinavia.

scanner [skáner] *nm* (*MÉD*) scanner.

scanographie [skánográfē] *nf* (*MÉD*) scanning; (*image*) scan.

scaphandre [skáfáṅdr(ə)] *nm* (*de plongeur*) diving suit; (*de cosmonaute*) space-suit; ~ **autonome** aqualung.

scaphandrier [skáfáṅdrēyā] *nm* diver.

scarabée [skárábā] *nm* beetle.

scarlatine [skárlátēṅ] *nf* scarlet fever.

scarole [skárol] *nf* endive.
scatologique [skátolozhĕk] *a* scatological, lavatorial.
sceau, x [sō] *nm* seal; (*fig*) stamp, mark; **sous le ~ du secret** under the seal of secrecy.
scélérat, e [sālárá, -át] *nm/f* villain, blackguard ♦ *a* villainous, blackguardly.
sceller [sālā] *vt* to seal.
scellés [sālā] *nmpl* seals.
scénario [sānáryō] *nm* (*CINÉMA*) screenplay, script; (*: idée, plan*) scenario; (*fig*) pattern; scenario.
scénariste [sānárēst(ə)] *nm/f* scriptwriter.
scène [sen] *nf* (*gén*) scene; (*estrade, fig: théâtre*) stage; **entrer en ~** to come on stage; **mettre en ~** (*THÉÂTRE*) to stage; (*CINÉMA*) to direct; (*fig*) to present, introduce; **sur le devant de la ~** (*en pleine actualité*) in the forefront; **porter à la ~** to adapt for the stage; **faire une ~ (à qn)** to make a scene (with sb); **~ de ménage** domestic fight *ou* scene.
scénique [sānēk] *a* (*effets*) theatrical; (*art*) scenic.
scepticisme [septēsēsm(ə)] *nm* skepticism (*US*), scepticism (*Brit*).
sceptique [septēk] *a* skeptical (*US*), sceptical (*Brit*) ♦ *nm/f* skeptic (*US*), sceptic (*Brit*).
sceptre [septr(ə)] *nm* skepter (*US*), sceptre (*Brit*).
schéma [shāmá] *nm* (*diagramme*) diagram, sketch; (*fig*) outline.
schématique [shāmátēk] *a* diagrammatic(al), schematic; (*fig*) oversimplified.
schématiquement [shāmátēkmáṅ] *ad* schematically, diagrammatically.
schématiser [shāmátēzā] *vt* to schematize; to (over)simplify.
schismatique [shēsmátēk] *a* schismatic.
schisme [shēsm(ə)] *nm* schism; rift, split.
schiste [shēst(ə)] *nm* schist.
schizophrène [skēzofren] *nm/f* schizophrenic.
schizophrénie [skēzofrānē] *nf* schizophrenia.
sciatique [syátēk] *a*: **nerf ~** sciatic nerve ♦ *nf* sciatica.
scie [sē] *nf* saw; (*fam: rengaine*) catchword, catch phrase; (*: personne*) bore; **~ à bois** wood saw; **~ circulaire** circular saw; **~ à découper** fretsaw; **~ à métaux** hacksaw; **~ sauteuse** jigsaw.
sciemment [syámáṅ] *ad* knowingly, wittingly.
science [syáṅs] *nf* science; (*savoir*) knowledge; (*savoir-faire*) art, skill; **~s humaines/sociales** social sciences; **~s naturelles** natural science *sg*, biology *sg*; **~s po** political studies.
science-fiction [syáṅsfēksyóṅ] *nf* science fiction.
scientifique [syáṅtēfēk] *a* scientific ♦ *nm/f* (*savant*) scientist; (*étudiant*) science student.
scientifiquement [syáṅtēfēkmáṅ] *ad* scientifically.
scier [syā] *vt* to saw; (*retrancher*) to saw off.
scierie [sērē] *nf* sawmill.
scieur [syœr] *nm*: **~ de long** pit sawyer.
Scilly [sēlē]: **les îles ~** the Scilly Isles, the Scillies, the Isles of Scilly.
scinder [saṅdá] *vt*, **se ~** *vi* to split (up).

scintillant, e [saṅtēyáṅ, -áṅt] *a* sparkling.
scintillement [saṅtēymáṅ] *nm* sparkling *q*.
scintiller [saṅtēyá] *vi* to sparkle.
scission [sēsyóṅ] *nf* split.
sciure [syür] *nf*: **~ (de bois)** sawdust.
sclérose [sklārōz] *nf* sclerosis; (*fig*) ossification; **~ en plaques (SEP)** multiple sclerosis (MS).
sclérosé, e [sklārōzā] *a* sclerosed, sclerotic; ossified.
scléroser [sklārōzā]: **se ~** *vi* to become sclerosed; (*fig*) to become ossified.
scolaire [skoler] *a* school *cpd*; (*péj*) schoolish; **l'année ~** the school year; (*à l'université*) the academic year; **en âge ~** of school age.
scolariser [skolárēzā] *vt* to provide with schooling (*ou* schools).
scolarité [skolárētā] *nf* schooling; **frais de ~** tuition (*US*), school fees (*Brit*).
scolastique [skolástēk] *a* (*péj*) scholastic.
scoliose [skolyōz] *nf* curvature of the spine, scoliosis.
scoop [skoōp] *nm* (*PRESSE*) scoop, exclusive.
scooter [skoōtœr] *nm* (motor) scooter.
scorbut [skorbüt] *nm* scurvy.
score [skor] *nm* score; (*électoral etc*) result.
scories [skorē] *nfpl* scoria *pl*.
scorpion [skorpyóṅ] *nm* (*signe*): **le S~** Scorpio, the Scorpion; **être du S~** to be Scorpio.
scotch [skotsh] *nm* (*whisky*) scotch, whisky; (*adhésif*) Scotch tape ® (*US*), Sellotape ® (*Brit*).
scotcher [skotshā] *vt* to scotchtape ® (*US*), sellotape ® (*Brit*).
scout, e [skoōt] *a*, *nm* scout.
scoutisme [skoōtēsm(ə)] *nm* (boy) scout movement; (*activités*) scouting.
scribe [skrēb] *nm* scribe; (*péj*) pencil pusher (*US*), penpusher (*Brit*).
scribouillard [skrēboōyár] *nm* pencil pusher (*US*), penpusher (*Brit*).
script [skrēpt] *nm* printing; (*CINÉMA*) (shooting) script.
script-girl [skrēptgœrl] *nf* continuity girl.
scriptural, e, aux [skrēptúrál, -ō] *a*: **monnaie ~e** bank money.
scrupule [skrüpül] *nm* scruple; **être sans ~s** to be unscrupulous; **se faire un ~ de qch** to have scruples *ou* qualms about doing sth.
scrupuleusement [skrüpülœzmáṅ] *ad* scrupulously.
scrupuleux, euse [skrüpülœ, -œz] *a* scrupulous.
scrutateur, trice [skrütátœr, -trēs] *a* searching ♦ *nm/f* canvasser (*US*), scrutineer (*Brit*).
scruter [skrütá] *vt* to search, scrutinize; (*l'obscurité*) to peer into; (*motifs, comportement*) to examine, scrutinize.
scrutin [skrütáṅ] *nm* (*vote*) ballot; (*ensemble des opérations*) poll; **~ proportionnel/majoritaire** election on a proportional/majority basis; **~ à deux tours** poll with two ballots *ou* rounds; **~ de liste** list system.
sculpter [skültá] *vt* to sculpt; (*suj: érosion*) to carve.
sculpteur [skültœr] *nm* sculptor.
sculptural, e, aux [skültürál, -ō] *a* sculptural; (*fig*) statuesque.

sculpture [skültür] *nf* sculpture; ~ **sur bois** wood carving.

sdb. *abr* = **salle de bain.**

SDN *sigle f* (= *Société des Nations*) League of Nations.

SE *sigle f* (= *Son Excellence*) HE.

se, s' [s(ə)] *pronom* (*emploi réfléchi*) oneself, *m* himself, *f* herself, *sujet non humain* itself; *pl* themselves; (: *réciproque*) one another, each other; (: *passif*): **cela se répare facilement** it is easily repaired; (: *possessif*): ~ **casser la jambe/laver les mains** to break one's leg/wash one's hands; *autres emplois pronominaux: voir le verbe en question.*

séance [sããns] *nf* (*d'assemblée, récréative*) meeting, session; (*de tribunal*) sitting, session; (*musicale*, CINÉMA, THÉÂTRE) performance; **ouvrir/lever la** ~ to open/close the meeting; ~ **tenante** forthwith.

séant, e [sãã, -ãnt] *a* seemly, fitting ♦ *nm* posterior.

seau, x [sō] *nm* bucket, pail; ~ **à glace** icebucket.

séburn [sãbom] *nm* sebum.

sec, sèche [sɛk, sɛsh] *a* dry; (*raisins, figues*) dried; (*cœur, personne: insensible*) hard, cold; (*maigre, déchaîné*) spare, lean; (*réponse, ton*) sharp, curt; (*démarrage*) sharp, sudden ♦ *nm*: **tenir au** ~ to keep in a dry place ♦ *ad* hard; (*démarrer*) sharply; **boire** ~ to be a heavy drinker; **je le bois** ~ I drink it straight *ou* neat; **à pied** ~ without getting one's feet wet; **à** ~ *a* dried up; (*à court d'argent*) broke.

SECAM [sɛkám] *sigle m* (= *procédé séquentiel à mémoire*) SECAM.

sécateur [sãkátœr] *nm* shears *pl*, pair of shears.

sécession [sãsãsyõn] *nf*: **faire** ~ to secede; **la guerre de S**~ the American Civil War.

séchage [sãsházh] *nm* drying; (*de bois*) seasoning.

sèche [sɛsh] *af voir* **sec** ♦ *nf* (*fam*) cigarette.

sèche-cheveux [sɛshshəvœ] *nm inv* hair dryer.

sèche-linge [sɛshlãnzh] *nm inv* (*machine*) clothes dryer.

sèche-mains [sɛshmãn] *nm inv* hand dryer.

sèchement [sɛshmãn] *ad* (*frapper etc*) sharply; (*répliquer etc*) dryly, sharply.

sécher [sãshā] *vt* to dry; (*dessécher: peau, blé*) to dry (out); (: *étang*) to dry up; (*bois*) to season; (*fam: classe, cours*) to skip, miss ♦ *vi* to dry; to dry out; to dry up; (*fam: candidat*) to be stumped; **se** ~ (*après le bain*) to dry o.s.

sécheresse [sɛshres] *nf* dryness; (*absence de pluie*) drought.

séchoir [sãshwàr] *nm* dryer.

second, e [səgõn, -õnd] *a* second ♦ *nm* (*assistant*) second in command; (*étage*) third floor (*US*), second floor (*Brit*); (NAVIG) first mate ♦ *nf* second; (SCOL: *degré*) ≈ tenth grade (*US*), ≈ fifth form (*Brit*); **en** ~**e** (*en second rang*) in second place; **voyager en** ~**e** to travel second-class; **doué de** ~**e vue** having (the gift of) second sight; **trouver son** ~ **souffle** (SPORT, *fig*) to get one's second wind;

être dans un état ~ to be in a daze (*ou* trance); **de** ~**e main** second-hand.

secondaire [səgõnder] *a* secondary.

seconder [səgõndā] *vt* to assist; (*favouriser*) to back.

secouer [səkwā] *vt* to shake; (*passagers*) to rock; (*traumatiser*) to shake (up); **se** ~ (*chien*) to shake itself; (*fam: se démener*) to shake o.s. up; ~ **la poussière d'un tapis** to shake the dust off a carpet; ~ **la tête** to shake one's head.

secourable [səkōōrábl(ə)] *a* helpful.

secourir [səkōōrēr] *vt* (*aller sauver*) to (go and) rescue; (*prodiguer des soins à*) to help, assist; (*venir en aide à*) to assist, aid.

secourisme [səkōōrēsm(ə)] *nm* (*premiers soins*) first aid; (*sauvetage*) lifesaving.

secouriste [səkōōrēst(ə)] *nm/f* first-aid worker.

secourons [səkōōrõn] *etc vb voir* **secourir.**

secours [səkōōr] *vb voir* **secourir** ♦ *nm* help, aid, assistance ♦ *nmpl* aid *sg*; **cela lui a été d'un grand** ~ this was a great help to him; **au** ~! help!; **appeler au** ~ to shout *ou* call for help; **appeler qn à son** ~ to call sb to one's assistance; **porter** ~ **à qn** to give sb assistance, help sb; **les premiers** ~ first aid *sg*; **le** ~ **en montagne** mountain rescue.

secouru, e [səkōōrü] *pp de* **secourir.**

secousse [səkōōs] *nf* jolt, bump; (*électrique*) shock; (*fig: psychologique*) jolt, shock; ~ **sismique** *ou* **tellurique** earth tremor.

secret, ète [səkrɛ, -et] *a* secret; (*fig: renfermé*) reticent, reserved ♦ *nm* secret; (*discrétion absolue*): **le** ~ secrecy; **en** ~ in secret, secretly; **au** ~ in solitary confinement; ~ **de fabrication** trade secret; ~ **professionnel** professional secrecy.

secrétaire [səkrɛter] *nm/f* secretary ♦ *nm* (*meuble*) secretary (*US*), writing desk; ~ **d'ambassade** embassy secretary; ~ **de direction** private *ou* personal secretary; ~ **d'État** ≈ Secretary of State (*US*), junior minister (*Brit*); ~ **général (SG)** Secretary-General; (COMM) company secretary; ~ **de mairie** town clerk; ~ **médicale** medical secretary; ~ **de rédaction** sub-editor.

secrétariat [s(ə)krātáryá] *nm* (*profession*) secretarial work; (*bureau: d'entreprise, d'école*) (secretary's) office; (*d'organisation internationale*) secretariat; (POL *etc*: *fonction*) secretaryship, office of Secretary.

secrètement [səkrɛtmãn] *ad* secretly.

sécréter [sãkrātā] *vt* to secrete.

sécrétion [sãkrāsyõn] *nf* secretion.

sectaire [sɛkter] *a* sectarian, bigoted.

sectarisme [sɛktáresm(ə)] *nm* sectarianism.

secte [sɛkt(ə)] *nf* sect.

secteur [sɛktœr] *nm* sector; (ADMIN) district; (ÉLEC) **branché sur le** ~ plugged into the mains (supply); **fonctionne sur pile et** ~ operates on DC or AC (*US*), battery or mains operated (*Brit*); **le** ~ **privé/public** (ÉCON) the private/public sector; **le** ~ **primaire/ tertiaire** the primary/tertiary sector.

section [sɛksyõn] *nf* section; (*de parcours d'autobus*) fare zone (*US*) *ou* stage (*Brit*); (MIL: *unité*) platoon; ~ **rythmique** rhythm section.

sectionner [sɛksyoná] *vt* to sever; **se** ~ *vi* to

be severed.

sectionneur [seksyonœr] *nm* (*ÉLEC*) isolation switch.

sectoriel, le [sektoryel] *a* sector-based.

sectoriser [sektorēzā] *vt* to divide into sectors.

sécu [sākü] *nf* (*fam*: = *sécurité sociale*) ≈ dole, ≈ Welfare (*US*).

séculaire [sākülɛr] *a* secular; (*très vieux*) age-old.

séculariser [sākülárēzā] *vt* to secularize.

séculier, ière [sākülyā, -yɛr] *a* secular.

sécurisant, e [sākürēzāñ, -āñt] *a* secure, giving a sense of security.

sécuriser [sākürēzā] *vt* to give a sense of security to.

sécurité [sākürētā] *nf* security; (*absence de danger*) safety; **impression de** ~ sense of security; **la** ~ **internationale** international security; **système de** ~ security (*ou* safety) system; **être en** ~ to be safe; **la** ~ **de l'emploi** job security; **la** ~ **routière** road safety; **la** ~ **sociale** ≈ (the) Welfare (*US*), ≈ (the) Social Security (*Brit*).

sédatif, ive [sādátēf, -ēv] *a*, *nm* sedative.

sédentaire [sādáñter] *a* sedentary.

sédiment [sādēmáñ] *nm* sediment; ~**s** *nmpl* (*alluvions*) sediment *sg*.

sédimentaire [sādēmáñter] *a* sedimentary.

séditieux, euse [sādēsyœ̄, -ēz] *a* insurgent; seditious.

sédition [sādēsyóñ] *nf* insurrection; sedition.

séducteur, trice [sādüktœr, -trēs] *a* seductive ♦ *nm/f* seducer/seductress.

séduction [sādüksyóñ] *nf* seduction; (*charme*, *attrait*) appeal, charm.

séduire [sādüēr] *vt* to charm; (*femme: abuser de*) to seduce; (*suj: chose*) to appeal to.

séduisant, e [sādüēzāñ, -āñt] *vb voir* **séduire** ♦ *a* (*femme*) seductive; (*homme, offre*) very attractive.

séduit, e [sādüē, -ēt] *pp de* **séduire**.

segment [segmáñ] *nm* segment; (*AUTO*): ~ **(de piston)** piston ring; ~ **de frein** brake shoe.

segmenter [segmáñtā] *vt*, **se** ~ *vi* to segment.

ségrégation [sāgrāgásyóñ] *nf* segregation.

ségrégationniste [sāgrāgásyonēst(ə)] *a* segregationist.

seiche [sesh] *nf* cuttlefish.

séide [sāēd] *nm* (*péj*) henchman.

seigle [segl(ə)] *nm* rye.

seigneur [senyœr] *nm* lord; **le S**~ the Lord.

seigneurial, e, aux [senyœryál, -ō] *a* lordly, stately.

sein [sañ] *nm* breast; (*entrailles*) womb; **au** ~ **de** *prép* (*équipe, institution*) within; (*flots, bonheur*) in the midst of; **donner le** ~ **à** (*bébé*) to feed (at the breast); to breast-feed; **nourrir au** ~ to breast-feed.

Seine [sen] *nf*: **la** ~ the Seine.

séisme [sāēsm(ə)] *nm* earthquake.

séismique *etc* [seismik] *voir* **sismique** *etc*.

SEITA [sāētā] *sigle f = Société d'exploitation industrielle des tabacs et allumettes*.

seize [sez] *num* sixteen.

seizième [sezyem] *num* sixteenth.

séjour [sāzhōōr] *nm* stay; (*pièce*) living room.

séjourner [sāzhōōrnā] *vi* to stay.

sel [sel] *nm* salt; (*fig*) wit; spice; ~ **de**

cuisine/de table cooking/table salt; ~ gemme rock salt; ~**s de bain** bath salts.

sélect, e [sālekt] *a* select.

sélectif, ive [sālektēf, -ēv] *a* selective.

sélection [sāleksyóñ] *nf* selection; **faire/opérer une** ~ **parmi** to make a selection from among; **épreuve de** ~ (*SPORT*) trial (for selection); ~ **naturelle** natural selection; ~ **professionnelle** professional recruitment.

selectionné, e [sāleksyonā] *a* (*joueur*) selected; (*produit*) specially selected.

sélectionner [sāleksyonā] *vt* to select.

sélectionneur, euse [sāleksyonœr, -ēz] *nm/f* selector.

sélectivement [sālektēvmáñ] *ad* selectively.

sélénologie [sālānolozhē] *nf* study of the moon, selenology.

self [self] *nm* (*fam*) self-service.

self-service [selfserves] *a* self-service ♦ *nm* self-service (*restaurant*); (*magasin*) self-service shop.

selle [sel] *nf* saddle; ~**s** *nfpl* (*MÉD*) stools; **aller à la** ~ (*MÉD*) to have a bowel movement; **se mettre en** ~ to mount, get into the saddle.

seller [sālā] *vt* to saddle.

sellette [selet] *nf*: **être sur la** ~ to be on the carpet (*fig*).

sellier [sālyā] *nm* saddler.

selon [səlóñ] *prép* according to; (*en se conformant à*) in accordance with; ~ **moi** as I see it; ~ **que** according to, depending on whether.

SEm *sigle f* (= *Son Éminence*) HE.

semailles [səmáy] *nfpl* sowing *sg*.

semaine [səmen] *nf* week; (*salaire*) week's wages *ou* pay, weekly wages *ou* pay; **en** ~ during the week, on weekdays; **à la petite** ~ from day to day; **la** ~ **sainte** Holy Week.

semainier [səmānyā] *nm* (*bracelet*) bracelet made up of seven bands; (*calendrier*) desk calendar (*US*) *ou* diary (*Brit*); (*meuble*) chest of (seven) drawers.

sémantique [sāmáñtēk] *a* semantic ♦ *nf* semantics *sg*.

sémaphore [sāmáfor] *nm* (*RAIL*) semaphore signal.

semblable [sáñblábl(ə)] *a* similar; (*de ce genre*): **de** ~**s mésaventures** such mishaps ♦ *nm* fellow creature *ou* man; ~ **à** similar to, like.

semblant [sáñbláñ] *nm*: **un** ~ **de vérité** a semblance of truth; **faire** ~ **(de faire)** to pretend (to do).

sembler [sáñblā] *vb avec attribut* to seem ♦ *vb impersonnel*: **il semble (bien) que/inutile de** it (really) seems *ou* appears that/useless to; **il me semble (bien) que** it (really) seems to me that, I (really) think (that); **il me semble le connaître** I think *ou* I've a feeling I know him; ~ **être** to seem to be; **comme bon lui semble** as he sees fit; **me semble- t-il, à ce qu'il me semble** it seems to me, to my mind.

semelle [səmel] *nf* sole; (*intérieure*) insole, inner sole; **battre la** ~ to stamp one's feet (to keep them warm); (*fig*) to hang around (waiting); ~**s compensées** platform soles.

semence [səmáñs] *nf* (*graine*) seed; (*clou*) tack.

semer [səmā] *vt* to sow; (*fig: éparpiller*) to scatter; (*confusion*) to spread; (: *poursuivants*) to lose, shake off; **~ la discorde/terreur parmi** to sow discord/terror among; **semé de** (*difficultés*) riddled with.

semestre [səmestr(ə)] *nm* half-year; (*SCOL*) semester.

semestriel, le [səmestrēyel] *a* half-yearly; semestral.

semeur, euse [səmœr, -ēz] *nm/f* sower.

semi-automatique [səmēotomátēk] *a* semi-automatic.

semiconducteur [səmēkôṅdüktœr] *nm* (*IN-FORM*) semiconductor.

sémillant, e [sāmēyāṅ, -áṅt] *a* vivacious; dashing.

séminaire [sāmēner] *nm* seminar; (*REL*) seminary.

séminariste [sāmēnárēst(ə)] *nm* seminarist.

sémiologie [sāmyolozhē] *nf* semiology.

semi-public, ique [səmēpüblēk] *a* (*JUR*) semipublic.

semi-remorque [səmērəmork(ə)] *nf* trailer ♦ *nm* semi(trailer) (*US*), articulated lorry (*Brit*).

semis [səmē] *nm* (*terrain*) seedbed, seed plot; (*plante*) seedling.

sémite [sāmēt] *a* Semitic.

sémitique [sāmētēk] *a* Semitic.

semoir [səmwár] *nm* seed-bag; seeder.

semonce [səmôṅs] *nf*: **un coup de ~** a warning shot.

semoule [səmōōl] *nf* semolina; **~ de riz** ground rice.

sempiternel, le [saṅpēternel] *a* eternal, never-ending.

sénat [sānà] *nm* senate.

sénateur [sānátœr] *nm* senator.

Sénégal [sānāgál] *nm*: **le ~** Senegal.

sénégalais, e [sānágále, -ez] *a* Senegalese.

sénevé [senvā] *nm* (*BOT*) mustard; (*graine*) mustard seed.

sénile [sānēl] *a* senile.

sénilité [sānēlētā] *nf* senility.

senior [sānyor] *nm/f* (*SPORT*) senior.

sens [sáṅ] *vb voir* **sentir** ♦ *nm* [sáṅs] (*PHYSIOL, instinct*) sense; (*signification*) meaning, sense; (*direction*) direction, way ♦ *nmpl* (*sensualité*) senses; **reprendre ses ~** to regain consciousness; **avoir le ~ des affaires/de la mesure** to have business sense/a sense of moderation; **ça n'a pas de ~** that doesn't make (any) sense; **en dépit du bon ~** contrary to all good sense; **tomber sous le ~** to stand to reason, be perfectly obvious; **en un ~, dans un ~** in a way; **en ce ~ que** in the sense that; **à mon ~** to my mind; **dans le ~ des aiguilles d'une montre** clockwise; **dans le ~ de la longeur/largeur** lengthwise/widthwise; **dans le mauvais ~** the wrong way; in the wrong direction; **bon ~** good sense; **~ commun** common sense; **~ dessus dessous** upside down; **~ interdit, ~ unique** one-way street.

sensass [sáṅsás] *a* (*fam*) fantastic.

sensation [sáṅsásyôṅ] *nf* sensation; **faire ~** to cause a sensation, create a stir; **à ~** (*péj*) sensational.

sensationnel, le [sáṅsásyonel] *a* sensational.

sensé, e [sáṅsā] *a* sensible.

sensibiliser [sáṅsēbēlēzā] *vt* to sensitize; **~ qn (à)** to make sb sensitive (to).

sensibilité [sáṅsēbēlētā] *nf* sensitivity; (*affectivité, émotivité*) sensitivity, sensibility.

sensible [sáṅsēbl(ə)] *a* sensitive; (*aux sens*) perceptible; (*appréciable: différence, progrès*) appreciable, noticeable; **~ à** sensitive to.

sensiblement [sáṅsēbləmáṅ] *ad* (*notablement*) appreciably, noticeably; (*à peu près*): **ils ont ~ le même poids** they weigh approximately the same.

sensiblerie [sáṅsēblərē] *nf* sentimentality; squeamishness.

sensitif, ive [sáṅsētēf, -ēv] *a* (*nerf*) sensory; (*personne*) oversensitive.

sensoriel, le [sáṅsoryel] *a* sensory, sensorial.

sensualité [sáṅsüálētā] *nf* sensuality, sensuousness.

sensuel, le [sáṅsüel] *a* sensual; sensuous.

sent [sáṅ] *vb voir* **sentir**.

sente [sáṅt] *nf* path.

sentence [sáṅtáṅs] *nf* (*jugement*) sentence; (*adage*) maxim.

sentencieux, euse [sáṅtáṅsyœ, -ēz] *a* sententious.

senteur [sáṅtœr] *nf* scent, perfume.

senti, e [sáṅtē] *a*: **bien ~** (*mots etc*) well-chosen.

sentier [sáṅtyā] *nm* path.

sentiment [sáṅtēmáṅ] *nm* feeling; (*conscience, impression*): **avoir le ~ de/que** to be aware of/have the feeling that; **recevez mes ~s respectueux** yours truly (*US*) *ou* faithfully (*Brit*); **faire du ~** (*péj*) to be sentimental; **si vous me prenez par les ~s** if you appeal to my feelings.

sentimental, e, aux [sáṅtēmáṅtál, -ō] *a* sentimental; (*vie, aventure*) love *cpd*.

sentimentalisme [sáṅtēmáṅtálēsm(ə)] *nm* sentimentalism.

sentimentalité [sáṅtēmáṅtálētā] *nf* sentimentality.

sentinelle [sáṅtēnel] *nf* sentry; **en ~** standing guard; (*soldat: en faction*) on sentry duty.

sentir [sáṅtēr] *vt* (*par l'odorat*) to smell; (*par le goût*) to taste; (*au toucher, fig*) to feel; (*répandre une odeur de*) to smell of; (: *ressemblance*) to smell like; (*avoir la saveur de*) to taste of; to taste like; (*fig: dénoter, annoncer*) to be indicative of; to smack of; to foreshadow ♦ *vi* to smell; **~ mauvais** to smell bad; **se ~ bien** to feel good; **se ~ mal** (*être indisposé*) to feel unwell *ou* ill; **se ~ le courage/la force de faire** to feel brave/strong enough to do; **ne plus se ~ de joie** to be beside o.s. with joy; **il ne peut pas le ~** (*fam*) he can't stand him.

seoir [swár]: **~ à** *vt* to become, befit; **comme il (leur) sied** as it is fitting (to them).

Seoul [sāōōl] *n* Seoul.

SEP *sigle f* (= *sclérose en plaques*) MS.

séparation [sāpárásyôṅ] *nf* separation; (*cloison*) division, partition; **~ de biens** division of property (*in marriage settlement*); **~ de corps** legal separation.

séparatiste [sāpárátēst(ə)] *a, nm/f* (*POL*) separatist.

séparé, e [săpárā] *a* (*appartements, pouvoirs*) separate; (*époux*) separated; ~ **de** separate from; separated from.

séparément [săpárāmáń] *ad* separately.

séparer [săpárā] *vt* (*gén*) to separate; (*suj: divergences etc*) to divide; to drive apart; (: *différences, obstacles*) to stand between; (*détacher*): ~ **qch de** to pull sth (off) from; (*dissocier*) to distinguish between; (*diviser*): ~ **qch par** to divide sth (up) with; ~ **une pièce en deux** to divide a room into two; **se** ~ (*époux*) to separate, part; (*prendre congé: amis etc*) to part, leave each other; (*adversaires*) to separate; (*se diviser: route, tige etc*) to divide; (*se détacher*): **se** ~ **(de)** to split off (from); to come off; **se** ~ **de** (*époux*) to separate *ou* part from; (*employé, objet personnel*) to part with.

sépia [săpyá] *nf* sepia.

sept [set] *num* seven.

septante [septáńt] *num* (*Belgique, Suisse*) seventy.

septembre [septáńbr(ə)] *nm* September; *voir aussi* **juillet**.

septennal, e, aux [septānál, -ō] *a* seven-year; (*festival*) seven-year, septennial.

septennat [sepātānā] *nm* seven-year term (of office); seven-year reign.

septentrional, e, aux [septáńtrēyonál, -ō] *a* northern.

septicémie [septēsāmē] *nf* blood poisoning, septicemia (*US*), septicaemia (*Brit*).

septième [setyem] *num* seventh; **être au** ~ **ciel** to be on cloud nine.

septique [septēk] *a*: **fosse** ~ septic tank.

septuagénaire [septüázhāner] *a*, *nm/f* septuagenarian.

sépulcral, e, aux [săpülkrál, -ō] *a* (*voix*) sepulchral.

sépulcre [săpülkr(ə)] *nm* sepulcher (*US*), sepulchre (*Brit*).

sépulture [săpültür] *nf* burial; (*tombeau*) burial place, grave.

séquelles [săkel] *nfpl* after-effects; (*fig*) aftermath *sg*; consequences.

séquence [săkáńs] *nf* sequence.

séquentiel, le [săkáńsyel] *a* sequential.

séquestration [săkestrâsyôń] *nf* illegal confinement; impounding.

séquestre [săkestr(ə)] *nm* impoundment; **mettre sous** ~ to impound.

séquestrer [săkestrā] *vt* (*personne*) to confine illegally; (*biens*) to impound.

serai [sərā] *etc vb voir* **être**.

sérail [sārăy] *nm* seraglio; harem; **rentrer au** ~ to return to the fold.

serbe [serb(ə)] *a* Serbian ♦ *nm* (*LING*) Serbian ♦ *nm/f*: **S**~ Serb.

Serbie [serbē] *nf*: **la** ~ Serbia.

serbo-croate [serbokroát] *a* Serbo-Croat, Serbo-Croatian ♦ *nm* (*LING*) Serbo-Croatian.

serein, e [sərań, -en] *a* serene; (*jugement*) dispassionate.

sereinement [sərenmáń] *ad* serenely.

sérénade [sārānád] *nf* serenade; (*fam*) hullabaloo.

sérénité [sārānētā] *nf* serenity.

serez [sərā] *vb voir* **être**.

serf, serve [ser, serv(ə)] *nm/f* serf.

serfouette [serfwet] *nf* weeding hoe.

serge [serzh(ə)] *nf* serge.

sergent [serzháń] *nm* sergeant.

sergent-chef [serzháńshef] *nm* staff sergeant.

sergent-major [serzháńmázhor] *nm* ≈ quartermaster sergeant.

sériciculture [sārēsēkültür] *nf* silkworm breeding, sericulture.

série [sārē] *nf* (*de questions, d'accidents, TV*) series *inv*; (*de clés, casseroles, outils*) set; (*catégorie: SPORT*) rank; class; **en** ~ in quick succession; (*COMM*) mass *cpd*; **de** ~ *a* standard; **hors** ~ (*COMM*) custom-built; (*fig*) outstanding; **imprimante** ~ (*INFORM*) serial printer; **soldes de fin de** ~**s** end of line special offers; ~ **noire** *nm* (crime) thriller ♦ *nf* (*suite de malheurs*) run of bad luck.

sérier [sāryā] *vt* to classify, sort out.

sérieusement [sāryœzmáń] *ad* seriously; reliably; responsibly; **il parle** ~ he's serious, he means it; ~**?** are you serious?, do you mean it?

sérieux, euse [sāryœ, -œz] *a* serious; (*élève, employé*) reliable, responsible; (*client, maison*) reliable, dependable; (*offre, proposition*) genuine, serious; (*grave, sévère*) serious, solemn; (*maladie, situation*) serious, grave; (*important*) considerable ♦ *nm* seriousness; reliability; **ce n'est pas** ~ (*raisonnable*) that won't do; **garder son** ~ to keep a straight face; **manquer de** ~ not to be very responsible (*ou* reliable); **prendre qch/qn au** ~ to take sth/sb seriously.

sérigraphie [sārēgráfē] *nf* silk screen printing.

serin [sərań] *nm* canary.

seriner [sərēnā] *vt*: ~ **qch à qn** to drum sth into sb.

seringue [sərań] *nf* syringe.

serions [səryôń] *etc vb voir* **être**.

serment [sermáń] *nm* (*juré*) oath; (*promesse*) pledge, vow; **prêter** ~ to take the *ou* an oath; **faire le** ~ **de** to take a vow to, swear to; **sous** ~ on *ou* under oath.

sermon [sermôń] *nm* sermon; (*péj*) sermon, lecture.

sermonner [sermonā] *vt* to lecture.

SERNAM [sernám] *sigle m* (= *Service national de messageries*) *rail delivery service*.

sérologie [sārolozhē] *nf* serology.

serpe [serp(ə)] *nf* billhook.

serpent [serpáń] *nm* snake; ~ **à sonnettes** rattlesnake; ~ **monétaire** (**européen**) (European) monetary snake.

serpenter [serpáńtā] *vi* to wind.

serpentin [serpáńtań] *nm* (*tube*) coil; (*ruban*) streamer.

serpillière [serpēyer] *nf* floorcloth.

serrage [serázh] *nm* tightening; **collier de** ~ clamp.

serre [ser] *nf* (*AGR*) greenhouse; ~ **chaude** hothouse; ~ **froide** unheated greenhouse.

serré, e [sārā] *a* (*tissu*) closely woven; (*réseau*) dense; (*écriture*) close; (*habits*) tight; (*fig: lutte, match*) tight, close-fought; (*passagers etc*) (tightly) packed; (*café*) strong ♦ *ad*: **jouer** ~ to play it close, play a close game; **écrire** ~ to write a cramped hand; **avoir la gorge** ~**e** to have a lump in one's throat.

serre-livres [sɛrlɛvr(ə)] *nm inv* bookends *pl.*

serrement [sɛrmɑ̃] *nm*: ~ **de main** handshake; ~ **de cœur** pang of anguish.

serrer [sɑrɑ̄] *vt* (*tenir*) to grip *ou* hold tight; (*comprimer, coincer*) to squeeze; (*poings, mâchoires*) to clench; (*suj: vêtement*) to be too tight for; to fit tightly; (*rapprocher*) to close up, move closer together; (*ceinture, nœud, frein, vis*) to tighten ♦ *vi*: ~ **à droite** to keep to the right; to move into the right-hand lane; **se** ~ (*se rapprocher*) to squeeze up; **se** ~ **contre qn** to huddle up to sb; **se** ~ **les coudes** to stick together, back one another up; **se** ~ **la ceinture** to tighten one's belt; ~ **la main à qn** to shake sb's hand; ~ **qn dans ses bras** to hug sb, clasp sb in one's arms; ~ **la gorge à qn** (*suj: chagrin*) to bring a lump to sb's throat; ~ **les dents** to clench *ou* grit one's teeth; ~ **qn de près** to follow close behind sb; ~ **le trottoir** to hug the curb; ~ **sa droite** to keep well to the right; ~ **la vis à qn** to crack down harder on sb; ~ **les rangs** to close ranks.

serres [sɛr] *nfpl* (*griffes*) claws, talons.

serre-tête [sɛrtɛt] *nm inv* (*bandeau*) headband; (*bonnet*) skullcap.

serrure [sɑrür] *nf* lock.

serrurerie [sɑrürrɛ̄] *nf* (*métier*) locksmith's trade; (*ferronnerie*) ironwork; ~ **d'art** ornamental ironwork.

serrurier [sɑrüryɑ̄] *nm* locksmith.

sers, sert [sɛr] *vb voir* **servir**.

sertir [sɛrtir] *vt* (*pierre*) to set; (*pièces métalliques*) to crimp.

sérum [sɑrom] *nm* serum; ~ **antivenimeux** snakebite serum; ~ **sanguin** (blood) serum; ~ **de vérité** truth serum.

servage [sɛrvɑzh] *nm* serfdom.

servant [sɛrvɑ̄] *nm* server.

servante [sɛrvɑ̄t] *nf* (maid)servant.

serve [sɛrv] *nf voir* **serf** ♦ *vb voir* **servir**.

serveur, euse [sɛrvœr, -œz] *nm/f* waiter/waitress ♦ *a*: **centre** ~ (*INFORM*) service center.

servi, e [sɛrvɛ̄] *a*: **être bien** ~ to get a large helping (*ou* helpings); **vous êtes** ~**?** are you being helped? (*US*) *ou* served? (*Brit*).

serviable [sɛrvyɑbl(ə)] *a* obliging, willing to help.

service [sɛrvɛ̄s] *nm* (*gén*) service; (*série de repas*): **premier** ~ first sitting; (*pourboire*) service (charge); (*assortiment de vaisselle*) set, service; (*linge de table*) set; (*bureau: de la vente etc*) department, section; (*travail*): **pendant le** ~ on duty; ~**s** *nmpl* (*travail, ÉCON*) services; ~ **compris/non compris** service included/not included; **faire le** ~ to serve; **être en** ~ **chez qn** (*domestique*) to be in sb's service; **être au** ~ **de** (*patron, patrie*) to be in the service of; **être au** ~ **de qn** (*collaborateur, voiture*) to be at sb's service; **porte de** ~ service (*US*) *ou* tradesman's (*Brit*) entrance; **rendre** ~ **à** to help; **il aime rendre** ~ he likes to help; **rendre un** ~ **à qn** to do sb a favor; **heures de** ~ hours of duty; **être de** ~ to be on duty; **reprendre du** ~ to get back into action; **avoir 25 ans de** ~ to have completed 25 years' service; **être/mettre en** ~ to be in/put into service *ou*

operation; **hors** ~ not in use; out of order; ~ **à thé/café** tea/coffee set *ou* service; ~ **après vente** (**SAV**) after-sales service; **en** ~ **commandé** on an official assignment; ~ **funèbre** funeral service; ~ **militaire** military service; ~ **d'ordre** police (*ou* stewards) in charge of maintaining order; ~**s publics** public services, (public) utilities; ~**s secrets** secret service *sg*; ~**s sociaux** social services.

serviette [sɛrvyɛt] *nf* (*de table*) (table) napkin, serviette; (*de toilette*) towel; (*porte-documents*) briefcase; ~ **éponge** terry towel; ~ **hygiénique** sanitary napkin (*US*) *ou* towel (*Brit*).

servile [sɛrvɛl] *a* servile.

servir [sɛrvɛr] *vt* (*gén*) to serve; (*dîneur: au restaurant*) to wait on; (*client: au magasin*) to serve, attend to; (*fig: aider*): ~ **qn** to aid sb; to serve sb's interests; to stand sb in good stead; (*COMM: rente*) to pay ♦ *vi* (*TENNIS*) to serve; (*CARTES*) to deal; (*être militaire*) to serve; ~ **qch à qn** to serve sb with sth; **qu'est-ce que je vous sers?** what can I get you?; **se** ~ (*prendre d'un plat*) to help o.s.; (*s'approvisionner*): **se** ~ **chez** to shop at; **se** ~ **de** (*plat*) to help o.s. to; (*voiture, outil, relations*) to use; ~ **à qn** (*diplôme, livre*) to be of use to sb; **ça m'a servi pour faire** it was useful to me when I did; I used it to do; ~ **à qch/à faire** (*outil etc*) to be used for sth/for doing; **ça peut** ~ it may come in handy; **ça peut encore** ~ it can still be used (*ou* of use); **à quoi cela sert-il (de faire)?** what's the use (of doing)?; **cela ne sert à rien** it's no use; ~ **(à qn) de** to serve as (for sb); ~ **à dîner (à qn)** to serve dinner (to sb).

serviteur [sɛrvɛtœr] *nm* servant.

servitude [sɛrvɛtüd] *nf* servitude; (*fig*) constraint; (*JUR*) easement.

servofrein [sɛrvofrɛ̄] *nm* power brake.

servomécanisme [sɛrvomɑkɑ̄nɛsm(ə)] *nm* servo mechanism.

ses [sɑ̄] *dét voir* **son**.

sésame [sɑzɑ́m] *nm* (*BOT*) sesame; (*graine*) sesame seed.

session [sɑsyɔ̄] *nf* session.

set [sɛt] *nm* set; (*napperon*) placemat; ~ **de table** set of placemats.

seuil [sœy] *nm* doorstep; (*fig*) threshold; **sur le** ~ **de sa maison** in the doorway of his house, on his doorstep; **au** ~ **de** (*fig*) on the threshold *ou* brink *ou* edge of; ~ **de rentabilité** (*COMM*) breakeven point.

seul, e [sœl] *a* (*sans compagnie*) alone; (*avec nuance affective: isolé*) lonely; (*unique*): **un** ~ **livre** only one book, a single book; **le** ~ **li-vre** the only book; ~ **ce livre, ce livre** ~ this book alone, only this book; **d'un** ~ **coup** (*soudainement*) all at once; (*à la fois*) at one blow ♦ *ad* (*vivre*) alone, on one's own; **parler tout** ~ to talk to oneself; **faire qch (tout)** ~ to do sth (all) on one's own *ou* (all) by oneself ♦ *nm, nf*: **il en reste un(e)** ~**(e)** there's only one left; **pas un(e)** ~**(e)** not a single; **à lui (tout)** ~ single-handed, on his own; ~ **à** ~ in private.

seulement [sœlmɑ̄] *ad* (*pas davantage*): ~ **5, 5** ~ only 5; (*exclusivement*): ~ **eux** only them, them alone; (*pas avant*): ~ **hier/à 10h** only yesterday/at 10 o'clock; (*mais, toutefois*): **il consent,** ~ **il demande des garanties** he agrees, only he wants guarantees; **non** ~ **... mais aussi** *ou* **encore** not only ... but also.

sève [sɛv] *nf* sap.

sévère [sāvɛr] *a* severe.

sévèrement [sāvermȧn] *ad* severely.

sévérité [sāvārētā] *nf* severity.

sévices [sāvēs] *nmpl* (physical) cruelty *sg*, ill treatment *sg*.

Séville [sāvēl] *n* Seville.

sévir [sāvēr] *vi* (*punir*) to use harsh measures, crack down; (*suj: fléau*) to rage, be rampant; ~ **contre** (*abus*) to deal ruthlessly with, crack down on.

sevrage [səvrȧzh] *nm* weaning; deprivation; (*d'un toxicomane*) withdrawal.

sevrer [səvrā] *vt* to wean; (*fig*): ~ **qn de** to deprive sb of.

sexagénaire [sɛgzázhānɛr] *a, nm/f* sexagenarian.

SExc *sigle f* (= *Son Excellence*) HE.

sexe [sɛks(ə)] *nm* sex; (*organe mâle*) member.

sexisme [sɛksēsm(ə)] *nm* sexism.

sexiste [sɛksēst(ə)] *a, nm* sexist.

sexologue [sɛksolog] *nm/f* sexologist, sex specialist.

sextant [sɛkstȧn] *nm* sextant.

sexualité [sɛksüálētā] *nf* sexuality.

sexué, e [sɛksüā] *a* sexual.

sexuel, le [sɛksüɛl] *a* sexual; **acte** ~ sex act.

sexuellement [sɛksüɛlmȧn] *ad* sexually.

seyant, e [sɛyȧn, -ȧnt] *vb voir* **seoir ♦** *a* becoming.

Seychelles [sȧshɛl] *nfpl*: **les** ~ the Seychelles.

SFIO *sigle f* (= *Section française de l'internationale ouvrière*) *former name of French Socialist Party.*

SG *sigle m* = **secrétaire général.**

SGEN *sigle m* (= *Syndicat général de l'éducation nationale*) *labor union.*

shaker [shekœr] *nm* (cocktail) shaker.

shampooiner [shȧnpwēnā] *vt* to shampoo.

shampooineur, euse [shȧnpwēnœr, -œz] *nm/f* (*personne*) shampooer.

shampooing [shȧnpwēn] *nm* shampoo; **se faire un** ~ to shampoo one's hair; ~ **colorant** color rinse; ~ **traitant** medicated shampoo.

Shetland [shɛtlȧnd] *n*: **les îles** ~ the Shetland Islands, Shetland.

shooter [shōōtā] *vi* (*FOOTBALL*) to shoot; **se** ~ (*drogué*) to mainline.

short [short] *nm* (pair of) shorts *pl*.

SI *sigle m* = **syndicat d'initiative.**

si [sē] *nm* (*MUS*) B; (*en chantant la gamme*) ti, te ♦ *ad* (*oui*) yes; (*tellement*) so ♦ *cj* if; (*d'opposition*): **s'il est amiable, eux par contre** ... whereas he's nice, they on the other hand ...; **Paul n'est pas venu,** ~**?** Paul didn't come, did he?; **je vous assure que** ~ I can assure you that it is (*ou* he did *etc*); ~ **seulement** if only; **(tant et)** ~ **bien que** so much so that; ~ **rapide qu'il soit** however fast he may be, fast though he is; **je me demande** ~ I wonder if *ou* whether.

siamois, e [syȧmwȧ, -wȧz] *a* Siamese; **frères/ sœurs** ~**(es)** Siamese twins.

Sibérie [sēbārē] *nf*: **la** ~ Siberia.

sibérien, ne [sēbāryȧn, -en] *a* Siberian ♦ *nm/f*: **S**~, **ne** Siberian.

sibyllin, e [sēbēlȧn, -ēn] *a* sibylline.

SICAV [sēkáv] *sigle f* (= *société d'investissement à capital variable*) open-ended investment trust; *share in such a trust.*

Sicile [sēsēl] *nf*: **la** ~ Sicily.

sicilien, ne [sēsēlyȧn, -en] *a* Sicilian.

SIDA, sida [sēdá] *nm* (= *syndrome immuno-déficitaire acquis*) AIDS *sg*.

sidéral, e, aux [sēdārál, -ō] *a* sidereal.

sidéré, e [sēdārā] *a* staggered.

sidérurgie [sēdārürzhē] *nf* steel industry.

sidérurgique [sēdārürzhēk] *a* steel *cpd*.

sidérurgiste [sēdārürzhēst(ə)] *nm/f* steel worker.

siècle [syɛkl(ə)] *nm* century; (*époque*): **le** ~ **des lumières/de l'atome** the age of enlightenment/atomic age; (*REL*): **le** ~ the world.

sied [syȧ] *vb voir* **seoir.**

siège [syɛzh] *nm* seat; (*d'entreprise*) head office; (*d'organisation*) headquarters *pl*; (*MIL*) siege; **lever le** ~ to raise the siege; **mettre le** ~ **devant** to besiege; **présentation par le** ~ (*MÉD*) breech position; ~ **avant/ arrière** (*AUTO*) front/back seat; ~ **baquet** bucket seat; ~ **social** head office.

siéger [syāzhā] *vi* (*assemblée, tribunal*) to sit; (*résider, se trouver*) to lie, be located.

sien, ne [syȧn, syen] *pronom*: **le(la)** ~**(ne), les** ~**s(**~**nes)** *m* his; **f** hers; *non humain* its; **y mettre du** ~ to pull one's weight; **faire des** ~**nes** (*fam*) to be up to one's (usual) tricks; **les** ~**s** (*sa famille*) one's family.

siérait [syȧrɛ] *etc vb voir* **seoir.**

Sierra Leone [syɛrȧlāon] *nf*: **la** ~ Sierra Leone.

sieste [syɛst(ə)] *nf* (afternoon) snooze *ou* nap, siesta; **faire la** ~ to have a snooze *ou* nap.

sieur [syœr] *nm*: **le** ~ **Thomas** Mr. Thomas; (*en plaisantant*) Master Thomas.

sifflant, e [sēflȧn, -ȧnt] *a* (*bruit*) whistling; (*toux*) wheezing; **(consonne)** ~**e** sibilant.

sifflement [sēfləmȧn] *nm* whistle, whistling *q*; wheezing *q*; hissing *q*.

siffler [sēflā] *vi* (*gén*) to whistle; (*avec un sifflet*) to blow (on) one's whistle; (*en respirant*) to wheeze; (*serpent, vapeur*) to hiss ♦ *vt* (*chanson*) to whistle; (*chien etc*) to whistle for; (*fille*) to whistle at; (*pièce, orateur*) to hiss, boo; (*faute*) to blow one's whistle at; (*fin du match, départ*) to blow one's whistle for; (*fam: verre, bouteille*) to guzzle.

sifflet [sēflɛ] *nm* whistle; ~**s** *nmpl* (*de mécontentement*) whistles, boos; **coup de** ~ whistle.

siffloter [sēflotā] *vi, vt* to whistle.

sigle [sēgl(ə)] *nm* acronym, (set of) initials *pl*.

signal, aux [sēnyál, -ō] *nm* (*signe convenu, appareil*) signal; (*indice, écriteau*) sign; **donner le** ~ **de** to give the signal for; ~ **d'alarme** alarm signal; ~ **d'alerte/de détresse** warning/distress signal; ~ **horaire** time signal; ~ **optique/sonore** warning light/sound; visual/acoustic signal; **signaux (lumineux)** (*AUTO*) traffic signals; **signaux routiers** road signs; (*lumineux*) traffic lights.

signalement [sĕnyàlmáñ] *nm* description, particulars *pl*.

signaler [sĕnyàlá] *vt* to indicate; to announce; to report; (*être l'indice de*) to indicate; (*faire remarquer*): ~ **qch à qn/à qn que** to point out sth to sb/to sb that; (*appeler l'attention sur*): ~ **qn à la police** to bring sb to the attention of the police; **se** ~ **par** to distinguish o.s. by; **se** ~ **à l'attention de qn** to attract sb's attention.

signalétique [sĕnyàlātĕk] *a*: **fiche** ~ description sheet.

signalisation [sĕnyàlĕzâsyóñ] *nf* signalling, signposting; **signals** *pl*; roadsigns *pl*; **panneau de** ~ roadsign.

signaliser [sĕnyàlĕzá] *vt* to put up roadsigns on; to put signals on.

signataire [sĕnyátɛr] *nm/f* signatory.

signature [sĕnyátür] *nf* signature; (*action*) signing.

signe [sĕny] *nm* sign; (*TYPO*) mark; **ne pas donner** ~ **de vie** to give no sign of life; **c'est bon** ~ it's a good sign; **c'est** ~ **que** it's a sign that; **faire un** ~ **de la main/tête** to give a sign with one's hand/shake one's head; **faire** ~ **à qn** (*fig*) to get in touch with sb; **faire** ~ **à qn d'entrer** to motion (to) sb to come in; **en** ~ **de** as a sign *ou* mark of; **le** ~ **de la croix** the sign of the Cross; ~ **de ponctuation** punctuation mark; ~ **du zodiaque** sign of the zodiac; ~**s particuliers** distinguishing marks.

signer [sĕnyá] *vt* to sign; **se** ~ *vi* to cross o.s.

signet [sĕnyɛ] *nm* bookmark.

significatif, ive [sĕnyĕfĕkàtĕf, -ĕv] *a* significant.

signification [sĕnyĕfĕkásyóñ] *nf* meaning.

signifier [sĕnyĕfyà] *vt* (*vouloir dire*) to mean, signify; (*faire connaître*): ~ **qch (à qn)** to make sth known (to sb); (*JUR*): ~ **qch à qn** to serve notice of sth on sb.

silence [sĕláñs] *nm* silence; (*MUS*) rest; **garder le** ~ **(sur qch)** to keep silent (about sth), say nothing (about sth); **passer sous** ~ to pass over (in silence); **réduire au** ~ to silence.

silencieusement [sĕláñsyœzmáñ] *ad* silently.

silencieux, euse [sĕláñsyœ̃, -œz] *a* quiet, silent ♦ *nm* (*d'arme à feu*) silencer; (*AUT*) muffler (*US*), silencer (*Brit*).

silex [sĕlɛks] *nm* flint.

silhouette [sĕlwɛt] *nf* outline, silhouette; (*lignes, contour*) outline; (*figure*) figure.

silice [sĕlĕs] *nf* silica.

siliceux, euse [sĕlĕsœ̃, -œz] *a* (*terrain*) chalky.

silicium [sĕlĕsyom] *nm* silicon; **plaquette de** ~ silicon chip.

silicone [sĕlĕkŏn] *nf* silicone.

silicose [sĕlĕkŏz] *nf* silicosis, dust disease.

sillage [sĕyázh] *nm* wake; (*fig*) trail; **dans le** ~ **de** (*fig*) in the wake of.

sillon [sĕyóñ] *nm* (*d'un champ*) furrow; (*de disque*) groove.

sillonner [sĕyoná] *vt* (*creuser*) to furrow; (*traverser*) to cross, criss-cross.

silo [sĕlŏ] *nm* silo.

simagrées [sĕmágrá] *nfpl* fuss *sg*; airs and graces.

simiesque [sĕmyɛsk(ə)] *a* monkey-like, ape-like.

similaire [sĕmĕlɛr] *a* similar.

similarité [sĕmĕlárĕtá] *nf* similarity.

simili [sĕmĕlĕ] *nm* imitation; (*TYPO*) halftone ♦ *nf* halftone engraving.

simili... [sĕmĕlĕ] *préfixe* imitation *cpd*, artificial.

similicuir [sĕmĕlĕkuĕr] *nm* imitation leather.

similigravure [sĕmĕlĕgrávür] *nf* halftone engraving.

similitude [sĕmĕlĕtüd] *nf* similarity.

simple [sáñpl(ə)] *a* (*gén*) simple; (*non multiple*) single; ~**s** *nmpl* (*MÉD*) medicinal plants; ~ **messieurs** *nm* (*TENNIS*) men's singles *sg*; **un** ~ **particulier** an ordinary citizen; **une** ~ **formalité** a mere formality; **cela varie du** ~ **au double** it can double, it can double the price *etc*; **dans le plus** ~ **appareil** in one's birthday suit; ~ **course** *a* single; ~ **d'esprit** *nm/f* simpleton; ~ **soldat** private.

simplement [sáñpləmáñ] *ad* simply.

simplet, te [sáñplɛ, -ɛt] *a* (*personne*) simpleminded.

simplicité [sáñplĕsĕtá] *nf* simplicity; **en toute** ~ quite simply.

simplification [sáñplĕfĕkâsyóñ] *nf* simplification.

simplifier [sáñplĕfyá] *vt* to simplify.

simpliste [sáñplĕst(ə)] *a* simplistic.

simulacre [sĕmülàkr(ə)] *nm* enactment; (*pej*): **un** ~ **de** a pretense (*US*) *ou* pretence (*Brit*) of, a sham.

simulateur, trice [sĕmülàtœr, -trĕs] *nm/f* shammer, pretender; (*qui se prétend malade*) malingerer ♦ *nm*: ~ **de vol** flight simulator.

simulation [sĕmülásyóñ] *nf* shamming, simulation; malingering.

simuler [sĕmülá] *vt* to sham, simulate.

simultané, e [sĕmültáná] *a* simultaneous.

simultanéité [sĕmültánáĕtá] *nf* simultaneity.

simultanément [sĕmültánámáñ] *ad* simultaneously.

Sinaï [sĕnáĕ] *nm*: **le** ~ Sinai.

sinapisme [sĕnápĕsm(ə)] *nm* (*MÉD*) mustard plaster (*US*) *ou* poultice (*Brit*).

sincère [sáñsɛr] *a* sincere; genuine; heartfelt; **mes** ~**s condoléances** my deepest sympathy.

sincèrement [sáñsɛrmáñ] *ad* sincerely; genuinely.

sincérité [sáñsárĕtá] *nf* sincerity; **en toute** ~ in all sincerity.

sinécure [sĕnákür] *nf* sinecure.

sine die [sĕnádyá] *ad* sine die, indefinitely.

sine qua non [sĕnákwànon] *a*: **condition** ~ indispensable condition.

Singapour [sáñgápŏŏr] *nm*: **le** ~ Singapore.

singe [sáñzh] *nm* monkey; (*de grande taille*) ape.

singer [sáñzhá] *vt* to ape, mimic.

singeries [sáñzhrĕ] *nfpl* antics; (*simagrées*) airs and graces.

singulariser [sáñgülárĕzá] *vt* to mark out; **se** ~ to call attention to o.s.

singularité [sáñgülárĕtá] *nf* peculiarity.

singulier, ière [sáñgülyá, -yɛr] *a* remarkable, singular; (*LING*) singular ♦ *nm* singular.

singulièrement [sáñgülyɛrmáñ] *ad* singularly, remarkably.

sinistre [sĕnĕstr(ǝ)] *a* sinister; (*intensif*): **un ~ imbécile** an incredible idiot ♦ *nm* (*incendie*) blaze; (*catastrophe*) disaster; (*ASSURANCES*) damage (*giving rise to a claim*).

sinistré, e [sĕnĕstrā] *a* disaster-stricken ♦ *nm/f* disaster victim.

sinistrose [sĕnĕstrōz] *nf* pessimism.

sino... [sĕnō] *préfixe*: **~-indien** Sino-Indian, Chinese-Indian.

sinon [sĕnôñ] *cj* (*autrement, sans quoi*) otherwise, or else; (*sauf*) except, other than; (*si ce n'est*) if not.

sinueux, euse [sĕnüœ̄, -œ̄z] *a* winding; (*fig*) tortuous.

sinuosités [sĕnüōzĕtā] *nfpl* winding *sg*, curves.

sinus [sĕnüs] *nm* (*ANAT*) sinus; (*GÉOM*) sine.

sinusite [sĕnüzĕt] *nf* sinusitis, sinus infection.

sionisme [syonĕsm(ǝ)] *nm* Zionism.

sioniste [syonĕst(ǝ)] *a, nm/f* Zionist.

siphon [sĕfôñ] *nm* (*tube, d'eau gazeuse*) siphon; (*d'évier etc*) trap, U-bend (*Brit*).

siphonner [sĕfonā] *vt* to siphon.

sire [sĕr] *nm* (*titre*): **S~** Sire; **un triste ~** an unsavory individual.

sirène [sĕren] *nf* siren; **~ d'alarme** fire alarm; (*pendant la guerre*) air-raid siren.

sirop [sĕrō] *nm* (*à diluer: de fruit etc*) syrup; (*boisson*) fruit drink; (*pharmaceutique*) syrup, mixture; **~ de menthe** mint syrup *ou* cordial; **~ contre la toux** cough syrup *ou* mixture.

siroter [sĕrotā] *vt* to sip.

sirupeux, euse [sĕrüpœ̄, -œ̄z] *a* syrupy.

sis, e [sĕ, sĕz] *a*: **~ rue de la Paix** located in the rue de la Paix.

sisal [sĕzàl] *nm* (*BOT*) sisal.

sismique [sĕsmĕk] *a* seismic.

sismographe [sĕsmogràf] *nm* seismograph.

sismologie [sĕsmolozhē] *nf* seismology.

site [sĕt] *nm* (*paysage, environnement*) setting; (*d'une ville etc: emplacement*) site; **~ (pittoresque)** beauty spot; **~s touristiques** places of interest; **~s naturels/historiques** natural/historic sites.

sitôt [sĕtō] *ad*: **~ parti** as soon as he *etc* had left; **~ après** straight after; **pas de ~** not for a long time; **~ (après) que** as soon as.

situation [sĕtüàsyoñ] *nf* (*gén*) situation; (*d'un édifice, d'une ville*) situation, position; (*emplacement*) location; **être en ~ de faire qch** to be in a position to do sth; **~ de famille** marital status.

situé, e [sĕtüā] *a*: **bien ~** well situated, in a good location; **~ à/près de** situated at/near.

situer [sĕtüā] *vt* to site, situate; (*en pensée*) to set, place; **se ~** *vi*: **se ~ à/près de** to be situated at/near.

SIVOM [sĕvom] *sigle m* (= *syndicat intercommunal à vocation multiple*) association of "communes".

six [sĕs] *num* six.

sixième [sĕzyem] *num* sixth.

skate (board) [skàt(bord)] *nm* (*SPORT*) skateboarding; (*planche*) skateboard.

sketch [sketsh] *nm* (variety) sketch.

ski [skē] *nm* (*objet*) ski; (*sport*) skiing; **faire du ~** to ski; **~ alpin** Alpine skiing; **~ courts** short skis; **~ évolutif** short ski method; **~ de fond** cross-country skiing; **~ nautique**

water-skiing; **~ de piste** downhill skiing; **~ de randonnée** cross-country skiing.

ski-bob [skēbob] *nm* skibob.

skier [skyā] *vi* to ski.

skieur, euse [skyœr, -œ̄z] *nm/f* skier.

skif(f) [skĕf] *nm* skiff.

slalom [slálom] *nm* slalom; **faire du ~ entre** to slalom between; **~ géant/spécial** giant/special slalom.

slave [sláv] *a* Slav(onic), Slavic ♦ *nm* (*LING*) Slavonic ♦ *nm/f*: **S~** Slav.

slip [slēp] *nm* (*sous-vêtement*) underpants *pl*, briefs *pl*; (*de bain: d'homme*) (bathing *ou* swimming) trunks *pl*; (: *du bikini*) (bikini) briefs *pl ou* bottoms *pl*.

slogan [slogáñ] *nm* slogan.

slovaque [slovák] *a* Slovak ♦ *nm* (*LING*) Slovak ♦ *nm/f*: **S~** Slovak.

Slovaquie [slovákē] *nf*: **la ~** Slovakia.

slovène [sloven] *a* Slovene.

Slovénie [slovänē] *nf*: **la ~** Slovenia.

SM *sigle f* (= *Sa Majesté*) HM.

SMAG [smág] *sigle m* = *salaire minimum agricole garanti*.

smasher [smáshā] *vi* to smash the ball ♦ *vt* (*balle*) to smash.

SME *sigle m* (= *Système monétaire européen*) EMS.

SMIC [smēk] *sigle m* = **salaire minimum interprofessionnel de croissance**.

smicard, e [smēkàr, -àrd(ǝ)] *nm/f* minimum wage earner.

smocks [smok] *nmpl* (*COUTURE*) smocking *q*.

smoking [smokĕng] *nm* tuxedo.

SMUR [smür] *sigle m* (= *service médical d'urgence et de réanimation*) specialist mobile emergency unit.

snack [snák] *nm* snack bar.

SNC *abr* = *service non compris*.

SNCB *sigle f* (= *Société nationale des chemins de fer belges*) Belgian railroad.

SNCF *sigle f* (= *Société nationale des chemins de fer français*) French railroad.

SNES [snes] *sigle m* (= *Syndicat national de l'enseignement secondaire*) secondary teachers' union.

SNE-sup [csenǝsüp] *sigle m* (= *Syndicat national de l'enseignement supérieur*) university teachers' union.

SNI *sigle m* (= *Syndicat national des instituteurs*) elementary teachers' union.

SNJ *sigle m* (= *Syndicat national des journalistes*) journalists' union.

snob [snob] *a* snobbish ♦ *nm/f* snob.

snober [snobā] *vt*: **~ qn** to give sb the cold shoulder, treat sb with disdain.

snobinard, e [snobĕnàr, -àrd(ǝ)] *nm/f* snooty *ou* stuck-up person.

snobisme *nm* snobbery.

SNSM *sigle f* (= *Société nationale de sauvetage en mer*) national sea-rescue association.

s.o. *abr* = *sans objet* no longer applicable.

sobre [sobr(ǝ)] *a* temperate, abstemious; (*élégance, style*) restrained, sober; **~ de** (*gestes, compliments*) sparing of.

sobrement [sobrǝmáñ] *ad* in moderation, abstemiously; soberly.

sobriété [sobrēyātā] *nf* temperance, abstemiousness; sobriety.

sobriquet [sobrĕke] *nm* nickname.

soc [sok] *nm* plowshare (*US*), ploughshare (*Brit*).

sociable [sosyàbl(ə)] *a* sociable.

social, e, aux [sosyàl, -ō] *a* social.

socialement [sosyàlmâń] *ad* socially.

socialisant, e [sosyàlēzâń, -âńt] *a* with socialist tendencies.

socialisation [sosyàlēzâsyôń] *nf* socialization.

socialiser [sosyàlēzā] *vt* to socialize.

socialisme [sosyàlēsm(ə)] *nm* socialism.

socialiste [sosyàlēst(ə)] *a*, *nm/f* socialist.

sociétaire [sosyàter] *nm/f* member.

société [sosyàtā] *nf* society; (*d'abeilles, de fourmis*) colony; (*sportive*) club; (*COMM*) company; **la bonne ~** polite society; **se plaire dans la ~ de** to enjoy the society of; **l'archipel de la S~** the Society Islands; **la ~ d'abondance/de consommation** the affluent/consumer society; **~ par actions** joint stock company; **~ anonyme (SA)** ≈ incorporated company (Inc.) (*US*), ≈ limited company (Ltd) (*Brit*); **~ d'investissement à capital variable (SICAV)** ≈ mutual fund (*US*), ≈ investment trust (*Brit*); **~ à responsabilité limitée (SARL)** *type of limited liability company* (*with non-negotiable shares*); **~ savante** learned society; **~ de services** service company.

socio-économique [sosyoākonomĕk] *a* socioeconomic.

sociolinguistique [sosyolàńgüēstĕk] *a* sociolinguistic.

sociologie [sosyolozhē] *nf* sociology.

sociologique [sosyolozhĕk] *a* sociological.

sociologue [sosyolog] *nm/f* sociologist.

socio-professionnel, le [sosyoprofesyonel] *a* socioprofessional.

socle [sokl(ə)] *nm* (*de colonne, statue*) plinth, pedestal; (*de lampe*) base.

socquette [soket] *nf* ankle sock.

soda [sodà] *nm* (*boisson*) fizzy drink, soda (*US*).

sodium [sodyom] *nm* sodium.

sodomie [sodomē] *nf* sodomy.

sœur [sœr] *nf* sister; (*religieuse*) nun, sister; **~ Élisabeth** (*REL*) Sister Elizabeth; **~ de lait** foster sister.

sofa [sofà] *nm* sofa.

Sofia [sofyà] *n* Sofia.

SOFRES [sofres] *sigle f* (= *Société française d'enquête par sondage*) *company which conducts opinion polls*.

soi [swà] *pronom* oneself; **cela va de ~** that *ou* it goes without saying, it stands to reason.

soi-disant [swàdēzâń] *a inv* so-called ♦ *ad* supposedly.

soie [swà] *nf* silk; (*de porc, sanglier: poil*) bristle.

soient [swà] *vb voir* être.

soierie [swàrē] *nf* (*industrie*) silk trade; (*tissu*) silk.

soif [swàf] *nf* thirst; (*fig*): **~ de** thirst *ou* craving for; **avoir ~** to be thirsty; **donner ~ à qn** to make sb thirsty.

soigné, e [swànyā] *a* (*tenue*) well-groomed, neat; (*travail*) careful, meticulous; (*fam*) whopping; stiff.

soigner [swànyā] *vt* (*malade, maladie: suj: docteur*) to treat; (: *suj: infirmière, mère*) to nurse, look after; (*blessé*) to tend; (*travail, détails*) to take care over; (*jardin, chevelure, invités*) to look after.

soigneur [swànyœr] *nm* (*CYCLISME, FOOTBALL*) trainer; (*BOXE*) second.

soigneusement [swànyœzmâń] *ad* carefully.

soigneux, euse [swànyœ̄, -œ̄z] *a* (*propre*) tidy, neat; (*méticuleux*) painstaking, careful; **~ de** careful with.

soi-même [swàmem] *pronom* oneself.

soin [swàń] *nm* (*application*) care; (*propreté, ordre*) tidiness, neatness; (*responsabilité*): **le ~ de qch** the care of sth; **~s** *nmpl* (*à un malade, blessé*) treatment *sg*, medical attention *sg*; (*attentions, prévenance*) care and attention *sg*; (*hygiène*) care *sg*; **~s de la chevelure/de beauté** hair/beauty care; **~s du corps/ménage** care of one's body/the home; **avoir** *ou* **prendre ~ de** to take care of, look after; **avoir** *ou* **prendre ~ de faire** to take care to do; **sans ~** *a* careless; untidy; **les premiers ~s** first aid *sg*; **aux bons ~s de c/o, care of; **être aux petits ~s pour qn** to wait on sb hand and foot, see to sb's every need; **confier qn aux ~s de qn** to hand sb over to sb's care.

soir [swàr] *nm*, *ad* evening; **le ~** in the evening(s); **ce ~** this evening, tonight; **à ce ~!** see you this evening (*ou* tonight)!; **la veille au ~** the previous evening; **sept/dix heures du ~** seven in the evening/ten at night; **le repas/journal du ~** the evening meal/newspaper; **dimanche ~** Sunday evening; **hier ~** yesterday evening; **demain ~** tomorrow evening, tomorrow night.

soirée [swàrā] *nf* evening; (*réception*) party; **donner en ~** (*film, pièce*) to give an evening performance of.

soit [swà] *vb voir* être; **~ un triangle ABC** let ABC be a triangle ♦ *cj* (*à savoir*) namely, to wit; (*ou*): **~ ... ~** either ... or ♦ *ad* so be it, very well; **~ que ... ~ que** *ou* ou que whether ... or whether.

soixantaine [swàsâńten] *nf*: **une ~ (de)** sixty or so, about sixty; **avoir la ~** to be around sixty.

soixante [swàsâńt] *num* sixty.

soixante-dix [swàsâńtdēs] *num* seventy.

soixante-dixième [swàsâńtdēzyem] *num* seventieth.

soixante-huitard, e [swàsâńtüetàr, -àrd(ə)] *a* relating to the demonstrations of May 1968 ♦ *nm/f* participant in the demonstrations of May 1968.

soixantième [swàsâńtyem] *num* sixtieth.

soja [sozhà] *nm*, soy, soya (*Brit*); (*graines*) soybeans *pl* (*US*), soya beans *pl* (*Brit*); **germes de ~** beansprouts.

sol [sol] *nm* ground; (*de logement*) floor; (*revêtement*) flooring *q*; (*territoire, AGR, GÉO*) soil; (*MUS*) G; (: *en chantant la gamme*) so(h).

solaire [soler] *a* solar, sun *cpd*.

solarium [solàryom] *nm* solarium.

soldat [soldà] *nm* soldier; **S~ inconnu** Unknown Warrior *ou* Soldier; **~ de plomb** tin *ou* toy soldier.

solde [sold(ə)] *nf* pay ♦ *nm* (*COMM*) balance; **~s** *nmpl ou nfpl* (*COMM*) sales; (*articles*) sale goods; **à la ~ de qn** (*péj*) in sb's pay; **~ créditeur/débiteur** credit/debit balance; **~ à payer** balance outstanding; **en ~** at sale price; **aux ~s** at the sales.

solder [soldā] *vt* (*compte*) to settle; (*marchandise*) to sell at sale price, sell off; **se ~ par** (*fig*) to end in; **article soldé (à) 10 F** item reduced to 10 F.

soldeur, euse [soldœr, -œz] *nm/f* (*COMM*) discounter.

sole [sol] *nf* sole *inv* (*fish*).

soleil [soley] *nm* sun; (*lumière*) sun(light); (*temps ensoleillé*) sun(shine); (*feu d'artifice*) pinwheel (*US*), Catherine wheel (*Brit*); (*ACROBATIE*) grand circle; (*BOT*) sunflower; **il y a** *ou* **il fait du ~** it's sunny; **au ~** in the sun; **en plein ~** in full sun; **le ~ levant/couchant** the rising/setting sun; **le ~ de minuit** the midnight sun.

solennel, le [solánel] *a* solemn; ceremonial.

solennellement [solánelmáñ] *ad* solemnly.

solenniser [solánēzā] *vt* to solemnize.

solennité [solánētā] *nf* (*d'une fête*) solemnity; **~s** *nfpl* (*formalités*) formalities.

solénoïde [solānoēd] *nm* (*ÉLEC*) solenoid.

solfège [solfezh] *nm* rudiments *pl* of music; (*exercices*) ear training *q*.

solfier [solfyā] *vt*: **~ un morceau** to sing a piece using the sol-fa.

soli [solē] *pl de* **solo**.

solidaire [solēder] *a* (*personnes*) who stand together, who show solidarity; (*pièces mécaniques*) interdependent; (*JUR*: *engagement*) binding on all parties; (*: débiteurs*) jointly liable; **être ~ de** (*collègues*) to stand by; (*mécanisme*) to be bound up with, be dependent on.

solidairement [solēdermáñ] *ad* jointly.

solidariser [solēdárēzā]: **se ~ avec** *vt* to show solidarity with.

solidarité [solēdárētā] *nf* (*entre personnes*) solidarity; (*de mécanisme, phénomènes*) interdependence; **par ~** (*avec*) (*cesser le travail etc*) in sympathy (with).

solide [solēd] *a* solid; (*mur, maison, meuble*) solid, sturdy; (*connaissances, argument*) sound; (*personne*) robust, sturdy; (*estomac*) strong ♦ *nm* solid; **avoir les reins ~s** (*fig*) to be in a good financial position; to have sound financial backing.

solidement [solēdmáñ] *ad* solidly; (*fermement*) firmly.

solidifier [solēdēfyā] *vt*, **se ~** *vi* to solidify.

solidité [solēdētā] *nf* solidity; sturdiness.

soliloque [solēlok] *nm* soliloquy.

soliste [solēst(ə)] *nm/f* soloist.

solitaire [solēter] *a* (*sans compagnie*) solitary, lonely; (*isolé*) solitary, isolated, lone; (*lieu*) lonely ♦ *nm/f* recluse; loner ♦ *nm* (*diamant, jeu*) solitaire.

solitude [solētüd] *nf* loneliness; (*paix*) solitude.

solive [solēv] *nf* joist.

sollicitations [solēsētásyóñ] *nfpl* (*requêtes*) entreaties, appeals; (*attractions*) enticements; (*TECH*) stress *sg*.

solliciter [solēsētā] *vt* (*personne*) to appeal to;

(*emploi, faveur*) to seek; (*moteur*) to prompt; (*suj: occupations, attractions etc*): **~ qn** to appeal to sb's curiosity *etc*; to entice sb; to make demands on sb's time; **~ qn de faire** to appeal to sb *ou* request sb to do.

sollicitude [solēsētüd] *nf* concern.

solo [solō] *nm*, *pl* **soli** [solē] (*MUS*) solo (*pl* -s *ou* soli).

solstice [solstēs] *nm* solstice; **~ d'hiver/d'été** winter/summer solstice.

solubilisé, e [solübēlēzā] *a* soluble.

soluble [solübl(ə)] *a* (*sucre, cachet*) soluble; (*problème etc*) soluble, solvable.

soluté [solütā] *nm* solution.

solution [solüsyóñ] *nf* solution; **~ de continuité** gap, break; **~ de facilité** easy way out.

solutionner [solüsyonā] *vt* to solve, find a solution for.

solvabilité [solvábēlētā] *nf* solvency.

solvable [solvábl(ə)] *a* solvent.

solvant [solváñ] *nm* solvent.

Somalie [somálē] *nf*: **la ~** Somalia.

somalien, ne [somályañ, -en] *a* Somalian.

sombre [sóñbr(ə)] *a* dark; (*fig*) somber (*US*), sombre (*Brit*), gloomy; (*sinistre*) awful, dreadful.

sombrer [sóñbrā] *vi* (*bateau*) to sink, go down; **~ corps et biens** to go down with all hands; **~ dans** (*misère, désespoir*) to sink into.

sommaire [somer] *a* (*simple*) basic; (*expéditif*) summary ♦ *nm* summary; **faire le ~ de** to make a summary of, summarize; **exécution ~** summary execution.

sommairement [somermáñ] *ad* basically; summarily.

sommation [somásyóñ] *nf* (*JUR*) summons *sg*; (*avant de faire feu*) warning.

somme [som] *nf* (*MATH*) sum; (*fig*) amount; (*argent*) sum, amount ♦ *nm*: **faire un ~** to have a (short) nap; **faire la ~ de** to add up; **en ~**, **~ toute** *ad* all in all.

sommeil [somey] *nm* sleep; **avoir ~** to be sleepy; **avoir le ~ léger** to be a light sleeper; **en ~** (*fig*) dormant.

sommeiller [somāyā] *vi* to doze; (*fig*) to lie dormant.

sommelier [somǝlyā] *nm* wine waiter.

sommer [somā] *vt*: **~ qn de faire** to command *ou* order sb to do; (*JUR*) to summon sb to do.

sommes [som] *vb voir* **être**; *voir aussi* **somme**.

sommet [some] *nm* top; (*d'une montagne*) summit, top; (*fig: de la perfection, gloire*) height; (*GÉOM: d'angle*) vertex (*pl* vertices); (*conférence*) summit (conference).

sommier [somyā] *nm* bedspring (*US*), bed base (*Brit*); (*ADMIN: registre*) register; **~ à ressorts** box spring (*US*), (interior sprung) divan base (*Brit*); **~ à lattes** slatted bedspring *ou* bed base.

sommité [somētā] *nf* prominent person, leading light.

somnambule [somnáñbül] *nm/f* sleepwalker.

somnambulisme [somnáñbülēsm(ə)] *nm* sleepwalking.

somnifère [somnēfer] *nm* sleeping drug; (*comprimé*) sleeping pill *ou* tablet.

somnolence [somnolãs] *nf* drowsiness.

somnolent, e [somnolãn, -ãnt] *a* sleepy, drowsy.

somnoler [somnolã] *vi* to doze.

somptuaire [sõnptüer] *a*: **lois** ~**s** sumptuary laws; **dépenses** ~**s** extravagant expenditure *sg*.

somptueusement [sõnptüœzmãn] *ad* sumptuously.

somptueux, euse [sõnptüœ, -œz] *a* sumptuous; (*cadeau*) lavish.

son [sõn], **sa** [sá], *pl* **ses** [sã] *dét* (*antécédent humain mâle*) his; (*: femelle*) her; (*: valeur indéfinie*) one's, his/her; (*: non humain*) its; *voir note sous* **il**.

son [sõn] *nm* sound; (*de blé etc*) bran; ~ **et lumière** *a inv* son et lumière.

sonar [sonàr] *nm* (*NAVIG*) sonar.

sonate [sonát] *nf* sonata.

sondage [sõndázh] *nm* (*de terrain*) boring, drilling; (*mer, atmosphère*) sounding; probe; (*enquête*) survey, sounding out of opinion; ~ **(d'opinion)** (opinion) poll.

sonde [sõnd] *nf* (*NAVIG*) lead *ou* sounding line; (*MÉTÉOROLOGIE*) sonde; (*MÉD*) probe; catheter; (*d'alimentation*) feeding tube; (*TECH*) borer, driller; (*de forage, sondage*) drill; (*pour fouiller etc*) probe; ~ **à avalanche** (*for probing snow and locating victims*); ~ **spatiale** probe.

sonder [sõndã] *vt* (*NAVIG*) to sound; (*atmosphère, plaie, bagages etc*) to probe; (*TECH*) to bore, drill; (*fig: personne*) to sound out; (*: opinion*) to probe; ~ **le terrain** (*fig*) to see how the land lies.

songe [sõnzh] *nm* dream.

songer [sõnzhã] *vi* to dream; ~ **à** (*rêver à*) to muse over, think over; (*penser à*) to think of; (*envisager*) to contemplate, think of, consider; ~ **que** to consider that; to think that.

songerie [sõnzhrã] *nf* reverie.

songeur, euse [sõnzhœr, -œz] *a* pensive; **ça me laisse** ~ that makes me wonder.

sonnailles [sonáy] *nfpl* jingle of bells.

sonnant, e [sonãn, -ãnt] *a*: **en espèces** ~**es et trébuchantes** in coin of the realm; **à 8 heures** ~**es** on the stroke of 8.

sonné, e [sonã] *a* (*fam*) cracked; (*passé*): **il est midi** ~ it's past twelve; **il a quarante ans bien** ~**s** he's well into his forties.

sonner [sonã] *vi* (*retentir*) to ring; (*donner une impression*) to sound ♦ *vt* (*cloche*) to ring; (*glas, tocsin*) to sound; (*portier, infirmière*) to ring for; (*messe*) to ring the bell for; (*fam: suj: choc, coup*) to knock out; ~ **du clairon** to sound the bugle; ~ **bien/mal/creux** to sound good/bad/hollow; ~ **faux** (*instrument*) to sound out of tune; (*rire*) to ring false; ~ **les heures** to strike the hours; **minuit vient de** ~ midnight has just struck; ~ **chez qn** to ring sb's doorbell, ring at sb's door.

sonnerie [sonrã] *nf* (*son*) ringing; (*sonnette*) bell; (*mécanisme d'horloge*) striking mechanism; ~ **d'alarme** alarm bell; ~ **de clairon** bugle call.

sonnet [sone] *nm* sonnet.

sonnette [sonet] *nf* bell; ~ **d'alarme** alarm bell; ~ **de nuit** night-bell.

sono [sonõ] *nf* (= *sonorisation*) PA (system).

sonore [sonor] *a* (*voix*) sonorous, ringing; (*salle, métal*) resonant; (*ondes, film, signal*) sound *cpd*; (*LING*) voiced; **effets** ~**s** sound effects.

sonorisation [sonorãzãsyõn] *nf* (*installations*) public address system.

sonoriser [sonorãzã] *vt* (*film, spectacle*) to add the sound track to; (*salle*) to fit with a public address system.

sonorité [sonorãtã] *nf* (*de piano, violon*) tone; (*de voix, mot*) sonority; (*d'une salle*) resonance; acoustics *pl*.

sonothèque [sonotek] *nf* sound library.

sont [sõn] *vb voir* **être**.

sophistication [sofẽstẽkãsyõn] *nf* sophistication.

sophistiqué, e [sofẽstẽkã] *a* sophisticated.

soporifique [soporẽfẽk] *a* soporific.

soprano [soprãnõ] *nm/f* soprano (*pl* -s).

sorbet [sorbe] *nm* sherbet (*US*), sorbet (*Brit*).

sorbetière [sorbətyer] *nf* ice-cream maker.

sorbier [sorbyã] *nm* service tree.

sorcellerie [sorselrã] *nf* witchcraft *q*, sorcery *q*.

sorcier, ière [sorsyã, -yer] *nm/f* sorcerer/witch *ou* sorceress ♦ *a*: **ce n'est pas** ~ (*fam*) it's as easy as pie.

sordide [sordẽd] *a* sordid; squalid.

Sorlingues [sorlãng] *nfpl*: **les (îles)** ~ the Scilly Isles, the Isles of Scilly, the Scillies.

sornettes [sornet] *nfpl* twaddle *sg*.

sort [sor] *vb voir* **sortir** ♦ *nm* (*fortune, destinée*) fate; (*condition, situation*) lot; (*magique*): **jeter un** ~ to cast a spell; **un coup du** ~ a blow dealt by fate; **le** ~ **en est jeté** the die is cast; **tirer au** ~ to draw lots; **tirer qch au** ~ to draw lots for sth.

sortable [sortãbl(ə)] *a*: **il n'est pas** ~ he doesn't know how to behave.

sortant, e [sortãn, -ãnt] *vb voir* **sortir** ♦ *a* (*numéro*) which comes up (*in a draw etc*); (*député, président*) outgoing.

sorte [sort(ə)] *vb voir* **sortir** ♦ *nf* sort, kind; **de la** ~ *ad* in that way; **en quelque** ~ in a way; **de** ~ **à** so as to, in order to; **de (telle)** ~ **que, en** ~ **que** (*de manière que*) so that; (*si bien que*) so much so that; **faire en** ~ **que** to see to it that.

sortie [sortã] *nf* (*issue*) way out, exit; (*MIL*) sortie; (*fig: verbale*) outburst, sally; (*: parole incongrue*) odd remark; (*d'un gaz, de l'eau*) outlet; (*promenade*) outing; (*le soir: au restaurant etc*) night out; (*de produits*) export; (*de capitaux*) outflow; (*COMM: somme*): ~**s** items of expenditure; outgoings *sans sg*; (*INFORM*) output; (*d'imprimante*) printout; **à sa** ~ as he went out *ou* left; **à la** ~ **de l'école/l'usine** (*moment*) after school/work; when school/the factory finishes; (*lieu*) at the school/factory gates; **à la** ~ **de ce nouveau modèle** when this new model comes (*ou* came) out, when they bring (*ou* brought) out this new model; ~ **de bain** (*vêtement*) bathrobe; "~ **de camions**" "vehicle exit"; ~ **papier** hard copy; ~ **de secours** emergency exit.

sortilège [sortãlczh] *nm* (magic) spell.

sortir [sortãr] *vi* (*gén*) to come out; (*partir, se*

promener, aller au spectacle etc) to go out; (*bourgeon, plante, numéro gagnant*) to come up ♦ *vt* (*gén*) to take out; (*produit, ouvrage, modèle*) to bring out; (*boniments, incongruités*) to come out with; (*INFORM*) to output; (*: sur papier*) to print out; (*fam: expulser*) to throw out ♦ *nm*: **au ~ de l'hiver/l'enfance** as winter/childhood nears its end; **~ qch de** to take sth out of; **~ qn d'embarras** to get sb out of trouble; **~ de** (*gén*) to leave; (*endroit*) to go (*ou* come) out of, leave; (*rainure etc*) to come out of; (*maladie*) to get over; (*époque*) to get through; (*cadre, compétence*) to be outside; (*provenir de: famille etc*) to come from; **~ de table** to leave the table; **~ du système** (*INFORM*) to log out; **~ de ses gonds** (*fig*) to fly off the handle; **se ~ de** (*affaire, situation*) to get out of; **s'en ~** (*malade*) to pull through; (*d'une difficulté etc*) to come through all right; to get through, be able to manage.

SOS *sigle m* mayday, SOS.
sosie [sozē] *nm* double.
sot, sotte [sō, sot] *a* silly, foolish ♦ *nm/f* fool.
sottement [sotmáñ] *ad* foolishly.
sottise [sotēz] *nf* silliness *q*, foolishness *q*; (*propos, acte*) silly *ou* foolish thing (to do *ou* say).
sou [soo] *nm*: **près de ses ~s** tight-fisted; **sans le ~** penniless; **~ à ~** penny by penny; **pas un ~ de bon sens** not a scrap *ou* an ounce of good sense; **de quatre ~s** worthless.
souahéli, e [swaālē] *a* Swahili ♦ *nm* (*LING*) Swahili.
soubassement [soobâsmáñ] *nm* base.
soubresaut [soobrəsō] *nm* (*de peur etc*) start; (*cahot: d'un véhicule*) jolt.
soubrette [soobret] *nf* soubrette, maidservant.
souche [soosh] *nf* (*d'arbre*) stump; (*de carnet*) stub; **dormir comme une ~** to sleep like a log; **de vieille ~** of old stock.
souci [soosē] *nm* (*inquiétude*) worry; (*préoccupation*) concern; (*BOT*) marigold; **se faire du ~** to worry; **avoir (le) ~ de** to have concern for; **par ~ de** for the sake of, out of concern for.
soucier [soosyā]: **se ~ de** *vt* to care about.
soucieux, euse [soosyœ̄, -ēz] *a* concerned, worried; **~ de** concerned about; **peu ~ de/que** caring little about/whether.
soucoupe [sookoop] *nf* saucer; **~ volante** flying saucer.
soudain, e [soodáñ, -en] *a* (*douleur, mort*) sudden ♦ *ad* suddenly, all of a sudden.
soudainement [soodenmáñ] *ad* suddenly.
soudaineté [soodentā] *nf* suddenness.
Soudan [soodáñ] *nm*: **le ~** the Sudan.
soudanais, e [soodáne, -ez] *a* Sudanese.
soude [sood] *nf* soda.
soudé, e [soodā] *a* (*fig: pétales, organes*) joined (together).
souder [soodā] *vt* (*avec fil à souder*) to solder; (*par soudure autogène*) to weld; (*fig*) to bind *ou* knit together; to fuse (together); **se ~** *vi* (*os*) to knit (together).
soudeur, euse [soodœr, -ēz] *nm/f* (*ouvrier*) welder.
soudoyer [soodwáyā] *vt* (*péj*) to bribe, buy over.

soudure [soodür] *nf* soldering; welding; (*joint*) soldered joint; weld; **faire la ~** (*COMM*) to fill a gap; (*fig: assurer une transition*) to bridge the gap.
souffert, e [soofer, -ert(ə)] *pp de* **souffrir**.
soufflage [sooflázh] *nm* (*du verre*) glass-blowing.
souffle [soofl(ə)] *nm* (*en expirant*) breath; (*en soufflant*) puff, blow; (*respiration*) breathing; (*d'explosion, de ventilateur*) blast; (*du vent*) blowing; (*fig*) inspiration; **retenir son ~** to hold one's breath; **avoir du/manquer de ~** to have a lot of/be short of breath; **être à bout de ~** to be out of breath; **avoir le ~ court** to be short-winded; **un ~ d'air** *ou* **de vent** a breath of air, a puff of wind; **~ au cœur** (*MÉD*) heart murmur.
soufflé, e [sooflā] *a* (*CULIN*) soufflé; (*fam: ahuri, stupéfié*) staggered ♦ *nm* (*CULIN*) soufflé.
souffler [sooflā] *vi* (*gén*) to blow; (*haleter*) to puff (and blow) ♦ *vt* (*feu, bougie*) to blow out; (*chasser: poussière etc*) to blow away; (*TECH: verre*) to blow; (*suj: explosion*) to destroy (with its blast); (*dire*): **~ qch à qn** to whisper sth to sb; (*fam: voler*): **~ qch à qn** to pinch sth from sb; **~ son rôle à qn** to prompt sb; **ne pas ~ mot** not to breathe a word; **laisser ~ qn** (*fig*) to give sb a breather.
soufflet [soofle] *nm* (*instrument*) bellows *pl*; (*entre wagons*) vestibule; (*COUTURE*) gusset; (*gifle*) slap (in the face).
souffleur, euse [sooflœr, -ēz] *nm/f* (*THÉÂTRE*) prompter; (*TECH*) glass-blower.
souffrance [soofráñs] *nf* suffering; **en ~** (*marchandise*) awaiting delivery; (*affaire*) pending.
souffrant, e [soofráñ, -âñt] *a* unwell.
souffre-douleur [soofrədoolœr] *nm inv* whipping boy, butt, underdog.
souffreteux, euse [soofrətœ̄, -ēz] *a* sickly.
souffrir [soofrēr] *vi* to suffer; (*éprouver des douleurs*) to be in pain ♦ *vt* to suffer, endure; (*supporter*) to bear, stand; (*admettre: exception etc*) to allow *ou* admit of; **~ de** (*maladie, froid*) to suffer from; **~ des dents** to have trouble with one's teeth; **ne pas pouvoir ~ qch/que** ... not to be able to endure *ou* bear sth/that ...; **faire ~ qn** (*suj: personne*) to make sb suffer; (*: dents, blessure etc*) to hurt sb.
soufre [soofr(ə)] *nm* sulfur (*US*), sulphur (*Brit*).
soufrer [soofrā] *vt* (*vignes*) to treat with sulphur *ou* sulfur.
souhait [swe] *nm* wish; **tous nos ~s de** good wishes *ou* our best wishes for; **riche etc à ~** as rich *etc* as one could wish; **à vos ~s!** bless you!
souhaitable [swetábl(ə)] *a* desirable.
souhaiter [swātā] *vt* to wish for; **~ le bonjour à qn** to bid sb good day; **~ la bonne année à qn** to wish sb a happy New Year; **il est à ~ que** it is to be hoped that.
souiller [sooyā] *vt* to dirty, soil; (*fig*) to sully, tarnish.
souillure [sooyür] *nf* stain.
soûl, e [soo, sool] *a* drunk; (*fig*): **~ de**

musique/plaisirs drunk with music/pleasure ♦ *nm*: **tout son ~** to one's heart's content.

soulagement [sŏŏlázhmáṅ] *nm* relief.

soulager [sŏŏlázhā] *vt* to relieve; **~ qn de** to relieve sb of.

soûler [sŏŏlā] *vt*: **~ qn** to get sb drunk; (*suj: boisson*) to make sb drunk; (*fig*) to make sb's head spin *ou* reel; **se ~** to get drunk; **se ~ de** (*fig*) to intoxicate o.s. with.

soûlerie [sŏŏlrē] *nf* (*péj*) drunken binge.

soulèvement [sŏŏlevmáṅ] *nm* uprising; (*GÉO*) upthrust.

soulever [sŏŏlvā] *vt* to lift; (*vagues, poussière*) to send up; (*peuple*) to stir up (to revolt); (*enthousiasme*) to arouse; (*question, débat, protestations, difficultés*) to raise; **se ~ vi** (*peuple*) to rise up; (*personne couchée*) to lift o.s. up; (*couvercle etc*) to lift; **cela me soulève le cœur** it makes me feel sick.

soulier [sŏŏlyā] *nm* shoe; **~s bas** low-heeled shoes; **~s plats/à talons** flat/heeled shoes.

souligner [sŏŏlēnyā] *vt* to underline; (*fig*) to emphasize, stress.

soumettre [sŏŏmctr] *vt* (*pays*) to subject, subjugate; (*rebelles*) to put down, subduc; **~ qn/qch à** to subject sb/sth to; **~ qch à qn** (*projet etc*) to submit sth to sb; **se ~ (à)** (*se rendre, obéir*) to submit (to); **se ~ à** (*formalités etc*) to submit to; (*régime etc*) to submit o.s. to.

soumis, e [sŏŏmē, -ēz] *pp de* **soumettre** ♦ *a* submissive; **revenus ~ à l'impôt** taxable income.

soumission [sŏŏmēsyôṅ] *nf* (*voir se soumettre*) submission; (*docilité*) submissiveness; (*COMM*) tender.

soumissionner [sŏŏmēsyonā] *vt* (*COMM: travaux*) to bid for, tender for.

soupape [sŏŏpáp] *nf* valve; **~ de sûreté** safety valve.

soupçon [sŏŏpsóṅ] *nm* suspicion; (*petite quantité*): **un ~ de** a hint *ou* touch of; **avoir ~ de** to suspect; **au dessus de tout ~** above (all) suspicion.

soupçonner [sŏŏpsonā] *vt* to suspect; **~ qn de qch/d'être** to suspect sb of sth/of being.

soupçonneux, euse [sŏŏpsonŏ̄, -ēz] *a* suspicious.

soupe [sŏŏp] *nf* soup; **~ au lait** *a inv* quick-tempered; **~ à l'oignon/de poisson** onion/fish soup; **~ populaire** soup kitchen.

soupente [sŏŏpáṅt] *nf* (*mansarde*) attic; (*placard*) closet (*US*) *ou* cupboard (*Brit*) under the stairs.

souper [sŏŏpā] *vi* to have supper ♦ *nm* supper; **avoir soupé de** (*fam*) to be sick and tired of.

soupeser [sŏŏpəzā] *vt* to weigh in one's hand(s), feel the weight of; (*fig*) to weigh (up (*Brit*)).

soupière [sŏŏpyer] *nf* (soup) tureen.

soupir [sŏŏpēr] *nm* sigh; (*MUS*) quarter rest (*US*), crotchet rest (*Brit*); **rendre le dernier ~** to breathe one's last.

soupirail, aux [sŏŏpēráy, -ō] *nm* (small) basement window.

soupirant [sŏŏpēráṅ] *nm* (*péj*) suitor, wooer.

soupirer [sŏŏpērā] *vi* to sigh; **~ après qch** to yearn for sth.

souple [sŏŏpl(ə)] *a* supple; (*col*) soft; (*fig: rè-* *glement, caractère*) flexible; (: *démarche, taille*) lithe, supple; **disque(tte) ~** (*INFORM*) floppy disk, diskette.

souplesse [sŏŏples] *nf* suppleness; flexibility.

source [sŏŏrs(ə)] *nf* (*point d'eau*) spring; (*d'un cours d'eau, fig*) source; **prendre sa ~ à/ dans** (*suj: cours d'eau*) to have its source at/ in; **tenir qch de bonne ~/de ~ sûre** to have sth on good authority/from a reliable source; **~ thermale/d'eau minérale** hot *ou* thermal/ mineral spring.

sourcier, ière [sŏŏrsyā, -yer] *nm* water diviner.

sourcil [sŏŏrsē] *nm* (eye)brow.

sourcilière [sŏŏrsēlyer] *af voir* **arcade**.

sourciller [sŏŏrsēyā] *vi*: **sans ~** without turning a hair *ou* batting an eyelid.

sourcilleux, euse [sŏŏrsēyŏ̄, -ēz] *a* (*hautain, sévère*) haughty, supercilious; (*pointilleux*) finicky, pernickety.

sourd, e [sŏŏr, sŏŏrd(ə)] *a* deaf; (*bruit, voix*) muffled; (*couleur*) muted; (*douleur*) dull; (*lutte*) silent, hidden; (*LING*) voiceless ♦ *nm/f* deaf person; **être ~ à** to be deaf to.

sourdement [sŏŏrdəmáṅ] *ad* (*avec un bruit sourd*) dully; (*secrètement*) silently.

sourdine [sŏŏrdēn] *nf* (*MUS*) mute; **en ~** *ad* softly, quietly; **mettre une ~ à** (*fig*) to tone down.

sourd-muet, sourde-muette [sŏŏrmüe, sŏŏrdmüet] *a* deaf-and-dumb ♦ *nm/f* deaf-mute.

sourdre [sŏŏrdr(ə)] *vi* (*eau*) to spring up; (*fig*) to rise.

souriant, e [sŏŏryáṅ, -áṅt] *vb voir* **sourire** ♦ *a* cheerful.

souricière [sŏŏrsyer] *nf* mousetrap; (*fig*) trap.

sourie [sŏŏrē] *etc vb voir* **sourire**.

sourire [sŏŏrēr] *nm* smile ♦ *vi* to smile; **~ à qn** to smile at sb; (*fig*) to appeal to sb; (: *chance*) to smile on sb; **faire un ~ à qn** to give sb a smile; **garder le ~** to keep smiling.

souris [sŏŏrē] *nf* mouse (*pl* mice); (*INFORM*) mouse.

sournois, e [sŏŏrnwá, -wáz] *a* deceitful, underhand.

sournoisement [sŏŏrnwázmáṅ] *ad* deceitfully.

sous [sŏŏ] *prép* (*gén*) under; **~ la pluie/ le soleil** in the rain/sunshine; **~ mes yeux** before my eyes; **~ terre** *a, ad* underground; **~ vide** *a, ad* vacuum-packed; **~ l'influence/ l'action de** under the influence of/by the action of; **~ antibiotiques/perfusion** on antibiotics/an I.V. (*US*) *ou* a drip (*Brit*); **~ cet angle/ce rapport** from this angle/in this respect; **~ peu** *ad* shortly, before long.

sous... [sŏŏ, sŏŏz + *vowel*] *préfixe* sub-; under....

sous-alimenté, e [sŏŏzálēmáṅtā] *a* undernourished.

sous-bois [sŏŏbwá] *nm inv* undergrowth.

sous-catégorie [sŏŏkátágorē] *nf* sub-category.

sous-chef [sŏŏshef] *nm* deputy chief, second in command; **~ de bureau** deputy head of department.

sous-comité [sŏŏkomētā] *nm* subcommittee.

sous-commission [sŏŏkomēsyôṅ] *nf* sub-committee.

sous-continent [sŏŏkôṅtēnáṅ] *nm* subcontinent.

sous-couche [sŏŏkŏŏsh] *nf* (*de peinture*) undercoat.

souscripteur, trice [sŏŏskrēptœr, -trēs] *nm/f* subscriber.

souscription [sŏŏskrēpsyŏ́n] *nf* subscription; **offert en** ~ available on subscription.

souscrire [sŏŏskrēr]: ~ **à** *vt* to subscribe to.

sous-cutané, e [sŏŏkütáná] *a* subcutaneous.

sous-développé, e [sŏŏdāvlopā] *a* underdeveloped.

sous-directeur, trice [sŏŏdērektœr, -trēs] *nm/f* assistant manager/manageress, submanager/manageress.

sous-emploi [sŏŏzáńplwá] *nm* underemployment.

sous-employé, e [sŏŏzáńplwáyā] *a* underemployed.

sous-ensemble [sŏŏzáńsáńbl(ǝ)] *nm* subset.

sous-entendre [sŏŏzáńtáńdr(ǝ)] *vt* to imply, infer.

sous-entendu, e [sŏŏzáńtáńdü] *a* implied; (*LING*) understood ♦ *nm* innuendo, insinuation.

sous-equipé, e [sŏŏzākēpā] *a* underequipped.

sous-estimer [sŏŏzestēmā] *vt* to underestimate.

sous-exploiter [sŏŏzāksplwátā] *vt* to underexploit.

sous-exposer [sŏŏzekspŏzā] *vt* to underexpose.

sous-fifre [sŏŏfēfr(ǝ)] *nm* (*péj*) underling.

sous-groupe [sŏŏgrŏŏp] *nm* subgroup.

sous-homme [sŏŏzom] *nm* subhuman.

sous-jacent, e [sŏŏzhásáń, -áńt] *a* underlying.

sous-lieutenant [sŏŏlyœ̄tnáń] *nm* second lieutenant (*US*), sub-lieutenant (*Brit*).

sous-locataire [sŏŏlokáter] *nm/f* subtenant.

sous-location [sŏŏlokásyŏ́n] *nf* subletting.

sous-louer [sŏŏlwā] *vt* to sublet.

sous-main [sŏŏmań] *nm inv* desk blotter; **en** ~ *ad* secretly.

sous-marin, e [sŏŏmáráń, -ēn] *a* (*flore, volcan*) submarine; (*navigation, pêche, explosif*) underwater ♦ *nm* submarine.

sous-médicalisé, e [sŏŏmādēkálēzā] *a* lacking adequate medical care.

sous-nappe [sŏŏnáp] *nf* table pad (*US*), undercloth (*Brit*).

sous-officier [sŏŏzofēsyā] *nm* ≈ noncommissioned officer (NCO).

sous-ordre [sŏŏzordr(ǝ)] *nm* subordinate; **créancier en** ~ creditor's creditor.

sous-payé, e [sŏŏpáyā] *a* underpaid.

sous-préfecture [sŏŏpráfektür] *nf* subprefecture.

sous-préfet [sŏŏpráfe] *nm* sub-prefect.

sous-production [sŏŏprodüksyŏ́n] *nf* underproduction.

sous-produit [sŏŏprodüē] *nm* by-product; (*fig: péj*) pale imitation.

sous-programme [sŏŏprográm] *nm* (*INFORM*) subroutine.

sous-pull [sŏŏpŏŏl] *nm* thin poloneck sweater.

sous-secrétaire [sŏŏsǝkrāter] *nm:* ~ **d'État** Under Secretary of State.

soussigné, e [sŏŏsēnyā] *a:* **je** ~ I the undersigned.

sous-sol [sŏŏsol] *nm* basement; (*GÉO*) subsoil.

sous-tasse [sŏŏtás] *nf* saucer.

sous-tendre [sŏŏtáńdr(ǝ)] *vt* to underlie.

sous-tltre [sŏŏtētr(ǝ)] *nm* subtitle.

sous-titré, e [sŏŏtētrā] *a* with subtitles.

soustraction [sŏŏstráksyŏ́n] *nf* subtraction.

soustraire [sŏŏstrer] *vt* to subtract, take away; (*dérober*): ~ **qch à qn** to remove sth from sb; ~ **qn à** (*danger*) to shield sb from; **se** ~ **à** (*autorité, obligation, devoir*) to elude, escape from.

sous-traitance [sŏŏtretáńs(ǝ)] *nf* subcontracting.

sous-traitant [sŏŏtretáń] *nm* subcontractor.

sous-traiter [sŏŏtrátā] *vt, vi* to subcontract.

soustrayais [sŏŏstreye] *etc vb voir* **soustraire**.

sous-verre [sŏŏver] *nm inv* glass mount.

sous-vêtement [sŏŏvetmáń] *nm* undergarment, item of underwear; ~**s** *nmpl* underwear *sg*.

soutane [sŏŏtán] *nf* cassock, soutane.

soute [sŏŏt] *nf* hold; ~ **à bagages** baggage hold.

soutenable [sŏŏtnábl(ǝ)] *a* (*opinion*) tenable, defensible.

soutenance [sŏŏtnáńs] *nf:* ~ **de thèse** ≈ defense (*US*), ≈ viva (voce) (*Brit*).

soutènement [sŏŏtenmáń] *nm:* **mur de** ~ retaining wall.

souteneur [sŏŏtnœr] *nm* procurer.

soutenir [sŏŏtnēr] *vt* to support; (*assaut, choc, regard*) to stand up to, withstand; (*intérêt, effort*) to keep up; (*assurer*): ~ **que** to maintain that; **se** ~ (*dans l'eau etc*) to hold o.s. up; (*être soutenable: point de vue*) to be tenable; (*s'aider mutuellement*) to stand by each other; ~ **la comparaison avec** to bear *ou* stand comparison with; ~ **le regard de qn** to be able to look sb in the face.

soutenu, e [sŏŏtnü] *pp de* **soutenir** ♦ *a* (*efforts*) sustained, unflagging; (*style*) elevated; (*couleur*) strong.

souterrain, e [sŏŏteráń, -en] *a* underground; (*fig*) subterranean ♦ *nm* underground passage.

soutien [sŏŏtyań] *nm* support; **apporter son** ~ **à** to lend one's support to; ~ **de famille** breadwinner.

soutiendrai [sŏŏtyáńdrā] *etc vb voir* **soutenir**.

soutien-gorge, *pl* **soutiens-gorge** [sŏŏtyańgorzh(ǝ)] *nm* bra; (*de maillot de bain*) top.

soutiens [sŏŏtyań], **soutint** [sŏŏtań] *etc vb voir* **soutenir**.

soutirer [sŏŏtērā] *vt:* ~ **qch à qn** to squeeze *ou* get sth out of sb.

souvenance [sŏŏvnáńs] *nf:* **avoir** ~ **de** to recollect.

souvenir [sŏŏvnēr] *nm* (*réminiscence*) memory; (*cadeau*) souvenir, keepsake; (*de voyage*) souvenir ♦ *vb:* **se** ~ **de** *vt* to remember; **se** ~ **que** to remember that; **garder le** ~ **de** to retain the memory of; **en** ~ **de** in memory *ou* remembrance of; **avec mes affectueux/meilleurs** ~**s**, ... with love from, .../regards, ...

souvent [sŏŏváń] *ad* often; **peu** ~ seldom, infrequently; **le plus** ~ more often than not, most often.

souvenu, e [sŏŏvǝnü] *pp de* **se souvenir**.

souverain, e [sŏŏvrań, -en] *a* sovereign; *(fig: mépris)* supreme ♦ *nm/f* sovereign, monarch.

souverainement [sŏŏvrenmáń] *ad (sans appel)* with sovereign power; *(extrêmement)* supremely, intensely.

souveraineté [sŏŏvrentä] *nf* sovereignty.

souviendrai [sŏŏvyańdrä], **souviens** [sŏŏvyań], **souvint** [sŏŏvań] *etc vb voir* **se souvenir.**

soviétique [sovyätēk] *a* a Soviet ♦ *nm/f*: **S~** Soviet citizen.

soviétiser [sovyätēzä] *vt* to sovietize.

soviétologue [sovyätolog] *nm/f* Kremlinologist.

soyeux, euse [swáyœ̄, -œ̄z] *a* silky.

soyez [swáyä] *etc vb voir* **être.**

SPA *sigle f* (− *Société protectrice des animaux*) ≈ SPCA *(US)*, ≈ RSPCA *(Brit)*.

spacieux, euse [spásyœ̄, -œ̄z] *a* spacious; roomy.

spaciosité [spásyozētä] *nf* spaciousness.

spaghettis [spágätē] *nmpl* spaghetti *sg.*

sparadrap [spárádrá] *nm* adhesive tape *(US)*, adhesive *ou* sticking plaster *(Brit)*.

Sparte [spárt(ə)] *nf* Sparta.

spartiate [spársyát] *a* Spartan; **~s** *nfpl (sandales)* Roman sandals.

spasme [spázm(ə)] *nm* spasm.

spasmodique [spázmodēk] *a* spasmodic.

spatial, e, aux [spásyál, -ō] *a (AVIAT)* space *cpd*; *(PSYCH)* spatial.

spatule [spátül] *nf (ustensile)* slice; spatula; *(bout)* tip.

speaker, ine [spēkœr, -krēn] *nm/f* announcer.

spécial, e, aux [spāsyál, -ō] *a* special; *(bizarre)* peculiar.

spécialement [spāsyálmáń] *ad* especially, particularly; *(tout exprès)* specially; **pas ~** not particularly.

spécialisation [spāsyálēzâsyóń] *nf* specialization.

spécialisé, e [spāsyálēzä] *a* specialized; **ordinateur ~** dedicated computer.

spécialiser [spāsyálēzä]: **se ~** *vi* to specialize.

spécialiste [spāsyálēst(ə)] *nm/f* specialist.

spécialité [spāsyálētä] *nf* specialty *(US)*, speciality *(Brit)*; *(SCOL)* major *(US)*, special field *(Brit)*; **~ pharmaceutique** patent medicine.

spécieux, euse [spāsyœ̄, -œ̄z] *a* specious.

spécification [spāsēfēkâsyóń] *nf* specification.

spécifier [spāsēfyä] *vt* to specify, state.

spécifique [spāsēfēk] *a* specific.

spécifiquement [spāsēfēkmáń] *ad (typiquement)* typically; *(tout exprès)* specifically.

spécimen [spāsēmen] *nm* specimen; *(revue etc)* specimen *ou* sample copy.

spectacle [spektákl(ə)] *nm (tableau, scène)* sight; *(représentation)* show; *(industrie)* show business, entertainment; **se donner en ~** *(péj)* to make a spectacle *ou* an exhibition of o.s; **pièce/revue à grand ~** spectacular (play/revue); **au ~ de ...** at the sight of ....

spectaculaire [spektákülœr] *a* spectacular.

spectateur, trice [spektátœr, -trēs] *nm/f (CINÉMA etc)* member of the audience; *(SPORT)* spectator; *(d'un événement)* onlooker, witness.

spectre [spektr(ə)] *nm (fantôme, fig)* specter *(US)*, spectre *(Brit)*; *(PHYSIQUE)* spectrum

(pl -a); **~ solaire** solar spectrum.

spéculateur, trice [spākülátœr, -trēs] *nm/f* speculator.

spéculatif, ive [spākülátēf, -ēv] *a* speculative.

spéculation [spākülâsyóń] *nf* speculation.

spéculer [spākülä] *vi* to speculate; **~ sur** *(COMM)* to speculate in; *(réfléchir)* to speculate on; *(tabler sur)* to bank *ou* rely on.

spéléologie [spālāolozhē] *nf (étude)* speleology; *(activité)* spelunking *(US)*, potholing *(Brit)*.

spéléologue [spālāolog] *nm/f* speleologist; spelunker *(US)*, potholer *(Brit)*.

spermatozoïde [spermátōzoēd] *nm* sperm, spermatozoon *(pl -zoa)*.

sperme [sperm(ə)] *nm* semen, sperm.

spermicide [spermēsēd] *a, nm* spermicide.

sphère [sfer] *nf* sphere.

sphérique [sfārēk] *a* spherical.

sphincter [sfańkter] *nm* sphincter.

sphinx [sfańks] *nm inv* sphinx; *(ZOOL)* hawkmoth.

spiral, aux [spērál, -ō] *nm* hairspring.

spirale [spērál] *nf* spiral; **en ~** in a spiral.

spire [spēr] *nf (d'une spirale)* turn; *(d'une coquille)* whorl.

spiritisme [spērētēsm(ə)] *nm* spiritualism, spiritism.

spirituel, le [spērētüel] *a* spiritual; *(fin, piquant)* witty; **musique ~le** sacred music; **concert ~** concert of sacred music.

spirituellement [spērētüelmáń] *ad* spiritually; wittily.

spiritueux [spērētüœ] *nm* spirit.

splendeur [splándœr] *nf* splendor *(US)*, splendour *(Brit)*.

splendide [oplândēd] *a* splendid, magnificent.

spolier [spolyä] *vt*: **~ qn (de)** to despoil sb (of).

spongieux, euse [spónzhyœ̄, -œ̄z] *a* spongy.

sponsor [spónsor] *nm* sponsor.

sponsoriser [spónsorēzä] *vt* to sponsor.

spontané, e [spóntánä] *a* spontaneous.

spontanément [spóntánámáń] *ad* spontaneously.

sporadique [sporádēk] *a* sporadic.

sport [spor] *nm* sport ♦ *a inv (vêtement)* casual; *(fair-play)* sporting; **faire du ~** to engage in sports; **~ individuel/d'équipe** individual/team sport; **~ de combat** combative sport; **~s d'hiver** winter sports.

sportif, ive [sportēf, -ēv] *a (journal, association, épreuve)* sports *cpd*; *(allure, démarche)* athletic; *(attitude, esprit)* sporting; **les résultats ~s** the sports results.

sportivement [sportēvmáń] *ad* sportingly.

sportivité [sportēvētä] *nf* sportsmanship.

spot [spot] *nm (lampe)* spot(light); *(annonce)*: **~ (publicitaire)** commercial (break).

spray [spre] *nm* spray, aerosol.

sprint [sprēnt] *nm* sprint; **piquer un ~** to put on a (final) spurt.

squale [skwál] *nm (type of)* shark.

square [skwár] *nm* public garden(s).

squash [skwásh] *nm* squash.

squatter *nm* [skwátœr] squatter ♦ *vt* [skwátä] to squat.

squelette [skəlet] *nm* skeleton.

squelettique [skəlätēk] *a* scrawny; *(fig)*

skimpy.
Sri Lanka [srēlåṅkå] *nm* Sri Lanka.
sri-lankais, e [srēlåṅkɛ, -cz] *a* Sri Lankan.
SS *sigle f* = **sécurité sociale**; (= *Sa Sainteté*) HH.
ss *abr* = **sous**.
S/S *sigle m* (= *steamship*) SS.
SSR *sigle f* (= *Société suisse romande*) the Swiss French-language broadcasting company.
stabilisateur, trice [stàbēlēzàtœr, -trēs] *a* stabilizing ♦ *nm* stabilizer; (*véhicule*) antiroll device; (*avion*) stabilizer (*US*), tailplane (*Brit*).
stabiliser [stàbēlēzå] *vt* to stabilize; (*terrain*) to consolidate.
stabilité [stàbēlētå] *nf* stability.
stable [stàbl(ə)] *a* stable, steady.
stade [stàd] *nm* (*SPORT*) stadium; (*phase, niveau*) stage.
stage [stàzh] *nm* training period; training course.
stagiaire [stàzhyer] *nm/f, a* trainee *(cpd)*.
stagnant, e [stàgnåṅ, -åṅt] *a* stagnant.
stagner [stàgnå] *vi* to stagnate.
stalactite [stàlàktēt] *nf* stalactite.
stalagmite [stàlàgmēt] *nf* stalagmite.
stalle [stàl] *nf* stall, box.
stand [ståṅd] *nm* (*d'exposition*) stand; (*de foire*) stall; ~ **de tir** (à *la foire, SPORT*) shooting gallery; ~ **de ravitaillement** pit.
standard [ståṅdàr] *a inv* standard ♦ *nm* (*type, norme*) standard; (*téléphonique*) switchboard.
standardiser [ståṅdàrdēzå] *vt* to standardize.
standardiste [ståṅdàrdēst(ə)] *nm/f* switchboard operator.
standing [ståṅdēng] *nm* standing; **immeuble de grand** ~ luxury apartment building (*US*), block of luxury flats (*Brit*).
star [stàr] *nf* star.
starlette [stàrlet] *nf* starlet.
starter [stàrter] *nm* (*AUTO*) choke; (*SPORT*: *personne*) starter; **mettre le** ~ to pull out the choke.
station [stàsyôṅ] *nf* station; (*de bus*) stop; (*de villégiature*) resort; (*posture*): **la** ~ **debout** standing, an upright posture; ~ **balnéaire** seaside resort; ~ **de graissage** lubrication bay; ~ **de lavage** carwash; ~ **de ski** ski resort; ~ **de sports d'hiver** winter sports resort; ~ **de taxis** taxi stand (*US*) *ou* rank (*Brit*); ~ **thermale** thermal spa.
stationnaire [stàsyoner] *a* stationary.
stationnement [stàsyonmåṅ] *nm* parking; **zone de** ~ **interdit** no parking area; ~ **alterné** parking on alternate sides.
stationner [stàsyonå] *vi* to park.
station-service [stàsyôṅservēs] *nf* service station.
statique [stàtēk] *a* static.
statisticien, ne [stàtēstēsyaṅ, -en] *nm/f* statistician.
statistique [stàtēstēk] *nf* (*science*) statistics *sg*; (*rapport, étude*) statistic ♦ *a* statistical; ~**s** *nfpl* (*données*) statistics *pl*.
statistiquement [stàtēstēkmåṅ] *ad* statistically.
statue [stàtü] *nf* statue.

statuer [stàtüå] *vi*: ~ **sur** to rule on, give a ruling on.
statuette [stàtüet] *nf* statuette.
statu quo [stàtükwō] *nm* status quo.
stature [stàtür] *nf* stature; **de haute** ~ of great stature.
statut [stàtü] *nm* status; ~**s** *nmpl* (*JUR, ADMIN*) statutes.
statutaire [stàtüter] *a* statutory.
Sté *abr* (= *société*) soc.
St(e) *abr* (= *Saint(e)*) St.
steak [stek] *nm* steak.
stèle [stel] *nf* stela, stele.
stellaire [stāler] *a* stellar.
stencil [stensēl] *nm* stencil.
sténodactylo [stānodàktēlō] *nf* stenographer (*US*), shorthand typist (*Brit*).
sténodactylographie [stānodàktēlogràfē] *nf* stenography (*US*), shorthand typing (*Brit*).
sténo(graphie) [stāno(gràfē)] *nf* shorthand; **prendre en** ~ to take down in shorthand.
sténographier [stānogràfyå] *vt* to take down in shorthand.
sténographique [stānogràfēk] *a* shorthand *cpd*.
stentor [ståṅtor] *nm*: **voix de** ~ stentorian voice.
stéphanois, e [stāfånwå, -wåz] *a* of *ou* from Saint-Étienne.
steppe [step] *nf* steppe.
stère [ster] *nm* stere.
stéréo(phonie) [stārāo(fonē)] *nf* stereo(phony); **émission en** ~ stereo broadcast.
stéréo(phonique) [stārāo(fonēk)] *a* stereo(phonic).
stéréoscope [stārāoskop] *nm* stereoscope.
stéréoscopique [stārāoskopēk] *a* stereoscopic.
stéréotype [stārāotēp] *nm* stereotype.
stéréotypé, e [stārāotēpå] *a* stereotyped.
stérile [stārēl] *a* sterile; (*terre*) barren; (*fig*) fruitless, futile.
stérilement [stārēlmåṅ] *ad* fruitlessly.
stérilet [stārēle] *nm* coil, loop.
stérilisateur [stārēlēzàtœr] *nm* sterilizer.
stérilisation [stārēlēzàsyôṅ] *nf* sterilization.
stériliser [stārēlēzå] *vt* to sterilize.
stérilité [stārēlētå] *nf* sterility.
sternum [sternom] *nm* breastbone, sternum.
stéthoscope [stātoskop] *nm* stethoscope.
stick [stēk] *nm* stick.
stigmates [stēgmàt] *nmpl* scars, marks; (*REL*) stigmata *pl*.
stigmatiser [stēgmàtēzå] *vt* to denounce, stigmatize.
stimulant, e [stēmülåṅ, -åṅt] *a* stimulating ♦ *nm* (*MÉD*) stimulant; (*fig*) stimulus (*pl* -i), incentive.
stimulateur [stēmülàtœr] *nm*: ~ **cardiaque** pacemaker.
stimulation [stēmülåsyôṅ] *nf* stimulation.
stimuler [stēmülå] *vt* to stimulate.
stimulus, i [stēmülüs, -ē] *nm* stimulus (*pl* -i).
stipulation [stēpülåsyôṅ] *nf* stipulation.
stipuler [stēpülå] *vt* to stipulate, specify.
stock [stok] *nm* stock; **en** ~ in stock.
stockage [stokåzh] *nm* stocking; storage.
stocker [stokå] *vt* to stock; (*déchets*) to store.
Stockholm [stokolm] *n* Stockholm.

stockiste |stokēst(ə)| *nm* dealer.

stoïcisme |stoēsēsm(ə)| *nm* stoicism.

stoïque |stoēk| *a* stoic, stoical.

stomacal, e, aux |stomákál, -ō| *a* gastric, stomach *cpd*.

stomatologie |stomátolozhē| *nf* stomatology.

stop |stop| *nm* (*AUTO*: écriteau) stop sign; (: *signal*) brake light; (*dans un télégramme*) stop ♦ *excl* stop!

stoppage |stopázh| *nm* invisible mending.

stopper |stopā| *vt* to stop, halt; (*COUTURE*) to mend ♦ *vi* to stop, halt.

store |stor| *nm* blind; (*de magasin*) shade, awning.

strabisme |stràbēsm(ə)| *nm* squint(ing).

strangulation |stràṅgülàsyôṅ| *nf* strangulation.

strapontin |stràpôṅtaṅ| *nm* jump *ou* foldaway seat.

Strasbourg |strázbōōr| *n* Strasbourg.

strass |strás| *nm* paste, strass.

stratagème |strátázhem| *nm* stratagem.

strate |strát| *nf* (*GÉO*) stratum, layer.

stratège |strátezh| *nm* strategist.

stratégie |strátāzhē| *nf* strategy.

stratégique |strátāzhēk| *a* strategic.

stratégiquement |strátāzhēkmáṅ| *ad* strategically.

stratifié, e |strátēfyā| *a* (*GÉO*) stratified; (*TECH*) laminated.

stratosphère |strátosfer| *nf* stratosphere.

stress |stres| *nm inv* stress.

stressant, e |tresáṅ, -áṅt| *a* stressful.

stresser |stresā| *vt* to stress, cause stress in.

strict, e |strēkt(ə)| *a* strict; (*tenue, décor*) severe, plain; **son droit le plus** ~ his most basic right; **dans la plus** ~**e intimité** strictly in private; **le** ~ **nécessaire/minimum** the bare essentials/minimum.

strictement |strēktəmáṅ| *ad* strictly; plainly.

strident, e |strēdáṅ, -áṅt| *a* shrill, strident.

stridulations |strēdülásyôṅ| *nfpl* stridulations, chirrings.

strie |strē| *nf* streak; (*ANAT, GÉO*) stria (*pl* -ae).

strier |strēyā| *vt* to streak; to striate.

strip-tease |strēptēz| *nm* striptease.

strip-teaseuse |strēptēzŏēz| *nf* stripper, striptease artist.

striures |strēyür| *nfpl* streaking *sg*.

strophe |strof| *nf* verse, stanza.

structure |strüktür| *nf* structure; ~**s d'accueil/touristiques** reception/tourist facilities.

structurer |strüktürā| *vt* to structure.

strychnine |strēknēn| *nf* strychnine.

stuc |stük| *nm* stucco.

studieusement |stüdyēzmáṅ| *ad* studiously.

studieux, euse |stüdyŏē, -ŏēz| *a* (*élève*) studious; (*vacances*) study *cpd*.

studio |stüdyō| *nm* (*logement*) studio apartment; (*d'artiste, TV etc*) studio (*pl* -s).

stupéfaction |stüpāfáksyôṅ| *nf* stupefaction, astonishment.

stupéfait, e |stüpáfe, -et| *a* astonished.

stupéfiant, e |stüpāfyáṅ, -áṅt| *a* stunning, astonishing ♦ *nm* (*MÉD*) drug, narcotic.

stupéfier |stüpáfyā| *vt* to stupefy; (*étonner*) to stun, astonish.

stupeur |stüpŏēr| *nf* (*inertie, insensibilité*)

stupor; (*étonnement*) astonishment, amazement.

stupide |stüpēd| *a* stupid; (*hébété*) stunned.

stupidement |stüpēdmáṅ| *ad* stupidly.

stupidité |stüpēdētā| *nf* stupidity *q*; (*propos, action*) stupid thing (to say *ou* do).

stups |stüp| *nmpl* (= *stupéfiants*): **brigade des** ~ narcotics bureau *ou* squad.

style |stēl| *nm* style; **meuble/robe de** ~ piece of period furniture/period dress; ~ **de vie** lifestyle.

stylé, e |stēlā| *a* well-trained.

stylet |stēle| *nm* (*poignard*) stiletto; (*CHIRURGIE*) stylet.

stylisé, e |stēlēzā| *a* stylized.

styliste |stēlēst(ə)| *nm/f* designer; stylist.

stylistique |stēlēstēk| *nf* stylistics *sg* ♦ *a* stylistic.

stylo |stēlō| *nm*: ~ **(à encre)** (fountain) pen; ~ **(à) bille** ballpoint pen.

stylo-feutre |stēlofŏētr(ə)| *nm* felt-tip pen.

su, e |sü| *pp de* **savoir** ♦ *nm*: **au** ~ **de** with the knowledge of.

suaire |süer| *nm* shroud.

suant, e |süáṅ, -áṅt| *a* sweaty.

suave |süáv| *a* (*odeur*) sweet; (*voix*) suave, smooth; (*coloris*) soft, mellow.

subalterne |sübáltern(ə)| *a* (*employé, officier*) junior; (*rôle*) subordinate, subsidiary ♦ *nm/f* subordinate, inferior.

subconscient |sübkôṅsyáṅ| *nm* subconscious.

subdiviser |sübdēvēzā| *vt* to subdivide.

subdivision |sübdēvēzyôṅ| *nf* subdivision.

subir |sübēr| *vt* (*affront, dégâts, mauvais traitements*) to suffer; (*influence, charme*) to be under, be subjected to; (*traitement, opération, châtiment*) to undergo; (*personne*) to suffer, be subjected to.

subit, e |sübē, -ēt| *a* sudden.

subitement |sübētmáṅ| *ad* suddenly, all of a sudden.

subjectif, ive |sübzhektēf, -ēv| *a* subjective.

subjectivement |sübzhektēvmáṅ| *ad* subjectively.

subjonctif |sübzhôṅktēt| *nm* subjunctive.

subjuguer |sübzhügā| *vt* to subjugate.

sublime |süblēm| *a* sublime.

sublimer |süblēmā| *vt* to sublimate.

submergé, e |sübmerzhā| *a* submerged; (*fig*): ~ **de** snowed under with; overwhelmed with.

submerger |sübmerzhā| *vt* to submerge; (*suj: foule*) to engulf; (*fig*) to overwhelm.

submersible |sübmersēbl(ə)| *nm* submarine.

subordination |sübordēnásyôṅ| *nf* subordination.

subordonné, e |sübordonā| *a, nm/f* subordinate; ~ **à** (*personne*) subordinate to; (*résultats etc*) subject to, depending on.

subordonner |sübordonā| *vt*: ~ **qn/qch à** to subordinate sb/sth to.

subornation |sübornásyôṅ| *nf* bribing.

suborner |sübornā| *vt* to bribe.

subrepticement |sübreptēsmáṅ| *ad* surreptitiously.

subroger |sübrozhā| *vt* (*JUR*) to subrogate.

subside |süpsēd| *nm* grant.

subsidiaire |süpsēdyer| *a* subsidiary; **question** ~ deciding question.

subsistance |süpzēstáṅs| *nf* subsistence;

pourvoir à la ~ **de qn** to keep sb, provide for sb's subsistence *ou* keep.

subsister [sübzēstā] *vi* (*rester*) to remain, subsist; (*vivre*) to live; (*survivre*) to live on.

substance [süpstáns] *nf* substance; **en** ~ in substance.

substantiel, le [süpstánsyel] *a* substantial.

substantif [süpstántēf] *nm* noun, substantive.

substantiver [süpstántēvā] *vt* to nominalize.

substituer [süpstētüā] *vt*: ~ **qn/qch à** to substitute sb/sth for; **se** ~ **à qn** (*représenter*) to substitute for sb; (*évincer*) to substitute o.s. for sb.

substitut [süpstētü] *nm* (*JUR*) assistant district attorney (*US*), deputy public prosecutor (*Brit*); (*succédané*) substitute.

substitution [süpstētüsyôñ] *nf* substitution.

subterfuge [süpterfüzh] *nm* subterfuge.

subtil, e [süptēl] *a* subtle.

subtilement [süptēlmáñ] *ad* subtly.

subtiliser [süptēlēzā] *vt*: ~ **qch (à qn)** to spirit sth away (from sb).

subtilité [süptēlētā] *nf* subtlety.

suburbain, e [sübürbañ, -en] *a* suburban.

subvenir [sübvənēr]: ~ **à** *vt* to meet.

subvention [sübvánsyôñ] *nf* subsidy, grant.

subventionner [sübvánsyonā] *vt* to subsidize.

subversif, ive [sübversēf, -ēv] *a* subversive.

subversion [sübversyôñ] *nf* subversion.

suc [sük] *nm* (*BOT*) sap; (*de viande, fruit*) juice; ~**s gastriques** gastric juices.

succédané [süksādánā] *nm* substitute.

succéder [süksādā]: ~ **à** *vt* (*directeur, roi etc*) to succeed; (*venir après: dans une série*) to follow, succeed; **se** ~ *vi* (*accidents, années*) to follow one another.

succès [sükse] *nm* success; **avec** ~ successfully; **sans** ~ unsuccessfully; **avoir du** ~ to be a success, be successful; **à** ~ successful; **livre à** ~ bestseller; ~ **de librairie** bestseller; ~ **(féminins)** conquests.

successeur [süksāser] *nm* successor.

successif, ive [süksāsēf, -ēv] *a* successive.

succession [süksāsyôñ] *nf* (*série, POL*) succession; (*JUR: patrimoine*) estate, inheritance; **prendre la** ~ **de** (*directeur*) to succeed, take over from; (*entreprise*) to take over.

successivement [süksāsēvmáñ] *ad* successively.

succinct, e [süksañ, -añt] *a* succinct.

succinctement [süksañtmáñ] *ad* succinctly.

succion [süksyôñ] *nf*: **bruit de** ~ sucking noise.

succomber [sükôñbā] *vi* to die, succumb; (*fig*): ~ **à** to give way to, succumb to.

succulent, e [sükülá, -áñt] *a* succulent.

succursale [sükürsál] *nf* branch; **magasin à** ~**s multiples** chain store.

sucer [süsā] *vt* to suck.

sucette [süset] *nf* (*bonbon*) lollipop; (*de bébé*) pacifier (*US*), dummy (*Brit*).

suçoter [süsotā] *vt* to suck.

sucre [sükr(ə)] *nm* (*substance*) sugar; (*morceau*) lump of sugar, sugar lump *ou* cube; ~ **de canne/betterave** cane/beet sugar; ~ **en morceaux/cristallisé/en poudre** lump *ou* cube/granulated/powdered (*US*) *ou* caster (*Brit*) sugar; ~ **glace** confectioners' (*US*) *ou* icing (*Brit*) sugar; ~ **d'orge** barley

sugar.

sucré, e [sükrā] *a* (*produit alimentaire*) sweetened; (*au goût*) sweet; (*péj*) sugary, honeyed.

sucrer [sükrā] *vt* (*thé, café*) to sweeten, put sugar in; ~ **qn** to put sugar in sb's tea (*ou* coffee *etc*); **se** ~ to help o.s. to sugar, have some sugar; (*fam*) to line one's pocket(s).

sucrerie [sükrərē] *nf* (*usine*) sugar refinery; ~**s** *nfpl* (*bonbons*) sweets, sweet things.

sucrier, ière [sükrēyā, -yer] *a* (*industrie*) sugar *cpd*; (*région*) sugar-producing ♦ *nm* (*fabricant*) sugar producer; (*récipient*) sugar bowl.

sud [süd] *nm*: **le** ~ the south ♦ *a inv* south; (*côte*) south, southern; **au** ~ (*situation*) in the south; (*direction*) to the south; **au** ~ **de** (to the) south of.

sud-africain, e [südáfrēkañ, -en] *a* South African ♦ *nm/f*: **Sud-Africain, e** South African.

sud-américain, e [südámārēkañ, -en] *a* South American ♦ *nm/f*: **Sud-Américain, e** South American.

sudation [südásyôñ] *nf* sweating, sudation.

sud-coréen, ne [südkorāañ, -en] *a* South Korean ♦ *nm/f*: **Sud-Coréen, ne** South Korean.

sud-est [südest] *nm, a inv* southeast.

sud-ouest [südwest] *nm, a inv* southwest.

sud-vietnamien, ne [südvyetnámyañ, -en] *a* South Vietnamese ♦ *nm/f*: **Sud-Vietnamien, ne** South Vietnamese.

Suède [süed] *nf*: **la** ~ Sweden.

suédois, e [süādwá, -wáz] *a* Swedish ♦ *nm* (*LING*) Swedish ♦ *nm/f*: **S**~, **e** Swede.

suer [süā] *vi* to sweat; (*suinter*) to ooze ♦ *vt* (*fig*) to exude; ~ **à grosses gouttes** to sweat profusely.

sueur [süer] *nf* sweat; **en** ~ sweating, in a sweat; **avoir des** ~**s froides** to be in a cold sweat.

suffire [süfēr] *vi* (*être assez*): ~ **(à qn/pour qch/pour faire)** to be enough *ou* sufficient (for sb/for sth/to do); (*satisfaire*): **cela lui suffit** he's content with this, this is enough for him; **se** ~ *vi* to be self-sufficient; **cela suffit pour les irriter/qu'ils se fâchent** it's enough to annoy them/for them to get angry; **il suffit d'une négligence/qu'on oublie pour que ...** it only takes one act of carelessness/one only needs to forget for ...; **ça suffit!** that's enough!, that'll do!

suffisamment [süfēzámáñ] *ad* sufficiently, enough; ~ **de** sufficient, enough.

suffisance [süfēzáñs] *nf* (*vanité*) self-importance, bumptiousness; (*quantité*): **en** ~ in plenty.

suffisant, e [süfēzáñ, -áñt] *a* (*temps, ressources*) sufficient; (*résultats*) satisfactory; (*vaniteux*) self-important, bumptious.

suffisons [süfēzôñ] *etc vb voir* **suffire**.

suffixe [süfēks(ə)] *nm* suffix.

suffocant, e [süfokáñ, -áñt] *a* (*étouffant*) suffocating; (*stupéfiant*) staggering.

suffocation [süfokásyôñ] *nf* suffocation.

suffoquer [süfokā] *vt* to choke, suffocate; (*stupéfier*) to stagger, astound ♦ *vi* to choke, suffocate; ~ **de colère/d'indignation** to choke with anger/indignation.

suffrage [süfräzh] *nm* (*POL*: *voix*) vote; (: *méthode*): ~ **universel/direct/indirect** universal/direct/indirect suffrage; (*du public etc*) approval *q*; ~**s exprimés** cast (*US*) *ou* valid (*Brit*) votes.

suggérer [sügzhārā] *vt* to suggest; ~ **que/de faire** to suggest that/doing.

suggestif, ive [sügzhestēf, -ēv] *a* suggestive.

suggestion [sügzhestyôn] *nf* suggestion.

suicidaire [süēsēder] *a* suicidal.

suicide [süēsēd] *nm* suicide ♦ *a*: **opération** ~ suicide mission.

suicidé, e [süēsēdā] *nm/f* suicide.

suicider [süēsēdā]: **se** ~ *vi* to commit suicide.

suie [süē] *nf* soot.

suif [süēf] *nm* tallow.

suinter [süantā] *vi* to ooze.

suis [süē] *vb voir* **être, suivre**.

suisse [süēs] *a* Swiss ♦ *nm* (*bedeau*) ≈ verger ♦ *nm/f*: **S**~ Swiss *pl inv* ♦ *nf*: **la S**~ Switzerland; **la S**~ **romande/allemande** French-speaking/German-speaking Switzerland; ~ **romand** Swiss French.

suisse-allemand, e [süēsálmán, -ánd] *a*, *nm/f* Swiss German.

Suissesse [süēses] *nf* Swiss (woman *ou* girl).

suit [süē] *vb voir* **suivre**.

suite [süēt] *nf* (*continuation: d'énumération etc*) rest, remainder; (: *de feuilleton*) continuation; (: *second film etc sur le même thème*) sequel; (*série: de maisons, succès*): **une** ~ **de** a series *ou* succession of; (*MATH*) series *sg*; (*conséquence*) result; (*ordre, liaison logique*) coherence; (*appartement, MUS*) suite; (*escorte*) retinue, suite; ~**s** *nfpl* (*d'une maladie etc*) effects; **prendre la** ~ **de** (*directeur etc*) to succeed, take over from; **faire** ~ **à** to follow; (*faisant*) ~ **à votre lettre du ...** with reference to your letter of the ...; **sans** ~ *a* incoherent, disjointed ♦ *ad* incoherently, disjointedly; **de** ~ *ad* (*d'affilée*) in succession; (*immédiatement*) at once; **par la** ~ afterwards, subsequently; **à la** ~ *ad* one after the other; **à la** ~ **de** (*derrière*) behind; (*en conséquence de*) following; **par** ~ **de** owing to, as a result of; **avoir de la** ~ **dans les idées** to show great singleness of purpose; **attendre la** ~ **des événements** to (wait and see) what happens.

suivant, e [süēván, -ánt] *vb voir* **suivre** ♦ *a* next, following; (*ci-après*): **l'exercice** ~ the following exercise ♦ *prép* (*selon*) according to; ~ **que** according to whether; **au** ~! next!

suive [süēv] *etc vb voir* **suivre**.

suiveur [süēvœr] *nm* (*CYCLISME*) (official) follower; (*péj*) (camp) follower.

suivi, e [süēvē] *pp de* **suivre** ♦ *a* (*régulier*) regular; (*COMM: article*) in general production; (*cohérent*) consistent; coherent ♦ *nm* follow-up; **très/peu** ~ (*cours*) well-/poorly-attended; (*mode*) widely/not widely adopted; (*feuilleton etc*) widely/not widely followed.

suivre [süēvr(ə)] *vt* (*gén*) to follow; (*SCOL: cours*) to attend; (: *leçon*) to follow, attend to; (: *programme*) to keep up with; (*COMM: article*) to continue to stock ♦ *vi* to follow; (*élève: écouter*) to attend, pay attention; (: *assimiler le programme*) to keep up, follow;

se ~ (*accidents, personnes, voitures etc*) to follow one after the other; (*raisonnement*) to be coherent; ~ **des yeux** to follow with one's eyes; **faire** ~ (*lettre*) to forward; ~ **son cours** (*suj: enquête etc*) to run *ou* take its course; **"à** ~**"** "to be continued".

sujet, te [süzhe, -et] *a*: **être** ~ **à** (*accidents*) to be prone to; (*vertige etc*) to be liable *ou* subject to ♦ *nm/f* (*d'un souverain*) subject ♦ *nm* subject; **un** ~ **de dispute/discorde/mécontentement** a cause for argument/dissension/dissatisfaction; **c'est à quel** ~**?** what is it about?; **avoir** ~ **de se plaindre** to have cause for complaint; **au** ~ **de** *prép* about; ~ **à caution** *a* questionable; ~ **de conversation** topic *ou* subject of conversation; ~ **d'examen** (*SCOL*) examination question; examination paper; ~ **d'expérience** (*BIO etc*) experimental subject.

sujétion [süzhāsyôn] *nf* subjection; (*fig*) constraint.

sulfater [sülfātā] *vt* to spray with copper sulphate.

sulfureux, euse [sülfürœ, -œz] *a* sulfurous (*US*), sulphurous (*Brit*).

sulfurique [sülfürēk] *a*: **acide** ~ sulfuric (*US*) *ou* sulphuric (*Brit*) acid.

sulfurisé, e [sülfürēzā] *a*: **papier** ~ wax (*US*) *ou* greaseproof (*Brit*) paper.

Sumatra [sümātrá] *nf* Sumatra.

summum [somom] *nm*: **le** ~ **de** the height of.

super [süper] *a inv* great, fantastic ♦ *nm* (= *supercarburant*) ≈ premium (*US*), ≈ 4-star (*Brit*).

superbe [süperb(ə)] *a* magnificent, superb ♦ *nf* arrogance.

superbement [süperbəmán] *ad* superbly.

supercarburant [süperkárbürán] *nm* ≈ premium gas (*US*), ≈ 4-star petrol (*Brit*).

supercherie [süpershərē] *nf* trick, trickery *q*; (*fraude*) fraud.

supérette [süpáret] *nf* minimarket.

superfétatoire [süperfātátwár] *a* superfluous.

superficie [süperfēsē] *nf* (*surface*) area; (*fig*) surface.

superficiel, le [süperfēsyel] *a* superficial.

superficiellement [süperfēsyelmán] *ad* superficially.

superflu, e [süperflü] *a* superfluous ♦ *nm*: **le** ~ the superfluous.

superforme [süperform(ə)] *nf* (*fam*) top form, excellent shape.

super-grand [süpergrán] *nm* superpower.

super-huit [süperüēt] *a*: **camera/film** ~ super-eight camera/film.

supérieur, e [süpáryœr] *a* (*lèvre, étages, classes*) upper; (*plus élevé: température, niveau*): ~ **(à)** higher (than); (*meilleur: qualité, produit*): ~ **(à)** superior (to); (*excellent, hautain*) superior ♦ *nm*, *nf* superior; **Mère** ~**e** Mother Superior; **à l'étage** ~ on the next floor up; ~ **en nombre** superior in number.

supérieurement [süpáryœrmán] *ad* exceptionally well, exceptionally + *adj*.

supériorité [süpáryorētā] *nf* superiority.

superlatif [süperlátēf] *nm* superlative.

supermarché [süpermárshā] *nm* supermarket.

superposable [süperpōzábl(ə)] *a* (*figures*) that

may be superimposed; (*lits*) stackable.

superposer [süperpōzā] *vt* to superpose; (*meubles, caisses*) to stack; (*faire chevaucher*) to superimpose; **se ~** (*images, souvenirs*) to be superimposed; **lits superposés** bunk beds.

superposition [süperpōzēsyôń] *nf* superposition; superimposition.

superpréfet [süperprāfe] *nm prefect in charge of a region.*

superproduction [süperprodüksyôń] *nf* (*film*) spectacular.

superpuissance [süperpüēsâńs] *nf* superpower.

supersonique [süpersonēk] *a* supersonic.

superstitieux, euse [süperstēsyœ̄, -œ̄z] *a* superstitious.

superstition [süperstēsyôń] *nf* superstition.

superstructure [süperstrüktür] *nf* superstructure.

supertanker [süpertâńkœr] *nm* supertanker.

superviser [süpervēzā] *vt* to supervise.

supervision [süpervēzyôń] *nf* supervision.

supplanter [süplâńtā] *vt* to supplant.

suppléance [süplāâńs] *nf* (*poste*) substitute teacher's post (*US*), supply post (*Brit*).

suppléant, e [süplāâń, -âńt] *a* (*juge, fonctionnaire*) deputy *cpd*; (*professeur*) substitute *cpd* (*US*), supply *cpd* (*Brit*) ♦ *nm/f* deputy; substitute *ou* supply teacher; **médecin ~** locum tenens.

suppléer [süplāā] *vt* (*ajouter: mot manquant etc*) to supply, provide; (*compenser: lacune*) to fill in; (*: défaut*) to make up for; (*remplacer: professeur*) to stand in for; (*: juge*) to deputize for; **~ à** *vt* to make up for; to substitute for.

supplément [süplāmâń] *nm* supplement; **un ~ de travail** extra *ou* additional work; **un ~ de frites** *etc* an extra portion of French fries *etc*; **un ~ de 100 F** a supplement of 100 F, an extra *ou* additional 100 F; **ceci est en ~** (*au menu etc*) this is extra, there is an extra charge for this; **~ d'information** additional information.

supplémentaire [süplāmâńter] *a* additional, further; (*train, bus*) relief *cpd*, extra.

supplétif, ive [süplātēf, -ēv] *a* (*MIL*) auxiliary.

suppliant, e [süplēyâń, -âńt] *a* imploring.

supplication [süplēkâsyôń] *nf* (*REL*) supplication; **~s** *nfpl* (*adjurations*) pleas, entreaties.

supplice [süplēs] *nm* (*peine corporelle*) torture *q*; form of torture; (*douleur physique, morale*) torture, agony; **être au ~** to be in agony.

supplier [süplēyā] *vt* to implore, beseech.

supplique [süplēk] *nf* petition.

support [süpor] *nm* support; (*pour livre, outils*) stand; **~ audio-visuel** audio-visual aid; **~ publicitaire** advertising medium.

supportable [süportábl(ə)] *a* (*douleur, température*) bearable; (*procédé, conduite*) tolerable.

supporter *nm* [süporter] supporter, fan ♦ *vt* [süportā] (*poids, poussée, SPORT: concurrent, équipe*) to support; (*conséquences, épreuve*) to bear, endure; (*défauts, personne*) to tolerate, put up with; (*suj: chose: chaleur etc*) to withstand; (*suj: personne: chaleur, vin*) to take.

supposé, e [süpōzā] *a* (*nombre*) estimated; (*auteur*) supposed.

supposer [süpōzā] *vt* to suppose; (*impliquer*) to presuppose; **en supposant** *ou* **à ~ que** supposing (that).

supposition [süpōzēsyôń] *nf* supposition.

suppositoire [süpōzētwár] *nm* suppository.

suppôt [süpō] *nm* (*péj*) henchman.

suppression [süprāsyôń] *nf* (*voir supprimer*) removal; deletion; cancellation; suppression.

supprimer [süprēmā] *vt* (*cloison, cause, anxiété*) to remove; (*clause, mot*) to delete; (*congés, service d'autobus etc*) to cancel; (*publication, article*) to suppress; (*emplois, privilèges, témoin gênant*) to do away with; **~ qch à qn** to deprive sb of sth.

suppurer [süpürā] *vi* to suppurate.

supputations [süpütâsyôń] *nfpl* calculations, reckonings.

supputer [süpütā] *vt* to calculate, reckon.

supranational, e, aux [süprànásyonál, -ō] *a* supranational.

suprématie [süprāmásē] *nf* supremacy.

suprême [süprem] *a* supreme.

suprêmement [süpremmâń] *ad* supremely.

sur [sür] *prép* (*gén*) on; (*par-dessus*) over; (*au-dessus*) above; (*direction*) towards; (*à propos de*) about, on; **un ~ 10** one out of 10, one in 10; (*SCOL*) one out of 10; **4m ~ 2** 4m by 2; **~ sa recommandation/leur invitation** on his (*ou* her) recommendation/their invitation; **avoir accident ~ accident** to have accident after accident; **je n'ai pas d'argent ~ moi** I haven't got any money with *ou* on me; **~ ce** *ad* hereupon.

sur, e [sür] *a* sour.

sûr, e [sür] *a* sure, certain; (*digne de confiance*) reliable; (*sans danger*) safe; **peu ~** unreliable; **~ de qch** sure *ou* certain of sth; **être ~ de qn** to be sure of sb; **~ et certain** absolutely certain; **~ de soi** self-assured, self-confident; **le plus ~ est de** the safest thing is to.

surabondant, e [sürábôńdâń, -âńt] *a* overabundant.

surabonder [sürábôńdā] *vi* to be overabundant; **~ de** to abound with, have an overabundance of.

suractivité [süráktēvētā] *nf* hyperactivity.

suraigu, ë [sürāgü] *a* very shrill.

surajouter [sürázhōōtā] *vt*: **~ qch à** to add sth to.

suralimenté, e [sürálēmâńtā] *a* (*personne*) overfed; (*moteur*) turbocharged.

suranné, e [süránā] *a* outdated, outmoded.

surarmement [sürárməmâń] *nm* (excess) stockpiling of arms (*ou* weapons).

surbaissé, e [sürbāsā] *a* lowered, low.

surcharge [sürshárzh(ə)] *nf* (*de passagers, marchandises*) excess load; (*de détails, d'ornements*) overabundance, excess; (*correction*) alteration; (*POSTES*) surcharge; **prendre des passagers en ~** to take on excess *ou* extra passengers; **~ de bagages** excess luggage; **~ de travail** extra work.

surchargé, e [sürshárzhā] *a* (*décoration, style*) over-elaborate, overfussy; (*voiture, emploi du temps*) overloaded.

surcharger [sürshárzhā] *vt* to overload; (*timbre-poste*) to surcharge; (*décoration*) to overdo.

surchauffe [sürshōf] *nf* overheating.

surchauffé, e [sürshōfā] *a* overheated; (*fig: imagination*) overactive.

surchoix [sürshwà] *a inv* top-quality.

surclasser [sürklâsā] *vt* to outclass.

surconsommation [sürkôṅsomâsyôṅ] *nf* (*ÉCON*) overconsumption.

surcoté, e [sürkotā] *a* overpriced.

surcouper [sürkōōpā] *vt* to overtrump.

surcroît [sürkrwá] *nm*: **un ~ de** additional + *nom*; **par** *ou* **de ~** moreover; **en ~** in addition.

surdi-mutité [sürdēmütētā] *nf*: **atteint de ~** deaf and dumb.

surdité [sürdētā] *nf* deafness; **atteint de ~ totale** profoundly deaf.

surdoué, e [surdwā] *a* gifted.

sureau, x [sürō] *nm* elder (tree).

sureffectif [sürāfektēf] *nm* overmanning.

surélever [sürelvā] *vt* to raise, heighten.

sûrement [sürmáṅ] *ad* reliably; safely, securely; (*certainement*) certainly; **~ pas** certainly not.

suremploi [süráṅplwá] *nm* (*ÉCON*) over-employment.

surenchère [süráṅsher] *nf* (*aux enchères*) higher bid; (*sur prix fixe*) overbid; (*fig*) overstatement; outbidding tactics *pl*; **~ de violence** build-up of violence; **~ électorale** political (*ou* electoral) one-upmanship.

surenchérir [süráṅshārēr] *vi* to bid higher; to raise one's bid; (*fig*) to try and outbid each other.

surent [sür] *vb voir* **savoir**.

suréquipé, e [sürākēpā] *a* overequipped.

surestimer [sürestēmā] *vt* (*tableau*) to overvalue; (*possibilité, personne*) to overestimate.

sûreté [sürtā] *nf* (*voir* **sûr**) reliability; safety; (*JUR*) guaranty; surety; **mettre en ~** to put in a safe place; **pour plus de ~** as an extra precaution; to be on the safe side; **la ~ de l'État** State security; **la S~** (**nationale**) *division of the Ministère de l'Intérieur heading all police forces except the gendarmerie and the Paris préfecture de police.*

surexcité, e [süreksētā] *a* overexcited.

surexploiter [süreksplwátā] *vt* to overexploit.

surexposer [sürekspōzā] *vt* to overexpose.

surf [sœrf] *nm* surfing; **faire du ~** to go surfing.

surface [sürfás] *nf* surface; (*superficie*) surface area; **faire ~** to surface; **en ~** *ad* near the surface; (*fig*) superficially; **la pièce fait 100m² de ~** the room has a surface area of 100m²; **~ de réparation** (*SPORT*) penalty area; **~ porteuse** *ou* **de sustentation** (*AVIAT*) airfoil (*US*), aerofoil (*Brit*).

surfait, e [sürfe, -et] *a* overrated.

surfiler [sürfēlā] *vt* (*COUTURE*) to oversew.

surfin, e [sürfaṅ, -ēn] *a* superfine.

surgélateur [sürzhālátœr] *nm* deep freeze.

surgelé, e [sürzhəlā] *a* (deep-)frozen.

surgeler [sürzhəlā] *vt* to (deep-)freeze.

surgir [sürzhēr] *vi* (*personne, véhicule*) to appear suddenly; (*jaillir*) to shoot up; (*montagne etc*) to rise up, loom up; (*fig: problème, conflit*) to arise.

surhomme [sürom] *nm* superman.

surhumain, e [sürümaṅ, -en] *a* superhuman.

surimposer [süraṅpōzā] *vt* to overtax.

surimpression [süraṅprāsyôṅ] *nf* (*PHOTO*) double exposure; **en ~** superimposed.

surimprimer [süraṅprēmā] *vt* to overstrike, overprint.

Surinam [sürēnám] *nm*: **le ~** Surinam.

surinfection [süraṅfeksyôṅ] *nf* (*MÉD*) secondary infection.

surjet [sürzhe] *nm* (*COUTURE*) overcast seam.

sur-le-champ [sürləshàṅ] *ad* immediately.

surlendemain [sürlàṅdmaṅ] *nm*: **le ~** (**soir**) two days later (in the evening); **le ~ de** two days after.

surligneur [sürlēnyœr] *nm* (*feutre*) highlighter (pen).

surmenage [sürmənázh] *nm* overwork; **le ~ intellectuel** mental fatigue.

surmené, e [sürmənā] *a* overworked.

surmener [sürmənā] *vt*, **se ~** *vi* to overwork.

surmonter [sürmôṅtā] *vt* (*suj: coupole etc*) to surmount, top; (*vaincre*) to overcome, surmount.

surmultiplié, c [sürmültēplcyā] *a*, *nf*: (**vitesse**) **~e** overdrive.

surnager [sürnázhā] *vi* to float.

surnaturel, le [sürnátürel] *a*, *nm* supernatural.

surnom [sürnôṅ] *nm* nickname.

surnombre [sürnôṅbr(ə)] *nm*: **être en ~** to be too many (*ou* one too many).

surnommer [sürnomā] *vt* to nickname.

surnuméraire [sürnümārer] *nm/f* supernumerary.

suroît [sürwà] *nm* sou'wester.

surpasser [sürpâsā] *vt* to surpass; **se ~** to surpass o.s., excel o.s.

surpayer [sürpáyā] *vt* (*personne*) to overpay; (*article etc*) to pay too much for.

surpeuplé, e [sürpœplā] *a* overpopulated.

surpeuplement [sürpœpləmàṅ] *nm* overpopulation.

surpiquer [sürpēkā] *vt* (*COUTURE*) to topstitch.

surpiqûre [sürpēkür] *nf* (*COUTURE*) topstitching.

surplace [sürplás] *nm*: **faire du ~** to mark time.

surplis [sürplē] *nm* surplice.

surplomb [sürplôṅ] *nm* overhang; **en ~** overhanging.

surplomber [sürplôṅbā] *vi* to be overhanging ♦ *vt* to overhang; (*dominer*) to tower above.

surplus [sürplü] *nm* (*COMM*) surplus; (*reste*): **~ de bois** wood left over; **au ~** moreover; **~ américains** American army surplus *sg*.

surpopulation [sürpopülâsyôṅ] *nf* overpopulation.

surprenant, e [sürprənàṅ, -àṅt] *vb voir* **surprendre** ♦ *a* amazing.

surprendre [sürpràṅdr(ə)] *vt* (*étonner, prendre à l'improviste*) to amaze, surprise; (*secret*) to discover; (*tomber sur: intrus etc*) to catch; (*fig*) to detect; to chance *ou* happen upon; (*clin d'œil*) to intercept; (*conversation*) to overhear; (*suj: orage, nuit etc*) to catch (out (*Brit*)), take by surprise; **~ la**

vigilance/bonne foi de qn to catch sb off guard/betray sb's good faith; **se ~ à faire** to catch *ou* find o.s. doing.

surprime [sürprēm] *nf* additional premium.

surpris, e [sürprē, -ēz] *pp de* **surprendre** ♦ *a:* **~ (de/que)** amazed *ou* surprised (at/that).

surprise [sürprēz] *nf* surprise; **faire une ~ à qn** to give sb a surprise; **voyage sans ~s** uneventful journey; **par ~** *ad* by surprise.

surprise-partie [sürprēzpártē] *nf* party.

surprit [sürprē] *vb voir* **surprendre**.

surproduction [sürprodüksyôn] *nf* overproduction.

surréaliste [sürrāálēst(ə)] *a, nm/f* surrealist.

sursaut [sürsō] *nm* start, jump; **~ de** (*énergie, indignation*) sudden fit *ou* burst of; **en ~** *ad* with a start.

sursauter [sürsōtā] *vi* to (give a) start, jump.

surseoir [sürswár]: **~ à** *vt* to defer; (*JUR*) to stay.

sursis [sürsē] *nm* (*JUR:* *gén*) suspended sentence; (*à l'exécution capitale, aussi fig*) reprieve; (*MIL*): **~ (d'appel** *ou* **d'incorporation)** deferment; **condamné à 5 mois (de prison) avec ~** given a 5-month suspended (prison) sentence.

sursitaire [sürsēter] *nm* (*MIL*) deferred draftee.

sursois [sürswà], **sursoyais** [sürswàyā] *etc vb voir* **surseoir**.

surtaxe [sürtáks(ə)] *nf* surcharge.

surtout [sürtōō] *ad* (*avant tout, d'abord*) above all; (*spécialement, particulièrement*) especially; **il aime le sport, ~ le football** he likes sports, especially football; **cet été, il a ~ fait de la pêche** this summer he went fishing more than anything (else); **~ pas d'histoires!** no fuss now!; **~, ne dites rien!** whatever you do - don't say anything!; **~ pas!** certainly *ou* definitely not!; **~ que ...** especially as ....

survécu, e [sürvākü] *pp de* **survivre**.

surveillance [sürveyáns] *nf* watch; (*POLICE, MIL*) surveillance; **sous ~ médicale** under medical supervision; **la ~ du territoire** internal security; *voir aussi* **DST**.

surveillant, e [sürvēyáń, -áńt] *nm/f* (*de prison*) guard, warder (*Brit*); (*SCOL*) monitor; (*de travaux*) supervisor, overseer.

surveiller [sürvāyā] *vt* (*enfant, élèves, bagages*) to watch, keep an eye on; (*malade*) to watch over; (*prisonnier, suspect*) to keep (a) watch on; (*territoire, bâtiment*) to (keep) watch over; (*travaux, cuisson*) to supervise; (*SCOL: examen*) to proctor (*US*), invigilate (*Brit*); **se ~** to keep a check *ou* watch on o.s.; **~ son langage/sa ligne** to watch one's language/figure.

survenir [sürvənēr] *vi* (*incident, retards*) to occur, arise; (*événement*) to take place; (*personne*) to appear, arrive.

survenu, e [sürv(ə)nü] *pp de* **survenir**.

survêt(ement) [sürvet(máń)] *nm* sweat suit (*US*), tracksuit (*Brit*).

survie [sürvē] *nf* survival; (*REL*) afterlife; **équipement de ~** survival equipment; **une ~ de quelques mois** a few more months of life.

surviens [sürvyań], **survint** [sürvań] *etc vb voir*

survenir.

survit [sōōrvē] *etc vb voir* **survivre**.

survitrage [sürvētrázh] *nm* insulating (window) (*US*), double-glazing (*Brit*).

survivance [sürvēváńs] *nf* relic.

survivant, e [sürvēváń, -áńt] *vb voir* **survivre** ♦ *nm/f* survivor.

survivre [sürvēvr(ə)] *vi* to survive; **~ à** *vt* (*accident etc*) to survive; (*personne*) to outlive; **la victime a peu de chance de ~** the victim has little hope of survival.

survol [sürvol] *nm* flying over.

survoler [sürvolā] *vt* to fly over; (*fig: livre*) to skim through; (*: question, problèmes*) to skim over.

survolté, e [sürvoltā] *a* (*ÉLEC*) stepped up, boosted; (*fig*) worked up.

sus [sü(s)]: **en ~ de** *prép* in addition to, over and above; **en ~** *ad* in addition; **~ à** *excl:* **~ au tyran!** at the tyrant! ♦ *vb* [sü] *voir* **savoir**.

susceptibilité [süseptēbēlētā] *nf* sensitivity *q*.

susceptible [süseptēbl(ə)] *a* touchy, sensitive; **~ d'amélioration** *ou* **d'être amélioré** that can be improved, open to improvement; **~ de faire** (*capacité*) able to do; (*probabilité*) liable to do.

susciter [süsētā] *vt* (*admiration*) to arouse; (*obstacles, ennuis*): **~ (à qn)** to create (for sb).

susdit, e [süsdē, -dēt] *a* aforesaid.

susmentionné, e [süsmáńsyonā] *a* abovementioned.

susnommé, e [süsnomā] *a* above-named.

suspect, e [süspe(kt), -ekt(ə)] *a* suspicious; (*témoignage, opinions, vin etc*) suspect ♦ *nm/f* suspect; **peu ~ de** most unlikely to be suspected of.

suspecter [süspektā] *vt* to suspect; (*honnêteté de qn*) to question, have one's suspicions about; **~ qn d'être/d'avoir fait qch** to suspect sb of being/having done sth.

suspendre [süspáńdr(ə)] *vt* (*accrocher: vêtement*): **~ qch (à)** to hang sth up (on); (*fixer: lustre etc*): **~ qch à** to hang sth from; (*interrompre, démettre*) to suspend; (*remettre*) to defer; **se ~ à** to hang from.

suspendu, e [süspáńdü] *pp de* **suspendre** ♦ *a* (*accroché*): **~ à** hanging on (*ou* from); (*perché*): **~ au-dessus de** suspended over; (*AUTO*): **bien/mal ~** with good/poor suspension; **être ~ aux lèvres de qn** to hang upon sb's every word.

suspens [süspáń]: **en ~** *ad* (*affaire*) in abeyance; **tenir en ~** to keep in suspense.

suspense [süspáńs] *nm* suspense.

suspension [süspáńsyôń] *nf* suspension; deferment; (*AUTO*) suspension; (*lustre*) pendant lamp; **en ~** in suspension, suspended; **~ d'audience** adjournment.

suspicieux, eux [süspēsyö́, -ēz] *a* suspicious.

suspicion [süspēsyôń] *nf* suspicion.

sustenter [süstáńtā]: **se ~** *vi* to take sustenance.

susurrer [süsürā] *vt* to whisper.

sut [sü] *vb voir* **savoir**.

suture [sütür] *nf:* **point de ~** stitch.

suturer [sütürā] *vt* to stitch up, suture.

suzeraineté [süzrentā] *nf* suzerainty.

svelte [svelt(ə)] *a* slender, svelte.

SVP *sigle* (= *s'il vous plaît*) please.

Swaziland [swàzēlånd] *nm*: **le** ~ Swaziland.

syllabe [sēlàb] *nf* syllable.

syllaber [sēlàbā] *vi* to pronounce syllable by syllable.

sylvestre [sēlvestr(ə)] *a*: **pin** ~ Scots pine, Scotch fir.

sylvicole [sēlvēkol] *a* forestry *cpd*.

sylviculteur [sēlvēkültœr] *nm* forester.

sylviculture [sēlvēkültür] *nf* forestry, silviculture.

symbole [sañbol] *nm* symbol; ~ **graphique** (*INFORM*) icon.

symbolique [sañbolēk] *a* symbolic; (*geste, offrande*) token *cpd*; (*salaire, dommages-intérêts*) nominal.

symboliquement [sañbolēkmåñ] *ad* symbolically.

symboliser [sañbolēzā] *vt* to symbolize.

symétrie [sēmātrē] *nf* symmetry.

symétrique [sēmātrēk] *a* symmetrical.

symétriquement [sēmātrēkmåñ] *ad* symmetrically.

sympa [sañpà] *a inv* (= *sympathique*) nice; friendly; good.

sympathie [sañpàtē] *nf* (*inclination*) liking; (*affinité*) fellow feeling; (*condoléances*) sympathy; **accueillir avec** ~ (*projet*) to receive favorably; **avoir de la** ~ **pour qn** to like sb, have a liking for sb; **témoignages de** ~ expressions of sympathy; **croyez à toute ma** ~ you have my deepest sympathy.

sympathique [sañpàtēk] *a* (*personne, figure*) nice, friendly, likeable; (*geste*) friendly; (*livre*) good; (*déjeuner*) nice; (*réunion, endroit*) pleasant, nice.

sympathisant, e [sañpàtēzåñ, -åñt] *nm/f* sympathizer.

sympathiser [sañpàtēzā] *vi* (*voisins etc*: *s'entendre*) to get along (well); (: *se fréquenter*) to socialize, see each other; ~ **avec** to get on *ou* along (well) with; to see, socialize with.

symphonie [sañfonē] *nf* symphony.

symphonique [sañfonēk] *a* (*orchestre, concert*) symphony *cpd*; (*musique*) symphonic.

symposium [sañpōzyom] *nm* symposium.

symptomatique [sañptomàtēk] *a* symptomatic.

symptôme [sañptōm] *nm* symptom.

synagogue [sēnàgog] *nf* synagogue.

synchrone [sañkron] *a* synchronous.

synchronique [sañkronēk] *a*: **tableau** ~ synchronic table of events.

synchronisation [sañkronēzàsyôñ] *nf* synchronization.

synchronisé, e [sañkronēzā] *a* synchronized.

synchroniser [sañkronēzā] *vt* to synchronize.

syncope [sañkop] *nf* (*MÉD*) blackout; (*MUS*) syncopation; **tomber en** ~ to faint, pass out.

syncopé, e [sañkopā] *a* syncopated.

syndic [sañdēk] *nm* managing agent.

syndical, e, aux [sañdēkàl, -ō] *a* (labor) union *cpd* (*US*), (trade-)union *cpd* (*Brit*); **centrale** ~**e** group of affiliated labor unions.

syndicalisme [sañdēkàlēsm(ə)] *nm* (*mouvement*) labor (*US*) *ou* trade (*Brit*) unionism; (*activités*) union(ist) activities *pl*.

syndicaliste [sañdēkàlēst(ə)] *nm/f* labor (*US*)

ou trade (*Brit*) unionist.

syndicat [sañdēkà] *nm* (*d'ouvriers, employés*) (labor (*US*) *ou* trade(s) (*Brit*)) union; (*autre association d'intérêts*) union, association; ~ **d'initiative (SI)** tourist office *ou* bureau; ~ **patronal** employers' association, federation of employers; ~ **de propriétaires** association of property owners.

syndiqué, e [sañdēkà] *a* belonging to a union; **non** ~ non-union.

syndiquer [sañdēkà]: **se** ~ *vi* to form a labor (*US*) *ou* trade (*Brit*) union; (*adhérer*) to join a labor *ou* trade union.

syndrome [sañdrōm] *nm* syndrome; ~ **prémenstruel** premenstrual syndrome (PMS).

synergie [sēnerzhē] *nf* synergy.

synode [sēnod] *nm* synod.

synonyme [sēnonēm] *a* synonymous ♦ *nm* synonym; ~ **de** synonymous with.

synopsis [sēnopsēs] *nm ou nf* synopsis.

synoptique [sēnoptēk] *a*: **tableau** ~ synoptic table.

synovie [sēnovē] *nf* synovia; **épanchement de** ~ water on the knee.

syntaxe [sañtàks(ə)] *nf* syntax.

synthèse [sañtez] *nf* synthesis (*pl* -es); **faire la** ~ **de** to synthesize.

synthétique [sañtātēk] *a* synthetic.

synthétiser [sañtātēzā] *vt* to synthesize.

synthétiseur [sañtātēzœr] *nm* (*MUS*) synthesizer.

syphilis [sēfēlēs] *nf* syphilis.

Syrie [sērē] *nf*: **la** ~ Syria.

syrien, ne [sēryañ, -en] *a* Syrian ♦ *nm/f*: **S~, ne** Syrian.

systématique [sēstāmàtēk] *a* systematic.

systématiquement [sēstāmàtēkmåñ] *ad* systematically.

systématiser [sēstāmàtēzā] *vt* to systematize.

système [sēstem] *nm* system; **le** ~ **D** resourcefulness; ~ **décimal** decimal system; ~ **expert** expert system; ~ **d'exploitation à disques** (*INFORM*) disk operating system; ~ **métrique** metric system; ~ **solaire** solar system.

T

T, t [tā] *nm inv* T, t ♦ *abr* (= *tonne*) t; **T comme Thérèse** T for Tommy.

t' [t(ə)] *pronom voir* **te**.

ta [tà] *dét voir* **ton**.

tabac [tàbà] *nm* tobacco; (*aussi*: **débit** *ou* **bureau de** ~) tobacco shop (*US*), tobacconist's (shop) (*Brit*) ♦ *a inv*: (**couleur**) ~ buff, tobacco *cpd*; **passer qn à** ~ to beat sb up; **faire un** ~ (*fam*) to be a big hit; ~ **blond/brun** light/dark tobacco; ~ **gris** shag; ~ **à priser** snuff.

tabagie [tàbàzhē] *nf* smoke den.

tabagisme [tàbàzhēsm(ə)] *nm* nicotine addiction.

tabasser [tàbásā] *vt* to beat up.

tabatière [tàbàtyer] *nf* snuffbox.

tabernacle [tàbernàkl(ə)] *nm* tabernacle.

table [tàbl(ə)] *nf* table; **avoir une bonne** ~ to keep a good table; **à** ~! dinner *etc* is ready!; **se mettre à** ~ to sit down to eat; (*fig: fam*) to come clean; **mettre** *ou* **dresser/desservir la** ~ to lay *ou* set/clear the table; **faire** ~ **rase de** to make a clean sweep of; ~ **basse** coffee table; ~ **de cuisson** (*à l'électricité*) hotplate; (*au gas*) gas burner; ~ **d'écoute** wire-tapping set; ~ **d'harmonie** sounding board; ~ **d'hôte** set menu; ~ **de lecture** turntable; ~ **des matières** (table of) contents *pl*; ~ **de multiplication** multiplication table; ~ **de nuit** *ou* **de chevet** bedside table; ~ **ronde** (*débat*) round table; ~ **roulante** serving cart (*US*), (tea) trolley (*Brit*); ~ **de toilette** washstand; ~ **traçante** (*INFORM*) plotter.

tableau, x [tàblō] *nm* (*ART*) painting; (*reproduction, fig*) picture; (*panneau*) board; (*schéma*) table, chart; ~ **d'affichage** bulletin board; ~ **de bord** dashboard; (*AVIAT*) instrument panel; ~ **de chasse** tally; ~ **de contrôle** console, control panel; ~ **de maître** masterpiece; ~ **noir** blackboard.

tablée [tàblā] *nf* (*personnes*) table.

tabler [tàblā] *vi*: ~ **sur** to count *ou* bank on.

tablette [tàblet] *nf* (*planche*) shelf (*pl* shelves); ~ **de chocolat** bar of chocolate.

tableur [tàblœr] *nm* (*INFORM*) spreadsheet.

tablier [tàblēyā] *nm* apron; (*de pont*) roadway; (*de cheminée*) (flue-)shutter.

tabou, e [tàbōō] *a*, *nm* taboo.

tabouret [tàbōōre] *nm* stool.

tabulateur [tàbūlátœr] *nm* (*TECH*) tabulator.

TAC *sigle m* (= *train-auto-couchettes*) carsleeper train.

tac [tàk] *nm*: **du** ~ **au** ~ **tit** for tat.

tache [tàsh] *nf* (*saleté*) stain, mark; (*ART, de couleur, lumière*) spot; splash, patch; **faire** ~ **d'huile** to spread, gain ground; ~ **de rousseur** *ou* **de son** freckle; ~ **de vin** (*sur la peau*) strawberry mark.

tâche [tàsh] *nf* task; **travailler à la** ~ to do piecework.

tacher [tàshā] *vt* to stain, mark; (*fig*) to sully, stain; **se** ~ *vi* (*fruits*) to become marked.

tâcher [tàshā] *vi*: ~ **de faire** to try to do, endeavor (*US*) *ou* endeavour (*Brit*) to do.

tâcheron [tàshróň] *nm* (*fig*) drudge.

tacheté, e [tàshtā] *a*: ~ **de** speckled *ou* spotted with.

tachisme [tàshēsm(ə)] *nm* (*PEINTURE*) tachisme.

tachygraphe [tàkēgráf] *nm* tachograph.

tachymètre [tàkēmetr(ə)] *nm* tachometer.

tacite [tàsēt] *a* tacit.

tacitement [tàsētmáň] *ad* tacitly.

taciturne [tàsētürn(ə)] *a* taciturn.

tacot [tàkō] *nm* (*péj: voiture*) clunker (*US*), banger (*Brit*).

tact [tàkt] *nm* tact; **avoir du** ~ to be tactful, have tact.

tacticien, ne [tàktēsyaň, -en] *nm/f* tactician.

tactile [tàktēl] *a* tactile.

tactique [tàktēk] *a* tactical ♦ *nf* (*technique*) tactics *sg*; (*plan*) tactic.

taffetas [tàftà] *nm* taffeta.

Tage [tàzh] *nm*: **le** ~ the (river) Tagus.

Tahiti [tàētē] *nf* Tahiti.

tahitien, ne [tàēsyaň, -en] *a* Tahitian.

taie [te] *nf*: ~ **(d'oreiller)** pillowslip, pillowcase.

taillader [tàyádā] *vt* to gash.

taille [tày] *nf* cutting; pruning; (*milieu du corps*) waist; (*hauteur*) height; (*grandeur*) size; **de** ~ **à faire** capable of doing; **de** ~ *a* sizeable; **quelle** ~ **faites-vous?** what size are you?

taillé, e [tàyā] *a* (*moustache, ongles, arbre*) trimmed; ~ **pour** (*fait pour, apte à*) cut out for; tailor-made for; ~ **en pointe** sharpened to a point.

taille-crayon(s) [tàykreyóň] *nm inv* pencil sharpener.

tailler [tàyā] *vt* (*pierre, diamant*) to cut; (*arbre, plante*) to prune; (*vêtement*) to cut out; (*crayon*) to sharpen; **se** ~ *vt* (*ongles, barbe*) to trim, cut; (*fig: réputation*) to gain, win ♦ *vi* (*fam: s'enfuir*) to beat it; ~ **dans** (*chair, bois*) to cut into; ~ **grand/petit** to be on the large/small side.

tailleur [tàyœr] *nm* (*couturier*) tailor; (*vêtement*) suit, costume; **en** ~ (*assis*) cross-legged; ~ **de diamants** diamond-cutter.

tailleur-pantalon [tàyœrpáňtálóň] *nm* pant(s) (*US*) *ou* trouser (*Brit*) suit.

taillis [tàyē] *nm* copse.

tain [taň] *nm* silvering; **glace sans** ~ two-way mirror.

taire [ter] *vt* to keep to o.s., conceal ♦ *vi*: **faire** ~ **qn** to make sb be quiet; (*fig*) to silence sb; **se** ~ *vi* (*s'arrêter de parler*) to fall silent, stop talking; (*ne pas parler*) to be silent *ou* quiet; (*s'abstenir de s'exprimer*) to keep quiet; (*bruit, voix*) to disappear; **tais-toi!**, **taisez-vous!** be quiet!

Taiwan [tàywàn] *nf* Taiwan.

talc [tàlk] *nm* talc, talcum powder.

talé, e [tàlā] *a* (*fruit*) bruised.

talent [tàláň] *nm* talent; **avoir du** ~ to be talented, have talent.

talentueux, euse [tàláňtüœ, -œz] *a* talented.

talion [tàlyóň] *nm*: **la loi du** ~ an eye for an eye.

talisman [tàlēsmáň] *nm* talisman.

talkie-walkie [tokēwokē] *nm* walkie-talkie.

taloche [tàlosh] *nf* (*fam: claque*) slap; (*TECH*) plaster float.

talon [tàlóň] *nm* heel; (*de chèque, billet*) stub; ~**s plats/aiguilles** flat/stiletto heels; **être sur les** ~**s de qn** to be on sb's heels; **tourner les** ~**s** to turn on one's heel; **montrer les** ~**s** (*fig*) to show a clean pair of heels.

talonner [tàlonā] *vt* to follow hard behind; (*fig*) to hound; (*RUGBY*) to heel.

talonnette [tàlonet] *nf* (*de chaussure*) heelpiece; (*de pantalon*) stirrup.

talquer [tàlkā] *vt* to put talc(um powder) on.

talus [tàlü] *nm* embankment; ~ **de remblai/déblai** embankment/excavation slope.

tamarin [tàmàraň] *nm* (*BOT*) tamarind.

tambour [tàňbōōr] *nm* (*MUS, aussi TECH*) drum; (*musicien*) drummer; (*porte*) revolving door(s *pl*); **sans** ~ **ni trompette** unobtrusively.

tambourin [tãṅbōōrãṅ] *nm* tambourine.
tambouriner [tãṅbōōrēnā] *vi*: ~ **contre** to drum against *ou* on.
tambour-major, *pl* **tambours-majors** [tãṅbōōrmàzhor] *nm* drum major.
tamis [tàmē] *nm* sieve.
Tamise [tàmēz] *nf*: **la** ~ the Thames.
tamisé, e [tàmēzā] *a* (*fig*) subdued, soft.
tamiser [tàmēzā] *vt* to sieve, sift.
tampon [tãṅpôṅ] *nm* (*de coton, d'ouate*) pad; (*aussi*: ~ **hygiénique** *ou* **périodique**) tampon; (*amortisseur*, *INFORM*: *aussi*: **mémoire** ~) buffer; (*bouchon*) plug, stopper; (*cachet, timbre*) stamp; (*CHIMIE*) buffer; ~ **buvard** blotter; ~ **encreur** inking pad; ~ (à **récurer**) scouring pad.
tamponné, e [tãṅponā] *a*: **solution** ~**e** buffer solution.
tamponner [tãṅponā] *vt* (*timbres*) to stamp; (*heurter*) to crash *ou* ram into; (*essuyer*) to mop up; **se** ~ (*voitures*) to crash (into each other).
tamponneuse [tãṅponēz] *af*: **autos** ~**s** dodgems, bumper cars.
tam-tam [tàmtàm] *nm* tomtom.
tancer [tãṅsā] *vt* to scold.
tanche [tãṅsh] *nf* tench.
tandem [tãṅdem] *nm* tandem; (*fig*) duo, pair.
tandis [tãṅdē]: ~ **que** *cj* while.
tangage [tãṅgàzh] *nm* pitching (and tossing).
tangent, e [tãṅzhãṅ, -ãṅt] *a* (*MATH*): ~ **à** tangentiel to; (*fam*: *de justesse*) close ♦ *nf* (*MATH*) tangent.
Tanger [tãṅzhā] *n* Tangier.
tangible [tãṅzhēbl(ə)] *a* tangible, concrete.
tango [tãṅgō] *nm* (*MUS*) tango ♦ *a inv* (*couleur*) bright orange.
tanguer [tãṅgā] *vi* to pitch (and toss).
tanière [tànyer] *nf* lair, den.
tanin [tànaṅ] *nm* tannin.
tank [tàṅk] *nm* tank.
tanker [tãṅker] *nm* tanker.
tanné, e [tànā] *a* weather-beaten.
tanner [tànā] *vt* to tan.
tannerie [tànrē] *nf* tannery.
tanneur [tànœr] *nm* tanner.
tant [tãṅ] *ad* so much; ~ **de** (*sable, eau*) so much; (*gens, livres*) so many; ~ **que** *cj* as long as; ~ **que** (*comparatif*) as much as; ~ **mieux** that's great; so much the better; ~ **mieux pour lui** good for him; ~ **pis** too bad; **un** ~ **soit peu** (*un peu*) a little bit; (*même un peu*) (even) remotely; ~ **bien que mal** as well as can be expected; ~ **s'en faut** far from it, not by a long way.
tante [tãṅt] *nf* aunt.
tantinet [tãṅtēne]: **un** ~ *ad* a tiny bit.
tantôt [tãṅtō] *ad* (*parfois*): ~ ... ~ now ... now; (*cet après-midi*) this afternoon.
Tanzanie [tãṅzànē] *nf*: **la** ~ Tanzania.
tanzanien, ne [tãṅzànyaṅ, -en] *a* Tanzanian.
TAO *sigle f* (= *traduction assistée par ordinateur*) MAT (= *machine-aided translation*).
taon [tãṅ] *nm* horsefly, gadfly.
tapage [tàpàzh] *nm* uproar, din; (*fig*) fuss, row; ~ **nocturne** (*JUR*) disturbance of the peace (*at night*).
tapageur, euse [tàpàzhœr, -œz] *a* (*bruyant*:

enfants etc) noisy; (*toilette*) loud, flashy; (*publicité*) obtrusive.
tape [tàp] *nf* slap.
tape-à-l'œil [tàpàlœy] *a inv* flashy, showy.
taper [tàpā] *vt* (*personne*) to clout; (*porte*) to bang, slam; (*dactylographier*) to type (out); (*INFORM*) to key(board); (*fam*: *emprunter*): ~ **qn de 10 F** to touch sb for 10 F, cadge 10 F off sb ♦ *vi* (*soleil*) to beat down; **se** ~ *vt* (*fam*: *travail*) to get landed with; (: *boire, manger*) to down; ~ **sur qn** to thump sb; (*fig*) to run sb down; ~ **sur qch** (*clou etc*) to hit sth; (*table etc*) to bang on sth; ~ **à** (*porte etc*) to knock on; ~ **dans** (*se servir*) to dig into; ~ **des mains/pieds** to clap one's hands/stamp one's feet; ~ (**à la machine**) to type.
tapi, e [tàpē] *a*: ~ **dans/derrière** (*blotti*) crouching *ou* cowering in/behind; (*caché*) hidden away in/behind.
tapinois [tàpēnwà]: **en** ~ *ad* stealthily.
tapioca [tàpyokà] *nm* tapioca.
tapir [tàpēr]: **se** ~ *vi* to hide away.
tapis [tàpē] *nm* carpet; (*de table*) cloth; **mettre sur le** ~ (*fig*) to bring up for discussion; **aller au** ~ (*BOXE*) to go down; **envoyer au** ~ (*BOXE*) to floor; ~ **roulant** conveyor belt; ~ **de sol** (*de tente*) groundsheet.
tapis-brosse [tàpēbros] *nm* doormat.
tapisser [tàpēsā] *vt* (*avec du papier peint*) to paper; (*recouvrir*): ~ **qch** (**de**) to cover sth (with).
tapisserie [tàpēsrē] *nf* (*tenture, broderie*) tapestry; (: *travail*) tapestry-making; (: *ouvrage*) tapestry work; (*papier peint*) wallpaper; (*fig*): **faire** ~ to sit out, be a wallflower.
tapissier, ière [tàpēsyā, -yer] *nm/f*: ~(**-décorateur**) upholsterer (and decorator).
tapoter [tàpotā] *vt* to pat, tap.
taquet [tàke] *nm* (*cale*) wedge; (*cheville*) peg.
taquin, e [tàkaṅ, -ēn] *a* teasing.
taquiner [tàkēnā] *vt* to tease.
taquinerie [tàkēnrē] *nf* teasing *q*.
tarabiscoté, e [tàràbēskotā] *a* over-ornate, fussy.
tarabuster [tàràbüstā] *vt* to bother, worry.
tarama [tàràmá] *nm* (*CULIN*) taramasalata.
tarauder [tàrōdā] *vt* (*TECH*) to tap; to thread; (*fig*) to pierce.
tard [tàr] *ad* late; **au plus** ~ at the latest; **plus** ~ later (on) ♦ *nm*: **sur le** ~ (*à une heure avancée*) late in the day; (*vers la fin de la vie*) late in life.
tarder [tàrdā] *vi* (*chose*) to be a long time coming; (*personne*): **à faire** to delay doing; **il me tarde d'être** I am longing to be; **sans (plus)** ~ without (further) delay.
tardif, ive [tàrdēf, -ēv] *a* (*heure, repas, fruit*) late; (*talent, goût*) late in developing.
tardivement [tàrdēvmãṅ] *ad* late.
tare [tàr] *nf* (*COMM*) tare; (*fig*) defect, taint, blemish.
targette [tàrzhet] *nf* (*verrou*) bolt.
targuer [tàrgā]: **se** ~ **de** *vt* to boast about.
tarif [tàrēf] *nm* (*liste*) price list; (*barème*) rate, rates *pl*; (: *de taxis etc*) fares *pl*; **voyager à plein** ~/**à** ~ **réduit** to travel at full/reduced fare.
tarifaire [tàrēfer] *a* (*voir tarif*) relating to

price lists *etc.*
tarifé, e [tárčfā] *a:* ~ **10 F** priced at 10 F.
tarifer [tárčfā] *vt* to fix the price *ou* rate for.
tarir [tárēr] *vi* to dry up, run dry ♦ *vt* to dry up.
tarot(s) [tárō] *nm(pl)* tarot cards.
tartare [tártár] *a (CULIN)* tartar(e).
tarte [tárt(ə)] *nf* tart; ~ **aux pommes/à la crème** apple/custard tart.
tartelette [tártəlet] *nf* tartlet.
tartine [tártēn] *nf* slice of bread (and butter (*ou* jam)); ~ **de miel** slice of bread and honey; ~ **beurrée** slice of bread and butter.
tartiner [tártēnā] *vt* to spread; **fromage à** ~ cheese spread.
tartre [tártr(ə)] *nm (des dents)* tartar; (*de chaudière*) fur, scale.
tas [tâ] *nm* heap, pile; *(fig)*: **un** ~ **de** heaps of, lots of; **en** ~ in a heap *ou* pile; **dans le** ~ *(fig)* in the crowd; among them; **formé sur le** ~ trained on the job.
Tasmanie [tásmánē] *nf:* **la** ~ Tasmania.
tasmanien, ne [tásmányań, -en] *a* Tasmanian.
tasse [tâs] *nf* cup; **boire la** ~ (*en se baignant*) to swallow a mouthful; ~ **à café/thé** coffee/teacup.
tassé, e [tâsā] *a:* **bien** ~ (*café etc*) strong.
tasseau, x [tâsō] *nm* length of wood.
tassement [tásmáń] *nm* (*de vertèbres*) compression; (*ÉCON, POL:* *ralentissement*) fall-off, slowdown; (*BOURSE*) dullness.
tasser [tâsā] *vt* (*terre, neige*) to pack down; (*entasser*): ~ **qch dans** to cram sth into; (*INFORM*) to pack; **se** ~ *vi* (*terrain*) to settle; (*personne: avec l'âge*) to shrink; *(fig)* to sort itself out, settle down.
tâter [tâtā] *vt* to feel; *(fig)* to sound out; ~ **de** (*prison etc*) to have a taste of; **se** ~ (*hésiter*) to be of (US) *ou* in (*Brit*) two minds; ~ **le terrain** *(fig)* to test the ground.
tatillon, ne [tátēyóń, -oń] *a* pernickety.
tâtonnement [tâtonmáń] *nm:* **par** ~**s** *(fig)* by trial and error.
tâtonner [tâtonā] *vi* to grope one's way along; *(fig)* to grope around (in the dark).
tâtons [tâtóń]: **à** ~ *ad:* **chercher/avancer à** ~ to grope around for/grope one's way forward.
tatouage [tátwàzh] *nm* tattooing; (*dessin*) tattoo.
tatouer [tátwā] *vt* to tattoo.
taudis [tōdē] *nm* hovel, slum.
taule [tōl] *nf* (*fam*) jail.
taupe [tōp] *nf* mole; (*peau*) moleskin.
taupinière [tōpēnyer] *nf* molehill.
taureau, x [torō] *nm* bull; (*signe*): **le T**~ Taurus, the Bull; **être du T**~ to be Taurus.
taurillon [torēyóń] *nm* bull-calf.
tauromachie [toromáshē] *nf* bullfighting.
taux [tō] *nm* rate; (*d'alcool*) level; ~ **d'escompte** discount rate; ~ **d'intérêt** interest rate; ~ **de mortalité** mortality rate.
tavelé, e [távlā] *a* marked.
taverne [távern(ə)] *nf* inn, tavern.
taxable [táksábl(ə)] *a* taxable.
taxation [táksâsyóń] *nf* taxation; (*TÉL*) charges *pl*.
taxe [táks(ə)] *nf* tax; (*douanière*) duty; **toutes** ~**s comprises (TTC)** inclusive of tax; ~ **de base** (*TÉL*) unit charge; ~ **de séjour** tourist

tax; ~ **à** *ou* **sur la valeur ajoutée (TVA)** value added tax (VAT).
taxer [táksā] *vt* (*personne*) to tax; (*produit*) to put a tax on, tax; *(fig)*: ~ **qn de** (*qualifier de*) to call sb + *attribut*; (*accuser de*) to accuse sb of, tax sb with.
taxi [táksē] *nm* taxi.
taxidermie [táksēdermē] *nf* taxidermy.
taximètre [táksēmetr(ə)] *nm* (taxi)meter.
taxiphone [táksēfon] *nm* pay phone.
tb *abr* (= *très bien*, = *très bon*) VG.
tbe *abr* (= *très bon état*) VGC, vgc.
TCA *sigle f* (= *taxe sur le chiffre d'affaires*) tax on turnover.
TCF *sigle m* (= *Touring Club de France*) ≈ AAA (*US*), ≈ AA *ou* RAC (*Brit*).
Tchad [tshád] *nm:* **le** ~ Chad.
tchadien, ne [tshádyań, -en] *a* Chad(ian), of *ou* from Chad.
tchao [tsháō] *excl* (*fam*) bye(-bye)!
tchécoslovaque [tshākoslovák] *a* Czechoslovak(ian) ♦ *nm/f:* **T**~ Czechoslovak(ian).
Tchécoslovaquie [tshākoslovákē] *nf:* **la** ~ Czechoslovakia.
tchèque [tshek] *a* Czech ♦ *nm* (*LING*) Czech ♦ *nm/f:* **T**~ Czech.
TCS *sigle m* (= *Touring Club de Suisse*) ≈ AAA (*US*), ≈ AA *ou* RAC (*Brit*).
TD *sigle mpl* = **travaux dirigés.**
TDF *sigle f* (= *Télévision de France*) French broadcasting authority.
te, t' [t(ə)] *pronom* you; (*réfléchi*) yourself.
té [tā] *nm* T-square.
technicien, ne [teknēsyań, -en] *nm/f* technician.
technicité [teknēsētā] *nf* technical nature.
technique [teknēk] *a* technical ♦ *nf* technique.
techniquement [teknēkmáń] *ad* technically.
technocrate [teknokrát] *nm/f* technocrat.
technocratie [teknokrásē] *nf* technocracy.
technologie [teknolozhē] *nf* technology.
technologique [teknolozhēk] *a* technological.
technologue [teknolog] *nm/f* technologist.
teck [tek] *nm* teak.
teckel [tākel] *nm* dachshund.
TEE *sigle m* = *Trans-Europ-Express.*
tee-shirt [tēshœrt] *nm* T-shirt, tee-shirt.
Téhéran [tāārâń] *n* Teheran.
teigne [teny] *vb voir* **teindre** ♦ *nf* (*ZOOL*) moth; (*MÉD*) ringworm.
teigneux, euse [tenyœ, -œz] *a* (*péj*) nasty, scabby.
teindre [tańdr(ə)] *vt* to dye; **se** ~ (**les cheveux**) to dye one's hair.
teint, e [tań, tańt] *pp de* **teindre** ♦ *a* dyed ♦ *nm* (*du visage: permanent*) complexion, coloring (*US*), colouring (*Brit*); (*momentané*) color (*US*), colour (*Brit*) ♦ *nf* shade, color, colour; *(fig: petite dose)*: **une** ~**e de** a hint of; **grand** ~ *a inv* colorfast (*US*), colourfast (*Brit*); **bon** ~ *a inv* (*couleur*) fast; (*tissu*) colorfast (*US*), colourfast (*Brit*); (*personne*) staunch, firm.
teinté, e [tańtā] *a* (*verres*) tinted; (*bois*) stained; ~ **acajou** mahogany-stained; ~ **de** *(fig)* tinged with.
teinter [tańtā] *vt* to tint; (*bois*) to stain; *(fig: d'ironie etc*) to tinge.
teinture [tańtür] *nf* dyeing; (*substance*) dye;

(*MÉD*): ~ **d'iode** tincture of iodine.

teinturerie [tɛ̃türrē] *nf* dry cleaner's.

teinturier, ière [tɛ̃türyā, -yer] *nm/f* dry cleaner.

tel, telle [tɛl] *a* (*pareil*) such; (*comme*): ~ **un/des** ... like a/like ...; (*indéfini*) such-and-such a, a given; (*intensif*): **un ~/de ~s** ... such (a)/such ...; **rien de** ~ nothing like it, no such thing; ~ **que** *cj* like, such as; ~ **quel** as it is *ou* stands (*ou* was *etc*).

tél. *abr* = *téléphone*.

Tel Aviv [tɛlávēv] *n* Tel Aviv.

télé [tālā] *nf* (= *télévision*) TV; **à la** ~ on TV *ou* telly.

télébenne [tālābɛn] *nm, nf* cable car, gondola.

télécabine [tālākábēn] *nm, nf* cable car, gondola.

télécarte [tālākárt(ə)] *nf* phonecard.

télécharger [tālāshárzhā] *vt* (*INFORM*) to download.

télécommande [tālākomáńd] *nf* remote control.

télécommander [tālākomáńdā] *vt* to operate by remote control, radio-control.

télécommunications [tālākomünēkásyóń] *nfpl* telecommunications.

télécopie [tālākopē] *nf* fax, telefax.

télécopieur [tālākopyœr] *nm* fax (machine).

télédétection [tālādāteksyóń] *nf* remote sensing.

télédiffuser [tālādēfüzā] *vt* to broadcast (on television).

télédiffusion [tālādēfüzyóń] *nf* television broadcasting.

télédistribution [tālādēstrēbüsyóń] *nf* cable TV

téléenseignement [tālāáńsenymáń] *nm* educational television (*US*), ≈ distance teaching (*ou* learning) (*Brit*).

téléférique [talafárēk] *nm* = **téléphérique**.

téléfilm [tālāfēlm] *nm* film made for TV, TV film.

télégramme [tālāgrám] *nm* telegram.

télégraphe [tālāgráf] *nm* telegraph.

télégraphie [tālāgráfē] *nf* telegraphy.

télégraphier [tālāgráfyā] *vt* to telegraph, cable.

télégraphique [tālāgráfēk] *a* telegraph *cpd*, telegraphic; (*fig*) telegraphic.

télégraphiste [tālāgráfēst(ə)] *nm/f* telegraphist.

téléguider [tālāgēdā] *vt* to operate by remote control, radio-control.

téléinformatique [tālāańformátēk] *nf* remote access computing.

téléjournal, aux [tālāzhōōrnàl, -ō] *nm* television news magazine program (*US*) *ou* programme (*Brit*).

télématique [tālāmátēk] *nf* telematics *sg* ♦ *a* telematic.

téléobjectif [tālāobzhektēf] *nm* telephoto lens *sg*.

télépathie [tālāpátē] *nf* telepathy.

téléphérique [tālāfárēk] *nm* cable-car.

téléphone [tālāfon] *nm* telephone; **avoir le** ~ to have a (tele)phone; **au** ~ on the phone; **les T~s** (the (tele)phone service *sg*; ~ **arabe** bush telegraph; ~ **manuel** manually-operated telephone system; ~ **rouge** hot line.

téléphoner [tālāfonā] *vt* to telephone ♦ *vi* to telephone; to make a phone call; ~ **à qn** to phone sb, give sb a ring.

téléphonique [tālāfonēk] *a* telephone *cpd*, phone *cpd*; **cabine** ~ (tele)phone booth *ou* box (*Brit*); **conversation/appel** ~ (tele)phone conversation/call.

téléphoniste [tālāfonēst(ə)] *nm/f* telephone operator; (*d'entreprise*) switchboard operator.

téléport [tālāpor] *nm* teleport.

téléprospection [tālāprospeksyóń] *nf* telephone selling.

télescope [tāleskop] *nm* telescope.

télescoper [tāleskopā] *vt* to smash up; **se** ~ (*véhicules*) to telescope.

télescopique [tāleskopēk] *a* telescopic.

téléscripteur [tālāskrēptœr] *nm* teleprinter.

télésiège [tālāsyezh] *nm* chairlift.

téléski [tālāskē] *nm* ski lift; ~ **à archets** T-bar tow; ~ **à perche** button lift.

téléspectateur, trice [tālāspektátœr, -trēs] *nm/f* (television) viewer.

télétraitement [tālātretmáń] *nm* remote processing.

télétransmission [tālātráńsmēsyóń] *nf* remote transmission.

télétype [tālātēp] *nm* teleprinter.

téléviser [tālāvēzā] *vt* to televise.

téléviseur [tālāvēzœr] *nm* television set.

télévision [tālāvēzyóń] *nf* television; (**poste de**) ~ television (set); **avoir la** ~ to have a television; **à la** ~ on television; ~ **par câble** cable television.

télex [tāleks] *nm* telex.

télexer [tālcksā] *vt* to telex.

télexiste [tālekoēst(ə)] *nm/f* telex operator.

telle [tɛl] *af voir* **tel**.

tellement [tɛlmáń] *ad* (*tant*) so much; (*si*) so; ~ **plus grand (que)** so much bigger (than); ~ **de** (*sable, eau*) so much; (*gens, livres*) so many; **il s'est endormi** ~ **il était fatigué** he was so tired (that) he fell asleep; **pas** ~ not really; **pas** ~ **fort/lentement** not (all) that strong/slowly; **il ne mange pas** ~ he doesn't eat (all that) much.

tellurique [tālürēk] *a*: **secousse** ~ earth tremor.

téméraire [tāmárer] *a* reckless, rash.

témérité [tāmārētā] *nf* recklessness, rashness.

témoignage [tāmwàny̌ázh] *nm* (*JUR*: *déclaration*) testimony *q*, evidence *q*; (*: faits*) evidence *q*; (*gén*: *rapport, récit*) account; (*fig*: *d'affection etc*) token, mark; expression.

témoigner [tāmwàny̌ā] *vt* (*manifester*: *intérêt, gratitude*) to show ♦ *vi* (*JUR*) to testify, give evidence; ~ **que** to testify that; (*fig*: *démontrer*) to reveal that, testify to the fact that; ~ **de** *vt* (*confirmer*) to bear witness to, testify to.

témoin [tāmwàń] *nm* witness; (*fig*) testimony; (*SPORT*) baton; (*CONSTR*) telltale ♦ *a* control *cpd*, test *cpd* ♦ *ad*: ~ **le fait que** ... (as) witness the fact that ...; **appartement-~** model apartment (*US*), show flat (*Brit*); **être** ~ **de** (*voir*) to witness; **prendre à** ~ to call to witness; ~ **à charge** witness for the prosecution; **T~ de Jehovah** Jehovah's Witness; ~ **de moralité** character reference; ~ **oculaire**

eyewitness.

tempe [tãɱp] *nf* (*ANAT*) temple.

tempérament [tãɱpārámãɱ] *nm* temperament, disposition; (*santé*) constitution; **à ~** (*vente*) on deferred (payment) terms; (*achat*) on the installment plan (*US*), by instalments; **avoir du ~** to be hot-blooded.

tempérance [tãɱpārãɱs] *nf* temperance; **société de ~** temperance society.

tempérant, e [tãɱpārãɱ, -ãɱt] *a* temperate.

température [tãɱpārátür] *nf* temperature; **prendre la ~ de** to take the temperature of; (*fig*) to gauge the feeling of; **avoir** *ou* **faire de la ~** to be running *ou* have a temperature.

tempéré, e [tãɱpārā] *a* temperate.

tempérer [tãɱpārā] *vt* to temper.

tempête [tãɱpet] *nf* storm; **~ de sable/neige** sand/snowstorm; **vent de ~** gale.

tempêter [tãɱpātā] *vi* to rant and rave.

temple [tãɱpl(ə)] *nm* temple; (*protestant*) church.

tempo [tempō] *nm* tempo (*pl* -s).

temporaire [tãɱporer] *a* temporary.

temporairement [tãɱporermãɱ] *ad* temporarily.

temporel, le [tãɱporel] *a* temporal.

temporisateur, trice [tãɱporēzátœr, -trēs] *a* temporizing, delaying.

temporiser [tãɱporēzā] *vi* to temporize, play for time.

temps [tãɱ] *nm* (*atmosphérique*) weather; (*durée*) time; (*époque*) time, times *pl*; (*LING*) tense; (*MUS*) beat; (*TECH*) stroke; **les ~ changent/sont durs** times are changing/hard; **il fait beau/mauvais ~** the weather is fine/bad; **avoir le ~/tout le ~/juste le ~** to have time/plenty of time/just enough time; **avoir fait son ~** (*fig*) to have had its (*ou* his *etc*) day; **en ~ de paix/guerre** in peacetime/wartime; **en ~ utile** *ou* **voulu** in due time *ou* course; **de ~ en ~**, **de ~ à autre** from time to time, now and again; **en même ~** at the same time; **à ~** (*partir, arriver*) in time; **à plein/mi-~** *ad*, *a* full-/part-time; **à ~ partiel** *ad*, *a* part-time; **dans le ~** at one time; **de tout ~** always; **du ~ que** at the time when, in the days when; **dans le** *ou* **du** *ou* **au ~ où** at the time when; **pendant ce ~** in the meantime; **~ d'accès** (*INFORM*) access time; **~ d'arrêt** pause, halt; **~ mort** (*SPORT*) time-out (*US*), stoppage (time) (*Brit*); (*COMM*) slack period; **~ partagé** (*INFORM*) time-sharing; **~ réel** (*INFORM*) real time.

tenable [tənábl(ə)] *a* bearable.

tenace [tənás] *a* tenacious, persistent.

ténacité [tənásētā] *nf* tenacity, persistence.

tenailler [tənáyā] *vt* (*fig*) to torment, torture.

tenailles [tənáy] *nfpl* pincers.

tenais [t(ə)ne] *etc vb voir* **tenir**.

tenancier, ière [tənãɱsyā, -yer] *nm/f* (*d'hôtel, de bistro*) manager/manageress.

tenant, e [tənãɱ, -ãɱt] *af voir* **séance** ♦ *nm/f* (*SPORT*): **~ du titre** title-holder ♦ *nm*: **d'un seul ~** in one piece; **les ~s et les aboutissants** (*fig*) the ins and outs.

tendance [tãɱdãɱs] *nf* (*opinions*) leanings *pl*, sympathies *pl*; (*inclination*) tendency; (*évolution*) trend; **~ à la hausse/baisse** upward/downward trend; **avoir ~ à** to have a

tendency to, tend to.

tendancieux, euse [tãɱdãɱsyœ, -œz] *a* tendentious.

tendeur [tãɱdœr] *nm* (*de vélo*) tension pulley (*US*), chain-adjuster (*Brit*); (*de câble*) wire-strainer; (*de tente*) runner; (*attache*) elastic strap.

tendon [tãɱdõɱ] *nm* tendon, sinew; **~ d'Achille** Achilles' tendon.

tendre [tãɱdr(ə)] *a* (*viande, légumes*) tender; (*bois, roche, couleur*) soft; (*affectueux*) tender, loving ♦ *vt* (*élastique, peau*) to stretch, draw tight; (*muscle*) to tense; (*donner*): **~ qch à qn** to hold sth out to sb; to offer sb sth; (*fig: piège*) to set, lay; (*tapisserie*): **tendu de soie** hung with silk, with silk hangings; **se ~** *vi* (*corde*) to tighten; (*relations*) to become strained; **~ à qch/à faire** to tend towards sth/to do; **~ l'oreille** to prick up one's ears; **~ la main/le bras** to hold out one's hand/stretch out one's arm; **~ la perche à qn** (*fig*) to throw sb a line.

tendrement [tãɱdrəmãɱ] *ad* tenderly, lovingly.

tendresse [tãɱdres] *nf* tenderness; **~s** *nfpl* (*caresses etc*) tenderness *q*, caresses.

tendu, e [tãɱdü] *pp de* **tendre** ♦ *a* tight; tensed; strained.

ténèbres [tānebr(ə)] *nfpl* darkness *sg*.

ténébreux, euse [tānābrœ, -œz] *a* obscure, mysterious; (*personne*) saturnine.

Ténérife [tānārēf] *nf* Tenerife.

teneur [tənœr] *nf* content, substance; (*d'une lettre*) terms *pl*, content; **~ en cuivre** copper content.

ténia [tānyá] *nm* tapeworm.

tenir [tənēr] *vt* to hold; (*magasin, hôtel*) to run; (*promesse*) to keep ♦ *vi* to hold; (*neige, gel*) to last; (*survivre*) to survive; **se ~** *vi* (*avoir lieu*) to be held, take place; (*être: personne*) to stand; **se ~ droit** to stand up (*ou* sit up) straight; **bien se ~** to behave well; **se ~ à qch** to hold on to sth; **s'en ~ à qch** to confine o.s. to sth; to stick to sth; **~ à** *vt* to be attached to, care about (*ou* for); (*avoir pour cause*) to be due to, stem from; **~ à faire** to want to do, be keen to do; **~ à ce que qn fasse qch** to be anxious that sb should do sth; **~ de** *vt* to partake of; (*ressembler à*) to take after; **ça ne tient qu'à lui** it is entirely up to him; **~ qn pour** to take sb for; **~ qch de qn** (*histoire*) to have heard *ou* learned sth from sb; (*qualité, défaut*) to have inherited *ou* got sth from sb; **~ les comptes** to keep the books; **~ un rôle** to play a part; **~ de la place** to take up space *ou* room; **~ l'alcool** to be able to hold a drink; **~ le coup** to hold out; **~ bon** to stand *ou* hold fast; **~ 3 jours/2 mois** (*résister*) to hold out *ou* last 3 days/2 months; **au chaud/à l'abri** to keep hot/under shelter *ou* cover; **~ prêt** to have ready; **~ sa langue** (*fig*) to hold one's tongue; **tiens** (*ou* **tenez**), **voilà le stylo** here's the pen!; **tiens, Alain!** look, here's Alain!; **tiens?** (*surprise*) really?; **tiens-toi bien!** (*pour informer*) brace yourself!, take a deep breath!

tennis [tānēs] *nm* tennis; (*aussi:* **court de ~**) tennis court ♦ *nmpl ou fpl* (*aussi:* **chaussures de ~**) tennis *ou* gym shoes; **~ de table** table tennis.

tennisman [tănēsmán] *nm* tennis player.

ténor [tānor] *nm* tenor.

tension [tãṅsyóṅ] *nf* tension; (*fig: des relations, de la situation*) tension; (*: concentration, effort*) strain; (*MÉD*) blood pressure; **faire** *ou* **avoir de la** ~ to have high blood pressure; ~ **nerveuse/raciale** nervous/racial tension.

tentaculaire [tãṅtáküler] *a* (*fig*) sprawling.

tentacule [tãṅtákül] *nm* tentacle.

tentant, e [tãṅtãṅ, -ãṅt] *a* tempting.

tentateur, trice [tãṅtátœr, -trēs] *a* tempting ♦ *nm* (*REL*) tempter.

tentation [tãṅtãsyóṅ] *nf* temptation.

tentative [tãṅtátēv] *nf* attempt, bid; ~ **d'évasion** escape attempt; ~ **de suicide** suicide attempt.

tente [tãṅt] *nf* tent; ~ **à oxygène** oxygen tent.

tenter [tãṅtā] *vt* (*éprouver, attirer*) to tempt; (*essayer*): ~ **qch/de faire** to attempt *ou* try sth/to do; **être tenté de** to be tempted to; ~ **sa chance** to try one's luck.

tenture [tãṅtür] *nf* hanging.

tenu, e [tãnü] *pp de* **tenir** ♦ *a* (*maison, comptes*): **bien** ~ well-kept; (*obligé*): ~ **de faire** under an obligation to do ♦ *nf* (*action de tenir*) running; keeping; holding; (*vêtements*) clothes *pl*, gear; (*allure*) dress *q*, appearance; (*comportement*) manners *pl*, behavior (*US*), behaviour (*Brit*); **être en** ~**e** to be dressed (up); **se mettre en** ~**e** to dress (up); **en grande** ~**e** in full dress; **en petite** ~**e** scantily dressed *ou* clad; **avoir de la** ~**e** to have good manners; (*journal*) to have a high standard; ~**e de combat** combat gear *ou* dress; ~**e de pompier** fireman's uniform; ~**e de route** (*AUTO*) road-holding; ~**e de soirée** evening dress; ~**e de sport/voyage** sports/traveling clothes *pl ou* gear *q*.

ténu, e [tānü] *a* (*indice, nuance*) tenuous, subtle; (*fil, objet*) fine; (*voix*) thin.

TEP *sigle m* = *Théâtre de l'Est parisien*.

ter [ter] *a*: **16** ~ **16b** *ou* B.

térébenthine [tārãḣãṅtēn] *nf*: (**essence de**) ~ (oil of) turpentine.

tergal [tergál] *nm* ® Terylene ®.

tergiversations [terzhēversãsyóṅ] *nfpl* shilly-shallying *q*.

tergiverser [terzhēversã] *vi* to shilly-shally.

terme [term(ǝ)] *nm* term; (*fin*) end; **être en bons/mauvais** ~**s avec qn** to be on good/bad terms with sb; **vente/achat à** ~ (*COMM*) forward sale/purchase; **au** ~ **de** at the end of; **en d'autres** ~**s** in other words; **moyen** ~ (*solution intermédiaire*) middle course; **à court/long** ~ *a* short-/long-term *ou* -range ♦ *ad* in the short/long term; **à** ~ *a* (*MÉD*) full-term ♦ *ad* sooner or later, eventually; (*MÉD*) at term; **avant** ~ (*MÉD*) *a* premature ♦ *ad* prematurely; **mettre un** ~ **à** to put an end *ou* a stop to; **toucher à son** ~ to be nearing its end.

terminaison [termēnezóṅ] *nf* (*LING*) ending.

terminal, e, aux [termēnál, -ō] *a* (*partie, phase*) final; (*MÉD*) terminal ♦ *nm* terminal ♦ *nf* (*SCOL*) ≈ twelfth grade (*US*), ≈ sixth form *ou* year (*Brit*).

terminer [termēnã] *vt* to end; (*travail, repas*) to finish; **se** ~ *vi* to end; **se** ~ **par** to end with.

terminologie [termēnolozhē] *nf* terminology.

terminus [termēnüs] *nm* terminal (*US*), terminus (*pl* -i) (*Brit*); ~! last stop!, end of the line!

termite [termēt] *nm* termite, white ant.

termitière [termētyer] *nf* anthill.

ternaire [terner] *a* compound.

terne [tern(ǝ)] *a* dull.

ternir [ternēr] *vt* to dull; (*fig*) to sully, tarnish; **se** ~ *vi* to become dull.

terrain [teraṅ] *nm* (*sol, fig*) ground; (*COMM*) land *q*, plot (of land); (*: à bâtir*) site; **sur le** ~ (*fig*) on the field; ~ **de football/rugby** football/rugby field (*US*) *ou* pitch (*Brit*); ~ **d'atterrissage** landing strip; ~ **d'aviation** airfield; ~ **de camping** campsite; **un** ~ **d'entente** an area of agreement; ~ **de golf** golf course; ~ **de jeu** playground; (*SPORT*) games field; ~ **de sport** sports ground; ~ **vague** waste ground *q*.

terrasse [terás] *nf* terrace; (*de café*) sidewalk (*US*) *ou* pavement (*Brit*) area, terrace; **à la** ~ (*café*) outside.

terrassement [terásmãṅ] *nm* earth-moving, earthworks *pl*; embankment.

terrasser [terásã] *vt* (*adversaire*) to floor, bring down; (*suj: maladie etc*) to lay low.

terrassier [terásyã] *nm* roadworker.

terre [ter] *nf* (*gén, aussi ÉLEC*) earth; (*substance*) soil, earth; (*opposé à mer*) land *q*; (*contrée*) land; ~**s** *nfpl* (*terrains*) lands, land *sg*; **travail de la** ~ work on the land; **en** ~ (*pipe, poterie*) clay *cpd*; **mettre en** ~ (*plante etc*) to plant; (*personne: enterrer*) to bury; **à** *ou* **par** ~ (*mettre, être*) on the ground (*ou* floor); (*jeter, tomber*) to the ground, down; ~ **à** ~ *a inv* down-to-earth, matter-of-fact; **la T**~ **Adélie** Adélie Coast *ou* Land; ~ **de bruyère** (heath-)peat; ~ **cuite** earthenware; terracotta; **la** ~ **ferme** dry land, terra firma; **la T**~ **de feu** Tierra del Fuego; ~ **glaise** clay; **la T**~ **promise** the Promised Land; **la T**~ **Sainte** the Holy Land.

terreau [terō] *nm* compost.

Terre-Neuve [ternœv] *nf*: **la** ~ (*aussi*: **l'île de** ~) Newfoundland.

terre-plein [terplaṅ] *nm* platform.

terrer [terã]: **se** ~ *vi* to hide away; to go into hiding.

terrestre [terestr(ǝ)] *a* (*surface*) earth's, of the earth; (*BOT, ZOOL, MIL*) land *cpd*; (*REL*) earthly, worldly.

terreur [terœr] *nf* terror *q*, fear.

terreux, euse [terœ, -œz] *a* muddy; (*goût*) earthy.

terrible [terēbl(ǝ)] *a* terrible, dreadful; (*fam: fantastique*) terrific.

terriblement [terēblǝmãṅ] *ad* (*très*) terribly, awfully.

terrien, ne [teryaṅ, -en] *a*: **propriétaire** ~ landowner ♦ *nm/f* (*habitant*) countryman/woman, man/woman of the soil; (*non martien etc*) earthling; (*non marin*) landsman.

terrier [teryã] *nm* burrow, hole; (*chien*) terrier.

terrifiant, e [terēfyãṅ, -ãṅt] *a* (*effrayant*) terrifying; (*extraordinaire*) terrible, awful.

terrifier [terēfyā] *vt* to terrify.
terril [terēl] *nm* slag heap.
terrine [terēn] *nf* (*récipient*) terrine; (*CULIN*) pâté.
territoire [terētwár] *nm* territory; **T~ des Afars et des Issas** French Territory of Afars and Issas.
territorial, e, aux [terētoryàl, -ō] *a* territorial; **eaux ~es** territorial waters; **armée ~e** regional defense force; **collectivités ~es** local and regional authorities.
terroir [terwár] *nm* (*AGR*) soil; (*région*) region; **accent du ~** country *ou* rural accent.
terroriser [terorēzā] *vt* to terrorize.
terrorisme [terorēsm(ə)] *nm* terrorism.
terroriste [terorēst(ə)] *nm/f* terrorist.
tertiaire [tersyer] *a* tertiary ♦ *nm* (*ÉCON*) tertiary sector, service industries *pl.*
tertre [tertr(ə)] *nm* hillock, mound.
tes [tā] *dét voir* **ton.**
tesson [tāsóṅ] *nm*: **~ de bouteille** piece of broken bottle.
test [test] *nm* test.
testament [testámáṅ] *nm* (*JUR*) will; (*fig*) legacy; (*REL*): **T~** Testament; **faire son ~** to make one's will.
testamentaire [testámáṅter] *a* of a will.
tester [testā] *vt* to test.
testicule [testēkül] *nm* testicle.
tétanos [tātánōs] *nm* tetanus.
têtard [tetár] *nm* tadpole.
tête [tet] *nf* head; (*cheveux*) hair *q*; (*visage*) face; (*longueur*): **gagner d'une (courte) ~** to win by a (short) head; (*FOOTBALL*) header; **de ~** *a* (*wagon etc*) front *cpd*; (*concurrent*) leading ♦ *ad* (*calculer*) in one's head, mentally; **par ~** (*par personne*) per head; **se mettre en ~ que** to get it into one's head that; **se mettre en ~ de faire** to take it into one's head to do; **prendre la ~ de qch** to take the lead in sth; **perdre la ~** (*fig*: *s'affoler*) to lose one's head; (: *devenir fou*) to go crazy; **ça ne va pas, la ~?** (*fam*) are you crazy?; **tenir ~ à qn** to stand up to *ou* defy sb; **la ~ en bas** with one's head down; **la ~ la première** (*tomber*) headfirst; **la ~ basse** hanging one's head; **avoir la ~ dure** (*fig*) to be thickheaded; **faire une ~** (*FOOTBALL*) to head the ball; **faire la ~** (*fig*) to sulk; **en ~** (*SPORT*) in the lead; at the front *ou* head; **de la ~ aux pieds** from head to toe; **~ d'affiche** (*THÉÂTRE etc*) headliner (*US*), top of the bill (*Brit*); **~ de bétail** head *inv* of cattle; **~ brulée** desperado; **~ chercheuse** homing device; **~ d'enregistrement** recording head; **~ de lecture** (playback) head; **~ de ligne** (*TRANSPORTS*) terminal (*US*), start of the line (*Brit*); **~ de liste** (*POL*) chief candidate; **~ de mort** skull and crossbones; **~ de pont** (*MIL*) bridge-ou beachhead; **~ de série** (*TENNIS*) seeded player, seed; **~ de Turc** (*fig*) whipping boy, butt; **~ de veau** (*CULIN*) calf's head.
tête-à-queue [tetàkœ] *nm inv*: **faire un ~** to spin around.
tête-à-tête [tetátet] *nm inv* tête-à-tête; (*service*) breakfast set for two; **en ~** in private, alone together.
tête-bêche [tetbesh] *ad* head to tail.

tétée [tātā] *nf* (*action*) sucking; (*repas*) nursing (*US*), feed (*Brit*).
téter [tātā] *vt*: **~ (sa mère)** to suck at one's mother's breast.
tétine [tātēn] *nf* teat; (*sucette*) pacifier (*US*), dummy (*Brit*).
téton [tātóṅ] *nm* breast.
têtu, e [tātü] *a* stubborn, pigheaded.
texte [tekst(ə)] *nm* text; (*SCOL*: *d'un devoir*) subject, topic; **apprendre son ~** (*THÉÂTRE*) to learn one's lines; **un ~ de loi** the wording of a law.
textile [tekstēl] *a* textile *cpd* ♦ *nm* textile; (*industrie*) textile industry.
textuel, le [tekstüel] *a* literal, word for word.
textuellement [tekstüelmáṅ] *ad* literally.
texture [tekstür] *nf* texture; (*fig*: *d'un texte, livre*) feel.
TF1 *sigle f* (= *Télévision française 1*) TV channel.
TG *sigle f* = Trésorerie générale.
TGI *sigle m* = tribunal de grande instance.
TGV *sigle m* = train à grande vitesse.
thaï, e [tác] *a* Thai ♦ *nm* (*LING*) Thai.
thaïlandais, e [tácláṅde, -ez] *a* Thai.
Thaïlande [tácláṅd] *nf*: **la ~** Thailand.
thalassothérapie [tálàsotārápē] *nf* sea-water therapy.
thé [tā] *nm* tea; (*réunion*) tea party; **prendre le ~** to have tea; **~ au lait/citron** tea with milk/lemon.
théâtral, e, aux [táátrál, -ō] *a* theatrical.
théâtre [táátr(ə)] *nm* theater (*US*), theatre (*Brit*); (*techniques, genre*) drama, theater; (*activité*) stage, theater; (*œuvres*) plays *pl*, dramatic works *pl*; (*fig*: *lieu*): **le ~ de** the scene of; (*péj*) histrionics *pl*, playacting; **faire du ~** (*en professionnel*) to be on the stage; (*en amateur*) to do some acting; **~ filmé** filmed stage productions *pl.*
thébain, e [tābaṅ, -en] *a* Theban.
Thèbes [teb] *n* Thebes.
théière [tāyer] *nf* teapot.
théine [tāēn] *nf* theine.
théisme [tāēsm(ə)] *nm* theism.
thématique [tāmátēk] *a* thematic.
thème [tem] *nm* theme; (*SCOL*: *traduction*) translation (*into the foreign language*); **~ astral** birth chart.
théocratie [tāokrásē] *nf* theocracy.
théologie [tāolozhē] *nf* theology.
théologien, ne [tāolozhyaṅ, -en] *nm* theologian.
théologique [tāolozhēk] *a* theological.
théorème [tāorem] *nm* theorem.
théoricien, ne [tāorēsyaṅ, -en] *nm/f* theoretician, theorist.
théorie [tāorē] *nf* theory; **en ~** in theory.
théorique [tāorēk] *a* theoretical.
théoriser [tāorēzā] *vi* to theorize.
thérapeutique [tārápœtēk] *a* therapeutic ♦ *nf* (*MÉD*: *branche*) therapeutics *sg*; (: *traitement*) therapy.
thérapie [tārápē] *nf* therapy.
thermal, e, aux [termál, -ō] *a* thermal; **station ~e** spa; **cure ~e** water cure.
thermes [term(ə)] *nmpl* thermal baths; (*romains*) thermae *pl.*
thermique [termēk] *a* (*énergie*) thermic;

(*unité*) thermal.

thermodynamique [termodēnámēk] *nf* thermodynamics *sg*.

thermomètre [termometr(ə)] *nm* thermometer.

thermonucléaire [termonükläer] *a* thermonuclear.

thermos [termōs] *nm ou nf* ®: **(bouteille)** ~ vacuum *ou* Thermos ® bottle (*US*) *ou* flask (*Brit*).

thermostat [termostá] *nm* thermostat.

thésauriser [tāzorēzā] *vi* to hoard money.

thèse [tez] *nf* thesis (*pl* theses).

Thessalie [tesálē] *nf*: **la** ~ Thessaly.

thessalien, ne [tesályań, -en] *a* Thessalian.

thibaude [tēbōd] *nf* carpet underlay.

thon [tôṅ] *nm* tuna (fish).

thoracique [torásēk] *a* thoracic.

thorax [toráks] *nm* thorax.

thrombose [trôṅbōz] *nf* thrombosis.

thym [taṅ] *nm* thyme.

thyroïde [tēroēd] *nf* thyroid (gland).

TI *sigle m* = **tribunal d'instance.**

tiare [tyàr] *nf* tiara.

Tibet [tēbe] *nm*: **le** ~ Tibet.

tibétain, e [tēbàtan, -en] *a* Tibetan.

tibia [tēbyá] *nm* shin; (*os*) shinbone, tibia.

Tibre [tēbr(ə)] *nm*: **le** ~ the Tiber.

tic [tēk] *nm* tic, (nervous) twitch; (*de langage etc*) mannerism.

ticket [tēke] *nm* ticket; ~ **de caisse** sales slip *ou* receipt; ~ **modérateur** *patient's contribution towards medical costs;* ~ **de quai** platform ticket; ~ **repas** luncheon voucher.

tic-tac [tēktàk] *nm inv* tick-tock.

tictaquer [tēktákā] *vi* to tick (away).

tiède [tyed] *a* (*bière etc*) lukewarm; (*thé, café etc*) tepid; (*bain, accueil, sentiment*) lukewarm; (*vent, air*) mild, warm ♦ *ad*: **boire** ~ to drink things lukewarm.

tièdement [tyedmáṅ] *ad* coolly, half-heartedly.

tiédir [tyādēr] *vi* (*se réchauffer*) to grow warmer; (*refroidir*) to cool.

tien, tienne [tyaṅ, tyen] *pronom*: **le** ~ (**la tienne**), **les** ~**s (tiennes)** yours; **à la tienne!** cheers!

tiendrai [tyaṅdrā] *etc vb voir* **tenir.**

tienne [tyen] *vb voir* **tenir** ♦ *pronom voir* **tien.**

tiens [tyaṅ] *vb, excl voir* **tenir.**

tierce [tyers(ə)] *af, nf voir* **tiers.**

tiercé [tyersā] *nm system of forecast betting giving first 3 horses.*

tiers, tierce [tyer, tyers(ə)] *a* third ♦ *nm* (*JUR*) third party; (*fraction*) third ♦ *nf* (*MUS*) third; (*CARTES*) tierce; **une tierce personne** a third party; **assurance au** ~ third-party insurance; **le** ~ **monde** the third world; ~ **payant** *direct payment by insurers of medical expenses;* ~ **provisionnel** *interim payment of tax.*

tiersmondisme [tyermóṅdēsm(ə)] *nm* support for the Third World.

TIG *sigle m* = **travail d'intérêt général.**

tige [tēzh] *nf* stem; (*baguette*) rod.

tignasse [tēnyás] *nf* (*péj*) shock *ou* mop of hair.

Tigre [tēgr(ə)] *nm*: **le** ~ the Tigris.

tigre [tēgr(ə)] *nm* tiger.

tigré, e [tēgrā] *a* (*rayé*) striped; (*tacheté*) spotted.

tigresse [tēgres] *nf* tigress.

tilleul [tēyœl] *nm* lime (tree), linden (tree); (*boisson*) lime(-blossom) tea.

tilt [tēlt(ə)] *nm*: **faire** ~ (*fig: échouer*) to miss the target; (*: inspirer*) to ring a bell.

timbale [taṅbál] *nf* (metal) tumbler; ~**s** *nfpl* (*MUS*) timpani, kettledrums.

timbrage [taṅbrázh] *nm*: **dispensé de** ~ post(age) paid.

timbre [taṅbr(ə)] *nm* (*tampon*) stamp; (*aussi*: ~-**poste**) (postage) stamp; (*cachet de la poste*) postmark; (*sonnette*) bell; (*MUS: de voix, instrument*) timbre, tone; ~ **dateur** date stamp.

timbré, e [taṅbrā] *a* (*enveloppe*) stamped; (*voix*) resonant; (*fam: fou*) cracked, nuts.

timbrer [taṅbrā] *vt* to stamp.

timide [tēmēd] *a* (*emprunté*) shy, timid; (*timoré*) timid, timorous.

timidement [tēmēdmáṅ] *ad* shyly; timidly.

timidité [tēmēdētā] *nf* shyness; timidity.

timonerie [tēmonrē] *nf* wheelhouse.

timonier [tēmonyā] *nm* helmsman.

timoré, e [tēmorā] *a* timorous.

tint [taṅ] *etc vb voir* **tenir.**

tintamarre [taṅtámár] *nm* din, uproar.

tintement [taṅtmáṅ] *nm* ringing, chiming; ~**s d'oreilles** ringing in the ears.

tinter [taṅtā] *vi* to ring, chime; (*argent, clefs*) to jingle.

Tipp-Ex [tēpeks] *nm* ® Liquid Paper ®, Tipp-Ex ® (*Brit*).

tique [tēk] *nf* tick (*insect*).

tiquer [tēkā] *vi* (*personne*) to make a face.

TIR *sigle mpl* (= *Transports internationaux routiers*) TIR.

tir [tēr] *nm* (*sport*) shooting; (*fait ou manière de tirer*) firing *q*; (*FOOTBALL*) shot; (*stand*) shooting gallery; ~ **d'obus/de mitraillette** shell/machine gun fire; ~ **à l'arc** archery; ~ **de barrage** barrage fire; ~ **au fusil** (rifle) shooting; ~ **au pigeon** (*d'argile*) trapshooting (*US*), clay pigeon shooting (*Brit*).

tirade [tērád] *nf* tirade.

tirage [tērázh] *nm* (*action*) printing; (*PHOTO*) print; (*INFORM*) printout; (*de journal*) circulation; (*de livre*) (print-)run; edition; (*de cheminée*) draft (*US*), draught (*Brit*); (*de loterie*) drawing (*US*), draw (*Brit*); (*fig: désaccord*) friction; ~ **au sort** drawing lots.

tiraillement [tēráymáṅ] *nm* (*douleur*) sharp pain; (*fig: doutes*) agony *q* of indecision; (*conflits*) friction *q*.

tirailler [tēráyā] *vt* to pull at, tug at; (*fig*) to gnaw at ♦ *vi* to fire at random.

tirailleur [tēráyœr] *nm* skirmisher.

tirant [tēráṅ] *nm*: ~ **d'eau** draft (*US*), draught (*Brit*).

tire [tēr] *nf*: **vol à la** ~ pickpocketing.

tiré [tērā] *a* (*visage, traits*) drawn ♦ *nm* (*COMM*) drawee; ~ **par les cheveux** far-fetched; ~ **à part** offprint.

tire-au-flanc [tēróflàṅ] *nm inv* (*péj*) shirker.

tire-bouchon [tērbōōshóṅ] *nm* corkscrew.

tire-bouchonner [tērbōōshonā] *vt* to twirl.

tire-d'aile [tērdel]: **à** ~ *ad* swiftly.

tire-fesses [tērfes] *nm inv* ski tow.

tire-lait [tērle] *nm inv* breast pump.

tire-larigot |tērlárēgō|: **à ~** *ad* as much as one likes, to one's heart's content.

tirelire |tērlēr| *nf* moneybox.

tirer |tērā| *vt* (*gén*) to pull; (*extraire*): **~ qch de** to take *ou* pull sth out of; to get sth out of; to extract sth from; (*tracer: ligne, trait*) to draw, trace; (*fermer: volet, porte, trappe*) to pull to, close; (: *rideau*) to draw; (*choisir: carte, conclusion, aussi* COMM: *chèque*) to draw; (*en faisant feu: balle, coup*) to fire; (: *animal*) to shoot; (*journal, livre, photo*) to print; (FOOTBALL: *corner etc*) to take ♦ *vi* (*faire feu*) to fire; (*faire du tir*, FOOTBALL) to shoot; (*cheminée*) to draw; **se ~** *vi* (*fam*) to push off; **s'en ~** to pull through; **~ sur** (*corde, poignée*) to pull on *ou* at; (*faire feu sur*) to shoot *ou* fire at; (*pipe*) to draw on; (*fig: avoisiner*) to verge *ou* border on; **~ 6 mètres** (NAVIG) to draw 6 meters of water; **~ son nom de** to take *ou* get its name from; **~ la langue** to stick out one's tongue; **~ qn de** (*embarras etc*) to help *ou* get sb out of; **~ à l'arc/la carabine** to shoot with a bow and arrow/with a rifle; **~ en longueur** to drag on; **~ à sa fin** to be drawing to an end; **~ les cartes** to read *ou* tell the cards.

tiret |tēre| *nm* dash; (*en fin de ligne*) hyphen.

tireur, euse |tērœr, -ø̄z| *nm/f* gunman; (COMM) drawer; **bon ~** good shot; **~ d'élite** marksman; **~ des cartes** fortuneteller.

tiroir |tērwár| *nm* drawer.

tiroir-caisse |tērwárkes| *nm* till.

tisane |tēzán| *nf* herb tea.

tison |tēzóṅ| *nm* brand.

tisonner |tēzonā| *vt* to poke.

tisonnier |tēzonyā| *nm* poker.

tissage |tēsazh| *nm* weaving *q*.

tisser |tēsā| *vt* to weave.

tisserand, e |tēsráṅ, -áṅd| *nm/f* weaver.

tissu |tēsü| *nm* fabric, material, cloth *q*; (*fig*) fabric; (ANAT, BIO) tissue; **~ de mensonges** web of lies.

tissu, e |tēsü| *a*: **~ de** woven through with.

tissu-éponge |tēsüäpôṅzh| *nm* terry cloth (US), (terry) towelling *q* (*Brit*).

titane |tētán| *nm* titanium.

titanesque |tētánesk(ə)| *a* titanic.

titiller |tētēlā| *vt* to titillate.

titre |tētr(ə)| *nm* (*gén*) title; (*de journal*) headline; (*diplôme*) qualification; (COMM) security; (CHIMIE) titer (*US*), titre (*Brit*); **en ~** (*champion, responsable*) official, recognized; **à juste ~** with just cause, rightly; **à quel ~?** on what grounds?; **à aucun ~** on no account; **au même ~ (que)** in the same way (as); **au ~ de la coopération** *etc* in the name of cooperation *etc*; **à ~ d'exemple** as an *ou* by way of an example; **à ~ exceptionnel** exceptionally; **à ~ d'information** for (your) information; **à ~ gracieux** free of charge; **à ~ d'essai** on a trial basis; **à ~ privé** in a private capacity; **~ courant** running head; **~ de propriété** title deed; **~ de transport** ticket.

titré, e |tētrā| *a* (*livre, film*) entitled; (*personne*) titled.

titrer |tētrā| *vt* (CHIMIE) to titrate; to assay; (PRESSE) to run as a headline; (*suj: vin*): **~ 10°** to be 10° proof.

titubant, e |tētübáṅ, -áṅt| *a* staggering, reeling.

tituber |tētübā| *vi* to stagger *ou* reel (along).

titulaire |tētüler| *a* (ADMIN) appointed, with tenure ♦ *nm* (ADMIN) incumbent; **être ~ de** to hold.

titulariser |tētülárēzā| *vt* to give tenure to.

TNP *sigle m* = *Théâtre national populaire*.

TNT *sigle m* (= *Trinitrotoluène*) TNT.

toast |tōst| *nm* slice *ou* piece of toast; (*de bienvenue*) (welcoming) toast; **porter un ~ à qn** to propose *ou* drink a toast to sb.

toboggan |tobogáṅ| *nm* toboggan; (*jeu*) slide; (AUTO) overpass (*US*), flyover (*Brit*); **~ de secours** (AVIAT) escape chute.

toc |tok| *nm*: **en ~** imitation *cpd*.

tocsin |toksaṅ| *nm* alarm (bell).

toge |tozh| *nf* toga; (*de juge*) gown.

Togo |togō| *nm*: **le ~** Togo.

togolais, e |togole, -ez| *a* Togolese.

tohu-bohu |toüboü| *nm* (*désordre*) confusion; (*tumulte*) commotion.

toi |twá| *pronom* you; **~, tu l'as fait?** did YOU do it?

toile |twál| *nf* (*matériau*) cloth *q*; (*bâche*) piece of canvas; (*tableau*) canvas; **grosse ~** canvas; **tisser sa ~** (*araignée*) to spin its web; **~ d'araignée** spider's web; (*au plafond etc: à enlever*) cobweb; **~ cirée** oilcloth; **~ émeri** emery cloth; **~ de fond** (*fig*) backdrop; **~ de jute** hessian; **~ de lin** linen; **~ de tente** canvas.

toilettage |twáletázh| *nm* grooming *q*; (*d'un texte*) tidying up.

toilette |twálet| *nf* wash; (*s'habiller et se préparer*) getting ready, washing and dressing; (*habits*) outfit; dress *q*; **~s** *nfpl* toilet *sg*; **les ~s des dames/messieurs** the ladies'/mens' (rest)room (*US*), the ladies'/gents' (toilets) (*Brit*); **faire sa ~** to get washed; **faire la ~ de** (*animal*) to groom; (*voiture etc*) to clean, wash; (*texte*) to tidy up; **articles de ~** toiletries; **~ intime** personal hygiene.

toi-même |twámem| *pronom* yourself.

toise |twáz| *nf*: **passer à la ~** to have one's height measured.

toiser |twázā| *vt* to eye up and down.

toison |twázóṅ| *nf* (*de mouton*) fleece; (*cheveux*) mane.

toit |twá| *nm* roof; **~ ouvrant** sun roof.

toiture |twátür| *nf* roof.

Tokyo |tokyō| *n* Tokyo.

tôle |tōl| *nf* sheet metal *q*; (*plaque*) steel (*ou* iron) sheet; **~s** *nfpl* (*carosserie*) body *sg*; panels; **~ d'acier** sheet steel *q*; **~ ondulée** corrugated iron.

Tolède |toled| *n* Toledo.

tolérable |tolārábl(ə)| *a* tolerable, bearable.

tolérance |tolāráṅs| *nf* tolerance; (*hors taxe*) allowance.

tolérant, e |tolāráṅ, -áṅt| *a* tolerant.

tolérer |tolārā| *vt* to tolerate; (ADMIN: *hors taxe etc*) to allow.

tôlerie |tōlrē| *nf* sheet metal manufacture; (*atelier*) sheet metal workshop; (*ensemble des tôles*) panels *pl*.

tollé |tolā| *nm*: **un ~ (de protestations)** a general outcry.

TOM |*parfois*: tom| *sigle m(pl)* = *territoire(s)*

d'outre-mer.

tomate [tɔmát] *nf* tomato.

tombal, e [tɔ̃bál] *a*: **pierre** ~**e** tombstone, gravestone.

tombant, e [tɔ̃bɑ̃ń, -ɑ̃nt] *a* (*fig*) drooping, sloping.

tombe [tɔ̃b] *nf* (*sépulture*) grave; (*avec monument*) tomb.

tombeau, x [tɔ̃bō] *nm* tomb; **à** ~ **ouvert** at breakneck speed.

tombée [tɔ̃bā] *nf*: **à la** ~ **du jour** *ou* **de la nuit** at the close of day, at nightfall.

tomber [tɔ̃bā] *vi* to fall ♦ *vt*: ~ **la veste** to slip off one's jacket; **laisser** ~ to drop; ~ **sur** *vt* (*rencontrer*) to come across; (*attaquer*) to set about; ~ **de fatigue/sommeil** to drop from exhaustion/be falling asleep on one's feet; ~ **à l'eau** (*fig*: *projet etc*) to fall through; ~ **en panne** to break down; ~ **juste** (*opération, calcul*) to come out right; ~ **en ruine** to fall into ruins; **ça tombe bien/mal** (*fig*) that's come at the right/wrong time; **il est bien/mal tombé** (*fig*) he's been lucky/unlucky.

tombereau, x [tɔ̃brō] *nm* tipcart.

tombeur [tɔ̃bœr] *nm* (*péj*) Casanova.

tombola [tɔ̃bɔlá] *nf* raffle, tombola (*Brit*).

Tombouctou [tɔ̃bŏŏktŏŏ] *n* Timbuktu.

tome [tom] *nm* volume.

tommette [tɔmet] *nf* hexagonal floor tile.

ton, ta, *pl* **tes** [tɔ̃, tá, tā] *dét* your.

ton [tɔ̃] *nm* (*gén*) tone; (*MUS*) key; (*couleur*) shade, tone; (*de la voix*: *hauteur*) pitch; **donner le** ~ to set the tone; **élever** *ou* **hausser le** ~ to raise one's voice; **de bon** ~ in good taste; **si vous le prenez sur ce** ~ if you're going to take it like that; ~ **sur** ~ in matching shades.

tonal, e [tɔnál] *a* tonal.

tonalité [tɔnálētā] *nf* (*au téléphone*) dial tone; (*MUS*) tonality; (: *ton*) key; (*fig*) tone.

tondeuse [tɔ̃dœz] *nf* (*à gazon*) (lawn)mower; (*du coiffeur*) clippers *pl*; (*pour la tonte*) shears *pl*.

tondre [tɔ̃dr(ə)] *vt* (*pelouse, herbe*) to mow; (*haie*) to cut, clip; (*mouton, toison*) to shear; (*cheveux*) to crop.

tondu, e [tɔ̃dü] *pp de* **tondre** ♦ *a* (*cheveux*) cropped; (*mouton, crâne*) shorn.

Tonga [tɔ̃gá]: **les îles** ~ Tonga.

tonicité [tɔnēsētā] *nf* (*MÉD*: *des tissus*) tone; (*fig*: *de l'air, la mer*) bracing effect.

tonifiant, e [tɔnēfyɑ̃ń, -ɑ̃nt] *a* invigorating, revivifying.

tonifier [tɔnēfyā] *vt* (*air, eau*) to invigorate; (*peau, organisme*) to tone up.

tonique [tɔnēk] *a* fortifying; (*personne*) dynamic ♦ *nm, nf* tonic.

tonitruant, e [tɔnētrüɑ̃ń, -ɑ̃nt] *a*: **voix** ~**e** thundering voice.

Tonkin [tɔ̃kań] *nm*: **le** ~ Tonkin, Tongking.

tonkinois, e [tɔ̃kēnwá, -wáz] *a* Tonkinese.

tonnage [tɔnázh] *nm* tonnage.

tonnant, e [tɔnɑ̃ń, -ɑ̃nt] *a* thunderous.

tonne [ton] *nf* metric ton, ton (*US*), tonne (*Brit*).

tonneau, x [tɔnō] *nm* (*à vin, cidre*) barrel; (*NAVIG*) ton; **faire des** ~**x** (*voiture, avion*) to roll over.

tonnelet [tɔnle] *nm* keg.

tonnelier [tɔnəlyā] *nm* cooper.

tonnelle [tɔnel] *nf* bower, arbor (*US*), arbour (*Brit*).

tonner [tɔnā] *vi* to thunder; (*parler avec véhémence*): ~ **contre qn/qch** to inveigh against sb/sth; **il tonne** it is thundering, there's some thunder.

tonnerre [tɔner] *nm* thunder; **coup de** ~ (*fig*) thunderbolt, bolt from the blue; **un** ~ **d'applaudissements** thunderous applause; **du** ~ *a* (*fam*) terrific.

tonsure [tɔ̃sür] *nf* bald patch; (*de moine*) tonsure.

tonte [tɔ̃t] *nf* shearing.

tonus [tɔnüs] *nm* (*des muscles*) tone; (*d'une personne*) dynamism.

top [top] *nm*: **au 3ème** ~ at the 3rd stroke ♦ *a*: ~ **secret** top secret ♦ *excl* go!

topaze [tɔpáz] *nf* topaz.

toper [tɔpā] *vi*: **tope-/topez-là** it's a deal!, you're on!

topinambour [tɔpēnɑ̃bŏŏr] *nm* Jerusalem artichoke.

topo [tɔpō] *nm* (*discours, exposé*) talk; (*fam*) spiel.

topographie [tɔpɔgráfē] *nf* topography.

topographique [tɔpɔgráfēk] *a* topographical.

toponymie [tɔpɔnēmē] *nf* study of place-names, toponymy.

toquade [tɔkád] *nf* fad, craze.

toque [tɔk] *nf* (*de fourrure*) fur hat; ~ **de jockey/juge** jockey's/judge's cap; ~ **de cuisinier** chef's hat.

toqué, e [tɔkā] *a* (*fam*) touched, cracked.

torche [torsh(ə)] *nf* torch; **se mettre en** ~ (*parachute*) to fail to open.

torcher [torshā] *vt* (*fam*) to wipe.

torchère [torsher] *nf* flare.

torchon [torshɔ̃ń] *nm* cloth, duster; (*à vaisselle*) dish (*US*) *ou* tea (*Brit*) towel.

tordre [tordr(ə)] *vt* (*chiffon*) to wring; (*barre, fig*: *visage*) to twist; **se** ~ *vi* (*barre*) to bend; (*roue*) to twist, buckle; (*ver, serpent*) to writhe; **se** ~ **le pied/bras** to twist one's foot/arm; **se** ~ **de douleur/rire** to writhe in pain/be doubled up with laughter.

tordu, e [tordü] *pp de* **tordre** ♦ *a* (*fig*) warped, twisted.

torero [tɔrārō] *nm* bullfighter.

tornade [tɔrnád] *nf* tornado.

toron [tɔrɔ̃ń] *nm* strand (of rope).

Toronto [tɔrɔ̃tō] *n* Toronto.

torontois, e [tɔrɔ̃twá, -wáz] *a* Torontonian ♦ *nm/f*: **T**~, **e** Torontonian.

torpeur [tɔrpœr] *nf* torpor, drowsiness.

torpille [tɔrpēy] *nf* torpedo.

torpiller [tɔrpēyā] *vt* to torpedo.

torpilleur [tɔrpēyœr] *nm* torpedo boat.

torréfaction [tɔrāfáksyɔ̃ń] *nf* roasting.

torréfier [tɔrāfyā] *vt* to roast.

torrent [tɔrɑ̃ń] *nm* torrent, mountain stream; (*fig*): **un** ~ **de** a torrent *ou* flood of; **il pleut à** ~**s** the rain is lashing down.

torrentiel, le [tɔrɑ̃syel] *a* torrential.

torride [tɔrēd] *a* torrid.

tors, torse *ou* **torte** [tɔr, tɔrs(ə) *ou* tɔrt(ə)] *a* twisted.

torsade [tɔrsád] *nf* twist; (*ARCHIT*) cable

molding (*US*) *ou* moulding (*Brit*).

torsader [torsàdā] *vt* to twist.

torse [tors(ə)] *nm* torso; (*poitrine*) chest.

torsion [torsyôñ] *nf* (*action*) twisting; (*TECH*, *PHYSIQUE*) torsion.

tort [tor] *nm* (*défaut*) fault; (*préjudice*) wrong *q*; ~**s** *nmpl* (*JUR*) fault *sg*; **avoir** ~ to be wrong; **être dans son** ~ to be in the wrong; **donner** ~ **à qn** to lay the blame on sb; (*fig*) to prove sb wrong; **causer du** ~ **à** to harm; to be harmful *ou* detrimental to; **en** ~ in the wrong, at fault; **à** ~ wrongly; **à** ~ **ou à raison** rightly or wrongly; **à** ~ **et à travers** wildly.

torte [tort(ə)] *af voir* **tors**.

torticolis [tortĕkolē] *nm* stiff neck.

tortiller [tortēyā] *vt* (*corde*, *mouchoir*) to twist; (*doigts*) to twiddle; **se** ~ *vi* to wriggle, squirm.

tortionnaire [torsyoner] *nm* torturer.

tortue [tortü] *nf* tortoise; (*fig*) slowpoke (*US*), slowcoach (*Brit*).

tortueux, euse [tortüœ̄, -œ̄z] *a* (*rue*) twisting; (*fig*) tortuous.

torture [tortür] *nf* torture.

torturer [tortürā] *vt* to torture; (*fig*) to torment.

torve [torv(ə)] *a*: **regard** ~ menacing *ou* grim look.

toscan, e [toskâñ, -àn] *a* Tuscan.

Toscane [toskàn] *nf*: **la** ~ Tuscany.

tôt [tō] *ad* early; ~ **ou tard** sooner or later; **si** ~ so early; (*déjà*) so soon; **au plus** ~ at the earliest, as soon as possible; **plus** ~ earlier; **il eut** ~ **fait de faire** ... he soon did ....

total, e, aux [totàl, -ō] *a*, *nm* total; **au** ~ in total *ou* all; (*fig*) all in all; **faire le** ~ to work out the total.

totalement [totàlmâñ] *ad* totally, completely.

totalisateur [totàlēzàtœr] *nm* adding machine.

totaliser [totàlēzā] *vt* to total (up).

totalitaire [totàlēter] *a* totalitarian.

totalitarisme [totàlētàrēsm(ə)] *nm* totalitarianism.

totalité [totàlētā] *nf*: **la** ~ **de**: **la** ~ **des élèves** all (of) the pupils; **la** ~ **de la population/ classe** the whole population/class; **en** ~ entirely.

totem [totem] *nm* totem.

toubib [tōōbēb] *nm* (*fam*) doctor.

touchant, e [tōōshâñ, -âñt] *a* touching.

touche [tōōsh] *nf* (*de piano, de machine à écrire*) key; (*de violon*) fingerboard; (*de télécommande etc*) key, button; (*PEINTURE etc*) stroke, touch; (*fig: de couleur, nostalgie*) touch, hint; (*RUGBY*) line-out; (*FOOTBALL*: *aussi*: **remise en** ~) throw-in; (*aussi*: **ligne de** ~) touchline; (*ESCRIME*) hit; **en** ~ in (*ou* into) touch; **avoir une drôle de** ~ to look a sight; ~ **de commande/de fonction/de retour** (*INFORM*) control/function/return key; ~ **à effleurement** *ou* **sensitive** touch-sensitive control *ou* key.

touche-à-tout [tōōshàtōō] *nm inv* (*péj: gén: enfant*) meddler; (: *fig: inventeur etc*) dabbler.

toucher [tōōshā] *nm* touch ♦ *vt* to touch; (*palper*) to feel; (*atteindre: d'un coup de feu etc*) to hit; (*affecter*) to touch, affect;

(*concerner*) to concern, affect; (*contacter*) to reach, contact; (*recevoir: récompense*) to receive, get; (: *salaire*) to draw, get; (*chèque*) to cash; (*aborder: problème, sujet*) to touch on; **au** ~ to the touch; by the feel; **se** ~ (*être en contact*) to touch; ~ **à** to touch; (*modifier*) to touch, tamper *ou* meddle with; (*traiter de, concerner*) to have to do with, concern; **je vais lui en** ~ **un mot** I'll have a word with him about it; ~ **au but** (*fig*) to near one's goal; ~ **à sa fin** to be drawing to a close.

touffe [tōōf] *nf* tuft.

touffu, e [tōōfü] *a* thick, dense; (*fig*) complex, involved.

toujours [tōōzhōōr] *ad* always; (*encore*) still; (*constamment*) forever; **depuis** ~ always; **essaie** ~ (you can) try anyway; **pour** ~ forever; ~ **est-il que** the fact remains that; ~ **plus** more and more.

toulonnais, e [tōōlone, -ez] *a* of *ou* from Toulon.

toulousain, e [tōōlōōzàñ, -en] *a* of *ou* from Toulouse.

toupet [tōōpe] *nm* tuft; (*fam*) nerve.

toupie [tōōpē] *nf* (spinning) top.

tour [tōōr] *nf* tower; (*immeuble*) high-rise building (*US*) *ou* block (*Brit*); (*ÉCHECS*) castle, rook ♦ *nm* (*excursion*: *à pied*) stroll, walk; (: *en voiture etc*) run, ride; (: *plus long*) trip; (*SPORT*: *aussi*: ~ **de piste**) lap; (*d'être servi ou de jouer etc, tournure, de vis ou clef*) turn; (*de roue etc*) revolution; (*circonférence*): **de 3 m de** ~ 3 m around, with a circumference *ou* girth of 3 m; (*POL*: *aussi*: ~ **de scrutin**) ballot; (*ruse, de prestidigitation, de cartes*) trick; (*de potier*) wheel; (*à bois, métaux*) lathe; **faire le** ~ **de** to go to (a)round; (*à pied*) to walk (a)round; (*fig*) to review; **faire le** ~ **de l'Europe** to tour Europe; **faire un** ~ to go for a walk; (*en voiture etc*) to go for a ride; **faire 2** ~**s** to go (a)round twice; (*hélice etc*) to turn *ou* revolve twice; **fermer à double** ~ *vi* to double-lock the door; **c'est au** ~ **de Renée** it's Renée's turn; **à** ~ **de rôle**, ~ **à** ~ in turn; **à** ~ **de bras** with all one's strength; (*fig*) non-stop, relentlessly; ~ **de taille/tête** waist/head measurement; ~ **de chant** song recital; ~ **de contrôle** *nf* control tower; ~ **de garde** turn of duty; ~ **d'horizon** (*fig*) general survey; ~ **de lit** valance; ~ **de main** dexterity, knack; **en un** ~ **de main** (as) quick as a flash; ~ **de passe-passe** trick, sleight of hand; ~ **de reins** sprained back.

tourangeau, elle, x [tōōrâñzhō, -el] *a* (*de la région*) of *ou* from Touraine; (*de la ville*) of *ou* from Tours.

tourbe [tōōrb(ə)] *nf* peat.

tourbière [tōōrbyer] *nf* peat bog.

tourbillon [tōōrbēyôñ] *nm* whirlwind; (*d'eau*) whirlpool; (*fig*) whirl, swirl.

tourbillonner [tōōrbēyonā] *vi* to whirl, swirl; (*objet, personne*) to whirl *ou* twirl round.

tourelle [tōōrel] *nf* turret.

tourisme [tōōrēsm(ə)] *nm* tourism; **agence de** ~ travel agency; **avion/voiture de** ~ private plane/car; **faire du** ~ to do some sightseeing, go touring.

touriste [tōōrēst(ə)] *nm/f* tourist.

touristique [tōōrēstēk] *a* tourist *cpd*; (*région*) touristic (*péj*), with tourist appeal.

tourment [tōōrmáṅ] *nm* torment.

tourmente [tōōrmáṅt] *nf* storm.

tourmenté, e [tōōrmáṅtā] *a* tormented, tortured; (*mer, période*) turbulent, tempestuous.

tourmenter [tōōrmáṅtā] *vt* to torment; **se ~** *vi* to fret, worry o.s.

tournage [tōōrnázh] *nm* (*d'un film*) shooting.

tournant, e [tōōrnáṅ, -áṅt] *a* (*feu, scène*) revolving; (*chemin*) winding; (*escalier*) spiral *cpd*; (*mouvement*) circling; *voir* **plaque**, **grève** ♦ *nm* (*de route*) curve (*US*), bend (*Brit*); (*fig*) turning point.

tourné, e [tōōrnā] *a* (*lait, vin*) sour; (*MENUISERIE: bois*) turned; (*fig: compliment*) well-phrased; **bien ~** (*personne*) shapely; **mal ~** (*lettre*) badly expressed; **avoir l'esprit mal ~** to have a dirty mind.

tournebroche [tōōrnəbrosh] *nm* roasting spit.

tourne-disque [tōōrnədēsk(ə)] *nm* record player.

tournedos [tōōrnədō] *nm* tournedos.

tournée [tōōrnā] *nf* (*du facteur etc*) round; (*d'artiste, politicien*) tour; (*au café*) round (of drinks); **~ électorale/musicale** election/concert tour; **faire la ~ de** to go (a)round.

tournemain [tōōrnəmaṅ]: **en un ~** *ad* in a flash.

tourner [tōōrnā] *vt* to turn; (*sauce, mélange*) to stir; (*contourner*) to get (a)round; (*CINÉMA*) to shoot, to make ♦ *vi* to turn; (*moteur*) to run; (*compteur*) to tick away; (*lait etc*) to turn (sour); (*fig: chance, vie*) to turn out; **se ~** *vi* to turn (a)round; **se ~ vers** to turn to; to turn towards; **bien ~** to turn out well; **~ autour de** to go (a)round; (*planète*) to revolve (a)round; (*péj*) to hang (a)round; **~ autour du pot** (*fig*) to go (a)round in circles; **~ à/en** to turn into; **~ à la pluie/au rouge** to turn rainy/red; **~ en ridicule** to ridicule; **~ le dos à** (*mouvement*) to turn one's back on; (*position*) to have one's back to; **~ court** to come to a sudden end; **se ~ les pouces** to twiddle one's thumbs; **~ la tête** to look away; **~ la tête à qn** (*fig*) to go to sb's head; **~ de l'œil** to pass out; **~ la page** (*fig*) to turn the page.

tournesol [tōōrnəsol] *nm* sunflower.

tourneur [tōōrnœr] *nm* turner; lathe-operator.

tournevis [tōōrnəvēs] *nm* screwdriver.

tourniquer [tōōrnēkā] *vi* to go (a)round in circles.

tourniquet [tōōrnēke] *nm* (*pour arroser*) sprinkler; (*portillon*) turnstile; (*présentoir*) revolving stand, spinner; (*CHIRURGIE*) tourniquet.

tournis [tōōrnē] *nm*: **avoir/donner le ~** to feel/make dizzy.

tournoi [tōōrnwá] *nm* tournament.

tournoyer [tōōrnwáyā] *vi* (*oiseau*) to wheel (a)round; (*fumée*) to swirl (a)round.

tournure [tōōrnür] *nf* (*LING: syntaxe*) turn of phrase; form; (: *d'une phrase*) phrasing; (*évolution*): **la ~ de qch** the way sth is developing; (*aspect*): **la ~ de** the look of; **la ~ des événements** the turn of events; **prendre ~** to take shape; **~ d'esprit** turn *ou* cast of mind.

tour-opérateur [tōōropārátœr] *nm* tour operator.

tourte [tōōrt(ə)] *nf* pie.

tourteau, x [tōōrtō] *nm* (*AGR*) oil cake, cattle-cake; (*ZOOL*) edible crab.

tourtereaux [tōōrtərō] *nmpl* lovebirds.

tourterelle [tōōrtərel] *nf* turtledove.

tourtière [tōōrtyer] *nf* pie tin (*US*) *ou* dish (*Brit*).

tous *dét* [tōō] , *pronom* [tōōs] *voir* **tout**.

Toussaint [tōōsaṅ] *nf*: **la ~** All Saints' Day.

tousser [tōōsā] *vi* to cough.

toussoter [tōōsotā] *vi* to have a slight cough; to cough a little; (*pour avertir*) to give a slight cough.

tout, e, *pl* **tous, toutes** [tōō, tōōs, toot] *dét* all; **~ le lait** all the milk, the whole of the milk; **~e la nuit** all night, the whole night; **~ le livre** the whole book; **~ un pain** a whole loaf; **tous les livres** all the books; **toutes les nuits** every night; **à ~ âge** at any age; **toutes les fois** every time; **toutes les 3/2 semaines** every third/other *ou* second week; **tous les 2** both *ou* each of us (*ou* them); **toutes les 3** all 3 of us (*ou* them); **~ le temps** all the time; (*sans cesse*) the whole time; **c'est ~ le contraire** it's quite the opposite; **il avait pour ~e nourriture** his only food was ♦ *pronom* everything, all; **tous, toutes** (of them); **je les vois tous** I can see them all *ou* all of them; **nous y sommes tous allés** all of us went, we all went; **en ~** in all; **en ~ et pour ~** all in all ♦ *ad* (*assez*) quite; (*très*) very; **~ en haut** right at the top; **le ~ premier** the very first; **le ~ livre ~ entier** the whole book; **~ court** quite simply; **~ seul** all alone; **~ droit** straight ahead; **~ en travaillant/mangeant** while working/eating, as *ou* while he *etc* works/eats ♦ *nm* whole; **le ~ all** of it (*ou* them), the whole lot; **le ~ est de** the main thing is to; **du ~ au ~** (*complètement*) utterly; **avoir ~ de**: **elle a ~ d'une mère** she's a real mother; **~ ce que ... all** that ...; **~ ce qu'il y a de plus aimable** the nicest possible, as nice as possible; **~ ou rien** all or nothing; **~ d'abord** first of all; **~ à coup** suddenly; **~ à fait** absolutely; **~ à l'heure** (*passé*) a short while ago; (*futur*) in a short while, shortly; **à ~ à l'heure!** see you later!; **~ de même** all the same; **~ le monde** everybody, everyone; **~ de suite** immediately, straightaway; **~ terrain** *ou* **tous terrains** *a inv* all-terrain.

tout-à-l'égout [tōōtálāgōō] *nm inv* sewer system.

toutefois [tōōtfwá] *ad* however.

toutou [tōōtōō] *nm* (*fam*) doggie.

tout-petit [tōōp(ə)tē] *nm* toddler.

tout-puissant, toute-puissante [tōōpüēsáṅ, tōōtpüēsáṅt] *a* all-powerful, omnipotent.

tout-venant [tōōvnáṅ] *nm*: **le ~** everyday stuff.

toux [tōō] *nf* cough.

toxémie [toksāmē] *nf* toxemia (*US*), toxaemia (*Brit*).

toxicité [toksēsētā] *nf* toxicity.

toxicomane [toksēkomán] *nm/f* drug addict.

toxicomanie [toksēkománē] *nf* drug addiction.

toxine [toksēn] *nf* toxin.

toxique [toksēk] *a* toxic, poisonous.

TP *sigle mpl* = **travaux pratiques, travaux publics** ♦ *sigle m* = **trésor public**.

TPG *sigle m* = **Trésorier-payeur général**.

tps *abr* = **temps**.

trac [trák] *nm* nerves *pl*; (*THÉÂTRE*) stage fright; **avoir le ~** to get an attack of nerves; to have stage fright; **tout à ~** all of a sudden.

traçant, e [trásáń, -áńt] *a*: **table ~e** (*INFORM*) (graph) plotter.

tracas [tráká] *nm* bother *q*, worry *q*.

tracasser [trákásā] *vt* to worry, bother; (*harceler*) to harass; **se ~** *vi* to worry o.s., fret.

tracasserie [trákásrē] *nf* annoyance *q*; harassment *q*.

tracassier, ière [trákásyā, -yer] *a* irksome.

trace [trás] *nf* (*empreintes*) tracks *pl*; (*marques, aussi fig*) mark; (*restes, vestige*) trace; (*indice*) sign; **suivre à la ~** to track; **~s de pas** footprints.

tracé [trásā] *nm* (*contour*) line; (*plan*) layout.

tracer [trásā] *vt* to draw; (*mot*) to trace; (*piste*) to open up; (*fig: chemin*) to show.

traceur [trásœr] *nm* (*INFORM*) plotter.

trachée(-artère) [tráshā(árter)] *nf* windpipe, trachea.

trachéite [trákāēt] *nf* tracheitis.

tract [trákt] *nm* tract, pamphlet; (*publicitaire*) handout.

tractations [tráktásyóń] *nfpl* dealings, bargaining *sg*.

tracter [tráktā] *vt* to tow.

tracteur [tráktœr] *nm* tractor.

traction [tráksyóń] *nf* traction; (*GYM*) pull-up; **~ avant/arrière** front-wheel/rear-wheel drive; **~ électrique** electric(al) traction *ou* haulage.

tradition [trádēsyóń] *nf* tradition.

traditionaliste [trádēsyonálēst(ə)] *a*, *nm/f* traditionalist.

traditionnel, le [trádēsyonel] *a* traditional.

traditionnellement [trádēsyonelmáń] *ad* traditionally.

traducteur, trice [trádüktœr, -trēs] *nm/f* translator.

traduction [trádüksyóń] *nf* translation.

traduire [trádüēr] *vt* to translate; (*exprimer*) to render, convey; **se ~ par** to find expression in; **~ en français** to translate into French; **~ en justice** to bring before the courts.

traduis [trádüē] *etc vb voir* **traduire**.

traduisible [trádüēzēbl(ə)] *a* translatable.

traduit, e [trádüē, -ēt] *pp de* **traduire**.

trafic [tráfēk] *nm* traffic; **~ d'armes** arms dealing; **~ de drogue** drug peddling.

trafiquant, e [tráfēkáń, -áńt] *nm/f* trafficker; dealer.

trafiquer [tráfēkā] *vt* (*péj*) to doctor, tamper with ♦ *vi* to traffic, to be engaged in trafficking.

tragédie [trázhādē] *nf* tragedy.

tragédien, ne [trázhādyań, -en] *nm/f* tragedian/tragedienne.

tragi-comique [trázhēkomēk] *a* tragi-comic.

tragique [trázhēk] *a* tragic ♦ *nm*: **prendre qch au ~** to make a tragedy out of sth.

tragiquement [trázhēkmáń] *ad* tragically.

trahir [tráēr] *vt* to betray; (*fig*) to give away, reveal; **se ~** to betray o.s., give o.s. away.

trahison [tráēzóń] *nf* betrayal; (*JUR*) treason.

traie [tre] *etc vb voir* **traire**.

train [trań] *nm* (*RAIL*) train; (*allure*) pace; (*fig: ensemble*) set; **être en ~ de faire qch** to be doing sth; **mettre qch en ~** to get sth under way; **mettre qn en ~** to put sb in good spirits; **se mettre en ~** (*commencer*) to get started; (*faire de la gymnastique*) to warm up; **se sentir en ~** to feel in good form; **aller bon ~** to make good progress; **~ avant/ arrière** front-wheel/rear-wheel axle assembly; **~ à grande vitesse (TGV)** high-speed train; **~ d'atterrissage** landing gear; **~- autos-couchettes** car-sleeper train; **~ électrique** (*jouet*) (electric) train set; **~ de pneus** set of tires (*US*) *ou* tyres (*Brit*); **~ de vie** style of living.

traînailler [trenâyā] *vi* = **traînasser**.

traînant, e [trenáń, -áńt] *a* (*voix, ton*) drawling.

traînard, e [trenár, -árd(ə)] *nm/f* (*péj*) slowpoke (*US*), slowcoach (*Brit*).

traînasser [trenásā] *vi* to dawdle.

traîne [tren] *nf* (*de robe*) train; **être à la ~** to be in tow; (*en arrière*) to lag behind; (*en désordre*) to be lying around.

traîneau, x [trenō] *nm* sleigh, sledge.

traînée [trenā] *nf* streak, trail; (*péj*) slut.

traîner [trenā] *vt* (*remorque*) to pull; (*enfant, chien*) to drag *ou* trail along; (*maladie*): **il traîne un rhume depuis l'hiver** he has a cold which has been dragging on since winter ♦ *vi* (*être en désordre*) to lie around; (*marcher lentement*) to dawdle (along); (*vagabonder*) to hang about; (*agir lentement*) to idle about; (*durer*) to drag on; **se ~** *vi* (*ramper*) to crawl along; (*marcher avec difficulté*) to drag o.s. along; (*durer*) to drag on; **se ~ par terre** to crawl (on the ground); **~ qn au cinéma** to drag sb to the cinema; **~ les pieds** to drag one's feet; **~ par terre** to trail on the ground; **~ en longueur** to drag out.

training [trenēng] *nm* (*pull*) tracksuit top; (*chaussure*) sneaker (*US*), trainer (*Brit*).

train-train [trańtrań] *nm* humdrum routine.

traire [trer] *vt* to milk.

trait, e [tre, -et] *pp de* **traire** ♦ *nm* (*ligne*) line; (*de dessin*) stroke; (*caractéristique*) feature, trait; (*flèche*) dart, arrow; shaft; **~s** *nmpl* (*du visage*) features; **d'un ~** (*boire*) in one gulp; **de ~** *a* (*animal*) draft (*US*), draught (*Brit*); **avoir ~ à** to concern; **~ pour ~** line for line; **~ de caractère** characteristic, trait; **~ d'esprit** flash of wit; **~ de génie** brain wave; **~ d'union** hyphen; (*fig*) link.

traitable [tretábl(ə)] *a* (*personne*) accommodating; (*sujet*) manageable.

traitant, e [tretáń, -áńt] *a*: **votre médecin ~** your usual *ou* family doctor; **shampooing ~** medicated shampoo; **crème ~e** conditioning cream, conditioner.

traite [tret] *nf* (*COMM*) draft; (*AGR*) milking; (*trajet*) stretch; **d'une (seule) ~** without stopping (once); **la ~ des noirs** the slave trade; **la ~ des blanches** the white slave trade.

traité [tretā] *nm* treaty.

traitement [tretmân] *nm* treatment; processing; (*salaire*) salary; **suivre un** ~ to undergo treatment; **mauvais** ~ ill-treatment; ~ **de données** *ou* **de l'information** (*INFORM*) data processing; ~ **par lots** (*INFORM*) batch processing; ~ **de texte** (*INFORM*) word processing.

traiter [trātā] *vt* (*gén*) to treat; (*TECH*: *matériaux*) to process, treat; (*INFORM*) to process; (*affaire*) to deal with, handle; (*qualifier*): ~ **qn d'idiot** to call sb a fool ♦ *vi* to deal; ~ **de** *vt* to deal with; **bien/mal** ~ to treat well/ill-treat.

traiteur [tretœr] *nm* caterer.

traître, esse [tretr(ə), -tres] *a* (*dangereux*) treacherous ♦ *nm* traitor; **prendre qn en** ~ to make an insidious attack on sb.

traîtrise [trātrēz] *nf* treachery.

trajectoire [tràzhektwàr] *nf* trajectory, path.

trajet [tràzhe] *nm* journey; (*itinéraire*) route; (*fig*) path, course.

tralala [tràlàlà] *nm* (*péj*) fuss.

tram [tràm] *nm* streetcar (*US*), tram (*Brit*).

trame [tràm] *nf* (*de tissu*) weft; (*fig*) framework; texture; (*TYPO*) screen.

tramer [tràmā] *vt* to plot, hatch.

trampoline [trânpolēn], **trampolino** [trânpolēnō] *nm* trampoline; (*SPORT*) trampolining.

tramway [tràmwe] *nm* tram(way); (*voiture*) streetcar (*US*), tram(car) (*Brit*).

tranchant, e [trânshân, -ânt] *a* sharp; (*fig*: *personne*) peremptory; (: *couleurs*) striking ♦ *nm* (*d'un couteau*) cutting edge; (*de la main*) edge; **à double** ~ (*argument*, *procédé*) double-edged.

tranche [trânsh] *nf* (*morceau*) slice; (*arête*) edge; (*partie*) section; (*série*) block; (*d'impôts*, *revenus etc*) bracket; (*loterie*) issue; ~ **d'âge** age bracket; ~ **(de silicium)** wafer.

tranché, e [trânshā] *a* (*couleurs*) distinct, sharply contrasted; (*opinions*) clear-cut, definite ♦ *nf* trench.

trancher [trânshā] *vt* to cut, sever; (*fig*: *résoudre*) to settle ♦ *vi* to be decisive; (*entre deux choses*) to settle the argument; ~ **avec** to contrast sharply with.

tranchet [trânshe] *nm* knife.

tranchoir [trânshwàr] *nm* chopper.

tranquille [trânkēl] *a* calm, quiet; (*enfant*, *élève*) quiet; (*rassuré*) easy in one's mind, with one's mind at rest; **se tenir** ~ (*enfant*) to be quiet; **avoir la conscience** ~ to have an easy conscience; **laisse-moi/laisse-ça** ~ leave me/it alone.

tranquillement [trânkēlmân] *ad* calmly.

tranquillisant, e [trânkēlēzân, -ânt] *a* (*nouvelle*) reassuring ♦ *nm* tranquillizer.

tranquilliser [trânkēlēzā] *vt* to reassure; **se** ~ to calm (o.s.) down.

tranquillité [trânkēlētā] *nf* quietness; peace (and quiet); **en toute** ~ with complete peace of mind; ~ **d'esprit** peace of mind.

transaction [trânzàksyôn] *nf* (*COMM*) transaction, deal.

transafricain, e [trânsàfrēkàn, -en] *a* transafrican.

transalpin, e [trânzàlpàn, -ēn] *a* transalpine.

transaméricain, e [trânzàmārēkàn, -en] *a* transamerican.

transat [trânzàt] *nm* deck chair ♦ *nf* = *course transatlantique*.

transatlantique [trânzàtlântēk] *a* transatlantic ♦ *nm* transatlantic liner.

transborder [trânsbordā] *vt* to tran(s)ship.

transcendant, e [trânsândân, -ânt] *a* (*PHILOSOPHIE*, *MATH*) transcendental; (*supérieur*) transcendent.

transcodeur [trânskodœr] *nm* compiler.

transcription [trânskrēpsyôn] *nf* transcription.

transcrire [trânskrēr] *vt* to transcribe.

transe [trâns] *nf*: **entrer en** ~ to go into a trance; ~**s** *nfpl* agony *sg*.

transfèrement [trânsfermân] *nm* transfer.

transférer [trânsfārā] *vt* to transfer.

transfert [trânsfer] *nm* transfer.

transfigurer [trânsfēgürā] *vt* to transform.

transfo [trânsfō] *nm* (= *transformateur*) transformer.

transformable [trânsformàbl(ə)] *a* convertible.

transformateur [trânsformàtœr] *nm* transformer.

transformation [trânsformàsyôn] *nf* transformation; (*RUGBY*) conversion; **industries de** ~ processing industries.

transformer [trânsformā] *vt* to transform, alter (*'alter' implique un changement moins radical*); (*matière première*, *appartement*, *RUGBY*) to convert; ~ **en** to transform into; to turn into; to convert into; **se** ~ *vi* to be transformed; to alter.

transfuge [trânsfüzh] *nm* renegade.

transfuser [trânsfüzā] *vt* to transfuse.

transfusion [trânsfüzyôn] *nf*: ~ **sanguine** blood transfusion.

transgresser [trânsgrāsā] *vt* to contravene, disobey.

transhumance [trânzümâns] *nf* transhumance, seasonal move to new pastures.

transi, e [trânzē] *a* numb (with cold), chilled to the bone.

transiger [trânzēzhā] *vi* to compromise, come to an agreement; ~ **sur** *ou* **avec qch** to compromise on sth.

transistor [trânzēstor] *nm* transistor.

transistorisé, e [trânzēstorēzā] *a* transistorized.

transit [trânzēt] *nm* transit; **de** ~ transit *cpd*; **en** ~ in transit.

transitaire [trânzēter] *nm/f* forwarding agent.

transiter [trânzētā] *vi* to pass in transit.

transitif, ive [trânzētēf, -ēv] *a* transitive.

transition [trânzēsyôn] *nf* transition; **de** ~ transitional.

transitoire [trânzētwàr] *a* (*mesure*, *gouvernement*) transitional, provisional; (*fugitif*) transient.

translucide [trânslüsēd] *a* translucent.

transmet [trânsme] *etc vb voir* **transmettre**.

transmettais [trânsmete] *etc vb voir* **transmettre**.

transmetteur [trânsmetœr] *nm* transmitter.

transmettre [trânsmetr(ə)] *vt* (*passer*): ~ **qch à qn** to pass sth on to sb; (*TECH*, *TÉL*, *MÉD*) to transmit; (*TV*, *RADIO*: *retransmettre*) to broadcast.

transmis, e [trânsmē, -ēz] *pp de* **transmettre**.

transmissible [trâńsmēsĕbl(ə)] *a* transmissible.

transmission [trâńsmēsyôń] *nf* transmission, passing on; (*AUTO*) transmission; ~**s** *nfpl* (*MIL*) ≈ signals corps; ~ **de données** (*INFORM*) data transmission; ~ **de pensée** thought transmission.

transocéanien, ne [trâńzosăányań, -en] *a*, **transocéanique** [trâńzosăánĕk] *a* transoceanic.

transparaître [trâńspárctr(ə)] *vi* to show (through).

transparence [trâńspáráńs] *nf* transparence; **par** ~ (*regarder*) against the light; (*voir*) showing through.

transparent, e [trâńspáráń, -áńt] *a* transparent.

transpercer [trâńspersă] *vt* to go through, pierce.

transpiration [trâńspērásyôń] *nf* perspiration.

transpirer [trâńspērā] *vi* to perspire; (*information, nouvelle*) to come to light.

transplant [trâńsplâń] *nm* transplant.

transplantation [trâńsplâńtâsyôń] *nf* transplant.

transplanter [trâńsplâńtā] *vt* (*MÉD, BOT*) to transplant; (*personne*) to uproot, move.

transport [trâńspor] *nm* transport; (*émotions*): ~ **de colère** fit of rage; ~ **de joie** transport of delight; ~ **de voyageurs/marchandises** passenger/goods transportation; ~**s en commun** public transport *sg*; ~**s routiers** trucking (*US*), haulage (*Brit*).

transportable [trâńsportâbl(ə)] *a* (*marchandises*) transportable; (*malade*) fit (enough) to be moved.

transporter [trâńsportā] *vt* to carry, move; (*COMM*) to transport, convey; (*fig*): ~ **qn (de joie)** to send sb into raptures; **se** ~ **quelque part** (*fig*) to let one's imagination carry one away (somewhere); ~ **qn à l'hôpital** to take sb to hospital.

transporteur [trâńsportœr] *nm* trucker (*US*), haulage contractor (*Brit*).

transposer [trâńspōzā] *vt* to transpose.

transposition [trâńspōzēsyôń] *nf* transposition.

transrhénan, e [trâńsrānáń, -áń] *a* beyond the Rhine.

transsaharien, ne [trâńssăáryań, -en] *a* trans-Saharan.

transsexuel, le [trâńsseksüel] *a*, *nm/f* transsexual.

transsibérien, ne [trâńssēbāryań, -en] *a* trans-Siberian.

transvaser [trâńsvázā] *vt* to decant.

transversal, e, aux [trâńsversál, -ō] *a* transverse, cross(-); (*route etc*) cross-country; (*mur, chemin, rue*) running at right angles; (*AUTO*): **axe** ~ main cross-country highway (*US*) *ou* road (*Brit*).

transversalement [trâńsversálmâń] *ad* crosswise.

trapèze [trápez] *nm* (*GÉOM*) trapezoid (*US*), trapezium (*Brit*); (*au cirque*) trapeze.

trapéziste [trápāzĕst(ə)] *nm/f* trapeze artist.

trappe [tráp] *nf* (*de cave, grenier*) trap door; (*piège*) trap.

trappeur [trápœr] *nm* trapper, fur trader.

trapu, e [trápü] *a* squat, stocky.

traquenard [tráknár] *nm* trap.

traquer [trákā] *vt* to track down; (*harceler*) to hound.

traumatisant, e [trōmátēzáń, -áńt] traumatic.

traumatiser [trōmátēzā] *vt* to traumatize.

traumatisme [trōmátēsm(ə)] *nm* traumatism; ~ **crânien** cranial traumatism.

traumatologie [trōmátolozhē] *nf* branch of medicine concerned with accidents.

travail, aux [tráváy, -ō] *nm* (*gén*) work; (*tâche, métier*) work *q*, job; (*ÉCON, MÉD*) labor (*US*), labour (*Brit*); (*INFORM*) job ♦ *nmpl* (*de réparation, agricoles etc*) work *sg*; (*sur route*) road construction (*US*) *ou* repairs, roadworks (*Brit*); (*de construction*) building (work) *sg*; **être/entrer en** ~ (*MÉD*) to be in/go into labor; **être sans** ~ (*employé*) to be out of work, be unemployed; ~ **d'intérêt général (TIG)** ≈ community service; ~ **(au) noir** moonlighting; ~ **posté** shiftwork; **travaux des champs** farmwork *sg*; **travaux dirigés (TD)** (*SCOL*) supervised practical work *sg*; **travaux forcés** hard labor *sg*; **travaux manuels** (*SCOL*) handicrafts; **travaux ménagers** housework *sg*; **travaux pratiques (TP)** (*gén*) practical work; (*en laboratoire*) lab (*US*), lab work (*Brit*); **travaux publics (TP)** ≈ public works *sg*.

travaillé, e [tráváyā] *a* (*style*) polished.

travailler [tráváyā] *vi* to work; (*bois*) to warp ♦ *vt* (*bois, métal*) to work; (*pâte*) to knead; (*objet d'art, discipline, fig: influencer*) to work on; **cela le travaille** it is on his mind; ~ **la terre** to work the land; ~ **son piano** to do one's piano practice; ~ **à** to work on; (*fig: contribuer à*) to work towards; ~ **à faire** to endeavor to do.

travailleur, euse [tráváyœr, -œz] *a* hardworking ♦ *nm/f* worker; ~ **de force** laborer (*US*), labourer (*Brit*); ~ **intellectuel** non-manual worker; ~ **social** social worker; **travailleuse familiale** social welfare worker in the home.

travailliste [tráváyēst(ə)] *a* ≈ Labour *cpd* (*Brit*) ♦ *nm/f* member of the Labour party (*Brit*).

travée [trávā] *nf* row; (*ARCHIT*) bay; span.

travelling [trávlĕng] *nm* (*chariot*) dolly; (*technique*) tracking; ~ **optique** zoom shots *pl*.

travelo [trávlō] *nm* (*fam*) (drag) queen.

travers [tráver] *nm* fault, failing; **en** ~ (**de**) across; **au** ~ (**de**) through; **de** ~ *a* askew ♦ *ad* sideways; (*fig*) the wrong way; **à** ~ through; **regarder de** ~ (*fig*) to look askance at.

traverse [trávers(ə)] *nf* (*de voie ferrée*) tie (*US*), sleeper (*Brit*); **chemin de** ~ shortcut.

traversée [tráversā] *nf* crossing.

traverser [tráversā] *vt* (*gén*) to cross; (*ville, tunnel, aussi: percer, fig*) to go through; (*suj: ligne, trait*) to run across.

traversin [tráversań] *nm* bolster.

travesti [trávestē] *nm* (*costume*) costume; (*artiste de cabaret*) female impersonator, drag artist; (*pervers*) transvestite.

travestir [trávestēr] *vt* (*vérité*) to misrepresent; **se** ~ (*costumer*) to dress up; (*artiste*) to put on drag; (*PSYCH*) to dress as a woman.

trayais [trɛyc] *etc vb voir* **traire.**

trayeuse [trcyɑ̃z] *nf* milking machine.

trébucher [trɑ̃büshɑ̃] *vi:* ~ **(sur)** to stumble (over), trip (over).

trèfle [trefl(ə)] *nm* (*BOT*) clover; (*CARTES*: *couleur*) clubs *pl*; (: *carte*) club; ~ **à quatre feuilles** four-leaf clover.

treillage [treyàzh] *nm* latticework.

treille [trcy] *nf* (*tonnelle*) vine arbor (*US*) *ou* arbour (*Brit*); (*vigne*) climbing vine.

treillis [trɑ̃yɛ̄] *nm* (*métallique*) wire netting; (*toile*) canvas; (*uniforme*) battle-dress.

treize [trez] *num* thirteen.

treizième [trezyem] *num* thirteenth.

tréma [trɑ̃mɑ̃] *nm* dieresis (*US*), diaeresis (*Brit*).

tremblant, e [trɑ̀nblɑ̀n, -ɑ̀nt] *a* trembling, shaking.

tremble [trɑ̀nbl(ə)] *nm* (*BOT*) aspen.

tremblé, c [trɑ̀nblɑ̃] *a* shaky.

tremblement [trɑ̀nbləmɑ̀n] *nm* trembling *q*, shaking *q*, shivering *q*; ~ **de terre** earthquake.

trembler [trɑ̀nblɑ̃] *vi* to tremble, shake; ~ **de** (*froid, fièvre*) to shiver *ou* tremble with; (*peur*) to shake *ou* tremble with; ~ **pour qn** to fear for sb.

trembloter [trɑ̀nblotɑ̃] *vi* to tremble *ou* shake slightly.

trémolo [trɑ̃molō] *nm* (*d'un instrument*) tremolo; (*de la voix*) quaver.

trémousser [trɑ̃moōsɑ̃]: **se** ~ *vi* to jig about, wriggle about.

trempe [trɑ̀np] *nf* (*fig*): **de cette/sa** ~ of this/his caliber (*US*) *ou* calibre (*Brit*).

trempé, e [trɑ̀npɑ̃] *a* soaking (wet), drenched; (*TECH*): **acier** ~ tempered steel.

tremper [trɑ̀npɑ̃] *vt* to soak, drench; (*aussi*: **faire** ~, **mettre à** ~) to soak; (*plonger*): ~ **qch dans** to dip sth in(to) ♦ *vi* to soak; (*fig*): ~ **dans** to be involved *ou* have a hand in; **se** ~ *vi* to have a quick dip; **se faire** ~ to get soaked *ou* drenched.

trempette [trɑ̀npet] *nf*: **faire** ~ to go paddling.

tremplin [trɑ̀nplɑ̀n] *nm* springboard; (*SKI*) ski jump.

trentaine [trɑ̀ntɛn] *nf* (*âge*): **avoir la** ~ to be around thirty; **une** ~ (**de**) thirty or so, about thirty.

trente [trɑ̀nt] *num* thirty; **voir** ~-**six chandelles** (*fig*) to see stars; **être/se mettre sur son** ~ **et un** to be/get dressed to kill; ~-**trois tours** *nm* long-playing record, LP.

trentième [trɑ̀ntyem] *num* thirtieth.

trépaner [trɑ̃pɑ̀nɑ̃] *vt* to trepan, trephine.

trépasser [trɑ̃pɑ̀sɑ̃] *vi* to pass away.

trépidant, e [trɑ̃pɛ̄dɑ̀n, -ɑ̀nt] *a* (*fig*: *rythme*) pulsating; (: *vie*) hectic.

trépidation [trɑ̃pɛ̄dɑ̀syōn] *nf* (*d'une machine, d'un moteur*) vibration; (*fig*: *de la vie*) whirl.

trépider [trɑ̃pɛ̄dɑ̃] *vi* to vibrate.

trépied [trɑ̃pyɑ̃] *nm* (*d'appareil*) tripod; (*meuble*) trivet.

trépigner [trɑ̃pɛ̄nyɑ̃] *vi* to stamp (one's feet).

très [tre] *ad* very; much + *pp*, highly + *pp*; ~ **beau/bien** very beautiful/well; ~ **critiqué** much criticized; ~ **industrialisé** highly industrialized; **j'ai** ~ **faim** I'm very hungry.

trésor [trɑ̄zor] *nm* treasure; (*ADMIN*) finances *pl*; (*d'un organisation*) funds *pl*; ~ **(public)** (**TP**) public revenue; (*service*) public revenue office.

trésorerie [trɑ̄zorrɛ̄] *nf* (*fonds*) funds *pl*; (*gestion*) accounts *pl*; (*bureaux*) accounts department; (*poste*) treasurership; **difficultés de** ~ cash problems, shortage of cash *ou* funds; ~ **générale** (**TG**) *local government finance office.*

trésorier, ière [trɑ̄zoryɑ̄, -yer] *nm/f* treasurer.

trésorier-payeur [trɑ̄zoryɑ̄peyœr] *nm:* ~ **général** (**TPG**) paymaster.

tressaillement [trɑ̄sɑ̄ymɑ̀n] *nm* shiver, shudder; quiver.

tressaillir [trɑ̄sɑ̀yɛ̄r] *vi* (*de peur etc*) to shiver, shudder; (*de joie*) to quiver.

tressauter [trɑ̄sōtɑ̃] *vi* to start, jump.

tresse [tres] *nf* (*de cheveux*) braid, plait; (*cordon, galon*) braid.

tresser [trɑ̄sɑ̃] *vt* (*cheveux*) to braid, plait; (*fil, jonc*) to plait; (*corbeille*) to weave; (*corde*) to twist.

tréteau, x [trɑ̄tō] *nm* trestle; **les** ~**x** (*fig*: *THÉÂTRE*) the boards.

treuil [trœy] *nm* winch.

trêve [trev] *nf* (*MIL, POL*) truce; (*fig*) respite; **sans** ~ unremittingly; ~ **de ...** enough of this ...; **les États de la T**~ the Trucial States.

tri [trɛ̄] *nm* (*voir trier*) sorting (out) *q*; selection; screening; (*INFORM*) sort; (*POSTES*: *action*) sorting; (: *bureau*) sorting office.

triage [trɛ̄yàzh] *nm* (*RAIL*) shunting; (*gare*) marshalling yard.

triangle [trɛ̄yɑ̀ngl(ə)] *nm* triangle; ~ **isocèle/équilatéral** isosceles/equilateral triangle; ~ **rectangle** right (*US*) *ou* right-angled (*Brit*) triangle.

triangulaire [trɛ̄yɑ̀ngülɛr] *a* triangular.

tribal, e, aux [trɛ̄bɑ̀l, -ō] *a* tribal.

tribord [trɛ̄bor] *nm*: **à** ~ to starboard, on the starboard side.

tribu [trɛ̄bü] *nf* tribe.

tribulations [trɛ̄bülɑ̀syōn] *nfpl* tribulations, trials.

tribunal, aux [trɛ̄bünɑ̀l, -ō] *nm* (*JUR*) court; (*MIL*) tribunal; ~ **de police/pour enfants** police/juvenile court; ~ **d'instance** (**TI**) ≈ district court (*US*), ≈ magistrates' court (*Brit*); ~ **de grande instance** (**TGI**) ≈ Supreme Court (*US*), ≈ High Court (*Brit*).

tribune [trɛ̄bün] *nf* (*estrade*) platform, rostrum; (*débat*) forum; (*d'église, de tribunal*) gallery; (*de stade*) stand; ~ **libre** (*PRESSE*) opinion column.

tribut [trɛ̄bü] *nm* tribute.

tributaire [trɛ̄büter] *a*: **être** ~ **de** to be dependent on; (*GÉO*) to be a tributary of.

tricentenaire [trɛ̄sɑ̀ntner] *nm* tercentenary, tricentennial.

tricher [trɛ̄shɑ̃] *vi* to cheat.

tricherie [trɛ̄shrɛ̄] *nf* cheating *q*.

tricheur, euse [trɛ̄shœr, -ɑ̄z] *nm/f* cheat.

trichromie [trɛ̄kromɛ̄] *nf* three-color (*US*) *ou* -colour (*Brit*) printing.

tricolore [trɛ̄kolor] *a* three-colored (*US*), three-coloured (*Brit*); (*français*: *drapeau*) red, white and blue; (: *équipe etc*) French.

tricot [trɛ̄kō] *nm* (*technique, ouvrage*) knitting *q*; (*tissu*) knitted fabric; (*vêtement*) jersey, sweater; **~ de corps** undershirt (*US*), vest (*Brit*).

tricoter [trēkotā] *vt* to knit; **machine/aiguille à ~** knitting machine/needle.

trictrac [trēktrák] *nm* backgammon.

tricycle [trēsēkl(ə)] *nm* tricycle.

triennal, e, aux [trēenál, -ō] *a* (*prix, foire, élection*) triennial; (*charge, mandat, plan*) three-year.

trier [trēyā] *vt* (*classer*) to sort (out); (*choisir*) to select; (*visiteurs*) to screen; (*POSTES, INFORM*) to sort.

trieur, euse [trēyœr, -ēz] *nm/f* sorter.

trigonométrie [trēgonomātrē] *nf* trigonometry.

trilingue [trēlaṅg] *a* trilingual.

trilogie [trēlozhē] *nf* trilogy.

trimbaler [traṅbálā] *vt* to cart around, trail along.

trimer [trēmā] *vi* to slave away.

trimestre [trēmestr(ə)] *nm* (*SCOL*) term; (*COMM*) quarter.

trimestriel, le [trēmestrēyel] *a* quarterly; (*SCOL*) final (*US*), end-of-term (*Brit*).

tringle [traṅgl(ə)] *nf* rod.

Trinité [trēnētā] *nf* Trinity.

Trinité et Tobago [trēnētāātobágō] *nf* Trinidad and Tobago.

trinquer [traṅkā] *vi* to clink glasses; (*fam*) to take the rap; **~ à qch/la santé de qn** to drink to sth/sb.

trio [trēyō] *nm* trio.

triolet [trēyole] *nm* (*MUS*) triplet.

triomphal, e, aux [trēyōṅfál, -ō] *a* triumphant, triumphal.

triomphant, e [trēyōṅfáṅ, -áṅt] *a* triumphant.

triomphateur, trice [trēyōṅfátœr, -trēs] *nm/f* (triumphant) victor.

triomphe [trēyōṅf] *nm* triumph; **être reçu/porté en ~** to be given a triumphant welcome/be carried shoulder-high in triumph.

triompher [trēyōṅfā] *vi* to triumph; **~ de** to triumph over, overcome.

triparti, e [trēpártē] *a* (*aussi:* **tripartite**: *réunion, assemblée*) tripartite, three-party.

triperie [trēprē] *nf* tripe shop.

tripes [trēp] *nfpl* (*CULIN*) tripe *sg*; (*fam*) guts.

triplace [trēplás] *a* three-seater *cpd*.

triple [trēpl(ə)] *a* (*à trois élements*) triple; (*trois fois plus grand*) treble ♦ *nm*: **le ~ (de)** (*comparaison*) three times as much (as); **en ~ exemplaire** in triplicate.

triplé [trēplā] *nm* triple success, hat-trick (*Brit*).

triplement [trēpləmáṅ] *ad* (*à un degré triple*) three times over; (*de trois façons*) in three ways; (*pour trois raisons*) on three counts ♦ *nm* trebling, threefold increase.

tripler [trēplā] *vi, vt* to triple, treble, increase threefold.

triplés, es [trēplā] *nm/fpl* triplets.

Tripoli [trēpolē] *n* Tripoli.

tripot [trēpō] *nm* (*péj*) dive.

tripotage [trēpotázh] *nm* (*péj*) hanky-panky.

tripoter [trēpotā] *vt* to fiddle with, finger ♦ *vi* (*fam*) to rummage about.

trique [trēk] *nf* cudgel.

trisannuel, le [trēzánüel] *a* triennial.

triste [trēst(ə)] *a* sad; (*péj*): **~ personnage/affaire** sorry individual/affair; **c'est pas ~!** (*fam*) it's something else!

tristement [trēstəmáṅ] *ad* sadly.

tristesse [trēstes] *nf* sadness.

triton [trētōṅ] *nm* triton.

triturer [trētürā] *vt* (*pâte*) to knead; (*objets*) to manipulate.

trivial, e, aux [trēvyál, -ō] *a* coarse, crude; (*commun*) mundane.

trivialité [trēvyálētā] *nf* coarseness, crudeness; mundaneness.

troc [trok] *nm* (*ÉCON*) barter; (*transaction*) exchange, swap.

troène [troen] *nm* privet.

troglodyte [troglodēt] *nm/f* cave dweller, troglodyte.

trognon [tronyōṅ] *nm* (*de fruit*) core; (*de légume*) stalk.

trois [trwȧ] *num* three.

trois-huit [trwȧüēt] *nm inv*: **faire les ~** to work eight-hour shifts (round the clock).

troisième [trwȧzyem] *num* third; **le ~ âge** the years of retirement.

troisièmement [trwȧzyemmáṅ] *ad* thirdly.

trois-quarts [trwȧkár] *nmpl*: **les ~ de** three-quarters of.

trolleybus [trolebüs] *nm* trolley bus.

trombe [trōṅb] *nf* waterspout; **des ~s d'eau** a downpour; **en ~** (*arriver, passer*) like a whirlwind.

trombone [trōṅbon] *nm* (*MUS*) trombone; (*de bureau*) paper clip; **~ à coulisse** slide trombone.

tromboniste [trōṅbonēst(ə)] *nm/f* trombonist.

trompe [trōṅp] *nf* (*d'éléphant*) trunk; (*MUS*) trumpet, horn; **~ d'Eustache** Eustachian tube; **~s utérines** Fallopian tubes.

trompe-l'œil [trōṅplœy] *nm*: **en ~** in trompe l'œil style.

tromper [trōṅpā] *vt* to deceive; (*fig: espoir, attente*) to disappoint; (*vigilance, poursuivants*) to elude; **se ~** *vi* to make a mistake, be mistaken; **se ~ de voiture/jour** to take the wrong car/get the day wrong; **se ~ de 3 cm/20 F** to be off by 3 cm/20 F.

tromperie [trōṅprē] *nf* deception, trickery *q*.

trompette [trōṅpet] *nf* trumpet; **en ~** (*nez*) turned-up.

trompettiste [trōṅpātēst(ə)] *nm/f* trumpet player.

trompeur, euse [trōṅpœr, -ēz] *a* deceptive, misleading.

tronc [trōṅ] *nm* (*BOT, ANAT*) trunk; (*d'église*) collection box; **~ d'arbre** tree trunk; **~ commun** (*SCOL*) common-core syllabus; **~ de cône** truncated cone.

tronche [trōṅsh] *nf* (*fam*) mug, face.

tronçon [trōṅsōṅ] *nm* section.

tronçonner [trōṅsonā] *vt* (*arbre*) to saw up; (*pierre*) to cut up.

tronçonneuse [trōṅsonēz] *nf* chain saw.

trône [trōn] *nm* throne; **monter sur le ~** to ascend the throne.

trôner [trōnā] *vi* (*fig*) to have the place of honor (*US*) *ou* honour (*Brit*).

tronquer [trōṅkā] *vt* to truncate; (*fig*) to curtail.

trop [trō] *ad vb +* too much, too *+ adjectif, adverbe*; **~ (nombreux)** too many; **~ peu**

(nombreux) too few; ~ **(souvent)** too often; ~ **(longtemps)** (for) too long; ~ **de** (*nombre*) too many; (*quantité*) too much; **de** ~, **en** ~: **des livres en** ~ a few books too many, a few extra books; **du lait en** ~ too much milk; **3 livres/5 F de** ~ 3 books too many/5 F too much.

trophée [trofā] *nm* trophy.

tropical, e, aux [tropēkál, -ō] *a* tropical.

tropique [tropēk] *nm* tropic; ~**s** *nmpl* tropics; ~ **du Cancer/Capricorne** Tropic of Cancer/Capricorn.

trop-plein [troplań] *nm* (*tuyau*) overflow *ou* outlet (pipe); (*liquide*) overflow.

troquer [trokā] *vt*: ~ **qch contre** to barter *ou* trade sth for; (*fig*) to swap sth for.

trot [trō] *nm* trot; **aller au** ~ to trot along; **partir au** ~ to set off at a trot.

trotter [trotā] *vi* to trot; (*fig*) to scamper along (*ou* about).

trotteuse [trotēz] *nf* (*de montre*) second hand.

trottiner [trotēnā] *vi* (*fig*) to scamper along (*ou* about).

trottinette [trotēnet] *nf* (child's) scooter.

trottoir [trotwar] *nm* sidewalk (*US*), pavement (*Brit*); **faire le** ~ (*péj*) to walk the streets; ~ **roulant** moving walkway.

trou [trōō] *nm* hole; (*fig*) gap; (*COMM*) deficit; ~ **d'aération** (air) vent; ~ **d'air** air pocket; ~ **de mémoire** blank, lapse of memory; ~ **noir** black hole; ~ **de la serrure** keyhole.

troublant, e [trōōblán, -ánt] *a* disturbing.

trouble [trōōbl(ə)] *a* (*liquide*) cloudy; (*image, mémoire*) indistinct, hazy; (*affaire*) shady, murky ♦ *ad* indistinctly ♦ *nm* (*désarroi*) distress, agitation; (*émoi sensuel*) turmoil, agitation; (*embarras*) confusion; (*zizanie*) unrest, discord; ~**s** *nmpl* (*POL*) disturbances, troubles, unrest *sg*; (*MÉD*) trouble *sg*, disorders; ~**s de la personnalité** personality problems; ~**s de la vision** eye trouble.

trouble-fête [trōōbləfet] *nm/f inv* spoilsport.

troubler [trōōblā] *vt* (*embarrasser*) to confuse, disconcert; (*émouvoir*) to agitate; to disturb; to perturb; (*perturber: ordre etc*) to disrupt, disturb; (*liquide*) to make cloudy; **se** ~ *vi* (*personne*) to become flustered *ou* confused; ~ **l'ordre public** to cause a breach of the peace.

troué, e [trōōā] *a* with a hole (*ou* holes) in it ♦ *nf* gap; (*MIL*) breach.

trouer [trōōā] *vt* to make a hole (*ou* holes) in; (*fig*) to pierce.

trouille [trōōy] *nf* (*fam*): **avoir la** ~ to be scared stiff, be scared out of one's wits.

troupe [trōōp] *nf* (*MIL*) troop; (*groupe*) troop, group; **la** ~ (*MIL*: *l'armée*) the army; (: *les simples soldats*) the troops *pl*; ~ **(de théâtre)** (theatrical) company; ~**s de choc** shock troops.

troupeau, x [trōōpō] *nm* (*de moutons*) flock; (*de vaches*) herd.

trousse [trōōs] *nf* case, kit; (*d'écolier*) pencil case; (*de docteur*) doctor's bag; **aux** ~**s de** (*fig*) on the heels *ou* tail of; ~ **à outils** tool-kit; ~ **de toilette** toilet *ou* sponge (*Brit*) bag.

trousseau, x [trōōsō] *nm* (*de mariée*) trousseau; ~ **de clefs** bunch of keys.

trouvaille [trōōvày] *nf* find; (*fig*: *idée, expression etc*) brainwave.

trouvé, e [trōōvā] *a*: **tout** ~ ready-made.

trouver [trōōvā] *vt* to find; (*rendre visite*): **aller/venir** ~ **qn** to go/come and see sb; **je trouve que** I find *ou* think that; ~ **à boire/critiquer** to find something to drink/criticize; ~ **asile/refuge** to find refuge/shelter; **se** ~ *vi* (*être*) to be; (*être soudain*) to find o.s.; **se** ~ **être/avoir** to happen to be/have; **il se trouve que** it happens that, it turns out that; **se** ~ **bien** to feel well; **se** ~ **mal** to pass out.

truand [trüán] *nm* villain, crook.

truander [trüándā] *vi* (*fam*) to cheat, swindle.

trublion [trüblēyóń] *nm* troublemaker.

truc [trük] *nm* (*astuce*) way, device; (*de cinéma, prestidigitateur*) trick effect; (*chose*) thing; (*machin*) thingumajig; **avoir le** ~ to have the knack; **c'est pas son** (*ou* **mon** etc) ~ (*fam*) it's not really his (*ou* my etc) thing.

truchement [trüshmáń] *nm*: **par le** ~ **de qn** through (the intervention of) sb.

trucider [trüsēdā] *vt* (*fam*) to do in, bump off.

truculent, e [trükülán, -áńt] *a* colorful (*US*), colourful (*Brit*).

truelle [trüel] *nf* trowel.

truffe [trüf] *nf* truffle; (*nez*) nose.

truffer [trüfā] *vt* (*CULIN*) to garnish with truffles; **truffé de** (*fig*: *citations*) peppered with; (: *pièges*) bristling with.

truie [trüē] *nf* sow.

truite [trüēt] *nf* trout *inv*.

truquage [trükázh] *nm* fixing; (*CINÉMA*) special effects *pl*.

truquer [trükā] *vt* (*élections, serrure, dés*) to fix; (*CINÉMA*) to use special effects in.

trust [trœst] *nm* (*COMM*) trust.

truster [trœstā] *vt* (*COMM*) to monopolize.

ts *abr* = **tous**.

tsar [dzár] *nm* tsar.

tsé-tsé [tsátsá] *nf*: **mouche** ~ tsetse fly.

TSF *sigle f* = *télégraphie sans fil*.

tsigane [tsēgàn] *a, nm/f* = **tzigane**.

TSVP *abr* (= *tournez s'il vous plaît*) PTO.

tt *abr* = **tout**.

TT(A) *sigle m* (= *transit temporaire (autorisé)*) vehicle registration for cars etc bought in France for export tax-free by non-residents.

TTC *abr* = **toutes taxes comprises**.

ttes *abr* = **toutes**.

TU *sigle m* = *temps universel*.

tu [tü] *pronom you* ♦ *nm*: **employer le** ~ to use the "tu" form.

tu, e [tü] *pp de* **taire**.

tuant, e [tüán, -áńt] *a* (*épuisant*) killing; (*énervant*) infuriating.

tuba [tübá] *nm* (*MUS*) tuba; (*SPORT*) snorkel.

tube [tüb] *nm* tube; (*de canalisation, métallique etc*) pipe; (*chanson, disque*) hit song *ou* record; ~ **digestif** alimentary canal, digestive tract; ~ **à essai** test tube.

tuberculeux, euse [tüberkülœ, -œz] *a* tubercular ♦ *nm/f* tuberculosis *ou* TB patient.

tuberculose [tüberkülōz] *nf* tuberculosis, TB.

tubulaire [tübüler] *a* tubular.

tubulure [tübülür] *nf* pipe; piping *q*; (*AUTO*): ~ **d'échappement/d'admission** exhaust/inlet manifold.

TUC [tük] *sigle m* (= *travail d'utilité collective*) *community work plan for the young unemployed.*

tuciste [tüsɛ̄st(ə)] *nm/f young person on a community work plan.*

tué, e [tüä] *nm/f*: **5** ~**s** 5 killed *ou* dead.

tue-mouche [tümōōsh] *a*: **papier** ~(**s**) flypaper.

tuer [tüä] *vt* to kill; **se** ~ (*se suicider*) to kill o.s.; (*dans un accident*) to be killed; **se** ~ **au travail** (*fig*) to work o.s. to death.

tuerie [türɛ̄] *nf* slaughter *q*, massacre.

tue-tête [tütɛt]: **à** ~ *ad* at the top of one's voice.

tueur [tücɛr] *nm* killer; ~ **à gages** hired killer.

tuile [tüɛ̈l] *nf* tile; (*fam*) bit of bad luck, blow.

tulipe [tülɛ̈p] *nf* tulip.

tuméfié, e [tümäfyä] *a* puffy, swollen.

tumeur [tümœr] *nf* growth, tumor (*US*), tumour (*Brit*).

tumulte [tümült(ə)] *nm* commotion, hubbub.

tumultueux, euse [tümültüœ̈, -œ̈z] *a* stormy, turbulent.

tuner [tüner] *nm* tuner.

tungstène [tœ̈ṅksten] *nm* tungsten.

tunique [tünɛ̈k] *nf* tunic; (*de femme*) smock, tunic.

Tunis [tünɛ̈s] *n* Tunis.

Tunisie [tünɛ̄zɛ̄] *nf*: **la** ~ Tunisia.

tunisien, ne [tünɛ̄zyaṅ, -en] *a* Tunisian ♦ *nm/f*: **T**~, **ne** Tunisian.

tunisois, e [tünɛ̄zwà, -wàz] *a* of *ou* from Tunis.

tunnel [tünel] *nm* tunnel.

TUP *sigle m* (= *titre universel de paiement*) ≈ payment slip.

turban [türbäṅ] *nm* turban.

turbin [türbaṅ] *nm* (*fam*) work *q*.

turbine [türbēn] *nf* turbine.

turbomoteur [türbomotœr] *nm* turbo(-boosted) engine.

turbopropulseur [türbopropülsœr] *nm* turboprop.

turboréacteur [türborääktœr] *nm* turbojet.

turbot [türbō] *nm* turbot.

turbotrain [türbotraṅ] *nm* turbotrain.

turbulences [türbülâṅs] *nfpl* (*AVIAT*) turbulence *sg*.

turbulent, e [türbüläṅ, -äṅt] *a* boisterous, unruly.

turc, turque [türk(ə)] *a* Turkish; (*w.-c.*) seatless ♦ *nm* (*LING*) Turkish ♦ *nm/f*: **T**~, **Turque** Turk/Turkish woman; **à la turque** *ad* (*assis*) cross-legged.

turf [türf] *nm* racing.

turfiste [türfɛ̈st(ə)] *nm/f* racegoer.

Turks et Caïques *ou* **Caicos** [türkäkäɛ̈k(os)] *nfpl* Turks and Caicos Islands.

turpitude [türpɛ̈tüd] *nf* base act, baseness *q*.

turque [türk(ə)] *af, nf voir* **turc**.

Turquie [türkɛ̄] *nf*: **la** ~ Turkey.

turquoise [türkwàz] *nf, a inv* turquoise.

tut [tü] *etc vb voir* **taire**.

tutelle [tütel] *nf* (*JUR*) guardianship; (*POL*) trusteeship; **sous la** ~ **de** (*fig*) under the supervision of.

tuteur, trice [tütœr, -trɛ̈s] *nm/f* (*JUR*) guardian; (*de plante*) stake, support.

tutoiement [tütwämäṅ] *nm* use of familiar

"tu" form.

tutoyer [tütwàyä] *vt*: ~ **qn** to address sb as "tu".

tutti quanti [tōōtɛ̈kwäṅtɛ̄] *nmpl*: **et** ~ and all the rest (of them).

tutu [tütü] *nm* (*DANSE*) tutu.

Tuvalu [tüvàlü] *nm*: **le** ~ Tuvalu.

tuyau, x [tüɛ̈yō] *nm* pipe; (*flexible*) tube; (*fam: conseil*) tip; (: *mise au courant*) gen *q*; ~ **d'arrosage** garden hose; ~ **d'échappement** exhaust pipe; ~ **d'incendie** fire hose.

tuyauté, e [tüɛ̈yōtä] *a* fluted.

tuyauterie [tüɛ̈yōtrɛ̄] *nf* piping *q*.

tuyère [tüɛ̈yer] *nf* nozzle.

TV [tävä] *nf* TV.

TVA *sigle f* = **taxe à** *ou* **sur la valeur ajoutée**.

tweed [twēd] *nm* tweed.

tympan [taṅpäṅ] *nm* (*ANAT*) eardrum.

type [tɛ̈p] *nm* type; (*personne, chose: représentant*) classic example, epitome; (*fam*) chap, guy ♦ *a* typical, standard; **avoir le** ~ **nordique** to be Nordic-looking.

typé, e [tɛ̈pä] *a* ethnic (*euph*).

typhoïde [tɛ̈foɛ̈d] *nf* typhoid (fever).

typhon [tɛ̈fóṅ] *nm* typhoon.

typhus [tɛ̈füs] *nm* typhus (fever).

typique [tɛ̈pɛ̈k] *a* typical.

typiquement [tɛ̈pɛ̈kmäṅ] *ad* typically.

typographe [tɛ̈pográf] *nm/f* typographer.

typographie [tɛ̈pográfɛ̄] *nf* typography; (*procédé*) letterpress (printing).

typographique [tɛ̈pográfɛ̈k] *a* typographical; letterpress *cpd*.

typologie [tɛ̈polozhɛ̄] *nf* typology.

tyran [tɛ̈räṅ] *nm* tyrant.

tyrannie [tɛ̈ranɛ̄] *nf* tyranny.

tyrannique [tɛ̈ranɛ̈k] *a* tyrannical.

tyranniser [tɛ̈ranɛ̈zä] *vt* to tyrannize.

Tyrol [tɛ̈rol] *nm*: **le** ~ the Tyrol.

tyrolien, ne [tɛ̈rolyaṅ, -en] *a* Tyrolean.

tzar [dzàr] *nm* = **tsar**.

tzigane [dzɛ̈gän] *a* gypsy, tzigane ♦ *nm/f* (Hungarian) gypsy, Tzigane.

U

U, u [ü] *nm inv* U, u ♦ *abr* (= *unité*) *10,000 francs*; **maison à vendre 50 U** house for sale: 500,000 francs; **U comme Ursule** U for Uncle.

ubiquité [übɛ̈küɛ̈tä] *nf*: **avoir le don d'**~ to be everywhere at once, be ubiquitous.

UDF *sigle f* (= *Union pour la démocratie française*) *political party.*

UEFA *sigle f* (= *Union of European Football Associations*) UEFA.

UER *sigle f* (= *unité d'enseignement et de recherche*) *old title of UFR*; (= *Union européenne de radiodiffusion*) EBU (= *European Broadcasting Union*).

UFC *sigle f* (= *Union fédérale des*

consommateurs) *national consumer group.*
UFR *sigle f* (= *unité de formation et de recherche*) ≈ *university department.*
UHF *sigle f* (= *ultra-haute fréquence*) UHF.
UHT *sigle* (= *ultra-haute température*) UHT.
UIT *sigle f* (= *Union internationale des télécommunications*) ITU (= *International Telecommunications Union*).
UJP *sigle f* (= *Union des jeunes pour le progrès*) *political party.*
Ukraine [ükrɛn] *nf:* **l'~** the Ukraine.
ukrainien, ne [ükrɛnyaɛ̃, -ɛn] *a* Ukrainian.
ulcère [ülsɛr] *nm* ulcer; **~ à l'estomac** stomach ulcer.
ulcérer [ülsārā] *vt* (*MÉD*) to ulcerate; (*fig*) to sicken, appall (*US*), appal (*Brit*).
ulcéreux, euse [ülsārœ̄, -œ̄z] *a* (*plaie, lésion*) ulcerous; (*membre*) ulcerated.
ULM *sigle m* (= *ultra léger motorisé*) ultralight (*US*), microlight (*Brit*).
ultérieur, e [ültāryœr] *a* later, subsequent; **remis à une date ~e** postponed to a later date.
ultérieurement [ültāryœrmāɛ̃] *ad* later.
ultimatum [ültēmátom] *nm* ultimatum.
ultime [ültēm] *a* final.
ultra... [ültrá] *préfixe* ultra....
ultramoderne [ültrámodern(ə)] ultramodern.
ultra-rapide [ültrárápēd] *a* ultrafast.
ultra-sensible [ültrásánsēbl(ə)] *a* (*PHOTO*) high-speed.
ultra-sons [ültrásóɛ̃] *nmpl* ultrasonics *sg.*
ultra-violet, te [ültrávyolɛ, -ɛt] *a* ultraviolet.
ululer [ülülā] *vi* = **hululer**.
un, une [œ̃, ün] *dét* a, an + *voyelle* ♦ *pronom, num, a* one; **l'~ l'autre, les ~s les autres** each other, one another; **l'~ ..., l'autre** (the) one ..., the other; **les ~s ..., les autres** some ..., others; **l'~ et l'autre** both (of them); **l'~ ou l'autre** either (of them); **l'~ des meilleurs** one of the best; **la une** (*PRESSE*) the front page.
unanime [ünánēm] *a* unanimous; **ils sont ~s (à penser que)** they are unanimous (in thinking that).
unanimement [ünánēmmāɛ̃] *ad* (*par tous*) unanimously; (*d'un commun accord*) with one accord.
unanimité [ünánēmētā] *nf* unanimity; **à l'~** unanimously; **faire l'~** to be approved unanimously.
UNEF [ünef] *sigle f* = *Union nationale des étudiants de France.*
UNESCO [üneskō] *sigle f* (= *United Nations Educational, Scientific and Cultural Organization*) UNESCO.
unetelle [üntel] *nf voir* **untel**.
UNI *sigle f* = *Union nationale interuniversitaire.*
uni, e [ünē] *a* (*ton, tissu*) plain; (*surface*) smooth, even; (*famille*) close(-knit); (*pays*) united.
UNICEF [ünēsef] *sigle m* (= *United Nations International Children's Emergency Fund*) UNICEF.
unième [ünyɛm] *num:* **vingt/trente et ~** twenty-/thirty-first; **cent ~** (one) hundred and first.
unificateur, trice [ünēfēkátœr, -trēs] *a* unify-

ing.
unification [ünēfēkásyōɛ̃] *nf* uniting; unification; standardization.
unifier [ünēfyā] *vt* to unite, unify; (*systèmes*) to standardize, unify; **s'~** to become united.
uniforme [ünēform(ə)] *a* (*mouvement*) regular, uniform; (*surface, ton*) even; (*objets, maisons*) uniform; (*fig: vie, conduite*) unchanging ♦ *nm* uniform; **être sous l'~** (*MIL*) to be serving in the military.
uniformément [ünēformāmāɛ̃] *ad* uniformly.
uniformiser [ünēformēzā] *vt* to make uniform; (*systèmes*) to standardize.
uniformité [ünēformētā] *nf* regularity; uniformity; evenness.
unijambiste [ünēzhánbēst(ə)] *nm/f* one-legged man/woman.
unilatéral, e, aux [ünēlátārál, -ō] *a* unilateral; **stationnement ~** parking on one side only.
unilatéralement [ünēlátárálmāɛ̃] *ad* unilaterally.
uninominal, e, aux [ünēnomēnál, -ō] *a* uncontested.
union [ünyōɛ̃] *nf* union; **~ conjugale** union of marriage; **~ de consommateurs** consumers' association; **~ libre** free love; **l'U~ des Républiques socialistes soviétiques (URSS)** the Union of Soviet Socialist Republics (USSR); **l'U~ soviétique** the Soviet Union.
unique [ünēk] *a* (*seul*) only; (*le même*): **un prix/système ~** a single price/system; (*exceptionnel*) unique; **ménage à salaire ~** one-salary family; **route à voie ~** single-lane road; **fils/fille ~** only son/daughter, only child; **~ en France** the only one of its kind in France.
uniquement [ünēkmāɛ̃] *ad* only, solely; (*juste*) only, merely.
unir [ünēr] *vt* (*nations*) to unite; (*éléments, couleurs*) to combine; (*en mariage*) to unite, join together; **~ qch à** to unite sth with; to combine sth with; **s'~** to unite; (*en mariage*) to be joined together; **s'~ à** *ou* **avec** to unite with.
unisexe [ünēseks] *a* unisex.
unisson [ünēsōɛ̃]: **à l'~** *ad* in unison.
unitaire [ünēter] *a* unitary; (*POL*) unitarian; **prix ~** unit price.
unité [ünētā] *nf* (*harmonie, cohésion*) unity; (*COMM, MIL, de mesure, MATH*) unit; **~ centrale (de traitement)** central processing unit (CPU); **~ de valeur (UV)** (university) course, credit.
univers [ünēver] *nm* universe.
universaliser [ünēversálēzā] *vt* to universalize.
universel, le [ünēversel] *a* universal; (*esprit*) all-embracing.
universellement [ünēverselmāɛ̃] *ad* universally.
universitaire [ünēversēter] *a* university *cpd*; (*diplôme, études*) academic, university *cpd* ♦ *nm/f* academic.
université [ünēversētā] *nf* university.
univoque [ünēvok] *a* unambiguous; (*MATH*) one-to-one.
UNR *sigle f* (= *Union pour la nouvelle république*) *former political party.*
UNSS *sigle f* = *Union nationale de sport scolaire.*

untel, unetelle [œ̃tel, ü̃tel] *nm/f* so-and-so.
uranium [üränyom] *nm* uranium.
urbain, e [ürbañ, -en] *a* urban, city *cpd*, town *cpd*; (*poli*) urbane.
urbanisation [ürbänēzâsyôn] *nf* urbanization.
urbaniser [ürbánēzä] *vt* to urbanize.
urbanisme [ürbánēsm(ə)] *nm* town planning.
urbaniste [ürbánēst(ə)] *nm/f* town planner.
urbanité [ürbánētä] *nf* urbanity.
urée [ürä] *nf* urea.
urémie [ürämē] *nf* uremia (*US*), uraemia (*Brit*).
urgence [ürzhâns] *nf* urgency; (*MÉD etc*) emergency; **d'~** *a* emergency *cpd* ♦ *ad* as a matter of urgency; **en cas d'~** in case of emergency; **service des ~s** emergency service.
urgent, e [ürzhâñ, -âñt] *a* urgent.
urinaire [ürēner] *a* urinary.
urinal, aux [ürēnál, -ō] *nm* (bed) urinal.
urine [ürēn] *nf* urine.
uriner [ürēnä] *vi* to urinate.
urinoir [ürēnwár] *nm* (public) urinal.
urne [ürn(ə)] *nf* (*électorale*) ballot box; (*vase*) urn; **aller aux ~s** (*voter*) to go to the polls.
urologie [ürolozhē] *nf* urology.
URSS [*parfois*: ürs] *sigle f* (= *Union des Républiques Socialistes Soviétiques*) USSR.
URSSAF [ürsáf] *sigle f* (= *Union pour le recouvrement de la sécurité sociale et des allocations familiales*) *administrative body responsible for social security funds and payments.*
urticaire [ürtēker] *nf* nettle rash, urticaria.
Uruguay [ürügwe] *nm*: **l'~** Uruguay.
uruguayen, ne [ürügwàyañ, -en] *a* Uruguayan ♦ *nm/f*: **U~, ne** Uruguayan.
us [üs] *nmpl*: **~ et coutumes** (habits and) customs.
US(A) *sigle mpl* (= *United States (of America)*) US(A).
usage [üzàzh] *nm* (*emploi, utilisation*) use; (*coutume*) custom; (*éducation*) (good) manners *pl*, (good) breeding; (*LING*): **l'~** usage; **faire ~ de** (*pouvoir, droit*) to exercise; **avoir l'~ de** to have the use of; **à l'~** *ad* with use; **à l'~ de** (*pour*) for (use of); **en ~** in use; **hors d'~** out of service; **à ~ interne** to be taken; **à ~ externe** for external use only.
usagé, e [üzàzhä] *a* (*usé*) worn; (*d'occasion*) used.
usager, ère [üzàzhä, -er] *nm/f* user.
usé, e [üzä] *a* worn (down *ou* out *ou* away); ruined; (*banal*) hackneyed.
user [üzä] *vt* (*outil*) to wear down; (*vêtement*) to wear out; (*matière*) to wear away; (*consommer: charbon etc*) to use; (*fig: santé*) to ruin; (: *personne*) to wear out; **s'~** *vi* to wear; to wear out; (*fig*) to decline; **s'~ à la tâche** to wear o.s. out with work; **~ de** *vt* (*moyen, procédé*) to use, employ; (*droit*) to exercise.
usine [üzēn] *nf* factory; **~ atomique** nuclear power plant; **~ à gaz** gasworks *sg*; **~ marémotrice** tidal power station.
usiner [üzēnä] *vt* (*TECH*) to machine; (*fabriquer*) to manufacture.
usité, e [üzētä] *a* in common use, common;

peu ~ rarely used.
ustensile [üstânsēl] *nm* implement; **~ de cuisine** kitchen utensil.
usuel, le [üzüel] *a* everyday, common.
usufruit [üzüfrüē] *nm* usufruct.
usuraire [üzürer] *a* usurious.
usure [üzür] *nf* wear; worn state; (*de l'usurier*) usury; **avoir qn à l'~** to wear sb down; **~ normale** normal wear and tear.
usurier, ière [üzüryä, -yer] *nm/f* usurer.
usurpateur, trice [üzürpátœr, -trēs] *nm/f* usurper.
usurper [üzürpä] *vt* to usurp.
ut [üt] *nm* (*MUS*) C.
UTA *sigle f* = *Union des transporteurs aériens*.
utérin, e [ütäran, -ēn] *a* uterine.
utérus [ütärüs] *nm* uterus, womb.
utile [ütēl] *a* useful; **~ à qn/qch** of use to sb/sth.
utilement [ütēlmáñ] *ad* usefully.
utilisable [ütēlēzábl(ə)] *a* usable.
utilisateur, trice [ütēlēzátœr, -trēs] *nm/f* user.
utilisation [ütēlēzásyôñ] *nf* use.
utiliser [ütēlēzä] *vt* to use.
utilitaire [ütēlēter] *a* utilitarian; (*objets*) practical ♦ *nm* (*INFORM*) utility.
utilité [ütēlētä] *nf* usefulness *q*; use; **jouer les ~s** (*THÉÂTRE*) to play bit parts; **reconnu d'~ publique** state-approved; **c'est d'une grande ~** it's extremely useful; **il n'y a aucune ~ à ...** there's no use in ....
utopie [ütopē] *nf* (*idée, conception*) utopian idea *ou* view; (*société etc idéale*) utopia.
utopiste [ütopēst(ə)] *nm/f* utopian.
UV *sigle f* (*SCOL*) = *unité de valeur*.
uvule [üvül] *nf* uvula.

V

V, v [vä] *nm inv* V, v ♦ *abr* (= *voir, verset*) v.; (= *vers*: *de poésie*) l.; (: *en direction de*) toward(s); **V comme Victor** V for Victor; **en ~** V-shaped; **encolure en ~** V-neck; **décolleté en ~** plunging neckline.
va [vá] *vb voir* **aller**.
vacance [vàkâñs] *nf* (*ADMIN*) vacancy; **~s** *nfpl* vacation *sg* (*US*), holiday(s *pl*) (*Brit*); **les grandes ~s** the summer vacation *ou* holidays; **prendre des/ses ~s** to take a vacation *ou* holiday/one's vacation *ou* holiday(s); **aller en ~s** to go on vacation *ou* holiday.
vacancier, ière [vàkáñsyä, -yer] *nm/f* vacationer (*US*), holiday-maker (*Brit*).
vacant, e [vàkáñ, -âñt] *a* vacant.
vacarme [vàkárm(ə)] *nm* row, din.
vacataire [vàkáter] *nm/f* temporary (employee); (*enseignement*) substitute (*US*) *ou* supply (*Brit*) teacher; (*UNIVERSITÉ*) part-time temporary lecturer.
vaccin [vàksañ] *nm* vaccine; (*opération*) vaccination.
vaccination [vàksēnásyôñ] *nf* vaccination.

vacciner [våksēnā] *vt* to vaccinate; *(fig)* to make immune; **être vacciné** *(fig)* to be immune.

vache [våsh] *nf* (*ZOOL*) cow; (*cuir*) cowhide ♦ *a* (*fam*) rotten, mean; ~ **à eau** (canvas) water bag; **(manger de la)** ~ **enragée** (to go through) hard times; ~ **à lait** (*péj*) sucker; ~ **laitière** dairy cow; **période des** ~**s maigres** lean times *pl*, lean period.

vachement [våshmåñ] *ad* (*fam*) damned, fantastically.

vacher, ère [våshå, -er] *nm/f* cowherd.

vacherie [våshrē] *nf* (*fam*) meanness *q*; (*action*) dirty trick; (*propos*) nasty remark.

vacherin [våshrañ] *nm* (*fromage*) vacherin cheese; (*gâteau*): ~ **glacé** vacherin (*type of cream gâteau*).

vachette [våshet] *nf* calfskin.

vacillant, e [våsēyåñ, -åñt] *a* wobbly; flickering; failing, faltering.

vaciller [våsēyā] *vi* to sway, wobble; (*bougie, lumière*) to flicker; (*fig*) to be failing, falter; ~ **dans ses réponses** to falter in one's replies; ~ **dans ses résolutions** to waver in one's resolutions.

~ **vacuité** [vakuētā] *nf* emptiness, vacuity.

vade-mecum [vådāmākom] *nm inv* pocketbook.

vadrouille [vådrōōy] *nf*: **être/partir en** ~ to be/go rambling around.

vadrouiller [vådrōōyā] *vi* to wander around *ou* about.

va-et-vient [våavyan] *nm inv* (*de pièce mobile*) to and fro (*ou* up and down) movement; (*de personnes, véhicules*) comings and goings *pl*, to-ings and fro-ings *pl*; (*ÉLEC*) two-way switch.

vagabond, e [vågåbóñ, -óñd] *a* wandering; (*imagination*) roaming, roving ♦ *nm* (*rôdeur*) tramp, vagrant; (*voyageur*) wanderer.

vagabondage [vågåbóñdåzh] *nm* roaming, wandering; (*JUR*) vagrancy.

vagabonder [vågåbóñdā] *vi* to roam, wander.

vagin [vázhañ] *nm* vagina.

vaginal, e, aux [våzhēnål, -ō] *a* vaginal.

vagissement [våzhēsmåñ] *nm* cry (*of newborn baby*).

vague [våg] *nf* wave ♦ *a* vague; (*regard*) faraway; (*manteau, robe*) loose(-fitting); (*quelconque*): **un** ~ **bureau/cousin** some office/cousin or other ♦ *nm*: **être dans le** ~ to be rather in the dark; **rester dans le** ~ to keep things rather vague; **regarder dans le** ~ to gaze into space; ~ **à l'âme** *nm* vague melancholy; ~ **d'assaut** *nf* (*MIL*) wave of assault; ~ **de chaleur** *nf* heat wave; ~ **de fond** *nf* ground swell; ~ **de froid** *nf* cold spell.

vaguelette [våglet] *nf* ripple.

vaguement [vågmåñ] *ad* vaguely.

vaillamment [våyåmåñ] *ad* bravely, gallantly.

vaillant, e [våyåñ, -åñt] *a* (*courageux*) brave, gallant; (*robuste*) vigorous, hale and hearty; **n'avoir plus un sou** ~ to be penniless.

vaille [våy] *vb voir* **valoir**.

vain, e [vañ, ven] *a* vain; **en** ~ *ad* in vain.

vaincre [vañkr(ə)] *vt* to defeat; (*fig*) to conquer, overcome.

vaincu, e [vañku] *pp de* **vaincre** ♦ *nm/f*

defeated party.

vainement [venmåñ] *ad* vainly.

vainquais [vañke] *etc vb voir* **vaincre.**

vainqueur [vañkœr] *nm* victor; (*SPORT*) winner ♦ *am* victorious.

vais [ve] *vb voir* **aller.**

vaisseau, x [vesō] *nm* (*ANAT*) vessel; (*NAVIG*) ship, vessel; ~ **spatial** spaceship.

vaisselier [vesəlyā] *nm* sideboard.

vaisselle [vesel] *nf* (*service*) dishes; (*plats etc à laver*) (dirty) dishes *pl*; **faire la** ~ to do the dishes.

val, vaux *ou* **vals** [vål, vō] *nm* valley.

valable [vålábl(ə)] *a* valid; (*acceptable*) decent, worthwhile.

valablement [vålábləmåñ] *ad* legitimately; (*de façon satisfaisante*) satisfactorily.

Valence [vålåñs] *n* (*en Espagne*) Valencia; (*en France*) Valence.

valent [vål] *etc vb voir* **valoir.**

valet [våle] *nm* valet; (*péj*) lackey; (*CARTES*) jack; ~ **de chambre** manservant, valet; ~ **de ferme** farmhand; ~ **de pied** footman.

valeur [vålœr] *nf* (*gén*) value; (*mérite*) worth, merit; (*COMM: titre*) security; **mettre en** ~ (*bien*) to exploit; (*terrain, région*) to develop; (*fig*) to highlight; to show off to advantage; **avoir de la** ~ to be valuable; **prendre de la** ~ to go up *ou* gain in value; **sans** ~ worthless; ~ **absolue** absolute value; ~ **d'échange** exchange value; ~ **nominale** face value; ~**s mobilières** transferable securities.

valeureux, euse [vålœrœ, -œz] *a* valorous.

valide [vålēd] *a* (*en bonne santé*) fit, well; (*indemne*) able-bodied, fit; (*valable*) valid.

valider [vålēdā] *vt* to validate.

validité [vålēdētā] *nf* validity.

valions [vålyóñ] *etc vb voir* **valoir.**

valise [vålēz] *nf* (suit)case; **faire sa** ~ to pack one's (suit)case; **la** ~ **(diplomatique)** the diplomatic pouch (*US*) *ou* bag (*Brit*).

vallée [vålā] *nf* valley.

vallon [vålóñ] *nm* small valley.

vallonné, e [vålonā] *a* undulating.

valoir [vålwår] *vi* (*être valable*) to hold, apply ♦ *vt* (*prix, valeur, effort*) to be worth; (*causer*): ~ **qch à qn** to earn sb sth; **se** ~ to be of equal merit; (*péj*) to be two of a kind; **faire** ~ (*droits, prérogatives*) to assert; (*domaine, capitaux*) to exploit; **faire** ~ **que** to point out that; **se faire** ~ to make the most of o.s.; **à** ~ on account; **à** ~ **sur** to be deducted from; **vaille que vaille** somehow or other; **cela ne me dit rien qui vaille** I don't like the look of it at all; **ce climat ne me vaut rien** this climate doesn't suit me; ~ **la peine** to be worth the trouble, be worth it; ~ **mieux: il vaut mieux se taire** it's better to say nothing; **il vaut mieux que je fasse/ comme ceci** it's better if I do/like this; **ça ne vaut rien** it's worthless; **que vaut ce candidat?** how good is this applicant?

valorisation [vålorēzåsyóñ] *nf* (economic) development; increased standing.

valoriser [vålorēzā] *vt* (*ÉCON*) to develop (the economy of); (*produit*) to increase the value of; (*PSYCH*) to increase the standing of; (*fig*) to highlight, bring out.

valse [vàls(ə)] *nf* waltz; **c'est la ~ des étiquettes** the prices don't stay the same from one moment to the next.

valser [vàlsā] *vi* to waltz; *(fig)*: **aller ~** to go flying.

valu, e [vàlü] *pp de* **valoir**.

valve [vàlv(ə)] *nf* valve.

vamp [vànp] *nf* vamp.

vampire [vànpēr] *nm* vampire.

van [vàn̄] *nm* horse trailer *(US) ou* box *(Brit)*.

vandale [vàndál] *nm/f* vandal.

vandalisme [vàndálēsm(ə)] *nm* vandalism.

vanille [vànēy] *nf* vanilla; **glace à la ~** vanilla ice cream.

vanillé, e [vànēyā] *a* vanilla *cpd.*

vanité [vànētā] *nf* vanity.

vaniteux, euse [vànētœ̄, -œ̄z] *a* vain, conceited.

vanne [vàn] *nf* gate; *(fam: remarque)* dig, (nasty) crack; **lancer une ~ à qn** to knock sb.

vanneau, x [vànō] *nm* lapwing.

vanner [vànā] *vt* to winnow.

vannerie [vànrē] *nf* basketwork.

vantail, aux [vàntày, -ō] *nm* door, leaf *(pl* leaves).

vantard, e [vàntàr, -àrd(ə)] *a* boastful.

vantardise [vàntàrdēz] *nf* boastfulness *q*; boast.

vanter [vàntā] *vt* to speak highly of, vaunt; **se ~** *vi* to boast, brag; **se ~ de** to pride o.s. on; *(péj)* to boast of.

Vanuatu [vànwàtōō] *nm*: **le ~** Vanuatu.

va-nu-pieds [vànüpyā] *nm/f inv* tramp, beggar.

vapeur [vàpœr] *nf* steam; *(émanation)* vapor *(US)*, vapour *(Brit)*, fumes *pl*; *(brouillard, buée)* haze; **~s** *nfpl (bouffées)* vapours, vapors; **à ~** steam-powered, steam *cpd*; **à toute ~** full steam ahead; *(fig)* at full tilt; **renverser la ~** to reverse engines; *(fig)* to backtrack, backpedal; **cuit à la ~** steamed.

vapocuisuer [vàpoküēzœr] *nm* pressure cooker.

vaporeux, euse [vàporœ̄, -œ̄z] *a (flou)* hazy, misty; *(léger)* filmy, gossamer *cpd.*

vaporisateur [vàporēzàtœr] *nm* spray.

vaporiser [vàporēzā] *vt (CHIMIE)* to vaporize; *(parfum etc)* to spray.

vaquer [vàkā] *vi (ADMIN)* to be on vacation; **~ à ses occupations** to attend to one's affairs, go about one's business.

varappe [vàràp] *nf* rock climbing.

varappeur, euse [vàràpœr, -œ̄z] *nm/f* (rock) climber.

varech [vàrek] *nm* wrack, kelp.

vareuse [vàrœ̄z] *nf (blouson)* pea jacket; *(d'uniforme)* tunic.

variable [vàryábl(ə)] *a* variable; *(temps, humeur)* changeable; *(TECH: à plusieurs positions etc)* adaptable; *(LING)* inflectional; *(divers: résultats)* varied, various ♦ *nf (IN-FORM, MATH)* variable.

variante [vàryànt] *nf* variant.

variation [vàryâsyôn̄] *nf* variation; changing *q*, change; *(MUS)* variation.

varice [vàrēs] *nf* varicose vein.

varicelle [vàrēsel] *nf* chickenpox.

varié, e [vàryā] *a* varied; *(divers)* various;

hors-d'œuvre **~s** selection of hors d'œuvres.

varier [vàryā] *vi* to vary; *(temps, humeur)* to change ♦ *vt* to vary.

variété [vàryātā] *nf* variety; **spectacle de ~s** variety show.

variole [vàryol] *nf* smallpox.

variqueux, euse [vàrēkœ̄, -œ̄z] *a* varicose.

Varsovie [vàrsovē] *n* Warsaw.

vas [và] *vb voir* **aller; ~-y!** [vazi] go on!

vasculaire [vàskuler] *a* vascular.

vase [vàz] *nm* vase ♦ *nf* silt, mud; **en ~ clos** in isolation; **~ de nuit** chamber pot; **~s communicants** communicating vessels.

vasectomie [vàzektomē] *nf* vasectomy.

vaseline [vàzlēn] *nf* Vaseline ®.

vaseux, euse [vàzœ̄, -œ̄z] *a* silty, muddy; *(fig: confus)* woolly, hazy; *(: fatigué)* peaky; *(: étourdi)* woozy.

vasistas [vàzēstàs] *nm* transom *(US)*, fanlight *(Brit)*.

vasque [vàsk(ə)] *nf (bassin)* basin; *(coupe)* bowl.

vaste [vàst(ə)] *a* vast, immense.

Vatican [vàtēkàn̄] *nm*: **le ~** the Vatican.

vaticiner [vàtēsēnā] *vi (péj)* to make pompous predictions.

va-tout [vàtōō] *nm*: **jouer son ~** to stake one's all.

vaudeville [vōdvēl] *nm* vaudeville, light comedy.

vaudrai [vōdrā] *etc vb voir* **valoir**.

vau-l'eau [vōlō]: **à ~** *ad* with the current; **s'en aller à ~** *(fig: projets)* to be adrift.

vaurien, ne [vōryàn̄, -en] *nm/f* good-for-nothing, guttersnipe.

vaut [vō] *vb voir* **valoir**.

vautour [vōtōōr] *nm* vulture.

vautrer [vōtrā]: **se ~** *vi*: **se ~ dans** to wallow in; **se ~ sur** to sprawl on.

vaux [vō] *pl de* **val** ♦ *vb voir* **valoir**.

va-vite [vàvēt]: **à la ~** *ad* in a rush.

vd *abr = vend*.

VDQS *abr (= vin délimité de qualité supérieure)* label guaranteeing quality of wine.

vds *abr = vends*.

veau, x [vō] *nm (ZOOL)* calf *(pl* calves); *(CULIN)* veal; *(peau)* calfskin; **tuer le ~ gras** to kill the fatted calf.

vecteur [vektœr] *nm* vector; *(MIL, BIO)* carrier.

vécu, e [vākü] *pp de* **vivre** ♦ *a (aventure)* real(-life).

vedettariat [vədetàryá] *nm* stardom; *(attitude)* acting like a star.

vedette [vədet] *nf (artiste etc)* star; *(canot)* patrol boat; launch; **avoir la ~** to get star billing; **mettre qn en ~** *(CINÉMA etc)* to give sb the starring role; *(fig)* to push sb into the limelight.

végétal, e, aux [vāzhātál, -ō] *a* vegetable ♦ *nm* vegetable, plant.

végétalien, ne [vāzhātályàn̄, -en] *a, nm/f* vegan.

végétarien, ne [vāzhātàryàn̄, -en] *a, nm/f* vegetarian.

végétarisme [vāzhātárēsm(ə)] *nm* vegetarianism.

végétatif, ive [vāzhātátēf, -ēv] *a*: **une vie ~ive** a vegetable existence.

végétation [vāzhātásyôṅ] *nf* vegetation; ~**s** *nfpl* (*MÉD*) adenoids.

végéter [vāzhātā] *vi* (*fig*) to vegetate; to stagnate.

véhémence [vāāmáṅs] *nf* vehemence.

véhément, e [vāāmáṅ, -áṅt] *a* vehement.

véhicule [vāékül] *nm* vehicle; ~ **utilitaire** commercial vehicle.

véhiculer [vāékülā] *vt* (*personnes, marchandises*) to transport, convey; (*fig*: *idées, substances*) to convey, serve as a vehicle for.

veille [vey] *nf* (*garde*) watch; (*PSYCH*) wakefulness; (*jour*): **la** ~ the day before, the previous day; **la** ~ **au soir** the previous evening; **la** ~ **de** the day before; **à la** ~ **de** on the eve of; **l'état de** ~ the waking state.

veillée [vāyā] *nf* (*soirée*) evening; (*réunion*) evening gathering; ~ **d'armes** night before combat; (*fig*) vigil; ~ (**mortuaire**) watch.

veiller [vāyā] *vi* (*rester debout*) to stay *ou* sit up; (*ne pas dormir*) to be awake; (*être de garde*) to be on watch; (*être vigilant*) to be watchful ♦ *vt* (*malade, mort*) to watch over, sit up with; ~ **à** *vt* to attend to, see to; ~ **à ce que** to make sure that, see to it that; ~ **sur** *vt* to keep a watch *ou* an eye on.

veilleur [vayœr] *nm*: ~ **de nuit** night watchman.

veilleuse [vāyœz] *nf* (*lampe*) night light; (*AUTO*) sidemarker light (*US*), sidelight (*Brit*); (*flamme*) pilot light; **en** ~ *a* (*lampe*) dimmed; (*fig*: *affaire*) shelved, set aside.

veinard, e [venár, -árd(ə)] *nm/f* (*fam*) lucky devil.

veine [ven] *nf* (*ANAT, du bois etc*) vein; (*filon*) vein, seam; (*fam*: *chance*): **avoir de la** ~ to be lucky; (*inspiration*) inspiration.

veiné, e [vānā] *a* veined; (*bois*) grained.

veineux, euse [vānœ, -œz] *a* venous.

vêler [vālā] *vi* to calve.

vélin [vālaṅ] *nm*: (**papier**) ~ vellum (paper).

véliplanchiste [vālēpláṅshēst(ə)] *nm/f* wind-surfer.

velléitaire [vālāēter] *a* irresolute, indecisive.

velléités [vālāētā] *nfpl* vague impulses.

vélo [vālō] *nm* bike, cycle; **faire du** ~ to go cycling.

véloce [vālos] *a* swift.

vélocité [vālosētā] *nf* (*MUS*) nimbleness, swiftness; (*vitesse*) velocity.

vélodrome [vālodrom] *nm* velodrome.

vélomoteur [vālomotœr] *nm* moped.

velours [vəlōōr] *nm* velvet; ~ **côtelé** corduroy.

velouté, e [vəlōōtā] *a* (*au toucher*) velvety; (*à la vue*) soft, mellow; (*au goût*) smooth, mellow ♦ *nm*: ~ **d'asperges/de tomates** cream of asparagus/tomato soup.

velu, e [vəlü] *a* hairy.

venaison [vənezôṅ] *nf* venison.

vénal, e, aux [vānál, -ō] *a* venal.

vénalité [vānálētā] *nf* venality.

venant [vənáṅ]: **à tout** ~ *ad* to all and sundry.

vendable [váṅdábl(ə)] *a* saleable, marketable.

vendange [váṅdáṅzh] *nf* (*opération, période*: *aussi*: ~**s**) grape harvest; (*raisins*) grape crop, grapes *pl*.

vendanger [váṅdáṅzhā] *vi* to harvest the grapes.

vendangeur, euse [váṅdáṅzhœr, -œz] *nm/f* grape-picker.

vendéen, ne [váṅdāaṅ, -en] *a* of *ou* from the Vendée.

vendeur, euse [váṅdœr, -œz] *nm/f* (*de magasin*) sales clerk (*US*), shop *ou* sales assistant (*Brit*); (*COMM*) salesman/woman ♦ *nm* (*JUR*) vendor, seller; ~ **de journaux** newspaper seller.

vendre [váṅdr(ə)] *vt* to sell; ~ **qch à qn** to sell sb sth; **cela se vend à la douzaine** these are sold by the dozen; **cela se vend bien** it's selling well; **"à** ~**"** "for sale".

vendredi [váṅdrədē] *nm* Friday; **V~ saint** Good Friday; *voir aussi* **lundi**.

vendu, e [váṅdü] *pp de* **vendre** ♦ *a* (*péj*) corrupt.

venelle [vənel] *nf* alley.

vénéneux, euse [vānānœ, -œz] *a* poisonous.

vénérable [vānārábl(ə)] *a* venerable.

vénération [vānārásyôṅ] *nf* veneration.

vénérer [vānārā] *vt* to venerate.

vénerie [venrē] *nf* hunting.

vénérien, ne [vānāryaṅ, -en] *a* venereal.

Venezuela [vānāzüelá] *nm*: **le** ~ Venezuela.

vénézuélien, ne [vānāzüälyaṅ, -en] *a* Venezuelan ♦ *nm/f*: **V~, ne** Venezuelan.

vengeance [váṅzháṅs] *nf* vengeance *q*, revenge *q*; (*acte*) act of vengeance *ou* revenge.

venger [váṅzhā] *vt* to avenge; **se** ~ *vi* to avenge o.s.; (*par rancune*) to take revenge; **se** ~ **de qch** to avenge o.s. for sth; to take one's revenge for sth; **se** ~ **de qn** to take revenge on sb; **se** ~ **sur** to wreak vengeance upon; to take revenge on *ou* through; to take it out on.

vengeur, eresse [váṅzhœr, -zhres] *a* vengeful ♦ *nm/f* avenger.

véniel, le [vānyel] *a* venial.

venimeux, euse [vənēmœ, -œz] *a* poisonous, venomous; (*fig*: *haineux*) venomous, vicious.

venin [vənaṅ] *nm* venom, poison; (*fig*) venom.

venir [vənēr] *vi* to come; ~ **de** to come from; ~ **de faire**: **je viens d'y aller/de le voir** I've just been there/seen him; **s'il vient à pleuvoir** if it should rain, if it happens to rain; **en** ~ **à faire**: **j'en viens à croire que** I am coming to believe that; **où veux-tu en** ~**?** what are you getting at?; **il en est venu à mendier** he has been reduced to begging; **en** ~ **aux mains** to come to blows; **les années/générations à** ~ the years/generations to come; **il me vient une idée** an idea has just occurred to me; **il me vient des soupçons** I'm beginning to be suspicious; **je te vois** ~ I know what you're after; **faire** ~ (*docteur, plombier*) to call (out); **d'où vient que ...?** how is it that ...?; ~ **au monde** to come into the world.

Venise [vənēz] *n* Venice.

vénitien, ne [vānēsyaṅ, -en] *a* Venetian.

vent [váṅ] *nm* wind; **il y a du** ~ it's windy; **c'est du** ~ it's all hot air; **au** ~ to windward; **sous le** ~ to leeward; **avoir le** ~ **debout/arrière** to head into the wind/have the wind astern; **dans le** ~ (*fam*) trendy; **prendre le** ~ (*fig*) to see which way the wind blows; **avoir** ~ **de** to get wind of; **contre** ~**s**

et marées come hell or high water.

vente [vãnt] *nf* sale; **la** ~ (*activité*) selling; (*secteur*) sales *pl*; **mettre en** ~ to put on sale; (*objets personnels*) to put up for sale; ~ **de charité** rummage (*US*) *ou* jumble (*Brit*) sale; ~ **par correspondance (VPC)** mail-order selling; ~ **aux enchères** auction.

venté, e [vãtã] *a* windswept, windy.

venter [vãtã] *vb impersonnel*: **il vente** the wind is blowing.

venteux, euse [vãtœ̃, -œ̃z] *a* windswept, windy.

ventilateur [vãtēlátœr] *nm* fan.

ventilation [vãtēlãsyõn] *nf* ventilation.

ventiler [vãtēlã] *vt* to ventilate; (*total, statistiques*) to break down.

ventouse [vãtōōz] *nf* (*ampoule*) cupping glass; (*de caoutchouc*) suction cup (*US*) *ou* pad (*Brit*); (*ZOOL*) sucker.

ventre [vãtr(ə)] *nm* (*ANAT*) stomach; (*fig*) belly; **prendre du** ~ to be getting a paunch; **avoir mal au** ~ to have (a) stomach ache.

ventricule [vãtrēkül] *nm* ventricle.

ventriloque [vãtrēlok] *nm/f* ventriloquist.

ventripotent, e [vãtrēpotãn, -ãnt] *a* potbellied.

ventru, e [vãtrü] *a* potbellied.

venu, e [vənü] *pp de* **venir** ♦ *a*: **être mal** ~ **à** *ou* **de faire** to have no grounds for doing, be in no position to do; **mal** ~ ill-timed, unwelcome; **bien** ~ timely, welcome ♦ *nf* coming.

vêpres [vepr(ə)] *nfpl* vespers.

ver [ver] *nm voir aussi* **vers**; worm; (*des fruits etc*) maggot; (*du bois*) woodworm *q*; ~ **blanc** May beetle grub; ~ **luisant** glow-worm; ~ **à soie** silkworm; ~ **solitaire** tapeworm; ~ **de terre** earthworm.

véracité [vãrãsētã] *nf* veracity.

véranda [vãrãndã] *nf* veranda(h).

verbal, e, aux [verbál, -ō] *a* verbal.

verbalement [verbálmãn] *ad* verbally.

verbaliser [verbálēzã] *vi* (*POLICE*) to report an offender; (*PSYCH*) to verbalize.

verbe [verb(ə)] *nm* (*LING*) verb; (*voix*): **avoir le** ~ **sonore** to have a sonorous tone (of voice); (*expression*): **la magie du** ~ the magic of language *ou* the word; (*REL*): **le V**~ the Word.

verbeux, euse [verbœ̃, -œ̃z] *a* verbose, wordy.

verbiage [verbyàzh] *nm* verbiage.

verdâtre [verdátr(ə)] *a* greenish.

verdeur [verdœr] *nf* (*vigueur*) vigor (*US*), vigour (*Brit*), vitality; (*crudité*) forthrightness; (*défaut de maturité*) tartness, sharpness.

verdict [verdēk(t)] *nm* verdict.

verdir [verdēr] *vi*, *vt* to turn green.

verdoyant, e [verdwáyãn, -ãnt] *a* green, verdant.

verdure [verdür] *nf* (*arbres, feuillages*) greenery; (*légumes verts*) green vegetables *pl*, greens *pl*.

véreux, euse [vãrœ̃, -œ̃z] *a* worm-eaten; (*malhonnête*) shady, corrupt.

verge [verzh(ə)] *nf* (*ANAT*) penis; (*baguette*) stick, cane.

verger [verzhã] *nm* orchard.

vergeture [verzhətür] *nf gén pl* stretch mark.

verglacé, e [verglásã] *a* icy, iced-over.

verglas [verglá] *nm* (black) ice.

vergogne [vergony]: **sans** ~ *ad* shamelessly.

véridique [vãrēdēk] *a* truthful.

verificateur, trice [vɛrēfēkátœr, -trēs] *nm/f* controller, checker ♦ *nf* (*machine*) verifier; ~ **des comptes** (*FINANCE*) auditor.

vérification [vãrēfēkásyõn] *nf* checking *q*, check; ~ **d'identité** identity check.

vérifier [vãrēfyã] *vt* to check; (*corroborer*) to confirm, bear out; (*INFORM*) to verify; **se** ~ *vi* to be confirmed *ou* verified.

vérin [vãrañ] *nm* jack.

véritable [vãrētábl(ə)] *a* real; (*ami, amour*) true; **un** ~ **désastre** an absolute disaster; **que le** ~ **X sorte du rang!** ≈ will the real X (please) stand up!

veritablement [verētáblemãn] *ad* (*effectivement*) really; (*absolument*) absolutely.

vérité [vãrētã] *nf* truth; (*d'un portrait*) lifelikeness; (*sincérité*) truthfulness, sincerity; **en** ~, **à la** ~ to tell the truth.

vermeil, le [vermey] *a* bright red, ruby red ♦ *nm* (*substance*) vermeil.

vermicelles [vermēsel] *nmpl* vermicelli *sg*.

vermifuge [vermēfüzh] *nm*: **poudre** ~ worm powder.

vermillon [vermēyõn] *a inv* vermilion, scarlet.

vermine [vermēn] *nf* vermin *pl*.

vermoulu, e [vermōōlü] *a* worm-eaten, with woodworm.

vermout(h) [vermōōt] *nm* vermouth.

verni, e [vernã] *a* varnished; glazed; (*fam*) lucky; **cuir** ~ patent leather; **souliers** ~s patent (leather) shoes.

vernir [vernēr] *vt* (*bois, tableau, ongles*) to varnish; (*poterie*) to glaze.

vernis [vernã] *nm* (*enduit*) varnish; glaze; (*fig*) veneer; ~ **à ongles** nail polish.

vernissage [vernēsázh] *nm* varnishing; glazing; (*d'une exposition*) preview.

vernisser [vernēsã] *vt* to glaze.

vérole [vãrol] *nf* (*variole*) smallpox; (*fam*: *syphilis*) pox.

Vérone [vãron] *n* Verona.

verrai [verã] *etc vb voir* **voir**.

verre [ver] *nm* glass; (*de lunettes*) lens *sg*; ~s *nmpl* (*lunettes*) glasses; **boire** *ou* **prendre un** ~ to have a drink; ~ **à vin/à liqueur** wine/liqueur glass; ~ **à dents** tooth mug; ~ **dépoli** frosted glass; ~ **de lampe** lamp glass *ou* chimney; ~ **de montre** watch crystal (*US*) *ou* glass (*Brit*); ~ **à pied** stemmed glass; ~s **de contact** contact lenses; ~s **fumés** tinted glasses.

verrerie [verrē] *nf* (*fabrique*) glassworks *sg*; (*activité*) glass-making, glass-working; (*objets*) glassware.

verrier [veryã] *nm* glass-blower.

verrière [veryer] *nf* (*grand vitrage*) window; (*toit vitré*) glass roof.

verrons [verõn] *etc vb voir* **voir**.

verroterie [verotrē] *nf* glass beads *pl*, glass jewelry (*US*) *ou* jewellery (*Brit*).

verrou [verōō] *nm* (*targette*) bolt; (*fig*) constriction; **mettre le** ~ to bolt the door; **mettre qn sous les** ~s to put sb behind bars.

verrouillage [verōōyázh] *nm* (*dispositif*) locking mechanism; (*AUTO*): ~ **central** central locking.

verrouiller [verōōyā] *vt* to bolt; to lock; (*MIL*: *brèche*) to close.

verrue [verü] *nf* wart; (*plantaire*) verruca; (*fig*) eyesore.

vers [ver] *nm* line ♦ *nmpl* (*poésie*) verse *sg* ♦ *prép* (*en direction de*) toward(s); (*près de*) around (about); (*temporel*) about, around.

versant [versán] *nm* slopes *pl*, side.

versatile [versátēl] *a* fickle, changeable.

verse [vers(ə)]: **à ~** *ad*: **il pleut à ~** it's pouring (with rain).

versé, e [versā] *a*: **être ~ dans** (*science*) to be (well-)versed in.

Verseau [versō] *nm*: **le ~** Aquarius, the water carrier; **être du ~** to be Aquarius.

versement [versəmán] *nm* payment; (*sur un compte*) deposit, remittance; **en 3 ~s** in 3 installments (*US*) *ou* instalments (*Brit*).

verser [versā] *vt* (*liquide, grains*) to pour; (*larmes, sang*) to shed; (*argent*) to pay; (*soldat: affecter*): **~ qn dans** to assign sb to ♦ *vi* (*véhicule*) to overturn; (*fig*): **~ dans** to lapse into; **~ à un compte** to pay into an account.

verset [verse] *nm* verse; versicle.

verseur [versœr] *am voir* **bec, bouchon**.

versifier [versēfyā] *vt* to put into verse ♦ *vi* to versify, write verse.

version [versyôn] *nf* version; (*SCOL*) translation (*into the mother tongue*); **film en ~ originale** film in the original language.

verso [versō] *nm* back; **voir au ~** see over(leaf).

vert, e [ver, vert(ə)] *a* green; (*vin*) young; (*vigoureux*) sprightly; (*cru*) forthright ♦ *nm* green; **dire des ~es (et des pas mûres)** to say some pretty spicy things; **il en a vu des ~es** he's seen a thing or two; **~ bouteille** *a inv* bottle-green; **~ d'eau** *a inv* sea-green; **~ pomme** *a inv* apple-green.

vert-de-gris [verdəgrē] *nm* verdigris ♦ *a inv* gray(ish)- (*US*) *ou* grey(ish)- (*Brit*) green.

vertébral, e, aux [vertābrál, -ō] *a* back *cpd*; *voir* **colonne**.

vertèbre [vertebr(ə)] *nf* vertebra (*pl* -ae).

vertébré, e [vertābrā] *a*, *nm* vertebrate.

vertement [vertəmán] *ad* (*réprimander*) sharply.

vertical, e, aux [vertēkál, -ō] *a*, *nf* vertical; **à la ~e** *ad* vertically.

verticalement [vertēkálmán] *ad* vertically.

verticalité [vertēkálētā] *nf* verticalness, verticality.

vertige [vertēzh] *nm* (*peur du vide*) vertigo; (*étourdissement*) dizzy spell; (*fig*) fever; **ça me donne le ~** it makes me dizzy; (*fig*) it makes my head spin *ou* reel.

vertigineux, euse [vertēzhēnœ, -œz] *a* (*hausse, vitesse*) breathtaking; (*altitude, gorge*) breathtakingly high (*ou* deep).

vertu [vertü] *nf* virtue; **une ~** a saint, a paragon of virtue; **avoir la ~ de faire** to have the virtue of doing; **en ~ de** *prép* in accordance with.

vertueusement [vertüœzmán] *ad* virtuously.

vertueux, euse [vertüœ, -œz] *a* virtuous.

verve [verv(ə)] *nf* witty eloquence; **être en ~** to be in brilliant form.

verveine [verven] *nf* (*BOT*) verbena, vervain;

(*infusion*) verbena tea.

vésicule [vāzēkül] *nf* vesicle; **~ biliaire** gallbladder.

vespasienne [vespázyen] *nf* urinal.

vespéral, e, aux [vespárál, -ō] *a* vespertine, evening *cpd*.

vessie [vāsē] *nf* bladder.

veste [vāst(ə)] *nf* jacket; **~ droite/croisée** single-/double-breasted jacket; **retourner sa ~** (*fig*) to turn one's coat.

vestiaire [vestyer] *nm* (*au théâtre etc*) cloakroom; (*de stade etc*) locker room (*US*), changing-room (*Brit*); (*métallique*): (**armoire**) **~** locker.

vestibule [vestēbül] *nm* hall.

vestige [vestēzh] *nm* (*objet*) relic; (*fragment*) trace; (*fig*) remnant, vestige; **~s** *nmpl* (*d'une ville*) remains; (*d'une civilisation, du passé*) remnants, relics.

vestimentaire [vestēmánter] *a* (*dépenses*) clothing; (*détail*) of dress; (*élégance*) sartorial.

veston [vestôn] *nm* jacket.

Vésuve [vāzüv] *nm*: **le ~** Vesuvius.

vêtais [vete] *etc vb voir* **vêtir**.

vêtement [vetmán] *nm* garment, item of clothing; (*COMM*): **le ~** the clothing industry; **~s** *nmpl* clothes; **~s de sport** sportswear *sg*, sports clothes.

vétéran [vātārán] *nm* veteran.

vétérinaire [vātārēner] *a* veterinary ♦ *nm/f* vet, veterinarian (*US*), veterinary surgeon (*Brit*).

vétille [vātēy] *nf* trifle, triviality.

vetilleux, euse [vātēyœ, -œz] *a* punctilious.

vêtir [vātēr] *vt* to clothe, dress; **se ~** to dress (o.s.).

vêtit [vātē] *etc vb voir* **vêtir**.

veto [vātō] *nm* veto; **opposer un ~ à** to veto.

vêtu, e [vetü] *pp de* **vêtir** ♦ *a*: **~ de** dressed in, wearing; **chaudement ~** warmly dressed.

vétuste [vātüst(ə)] *a* ancient, timeworn.

vétusté [vātüstā] *nf* age, delapidation.

veuf, veuve [vœf, vœv] *a* widowed ♦ *nm* widower ♦ *nf* widow.

veuille [vœy], **veuillez** [vœyā] *etc vb voir* **vouloir**.

veule [vœl] *a* spineless.

veulent [vœl] *etc vb voir* **vouloir**.

veulerie [vœlrē] *nf* spinelessness.

veut [vœ] *vb voir* **vouloir**.

veuvage [vœvázh] *nm* widowhood.

veuve [vœv] *af*, *nf voir* **veuf**.

veux [vœ] *vb voir* **vouloir**.

vexant, e [veksán, -ánt] *a* (*contrariant*) annoying; (*blessant*) upsetting.

vexations [veksâsyôn] *nfpl* humiliations.

vexatoire [veksâtwár] *a*: **mesures ~s** harassment *sg*.

vexer [veksā] *vt* to hurt, upset; **se ~** *vi* to be hurt, get upset.

VF *sigle f* (*CINÉMA*) = *version française*.

VHF *sigle f* (= *Very High Frequency*) VHF.

via [vyá] *prép* via.

viabiliser [vyábēlēzā] *vt* to provide with services (*water etc*).

viabilité [vyábēlētā] *nf* viability; (*d'un chemin*) practicability.

viable [vyábl(ə)] *a* viable.

viaduc [vyȧdük] *nm* viaduct.

viager, ère [vyȧzhä, -er] *a*: **rente** ~**ère** life annuity ♦ *nm*: **mettre en** ~ to sell in return for a life annuity.

viande [vyȧ̂nd] *nf* meat.

viatique [vyȧtĕk] *nm* (*REL*) viaticum; (*fig*) provisions *pl ou* money for the journey.

vibrant, e [vē̇brȧ̂n, -ȧ̂nt] vibrating; (*voix*) vibrant; (*émouvant*) emotive.

vibraphone [vē̇brȧfon] *nm* vibraphone, vibes *pl*.

vibration [vē̇brȧsyȯ̂n] *nf* vibration.

vibratoire [vē̇brȧtwȧr] *a* vibratory.

vibrer [vē̇brǡ] *vi* to vibrate; (*son, voix*) to be vibrant; (*fig*) to be stirred; **faire** ~ to (cause to) vibrate; to stir, thrill.

vibromasseur [vē̇bromȧsœr] *nm* vibrator.

vicaire [vē̇ker] *nm* curate.

vice... [vē̇s] *préfixe* vice-.

vice [vē̇s] *nm* vice; (*défaut*) fault; ~ **caché** (*COMM*) latent *ou* inherent defect; ~ **de forme** legal flaw *ou* irregularity.

vice-consul [vē̇skȯ̂nsül] *nm* vice-consul.

vice-président, e [vē̇sprȧzēdȧ̂n, -ȧ̂nt] *nm/f* vice-president; vice-chairman.

vice-roi [vē̇srwȧ] *nm* viceroy.

vice versa [vē̇sȧversȧ] *ad* vice versa.

vichy [vē̇shē̇] *nm* (*toile*) gingham; (*eau*) Vichy water; **carottes V**~ boiled carrots.

vichyssois, e [vē̇shē̇swȧ, -wȧz] *a* of *ou* from Vichy, Vichy *cpd* ♦ *nf* (*soupe*) vichyssoise (soup), *cream of leek and potato soup* ♦ *nm/f*: **V**~, **e** native *ou* inhabitant of Vichy.

vicié, e [vē̇syǡ] *a* (*air*) polluted, tainted; (*JUR*) invalidated.

vicier [vē̇syǡ] *vt* (*JUR*) to invalidate.

vicieux, euse [vē̇syœ̄, œ̄z] *a* (*pervers*) dirty(-minded); (*méchant*) nasty; (*fautif*) incorrect, wrong.

vicinal, e, aux [vē̇sēnȧl, -ō] *a*: **chemin** ~ by-road, byway.

vicissitudes [vē̇sēsētüd] *nfpl* (trials and) tribulations.

vicomte [vē̇kȯ̂nt] *nm* viscount.

vicomtesse [vē̇kȯ̂ntes] *nf* viscountess.

victime [vē̇ktēm] *nf* victim; (*d'accident*) casualty; **être (la)** ~ **de** to be the victim of; **être** ~ **d'une attaque/d'un accident** to suffer a stroke/be involved in an accident.

victoire [vē̇ktwȧr] *nf* victory.

victorieux, euse [vē̇ktoryœ̄, -œ̄z] *a* victorious; (*sourire, attitude*) triumphant.

victuailles [vē̇ktüȧy] *nfpl* provisions.

vidange [vē̇dȧ̂nzh] *nf* (*d'un fossé, réservoir*) emptying; (*AUTO*) oil change; (*de lavabo: bonde*) drain; ~**s** *nfpl* (*matières*) sewage *sg*; **faire la** ~ (*AUTO*) to change the oil, do an oil change; **tuyau de** ~ drain pipe.

vidanger [vē̇dȧ̂nzhǡ] *vt* to empty; **faire** ~ **la voiture** to have the oil changed in one's car.

vide [vē̇d] *a* empty ♦ *nm* (*PHYSIQUE*) vacuum; (*espace*) (empty) space, gap; (*sous soi: dans une falaise etc*) drop; (*futilité, néant*) void; ~ **de** empty of; (*de sens etc*) devoid of; **sous** ~ *ad* in a vacuum; **emballé sous** ~ vacuum packed; **regarder dans le** ~ to stare into space; **avoir peur du** ~ to be afraid of heights; **parler dans le** ~ to waste one's breath; **faire le** ~ (*dans son esprit*) to make

one's mind go blank; **faire le** ~ **autour de qn** to isolate sb; **à** ~ *ad* (*sans occupants*) empty; (*sans charge*) unladen; (*TECH*) without gripping *ou* being in gear.

vidé, e [vē̇dǡ] *a* (*épuisé*) done in, all in.

vidéo [vē̇dǡȯ] *nf*, *a inv* video; ~ **inverse** reverse video.

vidéocassette [vē̇dǡokȧset] *nf* video cassette.

vidéoclub [vē̇dǡoklœb] *nm* video club.

vidéodisque [vē̇dǡodĕsk] *nm* videodisc.

vlde-ordures [vē̇dordür] *nm inv* (garbage (*US*) *ou* rubbish (*Brit*)) chute.

vidéotex [vē̇dǡoteks] *nm* ℞ teletext.

vide-poches [vē̇dposh] *nm inv* tidy; (*AUTO*) glove compartment.

vide-pomme [vē̇dpom] *nm inv* apple corer.

vider [vē̇dǡ] *vt* to empty; (*CULIN: volaille, poisson*) to gut, clean; (*régler: querelle*) to settle; (*fatiguer*) to wear out; (*fam: expulser*) to throw out, chuck out; **se** ~ *vi* to empty; ~ **les lieux** to quit *ou* vacate the premises.

videur [vē̇dœr] *nm* (*de boîte de nuit*) bouncer.

vie [vē̇] *nf* life (*pl* lives); **être en** ~ to be alive; **sans** ~ lifeless; **à** ~ for life; **membre à** ~ life member; **dans la** ~ **courante** in everyday life; **avoir la** ~ **dure** to have nine lives; to die hard; **mener la** ~ **dure à qn** to make life miserable for sb.

vieil [vyey] *am voir* **vieux**.

vieillard [vyeyȧr] *nm* old man; **les** ~**s** old people, the elderly.

vieille [vyey] *af*, *nf voir* **vieux**.

vieilleries [vyeyrē̇] *nfpl* old things *ou* stuff *sg*.

vieillesse [vyeyes] *nf* old age; (*vieillards*): **la** ~ the old *pl*, the elderly *pl*.

vieilli, e [vyǡyē̇] *a* (*marqué par l'âge*) aged; (*suranné*) dated.

vieillir [vyǡyēr] *vi* (*prendre de l'âge*) to grow old; (*population, vin*) to age; (*doctrine, auteur*) to become dated ♦ *vt* to age; **il a beaucoup vleilli** he has aged a lot; **se** ~ to make o.s. older.

vieillissement [vyǡyēsmȧ̂n] *nm* growing old; aging.

vieillot, te [vyeyō, -ot] *a* antiquated, quaint.

vielle [vyel] *nf* hurdy-gurdy.

viendrai [vyǡndrǡ] *etc vb voir* **venir**.

Vienne [vyen] *n* (*en Autriche*) Vienna.

vienne [vyen], **viens** [vyȧ̂n] *etc vb voir* **venir**.

viennois, e [vyenwȧ, -wȧz] *a* Viennese.

vierge [vyerzh(ə)] *a* virgin; (*film*) blank; (*page*) clean, blank; (*jeune fille*): **être** ~ to be a virgin ♦ *nf* virgin; (*signe*): **la V**~ Virgo, the Virgin; **être de la V**~ to be Virgo; ~ **de** (*sans*) free from, unsullied by.

Viet-Nam, Vietnam [vyetnȧm] *nm*: **le** ~ Vietnam; **le** ~ **du Nord/du Sud** North/South Vietnam.

vietnamien, ne [vyetnȧmyȧ̂n, -en] *a* Vietnamese ♦ *nm* (*LING*) Vietnamese ♦ *nm/f*: **V**~, **ne** Vietnamese; **V**~, **ne du Nord/Sud** North/South Vietnamese.

vieux (vieil), vieille [vyœ̄, vyey] *a* old ♦ *nm/f* old man/woman ♦ *nmpl*: **les** ~ the old, old people; (*fam: parents*) the old folk *ou* ones; **un petit** ~ a little old man; **mon** ~/**ma vieille** (*fam*) old man/girl; **pauvre** ~ poor old soul; **prendre un coup de** ~ to put years on;

se faire ~ to make o.s. look older; **un** ~ **de la vieille** one of the old brigade; ~ **garçon** *nm* bachelor; ~ **jeu** *a inv* old-fashioned; ~ **rose** *a inv* old rose; **vieil or** *a inv* old gold; **vieille fille** *nf* spinster.

vif, vive [vēf, vēv] *a* (*animé*) lively; (*alerte*) sharp, quick; (*brusque*) sharp, brusque; (*aigu*) sharp; (*lumière, couleur*) brilliant; (*air*) crisp; (*vent, émotion*) keen; (*froid*) bitter; (*fort: regret, déception*) great, deep; (*vivant*): **brûlé** ~ burned alive; **eau vive** running water; **de vive voix** personally; **piquer qn au** ~ to cut sb to the quick; **tailler dans le** ~ to cut into the living flesh; **à** ~ (*plaie*) open; **avoir les nerfs à** ~ to be on edge; **sur le** ~ (*ART*) from life; **entrer dans le** ~ **du sujet** to get to the very heart of the matter.

vif-argent [vēfárzháń] *nm inv* quicksilver.

vigie [vēzhē] *nf* (*matelot*) lookout; (*poste*) look-out post, crow's nest.

vigilance [vēzhēláńs] *nf* vigilance.

vigilant, e [vēzhēláń, -áńt] *a* vigilant.

vigile [vēzhēl] *nm* (*veilleur de nuit*) (night) watchman; (*police privée*) vigilante.

vigne [vēny] *nf* (*plante*) vine; (*plantation*) vineyard; ~ **vierge** Virginia creeper.

vigneron [vēnyróń] *nm* wine grower.

vignette [vēnyet] *nf* (*motif*) vignette; (*de marque*) manufacturer's label *ou* seal; (*petite illustration*) (small) illustration; (*ADMIN*) ≈ (road) license plate sticker (*US*), ≈ tax disc (*Brit*); (*: sur médicament*) price label (*on medicines for reimbursement by Social Security*).

vignoble [vēnyobl(ə)] *nm* (*plantation*) vineyard; (*vignes d'une région*) vineyards *pl*.

vigoureusement [vēgōōrǽzmáń] *ad* vigorously.

vigoureux, euse [vēgōōrǽ, -ǽz] *a* vigorous, robust.

vigueur [vēgœr] *nf* vigor (*US*), vigour (*Brit*); **être/entrer en** ~ to be in/come into force; **en** ~ current.

vil, e [vēl] *a* vile, base; **à** ~ **prix** at a very low price.

vilain, e [vēlań, -en] *a* (*laid*) ugly; (*affaire, blessure*) nasty; (*pas sage: enfant*) naughty ♦ *nm* (*paysan*) villein, villain; **ça va tourner au** ~ things are going to turn nasty; ~ **mot** bad word.

vilebrequin [vēlbrəkań] *nm* (*outil*) (bit-)brace; (*AUTO*) crankshaft.

vilenie [vēlnē] *nf* vileness *q*, baseness *q*.

vilipender [vēlēpáńdā] *vt* to revile, vilify.

villa [vēlá] *nf* (detached) house.

village [vēlázh] *nm* village; ~ **de toile** tent village; ~ **de vacances** vacation (*US*) *ou* holiday (*Brit*) village.

villageois, e [vēlázhwá, -wáz] *a* village *cpd* ♦ *nm/f* villager.

ville [vēl] *nf* town; (*importante*) city; (*administration*): **la** ~ ≈ the Corporation; ≈ the (town) council; **aller en** ~ to go to town; **habiter en** ~ to live in town; ~ **nouvelle** new town.

ville-champignon, *pl* **villes-champignons** [vēlsháńpēnyóń] *nf* boom town.

ville-dortoir, *pl* **villes-dortoirs** [vēldortwár] *nf* bedroom community (*US*), dormitory town (*Brit*).

villégiature [vēlázhyátür] *nf* (*séjour*) vacation (*US*), holiday (*Brit*); (*lieu*) (vacation *ou* holiday) resort.

vin [vań] *nm* wine; **avoir le** ~ **gai/triste** to get happy/miserable after a few drinks; ~ **blanc/rosé/rouge** white/rosé/red wine; ~ **d'honneur** reception (*with wine and snacks*); ~ **de messe** communion wine; ~ **ordinaire** *ou* **de table** table wine; ~ **de pays** local wine.

vinaigre [vēnegr(ə)] *nm* vinegar; **tourner au** ~ (*fig*) to turn sour; ~ **de vin/d'alcool** wine/spirit vinegar.

vinaigrette [vēnegret] *nf* vinaigrette, French dressing.

vinaigrier [vēnegrēyā] *nm* (*fabricant*) vinegar-maker; (*flacon*) vinegar cruet *ou* bottle.

vinasse [vēnás] *nf* (*péj*) cheap wine.

vindicatif, ive [vańdēkátēf, -ēv] *a* vindictive.

vindicte [vańdēkt(ə)] *nf*: **désigner qn à la** ~ **publique** to expose sb to public condemnation.

vineux, euse [vēnœ̄, œ̄z] *a* win(e)y.

vingt [vań, vańt + *vowel and in 22, 23 etc*] *num* twenty; ~-**quatre heures sur** ~-**quatre** twenty-four hours a day, round the clock.

vingtaine [vańten] *nf*: **une** ~ (**de**) around twenty, twenty or so.

vingtième [vańtyem] *num* twentieth.

vinicole [vēnēkol] *a* (*production*) wine *cpd*; (*région*) wine-growing.

vinification [vēnēfēkásyôń] *nf* wine-making, wine production; (*des sucres*) vinification.

vinyle [vēnēl] *nm* vinyl.

viol [vyol] *nm* (*d'une femme*) rape; (*d'un lieu sacré*) violation.

violacé, e [vyolásā] *a* purplish, mauvish.

violation [vyolásyôń] *nf* desecration; violation; (*d'un droit*) breach.

violemment [vyolámáń] *ad* violently.

violence [vyoláńs] *nf* violence; ~**s** *nfpl* acts of violence; **faire** ~ **à qn** to do violence to sb; **se faire** ~ to force o.s.

violent, e [vyoláń, -áńt] *a* violent; (*remède*) drastic; (*besoin, désir*) intense, urgent.

violenter [vyoláńtā] *vt* to assault (sexually).

violer [vyolā] *vt* (*femme*) to rape; (*sépulture*) to desecrate, violate; (*loi, traité*) to violate.

violet, te [vyole, -et] *a, nm* purple, mauve ♦ *nf* (*fleur*) violet.

violeur [vyolœr] *nm* rapist.

violon [vyolôń] *nm* violin; (*dans la musique folklorique etc*) fiddle; (*fam: prison*) lockup; **premier** ~ first violin; ~ **d'Ingres** (artistic) hobby.

violoncelle [vyolôńsel] *nm* cello.

violoncelliste [vyolôńsālēst(ə)] *nm/f* cellist.

violoniste [vyolonēst(ə)] *nm/f* violinist, violin player; (*folklorique etc*) fiddler.

VIP *sigle m* (= *Very Important Person*) VIP.

vipère [vēper] *nf* viper, adder.

virage [vērázh] *nm* (*d'un véhicule*) turn; (*d'une route, piste*) curve (*US*), turn (*US*), bend (*Brit*); (*CHIMIE*) change in color (*US*) *ou* colour (*Brit*); (*de cuti-réaction*) positive reaction; (*PHOTO*) toning; (*fig: POL*) about-face (*US*), about-turn (*Brit*); **prendre un** ~

to go into a curve *ou* bend, take a curve *ou* bend; ~ **sans visibilité** blind curve *ou* bend.

viral, e, aux [vĕrăl, -ō] *a* viral.

virée [vĕrā] *nf* (*courte*) run; (: *à pied*) walk; (*longue*) trip; hike, walking tour.

virement [vĕrmáń] *nm* (*COMM*) transfer; ~ **bancaire** (bank) credit transfer, ≈ (bank) giro transfer (*Brit*); ~ **postal** Post office credit transfer, ≈ Girobank ® transfer (*Brit*).

virent [vĕr] *vb voir* **voir**.

virer [vĕrā] *vt* (*COMM*): ~ **qch (sur)** to transfer sth (into); (*PHOTO*) to tone; (*fam: renvoyer*) to sack, boot out ♦ *vi* to turn; (*CHIMIE*) to change color (*US*) *ou* colour (*Brit*); (*cuti-réaction*) to come up positive; (*PHOTO*) to tone; ~ **au bleu** to turn blue; ~ **de bord** to tack; (*fig*) to change tack; ~ **sur l'aile** to bank.

virevolte [vĕrvolt(ə)] *nf* twirl; (*d'avis, d'opinion*) about-face (*US*), about-turn (*Brit*).

virevolter [vĕrvoltā] *vi* to twirl around.

virginal, e, aux [vĕrzhēnăl, -ō] *a* virginal.

virginité [vĕrzhēnētā] *nf* virginity; (*fig*) purity.

virgule [vĕrgül] *nf* comma; (*MATH*) point; **4 ~ 2** 4 point 2; ~ **flottante** floating decimal.

viril, e [vĕrēl] *a* (*propre à l'homme*) masculine; (*énergique, courageux*) manly, virile.

viriliser [vĕrēlēzā] *vt* to make (more) manly *ou* masculine.

virilité [vĕrēlētā] *nf* (*attributs masculins*) masculinity; (*fermeté, courage*) manliness; (*sexuelle*) virility.

virologie [vĕrolozhē] *nf* virology.

virtualité [vĕrtüălētā] *nf* virtuality; potentiality.

virtuel, le [vĕrtüel] *a* potential; (*théorique*) virtual.

virtuellement [vĕrtüelmáń] *a* potentially; (*presque*) virtually.

virtuose [vĕrtüōz] *nm/f* (*MUS*) virtuoso; (*gén*) master.

virtuosité [vĕrtüōzētā] *nf* virtuosity; masterliness, masterful skills *pl*.

virulence [vĕrüláńs] *nf* virulence.

virulent, e [vĕrüláń, -áńt] *a* virulent.

virus [vĕrüs] *nm* virus.

vis *vb* [vē] *voir* **voir, vivre** ♦ *nf* [vēs] screw; ~ **à tête plate/ronde** flat-headed/round-headed screw; ~ **platinées** (*AUTO*) (contact) points; ~ **sans fin** worm, endless screw.

visa [vēză] *nm* (*sceau*) stamp; (*validation de passeport*) visa; ~ **de censure** (censor's) certificate.

visage [vēzázh] *nm* face; **à ~ découvert** (*franchement*) openly.

visagiste [vēzăzhēst(ə)] *nm/f* beautician.

vis-à-vis [vēzăvē] *ad* face to face ♦ *nm* person opposite; house *etc* opposite; ~ **de** *prép* opposite; (*fig*) towards, vis-à-vis; **en** ~ facing *ou* opposite each other; **sans** ~ (*immeuble*) with an open view.

viscéral, e, aux [vēsărăl, -ō] *a* (*fig*) deep-seated, deep-rooted.

viscères [vēsər] *nmpl* intestines, entrails.

viscose [vēskōz] *nf* viscose.

viscosité [vēskōzētā] *nf* viscosity.

visée [vēzā] *nf* (*avec une arme*) aiming; (*ARPENTAGE*) sighting; ~**s** *nfpl* (*intentions*)

designs; **avoir des** ~**s sur qn/qch** to have designs on sb/sth.

viser [vēză] *vi* to aim ♦ *vt* to aim at; (*concerner*) to be aimed *ou* directed at; (*apposer un visa sur*) to stamp, visa; ~ **à qch/faire** to aim at sth/at doing *ou* to do.

viseur [vēzœr] *nm* (*d'arme*) sight(s) (*pl*); (*PHOTO*) viewfinder.

visibilité [vēzēbēlētā] *nf* visibility; **sans** ~ (*pilotage, virage*) blind *cpd*.

visible [vēzēbl(ə)] *a* visible; (*disponible*): **est-il** ~**?** can he see me?, will he see visitors?

visiblement [vēzēbləmáń] *ad* visibly, obviously.

visière [vēzyer] *nf* (*de casquette*) peak; (*qui s'attache*) eyeshade.

vision [vēzyóń] *nf* vision; (*sens*) (eye)sight, vision; (*fait de voir*): **la** ~ **de** the sight of; **première** ~ (*CINÉMA*) first showing.

visionnaire [vēzyoner] *a, nm/f* visionary.

visionner [vēzyonā] *vt* to view.

visionneuse [vēzyonœz] *nf* viewer.

visite [vēzēt] *nf* visit; (*visiteur*) visitor; (*touristique: d'un musée etc*) tour; (*COMM: de représentant*) call; (*expertise, d'inspection*) inspection; (*médicale, à domicile*) visit, call; **la** ~ (*MÉD*) medical examination; (*MIL: d'entrée*) physical (examination); (: *quotidienne*) sick call (*US*) *ou* parade (*Brit*); **faire une** ~ **à qn** to call on sb, pay sb a visit; **rendre** ~ **à qn** to visit sb, pay sb a visit; **être en** ~ (**chez qn**) to be visiting (sb); **heures de** ~ (*hôpital, prison*) visiting hours; **le droit de** ~ (*JUR: aux enfants*) right of access, access; ~ **de douane** customs inspection *ou* examination.

visiter [vēzētā] *vt* to visit; (*musée, ville*) to visit, tour.

visiteur, euse [vēzētœr, -œz] *nm/f* visitor; ~ **des douanes** customs inspector; ~ **médical** medical rep(resentative); ~ **de prison** prison visitor.

vison [vēzóń] *nm* mink.

visqueux, euse [vēskœ, -œz] *a* viscous; (*péj*) gooey; (: *manières*) slimy.

visser [vēsā] *vt*: ~ **qch** (*fixer, serrer*) to screw sth on.

visu [vēzü]: **de** ~ *ad* with one's own eyes.

visualisation [vēzüălēzăsyóń] *nf* (*INFORM*) display; **ecran de** ~ visual display unit (VDU).

visualiser [vēzüălēzā] *vt* to visualize; (*INFORM*) to display, bring up on screen.

visuel, le [vēzüel] *a* visual ♦ *nm* (visual) display; (*INFORM*) visual display unit (VDU).

visuellement [vēzüelmáń] *ad* visually.

vit [vē] *vb voir* **voir, vivre**.

vital, e, aux [vētăl, -ō] *a* vital.

vitalité [vētălētā] *nf* vitality.

vitamine [vētămēn] *nf* vitamin.

vitaminé, e [vētămēnā] *a* with (added) vitamins.

vitaminique [vētămēnēk] *a* vitamin *cpd*.

vite [vēt] *ad* (*rapidement*) quickly, fast; (*sans délai*) quickly; soon; **faire** ~ (*agir rapidement*) to act fast; (*se dépêcher*) to be quick; **ce sera** ~ **fini** this will soon be finished; **viens** ~ come quick(ly).

vitesse [vētes] *nf* speed; (*AUTO: dispositif*) gear; **faire de la** ~ to speed, drive fast;

prendre qn de ~ to outstrip sb, get ahead of sb; **prendre de la** ~ to pick up *ou* gather speed; **à toute** ~ at full *ou* top speed; **en perte de** ~ *(avion)* losing lift; *(fig)* losing momentum; **changer de** ~ *(AUTO)* to change gear; ~ **acquise** momentum; ~ **de croisière** cruising speed; ~ **de pointe** top speed; ~ **du son** speed of sound.

viticole [vĕtĕkɔl] *a (industrie)* wine *cpd; (région)* wine-growing.

viticulteur [vĕtĕkültœr] *nm* wine grower.

viticulture [vĕtĕkültür] *nf* wine growing.

vitrage [vĕtràzh] *nm (cloison)* glass partition; *(toit)* glass roof; *(rideau)* net curtain.

vitrail, aux [vĕtrày, -ō] *nm* stained-glass window.

vitre [vĕtr(ə)] *nf* (window) pane; *(de portière, voiture)* window.

vitré, e [vĕtrā] *a* glass *cpd.*

vitrer [vĕtrā] *vt* to glaze.

vitreux, euse [vĕtrœ̄, -œ̄z] *a* vitreous; *(terne)* glassy.

vitrier [vĕtrēyā] *nm* glazier.

vitrifier [vĕtrĕfyā] *vt* to vitrify; *(parquet)* to glaze.

vitrine [vĕtrēn] *nf (devanture)* show *(US) ou* shop *(Brit)* window; *(étalage)* display; *(petite armoire)* display cabinet; **en** ~ in the window, on display; ~ **publicitaire** display case, showcase.

vitriol [vĕtrēyɔl] *nm* vitriol; **au** ~ *(fig)* vitriolic.

vitupérations [vĕtüpārâsyôṅ] *nfpl* invective *sg.*

vitupérer [vĕtüpārā] *vi* to rant and rave; ~ **contre** to rail against.

vivable [vĕvábl(ə)] *a (personne)* livable-with; *(endroit)* fit to live in.

vivace *a* [vĕvás] *(arbre, plante)* hardy; *(fig)* enduring ♦ *ad* [vĕvátshā] *(MUS)* vivace.

vivacité [vĕvásĕtā] *nf (voir vif)* liveliness, vivacity; sharpness; brilliance.

vivant, e [vĕvâṅ, -âṅt] *vb voir* **vivre** ♦ *a (qui vit)* living, alive; *(animé)* lively; *(preuve, exemple)* living; *(langue)* modern ♦ *nm*: **du** ~ **de qn** in sb's lifetime; **les** ~**s et les morts** the living and the dead.

vivarium [vĕváryom] *nm* vivarium.

vivats [vĕvá] *nmpl* cheers.

vive [vĕv] *af voir* **vif** ♦ *vb voir* **vivre** ♦ *excl*: ~ **le roi!** long live the king!; ~ **les vacances!** hurrah for the vacation! *(US) ou* holidays! *(Brit).*

vivement [vĕvmâṅ] *ad* vivaciously; sharply ♦ *excl*: ~ **les vacances!** I can't wait for the vacation! *(US) ou* holidays! *(Brit),* bring on vacation (time)!

vivier [vĕvyā] *nm (au restaurant etc)* fish tank; *(étang)* fishpond.

vivifiant, e [vĕvĕfyâṅ, -âṅt] *a* invigorating.

vivifier [vĕvĕfyā] *vt* to invigorate; *(fig: souvenirs, sentiments)* to liven up, enliven.

vivisection [vĕvĕsĕksyôṅ] *nf* vivisection.

vivoter [vĕvotā] *vi (personne)* to scrape a living, get by; *(fig: affaire etc)* to struggle along.

vivre [vĕvr(ə)] *vi, vt* to live ♦ *nm*: **le** ~ **et le logement** room and board ♦ ~**s** *nmpl* provisions, food supplies; **il vit encore** he is still alive; **se laisser** ~ to take life as it comes;

ne plus ~ *(être anxieux)* to be a bundle of nerves; **il a vécu** *(eu une vie aventureuse)* he has seen life; **ce régime a vécu** this regime has had its day; **être facile à** ~ to be easy to get along with; **faire** ~ **qn** *(pourvoir à sa subsistance)* to provide (a living) for sb; ~ **mal** *(chichement)* to have a meager existence; ~ **de** *(salaire etc)* to live on.

vivrier, ière [vĕvrēyā, -yer] *a* food-producing *cpd.*

vlan [vlâṅ] *excl* wham!, bang!

VO *sigle f (CINÉMA*: = *version originale)*: **voir un film en** ~ to see a film in its original language.

v° *abr* = **verso.**

vocable [vokábl(ə)] *nm* term.

vocabulaire [vokábüler] *nm* vocabulary.

vocal, e, aux [vokál, -ō] *a* vocal.

vocalique [vokálĕk] *a* vocalic, vowel *cpd.*

vocalise [vokálēz] *nf* singing exercise.

vocaliser [vokálēzā] *vi (LING)* to vocalize; *(MUS)* to do one's singing exercises.

vocation [vokâsyôṅ] *nf* vocation, calling; **avoir la** ~ to have a vocation.

vociférations [vosĕfārâsyôṅ] *nfpl* cries of rage, screams.

vociférer [vosĕfārā] *vi, vt* to scream.

vodka [vodká] *nf* vodka.

vœu, x [vœ̄] *nm* wish; *(à Dieu)* vow; **faire** ~ **de** to take a vow of; **avec tous nos** ~**x** with every good wish *ou* our best wishes; ~**x de bonheur** best wishes for your future happiness; ~**x de bonne année** best wishes for the New Year.

vogue [vog] *nf* fashion, vogue; **en** ~ in fashion, in vogue.

voguer [vogá] *vi* to sail.

voici [vwásĕ] *prép (pour introduire, désigner)* here is + *sg,* here are + *pl*; **et** ~ **que ... and** now it *(ou* he) ...; **il est parti** ~ **3 ans** he left 3 years ago; ~ **une semaine que je l'ai vue** it's a week since I've seen her; **me** ~ here I am; *voir aussi* **voilà.**

voie [vwá] *vb voir* **voir** ♦ *nf* way; *(RAIL)* track, line; *(AUTO)* lane; **par** ~ **buccale** *ou* **orale** orally; **par** ~ **rectale** rectally; **suivre la** ~ **hiérarchique** to go through official channels; **ouvrir/montrer la** ~ to open up/show the way; **être en bonne** ~ to be shaping up *ou* going well; **mettre qn sur la** ~ to put sb on the right track; **être en** ~ **d'achèvement/de rénovation** to be nearing completion/in the process of renovation; **à** ~ **étroite** narrow-gauge; **à** ~ **unique** single-track; **route à 2/3** ~**s** 2-/3-lane road; **par la** ~ **aérienne/ maritime** by air/sea; ~ **d'eau** *(NAVIG)* leak; ~ **express** expressway; ~ **de fait** *(JUR)* assault (and battery); ~ **ferrée** track; railroad *(US)*, railway line *(Brit)*; **par** ~ **ferrée** by rail, by railroad; ~ **de garage** *(RAIL)* siding; **la** ~ **lactée** the Milky Way; ~ **navigable** waterway; ~ **prioritaire** *(AUTO)* road with right of way; ~ **privée** private road; **la** ~ **publique** the public highway.

voilà [vwálá] *prép (en désignant)* there is + *sg,* there are + *pl*; **les** ~ *ou* **voici** here *ou* there they are; **en** ~ *ou* **voici un** here's one, there's one; ~ *ou* **voici deux ans** two years ago; ~ *ou* **voici deux ans que** it's two years since; **et** ~! there we are!; ~ **tout** that's all; "~ *ou* **voici**" *(en offrant etc)* "there *ou* here you are".

voilage [vwàlàzh] *nm (rideau)* sheer (curtain) *(US)*, net curtain *(Brit)*; *(tissu)* net.

voile [vwàl] *nm* veil; *(tissu léger)* sheer *(US)*, net *(Brit)* ♦ *nf* sail; *(sport)* sailing; **prendre le** ~ to take the veil; **mettre à la** ~ to set sail; ~ **du palais** *nm* soft palate, velum; ~ **au poumon** *nm* shadow on the lung.

voiler [vwàlā] *vt* to veil; *(PHOTO)* to fog; *(fausser: roue)* to buckle; *(: bois)* to warp; **se** ~ *vi (lune, regard)* to mist over; *(ciel)* to grow hazy; *(voix)* to become husky; *(roue, disque)* to buckle; *(planche)* to warp; **se** ~ **la face** to hide one's face.

voilette [vwàlet] *nf (hat)* veil.

voilier [vwàlyā] *nm* sailing ship; *(de plaisance)* sailboat *(US)*, sailing boat *(Brit)*.

voilure [vwàlür] *nf (de voilier)* sails *pl*; *(d'avion)* airfoils *pl (US)*, aerofoils *pl (Brit)*; *(de parachute)* canopy.

voir [vwàr] *vi, vt* to see; **se** ~: **se** ~ **critiquer/ transformer** to be criticized/transformed; **cela se voit** *(cela arrive)* it happens; *(c'est visible)* that's obvious, it shows; ~ **à faire qch** to see to it that sth is done; ~ **loin** *(fig)* to be farsighted; ~ **venir** *(fig)* to wait and see; **faire** ~ **qch à qn** to show sb sth; **en faire** ~ **à qn** *(fig)* to give sb a hard time; **ne pas pouvoir** ~ **qn** *(fig)* not to be able to stand sb; **regardez** ~ just look; **montrez** ~ show (me); **dites** ~ tell me; **voyons!** let's see now; *(indignation etc)* come (on) now!; **c'est à** ~! we'll see!; **c'est ce qu'on va** ~! we'll see about that!; **avoir quelque chose à** ~ **avec** to have something to do with; **ça n'a rien à** ~ **avec lui** that has nothing to do with him.

voire [vwàr] *ad* indeed; nay; or even.

voirie [vwàrē] *nf* highway maintenance; *(administration)* highway *(US)* ou highways *(Brit)* department; *(enlèvement des ordures)* garbage *(US)* ou refuse *(Brit)* collection.

vois [vwà] *vb voir* **voir**.

voisin, e [vwàzaṅ, -ēn] *a (proche)* neighboring *(US)*, neighbouring *(Brit)*; *(contigu)* next; *(ressemblant)* connected ♦ *nm/f* neighbor *(US)*, neighbour *(Brit)*; *(de table, de dortoir etc)* person next to me *(ou* him *etc)*; ~ **de palier** neighbor across the hall *(US)* ou landing *(Brit)*.

voisinage [vwàzēnàzh] *nm (proximité)* proximity; *(environs)* vicinity; *(quartier, voisins)* neighborhood *(US)*, neighbourhood *(Brit)*; **relations de bon** ~ neighborly terms.

voisiner [vwàzēnā] *vi*: ~ **avec** to be side by side with.

voit [vwà] *vb voir* **voir**.

voiture [vwàtür] *nf* car; *(wagon)* car *(US)*, carriage *(Brit)*; **en** ~! all aboard!; ~ **à bras** handcart; ~ **d'enfant** baby carriage *(US)*, pram *(Brit)*; ~ **d'infirme** wheelchair; ~ **de sport** sports car.

voiture-lit, *pl* **voitures-lits** [vwàtürlē] *nf* Pullman *(US)*, sleeper *(Brit)*.

voiture-restaurant, *pl* **voitures-restaurants** [vwàtürrestoràṅ] *nf* dining car.

voix [vwà] *nf* voice; *(POL)* vote; **la** ~ **de la**

conscience/raison the voice of conscience/ reason; **à haute** ~ aloud; **à** ~ **basse** in a low voice; **faire la grosse** ~ to speak gruffly; **avoir de la** ~ to have a good voice; **rester sans** ~ to be speechless; ~ **de basse/ténor** *etc* bass/tenor *etc* voice; **à 2/4** ~ *(MUS)* in 2/4 parts; **avoir** ~ **au chapitre** to have a say in the matter; **mettre aux** ~ to put to the vote.

vol [vol] *nm (mode de locomotion)* flying; *(trajet, voyage, groupe d'oiseaux)* flight; *(mode d'appropriation)* theft, stealing; *(larcin)* theft; **à** ~ **d'oiseau** as the crow flies; **au** ~: **attraper qch au** ~ to catch sth as it flies past; **saisir une remarque au** ~ to pick up a passing remark; **prendre son** ~ to take flight; **de haut** ~ *(fig)* of the highest order; **en** ~ in flight; ~ **avec effraction** breaking and entering *q*, break-in; ~ **à l'étalage** shoplifting *q*; ~ **libre** hang-gliding; ~ **à main armée** armed robbery; ~ **de nuit** night flight; ~ **plané** *(AVIAT)* glide, gliding *q*; ~ **à la tire** pickpocketing *q*; ~ **à voile** gliding.

vol. *abr (= volume)* vol.

volage [volàzh] *a* fickle.

volaille [volày] *nf (oiseaux)* poultry *pl*; *(viande)* poultry *q*; *(oiseau)* fowl.

volailler [volàyā] *nm* poulterer.

volant, e [volàṅ, -àṅt] *a voir* **feuille** *etc* ♦ *nm (d'automobile)* (steering) wheel; *(de commande)* wheel; *(objet lancé)* shuttlecock; *(jeu)* battledore and shuttlecock; *(bande de tissu)* flounce; *(feuillet détachable)* tear-off portion; **le personnel** ~, **les** ~**s** *(AVIAT)* the flight crew; ~ **de sécurité** *(fig)* reserve, margin, safeguard.

volatil, e [volàtēl] *a* volatile.

volatile [volàtēl] *nm (volaille)* bird; *(tout oiseau)* winged creature.

volatiliser [volàtēlēzā]: **se** ~ *vi (CHIMIE)* to volatilize; *(fig)* to vanish into thin air.

vol-au-vent [volōvàṅ] *nm inv* vol-au-vent.

volcan [volkàṅ] *nm* volcano; *(fig: personne)* hothead.

volcanique [volkànēk] *a* volcanic; *(fig: tempérament)* volatile.

volcanologue [volkànolog] *nm/f* vulcanologist.

volée [volā] *nf (groupe d'oiseaux)* flight, flock; *(TENNIS)* volley; ~ **de coups/de flèches** volley of blows/arrows; **à la** ~: **rattraper à la** ~ to catch in midair; **lancer à la** ~ to fling about; **semer à la** ~ to (sow) broadcast; **à toute** ~ *(sonner les cloches)* vigorously; *(lancer un projectile)* with full force; **de haute** ~ *(fig)* of the highest order.

voler [volā] *vi (avion, oiseau, fig)* to fly; *(voleur)* to steal ♦ *vt (objet)* to steal; *(personne)* to rob; ~ **en éclats** to smash to smithereens; ~ **de ses propres ailes** *(fig)* to stand on one's own two feet; ~ **au vent** to fly in the wind; ~ **qch à qn** to steal sth from sb.

volet [vole] *nm (de fenêtre)* shutter; *(AVIAT)* flap; *(de feuillet, document)* section; *(fig: d'un plan)* facet; **trié sur le** ~ hand-picked.

voleter [voltā] *vi* to flutter (about).

voleur, euse [volœr, -ēz] *nm/f* thief *(pl* thieves*)* ♦ *a* thieving.

volière [volyer] *nf* aviary.

volley(-ball) [vole(bōl)] *nm* volleyball.

volleyeur, euse [voleyœr, -ēz] *nm/f* volleyball

player.

volontaire [volôńter] *a (acte, activité)* voluntary; *(délibéré)* deliberate; *(caractère, personne: décidé)* self-willed ♦ *nm/f* volunteer.

volontairement [volôńtermâń] *ad* voluntarily; deliberately.

volontariat [volôńtáryá] *nm* voluntary service.

volontariste [volôńtárēst(ə)] *a, nm/f* voluntarist.

volonté [volôńtā] *nf (faculté de vouloir)* will; *(énergie, fermeté)* will(power); *(souhait, désir)* wish; **se servir/boire à** ~ to take/drink as much as one likes; **bonne** ~ goodwill, willingness; **mauvaise** ~ lack of goodwill, unwillingness.

volontiers [volôńtyā] *ad (de bonne grâce)* willingly; *(avec plaisir)* willingly, gladly; *(habituellement, souvent)* readily, willingly; "~" "with pleasure", "I'd be glad to".

volt [volt] *nm* volt.

voltage [voltázh] *nm* voltage.

volte-face [voltəfás] *nf inv* about-face *(US)*, about-turn *(Brit)*; *(fig)* about-turn, U-turn; **faire** ~ to do an about-face *ou* about-turn; to make a U-turn.

voltige [voltēzh] *nf (ÉQUITATION)* trick riding; *(au cirque)* acrobatics *sg*; *(AVIAT)* (aerial) acrobatics *sg*; **numéro de haute** ~ acrobatic act.

voltiger [voltēzhā] *vi* to flutter (about).

voltigeur [voltēzhœr] *nm (au cirque)* acrobat; *(MIL)* light infantryman.

voltmètre [voltmetr(ə)] *nm* voltmeter.

volubile [volübēl] *a* voluble.

volubilis [volübēlēs] *nm* convolvulus.

volume [volüm] *nm* volume; *(GÉOM: solide)* solid.

volumineux, euse [volümēnœ̄, -œ̄z] *a* voluminous, bulky.

volupté [volüptā] *nf* sensual delight *ou* pleasure.

voluptueusement [volüptüœ̄zmâń] *ad* voluptuously.

voluptueux, euse [volüptüœ̄, -œ̄z] *a* voluptuous.

volute [volüt] *nf (ARCHIT)* volute; ~ **de fumée** curl of smoke.

vomi [vomē] *nm* vomit.

vomir [vomēr] *vi* to vomit, be sick ♦ *vt* to vomit, bring up; *(fig)* to belch out, spew out; *(exécrer)* to loathe, abhor.

vomissement [vomēsmâń] *nm (action)* vomiting *q*; **des** ~**s** vomit.

vomissure [vomēsür] *nf* vomit *q*.

vomitif [vomētēf] *nm* emetic.

vont [vôń] *vb voir* aller.

vorace [vorás] *a* voracious.

voracement [vorásmâń] *ad* voraciously.

vos [vō] *dét voir* **votre.**

Vosges [vōzh] *nfpl:* **les** ~ the Vosges.

vosgien, ne [vōzhyań, -en] *a of ou* from the Vosges ♦ *nm/f* inhabitant *ou* native of the Vosges.

VOST *sigle f (CINÉMA:* = *version originale sous-titrée)* subtitled version.

votant, e [votâń, -âńt] *nm/f* voter.

vote [vot] *nm* vote; ~ **par correspondance** absentee ballot *(US)*, postal vote *(Brit)*; ~

par procuration proxy vote; ~ **à main levée** vote by show of hands; ~ **secret,** ~ **à bulletins secrets** secret ballot.

voter [votā] *vi* to vote ♦ *vt (loi, décision)* to vote for.

votre [votr(ə)], *pl* **vos** [vō] *dét* your.

vôtre [vōtr(ə)] *pronom:* **le** ~, **la** ~, **les** ~**s** yours; **les** ~**s** *(fig)* your family *ou* folks; **à la** ~ *(toast)* your (good) health!

voudrai [vōōdrā] *etc vb voir* **vouloir.**

voué, e [vwā] *a:* ~ **à** doomed to, destined for.

vouer [vwā] *vt:* ~ **qch à** *(Dieu/un saint)* to dedicate sth to; ~ **sa vie/son temps à** *(étude, cause etc)* to devote one's life/time to; ~ **une haine/amitié éternelle à qn** to vow undying hatred/friendship to sb.

vouloir [vōōlwâr] *vi* to show will, have willpower ♦ *vt* to want ♦ *nm:* **le bon** ~ **de qn** sb's goodwill; sb's pleasure; ~ **que qn fasse** to want sb to do; ~ **faire** to want to do; **je voudrais ceci** I would like this; **il voudrait que l'on vienne** he would like us to come; **le hasard a voulu que** fate decreed that; **la tradition veut que** tradition requires that; ... **qui se veut moderne** ... which purports to be modern; **veuillez attendre** please wait; **je veux bien** *(bonne volonté)* I'll be happy to; *(concession)* fair enough, that's fine; **si on veut, comme vous voudrez** as you wish; *(en quelque sorte)* if you like; **que me veut-il?** what does he want with me?; ~ **dire (que)** *(signifier)* to mean (that); **sans le** ~ *(involontairement)* without meaning to, unintentionally; ~ **qch à qn** to wish sth for sb; **en** ~ **à qn** to bear sb a grudge; **en** ~ **à qch** *(avoir des visées sur)* to be after sth; **s'en** ~ **de** to be annoyed with o.s. for; ~ **de qch/qn** *(accepter)* to want sth/sb.

voulu, e [vōōlü] *pp de* **vouloir** ♦ *a (requis)* required, requisite; *(délibéré)* deliberate, intentional.

voulus [vōōlü] *etc vb voir* **vouloir.**

vous [vōō] *pronom* you; *(objet indirect)* (to) you; *(réfléchi)* yourself *(pl* yourselves); *(réciproque)* each other ♦ *nm:* **employer le** ~ *(vouvoyer)* to use the "vous" form; ~**-même** yourself; ~**-mêmes** yourselves.

voûte [vōōt] *nf* vault; **la** ~ **céleste** the vault of heaven; ~ **du palais** *(ANAT)* roof of the mouth; ~ **plantaire** arch (of the foot).

voûté, e [vōōtā] *a* vaulted, arched; *(dos, personne)* bent, stooped.

voûter [vōōtā] *vt (ARCHIT)* to arch, vault; **se** ~ *vi (dos, personne)* to become stooped.

vouvoiement [vōōvwámâń] *nm* use of formal "vous" form.

vouvoyer [vōōvwáyā] *vt:* ~ **qn** to address sb as "vous".

voyage [vwàyázh] *nm* journey, trip; *(fait de voyager)*: **le** ~ travel, traveling *(US)*, travelling *(Brit)*; **partir/être en** ~ to go off/be away on a journey *ou* trip; **faire un** ~ to go on *ou* make a trip *ou* journey; **faire bon** ~ to have a good journey; **les gens du** ~ traveling people; ~ **d'agrément/d'affaires** pleasure/business trip; ~ **de noces** honeymoon; ~ **organisé** package tour.

voyager [vwàyázhā] *vi* to travel.

voyageur, euse [vwàyázhœr, -œ̄z] *nm/f*

traveler (*US*), traveller (*Brit*); (*passager*) passenger ♦ *a* (*tempérament*) nomadic, wayfaring; ~ **(de commerce)** traveling (*US*) *ou* travelling (*Brit*) salesman.

voyagiste [vwáyázhēst(ə)] *nm* tour operator.

voyais [vwàye] *etc vb voir* **voir.**

voyance [vwáyáńs] *nf* clairvoyance.

voyant, e [vwáyáń, -áńt] *a* (*couleur*) loud, gaudy ♦ *nm/f* (*personne qui voit*) sighted person ♦ *nm* (*signal*) (warning) light ♦ *nf* clairvoyant.

voyelle [vwáyɛl] *nf* vowel.

voyeur, euse [vwáyœr, -ēz] *nm/f* voyeur; peeping Tom.

voyons [vwáyóń] *etc vb voir* **voir.**

voyou [vwáyōō] *nm* lout, hoodlum; (*enfant*) guttersnipe.

VPC *sigle f* (= *vente par correspondance*) mail-order selling.

vrac [vrák]: **en** ~ *ad* higgledy-piggledy; (*COMM*) in bulk.

vrai, e [vrɛ] *a* (*véridique: récit, faits*) true; (*non factice, authentique*) real ♦ *nm*: **le** ~ the truth; **à** ~ **dire** to tell the truth; **il est** ~ **que** it is true that; **être dans le** ~ to be right.

vraiment [vrɛmáń] *ad* really.

vraisemblable [vrɛsáńblábl(ə)] *a* (*plausible*) likely, plausible; (*probable*) likely, probable.

vraisemblablement [vrɛsáńbláblǝmáń] *ad* in all likelihood, very likely.

vraisemblance [vrɛsáńbláńs] *nf* likelihood, plausibility; (*romanesque*) verisimilitude; **selon toute** ~ in all likelihood.

vraquier [vrákyā] *nm* freighter.

vrille [vrēy] *nf* (*de plante*) tendril; (*outil*) gimlet; (*spirale*) spiral; (*AVIAT*) spin.

vriller [vrēyā] *vt* to bore into, pierce.

vrombir [vróńbēr] *vi* to hum.

vrombissant, e [vróńbēsáń, -áńt] *a* humming.

vrombissement [vróńbēsmáń] *nm* hum(ming).

VRP *sigle m* (= *voyageur, représentant, placier*) (sales) rep.

vu [vü] *prép* (*en raison de*) in view of; ~ **que** in view of the fact that.

vu, e [vü] *pp de* **voir** ♦ *a*: **bien/mal** ~ (*personne*) well/poorly thought of; (*conduite*) good/bad form ♦ *nm*: **au** ~ **et au su de tous** openly and publicly; **ni** ~ **ni connu** what the eye doesn't see ...!, no one will be any the wiser; **c'est tout** ~ it's a foregone conclusion.

vue [vü] *nf* (*fait de voir*): **la** ~ **de** the sight of; (*sens, faculté*) (eye)sight; (*panorama, image, photo*) view; (*spectacle*) sight; ~**s** *nfpl* (*idées*) views; (*dessein*) designs; **perdre la** ~ to lose one's (eye)sight; **perdre de** ~ to lose sight of; **à la** ~ **de tous** in full view of everybody; **hors de** ~ out of sight; **à première** ~ at first sight; **connaître de** ~ to know by sight; **à** ~ (*COMM*) at sight; **tirer à** ~ to shoot on sight; **à** ~ **d'œil** *ad* visibly; (*à première vue*) at a quick glance; **avoir** ~ **sur** to have a view of; **en** ~ (*visible*) in sight; (*COMM*) in the public eye; **avoir qch en** ~ (*intentions*) to have one's sights on sth; **en** ~ **de faire** with the intention of doing, with a view to doing; ~ **d'ensemble** overall view; ~

de l'esprit theoretical view.

vulcaniser [vülkánēzā] *vt* to vulcanize.

vulcanologue [vulkánolog] *nm/f* = **volcanologue.**

vulgaire [vülgɛr] *a* (*grossier*) vulgar, coarse; (*trivial*) commonplace, mundane; (*péj: quelconque*): **de** ~**s touristes/chaises de cuisine** common tourists/kitchen chairs; (*BOT, ZOOL: non latin*) common.

vulgairement [vülgɛrmáń] *ad* vulgarly, coarsely; (*communément*) commonly.

vulgarisation [vülgárēzâsyóń] *nf*: **ouvrage de** ~ popularizing work, popularization.

vulgariser [vülgárēzā] *vt* to popularize.

vulgarité [vülgárētā] *nf* vulgarity, coarseness.

vulnérable [vülnārábl(ə)] *a* vulnerable.

vulve [vülv(ə)] *nf* vulva.

Vve *abr* = **veuve.**

VVF *sigle m* (= *village vacances famille*) state-subsidized vacation village.

vx *abr* = **vieux.**

W

W, w [dōōbləvā] *nm inv* W, w ♦ *abr* (= *watt*) W; **W comme William** W for William.

wagon [vàgóń] *nm* (*de voyageurs*) car (*US*), carriage (*Brit*); (*de marchandises*) truck, wagon.

wagon-citerne, *pl* **wagons-citernes** [vàgóńsētern(ə)] *nm* tanker.

wagon-lit, *pl* **wagons-lits** [vàgóńlē] *nm* Pullman (*US*), sleeper (*Brit*).

wagonnet [vàgone] *nm* small truck.

wagon-poste, *pl* **wagons-postes** [vàgóńpost(ə)] *nm* mail car (*US*) *ou* van (*Brit*).

wagon-restaurant, *pl* **wagons-restaurants** [vàgóńrestoráń] *nm* restaurant *ou* dining car.

walkman [wokmán] *nm* ® walkman ®, personal stereo.

Wallis et Futuna [wálēsáfütünä]: **les îles** ~ the Wallis and Futuna Islands.

wallon, ne [wálóń, -on] *a* Walloon ♦ *nm* (*LING*) Walloon ♦ *nm/f*: **W**~, **ne** Walloon.

waters [wáter] *nmpl* toilet *sg*.

watt [wàt] *nm* watt.

w.-c. [vāsā] *nmpl* toilet *sg*, lavatory *sg*.

week-end [wēkend] *nm* weekend.

western [western] *nm* western.

Westphalie [vesfálē] *nf*: **la** ~ Westphalia.

whisky, *pl* **whiskies** [wēskē] *nm* whiskey (*US, Ireland*), whisky (*Brit*).

Winchester [wēntshester]: **disque** ~ Winchester disk.

X

X, x [ĕks] *nm inv* X, x ♦ *sigle m* = *École Polytechnique*; **plainte contre X** (*JUR*) action against person or persons unknown; **X comme Xavier** X for Xmas.

xénophobe [ksānofob] *a* xenophobic ♦ *nm/f* xenophobe.

xérès [gzāres] *nm* sherry.

xylographie [ksēlográfē] *nf* xylography; (*image*) xylograph.

xylophone [ksēlofon] *nm* xylophone.

Y

Y, y [ēgrek] *nm inv* Y, y; **Y comme Yvonne** Y for Yoke.

y [ē] *ad* (*à cet endroit*) there; (*dessus*) on it (*ou* them); (*dedans*) in it (*ou* them) ♦ *pronom* (about *ou* on *ou* of) it : *vérifier la syntaxe du verbe employé*; **j'~ pense** I'm thinking about it; *voir aussi* **aller, avoir.**

yacht [yot] *nm* yacht.

yaourt [yàōōrt] *nm* yoghurt.

yaourtière [yàōōrtyer] *nf* yoghurt maker.

Yémen [yāmen] *nm:* **le ~** Yemen.

yéménite [yāmānēt] *a* Yemeni.

yeux [yœ̄] *pl de* **œil.**

yoga [yogá] *nm* yoga.

yoghourt [yogōōrt] *nm* = **yaourt.**

yole [yol] *nf* skiff.

yougoslave [yōōgosláv] *a* Yugoslav(ian) ♦ *nm/f:* **Y~** Yugoslav(ian).

Yougoslavie [yōōgoslávē] *nf:* **la ~** Yugoslavia.

youyou [yōōyōō] *nm* dinghy.

yo-yo [yōyō] *nm inv* yo-yo.

yucca [yōōká] *nm* yucca (tree *ou* plant).

Z

Z, z [zed] *nm inv* Z, z; **Z comme Zoé** Z for Zebra.

ZAC [zák] *sigle f* (= *zone d'aménagement concerté*) urban development zone.

ZAD [zád] *sigle f* (= *zone d'aménagement différé*) future development zone.

Zaïre [zàēr] *nm:* **le ~** Zaire.

zaïrois, e [zàērwá, -wáz] *a* Zairian (*US*), Zairese (*Brit*).

Zambèze [zánbez] *nm:* **le ~** the Zambezi.

Zambie [zánbē] *nf:* **la ~** Zambia.

zambien, ne [zánbyań, -en] *a* Zambian.

zèbre [zebr(ə)] *nm* (*ZOOL*) zebra.

zébré, e [zābrā] *a* striped, streaked.

zébrure [zābrür] *nf* stripe, streak.

zélateur, trice [zālátœr, -trēs] *nm/f* partisan, zealot.

zèle [zel] *nm* diligence, assiduousness; **faire du ~** (*péj*) to be overzealous.

zélé, e [zālā] *a* zealous.

zénith [zānēt] *nm* zenith.

ZEP [zep] *sigle f* (= *zone d'éducation prioritaire*) *area targeted for special help in education.*

zéro [zārō] *nm* zero; **au-dessous de ~** below zero (Centigrade), below freezing; **partir de ~** to start from scratch; **réduire à ~** to reduce to nothing; **trois (buts) à ~** three (goals to) nothing.

zeste [zest(ə)] *nm* peel, zest; **un ~ de citron** a piece of lemon peel.

zézaiement [zāzemáń] *nm* lisp.

zézayer [zāzāyā] *vi* to have a lisp.

ZI *sigle f* = **zone industrielle.**

zibeline [zeblēn] *nf* sable.

ZIF [zēf] *sigle f* (= *zone d'intervention foncière*) intervention zone.

zigouiller [zēgōōyā] *vt* (*fam*) to do in.

zigzag [zēgzág] *nm* zigzag.

zigzaguer [zēgzágā] *vi* to zigzag (along).

Zimbabwe [zēmbábwā] *nm:* **le ~** Zimbabwe.

zimbabwéen, ne [zēmbúbwūáń, -en] *nm* Zimbabwean.

zinc [zañg] *nm* (*CHIMIE*) zinc; (*comptoir*) bar, counter.

zinguer [zañgā] *vt* to cover with zinc.

zircon [zērkóń] *nm* zircon.

zizanie [zēzánē] *nf:* **semer la ~** to stir up ill feeling.

zizi [zēzē] *nm* (*fam*) peter (*US*), willy (*Brit*).

zodiaque [zodyák] *nm* zodiac.

zona [zōná] *nm* shingles *sg.*

zonage [zōnázh] *nm* (*ADMIN*) zoning.

zonard, e [zōnár, -árd] *nm/f* (*fam*) (young) hooligan *ou* thug.

zone [zōn] *nf* zone, area; (*INFORM*) field; (*quartiers*): **la ~** the slum belt; **de seconde ~** (*fig*) second-rate; **~ d'action** (*MIL*) sphere of activity; **~ bleue** ≈ restricted parking area; **~ d'extension** *ou* **d'urbanisation** urban development area; **~ franche** free zone; **~ industrielle (ZI)** industrial park (*US*) *ou* estate (*Brit*); **~ résidentielle** residential area.

zoner [zōnā] *vi* (*fam*) to hang around.

zoo [zōō] *nm* zoo.

zoologie [zoolozhē] *nf* zoology.

zoologique [zoolozhēk] *a* zoological.

zoologiste [zoolozhēst(ə)] *nm/f* zoologist.

zoom [zōōm] *nm* (*PHOTO*) zoom (lens).

ZUP [züp] *sigle f* (= *zone à urbaniser en priorité*) = **ZAC.**

Zurich [zürēk] *n* Zurich.

zut [züt] *excl* nuts! (*US*), dash (it)! (*Brit*).

ENGLISH-FRENCH
ANGLAIS-FRANÇAIS

A

A, a [ā] *n* (*letter*) A, a *m*; (*SCOL: mark*) A; (*MUS*): **A** la *m*; **A for Able** A comme Anatole; **A road** *n* (*Brit AUT*) route nationale; **A shares** *npl* (*Brit STOCK EXCHANGE*) actions *fpl* prioritaires.

a, an [ā, ə, an, ən] *definite article* un(e); **an apple** une pomme; **I haven't got ~ car** je n'ai pas de voiture; **he's ~ doctor** il est médecin; **3 ~ day/week** 3 par jour/semaine; **10 km an hour** 10 km à l'heure.

a. *abbr* = **acre.**

AA *n abbr* (*US*: = *Associate in/of Arts*) diplôme universitaire; (= *Alcoholics Anonymous*) AA; (= *anti-aircraft*) AA; (*Brit*: = *Automobile Association*) ≈ ACF *m*.

AAA [trip'əlā] *n abbr* (= *American Automobile Association*) ≈ ACF *m*; (*Brit*) = *Amateur Athletics Association*.

AAUP *n abbr* (= *American Association of University Professors*) *syndicat universitaire*.

AB *abbr* = **able-bodied seaman**; (*Canada*) = Alberta.

ABA *n abbr* = *American Bankers Association*; *American Bar Association*.

aback [əbak'] *ad*: **to be taken ~** être décontenancé(e).

abacus, *pl* **abaci** [ab'əkəs, ab'əsī] *n* boulier *m*.

abandon [əban'dən] *vt* abandonner ♦ *n* abandon *m*; **to ~ ship** évacuer le navire.

abandoned [əban'dənd] *a* (*child, house etc*) abandonné(e); (*unrestrained*) sans retenue.

abase [əbās'] *vt*: **to ~ o.s. (so far as to do)** s'abaisser (à faire).

abashed [əbasht'] *a* confus(e), embarrassé(e).

abate [əbāt'] *vi* s'apaiser, se calmer.

abatement [əbāt'mənt] *n*: **noise ~** lutte *f* contre le bruit.

abattoir [abətwâr'] *n* (*Brit*) abattoir *m*.

abbey [ab'ē] *n* abbaye *f*.

abbot [ab'ət] *n* père supérieur.

abbreviate [əbrē'vēāt] *vt* abréger.

abbreviation [əbrēvēā'shən] *n* abréviation *f*.

ABC [ābēsē'] *n abbr* (= *American Broadcasting Company*) *chaîne de télévision*.

abdicate [ab'dikāt] *vt, vi* abdiquer.

abdication [abdikā'shən] *n* abdication *f*.

abdomen [ab'dəmən] *n* abdomen *m*.

abdominal [abdâm'ənəl] *a* abdominal(e).

abduct [abdukt'] *vt* enlever.

abduction [abduk'shən] *n* enlèvement *m*.

aberration [abərā'shən] *n* anomalie *f*; **in a moment of mental ~** dans un moment d'égarement.

abet [əbet'] *vt see* **aid.**

abeyance [əbā'əns] *n*: **in ~** (*law*) en désuétude; (*matter*) en suspens.

abhor [abhôr'] *vt* abhorrer, exécrer.

abhorrent [abhôr'ənt] *a* odieux(euse), exécrable.

abide [əbīd'] *vt* souffrir, supporter.
  abide by *vt fus* observer, respecter.

ability [əbil'itē] *n* compétence *f*; capacité *f*; (*skill*) talent *m*; **to the best of my ~** de mon mieux.

abject [ab'jckt] *a* (*poverty*) sordide; (*coward*) méprisable; **an ~ apology** les excuses les plus plates.

ablaze [əblāz'] *a* en feu, en flammes; **~ with light** resplendissant de lumière.

able [ā'bəl] *a* compétent(e); **to be ~ to do sth** pouvoir faire qch, être capable de faire qch.

able-bodied [ā'bəlbâd'ēd] *a* robuste; **~ seaman** matelot breveté.

ably [ā'blē] *ad* avec compétence *or* talent, habilement.

ABM *n abbr* = *anti-ballistic missile.*

abnormal [abnôr'məl] *a* anormal(e).

abnormality [abnôrmal'ətē] *n* (*condition*) caractère anormal; (*instance*) anomalie *f*.

aboard [əbôrd'] *ad* à bord ♦ *prep* à bord de; (*train*) dans.

abode [əbōd'] *n* (*old*) demeure *f*; (*LAW*): **of no fixed ~** sans domicile fixe.

abolish [əbâl'ish] *vt* abolir.

abolition [abəlish'ən] *n* abolition *f*.

abominable [əbâm'inəbəl] *a* abominable.

aborigine [abərij'ənē] *n* aborigène *m/f*.

abort [əbôrt'] *vt* (*MED, fig*) faire avorter; (*COMPUT*) abandonner.

abortion [əbôr'shən] *n* avortement *m*; **to have an ~** se faire avorter.

abortive [əbôr'tiv] *a* manqué(e).

abound [əbound'] *vi* abonder; **to ~ in** abonder en, regorger de.

about [əbout'] *prep* au sujet de, à propos de ♦ *ad* environ; (*here and there*) de côté et d'autre, çà et là; **do something ~ it!** faites quelque chose!; **it takes ~ 10 hours** ça prend environ *or* à peu près 10 heures, ça prend une dizaine d'heures; **at ~ 2 o'clock** vers 2 heures; **it's just ~ finished** c'est presque fini; **it's ~ here** c'est par ici, c'est dans les parages; **to walk ~ the town** se promener dans *or* à travers la ville; **they left all their things lying ~** ils ont laissé traîner toutes leurs affaires; **to be ~ to: he was ~ to cry** il allait pleurer, il était sur le point de pleurer; **I'm not ~ to do all that for nothing** (*col*) je ne vais quand même pas faire tout ça pour rien; **what** *or* **how ~ doing this?** et si on faisait ça?

about-face [əbout'fās] *n* (*US: MIL*) demi-tour *m*; (*: fig*) volte-face *f*.

about-turn [əbout'tûrn] *n* (*Brit*) = **about-face.**

above [əbuv'] *ad* au-dessus ♦ *prep* au-dessus de; **mentioned ~** mentionné ci-dessus;

costing ~ **$10** coûtant plus de 10 dollars; ~ **all** par-dessus tout, surtout.

aboveboard [əbuv'bôrd] *a* franc(franche), loyal(e); honnête.

abrasion [əbrā'zhən] *n* frottement *m*; (*on skin*) écorchure *f*.

abrasive [əbrā'siv] *a* abrasif(ive); (*fig*) caustique, agressif(ive).

abreast [əbrest'] *ad* de front; **to keep ~ of** se tenir au courant de.

abridge [əbrij'] *vt* abréger.

abroad [əbrôd'] *ad* à l'étranger; **there is a rumor ~ that...** (*fig*) le bruit court que....

abrupt [əbrupt'] *a* (*steep, blunt*) abrupt(e); (*sudden, gruff*) brusque.

abscess [ab'ses] *n* abcès *m*.

abscond [abskând'] *vi* disparaître, s'enfuir.

absence [ab'səns] *n* absence *f*; **in the ~ of** (*person*) en l'absence de; (*thing*) faute de.

absent [ab'sənt] *a* absent(e); **~ without leave (AWOL)** (*MIL*) en absence irrégulière.

absentee [absəntē'] *n* absent/e.

absentee ballot *n* (*US*) vote *m* par correspondance.

absenteeism [absəntē'izəm] *n* absentéisme *m*.

absent-minded [ab'səntmīn'did] *a* distrait(e).

absent-mindedness [ab'səntmīn'didnis] *n* distraction *f*.

absolute [ab'səlōōt] *a* absolu(e).

absolutely [absəlōōt'lē] *ad* absolument.

absolve [abzâlv'] *vt*: **to ~ sb (from)** (*sin etc*) absoudre qn (de); **to ~ sb from** (*oath*) délier qn de.

absorb [absôrb'] *vt* absorber; **to be ~ed in a book** être plongé(e) dans un livre.

absorbent [absôr'bənt] *a* absorbant(e).

absorbent cotton *n* (*US*) coton *m* hydrophile.

absorbing [absôr'bing] *a* absorbant(e); (*book, film etc*) captivant(e).

absorption [absôrp'shən] *n* absorption *f*.

abstain [abstān'] *vi*: **to ~ (from)** s'abstenir (de).

abstemious [abstē'mēəs] *a* sobre, frugal(e).

abstention [absten'shən] *n* abstention *f*.

abstinence [ab'stənəns] *n* abstinence *f*.

abstract *a, n* [ab'strakt] *a* abstrait(e) ♦ *n* (*summary*) résumé *m* ♦ *vt* [abstrakt'] extraire.

absurd [absûrd'] *a* absurde.

absurdity [absûr'dətē] *n* absurdité *f*.

Abu Dhabi [âb'ōō dâ'bē] *n* Ab(o)u Dhabî *m*.

abundance [əbun'dəns] *n* abondance *f*.

abundant [əbun'dənt] *a* abondant(e).

abuse *n* [əbyōōs'] insultes *fpl*, injures *fpl*; (*of power etc*) abus *m* ♦ *vt* [əbyōōz'] abuser de; **to be open to ~** se prêter à des abus.

abusive [əbyōō'siv] *a* grossier(ière), injurieux(euse).

abysmal [əbiz'məl] *a* exécrable; (*ignorance etc*) sans bornes.

abyss [əbis'] *n* abîme *m*, gouffre *m*.

AC *abbr* (= *alternating current*) courant alternatif ♦ *n abbr* (*US*) = *athletic club*.

a/c *abbr* (*BANKING etc*) = *account, account current*.

academic [akədəm'ik] *a* universitaire; (*pej: issue*) oiseux(euse), purement théorique ♦ *n* universitaire *m/f*; **~ freedom** liberté *f* académique.

academic year *n* année *f* universitaire.

academy [əkad'əmē] *n* (*learned body*) académie *f*; (*school*) collège *m*; **military/naval ~** école militaire/navale; **~ of music** conservatoire *m*.

accede [aksēd'] *vi*: **to ~ to** (*request, throne*) accéder à.

accelerate [aksel'ərāt] *vt, vi* accélérer.

acceleration [akselərā'shən] *n* accélération *f*.

accelerator [aksel'ərātûr] *n* accélérateur *m*.

accent [ak'sent] *n* accent *m*.

accentuate [aksen'chōōāt] *vt* (*syllable*) accentuer; (*need, difference etc*) souligner.

accept [aksept'] *vt* accepter.

acceptable [aksep'təbəl] *a* acceptable.

acceptance [aksep'təns] *n* acceptation *f*; **to meet with general ~** être favorablement accueilli par tous.

access [ak'ses] *n* accès *m* ♦ *vt* (*COMPUT*) accéder à; **to have ~ to** (*information, library etc*) avoir accès à, pouvoir utiliser *or* consulter; (*person*) avoir accès auprès de; **the burglars gained ~ through a window** les cambrioleurs sont entrés par une fenêtre.

accessible [akses'əbəl] *a* accessible.

accession [aksesh'ən] *n* accession *f*; (*of king*) avènement *m*; (*to library*) acquisition *f*.

accessory [akses'ûrē] *n* accessoire *m*; **toilet accessories** (*Brit*) articles *mpl* de toilette.

access road *n* (*Brit*) voie *f* d'accès; (: *to freeway*) bretelle *f* de raccordement.

access time *n* (*COMPUT*) temps *m* d'accès.

accident [ak'sidənt] *n* accident *m*; (*chance*) hasard *m*; **to meet with** *or* **to have an ~** avoir un accident; **~s at work** accidents du travail; **by ~** par hasard; (*not deliberately*) accidentellement.

accidental [aksidən'təl] *a* accidentel(le).

accidentally [aksiden'təlē] *ad* accidentellement.

accident insurance *n* assurance *f* accident.

accident-prone [ak'sidəntprōn'] *a* sujet(te) aux accidents.

acclaim [əklām'] *vt* acclamer ♦ *n* acclamation *f*.

acclamation [akləmā'shən] *n* (*approval*) acclamation *f*; (*applause*) ovation *f*.

acclimate [əklī'mit] *vt* (*US*): **to become ~d** s'acclimater.

acclimatize [əklī'mətīz] *vt* (*Brit*) = **acclimate**.

accolade [akəlād'] *n* accolade *f*; (*fig*) marque *f* d'honneur.

accommodate [əkâm'ədāt] *vt* loger, recevoir; (*oblige, help*) obliger; (*adapt*): **to ~ one's plans to** adapter ses projets à; **this car ~s 4 people comfortably** on tient confortablement à 4 dans cette voiture.

accommodating [əkâm'ədāting] *a* obligeant(e), arrangeant(e).

accommodations, (*Brit*) accommodation [əkâmədā'shən(z)] *n(pl)* logement *m*; **he's found ~** il a trouvé à se loger; **they have ~ for 500** ils peuvent recevoir 500 personnes, il y a de la place pour 500 personnes.

accompaniment [əkum'pənimənt] *n* accompagnement *m*.

accompanist [əkum'pənist] *n* accompagnateur/trice.

accompany [əkum'pənē] *vt* accompagner.
accomplice [əkâm'plis] *n* complice *m/f*.
accomplish [əkâm'plish] *vt* accomplir.
accomplished [əkâm'plisht] *a* accompli(e).
accomplishment [əkâm'plishmənt] *n* accomplissement *m*; (*achievement*) réussite *f*; **~s** *npl* (*skills*) talents *mpl*.
accord [əkôrd'] *n* accord *m* ♦ *vt* accorder; **of his own ~** de son plein gré; **with one ~** d'un commun accord.
accordance [əkôr'dəns] *n*: **in ~ with** conformément à.
according [əkôr'ding] : **~ to** *prep* selon; **~ to plan** comme prévu.
accordingly [əkôr'dinglē] *ad* en conséquence.
accordion [əkôr'dēən] *n* accordéon *m*.
accost [əkôst'] *vt* accoster, aborder.
account [əkount'] *n* (*COMM*) compte *m*; (*report*) compte rendu, récit *m*; **~s** *npl* (*BOOK-KEEPING*) comptabilité *f*, comptes; **to keep an ~ of** noter; **to bring sb to ~ for** sth/for having done sth amener qn à rendre compte de qch/d'avoir fait qch; **by all ~s** au dire de tous; **of little ~** de peu d'importance; **to pay $5 on ~** verser un acompte de 5 dollars; **to buy sth on ~** acheter qch à crédit; **on no ~** en aucun cas; **on ~ of** à cause de; **to take into ~, take ~ of** tenir compte de.
account for *vt fus* expliquer, rendre compte de; **all the children were ~ed for** aucun enfant ne manquait; **4 people are still not ~ed for** on n'a toujours pas retrouvé 4 personnes.
accountability [əkountəbil'ətē] *n* responsabilité *f*; (*financial, political*) transparence *f*.
accountable [əkoun'təbəl] *a* responsable.
accountancy [əkoun'tənsē] *n* comptabilité *f*.
accountant [əkoun'tənt] *n* comptable *m/f*.
accounting [əkoun'ting] *n* comptabilité *f*.
accounting period *n* exercice financier, période *f* comptable.
account number *n* numéro *m* de compte.
account payable *n* compte *m* fournisseurs.
account receivable *n* compte *m* clients.
accredited [əkred'itid] *a* (*person*) accrédité(e).
accretion [əkrē'shən] *n* accroissement *m*.
accrue [əkrōō'] *vi* s'accroître; (*mount up*) s'accumuler; **to ~ to** s'ajouter à; **~d interest** intérêt couru.
acct. *abbr* = **account; accountant.**
accumulate [əkyōōm'yəlāt] *vt* accumuler, amasser ♦ *vi* s'accumuler, s'amasser.
accumulation [əkyōōmyəlā'shən] *n* accumulation *f*.
accuracy [ak'yūrəsē] *n* exactitude *f*, précision *f*.
accurate [ak'yūrit] *a* exact(e), précis(e).
accurately [ak'yūritlē] *ad* avec précision.
accusation [akyōōzā'shən] *n* accusation *f*.
accusative [əkyōō'zətiv] *n* (*LING*) accusatif *m*.
accuse [əkyōōz'] *vt* accuser.
accused [əkyōōzd'] *n* accusé/e.
accustom [əkus'təm] *vt* accoutumer, habituer; **to ~ o.s. to sth** s'habituer à qch.
accustomed [əkus'təmd] *a* (*usual*) habituel(le); **~ to** habitué(e) *or* accoutumé(e) à.
AC/DC *abbr* = **alternating current/direct**

current.
ACE [ās] *n abbr* = **American Council on Education.**
ace [ās] *n* as *m*; **within an ~ of** à deux doigts *or* un cheveu de.
Ace bandage *n* ® (*US*) bande *f* Velpeau ®.
acerbic [əsûr'bik] *a* (*also fig*) acerbe.
acetate [as'itāt] *n* acétate *m*.
ache [āk] *n* mal *m*, douleur *f* ♦ *vi* (*be sore*) faire mal, être douloureux(euse); (*yearn*): **to ~ to do sth** mourir d'envie de faire qch; **I've got a stomach~** *or* (*Brit*) **stomach ~** j'ai mal à l'estomac; **my head ~s** j'ai mal à la tête; **I'm aching all over** j'ai mal partout.
achieve [əchēv'] *vt* (*aim*) atteindre; (*victory, success*) remporter, obtenir; (*task*) accomplir.
achievement [əchēv'mənt] *n* exploit *m*, réussite *f*; (*of aims*) réalisation *f*.
acid [as'id] *a, n* acide (*m*).
acidity [əsid'itē] *n* acidité *f*.
acid rain *n* pluie(s) *f(pl)* acide(s).
acknowledge [aknâl'ij] *vt* (*also*: **~ receipt of**) accuser réception de; (*fact*) reconnaître.
acknowledgement [aknâl'ijmənt] *n* accusé *m* de réception; **~s** (*in book*) remerciements *mpl*.
ACLU *n abbr* (= *American Civil Liberties Union*) *ligue des droits de l'homme*.
acme [ak'mē] *n* point culminant.
acne [ak'nē] *n* acné *m*.
acorn [ā'kôrn] *n* gland *m*.
acoustic [əkōōs'tik] *a* acoustique.
acoustic coupler [əkōōs'tik kup'lûr] *n* (*COMPUT*) coupleur *m* acoustique.
acoustics [əkōōs'tiks] *n, npl* acoustique *f*.
acoustic screen *n* panneau *m* d'isolation phonique.
acquaint [əkwānt'] *vt*: **to ~ sb with sth** mettre qn au courant de qch; **to be ~ed with** (*person*) connaître; (*fact*) savoir.
acquaintance [əkwān'təns] *n* connaissance *f*; **to make sb's ~** faire la connaissance de qn.
acquiesce [əkwēes'] *vi* (*agree*): **to ~ (in)** acquiescer (à).
acquire [əkwī'ûr] *vt* acquérir.
acquired [əkwī'ûrd] *a* acquis(e); **an ~ taste** un goût acquis.
acquisition [akwizish'ən] *n* acquisition *f*.
acquisitive [əkwiz'ətiv] *a* qui a l'instinct de possession *or* de la propriété.
acquit [əkwit'] *vt* acquitter; **to ~ o.s. well** s'en tirer très honorablement.
acquittal [əkwit'əl] *n* acquittement *m*.
acre [ā'kûr] *n* acre *f* (= *4047 m²*).
acreage [ā'kûrij] *n* superficie *f*.
acrid [ak'rid] *a* (*smell*) âcre; (*fig*) mordant(e).
acrimonious [akrəmō'nēəs] *a* acrimonieux(euse), aigre.
acrobat [ak'rəbat] *n* acrobate *m/f*.
acrobatic [akrəbat'ik] *a* acrobatique.
acrobatics [akrəbat'iks] *n, npl* acrobatie *f*.
Acropolis [əkrâp'əlis] *n*: **the ~** l'Acropole *f*.
across [əkrôs'] *prep* (*on the other side*) de l'autre côté de; (*crosswise*) en travers de ♦ *ad* de l'autre côté; en travers; **to walk ~ (the road)** traverser (la route); **to take sb ~ the road** faire traverser la route à qn; **a road ~ the wood** une route qui traverse le

bois; **the lake is 12 km** ~ le lac fait 12 km de large; ~ **from** en face de; **to get sth** ~ **(to sb)** faire comprendre qch (à qn).

acrylic [əkril'ik] *a, n* acrylique *(m)*.

ACT *n abbr* (= *American College Test*) *examen de fin d'études secondaires.*

act [akt] *n* acte *m*, action *f*; (*THEATER*: *part of play*) acte; (*: of performer*) numéro *m*; (*LAW*) loi *f* ♦ *vi* agir; (*THEATER*) jouer; (*pretend*) jouer la comédie ♦ *vt* (*rôle*) jouer, tenir; ~ **of God** (*LAW*) catastrophe naturelle; **to catch sb in the** ~ prendre qn sur le fait; **it's only an** ~ c'est du cinéma; **to** ~ **Hamlet** tenir *or* jouer le rôle d'Hamlet; **to** ~ **the fool** (*Brit*) faire l'idiot; **to** ~ **as** servir de; **it** ~**s as a deterrent** cela a un effet dissuasif; ~**ing in my capacity as chairman, I** ... en ma qualité de président, je ....

act on *vt*: **to** ~ **on sth** agir sur la base de qch.

act out *vt* (*event*) raconter en mimant; (*fantasies*) réaliser.

act up *vi* (*cause trouble*) faire des siennes.

acting [ak'ting] *a* suppléant(e), par intérim ♦ *n* (*of actor*) jeu *m*; (*activity*): **to do some** ~ faire du théâtre (*or* du cinéma); **he is the** ~ **manager** il remplace (provisoirement) le directeur.

action [ak'shən] *n* action *f*; (*MIL*) combat(s) *m(pl)*; (*LAW*) procès *m*, action en justice; **to bring an** ~ **against sb** (*LAW*) poursuivre qn en justice, intenter un procès contre qn; **killed in** ~ (*MIL*) tué au champ d'honneur; **out of** ~ hors de combat; (*machine etc*) hors d'usage; **to take** ~ agir, prendre des mesures; **to put a plan into** ~ mettre un projet à exécution.

action replay *n* (*Brit TV*) retour *m* sur une séquence.

activate [ak'təvāt] *vt* (*mechanism*) actionner, faire fonctionner; (*CHEMISTRY, PHYSICS*) activer.

active [ak'tiv] *a* actif(ive); (*volcano*) en activité; **to play an** ~ **part in** jouer un rôle actif dans.

active duty (AD) *n* (*US MIL*) campagne *f*.

actively [ak'tivlē] *ad* activement.

active partner *n* (*COMM*) associé/e.

active service *n* (*Brit MIL*) campagne *f*.

activist [ak'tivist] *n* activiste *m/f*.

activity [aktiv'ətē] *n* activité *f*.

actor [ak'tûr] *n* acteur *m*.

actress [ak'tris] *n* actrice *f*.

actual [ak'chōōəl] *a* réel(le), véritable.

actually [ak'chōōəlē] *ad* réellement, véritablement; (*in fact*) en fait.

actuary [ak'chōōārē] *n* actuaire *m*.

actuate [ak'chōōāt] *vt* déclencher, actionner.

acuity [əkyōō'itē] *n* acuité *f*.

acumen [əkyōō'mən] *n* perspicacité *f*; **business** ~ sens *m* des affaires.

acupuncture [ak'yōōpungkchûr] *n* acuponcture *f*.

acute [əkyōōt'] *a* aigu(ë); (*mind, observer*) pénétrant(e).

AD *ad abbr* (= *Anno Domini*) ap. J.-C. ♦ *n abbr* (*US MIL*) = **active duty.**

ad [ad] *n abbr* = **advertisement.**

adamant [ad'əmənt] *a* inflexible.

Adam's apple [ad'əms ap'əl] *n* pomme *f* d'Adam.

adapt [ədapt'] *vt* adapter ♦ *vi*: **to** ~ **(to)** s'adapter (à).

adaptability [ədaptəbil'ətē] *n* faculté *f* d'adaptation.

adaptable [ədap'təbəl] *a* (*device*) adaptable; (*person*) qui s'adapte facilement.

adaptation [ədəptā'shən] *n* adaptation *f*.

adapter [ədap'tûr] *n* (*ELEC*) adapteur *m*.

ADC *n abbr* (*MIL*) = *aide-de-camp*; (*US*: = *Aid to Dependent Children*) *aide pour enfants assistés.*

add [ad] *vt* ajouter; (*figures*) additionner ♦ *vi*: **to** ~ **to** (*increase*) ajouter à, accroître.

add on *vt* ajouter.

add up *vt* (*figures*) additionner ♦ *vi* (*fig*): **it doesn't** ~ **up** cela ne rime à rien; **it doesn't** ~ **up to much** ça n'est pas grand'chose.

adder [ad'ûr] *n* vipère *f*.

addict [ad'ikt] *n* toxicomane *m/f*; (*fig*) fanatique *m/f*; **heroin** ~ héroïnomane *m/f*; **drug** ~ drogué/e *m/f*.

addicted [ədik'tid] *a*: **to be** ~ **to** (*drink etc*) être adonné(e) à; (*fig*: *football etc*) être un(e) fanatique de.

addiction [ədik'shən] *n* (*MED*) dépendance *f*.

adding machine [ad'ing mashēn'] *n* machine *f* à calculer.

Addis Ababa [ad'is âb'əbâ] *n* Addis Abeba, Addis Ababa.

addition [ədish'ən] *n* addition *f*; **in** ~ de plus, de surcroît; **in** ~ **to** en plus de.

additional [ədish'ənəl] *a* supplémentaire.

additive [ad'ətiv] *n* additif *m*.

addled [ad'əld] *a* (*Brit*: *egg*) pourri(e).

address [ədres'] *n* adresse *f*; (*talk*) discours *m*, allocution *f* ♦ *vt* adresser; (*speak to*) s'adresser à; **form of** ~ titre *m*; **what form of** ~ **do you use for...?** comment s'adresse-t-on à...?; **to** ~ **(o.s. to)** (*problem, issue*) aborder qch; **absolute/relative** ~ (*COMPUT*) adresse absolue/relative.

Aden [â'dən] *n*: **Gulf of** ~ Golfe *m* d'Aden.

adenoids [ad'ənoidz] *npl* végétations *fpl*.

adept [ədept'] *a*: ~ **at** expert(e) à *or* en.

adequate [ad'əkwit] *a* (*enough*) suffisant(e); **to feel** ~ **to the task** se sentir à la hauteur de la tâche.

adequately [ad'əkwitlē] *ad* de façon adéquate.

adhere [adhēr'] *vi*: **to** ~ **to** adhérer à; (*fig: rule, decision*) se tenir à.

adhesion [adhē'zhən] *n* adhésion *f*.

adhesive [adhē'siv] *a* adhésif(ive) ♦ *n* adhésif *m*; ~ **tape** (*US*) sparadrap *m*; (*Brit*) ruban adhésif.

ad hoc [ad hâk'] *a* (*decision*) de circonstance; (*committee*) ad hoc.

ad infinitum [ad infənī'təm] *ad* à l'infini.

adjacent [əjā'sənt] *a* adjacent(e), contigu(ë); ~ **to** adjacent à.

adjective [aj'iktiv] *n* adjectif *m*.

adjoin [əjoin'] *vt* jouxter.

adjoining [əjoi'ning] *a* voisin(e), adjacent(e), attenant(e) ♦ *prep* voisin de, adjacent à.

adjourn [əjûrn'] *vt* ajourner ♦ *vi* suspendre la séance; lever la séance; clore la session; (*go*) se retirer; **to** ~ **a meeting till the following week** reporter une réunion à la semaine suivante.

adjournment [əjûrn'mənt] n (*period*) ajourne-ment m.

Adjt abbr (MIL: = adjutant) Adj.

adjudicate [əjōō'dikāt] vt (*contest*) juger; (*claim*) statuer (sur) ♦ vi se prononcer.

adjudication [əjōōdikā'shən] n (LAW) juge-ment m.

adjust [əjust'] vt ajuster, régler; rajuster ♦ vi: **to ~ (to)** s'adapter (à).

adjustable [əjust'əbəl] a réglable.

adjuster [əjust'ûr] n see **loss**.

adjustment [əjust'mənt] n ajustage m, réglage m; (of prices, wages) rajustement m; (of person) adaptation f.

adjutant [aj'ətənt] n adjudant m.

ad-lib [adlib'] vt, vi improviser ♦ n improvisa-tion f ♦ ad: **ad lib** à volonté, à discrétion.

adman [ad'man] n (col) publicitaire m.

admin [ad'min] n abbr (col) = **administration**.

administer [admin'istûr] vt administrer; (justice) rendre.

administration [administrā'shən] n adminis-tration f; **the A~** (US) le gouvernement.

administrative [admin'istrātiv] a administra-tif(ive).

administrator [admin'istrātûr] n administrateur/trice.

admirable [ad'mûrəbəl] a admirable.

admiral [ad'mûrəl] n amiral m.

Admiralty [ad'mûrəltē] n (Brit: also: ~ **Board**) ministère m de la Marine.

admiration [admərā'shən] n admiration f.

admire [admī'ûr] vt admirer.

admirer [admī'ərûr] n admirateur/trice.

admission [admish'ən] n admission f; (to exhi-bition, night club etc) entrée f; (confession) aveu m; **"~ free"**, **"free ~"** "entrée libre"; **by his own ~** de son propre aveu.

admit [admit'] vt laisser entrer; admettre; (agree) reconnaître, admettre; **"children not ~ted"** "entrée interdite aux enfants"; **this ticket ~s two** ce billet est valable pour deux personnes; **I must ~ that...** je dois admettre or reconnaître que,....

admit of vt fus admettre, permettre.

admit to vt fus reconnaître, avouer.

admittance [admit'əns] n admission f, (droit m d')entrée f; **"no ~"** "défense d'entrer".

admittedly [admit'idlē] ad il faut en convenir.

admonish [admân'ish] vt donner un avertisse-ment à; réprimander.

ad nauseam [ad nô'zēəm] ad à satiété.

ado [ədōō'] n: **without further ~** sans plus de cérémonies.

adolescence [adəles'əns] n adolescence f.

adolescent [adəles'ənt] a, n adolescent(e).

adopt [ədápt'] vt adopter.

adopted [ədáp'tid] a adoptif(ive), adopté(e).

adoption [ədáp'shən] n adoption f.

adore [ədôr'] vt adorer.

adoringly [ədôr'inglē] ad avec adoration.

adorn [ədôrn'] vt orner.

adornment [ədôrn'mənt] n ornement m.

ADP n abbr = **automatic data processing**.

adrenalin [ədren'əlin] n adrénaline f; **to get the ~ going** faire monter le taux d'adrénali-ne.

Adriatic (Sea) [ādrēat'ik (sē')] n Adriatique f.

adrift [ədrift'] ad à la dérive; **to come ~** (boat) aller à la dérive; (wire, rope, fasten-ing etc) se défaire.

adroit [ədroit'] a adroit(e), habile.

adult [ədult'] n adulte m/f.

adult education n éducation f des adultes.

adulterate [ədul'tûrāt] vt frelater, falsifier.

adultery [ədul'tûrē] n adultère m.

adulthood [ədult'hōōd] n âge m adulte.

advance [advans'] n avance f ♦ vt avancer ♦ vi s'avancer; **in ~** en avance, d'avance; **to make ~s to sb** (gen) faire des propositions à qn; (amorously) faire des avances à qn.

advanced [advanst'] a avancé(e); (SCOL: studies) supérieur(e); **~ in years** d'un âge avancé.

advancement [advans'mənt] n avancement m.

advance notice n préavis m.

advantage [advan'tij] n (also TENNIS) avanta-ge m; **to take ~ of** profiter de; **it's to our ~** c'est notre intérêt; **it's to our ~ to ... nous avons intérêt à ....**

advantageous [advəntā'jəs] a avanta-geux(euse).

advent [ad'vent] n avènement m, venue f; **A~** (REL) Avent m.

Advent calendar n calendrier m de l'avent.

adventure [adven'chûr] n aventure f.

adventurous [adven'chûrəs] a aventu-reux(euse).

adverb [ad'vûrb] n adverbe m.

adversary [ad'vûrsārē] n adversaire m/f.

adverse [advûrs'] a contraire, adverse; **~ to** hostile à; **in ~ circumstances** dans l'adversi-té.

adversity [advûr'sitē] n adversité f.

advert [ad'vûrt] n abbr (Brit) = **advertise-ment**.

advertise [ad'vûrtīz] vi (vt) faire de la publici-té or de la réclame (pour); (in classified ads etc) mettre une annonce (pour vendre); **to ~ for** (staff) recruter par (voie d')annonce.

advertisement [advûrtīz'mənt] n (COMM) ré-clame f, publicité f; (in classified ads etc) annonce f.

advertiser [ad'vûrtīzûr] n annonceur m.

advertising [ad'vûrtīzing] n publicité f.

advertising agency n agence f de publicité.

advertising campaign n campagne f de pu-blicité.

advice [advīs'] n conseils mpl; (notification) avis m; **piece of ~** conseil; **to ask (sb) for ~** demander conseil (à qn); **to seek legal ~** consulter un avocat.

advice slip n avis m d'expédition.

advisable [advī'zəbəl] a recommandable, indi-qué(e).

advise [advīz'] vt conseiller; **to ~ sb of sth** aviser or informer qn de qch; **to ~ sb against sth** déconseiller qch à qn; **to ~ sb against doing sth** conseiller à qn de ne pas faire qch; **you would be well/ill ~d to go** vous feriez mieux d'y aller/de ne pas y aller, vous auriez intérêt à y aller/à ne pas y aller.

advisedly [advī'zidlē] ad (deliberately) délibé-rément.

adviser [advī'zûr] n conseiller/ère.

advisory [advī'zûrē] a consultatif(ive); **in an ~ capacity** à titre consultatif.

advocate n [ad'vəkit] (upholder) défenseur m, avocat/e ♦ vt [ad'vəkāt] recommander, prôner; **to be an ~ of** être partisan/e de.
advt. abbr = **advertisement.**
AEA n abbr (Brit: = Atomic Energy Authority) ≈ AEN f (= Agence pour l'énergie nucléaire).
AEC n abbr (US: = Atomic Energy Commission) ≈ AEN f (= Agence pour l'énergie nucléaire).
Aegean (Sea) [ijē'ən (sē')] n mer f Égée.
aegis [ē'jis] n: **under the ~ of** sous l'égide de.
aeon [ē'ən] n (Brit) = **eon.**
aerial [ār'ēəl] n antenne f ♦ a aérien(ne).
aerie [ār'ē] n (US) aire f.
aerobatics [ārəbat'iks] npl acrobaties aériennes.
aerobics [ārō'biks] n aérobic m.
aerodrome [ār'ədrōm] n (Brit) aérodrome m.
aerodynamic [ārōdīnam'ik] a aérodynamique.
aerogramme [ār'əgram] n aérogramme m.
aeronautics [ārənô'tiks] n aéronautique f.
aeroplane [ār'əplān] n (Brit) avion m.
aerosol [ār'əsôl] n aérosol m.
aerospace industry [ār'əspās in'dəstrē] n (industrie) aérospatiale.
aesthetic [esthet'ik] a (Brit) = **esthetic.**
afar [əfâr'] ad: **from ~** de loin.
AFB n abbr (US) = **Air Force Base.**
AFDC n abbr (US: = Aid to Families with Dependent Children) aide pour enfants assistés.
affable [af'əbəl] a affable.
affair [əfâr'] n affaire f; (also: **love ~**) liaison f; aventure f; **~s** (business) affaires f.
affect [əfekt'] vt affecter.
affectation [afektā'shən] n affectation f.
affected [əfek'tid] a affecté(e).
affection [əfek'shən] n affection f.
affectionate [əfek'shənit] a affectueux(euse).
affectionately [əfek'shənitlē] ad affectueusement.
affidavit [afidā'vit] n (LAW) déclaration écrite sous serment.
affiliated [əfil'ēātid] a affilié(e); **~ company** filiale f.
affinity [əfin'ətē] n affinité f.
affirm [əfûrm'] vt affirmer.
affirmation [afûrmā'shən] n affirmation f, assertion f.
affirmative [əfûr'mətiv] a affirmatif(ive) ♦ n: **in the ~** dans or par l'affirmative.
affix [əfiks'] vt apposer, ajouter.
afflict [əflikt'] vt affliger.
affliction [əflik'shən] n affliction f.
affluence [af'lōōəns] n aisance f, opulence f.
affluent [af'lōōənt] a opulent(e); (person) dans l'aisance, riche; **the ~ society** la société d'abondance.
afford [əfôrd'] vt (goods etc) avoir les moyens d'acheter or d'entretenir; (behavior): **can we ~ a car?** avons-nous de quoi acheter or les moyens d'acheter une voiture?; **I can't ~ the time** je n'ai vraiment pas le temps.
affront [əfrunt'] n affront m.
affronted [əfrun'tid] a insulté(e).
Afghan [af'gan] a afghan(e) ♦ n Afghan/e.
Afghanistan [afgan'istan] n Afghanistan m.
afield [əfēld'] ad: **far ~** loin.

AFL-CIO n abbr (= American Federation of Labor and Congress of Industrial Organizations) confédération syndicale.
afloat [əflōt'] a à flot ♦ ad: **to stay ~** surnager; **to keep/get a business ~** maintenir à flot/lancer une affaire.
afoot [əfōōt'] ad: **there is something ~** il se prépare quelque chose.
aforementioned [əfôr'menshənd] a, **aforesaid** [əfôr'sed] a susdit(e), susmentionné(e).
afraid [əfrād'] a effrayé(e); **to be ~ of** or to avoir peur de; **I am ~ that** je crains que + sub; **I'm ~ so/not** oui/non, malheureusement.
afresh [əfresh'] ad de nouveau.
Africa [af'rika] n Afrique f.
African [af'rikən] a africain(e) ♦ n Africain/e.
Afrikaans [afrikäns'] n afrikaans m.
Afrikaner [afrikä'nûr] n Afrikaner or Afrikander m/f.
Afro-American [af'rōəmär'ikən] a afro-américain(e).
AFT n abbr (= American Federation of Teachers) syndicat enseignant.
aft [aft] ad à l'arrière, vers l'arrière.
after [af'tûr] prep, ad après ♦ cj après que, après avoir or être + pp; **~ dinner** après (le) dîner; **the day ~ tomorrow** après demain; **quarter ~ two** (US) deux heures et quart; **what/who are you ~?** que/qui cherchez-vous?; **the police are ~ him** la police est à ses trousses; **~ you!** après vous!; **~ all** après tout.
aftercare [af'tûrkär] n (MED) post-cure f.
after-effects [af'tûrifekts] npl répercussions fpl; (of illness) séquelles fpl, suites fpl.
afterlife [af'tûrlīf] n vie future.
aftermath [af'tûrmath] n conséquences fpl; **in the ~ of** dans les mois or années etc qui suivirent, au lendemain de.
afternoon [aftûrnōōn'] n après-midi m or f; **good ~!** bonjour!; (goodbye) au revoir!
after-sales service [af'tûrsālz sûr'vis] n (Brit) service m après-vente, SAV m.
after-shave (lotion) [af'tûrshāv (lō'shən)] n lotion f après-rasage.
aftershock [af'tûrshâk] n réplique f (sismique).
afterthought [af'tûrthôt] n: **I had an ~** il m'est venu une idée après coup.
afterwards [af'tûrwûrdz] ad après.
again [əgen'] ad de nouveau, encore une fois; **to begin/see ~** recommencer/revoir; **not ... ~** ne ... plus; **~ and ~** à plusieurs reprises; **he's opened it ~** il l'a rouvert, il l'a de nouveau or l'a encore ouvert; **now and ~** de temps à autre.
against [əgenst'] prep contre; **~ a blue background** sur un fond bleu; **(over) ~** contre.
age [āj] n âge m ♦ vt, vi vieillir; **what ~ is he?** quel âge a-t-il?; **he is 20 years of ~** il a 20 ans; **under ~** mineur(e); **to come of ~** atteindre sa majorité; **it's been ~s since** ça fait une éternité que ... ne.
aged [ājd] a âgé(e); **~ 10** âgé de 10 ans; **the ~** [ā'jid] npl les personnes âgées.
age group n tranche f d'âge; **the 40 to 50 ~** la tranche d'âge des 40 à 50 ans.
ageless [āj'lis] a sans âge.
age limit n limite f d'âge.

agency [ā'jənsē] *n* agence *f*; **through** *or* **by the** ~ **of** par l'entremise *or* l'action de.

agenda [əjen'də] *n* ordre *m* du jour; **on the** ~ à l'ordre du jour.

agent [ā'jənt] *n* agent *m*.

aggravate [ag'rəvāt] *vt* aggraver; (*annoy*) exaspérer, agacer.

aggravation [agrəvā'shən] *n* agacements *mpl*.

aggregate [ag'rəgit] *n* ensemble *m*, total *m*; **on** ~ (*SPORT*) au total des points.

aggression [əgresh'ən] *n* agression *f*.

aggressive [əgres'iv] *a* agressif(ive).

aggressiveness [əgres'ivnis] *n* agressivité *f*.

aggrieved [əgrēvd'] *a* chagriné(e), affligé(e).

aghast [əgast'] *a* consterné(e), atterré(e).

agile [aj'əl] *a* agile.

agitate [aj'ətāt] *vt* rendre inquiet(ète) *or* agité(e) ♦ *vi* faire de l'agitation (politique); **to** ~ **for** faire campagne pour.

agitator [aj'itātûr] *n* agitateur/trice (politique).

AGM *n abbr* (*Brit*) = **annual general meeting.**

ago [əgō'] *ad*: **2 days** ~ il y a 2 jours; **not long** ~ il n'y a pas longtemps; **as long** ~ **as 1960** déjà en 1960; **how long** ~? il y a combien de temps (de cela)?

agog [əgâg'] *a*: (**all**) ~ en émoi.

agonize [ag'ənīz] *vi*: **he** ~**d over the problem** ce problème lui a causé bien du tourment.

agonizing [ag'ənīzing] *a* angoissant(e); (*cry*) déchirant(e).

agony [ag'ənē] *n* grande souffrance *or* angoisse; **to be in** ~ souffrir le martyre.

agony column *n* courrier *m* du cœur.

agree [əgrē'] *vt* (*price*) convenir de ♦ *vi*: **to** ~ (**with**) (*person*) être d'accord (avec); (*statements etc*) concorder (avec); (*LING*) s'accorder (avec); **to** ~ **to do** accepter de *or* consentir à faire; **to** ~ **to sth** consentir à qch; **to** ~ **that** (*admit*) convenir *or* reconnaître que; **it was** ~**d that ...** il a été convenu que ...; **they** ~ **on this** ils sont d'accord sur ce point; **they** ~**d on going/a price** ils se mirent d'accord pour y aller/sur un prix; **garlic doesn't** ~ **with me** je ne supporte pas l'ail.

agreeable [əgrē'əbəl] *a* (*pleasant*) agréable; (*willing*) consentant(e), d'accord; **are you** ~ **to this?** est-ce que vous êtes d'accord?

agreed [əgrēd'] *a* (*time*, *place*) convenu(e); **to be** ~ être d'accord.

agreement [əgrē'mənt] *n* accord *m*; **in** ~ d'accord; **by mutual** ~ d'un commun accord.

agricultural [agrəkul'chûrəl] *a* agricole.

agriculture [ag'rəkulchûr] *n* agriculture *f*.

aground [əground'] *ad*: **to run** ~ s'échouer.

agt. *abbr* = **agent.**

ahead [əhed'] *ad* en avant; devant; **go right** *or* **straight** ~ allez tout droit; **go** ~! (*fig*) allez-y!; ~ **of** devant; (*fig: schedule etc*) en avance sur; ~ **of time** en avance; **they were (right)** ~ **of us** ils nous précédaient (de peu), ils étaient (juste) devant nous.

AI *n abbr* = *Amnesty International*; (*COMPUT*) = **artificial intelligence.**

AID *n abbr* (= *artificial insemination by donor*) IAD *f*; (*US*: = *Agency for International Development*) *agence pour le développement international*.

aid [ād] *n* aide *f* ♦ *vt* aider; **with the** ~ **of** avec l'aide de; **in** ~ **of** en faveur de; **to** ~ **and abet** (*LAW*) se faire le complice de.

aide [ād] *n* (*person*) assistant/e.

AIDS [ādz] *n abbr* (= *acquired immune deficiency syndrome*) SIDA *m*.

AIH *n abbr* (= *artificial insemination by husband*) IAC *f*.

ailment [āl'mənt] *n* affection *f*.

aim [ām] *n* but *m* ♦ *vt*: **to** ~ **sth at** (*gun*, *camera*) braquer *or* pointer qch sur, diriger qch contre; (*missile*) pointer qch vers *or* sur; (*remark*, *blow*) destiner *or* adresser qch à ♦ *vi* (*also*: **to take** ~) viser; **to** ~ **at** viser; (*fig*) viser (à); avoir pour but *or* ambition; **to** ~ **to do** avoir l'intention de faire.

aimless [ām'lis] *a* sans but.

aimlessly [ām'lislē] *ad* sans but.

ain't [ānt] (*col*) = **am not, aren't, isn't.**

air [är] *n* air *m* ♦ *vt* aérer; (*idea*, *grievance*, *views*) mettre sur le tapis; (*knowledge*) faire étalage de ♦ *cpd* (*currents*, *attack etc*) aérien(ne); **by** ~ par avion; **to be on the** ~ (*RADIO*, *TV*: *program*) être diffusé(e); (: *station*) émettre.

air base *n* base aérienne.

air bed *n* (*Brit*) matelas *m* pneumatique.

airborne [är'hôrn] *a* (*plane*) en vol; (*troops*) aeroporté(e); (*particles*) dans l'air; **as soon as the plane was** ~ dès que l'avion eut décollé.

air cargo *n* fret aérien.

air-conditioned [är'kəndishənd] *a* climatisé(e), a air conditionné.

air conditioning [är' kəndish'əning] *n* climatisation *f*.

air-cooled [är'kōōld] *a* à refroidissement à air.

aircraft [är'kraft] *n* (*pl inv*) avion *m*.

aircraft carrier *n* porte-avions *m inv*.

air cushion *n* coussin *m* d'air.

airdrome [är'drōm] *n* (*US*) aérodrome *m*.

airfield [är'fēld] *n* terrain *m* d'aviation.

Air Force *n* Armée *f* de l'air.

air freight *n* fret aérien.

air gun *n* fusil *m* à air comprimé.

air hostess *n* (*Brit*) hôtesse *f* de l'air.

airily [är'ilē] *ad* d'un air dégagé.

airing [är'ing] *n*: **to give an** ~ **to** aérer; (*fig: ideas*, *views etc*) mettre sur le tapis.

air letter *n* aérogramme *m*.

airlift [är'lift] *n* pont aérien.

airline [är'līn] *n* ligne aérienne, compagnie aérienne.

airliner [är'līnûr] *n* avion *m* de ligne.

airlock [är'läk] *n* sas *m*.

airmail [är'māl] *n*: **by** ~ par avion.

air mattress *n* matelas *m* pneumatique.

airplane [är'plān] *n* (*US*) avion *m*.

airport [är'pôrt] *n* aéroport *m*.

air raid *n* attaque aérienne.

airsick [är'sik] *a*: **to be** ~ avoir le mal de l'air.

airstrip [är'strip] *n* terrain *m* d'atterrissage.

air terminal *n* aérogare *f*.

airtight [är'tīt] *a* hermétique.

air traffic control *n* contrôle *m* de la navigation aérienne.

air traffic controller *n* aiguilleur *m* du ciel.

air waybill [är' wā'bil] *n* lettre *f* de transport aérien.

airy [är'ē] *a* bien aéré(e); *(manners)* dégagé(e).

aisle [īl] *n* *(of church)* allée centrale; nef latérale; *(in theater)* allée *f*; *(on plane)* couloir *m*.

ajar [əjâr'] *a* entrouvert(e).

AK *abbr (US MAIL)* = *Alaska*.

aka *abbr* (= *also known as*) alias.

akin [əkin'] *a*: ~ **to** semblable à, du même ordre que.

AL *abbr (US MAIL)* = *Alabama*.

ALA *n abbr* = *American Library Association*.

Ala. *abbr (US)* = *Alabama*.

alacrity [əlak'ritē] *n*: **with** ~ avec empressement, promptement.

alarm [əlârm'] *n* alarme *f* ♦ *vt* alarmer.

alarm clock *n* réveille-matin *m*, réveil *m*.

alarming [əlâr'ming] *a* alarmant(e).

alarmist [əlâr'mist] *n* alarmiste *m/f*.

Alas. *abbr (US)* = *Alaska*.

alas [əlas'] *excl* hélas.

Alaska [əlas'kə] *n* Alaska *m*.

Albania [albā'nēə] *n* Albanie *f*.

Albanian [albā'nēən] *a* albanais(e) ♦ *n* Albanais/e; *(LING)* albanais *m*.

albeit [ôlbē'it] *cj* bien que + *sub*, encore que + *sub*.

album [al'bəm] *n* album *m*.

albumen [albyōō'mən] *n* albumine *f*; *(of egg)* albumen *m*.

alchemy [al'kəmē] *n* alchimie *f*.

alcohol [al'kəhôl] *n* alcool *m*.

alcoholic [alkəhôl'ik] *a, n* alcoolique *(m/f)*.

alcoholism [al'kəhôlizəm] *n* alcoolisme *m*.

alcove [al'kōv] *n* alcôve *f*.

ald. *abbr* = **alderman**.

alderman [ôl'dûrmən] *n* conseiller municipal *(en Angleterre)*.

ale [āl] *n* bière *f*.

alert [əlûrt'] *a* alerte, vif(vive); *(watchful)* vigilant(e) ♦ *n* alerte *f* ♦ *vt*: **to** ~ **sb (to sth)** attirer l'attention de qn (sur qch); **to** ~ **sb to the dangers of sth** avertir qn des dangers de qch; **on the** ~ sur le qui-vive; *(MIL)* en état d'alerte.

Aleutian Islands [əlōō'shən ī'ləndz] *npl* îles Aléoutiennes.

Alexandria [aligzan'drēə] *n* Alexandrie.

alfresco [alfres'kō] *a, ad* en plein air.

algebra [al'jəbrə] *n* algèbre *m*.

Algeria [aljē'rēə] *n* Algérie *f*.

Algerian [aljə'rēən] *a* algérien(ne) ♦ *n* Algérien/ne.

Algiers [aljērz'] *n* Alger *f*.

algorithm [al'gəriḥəm] *n* algorithme *m*.

alias [ā'lēəs] *ad* alias ♦ *n* faux nom, nom d'emprunt.

alibi [al'əbī] *n* alibi *m*.

alien [āl'yən] *n* étranger/ère ♦ *a*: ~ **(to)** étranger(ère) (à).

alienate [āl'yənāt] *vt* aliéner; *(subj: person)* s'aliéner.

alienation [ālyənā'shən] *n* aliénation *f*.

alight [əlīt'] *a, ad* en feu ♦ *vi* mettre pied à terre; *(passenger)* descendre; *(bird)* se poser.

align [əlīn'] *vt* aligner.

alignment [əlīn'mənt] *n* alignement *m*; **it's out of** ~ **(with)** ce n'est pas aligné (avec).

alike [əlīk'] *a* semblable, pareil(le) ♦ *ad* de même; **to look** ~ se ressembler.

alimony [al'əmōnē] *n* *(payment)* pension *f* alimentaire.

alive [əlīv'] *a* vivant(e); *(active)* plein(e) de vie; ~ **with** grouillant(e) de; ~ **to** sensible à.

alkali [al'kəlī] *n* alcali *m*.

all [ôl] *a* tout(e), tous(toutes) *pl* ♦ *pronoun* tout *m*; *(pl)* tous(toutes) ♦ *ad* tout; ~ **wrong/ alone** tout faux/seul; ~ **the time/his life** tout le temps/toute sa vie; ~ **five (of them)** tous les cinq; ~ **five girls** les cinq filles; ~ **of them**, tous, toutes; ~ **of it** tout; ~ **of us** went nous y sommes tous allés; ~ **day** toute la journée; **is that** ~? c'est tout?; *(in store)* ce sera tout?; **for** ~ **their efforts** malgré tous leurs efforts; **not as hard** *etc* **as** ~ **that** pas si dur *etc* que ça; **at** ~: **not at** ~ *(in answer to question)* pas du tout; *(in answer to thanks)* je vous en prie!; **I'm not at** ~ **tired** je ne suis pas du tout fatigué; **anything at** ~ **will do** n'importe quoi fera l'affaire; ~ **but** presque, pratiquement; **to be** ~ **in** *(col)* être complètement à plat; ~ **in** ~ en somme, somme toute, finalement; ~ **out** *ad* à fond.

all-around [ôl'əround] *a* compétent(e) dans tous les domaines; *(athlete etc)* complet (ète).

allay [əlā'] *vt* *(fears)* apaiser, calmer.

all clear *n* *(also fig)* fin *f* d'alerte.

allegation [aləgā'shən] *n* allégation *f*.

allege [əlej'] *vt* alléguer, prétendre; **he is** ~**d to have said** il aurait dit.

alleged [əlejd'] *a* prétendu(e).

allegedly [əlej'idlē] *ad* à ce que l'on prétend, paraît-il.

allegiance [əlē'jəns] *n* fidélité *f*, obéissance *f*.

allegory [al'əgôrē] *n* allégorie *f*.

all-embracing [ôl'embrās'ing] *a* universel(le).

allergic [əlûr'jik] *a*: ~ **to** allergique à.

allergy [al'ûrjē] *n* allergie *f*.

alleviate [əlē'vēāt] *vt* soulager, adoucir.

alley [al'ē] *n* ruelle *f*; *(in garden)* allée *f*.

alliance [əlī'əns] *n* alliance *f*.

allied [əlīd'] *a* allié(e).

alligator [al'əgātûr] *n* alligator *m*.

all-important [ôl'impôr'tənt] *a* capital(e), crucial(e).

all-inclusive [ôl'inklōō'siv] *a* *(also ad: charge)* tout compris.

all-in wrestling [ôl'in res'ling] *n* *(Brit)* catch *m*.

alliteration [əlitərā'shən] *n* allitération *f*.

all-night [ôl'nīt] *a* ouvert(e) *or* qui dure toute la nuit.

allocate [al'əkāt] *vt* *(share out)* répartir, distribuer; *(duties)*: **to** ~ **sth to** assigner *or* attribuer qch à; *(sum, time)*: **to** ~ **sth to** allouer qch à; **to** ~ **sth for** affecter qch à.

allocation [aləkā'shən] *n* *(see vb)* répartition *f*; attribution *f*; allocation *f*; affectation *f*; *(money)* crédit(s) *m(pl)*, somme(s) allouée(s).

allot [əlât'] *vt* *(share out)* répartir, distribuer; *(time)*: **to** ~ **sth to** allouer qch à; *(duties)*: **to** ~ **sth to** assigner qch à; **in the** ~**ted time** dans le temps imparti.

allotment [əlât'mənt] *n* *(share)* part *f*; *(Brit:*

garden) lopin *m* de terre (*loué à la municipalité*).

all-out |ôl'out'| *a* (*effort etc*) total(e).

allow [əlou'] *vt* (*practice, behavior*) permettre, autoriser; (*sum to spend etc*) accorder, allouer; (*sum, time estimated*) compter, prévoir; (*concede*): **to ~ that** convenir que; **to ~ sb to do** permettre à qn de faire, autoriser qn à faire; **he is ~ed to ...** on lui permet de ...; **smoking is not ~ed** il est interdit de fumer; **we must ~ 3 days for the journey** il faut compter 3 jours pour le voyage. **allow for** *vt fus* tenir compte de.

allowance [əlou'əns] *n* (*money received*) allocation *f*; (: *from parent etc*) subside *m*; (: *for expenses*) indemnité *f*; (*TAX*) somme *f* déductible du revenu imposable, abattement *m*; **to make ~s for** tenir compte de.

alloy [al'oi] *n* alliage *m*.

all right *ad* (*feel, work*) bien; (*as answer*) d'accord.

all-rounder [ôlroun'dûr] *n* (*Brit*): **to be a good ~** être doué(e) en tout.

allspice [ôl'spīs] *n* poivre *m* de la Jamaïque.

all-time [ôl'tīm] *a* (*record*) sans précédent, absolu(e).

allude [əlōōd'] *vi*: **to ~ to** faire allusion à.

alluring [əlōō'ring] *a* séduisant(e), alléchant(e).

allusion [əlōō'zhən] *n* allusion *f*.

alluvium [əlōō'vēəm] *n* alluvions *fpl*.

ally *n* [al'ī] allié *m* ♦ *vt* [əlī']: **to ~ o.s. with** s'allier avec.

almighty [ôlmī'tē] *a* tout-puissant.

almond [â'mənd] *n* amande *f*.

almost [ôl'mōst] *ad* presque; **he ~ fell** il a failli tomber.

alms [âmz] *n* aumône(s) *f(pl)*.

aloft [əlôft'] *ad* en haut, en l'air; (*NAUT*) dans la mâture.

alone [əlōn'] *a, ad* seul(e); **to leave sb ~** laisser qn tranquille; **to leave sth ~** ne pas toucher à qch; **let ~ ...** sans parler de ...; encore moins ....

along [əlông'] *prep* le long de ♦ *ad*: **is he coming ~?** vient-il avec nous?; **he was hopping/limping ~** il venait *or* avançait en sautillant/boitant; **~ with** avec, en plus de; (*person*) en compagnie de.

alongside [əlông'sīd'] *prep* le long de; au côté de ♦ *ad* à bord à bord; côte à côte; **we brought our boat ~** (*of a pier, shore etc*) nous avons accosté.

aloof [əlōōf'] *a, ad* à distance, à l'écart; **to stand ~** se tenir à l'écart *or* à distance.

aloofness [əlōōf'nis] *n* réserve (hautaine), attitude distante.

aloud [əloud'] *ad* à haute voix.

alphabet [al'fəbet] *n* alphabet *m*.

alphabetical [alfəbet'ikəl] *a* alphabétique; **in ~ order** par ordre alphabétique.

alphanumeric [alfənōōmär'ik] *a* alphanumérique.

alpine [al'pīn] *a* alpin(e), alpestre; **~ hut** cabane *f or* refuge *m* de montagne; **~ pasture** pâturage *m* (de montagne); **~ skiing** ski alpin.

Alps [alps] *npl*: **the ~** les Alpes *fpl*.

already [ôlred'ē] *ad* déjà.

alright [ôlrīt'] *ad* = **all right.**

Alsace [alsās'] *n* Alsace *f*.

Alsatian [alsā'shən] *a* alsacien(ne), d'Alsace ♦ *n* Alsacien/ne; (*Brit: dog*) berger allemand.

also [ôl'sō] *ad* aussi.

Alta. *abbr* (*Canada*) = *Alberta.*

altar [ôl'tûr] *n* autel *m*.

alter [ôl'tûr] *vt, vi* changer, modifier.

alteration [ôltərā'shən] *n* changement *m*, modification *f*; **~s** (*SEWING*) retouches *fpl*; (*ARCHIT*) modifications *fpl*; **timetable subject to ~** horaires sujets à modifications.

alternate *a* [ôl'tûrnit] alterné(e), alternant(e), alternatif(ive) ♦ *vi* [ôl'tûrnāt] alterner; **on ~ days** un jour sur deux, tous les deux jours.

alternately [ôl'tûrnitlē] *ad* alternativement, en alternant.

alternating [ôl'tûrnāting] *a* (*current*) alternatif(ive).

alternative [ôltûr'nətiv] *a* (*solutions*) interchangeable, possible; (*solution*) autre, de remplacement; (*energy*) doux(douce); (*society*) parallèle ♦ *n* (*choice*) alternative *f*; (*other possibility*) autre possibilité *f*.

alternatively [ôltûr'nətivlē] *ad*: **~ one could** une autre *or* l'autre solution serait de.

alternator [ôl'tûrnātûr] *n* (*AUT*) alternateur *m*.

although [ôlthō'] *cj* bien que + *sub*.

altitude [al'tətōōd] *n* altitude *f*.

alto [al'tō] *n* (*female*) contralto *m*; (*male*) haute-contre *f*.

altogether [ôltəgeth'ûr] *ad* entièrement, tout à fait; (*on the whole*) tout compte fait; (*in all*) en tout; **how much is that ~?** ça fait combien en tout?

altruistic [altrōōis'tik] *a* altruiste.

aluminium *etc* [alōōmin'ēəm] (*Brit*) = **aluminum** *etc*.

aluminum [əlōō'mənəm] *n* (*US*) aluminium *m*.

aluminum foil *n* papier *m* d'alu.

alumnus [əlum'nəs] *n* (*US*) ancien(ne) élève.

always [ôl'wāz] *ad* toujours.

AM *abbr* = *amplitude modulation.*

am [am] *vb see* **be.**

a.m. *ad abbr* (= *ante meridiem*) du matin.

AMA *n abbr* = *American Medical Association.*

amalgam [əmal'gəm] *n* amalgame *m*.

amalgamate [əmal'gəmāt] *vt, vi* fusionner.

amalgamation [əmalgəmā'shən] *n* fusion *f*; (*COMM*) fusionnement *m*.

amass [əmas'] *vt* amasser.

amateur [am'əchûr] *n* amateur *m* ♦ *a* (*SPORT*) amateur *inv*; **~ dramatics** le théâtre amateur.

amateurish [aməchōō'rish] *a* (*pej*) d'amateur, un peu amateur.

amaze [əmāz'] *vt* surprendre, étonner; **to be ~d (at)** être surpris *or* étonné (de).

amazement [əmāz'mənt] *n* surprise *f*, étonnement *m*.

amazing [əmā'zing] *a* étonnant(e), incroyable; (*bargain, offer*) exceptionnel(le).

amazingly [əmā'zinglē] *ad* incroyablement.

Amazon [am'əzän] *n* (*GEO, MYTHOLOGY*) Amazone *f* ♦ *cpd* amazonien(ne), de l'Amazone; **the ~ basin** le bassin de l'Amazone; **the ~ jungle** la forêt amazonienne.

Amazonian [aməzō'nēən] *a* amazonien(ne).

ambassador [ambas'ədûr] *n* ambassadeur *m*.

amber |am'bûr| *n* ambre *m*; **at ~** (*Brit AUT*) à l'orange.
ambidextrous |ambidek'strəs| *a* ambidextre.
ambience |am'bēəns| *n* ambiance *f*.
ambiguity |ambəgyōō'itē| *n* ambiguïté *f*.
ambiguous |ambig'yōōəs| *a* ambigu(ë).
ambition |ambish'ən| *n* ambition *f*.
ambitious |ambish'əs| *a* ambitieux(euse).
ambivalent |ambiv'ələnt| *a* (*attitude*) ambivalent(e).
amble |am'bəl| *vi* (*also*: **to ~ along**) aller d'un pas tranquille.
ambulance |am'byələns| *n* ambulance *f*.
ambush |am'bōōsh| *n* embuscade *f* ♦ *vt* tendre une embuscade à.
ameba |əmē'bə| *n* (*US*) = **amoeba**.
ameliorate |əmēl'yərāt| *vt* améliorer.
amen |ā'men'| *excl* amen.
amenable |əmē'nəbəl| *a*: **~ to** (*advice etc*) disposé(e) à écouter *or* suivre; **~ to the law** responsable devant la loi.
amend |əmend'| *vt* (*law*) amender; (*text*) corriger; (*habits*) réformer ♦ *vi* s'amender, se corriger; **to make ~s** réparer ses torts, faire amende honorable.
amendment |əmend'mənt| *n* (*to law*) amendement *m*; (*to text*) correction *f*.
amenities |əmen'itēz| *npl* aménagements *mpl*, équipements *mpl*.
amenity |əmen'itē| *n* charme *m*, agrément *m*.
America |əmär'ikə| *n* Amérique *f*.
American |əmär'ikən| *a* américain(e) ♦ *n* Américain/e.
americanize |əmär'ikənīz| *vt* américaniser.
Amerindian |əmərin'dēən| *a* amérindien(ne) ♦ *n* Amérindien/ne.
amethyst |am'ithist| *n* améthyste *f*.
Amex |am'eks| *n abbr* = *American Stock Exchange*.
amiable |ā'mēəbəl| *a* aimable, affable.
amicable |am'ikəbəl| *a* amical(e).
amid(st) |əmid(st)'| *prep* parmi, au milieu de.
amiss |əmis'| *a, ad*: **there's something ~** il y a quelque chose qui ne va pas *or* qui cloche; **to take sth ~** prendre qch mal *or* de travers.
ammo |am'ō| *n abbr* (*col*) = **ammunition**.
ammonia |əmōn'yə| *n* (*gas*) ammoniac *m*; (*liquid*) ammoniaque *f*.
ammunition |amyənish'ən| *n* munitions *fpl*; (*fig*) arguments *mpl*.
ammunition dump *n* dépôt *m* de munitions.
amnesia |amnē'zhə| *n* amnésie *f*.
amnesty |am'nistē| *n* amnistie *f*; **to grant an ~** to accorder une amnistie à.
amoeba |əmē'bə| *n* amibe *f*.
amok |əmuk'| *ad*: **to run ~** être pris(e) d'un accès de folie furieuse.
among(st) |əmung(st)'| *prep* parmi, entre.
amoral |āmôr'əl| *a* amoral(e).
amorous |am'ûrəs| *a* amoureux(euse).
amorphous |əmôr'fəs| *a* amorphe.
amortization |əmûrtəzā'shən| *n* (*COMM*) amortissement *m*.
amount |əmount'| *n* (*sum of money*) somme *f*; (*total*) montant *m*; (*quantity*) quantité *f*; nombre *m* ♦ *vi*: **to ~ to** (*total*) s'élever à; (*be same as*) équivaloir à, revenir à; **this ~s to a refusal** cela équivaut à un refus; **the total ~** (*of money*) le montant total.

amp(ere) |am'pēr| *n* ampère *m*; **a 13 amp plug** une fiche de 13 A.
ampersand |am'pûrsand| *n* signe &, "et" commercial.
amphibian |amfib'ēən| *n* batracien *m*.
amphibious |amfib'ēəs| *a* amphibie.
amphitheater, (*Brit*) **amphitheatre** |am'fəthēətûr| *n* amphithéâtre *m*.
ample |am'pəl| *a* ample; spacieux(euse); (*enough*): **this is ~** c'est largement suffisant; **to have ~ time/room** avoir bien assez de temps/place, avoir largement le temps/la place.
amplifier |am'pləfîûr| *n* amplificateur *m*.
amplify |am'pləfī| *vt* amplifier.
amply |am'plē| *ad* amplement, largement.
ampule, (*Brit*) **ampoule** |am'pyōōl| *n* (*MED*) ampoule *f*.
amputate |am'pyōōtāt| *vt* amputer.
Amsterdam |am'stûrdam| *n* Amsterdam.
amt *abbr* = **amount**.
amuck |əmuk'| *ad* = **amok**.
amuse |əmyōōz'| *vt* amuser; **to ~ o.s. with sth/by doing sth** se divertir avec qch/à faire qch; **to be ~d at** être amusé par; **he was not ~d** il n'a pas apprécié.
amusement |əmyōōz'mənt| *n* amusement *m*.
amusement arcade *n* salle *f* de jeu.
amusement park *n* parc *m* d'attractions.
amusing |əmyōō'zing| *a* amusant(e), divertissant(e).
an |an, ən, n| *definite article see* **a**.
ANA *n abbr* = *American Newspaper Association; American Nurses Association.*
anachronism |ənak'rənizəm| *n* anachronisme *m*.
anaemia |ənē'mēə| *etc* (*Brit*) = **anemia**.
anaesthetic |anisthet'ik| (*Brit*) *a, n* = **anesthetic**.
anaesthetist |ənēs'thətist| *n* (*Brit*) anesthésiste *m/f*.
anagram |an'əgram| *n* anagramme *m*.
analgesic |anəljē'zik| *a, n* analgésique (*m*).
analog(ue) |an'əlôg| *a* (*watch, computer*) analogique.
analogy |ənal'əjē| *n* analogie *f*; **to draw an ~ between** établir une analogie entre.
analyse |an'əlīz| *vt* (*Brit*) = **analyze**.
analysis, *pl* **analyses** |ənal'isis, -sēz| *n* analyse *f*; **in the last ~** en dernière analyse.
analyst |an'əlist| *n* (*political ~ etc*) analyste *m/f*; (*US*) psychanalyste *m/f*.
analytic(al) |anəlit'ik(əl)| *a* analytique.
analyze |an'əlīz| *vt* (*US*) analyser.
anarchist |an'ûrkist| *a, n* anarchiste (*m/f*).
anarchy |an'ûrkē| *n* anarchie *f*.
anathema |ənath'əmə| *n*: **it is ~ to him** il a cela en abomination.
anatomical |anətâm'ikəl| *a* anatomique.
anatomy |ənat'əmē| *n* anatomie *f*.
ANC *n abbr* (= *African National Congress*) ANC *m*.
ancestor |an'sestûr| *n* ancêtre *m*, aïeul *m*.
ancestral |anses'trəl| *a* ancestral(e).
ancestry |an'sestrē| *n* ancêtres *mpl*; ascendance *f*.
anchor |ang'kûr| *n* ancre *f* ♦ *vi* (*also*: **to drop ~**) jeter l'ancre, mouiller ♦ *vt* mettre à l'ancre.

anchorage [ang'kûrij] n mouillage m, ancrage m.

anchovy [an'chōvē] n anchois m.

ancient [ān'shənt] a ancien(ne), antique; (fig) d'un âge vénérable, antique; ~ **monument** monument m historique.

ancillary [an'səlärē] a auxiliaire.

and [and] cj et; ~ **so on** et ainsi de suite; **try** ~ **come** tâchez de venir; **come** ~ **sit here** venez vous asseoir ici; **better** ~ **better** de mieux en mieux; **more** ~ **more** de plus en plus.

Andes [an'dēz] npl: **the** ~ les Andes fpl.

anecdote [an'ikdōt] n anecdote f.

anemia [ənē'mēə] n (US) anémie f.

anemic [ənē'mik] a (US) anémique.

anemone [ənem'ənē] n (BOT) anémone f; **sea** ~ anémone de mer.

anesthesiologist [an'isthēzēăl'əjist] n (US) anesthésiste m/f.

anesthetic [anisthet'ik] (US) a, n anesthésique (m); **under the** ~ sous anesthésie; **local/ general** ~ anesthésie locale/générale.

anew [ənōō'] ad à nouveau.

angel [ān'jəl] n ange m.

anger [ang'gûr] n colère f ♦ vt mettre en colère, irriter.

angina [anji'nə] n angine f de poitrine.

angle [ang'gəl] n angle m ♦ vi: **to** ~ **for** (trout) pêcher; (compliments) chercher, quêter; **from their** ~ de leur point de vue.

angler [ang'glûr] n pêcheur/euse à la ligne.

Anglican [ang'glikən] a, n anglican(e).

anglicize [ang'gləsīz] vt angliciser.

angling [ang'gling] n pêche f à la ligne.

Anglo- [un'glō] prefix anglo(-).

Anglo-French [an'glōfrench'] a anglo-français(e).

Anglo-Saxon [an'glōsak'sən] a, n anglo-saxon(ne).

Angola [anggō'lə] n Angola m.

Angolan [anggō'lən] a angolais(e) ♦ n Angolais/e.

angrily [ang'grilē] ad avec colère.

angry [ang'grē] a en colère, furieux(euse); **to be** ~ **with sb/at sth** être furieux contre qn/ de qch; **to get** ~ se fâcher, se mettre en colère; **to make sb** ~ mettre qn en colère.

anguish [ang'gwish] n angoisse f.

angular [ang'gyəlûr] a anguleux(euse).

animal [an'əməl] n animal m ♦ a animal(e).

animal spirits npl entrain m, vivacité f.

animate vt [an'əmāt] animer ♦ a [an'əmit] animé(e), vivant(e).

animated [an'əmātid] a animé(e).

animosity [anəmâs'ətē] n animosité f.

aniseed [an'isēd] n anis m.

Ankara [ang'kûrə] n Ankara.

ankle [ang'kəl] n cheville f.

ankle socks npl socquettes fpl.

annex n [an'eks] (also: Brit: **annexe**) annexe f ♦ vt [əneks'] annexer.

annexation [anəksā'shən] n annexion f.

annihilate [ənī'əlāt] vt annihiler, anéantir.

anniversary [anəvûr'sûrē] n anniversaire m.

anniversary dinner n dîner commémoratif or anniversaire.

annotate [an'ōtāt] vt annoter.

announce [ənouns'] vt annoncer; (birth, death) faire part de; **he** ~**d that he wasn't going** il a déclaré qu'il n'irait pas.

announcement [ənouns'mənt] n annonce f; (for births etc: in newspaper) avis m de faire-part; (: letter, card) faire-part m; **I'd like to make an** ~ j'ai une communication à faire.

announcer [ənoun'sûr] n (RADIO, TV: between programs) speaker/ine; (: in a program) présentateur/trice.

annoy [ənoi'] vt agacer, ennuyer, contrarier; **to be** ~**ed (at sth/with sb)** être en colère or irrité (contre qch/qn); **don't get** ~**ed!** ne vous fâchez pas!

annoyance [ənoi'əns] n mécontentement m, contrariété f.

annoying [ənoi'ing] a ennuyeux(euse), agaçant(e), contrariant(e).

annual [an'yōōəl] a annuel(le) ♦ n (BOT) plante annuelle; (book) album m.

annual general meeting (AGM) n (Brit) assemblée générale annuelle (AGA).

annually [an'yōōəlē] ad annuellement.

annual report n rapport annuel.

annuity [ənōō'itē] n rente f; **life** ~ rente viagère.

annul [ənul'] vt annuler; (law) abroger.

annulment [ənul'mənt] n (see vb) annulation f; abrogation f.

annum [an'əm] n see **per annum**.

Annunciation [ənunsēā'shən] n Annonciation f.

anode [an'ōd] n anode f.

anoint [ənoint'] vt oindre.

anomalous [ənâm'ələs] a anormal(e).

anomaly [ənâm'əlē] n anomalie f.

anon. [ənûn'] abbr = **anonymous**.

anonymity [anənim'itē] n anonymat m.

anonymous [ənân'əməs] a anonyme; **to re-main** ~ garder l'anonymat.

anorak [ân'ərâk] n anorak m.

anorexia [anərek'sēə] n (also: ~ **nervosa**) anorexie f.

another [ənuth'ûr] a: ~ **book** (one more) un autre livre, encore un livre, un livre de plus; (a different one) un autre livre; ~ **drink?** encore un verre?; **in** ~ **5 years** dans 5 ans ♦ pronoun un(e) autre, encore un(e), un(e) de plus; **some actor or** ~ un certain acteur, je ne sais quel acteur; see also **one**.

ANSI n abbr (= American National Standards Institute) association de normalisation.

answer [an'sûr] n réponse f; (to problem) solution f ♦ vi répondre ♦ vt (reply to) répondre à; (problem) résoudre; (prayer) exaucer; **to** ~ **the phone** répondre (au téléphone); **in** ~ **to your letter** suite à or en réponse à votre lettre; **to** ~ **the bell** or **the door** aller or venir ouvrir (la porte).

answer back vi répondre, répliquer.

answer for vt fus répondre de, se porter garant de; (crime, one's actions) répondre de.

answer to vt fus (description) répondre or correspondre à.

answerable [an'sûrəbəl] a: ~ **(to sb/for sth)** responsable (devant qn/de qch); **I am** ~ **to no one** je n'ai de comptes à rendre à personne.

answering machine [an'sûring məshēn'] n ré-

pondeur *m*.
ant |ant| *n* fourmi *f*.
ANTA *n abbr = American National Theatre and Academy.*
antagonism |antag'ənizəm| *n* antagonisme *m*.
antagonist |antag'ənist| *n* antagoniste *m/f*, adversaire *m/f*.
antagonistic |antagənis'tik| *a (attitude, feelings)* hostile.
antagonize |antag'ənīz| *vt* éveiller l'hostilité de, contrarier.
Antarctic |antârk'tik| *a* antarctique, austral(e) ♦ *n*: **the** ~ l'Antarctique *m*.
Antarctica |antârk'tikə| *n* Antarctique *m*, Terres Australes.
Antarctic Circle *n* cercle *m* Antarctique.
Antarctic Ocean *n* océan *m* Antarctique *or* Austral.
ante |an'tē| *n*: **to up the** ~ faire monter les enjeux.
ante... *prefix* anté..., anti..., pré....
anteater |ant'ētûr| *n* fourmilier *m*, tamanoir *m*.
antecedent |antisē'dənt| *n* antécédent *m*.
antechamber |an'tēchāmbûr| *n* antichambre *f*.
antelope |an'təlōp| *n* antilope *f*.
antenatal |antēnā'təl| *a (Brit)* = **prenatal**.
antenna, *pl* ~**e** |anten'ə, -ē| *n* antenne *f*; *(US TV)* antenne intérieure.
anthem |an'thəm| *n* motet *m*; **national** ~ hymne national.
anthill |ant-hil'| *n* fourmilière *f*.
anthology |anthâl'əjē| *n* anthologie *f*.
anthropologist |anthrəpâl'əjist| *n* anthropologue *m/f*.
anthropology |anthrəpâl'əjē| *n* anthropologie *f*.
anti- |an'tī| *prefix* anti-.
antiaircraft |antiär'kraft| *a* antiaérien(ne).
antiaircraft defense *n* défense *f* contre avions, DCA *f*.
antiballistic |antēbəlis'tik| *a* antibalistique.
antibiotic |antēbīât'ik| *a, n* antibiotique *(m)*.
antibody |an'tēbâdē| *n* anticorps *m*.
anticipate |antis'əpāt| *vt* s'attendre à, prévoir; *(wishes, request)* aller au devant de, devancer; **this is worse than I** ~**d** c'est pire que je ne pensais; **as** ~**d** comme prévu.
anticipation |antisəpā'shən| *n* attente *f*; **thanking you in** ~ en vous remerciant d'avance, avec mes remerciements anticipés.
anticlimax |antēklī'maks| *n* réalisation décevante d'un événement que l'on escomptait important, intéressant etc.
anticlockwise |antēklâk'wīz| *a (Brit)* dans le sens inverse des aiguilles d'une montre.
antics |an'tiks| *npl* singeries *fpl*.
anticyclone |antēsī'klōn| *n* anticyclone *m*.
antidote |an'tidōt| *n* antidote *m*, contrepoison *m*.
antifreeze |an'tēfrēz| *n* antigel *m*.
antihistamine |antēhis'təmēn| *n* antihistaminique *m*.
Antilles |antil'ēz| *npl*: **the** ~ les Antilles *fpl*.
antipathy |antip'əthē| *n* antipathie *f*.
Antipodean |antipədē'ən| *a* australien(ne) et néozélandais(e), d'Australie et de Nouvelle-Zélande.
Antipodes |antip'ədēz| *npl*: **the** ~ l'Australie *f*

et la Nouvelle-Zélande.
antiquarian |antəkwär'ēən| *a*: ~ **bookshop** librairie *f* d'ouvrages anciens ♦ *n* expert *m* en objets *or* livres anciens; amateur *m* d'antiquités.
antiquated |an'təkwātid| *a* vieilli(e), suranné(e), vieillot(te).
antique |antēk'| *n* objet *m* d'art ancien, meuble ancien *or* d'époque, antiquité *f* ♦ *a* ancien(ne); *(pre-medieval)* antique.
antique dealer *n* antiquaire *m/f*.
antique shop *n* magasin *m* d'antiquités.
antiquity |antik'witē| *n* antiquité *f*.
anti-Semitic |an'tisəmit'ik| *a* antisémite.
anti-Semitism |antīsem'itizəm| *n* antisémitisme *m*.
antiseptic |antēsep'tik| *a, n* antiseptique *(m)*.
antisocial |antēsō'shəl| *a* peu liant(e), sauvage, insociable; *(against society)* antisocial(e).
antitank |antētangk'| *a* antichar.
antithesis, *pl* **antitheses** |antith'əsis, -sēz| *n* antithèse *f*.
antitrust |antētrust'| *a*: ~ **legislation** loi *f* anti-trust.
antlers |ant'lûrz| *npl* bois *mpl*, ramure *f*.
Antwerp |ant'wûrp| *n* Anvers.
anus |ā'nəs| *n* anus *m*.
anvil |an'vil| *n* enclume *f*.
anxiety |angzī'ətē| *n* anxiété *f*; *(keenness)*: ~ **to do** grand désir *or* impatience *f* de faire.
anxious |angk'shəs| *a* anxieux(euse), (très) inquiet(ète); *(keen)*: ~ **to do/that** qui tient beaucoup à faire/à ce que; impatient(e) de faire/que; **I'm very** ~ **about you** je me fais beaucoup de souci pour toi.
anxiously |angk'shəslē| *ad* anxieusement.
any |en'ē| *a (in negative and interrogative sentences = some)* de, d'; du, de l', de la, des; *(no matter which)* n'importe quel(le), quelconque; *(each and every)* tout(e), chaque; **I haven't** ~ **money/books** je n'ai pas d'argent/de livres; **have you** ~ **butter/children?** avez-vous du beurre/des enfants?; **without** ~ **difficulty** sans la moindre difficulté; **come (at)** ~ **time** venez à n'importe quelle heure; **at** ~ **moment** à tout moment, d'un instant à l'autre; ~ **day now** d'un jour à l'autre; **in** ~ **case** de toute façon; *(at least)* en tout cas; **at** ~ **rate** de toute façon ♦ *pronoun* n'importe lequel(laquelle); *(anybody)* n'importe qui; *(in negative and interrogative sentences)*: **I haven't** ~ je n'en ai pas, je n'en ai aucun; **have you got** ~? en avez-vous?; **can** ~ **of you sing?** est-ce que l'un d'entre vous *or* quelqu'un parmi vous sait chanter? ♦ *ad (in negative sentences)* nullement, aucunement; *(in interrogative and conditional constructions)* un peu; tant soit peu; **I can't hear him** ~ **more** je ne l'entends plus; **are you feeling** ~ **better?** vous sentez-vous un peu mieux?; **do you want** ~ **more soup?** voulez-vous encore un peu de soupe?
anybody |en'ēbâdē| *pronoun* n'importe qui; *(in interrogative sentences)* quelqu'un; *(in negative sentences)* **I don't see** ~ je ne vois personne.
anyhow |en'ēhou| *ad* quoi qu'il en soit; *(haphazardly)* n'importe comment; **I shall go** ~

j'irai de toute façon.

anyone [en'ēwun] = **anybody.**

anyplace [en'ēplās] *ad* (*US*) = **anywhere.**

anything [en'ēthing] *pronoun* n'importe quoi; (*in interrogative sentences*) quelque chose; (*in negative sentences*): **I don't want** ~ je ne veux rien; ~ **else?** (*in store*) et avec ça?

anytime [en'ētīm] *ad* n'importe quand.

anyway [en'ēwā] *ad* de toute façon.

anywhere [en'ēhwär] *ad* n'importe où; (*in interrogative sentences*) quelque part; (*in negative sentences*): **I don't see him** ~ je ne le vois nulle part; ~ **in the world** n'importe où dans le monde.

Anzac [an'zak] *n abbr* (= *Australia-New Zealand Army Corps*) soldat du corps *ANZAC.*

apart [əpärt'] *ad* (*to one side*) à part; de côté; à l'écart; (*separately*) séparément; **10 miles/a long way** ~ à 10 milles/très éloignés l'un de l'autre; **they are living** ~ ils sont séparés; ~ **from** *prep* à part, excepté.

apartheid [əpärt'hīt] *n* apartheid *m.*

apartment [əpärt'mənt] *n* appartement *m*, logement *m.*

apartment building *or* **block** *or* **house** *n* immeuble *m*; maison divisée en appartements.

apathetic [apəthet'ik] *a* apathique, indifférent(e).

apathy [ap'əthē] *n* apathie *f*, indifférence *f.*

APB *n abbr* (*US*: = *all points bulletin*) expression de la police signifiant 'découvrir et appréhender le suspect'.

ape [āp] *n* (grand) singe ♦ *vt* singer.

Apennines [ap'əninz] *npl*: **the** ~ les Apennins *mpl.*

aperitif [əpārētēf'] *n* apéritif *m.*

aperture [ap'ùrchûr] *n* orifice *m*, ouverture *f*; (*PHOT*) ouverture (du diaphragme).

APEX [ā'peks] *n abbr* (*AVIAT*: = *advance purchase excursion*) APEX *m.*

apex [ā'peks] *n* sommet *m.*

aphid [ā'fid] *n* puceron *m.*

aphrodisiac [afrədiz'eak] *a, n* aphrodisiaque *(m).*

API *n abbr* = *American Press Institute.*

apiece [əpēs'] *ad* (*for each person*) chacun(e), par tête; (*for each item*) chacun(e), (la) pièce.

aplomb [əplām'] *n* sang-froid *m*, assurance *f.*

APO *n abbr* (*US*: = *Army Post Office*) service postal de l'armée.

apocalypse [əpāk'əlips] *n* apocalypse *f.*

apolitical [āpəlit'ikəl] *a* apolitique.

apologetic [əpāləjet'ik] *a* (*tone, letter*) d'excuse; **to be very** ~ **about** s'excuser vivement de.

apologetically [əpāləjet'iklē] *ad* (*say*) en s'excusant.

apologize [əpāl'əjīz] *vi*: **to** ~ **(for sth to sb)** s'excuser (de qch auprès de qn), présenter des excuses (à qn pour qch).

apology [əpāl'əjē] *n* excuses *fpl*; **to send one's apologies** envoyer une lettre *or* un mot d'excuse, s'excuser (de ne pas pouvoir venir); **please accept my apologies** vous voudrez bien m'excuser.

apoplectic [apəplek'tik] *a* (*MED*) apoplectique;

(*col*): ~ **with rage** fou(folle) de rage.

apoplexy [ap'əpleksē] *n* apoplexie *f.*

apostle [əpás'əl] *n* apôtre *m.*

apostrophe [əpás'trəfē] *n* apostrophe *f.*

Appalachian Mountains [apəlā'chēən moun'tənz] *npl*: **the** ~ les (monts *mpl*) Appalaches.

appall, (*Brit*) **appal** [əpôl'] *vt* consterner, atterrer; horrifier.

appalling [əpôl'ing] *a* épouvantable; (*stupidity*) consternant(e); **she's an** ~ **cook** c'est une très mauvaise cuisinière.

apparatus [apərat'əs] *n* appareil *m*, dispositif *m*; (*in gymnasium*) agrès *mpl.*

apparel [əpar'əl] *n* (*US*) habillement *m*, confection *f.*

apparent [əpar'ənt] *a* apparent(e); **it is** ~ **that** il est évident que.

apparently [əpar'əntlē] *ad* apparemment.

apparition [apərish'ən] *n* apparition *f.*

appeal [əpēl'] *vi* (*LAW*) faire *or* interjeter appel ♦ *n* (*LAW*) appel *m*; (*request*) appel; prière *f*; (*charm*) attrait *m*, charme *m*; **to** ~ **for** demander (instamment); implorer; **to** ~ **to** (*subj: person*) faire appel à; (*subj: thing*) plaire à; **to** ~ **to sb for mercy** implorer la pitié de qn, prier *or* adjurer qn d'avoir pitié; **it doesn't** ~ **to me** cela ne m'attire pas; **right of** ~ droit *m* de recours.

appealing [əpē'ling] *a* (*nice*) attrayant(e); (*touching*) attendrissant(e).

appear [əpēr'] *vi* apparaître, se montrer; (*LAW*) comparaître; (*publication*) paraître, sortir, être publié(e); (*seem*) paraître, sembler; **it would** ~ **that** il semble que; **to** ~ **in Hamlet** jouer dans Hamlet; **to** ~ **on IV** passer à la télé.

appearance [əpē'rəns] *n* apparition *f*; parution *f*; (*look, aspect*) apparence *f*, aspect *m*; **to put in** *or* **make an** ~ faire acte de présence; (*THEATER*): **by order of** ~ par ordre d'entrée en scène; **to keep up** ~**s** sauver les apparences; **to** ~ **s** selon toute apparence.

appease [əpēz'] *vt* apaiser, calmer.

appeasement [əpēz'mənt] *n* (*POL*) apaisement *m.*

appellate court [əpel'it kôrt] *n* (*US*) cour *f* d'appel.

append [əpend'] *vt* (*COMPUT*) ajouter (à la fin d'un fichier).

appendage [əpen'dij] *n* appendice *m.*

appendicitis [əpendisī'tis] *n* appendicite *f.*

appendix, *pl* **appendices** [əpen'diks, -disēz] *n* appendice *m*; **to have one's** ~ **out** se faire opérer de l'appendicite.

appetite [ap'itit] *n* appétit *m*; **that walk has given me an** ~ cette promenade m'a ouvert l'appétit.

appetizer [ap'itīzûr] *n* (*food*) amuse-gueule *m*; (*drink*) apéritif *m.*

appetizing [ap'itīzing] *a* appétissant(e).

applaud [əplôd'] *vt, vi* applaudir.

applause [əplôz'] *n* applaudissements *mpl.*

apple [ap'əl] *n* pomme *f*; (*also*: ~ **tree**) pommier *m*; **it's the** ~ **of my eye** j'y tiens comme à la prunelle de mes yeux.

apple turnover *n* chausson *m* aux pommes.

appliance [əplī'əns] *n* appareil *m*; **electrical** ~**s** l'électroménager *m.*

applicable [ap'likəbəl] *a* applicable; **the law is ~ from January** la loi entre en vigueur au mois de janvier; **to be ~ to** valoir pour.

applicant [ap'likənt] *n*: ~ **(for)** (*ADMIN*: *for benefit etc*) demandeur/euse (de); (*for post*) candidat/e (à).

application [aplikā'shən] *n* application *f*; (*for a job, a grant etc*) demande *f*; candidature *f*; **on ~** sur demande.

application form *n* formulaire *m* de demande.

application program *n* (*COMPUT*) programme *m* d'application.

applications package [aplikā'shənz pak'ij] *n* (*COMPUT*) progiciel *m* d'application.

applied [əplīd'] *a* appliqué(e); ~ **arts** *npl* arts décoratifs.

apply [əplī'] *vt*: **to ~ to** (*paint, ointment*) appliquer (sur); (*theory, technique*) appliquer (à) ♦ *vi*: **to ~ to** (*ask*) s'adresser à; (*be suitable for, relevant to*) s'appliquer à, être valable pour; **to ~ (for)** (*permit, grant*) faire une demande (en vue d'obtenir); (*job*) poser sa candidature (pour), faire une demande d'emploi (concernant); **to ~ the brakes** actionner les freins, freiner; **to ~ o.s. to** s'appliquer à.

appoint [əpoint'] *vt* nommer, engager; (*date, place*) fixer, désigner.

appointee [əpointē'] *n* personne nommée; candidat retenu.

appointment [əpoint'mənt] *n* (*to post*) nomination *f*; (*arrangement to meet*) rendez-vous *m*; **to make an ~ (with)** prendre rendez-vous (avec); **by ~** sur rendez-vous.

appointment book *n* agenda *m*.

apportion [əpôr'shən] *vt* (*share out*) répartir, distribuer; **to ~ sth to sb** attribuer *or* assigner *or* allouer qch à qn.

appraisal [əprā'zəl] *n* évaluation *f*.

appraise [əprāz'] *vt* (*value*) estimer; (*situation etc*) évaluer.

appreciable [əprē'shēəbəl] *a* appréciable.

appreciate [əprē'shēāt] *vt* (*like*) apprécier, faire cas de; (*be grateful for*) être reconnaissant(e) de; (*assess*) évaluer; (*be aware of*) comprendre, se rendre compte de ♦ *vi* (*FINANCE*) prendre de la valeur; **I ~ your help** je vous remercie pour votre aide.

appreciation [əprēshēā'shən] *n* appréciation *f*; (*gratitude*) reconnaissance *f*; (*FINANCE*) hausse *f*, valorisation *f*.

appreciative [əprē'shətiv] *a* (*person*) sensible; (*comment*) élogieux(euse).

apprehend [aprihend'] *vt* appréhender, arrêter; (*understand*) comprendre.

apprehension [aprihen'shən] *n* appréhension *f*, inquiétude *f*.

apprehensive [aprihen'siv] *a* inquiet(ète), appréhensif(ive).

apprentice [əpren'tis] *n* apprenti *m* ♦ *vt*: **to be ~d to** être en apprentissage chez.

apprenticeship [əpren'tisship] *n* apprentissage *m*; **to serve one's ~** faire son apprentissage.

approach [əprōch'] *vi* approcher ♦ *vt* (*come near*) approcher de; (*ask, apply to*) s'adresser à; (*subject, passer-by*) aborder ♦ *n* approche *f*; accès *m*, abord *m*; démarche *f* (*auprès de qn*); démarche (*intellectuelle*); **to**

~ sb about sth aller *or* venir voir qn pour qch.

approachable [əprō'chəbəl] *a* accessible.

approbation [aprəbā'shən] *n* approbation *f*.

appropriate *vt* [əprōp'rēāt] (*take*) s'approprier; (*allot*): **to ~ sth for** affecter qch à ♦ *a* [əprōp'rēit] qui convient, approprié(e); (*timely*) opportun(e); **~ for** *or* **to** approprié à; **it would not be ~ for me to comment** il ne me serait pas approprié de commenter.

appropriately [əprōp'rēitlē] *ad* pertinemment, avec à-propos.

appropriation [əprōprēā'shən] *n* dotation *f*, affectation *f*.

approval [əprōō'vəl] *n* approbation *f*; **to meet with sb's ~** (*proposal etc*) recueillir l'assentiment de qn; **on ~** (*COMM*) à l'examen.

approve [əprōōv'] *vt* approuver.

approve of *vt fus* approuver.

approvingly [əprōō'vinglē] *ad* d'un air approbateur.

approx. *abbr* (= *approximately*) env.

approximate *a* [əprāk'səmit] approximatif(ive) ♦ *vt* [əprāk'səmāt] se rapprocher de; être proche de.

approximation [əprāksəmā'shən] *n* approximation *f*.

appt. *abbr* (*US*) = **appointment**.

Apr. *abbr* = **April**.

apr *n abbr* (= *annual percentage rate*) taux (d'intérêt) annuel.

apricot [ap'rikāt] *n* abricot *m*.

April [āp'rəl] *n* avril *m*; **~ fool!** poisson d'avril!; *for phrases see also* **July**.

April Fool's Day *n* le premier avril.

apron [ā'prən] *n* tablier *m*; (*AVIAT*) aire *f* de stationnement.

apse [aps] *n* (*ARCHIT*) abside *f*.

Apt. *abbr* (= *apartment*) appt.

apt [apt] *a* (*suitable*) approprié(e); (*able*): **~ (at)** doué(e) (pour); apte (à); (*likely*): **~ to do** susceptible de faire; ayant tendance à faire.

aptitude [ap'tətōōd] *n* aptitude *f*.

aptitude test *n* test *m* d'aptitude.

aptly [apt'lē] *ad* (fort) à propos.

aqualung [ak'wəlung] *n* scaphandre *m* autonome.

aquarium [əkwär'ēəm] *n* aquarium *m*.

Aquarius [əkwär'ēəs] *n* le Verseau; **to be ~** être du Verseau.

aquatic [əkwat'ik] *a* aquatique; (*sport*) nautique.

aqueduct [ak'widukt] *n* aqueduc *m*.

AR *abbr* (*US MAIL*) = *Arkansas*.

Arab [ar'əb] *n* Arabe *m/f* ♦ *a* arabe.

Arabia [ərā'bēə] *n* Arabie *f*.

Arabian [ərā'bēən] *a* arabe.

Arabian Desert *n* désert *m* d'Arabie.

Arabian Sea *n* mer *f* d'Arabie.

Arabic [ar'əbik] *a*, *n* arabe (*m*).

Arabic numerals *npl* chiffres *mpl* arabes.

arable [ar'əbəl] *a* arable.

arbiter [âr'bitûr] *n* arbitre *m*.

arbitrary [âr'bitrārē] *a* arbitraire.

arbitrate [âr'bitrāt] *vi* arbitrer; trancher.

arbitration [ârbitrā'shən] *n* arbitrage *m*; **the dispute went to ~** le litige a été soumis à arbitrage.

arbitrator [âr'bitrātûr] *n* arbitre *m*, médiateur/ trice.

ARC *n abbr* = *American Red Cross.*

arc [ârk] *n* arc *m*.

arcade [ârkād'] *n* arcade *f*; *(passage with stores)* passage *m*, galerie *f*.

arch [ârch] *n* arche *f*; *(of foot)* cambrure *f*, voûte *f* plantaire ♦ *vt* arquer, cambrer ♦ *a* malicieux(euse) ♦ *prefix:* ~(-) achevé(e); par excellence; **pointed** ~ ogive *f*.

archaeology [ârkēâl'əjē] *etc* = **archeology** *etc*.

archaic [ârkā'ik] *a* archaïque.

archangel [ârkān'jəl] *n* archange *m*.

archbishop [ârchbish'əp] *n* archevêque *m*.

archenemy [ârch'en'əmē] *n* ennemi *m* de toujours *or* par excellence.

archeological [ârkēəlâj'ikəl] *a* archéologique.

archeologist [ârkēâl'əjist] *n* archéologue *m/f*.

archeology [ârkēâl'əjē] *n* archéologie *f*.

archer [âr'chûr] *n* archer *m*.

archery [âr'chûrē] *n* tir *m* à l'arc.

archetypal [âr'kitīpəl] *a* archétype.

archetype [âr'kitīp] *n* prototype *m*, archétype *m*.

archipelago [ârkəpel'əgō] *n* archipel *m*.

architect [âr'kitekt] *n* architecte *m*.

architectural [âr'kitekchûrəl] *a* architectural(e).

architecture [âr'kitekchûr] *n* architecture *f*.

archive file [âr'kīv fīl'] *n (COMPUT)* fichier *m* d'archives.

archives [âr'kīvz] *npl* archives *fpl*.

archivist [âr'kəvist] *n* archiviste *m/f*.

archway [ârch'wā] *n* voûte *f*, porche voûté *or* cintré.

Arctic [ârk'tik] *a* arctique ♦ *n*: **the** ~ l'Arctique *m*.

Arctic Circle *n* cercle *m* Arctique.

Arctic Ocean *n* océan *m* Arctique.

ARD *n abbr (US MED)* = *acute respiratory disease.*

ardent [âr'dənt] *a* fervent(e).

ardor, (Brit) ardour [âr'dûr] *n* ardeur *f*.

arduous [âr'jōōəs] *a* ardu(e).

are [âr] *vb see* **be.**

area [är'ēə] *n (GEOM)* superficie *f*; *(zone)* région *f*; *(: smaller)* secteur *m*; **dining** ~ coin *m* salle à manger; **the New York** ~ la région new-yorkaise.

area code *n (TEL)* indicatif *m* de zone.

arena [ərē'nə] *n* arène *f*.

aren't [ârnt] = **are not.**

Argentina [ârjəntē'nə] *n* Argentine *f*.

Argentinian [ârjəntin'ēən] *a* argentin(e) ♦ *n* Argentin/e.

arguable [âr'gyōōəbəl] *a* discutable, contestable; **it is** ~ **whether** on peut se demander si.

arguably [âr'gyōōəblē] *ad*: **it is** ~ ... on peut soutenir que c'est ....

argue [âr'gyōō] *vi (quarrel)* se disputer; *(reason)* argumenter ♦ *vt (debate: case, matter)* débattre; **to** ~ **about sth (with sb)** se disputer (avec qn) au sujet de qch; **to** ~ **that** objecter *or* alléguer que, donner comme argument que.

argument [âr'gyəmənt] *n (reasons)* argument *m*; *(quarrel)* dispute *f*, discussion *f*; *(debate)* discussion, controverse *f*; ~ **for/against** argument pour/contre.

argumentative [ârgyəmen'tətiv] *a* ergoteur(euse), raisonneur(euse).

aria [âr'ēə] *n* aria *f*.

arid [ar'id] *a* aride.

aridity [ərid'itē] *n* aridité *f*.

Aries [är'ēz] *n* le Bélier; **to be** ~ être du Bélier.

arise, *pt* **arose,** *pp* **arisen** [ərīz', ərōz', əriz'ən] *vi* survenir, se présenter; **to** ~ **from** résulter de; **should the need** ~ en cas de besoin.

aristocracy [aristâk'rəsē] *n* aristocratie *f*.

aristocrat [əris'təkrat] *n* aristocrate *m/f*.

aristocratic [əristəkrat'ik] *a* aristocratique.

arithmetic [ərith'mətik] *n* arithmétique *f*.

arithmetical [arithmet'ikəl] *a* arithmétique.

Ariz. *abbr (US)* = *Arizona.*

Ark. *abbr (US)* = *Arkansas.*

ark [ârk] *n*: **Noah's A~** l'Arche *f* de Noé.

arm [ârm] *n* bras *m* ♦ *vt* armer; ~ **in** ~ bras dessus bras dessous.

armaments [âr'məmənts] *npl (weapons)* armement *m*.

armband [ârm'band] *n* brassard *m*.

armchair [ârm'chär] *n* fauteuil *m*.

armed [ârmd] *a* armé(e); **the** ~ **forces** les forces armées.

armed robbery *n* vol *m* à main armée.

Armenia [ârmē'nēə] *n* Arménie *f*.

Armenian [ârmē'nēən] *a* arménien(ne) ♦ *n* Arménien/ne; *(LING)* arménien *m*.

armful [ârm'fəl] *n* brassée *f*.

armistice [âr'mistis] *n* armistice *m*.

armor [âr'mûr] *n (US)* armure *f*; *(also:* ~-**plating)** blindage *m*; *(MIL: tanks)* blindés *mpl*.

armored car [ârmûrd kâr'] *n* véhicule blindé.

armory [âr'mûrē] *n* arsenal *m*.

armour *etc* [âr'mûr] *(Brit)* = **armor** *etc*.

armpit [ârm'pit] *n* aisselle *f*.

armrest [ârm'rest] *n* accoudoir *m*.

arms [ârmz] *npl (weapons, HERALDRY)* armes *fpl*.

arms control *n* contrôle *m* des armements.

arms race *n* course *f* aux armements.

army [âr'mē] *n* armée *f*.

aroma [ərō'mə] *n* arôme *m*.

aromatic [ârəmat'ik] *a* aromatique.

arose [ərōz'] *pt of* **arise.**

around [əround'] *ad* (tout) autour; *(nearby)* dans les parages ♦ *prep* autour de; *(fig: about)* environ; vers; **is he** ~? est-il dans les parages *or* là?; **it's the other way** ~ c'est l'inverse; **all** ~ tout autour; **the long way** ~ (par) le chemin le plus long; **it's just** ~ **the corner** c'est juste après le coin; *(fig)* c'est tout près; **to ask sb** ~ inviter qn (chez soi); **I'll be** ~ **at 6 o'clock** je serai là à six heures; **to go** ~ faire le tour *or* un détour; **to go** ~ **to sb's (house)** aller chez qn; **to go** ~ **an obstacle** contourner un obstacle; **go** ~ **the back** passez par derrière; **to go** ~ **a house** visiter une maison, faire le tour d'une maison; **enough to go** ~ assez pour tout le monde; ~ **the clock** 24 heures sur 24.

arouse [ərouz'] *vt (sleeper)* éveiller; *(curiosity, passions)* éveiller, susciter; exciter.

arpeggio [ârpej'ēō] *n* arpège *m*.

arrange [ərānj'] *vt* arranger; *(program)* arrêter, convenir de ◆ *vi*: **we have ~d for a car to pick you up** nous avons prévu qu'une voiture vienne vous prendre; **it was ~d that...** il a été convenu que..., il a été décidé que...; **to ~ to do sth** prévoir de faire qch.

arrangement [ərānj'mənt] *n* arrangement *m*; *(plans etc)*: **~s** dispositions *fpl*; **to come to an ~ (with sb)** se mettre d'accord (avec qn); **home deliveries by ~** livraison à domicile sur demande; **I'll make ~s for you to be met** je vous enverrai chercher.

array [ərā'] *n (of objects)* déploiement *m*, étalage *m*; *(MATH, COMPUT)* tableau *m*.

arrears [ərērz'] *npl* arriéré *m*; **to be in ~ with one's rent** devoir un arriéré de loyer, être en retard pour le paiement de son loyer.

arrest [ərest'] *vt* arrêter; *(sb's attention)* retenir, attirer ◆ *n* arrestation *f*; **under ~** en état d'arrestation.

arresting [əres'ting] *a (fig: beauty)* saisissante(e); *(: charm, candor)* désarmant(e).

arrival [ərī'vəl] *n* arrivée *f*; *(COMM)* arrivage *m*; *(person)* arrivant/e; **new ~** nouveau venu/nouvelle venue.

arrive [ərīv'] *vi* arriver.
   arrive at *vt fus (fig)* parvenir à.

arrogance [ar'əgəns] *n* arrogance *f*.

arrogant [ar'əgənt] *a* arrogant(e).

arrow [ar'ō] *n* flèche *f*.

arse [ârs] *n (Brit col!)* cul *m* (!).

arsenal [âr'sənəl] *n* arsenal *m*.

arsenic [âr'sənik] *n* arsenic *m*.

arson [âr'sən] *n* incendie criminel.

art [ârt] *n* art *m*; *(craft)* métier *m*; **work of ~** œuvre *f* d'art.

artefact [âr'təfakt] *n (Brit)* = **artifact**.

arterial [ârtē'rēəl] *a (ANAT)* artériel(le); *(road etc)* à grande circulation.

artery [âr'tûrē] *n* artère *f*.

artful [ârt'fəl] *a* rusé(e).

art gallery *n* musée *m* d'art; *(small and private)* galerie *f* de peinture.

arthritis [ârthrī'tis] *n* arthrite *f*.

artichoke [âr'tichōk] *n* artichaut *m*; **Jerusalem ~** topinambour *m*.

article [âr'tikəl] *n* article *m*; *(Brit LAW: training)*: **~s** *npl* = stage *m*; **~s of clothing** vêtements *mpl*.

articles of association *npl (COMM)* statuts *mpl* d'une société.

articulate *a* [ârtik'yəlit] *(person)* qui s'exprime clairement et aisément; *(speech)* bien articulé(e), prononcé(e) clairement ◆ *vi* [ârtik'yəlāt] articuler, parler distinctement.

articulated lorry [ârtik'yəlātid lôr'ē] *n (Brit)* (camion *m*) semi-remorque *m*.

artifact [âr'təfakt] *n (US)* objet fabriqué.

artifice [âr'təfis] *n* ruse *f*.

artificial [ârtəfish'əl] *a* artificiel(le).

artificial insemination [ârtəfish'əl insemənā'shən] *n* insémination artificielle.

artificial intelligence (AI) *n* intelligence artificielle (IA).

artificial respiration *n* respiration artificielle.

artillery [ârtil'ûrē] *n* artillerie *f*.

artisan [âr'tizən] *n* artisan/e.

artist [âr'tist] *n* artiste *m/f*.

artistic [ârtis'tik] *a* artistique.

artistry [âr'tistrē] *n* art *m*, talent *m*.

artless [ârt'lis] *a* naïf(naïve), simple, ingénu(e).

arts [ârts] *npl (SCOL)* lettres *fpl*.

art school *n* ≃ école *f* des beaux-arts.

ARV *n abbr (= American Revised Version)* traduction américaine de la Bible.

AS *n abbr (US SCOL:* = *Associate in/of Science)* diplôme universitaire ◆ *abbr (US MAIL)* = American Samoa.

as [az] *cj (cause)* comme, puisque; *(time: moment)* alors que, comme; *(: duration)* tandis que; *(manner)* comme ◆ *prep (in the capacity of)* en tant que, en qualité de; **~ big ~** aussi grand que; **twice ~ big ~** deux fois plus grand que; **big ~ it is** si grand que ce soit; **much ~ I like them, I ...** je les aime bien, mais je ...; **~ the years went by** à mesure que les années passaient; **~ she said** comme elle l'avait dit; **he gave it to me ~ a present** il m'en a fait cadeau; **~ if** *or* **though** comme si; **~ for** *or* **to** en ce qui concerne, quant à; **~** *or* **so long ~** *cj* à condition que; **~ much/many (~)** autant (que); **~ soon ~** *cj* aussitôt que, dès que; **~ soon ~ possible** aussitôt *or* dès que possible; **~ such** *ad* en tant que tel(le); **~ well** *ad* aussi; **~ well ~** *cj* en plus de, en même temps que; *see also* **so, such**.

ASA *n abbr (= American Standards Association)* association de normalisation.

a.s.a.p. *abbr* = **as soon as possible**.

asbestos [asbes'təs] *n* asbeste *m*, amiante *m*.

ascend [əsend'] *vt* gravir.

ascendancy [əsen'dənsē] *n* ascendant *m*.

ascendant [əsen'dənt] *n*: **to be in the ~** monter.

ascension [əsen'shən] *n*: **the A~** *(REL)* l'Ascension *f*.

Ascension Island *n* île *f* de l'Ascension.

ascent [əsent'] *n* ascension *f*.

ascertain [asûrtān'] *vt* s'assurer de, vérifier; établir.

ascetic [əset'ik] *a* ascétique.

asceticism [əset'isizəm] *n* ascétisme *m*.

ASCII [as'kē] *n abbr (= American Standard Code for Information Interchange)* ASCII.

ascribe [əskrīb'] *vt*: **to ~ sth to** attribuer qch à; *(blame)* imputer qch à.

ASCU *n abbr (US)* = *Association of State Colleges and Universities*.

ASE *n abbr* = *American Stock Exchange*.

ash [ash] *n (dust)* cendre *f*; *(also: ~ tree)* frêne *m*.

ashamed [əshāmd'] *a* honteux(euse), confus(e); **to be ~ of** avoir honte de; **to be ~ (of o.s.) for having done** avoir honte d'avoir fait.

ashen [ash'ən] *a (pale)* cendreux(euse), blême.

ashore [əshôr'] *ad* à terre; **to go ~** aller à terre, débarquer.

ashtray [ash'trā] *n* cendrier *m*.

Ash Wednesday *n* mercredi *m* des Cendres.

Asia [ā'zhə] *n* Asie *f*.

Asia Minor *n* Asie Mineure.

Asian [ā'zhən] *n* Asiatique *m/f* ◆ *a* asiatique.

Asiatic [āzhēat'ik] *a* asiatique.

aside [əsīd'] *ad* de côté; à l'écart ◆ *n* aparté

m; ~ **from** *prep* à part, excepté.

ask [ask] *vt* demander; *(invite)* inviter; **to ~ sb sth/to do sth** demander à qn qch/de faire qch; **to ~ sb the time** demander l'heure à qn; **to ~ sb about sth** questionner qn au sujet de qch; se renseigner auprès de qn au sujet de qch; **to ~ about the price** s'informer du prix, se renseigner au sujet du prix; **to ~ (sb) a question** poser une question (à qn); **to ~ sb out to dinner** inviter qn au restaurant.

ask after *vt fus* demander des nouvelles de.

ask for *vt fus* demander; **it's just ~ing for trouble** *or* **for it** ce serait chercher des ennuis.

askance [əskans'] *ad*: **to look ~ at sb** regarder qn de travers *or* d'un œil désapprobateur.

askew [əskyōō'] *ad* de travers, de guinguois.

asking price [as'king prīs] *n* prix demandé.

asleep [əslēp'] *a* endormi(e); **to be ~** dormir, être endormi; **to fall ~** s'endormir.

asp [asp] *n* aspic *m*.

asparagus [əspar'əgəs] *n* asperges *fpl*.

asparagus tips *npl* pointes *fpl* d'asperges.

ASPCA *n abbr* (– *American Society for the Prevention of Cruelty to Animals*) ≈ SPA *f*.

aspect [as'pekt] *n* aspect *m*; *(direction in which a building etc faces)* orientation *f*, exposition *f*.

aspersions [əspûr'zhənz] *npl*: **to cast ~ on** dénigrer.

asphalt [as'fôlt] *n* asphalte *m*.

asphyxiate [asfik'sēāt] *vt* asphyxier.

asphyxiation [asfiksēā'shən] *n* asphyxie *f*.

aspirate *vt* [as'pûrāt] aspirer ♦ *a* [as'pûrit] aspiré(e).

aspiration [aspərā'shən] *n* aspiration *f*.

aspire [əspī'ûr] *vi*: **to ~ to** aspirer à.

aspirin [as'pûrin] *n* aspirine *f*.

ass [as] *n* âne *m*; *(col)* imbécile *m/f*; *(US col!)* cul *m* (*!*); **kiss my ~!** *(US col!)* va te faire foutre (*!*).

assail [əsāl'] *vt* assaillir.

assailant [əsā'lənt] *n* agresseur *m*; assaillant *m*.

assassin [əsas'in] *n* assassin *m*.

assassinate [əsas'ənāt] *vt* assassiner.

assassination [əsasinā'shən] *n* assassinat *m*.

assault [əsôlt'] *n* (*MIL*) assaut *m*; *(gen: attack)* agression *f*; *(LAW)*: **~ (and battery)** voies *fpl* de fait, coups *mpl* et blessures *fpl* ♦ *vt* attaquer; *(sexually)* violenter.

assemble [əsem'bəl] *vt* assembler ♦ *vi* s'assembler, se rassembler.

assembly [əsem'blē] *n* *(meeting)* rassemblement *m*; *(construction)* assemblage *m*.

assembly language *n* (*COMPUT*) langage *m* d'assemblage.

assembly line *n* chaîne *f* de montage.

assent [əsent'] *n* assentiment *m*, consentement *m* ♦ *vi*: **to ~ (to sth)** donner son assentiment (à qch), consentir (à qch).

assert [əsûrt'] *vt* affirmer, déclarer; établir; **to ~ o.s.** s'imposer.

assertion [əsûr'shən] *n* assertion *f*, affirmation *f*.

assertive [əsûr'tiv] *a* assuré(e); péremptoire.

assess [əses'] *vt* évaluer, estimer; *(tax, damages)* établir *or* fixer le montant de; *(property*

etc: for tax) calculer la valeur imposable de.

assessment [əses'mənt] *n* évaluation *f*, estimation *f*; *(judgment)*: **~ (of)** jugement *m or* opinion *f* (sur).

assessor [əses'ûr] *n* expert *m* *(en matière d'impôt et d'assurance)*.

asset [as'et] *n* avantage *m*, atout *m*; *(person)* atout; **~s** *npl* (*COMM*) capital *m*; avoir(s) *m(pl)*; actif *m*.

asset-stripping [as'etstriping] *n* (*COMM*) récupération *f* (et démantèlement *m*) d'une entreprise en difficulté.

assiduous [əsij'ōōəs] *a* assidu(e).

assign [əsīn'] *vt* *(date)* fixer, arrêter; *(task)*: **to ~ sth to** assigner qch à; *(resources)*: **to ~ sth to** affecter qch à; *(cause, meaning)*: **to ~ sth to** attribuer qch à.

assignment [əsīn'mənt] *n* tâche *f*, mission *f*; *(SCOL)* devoir *m*.

assimilate [əsim'əlāt] *vt* assimiler.

assimilation [əsiməlā'shən] *n* assimilation *f*.

assist [əsist'] *vt* aider, assister; *(injured person etc)* secourir.

assistance [əsis'təns] *n* aide *f*, assistance *f*; secours *mpl*.

assistant [əsis'tənt] *n* assistant/e, adjoint/e; *(Brit: also:* **shop ~**) vendeur/euse.

assistant manager *n* sous-directeur *m*.

assizes [əsī'ziz] *npl* assises *fpl*.

associate *a, n* [əsō'shēit] associé(e) ♦ *vb* [əsō'shēāt] *vt* associer ♦ *vi*: **to ~ with sb** fréquenter qn; **~ director** directeur adjoint; **~d company** société affiliée.

association [əsōsēā'shən] *n* association *f*; **in ~ with** en collaboration avec.

association football *n* (*Brit*) football *m*.

assorted [əsôr'tid] *a* assorti(e); **in ~ sizes** en plusieurs tailles.

assortment [əsôrt'mənt] *n* assortiment *m*.

Asst. *abbr* = **assistant**.

assuage [əswāj'] *vt* *(grief, pain)* soulager; *(thirst, appetite)* assouvir.

assume [əsōōm'] *vt* supposer; *(responsibilities etc)* assumer; *(attitude, name)* prendre, adopter.

assumed name [əsōōmd' nām'] *n* nom *m* d'emprunt.

assumption [əsump'shən] *n* supposition *f*, hypothèse *f*; **on the ~ that** dans l'hypothèse où; *(on condition that)* à condition que.

assurance [əshōōr'əns] *n* assurance *f*; **I can give you no ~s** je ne peux rien vous garantir.

assure [əshōōr'] *vt* assurer.

AST *abbr* (*US:* = *Atlantic Standard Time*) heure d'hiver de la Nouvelle-Écosse.

asterisk [as'tûrisk] *n* astérisque *m*.

astern [əstûrn'] *ad* à l'arrière.

asteroid [as'təroid] *n* astéroïde *m*.

asthma [az'mə] *n* asthme *m*.

asthmatic [azmat'ik] *a, n* asthmatique *(m/f)*.

astigmatism [əstig'mətizəm] *n* astigmatisme *m*.

astir [əstûr'] *ad* en émoi.

ASTM *abbr* = *American Society for Testing Materials*.

astonish [əstân'ish] *vt* étonner, stupéfier.

astonishing [əstân'ishing] *a* étonnant(e), stupéfiant(e); **I find it ~ that** ... je trouve incroyable que ....

astonishingly [əstân'ishinglē] *ad* incroyablement.

astonishment [əstân'ishmənt] *n* (grand) étonnement, stupéfaction *f*.

astound [əstound'] *vt* stupéfier, sidérer.

astray [əstrā'] *ad*: **to go ~** s'égarer; (*fig*) quitter le droit chemin; **to go ~ in one's calculations** faire fausse route dans ses calculs.

astride [əstrīd'] *ad* à cheval ♦ *prep* à cheval sur.

astringent [əstrin'jənt] *a* astringent(e) ♦ *n* astringent *m*.

astrologer [astrâl'əjûr] *n* astrologue *m*.

astrology [əstrâl'əjē] *n* astrologie *f*.

astronaut [as'trənôt] *n* astronaute *m/f*.

astronomer [əstrân'əmûr] *n* astronome *m*.

astronomical [astrənâm'ikəl] *a* astronomique.

astronomy [əstrân'əmē] *n* astronomie *f*.

astrophysics [astrōfiz'iks] *n* astrophysique *f*.

astute [əstōōt'] *a* astucieux(euse), malin(igne).

asunder [əsun'dûr] *ad*: **to tear ~** déchirer.

ASV *n abbr* (= *American Standard Version*) traduction de la Bible.

asylum [əsi'ləm] *n* asile *m*; **to seek political ~** demander l'asile politique.

asymmetric(al) [āsəmet'rik(əl)] *a* asymétrique.

at [at] *prep* à; (*because of: following surprised, annoyed etc*) de; par; **~ the top** au sommet; **~ Pierre's** chez Pierre; **~ the baker's** chez le boulanger, à la boulangerie; **~ times** parfois; **~ 4 o'clock** à 4 heures; **~ night** la nuit; (*in the evening*) le soir; **~ $1 a kilo** un dollar le kilo; **two ~ a time** deux à la fois; **~ full speed** à toute vitesse.

ate [āt] *pt of* **eat**.

atheism [ā'thēizəm] *n* athéisme *m*.

atheist [ā'thēist] *n* athée *m/f*.

Athenian [əthē'nēən] *a* athénien(ne) ♦ *n* Athénien/ne.

Athens [ath'ənz] *n* Athènes.

athlete [ath'lēt] *n* athlète *m/f*.

athletic [athlet'ik] *a* athlétique.

athletics [athlet'iks] *n* athlétisme *m*.

Atlantic [atlan'tik] *a* atlantique ♦ *n*: **the ~ (Ocean)** l'Atlantique *m*, l'océan *m* Atlantique.

atlas [at'ləs] *n* atlas *m*.

Atlas Mountains *npl*: **the ~** les monts *mpl* de l'Atlas, l'Atlas *m*.

A.T.M. *abbr* (= *Automated Teller Machine*) guichet *m* automatique.

atmosphere [at'məsfēr] *n* atmosphère *f*; (*air*) air *m*.

atmospheric [atməsfär'ik] *a* atmosphérique.

atmospherics [atməsfär'iks] *n* (*RADIO*) parasites *mpl*.

atoll [at'ôl] *n* atoll *m*.

atom [at'əm] *n* atome *m*.

atomic [ətâm'ik] *a* atomique.

atom(ic) bomb *n* bombe *f* atomique.

atomizer [at'əmīzûr] *n* atomiseur *m*.

atone [ətōn'] *vi*: **to ~ for** expier, racheter.

atonement [ətōn'mənt] *n* expiation *f*.

ATP *n abbr* (= *Association of Tennis Professionals*) ATP *f* (= *Association des tennismen professionnels*).

atrocious [ətrō'shəs] *a* (*very bad*) atroce, exécrable.

atrocity [ətrâs'itē] *n* atrocité *f*.

atrophy [at'rəfē] *n* atrophie *f* ♦ *vt* atrophier ♦ *vi* s'atrophier.

attach [ətach'] *vt* (*gen*) attacher; (*document, letter*) joindre; (*employee, troops*) affecter; **to be ~ed to sb/sth** (*to like*) être attaché à qn/qch; **the ~ed letter** la lettre ci-jointe.

attaché [atashā'] *n* attaché *m*.

attaché case *n* mallette *f*, attaché-case *m*.

attachment [ətach'mənt] *n* (*tool*) accessoire *m*; (*love*): **~ (to)** affection *f* (pour), attachement *m* (à).

attack [ətak'] *vt* attaquer; (*task etc*) s'attaquer à ♦ *n* attaque *f*; (*also*: **heart ~**) crise *f* cardiaque.

attacker [ətak'ûr] *n* attaquant *m*; agresseur *m*.

attain [ətān'] *vt* (*also*: **to ~ to**) parvenir à, atteindre; acquérir.

attainments [ətān'mənts] *npl* connaissances *fpl*, résultats *mpl*.

attempt [ətempt'] *n* tentative *f* ♦ *vt* essayer, tenter; **~ed theft** *etc* (*LAW*) tentative de vol *etc*; **to make an ~ on sb's life** attenter à la vie de qn; **he made no ~ to help** il n'a rien fait pour m'aider (*or* l'aider *etc*).

attend [ətend'] *vt* (*course*) suivre; (*meeting, talk*) assister à; (*school, church*) aller à, fréquenter; (*patient*) soigner, s'occuper de; **to ~ (up)on** servir; être au service de.

attend to *vt fus* (*needs, affairs etc*) s'occuper de; (*customer*) s'occuper de, servir.

attendance [əten'dəns] *n* (*being present*) présence *f*; (*people present*) assistance *f*.

attendant [əten'dənt] *n* employé/e; gardien/ne ♦ *a* concomitant(e), qui accompagne *or* s'ensuit.

attention [əten'shən] *n* attention *f*; **~s** attentions *fpl*, prévenances *fpl*; **~!** (*MIL*) garde-à-vous!; **at ~** (*MIL*) au garde-à-vous; **for the ~ of** (*ADMIN*) à l'attention de; **it has come to my ~ that ...** je constate que ....

attentive [əten'tiv] *a* attentif(ive); (*kind*) prévenant(e).

attentively [əten'tivlē] *ad* attentivement, avec attention.

attenuate [əten'yōōāt] *vt* atténuer ♦ *vi* s'atténuer.

attest [ətest'] *vi*: **to ~ to** témoigner de, attester (de).

attic [at'ik] *n* grenier *m*, combles *mpl*.

attire [ətīûr'] *n* habit *m*, atours *mpl*.

attitude [at'ətōōd] *n* (*behavior*) attitude *f*, manière *f*; (*posture*) pose *f*, attitude; (*view*): **~ (to)** attitude (envers).

attorney [ətûr'nē] *n* (*US: lawyer*) avocat *m*; (*having proxy*) mandataire *m*; **power of ~** procuration *f*.

Attorney General *n* (*US*) ≈ garde *m* des Sceaux, ministre *m* de la Justice; (*Brit*) procureur général.

attract [ətrakt'] *vt* attirer.

attraction [ətrak'shən] *n* (*gen pl: pleasant things*) attraction *f*, attrait *m*; (*PHYSICS*) attraction; (*fig: towards sth*) attirance *f*.

attractive [ətrak'tiv] *a* séduisant(e), attrayant(e).

attribute *n* [at'rəbyōōt] attribut *m* ♦ *vt* [ətrib'yōōt]: **to ~ sth to** attribuer qch à.

attrition [ətrish'ən] *n*: **war of ~** guerre *f* d'usure.

atty *abbr* (*US*) = **attorney**.

Atty. Gen. *abbr* = **Attorney General.**

ATV *n abbr* (= *all terrain vehicle*) véhicule *m* tout-terrain.

aubergine [ō'bûrzhēn] *n* aubergine *f*.

auburn [ô'bûrn] *a* auburn *inv*, châtain roux *inv*.

auction [ôk'shən] *n* (*also*: **sale by ~**) vente *f* aux enchères ♦ *vt* (*also*: **to sell by ~**) vendre aux enchères; (*also*: **to put up for ~**) mettre aux enchères.

auctioneer [ôkshənēr'] *n* commissaire-priseur *m*.

auction room *n* salle *f* des ventes.

aud. *abbr* = **audit; auditor.**

audacious [ôdā'shəs] *a* impudent(e); audacieux(euse), intrépide.

audacity [ôdas'itē] *n* impudence *f*; audace *f*.

audible [ôd'əbəl] *a* audible.

audience [ôd'ēəns] *n* (*people*) assistance *f*, auditoire *m*; auditeurs *mpl*; spectateurs *mpl*; (*interview*) audience *f*.

audiovisual [ôd'ēōvizh'ōōəl] *a* audiovisuel(le); **~ aids** supports *or* moyens audiovisuels.

audit [ôd'it] *n* vérification *f* des comptes, apurement *m* ♦ *vt* vérifier, apurer.

audition [ôdish'ən] *n* audition *f* ♦ *vi* auditionner.

auditor [ô'ditûr] *n* vérificateur *m* des comptes; (*US*: *SCOL*) auditeur/trice libre.

auditorium [ôditôr'ēəm] *n* auditorium *m*, salle *f* de concert *or* de spectacle; (*US*: *SCOL*) ampithéâtre *m*.

Aug. *abbr* = **August.**

augment [ôgment'] *vt, vi* augmenter.

augur [ô'gûr] *vt* (*be a sign of*) présager, annoncer ♦ *vi*: **it ~s well** c'est bon signe *or* de bon augure, cela s'annonce bien.

August [ôg'əst] *n* août *m*; *for phrases see also* **July.**

august [ôgust'] *a* majestueux(euse), imposant(e).

aunt [ant] *n* tante *f*.

auntie, aunty [an'tē] *n dimunutive of* **aunt.**

au pair [ô pär'] *n* (*also*: **~ girl**) jeune fille *f* au pair.

aura [ô'rə] *n* atmosphère *f*.

auspices [ôs'pisiz] *npl*: **under the ~ of** sous les auspices de.

auspicious [ôspish'əs] *a* de bon augure, propice.

austere [ôstēr'] *a* austère.

austerity [ôstär'itē] *n* austérité *f*.

Australasia [ôstrəlā'zhə] *n* Australasie *f*.

Australia [ôstrāl'yə] *n* Australie *f*.

Australian [ôstrāl'yən] *a* australien(ne) ♦ *n* Australien/ne.

Austria [ôs'trēə] *n* Autriche *f*.

Austrian [ôs'trēən] *a* autrichien(ne) ♦ *n* Autrichien/ne.

authentic [ôthen'tik] *a* authentique.

authenticate [ôthen'tikāt] *vt* établir l'authenticité de.

authenticity [ôthəntis'itē] *n* authenticité *f*.

author [ô'thûr] *n* auteur *m*.

authoritarian [əthôritär'ēən] *a* autoritaire.

authoritative [əthôr'itātiv] *a* (*account*) digne de foi; (*study, treatise*) qui fait autorité; (*manner*) autoritaire.

authority [əthôr'itē] *n* autorité *f*; (*permission*) autorisation (formelle); **the authorities** les autorités, l'administration *f*; **to have ~ to do sth** être habilité à faire qch.

authorization [ôthûrəzā'shən] *n* autorisation *f*.

authorize [ô'thərīz] *vt* autoriser.

authorized capital [ô'thərīzd kap'ətəl] *n* (*COMM*) capital social.

authorship [ô'thûrship] *n* paternité *f* (*littéraire etc*).

autistic [ôtis'tik] *a* autistique.

autobiography [ôtəbīāg'rəfē] *n* autobiographie *f*.

autocratic [ôtəkrat'ik] *a* autocratique.

autograph [ô'təgraf] *n* autographe *m* ♦ *vt* signer, dédicacer.

automat [ô'təmat] *n* (*vending machine*) distributeur *m* (automatique); (*US*: *place*) cafétéria *f* avec distributeurs automatiques.

automated [ô'təmātid] *a* automatisé(e).

automatic [ôtəmat'ik] *a* automatique ♦ *n* (*gun*) automatique *m*; (*washing machine*) lave-linge *m* automatique; (*AUT*) voiture *f* à transmission automatique.

automatically [ôtəmat'iklē] *ad* automatiquement.

automatic data processing (ADP) *n* traitement *m* automatique des données.

automation [ôtəmā'shən] *n* automatisation *f*.

automaton, pl automata [ôtâm'ətân, tə] *n* automate *m*.

automobile [ôtəməbēl'] *n* (*US*) automobile *f*.

autonomous [ôtân'əməs] *a* autonome.

autonomy [ôtân'əmē] *n* autonomie *f*.

autopsy [ô'tâpsē] *n* autopsie *f*.

autumn [ô'təm] *n* automne *m*.

auxiliary [ôgzil'yûrē] *a*, *n* auxiliaire (*m/f*).

AV *n abbr* (= *Authorized Version*) traduction anglaise de la Bible ♦ *abbr* = **audiovisual.**

Av. *abbr* (= *avenue*) Av.

avail [əvāl'] *vt*: **to ~ o.s. of** user de; profiter de ♦ *n*: **to no ~** sans résultat, en vain, en pure perte.

availability [əvāləbil'ətē] *n* disponibilité *f*.

available [əvā'ləbəl] *a* disponible; **every ~ means** tous les moyens possibles *or* à sa (*or* notre *etc*) disposition; **is the manager ~?** est-ce que le directeur peut (me) recevoir?; (*on phone*) pourrais-je parler au directeur?; **to make sth ~ to sb** mettre qch à la disposition de qn.

avalanche [av'əlanch] *n* avalanche *f*.

avant-garde [avântgârd'] *a* d'avant-garde.

avaricious [avərish'əs] *a* âpre au gain.

avdp. *abbr* = *avoirdupois*.

Ave. *abbr* (= *avenue*) Av.

avenge [əvenj'] *vt* venger.

avenue [av'ənōō] *n* avenue *f*.

average [av'ûrij] *n* moyenne *f* ♦ *a* moyen(ne) ♦ *vt* (*a certain figure*) atteindre *or* faire *etc* en moyenne; **on (the) ~** en moyenne; **above/below (the) ~** au-dessus/en-dessous de la moyenne.

average out *vi*: **to ~ out at** représenter en moyenne, donner une moyenne de.

averse [əvûrs'] *a*: **to be ~ to sth/doing** éprouver une forte répugnance envers qch/à faire; **I wouldn't be ~ to a drink** un petit verre ne serait pas de refus, je ne dirais pas non à un petit verre.

aversion [əvûr'zhən] *n* aversion *f*, répugnance *f*.

avert [əvûrt'] *vt* prévenir, écarter; *(one's eyes)* détourner.

aviary [ā'vēārē] *n* volière *f*.

aviation [āvēā'shən] *n* aviation *f*.

avid [av'id] *a* avide.

avidly [av'idlē] *ad* avidement, avec avidité.

avocado [avəkád'ō] *n* avocat *m*.

avoid [əvoid'] *vt* éviter.

avoidable [əvoid'əbəl] *a* évitable.

avoidance [əvoid'əns] *n le fait d'éviter.*

avowed [əvoud'] *a* déclaré(e).

AVP *n abbr* (*US*) = *assistant vice-president.*

AWACS [ā'waks] *n abbr* (= *airborne warning and control system*) AWACS *(système aéroporté d'alerte et de contrôle).*

await [əwāt'] *vt* attendre; **~ing attention/ delivery** *(COMM)* en souffrance; **long ~ed** tant attendu(e).

awake [əwāk'] *a* éveillé(e); *(fig)* en éveil ♦ *vb* (*pt* **awoke** [əwōk'], *pp* **awaked**, **awoken** [əwō'kən]) *vt* éveiller ♦ *vi* s'éveiller; **~ to** conscient de; **he was still ~** il ne dormait pas encore.

awakening [əwā'kəning] *n* réveil *m*.

award [əwôrd'] *n* récompense *f*, prix *m* ♦ *vt* (*prize*) décerner; (*LAW*: *damages*) accorder.

aware [əwär'] *a*: **~ of** (*conscious*) conscient(e) de; (*informed*) au courant de; **to become ~ of** avoir conscience de, prendre conscience de; se rendre compte de; **politically/socially ~** sensibilisé(e) aux *or* ayant pris conscience des problèmes politiques/sociaux; **I am fully ~ that** je me rends parfaitement compte que.

awareness [əwär'nis] *n* conscience *f*, connaissance *f*; **to develop people's ~ (of)** sensibiliser le public (à).

awash [əwâsh'] *a* recouvert(e) (d'eau); **~ with** inondé(e) de.

away [əwā'] *a*, *ad* (au) loin; absent(e); **two kilometers ~** à (une distance de) deux kilomètres, à deux kilomètres de distance; **two hours ~ by car** à deux heures de voiture *or* de route; **the vacation was two weeks ~** il restait deux semaines jusqu'aux vacances; **~ from** loin de; **he's ~ for a week** il est parti (pour) une semaine; **he's ~ in Milan** il est (parti) à Milan; **to take ~** *vt* emporter; **to pedal/work/laugh** *etc* **~** *la particule indique la constance et l'énergie de l'action*: il pédalait *etc* tant qu'il pouvait; **to fade/wither** *etc* **~** *la particule renforce l'idée de la disparition, l'éloignement.*

away game *n* (*SPORT*) match *m* à l'extérieur.

awe [ô] *n* respect mêlé de crainte, effroi mêlé d'admiration.

awe-inspiring [ô'inspīúring], **awesome** [ô'səm] *a* impressionnant(e).

awestruck [ô'struk] *a* frappé(e) d'effroi.

awful [ô'fəl] *a* affreux(euse); **an ~ lot of** énormément de.

awfully [ô'fəlē] *ad* (*very*) terriblement, vraiment.

awhile [əhwīl'] *ad* un moment, quelque temps.

awkward [ôk'wûrd] *a* (*clumsy*) gauche, maladroit(e); (*inconvenient*) malaisé(e), d'emploi malaisé, peu pratique; (*embarrassing*) gênant(e), délicat(e); (*difficult: problem, task*) délicat, difficile.

awkwardness [ôk'wûrdnis] *n* (*embarrassment*) gêne *f*.

awl [ôl] *n* alêne *f*.

awning [ô'ning] *n* (*of tent*) auvent *m*; (*of store*) store *m*; (*of hotel etc*) marquise *f* (de toile).

awoke [əwōk'] *pt of* **awake**.

awoken [əwō'kən] *pp of* **awake**.

AWOL [ā'wôl] *abbr* (*MIL*) = *absent without leave.*

awry [ərī'] *ad*, *a* de travers; **to go ~** mal tourner.

ax, (*Brit*) **axe** [aks] *n* hache *f* ♦ *vt* (*employee*) renvoyer; (*project etc*) abandonner; (*jobs*) supprimer; **to have an ~ to grind** (*fig*) prêcher pour son saint.

axes [ak'sēz] *npl of* **axis**.

axiom [ak'sēəm] *n* axiome *m*.

axiomatic [aksēəmat'ik] *a* axiomatique.

axis, *pl* **axes** [ak'sis, -sēz] *n* axe *m*.

axle [ak'səl] *n* (*also:* **~-tree**) essieu *m*.

ay(e) [ī'] *excl* (*yes*) oui ♦ *n*: **the ~s** les oui.

AYH *n abbr* = *American Youth Hostels.*

AZ *abbr* (*US MAIL*) = *Arizona.*

azalea [əzāl'yə] *n* azalée *f*.

Azores [əzôrz'] *npl*: **the ~** les Açores *fpl.*

Aztec [az'tek] *a* aztèque ♦ *n* Aztèque *m/f.*

azure [azh'ûr] *a* azuré(e).

B

B, b [bē] *n* (*letter*) B, b *m*; (*SCOL*: *mark*) B; (*MUS*): **B** si *m*; **B for Baker** B comme Berthe; **B road** *n* (*Brit AUT*) route départementale.

b. *abbr* = *born.*

BA *n abbr* (*SCOL*) = *Bachelor of Arts.*

babble [bab'əl] *vi* babiller ♦ *n* babillage *m.*

baboon [babōōn'] *n* babouin *m.*

baby [bā'bē] *n* bébé *m.*

baby buggy [bā'bē bug'ē] *n* voiture *f* d'enfant.

baby carriage *n* (*US*) voiture *f* d'enfant.

baby grand *n* (*also:* **~ piano**) (piano *m*) demi-queue *m.*

babyhood [bā'bēhōōd] *n* petite enfance.

babyish [bā'bēish] *a* enfantin(e), de bébé.

baby-minder [bā'bēmīndûr] *n* (*Brit*) gardienne *f* (d'enfants).

baby-sit [bā'bēsit] *vi* garder les enfants.

baby-sitter [bā'bēsitûr] *n* baby-sitter *m/f.*

bachelor [bach'əlûr] *n* célibataire *m*; **B~ of Arts/Science (BA/BSc)** ≈ licencié/e ès *or* en lettres/sciences; **B~ of Arts/Science degree**

(BA/BSc) *n* ≈ licence *f* ès *or* en lettres/sciences.
bachelorhood [bach'əlûrhōōd] *n* célibat *m*.
bachelor party *n* (*US*) enterrement *m* de vie de garçon.
back [bak] *n* (*of person, horse*) dos *m*; (*of hand*) dos, revers *m*; (*of house*) derrière *m*; (*of car, train*) arrière *m*; (*of chair*) dossier *m*; (*of page*) verso *m*; (*SPORT*) arrière *m*; **to have one's ~ to the wall** (*fig*) être au pied du mur; **~ to front** à l'envers ♦ *vt* (*financially*) soutenir (financièrement); (*candidate*: *also*: **~ up**) soutenir, appuyer; (*horse*: *at races*) parier *or* miser sur; (*car*) (faire) reculer ♦ *vi* reculer; (*car etc*) faire marche arrière ♦ *a* (*in compounds*) de derrière, à l'arrière; **~ seats/wheels** (*AUT*) sièges *mpl*/roues *fpl* arrière; **~ payments/rent** arriéré *m* de paiements/loyer; **~ garden/room** jardin/pièce sur l'arrière; **to take a ~ seat** (*fig*) se contenter d'un second rôle, être relégué(e) au second plan ♦ *ad* (*not forward*) en arrière; (*returned*): **he's ~** il est rentré, il est de retour; **when will you be ~?** quand seras-tu de retour?; **he ran ~** il est revenu en courant; (*restitution*): **throw the ball ~** renvoie la balle; **can I have it ~?** puis-je le ravoir?, peux tu me le rendre?; (*again*): **he called ~** il a rappelé.
back down *vi* rabattre de ses prétentions.
back on to *vt fus*: **the house ~s on to the golf course** la maison donne derrière sur le terrain de golf.
back out *vi* (*of promise*) se dédire.
back up *vt* (*COMPUT*) faire une copie de sauvegarde de.
backache [bak'āk] *n* maux *mpl* de reins.
backbencher [bak'benchûr] *n* (*Brit*) membre du parlement sans portefeuille.
backbiting [bak'bīting] *n* médisance(s) *f(pl)*.
backbone [bak'bōn] *n* colonne vertébrale, épine dorsale; **he's the ~ of the organization** c'est sur lui que repose l'organisation.
back burner *n*: **to put sth on the ~** mettre qch en veilleuse *or* en attente.
backcomb [bak'kōm] *vt* (*Brit*) crêper.
backdate [bakdāt'] *vt* (*letter*) antidater; **~d pay raise** augmentation *f* avec effet rétroactif.
backdrop [bak'dräp] *n* toile *f* de fond.
backer [bak'ûr] *n* partisan *m*; (*COMM*) commanditaire *m*.
backfire [bak'fiûr] *vi* (*AUT*) pétarader; (*plans*) mal tourner.
backgammon [bak'gamən] *n* trictrac *m*.
background [bak'ground] *n* arrière-plan *m*; (*of events*) situation *f*, conjoncture *f*; (*basic knowledge*) éléments *mpl* de base; (*experience*) formation *f* ♦ *cpd* (*noise, music*) de fond; **~ reading** lecture(s) générale(s) (sur un sujet); **family ~** milieu familial.
backhand [bak'hand] *n* (*TENNIS*: *also*: **~hand stroke**) revers *m*.
backhanded [bak'handid] *a* (*fig*) déloyal(e); équivoque.
backhander [bak'handûr] *n* (*Brit*: *bribe*) pot-de-vin *m*.
backing [bak'ing] *n* (*fig*) soutien *m*, appui *m*; (*COMM*) soutien (financier); (*MUS*) accompa-

gnement *m*.
backlash [bak'lash] *n* contre-coup *m*, répercussion *f*.
backlog [bak'lôg] *n*: **~ of work** travail *m* en retard.
back number *n* (*of magazine etc*) vieux numéro.
backpack [bak'pak] *n* sac *m* à dos.
backpacker [bak'pakûr] *n* randonneur/euse.
back pay *n* rappel *m* de salaire.
backpedal [bak'pedəl] *vi* (*fig*) faire marche arrière.
backside [bak'sīd] *n* (*col*) derrière *m*, postérieur *m*.
backslash [bak'slash] *n* barre oblique inversée.
backslide [bak'slīd] *vi* retomber dans l'erreur.
backspace [bak'spās] *vi* (*in typing*) appuyer sur la touche retour.
backstage [bak'stāj'] *ad* dans les coulisses.
back-street [bak'strēt] *a* (*abortion*) clandestin(e); **~ abortionist** avorteur/euse (clandestin).
backstroke [bak'strōk] *n* dos crawlé.
backtalk [bak'tôk] *n* (*col*) impertinences *fpl*.
backtrack [bak'trak] *vi* (*Brit fig*) = **backpedal**.
backup [bak'up] *a* (*train, plane*) supplémentaire, de réserve; (*COMPUT*) de sauvegarde ♦ *n* (*support*) appui *m*, soutien *m*; (*COMPUT*: *also*: **~ file**) sauvegarde *f*.
back-up lights [bak'up līts] *npl* (*US AUT*) feux *mpl* de marche arrière *or* de recul.
backward [bak'wûrd] *a* (*movement*) en arrière; (*measure*) rétrograde; (*person, country*) arriéré(e); attardé(e); (*shy*) hésitant(e); **~ and forward movement** mouvement de va-et-vient.
backwards [bak'wûrdz] *ad* (*move, go*) en arrière; (*read a list*) à l'envers, à rebours; (*fall*) à la renverse; (*walk*) à reculons; (*in time*) en arrière, vers le passé; **to know sth ~ and forwards** *or* (*Brit*) **~** (*col*) connaître qch sur le bout des doigts.
backwater [bak'wôtûr] *n* (*fig*) coin reculé; bled perdu.
backyard [bak'yârd] *n* arrière-cour *f*.
bacon [bā'kən] *n* bacon *m*, lard *m*.
bacteria [baktē'reə] *npl* bactéries *fpl*.
bacteriology [baktēreāl'əjē] *n* bactériologie *f*.
bad [bad] *a* mauvais(e); (*child*) vilain(e); (*meat, food*) gâté(e), avarié(e); **his ~ leg** sa jambe malade; **to go ~** (*meat, food*) se gâter; (*milk*) tourner; **to have a ~ time of it** traverser une mauvaise passe; **I feel ~ about it** (*guilty*) j'ai un peu mauvaise conscience; **~ debt** créance douteuse; **in ~ faith** de mauvaise foi.
bade [bad] *pt of* **bid**.
bad feeling *n* ressentiment *m*, rancune *f*.
badge [baj] *n* insigne *m*; (*of policeman*) plaque *f*; (*stick-on, sew-on*) badge *m*.
badger [baj'ûr] *n* blaireau *m* ♦ *vt* harceler.
badly [bad'lē] *ad* (*work, dress etc*) mal; **~ wounded** grièvement blessé; **he needs it ~** il en a absolument besoin; **things are going ~** les choses vont mal; **~ off** *a*, *ad* dans la gêne.
bad-mannered [badman'ûrd] *a* mal élevé(e).
badminton [bad'mintən] *n* badminton *m*.
bad-mouth [bad'mouth'] *vt* (*US*) critiquer, dé-

nigrer.

bad-smelling [bad'sme'ling] *a* malodorant(e).

bad-tempered [had'tem'pûrd] *a* (*by nature*) ayant mauvais caractère; (*on one occasion*) de mauvaise humeur.

baffle [baf'əl] *vt* (*puzzle*) déconcerter.

baffling [baf'ling] *a* déroutant(e), déconcertant(e).

bag [bag] *n* sac *m*; (*of hunter*) gibecière *f*, chasse *f* ♦ *vt* (*col: take*) empocher; s'approprier; (*TECH*) mettre en sacs; ~s of (*col: lots of*) des masses de; **to pack one's ~s** faire ses valises *or* bagages; **~s under the eyes** poches *fpl* sous les yeux.

bagful [bag'fal] *n* plein sac.

baggage [bag'ij] *n* bagages *mpl*.

baggage check *n* bulletin *m* de consigne.

baggage claim *n* (*at airport*) livraison *f* des bagages.

baggy [bag'ē] *a* avachi(e), qui fait des poches.

Baghdad [bag'dad] *n* Baghdâd, Bagdad.

bagpipes [bag'pīps] *npl* cornemuse *f*.

bag-snatcher [bag'snachûr] *n* (*Brit*) voleur *m* à l'arraché.

Bahamas [bəham'əz] *npl*: **the** ~ les Bahamas *fpl*.

Bahrain [bârân'] *n* Bahreïn *m*.

bail [bāl] *n* caution *f* ♦ *vt* (*prisoner: also:* **grant** ~ **to**) mettre en liberté sous caution; (*boat: also:* ~ **out**) écoper; **to be released on** ~ être libéré(e) sous caution.

bail out *vt* (*prisoner*) payer la caution de; (*NAUT: water, boat*) écoper ♦ *vi* (*of a plane*) sauter en parachute.

bailiff [bā'lif] *n* huissier *m*.

bait [bāt] *n* appât *m* ♦ *vt* appâter; (*fig*) tourmenter.

bake [bāk] *vt* (*faire*) cuire au four ♦ *vi* (*bread etc*) cuire (au four); (*make cakes etc*) faire de la pâtisserie.

baked beans [bākt bēnz] *npl* haricots blancs à la sauce tomate.

baker [bā'kûr] *n* boulanger *m*.

bakery [bā'kûrē] *n* boulangerie *f*; boulangerie industrielle.

baking [bā'king] *n* cuisson *f*.

baking dish, baking pan *n* (*US*) plat *m* pour le four.

baking powder *n* levure *f* (chimique).

baking sheet *n* plaque *f* à gâteaux.

baking tin *n* (*Brit: for cake*) moule *m* à gâteaux; (: *for meat*) plat *m* pour le four.

baking tray *n* (*Brit*) = **baking sheet**.

balaclava [baləklâv'ə] *n* (*also:* ~ **helmet**) passe-montagne *m*.

balance [bal'əns] *n* équilibre *m*; (*COMM: sum*) solde *m*; (*scales*) balance *f* ♦ *vt* mettre *or* faire tenir en équilibre; (*pros and cons*) peser; (*budget*) équilibrer; (*account*) balancer; (*compensate*) compenser, contrebalancer; ~ **of trade/payments** balance commerciale/des comptes *or* paiements; ~ **carried forward** solde *m* à reporter; ~ **brought forward** solde reporté; **to** ~ **the books** arrêter les comptes, dresser le bilan.

balanced [bal'ənst] *a* (*personality, diet*) équilibré(e).

balance sheet *n* bilan *m*.

balance wheel *n* balancier *m*.

balcony [bal'kənē] *n* balcon *m*; **first** ~ (*US*) premier balcon.

bald [bôld] *a* chauve; (*tire*) lisse.

baldness [bôld'nis] *n* calvitie *f*.

bale [bāl] *n* balle *f*, ballot *m*.

bale out (*Brit*) *vi* (*of a plane*) sauter en parachute ♦ *vt* (*NAUT: water, boat*) écoper.

Balearic Islands [balēār'ək ī'ləndz] *npl*: **the** ~ les (îles *fpl*) Baléares.

baleful [bāl'fəl] *a* funeste, maléfique.

balk [bôk] *vi*: **to** ~ (**at**) (*person*) regimber (contre); (*horse*) se dérober (devant).

Balkan [bôl'kən] *a* balkanique ♦ *n*: **the** ~**s** les Balkans *mpl*.

ball [bôl] *n* boule *f*; (*football*) ballon *m*; (*for tennis, golf*) balle *f*; (*dance*) bal *m*; **to play** ~ (**with sb**) jouer au ballon (*or* à la balle) (avec qn); (*fig*) coopérer (avec qn); **to be on the** ~ (*fig: competent*) être à la hauteur; (: *alert*) être éveillé(e), être vif(vive); **to start the** ~ **rolling** (*fig*) commencer; **the** ~ **is in their court** (*fig*) la balle est dans leur camp.

ballad [bal'əd] *n* ballade *f*.

ballast [bal'əst] *n* lest *m*.

ball bearing *n* roulement *m* à billes.

ball cock *n* robinet *m* à flotteur.

ballerina [balərē'nə] *n* ballerine *f*.

ballet [balā'] *n* ballet *m*; (*art*) danse *f* (classique).

ballet dancer *n* danseur/euse de ballet.

ballistic [bəlis'tik] *a* balistique.

ballistics [bəlis'tiks] *n* balistique *f*.

balloon [bəlōōn'] *n* ballon *m*; (*in comic strip*) bulle *f* ♦ *vi* gonfler.

balloonist [bəlōō'nist] *n* aéronaute *m/f*.

ballot [bal'ət] *n* scrutin *m*; (*US*: ~ **paper**) bulletin *m* de vote.

ballot box *n* urne (électorale).

ballot paper *n* bulletin *m* de vote.

ballpark [bôl'pârk] *n* (*US*) stade *m* de baseball.

ballpark figure *n* (*col*) chiffre approximatif.

ball-point (pen) [bôl'point (pen')] *n* stylo *m* à bille.

ballroom [bôl'rōōm] *n* salle *f* de bal.

balls [bôlz] *npl* (*col!*) couilles *fpl* (!).

balm [bâm] *n* baume *m*.

balmy [bâ'mē] *a* (*breeze, air*) doux(douce).

balsam [bôl'səm] *n* baume *m*.

balsa (wood) [bôl'sə (wōōd)] *n* balsa *m*.

Baltic [bôl'tik] *a, n*: **the** ~ (**Sea**) la (mer) Baltique.

balustrade [bal'əstrād] *n* balustrade *f*.

bamboo [bambōō'] *n* bambou *m*.

bamboozle [bambōō'zəl] *vt* (*col*) embobiner.

ban [ban] *n* interdiction *f* ♦ *vt* interdire.

banal [bənal'] *a* banal(e).

banana [bənan'ə] *n* banane *f*.

band [band] *n* bande *f*; (*at a dance*) orchestre *m*; (*MIL*) musique *f*, fanfare *f*.

band together *vi* se liguer.

bandage [ban'dij] *n* bandage *m*, pansement *m* ♦ *vt* (*wound, leg*) mettre un pansement *or* un bandage sur; (*person*) mettre un pansement *or* un bandage à.

Band-Aid [band'ād] *n* ® (*US*) pansement adhésif.

bandit [ban'dit] *n* bandit *m*.

bandstand [band'stand] *n* kiosque *m* (à musique).

bandwagon [band'wagən] *n*: **to jump on the** ~ (*fig*) monter dans *or* prendre le train en marche.

bandy [ban'dē] *vt* (*jokes, insults*) échanger.
bandy about *vt* employer à tout bout de champ *or* à tort et à travers.

bandy-legged [ban'dēlegid] *a* aux jambes arquées.

bane [bān] *n*: **it** (*or* **he** *etc*) **is the** ~ **of my life** c'est (*or* il est *etc*) le drame de ma vie.

bang [bang] *n* détonation *f*; (*of door*) claquement *m*; (*blow*) coup (violent) ♦ *vt* frapper (violemment); (*door*) claquer ♦ *vi* détoner; claquer; **to** ~ **at the door** cogner à la porte; **to** ~ **into sth** se cogner contre qch.

banger [bang'ûr] *n* (*Brit: car: also:* **old** ~) (vieux) tacot; (*Brit col: sausage*) saucisse *f*; (*firework*) pétard *m*.

Bangkok [bang'kâk] *n* Bangkok.

Bangladesh [banggladesh'] *n* Bangladesh *m*.

bangle [bang'gəl] *n* bracelet *m*.

bangs [bangz] *npl* (*US: hair*) frange *f*.

banish [ban'ish] *vt* bannir.

banister(s) [ban'istûr(z)] *n(pl)* rampe *f* (d'escalier).

banjo, ~**es** *or* ~**s** [ban'jō] *n* banjo *m*.

bank [bangk] *n* banque *f*; (*of river, lake*) bord *m*, rive *f*; (*of earth*) talus *m*, remblai *m* ♦ *vi* (*AVIAT*) virer sur l'aile; (*COMM*): **they** ~ **with Pitt's** leur banque *or* banquier est Pitt's.
bank on *vt fus* miser *or* tabler sur.

bank account *n* compte *m* en banque.

bank card *n* carte d'identité bancaire.

bank charges *npl* frais *mpl* de banque.

bank draft *n* traite *f* bancaire.

banker [bangk'ûr] *n* banquier *m*; ~**'s order** (*Brit*) ordre *m* de virement.

Bank holiday *n* (*Brit*) jour férié (*où les banques sont fermées*).

banking [bangk'ing] *n* opérations *fpl* bancaires; profession *f* de banquier.

banking hours *npl* heures *fpl* d'ouverture des banques.

bank loan *n* prêt *m* bancaire.

bank manager *n* directeur *m* d'agence (bancaire).

banknote [bangk'nōt] *n* billet *m* de banque.

bank rate *n* taux *m* de l'escompte.

bankrupt [bangk'rupt] *n* failli/e ♦ *a* en faillite; **to go** ~ faire faillite.

bankruptcy [bangk'ruptsē] *n* faillite *f*.

bank statement *n* relevé *m* de compte.

banner [ban'ûr] *n* bannière *f*.

bannister(s) [ban'istûr(z)] *n(pl)* = **banister(s)**.

banns [banz] *npl* bans *mpl* (de mariage).

banquet [bang'kwit] *n* banquet *m*, festin *m*.

bantamweight [ban'təmwāt] *n* poids *m* coq *inv*.

banter [ban'tûr] *n* badinage *m*.

BAOR *n abbr* (= *British Army of the Rhine*) *forces britanniques en Allemagne*.

baptism [bap'tizəm] *n* baptême *m*.

Baptist [bap'tist] *n* baptiste *m/f*.

baptize [baptīz'] *vt* baptiser.

bar [bâr] *n* barre *f*; (*of window etc*) barreau *m*; (*of chocolate*) tablette *f*, plaque *f*; (*fig*) obstacle *m*; mesure *f* d'exclusion; (*place*)

bar *m*; (*counter*) comptoir *m*, bar; (*MUS*) mesure *f* ♦ *vt* (*road*) barrer; (*window*) munir de barreaux; (*person*) exclure; (*activity*) interdire; ~ **of soap** savonnette *f*; **behind** ~**s** (*prisoner*) derrière les barreaux; **the B**~ (*LAW*) le barreau; ~ **none** sans exception.

Barbados [bârbā'dōs] *n* Barbade *f*.

barbaric [bârbar'ik] *a* barbare.

barbarous [bâr'bûrəs] *a* barbare, cruel(le).

barbecue [bâr'bəkyōō] *n* barbecue *m*.

barbed wire [bârbd wīûr] *n* fil *m* de fer barbelé.

barber [bâr'bûr] *n* coiffeur *m* (pour hommes).

barbiturate [bârbich'ûrit] *n* barbiturique *m*.

Barcelona [bârsəlō'nə] *n* Barcelone.

bar chart *n* diagramme *m* en bâtons.

bar code *n* code *m* à barres.

bare [bär] *a* nu(e) ♦ *vt* mettre à nu, dénuder; (*teeth*) montrer; **the** ~ **essentials** le strict nécessaire.

bareback [bär'bak] *ad* à cru, sans selle.

barefaced [bär'fāst] *a* impudent(e), effronté(e).

barefoot [bär'fōōt] *a, ad* nu-pieds, (les) pieds nus.

bareheaded [bär'hedid] *a, ad* nu-tête, (la) tête nue.

barely [bär'lē] *ad* à peine.

Barents Sea [bär'ənts sē] *n*: **the** ~ la mer de Barents.

bargain [bâr'gin] *n* (*transaction*) marché *m*; (*good buy*) affaire *f*, occasion *f* ♦ *vi* (*haggle*) marchander; (*trade*) négocier, traiter; **into the** ~ par-dessus le marché.
bargain for *vi* (*col*): **he got more than he** ~**ed for!** il en a eu pour son argent!

bargaining [bâr'gining] *n* marchandage *m*; négociations *fpl*.

barge [bârj] *n* péniche *f*.
barge in *vi* (*walk in*) faire irruption; (*interrupt talk*) intervenir mal à propos.
barge into *vt fus* rentrer dans.

baritone [bar'itōn] *n* baryton *m*.

barium meal [bar'ēəm mēl'] *n* (bouillie *f* de) sulfate *m* de baryum.

bark [bârk] *n* (*of tree*) écorce *f*; (*of dog*) aboiement *m* ♦ *vi* aboyer.

barley [bâr'lē] *n* orge *f*.

barley sugar *n* sucre *m* d'orge.

barmaid [bâr'mād] *n* serveuse *f* (de bar), barmaid *f*.

barman [bâr'mən] *n* serveur *m* (de bar), barman *m*.

barn [bârn] *n* grange *f*.

barnacle [bâr'nəkəl] *n* anatife *m*, bernache *f*.

barometer [bərâm'itûr] *n* baromètre *m*.

baron [bar'ən] *n* baron *m*; **the press/oil** ~**s** les magnats *mpl or* barons *mpl* de la presse/du pétrole.

baroness [bar'ənis] *n* baronne *f*.

barracks [bar'əks] *npl* caserne *f*.

barrage [bərâzh'] *n* (*MIL*) tir *m* de barrage; (*dam*) barrage *m*; **a** ~ **of questions** un feu roulant de questions.

barrel [bar'əl] *n* tonneau *m*; (*of gun*) canon *m*.

barrel organ *n* orgue *m* de Barbarie.

barren [bar'ən] *a* stérile; (*hills*) aride.

barrette [bəret'] *n* (*US*) barrette *f*.

barricade [bar'əkād] *n* barricade *f* ♦ *vt* barricader.

barrier [bar'ēûr] *n* barrière *f*; (*Brit*: *also*: **crash ~**) rail *m* de sécurité.

barring [bâr'ing] *prep* sauf.

barrister [bar'istûr] *n* (*Brit*) avocat (plaidant).

barrow [bar'ō] *n* (*cart*) charrette *f* à bras.

barstool [bâr'stōōl] *n* tabouret *m* de bar.

bartender [bâr'tendûr] *n* (*US*) serveur *m* (de bar), barman *m*.

barter [bâr'tûr] *n* échange *m*, troc *m* ♦ *vt*: to ~ sth for échanger qch contre.

base [bās] *n* base *f* ♦ *vt* (*troops*): to be ~d at être basé(e) à; (*opinion, belief*): to ~ sth on baser *or* fonder qch sur ♦ *a* vil(e), bas(se); **coffee-~d** à base de café; **a Paris-~d firm** une maison opérant de Paris *or* dont le siège est à Paris; **I'm ~d in New York** je suis basé(e) à New York.

baseball [bās'bôl] *n* base-ball *m*.

baseboard [bās'bôrd] *n* (*US*) plinthe *f*.

base camp *n* camp *m* de base.

Basel [bâz'əl] *n* = **Basle**.

basement [bās'mənt] *n* sous-sol *m*.

base pay *n* (*US*) salaire *m* de base.

base rate *n* taux *m* de base.

bases [bā'sēz] *npl of* **basis**; [bā'siz] *npl of* **base**.

bash [bash] *vt* (*col*) frapper, cogner ♦ *n*: **I'll have a ~ (at it)** (*col*) je vais essayer un coup; **~ed in** *a* enfoncé(e), défoncé(e).

bash up *vt* (*col*: *car*) bousiller; (: *Brit*: *person*) tabasser.

bashful [bash'fəl] *a* timide; modeste.

bashing [bash'ing] *n* (*col*) raclée *f*; **Paki-~** (*Brit*) ≈ ratonnade *f*.

BASIC [bā'sik] *n* (*COMPUT*) BASIC *m*.

basic [bā'sik] *a* (*precautions, rules*) élémentaire; (*principles, research*) fondamental(e); (*vocabulary, salary*) de base; réduit(e) au minimum, rudimentaire.

basically [bā'siklē] *ad* (*really*) en fait; (*essentially*) fondamentalement.

basic rate *n* (*of tax*) première tranche d'imposition.

basil [baz'əl] *n* basilic *m*.

basin [bā'sin] *n* (*vessel, also GEO*) cuvette *f*, bassin *m*; (*Brit*: *for food*) bol *m*; (: *bigger*) saladier *m*; (*also*: **wash~**) lavabo *m*.

basis, *pl* **bases** [bā'sis, -sēz] *n* base *f*; **on the ~ of what you've said** d'après ce que *or* compte tenu de ce que vous dites.

bask [bask] *vi*: to ~ **in the sun** se chauffer au soleil.

basket [bas'kit] *n* corbeille *f*; (*with handle*) panier *m*.

basketball [bas'kitbôl] *n* basket-ball *m*.

basketball player *n* basketteur/euse.

Basle [baz'əl] *n* Bâle.

Basque [bask] *a* basque ♦ *n* Basque *m/f*.

bass [bās] *n* (*MUS*) basse *f*.

bass clef [bās klef] *n* clé *f* de fa.

bassoon [basōōn'] *n* basson *m*.

bastard [bas'tûrd] *n* enfant naturel(le), bâtard/e; (*col!*) salaud *m* (!).

baste [bāst] *vt* (*CULIN*) arroser; (*SEWING*) bâtir, faufiler.

bastion [bas'chən] *n* bastion *m*.

bat [bat] *n* chauve-souris *f*; (*for baseball etc*) batte *f*; (*Brit*: *for table tennis*) raquette *f* ♦ *vt*: **he didn't ~ an eyelid** il n'a pas sourcillé

or bronché; **to take off like a ~ out of hell** filer comme un zèbre.

batch [bach] *n* (*of bread*) fournée *f*; (*of papers*) liasse *f*; (*of applicants, letters*) paquet *m*; (*of work*) monceau *m*; (*of goods*) lot *m*.

batch processing *n* (*COMPUT*) traitement *m* par lot.

bated [bā'tid] *a*: **with ~ breath** en retenant son souffle.

bath [bath, *pl* bathz] *n* bain *m*; (*bathtub*) baignoire *f* ♦ *vt* baigner, donner un bain à; **to have a ~** prendre un bain; *see also* **baths**.

bathe [bāth] *vi* se baigner ♦ *vt* baigner; (*wound etc*) laver.

bather [bāth'ûr] *n* baigneur/euse.

bathing [bā'thing] *n* baignade *f*.

bathing cap *n* bonnet *m* de bain.

bathing suit *n* maillot *m* (de bain).

bathmat [bath'mat] *n* tapis *m* de bain.

bathrobe [bath'rōb] *n* peignoir *m* de bain.

bathroom [bath'rōōm] *n* salle *f* de bains.

baths [bathz] *npl* établissement *m* de bains(-douches).

bath towel [bath' toul] *n* serviette *f* de bain.

bathtub [bath'tub] *n* baignoire *f*.

baton [batân'] *n* bâton *m*; (*MUS*) baguette *f*; (*club*) matraque *f*.

battalion [bətal'yən] *n* bataillon *m*.

batten [bat'ən] *n* (*CARPENTRY*) latte *f*; (*NAUT*: *on sail*) latte de voile.

batten down *vt* (*NAUT*): **to ~ down the hatches** fermer les écoutilles.

batter [bat'ûr] *vt* battre ♦ *n* pâte *f* à frire.

battered [bat'ûrd] *a* (*hat, pan*) cabossé(e); ~ **wife/child** épouse/enfant maltraité(e) *or* martyr(e).

battering ram [bat'ûring ram] *n* bélier *m* (*fig*).

battery [bat'ûrē] *n* batterie *f*; (*of torch*) pile *f*.

battery charger *n* chargeur *m*.

battery farming *n* élevage *m* en batterie.

battle [bat'əl] *n* bataille *f*, combat *m* ♦ *vi* se battre, lutter; **that's half the ~** (*fig*) c'est déjà bien; **it's a or we're fighting a losing ~** (*fig*) c'est perdu d'avance, c'est peine perdue.

battle dress *n* tenue *f* de campagne *or* d'assaut.

battlefield [bat'əlfēld] *n* champ *m* de bataille.

battlements [bat'əlmənts] *npl* remparts *mpl*.

battleship [bat'əlship] *n* cuirassé *m*.

bauble [bô'bəl] *n* babiole *f*.

baud [bôd] *n* (*COMPUT*) baud *m*.

baud rate *n* (*COMPUT*) vitesse *f* de transmission.

baulk [bôk] *vi* = **balk**.

bauxite [bôk'sīt] *n* bauxite *f*.

Bavaria [bəvär'ēə] *n* Bavière *f*.

Bavarian [bəvär'ēən] *a* bavarois(e) ♦ *n* Bavarois/e.

bawdy [bô'dē] *a* paillard(e).

bawl [bôl] *vi* hurler, brailler.

bawl out *vt fus* (*col*) engueuler.

bay [bā] *n* (*of sea*) baie *f*; (*Brit*: *for parking*) place *f* de stationnement; (: *for loading*) aire *f* de chargement; (*horse*) bai/e *m/f*; **to hold sb at ~** tenir qn à distance *or* en échec.

bay leaf *n* laurier *m*.

bayonet [bā'ənet] *n* baïonnette *f*.

bay tree *n* laurier *m*.

bay window *n* baie vitrée.
bazaar [bɔzâr'] *n* bazar *m*; vente *f* de charité.
bazooka [bɔzoō'kɔ] *n* bazooka *m*.
B & B *n abbr* = **bed and breakfast**.
BBA *n abbr* (*US*: = *Bachelor of Business Administration*) licencié/e en administration des affaires.
BBB *n abbr* (*US*: = *Better Business Bureau*) organisme de défense du consommateur.
BBC *n abbr* (= *British Broadcasting Corporation*) office de la radiodiffusion et télévision britannique.
BC *ad abbr* (= *before Christ*) av. J.-C. ♦ *abbr* (*Canada*) = *British Columbia* ♦ *n abbr* (*US*) = *Bachelor of Commerce*.
BCG *n abbr* (= *Bacillus Calmette-Guérin*) BCG *m*.
BD *n abbr* (= *Bachelor of Divinity*) diplôme universitaire.
B/D *abbr* = **bank draft**.
BDS *n abbr* (= *Bachelor of Dental Surgery*) diplôme universitaire.
be, *pt* **was, were**, *pp* **been** [bē, wuz, wûr, bēn] *vi* être; **how are you?** comment allez-vous?; **I am warm** j'ai chaud; **it is cold** il fait froid; **how much is it?** combien ça coûte?; **what are you doing?** que faites-vous?; **he is four (years old)** il a quatre ans; **it's 8 o'clock** il est 8 heures; **2 and 2 are 4** 2 et 2 font 4; **where have you been?** où êtes-vous allé(s)?; **I've been waiting for her for two hours** cela fait deux heures que je l'attends, je l'attends depuis deux heures; **to ~ killed** être tué, se faire tuer; **he is nowhere to ~ found** on ne sait pas où il se trouve; **the car is to ~ sold** la voiture est à vendre; **he was to have come yesterday** il devait venir hier; **if I were you, I ...** à votre place, je ..., si j'étais vous, je ...; **am I to understand that ...?** dois-je comprendre que ...?
B/E *abbr* = **bill of exchange**.
beach [bēch] *n* plage *f* ♦ *vt* échouer.
beachcomber [bēch'kōmûr] *n* ramasseur *m* d'épaves; (*fig*) glandeur *m*.
beachwear [bēch'wär] *n* tenues *fpl* de plage.
beacon [bē'kən] *n* (*lighthouse*) fanal *m*; (*marker*) balise *f*; (*also:* **radio ~**) radiophare *m*.
bead [bēd] *n* perle *f*; (*of dew, sweat*) goutte *f*; **~s** (*necklace*) collier *m*.
beady [bē'dē] *a:* **~ eyes** yeux *mpl* de fouine.
beagle [bē'gəl] *n* beagle *m*.
beak [bēk] *n* bec *m*; (*US col: nose*) blair *m*.
beaker [bē'kûr] *n* gobelet *m*.
beam [bēm] *n* poutre *f*; (*of light*) rayon *m*; (*RADIO*) faisceau *m* radio ♦ *vi* rayonner; **to drive on high** *or* (*Brit*) **full ~** rouler en pleins phares.
beaming [bē'ming] *a* (*sun, smile*) radieux(euse).
bean [bēn] *n* haricot *m*; (*of coffee*) grain *m*.
bean sprouts *npl* pousses *fpl* (de soja).
bear [bär] *n* ours *m*; (*STOCK EXCHANGE*) baissier *m* ♦ *vb* (*pt* **bore**, *pp* **borne** [bôr, bôrn]) *vt* porter; (*endure*) supporter; (*traces, signs*) porter; (*COMM: interest*) rapporter ♦ *vi:* **to ~ right/left** obliquer à droite/gauche, se diriger vers la droite/gauche; **to ~ the re-**

sponsibility of assumer la responsabilité de; **to ~ comparison with** soutenir la comparaison avec; **I can't ~ him** je ne peux pas le supporter *or* souffrir; **to bring pressure to ~ on sb** faire pression sur qn.
bear out *vt* (*theory, suspicion*) confirmer.
bear up *vi* supporter, tenir le coup; **he bore up well** il a tenu le coup.
bear with *vt fus* (*sb's moods, temper*) supporter; **~ with me a minute** un moment, s'il vous plaît.
bearable [bär'əbəl] *a* supportable.
beard [bērd] *n* barbe *f*.
bearded [bērd'id] *a* barbu(e).
bearer [bär'ûr] *n* porteur *m*; (*of passport etc*) titulaire *m/f*.
bearing [bär'ing] *n* maintien *m*, allure *f*; (*connection*) rapport *m*; (*TECH*): **~s** *npl* roulement *m* (à billes); **to take a ~** faire le point; **to find one's ~s** s'orienter.
beast [bēst] *n* bête *f*; (*col*): **he's a ~** c'est une brute.
beastly [bēst'lē] *a* infect(e).
beat [bēt] *n* battement *m*; (*MUS*) temps *m*, mesure *f*; (*of policeman*) ronde *f* ♦ *vt* (*pt* **beat**, *pp* **beaten**) battre ♦ *a* (*US col*) crevé(e); **off the ~en track** hors des chemins *or* sentiers battus; **to ~ around the bush** tourner autour du pot; **to ~ time** battre la mesure; **that ~s everything!** c'est le comble!
beat down *vt* (*door*) enfoncer; (*price*) faire baisser; (*seller*) faire descendre ♦ *vi* (*rain*) tambouriner; (*sun*) taper.
beat off *vt* repousser.
beat up *vt* (*eggs*) battre; (*col: person*) tabasser.
beater [bē'tûr] *n* (*for eggs, cream*) fouet *m*, batteur *m*.
beating [bē'ting] *n* raclée *f*.
beat-up [bēt'up] *a* (*col*) déglingué(e).
beautician [byoōtish'ən] *n* esthéticien/ne.
beautiful [byoō'təfəl] *a* beau(belle).
beautifully [byoō'təfəlē] *ad* admirablement.
beautify [byoō'təfī] *vt* embellir.
beauty [byoō'tē] *n* beauté *f*; **the ~ of it is that ...** le plus beau, c'est que ....
beauty contest *n* concours *m* de beauté.
beauty queen *n* reine *f* de beauté.
beauty salon [byoō'tē sal'ân] *n* institut *m* de beauté.
beauty spot *n* grain *m* de beauté; (*Brit TOURISM*) site naturel (d'une grande beauté).
beaver [bē'vûr] *n* castor *m*.
becalmed [bikâmd'] *a* immobilisé(e) par le calme plat.
became [bikām'] *pt of* **become**.
because [bikôz'] *cj* parce que; **~ of** *prep* à cause de.
beck [bek] *n:* **to be at sb's ~ and call** être à l'entière disposition de qn.
beckon [bek'ən] *vt* (*also:* **~ to**) faire signe (de venir) à.
become [bikum'] *vt* (*irg: like* **come**) devenir; **to ~ fat/thin** grossir/maigrir; **to ~ angry** se mettre en colère; **it became known that** on apprit que; **what has ~ of him?** qu'est-il devenu?
becoming [bikum'ing] *a* (*behavior*) convena-

ble, bienséant(e); (*clothes*) seyant(e).

BEd *n abbr* (= *Bachelor of Education*) diplôme d'aptitude à l'enseignement.

bed [bed] *n* lit *m*; (*of flowers*) parterre *m*; (*of coal, clay*) couche *f*; (*of sea, lake*) fond *m*; **to go to ~** aller se coucher.
bed down *vi* se coucher.

bed and breakfast (B & B) *n* (*terms*) chambre et petit déjeuner; (*place*) ≈ chambre *f* d'hôte.

bedbug [bed'bug] *n* punaise *f*.

bedclothes [bed'klōz] *npl* couvertures *fpl* et draps *mpl*.

bedcover [bed'kuvûr] *n* couvre-lit *m*, dessus-de-lit *m*.

bedding [bed'ing] *n* literie *f*.

bedevil [bidev'əl] *vt* (*harass*) harceler; **to be ~led by** être victime de.

bedfellow [bed'felō] *n*: **they are strange ~s** (*fig*) ça fait un drôle de mélange.

bedlam [bed'ləm] *n* chahut *m*, cirque *m*.

bedpan [bed'pan] *n* bassin *m* (hygiénique).

bedpost [bed'pōst] *n* colonne *f* de lit.

bedraggled [bidrag'əld] *a* dépenaillé(e), les vêtements en désordre.

bedridden [bed'ridən] *a* cloué(e) au lit.

bedrock [bed'râk] *n* (*fig*) principes essentiels *or* de base, essentiel *m*; (*GEO*) roche *f* en place, socle *m*.

bedroom [bed'rōōm] *n* chambre *f* (à coucher).

Beds [bedz] *abbr* (*Brit*) = Bedfordshire.

bedside [bed'sīd] *n*: **at sb's ~** au chevet de qn ♦ *cpd* (*book, lamp*) de chevet.

bedsit(ter) [bed'sit(ûr)] *n* (*Brit*) chambre meublée, studio *m*.

bedspread [bed'spred] *n* couvre-lit *m*, dessus-de-lit *m*.

bedtime [bed'tīm] *n*: **it's ~** c'est l'heure de se coucher.

bee [bē] *n* abeille *f*; **to have a ~ in one's bonnet (about sth)** être obnubilé(e) (par qch).

beech [bēch] *n* hêtre *m*.

beef [bēf] *n* bœuf *m*.
beef up *vt* (*col: support*) renforcer; (: *essay*) étoffer.

beefburger [bēf'bûrgûr] *n* hamburger *m*.

beefeater [bēf'ētûr] *n* hallebardier *m* (de la tour de Londres).

beehive [bē'hīv] *n* ruche *f*.

beeline [bē'līn] *n*: **to make a ~ for** se diriger tout droit vers.

been [bin] *pp* of **be**.

beeper [bēp'ûr] *n* (*of doctor etc*) bip *m*.

beer [bēr] *n* bière *f*.

beer can *n* canette *f* de bière.

beet [bēt] *n* (*US*) betterave *f*.

beetle [bēt'əl] *n* scarabée *m*, coléoptère *m*.

beetroot [bēt'rōōt] *n* (*Brit*) betterave *f*.

befall [bifôl'] *vi*(*vt*) (*irg: like* **fall**) advenir (à).

befit [bifit'] *vt* seoir à.

before [bifôr'] *prep* (*of time*) avant; (*of space*) devant ♦ *cj* avant que + *sub*; avant de ♦ *ad* avant; **~ going** avant de partir; **~ she goes** avant qu'elle (ne) parte; **the week ~** la semaine précédente *or* d'avant; **I've seen it ~** je l'ai déjà vu; **I've never seen it ~** c'est la première fois que je le vois.

beforehand [bifôr'hand] *ad* au préalable, à

l'avance.

befriend [bifrend'] *vt* venir en aide à; traiter en ami.

befuddled [bifud'əld] *a*: **to be ~** avoir les idées brouillées.

beg [beg] *vi* mendier ♦ *vt* mendier; (*favor*) quémander, solliciter; (*entreat*) supplier; **I ~ your pardon** (*apologizing*) excusez-moi; (: *not hearing*) pardon?; **that ~s the question of** ... cela soulève la question de ..., cela suppose réglée la question de ....

began [bigan'] *pt of* **begin**.

beggar [beg'ûr] *n* (*also:* **~man**, **~woman**) mendiant/e.

begin, *pt* **began,** *pp* **begun** [bigin', bigan', bigun'] *vt*, *vi* commencer; **to ~ doing** *or* **to do sth** commencer à faire qch; **~ning (from) Monday** à partir de lundi; **I can't ~ to thank you** je ne saurais vous remercier; **to ~ with** d'abord, pour commencer.

beginner [bigin'ûr] *n* débutant/e.

beginning [bigin'ing] *n* commencement *m*, début *m*; **right from the ~** dès le début.

begrudge [bigruj'] *vt*: **to ~ sb sth** envier qch à qn; donner qch à contrecœur *or* à regret à qn.

beguile [bigīl'] *vt* (*enchant*) enjôler.

beguiling [bigī'ling] *a* (*charming*) séduisant(e), enchanteur(eresse).

begun [bigun'] *pp of* **begin**.

behalf [bihaf'] *n*: **in ~ of,** (*Brit*) **on ~ of** de la part de; au nom de; pour le compte de.

behave [bihāv'] *vi* se conduire, se comporter; (*well: also:* **~ o.s.**) se conduire bien *or* comme il faut.

behavior, (*Brit*) **behaviour** [bihāv'yûr] *n* comportement *m*, conduite *f*.

behead [bihed'] *vt* décapiter.

beheld [biheld'] *pt*, *pp of* **behold**.

behind [bihīnd'] *prep* derrière; (*time*) en retard sur ♦ *ad* derrière; en retard ♦ *n* derrière *m*; **~ the scenes** dans les coulisses; **to leave sth ~** (*forget*) oublier de prendre qch; **to be ~ (schedule) with sth** être en retard dans qch.

behold [bihōld'] *vt* (*irg: like* **hold**) apercevoir, voir.

beige [bāzh] *a* beige.

being [bē'ing] *n* être *m*; **to come into ~** prendre naissance.

Beirut [bārōōt'] *n* Beyrouth.

belated [bilā'tid] *a* tardif(ive).

belch [belch] *vi* avoir un renvoi, roter ♦ *vt* (*also:* **~ out:** *smoke etc*) vomir, cracher.

beleaguered [bilē'gûrd] *a* (*city*) assiégé(e); (*army*) cerné(e); (*fig*) sollicité(e) de toutes parts.

Belfast [bel'fast] *n* Belfast.

belfry [bel'frē] *n* beffroi *m*.

Belgian [bel'jən] *a* belge, de Belgique ♦ *n* Belge *m/f*.

Belgium [bel'jəm] *n* Belgique *f*.

Belgrade [belgrād'] *n* Belgrade.

belie [bilī'] *vt* démentir; (*give false impression of*) occulter.

belief [bilēf'] *n* (*opinion*) conviction *f*; (*trust, faith*) foi *f*; (*acceptance as true*) croyance *f*; **it's beyond ~** c'est incroyable; **in the ~ that** dans l'idée que.

believable [bilēv'əbəl] *a* croyable.

believe [bilēv'] *vt, vi* croire, estimer; **to ~ in** (*God*) croire en; (*ghosts, method*) croire à; **I don't ~ in corporal punishment** je ne suis pas partisan des châtiments corporels; **he is ~d to be abroad** il serait à l'étranger.

believer [bilēv'ûr] *n* (*in idea, activity*): **~ in** partisan/e de; (*REL*) croyant/e.

belittle [bilit'əl] *vt* déprécier, rabaisser.

Belize [bəlēz'] *n* Bélize *m*.

bell [bel] *n* cloche *f*; (*small*) clochette *f*, grelot *m*; (*on door*) sonnette *f*; (*electric*) sonnerie *f*; **that rings a ~** (*fig*) cela me rappelle qch.

bell-bottoms [bel'bâtəmz] *npl* pantalon *m* à pattes d'éléphant.

bellhop [bel'hâp] (*Brit*) **bellboy** [bel'boi] *n* groom *m*, chasseur *m*.

belligerent [bəlij'ûrənt] *a* (*at war*) belligérant(e); (*fig*) agressif(ive).

bellow [bel'ō] *vi* mugir; beugler ♦ *vt* (*orders*) hurler.

bellows [bel'ōz] *npl* soufflet *m*.

belly [bel'ē] *n* ventre *m*.

bellyache [bel'ēāk] *n* (*col*) colique *f* ♦ *vi* ronchonner.

bellybutton [bel'ēbutən] *n* nombril *m*.

belong [bilóng'] *vi*: **to ~ to** appartenir à; (*club etc*) faire partie de; **this book ~s here** ce livre va ici, la place de ce livre est ici.

belongings [bilóng'ingz] *npl* affaires *fpl*, possessions *fpl*; **personal ~** effets personnels.

beloved [biluv'id] *a* (bien-)aimé(e), chéri(e) ♦ *n* bien-aimé/e.

below [bilō'] *prep* sous, au-dessous de ♦ *ad* en dessous; en contre-bas; **see ~** voir plus bas *or* plus loin *or* ci-dessous; **temperatures ~ normal** températures inférieures à la normale.

belt [belt] *n* ceinture *f*; (*TECH*) courroie *f* ♦ *vt* (*thrash*) donner une raclée à; **industrial ~** zone industrielle.

belt out *vt* (*song*) chanter à tue-tête *or* à pleins poumons.

belt up *vi* (*Brit col*) la boucler.

beltway [belt'wā] *n* (*US AUT*) route *f* de ceinture; (: *freeway*) périphérique *m*.

bemoan [bimōn'] *vt* se lamenter sur.

bemused [bimyōōzd'] *a* médusé(e).

bench [bench] *n* banc *m*; (*in workshop*) établi *m*; **the B~** (*LAW*) la magistrature, la Cour.

bench mark *n* repère *m*.

bend [bend] *vb* (*pt, pp* **bent** [bent]) *vt* courber; (*leg, arm*) plier ♦ *vi* se courber ♦ *n* (*Brit*: *in road*) virage *m*, tournant *m*; (*in pipe, river*) coude *m*.

bend down *vi* se baisser.

bend over *vi* se pencher.

bends [bendz] *npl* (*MED*) maladie *f* des caissons.

beneath [binēth'] *prep* sous, au-dessous de; (*unworthy of*) indigne de ♦ *ad* dessous, au-dessous, en bas.

benefactor [ben'əfaktûr] *n* bienfaiteur *m*.

benefactress [ben'əfaktris] *n* bienfaitrice *f*.

beneficial [benəfish'əl] *a*: **~ (to)** salutaire (pour), bénéfique (à).

beneficiary [benəfish'ēârē] *n* (*LAW*) bénéficiaire *m/f*.

benefit [ben'əfit] *n* avantage *m*, profit *m*;

(*allowance of money*) allocation *f* ♦ *vt* faire du bien à, profiter à ♦ *vi*: **he'll ~ from it** cela lui fera du bien, il y gagnera *or* s'en trouvera bien.

benefit performance *n* représentation *f or* gala *m* de bienfaisance.

benefit society *n* (*US*) société *f* mutualiste.

Benelux [ben'əluks] *n* Bénélux *m*.

benevolent [bənev'ələnt] *a* bienveillant(e).

BEng *n abbr* (= *Bachelor of Engineering*) diplôme universitaire.

benign [binīn'] *a* (*person, smile*) bienveillant(e), affable; (*MED*) bénin(igne).

bent [bent] *pt, pp of* **bend** ♦ *n* inclination *f*, penchant *m* ♦ *a* (*wire, pipe*) coudé(e); (*col*: *dishonest*) véreux(euse); **to be ~ on** être résolu(e) à.

bequeath [bikwēth'] *vt* léguer.

bequest [bikwest'] *n* legs *m*.

bereaved [birēvd'] *n*: **the ~** la famille du disparu ♦ *a* endeuillé(e).

bereavement [birēv'mənt] *n* deuil *m*.

beret [bərā'] *n* béret *m*.

Bering Sea [bar'ing sē] *n*: **the ~** la mer de Béring.

Berks *abbr* (*Brit*) = *Berkshire*.

Berlin [bûrlin'] *n* Berlin; **East/West ~** Berlin Est/Ouest.

berm [bûrm] *n* (*US AUT*) accotement *m*.

Bermuda [bûrmŏŏ'də] *n* Bermudes *fpl*.

Bermuda shorts *npl* bermuda *m*.

Bern [bûrn] *n* Berne.

berry [bär'ē] *n* baie *f*.

berserk [bûrsûrk'] *a*: **to go ~** être pris(e) d'une rage incontrôlable; se déchaîner.

berth [bûrth] *n* (*bed*) couchette *f*; (*for ship*) poste *m* d'amarrage, mouillage *m* ♦ *vi* (*in harbor*) venir à quai; (*at anchor*) mouiller; **to give sb a wide ~** (*fig*) éviter qn.

beseech, *pt, pp* **besought** [bisēch', bisôt'] *vt* implorer, supplier.

beset, *pt, pp* **beset** [biset'] *vt* assaillir ♦ *a*: **~ with** semé(e) de.

besetting [biset'ing] *a*: **his ~ sin** son vice, son gros défaut.

beside [bisīd'] *prep* à côté de; (*compared with*) par rapport à; **that's ~ the point** ça n'a rien à voir; **to be ~ o.s. (with anger)** être hors de soi.

besides [bisīdz'] *ad* en outre, de plus ♦ *prep* en plus de; (*except*) excepté.

besiege [bisēj'] *vt* (*town*) assiéger; (*fig*) assaillir.

besotted [bisât'id] *a*: **~ with** entiché(e) de.

besought [bisôt'] *pt, pp of* **beseech**.

bespectacled [bispek'təkəld] *a* à lunettes.

best [best] *a* meilleur(e) ♦ *ad* le mieux; **the ~ part of** (*quantity*) le plus clair de, la plus grande partie de; **at ~** au mieux; **to make the ~ of sth** s'accommoder de qch (du mieux que l'on peut); **to do one's ~** faire de son mieux; **to the ~ of my knowledge** pour autant que je sache; **to the ~ of my ability** du mieux que je pourrai; **he's not exactly patient at the ~ of times** il n'est jamais spécialement patient; **the ~ thing to do is ...** le mieux, c'est de ....

best man *n* garçon *m* d'honneur.

bestow [bistō'] *vt* accorder; (*title*) conférer.

best seller n bestseller m, succès m de librairie.
bet [bɛt] n pari m ♦ vt, vi (pt, pp **bet** or **betted**) parier; **it's a safe** ~ (fig) il y a de fortes chances.
Bethlehem [bɛth'lēəm] n Bethléem.
betray [bitrā'] vt trahir.
betrayal [bitrā'əl] n trahison f.
better [bɛt'ûr] a meilleur(e) ♦ ad mieux ♦ vt améliorer ♦ n: **to get the** ~ **of** triompher de, l'emporter sur; **a change for the** ~ une amélioration; **I had** ~ **go** il faut que je m'en aille; **you had** ~ **do it** vous feriez mieux de le faire; **he thought** ~ **of it** il s'est ravisé; **to get** ~ aller mieux; s'améliorer; **that's** ~! c'est mieux!; ~ **off** a plus à l'aise financièrement; (fig): **you'd be** ~ **off this way** vous vous en trouveriez mieux ainsi, ce serait mieux or plus pratique ainsi.
betting [bɛt'ing] n paris mpl.
betting shop n (Brit) bureau m de paris.
between [bitwēn'] prep entre ♦ ad au milieu, dans l'intervalle; **the road** ~ **here and Chicago** la route d'ici à Chicago; **we only had 5** ~ **us** nous n'en avions que 5 en tout.
bevel [bɛv'əl] n (also: ~ **edge**) biseau m.
beverage [bɛv'ûrij] n boisson f (gén sans alcool).
bevy [bɛv'ē] n: **a** ~ **of** un essaim or une volée de.
bewail [biwāl'] vt se lamenter sur.
beware [biwār'] vt, vi: **to** ~ **(of)** prendre garde (à).
bewildered [biwil'dûrd] a dérouté(e), ahuri(e).
bewildering [biwil'dûring] a déroutant(e), ahurissant(e).
bewitching [biwich'ing] a enchanteur(teresse).
beyond [bēând'] prep (in space) au-delà de; (exceeding) au-dessus de ♦ ad au-delà; ~ **doubt** hors de doute; ~ **repair** irréparable.
b/f abbr = brought forward.
BFPO n abbr (= British Forces Post Office) service postal de l'armée.
bhp n abbr (AUT: = brake horsepower) puissance f aux freins.
bi... [bī] prefix bi....
biannual [bīan'yōōəl] a semestriel(le).
bias [bī'əs] n (prejudice) préjugé m, parti pris; (preference) prévention f.
bias(s)ed [bī'əst] a partial(e), montrant un parti pris; **to be** ~ **against** avoir un préjugé contre.
bib [bib] n bavoir m, bavette f.
Bible [bī'bəl] n Bible f.
bibliography [biblēâg'rəfē] n bibliographie f.
bicarbonate of soda [bīkâr'bənit əv sō'də] n bicarbonate m de soude.
bicentenary [bīsen'tənārē] n bicentenaire m.
bicentennial [bīsenten'ēəl] n = **bicentenary**.
biceps [bī'seps] n biceps m.
bicker [bik'ûr] vi se chamailler.
bicycle [bī'sikəl] n bicyclette f.
bicycle path n piste f cyclable.
bicycle pump n pompe f à vélo.
bicycle track n piste f cyclable.
bid [bid] n offre f; (at auction) enchère f; (attempt) tentative f ♦ vb (pt **bid** or **bade** [bad], pp **bid** or **bidden** [bid'n]) vi faire une

enchère or offre ♦ vt faire une enchère or offre de; **to** ~ **sb good day** souhaiter le bonjour à qn.
bidder [bid'ûr] n: **the highest** ~ le plus offrant.
bidding [bid'ing] n enchères fpl.
bide [bīd] vt: **to** ~ **one's time** attendre son heure.
bidet [bēdā'] n bidet m.
bidirectional [bīdirek'shənəl] a bidirectionnel(le).
biennial [bīen'ēəl] a biennal(e), bisannuel(le) ♦ n biennale f; (plant) plante bisannuelle.
bier [bēr] n bière f (cercueil).
bifocals [bīfō'kəlz] npl lunettes fpl à double foyer.
big [big] a grand(e); gros(se); **to do things in a** ~ **way** faire les choses en grand.
bigamy [big'əmē] n bigamie f.
big dipper [big dip'ûr] n (Brit) montagnes fpl russes.
big end n (Brit AUT) tête f de bielle.
bigheaded [big'hedid] a prétentieux(euse).
big-hearted [big'hâr'tid] a au grand cœur.
bigot [big'ət] n fanatique m/f, sectaire m/f.
bigoted [big'ətid] a fanatique, sectaire.
bigotry [big'ətrē] n fanatisme m, sectarisme m.
big toe n gros orteil.
big top n grand chapiteau.
big wheel n (Brit: at fair) grande roue.
bigwig [big'wig] n (col) grosse légume, huile f.
bike [bīk] n vélo m, bécane f.
bike rack n (US) râtelier m á bicyclette.
bikeway [bīk'wā] n (US) piste f cyclable.
bikini [bikē'nē] n bikini m.
bilateral [bīlat'ûrəl] a bilatéral(e).
bile [bīl] n bile f.
bilingual [bīling'gwəl] a bilingue.
bilious [bil'yəs] a bilieux(euse); (fig) maussade, irritable.
bill [bil] n note f, facture f; (POL) projet m de loi; (US: bank note) billet m (de banque); (in restaurant) addition f, note f; (notice) affiche f; (THEATER): **on the** ~ à l'affiche; (of bird) bec m ♦ vt (item) facturer; (customer) remettre la facture à; **may I have the** ~ **please?** (est-ce que je peux avoir) l'addition, s'il vous plaît?; **"post no** ~**s"** "défense d'afficher"; **to fit** or **fill the** ~ (fig) faire l'affaire; ~ **of exchange** lettre f de change; ~ **of lading** connaissement m; ~ **of sale** contrat m de vente.
billboard [bil'bôrd] n panneau m d'affichage.
billet [bil'it] n cantonnement m (chez l'habitant) ♦ vt (troops) cantonner.
billfold [bil'fōld] n (US) portefeuille m.
billiards [bil'yûrdz] n (jeu m de) billard m.
billion [bil'yən] n (US) milliard m; (Brit) billion m (million de millions).
billionaire [bilyənär'] n ≈ milliardaire m/f.
billow [bil'ō] n nuage m ♦ vi (smoke) s'élever en nuage; (sail) se gonfler.
billy [bil'ē] n (US) matraque f.
billy goat [bil'ē gōt] n bouc m.
bin [bin] n boîte f; (Brit: also: **dust~, litter~**) poubelle f; (for coal) coffre m.
binary [bī'nûrē] a binaire.
bind, pt, pp bound [bīnd, bound] vt attacher;

(*book*) relier; (*oblige*) obliger, contraindre.
bind over *vt* (*LAW*) mettre en liberté conditionnelle.
bind up *vt* (*wound*) panser; **to be bound up in** (*work, research etc*) être complètement absorbé par, être accroché par; **to be bound up with** (*person*) être accroché à.
binder [bīn'dûr] *n* (*file*) classeur *m*.
binding [bīn'ding] *n* (*of book*) reliure *f* ♦ *a* (*contract*) qui constitue une obligation.
binge [binj] *n* (*col*): **to go on a** ~ faire la bringue.
bingo [bing'gō] *n* sorte de jeu de loto pratiqué dans des établissements publics.
binoculars [bənäk'yəlûrz] *npl* jumelles *fpl*.
biochemistry [bīōkem'istrē] *n* biochimie *f*.
biodegradable [bīōdigrā'dəbəl] *a* biodégradable.
biographer [bīäg'rəfûr] *n* biographe *m/f*.
biographic(al) [bīəgraf'ik(əl)] *a* biographique.
biography [bīäg'rəfē] *n* biographie *f*.
biological [bīəlâj'ikəl] *a* biologique.
biologist [bīäl'əjist] *n* biologiste *m/f*.
biology [bīäl'əjē] *n* biologie *f*.
biophysics [bīōfiz'iks] *n* biophysique *f*.
biopsy [bī'âpsē] *n* biopsie *f*.
biorhythm [bī'ōrithəm] *n* biorythme *m*.
biotechnology [bīōteknäl'əjē] *n* biotechnologie *f*.
birch [bûrch] *n* bouleau *m*.
bird [bûrd] *n* oiseau *m*; (*Brit col*: *girl*) nana *f*.
bird's-eye view [bûrdz'ī vyōō'] *n* vue *f* à vol d'oiseau; (*fig*) vue d'ensemble or générale.
bird watcher [bûrd' wâch'ûr] *n* ornithologue *m/f* amateur.
Biro [bē'rō] *n* ® (*Brit*) stylo *m* à bille.
birth [bûrth] *n* naissance *f*; **to give** ~ **to** donner naissance à, mettre au monde; (*animal*) mettre bas.
birth certificate *n* acte *m* de naissance.
birth control *n* limitation *f* des naissances; méthode(s) contraceptive(s).
birthday [bûrth'dā] *n* anniversaire *m*.
birthmark [bûrth'märk] *n* envie *f*, tache *f* de vin.
birthplace [bûrth'plās] *n* lieu *m* de naissance.
birth rate [bûrth rāt] *n* (taux *m* de) natalité *f*.
Biscay [bis'kā] *n*: **the Bay of** ~ le golfe de Gascogne.
biscuit [bis'kit] *n* (*US*) petit pain au lait; (*Brit*) biscuit *m*.
bisect [bīsekt'] *vt* couper *or* diviser en deux.
bishop [bish'əp] *n* évêque *m*; (*CHESS*) fou *m*.
bison [bī'sən] *n* bison *m*.
bit [bit] *pt of* **bite** ♦ *n* morceau *m*; (*of tool*) mèche *f*; (*of horse*) mors *m*; (*COMPUT*) bit *m*, élément *m* binaire; **a** ~ **of** un peu de; **a** ~ **mad/dangerous** un peu fou/risqué; ~ **by** ~ petit à petit; **to come to** ~s (*break*) tomber en morceaux, se déglinguer; **bring all your** ~s **and pieces** apporte toutes tes affaires; **to do one's** ~ y mettre du sien.
bitch [bich] *n* (*dog*) chienne *f*; (*col!*) salope *f* (!), garce *f*.
bite [bīt] *vt, vi* (*pt* **bit**, *pp* **bitten** [bit, bit'ən]) mordre ♦ *n* morsure *f*; (*insect* ~) piqûre *f*; (*mouthful*) bouchée *f*; **let's have a** ~ **(to eat)** mangeons un morceau; **to** ~ **one's nails** se ronger les ongles.

biting [bī'ting] *a* mordant(e).
bit part *n* (*THEATER*) petit rôle.
bitten [bit'ən] *pp of* **bite**.
bitter [bit'ûr] *a* amer(ère); (*criticism*) cinglant(e); (*icy: weather, wind*) glacial(e) ♦ *n* (*Brit: beer*) bière *f* (à forte teneur en houblon); **to the** ~ **end** jusqu'au bout.
bitterly [bit'ûrlē] *ad* (*complain, weep*) amèrement; (*oppose, criticize*) durement, âprement; (*jealous, disappointed*) horriblement; **it's** ~ **cold** il fait un froid de loup.
bitterness [bit'ûrnis] *n* amertume *f*; goût amer.
bittersweet [bit'ûrswēt] *a* aigre-doux(douce).
bitty [bit'ē] *a* (*US: tiny*) minuscule; (*Brit col*) décousu(e).
bitumen [bitōō'mən] *n* bitume *m*.
bivouac [biv'ōoak] *n* bivouac *m*.
bizarre [bizâr'] *a* bizarre.
bk *abbr* = **bank, book.**
BL *n abbr* (= *Bachelor of Law(s), Bachelor of Letters*) diplôme universitaire.
b/l *abbr* = **bill of lading.**
blab [blab] *vi* jaser, trop parler ♦ *vt* (*also*: ~ **out**) laisser échapper, aller raconter.
black [blak] *a* noir(e) ♦ *n* (*color*) noir *m*; (*person*): **B**~ noir/e ♦ *vt* (*shoes*) cirer; (*Brit INDUSTRY*) boycotter; **to give sb a** ~ **eye** pocher l'œil à qn, faire un œil au beurre noir à qn; ~ **coffee** café noir; **there it is in** ~ **and white** (*fig*) c'est écrit noir sur blanc; **to be in the** ~ (*in credit*) avoir un compte créditeur; ~ **and blue** a couvert(e) de bleus.
black out *vi* (*faint*) s'évanouir.
black belt *n* (*US*) région à forte population noire.
blackberry [blak'bärē] *n* mûre *f*.
blackbird [blak'bûrd] *n* merle *m*.
blackboard [blak'bôrd] *n* tableau noir.
black box *n* (*AVIAT*) boîte noire.
blackcurrant [blakkur'ənt] *n* cassis *m*.
black economy *n* (*Brit*) travail *m* au noir.
blacken [blak'ən] *vt* noircir.
Black Forest *n*: **the** ~ la Forêt Noire.
blackhead [blak'hed] *n* point noir.
black ice *n* verglas *m*.
blackjack [blak'jak] *n* (*CARDS*) vingt-et-un *m*; (*US: billy*) matraque *f*.
blackleg [blak'leg] *n* (*Brit*) briseur *m* de grève, jaune *m*.
blacklist [blak'list] *n* liste noire ♦ *vt* mettre sur la liste noire.
blackmail [blak'māl] *n* chantage *m* ♦ *vt* faire chanter, soumettre au chantage.
blackmailer [blak'mālûr] *n* maître-chanteur *m*.
black market *n* marché noir.
blackout [blak'out] *n* panne *f* d'électricité; (*in wartime*) black-out *m*; (*TV*) interruption *f* d'émission; (*fainting*) syncope *f*.
Black Sea *n*: **the** ~ la mer Noire.
black sheep *n* brebis galeuse.
blacksmith [blak'smith] *n* forgeron *m*.
black spot *n* (*Brit AUT*) point noir.
bladder [blad'ûr] *n* vessie *f*.
blade [blād] *n* lame *f*; (*of oar*) plat *m*; ~ **of grass** brin *m* d'herbe.
blame [blām] *n* faute *f*, blâme *m* ♦ *vt*: **to** ~ **sb/sth for sth** attribuer à qn/qch la responsabilité de qch; reprocher qch à qn/qch; **who's**

to ~? qui est le fautif *or* coupable *or* responsable?; **I'm not to** ~ ce n'est pas ma faute.
blameless [blām'lis] *a* irréprochable.
blanch [blanch] *vi* (*person, face*) blêmir ♦ *vt* (*CULIN*) blanchir.
bland [bland] *a* affable; (*taste*) doux(douce), fade.
blank [blangk] *a* blanc(blanche); (*look*) sans expression, dénué(e) d'expression ♦ *n* espace *m* vide, blanc *m*; (*cartridge*) cartouche *f* à blanc; **we drew a** ~ (*fig*) nous n'avons abouti à rien.
blank check *n* chèque *m* en blanc; **to give sb a** ~ **to do** ... (*fig*) donner carte blanche à qn pour faire ....
blanket [blang'kit] *n* couverture *f* ♦ *a* (*statement, agreement*) global(e), de portée générale.
blare [blär] *vi* (*brass band, horns, radio*) beugler.
blarney [blär'nē] *n* boniment *m*.
blasé [blâzā'] *a* blasé(e).
blasphemous [blas'fəməs] *a* (*words*) blasphématoire; (*person*) blasphémateur(trice).
blasphemy [blas'fəmē] *n* blasphème *m*.
blast [blast] *n* explosion *f*; (*shock wave*) souffle *m*; (*of air, steam*) bouffée *f* ♦ *vt* faire sauter *or* exploser ♦ *excl* (*Brit col*) zut!; **(at) full** ~ (*play music etc*) à plein volume.
  blast off *vi* (*SPACE*) décoller.
blast-off [blast'ôf] *n* (*SPACE*) lancement *m*.
blatant [blā'tənt] *a* flagrant(e), criant(e).
blatantly [blā'təntlē] *ad* (*lie*) ouvertement; **it's** ~ **obvious** c'est l'évidence même.
blaze [blāz] *n* (*fire*) incendie *m*; (*flames: of fire, sun etc*) embrasement *m*; (: *in hearth*) flamme *f*, flambée *f*; (*fig*) flamboiement *m* ♦ *vi* (*fire*) flamber; (*fig*) flamboyer, resplendir ♦ *vt*: **to** ~ **a trail** (*fig*) montrer la voie; **in a** ~ **of publicity** à grand renfort de publicité.
blazer [blā'zûr] *n* blazer *m*.
bleach [blēch] *n* (*also:* **household** ~) eau *f* de Javel ♦ *vt* (*linen*) blanchir.
bleached [blēcht] *a* (*hair*) oxygéné(e), décoloré(e).
bleachers [blē'chûrz] *npl* (*US SPORT*) gradins *mpl* (*en plein soleil*).
bleak [blēk] *a* morne, désolé(e); (*weather*) triste, maussade; (*smile*) lugubre; (*prospect, future*) morose.
bleary-eyed [blē'rēïd] *a* aux yeux pleins de sommeil.
bleat [blēt] *n* bêlement *m* ♦ *vi* bêler.
bleed, *pt, pp* **bled** [blēd, bled] *vt* saigner; (*brakes, radiator*) purger ♦ *vi* saigner; **my nose is** ~**ing** je saigne du nez.
bleeper [blē'pûr] *n* (*Brit: of doctor etc*) bip *m*.
blemish [blem'ish] *n* défaut *m*; (*on reputation*) tache *f*.
blend [blend] *n* mélange *m* ♦ *vt* mélanger ♦ *vi* (*colors etc*) se mélanger, se fondre, s'allier.
blender [blen'dûr] *n* (*CULIN*) mixeur *m*.
bless, *pt, pp* **blessed** *or* **blest** [bles, blest] *vt* bénir; **to be** ~**ed with** avoir le bonheur de jouir de *or* d'avoir.
blessed [bles'id] *a* (*REL: holy*) béni(e); (*happy*) bienheureux(euse); **it rains every** ~ **day** il ne se passe pas de jour sans qu'il ne

pleuve.
blessing [bles'ing] *n* bénédiction *f*; bienfait *m*; **to count one's** ~**s** s'estimer heureux; **it was a** ~ **in disguise** c'est un bien pour un mal.
blew [blōō] *pt of* **blow**.
blight [blīt] *n* (*of plants*) rouille *f* ♦ *vt* (*hopes etc*) anéantir, briser.
blind [blīnd] *a* aveugle ♦ *n* (*for window*) store *m* ♦ *vt* aveugler; **to turn a** ~ **eye (on** *or* **to)** fermer les yeux (sur).
blind alley *n* impasse *f*.
blind corner *n* virage *m* sans visibilité.
blinders [blīn'dûrz] *npl* (*US*) œillères *fpl*.
blindfold [blīnd'fōld] *n* bandeau *m* ♦ *a, ad* les yeux bandés ♦ *vt* bander les yeux à.
blindly [blīnd'lē] *ad* aveuglément.
blindness [blīnd'nis] *n* cécité *f*; (*fig*) aveuglement *m*.
blind spot *n* (*AUT etc*) angle *m* aveugle; (*fig*) angle mort.
blink [blingk] *vi* cligner des yeux; (*light*) clignoter ♦ *n*: **the TV's on the** ~ (*col*) la télé ne va pas tarder à nous lâcher.
blinkers [blingk'ûrz] *npl* (*Brit*) œillères *fpl*.
bliss [blis] *n* félicité *f*, bonheur *m* sans mélange.
blissful [blis'fəl] *a* (*event, day*) merveilleux(euse); (*smile*) de bonheur; **a** ~ **sigh** un soupir d'aise; **in** ~ **ignorance** dans une ignorance béate.
blissfully [blis'fəlē] *ad* (*smile*) béatement; (*happy*) merveilleusement.
blister [blis'tûr] *n* (*on skin*) ampoule *f*, cloque *f*; (*on paintwork*) boursouflure *f* ♦ *vi* (*paint*) se boursoufler, se cloquer.
blithely [blīth'lē] *ad* (*unconcernedly*) tranquillement; (*joyfully*) gaiement.
blithering [blith'ûring] *a* (*col*): **this** ~ **idiot** cet espèce d'idiot.
BLit(t) *n abbr* (= *Bachelor of Literature*) diplôme universitaire.
blitz [blits] *n* bombardement (aérien); **to have a** ~ **on sth** (*fig*) s'attaquer à qch.
blizzard [bliz'ûrd] *n* blizzard *m*, tempête *f* de neige.
BLM *n abbr* (*US*: = *Bureau of Land Management*) ≈ les domaines.
bloated [blō'tid] *a* (*face*) bouffi(e); (*stomach*) gonflé(e).
blob [blâb] *n* (*drop*) goutte *f*; (*stain, spot*) tache *f*.
bloc [blâk] *n* (*POL*) bloc *m*.
block [blâk] *n* bloc *m*; (*in pipes*) obstruction *f*; (*toy*) cube *m*; (*of buildings*) pâté *m* (de maisons) ♦ *vt* bloquer; (*COMPUT*) grouper; ~ **of flats** (*Brit*) immeuble (locatif); **3** ~**s from here** à trois rues d'ici; **mental** ~ blocage *m*; ~ **and tackle** (*TECH*) palan *m*.
  block up *vt* boucher.
blockade [blâkād'] *n* blocus *m* ♦ *vt* faire le blocus de.
blockage [blâk'ij] *n* obstruction *f*.
block booking *n* réservation *f* en bloc.
blockbuster [blâk'bustûr] *n* (*film, book*) grand succès.
block capitals *npl* (*Brit*) majuscules *fpl* d'imprimerie.
blockhead [blâk'hed] *n* imbécile *m/f*.
block letters *npl* majuscules *fpl*.

block release n (*Brit*) congé m de formation.
block vote n (*Brit*) vote m de délégation.
bloke [blōk] n (*Brit col*) type m.
blonde [blând] a, n blond(e).
blood [blud] n sang m.
bloodcurdling [blud'kûrdling] a à vous glacer le sang.
blood donor n donneur/euse de sang.
blood group n groupe sanguin.
bloodhound [blud'hound] n limier m.
bloodless [blud'lis] a (*victory*) sans effusion de sang; (*pale*) anémié(e).
bloodletting [blud'leting] n (*MED*) saignée f; (*fig*) effusion f de sang, représailles fpl.
blood poisoning n empoisonnement m du sang.
blood pressure n tension (artérielle); **to have high/low** ~ faire de l'hypertension/ l'hypotension.
blood sausage n (*US*) boudin m.
bloodshed [blud'shcd] n effusion f de sang, carnage m.
bloodshot [blud'shât] a: ~ **eyes** yeux injectés de sang.
bloodstained [blud'stând] a taché(e) de sang.
bloodstream [blud'strēm] n sang m, système sanguin.
blood test n analyse f de sang.
bloodthirsty [blud'thûrstē] a sanguinaire.
blood transfusion n transfusion f de sang.
blood vessel n vaisseau sanguin.
bloody [blud'ē] a sanglant(e); (*Brit col!*): **this** ~ ... ce foutu ..., ce putain de ... (!); ~ **strong/good** (*col!*) vachement or sacrément fort/bon.
bloody-minded [blud'ēmīn'did] a (*Brit col*) contrariant(e), obstiné(e).
bloom [blōōm] n fleur f; (*fig*) épanouissement m ♦ vi être en fleur; (*fig*) s'épanouir; être florissant(e).
blossom [blâs'əm] n fleur(s) f(pl) ♦ vi être en fleurs; (*fig*) s'épanouir; **to** ~ **into** (*fig*) devenir.
blot [blât] n tache f ♦ vt tacher; (*ink*) sécher; **to be a** ~ **on the landscape** gâcher le paysage.
blot out vt (*memories*) effacer; (*view*) cacher, masquer; (*nation, city*) annihiler.
blotchy [blâch'ē] a (*complexion*) couvert(e) de marbrures.
blotter [blât'ûr] n, **blotting paper** [blât'ing pā'pûr] n buvard m.
blouse [blous] n (*feminine garment*) chemisier m, corsage m.
blow [blō] n coup m ♦ vb (*pt* **blew**, *pp* **blown** [blōō, bloun]) vi souffler ♦ vt (*glass*) souffler; (*fuse*) faire sauter; **to** ~ **one's nose** se moucher; **to** ~ **a whistle** siffler; **to come to** ~**s** en venir aux coups.
blow away vi s'envoler ♦ vt chasser, faire s'envoler.
blow down vt faire tomber, renverser.
blow off vi s'envoler ♦ vt (*hat*) emporter; (*ship*): **to** ~ **off course** faire dévier.
blow out vi (*tire*) éclater; (*fuse*) sauter.
blow over vi s'apaiser.
blow up vi exploser, sauter ♦ vt faire sauter; (*tire*) gonfler; (*PHOT*) agrandir.
blow-dry [blō'drī] n (*hairstyle*) brushing m ♦

vt faire un brushing à.
blowfly [blō'flī] n (*US*) mouche f á viande.
blowout [blō'out] n (*of tire*) éclatement m; (*col: big meal*) gueuleton m.
blowtorch [blō'tôrch] n chalumeau m.
BLS n abbr (*US*) = *Bureau of Labor Statistics*.
BLT n abbr = *bacon, lettuce and tomato* (*sandwich*).
blubber [blub'ûr] n blanc m de baleine ♦ vi (*pej*) pleurer comme un veau.
bludgeon [bluj'ən] n gourdin m, trique f.
blue [blōō] a bleu(e); ~ **film/joke** film m/ histoire f pornographique; (**only**) **once in a** ~ **moon** tous les trente-six du mois; **out of the** ~ (*fig*) à l'improviste, sans qu'on si attende.
blue baby n enfant bleu(e).
bluebell [blōō'bcl] n jacinthe f des bois.
blueberry [blōō'bärē] n (*US*) myrtille f.
bluebottle [blōō'bâtəl] n mouche f à viande.
blue cheese n (fromage) bleu m.
blue-chip [blōō'chip'] a: ~ **investment** investissement m de premier ordre.
blue-collar worker [blōō'kâl'ûr wûr'kûr] n ouvrier/ère, col bleu.
blue jeans npl blue-jeans mpl.
blueprint [blōō'print] n bleu m; (*fig*) projet m, plan directeur.
blues [blōōz] npl: **the** ~ (*MUS*) le blues; **to have the** ~ (*col: feeling*) avoir le cafard.
bluff [bluf] vi bluffer ♦ n bluff m; (*cliff*) promontoire m, falaise f ♦ a (*person*) bourru(e), brusque; **to call sb's** ~ mettre qn au défi d'exécuter ses menaces.
blunder [blun'dûr] n gaffe f, bévue f ♦ vi faire une gaffe or une bévue; **to** ~ **into sb/sth** buter contre qn/qch.
blunt [blunt] a émoussé(e), peu tranchant(e); (*pencil*) mal taillé(e); (*person*) brusque, ne mâchant pas ses mots ♦ vt émousser; ~ **instrument** (*LAW*) instrument contondant.
bluntly [blunt'lē] ad carrément, sans prendre de gants.
bluntness [blunt'nis] n (*of person*) brusquerie f, franchise brutale.
blur [blûr] n tache or masse floue or confuse ♦ vt brouiller, rendre flou(e).
blurb [blûrb] n (*for book*) texte m de présentation; (*pej*) baratin m.
blurred [blûrd] a flou(e).
blurt [blûrt]: **to** ~ **out** vt (*reveal*) lâcher; (*say*) balbutier, dire d'une voix entrecoupée.
blush [blush] vi rougir ♦ n rougeur f.
blusher [blush'ûr] n rouge m à joues.
bluster [blus'tûr] n paroles fpl en l'air; (*boasting*) fanfaronnades fpl; (*threats*) menaces fpl en l'air ♦ vi parler en l'air; fanfaronner.
blustering [blus'tûring] a fanfaron(ne).
blustery [blus'tûrē] a (*weather*) à bourrasques.
Blvd abbr (= *boulevard*) Bd.
BM n abbr (*SCOL*: = *Bachelor of Medicine*) diplôme universitaire.
BMA n abbr = *British Medical Association*.
BMus n abbr (= *Bachelor of Music*) diplôme universitaire.
BO n abbr (*col*: = *body odor*) odeurs corporelles; (*US*) = **box office**.
boar [bôr] n sanglier m.
board [bôrd] n planche f; (*on wall*) panneau

m; (*for chess etc*) plateau *m*; (*committee*) conseil *m*, comité *m*; (*in firm*) conseil d'administration; (*NAUT, AVIAT*): **on ~ à bord ♦** *vt* (*ship*) monter à bord de; (*train*) monter dans; **full ~** (*Brit*) pension complète; **half ~** (*Brit*) demi-pension *f*; **~ and lodging** *n* chambre *f* avec pension; **with ~ and lodging** logé nourri; **above ~** (*fig*) régulier(ère); **across the ~** (*fig: ad*) systématiquement; (*: a*) de portée générale; **to go by the ~** être abandonné(e); (*be unimportant*) compter pour rien, n'avoir aucune importance.
  board up *vt* (*door*) condamner (*au moyen de planches, de tôle*).
boarder [bôr'dûr] *n* pensionnaire *m/f*; (*SCOL*) interne *m/f*, pensionnaire.
board game *n* jeu *m* de société.
boarding house [bôr'ding hous] *n* pension *f*.
boarding pass [bôr'ding pas] *n* (*AVIAT, NAUT*) carte *f* d'embarquement.
boarding school [bôr'ding skōōl] *n* internat *m*, pensionnat *m*.
board meeting *n* réunion *f* du conseil d'administration.
board room *n* salle *f* du conseil d'administration.
boardwalk [bôrd'wôk] *n* (*US*) cheminement *m* en planches.
boast [bōst] *vi*: **to ~ (about** *or* **of)** se vanter (de) **♦** *vt* s'enorgueillir de **♦** *n* vantardise *f*; sujet *m* d'orgueil *or* de fierté.
boastful [bōst'fəl] *a* vantard(e).
boastfulness [bōst'fəlnis] *n* vantardise *f*.
boat [bōt] *n* bateau *m*; (*small*) canot *m*; barque *f*; **to go by ~** aller en bateau; **to be in the same ~** (*fig*) être logé à la même enseigne.
boater [bō'tûr] *n* (*hat*) canotier *m*.
boating [bō'ting] *n* canotage *m*.
boatswain [bō'sən] *n* maître *m* d'équipage.
bob [bâb] *vi* (*boat, cork on water*: *also*: **~ up and down**) danser, se balancer **♦** *n* (*Brit col*) = **shilling**.
  bob up *vi* surgir *or* apparaître brusquement.
bobbin [bâb'in] *n* bobine *f*; (*of sewing machine*) navette *f*.
bobby [bâb'ē] *n* (*Brit col*) ≈ agent *m* (de police).
bobby pin [bâb'ē pin] *n* pince *f* à cheveux.
bobsled [bâb'sled], (*Brit*) **bobsleigh** [bâb'slā] *n* bob *m*.
bode [bōd] *vi*: **to ~ well/ill (for)** être de bon/mauvais augure (pour).
bodice [bâd'is] *n* corsage *m*.
bodily [bâd'əlē] *a* corporel(le); (*pain, comfort*) physique; (*needs*) matériel(le) **♦** *ad* (*carry, lift*) dans ses bras.
body [bâd'ē] *n* corps *m*; (*of car*) carrosserie *f*; (*of plane*) fuselage *m*; (*fig: society*) organe *m*, organisme *m*; (*: quantity*) ensemble *m*, masse *f*; (*of wine*) corps; (*also*: **~ stocking**) body *m*; **ruling ~** organe directeur; **in a ~** en masse, ensemble; (*speak*) comme un seul et même homme.
body-building [bâd'ēbil'ding] *n* body-building *m*, culturisme *m*.
bodyguard [bâd'ēgârd] *n* garde *m* du corps.

body repairs *npl* travaux *mpl* de carrosserie.
bodywork [bâd'ēwûrk] *n* carrosserie *f*.
boffin [bâf'in] *n* (*Brit*) savant *m*.
bog [bâg] *n* tourbière *f* **♦** *vt*: **to get ~ged down (in)** (*fig*) s'enliser (dans).
boggle [bâg'əl] *vi*: **the mind ~s** c'est incroyable, on en reste sidéré.
bogie [bō'gē] *n* bogie *m*.
Bogotá [bōgətâ'] *n* Bogotá.
bogus [bō'gəs] *a* bidon *inv*; fantôme.
Bohemia [bōhē'mēə] *n* Bohême *f*.
Bohemian [bōhē'mēən] *a* bohémien(ne) **♦** *n* Bohémien/ne; (*gipsy: also*: **b~**) bohémien/ne.
boil [boil] *vt* (faire) bouillir **♦** *vi* bouillir **♦** *n* (*MED*) furoncle *m*; **to come to a** *or* (*Brit*) **the ~** bouillir; **to bring to a** *or* (*Brit*) **the ~** porter à ébullition; **~ed egg** œuf *m* à la coque; **~ed potatoes** pommes *fpl* à l'anglaise *or* à l'eau.
  boil down *vi* (*fig*): **to ~ down to** se réduire *or* ramener à.
  boil over *vi* déborder.
boiler [boi'lûr] *n* chaudière *f*.
boiler suit *n* (*Brit*) bleu *m* de travail, combinaison *f*.
boiling [boi'ling] *a*: **I'm ~ (hot)** (*col*) je crève de chaud.
boiling point *n* point *m* d'ébullition.
boisterous [bois'tûrəs] *a* bruyant(e), tapageur(euse).
bold [bōld] *a* hardi(e), audacieux(euse); (*pej*) effronté(e); (*outline, color*) franc(franche), tranché(e), marqué(e).
boldness [bōld'nis] *n* hardiesse *f*, audace *f*; aplomb *m*, effronterie *f*.
bold type *n* (*TYP*) caractères *mpl* gras.
Bolivia [bōliv'ēə] *n* Bolivie *f*.
Bolivian [bōliv'ēən] *a* bolivien(ne) **♦** *n* Bolivien/ne.
bollard [bâl'ûrd] *n* (*NAUT*) bitte *f* d'amarrage; (*Brit AUT*) borne lumineuse *or* de signalisation.
bolster [bōl'stûr] *n* traversin *m*.
  bolster up *vt* soutenir.
bolt [bōlt] *n* verrou *m*; (*with nut*) boulon *m* **♦** *ad*: **~ upright** droit(e) comme un piquet **♦** *vt* verrouiller; (*food*) engloutir **♦** *vi* se sauver, filer (comme une flèche); **a ~ from the blue** (*fig*) un coup de tonnerre dans un ciel bleu.
bomb [bâm] *n* bombe *f* **♦** *vt* bombarder.
bombard [bâmbârd'] *vt* bombarder.
bombardment [bâmbârd'mənt] *n* bombardement *m*.
bombastic [bâmbas'tik] *a* grandiloquent(e), pompeux(euse).
bomb disposal *n*: **~ unit** section *f* de déminage; **~ expert** artificier *m*.
bomber [bâm'ûr] *n* caporal *m* d'artillerie; (*AVIAT*) bombardier *m*; (*terrorist*) poseur *m* de bombes.
bombing [bâm'ing] *n* bombardement *m*.
bombshell [bâm'shel] *n* obus *m*; (*fig*) bombe *f*.
bomb site *n* zone *f* de bombardement.
bona fide [bō'nə fīd'] *a* de bonne foi; (*offer*) sérieux(euse).
bonanza [bənan'zə] *n* filon *m*.
bond [bând] *n* lien *m*; (*binding promise*) engagement *m*, obligation *f*; (*FINANCE*) obliga-

tion; **in ~** (*of goods*) en entrepôt.
bondage [bân'dij] *n* esclavage *m*.
bonded warehouse [bán'did wär'hous] *n* entrepôt *m* sous douanes.
bone [bōn] *n* os *m*; (*of fish*) arête *f* ♦ *vt* désosser; ôter les arêtes de.
　bone up on *vt* bûcher.
bone china *n* porcelaine *f* tendre.
bone-dry [bōn'drī'] *a* absolument sec(sèche).
bone idle *a* fainéant(e).
boner [bō'nûr] *n* (*US*) gaffe *f*, bourde *f*.
bonfire [bân'fiûr] *n* feu *m* (de joie); (*for garbage*) feu.
Bonn [bân] *n* Bonn.
bonnet [bân'it] *n* bonnet *m*; (*Brit: of car*) capot *m*.
bonny [bân'ē] *a* (*Scottish*) joli(e).
bonus [bō'nəs] *n* prime *f*, gratification *f*; (*on wages*) prime.
bony [bō'nē] *a* (*arm, face*, MED: *tissue*) osseux(euse); (*thin: person*) squelettique; (*meat*) plein(e) d'os; (*fish*) plein d'arêtes.
boo [bōō] *excl* hou!, peuh! ♦ *vt* huer ♦ *n* huée *f*.
boob [bōōb] *n* (*col: breast*) nichon *m*; (*: Brit: mistake*) gaffe *f*.
boo-boo [bōō'bōō] *n* gaffe *f*.
booby prize [bōō'bē prīz] *n* timbale *f* (*ironique*).
booby trap [bōō'bē trap] *n* guet-apens *m*.
booby-trapped [bōō'bētrapt] *a* piégé(e).
book [bōōk] *n* livre *m*; (*of stamps etc*) carnet *m*; (*COMM*): **~s** comptes *mpl*, comptabilité *f* ♦ *vt* (*ticket*) prendre; (*seat, room*) réserver; (*driver*) dresser un procès-verbal à; (*soccer player*) prendre le nom de, donner un carton à; **to keep the ~s** tenir la comptabilité; **by the ~** a la lettre, selon les règles; **to throw the ~ at sb** passer un savon à qn.
　book in *vi* (*Brit: at hotel*) prendre sa chambre.
　book up *vt* réserver; **all seats are ~ed up** tout est pris, c'est complet; **the hotel is ~ed up** l'hôtel est complet.
bookable [bōōk'əbəl] *a*: **seats are ~** on peut réserver ses places.
bookcase [bōōk'kās] *n* bibliothèque *f* (*meuble*).
book ends *npl* serre-livres *m inv*.
booking [bōōk'ing] *n* (*Brit*) réservation *f*.
booking office [bōōk'ing ôf'is] *n* (*Brit*) bureau *m* de location.
book-keeping [bōōkkē'ping] *n* comptabilité *f*.
booklet [bōōk'lit] *n* brochure *f*.
bookmaker [bōōk'mākûr] *n* bookmaker *m*.
bookseller [bōōk'selûr] *n* libraire *m/f*.
bookshop [bōōk'shåp] *n* librairie *f*.
bookstall [bōōk'stôl] *n* (*Brit*) kiosque *m* à journaux.
bookstore [bōōk'stôr] *n* librairie *f*.
book token *n* (*Brit*) bon-cadeau *m* (pour un livre).
book value *n* valeur *f* comptable.
boom [bōōm] *n* (*noise*) grondement *m*; (*busy period*) boom *m*, vague *f* de prospérité ♦ *vi* gronder; prospérer.
boomerang [bōō'mərang] *n* boomerang *m*.
boom town *n* ville *f* en plein essor.
boon [bōōn] *n* bénédiction *f*, grand avantage.

boorish [bōō'rish] *a* grossier(ère), rustre.
boost [bōōst] *n* stimulant *m*, remontant *m* ♦ *vt* stimuler; **to give a ~ to sb's spirits** *or* **to sb** remonter le moral à qn.
booster [bōōs'tûr] *n* (*TV*) amplificateur *m* (de signal); (*ELEC*) survolteur *m*; (*also:* **~ rocket**) booster *m*; (*MED: vaccine*) rappel *m*.
booster seat *n* (*Brit* AUT: *for children*) siège *m* rehausseur.
boot [bōōt] *n* botte *f*; (*for hiking*) chaussure *f* (de marche); (*for football etc*) soulier *m*; (*ankle ~*) bottine *f*; (*US: also:* **Denver ~**) sabot *m* (de Denver); (*Brit: of car*) coffre *m* ♦ *vt* (*COMPUT*) lancer, mettre en route; **to ~** (*in addition*) par-dessus le marché, en plus; **to give sb the ~** (*col*) flanquer qn dehors, virer qn.
booth [bōōth] *n* (*at fair*) baraque (foraine); (*of cinema, telephone etc*) cabine *f*; (*also:* **voting ~**) isoloir *m*.
bootleg [bōōt'leg] *a* de contrebande; **~ record** enregistrement *m* pirate.
bootlicker [bōōt'likûr] *n* (*col*) fayot *m*.
booty [bōō'tē] *n* butin *m*.
booze [bōōz] (*col*) *n* boissons *fpl* alcooliques, alcool *m* ♦ *vi* boire, picoler.
boozer [bōōz'ûr] *n* (*col: person*): **he's a ~** il picole pas mal.
border [bôr'dûr] *n* bordure *f*; bord *m*; (*of a country*) frontière *f*.
　border on *vt fus* être voisin(e) de, toucher à.
borderline [bôr'dûrlīn] *n* (*fig*) ligne *f* de démarcation ♦ *a*: **~ case** cas *m* limite.
bore [bôr] *pt of* **bear** ♦ *vt* (*hole*) percer; (*person*) ennuyer, raser ♦ *n* (*person*) raseur/euse; (*of gun*) calibre *m*; **he's ~d to tears** *or* **~d to death** *or* **~d stiff** il s'ennuie à mourir.
boredom [bôr'dəm] *n* ennui *m*.
boring [bôr'ing] *a* ennuyeux(euse).
born [bôrn] *a*: **to be ~** naître; **I was ~ in 1960** je suis né en 1960; **~ blind** aveugle de naissance; **a ~ comedian** un comédien-né.
borne [bôrn] *pp of* **bear**.
Borneo [bôr'nēo] *n* Bornéo *f*.
borough [bur'ə] *n* municipalité *f*.
borrow [bar'ō] *vt*: **to ~ sth (from sb)** emprunter qch (à qn); **may I ~ your car?** est-ce que je peux vous emprunter votre voiture?
borrower [bar'ōûr] *n* emprunteur/euse.
borrowing [bâr'ōing] *n* emprunt(s) *m(pl)*.
bosom [bōōz'əm] *n* poitrine *f*; (*fig*) sein *m*.
bosom friend *n* ami/e intime.
boss [bôs] *n* patron/ne ♦ *vt* (*also:* **~ around**) mener à la baguette.
bossy [bôs'ē] *a* autoritaire.
bosun [bō'sən] *n* maître *m* d'équipage.
botanical [bətan'ikəl] *a* botanique.
botanist [bât'ənist] *n* botaniste *m/f*.
botany [bât'ənē] *n* botanique *f*.
botch [bâch] *vt* (*also:* **~ up**) saboter, bâcler.
both [bōth] *a* les deux, l'un(e) et l'autre ♦ *pronoun*: **~** (**of them**) les deux, tous(toutes) (les) deux, l'un(e) et l'autre; **~ of us went**, **we ~ went** nous y sommes allés tous les deux ♦ *ad*: **they sell ~ the fabric and the finished curtains** ils vendent (et) le tissu et les rideaux (finis), ils vendent à la fois le

tissu et les rideaux (finis).

bother [bâth'ûr] *vt* (*worry*) tracasser; (*needle, bait*) importuner, ennuyer; (*disturb*) déranger ♦ *vi* (*also*: ~ **o.s.**) se tracasser, se faire du souci ♦ *n*: **it is a ~ to have to do** c'est vraiment ennuyeux d'avoir à faire ♦ *excl* zut!; **to ~ doing** prendre la peine de faire; **I'm sorry to ~ you** excusez-moi de vous déranger; **please don't ~** ne vous dérangez pas; **don't ~** ce n'est pas la peine; **it's no ~** aucun problème.

Botswana [bâchwân'ə] *n* Botswana *m*.

bottle [bât'əl] *n* bouteille *f*; (*baby's*) biberon *m*; (*of perfume, medicine*) flacon *m* ♦ *vt* mettre en bouteille(s); **~ of wine/milk** bouteille de vin/lait; **wine/milk ~** bouteille à vin/lait.

bottle up *vt* refouler, contenir.

bottleneck [bât'əlnɛk] *n* étranglement *m*.

bottle opener *n* ouvre-bouteille *m*.

bottom [bât'əm] *n* (*of container, sea etc*) fond *m*; (*buttocks*) derrière *m*; (*of page, list*) bas *m*; (*of chair*) siège *m*; (*of mountain, tree, hill*) pied *m* ♦ *a* du fond; du bas; **to get to the ~ of sth** (*fig*) découvrir le fin fond de qch.

bottomless [bât'əmlis] *a* sans fond, insondable.

bottom line *n* (*fig*): **the ~ is** ... l'essentiel *m* est ....

bough [bou] *n* branche *f*, rameau *m*.

bought [bôt] *pt*, *pp* of **buy.**

bouillon cube [bool'yən kyoob] *n* (*US CULIN*) bouillon-cube *m*.

boulder [bōl'dûr] *n* gros rocher (*gén lisse, arrondi*).

bounce [bouns] *vi* (*ball*) rebondir; (*check*) être refusé (*étant sans provision*); (*also*: **to ~ forward/out** *etc*) bondir, s'élancer ♦ *vt* faire rebondir ♦ *n* (*rebound*) rebond *m*; **he's got plenty of ~** (*fig*) il est plein d'entrain *or* d'allant.

bouncer [boun'sûr] *n* (*col*) videur *m*.

bound [bound] *pt*, *pp* of **bind** ♦ *n* (*gen pl*) limite *f*; (*leap*) bond *m* ♦ *vt* (*leap*) bondir; (*limit*) borner ♦ *a*: **to be ~ to do sth** (*obliged*) être obligé(e) *or* avoir obligation de faire qch; **he's ~ to fail** (*likely*) il est sûr d'échouer, son échec est inévitable *or* assuré; **~ for** à destination de; **out of ~s** dont l'accès est interdit.

boundary [boun'dûrē] *n* frontière *f*.

boundless [bound'lis] *a* illimité(e), sans bornes.

bountiful [boun'təfəl] *a* (*person*) généreux(euse); (*God*) bienfaiteur(trice); (*supply*) ample.

bounty [boun'tē] *n* (*generosity*) générosité *f*.

bouquet [bookā'] *n* bouquet *m*.

bourbon [bûr'bən] *n* (*US*: *also*: **~ whiskey**) bourbon *m*.

bourgeois [boor'zhwâ] *a*, *n* bourgeois(e).

bout [bout] *n* période *f*; (*of malaria etc*) accès *m*, crise *f*, attaque *f*; (*BOXING etc*) combat *m*, match *m*.

boutique [bootēk'] *n* boutique *f*.

bow [bō] *n* nœud *m*; (*weapon*) arc *m*; (*MUS*) archet *m*; [bou] (*with body*) révérence *f*, inclination *f* (*du buste or corps*); (*NAUT*: *also*: **~s**) proue *f* ♦ *vi* [bou] faire une révérence,

s'incliner; (*yield*): **to ~ to** *or* **before** s'incliner devant, se soumettre à; **to ~ to the inevitable** accepter l'inévitable *or* l'inéluctable.

bowels [bou'əlz] *npl* intestins *mpl*; (*fig*) entrailles *fpl*.

bowl [bōl] *n* (*for eating*) bol *m*; (*for washing*) cuvette *f*; (*ball*) boule *f*; (*of pipe*) fourneau *m*; (*US*: *stadium*) stade *m* ♦ *vi* (*CRICKET*) lancer (la balle).

bowl over *vt* (*fig*) renverser.

bow-legged [bō'lɛgid] *a* aux jambes arquées.

bowler [bō'lûr] *n* joueur *m* de boules; (*CRICKET*) lanceur *m* (de la balle); (*Brit*: *also*: **~ hat**) (chapeau *m*) melon *m*.

bowling [bō'ling] *n* (*game*) jeu *m* de boules; jeu de quilles.

bowling alley *n* bowling *m*.

bowling green *n* terrain *m* de boules (*gazonné et carré*).

bowls [bōlz] *n* (jeu *m* de) boules *fpl*.

bow tie [bō tī] *n* nœud *m* papillon.

box [bâks] *n* boîte *f*; (*also*: **cardboard ~**) carton *m*; (*crate*) caisse *f*; (*THEATER*) loge *f*; (*Brit AUT*) intersection *f* (*matérialisée par des marques au sol*) ♦ *vt* mettre en boîte; (*SPORT*) boxer avec ♦ *vi* boxer, faire de la boxe.

boxcar [bâks'kâr] *n* (*RAIL*) wagon couvert.

boxer [bâk'sûr] *n* (*person*) boxeur *m*; (*dog*) boxer *m*.

boxing [bâk'sing] *n* (*sport*) boxe *f*.

Boxing Day *n* (*Brit*) le lendemain de Noël.

boxing gloves *npl* gants *mpl* de boxe.

boxing ring *n* ring *m*.

box number *n* (*Brit*: *for advertisements*) numéro *m* d'annonce.

box office *n* bureau *m* de location.

boy [boi] *n* garçon *m*.

boycott [boi'kât] *n* boycottage *m* ♦ *vt* boycotter.

boyfriend [boi'frend] *n* (petit) ami.

boyish [boi'ish] *a* d'enfant, de garçon.

Bp *abbr* = **bishop.**

BPOE *n abbr* (*US*: = *Benevolent and Protective Order of Elks*) association charitable.

BR *abbr* = **British Rail.**

bra [brâ] *n* soutien-gorge *m*.

brace [brās] *n* attache *f*, agrafe *f*; (*on teeth*) appareil *m* (dentaire); (*tool*) vilbrequin *m*; (*TYP*: *also*: **~ bracket**) accolade *f* ♦ *vt* consolider, soutenir; **to ~ o.s.** (*fig*) se préparer mentalement.

bracelet [brās'lit] *n* bracelet *m*.

braces [brā'siz] *npl* (*on teeth*) appareil *m* (dentaire); (*Brit*) bretelles *fpl*.

bracing [brā'sing] *a* tonifiant(e), tonique.

bracken [brak'ən] *n* fougère *f*.

bracket [brak'it] *n* (*TECH*) tasseau *m*, support *m*; (*group*) classe *f*, tranche *f*; (*also*: *Brit*: **brace ~**) accolade *f*; (*also*: **square ~**) crochet *m* ♦ *vt* mettre entre parenthèses; (*fig*: *also*: **~ together**) regrouper; **income ~** tranche *f* des revenus; **in ~s** entre parenthèses (*or* crochets).

brackish [brak'ish] *a* (*water*) saumâtre.

brag [brag] *vi* se vanter.

braid [brād] *n* (*trimming*) galon *m*; (*of hair*)

tresse *f*, natte *f*.
Braille [brāl] *n* braille *m*.
brain [brān] *n* cerveau *m*; ~**s** *npl* cervelle *f*;
he's got ~s il est intelligent.
brainchild [brān'chīld] *n* trouvaille
(personnelle), invention *f*.
brainless [brān'lis] *a* sans cervelle, stupide.
brainstorm [brān'stôrm] *n* (*fig*) moment *m*
d'égarement; (*US: brain wave*) idée *f* de génie.
brainwash [brān'wâsh] *vt* faire subir un lavage de cerveau à.
brain wave *n* idée *f* de génie.
brainy [brā'nē] *a* intelligent(e), doué(e).
braise [brāz] *vt* braiser.
brake [brāk] *n* (*on vehicle*) frein *m* ♦ *vt*, *vi*
freiner.
brake light *n* feu *m* de stop.
brake pedal *n* pédale *f* de frein.
bramble [bram'bəl] *n* ronces *fpl*; (*fruit*) mûre
f.
bran [bran] *n* son *m*.
branch [branch] *n* branche *f*; (*COMM*)
succursale *f*; (*: bank*) agence *f*; (*of association*) section locale ♦ *vi* bifurquer.
branch out *vi* diversifier ses activités; **to ~
out into** étendre ses activités à.
branch line *n* (*RAIL*) bifurcation *f*, embranchement *m*.
branch manager *n* directeur/trice de
succursale (*or* d'agence).
brand [brand] *n* marque (commerciale) ♦ *vt*
(*cattle*) marquer (au fer rouge); (*fig: pej*):
to ~ sb a communist *etc* traiter *or* qualifier
qn de communiste *etc*.
brandish [bran'dish] *vt* brandir.
brand name *n* nom *m* de marque.
brand-new [brand'nōō'] *a* tout(e) neuf(neuve),
flambant neuf(neuve).
brandy [bran'dē] *n* cognac *m*, fine *f*.
brash [brash] *a* effronté(e).
Brasilia [brəzil'ēə] *n* Brasilia.
brass [bras] *n* cuivre *m* (jaune), laiton *m*; **the
~** (*MUS*) les cuivres.
brass band *n* fanfare *f*.
brassière [brəzēr'] *n* soutien-gorge *m*.
brass knuckles *npl* coup-de-poing américain.
brass tacks *npl*: **to get down to ~** en venir
au fait.
brat [brat] *n* (*pej*) mioche *m/f*, môme *m/f*.
bravado [brəvá'dō] *n* bravade *f*.
brave [brāv] *a* courageux(euse), brave ♦ *n*
guerrier indien ♦ *vt* braver, affronter.
bravery [brā'vûrē] *n* bravoure *f*, courage *m*.
bravo [brá'vō] *excl* bravo!
brawl [brôl] *n* rixe *f*, bagarre *f* ♦ *vi* se bagarrer.
brawn [brôn] *n* muscle *m*; (*Brit: meat*) fromage *m* de tête.
brawny [brô'nē] *a* musclé(e), costaud(e).
bray [brā] *n* braiement *m* ♦ *vi* braire.
brazen [brā'zən] *a* impudent(e), effronté(e) ♦
vt: **to ~ it out** payer d'effronterie, crâner.
brazier [brā'zhûr] *n* brasero *m*.
Brazil [brəzil'] *n* Brésil *m*.
Brazilian [brəzil'ēən] *a* brésilien(ne) ♦ *n*
Brésilien/ne.
Brazil nut *n* noix *f* du Brésil.
breach [brēch] *vt* ouvrir une brèche dans ♦ *n*

(*gap*) brèche *f*; (*estrangement*) brouille *f*;
(*breaking*): ~ **of contract** rupture *f* de
contrat; ~ **of the peace** attentat *m* à l'ordre
public; ~ **of trust** abus *m* de confiance.
bread [bred] *n* pain *m*; (*col: money*) fric *m*;
~ **and butter** *n* tartines (beurrées); (*fig*)
subsistance *f*; **to earn one's daily ~** gagner
son pain; **to know which side one's ~ is
buttered (on)** savoir où est son avantage *or*
intérêt.
breadbin [bred'bin] *n* (*Brit*) boîte *f* or huche *f*
à pain.
breadboard [bred'bôrd] *n* planche *f* à pain;
(*COMPUT*) montage expérimental.
breadbox [bred'bâks] *n* (*US*) boîte *f* or huche *f*
à pain.
breadcrumbs [bred'krumz] *npl* miettes *fpl* de
pain; (*CULIN*) chapelure *f*, panure *f*.
breadline [bred'līn] *n*: **to be on the ~** être
sans le sou *or* dans l'indigence.
breadth [bredth] *n* largeur *f*.
breadwinner [bred'winûr] *n* soutien *m* de famille.
break [brāk] *vb* (*pt* **broke** [brōk], *pp* **broken**
[brō'kən]) *vt* casser, briser; (*promise*) rompre; (*law*) violer ♦ *vi* (se) casser, se briser;
(*weather*) tourner ♦ *n* (*gap*) brèche *f*;
(*fracture*) cassure *f*; (*rest*) interruption *f*,
arrêt *m*; (*: short*) pause *f*; (*: at school*) récréation *f*; (*chance*) chance *f*, occasion *f* favorable; **to ~ one's leg** *etc* se casser la
jambe *etc*; **to ~ a record** battre un record;
to ~ the news to sb annoncer la nouvelle à
qn; **to ~ with sb** rompre avec qn; **to ~
even** *vi* rentrer dans ses frais; **to ~ free** *or*
loose *vi* se dégager, s'échapper; **to take a ~**
(*few minutes*) faire une pause, s'arrêter cinq
minutes; (*vacation*) prendre un peu de repos;
without a ~ sans interruption, sans arrêt.
break down *vt* (*door etc*) enfoncer; (*resistance*) venir à bout de; (*figures, data*) décomposer, analyser ♦ *vi* s'effondrer; (*MED*)
faire une dépression (nerveuse); (*AUT*)
tomber en panne.
break in *vt* (*horse etc*) dresser; (*US: car*)
roder ♦ *vi* (*burglar*) entrer par effraction.
break into *vt fus* (*house*) s'introduire *or* pénétrer par effraction dans.
break off *vi* (*speaker*) s'interrompre;
(*branch*) se rompre ♦ *vt* (*talks, engagement*)
rompre.
break open *vt* (*door etc*) forcer, fracturer.
break out *vi* éclater, se déclarer; **to ~ out
in spots** se couvrir de boutons.
break through *vi*: **the sun broke through**
le soleil a fait son apparition ♦ *vt fus* (*defenses, barrier*) franchir; (*crowd*) se frayer
un passage à travers.
break up *vi* (*partnership*) cesser, prendre
fin; (*marriage*) se briser; (*friends*) se séparer ♦ *vt* fracasser, casser; (*fight etc*)
interrompre, faire cesser; (*marriage*) désunir.
breakable [brā'kəbəl] *a* cassable, fragile ♦ *n*:
~**s** objets *mpl* fragiles.
breakage [brā'kij] *n* casse *f*; **to pay for ~s**
payer la casse.
breakaway [brā'kəwā] *a* (*group etc*) dissi-
dent(e).

breakdown [brāk'doun] *n* (*AUT*) panne *f*; (*in communications*) rupture *f*; (*MED*: *also*: **nervous ~**) dépression (nerveuse); (*of figures*) ventilation *f*, répartition *f*.

breakdown service *n* (*Brit*) service *m* de dépannage.

breakdown van *n* (*Brit*) dépanneuse *f*.

breaker [brā'kûr] *n* brisant *m*.

breakeven [brākē'vən] *cpd*: **~ chart** *n* graphique *m* de rentabilité; **~ point** *n* seuil *m* de rentabilité.

breakfast [brek'fəst] *n* petit déjeuner *m*.

breakfast cereal *n* céréales *fpl*.

break-in [brāk'in] *n* cambriolage *m*.

breaking point [brā'king point] *n* limites *fpl*.

breakthrough [brāk'thrōō] *n* percée *f*.

break-up [brāk'up] *n* (*of partnership, marriage*) rupture *f*.

break-up value *n* (*Brit COMM*) valeur *f* de liquidation.

breakwater [brāk'wôtûr] *n* brise-lames *m inv*, digue *f*.

breast [brest] *n* (*of woman*) sein *m*; (*chest*) poitrine *f*.

breast-feed [brest'fēd] *vt*, *vi* (*irg*: *like* **feed**) allaiter.

breast pocket *n* poche *f* (de) poitrine.

breaststroke [brest'strōk] *n* brasse *f*.

breath [breth] *n* haleine *f*, souffle *m*; **to go out for a ~ of air** sortir prendre l'air; **out of ~** à bout de souffle, essoufflé(e).

Breathalyzer [breth'əlīzûr] *n* ® alcootest *m*.

breathe [brēth] *vt*, *vi* respirer; **I won't ~ a word about it** je n'en soufflerai pas mot, je n'en dirai rien à personne.

breathe in *vi* inspirer ♦ *vt* aspirer.

breathe out *vt*, *vi* expirer.

breather [brē'thûr] *n* moment *m* de repos *or* de répit.

breathing [brē'thing] *n* respiration *f*.

breathing space *n* (*fig*) (moment *m* de) répit *m*.

breathless [breth'lis] *a* essoufflé(e), haletant(e); oppressé(e); **~ with excitement** le souffle coupé par l'émotion.

breathtaking [breth'tāking] *a* stupéfiant(e), à vous couper le souffle.

breed [brēd] *vb* (*pt*, *pp* **bred** [bred]) *vt* élever, faire l'élevage de; (*fig*: *hate, suspicion*) engendrer ♦ *vi* se reproduire ♦ *n* race *f*, variété *f*.

breeder [brē'dûr] *n* (*person*) éleveur *m*; (*PHYSICS*: *also*: **~ reactor**) (réacteur *m*) surrégénérateur *m*.

breeding [brē'ding] *n* reproduction *f*; élevage *m*; (*upbringing*) éducation *f*.

breeze [brēz] *n* brise *f*.

breezeblock [brēz'blâk] *n* (*Brit*) parpaing *m*.

breezy [brē'zē] *a* frais(fraîche); aéré(e); désinvolte, jovial(e).

Breton [bret'ən] *a* breton(ne) ♦ *n* Breton/ne; (*LING*) breton *m*.

brevity [brev'itē] *n* brièveté *f*.

brew [brōō] *vt* (*tea*) faire infuser; (*beer*) brasser; (*plot*) tramer, préparer ♦ *vi* (*tea*) infuser; (*beer*) fermenter; (*fig*) se préparer, couver.

brewer [brōō'ûr] *n* brasseur *m*.

brewery [brōō'ûrē] *n* brasserie *f* (*fabrique*).

briar [brī'ûr] *n* (*thorny bush*) ronces *fpl*; (*wild rose*) églantine *f*.

bribe [brīb] *n* pot-de-vin *m* ♦ *vt* acheter; soudoyer; **to ~ sb to do sth** soudoyer qn pour qu'il fasse qch.

bribery [brī'bûrē] *n* corruption *f*.

bric-a-brac [brik'əbrak] *n* bric-à-brac *m*.

brick [brik] *n* brique *f*.

bricklayer [brik'lāûr] *n* maçon *m*.

brickwork [brik'wûrk] *n* briquetage *m*, maçonnerie *f*.

brickyard [brik'yârd] *n* briqueterie *f*.

bridal [brīd'əl] *a* nuptial(e); **~ party** noce *f*.

bride [brīd] *n* mariée *f*, épouse *f*.

bridegroom [brīd'grōōm] *n* marié *m*, époux *m*.

bridesmaid [brīdz'mād] *n* demoiselle *f* d'honneur.

bridge [brij] *n* pont *m*; (*NAUT*) passerelle *f* (de commandement); (*of nose*) arête *f*; (*CARDS, DENTISTRY*) bridge *m* ♦ *vt* (*river*) construire un pont sur; (*gap*) combler.

bridge loan, (*Brit*) **bridging loan** [brij'ing lōn] *n* prêt *m* relais.

bridle [brīd'əl] *n* bride *f* ♦ *vt* refréner, mettre la bride à; (*horse*) brider.

bridle path *n* piste *or* allée cavalière.

brief [brēf] *a* bref(brève) ♦ *n* (*LAW*) dossier *m*, cause *f* ♦ *vt* (*MIL etc*) donner des instructions à; **in ~ ...** (en) bref ...; **to ~ sb (about sth)** mettre qn au courant (de qch).

briefcase [brēf'kās] *n* serviette *f*; porte-documents *m inv*.

briefing [brē'fing] *n* instructions *fpl*.

briefly [brēf'lē] *ad* brièvement; (*visit*) en coup de vent; **to glimpse ~** entrevoir.

briefness [brēf'nis] *n* brièveté *f*.

briefs [brēfs] *npl* slip *m*.

Brig. *abbr* = **brigadier**.

brigade [brigād'] *n* (*MIL*) brigade *f*.

brigadier [brigədi'ûr] *n* brigadier général.

bright [brīt] *a* brillant(e); (*room, weather*) clair(e); (*person*) intelligent(e), doué(e); (*color*) vif(vive); **to look on the ~ side** regarder le bon côté des choses.

brighten [brīt'ən] (*also*: **~ up**) *vt* (*room*) éclaircir; égayer ♦ *vi* s'éclaircir; (*person*) retrouver un peu de sa gaieté.

brightly [brīt'lē] *ad* brillamment.

brilliance [bril'yəns] *n* éclat *m*; (*fig*: *of person*) brio *m*.

brilliant [bril'yənt] *a* brillant(e).

brim [brim] *n* bord *m*.

brimful [brim'fōōl'] *a* plein(e) à ras bord; (*fig*) débordant(e).

brine [brīn] *n* eau salée; (*CULIN*) saumure *f*.

bring, *pt*, *pp* **brought** [bring, brôt] *vt* (*thing*) apporter; (*person*) amener; **to ~ sth to an end** mettre fin à qch; **I can't ~ myself to fire him** je ne peux me résoudre à le mettre à la porte.

bring about *vt* provoquer, entraîner.

bring around *vt* (*US*: *unconscious person*) ranimer.

bring back *vt* rapporter; (*person*) ramener.

bring down *vt* (*lower*) abaisser; (*shoot down*) abattre; (*government*) faire s'effondrer.

bring forward *vt* avancer; (*BOOK-*

KEEPING) reporter.
bring in vt (*person*) faire entrer; (*object*) rentrer; (*POL: legislation*) introduire; (*LAW: verdict*) rendre; (*produce: income*) rapporter.
bring off vt (*task, plan*) réussir, mener à bien; (*deal*) mener à bien.
bring out vt (*meaning*) faire ressortir, mettre en relief; (*new product, book*) sortir.
bring round, bring to vt (*Brit*) = **bring around.**
bring up vt élever; (*question*) soulever; (*food: vomit*) vomir, rendre.
brink [bringk] n bord m; **on the ~ of doing** sur le point de faire, à deux doigts de faire; **she was on the ~ of tears** elle était au bord des larmes.
brisk [brisk] a vif(vive); (*abrupt*) brusque; (*trade etc*) actif(ive); **to go for a ~ walk** se promener d'un bon pas; **business is ~** les affaires marchent (bien).
bristle [bris'əl] n poil m ♦ vi se hérisser; **bristling with** hérissé(e) de.
bristly [bris'lē] a (*beard, hair*) hérissé(e); **your chin's all ~** ton menton gratte.
Brit [brɪt] n abbr (*col:* = *British person*) Britannique m/f.
Britain [brit'in] n (*also:* **Great ~**) la Grande-Bretagne; **in ~** en Grande-Bretagne.
British [brit'ish] a britannique; **the ~** npl les Britanniques mpl; **the ~ Isles** les îles fpl Britanniques.
British Rail (BR) n compagnie ferroviaire britannique, ≈ SNCF f.
Briton [brit'ən] n Britannique m/f.
Brittany [brit'ənē] n Bretagne f.
brittle [brit'əl] a cassant(e), fragile.
Br(o). abbr (*REL*) = **brother.**
broach [brōch] vt (*subject*) aborder.
broad [brôd] a large; (*distinction*) général(e); (*accent*) prononcé(e) ♦ n (*US col*) nana f; **~ hint** allusion transparente; **in ~ daylight** en plein jour; **the ~ outlines** les grandes lignes.
broad bean n fève f.
broadcast [brôd'kast] n émission f ♦ vb (*pt, pp* **broadcast**) vt radiodiffuser; téléviser ♦ vi émettre.
broadcasting [brôd'kasting] n radiodiffusion f; télévision f.
broadcasting station n station f de radio (*or* de télévision).
broaden [brôd'ən] vt élargir ♦ vi s'élargir.
broadly [brôd'lē] ad en gros, généralement.
broad-minded [brôd'mīn'did] a large d'esprit.
broccoli [brâk'əlē] n brocoli m.
brochure [brōshoor'] n prospectus m, dépliant m.
brogue [brōg] n (*accent*) accent régional; (*shoe*) (*sorte de*) chaussure basse de cuir épais.
broil [broil] vt griller.
broiler [broi'lûr] n (*fowl*) poulet m (à rôtir).
broke [brōk] pt of **break** ♦ a (*col*) fauché(e); **to go ~** (*business*) faire faillite.
broken [brō'kən] pp of **break** ♦ a (*stick, leg etc*) cassé(e); (*promise, vow*) rompu(e); **a ~ marriage** un couple dissocié; **a ~ home** un foyer désuni; **in ~ French/English** dans un français/anglais approximatif or hésitant.

broken-down [brō'kəndoun'] a (*car*) en panne; (*machine*) fichu(e); (*house*) en ruines.
brokenhearted [brō'kənhâr'tid] a (ayant) le cœur brisé.
broker [brō'kûr] n courtier m.
brokerage [brō'kûrij] n courtage m; (*US: payment*) commission f.
brolly [brâl'ē] n (*Brit col*) pépin m, parapluie m.
bronchitis [brângkī'tis] n bronchite f.
bronze [brânz] n bronze m.
bronzed [brânzd] a bronzé(e), hâlé(e).
brooch [brōch] n broche f.
brood [brood] n couvée f ♦ vi (*hen, storm*) couver; (*person*) méditer (sombrement), ruminer.
broody [broo'dē] a (*fig*) taciturne, mélancolique.
brook [brook] n ruisseau m.
broom [broom] n balai m.
broomstick [broom'stik] n manche m à balai.
Bros. abbr (*COMM* = *brothers*) Frères.
broth [brôth] n bouillon m de viande et de légumes.
brothel [brâth'əl] n maison close, bordel m.
brother [bruth'ûr] n frère m.
brotherhood [bruth'ûrhood] n fraternité f.
brother-in-law [bruth'ûrinlô] n beau-frère m.
brotherly [bruth'ûrlē] a fraternel(le).
brought [brôt] pt, pp of **bring.**
brow [brou] n front m; (*rare: gen:* **eye~**) sourcil m; (*of hill*) sommet m.
browbeat [brou'bēt] vt intimider, brusquer.
brown [broun] a brun(e), marron inv; (*hair*) châtain inv; (*rice, bread, flour*) complet(ète) ♦ n (*color*) brun m, marron m ♦ vt brunir; (*CULIN*) faire dorer, faire roussir; **to go ~** (*person*) bronzer; (*leaves*) jaunir.
brownie [brou'nē] n jeannette f, éclaireuse (cadette); (*US: cake*) gâteau au chocolat et aux noix.
brownnose(r) [broun'nōz(ûr)] n (*US col*) fayot m.
brown paper n papier m d'emballage, papier kraft.
brown sugar n cassonade f.
browse [brouz] vi (*among books*) bouquiner, feuilleter les livres; (*animal*) paître; **to ~ through a book** feuilleter un livre.
bruise [brooz] n bleu m, ecchymose f, contusion f ♦ vt contusionner, meurtrir ♦ vi (*fruit*) se taler, se meurtrir; **to ~ one's arm** se faire un bleu au bras.
brunch [brunch] n brunch m.
brunette [broonet'] n (*femme*) brune.
brunt [brunt] n: **the ~ of** (*attack, criticism etc*) le plus gros de.
brush [brush] n brosse f; (*quarrel*) accrochage m, prise f de bec ♦ vt brosser; (*also:* **~ past, ~ against**) effleurer, frôler; **to have a ~ with sb** s'accrocher avec qn; **to have a ~ with the police** avoir maille à partir avec la police.
brush aside vt écarter, balayer.
brush up vt (*knowledge*) rafraîchir, réviser.
brushed [brusht] a (*TECH: steel, chrome etc*) brossé(e); (*nylon, denim etc*) gratté(e).

brush-off [brush'ôf] *n* (*col*): **to give sb the** ~ envoyer qn promener.

brushwood [brush'wŏŏd] *n* broussailles *fpl*, taillis *m*.

brusque [brusk] *a* (*person, manner*) brusque, cassant(e); (*tone*) sec(sèche), cassant(e).

Brussels [brus'əlz] *n* Bruxelles.

Brussels sprout *n* chou *m* de Bruxelles.

brutal [brŏŏt'əl] *a* brutal(e).

brutality [brŏŏtal'itē] *n* brutalité *f*.

brute [brŏŏt] *n* brute *f* ♦ *a*: **by** ~ **force** par la force.

brutish [brŏŏ'tish] *a* grossier(ère), brutal(e).

BS *n* *abbr* (*US*: = *Bachelor of Science*) diplôme universitaire.

bs *abbr* = **bill of sale**.

BSc *n* *abbr* = **Bachelor of Science**.

BSI *n* *abbr* (= *British Standards Institution*) association de normalisation.

BST *abbr* (= *British Summer Time*) heure *f* d'été.

btu *n* *abbr* (= *British thermal unit*) btu (= *1054,2 joules*).

bubble [bub'əl] *n* bulle *f* ♦ *vi* bouillonner, faire des bulles; (*sparkle, fig*) pétiller.

bubble bath *n* bain moussant.

Bucharest [bŏŏ'kərest] *n* Bucarest.

buck [buk] *n* mâle *m* (*d'un lapin, lièvre, daim etc*); (*US col*) dollar *m* ♦ *vi* ruer, lancer une ruade; **to pass the** ~ **(to sb)** se décharger de la responsabilité (sur qn).

buck up *vi* (*cheer up*) reprendre du poil de la bête, se remonter ♦ *vt*: **to** ~ **one's ideas up** se reprendre.

bucket [buk'it] *n* seau *m*.

buckle [buk'əl] *n* boucle *f* ♦ *vt* boucler, attacher; (*warp*) tordre, gauchir; (: *wheel*) voiler.

buckle down *vi* s'y mettre.

buckle up *vi* (*AUT*) attacher sa ceinture.

Bucks *abbr* (*Brit*) = **Buckinghamshire**.

bud [bud] *n* bourgeon *m*; (*of flower*) bouton *m* ♦ *vi* bourgeonner; (*flower*) éclore.

Budapest [bŏŏ'dəpest] *n* Budapest.

Buddha [bŏŏ'də] *n* Bouddha *m*.

Buddhism [bŏŏ'dizəm] *n* bouddhisme *m*.

Buddhist [bŏŏ'dist] *a* bouddhiste ♦ *n* Bouddhiste *m/f*.

budding [bud'ing] *a* (*flower*) en bouton; (*poet etc*) en herbe; (*passion etc*) naissant(e).

buddy [bud'ē] *n* (*US*) copain *m*.

budge [buj] *vt* faire bouger ♦ *vi* bouger.

budgerigar [buj'ûrēgâr] *n* perruche *f*.

budget [buj'it] *n* budget *m* ♦ *vi*: **to** ~ **for sth** inscrire qch au budget; **I'm on a tight** ~ je dois faire attention à mon budget.

budgie [buj'ē] *n* = **budgerigar**.

Buenos Aires [bwā'nəs ī'riz] *n* Buenos Aires.

buff [buf] *a* (couleur *f*) chamois *m* ♦ *n* (*enthusiast*) mordu/e.

buffalo, *pl* ~ *or* ~**es** [buf'əlō] *n* buffle *m*; (*US*) bison *m*.

buffer [buf'ûr] *n* tampon *m*; (*COMPUT*) mémoire *f* tampon.

buffering [buf'ûring] *n* (*COMPUT*) mise *f* en mémoire tampon.

buffer state *n* état *m* tampon.

buffet *n* [bŏŏfā'] (*food, Brit*: *bar*) buffet *m* ♦ *vt* [buf'it] gifler, frapper; secouer, ébranler.

buffet car [bŏŏfā' kâr] *n* (*Brit RAIL*) voiture-bar *f*.

buffet lunch [bŏŏfā' lunch] *n* lunch *m*.

buffoon [bufŏŏn'] *n* buffon *m*, pitre *m*.

bug [bug] *n* (*insect*) punaise *f*; (: *gen*) insecte *m*, bestiole *f*; (*fig: germ*) virus *m*, microbe *m*; (*spy device*) dispositif *m* d'écoute (électronique), micro clandestin; (*COMPUT*: *of program*) erreur *f*; (: *of equipment*) défaut *m* ♦ *vt* (*room*) poser des micros dans; (*col*: *annoy*) embêter; **I've got the travel** ~ (*fig*) j'ai le virus du voyage.

bugbear [bug'bär] *n* cauchemar *m*, bête noire.

bugle [byŏŏ'gəl] *n* clairon *m*.

build [bild] *n* (*of person*) carrure *f*, charpente *f* ♦ *vt* (*pt, pp* **built** [bilt]) construire, bâtir.

build on *vt fus* (*fig*) tirer parti de, partir de.

build up *vt* accumuler, amasser; (*business*) développer; (*reputation*) bâtir; (*increase*: *production*) développer, accroître.

builder [bil'dûr] *n* entrepreneur *m*.

building [bil'ding] *n* construction *f*; (*structure*) bâtiment *m*, construction; (: *residential, offices*) immeuble *m*.

building contractor *n* entrepreneur *m* (en bâtiment).

building industry *n* (industrie *f* du) bâtiment *m*.

building site *n* chantier *m* (de construction).

building society *n* (*Brit*) société *f* de crédit immobilier.

building trade *n* = **building industry**.

build-up [bild'up] *n* (*of gas etc*) accumulation *f*; (*publicity*): **to give sb/sth a good** ~ faire de la pub pour qn/qch.

built [bilt] *pt, pp of* **build**.

built-in [bilt'in'] *a* (*closet*) encastré(e); (*device*) incorporé(e); intégré(e).

built-up area [bilt'up âr'ēə] *n* agglomération (urbaine); zone urbanisée.

bulb [bulb] *n* (*BOT*) bulbe *m*, oignon *m*; (*ELEC*) ampoule *f*.

bulbous [bul'bəs] *a* bulbeux(euse).

Bulgaria [bulgär'ēə] *n* Bulgarie *f*.

Bulgarian [bulgär'ēən] *a* bulgare ♦ *n* Bulgare *m/f*; (*LING*) bulgare *m*.

bulge [bulj] *n* renflement *m*, gonflement *m*; (*in birth rate, sales*) brusque augmentation *f* ♦ *vi* faire saillie; présenter un renflement; **to be bulging with** être plein(e) à craquer de.

bulk [bulk] *n* masse *f*, volume *m*; **in** ~ (*COMM*) en gros, en vrac; **the** ~ **of** la plus grande *or* grosse partie de.

bulk buying [bulk bī'ing] *n* achat *m* en gros.

bulkhead [bulk'hed] *n* cloison *f* (étanche).

bulky [bul'kē] *a* volumineux(euse), encombrant(e).

bull [bŏŏl] *n* taureau *m*; (*STOCK EXCHANGE*) haussier *m*; (*REL*) bulle *f*.

bulldog [bŏŏl'dôg] *n* bouledogue *m*.

bulldoze [bŏŏl'dōz] *vt* passer *or* raser au bulldozer; **I was** ~**d into doing it** (*fig col*) on m'a forcé la main.

bulldozer [bŏŏl'dōzûr] *n* bulldozer *m*.

bullet [bŏŏl'it] *n* balle *f* (*de fusil etc*).

bulletin [bŏŏl'itən] *n* bulletin *m*, communiqué *m*.

bulletin board *n* panneau *m* d'affichage;

(*COMPUT*) messagerie *f* (électronique).
bulletproof [bōol'itprōōf] *a* à l'épreuve des balles; ~ **vest** gilet *m* pare-balles.
bullfight [bōol'fīt] *n* corrida *f*, course *f* de taureaux.
bullfighter [bōol'fītûr] *n* torero *m*.
bullfighting [bōol'fīting] *n* tauromachie *f*.
bullhorn [bōol'hôrn] *n* (*US*) porte-voix *m inv*.
bullion [bōol'yən] *n* or *m* or argent *m* en lingots.
bullock [bōol'ək] *n* bœuf *m*.
bullring [bōol'ring] *n* arène *f*.
bull's-eye [bōolz'ī] *n* centre *m* (*de la cible*).
bully [bōol'ē] *n* brute *f*, tyran *m* ♦ *vt* tyranniser, rudoyer; (*frighten*) intimider.
bullying [bōol'ēing] *n* brimades *fpl*.
bum [bum] *n* (*col: backside*) derrière *m*; (*: tramp*) vagabond/e, traîne-savates *m/f inv*; (*: idler*) glandeur *m*.
bum around *vi* (*col*) vagabonder.
bumblebee [bum'bəlbē] *n* bourdon *m*.
bumf [bumf] *n* (*Brit col: forms etc*) paperasses *fpl*.
bump [bump] *n* (*blow*) coup *m*, choc *m*; (*jolt*) cahot *m*; (*on road etc, on head*) bosse *f* ♦ *vt* heurter, cogner; (*car*) emboutir.
bump along *vi* avancer en cahotant.
bump into *vt fus* rentrer dans, tamponner; (*col: meet*) tomber sur.
bumper [bum'pûr] *n* pare-chocs *m inv* ♦ *a*: ~ **crop/harvest** récolte/moisson exceptionnelle.
bumper cars *npl* autos tamponneuses.
bumptious [bump'shəs] *a* suffisant(e), prétentieux(euse).
bumpy [bum'pē] *a* cahoteux(euse); **it was a ~ flight/ride** on a été secoués dans l'avion/la voiture.
bun [bun] *n* petit pain au lait; (*of hair*) chignon *m*.
bunch [bunch] *n* (*of flowers*) bouquet *m*; (*of keys*) trousseau *m*; (*of bananas*) régime *m*; (*of people*) groupe *m*; ~ **of grapes** grappe *f* de raisin.
bundle [bun'dəl] *n* paquet *m* ♦ *vt* (*also*: ~ **up**) faire un paquet de; (*put*): **to** ~ **sth/sb into** fourrer *or* enfourner qch/qn dans.
bundle off *vt* (*person*) faire sortir (en toute hâte); expédier.
bundle out *vt* éjecter, sortir (sans ménagements).
bung [bung] *n* bonde *f*, bouchon *m* ♦ *vt* (*Brit: throw: also*: ~ **into**) flanquer; (*also*: ~ **up**: *pipe, hole*) boucher.
bungalow [bung'gəlō] *n* bungalow *m*.
bungle [bung'gəl] *vt* bâcler, gâcher.
bunion [bun'yən] *n* oignon *m* (*au pied*).
bunk [bungk] *n* couchette *f*.
bunk beds *npl* lits superposés.
bunker [bung'kûr] *n* (*coal store*) soute *f* à charbon; (*MIL, GOLF*) bunker *m*.
bunny [bun'ē] *n* (*also*: ~ **rabbit**) Jeannot *m* lapin.
bunny girl *n* hôtesse *f* de cabaret.
bunny hill *n* (*US SKI*) piste *f* pour débutants.
bunting [bun'ting] *n* pavoisement *m*, drapeaux *mpl*.
buoy [bōō'ē] *n* bouée *f*.
buoy up *vt* faire flotter; (*fig*) soutenir, épauler.

buoyancy [boi'ənsē] *n* (*of ship*) flottabilité *f*.
buoyant [boi'ənt] *a* (*ship*) flottable; (*carefree*) gai(e), plein(e) d'entrain; (*COMM: market*) actif(ive); (*: prices, currency*) soutenu(e).
burden [bûr'dən] *n* fardeau *m*, charge *f* ♦ *vt* charger; (*oppress*) accabler, surcharger; **to be a** ~ **to sb** être un fardeau pour qn.
bureau, *pl* ~**x** [byōōr'ō, z] *n* (*US: chest of drawers*) commode *f*; (*Brit: writing desk*) bureau *m*, secrétaire *m*; (*office*) bureau, office *m*.
bureaucracy [byōōrâk'rəsē] *n* bureaucratie *f*.
bureaucrat [byōōr'əkrat] *n* bureaucrate *m/f*, rond-de-cuir *m*.
bureaucratic [byōōrəkrat'ik] *a* bureaucratique.
burgeon [bûr'jən] *vi* (*fig*) être en expansion rapide.
burglar [bûr'glûr] *n* cambrioleur *m*.
burglar alarm *n* sonnerie *f* d'alarme.
burglarize [bûr'glərīz] *vt* (*US*) cambrioler.
burglary [bûr'glûrē] *n* cambriolage *m*.
burgle [bûr'gəl] *vt* cambrioler.
Burgundy [bûr'gəndē] *n* Bourgogne *f*.
burial [bär'ēəl] *n* enterrement *m*.
burial ground *n* cimetière *m*.
burlesque [bûrlesk'] *n* caricature *f*, parodie *f*.
burly [bûr'lē] *a* de forte carrure, costaud(e).
Burma [bûr'mə] *n* Birmanie *f*.
Burmese [bûrmēz'] *a* birman(e), de Birmanie ♦ *n* (*pl inv*) Birman(e); (*LING*) birman *m*.
burn [bûrn] *vt*, *vi* (*pt*, *pp* **burned** *or* **burnt** [bûrnt]) brûler ♦ *n* brûlure *f*; **the cigarette** ~**ed a hole in her dress** la cigarette a fait un trou dans sa robe; **I've** ~**ed myself!** je me suis brûlé(e)!
burn down *vt* incendier, détruire par le feu.
burn out *vt* (*subj: writer etc*): **to** ~ **o.s. out** s'user (à force de travailler).
burner [bûr'nûr] *n* brûleur *m*.
burning [bûr'ning] *a* (*building, forest*) en flammes; (*issue, question*) brûlant(e).
burnish [bûr'nish] *vt* polir.
burnt [bûrnt] *pt*, *pp* of **burn**.
burp [bûrp] (*col*) *n* rot *m* ♦ *vi* roter.
burrow [bûr'ō] *n* terrier *m* ♦ *vt* creuser.
bursar [bûr'sûr] *n* économe *m/f*; (*Brit: student*) boursier/ère.
bursary [bûr'sûrē] *n* (*Brit*) bourse *f* (d'études).
burst [bûrst] *vb* (*pt*, *pp* **burst**) *vt* faire éclater ♦ *vi* éclater ♦ *n* explosion *f*; (*also*: ~ **pipe**) fuite *f* (*due à une rupture*); ~ **of energy** déploiement soudain d'énergie, activité soudaine; ~ **of laughter** éclat *m* de rire; **a** ~ **of applause** une salve d'applaudissement; **a** ~ **of speed** une pointe de vitesse; ~ **blood vessel** rupture *f* de vaisseau sanguin; **the river has** ~ **its banks** le cours d'eau est sorti de son lit; **to** ~ **into flames** s'enflammer soudainement; **to** ~ **out laughing** éclater de rire; **to** ~ **into tears** fondre en larmes; **to** ~ **open** *vi* s'ouvrir violemment *or* soudainement; **to be** ~**ing with** être plein(e) (à craquer) de; regorger de.
burst into *vt fus* (*room etc*) faire irruption dans.
burst out of *vt fus* sortir précipitamment de.
bury [bär'ē] *vt* enterrer; **to** ~ **one's face in**

one's hands se couvrir le visage de ses mains; **to ~ one's head in the sand** (fig) pratiquer la politique de l'autruche; **to ~ the hatchet** (fig) enterrer la hache de guerre.

bus, ~**es** [bus] n autobus m; autocar m.

bush [boosh] n buisson m; (scrub land) brousse f.

bushel [boosh'əl] n boisseau m.

bushy [boosh'ē] a broussailleux(euse), touffu(e).

busily [biz'ilē] ad: **to be ~ doing sth** s'affairer à faire qch.

business [biz'nis] n (matter, firm) affaire f; (trading) affaires fpl; (job, duty) travail m; **to be away on ~** être en déplacement d'affaires; **I'm here on ~** je suis là pour affaires; **he's in the insurance/transport ~** il est dans les assurances/les transports; **to do ~ with sb** traiter avec qn; **it's none of my ~** cela ne me regarde pas, ce ne sont pas mes affaires; **he means ~** il ne plaisante pas, il est sérieux.

business address n adresse professionnelle or au bureau.

business card n carte f de visite (professionnelle).

business corporation n (US) ≈ société f anonyme (SA) (cotée en bourse).

business hours npl heures fpl ouvrables.

businesslike [biz'nislīk] a sérieux(euse); efficace.

businessman [biz'nisman] n homme m d'affaires.

business school n école f de commerce.

business suit n complet m.

business trip n voyage m d'affaires.

businesswoman [biz'niswooman] n femme f d'affaires.

busker [bus'kûr] n (Brit) artiste ambulant(e).

bus lane n voie réservée aux autobus.

bus shelter n abribus m.

bus station n gare routière.

bus stop n arrêt m d'autobus.

bust [bust] n buste m ♦ a (col: broken) fichu(e), fini(e) ♦ vt (col: POLICE: arrest) pincer; **to go ~** faire faillite.

bustle [bus'əl] n remue-ménage m, affairement m ♦ vi s'affairer, se démener.

bustling [bus'ling] a (person) affairé(e); (town) très animé(e).

bust-up [bust'up] n (Brit col) engueulade f.

busy [biz'ē] a occupé(e); (store, street) très fréquenté(e); (US: telephone, line) occupé ♦ vt: **to ~ o.s.** s'occuper; **he's a ~ man** (normally) c'est un homme très pris; (temporarily) il est très pris.

busybody [biz'ēbâdē] n mouche f du coche, âme f charitable.

busy signal n (US) tonalité f occupé.

but [but] cj mais ♦ prep excepté, sauf; **nothing ~** rien d'autre que; **~ for** sans, si ce n'était pour; **no one ~ him** lui seul; **all ~ finished** pratiquement fini; **anything ~ finished** tout sauf fini, très loin d'être fini.

butane [byoo'tān] n (also: **~ gas**) butane m.

butcher [booch'ûr] n boucher m ♦ vt massacrer; (cattle etc for meat) tuer; **~'s (shop)** boucherie f.

butler [but'lûr] n maître m d'hôtel.

butt [but] n (cask) gros tonneau; (thick end) (gros) bout; (of gun) crosse f; (of cigarette) mégot m; (US col) derrière m; (Brit fig: target) cible f ♦ vt donner un coup de tête à.

butt in vi (interrupt) interrompre.

butter [but'ûr] n beurre m ♦ vt beurrer.

buttercup [but'ûrkup] n bouton m d'or.

butter dish n beurrier m.

butterfingers [but'ûrfinggûrz] n (col) maladroit/e.

butterfly [but'ûrflī] n papillon m; (SWIMMING: also: **~ stroke**) brasse f papillon.

buttocks [but'əks] npl fesses fpl.

button [but'ən] n bouton m ♦ vt (also: **~ up**) boutonner ♦ vi se boutonner.

buttonhole [but'ənhōl] n boutonnière f ♦ vt accrocher, arrêter, retenir.

buttress [but'tris] n contrefort m.

buxom [buk'səm] a aux formes avantageuses or épanouies, bien galbé(e).

buy [bī] vb (pt, pp **bought** [bôt]) vt acheter; (COMM: company) (r)acheter ♦ n: **that was a good/bad ~** c'était un bon/mauvais achat; **to ~ sb sth/sth from sb** acheter qch à qn; **to ~ sb a drink** offrir un verre or à boire à qn.

buy back vt racheter.

buy in vt (Brit: goods) acheter, faire venir.

buy into vt fus (COMM) acheter des actions de.

buy off vt (bribe) acheter.

buy out vt (partner) désintéresser; (business) racheter.

buy up vt acheter en bloc, rafler.

buyer [bī'ûr] n acheteur/euse; **~'s market** marché m favorable aux acheteurs.

buzz [buz] n bourdonnement m; (col: phone call) coup m de fil ♦ vi bourdonner ♦ vt (call on intercom) appeler; (with buzzer) sonner; (AVIAT: plane, building) raser; **my head is ~ing** j'ai la tête qui bourdonne.

buzz off vi (col) s'en aller, ficher le camp.

buzzard [buz'ûrd] n buse f.

buzzer [buz'ûr] n timbre m électrique.

buzz word n (col) mot m à la mode or dans le vent.

by [bī] prep par; (beside) à côté de; au bord de; (before): **~ 4 o'clock** avant 4 heures, d'ici 4 heures; **~ this time tomorrow** demain à la même heure ♦ ad see **pass, go** etc; **a picture ~ Picasso** un tableau de Picasso; **surrounded ~ enemies** entouré d'ennemis; **~ bus/car** en autobus/voiture; **paid ~ the hour** payé à l'heure; **to increase** etc **~ the hour** augmenter etc d'heure en heure; **~ the kilo/meter** au kilo/mètre; **to pay ~ check** payer par chèque; **a room 3 meters ~ 4** une pièce de 3 mètres sur 4; **the bullet missed him ~ inches** la balle est passée à quelques centimètres de lui; **~ saving hard, he ...** à force d'économiser, il ...; **(all) ~ oneself** tout(e) seul(e); **~ the way** à propos; **~ and large** dans l'ensemble; **~ and** bientôt.

bye(-bye) [bī'(bī')] excl au revoir!, salut!

by(e)-law [bī'lô] n arrêté municipal.

by-election [bī'ilekshən] n élection (législative) partielle.

bygone [bī'gôn] a passé(e) ♦ n: **let ~s be ~s** passons l'éponge, oublions le passé.

bypass [bī'pas] n (route f de) contournement m; (MED) pontage m ♦ vt éviter.

by-product [bī'prȧdəkt] n sous-produit m, dérivé m; (fig) conséquence f secondaire, retombée f.

bystander [bī'standûr] n spectateur/trice, badaud/e.

byte [bīt] n (COMPUT) octet m.

byway [bī'wā] n chemin détourné.

byword [bī'wûrd] n: **to be a ~ for** être synonyme de (fig).

by-your-leave [bīyo͞orlēv'] n: **without so much as a ~** sans même demander la permission.

C

C, c [sē] n (letter) C, c m; (SCOL: grade) C; (MUS): **C do** m; **C for Charlie** C comme Célestin.

C abbr (= Celsius, centigrade) C.

c [sē] abbr (= century) s.; (= circa) v.; (US etc) = **cent(s)**.

CA n abbr = Central America; – **chartered accountant** ♦ abbr (US MAIL) = California.

ca. abbr (= circa) v.

c/a abbr = capital account, credit account, current account.

CAA n abbr (Brit: = Civil Aviation Authority) direction de l'aviation civile.

cab [kab] n taxi m; (of train, truck) cabine f; (horse-drawn) fiacre m.

cabaret [kabərā'] n attractions fpl, spectacle m de cabaret.

cabbage [kab'ij] n chou m.

cabin [kab'in] n cabane f, hutte f; (on ship) cabine f.

cabin cruiser n yacht m (à moteur).

cabinet [kab'ənit] n (POL) cabinet m; (furniture) petit meuble à tiroirs et rayons; (also: **display ~**) vitrine f, petite armoire vitrée.

cabinet-maker [kab'ənitmākûr] n ébéniste m.

cabinet minister n ministre m (membre du cabinet).

cable [kā'bəl] n câble m ♦ vt câbler, télégraphier.

cable car n téléphérique m.

cablegram [kā'bəlgram] n câblogramme m.

cable railway n (Brit) funiculaire m.

cable television n télévision f par câble.

caboose [kəbo͞os'] n (US: RAIL) fourgon m.

cache [kash] n cachette f; **a ~ of food** etc un dépôt secret de provisions etc, une cachette contenant des provisions etc.

cackle [kak'əl] vi caqueter.

cactus, pl cacti [kak'təs, kak'tī] n cactus m.

CAD n abbr (= computer-aided design) CAO f.

caddie [kad'ē] n caddie m.

cadet [kədet'] n (MIL) élève m officier; **police ~** élève agent de police.

cadge [kaj] vt (col) se faire donner; **to ~ a meal (off sb)** se faire inviter à manger (par qn).

cadger [kaj'ûr] n pique-assiette m/f inv, tapeur/euse.

cadre [kȧd'rə] n cadre m.

Caesarean [sizār'ēən] a (Brit) = **Cesarean**.

CAF abbr (= cost and freight) C et F.

café [kafā'] n ≈ café(-restaurant) m (sans alcool).

cafeteria [kafitē'rēə] n cafétéria f.

caffein(e) [ka'fēn] n caféine f.

cage [kāj] n cage f ♦ vt mettre en cage.

cagey [kā'jē] a (col) réticent(e); méfiant(e).

cagoule [kəgo͞ol'] n K-way m ®.

CAI n abbr (= computer-aided instruction) EAO m.

Cairo [kī'rō] n le Caire.

cajole [kəjōl'] vt couvrir de flatteries or de gentillesses.

cake [kāk] n gâteau m; **~ of soap** savonnette f; **it's a piece of ~** (col) c'est un jeu d'enfant; **he wants to have his ~ and eat it too** (fig) il veut tout avoir.

caked [kākt] a: **~ with** raidi(e) par, couvert(e) d'une croûte de.

cake pan n (US) moule m à gâteaux.

Cal. abbr (US) = California.

calamitous [kəlam'itəs] a catastrophique, désastreux(euse).

calamity [kəlam'itē] n calamité f, désastre m.

calcium [kal'sēəm] n calcium m.

calculate [kal'kyəlāt] vt calculer; (estimate: chances, effect) évaluer.

calculate on vt fus: **to ~ on sth/on doing sth** compter sur qch/faire qch.

calculated [kal'kyəlātid] a (insult, action) délibéré(e); **a ~ risk** un risque pris en toute connaissance de cause.

calculating [kal'kyəlāting] a calculateur(trice).

calculation [kalkyəlā'shən] n calcul m.

calculator [kal'kyəlātûr] n machine f à calculer, calculatrice f.

calculus [kal'kyələs] n analyse f (mathématique), calcul infinitésimal; **integral/ differential ~** calcul intégral/différentiel.

calendar [kal'əndûr] n calendrier m.

calendar month n mois m (de calendrier).

calendar year n année civile.

calf, pl calves [kaf, kavz] n (of cow) veau m; (of other animals) petit m; (also: **~skin**) veau m, vachette f; (ANAT) mollet m.

caliber [kal'əbûr] n (US) calibre m.

calibrate [kal'əbrāt] vt (gun etc) calibrer; (scale of measuring instrument) étalonner.

calibre [kal'əbûr] n (Brit) = **caliber**.

calico [kal'ikō] n (US) indienne f; (Brit) calicot m.

Calif. abbr (US) = California.

California [kaləfôr'nyə] n Californie f.

calipers [kal'əpûrz] npl (US MATH) compas m; (: MED) appareil m orthopédique; gouttière f; étrier m.

call [kôl] vt (gen, also TEL) appeler; (announce: flight) annoncer; (meeting) convoquer; (strike) lancer ♦ vi appeler; (visit: also: **~ in; to ~ (for)** passer (prendre) ♦ n (shout) appel m, cri m; (summons: for flight etc, fig: lure) appel; (visit) visite f; (also: **telephone ~**) coup m de téléphone; communication f; **to be on ~** être de permanence; **she's** ~ed Suzanne elle s'appelle Suzanne; **who is** ~ing? (*TEL*) qui est à l'appareil?; **New York** ~ing (*RADIO*) ici New York; **please give me a** ~ **at 7** appelez-moi à 7 heures; **to make a** ~ téléphoner, passer un coup de fil; **to pay a** ~ **on sb** rendre visite à qn, passer voir qn; **there's not much** ~ **for these items** ces articles ne sont pas très demandés.

call at *vt fus* (*subj: ship*) faire escale à; (: *train*) s'arrêter à.

call back *vi* (*return*) repasser; (*TEL*) rappeler ♦ *vt* (*TEL*) rappeler.

call for *vt fus* demander.

call in *vt* (*doctor, expert, police*) appeler, faire venir.

call off *vt* annuler; **the strike was** ~ed **off** l'ordre de grève a été rapporté.

call on *vt fus* (*visit*) rendre visite à, passer voir; (*request*): **to** ~ **on sb to do** inviter qn à faire.

call out *vi* pousser un cri *or* des cris ♦ *vt* (*doctor, police, troops*) appeler.

call up *vt* (*MIL*) appeler, mobiliser.

callbox [kôl'bâks] *n* (*Brit*) cabine *f* téléphonique.

caller [kôl'ûr] *n* personne *f* qui appelle; visiteur *m*; **hold the line,** ~! (*TEL*) ne quittez pas, Monsieur (*or* Madame)!

call girl *n* call-girl *f*.

call-in [kôl'in] *n* (*US RADIO, TV*) programme *m* à ligne ouverte.

calling [kôl'ing] *n* vocation *f*; (*trade, occupation*) état *m*.

calling card *n* (*US*) carte *f* de visite.

callipers [kal'əpûrz] *npl* (*Brit*) = **calipers**.

callous [kal'əs] *a* dur(e), insensible.

callousness [kal'əsnis] *n* dureté *f*, manque *m* de cœur, insensibilité *f*.

callow [kal'ō] *a* sans expérience (de la vie).

calm [kâm] *a* calme ♦ *n* calme *m* ♦ *vt* calmer, apaiser.

calm down *vi* se calmer, s'apaiser ♦ *vt* calmer, apaiser.

calmly [kâm'lē] *ad* calmement, avec calme.

calmness [kâm'nis] *n* calme *m*.

Calor gas [kā'lûr gas] *n* ® (*Brit*) butane *m*, butagaz *m* ®.

calorie [kal'ûrē] *n* calorie *f*; **low** ~ **product** produit *m* pauvre en calories.

calve [kav] *vi* vêler, mettre bas.

calves [kavz] *npl of* **calf**.

CAM *n abbr* (= *computer-aided manufacturing*) FAO *f*.

camber [kam'bûr] *n* (*of road*) bombement *m*.

Cambodia [kambō'dēə] *n* Cambodge *m*.

Cambodian [kambō'dēən] *a* cambodgien(ne) ♦ *n* Cambodgien/ne.

Cambs *abbr* (*Brit*) = *Cambridgeshire*.

camcorder [kam'kôrdûr] *n* caméscope *m*.

came [kām] *pt of* **come**.

camel [kam'əl] *n* chameau *m*.

cameo [kam'ēō] *n* camée *m*.

camera [kam'ûrə] *n* appareil-photo *m*; (*CINEMA, TV*) caméra *f*; **35mm** ~ appareil 24 x 36 *or* petit format.

cameraman [kam'ûrəman] *n* caméraman *m*.

Cameroon, Cameroun [kamərōōn'] *n* Cameroun *m*.

camouflage [kam'əflâzh] *n* camouflage *m* ♦ *vt* camoufler.

camp [kamp] *n* camp *m* ♦ *vi* camper; **to go** ~ing faire du camping.

campaign [kampān'] *n* (*MIL, POL etc*) campagne *f* ♦ *vi* (*also fig*) faire campagne; **to** ~ **for/against** militer pour/contre.

campaigner [kampān'ûr] *n*: ~ **for** partisan/e de; ~ **against** opposant/e à.

camp bed *n* lit *m* de camp.

camper [kam'pûr] *n* campeur/euse; (*vehicle*) camping-car *m*.

camping [kam'ping] *n* camping *m*.

camp(ing) site *n* (terrain *m* de) camping *m*.

campus [kam'pəs] *n* campus *m*.

camshaft [kam'shaft] *n* arbre *m* à came.

can [kan] *auxiliary vb see next headword* ♦ *n* (*of milk, oil, water*) bidon *m*; (*of fruit, soup etc*) boîte *f* (de conserve) ♦ *vt* mettre en conserve; **a** ~ **of beer** une canette de bière; **he had to carry the** ~ (*Brit col*) on lui a fait porter le chapeau.

can [kan] *n, vt see previous headword* ♦ *auxiliary vb* (*gen*) pouvoir; (*know how to*) savoir; **I** ~ **swim** *etc* je sais nager *etc*; **I** ~ **speak French** je parle français; **I** ~**'t see you** je ne vous vois pas; **could I have a word with you?** est-ce que je pourrais vous parler un instant?; **he could be in the library** il est peut-être dans la bibliothèque; **they could have forgotten** ils ont pu oublier.

Canada [kan'ədə] *n* Canada *m*.

Canadian [kənā'dēən] *a* canadien(ne) ♦ *n* Canadien/ne.

canal [kənal'] *n* canal *m*.

canary [kənär'ē] *n* canari *m*, serin *m*.

Canary Islands, Canaries [kənär'ēz] *npl*: **the** ~ les (îles *fpl*) Canaries *fpl*.

Canberra [kan'bärə] *n* Canberra *f*.

cancel [kan'səl] *vt* annuler; (*train*) supprimer; (*party, appointment*) décommander; (*cross out*) barrer, rayer; (*stamp*) oblitérer; (*check*) faire opposition à.

cancel out *vt* annuler; **they** ~ **each other out** ils s'annulent.

cancellation [kansəlā'shən] *n* annulation *f*; suppression *f*; oblitération *f*; (*TOURISM*) réservation annulée, client *etc* qui s'est décommandé.

cancer [kan'sûr] *n* cancer *m*; **C**~ (*sign*) Cancer; **to be C**~ être du Cancer.

cancerous [kan'sûrəs] *a* cancéreux(euse).

cancer patient *n* cancéreux/euse.

cancer research *n* recherche *f* contre le cancer.

C and F *abbr* (= *cost and freight*) C et F.

candid [kan'did] *a* (très) franc(franche), sincère.

candidacy [kan'didəsē] *n* candidature *f*.

candidate [kan'didāt] *n* candidat/e.

candied [kan'dēd] *a* confit(e); ~ **apple** (*US*) pomme caramélisée.

candle [kan'dəl] *n* bougie *f*; (*of tallow*) chandelle *f*; (*in church*) cierge *m*.

candlelight [kan'dəllīt] *n*: **by** ~ à la lumière d'une bougie; (*dinner*) aux chandelles.

candlestick [kan'dəlstik] *n* (*also*: **candle holder**) bougeoir *m*; (*bigger, ornate*) chandelier *m*.

candor, (*Brit*) **candour** [kan'dûr] *n* (grande) franchise *or* sincérité.

candy [kan'dē] *n* sucre candi; (*US*) bonbon *m*.

candy-floss [kan'dēflôs] *n* (*Brit*) barbe *f* à papa.

candy store *n* (*US*) confiserie *f*.

cane [kān] *n* canne *f*; (*for baskets, chairs etc*) rotin *m* ♦ *vt* (*Brit SCOL*) administrer des coups de bâton à.

canine [kā'nīn] *a* canin(e).

canister [kan'istûr] *n* boîte *f* (*gén en métal*).

cannabis [kan'əbis] *n* (*drug*) cannabis *m*; (*also:* ~ **plant**) chanvre indien.

canned [kand] *a* (*food*) en boîte, en conserve; (*col: music*) enregistré(e); (*US col: worker*) mis(e) à la porte; (*Brit col: drunk*) bourré(e).

cannibal [kan'əbəl] *n* cannibale *m/f*, anthropophage *m/f*.

cannibalism [kan'əbəlizəm] *n* cannibalisme *m*, anthropophagie *f*.

cannon, *pl* ~ *or* ~**s** [kan'ən] *n* (*gun*) canon *m*.

cannonball [kan'ənbôl] *n* boulet *m* de canon.

cannon fodder *n* chair *f* à canon.

cannot [kan'ât] = **can not.**

canny [kan'ē] *a* madré(e), finaud(e).

canoe [kənōō'] *n* pirogue *f*; (*SPORT*) canoë *m*.

canoeing [kənōō'ing] *n* (*sport*) canoë *m*.

canoeist [kənōō'ist] *n* canoéiste *m/f*.

canon [kan'ən] *n* (*clergyman*) chanoine *m*; (*standard*) canon *m*.

canonize [kan'ənīz] *vt* canoniser.

can opener [kan ō'pənûr] *n* ouvre-boîte *m*.

canopy [kan'əpē] *n* baldaquin *m*; dais *m*.

cant [kant] *n* jargon *m* ♦ *vt, vi* pencher.

can't [kant] = **can not.**

cantankerous [kantang'kûrəs] *a* querelleur(euse), acariâtre.

canteen [kantēn'] *n* cantine *f*; (*Brit: of cutlery*) ménagère *f*.

canter [kan'tûr] *n* petit galop ♦ *vi* aller au petit galop.

cantilever [kan'təlevûr] *n* porte-à-faux *m inv*.

canvas [kan'vəs] *n* (*gen*) toile *f*; **under** ~ (*camping*) sous la tente; (*NAUT*) toutes voiles dehors.

canvass [kan'vəs] *vt* (*POL: district*) faire la tournée électorale dans; (*: person*) solliciter le suffrage de; (*COMM: district*) prospecter; (*citizens, opinions*) sonder.

canvasser [kan'vəsûr] *n* (*POL*) agent électoral; (*COMM*) démarcheur *m*.

canvassing [kan'vəsing] *n* (*POL*) prospection électorale, démarchage électoral; (*COMM*) démarchage, prospection.

canyon [kan'yən] *n* cañon *m*, gorge (profonde).

CAP *n abbr* (*Brit: = Common Agricultural Policy*) PAC *f*.

cap [kap] *n* casquette *f*; (*for swimming*) bonnet *m* de bain; (*of pen*) capuchon *m*; (*of bottle*) capsule *f*; (*Brit: contraceptive: also:* **Dutch** ~) diaphragme *m*; (*: SOCCER*) sélection *f* pour l'équipe nationale ♦ *vt* capsuler; (*outdo*) surpasser; ~**ped with** coiffé(e) de; **and to** ~ **it all, he ...** (*Brit*) pour couronner le tout, il ....

capability [kāpəbil'ətē] *n* aptitude *f*, capacité *f*.

capable [kā'pəbəl] *a* capable; ~ **of** (*interpre-*

tation etc) susceptible de.

capacious [kəpā'shəs] *a* vaste.

capacity [kəpas'itē] *n* (*of container*) capacité *f*, contenance *f*; (*ability*) aptitude *f*; **filled to** ~ plein(e); **in his** ~ **as** en sa qualité de; **this work is beyond my** ~ ce travail dépasse mes capacités; **in an advisory** ~ à titre consultatif; **to work at full** ~ travailler à plein rendement.

cape [kāp] *n* (*garment*) cape *f*; (*GEO*) cap *m*.

Cape of Good Hope *n* cap *m* de Bonne Espérance.

caper [kā'pûr] *n* (*CULIN: also:* ~**s**) câpre *f*.

Cape Town *n* Le Cap.

capita [kap'itə] *see* **per capita.**

capital [kap'itəl] *n* (*also:* ~ **city**) capitale *f*; (*money*) capital *m*; (*also:* ~ **letter**) majuscule *f*.

capital account *n* balance *f* des capitaux; (*of country*) compte capital.

capital allowance *n* provision *f* pour amortissement.

capital assets *npl* immobilisations *fpl*.

capital expenditure *n* dépenses *fpl* d'équipement.

capital gains tax *n* impôt *m* sur les plus-values.

capital goods *n* biens *mpl* d'équipement.

capital-intensive [kap'itəlintensiv] *a* à forte proportion de capitaux.

capitalism [kap'itəlizəm] *n* capitalisme *m*.

capitalist [kap'itəlist] *a, n* capitaliste (*m/f*).

capitalize [kap'itəlīz] *vt* (*provide with capital*) financer.

capitalize on *vt fus* (*fig*) profiter de.

capital punishment *n* peine capitale.

capitulate [kəpich'ōōlāt] *vi* capituler.

capitulation [kəpichōōlā'shən] *n* capitulation *f*.

capricious [kəprish'əs] *a* capricieux(euse), fantasque.

Capricorn [kap'rikôrn] *n* le Capricorne; **to be** ~ être du Capricorne.

caps [kaps] *abbr* = **capital letters.**

capsize [kap'sīz] *vt* faire chavirer ♦ *vi* chavirer.

capstan [kap'stən] *n* cabestan *m*.

capsule [kap'səl] *n* capsule *f*.

Capt. *abbr* (= *captain*) Cne.

captain [kap'tin] *n* capitaine *m* ♦ *vt* commander, être la capitaine de.

caption [kap'shən] *n* légende *f*.

captivate [kap'təvāt] *vt* captiver, fasciner.

captive [kap'tiv] *a, n* captif(ive).

captivity [kaptiv'ətē] *n* captivité *f*.

captor [kap'tûr] *n* (*unlawful*) ravisseur *m*; (*lawful*): **his** ~**s** les gens (*or* ceux *etc*) qui l'ont arrêté.

capture [kap'chûr] *vt* capturer, prendre; (*attention*) capter ♦ *n* capture *f*.

car [kâr] *n* voiture *f*, auto *f*; (*US RAIL*) wagon *m*, voiture; **by** ~ en voiture.

Caracas [kərak'əs] *n* Caracas.

carafe [kəraf'] *n* carafe *f*.

carafe wine *n* (*in restaurant*) ≈ vin ouvert.

caramel [kar'əməl] *n* caramel *m*.

carat [kar'ət] *n* carat *m*; **18** ~ **gold** or *m* à 18 carats.

caravan [kar'əvan] *n* (*Brit: camper*) caravane *f*.

caravan site *n* (*Brit*) camping *m* pour caravanes.

caraway [kar'əwã] *n:* ~ **seed** graine *f* de cumin, cumin *m*.

carbohydrates [kârbōhī'drãts] *npl* (*foods*) aliments *mpl* riches en hydrate de carbone.

carbolic acid [kârbál'ik as'id] *n* phénol *m*.

carbon [kâr'bən] *n* carbone *m*.

carbonated [kâr'bənãtid] *a* (*drink*) gazeux(euse).

carbon copy *n* carbone *m*.

carbon dioxide *n* gas *m* carbonique, dioxyde *m* de carbone.

carbon paper *n* papier *m* carbone.

carbon ribbon *n* ruban *m* carbone.

carburetor, (*Brit*) **carburettor** [kâr'bərātûr] *n* carburateur *m*.

carcass [kâr'kəs] *n* carcasse *f*.

carcinogenic [kârsinəjen'ik] *a* cancérigène.

card [kârd] *n* carte *f*; (*membership* ~) carte d'adhérent; **to play** ~s jouer aux cartes.

cardamom [kâr'dəməm] *n* cardamome *f*.

cardboard [kârd'bôrd] *n* carton *m*.

cardboard box *n* (boîte *f* en) carton *m*.

card-carrying member [kârd'karēing mem'bûr] *n* membre actif.

card game *n* jeu *m* de cartes.

cardiac [kâr'dēak] *a* cardiaque.

cardigan [kâr'digən] *n* cardigan *m*.

cardinal [kâr'dənəl] *a* cardinal(e) ♦ *n* cardinal *m*.

card index *n* fichier *m* (alphabétique).

Cards *abbr* (*Brit*) = *Cardiganshire*.

cardsharp [kârd'shârp] *n* tricheur/euse professionnel(le).

CARE *n abbr* (= *Cooperative for American Relief Everywhere*) association charitable.

care [kâr] *n* soin *m*, attention *f*; (*worry*) souci *m* ♦ *vi:* **to** ~ **about** se soucier de, s'intéresser à; **would you** ~ **to/for ...?** voulez-vous ...?; **I wouldn't** ~ **to do it** je n'aimerais pas le faire; **in sb's** ~ à la garde de qn, confié à qn; ~ **of (c/o)** (*on letter*) aux bons soins de; "**handle with** ~" "fragile"; **to take** ~ **(to do)** faire attention (à faire); **to take** ~ **of** *vt* s'occuper de, prendre soin de; (*details, arrangements*) s'occuper de; **the child has been taken into** ~ l'enfant a été placé en institution; **I don't** ~ ça m'est bien égal, peu m'importe; **I could** ~ **less,** (*Brit*) **I couldn't** ~ **less** cela m'est complètement égal, je m'en fiche complètement.

care for *vt fus* s'occuper de; (*like*) aimer.

careen [kərēn'] *vi* (*ship*) donner de la bande ♦ *vt* caréner, mettre en carène.

career [kərēr'] *n* carrière *f* ♦ *vi* (*also:* ~ **along**) aller à toute allure.

career counselor *n* counseiller/ère d'orientation (professionnelle).

career girl *n* jeune fille *f* (*or* femme *f*) qui veut faire carrière.

careers officer *n* (*Brit*) conseiller/ère d'orientation (professionnelle).

carefree [kâr'frē] *a* sans souci, insouciant(e).

careful [kâr'fəl] *a* soigneux(euse); (*cautious*) prudent(e); **(be)** ~! (fais) attention!; **to be** ~ **with one's money** regarder à la dépense.

carefully [kâr'fəlē] *ad* avec soin, soigneusement; prudemment.

careless [kâr'lis] *a* négligent(e); (*heedless*) insouciant(e).

carelessly [kâr'lislē] *ad* négligemment; avec insouciance.

carelessness [kâr'lisnis] *n* manque *m* de soin, négligence *f*; insouciance *f*.

caress [kəres'] *n* caresse *f* ♦ *vt* caresser.

caretaker [kâr'tākûr] *n* gardien/ne, concierge *m/f*.

caretaker government *n* gouvernement *m* intérimaire.

car ferry *n* (*on sea*) ferry(-boat) *m*; (*on river*) bac *m*.

cargo, *pl* ~**es** [kâr'gō] *n* cargaison *f*, chargement *m*.

cargo boat *n* cargo *m*.

cargo plane *n* avion-cargo *m*.

car hire *n* (*Brit*) location *f* de voitures.

Caribbean [karəbē'ən] *a* des Caraïbes; **the** ~ **(Sea)** la mer des Antilles *or* des Caraïbes.

caricature [kar'əkəchûr] *n* caricature *f*.

caring [kâr'ing] *a* (*person*) bienveillant(e); (*society, organization*) humanitaire.

carnage [kâr'nij] *n* carnage *m*.

carnal [kâr'nəl] *a* charnel(le).

carnation [kârnā'shən] *n* œillet *m*.

carnival [kâr'nəvəl] *n* (*public celebration*) carnaval *m*; (*US*) fête foraine.

carnivorous [kârniv'ûrəs] *a* carnivore, carnassier(ière).

carol [kar'əl] *n:* **(Christmas)** ~ chant *m* de Noël.

carouse [kərouz'] *vi* faire la bringue.

carousel [karəsel'] *n* (*US*) manège *m*.

carp [kârp] *n* (*fish*) carpe *f*.

carp at *vt fus* critiquer.

car park *n* (*Brit*) parking *m*, parc *m* de stationnement.

carpenter [kâr'pəntûr] *n* charpentier *m*.

carpentry [kâr'pəntrē] *n* charpenterie *f*, métier *m* de charpentier; (*woodwork: at school etc*) menuiserie *f*.

carpet [kâr'pit] *n* tapis *m* ♦ *vt* recouvrir (d'un tapis).

carpet slippers *npl* pantoufles *fpl*.

carpet sweeper [kâr'pit swē'pûr] *n* balai *m* mécanique.

car phone *n* téléphone *m* de voiture.

car rental *n* (*US*) location *f* de voitures.

carriage [kar'ij] *n* voiture *f*; (*of goods*) transport *m*; (: *cost*) port *m*; (*of typewriter*) chariot *m*; (*bearing*) maintien *m*, port *m*; ~ **forward** port dû; ~ **free** franco de port; ~ **paid** (en) port payé.

carriage return *n* retour *m* à la ligne.

carriageway [kar'ijwã] *n* (*Brit: part of road*) chaussée *f*.

carrier [kar'ēûr] *n* transporteur *m*, camionneur *m*; (*MED*) porteur/euse; (*NAUT*) porte-avions *m inv*.

carrier bag *n* (*Brit*) sac *m* en papier *or* en plastique.

carrier pigeon *n* pigeon voyageur.

carrion [kar'ēən] *n* charogne *f*.

carrot [kar'ət] *n* carotte *f*.

carry [kar'ē] *vt* (*subj: person*) porter; (: *vehicle*) transporter; (*a motion, bill*) voter, adopter; (*MATH: figure*) retenir; (*COMM: interest*) rapporter; (*involve: responsibilities* *etc*) comporter, impliquer ♦ *vi* (*sound*) porter; **to be carried away** (*fig*) s'emballer, s'enthousiasmer; **this loan carries 10% interest** ce prêt est à 10% (d'intérêt).

carry forward *vt* (*gen*, BOOK-KEEPING) reporter.

carry on *vi* (*continue*): **to ~ on with sth/doing** continuer qch/à faire; (*col*: *make a fuss*) faire des histoires ♦ *vt* entretenir, poursuivre.

carry out *vt* (*orders*) exécuter; (*investigation*) effectuer; (*idea, threat*) mettre à exécution.

carryall [kar'ēól] *n* (*US*) fourre-tout *m inv*.

carrycot [kar'ēkàt] *n* (*Brit*) porte-bébé *m*.

carry-on [kar'ēân] *n* (*Brit col*: *fuss*) histoires *fpl*; (*: annoying behavior*) cirque *m*, cinéma *m*.

cart [kàrt] *n* charrette *f*; (*US*: *for shopping*) chariot *m*, caddie *m* ♦ *vt* transporter.

carte blanche [kàrt' blânsh'] *n*: **to give sb ~** donner carte blanche à qn.

cartel [kârtel'] *n* (COMM) cartel *m*.

cartilage [kâr'təlij] *n* cartilage *m*.

cartographer [kârtâg'rəfûr] *n* cartographe *m/f*.

cartography [kârtâg'rəfē] *n* cartographie *f*.

carton [kâr'tən] *n* (*box*) carton *m*; (*of yogurt*) pot *m* (en carton); (*of cigarettes*) cartouche *f*.

cartoon [kârtōōn'] *n* (PRESS) dessin *m* (humoristique); (*satirical*) caricature *f*; (*comic strip*) bande dessinée; (CINEMA) dessin animé.

cartoonist [kârtōō'nist] *n* dessinateur/trice humoristique, caricaturiste *m/f*; auteur *m* de dessins animés; auteur de bandes dessinées.

cartridge [kâr'trij] *n* (*for gun, pen*) cartouche *f*; (*for camera*) chargeur *m*; (*music tape*) cassette *f*; (*of record player*) cellule *f*.

cartwheel [kârt'hwēl] *n* roue *f*; **to turn a ~** faire la roue.

carve [kârv] *vt* (*meat*: *also*: **~ up**) découper; (*wood, stone*) tailler, sculpter.

carving [kâr'ving] *n* (*in wood etc*) sculpture *f*.

carving knife *n* couteau *m* à découper.

car wash *n* station *f* de lavage (de voitures).

Casablanca [kasəblang'kə] *n* Casablanca.

cascade [kaskād'] *n* cascade *f* ♦ *vi* tomber en cascade.

case [kās] *n* cas *m*; (LAW) affaire *f*, procès *m*; (*box*) caisse *f*, boîte *f*, étui *m*; (*Brit*: *also*: **suit~**) valise *f*; (TYP): **lower/upper ~** minuscule *f*/majuscule *f*; **to have a good ~** avoir de bons arguments; **there's a strong ~ for reform** il y aurait lieu d'engager une réforme; **in ~ of** en cas de; **in ~ he** au cas où il; **just in ~** à tout hasard.

case-hardened [kās'hâr'dənd] *a* endurci(e).

case history *n* (MED) dossier médical, antécédents médicaux.

case study *n* étude *f* de cas.

cash [kash] *n* argent *m*; (COMM) argent liquide, numéraire *m*; liquidités *fpl*; (*: in payment*) argent comptant, espèces *fpl* ♦ *vt* encaisser; **to pay (in) ~** payer (en argent) comptant *or* en espèces; **~ on delivery (COD)** (COMM) payable *or* paiement à la livraison; **to be short of ~** être à court d'argent.

cash in *vt* (*insurance policy etc*) toucher.

cash in on *vt fus* profiter de.

cash account *n* compte *m* caisse.

cashbook [kash'bŏŏk] *n* livre *m* de caisse.

cash box *n* caisse *f*.

cash card *n* carte de retrait *or* accréditive.

cash desk *n* (*Brit*) caisse *f*.

cash discount *n* escompte *m* de caisse (pour paiement au comptant), remise *f* au comptant.

cash dispenser *n* distributeur *m* automatique de billets.

cashew [kash'ōō] *n* (*also*: **~ nut**) noix *f* de cajou.

cash flow *n* cash-flow *m*, marge brute d'autofinancement.

cashier [kashi'ûr] *n* caissier/ère ♦ *vt* (MIL) destituer, casser.

cashmere [kazh'mēr] *n* cachemire *m*.

cash payment *n* paiement comptant, versement *m* en espèces.

cash price *n* prix comptant.

cash register *n* caisse enregistreuse.

cash sale *n* vente *f* au comptant.

casing [kā'sing] *n* revêtement (protecteur), enveloppe (protectrice).

casino [kəsē'nō] *n* casino *m*.

cask [kask] *n* tonneau *m*.

casket [kas'kit] *n* coffret *m*; (*US*: *coffin*) cercueil *m*.

Caspian Sea [kas'pēən sē'] *n*: **the ~** la mer Caspienne.

casserole [kas'ərōl] *n* cocotte *f*; (*food*) ragoût *m* (en cocotte).

cassette [kəset'] *n* cassette *f*, musicassette *f*.

cassette deck *n* platine *f* cassette.

cassette player *n* lecteur *m* de cassettes.

cassette recorder *n* magnétophone *m* à cassettes.

cast [kast] *vb* (*pt, pp* **cast**) *vt* (*throw*) jeter; (*shed*) perdre; se dépouiller de; (*metal*) couler, fondre; (THEATER): **to ~ sb as Hamlet** attribuer à qn le rôle d'Hamlet ♦ *n* (THEATER) distribution *f*; (*mold*) moule *m*; (*also*: **plaster ~**) plâtre *m*; **to ~ one's vote** voter, exprimer son suffrage.

cast aside *vt* (*reject*) rejeter.

cast off *vi* (NAUT) larguer les amarres; (KNITTING) arrêter les mailles ♦ *vt* (KNITTING) arrêter.

cast on (KNITTING) *vt* monter ♦ *vi* monter les mailles.

castanets [kastənets'] *npl* castagnettes *fpl*.

castaway [kas'təwā] *n* naufragé/e.

caste [kast] *n* caste *f*, classe sociale.

caster sugar [kas'tûr shŏŏg'ûr] *n* (*Brit*) sucre *m* semoule.

casting vote [kas'ting vōt'] *n* (*Brit*) voix prépondérante (*pour départager*).

cast iron *n* fonte *f* ♦ *a*: **cast-iron** (*fig*: *will*) de fer; (*: alibi*) en béton.

castle [kas'əl] *n* château-fort *m*; (*manor*) château *m*.

castor [kas'tûr] *n* (*wheel*) roulette *f*.

castor oil *n* huile *f* de ricin.

castrate [kas'trāt] *vt* châtrer.

casual [kazh'ōōəl] *a* (*by chance*) de hasard, fait(e) au hasard, fortuit(e); (*irregular*: *work etc*) temporaire; (*unconcerned*) désinvolte; **~ wear** vêtements *mpl* sport *inv*.

casual labor n main-d'œuvre f temporaire.
casually [kazh'ōōəlē] ad avec désinvolture, négligemment; (by chance) fortuitement.
casualty [kazh'ōōəltē] n accidenté/e, blessé/e; (dead) victime f, mort/e; **heavy casualties** lourdes pertes.
casualty ward n (Brit) service m des urgences.
cat [kat] n chat m.
catacombs [kat'əkōmz] npl catacombes fpl.
catalog, (Brit) **catalogue** [kat'əlôg] n catalogue m ♦ vt cataloguer.
catalyst [kat'əlist] n catalyseur m.
catalytic converter [katelit'ik kânvûrt'ûr] n (AUT) pot m catalytique.
catapult [kat'əpult] n lance-pierres m inv, fronde m; (HIST) catapulte f.
cataract [kat'ərakt] n (also MED) cataracte f.
catarrh [kətâr'] n rhume m chronique, catarrhe f.
catastrophe [kətas'trəfē] n catastrophe f.
catastrophic [katəstrâf'ik] a catastrophique.
catcall [kat'kôl] n (at meeting etc) sifflet m.
catch [kach] vb (pt, pp **caught** [kôt]) vt (ball, train, thief, cold) attraper; (person: by surprise) prendre, surprendre; (understand) saisir; (get entangled) accrocher ♦ vi (fire) prendre; (get entangled) s'accrocher ♦ n (fish etc caught) prise f; (thief etc caught) capture f; (trick) attrape f; (TECH) loquet m; cliquet m; **to ~ sb's attention** or **eye** attirer l'attention de qn; **to ~ fire** prendre feu; **to ~ sight of** apercevoir.
catch on vi (become popular) prendre; (understand): **to ~ on (to sth)** saisir (qch).
catch out vt (Brit fig: with trick question) prendre en défaut.
catch up vi se rattraper, combler son retard ♦ vt (also: ~ **up with**) rattraper.
catching [kach'ing] a (MED) contagieux(euse).
catchment area [kach'mənt är'ēə] n (Brit SCOL) aire f de recrutement; (GEO) bassin m hydrographique.
catch phrase n slogan m; expression toute faite.
catch-22 [kach'twentētōō'] n: **it's a ~ situation** c'est (une situation) sans issue.
catchy [kach'ē] a (tune) facile à retenir.
cat door n (US) chatière f.
catechism [kat'əkizəm] n catéchisme m.
categoric(al) [katəgôr'ik(əl)] a catégorique.
categorize [kat'əgərīz] vt classer par catégories.
category [kat'əgôrē] n catégorie f.
cater [kā'tûr] vi (provide food): **to ~ (for)** préparer des repas (pour), se charger de la restauration (pour).
cater to vt fus (needs) satisfaire, pourvoir à; (: readers, consumers) s'adresser à, pourvoir aux besoins de.
caterer [kā'tûrûr] n traiteur m; fournisseur m.
catering [kā'tûring] n restauration f; approvisionnement m, ravitaillement m.
caterpillar [kat'ûrpilûr] n chenille f ♦ cpd (vehicle) à chenille; ~ **track** n chenille f.
cathedral [kəthē'drəl] n cathédrale f.
cathode [kath'ōd] n cathode f.
cathode ray tube [kath'ōd rā' tōōb] n tube m cathodique.

catholic [kath'əlik] a éclectique; universel(le); libéral(e); **C~** a, n (REL) catholique (m/f).
cat's-eye [kats'ī'] n (Brit AUT) (clou m à) catadioptre m.
catsup [kat'səp] n (US) ketchup m.
cattle [kat'əl] npl bétail m, bestiaux mpl.
catty [kat'ē] a méchant(e).
CATV n abbr (US: = community antenna television) télédistribution f.
Caucasian [kôkā'zhən] a, n caucasien(ne).
Caucasus [kôk'əsəs] n Caucase m.
caucus [kô'kəs] n (US POL) comité électoral (pour désigner des candidats); (Brit POL: group) comité local (d'un parti politique).
caught [kôt] pt, pp of **catch**.
cauliflower [kô'ləflouûr] n chou-fleur m.
cause [kôz] n cause f ♦ vt causer; **there is no ~ for concern** il n'y a pas lieu de s'inquiéter; **to ~ sth to be done** faire faire qch; **to ~ sb to do sth** faire faire qch à qn.
causeway [kôz'wā] n chaussée (surélevée).
caustic [kôs'tik] a caustique.
caution [kô'shən] n prudence f; (warning) avertissement m ♦ vt avertir, donner un avertissement à.
cautious [kô'shəs] a prudent(e).
cautiously [kô'shəslē] ad prudemment, avec prudence.
cautiousness [kô'shəsnis] n prudence f.
cavalier [kavəliûr'] a cavalier(ère), désinvolte ♦ n (knight) cavalier m.
cavalry [kav'əlrē] n cavalerie f.
cave [kāv] n caverne f, grotte f ♦ vi: **to go caving** faire de la spéléo(logie).
cave in vi (roof etc) s'effondrer.
caveman [kāv'mən] n homme m des cavernes.
cavern [kav'ûrn] n caverne f.
caviar(e) [kav'ēâr] n caviar m.
cavity [kav'itē] n cavité f.
cavity wall insulation n isolation f des murs creux.
cavort [kəvôrt'] vi cabrioler, faire des cabrioles.
cayenne [kīen'] n (also: ~ **pepper**) poivre m de cayenne.
CB n abbr (= Citizens' Band (Radio)) CB f
CBC n abbr (= Canadian Broadcasting Corporation) organisme m de radiodiffusion.
CBI n abbr (= Confederation of British Industry) ≈ CNPF m (= Conseil national du patronat français).
CBS n abbr (US: = Columbia Broadcasting System) chaîne de télévision.
cc abbr (= cubic centimeter) cm³; (on letter etc) = **carbon copy**.
CCA n abbr (US: = Circuit Court of Appeals) cour d'appel itinérante.
CCC n abbr (US: = Commodity Credit Corporation) organisme m d'aide aux prix agricoles.
CCU n abbr (US: = coronary care unit) unité f de soins cardiologiques.
CD n abbr (= compact disc) CD m; (MIL) = Civil Defense (US), Civil Defence (Corps) (Brit) ♦ abbr (Brit: = Corps Diplomatique) CD.
CDC n abbr (US) = center for disease control.
Cdr. abbr (= commander) Cdt.
CDV n abbr (= compact disc video) CDV m.

CDW *n abbr* = **collision damage waiver.**
cease [sēs] *vt, vi* cesser.
ceasefire [sēs'fiûr'] *n* cessez-le-feu *m*.
ceaseless [sēs'lis] *a* incessant(e), continuel(le).
CED *n abbr* (*US*) = *Committee for Economic Development.*
cedar [sē'dûr] *n* cèdre *m*.
cede [sēd] *vt* céder.
cedilla [sidil'ə] *n* cédille *f*.
CEEB *n abbr* (*US*: = *College Entry Examination Board*) commission d'admission dans l'enseignement supérieur.
ceiling [sē'ling] *n* (*also fig*) plafond *m*.
celebrate [sel'əbrāt] *vt, vi* célébrer.
celebrated [sel'əbrātid] *a* célèbre.
celebration [seləbrā'shən] *n* célébration *f*.
celebrity [səleb'ritē] *n* célébrité *f*.
celeriac [səlär'ēak] *n* céleri(-rave) *m*.
celery [sel'ûrē] *n* céleri *m* (en branches).
celestial [səles'chəl] *a* céleste.
celibacy [sel'əbəsē] *n* célibat *m*.
cell [sel] *n* (*gen*) cellule *f*; (*ELEC*) élément *m* (*de pile*).
cellar [sel'ûr] *n* cave *f*.
cellophane [sel'əfān] *n* ® cellophane *f* ®.
cellular [sel'yələr] *a* cellulaire.
Celluloid [sel'yəloid] *n* ® celluloïd *m* ®.
cellulose [sel'yəlōs] *n* cellulose *f*.
Celsius [sel'sēəs] *a* Celsius *inv*.
Celt [selt, kelt] *n* Celte *m/f*.
Celtic [sel'tik, kel'tik] *a* celte, celtique ♦ *n* (*LING*) celtique *m*.
cement [siment'] *n* ciment *m* ♦ *vt* cimenter.
cement mixer *n* bétonnière *f*.
cemetery [sem'itärē] *n* cimetière *m*.
cenotaph [sen'ətaf] *n* cénotaphe *m*.
censor [sen'sûr] *n* censeur *m* ♦ *vt* censurer.
censorship [sen'sûrship] *n* censure *f*.
censure [sen'shûr] *vt* blâmer, critiquer.
census [sen'səs] *n* recensement *m*.
cent [sent] *n* (*US: coin*) cent *m* (= *1:100 du dollar*); *see also* **percent.**
centenary [sen'tənärē] *n* centenaire *m*.
centennial [senten'ēəl] *n* = **centenary.**
center [sen'tûr] (*US*) *n* centre *m* ♦ *vt* centrer; (*PHOT*) cadrer; (*concentrate*): **to ~ on** centrer sur.
centerfold [sen'tûrfōld] *n* (*PRESS*) pages centrales détachables (*avec photo de pin up*).
center forward *n* (*SPORT*) avant-centre *m*.
center half *n* (*SPORT*) demi-centre *m*.
centerpiece [sen'tûrpēs] *n* milieu *m* de table; (*fig*) pièce maitresse.
centigrade [sen'tigrād] *a* centigrade.
centiliter, (*Brit*) **centilitre** [sen'tələtûr] *n* centilitre *m*.
centimeter, (*Brit*) **centimetre** [sen'təmētûr] *n* centimètre *m*.
centipede [sen'təpēd] *n* mille-pattes *m inv*.
central [sen'trəl] *a* central(e).
Central African Republic *n* République Centrafricaine.
central heating *n* chauffage central.
centralize [sen'trəliz] *vt* centraliser.
central processing unit (CPU) *n* (*COMPUT*) unité centrale (de traitement).
central reservation *n* (*Brit AUT*) terre-plein central.

centre [sen'tûr] *etc* (*Brit*) = **center** *etc.*
centrifugal [sentrif'əgəl] *a* centrifuge.
centrifuge [sen'trəfyōōj] *n* centrifugeuse *f*.
century [sen'chûrē] *n* siècle *m*; **in the twentieth ~** au vingtième siècle.
CEO *n abbr* = **chief executive officer.**
ceramic [səram'ik] *a* céramique.
cereal [sēr'ēəl] *n* céréale *f*.
cerebral [sär'əbrəl] *a* cérébral(e).
ceremonial [särəmō'nēəl] *n* cérémonial *m*; (*rite*) rituel *m*.
ceremony [sär'əmōnē] *n* cérémonie *f*; **to stand on ~** faire des façons.
certain [sûr'tən] *a* certain(e); **to make ~ of** s'assurer de; **for ~** certainement, sûrement.
certainly [sûr'tənlē] *ad* certainement.
certainty [sûr'təntē] *n* certitude *f*.
certificate [sûrtif'əkit] *n* certificat *m*.
certified letter [sûr'təfīd let'ûr] *n* (*US*) lettre recommandée.
certified public accountant (CPA) *n* (*US*) expert-comptable *m*.
certify [sûr'təfī] *vt* certifier ♦ *vi*: **to ~ to** attester.
cervical [sûr'vikəl] *a*: **~ cancer** cancer *m* du col de l'utérus; **~ smear** frottis vaginal.
cervix [sûr'viks] *n* col *m* de l'utérus.
Cesarean [sizär'ēən] *a* (*US*): **~ (section)** césarienne *f*.
cessation [sesā'shən] *n* cessation *f*, arrêt *m*.
cesspit [ses'pit] *n* fosse *f* d'aisance.
CET *abbr* (= *Central European Time*) heure *d'Europe centrale.*
Ceylon [silän'] *n* Ceylan *m*.
cf. *abbr* (= *compare*) cf., voir.
C.F. *abbr* (= *cost and freight*) coût *m* et fret *m*.
c/f *abbr* (*COMM*) = *carried forward.*
cfc *n abbr* = *chlorofluorocarbon*) CFC.
C.F.I. *abbr* (= *cost, freight and insurance*) CAF.
CG *n abbr* (*US*) = **coastguard.**
cg *abbr* (= *centigram*) cg.
ch *abbr* (*Brit*: = *central heating*) c.c.
ch. *abbr* (= *chapter*) chap.
Chad [chad] *n* Tchad *m*.
chafe [chāf] *vt* irriter, frotter contre ♦ *vi* (*fig*): **to ~ against** se rebiffer contre, regimber contre.
chaffinch [chaf'inch] *n* pinson *m*.
chagrin [shəgrin'] *n* contrariété *f*, déception *f*.
chain [chān] *n* (*gen*) chaîne *f* ♦ *vt* (*also*: **~ up**) enchaîner, attacher (avec une chaîne).
chain reaction *n* réaction *f* en chaîne.
chain-smoke [chān'smōk] *vi* fumer cigarette sur cigarette.
chain store *n* magasin *m* à succursales multiples.
chair [chär] *n* chaise *f*; (*armchair*) fauteuil *m*; (*of university*) chaire *f* ♦ *vt* (*meeting*) présider; **the ~** (*US: electric ~*) la chaise électrique.
chairlift [chär'lift] *n* télésiège *m*.
chairman [chär'mən] *n* président *m*.
chairperson [chär'pûrsən] *n* président/e.
chairwoman [chär'woomən] *n* présidente *f*.
chalet [shalā'] *n* chalet *m*.
chalice [chal'is] *n* calice *m*.
chalk [chôk] *n* craie *f*.

chalk up *vt* écrire à la craie; (*fig: success etc*) remporter.

challenge [chal'inj] *n* défi *m* ♦ *vt* défier; (*statement, right*) mettre en question, contester; **to ~ sb to a fight/game** inviter qn à se battre/à jouer (*sous forme d'un défi*); **to ~ sb to do** mettre qn au défi de faire.

challenger [chal'injûr] *n* (*SPORT*) challenger *m*.

challenging [chal'injing] *a* de défi, provocateur(trice).

chamber [chām'bûr] *n* chambre *f*; **~ of commerce** chambre de commerce.

chambermaid [chām'bûrmād] *n* femme *f* de chambre.

chamber music *n* musique *f* de chambre.

chamber pot *n* pot *m* de chambre.

chameleon [kəmē'lēən] *n* caméléon *m*.

chamois [sham'ē] *n* chamois *m*.

chamois leather [sham'ē leth'ûr] *n* peau *f* de chamois.

champagne [shampān'] *n* champagne *m*.

champion [cham'pēən] *n* (*also of cause*) champion/ne ♦ *vt* défendre.

championship [cham'pēənship] *n* championnat *m*.

chance [chans] *n* hasard *m*; (*opportunity*) occasion *f*, possibilité *f*; (*hope, likelihood*) chance *f* ♦ *vt* (*risk*): **to ~ it** risquer (le coup), essayer; (*happen*): **to ~ to do** faire par hasard ♦ *a* fortuit(e), de hasard; **there is little ~ of his coming** il est peu probable *or* il y a peu de chances qu'il vienne; **to take a ~** prendre un risque; **it's the ~ of a lifetime** c'est une occasion unique; **by ~** par hasard.

chance (up)on *vt fus* (*person*) tomber sur, rencontrer par hasard; (*thing*) trouver par hasard.

chancel [chan'səl] *n* chœur *m*.

chancellor [chan'səlûr] *n* chancelier *m*; **C~ of the Exchequer** (*Brit*) chancelier de l'Échiquier.

chandelier [shandəliûr'] *n* lustre *m*.

change [chānj] *vt* (*alter, replace, COMM: money*) changer; (*switch, substitute: gear, hands, trains, clothes, one's name etc*) changer de; (*transform*): **to ~ sb into** changer *or* transformer qn en ♦ *vi* (*gen*) changer; (*change clothes*) se changer; (*be transformed*): **to ~ into** se changer *or* transformer en ♦ *n* changement *m*; (*money*) monnaie *f*; **to ~ one's mind** changer d'avis; **she ~d into an old skirt** elle (s'est changée et) a enfilé une vieille jupe; **a ~ of clothes** des vêtements de rechange; **for a ~** pour changer; **small ~** petite monnaie; **to give sb ~ for $10** faire à qn la monnaie de 10 dollars.

changeable [chān'jəbəl] *a* (*weather*) variable; (*person*) d'humeur changeante.

change machine *n* distributeur *m* de monnaie.

changeover [chānj'ōvûr] *n* (*to new system*) changement *m*, passage *m*.

changing [chān'jing] *a* changeant(e).

changing room *n* (*Brit: in store*) salon *m* d'essayage; (*: SPORT*) vestiaire *m*.

channel [chan'əl] *n* (*TV*) chaîne *f*; (*waveband, groove, fig: medium*) canal *m*; (*of river, sea*)

chenal *m* ♦ *vt* canaliser; (*fig: interest, energies*): **to ~ into** diriger vers; **through the usual ~s** en suivant la filière habituelle; **green/red ~** (*CUSTOMS*) couloir *m or* sortie *f* "rien à déclarer"/"marchandises à déclarer"; **the (English) C~** la Manche.

Channel Islands *npl*: **the ~** les îles de la Manche, les îles anglo-normandes.

chant [chant] *n* chant *m*; mélopée *f*; psalmodie *f* ♦ *vt* chanter, scander; psalmodier.

chaos [kā'âs] *n* chaos *m*.

chaotic [kāāt'ik] *a* chaotique.

chap [chap] *n* (*Brit col: man*) type *m*; (*term of address*): **old ~** mon vieux ♦ *vt* (*skin*) gercer, crevasser.

chapel [chap'əl] *n* chapelle *f*.

chaperon [shap'ərōn] *n* chaperon *m* ♦ *vt* chaperonner.

chaplain [chap'lin] *n* aumônier *m*.

chapter [chap'tûr] *n* chapitre *m*.

char [châr] *vt* (*burn*) carboniser ♦ *vi* (*Brit: cleaner*) faire des ménages ♦ *n* (*Brit*) = **charlady.**

character [kar'iktûr] *n* caractère *m*; (*in novel, film*) personnage *m*; (*eccentric*) numéro *m*, phénomène *m*; **a person of good ~** une personne bien.

character code *n* (*COMPUT*) code *m* de caractère.

characteristic [kariktəris'tik] *a*, *n* caractéristique (*f*).

characterize [kar'iktərīz] *vt* caractériser; **to ~ (as)** définir (comme).

charade [shərād'] *n* charade *f*.

charcoal [châr'kōl] *n* charbon *m* de bois.

charge [chârj] *n* accusation *f*; (*LAW*) inculpation *f*; (*cost*) prix (demandé); (*of gun, battery, MIL: attack*) charge *f* ♦ *vt* (*LAW*): **to ~ sb (with)** inculper qn (de); (*gun, battery, MIL: enemy*) charger; (*customer, sum*) faire payer ♦ *vi* (*gen with: up, along etc*) foncer; **~s** *npl*: **bank/labor ~s** frais *mpl* de banque/main-d'œuvre; **to ~ in/out** entrer/sortir en trombe; **to ~ down/up** dévaler/grimper à toute allure; **is there a ~?** doit-on payer?; **there's no ~** c'est gratuit, on ne fait pas payer; **extra ~** supplément *m*; **to take ~ of** se charger de; **to be in ~ of** être responsable de, s'occuper de; **to have ~ of sb** avoir la charge de qn; **they ~d us $10 for the meal** ils nous ont fait payer le repas 10 dollars, ils nous ont compté 10 dollars pour le repas; **how much do you ~ for this repair?** combien demandez-vous pour cette réparation?; **to ~ an expense (up) to sb** mettre une dépense sur le compte de qn; **~ it to my account** facturez-le sur mon compte.

charge account *n* compte *m* client.

charge card *n* carte *f* de client (*émise par un grand magasin*).

chargehand [chârj'hand] *n* (*Brit*) chef *m* d'équipe.

charger [châr'jûr] *n* (*also:* **battery ~**) chargeur *m*; (*old: warhorse*) cheval *m* de bataille.

charitable [char'itəbəl] *a* charitable.

charity [char'itē] *n* charité *f*; (*organization*) institution *f* charitable *or* de bienfaisance, œuvre *f* (de charité).

charlady [châr'lādē] *n* (*Brit*) femme *f* de ménage.

charm [chârm] *n* charme *m* ♦ *vt* charmer, enchanter.

charm bracelet *n* bracelet *m* à breloques.

charming [châr'ming] *a* charmant(e).

chart [chârt] *n* tableau *m*, diagramme *m*; graphique *m*; (*map*) carte marine; (*weather* ~) carte *f* du temps ♦ *vt* dresser *or* établir la carte de; (*sales, progress*) établir la courbe de; **to be on** *or* (*Brit*) **in the** ~**s** (*record, pop group*) figurer au hit-parade.

charter [châr'tûr] *vt* (*plane*) affréter ♦ *n* (*document*) charte *f*; **on** ~ (*plane*) affrété(e).

chartered accountant (CA) [châr'tûrd əkoun'tənt] *n* expert-comptable *m*.

charter flight *n* charter *m*.

charwoman [châr'wōōmən] *n* = **charlady**.

chase [chās] *vt* poursuivre, pourchasser ♦ *n* poursuite *f*, chasse *f*.

chase down *vt* (*US: person*) relancer; (*: information*) rechercher.

chase up *vt* (*Brit*) = **chase down**.

chasm [kaz'əm] *n* gouffre *m*, abîme *m*.

chassis [shas'ē] *n* châssis *m*.

chastened [chā'sənd] *a* assagi(e), rappelé(e) à la raison.

chastening [chā'səning] *a* qui fait réfléchir.

chastise [chastīz'] *vt* punir, châtier; corriger.

chastity [chas'titē] *n* chasteté *f*.

chat [chat] *vi* (*also*: **have a** ~) bavarder, causer ♦ *n* conversation *f*.

chat up *vt* (*Brit col: girl*) baratiner.

chat show *n* (*Brit*) entretien télévisé.

chattel [chat'əl] *see* **goods**.

chatter [chat'ûr] *vi* (*person*) bavarder, papoter ♦ *n* bavardage *m*, papotage *m*; **my teeth are** ~**ing** je claque des dents.

chatterbox [chat'ûrbâks] *n* moulin *m* à paroles, babillard/e.

chatty [chat'ē] *a* (*style*) familier(ière); (*person*) enclin(e) à bavarder *or* au papotage.

chauffeur [shō'fûr] *n* chauffeur *m* (de maître).

chauvinism [shō'vənizəm] *n* (*also*: **male** ~) phallocratie *f*, machisme *m*; (*nationalism*) chauvinisme *m*.

chauvinist [shō'vənist] *n* (*also*: **male** ~) phallocrate *m*, macho *m*; (*nationalist*) chauvin/e.

ChE *abbr* = *chemical engineer*.

cheap [chēp] *a* bon marché *inv*, pas cher(chère); (*reduced: ticket*) à prix réduit; (*: fare*) réduit(e); (*joke*) facile, d'un goût douteux; (*poor quality*) à bon marché, de qualité médiocre ♦ *ad* à bon marché, pour pas cher; ~**er** à moins cher(chère).

cheapen [chē'pən] *vt* rabaisser, déprécier.

cheaply [chēp'lē] *ad* à bon marché, à bon compte.

cheat [chēt] *vi* tricher; (*in exam*) copier ♦ *vt* tromper, duper; (*rob*) escroquer ♦ *n* tricheur/euse; escroc *m*; (*trick*) duperie *f*, tromperie *f*; **to** ~ **on sb** (*col: husband, wife etc*) tromper qn.

cheating [chēt'ing] *n* tricherie *f*.

check [chek] *vt* vérifier; (*passport, ticket*) contrôler; (*halt*) enrayer; (*restrain*) maîtriser ♦ *vi* (*official etc*) se renseigner ♦ *n* vé-

rification *f*; contrôle *m*; (*curb*) frein *m*; (*bill*) addition *f*; (*pattern: gen pl*) carreaux *mpl*; (*US*) chèque *m* ♦ *a* (*also*: ~**ed**: *pattern, cloth*) à carreaux; **to** ~ **with sb** demander à qn; **to keep a** ~ **on sb/sth** surveiller qn/qch; **to pay by** ~ payer par chèque.

check in *vi* (*in hotel*) remplir sa fiche (d'hôtel); (*at airport*) se présenter à l'enregistrement ♦ *vt* (*baggage*) (faire) enregistrer.

check off *vt* cocher.

check out *vi* (*in hotel*) régler sa note ♦ *vt* (*baggage*) retirer; (*investigate: story*) vérifier; (*person*) prendre des renseignements sur.

check up *vi*: **to** ~ **up (on sth)** vérifier (qch); **to** ~ **up on sb** se renseigner sur le compte de qn.

checkbook [chek'bŏŏk] *n* chéquier *m*, carnet *m* de chèques.

checkerboard [chek'ərbôrd] *n* damier *m*.

checkered [chek'ûrd] *a* (*fig*) varié(e).

checkers [chek'ûrz] *n* (*US*) (jeu *m* de) dames.

check guarantee card *n* (*US*) carte *f* (d'identité) bancaire.

check-in [chek'in] *n* (*also*: ~ **desk**: *at airport*) enregistrement *m*.

checking account [chek'ing əkount'] *n* (*US*) compte courant.

checklist [chek'list] *n* liste *f* de contrôle.

checkmate [chek'māt] *n* échec et mat *m*.

checkout [chek'out] *n* (*in supermarket*) caisse *f*.

checkpoint [chek'point] *n* contrôle *m*.

checkroom [chek'rōōm] *n* (*US*) vestiaire *m*.

checkup [chek'up] *n* (*MED*) examen médical, check-up *m*.

cheek [chēk] *n* joue *f*; (*impudence*) toupet *m*, culot *m*.

cheekbone [chēk'bōn] *n* pommette *f*.

cheeky [chē'kē] *a* effronté(e), culotté(e).

cheep [chēp] *n* (*of bird*) piaulement *m* ♦ *vi* piauler.

cheer [chēr] *vt* acclamer, applaudir; (*gladden*) réjouir, réconforter ♦ *vi* applaudir ♦ *n* (*gen pl*) acclamations *fpl*, applaudissements *mpl*; bravos *mpl*, hourras *mpl*; ~**s!** (à votre) santé!

cheer on *vt* encourager (par des cris *etc*).

cheer up *vi* se dérider, reprendre courage ♦ *vt* remonter le moral à *or* de, dérider, égayer.

cheerful [chēr'fəl] *a* gai(e), joyeux(euse).

cheerfulness [chēr'fəlnis] *n* gaieté *f*, bonne humeur.

cheerio [chēr'ēō] *excl* (*Brit*) salut!, au revoir!

cheerless [chēr'lis] *a* sombre, triste.

cheese [chēz] *n* fromage *m*.

cheeseboard [chēz'bôrd] *n* plateau *m* à fromages; (*with cheese on it*) plateau *m* de fromages.

cheesecake [chēz'kāk] *n* tarte *f* au fromage.

cheetah [chē'tə] *n* guépard *m*.

chef [shef] *n* chef (cuisinier).

chemical [kem'ikəl] *a* chimique ♦ *n* produit *m* chimique.

chemist [kem'ist] *n* (*Brit*: *pharmacist*) pharmacien/ne; (*scientist*) chimiste *m/f*; ~**'s (shop)** *n* (*Brit*) pharmacie *f*.

chemistry [kem'istrē] *n* chimie *f*.

cheque [chck] *etc* (*Brit*) = **check.**
cheque card *n* (*Brit*) carte *f* (d'identité) bancaire.
chequered [chck'ûrd] *a* (*Brit*) = **checkered.**
cherish [chär'ish] *vt* chérir; (*hope etc*) entretenir.
cheroot [shərōōt'] *n* cigare *m* de Manille.
cherry [chär'ē] *n* cerise *f*.
Ches *abbr* (*Brit*) = *Cheshire.*
chess [ches] *n* échecs *mpl.*
chessboard [ches'bôrd] *n* échiquier *m.*
chessman [ches'man] *n* pièce *f* (de jeu d'échecs).
chessplayer [ches'plāûr] *n* joueur/euse d'échecs.
chest [chest] *n* poitrine *f*; (*box*) coffre *m*, caisse *f*; **to get sth off one's ~** (*col*) vider son sac; **~ of drawers** *n* commode *f.*
chest measurement *n* tour *m* de poitrine.
chestnut [ches'nut] *n* châtaigne *f*; (*also: ~ tree*) châtaignier *m*; (*color*) châtain *m* ♦ *a* (*hair*) châtain *inv*; (*horse*) alezan.
chew [chōō] *vt* mâcher.
chewing gum [chōō'ing gum] *n* chewing-gum *m.*
chic [shēk] *a* chic *inv*, élégant(e).
chick [chik] *n* poussin *m*; (*col*) pépée *f.*
chicken [chik'ən] *n* poulet *m*; (*col: coward*) poule mouillée.
chicken out *vi* (*col*) se dégonfler.
chicken feed *n* (*fig*) broutilles *fpl*, bagatelle *f.*
chickenpox [chik'ənpâks] *n* varicelle *f.*
chick pea [chik pē] *n* pois *m* chiche.
chicory [chik'ûrē] *n* (*for coffee*) chicorée *f*; (*salad*) endive *f.*
chide [chīd] *vt* réprimander, gronder.
chief [chēf] *n* chef *m* ♦ *a* principal(e); **C~ of Staff** (*MIL*) chef d'État-major.
chief constable *n* (*Brit*) ≈ préfet *m* de police.
chief executive officer, chief executive *n* directeur général.
chiefly [chēf'lē] *ad* principalement, surtout.
chiffon [shifân'] *n* mousseline *f* de soie.
chilblain [chil'blān] *n* engelure *f.*
child, *pl* **~ren** [chīld, chil'drən] *n* enfant *m/f.*
childbirth [chīld'bûrth] *n* accouchement *m.*
childhood [chīld'hōōd] *n* enfance *f.*
childish [chīl'dish] *a* puéril(e), enfantin(e).
childless [chīld'lis] *a* sans enfants.
childlike [chīld'līk] *a* innocent(e), pur(e).
child minder *n* (*Brit*) garde *f* d'enfants.
Chile [chil'ē] *n* Chili *m.*
Chilean [chēl'āən] *a* chilien(ne) ♦ *n* Chilien/ne.
chili, (*Brit*) **chilli** [chil'ē] *n* piment *m* (rouge).
chill [chil] *n* froid *m*; (*MED*) refroidissement *m*, coup *m* de froid ♦ *a* froid(e), glacial(e) ♦ *vt* faire frissonner; refroidir; (*CULIN*) mettre au frais, rafraîchir; **"serve ~ed"** "à servir frais".
chilly [chil'ē] *a* froid(e), glacé(e); (*sensitive to cold*) frileux(euse); **to feel ~** avoir froid.
chime [chīm] *n* carillon *m* ♦ *vi* carillonner, sonner.
chimney [chim'nē] *n* cheminée *f.*
chimney sweep *n* ramonneur *m.*
chimpanzee [chimpanzē'] *n* chimpanzé *m.*
chin [chin] *n* menton *m.*
China [chī'nə] *n* Chine *f.*

china *n* porcelaine *f*; (vaisselle *f* en) porcelaine.
Chinese [chīnēz'] *a* chinois(e) ♦ *n* (*pl inv*) Chinois/e; (*LING*) chinois *m.*
chink [chingk] *n* (*opening*) fente *f*, fissure *f*; (*noise*) tintement *m.*
chip [chip] *n* (*gen pl: US: also: **potato ~***) chip *m*; (: *Brit CULIN*) frite *f*; (*of wood*) copeau *m*; (*of glass, stone*) éclat *m*; (*also: **micro~***) puce *f*; (*in gambling*) fiche *f* ♦ *vt* (*cup, plate*) ébrécher; **when the ~s are down** (*fig*) au moment critique.
chip in *vi* (*col*) mettre son grain de sel.
chipboard [chip'bôrd] *n* (*Brit*) aggloméré *m*, panneau *m* de particules.
chipmunk [chip'mungk] *n* suisse *m* (*animal*).
chiropodist [kirâp'ədist] *n* (*Brit*) pédicure *m/f.*
chiropody [kirâp'ədē] *n* (*Brit*) pédicurie *f.*
chirp [chûrp] *n* pépiement *m*, gazouillis *m*; (*of crickets*) stridulation *f* ♦ *vi* pépier, gazouiller; chanter, striduler.
chirpy [chûr'pē] *a* (*col*) plein(e) d'entrain, tout guilleret(te).
chisel [chiz'əl] *n* ciseau *m.*
chit [chit] *n* mot *m*, note *f.*
chitchat [chit'chat] *n* bavardage *m*, papotage *m.*
chivalrous [shiv'əlrəs] *a* chevaleresque.
chivalry [shiv'əlrē] *n* chevalerie *f*; esprit *m* chevaleresque.
chives [chīvz] *npl* ciboulette *f*, civette *f.*
chloride [klôr'īd] *n* chlorure *m.*
chlorinate [klôr'ənāt] *vt* chlorer.
chlorine [klôr'ēn] *n* chlore *m.*
chock [châk] *n* cale *f.*
chock-a-block [châk'əblâk'], **chock-full** [châk'fōōl] *a* plein(e) à craquer.
chocolate [chôk'əlit] *n* chocolat *m.*
choice [chois] *n* choix *m* ♦ *a* de choix; **by** *or* **from ~** par choix; **a wide ~** un grand choix.
choir [kwī'ûr] *n* chœur *m*, chorale *f.*
choirboy [kwī'ûr'boi] *n* jeune choriste *m*, petit chanteur.
choke [chōk] *vi* étouffer ♦ *vt* étrangler; étouffer; (*block*) boucher, obstruer ♦ *n* (*AUT*) starter *m.*
cholera [kâl'ərə] *n* choléra *m.*
cholesterol [kəles'tərôl] *n* cholestérol *m.*
choose, *pt* **chose,** *pp* **chosen** [chōōz, chōz, chō'zən] *vt* choisir ♦ *vi:* **to ~ between** choisir entre; **to ~ from** choisir parmi; **to ~ to do** décider de faire, juger bon de faire.
choosy [chōō'zē] *a:* **(to be) ~** (faire le) difficile.
chop [châp] *vt* (*wood*) couper (à la hache); (*CULIN: also: ~ up*) couper (fin), émincer, hacher (en morceaux) ♦ *n* coup *m* (de hache, du tranchant de la main); (*CULIN*) côtelette *f*; **to get the ~** (*Brit col: project*) tomber à l'eau; (: *person: be sacked*) se faire renvoyer.
chop down *vt* (*tree*) abattre.
chopper [châp'ûr] *n* (*helicopter*) hélicoptère *m*, hélico *m.*
choppy [châp'ē] *a* (*sea*) un peu agité(e).
chops [châps] *npl* (*jaws*) mâchoires *fpl*; babines *fpl.*
chopsticks [châp'stiks] *npl* baguettes *fpl.*
choral [kôr'əl] *a* choral(e), chanté(e) en

chœur.

chord [kôrd] n (MUS) accord m.

chore [chôr] n travail m de routine; **household** ~s travaux mpl du ménage.

choreographer [kórēåg'rəfûr] n choréographe m/f.

chorister [kôr'istûr] n choriste m/f.

chortle [chôr'təl] vi glousser.

chorus [kôr'əs] n chœur m; (repeated part of song, also fig) refrain m.

chose [chōz] pt of **choose**.

chosen [chō'zən] pp of **choose**.

chow [chou] n (dog) chow-chow m.

chowder [chou'dûr] n soupe f de poisson.

Christ [krīst] n Christ m.

christen [kris'ən] vt baptiser.

christening [kris'əning] n baptême m.

Christian [kris'chən] a, n chrétien(ne).

Christianity [krischēan'itē] n christianisme m; chrétienté f.

Christian name n prénom m.

Christmas [kris'məs] n Noël m or f; **happy** or **merry** ~! joyeux Noël!

Christmas card n carte f de Noël.

Christmas Day n le jour de Noël.

Christmas Eve n la veille de Noël; la nuit de Noël.

Christmas Island n île f Christmas.

Christmas tree n arbre m de Noël.

Christmas tree lights npl guirlande lumineuse.

chrome [krōm] n = **chromium**.

chromium [krō'mēəm] n chrome m; (also: ~ **plating**) chromage m.

chromosome [krō'məsōm] n chromosome m.

chronic [krân'ik] a chronique; (fig: liar, smoker) invétéré(e).

chronicle [krân'ikəl] n chronique f.

chronological [krânəlâj'ikəl] a chronologique.

chrysanthemum [krisan'thəməm] n chrysanthème m.

chubby [chub'ē] a potelé(e), rondelet(te).

chuck [chuk] vt lancer, jeter; **to** ~ (**up** or **in**) vt (Brit: job) lâcher; (: person) plaquer. **chuck out** vt flanquer dehors or à la porte.

chuckle [chuk'əl] vi glousser.

chug [chug] vi faire teuf-teuf; souffler.

chum [chum] n copain/copine.

chump [chump] n (col) imbécile m/f, crétin/e.

chunk [chungk] n gros morceau; (of bread) quignon m.

chunky [chung'kē] a (furniture etc) massif(ive); (person) trapu(e); (knitwear) en grosse laine.

church [chûrch] n église f; **the C~ of England** l'Église anglicane.

churchyard [chûrch'yârd] n cimetière m.

churlish [chûr'lish] a grossier(ère); hargneux(euse).

churn [chûrn] n (for butter) baratte f; (for transport: also: **milk** ~) (grand) bidon à lait. **churn out** vt débiter.

chute [shōōt] n glissoire f; (also: **garbage** ~) vide-ordures m inv; (Brit: children's slide) toboggan m.

chutney [chut'nē] n chutney m.

CIA n abbr (US: = Central Intelligence Agency) CIA f.

CID n abbr (Brit: = Criminal Investigation De-

partment) ≈ P.J. f (= police judiciaire).

cider [sī'dûr] n cidre m.

CIF abbr (= cost, insurance and freight) CAF.

cigar [sigâr'] n cigare m.

cigarette [sigəret'] n cigarette f.

cigarette butt, (Brit) **cigarette end** n mégot m.

cigarette case n étui m à cigarettes.

cigarette holder n fume-cigarettes m inv.

C in C abbr = **commander in chief**.

cinch [sinch] n (col): **it's a** ~ c'est du gâteau, c'est l'enfance de l'art.

cinder [sin'dûr] n cendre f.

cinder block [sindûr blâk] n (US) parpaing m.

Cinderella [sindərēl'ə] n Cendrillon.

cine-camera [sin'ēkamûrə] n (Brit) caméra f.

cine-film [sin'ēfilm] n (Brit) film m.

cinema [sin'əmə] n cinéma m.

cinnamon [sin'əmən] n cannelle f.

cipher [sī'fûr] n code secret; (fig: faceless employee etc) numéro m; **in** ~ codé(e).

circa [sûr'kə] prep circa, environ.

circle [sûr'kəl] n cercle m; (in cinema) balcon m ♦ vi faire or décrire des cercles ♦ vt (surround) entourer, encercler; (move around) faire le tour de, tourner autour de.

circuit [sûr'kit] n circuit m.

circuit board n plaquette f.

circuit court n (US) ≈ Cour f d'assises.

circuitous [sûrkyōō'itəs] a indirect(e), qui fait un détour.

circular [sûr'kyəlûr] a circulaire ♦ n circulaire f; (as advertisement) prospectus m.

circulate [sûr'kyəlāt] vi circuler ♦ vt faire circuler.

circulation [sûrkyəlā'shən] n circulation f; (of newspaper) tirage m.

circumcise [sûr'kəmsīz] vt circoncire.

circumference [sûrkum'fûrəns] n circonférence f.

circumflex [sûr'kəmfleks] n (also: ~ **accent**) accent m circonflexe.

circumscribe [sûr'kəmskrīb'] vt circonscrire.

circumspect [sûr'kəmspekt] a circonspect(e).

circumstances [sûr'kəmstansiz] npl circonstances fpl; (financial condition) moyens mpl, situation financière; **under the** ~ dans ces conditions; **under no** ~ en aucun cas, sous aucun prétexte.

circumstantial [sûrkəmstan'shəl] a (report, statement) circonstancié(e); ~ **evidence** preuve indirecte.

circumvent [sûrkəmvent'] vt (rule etc) tourner.

circus [sûr'kəs] n cirque m; (also: **C~**: in place names) place f.

cistern [sis'tûrn] n réservoir m (d'eau); (Brit: in toilet) réservoir de la chasse d'eau.

citation [sītā'shən] n citation f; (US) P.-V. m.

cite [sīt] vt citer.

citizen [sit'əzən] n (POL) citoyen/ne; (resident): **the** ~s **of this town** les habitants de cette ville.

citizenship [sit'əzənship] n citoyenneté f.

citric [sit'rik] a: ~ **acid** acide m citrique.

citrus fruit [sit'rəs frōōt] n agrume m.

city [sit'ē] n ville f, cité f.

city center n centre m de la ville, centre-ville m.

city hall n (US) hôtel m de ville.
city plan n plan m de ville.
city planner n (US) urbaniste m/f.
city planning n (US) urbanisme m.
civic [siv'ik] a civique.
civil [siv'əl] a civil(e); (polite) poli(e), civil.
civil disobedience n désobéissance civile.
civil engineer n ingénieur civil.
civil engineering n génie civil, travaux publics.
civilian [sivil'yən] a, n civil(e).
civilization [sivələzā'shən] n civilisation f.
civilized [siv'əlīzd] a civilisé(e); (fig) où règnent les bonnes manières, empreint(e) d'une courtoisie de bon ton.
civil law n code civil; (study) droit civil.
civil rights npl droits mpl civiques.
civil servant n fonctionnaire m/f.
Civil Service n fonction publique, administration f.
civil war n guerre civile.
cl abbr (= centiliter) cl.
clad [klad] a: ~ (in) habillé(e) de, vêtu(e) de.
claim [klām] vt (rights etc) revendiquer; (compensation) réclamer; **to ~ that/to be** prétendre que/être ♦ vi (for insurance) faire une déclaration de sinistre ♦ n revendication f; prétention f; (right) droit m; (for expenses) note f de frais; **(insurance)** ~ demande f d'indemnisation, déclaration f de sinistre; **to put in a ~ for** (pay raise etc) demander.
claimant [klā'mənt] n (ADMIN, LAW) requérant/e.
claim form n (gen) formulaire m de demande.
clairvoyant [klärvoi'ənt] n voyant/e, extralucide m/f.
clam [klam] n palourde f.
   clam up vi (col) la boucler.
clamber [klam'bûr] vi grimper, se hisser.
clammy [klam'ē] a humide et froid(e) (au toucher), moite.
clamor, (Brit) **clamour** [klam'ûr] n (noise) clameurs fpl; (protest) protestations bruyantes ♦ vi: **to ~ for sth** réclamer qch à grands cris.
clamp [klamp] n étau m à main; agrafe f, crampon m ♦ vt serrer; cramponner.
   clamp down on vt fus sévir contre, prendre des mesures draconiennes à l'égard de.
clan [klan] n clan m.
clandestine [klandes'tin] a clandestin(e).
clang [klang] n bruit m or fracas m métallique ♦ vi émettre un bruit or fracas métallique.
clansman [klanz'mən] n membre m d'un clan (écossais).
clap [klap] vi applaudir ♦ vt: **to ~ (one's hands)** battre des mains ♦ n claquement m; tape f; **a ~ of thunder** un coup de tonnerre.
clapping [klap'ing] n applaudissements mpl.
claret [klar'it] n (vin m de) bordeaux m (rouge).
clarification [klarəfəkā'shən] n (fig) clarification f, éclaircissement m.
clarify [klar'əfī] vt clarifier.
clarinet [klarənet'] n clarinette f.
clarity [klar'itē] n clarté f.
clash [klash] n (sound) choc m, fracas m;

(with police) affrontement m; (fig) conflit m ♦ vi se heurter; être or entrer en conflit; (dates, events) tomber en même temps.
clasp [klasp] n fermoir m ♦ vt serrer, étreindre.
class [klas] n (gen) classe f; (group, category) catégorie f ♦ vt classer, classifier.
class-conscious [klas'kân'shəs] a conscient(e) de son appartenance sociale.
class consciousness n conscience f de classe.
classic [klas'ik] a classique ♦ n (author) classique m; (race etc) classique f.
classical [klas'ikəl] a classique.
classics [klas'iks] npl (SCOL) lettres fpl classiques.
classification [klasəfəkā'shən] n classification f.
classified [klas'əfīd] a (information) secret(ète); ~ **ads** petites annonces.
classify [klas'əfī] vt classifier, classer.
classmate [klas'māt] n camarade m/f de classe.
classroom [klas'rōōm] n (salle f de) classe f.
clatter [klat'ûr] n cliquetis m ♦ vi cliqueter.
clause [klôz] n clause f; (LING) proposition f.
claustrophobia [klôstrəfō'bēə] n claustrophobie f.
claw [klô] n griffe f; (of bird of prey) serre f; (of lobster) pince f ♦ vt griffer; déchirer.
clay [klā] n argile f.
clean [klēn] a propre; (clear, smooth) net(te) ♦ vt nettoyer ♦ ad: **he ~ forgot** il a complètement oublié; **to come ~** (col: admit guilt) se mettre à table; **to ~ one's teeth** (Brit) se laver les dents; ~ **driving record** permis où n'est portée aucune indication de contravention.
   clean off vt enlever.
   clean out vt nettoyer (à fond).
   clean up vt nettoyer; (fig) remettre de l'ordre dans ♦ vi (fig: make profit): **to ~ up on** faire son beurre avec.
clean-cut [klēn'kut'] a (man) soigné; (situation etc) bien délimité(e), net(te), clair(e).
cleaner [klē'nûr] n (person) nettoyeur/euse, femme f de ménage; (also: **dry ~er**) teinturier/ière; (product) détachant m.
cleaning [klē'ning] n nettoyage m.
cleaning lady or **woman** n femme f de ménage.
cleanliness [klen'lēnis] n propreté f.
cleanly [klēn'lē] ad proprement; nettement.
cleanse [klenz] vt nettoyer; purifier.
cleanser [klen'zûr] n détergent m; (for face) démaquillant m.
clean-shaven [klēn'shā'vən] a rasé(e) de près.
cleansing department [klen'zing dipârt'mənt] n (Brit) service m de voirie.
clean-up [klēn'up] n nettoyage m.
clear [klī'ûr] a clair(e); (road, way) libre, dégagé(e); (profit, majority) net(te) ♦ vt dégager, déblayer, débarrasser; (room etc: of people) faire évacuer; (woodland) défricher; (check) compenser; (COMM: goods) liquider; (LAW: suspect) innocenter; (obstacle) franchir or sauter sans heurter ♦ vi (weather) s'éclaircir; (fog) se dissiper ♦ ad: ~ **of** à distance de, à l'écart de ♦ n: **to be in the ~**

(*out of debt*) être dégagé(e) de toute dette; (*out of suspicion*) être lavé(e) de tout soupçon; (*out of danger*) être hors de danger; **to ~ the table** débarrasser la table, desservir; **to ~ one's throat** s'éclaircir la gorge; **to ~ a profit** faire un bénéfice net; **to make o.s. ~** se faire bien comprendre; **to make it ~ to sb that ...** bien faire comprendre à qn que ...; **I have a ~ day tomorrow** (*Brit*) je n'ai rien de prévu demain; **to keep ~ of sb/sth** (*Brit*) éviter qn/qch.

clear off *vi* (*Brit col*) = **clear out.**

clear out *vi* (*US col*) dégager.

clear up *vi* s'éclaircir, se dissiper ♦ *vt* ranger, mettre en ordre; (*mystery*) éclaircir, résoudre.

clearance [klē'rəns] *n* (*removal*) déblayage *m*; (*free space*) dégagement *m*; (*permission*) autorisation *f*.

clearance sale *n* (*COMM*) liquidation *f*.

clear-cut [kli'ûrkut'] *a* précise(e), nettement défini(e).

clearing [klē'ring] *n* (*in forest*) clairière *f*; (*Brit BANKING*) compensation *f*, clearing *m*.

clearing bank *n* (*Brit*) banque *f* qui appartient à une chambre de compensation.

clearly [kli'ûrlē] *ad* clairement; (*obviously*) de toute évidence.

clearway [klēr'wā] *n* (*Brit*) route *f* à stationnement interdit.

cleavage [klē'vij] *n* (*of dress*) décolleté *m*.

cleaver [klē'vûr'] *n* fendoir *m*, couperet *m*.

clef [klef] *n* (*MUS*) clé *f*.

cleft [kleft] *n* (*in rock*) crevasse *f*, fissure *f*.

clemency [klem'ənsē] *n* clémence *f*.

clement [klem'ənt] *a* (*weather*) clément(e).

clench [klench] *vt* serrer.

clergy [klûr'jē] *n* clergé *m*.

clergyman [klûr'jēmən] *n* ecclésiastique *m*.

clerical [klär'ikəl] *a* de bureau, d'employé de bureau; (*REL*) clérical(e), du clergé.

clerk [klûrk] *n* employé/e de bureau; (*US: salesman/woman*) vendeur/euse; **C~ of Court** (*LAW*) greffier *m* (du tribunal).

clever [klev'ûr] *a* (*mentally*) intelligent(e); (*deft, crafty*) habile, adroit(e); (*device, arrangement*) ingénieux(euse), astucieux(euse).

clew [klōō] *n* (*US*) = **clue.**

cliché [kleshā'] *n* cliché *m*.

click [klik] *vi* faire un bruit sec *or* un déclic ♦ *vt*: **to ~ one's tongue** faire claquer sa langue; **to ~ one's heels** claquer des talons.

client [klī'ənt] *n* client/e.

clientele [klīəntel'] *n* clientèle *f*.

cliff [klif] *n* falaise *f*.

cliffhanger [klif'hangûr] *n* (*TV, fig*) histoire pleine de suspense.

climactic [klīmak'tik] *a* à son point culminant, culminant(e).

climate [klī'mit] *n* climat *m*.

climax [klī'maks] *n* apogée *m*, point culminant; (*sexual*) orgasme *m*.

climb [klīm] *vi* grimper, monter; (*plane*) prendre de l'altitude ♦ *vt* gravir, escalader, monter sur ♦ *n* montée *f*, escalade *f*; **to ~ over a wall** passer par dessus un mur.

climb down *vi* (re)descendre; (*Brit fig*) rabattre de ses prétentions.

climbdown [klīm'doun] *n* (*Brit*) reculade *f*.

climber [klī'mûr] *n* (*also:* **rock ~**) grimpeur/euse, varappeur/euse.

climbing [klī'ming] *n* (*also:* **rock ~**) escalade *f*, varappe *f*.

clinch [klinch] *vt* (*deal*) conclure, sceller.

cling, *pt*, *pp* **clung** [kling, klung] *vi*: **to ~ (to)** se cramponner (à), s'accrocher (à); (*of clothes*) coller (à).

clinic [klin'ik] *n* clinique *f*; centre médical; (*session:* MED) consultation(s) *f(pl)*, séance(s) *f(pl)*; (*: SPORT*) séance(s) de perfectionnement.

clinical [klin'ikəl] *a* clinique; (*fig*) froid(e).

clink [klingk] *vi* tinter, cliqueter.

clip [klip] *n* (*for hair*) barrette *f*; (*also:* **paper ~**) trombone *m*; (*clamp*) pince *f* de bureau; (*holding hose etc*) collier *m or* bague *f* (métallique) de serrage ♦ *vt* (*also:* **~ together**) *papers*) attacher; (*hair, nails*) couper; (*hedge*) tailler.

clippers [klip'ûrz] *npl* tondeuse *f*; (*also:* **nail ~**) coupe-ongles *m inv*.

clipping [klip'ing] *n* (*from newspaper*) coupure *f* de journal.

clique [klēk] *n* clique *f*, coterie *f*.

cloak [klōk] *n* grande cape.

cloakroom [klōk'rōōm] *n* (*for coats etc*) vestiaire *m*; (*Brit: W.C.*) toilettes *fpl*.

clock [klâk] *n* (*large*) horloge *f*; (*small*) pendule *f*; **around the ~** (*work etc*) vingt-quatre heures sur vingt-quatre; **to sleep around the ~** faire le tour du cadran; **30,000 on the ~** (*Brit AUT*) 30 000 km au compteur; **to work against the ~** faire la course contre la montre.

clock in, clock on *vi* pointer (en arrivant).

clock off, clock out *vi* pointer (en partant).

clock up *vt* (*miles, hours etc*) faire.

clockwise [klâk'wīz] *ad* dans le sens des aiguilles d'une montre.

clockwork [klâk'wûrk] *n* mouvement *m* (d'horlogerie); rouages *mpl*, mécanisme *m* ♦ *a* (*toy, train*) mécanique.

clod [klâd] *n* (*col*) lourdaud *m*, balourd *m*.

clog [klâg] *n* sabot *m* ♦ *vt* boucher, encrasser ♦ *vi* se boucher, s'encrasser.

cloister [klois'tûr] *n* cloître *m*.

clone [klōn] *n* clone *m*.

close *a, ad and derivatives* [klōs] *a* (*near*): **~ (to)** près (de), proche (de); (*writing, texture*) serré(e); (*watch*) étroit(e), strict(e); (*examination*) attentif(ive), minutieux(euse); (*weather*) lourd(e), étouffant(e); (*room*) mal aéré(e) ♦ *ad* près, à proximité; **~ to** *prep* près de; **~ by, ~ at hand** *a, ad* tout(e) près; **how ~ is Philadelphia to New York?** combien de kilomètres y-a-t-il entre Philadelphie et New York?; **a ~ friend** un ami intime; **to have a ~ shave** (*fig*) l'échapper belle; **at ~ quarters** tout près, à côté ♦ *vb and derivatives* [klōz] *vt* fermer; (*bargain, deal*) conclure ♦ *vi* (*store etc*) fermer; (*lid, door etc*) se fermer; (*end*) se terminer, se conclure ♦ *n* (*end*) conclusion *f*; **to bring sth to a ~** mettre fin à qch.

close down *vt, vi* fermer (*définitivement*).

close in *vi* (*hunters*) approcher; (*night, fog*) tomber; **the days are closing in** les jours

raccourcissent; **to ~ in on sb** cerner qn.
close off *vt* (*area*) boucler.
closed [klōzd] *a* (*store etc*) fermé(e); (*road*) fermé à la circulation.
closed-circuit [klōzdsûr'kit] *a*: **~ television** télévision *f* en circuit fermé.
closed shop *n* organisation *f* qui n'admet que des travailleurs syndiqués.
close-knit [klōs'nit'] *a* (*family, community*) très uni(e).
closely [klōs'lē] *ad* (*examine, watch*) de près; **we are ~ related** nous sommes proches parents; **a ~ guarded secret** un secret bien gardé.
closet [klâz'it] *n* placard *m*, réduit *m*; (*for hanging clothes*) penderie *f*.
close-up [klōs'up] *n* gros plan.
closing [klō'zing] *a* (*stages, remarks*) final(e); **~ price** (*STOCK EXCHANGE*) cours *m* de clôture.
closure [klō'zhûr] *n* fermeture *f*.
clot [klât] *n* (*gen*: **blood ~**) caillot *m*; (*col*: *person*) ballot *m* ♦ *vi* (*blood*) former des caillots; (: *external bleeding*) se coaguler.
cloth [klôth] *n* (*material*) tissu *m*, étoffe *f*; (*Brit*: *also*: **tea~**) torchon *m*; lavette *f*; (*also*: **table~**) nappe *f*.
clothe [klōth] *vt* habiller, vêtir.
clothes [klōz] *npl* vêtements *mpl*, habits *mpl*; **to put one's ~ on** s'habiller; **to take one's ~ off** enlever ses vêtements.
clothes brush *n* brosse *f* à habits.
clothes line *n* corde *f* (à linge).
clothes pin, (*Brit*) **clothes peg** *n* pince *f* à linge.
clothing [klō'thing] *n* = **clothes.**
clotted cream [klât'id krēm'] *n* (*Brit*) crème caillée.
cloud [kloud] *n* nuage *m* ♦ *vt* (*liquid*) troubler; **to ~ the issue** brouiller les cartes; **every ~ has a silver lining** (*proverb*) à quelque chose malheur est bon (*proverbe*).
cloud over *vi* se couvrir; (*fig*) s'assombrir.
cloudburst [kloud'bûrst] *n* violente averse.
cloudland [kloud'land] *n* (*US*) monde *m* imaginaire.
cloudy [klou'dē] *a* nuageux(euse), couvert(e); (*liquid*) trouble.
clout [klout] *n* (*blow*) taloche *f*; (*fig*) pouvoir *m* ♦ *vt* flanquer une taloche à.
clove [klōv] *n* clou *m* de girofle; **~ of garlic** gousse *f* d'ail.
clover [klō'vûr] *n* trèfle *m*.
cloverleaf [klō'vûrlēf] *n* feuille *f* de trèfle; (*AUT*) croisement *m* en trèfle.
clown [kloun] *n* clown *m* ♦ *vi* (*also*: **~ around**) faire le clown.
cloying [kloi'ing] *a* (*taste, smell*) écœurant(e).
CLU *n abbr* (*US*: = *Chartered Life Underwriter*) spécialiste agréé en assurance-vie.
club [klub] *n* (*society*) club *m*; (*weapon*) massue *f*, matraque *f*; (*also*: **golf ~**) club ♦ *vt* matraquer ♦ *vi*: **to ~ together** s'associer; **~s** *npl* (*CARDS*) trèfle *m*.
club car *n* (*US RAIL*) wagon-restaurant *m*.
clubhouse [klub'hous] *n* pavillon *m*.
cluck [kluk] *vi* glousser.
clue [klōō] *n* indice *m*; (*in crosswords*) définition *f*; **I haven't a ~** je n'en ai pas la moin-

dre idée.
clued in [klōōd in] *a* (*US col*) (vachement) calé(e).
clued up [klōōd up] *a* (*Brit col*) = **clued in.**
clump [klump] *n*: **~ of trees** bouquet *m* d'arbres.
clumsy [klum'zē] *a* (*person*) gauche, maladroit(e); (*object*) malcommode, peu maniable.
clung [klung] *pt, pp of* **cling.**
clunker [klunk'ûr] *n* (*US col*: *car*) (vieux) tacot.
cluster [klus'tûr] *n* (petit) groupe ♦ *vi* se rassembler.
clutch [kluch] *n* (*grip, grasp*) étreinte *f*, prise *f*; (*AUT*) embrayage *m* ♦ *vt* agripper, serrer fort; **to let out the ~** (*AUT*) débrayer; **to ~ at** se cramponner à.
clutter [klut'ûr] *vt* (*also*: **~ up**) encombrer ♦ *n* désordre *m*, fouillis *m*.
CM *abbr* (*US MAIL*) = *North Marianna Islands.*
cm *abbr* (= *centimeter*) cm.
CND *n abbr* = *Campaign for Nuclear Disarmament.*
CO *n abbr* (= *commanding officer*) Cdt ♦ *abbr* (*US MAIL*) = *Colorado.*
Co. *abbr* = **company, county.**
c/o *abbr* (= *care of*) c/o, aux bons soins de.
coach [kōch] *n* (*bus*) autocar *m*; (*horse-drawn*) diligence *f*; (*of train*) voiture *f*, wagon *m*; (*SPORT*: *trainer*) entraîneur/euse; (*school*: *tutor*) répétiteur/trice ♦ *vt* entraîner; donner des leçons particulières à.
coach trip *n* excursion *f* en car.
coagulate [kōag'yəlāt] *vt* coaguler ♦ *vi* se coaguler.
coal [kōl] *n* charbon *m*.
coalfield [kōl'fēld] *n* bassin houiller.
coalition [kōəlish'ən] *n* coalition *f*.
coalman [kōl'mən], **coal merchant** *n* charbonnier *m*, marchand *m* de charbon.
coal mine *n* mine *f* de charbon.
coal miner *n* mineur *m*.
coal mining *n* extraction *f* du charbon.
coarse [kôrs] *a* grossier(ère), rude; (*vulgar*) vulgaire.
coast [kōst] *n* côte *f* ♦ *vi* (*with cycle etc*) descendre en roue libre.
coastal [kōs'təl] *a* côtier(ère).
coaster [kōs'tûr] *n* (*NAUT*) caboteur *m*; (*for glass*) dessous *m* de verre.
coastguard [kōst'gârd] *n* garde-côte *m*.
coastline [kōst'līn] *n* côte *f*, littoral *m*.
coat [kōt] *n* manteau *m*; (*of animal*) pelage *m*, poil *m*; (*of paint*) couche *f* ♦ *vt* couvrir, enduire; **~ of arms** *n* blason *m*, armoiries *fpl*.
coated [kō'tid] (*US*) *a*: **to have a ~ tongue** avoir la langue pâteuse.
coat hanger *n* cintre *m*.
coating [kō'ting] *n* couche *f*, enduit *m*.
co-author [kō'ô'thûr] *n* co-auteur *m*.
coax [kōks] *vt* persuader par de cajoleries.
cob [kâb] *n* see **corn.**
cobbler [kâb'lûr] *n* cordonnier *m*.
cobbles [kâb'əlz], **cobblestones** [kâb'əlstōnz] *npl* pavés (ronds).
COBOL [kō'bôl] *n* COBOL *m*.

cobra [kōb'rə] n cobra m.
cobweb [kâb'web] n toile f d'araignée.
cocaine [kōkān'] n cocaïne f.
cock [kâk] n (rooster) coq m; (male bird) mâle m ♦ vt (gun) armer; **to ~ one's ears** (fig) dresser l'oreille.
cock-a-hoop [kâkəhōōp'] a jubilant(e).
cockerel [kâk'ûrəl] n jeune coq m.
cockeyed [kâk'īd] a (fig) de travers; qui louche; qui ne tient pas debout (fig).
cockle [kâk'əl] n coque f.
cockney [kâk'nē] n cockney m/f (habitant des quartiers populaires de l'East End de Londres), ≈ faubourien/ne.
cockpit [kâk'pit] n (in aircraft) poste m de pilotage, cockpit m.
cockroach [kâk'rōch] n cafard m, cancrelat m.
cocktail [kâk'tāl] n cocktail m; **shrimp ~**, (Brit) **prawn ~** cocktail de crevettes.
cocktail cabinet [kâk'tāl] n (meuble-)bar m.
cocktail party n cocktail m.
cocktail shaker [kâk'tāl shā'kûr] n shaker m.
cocoa [kō'kō] n cacao m.
coconut [kō'kənut] n noix f de coco.
cocoon [kəkōōn'] n cocon m.
COD abbr = **cash on delivery, collect on delivery** (US).
cod [kâd] n morue (fraîche), cabillaud m.
code [kōd] n code m; **~ of behavior** règles fpl de conduite; **~ of practice** déontologie f.
codeine [kō'dēn] n codéine f.
codicil [kâd'isəl] n codicille m.
codify [kâd'əfī] vt codifier.
cod-liver oil [kâd'livûr oil] n huile f de foie de morue.
co-driver [kōdrī'vûr] n (in race) copilote m; (of truck) deuxième chauffeur m.
co-ed [kōed'] a abbr = **coeducational** ♦ n abbr (US: female student) étudiante d'une université mixte; (Brit: school) école f mixte.
coeducational [kōejōōkā'shənəl] a mixte.
coerce [kōûrs'] vt contraindre.
coercion [kōûr'shən] n contrainte f.
coexistence [kōigzis'təns] n coexistence f.
C. of C. n abbr = **chamber of commerce.**
C of E abbr = **Church of England.**
coffee [kôf'ē] n café m; **~ with cream** (café-)crème m.
coffee bar n (Brit) café m.
coffee bean n grain m de café.
coffee break n pause-café f.
coffeecake [kôf'ēkāk] n (US) ≈ petit pain aux raisins.
coffee cup n tasse f à café.
coffeepot [kôf'ēpât] n cafetière f.
coffee table n (petite) table basse.
coffin [kôf'in] n cercueil m.
cog [kâg] n dent f (d'engrenage).
cogent [kō'jənt] a puissant(e), convaincant(e).
cognac [kōn'yak] n cognac m.
cogwheel [kâg'hwēl] n roue dentée.
cohabit [kōhab'it] vi (formal): **to ~ (with sb)** cohabiter (avec qn).
coherent [kōhē'rənt] a cohérent(e).
cohesion [kōhē'zhən] n cohésion f.
cohesive [kōhē'siv] a (fig) cohésif(ive).
coil [koil] n rouleau m, bobine f; (one loop) anneau m, spire f; (of smoke) volute f;

(contraceptive) stérilet m ♦ vt enrouler.
coin [koin] n pièce f de monnaie ♦ vt (word) inventer.
coinage [koi'nij] n monnaie f, système m monétaire.
coincide [kōinsīd'] vi coïncider.
coincidence [kōin'sidəns] n coïncidence f.
coin-operated [koinâp'ərātid] a (machine, launderette) automatique.
coin purse n (US) porte-monnaie m inv.
coke [kōk] n coke m; (®: Coca-Cola) coca m.
Col. abbr (US) = Colorado; (= colonel) Col.
COLA n abbr (US: = cost-of-living adjustment) réajustement (des salaires, indemnités etc) en fonction du coût de la vie.
colander [kâl'əndûr] n passoire f (à légumes).
cold [kōld] a froid(e) ♦ n froid m; (MED) rhume m; **it's ~** il fait froid; **to be ~** avoir froid; **to catch ~** prendre or attraper froid; **to catch a ~** s'enrhumer, attraper un rhume; **in ~ blood** de sang-froid; **to have ~ feet** avoir froid aux pieds; (fig) avoir la frousse or la trouille; **to give sb the ~ shoulder** battre froid à qn.
cold-blooded [kōld'blud'id] a (ZOOL) à sang froid.
cold cream n crème f de soins.
cold cuts npl viandes froides.
coldly [kōld'lē] ad froidement.
cold sore n bouton m de fièvre.
coleslaw [kōl'slô] n sorte de salade de chou cru.
colic [kâl'ik] n colique(s) f(pl).
collaborate [kəlab'ərāt] vi collaborer.
collaboration [kəlabərā'shən] n collaboration f.
collaborator [kəlab'ərātûr] n collaborateur/trice.
collage [kəlâzh'] n (ART) collage m.
collagen [kâl'əjən] n collagène m.
collapse [kəlaps'] vi s'effondrer, s'écrouler ♦ n effondrement m, écroulement m; (of government) chute f.
collapsible [kəlaps'əbəl] a pliant(e); télescopique.
collar [kâl'ûr] n (of coat, shirt) col m; (for dog) collier m; (TECH) collier, bague f ♦ vt (col: person) pincer.
collarbone [kâl'ûrbōn] n clavicule f.
collate [kəlāt'] vt collationner.
collateral [kəlat'ərəl] n nantissement m.
collation [kəlā'shən] n collation f.
colleague [kâl'ēg] n collègue m/f.
collect [kəlekt'] vt rassembler; (pick up) ramasser; (as a hobby) collectionner; (Brit: call for) (passer) prendre; (mail) faire la levée de, ramasser; (money owed) encaisser; (donations, subscriptions) recueillir ♦ vi (people) se rassembler; (dust, dirt) s'amasser; **to ~ one's thoughts** réfléchir, réunir ses idées; **~ on delivery (COD)** (US COMM) payable or paiement à la livraison; **to call ~** (US TEL) téléphoner en PCV.
collect call n (US TEL) communication f en PCV.
collected [kəlek'tid] a: **~ works** œuvres complètes.
collection [kəlek'shən] n collection f; (of mail) levée f; (for money) collecte f, quête f.

collective [kəlek'tiv] *a* collectif(ive) ♦ *n* collectif *m*.

collective bargaining *n* convention collective.

collector [kəlek'tûr] *n* collectionneur *m*; (*of taxes*) percepteur *m*; (*of rent, cash*) encaisseur *m*; ~'s **item** *or* **piece** pièce *f* de collection.

college [kâl'ij] *n* collège *m*; (*of technology, agriculture etc*) institut *m*; **to go to** ~ faire des études supérieures; ~ **of education** ≈ école normale.

collide [kəlīd'] *vi*: **to** ~ **(with)** entrer en collision (avec).

collie [kâl'ē] *n* (*dog*) colley *m*.

colliery [kâl'yûrē] *n* (*Brit*) mine *f* de charbon, houillère *f*.

collision [kəlizh'ən] *n* collision *f*, heurt *m*; **to be on a** ~ **course** aller droit à la collision; (*fig*) aller vers l'affrontement.

collision damage waiver *n* (*INSURANCE*) rachat *m* de franchise.

colloquial [kəlō'kwēəl] *a* familier(ère).

collusion [kəlōō'zhən] *n* collusion *f*; **in** ~ **with** en complicité avec.

Colo. *abbr* (*US*) = *Colorado*.

cologne [kəlōn'] *n* (*also:* **eau de** ~) eau *f* de cologne.

Colombia [kəlum'bēə] *n* Colombie *f*.

Colombian [kəlum'bēən] *a* colombien(ne) ♦ *n* Colombien/ne.

colon [kō'lən] *n* (*sign*) deux-points *mpl*; (*MED*) côlon *m*.

colonel [kûr'nəl] *n* colonel *m*.

colonial [kəlō'nēəl] *a* colonial(e).

colonize [kâl'ənīz] *vt* coloniser.

colony [kâl'ənē] *n* colonie *f*.

color [kul'ûr] (*US*) *n* couleur *f* ♦ *vt* colorer; peindre; (*with crayons*) colorier; (*news*) fausser, exagérer ♦ *vi* rougir ♦ *cpd* (*film, photograph, television*) en couleur; ~**s** *npl* (*of party, club*) couleurs *fpl*.

Colorado beetle [kâlərâd'ō bē'təl] *n* doryphore *m*.

color bar *n* discrimination raciale (*dans un établissement etc*).

color-blind [kul'ûrblīnd] *a* daltonien(ne).

colored [kul'ûrd] *a* coloré(e); (*photo*) en couleur ♦ *n*: ~**s** personnes *fpl* de couleur.

colorful [kul'ûrfəl] *a* coloré(e), vif(vive); (*personality*) pittoresque, haut(e) en couleurs.

coloring [kul'ûring] *n* colorant *m*; (*complexion*) teint *m*.

color scheme *n* combinaison *f* de(s) couleur(s).

colossal [kəlâs'əl] *a* colossal(e).

colour [kul'ûr] *etc* (*Brit*) = **color** *etc*.

colt [kōlt] *n* poulain *m*.

column [kâl'əm] *n* colonne *f*; (*fashion* ~, *sports* ~ *etc*) rubrique *f*; **the editorial** ~ l'éditorial *m*.

columnist [kâl'əmist] *n* rédacteur/trice d'une rubrique.

coma [kō'mə] *n* coma *m*.

comb [kōm] *n* peigne *m* ♦ *vt* (*hair*) peigner; (*area*) ratisser, passer au peigne fin.

combat *n* [kâm'bat] combat *m* ♦ *vt* [kəmbat'] combattre, lutter contre.

combination [kâmbənā'shən] *n* (*gen*) combinaison *f*.

combination lock *n* serrure *f* à combinaison.

combine *vb* [kəmbīn'] *vt* combiner; (*one quality with another*): **to** ~ **sth with sth** joindre qch à qch, allier qch à qch ♦ *vi* s'associer; (*CHEMISTRY*) se combiner ♦ *n* [kâm'bīn] association *f*; (*ECON*) trust *m*; **a** ~**d effort** un effort conjugué.

combine (harvester) *n* moissonneuse-batteuse(-lieuse) *f*.

combo [kâm'bō] *n* (*JAZZ etc*) groupe *m* de musiciens.

combustible [kəmbus'təbəl] *a* combustible.

combustion [kəmbus'chən] *n* combustion *f*.

come, *pt* **came,** *pp* **come** [kum, kām] *vi* venir; (*col: sexually*) jouir; ~ **with me** suivez-moi; **we've just** ~ **from Paris** nous arrivons de Paris; ... **what might** ~ **of it** ... ce qui pourrait en résulter, ... ce qui pourrait advenir *or* se produire; **to** ~ **into sight** *or* **view** apparaître; **to** ~ **to** (*decision etc*) parvenir *or* arriver à; **to** ~ **undone/loose** se défaire/desserrer; **coming!** j'arrive!; **if it** ~**s to it** s'il le faut, dans le pire des cas.

come about *vi* se produire, arriver.

come across *vt fus* rencontrer par hasard, tomber sur ♦ *vi*: **to** ~ **across well/badly** faire une bonne/mauvaise impression.

come along *vi* (*pupil, work*) faire des progrès, avancer; ~ **along!** viens!; allons!, allez!

come apart *vi* s'en aller en morceaux; se détacher.

come around *vi* (*US: after faint, operation*) revenir à soi, reprendre connaissance.

come away *vi* partir, s'en aller; (*become detached*) se détacher.

come back *vi* revenir; (*reply*): **can I** ~ **back to you on that one?** est-ce qu'on peut revenir là-dessus plus tard?

come by *vt fus* (*acquire*) obtenir, se procurer.

come down *vi* descendre; (*prices*) baisser; (*buildings*) s'écrouler; (*: be demolished*) être démoli(e).

come forward *vi* s'avancer; (*make o.s. known*) se présenter, s'annoncer.

come from *vt fus* venir de; (*place*) venir de, être originaire de.

come in *vi* entrer.

come in for *vt fus* (*criticism etc*) être l'objet de.

come into *vt fus* (*money*) hériter de.

come off *vi* (*button*) se détacher; (*stain*) s'enlever; (*attempt*) réussir.

come on *vi* (*lights, electricity*) s'allumer; (*central heating*) se mettre en marche; (*pupil, work, project*) faire des progrès, avancer; ~ **on!** viens!; allons!, allez!

come out *vi* sortir; (*book*) paraître; (*strike*) cesser le travail, se mettre en grève.

come over *vt fus*: **I don't know what's** ~ **over him!** je ne sais pas ce qui lui a pris!

come round *vi* (*Brit*) = **come around**.

come through *vi* (*survive*) s'en sortir; (*telephone call*): **the call came through** l'appel est bien parvenu.

come to *vi* revenir à soi; (*add up to:*

amount): **how much does it ~ to?** ça fait combien?
come under *vt fus* (*heading*) se trouver sous; (*influence*) subir.
come up *vi* monter.
come up against *vt fus* (*resistance, difficulties*) rencontrer.
come up to *vt fus* arriver à; **the film didn't ~ up to our expectations** le film nous a déçu.
come up with *vt fus*: **he came up with an idea** il a eu une idée, il a proposé quelque chose.
come upon *vt fus* tomber sur.
comeback [kum'bak] *n* (*reaction*) réaction *f*; (*response*) réponse *f*; (*THEATER etc*) rentrée *f*.
Comecon [kâm'əkân] *n abbr* (= *Council for Mutual Economic Aid*) COMECON *m*.
comedian [kəmē'dēən] *n* (*in music hall etc*) comique *m*; (*THEATER*) comédien *m*.
comedienne [kəmēdēen'] *n* comique *f*.
comedown [kum'doun] *n* déchéance *f*.
comedy [kâm'idē] *n* comédie *f*.
comet [kâm'it] *n* comète *f*.
comeuppance [kumup'əns] *n*: **to get one's ~** recevoir ce qu'on mérite.
comfort [kum'fûrt] *n* confort *m*, bien-être *m*; (*solace*) consolation *f*, réconfort *m* ♦ *vt* consoler, réconforter.
comfortable [kum'fûrtəbəl] *a* confortable; **I don't feel very ~ about it** cela m'inquiète un peu.
comfortably [kum'fûrtəblē] *ad* (*sit*) confortablement; (*live*) à l'aise.
comforter [kum'fûrtûr] *n* (*US*) édredon *m*.
comforts [kum'fûrts] *npl* aises *fpl*.
comfort station *n* (*US*) toilettes *fpl*.
comic [kâm'ik] *a* comique ♦ *n* comique *m*; (*magazine*) illustré *m*.
comical [kâm'ikəl] *a* amusant(e).
comic strip *n* bande dessinée.
coming [kum'ing] *n* arrivée *f* ♦ *a* (*next*) prochain(e); (*future*) à venir; **in the ~ weeks** dans les prochaines semaines.
coming(s) and going(s) *n(pl)* va-et-vient *m inv*.
Comintern [kâm'intûrn] *n* Comintern *m*.
comma [kâm'ə] *n* virgule *f*.
command [kəmand'] *n* ordre *m*, commandement *m*; (*MIL*: *authority*) commandement; (*mastery*) maîtrise *f*; (*COMPUT*) commande *f* ♦ *vt* (*troops*) commander; (*be able to get*) (pouvoir) disposer de, avoir à sa disposition; (*deserve*) avoir droit à; **to ~ sb to do** donner l'ordre *or* commander à qn de faire; **to have/take ~ of** avoir/prendre le commandement de; **to have at one's ~** (*money, resources etc*) disposer de.
commandeer [kâməndēr'] *vt* réquisitionner (par la force).
commander [kəman'dûr] *n* chef *m*; (*MIL*) commandant *m*.
commander in chief *n* (*MIL*) commandant *m* en chef.
commanding [kəman'ding] *a* (*appearance*) imposant(e); (*voice, tone*) autoritaire; (*lead, position*) dominant(e).
commanding officer *n* commandant *m*.

commandment [kəmand'mənt] *n* (*REL*) commandement *m*.
command module *n* (*SPACE*) module *m* de commande.
commando [kəman'dō] *n* commando *m*; membre *m* d'un commando.
commemorate [kəmem'ərāt] *vt* commémorer.
commemoration [kəmemərā'shən] *n* commémoration *f*.
commemorative [kəmem'ərātiv] *a* commémoratif(ive).
commence [kəmens'] *vt, vi* commencer.
commend [kəmend'] *vt* louer; recommander.
commendable [kəmend'əbəl] *a* louable.
commendation [kâməndā'shən] *n* éloge *m*; recommandation *f*.
commensurate [kəmen'sərit] *a*: **~ with/to** en rapport avec/selon.
comment [kâm'ent] *n* commentaire *m* ♦ *vi* faire des remarques *or* commentaires; **to ~ on** faire des remarques sur; **to ~ that** faire remarquer que; **"no ~"** "je n'ai rien à déclarer".
commentary [kâm'əntärē] *n* commentaire *m*; (*SPORT*) reportage *m* (en direct).
commentator [kâm'əntātûr] *n* commentateur *m*; (*SPORT*) reporter *m*.
commerce [kâm'ûrs] *n* commerce *m*.
commercial [kəmûr'shəl] *a* commercial(e) ♦ *n* (*TV*: *also*: **~ break**) annonce *f* publicitaire, spot *m* (publicitaire).
commercial bank *n* banque *f* d'affaires.
commercialism [kəmûr'shəlizəm] *n* mercantilisme *m*.
commercialize [kəmûr'shəlīz] *vt* commercialiser.
commercial television *n* publicité *f* à la télévision; chaînes indépendantes (financées par la publicité).
commercial vehicle *n* véhicule *m* utilitaire.
commiserate [kəmiz'ərāt] *vi*: **to ~ with sb** témoigner de la sympathie pour qn.
commission [kəmish'ən] *n* (*committee; fee; also for salesman*) commission *f*; (*order for work of art etc*) commande *f* ♦ *vt* (*MIL*) nommer (à un commandement); (*work of art*) commander, charger un artiste de l'exécution de; **out of ~** (*NAUT*) hors de service; (*machine*) hors service; **I get 10% ~** je reçois une commission de 10%.
commissionaire [kəmishənär'] *n* (*Brit*: *at store, cinema etc*) portier *m* (en uniforme).
commissioner [kəmish'ənûr] *n* membre *m* d'une commission; (*POLICE*) préfet *m* (de police).
commit [kəmit'] *vt* (*act*) commettre; (*to sb's care*) confier (à); **to ~ o.s. (to do)** s'engager (à faire); **to ~ suicide** se suicider; **to ~ to writing** coucher par écrit; **to ~ sb for trial** traduire qn en justice.
commitment [kəmit'mənt] *n* engagement *m*; (*obligation*) responsabilité(s) *f(pl)*.
committed [kəmit'id] *a* (*writer, politician etc*) engagé(e).
committee [kəmit'ē] *n* comité *m*; commission *f*; **to be on a ~** siéger dans un comité (*or* une commission).
committee meeting *n* réunion *f* de comité *or* commission.

commodity [kəmâd'itē] *n* produit *m*, marchandise *f*, article *m*; (*food*) denrée *f*.
commodity exchange *n* bourse *f* de marchandises.
common [kâm'ən] *a* (*gen, also pej*) commun(e); (*usual*) courant(e) ♦ *n* terrain communal; **in ~** en commun; **in ~ use** d'un usage courant; **it's ~ knowledge that** il est bien connu *or* notoire que; **to the ~ good** pour le bien de tous, dans l'intérêt général.
commoner [kâm'ənûr] *n* roturier/ière.
common ground *n* (*fig*) terrain *m* d'entente.
common law *n* droit coutumier.
common-law [kâm'ənlô'] *a*: **~ wife** épouse *f* de facto.
commonly [kâm'ənlē] *ad* communément, généralement; couramment.
Common Market *n* Marché commun.
commonplace [kâm'ənplâs] *a* banal(e), ordinaire.
common room *n* (*Brit*) salle commune.
Commons [kâm'ənz] *npl* (*Brit POL*): **the (House of) ~** la chambre des Communes.
commons [kâm'ənz] *n sg* (*US UNIV*) réfectoire *m*.
common sense *n* bon sens.
common stock *n* (*US FINANCE*) actions *fpl* ordinaires.
Commonwealth [kâm'ənwelth] *n*: **the ~** le Commonwealth.
commotion [kəmō'shən] *n* désordre *m*, tumulte *m*.
communal [kəmyoo'nəl] *a* (*life*) communautaire; (*for common use*) commun(e).
commune *n* [kâm'yoon] (*group*) communauté *f* ♦ *vi* [kəmyoon'] : **to ~ with** converser intimement avec; communier avec.
communicate [kəmyoo'nikāt] *vt* communiquer, transmettre ♦ *vi*: **to ~ (with)** communiquer (avec).
communication [kəmyoonikā'shən] *n* communication *f*.
communication cord *n* (*Brit*) sonnette *f* d'alarme.
communications network *n* réseau *m* de communications.
communications satellite *n* satellite *m* de télécommunications.
communicative [kəmyoo'nikātiv] *a* communicatif(ive).
communion [kəmyoon'yən] *n* (*also*: **Holy C~**) communion *f*.
communiqué [kəmyoonikā'] *n* communiqué *m*.
communism [kâm'yənizəm] *n* communisme *m*.
communist [kâm'yənist] *a, n* communiste (*m/f*).
community [kəmyoo'nitē] *n* communauté *f*.
community center *n* foyer socio-éducatif, centre *m* de loisirs.
community chest *n* (*US*) fonds commun.
community health center *n* centre médico-social.
community spirit *n* solidarité *f*.
commutation ticket [kâmyətā'shən tik'it] *n* (*US*) carte *f* d'abonnement.
commute [kəmyoot'] *vi* faire le trajet journalier (de son domicile à un lieu de travail assez éloigné) ♦ *vt* (*LAW*) commuer; (*MATH: terms etc*) opérer la commutation de.
commuter [kəmyoot'ûr] *n* banlieusard/e (qui ... *see vi*).
compact [kâm'pakt] *a* compact(e) ♦ *n* contrat *m*, entente *f*; (*also*: **powder ~**) poudrier *m*.
compact disc [kâm'pakt disk] *n* disque compact.
companion [kəmpan'yən] *n* compagnon/compagne.
companionship [kəmpan'yənship] *n* camaraderie *f*.
companionway [kəmpan'yənwā] *n* (*NAUT*) escalier *m* des cabines.
company [kum'pənē] *n* (*also COMM, MIL, THEATER*) compagnie *f*; **he's good ~** il est d'une compagnie agréable; **we have ~** nous avons de la visite; **to keep sb ~** tenir compagnie à qn; **to part ~ with** se séparer de; **Smith and C~** Smith et Compagnie.
company car *n* voiture *f* de fonction.
company director *n* administrateur/trice.
company secretary *n* (*Brit COMM*) secrétaire général (*d'une société*).
comparable [kâm'pûrəbəl] *a* comparable.
comparative [kəmpar'ətiv] *a* comparatif(ive); (*relative*) relatif(ive).
comparatively [kəmpar'ətivlē] *ad* (*relatively*) relativement.
compare [kəmpär'] *vt*: **to ~ sth/sb with/to** comparer qch/qn avec *or* et/à ♦ *vi*: **to ~ (with)** se comparer (à); être comparable (à); **how do the prices ~?** comment sont les prix?, est-ce que les prix sont comparables?; **~d with** *or* **to** par rapport à.
comparison [kəmpar'isən] *n* comparaison *f*; **in ~ (with)** en comparaison (de).
compartment [kəmpârt'mənt] *n* (*also RAIL*) compartiment *m*.
compass [kum'pəs] *n* boussole *f*; **within the ~ of** dans les limites de.
compasses [kum'pəsiz] *npl* compas *m*.
compassion [kəmpash'ən] *n* compassion *f*, humanité *f*.
compassionate [kəmpash'ənit] *a* accessible à la compassion, au cœur charitable et bienveillant; **on ~ grounds** pour raisons personnelles *or* de famille.
compatibility [kəmpatəbil'ətē] *n* compatibilité *f*.
compatible [kəmpat'əbəl] *a* compatible.
compel [kəmpel'] *vt* contraindre, obliger.
compelling [kəmpel'ing] *a* (*fig: argument*) irrésistible.
compendium [kəmpen'dēəm] *n* (*summary*) abrégé *m*.
compensate [kâm'pənsāt] *vt* indemniser, dédommager ♦ *vi*: **to ~ for** compenser.
compensation [kâmpənsā'shən] *n* compensation *f*; (*money*) dédommagement *m*, indemnité *f*.
compère [kâm'pär] *n* (*Brit*) présentateur/trice, animateur/trice.
compete [kəmpēt'] *vi* (*take part*) concourir; (*vie*): **to ~ (with)** rivaliser (avec), faire concurrence (à).
competence [kâm'pitəns] *n* compétence *f*, aptitude *f*.
competent [kâm'pitənt] *a* compétent(e), capa-

ble.

competition [kåmpitish'ən] _n_ compétition _f_, concours _m_; (_ECON_) concurrence _f_; **in** ~ **with** en concurrence avec.

competitive [kəmpet'ətiv] _a_ (_ECON_) concurrentiel(le); (_sports_) de compétition.

competitive examination _n_ concours _m_.

competitor [kəmpet'itûr] _n_ concurrent/e.

compile [kəmpīl'] _vt_ compiler.

complacency [kəmplā'sənsē] _n_ contentement _m_ de soi, autosatisfaction _f_.

complacent [kəmplā'sənt] _a_ (trop) content(e) de soi.

complain [kəmplān'] _vi_: **to** ~ **(about)** se plaindre (de); (_in store etc_) réclamer (au sujet de).

complain of _vt fus_ (_MED_) se plaindre de.

complaint [kəmplānt'] _n_ plainte _f_; (_in store etc_) réclamation _f_; (_MED_) affection _f_.

complement _n_ [kâm'pləmənt] complément _m_; (_esp of ship's crew etc_) effectif complet ♦ _vt_ [kâm'pləmənt] compléter.

complementary [kâmpləmən'tûrē] _a_ complémentaire.

complete [kəmplēt'] _a_ complet(ète) ♦ _vt_ achever, parachever; (_a form_) remplir.

completely [kəmplēt'lē] _ad_ complètement.

completion [kəmplē'shən] _n_ achèvement _m_; **to be nearing** ~ être presque terminé; **on** ~ **of contract** dès signature du contrat.

complex [kâmpleks'] _a_ complexe ♦ _n_ (_PSYCH_, _buildings etc_) complexe _m_.

complexion [kəmplek'shən] _n_ (_of face_) teint _m_; (_of event etc_) aspect _m_, caractère _m_.

complexity [kəmplek'sitē] _n_ complexité _f_.

compliance [kəmplī'əns] _n_ (_submission_) docilité _f_; (_agreement_): ~ **with** le fait de se conformer à; **in** ~ **with** en conformité avec, conformément à.

compliant [kəmplī'ənt] _a_ docile, très accommodant(e).

complicate [kâm'pləkāt] _vt_ compliquer.

complicated [kâm'pləkātid] _a_ compliqué(e).

complication [kâmpləkā'shən] _n_ complication _f_.

complicity [kəmplis'ətē] _n_ complicité _f_.

compliment _n_ [kâm'pləmənt] compliment _m_ ♦ _vt_ [kâm'pləmənt] complimenter; ~**s** _npl_ compliments _mpl_, hommages _mpl_; vœux _mpl_; **to pay sb a** ~ faire _or_ adresser un compliment à qn; **to** ~ **sb (on sth/on doing sth)** féliciter qn (pour qch/de faire qch).

complimentary [kâmpləmen'tûrē] _a_ flatteur(euse); (_free_) à titre gracieux.

complimentary ticket _n_ billet _m_ de faveur.

compliments card, (_Brit_) **compliments slip** _n_ fiche _f_ de transmission.

comply [kəmplī'] _vi_: **to** ~ **with** se soumettre à, se conformer à.

component [kəmpō'nənt] _a_ composant(e), constituant(e) ♦ _n_ composant _m_, élément _m_.

compose [kəmpōz'] _vt_ composer; **to** ~ **o.s.** se calmer, se maîtriser; prendre une contenance.

composed [kəmpōzd'] _a_ calme, posé(e).

composer [kəmpō'zûr] _n_ (_MUS_) compositeur _m_.

composite [kəmpâz'it] _a_ composite; (_BOT_, _MATH_) composé(e).

composition [kâmpəzish'ən] _n_ composition _f_.

compost [kâm'pōst] _n_ compost _m_.

composure [kəmpō'zhûr] _n_ calme _m_, maîtrise _f_ de soi.

compound [kâm'pound] _n_ (_CHEM_, _LING_) composé _m_; (_enclosure_) enclos _m_, enceinte _f_ ♦ _a_ composé(e) ♦ _vt_ [kəmpound'] (_fig: problem etc_) aggraver.

compound fracture _n_ fracture compliquée.

compound interest _n_ intérêt composé.

comprehend [kâmprihend'] _vt_ comprendre.

comprehension [kâmprihen'shən] _n_ compréhension _f_.

comprehensive [kâmprihen'siv] _a_ (très) complet(ète).

comprehensive insurance policy _n_ assurance _f_ tous risques.

comprehensive (school) _n_ (_Brit_) école secondaire non sélective avec libre circulation d'une section à l'autre, ≈ CES _m_.

compress _vt_ [kəmpres'] comprimer ♦ _n_ [kâm'pres] (_MED_) compresse _f_.

compression [kəmpresh'ən] _n_ compression _f_.

comprise [kəmprīz'] _vt_ (_also:_ **be** ~**d of**) comprendre.

compromise [kâm'prəmīz] _n_ compromis _m_ ♦ _vt_ compromettre ♦ _vi_ transiger, accepter un compromis ♦ _cpd_ (_decision, solution_) de compromis.

compulsion [kəmpul'shən] _n_ contrainte _f_, force _f_; **under** ~ sous la contrainte.

compulsive [kəmpul'siv] _a_ (_PSYCH_) compulsif(ive); **he's a** ~ **smoker** c'est un fumeur invétéré.

compulsory [kəmpul'sûrē] _a_ obligatoire.

compulsory purchase _n_ (_Brit_) expropriation _f_.

compunction [kəmpungk'shən] _n_ scrupule _m_; **to have no** ~ **about doing sth** n'avoir aucun scrupule à faire qch.

computer [kəmpyōō'tûr] _n_ ordinateur _m_; (_mechanical_) calculatrice _f_.

computerize [kəmpyōō'tərīz] _vt_ traiter _or_ automatiser par ordinateur.

computer language _n_ langage _m_ machine _or_ informatique.

computer peripheral _n_ périphérique _m_.

computer program _n_ programme _m_ informatique.

computer programmer _n_ programmeur/euse.

computer programming _n_ programmation _f_.

computer science _n_ informatique _f_.

computer scientist _n_ informaticien/ne.

computing [kəmpyōō'ting] _n_ informatique _f_.

comrade [kâm'rad] _n_ camarade _m/f_.

comradeship [kâm'rədship] _n_ camaraderie _f_.

comsat [kâm'sat] _n_ _abbr_ = **communications satellite**.

con [kân] _vt_ duper; escroquer ♦ _n_ escroquerie _f_; **to** ~ **sb into doing sth** tromper qn pour lui faire faire qch.

concave [kânkāv'] _a_ concave.

conceal [kənsēl'] _vt_ cacher, dissimuler.

concede [kənsēd'] _vt_ concéder ♦ _vi_ céder.

conceit [kənsēt'] _n_ vanité _f_, suffisance _f_, prétention _f_.

conceited [kənsē'tid] _a_ vaniteux(euse),

suffisant(e).

conceivable [kənsēv'əbəl] *a* concevable, imaginable; **it is ~ that** il est concevable que.

conceivably [kənsēv'əblē] *ad*: **he may ~ be right** il n'est pas impossible qu'il ait raison.

conceive [kənsēv'] *vt* concevoir ♦ *vi*: **to ~ of sth/of doing sth** imaginer qch/de faire qch.

concentrate [kân'səntrāt] *vi* se concentrer ♦ *vt* concentrer.

concentration [kânsəntrā'shən] *n* concentration *f*.

concentration camp *n* camp *m* de concentration.

concentric [kənsen'trik] *a* concentrique.

concept [kân'sept] *n* concept *m*.

conception [kənsep'shən] *n* conception *f*; (*idea*) idée *f*.

concern [kənsûrn'] *n* affaire *f*; (*COMM*) entreprise *f*, firme *f*; (*anxiety*) inquiétude *f*, souci *m* ♦ *vt* concerner; **to be ~ed (about)** s'inquiéter (de), être inquiet(ète) (au sujet de); **"to whom it may ~"** "à qui de droit"; **as far as I am ~ed** en ce qui me concerne; **to be ~ed with** (*person: involved with*) s'occuper de; **the department ~ed** (*under discussion*) le service en question; (*involved*) le service concerné.

concerning [kənsûr'ning] *prep* en ce qui concerne, à propos de.

concert [kân'sûrt] *n* concert *m*; **in ~** à l'unisson, en chœur; ensemble.

concerted [kənsûr'tid] *a* concerté(e).

concert hall *n* salle *f* de concert.

concertina [kânsûrtē'nə] *n* concertina *m* ♦ *vi* se télescoper, se caramboler.

concertmaster [kân'sûrtmastûr] *n* (*US*) premier violon.

concerto [kənchär'tō] *n* concerto *m*.

concession [kənsesh'ən] *n* concession *f*.

concessionaire [kənseshənär'] *n* concessionnaire *m/f*.

concessionary [kənsesh'ənärē] *a* (*ticket, fare*) à tarif réduit.

conciliation [kənsilēā'shən] *n* conciliation *f*, apaisement *m*.

conciliatory [kənsil'ēətôrē] *a* conciliateur(trice); conciliant(e).

concise [kənsīs'] *a* concis(e).

conclave [kân'klāv] *n* assemblée secrète; (*REL*) conclave *m*.

conclude [kənklōōd'] *vt* conclure ♦ *vi* (*speaker*) conclure; (*events*): **to ~ (with)** se terminer (par).

conclusion [kənklōō'zhən] *n* conclusion *f*; **to come to the ~ that** (en) conclure que.

conclusive [kənklōō'siv] *a* concluant(e), définitif(ive).

concoct [kənkâkt'] *vt* confectionner, composer.

concoction [kənkâk'shən] *n* (*food, drink*) mélange *m*.

concord [kân'kôrd] *n* (*harmony*) harmonie *f*; (*treaty*) accord *m*.

concourse [kân'kôrs] *n* (*hall*) hall *m*, salle *f* des pas perdus; (*crowd*) affluence *f*; multitude *f*.

concrete [kân'krēt] *n* béton *m* ♦ *a* concret(ète); (*CONSTR*) en béton.

concrete mixer *n* bétonnière *f*.

concur [kənkûr'] *vi* être d'accord.

concurrently [kənkûr'əntlē] *ad* simultanément.

concussion [kənkush'ən] *n* (*MED*) commotion (cérébrale).

condemn [kəndem'] *vt* condamner.

condemnation [kândemnā'shən] *n* condamnation *f*.

condensation [kândensā'shən] *n* condensation *f*.

condense [kəndens'] *vi* se condenser ♦ *vt* condenser.

condensed milk [kəndenst' milk'] *n* lait concentré (sucré).

condescend [kândisend'] *vi* condescendre, s'abaisser; **to ~ to do sth** daigner faire qch.

condescending [kândisen'ding] *a* condescendant(e).

condition [kəndish'ən] *n* condition *f*; (*disease*) maladie *f* ♦ *vt* déterminer, conditionner; **in good/poor ~** en bon/mauvais état; **a heart ~** une maladie cardiaque; **weather ~s** conditions *fpl* météorologiques; **on ~ that** à condition que + *sub*, à condition de.

conditional [kəndish'ənəl] *a* conditionnel(le); **to be ~ upon** dépendre de.

conditioner [kəndish'ənûr] *n* (*for hair*) baume démêlant.

condolences [kəndō'lənsiz] *npl* condoléances *fpl*.

condom [kân'dəm] *n* préservatif *m*.

condo(minium) [kân'dō(min'ēəm)] *n* (*US: building*) immeuble *m* (en copropriété); (*: rooms*) appartement *m* (dans un immeuble en copropriété).

condone [kəndōn'] *vt* fermer les yeux sur, approuver (tacitement).

conducive [kəndōō'siv] *a*: **~ to** favorable à, qui contribue à.

conduct *n* [kân'dukt] conduite *f* ♦ *vt* [kəndukt'] conduire; (*manage*) mener, diriger; (*MUS*) diriger; **to ~ o.s.** se conduire, se comporter.

conductor [kənduk'tûr] *n* (*of orchestra*) chef *m* d'orchestre; (*on bus*) receveur *m*; (*US: on train*) chef *m* de train; (*ELEC*) conducteur *m*.

conductress [kənduk'tris] *n* (*on bus*) receveuse *f*.

conduit [kân'dōōwit] *n* conduit *m*, tuyau *m*; tube *m*.

cone [kōn] *n* cône *m*; (*for ice-cream*) cornet *m*; (*BOT*) pomme *f* de pin, cône.

confectioner [kənfek'shənûr] *n* (*of cakes*) pâtissier/ière; (*of sweets*) confiseur/euse; **~'s (shop)** confiserie(-pâtisserie).

confectioner's sugar *n* (*US*) sucre *m* glace.

confectionery [kənfek'shənärē] *n* (*cakes*) pâtisserie *f*; (*sweets*) confiserie *f*.

confederate [kənfed'ûrit] *a* confédéré(e) ♦ *n* (*pej*) acolyte *m*; (*US HIST*) confédéré/e.

confederation [kənfedərā'shən] *n* confédération *f*.

confer [kənfûr'] *vt*: **to ~ sth on** conférer qch à ♦ *vi* conférer, s'entretenir; **to ~ (with sb about sth)** s'entretenir (de qch avec qn).

conference [kân'fûrəns] *n* conférence *f*; **to be in ~** être en réunion *or* en conférence.

conference room *n* salle *f* de conférence.

confess [kənfes'] *vt* confesser, avouer ♦ *vi* se confesser.

confession [kənfesh'ən] *n* confession *f*.

confessional [kənfesh'ənəl] *n* confessional *m*.

confessor [kənfes'ûr] *n* confesseur *m*.
confetti [kənfet'ē] *n* confettis *mpl*.
confide [kənfīd'] *vi*: **to ~ in** s'ouvrir à, se confier à.
confidence [kân'fidəns] *n* confiance *f*; (*also*: **self-~**) assurance *f*, confiance en soi; (*secret*) confidence *f*; **to have (every) ~ that** être certain que; **motion of no ~** motion *f* de censure; **to tell sb sth in strict ~** dire qch à qn en toute confidence.
confidence game *n* escroquerie *f*.
confident [kân'fidənt] *a* sûr(e), assuré(e).
confidential [kânfiden'shəl] *a* confidentiel(le); (*secretary*) particulier(ère).
confidentiality [kânfidenshēal'itē] *n* confidentialité *f*.
configuration [kənfigyərā'shən] *n* (*also* COMPUT) configuration *f*.
confine [kənfīn'] *vt* limiter, borner; (*shut up*) confiner, enfermer; **to ~ o.s. to doing sth/ to sth** se contenter de faire qch/se limiter à qch.
confined [kənfīnd'] *a* (*space*) restreint(e), réduit(e).
confinement [kənfīn'mənt] *n* emprisonnement *m*, détention *f*; (MIL) consigne *f* (au quartier); (MED) accouchement *m*.
confines [kân'fīnz] *npl* confins *mpl*, bornes *fpl*.
confirm [kənfûrm'] *vt* (*report*, REL) confirmer; (*appointment*) ratifier.
confirmation [kânfûrmā'shən] *n* confirmation *f*; ratification *f*.
confirmed [kənfûrmd'] *a* invétéré(e), incorrigible.
confiscate [kân'fiskāt] *vt* confisquer.
confiscation [kânfiskā'shən] *n* confiscation *f*.
conflagration [kânfləgrā'shən] *n* incendie *m*; (*fig*) conflagration *f*.
conflict *n* [kân'flikt] conflit *m*, lutte *f* ♦ *vi* [kənflikt'] être *or* entrer en conflit; (*opinions*) s'opposer, se heurter.
conflicting [kənflik'ting] *a* contradictoire.
conform [kənfôrm'] *vi*: **to ~ (to)** se conformer (à).
conformist [kənfôr'mist] *n* conformiste *m/f*.
confound [kənfound'] *vt* confondre; (*amaze*) rendre perplexe.
confounded [kənfoun'did] *a* maudit(e), sacré(e).
confront [kənfrunt'] *vt* confronter, mettre en présence; (*enemy*, *danger*) affronter, faire face à.
confrontation [kânfrəntā'shən] *n* confrontation *f*.
confuse [kənfyōōz'] *vt* embrouiller; (*one thing with another*) confondre.
confused [kənfyōōzd'] *a* (*person*) dérouté(e), désorienté(e); (*situation*) embrouillé(e).
confusing [kənfyōō'zing] *a* peu clair(e), déroutant(e).
confusion [kənfyōō'zhən] *n* confusion *f*.
congeal [kənjēl'] *vi* (*oil*) se figer; (*blood*) se coaguler.
congenial [kənjēn'yəl] *a* sympathique, agréable.
congenital [kənjen'itəl] *a* congénital(e).
conger eel [kâng'gûr ēl] *n* congre *m*.
congested [kənjes'tid] *a* (MED) congestionné(e); (*fig*) surpeuplé(e); con-

gestionné; bloqué(e); (*telephone lines*) encombré(e).
congestion [kənjes'chən] *n* congestion *f*; (*fig*) encombrement *m*.
conglomerate [kənglâm'ûrit] *n* (COMM) conglomérat *m*.
conglomeration [kənglâmərā'shən] *n* groupement *m*; agglomération *f*.
Congo [kâng'gō] *n* (*state*) (république *f* du) Congo.
congratulate [kəngrach'ōōlāt] *vt*: **to ~ sb (on)** féliciter qn (de).
congratulations [kəngrachōōlā'shənz] *npl*: **~ (on)** félicitations *fpl* (pour) ♦ *excl*: **~!** (toutes mes) félicitations!
congregate [kâng'grəgāt] *vi* se rassembler, se réunir.
congregation [kânggrəgā'shən] *n* assemblée *f* (des fidèles).
congress [kâng'gris] *n* congrès *m*.
congressman [kâng'grismən], **congress-woman** [kâ'ng'griswōōmən] *n* (US) membre *m* du Congrès.
conical [kân'ikəl] *a* (de forme) conique.
conifer [kō'nitûr] *n* conifère *m*.
coniferous [kōnif'ûrəs] *a* (*forest*) de conifères.
conjecture [kənjek'chûr] *n* conjecture *f* ♦ *vt*, *vi* conjecturer.
conjugal [kân'jəgəl] *a* conjugal(e).
conjugate [kân'jəgāt] *vt* conjuguer.
conjugation [kânjəgā'shən] *n* conjugaison *f*.
conjunction [kənjungk'shən] *n* conjonction *f*; **in ~ with** (conjointement) avec.
conjunctivitis [kənjungktəvī'tis] *n* conjonctivite *f*.
conjure [kân'jûr] *vt* faire apparaître (par la prestidigitation); [kənjōōr'] conjurer, supplier ♦ *vi* faire des tours de passe-passe.
conjure up *vt* (*ghost*, *spirit*) faire apparaître; (*memories*) évoquer.
conjurer [kân'jûrûr] *n* prestidigitateur *m*, illusionniste *m/f*.
conjuring trick [kân'jûring trik] *n* tour *m* de prestidigitation.
conker [kâng'kû] *n* (*Brit*) marron *m* (d'Inde).
conk out [kângk out] *vi* (*col*) tomber *or* rester en panne.
con man *n* escroc *m*.
Conn. *abbr* (US) = Connecticut.
connect [kənekt'] *vt* joindre, relier; (ELEC) connecter; (*fig*) établir un rapport entre, faire un rapprochement entre ♦ *vi* (*train*): **to ~ with** assurer la correspondance avec; **to be ~ed with** avoir un rapport avec; (*have dealings with*) avoir des rapports avec, être en relation avec; **I am trying to ~ you** (TEL) j'essaie d'obtenir votre communication.
connection [kənek'shən] *n* relation *f*, lien *m*; (ELEC) connexion *f*; (TEL) communication *f*; (*train etc*) correspondance *f*; **in ~ with** à propos de; **what is the ~ between them?** quel est le lien entre eux?; **business ~s** relations d'affaires; **to miss/get one's ~** (*train etc*) rater/avoir sa correspondance.
connexion [kənek'shən] *n* (*Brit*) = connection.
conning tower [kân'ing tou'ûr] *n* kiosque *m* (de sous-marin).
connive [kənīv'] *vi*: **to ~ at** se faire le compli-

ce de.

connoisseur [kânisûr'] *n* connaisseur *m*.

connotation [kânətā'shən] *n* connotation *f*, implication *f*.

connubial [kənoo̅'bēəl] *a* conjugal(e).

conquer [kâng'kûr] *vt* conquérir; *(feelings)* vaincre, surmonter.

conqueror [kâng'kûrûr] *n* conquérant *m*, vainqueur *m*.

conquest [kân'kwest] *n* conquête *f*.

cons [kânz] *npl see* **pro.**

conscience [kân'shəns] *n* conscience *f*; **in all** ~ en conscience.

conscientious [kânshēen'shəs] *a* consciencieux(euse); *(scruple, objection)* de conscience.

conscientious objector *n* objecteur *m* de conscience.

conscious [kân'shəs] *a* conscient(e); *(deliberate: insult, error)* délibéré(e); **to become** ~ **of sth/that** prendre conscience de qch/que.

consciousness [kân'shəsnis] *n* conscience *f*; *(MED)* connaissance *f*; **to lose/regain** ~ perdre/reprendre connaissance.

conscript [kân'skript] *(Brit)* *n* conscrit *m*.

conscription [kənskrip'shən] *n* conscription *f*.

consecrate [kân'səkrāt] *vt* consacrer.

consecutive [kənsek'yətiv] *a* consécutif(ive); **on three** ~ **occasions** trois fois de suite.

consensus [kənsen'səs] *n* consensus *m*; **the** ~ **(of opinion)** le consensus (d'opinion).

consent [kənsent'] *n* consentement *m* ♦ *vi*: **to** ~ **(to)** consentir (à); **age of** ~ âge nubile (légal); **by common** ~ d'un commun accord.

consequence [kân'səkwens] *n* suites *fpl*, conséquence *f*; importance *f*; **in** ~ en conséquence, par conséquent.

consequently [kân'səkwentlē] *ad* par conséquent, donc.

conservation [kânsûrvā'shən] *n* préservation *f*, protection *f*; *(also:* **nature** ~) défense *f* de l'environnement; **energy** ~ économies *fpl* d'énergie.

conservationist [kânsûrvā'shənist] *n* protecteur/trice de la nature.

conservative [kənsûr'vətiv] *a* conservateur(trice); *(cautious)* prudent(e); **C**~ *a*, *n (Brit POL)* conservateur(trice).

conservatory [kənsûr'vətôrē] *n (greenhouse)* serre *f*.

conserve *vt* [kənsûrv'] conserver, préserver; *(supplies, energy)* économiser ♦ *n* [kân'sûrv] confiture *f*, conserve *f* (de fruits).

consider [kənsid'ûr] *vt* considérer, réfléchir à; *(take into account)* penser à, prendre en considération; *(regard, judge)* considérer, estimer; ~ **doing sth** envisager de faire qch; ~ **yourself lucky** estimez-vous heureux; **all things** ~**ed** (toute) réflexion faite.

considerable [kənsid'ûrəbəl] *a* considérable.

considerably [kənsid'ûrəblē] *ad* nettement.

considerate [kənsid'ûrit] *a* prévenant(e), plein(e) d'égards.

consideration [kənsidərā'shən] *n* considération *f*; *(reward)* rétribution *f*, rémunération *f*; **out of** ~ **for** par égard pour; **under** ~ à l'étude; **my first** ~ **is my family** ma famille passe avant tout le reste.

considering [kənsid'ûring] *prep*: ~ **(that)**

étant donné (que).

consign [kənsīn'] *vt* expédier, livrer.

consignee [kânsīnē'] *n* destinataire *m/f*.

consignment [kənsīn'mənt] *n* arrivage *m*, envoi *m*.

consignment note *n (Brit COMM)* bordereau *m* d'expédition.

consignor [kənsī'nûr] *n* expéditeur/trice.

consist [kənsist'] *vi*: **to** ~ **of** consister en, se composer de.

consistency [kənsis'tənsē] *n* consistance *f*; *(fig)* cohérence *f*.

consistent [kənsis'tənt] *a* logique, cohérent(e); ~ **with** compatible avec, en accord avec.

consolation [kânsəlā'shən] *n* consolation *f*.

console *vt* [kənsōl'] consoler ♦ *n* [kân'sōl] console *f*.

consolidate [kənsâl'idāt] *vt* consolider.

consommé [kânsəmā'] *n* consommé *m*.

consonant [kân'sənənt] *n* consonne *f*.

consort *n* [kân'sôrt] époux/épouse; **prince** ~ prince *m* consort ♦ *vi* [kənsôrt'] *(often pej)*: **to** ~ **with sb** frayer avec qn.

consortium [kənsôr'shēəm] *n* consortium *m*, comptoir *m*.

conspicuous [kənspik'yōōəs] *a* voyant(e), qui attire la vue *or* l'attention; **to make o.s.** ~ se faire remarquer.

conspiracy [kənspir'əsē] *n* conspiration *f*, complot *m*.

conspiratorial [kənspirətôr'ēəl] *a (behavior)* de conspirateur; *(glance)* conspirateur(trice).

conspire [kənspī'ûr] *vi* conspirer, comploter.

constable [kân'stəbəl] *n (Brit)* ≈ agent *m* de police, gendarme *m*.

constabulary [kənstab'yəlärē] *n* ≈ police *f*, gendarmerie *f*.

constant [kân'stənt] *a* constant(e); incessant(e).

constantly [kân'stəntlē] *ad* constamment, sans cesse.

constellation [kânstəlā'shən] *n* constellation *f*.

consternation [kânstûrnā'shən] *n* consternation *f*.

constipated [kân'stəpātid] *a* constipé(e).

constipation [kânstəpā'shən] *n* constipation *f*.

constituency [kənstich'ōōənsē] *n* circonscription électorale; *(people)* électorat *m*.

constituency party *n* section locale (d'un parti).

constituent [kənstich'ōōənt] *n* électeur/trice; *(part)* élément constitutif, composant *m*.

constitute [kân'stitōōt] *vt* constituer.

constitution [kânstitōō'shən] *n* constitution *f*.

constitutional [kânstitōō'shənəl] *a* constitutionnel(le).

constrain [kənstrān'] *vt* contraindre, forcer.

constrained [kənstrānd'] *a* contraint(e), gêné(e).

constraint [kənstrānt'] *n* contrainte *f*; *(embarrassment)* gêne *f*.

constrict [kənstrikt'] *vt* rétrécir, resserrer; gêner, limiter.

construct [kənstrukt'] *vt* construire.

construction [kənstruk'shən] *n* construction *f*; *(fig: interpretation)* interprétation *f*; **under** ~ *(building etc)* en construction.

construction industry *n* (industrie *f* du) bâtiment.

constructive [kənstruk'tiv] *a* constructif(ive).
construe [kənstrōō'] *vt* analyser, expliquer.
consul [kån'səl] *n* consul *m*.
consulate [kån'səlit] *n* consulat *m*.
consult [kənsult'] *vt* consulter; **to ~ sb (about sth)** consulter qn (à propos de qch).
consultancy [kənsul'tənsē] *n* service *m* de conseils.
consultancy fee *n* honoraires *mpl* d'expert.
consultant [kənsul'tənt] *n* (*MED*) médecin consultant; (*other specialist*) consultant *m*, (expert-)conseil *m* ♦ *cpd:* **~ engineer** *n* ingénieur-conseil *m*; **~ pediatrician** *n* pédiatre *m*; **legal/management ~** conseiller *m* juridique/en gestion.
consultation [kånsəltā'shən] *n* consultation *f*; **in ~ with** en consultation avec.
consulting room [kənsul'ting rōōm] *n* cabinet *m* de consultation.
consume [kənsōōm'] *vt* consommer.
consumer [kənsōō'mûr] *n* consommateur/trice; (*of electricity, gas etc*) usager *m*.
consumer credit *n* crédit *m* aux consommateurs.
consumer durables *npl* biens *mpl* de consommation durables.
consumer goods *npl* biens *mpl* de consommation.
consumerism [kənsōō'mərizəm] *n* (*consumer protection*) défense *f* du consommateur; (*ECON*) consumérisme *m*.
consumer society *n* société *f* de consommation.
consummate [kån'səmāt] *vt* consommer.
consumption [kənsump'shən] *n* consommation *f*; (*MED*) consomption *f* (pulmonaire); **not fit for human ~** non comestible.
cont. *abbr* = **continued.**
contact [kån'takt] *n* contact *m*; (*person*) connaissance *f*, relation *f* ♦ *vt* se mettre en contact *or* en rapport avec; **to be in ~ with sb/sth** être en contact avec qn/qch; **business ~s** relations *fpl* d'affaires, contacts *mpl*.
contact lenses *npl* verres *mpl* de contact.
contagious [kəntā'jəs] *a* contagieux(euse).
contain [kəntān'] *vt* contenir; **to ~ o.s.** se contenir, se maîtriser.
container [kəntā'nûr] *n* récipient *m*; (*for shipping etc*) conteneur *m*.
containerize [kəntā'nərīz] *vt* conteneuriser.
contaminate [kəntam'ənāt] *vt* contaminer.
contamination [kəntamənā'shən] *n* contamination *f*.
cont'd *abbr* = **continued.**
contemplate [kån'təmplāt] *vt* contempler; (*consider*) envisager.
contemplation [kåntəmplā'shən] *n* contemplation *f*.
contemporary [kəntem'pərärē] *a* contemporain(e); (*design, wallpaper*) moderne ♦ *n* contemporain/e.
contempt [kəntempt'] *n* mépris *m*, dédain *m*; **~ of court** (*LAW*) outrage *m* à l'autorité de la justice.
contemptible [kəntemp'təbəl] *a* méprisable, vil(e).
contemptuous [kəntemp'chōōəs] *a* dédaigneux(euse), méprisant(e).
contend [kəntend'] *vt:* **to ~ that** soutenir *or*

prétendre que ♦ *vi:* **to ~ with** (*compete*) lutter avec; **to have to ~ with** (*be faced with*) avoir affaire à, être aux prises avec.
contender [kəntend'ûr] *n* prétendant/e; candidat/e.
content [kəntent'] *a* content(e), satisfait(e) ♦ *vt* contenter, satisfaire ♦ *n* [kån'tent] contenu *m*; teneur *f*; **~s** *npl* contenu *m*; **(table of) ~s** table *f* des matières; **to be ~ with** se contenter de; **to ~ o.s. with sth/with doing sth** se contenter de qch/de faire qch.
contented [kənten'tid] *a* content(e), satisfait(e).
contentedly [kənten'tidlē] *ad* avec un sentiment de (profonde) satisfaction.
contention [kənten'shən] *n* dispute *f*, contestation *f*; (*argument*) assertion *f*, affirmation *f*; **bone of ~** sujet *m* de discorde.
contentious [kənten'shəs] *a* querelleur(euse); litigieux(euse).
contentment [kəntent'mənt] *n* contentement *m*, satisfaction *f*.
contest *n* [kån'test] combat *m*, lutte *f*; (*competition*) concours *m* ♦ *vt* [kəntest'] contester, discuter; (*compete for*) disputer; (*LAW*) attaquer.
contestant [kəntes'tənt] *n* concurrent/e; (*in fight*) adversaire *m/f*.
context [kån'tekst] *n* contexte *m*; **in/out of ~** dans le/hors contexte.
continent [kån'tənənt] *n* continent *m*; **the C~** l'Europe continentale; **on the C~** en Europe (continentale).
continental [kåntənen'təl] *a* continental(e) ♦ *n* (*Brit*) Européen/ne (continental(e)).
continental breakfast *n* café (*or* thé) complet.
continental quilt *n* (*Brit*) couette *f*.
contingency [kəntin'jənsē] *n* éventualité *f*, événement imprévu.
contingency plan *n* plan *m* d'urgence.
contingent [kəntin'jənt] *a* contingent(e) ♦ *n* contingent *m*; **to be ~ upon** dépendre de.
continual [kəntin'yōōəl] *a* continuel(le).
continually [kəntin'yōōəlē] *ad* continuellement, sans cesse.
continuation [kəntinyōōā'shən] *n* continuation *f*; (*after interruption*) reprise *f*; (*of story*) suite *f*.
continue [kəntin'yōō] *vi* continuer ♦ *vt* continuer; (*start again*) reprendre; **to be ~d** (*story*) à suivre; **~d on page 10** suite page 10.
continuity [kåntənōō'itē] *n* continuité *f*; (*CINEMA*) script *m*.
continuous [kəntin'yōōəs] *a* continu(e), permanent(e); **~ performance** (*CINEMA*) séance permanente.
continuously [kəntin'yōōəslē] *ad* (*repeatedly*) continuellement; (*uninterruptedly*) sans interruption.
contort [kəntôrt'] *vt* tordre, crisper.
contortion [kəntôr'shən] *n* crispation *f*, torsion *f*; (*of acrobat*) contorsion *f*.
contortionist [kəntôr'shənist] *n* contorsionniste *m/f*.
contour [kån'tōōr] *n* contour *m*, profil *m*; (*also:* **~ line**) courbe *f* de niveau.
contraband [kån'trəband] *n* contrebande *f* ♦ *a* de contrebande.

contraception [kåntrəsep'shən] *n* contraception *f*.

contraceptive [kåntrəsep'tiv] *a* contraceptif(ive), anticonceptionnel(le) ♦ *n* contraceptif *m*.

contract [kån'trakt] *n* contrat *m* ♦ *cpd (price, date)* contractuel(le); *(work)* à forfait ♦ *vb* [kəntrakt'] *vi (become smaller)* se contracter, se resserrer; *(COMM)*: **to ~ to do sth** s'engager (par contrat) à faire qch ♦ *vt* contracter; **~ of employment/service** contrat de travail/de service.

contraction [kəntrak'shən] *n* contraction *f*; *(LING)* forme contractée.

contractor [kån'traktür] *n* entrepreneur *m*.

contractual [kəntrak'chōōəl] *a* contractuel(le).

contradict [kåntrədikt'] *vt* contredire; *(be contrary to)* démentir, être en contradiction avec.

contradiction [kåntrədik'shən] *n* contradiction *f*; **to be in ~ with** contredire, être en contradiction avec.

contradictory [kåntrədik'tûrē] *a* contradictoire.

contralto [kəntral'tō] *n* contralto *m*.

contraption [kəntrap'shən] *n (pej)* machin *m*, truc *m*.

contrary [kån'trärē] *a* contraire, opposé(e); *(perverse)* contrariant(e), entêté(e) ♦ *n* contraire *m*; **on the ~** au contraire; **unless you hear to the ~** sauf avis contraire; **~ to what we thought** contrairement à ce que nous pensions.

contrast *n* [kån'trast] contraste *m* ♦ *vt* [kəntrast'] mettre en contraste, contraster; **in ~ to** *or* **with** contrairement à, par opposition à.

contrasting [kəntras'ting] *a* opposé(e), contrasté(e).

contravene [kåntrəvēn'] *vt* enfreindre, violer, contrevenir à.

contravention [kåntrəven'shən] *n*: **~ (of)** infraction *f* (à).

contribute [kəntrib'yōōt] *vi* contribuer ♦ *vt*: **to ~ $10/an article to** donner 10 dollars/un article à; **to ~ to** *(gen)* contribuer à; *(newspaper)* collaborer à; *(discussion)* prendre part à.

contribution [kåntrəbyōō'shən] *n* contribution *f*.

contributor [kəntrib'yətûr] *n (to newspaper)* collaborateur/trice.

contributory [kəntrib'yətôrē] *a (cause)* annexe; **it was a ~ factor in** ... ce facteur a contribué à ....

contributory pension plan *n* régime *m* de retraite salariale.

contrite [kəntrīt'] *a* contrit(e).

contrivance [kəntrī'vəns] *n (scheme)* machination *f*, combinaison *f*; *(device)* appareil *m*, dispositif *m*.

contrive [kəntrīv'] *vt* combiner, inventer ♦ *vi*: **to ~ to do** s'arranger pour faire, trouver le moyen de faire.

control [kəntrōl'] *vt* maîtriser; *(check)* contrôler ♦ *n* maîtrise *f*; **~s** *npl* commandes *fpl*; **to take ~ of** se rendre maître de; *(COMM)* acquérir une participation majoritaire dans; **to be in ~ of** être maître de, maîtriser; *(in charge of)* être responsable de; **to ~ o.s.** se contrôler; **everything is under ~** j'ai (*or* il a *etc*) la situation en main; **the car went out of ~** j'ai (*or* il a *etc*) perdu le contrôle du véhicule; **beyond our ~** indépendant(e) de notre volonté.

control key *n (COMPUT)* touche *f* de commande.

controller [kəntrō'lûr] *n* contrôleur *m*.

controlling interest [kəntrō'ling in'trist] *n (COMM)* participation *f* majoritaire.

control panel *n (on aircraft, ship, TV etc)* tableau *m* de commandes.

control point *n* (poste *m* de) contrôle *m*.

control room *n (NAUT, MIL)* salle *f* des commandes; *(RADIO, TV)* régie *f*.

control tower *n (AVIAT)* tour *f* de contrôle.

control unit *n (COMPUT)* unité *f* de contrôle.

controversial [kåntrəvûr'shəl] *a* discutable, controversé(e).

controversy [kån'trəvûrsē] *n* controverse *f*, polémique *f*.

conurbation [kånûrbā'shən] *n* conurbation *f*.

convalesce [kånvəles'] *vi* relever de maladie, se remettre (d'une maladie).

convalescence [kånvəles'əns] *n* convalescence *f*.

convalescent [kånvəles'ənt] *a*, *n* convalescent(e).

convector [kənvek'tûr] *n* radiateur *m* à convection, appareil *m* de chauffage par convection.

convene [kənvēn'] *vt* convoquer, assembler ♦ *vi* se réunir, s'assembler.

convener [kənvē'nûr] *n* organisateur *m*.

convenience [kənvēn'yəns] *n* commodité *f*; **at your ~** quand *or* comme cela vous convient; **at your earliest ~** *(COMM)* dans les meilleurs délais, le plus tôt possible; **all modern ~s** avec tout le confort moderne, tout confort.

convenience foods *npl* plats cuisinés.

convenient [kənvēn'yənt] *a* commode; **if it is ~ to you** si cela vous convient, si cela ne vous dérange pas.

conveniently [kənvēn'yəntlē] *ad (happen)* à pic; *(situated)* commodément.

convent [kån'vent] *n* couvent *m*.

convention [kənven'shən] *n* convention *f*.

conventional [kənven'shənəl] *a* conventionnel(le).

convent school *n* couvent *m*.

converge [kənvûrj'] *vi* converger.

conversant [kənvûr'sənt] *a*: **to be ~ with** s'y connaître en; être au courant de.

conversation [kånvûrsā'shən] *n* conversation *f*.

conversational [kånvûrsā'shənəl] *a* de la conversation; *(COMPUT)* conversationnel(le).

conversationalist [kånvûrsāsh'nəlist] *n* brillant(e) causeur/euse.

converse *n* [kån'vûrs] contraire *m*, inverse *m* ♦ *vi* [kənvûrs']: **to ~ (with sb about sth)** s'entretenir (avec qn de qch).

conversely [kənvûrs'lē] *ad* inversement, réciproquement.

conversion [kənvûr'zhən] *n* conversion *f*; *(Brit: of house)* transformation *f*, aménagement *m*.

conversion table *n* table *f* de conversion.

convert vt [kənvûrt'] (REL, COMM) convertir; (alter) transformer, aménager; (RUGBY) transformer ♦ n [kân'vûrt] converti/e.
convertible [kənvûr'təbəl] a convertible ♦ n (voiture f) décapotable f.
convex [kânveks'] a convexe.
convey [kənvā'] vt transporter; (thanks) transmettre; (idea) communiquer.
conveyance [kənvā'əns] n (of goods) transport m de marchandises; (vehicle) moyen m de transport.
conveyancing [kənvā'ənsing] n (LAW) rédaction f des actes de cession de propriété.
conveyor belt [kənvā'ûr belt] n convoyeur m, tapis roulant.
convict vt [kənvikt'] déclarer (or reconnaître) coupable ♦ n [kân'vikt] forçat m, convict m.
conviction [kənvik'shən] n condamnation f; (belief) conviction f.
convince [kənvins'] vt convaincre, persuader; **to ~ sb (of sth/that)** persuader qn (de qch/que).
convincing [kənvin'sing] a persuasif(ive), convaincant(e).
convincingly [kənvin'singlē] ad de façon convaincante.
convivial [kənviv'ēəl] a joyeux(euse), plein(e) d'entrain.
convoluted [kân'vəlootid] a (shape) tarabiscoté(e); (argument) compliqué(e).
convoy [kân'voi] n convoi m.
convulse [kənvuls'] vt ébranler; **to be ~d with laughter** se tordre de rire.
convulsion [kənvul'shən] n convulsion f.
coo [koo] vi roucouler.
cook [kook] vt (faire) cuire ♦ vi cuire; (person) faire la cuisine ♦ n cuisinier/ière.
cook up vt (col: excuse, story) inventer.
cookbook [kook'book] n livre m de cuisine.
cooker [kook'ûr] n cuisinière f.
cookery [kook'ûrē] n cuisine f.
cookery book n (Brit) = **cookbook**.
cookie [kook'ē] n (US) biscuit m, petit gâteau sec.
cookie sheet n (US) plaque f à gâteaux.
cooking [kook'ing] n cuisine f ♦ cpd (apples, chocolate) à cuire; (utensils, salt) de cuisine.
cookout [kook'out] n (US) barbecue m.
cool [kool] a frais(fraîche); (not afraid) calme; (unfriendly) froid(e); (impertinent) effronté(e) ♦ vt, vi rafraîchir, refroidir; **it's ~** (weather) il fait frais; **to keep sth ~** or **in a ~ place** garder or conserver qch au frais.
cool down vi refroidir; (fig: person, situation) se calmer.
cooler [koo'lûr], (Brit) **cool box** n boîte f isotherme.
cooling tower [koo'ling tou'ûr] n refroidisseur m.
coolly [koo'lē] ad (calmly) calmement; (audaciously) sans se gêner; (unenthusiastically) froidement.
coolness [kool'nis] n fraîcheur f; sang-froid m, calme m; froideur f.
coop [koop] n poulailler m ♦ vt: **to ~ up** (fig) cloîtrer, enfermer.
co-op [kō'âp] n abbr (= cooperative (society)) coop f.
cooperate [kōâp'ərāt] vi coopérer, collaborer.

cooperation [kōâpərā'shən] n coopération f, collaboration f.
cooperative [kōâp'rətiv] a coopératif(ive) ♦ n coopérative f.
co-opt [kōâpt'] vt: **to ~ sb onto a committee** coopter qn pour faire partie d'un comité.
coordinate vt [kōôr'dənāt] coordonner ♦ n [kōôr'dənit] (MATH) coordonnée f; **~s** npl (clothes) ensemble m, coordonnés mpl.
coordination [kōôrdənā'shən] n coordination f.
coot [koot] n foulque f.
co-ownership [kōō'nûrship] n copropriété f.
cop [kâp] n (col) flic m.
cope [kōp] vi s'en sortir, tenir le coup; **to ~ with** faire face à; (take care of) s'occuper de.
Copenhagen [kōpenhā'gən] n Copenhague f.
copier [kâp'ēûr] n (also: **photo~**) copieur m.
copilot [kōpi'lət] n copilote m.
copious [kō'pēəs] a copieux(euse), abondant(e).
copper [kâp'ûr] n cuivre m; (col: policeman) flic m; **~s** npl petite monnaie.
copse [kâps] n taillis m.
copulate [kâp'yəlāt] vi copuler.
copy [kâp'ē] n copie f; (book etc) exemplaire m; (material: for printing) copie ♦ vt copier; (imitate) imiter; **to make good** (PRESS) faire un bon sujet d'article.
copy out vt copier.
copycat [kâp'ēkat] n (pej) copieur/euse.
copyright [kâp'ērit] n droit m d'auteur, copyright m; **~ reserved** tous droits (de reproduction) réservés.
copy typist n dactylo m/f.
copywriter [kâp'ēritûr] n rédacteur/trice publicitaire.
coral [kôr'əl] n corail m.
coral reef n récif m de corail.
Coral Sea n: **the ~** la mer de Corail.
cord [kôrd] n corde f; (fabric) velours côtelé; whipcord m; corde f; (ELEC) cordon m (d'alimentation), fil m (électrique); **~s** npl (pants) pantalon m de velours côtelé.
cordial [kôr'jəl] a cordial(e), chaleureux(euse) ♦ n sirop m; cordial m.
cordless [kôrd'lis] a sans fil.
cordon [kôr'dən] n cordon m.
cordon off vt (area) interdire l'accès à; (crowd) tenir à l'écart.
corduroy [kôr'dəroi] n velours côtelé.
CORE n abbr (US) = Congress of Racial Equality.
core [kôr] n (of fruit) trognon m, cœur m; (TECH: also of earth) noyau m; (of nuclear reactor, fig: of problem etc) cœur ♦ vt enlever le trognon or le cœur de; **rotten to the ~** complètement pourri.
Corfu [kôr'foo] n Corfou.
coriander [kôrēan'dûr] n coriandre f.
cork [kôrk] n liège m; (of bottle) bouchon m.
corkscrew [kôrk'skroo] n tire-bouchon m.
corky [kôr'kē] a (Brit) **corked** [kôrkt] a (wine) qui sent le bouchon.
corm [kôrm] n bulbe m.
cormorant [kôr'mûrənt] n cormorant m.
Corn abbr (Brit) = Cornwall.
corn [kôrn] n (US: maize) maïs m; (Brit: wheat) blé m; (on foot) cor m; **~ on the cob**

(*CULIN*) épi *m* de maïs au naturel.

cornea [kôr'nēə] *n* cornéc *f*.

corned beef [kôrnd bēf] *n* corned-beef *m*.

corner [kôr'nûr] *n* coin *m*; (*AUT*) tournant *m*, virage *m*; (*SOCCER*: *also*: ~ **kick**) corner *m* ♦ *vt* acculer, mettre au pied du mur; coincer; (*COMM*: *market*) accaparer ♦ *vi* prendre un virage; **to cut** ~**s** (*fig*) prendre des raccourcis.

corner flag *n* (*SOCCER*) piquet *m* de coin.

corner kick *n* (*SOCCER*) corner *m*.

cornerstone [kôr'nûrstōn] *n* pierre *f* angulaire.

cornet [kôrnet'] *n* (*MUS*) cornet *m* à pistons; (*Brit*: *of ice-cream*) cornet (de glace).

cornflakes [kôrn'flāks] *npl* cornflakes *mpl*.

cornflour [kôrn'flouûr] *n* (*Brit*) farine *f* de maïs, maïzena *f* ®.

cornice [kôr'nis] *n* corniche *f*.

corn oil *n* huile *f* de maïs.

cornstarch [kôrn'stárch] *n* (*US*) farine *f* de maïs, maïzena *f* ®.

cornucopia [kôrnəkō'pēə] *n* corne *f* d'abondance.

corny [kôr'nē] *a* (*col*) rebattu(e), galvaudé(e).

corollary [kôr'əlärē] *n* corollaire *m*.

coronary [kôr'ənärē] *n*: ~ **(thrombosis)** infarctus *m* (du myocarde), thrombose *f* coronaire.

coronation [kôrənā'shən] *n* couronnement *m*.

coroner [kôr'ənûr] *n* coroner *m*.

coronet [kôr'ənit] *n* couronne *f*.

Corp. *abbr* = **corporation**.

corporal [kôr'pûrəl] *n* caporal *m*, brigadier *m* ♦ *a*: ~ **punishment** châtiment corporel.

corporate [kôr'pərit] *a* en commun; (*COMM*) constitué(e) (en corporation).

corporate identity, corporate image *n* (*of organization*) image *f* de l'entreprise.

corporation [kôrpərā'shən] *n* (*of town*) municipalité *f*, conseil municipal; (*COMM*) société *f*.

corporation tax *n* ≈ impôt *m* sur les bénéfices.

corps [kôr], *pl* **corps** [kôrz] *n* corps *m*; **the press** ~ la presse.

corpse [kôrps] *n* cadavre *m*.

corpuscle [kôr'pəsəl] *n* corpuscule *m*.

corral [kəral'] *n* corral *m*.

correct [kərekt'] *a* (*accurate*) correct(e), exact(e); (*proper*) correct, convenable ♦ *vt* corriger; **you are** ~ vous avez raison.

correction [kərek'shən] *n* correction *f*.

correlate [kôr'əlāt] *vt* mettre en corrélation ♦ *vi*: **to** ~ **with** correspondre à.

correlation [kôrəlā'shən] *n* corrélation *f*.

correspond [kôrəspånd'] *vi* correspondre.

correspondence [kôrəspån'dəns] *n* correspondance *f*.

correspondence column *n* (*PRESS*) courrier *m* des lecteurs.

correspondence course *n* cours *m* par correspondance.

correspondent [kôrəspån'dənt] *n* correspondant/e.

corridor [kôr'idûr] *n* couloir *m*, corridor *m*.

corroborate [kəráb'ərāt] *vt* corroborer, confirmer.

corrode [kərōd'] *vt* corroder, ronger ♦ *vi* se corroder.

corrosion [kərō'zhən] *n* corrosion *f*.

corrosive [kərō'siv] *a* corrosif(ive).

corrugated [kôr'əgātid] *a* plissé(e); ondulé(e).

corrugated iron *n* tôle ondulée.

corrupt [kərupt'] *a* corrompu(e) ♦ *vt* corrompre; (*data*) altérer; ~ **practices** (*dishonesty, bribery*) malversation *f*.

corruption [kərup'shən] *n* corruption *f*; altération *f* (de données).

corset [kôr'sit] *n* corset *m*.

Corsica [kôr'sikə] *n* Corse *f*.

Corsican [kôr'sikən] *a* corse ♦ *n* Corse *m/f*.

cortège [kôrtezh'] *n* cortège *m* (*gén funèbre*).

cortisone [kôr'tisōn] *n* cortisone *f*.

coruscating [kôr'əskāting] *a* scintillant(e).

c.o.s. *abbr* (= *cash on shipment*) paiement *m* à l'expédition.

cosh [kâsh] *n* (*Brit*) matraque *f*.

cosignatory [kōsig'nətôrē] *n* cosignataire *m/f*.

cosiness [kō'zēnis] *n* (*Brit*) = **coziness**.

cos lettuce [kâs let'is] *n* (laitue *f*) romaine *f*.

cosmetic [kâzmet'ik] *n* produit *m* de beauté, cosmétique *m* ♦ *a* (*preparation*) cosmétique; (*surgery*) esthétique; (*fig: reforms*) symbolique, superficiel(le).

cosmic [kâz'mik] *a* cosmique.

cosmonaut [kâz'mənôt] *n* cosmonaute *m/f*.

cosmopolitan [kâzməpâl'itən] *a* cosmopolite.

cosmos [kâz'məs] *n* cosmos *m*.

cosset [kâs'it] *vt* choyer, dorloter.

cost [kôst] *n* coût *m* ♦ *vb* (*pt, pp* **cost**) *vi* coûter ♦ *vt* établir or calculer le prix de revient de; ~**s** *npl* (*LAW*) dépens *mpl*; **how much does it** ~? combien ça coûte?; **it** ~**s $5/too much** cela coûte 5 dollars/trop cher; **what will it** ~ **to have it repaired?** combien cela coûtera de le faire réparer?; **it** ~ **him his life/job** ça lui a coûté la vie/son emploi; **the** ~ **of living** le coût de la vie; **at all** ~**s** coûte que coûte, à tout prix.

cost accountant *n* analyste *m/f* de coûts.

co-star [kō'stár] *n* partenaire *m/f*.

Costa Rica [kâs'tə rē'kə] *n* Costa Rica *m*.

cost center *n* centre *m* de coût.

cost control *n* contrôle *m* des coûts.

cost-effective [kôstifek'tiv] *a* rentable.

cost-effectiveness [kôstifek'tivnis] *n* rentabilité *f*.

costing [kôs'ting] *n* calcul *m* du prix de revient.

costly [kôst'lē] *a* coûteux(euse).

cost-of-living [kôstəvliv'ing] *a*: ~ **allowance** indemnité *f* de vie chère; ~ **index** indice *m* du coût de la vie.

cost price *n* (*Brit*) prix coûtant or de revient.

costume [kâs'tōōm] *n* costume *m*; (*lady's suit*) tailleur *m*; (*Brit*: *also*: **swimming** ~) maillot *m* (de bain).

costume ball *n* bal masqué or costumé.

costume jewelry *n* bijoux *mpl* de fantaisie.

cosy [kō'zē] *a* (*Brit*) = **cozy**.

cot [kât] *n* (*US*: *camp bed*) lit de camp; (*Brit*: *child's*) lit *m* d'enfant, petit lit.

cottage [kât'ij] *n* petite maison (à la campagne), cottage *m*.

cottage cheese *n* fromage blanc (*maigre*).

cottage industry *n* industrie familiale or artisanale.

cottage pie n (Brit) ≈ hachis m Parmentier.
cotton [kát'ən] n coton m; (MED) ouate f, coton m hydrophile; ~ **dress** etc robe etc en or de coton.
  cotton on vi (Brit col): **to ~ on (to sth)** piger (qch).
cotton candy n (US) barbe f à papa.
cotton wool n (Brit) ouate f, coton m hydrophile.
couch [kouch] n canapé m; divan m; (doctor's) table f d'examen; (psychiatrist's) divan ♦ vt formuler, exprimer.
couchette [kōōshet'] n (Brit) couchette f.
cough [kôf] vi tousser ♦ n toux f.
cough drop n pastille f pour or contre la toux.
cough syrup n sirop m pour la toux.
could [kōōd] pt of **can**.
couldn't [kōōd'ənt] = **could not**.
council [koun'səl] n conseil m; **city** or **town** ~ conseil municipal; **C~ of Europe** Conseil de l'Europe.
council estate n (Brit) (quartier m or zone f de) logements loués à/par la municipalité.
council house n (Brit) maison f (à loyer modéré) louée par la municipalité.
councilor, (Brit) **councillor** [koun'səlûr] n conseiller/ère.
counsel [koun'səl] n consultation f, délibération f; (person) avocat/e ♦ vt: **to ~ sth/sb to do sth** conseiller qch/à qn de faire qch; ~ **for the defense/the prosecution** (avocat de la) défense/avocat du ministère public.
counselor, (Brit) **counsellor** [koun'səlûr] n conseiller/ère; (US LAW) avocat m.
count [kount] vt, vi compter ♦ n compte m; (nobleman) comte m; **to ~ (up) to 10** compter jusqu'à 10; **to keep ~ of sth** tenir le compte de qch; **not ~ing the children** sans compter les enfants; **10 ~ing him** 10 avec lui, 10 en le comptant; **to ~ the cost of** établir le coût de; **it ~s for very little** cela n'a pas beaucoup d'importance; ~ **yourself lucky** estimez-vous heureux.
  count on vt fus compter sur; **to ~ on doing sth** compter faire qch.
  count up vt compter, additionner.
countdown [kount'doun] n compte m à rebours.
countenance [koun'tənəns] n expression f ♦ vt approuver.
counter [koun'tûr] n comptoir m; (in post office, bank) guichet m; (in game) jeton m ♦ vt aller à l'encontre de, opposer; (blow) parer ♦ ad: ~ **to** à l'encontre de; contrairement à; **to buy under the** ~ (fig) acheter sous le manteau or en sous-main; **to ~ sth with sth/by doing sth** contrer or riposter à qch par qch/en faisant qch.
counteract [kountûrakt'] vt neutraliser, contrebalancer.
counterattack n [koun'tûrətak] contre-attaque f ♦ vi [kountûrətak'] contre-attaquer.
counterbalance [kountûrbal'əns] vt contrebalancer, faire contrepoids à.
counterclockwise [kountûrklâk'wīz] ad dans le sens inverse des aiguilles d'une montre.
counterespionage [kountûres'pēənâzh] n contre-espionnage m.

counterfeit [koun'tûrfit] n faux m, contrefaçon f ♦ vt contrefaire ♦ a faux(fausse).
counterfoil [koun'tûrfoil] n talon m, souche f.
counterintelligence [kountûrintel'ijəns] n contre-espionnage m.
countermand [kountûrmand'] vt annuler.
countermeasure [koun'tûrmezhûr] n contremesure f.
counteroffensive [kountûrəfen'siv] n contre-offensive f.
counterpane [koun'tûrpān] n dessus-de-lit m.
counterpart [koun'tûrpârt] n (of document etc) double m; (of person) homologue m/f.
counterproductive [kountûrprəduk'tiv] a contre-productif(ive).
counterproposal [koun'tûrprəpōzəl] n contre-proposition f.
countersign [koun'tûrsīn] vt contresigner.
countersink [koun'tûrsingk] vt (hole) fraiser.
countess [koun'tis] n comtesse f.
countless [kount'lis] a innombrable.
countrified [kun'trəfīd] a rustique, à l'air campagnard.
country [kun'trē] n pays m; (native land) patrie f; (as opposed to town) campagne f; (region) région f, pays; **in the** ~ à la campagne; **mountainous** ~ pays de montagne, région montagneuse.
country and western (music) n musique f country.
country dancing n (Brit) danse f folklorique.
country house n manoir m, (petit) château.
countryman [kun'trēmən] n (national) compatriote m; (rural) habitant m de la campagne, campagnard m.
countryside [kun'trēsīd] n campagne f.
country-wide [kun'trēwīd] a s'étendant à l'ensemble du pays; (problem) à l'échelle du pays entier ♦ ad à travers or dans tout le pays.
county [koun'tē] n comté m.
county seat n chef-lieu m.
coup, ~**s** [kōō, -z] n beau coup; (also: ~ **d'état**) coup d'Etat.
coupé [kōōpā'] n (AUT) coupé m.
couple [kup'əl] n couple m ♦ vt (carriages) atteler; (TECH) coupler; (ideas, names) associer; **a** ~ **of** deux; (a few) deux ou trois.
couplet [kup'lit] n distique m.
coupling [kup'ling] n (RAIL) attelage m.
coupon [kōō'pân] n (voucher) bon-prime m, bon-réclame m; (detachable form) coupon m détachable, coupon-réponse m; (FINANCE) coupon.
courage [kûr'ij] n courage m.
courageous [kərā'jəs] a courageux(euse).
courgette [kōōrzhet'] n (Brit) courgette f.
courier [kûr'ēûr] n messager m, courrier m; (for tourists) accompagnateur/trice.
course [kôrs] n cours m; (of ship) route f; (for golf) terrain m; (part of meal) plat m; **first** ~ entrée f; **of** ~ bien sûr; **(no) of** ~ **not!** bien sûr que non!, évidemment que non!; **in the** ~ **of the next few days** au cours des prochains jours; **in due** ~ en temps utile or voulu; ~ **(of action)** parti m, ligne f de conduite; **the best** ~ **would be to** ... le mieux serait de ...; **we have no other** ~ **but to** ... nous n'avons pas d'autre solution

que de ...; ~ **of lectures** série *f* de conférences; ~ **of treatment** (*MED*) traitement *m*.

court [kôrt] *n* cour *f*; (*LAW*) cour, tribunal *m*;
(*TENNIS*) court *m* ♦ *vt* (*woman*) courtiser,
faire la cour à; (*fig: favor, popularity*) rechercher; (: *death, disaster*) courir après,
flirter avec; **out of** ~ (*LAW: settle*) à l'amiable; **to take to** ~ actionner *or* poursuivre en
justice; ~ **of appeal** cour d'appel.

courteous [kûr'tēəs] *a* courtois(e), poli(e).

courtesan [kôr'tizən] *n* courtisane *f*.

courtesy [kûr'tisē] *n* courtoisie *f*, politesse *f*;
by ~ **of** avec l'aimable autorisation de.

courtesy bus *n* navette gratuite.

courtesy light *n* (*AUT*) plafonnier *m*.

courtesy van *n* (*US*) navette gratuite.

courthouse [kôrt'hous] *n* (*US*) palais *m* de
justice.

courtier [kôr'tēûr] *n* courtisan *m*, dame *f* de
cour.

court martial, *pl* **courts martial** *n* cour
martiale, conseil *m* de guerre.

courtroom [kôrt'rōōm] *n* salle *f* de tribunal.

court shoe *n* (*Brit*) escarpin *m*.

courtyard [kôrt'yârd] *n* cour *f*.

cousin [kuz'in] *n* cousin/e.

cove [kōv] *n* petite baie, anse *f*.

covenant [kuv'ənənt] *n* contrat *m*, engagement *m*.

Coventry [kuv'intrē] *n*: **to send sb to** ~ (*fig*)
mettre qn en quarantaine.

cover [kuv'ûr] *vt* couvrir; (*PRESS: report on*)
faire un reportage sur ♦ *n* (*for bed, of book,*
COMM, INSURANCE) couverture *f*; (*of pan*)
couvercle *m*; (*over furniture*) housse *f*;
(*shelter*) abri *m*; **to take** ~ se mettre à
l'abri; **under** ~ à l'abri; **under** ~ **of dark-**
ness à la faveur de la nuit; **under separate**
~ (*COMM*) sous pli séparé; **$10 will** ~ **every-**
thing 10 dollars suffiront (pour tout payer).

cover up *vt* (*person, object*): **to** ~ **up**
(with) couvrir (de); (*fig: truth, facts*)
occulter; **to** ~ **up for sb** (*fig*) couvrir qn.

coverage [kuv'ûrij] *n* (*in media*) reportage *m*;
(*INSURANCE*) couverture *f*.

coveralls [kuv'ûrôlz] *npl* bleu *m* de travail,
combinaison *f*.

cover charge *n* couvert *m* (*supplément à*
payer).

covering [kuv'ûring] *n* couverture *f*, enveloppe
f.

cover letter, (*Brit*) **covering letter** *n* lettre
explicative.

cover note *n* (*INSURANCE*) police *f* provisoire.

cover price *n* prix *m* de l'exemplaire.

covert [kō'vûrt] *a* (*threat*) voilé(e), caché(e);
(*attack*) indirect(e); (*glance*) furtif(ive).

cover-up [kuv'ûrup] *n* tentative *f* pour étouffer
une affaire.

covet [kuv'it] *vt* convoiter.

cow [kou] *n* vache *f* ♦ *cpd* femelle ♦ *vt* effrayer, intimider.

coward [kou'ûrd] *n* lâche *m/f*.

cowardice [kou'ûrdis] *n* lâcheté *f*.

cowardly [kou'ûrdlē] *a* lâche.

cowboy [kou'boi] *n* cow-boy *m*.

cower [kou'ûr] *vi* se recroqueviller; trembler.

cowshed [kou'shed] *n* étable *f*.

cowslip [kou'slip] *n* (*BOT*) (fleur *f* de) coucou

m.

coxswain [kâk'sin] *n* (*abbr:* **cox**) barreur *m*;
(*of ship*) patron *m*.

coy [koi] *a* faussement effarouché(e) *or* timide.

coyote [kīōt'ē] *n* coyote *m*.

coziness [kō'zēnis] *n* (*US*) atmosphère
douillette, confort *m*.

cozy [kō'zē] *a* (*US: bed*) douillet(te); (: *scarf,*
gloves) bien chaud(e); (: *atmosphere*) cha-
leureux(euse); (: *room*) mignon(ne).

CP *n abbr* (= *Communist Party*) PC *m*.

cp. *abbr* (= *compare*) cf.

c/p *abbr* (*Brit*) = **carriage paid.**

CPA *n abbr* (*US*) = **certified public**
accountant.

CPI *n abbr* (= *Consumer Price Index*) IPC *m*.

Cpl. *abbr* (= *corporal*) C/C.

CP/M *n abbr* (= *Central Program for Micro-*
processors) CP/M *m*.

c.p.s. *abbr* (= *characters per second*)
caractères/seconde.

CPU *n abbr* = **central processing unit.**

cr. *abbr* = **credit, creditor.**

crab [krab] *n* crabe *m*.

crab apple *n* pomme *f* sauvage.

crack [krak] *n* fente *f*, fissure *f*; (*in bone, dish,*
glass) fêlure *f*; (*in wall*) lézarde *f*; (*noise*)
craquement *m*, coup (sec); (*joke*) plaisanterie *f*; (*col: attempt*): **to have a** ~ **(at sth)**
essayer (qch); (*DRUGS*) crack *m* ♦ *vt* fendre,
fissurer; fêler; lézarder; (*whip*) faire claquer; (*nut*) casser; (*solve*) résoudre, trouver
la clef de; déchiffrer ♦ *cpd* (*athlete*) de première classe, d'élite; **to** ~ **jokes** (*col*) raconter des blagues; **to get** ~**ing** (*col*) s'y
mettre, se magner.

crack down on *vt fus* (*crime*) sévir
contre, réprimer; (*spending*) mettre un frein
à.

crack up *vi* être au bout de son rouleau,
flancher.

crackdown [krak'doun] *n*: ~ **(on)** (*on crime*)
répression *f* (de); (*on spending*) restrictions
fpl (de).

cracked [krakt] *a* (*col*) toqué(e), timbré(e).

cracker [krak'ûr] *n* pétard *m*; (*cookie*) biscuit
(salé), craquelin *m*; (*Christmas* ~) diablotin
m.

crackle [krak'əl] *vi* crépiter, grésiller.

crackling [krak'ling] *n* crépitement *m*, grésillement *m*; (*on radio, telephone*) grésillement *m*,
friture *f*; (*of pork*) couenne *f*.

cradle [krā'dəl] *n* berceau *m* ♦ *vt* (*child*)
bercer; (*object*) tenir dans ses bras.

craft [kraft] *n* métier (artisanal); (*cunning*)
ruse *f*, astuce *f*; (*boat*) embarcation *f*, barque
f.

craftsman [krafts'mən] *n* artisan *m*, ouvrier
(qualifié).

craftsmanship [krafts'mənship] *n* métier *m*,
habileté *f*.

crafty [kraf'tē] *a* rusé(e), malin(igne), astu-
cieux(euse).

crag [krag] *n* rocher escarpé.

craggy [krag'ē] *a* escarpé(e), rocheux(euse).

cram [kram] *vt* (*fill*): **to** ~ **sth with** bourrer
qch de; (*put*): **to** ~ **sth into** fourrer qch
dans.

cramming [kram'ing] *n* (*for exams*) bachotage

m.

cramp [kramp] *n* crampe *f* ♦ *vt* gêner, entraver.

cramped [krampt] *a* à l'étroit, très serré(e).

crampon [kram'pän] *n* crampon *m*.

cranberry [kran'bärē] *n* canneberge *f*.

crane [krān] *n* grue *f* ♦ *vt*, *vi*: **to ~ forward**, **to ~ one's neck** allonger le cou.

cranium, *pl* **crania** [krā'nēəm, krā'nēə] *n* boîte crânienne.

crank [krangk] *n* manivelle *f*; (*person*) excentrique *m*/*f*.

crankshaft [krangk'shaft] *n* vilebrequin *m*.

cranky [krang'kē] *a* excentrique, loufoque; (*bad-tempered*) grincheux(euse), revêche.

cranny [kran'ē] *n see* **nook**.

crap [krap] *n* (*col!*) conneries *fpl* (*!*); **to have a ~** chier (*!*).

crash [krash] *n* fracas *m*; (*of car, plane*) collision *f*; (*of business*) faillite *f*; (*STOCK EXCHANGE*) krach *m* ♦ *vt* (*plane*) écraser ♦ *vi* (*plane*) s'écraser; (*two cars*) se percuter, s'emboutir; (*fig*) s'effondrer; **to ~ into** se jeter *or* se fracasser contre; **he ~ed the car into a wall** il s'est écrasé contre un mur avec sa voiture.

crash barrier *n* (*Brit AUT*) rail *m* de sécurité.

crash course *n* cours intensif.

crash helmet *n* casque (protecteur).

crash landing *n* atterrissage forcé *or* en catastrophe.

crass [kras] *a* grossier(ière), crasse.

crate [krāt] *n* cageot *m*.

crater [krā'tûr] *n* cratère *m*.

cravat(e) [krəvat'] *n* foulard (noué autour du cou).

crave [krāv] *vt*, *vi*: **to ~ for** désirer violemment, avoir un besoin physiologique de, avoir une envie irrésistible de.

craving [krā'ving] *n*: **~ (for)** (*for food, cigarettes etc*) envie *f* irrésistible (de).

crawfish [krô'fish] *n* (*US*) = **crayfish**.

crawl [krôl] *vi* ramper; (*vehicle*) avancer au pas ♦ *n* (*SWIMMING*) crawl *m*; **to ~ to sb** (*col*) faire de la lèche à qn.

crayfish [krā'fish] *n* (*pl inv*) (*freshwater*) écrevisse *f*; (*saltwater*) langoustine *f*.

crayon [krā'án] *n* crayon *m* (de couleur).

craze [krāz] *n* engouement *m*.

crazed [krāzd] *a* (*look, person*) affolé(e); (*pottery, glaze*) craquelé(e).

crazy [krā'zē] *a* fou(folle); **to go ~** devenir fou; **to be ~ about sb** (*col*) aimer qn à la folie; **he's ~ about skiing** (*col*) c'est un fana(tique) de ski.

crazy paving *n* (*Brit*) dallage irrégulier (en pierres plates).

CRC *n abbr* (*US*) = *Civil Rights Commission*.

creak [krēk] *vi* (*hinge*) grincer; (*floor, shoes*) craquer.

cream [krēm] *n* crème *f* ♦ *a* (*color*) crème *inv*; **whipped ~** crème fouettée.

cream cake *n* (*Brit*) (petit) gâteau à la crème.

cream cheese *n* fromage *m* à la crème, fromage blanc.

creamery [krē'mûrē] *n* (*store*) crémerie *f*; (*factory*) laiterie *f*.

creamy [krē'mē] *a* crémeux(euse).

crease [krēs] *n* pli *m* ♦ *vt* froisser, chiffonner ♦ *vi* se froisser, se chiffonner.

crease-resistant [krēsrizis'tənt] *a* infroissable.

create [krēā'] *vt* créer; (*impression, fuss*) faire.

creation [krēā'shən] *n* création *f*.

creative [krēā'tiv] *a* créateur(trice).

creativity [krēātiv'ətē] *n* créativité *f*.

creator [krēā'tûr] *n* créateur/trice.

creature [krē'chûr] *n* créature *f*.

crèche, creche [kresh] *n* (*Brit*) garderie *f*, crèche *f*.

credence [krēd'əns] *n* croyance *f*, foi *f*.

credentials [kriden'shəlz] *npl* (*papers*) références *fpl*; (*letters of reference*) pièces justificatives.

credibility [kredəbil'ətē] *n* crédibilité *f*.

credible [kred'əbəl] *a* digne de foi, crédible.

credit [kred'it] *n* crédit *m*; (*SCOL*) unité *f* de valeur ♦ *vt* (*COMM*) créditer; (*believe: also*: **give ~ to**) ajouter foi à, croire; **to ~ sb with** (*fig*) prêter *or* attribuer à qn; **to ~ $50 to sb** créditer (le compte de) qn de 50 dollars; **to be in ~** (*person, bank account*) être créditeur(trice); **on ~** à crédit; **to one's ~** à son honneur; à son actif; **to take the ~ for** s'attribuer le mérite de; **it does him ~** cela lui fait honneur.

creditable [kred'itəbəl] *a* honorable, estimable.

credit account *n* compte *m* client.

credit agency *n* (*Brit*) agence *f* de renseignements commerciaux.

credit balance *n* solde créditeur.

credit bureau *n* (*US*) agence *f* de renseignements commerciaux.

credit card *n* carte *f* de crédit.

credit control *n* suivi *m* des factures.

credit facilities *npl* facilités *fpl* de paiement.

credit limit *n* limite *f* de crédit.

credit note *n* (*Brit*) avoir *m*.

creditor [kred'itûr] *n* créancier/ière.

credit rating *n* réputation *f* de solvabilité.

credits [kred'its] *npl* (*CINEMA*) générique *m*.

credit transfer *n* virement *m*.

creditworthy [kred'itwûrᵺē] *a* solvable.

credulity [krədōō'litē] *n* crédulité *f*.

creed [krēd] *n* croyance *f*; credo *m*, principes *mpl*.

creek [krēk] *n* crique *f*, anse *f*; (*US*) ruisseau *m*, petit cours d'eau.

creel [krēl] *n* panier *m* de pêche; (*also*: **lobster ~**) panier à homards.

creep [krēp], *pt, pp* **crept** [krēp, krept] *vi* ramper; (*fig*) se faufiler, se glisser; (*plant*) grimper ♦ *n* (*col*) saligaud *m*; **he's a ~** c'est un type puant; **it gives me the ~s** cela me fait froid dans le dos; **to ~ up on sb** s'approcher furtivement de qn.

creeper [krē'pûr] *n* plante grimpante.

creepers [krē'pûrz] *npl* (*US: for baby*) barboteuse *f*.

creepy [krē'pē] *a* (*frightening*) qui fait frissonner, qui donne la chair de poule.

creepy-crawly [krē'pēkrôlē] *n* (*col*) bestiole *f*.

cremate [krē'māt] *vt* incinérer.

cremation [krimā'shən] *n* incinération *f*.

crematorium, *pl* **crematoria** [kremətôr'ēəm, -tôr'ēə] *n* four *m* crématoire.

creosote [krē'əsōt] *n* créosote *f*.

crêpe [krāp] *n* crêpe *m*.
crêpe bandage *n* (*Brit*) bande *f* Velpeau ®.
crêpe paper *n* papier *m* crépon.
crêpe sole *n* semelle *f* de crêpe.
crept [krɛpt] *pt, pp of* **creep**.
crescendo [krishen'dō] *n* crescendo *m*.
crescent [krɛs'ənt] *n* croissant *m*; (*street*) rue *f* (*en arc de cercle*).
cress [krɛs] *n* cresson *m*.
crest [krɛst] *n* crête *f*; (*of helmet*) cimier *m*; (*of coat of arms*) timbre *m*.
crestfallen [krɛst'fôlən] *a* déconfit(e), découragé(e).
Crete [krēt] *n* Crète *f*.
crevasse [krəvas'] *n* crevasse *f*.
crevice [krɛv'is] *n* fissure *f*, lézarde *f*, fente *f*.
crew [krōō] *n* équipage *m*; (*CINEMA*) équipe *f* (de tournage); (*gang*) bande *f*.
crew cut *n*: **to have a** ~ avoir les cheveux en brosse.
crew neck *n* col ras.
crib [krib] *n* lit *m* d'enfant ♦ *vt* (*col*) copier.
cribbage [krib'ij] *n* sorte de jeu de cartes.
crick [krik] *n* crampe *f*; ~ **in the neck** torticolis *m*.
cricket [krik'it] *n* (*insect*) grillon *m*, cri-cri *m inv*; (*game*) cricket *m*.
cricketer [krik'itûr] *n* joueur *m* de cricket.
crime [krīm] *n* crime *m*; **minor** ~ délit *m or* infraction *f* mineur(e).
crime wave *n* poussée *f* de la criminalité.
criminal [krim'ənəl] *a, n* criminel(le).
crimp [krimp] *vt* friser, frisotter.
crimson [krim'zən] *a* cramoisi(e).
cringe [krinj] *vi* avoir un mouvement de recul; (*fig*) s'humilier, ramper.
crinkle [kriŋ'kəl] *vt* froisser, chiffonner.
cripple [krip'əl] *n* boiteux/euse, infirme *m/f* ♦ *vt* estropier, paralyser; (*ship, plane*) immobiliser; (*production, exports*) paralyser; ~**d with rheumatism** perclus(e) de rhumatismes.
crippling [krip'liŋ] *a* (*disease*) handicapant(e); (*taxation, debts*) écrasant(e).
crisis, *pl* **crises** [krī'sis, -sēz] *n* crise *f*.
crisp [krisp] *a* croquant(e); (*fig*) vif(vive), brusque.
crisps [krisps] *npl* (*Brit*) (pommes) chips *fpl*.
crisscross [kris'krôs] *a* entrecroisé(e), en croisillons ♦ *vt* sillonner; ~ **pattern** croisillons *mpl*.
criterion, *pl* **criteria** [krītēr'ēən, -tēr'ēə] *n* critère *m*.
critic [krit'ik] *n* critique *m/f*.
critical [krit'ikəl] *a* critique; **to be** ~ **of sb/sth** critiquer qn/qch.
critical list *n* (*MED*): **on the** ~ dans un état critique.
critically [krit'iklē] *ad* (*examine*) d'un œil critique; (*speak*) sévèrement; ~ **ill** gravement malade.
criticism [krit'isizəm] *n* critique *f*.
criticize [krit'əsīz] *vt* critiquer.
croak [krōk] *vi* (*frog*) coasser; (*raven*) croasser.
crochet [krōshā'] *n* travail *m* au crochet.
crock [krák] *n* cruche *f*; (*col: also:* **old** ~) épave *f*.
crockery [krák'ûrē] *n* vaisselle *f*.

crocodile [krák'ədīl] *n* crocodile *m*.
crocus [krō'kəs] *n* crocus *m*.
croft [krôft] *n* (*Brit*) petite ferme.
crone [krōn] *n* vieille bique, (vieille) sorcière.
crony [krō'nē] *n* copain/copine.
crook [krōōk] *n* escroc *m*; (*of shepherd*) houlette *f*.
crooked [krōōk'id] *a* courbé(e), tordu(e); (*action*) malhonnête.
crop [kráp] *n* (*produce*) culture *f*; (*amount produced*) récolte *f*; (*riding* ~) cravache *f*; (*of bird*) jabot *m* ♦ *vt* (*hair*) tondre; (*subj: animals: grass*) brouter.
crop up *vi* surgir, se présenter, survenir.
cropper [kráp'ûr] *n*: **to come a** ~ (*col*) faire la culbute, s'étaler.
crop spraying [kráp sprā'ing] *n* pulvérisation *f* des cultures.
croquet [krōkā'] *n* croquet *m*.
croquette [krōket'] *n* croquette *f*.
cross [krôs] *n* croix *f*; (*BIOL*) croisement *m* ♦ *vt* (*street etc*) traverser; (*arms, legs, BIOL*) croiser; (*check*) barrer; (*thwart: person, plan*) contrarier ♦ *vi*: **the boat** ~**es from ... to ...** le bateau fait la traversée de ... à ... ♦ *a* en colère, fâché(e); **to** ~ **o.s.** se signer, faire le signe de (la) croix; **we have a** ~**ed line** (*Brit: on telephone*) il y a des interférences; **they've got their wires** ~**ed** (*fig*) il y a un malentendu entre eux; **to be/get** ~ **with sb (about sth)** être en colère/se fâcher contre qn (à propos de qch).
cross out *vt* barrer, biffer.
cross over *vi* traverser.
crossbar [krôs'bâr] *n* barre transversale.
crossbreed [krôs'brēd] *n* hybride *m*, métis/se.
cross-Channel ferry [krôs'chanəl fär'ē] *n* ferry *m* qui fait la traversée de la manche.
cross-check [krôs'chek] *n* recoupement *m* ♦ *vi* vérifier par recoupement.
cross-country (race) [krôs'kun'trē (rās)] *n* cross(-country) *m*.
cross-examination [krôs'igzamənā'shən] *n* (*LAW*) examen *m* contradictoire (*d'un témoin*).
cross-examine [krôs'igzam'in] *vt* (*LAW*) faire subir un examen contradictoire à.
cross-eyed [krôs'īd] *a* qui louche.
crossfire [krôs'fīûr] *n* feux croisés.
crossing [krôs'ing] *n* croisement *m*, carrefour *m*; (*sea passage*) traversée *f*; (*also:* **pedestrian** ~) passage clouté.
cross-purposes [krôs'pûr'pəsiz] *npl*: **to be at** ~ **with sb** comprendre qn de travers; **we're (talking) at** ~ on ne parle pas de la même chose.
cross-reference [krôs'ref'ûrəns] *n* renvoi *m*, référence *f*.
crossroads [krôs'rōdz] *n* carrefour *m*.
cross section *n* (*BIOL*) coupe transversale; (*in population*) échantillon *m*.
crosswalk [krôs'wôk] *n* (*US*) passage clouté.
crosswind [krôs'wind] *n* vent *m* de travers.
crosswise [krôs'wīz] *ad* en travers.
crossword [krôs'wûrd] *n* mots croisés *mpl*.
crotch [krách] *n* (*of garment*) entre-jambes *m inv*.
crotchet [krách'it] *n* (*MUS*) noire *f*.
crotchety [krách'ətē] *a* (*person*) grognon(ne),

grincheux(euse).

crouch [krouch] *vi* s'accroupir; se tapir; se ramasser.

croup [kroop] *n* (*MED*) croup *m*.

crouton [kroo'tân] *n* croûton *m*.

crow [krō] *n* (*bird*) corneille *f*; (*of cock*) chant *m* du coq, cocorico *m* ♦ *vi* (*cock*) chanter; (*fig*) pavoiser, chanter victoire.

crowbar [krō'bâr] *n* levier *m*.

crowd [kroud] *n* foule *f* ♦ *vt* bourrer, remplir ♦ *vi* affluer, s'attrouper, s'entasser; **~s of people** une foule de gens.

crowded [krou'did] *a* bondé(e), plein(e); **~ with** plein de.

crowd scene *n* (*CINEMA, THEATER*) scène *f* de foule.

crown [kroun] *n* couronne *f*; (*of head*) sommet *m* de la tête, calotte crânienne; (*of hat*) fond *m*; (*of hill*) sommet *m* ♦ *vt* (*also tooth*) couronner.

crown court *n* (*Brit*) ≈ Cour *f* d'assises.

crowning [krou'ning] *a* (*achievement, glory*) suprême.

crown jewels *npl* joyaux *mpl* de la Couronne.

crown prince *n* prince héritier.

crow's-feet [krōz'fēt] *npl* pattes *fpl* d'oie (*fig*).

crow's-nest [krōz'nest] *n* (*on sailing-ship*) nid *m* de pie.

crucial [kroo'shəl] *a* crucial(e), décisif(ive); **~ to** essentiel(le) à.

crucifix [kroo'səfiks] *n* crucifix *m*.

crucifixion [kroosəfik'shən] *n* crucifiement *m*, crucifixion *f*.

crucify [kroo'səfī] *vt* crucifier, mettre en croix; (*fig*) crucifier.

crude [krood] *a* (*materials*) brut(e); non raffiné(e); (*basic*) rudimentaire, sommaire; (*vulgar*) cru(e), grossier(ière).

crude (oil) *n* (pétrole) brut *m*.

cruel [kroo'əl] *a* cruel(le).

cruelty [kroo'əltē] *n* cruauté *f*.

cruet [kroo'it] *n* huilier *m*; vinaigrier *m*.

cruise [krooz] *n* croisière *f* ♦ *vi* (*ship*) croiser; (*car*) rouler; (*aircraft*) voler; (*taxi*) être en maraude.

cruise missile *n* missile *m* de croisière.

cruiser [kroo'zûr] *n* croiseur *m*.

cruise ship *n* vapeur *m* de plaisance.

cruising speed [kroo'zing spēd] *n* vitesse *f* de croisière.

crumb [krum] *n* miette *f*.

crumble [krum'bəl] *vt* émietter ♦ *vi* s'émietter; (*plaster etc*) s'effriter; (*land, earth*) s'ébouler; (*building*) s'écrouler, crouler; (*fig*) s'effondrer.

crumbly [krum'blē] *a* friable.

crummy [krum'ē] *a* (*col*) minable; (*: unwell*) mal fichu(e), patraque.

crumpet [krum'pit] *n* petite crêpe (épaisse).

crumple [krum'pəl] *vt* froisser, friper.

crunch [krunch] *vt* croquer; (*underfoot*) faire craquer, écraser; faire crisser ♦ *n* (*fig*) instant *m or* moment *m* critique, moment de vérité.

crunchy [krun'chē] *a* croquant(e), croustillant(e).

crusade [kroosād'] *n* croisade *f* ♦ *vi* (*fig*): **to ~ for/against** partir en croisade pour/contre.

crusader [kroosā'dûr] *n* croisé *m*; (*fig*): **~**

(for) champion *m* (de).

crush [krush] *n* foule *f*, cohue *f*; (*love*): **to have a ~ on sb** avoir le béguin pour qn ♦ *vt* écraser; (*crumple*) froisser; (*grind, break up: garlic, ice*) piler; (*: grapes*) presser.

crushing [krush'ing] *a* écrasant(e).

crust [krust] *n* croûte *f*.

crustacean [krustā'shən] *n* crustacé *m*.

crusty [krus'tē] *a* (*loaf*) croustillant(e).

crutch [kruch] *n* béquille *f*; (*TECH*) support *m*; (*also:* **crotch**) entrejambe *m*.

crux [kruks] *n* point crucial.

cry [krī] *vi* pleurer; (*shout: also:* **~ out**) crier ♦ *n* cri *m*; **what are you ~ing about?** pourquoi pleures-tu?; **to ~ for help** appeler à l'aide; **she had a good ~** elle a pleuré un bon coup; **it's a far ~ from ...** (*fig*) on est loin de ....

cry off *vi* (*Brit*) se dédire; se décommander.

crying [krī'ing] *a* (*fig*) criant(e), flagrant(e).

crypt [kript] *n* crypte *f*.

cryptic [krip'tik] *a* énigmatique.

crystal [kris'təl] *n* cristal *m*.

crystal-clear [kris'təlkli'ûr] *a* clair(e) comme de l'eau de roche.

crystallize [kris'təlīz] *vt* cristalliser ♦ *vi* (se) cristalliser; **~d fruits** (*Brit*) fruits confits.

CSA *n abbr* = *Confederate States of America*.

CS gas [sē'es gas'] *n* (*Brit*) gaz *m* C.S.

CST *abbr* (*US:* = *Central Standard Time*) fuseau horaire.

CT *abbr* (*US MAIL*) = *Connecticut*.

ct *abbr* = *carat*.

Ct. *abbr* (*US*) = *Connecticut*.

cu. *abbr* = *cubic*.

cub [kub] *n* petit *m* (*d'un animal*); (*also:* **~ scout**) louveteau *m*.

Cuba [kyoo'bə] *n* Cuba *m*.

Cuban [kyoo'bən] *a* cubain(e) ♦ *n* Cubain/e.

cubbyhole [kub'ēhōl] *n* cagibi *m*.

cube [kyoob] *n* cube *m* ♦ *vt* (*MATH*) élever au cube.

cube root *n* racine *f* cubique.

cubic [kyoo'bik] *a* cubique; **~ meter** *etc* mètre *m etc* cube; **~ capacity** (*AUT*) cylindrée *f*.

cubicle [kyoo'bikəl] *n* box *m*, cabine *f*.

cuckoo [koo'koo] *n* coucou *m*.

cuckoo clock *n* (pendule *f* à) coucou *m*.

cucumber [kyoo'kumbûr] *n* concombre *m*.

cud [kud] *n*: **to chew the ~** ruminer.

cuddle [kud'əl] *vt* câliner, caresser ♦ *vi* se blottir l'un contre l'autre.

cuddly [kud'lē] *a* câlin(e).

cudgel [kuj'əl] *n* gourdin *m* ♦ *vt*: **to ~ one's brains** se creuser la tête.

cue [kyoo] *n* queue *f* de billard; (*THEATER etc*) signal *m*.

cuff [kuf] *n* (*of shirt, coat etc*) poignet *m*, manchette *f*; (*US: on pants*) revers *m*; (*blow*) gifle *f* ♦ *vt* gifler; **off the ~** *ad* de chic, à l'improviste.

cuff link *n* bouton *m* de manchette.

cu. in. *abbr* = *cubic inches*.

cuisine [kwizēn'] *n* cuisine *f*, art *m* culinaire.

cul-de-sac [kul'dəsak'] *n* cul-de-sac *m*, impasse *f*.

culinary [kyoo'lənärē] *a* culinaire.

cull [kul] *vt* sélectionner; (*kill selectively*) pratiquer l'abattage sélectif de.

culminate [kul'mənāt] *vi*: **to ~ in** finir *or* se terminer par; (*lead to*) mener à.

culmination [kulmənā'shən] *n* point culminant.

culotte [kyōōlât'] *n* (*US*) jupe-culotte *f*.

culottes [kyōōlâts'] *npl* (*Brit*) jupe-culotte *f*.

culpable [kul'pəbəl] *a* coupable.

culprit [kul'prit] *n* coupable *m/f*.

cult [kult] *n* culte *m*.

cult figure *n* idole *f*.

cultivate [kul'təvāt] *vt* (*also fig*) cultiver.

cultivation [kultəvā'shən] *n* culture *f*.

cultural [kul'chūrəl] *a* culturel(le).

culture [kul'chūr] *n* (*also fig*) culture *f*.

cultured [kul'chūrd] *a* cultivé(e) (*fig*).

cumbersome [kum'būrsəm] *a* encombrant(e), embarrassant(e).

cumin [kyōōm'in] *n* (*spice*) cumin *m*.

cumulative [kyōōm'yələtiv] *a* cumulatif(ive).

cunning [kun'ing] *n* ruse *f*, astuce *f* ♦ *a* rusé(e), malin(igne); (*clever: device, idea*) astucieux(euse).

cup [kup] *n* tasse *f*; (*prize, event*) coupe *f*; (*of bra*) bonnet *m*; **a ~ of tea** une tasse de thé.

cupboard [kub'ûrd] *n* placard *m*.

Cupid [kyōō'pid] *n* Cupidon *m*; (*figurine*) amour *m*.

cupidity [kyōōpid'itē] *n* cupidité *f*.

cupola [kyōō'pələ] *n* coupole *f*.

curable [kyōō'rəbəl] *a* guérissable, curable.

curate [kyōō'rit] *n* vicaire *m*.

curator [kyōōrā'tûr] *n* conservateur *m* (*d'un musée etc*).

curb [kûrb] *vt* refréner, mettre un frein à; (*expenditure*) limiter, juguler ♦ *n* frein *m* (*fig*); (*US*) bordure *f* du trottoir.

curd cheese [kûrd chēz] *n ~* fromage blanc.

curdle [kûr'dəl] *vi* (se) cailler.

curds [kûrdz] *npl* lait caillé.

cure [kyōōr] *vt* guérir; (*CULIN*) saler; fumer; sécher ♦ *n* remède *m*; **to be ~d of sth** être guéri de qch.

cure-all [kyōōr'ól] *n* (*also fig*) panacée *f*.

curfew [kûr'fyōō] *n* couvre-feu *m*.

curio [kyōō'rēō] *n* bibelot *m*, curiosité *f*.

curiosity [kyōōrēâs'ətē] *n* curiosité *f*.

curious [kyōō'rēəs] *a* curieux(euse); **I'm ~ about him** il m'intrigue.

curiously [kyōō'rēəslē] *ad* curieusement; (*inquisitively*) avec curiosité; **~ enough, ...** bizarrement ....

curl [kûrl] *n* boucle *f* (de cheveux); (*of smoke etc*) volute *f* ♦ *vt, vi* boucler; (*tightly*) friser.

curl up *vi* s'enrouler; se pelotonner.

curler [kûr'lûr] *n* bigoudi *m*, rouleau *m*; (*SPORT*) joueur/euse de curling.

curlew [kûr'lōō] *n* courlis *m*.

curling [kûr'ling] *n* (*sport*) curling *m*.

curling iron *n* (*US*) fer *m* à friser.

curling tongs *npl* (*Brit*) = **curling iron**.

curly [kûr'lē] *a* bouclé(e); (*tightly curled*) frisé(e).

currant [kûr'ənt] *n* raisin *m* de Corinthe, raisin sec.

currency [kûr'ənsē] *n* monnaie *f*; **foreign ~** devises étrangères, monnaie étrangère; **to gain ~** (*fig*) s'accréditer.

current [kûr'ənt] *n* courant *m* ♦ *a* courant(e); (*tendency, price, event*) actuel(le); **direct/**

alternating ~ (*ELEC*) courant continu/alternatif; **the ~ issue of a magazine** le dernier numéro d'un magazine, **in ~ use** d'usage courant.

current account *n* (*Brit*) compte courant.

current affairs *npl* (questions *fpl* d')actualité *f*.

current assets *npl* (*COMM*) actif *m* disponible.

current liabilities *npl* (*COMM*) passif *m* exigible.

currently [kûr'əntlē] *ad* actuellement.

curriculum, *pl* **~s** *or* **curricula** [kərik'yələm, -yələ] *n* programme *m* d'études.

curriculum vitae (CV) [kərik'yələm vē'tī] *n* curriculum vitae (CV) *m*.

curry [kûr'ē] *n* curry *m* ♦ *vt*: **to ~ favor with** chercher à gagner la faveur *or* à s'attirer les bonnes grâces de; **chicken ~** curry de poulet, poulet *m* au curry.

curry powder *n* poudre *f* de curry.

curse [kûrs] *vi* jurer, blasphémer ♦ *vt* maudire ♦ *n* malédiction *f*; fléau *m*; (*swearword*) juron *m*.

cursor [kûr'sûr] *n* (*COMPUT*) curseur *m*.

cursory [kûr'sûrē] *a* superficiel(le), hâtif(ive).

curt [kûrt] *a* brusque, sec(sèche).

curtail [kûrtāl'] *vt* (*visit etc*) écourter; (*expenses etc*) réduire.

curtain [kûr'tən] *n* rideau *m*; **to draw the ~s** (*together*) fermer *or* tirer les rideaux; (*apart*) ouvrir les rideaux.

curtain call *n* (*THEATER*) rappel *m*.

curts(e)y [kûrt'sē] *n* révérence *f* ♦ *vi* faire une révérence.

curvature [kûr'vəchûr] *n* courbure *f*.

curve [kûrv] *n* courbe *f*; (*in the road*) tournant *m*, virage *m* ♦ *vt* courber ♦ *vi* se courber; (*road*) faire une courbe.

curved [kûrvd] *a* courbe.

cushion [kōōsh'ən] *n* coussin *m* ♦ *vt* (*seat*) rembourrer; (*shock*) amortir.

cushy [kōōsh'ē] *a* (*col*): **a ~ job** un boulot de tout repos.

custard [kus'tûrd] *n* (*for pouring*) crème anglaise.

custodian [kustō'dēən] *n* gardien/ne; (*of collection etc*) conservateur/trice.

custody [kus'tədē] *n* (*of child*) garde *f*; (*for offenders*) détention préventive; **to take sb into ~** placer qn en détention préventive; **in the ~ of** sous la garde de.

custom [kus'təm] *n* coutume *f*, usage *m*; (*LAW*) droit coutumier, coutume; (*COMM*) clientèle *f*.

customary [kus'təmārē] *a* habituel(le); **it is ~ to do it** l'usage veut qu'on le fasse.

custom-built [kus'təmbilt'] *a see* **custom-made**.

customer [kus'təmûr] *n* client/e; **he's a tough ~** (*col*) ce n'est pas quelqu'un de facile.

customer profile *n* profil *m* du client.

customer service *n* service *m* après-vente, SAV *m*.

customized [kus'təmīzd] *a* personnalisé(e).

custom-made [kus'təmmād'] *a* (*clothes*) fait(e) sur mesure; (*other goods: also:* **custom-built**) hors série, fait(e) sur commande.

customs [kus'təmz] *npl* douane *f*; **to go through (the)** ~ passer la douane.
Customs and Excise *n* (*Brit*) administration *f* des douanes.
customs duty *n* droits *mpl* de douane.
customs officer *n* douanier *m*.
cut [kut] *vb* (*pt, pp* **cut**) *vt* couper; (*meat*) découper; (*shape, make*) tailler; couper; creuser; graver; (*reduce*) réduire; (*col: lecture, appointment*) manquer ♦ *vi* couper; (*intersect*) se couper ♦ *n* (*gen*) coupure *f*; (*of clothes*) coupe *f*; (*of jewel*) taille *f*; (*in salary etc*) réduction *f*; (*of meat*) morceau *m*; **cold** ~**s** *npl* viandes froides; **to** ~ **teeth** (*baby*) faire ses dents; **to** ~ **a tooth** percer une dent; **to** ~ **one's finger** se couper le doigt; **to get one's hair** ~ se faire couper les cheveux; **to** ~ **sth short** couper court à qch.
cut back *vt* (*plants*) tailler; (*production, expenditure*) réduire.
cut down *vt* (*tree*) abattre; (*reduce*) réduire; **to** ~ **sb down to size** (*fig*) remettre qn à sa place.
cut down on *vt fus* réduire.
cut in *vi* (*interrupt: conversation*): **to** ~ **in (on)** couper la parole (à); (*AUT*) faire une queue de poisson.
cut off *vt* couper; (*fig*) isoler; **we've been** ~ **off** (*TEL*) nous avons été coupés.
cut out *vt* (*picture etc*) découper; (*remove*) ôter; supprimer.
cut up *vt* découper.
cut and dried [kutəndrīd'] *a* (*also:* **cut-and-dry**) tout(e) fait(e), tout(e) décidé(e).
cutaway [kut'əwa] *a, n:* ~ **(drawing)** écorché *m*.
cutback [kut'bak] *n* réduction *f*.
cute [kyōōt] *a* mignon(ne), adorable; (*clever*) rusé(e), astucieux(euse).
cut glass *n* cristal taillé.
cuticle [kyōō'tikəl] *n* (*on nail*): ~ **remover** repousse-peaux *m inv*.
cutlery [kut'lûrē] *n* couverts *mpl*; (*trade*) coutellerie *f*.
cutlet [kut'lit] *n* côtelette *f*.
cutoff [kut'ôf] *n* (*also:* ~ **point**) seuil-limite *m*.
cutoff switch *n* interrupteur *m*.
cutout [kut'out] *n* coupe-circuit *m inv*; (*paper figure*) découpage *m*.
cut-price [kut'prīs] *a* (*Brit*) = **cut-rate**.
cut-rate [kut'rāt] *a* (*US*) au rabais, à prix réduit.
cutthroat [kut'thrōt] *n* assassin *m* ♦ *a:* ~ **competition** concurrence *f* sauvage.
cutting [kut'ing] *a* tranchant(e), coupant(e); (*fig*) cinglant(e), mordant(e) ♦ *n* (*Brit: from newspaper*) coupure *f* (de journal); (: *RAIL*) tranchée *f*; (*CINEMA*) montage *m*.
cuttlefish [kut'əlfish] *n* seiche *f*.
CV *n abbr* = **curriculum vitae**.
C & W *n abbr* = **country and western** (music).
cwt. *abbr* = **hundredweight**.
cyanide [sī'ənīd] *n* cyanure *m*.
cybernetics [sībûrnet'iks] *n* cybernétique *f*.
cyclamen [sik'ləmən] *n* cyclamen *m*.
cycle [sī'kəl] *n* cycle *m* ♦ *vi* faire de la bicyclette.
cycle race *n* course *f* cycliste.

cycle rack *n* (*Brit*) râtelier *m* à bicyclette.
cycling [sīk'ling] *n* cyclisme *m*; **to go on a** ~ **tour** faire du cyclotourisme.
cyclist [sīk'list] *n* cycliste *m/f*.
cyclone [sīk'lōn] *n* cyclone *m*.
cygnet [sig'nit] *n* jeune cygne *m*.
cylinder [sil'indûr] *n* cylindre *m*.
cylinder block *n* bloc-cylindres *m*.
cylinder capacity *n* cylindrée *f*.
cylinder head *n* culasse *f*.
cylinder-head gasket [sil'indûrhed gas'kit] *n* joint *m* de culasse.
cymbals [sim'bəlz] *npl* cymbales *fpl*.
cynic [sin'ik] *n* cynique *m/f*.
cynical [sin'ikəl] *a* cynique.
cynicism [sin'əsizəm] *n* cynisme *m*.
CYO *n abbr* (*US:* = *Catholic Youth Organization*) ≈ JC *f*.
cypress [sī'pris] *n* cyprès *m*.
Cypriot [sip'rēət] *a* cypriote, chypriote ♦ *n* Cypriote *m/f*, Chypriote *m/f*.
Cyprus [sip'rəs] *n* Chypre *f*.
cyst [sist] *n* kyste *m*.
cystitis [sistī'tis] *n* cystite *f*.
CZ *n abbr* (*US:* = *Canal Zone*) zone du canal de Panama.
czar [zâr] *n* tsar *m*.
Czech [chek] *a* tchèque ♦ *n* Tchèque *m/f*; (*LING*) tchèque *m*.
Czechoslovak [chekəslō'vak] *a, n* = **Czechoslovakian**.
Czechoslovakia [chekəsləvâk'ēə] *n* Tchécoslovaquie *f*.
Czechoslovakian [chekəsləvâk'ēən] *a* tchécoslovaque ♦ *n* Tchécoslovaque *m/f*.

D

D, d [dē] *n* (*letter*) D, d *m*; (*MUS*): **D** ré *m*; **D for Dog** D comme Désirée.
D [dē] *abbr* (*US POL*) = **democrat(ic)**.
d. *abbr* = **died**.
DA *n abbr* (*US*) = **district attorney**.
dab [dab] *vt* (*eyes, wound*) tamponner; (*paint, cream*) appliquer (par petites touches *or* rapidement); **a** ~ **of paint** un petit coup de peinture.
dabble [dab'əl] *vi:* **to** ~ **in** faire *or* se mêler *or* s'occuper un peu de.
Dacca [dak'ə] *n* Dacca.
dachshund [dâks'ōōnd] *n* teckel *m*.
dad, daddy [dad, dad'ē] *n* papa *m*.
daddy-long-legs [dadēlông'legz] *n* tipule *f*; faucheux *m*.
daffodil [daf'ədil] *n* jonquille *f*.
daft [daft] *a* (*col*) idiot(e), stupide; **to be** ~ **about** être toqué(e) *or* mordu(e) de.
dagger [dag'ûr] *n* poignard *m*; **to be at** ~**s drawn with sb** (*Brit*) être à couteaux tirés avec qn; **to look** ~**s at sb** foudroyer qn du regard.
dahlia [dal'yə] *n* dahlia *m*.

daily [dā'lē] *a* quotidien(ne), journalier(ière) ♦ *n* quotidien *m*; (*Brit: domestic help*) femme *f* de ménage (*à la journée*) ♦ *ad* tous les jours; **twice** ~ deux fois par jour.

dainty [dān'tē] *a* délicat(e), mignon(ne).

dairy [dār'ē] *n* (*store*) crémerie *f*, laiterie *f*; (*on farm*) laiterie ♦ *a* laitier(ière).

dairy cow *n* vache laitière.

dairy farm *n* exploitation *f* pratiquant l'élevage laitier.

dairy produce *n* produits laitiers.

dais [dā'is] *n* estrade *f*.

daisy [dā'zē] *n* pâquerette *f*.

daisy wheel *n* (*on printer*) marguerite *f*.

daisy-wheel printer [dā'zēhwēl prin'tûr] *n* imprimante *f* à marguerite.

Dakar [dákâr'] *n* Dakar.

dale [dāl] *n* vallon *m*.

dally [dal'ē] *vi* musarder, flâner.

dalmatian [dalmā'shən] *n* (*dog*) dalmatien/ne.

dam [dam] *n* barrage *m*; (*reservoir*) réservoir *m*, lac *m* de retenue ♦ *vt* endiguer.

damage [dam'ij] *n* dégâts *mpl*, dommages *mpl*; (*fig*) tort *m* ♦ *vt* endommager, abîmer; (*fig*) faire du tort à; ~ **to property** dégâts matériels.

damages [dam'ijiz] *npl* (*LAW*) dommages-intérêts *mpl*; **to pay $5000 in** ~ payer 5000 dollars de dommages-intérêts.

damaging [dam'ijing] *a*: ~ (**to**) préjudiciable (à), nuisible (à).

Damascus [dəmas'kəs] *n* Damas.

dame [dām] *n* (*title*) *titre porté par une femme décorée de l'ordre de l'Empire Britannique ou d'un ordre de chevalerie; titre porté par la femme ou la veuve d'un chevalier ou baronnet;* (*THEATER*) vieille dame (*rôle comique joué par un homme*).

damn [dam] *vt* condamner; (*curse*) maudire ♦ *n* (*col*): **I don't give a** ~ je m'en fous ♦ *a* (*col*): **this** ~ ... ce sacré *or* foutu ...; ~ (**it)!** zut!

damnable [dam'nəbəl] *a* (*col: behavior*) odieux(euse), détestable; (*: weather*) épouvantable, abominable.

damnation [damnā'shən] *n* (*REL*) damnation *f* ♦ *excl* (*col*) malédiction!, merde!

damning [dam'ing] *a* (*evidence*) accablant(e).

damp [damp] *a* humide ♦ *n* humidité *f* ♦ *vt* (*also:* ~**en:** *cloth, rag*) humecter; (*: enthusiasm etc*) refroidir.

dampcourse [damp'kôrs] *n* (*Brit*) couche isolante (contre l'humidité).

damper [dam'pûr] *n* (*MUS*) étouffoir *m*; (*of fire*) registre *m*; **to put a** ~ **on** (*fig: atmosphere, enthusiasm*) refroidir.

dampness [damp'nis] *n* humidité *f*.

damson [dam'zən] *n* prune *f* de Damas.

dance [dans] *n* danse *f*; (*ball*) bal *m* ♦ *vi* danser; **to** ~ **about** sautiller, gambader.

dance hall *n* salle *f* de bal, dancing *m*.

dancer [dan'sûr] *n* danseur/euse.

dancing [dan'sing] *n* danse *f*.

D and C *n abbr* (*Brit MED*: = *dilation and curettage*) curetage *m*.

dandelion [dan'dəlīən] *n* pissenlit *m*.

dandruff [dan'drəf] *n* pellicules *fpl*.

dandy [dan'dē] *n* dandy *m*, élégant *m* ♦ *a* (*US col*) fantastique, super.

Dane [dān] *n* Danois/e.

danger [dān'jûr] *n* danger *m*; **there is a** ~ **of fire** il y a (un) risque d'incendie; **in** ~ en danger; **he was in** ~ **of falling** il risquait de tomber; **out of** ~ hors de danger.

danger list *n* (*Brit MED*): **on the** ~ dans un état critique.

dangerous [dān'jûrəs] *a* dangereux(euse).

dangerously [dān'jûrəslē] *ad* dangereusement; ~ **ill** très gravement malade, en danger de mort.

danger zone *n* zone dangereuse.

dangle [dang'gəl] *vt* balancer; (*fig*) faire miroiter ♦ *vi* pendre, se balancer.

Danish [dā'nish] *a* danois(e) ♦ *n* (*LING*) danois *m*.

Danish pastry *n* feuilleté *m* (*recouvert d'un glaçage et fourré aux fruits etc*).

dank [dangk] *a* froid(e) et humide.

Danube [dan'yōōb] *n*: **the** ~ le Danube.

dapper [dap'ûr] *a* pimpant(e).

Dardanelles [dârdənelz'] *npl* Dardanelles *fpl*.

dare [dār] *vt*: **to** ~ **sb to do** défier qn *or* mettre qn au défi de faire ♦ *vi*: **to** ~ (**to**) **do sth** oser faire qch; **I** ~**n't tell him** (*Brit*) je n'ose pas le lui dire; **I** ~ **say he'll turn up** il est probable qu'il viendra.

daredevil [dār'devəl] *n* casse-cou *m inv*.

Dar es Salaam [dâr es səlâm'] *n* Dar-es-Salaam, Dar-es-Salam.

daring [dār'ing] *a* hardi(e), audacieux(euse) ♦ *n* audace *f*, hardiesse *f*.

dark [dârk] *a* (*night, room*) obscur(e), sombre; (*color, complexion*) foncé(e), sombre; (*fig*) sombre ♦ *n*: **in the** ~ dans le noir; **in the** ~ **about** (*fig*) ignorant tout de; **after** ~ après la tombée de la nuit; **it is/is getting** ~ il fait nuit/commence à faire nuit.

dark chocolate *n* chocolat *m* à croquer.

darken [dâr'kən] *vt* obscurcir, assombrir ♦ *vi* s'obscurcir, s'assombrir.

dark glasses *npl* lunettes noires.

darkly [dârk'lē] *ad* (*gloomily*) mélancoliquement; (*in a sinister way*) lugubrement.

darkness [dârk'nis] *n* obscurité *f*.

darkroom [dârk'rōōm] *n* chambre noire.

darling [dâr'ling] *a*, *n* chéri(e).

darn [dârn] *vt* repriser.

dart [dârt] *n* fléchette *f* ♦ *vi*: **to** ~ **towards** (*also:* **make a** ~ **towards**) se précipiter *or* s'élancer vers; **to** ~ **away/along** partir/passer comme une flèche.

dartboard [dârt'bôrd] *n* cible *f* (de jeu de fléchettes).

darts [dârts] *n* jeu *m* de fléchettes.

dash [dash] *n* (*sign*) tiret *m*; (*small quantity*) goutte *f*, larme *f* ♦ *vt* (*missile*) jeter *or* lancer violemment; (*hopes*) anéantir ♦ *vi*: **to** ~ **towards** (*also:* **make a** ~ **towards**) se précipiter *or* se ruer vers; **a** ~ **of soda** un peu d'eau gazeuse.

dash away *vi* partir à toute allure.

dashboard [dash'bôrd] *n* (*AUT*) tableau *m* de bord.

dashing [dash'ing] *a* fringant(e).

dastardly [das'tûrdlē] *a* lâche.

data [dā'tə] *npl* données *fpl*.

database [dā'təbās] *n* base *f* de données.

data capture n saisie f de données.
data processing n traitement m (électronique) de l'information.
data transmission n transmission f de données.
date [dāt] n date f; (*appointment*) rendez-vous m; (*fruit*) datte f ♦ vt dater; (*col: girl etc*) sortir avec; **what's the ~ today?** quelle date sommes-nous aujourd'hui?; **~ of birth** date de naissance; **closing ~** date de clôture; **to ~ ad** à ce jour; **out of ~** périmé(e); **up to ~** à la page; mis(e) à jour; moderne; **to bring up to ~** (*correspondence, information*) mettre à jour; (*method*) moderniser; (*person*) mettre au courant; **letter ~d July 5th** lettre (datée) du 5 juillet.
dated [dā'tid] a démodé(e).
dateline [dāt'līn] n ligne f de changement de date.
date stamp n timbre-dateur m.
daub [dôb] vt barbouiller.
daughter [dôt'ûr] n fille f.
daughter-in-law [dô'tûrinlô] n belle-fille f, bru f.
daunt [dônt] vt intimider, décourager.
daunting [dôn'ting] a décourageant(e), intimidant(e).
dauntless [dônt'lis] a intrépide.
dawdle [dôd'əl] vi traîner, lambiner; **to ~ over one's work** traînasser or lambiner sur son travail.
dawn [dôn] n aube f, aurore f ♦ vi (*day*) se lever, poindre; (*fig*) naître, se faire jour; **at ~** à l'aube; **from ~ to dusk** du matin au soir; **it ~ed on him that** ... il lui vint à l'esprit que ....
day [dā] n jour m; (*as duration*) journée f; (*period of time, age*) époque f, temps m; **the ~ before** la veille, le jour précédent; **the ~ after, the following ~** le lendemain, le jour suivant; **the ~ before yesterday** avant-hier; **the ~ after tomorrow** après-demain; (on) **the ~ that** ... le jour où ...; **~ by ~** jour après jour; **by ~** de jour; **paid by the ~** payé(e) à la journée; **these ~s, in the present ~** de nos jours, à l'heure actuelle.
daybreak [dā'brāk] n point m du jour.
day-care center [dā'kär sen'tûr] n garderie f, crèche f.
daydream [dā'drēm] n rêverie f ♦ vi rêver (tout éveillé).
daylight [dā'līt] n (lumière f du) jour m.
Daylight Saving Time n (US) heure f d'été.
day nursery n garderie f, crèche f.
day release n (*Brit*): **to be on ~** avoir une journée de congé pour formation professionnelle.
day return (ticket) n (*Brit*) billet m d'aller-retour (valable pour la journée).
day shift n équipe f de jour.
day student n (*at school*) externe m/f.
daytime [dā'tīm] n jour m, journée f.
day-to-day [dātōōdā'] a (*routine, expenses*) journalier(ière); **on a ~ basis** au jour le jour.
day trip n excursion f (d'une journée).
day-tripper [dā'trip'ûr] n excursionniste m/f.
daze [dāz] vt (*subj: drug*) hébéter; (: *blow*) étourdir ♦ n: **in a ~** hébété(e); étourdi(e).

dazzle [daz'əl] vt éblouir, aveugler.
dazzling [daz'ling] a (*light*) aveuglant(e), éblouissant(e); (*fig*) éblouissant(e).
DC abbr (*ELEC*) = **direct current**; (*US MAIL*) = *District of Columbia*.
DD n abbr (= *Doctor of Divinity*) titre universitaire.
D/D abbr = **demand draft**; = **direct debit**.
D-day [dē'dā] n le jour J.
DDS n abbr (*US*: = *Doctor of Dental Science, Doctor of Dental Surgery*) titres universitaires.
DDT n abbr (= *dichlorodiphenyl trichloroethane*) DDT m.
DE abbr (*US MAIL*) = *Delaware*.
DEA n abbr (*US*: = *Drug Enforcement Administration*) ≈ brigade f des stupéfiants.
deacon [dē'kən] n diacre m.
dead [ded] a mort(e); (*numb*) engourdi(e), insensible; (*battery*) plat(e) ♦ ad absolument, complètement; **the ~** npl les morts; **he was shot ~** il a été tué d'un coup de revolver; **~ on time** à l'heure pile; **~ tired** éreinté(e), complètement fourbu(e); **to stop ~** s'arrêter pile or net; **the line has gone ~** (*TEL*) on n'entend plus rien.
deaden [ded'ən] vt (*blow, sound*) amortir; (*make numb*) endormir, rendre insensible.
dead end n impasse f.
dead-end [ded end'] a: **a ~ job** un emploi or poste sans avenir.
dead heat n (*SPORT*): **to finish in a ~** terminer ex-aequo.
dead-letter office [ded'let'ûr ôf'is] n ~ centre m de recherche du courrier.
deadline [ded'līn] n date f or heure f limite; **to work to a ~** avoir des délais stricts à respecter.
deadlock [ded'läk] n impasse f (*fig*).
dead loss n (*col*): **to be a ~** (*person*) n'être bon(bonne) à rien; (*thing*) ne rien valoir.
deadly [ded'lē] a mortel(le); (*weapon*) meurtrier(ière); **~ dull** ennuyeux(euse) à mourir, mortellement ennuyeux.
deadpan [ded'pan] a impassible; (*humor*) pince-sans-rire inv.
Dead Sea n: **the ~** la mer Morte.
dead season n (*TOURISM*) morte saison.
deaf [def] a sourd(e); **to turn a ~ ear to sth** faire la sourde oreille à qch.
deaf-and-dumb [def'əndum'] a sourd(e)-muet(te); **~ alphabet** alphabet m des sourds-muets.
deafen [def'ən] vt rendre sourd(e); (*fig*) assourdir.
deafening [def'əning] a assourdissant(e).
deaf-mute [def'myōōt'] n sourd/e-muet/te.
deafness [def'nis] n surdité f.
deal [dēl] n affaire f, marché m ♦ vt (*pt, pp dealt* [delt]) (*blow*) porter; (*cards*) donner, distribuer; **to strike a ~ with sb** faire or conclure un marché avec qn; **it's a ~!** (*col*) marché conclu!, tope-là!, tape-là!; **he got a bad ~ from them** ils ont mal agi envers lui; **he got a fair ~ from them** ils ont agi loyalement envers lui; **a good ~** (*a lot*) beaucoup; **a good ~ of, a great ~ of** beaucoup de, énormément de.
deal in vt fus (*COMM*) faire le commerce

de, être dans le commerce de.

deal with *vt fus* (*COMM*) traiter avec; (*handle*) s'occuper *or* se charger de; (*be about: book etc*) traiter de.

dealer [dē'lûr] *n* marchand *m*.

dealership [dē'lûrship] *n* concession *f*.

dealings [dē'lingz] *npl* (*in goods, shares*) opérations *fpl*, transactions *fpl*; (*relations*) relations *fpl*, rapports *mpl*.

dean [dēn] *n* (*US SCOL*) conseiller/ère (principal(e)) d'éducation; (*REL, Brit SCOL*) doyen *m*.

dear [dēr] *a* cher(chère); (*expensive*) cher, coûteux(euse) ♦ *n*: **my ~** mon cher/ma chère; **~ me!** mon Dieu!; **D~ Sir/Madam** (*in letter*) Monsieur/Madame; **D~ Mr/Mrs X** Cher Monsieur/Chère Madame X.

dearly [dēr'lē] *ad* (*love*) tendrement; (*pay*) cher.

dearth [dûrth] *n* disette *f*, pénurie *f*.

death [deth] *n* mort *f*; (*ADMIN*) décès *m*.

deathbed [deth'bed] *n* lit *m* de mort.

death certificate *n* acte *m* de décès.

deathly [deth'lē] *a* de mort ♦ *ad* comme la mort.

death penalty *n* peine *f* de mort.

death rate *n* taux *m* de mortalité.

death sentence *n* condamnation *f* à mort.

deathtrap [deth'trap] *n* endroit (*or* véhicule *etc*) dangereux; (*AUT*) point noir.

debar [dibâr'] *vt*: **to ~ sb from a club** *etc* exclure qn d'un club *etc*; **to ~ sb from doing** interdire à qn de faire.

debase [dibās'] *vt* (*currency*) déprécier, dévaloriser; (*person*) abaisser, avilir.

debatable [dibā'təbəl] *a* discutable, contestable; **it is ~ whether** ... il est douteux que ....

debate [dibāt'] *n* discussion *f*, débat *m* ♦ *vt* discuter, débattre ♦ *vi* (*consider*): **to ~ whether** se demander si.

debauchery [debô'chûrē] *n* débauche *f*.

debenture [diben'chûr] *n* (*COMM*) obligation *f*.

debilitate [dibil'ətāt] *vt* débiliter.

debit [deb'it] *n* débit *m* ♦ *vt*: **to ~ a sum to sb** *or* **to sb's account** porter une somme au débit de qn, débiter qn d'une somme.

debit balance *n* solde débiteur.

debit note *n* note *f* de débit.

debrief [dēbrēf'] *vt* demander un compte rendu de fin de mission à.

debriefing [dēbrēf'ing] *n* compte rendu *m*.

debris [dəbrē'] *n* débris *mpl*, décombres *mpl*.

debt [det] *n* dette *f*; **to be in ~** avoir des dettes, être endetté(e); **bad ~** créance *f* irrécouvrable.

debt collector *n* agent *m* de recouvrements.

debtor [det'ûr] *n* débiteur/trice.

debug [dēbug'] *vt* (*COMPUT*) déverminer.

debunk [dibungk'] *vt* (*theory, claim*) montrer le ridicule de.

debut [dābyōō'] *n* début(s) *m(pl)*.

debutante [debyōōtânt'] *n* débutante *f*.

Dec. *abbr* (= *december*) déc.

decade [dek'ād] *n* décennie *f*, décade *f*.

decadence [dek'ədəns] *n* décadence *f*.

decadent [dek'ədənt] *a* décadent(e).

decaffeinated [dēkaf'ənātid] *a* décaféiné(e).

decamp [dikamp'] *vi* (*col*) décamper, filer.

decant [dikant'] *vt* (*wine*) décanter.

decanter [dikan'tûr] *n* carafe *f*.

decarbonize [dēkâr'bənīz] *vt* (*AUT*) décalaminer.

decay [dikā'] *n* décomposition *f*, pourrissement *m*; (*fig*) déclin *m*, délabrement *m*; (*also*: **tooth ~**) carie *f* (dentaire) ♦ *vi* (*rot*) se décomposer, pourrir; (*fig*) se délabrer; décliner; se détériorer.

decease [disēs'] *n* décès *m*.

deceased [disēst'] *n*: **the ~** le/la défunt/e.

deceit [disēt'] *n* tromperie *f*, supercherie *f*.

deceitful [disēt'fəl] *a* trompeur(euse).

deceive [disēv'] *vt* tromper; **to ~ o.s.** s'abuser.

decelerate [dēsel'ərāt] *vt, vi* ralentir.

December [disem'bûr] *n* décembre *m*; *for phrases see also* **July.**

decency [dē'sənsē] *n* décence *f*.

decent [dē'sənt] *a* décent(e), convenable; **they were very ~ about it** ils se sont montrés très chics.

decently [dē'səntlē] *ad* (*respectably*) décemment, convenablement; (*kindly*) décemment.

decentralization [dēsentrəlizā'shən] *n* décentralisation *f*.

decentralize [dēsen'trəlīz] *vt* décentraliser.

deception [disep'shən] *n* tromperie *f*.

deceptive [disep'tiv] *a* trompeur(euse).

decibel [des'əbəl] *n* décibel *m*.

decide [disīd'] *vt* (*person*) décider; (*question, argument*) trancher, régler ♦ *vi* se décider, décider; **to ~ to do/that** décider de faire/que; **to ~ on** décider, se décider pour; **to ~ on doing** décider de faire; **to ~ against doing** décider de ne pas faire.

decided [disī'did] *a* (*resolute*) résolu(e), décidé(e); (*clear, definite*) net(te), marqué(e).

decidedly [disī'didlē] *ad* résolument; incontestablement, nettement.

deciding [disī'ding] *a* décisif(ive); **~ vote** voix prépondérante (*pour départager*).

deciduous [disij'ōōəs] *a* à feuilles caduques.

decimal [des'əməl] *a* décimal(e) ♦ *n* décimale *f*; **to 3 ~ places** (jusqu')à la troisième décimale.

decimalize [des'əməlīz] *vt* décimaliser.

decimal point *n* ~ virgule *f*.

decimate [des'əmāt] *vt* décimer.

decipher [disī'fûr] *vt* déchiffrer.

decision [disizh'ən] *n* décision *f*; **to make a ~** prendre une décision.

decisive [disī'siv] *a* décisif(ive); (*influence*) décisif, déterminant(e); (*manner, person*) décidé(e), catégorique; (*reply*) ferme, catégorique.

deck [dek] *n* (*NAUT*) pont *m*; (*of bus*): **top ~** impériale *f*; (*of cards*) jeu *m*; **to go up on ~** monter sur le pont; **below ~** dans l'entrepont; **record/cassette ~** platine-disques/-cassettes *f*.

deck chair *n* chaise longue.

deck hand *n* matelot *m*.

declaration [deklərā'shən] *n* déclaration *f*.

declare [diklär'] *vt* déclarer.

declassify [dēklas'əfī] *vt* rendre accessible au public *or* à tous.

decline [diklīn'] *n* (*decay*) déclin *m*; (*lessening*) baisse *f* ♦ *vt* refuser, décliner ♦ *vi* décliner; être en baisse, baisser; ~ **in living standards** baisse du niveau de vie; **to ~ to do sth** refuser (poliment) de faire qch.

declutch [dēkluch'] vi (Brit) débrayer.

decode [dēkōd'] vt décoder.

decoder [dēkō'dûr] n décodeur m.

decompose [dēkəmpōz'] vi se décomposer.

decomposition [dēkámpəzish'ən] n décomposition f.

decompression [dēkəmpresh'ən] n décompression f.

decompression chamber n caisson m de décompression.

decongestant [dēkənjes'tənt] n décongestif m.

decontaminate [dēkəntam'ənāt] vt décontaminer.

decontrol [dēkəntrōl'] vt (Brit: prices etc) libérer.

décor [dākôr'] n décor m.

decorate [dek'ərāt] vt (adorn, give a medal to) décorer; (paint and paper) peindre et tapisser.

decoration [dekərā'shən] n (medal etc, adornment) décoration f.

decorative [dek'ûrətiv] a décoratif(ive).

decorator [dek'ərātûr] n peintre m en bâtiment.

decorum [dikôr'əm] n décorum m, bienséance f.

decoy [de'koi] n piège m; **they used him as a ~ for the enemy** ils se sont servis de lui pour attirer l'ennemi.

decrease n [de'krēs] diminution f ♦ vt, vi [dikrēs'] diminuer; **to be on the ~** diminuer, être en diminution.

decreasing [dikrēs'ing] a en voie de diminution.

decree [dikrē'] n (POL, REL) décret m; (LAW) arrêt m, jugement m ♦ vt: **to ~ (that)** décréter (que), ordonner (que); **~ absolute** jugement définitif (de divorce); **~ nisi** jugement provisoire de divorce.

decrepit [dikrep'it] a (person) décrépit(e); (building) délabré(e).

decry [dikrī'] vt condamner ouvertement, déplorer; (disparage) dénigrer, décrier.

dedicate [ded'ikāt] vt consacrer; (book etc) dédier.

dedicated [ded'ikātid] a (person) dévoué(e); (COMPUT) spécialise(e), dédié(e); **~ word processor** station f de traitement de texte.

dedication [dedikā'shən] n (devotion) dévouement m; (in book) dédicace f.

deduce [didōōs'] vt déduire, conclure.

deduct [didukt'] vt: **to ~ sth (from)** déduire qch (de), retrancher qch (de); (from wage etc) prélever qch (sur), retenir qch (sur).

deduction [diduk'shən] n (deducting) déduction f; (from wage etc) prélèvement m, retenue f; (deducing) déduction, conclusion f.

deed [dēd] n action f, acte m; (LAW) acte notarié, contrat m; **~ of covenant** (acte m de) donation f.

deem [dēm] vt (formal) juger, estimer; **to ~ it wise to do** juger bon de faire.

deep [dēp] a (water, sigh, sorrow, thoughts) profond(e); (voice) grave ♦ ad: **~ in snow** recouvert(e) d'une épaisse couche de neige; **spectators stood 20 ~** il y avait 20 rangs de spectateurs; **knee-~ in water** dans l'eau jusqu'aux genoux; **4 meters ~** de 4 mètres de profondeur; **he took a ~ breath** il inspira profondément, il prit son souffle.

deepen [dē'pən] vt (hole) approfondir ♦ vi s'approfondir; (darkness) s'épaissir.

deep-freeze [dēp'frēz'] n congélateur m ♦ vt surgeler.

deep-fry [dēp'frī'] vt faire frire (dans une friteuse).

deep fryer [dēp' frī'ûr] n friteuse f.

deeply [dēp'lē] ad profondément; (dig) en profondeur; (regret, interest) vivement.

deep-rooted [dēp'rōō'tid] a (prejudice) profondément enraciné(e); (affection) profond(e); (habit) invétéré(e).

deep-sea [dēp'sē'] a: **~ diver** plongeur sous-marin; **~ diving** n plongée sous-marine.

deep-sea fishing n pêche hauturière.

deep-seated [dēp'sē'tid] a (beliefs) profondément enraciné(e).

deep-set [dēp'set] a (eyes) enfoncé(e).

deer [dēr] n (pl inv): **the ~** les cervidés mpl (ZOOL); **(red)** ~ cerf m; **(fallow)** ~ daim m; **(roe)** ~ chevreuil m.

deerskin [dēr'skin] n peau f de daim.

deerstalker [dēr'stôkûr] n (person) chasseur m de cerf; (hat) casquette f à la Sherlock Holmes.

deface [difās'] vt dégrader; barbouiller; rendre illisible.

defamation [defəmā'shən] n diffamation f.

defamatory [difam'ətôrē] a diffamatoire, diffamant(e).

default [difôlt'] vi (LAW) faire défaut; (gen) manquer à ses engagements ♦ n (COMPUT: also: **~ value**) valeur f par défaut; **by ~** (LAW) par défaut, par contumace; (SPORT) par forfait; **to ~ on a debt** ne pas s'acquitter d'une dette.

defaulter [difôlt'ûr] n (on debt) débiteur défaillant.

default option n (COMPUT) option f par défaut.

defeat [difēt'] n défaite f ♦ vt (team, opponents) battre; (fig: plans, efforts) faire échouer.

defeatism [difē'tizəm] n défaitisme m.

defeatist [difē'tist] a, n défaitiste (m/f).

defect n [dē'fekt] défaut m ♦ vi [difekt']: **to ~ to the enemy/the West** passer à l'ennemi/l'Ouest; **physical ~** malformation f, vice m de conformation; **mental ~** anomalie or déficience mentale.

defective [difek'tiv] a défectueux(euse).

defector [difek'tûr] n transfuge m/f.

defence [difens'] n (Brit) = **defense**; **the Ministry of D~** le ministère de la Défense nationale.

defend [difend'] vt défendre; (decision, action, opinion) justifier, défendre.

defendant [difen'dənt] n défendeur/deresse; (in criminal case) accusé/e, prévenu/e.

defender [difen'dûr] n défenseur m.

defending champion [difen'ding cham'pēən] n (SPORT) champion m en titre.

defending counsel [difen'ding koun'səl] n (Brit LAW) avocat m de la défense.

defense [difens'] n (US) défense f; **in ~ of**

pour défendre; **the Department of D**~ le ministère de la Défense nationale.

defense counsel *n* (*US*) avocat *m* de la défense.

defenseless [difens'lis] *a* sans défense.

defensive [difɛn'siv] *a* défensif(ive) ♦ *n* défensive *f*; **on the** ~ sur la défensive.

defer [difûr'] *vt* (*postpone*) différer, ajourner ♦ *vi* (*submit*): **to** ~ **to sb/sth** déférer à qn/qch, s'en remettre à qn/qch.

deference [dɛf'ûrəns] *n* déférence *f*, égards *mpl*; **out of** *or* **in** ~ **to** par déférence *or* égards pour.

defiance [difî'əns] *n* défi *m*; **in** ~ **of** au mépris de.

defiant [difî'ənt] *a* provocant(e), de défi.

defiantly [difî'əntlē] *ad* d'un air (*or* d'un ton) de défi.

deficiency [difish'ənsē] *n* insuffisance *f*, déficience *f*; carence *f*; (*COMM*) déficit *m*, découvert *m*.

deficiency disease *n* maladie *f* de carence.

deficient [difish'ənt] *a* insuffisant(e); défectueux(euse); déficient(e); **to be** ~ **in** manquer de.

deficit [dɛf'isit] *n* déficit *m*.

defile [difīl'] *vt* souiller ♦ *vi* défiler ♦ *n* défilé *m*.

define [difīn'] *vt* définir.

definite [dɛf'ənit] *a* (*fixed*) défini(e), (bien) déterminé(e); (*clear, obvious*) net(te), manifeste; (*LING*) défini(e); **he was** ~ **about it** il a été catégorique; il était sûr de son fait.

definitely [dɛf'ənitlē] *ad* sans aucun doute.

definition [dɛfənish'ən] *n* définition *f*.

definitive [difin'ətiv] *a* définitif(ive).

deflate [diflāt'] *vt* dégonfler; (*pompous person*) rabattre le caquet à; (*ECON*) provoquer la déflation de; (*: prices*) faire tomber *or* baisser.

deflation [diflā'shən] *n* (*ECON*) déflation *f*.

deflationary [diflā'shənârē] *a* (*ECON*) déflationniste.

deflect [diflɛkt'] *vt* détourner, faire dévier.

defog [dēfôg'] *vt* (*US AUT*) désembuer.

defogger [dēfôg'ûr] *n* (*US AUT*) dispositif *m* anti-buée *inv*.

deforestation [dēfôristā'shən] *n* déboisement *m*.

deform [difôrm'] *vt* déformer.

deformed [difôrmd'] *a* difforme.

deformity [difôr'mitē] *n* difformité *f*.

defraud [difrôd'] *vt* frauder; **to** ~ **sb of sth** soutirer qch malhonnêtement à qn; escroquer qch à qn; frustrer qn de qch.

defray [difrā'] *vt*: **to** ~ **sb's expenses** défrayer qn (de ses frais), rembourser *or* payer à qn ses frais.

defrost [difrôst'] *vt* (*fridge*) dégivrer; (*frozen food*) décongeler.

deft [dɛft] *a* adroit(e), preste.

defunct [difungkt'] *a* défunt(e).

defuse [dēfyōōz'] *vt* désamorcer.

defy [difī'] *vt* défier; (*efforts etc*) résister à.

degenerate *vi* [dijen'ûrāt] dégénérer ♦ *a* [dijen'ûrit] dégénéré(e).

degradation [dɛgrədā'shən] *n* dégradation *f*.

degrade [digrād'] *vt* dégrader.

degrading [digrā'ding] *a* dégradant(e).

degree [digrē'] *n* degré *m*; (*SCOL*) diplôme *m* (universitaire); **10** ~**s below (zero)** 10 degrés au-dessous de zéro; **a (first)** ~ **in math** une licence en maths; **a considerable** ~ **of risk** un considérable facteur *or* élément de risque; **by** ~**s** (*gradually*) par degrés; **to some** ~, **to a certain** ~ jusqu'à un certain point, dans une certaine mesure.

dehydrated [dēhī'drātid] *a* déshydraté(e); (*milk, eggs*) en poudre.

dehydration [dēhīdrā'shən] *n* déshydratation *f*.

de-ice [dēīs'] *vt* (*windscreen*) dégivrer.

de-icer [dēī'sûr] *n* dégivreur *m*.

deign [dān] *vi*: **to** ~ **to do** daigner faire.

deity [dē'itē] *n* divinité *f*; dieu *m*, déesse *f*.

dejected [dijek'tid] *a* abattu(e), déprimé(e).

dejection [dijek'shən] *n* abattement *m*, découragement *m*.

Del. *abbr* (*US*) = *Delaware*.

del. *abbr* = **delete**.

delay [dilā'] *vt* (*journey, operation*) retarder, différer; (*travelers, trains*) retarder; (*payment*) différer ♦ *vi* s'attarder ♦ *n* délai *m*, retard *m*; **without** ~ sans délai, sans tarder.

delayed-action [dilād'ak'shən] *a* à retardement.

delectable [dilek'təbəl] *a* délicieux(euse).

delegate *n* [del'əgit] délégué/e ♦ *vt* [del'əgāt] déléguer; **to** ~ **sth to sb/sb to do sth** déléguer qch à qn/qn pour faire qch.

delegation [deləgā'shən] *n* délégation *f*.

delete [dilēt'] *vt* rayer, supprimer; (*COMPUT*) effacer.

Delhi [del'ē] *n* Delhi.

deliberate *a* [dilib'ûrit] (*intentional*) délibéré(e); (*slow*) mesuré(e) ♦ *vi* [dilib'ûrāt] délibérer, réfléchir.

deliberately [dilib'ûritlē] *ad* (*on purpose*) exprès, délibérément.

deliberation [dilibûrā'shən] *n* délibération *f*, réflexion *f*; (*gen pl: discussion*) délibérations, débats *mpl*.

delicacy [del'əkəsē] *n* délicatesse *f*; (*choice food*) mets fin *or* délicat, friandise *f*.

delicate [del'əkit] *a* délicat(e).

delicately [del'əkitlē] *ad* délicatement; (*act, express*) avec délicatesse, avec tact.

delicatessen [delikətes'ən] *n* épicerie fine.

delicious [dilish'əs] *a* délicieux(euse), exquis(e).

delight [dilīt'] *n* (grande) joie, grand plaisir ♦ *vt* enchanter; **a** ~ **to the eyes** un régal *or* plaisir pour les yeux; **to take** ~ **in** prendre grand plaisir à; **to be the** ~ **of** faire les délices *or* la joie de.

delighted [dilī'tid] *a*: ~ **(at** *or* **with sth)** ravi(e) (de qch); **to be** ~ **to do sth/that** être enchanté(e) *or* ravi(e) de faire qch/que; **I'd be** ~ j'en serais enchanté *or* ravi.

delightful [dilīt'fəl] *a* (*person, child*) absolument charmant(e), adorable; (*evening, view*) merveilleux(euse); (*meal*) délicieux(euse).

delimit [dilim'it] *vt* délimiter.

delineate [dilin'ēāt] *vt* tracer, esquisser; (*fig*) dépeindre, décrire.

delinquency [diling'kwənsē] *n* délinquance *f*.

delinquent [diling'kwint] *a, n* délinquant(e).

delirious [dilēr'ēəs] *a* (*MED, fig*) délirant(e); **to be** ~ délirer.

delirium [dilēr'ēəm] *n* délire *m*.

deliver [diliv'ûr] *vt* (*mail*) distribuer; (*goods*) livrer; (*message*) remettre; (*speech*) prononcer; (*warning, ultimatum*) lancer; (*free*) délivrer; (*MED*) accoucher; **to ~ the goods** (*fig*) tenir ses promesses.

deliverance [diliv'ûrəns] *n* délivrance *f*, libération *f*.

delivery [diliv'ûrē] *n* (*of mail*) distribution *f*; (*of goods*) livraison *f*; (*of speaker*) élocution *f*; (*MED*) accouchement *m*; **to take ~ of** prendre livraison de.

delivery slip *n* bon *m* de livraison.

delivery truck, (*Brit*) **delivery van** *n* fourgonnette *f or* camionnette *f* de livraison.

delouse [dēlous'] *vt* épouiller, débarrasser de sa (*or* leur *etc*) vermine.

delta [del'tə] *n* delta *m*.

delude [dilood'] *vt* tromper, leurrer; **to ~ o.s.** se leurrer, se faire des illusions.

deluge [del'yooj] *n* déluge *m* ♦ *vt* (*fig*): **to ~ (with)** inonder (de).

delusion [diloo'zhən] *n* illusion *f*; **to have ~s of grandeur** être un peu mégalomane.

de luxe [dəluks'] *a* de luxe.

delve [delv] *vi*: **to ~ into** fouiller dans.

Dem. *abbr* (*US POL*) = **democrat(ic)**.

demagogue [dem'əgôg] *n* démagogue *m/f*.

demand [dimand'] *vt* réclamer, exiger; (*need*) exiger, requérir ♦ *n* exigence *f*; (*claim*) revendication *f*; (*ECON*) demande *f*; **to ~ sth (from *or* of sb)** exiger qch (de qn), réclamer qch (à qn), **in ~** demandé(e), recherché(e); **on ~** sur demande.

demand draft *n* bon *m* à vue.

demanding [dimand'ing] *a* (*person*) exigeant(e); (*work*) astreignant(e).

demarcation [demârkā'shən] *n* démarcation *f*.

demarcation dispute *n* (*INDUSTRY*) conflit *m* d'attributions.

demean [dimēn'] *vt*: **to ~ o.s.** s'abaisser.

demeanor, (*Brit*) **demeanour** [dimē'nûr] *n* comportement *m*; maintien *m*.

demented [dimen'tid] *a* dément(e), fou(folle).

demilitarized zone [dēmil'itərīzd zōn'] *n* zone démilitarisée.

demise [dimīz'] *n* décès *m*.

demist [dēmist'] *vt* (*Brit AUT*) désembuer.

demister [dimis'tûr] *n* (*Brit AUT*) dispositif *m* anti-buée *inv*.

demo [dem'ō] *n abbr* (*col*: = *demonstration*) manif *f*.

demobilize [dēmō'bəlīz] *vt* démobiliser.

democracy [dimâk'rəsē] *n* démocratie *f*.

democrat [dem'əkrat] *n* (*also*: *POL*: **D~**) démocrate *m/f*.

democratic [deməkrat'ik] *a* démocratique.

demography [dimâg'rəfē] *n* démographie *f*.

demolish [dimâl'ish] *vt* démolir.

demolition [deməlish'ən] *n* démolition *f*.

demon [dē'mən] *n* démon *m* ♦ *cpd*: **a ~ squash player** un crack en squash; **a ~ driver** un fou du volant.

demonstrate [dem'ənstrāt] *vt* démontrer, prouver ♦ *vi*: **to ~ (for/against)** manifester (en faveur de/contre).

demonstration [demənstrā'shən] *n* démonstration *f*; (*POL etc*) manifestation *f*; **to hold a ~** (*POL etc*) organiser une manifestation, ma-

nifester.

demonstrative [dimân'strətiv] *a* démonstratif(ive).

demonstrator [dem'ənstrātûr] *n* (*POL etc*) manifestant/e; (*COMM*: *sales person*) vendeur/euse; (: *car, computer etc*) modèle *m* de démonstration.

demoralize [dimôr'əlīz] *vt* démoraliser.

demote [dimōt'] *vt* rétrograder.

demotion [dimō'shən] *n* rétrogradation *f*.

demur [dimûr'] *vi*: **to ~ (at sth)** hésiter (devant qch); (*object*) élever des objections (contre qch) ♦ *n*: **without ~** sans hésiter; sans faire de difficultés.

demure [dimyoor'] *a* sage, réservé(e); d'une modestie affectée.

demurrage [dimûr'ij] *n* droits *mpl* de magasinage; surestarie *f*.

den [den] *n* tanière *f*, antre *m*.

denationalization [dēnashnəlizā'shən] *n* dénationalisation *f*.

denationalize [dēnash'nəlīz] *vt* dénationaliser.

denial [dinī'əl] *n* (*of accusation*) démenti *m*; (*of rights, guilt, truth*) dénégation *f*.

denier [den'yûr] *n* denier *m*; **15 ~ stockings** bas de 15 deniers.

denigrate [den'əgrāt] *vt* dénigrer.

denim [den'əm] *n* coton émerisé.

denim jacket *n* veste *f* en jean.

denims [den'əmz] *npl* (blue-)jeans *mpl*.

denizen [den'izən] *n* (*inhabitant*) habitant/e; (*foreigner*) étranger/ère.

Denmark [den'mârk] *n* Danemark *m*.

denomination [dinâmənā'shən] *n* (*money*) valeur *f*; (*REL*) confession *f*; culte *m*.

denominator [dinâm'ənātûr] *n* dénominateur *m*.

denote [dinōt'] *vt* dénoter.

denounce [dinouns'] *vt* dénoncer.

dense [dens] *a* dense; (*col*: *stupid*) obtus(e), dur(e) *or* lent(e) à la comprendre.

densely [dens'lē] *ad*: **~ wooded** couvert(e) d'épaisses forêts; **~ populated** à forte densité (de population), très peuplé(e).

density [den'sitē] *n* densité *f*; **single/double ~ disk** (*COMPUT*) disquette *f* (à) simple/double densité.

dent [dent] *n* bosse *f* ♦ *vt* (*also*: **make a ~ in**) cabosser; **to make a ~ in** (*fig*) entamer.

dental [den'təl] *a* dentaire.

dental surgeon *n* (chirurgien/ne) dentiste.

dentifrice [den'təfris] *n* dentifrice *m*.

dentist [den'tist] *n* dentiste *m/f*; **~'s office** *or* (*Brit*) **surgery** cabinet *m* de dentiste.

dentistry [den'tistrē] *n* art *m* dentaire.

denture(s) [den'chûr(z)] *n(pl)* dentier *m*.

denunciation [dinunsēā'shən] *n* dénonciation *f*.

deny [dinī'] *vt* nier; (*refuse*) refuser; (*disown*) renier; **he denies having said it** il nie l'avoir dit.

deodorant [dēō'dûrənt] *n* désodorisant *m*, déodorant *m*.

depart [dipârt'] *vi* partir; **to ~ from** (*leave*) quitter, partir de; (*fig: differ from*) s'écarter de.

department [dipârt'mənt] *n* (*COMM*) rayon *m*; (*SCOL*) section *f*; (*POL*) ministère *m*, département *m*; **that's not my ~** (*fig*) ce n'est pas mon domaine *or* ma compétence, ce n'est pas mon rayon; **D~ of State** (*US*) Département d'Etat.

departmental [dēpârtmen'təl] *a* d'une *or* de la section; d'un *or* du ministère, d'un *or* du département; **~ manager** chef *m* de service; (*in shop*) chef de rayon.

department store *n* grand magasin.

departure [dipâr'chûr] *n* départ *m*; (*fig*): **~ from** écart *m* par rapport à; **a new ~** une nouvelle voie.

departure lounge *n* salle *f* de départ.

depend [dipend'] *vi*: **to ~ (up)on** dépendre de; (*rely on*) compter sur; (*financially*) dépendre (financièrement) de, être à la charge de; **it ~s** cela dépend; **~ing on the result ...** selon le résultat ....

dependable [dipen'dəbəl] *a* sûr(e), digne de confiance.

dependant [dipen'dənt] *n* personne *f* à charge.

dependence [dipen'dəns] *n* dépendance *f*.

dependent [dipen'dənt] *a*: **to be ~ (on)** dépendre (de) ♦ *n* = **dependant**.

depict [dipikt'] *vt* (*in picture*) représenter; (*in words*) (dé)peindre, décrire.

depilatory [dipil'ətôrē] *n* (*also*: **~ cream**) dépilatoire *m*, crème *f* à épiler.

deplane [dēplān'] *vi* (*US*) débarquer.

depleted [diplēt'id] *a* (considérablement) réduit(e) *or* diminué(e).

deplorable [diplôr'əbəl] *a* déplorable, lamentable.

deplore [diplôr'] *vt* déplorer.

deploy [diploi'] *vt* déployer.

depopulate [dipâp'yəlāt] *vt* dépeupler.

depopulation [dipâpyəlā'shən] *n* dépopulation *f*, dépeuplement *m*.

deport [dipôrt'] *vt* déporter, expulser.

deportation [dēpôrtā'shən] *n* déportation *f*, expulsion *f*.

deportation order *n* arrêté *m* d'expulsion.

deportment [dipôrt'mənt] *n* maintien *m*, tenue *f*.

depose [dipōz'] *vt* déposer.

deposit [dipâz'it] *n* (*CHEMISTRY, COMM, GEO*) dépôt *m*; (*of ore, oil*) gisement *m*; (*part payment*) arrhes *fpl*, acompte *m*; (*on bottle etc*) consigne *f*; (*for rented goods etc*) cautionnement *m*, garantie *f* ♦ *vt* déposer; (*valuables*) mettre *or* laisser en dépôt; **to put down a ~ of $50** verser 50 dollars d'arrhes *or* d'acompte; laisser 50 dollars en garantie.

deposit account *n* compte *m* de dépôt.

depositor [dipâz'itûr] *n* déposant/e.

depository [dipâz'itôrē] *n* (*person*) dépositaire *m/f*; (*place*) dépôt *m*.

depot [dē'pō] *n* dépôt *m*.

depraved [diprāvd'] *a* dépravé(e), perverti(e).

depravity [diprav'itē] *n* dépravation *f*.

deprecate [dep'rəkāt] *vt* désapprouver.

deprecating [dep'rəkāting] *a* (*disapproving*) désapprobateur(trice); (*apologetic*): **a ~ smile** un sourire d'excuse.

depreciate [diprē'shēāt] *vt* déprécier ♦ *vi* se déprécier, se dévaloriser.

depreciation [diprēshēā'shən] *n* dépréciation *f*.

depress [dipres'] *vt* déprimer; (*press down*) appuyer sur, abaisser.

depressant [dipres'ənt] *n* (*MED*) dépresseur *m*.

depressed [diprest'] *a* (*person*) déprimé(e), abattu(e); (*area*) en déclin, touché(e) par le sous-emploi; (*COMM: market, trade*) maussade; **to get ~** se démoraliser, se laisser abattre.

depressing [dipres'ing] *a* déprimant(e).

depression [dipresh'ən] *n* (*also ECON*) dépression *f*.

deprivation [deprəvā'shən] *n* privation *f*; (*loss*) perte *f*.

deprive [diprīv'] *vt*: **to ~ sb of** priver qn de; enlever à qn.

deprived [diprīvd'] *a* déshérité(e).

dept. *abbr* (= *department*) dép., dépt.

depth [depth] *n* profondeur *f*; **in the ~s of** au fond de; au cœur de; au plus profond de; **at a ~ of 3 meters** à 3 mètres de profondeur; **to be out of one's ~** (*swimmer*) ne plus avoir pied; (*fig*) être dépassé(e), nager; **to study sth in ~** étudier qch en profondeur.

depth charge *n* grenade sous-marine.

deputation [depyətā'shən] *n* députation *f*, délégation *f*.

deputize [dep'yətīz] *vi*: **to ~ for** assurer l'intérim de.

deputy [dep'yətē] *a*: **~ chairman** vice-président *m*; **~ head** (*SCOL*) directeur/trice adjoint(e), sous-directeur/trice; **~ leader** (*Brit POL*) vice-président/e, secrétaire adjoint/e ♦ *n* (*replacement*) suppléant/e, intérimaire *m/f*; (*second in command*) adjoint/e.

derail [dirāl'] *vt* faire dérailler; **to be ~ed** dérailler.

derailment [dirāl'mənt] *n* déraillement *m*.

deranged [dirānjd'] *a*: **to be (mentally) ~** avoir le cerveau dérangé.

derby (hat) [dûr'be (hat)] *n* (*US*) (chapeau *m*) melon *m*.

Derbys *abbr* (*Brit*) = *Derbyshire*.

deregulate [dēreg'yəlāt] *vt* libérer, dérégler.

deregulation [dēregyəlā'shən] *n* libération *f*, dérèglement *m*.

derelict [där'əlikt] *a* abandonné(e), à l'abandon.

deride [dirīd'] *vt* railler.

derision [dirizh'ən] *n* dérision *f*.

derisive [dirī'siv] *a* moqueur(euse), railleur(euse).

derisory [dirī'sûrē] *a* (*sum*) dérisoire; (*smile, person*) moqueur(euse), railleur(euse).

derivation [därəvā'shən] *n* dérivation *f*.

derivative [diriv'ətiv] *n* dérivé *m* ♦ *a* dérivé(e).

derive [dirīv'] *vt*: **to ~ sth from** tirer qch de; trouver qch dans ♦ *vi*: **to ~ from** provenir de, dériver de.

dermatitis [dûrmətī'tis] *n* dermatite *f*.

dermatology [dûrmətâl'əjē] *n* dermatologie *f*.

derogatory [dirâg'ətôrē] *a* désobligeant(e); péjoratif(ive).

derrick [där'ik] *n* mât *m* de charge; derrick *m*.

derv [dûrv] *n* (*Brit*) gas-oil *m*, diesel *m*.

DES *n abbr* (*Brit*: = *Department of Education and Science*) ministère *de l'éducation nationale et des sciences*.

desalination [dēsalənā'shən] *n* dessalement *m*, dessalage *m*.

descend [disend'] *vt, vi* descendre; **to ~ from**

descendre de, être issu(e) de; **in ~ing order of importance** par ordre d'importance décroissante.

descend on *vt fus* (*subj: enemy, angry person*) tomber *or* sauter sur; (: *misfortune*) s'abattre sur; (: *gloom, silence*) envahir; **visitors ~ed (up)on us** des gens sont arrivés chez nous à l'improviste.

descendant [disen'dənt] *n* descendant/e.

descent [disent'] *n* descente *f*; (*origin*) origine *f*.

describe [diskrīb'] *vt* décrire.

description [diskrip'shən] *n* description *f*; (*sort*) sorte *f*, espèce *f*; **of every ~** de toutes sortes.

descriptive [diskrip'tiv] *a* descriptif(ive).

desecrate [des'əkrāt] *vt* profaner.

desert *n* [dez'ûrt] désert *m* ♦ *vb* [dizûrt'] *vt* déserter, abandonner ♦ *vi* (*MIL*) déserter.

deserter [dizûr'tûr] *n* déserteur *m*.

desertion [dizûr'shən] *n* désertion *f*.

desert island *n* île déserte.

deserts [dizûrts'] *npl:* **to get one's just ~** n'avoir que ce qu'on mérite.

deserve [dizûrv'] *vt* mériter.

deservedly [dizûr'vidlē] *ad* à juste titre, à bon droit.

deserving [dizûr'ving] *a* (*person*) méritant(e); (*action, cause*) méritoire.

desiccated [des'əkātid] *a* séché(e).

design [dizīn'] *n* (*sketch*) plan *m*, dessin *m*; (*layout, shape*) conception *f*, ligne *f*; (*pattern*) dessin *m*, motif(s) *m(pl)*; (*of dress, car*) modèle *m*; (*art*) design *m*, stylisme *m*; (*intention*) dessein *m* ♦ *vt* dessiner; (*plan*) concevoir; **to have ~s on** avoir des visées sur; **well-~ed** *a* bien conçu(e); **industrial ~** esthétique industrielle.

designate *vt* [dez'ignāt] désigner ♦ *a* [dez'ignit] désigné(e).

designation [dezignā'shən] *n* désignation *f*.

designer [dizī'nûr] *n* (*ARCHIT, ART*) dessinateur/trice; (*INDUSTRY*) concepteur *m*, designer *m*; (*FASHION*) modéliste *m/f*.

desirability [dizīrəbil'ətē] *n* avantage *m*; attrait *m*.

desirable [dizī'ûrəbəl] *a* désirable; **it is ~ that** il est souhaitable que.

desire [dizī'ûr] *n* désir *m* ♦ *vt* désirer, vouloir; **to ~ to do sth/that** désirer faire qch/que.

desirous [dizī'ûrəs] *a* ~ **of** désireux(euse) de.

desk [desk] *n* (*in office*) bureau *m*; (*for pupil*) pupitre *m*; (*Brit: in store, restaurant*) caisse *f*; (*in hotel, at airport*) réception *f*.

desktop publishing [desk'tâp pub'lishing] *n* publication assistée par ordinateur, PAO *f*.

desolate [des'əlit] *a* désolé(e).

desolation [desəlā'shən] *n* désolation *f*.

despair [dispär'] *n* désespoir *m* ♦ *vi:* **to ~ of** désespérer de; **to be in ~** être au désespoir.

despatch [dispach'] *n*, *vt* = **dispatch**.

desperate [des'pûrit] *a* désespéré(e); (*fugitive*) prêt(e) à tout; (*measures*) désespéré, extrême; **we are getting ~** nous commençons à désespérer.

desperately [des'pûritlē] *ad* désespérément; (*very*) terriblement, extrêmement; **~ ill** très gravement malade.

desperation [despərā'shən] *n* désespoir *m*; **in**

~ en désespoir de cause.

despicable [des'pikəbəl] *a* méprisable.

despise [dispīz'] *vt* mépriser, dédaigner.

despite [dispīt'] *prep* malgré, en dépit de.

despondent [dispân'dənt] *a* découragé(e), abattu(e).

despot [des'pət] *n* despote *m/f*.

dessert [dizûrt'] *n* dessert *m*.

dessertspoon [dizûrt'spōōn] *n* cuiller *f* à dessert.

destabilize [dēsta'bəlīz] *vt* déstabiliser.

destination [destənā'shən] *n* destination *f*.

destine [des'tin] *vt* destiner.

destined [des'tind] *a:* **to be ~ to do sth** être destiné(e) à faire qch; **~ for New York** à destination de New York.

destiny [des'tənē] *n* destinée *f*, destin *m*.

destitute [des'titōōt] *a* indigent(e), dans le dénuement; **~ of** dépourvu(e) *or* dénué(e) de.

destroy [distroi'] *vt* détruire.

destroyer [distroi'ûr] *n* (*NAUT*) contre-torpilleur *m*.

destruction [distruk'shən] *n* destruction *f*.

destructive [distruk'tiv] *a* destructeur(trice).

desultory [des'əltôrē] *a* (*reading, conversation*) décousu(e); (*contact*) irrégulier(ière).

detach [ditach'] *vt* détacher.

detachable [ditach'əbəl] *a* amovible, détachable.

detached [ditacht'] *a* (*attitude*) détaché(e).

detached house *n* (*Brit*) pavillon *m*, maison(nette) (individuelle).

detachment [ditach'mənt] *n* (*MIL*) détachement *m*; (*fig*) détachement, indifférence *f*.

detail [ditāl'] *n* détail *m*; (*MIL*) détachement *m* ♦ *vt* raconter en détail, énumérer; (*MIL*): **to ~ sb (for)** affecter qn (à), détacher qn (pour); **in ~** en détail; **to go into ~(s)** entrer dans les détails.

detailed [ditāld'] *a* détaillé(e).

detain [ditān'] *vt* retenir; (*in captivity*) détenir; (*in hospital*) hospitaliser.

detainee [dētānē'] *n* détenu/e.

detect [ditekt'] *vt* déceler, percevoir; (*MED, POLICE*) dépister; (*MIL, RADAR, TECH*) détecter.

detection [ditek'shən] *n* découverte *f*; (*MED, POLICE*) dépistage *m*; (*MIL, RADAR, TECH*) détection *f*; **to escape ~** échapper aux recherches, éviter d'être découvert(e); (*mistake*) passer inaperçu(e); **crime ~** le dépistage des criminels.

detective [ditek'tiv] *n* agent *m* de la sûreté, policier *m*; **private ~** détective privé.

detective story *n* roman policier.

detector [ditek'tûr] *n* détecteur *m*.

détente [dātänt'] *n* détente *f*.

detention [diten'chən] *n* détention *f*; (*SCOL*) retenue *f*, consigne *f*.

deter [ditûr'] *vt* dissuader.

detergent [ditûr'jənt] *n* détersif *m*, détergent *m*.

deteriorate [ditē'rēərāt] *vi* se détériorer, se dégrader.

deterioration [ditērēərā'shən] *n* détérioration *f*.

determination [ditûrmənā'shən] *n* détermination *f*.

determine [ditûr'min] *vt* déterminer; **to ~ to**

do résoudre de faire, se déterminer à faire.

determined [ditûr'mind] *a* (*person*) déterminé(e), décidé(e); (*quantity*) déterminé, établi(e); (*effort*) très gros(se).

deterrence [ditûr'əns] *n* dissuasion *f*.

deterrent [ditûr'ənt] *n* effet *m* de dissuasion; force *f* de dissuasion; **to act as a** ~ avoir un effet dissuasif.

detest [ditest'] *vt* détester, avoir horreur de.

detestable [dites'təbəl] *a* détestable, odieux(euse).

detonate [det'ənāt] *vi* exploser ♦ *vt* faire exploser *or* détoner.

detonator [det'ənātûr] *n* détonateur *m*.

detour [dē'tōōr] *n* détour *m*; (*US* AUT: *diversion*) déviation *f*.

detract [ditrakt'] *vt*: **to** ~ **from** (*quality, pleasure*) diminuer; (*reputation*) porter atteinte à.

detractor [ditrak'tûr] *n* détracteur/trice.

detriment [det'rəmənt] *n*: **to the** ~ **of** au détriment de, au préjudice de; **without** ~ **to** sans porter atteinte *or* préjudice à, sans conséquences fâcheuses pour.

detrimental [detrəmen'təl] *a*: ~ **to** préjudiciable *or* nuisible à.

deuce [dōōs] *n* (*TENNIS*) égalité *f*.

devaluation [dēvalyōōā'shən] *n* dévaluation *f*.

devalue [dēval'yōō] *vt* dévaluer.

devastate [dev'əstāt] *vt* dévaster; **he was** ~**d by the news** cette nouvelle lui a porté un coup terrible.

devastating [dev'əstāting] *a* dévastateur(trice).

devastation [devəstā'shən] *n* dévastation *f*.

develop [divel'əp] *vt* (*gen*) développer; (*habit*) contracter; (*resources*) mettre en valeur, exploiter; (*land*) aménager ♦ *vi* se développer; (*situation, disease: evolve*) évoluer; (*facts, symptoms: appear*) se manifester, se produire; **to** ~ **a taste for sth** prendre goût à qch; **to** ~ **into** devenir.

developer [divel'əpûr] *n* (*PHOT*) révélateur *m*; (*of land*) promoteur *m*; (*also:* **property** ~) promoteur immobilier.

developing country [divel'əping kun'trē] *n* pays *m* en voie de développement.

development [divel'əpmənt] *n* développement *m*; (*of affair, case*) rebondissement *m*, fait(s) nouveau(x).

development area *n* zone *f* à urbaniser.

deviate [dē'vēāt] *vi*: **to** ~ **(from)** dévier (de).

deviation [dēvēā'shən] *n* déviation *f*.

device [divīs'] *n* (*scheme*) moyen *m*, expédient *m*; (*apparatus*) engin *m*, dispositif *m*; **explosive** ~ engin explosif.

devil [dev'əl] *n* diable *m*; démon *m*.

devilish [dev'əlish] *a* diabolique.

devil-may-care [dev'əlmākär'] *a* je-m'en-foutiste.

devious [dē'vēəs] *a* (*means*) détourné(e); (*person*) sournois(e), dissimulé(e).

devise [divīz'] *vt* imaginer, concevoir.

devoid [divoid'] *a*: ~ **of** dépourvu(e) de, dénué(e) de.

devolution [devəlōō'shən] *n* (*POL*) décentralisation *f*.

devolve [divälv'] *vi*: **to** ~ **(up)on** retomber sur.

devote [divōt'] *vt*: **to** ~ **sth to** consacrer qch à.

devoted [divōt'id] *a* dévoué(e); **to be** ~ **to** être dévoué(e) *or* très attaché(e) à; (*subj: book etc*) être consacré(e) à.

devotee [devōtē'] *n* (*REL*) adepte *m/f*; (*MUS, SPORT*) fervent/e.

devotion [divō'shən] *n* dévouement *m*, attachement *m*; (*REL*) dévotion *f*, piété *f*.

devour [divou'ûr] *vt* dévorer.

devout [divout'] *a* pieux(euse), dévot(e).

dew [dōō] *n* rosée *f*.

dexterity [dekstär'itē] *n* dextérité *f*, adresse *f*.

dext(e)rous [dek'strəs] *a* adroit(e).

dg *abbr* (= *decigram*) dg.

diabetes [dīəbē'tis] *n* diabète *m*.

diabetic [dīəbet'ik] *n* diabétique *m/f* ♦ *a* (*person*) diabétique; (*chocolate, jam*) pour diabétiques.

diabolical [dīəbâl'ikəl] *a* diabolique; (*col: dreadful*) infernal(e), atroce.

diaeresis [dīär'əsis] *n* tréma *m*.

diagnose [dīəgnōs'] *vt* diagnostiquer.

diagnosis, *pl* **diagnoses** [dīəgnō'sis, -sēz] *n* diagnostic *m*.

diagonal [dīag'ənəl] *a* diagonal(e) ♦ *n* diagonale *f*.

diagram [dī'əgram] *n* diagramme *m*, schéma *m*.

dial [dīl] *n* cadran *m* ♦ *vt* (*number*) faire, composer; **to** ~ **a wrong number** faire un faux numéro; **can I** ~ **New York direct?** puis-je *or* est-ce-que je peux avoir New York par l'automatique?

dial. *abbr* = **dialect**.

dial code, (*Brit*) **dialling code** [dī'ling kōd] *n* indicatif *m* (téléphonique).

dial tone, (*Brit*) **dialling tone** [dī'ling tōn] *n* tonalité *f*.

dialect [dī'əlekt] *n* dialecte *m*.

dialogue [dī'əlóg] *n* dialogue *m*.

dialysis [dīal'isis] *n* dialyse *f*.

diameter [dīam'itûr] *n* diamètre *m*.

diametrically [dīəmet'riklē] *ad*: ~ **opposed (to)** diamétralement opposé(e) (à).

diamond [dī'mənd] *n* diamant *m*; (*shape*) losange *m*; ~**s** *npl* (*CARDS*) carreau *m*.

diamond ring *n* bague *f* de diamant(s).

diaper [dī'pûr] *n* (*US*) couche *f*.

diaphragm [dī'əfram] *n* diaphragme *m*.

diarrhea, (*Brit*) **diarrhoea** [dīərē'ə] *n* diarrhée *f*.

diary [dī'ûrē] *n* (*daily account*) journal *m*; (*book*) agenda *m*; **to keep a** ~ tenir un journal.

diatribe [dī'ətrīb] *n* diatribe *f*.

dice [dīs] *n* (*pl inv*) dé *m* ♦ *vt* (*CULIN*) couper en dés *or* en cubes.

dichotomy [dīkât'əmē] *n* dichotomie *f*.

Dictaphone [dik'təfōn] *n* ® Dictaphone *m* ®.

dictate *vt* [diktāt'] dicter ♦ *vi*: **to** ~ **to** (*person*) imposer sa volonté à, régenter; **I won't be** ~**d to** je n'ai d'ordres à recevoir de personne ♦ *n* [dik'tāt] injonction *f*.

dictation [diktā'shən] *n* dictée *f*; **at** ~ **speed** à une vitesse de dictée.

dictator [dik'tātûr] *n* dictateur *m*.

dictatorship [dik'tātûrship] *n* dictature *f*.

diction [dik'shən] *n* diction *f*, élocution *f*.

dictionary [dik'shənärē] *n* dictionnaire *m*.
did [did] *pt* of **do**.
didactic [dīdak'tik] *a* didactique.
die [dī] *n* (*pl:* **dice**) dé *m*; (*pl:* **dies**) coin *m*; matrice *f*; étampe *f* ♦ *vi:* **to** ~ (**of** *or* **from**) mourir (de); **to be dying** (de); **to be dying for sth** avoir une envie folle de qch; **to be dying to do sth** mourir d'envie de faire qch.
   die away *vi* s'éteindre.
   die down *vi* se calmer, s'apaiser.
   die out *vi* disparaître, s'éteindre.
diehard [dī'hârd] *n* réactionnaire *m/f*, jusqu'au-boutiste *m/f*.
dieresis [dīär'əsis] *n* tréma *m*.
diesel [dē'zəl] *n* diesel *m*.
diesel engine *n* moteur *m* diesel.
diesel fuel, diesel oil *n* carburant *m* diesel.
diet [dī'ət] *n* alimentation *f*; (*restricted food*) régime *m* ♦ *vi* (*also:* **be on a** ~) suivre un régime; **to live on a** ~ se nourrir de.
dietician [dīətish'ən] *n* diététicien/ne.
differ [dif'ûr] *vi:* **to** ~ **from sth** être différent(e) de; différer de; **to** ~ **from sb over sth** ne pas être d'accord avec qn au sujet de qch.
difference [dif'ûrəns] *n* différence *f*; (*quarrel*) différend *m*, désaccord *m*; **it makes no** ~ **to me** cela m'est égal, cela m'est indifférent; **to settle one's** ~**s** résoudre la situation.
different [dif'ûrənt] *a* différent(e).
differential [difəren'chəl] *n* (*AUT, wages*) différentiel *m*.
differentiate [difərən'chēāt] *vt* différencier ♦ *vi* se différencier; **to** ~ **between** faire une différence entre.
differently [dif'ûrəntlē] *ad* différemment.
difficult [dif'əkult] *a* difficile; ~ **to understand** difficile à comprendre.
difficulty [dif'əkultē] *n* difficulté *f*; **to have difficulties with** avoir des ennuis *or* problèmes avec; **to be in** ~ avoir des difficultés, avoir des problèmes.
diffidence [dif'idəns] *n* manque *m* de confiance en soi, manque d'assurance.
diffident [dif'idənt] *a* qui manque de confiance *or* d'assurance, peu sûr(e) de soi.
diffuse *a* [difyōōs'] diffus(e) ♦ *vt* [difyōōz'] diffuser, répandre.
dig [dig] *vt* (*pt, pp* **dug** [dug]) (*hole*) creuser; (*garden*) bêcher ♦ *n* (*prod*) coup *m* de coude; (*fig*) coup de griffe *or* de patte; (*ARCHEOLOGY*) fouille *f*; **to** ~ **into** (*snow, soil*) creuser; **to** ~ **into one's pockets for sth** fouiller dans ses poches pour chercher *or* prendre qch; **to** ~ **one's nails into** enfoncer ses ongles dans.
   dig in (*also:* ~ **o.s. in**: *MIL*) se retrancher; (: *fig*) tenir bon, se braquer; (*col: eat*) attaquer (un repas *or* un plat *etc*) ♦ *vt* (*compost*) bien mélanger à la bêche; (*knife, claw*) enfoncer; **to** ~ **in one's heels** (*fig*) se braquer, se buter.
   dig out *vt* (*survivors, car from snow*) sortir *or* dégager (à coups de pelles *or* pioches).
   dig up *vt* déterrer.
digest *vt* [dijest'] digérer ♦ *n* [dī'jest] sommaire *m*, résumé *m*.
digestible [dijes'təbəl] *a* digestible.
digestion [dijes'chən] *n* digestion *f*.

digestive [dijes'tiv] *a* digestif(ive).
digit [dij'it] *n* chiffre *m* (*de 0 à 9*); (*finger*) doigt *m*.
digital [dij'itəl] *a* digital(e); (*watch*) à affichage numérique *or* digital.
dignified [dig'nəfīd] *a* digne.
dignitary [dig'nitärē] *n* dignitaire *m*.
dignity [dig'nitē] *n* dignité *f*.
digress [digres'] *vi:* **to** ~ **from** s'écarter de, s'éloigner de.
digression [digresh'ən] *n* digression *f*.
digs [digz] *npl* (*Brit col*) piaule *f*, chambre meublée.
dike [dīk] *n* (*embankment*) digue *f*.
dilapidated [dilap'ədātid] *a* délabré(e).
dilate [dīlāt'] *vt* dilater ♦ *vi* se dilater.
dilatory [dil'ətôrē] *a* dilatoire.
dilemma [dilem'ə] *n* dilemme *m*; **to be in a** ~ être pris dans un dilemme.
diligent [dil'ijənt] *a* appliqué(e), assidu(e).
dill [dil] *n* aneth *m*.
dilly-dally [dil'ēdalē] *vi* hésiter, tergiverser; traînasser, lambiner.
dilute [dilōōt'] *vt* diluer ♦ *vi* dilué(e).
dim [dim] *a* (*light, eyesight*) faible; (*memory, outline*) vague, indécis(e); (*stupid*) borné(e), obtus(e) ♦ *vt* (*light*) réduire, baisser; (*US AUT*) mettre en code, baisser; **to take a** ~ **view of sth** voir qch d'un mauvais œil.
dime [dīm] *n* (*US*) = *10 cents*.
dimension [dimen'chən] *n* dimension *f*.
diminish [dimin'ish] *vt, vi* diminuer.
diminished [dimin'isht] *a:* ~ **responsibility** (*LAW*) responsabilité atténuée.
diminutive [dimin'yətiv] *a* minuscule, tout(e) petit(e) ♦ *n* (*LING*) diminutif *m*.
dimly [dim'lē] *ad* faiblement; vaguement.
dimmers [dim'ûrz] *npl* (*US AUT*) phares *mpl* code *inv*; (: *parking lights*) feux *mpl* de position.
dimple [dim'pəl] *n* fossette *f*.
dim-witted [dim'witid] *a* (*col*) stupide, borné(e).
din [din] *n* vacarme *m* ♦ *vt:* **to** ~ **sth into sb** (*col*) enfoncer qch dans la tête *or* la caboche de qn.
dine [dīn] *vi* dîner.
diner [dīn'ûr] *n* (*person*) dîneur/euse; (*RAIL*) = **dining car**; (*US: eating place*) petit restaurant.
dinghy [ding'ē] *n* youyou *m*; (*inflatable*) canot *m* pneumatique; (*also:* **sailing** ~) voilier *m*, dériveur *m*.
dingy [din'jē] *a* miteux(euse), minable.
dining car [dīn'ing kâr] *n* voiture-restaurant *f*, wagon-restaurant *m*.
dining room [dīn'ing rōōm] *n* salle *f* à manger.
dinner [din'ûr] *n* dîner *m*; (*public*) banquet *m*; ~**'s ready!** à table!
dinner jacket *n* smoking *m*.
dinner party *n* dîner *m*.
dinner time *n* heure *f* du dîner.
dinosaur [dī'nəsôr] *n* dinosaure *m*.
dint [dint] *n:* **by** ~ **of (doing) sth** à force de (faire) qch.
diocese [dī'əsēs] *n* diocèse *m*.
dioxide [dīāk'sīd] *n* dioxyde *m*.
dioxin [dīāks'in] *n* dioxine *f*.

dip [dip] *n* déclivité *f*; (*in sea*) baignade *f*, bain *m* ♦ *vt* tremper, plonger; (*Brit AUT: lights*) mettre en code, baisser ♦ *vi* plonger.

diphtheria [dipthē'rēə] *n* diphtérie *f*.

diphthong [dif'thông] *n* diphtongue *f*.

diploma [diplō'mə] *n* diplôme *m*.

diplomacy [diplō'məsē] *n* diplomatie *f*.

diplomat [dip'ləmat] *n* diplomate *m*.

diplomatic [dipləmat'ik] *a* diplomatique; **to break off ~ relations (with)** rompre les relations diplomatiques (avec).

diplomatic corps *n* corps *m* diplomatique.

dipstick [dip'stik] *n* (*AUT*) jauge *f* de niveau d'huile.

dipswitch [dip'swich] *n* (*Brit AUT*) commutateur *m* de code.

dire [dī'ûr] *a* extrême, affreux(euse).

direct [direkt'] *a* direct(e); (*manner, person*) direct, franc(franche) ♦ *vt* diriger, orienter; **can you ~ me to ...?** pouvez-vous m'indiquer le chemin de ...?; **to ~ sb to do sth** ordonner à qn de faire qch.

direct cost *n* (*COMM*) coût *m* variable.

direct current *n* (*ELEC*) courant continu.

direct debit *n* (*BANKING*) prélèvement *m* automatique.

direct dialling [direkt' dī'ling] *n* (*TEL*) automatique *m*.

direct hit *n* (*MIL*) coup *m* au but, touché *m*.

direction [direk'shən] *n* direction *f*; (*THEATER*) mise *f* en scène; (*CINEMA, TV*) réalisation *f*; **~s** *npl* (*instructions: to a place*) indications *fpl*; **~s for use** mode *m* d'emploi; **to ask for ~s** demander sa route *or* son chemin; **sense of ~** sens *m* de l'orientation; **in the ~ of** dans la direction de, vers.

directive [direk'tiv] *n* directive *f*; **a government ~** une directive du gouvernement.

directly [direkt'lē] *ad* (*in straight line*) directement, tout droit; (*at once*) tout de suite, immédiatement.

direct mail *n* vente *f* par publicité directe.

direct mailshot *n* (*Brit*) publicité postale.

directness [direkt'nis] *n* (*of person, speech*) franchise *f*.

director [direk'tûr] *n* directeur *m*; (*board member*) administrateur *m*; (*THEATER*) metteur *m* en scène; (*CINEMA, TV*) réalisateur/trice; **D~ of Public Prosecutions** (*Brit*) ≈ procureur général.

directory [direk'tûrē] *n* annuaire *m*; (*also: street ~*) indicateur *m* de rues; (*also: trade ~*) annuaire du commerce; (*COMPUT*) répertoire *m*.

directory assistance, (*Brit*) **directory enquiries** *n* (*TEL: service*) renseignements *mpl*.

dirt [dûrt] *n* saleté *f*; (*mud*) boue *f*; **to treat sb like ~** traiter qn comme un chien.

dirt-cheap [dûrt'chēp'] *a* (ne) coûtant presque rien.

dirt road *n* chemin non macadamisé *or* non revêtu.

dirty [dûr'tē] *a* sale ♦ *vt* salir; **~ story** histoire cochonne; **~ trick** coup tordu.

disability [disəbil'ətē] *n* invalidité *f*, infirmité *f*.

disability allowance *n* allocation *f* d'invalidité *or* d'infirmité.

disable [disā'bəl] *vt* (*subj: illness, accident*) rendre *or* laisser infirme; (*tank, gun*) mettre

hors d'action.

disabled [disā'bəld] *a* infirme, invalide; (*maimed*) mutilé(e); (*through illness, old age*) impotent(e).

disadvantage [disədvan'tij] *n* désavantage *m*, inconvénient *m*.

disadvantaged [disədvan'tijd] *a* (*person*) désavantagé(e).

disadvantageous [disadvəntā'jəs] *a* désavantageux(euse).

disaffected [disəfek'tid] *a:* **~ (to or towards)** mécontent(e) (de).

disaffection [disəfek'shən] *n* désaffection *f*, mécontentement *m*.

disagree [disəgrē'] *vi* (*differ*) ne pas concorder; (*be against, think otherwise*): **to ~ (with)** ne pas être d'accord (avec); **garlic ~s with me** l'ail ne me convient pas, je ne supporte pas l'ail.

disagreeable [disəgrē'əbəl] *a* désagréable.

disagreement [disəgrē'mənt] *n* désaccord *m*, différend *m*.

disallow [disəlou'] *vt* rejeter, désavouer.

disappear [disəpi'ûr] *vi* disparaître.

disappearance [disəpi'ûrəns] *n* disparition *f*.

disappoint [disəpoint'] *vt* décevoir.

disappointed [disəpoin'tid] *a* déçu(e).

disappointing [disəpoin'ting] *a* décevant(e).

disappointment [disəpoint'mənt] *n* déception *f*.

disapproval [disəprōō'vəl] *n* désapprobation *f*.

disapprove [disəprōōv'] *vi:* **to ~ of** désapprouver.

disapproving [disəprōō'ving] *a* désapprobateur(trice), de désapprobation.

disarm [disârm'] *vt* désarmer.

disarmament [disâr'məmənt] *n* désarmement *m*.

disarming [disârm'ing] *a* (*smile*) désarmant(e).

disarray [disərā'] *n* désordre *m*, confusion *f*; **in ~** (*troops*) en déroute; (*thoughts*) embrouillé(e); (*clothes*) en désordre; **to throw into ~** semer la confusion *or* le désordre dans (*or* parmi).

disaster [dizas'tûr] *n* catastrophe *f*, désastre *m*.

disastrous [dizas'trəs] *a* désastreux(euse).

disband [disband'] *vt* démobiliser; disperser ♦ *vi* se séparer; se disperser.

disbelief [disbilēf'] *n* incrédulité *f*; **in ~** avec incrédulité.

disbelieve [disbilēv'] *vt* (*person*) ne pas croire; (*story*) mettre en doute; **I don't ~ you** je veux bien vous croire.

disc [disk] *n* (*Brit*) disque *m*.

disc. *abbr* (*COMM*) = **discount**.

discard [diskârd'] *vt* (*old things*) se défaire de, mettre au rencart *or* au rebut; (*fig*) écarter, renoncer à.

disc brake [disk brāk] *n* frein *m* à disque.

discern [disûrn'] *vt* discerner, distinguer.

discernible [disûr'nəbəl] *a* discernable, perceptible; (*object*) visible.

discerning [disûr'ning] *a* judicieux(euse), perspicace.

discharge *vt* [dischârj'] (*duties*) s'acquitter de; (*settle: debt*) s'acquitter de, régler; (*waste etc*) déverser; décharger; (*ELEC, MED*) émettre; (*patient*) renvoyer (chez lui); (*employee, soldier*) congédier, licencier; (*defendant*) relaxer, élargir ♦ *n* [dis'chârj] (*ELEC, MED etc*) émission *f*; (*also*: **vaginal ~**) pertes blanches; (*dismissal*) renvoi *m*; licenciement *m*; élargissement *m*; **to ~ one's gun** faire feu; **~d bankrupt** failli/e réhabilité(e).

disciple [disï'pəl] *n* disciple *m*.

disciplinary [dis'əplənärē] *a* disciplinaire; **to take ~ action against sb** prendre des mesures disciplinaires à l'encontre de qn.

discipline [dis'əplin] *n* discipline *f* ♦ *vt* discipliner; (*punish*) punir; **to ~ o.s. to do sth** s'imposer *or* s'astreindre à une discipline pour faire qch.

disc jockey (DJ) *n* disque-jockey *m* (DJ).

disclaim [disklām'] *vt* désavouer, dénier.

disclaimer [disklām'ûr] *n* démenti *m*, dénégation *f*; **to issue a ~** publier un démenti.

disclose [disklōz'] *vt* révéler, divulguer.

disclosure [disklō'zhûr] *n* révélation *f*, divulgation *f*.

disco [dis'kō] *n abbr* = **discothèque**.

discolor [diskul'ûr] (*US*) *vt* décolorer; (*sth white*) jaunir ♦ *vi* se décolorer; jaunir.

discoloration [diskulərā'shən] *n* décoloration *f*; jaunissement *m*.

discolored [diskul'ûrd] *a* décoloré(e); jauni(e).

discolour [diskul'ûr] *etc* (*Brit*) = **discolor** *etc*.

discomfort [diskum'fûrt] *n* malaise *m*, gêne *f*; (*lack of comfort*) manque *m* de confort.

disconcert [diskənsûrt'] *vt* déconcerter, décontenancer.

disconnect [diskənekt'] *vt* détacher; (*ELEC, RADIO*) débrancher; (*gas, water*) couper.

disconnected [diskənekt'id] *a* (*speech, thoughts*) décousu(e), peu cohérent(e).

disconsolate [diskân'səlit] *a* inconsolable.

discontent [diskəntent'] *n* mécontentement *m*.

discontented [diskəntent'id] *a* mécontent(e).

discontinue [diskəntin'yōō] *vt* cesser, interrompre; "**~d**" (*COMM*) "fin de série".

discord [dis'kôrd] *n* discorde *f*, dissension *f*; (*MUS*) dissonance *f*.

discordant [diskôr'dənt] *a* discordant(e), dissonant(e).

discothèque [dis'kōtek] *n* discothèque *f*.

discount *n* [dis'kount] remise *f*, rabais *m* ♦ *vt* [diskount'] (*report etc*) ne pas tenir compte de; **to give sb a ~ on sth** faire une remise *or* un rabais à qn sur qch; **~ for cash** escompte *f* au comptant; **at a ~** avec une remise *or* réduction, au rabais.

discount house *n* (*FINANCE*) banque *f* d'escompte; (*COMM: also*: **discount store**) magasin *m* de discount.

discount rate *n* taux *m* de remise.

discourage [diskûr'ij] *vt* décourager; (*dissuade, deter*) dissuader, décourager.

discouragement [diskûr'ijmənt] *n* (*depression*) découragement *m*; **to act as a ~ to sb** dissuader qn.

discouraging [diskûr'ijing] *a* décourageant(e).

discourteous [diskûr'tēəs] *a* incivil(e), discourtois(e).

discover [diskuv'ûr] *vt* découvrir.

discovery [diskuv'ûrē] *n* découverte *f*.

discredit [diskred'it] *vt* mettre en doute; discréditer ♦ *n* discrédit *m*.

discreet [diskrēt'] *a* discret(ète).

discreetly [diskrēt'lē] *ad* discrètement.

discrepancy [diskrep'ənsē] *n* divergence *f*, contradiction *f*.

discretion [diskresh'ən] *n* discrétion *f*; **use your own ~** à vous de juger.

discretionary [diskresh'ənärē] *a* (*powers*) discrétionnaire.

discriminate [diskrim'ənāt] *vi*: **to ~ between** établir une distinction entre, faire la différence entre; **to ~ against** pratiquer une discrimination contre.

discriminating [diskrim'ənāting] *a* qui a du discernement.

discrimination [diskrimənā'shən] *n* discrimination *f*; (*judgment*) discernement *m*; **racial/sexual ~** discrimination raciale/sexuelle.

discus [dis'kəs] *n* disque *m*.

discuss [diskus'] *vt* discuter de; (*debate*) discuter.

discussion [diskush'ən] *n* discussion *f*; **under ~** en discussion.

disdain [disdān'] *n* dédain *m*.

disease [dizēz'] *n* maladie *f*.

diseased [dizēzd'] *a* malade.

disembark [disembârk'] *vt, vi* débarquer.

disembarkation [disembârkā'shən] *n* débarquement *m*.

disembodied [disembâd'ēd] *a* désincarné(e).

disembowel [disembou'əl] *vt* éviscérer, étriper.

disenchanted [disenchan'tid] *a*: **~ (with)** désenchanté(e) (de), désabusé(e) (de).

disenfranchise [disenfran'chīz] *vt* priver du droit de vote; (*COMM*) retirer la franchise à.

disengage [disengāj'] *vt* dégager; (*TECH*) déclencher; **to ~ the clutch** (*AUT*) débrayer.

disengagement [disengāj'mənt] *n* (*POL*) désengagement *m*.

disentangle [disentang'gəl] *vt* démêler.

disfavor, (*Brit*) **disfavour** [disfā'vûr] *n* défaveur *f*; disgrâce *f*.

disfigure [disfig'yûr] *vt* défigurer.

disgorge [disgôrj'] *vt* déverser.

disgrace [disgrās'] *n* honte *f*; (*disfavor*) disgrâce *f* ♦ *vt* déshonorer, couvrir de honte.

disgraceful [disgrās'fəl] *a* scandaleux(euse), honteux(euse).

disgruntled [disgrun'təld] *a* mécontent(e).

disguise [disgīz'] *n* déguisement *m* ♦ *vt* déguiser; (*voice*) déguiser, contrefaire; (*feelings etc*) masquer, dissimuler; **in ~** déguisé(e); **to ~ o.s. as** se déguiser en; **there's no disguising the fact that ...** on ne peut pas se dissimuler que ....

disgust [disgust'] *n* dégoût *m*, aversion *f* ♦ *vt* dégoûter, écœurer.

disgusting [disgus'ting] *a* dégoûtant(e), révoltant(e).

dish [dish] *n* plat *m*; **to do** *or* **wash the ~es** faire la vaisselle.

dish out *vt* distribuer.

dish up *vt* servir; (*facts, statistics*) sortir, débiter.

dishcloth [dish'klôth] *n* (*for drying*) torchon *m*; (*for washing*) lavette *f*.

dishearten [dis·hâr'tən] *vt* décourager.

disheveled, (*Brit*) **dishevelled** [dishev'əld] *a* ébouriffé(e); décoiffé(e); débraillé(e).

dishonest [disân'ist] *a* malhonnête.

dishonesty [disân'istē] *n* malhonnêteté *f.*

dishonor [disân'ûr] *n* (*US*) déshonneur *m.*

dishonorable [disân'ûrəbəl] *a* déshonorant(e).

dishonour [disân'ûr] *etc* (*Brit*) = **dishonor** *etc.*

dish soap *n* (*US*) produit *m* pour la vaisselle.

dishtowel [dish'touəl] *n* torchon *m* (à vaisselle).

dishwasher [dish'wâshûr] *n* lave-vaisselle *m*; (*person*) plongeur/euse.

dishwashing liquid [dish'wâshing lik'wid] *n* produit *m* pour la vaisselle.

disillusion [disilōō'zhən] *vt* désabuser, désenchanter ♦ *n* désenchantement *m*; **to become ~ed (with)** perdre ses illusions (en ce qui concerne).

disillusionment [disilōō'zhənmənt] *n* désillusionnement *m*, désillusion *f.*

disincentive [disinsen'tiv] *n*: **it's a ~** c'est dé-motivant; **to be a ~ to sb** démotiver qn.

disinclined [disinklīnd'] *a*: **to be ~ to do sth** être peu disposé(e) *or* peu enclin(e) à faire qch.

disinfect [disinfekt'] *vt* désinfecter.

disinfectant [disinfek'tənt] *n* désinfectant *m.*

disinflation [disinflā'shən] *n* désinflation *f.*

disinherit [disinhär'it] *vt* déshériter.

disintegrate [disin'təgrāt] *vi* se désintégrer.

disinterested [disin'tristid] *a* désintéressé(e).

disjointed [disjoint'id] *a* décousu(e), incohérent(e).

disk [disk] *n* disque *m*; (*COMPUT*) disquette *f*; **single-/double-sided ~** disquette une face/ double face.

disk drive *n* lecteur *m* de disquette.

diskette [disket'] *n* (*COMPUT*) disquette *f.*

disk operating system (DOS) *n* système *m* d'exploitation à disques (DOS).

dislike [dislīk'] *n* aversion *f*, antipathie *f* ♦ *vt* ne pas aimer; **to take a ~ to sb/sth** prendre qn/qch en grippe; **I ~ the idea** l'idée me déplaît.

dislocate [dis'lōkāt] *vt* disloquer, déboîter; (*services etc*) désorganiser; **he has ~d his shoulder** il s'est disloqué l'épaule.

dislodge [disläj'] *vt* déplacer, faire bouger; (*enemy*) déloger.

disloyal [disloi'əl] *a* déloyal(e).

dismal [diz'məl] *a* lugubre, maussade.

dismantle [disman'təl] *vt* démonter; (*fort, warship*) démanteler.

dismast [dismast'] *vt* démâter.

dismay [dismā'] *n* consternation *f* ♦ *vt* consterner; **much to my ~** à ma grande consternation, à ma grande inquiétude.

dismiss [dismis'] *vt* congédier, renvoyer; (*idea*) écarter; (*LAW*) rejeter ♦ *vi* (*MIL*) rompre les rangs.

dismissal [dismis'əl] *n* renvoi *m.*

dismount [dismount'] *vi* mettre pied à terre.

disobedience [disəbē'dēəns] *n* désobéissance *f.*

disobedient [disəbē'dēənt] *a* désobéissant(e), indiscipliné(e).

disobey [disəbā'] *vt* désobéir à; (*rule*) transgresser, enfreindre.

disorder [disôr'dûr] *n* désordre *m*; (*rioting*) désordres *mpl*; (*MED*) troubles *mpl.*

disorderly [disôr'dûrlē] *a* (*room*) en désordre; (*behavior, retreat, crowd*) désordonné(e).

disorderly conduct *n* (*LAW*) conduite *f* contraire aux bonnes mœurs.

disorganized [disôr'gənīzd] *a* désorganisé(e).

disorientated [disô'rēintātid] *a* désorienté(e).

disown [disōn'] *vt* renier.

disparaging [dispar'ijing] *a* désobligeant(e); **to be ~ about sb/sth** faire des remarques désobligeantes sur qn/qch.

disparate [dis'pûrit] *a* disparate.

disparity [dispar'itē] *n* disparité *f.*

dispassionate [dispash'ənit] *a* calme, froid(e); impartial(e), objectif(ive).

dispatch [dispach'] *vt* expédier, envoyer; (*deal with: business*) régler, en finir avec ♦ *n* envoi *m*, expédition *f*; (*MIL, PRESS*) dépêche *f.*

dispatch department *n* service *m* des expéditions.

dispatch rider *n* (*MIL*) estafette *f.*

dispel [dispel'] *vt* dissiper, chasser.

dispensary [dispen'sûrē] *n* pharmacie *f*; (*in chemist's*) officine *f.*

dispense [dispens'] *vt* distribuer, administrer; (*medicine*) préparer (et vendre); **to ~ sb from** dispenser qn de.

dispense with *vt fus* se passer de; (*make unnecessary*) rendre superflu(e).

dispenser [dispen'sûr] *n* (*device*) distributeur *m.*

dispensing chemist [dispen'sing kem'ist] *n* (*Brit*) pharmacie *f.*

dispersal [dispûr'səl] *n* dispersion *f*; (*ADMIN*) déconcentration *f.*

disperse [dispûrs'] *vt* disperser; (*knowledge*) disséminer ♦ *vi* se disperser.

dispirited [dispir'itid] *a* découragé(e), déprimé(e).

displace [displās'] *vt* déplacer.

displaced person [displāst' pûr'sən] *n* (*POL*) personne déplacée.

displacement [displās'mənt] *n* déplacement *m.*

display [displā'] *n* (*of goods*) étalage *m*; affichage *m*; (*computer ~: information*) visualisation *f*; (*: device*) visuel *m*; (*of feeling*) manifestation *f*; (*pej*) ostentation *f*; (*show, spectacle*) spectacle *m*; (*military ~*) parade *f* militaire ♦ *vt* montrer; (*goods*) mettre à l'étalage, exposer; (*results, departure times*) afficher; (*pej*) faire étalage de; **on ~** (*exhibits*) exposé(e), exhibé(e); (*goods*) à l'étalage.

display advertising *n* publicité rédactionnelle.

displease [displēz'] *vt* mécontenter, contrarier; **~d with** mécontent(e) de.

displeasure [displezh'ûr] *n* mécontentement *m.*

disposable [dispō'zəbəl] *a* (*pack etc*) jetable; (*income*) disponible; **~ diaper** couche *f* à jeter, couche-culotte *f.*

disposal [dispō'zəl] *n* (*availability, arrangement*) disposition *f*; (*of property etc: by selling*) vente *f*; (*: by giving away*) cession *f*; (*of garbage*) évacuation *f*, destruction *f*; **at one's ~** à sa disposition; **to put sth at sb's**

~ mettre qch à la disposition de qn.

dispose [dispōz'] *vt* disposer.

dispose of *vt fus* (*time, money*) disposer de; (*unwanted goods*) se débarrasser de, se défaire de; (*COMM: stock*) écouler, vendre; (*problem*) expédier.

disposed [dispōzd'] *a*: ~ **to do** disposé(e) à faire.

disposition [dispəzish'ən] *n* disposition *f*; (*temperament*) naturel *m*.

dispossess [dispəzes'] *vt*: **to** ~ **sb (of)** déposséder qn (de).

disproportion [dishprəpôr'shən] *n* disproportion *f*.

disproportionate [disprəpôr'shənit] *a* disproportionné(e).

disprove [disprōōv'] *vt* réfuter.

dispute [dispyōōt'] *n* discussion *f*; (*also:* **industrial** ~) conflit *m* ♦ *vt* contester; (*matter*) discuter; (*victory*) disputer; **to be in** *or* **under** ~ (*matter*) être en discussion; (*territory*) être contesté(e).

disqualification [diskwôləfəkā'shən] *n* disqualification *f*; ~ **(from driving)** (*Brit*) retrait *m* du permis (de conduire).

disqualify [diskwôl'əfī] *vt* (*SPORT*) disqualifier; **to** ~ **sb for sth/from doing** (*status, situation*) rendre qn inapte à qch/à faire; (*authority*) **to** ~ **sb (from driving)** (*Brit*) retirer à qn son permis (de conduire).

disquiet [diskwī'it] *n* inquiétude *f*, trouble *m*.

disquieting [diskwī'iting] *a* inquiétant(e), alarmant(e).

disregard [disrigard'] *vt* ne pas tenir compte de ♦ *n* (*indifference*): ~ **(for)** (*feelings*) indifférence *f* (pour), insensibilité *f* (à); (*danger, money*) mépris *m* (pour).

disrepair [disripär'] *n* mauvais état; **to fall into** ~ (*building*) tomber en ruine; (*street*) se dégrader.

disreputable [disrep'yətəbəl] *a* (*person*) de mauvaise réputation, peu recommandable; (*behavior*) déshonorant(e); (*area*) mal famé(e), louche.

disrepute [disripyōōt'] *n* déshonneur *m*, discrédit *m*; **to bring into** ~ faire tomber dans le discrédit.

disrespectful [disrispekt'fəl] *a* irrespectueux(euse).

disrupt [disrupt'] *vt* (*plans, meeting, lesson*) perturber, déranger.

disruption [disrup'shən] *n* perturbation *f*, dérangement *m*.

disruptive [disrup'tiv] *a* perturbateur(trice).

dissatisfaction [dissatisfak'shən] *n* mécontentement *m*, insatisfaction *f*.

dissatisfied [dissat'isfīd] *a*: ~ **(with)** mécontent(e) *or* insatisfait(e) (de).

dissect [disekt'] *vt* disséquer; (*fig*) disséquer, éplucher.

disseminate [disem'ənāt] *vt* disséminer.

dissent [disent'] *n* dissentiment *m*, différence *f* d'opinion.

dissenter [disen'tûr] *n* (*REL, POL etc*) dissident/e.

dissertation [disûrtā'shən] *n* (*SCOL*) mémoire *m*.

disservice [dissûr'vis] *n*: **to do sb a** ~ rendre

un mauvais service à qn; desservir qn.

dissident [dis'idənt] *a, n* dissident(e).

dissimilar [disim'ilûr] *a*: ~ **(to)** dissemblable (à), différent(e) (de).

dissipate [dis'əpāt] *vt* dissiper; (*energy, efforts*) disperser.

dissipated [dis'əpātid] *a* dissolu(e); débauché(e).

dissociate [disō'shēāt] *vt* dissocier; **to** ~ **o.s. from** se désolidariser de.

dissolute [dis'əlōōt] *a* débauché(e), dissolu(e).

dissolution [disəlōō'shən] *n* dissolution *f*.

dissolve [dizálv'] *vt* dissoudre ♦ *vi* se dissoudre, fondre; (*fig*) disparaître.

dissuade [diswād'] *vt*: **to** ~ **sb (from)** dissuader qn (de).

distaff [dis'taf] *n*: ~ **side** côté maternel.

distance [dis'təns] *n* distance *f*; **what's the** ~ **to Chicago?** à quelle distance se trouve Chicago?; **it's within walking** ~ on peut y aller à pied; **in the** ~ au loin.

distant [dis'tənt] *a* lointain(e), éloigné(e); (*manner*) distant(e), froid(e).

distaste [distāst'] *n* dégoût *m*.

distasteful [distāst'fəl] *a* déplaisant(e), désagréable.

Dist. Atty. *abbr* (*US*) = **district attorney**.

distemper [distem'pûr] *n* (*paint*) détrempe *f*, badigeon *m*; (*of dogs*) maladie *f* de Carré.

distended [distend'id] *a* (*stomach*) dilaté(e).

distil(l) [distil'] *vt* distiller.

distillery [distil'ûrē] *n* distillerie *f*.

distinct [distingkt'] *a* distinct(e); (*preference, progress*) marqué(e); **as** ~ **from** par opposition à, en contraste avec.

distinction [distingk'shən] *n* distinction *f*; (*in exam*) mention *f* très bien; **to draw a** ~ **between** faire une distinction entre; **a writer of** ~ un écrivain réputé.

distinctive [distingk'tiv] *a* distinctif(ive).

distinctly [distingkt'lē] *ad* distinctement; (*specify*) expressément.

distinguish [disting'gwish] *vt* distinguer; **to** ~ **between** (*concepts*) distinguer entre, faire une distinction entre; **to** ~ **o.s.** se distinguer.

distinguished [disting'gwisht] *a* (*eminent, refined*) distingué(e); (*career*) remarquable, brillant(e).

distinguishing [disting'gwishing] *a* (*feature*) distinctif(ive), caractéristique.

distort [distôrt'] *vt* déformer.

distortion [distôr'shən] *n* déformation *f*.

distr. *abbr* = **distribution; distributor**.

distract [distrakt'] *vt* distraire, déranger.

distracted [distrak'tid] *a* (*look etc*) éperdu(e), égaré(e).

distraction [distrak'shən] *n* distraction *f*, dérangement *m*; **to drive sb to** ~ rendre qn fou(folle).

distraught [distrôt'] *a* éperdu(e).

distress [distres'] *n* détresse *f*; (*pain*) douleur *f* ♦ *vt* affliger; **in** ~ (*ship*) en perdition; (*plane*) en détresse.

distressing [distres'ing] *a* douloureux(euse), pénible, affligeant(e).

distress signal *n* signal *m* de détresse.

distribute [distrib'yōōt] *vt* distribuer.

distribution [distrəbyōō'shən] *n* distribution *f*.

distribution cost *n* coût *m* de distribution.

distributor [distrib'yətûr'] *n* (*gen*, *TECH*) distri-buteur *m*; (*COMM*) concessionnaire *m/f*.

district [dis'trıkt] *n* (*of country*) région *f*; (*of town*) quartier *m*; (*ADMIN*) district *m*.

district attorney *n* (*US*) ≈ procureur *m* de la République.

district council *n* (*Brit*) ≈ conseil municipal.

district nurse *n* (*Brit*) infirmière visiteuse.

distrust [distrust'] *n* méfiance *f*, doute *m* ♦ *vt* se méfier de.

distrustful [distrust'fəl] *a* méfiant(e).

disturb [distûrb'] *vt* troubler; (*inconvenience*) déranger; **sorry to ~ you** excusez-moi de vous déranger.

disturbance [distûr'bəns] *n* dérangement *m*; (*political etc*) troubles *mpl*; (*by drunks etc*) tapage *m*; **to cause a ~** troubler l'ordre pu-blic; **~ of the peace** (*LAW*) tapage injurieux *or* nocturne.

disturbed [distûrbd'] *a* agité(e), troublé(e); **to be mentally/emotionally ~** avoir des problè-mes psychologiques/affectifs.

disturbing [distûrb'ing] *a* troublant(e), inquié-tant(e).

disuse [disyōōs'] *n*: **to fall into ~** tomber en désuétude.

disused [disyōōzd'] *a* désaffecté(e).

ditch [dich] *n* fossé *m* ♦ *vt* (*col*) abandonner.

dither [dith'ûr] *vi* hésiter.

ditto [dit'ō] *ad* idem.

divan [divan'] *n* divan *m*.

divan bed *n* divan-lit *m*.

dive [dīv] *n* plongeon *m*; (*of submarine*) plongée *f*; (*AVIAT*) piqué *m*; (*pej*: *café, bar etc*) bouge *m* ♦ *vi* plonger.

diver [dī'vûr] *n* plongeur *m*.

diverge [divûrj'] *vi* diverger.

divergent [divûr'jənt] *a* divergent(e).

diverse [divûrs'] *a* divers(e).

diversification [divûrsəfəkā'shən] *n* diversifica-tion *f*.

diversify [divûr'səfī] *vt* diversifier.

diversion [divûr'zhən] *n* (*distraction*, *MIL*) di-version *f*; (*Brit AUT*) déviation *f*.

diversity [divûr'sitē] *n* diversité *f*, variété *f*.

divert [divûrt'] *vt* (*plane*) dérouter; (*train, river*) détourner; (*amuse*) divertir; (*Brit*: *traffic*) dévier.

divest [divest'] *vt*: **to ~ sb of** dépouiller qn de.

divide [divīd'] *vt* diviser; (*separate*) séparer ♦ *vi* se diviser; **to ~ (between** *or* **among)** ré-partir *or* diviser (entre); **40 ~d by 5** 40 divi-sé par 5.

divide out *vt*: **to ~ out (between** *or* **among)** distribuer *or* répartir (entre).

divided [divīd'id] *a* (*fig*: *country, couple*) dés-uni(e); (*opinions*) partagé(e).

dividend [div'idend] *n* dividende *m*.

dividend cover *n* rapport *m* dividendes-résultat.

dividers [divī'dûrz] *npl* compas *m* à pointes sè-ches; (*between pages*) feuillets *mpl* interca-laires.

divine [divīn'] *a* divin(e) ♦ *vt* (*future*) prédire; (*truth*) deviner, entrevoir; (*water, metal*) dé-tecter la présence de (*par l'intermédiaire de la radiesthésie*).

diving [dī'ving] *n* plongée (sous-marine).

diving board [dī'ving bōrd] *n* plongeoir *m*.

diving suit *n* scaphandre *m*.

divinity [divin'ətē] *n* divinité *f*; (*as study*) théologie *f*.

division [divizh'ən] *n* (*also Brit SOCCER*) divi-sion *f*; (*separation*) séparation *f*; (*Brit POL*) vote *m*; **~ of labor** division du travail.

divisive [divī'siv] *a* qui entraîne la division, qui crée des dissensions.

divorce [divôrs'] *n* divorce *m* ♦ *vt* divorcer d'avec.

divorced [divôrst'] *a* divorcé(e).

divorcee [divôrsē'] *n* divorcé/e.

divulge [divulj'] *vt* divulguer, révéler.

DIY *a*, *n abbr* (*Brit*) = **do-it-yourself**.

dizziness [diz'ēnis] *n* vertige *m*, étourdisse-ment *m*.

dizzy [diz'ē] *a* (*height*) vertigineux(euse); **to make sb ~** donner le vertige à qn; **I feel ~** la tête me tourne, j'ai la tête qui tourne.

DJ *n abbr* = **disc jockey**.

Djakarta [jəkâr'tə] *n* Djakarta.

DJIA *n abbr* (*US STOCK EXCHANGE*) = *Dow-Jones Industrial Average*.

dl *abbr* (= *decilitre*) dl.

DLit(t) *n abbr* (= *Doctor of Literature, Doctor of Letters*) *titre universitaire*.

DLO *n abbr* = **dead-letter office**.

dm *abbr* (= *decimetre*) dm.

DMus *n abbr* (= *Doctor of Music*) *titre uni-versitaire*.

DMZ *n abbr* = **demilitarized zone**.

DNA *n abbr* (= *deoxyribonucleic acid*) ADN *m*.

do [dōō] *abbr* (= *ditto*) d°.

do [dōō] *vt, vi* (*pt* **did** [did], *pp* **done** [dun]) fai-re; (*visit*: *city, museum*) faire, visiter ♦ *n* (*col*: *party*) fête *f*, soirée *f*; (: *formal gath-ering*) réception *f*; **he didn't laugh** il n'a pas ri; **~ you want any?** en voulez-vous?, est-ce que vous en voulez?; **she swims better than I ~** elle nage mieux que moi; **he laughed, didn't he?** il a ri, n'est-ce pas?; **~ they?** ah oui?, vraiment?; **who broke it? - I did** qui l'a cassé? - (c'est) moi; **~ you agree? - I ~** êtes-vous d'accord? - oui; **you speak better than I ~** tu parles mieux que moi; **so does he** lui aussi; **DO come!** je t'en prie, viens, il faut absolument que tu viennes; **I DO wish I could go** j'aimerais tant y aller; **but I DO like it!** mais si, je l'aime!; **to ~ one's nails/ teeth** se faire les ongles/brosser les dents; **to ~ one's hair** se coiffer; **will it ~?** est-ce que ça ira?; **that'll ~!** (*in annoyance*) ça suffit!, c'en est assez!; **to make ~ (with)** se contenter (de); **to ~ without sth** se passer de qch; **what did he ~ with the cat?** qu'a-t-il fait du chat?; **what has that got to ~ with it?** quel rapport y-a-t-il?, qu'est-ce que cela vient faire là-dedans?

do away with *vt fus* supprimer, abolir; (*kill*) supprimer.

do up *vt* remettre à neuf; **to ~ o.s. up** se faire beau(belle).

do with *vt fus*: **I could ~ with a drink** je prendrais bien un verre; **I could ~ with some help** j'aurais bien besoin d'un petit coup de main; **it could ~ with a wash** ça ne lui ferait pas de mal d'être lavé.

DOA *abbr* (= *dead on arrival*) décédé(e) à

l'admission.

d.o.b. *abbr* = **date of birth.**

docile [dâs'əl] *a* docile.

dock [dâk] *n* dock *m*; *(wharf)* quai *m*; *(LAW)* banc *m* des accusés ♦ *vi* se mettre à quai ♦ *vt*: **they ~ed a third of his wages** ils lui ont retenu *or* décompté un tiers de son salaire.

dock dues *npl* droits *mpl* de bassin.

docker [dâk'ûr] *n* docker *m*.

docket [dâk'it] *n* bordereau *m*; *(on parcel etc)* étiquette *f or* fiche *f* *(décrivant le contenu d'un paquet etc)*.

dockyard [dâk'yârd] *n* chantier *m* de construction navale.

doctor [dâk'tûr] *n* médecin *m*, docteur *m*; *(PhD etc)* docteur ♦ *vt (cat)* couper; *(interfere with: food)* altérer; *(: drink)* frelater; *(: text, document)* arranger; **~'s office** *or* *(Brit)* **surgery** cabinet *m* de consultation; **D~ of Philosophy (PhD)** doctorat *m*; titulaire *m/f* d'un doctorat.

doctorate [dâk'tûrit] *n* doctorat *m*.

doctrine [dâk'trin] *n* doctrine *f*.

document *n* [dâk'yəmənt] document *m* ♦ *vt* [dâk'yəment] documenter.

documentary [dâkyəmen'tûrē] *a*, *n* documentaire *(m)*.

documentation [dâkyəməntā'shən] *n* documentation *f*.

DOD *n abbr (US)* = ~~Department of Defense~~.

doddering [dâd'ûring] *a (senile)* gâteux(euse).

Dodecanese (Islands) [dōdekənēs' (ī'ləndz)] *n(pl)* Dodécanèse *m*.

dodge [dâj] *n* truc *m*; combine *f* ♦ *vt* esquiver, éviter ♦ *vi* faire un saut de côté; *(SPORT)* faire une esquive; **to ~ out of the way** s'esquiver; **to ~ through the traffic** se faufiler *or* faire de savantes manœuvres entre les voitures.

dodgems [dâj'əmz] *npl* autos tamponneuses.

DOE *n abbr (US)* = **Department of Energy;** *(Brit)* = **Department of the Environment.**

doe [dō] *n (deer)* biche *f*; *(rabbit)* lapine *f*.

does [duz] *see* **do.**

doesn't [duz'nt] = **does not.**

dog [dôg] *n* chien/ne ♦ *vt (follow closely)* suivre de près, ne pas lâcher d'une semelle; *(fig: memory etc)* poursuivre, harceler; **to go to the ~s** *(nation etc)* aller à vau-l'eau.

dog biscuits *npl* biscuits *mpl* pour chien.

dog collar *n* collier *m* de chien; *(fig)* faux-col *m* d'ecclésiastique.

dog-eared [dôg'ērd] *a* corné(e).

dog food *n* nourriture *f* pour les chiens *or* le chien.

dogged [dôg'id] *a* obstiné(e), opiniâtre.

dogma [dôg'mə] *n* dogme *m*.

dogmatic [dôgmat'ik] *a* dogmatique.

do-gooder [dōōgōōd'ûr] *n (pej)* faiseur/euse de bonnes œuvres.

dogsbody [dôgz'bâdē] *n (Brit)* bonne *f* à tout faire, tâcheron *m*.

dog tag *n (US)* plaque *f* d'identité.

doing [dōō'ing] *n*: **this is your ~** c'est votre travail, c'est vous qui avez fait ça.

doings [dōō'ingz] *npl* activités *fpl*.

do-it-yourself [dōō'ityōōrself'] *n* bricolage *m*.

do-it-yourselfer [dōō'ityōōrself'ûr] *n* bricoleur *m*, euse *f*.

doldrums [dōl'drəmz] *npl*: **to be in the ~** avoir le cafard; être dans le marasme.

dole [dōl] *n (payment)* allocation *f* de chômage; **on the ~** au chômage.

dole out *vt* donner au compte-goutte.

doleful [dōl'fəl] *a* triste, lugubre.

doll [dâl] *n* poupée *f*.

doll up *vt*: **to ~ o.s. up** se faire beau(belle).

dollar [dâl'ûr] *n* dollar *m*.

dollar area *n* zone *f* dollar.

dolphin [dâl'fin] *n* dauphin *m*.

domain [dōmān'] *n (also fig)* domaine *m*.

dome [dōm] *n* dôme *m*.

domestic [dəmes'tik] *a (duty, happiness)* familial(e); *(policy, affairs, flights)* intérieur(e); *(news)* national(e); *(animal)* domestique.

domesticated [dəmes'tikātid] *a* domestiqué(e); *(pej)* d'intérieur; **he's very ~** il participe volontiers aux tâches ménagères; question ménage, il est très organisé.

domesticity [dōmestis'itē] *n* vie *f* de famille.

domestic servant *n* domestique *m/f*.

domicile [dâm'isīl] *n* domicile *m*.

dominant [dâm'ənənt] *a* dominant(e).

dominate [dâm'ənāt] *vt* dominer.

domination [dâmənā'shən] *n* domination *f*.

domineering [dâmənēr'ing] *a* dominateur(trice), autoritaire.

Dominican Republic [dəmin'əkən ripub'lik] *n* République Dominicaine.

dominion [dəmin'yən] *n* domination *f*; territoire *m*; dominion *m*.

domino, **~es** [dâm'ənō] *n* domino *m*; **~es** *n (game)* dominos *mpl*.

don [dân] *n (Brit)* professeur *m* d'université ♦ *vt* revêtir.

donate [dō'nāt] *vt* faire don de, donner.

donation [dōnā'shən] *n* donation *f*, don *m*.

done [dun] *pp of* **do.**

donkey [dâng'kē] *n* âne *m*.

donkey-work [dâng'kēwûrk] *n (Brit col)* le gros du travail, le plus dur (du travail).

donor [dō'nûr] *n (of blood etc)* donneur/euse; *(to charity)* donateur/trice.

don't [dōnt] = **do not.**

donut [dō'nut] *n (US)* = **doughnut.**

doodle [dōōd'əl] *n* griffonnage *m*, gribouillage *m* ♦ *vi* griffonner, gribouiller.

doom [dōōm] *n (fate)* destin *m*; *(ruin)* ruine *f* ♦ *vt*: **to be ~ed (to failure)** être voué(e) à l'échec.

doomsday [dōōmz'dā] *n* le Jugement dernier.

door [dôr] *n* porte *f*; *(of vehicle)* portière *f*, porte; **to go from ~ to ~** aller de porte en porte.

doorbell [dôr'bel] *n* sonnette *f*.

door handle *n* poignée *f* de porte.

doorman [dôr'man] *n (in hotel)* portier *m*; *(in block of flats)* concierge *m*.

doormat [dôr'mat] *n* paillasson *m*.

doorpost [dôr'pōst] *n* montant *m* de porte.

doorstep [dôr'step] *n* pas *m* de (la) porte, seuil *m*.

door-to-door [dôr'tədôr'] *a*: **~ selling** vente *f* à domicile.

doorway [dôr'wā] *n (embrasure *f* de) porte *f*.

dope [dōp] *n (col)* drogue *f*; *(: information)* tuyaux *mpl*, rancards *mpl*; *(: fool)* andouille

f ♦ vt (horse etc) doper.
dopey [dō'pē] *a (col)* à moitié endormi(e).
dormant [dôr'mənt] *a* assoupi(e), en veilleuse; *(rule, law)* inappliqué(e).
dormer [dôr'mûr] *n (also:* ~ **window)** lucarne *f.*
dormice [dôr'mīs] *npl of* **dormouse.**
dormitory [dôr'mitôrē] *n* dortoir *m; (US: for students)* foyer *m* d'étudiants.
dormouse, *pl* **dormice** [dôr'mous, -mīs] *n* loir *m.*
Dors *abbr (Brit)* = Dorset.
DOS [dŏs] *n abbr* = **disk operating system.**
dosage [dō'sij] *n* dose *f;* dosage *m; (on label)* posologie *f.*
dose [dŏs] *n* dose *f; (Brit: bout)* attaque *f ♦ vt:* to ~ o.s. se bourrer de médicaments; **a** ~ **of flu** une belle *or* bonne grippe.
doss house [dâs' hous] *n (Brit)* asile *m* de nuit.
dossier [dâs'ēā] *n* dossier *m.*
DOT *n abbr (US)* = **Department of Transportation.**
dot [dât] *n* point *m ♦ vt:* ~**ted with** parsemé(e) de; **on the** ~ à l'heure tapante.
dot command *n (COMPUT)* commande précédée d'un point.
dote [dōt]: **to** ~ **on** *vt fus* être fou(folle) de.
dot-matrix printer [dâtmāt'riks prin'tûr] *n* imprimante matricielle.
dotted line [dât'id līn'] *n* ligne pointillée; *(AUT)* ligne discontinue; **to sign on the** ~ signer à l'endroit indiqué *or* sur la ligne pointillée; *(fig)* donner son consentement.
dotty [dât'ē] *a (col)* loufoque, farfelu(e).
double [dub'əl] *a* double ♦ *ad (fold)* en deux; *(twice):* **to cost** ~ **(sth)** coûter le double (de qch) *or* deux fois plus (que qch) ♦ *n* double *m; (CINEMA)* doublure *f ♦ vt* doubler; *(fold)* plier en deux ♦ *vi* doubler; *(have two uses):* **to** ~ **as** servir aussi de; **it's spelled with a** ~ **"l"** ça s'écrit avec deux "l"; **on the** ~ au pas de course.
    double back *vi (person)* revenir sur ses pas.
    double up *vi (bend over)* se courber, se plier; *(share room)* partager la chambre.
double bass *n* contrebasse *f.*
double bed *n* grand lit.
double bend *n (Brit)* virage *m* en S.
double-breasted [dub'əlbres'tid] *a* croisé(e).
double-check [dub'əlchek'] *vt, vi* revérifier.
double-clutch [dub'əlkluch'] *vi (US)* faire un double débrayage.
double cream *n (Brit)* crème fraîche épaisse.
doublecross [dub'əlkrôs'] *vt* doubler, trahir.
doubledecker [dubəldek'ûr] *n* autobus *m* à impériale.
double-declutch [dub'əldēkluch'] *vi (Brit)* faire un double débrayage.
double exposure *n (PHOT)* surimpression *f.*
double glazing [dub'əl glāz'ing] *n (Brit)* double vitrage *m.*
double-page [dub'əlpāj] *a:* ~ **spread** publicité *f* en double page.
double parking *n* stationnement *m* en double file.
double room *n* chambre *f* pour deux.

doubles [dub'əlz] *n (TENNIS)* double *m.*
doubly [dub'lē] *ad* doublement, deux fois plus.
doubt [dout] *n* doute *m ♦ vt* douter de; **without (a)** ~ sans aucun doute; **beyond** ~ *ad* indubitablement ♦ *a* indubitable; **to** ~ **that** douter que; **I** ~ **it very much** j'en doute fort.
doubtful [dout'fəl] *a* douteux(euse); *(person)* incertain(e); **to be** ~ **about sth** avoir des doutes sur qch, ne pas être convaincu de qch; **I'm a bit** ~ je n'en suis pas certain *or* sûr.
doubtless [dout'lis] *ad* sans doute, sûrement.
dough [dō] *n* pâte *f; (col: money)* fric *m,* pognon *m.*
doughnut [dō'nut] *n* beignet *m.*
dour [dōōr] *a* austère.
douse [dous] *vt (with water)* tremper, inonder; *(flames)* éteindre.
dove [duv] *n* colombe *f.*
Dover [dō'vûr] *n* Douvres *f.*
dovetail [duv'tāl] *n:* ~ **joint** assemblage *m* à queue d'aronde ♦ *vi (fig)* concorder.
dowager [dou'əjûr] *n* douairière *f.*
dowdy [dou'dē] *a* démodé(e); mal fagoté(e).
Dow-Jones average [dou'jōnz' av'ûrij] *n (US)* indice boursier Dow-Jones.
down [doun] *n (fluff)* duvet *m; (hill)* colline (dénudée) ♦ *ad* en bas ♦ *prep* en bas de ♦ *vt (enemy)* abattre; *(col: drink)* siffler; ~ **there** là-bas (en bas), là au fond; ~ **here** ici en bas; **the price of meat is** ~ le prix de la viande a baissé; **I've got it** ~ **in my diary** c'est inscrit dans mon agenda; **to pay $2** ~ verser 2 dollars d'arrhes *or* en acompte; **England is two goals** ~ l'Angleterre a deux buts de retard; **to** ~ **tools** *(Brit)* cesser le travail; ~ **with X!** à bas X!
down-and-out [doun'ənout] *n (tramp)* clochard(e).
down-at-heel(s) [dounat·hēl(z)'] *a (fig)* miteux(euse).
downbeat [doun'bēt] *n (MUS)* temps frappé ♦ *a* sombre, négatif(ive).
downcast [doun'kast] *a* démoralisé(e).
downer [dou'nûr] *n (col: drug)* tranquillisant *m;* **to be on a** ~ *(depressed)* flipper.
downfall [doun'fôl] *n* chute *f;* ruine *f.*
downgrade [doun'grād] *vt* déclasser.
downhearted [doun'hâr'tid] *a* découragé(e).
downhill [doun'hil'] *ad (face, look)* en aval, vers l'aval; *(roll, go)* vers le bas, en bas ♦ *n (SKI: also:* ~ **race)** descente *f;* **to go** ~ descendre; *(business)* péricliter, aller à vau-l'eau.
Downing Street [dou'ning strēt] *n (Brit):* **10** ~ résidence du Premier ministre.
download [doun'lōd] *vt* télécharger.
down-market [dounmâr'kit] *a (Brit: product)* bas de gamme *inv.*
down payment *n* acompte *m.*
downplay [doun'plā] *vt (US)* minimiser (l'importance de).
downpour [doun'pôr] *n* pluie torrentielle, déluge *m.*
downright [doun'rit] *a* franc(franche); *(refusal)* catégorique.
Down's syndrome [dounz' sin'drōm] *n (MED)* trisomie *f,* mongolisme *m.*
downstairs [doun'stärz'] *ad (on or to ground*

floor) au rez-de-chaussée; (*on or to floor below*) à l'étage inférieur; **to come ~, to go ~** descendre (l'escalier).
downstream [doun'strēm'] *ad* en aval.
downtime [doun'tīm] *n* (*of machine etc*) temps mort; (*of person*) temps d'arrêt.
down-to-earth [dountōōûrth'] *a* terre à terre *inv*.
downtown [doun'toun'] *ad* en ville ♦ *a* (*US*): ~ **Chicago** le centre commerçant de Chicago.
downtrodden [doun'trâdən] *a* opprimé(e).
down under *ad* en Australie (*or* Nouvelle Zélande).
downward [doun'wûrd] *a* vers le bas; **a ~ trend** une tendance à la baisse, une diminution progressive.
downward(s) [doun'wûrd(z)] *ad* vers le bas.
dowry [dou'rē] *n* dot *f*.
doz. *abbr* (= *dozen*) douz.
doze [dōz] *vi* sommeiller.
doze off *vi* s'assoupir.
dozen [duz'ən] *n* douzaine *f*; **a ~ books** une douzaine de livres; **80¢ a ~** 80¢ la douzaine; **~s of times** des centaines de fois.
DPh, DPhil *n abbr* (= *Doctor of Philosophy*) *litre universitaire*.
DPP *n abbr* (*Brit*) = **Director of Public Prosecutions.**
DPT *n abbr* (*MED*: = *diphtheria, pertussis, letanus*) DCT *m*.
DPW *n abbr* (*US*) = *Department of Public Works.*
Dr, Dr. *abbr* (= *doctor*) Dr.
Dr. *abbr* (*in street names*) = **drive.**
dr *abbr* (*COMM*) = **debtor.**
drab [drab] *a* terne, morne.
draft [draft] *n* brouillon *m*; (*of contract, document*) version *f* préliminaire; (*COMM*) traite *f*; (*US: MIL*) contingent *m*; (*: call-up*) conscription *f*; (*: of air*) courant *m* d'air; (*: of chimney*) tirage *m*; (*: NAUT*) tirant *m* d'eau ♦ *vt* faire le brouillon de; (*document, report*) rédiger une version préliminaire de; **on ~** (*beer*) à la pression.
draftee [draftē'] *n* (*US MIL*) appelé *m*.
draftsman [drafts'mən] *n* (*US*) dessinateur/trice (industriel(le)).
draftsmanship [drafts'mənship] *n* (*US: technique*) dessin industriel; (*: art*) graphisme *m*.
drag [drag] *vt* traîner; (*river*) draguer ♦ *vi* traîner ♦ *n* (*AVIAT, NAUT*) résistance *f*, (*col: person*) raseur/euse; (*: task etc*) corvée *f*; (*women's clothing*): **in ~** (en) travesti.
drag away *vt*: **to ~ away (from)** arracher *or* emmener de force (de).
drag on *vi* s'éterniser.
dragnet [drag'net] *n* drège *f*; (*fig*) piège *m*, filets *mpl*.
dragon [drag'ən] *n* dragon *m*.
dragonfly [drag'ənflī] *n* libellule *f*.
dragoon [drəgōōn'] *n* (*cavalryman*) dragon *m* ♦ *vt*: **to ~ sb into doing sth** (*Brit*) forcer qn à faire qch.
drain [drān] *n* égout *m*; (*on resources*) saignée *f* ♦ *vt* (*land, marshes*) drainer, assécher; (*vegetables*) égoutter; (*reservoir etc*) vider ♦ *vi* (*water*) s'écouler; **to feel ~ed (of energy** *or* **emotion)** être miné(e).
drainage [drā'nij] *n* système *m* d'égouts.

drainboard [drān'bôrd], (*Brit*) **draining board** [drā'ning bôrd] *n* égouttoir *m*.
drainpipe [drān'pīp] *n* tuyau *m* d'écoulement.
drake [drāk] *n* canard *m* (mâle).
dram [dram] *n* petit verre.
drama [drâm'ə] *n* (*art*) théâtre *m*, art *m* dramatique; (*play*) pièce *f*; (*event*) drame *m*.
dramatic [drəmat'ik] *a* (*THEATER*) dramatique; (*impressive*) spectaculaire.
dramatically [drəmat'iklē] *ad* de façon spectaculaire.
dramatist [dram'ətist] *n* auteur *m* dramatique.
dramatize [dram'ətīz] *vt* (*events etc*) dramatiser; (*adapt*) adapter pour la télévision (*or* pour l'écran).
drank [drangk] *pt of* **drink.**
drape [drāp] *vt* draper.
drapes [drāps] *npl* (*US*) rideaux *mpl*.
drastic [dras'tik] *a* (*measures*) d'urgence, énergique; (*change*) radical(e).
drastically [dras'tiklē] *ad* radicalement.
draught [draft] *n* (*Brit*) courant *m* d'air; (*of chimney*) tirage *m*; (*NAUT*) tirant *m* d'eau; **on ~** (*beer*) à la pression.
draughtboard [draft'bôrd] *n* (*Brit*) damier *m*.
draughts [drafts] *n* (*Brit*) (jeu *m* de) dames *fpl*.
draughtsman [drafts'mən] *etc* (*Brit*) = **draftsman** *etc*.
draw [drô] *vb* (*pt* **drew**, *pp* **drawn** [drōō, drôn]) *vt* tirer; (*attract*) attirer; (*picture*) dessiner; (*line, circle*) tracer; (*money*) retirer; (*comparison, distinction*): **to ~ (between)** faire (entre) ♦ *vi* (*SPORT*) faire match nul ♦ *n* match nul; (*lottery*) loterie *f*; (*: picking of ticket*) tirage *m* au sort; **to ~ to a close** toucher à *or* tirer à sa fin; **to ~ near** *vi* s'approcher; approcher.
draw back *vi* (*move back*): **to ~ back (from)** reculer (de).
draw in *vi* (*Brit: car*) s'arrêter le long du trottoir; (*: train*) entrer en gare *or* dans la station.
draw on *vt* (*resources*) faire appel à; (*imagination, person*) avoir recours à, faire appel à.
draw out *vi* (*lengthen*) s'allonger ♦ *vt* (*money*) retirer.
draw up *vi* (*stop*) s'arrêter ♦ *vt* (*document*) établir, dresser; (*plans*) formuler, dessiner.
drawback [drô'bak] *n* inconvénient *m*, désavantage *m*.
drawbridge [drô'brij] *n* pont-levis *m*.
drawee [drôē'] *n* tiré *m*.
drawer [drôr] *n* tiroir *m*; [drô'ûr] (*of check*) tireur *m*.
drawing [drô'ing] *n* dessin *m*.
drawing board *n* planche *f* à dessin.
drawing pin *n* (*Brit*) punaise *f*.
drawing room *n* salon *m*.
drawl [drôl] *n* accent traînant.
drawn [drôn] *pp of* **draw** ♦ *a* (*haggard*) tiré(e), crispé(e).
drawstring [drô'string] *n* cordon *m*.
dread [dred] *n* épouvante *f*, effroi *m* ♦ *vt* redouter, appréhender.
dreadful [dred'fəl] *a* épouvantable, affreux(euse).
dream [drēm] *n* rêve *m* ♦ *vt, vi* (*pt, pp*

dreamed or **dreamt** [dremt]) rêver; **to have a ~ about sb/sth** rêver à qn/qch; **sweet ~s!** faites de beaux rêves!
dream up vt inventer.
dreamer [drē'mûr] n rêveur/euse.
dream world n monde m imaginaire.
dreamy [drē'mē] a (absent-minded) rêveur(euse).
dreary [drēr'ē] a triste; monotone.
dredge [drej] vt draguer.
dredge up vt draguer; (fig: unpleasant facts) (faire) ressortir.
dredger [drej'ûr] n (ship) dragueur m; (machine) drague f; (for sugar) saupoudreuse f.
dregs [dregz] npl lie f.
drench [drench] vt tremper; **~ed to the skin** trempé(e) jusqu'aux os.
dress [dres] n robe f; (clothing) habillement m, tenue f ♦ vt habiller; (wound) panser; (food) préparer ♦ vi: **she ~es very well** elle s'habille très bien; **to ~ o.s.**, **to get ~ed** s'habiller; **to ~ a shop window** faire l'étalage or la vitrine.
dress up vi s'habiller; (in fancy dress) se déguiser.
dress circle n (Brit) premier balcon.
dress designer n modéliste m/f, dessinateur/trice de mode.
dresser [dres'ûr] n (THEATER) habilleur/euse; (also: **window ~**) étalagiste m/f; (furniture) vaisselier m.
dressing [dres'ing] n (MED) pansement m; (CULIN) sauce f, assaisonnement m.
dressing gown n (Brit) robe f de chambre.
dressing room n (THEATER) loge f; (SPORT) vestiaire m.
dressing table n coiffeuse f.
dressmaker [dres'mākûr] n couturière f.
dressmaking [dres'māking] n couture f; travaux mpl de couture.
dress rehearsal n (répétition f) générale.
dress shirt n chemise f à plastron.
dressy [dres'ē] a (col: clothes) (qui fait) habillé(e).
drew [drōō] pt of **draw**.
dribble [drib'əl] vi tomber goutte à goutte; (baby) baver ♦ vt (ball) dribbler.
dried [drīd] a (fruit, beans) sec(sèche); (eggs, milk) en poudre.
drier [drī'ûr] n = **dryer**.
drift [drift] n (of current etc) force f; direction f; (of sand etc) amoncellement m; (of snow) rafale f; coulée f; (: on ground) congère f; (general meaning) sens général ♦ vi (boat) aller à la dérive, dériver; (sand, snow) s'amonceler, s'entasser; **to let things ~** laisser les choses aller à la dérive; **to ~ apart** (friends, lovers) s'éloigner l'un de l'autre; **I get** or **catch your ~** je vois en gros ce que vous voulez dire.
drifter [drif'tûr] n personne f sans but dans la vie.
driftwood [drift'wood] n bois flotté.
drill [dril] n perceuse f; (bit) foret m; (of dentist) roulette f, fraise f; (MIL) exercice m ♦ vt percer; (soldiers) faire faire l'exercice à; (pupils: in grammar) faire faire des exercices à ♦ vi (for oil) faire un or des forage(s).

drilling [dril'ing] n (for oil) forage m.
drilling rig n (on land) tour f (de forage), derrick m; (at sea) plate-forme f de forage.
drily [drī'lē] ad = **dryly**.
drink [dringk] n boisson f ♦ vt, vi (pt **drank**, pp **drunk** [drangk, drungk]) boire; **to have a ~ of water** boire quelque chose, boire un verre; **a ~ of water** un verre d'eau; **would you like something to ~?** aimeriez-vous boire quelque chose?; **we had ~s before lunch** on a pris l'apéritif.
drink in vt (fresh air) inspirer profondément; (story) avaler, ne pas perdre une miette de; (sight) se remplir la vue de.
drinkable [dring'kəbəl] a (not dangerous) potable; (palatable) buvable.
drinker [dring'kûr] n buveur/euse.
drinking [dring'king] n (drunkenness) boisson f, alcoolisme m.
drinking fountain n (in park etc) fontaine publique; (in building) jet m d'eau potable.
drinking water n eau f potable.
drip [drip] n goutte f; (sound: of water etc) bruit m de l'eau qui tombe goutte à goutte; (Brit MED) goutte-à-goutte m inv, perfusion f; (col: person) lavette f, nouille f ♦ vi tomber goutte à goutte; (washing) s'égoutter; (wall) suinter.
drip-dry [drip'drī] a (shirt) sans repassage.
drip-feed [drip'fēd] vt (Brit) alimenter au goutte-à-goutte or par perfusion.
dripping [drip'ing] n graisse f de rôti ♦ a: **~ wet** trempé(e).
drive [drīv] n promenade f or trajet m en voiture; (also: **~way**) allée f; (energy) dynamisme m, énergie f; (PSYCH) besoin m; pulsion f; (push) effort (concerté); campagne f; (SPORT) drive m; (TECH) entraînement m; traction f; transmission f ♦ vb (pt **drove**, pp **driven** [drōv, driv'ən]) vt conduire; (nail) enfoncer; (push) chasser, pousser; (TECH: motor) actionner; entraîner; (COMPUT: also: **disk ~**) lecteur m de disquette ♦ vi (be at the wheel) conduire; (travel by car) aller en voiture; **to go for a ~** aller faire une promenade en voiture; **it's 3 hours' ~ from Philadelphia** Philadelphie est à 3 heures de route; **left-/right-hand ~** (AUT) conduite f à gauche/droite; **front-/rear-wheel ~** (AUT) traction f avant/arrière; **to ~ sb to (do) sth** pousser or conduire qn à (faire) qch; **to ~ sb mad** rendre qn fou(folle).
drive at vt fus (fig: intend, mean) vouloir dire, en venir à.
drive on vi poursuivre sa route, continuer; (after stopping) reprendre sa route, repartir ♦ vt (incite, encourage) inciter.
drive-in [drīv'in] a, n (esp US) drive-in (m).
drive-in window n (US) guichet-auto m.
drivel [driv'əl] n (col) idioties fpl, imbécillités fpl.
driven [driv'ən] pp of **drive**.
driver [drī'vûr] n conducteur/trice; (of taxi, bus) chauffeur m.
driver's license n (US) permis m de conduire.
driveway [drīv'wā] n allée f.
driving [drī'ving] a: **~ rain** n pluie battante ♦ n conduite f.

driving belt *n* courroie *f* de transmission.
driving force *n* locomotive *f*, élément *m* dynamique.
driving instructor *n* moniteur *m* d'auto-école.
driving lesson *n* leçon *f* de conduite.
driving licence *n* (*Brit*) permis *m* de conduire.
driving school *n* auto-école *f*.
driving test *n* examen *m* du permis de conduire.
drizzle [driz'əl] *n* bruine *f*, crachin *m* ♦ *vi* bruiner.
droll [drōl] *a* drôle.
dromedary [drâm'idārē] *n* dromadaire *m*.
drone [drōn] *vi* (*bee*) bourdonner; (*engine etc*) ronronner; (*also:* ~ **on**) parler d'une voix monocorde ♦ *n* bourdonnement *m*; ronronnement *m*; (*male bee*) faux-bourdon *m*.
drool [drōōl] *vi* baver; **to** ~ **over sb/sth** (*fig*) baver d'admiration *or* être en extase devant qn/qch.
droop [drōōp] *vi* s'affaisser; tomber.
drop [drâp] *n* goutte *f*; (*fall: also in price*) baisse *f*; (: *in salary*) réduction *f*; (*also:* **parachute** ~) saut *m*; (*of cliff*) dénivellation *f*; à-pic *m* ♦ *vt* laisser tomber; (*voice, eyes, price*) baisser; (*set down from car*) déposer ♦ *vi* (*wind, temperature, price, voice*) tomber; (*numbers, attendance*) diminuer; ~**s** *npl* (*MED*) gouttes; **cough** ~**s** pastilles *fpl* pour la toux; **a** ~ **of 10%** une baisse (*or* réduction) de 10%; **to** ~ **anchor** jeter l'ancre; **to** ~ **sb a line** mettre un mot à qn.
drop in *vi* (*col: visit*): **to** ~ **in (on)** faire un saut (chez), passer (chez).
drop off *vi* (*sleep*) s'assoupir ♦ *vt*: **to** ~ **sb off** déposer qn.
drop out *vi* (*withdraw*) se retirer; (*student etc*) abandonner, décrocher.
droplet [drâp'lit] *n* gouttelette *f*.
dropout [drâp'out] *n* (*from society*) marginal/e; (*from university*) drop-out *m/f*, dropé/e.
dropper [drâp'ûr] *n* (*MED etc*) compte-gouttes *m inv*.
droppings [drâp'ingz] *npl* crottes *fpl*.
dross [drôs] *n* déchets *mpl*; rebut *m*.
drought [drout] *n* sécheresse *f*.
drove [drōv] *pt of* **drive** ♦ *n*: ~**s of people** une foule de gens.
drown [droun] *vt* noyer; (*also:* ~ **out**: *sound*) couvrir, étouffer ♦ *vi* se noyer.
drowse [drouz] *vi* somnoler.
drowsy [drou'zē] *a* somnolent(e).
drudge [druj] *n* bête *f* de somme (*fig*).
drudgery [druj'ûrē] *n* corvée *f*.
drug [drug] *n* médicament *m*; (*narcotic*) drogue *f* ♦ *vt* droguer; **he's on** ~**s** il se drogue; (*MED*) il est sous médication.
drug addict *n* toxicomane *m/f*.
druggist [drug'ist] *n* (*US*) pharmacien/ne-droguiste.
drug peddler *n* revendeur/euse de drogue.
drugstore [drug'stôr] *n* pharmacie-droguerie *f*, drugstore *m*.
drum [drum] *n* tambour *m*; (*for oil, gasoline*) bidon *m* ♦ *vt*: **to** ~ **one's fingers on the table** pianoter *or* tambouriner sur la table; ~**s** *npl* (*MUS*) batterie *f*.

drum up *vt* (*enthusiasm, support*) susciter, rallier.
drummer [drum'ûr] *n* (joueur *m* de) tambour *m*.
drum roll *n* roulement *m* de tambour.
drumstick [drum'stik] *n* (*MUS*) baguette *f* de tambour; (*of chicken*) pilon *m*.
drunk [drungk] *pp of* **drink** ♦ *a* ivre, soûl(e) ♦ *n* soûlard/e; homme/femme soûl(e); **to get** ~ s'enivrer, se soûler.
drunkard [drung'kûrd] *n* ivrogne *m/f*.
drunken [drung'kən] *a* ivre, soûl(e); (*habitual*) ivrogne, d'ivrogne; ~ **driving** conduite *f* en état d'ivresse.
drunkenness [drung'kənnis] *n* ivresse *f*; ivrognerie *f*.
dry [drī] *a* sec(sèche); (*day*) sans pluie; (*humor*) pince-sans-rire; (*uninteresting*) aride, rébarbatif(ive) ♦ *vt* sécher; (*clothes*) faire sécher ♦ *vi* sécher; **on** ~ **land** sur la terre ferme; **to** ~ **one's hands/hair/eyes** se sécher les mains/les cheveux/les yeux.
dry up *vi* (*also fig: source of supply, imagination*) se tarir; (: *speaker*) sécher, rester sec.
dry-clean [drī'klēn'] *vt* nettoyer à sec.
dry-cleaner [drī'klē'nûr] *n* teinturier *m*.
dry-cleaner's [drī'klē'nûrz] *n* teinturerie *f*.
dry-cleaning [drī'klē'ning] *n* nettoyage *m* à sec.
dry dock *n* (*NAUT*) cale sèche, bassin *m* de radoub.
dryer [drī'ûr] *n* séchoir *m*; (*spin-*~) essoreuse *f*.
dry goods *npl* (*COMM*) textiles *mpl*, mercerie *f*.
dry goods store *n* (*US*) magasin *m* de nouveautés.
dry ice *n* neige *f* carbonique.
dryly [drī'lē] *ad* sèchement; d'un ton pince-sans-rire.
dryness [drī'nis] *n* sécheresse *f*.
dry rot *n* pourriture sèche (*du bois*).
dry run *n* (*fig*) essai *m*.
dry ski slope *n* piste (de ski) artificielle.
DSc *n abbr* (= *Doctor of Science*) titre universitaire.
DSS *n abbr* (*Brit*) = **Department of Social Security.**
DST *abbr* (*US:* = *Daylight Saving Time*) heure d'été.
DT *n abbr* (*COMPUT*) = **data transmission.**
DTI *n abbr* (*Brit*) = **Department of Trade and Industry.**
DT's *n abbr* (*col:* = *delirium tremens*) delirium tremens *m*.
dual [dōō'əl] *a* double.
dual carriageway *n* (*Brit*) route *f* à quatre voies.
dual-control [dōō'əlkəntrōl'] *a* à doubles commandes.
dual nationality *n* double nationalité *f*.
dual-purpose [dōō'əlpûr'pəs] *a* à double emploi.
dubbed [dubd] *a* (*CINEMA*) doublé(e); (*nicknamed*) surnommé(e).
dubious [dōō'bēəs] *a* hésitant(e), incertain(e); (*reputation, company*) douteux(euse); **I'm very** ~ **about it** j'ai des doutes sur la

question, je n'en suis pas sûr du tout.
Dublin [dub'lin] *n* Dublin.
Dubliner [dub'linûr] *n* habitant/e de Dublin; originaire *m/f* de Dublin.
duchess [duch'is] *n* duchesse *f*.
duck [duk] *n* canard *m* ♦ *vi* se baisser vivement, baisser subitement la tête ♦ *vt* plonger dans l'eau.
duckling [duk'ling] *n* caneton *m*.
duct [dukt] *n* conduite *f*, canalisation *f*; (*ANAT*) conduit *m*.
dud [dud] *n* (*shell*) obus non éclaté; (*object, tool*): **it's a ~** c'est de la camelote, ça ne marche pas ♦ *a* (*Brit: check*) sans provision; (: *note, coin*) faux(fausse).
dude [dood] *n* (*US col*) coco *m*.
due [doo] *a* dû(due); (*expected*) attendu(e); (*fitting*) qui convient ♦ *n* dû *m* ♦ *ad*: **~ north** droit vers le nord; **~s** *npl* (*for club, union*) cotisation *f*; (*in harbor*) droits *mpl* (de port); **in ~ course** en temps utile *or* voulu; (*in the end*) finalement; **~ to** dû à; causé par; **the rent is ~ on the 30th** il faut payer le loyer le 30; **the train is ~ at 8** le train est attendu à 8h; **she is ~ back tomorrow** elle doit rentrer demain; **I am ~ 6 days' leave** j'ai droit à 6 jours de congé.
due date *n* date *f* d'échéance.
duel [doo'əl] *n* duel *m*.
duet [dooet'] *n* duo *m*.
duff [duf] *a* (*Brit col*) nullard(e), nul(le).
duffelbag, duffle bag [duf'əlbag] *n* sac marin.
duffelcoat, duffle coat [duf'əlkōt] *n* duffel-coat *m*.
duffer [duf'ûr] *n* (*col*) nullard/e.
dug [dug] *pt, pp of* **dig**.
duke [dook] *n* duc *m*.
dull [dul] *a* (*boring*) ennuyeux(euse); (*slow*) borné(e); (*lackluster*) morne, terne; (*sound, pain*) sourd(e); (*weather, day*) gris(e), maussade; (*blade*) émoussé(e) ♦ *vt* (*pain, grief*) atténuer; (*mind, senses*) engourdir.
duly [doo'lē] *ad* (*on time*) en temps voulu; (*as expected*) comme il se doit.
dumb [dum] *a* muet(te); (*stupid*) bête; **to be struck ~** (*fig*) rester abasourdi(e), être sidéré(e).
dumbbell [dum'bel] *n* (*SPORT*) haltère *m*; (*fig*) gourde *f*.
dumbfounded [dumfound'id] *a* sidéré(e).
dummy [dum'ē] *n* (*tailor's model*) mannequin *m*; (*SPORT*) feinte *f*; (*Brit: for baby*) tétine *f* ♦ *a* faux(fausse), factice.
dummy run *n* essai *m*.
dump [dump] *n* tas *m* d'ordures; (*place*) décharge (publique); (*MIL*) dépôt *m*; (*COMPUT*) listage *m* (de la mémoire) ♦ *vt* (*put down*) déposer; déverser; (*get rid of*) se débarrasser de; (*COMPUT*) lister; (*COMM: goods*) vendre à perte (*sur le marché extérieur*); **to be (down) in the ~s** (*col*) avoir le cafard, broyer du noir.
dumping [dum'ping] *n* (*ECON*) dumping *m*; (*of garbage*): **"no ~"** "décharge interdite".
dumpling [dump'ling] *n* boulette *f* (de pâte).
dumpy [dump'ē] *a* courtaud(e), boulot(te).
dunce [duns] *n* âne *m*, cancre *m*.
dune [doon] *n* dune *f*.
dung [dung] *n* fumier *m*.

dungarees [dunggərēz'] *npl* bleu(s) *m(pl)*; (*for child, woman*) salopette *f*.
dungeon [dun'jən] *n* cachot *m*.
dunk [dungk] *vt* tremper.
Dunkirk [dun'kûrk] *n* Dunkerque.
duo [doo'ō] *n* (*gen, MUS*) duo *m*.
duodenal [dooədē'nəl] *a* duodénal(e); **~ ulcer** ulcère *m* du duodénum.
dupe [doop] *n* dupe *f* ♦ *vt* duper, tromper.
duplex [doo'pleks] *n* (*US: also:* **~ apartment**) duplex *m*.
duplicate [doo'plikit] *n* double *m*, copie exacte; (*copy of letter etc*) duplicata *m* ♦ *a* (*copy*) en double ♦ *vt* [doo'plikāt] faire un double de; (*on machine*) polycopier; **in ~** en deux exemplaires, en double; **~ key** double *m* de la (*or* d'une) clé.
duplicating machine [doo'plikāting məshēn'], **duplicator** [doo'plikātûr] *n* duplicateur *m*.
duplicity [dooplis'ətē] *n* duplicité *f*, fausseté *f*.
Dur *abbr* (*Brit*) = *Durham*.
durability [doorəbil'ətē] *n* solidité *f*; durabilité *f*.
durable [door'əbəl] *a* durable; (*clothes, metal*) résistant(e), solide.
duration [doorā'shən] *n* durée *f*.
duress [doores'] *n*: **under ~** sous la contrainte.
Durex [doo'reks] *n* ® (*Brit*) préservatif (masculin).
during [door'ing] *prep* pendant, au cours de.
dusk [dusk] *n* crépuscule *m*.
dusky [dus'kē] *a* sombre.
dust [dust] *n* poussière *f* ♦ *vt* (*furniture*) essuyer, épousseter; (*cake etc*): **to ~ with** saupoudrer de.
dust off *vt* (*also fig*) dépoussiérer.
dustbin [dust'bin] *n* (*Brit*) poubelle *f*.
duster [dus'tûr] *n* chiffon *m*.
dust jacket *n* jacquette *f*.
dustman [dust'man] *n* (*Brit*) boueux *m*, éboueur *m*.
dustpan [dust'pan] *n* pelle *f* à poussière.
dusty [dus'tē] *a* poussiéreux(euse).
Dutch [duch] *a* hollandais(e), néerlandais(e) ♦ *n* (*LING*) hollandais *m*, néerlandais *m* ♦ *ad*: **to go ~** *or* **d~** partager les frais; **the ~** *npl* les Hollandais, les Néerlandais.
Dutch auction *n* enchères *fpl* à la baisse.
Dutchman [duch'mən], **Dutchwoman** [duch'woomən] *n* Hollandais/e.
dutiable [doo'tēəbəl] *a* taxable; soumis(e) à des droits de douane.
dutiful [doo'tifəl] *a* (*child*) respectueux(euse); (*husband, wife*) plein(e) d'égards, prévenant(e); (*employee*) consciencieux (euse).
duty [doo'tē] *n* devoir *m*; (*tax*) droit *m*, taxe *f*; **duties** *npl* fonctions *fpl*; **to make it one's ~ to do sth** se faire un devoir de faire qch; **to pay ~ on sth** payer un droit *or* une taxe sur qch; **on ~** de service; (*at night etc*) de garde; **off ~** libre, pas de service *or* de garde.
duty-free [doo'tēfrē'] *a* exempté(e) de douane, hors-taxe; **~ shop** boutique *f* hors-taxe.
duty officer *n* (*MIL etc*) officier *m* de permanence.
duvet [doo'vā] *n* (*Brit*) couette *f*.

DV *abbr* (= *Deo volente*) si Dieu le veut.
DVM *n abbr* (*US*: = *Doctor of Veterinary Medicine*) *titre universitaire*.
dwarf |dwôrf| *n* nain/e ♦ *vt* écraser.
dwell, *pt, pp* **dwelt** |dwel, dwelt| *vi* demeurer.
dwell on *vt fus* s'étendre sur.
dweller |dwel'ûr| *n* habitant/e.
dwelling |dwel'ing| *n* habitation *f,* demeure *f.*
dwindle |dwin'dəl| *vi* diminuer, décroître.
dwindling |dwin'dling| *a* décroissant(e), en diminution.
dye |dī| *n* teinture *f* ♦ *vt* teindre; **hair** ~ teinture pour les cheveux.
dyestuffs |dī'stufs| *npl* colorants *mpl.*
dying |dī'ing| *a* mourant(e), agonisant(e).
dyke |dīk| *n* (*embankment*) digue *f.*
dynamic |dīnam'ik| *a* dynamique.
dynamics |dīnam'iks| *n or npl* dynamique *f.*
dynamite |dī'nəmīt| *n* dynamite *f* ♦ *vt* dynamiter, faire sauter à la dynamite.
dynamo |dī'nəmō| *n* dynamo *f.*
dynasty |dī'nəstē| *n* dynastie *f.*
dysentery |dis'əntärē| *n* dysenterie *f.*
dyslexia |dislek'sēə| *n* dyslexie *f.*
dyslexic |dislek'sik| *a, n* dyslexique *m/f.*
dyspepsia |dispep'shə| *n* dyspepsie *f.*
dystrophy |dis'trəfē| *n* dystrophie *f;* **muscular** ~ dystrophie musculaire.

E

E, e |ē| *n* (*letter*) E, e *m;* (*MUS*): **E** mi *m;* **E for Easy** E comme Eugène.
E |ē| *abbr* (= *east*) E.
E111 *n abbr* (*Brit*: *also*: **form** ~) formulaire *m* E111.
ea. *abbr* = **each.**
E.A. *n abbr* (*US*: = *educational age*) niveau scolaire.
each |ēch| *a* chaque ♦ *pronoun* chacun(e); ~ **one** chacun(e); ~ **other** se (*or* nous *etc*); **they hate** ~ **other** ils se détestent (mutuellement); **you are jealous of** ~ **other** vous êtes jaloux l'un de l'autre; ~ **day** chaque jour, tous les jours; **they have 2 books** ~ ils ont 2 livres chacun; **they cost $5** ~ ils coûtent 5 dollars (la) pièce; ~ **of us** chacun(e) de nous.
eager |ē'gûr| *a* impatient(e); avide; ardent(e), passionné(e); (*keen: pupil*) plein(e) d'enthousiasme, qui se passionne pour les études; **to be** ~ **to do sth** être impatient de faire qch, brûler de faire qch; désirer vivement faire qch; **to be** ~ **for** désirer vivement, être avide de.
eagle |ē'gəl| *n* aigle *m.*
E and OE *abbr* = **errors and omissions excepted.**
ear |ēr| *n* oreille *f;* (*of corn*) épi *m;* **up to one's** ~**s in debt** endetté(e) jusqu'au cou.
earache |ēr'āk| *n* douleurs *fpl* aux oreilles.
eardrum |ēr'drum| *n* tympan *m.*

earl |ûrl| *n* comte *m.*
earlier |ûr'lēûr| *a* (*date etc*) plus rapproché(e); (*edition etc*) plus ancien(ne), antérieur(e) ♦ *ad* plus tôt.
early |ûr'lē| *ad* tôt, de bonne heure; (*ahead of time*) en avance ♦ *a* précoce; qui se manifeste (*or* se fait) tôt *or* de bonne heure; (*Christians, settlers*) premier(ière); **have an** ~ **night/start** couchez-vous/partez tôt *or* de bonne heure; **take the** ~ **train** prenez le premier train; **in the** ~ *or* ~ **in the spring/19th century** au début *or* commencement du printemps/19ème siècle; **you're** ~! tu es en avance!; ~ **in the morning** tôt le matin; **she's in her** ~ **forties** elle a un peu plus de quarante ans *or* de la quarantaine; **at your earliest convenience** (*COMM*) dans les meilleurs délais.
early retirement *n* retraite anticipée.
early warning system *n* système *m* de première alerte.
earmark |ēr'märk| *vt*: **to** ~ **sth for** réserver *or* destiner qch à.
earn |ûrn| *vt* gagner; (*COMM*: *yield*) rapporter; **to** ~ **one's living** gagner sa vie; **this** ~**ed him much praise, he** ~**ed much praise for this** ceci lui a valu de nombreux éloges; **he's** ~**ed his rest/reward** il mérite *or* a bien mérité *or* a bien gagné son repos/sa récompense.
earned income |ûrnd' in'kum| *n* revenu *m* du travail.
earnest |ûr'nist| *a* sérieux(euse) ♦ *n* (*also*: ~ **money**) acompte *m,* arrhes *fpl;* **in** ~ *ad* sérieusement, pour de bon.
earnings |ûr'ningz| *npl* salaire *m;* gains *mpl;* (*of company etc*) profits *mpl,* bénéfices *mpl.*
ear, nose and throat specialist *n* oto-rhino-laryngologiste *m/f.*
earphones |ēr'fōnz| *npl* écouteurs *mpl.*
earplugs |ēr'plugz| *npl* boules *fpl* Quiès ®; (*to keep out water*) protège-tympans *mpl.*
earring |ēr'ring| *n* boucle *f* d'oreille.
earshot |ēr'shât| *n*: **out of/within** ~ hors de portée/à portée de la voix.
earth |ûrth| *n* (*gen, also Brit ELEC*) terre *f;* (*of fox etc*) terrier *m* ♦ *vt* (*Brit ELEC*) relier à la terre.
earthenware |ûr'thənwär| *n* poterie *f;* faïence *f* ♦ *a* de *or* en faïence.
earthly |ûrth'lē| *a* terrestre; ~ **paradise** paradis *m* terrestre; **there is no** ~ **reason to think** ... il n'y a absolument aucune raison *or* pas la moindre raison de penser ....
earthquake |ûrth'kwāk| *n* tremblement *m* de terre, séisme *m.*
earth tremor *n* secousse *f* sismique.
earthworks |ûrth'wûrks| *npl* travaux *mpl* de terrassement.
earthworm |ûrth'wûrm| *n* ver *m* de terre.
earthy |ûr'thē| *a* (*fig*) terre à terre *inv;* truculent(e).
earwax |ēr'waks| *n* cérumen *m.*
earwig |ēr'wig| *n* perce-oreille *m.*
ease |ēz| *n* facilité *f,* aisance *f* ♦ *vt* (*soothe*) calmer; (*loosen*) relâcher, détendre; (*help pass*): **to** ~ **sth in/out** faire pénétrer/sortir qch délicatement *or* avec douceur; faciliter la pénétration/la sortie de qch ♦ *vi* (*situation*) se

détendre; **with** ~ sans difficulté, aisément; **life of** ~ vie oisive; **at** ~ à l'aise; (*MIL*) au repos.

ease off, ease up *vi* diminuer; (*slow down*) ralentir; (*relax*) se détendre.

easel [ē'zəl] *n* chevalet *m*.

easily [ē'zilē] *ad* facilement.

easiness [ē'zēnis] *n* facilité *f*; (*of manner*) aisance *f*; nonchalance *f*.

east [ēst] *n* est *m* ♦ *a* d'est ♦ *ad* à l'est, vers l'est; **the E~** l'Orient *m*; (*POL*) les pays *mpl* de l'Est.

Easter [ēs'tûr] *n* Pâques *fpl* ♦ *a* (*vacation*) de Pâques, pascal(e).

Easter egg *n* œuf *m* de Pâques.

Easter Island *n* île *f* de Pâques.

easterly [ēs'tûrlē] *a* d'est.

Easter Monday *n* le lundi de Pâques.

eastern [ēs'tûrn] *a* de l'est, oriental(e); **E~ Europe** l'Europe de l'Est; **the E~ bloc** (*POL*) les pays *mpl* de l'est.

Easter Sunday *n* le dimanche de Pâques.

East Germany *n* Allemagne *f* de l'Est.

eastward(s) [ēst'wûrd(z)] *ad* vers l'est, à l'est.

easy [ē'zē] *a* facile; (*manner*) aisé(e) ♦ *ad*: **to take it** *or* **things** ~ ne pas se fatiguer; (*not worry*) ne pas (trop) s'en faire; **payment on** ~ **terms** (*COMM*) facilités *fpl* de paiement; **that's easier said than done** c'est plus facile à dire qu'à faire, c'est vite dit; **I'm** ~ (*col*) ça m'est égal.

easy chair *n* fauteuil *m*.

easy-going [ē'zēgō'ing] *a* accommodant(e), facile à vivre.

eat, *pt* **ate**, *pp* **eaten** [ēt, āt, ē'tən] *vt*, *vi* manger.

eat away *vt* (*subj: sea*) saper, éroder; (*: acid*) ronger, corroder.

eat away at, eat into *vt fus* ronger, attaquer.

eat out *vi* manger au restaurant.

eat up *vt* (*food*) finir (de manger); **it** ~**s up electricity** ça bouffe du courant, ça consomme beaucoup d'électricité.

eatable [ē'təbəl] *a* mangeable; (*safe to eat*) comestible.

eau de Cologne [ō' də kəlōn'] *n* eau *f* de Cologne.

eaves [ēvz] *npl* avant-toit *m*.

eavesdrop [ēvz'dräp] *vi*: **to** ~ **(on)** écouter de façon indiscrète.

ebb [eb] *n* reflux *m* ♦ *vi* refluer; (*fig: also:* ~ **away**) décliner; **the** ~ **and flow** le flux et le reflux; **to be at a low** ~ (*fig*) être bien bas(se), ne pas aller bien fort.

ebb tide *n* marée descendante, reflux *m*.

ebony [eb'ənē] *n* ébène *f*.

ebullient [ibul'yənt] *a* exubérant(e).

EC *n abbr* (= *European Community*) CE *f* (= *Communauté européenne*).

eccentric [iksen'trik] *a, n* excentrique (*m/f*).

ecclesiastic(al) [iklēzēas'tik(əl)] *a* ecclésiastique.

ECG *n abbr* = **electrocardiogram**.

ECGD *n abbr* (= *Export Credits Guarantee Department*) *service de garantie financière à l'exportation*.

echo, ~**es** [ek'ō] *n* écho *m* ♦ *vt* répéter; faire chorus avec ♦ *vi* résonner; faire écho.

éclair [iklär'] *n* éclair *m* (*CULIN*).

eclipse [iklips'] *n* éclipse *f* ♦ *vt* éclipser.

ECM *n abbr* (*US*) = *European Common Market*.

ecologist [ikâl'əjist] *n* écologiste *m/f*.

ecology [ikál'əjē] *n* écologie *f*.

economic [ēkənâm'ik] *a* économique; (*profitable*) rentable.

economical [ēkənâm'ikəl] *a* économique; (*person*) économe.

economically [ēkənâm'iklē] *ad* économiquement.

economics [ēkənâm'iks] *n* économie *f* politique ♦ *npl* côté *m* or aspect *m* économique.

economist [ikân'əmist] *n* économiste *m/f*.

economize [ikân'əmīz] *vi* économiser, faire des économies.

economy [ikân'əmē] *n* économie *f*; **economies of scale** économies d'échelle.

economy class *n* (*AVIAT etc*) classe *f* touriste.

economy size *n* taille *f* économique.

ecosystem [ek'ōsistəm] *n* écosystème *m*.

ECSC *n abbr* (= *European Coal & Steel Community*) CECA *f* (= *Communauté européenne du charbon et de l'acier*).

ecstasy [ek'stəsē] *n* extase *f*; **to go into ecstasies over** s'extasier sur.

ecstatic [ekstat'ik] *a* extatique, en extase.

ECT *n abbr* = **electroconvulsive therapy**.

ECU *n abbr* (= *European Currency Unit*) ECU *m*.

Ecuador [ek'wədōr] *n* Équateur *m*.

ecumenical [ekyōōmen'ikəl] *a* œcuménique.

eczema [ek'səmə] *n* eczéma *m*.

eddy [ed'ē] *n* tourbillon *m*.

edge [ej] *n* bord *m*; (*of knife etc*) tranchant *m*, fil *m* ♦ *vt* border ♦ *vi*: **to** ~ **forward** avancer petit à petit; **to** ~ **away from** s'éloigner furtivement de; **on** ~ (*fig*) = **edgy**; **to have the** ~ **on** (*fig*) l'emporter (de justesse) sur, être légèrement meilleur que.

edgeways [ej'wāz] *ad* latéralement; **he couldn't get a word in** ~ il ne pouvait pas placer un mot.

edging [ej'ing] *n* bordure *f*.

edgy [ej'ē] *a* crispé(e), tendu(e).

edible [ed'əbəl] *a* comestible; (*meal*) mangeable.

edict [ē'dikt] *n* décret *m*.

edifice [ed'əfis] *n* édifice *m*.

edifying [ed'əfiing] *a* édifiant(e).

Edinburgh [ed'ənbûrə] *n* Edimbourg.

edit [ed'it] *vt* éditer; (*magazine*) diriger; (*newspaper*) être le rédacteur *or* la rédactrice en chef de.

edition [idish'ən] *n* édition *f*.

editor [ed'itûr] *n* (*in newspaper*) rédacteur/trice; rédacteur/trice en chef; (*of sb's work*) éditeur/trice; (*also:* **film** ~) monteur/euse.

editorial [editôr'ēəl] *a* de la rédaction, éditorial(e) ♦ *n* éditorial *m*; **the** ~ **staff** la rédaction.

EDP *n abbr* = **electronic data processing**.

EDT *abbr* (*US:* = *Eastern Daylight Time*) *heure d'été de New York*.

educate [ej'ōōkāt] *vt* instruire; éduquer; ~**d at ...** qui a fait ses études à ....

education [ejōōkā'shən] *n* éducation *f*;

(*schooling*) enseignement *m*, instruction *f*; (*at university: subject etc*) pédagogie *f*; **elementary** *or* (*Brit*) **primary/secondary** ~ instruction *f* primaire/secondaire.

educational [cjōōkā'shənəl] *a* pédagogique; scolaire; (*useful*) instructif(ive); (*games, toys*) éducatif(ive); ~ **technology** technologie *f* de l'enseignement.

Edwardian [edwôr'dēən] *a* de l'époque du roi Edouard VII, des années 1900.

EE *abbr* = **electrical engineer**.

EEC *n abbr* (= *European Economic Community*) C.E.E. *f* (= *Communauté économique européenne*).

EEG *n abbr* = **electroencephalogram**.

eel [ēl] *n* anguille *f*.

EENT *n abbr* (*US MED*) = *eye, ear, nose and throat*.

EEOC *n abbr* (*US*) = **Equal Employment Opportunity Commission**.

eerie [ē'rē] *a* inquiétant(e), spectral(e), surnaturel(le).

EET *abbr* (= *Eastern European Time*) HEO (= *heure d'Europe orientale*).

effect [ifekt'] *n* effet *m* ♦ *vt* effectuer; **to take** ~ (*LAW*) entrer en vigueur, prendre effet; (*drug*) agir, faire son effet; **to put into** ~ (*plan*) mettre en application *or* à exécution; **to have an** ~ **on sb/sth** avoir *or* produire un effet sur qn/qch; **in** ~ en fait; **his letter is to the** ~ **that** ... sa lettre nous apprend que ....

effective [ifek'tiv] *a* efficace; (*striking: display, outfit*) frappant(e), qui produit *or* fait de l'effet; **to become** ~ (*LAW*) entrer en vigueur, prendre effet; ~ **date** date *f* d'effet *or* d'entrée en vigueur.

effectively [ifek'tivlē] *ad* efficacement; (*strikingly*) d'une manière frappante, avec beaucoup d'effet; (*in reality*) effectivement, en fait.

effectiveness [ifek'tivnis] *n* efficacité *f*.

effects [ifekts'] *npl* (*THEATER*) effets *mpl*; (*property*) effets, affaires *fpl*.

effeminate [ifem'ənit] *a* efféminé(e).

effervescent [efûrves'ənt] *a* effervescent(e).

efficacy [ef'ikəsē] *n* efficacité *f*.

efficiency [ifish'ənsē] *n* efficacité *f*; rendement *m*.

efficiency apartment *n* (*US*) studio *m* avec coin cuisine.

efficient [ifish'ənt] *a* efficace; (*machine, car*) d'un bon rendement.

efficiently [ifish'əntlē] *ad* efficacement.

effigy [ef'ijē] *n* effigie *f*.

effluent [ef'lōōənt] *n* effluent *m*.

effort [ef'ûrt] *n* effort *m*; **to make an** ~ **to do sth** faire *or* fournir un effort pour faire qch.

effortless [ef'ûrtlis] *a* sans effort, aisé(e).

effrontery [ifrun'tûrē] *n* effronterie *f*.

effusive [ifyōō'siv] *a* (*person*) expansif(ive); (*welcome*) chaleureux(euse).

EFL *n abbr* (*SCOL*) = *English as a foreign language*.

EFT *n abbr* (*US*: = *electronic funds transfer*) transfert *m* électronique de fonds.

EFTA [ef'tə] *n abbr* (= *European Free Trade Association*) AELE *f* (= *Association européenne de libre échange*).

e.g. *ad abbr* (= *exempli gratia*) par exemple,

p. ex.

egalitarian [igalitär'ēən] *a* égalitaire.

egg [eg] *n* œuf *m*.
  egg on *vt* pousser.
eggcup [eg'kup] *n* coquetier *m*.
eggplant [eg'plant] *n* aubergine *f*.
eggshell [eg'shel] *n* coquille *f* d'œuf ♦ *a* (*color*) blanc cassé *inv*.
egg white *n* blanc *m* d'œuf.
egg yolk *n* jaune *m* d'œuf.
ego [ē'gō] *n* moi *m*.
egoism [ē'gōizəm] *n* égoïsme *m*.
egoist [ē'gōist] *n* égoïste *m/f*.
egotism [ē'gətizəm] *n* égotisme *m*.
egotist [ē'gətist] *n* égocentrique *m/f*.
Egypt [ē'jipt] *n* Egypte *f*.
Egyptian [ijip'shən] *a* égyptien(ne) ♦ *n* Egyptien/ne.
eiderdown [ī'dûrdoun] *n* édredon *m*.
eight [āt] *num* huit.
eighteen [ā'tēn'] *num* dix-huit.
eighth [ātth] *num* huitième.
eighth note *n* (*US*) croche *f*.
eighty [ā'tē] *num* quatre-vingt(s).
Eire [ār'ə] *n* République *f* d'Irlande.
either [ē'thûr] *a* l'un ou l'autre; (*both, each*) chaque; **on** ~ **side** de chaque côté ♦ *pronoun*: ~ (**of them**) l'un ou l'autre; **I don't like** ~ je n'aime ni l'un ni l'autre ♦ *ad* non plus; **no, I don't** ~ moi non plus ♦ *cj*: ~ **good or bad** ou bon ou mauvais, soit bon soit mauvais; **I haven't seen** ~ **one or the other** je n'ai vu ni l'un ni l'autre.
ejaculation [ijakyəlā'shən] *n* (*PHYSIOL*) éjaculation *f*.
eject [ijekt'] *vt* expulser; éjecter ♦ *vi* (*pilot*) s'éjecter.
ejector seat [ijek'tûr sēt] *n* siège *m* éjectable.
eke [ēk]: **to** ~ **out** *vt* faire durer; augmenter.
EKG *n abbr* (*US*) = **electrocardiogram**.
el [el] *n abbr* (*US col*) = **elevated railroad**.
elaborate *a* [ilab'ûrit] compliqué(e), recherché(e), minutieux(euse) ♦ *vb* [ilab'ûrāt] *vt* élaborer ♦ *vi* entrer dans les détails.
elapse [ilaps'] *vi* s'écouler, passer.
elastic [ilas'tik] *a, n* élastique (*m*).
elastic band *n* (*Brit*) élastique *m*.
elasticity [ilastis'itē] *n* élasticité *f*.
elated [ilā'tid] *a* transporté(e) de joie.
elation [ilā'shən] *n* (grande) joie, allégresse *f*.
elbow [el'bō] *n* coude *m* ♦ *vt*: **to** ~ **one's way through the crowd** se frayer un passage à travers la foule (en jouant des coudes).
elder [el'dûr] *a* aîné(e) ♦ *n* (*tree*) sureau *m*; **one's** ~**s** ses aînés.
elderly [el'dûrlē] *a* âgé(e) ♦ *npl*: **the** ~ les personnes âgées.
eldest [el'dist] *a, n*: **the** ~ (**child**) l'aîné(e) (des enfants).
elect [ilekt'] *vt* élire; (*choose*): **to** ~ **to do** choisir de faire ♦ *a*: **the president** ~ le président désigné.
election [ilek'shən] *n* élection *f*; **to hold an** ~ procéder à une élection.
election campaign *n* campagne électorale.
electioneering [ilekshənē'ring] *n* propagande électorale, manœuvres électorales.
elective [ilek'tiv] *n* (*SCOL*) cours facultatif.
elector [ilek'tûr] *n* électeur/trice.

electoral [ilek'tûrəl] *a* électoral(e).
electoral college *n* collège électoral.
electoral roll *n* (*Brit*) liste électorale.
electorate [ilek'tûrit] *n* électorat *m*.
electric [ilek'trik] *a* électrique.
electrical [ilek'trikəl] *a* électrique.
electrical engineer *n* ingénieur électricien.
electrical failure *n* panne d'électricité *or* de courant.
electric blanket *n* couverture chauffante.
electric chair *n* chaise *f* électrique.
electric current *n* courant *m* électrique.
electrician [ilektrish'ən] *n* électricien *m*.
electricity [ilektris'ətē] *n* électricité *f*; **to switch on/off the ~** rétablir/couper le courant.
electric light *n* lumière *f* électrique.
electric shock *n* choc *m or* décharge *f* électrique.
electrify [ilek'trəfī] *vt* (*RAIL*) électrifier; (*audience*) électriser.
electro... [ilek'trō] *prefix* électro....
electrocardiogram (**ECG**) [ilektrōkâr'dēəgram] *n* électrocardiogramme *m* (ECG).
electro-convulsive therapy [ilek'trōkənvul'siv thär'əpē] *n* électrochocs *mpl*.
electrocute [ilek'trəkyōōt] *vt* électrocuter.
electrode [ilek'trōd] *n* électrode *f*.
electroencephalogram (**EEG**) [ilektrōensef'ələgram] *n* électroencéphalogramme *m* (EEG).
electrolysis [ilektrâl'isis] *n* électrolyse *f*.
electromagnetic [ilektrōmagnet'ik] *a* électromagnétique.
electron [ilek'trân] *n* électron *m*.
electronic [ilektrân'ik] *a* électronique.
electronic data processing (**EDP**) *n* traitement *m* électronique des données.
electronic mail *n* courrier *m* électronique.
electronics [ilektrân'iks] *n* électronique *f*.
electron microscope *n* microscope *m* électronique.
electroplated [ilek'trəplātid] *a* plaqué(e) *or* doré(e) *or* argenté(e) par galvanoplastie.
electrotherapy [ilektrōthär'əpē] *n* électrothérapie *f*.
elegance [el'əgəns] *n* élégance *f*.
elegant [el'əgənt] *a* élégant(e).
element [el'əmənt] *n* (*gen*) élément *m*; (*of heater, kettle etc*) résistance *f*.
elementary [elimen'tûrē] *a* élémentaire; (*school, education*) primaire.
elephant [el'əfənt] *n* éléphant *m*.
elevate [el'əvāt] *vt* élever.
elevated railroad [el'əvātid rāl'rōd] *n* (*US*) métro aérien.
elevation [eləvā'shən] *n* élévation *f*; (*height*) altitude *f*.
elevator [el'əvātûr] *n* élévateur *m*, montecharge *m inv*; (*US*) ascenseur *m*.
eleven [ilev'ən] *num* onze.
elevenses [ilev'ənziz] *npl* (*Brit*) ≈ pause-café *f*.
eleventh [ilev'ənth] *a* onzième; **at the ~ hour** (*fig*) à la dernière minute.
elf, *pl* **elves** [elf, elvz] *n* lutin *m*.
elicit [ilis'it] *vt*: **to ~ (from)** obtenir (de); tirer (de).
eligible [el'ijəbəl] *a* éligible; (*for membership*)

admissible; **~ for a pension** ayant droit à la retraite.
eliminate [əlim'ənāt] *vt* éliminer.
elimination [əlimənā'shən] *n* élimination *f*; **by process of ~** par élimination.
élite [ilēt'] *n* élite *f*.
élitist [ilē'tist] *a* (*pej*) élitiste.
elixir [ilik'sûr] *n* élixir *m*.
Elizabethan [ilizəbē'thən] *a* élisabéthain(e).
ellipse [ilips'] *n* ellipse *f*.
elliptical [ilip'tikəl] *a* elliptique.
elm [elm] *n* orme *m*.
elocution [eləkyōō'shən] *n* élocution *f*.
elongated [ilông'gātid] *a* étiré(e), allongé(e).
elope [ilōp'] *vi* (*lovers*) s'enfuir (ensemble).
elopement [ilōp'mənt] *n* fugue amoureuse.
eloquence [el'əkwəns] *n* éloquence *f*.
eloquent [el'əkwənt] *a* éloquent(e).
else [els] *ad* d'autre; **something ~** quelque chose d'autre, autre chose; **somewhere ~** ailleurs, autre part; **everywhere ~** partout ailleurs; **everyone ~** tous les autres; **nothing ~** rien d'autre; **is there anything ~ I can do?** est-ce que je peux faire quelque chose d'autre?; **where ~?** à quel autre endroit?; **little ~** pas grand-chose d'autre.
elsewhere [els'hwär] *ad* ailleurs, autre part.
ELT *n abbr* (*SCOL*) = *English Language Teaching*.
elucidate [ilōō'sidāt] *vt* élucider.
elude [ilōōd'] *vt* échapper à; (*question*) éluder.
elusive [ilōō'siv] *a* insaisissable; (*answer*) évasif(ive).
elves [elvz] *npl of* **elf**.
emaciated [imā'shēātid] *a* émacié(e), décharné(e).
emanate [em'ənāt] *vi*: **to ~ from** émaner de.
emancipate [iman'səpāt] *vt* émanciper.
emancipation [imansəpā'shən] *n* émancipation *f*.
emasculate [imas'kyəlāt] *vt* émasculer.
embalm [embâm'] *vt* embaumer.
embankment [embangk'mənt] *n* (*of road, railway*) remblai *m*, talus *m*; (*riverside*) berge *f*, quai *m*; (*dyke*) digue *f*.
embargo, ~es [embâr'gō] *n* (*COMM, NAUT*) embargo *m* ♦ *vt* frapper d'embargo, mettre l'embargo sur; **to put an ~ on sth** mettre l'embargo sur qch.
embark [embârk'] *vi*: **to ~ (on)** (s')embarquer (à bord de *or* sur) ♦ *vt* embarquer; **to ~ on** (*journey etc*) commencer, entreprendre; (*fig*) se lancer *or* s'embarquer dans.
embarkation [embârkā'shən] *n* embarquement *m*.
embarkation card *n* carte *f* d'embarquement.
embarrass [embar'əs] *vt* embarrasser, gêner; **to be ~ed** être gêné(e).
embarrassing [embar'əsing] *a* gênant(e), embarrassant(e).
embarrassment [embar'əsmənt] *n* embarras *m*, gêne *f*.
embassy [em'bəsē] *n* ambassade *f*; **the French E~** l'ambassade de France.
embed [embed'] *vt* enfoncer; sceller.
embellish [embel'ish] *vt* embellir; enjoliver.
embers [em'bûrz] *npl* braise *f*.
embezzle [embez'əl] *vt* détourner.

embezzlement [embez'əlmənt] *n* détournement *m* (de fonds).

embezzler [embez'lûr] *n* escroc *m*.

embitter [embit'ûr] *vt* aigrir; envenimer.

emblem [em'bləm] *n* emblème *m*.

embodiment [embâd'ēmənt] *n* personification *f*, incarnation *f*.

embody [embâd'ē] *vt* (*features*) réunir, comprendre; (*ideas*) formuler, exprimer.

embolden [embōl'dən] *vt* enhardir.

embolism [em'bəlizəm] *n* embolie *f*.

embossed [embôst'] *a* repoussé(e); gaufré(e); ~ **with** où figure(nt) en relief.

embrace [embrās'] *vt* embrasser, étreindre; (*include*) embrasser, couvrir, comprendre ♦ *vi* s'embrasser, s'étreindre ♦ *n* étreinte *f*.

embroider [embroi'dûr] *vt* broder; (*fig: story*) enjoliver.

embroidery [embroi'dûrē] *n* broderie *f*.

embroil [embroil'] *vt*: **to become ~ed (in sth)** se retrouver mêlé(e) (à qch), se laisser entraîner (dans qch).

embryo [em'brēō] *n* (*also fig*) embryon *m*.

emcee [em'sē'] *n* (*US: col*) animateur/trice, présentateur/trice.

emend [imend'] *vt* (*text*) corriger.

emerald [em'ûrəld] *n* émeraude *f*.

emerge [imûrj'] *vi* apparaître, surgir; **it ~s that** (*Brit*) Il ressort que.

emergence [imûr'jəns] *n* apparition *f*; (*of nation*) naissance *f*.

emergency [imûr'jənsē] *n* urgence *f*; **in an ~** en cas d'urgence; **state of ~** état *m* d'urgence.

emergency exit *n* sortie *f* de secours.

emergency flasher *n* (*US: AUT*) feux mpl de détresse.

emergency landing *n* atterrissage forcé.

emergency lane *n* (*US AUT*) accotement stabilisé.

emergency road service *n* (*US*) service *m* de dépannage.

emergency service *n* service *m* d'urgence.

emergency stop *n* (*AUT*) arrêt *m* d'urgence.

emergent [imûr'jənt] *a*: ~ **nation** pays *m* en voie de développement.

emery board [em'ûrē bōrd] *n* lime *f* à ongles (*en carton émerisé*).

emery paper [em'ûrē pāpûr] *n* papier *m* (d')émeri.

emetic [imet'ik] *n* vomitif *m*, émétique *m*.

emigrant [em'əgrənt] *n* émigrant/e.

emigrate [em'əgrāt] *vi* émigrer.

emigration [eməgrā'shən] *n* émigration *f*.

émigré [emigrā'] *n* émigré/e.

eminence [em'ənəns] *n* éminence *f*.

eminent [em'ənənt] *n* éminent(e).

eminently [em'ənəntlē] *ad* éminemment, admirablement.

emirate [emē'rit] *n* émirat *m*.

emission [imish'ən] *n* émission *f*.

emit [imit'] *vt* émettre.

emolument [imâl'yəmənt] *n* (*often pl: formal*) émoluments *mpl*; (*fee*) honoraires *mpl*; (*salary*) traitement *m*.

emotion [imō'shən] *n* sentiment *m*; (*as opposed to reason*) émotion *f*, sentiments.

emotional [imō'shənəl] *a* (*person*) émotif(ive), très sensible; (*scene*) émouvant(e); (*tone,*

speech) qui fait appel aux sentiments.

emotionally [imō'shənəlē] *ad* (*behave*) émotivement; (*be involved*) affectivement; (*speak*) avec émotion; ~ **disturbed** qui souffre de troubles de l'affectivité.

emotive [imō'tiv] *a* émotif(ive); ~ **power** capacité *f* d'émouvoir *or* de toucher.

empathy [em'pəthē] *n* communion *f* d'idées *or* de sentiments; empathie *f*; **to feel ~ with sb** se mettre à la place de qn.

emperor [em'pûrûr] *n* empereur *m*.

emphasis, *pl* **-ases** [em'fəsis, -sēz] *n* accent *m*; force *f*, insistance *f*; **to lay** *or* **place ~ on sth** (*fig*) mettre l'accent sur, insister sur; **the ~ is on reading** la lecture tient une place primordiale, on accorde une importance particulière à la lecture.

emphasize [em'fəsiz] *vt* (*syllable, word, point*) appuyer *or* insister sur; (*feature*) souligner, accentuer.

emphatic [əmfat'ik] *a* (*strong*) énergique, vigoureux(euse); (*unambiguous, clear*) catégorique.

emphatically [əmfat'iklē] *ad* avec vigueur *or* énergie; catégoriquement.

empire [em'pīûr] *n* empire *m*.

empirical [empir'ikəl] *a* empirique.

employ [emploi'] *vt* employer; **he's ~ed in a bank** il est employé de banque, il travaille dans une banque.

employee [emploi'ē] *n* employé/e.

employer [emploi'ûr] *n* employeur/euse.

employment [emploi'mənt] *n* emploi *m*; **to find ~** trouver un emploi *or* du travail; **without ~** au chômage, sans emploi; **place of ~** lieu *m* de travail.

employment agency *n* agence *f* *or* bureau *m* de placement.

empower [empou'ûr] *vt*: **to ~ sb to do** autoriser *or* habiliter qn à faire.

empress [em'pris] *n* impératrice *f*.

emptiness [emp'tēnis] *n* vide *m*.

empty [emp'tē] *a* vide; (*street, area*) désert(e); (*threat, promise*) en l'air, vain(e) ♦ *n* (*bottle*) bouteille *f* vide ♦ *vt* vider ♦ *vi* se vider; (*liquid*) s'écouler; **on an ~ stomach** à jeun; **to ~ into** (*river*) se jeter dans, se déverser dans.

empty-handed [emp'tēhan'did] *a* les mains vides.

empty-headed [emp'tēhed'id] *a* écervelé(e), qui n'a rien dans la tête.

EMT *n abbr* = **emergency medical technician**.

emulate [em'yəlāt] *vt* rivaliser avec, imiter.

emulsion [imul'shən] *n* émulsion *f*; (*also:* ~ **paint**) peinture mate.

enable [enā'bəl] *vt*: **to ~ sb to do** permettre à qn de faire, donner à qn la possibilité de faire.

enact [enakt'] *vt* (*LAW*) promulguer; (*play, scene*) jouer, représenter.

enamel [inam'əl] *n* émail *m*.

enamel paint *n* peinture émaillée.

enamored, (*Brit*) **enamoured** [enam'ûrd] *a*: ~ **of** amoureux(euse) de; (*idea*) enchanté(e) par.

encampment [enkamp'mənt] *n* campement *m*.

encased [enkāst'] *a*: ~ **in** enfermé(e) dans, recouvert(e) de.

enchant [ɛnchant'] *vt* enchanter.
enchanting [ɛnchan'ting] *a* ravissant(e), enchanteur(eresse).
encircle [ɛnsûr'kəl] *vt* entourer, encercler.
enc(l). *abbr* (*on letters etc*: = *enclosed, enclosure*) PJ.
enclose [ɛnklōz'] *vt* (*land*) clôturer; (*letter etc*): **to ~ (with)** joindre (à); **please find ~d** veuillez trouver ci-joint.
enclosure [ɛnklō'zhûr] *n* enceinte *f*; (*in letter etc*) annexe *f*.
encoder [ɛnkō'dûr] *n* (*COMPUT*) encodeur *m*.
encompass [ɛnkum'pəs] *vt* encercler, entourer; (*include*) contenir, inclure.
encore [āng'kôr] *excl*, *n* bis (*m*).
encounter [ɛnkoun'tûr] *n* rencontre *f* ♦ *vt* rencontrer.
encourage [ɛnkûr'ij] *vt* encourager; (*industry, growth*) favoriser; **to ~ sb to do sth** encourager qn à faire qch.
encouragement [ɛnkûr'ijmənt] *n* encouragement *m*.
encouraging [ɛnkûr'ijing] *a* encourageant(e).
encroach [ɛnkrōch'] *vi*: **to ~ (up)on** empiéter sur.
encrust [ɛnkrust'] *vt*: **~ed (with)** incrusté(e) (de).
encumber [ɛnkum'bûr] *vt*: **to be ~ed with** (*luggage*) être encombré(e) de; (*debts*) être grevé(e) de.
encyclop(a)edia [ɛnsīkləpē'dēa] *n* encyclopédie *f*.
end [ɛnd] *n* (*gen, also: aim*) fin *f*; (*of table, street, line, rope etc*) bout *m*, extrémité *f*; (*of pointed object*) pointe *f*; (*of town*) bout ♦ *vt* terminer; (*also*: **bring to an ~, put an ~ to**) mettre fin à ♦ *vi* se terminer, finir; **from ~ to ~** d'un bout à l'autre; **to come to an ~** prendre fin; **to be at an ~** être fini(e), être terminé(e); **in the ~** finalement; **on ~** (*object*) debout, dressé(e); **to stand on ~** (*hair*) se dresser sur la tête; **for 5 hours on ~** durant 5 heures d'affilée or de suite; **for hours on ~** pendant des heures (et des heures); **at the ~ of the day** (*Brit fig*) en fin de compte; **to this ~, with this ~ in view** à cette fin, dans ce but.
end up *vi*: **to ~ up in** finir or se terminer par; (*place*) finir or aboutir à.
endanger [ɛndān'jûr] *vt* mettre en danger; **an ~ed species** une espèce en voie de disparition.
endear [ɛndēr'] *vt*: **to ~ o.s. to sb** se faire aimer de qn.
endearing [ɛndēr'ing] *a* attachant(e).
endearment [ɛndēr'mənt] *n*: **to whisper ~s** murmurer des mots or choses tendres; **term of ~** terme *m* d'affection.
endeavor, (*Brit*) **endeavour** [ɛndev'ûr] *n* tentative *f*, effort *m* ♦ *vi*: **to ~ to do** tenter or s'efforcer de faire.
endemic [ɛndem'ik] *a* endémique.
ending [ɛn'ding] *n* dénouement *m*, conclusion *f*; (*LING*) terminaison *f*.
endive [ɛn'dīv] *n* (*curly*) chicorée *f*; (*smooth, flat*) endive *f*.
endless [ɛnd'lis] *a* sans fin, interminable; (*patience, resources*) inépuisable, sans limites; (*possibilities*) illimité(e).

endorse [ɛndôrs'] *vt* (*check*) endosser; (*approve*) appuyer, approuver, sanctionner.
endorsee [ɛndôrsē'] *n* bénéficiaire *m/f*, endossataire *m/f*.
endorsement [ɛndôrs'mənt] *n* (*approval*) caution *f*, aval *m*; (*signature*) endossement *m*; (*Brit: on driver's license*) contravention *f* (*portée au permis de conduire*).
endorser [ɛndôrs'ûr] *n* avaliste *m*, endosseur *m*.
endow [ɛndou'] *vt* (*provide with money*) faire une donation à, doter; (*equip*): **to ~ with** gratifier de, doter de.
endowment [ɛndou'mənt] *n* dotation *f*.
endowment insurance *n* assurance *f* mixte.
end product *n* (*INDUSTRY*) produit fini; (*fig*) résultat *m*, aboutissement *m*.
end result *n* résultat final.
endurable [ɛndōō'rəbəl] *a* supportable.
endurance [ɛndōō'əns] *n* endurance *f*, résistance *f*; patience *f*.
endurance test *n* test *m* d'endurance.
endure [ɛndōōr'] *vt* supporter, endurer ♦ *vi* durer.
end user *n* (*COMPUT*) utilisateur final.
enema [ɛn'əmə] *n* (*MED*) lavement *m*.
enemy [ɛn'əmē] *a*, *n* ennemi(e); **to make an ~ of sb** se faire un(e) ennemi(e) de qn, se mettre qn à dos.
energetic [ɛnûrjet'ik] *a* énergique; (*activity*) très actif(ive), qui fait se dépenser (physiquement).
energy [ɛn'ûrjē] *n* énergie *f*; **Department of E~** ministère *m* de l'Energie.
energy crisis *n* crise *f* de l'énergie.
energy-saving [ɛn'ûrjēsāving] *a* (*policy*) d'économie d'énergie; (*device*) qui permet de réaliser des économies d'énergie.
enervating [ɛn'ûrvāting] *a* débilitant(e), affaiblissant(e).
enforce [ɛnfôrs'] *vt* (*LAW*) appliquer, faire respecter.
enforced [ɛnfôrst'] *a* forcé(e).
enfranchise [ɛnfran'chīz] *vt* accorder le droit de vote à; (*set free*) affranchir.
engage [ɛngāj'] *vt* engager; (*MIL*) engager le combat avec; (*lawyer*) prendre ♦ *vi* (*TECH*) s'enclencher, s'engrener; **to ~ in** se lancer dans; **to ~ sb in conversation** engager la conversation avec qn.
engaged [ɛngājd'] *a* (*betrothed*) fiancé(e); (*Brit: busy, in use*) occupé(e); **to get ~** se fiancer; **he is ~ in research/a survey** il fait de la recherche/une enquête.
engaged tone *n* (*Brit TEL*) tonalité *f* occupé.
engagement [ɛngāj'mənt] *n* obligation *f*, engagement *m*; (*appointment*) rendez-vous *m inv*; (*to marry*) fiançailles *fpl*; (*MIL*) combat *m*; **I have a previous ~** j'ai déjà un rendez-vous, je suis déjà prise(e).
engagement ring *n* bague *f* de fiançailles.
engaging [ɛngā'jing] *a* engageant(e), attirant(e).
engender [ɛnjen'dûr] *vt* produire, causer.
engine [ɛn'jən] *n* (*AUT*) moteur *m*; (*RAIL*) locomotive *f*.
engine driver *n* (*Brit: of train*) mécanicien *m*.
engineer [ɛnjənēr'] *n* ingénieur *m*; (*US RAIL*)

mécanicien *m*; (*Brit*: *for domestic appliances*) réparateur *m*; **civil/mechanical** ~ ingénieur des Travaux Publics *or* des Ponts et Chaussées/mécanicien.

engineering [enjənēr'ing] *n* engineering *m*, ingénierie *f*; (*of bridges, ships*) génie *m*; (*of machine*) mécanique *f* ♦ *cpd*: ~ **works** *or* **factory** atelier *m* de construction mécanique.

engine failure *n* panne *f*.

engine trouble *n* ennuis *mpl* mécaniques.

England [ing'glənd] *n* Angleterre *f*.

English [ing'glish] *a* anglais(e) ♦ *n* (*LING*) anglais *m*; **the** ~ *npl* les Anglais; **an** ~ **speaker** un anglophone.

English Channel *n*: **the** ~ la Manche.

English horn *n* (*US*) cor anglais.

Englishman [ing'glishmən], **Englishwoman** [ing'glishwōomən] *n* Anglais/e.

English-speaking [ing'glishspē'king] *a* qui parle anglais; anglophone.

engrave [engrāv'] *vt* graver.

engraving [engrā'ving] *n* gravure *f*.

engrossed [engrōst'] *a*: ~ **in** absorbé(e) par, plongé(e) dans.

engulf [engulf'] *vt* engloutir.

enhance [enhans'] *vt* rehausser, mettre en valeur; (*position*) améliorer; (*reputation*) ac croître.

enigma [ənig'mə] *n* énigme *f*.

enigmatic [enigmat'ik] *a* énigmatique.

enjoy [enjoi'] *vt* aimer, prendre plaisir à; (*have benefit of: health, fortune*) jouir de; (*success*) connaître; **to** ~ **o.s.** s'amuser.

enjoyable [enjoi'əbəl] *a* agréable.

enjoyment [enjoi'mənt] *n* plaisir *m*.

enlarge [enlârj'] *vt* accroître; (*PHOT*) agrandir ♦ *vi*: **to** ~ **on** (*subject*) s'étendre sur.

enlarged [enlârjd'] *a* (*edition*) augmenté(e); (*MED*: *organ, gland*) anormalement gros(se), hypertrophié(e).

enlargement [enlârj'mənt] *n* (*PHOT*) agrandissement *m*.

enlighten [enlīt'ən] *vt* éclairer.

enlightened [enlīt'ənd] *a* éclairé(e).

enlightening [enlīt'əning] *a* instructif(ive), ré vélateur(trice).

enlightenment [enlīt'ənmənt] *n* édification *f*; éclaircissements *mpl*; (*HIST*): **the E~** ≈ le Siècle des lumières.

enlist [enlist'] *vt* recruter; (*support*) s'assurer ♦ *vi* s'engager; **~ed man** (*US MIL*) simple soldat *m*.

enliven [enlī'vən] *vt* animer, égayer.

enmity [en'mitē] *n* inimitié *f*.

ennoble [ennō'bəl] *vt* (*with title*) anoblir.

enormity [inôr'mitē] *n* énormité *f*.

enormous [inôr'məs] *a* énorme.

enormously [inôr'məslē] *ad* (*increase*) dans des proportions énormes; (*rich*) extrêmement.

enough [inuf'] *a*, *n*: ~ **time/books** assez *or* suffisamment de temps/livres; **have you got** ~**?** (en) avez-vous assez?; **will 5 be** ~**?** est-ce que 5 suffiront?, est-ce qu'il y en aura assez avec 5?; **that's** ~**!** ça suffit!, assez!; **that's** ~**, thanks** cela suffit *or* c'est assez, merci; **I've had** ~**!** je n'en peux plus! ♦ *ad*: **big** ~ assez *or* suffisamment grand; **he has not worked** ~ il n'a pas assez *or*

suffisamment travaillé, il n'a pas travaillé assez *or* suffisamment; ~**!** assez!, ça suffit!; **it's hot** ~ **(as it is)!** il fait assez chaud comme ça!; **he was kind** ~ **to lend me the money** il a eu la gentillesse de me prêter l'argent; **... which, funnily** ~ **...** qui, chose curieuse.

enquire [enkwī'ûr] *vt*, *vi* = **inquire**.

enrage [enrāj'] *vt* mettre en fureur *or* en rage, rendre furieux(euse).

enrich [enrich'] *vt* enrichir.

enroll, (*Brit*) enrol [enrōl'] *vt* inscrire ♦ *vi* s'inscrire.

enrol(l)ment [enrōl'mənt] *n* inscription *f*.

en route [ôn rōōt'] *ad* en route, en chemin; ~ **for** *or* **to** en route vers, à destination de.

ensconced [enskânst'] *a*: ~ **in** bien calé(e) dans.

enshrine [enshrīn'] *vt* (*fig*) préserver.

ensign [en'sən] *n* (*NAUT*) enseigne *f*, pavillon *m*.

enslave [enslāv'] *vt* asservir.

ensue [ensōō'] *vi* s'ensuivre, résulter.

ensure [enshōōr'] *vt* assurer, garantir; **to** ~ **that** s'assurer que.

ENT *n abbr* (= *Ear, Nose & Throat*) ORL *f*.

entail [entāl'] *vt* entraîner, nécessiter.

entangle [entang'gəl] *vt* emmêler, embrouiller; **to become** ~**d in sth** (*fig*) se laisser entraîner *or* empêtrer dans qch.

enter [en'tûr] *vt* (*room*) entrer dans, pénétrer dans; (*club, army*) entrer à; (*profession*) embrasser; (*competition*) s'inscrire à *or* pour; (*sb for a competition*) (faire) inscrire; (*write down*) inscrire, noter; (*COMPUT*) entrer, introduire ♦ *vi* entrer.

enter for *vt fus* s'inscrire à, se présenter pour *or* à.

enter into *vt fus* (*explanation*) se lancer dans; (*negotiations*) entamer; (*debate*) prendre part à; (*agreement*) conclure.

enter (up)on *vt fus* commencer.

enteritis [entərī'tis] *n* entérite *f*.

enterprise [en'tûrprīz] *n* (*company, undertaking*) entreprise *f*; (*initiative*) (esprit *m* d')initiative *f*.

enterprising [en'tûrprīzing] *a* entreprenant(e), dynamique.

entertain [entûrtān'] *vt* amuser, distraire; (*invite*) recevoir (à dîner); (*idea, plan*) envisager.

entertainer [entûrtān'ûr] *n* artiste *m/f* de variétés.

entertaining [entûrtā'ning] *a* amusant(e), distrayant(e) ♦ *n*: **to do a lot of** ~ beaucoup recevoir.

entertainment [entûrtān'mənt] *n* (*amusement*) distraction *f*, divertissement *m*, amusement *m*; (*show*) spectacle *m*.

entertainment allowance *n* frais *mpl* de représentation.

enthralling [enthrôl'ing] *a* captivant(e), enchanteur(eresse).

enthuse [enthōōz'] *vi*: **to** ~ **about** *or* **over** parler avec enthousiasme de.

enthusiasm [enthōō'zēazəm] *n* enthousiasme *m*.

enthusiast [enthōō'zēast] *n* enthousiaste *m/f*; **a jazz** *etc* ~ un fervent *or* passionné du jazz *etc.*

enthusiastic [enthōōzēas'tik] *a* enthousiaste; **to be ~ about** être enthousiasmé(e) par.

entice [entīs'] *vt* attirer, séduire.

enticing [entī'sing] *a* (*person, offer*) séduisant(e); (*food*) alléchant(e).

entire [entī'ûr] *a* (tout) entier(ère).

entirely [entīûr'lē] *ad* entièrement, complètement.

entirety [entīr'tē] *n*: **in its ~** dans sa totalité.

entitle [entīt'əl] *vt* (*allow*): **to ~ sb to do** donner (le) droit à qn de faire; **to ~ sb to sth** donner droit à qch à qn.

entitled [entīt'əld] *a* (*book*) intitulé(e); **to be ~ to sth/to do sth** avoir droit à qch/le droit de faire qch.

entity [en'titē] *n* entité *f*.

entrails [en'trālz] *npl* entrailles *fpl*.

entrance *n* [en'trəns] entrée *f* ♦ *vt* [entrans'] enchanter, ravir; **to gain ~ to** (*university etc*) être admis à.

entrance examination *n* examen *m* d'entrée *or* d'admission.

entrance fee *n* droit *m* d'inscription; (*to museum etc*) prix *m* d'entrée.

entrance ramp *n* (*US AUT*) bretelle *f* d'accès.

entrancing [entrans'ing] *a* enchanteur(teresse), ravissant(e).

entrant [en'trənt] *n* (*in race etc*) participant/e, concurrent/e; (*Brit: in exam*) candidat/e.

entreat [entrēt'] *vt* supplier.

entreaty [entrē'tē] *n* supplication *f*, prière *f*.

entrée [ántrā'] *n* (*CULIN*) entrée *f*.

entrenched [entrencht'] *a* retranché(e).

entrepreneur [ántrəprənûr'] *n* entrepreneur *m*.

entrepreneurial [ántrəprənûr'ēəl] *a* animé(e) d'un esprit d'entreprise.

entrust [entrust'] *vt*: **to ~ sth to** confier qch à.

entry [en'trē] *n* entrée *f*; (*in register, diary*) inscription *f*; (*in ledger*) écriture *f*; **"no ~"** "défense d'entrer", "entrée interdite"; (*AUT*) "sens interdit"; **single/double ~ bookkeeping** comptabilité *f* en partie simple/double.

entry form *n* feuille *f* d'inscription.

entry phone *n* (*Brit*) interphone *m* (à l'entrée d'un immeuble).

entwine [entwīn'] *vt* entrelacer.

enumerate [inōō'mərāt] *vt* énumérer.

enunciate [inun'sēāt] *vt* énoncer; prononcer.

envelop [envel'əp] *vt* envelopper.

envelope [en'vəlōp] *n* enveloppe *f*.

enviable [en'vēəbəl] *a* enviable.

envious [en'vēəs] *a* envieux(euse).

environment [envī'rənmənt] *n* milieu *m*; environnement *m*; **Department of the E~** (*Brit*) ministère de l'équipement et de l'aménagement du territoire.

environmental [envīrənmen'təl] *a* écologique, relatif(ive) à l'environnement; **~ studies** (*in school etc*) écologie *f*.

environmentalist [envīrənmen'təlist] *n* écologiste *m/f*.

Environmental Protection Agency (EPA) *n* (*US*) ≈ ministère *m* de l'Environnement.

envisage [enviz'ij] *vt* envisager; prévoir.

envision [envizh'ən] *vt* envisager, concevoir.

envoy [en'voi] *n* envoyé/e.

envy [en'vē] *n* envie *f* ♦ *vt* envier; **to ~ sb sth** envier qch à qn.

enzyme [en'zīm] *n* enzyme *m*.

eon [ē'ən] *n* (*US*) éternité *f*.

EPA *n abbr* (*US*) = **Environmental Protection Agency.**

ephemeral [ifem'ûrəl] *a* éphémère.

epic [ep'ik] *n* épopée *f* ♦ *a* épique.

epicenter, (*Brit*) **epicentre** [ep'isentûr] *n* épicentre *m*.

epidemic [epidem'ik] *n* épidémie *f*.

epilepsy [ep'əlepsē] *n* épilepsie *f*.

epileptic [epəlep'tik] *a*, *n* épileptique (*m/f*).

epilogue [ep'əlôg] *n* épilogue *m*.

episcopal [ipis'kəpəl] *a* épiscopal(e).

episode [ep'isōd] *n* épisode *m*.

epistle [ipis'əl] *n* épître *f*.

epitaph [ep'itaf] *n* épitaphe *f*.

epithet [ep'əthet] *n* épithète *f*.

epitome [ipit'əmē] *n* (*fig*) quintessence *f*, type *m*.

epitomize [ipit'əmīz] *vt* (*fig*) illustrer, incarner.

epoch [ep'ək] *n* époque *f*, ère *f*.

epoch-making [ep'əkmāking] *a* qui fait époque.

eponymous [epán'əməs] *a* de ce *or* du même nom, éponyme.

equable [ck'wəbəl] *a* égal(e); de tempérament égal.

equal [ē'kwəl] *a* égal(e) ♦ *n* égal/e ♦ *vt* égaler; **~ to** (*task*) à la hauteur de; **~ to doing** de taille à *or* capable de faire.

equality [ikwál'itē] *n* égalité *f*.

equalize [ē'kwəlīz] *vt*, *vi* égaliser.

equalizer [ē'kwəlīzûr] *n* but égalisateur.

equally [ē'kwəlē] *ad* également; (*just as*) tout aussi; **they are ~ clever** ils sont tout aussi intelligents.

Equal Employment Opportunity Commission, (*Brit*) **Equal Opportunities Commission** *n commission pour la non discrimination dans l'emploi.*

equal(s) sign [ē'kwəl(z) sīn] *n* signe *m* d'égalité.

equanimity [ēkwənim'itē] *n* égalité *f* d'humeur.

equate [ikwāt'] *vt*: **to ~ sth with** comparer qch à; assimiler qch à; **to ~ sth to** mettre qch en équation avec; égaler qch à.

equation [ikwā'zhən] *n* (*MATH*) équation *f*.

equator [ikwā'tûr] *n* équateur *m*.

equatorial [ēkwətôr'ēəl] *a* équatorial(e).

Equatorial Guinea *n* Guinée équatoriale.

equestrian [ikwes'trēən] *a* équestre ♦ *n* écuyer/ère, cavalier/ère.

equilibrium [ēkwəlib'rēəm] *n* équilibre *m*.

equinox [ē'kwənáks] *n* équinoxe *m*.

equip [ikwip'] *vt* équiper; **to ~ sb/sth with** équiper *or* munir qn/qch de; **he is well ~ped for the job** il a les compétences *or* les qualités requises pour ce travail.

equipment [ikwip'mənt] *n* équipement *m*; (*electrical etc*) appareillage *m*, installation *f*.

equitable [ck'witəbəl] *a* équitable.

equities [ck'witēz] *npl* (*Brit COMM*) actions cotées en Bourse.

equity [ɛk'witē] n équité f.

equity capital n capitaux mpl propres.

equivalent [ikwiv'ələnt] a équivalent(e) ♦ n équivalent m; **to be ~ to** équivaloir à, être équivalent(e) à.

equivocal [ikwiv'əkəl] a équivoque; (open to suspicion) douteux(euse).

equivocate [ikwiv'əkāt] vi user de faux-fuyants; éviter de répondre.

equivocation [ikwivəkā'shən] n équivoque f.

ER abbr (Brit: = Elizabeth Regina) la reine Élisabeth.

ERA n abbr (US POL: = Equal Rights Amendment) amendement sur l'égalité des droits des femmes.

era [ē'rə] n ère f, époque f.

eradicate [irad'ikāt] vt éliminer.

erase [irās'] vt effacer.

eraser [irā'sûr] n gomme f.

erect [irɛkt'] a droit(e) ♦ vt construire; (monument) ériger, élever; (tent etc) dresser.

erection [irɛk'shən] n (PHYSIOL) érection f; (of building) construction f; (of machinery etc) installation f.

ergonomics [ûrgənâm'iks] n ergonomie f.

ERISA n abbr (US: = Employee Retirement Income Security Act) loi sur les pensions de retraite.

ermine [ûr'min] n hermine f.

erode [irōd'] vt éroder; (metal) ronger.

erosion [irō'zhən] n érosion f.

erotic [irât'ik] a érotique.

eroticism [irât'isizəm] n érotisme m.

err [ûr] vi se tromper; (REL) pécher.

errand [är'ənd] n course f, commission f; **to run ~s** faire des courses; **~ of mercy** mission f de charité, acte m charitable.

errand boy n garçon m de courses.

erratic [irat'ik] a irrégulier(ière); inconstant(e).

erroneous [irō'nēəs] a erroné(e).

error [är'ûr] n erreur f; **typing/spelling ~** faute f de frappe/d'orthographe; **in ~** par erreur, par méprise; **~s and omissions excepted** sauf erreur ou omission.

error message n (COMPUT) message m d'erreur.

erstwhile [ûrst'hwīl] a précédent(e), d'autrefois.

erudite [är'yōōdīt] a savant(e).

erupt [irupt'] vi entrer en éruption; (fig) éclater, exploser.

eruption [irup'shən] n éruption f; (of anger, violence) explosion f.

ESA n abbr (= European Space Agency) ASE f (= Agence spatiale européenne).

escalate [ɛs'kəlāt] vi s'intensifier; (costs) monter en flèche.

escalation [ɛs'kəlāshən] n escalade f.

escalation clause [ɛskəlā'shən klōz] n clause f d'indexation.

escalator [ɛs'kəlātûr] n escalier roulant.

escapade [ɛs'kəpād] n fredaine f; équipée f.

escape [ɛskāp'] n évasion f, fuite f; (of gas etc) fuite; (TECH) échappement m ♦ vi s'échapper, fuir; (from jail) s'évader; (fig) s'en tirer, en réchapper; (leak) fuir; s'échapper ♦ vt échapper à; **to ~ from** (person) échapper à; (place) s'échapper de;

(fig) fuir; **to ~ to** (another place) fuir à, s'enfuir à; **to ~ to safety** se réfugier dans or gagner un endroit sûr; **to ~ notice** passer inaperçu(e).

escape artist n virtuose m/f de l'évasion.

escape clause n clause f dérogatoire.

escape key n (COMPUT) touche f d'échappement.

escape route n (from fire) issue f de secours; (of prisoners etc) voie empruntée pour s'échapper.

escapism [ɛskā'pizəm] n évasion f (fig).

escapist [ɛskā'pist] a (literature) d'évasion ♦ n personne f qui se réfugie hors de la réalité.

escapologist [ɛskəpâl'əjist] n (Brit) = **escape artist**.

escarpment [ɛskârp'mənt] n escarpement m.

eschew [ɛschōō'] vt éviter.

escort vt [ɛskôrt'] escorter ♦ n [ɛs'kôrt] escorte f; (to dance etc): **her ~** son compagnon or cavalier; **his ~** sa compagne.

escort agency n bureau m d'hôtesses.

Eskimo [ɛs'kəmō] a esquimau(de), eskimo ♦ n Esquimau/de; (LING) esquimau m.

ESL n abbr (SCOL) = English as a Second Language.

esophagus [isâf'əgəs] n (US) oesophage m.

esoteric [ɛsətär'ik] a ésotérique.

ESP n abbr = **extrasensory perception**.

esp. abbr = **especially**.

especially [ɛspesh'əlē] ad (specifically) spécialement, exprès; (more than usually) particulièrement; (above all) particulièrement, surtout.

espionage [ɛs'pēənâzh] n espionnage m.

esplanade [ɛsplənād'] n esplanade f.

espouse [ɛspouz'] vt épouser, embrasser.

Esquire [ɛs'kwiûr] n (Brit: abbr **Esq.**): J. Brown, **~** Monsieur J. Brown.

essay [ɛs'ā] n (SCOL) dissertation f; (LITERATURE) essai m; (attempt) tentative f.

essence [ɛs'əns] n essence f; (fig): **speed is of the ~** l'essentiel, c'est la rapidité.

essential [əsen'chəl] a essentiel(le); (basic) fondamental(e) ♦ n élément essentiel; **it is ~ that** il est essentiel or primordial que.

essentially [əsen'chəlē] ad essentiellement.

EST abbr (US: = Eastern Standard Time) heure d'hiver de New York.

est. abbr = **established, estimate(d)**.

establish [əstab'lish] vt établir; (business) fonder, créer; (one's power etc) asseoir, affermir.

establishment [əstab'lishmənt] n établissement m; création f; (institution) établissement; **the E~** les pouvoirs établis; l'ordre établi.

estate [əstāt'] n (land) domaine m, propriété f; (LAW) biens mpl, succession f; (Brit: also: **housing ~**) lotissement m.

estate agent n (Brit) agent immobilier.

estate car n (Brit) break m.

esteem [əstēm'] n estime f ♦ vt estimer; apprécier; **to hold sb in high ~** tenir qn en haute estime.

esthetic [esthet'ik] a (US) esthétique.

estimate n [ɛs'təmit] estimation f; (COMM) devis m ♦ vt [ɛs'təmāt] estimer; **to give sb an**

~ **of** faire *or* donner un devis à qn pour; **at a rough** ~ approximativement.

estimation [ɛstəmā'shən] *n* opinion *f*; estime *f*; **in my** ~ à mon avis, selon moi.

estimator [ɛs'təmātûr] *n* personne *f* qui évalue.

Estonia [ɛstō'nēə] *n* Estonie *f*.

estranged [ɛstrānjd'] *a* (*couple*) séparé(e); (*husband, wife*) dont on s'est séparé(e).

estrangement [ɛstrānj'mənt] *n* (*from wife, family*) séparation *f*.

estrogen [ɛs'trəjən] *n* (*US*) oestrogène.

estuary [ɛs'chōōārē] *n* estuaire *m*.

ETA *n abbr* (= *estimated time of arrival*) HPA *f* (= *heure probable d'arrivée*).

et al. [ɛt âl] *abbr* (= *et alii: and others*) et coll.

etc. *abbr* (= *et cetera*) etc.

etch [ɛch] *vt* graver à l'eau forte.

etching [ɛch'ing] *n* eau-forte *f*.

ETD *n abbr* (= *estimated time of departure*) HPA *f* (= *heure probable de départ*).

eternal [itûr'nəl] *a* éternel(le).

eternity [itûr'nitē] *n* éternité *f*.

ether [ē'thûr] *n* éther *m*.

ethereal [ithēr'ēəl] *a* éthéré(e).

ethical [ɛth'ikəl] *a* moral(e).

ethics [ɛth'iks] *n* éthique *f* ♦ *npl* moralité *f*.

Ethiopia [ēthēō'pēə] *n* Ethiopie *f*.

Ethiopian [ēthēō'pēən] *a* éthiopien(ne) ♦ *n* Ethiopien/ne.

ethnic [ɛth'nik] *a* ethnique; (*clothes, food*) folklorique, exotique: *propre aux minorités ethniques non-occidentales.*

ethnology [ɛthnâl'əjē] *n* ethnologie *f*.

ethos [ē'thâs] *n* (système *m* de) valeurs *fpl*.

etiquette [ɛt'əkit] *n* convenances *fpl*, étiquette *f*.

ETV *n abbr* (*US*: = *Educational Television*) télévision scolaire.

etymology [ɛtəmâl'əjē] *n* étymologie *f*.

eucalyptus [yōōkəlip'təs] *n* eucalyptus *m*.

eulogy [yōō'ləjē] *n* éloge *m*.

euphemism [yōō'fəmizəm] *n* euphémisme *m*.

euphemistic [yōōfəmis'tik] *a* euphémique.

euphoria [yōōfôr'ēə] *n* euphorie *f*.

Eurasia [yōōrā'zhə] *n* Eurasie *f*.

Eurasian [yōōrā'zhən] *a* eurasien(ne); (*continent*) eurasiatique ♦ *n* Eurasien/ne.

Euratom [yōōrat'əm] *n abbr* (= *European Atomic Energy Community*) EURATOM *f*.

Euro... [yōō'rō] *prefix* euro....

Eurocheque [yōō'rōchɛk] *n* (*Brit*) eurochèque *m*.

Eurocrat [yōō'rəkrat] *n* eurocrate *m/f*.

Eurodollar [yōō'rōdâlûr] *n* eurodollar *m*.

Europe [yōō'rəp] *n* Europe *f*.

European [yōōrəpē'ən] *a* européen(ne) ♦ *n* Européen/ne.

European Court of Justice *n* Cour *f* de Justice de la CEE.

euthanasia [yōōthənā'zhə] *n* euthanasie *f*.

evacuate [ivak'yōōāt] *vt* évacuer.

evacuation [ivakyōōā'shən] *n* évacuation *f*.

evade [ivād'] *vt* échapper à; (*question etc*) éluder; (*duties*) se dérober à.

evaluate [ival'yōōāt] *vt* évaluer.

evangelist [ivan'jəlist] *n* évangéliste *m*.

evangelize [ivan'jəlīz] *vt* évangéliser, prêcher l'Evangile à.

evaporate [ivap'ərāt] *vi* s'évaporer ♦ *vt* faire évaporer.

evaporated milk [ivap'ərātid milk'] *n* lait condensé (non sucré).

evaporation [ivapərā'shən] *n* évaporation *f*.

evasion [ivā'zhən] *n* dérobade *f*; (*excuse*) faux-fuyant *m*.

evasive [ivā'siv] *a* évasif(ive).

eve [ēv] *n*: **on the** ~ **of** à la veille de.

even [ē'vən] *a* régulier(ière), égal(e); (*number*) pair(e) ♦ *ad* même; ~ **if** même si + *indicative*; ~ **though** quand (bien) même + *conditional*, alors même que + *conditional*; ~ **more** encore plus; ~ **faster** encore plus vite; ~ **so** quand même; **not** ~ pas même; **to break** ~ s'y retrouver, équilibrer ses comptes; **to get** ~ **with sb** prendre sa revanche sur qn.

even out *vi* s'égaliser.

evening [ēv'ning] *n* soir *m*; (*as duration, event*) soirée *f*; **in the** ~ le soir; **this** ~ ce soir; **tomorrow/yesterday** ~ demain/hier soir.

evening class *n* cours *m* du soir.

evening dress *n* (*man's*) habit *m* de soirée, smoking *m*; (*woman's*) robe *f* de soirée.

evenly [ē'vənlē] *ad* uniformément, également; (*space*) régulièrement.

evensong [ē'vənsông] *n* office *m* du soir.

event [ivɛnt'] *n* événement *m*; (*SPORT*) épreuve *f*; **in the course of** ~s par la suite; **in the** ~ **of** en cas de; **in the** ~ en réalité, en fait; **in any** ~ en tout cas, de toute manière.

eventful [ivɛnt'fəl] *a* mouvementé(e).

eventual [ivɛn'chōōəl] *a* final(e).

eventuality [ivɛnchōōal'itē] *n* possibilité *f*, éventualité *f*.

eventually [ivɛn'chōōəlē] *ad* finalement.

ever [ɛv'ûr] *ad* jamais; (*at all times*) toujours; **the best** ~ le meilleur qu'on ait jamais vu; **did you** ~ **meet him?** est-ce qu'il vous est arrivé de le rencontrer?; **have you** ~ **been there?** y êtes-vous déjà allé?; **for** ~ pour toujours; **hardly** ~ ne ... presque jamais; ~ **since** *ad* depuis ♦ *cj* depuis que; ~ **so pretty** si joli; **thank you** ~ **so much** merci mille fois; **yours** ~ (*Brit*: *in letters*) cordialement vôtre.

Everest [ɛv'ûrist] *n* (*also*: **Mount** ~) le mont Everest, l'Everest *m*.

evergreen [ɛv'ûrgrēn] *n* arbre *m* à feuilles persistantes.

everlasting [ɛvûrlas'ting] *a* éternel(le).

every [ɛv'rē] *a* chaque; ~ **day** tous les jours, chaque jour; ~ **other/third day** tous les deux/trois jours; ~ **other car** une voiture sur deux; ~ **now and then** de temps en temps; **I have** ~ **confidence in him** j'ai entièrement *or* pleinement confiance en lui.

everybody [ɛv'rēbâdē] *pronoun* tout le monde, tous *pl*; ~ **knows about it** tout le monde le sait; ~ **else** tous les autres.

everyday [ɛv'rēdā] *a* (*expression*) courant(e), d'usage courant; (*use*) courant; (*occurrence, experience*) de tous les jours, ordinaire.

everyone [ɛv'rēwun] *pronoun* = **everybody**.

everything [ɛv'rēthing] *pronoun* tout; ~ **is ready** tout est prêt; **he did** ~ **possible** il a fait tout son possible.

everywhere [ɛv'rēhwär] *ad* partout; ~ **you go you meet ...** où qu'on aille, on rencontre ....

evict [ivikt'] *vt* expulser.

eviction [ivik'shən] *n* expulsion *f*.

eviction notice *n* préavis *m* d'expulsion.

evidence [ɛv'idəns] *n* (*proof*) preuve(s) *f(pl)*; (*of witness*) témoignage *m*; (*sign*): **to show** ~ **of** donner des signes de; **to give** ~ témoigner, déposer; **in** ~ (*obvious*) en évidence; en vue.

evident [ɛv'idənt] *a* évident(e).

evidently [ɛv'idəntlē] *ad* de toute évidence.

evil [ē'vəl] *a* mauvais(e) ♦ *n* mal *m*.

evince [ivins'] *vt* manifester.

evocative [ivȧk'ətiv] *a* évocateur(trice).

evoke [ivōk'] *vt* évoquer; (*admiration*) susciter.

evolution [ɛvəlōō'shən] *n* évolution *f*.

evolve [ivȧlv'] *vt* élaborer ♦ *vi* évoluer, se transformer.

ewe [yōō] *n* brebis *f*.

ewer [yōō'ûr] *n* broc *m*.

ex- [ɛks] *prefix* (*former*: *husband*, *president etc*) ex-; (*out of*): **the price** ~**works** le prix départ usine.

exacerbate [igzas'ûrbāt] *vt* (*pain*) exacerber, accentuer; (*fig*) aggraver.

exact [igzakt'] *a* exact(e) ♦ *vt*: **to** ~ **sth (from)** extorquer qch (à); exiger qch (de).

exacting [igzak'ting] *a* exigeant(e); (*work*) fatigant(e).

exactitude [igzakt'ətōōd] *n* exactitude *f*, précision *f*.

exactly [igzakt'lē] *ad* exactement; ~! parfaitement!, précisément!

exaggerate [igzaj'ərāt] *vt*, *vi* exagérer.

exaggeration [igzajərā'shən] *n* exagération *f*.

exalted [igzôl'tid] *a* (*rank*) élevé(e); (*person*) haut placé(e); (*elated*) exalté(e).

exam [igzam'] *n* abbr (SCOL) = **examination**.

examination [igzamənā'shən] *n* (SCOL, MED) examen *m*; **to take an** ~ passer un examen; **the matter is under** ~ la question est à l'examen.

examine [igzam'in] *vt* (*gen*) examiner; (SCOL, LAW: *person*) interroger; (*inspect*: *machine, premises*) inspecter; (*passport*) contrôler; (*luggage*) fouiller.

examiner [igzam'inûr] *n* examinateur/trice.

example [igzam'pəl] *n* exemple *m*; **for** ~ par exemple; **to set a good/bad** ~ donner le bon/mauvais exemple.

exasperate [igzas'pərāt] *vt* exaspérer, agacer.

exasperation [igzaspərā'shən] *n* exaspération *f*, irritation *f*.

excavate [ɛks'kəvāt] *vt* excaver; (*object*) mettre au jour.

excavation [ɛks'kəvā'shən] *n* excavation *f*.

excavator [ɛks'kəvātûr] *n* excavateur *m*, excavatrice *f*.

exceed [iksēd'] *vt* dépasser; (*one's powers*) outrepasser.

exceedingly [iksē'dinglē] *ad* excessivement.

excel [iksɛl'] *vi* exceller ♦ *vt* surpasser.

excellence [ɛk'sələns] *n* excellence *f*.

Excellency [ɛk'sələnsē] *n*: **His** ~ son Excellence *f*.

excellent [ɛk'sələnt] *a* excellent(e).

except [iksɛpt'] *prep* (*also*: ~ **for**, ~**ing**) sauf,

excepté, à l'exception de ♦ *vt* excepter; ~ **if/ when** sauf si/quand; ~ **that** excepté que, si ce n'est que.

exception [iksɛp'shən] *n* exception *f*; **to take** ~ **to** s'offusquer de; **with the** ~ **of** à l'exception de.

exceptional [iksɛp'shənəl] *a* exceptionnel(le).

excerpt [ɛk'sûrpt] *n* extrait *m*.

excess [ɛkses'] *n* excès *m*; **in** ~ **of** plus de.

excess baggage *n* excédent *m* de bagages.

excess fare *n* supplément *m*.

excessive [ikses'iv] *a* excessif(ive).

excess supply *n* suroffre *f*, offre *f* excédentaire.

exchange [ikschānj'] *n* échange *m*; (*also*: **telephone** ~) central *m* ♦ *vt*: **to** ~ **(for)** échanger (contre); **in** ~ **for** en échange de; **foreign** ~ (COMM) change *m*.

exchange control *n* contrôle *m* des changes.

exchange market *n* marché *m* des changes.

exchange rate *n* taux *m* de change.

exchequer [ɛks'chekûr] *n* (*Brit*) Échiquier *m*, ≈ ministère *m* des Finances.

excisable [iksī'zəbəl] *a* taxable.

excise *n* [ɛk'sīz] taxe *f* ♦ *vt* [iksīz'] exciser.

excise duties *npl* impôts indirects.

excitable [iksī'təbəl] *a* excitable, nerveux(euse).

excite [iksīt'] *vt* exciter; **to get** ~**d** s'exciter.

excitement [iksīt'mənt] *n* excitation *f*.

exciting [iksī'ting] *a* passionnant(e).

excl. *abbr* = **excluding, exclusive (of)**.

exclaim [iksklām'] *vi* s'exclamer.

exclamation [ɛkskləmā'shən] *n* exclamation *f*.

exclamation mark *n* point *m* d'exclamation.

exclude [iksklōōd'] *vt* exclure.

excluding [iksklōō'ding] *prep*: ~ **VAT** la TVA non comprise.

exclusion [iksklōō'zhən] *n* exclusion *f*; **to the** ~ **of** à l'exclusion de.

exclusion clause *n* clause *f* d'exclusion.

exclusive [iksklōō'siv] *a* exclusif(ive); (*club, district*) sélect(e); (*item of news*) en exclusivité ♦ *ad* (COMM) exclusivement, non inclus; ~ **of VAT** TVA non comprise; ~ **of postage** (les) frais de poste non compris; **from 1st to 15th March** ~ du 1er au 15 mars exclusivement *or* exclu; ~ **rights** (COMM) exclusivité *f*.

exclusively [iksklōō'sivlē] *ad* exclusivement.

excommunicate [ɛkskəmyōō'nəkāt] *vt* excommunier.

excrement [ɛks'krəmənt] *n* excrément *m*.

excruciating [ikskrōō'shēāting] *a* atroce, déchirant(e).

excursion [ikskûr'zhən] *n* excursion *f*.

excursion ticket *n* billet *m* à tarif excursion.

excusable [ikskyōō'zəbəl] *a* excusable.

excuse *n* [ikskyōōs'] excuse *f* ♦ *vt* [ikskyōōz'] excuser; (*justify*) excuser, justifier; **to** ~ **sb from** (*activity*) dispenser qn de; ~ **me!** excusez-moi!, pardon!; **now if you will** ~ **me, ...** maintenant, si vous (le) permettez ...; **to make** ~**s for sb** trouver des excuses à qn; **to** ~ **o.s. for sth/for doing sth** s'excuser de/ d'avoir fait qch.

ex-directory [ɛksdirɛk'tûrē] *a* (*Brit*): ~ **(phone) number** numéro *m* (de téléphone) sur la liste rouge.

exec. [igzek'] *abbr* = **executive.**
execute [ek'səkyōōt] *vt* exécuter.
execution [eksəkyōō'shən] *n* exécution *f*.
executioner [eksəkyōō'shənûr] *n* bourreau *m*.
executive [igzek'yətiv] *n* (*COMM*) cadre *m*; (*POL*) exécutif *m* ♦ *a* exécutif(ive); (*position, job*) de cadre; (*secretary*) de direction; (*offices*) de la direction; (*car, plane*) de fonction.
executive director *n* administrateur/trice.
executor [igzek'yətûr] *n* exécuteur/trice testamentaire.
exemplary [igzem'plûrē] *a* exemplaire.
exemplify [igzem'pləfī] *vt* illustrer.
exempt [igzempt'] *a*: ~ **from** exempté(e) *or* dispensé(e) de ♦ *vt*: **to** ~ **sb from** exempter *or* dispenser qn de.
exemption [igzemp'shən] *n* exemption *f*, dispense *f*.
exercise [ek'sûrsīz] *n* exercice *m* ♦ *vt* exercer; (*patience etc*) faire preuve de; (*dog*) promener ♦ *vi* prendre de l'exercice.
exercise book *n* cahier *m*.
exert [igzûrt'] *vt* exercer, employer; (*strength, force*) employer; **to** ~ **o.s.** se dépenser.
exertion [igzûr'shən] *n* effort *m*.
ex gratia [eks grā'tēə] *a*: ~ **payment** gratification *f*.
exhale [eks·hāl'] *vt* expirer; exhaler ♦ *vi* expirer.
exhaust [igzôst'] *n* (*also*: ~ **fumes**) gaz *mpl* d'échappement; (*also*: ~ **pipe**) tuyau *m* d'échappement ♦ *vt* épuiser; **to** ~ **o.s.** s'épuiser.
exhausted [igzôs'tid] *a* épuisé(e).
exhausting [igzôs'ting] *a* épuisant(e).
exhaustion [igzôs'chən] *n* épuisement *m*; **nervous** ~ fatigue nerveuse.
exhaustive [igzôs'tiv] *a* très complet(ète).
exhibit [igzib'it] *n* (*ART*) pièce *f or* objet *m* exposé(e); (*LAW*) pièce à conviction ♦ *vt* exposer; (*courage, skill*) faire preuve de.
exhibition [eksəbish'ən] *n* exposition *f*; ~ **of temper** manifestation *f* de colère.
exhibitionist [eksəbish'ənist] *n* exhibitionniste *m/f*.
exhibitor [igzib'ətûr] *n* exposant/e.
exhilarating [igzil'ərāting] *a* grisant(e); stimulant(e).
exhilaration [igzilərā'shən] *n* euphorie *f*, ivresse *f*.
exhort [igzôrt'] *vt* exhorter.
exile [eg'zīl] *n* exil *m*; (*person*) exilé/e ♦ *vt* exiler; **in** ~ en exil.
exist [igzist'] *vi* exister.
existence [igzis'təns] *n* existence *f*; **to be in** ~ exister.
existentialism [egzisten'chəlizəm] *n* existentialisme *m*.
existing [igzis'ting] *a* (*laws*) existant(e); (*system, regime*) actuel(le).
exit [eg'zit] *n* sortie *f* ♦ *vi* (*COMPUT, THEATER*) sortir.
exit poll *n* (*POL*) sondage *m* à la sortie des bureaux de vote.
exit ramp *n* (*US AUT*) bretelle *f* d'accès.
exit visa *n* visa *m* de sortie.
exodus [ek'sədəs] *n* exode *m*.
ex officio [eks əfish'ēō] *a*, *ad* d'office, de droit.

exonerate [igzàn'ərāt] *vt*: **to** ~ **from** disculper de.
exorbitant [igzôr'bətənt] *a* (*price*) exorbitant(e), excessif(ive); (*demands*) exorbitant, démesuré(e).
exorcize [ek'sôrsīz] *vt* exorciser.
exotic [igzát'ik] *a* exotique.
exp. *abbr* = **expenses; expired; export; express.**
expand [ikspand'] *vt* (*area*) agrandir; (*quantity*) accroître; (*influence etc*) étendre ♦ *vi* (*population, production*) s'accroître; (*trade, influence etc*) se développer, s'étendre; (*gas, metal*) se dilater; **to** ~ **on** (*notes, story etc*) développer.
expanse [ikspans'] *n* étendue *f*.
expansion [ikspan'chən] *n* (*see expand*) développement *m*; accroissement *m*; extension *f*; dilatation *f*.
expansionism [ikspan'chənizəm] *n* expansionnisme *m*.
expansionist [ikspan'chənist] *a* expansionniste.
expatriate *n* [ekspā'trēit] expatrié/e ♦ *vt* [ekspā'trēāt] expatrier, exiler.
expect [ikspekt'] *vt* (*anticipate*) s'attendre à, s'attendre à ce que + *sub*; (*count on*) compter sur, escompter; (*hope for*) espérer; (*require*) demander, exiger; (*suppose*) supposer; (*await, also baby*) attendre ♦ *vi*: **to be** ~**ing** être enceinte; **to** ~ **sb to do** (*anticipate*) s'attendre à ce que qn fasse; (*demand*) attendre de qn qu'il fasse; **to** ~ **to do sth** penser *or* compter faire qch, s'attendre à faire qch; **as** ~**ed** comme prévu; **I** ~ **so** je crois que oui, je crois bien.
expectancy [ikspek'tənsē] *n* attente *f*; **life** ~ espérance *f* de vie.
expectant [ikspek'tənt] *a* qui attend (quelque chose); ~ **mother** future maman.
expectantly [ikspek'təntlē] *ad* (*look, listen*) avec l'air d'attendre quelque chose.
expectation [ikspektā'shən] *n* attente *f*, prévisions *fpl*; espérance(s) *f(pl)*; **in** ~ **of** dans l'attente de, en prévision de; **against** *or* **contrary to all** ~**(s)** contre toute attente, contrairement à ce qu'on attendait; **to come** *or* **live up to sb's** ~**s** répondre à l'attente *or* aux espérances de qn.
expedience, expediency [ikspē'dēəns, ikspē'dēənsē] *n* opportunité *f*; convenance *f* (du moment); **for the sake of** ~ parce que c'est (*or* c'était) plus simple *or* plus commode.
expedient [ikspē'dēənt] *a* indiqué(e), opportun(e); commode ♦ *n* expédient *m*.
expedite [ek'spidīt] *vt* hâter; expédier.
expedition [ekspidish'ən] *n* expédition *f*.
expeditionary force [ekspədish'ənārē fôrs] *n* corps *m* expéditionnaire.
expeditious [ekspidish'əs] *a* expéditif(ive), prompt(e).
expel [ikspel'] *vt* chasser, expulser; (*SCOL*) renvoyer, exclure.
expend [ikspend'] *vt* consacrer; (*use up*) dépenser.
expendable [ikspen'dəbəl] *a* remplaçable.
expenditure [ikspen'dichûr] *n* dépense *f*; dépenses *fpl*.
expense [ikspens'] *n* (*cost*) coût *m*; (*spending*)

dépense f, frais mpl; ~s npl frais mpl; dépenses; **to go to the** ~ **of** faire la dépense de; **at great/little** ~ à grands/peu de frais; **at the** ~ **of** aux frais de; (fig) aux dépens de.

expense account n (note f de) frais mpl.

expensive [ikspen'siv] a cher(chère), coûteux(euse); **to be** ~ coûter cher; ~ **tastes** goûts mpl de luxe.

experience [ikspēr'ēəns] n expérience f ♦ vt connaître; éprouver; **to know by** ~ savoir par expérience.

experienced [ikspēr'ēənst] a expérimenté(e).

experiment n [ikspär'əmənt] expérience f ♦ vi [ikspär'əment] faire une expérience; **to** ~ **with** expérimenter; **to perform** or **carry out an** ~ faire une expérience; **as an** ~ à titre d'expérience.

experimental [ikspärəmen'təl] a expérimental(e).

expert [ek'spûrt] a expert(e) ♦ n expert m; ~ **in** or **at doing sth** spécialiste de qch; an ~ **on sth** un spécialiste de qch; ~ **witness** (LAW) expert m.

expertise [ekspûrtēz'] n (grande) compétence.

expiration [ekspərā'shən] n expiration f.

expire [ikspī'ûr] vi expirer.

expiry [ikspīûr'ē] n (Brit) expiration f.

explain [iksplān'] vt expliquer.

explain away vt justifier, excuser.

explanation [eksplənā'shən] n explication f; **to find an** ~ **for sth** trouver une explication à qch.

explanatory [iksplan'ətôrē] a explicatif(ive).

explicit [iksplis'it] a explicite; (definite) formel(le).

explode [iksplōd'] vi exploser ♦ vt faire exploser; (fig: theory) démolir; **to** ~ **a myth** détruire un mythe.

exploit n [eks'ploit] exploit m ♦ vt [iksploit'] exploiter.

exploitation [eksploitā'shən] n exploitation f.

exploration [eksplərā'shən] n exploration f.

exploratory [iksplôr'ətôrē] a (fig: talks) préliminaire; ~ **operation** (MED) intervention f (à visée) exploratrice.

explore [iksplôr'] vt explorer; (possibilities) étudier, examiner.

explorer [iksplôr'ûr] n explorateur/trice.

explosion [iksplō'zhən] n explosion f.

explosive [iksplō'siv] a explosif(ive) ♦ n explosif m.

exponent [ekspō'nent] n (of school of thought etc) interprète m, représentant m; (MATH) exposant m.

export vt [ikspôrt'] exporter ♦ n [eks'pôrt] exportation f ♦ cpd d'exportation.

exportation [ekspôrtā'shən] n exportation f.

exporter [ekspôr'tûr] n exportateur m.

export license n licence f d'exportation.

expose [ikspōz'] vt exposer; (unmask) démasquer, dévoiler; **to** ~ **o.s.** (LAW) commettre un outrage à la pudeur.

exposed [ikspōzd'] a (land, house) exposé(e); (ELEC: wire) à nu; (pipe, beam) apparent(e).

exposition [ekspəzish'ən] n exposition f.

exposure [ikspō'zhûr] n exposition f; (PHOT) (temps m de) pose f; (: shot) pose; **suffering from** ~ (MED) souffrant des effets du froid et de l'épuisement; **to die of** ~ (MED) mourir de froid.

exposure meter n posemètre m.

expound [ikspound'] vt exposer, expliquer.

express [ikspres'] a (definite) formel(le), exprès(esse); (Brit: letter etc) exprès inv ♦ n (train) rapide m ♦ ad (send) exprès ♦ vt exprimer; **to** ~ **o.s.** s'exprimer; **to send sth** ~ envoyer qch exprès.

expression [ikspresh'ən] n expression f.

expressionism [ikspresh'ənizəm] n expressionnisme m.

expressive [ikspres'iv] a expressif(ive).

expressly [ikspres'lē] ad expressément, formellement.

expressway [ikspres'wā] n voie f express (à plusieurs files).

expropriate [eksprōp'rēāt] vt exproprier.

expulsion [ikspul'shən] n expulsion f; renvoi m.

exquisite [ekskwiz'it] a exquis(e).

ex-serviceman [ekssûr'vismən] n (Brit) ancien combattant.

ext. abbr (TEL) = **extension.**

extemporize [ikstem'pərīz] vi improviser.

extend [ikstend'] vt (visit, street) prolonger; (deadline) reporter, remettre; (building) agrandir; (offer) présenter, offrir; (COMM: credit) accorder ♦ vi (land) s'étendre.

extension [iksten'chən] n (see extend) prolongation f; agrandissement m; (building) annexe f; (to wire, table) rallonge f; (telephone: in offices) poste m; (: in private house) téléphone m supplémentaire; ~ **3718** (TEL) poste 3718.

extension cord n (ELEC) rallonge f.

extensive [iksten'siv] a étendu(e), vaste; (damage, alterations) considérable; (inquiries) approfondi(e); (use) largement répandu(e).

extensively [iksten'sivlē] ad (altered, damaged etc) considérablement; **he's traveled** ~ il a beaucoup voyagé.

extent [ikstent'] n étendue f; (degree: of damage, loss) importance f, **to some** ~ dans une certaine mesure; **to a certain** ~ dans une certaine mesure, jusqu'à un certain point; **to a large** ~ en grande partie; **to what** ~? dans quelle mesure?, jusqu'à quel point?; **to such an** ~ **that** ... à tel point que ....

extenuating [iksten'yōōāting] a: ~ **circumstances** circonstances atténuantes.

exterior [ikstēr'ēûr] a extérieur(e), du dehors ♦ n extérieur m; dehors m.

exterminate [ikstûr'mənāt] vt exterminer.

extermination [ikstûrmənā'shən] n extermination f.

extern [eks'tûrn] n (US) externe m/f.

external [ikstûr'nəl] a externe ♦ n: **the** ~**s** les apparences fpl; **for** ~ **use only** (MED) à usage externe.

externally [ikstûr'nəlē] ad extérieurement.

extinct [ikstingkt'] a éteint(e).

extinction [ikstingk'shən] n extinction f.

extinguish [iksting'gwish] vt éteindre.

extinguisher [iksting'gwishûr] n extincteur m.

extoll, (Brit) **extol** [ikstōl'] vt (merits) chanter, prôner; (person) chanter les louanges de.

extort [ikstôrt'] *vt*: **to** ~ **sth (from)** extorquer qch (à).

extortion [ikstôr'shən] *n* extorsion *f*.

extortionate [ikstôr'shənit] *a* exorbitant(e).

extra [ek'strə] *a* supplémentaire, de plus ♦ *ad* (*in addition*) en plus ♦ *n* supplément *m*; (*THEATER*) figurant/e; **wine will cost** ~ le vin sera en supplément; ~ **large sizes** très grandes tailles.

extra... *prefix* extra....

extract *vt* [ikstrakt'] extraire; (*tooth*) arracher; (*money, promise*) soutirer ♦ *n* [eks'trakt] extrait *m*.

extraction [ikstrak'shən] *n* (*also descent*) extraction *f*.

extracurricular [ekstrəkərik'yəlûr] *a* (*SCOL*) parascolaire.

extradite [eks'trədit] *vt* extrader.

extradition [ekstrədish'ən] *n* extradition *f*.

extramarital [ekstrəmar'itəl] *a* extraconjugal(e).

extramural [ekstrəmyōōr'əl] *a* hors-faculté *inv*.

extraneous [ikstrā'nēəs] *a*: ~ **to** étranger(ère) à.

extraordinary [ikstrôr'dənärē] *a* extraordinaire; **the** ~ **thing is that** ... le plus étrange *or* étonnant c'est que ....

extraordinary general meeting *n* assemblée générale extraordinaire.

extrapolation [ikstrapəlā'shən] *n* extrapolation *f*.

extrasensory perception (ESP) [ekstrəsen'sûrē pûrsep'shən] *n* perception extra-sensorielle.

extra time *n* (*SOCCER*) prolongations *fpl*.

extravagance [ikstrav'əgəns] *n* (*excessive spending*) prodigalités *fpl*; (*thing bought*) folie *f*, dépense excessive *or* exagérée.

extravagant [ikstrav'əgənt] *a* extravagant(e); (*in spending: person*) prodigue, dépensier(ière); (: *tastes*) dispendieux(euse).

extreme [ikstrēm'] *a*, *n* extrême *(m)*; **the** ~ **left/right** (*POL*) l'extrême gauche *f*/droite *f*; ~**s of temperature** différences *fpl* extrêmes de température.

extremely [ikstrēm'lē] *ad* extrêmement.

extremist [ikstrē'mist] *a*, *n* extrémiste *(m/f)*.

extremity [ikstrem'itē] *n* extrémité *f*.

extricate [ek'strikāt] *vt*: **to** ~ **sth (from)** dégager qch (de).

extrovert [ek'strōvûrt] *n* extraverti/e.

exuberance [igzōō'bûrəns] *n* exubérance *f*.

exuberant [igzōō'bûrənt] *a* exubérant(e).

exude [igzōōd'] *vt* exsuder; (*fig*) respirer; **the charm** *etc* **he** ~**s** le charme *etc* qui émane de lui.

exult [igzult'] *vi* exulter, jubiler.

exultant [igzul'tənt] *a* (*shout, expression*) de triomphe; **to be** ~ jubiler, triompher.

exultation [egzultā'shən] *n* exultation *f*, jubilation *f*.

eye [ī] *n* œil *m* (*pl* yeux); (*of needle*) trou *m*, chas *m* ♦ *vt* examiner; **as far as the** ~ **can see** à perte de vue; **to keep an** ~ **on** surveiller; **to have an** ~ **for sth** avoir l'œil pour qch; **in the public** ~ en vue; **there's more to this than meets the** ~ ce n'est pas aussi simple que cela paraît.

eyeball [ī'bôl] *n* globe *m* oculaire.

eyebath [ī'bath] *n* (*Brit*) = **eye cup.**

eyebrow [ī'brou] *n* sourcil *m*.

eyebrow pencil *n* crayon *m* à sourcils.

eye-catching [ī'kaching] *a* voyant(e), accrocheur(euse).

eye cup *n* (*US*) œillère *f* (*pour bains d'œil*).

eyedrops [ī'drāps] *npl* gouttes *fpl* pour les yeux.

eyeglass [ī'glas] *n* monocle *m*.

eyelash [ī'lash] *n* cil *m*.

eyelet [ī'lit] *n* œillet *m*.

eye-level [ī'levəl] *a* en hauteur.

eyelid [ī'lid] *n* paupière *f*.

eyeliner [ī'līnûr] *n* eye-liner *m*.

eye-opener [ī'ōpənûr] *n* révélation *f*.

eyeshadow [ī'shadō] *n* ombre *f* à paupières.

eyesight [ī'sīt] *n* vue *f*.

eyesore [ī'sôr] *n* horreur *f*, chose *f* qui dépare *or* enlaidit.

eyestrain [ī'strān] *a*: **to get** ~ se fatiguer la vue *or* les yeux.

eye test *n* examen *m* de la vue.

eyetooth *pl* **-teeth** [ī'tōōth, -tēth] *n* canine supérieure; **to give one's eyeteeth for sth/to do sth** (*fig*) donner n'importe quoi pour qch/pour faire qch.

eyewash [ī'wāsh] *n* bain *m* d'œil; (*fig*) frime *f*.

eye witness *n* témoin *m* oculaire.

eyrie [är'ē] *n* aire *f*.

F

F, f [ef] *n* (*letter*) F, f *m*; (*MUS*): **F** fa *m*; **F for Fox** F comme François.

F [ef] *abbr* (= *Fahrenheit*) F.

FA *n abbr* (*Brit*: = *Football Association*) fédération de football.

FAA *n abbr* (*US*) = *Federal Aviation Administration.*

fable [fā'bəl] *n* fable *f*.

fabric [fab'rik] *n* tissu *m* ♦ *cpd*: ~ **ribbon** *n* (*for typewriter*) ruban *m* (en) tissu.

fabricate [fab'rikāt] *vt* fabriquer, inventer.

fabrication [fabrikā'shən] *n* fabrication *f*, invention *f*.

fabulous [fab'yələs] *a* fabuleux(euse); (*col: super*) formidable, sensationnel(le).

façade [fəsâd'] *n* façade *f*.

face [fās] *n* visage *m*, figure *f*; expression *f*; grimace *f*; (*of clock*) cadran *m*; (*of building*) façade *f*; (*side, surface*) face *f*; (*in mine*) front *m* de taille ♦ *vt* faire face à; (*facts etc*) accepter; ~ **down** (*person*) à plat ventre; (*card*) face en dessous; **to lose/save** ~ perdre/sauver la face; **to make a** ~ faire une grimace; **in the** ~ **of** (*difficulties etc*) face à, devant; **on the** ~ **of it** à première vue.

face up to *vt fus* faire face à, affronter.

facecloth [fās'klôth] *n* gant *m* de toilette.

face cream *n* crème *f* pour le visage.

face lift *n* lifting *m*; (*of façade etc*) ravalement *m*, retapage *m*.

face powder *n* poudre *f* (pour le visage).

face-saving [fās'sāving] *a* qui sauve la face.

facet [fas'it] *n* facette *f*.

facetious [fəsē'shəs] *a* facétieux(euse).

face-to-face [fās'təfās'] *ad* face à face.

face value [fās val'yōō] *n* (*of coin*) valeur nominale; **to take sth at ~** (*fig*) prendre qch pour argent comptant.

facia [fā'shēə] *n* = **fascia**.

facial [fā'shəl] *a* facial(e) ♦ *n* soin complet du visage.

facile [fas'əl] *a* facile.

facilitate [fəsil'ətāt] *vt* faciliter.

facility [fəsil'ətē] *n* facilité *f*; **facilities** *npl* installations *fpl*, équipement *m*; **credit facilities** facilités de paiement.

facing [fā'sing] *prep* face à, en face de ♦ *n* (*of wall etc*) revêtement *m*; (*SEWING*) revers *m*.

facsimile [faksim'əlē] *n* (*exact replica*) fac-similé *m*; (*also:* **~ machine**) télécopieur *m*; (*transmitted document*) télécopie *f*.

fact [fakt] *n* fait *m*; **in ~** en fait; **to know for a ~ that** ... savoir pertinemment que ....

fact-finding [takt'fīnding] *a*: **a ~ tour** *or* **mission** une mission d'enquête.

faction [fak'shən] *n* faction *f*.

factor [fak'tûr] *n* facteur *m*; (*COMM*) factor *m*, société *f* d'affacturage; (*: agent*) dépositaire *m/f* ♦ *vi* faire du factoring; **safety ~** facteur de sécurité.

factory [fak'tûrē] *n* usine *f*, fabrique *f*.

factory farming *n* (*Brit*) élevage industriel.

factory ship *n* navire-usine *m*.

factual [fak'chōōəl] *a* basé(e) sur les faits.

faculty [fak'əltē] *n* faculté *f*; (*US: teaching staff*) corps enseignant.

fad [fad] *n* (*col*) manie *f*; engouement *m*.

fade [fād] *vi* se décolorer, passer; (*light, sound, hope*) s'affaiblir, disparaître; (*flower*) se faner.

fade in *vt* (*picture*) ouvrir en fondu; (*sound*) monter progressivement.

fade out *vt* (*picture*) fermer en fondu; (*sound*) baisser progressivement.

faeces [fē'sēz] *npl* (*Brit*) = **feces**.

fag [fag] *n* (*US col: homosexual*) pédé *m*; (*Brit col: cigarette*) sèche *f*; (*: chore*): **what a ~!** quelle corvée!

fag end *n* (*Brit col*) mégot *m*.

fail [fāl] *vt* (*exam*) échouer à; (*candidate*) recaler; (*subj: courage, memory*) faire défaut à ♦ *vi* échouer; (*supplies*) manquer; (*eyesight, health, light: also:* **be ~ing**) baisser, s'affaiblir; (*brakes*) lâcher; **to ~ to do sth** (*neglect*) négliger de *or* ne pas faire qch; (*be unable*) ne pas arriver *or* parvenir à faire qch; **without ~** à coup sûr; sans faute.

failing [fā'ling] *n* défaut *m* ♦ *prep* faute de; **~ that** à défaut, sinon.

failsafe [fāl'sāf] *a* (*device etc*) à sûreté intégrée.

failure [fāl'yûr] *n* échec *m*; (*person*) raté/e; (*mechanical etc*) défaillance *f*; **his ~ to turn up** le fait de n'être pas venu *or* qu'il ne soit pas venu.

faint [fānt] *a* faible; (*recollection*) vague; (*mark*) à peine visible; (*smell, breeze, trace*) léger(ère) ♦ *n* évanouissement *m* ♦ *vi* s'éva-

nouir; **to feel ~** défaillir.

faint-hearted [fānt'hár'tid] *a* pusillanime.

faintly [fānt'lē] *ad* faiblement; vaguement.

faintness [fānt'nis] *n* faiblesse *f*.

fair [fär] *a* équitable, juste; (*reasonable*) correct(e), honnête; (*hair*) blond(e); (*skin, complexion*) pâle, blanc(blanche); (*weather*) beau(belle); (*good enough*) assez bon(ne) ♦ *ad*: **to play ~** jouer franc jeu ♦ *n* foire *f*; (*carnival*) fête (foraine); (*also:* **trade ~**) foire(-exposition) commerciale; **it's not ~!** ce n'est pas juste!; **a ~ amount of** une quantité considérable de.

fairground [fär'ground] *n* champ *m* de foire.

fair-haired [fär'härd] *a* (*person*) aux cheveux clairs, blond(e).

fairly [fär'lē] *ad* équitablement; (*quite*) assez; **I'm ~ sure** j'en suis quasiment *or* presque sûr.

fairness [fär'nis] *n* (*of trial etc*) justice *f*, équité *f*; (*of person*) sens *m* de la justice; **in all ~** en toute justice.

fair play *n* fair play *m*.

fair trade *n* (*US*) vente *au détail á prix imposé*.

fairy [fär'ē] *n* fée *f*.

fairy godmother *n* bonne fée.

fairy tale *n* conte *m* de fées.

faith [fāth] *n* foi *f*; (*trust*) confiance *f*; (*sect*) culte *m*, religion *f*; **to have ~ in sb/sth** avoir confiance en sb/qch.

faithful [fāth'fəl] *a* fidèle.

faithfully [fāth'fəlē] *ad* fidèlement; **yours ~** (*Brit: in letters*) veuillez agréer l'expression de mes salutations les plus distinguées.

faith healer [fāth' he'lur] *n* guérisseur/euse.

fake [fāk] *n* (*painting etc*) faux *m*; (*photo*) trucage *m*; (*person*) imposteur *m* ♦ *a* faux(fausse) ♦ *vt* (*emotions*) simuler; (*photo*) truquer; (*story*) fabriquer; **his illness is a ~** sa maladie est une comédie *or* de la simulation.

falcon [fal'kən] *n* faucon *m*.

Falkland Islands [fôlk'lənd i'ləndz] *npl*: **the ~** les Malouines *fpl*, les îles *fpl* Falkland.

fall [fôl] *n* chute *f*; (*decrease*) baisse *f*; (*US*) automne *m* ♦ *vi* (*pt* **fell**, *pp* **fallen** [fel, fôl'ən]) tomber; **~s** *npl* (*waterfall*) chute *f* d'eau, cascade *f*; **to ~ flat** *vi* (*on one's face*) tomber de tout son long, s'étaler; (*joke*) tomber à plat; (*plan*) échouer; **to ~ short of** (*sb's expectations*) ne pas répondre à; **a ~ of snow** (*Brit*) une chute de neige.

fall apart *vi* tomber en morceaux; (*col: emotionally*) craquer.

fall back *vi* reculer, se retirer.

fall back on *vt fus* se rabattre sur; **to have something to ~ back on** (*money etc*) avoir quelque chose en réserve; (*job etc*) avoir une solution de rechange.

fall behind *vi* prendre du retard.

fall down *vi* (*person*) tomber; (*building, hopes*) s'effondrer, s'écrouler.

fall for *vt fus* (*trick*) se laisser prendre à; (*person*) tomber amoureux(euse) de.

fall in *vi* s'effondrer; (*MIL*) se mettre en rangs.

fall in with *vt fus* (*sb's plans etc*) accepter.

fall off *vi* tomber; (*diminish*) baisser, dimi-

nuer.
fall out vi (*friends etc*) se brouiller.
fall over vi tomber (par terre).
fall through vi (*plan, project*) tomber à l'eau.
fallacy [fal'əsē] n erreur f, illusion f.
fallback [fôl'bak] a: ~ **position** position f de repli.
fallen [fôl'ən] pp of **fall**.
fallible [fal'əbəl] a faillible.
fallopian tube [fəlō'pēən tōōb'] n (ANAT) trompe f de Fallope.
fallout [fôl'out] n retombées (radioactives).
fallout shelter n abri m anti-atomique.
fallow [fal'ō] a en jachère; en friche.
false [fôls] a faux(fausse); **under ~ pretenses** sous un faux prétexte.
false alarm n fausse alerte.
falsehood [fôls'hōōd] n mensonge m.
falsely [fôls'lē] ad (*accuse*) à tort.
false teeth npl fausses dents.
falsify [fôl'səfī] vt falsifier; (*accounts*) maquiller.
falter [fôl'tûr] vi chanceler, vaciller.
fame [fām] n renommée f, renom m.
familiar [fəmil'yûr] a familier(ière); **to be ~ with sth** connaître qch; **to make o.s. ~ with sth** se familiariser avec qch; **to be on ~ terms with sb** bien connaître qn.
familiarity [fəmilēar'ətē] n familiarité f.
familiarize [fəmil'yərīz] vt familiariser.
family [fam'lē] n famille f.
family allowance n allocations familiales.
family business n entreprise familiale.
family doctor n médecin m de famille.
family life n vie f de famille.
family planning clinic n centre m de planning familial.
family tree n arbre m généalogique.
famine [fam'in] n famine f.
famished [fam'isht] a affamé(e); **I'm ~!** (*col*) je meurs de faim!
famous [fā'məs] a célèbre.
famously [fā'məslē] ad (*get on*) fameusement, à merveille.
fan [fan] n (*folding*) éventail m; (ELEC) ventilateur m; (*person*) fan m, admirateur/trice; (: SPORT) supporter m/f ♦ vt éventer; (*fire, quarrel*) attiser.
fan out vi se déployer (en éventail).
fanatic [fənat'ik] n fanatique m/f.
fanatical [fənat'ikəl] a fanatique.
fan belt n courroie f de ventilateur.
fancied [fan'sēd] a imaginaire.
fanciful [fan'sifəl] a fantaisiste.
fancy [fan'sē] n fantaisie f, envie f; imagination f ♦ cpd (de) fantaisie inv ♦ vt (*feel like, want*) avoir envie de; (*imagine*) imaginer; **to take a ~ to** se prendre d'affection pour; s'enticher de; **it took or caught my ~** ça m'a plu; **when the ~ takes him** quand ça lui prend; **to ~ that ...** se figurer or s'imaginer que ...; **he fancies her** (*Brit*) elle lui plaît.
fancy dress n déguisement m, travesti m.
fancy-dress ball [fan'sedres bôl'] n (*Brit*) bal masqué or costumé.
fancy goods npl articles mpl (de) fantaisie.
fanfare [fan'fär] n fanfare f (*musique*).
fanfold paper [fan'fōld pā'pûr] n papier m à

pliage accordéon.
fang [fang] n croc m; (*of snake*) crochet m.
fan heater n (*Brit*) radiateur soufflant.
fanlight [fan'lit] n imposte f.
fantasize [fan'təsīz] vi fantasmer.
fantastic [fantas'tik] a fantastique.
fantasy [fan'təsē] n imagination f, fantaisie f; fantasme m.
FAO n abbr (= *Food and Agriculture Organization*) FAO f.
far [fâr] a: **the ~ side/end** l'autre côté/bout; **the ~ left/right** (POL) l'extrême gauche f/ droite f ♦ ad loin; **is it ~ to Boston?** est-ce qu'on est loin de Boston?; **it's not ~ (from here)** ce n'est pas loin (d'ici); ~ **away**, ~ **off** au loin, dans le lointain; ~ **better** beaucoup mieux; ~ **from** loin de; **by ~** de loin, de beaucoup; **as ~ back as the 13th century** dès le 13e siècle; **go as ~ as the farm** allez jusqu'à la ferme; **as ~ as I know** pour autant que je sache; **as ~ as possible** dans la mesure du possible; **how ~ have you got with your work?** où en êtes-vous dans votre travail?
faraway [fâr'əwā] a lointain(e); (*look*) absent(e).
farce [fârs] n farce f.
farcical [fâr'sikəl] a grotesque.
fare [fär] n (*on trains, buses*) prix m du billet; (*in taxi*) prix de la course; (*passenger in taxi*) client m; (*food*) table f, chère f ♦ vi se débrouiller.
Far East n: **the ~** l'Extrême-Orient m.
farewell [fär'wel'] excl, n adieu (m) ♦ cpd [fär'wel] (*party etc*) d'adieux.
far-fetched [fâr'fecht'] a exagéré(e), poussé(e).
farm [fârm] n ferme f ♦ vt cultiver.
farm out vt (*work etc*) distribuer.
farmer [fâr'mûr] n fermier/ière; cultivateur/ trice.
farmhand [fârm'hand] n ouvrier/ière agricole.
farmhouse [fârm'hous] n (maison f de) ferme f.
farming [fâr'ming] n agriculture f; **intensive ~** culture intensive; **sheep ~** élevage m du mouton.
farm laborer n = **farmhand**.
farmland [fârm'land] n terres cultivées or arables.
farm produce n produits mpl agricoles.
farm worker n = **farmhand**.
farmyard [fârm'yârd] n cour f de ferme.
Faroe Islands [farō' i'landz] npl, **Faroes** [farōz'] npl: **the ~** les îles fpl Féroé or Faeroe.
far-reaching [fâr'rē'ching] a d'une grande portée.
farsighted [fâr'sī'tid] a presbyte; (*fig*) prévoyant(e), qui voit loin.
fart [fârt] (*col!*) n pet m ♦ vi péter.
farther [fâr'thûr] ad plus loin ♦ a plus eloigné(e), plus lointain(e).
farthest [fâr'thist] superlative of **far**.
FAS abbr (= *free alongside ship*) FLB.
fascia [fā'shēə] n (AUT) (garniture f du) tableau m de bord.
fascinate [fas'ənāt] vt fasciner, captiver.
fascinating [fas'ənāting] a fascinant(e).

fascination [fasənā'shən] *n* fascination *f*.

fascism [fash'izəm] *n* fascisme *m*.

fascist [fash'ist] *a*, *n* fasciste *(m/f)*.

fashion [fash'ən] *n* mode *f*; *(manner)* façon *f*, manière *f* ♦ *vt* façonner; **in** ~ à la mode; **out of** ~ démodé(e); **in the Greek** ~ à la grecque; **after a** ~ *(finish, manage etc)* tant bien que mal.

fashionable [fash'ənəbəl] *a* à la mode.

fashion designer *n* (grand(e)) couturier/ière.

fashion show *n* défilé *m* de mannequins *or* de mode.

fast [fast] *a* rapide; *(clock)*: **to be** ~ avancer; *(dye, color)* grand *or* bon teint *inv* ♦ *ad* vite, rapidement; *(stuck, held)* solidement ♦ *n* jeûne *m* ♦ *vi* jeûner; **my watch is 5 minutes** ~ ma montre avance de 5 minutes; ~ **asleep** profondément endormi; **as** ~ **as I can** aussi vite que je peux.

fasten [fas'ən] *vt* attacher, fixer; *(coat)* attacher, fermer ♦ *vi* se fermer, s'attacher.

fasten (up)on *vt fus (idea)* se cramponner à.

fastener [fas'ənûr], **fastening** [fas'əning] *n* fermeture *f*, attache *f*; *(Brit: zip* ~) fermeture éclair *inv* ® *or* à glissière.

fast food *n* fast food *m*, restauration *f* rapide.

fastidious [fastid'ēəs] *a* exigeant(e), difficile.

fast lane *n* *(AUT:* in Britain) voie *f* de droite.

fat [fat] *a* gros(se) ♦ *n* graisse *f*; *(on meat)* gras *m*; **to live off the** ~ **of the land** vivre grassement.

fatal [fāt'əl] *a* fatal(e); *(leading to death)* mortel(le).

fatalism [fāt'əlizəm] *n* fatalisme *m*.

fatality [fātal'itē] *n* *(road death etc)* victime *f*, décès *m*.

fatally [fāt'əlē] *ad* fatalement; mortellement.

fate [fāt] *n* destin *m*; *(of person)* sort *m*; **to meet one's** ~ trouver la mort.

fated [fā'tid] *a* *(person)* condamné(e); *(project)* voué(e) à l'échec.

fateful [fāt'fəl] *a* fatidique.

father [fâ'thûr] *n* père *m*.

Father Christmas *n* (Brit) le Père Noël.

fatherhood [fâ'thûrhood] *n* paternité *f*.

father-in-law [fâ'thûrinlô] *n* beau-père *m*.

fatherland [fâ'thûrland] *n* (mère *f*) patrie *f*.

fatherly [fâ'thûrlē] *a* paternel(le).

fathom [fath'əm] *n* brasse *f* (= *1828 mm*) ♦ *vt* *(mystery)* sonder, pénétrer.

fatigue [fətēg'] *n* fatigue *f*; *(MIL)* corvée *f*; **metal** ~ fatigue du métal.

fatness [fat'nis] *n* corpulence *f*, grosseur *f*.

fatten [fat'ən] *vt*, *vi* engraisser; **chocolate is** ~**ing** le chocolat fait grossir.

fatty [fat'ē] *a* *(food)* gras(se) ♦ *n* *(col)* gros/grosse.

fatuous [fach'ōōəs] *a* stupide.

faucet [fô'sit] *n* *(US)* robinet *m*.

fault [fôlt] *n* faute *f*; *(defect)* défaut *m*; *(GEO)* faille *f* ♦ *vt* trouver des défauts à, prendre en défaut; **it's my** ~ c'est de ma faute; **to find** ~ **with** trouver à redire *or* à critiquer à; **at** ~ fautif(ive), coupable; **to a** ~ à l'excès.

faultless [fôlt'lis] *a* impeccable; irréprochable.

faulty [fôl'tē] *a* défectueux(euse).

fauna [fôn'ə] *n* faune *f*.

faux pas [fō pä'] *n* impair *m*, bévue *f*, gaffe *f*.

favor [fā'vûr] *(US)* *n* faveur *f*; *(help)* service *m* ♦ *vt* *(proposition)* être en faveur de; *(pupil etc)* favoriser; *(team, horse)* donner gagnant; **to do sb a** ~ rendre un service à qn; **in** ~ **of** en faveur de; **to be in** ~ **of sth/of doing sth** être partisan de qch/de faire qch; **to find** ~ **with sb** trouver grâce aux yeux de qn.

favorable [fā'vûrəbəl] *a* favorable; *(price)* avantageux(euse).

favorably [fā'vûrəblē] *ad* favorablement.

favorite [fā'vûrit] *a*, *n* favori(te).

favoritism [fā'vûritizəm] *n* favoritisme *m*.

favour [fā'vûr] *etc* (Brit) = **favor** *etc*.

fawn [fôn] *n* faon *m* ♦ *a* *(also:* ~**-colored)** fauve ♦ *vi:* **to** ~ **(up)on** flatter servilement.

fax [faks] *n* *(document)* télécopie *f*; *(machine)* télécopieur *m* ♦ *vt* envoyer par télécopie.

fazed [fāzd] *a* *(col)* déconcerté(e).

FBI *n abbr* *(US:* = *Federal Bureau of Investigation)* FBI *m*.

FCA *n abbr* *(US)* = *Farm Credit Administration.*

FCC *n abbr* *(US)* = *Federal Communications Commission.*

FCO *n abbr* *(Brit:* = *Foreign and Commonwealth Office) ministère des Affaires étrangères et du Commonwealth.*

FD *n abbr* *(US)* = **fire department.**

FDA *n abbr* *(US:* = *Food and Drug Administration) office de contrôle des produits pharmaceutiques et alimentaires.*

FDIC *n abbr* *(US:* = *Federal Deposit Insurance Corporation) organisme fédéral assurant les dépôts des banques.*

fear [fēr] *n* crainte *f*, peur *f* ♦ *vt* craindre ♦ *vi:* **to** ~ **for** craindre pour; **to** ~ **that** craindre que; ~ **of heights** vertige *m*; **for** ~ **of** de peur que + *sub or* de + *infinitive*.

fearful [fēr'fəl] *a* craintif(ive); *(sight, noise)* affreux(euse), épouvantable; **to be** ~ **of** avoir peur de, craindre.

fearfully [fēr'fəlē] *ad* *(timidly)* craintivement; *(col: very)* affreusement.

fearless [fēr'lis] *a* intrépide, sans peur.

fearsome [fēr'səm] *a* *(opponent)* redoutable; *(sight)* épouvantable.

feasibility [fēzəbil'ətē] *n* *(of plan)* possibilité *f* de réalisation, faisabilité *f*.

feasibility study *n* étude *f* de faisabilité.

feasible [fē'zəbəl] *a* faisable, réalisable.

feast [fēst] *n* festin *m*, banquet *m*; *(REL: also:* ~ **day)** fête *f* ♦ *vi* festoyer; **to** ~ **on** se régaler de.

feat [fēt] *n* exploit *m*, prouesse *f*.

feather [feth'ûr] *n* plume *f* ♦ *vt:* **to** ~ **one's nest** *(fig)* faire sa pelote ♦ *cpd (bed etc)* de plumes.

featherweight [feth'ûrwāt] *n* poids *m* plume *inv*.

feature [fē'chûr] *n* caractéristique *f*; *(article)* chronique *f*, rubrique *f* ♦ *vt* *(subj: film)* avoir pour vedette(s) ♦ *vi* figurer (en bonne place); ~**s** *npl (of face)* traits *mpl*; **a (special)** ~ **on sth/sb** un reportage sur qch/qn; **it** ~**d prominently in** .... cela a figuré en bonne place sur *or* dans ....

feature film *n* long métrage *m*.

featureless [fē'chûrlis] *a* anonyme, sans traits

distinctifs.
Feb. *abbr* (= *February*) fév.
February [feb'yəwārē] *n* février *m*; *for phrases see also* **July**.
feces [fē'sēz] *npl* (*US*) féces *fpl*.
feckless [fek'lis] *a* inepte.
Fed *abbr* (*US*) = **federal, federation.**
fed [fed] *pt, pp of* **feed; to be ~ up** en avoir marre *or* plein le dos.
Fed. [fed] *n abbr* (*US col*) = **Federal Reserve Board.**
federal [fed'ûrəl] *a* fédéral(e).
Federal Republic of Germany (FRG) *n* République fédérale d'Allemagne (RFA).
Federal Reserve Board *n* (*US*) *organe de contrôle de la banque centrale américaine.*
Federal Trade Commission (FTC) *n* (*US*) *organisme de protection contre les pratiques commerciales abusives.*
federation [fedərā'shən] *n* fédération *f*.
fedora [fədôr'ə] *n* (*US*) chapeau mou, feutre *m*.
fee [fē] *n* rémunération *f*; (*of doctor, lawyer*) honoraires *mpl*; (*of school, college etc*) frais *mpl* de scolarité; (*for examination*) droits *mpl*; **entrance/membership** ~ droit d'entrée/d'inscription; **for a small** ~ pour une somme modique.
feeble [fē'bəl] *a* faible.
feeble-minded [fē'bəlmīndid] *a* faible d'esprit.
feed [fēd] *n* (*of baby*) tétée *f*; (*of animal*) fourrage *m*; pâture *f*; (*on printer*) mécanisme *m* d'alimentation ♦ *vt* (*pt, pp* **fed** [fed]) nourrir; (*horse etc*) donner à manger à; (*machine*) alimenter; (*data etc*): **to ~ sth into** fournir qch à, introduire qch dans.
  feed back *vt* (*results*) donner en retour.
  feed on *vt fus* se nourrir de.
feedback [fēd'bak] *n* feed-back *m*; (*from person*) réactions *fpl*.
feeder [fē'dûr] *n* (*bib*) bavette *f*.
feeding bottle [fē'ding bât'əl] *n* (*Brit*) biberon *m*.
feel [fēl] *n* sensation *f* ♦ *vt* (*pt, pp* **felt** [felt]) (*touch*) toucher; tâter, palper; (*cold, pain*) sentir; (*grief, anger*) ressentir, éprouver; (*think, believe*): **to ~ (that)** trouver que; **I ~ that you ought to do it** il me semble que vous devriez le faire; **to ~ hungry/cold** avoir faim/froid; **to ~ lonely/better** se sentir seul/mieux; **I don't ~ well** je ne me sens pas bien; **to ~ sorry for** avoir pitié de; **it ~s soft** c'est doux au toucher; **it ~s colder here** je trouve qu'il fait plus froid ici; **it ~s like velvet** on dirait du velours, ça ressemble au velours; **to ~ like** (*want*) avoir envie de; **to ~ around** fouiller, tâtonner; **to get the ~ of sth** (*fig*) s'habituer à qch.
feeler [fē'lûr] *n* (*of insect*) antenne *f*; (*fig*): **to put out a ~** *or* **~s** tâter le terrain.
feeling [fē'ling] *n* sensation *f*, sentiment *m*; (*impression*) sentiment; **to hurt sb's ~s** froisser qn; **~s ran high about it** cela a déchaîné les passions; **what are your ~s about the matter?** quel est votre sentiment sur cette question?; **my ~ is that ...** j'estime que ...; **I have a ~ that ...** j'ai l'impression que ....
feet [fēt] *npl of* **foot.**

feign [fān] *vt* feindre, simuler.
felicitous [filis'itəs] *a* heureux(euse).
fell [fel] *pt of* **fall** ♦ *vt* (*tree*) abattre ♦ *a*: **with one ~ blow** d'un seul coup.
fellow [fel'ō] *n* type *m*; (*comrade*) compagnon *m*; (*of learned society*) membre *m*; (*of university*) universitaire *m/f* (membre du conseil) ♦ *cpd*: **their ~ prisoners/students** leurs camarades prisonniers/étudiants; **his ~ workers** ses collègues *mpl* (de travail).
fellow citizen *n* concitoyen/ne.
fellow countryman *n* compatriote *m*.
fellow feeling *n* sympathie *f*.
fellow men *npl* semblables *mpl*.
fellowship [fel'ōship] *n* (*society*) association *f*; (*comradeship*) amitié *f*, camaraderie *f*; (*SCOL*) sorte de bourse universitaire.
fellow traveler *n* compagnon/compagne de route; (*POL*) communisant/e.
fell-walking [fel'wôking] *n* (*Brit*) randonnée *f* en montagne.
felon [fel'ən] *n* (*LAW*) criminel/le.
felony [fel'ənē] *n* (*LAW*) crime *m*, forfait *m*.
felt [felt] *pt, pp of* **feel** ♦ *n* feutre *m*.
felt-tip pen [felt'tip pen'] *n* stylo-feutre *m*.
female [fē'māl] *n* (*ZOOL*) femelle *f*; (*pej: woman*) bonne femme ♦ *a* (*BIOL, ELEC*) femelle; (*sex, character*) féminin(e); (*vote etc*) des femmes; (*child etc*) du sexe féminin; **male and ~ students** étudiants et étudiantes.
female impersonator *n* (*THEATER*) travesti *m*.
feminine [fem'ənin] *a* féminin(e) ♦ *n* féminin *m*.
femininity [femənin'ətē] *n* féminité *f*.
feminism [fem'ənizəm] *n* féminisme *m*.
feminist [fem'ənist] *n* féministe *m/f*.
fence [fens] *n* barrière *f*; (*SPORT*) obstacle *m*; (*col: person*) receleur/euse ♦ *vt* (*also:* ~ **in**) clôturer ♦ *vi* faire de l'escrime; **to sit on the ~** (*fig*) ne pas se mouiller.
fencing [fen'sing] *n* (*sport*) escrime *m*.
fend [fend] *vi*: **to ~ for o.s.** se débrouiller (tout seul).
  fend off *vt* (*attack etc*) parer.
fender [fen'dûr] *n* (*of fireplace*) garde-feu *m inv*; (*on boat*) défense *f*; (*US AUT*) garde-boue *m*.
fennel [fen'əl] *n* fenouil *m*.
FEPC *n abbr* (*US*: = *Fair Employment Practices Committee*) *commission f pour l'égalité des chances dans le travail.*
FERC *n abbr* (*US*) = *Federal Energy Regulatory Commission.*
ferment *vi* [fûrment'] fermenter ♦ *n* [fûr'ment] agitation *f*, effervescence *f*.
fermentation [fûrmentā'shən] *n* fermentation *f*.
fern [fûrn] *n* fougère *f*.
ferocious [fərō'shəs] *a* féroce.
ferocity [fəräs'itē] *n* férocité *f*.
ferret [fär'it] *n* furet *m*.
  ferret around *vi* fureter.
  ferret out *vt* dénicher.
Ferris wheel [fär'is hwēl] *n* (*at fair*) grande roue.
ferry [fär'ē] *n* (*small*) bac *m*; (*large: also:* ~**boat**) ferry(-boat) *m* ♦ *vt* transporter; **to ~**

sth/sb **across** or **over** faire traverser qch/qn.
ferryman [fär'ēmən] n passeur m.
fertile [fûr'təl] a fertile; (BIOL) fécond(e); ~
period période f de fécondité.
fertility [fûrtil'ətē] n fertilité f; fécondité f.
fertility drug n médicament m contre la stérilité.
fertilize [fûr'təliz] vt fertiliser; féconder.
fertilizer [fûr'təlizûr] n engrais m.
fervent [fûr'vənt] a fervent(e), ardent(e).
fervor, (Brit) **fervour** [fûr'vûr] n ferveur f.
fester [fes'tûr] vi suppurer.
festival [fes'təvəl] n (REL) fête f; (ART, MUS)
festival m.
festive [fes'tiv] a de fête; **the ~ season** (Brit:
Christmas) la période des fêtes.
festivities [festiv'itēz] npl réjouissances fpl.
festoon [festōōn'] vt: **to ~ with** orner de.
FET n abbr (US: = Federal Excise Tax) excise
fédérale.
fetal [fēt'l] a (US) fœtal(e).
fetch [fech] vt aller chercher; (Brit: sell for)
se vendre.
fetching [fech'ing] a charmant(e).
fête [fet] n fête f, kermesse f.
fetid [fet'id] a fétide.
fetish [fet'ish] n fétiche m.
fetter [fet'ûr] vt entraver.
fetters [fet'ûrz] npl chaînes fpl.
fettle [fet'əl] n (Brit): **in fine ~** en bonne
forme.
fetus [fē'təs] n (US) foetus m.
feud [fyōōd] n dispute f, dissension f ♦ vi se
disputer, se quereller; **a family ~** une querelle de famille.
feudal [fyōōd'əl] a féodal(e).
feudalism [fyōō'dəlizəm] n féodalité f.
fever [fē'vûr] n fièvre f; **he has a ~** il a de la
fièvre.
feverish [fē'vûrish] a fiévreux(euse), fébrile.
few [fyōō] a peu de ♦ pronoun: **~ succeed** il y
en a peu qui réussissent, (bien) peu
réussissent; **they were ~** ils étaient peu
(nombreux), il y en avait peu; **a ~ ...**
quelques ...; **I know a ~** j'en connais
quelques-uns; **quite a ~ ...** un certain nombre
de ..., pas mal de ...; **in the next ~ days**
dans les jours qui viennent; **in the past ~**
days ces derniers jours; **every ~ days/**
months tous les deux ou trois jours/mois; **a**
~ more ... encore quelques ..., quelques ... de
plus.
fewer [fyōō'úr] a moins de ♦ pronoun moins;
they are ~ now il y en a moins maintenant,
ils sont moins (nombreux) maintenant.
fewest [fyōō'ist] a le moins nombreux.
FFA n abbr = Future Farmers of America.
FHA n abbr (US: = Federal Housing Administration) office fédéral du logement.
fiancé [fēänsā'] n fiancé m.
fiancée [fēänsā'] n fiancée f.
fiasco [fēas'kō] n fiasco m.
fib [fib] n bobard m.
fiber [fī'bûr] n (US) fibre f.
fiberboard [fī'bûrbôrd] n panneau m de fibres.
fiber-glass [fī'bûrglas] n fibre de verre.
fibre [fī'bûr] etc (Brit) = **fiber** etc.
fibrositis [fībrəsī'tis] n aponévrosite f.
FIC n abbr (US: = Federal Information

Centers) centre fédéral d'information au public.
FICA n abbr (US) = Federal Insurance Contributions Act.
fickle [fik'əl] a inconstant(e), volage, capri-
cieux(euse).
fiction [fik'shən] n romans mpl, littérature f romanesque; (invention) fiction f.
fictional [fik'shənəl] a fictif(ive).
fictionalize [fik'shənəliz] vt romancer.
fictitious [fiktish'əs] a fictif(ive), imaginaire.
fiddle [fid'əl] n (MUS) violon m; (cheating)
combine f; escroquerie f ♦ vt (Brit:
accounts) falsifier, maquiller; **to work a ~**
traficoter.
fiddle with vt fus tripoter.
fiddler [fid'lûr] n violoniste m/f.
fiddly [fid'lē] a (task) minutieux(euse).
fidelity [fidel'itē] n fidélité f.
fidget [fij'it] vi se trémousser, remuer.
fidgety [fij'itē] a agité(e), qui a la bougeotte.
fiduciary [fidōō'shēärē] n agent m fiduciaire.
field [fēld] n champ m; (fig) domaine m,
champ; (SPORT: ground) terrain m;
(COMPUT) champ, zone f; **to lead the ~**
(SPORT, COMM) dominer; **the children had a**
~ day (fig) c'était un grand jour pour les
enfants.
field glasses npl jumelles fpl.
field marshal n maréchal m.
fieldwork [fēld'wûrk] n travaux mpl pratiques
(or recherches fpl) sur le terrain.
fiend [fēnd] n démon m.
fiendish [fēn'dish] a diabolique.
fierce [fērs] a (look) féroce, sauvage; (wind,
attack) (très) violent(e); (fighting, enemy)
acharné(e).
fiery [fī'ûrē] a ardent(e), brûlant(e); fou-
gueux(euse).
FIFA [fē'fa] n abbr (= Fédération Internationale de Football Association) FIFA f.
fifteen [fif'tēn'] num quinze.
fifth [fifth] num cinquième.
fiftieth [fif'tēith] num cinquantième.
fifty [fif'tē] num cinquante.
fifty-fifty [fif'tēfif'tē] ad: **to share ~ with sb**
partager moitié-moitié avec qn ♦ a: **to have**
a ~ chance (of success) avoir une chance
sur deux (de réussir).
fig [fig] n figue f.
fight [fīt] n bagarre f; (MIL) combat m;
(against cancer etc) lutte f ♦ vb (pt, pp
fought [fôt]) vt se battre contre; (cancer,
alcoholism) combattre, lutter contre; (LAW:
case) défendre ♦ vi se battre; (fig): **to ~**
(for/against) lutter (pour/contre).
fighter [fī'tûr] n lutteur m (fig); (plane)
chasseur m.
fighter pilot n pilote m de chasse.
fighting [fī'ting] n combats mpl; (brawls) ba-
garres fpl.
figment [fig'mənt] n: **a ~ of the imagination**
une invention.
figurative [fig'yûrətiv] a figuré(e).
figure [fig'yûr] n (DRAWING, GEOM) figure f;
(number, cipher) chiffre m; (body, outline)
silhouette f, ligne f, formes fpl; (person)
personnage m ♦ vt (US) supposer ♦ vi
(appear) figurer; (US: make sense) s'expli-

quer; **public ~** personnalité *f*; **~ of speech** figure *f* de rhétorique.

figure on *vt fus* (*US*): **to ~ on doing** compter faire.

figure out *vt* arriver à comprendre; calculer.

figurehead [fig'yûrhed] *n* (*NAUT*) figure *f* de proue; (*pej*) prête-nom *m*.

figure skating *n* figures imposées (*en patinage*); patinage *m* artistique.

Fiji (Islands) [fē'jē (i'ləndz)] *n(pl)* (îles *fpl*) Fi(d)ji *fpl*.

filament [fil'əmənt] *n* filament *m*.

filch [filch] *vt* (*col: steal*) voler, chiper.

file [fīl] *n* (*tool*) lime *f*; (*dossier*) dossier *m*; (*folder*) dossier, chemise *f*; (*: binder*) classeur *m*; (*COMPUT*) fichier *m*; (*row*) file *f* ♦ *vt* (*nails, wood*) limer; (*papers*) classer; (*LAW: claim*) faire enregistrer; déposer ♦ *vi*: **to ~ in/out** entrer/sortir l'un derrière l'autre; **to ~ past** défiler devant; **to ~ a suit against sb** (*LAW*) intenter un procès à qn.

file name *n* (*COMPUT*) nom *m* de fichier.

filibuster [fil'əbustûr] (*esp US POL*) *n* (*also:* **~er**) obstructionniste *m/f* ♦ *vi* faire de l'obstructionnisme.

filing [fī'ling] *n* (*travaux mpl* de) classement *m*; **~s** *npl* limaille *f*.

filing cabinet *n* classeur *m* (*meuble*).

filing clerk *n* documentaliste *m/f*.

Filipino [filəpē'nō] *n* (*person*) Philippin/e; (*LING*) tagalog *m*.

fill [fil] *vt* remplir; (*vacancy*) pourvoir à; (*tooth*) plomber ♦ *n*: **to eat one's ~** manger à sa faim.

fill in *vt* (*hole*) boucher; (*form*) remplir; (*details, report*) compléter.

fill out *vt* (*form, receipt*) remplir.

fill up *vt* remplir ♦ *vi* (*AUT*) faire le plein; **~ it up, please** (*AUT*) le plein, s'il vous plaît.

fillet [filā'] *n* filet *m* ♦ *vt* préparer en filets.

fillet steak *n* filet *m* de bœuf, tournedos *m*.

filling [fil'ing] *n* (*CULIN*) garniture *f*, farce *f*; (*for tooth*) plombage *m*.

filling station *n* station *f* d'essence.

fillip [fil'əp] *n* coup *m* de fouet (*fig*).

filly [fil'ē] *n* pouliche *f*.

film [film] *n* film *m*; (*PHOT*) pellicule *f*, film ♦ *vt* (*scene*) filmer.

film star *n* vedette *f* de cinéma.

filmstrip [film'strip] *n* (film *m* pour) projection *f* fixe.

film studio *n* studio *m* (de cinéma).

filter [fil'tûr] *n* filtre *m* ♦ *vt* filtrer.

filter coffee *n* café *m* filtre.

filter lane *n* (*Brit AUT*) voie *f* de sortie.

filter tip *n* bout *m* filtre.

filter-tipped [fil'tûrtipt] *a* à bout filtre.

filth [filth] *n* saleté *f*.

filthy [fil'thē] *a* sale, dégoûtant(e); (*language*) ordurier(ière), grossier(ière).

fin. *abbr* **= finance.**

fin [fin] *n* (*of fish*) nageoire *f*.

final [fī'nəl] *a* final(e), dernier(ière); (*decision, answer*) définitif(ive) ♦ *n* (*SPORT*) finale *f*; **~s** *npl* (*SCOL*) examens *mpl* de dernière année; **~ demand** (*on invoice etc*) dernier rappel.

finale [final'ē] *n* finale *m*.

finalist [fī'nəlist] *n* (*SPORT*) finaliste *m/f*.

finalize [fī'nəlīz] *vt* mettre au point.

finally [fī'nəlē] *ad* (*lastly*) en dernier lieu; (*eventually*) enfin, finalement; (*irrevocably*) définitivement.

finance *n* [fī'nans] finance *f* ♦ *vt* [finans'] financer; **~s** *npl* finances *fpl*.

financial [finan'chəl] *a* financier(ière); **~ statement** bilan *m*, exercice financier.

financially [finan'chəlē] *ad* financièrement.

financial year *n* année *f* budgétaire.

financier [finansiûr'] *n* financier *m*.

find [fīnd] *vt* (*pt, pp* **found** [found]) trouver; (*lost object*) retrouver ♦ *n* trouvaille *f*, découverte *f*; **to ~ sb guilty** (*LAW*) déclarer qn coupable; **to ~ (some) difficulty in doing sth** avoir du mal à faire qch.

find out *vt* se renseigner sur; (*truth, secret*) découvrir; (*person*) démasquer ♦ *vi*: **to ~ out about** se renseigner sur; (*by chance*) apprendre.

findings [fīn'dingz] *npl* (*LAW*) conclusions *fpl*, verdict *m*; (*of report*) constatations *fpl*.

fine [fīn] *a* beau(belle); excellent(e); (*subtle, not coarse*) fin(e) ♦ *ad* (*well*) très bien; (*small*) fin, finement ♦ *n* (*LAW*) amende *f*; contravention *f* ♦ *vt* (*LAW*) condamner à une amende; donner une contravention à; **he's ~** il va bien; **the weather is ~** il fait beau; **you're doing ~** c'est bien, vous vous débrouillez bien; **to cut it ~** calculer un peu juste.

fine arts *npl* beaux-arts *mpl*.

finery [fī'nûrē] *n* parure *f*.

finesse [fines'] *n* finesse *f*, élégance *f*.

fine-tooth comb [fīn'tōōth kōm] *n*: **to go through sth with a ~** (*fig*) passer qch au peigne fin *or* au crible.

finger [fing'gûr] *n* doigt *m* ♦ *vt* palper, toucher.

fingernail [fing'gûrnāl] *n* ongle *m* (de la main).

fingerprint [fing'gûrprint] *n* empreinte digitale ♦ *vt* (*person*) prendre les empreintes digitales de.

fingerstall [fing'gûrstôl] *n* doigtier *m*.

fingertip [fing'gûrtip] *n* bout *m* du doigt; (*fig*): **to have sth at one's ~s** avoir qch à sa disposition; (*knowledge*) savoir qch sur le bout du doigt.

finicky [fin'ikē] *a* tatillon(ne), méticuleux(euse); minutieux(euse).

finish [fin'ish] *n* fin *f*; (*SPORT*) arrivée *f*; (*polish etc*) finition *f* ♦ *vt* finir, terminer ♦ *vi* finir, se terminer; (*session*) s'achever; **to ~ doing sth** finir de faire qch; **to ~ third** arriver *or* terminer troisième.

finish off *vt* finir, terminer; (*kill*) achever.

finish up *vi, vt* finir.

finished product [fin'isht präd'əkt] *n* produit fini.

finishing line [fin'ishing līn] *n* ligne *f* d'arrivée.

finishing school [fin'ishing skōōl] *n* institution privée (*pour jeunes filles*).

finite [fī'nīt] *a* fini(e); (*verb*) conjugué(e).

Finland [fin'lənd] *n* Finlande *f*.

Finn [fin] *n* Finnois/e; Finlandais/e.

Finnish [fin'ish] *a* finnois(e); finlandais(e) ♦ *n* (*LING*) finnois *m*.

fiord [fyôrd] *n* fjord *m*.

fir |fûr| *n* sapin *m*.

fire |fî'ûr| *n* feu *m*; incendie *m* ♦ *vt* (*discharge*): **to ~ a gun** tirer un coup de feu; (*fig*) enflammer, animer; (*dismiss*) mettre à la porte, renvoyer ♦ *vi* tirer, faire feu ♦ *cpd*: **~ hazard, ~ risk: that's a ~ hazard** *or* **risk** cela présente un risque d'incendie; **on ~** en feu; **to set ~ to sth, set sth on ~** mettre le feu à qch; **insured against ~** assuré contre l'incendie.

fire alarm *n* avertisseur *m* d'incendie.

firearm |fîûr'ârm| *n* arme *f* à feu.

fire brigade *n* (*Brit*) = **fire department**.

fire chief *n* (*US*) capitaine *m* des pompiers.

fire department *n* (*US*) (*régiment m* de sapeurs-)pompiers *mpl*.

fire engine *n* pompe *f* à incendie.

fire escape *n* escalier *m* de secours.

fire extinguisher *n* extincteur *m*.

fire insurance *n* assurance *f* incendie.

fireman |fîûr'mən| *n* pompier *m*.

fire master *n* (*Brit*) = **fire chief**.

fireplace |fîûr'plās| *n* cheminée *f*.

fireplug |fî'ûrplug| *n* (*US*) bouche *f* d'incendie.

fireproof |fîûr'prōōf| *a* ignifuge.

fire regulations *npl* consignes *fpl* en cas d'incendie.

fire screen *n* (*decorative*) écran *m* de cheminée; (*for protection*) garde-feu *m inv*.

fireside |fîûr'sīd| *n* foyer *m*, coin *m* du feu.

fire station *n* caserne *f* de pompiers.

firewood |fîûr'wōōd| *n* bois *m* de chauffage.

firework |fîûr'wûrk| *n* feu *m* d'artifice; **~s** *npl* (*display*) feu(x) d'artifice.

firing |fîûr'ing| *n* (*MIL*) feu *m*, tir *m*.

firing squad *n* peloton *m* d'exécution.

firm |fûrm| *a* ferme ♦ *n* compagnie *f*, firme *f*.

firmly |fûrm'lē| *ad* fermement.

firmness |fûrm'nis| *n* fermeté *f*.

first |fûrst| *a* premier(ière) ♦ *ad* (*before others*) le premier, la première; (*before other things*) en premier, d'abord; (*when listing reasons etc*) en premier lieu, premièrement ♦ *n* (*person: in race*) premier/ière; (*AUT*) première *f*; **the ~ of January** le premier janvier; **at ~** au commencement, au début; **~ of all** tout d'abord, pour commencer; **in the ~ instance** en premier lieu; **I'll do it ~ thing tomorrow** je le ferai tout de suite demain matin.

first aid *n* premiers secours *or* soins.

first-aid kit |fûrstād' kit| *n* trousse *f* à pharmacie.

first-class |fûrst'klas'| *a* de première classe.

first-class mail *n* courrier *m* rapide.

first-hand |fûrst'hand'| *a* de première main.

first lady *n* (*US*) femme *f* du président.

firstly |fûrst'lē| *ad* premièrement, en premier lieu.

first name *n* prénom *m*.

first night *n* (*THEATER*) première *f*.

first-rate |fûrst'rāt'| *a* excellent(e).

fir tree *n* sapin *m*.

fiscal |fis'kəl| *a* fiscal(e); **~ year** exercice financier.

fish |fish| *n* (*pl inv*) poisson *m*; poissons *mpl* ♦ *vt, vi* pêcher; **to ~ a river** pêcher dans une rivière; **to go ~ing** aller à la pêche.

fisherman |fish'ûrmən| *n* pêcheur *m*.

fishery |fish'ûrē| *n* pêcherie *f*.

fish factory *n* (*Brit*) conserverie *f* de poissons.

fish farm *n* établissement *m* piscicole.

fish fingers *npl* (*Brit*) = **fish sticks**.

fish hook *n* hameçon *m*.

fishing boat |fish'ing bōt| *n* barque *f* de pêche.

fishing industry *n* industrie *f* de la pêche.

fishing line *n* ligne *f* (de pêche).

fishing rod *n* canne *f* à pêche.

fishing tackle *n* attirail *m* de pêche.

fish market *n* marché *m* au poisson.

fishmonger |fish'munggûr| *n* marchand *m* de poisson; **~'s (shop)** poissonnerie *f*.

fish slice *n* (*Brit*) pelle *f* à poisson.

fish sticks *npl* bâtonnets de poisson (congelés).

fishy |fish'ē| *a* (*fig*) suspect(e), louche.

fission |fish'ən| *n* fission *f*; **atomic** *or* **nuclear ~** fission nucléaire.

fissure |fish'ûr| *n* fissure *f*.

fist |fist| *n* poing *m*.

fistfight |fist'fīt| *n* pugilat *m*, bagarre *f* (à coups de poing).

fit |fit| *a* (*MED, SPORT*) en (bonne) forme; (*proper*) convenable; approprié(e) ♦ *vt* (*subj: clothes*) aller à; (*adjust*) ajuster; (*put in, attach*) installer, poser; adapter; (*equip*) équiper, garnir, munir ♦ *vi* (*clothes*) aller; (*parts*) s'adapter; (*in space, gap*) entrer, s'adapter ♦ *n* (*MED*) accès *m*, crise *f*; (*of coughing*) quinte *f*; **~ to** en état de; **~ for** digne de; apte à; **to keep ~** se maintenir en forme; **this dress is a tight/good ~** cette robe est un peu juste/(me) va très bien; **a ~ of anger** un accès de colère; **to have a ~** (*MED*) faire *or* avoir une crise; (*col*) piquer une crise; **by ~s and starts** par à-coups.

fit in *vi* s'accorder; (*person*) s'adapter.

fit out *vt* équiper.

fitful |fit'fəl| *a* intermittent(e).

fitment |fit'mənt| *n* (*Brit*) meuble encastré, élément *m*.

fitness |fit'nis| *n* (*MED*) forme *f* physique; (*of remark*) à-propos *m*, justesse *f*.

fitted kitchen |fit'id kich'ən| *n* (*Brit*) cuisine équipée.

fitter |fit'ûr| *n* monteur *m*; (*DRESSMAKING*) essayeur/euse.

fitting |fit'ing| *a* approprié(e) ♦ *n* (*of dress*) essayage *m*; (*of piece of equipment*) pose *f*, installation *f*.

fitting room *n* (*in shop*) cabine *f* d'essayage.

fittings |fit'ingz| *npl* installations *fpl*.

five |fīv| *num* cinq.

five-day week |fīv'dā wēk'| *n* semaine *f* de cinq jours.

fiver |fī'vûr| *n* (*col: US*) billet de cinq dollars; (: *Brit*) billet *m* de cinq livres.

fix |fiks| *vt* fixer; (*sort out*) arranger; (*mend*) réparer; (*make ready: meal, drink*) préparer; (*castrate*) châtrer, castrer; (*col: game etc*) truquer ♦ *n*: **to be in a ~** être dans le pétrin.

fix up *vt* (*meeting*) arranger; **to ~ sb up with sth** faire avoir qch à qn.

fixation |fiksā'shən| *n* (*PSYCH*) fixation *f*; (*fig*) obsession *f*.

fixed [fikst] *a* (*prices etc*) fixe; **there's a ~ charge** il y a un prix forfaitaire; **how are you ~ for money?** (*col*) question fric, ça va?
fixed assets *npl* immobilisations *fpl*.
fixture [fiks'chûr] *n* installation *f* (fixe); (*SPORT*) rencontre *f* (au programme).
fizz [fiz] *vi* pétiller.
fizzle [fiz'əl] *vi* pétiller.
fizzle out *vi* rater.
fizzy [fiz'ē] *a* pétillant(e); gazeux(euse).
fjord [fyôrd] *n* = **fiord**.
FL *abbr* (*US MAIL*) = *Florida*.
Fla. *abbr* (*US*) = *Florida*.
flabbergasted [flab'ûrgastid] *a* sidéré(e), ahuri(e).
flabby [flab'ē] *a* mou(molle).
flag [flag] *n* drapeau *m*; (*also*: **~stone**) dalle *f* ♦ *vi* faiblir; fléchir; **~ of convenience** pavillon *m* de complaisance.
flag down *vt* héler, faire signe (de s'arrêter) à.
flagon [flag'ən] *n* bonbonne *f*.
flagpole [flag'pōl] *n* mât *m*.
flagrant [flāg'rənt] *a* flagrant(e).
flag stop *n* (*US: for bus*) arrêt facultatif.
flair [flâr] *n* flair *m*.
flak [flak] *n* (*MIL*) tir antiaérien; (*col: criticism*) critiques *fpl*.
flake [flāk] *n* (*of rust, paint*) écaille *f*; (*of snow, soap powder*) flocon *m* ♦ *vi* (*also*: **~ off**) s'écailler.
flaky [flā'kē] *a* (*paintwork*) écaillé(e); (*skin*) desquamé(e); (*Brit: pastry*) feuilleté(e).
flamboyant [flamboi'ənt] *a* flamboyant(e), éclatant(e); (*person*) haut(e) en couleur.
flame [flām] *n* flamme *f*.
flamingo [fləming'gō] *n* flamant *m* (rose).
flammable [flam'əbəl] *a* inflammable.
flan [flan] *n* tarte *f*.
Flanders [flan'dûrz] *n* Flandre(s) *f(pl)*.
flange [flanj] *n* boudin *m*; collerette *f*.
flank [flangk] *n* flanc *m* ♦ *vt* flanquer.
flannel [flan'əl] *n* (*Brit: also*: **face ~**) gant *m* de toilette; (*fabric*) flanelle *f*; (*Brit col*) baratin *m*; **~s** *npl* pantalon *m* de flanelle.
flap [flap] *n* (*of pocket, envelope*) rabat *m* ♦ *vt* (*wings*) battre (de) ♦ *vi* (*sail, flag*) claquer; (*col: also*: **be in a ~**) paniquer.
flapjack [flap'jak] *n* (*US*) ≈ crêpe *f*; (*Brit: biscuit*) galette *f*.
flare [flâr] *n* fusée éclairante; (*in skirt etc*) évasement *m*.
flare up *vi* s'embraser; (*fig: person*) se mettre en colère, s'emporter; (*: revolt*) éclater.
flared [flârd] *a* (*trousers*) à jambes évasées; (*skirt*) évasé(e).
flash [flash] *n* éclair *m*; (*also*: **news ~**) flash *m* (d'information); (*PHOT*) flash ♦ *vt* (*switch on*) allumer (brièvement); (*direct*): **to ~ sth at** braquer qch sur; (*flaunt*) étaler, exhiber; (*send: message*) câbler ♦ *vi* briller; jeter des éclairs; (*light on ambulance etc*) clignoter; **in a ~** en un clin d'œil; **to ~ one's headlights** faire un appel de phares; **he ~ed by** or **past** il passa (devant nous) comme un éclair.
flashback [flash'bak] *n* flashback *m*, retour *m* en arrière.

flashbulb [flash'bulb] *n* ampoule *f* de flash.
flash card *n* (*SCOL*) carte *f* (*support visuel*).
flashcube [flash'kyoōb] *n* cube-flash *m*.
flasher [flash'ûr] *n* (*AUT*) clignotant *m*.
flashlight [flash'līt] *n* lampe *f* de poche.
flash point *n* point *m* d'ignition; (*fig*): **to be at ~** être sur le point d'exploser.
flashy [flash'ē] *a* (*pej*) tape-à-l'œil *inv*, tapageur(euse).
flask [flask] *n* flacon *m*, bouteille *f*; (*CHEMISTRY*) ballon *m*; (*also*: **vacuum ~**) bouteille *f* thermos ®.
flat [flat] *a* plat(e); (*tire*) dégonflé(e), à plat; (*denial*) catégorique; (*MUS*) bémolisé(e); (*: voice*) faux(fausse) ♦ *n* (*Brit: rooms*) appartement *m*; (*AUT*) crevaison *f*, pneu crevé; (*MUS*) bémol *m*; **~ out** (*work*) sans relâche; (*race*) à fond; **~ rate of pay** (*COMM*) (salaire *m*) fixe.
flat-footed [flat'foōtid] *a*: **to be ~** avoir les pieds plats.
flatly [flat'lē] *ad* catégoriquement.
flatmate [flat'māt] *n* (*Brit*): **he's my ~** il partage l'appartement avec moi.
flatness [flat'nis] *n* (*of land*) absence *f* de relief, aspect plat.
flatten [flat'ən] *vt* (*also*: **~ten out**) aplatir; (*house, city*) raser.
flatter [flat'ûr] *vt* flatter.
flatterer [flat'ûrûr] *n* flatteur *m*.
flattering [flat'ûring] *a* flatteur(euse); (*clothes etc*) seyant(e).
flattery [flat'ûrē] *n* flatterie *f*.
flatulence [flach'ələns] *n* flatulence *f*.
flaunt [flônt] *vt* faire étalage de.
flavor [flā'vûr] (*US*) *n* goût *m*, saveur *f*; (*of ice cream etc*) parfum *m* ♦ *vt* parfumer, aromatiser; **vanilla-~ed** à l'arôme de vanille, vanillé(e); **to give** or **add ~ to** donner du goût à, relever.
flavoring [flā'vûring] *n* arôme *m* (synthétique).
flavour [flā'vûr] *etc* (*Brit*) = **flavor** *etc*.
flaw [flô] *n* défaut *m*.
flawless [flô'lis] *a* sans défaut.
flax [flaks] *n* lin *m*.
flaxen [flaks'ən] *a* blond(e).
flea [flē] *n* puce *f*.
flea market *n* marché *m* aux puces.
fleck [flek] *n* (*of dust*) particule *f*; (*of mud, paint, color*) tacheture *f*, moucheture *f* ♦ *vt* tacher, éclabousser; **brown ~ed with white** brun moucheté de blanc.
fledg(e)ling [flej'ling] *n* oisillon *m*.
flee [flē], *pt*, *pp* **fled** [fled] *vt* fuir, s'enfuir de ♦ *vi* fuir, s'enfuir.
fleece [flēs] *n* toison *f* ♦ *vt* (*col*) voler, filouter.
fleecy [flē'sē] *a* (*blanket*) moelleux(euse); (*cloud*) floconneux(euse).
fleet [flēt] *n* flotte *f*; (*of trucks, cars etc*) parc *m*; convoi *m*.
fleeting [flē'ting] *a* fugace, fugitif(ive); (*visit*) très bref(brève).
Flemish [flem'ish] *a* flamand(e) ♦ *n* (*LING*) flamand *m*; **the ~** *npl* les Flamands.
flesh [flesh] *n* chair *f*.
flesh wound *n* blessure superficielle.
flew [floō] *pt* of **fly**.
flex [fleks] *n* fil *m* or câble *m* électrique (souple) ♦ *vt* fléchir; (*muscles*) tendre.

flexibility [fleksəbil'ətē] n flexibilité f.

flexible [flek'səbəl] a flexible; (person, schedule) souple.

flick [flik] n petite tape; chiquenaude f; sursaut m.

 flick through vt fus feuilleter.

flicker [flik'ûr] vi vaciller ♦ n vacillement m; **a ~ of light** une brève lueur.

flick knife n (Brit) couteau m à cran d'arrêt.

flier [flī'ûr] n aviateur m.

flight [flīt] n vol m; (escape) fuite f; (also: ~ of steps) escalier m; **to take ~** prendre la fuite; **to put to ~** mettre en fuite.

flight attendant n steward m, hôtesse f de l'air.

flight crew n équipage m.

flight deck n (AVIAT) poste m de pilotage; (NAUT) pont m d'envol.

flight recorder n enregistreur m de vol.

flimsy [flim'zē] a (partition, fabric) peu solide, mince; (excuse) pauvre, mince.

flinch [flinch] vi tressaillir; **to ~ from** se dérober à, reculer devant.

fling [fling] vt (pt, pp **flung** [flung]) jeter, lancer ♦ n (love affair) brève liaison, passade f.

flint [flint] n silex m; (in lighter) pierre f (à briquet).

flip [flip] n chiquenaude f ♦ vt donner une chiquenaude à; (US: flapjack) faire sauter ♦ vi: **to ~ for sth** (US) jouer qch à pile ou face.

 flip through vt fus feuilleter.

flippant [flip'ənt] a désinvolte, irrévérencieux(euse).

flipper [flip'ûr] n (of animal) nageoire f; (for swimmer) palme f.

flip side n (of record) deuxième face f.

flirt [flûrt] vi flirter ♦ n flirteuse f.

flirtation [flûrtā'shən] n flirt m.

flit [flit] vi voleter.

float [flōt] n flotteur m; (in procession) char m; (sum of money) réserve f ♦ vi flotter; (bather) flotter, faire la planche ♦ vt faire flotter; (loan, business, idea) lancer.

floating [flō'ting] a flottant(e); **~ vote** voix flottante; **~ voter** électeur indécis.

flock [fläk] n troupeau m; (of birds) vol m; (of people) foule f.

floe [flō] n (also: **ice ~**) iceberg m.

flog [flåg] vt fouetter.

flood [flud] n inondation f; (of words, tears etc) flot m, torrent m ♦ vt inonder; (AUT: carburetor) noyer; **to ~ the market** (COMM) inonder le marché; **in ~** en crue.

flooding [flud'ing] n inondation f.

floodlight [flud'līt] n projecteur m ♦ vt éclairer aux projecteurs, illuminer.

floodlit [flud'līt] pt, pp of **floodlight** ♦ a illuminé(e).

flood tide n marée montante.

floor [flôr] n sol m; (story) étage m; (of sea, valley) fond m; (fig: at meeting): **the ~** l'assemblée f, les membres mpl de l'assemblée ♦ vt terrasser; (baffle) désorienter; **on the ~** par terre; **first ~**, (Brit) **ground ~** rez-de-chaussée m; **second ~**, (Brit) **first ~** premier étage; **top ~** dernier étage; **to have the ~** (speaker) avoir la parole.

floorboard [flôr'bôrd] n planche f (du plancher).

flooring [flôr'ing] n sol m; (wooden) plancher m; (material to make floor) matériau(x) m(pl) pour planchers; (covering) revêtement m de sol.

floor lamp n (US) lampadaire m.

floor show n spectacle m de variétés.

floorwalker [flôr'wôkûr] n (esp US) surveillant m (de grand magasin).

flop [flåp] n fiasco m ♦ vi (fail) faire fiasco.

flophouse [flåp'hous] n (US) asile m de nuit.

floppy [flåp'ē] a lâche, flottant(e); **~ hat** chapeau m à bords flottants.

floppy disk n disquette f, disque m souple.

flora [flôr'ə] n flore f.

floral [flôr'əl] a floral(e).

Florence [flär'əns] n Florence.

florid [flôr'id] a (complexion) fleuri(e); (style) plein(e) de fioritures.

florist [flôr'ist] n fleuriste m/f; **~'s (shop)** magasin m or boutique f de fleuriste.

flotation [flōtā'shən] n (of shares) émission f; (of company) lancement m (en Bourse).

flounce [flouns] n volant m.

 flounce out vi sortir dans un mouvement d'humeur.

flounder [floun'dûr] n (ZOOL) flet m ♦ vi patauger.

flour [flou'ûr] n farine f.

flourish [flûr'ish] vi prospérer ♦ vt brandir ♦ n fioriture f; (of trumpets) fanfare f.

flourishing [flûr'ishing] a prospère, florissant(e).

flout [flout] vt se moquer de, faire fi de.

flow [flō] n (of water, traffic etc) écoulement m; (tide, influx) flux m; (of orders, letters etc) flot m; (of blood, ELEC) circulation f; (of river) courant m ♦ vi couler; (traffic) s'écouler; (robes, hair) flotter.

flow chart, flow diagram n organigramme m.

flower [flou'ûr] n fleur f ♦ vi fleurir; **in ~** en fleur.

flower bed n plate-bande f.

flowerpot [flou'ûrpät] n pot m (à fleurs).

flowery [flou'ûrē] a fleuri(e).

flown [flōn] pp of **fly**.

flu [flōō] n grippe f.

fluctuate [fluk'chōōāt] vi varier, fluctuer.

fluctuation [flukchōō'shən] n fluctuation f, variation f.

flue [flōō] n conduit m.

fluency [flōō'ənsē] n facilité f, aisance f.

fluent [flōō'ənt] a (speech, style) coulant(e), aisé(e); **he's a ~ speaker/reader** il s'exprime/lit avec aisance or facilité; **he speaks ~ French, he's ~ in French** il parle le français couramment.

fluently [flōō'əntlē] ad couramment; avec aisance or facilité.

fluff [fluf] n duvet m; peluche f.

fluffy [fluf'ē] a duveteux(euse); pelucheux(euse).

fluid [flōō'id] n fluide m; (in diet) liquide m ♦ a fluide.

fluid ounce n (Brit) = 0.028 l; 0.05 pints.

fluke [flōōk] n (col) coup m de veine.

flummox [flum'əks] vt dérouter, déconcerter.

flung [flung] pt, pp of **fling**.

flunky [flung'kē] n larbin m.
fluorescent [flo͞oərɛs'ənt] a fluorescent(e).
fluoride [flo͞o'ərīd] n fluor m.
fluorine [flo͞o'ərēn] n fluor m.
flurry [flûr'ē] n (of snow) rafale f, bourrasque f; ~ **of activity/excitement** affairement m/ excitation f soudain(e).
flush [flush] n rougeur f; (fig) éclat m; afflux m ♦ vt nettoyer à grande eau; (also: ~ **out**) débusquer ♦ vi rougir ♦ a (col) en fonds; (level): ~ **with** au ras de, de niveau avec; **to** ~ **the toilet** tirer la chasse (d'eau).
flushed [flusht] a (tout(e)) rouge.
fluster [flus'tûr] n agitation f, trouble m.
flustered [flus'tûrd] a énervé(e).
flute [flo͞ot] n flûte f.
fluted [flo͞o'tid] a cannelé(e).
flutter [flut'ûr] n agitation f; (of wings) battement m ♦ vi battre des ailes, voleter; (person) aller et venir dans une grande agitation.
flux [fluks] n: **in a state of** ~ fluctuant sans cesse.
fly [flī] n (insect) mouche f; (on trousers: also: **flies**) braguette f ♦ vb (pt **flew**, pp **flown** [flo͞o, flōn]) vt (plane) piloter; (passengers, cargo) transporter (par avion); (distances) parcourir ♦ vi voler; (passengers) aller en avion; (escape) s'enfuir, fuir; (flag) se déployer; **to** ~ **open** s'ouvrir brusquement; **to** ~ **off the handle** s'énerver, s'emporter.
fly away vi s'envoler.
fly in vi (plane) atterrir; (person): **he flew in yesterday** il est arrivé hier (par avion).
fly off vi s'envoler.
fly out vi (see fly in) s'envoler; partir (par avion).
fly-fishing [flī'fishing] n pêche f à la mouche.
flying [flī'ing] n (activity) aviation f ♦ a: ~ **visit** visite f éclair inv; **with** ~ **colors** haut la main; **he doesn't like** ~ il n'aime pas voyager en avion.
flying buttress n arc-boutant m.
flying saucer n soucoupe volante.
flying squad n (MIL etc) brigade volante.
flying start n: **to get off to a** ~ faire un excellent départ.
flyleaf [flī'lēf] n page f de garde.
flyover [flī'ōvûr] n défilé aérien; (Brit: overpass) saut-de-mouton m, pont autoroutier.
flypast [flī'past] n défilé aérien.
flysheet [flī'shēt] n (for tent) double toit m.
flywheel [flī'hwēl] n volant m (de commande).
FM abbr (RADIO) = **frequency modulation**; (Brit MIL) = **field marshal**.
FMB n abbr (US) = Federal Maritime Board.
FMCS n abbr (US: = Federal Mediation and Conciliation Services) organisme de conciliation en cas de conflits du travail.
foal [fōl] n poulain m.
foam [fōm] n écume f; (on beer) mousse f; (also: **plastic** ~) mousse cellulaire or de plastique ♦ vi écumer; (soapy water) mousser.
foam rubber n caoutchouc m mousse.
FOB abbr (= free on board) fob.
fob [fâb] n (also: **watch** ~) chaîne f, ruban m ♦ vt: **to** ~ **sb off with** refiler à qn; se dé-

barrasser de qn avec.
foc abbr (Brit) = **free of charge**.
focal [fō'kəl] a (also fig) focal(e).
focal point n foyer m; (fig) centre m de l'attention, point focal.
focus [fō'kəs] n (pl: ~**es**) foyer m; (of interest) centre m ♦ vt (field glasses etc) mettre au point; (light rays) faire converger ♦ vi: **to** ~ **(on)** (with camera) régler la mise au point (sur); (person) fixer son regard (sur); **in** ~ au point; **out of** ~ pas au point.
fodder [fâd'ûr] n fourrage m.
FOE n abbr (= Friends of the Earth) AT mpl (= Amis de la Terre); (US: = Fraternal Order of Eagles) organisation charitable.
foe [fō] n ennemi m.
foetus [fē'təs] etc n (Brit) = **fetus** etc.
fog [fôg] n brouillard m.
fog up vi (windows) s'embuer.
fogbound [fôg'bound] a bloqué(e) par le brouillard.
foggy [fôg'ē] a: **it's** ~ il y a du brouillard.
fog light n (AUT) phare m anti-brouillard.
foible [foi'bəl] n faiblesse f.
foil [foil] vt déjouer, contrecarrer ♦ n feuille f de métal; (kitchen ~) papier m d'alu(minium); (FENCING) fleuret m; **to act as a** ~ **to** (fig) servir de repoussoir or de faire valoir à.
foist [foist] vt: **to** ~ **sth on sb** imposer qch à qn.
fold [fōld] n (bend, crease) pli m; (AGR) parc m à moutons; (fig) bercail m ♦ vt plier; **to** ~ **one's arms** croiser les bras.
fold up vi (map etc) se plier, se replier; (business) fermer boutique ♦ vt (map etc) plier, replier.
folder [fōl'dûr] n (for papers) chemise f; (: binder) classeur m; (brochure) dépliant m.
folding [fōl'ding] a (chair, bed) pliant(e).
foliage [fō'lēij] n feuillage m.
folk [fōk] npl gens mpl ♦ cpd folklorique; ~**s** npl famille f, parents mpl.
folklore [fōk'lôr] n folklore m.
folksong [fōk'sông] n chanson f folklorique; (contemporary) chanson folk inv.
follow [fâl'ō] vt suivre ♦ vi suivre; (result) s'ensuivre; **to** ~ **sb's advice** suivre les conseils de qn; **I don't quite** ~ **you** je ne vous suis plus; **to** ~ **in sb's footsteps** emboîter le pas à qn; (fig) suivre les traces de qn; **it** ~**s that ...** de ce fait, il s'ensuit que ...; **he** ~**ed suit** il fit de même.
follow out vt (idea, plan) poursuivre, mener à terme.
follow through vt = **follow out**.
follow up vt (victory) tirer parti de; (letter, offer) donner suite à; (case) suivre.
follower [fâl'ōûr] n disciple m/f, partisan/e.
following [fâl'ōing] a suivant(e) ♦ n partisans mpl, disciples mpl.
follow-up [fâl'ōup] n suite f; suivi m.
folly [fâl'ē] n inconscience f; sottise f; (building) folie f.
fond [fând] a (memory, look) tendre, affectueux(euse); **to be** ~ **of** aimer beaucoup.
fondle [fân'dəl] vt caresser.
fondly [fând'lē] ad (lovingly) tendrement;

(*naïvely*) naïvement.

fondness [fând'nis] *n* (*for things*) attachement *m*; (*for people*) sentiments affectueux; **a special ~ for** une prédilection pour.

font [fânt] *n* (*REL*) fonts baptismaux; (*TYP*) police *f* de caractères.

food [fōōd] *n* nourriture *f*.

food mixer *n* mixeur *m*.

food poisoning *n* intoxication *f* alimentaire.

food processor [fōōd prâs'esûr] *n* robot *m* de cuisine.

foodstuffs [fōōd'stufs] *npl* denrées *fpl* alimentaires.

fool [fōōl] *n* idiot/e; (*HIST*: *of king*) bouffon *m*, fou *m*; (*CULIN*) purée *f* de fruits à la crème ♦ *vt* berner, duper ♦ *vi* (*also*: ~ **around**) faire l'idiot *or* l'imbécile; **to make a ~ of sb** (*ridicule*) ridiculiser qn; (*trick*) avoir *or* duper qn; **to make a ~ of o.s.** se couvrir de ridicule; **you can't ~ me** vous (ne) me la ferez pas, on (ne) me la fait pas.

fool about, fool around *vi* (*pej*: *waste time*) traînailler, glandouiller; (: *behave foolishly*) faire l'imbécile.

foolhardy [fōōl'hârdē] *a* téméraire, imprudent(e).

foolish [fōō'lish] *a* idiot(e), stupide; (*rash*) imprudent(e).

foolishly [fōō'lishlē] *ad* stupidement.

foolishness [fōō'lishnis] *n* idiotie *f*, stupidité *f*.

foolproof [fōōl'prōōf] *a* (*plan etc*) infaillible.

foolscap [fōōlz'kap] *n* ≈ papier *m* ministre.

foot [fōōt] *n* (*pl*: **feet**) pied *m*; (*measure*) pied (= *304 mm*; *12 inches*); (*of animal*) patte *f* ♦ *vt* (*bill*) casquer, payer; **on ~** à pied; **to find one's feet** (*fig*) s'acclimater; **to put one's ~ down** (*AUT*) appuyer sur le champignon; (*say no*) s'imposer.

footage [fōōt'ij] *n* (*CINEMA*: *length*) ≈ métrage *m*; (: *material*) séquences *fpl*.

foot and mouth (disease) *n* fièvre aphteuse.

football [fōōt'bôl] *n* ballon *m* (de football); (*sport*: *US*) football américain; (: *Brit*) football *m*, foot *m*.

footballer [fōōt'bôlûr] *n* (*Brit*) = **football player**.

football field *n* terrain *m* de football.

football game *n* match *m* de football.

football player *n* footballeur *m*, joueur *m* de football.

footbrake [fōōt'brāk] *n* frein *m* à pied.

footbridge [fōōt'brij] *n* passerelle *f*.

foothills [fōōt'hilz] *npl* contreforts *mpl*.

foothold [fōōt'hōld] *n* prise *f* (de pied).

footing [fōōt'ing] *n* (*fig*) position *f*; **to lose one's ~** perdre pied; **on an equal ~** sur pied d'égalité.

footlights [fōōt'līts] *npl* rampe *f*.

footman [fōōt'mən] *n* laquais *m*.

footnote [fōōt'nōt] *n* note *f* (en bas de page).

footpath [fōōt'path] *n* sentier *m*; (*in street*) trottoir *m*.

footprint [fōōt'print] *n* trace *f* (de pied).

footrest [fōōt'rest] *n* marchepied *m*.

footsore [fōōt'sôr] *a* aux pieds endoloris.

footstep [fōōt'step] *n* pas *m*.

footwear [fōōt'weûr] *n* chaussure(s) *f(pl)* (*terme générique en anglais*).

FOR *abbr* (= *free on rail*) franco wagon.

for [fôr] *prep* pour; (*during*) pendant; (*in spite of*) malgré ♦ *cj* car; **I haven't seen him ~ a week** je ne l'ai pas vu depuis une semaine, cela fait une semaine que je ne l'ai pas vu; **I'll be away ~ 3 weeks** je serai absent pendant 3 semaines; **he went down ~ the paper** il est descendu chercher le journal; **I sold it for $5** je l'ai vendu 5 dollars; **~ sale** à vendre; **the train ~ Ohio** le train pour Ohio; **it's time ~ lunch** c'est l'heure de déjeuner; **what ~?** (*why*) pourquoi?; (*to what end*) pourquoi faire?, à quoi bon?; **what's this button ~?** à quoi sert ce bouton?; **~ all that** malgré cela, néamoins; **there's nothing ~ it but to jump** (*Brit*) il n'y a plus qu'à sauter.

forage [fôr'ij] *n* fourrage *m* ♦ *vi* fourrager, fouiller.

forage cap *n* (*Brit*) calot *m*.

foray [fôr'ā] *n* incursion *f*.

forbad(e) [fûrbād] *pt of* **forbid**.

forbearing [fôrbär'ing] *a* patient(e), tolérant(e).

forbid [fûrbid'] *pt* **forbad(e)**, *pp* **forbidden** [fûrbid', -bād', -bid'n] *vt* défendre, interdire; **to ~ sb to do** défendre *or* interdire à qn de faire.

forbidden [fûrbid'ən] *a* défendu(e).

forbidding [fûrbid'ing] *a* d'aspect *or* d'allure sévère *or* sombre.

force [fôrs] *n* force *f* ♦ *vt* forcer; **the Armed F~s** *npl* l'armée *f*; **to ~ sb to do sth** forcer qn à faire qch; **in ~** en force; **to come into ~** entrer en vigueur; **a ~ 5 wind** un vent de force 5; **the sales ~** (*COMM*) la force de vente; **to join ~s** unir ses forces.

force back *vt* (*crowd, enemy*) repousser; (*tears*) retouler.

force down *vt* (*food*) se forcer à manger.

forced [fôrst] *a* forcé(e).

force-feed [fôrs'fēd] *vt* nourrir de force.

forceful [fôrs'fəl] *a* énergique, volontaire.

forceps [fôr'səps] *npl* forceps *m*.

forcibly [fôr'səblē] *ad* par la force, de force; (*vigorously*) énergiquement.

ford [fôrd] *n* gué *m* ♦ *vt* passer à gué.

fore [fôr] *n*: **to the ~** en évidence.

forearm [fôr'ârm] *n* avant-bras *m inv*.

forebear [fôr'beûr] *n* ancêtre *m*.

foreboding [fôrbō'ding] *n* pressentiment *m* (néfaste).

forecast [fôr'kast] *n* prévision *f*; (*also*: **weather ~**) prévisions météorologiques, météo *f* ♦ *vt* (*irg*: *like* **cast**) prévoir.

foreclose [fôrklōz'] *vt* (*LAW*: *also*: ~ **on**) saisir.

foreclosure [fôrklō'zhûr] *n* saisie *f* du bien hypothéqué.

forecourt [fôr'kôrt] *n* (*of garage*) devant *m*.

forefathers [fôr'fâ\th\ûrz] *npl* ancêtres *mpl*.

forefinger [fôr'finggûr] *n* index *m*.

forefront [fôr'frunt] *n*: **in the ~ of** au premier rang *or* plan de.

forego *pt* **forewent**, *pp* **foregone** [fôrgō', -went', -gôn'] *vt* = **forgo**.

foregoing [fôrgō'ing] *a* susmentionné(e) ♦ *n*: **the ~** ce qui précède.

foregone [fôrgôn'] *a*: **it's a ~ conclusion** c'est à prévoir, c'est couru d'avance.

foreground [fôr'ground] *n* premier plan ♦ *cpd* (*COMPUT*) prioritaire.

forehand [fôr'hand] *n* (*TENNIS*) coup droit.

forehead [fôr'hed] *n* front *m*.

foreign [fôr'in] *a* étranger(ère); (*trade*) extérieur(e).

foreign body *n* corps étranger.

foreign currency *n* devises étrangères.

foreigner [fôr'ənûr] *n* étranger/ère.

foreign exchange *n* (*system*) change *m*; (*money*) devises *fpl*.

foreign exchange market *n* marché *m* des devises.

foreign exchange rate *n* cours *m* des devises.

foreign investment *n* investissement *m* à l'étranger.

Foreign Office *n* (*Brit*) ministère *m* des Affaires étrangères.

foreign secretary *n* (*Brit*) ministre *m* des Affaires étrangères.

foreleg [fôr'leg] *n* patte *f* de devant; jambe antérieure.

foreman [fôr'mən] *n* contremaître *m*; (*LAW: of jury*) président *m* (du jury).

foremost [fôr'mōst] *a* le(la) plus en vue; premier(ière) ♦ *ad*: **first and** ~ avant tout, tout d'abord.

forename [fôr'nām] *n* prénom *m*.

forensic [fəren'sik] *a*: ~ **medicine** médecine légale; ~ **expert** expert *m* de la police, expert légiste.

forerunner [fôr'runûr] *n* précurseur *m*.

foresee, *pt* **foresaw**, *pp* **foreseen** [fôrsē', -sô', -sēn'] *vt* prévoir.

foreseeable [fôrsē'əbəl] *a* prévisible.

foreshadow [fôrshad'ō] *vt* présager, annoncer, laisser prévoir.

foreshorten [fôrshôr'tən] *vt* (*figure, scene*) réduire, faire en raccourci.

foresight [fôr'sīt] *n* prévoyance *f*.

foreskin [fôr'skin] *n* (*ANAT*) prépuce *m*.

forest [fôr'ist] *n* forêt *f*.

forestall [fôrstôl'] *vt* devancer.

forestry [fôr'istrē] *n* sylviculture *f*.

foretaste [fôr'tāst] *n* avant-goût *m*.

foretell, *pt*, *pp* **foretold** [fôrtel', -tōld'] *vt* prédire.

forethought [fôr'thôt] *n* prévoyance *f*.

forever [fôrev'ûr] *ad* pour toujours; (*fig*) continuellement.

forewarn [fôrwôrn'] *vt* avertir.

forewent [fôrwent'] *pt of* **forego**.

foreword [fôr'wûrd] *n* avant-propos *m inv*.

forfeit [fôr'fit] *n* prix *m*, rançon *f* ♦ *vt* perdre; (*one's life, health*) payer de.

forgave [fôrgāv'] *pt of* **forgive**.

forge [fôrj] *n* forge *f* ♦ *vt* (*signature*) contrefaire; (*wrought iron*) forger; **to** ~ **documents/ a will** fabriquer de faux papiers/un faux testament; **to** ~ **money** (*Brit*) fabriquer de la fausse monnaie.

forge ahead *vi* pousser de l'avant, prendre de l'avance.

forger [fôr'jûr] *n* faussaire *m*.

forgery [fôr'jûrē] *n* faux *m*, contrefaçon *f*.

forget, *pt* **forgot**, *pp* **forgotten** [fûrget', -gât', -gât'ən] *vt*, *vi* oublier.

forgetful [fûrget'fəl] *a* distrait(e), étourdi(e); ~ **of** oublieux(euse) de.

forgetfulness [fûrget'fəlnis] *n* tendance *f* aux oublis; (*oblivion*) oubli *m*.

forget-me-not [fûrget'mēnât] *n* myosotis *m*.

forgive, *pt* **forgave**, *pp* **forgiven** [fûrgiv', -gāv', -giv'ən] *vt* pardonner; **to** ~ **sb for sth/for doing sth** pardonner qch à qn/à qn de faire qch.

forgiveness [fûrgiv'nis] *n* pardon *m*.

forgiving [fûrgiv'ing] *a* indulgent(e).

forgo, *pt* **forwent**, *pp* **forgone** [fôrgō', -went', -gôn'] *vt* renoncer à.

forgot [fûrgât'] *pt of* **forget**.

forgotten [fûrgât'ən] *pp of* **forget**.

fork [fôrk] *n* (*for eating*) fourchette *f*; (*for gardening*) fourche *f*; (*of roads*) bifurcation *f*; (*of railways*) embranchement *m* ♦ *vi* (*road*) bifurquer.

fork out (*col: pay*) *vt* allonger, se fendre de ♦ *vi* casquer.

forked [fôrkt] *a* (*lightning*) en zigzags, ramifié(e).

forklift truck [fôrk'lift truk'] *n* chariot élévateur.

forlorn [fôrlôrn'] *a* abandonné(e), délaissé(e); (*hope, attempt*) désespéré(e).

form [fôrm] *n* forme *f*; (*Brit SCOL*) classe *f*; (*questionnaire*) formulaire *m* ♦ *vt* former; **in the** ~ **of** sous forme de; **to** ~ **part of sth** faire partie de qch; **to be in good** ~ (*SPORT, fig*) être en forme; **in top** ~ en pleine forme.

formal [fôr'məl] *a* (*offer, receipt*) en bonne et due forme; (*person*) cérémonieux(euse), à cheval sur les convenances; (*occasion, dinner*) officiel(le); (*ART, PHILOSOPHY*) formel(le); ~ **dress** tenue *f* de cérémonie; (*evening dress*) tenue de soirée.

formality [fôrmal'itē] *n* formalité *f*; cérémonie(s) *f(pl)*.

formalize [fôr'məlīz] *vt* officialiser.

formally [fôr'məlē] *ad* officiel[l]ement; formellement; cérémonieusement.

format [fôr'mat] *n* format *m* ♦ *vt* (*COMPUT*) formater.

formation [fôrmā'shən] *n* formation *f*.

formative [fôr'mətiv] *a*: ~ **years** années *fpl* d'apprentissage (*fig*) or de formation (*d'un enfant, d'un adolescent*).

former [fôr'mûr] *a* ancien(ne) (*before n*), précédent(e); **the** ~ **... the latter** le premier ... le second, celui-là ... celui-ci; **the** ~ **president** l'ex-président.

formerly [fôr'mûrlē] *ad* autrefois.

form feed *n* (*on printer*) alimentation *f* en feuilles.

formidable [fôr'midəbəl] *a* redoutable.

formula [fôr'myələ] *n* formule *f*; **F~ One** (*AUT*) Formule un.

formulate [fôr'myəlāt] *vt* formuler.

fornicate [fôr'nikāt] *vi* forniquer.

forsake, *pt* **forsook**, *pp* **forsaken** [fôrsāk', -sōōk, -sā'kən] *vt* abandonner.

fort [fôrt] *n* fort *m*; **to hold the** ~ (*fig*) assurer la permanence.

forte [fôr'tā] *n* (point) fort *m*.

forth [fôrth] *ad* en avant; **to go back and** ~ aller et venir; **and so** ~ et ainsi de suite.

forthcoming [fôrth'kum'ing] *a* qui va paraître *or* avoir lieu prochainement; (*character*) ouvert(e), communicatif(ive).

forthright [fôrth'rīt] *a* franc(franche), direct(e).

forthwith [fôrthwith'] *ad* sur le champ.

fortieth [fôr'tēith] *num* quarantième.

fortification [fôrtəfəkā'shən] *n* fortification *f*.

fortified wine [fôr'təfīd wīn'] *n* vin liquoreux *or* de liqueur.

fortify [fôr'təfī] *vt* fortifier.

fortitude [fôr'tətōod] *n* courage *m*, force *f* d'âme.

fortnight [fôrt'nīt] *n* (*Brit*) quinzaine *f*, quinze jours *mpl*; **it's a ~ since** ... il y a quinze jours que ....

fortnightly [fôrt'nītlē] (*Brit*) *a* bimensuel(le) ♦ *ad* tous les quinze jours.

FORTRAN [fôr'tran] *n* FORTRAN *m*.

fortress [fôr'tris] *n* forteresse *f*.

fortuitous [fôrtōō'itəs] *a* fortuit(e).

fortunate [fôr'chənit] *a*: **to be ~** avoir de la chance; **it is ~ that** c'est une chance que, il est heureux que.

fortunately [fôr'chənitlē] *ad* heureusement, par bonheur.

fortune [fôr'chən] *n* chance *f*; (*wealth*) fortunc *f*; **to make a ~** faire fortune.

fortuneteller [fôr'chəntelûr] *n* diseuse *f* de bonne aventure.

forty [fôr'tē] *num* quarante.

forum [fôr'əm] *n* forum *m*, tribune *f*.

forward [fôr'wûrd] *a* (*movement, position*) en avant, vers l'avant; (*not shy*) effronté(e); (*COMM: delivery, sales, exchange*) à terme ♦ *ad* en avant ♦ *n* (*SPORT*) avant *m* ♦ *vt* (*letter*) faire suivre; (*parcel, goods*) expédier; (*fig*) promouvoir, contribuer au développement *or* à l'avancement de; **to move ~** avancer; **"please ~"** "prière de faire suivre".

forward(s) [fôr'wûrd(z)] *ad* en avant.

forwent [fôrwent'] *pt of* **forgo**.

fossil [fâs'əl] *a, n* fossile (*m*); **~ fuel** combustible *m* fossile.

foster [fôs'tûr] *vt* encourager, favoriser.

foster brother *n* frère adoptif; frère de lait.

foster child *n* enfant adopté.

foster mother *n* mère adoptive; mère nourricière.

fought [fôt] *pt, pp of* **fight**.

foul [foul] *a* (*weather, smell, food*) infect(e); (*language*) ordurier(ière); (*deed*) infâme ♦ *n* (*SPORT*) faute *f* ♦ *vt* salir, encrasser; (*player*) commettre une faute sur; (*entangle: anchor, propeller*) emmêler.

foul play *n* (*SPORT*) jeu déloyal; **~ is not suspected** la mort (*or* l'incendie *etc*) n'a pas de causes suspectes, on écarte l'hypothèse d'un meurtre (*or* d'un acte criminel).

found [found] *pt, pp of* **find** ♦ *vt* (*establish*) fonder.

foundation [foundā'shən] *n* (*act*) fondation *f*; (*base*) fondement *m*; (*also:* **~ cream**) fond *m* de teint; **~s** *npl* (*of building*) fondations *fpl*; **to lay the ~s** (*fig*) poser les fondements.

foundation stone *n* première pierre.

founder [foun'dûr] *n* fondateur *m* ♦ *vi* couler, sombrer.

founding [foun'ding] *a*: **~ fathers** (*esp US*) pères *mpl* fondateurs; **~ member** membre *m*

fondateur.

foundry [foun'drē] *n* fonderie *f*.

fount [fount] *n* source *f*; (*Brit TYP*) fonte *f*.

fountain [foun'tin] *n* fontaine *f*.

fountain pen *n* stylo *m* (à encre).

four [fôr] *num* quatre; **on all ~s** à quatre pattes.

four-poster [fôr'pōs'tûr] *n* (*also:* **~ bed**) lit *m* à baldaquin.

foursome [fôr'səm] *n* partie *f* à quatre; sortie *f* à quatre.

fourteen [fôr'tēn'] *num* quatorze.

fourth [fôrth] *num* quatrième ♦ *n* (*AUT: also:* **~ gear**) quatrième *f*.

four-wheel drive [fôr'hwēl drīv'] *n* (*AUT*): **with ~** à quatre roues motrices.

fowl [foul] *n* volaille *f*.

fox [fâks] *n* renard *m* ♦ *vt* mystifier.

fox fur *n* renard *m*.

foxglove [fâks'gluv] *n* (*BOT*) digitale *f*.

fox-hunting [fâks'hunting] *n* chasse *f* au renard.

foyer [foi'ûr] *n* vestibule *m*; (*THEATER*) foyer *m*.

FP *n* *abbr* (*US*) = **fireplug**; (*Brit*) = *former pupil*.

Fr. *abbr* (= *father*: *REL*) P; (= *friar*) F.

fr. *abbr* (= *franc*) F.

fracas [trä'kəs] *n* bagarre *f*.

fraction [frak'shən] *n* fraction *f*.

fractionally [frak'shənəlē] *ad*: **~ smaller** *etc* un poil plus petit *etc*.

fractious [frak'shəs] *a* grincheux(euse).

fracture [frak'chûr] *n* fracture *f* ♦ *vt* fracturer.

fragile [fraj'əl] *a* fragile.

fragment [frag'mənt] *n* fragment *m*.

fragmentary [frag'məntärē] *a* fragmentaire.

fragrance [frā'grəns] *n* parfum *m*.

fragrant [frā'grənt] *a* parfumé(e), odorant(e).

frail [frāl] *a* fragile, délicat(e).

frame [frām] *n* (*of building*) charpente *f*; (*of human, animal*) charpente, ossature *f*; (*of picture*) cadre *m*; (*of door, window*) encadrement *m*, chambranle *m*; (*of spectacles: also:* **~s**) monture *f* ♦ *vt* encadrer; (*theory, plan*) construire, élaborer; **to ~ sb** (*col*) monter un coup contre qn; **~ of mind** disposition *f* d'esprit.

framework [frām'wûrk] *n* structure *f*.

France [frans] *n* la France; **in ~** en France.

franchise [fran'chīz] *n* (*POL*) droit *m* de vote; (*COMM*) franchise *f*.

franchisee [franchizē'] *n* franchisé *m*.

franchiser [fran'chīzûr] *n* franchiseur *m*.

frank [frangk] *a* franc(franche) ♦ *vt* (*letter*) affranchir.

Frankfurt [frangk'fûrt] *n* Francfort.

frankly [frangk'lē] *ad* franchement.

frankness [frangk'nis] *n* franchise *f*.

frantic [fran'tik] *a* (*desperate: need, desire*) effréné(e); (*person*) hors de soi.

frantically [fran'tiklē] *ad* frénétiquement.

fraternal [frətûr'nəl] *a* fraternel(le).

fraternity [frətûr'nitē] *n* (*club*) communauté *f*, confrérie *f*; (*spirit*) fraternité *f*.

fraternize [frat'ûrnīz] *vi* fraterniser.

fraud [frôd] *n* supercherie *f*, fraude *f*, tromperie *f*; (*person*) imposteur *m*.

fraudulent [frô'jələnt] *a* frauduleux(euse).

fraught [frôt] *a* (*tense: person*) très tendu(e); (: *situation*) pénible; ~ **with** (*difficulties etc*) chargé(e) de, plein(e) de.

fray [frā] *n* bagarre *f*; (*MIL*) combat *m* ♦ *vt* effilocher ♦ *vi* s'effilocher; **tempers were** ~**ed** les gens commençaient à s'énerver; **her nerves were** ~**ed** elle était à bout de nerfs.

FRB *n abbr* (*US*) = **Federal Reserve Board**.

freak [frēk] *n* (*also cpd*) phénomène *m*, créature ou événement exceptionnel par sa rareté, son caractère d'anomalie; (*pej: fanatic*): **health** ~ fana *m/f* or obsédé/e de l'alimentation saine (*or* de la forme physique).

freak out *vi* (*col: drop out*) se marginaliser; (: *on drugs*) se défoncer.

freakish [frēk'ish] *a* insolite; anormal(e).

freckle [frek'əl] *n* tache *f* de rousseur.

free [frē] *a* libre; (*gratis*) gratuit(e); (*liberal*) généreux(euse), large ♦ *vt* (*prisoner etc*) libérer; (*jammed object or person*) dégager; **to give sb a** ~ **hand** donner carte blanche à qn; ~ **and easy** sans façon, décontracté(e); **admission** ~ entrée libre; ~ (**of charge**) *ad* gratuitement.

-free *suffix*: **additive**~ sans additif; **tax**~ exonéré(e) d'impôt.

freebie [frē'bē] *n* (*col*): **it's a** ~ c'est gratuit.

freedom [frē'dəm] *n* liberté *f*.

freedom fighter *n* combattant *m* de la liberté.

free enterprise *n* libre entreprise *f*.

free-for-all [frē'fúrôl'] *n* mêlée générale.

free gift *n* prime *f*.

freehold [frē'hōld] *n* propriété foncière libre.

free kick *n* (*SPORT*) coup franc.

freelance [frē'lans] *a* (*journalist etc*) indépendant(e); (*work*) à la pige, à la tâche.

freeloader [frē'lōdûr] *n* (*pej*) parasite *m*.

freely [frē'lē] *ad* librement; (*liberally*) libéralement.

freemason [frē'māsən] *n* franc-maçon *m*.

freemasonry [frē'māsənrē] *n* franc-maçonnerie *f*.

free-range [frē'rānj] *a* (*Brit: eggs*) de ferme.

free sample *n* échantillon gratuit.

free speech *n* liberté *f* d'expression.

freestyle wrestling [frē'stīl res'ling] *n* (*US*) catch *m*.

free trade *n* libre-échange *m*.

freeway [frē'wā] *n* (*US*) autoroute *f*.

freewheel [frē'hwēl'] *vi* descendre en roue libre.

freewheeling [frē'hwē'ling] *a* indépendant(e), libre.

free will *n* libre arbitre *m*; **of one's own** ~ de son plein gré.

freeze [frēz] *vb* (*pt* **froze**, *pp* **frozen** [frōz, frō'zən]) *vi* geler ♦ *vt* geler; (*food*) congeler; (*prices, salaries*) bloquer, geler ♦ *n* gel *m*; blocage *m*.

freeze over *vi* (*river*) geler; (*windshield*) se couvrir de givre *or* de glace.

freeze up *vi* geler.

freeze-dried [frēz'drīd'] *a* lyophilisé(e).

freezer [frē'zûr] *n* congélateur *m*.

freezing [frē'zing] *a*: ~ (**cold**) (*room etc*) glacial(e); (*person, hands*) gelée(e), glacé(e) ♦ *n*: **3 degrees below** ~ 3 degrés au-dessous de zéro.

freezing point *n* point *m* de congélation.

freight [frāt] *n* (*goods*) fret *m*, cargaison *f*; (*money charged*) fret, prix *m* du transport; ~ **forward** port dû; ~ **inward** port payé par le destinataire.

freighter [frā'tûr] *n* (*NAUT*) cargo *m*.

freight forwarder [frāt' fôr'wûrdûr] *n* transitaire *m*.

freight train *n* (*US*) train *m* de marchandises.

French [french] *a* français(e) ♦ *n* (*LING*) français *m*; **the** ~ *npl* les Français.

French bean *n* (*Brit*) haricot vert.

French Canadian *a* canadien(ne) français(e) ♦ *n* Canadien/ne français(e); (*LING*) français canadien.

French dressing *n* (*CULIN*) vinaigrette *f*.

French fries [french frīz] *npl* (pommes de terre *fpl*) frites.

French Guiana [french gēan'ə] *n* Guyane française.

Frenchman [french'mən] *n* Français *m*.

French Riviera *n*: **the** ~ la Côte d'Azur.

French window *n* porte-fenêtre *f*.

Frenchwoman [french'woomən] *n* Française *f*.

frenetic [frənet'ik] *a* frénétique.

frenzy [fren'zē] *n* frénésie *f*.

frequency [frē'kwənsē] *n* fréquence *f*.

frequency modulation (FM) *n* modulation *f* de fréquence (FM, MF).

frequent *a* [frē'kwint] fréquent(e) ♦ *vt* [frikwent'] fréquenter.

frequently [frē'kwintlē] *ad* fréquemment.

fresco [fres'kō] *n* fresque *f*.

fresh [fresh] *a* frais(fraîche); (*new*) nouveau(nouvelle); (*cheeky*) familier(ière), culotté(e); **to make a** ~ **start** prendre un nouveau départ.

freshen [fresh'ən] *vi* (*wind, air*) fraîchir.

freshen up *vi* faire un brin de toilette.

freshener [fresh'ənûr] *n*: **skin** ~ astringent *m*; **air** ~ désodorisant *m*.

fresher [fresh'ûr] *n* (*Brit SCOL: col*) = **freshman**.

freshly [fresh'lē] *ad* nouvellement, récemment.

freshman [fresh'mən] *n* (*SCOL*) bizuth *m*, étudiant/e de première année.

freshness [fresh'nis] *n* fraîcheur *f*.

freshwater [fresh'wôtûr] *a* (*fish*) d'eau douce.

fret [fret] *vi* s'agiter, se tracasser.

fretful [fret'fəl] *a* (*child*) grincheux(euse).

Freudian [froi'dēən] *a* freudien(ne); ~ **slip** lapsus *m*.

FRG *n abbr* (= *Federal Republic of Germany*) RFA *f*.

Fri. *abbr* (= *Friday*) ve.

friar [frī'ûr] *n* moine *m*, frère *m*.

friction [frik'shən] *n* friction *f*, frottement *m*.

friction feed *n* (*on printer*) entraînement *m* par friction.

Friday [frī'dā] *n* vendredi *m*; *for phrases see also* **Tuesday**.

fridge [frij] *n* (*Brit*) frigo *m*, frigidaire *m* ®.

fried [frīd] *pt, pp of* **fry** ♦ *a* frit(e); ~ **egg** œuf *m* sur le plat.

friend [frend] *n* ami/e; **to make** ~**s with** se lier (d'amitié) avec.

friendliness [frend'lēnis] *n* attitude amicale.

friendly [frend'lē] *a* amical(e); (*kind*) sympathique, gentil(le); (*POL*: *country, government*) ami(e) ♦ *n* (*also*: ~ **match**) match amical; **to be** ~ **with** être ami(e) avec; **to be** ~ **to** être bien disposé(e) à l'égard de.

friendly society *n* (*Brit*) société *f* mutualiste.

friendship [frend'ship] *n* amitié *f*.

frieze [frēz] *n* frise *f*, bordure *f*.

frigate [frig'it] *n* (*NAUT*: *modern*) frégate *f*.

fright [frīt] *n* peur *f*, effroi *m*; **to take** ~ prendre peur, s'effrayer; **she looks a** ~ elle a l'air d'un épouvantail.

frighten [frīt'ən] *vt* effrayer, faire peur à.
  frighten away, frighten off *vt* (*birds, children etc*) faire fuir, effaroucher.

frightened [frīt'ənd] *a*: **to be** ~ (**of**) avoir peur (de).

frightening [frīt'ning] *a* effrayant(e).

frightful [frīt'fəl] *a* affreux(euse).

frightfully [frīt'fəlē] *ad* affreusement.

frigid [frij'id] *a* (*woman*) frigide.

frigidity [frijid'itē] *n* frigidité *f*.

frill [fril] *n* (*of dress*) volant *m*; (*of shirt*) jabot *m*; **without** ~**s** (*fig*) sans manières.

fringe [frinj] *n* frange *f*; (*edge: of forest etc*) bordure *f*; (*fig*): **on the** ~ en marge.

fringe benefits *npl* avantages sociaux *or* en nature.

fringe theatre *n* (*Brit*) théâtre *m* d'avant-garde.

frisk [frisk] *vt* fouiller.

frisky [fris'kē] *a* vif(vive), sémillant(e).

fritter [frit'ûr] *n* beignet *m*.
  fritter away *vt* gaspiller.

frivolity [frəvâl'itē] *n* frivolité *f*.

frivolous [friv'ələs] *a* frivole.

frizzy [friz'ē] *a* crépu(e).

fro [frō] *see* **to.**

frock [frâk] *n* robe *f*.

frog [frôg] *n* grenouille *f*; **to have a** ~ **in one's throat** avoir un chat dans la gorge.

frogman [frôg'man] *n* homme-grenouille *m*.

frogmarch [frôg'mârch] *vt* (*Brit*): **to** ~ **sb in/out** faire entrer/sortir qn de force.

frolic [frâl'ik] *n* ébats *mpl* ♦ *vi* folâtrer, batifoler.

from [frum] *prep* de; **where is he** ~? d'où est-il?; **where has he come** ~? d'où arrive-t-il?; **(as)** ~ **Friday** à partir de vendredi; **a telephone call** ~ **Mr.** Smith un appel de M. Smith; **prices range** ~ **$10 to $50** les prix vont de 10 dollars à 50 dollars; ~ **what he says** d'après ce qu'il dit.

frond [frând] *n* fronde *f*.

front [frunt] *n* (*of house, dress*) devant *m*; (*of coach, train*) avant *m*; (*of book*) couverture *f*; (*promenade: also*: **sea** ~) bord *m* de mer; (*MIL, POL, METEOROLOGY*) front *m*; (*fig: appearances*) contenance *f*, façade *f* ♦ *a* de devant; premier(ière) ♦ *vi*: **to** ~ **onto sth** donner sur qch; **in** ~ (**of**) devant.

frontage [frun'tij] *n* façade *f*; (*of shop*) devanture *f*.

frontal [frun'təl] *a* frontal(e).

front bench *n* (*Brit POL*) les dirigeants du parti au pouvoir ou de l'opposition.

front desk *n* (*in hotel, at doctor's*) réception *f*.

front door *n* porte *f* d'entrée; (*of car*) portière *f* avant.

frontier [fruntēûr'] *n* frontière *f*.

frontispiece [frun'tispēs] *n* frontispice *m*.

front page *n* première page.

front room *n* pièce *f* de devant, salon *m*.

front runner *n* (*fig*) favori/te.

front-wheel drive [frunt'hwēl drīv] *n* traction *f* avant.

frost [frôst] *n* gel *m*, gelée *f*; (*also*: **hoar**~) givre *m* ♦ *vt* (*cake*) glacer.

frostbite [frôst'bīt] *n* gelures *fpl*.

frosted [frôs'tid] *a* (*glass*) dépoli(e); (*esp US: cake*) glacé(e).

frosting [frôs'ting] *n* (*esp US: on cake*) glaçage *m*.

frosty [frôs'tē] *a* (*window*) couvert(e) de givre; (*welcome*) glacial(e).

froth [frôth] *n* mousse *f*; écume *f*.

frown [froun] *n* froncement *m* de sourcils ♦ *vi* froncer les sourcils.
  frown on *vt* (*fig*) désapprouver.

froze [frōz] *pt of* **freeze.**

frozen [frō'zən] *pp of* **freeze** ♦ *a* (*food*) congelé(e); (*COMM: assets*) gelé(e).

FRS *n abbr* (*US: = Federal Reserve System*) banque centrale américaine.

frugal [frōō'gəl] *a* frugal(e).

fruit [frōōt] *n* (*pl inv*) fruit *m*.

fruiterer [frōōt'ərûr] *n* fruitier *m*, marchand/e de fruits; ~**'s (shop)** fruiterie *f*.

fruitful [frōōt'fəl] *a* fructueux(euse); (*plant, soil*) fécond(e).

fruition [frōōish'ən] *n*: **to come to** ~ se réaliser.

fruit juice *n* jus *m* de fruit.

fruitless [frōōt'lis] *a* (*fig*) vain(e), infructueux(euse).

fruit machine *n* (*Brit*) machine *f* à sous.

fruit salad *n* salade *f* de fruits.

frump [frump] *n* mocheté *f*.

frustrate [frus'trāt] *vt* frustrer; (*plot, plans*) faire échouer.

frustrated [frus'trātid] *a* frustré(e).

frustrating [frus'trāting] *a* (*job*) frustrant(e); (*day*) démoralisant(e).

frustration [frustrā'shən] *n* frustration *f*.

fry, *pt, pp* **fried** [frī, frīd] *vt* (faire) frire; **the small** ~ le menu fretin.

frying pan [frī'ing pan] *n* poêle *f* (à frire).

FSLIC *n abbr* (*US: = Federal Savings and Loan Insurance Corporation*) organisme fédéral assurant les dépôts des associations d'épargne et de prêt.

FT *n abbr* (*Brit: = Financial Times*) journal financier; **the** ~ **index** l'indice boursier du Financial Times.

ft. *abbr* = **foot, feet.**

FTC *n abbr* (*US*) = **Federal Trade Commission.**

fuchsia [fyōō'sha] *n* fuchsia *m*.

fuck [fuk] *vt, vi* (*col!*) baiser (!); ~ **off!** fous le camp! (!).

fuddled [fud'əld] *a* (*muddled*) embrouillé(e), confus(e).

fuddy-duddy [fud'ēdudē] *a* (*pej*) vieux jeu *inv*, ringard(e).

fudge [fuj] *n* (*CULIN*) sorte *f* de confiserie à

base de sucre, de beurre et de lait ♦ vt (issue, problem) esquiver.

fuel [fyōo'əl] n (for heating) combustible m; (for propelling) carburant m.

fuel oil n mazout m.

fuel pump n (AUT) pompe f d'alimentation.

fuel tank n cuve f à mazout, citerne f; (in vehicle) réservoir m de or à carburant.

fug [fug] n (Brit) puanteur f, odeur f de renfermé.

fugitive [fyōo'jətiv] n fugitif/ive.

fulfill, (Brit) **fulfil** [fōolfil'] vt (function) remplir; (order) exécuter; (wish, desire) satisfaire, réaliser.

fulfilled [fōolfild'] a (person) comblé(e), épanoui(e).

fulfillment [fōolfil'mənt] n (of wishes) réalisation f.

full [fōol] a plein(e); (details, information) complet(ète); (price) fort(e), normal(e); (skirt) ample, large ♦ ad: **to know ~ well that** savoir fort bien que; **~ (up)** (hotel etc) complet(ète); **I'm ~ (up)** j'ai bien mangé; **~ employment/fare** plein emploi/tarif; **a ~ two hours** deux bonnes heures; **at ~ speed** à toute vitesse; **in ~** (reproduce, quote, pay) intégralement; (write name etc) en toutes lettres.

fullback [fōol'bak] n (RUGBY, SOCCER) arrière m.

full-blooded [fōol'blud'id] a (vigorous) vigoureux(euse).

full-cream [fōol'krēm] a: **~ milk** (Brit) lait entier.

full-fledged [fōol'flejd'] a (US: teacher, barrister) diplômé(e); (: citizen, member) à part entière.

full-grown [fōol'grōn'] a arrivé(e) à maturité, adulte.

full-length [fōol'lengkth'] a (portrait) en pied; **~ film** long métrage.

full moon n pleine lune.

full-scale [fōol'skāl'] a (model) grandeur nature inv; (search, retreat) complet(ète), total(e).

full-sized [fōol'sīzd] a (portrait etc) grandeur nature inv.

full stop n (Brit) point m.

full-time [fōol'tīm] a (work) à plein temps ♦ n (SPORT) fin f du match.

fully [fōol'ē] ad entièrement, complètement; (at least): **~ as big** au moins aussi grand.

fully-fledged [fōol'ēflejd'] a (Brit) = **full-fledged.**

fulsome [fōol'səm] a (pej: praise) excessif(ive); (: manner) exagéré(e).

fumble [fum'bəl] vi fouiller, tâtonner ♦ vt (ball) mal réceptionner, cafouiller.

fumble with vt fus tripoter.

fume [fyōom] vi rager; **~s** npl vapeurs fpl, émanations fpl, gaz mpl.

fumigate [fyōo'məgāt] vt désinfecter (par fumigation).

fun [fun] n amusement m, divertissement m; **to have ~** s'amuser; **for ~** pour rire; **it's not much ~** ce n'est pas très drôle or amusant; **to make ~ of** se moquer de.

function [fungk'shən] n fonction f; (reception, dinner) cérémonie f, soirée officielle ♦ vi

fonctionner; **to ~ as** faire office de.

functional [fungk'shənəl] a fonctionnel(le).

function key n (COMPUT) touche f de fonction.

fund [fund] n caisse f, fonds m; (source, store) source f, mine f; **~s** npl fonds mpl.

fundamental [fundəmen'təl] a fondamental(e); **~s** npl principes mpl de base.

fundamentalist [fundəmen'təlist] intégriste m/f.

fundamentally [fundəmen'təlē] ad fondamentalement.

fund-raising [fund'rāzing] n collecte f de fonds.

funeral [fyōo'nûrəl] n enterrement m, obsèques fpl (more formal occasion).

funeral director n entrepreneur m des pompes funèbres.

funeral home, (Brit) **funeral parlour** n dépôt m mortuaire.

funeral service n service m funèbre.

funereal [fyōonē'rēəl] a lugubre, funèbre.

funfair [fun'fär] n (Brit) fête (foraine).

fungus, pl **fungi** [fung'gəs, -jī] n champignon m; (mould) moisissure f.

funicular [fyōonik'yəlûr] n (also: **~ railway**) funiculaire m.

funnel [fun'əl] n entonnoir m; (of ship) cheminée f.

funnily [fun'ilē] ad (see funny) drôlement; curieusement.

funny [fun'ē] a amusant(e), drôle; (strange) curieux(euse), bizarre.

funny bone n endroit sensible du coude.

fur [fûr] n fourrure f; (Brit: in kettle etc) (dépôt m de) tartre m.

fur coat n manteau m de fourrure.

furious [fyōor'ēəs] a furieux(euse); (effort) acharné(e); **to be ~ with sb** être dans une fureur noire contre qn.

furiously [fyōor'ēəslē] ad furieusement; avec acharnement.

furl [fûrl] vt rouler; (NAUT) ferler.

furlong [fûr'lông] n = 201.17 m (terme d'hippisme).

furlough [fûr'lō] n permission f, congé m.

furnace [fûr'nis] n fourneau m.

furnish [fûr'nish] vt meubler; (supply) fournir; **~ed apartment** meublé m.

furnishings [fûr'nishingz] npl mobilier m, articles mpl d'ameublement.

furniture [fûr'nichûr] n meubles mpl, mobilier m; **piece of ~** meuble m.

furniture mover n déménageur m.

furniture polish n encaustique f.

furore [fyōor'ôr] n (protests) protestations fpl.

furrier [fûr'ēûr] n fourreur m.

furrow [fûr'ō] n sillon m.

furry [fûr'ē] a (animal) à fourrure; (toy) en peluche.

further [fûr'thûr] a supplémentaire, autre; nouveau(nouvelle) ♦ ad plus loin; (more) davantage; (moreover) de plus ♦ vt faire avancer or progresser, promouvoir; **how much ~ is it?** quelle distance or combien reste-t-il à parcourir?; **until ~ notice** jusqu'à nouvel ordre or avis; **~ to your letter of ...** (Brit COMM) suite à votre lettre du ....

further education n enseignement m postscolaire (*recyclage, formation profes-sionnelle*).

furthermore [fûr'thûrmôr] *ad* de plus, en outre.

furthermost [fûr'thûrmōst] *a* le(la) plus éloigné(e).

furthest [fûr'thist] *superlative of* **far**.

furtive [fûr'tiv] *a* furtif(ive).

furtively [fûr'tivlē] *ad* furtivement.

fury [fyŏor'ē] *n* fureur *f*.

fuse [fyŏoz] *n* fusible *m*; (*Brit: for bomb etc*) amorce *f*, détonateur *m* ♦ *vt, vi* (*metal*) fondre; (*fig*) fusionner; (*Brit* ELEC): **to ~ the lights** faire sauter les fusibles *or* les plombs; **a ~ has blown** un fusible a sauté.

fuse box *n* boîte *f* à fusibles.

fuselage [fyŏo'sәlàzh] *n* fuselage *m*.

fuse wire *n* fusible *m*.

fusillade [fyŏos'әlād] *n* fusillade *f*; (*fig*) feu roulant.

fusion [fyŏo'zhәn] *n* fusion *f*.

fuss [fus] *n* (*anxiety, excitement*) chichis *mpl*, façons *fpl*; (*commotion*) tapage *m*; (*complaining, trouble*) histoire(s) *f(pl)* ♦ *vi* faire des histoires ♦ *vt* (*person*) embêter; **to make a ~** faire des façons (*or* des histoires).

fuss over *vt fus* (*person*) dorloter.

fussy [fus'ē] *a* (*person*) tatillon(ne), difficile; chichiteux(euse); (*dress, style*) tarabiscoté(e); **I'm not ~** (*col*) ça m'est égal.

futile [fyŏotil'] *a* futile.

futility [fyŏotil'әtē] *n* futilité *f*.

future [fyŏo'chûr] *a* futur(e) ♦ *n* avenir *m*; (LING) futur *m*; **in (the) ~** à l'avenir; **in the near/immediate ~** dans un avenir proche/immédiat.

futures [fyŏo'chûrz] *npl* (COMM) opérations *fpl* à terme.

futuristic [fyŏochәris'tik] *a* futuriste.

fuze [fyŏoz] (US) *n* (*for bomb etc*) amorce *f*, détonateur *m* ♦ *vt, vi* = **fuse**.

fuzzy [fuz'ē] *a* (PHOT) flou(e); (*hair*) crépu(e).

fwd. *abbr* = **forward**.

fwy *abbr* (US) = **freeway**.

FY *abbr* = **fiscal year**.

FYI *abbr* = **for your information**.

G

G, g [jē] *n* (*letter*) G, g *m*; (MUS): **G** sol *m*; **G for George** G comme Gaston.

G [jē] *n abbr* (US CINEMA: = *general (audience*) ≈ tous publics; (*Brit* SCOL: = *good*) b (= *bien*).

g [jē] *abbr* (= *gram, gravity*) g.

GA *abbr* (US MAIL) = *Georgia*.

gab [gab] *n* (*col*): **to have the gift of the ~** avoir la langue bien pendue.

gabble [gab'әl] *vi* bredouiller; jacasser.

gaberdine [gab'ûrdēn] *n* gabardine *f*.

gable [gā'bәl] *n* pignon *m*.

Gabon [gābán'] *n* Gabon *m*.

gad about [gad әbout'] *vi* (*col*) se balader.

gadget [gaj'it] *n* gadget *m*.

Gaelic [gā'lik] *a, n* gaélique (*m*).

gaffe [gaf] *n* gaffe *f*.

gag [gag] *n* bâillon *m*; (*joke*) gag *m* ♦ *vt* bâillonner.

gaga [gâ'gâ] *a*: **to go ~** devenir gaga *or* gâteux(euse).

gage [gāj] *n, vt* (US) = **gauge**.

gaiety [gā'әtē] *n* gaieté *f*.

gaily [gā'lē] *ad* gaiement.

gain [gān] *n* gain *m*, profit *m* ♦ *vt* gagner ♦ *vi* (*watch*) avancer; **to ~ in/by** gagner en/à; **to ~ 3lbs (in weight)** prendre 3 livres; **to ~ ground** gagner du terrain.

gainful [gān'fәl] *a* profitable, lucratif(ive).

gainsay [gānsā'] *vt irg* (*like* **say**) contredire; nier.

gait [gāt] *n* démarche *f*.

gal. *abbr* = **gallon**.

gala [gā'lә] *n* gala *m*; **swimming ~** grand concours de natation.

Galapagos (Islands) [gәlà'pәgōs (i'lәndz)] *npl*: **the ~** les (îles *fpl*) Galapagos *fpl*.

galaxy [gal'әksē] *n* galaxie *f*.

gale [gāl] *n* coup *m* de vent; **~ force 10** vent *m* de force 10.

gall [gôl] *n* (ANAT) bile *f*; (*fig*) effronterie *f* ♦ *vt* ulcérer, irriter.

gall. *abbr* = **gallon**.

gallant [gal'әnt] *a* vaillant(e), brave; [gәlânt'] (*towards ladies*) empressé(e), galant(e).

gallantry [gal'әntrē] *n* bravoure *f*, vaillance *f*; empressement *m*, galanterie *f*.

gall bladder *n* vésicule *f* biliaire.

galleon [gal'ēәn] *n* galion *m*.

gallery [gal'ûrē] *n* galerie *f*; (*for spectators*) tribune *f*; (*: in theater*) dernier balcon; (*also:* **art ~**) musée *m*; (*: private*) galerie.

galley [gal'ē] *n* (*ship's kitchen*) cambuse *f*; (*ship*) galère *f*; (*also:* **~ proof**) placard *m*, galée *f*.

Gallic [gal'ik] *a* (*of Gaul*) gaulois(e); (*French*) français(e).

galling [gô'ling] *a* irritant(e).

gallon [gal'әn] *n* gallon *m* (= *8 pints; US* = *3.785 l; Brit* = *4.543 l*).

gallop [gal'әp] *n* galop *m* ♦ *vi* galoper; **~ing inflation** inflation galopante.

gallows [gal'ōz] *n* potence *f*.

gallstone [gôl'stōn] *n* calcul *m* (biliaire).

galore [gәlôr'] *ad* en abondance, à gogo.

galvanize [gal'vәnīz] *vt* galvaniser; (*fig*): **to ~ sb into action** galvaniser qn.

Gambia [gam'bēә] *n* Gambie *f*.

gambit [gam'bit] *n* (*fig*): (**opening**) **~** manœuvre *f* stratégique.

gamble [gam'bәl] *n* pari *m*, risque calculé ♦ *vt, vi* jouer; **to ~ on the Stock Exchange** jouer en *or* à la Bourse; **to ~ on** (*fig*) miser sur.

gambler [gam'blûr] *n* joueur *m*.

gambling [gam'bling] *n* jeu *m*.

gambol [gam'bәl] *vi* gambader.

game [gām] *n* jeu *m*; (*event*) match *m*; (HUNTING) gibier *m* ♦ *a* brave; (*ready*): **to be ~ (for sth/to do)** être prêt(e) (à qch/à faire), se sentir de taille (à faire); **a ~ of**

football/tennis une partie de football/tennis; **~s** (*SCOL*) sport *m*; **big ~** gros gibier.

game bird *n* gibier *m* à plume.

gamekeeper [gām'kēpúr] *n* garde-chasse *m*.

gamely [gām'lē] *ad* vaillamment.

game reserve *n* réserve animalière.

gamesmanship [gāmz'mənship] *n* roublardise *f*.

gammon [gam'ən] *n* (*bacon*) quartier *m* de lard fumé; (*ham*) jambon fumé.

gamut [gam'ət] *n* gamme *f*.

gang [gang] *n* bande *f*, groupe *m* ♦ *vi*: **to ~ up on sb** se liguer contre qn.

Ganges [gan'jēz] *n*: **the ~** le Gange.

gangling [gang'gling] *a* dégingandé(e).

gangplank [gang'plangk] *n* passerelle *f*.

gangrene [gang'grēn] *n* gangrène *f*.

gangster [gang'stúr] *n* gangster *m*, bandit *m*.

gangway [gang'wā] *n* passerelle *f*; (*Brit: of bus*) couloir central.

gantry [gan'trē] *n* portique *m*; (*for rocket*) tour *f* de lancement.

GAO *n abbr* (*US*: = *General Accounting Office*) ≈ Cour *f* des comptes.

gaol [jāl] *n, vt* (*Brit*) = **jail**.

gap [gap] *n* trou *m*; (*in time*) intervalle *m*; (*fig*) lacune *f*; vide *m*.

gape [gāp] *vi* être *or* rester bouche bée.

gaping [gā'ping] *a* (*hole*) béant(e).

garage [gərāzh'] *n* garage *m*.

garb [gârb] *n* tenue *f*, costume *m*.

garbage [gâr'bij] *n* ordures *fpl*, détritus *mpl*; (*fig: col*) conneries *fpl*.

garbage can *n* (*US*) poubelle *f*, boîte *f* à ordures.

garbage disposal unit *n* (*US*) broyeur *m* d'ordures.

garbage dump *n* (*US: in town*) décharge publique, dépotoir *m*.

garbageman [gâr'bijman] *n* (*US*) éboueur *m*.

garbled [gâr'bəld] *a* déformé(e); faussé(e).

garden [gâr'dən] *n* jardin *m* ♦ *vi* jardiner; **~s** *npl* (*public*) jardin public; (*private*) parc *m*.

garden center *n* garden-centre *m*, pépinière *f*.

gardener [gârd'núr] *n* jardinier *m*.

gardening [gâr'dəning] *n* jardinage *m*.

gargle [gâr'gəl] *vi* se gargariser ♦ *n* gargarisme *m*.

gargoyle [gâr'goil] *n* gargouille *f*.

garish [gär'ish] *a* criard(e), voyant(e).

garland [gâr'lənd] *n* guirlande *f*; couronne *f*.

garlic [gâr'lik] *n* ail *m*.

garment [gâr'mənt] *n* vêtement *m*.

garner [gâr'núr] *vt* engranger, amasser.

garnish [gâr'nish] *vt* garnir.

garret [gar'it] *n* mansarde *f*.

garrison [gar'isən] *n* garnison *f* ♦ *vt* mettre en garnison, stationner.

garrison cap *n* (*US*) calot *m*.

garrulous [gar'ələs] *a* volubile, loquace.

garter [gâr'túr] *n* jarretière *f*; (*US: suspender*) jarretelle *f*.

garter belt *n* (*US*) porte-jarretelles *m inv*.

gas [gas] *n* gaz *m*; (*used as anesthetic*): **to be given ~** se faire endormir; (*US: gasoline*) essence *f* ♦ *vt* asphyxier; (*MIL*) gazer.

gas can *n* (*US*) bidon *m* à essence.

Gascony [gas'kənē] *n* Gascogne *f*.

gas cylinder *n* bouteille *f* de gaz.

gaseous [gas'ēəs] *a* gazeux(euse).

gash [gash] *n* entaille *f*; (*on face*) balafre *f* ♦ *vt* taillader; balafrer.

gasket [gas'kit] *n* (*AUT*) joint *m* de culasse.

gas mask *n* masque *m* à gaz.

gas meter *n* compteur *m* à gaz.

gas(oline) [gas(əlēn')] *n* (*US*) essence *f*.

gasp [gasp] *vi* haleter; (*fig*) avoir le souffle coupé.

gasp out *vt* (*say*) dire dans un souffle *or* d'une voix entrecoupée.

gas pedal *n* (*US*) accélérateur *m*.

gas-permeable [gaspûr'mēəbəl] *a* (*contact lenses*) perméable à l'air.

gas pump *n* (*US*) pompe *f* à essence.

gas ring *n* brûleur *m*.

gas station *n* (*US*) station-service *f*.

gas stove *n* réchaud *m* à gaz; (*cooker*) cuisinière *f* à gaz.

gassy [gas'ē] *a* gazeux(euse).

gas tank *n* (*US AUT*) réservoir *m* d'essence.

gas tap *n* bouton *m* (de cuisinière à gaz); (*on pipe*) robinet *m* à gaz.

gastric [gas'trik] *a* gastrique.

gastric ulcer *n* ulcère *m* de l'estomac.

gastroenteritis [gastrōentərī'tis] *n* gastroentérite *f*.

gastronomy [gastrân'əmē] *n* gastronomie *f*.

gasworks [gas'wûrks] *n, npl* usine *f* à gaz.

gate [gāt] *n* (*of garden*) portail *m*; (*of farm, at level crossing*) barrière *f*; (*of building, town, at airport*) porte *f*; (*of lock*) vanne *f*.

gateau, *pl* **~x** [gatō', z] *n* (*Brit*) gros gâteau à la crème.

gate-crash [gāt'krash] *vt* s'introduire sans invitation dans.

gate-crasher [gāt'krashûr] *n* intrus/e.

gateway [gāt'wā] *n* porte *f*.

gather [gath'ûr] *vt* (*flowers, fruit*) cueillir; (*pick up*) ramasser; (*assemble*) rassembler, réunir; recueillir; (*understand*) comprendre ♦ *vi* (*assemble*) se rassembler; (*dust*) s'amasser; (*clouds*) s'amonceler; **to ~ (from/that)** conclure *or* déduire (de/que); **as far as I can ~** d'après ce que je comprends; **to ~ speed** prendre de la vitesse.

gathering [gath'ûring] *n* rassemblement *m*.

GATT [gat] *n abbr* (= *General Agreement on Tariffs and Trade*) GATT *m*.

gauche [gōsh] *a* gauche, maladroit(e).

gaudy [gô'dē] *a* voyant(e).

gauge [gāj] *n* (*standard measure*) calibre *m*; (*RAIL*) écartement *m*; (*instrument*) jauge *f* ♦ *vt* jauger; (*fig: sb's capabilities, character*) juger de; **to ~ the right moment** calculer le moment propice; **gas ~**, (*Brit*) **petrol ~** jauge d'essence.

Gaul [gôl] *n* (*country*) Gaule *f*; (*person*) Gaulois/e.

gaunt [gônt] *a* décharné(e); (*grim, desolate*) désolé(e).

gauntlet [gônt'lit] *n* (*fig*): **to throw down the ~** jeter le gant; **to run the ~ through an angry crowd** se frayer un passage à travers une foule hostile *or* entre deux haies de manifestants *etc* hostiles.

gauze [gôz] *n* gaze *f*.

gave [gāv] *pt of* **give**.

gavel [gav'əl] *n* marteau *m*.
gawky [gô'kē] *a* dégingandé(e), godiche.
gawp [gôp] *vi*: **to ~ at** regarder bouche bée.
gay [gā] *a* (*homosexual*) homosexuel(le); (*slightly old-fashioned: cheerful*) gai(e), réjoui(e); (*color*) gai, vif(vive).
gaze [gāz] *n* regard *m* fixe ♦ *vi*: **to ~ at** *vt* fixer du regard.
gazelle [gəzel'] *n* gazelle *f*.
gazette [gəzet'] *n* (*newspaper*) gazette *f*; (*official publication*) journal officiel.
gazetteer [gazitēr'] *n* dictionnaire *m* géographique.
GB *abbr* = **Great Britain**.
GCE *n abbr* (*Brit*) = *General Certificate of Education*.
GCSE *n abbr* (*Brit*) = *General Certificate of Secondary Education*.
Gdns. *abbr* = *Gardens*.
GDP *n abbr* = **gross domestic product**.
GDR *n abbr* (= *German Democratic Republic*) RDA *f*.
gear [gēr] *n* matériel *m*, équipement *m*; (*TECH*) engrenage *m*; (*AUT*) vitesse *f* ♦ *vt* (*fig: adapt*) adapter; **high** *or* (*Brit*) **top/low/bottom ~** quatrième (*or* cinquième)/deuxième/première vitesse; **in ~** en prise; **out of ~** au point mort; **our service is ~ed to meet the needs of the disabled** notre service répond dc façon spécifique aux besoins des handicapés.
  gear up *vi*: **to ~ up (to do)** se préparer (à faire).
gear box *n* boîte *f* de vitesse.
gear shift, (*Brit*) **gear lever** *n* levier *m* de vitesse.
GED *n abbr* (*US SCOL*) = *general educational development*.
geese [gēs] *npl of* **goose**.
Geiger counter [gī'gûr koun'tûr] *n* compteur *m* Geiger.
gel [jel] *n* gelée *f*; (*CHEMISTRY*) colloïde *m*.
gelatin(e) [jel'atin] *n* gélatine *f*.
gelignite [jel'ignīt] *n* plastic *m*.
gem [jem] *n* pierre précieuse.
Gemini [jem'əni] *n* les Gémeaux *mpl*; **to be ~** être des Gémeaux.
gen [jen] *n* (*Brit col*): **to give sb the ~ on sth** mettre qn au courant de qch.
Gen. *abbr* (*MIL*: = *general*) Gal.
gen. *abbr* (= *general, generally*) gén.
gender [jen'dûr] *n* genre *m*.
gene [jēn] *n* (*BIOL*) gène *m*.
genealogy [jēnēâl'əjē] *n* généalogie *f*.
general [jen'ûrəl] *n* général *m* ♦ *a* général(e); **in ~** en général; **the ~ public** le grand public; **~ audit** (*COMM*) vérification annuelle.
general anesthetic *n* anesthésie générale.
general delivery *n* (*US*) poste restante.
general election *n* élection(s) législative(s).
generalization [jenûrələzā'shən] *n* généralisation *f*.
generalize [jen'ûrəlīz] *vi* généraliser.
generally [jen'ûrəlē] *ad* généralement.
general manager *n* directeur général.
general practitioner (GP) *n* généraliste *m/f*; **who's your GP?** qui est votre médecin traitant?
general strike *n* grève générale.

generate [jen'ərāt] *vt* engendrer; (*electricity*) produire.
generation [jenərā'shən] *n* génération *f*; (*of electricity etc*) production *f*.
generator [jen'ərātûr] *n* générateur *m*.
generic [jənär'ik] *a* générique.
generosity [jenərâs'ətē] *n* générosité *f*.
generous [jen'ûrəs] *a* généreux(euse); (*copious*) copieux(euse).
genesis [jen'əsis] *n* genèse *f*.
genetic [jinet'ik] *a* génétique; **~ engineering** génie *m* génétique.
genetics [jənet'iks] *n* génétique *f*.
Geneva [jənē'və] *n* Genève; **Lake ~** le lac Léman.
genial [jē'nēəl] *a* cordial(e), chaleureux(euse); (*climate*) clément(e).
genitals [jen'itəlz] *npl* organes génitaux.
genitive [jen'ətiv] *n* génitif *m*.
genius [jēn'yəs] *n* génie *m*.
Genoa [jen'əwə] *n* Gênes.
genocide [jen'əsid] *n* génocide *m*.
genteel [jentēl'] *a* de bon ton, distingué(e).
gentle [jen'təl] *a* doux(douce).
gentleman [jen'təlmən] *n* monsieur *m*; (*well-bred man*) gentleman *m*; **~'s agreement** gentleman's agreement *m*.
gentlemanly [jen'təlmənlē] *a* bien élevé(e).
gentleness [jen'təlnis] *n* douceur *f*.
gently [jen'tlē] *ad* doucement.
gentry [jen'trē] *n* petite noblesse.
genuine [jen'yōōin] *a* véritable, authentique; (*person, emotion*) sincère.
genuinely [jen'yōōinlē] *ad* sincèrement, vraiment.
geographer [jēâg'rəfûr] *n* géographe *m/f*.
geographic(al) [jēəgraf'ik(əl)] *a* géographique.
geography [jēâg'rəfē] *n* géographie *f*.
geological [jēəlâj'ikəl] *a* géologique.
geologist [jēâl'əjist] *n* géologuc *m/f*.
geology [jēâl'əjē] *n* géologie *f*.
geometric(al) [jēəmet'rik(əl)] *a* géométrique.
geometry [jēâm'ətrē] *n* géométrie *f*.
geranium [jərā'nēəm] *n* géranium *m*.
geriatric [järēat'rik] *a* gériatrique.
germ [jûrm] *n* (*MED*) microbe *m*; (*BIO, fig*) germe *m*.
German [jûr'mən] *a* allemand(e) ♦ *n* Allemand/e; (*LING*) allemand *m*.
German measles *n* rubéole *f*.
German shepherd *n* (*US: dog*) berger allemand.
Germany [jûr'mənē] *n* Allemagne *f*.
germination [jûrmənā'shən] *n* germination *f*.
germ warfare *n* guerre *f* bactériologique.
gerrymandering [jär'ēmandûring] *n* tripotage *m* du découpage électoral.
gestation [jestā'shən] *n* gestation *f*.
gesticulate [jestik'yəlāt] *vi* gesticuler.
gesture [jes'chûr] *n* geste *m*; **as a ~ of friendship** en témoignage d'amitié.
get, *pt, pp* **got**, (*US*) *pp* **gotten** [get, gât, gât'ən] *vt* (*obtain*) avoir, obtenir; (*receive*) recevoir; (*find*) trouver, acheter; (*catch*) attraper; (*fetch*) aller chercher; (*take, move*) emmener; (*understand*) comprendre, saisir; (*have*): **to have got** avoir; (*become*): **to ~ rich/old** s'enrichir/vieillir; (*col: annoy*): **he really ~s me!** il me porte sur les nerfs! ♦ *vi*

(go): **to** ~ **to** *(place)* aller à; arriver à; parvenir à; *(modal auxiliary vb)*: **you've got to do it** il faut que vous le fassiez; **he got across the bridge/under the fence** il a traversé le pont/est passé par-dessous la barrière; **to** ~ **sth for sb** obtenir qch pour qn, procurer qch à qn; *(fetch)* aller chercher qch (pour qn); ~ **me Mr Jones, please** *(TEL)* appelez-moi Mr Jones (au téléphone), s'il vous plaît; **can I** ~ **you a drink?** puis-je vous offrir quelque chose à boire?; **to** ~ **ready/ washed/shaved** *etc* se préparer/laver/raser *etc*; **to** ~ **sth done** *(do)* faire qch; arriver à faire qch; *(have done)* faire faire qch; **to** ~ **sth/sb ready** préparer qch/qn; **to** ~ **one's hair cut** se faire couper les cheveux; **to** ~ **sb to do sth** faire faire qch à qn; **to** ~ **sth through/out** faire passer qch par/sortir qch de; **let's** ~ **going** *or* **started!** allons-y!

get about *vi* se déplacer; *(news)* se répandre.

get across *vt*: **to** ~ **across (to)** *(message, meaning)* faire passer (à) ♦ *vi*: **to** ~ **across to** *(subj: speaker)* se faire comprendre (par).

get along *vi* *(agree)*: **to** ~ **along (with)** s'entendre (avec); *(depart)* s'en aller; *(manage)* = **to get by**.

get around *vi*: **to** ~ **around to doing sth** se mettre (finalement) à faire qch ♦ *vt fus* contourner; *(fig: person)* entortiller.

get at *vt fus* *(attack)* s'en prendre à; *(reach)* attraper, atteindre; **what are you ~ting at?** à quoi voulez-vous en venir?

get away *vi* partir, s'en aller; *(escape)* s'échapper.

get away with *vt fus* en être quitte pour; se faire passer *or* pardonner.

get back *vi* *(return)* rentrer ♦ *vt* récupérer, recouvrer; **to** ~ **back to** *(start again)* retourner *or* revenir à; *(contact again)* recontacter.

get back at *vt fus* *(col)*: **to** ~ **back at sb** rendre la monnaie de sa pièce à qn.

get by *vi* *(pass)* passer; *(manage)* se débrouiller; **I can** ~ **by in Dutch** je me débrouille en hollandais.

get down *vi*, *vt fus* descendre ♦ *vt* descendre; *(depress)* déprimer.

get down to *vt fus* *(work)* se mettre à (faire); **to** ~ **down to business** passer aux choses sérieuses.

get in *vi* entrer; *(train)* arriver; *(arrive home)* rentrer ♦ *vt* *(bring in: harvest)* rentrer; *(: coal)* faire rentrer; *(: supplies)* faire des provisions de.

get into *vt fus* entrer dans; *(vehicle)* monter dans; *(clothes)* mettre, enfiler; **to** ~ **into bed/a rage** se mettre au lit/en colère.

get off *vi* *(from train etc)* descendre; *(depart: person, car)* s'en aller; *(escape)* s'en tirer ♦ *vt* *(remove: clothes, stain)* enlever; *(send off)* expédier; *(have as leave: day, time)*: **we got 2 days off** nous avons eu 2 jours de congé ♦ *vt fus* *(train, bus)* descendre de; **to** ~ **off to a good start** *(fig)* prendre un bon départ.

get on *vi* *(at exam etc)* se débrouiller; *(agree)*: **to** ~ **on (with)** s'entendre (avec) ♦

vt fus monter dans; *(horse)* monter sur; **how are you ~ting on?** comment ça va?

get on to *vt fus* *(Brit: deal with: problem)* s'occuper de; *(: contact: person)* contacter.

get out *vi* sortir; *(of vehicle)* descendre; *(news etc)* s'ébruiter ♦ *vt* sortir.

get out of *vt fus* sortir de; *(duty etc)* échapper à, se soustraire à.

get over *vt fus* *(illness)* se remettre de ♦ *vt* *(communicate: idea etc)* communiquer; *(finish)*: **let's** ~ **it over (with)** finissons-en.

get round *vi*, *vt fus* *(Brit)* = **get around**.

get through *vi* *(TEL)* avoir la communication ♦ *vt fus* *(finish: work, book)* finir, terminer.

get through to *vt fus* *(TEL)* atteindre.

get together *vi* se réunir ♦ *vt* rassembler.

get up *vi* *(rise)* se lever ♦ *vt fus* monter.

get up to *vt fus* *(reach)* arriver à; *(Brit: prank etc)* faire.

getaway [get'əwā] *n* fuite *f*.

getaway car *n* voiture prévue pour prendre la fuite.

get-together [get'təgeṭhûr] *n* petite réunion, petite fête.

get-up [get'up] *n* *(col: outfit)* accoutrement *m*.

get-well card [getwel' kârd] *n* carte *f* de vœux de bon rétablissement.

geyser [gī'zûr] *n* *(GEO)* geyser *m*.

Ghana [gán'ə] *n* Ghana *m*.

Ghanaian [gənā'ēən] *a* ghanéen(ne) ♦ *n* Ghanéen/ne.

ghastly [gast'lē] *a* atroce, horrible; *(pale)* livide, blême.

gherkin [gûr'kin] *n* cornichon *m*.

ghetto [get'ō] *n* ghetto *m*.

ghetto blaster [get'ō blast'ûr] *n* *(col)* grosse radio-cassette.

ghost [gōst] *n* fantôme *m*, revenant *m* ♦ *vt* *(sb else's book)* écrire.

ghostly [gōst'lē] *a* fantomatique.

ghostwriter [gōst'rītûr] *n* nègre *m* *(fig)*.

ghoul [gōōl] *n* *(ghost)* vampire *m*.

ghoulish [gōōl'ish] *a* *(tastes etc)* morbide.

GHQ *n abbr* *(MIL: = general headquarters)* GQG *m*.

GI *n abbr* *(US col: = government issue)* soldat *de l'armée américaine*, GI *m*.

giant [jī'ənt] *n* géant/e ♦ *a* géant(e), énorme; ~ **(size) packet** paquet géant.

gibber [jib'ûr] *vi* émettre des sons inintelligibles.

gibberish [jib'ûrish] *n* charabia *m*.

gibe [jīb] *n* sarcasme *m* ♦ *vi*: **to** ~ **at** railler.

giblets [jib'lits] *npl* abats *mpl*.

Gibraltar [jibrôl'tûr] *n* Gibraltar *m*.

giddiness [gid'ēnis] *n* vertige *m*.

giddy [gid'ē] *a* *(dizzy)*: **to be** *(or* **feel)** ~ avoir le vertige; *(height)* vertigineux(euse); *(thoughtless)* sot(te), étourdi(e).

gift [gift] *n* cadeau *m*, présent *m*; *(donation)* don *m*; *(COMM: also:* **free** ~) cadeau(-réclame) *m*; *(talent)*: **to have a** ~ **for sth** avoir des dons pour *or* le don de qch.

gift certificate *n* *(US)* bon *m* d'achat.

gifted [gif'tid] *a* doué(e).

gift token *n* *(Brit)* bon *m* d'achat.

gig [gig] *n* *(col: of musician)* gig *f*.

gigantic [jīgan'tik] *a* gigantesque.

giggle [gig'əl] *vi* pouffer, ricaner sottement ♦ *n* petit rire sot, ricanement *m*.

GIGO [gīg'ō] *abbr* (*COMPUT col*: = *garbage in, garbage out*) qualité d'entrée = qualité de sortie.

gild [gild] *vt* dorer.

gill [jil] *n* (*measure*) = *0.25 pints* (*US = 0.118 l*; *Brit = 0.148 l*).

gills [gilz] *npl* (*of fish*) ouïes *fpl*, branchies *fpl*.

gilt [gilt] *n* dorure *f* ♦ *a* doré(e).

gilt-edged [gilt'ejd] *a* (*stocks, securities*) de premier ordre.

gimlet [gim'lit] *n* vrille *f*.

gimmick [gim'ik] *n* truc *m*; **sales** ~ offre promotionnelle.

gin [jin] *n* gin *m*.

ginger [jin'jûr] *n* gingembre *m*.

ginger up *vt* secouer; animer.

ginger ale, ginger beer *n* boisson gazeuse au gingembre.

gingerbread [jin'jûrbred] *n* pain *m* d'épices.

ginger group *n* (*Brit*) groupe *m* de pression.

ginger-haired [jin'jûrhärd] *a* roux(rousse).

gingerly [jin'jûrlē] *ad* avec précaution.

gingham [ging'əm] *n* vichy *m*.

gipsy [jip'sē] *n* = **gypsy**.

giraffe [jəraf'] *n* girafe *f*.

girder [gûr'dûr] *n* poutrelle *f*.

girdle [gûr'dəl] *n* (*corset*) gaine *f* ♦ *vt* ceindre.

girl [gûrl] *n* fille *f*, fillette *f*; (*young unmarried woman*) jeune fille; (*daughter*) fille; **an English** ~ une jeune Anglaise; **a little English** ~ une petite Anglaise.

girl Friday *n* aide *f* de bureau.

girlfriend [gûrl'frend] *n* (*of girl*) amie *f*; (*of boy*) petite amie.

girlish [gûr'lish] *a* de jeune fille.

Girl Scout *n* (*US*) guide *f*.

Giro [jī'rō] *n*: **the National** ~ (*Brit*) ≈ les comptes chèques postaux.

giro [jī'rō] *n* (*Brit: bank* ~) virement *m* bancaire; (: *post office* ~) mandat *m*.

girth [gûrth] *n* circonférence *f*; (*of horse*) sangle *f*.

gist [jist] *n* essentiel *m*.

give [giv] *n* (*of fabric*) élasticité *f* ♦ *vb* (*pt* **gave**, *pp* **given** [gāv, giv'ən]) *vt* donner ♦ *vi* (*break*) céder; (*stretch: fabric*) se prêter; **to** ~ **sb sth**, ~ **sth to sb** donner qch à qn; **to** ~ **a cry/sigh** pousser un cri/un soupir; **how much did you** ~ **for it?** combien (l')avez-vous payé?; **12 o'clock**, ~ **or take a few minutes** midi, à quelques minutes près; **to** ~ **way** *vi* céder; (*Brit AUT*) donner la priorité.

give away *vt* donner; (*give free*) faire cadeau de; (*betray*) donner, trahir; (*disclose*) révéler; (*bride*) conduire à l'autel.

give back *vt* rendre.

give in *vi* céder ♦ *vt* donner.

give off *vt* dégager.

give out *vt* (*food etc*) distribuer; (*news*) annoncer ♦ *vi* (*be exhausted: supplies*) s'épuiser; (*fail*) lâcher.

give up *vi* renoncer ♦ *vt* renoncer à; **to** ~ **up smoking** arrêter de fumer; **to** ~ **o.s. up** se rendre.

give-and-take [giv'əntāk'] *n* concessions mutuelles.

giveaway [giv'əwā] *n* (*col*): **her expression was a** ~ son expression la trahissait; **the exam was a** ~! cet examen, c'était du gâteau! ♦ *cpd*: ~ **prices** prix sacrifiés.

given [giv'ən] *pp of* **give** ♦ *a* (*fixed: time, amount*) donné(e), déterminé(e) ♦ *cj*: ~ **the circumstances** ... étant donné les circonstances ..., vu les circonstances ...; ~ **that** ... étant donné que ....

glacial [glā'shəl] *a* (*GEO*) glaciaire; (*wind, weather*) glacial(e).

glacier [glā'shûr] *n* glacier *m*.

glad [glad] *a* content(e); **to be** ~ **about sth/ that** être heureux(euse) *or* bien content de qch/que; **I was** ~ **of his help** (*Brit*) j'étais bien content de (pouvoir compter sur) son aide *or* qu'il m'aide.

gladden [glad'ən] *vt* réjouir.

glade [glād] *n* clairière *f*.

gladioli [gladō'lē] *npl* glaïeuls *mpl*.

gladly [glad'lē] *ad* volontiers.

glamorous [glam'ûrəs] *a* séduisant(e).

glamour [glam'ûr] *n* éclat *m*, prestige *m*.

glance [glans] *n* coup *m* d'œil ♦ *vi*: **to** ~ **at** jeter un coup d'œil à.

glance off *vt fus* (*bullet*) ricocher sur.

glancing [glan'sing] *a* (*blow*) oblique.

gland [gland] *n* glande *f*.

glandular [glan'jəlûr] *a*: ~ **fever** (*Brit*) mononucléose infectieuse.

glare [glä] *n* lumière éblouissante ♦ *vi* briller d'un éclat aveuglant; **to** ~ **at** lancer un *or* des regard(s) furieux à.

glaring [glär'ing] *a* (*mistake*) criant(e), qui saute aux yeux.

glass [glas] *n* verre *m*; (*also*: **looking** ~) miroir *m*.

glass-blowing [glas'blōing] *n* soufflage *m* (du verre).

glasses [glas'iz] *npl* lunettes *fpl*.

glass fiber *n* fibre *f* de verre.

glasshouse [glas'hous] *n* (*Brit*) serre *f*.

glassware [glas'wär] *n* verrerie *f*.

glassy [glas'ē] *a* (*eyes*) vitreux(euse).

glaze [glāz] *vt* (*door*) vitrer; (*pottery*) vernir; (*CULIN*) glacer ♦ *n* vernis *m*; (*CULIN*) glaçage *m*.

glazed [glāzd] *a* (*eye*) vitreux(euse); (*pottery*) verni(e); (*tiles*) vitrifié(e).

glazier [glā'zhûr] *n* vitrier *m*.

gleam [glēm] *n* lueur *f* ♦ *vi* luire, briller; **a** ~ **of hope** une lueur d'espoir.

gleaming [glē'ming] *a* luisant(e).

glean [glēn] *vt* (*information*) recueillir.

glee [glē] *n* joie *f*.

gleeful [glē'fəl] *a* joyeux(euse).

glen [glen] *n* vallée *f*.

glib [glib] *a* qui a du bagou; facile.

glide [glīd] *vi* glisser; (*AVIAT, bird*) planer ♦ *n* glissement *m*; vol plané.

glider [glī'dûr] *n* (*AVIAT*) planeur *m*.

gliding [glī'ding] *n* (*AVIAT*) vol *m* à voile.

glimmer [glim'ûr] *vi* luire ♦ *n* lueur *f*.

glimpse [glimps] *n* vision passagère, aperçu *m* ♦ *vt* entrevoir, apercevoir; **to catch a** ~ **of** entrevoir.

glint [glint] *n* éclair *m* ♦ *vi* étinceler.

glisten [glis'ən] *vi* briller, luire.

glitter [glit'ûr] *vi* scintiller, briller ♦ *n* scintillement *m*.

glitz |glits| *n* (*col*) clinquant *m*.
gloat |glōt| *vi*: **to ~ (over)** jubiler (à propos de).
global |glō'bəl| *a* (*world-wide*) mondial(e); (*overall*) global(e).
globe |glōb| *n* globe *m*.
globe-trotter |glōb'trátûr| *n* globe-trotter *m*.
globule |glâb'yōōl| *n* (*ANAT*) globule *m*; (*of water etc*) gouttelette *f*.
gloom |glōōm| *n* obscurité *f*; (*sadness*) tristesse *f*, mélancolie *f*.
gloomy |glōō'mē| *a* sombre, triste, mélancolique; **to feel ~** avoir *or* se faire des idées noires.
glorification |glôrəfəkā'shən| *n* glorification *f*.
glorify |glôr'əfī| *vt* glorifier.
glorious |glôr'ēəs| *a* glorieux(euse); (*beautiful*) splendide.
glory |glôr'ē| *n* gloire *f*; splendeur *f* ♦ *vi*: **to ~ in** se glorifier de.
glory hole *n* (*col*) capharnaüm *m*.
Glos *abbr* (*Brit*) = *Gloucestershire*.
gloss |glôs| *n* (*shine*) brillant *m*, vernis *m*; (*also*: **~ paint**) peinture brillante *or* laquée.
gloss over *vt fus* glisser sur.
glossary |glâs'ûrē| *n* glossaire *m*, lexique *m*.
glossy |glâs'ē| *a* brillant(e), luisant(e) ♦ *n* (*also*: **~ magazine**) revue *f* de luxe.
glove |gluv| *n* gant *m*.
glove compartment *n* (*AUT*) boîte *f* à gants, vide-poches *m inv*.
glow |glō| *vi* rougeoyer; (*face*) rayonner ♦ *n* rougeoiement *m*.
glower |glou'ûr| *vi* lancer des regards mauvais.
glowing |glō'ing| *a* (*fire*) rougeoyant(e); (*complexion*) éclatant(e); (*report, description etc*) dithyrambique.
glow-worm |glō'wûrm| *n* ver luisant.
glucose |glōō'kōs| *n* glucose *m*.
glue |glōō| *n* colle *f* ♦ *vt* coller.
glue-sniffing |glōō'snifing| *n* inhalation *f* de colle.
glum |glum| *a* maussade, morose.
glut |glut| *n* surabondance *f* ♦ *vt* rassasier; (*market*) encombrer.
glutinous |glōōt'nəs| *a* visqueux(euse).
glutton |glut'ən| *n* glouton/ne; **a ~ for work** un bourreau de travail.
gluttonous |glut'ənəs| *a* glouton(ne).
gluttony |glut'ənē| *n* gloutonnerie *f*; (*sin*) gourmandise *f*.
glycerin(e) |glis'ûrin| *n* glycérine *f*.
gm *abbr* (= *gram*) g.
GMAT *n abbr* (*US*: = *Graduate Management Admissions Test*) examen d'admission dans le 2e cycle de l'enseignement supérieur.
GMT *abbr* (= *Greenwich Mean Time*) GMT.
gnarled |nârld| *a* noueux(euse).
gnash |nash| *vt*: **to ~ one's teeth** grincer des dents.
gnat |nat| *n* moucheron *m*.
gnaw |nô| *vt* ronger.
gnome |nōm| *n* gnome *m*, lutin *m*.
GNP *n abbr* = **gross national product**.
go |gō| *vb* (*pt* **went**, *pp* **gone** |went, gôn|) *vi* aller; (*depart*) partir, s'en aller; (*work*) marcher; (*be sold*): **to ~ for $10** se vendre 10 dollars; (*fit, suit*): **to ~ with** aller avec; (*be-*

come): **to ~ pale/moldy** pâlir/moisir; (*break etc*) céder ♦ *n* (*pl*: **~es**): **to have a ~ (at)** essayer (de faire); **to be on the ~** être en mouvement; **whose ~ is it?** à qui est-ce de jouer?; **to ~ by car/on foot** aller en voiture/à pied; **he's ~ing to do** il va faire, il est sur le point de faire; **to ~ for a walk** aller se promener; **to ~ dancing/shopping** aller danser/faire les courses; **to ~ looking for sb/sth** aller *or* partir à la recherche de qn/qch; **to ~ to sleep** s'endormir; **to ~ and see sb, to ~ to see sb** aller voir qn; **how is it ~ing?** comment ça marche?; **how did it ~?** comment est-ce que ça s'est passé?; **to ~ round the back/by the shop** passer par derrière/devant le magasin; **my voice has gone** j'ai une extinction de voix; **the cake is all gone** il n'y a plus de gâteau; **I'll take whatever is ~ing** (*Brit*) je prendrai ce qu'il y a (*or* ce que vous avez); **... to ~** (*US*: *food*) ... à emporter.
go about *vt fus*: **how do I ~ about this?** comment dois-je m'y prendre (pour faire ceci)? ♦ *vi* (*Brit*) = **go around**; **to ~ about one's business** s'occuper de ses affaires.
go after *vt fus* (*pursue*) poursuivre, courir après; (*job, record etc*) essayer d'obtenir.
go against *vt fus* (*be unfavorable to*) être défavorable à; (*be contrary to*) être contraire à.
go ahead *vi* (*make progress*) avancer; (*get going*) y aller.
go along *vi* aller, avancer ♦ *vt fus* longer, parcourir; **as you ~ along (with your work)** au fur et à mesure (de votre travail); **to ~ along with** (*accompany*) accompagner; (*agree with: idea*) être d'accord sur; (: *person*) suivre.
go around *vi* (*circulate: news, rumor*) circuler; (*revolve*) tourner; (*wander around*) aller çà et là; (*visit*): **to ~ around to sb's** passer chez qn; aller chez qn; (*make a detour*): **to ~ around (by)** faire un détour (par); (*suffice*) suffire (pour tout le monde).
go away *vi* partir, s'en aller.
go back *vi* rentrer; revenir; (*go again*) retourner.
go back on *vt fus* (*promise*) revenir sur.
go by *vi* (*years, time*) passer, s'écouler ♦ *vt fus* s'en tenir à; (*believe*) en croire.
go down *vi* descendre; (*ship*) couler; (*sun*) se coucher ♦ *vt fus* descendre; **that should ~ down well with him** (*fig*) ça devrait lui plaire.
go for *vt fus* (*fetch*) aller chercher; (*like*) aimer; (*attack*) s'en prendre à; attaquer.
go in *vi* entrer.
go in for *vt fus* (*competition*) se présenter à; (*like*) aimer.
go into *vt fus* entrer dans; (*investigate*) étudier, examiner; (*embark on*) se lancer dans.
go off *vi* partir, s'en aller; (*food*) se gâter; (*bomb*) sauter; (*lights etc*) s'éteindre; (*event*) se dérouler ♦ *vt fus* ne plus aimer, ne plus avoir envie de; **the gun went off** le coup est parti; **to ~ off to sleep** s'endormir; **the party went off well** la fête s'est bien passée *or* était très réussie.

go on *vi* continuer; (*happen*) se passer; (*lights*) s'allumer ♦ *vt fus* (*be guided by: evidence etc*) se fonder sur; **to ~ on doing** continuer à faire; **what's ~ing on here?** qu'est-ce qui se passe ici?

go on at *vt fus* (*nag*) tomber sur le dos de.

go on with *vt fus* poursuivre, continuer.

go out *vi* sortir; (*fire, light*) s'éteindre; (*tide*) descendre; **to ~ out with sb** sortir avec qn.

go over *vi* (*ship*) chavirer ♦ *vt fus* (*check*) revoir, vérifier; **to ~ over sth in one's mind** repasser qch dans son esprit.

go round *vi* (*Brit*) = **go around**.

go through *vt fus* (*town etc*) traverser; (*search through*) fouiller; (*examine: list, book*) lire *or* regarder en détail, éplucher; (*perform: lesson*) réciter; (*: formalities*) remplir; (*: program*) exécuter.

go through with *vt fus* (*plan, crime*) aller jusqu'au bout de.

go under *vi* (*sink: also fig*) couler; (*: person*) succomber.

go up *vi* monter; (*price*) augmenter ♦ *vt fus* gravir; **to ~ up in flames** flamber, s'enflammer brusquement.

go without *vt fus* se passer de.

goad [gōd] *vt* aiguillonner.

go-ahead [gō'əhed] *a* dynamique, entreprenant(e) ♦ *n* feu vert.

goal [gōl] *n* but *m*.

goalkeeper [gōl'kēpûr] *n* gardien *m* de but.

goal post *n* poteau *m* de but.

goat [gōt] *n* chèvre *f*.

gobble [gâb'əl] *vt* (*also:* **~ down, ~ up**) engloutir.

gobbledygook [gâb'əldēgōōk] *n* charabia *m*.

go-between [gō'bitwēn] *n* médiateur *m*.

Gobi Desert [gō'bē dez'ûrt] *n* désert *m* de Gobi.

goblet [gâb'lit] *n* goblet *m*.

goblin [gâb'lin] *n* lutin *m*.

go-cart [gō'kârt] *n* kart *m* ♦ *cpd:* **~ racing** *n* karting *m*.

god [gâd] *n* dieu *m*; **G~** Dieu.

godchild [gâd'chīld] *n* filleul/e.

goddamn [gâd'dam'] *n* (*US col!*): **this ~** ... ce foutu ..., ce putain de ....

goddaughter [gâd'dôtûr] *n* filleule *f*.

goddess [gâd'is] *n* déesse *f*.

godfather [gâd'fâthûr] *n* parrain *m*.

godforsaken [gâd'fûrsā'kən] *a* maudit(e).

godmother [gâd'muthûr] *n* marraine *f*.

godparents [gâd'pärənts] *npl:* **the ~** le parrain et la marraine.

godsend [gâd'send] *n* aubaine *f*.

godson [gâd'sun] *n* filleul *m*.

goes [gōz] *vb see* **go**.

gofer [gō'fûr] *n* (*US*) bonne *f* à tout faire, tâcheron *m*.

go-getter [gō'get'ûr] *n* arriviste *m/f*.

goggle [gâg'əl] *vi:* **to ~ at** regarder avec des yeux ronds.

goggles [gâg'əlz] *npl* lunettes *fpl* (protectrices) (*de motocycliste etc*).

going [gō'ing] *n* (*conditions*) état *m* du terrain ♦ *a:* **the ~ rate** le tarif (en vigueur); **a ~ concern** une affaire prospère; **it was slow ~** les progrès étaient lents, ça n'avançait pas vite.

goings-on [gō'ingzân'] *npl* (*col*) manigances *fpl*.

go-kart [gō'kârt] *n* = **go-cart**.

gold [gōld] *n or m* ♦ *a* en or; (*reserves*) d'or.

golden [gōl'dən] *a* (*made of gold*) en or; (*gold in color*) doré(e).

golden age *n* âge *m* d'or.

golden rule *n* règle *f* d'or.

goldfish [gōld'fish] *n* poisson *m* rouge.

gold leaf *n or m* en feuille.

gold medal *n* (*SPORT*) médaille *f* d'or.

goldmine [gōld'mīn] *n* mine *f* d'or.

gold-plated [gōldplā'tid] *a* plaqué(e) or *inv*.

goldsmith [gōld'smith] *n* orfèvre *m*.

gold standard *n* étalon-or *m*.

golf [gâlf] *n* golf *m*.

golf ball *n* balle *f* de golf; (*on typewriter*) boule *f*.

golf club *n* club *m* de golf; (*stick*) club *m*, crosse *f* de golf.

golf course *n* terrain *m* de golf.

golfer [gâl'fûr] *n* joueur/euse de golf.

gondola [gân'dələ] *n* gondole *f*.

gondolier [gândəliûr'] *n* gondolier *m*.

gone [gôn] *pp of* **go** ♦ *a* parti(e).

gong [gông] *n* gong *m*.

good [gōōd] *a* bon(ne); (*kind*) gentil(le); (*child*) sage ♦ *n* bien *m*; **~!** bon!, très bien!; **to be ~ at** être bon en; **it's ~ for you** c'est bon pour vous; **it's a ~ thing you were there** heureusement que vous étiez là; **she is ~ with children/her hands** elle sait bien s'occuper des enfants/sait se servir de ses mains; **to feel ~** se sentir bien; **it's ~ to see you** ça me fait plaisir de vous voir, je suis content de vous voir; **he's up to no ~** il prépare quelque mauvais coup; **it's no ~ complaining** cela ne sert à rien de se plaindre; **for the common ~** dans l'intérêt commun; **for ~** (*for ever*) pour de bon, une fois pour toutes; **would you be ~ enough to ...?** auriez-vous la bonté *or* l'amabilité de ...?; **that's very ~ of you** c'est très gentil de votre part, **is this any~?** (*will it do?*) est-ce que ceci fera l'affaire?, est-ce que cela peut vous rendre service?; (*what's it like?*) qu'est-ce que ça vaut?; **a ~ deal (of)** beaucoup (de); **a ~ many** beaucoup (de); **~ morning/afternoon!** bonjour!; **~ evening!** bonsoir!; **~ night!** bonsoir!; (*on going to bed*) bonne nuit!

goodbye [gōōdbī'] *excl* au revoir!; **to say ~ to** dire au revoir à.

good faith *n* bonne foi.

good-for-nothing [gōōd'fərnuth'ing] *a* bon(ne) *or* propre à rien.

Good Friday *n* Vendredi saint.

good-humored [gōōd'hyōō'mûrd] *a* (*person*) jovial(e); (*remark, joke*) sans malice.

good-looking [gōōd'lōōk'ing] *a* bien *inv*.

good-natured [gōōd'nā'chûrd] *a* (*person*) qui a un bon naturel; (*discussion*) enjoué(e).

goodness [gōōd'nis] *n* (*of person*) bonté *f*; **for ~ sake!** je vous en prie!; **~ gracious!** mon Dieu!

goods [gōōdz] *npl* marchandise *f*, articles *mpl*; (*COMM etc*) marchandises; **~ and chattels** biens *mpl* et effets *mpl*.

goods train n (*Brit*) train m de marchandises.

goodwill [gŏŏd'wil'] n bonne volonté; (*COMM*) réputation f (auprès de la clientèle).

goody-goody [gŏŏd'ēgŏŏd'ē] n (*pej*) petit saint, sainte nitouche.

goof [gŏŏf] vi (*US col*) gaffer.

goose, pl **geese** [gŏŏs, gēs] n oie f.

gooseberry [gŏŏs'bärē] n groseille f à maquereau; **to play** ~ (*Brit*) tenir la chandelle.

gooseflesh [gŏŏs'flesh] n, **goosepimples** [gŏŏs'pimpəlz] npl chair f de poule.

goose step n (*MIL*) pas m de l'oie.

GOP n abbr (*US POL:* col: = *Grand Old Party*) parti républicain.

gore [gôr] vt encorner ♦ n sang m.

gorge [gôrj] n gorge f ♦ vt: **to** ~ **o.s.** **(on)** se gorger (de).

gorgeous [gôr'jəs] a splendide, superbe.

gorilla [gəril'ə] n gorille m.

gorse [gôrs] n ajoncs mpl.

gory [gôr'ē] a sanglant(e).

go-slow [gō'slō'] n (*Brit*) grève perlée.

gospel [gâs'pəl] n évangile m.

gossamer [gâs'əmûr] n (*cobweb*) fils mpl de la vierge; (*light fabric*) étoffe très légère.

gossip [gâs'əp] n bavardages mpl; (*malicious*) commérage m, cancans mpl; (*person*) commère f ♦ vi bavarder; cancaner, faire des commérages; **a piece of** ~ un ragot, un racontar.

gossip column n (*PRESS*) échos mpl.

got [gât] pt, pp of **get.**

Gothic [gâth'ik] a gothique.

gotten [gât'ən] (*US*) pp of **get.**

gouge [gouj] vt (*also:* ~ **out:** *hole etc*) évider; (: *initials*) tailler; **to** ~ **sb's eyes out** crever les yeux à qn.

gourd [gôrd] n calebasse f, gourde f.

gourmet [gŏŏrmā'] n gourmet m, gastronome m/f.

gout [gout] n goutte f.

govern [guv'ûrn] vt (*gen, LING*) gouverner.

governess [guv'ûrnis] n gouvernante f.

governing [guv'ûrning] a (*POL*) au pouvoir, au gouvernement; ~ **body** conseil m d'administration.

government [guv'ûrnmənt] n gouvernement m; (*Brit: ministers*) ministère m ♦ cpd de l'Etat; **local** ~ administration locale.

governmental [guvûrnmen'təl] a gouvernemental(e).

government housing n (*US*) logements sociaux.

government stock n titres mpl d'État.

governor [guv'ûrnûr] n (*of colony, state, bank*) gouverneur m; (*of school, hospital etc*) administrateur/trice; (*Brit: of prison*) directeur/trice.

Govt abbr (= *government*) gvt.

gown [goun] n robe f; (*of teacher; Brit: of judge*) toge f.

GP n abbr (*MED*) = **general practitioner.**

GPO n abbr (*US*) = *Government Printing Office.*

gr. abbr (*COMM*) = **gross.**

grab [grab] vt saisir, empoigner; (*property, power*) se saisir de ♦ vi: **to** ~ **at** essayer de saisir.

grace [grās] n grâce f ♦ vt honorer; **5 days'** ~ répit m de 5 jours; **to say** ~ dire le bénédicité; (*after meal*) dire les grâces; **with a good/bad** ~ de bonne/mauvaise grâce; **his sense of humor is his saving** ~ il se rachète par son sens de l'humour.

graceful [grās'fəl] a gracieux(euse), élégant(e).

gracious [grā'shəs] a (*kind*) charmant(e), bienveillant(e); (*elegant*) plein(e) d'élégance, d'une grande élégance; (*formal: pardon etc*) miséricordieux(euse) ♦ excl: **(good)** ~! mon Dieu!

gradation [grādā'shən] n gradation f.

grade [grād] n (*COMM*) qualité f; calibre m; catégorie f; (*in hierarchy*) grade m, échelon m; (*US: SCOL*) note f; classe f; (: *gradient*) pente f ♦ vt classer; calibrer; graduer; **to make the** ~ (*fig*) réussir.

grade crossing n (*US*) passage m à niveau.

grade school n (*US*) école f primaire.

gradient [grā'dēənt] n inclinaison f, pente f; (*GEOM*) gradient m.

gradual [graj'ōōəl] a graduel(le), progressif(ive).

gradually [graj'ōōəlē] ad peu à peu, graduellement.

graduate n [graj'ōōit] diplômé/e d'université; (*US*) diplômé/e de fin d'études ♦ vi [graj'ōōāt] obtenir un diplôme d'université (*or* de fin d'études).

graduated pension [graj'ōōātid pen'shən] n retraite calculée en fonction des derniers salaires.

graduation [grajōōā'shən] n cérémonie f de remise des diplômes.

graffiti [grətē'tē] npl graffiti mpl.

graft [graft] n (*AGR, MED*) greffe f; (*bribery*) corruption f ♦ vt greffer; **hard** ~ (*Brit col*) boulot acharné.

grain [grān] n grain m; (*no pl: cereals*) céréales fpl; (*US*) blé m; **it goes against the** ~ cela va à l'encontre de sa (*or* ma *etc*) nature.

gram [gram] n gramme m.

grammar [gram'ûr] n grammaire f.

grammatical [grəmat'ikəl] a grammatical(e).

gramme [gram] n – **gram.**

granary [grā'nûrē] n grenier m.

grand [grand] a splendide, imposant(e); (*terrific*) magnifique, formidable; (*also humorous: gesture etc*) noble ♦ n (*col: thousand*) mille livres fpl (*or* dollars *mpl*).

grandchildren [gran'chil'drən] npl petits-enfants mpl.

granddad [gran'dad] n grand-papa m.

granddaughter [gran'dôtûr] n petite-fille f.

grandeur [gran'jûr] n magnificence f, splendeur f; (*of position etc*) éminence f.

grandfather [gran'fâthûr] n grand-père m.

grandiose [gran'dēōs] a grandiose; (*pej*) pompeux(euse).

grand jury n (*US*) jury m d'accusation (*formé de 12 à 23 jurés*).

grandma [gran'mə] n grand-maman f.

grandmother [gran'muthûr] n grand-mère f.

grandpa [gran'pə] n = **granddad.**

grandparent [gran'pärənt] n grand-père/grand-mère.

grand piano n piano m à queue.

Grand Prix [grand prē'] n (AUT) grand prix automobile.

grandson [gran'sun] n petit-fils m.

grandstand [gran'stand] n (SPORT) tribune f.

grand total n total général.

granite [gran'it] n granit m.

granny [gran'ē] n grand-maman f.

grant [grant] vt accorder; (a request) accéder à; (admit) concéder ♦ n (SCOL) bourse f; (ADMIN) subside m, subvention f; **to take sth for ~ed** considérer qch comme acquis; **to ~ that** admettre que.

granulated [gran'yəlātid] a: **~ sugar** sucre m en poudre.

granule [gran'yōōl] n granule m.

grape [grāp] n raisin m; **a bunch of ~s** une grappe de raisin.

grapefruit [grāp'frōōt] n pamplemousse m.

grapevine [grāp'vīn] n vigne f; **I heard it on the ~** (fig) je l'ai appris par le téléphone arabe.

graph [graf] n graphique m, courbe f.

graphic [graf'ik] a graphique; (vivid) vivant(e).

graphic designer n graphiste m/f.

graphics [graf'iks] n (art) arts mpl graphiques; (process) graphisme m; (pl: drawings) illustrations fpl.

graphite [graf'īt] n graphite m.

graph paper n papier millimétré.

grapple [grap'əl] vi: **to ~ with** être aux prises avec.

grappling iron [grap'ling ī'ûrn] n (NAUT) grappin m.

grasp [grasp] vt saisir, empoigner; (understand) saisir, comprendre ♦ n (grip) prise f; (fig) compréhension f, connaissance f; **to have sth within one's ~** avoir qch à sa portée; **to have a good ~ of sth** (fig) bien comprendre qch.

grasp at vt fus (rope etc) essayer de saisir; (fig: opportunity) sauter sur.

grasping [gras'ping] a avide.

grass [gras] n herbe f; (Brit col: informer) mouchard/e; (: ex-terrorist) balanceur/euse.

grasshopper [gras'hâpûr] n sauterelle f.

grassland [gras'land] n prairie f.

grass roots npl (fig) base f.

grass snake n couleuvre f.

grassy [gras'ē] a herbeux(euse).

grate [grāt] n grille f de cheminée ♦ vi grincer ♦ vt (CULIN) râper.

grateful [grāt'fəl] a reconnaissant(e).

gratefully [grāt'fəlē] ad avec reconnaissance.

grater [grā'tûr] n râpe f.

gratification [gratəfəkā'shən] n satisfaction f.

gratify [grat'əfī] vt faire plaisir à; (whim) satisfaire.

gratifying [grat'əfīing] a agréable; satisfaisant(e).

grating [grā'ting] n (iron bars) grille f ♦ a (noise) grinçant(e).

gratitude [grat'ətōōd] n gratitude f.

gratuitous [grətōō'itəs] a gratuit(e).

gratuity [grətōō'itē] n pourboire m.

grave [grāv] n tombe f ♦ a grave, sérieux(euse).

gravedigger [grāv'digûr] n fossoyeur m.

gravel [grav'əl] n gravier m.

gravely [grāv'lē] ad gravement, sérieusement; **~ ill** gravement malade.

gravestone [grāv'stōn] n pierre tombale.

graveyard [grāv'yârd] n cimetière m.

gravitate [grav'ətāt] vi graviter.

gravity [grav'itē] n (PHYSICS) gravité f; pesanteur f; (seriousness) gravité, sérieux m.

gravy [grā'vē] n jus m (de viande); sauce f (au jus de viande).

gravy boat n saucière f.

gravy train n (col): **to ride the ~** avoir une bonne planque.

gray [grā] a (US) gris(e); (dismal) sombre; **to go ~** (commencer à) grisonner.

gray-haired [grā'hârd] a aux cheveux gris.

grayhound [grā'hound] n lévrier m.

graze [grāz] vi paître, brouter ♦ vt (touch lightly) frôler, effleurer; (scrape) écorcher ♦ n écorchure f.

grazing [grā'zing] n (pasture) pâturage m.

grease [grēs] n (fat) graisse f; (lubricant) lubrifiant m ♦ vt graisser; lubrifier; **to ~ the skids** (US: fig) huiler les rouages.

grease gun n graisseur m.

greasepaint [grēs'pānt] n produits mpl de maquillage.

greaseproof paper [grēs'prōōf pā'pûr] n (Brit) papier sulfurisé.

greasy [grē'sē] a gras(se), graisseux(euse); (hands, clothes) graisseux; (Brit: road, surface) glissant(e).

great [grāt] a grand(e); (heat, pain etc) très fort(e), intense; (col) formidable; **they're ~ friends** ils sont très amis, ce sont de grands amis; **we had a ~ time** nous nous sommes bien amusés, **it was ~!** c'était fantastique or super!; **the ~ thing is that** ... ce qu'il y a de vraiment bien c'est que ....

Great Barrier Reef n: **the ~** la Grande Barrière.

Great Britain n Grande-Bretagne f.

great-grandchild, pl **-children** [grāt'gran'chīld, -chil'drən] n arrière-petit(e)-enfant.

great-grandfather [grāt'gran'fâthûr] n arrière-grand-père m.

great-grandmother [grāt'gran'muthûr] n arrière-grand-mère f.

Great Lakes npl: **the ~** les Grands Lacs.

greatly [grāt'lē] ad très, grandement; (with verbs) beaucoup.

greatness [grāt'nis] n grandeur f.

Grecian [grē'shən] a grec(grecque).

Greece [grēs] n Grèce f.

greed [grēd] n (also: ~iness) avidité f; (for food) gourmandise f.

greedily [grē'dilē] ad avidement; avec gourmandise.

greedy [grē'dē] a avide; gourmand(e).

Greek [grēk] a grec(grecque) ♦ n Grec/Grecque; (LING) grec m; **ancient/modern ~** grec classique/moderne.

green [grēn] a vert(e); (inexperienced) (bien) jeune, naïf(ïve) ♦ n (color, of golf course) vert m; (stretch of grass) pelouse f; (also: village ~) ≈ place f du village; **~s** npl légumes verts; **to have a ~ thumb** or (Brit) **~ fingers** (fig) avoir le pouce vert.

greenback [grēn'bak] n (US col) billet m d'un dollar, dolluche m (col).

green bean *n* haricot vert.
green belt *n* (*round town*) ceinture verte.
green card *n* permis *m* de travail; (*Brit AUT*) carte verte.
greenery [grē'nûrē] *n* verdure *f*.
greenfly [grēn'flī] *n* (*Brit*) puceron *m*.
greengage [grēn'gāj] *n* reine-claude *f*.
greengrocer [grēn'grōsûr] *n* (*Brit*) marchand *m* de fruits et légumes.
greenhouse [grēn'hous] *n* serre *f*.
greenhouse effect *n* effet *m* de serre.
greenish [grē'nish] *a* verdâtre.
Greenland [grēn'lənd] *n* Groenland *m*.
Greenlander [grēn'ləndûr] *n* Groenlandais/e.
green pepper *n* poivron (vert).
green pound *n* (*ECON*) livre verte.
greet [grēt] *vt* accueillir.
greeting [grē'ting] *n* salutation *f*; **Christmas/birthday** ~**s** souhaits *mpl* de Noël/de bon anniversaire.
greeting(s) card *n* carte *f* de vœux.
gregarious [grigär'ēəs] *a* grégaire; sociable.
grenade [grinād'] *n* (*also:* **hand** ~) grenade *f*.
grew [grōō] *pt of* **grow**.
grey [grā] *etc a* (*Brit*) = **gray** *etc*.
grid [grid] *n* grille *f*; (*ELEC*) réseau *m*; (*US AUT*) intersection *f* (*matérialisée par des marques au sol*).
griddle [grid'əl] *n* (*on stove*) plaque chauffante.
gridiron [grid'īûrn] *n* gril *m*.
grief [grēf] *n* chagrin *m*, douleur *f*; **to come to** ~ (*plan*) échouer; (*person*) avoir un malheur.
grievance [grē'vəns] *n* doléance *f*, grief *m*; (*cause for complaint*) grief.
grieve [grēv] *vi* avoir du chagrin; se désoler ♦ *vt* faire de la peine à, affliger; **to** ~ **at** se désoler de; pleurer.
grievous [grē'vəs] *a* grave; cruel(le); ~ **bodily harm** (*LAW*) coups *mpl* et blessures *fpl*.
grill [gril] *n* (*on stove*) gril *m* ♦ *vt* griller; (*question*) interroger longuement, cuisiner.
grille [gril] *n* grillage *m*; (*AUT*) calandre *f*.
grill(room) [gril'(rōōm)] *n* rôtisserie *f*.
grim [grim] *a* sinistre, lugubre.
grimace [grim'əs] *n* grimace *f* ♦ *vi* grimacer, faire une grimace.
grime [grīm] *n* crasse *f*.
grimy [grī'mē] *a* crasseux(euse).
grin [grin] *n* large sourire *m* ♦ *vi* sourire; **to** ~ (**at**) faire un grand sourire (à).
grind [grīnd] *vb* (*pt, pp* **ground** [ground]) *vt* écraser; (*coffee, pepper etc*) moudre; (*US: meat*) hacher; (*make sharp*) aiguiser; (*polish: gem, lens*) polir ♦ *vi* (*car gears*) grincer ♦ *n* (*work*) corvée *f*; **to** ~ **one's teeth** grincer des dents; **to** ~ **to a halt** (*vehicle*) s'arrêter dans un grincement de freins; (*fig*) s'arrêter, s'immobiliser; **the daily** ~ (*col*) le train-train quotidien.
grinder [grīn'dûr] *n* (*machine: for coffee*) moulin *m* (à café *m*); (*: for meat*) hachoir *m*; (*: for waste disposal etc*) broyeur *m*.
grindstone [grīnd'stōn] *n*: **to keep one's nose to the** ~ travailler sans relâche.
grip [grip] *n* (*control, grasp*) étreinte *f*; (*hold*) prise *f*; (*handle*) poignée *f*; (*carryall*) sac *m* de voyage ♦ *vt* saisir, empoigner; étreindre;

to come to ~**s with** se colleter avec, en venir aux prises avec; **to** ~ **the road** (*AUT*) adhérer à la route; **to lose one's** ~ lâcher prise; (*fig*) perdre les pédales, être dépassé(e).
gripe [grīp] *n* (*MED*) coliques *fpl*; (*col: complaint*) ronchonnement *m*, rouspétance *f* ♦ *vi* (*col*) râler.
gripping [grip'ing] *a* prenant(e), palpitant(e).
grisly [griz'lē] *a* sinistre, macabre.
grist [grist] *n* (*fig*): **it's (all)** ~ **to his mill** ça l'arrange, ça apporte de l'eau à son moulin.
gristle [gris'əl] *n* cartilage *m* (*de poulet etc*).
grit [grit] *n* gravillon *m*; (*courage*) cran *m* ♦ *vt* (*road*) sabler; **to** ~ **one's teeth** serrer les dents; **to have a piece of** ~ **in one's eye** (*Brit*) avoir une poussière *or* une saleté dans l'œil.
grits [grits] *npl* (*US*) gruau *m* de maïs.
grizzle [griz'əl] *vi* (*Brit*) pleurnicher.
grizzly [griz'lē] *n* (*also:* ~ **bear**) grizzli *m*, ours gris.
groan [grōn] *n* gémissement *m*; grognement *m* ♦ *vi* gémir; grogner.
grocer [grō'sûr] *n* épicier *m*; **at the** ~**'s** à l'épicerie, chez l'épicier.
groceries [grō'sûrēz] *npl* provisions *fpl*.
grocery [grō'sûrē] *n* (*also:* ~ **store**) épicerie *f*.
grog [grâg] *n* grog *m*.
groggy [grâg'ē] *a* groggy *inv*.
groin [groin] *n* aine *f*.
groom [grōōm] *n* palefrenier *m*; (*also:* **bride**~) marié *m* ♦ *vt* (*horse*) panser; (*fig*): **to** ~ **sb for** former qn pour.
groove [grōōv] *n* sillon *m*, rainure *f*.
grope [grōp] *vi* tâtonner; **to** ~ **for** *vt fus* chercher à tâtons.
grosgrain [grō'grān] *n* gros-grain *m*.
gross [grōs] *a* grossier(ière); (*COMM*) brut(e) ♦ *n* (*pl inv*) (*twelve dozen*) grosse *f* ♦ *vt* (*COMM*): **to** ~ **$500,000** gagner 500,000 dollars avant impôt.
gross domestic product (GDP) *n* produit brut intérieur (PIB).
grossly [grōs'lē] *ad* (*greatly*) très, grandement.
gross national product (GNP) *n* produit national brut (PNB).
grotesque [grōtesk'] *a* grotesque.
grotto [grât'ō] *n* grotte *f*.
grotty [grât'ē] *a* (*Brit col*) minable.
grouch [grouch] (*col*) *vi* rouspéter ♦ *n* (*person*) rouspéteur/euse.
ground [ground] *pt, pp of* **grind** ♦ *n* sol *m*, terre *f*; (*land*) terrain *m*, terres *fpl*; (*SPORT*) terrain; (*reason: gen pl*) raison *f*; (*US: also:* ~ **wire**) terre *f* ♦ *vt* (*plane*) empêcher de décoller, retenir au sol; (*US ELEC*) équiper d'une prise de terre, mettre à la terre ♦ *vi* (*ship*) s'échouer ♦ *a* (*coffee etc*) moulu(e); (*US: meat*) haché(e); ~**s** *npl* (*gardens etc*) parc *m*, domaine *m*; (*of coffee*) marc *m*; **on the** ~, **to the** ~ par terre; **below** ~ sous terre; **to gain/lose** ~ gagner/perdre du terrain; **common** ~ terrain d'entente; **he covered a lot of** ~ **in his lecture** sa conférence a traité un grand nombre de questions *or* la question en profondeur.
ground cloth *n* (*US*) tapis *m* de sol.

ground control n (AVIAT. SPACE) centre m de contrôle (au sol).
ground floor n (Brit) rez-de-chaussée m.
grounding [groun'ding] n (in education) connaissances fpl de base.
groundless [ground'lis] a sans fondement.
ground meat n (US) viande hachée, hachis m.
groundnut [ground'nut] n arachide f.
ground rent n (Brit) fermage m.
groundsheet [ground'shēt] n (Brit) = **ground cloth.**
groundskeeper [groundz'kēpûr] n (US: SPORT) gardien m de stade.
groundsman [groundz'mən], n (Brit) = **groundskeeper.**
ground staff n équipage m au sol.
groundswell [ground'swel] n lame f or vague f de fond.
ground-to-ground [ground'təground'] a: ~ missile missile m sol-sol.
groundwork [ground'wûrk] n préparation f.
group [grōōp] n groupe m ♦ vt (also: ~ together) grouper ♦ vi (also: ~ together) se grouper.
grouse [grous] n (pl inv) (bird) grouse f (sorte de coq de bruyère) ♦ vi (complain) rouspéter, râler.
grove [grōv] n bosquet m.
grovel [gruv'əl] vi (fig): to ~ (before) ramper (devant).
grow, pt **grew,** pp **grown** [grō, grōō, grōn] vi (plant) pousser, croître; (person) grandir; (increase) augmenter, se développer; (become): to ~ rich/weak s'enrichir/s'affaiblir ♦ vt cultiver, faire pousser.
grow apart vi (fig) se détacher (l'un de l'autre).
grow away from vt fus (fig) s'éloigner de.
grow on vt fus: that painting is ~ing on me je finirai par aimer ce tableau.
grow out of vt fus (clothes) devenir trop grand pour; (habit) perdre (avec le temps); he'll ~ out of it ça lui passera.
grow up vi grandir.
grower [grō'ûr] n producteur m; (AGR) cultivateur/trice.
growing [grō'ing] a (fear, amount) croissant(e), grandissant(e); ~ pains (MED) fièvre f de croissance; (fig) difficultés fpl de croissance.
growl [groul] vi grogner.
grown [grōn] pp of **grow** ♦ a adulte.
grown-up [grōn'up'] n adulte m/f, grande personne.
growth [grōth] n croissance f, développement m; (what has grown) pousse f; poussée f; (MED) grosseur f, tumeur f.
growth rate n taux m de croissance.
grub [grub] n larve f; (col: food) bouffe f.
grubby [grub'ē] a crasseux(euse).
grudge [gruj] n rancune f ♦ vt: to ~ sb sth donner qch à qn à contre-cœur; reprocher qch à qn; to bear sb a ~ (for) garder rancune or en vouloir à qn (de); he ~s spending il rechigne à dépenser.
grudgingly [gruj'inglē] ad à contre-cœur, de mauvaise grâce.
gruel(l)ing [grōō'əling] a exténuant(e).
gruesome [grōō'səm] a horrible.

gruff [gruf] a bourru(e).
grumble [grum'bəl] vi rouspéter, ronchonner.
grumpy [grum'pē] a grincheux(euse).
grunt [grunt] vi grogner ♦ n grognement m.
GSA n abbr (US) = General Services Administration.
G-string [jē'string] n (garment) cache-sexe m inv.
GSUSA n abbr = Girl Scouts of the United States of America.
GU abbr (US MAIL) = Guam.
guarantee [garəntē'] n garantie f ♦ vt garantir; he can't ~ (that) he'll come il n'est pas absolument certain de pouvoir venir.
guarantor [gar'əntôr] n garant/e.
guard [gârd] n garde f, surveillance f; (squad, BOXING, FENCING) garde f; (one man) garde m; (in prison) gardien/ne; (Brit RAIL) chef m de train; (safety device: on machine) dispositif m de sûreté; (also: fire~) garde-feu m inv ♦ vt garder, surveiller; (protect): to ~ (against or from) protéger (contre); to be on one's ~ (fig) être sur ses gardes.
guard against vi: to ~ against doing sth se garder de faire qch.
guard dog n chien m de garde.
guarded [gâr'did] a (fig) prudent(e).
guardian [gâr'dēən] n gardien/ne; (of minor) tuteur/trice.
guardrail [gârd'rāl] n rail m de sécurité.
guard's van [gârdz' van] n (Brit RAIL) fourgon m.
Guatemala [gwâtəmâl'ə] n Guatémala m.
guerrilla [gəril'ə] n guérillero m.
guerrilla warfare n guérilla f.
guess [ges] vi deviner ♦ vt deviner; (US) croire, penser ♦ n supposition f, hypothèse f; to take or have a ~ essayer de deviner; to keep sb ~ing laisser qn dans le doute or l'incertitude, tenir qn en haleine.
guesstimate [ges'timit] n (col) estimation f.
guesswork [ges'wûrk] n hypothèse f; I got the answer by ~ j'ai deviné la réponse.
guest [gest] n invité/e; (in hotel) client/e; be my ~ faites comme chez vous.
guest book n livre m d'or.
guesthouse [gest'hous] n pension f.
guest room n chambre f d'amis.
guffaw [gufô'] n gros rire ♦ vi pouffer de rire.
guidance [gid'əns] n conseils mpl; under the ~ of conseillé(e) or encadré(e) par, sous la conduite de; vocational ~ orientation professionnelle; marriage ~ conseils conjugaux.
guide [gīd] n (person, book etc) guide m; (Brit: also: girl ~) guide f ♦ vt guider; to be ~d by sb/sth se laisser guider par qn/qch.
guidebook [gīd'bŏŏk] n guide m.
guided missile [gī'did mis'əl] n missile téléguidé.
guide dog n chien m d'aveugle.
guided tour [gīd'id tŏŏr] n visite guidée.
guidelines [gīd'līnz] npl (fig) instructions générales, conseils mpl.
guild [gild] n corporation f; cercle m, association f.
guile [gīl] n astuce f.
guileless [gīl'lis] a candide.
guillotine [gil'ətēn] n guillotine f; (for paper) massicot m.

guilt [gilt] *n* culpabilité *f*.
guilty [gil'tē] *a* coupable; **to plead ~/not ~** plaider coupable/non coupable; **to feel ~ about doing sth** avoir mauvaise conscience à faire qch.
Guinea [gin'ē] *n*: **Republic of ~** (République *f* de) Guinée *f*.
guinea pig *n* cobaye *m*.
guise [gīz] *n* aspect *m*, apparence *f*.
guitar [gitâr'] *n* guitare *f*.
guitarist [gitâr'ist] *n* guitariste *m/f*.
gulch [gulch] *n* (*US*) ravin *m*.
gulf [gulf] *n* golfe *m*; (*abyss*) gouffre *m*; **the (Persian) G~** le golfe Persique.
Gulf States *npl*: **the ~** (*in Middle East*) les pays *mpl* du Golfe.
Gulf Stream *n*: **the ~** le Gulf Stream.
gull [gul] *n* mouette *f*.
gullet [gul'it] *n* gosier *m*.
gullibility [guləbil'ətē] *n* crédulité *f*.
gullible [gul'əbəl] *a* crédule.
gully [gul'ē] *n* ravin *m*; ravine *f*; couloir *m*.
gulp [gulp] *vi* avaler sa salive; (*from emotion*) avoir la gorge serrée, s'étrangler ♦ *vt* (*also: ~ down*) avaler ♦ *n* (*of drink*) gorgée *f*; **at one ~** d'un seul coup.
gum [gum] *n* (*ANAT*) gencive *f*; (*glue*) colle *f*; (*sweet*) boule *f* de gomme; (*also: chewing-~*) chewing-gum *m* ♦ *vt* coller.
gum up *vt*: **to ~ up the works** (*col*) bousiller tout.
gumboil [gum'boil] *n* abcès *m* dentaire.
gumboots [gum'boots] *npl* (*Brit*) bottes *fpl* en caoutchouc.
gun [gun] *n* (*small*) revolver *m*, pistolet *m*; (*rifle*) fusil *m*, carabine *f*; (*cannon*) canon *m* ♦ *vt* (*also: ~ down*) abattre; **to stick to one's ~s** (*fig*) ne pas en démordre.
gunboat [gun'bōt] *n* canonnière *f*.
gun dog *n* chien *m* de chasse.
gunfire [gun'fīûr] *n* fusillade *f*.
gunk [gungk] *n* (*col*) saleté *f*.
gunman [gun'mən] *n* bandit armé.
gunner [gun'ûr] *n* artilleur *m*.
gunpoint [gun'point] *n*: **at ~** sous la menace du pistolet (*or* fusil).
gunpowder [gun'poudûr] *n* poudre *f* à canon.
gunrunner [gun'runûr] *n* trafiquant *m* d'armes.
gunrunning [gun'runing] *n* trafic *m* d'armes.
gunshot [gun'shât] *n* coup *m* de feu; **within ~** à portée de fusil.
gunsmith [gun'smith] *n* armurier *m*.
gurgle [gûr'gəl] *n* gargouillis *m* ♦ *vi* gargouiller.
guru [goo'roo] *n* gourou *m*.
gush [gush] *n* jaillissement *m*, jet *m* ♦ *vi* jaillir; (*fig*) se répandre en effusions.
gusset [gus'it] *n* gousset *m*, soufflet *m*; (*in tights, pants*) entre-jambes *m*.
gust [gust] *n* (*of wind*) rafale *f*; (*of smoke*) bouffée *f*.
gusto [gus'tō] *n* enthousiasme *m*.
gut [gut] *n* intestin *m*, boyau *m*; (*MUS etc*) boyau ♦ *vt* (*poultry, fish*) vider; (*building*) ne laisser que les murs de; **~s** *npl* boyaux *mpl*; (*col: courage*) cran *m*; **to hate sb's ~s** ne pas pouvoir voir qn en peinture *or* sentir qn.
gut reaction *n* réaction instinctive.

gutter [gut'ûr] *n* (*of roof*) gouttière *f*; (*in street*) caniveau *m*; (*fig*) ruisseau *m*.
guttural [gut'ûrəl] *a* guttural(e).
guy [gī] *n* (*also: ~rope*) corde *f*; (*col: man*) type *m*; (*figure*) effigie de Guy Fawkes.
Guyana [gēân'ə] *n* Guyane *f*.
guzzle [guz'əl] *vi* s'empiffrer ♦ *vt* avaler gloutonnement.
gym [jim] *n* (*also: gymnasium*) gymnase *m*; (*also: gymnastics*) gym *f*.
gymkhana [jimkâ'nə] *n* gymkhana *m*.
gymnasium [jimnā'zēəm] *n* gymnase *m*.
gymnast [jim'nast] *n* gymnaste *m/f*.
gymnastics [jimnas'tiks] *n*, *npl* gymnastique *f*.
gym shoes *npl* chaussures *fpl* de gym(nastique).
gym slip *n* (*Brit*) tunique *f* (d'écolière).
gynecologist, (*Brit*) **gynaecologist** [gīnəkâl'əjist] *n* gynécologue *m/f*.
gynecology, (*Brit*) **gynaecology** [gīnəkâl'əjē] *n* gynécologie *f*.
gypsy [jip'sē] *n* gitan/e, bohémien/ne ♦ *cpd*: **~ caravan** *n* roulotte *f*.
gyrate [jī'rāt] *vi* tournoyer.
gyroscope [jī'rəskōp] *n* gyroscope *m*.

H

H, h [āch] *n* (*letter*) H, h *m*; **H for How** H comme Henri.
habeas corpus [hā'bēəs kôr'pəs] *n* (*LAW*) habeas corpus *m*.
haberdashery [hab'ûrdashûrē] *n* (*Brit*) mercerie *f*.
habit [hab'it] *n* habitude *f*; (*costume*) habit *m*, tenue *f*; **to get out of/into the ~ of doing sth** perdre/prendre l'habitude de faire qch.
habitable [hab'itəbəl] *a* habitable.
habitat [hab'itat] *n* habitat *m*.
habitation [habitā'shən] *n* habitation *f*.
habitual [həbich'ooəl] *a* habituel(le); (*drinker, liar*) invétéré(e).
habitually [həbich'ooəlē] *ad* habituellement, d'habitude.
hack [hak] *vt* hacher, tailler ♦ *n* (*cut*) entaille *f*; (*blow*) coup *m*; (*pej: writer*) nègre *m*; (*old horse*) canasson *m*.
hacker [hak'ûr] *n* (*COMPUT*) pirate *m* informatique.
hackles [hak'əlz] *npl*: **to make sb's ~ rise** (*fig*) mettre qn hors de soi.
hackney cab [hak'nē kab] *n* fiacre *m*.
hackneyed [hak'nēd] *a* usé(e), rebattu(e).
had [had] *pt, pp of* **have**.
haddock, *pl* **~** *or* [had'ək] **~s** *n* églefin *m*; **smoked ~** haddock *m*.
hadn't [had'ənt] = **had not**.
haematology [hēmətâl'əjē] *n* (*Brit*) hématologie *f*.
haemoglobin [hē'məglōbin] *n* (*Brit*) hémoglobine *f*.
haemophilia [hēməfil'ēə] *n* (*Brit*) hémophilie

f.

haemorrhage [hem'ûrij] *n* (*Brit*) hémorragie*f.*

haemorrhoids [hem'ɔroidz] *npl* (*Brit*) hémorroïdes *fpl.*

hag [hag] *n* (*ugly*) vieille sorcière; (*nasty*) chameau *m*, harpie *f*; (*witch*) sorcière.

haggard [hag'ûrd] *a* hagard(e), égaré(e).

haggis [hag'is] *n* haggis *m*.

haggle [hag'əl] *vi* marchander; **to** ~ **over** chicaner sur.

haggling [hag'ling] *n* marchandage *m*.

Hague [hāg] *n*: **The** ~ La Haye.

hail [hāl] *n* grêle *f* ♦ *vt* (*call*) héler; (*greet*) acclamer ♦ *vi* grêler; (*originate*): **he** ~**s from Scotland** il est originaire d'Écosse.

hailstone [hāl'stōn] *n* grêlon *m*.

hailstorm [hāl'stôrm] *n* averse *f* de grêle.

hair [hâr] *n* cheveux *mpl*; (*on body*) poils *mpl*, pilosité *f*; (*single hair: on head*) cheveu *m*; (: *on body*) poil *m*; **to do one's** ~ se coiffer.

hairbrush [hâr'brush] *n* brosse *f* à cheveux.

haircut [hâr'kut] *n* coupe *f* (de cheveux).

hairdo [hâr'dōō] *n* coiffure *f*.

hairdresser [hâr'dresûr] *n* coiffeur/euse.

hair dryer *n* sèche-cheveux *m*.

hair gel *n* gel *m*.

hairgrip [hâr'grip] *n* (*Brit*) pince *f* à cheveux.

hairline [hâr'līn] *n* naissance *f* des cheveux.

hairline fracture *n* fêlure *f*.

hairnet [hâr'net] *n* résille *f*.

hair oil *n* huile *f* capillaire.

hairpiece [hâr'pēs] *n* postiche *m*.

hairpin [hâr'pin] *n* épingle *f* à cheveux.

hairpin curve, (*Brit*) **hairpin bend** *n* virage *m* en épingle à cheveux.

hair-raising [hâr'rāzing] *a* à (vous) faire dresser les cheveux sur la tête.

hair remover *n* dépilateur *m*.

hair spray *n* laque *f* (pour les cheveux).

hairstyle [hâr'stīl] *n* coiffure *f*.

hairy [hâr'ē] *a* poilu(e); chevelu(e); (*fig*) effrayant(e).

Haiti [hā'tē] *n* Haïti *m*.

hake [hāk] *n* colin *m*, merlu *m*.

halcyon [hal'sēən] *a* merveilleux(euse).

hale [hāl] *a*: ~ **and hearty** robuste, en pleine santé.

half [haf] *n* (*pl* **halves** [havz]) moitié *f*; (*SPORT*: *of match*) mi-temps *f*; (: *of ground*) moitié (du terrain) ♦ *a* demi(e) ♦ *ad* (à) moitié, à demi; ~ **an hour** une demi-heure; ~ **a dozen** une demi-douzaine; ~ **a pound** une demi-livre, ≈ 250 g; **two and a** ~ deux et demi; **a week and a** ~ une semaine et demie; ~ (**of it**) la moitié; ~ (**of**) la moitié de; ~ **the amount of** la moitié de; **to cut sth in** ~ couper qch en deux; ~ **after three** trois heures et demie; ~ **empty/closed** à moitié vide/fermé; **to go halves (with sb)** se mettre de moitié avec qn.

halfback [haf'bak] *n* (*SPORT*) demi *m*.

half-baked [haf'bākt'] *a* (*col*: *idea, scheme*) qui ne tient pas debout.

half-breed [haf'brēd] *n* = **halfcaste**.

half-brother [haf'bruth'ûr] *n* demi-frère *m*.

half-caste [haf'kast] *n* métis/se.

half-hearted [haf'hâr'tid] *a* tiède, sans enthousiasme.

half-hour [haf'our'] *n* demi-heure *f*.

half-mast [haf'mast'] *n*: **at** ~ (*flag*) en berne, à mi-mât.

half note *n* (*US*) blanche *f*.

halfpenny [hā'pənē] *n* demi-penny *m*.

half-price [haf'prīs'] *a* à moitié prix ♦ *ad* (*also*: **at** ~) à moitié prix.

half term *n* (*Brit SCOL*) congé *m* de demi-trimestre.

half-time [haf'tīm'] *n* mi-temps *f*.

halfway [haf'wā'] *ad* à mi-chemin; **to meet sb** ~ (*fig*) parvenir à un compromis avec qn.

half-yearly [haf'yēr'lē] *ad* deux fois par an ♦ *a* semestriel(le).

halibut [hal'əbət] *n* (*pl inv*) flétan *m*.

halitosis [halitō'sis] *n* mauvaise haleine.

hall [hôl] *n* salle *f*; (*entrance way*) hall *m*, entrée *f*; (*corridor*) couloir *m*; (*mansion*) château *m*, manoir *m*; ~ **of residence** *n* (*Brit*) pavillon *m* or résidence *f* universitaire.

hallmark [hôl'márk] *n* poinçon *m*; (*fig*) marque *f*.

hallo [həlō'] *excl* (*Brit*) = **hello**.

Hallowe'en [haləwēn'] *n* veille *f* de la Toussaint.

hallucination [həlōōsənā'shən] *n* hallucination *f*.

hallway [hôl'wā] *n* vestibule *m*; couloir *m*.

halo [hā'lō] *n* (*of saint etc*) auréole *f*; (*of sun*) halo *m*.

halt [hôlt] *n* halte *f*, arrêt *m* ♦ *vt* faire arrêter ♦ *vi* faire halte, s'arrêter; **to call a** ~ **to sth** (*fig*) mettre fin à qch.

halter [hôl'tûr] *n* (*for horse*) licou *m*.

halterneck [hôl'tûrnek] *a* (*Brit*: *dress*) (avec) dos nu *inv*.

halve [hav] *vt* (*apple, etc*) partager *or* diviser en deux; (*reduce by half*) réduire de moitié.

halves [havz] *npl of* **half**.

ham [ham] *n* jambon *m*; (*col*: *also*: **radio** ~) radio-amateur *m*; (: *also*: ~ **actor**) cabotin/e.

Hamburg [ham'bûrg] *n* Hambourg.

hamburger [ham'bûrgûr] *n* hamburger *m*.

ham-handed [ham'handid] *a* maladroit(e).

hamlet [ham'lit] *n* hameau *m*.

hammer [ham'ûr] *n* marteau *m* ♦ *vt* (*fig*) éreinter, démolir ♦ *vi* (*at door*) frapper à coups redoublés; **to** ~ **a point home to sb** faire rentrer qch dans la tête de qn.

hammer out *vt* (*metal*) étendre au marteau; (*fig: solution*) élaborer.

hammock [ham'ək] *n* hamac *m*.

hamper [ham'pûr] *vt* gêner ♦ *n* panier *m* (d'osier).

hamster [ham'stûr] *n* hamster *m*.

hamstring [ham'string] *n* (*ANAT*) tendon *m* du jarret.

hand [hand] *n* main *f*; (*of clock*) aiguille *f*; (*handwriting*) écriture *f*; (*at cards*) jeu *m*; (*measurement: of horse*) paume *f*; (*worker*) ouvrier/ière *f* vt passer, donner; **to give sb a** ~ donner un coup de main à qn; **at** ~ à portée de la main; **in** ~ en main; (*work*) en cours; **we have the situation in** ~ nous avons la situation bien en main; **to be on** ~ (*person*) être disponible; (*emergency services*) se tenir prêt(e) (à intervenir); **to** ~ (*information etc*) sous la main, à portée de la main; **to force sb's** ~ forcer la main à qn; **to have a free** ~ avoir carte blanche; **to**

have sth in one's ~ tenir qch à la main; **on the one** ~ ..., **on the other** ~ d'une part ..., d'autre part.

hand down vt passer; (tradition, heirloom) transmettre; (US: sentence, verdict) prononcer.

hand in vt remettre.

hand out vt distribuer.

hand over vt remettre; (powers etc) transmettre.

hand round vt (Brit: information) faire circuler; (: chocolates etc) faire passer.

handbag [hand'bag] n sac m à main.

handball [hand'bôl] n handball m.

hand basin n lavabo m.

handbook [hand'bōōk] n manuel m.

handbrake [hand'brāk] n frein m à main.

hand cream n crème f pour les mains.

handcuffs [hand'kufs] npl menottes fpl.

handful [hand'fōōl] n poignée f.

handicap [han'dēkap] n handicap m ♦ vt handicaper; **mentally/physically** ~ped handicapé(e) mentalement/physiquement.

handicraft [han'dēkraft] n travail m d'artisanat, technique artisanale.

handiwork [han'dēwûrk] n ouvrage m; **this looks like his** ~ (pej) ça a tout l'air d'être son œuvre.

handkerchief [hang'kûrchif] n mouchoir m.

handle [han'dəl] n (of door etc) poignée f; (of cup etc) anse f; (of knife etc) manche m; (of saucepan) queue f; (for winding) manivelle f ♦ vt toucher, manier; (deal with) s'occuper de; (treat: people) prendre; "~ with care" "fragile".

handlebar(s) [han'dəlbâr(z)] n(pl) guidon m.

handling charges [hand'ling châr'jəz] npl frais mpl de manutention; (BANKING) agios mpl.

hand luggage n bagages mpl à main.

handmade [hand'mād'] a fait(e) à la main.

handout [hand'out] n documentation f, prospectus m; (press ~) communiqué m de presse.

hand-picked [hand'pikt'] a (produce) cueilli(e) à la main; (staff etc) trié(e) sur le volet.

handrail [hand'rāl] n (on staircase etc) rampe f, main courante.

handshake [hand'shāk] n poignée f de main; (COMPUT) établissement m de la liaison.

handsome [han'səm] a beau(belle); (gift) généreux(euse); (profit) considérable.

hands-on [handz'än] a: ~ **experience** expérience f sur le tas.

handstand [hand'stand] n: **to do a** ~ faire l'arbre droit.

hand-to-mouth [hand'təmouth'] a (existence) au jour le jour.

handwriting [hand'rīting] n écriture f.

handwritten [hand'ritən] a manuscrit(e), écrit(e) à la main.

handy [han'dē] a (person) adroit(e); (close at hand) sous la main; (convenient) pratique; **to come in** ~ être (or s'avérer) utile.

handyman [han'dēman] n bricoleur m; (servant) homme m à tout faire.

hang, pt, pp **hung** [hang, hung] vt accrocher; (criminal: pt, pp **hanged**) pendre ♦ vi pendre; (hair, drapery) tomber; **to get the** ~ of (doing) sth (col) attraper le coup pour faire qch.

hang about vi flâner, traîner.

hang back vi (hesitate): **to** ~ **back (from doing)** être réticent(e) (pour faire).

hang on vi (wait) attendre ♦ vt fus (depend on) dépendre de; **to** ~ **on to** (keep hold of) ne pas lâcher; (keep) garder.

hang out vt (washing) étendre (dehors) ♦ vi pendre; (col: live) habiter, percher.

hang together vi (argument etc) se tenir, être cohérent(e).

hang up vi (TEL) raccrocher ♦ vt accrocher, suspendre; **to** ~ **up on sb** (TEL) raccrocher au nez de qn.

hangar [hang'ûr] n hangar m.

hangdog [hang'dôg] a (look, expression) de chien battu.

hanger [hang'ûr] n cintre m, portemanteau m.

hanger-on [hang'ûrân'] n parasite m.

hang-gliding [hang'glīding] n vol m libre or sur aile delta.

hanging [hang'ing] n (execution) pendaison f.

hangman [hang'mən] n bourreau m.

hangover [hang'ōvûr] n (after drinking) gueule f de bois.

hang-up [hang'up] n complexe m.

hank [hangk] n écheveau m.

hanker [hang'kûr] vi: **to** ~ **after** avoir envie de.

hankie, hanky [hang'kē] n abbr = **handkerchief.**

hanky-panky [hang'kēpang'kē] n (pej) tripotage m.

Hants abbr (Brit) = Hampshire.

haphazard [hap'haz'ûrd] a fait(e) au hasard, fait(e) au petit bonheur.

hapless [hap'lis] a malheureux(euse).

happen [hap'ən] vi arriver, se passer, se produire; **what's** ~**ing?** que se passe-t-il?; **she** ~**ed to be free** il s'est trouvé (or se trouvait) qu'elle était libre; **if anything** ~**ed to him** s'il lui arrivait quoi que ce soit; **as it** ~**s** justement.

happen (up)on vt fus tomber sur.

happening [hap'əning] n événement m.

happily [hap'ilē] ad heureusement.

happiness [hap'ēnis] n bonheur m.

happy [hap'ē] a heureux(euse); ~ **with** (arrangements etc) satisfait(e) de; **yes, I'd be** ~ **to** oui, avec plaisir or (bien) volontiers; ~ **birthday!** bon anniversaire!; ~ **Christmas/New Year!** joyeux Noël/bonne année!

happy-go-lucky [hap'ēgōluk'ē] a insouciant(e).

harangue [hərang'] vt haranguer.

harass [həras'] vt accabler, tourmenter.

harassed [hərast'] a tracassé(e).

harassment [həras'mənt] n tracasseries fpl.

harbor, (Brit) harbour [hâr'bûr] n port m ♦ vt héberger, abriter; (hopes, suspicions) entretenir; **to** ~ **a grudge against sb** en vouloir à qn.

harbo(u)r dues npl droits mpl de port.

harbo(u)r master n capitaine m du port.

hard [hârd] a dur(e) ♦ ad (work) dur; (think, try) sérieusement; **to look** ~ **at** regarder fixement; regarder de près; **to drink** ~ boire sec; ~ **luck!** pas de veine!; **no** ~ **feelings!** sans rancune!; **to be** ~ **of hearing** être dur(e) d'oreille; **to be** ~ **on sb** être dur(e) avec qn; **I find it** ~ **to believe that** ... je n'arrive pas à croire que ....

hard-and-fast [hârd'ənfast] *a* strict(e), absolu(e).

hardback [hârd'bak] *n* livre relié.

hardboard [hârd'bôrd] *n* Isorel *m* ®.

hard-boiled egg [hârd'boild' eg] *n* œuf dur.

hard cash *n* espèces *fpl*.

hard copy *n* (*COMPUT*) sortie *f* or copie *f* papier.

hard-core [hârd'kôr'] *a* (*pornography*) (dit(e)) dur(e); (*supporters*) inconditionnel(le).

hard court *n* (*TENNIS*) court *m* en dur.

hard disk *n* (*COMPUT*) disque dur.

harden [hâr'dən] *vt* durcir; (*steel*) tremper; (*fig*) endurcir ♦ *vi* (*substance*) durcir.

hardened [hâr'dənd] *a* (*criminal*) endurci(e); **to be** ~ **to sth** s'être endurci(e) à qch, être (devenu(e)) insensible à qch.

hardening [hâr'dəning] *n* durcissement *m*.

hard-headed [hârd'hed'id] *a* réaliste; décidé(e).

hard-hearted [hârd'hâr'tid] *a* dur(e), impitoyable.

hard labor *n* travaux forcés.

hardliner [hârdlī'nûr] *n* intransigeant/e, dur/e.

hardly [hârd'lē] *ad* (*scarcely*) à peine; (*harshly*) durement; **it's** ~ **the case** ce n'est guère le cas; ~ **anywhere/ever** presque nulle part/jamais; **I can** ~ **believe it** j'ai du mal à le croire.

hardness [hârd'nis] *n* dureté *f*.

hard sell *n* vente agressive.

hardship [hârd'ship] *n* epreuves *fpl*; privations *fpl*.

hard shoulder *n* (*AUT*) accotement stabilisé.

hard up *a* (*col*) fauché(e).

hardware [hârd'wär] *n* quincaillerie *f*; (*COMPUT*) matériel *m*.

hardware dealer *n* (*US*) marchand *m* de couleurs.

hardware shop *n* quincaillerie *f*.

hard-wearing [hârd'wär'ing] *a* solide.

hard-working [hârd'wûr'king] *a* travailleur(euse), consciencieux(euse).

hardy [hâr'dē] *a* robuste; (*plant*) résistant(e) au gel.

hare [här] *n* lièvre *m*.

harebrained [här'brānd] *a* farfelu(e); écervelé(e).

harelip [här'lip] *n* (*MED*) bec-de-lièvre *m*.

harem [här'əm] *n* harem *m*.

hark back [hârk bak] *vi*: **to** ~ **back to** (en) revenir toujours à.

harm [hârm] *n* mal *m*; (*wrong*) tort *m* ♦ *vt* (*person*) faire du mal or du tort à; (*thing*) endommager; **to mean no** ~ ne pas avoir de mauvaises intentions; **there's no** ~ **in trying** on peut toujours essayer; **out of** ~**'s way** à l'abri du danger, en lieu sûr.

harmful [hârm'fəl] *a* nuisible.

harmless [hârm'lis] *a* inoffensif(ive); sans méchanceté.

harmonic [hârmân'ik] *a* harmonique.

harmonica [hârmân'ika] *n* harmonica *m*.

harmonics [hârmân'iks] *npl* harmoniques *mpl* or *fpl*.

harmonious [hârmō'nēəs] *a* harmonieux(euse).

harmonium [hârmō'nēəm] *n* harmonium *m*.

harmonize [hâr'mənīz] *vt* harmoniser ♦ *vi* s'harmoniser.

harmony [hâr'mənē] *n* harmonie *f*.

harness [hâr'nis] *n* harnais *m* ♦ *vt* (*horse*) harnacher; (*resources*) exploiter.

harp [hârp] *n* harpe *f* ♦ *vi*: **to** ~ **on about** parler tout le temps de.

harpist [hâr'pist] *n* harpiste *m*/*f*.

harpoon [hârpōōn'] *n* harpon *m*.

harpsichord [hârp'sikôrd] *n* clavecin *m*.

harrow [har'ō] *n* (*AGR*) herse *f*.

harrowing [har'ōing] *a* déchirant(e).

harry [har'ē] *vt* (*MIL*, *fig*) harceler.

harsh [hârsh] *a* (*hard*) dur(e), sévère; (*rough: surface*) rugueux(euse); (: *sound*) discordant(e); (: *taste*) âpre.

harshly [hârsh'lē] *ad* durement, sévèrement.

harshness [hârsh'nis] *n* dureté *f*, sévérité *f*.

harvest [hâr'vist] *n* (*of corn*) moisson *f*; (*of fruit*) récolte *f*; (*of grapes*) vendange *f* ♦ *vi*, *vt* moissonner; récolter; vendanger.

harvester [hâr'vistûr] *n* (*machine*) moissonneuse *f*; (*also:* **combine** ~) moissonneuse-batteuse(-lieuse) *f*; (*person*) moissonneur/euse.

has [haz] *vb see* **have**.

has-been [haz'bin] *n* (*col: person*): **he/she's a** ~ il/elle a fait son temps *or* est fini(e).

hash [hash] *n* (*CULIN*) hachis *m*; (*fig: mess*) gâchis *m* ♦ *n abbr* (*col*) = **hashish**.

hashish [hash'ēsh] *n* haschisch *m*.

hasn't [haz'ənt] = **has not**.

hassle [has'əl] *n* (*col: fuss*) histoire(s) *f(pl)*.

haste [hāst] *n* hâte *f*, précipitation *f*; **in** ~ à la hâte, précipitemment.

hasten [hā'sən] *vt* hâter, accélérer ♦ *vi* se hâter, s'empresser; **I** ~ **to add that** ... je m'empresse d'ajouter que ....

hastily [hās'tilē] *ad* à la hâte, précipitamment.

hasty [hās'tē] *a* hâtif(ive), précipité(e).

hat [hat] *n* chapeau *m*.

hatbox [hat'bâks] *n* carton *m* à chapeau.

hatch [hach] *n* (*NAUT: also:* ~**way**) écoutille *f* ♦ *vi* éclore ♦ *vt* faire éclore; (*fig: scheme*) tramer, ourdir.

hatchback [hach'bak] *n* (*AUT*) modèle *m* avec hayon arrière.

hatchet [hach'it] *n* hachette *f*.

hate [hāt] *vt* haïr, détester ♦ *n* haine *f*; **to** ~ **to do** *or* **doing** détester faire; **I** ~ **to trouble you, but** ... désolé de vous déranger, mais ....

hateful [hāt'fəl] *a* odieux(euse), détestable.

hatred [hā'trid] *n* haine *f*.

hat trick *n* (*Brit SPORT, also fig*): **to get a** ~ réussir trois coups (*or* gagner trois matchs *etc*) consécutifs.

haughty [hô'tē] *a* hautain(e), arrogant(e).

haul [hôl] *vt* traîner, tirer; (*by truck*) camionner; (*NAUT*) haler ♦ *n* (*of fish*) prise *f*; (*of stolen goods etc*) butin *m*.

haulage [hô'lij] *n* transport routier.

haulage contractor *n* (*company*) entreprise *f* de transport (routier); (*person*) transporteur routier.

hauler [hô'lûr], (*Brit*) **haulier** [hôl'êûr] *n* transporteur (routier), camionneur *m*.

haunch [hônch] *n* hanche *f*.

haunt [hônt] *vt* (*subj: ghost, fear*) hanter; (: *person*) fréquenter ♦ *n* repaire *m*.

haunted [hôn'tid] *a* (*castle etc*) hanté(e); (*look*) égaré(e), hagard(e).

haunting [hôn'ting] *a* (*sight, music*) obsédant(e).

Havana [həvan'ə] *n* La Havane.

have, *pt, pp* **had** [hav, had] *vt* avoir; (*meal, shower*) prendre ♦ *auxiliary vb*: **to ~ eaten** avoir mangé; **to ~ arrived** être arrivé(e); **to ~ breakfast** prendre son petit déjeuner; **to ~ lunch** déjeuner; **to ~ dinner** dîner; **I'll ~ a coffee** je prendrai un café; **to ~ an operation** se faire opérer; **to ~ a party** donner une réception *or* une soirée; **to ~ sth done** faire faire qch; **he had a suit made** il s'est fait faire un costume; **let me ~ a try** laissez-moi essayer; **she has to do it** il faut qu'elle le fasse, elle doit le faire; **I had better leave** je ferais mieux de partir; **I won't ~ it** cela ne se passera pas ainsi; **he's been had** (*col*) il s'est fait avoir *or* rouler.

have in *vt*: **to ~ it in for sb** (*col*) avoir une dent contre qn.

have on *vt*: **~ you anything on tomorrow?** (*Brit*) est-ce que vous êtes pris demain?; **I don't ~ any money on me** je n'ai pas d'argent sur moi; **to ~ sb on** (*Brit col*) faire marcher qn.

have out *vt*: **to ~ it out with sb** s'expliquer (franchement) avec qn.

haven [hā'vən] *n* port *m*; (*fig*) havre *m*.

haversack [hav'ûrsak] *n* sac *m* à dos.

haves [havz] *npl* (*col*): **the ~ and have-nots** les riches et les pauvres.

havoc [hav'ək] *n* ravages *mpl*; **to play ~ with** (*fig*) désorganiser; détraquer.

Hawaii [həwī'yē] *n* (*îles fpl*) Hawaii *m*.

Hawaiian [həwī'ən] *a* hawaïen(ne) ♦ *n* Hawaïen/ne; (*LING*) hawaïen *m*.

hawk [hôk] *n* faucon *m* ♦ *vt* (*goods for sale*) colporter.

hawker [hô'kûr] *n* colporteur *m*.

hawthorn [hô'thôrn] *n* aubépine *f*.

hay [hā] *n* foin *m*.

hay fever *n* rhume *m* des foins.

haystack [hā'stak] *n* meule *f* de foin.

haywire [hā'wiûr] *a* (*col*): **to go ~** perdre la tête; mal tourner.

hazard [haz'ûrd] *n* (*chance*) hasard *m*, chance *f*; (*risk*) danger *m*, risque *m* ♦ *vt* risquer, hasarder; **to be a health/fire ~** présenter un risque d'incendie/pour la santé; **to ~ a guess** émettre *or* hasarder une hypothèse.

hazardous [haz'ûrdəs] *a* hasardeux(euse), risqué(e).

hazardous pay *n* (*US*) prime *f* de risque.

hazard warning lights *npl* (*Brit: AUT*) feux *mpl* de détresse.

haze [hāz] *n* brume *f*.

hazel [hā'zəl] *n* (*tree*) noisetier *m* ♦ *a* (*eyes*) noisette *inv*.

hazelnut [hā'zəlnut] *n* noisette *f*.

hazy [hā'zē] *a* brumeux(euse); (*idea*) vague; (*photograph*) flou(e).

H-bomb [āch'bâm] *n* bombe *f* H.

h & c *abbr* (*Brit*) = *hot and cold (water)*.

HE *abbr* = *high explosive*; (*REL, DIPLOMACY*) = *His (or Her) Excellency*.

he [hē] *pronoun* il; **it is ~ who** ... c'est lui qui ...; **here ~ is** le voici; **~-bear** *etc* ours *etc* mâle.

head [hed] *n* tête *f*; (*leader*) chef *m* ♦ *vt* (*list*) être en tête de; (*group*) être à la tête de; **~s** (*on coin*) (le côté) face; **~s or tails** pile ou face; **~ first** la tête la première; **~ over heels in love** follement *or* éperdument amoureux(euse); **to ~ the ball** faire une tête; **10 francs a** *or* **per ~** 10 F par personne; **to sit at the ~ of the table** présider la tablée; **to have a ~ for business** avoir des dispositions pour les affaires; **to have no ~ for heights** (*Brit*) être sujet(te) au vertige; **to come to a ~** (*fig: situation etc*) devenir critique.

head for *vt fus* se diriger vers.

head off *vt* (*threat, danger*) détourner.

headache [hed'āk] *n* mal *m* de tête; **to have a ~** avoir mal à la tête.

headcheese [hed'chēz] *n* (*US*) fromage *m* de tête.

head cold *n* rhume *m* de cerveau.

headdress [hed'dres] *n* coiffure *f*.

header [hed'ûr] *n* (*Brit col: SOCCER*) (coup *m* de) tête *f*; (: *fall*) chute *f* (*or* plongeon *m*) la tête la première.

headhunter [hed'huntûr] *n* chasseur *m* de têtes.

heading [hed'ing] *n* titre *m*; (*subject title*) rubrique *f*.

headlamp [hed'lamp] *n* (*Brit*) = **headlight**.

headland [hed'land] *n* promontoire *m*, cap *m*.

headlight [hed'līt] *n* phare *m*.

headline [hed'līn] *n* titre *m*; **to make the ~** être à la une des journaux.

headlong [hed'lông] *ad* (*fall*) la tête la première; (*rush*) tête baissée.

headmaster [hed'mas'tûr] *n* (*Brit*) directeur *m*, proviseur *m*.

headmistress [hed'mis'tris] *n* (*Brit*) directrice *f*.

head office *n* siège *m*, direction *f* (générale).

head-on [hed'ân'] *a* (*collision*) de plein fouet.

headphones [hed'fōnz] *npl* casque *m* (à écouteurs).

headquarters (HQ) [hed'kwôrtûrz] *npl* (*of business*) siège *m*, direction *f* (générale); (*MIL*) quartier général.

headrest [hed'rest] *n* appui-tête *m*.

headroom [hed'rōom] *n* (*in car*) hauteur *f* de plafond; (*under bridge*) hauteur limite; dégagement *m*.

headscarf [hed'skârf] *n* foulard *m*.

headset [hed'set] *n* = **headphones**.

headstone [hed'stōn] *n* (*on grave*) pierre tombale.

headstrong [hed'strông] *a* têtu(e), entêté(e).

head waiter *n* maître *m* d'hôtel.

headway [hed'wā] *n*: **to make ~** avancer, faire des progrès.

headwind [hed'wind] *n* vent *m* contraire.

heady [hed'ē] *a* capiteux(euse); enivrant(e).

heal [hēl] *vt, vi* guérir.

health [helth] *n* santé *f*; **Department of H~** (*US*) ≈ ministère *m* de la Santé.

health benefit *n* (*US*) (prestations *fpl* de

l')assurance-maladie f.
health centre n (Brit) centre m de santé.
health food(s) n(pl) aliment(s) naturel(s).
health food store n magasin m diététique.
health hazard n risque m pour la santé.
Health Service n: **the ~** (Brit) ≈ la Sécurite Sociale.
healthy [hel'thē] a (person) en bonne santé; (climate, food, attitude etc) sain(e).
heap [hēp] n tas m, monceau m ♦ vt entasser, amonceler; **~s (of)** (col: lots) des tas (de); **to ~ favors/praise/gifts** etc **on sb** combler qn de faveurs/d'éloges/de cadeaux etc.
hear, pt, pp **heard** [hēr, hûrd] vt entendre; (news) apprendre; (lecture) assister à, écouter ♦ vi entendre; **to ~ about** entendre parler de; (have news of) avoir des nouvelles de; **did you ~ about the move?** tu es au courant du déménagement?; **to ~ from sb** recevoir des nouvelles de qn; **I've never heard of that book** je n'ai jamais entendu parler de ce livre.
hear out vt écouter jusqu'au bout.
hearing [hē'ring] n (sense) ouïe f; (of witnesses) audition f; (of a case) audience f; (of committee) séance f; **to give sb a ~** écouter ce que qn a à dire.
hearing aid n appareil m acoustique.
hearsay [hēr'sā] n on-dit mpl, rumeurs fpl; **by ~** ad par ouï-dire.
hearse [hûrs] n corbillard m.
heart [hârt] n cœur m; **~s** npl (CARDS) cœur; **at ~** au fond, by **~** (learn, know) par cœur; **to have a weak ~** avoir le cœur malade, avoir des problèmes de cœur; **to lose ~** perdre courage, se décourager; **to take ~** prendre courage; **to set one's ~ on sth/on doing sth** vouloir absolument qch/faire qch; **the ~ of the matter** le fond du problème.
heart attack n crise f cardiaque.
heartbeat [hârt'bēt] n battement m de cœur.
heartbreak [hârt'brāk] n immense chagrin m.
heartbreaking [hârt'brāking] a navrant(e), déchirant(e).
heartbroken [hârt'brōkən] a: **to be ~** avoir beaucoup de chagrin.
heartburn [hârt'bûrn] n brûlures fpl d'estomac.
heartening [hâr'təning] a encourageant(e), réconfortant(e).
heart failure n (MED) arrêt m du cœur.
heartfelt [hârt'felt] a sincère.
hearth [hârth] n foyer m, cheminée f.
heartily [hâr'təlē] ad chaleureusement; (laugh) de bon cœur; (eat) de bon appétit; **to agree ~** être entièrement d'accord; **to be ~ sick of** (Brit) en avoir ras le bol de.
heartland [hârt'land] n centre m, cœur m; **France's ~s** la France profonde.
heartless [hârt'lis] a sans cœur, insensible; cruel(le).
heart-to-heart [hârt'təhârt'] a, ad à cœur ouvert.
heart transplant n greffe f du cœur.
heartwarming [hârt'wôrming] a réconfortant(e).
hearty [hâr'tē] a chaleureux(euse); robuste; vigoureux(euse).
heat [hēt] n chaleur f; (fig) ardeur f; feu m;

(SPORT: also: **qualifying ~**) éliminatoire f; (ZOOL): **in** or (Brit) **on ~** en chaleur ♦ vt chauffer.
heat up vi (liquids) chauffer; (room) se réchauffer ♦ vt réchauffer.
heated [hē'tid] a chauffé(e); (fig) passionné(e); échauffé(e), excité(e).
heater [hē'tûr] n appareil m de chauffage; radiateur m.
heath [hēth] n (Brit) lande f.
heathen [hē'thən] a, n païen(ne).
heather [heth'ûr] n bruyère f.
heating [hē'ting] n chauffage m.
heat-resistant [hēt'rizistənt] a résistant(e) à la chaleur.
heatstroke [hēt'strōk] n coup m de chaleur.
heat wave n vague f de chaleur.
heave [hēv] vt soulever (avec effort) ♦ vi se soulever; (retch) avoir des haut-le-cœur ♦ n (push) poussée f; **to ~ a sigh** pousser un gros soupir.
heaven [hev'ən] n ciel m, paradis m; **~ forbid!** surtout pas!; **thank ~!** Dieu merci!; **for ~'s sake!** (pleading) je vous en prie!; (protesting) mince alors!
heavenly [hev'ənlē] a céleste, divin(e).
heavily [hev'ilē] ad lourdement; (drink, smoke) beaucoup; (sleep, sigh) profondément.
heavy [hev'ē] a lourd(e); (work, rain, user, eater) gros(se); (drinker, smoker) grand(e); **it's ~ going** ça ne va pas tout seul, c'est pénible.
heavy cream n (US) crème fraîche épaisse.
heavy-duty [hev'ēdōō'tē] a à usage intensif.
heavy goods vehicle (HGV) n (Brit) poids lourd m (P L.).
heavy-handed [hev'ēhan'did] a (fig) maladroit(e), qui manque de tact.
heavyweight [hev'ēwāt] n (SPORT) poids lourd.
Hebrew [hē'brōō] a hébraïque ♦ n (LING) hébreu m.
heckle [hek'əl] vt interpeller (un orateur).
heckler [hek'lûr] n interrupteur m; élément m perturbateur.
hectic [hek'tik] a agité(e), trépidant(e); (busy) trépidant.
hector [hek'tûr] vt rudoyer, houspiller.
he'd [hēd] = **he would, he had**.
hedge [hej] n haie f ♦ vi se défiler; **to ~ one's bets** (fig) se couvrir; **as a ~ against inflation** pour se prémunir contre l'inflation.
hedge in vt entourer d'une haie.
hedgehog [hej'hâg] n hérisson m.
hedgerow [hej'rō] n haie(s) f(pl).
hedonism [hē'dənizm] n hédonisme m.
heed [hēd] vt (also: **take ~ of**) tenir compte de, prendre garde à.
heedless [hēd'lis] a insouciant(e).
heel [hēl] n talon m ♦ vt (shoe) retalonner; **to bring to ~** (dog) faire venir à ses pieds; (fig: person) rappeler à l'ordre; **to take to one's ~s** prendre ses jambes à son cou.
hefty [hef'tē] a (person) costaud(e); (parcel) lourd(e); (piece, price) gros(se).
heifer [hef'ûr] n génisse f.
height [hīt] n (of person) taille f, grandeur f; (of object) hauteur f; (of plane, mountain)

altitude *f*; (*high ground*) hauteur, éminence *f*; (*fig: of glory*) sommet *m*; (: *of stupidity*) comble *m*; **what ~ are you?** combien mesurez-vous?, quelle est votre taille?; **of average ~** de taille moyenne; **to be afraid of ~s** être sujet(te) au vertige; **it's the ~ of fashion** c'est le dernier cri.

heighten [hīt'ən] *vt* hausser, surélever; (*fig*) augmenter.

heinous [hā'nəs] *a* odieux(euse), atroce.

heir [är] *n* héritier *m*.

heir apparent *n* héritier présomptif.

heiress [är'is] *n* héritière *f*.

heirloom [är'lōōm] *n* meuble *m* (*or* bijou *m or* tableau *m*) de famille.

heist [hīst] *n* (*US col: hold-up*) casse *m*.

held [held] *pt, pp of* **hold**.

helicopter [hel'əkâptûr] *n* hélicoptère *m*.

heliport [hel'əpôrt] *n* (*AVIAT*) héliport *m*.

helium [hē'lēəm] *n* hélium *m*.

hell [hel] *n* enfer *m*; **a ~ of a** ... (*col*) un(e) sacré(e) ...; **oh ~!** (*col*) merde!

he'll [hēl] = **he will, he shall**.

hellish [hel'ish] *a* infernal(e).

hello [helō'] *excl* bonjour!; salut! (*to sb one addresses as 'tu'*); (*surprise*) tiens!

hell's angel [helz ān'jəl] *n* blouson *m* noir.

helm [helm] *n* (*NAUT*) barre *f*.

helmet [hel'mit] *n* casque *m*.

helmsman [helmz'mən] *n* timonier *m*.

help [help] *n* aide *f*; (*cleaner*) femme *f* de ménage; (*assistant etc*) employé/e ♦ *vt* aider; **~!** au secours!; **~ yourself (to bread)** servez-vous (de pain); **are you being ~ed?** (*US*) est-ce qu'on s'occupe de vous?; **can I ~ you?** (*in store*) vous désirez?; **with the ~ of** (*person*) avec l'aide de; (*tool etc*) à l'aide de; **to be of ~ to sb** être utile à qn; **"~ wanted"** (*US PRESS*) "offres d'emploi"; **to ~ sb (to) do sth** aider qn à faire qch; **I can't ~ saying** je ne peux pas m'empêcher de dire; **he can't ~ it** il n'y peut rien.

helper [hel'pûr] *n* aide *m/f*, assistant/e.

helpful [help'fəl] *a* serviable, obligeant(e); (*useful*) utile.

helping [hel'ping] *n* portion *f*.

helpless [help'lis] *a* impuissant(e); (*baby*) sans défense.

helplessly [help'lislē] *ad* (*watch*) sans pouvoir rien faire.

Helsinki [hel'singkē] *n* Helsinki.

helter-skelter [hel'tûrskel'tûr] *n* (*Brit: at amusement park*) toboggan *m*.

hem [hem] *n* ourlet *m* ♦ *vt* ourler.

hem in *vt* cerner; **to feel ~med in** (*fig*) avoir l'impression d'étouffer, se sentir oppressé(e) *or* écrasé(e).

he-man [hē'man] *n* (*col*) macho *m*.

hematology [hēmətâl'əjē] *n* hématologie *f*.

hemisphere [hem'isfēr] *n* hémisphère *m*.

hemlock [hem'lâk] *n* ciguë *f*.

hemoglobin [hē'məglōbin] *n* hémoglobine *f*.

hemophilia [hēməfil'ēə] *n* hémophilie *f*.

hemorrhage [hem'ûrij] *n* hémorragie *f*.

hemorrhoids [hem'əroidz] *npl* hémorroïdes *fpl*.

hemp [hemp] *n* chanvre *m*.

hen [hen] *n* poule *f*; (*female bird*) femelle *f*.

hence [hens] *ad* (*therefore*) d'où, de là; **2**

years ~ d'ici 2 ans.

henceforth [hens'fôrth] *ad* dorénavant.

henchman [hench'mən] *n* (*pej*) acolyte *m*, séide *m*.

henna [hen'ə] *n* henné *m*.

hen party *n* (*col*) réunion *f or* fête *f* entre femmes.

henpecked [hen'pekt] *a* dominé par sa femme.

hepatitis [hepətī'tis] *n* hépatite *f*.

her [hûr] *pronoun* (*direct*) la, l' + *vowel or h mute*; (*indirect*) lui; (*stressed, after prep*) elle; *see note at* **she** ♦ *a* son(sa), ses *pl*; **I see ~** je la vois; **give ~ a book** donne-lui un livre; **after ~** après elle.

herald [här'əld] *n* héraut *m* ♦ *vt* annoncer.

heraldic [hiral'dik] *a* héraldique.

heraldry [här'əldrē] *n* héraldique *f*; (*coat of arms*) blason *m*.

herb [ûrb] *n* herbe *f*; **~s** *npl* (*CULIN*) fines herbes.

herbaceous [hûrbā'shəs] *a* herbacé(e).

herbal [hûr'bəl] *a* à base de plantes; **~ tea** tisane *f*.

herbicide [hûr'bisīd] *n* herbicide *m*.

herd [hûrd] *n* troupeau *m*; (*of wild animals, swine*) troupeau, troupe *f* ♦ *vt* (*drive: animals, people*) mener, conduire; (*gather*) rassembler; **~ed together** parqués (comme du bétail).

here [hēr] *ad ici* ♦ *excl* tiens!, tenez!; **~!** présent!; **~ is, ~ are** voici; **~'s my sister** voici ma sœur; **~ he/she is** le/la voici; **~ she comes** la voici qui vient; **come ~!** viens ici!; **~ and there** ici et là.

hereabouts [hē'rəbouts] *ad* par ici, dans les parages.

hereafter [hēraf'tûr] *ad* après, plus tard; ci-après ♦ *n:* **the ~** l'au-delà *m*.

hereby [hērbī'] *ad* (*in letter*) par la présente.

hereditary [həred'itärē] *a* héréditaire.

heredity [həred'itē] *n* hérédité *f*.

heresy [här'isē] *n* hérésie *f*.

heretic [här'itik] *n* hérétique *m/f*.

heretical [həret'ikəl] *a* hérétique.

herewith [hērwith'] *ad* avec ceci, ci-joint.

heritage [här'itij] *n* héritage *m*, patrimoine *m*; **our national ~** notre patrimoine national.

hermetically [hûrmet'ikle] *ad* hermétiquement; **~ sealed** hermétiquement fermé *or* clos.

hermit [hûr'mit] *n* ermite *m*.

hernia [hûr'nēə] *n* hernie *f*.

hero, *pl* **~es** [hē'rō] *n* héros *m*.

heroic [hirō'ik] *a* héroïque.

heroin [här'ōin] *n* héroïne *f*.

heroin addict *n* héroïnomane *m/f*.

heroine [här'ōin] *n* héroïne *f* (*femme*).

heroism [här'ōizəm] *n* héroïsme *m*.

heron [här'ən] *n* héron *m*.

hero worship *n* culte *m* (du héros).

herring [här'ing] *n* hareng *m*.

hers [hûrz] *pronoun* le(la) sien(ne), les siens(siennes); **a friend of ~** un(e) ami(e) à elle, un(e) de ses ami(e)s; **this is ~** c'est à elle, c'est le sien.

herself [hûrself'] *pronoun* (*reflexive*) se; (*emphatic*) elle-même; (*after prep*) elle.

Herts *abbr* (*Brit*) = Hertfordshire.

he's [hēz] = **he is, he has.**
hesitant [hez'ətənt] *a* hésitant(e), indécis(e);
to be ~ about doing sth hésiter à faire qch.
hesitate [hez'ətāt] *vi*: **to ~ (about/to do)** hésiter (sur/à faire).
hesitation [hezətā'shən] *n* hésitation *f*; **I have
no ~ in saying (that)** ... je n'hésiterai pas à
dire (que) ....
hessian [hesh'ən] *n* (toile *f* de) jute *m*.
heterogeneous [hetûrəjē'nēəs] *a* hétérogène.
heterosexual [hetûrəsek'shōōəl] *a*, *n* hétéro-
sexuel(le).
het up [het up] *a* (*col*) agité(e), excité(e).
HEW *n abbr* (*US*: *formerly*: = *Department of
Health, Education and Welfare*) ministère de
la santé publique, de l'enseignement et du
bien-être.
hew [hyōō] *vt* tailler (*à la hache*).
hex [heks] (*US*) *n* sort *m* ♦ *vt* jeter un sort sur.
hexagon [hek'səgən] *n* hexagone *m*.
hexagonal [heksag'ənəl] *a* hexagonal(e).
hey [hā] *excl* hé!
heyday [hā'dā] *n*: **the ~ of** l'âge *m* d'or de,
les beaux jours de.
HF *n abbr* (- *high frequency*) HF *f*.
HGV *n abbr* (*Brit*) = **heavy goods vehicle.**
HI *abbr* (*US MAIL.*) = *Hawaii.*
hi [hī] *excl* salut!
hiatus [hīā'təs] *n* trou *m*, lacune *f*; (*LING*) hiatus *m*.
hibernate [hī'bûrnāt] *vi* hiberner.
hibernation [hībûrnā'shən] *n* hibernation *f*.
hiccough, hiccup [hik'up] *vi* hoqueter ♦ *n* hoquet *m*; **to have (the) ~s** avoir le hoquet.
hick [hik] *n* (*US*) rustre *m*, péquenaud *m*.
hid [hid] *pt of* **hide.**
hidden [hid'ən] *pp of* **hide** ♦ *a*: **there are no ~
extras** absolument tout est compris dans le
prix.
hide [hīd] *n* (*skin*) peau *f* ♦ *vb* (*pt* **hid,** *pp*
hidden [hid, hid'ən]) *vt*: **to ~ sth (from sb)**
cacher qch (à qn); (*feelings, truth*) dissimuler qch (à qn) ♦ *vi*: **to ~ (from sb)** se cacher
de qn.
hide-and-seek [hīd'ənsēk'] *n* cache-cache *m*.
hideaway [hīd'əwā] *n* cachette *f*.
hideous [hid'ēəs] *a* hideux(euse); atroce.
hide-out [hīd'out] *n* cachette *f*.
hiding [hī'ding] *n* (*beating*) correction *f*, volée
f de coups; **to be in ~** (*concealed*) se tenir
caché(e).
hiding place *n* cachette *f*.
hierarchy [hī'ərârkē] *n* hiérarchie *f*.
hieroglyphic [hīûrəglif'ik] *a* hiéroglyphique;
~s *npl* hiéroglyphes *mpl*.
hi-fi [hī'fī'] *a*, *n abbr* (= *high fidelity*) hi-fi (*f*)
inv.
higgledy-piggledy [hig'əldēpig'əldē] *ad* pêle-
mêle, dans le plus grand désordre.
high [hī] *a* haut(e); (*speed, respect, number*)
grand(e); (*price*) élevé(e); (*wind*) fort(e),
violent(e); (*voice*) aigu(aiguë); (*col: person:
on drugs*) défoncé(e), fait(e); (*: on drink*)
soûl(e), bourré(e); (*Brit CULIN: meat, game*)
faisandé(e); (*: spoilt*) avarié(e) ♦ *ad* haut,
en haut ♦ *n*: **exports have reached a new ~**
les exportations ont atteint un nouveau record; **20 m ~** haut(e) de 20 m; **to pay a ~
price for sth** payer cher pour qch.

highball [hī'bôl] *n* (*US*) whisky *m* à l'eau avec
des glaçons.
highboy [hī'boi] *n* (*US*) grande commode.
highbrow [hī'brou] *a*, *n* intellectuel(le).
highchair [hī'chär] *n* chaise haute (*pour
enfant*).
high-class [hī'klas'] *a* (*neighborhood, hotel*)
chic *inv*, de grand standing; (*performance
etc*) de haut niveau.
high court *n* (*LAW*) cour *f* suprême.
higher [hī'ûr] *a* (*form of life, study etc*) supé-
rieur(e) ♦ *ad* plus haut.
higher education *n* études supérieures.
high finance *n* la haute finance.
high-flier [hī'flī'ûr] *n* étudiant/e (*or* employé/e)
particulièrement doué(e) et ambitieux(euse).
high-flying [hī'flī'ing] *a* (*fig*) ambitieux(euse),
de haut niveau.
high-handed [hī'han'did] *a* très autoritaire;
très cavalier(ière).
high-heeled [hī'hēld] *a* à hauts talons.
highjack [hī'jak] *n*, *vt* = **hijack.**
high jump *n* (*SPORT*) saut *m* en hauteur.
highlands [hī'ləndz] *npl* région montagneuse.
high-level [hī'levəl] *a* (*talks etc*) à un haut niveau; **~ language** (*COMPUT*) langage évolué.
highlight [hī'līt] *n* (*fig: of event*) point culminant ♦ *vt* faire ressortir, souligner; **~s** *npl*
(*hairstyle*) reflets *mpl*.
highlighter [hī'lītûr] *n* (*pen*) surligneur (lumineux).
highly [hī'lē] *ad* très, fort, hautement; **~ paid**
très bien payé(e); **to speak ~ of** dire beaucoup de bien de.
highly-strung [hī'lēstrung'] *a* (*Brit*) = **high-
strung.**
High Mass *n* grand-messe *f*.
highness [hī'nis] *n* hauteur *f*; **Her H~** son
Altesse *f*.
high-pitched [hī'picht'] *a* aigu(ë).
high-powered [hī'pou'ûrd] *a* (*engine*)
performant(e); (*fig: person*) dynamique; (*:
job, businessman*) très important(e).
high-pressure [hī'presh'ûr] *a* à haute pression.
high-rise block [hī'rīz'blák] *n* tour *f* (d'habitation).
high school *n* lycée *m*; (*US*) établissement *m*
d'enseignement secondaire.
high season *n* haute saison.
high spirits *npl* pétulance *f*; **to be in ~** être
plein(e) d'entrain.
high street *n* (*Brit*) grand-rue *f*.
high-strung [hī'strung'] *a* (*US*) nerveux(euse),
toujours tendu(e).
highway [hī'wā] *n* grand'route *f*, route nationale; **it's ~ robbery!** c'est le coup de barre!
Highway Code *n* (*Brit*) code *m* de la route.
highwayman [hī'wāmən] *n* voleur *m* de grand
chemin.
hijack [hī'jak] *vt* détourner (*par la force*) ♦ *n*
(*also*: **~ing**) détournement *m* (d'avion).
hijacker [hī'jakûr] *n* auteur *m* d'un détournement d'avion, pirate *m* de l'air.
hike [hīk] *vi* aller à pied ♦ *n* excursion *f* à
pied, randonnée *f*; (*col: in prices etc*)
augmentation *f* ♦ *vt* (*col*) augmenter.
hiker [hī'kûr] *n* promeneur/euse, excursionniste
m/f.
hiking [hī'king] *n* excursions *fpl* à pied,

randonnée *f*.
hilarious [hilär'ēəs] *a* (*behavior, event*) désopilant(e).
hilarity [hilar'itē] *n* hilarité *f*.
hill [hil] *n* colline *f*; (*fairly high*) montagne *f*; (*on road*) côte *f*.
hillbilly [hil'bilē] *n* (*US*) montagnard/e du sud des USA; (*pej*) péquenaud *m*.
hillock [hil'ək] *n* petite colline, butte *f*.
hillside [hil'sīd] *n* (flanc *m* de) coteau *m*.
hill start *n* (*AUT*) démarrage *m* en côte.
hilly [hil'ē] *a* vallonné(e); montagneux(euse); (*road*) à fortes côtes.
hilt [hilt] *n* (*of sword*) garde *f*; **to the ~** (*fig: support*) à fond.
him [him] *pronoun* (*direct*) le, l' + *vowel or h mute*; (*stressed, indirect, after prep*) lui; **I see ~** je le vois; **give ~ a book** donne-lui un livre; **after ~** après lui.
Himalayas [himəlā'əz] *npl*: **the ~** l'Himalaya *m*.
himself [himself'] *pronoun* (*reflexive*) se; (*emphatic*) lui-même; (*after prep*) lui.
hind [hīnd] *a* de derrière ♦ *n* biche *f*.
hinder [hin'dûr] *vt* gêner; (*delay*) retarder; (*prevent*): **to ~ sb from doing** empêcher qn de faire.
hindquarters [hīnd'kwôrtûrz] *npl* (*ZOOL*) arrière-train *m*.
hindrance [hin'drəns] *n* gêne *f*, obstacle *m*.
hindsight [hīnd'sīt] *n* bon sens après coup; **with the benefit of ~** avec du recul, rétrospectivement.
Hindu [hin'dōō] *n* Hindou/e.
hinge [hinj] *n* charnière *f* ♦ *vi* (*fig*): **to ~ on** dépendre de.
hint [hint] *n* allusion *f*; (*advice*) conseil *m* ♦ *vt*: **to ~ that** insinuer que ♦ *vi*: **to ~ at** faire une allusion à; **to drop a ~** faire une allusion *or* insinuation; **give me a ~** (*clue*) mettez-moi sur la voie, donnez-moi une indication.
hip [hip] *n* hanche *f*; (*BOT*) fruit *m* de l'églantier *or* du rosier.
hip flask *n* flacon *m* (pour la poche).
hippie, hippy [hip'ē] *n* hippie *m/f*.
hip pocket *n* poche-revolver *f*.
hippopotamus, *pl* **~es** *or* **hippopotami** [hipəpât'əməs, -pât'əmī] *n* hippopotame *m*.
hippy [hip'ē] *n* = **hippie**.
hire [hīûr] *vt* (*Brit: car, equipment*) louer; (*worker*) embaucher, engager ♦ *n* location *f*; **for ~** à louer; (*taxi*) libre; **on ~** en location.
hire out *vt* louer.
hire(d) car *n* (*Brit*) voiture louée.
hire purchase (H.P.) *n* (*Brit*) achat *m* (*or* vente *f*) à tempérament *or* crédit; **to buy sth on ~** acheter qch en location-vente.
his [hiz] *pronoun* le(la) sien(ne), les siens(siennes) ♦ *a* son(sa), ses *pl*; **this is ~** c'est à lui, c'est le sien.
hiss [his] *vi* siffler ♦ *n* sifflement *m*.
histogram [his'təgram] *n* histogramme *m*.
historian [histôr'ēən] *n* historien/ne.
historic(al) [histôr'ik(əl)] *a* historique.
history [his'tûrē] *n* histoire *f*; **medical ~** (*of patient*) passé médical.
histrionics [histrēân'iks] *n* gestes *mpl* dramatiques, cinéma *m* (*fig*).

hit [hit] *vt* (*pt, pp* **hit**) frapper; (*knock against*) cogner; (*reach: target*) atteindre, toucher; (*collide with: car*) entrer en collision avec, heurter; (*fig: affect*) toucher; (*find*) tomber sur ♦ *n* coup *m*; (*success*) coup réussi; succès *m*; (*song*) chanson *f* à succès, tube *m*; **to ~ it off with sb** bien s'entendre avec qn; **to ~ the road** (*col*) se mettre en route.
hit back *vi*: **to ~ back at sb** prendre sa revanche sur qn.
hit out at *vt fus* envoyer un coup à; (*fig*) attaquer.
hit (up)on *vt fus* (*answer*) trouver (par hasard); (*solution*) tomber sur (par hasard).
hit-and-run driver [hit'ənrun' drī'vûr] *n* chauffard *m*.
hitch [hich] *vt* (*fasten*) accrocher, attacher; (*also: ~ up*) remonter d'une saccade ♦ *n* (*knot*) nœud *m*; (*difficulty*) anicroche *f*, contretemps *m*; **to ~ a lift** faire du stop; **technical ~** incident *m* technique.
hitch up *vt* (*horse, cart*) atteler; *see also* **hitch**.
hitchhike [hich'hīk] *vi* faire de l'auto-stop.
hitchhiker [hich'hīkûr] *n* auto-stoppeur/euse.
hi-tech [hī'tek'] *a* à la pointe de la technologie, technologiquement avancé(e) ♦ *n* high-tech *m*.
hitherto [hith'ûrtōō] *ad* jusqu'ici, jusqu'à présent.
hit man *n* tueur *m*.
hit-or-miss [hit'ərmis'] *a* fait(e) au petit bonheur; **it's ~ whether...** il est loin d'être certain que... + *sub*.
hit parade *n* hit parade *m*.
hive [hīv] *n* ruche *f*; **the shop was a ~ of activity** (*fig*) le magasin était une véritable ruche.
hive off *vt* (*col*) mettre à part, séparer.
hl *abbr* (= *hectoliter*) hl.
HM *abbr* (= *His* (*or Her*) *Majesty*) SM.
HMG *abbr* (*Brit*) = *His* (*or Her*) *Majesty's Government*.
HMO *n abbr* (*US*: = *health maintenance organization*) organisme médical assurant un forfait entretien de santé.
HMS *abbr* (*Brit*) = *His* (*or Her*) *Majesty's Ship*.
hoard [hôrd] *n* (*of food*) provisions *fpl*, réserves *fpl*; (*of money*) trésor *m* ♦ *vt* amasser.
hoarding [hôr'ding] *n* (*Brit*) panneau *m* d'affichage *or* publicitaire.
hoarfrost [hôr'frâst] *n* givre *m*.
hoarse [hôrs] *a* enroué(e).
hoax [hōks] *n* canular *m*.
hob [hâb] *n* plaque chauffante.
hobble [hâb'əl] *vi* boitiller.
hobby [hâb'ē] *n* passe-temps favori.
hobbyhorse [hâb'ēhôrs] *n* cheval *m* à bascule; (*fig*) dada *m*.
hobnob [hâb'nâb] *vi*: **to ~ with** frayer avec, fréquenter.
hobo [hō'bō] *n* (*US*) vagabond *m*.
hock [hâk] *n* (*of animal*, *CULIN*) jarret *m*; (*Brit: wine*) vin *m* du Rhin; (*col*): **to be in ~** (*person*) avoir des dettes; (*object*) être en gage *or* au clou.

hockey [hák'ē] *n* hockey *m*.

hocus-pocus [hō'kəspō'kəs] *n* (*trickery*) supercherie *f*; (*words: of magician*) formules *fpl* magiques; (*: jargon*) galimatias *m*.

hodgepodge [háj'páj] *n* mélange *m* hétéroclite.

hoe [hō] *n* houe *f*, binette *f* ♦ *vt* (*ground*) biner; (*plants etc*) sarcler.

hog [hóg] *n* sanglier *m* ♦ *vt* (*fig*) accaparer; **to go the whole** ~ aller jusqu'au bout.

hoist [hoist] *n* palan *m* ♦ *vt* hisser.

hold [hōld] *vb* (*pt, pp* **held** [held]) *vt* tenir; (*contain*) contenir; (*keep back*) retenir; (*believe*) maintenir; considérer; (*possess*) avoir; détenir ♦ *vi* (*withstand pressure*) tenir (bon); (*be valid*) valoir ♦ *n* prise *f*; (*fig*) influence *f*; (NAUT) cale *f*; **to catch** *or* **get (a)** ~ **of** saisir; **to get** ~ **of** (*fig*) trouver; **to get** ~ **of o.s.** se contrôler; ~ **the line!** (TEL) ne quittez pas!; **to** ~ **one's own** (*fig*) (bien) se défendre; **to** ~ **office** (POL) avoir un portefeuille; **to** ~ **firm** *or* **fast** tenir bon; **he** ~**s the view that ...** il pense *or* estime que ..., d'après lui ...; **to** ~ **sb responsible for sth** tenir qn pour responsable de qch.

hold back *vt* retenir; (*secret*) cacher; **to** ~ **sb back from doing sth** empêcher qn de faire qch.

hold down *vt* (*person*) maintenir à terre; (*job*) occuper.

hold forth *vi* pérorer.

hold off *vt* tenir à distance ♦ *vi* (*rain*): **if the rain** ~**s off** s'il ne pleut pas, s'il ne se met pas à pleuvoir.

hold on *vi* tenir bon; (*wait*) attendre; ~ **on!** (TEL) ne quittez pas!

hold on to *vt fus* se cramponner à; (*keep*) conserver, garder.

hold out *vt* offrir ♦ *vi* (*resist*): **to** ~ **out (against)** résister (devant), tenir bon (devant).

hold over *vt* (*meeting etc*) ajourner, reporter.

hold up *vt* (*raise*) lever; (*support*) soutenir; (*delay*) retarder; (*: traffic*) ralentir; (*rob*) braquer.

holdall [hōld'ôl] *n* (*Brit*) fourre-tout *m inv*.

holder [hōl'dûr] *n* (*of ticket, record*) détenteur/trice; (*of office, title, passport etc*) titulaire *m/f*.

holding [hōl'ding] *n* (*share*) intérêts *mpl*; (*farm*) ferme *f*.

holding company *n* holding *m*.

holdup [hōld'up] *n* (*robbery*) hold-up *m*; (*delay*) retard *m*; (*in traffic*) embouteillage *m*.

hole [hōl] *n* trou *m* ♦ *vt* trouer, faire un trou dans; ~ **in the heart** (MED) communication *f* interventriculaire; **to pick** ~**s (in)** (*fig*) chercher des poux (dans).

hole up *vi* se terrer.

holiday [hál'idā] *n* (*Brit: vacation*) vacances *fpl*; (*day off*) jour *m* de congé; (*public*) jour férié; **to be on** ~ être en congé; **tomorrow is a** ~ demain c'est fête, on a congé demain.

holiday camp *n* (*Brit: for children*) colonie *f* de vacances; (*: also:* **holiday centre**) camp *m* de vacances.

holidaymaker [hál'idāmākûr] *n* (*Brit*) vacancier/ière.

holiday pay *n* (*Brit*) paie *f* des vacances.

holiday resort *n* centre *m* de villégiature *or* de vacances.

holiday season *n* (US) fêtes *fpl* de fin d'année; (*Brit*) période *f* des vacances.

holiness [hō'lēnis] *n* sainteté *f*.

Holland [hál'ənd] *n* Hollande *f*.

hollow [hál'ō] *a* creux(euse); (*fig*) faux(fausse) ♦ *n* creux *m*; (*in land*) dépression *f* (de terrain), cuvette *f* ♦ *vt*: **to** ~ **out** creuser, évider.

holly [hál'ē] *n* houx *m*.

hollyhock [hál'ēhák] *n* rose trémière.

holocaust [hál'əkôst] *n* holocauste *m*.

holster [hōl'stûr] *n* étui *m* de revolver.

holy [hō'lē] *a* saint(e); (*bread, water*) bénit(e); (*ground*) sacré(e).

Holy Communion *n* la (sainte) communion.

Holy Ghost, Holy Spirit *n* Saint-Esprit *m*.

Holy Land *n*: **the** ~ la Terre Sainte.

holy orders *npl* ordres (majeurs).

homage [hám'ij] *n* hommage *m*; **to pay** ~ **to** rendre hommage à.

home [hōm] *n* foyer *m*, maison *f*; (*country*) pays natal, patrie *f*; (*institution*) maison ♦ *a* de famille; (ECON, POL) national(e), intérieur(e); (SPORT: *team*) qui reçoit; (*: match, win*) sur leur (*or* notre) terrain ♦ *ad* chez soi, à la maison; au pays natal; (*right in: nail etc*) à fond; **at** ~ chez soi, à la maison; **to go** (*or* **come**) ~ rentrer (chez soi), rentrer à la maison (*or* au pays); **make yourself at** ~ faites comme chez vous; **near my** ~ près de chez moi.

home in on *vt fus* (*missiles*) se diriger automatiquement vers *or* sur.

home address *n* domicile permanent.

home-brew [hōm'brōō'] *n* vin *m* (*or* bière *f*) maison.

homecoming [hōm'kuming] *n* retour *m* (au bercail).

home computer *n* ordinateur *m* domestique.

home economics *n* économie *f* domestique.

home furnishings [hōm fûr'nishingz] *npl* (*drapes etc*) tissus *mpl* d'ameublement.

home-grown [hōm'grōn'] *a* (*not foreign*) du pays; (*from garden*) du jardin.

homeland [hōm'land] *n* patrie *f*.

homeless [hōm'lis] *a* sans foyer, sans abri; **the** ~ *npl* les sans-abri *mpl*.

home loan *n* prêt *m* sur hypothèque.

homely [hōm'lē] *a* simple, sans prétention; accueillant(e).

home-made [hōm'mād'] *a* fait(e) à la maison.

Home Office *n* (*Brit*) ministère *m* de l'Intérieur.

homeopath [hō'mēəpath] *n* homéopath *m/f*.

homeopathy [hōmēáp'əthē] *n* homéopathe *f*.

homeowner [hōm'ōnûr] *n* propriétaire occupant.

home rule *n* autonomie *f*.

Home Secretary *n* (*Brit*) ministre *m* de l'Intérieur.

homesick [hōm'sik] *a*: **to be** ~ avoir le mal du pays; (*missing one's family*) s'ennuyer de sa famille.

homestead [hōm'sted] *n* propriété *f*; (*farm*) ferme *f*.

home town *n* ville natale.

homeward [hōm'wûrd] *a (journey)* du retour.
homeward(s) [hōm'wûrd(z)] *ad* vers la maison.
homework [hōm'wûrk] *n* devoirs *mpl.*
homicidal [hámisīd'əl] *a* homicide.
homicide [hám'isīd] *n (US)* homicide *m.*
homily [hám'ilē] *n* homélie *f.*
homing [hō'ming] *a (device, missile)* à tête chercheuse; ~ **pigeon** pigeon voyageur.
homoeopathy [hōmēáp'əthē] *etc (Brit)* = **homeopathy** *etc.*
homogeneous [hōməjē'nēəs] *a* homogène.
homogenize [həmáj'əniz] *vt* homogénéiser.
homosexual [hōməsek'shōōəl] *a, n* homosexuel(le).
Hon. *abbr* (= *honorable, honorary*) *dans un titre.*
Honduras [hundōō'rəs] *n* Honduras *m.*
hone [hōn] *n* pierre *f* à aiguiser ♦ *vt* affûter, aiguiser.
honest [ân'ist] *a* honnête; *(sincere)* franc(franche); **to be quite** ~ **with you** ... à dire vrai ....
honestly [ân'istlē] *ad* honnêtement; franchement.
honesty [ân'istē] *n* honnêteté *f.*
honey [hun'ē] *n* miel *m*; *(US col: darling)* chéri/e.
honeycomb [hun'ēkōm] *n* rayon *m* de miel; *(pattern)* nid *m* d'abeilles, motif alvéolé ♦ *vt (fig)*: **to** ~ **with** cribler de.
honeymoon [hun'ēmōōn] *n* lune *f* de miel, voyage *m* de noces.
honeysuckle [hun'ēsukəl] *n* chèvrefeuille *m.*
Hong Kong [hâng' kông'] *n* Hong Kong.
honk [hângk] *n (AUT)* coup *m* de klaxon ♦ *vi* klaxonner.
Honolulu [hânəlōō'lōō] *n* Honolulu.
honor [ân'ûr] *(US) vt* honorer ♦ *n* honneur *m*; **in** ~ **of** en l'honneur de.
honorable [ân'ûrəbəl] *a* honorable.
honorary [ân'ərārē] *a* honoraire; *(duty, title)* honorifique.
honor-bound [an'ûrbound'] *a*: **to be** ~ **to do** se devoir de faire.
honors degree *n (SCOL)* licence *avec mention.*
honour [ân'ûr] *etc (Brit)* = **honor** *etc.*
Hons. *abbr (SCOL)* = **honors degree.**
hood [hōōd] *n* capuchon *m*; *(US AUT)* capot *m*; *(Brit AUT)* capote *f*; *(col)* truand *m.*
hoodlum [hōōd'ləm] *n* truand *m.*
hoodwink [hōōd'wingk] *vt* tromper.
hoof, *pl* ~**s** *or* **hooves** [hōōf, hōōvz] *n* sabot *m.*
hook [hōōk] *n* crochet *m*; *(on dress)* agrafe *f*; *(for fishing)* hameçon *m* ♦ *vt* accrocher; *(dress)* agrafer; ~ **and eye** agrafe; **by** ~ **or by crook** de gré ou de force, coûte que coûte; **to be** ~**ed** *(col)* être accroché(e) (par); *(person)* être dingue (de).
hook up *vt (RADIO, TV etc)* faire un duplex entre.
hooker [hōōk'ûr] *n (col: pej)* putain *f.*
hooky [hōōk'ē] *n*: **to play** ~ faire l'école buissonnière.
hooligan [hōō'ligən] *n* voyou *m.*
hoop [hōōp] *n* cerceau *m*; *(of barrel)* cercle *m.*
hoot [hōōt] *vi (siren)* mugir; *(owl)* hululer;

(Brit AUT) klaxonner ♦ *vt (jeer at)* huer ♦ *n* huée *f*; coup *m* de klaxon; mugissement *m*; hululement *m*; **to** ~ **with laughter** rire aux éclats.
hooter [hōō'tûr] *n (NAUT, factory)* sirène *f*; *(Brit AUT)* klaxon *m.*
hoover [hōō'vûr] ® *(Brit) n* aspirateur *m* ♦ *vt (room)* passer l'aspirateur dans; *(carpet)* passer l'aspirateur sur.
hooves [hōōvz] *npl of* **hoof.**
hop [háp] *vi* sauter; *(on one foot)* sauter à cloche-pied ♦ *n* saut *m.*
hope [hōp] *vt, vi* espérer ♦ *n* espoir *m*; **I** ~ **so** je l'espère; **I** ~ **not** j'espère que non.
hopeful [hōp'fəl] *a (person)* plein(e) d'espoir; *(situation)* prometteur(euse), encourageant(e); **I'm** ~ **that she'll manage to come** j'ai bon espoir qu'elle pourra venir.
hopefully [hōp'fəlē] *ad* avec espoir, avec optimisme; ~, **they'll come back** espérons bien qu'ils reviendront.
hopeless [hōp'lis] *a* désespéré(e), sans espoir; *(useless)* nul(le).
hopelessly [hōp'lislē] *ad (live etc)* sans espoir; ~ **confused** *etc* complètement désorienté *etc.*
hopper [háp'ûr] *n (chute)* trémie *f.*
hops [háps] *npl* houblon *m.*
horde [hôrd] *n* horde *f.*
horizon [hərī'zən] *n* horizon *m.*
horizontal [hôrizân'təl] *a* horizontal(e).
hormone [hôr'mōn] *n* hormone *f.*
horn [hôrn] *n* corne *f*; *(MUS)* cor *m*; *(AUT)* klaxon *m.*
horned [hôrnd] *a (animal)* à cornes.
hornet [hôr'nit] *n* frelon *m.*
horny [hôr'nē] *a* corné(e); *(hands)* calleux(euse); *(col: aroused)* excité(e).
horoscope [hôr'əskōp] *n* horoscope *m.*
horrendous [hôren'dəs] *a* horrible, affreux(euse).
horrible [hôr'əbəl] *a* horrible, affreux(euse).
horrid [hôr'id] *a* méchant(e), désagréable.
horrific [hôrif'ik] *a* horrible.
horrify [hôr'əfī] *vt* horrifier.
horrifying [hôr'əfīing] *a* horrifiant(e).
horror [hôr'ûr] *n* horreur *f.*
horror film *n* film *m* d'épouvante.
horror-struck [hôr'ûrstruk], **horror-stricken** [hôr'ûrstrikən] *a* horrifié(e).
hors d'œuvre [ôr dûrv'] *n* hors d'œuvre *m.*
horse [hôrs] *n* cheval *m.*
horseback [hôrs'bak]: **on** ~ *a, ad* à cheval; **to go** ~ **riding** faire du cheval.
horsebox [hôrs'bâks] *n (Brit)* = **horse trailer.**
horse chestnut *n* marron *m* (d'Inde).
horse-drawn [hôrs'drôn] *a* tiré(e) par des chevaux.
horsefly [hôrs'flī] *n* taon *m.*
horseman [hôrs'mən] *n* cavalier *m.*
horsemanship [hôrs'mənship] *n* talents *mpl* de cavalier.
horseplay [hôrs'plā] *n* chahut *m (blagues etc).*
horsepower (hp) [hôrs'pouûr] *n* puissance *f* (en chevaux); cheval-vapeur *m* (CV).
horse racing *n* courses *fpl* de chevaux.
horseradish [hôrs'radish] *n* raifort *m.*
horseshoe [hôrs'shōō] *n* fer *m* à cheval.
horse show *n* concours *m* hippique.

horse-trading [hôrs'trāding] *n* maquignonage *m*.

horse trailer *n* (*US*) van *m*.

horse trials *npl* = **horse show**.

horsewhip [hôrs'hwip] *vt* cravacher.

horsewoman [hôrs'wŏŏmən] *n* cavalière *f*.

horsey [hôr'sē] *a* féru(e) d'équitation *or* de cheval; (*appearance*) chevalin(e).

horticulture [hôr'təkulchûr] *n* horticulture *f*.

hose [hōz] *n* (*also*: ~**pipe**) tuyau *m*; (*also*: **garden** ~) tuyau d'arrosage.
hose down *vt* laver au jet.

hosiery [hō'zhûrē] *n* (*in store*) (rayon *m* des) bas *mpl*.

hospice [hâs'pis] *n* hospice *m*.

hospitable [hâspit'əbəl] *a* hospitalier(ière).

hospital [hâs'pitəl] *n* hôpital *m*; **in the** ~, (*Brit*) **in** ~ à l'hôpital.

hospitality [hâspətal'itē] *n* hospitalité *f*.

hospitalize [hâs'pitəlīz] *vt* hospitaliser.

host [hōst] *n* hôte *m*; (*in hotel etc*) patron *m*; (*TV, RADIO*) présentateur/trice, animateur/ trice; (*large number*): **a** ~ **of** une foule de; (*REL*) hostie *f* ♦ *vt* (*TV program*) présenter, animer.

hostage [hâs'tij] *n* otage *m*.

host country *n* pays *m* d'accueil, pays-hôte *m*.

hostel [hâs'təl] *n* foyer *m*; (*also*: **youth** ~) auberge *f* de jeunesse.

hostelling [hâs'təling] *n*: **to go (youth)** ~ faire une virée *or* randonnée en séjournant dans des auberges de jeunesse.

hostess [hōs'tis] *n* hôtesse *f*; (*AVIAT*) hôtesse de l'air; (*in nightclub*) entraîneuse *f*.

hostile [hâs'təl] *a* hostile.

hostility [hâstil'ətē] *n* hostilité *f*.

hot [hât] *a* chaud(e); (*as opposed to only warm*) très chaud; (*spicy*) fort(e); (*fig*) acharné(e); brûlant(e); violent(e); passionné(e); **to be** ~ (*person*) avoir chaud; (*thing*) être (très) chaud; (*weather*) faire chaud.
hot up (*Brit col*) *vi* (*situation*) devenir tendu(e); (*partly*) s'animer ♦ *vt* (*pace*) accélérer, forcer; (*engine*) gonfler.

hot-air balloon [hâtär' bəlōōn'] *n* montgolfière *f*, ballon *m*.

hotbed [hât'bed] *n* (*fig*) foyer *m*, pépinière *f*.

hotchpotch [hâch'pâch] *n* (*Brit*) = **hodgepodge**.

hot dog *n* hot-dog *m*.

hotel [hōtel'] *n* hôtel *m*.

hotelier [ōtelyā'] *n* hôtelier/ière.

hotel industry *n* industrie hôtelière.

hotel room *n* chambre *f* d'hôtel.

hotfoot [hât'fŏŏt] *ad* à toute vitesse.

hotheaded [hât'hedid] *a* impétueux(euse).

hothouse [hât'hous] *n* serre chaude.

hot line [hât līn] *n* (*POL*) téléphone *m* rouge, ligne directe.

hotly [hât'lē] *ad* passionnément, violemment.

hot pad *n* (*US*) dessous-de-plat *m inv*.

hotplate [hât'plāt] *n* (*on stove*) plaque chauffante.

hotpot [hât'pât] *n* (*Brit CULIN*) ragoût *m*.

hot seat *n* (*fig*) poste chaud.

hot spot *n* point chaud.

hot spring *n* source thermale.

hot-tempered [hât'tem'pûrd] *a* emporté(e).

hot-water bottle [hâtwôt'ûr bâtəl] *n* bouillotte *f*.

hound [hound] *vt* poursuivre avec acharnement ♦ *n* chien courant; **the** ~**s** la meute.

hour [ou'ûr] *n* heure *f*; **at 30 miles an** ~ ≈ à 50 km à l'heure; **lunch** ~ heure du déjeuner; **to pay sb by the** ~ payer qn à l'heure.

hourly [ouûr'lē] *a* toutes les heures; (*rate*) horaire; ~ **paid** *a* payé(e) à l'heure.

house *n* [hous] (*pl*: ~**s** [hou'zəz]) maison *f*; (*POL*) chambre *f*; (*THEATER*) salle *f*; auditoire *m* ♦ *vt* [houz] (*person*) loger, héberger; **at** (*or* **to**) **my** ~ chez moi; **the H**~ (**of Representatives**) (*US*) la Chambre des représentants; **the H**~ (**of Commons**) (*Brit*) la Chambre des communes; **on the** ~ (*fig*) aux frais de la maison.

house arrest *n* assignation *f* à domicile.

houseboat [hous'bōt] *n* bateau (aménagé en habitation).

housebound [hous'bound] *a* confiné(e) chez soi.

housebreaking [hous'brāking] *n* cambriolage *m* (avec effraction).

house-broken [hous'brōkən] *a* (*US: animal*) propre.

housecoat [hous'kōt] *n* peignoir *m*.

household [hous'hōld] *n* ménage *m*; (*people*) famille *f*, maisonnée *f*; ~ **name** nom connu de tout le monde.

householder [hous'hōldûr] *n* propriétaire *m/f*; (*head of house*) chef *m* de ménage *or* de famille.

house hunting *n*: **to go** ~ se mettre en quête d'une maison (*or* d'un appartement).

houcokoopor [hous'kēpûr] *n* gouvernante *f*.

housekeeping [hous'kēping] *n* (*work*) ménage *m*; (*also*: ~ **money**) argent *m* du ménage; (*COMPUT*) gestion *f* (des disques).

houseman [hous'mən] *n* (*Brit MED*) ≈ interne *m*.

house-proud [hous'proud] *a* qui tient à avoir une maison impeccable.

house-to-house [hous'təhous'] *a* (*enquiries etc*) chez tous les habitants (du quartier *etc*).

house-trained [hous'trānd] *a* (*Brit*) = **housebroken**.

house-warming [hous'wôrming] *n* (*also*: ~ **party**) pendaison *f* de crémaillère.

housewife [hous'wīf] *n* ménagère *f*; femme *f* du foyer.

housework [hous'wûrk] *n* (travaux *mpl* du) ménage *m*.

housing [hou'zing] *n* logement *m* ♦ *cpd* (*problem, shortage*) de *or* du logement.

housing association *n* fondation *f* charitable fournissant des logements.

housing conditions *npl* conditions *fpl* de logement.

housing development, (Brit) housing estate *n* cité *f*; lotissement *m*.

hovel [huv'əl] *n* taudis *m*.

hover [huv'ûr] *vi* planer; **to** ~ **around sb** rôder *or* tourner autour de qn.

hovercraft [huv'ûrkraft] *n* aéroglisseur *m*.

hoverport [huv'ûrpôrt] *n* hoverport *m*.

how [hou] *ad* comment; ~ **are you?** comment allez-vous?; ~ **do you do?** bonjour; (*on* *being introduced*) enchanté(e); ~ **far is it to ...?** combien y a-t-il jusqu'à ...?; ~ **long have you been here?** depuis combien de temps êtes-vous là?; ~ **lovely!** que *or* comme c'est joli!; ~ **many/much?** combien?; ~ **many people/much milk** combien de gens/lait; ~ **old are you?** quel âge avez-vous?; ~**'s life?** (*col*) comment ça va?; ~ **about a drink?** si on buvait quelque chose?; ~ **is it that ...?** comment se fait-il que ... | *sub?*

however [houev'ûr] *cj* pourtant, cependant ♦ *ad* de quelque façon *or* manière que + *sub*; (+ *adjective*) quelque *or* si ... que + *sub*; (*in questions*) comment.

howitzer [hou'itsûr] *n* (*MIL*) obusier *m*.

howl [houl] *n* hurlement *m* ♦ *vi* hurler.

howler [hou'lûr] *n* gaffe *f*, bourde *f*.

HP *n abbr* (*Brit*) = **hire purchase.**

hp *abbr* (*AUT*) = **horsepower.**

HQ *n abbr* (= *headquarters*) QG *m*.

HR *n abbr* (*US*) = **House of Representatives.**

HRH *abbr* (= *His* (*or Her*) *Royal Highness*) SAR.

hr(s) *abbr* (= *hour(s)*) h.

HS *abbr* (*US*) = **high school.**

HST *abbr* (*US*: = *Hawaiian Standard Time*) heure de Hawaii.

hub [hub] *n* (*of wheel*) moyeu *m*; (*fig*) centre *m*, foyer *m*.

hubbub [hub'ub] *n* brouhaha *m*.

hub cap *n* (*AUT*) enjoliveur *m*.

HUD *n abbr* (*US*: = *Department of Housing and Urban Development*) ministère de l'urbanisme et du logement).

huddle [hud'əl] *vi*: **to ~ together** se blottir les uns contre les autres.

hue [hyōō] *n* teinte *f*, nuance *f*; ~ **and cry** *n* tollé (général), clameur *f*.

huff [huf] *n*: **in a ~** fâché(e); **to get into a ~** prendre la mouche.

hug [hug] *vt* serrer dans ses bras; (*shore, curb*) serrer ♦ *n* étreinte *f*; **to give sb a ~** serrer qn dans ses bras.

huge [hyōōj] *a* énorme, immense.

hulk [hulk] *n* (*ship*) vieux rafiot; (*car, building*) carcasse *f*; (*person*) mastodonte *m*, malabar *m*.

hulking [hul'king] *a* balourd(e).

hull [hul] *n* (*of ship, nuts*) coque *f*; (*of peas*) cosse *f*.

hullabaloo [huləbəlōō'] *n* (*col: noise*) tapage *m*, raffut *m*.

hullo [hələ̄'] *excl* = **hello.**

hum [hum] *vt* (*tune*) fredonner ♦ *vi* fredonner; (*insect*) bourdonner; (*plane, tool*) vrombir ♦ *n* fredonnement *m*; bourdonnement *m*; vrombissement *m*.

human [hyōō'mən] *a* humain(e) ♦ *n* (*also: ~ being*) être humain.

humane [hyōōmān'] *a* humain(e), humanitaire.

humanism [hyōō'mənizəm] *n* humanisme *m*.

humanitarian [hyōōmanitâr'ēən] *a* humanitaire.

humanity [hyōōman'itē] *n* humanité *f*.

humanly [hyōō'mənlē] *ad* humainement.

humanoid [hyōō'mənoid] *a*, *n* humanoïde (*m/f*).

humble [hum'bəl] *a* humble, modeste ♦ *vt* hu-

milier.

humbly [hum'blē] *ad* humblement, modestement.

humbug [hum'bug] *n* fumisterie *f*; (*Brit: candy*) bonbon *m* à la menthe.

humdrum [hum'drum] *a* monotone, routinier(ière).

humid [hyōō'mid] *a* humide.

humidifier [hyōōmid'əfīûr] *n* humidificateur *m*.

humidity [hyōōmid'ətē] *n* humidité *f*.

humiliate [hyōōmil'ēāt] *vt* humilier.

humiliation [hyōōmilēā'shən] *n* humiliation *f*.

humility [hyōōmil'ətē] *n* humilité *f*.

humor [hyōō'mûr] (*US*) *n* humour *m*; (*mood*) humeur *f* ♦ *vt* (*person*) faire plaisir à; se prêter aux caprices de; **sense of ~** sens *m* de l'humour; **to be in a good/bad ~** être de bonne/mauvaise humeur.

humorist [hyōō'mûrist] *n* humoriste *m/f*.

humorless [hyōō'mûrlis] *a* dépourvu(e) d'humour.

humorous [hyōō'mûrəs] *a* humoristique; (*person*) plein(e) d'humour.

humour [hyōō'mûr] *etc* (*Brit*) = **humor** *etc*.

hump [hump] *n* bosse *f*.

humpback [hump'bak] *n* bossu/e.

humus [hyōō'məs] *n* humus *m*.

hunch [hunch] *n* bosse *f*; (*premonition*) intuition *f*; **I have a ~ that** j'ai (comme une vague) idée que.

hunchback [hunch'bak] *n* bossu/e.

hunched [huncht] *a* arrondi(e), voûté(e).

hundred [hun'drid] *num* cent; **about a ~ people** une centaine de personnes; ~**s of people** des centaines de gens; **I'm a ~ per cent sure** j'en suis absolument certain.

hundredweight [hun'dridwāt] *n* (*US*) = 45.3 *kg; 100 lb*; (*Brit*) = 50.8 *kg; 112 lb*.

hung [hung] *pt, pp of* **hang.**

Hungarian [hunggär'ēən] *a* hongrois(e) ♦ *n* Hongrois/e; (*LING*) hongrois *m*.

Hungary [hung'gûrē] *n* Hongrie *f*.

hunger [hung'gûr] *n* faim *f* ♦ *vi*: **to ~ for** avoir faim de, désirer ardemment.

hunger strike *n* grève *f* de la faim.

hungrily [hung'grilē] *ad* voracement; (*fig*) avidement.

hungry [hung'grē] *a* affamé(e); **to be ~** avoir faim; ~ **for** (*fig*) avide de.

hung up *a* (*col*) complexé(e), bourré(e) de complexes.

hunk [hungk] *n* gros morceau; (*col: man*) beau mec.

hunt [hunt] *vt* (*seek*) chercher; (*SPORT*) chasser ♦ *vi* chasser ♦ *n* chasse *f*.

hunt down *vt* pourchasser.

hunter [hun'tûr] *n* chasseur *m*; (*Brit: horse*) cheval *m* de chasse.

hunting [hun'ting] *n* chasse *f*.

hurdle [hûr'dəl] *n* (*for fences*) claie *f*; (*SPORT*) haie *f*; (*fig*) obstacle *m*.

hurl [hûrl] *vt* lancer (avec violence).

hurrah, hurray [hərâ', hərā'] *n* hourra *m*.

hurricane [hûr'əkān] *n* ouragan *m*.

hurried [hûr'ēd] *a* pressé(e), précipité(e); (*work*) fait(e) à la hâte.

hurriedly [hûr'ēdlē] *ad* précipitamment, à la hâte.

hurry [hûr'ē] *n* hâte *f*, précipitation *f* ♦ *vi* se

presser, se dépêcher ♦ *vt* (*person*) faire presser, faire se dépêcher; (*work*) presser; **to be in a** ~ être pressé(e); **to do sth in a** ~ faire qch en vitesse; **to** ~ **in/out** entrer/ sortir précipitamment; **to** ~ **home** se dépêcher de rentrer.
hurry along *vi* marcher d'un pas pressé.
hurry away, hurry off *vi* partir précipitamment.
hurry up *vi* se dépêcher.
hurt [hûrt] *vb* (*pt, pp* **hurt**) *vt* (*cause pain to*) faire mal à; (*injure, fig*) blesser; (*damage: business, interests etc*) nuire à, faire du tort à ♦ *vi* faire mal ♦ *a* blessé(e); **I** ~ **my arm** je me suis fait mal au bras; **where does it** ~? où avez-vous mal?, où est-ce que ça vous fait mal?
hurtful [hûrt'fəl] *a* (*remark*) blessant(e).
hurtle [hûr'təl] *vt* lancer (de toutes ses forces) ♦ *vi*: **to** ~ **past** passer en trombe; **to** ~ **down** dégringoler.
husband [huz'bənd] *n* mari *m*.
hush [hush] *n* calme *m*, silence *m* ♦ *vt* faire taire; ~**!** chut!
hush up *vt* (*fact*) étouffer.
hush-hush [hush'hush] *a* (*col*) ultra-secret(ète).
husk [husk] *n* (*of wheat*) balle *f*; (*of rice, maize*) enveloppe *f*; (*of peas*) cosse *f*.
husky [hus'kē] *a* rauque; (*burly*) costaud(e) ♦ *n* chien *m* esquimau *or* de traîneau.
hustings [hus'tingz] *npl* (*Brit POL*) plate-forme électorale.
hustle [hus'əl] *vt* pousser, bousculer ♦ *n* bousculade *f*; ~ **and bustle** *n* tourbillon *m* (d'activité).
hut [hut] *n* hutte *f*; (*shed*) cabane *f*.
hutch [huch] *n* clapier *m*.
hyacinth [hī'əsinth] *n* jacinthe *f*.
hybrid [hī'brid] *a, n* hybride (*m*).
hydrant [hī'drənt] *n* prise *f* d'eau; (*also*: **fire** ~) bouche *f* d'incendie.
hydraulic [hīdrô'lik] *a* hydraulique.
hydraulics [hīdrô'liks] *n* hydraulique *f*.
hydrochloric [hīdrəklôr'ik] *a*: ~ **acid** acide *m* chlorhydrique.
hydroelectric [hīdrōilek'trik] *a* hydro-électrique.
hydrofoil [hī'drəfoil] *n* hydrofoil *m*.
hydrogen [hī'drəjən] *n* hydrogène *m*.
hydrogen bomb *n* bombe *f* à hydrogène.
hydrophobia [hīdrəfō'bēə] *n* hydrophobie *f*.
hydroplane [hī'drəplān] *n* (*seaplane*) hydravion *m*; (*jetfoil*) hydroglisseur *m*.
hyena [hīē'nə] *n* hyène *f*.
hygiene [hī'jēn] *n* hygiène *f*.
hygienic [hījēen'ik] *a* hygiénique.
hymn [him] *n* hymne *m*; cantique *m*.
hype [hīp] *n* (*col*) matraquage *m* publicitaire *or* médiatique.
hyperactive [hīpûrak'tiv] *a* hyperactif(ive).
hypermarket [hī'pûrmârkit] *n* (*Brit*) hypermarché *m*.
hypertension [hīpûrten'chən] *n* (*MED*) hypertension *f*.
hyphen [hī'fən] *n* trait *m* d'union.
hypnosis [hipnō'sis] *n* hypnose *f*.
hypnotic [hipnât'ik] *a* hypnotique.
hypnotism [hip'nətizəm] *n* hypnotisme *m*.

hypnotist [hip'nətist] *n* hypnotiseur/euse.
hypnotize [hip'nətīz] *vt* hypnotiser.
hypoallergenic [hīpōalûrjen'ik] *a* hypoallergique.
hypochondriac [hīpəkân'drēak] *n* hypocondriaque *m/f*.
hypocrisy [hipâk'rəsē] *n* hypocrisie *f*.
hypocrite [hip'əkrit] *n* hypocrite *m/f*.
hypocritical [hipəkrit'ikəl] *a* hypocrite.
hypodermic [hīpədûr'mik] *a* hypodermique ♦ *n* (*syringe*) seringue *f* hypodermique.
hypothermia [hīpōthûr'mēə] *n* hypothermie *f*.
hypothesis, *pl* hypotheses [hīpâth'əsis, -sēz] *n* hypothèse *f*.
hypothetic(al) [hīpəthet'ik(əl)] *a* hypothétique.
hysterectomy [histərek'təmē] *n* hystérectomie *f*.
hysteria [histē'rēə] *n* hystérie *f*.
hysterical [histâr'ikəl] *a* hystérique; **to become** ~ avoir une crise de nerfs.
hysterics [histâr'iks] *npl* (*violente*) crise de nerfs; (*laughter*) crise de rire; **to have** ~ avoir une crise de nerfs; attraper un fou rire.
Hz *abbr* (= *hertz*) Hz.

I

I, i [ī] *n* (*letter*) I, i *m*; **I for Item** I comme Irma.
I [ī] *pronoun* je; (*before vowel*) j'; (*stressed*) moi ♦ *abbr* (= *island, isle*) I; (*US*) = **interstate (highway)**.
IA *abbr* (*US MAIL*) = *Iowa*.
IAEA *n abbr* = **International Atomic Energy Agency**.
IBA *n abbr* (*Brit*: = *Independent Broadcasting Authority*) ≈ CNCL *f* (= *Commission nationale de la communication audio-visuelle*).
Iberian [ībēr'ēən] *a* ibérique, ibérien(ne).
Iberian Peninsula *n*: **the** ~ la péninsule Ibérique.
IBEW *n abbr* (*US*: = *International Brotherhood of Electrical Workers*) syndicat international des électriciens.
i/c *abbr* (*Brit*) = **in charge**.
ICC *n abbr* (= *International Chamber of Commerce*) CCI *f*; (*US*) = *Interstate Commerce Commission*.
ice [īs] *n* glace *f*; (*on road*) verglas *m* ♦ *vt* (*cake*) glacer; (*drink*) faire rafraîchir ♦ *vi* (*also*: ~ **over**) geler; (*also*: ~ **up**) se givrer; **to put sth on** ~ (*fig*) mettre qch en attente.
Ice Age *n* ère *f* glaciaire.
ice ax (*Brit*) **ice axe** *n* piolet *m*.
iceberg [īs'bûrg] *n* iceberg *m*; **the tip of the** ~ (*also fig*) la partie émergée de l'iceberg.
icebox [īs'bâks] *n* (*US*) réfrigérateur *m*; (*Brit*) compartiment *m* à glace; (*insulated box*) glacière *f*.
icebreaker [īs'brākûr] *n* brise-glace *m*.
ice bucket *n* seau *m* à glace.
ice-cold [īs'kōld'] *a* glacé(e).

ice cream n glace f.

ice cube n glaçon m.

iced [īst] a (drink) frappé(e); (coffee, tea, also cake) glacé(e).

ice hockey n hockey m sur glace.

Iceland [īs'lənd] n Islande f.

Icelander [īs'landúr] n Islandais/e.

Icelandic [īslan'dik] a islandais(e) ♦ n (LING) islandais m.

ice lolly [īs lôl'ē] n (Brit) Esquimau m ®.

ice pick n pic m à glace.

ice rink n patinoire f.

ice-skate [īs'skāt] n patin m à glace ♦ vi faire du patin à glace.

ice-skating [īs'skāting] n patinage m (sur glace).

icicle [ī'sikəl] n glaçon m (naturel).

icing [ī'sing] n (AVIAT etc) givrage m; (CULIN) glaçage m.

icing sugar n (Brit) sucre m glace.

ICJ n abbr = International Court of Justice.

icon [ī'kân] n icône f.

ICR n abbr (US) = Institute for Cancer Research.

ICU n abbr = intensive care unit.

icy [ī'sē] a glacé(e); (road) verglacé(e); (weather, temperature) glacial(e).

ID abbr (US MAIL) = Idaho.

I'd [īd] = I would, I had.

Ida. abbr (US) = Idaho.

ID card n carte f d'identité.

idea [īdē'ə] n idée f; **good ~!** bonne idée!; **to have an ~ that ...** avoir idée que ...; **I haven't the least ~** je n'ai pas la moindre idée.

ideal [īdē'əl] n idéal m ♦ a idéal(e).

idealist [īdē'əlist] n idéaliste m/f.

ideally [īdē'əlē] ad idéalement, dans l'idéal; **~ the book should have ...** l'idéal serait que le livre ait ....

identical [īden'tikəl] a identique.

identification [īdentəfəkā'shən] n identification f; **means of ~** pièce f d'identité.

identify [īden'təfī] vt identifier ♦ vi: **to ~ with** s'identifier à.

Identikit [īden'təkit] n ® (Brit): **~ (picture)** portrait-robot m.

identity [īden'titē] n identité f.

identity card n (Brit) carte f d'identité.

identity parade n (Brit) parade f d'identification.

ideological [īdēəlâj'ikəl] a idéologique.

ideology [īdēâl'əjē] n idéologie f.

idiocy [id'ēəsē] n idiotie f, stupidité f.

idiom [id'ēəm] n langue f, idiome m; (phrase) expression f idiomatique.

idiomatic [idēəmat'ik] a idiomatique.

idiosyncrasy [idēəsing'krəsē] n particularité f, caractéristique f.

idiot [id'ēət] n idiot/e, imbécile m/f.

idiotic [idēāt'ik] a idiot(e), bête, stupide.

idle [ī'dəl] a sans occupation, désœuvré(e); (lazy) oisif(ive), paresseux(euse) (unemployed) au chômage; (machinery) au repos; (question, pleasures) vain(e), futile ♦ vi (engine) tourner au ralenti; **to lie ~** être arrêté, ne pas fonctionner.

   idle away vt: **to ~ away one's time** passer son temps à ne rien faire.

idleness [ī'dəlnis] n désœuvrement m; oisi-

veté f.

idler [īd'lûr] n désœuvré/e; oisif/ive.

idle time n (COMM) temps mort.

idol [ī'dəl] n idole f.

idolize [ī'dəlīz] vt idolâtrer, adorer.

idyllic [īdil'ik] a idyllique.

i.e. abbr (= id est: that is) c. à d., c'est-à-dire.

if [if] cj si ♦ n: **there are a lot of ~s and buts** il y a beaucoup de si mpl et de mais mpl; **I'd be pleased ~ you could do it** je serais très heureux si vous pouviez le faire; **~ necessary** si nécessaire, le cas échéant; **~ only he were here** si seulement il était là; **~ only to show him my gratitude** ne serait-ce que pour lui témoigner ma gratitude.

igloo [ig'lōō] n igloo m.

ignite [ignīt'] vt mettre le feu à, enflammer ♦ vi s'enflammer.

ignition [ignish'ən] n (AUT) allumage m; **to switch on/off the ~** mettre/couper le contact.

ignition key n (AUT) clé f de contact.

ignoble [ignō'bəl] a ignoble, indigne.

ignominious [ignəmin'ēəs] a honteux(euse), ignominieux(euse).

ignoramus [ignərā'məs] n personne f ignare.

ignorance [ig'nûrəns] n ignorance f; **to keep sb in ~ of sth** tenir qn dans l'ignorance de qch.

ignorant [ig'nûrənt] a ignorant(e); **to be ~ of** (subject) ne rien connaître en; (events) ne pas être au courant de.

ignore [ignôr'] vt ne tenir aucun compte de, ne pas relever; (person) faire semblant de ne pas reconnaître, ignorer; (fact) méconnaître.

ikon [ī'kân] n = **icon.**

IL abbr (US MAIL) = Illinois.

ILA n abbr (US: = International Longshoremen's Association) syndicat international des dockers.

ILGWU n abbr (US: = International Ladies' Garment Workers Union) syndicat des employés de l'habillement féminin.

Ill. abbr (US) = Illinois.

ill [il] a (sick) malade; (bad) mauvais(e) ♦ n mal m ♦ ad: **to speak/think ~ of sb** dire/penser du mal de qn; **to take or be taken ~** tomber malade.

I'll [īl] = I will, I shall.

ill-advised [il'ədvīzd'] a (decision) peu judicieux(euse); (person) malavisé(e).

ill-at-ease [il'ətēz'] a mal à l'aise.

ill-considered [il'kənsid'ûrd] a (plan) inconsidéré(e), irréfléchi(e).

ill-disposed [il'dispōzd'] a: **to be ~ towards sb/sth** être mal disposé(e) envers qn/qch.

illegal [ilē'gəl] a illégal(e).

illegally [ilē'gəlē] ad illégalement.

illegible [ilej'əbəl] a illisible.

illegitimate [ilijit'əmit] a illégitime.

ill-fated [il'fā'tid] a malheureux(euse); (day) néfaste.

ill-favored, (Brit) **ill-favoured** [il'fā'vûrd] a déplaisant(e).

ill feeling n (Brit) ressentiment m, rancune f.

ill-gotten [il'gât'ən] a (gains etc) mal acquis(e).

illicit [ilis'it] a illicite.

ill-informed [il'infôrmd'] a (judgment) erroné(e); (person) mal renseigné(e).

illiterate [ilit'ûrit] a illettré(e); (letter) plein(e) de fautes.

ill-mannered [il'man'ûrd] a impoli(e), grossier(ière).

illness [il'nis] n maladie f.

illogical [ilâj'ikəl] a illogique.

ill-suited [il'sōō'tid] a (couple) mal assorti(e); **he is ~ to the job** il n'est pas vraiment fait pour ce travail.

ill-timed [il'tīmd] a inopportun(e).

ill-treat [il'trēt] vt maltraiter.

ill-treatment [il'trēt'mənt] n mauvais traitement.

illuminate [ilōō'mənāt] vt (room, street) éclairer; (building) illuminer; **~d sign** n enseigne lumineuse.

illuminating [ilōō'mənāting] a éclairant(e).

illumination [ilōōmənā'shən] n éclairage m; illumination f.

illusion [ilōō'zhən] n illusion f; **to be under the ~ that** avoir l'illusion que.

illusive [ilōō'siv], **illusory** [ilōō'sərē] a illusoire.

illustrate [il'əstrāt] vt illustrer.

illustration [iləstrā'shən] n illustration f.

Illustrator [il'əstrātûr] n illustrateur/trice.

illustrious [ilus'trēəs] a illustre.

ill will n malveillance f.

ILO n abbr (= International Labour Organization) OIT f.

ILWU n abbr (US: = International Longshoremen's and Warehousemen's Union) syndicat international des dockers et des magaziniers.

I'm [īm] = **I am**.

image [im'ij] n image f; (public face) image de marque.

imagery [im'ijrē] n images fpl.

imaginable [imaj'ənəbəl] a imaginable.

imaginary [imaj'ənārē] a imaginaire.

imagination [imajanā'shən] n imagination f.

imaginative [imaj'ənətiv] a imaginatif(ive), plein(e) d'imagination.

imagine [imaj'in] vt s'imaginer; (suppose) imaginer, supposer.

imbalance [imbal'əns] n déséquilibre m.

imbecile [im'bəsil] n imbécile m/f.

imbue [imbyōō'] vt: **to ~ sth with** imprégner qch de.

IMF n abbr = **International Monetary Fund**.

imitate [im'ətāt] vt imiter.

imitation [imətā'shən] n imitation f.

imitator [im'ətātûr] n imitateur/trice.

immaculate [imak'yəlit] a impeccable; (REL) immaculé(e).

immaterial [imətē'rēəl] a sans importance, insignifiant(e).

immature [imətōōr'] a (fruit) qui n'est pas mûr(e); (person) qui manque de maturité.

immaturity [imətōō'ritē] n immaturité f.

immeasurable [imezh'ûrəbəl] a incommensurable.

immediacy [imē'dēəsē] n (of events etc) caractère or rapport immédiat; (of needs) urgence f.

immediate [imē'dēit] a immédiat(e).

immediately [imē'dēitlē] ad (at once) immédiatement; **~ next to** juste à côté de.

immense [imens'] a immense; énorme.

immensity [imen'sitē] n immensité f.

immerse [imûrs'] vt immerger, plonger; **to ~ sth in** plonger qch dans.

immersion heater [imûr'zhən hē'tûr] n chauffe-eau m électrique.

immigrant [im'əgrənt] n immigrant/e; (already established) immigré/e.

immigration [iməgrā'shən] n immigration f.

immigration authorities npl service m de l'immigration.

immigration laws npl lois fpl sur l'immigration.

imminent [im'ənənt] a imminent(e).

immobile [imō'bəl] a immobile.

immobilize [imō'bəlīz] vt immobiliser.

immoderate [imâd'ûrit] a immodéré(e), démesuré(e).

immodest [imâd'ist] a (indecent) indécent(e); (boasting) pas modeste, présomptueux(euse).

immoral [imôr'əl] a immoral(e).

immorality [iməral'itē] n immoralité f.

immortal [imôr'təl] a, n immortel(le).

immortalize [imôr'təlīz] vt immortaliser.

immovable [imōō'vəbəl] a (object) fixe; immobilier(ière); (person) inflexible; (opinion) immuable.

immune [imyōōn'] a: **~ (to)** immunisé(e) (contre).

immunity [imyōō'nitē] n immunité f; **diplomatic ~** immunité diplomatique.

immunization [imyōōnəzā'shən] n immunisation f.

immunize [im'yənīz] vt immuniser.

imp [imp] n (small devil) lutin m; (child) petit diable.

impact [im'pakt] n choc m, impact m; (fig) impact.

impair [impâr'] vt détériorer, diminuer.

impale [impāl'] vt empaler.

impart [impârt'] vt (make known) communiquer, transmettre; (bestow) confier, donner.

impartial [impâr'shəl] a impartial(e).

impartiality [impârshēal'itē] n impartialité f.

impassable [impas'əbəl] a infranchissable; (road) impraticable.

impasse [im'pas] n (fig) impasse f.

impassioned [impash'ənd] a passionné(e).

impassive [impas'iv] a impassible.

impatience [impā'shəns] n impatience f.

impatient [impā'shənt] a impatient(e); **to get or grow ~** s'impatienter.

impeach [impēch'] vt accuser, attaquer; (public official) mettre en accusation.

impeachment [impēch'mənt] n (LAW) (mise f en) accusation f.

impeccable [impek'əbəl] a impeccable, parfait(e).

impecunious [impəkyōō'nēəs] a sans ressources.

impede [impēd'] vt gêner.

impediment [imped'əmənt] n obstacle m; (also: speech ~) défaut m d'élocution.

impel [impel'] vt (force): **to ~ sb (to do sth)** forcer qn (à faire qch).

impending [impen'ding] a imminent(e).

impenetrable [impen'itrəbəl] a impénétrable.

imperative [impâr'ətiv] a nécessaire; urgent(e), pressant(e); (tone) impérieux(euse) ♦ n (LING) impératif m.

imperceptible [impûrsep'təbəl] a imperceptible.

imperfect [impûr'fĭkt] *a* imparfait(e); (*goods etc*) défectueux(euse) ♦ *n* (*LING*: *also*: ~ **tense**) imparfait *m*.

imperfection [impûrfɛk'shən] *n* imperfection *f*; défectuosité *f*.

imperial [impēr'ēəl] *a* impérial(e); (*Brit*: *measure*) légal(e).

imperialism [impēr'ēəlizəm] *n* impérialisme *m*.

imperil [impär'əl] *vt* mettre en péril.

imperious [impēr'ēəs] *a* impérieux(euse).

impersonal [impûr'sənəl] *a* impersonnel(le).

impersonate [impûr'sənāt] *vt* se faire passer pour; (*THEATER*) imiter.

impersonation [impûrsənā'shən] *n* (*LAW*) usurpation *f* d'identité; (*THEATER*) imitation *f*.

impersonator [impûr'sənâtûr] *n* imposteur *m*; (*THEATER*) imitateur/trice.

impertinence [impûr'tənəns] *n* impertinence *f*, insolence *f*.

impertinent [impûr'tənənt] *a* impertinent(e), insolent(e).

imperturbable [impûrtûr'bəbəl] *a* imperturbable.

impervious [impûr'vēəs] *a* imperméable; (*fig*): ~ **to** insensible à; inaccessible à.

impetuous [impech'ōōəs] *a* impétueux(euse), fougueux(euse).

impetus [im'pitəs] *n* impulsion *f*; (*of runner*) élan *m*.

impinge [impinj'] : **to** ~ **on** *vt fus* (*person*) affecter, toucher; (*rights*) empiéter sur.

impish [imp'ish] *a* espiègle.

implacable [implak'əbəl] *a* implacable.

implant [implant'] *vt* (*MED*) implanter; (*fig*) inculquer.

implausible [implô'zəbəl] *a* peu plausible.

implement *n* [im'pləmənt] outil *m*, instrument *m*; (*for cooking*) ustensile *m* ♦ *vt* [im'pləment] exécuter, mettre à effet.

implicate [im'plikāt] *vt* impliquer, compromettre.

implication [implikā'shən] *n* implication *f*; **by** ~ indirectement.

implicit [implis'it] *a* implicite; (*complete*) absolu(e), sans réserve.

implicitly [implis'itlē] *ad* implicitement; absolument, sans réserve.

implore [implôr'] *vt* implorer, supplier.

imply [implī'] *vt* (*hint*) suggérer, laisser entendre; (*mean*) indiquer, supposer.

impolite [impəlīt'] *a* impoli(e).

imponderable [impân'dûrəbəl] *a* impondérable.

import *vt* [impôrt'] importer ♦ *n* [im'pôrt] (*COMM*) importation *f*; (*meaning*) portée *f*, signification *f* ♦ *cpd* (*duty, license etc*) d'importation.

importance [impôr'təns] *n* importance *f*; **to be of great/little** ~ avoir beaucoup/peu d'importance.

important [impôr'tənt] *a* important(e); **it is** ~ **that** il importe que, il est important que; **it's not** ~ c'est sans importance, ce n'est pas important.

importantly [impôr'təntlē] *ad* (*with an air of importance*) d'un air important;

(*essentially*): **but, more** ~ ... mais, (ce qui est) plus important encore ....

importation [impôrtā'shən] *n* importation *f*.

imported [impôr'tid] *a* importé(e), d'importation.

importer [impôr'tûr] *n* importateur/trice.

impose [impōz'] *vt* imposer ♦ *vi*: **to** ~ **on sb** abuser de la gentillesse de qn.

imposing [impō'zing] *a* imposant(e), impressionnant(e).

imposition [impəzish'ən] *n* (*of tax etc*) imposition *f*; **to be an** ~ **on** (*person*) abuser de la gentillesse *or* la bonté de.

impossibility [impâsəbil'itē] *n* impossibilité *f*.

impossible [impâs'əbəl] *a* impossible; **it is** ~ **for me to leave** il m'est impossible de partir.

impostor [impâs'tûr] *n* imposteur *m*.

impotence [im'pətəns] *n* impuissance *f*.

impotent [im'pətənt] *a* impuissant(e).

impound [impound'] *vt* confisquer, saisir.

impoverished [impâv'ûrisht] *a* pauvre, appauvri(e).

impracticable [imprak'tikəbəl] *a* impraticable.

impractical [imprak'tikəl] *a* pas pratique; (*person*) qui manque d'esprit pratique.

imprecise [imprisīs'] *a* imprécis(e).

impregnable [impreg'nəbəl] *a* (*fortress*) imprenable; (*fig*) inattaquable; irréfutable.

impregnate [impreg'nāt] *vt* imprégner; (*fertilize*) féconder.

impresario [imprəsâ'rēō] *n* impresario *m*.

impress [impres'] *vt* impressionner, faire impression sur; (*mark*) imprimer, marquer; **to** ~ **sth on sb** faire bien comprendre qch à qn.

impression [impresh'ən] *n* impression *f*; (*of stamp, seal*) empreinte *f*; **to make a good/bad** ~ **on sb** faire bonne/mauvaise impression sur qn; **to be under the** ~ **that** avoir l'impression que.

impressionable [impresh'ənəbəl] *a* impressionnable, sensible.

impressionist [impresh'ənist] *n* impressionniste *m/f*.

impressive [impres'iv] *a* impressionnant(e).

imprint [im'print] *n* empreinte *f*; (*PUBLISHING*) notice *f*; (: *label*) nom *m* (de collection *or* d'éditeur).

imprinted [imprin'tid] *a*: ~ **on** imprimé(e) sur; (*fig*) imprimé(e) *or* gravé(e) dans.

imprison [impriz'ən] *vt* emprisonner, mettre en prison.

imprisonment [impriz'ənmənt] *n* emprisonnement *m*.

improbable [imprâb'əbəl] *a* improbable; (*excuse*) peu plausible.

impromptu [imprâmp'tōō] *a* impromptu(e) ♦ *ad* impromptu.

improper [imprâp'ûr] *a* (*wrong*) incorrect(e); (*unsuitable*) déplacé(e), de mauvais goût; indécent(e).

impropriety [imprəprī'ətē] *n* inconvenance *f*; (*of expression*) impropriété *f*.

improve [improōv'] *vt* améliorer ♦ *vi* s'améliorer; (*pupil etc*) faire des progrès.

improve (up)on *vt fus* (*offer*) enchérir sur.

improvement [improōv'mənt] *n* amélioration *f*; (*of pupil etc*) progrès *m*; **to make ~s to** apporter des améliorations à.

improvisation [imprəvəzā'shən] *n* improvisa-

tion *f.*
improvise [im'prəvīz] *vt, vi* improviser.
imprudence [improōd'əns] *n* imprudence *f.*
imprudent [improōd'ənt] *a* imprudent(e).
impudent [im'pyədənt] *a* impudent(e).
impugn [impyoōn'] *vt* contester, attaquer.
impulse [im'puls] *n* impulsion *f;* **on** ~ impulsivement, sur un coup de tête.
impulse buying [im'puls bī'ing] *n* achat *m* d'impulsion.
impulsive [impul'siv] *a* impulsif(ive).
impunity [impyoō'nitē] *n:* **with** ~ impunément.
impure [impyoōr'] *a* impur(e).
impurity [impyoōr'itē] *n* impureté *f.*
IN *abbr* (*US MAIL*) = *Indiana.*
in [in] *prep* dans; (*with time: during, within*): ~ **May/2 days** en mai/2 jours; (: *after*): ~ **2 weeks** dans 2 semaines; (*with substance*) en; (*with town*) à; (*with country*): **it's** ~ **France/Portugal** c'est en France/au Portugal ♦ *ad* dedans, à l'intérieur; (*fashionable*) à la mode; **is he** ~? est-il là?; ~ **the United States** aux États-Unis; ~ **1992** en 1992; ~ **spring/fall** au printemps/en automne; ~ **the morning** le matin; dans la matinée; ~ **the country** à la campagne; ~ **town** en ville; ~ **here/there** ici/là(-dedans); ~ **the sun** au soleil; ~ **the rain** sous la pluie; ~ **French** en français; ~ **writing** par écrit; ~ **pencil** au crayon; **to pay** ~ **dollars** payer en dollars; **a man** ~ **10** un homme sur 10; **once** ~ **a hundred years** une fois tous les cent ans; ~ **hundreds** par centaines; **the best pupil** ~ **the class** le meilleur élève de la classe; **to be** ~ **insurance/publishing** être dans l'assurance/l'édition; ~ **saying this** en disant ceci; **their party is** ~ leur parti est au pouvoir; **to ask sb** ~ inviter qn à entrer; **to run/limp** *etc* ~ entrer en courant/boitant *etc*; **the** ~**s and outs of** les tenants et aboutissants de.
in., ins *abbr* = **inch(es).**
inability [inəbil'ətē] *n* incapacité *f;* ~ **to pay** incapacité de payer.
inaccessible [inakses'əbəl] *a* inaccessible.
inaccuracy [inak'yûrəsē] *n* inexactitude *f;* manque *m* de précision.
inaccurate [inak'yûrit] *a* inexact(e); (*person*) qui manque de précision.
inaction [inak'shən] *n* inaction *f,* inactivité *f.*
inactivity [inaktiv'itē] *n* inactivité *f.*
inadequacy [inad'əkwəsē] *n* insuffisance *f.*
inadequate [inad'əkwit] *a* insuffisant(e), inadéquat(e).
inadmissible [inədmis'əbəl] *a* (*behavior*) inadmissible; (*LAW: evidence*) irrecevable.
inadvertent [inədvûr'tənt] *a* (*mistake*) commis(e) par inadvertance.
inadvertently [inədvûr'təntlē] *ad* par mégarde.
inadvisable [inədvī'zəbəl] *a* à déconseiller; **it is** ~ **to** il est déconseillé de.
inane [inān'] *a* inepte, stupide.
inanimate [inan'əmit] *a* inanimé(e).
inapplicable [inap'likəbəl] *a* inapplicable.
inappropriate [inəprō'prēit] *a* inopportun(e), mal à propos; (*word, expression*) impropre.
inapt [inapt'] *a* inapte; peu approprié(e).

inaptitude [inap'tətoōd] *n* inaptitude *f.*
inarticulate [inârtik'yəlit] *a* (*person*) qui s'exprime mal; (*speech*) indistinct(e).
inasmuch as [inəzmuch' az] *ad* dans la mesure où; (*seeing that*) attendu que.
inattention [inəten'chən] *n* manque *m* d'attention.
inattentive [inəten'tiv] *a* inattentif(ive), distrait(e);*r* négligent(e).
inaudible [inô'dəbəl] *a* inaudible.
inaugural [inô'gyûrəl] *a* inaugural(e).
inaugurate [inô'gyərāt] *vt* inaugurer; (*president, official*) investir de ses fonctions.
inauguration [inôgyərā'shən] *n* inauguration *f;* investiture *f.*
inauspicious [inôspish'əs] *a* peu propice.
in-between [in'bitwēn'] *a* entre les deux.
inborn [in'bôrn] *a* (*feeling*) inné(e); (*defect*) congénital(e).
inbred [in'bred] *a* inné(e), naturel(le); (*family*) consanguin(e).
inbreeding [in'brēding] *n* croisement *m* d'animaux de même souche; unions consanguines.
Inc. *abbr* = **incorporated.**
Inca [ing'kə] *a* (*also:* ~**n**) inca *inv* ♦ *n* Inca *m/ f.*
incalculable [inkal'kyələbəl] *a* incalculable.
incapability [inkāpəbil'ətē] *n* incapacité *f.*
incapable [inkā'pəbəl] *a:* ~ (**of**) incapable (de).
incapacitate [inkəpas'ətāt] *vt:* **to** ~ **sb from doing** rendre qn incapable de faire.
incapacitated [inkəpas'ətātid] *a* (*LAW*) frappé(e) d'incapacité.
incapacity [inkəpas'itē] *n* incapacité *f.*
incarcerate [inkâr'sûrit] *vt* incarcérer.
incarnate *a* [inkâr'nit] incarné(e) ♦ *vt* [inkâr'nāt] incarner.
incarnation [inkârnā'shən] *n* incarnation *f.*
incendiary [insen'dēārē] *a* incendiaire ♦ *n* (*bomb*) bombe *f* incendiaire.
incense *n* [in'sens] encens *m* ♦ *vt* [insens'] (*anger*) mettre en colère.
incense burner *n* encensoir *m.*
incentive [insen'tiv] *n* encouragement *m,* raison *f* de se donner de la peine.
incentive scheme *n* système *m* de primes d'encouragement.
inception [insep'shən] *n* commencement *m,* début *m.*
incessant [inses'ənt] *a* incessant(e).
incessantly [inses'əntlē] *ad* sans cesse, constamment.
incest [in'sest] *n* inceste *m.*
inch [inch] *n* pouce *m* (= *25 mm; 12 in a foot*); **within an** ~ **of** à deux doigts de; **he wouldn't give an** ~ (*fig*) il n'a pas voulu céder d'un pouce *or* faire la plus petite concession.
inch forward *vi* avancer petit à petit.
incidence [in'sidəns] *n* (*of crime, disease*) fréquence *f.*
incident [in'sidənt] *n* incident *m;* (*in book*) péripétie *f.*
incidental [insiden'təl] *a* accessoire; (*unplanned*) accidentel(le); ~ **to** qui accompagne; ~ **expenses** faux frais *mpl.*
incidentally [insiden'təlē] *ad* (*by the way*) à propos.

incidental music *n* musique *f* de fond.
incinerate [insin'ərāt] *vt* incinérer.
incinerator [insin'ərātûr] *n* incinérateur *m*.
incipient [insip'ēənt] *a* naissant(e).
incision [insizh'ən] *n* incision *f*.
incisive [insī'siv] *a* incisif(ive); mordant(e).
incisor [insī'zúr] *n* incisive *f*.
incite [insīt'] *vt* inciter, pousser.
incl. *abbr* = **including, inclusive (of)**.
inclement [inklem'ənt] *a* inclément(e), rigoureux(euse).
inclination [inklənā'shən] *n* inclination *f*.
incline *n* [in'klīn] pente *f*, plan incliné ♦ *vb* [inklīn'] *vt* incliner ♦ *vi*: **to ~ to** avoir tendance à; **to be ~d to do** être enclin(e) à faire; (*have a tendency to do*) avoir tendance à faire; **to be well ~d towards sb** être bien disposé(e) à l'égard de qn.
include [inklōōd'] *vt* inclure, comprendre; **the tip is/is not ~d** le service est compris/n'est pas compris.
including [inklōōd'ing] *prep* y compris; **~ tip** service compris.
inclusion [inklōō'zhən] *n* inclusion *f*.
inclusive [inklōō'siv] *a* inclus(e), compris(e); **$50 ~ of all surcharges** 50 dollars tous frais compris.
inclusive terms *npl* (*Brit*) prix tout compris.
incognito [inkägnē'tō] *ad* incognito.
incoherent [inkōhē'rənt] *a* incohérent(e).
income [in'kum] *n* revenu *m*; **gross/net ~** revenu brut/net; **~ and expenditure account** compte *m* de recettes et de dépenses.
income tax *n* impôt *m* sur le revenu.
income tax auditor, (*Brit*) **income tax inspector** *n* inspecteur *m* des contributions directes.
income tax return *n* déclaration *f* des revenus.
incoming [in'kuming] *a* (*passengers, mail*) à l'arrivée; (*government, tenant*) nouveau(nouvelle); **~ tide** marée montante.
incommunicado [inkəmyōōnəkä'dō] *a*: **to hold sb ~** tenir qn au secret.
incomparable [inkâm'pûrəbəl] *a* incomparable.
incompatible [inkəmpat'əbəl] *a* incompatible.
incompetence [inkâm'pitəns] *n* incompétence *f*, incapacité *f*.
incompetent [inkâm'pitənt] *a* incompétent(e), incapable.
incomplete [inkəmplēt'] *a* incomplet(ète).
incomprehensible [inkâmprihen'səbəl] *a* incompréhensible.
inconceivable [inkənsē'vəbəl] *a* inconcevable.
inconclusive [inkənklōō'siv] *a* peu concluant(e); (*argument*) peu convaincant(e).
incongruous [inkâng'grōōəs] *a* peu approprié(e); (*remark, act*) incongru(e), déplacé(e).
inconsequential [inkânsəkwen'chəl] *a* sans importance.
inconsiderable [inkənsid'ûrəbəl] *a*: **not ~** non négligeable.
inconsiderate [inkənsid'ûrit] *a* (*action*) inconsidéré(e); (*person*) qui manque d'égards.
inconsistency [inkənsis'tənsē] *n* (*of actions etc*) inconséquence *f*; (*of work*) irrégularité

f; (*of statement etc*) incohérence *f*.
inconsistent [inkənsis'tənt] *a* inconséquent(e); irregulier(ière); peu cohérent(e); **~ with** en contradiction avec.
inconsolable [inkənsō'ləbəl] *a* inconsolable.
inconspicuous [inkənspik'yōōəs] *a* qui passe inaperçu(e); (*color, dress*) discret(ète); **to make o.s. ~** ne pas se faire remarquer.
inconstant [inkân'stənt] *a* inconstant(e); variable.
incontinence [inkân'tənəns] *n* incontinence *f*.
incontinent [inkân'tənənt] *a* incontinent(e).
incontrovertible [inkântrəvûr'təbəl] *a* irréfutable.
inconvenience [inkənvēn'yəns] *n* inconvénient *m*; (*trouble*) dérangement *m* ♦ *vt* déranger; **don't ~ yourself** ne vous dérangez pas.
inconvenient [inkənvēn'yənt] *a* malcommode; (*time, place*) mal choisi(e), qui ne convient pas; **that time is very ~ for me** c'est un moment qui ne me convient pas du tout.
incorporate [inkôr'pûrāt] *vt* incorporer; (*contain*) contenir ♦ *vi* fusionner; (*two firms*) se constituer en société.
incorporated [inkôr'pərātid] *a*: **~ company** (*US: abbr* **Inc.**) ≈ société *f* anonyme (S.A.).
incorrect [inkərekt'] *a* incorrect(e); (*opinion, statement*) inexact(e).
incorrigible [inkôr'ijəbəl] *a* incorrigible.
incorruptible [inkərup'təbəl] *a* incorruptible.
increase *n* [in'krēs] augmentation *f* ♦ *vi, vt* [inkrēs'] augmenter; **an ~ of 5%** une augmentation de 5%; **to be on the ~** être en augmentation.
increasing [inkrēs'ing] *a* croissant(e).
increasingly [inkrēs'inglē] *ad* de plus en plus.
incredible [inkred'əbəl] *a* incroyable.
incredulous [inkrej'ələs] *a* incrédule.
increment [in'krəmənt] *n* augmentation *f*.
incriminate [inkrim'ənāt] *vt* incriminer, compromettre.
incriminating [inkrim'ənāting] *a* compromettant(e).
incrust [inkrust'] *vt* = **encrust**.
incubate [in'kyəbāt] *vt* (*egg*) couver, incuber ♦ *vi* (*eggs*) couver; (*disease*) couver.
incubation [inkyəbā'shən] *n* incubation *f*.
incubation period *n* période *f* d'incubation.
incubator [in'kyəbātûr] *n* incubateur *m*; (*for babies*) couveuse *f*.
inculcate [in'kulkāt] *vt*: **to ~ sth in sb** inculquer qch à qn.
incumbent [inkum'bənt] *a*: **it is ~ on him to ...** il lui incombe *or* appartient de ... ♦ *n* titulaire *m/f*.
incur [inkûr'] *vt* (*expenses*) encourir; (*anger, risk*) s'exposer à; (*debt*) contracter; (*loss*) subir.
incurable [inkyōōr'əbəl] *a* incurable.
incursion [inkûr'zhən] *n* incursion *f*.
Ind. *abbr* (*US*) = *Indiana*.
indebted [indet'id] *a*: **to be ~ to sb (for)** être redevable à qn (de).
indecency [indē'sənsē] *n* indécence *f*.
indecent [indē'sənt] *a* indécent(e), inconvenant(e).
indecent assault *n* (*Brit*) attentat *m* à la pudeur.
indecent exposure *n* outrage *m* public à la

pudeur.
indecipherable [indisī'fûrəbəl] *a* indéchiffrable.
indecision [indisizh'ən] *n* indécision *f*.
indecisive [indisī'siv] *a* indécis(e); (*discussion*) peu concluant(e).
indeed [indēd'] *ad* en effet, effectivement; (*furthermore*) d'ailleurs; **yes ~!** certainement!
indefatigable [indifat'əgəbəl] *a* infatigable.
indefensible [indifen'səbəl] *a* (*conduct*) indéfendable.
indefinable [indifī'nəbəl] *a* indéfinissable.
indefinite [indef'ənit] *a* indéfini(e); (*answer*) vague; (*period, number*) indéterminé(e).
indefinitely [indef'ənitlē] *ad* (*wait*) indéfiniment; (*speak*) vaguement, avec imprécision.
indelible [indel'əbəl] *a* indélébile.
indelicate [indel'əkit] *a* (*tactless*) indélicat(e), grossier(ière); (*not polite*) inconvenant(e), malséant(e).
indemnify [indem'nəfī] *vt* indemniser, dédommager.
indemnity [indem'nitē] *n* (*insurance*) assurance *f*, garantie *f*; (*compensation*) indemnité *f*.
indent [indent'] *vt* (*text*) commencer en retrait.
indentation [indentā'shən] *n* découpure *f*; (*TYP*) alinéa *m*; (*on metal*) bosse *f*.
independence [indipen'dəns] *n* indépendance *f*.
independent [indipen'dənt] *a* indépendant(e); **to become ~** s'affranchir.
independently [indipen'dəntlē] *ad* de façon indépendante; **~ of** indépendamment de.
indescribable [indiskrī'bəbəl] *a* indescriptible.
indeterminate [inditûr'mənit] *a* indéterminé(e).
index [in'deks] *n* (*pl*: **~es**: *in book*) index *m*; (*: in library etc*) catalogue *m*; (*pl*: **indices** [in'dīsēz]) (*ratio, sign*) indice *m*.
index card *n* fiche *f*.
indexed [in'dekst] *a* (*US*) indexé(e) (sur le coût de la vie *etc*).
index finger *n* index *m*.
index-linked [in'dekslingkt'] *a* (*Brit*) = **indexed**.
India [in'dēə] *n* Inde *f*.
Indian [in'dēən] *a* indien(ne) ♦ *n* Indien/ne.
Indian ink *n* encre *f* de Chine.
Indian Ocean *n*: **the ~** l'océan Indien.
Indian summer *n* (*fig*) été indien, beaux jours en automne.
India paper *n* papier *m* bible.
indicate [in'dikāt] *vt* indiquer ♦ *vi* (*Brit AUT*): **to ~ left/right** mettre son clignotant à gauche/à droite.
indication [indikā'shən] *n* indication *f*, signe *m*.
indicative [indik'ətiv] *a* indicatif(ive) ♦ *n* (*LING*) indicatif *m*; **to be ~ of sth** être symptomatique de qch.
indicator [in'dikātûr] *n* (*sign*) indicateur *m*; (*Brit AUT*) clignotant *m*.
indices [in'dīsēz] *npl of* **index**.
indict [indīt'] *vt* accuser.
indictable [indīt'əbəl] *a* (*person*) passible de poursuites; **~ offense** délit *m* tombant sous

le coup de la loi.
indictment [indīt'mənt] *n* accusation *f*.
indifference [indif'ûrəns] *n* indifférence *f*.
indifferent [indif'ûrənt] *a* indifférent(e); (*poor*) médiocre, quelconque.
indigenous [indij'ənəs] *a* indigène.
indigestible [indijes'təbəl] *a* indigeste.
indigestion [indijes'chən] *n* indigestion *f*, mauvaise digestion.
indignant [indig'nənt] *a*: **~ (at sth/with sb)** indigné(e) (de qch/contre qn).
indignation [indignā'shən] *n* indignation *f*.
indignity [indig'nitē] *n* indignité *f*, affront *m*.
indigo [in'dəgō] *a* indigo *inv* ♦ *n* indigo *m*.
indirect [indirekt'] *a* indirect(e).
indirectly [indirekt'lē] *ad* indirectement.
indiscreet [indiskrēt'] *a* indiscret(ète); (*rash*) imprudent(e).
indiscretion [indiskresh'ən] *n* (*see indiscreet*) indiscrétion *f*; imprudence *f*.
indiscriminate [indiskrim'ənit] *a* (*person*) qui manque de discernement; (*admiration*) aveugle; (*killings*) commis(e) au hasard.
indispensable [indispen'səbəl] *a* indispensable.
indisposed [indispōzd'] *a* (*unwell*) indisposé(e), souffrant(e).
indisposition [indispəzish'ən] *n* (*illness*) indisposition *f*, malaise *m*.
indisputable [indispyōō'təbəl] *a* incontestable, indiscutable.
indistinct [indistingkt'] *a* indistinct(e); (*memory, noise*) vague.
indistinguishable [indisting'gwishəbəl] *a* impossible à distinguer.
individual [indəvij'ōōəl] *n* individu *m* ♦ *a* individuel(le); (*characteristic*) particulier(ière), original(e).
individualist [indəvij'ōōəlist] *n* individualiste *m/f*.
individuality [indəvijōōal'itē] *n* individualité *f*.
individually [indəvij'ōōəlē] *ad* individuellement.
indivisible [indəviz'əbəl] *a* indivisible; (*MATH*) insécable.
Indo-China [in'dōchī'nə] *n* Indochine *f*.
indoctrinate [indâk'trənāt] *vt* endoctriner.
indoctrination [indâktrənā'shən] *n* endoctrinement *m*.
indolent [in'dələnt] *a* indolent(e), nonchalant(e).
Indonesia [indənē'zhə] *n* Indonésie *f*.
Indonesian [indənē'zhən] *a* indonésien(ne) ♦ *n* Indonésien/ne.
indoor [in'dôr] *a* d'intérieur; (*plant*) d'appartement; (*swimming pool*) couvert(e); (*sport, games*) pratiqué(e) en salle.
indoors [indôrz'] *ad* à l'intérieur; (*at home*) à la maison.
indubitable [indōō'bitəbəl] *a* indubitable, incontestable.
induce [indōōs'] *vt* persuader; (*bring about*) provoquer; **to ~ sb to do sth** inciter *or* pousser qn à faire qch.
inducement [indōōs'mənt] *n* incitation *f*; (*incentive*) but *m*; (*pej: bribe*) pot-de-vin *m*.
induct [indukt'] *vt* établir dans ses fonctions; (*fig*) initier.
induction [induk'shən] *n* (*MED: of birth*)

accouchement provoqué.

induction course n (*Brit*) stage m de mise au courant.

indulge [indulj'] vt (*whim*) céder à, satisfaire; (*child*) gâter ♦ vi: **to ~ in sth** s'offrir qch, se permettre qch; **se livrer à** qch.

indulgence [indul'jəns] n fantaisie f (que l'on s'offre); (*leniency*) indulgence f.

indulgent [indul'jənt] a indulgent(e).

industrial [indus'trēəl] a industriel(le); (*injury*) du travail; (*dispute*) ouvrier(ière).

industrial action n (*Brit*) action revendicative.

industrial estate n (*Brit*) zone industrielle.

industrialist [indus'trēəlist] n industriel m.

industrialize [indus'trēəlīz] vt industrialiser.

industrial park n (*US*) zone industrielle.

industrial relations npl relations fpl dans l'entreprise.

industrial tribunal n (*Brit*) ≈ conseil m de prud'hommes.

industrial unrest n (*Brit*) agitation sociale, conflits sociaux.

industrious [indus'trēəs] a travailleur(euse).

industry [in'dəstrē] n industrie f; (*diligence*) zèle m, application f.

inebriated [inēb'rēātid] a ivre.

inedible [ined'əbəl] a immangeable; (*plant etc*) non comestible.

ineffective [inifek'tiv], **ineffectual** [inefek'chooəl] a inefficace; incompétent(e).

inefficiency [inifish'ənsē] n inefficacité f.

inefficient [inifish'ənt] a inefficace.

inelegant [inel'əgənt] a peu élégant(e), inélégant(e).

ineligible [inel'ijəbəl] a (*candidate*) inéligible; **to be ~ for sth** ne pas avoir droit à qch.

inept [inept'] a inepte.

ineptitude [inep'tətōōd] n ineptie f.

inequality [inikwâl'itē] n inégalité f.

inequitable [inek'witəbəl] a inéquitable, inique.

ineradicable [inirad'ikəbəl] a indéracinable, tenace.

inert [inûrt'] a inerte.

inertia [inûr'shə] n inertie f.

inertia-reel seat belt [inûr'shərēl sēt' belt] n ceinture f de sécurité à enrouleur.

inescapable [inəskā'pəbəl] a inéluctable, inévitable.

inessential [inisen'chəl] a superflu(e).

inestimable [ines'təməbəl] a inestimable, incalculable.

inevitable [inev'itəbəl] a inévitable.

inevitably [inev'itəblē] ad inévitablement, fatalement.

inexact [in'igzakt'] a inexact(e).

inexcusable [inikskyōō'zəbəl] a inexcusable.

inexhaustible [inigzôs'təbəl] a inépuisable.

inexorable [inek'sûrəbəl] a inexorable.

inexpensive [inikspen'siv] a bon marché inv.

inexperience [inikspēr'ēəns] n inexpérience f, manque m d'expérience.

inexperienced [inikspēr'ēənst] a inexpérimenté(e); **to be ~ in sth** manquer d'expérience dans qch.

inexplicable [ineks'plikəbəl] a inexplicable.

inexpressible [inikspres'əbəl] a inexprimable; indicible.

inextricable [ineks'trikəbəl] a inextricable.

infallibility [infaləbil'ətē] n infaillibilité f.

infallible [infal'əbəl] a infaillible.

infamous [in'fəməs] a infâme, abominable.

infamy [in'fəmē] n infamie f.

infancy [in'fənsē] n petite enfance, bas âge; (*fig*) enfance, débuts mpl.

infant [in'fənt] n (*baby*) nourrisson m; (*young child*) petit(e) enfant.

infantile [in'fəntīl] a infantile.

infant mortality n mortalité f infantile.

infantry [in'fəntrē] n infanterie f.

infantryman [in'fəntrēmən] n fantassin m.

infant school n (*Brit*) classes fpl préparatoires (*entre 5 et 7 ans*).

infatuated [infach'ōōātid] a: **~ with** entiché(e) de; **to become ~ (with sb)** s'enticher (de qn).

infatuation [infachōōā'shən] n toquade f; engouement m.

infect [infekt'] vt infecter, contaminer; (*fig: pej*) corrompre; **~ed with** (*illness*) atteint(e) de; **to become ~ed** (*wound*) s'infecter.

infection [infek'shən] n infection f; contagion f.

infectious [infek'shəs] a infectieux(euse); (*also fig*) contagieux(euse).

infer [infûr'] vt: **to ~ (from)** conclure (de), déduire (de).

inference [in'fûrəns] n conclusion f, déduction f.

inferior [infē'rēûr] a inférieur(e); (*goods*) de qualité inférieure ♦ n inférieur/e; (*in rank*) subalterne m/f; **to feel ~** avoir un sentiment d'infériorité.

inferiority [infērēôr'itē] n infériorité f.

inferiority complex n complexe m d'infériorité.

infernal [infûr'nəl] a infernal(e).

infernally [infûr'nəlē] ad abominablement.

inferno [infûr'nō] n enfer m; brasier m.

infertile [infûr'təl] a stérile.

infertility [infûrtil'ətē] n infertilité f, stérilité f.

infested [infes'tid] a: **~ (with)** infesté(e) (de).

infidelity [infidel'itē] n infidélité f.

infighting [in'fīting] n querelles fpl internes.

infiltrate [infil'trāt] vt (*troops etc*) faire s'infiltrer; (*enemy line etc*) s'infiltrer dans ♦ vi s'infiltrer.

infinite [in'fənit] a infini(e); (*time, money*) illimité(e).

infinitely [in'fənitlē] ad infiniment.

infinitesimal [infinites'əməl] a infinitésimal(e).

infinitive [infin'ətiv] n infinitif m.

infinity [infin'ətē] n infinité f; (*also* MATH) infini m.

infirm [infûrm'] a infirme.

infirmary [infûr'mûrē] n hôpital m; (*in school, factory*) infirmerie f.

infirmity [infûr'mitē] n infirmité f.

inflamed [inflāmd'] a enflammé(e).

inflammable [inflam'əbəl] a inflammable.

inflammation [infləmā'shən] n inflammation f.

inflammatory [inflam'ətôrē] a (*speech*) incendiaire.

inflatable [inflā'təbəl] a gonflable.

inflate [inflāt'] vt (*tire, balloon*) gonfler; (*fig*) grossir; gonfler; faire monter.

inflated [inflā'tid] a (*style*) enflé(e); (*value*)

exagéré(e).

inflation [inflā'shən] n (ECON) inflation f.

inflationary [inflā'shənārē] a inflationniste.

inflection [inflek'shən] n inflexion f; (ending) désinence f.

inflexible [inflek'səbəl] a inflexible, rigide.

inflict [inflikt'] vt: **to ~ on** infliger à.

infliction [inflik'shən] n infliction f; affliction f.

in-flight [in'flīt] a (refuelling) en vol; (service etc) à bord.

inflow [in'flō] n afflux m.

influence [in'flooəns] n influence f ♦ vt influencer; **under the ~ of** sous l'effet de; **under the ~ of drink** en état d'ébriété.

influential [inflooen'chəl] a influent(e).

influenza [inflooen'zə] n grippe f.

influx [in'fluks] n afflux m.

inform [infôrm'] vt: **to ~ sb (of)** informer or avertir qn (de) ♦ vi: **to ~ on sb** dénoncer qn, informer contre qn; **to ~ sb about** renseigner qn sur, mettre qn au courant de.

informal [infôr'məl] a (person, manner) simple, sans cérémonie; (announcement, visit) non officiel(le); **"dress ~"** "tenue de ville".

informality [informal'itē] n simplicité f, absence f de cérémonie; caractère non officiel.

informal language n langage m de la conversation.

informally [infôr'məlē] ad sans cérémonie, en toute simplicité; non officiellement.

informant [intôr'mənt] n informateur/trice.

information [infurmā'shən] n information(s) f(pl); renseignements mpl; (knowledge) connaissances fpl; **to get ~ on** se renseigner sur; **a piece of ~** un renseignement; **for your ~** à titre d'information.

information bureau n bureau m de renseignements.

information desk n guichet m de renseignements.

information processing n traitement m de l'information.

information retrieval n recherche f (informatique) de renseignements.

information technology (IT) n informatique f.

informative [infôr'mətiv] a instructif(ive).

informed [infôrmd'] a (bien) informé(e); **an ~ guess** une hypothèse fondée sur la connaissance des faits.

informer [infôr'mûr] n dénonciateur/trice; (also: **police ~**) indicateur/trice.

infra dig [in'frə dig] a abbr (col: = infra dignitatem) au-dessous de ma (or sa etc) dignité.

infra-red [in'frəred'] a infrarouge.

infrastructure [in'frəstruk'chûr] n infrastructure f.

infrequent [infrē'kwint] a peu fréquent(e), rare.

infringe [infrinj'] vt enfreindre ♦ vi: **to ~ on** empiéter sur.

infringement [infrinj'mənt] n: **~ (of)** infraction f (à).

infuriate [infyoor'ēāt] vt mettre en fureur.

infuriating [infyoor'ēāting] a exaspérant(e).

infuse [infyooz'] vt: **to ~ sb with sth** (fig) insuffler qch à qn.

infusion [infyoo'zhən] n (tea etc) infusion f.

ingenious [injēn'yəs] a ingénieux(euse).

ingenuity [injənoo'itē] n ingéniosité f.

ingenuous [injen'yooəs] a franc(franche), ouvert(e).

ingot [ing'gət] n lingot m.

ingrained [ingrānd'] a enraciné(e).

ingratiate [ingrā'shēāt] vt: **to ~ o.s. with** s'insinuer dans les bonnes grâces de, se faire bien voir de.

ingratiating [ingrā'shēāting] a (smile, speech) insinuant(e); (person) patelin(e).

ingratitude [ingrat'ətood] n ingratitude f.

ingredient [ingrē'dēənt] n ingrédient m; élément m.

ingrowing [in'grōing], **ingrown** [in'grōn] a: **~ toenail** ongle incarné.

inhabit [inhab'it] vt habiter.

inhabitable [inhab'itəbəl] a habitable.

inhabitant [inhab'ətənt] n habitant/e.

inhale [inhāl'] vt inhaler; (perfume) respirer ♦ vi (in smoking) avaler la fumée.

inherent [inhār'ent] a: **~ (in or to)** inhérent(e) (à).

inherently [inhār'entlē] ad (easy, difficult) en soi; (lazy) fondamentalement.

inherit [inhār'it] vt hériter (de).

inheritance [inhār'itəns] n héritage m; **law of ~** droit m de la succession.

inheritance tax n droits mpl de succession.

inhibit [inhib'it] vt (PSYCH) inhiber; **to ~ sb from doing** empêcher or retenir qn de faire.

inhibited [inhib'itid] a (person) inhibé(e).

inhibiting [inhib'iting] a gênant(e).

inhibition [inibish'ən] n inhibition f.

inhospitable [inhäspit'əbəl] a inhospitalier(lère).

inhuman [inhyoo'mən] a inhumain(e).

inhumane [inhyoomān'] a inhumain(e).

inimitable [inim'itəbəl] a inimitable.

iniquity [inik'witē] n iniquité f.

initial [inish'əl] a initial(e) ♦ n initiale f ♦ vt parafer; **~s** npl initiales fpl; (as signature) parafe m.

initialize [inish'əlīz] vt (COMPUT) initialiser.

initially [inish'əlē] ad initialement, au début.

initiate [inish'ēāt] vt (start) entreprendre; amorcer; lancer; (person) initier; **to ~ sb into a secret** initier qn à un secret; **to ~ proceedings against sb** (LAW) intenter une action à qn, engager des poursuites contre qn.

initiation [inishēā'shən] n (into secret etc) initiation f.

initiative [inish'ēətiv] n initiative f; **to take the ~** prendre l'initiative.

inject [injekt'] vt (liquid, fig: money) injecter; (person) faire une piqûre à.

injection [injek'shən] n injection f, piqûre f; **to have an ~** se faire faire une piqûre.

injudicious [injōōdish'əs] a peu judicieux(euse).

injunction [injungk'shən] n (LAW) injonction f, ordre m.

injure [in'jûr] vt blesser; (wrong) faire du tort à; (damage: reputation etc) compromettre; (feelings) heurter; **to ~ o.s.** se blesser.

injured [in'jûrd] a (person, leg etc) blessé(e); (tone, feelings) offensé(e); **~ party** (LAW)

injurious 158 insight

partie lésée.

injurious [injōōr'ēəs] *a*: ~ **(to)** préjudiciable (à).

injury [in'jûrē] *n* blessure *f*; (*wrong*) tort *m*; **to escape without** ~ s'en sortir sain et sauf.

injury time *n* (*SPORT*) arrêts *mpl* de jeu.

injustice [injus'tis] *n* injustice *f*; **you do me an** ~ vous êtes injuste envers moi.

ink [ingk] *n* encre *f*.

ink-jet printer [ingk'jet prin'tûr] *n* imprimante *f* à jet d'encre.

inkling [ingk'ling] *n* soupçon *m*, vague idée *f*.

inkpad [ingk'pad] *n* tampon *m* encreur.

inky [ing'kē] *a* taché(e) d'encre.

inlaid [in'lād] *a* incrusté(e); (*table etc*) marqueté(e).

inland [in'land] *a* intérieur(e) ♦ *ad* à l'intérieur, dans les terres; ~ **waterways** canaux *mpl* et rivières *fpl*.

Inland Revenue *n* (*Brit*) fisc *m*.

in-laws [in'lôz] *npl* beaux-parents *mpl*; belle famille.

inlet [in'let] *n* (*GEO*) crique *f*.

inlet pipe *n* (*TECH*) tuyau *m* d'arrivée.

inmate [in'māt] *n* (*in prison*) détenu/e; (*in asylum*) interné/e.

inmost [in'mōst] *a* le(la) plus profond(e).

inn [in] *n* auberge *f*.

innards [in'ûrdz] *npl* (*col*) entrailles *fpl*.

innate [ināt'] *a* inné(e).

inner [in'ûr] *a* intérieur(e).

inner city *n* (vieux quartiers du) centre urbain (*souffrant souvent de délabrement, d'embouteillages etc*).

innermost [in'ûrmōst] *a* le(la) plus profond(e).

inner tube *n* (*of tire*) chambre *f* à air.

innings [in'ingz] *n* (*SPORT*) tour *m* de batte.

innocence [in'əsəns] *n* innocence *f*.

innocent [in'əsənt] *a* innocent(e).

innocuous [inäk'yōōəs] *a* inoffensif(ive).

innovation [inəvā'shən] *n* innovation *f*.

innuendo, ~es [inyōōen'dō] *n* insinuation *f*, allusion (malveillante).

Innuit [in'ōōwit] *a* esquimau(de), eskimo ♦ *n* Esquimau/de.

innumerable [inōō'mûrəbəl] *a* innombrable.

inoculate [inäk'yəlāt] *vt*: **to** ~ **sb with sth** inoculer qch à qn; **to** ~ **sb against sth** vacciner qn contre qch.

inoculation [inâkyəlā'shən] *n* inoculation *f*.

inoffensive [inəfen'siv] *a* inoffensif(ive).

inopportune [inâpûrtōōn'] *a* inopportun(e).

inordinate [inôr'dənit] *a* démesuré(e).

inordinately [inôr'dənitlē] *ad* démesurément.

inorganic [inôrgan'ik] *a* inorganique.

inpatient [in'pāshənt] *n* malade hospitalisé(e).

input [in'pŏŏt] *n* (*ELEC*) énergie *f*, puissance *f*; (*of machine*) consommation *f*; (*of computer*) information fournie ♦ *vt* (*COMPUT*) introduire, entrer.

inquest [in'kwest] *n* enquête (criminelle).

inquire [inkwīûr'] *vi* demander ♦ *vt* demander, s'informer de; **to** ~ **about** s'informer de, se renseigner sur; **to** ~ **when/where/whether** demander quand/où/si.

inquire after *vt fus* demander des nouvelles de.

inquire into *vt fus* faire une enquête sur.

inquiring [inkwīûr'ing] *a* (*mind*) curieux(euse), investigateur(trice).

inquiry [inkwīûr'ē] *n* demande *f* de renseignements; (*LAW*) enquête *f*, investigation *f*; **to hold an** ~ **into sth** enquêter sur qch.

inquiry desk *n* (*Brit*) guichet *m* de renseignements.

inquiry office *n* (*Brit*) bureau *m* de renseignements.

inquisition [inkwizish'ən] *n* enquête *f*, investigation *f*; (*REL*): **the l~** l'Inquisition *f*.

inquisitive [inkwiz'ətiv] *a* curieux(euse).

inroads [in'rōdz] *npl*: **to make** ~ **into** (*savings, supplies*) entamer.

insane [insān'] *a* fou(folle); (*MED*) aliéné(e).

insanitary [insan'itärē] *a* insalubre.

insanity [insan'itē] *n* folie *f*; (*MED*) aliénation (mentale).

insatiable [insā'shəbəl] *a* insatiable.

inscribe [inskrīb'] *vt* inscrire; (*book etc*): **to** ~ **(to sb)** dédicacer (à qn).

inscription [inskrip'shən] *n* inscription *f*; (*in book*) dédicace *f*.

inscrutable [inskrōō'təbəl] *a* impénétrable.

inseam [in'sēm] *n* (*US*): ~ **measurement** hauteur *f* d'entre-jambe.

insect [in'sekt] *n* insecte *m*.

insect bite *n* piqûre *f* d'insecte.

insecticide [insek'tisīd] *n* insecticide *m*.

insect repellent *n* crème *f* anti-insectes.

insecure [insikyōōr'] *a* peu solide; peu sûr(e); (*person*) anxieux(euse).

insecurity [insikyōōr'itē] *n* insécurité *f*.

insensible [insen'səbəl] *a* insensible; (*unconscious*) sans connaissance.

insensitive [insen'sətiv] *a* insensible.

insensitivity [insensətiv'itē] *n* insensibilité *f*.

inseparable [insep'ûrəbəl] *a* inséparable.

insert *vt* [insûrt'] insérer ♦ *n* [in'sûrt] insertion *f*.

insertion [insûr'shən] *n* insertion *f*.

in-service [in'sûr'vis] *a* (*training*) continu(e); (*course*) d'initiation; de perfectionnement; de recyclage.

inshore [in'shôr] *a* côtier(ière) ♦ *ad* près de la côte; vers la côte.

inside [in'sīd'] *n* intérieur *m*; (*of road*: *US, Europe etc*) côté *m* droit (*de la route*); (: *Brit*) côté *m* gauche (*de la route*) ♦ *a* intérieur(e) ♦ *ad* à l'intérieur, dedans ♦ *prep* à l'intérieur de; (*of time*): ~ **10 minutes** en moins de 10 minutes; ~**s** *npl* (*col*) intestins *mpl*; ~ **out** *ad* à l'envers; **to turn sth** ~ **out** retourner qch; **to know sth** ~ **out** connaître qch à fond *or* comme sa poche; ~ **information** renseignements *mpl* à la source; ~ **story** histoire racontée par un témoin.

inside forward *n* (*SPORT*) intérieur *m*.

inside lane *n* (*AUT*: *in US, Europe*) voie *f* de droite; (: *in Britain*) voie *f* de gauche.

inside leg measurement *n* (*Brit*) hauteur *f* d'entre-jambe.

insider [insī'dûr] *n* initié/e.

insider dealing *n* (*STOCK EXCHANGE*) délit *m* d'initié(s).

insidious [insid'ēəs] *a* insidieux(euse).

insight [in'sīt] *n* perspicacité *f*; (*glimpse, idea*) aperçu *m*; **to gain (an)** ~ **into** parvenir à comprendre.

insignia [insig'nēə] *npl* insignes *mpl*.
insignificant [insignif'ikənt] *a* insignifiant(e).
insincere [insinsēr'] *a* hypocrite.
insincerity [insinsär'itē] *n* manque *m* de sincérité, hypocrisie *f*.
insinuate [insin'yōōāt] *vt* insinuer.
insinuation [insinyōōā'shən] *n* insinuation *f*.
insipid [insip'id] *a* insipide, fade.
insist [insist'] *vi* insister; **to ~ on doing** insister pour faire; **to ~ that** insister pour que; (*claim*) maintenir *or* soutenir que.
insistence [insis'təns] *n* insistance *f*.
insistent [insis'tənt] *a* insistant(e), pressant(e).
insole [in'sōl] *n* semelle intérieure; (*fixed part of shoe*) première *f*.
insolence [in'sələns] *n* insolence *f*.
insolent [in'sələnt] *a* insolent(e).
insoluble [insâl'yəbəl] *a* insoluble.
insolvency [insâl'vənsē] *n* insolvabilité *f*; faillite *f*.
insolvent [insâl'vənt] *a* insolvable; (*bankrupt*) en faillite.
insomnia [insâm'nēə] *n* insomnie *f*.
insomniac [insâm'nēak] *n* insomniaque *m/f*.
inspect [inspekt'] *vt* inspecter; (*Brit: ticket*) contrôler.
inspection [inspek'shən] *n* inspection *f*; contrôle *m*.
inspector [inspek'tûr] *n* inspecteur/trice; contrôleur/euse.
inspiration [inspərā'shən] *n* inspiration *f*.
inspire [inspīūr'] *vt* inspirer.
inspired [inspīūrd'] *a* (*writer, book etc*) inspiré(e); **in an ~ moment** dans un moment d'inspiration.
inspiring [inspīūr'ing] *a* inspirant(e).
inst. *abbr* (*Brit COMM*: = *instant*): **of the 16th ~** du 16 courant.
instability [instəbil'ətē] *n* instabilité *f*.
install [instôl'] *vt* installer.
installation [instəlā'shən] *n* installation *f*.
installment, (*Brit*) **instalment** [instôl'mənt] *n* acompte *m*, versement partiel; (*of TV serial etc*) épisode *m*; **in ~s** (*pay*) à tempérament; (*receive*) en plusieurs fois.
installment plan *n* (*US*) achat *m* (*or* vente *f*) à tempérament *or* crédit.
instance [in'stəns] *n* exemple *m*; **for ~** par exemple; **in many ~s** dans bien des cas; **in that ~** dans ce cas; **in the first ~** tout d'abord, en premier lieu.
instant [in'stənt] *n* instant *m* ♦ *a* immédiat(e); urgent(e); (*coffee, food*) instantané(e), en poudre; **the 10th ~** le 10 courant.
instantaneous [instəntā'nēəs] *a* instantané(e).
instantly [in'stəntlē] *ad* immédiatement, tout de suite.
instant replay *n* (*US TV*) retour *m* sur une séquence.
instead [insted'] *ad* au lieu de cela; **~ of** au lieu de; **~ of sb** à la place de qn.
instep [in'step] *n* cou-de-pied *m*; (*of shoe*) cambrure *f*.
instigate [in'stəgāt] *vt* (*rebellion, strike, crime*) inciter à; (*new ideas etc*) susciter.
instigation [instəgā'shən] *n* instigation *f*; **at sb's ~** à l'instigation de qn.
instill, (*Brit*) **instil** [instil'] *vt*: **to ~ (into)**

inculquer (à); (*courage*) insuffler (à).
instinct [in'stingkt] *n* instinct *m*.
instinctive [instingk'tiv] *a* instinctif(ive).
instinctively [instingk'tivlē] *ad* instinctivement.
institute [in'stitōōt] *n* institut *m* ♦ *vt* instituer, établir; (*inquiry*) ouvrir; (*proceedings*) entamer.
institution [institōō'shən] *n* institution *f*; (*school*) établissement *m* (scolaire); (*for care*) établissement (psychiatrique *etc*).
institutional [institōō'shənəl] *a* institutionnel(le); **~ care** soins *mpl* fournis par un établissement médico-social.
instruct [instrukt'] *vt* instruire, former; **to ~ sb in sth** enseigner qch à qn; **to ~ sb to do** charger qn *or* ordonner à qn de faire.
instruction [instruk'shən] *n* instruction *f*; **~s** *npl* directives *fpl*; **~s for use** mode *m* d'emploi.
instruction book *n* manuel *m* d'instructions.
instructive [instruk'tiv] *a* instructif(ive).
instructor [instruk'tûr] *n* professeur *m*; (*for skiing, driving*) moniteur *m*.
instrument [in'strəmənt] *n* instrument *m*.
instrumental [instrəmen'təl] *a* (*MUS*) instrumental(e); **to be ~ in sth/in doing sth** contribuer à qch/à faire qch.
instrumentalist [instrəmen'təlist] *n* instrumentiste *m/f*.
instrument panel *n* tableau *m* de bord.
insubordinate [insəbôr'dənit] *a* insubordonné(e).
insubordination [insəbôrdənā'shən] *n* insubordination *f*.
insufferable [insuf'ûrəbəl] *a* insupportable.
insufficient [insəfish'ənt] *a* insuffisant(e).
insufficiently [insəfish'əntlē] *ad* insuffisamment.
insular [in'sələr] *a* insulaire; (*outlook*) étroit(e); (*person*) aux vues étroites.
insulate [in'səlāt] *vt* isoler; (*against sound*) insonoriser.
insulating tape [in'səlāting tāp] *n* ruban isolant.
insulation [insəlā'shən] *n* isolation *f*; insonorisation *f*.
insulin [in'səlin] *n* insuline *f*.
insult *n* [in'sult] insulte *f*, affront *m* ♦ *vt* [insult'] insulter, faire un affront à.
insulting [insul'ting] *a* insultant(e), injurieux(euse).
insuperable [insōō'pûrəbəl] *a* insurmontable.
insurance [inshûr'əns] *n* assurance *f*; **fire/life ~** assurance-incendie/-vie; **to take out ~ (against)** s'assurer (contre).
insurance agent *n* agent *m* d'assurances.
insurance broker *n* courtier *m* en assurances.
insurance policy *n* police *f* d'assurance.
insurance premium *n* prime *f* d'assurance.
insure [inshōōr'] *vt* assurer; **to ~ sb/sb's life** assurer qn/la vie de qn; **to be ~d for $5000** être assuré(e) pour 5000 dollars.
insured [inshōōrd'] *n*: **the ~** l'assuré/e.
insurer [inshōō'rûr] *n* assureur *m*.
insurgent [insûr'jənt] *a*, *n* insurgé(e).
insurmountable [insûrmoun'təbəl] *a* insurmontable.

insurrection [insərek'shən] n insurrection f.

intact [ɪntakt'] a intact(e).

intake [in'tāk] n (TECH) admission f; adduction f; (of food) consommation f; (Brit SCOL): **an ~ of 200 a year** 200 admissions par an.

intangible [intan'jəbəl] a intangible; (assets) immatériel(le).

integral [in'təgrəl] a intégral(e); (part) inté-grant(e).

integrate [in'təgrāt] vt intégrer ♦ vi s'intégrer.

integrated circuit [in'təgrātid sûr'kit] n (COMPUT) circuit intégré.

integration [intəgrā'shən] n intégration f; **ra-cial ~** intégration raciale.

integrity [integ'ritē] n intégrité f.

intellect [in'təlekt] n intelligence f.

intellectual [intəlek'chōōəl] a, n intel-lectuel(le).

intelligence [intel'ijəns] n intelligence f; (MIL etc) informations fpl, renseignements mpl.

intelligence quotient (IQ) n quotient intellectuel (QI).

Intelligence Service n services mpl de renseignements.

intelligence test n test m d'intelligence.

intelligent [intel'ijənt] a intelligent(e).

intelligently [intel'ijəntlē] ad intelligemment.

intelligible [intel'ijəbəl] a intelligible.

intemperate [intem'pûrit] a immodéré(e); (drinking too much) adonné(e) à la boisson.

intend [intend'] vt (gift etc): **to ~ sth for** des-tiner qch à; **to ~ to do** avoir l'intention de faire.

intended [inten'did] a (insult) intentionnel(le); (journey) projeté(e); (effect) voulu(e).

intense [intens'] a intense; (person) véhé-ment(e).

intensely [intens'lē] ad intensément; (moving) profondément.

intensify [inten'səfī] vt intensifier.

intensity [inten'sitē] n intensité f.

intensive [inten'siv] a intensif(ive).

intensive care n: **to be in ~** être en réani-mation; **~ unit** n service m de réanimation.

intent [intent'] n intention f ♦ a attentif(ive), absorbé(e); **to all ~s and purposes** en fait, pratiquement; **to be ~ on doing sth** être (bien) décidé à faire qch.

intention [inten'chən] n intention f.

intentional [inten'chənəl] a intentionnel(le), délibéré(e).

intently [intent'lē] ad attentivement.

inter [intûr'] vt enterrer.

interact [intûrakt'] vi avoir une action récipro-que.

interaction [intûrak'shən] n interaction f.

interactive [intûrak'tiv] a interactif(ive).

intercede [intûrsēd'] vi: **to ~ with sb/on be-half of sb** intercéder auprès de qn/en faveur de qn.

intercept [intûrsept'] vt intercepter; (person) arrêter au passage.

interception [intûrsep'shən] n interception f.

interchange n [in'tûrchānj] (exchange) échange m; (on freeway) échangeur m ♦ vt [intûrchānj'] échanger; mettre à la place l'un(e) de l'autre.

interchangeable [intûrchān'jəbəl] a inter-changeable.

intercity [in'tûrsitē] a: **~ (train)** train m rapi-de.

intercom [in'tûrkâm] n interphone m.

interconnect [intûrkənekt'] vi (rooms) communiquer.

intercontinental [intûrkântənen'təl] a intercontinental(e).

intercourse [in'tûrkôrs] n rapports mpl; **sex-ual ~** rapports sexuels.

interdependent [intûrdipen'dənt] a interdé-pendant(e).

interest [in'trist] n intérêt m; (COMM: stake, share) participation f, intérêts mpl ♦ vt inté-resser; **compound/simple ~** intérêt composé/simple; **American ~s in the Middle East** les intérêts américains au Moyen-Orient; **his main ~ is ...** ce qui l'intéresse le plus est ....

interested [in'tristid] a intéressé(e); **to be ~ in** s'intéresser à.

interest-free [in'tristfrē] a sans intérêt.

interesting [in'tristing] a intéressant(e).

interest rate n taux m d'intérêt.

interface [in'tûrfās] n (COMPUT) interface f.

interfere [intûrfēr'] vi: **to ~ in** (quarrel, other people's business) se mêler à; **to ~ with** (object) tripoter, toucher à; (plans) contre-carrer; (duty) être en conflit avec; **don't ~** mêlez-vous de vos affaires.

interference [intûrfēr'əns] n (gen) intrusion f; (PHYSICS) interférence f; (RADIO, TV) para-sites mpl.

interfering [intûrfēr'ing] a importun(e).

interim [in'tûrim] a provisoire; (post) intéri-maire ♦ n: **in the ~** dans l'intérim.

interior [intē'rēûr] n intérieur m ♦ a inté-rieur(e).

interior decorator, interior designer n décorateur/trice d'intérieur.

interjection [intûrjek'shən] n interjection f.

interlock [intûrlâk'] vi s'enclencher ♦ vt en-clencher.

interloper [in'tûrlō'pûr] n intrus/e.

interlude [in'tûrlōōd] n intervalle m; (THEA-TER) intermède m.

intermarry [intûrmar'ē] vi former des alliances entre familles (or tribus); former des unions consanguines.

intermediary [intûrmē'dēârē] n intermédiaire m/f.

intermediate [intûrmē'dēit] a intermédiaire; (SCOL: course, level) moyen(ne).

interminable [intûr'mənəbəl] a sans fin, interminable.

intermission [intûrmish'ən] n pause f; (THEA-TER, CINEMA) entracte m.

intermittent [intûrmit'ənt] a intermittent(e).

intermittently [intûrmit'əntlē] ad par intermittence, par intervalles.

intern vt [intûrn'] interner ♦ n [in'tûrn] (US) interne m/f.

internal [intûr'nəl] a interne; (dispute, reform etc) intérieur(e); **~ injuries** lésions fpl internes.

internally [intûr'nəlē] ad intérieurement; **"not to be taken ~"** "pour usage externe".

Internal Revenue (Service) (IRS) n (US) fisc m.

international [intûrnash'ənəl] _a_ international(e) ♦ _n_ (_Brit SPORT_) international _m_.

International Atomic Energy Agency (IAEA) _n_ Agence Internationale de l'Energie Atomique (AIEA).

International Court of Justice (ICJ) _n_ Cour internationale de justice (CIJ).

international date line _n_ ligne _f_ de changement de date.

internationally [intûrnash'ənəlē] _ad_ dans le monde entier.

International Monetary Fund (IMF) _n_ Fonds _m_ monétaire international (FMI).

internecine [intûrnē'sīn] _a_ mutuellement destructeur(trice).

internee [intûrnē'] _n_ interné/e.

Internment [intûrn'mənt] _n_ internement _m_.

interplay [in'tûrplā] _n_ effet _m_ réciproque, jeu _m_.

Interpol [in'tûrpōl] _n_ Interpol _m_.

interpret [intûr'prit] _vt_ interpréter ♦ _vi_ servir d'interprète.

interpretation [intûrpritā'shən] _n_ interprétation _f_.

interpreter [intûr'pritûr] _n_ interprète _m/f_.

interpreting [intûr'priting] _n_ (_profession_) interprétariat _m_.

interrelated [intərilā'tid] _a_ en corrélation, en rapport étroit.

interrogate [intär'əgāt] _vt_ interroger; (_suspect etc_) soumettre à un interrogatoire.

interrogation [intärəgā'shən] _n_ interrogation _f_; interrogatoire _m_.

interrogative [intərâg'ətiv] _a_ interrogateur(trice) ♦ _n_ (_LING_) interrogatif _m_.

interrogator [intär'əgātûr] _n_ interrogateur/trice.

interrupt [intərupt'] _vt_ interrompre.

interruption [intərup'shən] _n_ interruption _f_.

intersect [intûrsekt'] _vt_ couper, croiser; (_MATH_) intersecter ♦ _vi_ se croiser, se couper; s'intersecter.

intersection [intûrsek'shən] _n_ intersection _f_; (_of roads_) croisement _m_.

intersperse [intûrspûrs'] _vt_: **to ~ with** parsemer de.

interstate (highway) [in'tûrstāt (hī'wā)] _n_ (_US_) route nationale.

intertwine [intûrtwīn'] _vt_ entrelacer ♦ _vi_ s'entrelacer.

interval [in'tûrvəl] _n_ intervalle _m_; (_Brit: THEATER_) entracte _m_; (: _SPORT_) mi-temps _f_; **bright ~s** (_in weather_) éclaircies _fpl_; **at ~s** par intervalles.

intervene [intûrvēn'] _vi_ (_time_) s'écouler (entre-temps); (_event_) survenir; (_person_) intervenir.

intervention [intûrven'chən] _n_ intervention _f_.

interview [in'tûrvyōo] _n_ (_RADIO, TV etc_) interview _f_; (_for job_) entrevue _f_ ♦ _vt_ interviewer; avoir une entrevue avec.

interviewer [in'tûrvyōoûr] _n_ interviewer _m_.

intestate [intes'tāt] _a_ intestat.

intestinal [intes'tənəl] _a_ intestinal(e).

intestine [intes'tin] _n_ intestin _m_; **large ~** gros intestin; **small ~** intestin grêle.

intimacy [in'təməsē] _n_ intimité _f_.

intimate _a_ [in'təmit] intime; (_knowledge_) approfondi(e) ♦ _vt_ [in'təmāt] suggérer, laisser entendre; (_announce_) faire savoir.

intimately [in'təmitlē] _ad_ intimement.

intimation [intəmā'shən] _n_ annonce _f_.

intimidate [intim'idāt] _vt_ intimider.

intimidation [intimidā'shən] _n_ intimidation _f_.

into [in'tōo] _prep_ dans; **~ pieces/French** en morceaux/français; **to change pounds ~ dollars** changer des livres en dollars.

intolerable [intâl'ûrəbəl] _a_ intolérable.

intolerance [intâl'ûrəns] _n_ intolérance _f_.

intolerant [intâl'ûrənt] _a_: **~ (of)** intolérant(e) (de); (_MED_) intolérant (à).

intonation [intōnā'shən] _n_ intonation _f_.

intoxicate [intâk'sikāt] _vt_ enivrer.

intoxicated [intâk'sikātid] _a_ ivre.

intoxication [intâksikā'shən] _n_ ivresse _f_.

intractable [intrak'təbəl] _a_ (_child, temper_) indocile, insoumis(e); (_problem_) insoluble; (_illness_) incurable.

intransigent [intran'sijənt] _a_ intransigeant(e).

intransitive [intran'sətiv] _a_ intransitif(ive).

intra-uterine device (IUD) [intrəyōo'tûrin divīs'] _n_ dispositif intra-utérin (DIU), stérilet _m_.

intravenous [intrəvē'nəs] _a_ intraveineux(euse).

in-tray [in'trā] _n_ courrier _m_ "arrivée".

intrepid [intrep'id] _a_ intrépide.

intricacy [in'trəkəsē] _n_ complexité _f_.

intricate [in'trəkit] _a_ complexe, compliqué(e).

intrigue [intrēg'] _n_ intrigue _f_ ♦ _vt_ intriguer ♦ _vi_ intriguer, comploter.

intriguing [intrē'ging] _a_ fascinant(e).

intrinsic [intrin'sik] _a_ intrinsèque.

introduce [intrədōos'] _vt_ introduire; **to ~ sb (to sb)** présenter qn (à qn); **to ~ sb to** (_pastime, technique_) initier qn à; **may I ~ ...?** je vous présente ....

introduction [intrəduk'shən] _n_ introduction _f_; (_of person_) présentation _f_; **a letter of ~** une lettre de recommendation.

introductory [intrəduk'tûrē] _a_ préliminaire, introductif(ive); **~ remarks** remarques _fpl_ liminaires; **an ~ offer** une offre de lancement.

introspection [intrəspek'shən] _n_ introspection _f_.

introspective [intrəspek'tiv] _a_ introspectif(ive).

introvert [in'trəvûrt] _a, n_ introverti(e).

intrude [intrōod'] _vi_ (_person_) être importun(e); **to ~ on** _or_ **into** (_conversation etc_) s'immiscer dans; **am I intruding?** est-ce que je vous dérange?

intruder [intrōo'dûr] _n_ intrus/e.

intrusion [intrōo'zhən] _n_ intrusion _f_.

intrusive [intrōo'siv] _a_ importun(e), gênant(e).

intuition [intōoish'ən] _n_ intuition _f_.

intuitive [intōo'ətiv] _a_ intuitif(ive).

inundate [in'undāt] _vt_: **to ~ with** inonder de.

inure [inyōor'] _vt_: **to ~ (to)** habituer (à).

invade [invād'] _vt_ envahir.

invader [invā'dûr] _n_ envahisseur _m_.

invalid _n_ [in'vəlid] malade _m/f_; (_with disability_) invalide _m/f_ ♦ _a_ [inval'id] (_not valid_) invalide, non valide.

invalidate [inval'idāt] _vt_ invalider, annuler.

invalid chair _n_ (_Brit_) fauteuil _m_ d'infirme.

invaluable [inval'yōoəbəl] _a_ inestimable, inappréciable.

invariable [invär'ēəbəl] *a* invariable; *(fig)* immanquable.
invariably [invär'ēəblē] *ad* invariablement; **she is ~ late** elle est toujours en retard.
invasion [invā'zhən] *n* invasion *f*.
invective [invek'tiv] *n* invective *f*.
inveigle [invē'gəl] *vt*: **to ~ sb into (doing) sth** amener qn à (faire) qch (par la ruse *or* la flatterie).
invent [invent'] *vt* inventer.
invention [inven'chən] *n* invention *f*.
inventive [inven'tiv] *a* inventif(ive).
inventiveness [inven'tivnis] *n* esprit inventif *or* d'invention.
inventor [inven'tûr] *n* inventeur/trice.
inventory [in'vəntôrē] *n* inventaire *m*.
inventory control *n* (COMM) contrôle *m* des stocks.
inverse [invûrs'] *a* inverse ♦ *n* inverse *m*, contraire *m*; **in ~ proportion (to)** inversement proportionel(le) (à).
inversely [invûrs'lē] *ad* inversement.
invert [invûrt'] *vt* intervertir; *(cup, object)* retourner.
invertebrate [invûr'tərit] *n* invertébré *m*.
inverted commas [invûr'tid kâm'əz] *npl* (Brit) guillemets *mpl*.
invest [invest'] *vt* investir; *(endow)*: **to ~ sb with sth** conférer qch à qn ♦ *vi* faire un investissement, investir; **to ~ in** placer de l'argent *or* investir dans; *(acquire)* s'offrir, faire l'acquisition de.
investigate [inves'təgāt] *vt* étudier, examiner; *(crime)* faire une enquête sur.
investigation [inves'təgāshən] *n* examen *m*; *(of crime)* enquête *f*, investigation *f*.
investigative [inves'təgātiv] *a*: **~ journalism** journalisme *m* d'enquête.
investigator [inves'təgātûr] *n* investigateur/trice; **private ~** détective privé.
investiture [inves'tichûr] *n* investiture *f*.
investment [invest'mənt] *n* investissement *m*, placement *m*.
investment income *n* revenu *m* de placement.
investment trust *n* société *f* d'investissements.
investor [inves'tûr] *n* épargnant/e; *(shareholder)* actionnaire *m/f*.
inveterate [invet'ûrit] *a* invétéré(e).
invidious [invid'ēəs] *a* injuste; *(task)* déplaisant(e).
invigilator [invij'əlātûr] *n* (Brit) surveillant *m* (d'examen).
invigorating [invig'ərāting] *a* vivifiant(e); stimulant(e).
invincible [invin'səbəl] *a* invincible.
inviolate [invī'əlit] *a* inviolé(e).
invisible [inviz'əbəl] *a* invisible.
invisible ink *n* encre *f* sympathique.
invisible mending *n* stoppage *m*.
invitation [invitā'shən] *n* invitation *f*; **by ~ only** sur invitation; **at sb's ~** à la demande de qn.
invite [invīt'] *vt* inviter; *(opinions etc)* demander; *(trouble)* chercher; **to ~ sb (to do)** inviter qn (à faire); **to ~ sb to dinner** inviter qn à dîner.
invite out *vt* inviter (à sortir).

invite over *vt* inviter (chez soi).
inviting [invī'ting] *a* engageant(e), attrayant(e); *(gesture)* encourageant(e).
invoice [in'vois] *n* facture *f* ♦ *vt* facturer; **to ~ sb for goods** facturer des marchandises à qn.
invoke [invōk'] *vt* invoquer.
involuntary [invâl'əntärē] *a* involontaire.
involve [invâlv'] *vt* *(entail)* impliquer; *(concern)* concerner; *(require)* nécessiter; **to ~ sb in** *(theft etc)* impliquer qn dans; *(activity, meeting)* faire participer qn à.
involved [invâlvd'] *a* complexe; **to feel ~** se sentir concerné(e); **to become ~** *(in love etc)* s'engager.
involvement [invâlv'mənt] *n* *(personal role)* participation *f*; *(of resources, funds)* mise *f* en jeu.
invulnerable [invul'nûrəbəl] *a* invulnérable.
inward [in'wûrd] *a* *(movement)* vers l'intérieur; *(thought, feeling)* profond(e), intime.
inwardly [in'wûrdlē] *ad* *(feel, think etc)* secrètement, en son for intérieur.
inward(s) [in'wûrd(z)] *ad* vers l'intérieur.
I/O *abbr* *(COMPUT:* = *input/output)* E/S.
IOC *n* *abbr* (= *International Olympic Committee)* CIO *m* (= *Comité international olympique)*.
iodine [ī'ədīn] *n* iode *m*.
ion [ī'ən] *n* ion *m*.
Ionian Sea [īō'nēən sē] *n*: **the ~** la mer Ionienne.
iota [īō'tə] *n* *(fig)* brin *m*, grain *m*.
IOU *n* *abbr* (= *I owe you)* reconnaissance *f* de dette.
IOW *abbr* (Brit) = *Isle of Wight.*
IPA *n* *abbr* (– *International Phonetic Alphabet)* A.P.I. *m*.
IQ *n* *abbr* = **intelligence quotient.**
IRA *n* *abbr* (= *Irish Republican Army)* IRA *f*; *(US)* = *individual retirement account.*
Iran [iran'] *n* Iran *m*.
Iranian [irā'nēən] *a* iranien(ne) ♦ *n* Iranien/ne; *(LING)* iranien *m*.
Iraq [irak'] *n* Irak *m*.
Iraqi [irâk'ē] *a* irakien(ne) ♦ *n* Irakien/ne; *(LING)* irakien *m*.
irascible [iras'əbəl] *a* irascible.
irate [īrāt'] *a* courroucé(e).
Ireland [īûr'lənd] *n* Irlande *f*; **Republic of ~** République *f* d'Irlande.
iris, ~es [ī'ris] *n* iris *m*.
Irish [ī'rish] *a* irlandais(e) ♦ *n* *(LING)* irlandais *m*; **the ~** *npl* les Irlandais.
Irishman [ī'rishmən] *n* Irlandais *m*.
Irish Sea *n*: **the ~** la mer d'Irlande.
Irishwoman [ī'rishwŏŏmən] *n* Irlandaise *f*.
irk [ûrk] *vt* ennuyer.
irksome [ûrk'səm] *a* ennuyeux(euse).
IRO *n* *abbr* (US) = *International Refugee Organization.*
iron [ī'ûrn] *n* fer *m*; *(for clothes)* fer *m* à repasser ♦ *a* de *or* en fer ♦ *vt* *(clothes)* repasser; **~s** *npl* *(chains)* fers *mpl*, chaînes *fpl*.
iron out *vt* *(crease)* faire disparaître au fer; *(fig)* aplanir; faire disparaître.
Iron Curtain *n*: **the ~** le rideau de fer.
iron foundry *n* fonderie *f* de fonte.
ironic(al) [īrân'ik(əl)] *a* ironique.

ironically [īrân'iklē] *ad* ironiquement.
ironing [ī'ûrning] *n* repassage *m*.
ironing board *n* planche *f* à repasser.
ironmonger [ī'ûrnmunggûr] *n* (*Brit*) quincailler *m*; ~'s (shop) quincaillerie *f*.
iron ore [ī'ûrn ôr] *n* minerai *m* de fer.
ironworks [ī'ûrnwûrks] *n* usine *f* sidérurgique.
irony [ī'rənē] *n* ironie *f*.
irrational [irash'ənəl] *a* irrationnel(le); déraisonnable; qui manque de logique.
irreconcilable [irek'ənsīləbəl] *a* irréconciliable; (*opinion*): ~ with inconciliable avec.
irredeemable [iridē'məbəl] *a* (*COMM*) non remboursable.
irrefutable [irifyōō'təbəl] *a* irréfutable.
irregular [ircg'yəlûr] *a* irrégulier(ière).
irregularity [iregyəlar'itē] *n* irrégularité *f*.
irrelevance [irel'əvəns] *n* manque *m* de rapport *or* d'à-propos.
irrelevant [irel'əvənt] *a* sans rapport, hors de propos.
irreligious [irilij'əs] *a* irréligieux(euse).
irreparable [irep'ûrəbəl] *a* irréparable.
irreplaceable [iriplā'səbəl] *a* irremplaçable.
irrepressible [iripres'əbəl] *a* irrépressible.
irreproachable [iriprō'chəbəl] *a* irréprochable.
irresistible [irizis'təbəl] *a* irrésistible.
irresolute [irez'əlōōt] *a* irrésolu(e), indécis(e).
irrespective [irispek'tiv] : ~ of *prep* sans tenir compte de.
irresponsible [irispân'səbəl] *a* (*act*) irréfléchi(e); (*person*) qui n'a pas le sens des responsabilités.
irretrievable [iritrē'vəhəl] *a* irréparable, irrémédiable; (*object*) introuvable.
irreverent [irev'ûrənt] *a* irrévérencieux(euse).
irrevocable [irev'əkəbəl] *a* irrévocable.
irrigate [ir'igāt] *vt* irriguer.
irrigation [irigā'shən] *n* irrigation *f*.
irritable [ir'itəbəl] *a* irritable.
irritate [ir'ətāt] *vt* irriter.
irritation [iritā'shən] *n* irritation *f*.
IRS *n abbr* (*US*) = **Internal Revenue Service**.
is [iz] *vb see* **be**.
ISBN *n abbr* (= *International Standard Book Number*) ISBN *m*.
Islam [iz'lâm] *n* Islam *m*.
island [ī'lənd] *n* île *f*; (*also*: **traffic** ~) refuge *m* (pour piétons).
islander [ī'ləndûr] *n* habitant/e d'une île, insulaire *m/f*.
isle [īl] *n* île *f*.
isn't [iz'ənt] = **is not**.
isolate [ī'səlāt] *vt* isoler.
isolated [ī'səlātid] *a* isolé(e).
isolation [īsəlā'shən] *n* isolement *m*.
isolationism [īsəlā'shənizəm] *n* isolationnisme *m*.
isotope [ī'sətōp] *n* isotope *m*.
Israel [iz'rāəl] *n* Israël *m*.
Israeli [izrā'lē] *a* israélien(ne) ♦ *n* Israélien/ne.
issue [ish'ōō] *n* question *f*, problème *m*; (*outcome*) résultat *m*, issue *f*; (*of banknotes etc*) émission *f*; (*of newspaper etc*) numéro *m*; (*offspring*) descendance *f* ♦ *vt* (*rations, equipment*) distribuer; (*orders*) donner; (*book*) faire paraître, publier; (*banknotes, checks, stamps*) émettre, mettre en circulation ♦ *vi*: **to** ~ **from** provenir de; **at** ~ en

jeu, en cause; **to avoid the** ~ éluder le problème; **to take** ~ **with sb (over sth)** exprimer son désaccord avec qn (sur qch); **to make an** ~ **of sth** faire de qch un problème; **to confuse** *or* **obscure the** ~ embrouiller la question.
Istanbul [istambōōl'] *n* Istamboul, Istanbul.
isthmus [is'məs] *n* isthme *m*.
IT *n abbr* = **information technology**.
it [it] *pronoun* (*subject*) il(elle); (*direct object*) le(la), l'; (*indirect object*) lui; (*impersonal*) il; ce, cela, ça; **of** ~, **from** ~, **about** ~, **out of** ~ *etc* en; **in** ~, **to** ~, **at** ~ *etc* y; **above** ~, **over** ~ (au-)dessus; **below** ~, **under** ~ (en-)dessous; **in front of/behind** ~ devant/derrière; **who is** ~? qui est-ce?; ~'s **me** c'est moi; **what is** ~? qu'est-ce que c'est?; **where is** ~? où est-ce?, où est-ce que c'est?; ~'s **Friday tomorrow** demain, c'est vendredi; ~'s **raining** il pleut; ~'s **6 o'clock** il est 6 heures; ~'s **2 hours by train** c'est à 2 heures de train; **I've come from** ~ j'en viens; **it's on** ~ c'est dessus; **he's proud of** ~ il en est fier; **he agreed to** ~ il y a consenti.
Italian [ital'yən] *a* Italien(ne) ♦ *n* Italien/ne; (*LING*) italien *m*.
italic [ital'ik] *a* italique; ~s *npl* italique *m*.
Italy [it'əlē] *n* Italie *f*.
itch [ich] *n* démangeaison *f* ♦ *vi* (*person*) éprouver des démangeaisons; (*part of body*) démanger; **I'm** ~**ing to do** l'envie me démange de faire.
itching [ich'ing] *n* démangeaison *f*.
itchy [ich'ē] *a* qui démange; **my back is** ~ j'ai le dos qui me démange.
it'd [it'əd] = **it would**, **it had**.
item [ī'təm] *n* (*gen*) article *m*; (*on agenda*) question *f*, point *m*; (*in program*) numéro *m*; (*also*: **news** ~) nouvelle *f*; ~s **of clothing** articles vestimentaires.
itemize [ī'təmīz] *vt* détailler, spécifier.
itinerant [ītin'ûrənt] *a* itinérant(e); (*musician*) ambulant(e).
itinerary [ītin'ərārē] *n* itinéraire *m*.
it'll [it'əl] = **it will**, **it shall**.
its [its] *a* son(sa), ses *pl* ♦ *pronoun* le(la) sien(ne), les siens(siennes).
it's [its] = **it is**, **it has**.
itself [itself'] *pronoun* (*emphatic*) lui-même(elle-même); (*reflexive*) se.
ITV *n abbr* (*Brit*: = *Independent Television*) chaîne de télévision commerciale.
IUD *n abbr* = **intra-uterine device**.
I.V. *n* (*US MED*) goutte-à-goutte *m inv*, perfusion *f*; **to put sb on an** ~ alimenter qn au goutte-à-goutte *or* par perfusion.
I've [īv] = **I have**.
ivory [ī'vûrē] *n* ivoire *m*.
Ivory Coast *n* Côte *f* d'Ivoire.
ivory tower *n* (*fig*) tour *f* d'ivoire.
ivy [ī'vē] *n* lierre *m*.
Ivy League *n* (*US*) *les grandes universités du nord-est des États Unis* (*Harvard, Yale, Princeton etc*).

J

J, j [jā] n (*letter*) J, j m; **J for Jig** J comme Joseph.
JA n abbr = **judge advocate**.
J/A abbr = **joint account**.
jab [jab] vt: **to ~ sth into** enfoncer or planter qch dans ♦ n coup m; (*MED col*) piqûre f.
jabber [jab'ûr] vt, vi bredouiller, baragouiner.
jack [jak] n (*AUT*) cric m; (*Brit BOWLS*) cochonnet m; (*CARDS*) valet m.
  jack in vt (*col*) laisser tomber.
  jack up vt soulever (au cric).
jackal [jak'əl] n chacal m.
jackass [jak'as] n (*also fig*) âne m.
jackdaw [jak'dô] n choucas m.
jacket [jak'it] n veste f, veston m; (*of boiler etc*) enveloppe f; (*of book*) couverture f, jaquette f.
jack-in-the-box [jak'intḥəbâks] n diable m à ressort.
jackknife [jak'nīf] n couteau m de poche ♦ vi: **the truck ~d** la remorque (du camion) s'est mise en travers.
jack-of-all-trades [jak'əvôltrādz'] n bricoleur m.
jack plug n (*Brit*) jack m.
jackpot [jak'pät] n gros lot.
jacuzzi [jəkōō'zē] n ℞ jacuzzi m ℞.
jade [jād] n (*stone*) jade m.
jaded [jā'did] a ereinté(e), fatigué(e).
JAG n abbr = **Judge Advocate General**.
jagged [jag'id] a dentelé(e).
jaguar [jag'wâr] n jaguar m.
jail [jāl] n prison f ♦ vt emprisonner, mettre en prison.
jailbird [jāl'bûrd] n récidiviste m/f.
jailbreak [jāl'brāk] n évasion f.
jailer [jā'lûr] n geôlier/ière.
jalopy [jəláp'ē] n (*col*) vieux clou.
jam [jam] n confiture f; (*of shoppers etc*) cohue f; (*also*: **traffic ~**) embouteillage m ♦ vt (*passage etc*) encombrer, obstruer; (*mechanism, drawer etc*) bloquer, coincer; (*RADIO*) brouiller ♦ vi (*mechanism, sliding part*) se coincer, se bloquer; (*gun*) s'enrayer; **to get sb out of a ~** (*col*) sortir qn du pétrin; **to ~ sth into** entasser or comprimer qch dans; enfoncer qch dans; **the telephone lines are ~med** les lignes (téléphoniques) sont encombrées.
Jamaica [jəmā'kə] n Jamaïque f.
Jamaican [jəmā'kən] a jamaïquain(e) ♦ n Jamaïquain/e.
jamb [jam] n jambage m.
jam-packed [jam'pakt'] a: **~ (with)** bourré(e) (de).
jam session n jam session f.
Jan. abbr (= *January*) janv.
jangle [jang'gəl] vi cliqueter.
janitor [jan'itûr] n (*caretaker*) huissier m;

concierge m.
January [jan'yōōwärē] n janvier m; *for phrases see also* **July**.
Japan [jəpan'] n Japon m.
Japanese [japənēz'] a japonais(e) ♦ n (*pl inv*) Japonais/e; (*LING*) japonais m.
jar [jâr] n (*container*) pot m, bocal m ♦ vi (*sound*) produire un son grinçant or discordant; (*colors etc*) détonner, jurer ♦ vt (*shake*) ébranler, secouer.
jargon [jâr'gən] n jargon m.
jarring [jâr'ing] a (*sound, color*) discordant(e).
Jas. abbr = *James*.
jasmin(e) [jaz'min] n jasmin m.
jaundice [jôn'dis] n jaunisse f.
jaundiced [jôn'dist] a (*fig*) envieux(euse), désapprobateur(trice).
jaunt [jônt] n balade f.
jaunty [jôn'tē] a enjoué(e); désinvolte.
Java [jâv'ə] n Java f.
javelin [jav'lin] n javelot m.
jaw [jô] n mâchoire f.
jawbone [jô'bōn] n maxillaire m.
jay [jā] n geai m.
jaywalker [jā'wôkûr] n piéton indiscipliné.
jazz [jaz] n jazz m.
  jazz up vt animer, égayer.
jazz band n orchestre m or groupe m de jazz.
jazzy [jaz'ē] a bariolé(e), tapageur(euse).
JCC n abbr (*US*) = *Junior Chamber of Commerce*.
JCS n abbr (*US*) = *Joint Chiefs of Staff*.
JD n abbr (*US*) = *Doctor of Laws*) titre universitaire; (: = *Justice Department*) ministère de la Justice.
jealous [jel'əs] a jaloux(ouse).
jealously [jel'əslē] ad jalousement.
jealousy [jel'əsē] n jalousie f.
jeans [jēnz] npl (blue-)jean m.
jeep [jēp] n jeep f.
jeer [jēr] vi: **to ~ (at)** huer; se moquer cruellement (de), railler.
jeering [jē'ring] a railleur(euse), moqueur(euse) ♦ n huées fpl.
jeers [jērz] npl huées fpl; sarcasmes mpl.
jelly [jel'ē] n gelée f.
jellyfish [jel'ēfish] n méduse f.
jeopardize [jep'ûrdīz] vt mettre en danger or péril.
jeopardy [jep'ûrdē] n: **in ~** en danger or péril.
jerk [jûrk] n secousse f; saccade f; sursaut m, spasme m; (*col*) pauvre type m; (: *idiot*) andouille f ♦ vt donner une secousse à ♦ vi (*vehicles*) cahoter.
jerkin [jûr'kin] n blouson m.
jerky [jûr'kē] a saccadé(e); cahotant(e).
jerry-built [jär'ēbilt] a de mauvaise qualité.
jerry can [jär'ē kan] n bidon m.
jersey [jûr'zē] n tricot m; (*fabric*) jersey m.
Jerusalem [jərōō'sələm] n Jérusalem.
jest [jest] n plaisanterie f; **in ~** en plaisantant.
jester [jes'tûr] n (*HIST*) plaisantin m.
Jesus [jē'səs] n Jésus; **~ Christ** Jésus-Christ.
jet [jet] n (*of gas, liquid*) jet m; (*AUT*) gicleur m; (*AVIAT*) avion m à réaction, jet m.
jet-black [jet'blak'] a (d'un noir) de jais.
jet engine n moteur m à réaction.
jet lag n décalage m horaire.
jetsam [jet'səm] n objets jetés à la mer (et re-

jetés sur la côte).
jettison [jɛt'əsən] *vt* jeter par-dessus bord.
jetty [jɛt'ē] *n* jetée *f*, digue *f*.
Jew [jōō] *n* Juif *m*.
jewel [jōō'əl] *n* bijou *m*, joyau *m*.
jeweler, (*Brit*) **jeweller** [jōō'əlûr] *n* bijoutier/
ière, joaillier *m*; ~'s (shop) *n* bijouterie *f*,
joaillerie *f*.
jewelry, (*Brit*) **jewellery** [jōō'əlrē] *n* bijoux
mpl.
Jewess [jōō'is] *n* Juive *f*.
Jewish [jōō'ish] *a* juif(juive).
JFK *n abbr* (*US*) = *John Fitzgerald Kennedy
International Airport.*
jib [jib] *n* (*NAUT*) foc *m*; (*of crane*) flèche *f* ♦
vi (*horse*) regimber; **to** ~ **at doing sth** rechigner à faire qch.
jibe [jīb] *n* sarcasme *m*.
jiffy [jif'ē] *n* (*col*): **in a** ~ en un clin d'œil.
jig [jig] *n* (*dance, tunc*) gigue *m*.
jigsaw [jig'sô] *n* (*also:* ~ **puzzle**) puzzle *m*;
(*tool*) scie sauteuse.
jilt [jilt] *vt* laisser tomber, plaquer.
jingle [jing'gəl] *n* (*advertising* ~) couplet *m* publicitaire ♦ *vi* cliqueter, tinter.
jingoism [jing'gōizəm] *n* chauvinisme *m*.
jinx [jingks] *n* (*col*) (mauvais) sort.
jitters [jit'ûrz] *npl* (*col*): **to get the** ~ avoir la
trouille *or* la frousse.
jittery [jit'ûrē] *a* (*col*) froussard(e).
jiujitsu [jōōjit'sōō] *n* jiu-jitsu *m*.
job [jâb] *n* travail *m*; (*employment*) emploi *m*,
poste *m*, place *f*; **a part-time/full-time** ~ un
emploi à temps partiel/à plein temps; **he's
only doing his** ~ il fait son boulot; **it's a
good** ~ **that** ... c'est heureux *or* c'est une
chance que ...; **just the** ~! (c'est) juste *or*
exactement ce qu'il faut!
job action *n* (*US*) action revendicative.
jobber [jâb'ûr] *n* (*Brit STOCK EXCHANGE*) négociant *m* en titres.
jobbing [jâb'ing] *a* (*Brit: workman*) à la
tâche, à la journée.
Jobcentre [jâb'sentûr] *n* (*Brit*) agence *f* pour
l'emploi.
job creation scheme *n* (*Brit*) plan *m* pour
la création d'emplois.
job description *n* description *f* du poste.
jobless [jâb'lis] *a* sans travail, au chômage.
job lot *n* lot *m* (d'articles divers).
job satisfaction *n* satisfaction professionnelle.
job security *n* sécurité *f* de l'emploi.
job specification *n* caractéristiques *fpl* du
poste.
jockey [jâk'ē] *n* jockey *m* ♦ *vi*: **to** ~ **for position** manœuvrer pour être bien placé.
jocular [jâk'yəlûr] *a* jovial(e), enjoué(e); facé-
tieux(euse).
jog [jâg] *vt* secouer ♦ *vi* (*SPORT*) faire du
jogging; **to** ~ **along** cahoter; trotter; **to** ~
sb's memory rafraîchir la mémoire de qn.
jogger [jâg'ûr] *n* jogger *m/f*.
jogging [jâg'ing] *n* jogging *m*.
john [jân] *n* (*US col*) w.-c. *mpl*, petit coin.
join [join] *vt* unir, assembler; (*become
member of*) s'inscrire à; (*meet*) rejoindre,
retrouver; se joindre à ♦ *vi* (*roads, rivers*) se
rejoindre, se rencontrer ♦ *n* raccord *m*; **will**

you ~ **us for dinner?** vous dînerez bien avec
nous?; **I'll** ~ **you later** je vous rejoindrai plus
tard; **to** ~ **forces (with)** s'associer (à).
join in *vi* se mettre de la partie ♦ *vt* se mêler à.
join up *vi* s'engager.
joiner [joi'nûr] *n* menuisier *m*.
joinery [joi'nûrē] *n* menuiserie *f*.
joint [joint] *n* (*TECH*) jointure *f*; joint *m*;
(*ANAT*) articulation *f*, jointure; (*Brit CULIN*)
rôti *m*; (*col: place*) boîte *f* ♦ *a* commun(e);
(*committee*) mixte, paritaire; ~ **responsibility** coresponsabilité *f*.
joint account (J/A) *n* compte joint.
jointly [joint'lē] *ad* ensemble, en commun.
joint ownership *n* copropriété *f*.
joint-stock company [joint'stâk' kum'pənē] *n*
société *f* par actions.
joint venture *n* entreprise commune.
joist [joist] *n* solive *f*.
joke [jōk] *n* plaisanterie *f*; (*also:* **practical** ~)
farce *f* ♦ *vi* plaisanter; **to play a** ~ **on** jouer
un tour à, faire une farce à.
joker [jō'kûr] *n* plaisantin *m*, blagueur/euse;
(*CARDS*) joker *m*.
joking [jō'king] *n* plaisanterie *f*.
jollity [jâl'itē] *n* réjouissances *fpl*, galeté *f*.
jolly [jâl'ē] *a* gai(e), enjoué(e) ♦ *ad* (*Brit col*)
rudement, drôlement; ~ **good!** (*Brit*) formidable!
jolt [jōlt] *n* cahot *m*, secousse *f* ♦ *vt* cahoter,
secouer.
Jordan [jôr'dun] *n* (*country*) Jordanie *f*; (*river*) Jourdain *m*.
Jordanian [jôrdā'nēən] *a* jordanien(ne) ♦ *n*
Jordanien/ne.
joss stick [jâs stik] *n* bâton *m* d'encens.
jostle [jâs'əl] *vt* bousculer, pousser ♦ *vi* jouer
des coudes.
jot [jât] *n*: **not one** ~ pas un brin.
jot down *vt* inscrire rapidement, noter.
jotter [jât'ûr] *n* (*Brit*) cahier *m* (de brouillon);
bloc-notes *m*.
journal [jûr'nəl] *n* journal *m*.
journalese [jûrnəlēz'] *n* (*pej*) style *m* journalistique.
journalism [jûr'nəlizəm] *n* journalisme *m*.
journalist [jûr'nəlist] *n* journaliste *m/f*.
journey [jûr'nē] *n* voyage *m*; (*distance covered*) trajet *m*; **a 5-hour** ~ un voyage de 5
heures ♦ *vi* voyager.
jovial [jō'vēəl] *a* jovial(e).
jowl [joul] *n* mâchoire *f* (*inférieure*); bajoue *f*.
joy [joi] *n* joie *f*.
joyful [joi'fəl], **joyous** [joi'əs] *a* joyeux(euse).
joy ride *n* virée *f* (*gén avec une voiture volée*).
joystick [joi'stik] *n* (*AVIAT*) manche *m* à balai;
(*COMPUT*) manche à balai, manette *f* (de
jeu).
JP *n abbr* = **Justice of the Peace.**
Jr. *abbr* = **junior.**
JTPA *n abbr* (*US*: = *Job Training Partnership
Act*) programme gouvernemental de formation.
jubilant [jōō'bələnt] *a* triomphant(e); ré-
joui(e).
jubilation [jōōbəlā'shən] *n* jubilation *f*.
jubilee [jōō'bəlē] *n* jubilé *m*; **silver** ~ (jubilé

du) vingt-cinquième anniversaire.

judge [juj] *n* juge *m* ♦ *vt* juger; (*estimate: weight, size etc*) apprécier; (*consider*) estimer ♦ *vi*: **judging** *or* **to ~ by his expression** d'après son expression; **as far as I can ~** autant que je puisse en juger; **I ~d it necessary to inform him** j'ai jugé nécessaire de l'informer.

judge advocate (JA) *n* (*MIL*) magistrat *m* militaire.

Judge Advocate General (JAG) *n* (*MIL*) magistrat *m* militaire en chef.

judg(e)ment [juj'mənt] *n* jugement *m*; (*punishment*) châtiment *m*; **in my ~** à mon avis; **to pass ~ on** (*LAW*) prononcer un jugement (sur).

judicial [jōōdish'əl] *a* judiciaire; (*fair*) impartial(e).

judiciary [jōōdish'ēārē] *n* (pouvoir *m*) judiciaire *m*.

judicious [jōōdish'əs] *a* judicieux(euse).

judo [jōō'dō] *n* judo *m*.

jug [jug] *n* pot *m*, cruche *f*.

juggernaut [jug'ûrnôt] *n* (*Brit*: *huge truck*) mastodonte *m*.

juggle [jug'əl] *vi* jongler.

juggler [jug'lûr] *n* jongleur *m*.

Jugoslav [yōō'gōslàv] *a*, *n* = **Yugoslav**.

jugular [jug'yəlûr] *a*: **~ (vein)** veine *f* jugulaire.

juice [jōōs] *n* jus *m*; (*col: gas*): **we've run out of ~** c'est la panne sèche.

juicy [jōō'sē] *a* juteux(euse).

jukebox [jōōk'bàks] *n* juke-box *m*.

Jul. *abbr* (= *July*) juil.

July [julī'] *n* juillet *m*; **the first of ~** le premier juillet; **(on) the eleventh of ~** le onze juillet; **in the month of ~** au mois de juillet; **at the beginning/end of ~** au début/à la fin (du mois) de juillet, début/fin juillet; **in the middle of ~** au milieu (du mois) de juillet, à la mi-juillet; **during ~** pendant le mois de juillet; **in ~ of next year** en juillet de l'année prochaine; **each** *or* **every ~** tous les ans *or* chaque année en juillet; **~ was wet this year** il a beaucoup plu cette année en juillet.

jumble [jum'bəl] *n* fouillis *m* ♦ *vt* (*also*: **~ up**, **~ together**) mélanger, brouiller.

jumble sale *n* (*Brit*) vente *f* de charité.

jumbo [jum'bō] *a*: **~ jet** (avion) gros porteur (à réaction); **~ size** format maxi *or* extragrand.

jump [jump] *vi* sauter, bondir; (*start*) sursauter; (*increase*) monter en flèche ♦ *vt* sauter, franchir ♦ *n* saut *m*, bond *m*; sursaut *m*; (*fence*) obstacle *m*.

jump about *vi* sautiller.

jump at *vt fus* (*fig*) sauter sur; **he ~ed at the offer** il s'est empressé d'accepter la proposition.

jump down *vi* sauter (pour descendre).

jump up *vi* se lever (d'un bond).

jumped-up [jumpt'up] *a* (*Brit pej*) parvenu(e).

jumper [jum'pûr] *n* (*US: pinafore dress*) robe-chasuble *f*; (*Brit*: *pullover*) pull-over *m*; (*SPORT*) sauteur/euse.

jumper cables, (*Brit*) **jump leads** *npl* câbles *mpl* de démarrage.

jump rope *n* (*US*) corde *f* à sauter.

jump suit *n* combinaison *f* (d'aviateur).

Jumpy [jum'pē] *a* nerveux(euse), agité(e).

Jun. *abbr* = **June**.

Jun., Junr *abbr* = **junior**.

junction [jungk'shən] *n* (*of rails*) embranchement *m*; (*Brit*: *of roads*) carrefour *m*.

juncture [jungk'chûr] *n*: **at this ~** à ce moment-là, sur ces entrefaites.

June [jōōn] *n* juin *m*; *for phrases see also* **July**.

jungle [jung'gəl] *n* jungle *f*.

junior [jōōn'yûr] *a*, *n*: **he's ~ to me (by 2 years)**, **he's my ~ (by 2 years)** il est mon cadet (de 2 ans), il est plus jeune que moi (de 2 ans); **he's ~ to me** (*seniority*) il est en dessous de moi (dans la hiérarchie), j'ai plus d'ancienneté que lui.

junior executive *n* cadre moyen.

junior high school *n* (*US*) ≈ collège *m* d'enseignement secondaire.

junior partner *n* associé(-adjoint) *m*.

junior school *n* (*Brit*) école *f* primaire, cours moyen.

junior sizes *npl* (*COMM*) tailles *fpl* fillettes/garçonnets.

juniper [jōō'nəpûr] *n*: **~ berry** baie *f* de genièvre.

junk [jungk] *n* (*trash*) bric-à-brac *m inv*; (*ship*) jonque *f* ♦ *vt* (*col*) abandonner, mettre au rancart.

junk dealer *n* brocanteur/euse.

junket [jung'kit] *n* (*CULIN*) lait caillé; (*Brit col*): **to go on a ~**, **go ~ing** voyager aux frais de la princesse.

junk foods *npl* snacks *mpl* (vite prêts).

junkie [jung'kē] *n* (*col*) junkie *m*, drogué/e.

junk room *n* débarras *m*.

junk shop *n* (boutique *f* de) brocanteur *m*.

junkyard [jungk'yârd] *n* parc *m* à ferrailles; (*for cars*) cimetière *m* de voitures.

junta [hōōn'tə] *n* junte *f*.

Jupiter [jōō'pitûr] *n* (*planet*) Jupiter *f*.

jurisdiction [jōōrisdik'shən] *n* juridiction *f*; **it falls** *or* **comes within/outside our ~** cela est/n'est pas de notre compétence *or* ressort.

jurisprudence [jōōrisprōōd'əns] *n* jurisprudence *f*.

juror [jōō'rûr] *n* juré *m*.

jury [jōō'rē] *n* jury *m*.

jury box *n* banc *m* des jurés.

juryman [jōōr'ēmən] *n* = **juror**.

just [just] *a* juste ♦ *ad*: **he's ~ done it/left** il vient de le faire/partir; **~ as I expected** exactement *or* précisément comme je m'y attendais; **~ right/two o'clock** exactement *or* juste ce qu'il faut/deux heures; **we were ~ going** nous partions; **I was ~ about to phone** j'allais téléphoner; **~ as he was leaving** au moment *or* à l'instant précis où il partait; **~ before/enough/here** juste avant/assez/là; **it's ~ me/a mistake** ce n'est que moi/(rien) qu'une erreur; **~ missed/caught** manqué/attrapé de justesse; **~ listen to this!** écoutez un peu ça!; **~ ask someone the way** vous n'avez qu'à demander votre chemin à quelqu'un; **it's ~ as good** c'est (vraiment) aussi bon; **it's ~ as well that you ...** heureusement que vous ...; **not ~ now** pas tout de suite; ~ **a minute!**, ~ **one moment!** un instant (s'il vous plaît)!

justice [jus'tis] *n* justice *f*; **this photo doesn't do you** ~ cette photo ne vous avantage pas.

Justice of the Peace (JP) *n* juge *m* de paix.

justifiable [jus'tifiəbəl] *a* justifiable.

justifiably [jus'təfiəblē] *ad* légitimement, à juste titre.

justification [justəfəkā'shən] *n* justification *f*.

justify [jus'təfī] *vt* justifier; **to be justified in doing sth** être en droit de faire qch.

justly [just'lē] *ad* avec raison, justement.

justness [just'nis] *n* justesse *f*.

jut [jut] *vi* (*also*: ~ **out**) dépasser, faire saillie.

jute [jōōt] *n* jute *m*.

juvenile [jōō'vənəl] *a* juvénile; (*court, books*) pour enfants ♦ *n* adolescent/e.

juvenile delinquency *n* délinquance *f* juvénile.

juxtapose [jukstəpōz'] *vt* juxtaposer.

juxtaposition [jukstəpəzish'ən] *n* juxtaposition *f*.

K

K, k [kā] *n* (*letter*) K, k *m*; **K for King** K comme Kléber.

K [ka] *abbr* (= *kilobyte*) Ko ♦ *n* *abbr* (= *one thousand*) K.

kaftan [kaf'tən] *n* cafetan *m*.

Kalahari Desert [kâləhâr'ē dez'ûrt] *n* désert *m* de Kalahari.

kale [kāl] *n* chou frisé.

kaleidoscope [kəlī'dəskōp] *n* kaléidoscope *m*.

Kampala [kâmpâl'ə] *n* Kampala.

Kampuchea [kampōōchē'ə] *n* Kampuchéa *m*.

kangaroo [kanggərōō'] *n* kangourou *m*.

Kans. *abbr* (*US*) = *Kansas*.

kaput [kəpōōt'] *a* (*col*) kapout, capout.

karate [kərâ'tē] *n* karaté *m*.

Kashmir [kash'mēr] *n* Cachemire *m*.

kd *abbr* (*US*: = *knocked down*) en pièces détachées.

kebab [kəbâb'] *n* kébab *m*.

keel [kēl] *n* quille *f*; **on an even** ~ (*fig*) à flot.

keel over *vi* (*NAUT*) chavirer, dessaler; (*person*) tomber dans les pommes.

keen [kēn] *a* (*interest, desire, competition*) vif(vive); (*eye, intelligence*) pénétrant(e); (*edge*) effilé(e); (*eager*) plein(e) d'enthousiasme; **to be** ~ **to do** *or* **on doing sth** désirer vivement faire qch, tenir beaucoup à faire qch; **to be** ~ **on sth/sb** aimer beaucoup qch/qn; **I'm not** ~ **on going** je ne suis pas chaud pour aller, je n'ai pas très envie d'y aller.

keenly [kēn'lē] *ad* (*enthusiastically*) avec enthousiasme; (*feel*) vivement, profondément; (*look*) intensément.

keenness [kēn'nis] *n* (*eagerness*) enthousiasme *m*; ~ **to do** vif désir de faire.

keep [kēp] *vb* (*pt, pp* **kept** [kept]) *vt* (*retain,*

preserve) garder; (*hold back*) retenir; (*a store, the books, a diary*) tenir; (*feed: one's family etc*) entretenir, assurer la subsistance de; (*a promise*) tenir; (*chickens, bees, pigs etc*) élever ♦ *vi* (*food*) se conserver; (*remain: in a certain state or place*) rester ♦ *n* (*of castle*) donjon *m*; (*food etc*): **enough for his** ~ assez pour (assurer) sa subsistance; **to** ~ **doing sth** continuer à faire qch; faire qch continuellement; **to** ~ **sb from doing/sth from happening** empêcher qn de faire *or* que qn (ne) fasse/que qch (n')arrive; **to** ~ **sb happy/a place tidy** faire que qn soit content/qu'un endroit reste propre; **to** ~ **sb waiting** faire attendre qn; **to** ~ **an appointment** ne pas manquer un rendez-vous; **to** ~ **a record of sth** prendre note de qch; **to** ~ **sth to o.s.** garder qch pour soi, tenir qch secret; **to** ~ **sth (back) from sb** cacher qch à qn; **to** ~ **time** (*clock*) être à l'heure, ne pas retarder.

keep away *vt*: **to** ~ **sth/sb away from sb** tenir qch/qn éloigné de qn ♦ *vi*: **to** ~ **away (from)** ne pas s'approcher (de).

keep back *vt* (*crowds, tears, money*) retenir ♦ *vi* rester en arrière.

keep down *vt* (*control: prices, spending*) empêcher d'augmenter, limiter; (*retain: food*) garder ♦ *vi* (*person*) rester assis(e); rester par terre.

keep in *vt* (*invalid, child*) garder à la maison; ♦ *vi* (*col*): **to** ~ **in with sb** rester en bons termes avec qn.

keep off *vi* ne pas s'approcher de; "~ **off the grass**" "pelouse interdite".

keep on *vi* continuer; **to** ~ **on doing** continuer à faire.

keep out *vt* empêcher d'entrer ♦ *vi* rester en dehors; "~ **out**" "défense d'entrer".

keep up *vt* se maintenir; (*fig: in comprehension*) suivre ♦ *vt* continuer, maintenir; **to** ~ **up with** se maintenir au niveau de; **to** ~ **up with sb** (*in race etc*) aller aussi vite que qn, être du même niveau que qn.

keeper [kē'pûr] *n* gardien/ne.

keep-fit [kēp'fit'] *n* (*Brit*) gymnastique *f* de maintien.

keeping [kē'ping] *n* (*care*) garde *f*; **in** ~ **with** à l'avenant de; en accord avec.

keeps [kēps] *n*: **for** ~**s** (*col*) pour de bon, pour toujours.

keepsake [kēp'sāk] *n* souvenir *m*.

keg [keg] *n* barrique *f*, tonnelet *m*.

Ken. *abbr* (*US*) = *Kentucky*.

kennel [ken'əl] *n* niche *f*; ~**s** *npl* chenil *m*.

Kenya [ken'yə] *n* Kenya *m*.

Kenyan [ken'yən] *a* Kenyen(ne) ♦ *n* Kenyen/ne.

kept [kept] *pt, pp of* **keep**.

kerb [kûrb] *n* (*Brit*) bordure *f* du trottoir.

kernel [kûr'nəl] *n* amande *f*; (*fig*) noyau *m*.

kerosene [kär'əsēn] *n* kérosène *m*.

ketchup [kech'əp] *n* ketchup *m*.

kettle [ket'əl] *n* bouilloire *f*.

kettle drums *npl* timbales *fpl*.

key [kē] *n* (*gen, MUS*) clé *f*; (*of piano, typewriter*) touche *f*; (*on map*) légende *f* ♦ *cpd* (-)clé.

key in *vt* (*text*) introduire au clavier.

keyboard [kē'bôrd] *n* clavier *m* ♦ *vt* (*text*)

saisir.

keyed up [kēd up] *a*: **to be (all)** ~ être surexcité(e).

keyhole [kē'hōl] *n* trou *m* de la serrure.

keynote [kē'nōt] *n* (*MUS*) tonique *f*; (*fig*) note dominante.

keypad [kē'pad] *n* pavé *m* numérique.

key ring *n* porte-clés *m*.

keystroke [kē'strōk] *n* frappe *f*.

kg *abbr* (= *kilogram*) K.

KGB *n abbr* KGB *m*.

khaki [kak'ē] *a*, *n* kaki *(m)*.

kibbutz [kibōōts'] *n* kibboutz *m*.

kick [kik] *vt* donner un coup de pied à ♦ *vi* (*horse*) ruer ♦ *n* coup *m* de pied; (*of rifle*) recul *m*; (*col*: *thrill*): **he does it for** ~**s** il le fait parce que ça l'excite, il le fait pour le plaisir.

  kick around *vi* (*col*) traîner.

  kick off *vi* (*SPORT*) donner le coup d'envoi.

kickoff [kik'ôf] *n* (*SPORT*) coup *m* d'envoi.

kick-start [kik'stárt] *n* (*Brit*: *also*: ~**er**) lanceur *m* au pied.

kid [kid] *n* (*col*: *child*) gamin/e, gosse *m/f*; (*animal*, *leather*) chevreau *m* ♦ *vi* (*col*) plaisanter, blaguer.

kidnap [kid'nap] *vt* enlever, kidnapper.

kidnap(p)er [kid'napûr] *n* ravisseur/euse.

kidnap(p)ing [kid'naping] *n* enlèvement *m*.

kidney [kid'nē] *n* (*ANAT*) rein *m*; (*CULIN*) rognon *m*.

kidney bean *n* haricot *m* rouge.

kidney machine *n* (*MED*) rein artificiel.

Kilimanjaro [kiləmənjâr'ō] *n*: **Mount** ~ Kilimandjaro *m*.

kill [kil] *vt* tuer; (*fig*) faire échouer; détruire; supprimer ♦ *n* mise *f* à mort; **to** ~ **time** tuer le temps.

  kill off *vt* exterminer; (*fig*) éliminer.

killer [kil'ûr] *n* tueur/euse; meurtrier/ière.

killing [kil'ing] *n* meurtre *m*; tuerie *f*, massacre *m*; (*col*): **to make a** ~ se remplir les poches, réussir un beau coup ♦ *a* (*col*) tordant(e).

killjoy [kil'joi] *n* rabat-joie *m inv*.

kiln [kiln] *n* four *m*.

kilo [kē'lō] *n abbr* (= *kilogram*) kilo *m*.

kilobyte [kil'əbīt] *n* kilo-octet *m*.

kilogram, (*Brit***) kilogramme** [kil'əgram] *n* kilogramme *m*.

kilometer, (*Brit***) kilometre** [kil'əmētûr] *n* kilomètre *m*.

kilowatt [kil'əwât] *n* kilowatt *m*.

kilt [kilt] *n* kilt *m*.

kilter [kil'tûr] *n*: **out of** ~ déréglé(e), détraqué(e).

kimono [kimō'nō] *n* kimono *m*.

kin [kin] *n see* **next**, **kith**.

kind [kīnd] *a* gentil(le), aimable ♦ *n* sorte *f*, espèce *f*; (*species*) genre *m*; **to be two of a** ~ se ressembler; **would you be** ~ **enough to ...?, would you be so** ~ **as to ...?** auriez-vous la gentillesse *or* l'obligeance de ...?; **it's very** ~ **of you (to do)** c'est très aimable à vous (de faire); **in** ~ (*COMM*) en nature; (*fig*): **to repay sb in** ~ rendre la pareille à qn.

kindergarten [kin'dûrgârtən] *n* jardin *m* d'enfants.

kind-hearted [kīnd'hâr'tid] *a* bon(bonne).

kindle [kin'dəl] *vt* allumer, enflammer.

kindling [kind'ling] *n* petit bois.

kindly [kīnd'lē] *a* bienveillant(e), plein(e) de gentillesse ♦ *ad* avec bonté; **will you** ~ ... auriez-vous la bonté *or* l'obligeance de ...; **he didn't take it** ~ il l'a mal pris.

kindness [kīnd'nis] *n* bonté *f*, gentillesse *f*.

kindred [kin'drid] *a* apparenté(e); ~ **spirit** âme *f* sœur.

kinetic [kinet'ik] *a* cinétique.

king [king] *n* roi *m*.

kingdom [king'dəm] *n* royaume *m*.

kingfisher [king'fishûr] *n* martin-pêcheur *m*.

kingpin [king'pin] *n* (*TECH*) pivot *m*; (*fig*) cheville ouvrière.

king-size(d) [king'sīz(d)] *a* (*cigarette*) (format) extra-long(longue).

kink [kingk] *n* (*of rope*) entortillement *m*; (*in hair*) ondulation *f*; (*col*: *fig*) aberration *f*.

kinky [king'kē] *a* (*fig*) excentrique; (*pej*) aux goûts spéciaux.

kinship [kin'ship] *n* parenté *f*.

kinsman [kinz'mən] *n* parent *m*.

kinswoman [kinz'wōōmən] *n* parente *f*.

kiosk [kēâsk'] *n* kiosque *m*; (*Brit*: *also*: **telephone** ~) cabine *f* (téléphonique); (: *also*: **newspaper** ~) kiosque à journaux.

kipper [kip'ûr] *n* hareng fumé et salé.

kiss [kis] *n* baiser *m* ♦ *vt* embrasser; **to** ~ **(each other)** s'embrasser; **to** ~ **sb goodbye** dire au revoir à qn en l'embrassant; ~ **of life** *n* (*Brit*) bouche à bouche *m*.

kit [kit] *n* équipement *m*, matériel *m*; (*set of tools etc*) trousse *f*; (*for assembly*) kit *m*; **tool** ~ nécessaire *m* à outils.

  kit out *vt* (*Brit*) équiper.

kitbag [kit'bag] *n* sac *m* de voyage *or* de marin.

kitchen [kich'ən] *n* cuisine *f*.

kitchen garden *n* jardin *m* potager.

kitchen sink *n* évier *m*.

kitchen unit *n* (*Brit*) élément *m* de cuisine.

kitchenware [kich'ənwär] *n* vaisselle *f*; ustensiles *mpl* de cuisine.

kite [kīt] *n* (*toy*) cerf-volant *m*; (*ZOOL*) milan *m*.

kith [kith] *n*: ~ **and kin** parents et amis *mpl*.

kitten [kit'ən] *n* petit chat, chaton *m*.

kitty [kit'ē] *n* (*money*) cagnotte *f*.

KKK *n abbr* (*US*) = *Ku Klux Klan*.

Kleenex [klē'neks] *n* ® Kleenex *m* ®.

kleptomaniac [kleptəmā'nēak] *n* kleptomane *m/f*.

km *abbr* (= *kilometer*) km.

km/h *abbr* (= *kilometers per hour*) km/h.

knack [nak] *n*: **to have the** ~ **(of doing)** avoir le coup (pour faire); **there's a** ~ il y a un coup à prendre *or* une combine.

knapsack [nap'sak] *n* musette *f*.

knave [nāv] *n* (*CARDS*) valet *m*.

knead [nēd] *vt* pétrir.

knee [nē] *n* genou *m*.

kneecap [nē'kap] *n* rotule *f*.

knee-deep [nē'dēp] *a*: **the water was** ~ l'eau arrivait aux genoux.

kneel, *pt*, *pp* knelt [nēl, nelt] *vi* (*also*: ~ **down**) s'agenouiller.

kneepad [nē'pad] *n* genouillère *f*.

knell [nel] *n* glas *m*.

knelt [nelt] *pt, pp of* **kneel**.

knew [nōō] *pt of* **know**.

knickers [nik'ûrz] *npl* (*Brit*) culotte *f* (de femme).

knick-knack [nik'nak] *n* colifichet *m*.

knife [nīf] *n* (*pl* **knives**) couteau *m* ♦ *vt* poignarder, frapper d'un coup de couteau; ~, **fork and spoon** couvert *m*.

knight [nīt] *n* chevalier *m*; (*CHESS*) cavalier *m*.

knighthood [nīt'hōōd] *n* chevalerie *f*; (*title*): **to get a** ~ être fait chevalier.

knit [nit] *vt* tricoter; (*fig*): **to** ~ **together** unir ♦ *vi* (*broken bones*) se ressouder.

knitted [nit'id] *a* en tricot.

knitting [nit'ing] *n* tricot *m*.

knitting machine *n* machine *f* à tricoter.

knitting needle *n* aiguille *f* à tricoter.

knitting pattern *n* modèle *m* (pour tricot).

knitwear [nit'wär] *n* tricots *mpl*, lainages *mpl*.

knives [nīvz] *npl of* **knife**.

knob [nâb] *n* bouton *m*; (*Brit*): **a** ~ **of butter** une noix de beurre.

knobby [nâb'ē], (*Brit*) **knobbly** [nâb'lē] *a* (*wood, surface*) noueux(euse); (*knees*) noueux.

knock [nâk] *vt* frapper; (*make: hole etc*): **to** ~ **a hole in** faire un trou dans, trouer; (*Brit: force: nail etc*): **to** ~ **a nail into** enfoncer un clou dans; (*fig: col*) dénigrer ♦ *vi* (*engine*) cogner; (*at door etc*): **to** ~ **at/on** frapper à/sur ♦ *n* coup *m*; **he** ~**ed at the door** il frappa à la porte.

knock down *vt* renverser; (*price*) réduire.

knock off *vi* (*col: finish*) s'arrêter (de travailler) ♦ *vt* (*vase, object*) faire tomber; (*fig: from price etc*): **to** ~ **off $10** faire une remise de 10 dollars; (*col: steal*) piquer.

knock out *vt* assommer; (*BOXING*) mettre k.-o.

knock over *vt* (*object*) faire tomber; (*pedestrian*) renverser.

knockdown [nâk'doun] *a* (*price*) sacrifié(e); (*furniture etc*) démontable.

knocker [nâk'ûr] *n* (*on door*) heurtoir *m*.

knock-for-knock [nâk'fûrnâk'] *a* (*Brit*): ~ **agreement** convention entre compagnies d'assurances par laquelle chacune s'engage à dédommager son propre client.

knocking [nâk'ing] *n* coups *mpl*.

knock-kneed [nâk'nēd] *a* aux genoux cagneux.

knock-on effect [nâk'ân ifekt'] *n* répercussions *fpl* en chaîne.

knockout [nâk'out] *n* (*BOXING*) knock-out *m*, K.-O. *m*.

knot [nât] *n* (*gen*) nœud *m* ♦ *vt* nouer; **to tie a** ~ faire un nœud.

knotty [nât'ē] *a* (*fig*) épineux(euse).

know [nō] *vt* (*pt* **knew**, *pp* **known** [nōō, nōn]) savoir; (*person, place*) connaître; **to** ~ **that** savoir que; **to** ~ **how to do** savoir faire; **to** ~ **about/of sth** être au courant de/connaître qch; **to get to** ~ **sth** (*fact*) apprendre qch; (*place*) apprendre à connaître qch; **I don't** ~ **him** je ne le connais pas; **to** ~ **right from wrong** savoir distinguer le bon du mauvais; **as far as I** ~ ... à ma connaissance ...,

autant que je sache ....

know-all [nō'ôl] *n* (*Brit*) = **know-it-all**.

know-how [nō'hou] *n* savoir-faire *m*, technique *f*, compétence *f*.

knowing [nō'ing] *a* (*look etc*) entendu(e).

knowingly [nō'inglē] *ad* sciemment; d'un air entendu.

know-it-all [nō'itôl] *n* (*US pej*) je-sais-tout *m/f*.

knowledge [nâl'ij] *n* connaissance *f*; (*learning*) connaissances, savoir *m*; **to have no** ~ **of** ignorer; **not to my** ~ pas à ma connaissance; **without my** ~ à mon insu; **to have a working** ~ **of French** se débrouiller en français; **it is common** ~ **that** ... chacun sait que ...; **it has come to my** ~ **that** ... j'ai appris que ....

knowledgeable [nâl'ijəbəl] *a* bien informé(e).

known [nōn] *pp of* **know** ♦ *a* (*thief, facts*) notoire; (*expert*) célèbre.

knuckle [nuk'əl] *n* articulation *f* (des phalanges), jointure *f*.

knuckle under *vi* (*col*) céder.

knuckle-duster [nuk'əldustûr] *n* coup-de-poing américain.

KO *abbr* (= *knock out*) *n* K.-O. *m* ♦ *vt* mettre K.-O.

koala [kōâl'ə] *n* (*also*: ~ **bear**) koala *m*.

kook [kōōk] *n* (*US col*) loufoque *m/f*.

Koran [kôrân'] *n* Coran *m*.

Korea [kôrē'ə] *n* Corée *f*; **North/South** ~ Corée du Nord/Sud.

Korean [kôrē'ən] *a* coréen(ne) ♦ *n* Coréen/ne.

kosher [kō'shûr] *a* kascher *inv*.

kowtow [kou'tou] *vi*: **to** ~ **to sb** s'aplatir devant qn.

Kremlin [krem'lin] *n*: **the** ~ **le** Kremlin.

KS *abbr* (*US MAIL*) = *Kansas*.

Kuala Lumpur [kōōâ'lə lōōm'pōōr] *n* Kuala Lumpur.

kudos [kyōō'dōs] *n* gloire *f*, lauriers *mpl*.

Kuwait [kōōwāt'] *n* Koweït *f*, Kuweit *f*.

Kuwaiti [kōōât'ē] *a* koweïtien(ne) ♦ *n* Koweïtien/ne.

kW *abbr* (= *kilowatt*) kW.

KY *abbr* (*US MAIL*) = *Kentucky*.

L

L, l [el] *n* (*letter*) L, l *m*; **L for Love** L comme Louis.

L *abbr* (= *lake, large*) L; (= *left*) g; (*Brit AUT*: = *learner*) signale un conducteur débutant.

l *abbr* (= *liter*) l.

La. *abbr* (*US*) = *Louisiana*.

LA *n abbr* (*US*) = *Los Angeles* ♦ *abbr* (*US MAIL*) = *Louisiana*.

Lab. *abbr* (*Canada*) = *Labrador*.

lab [lab] *n abbr* (= *laboratory*) labo *m*.

label [lā'bəl] *n* étiquette *f*; (*brand: of record*) marque *f* ♦ *vt* étiqueter; **to** ~ **sb a** ... qualifier qn de ....

labor |lā'bûr| (US) n (task) travail m; (workmen) main-d'œuvre f; (MED) travail, accouchement m ♦ vi: **to ~ (at)** travailler dur (à), peiner (sur); **in ~** (MED) en travail.

laboratory |lab'rətôrē| n laboratoire m.

labor camp n camp m de travaux forcés.

labor cost n coût m de la main-d'œuvre; coût de la façon.

Labor Day n fête f du travail.

labor dispute n conflit social.

labored |lā'bûrd| a lourd(e), laborieux(euse); (breathing) difficile, pénible; (style) lourd, embarrassé(e).

laborer |lā'bûrûr| n manœuvre m; (on farm) ouvrier m agricole.

labor force n main-d'œuvre f.

labor-intensive |lā'bûrintensiv| a intensif(ive) en main-d'œuvre.

laborious |ləbôr'ēəs| a laborieux(euse).

labor market n marché m du travail.

labor pains npl douleurs fpl de l'accouchement.

labor relations npl relations fpl dans l'entreprise.

labor-saving |lā'bûrsā'ving| a qui simplifie le travail.

labor union n (US) syndicat m.

labor unrest n agitation sociale.

Labour |lā'bûr| n (Brit POL): **also: the ~ Party**) le parti travailliste, les travaillistes mpl.

labour etc |lā'bûr| (Brit) = **labor** etc.

labyrinth |lab'ûrinth| n labyrinthe m, dédale m.

lace |lās| n dentelle f; (of shoe etc) lacet m ♦ vt (shoe) lacer; (drink) arroser, corser.

lacemaking |lās'māking| n fabrication f de dentelle.

laceration |lasərā'shən| n lacération f.

lace-up |lās'up| a (shoes etc) à lacets.

lack |lak| n manque m ♦ vt manquer de; **through** or **for ~ of** faute de, par manque de; **to be ~ing** manquer, faire défaut; **to be ~ing in** manquer de.

lackadaisical |lakədā'zikəl| a nonchalant(e), indolent(e).

lackey |lak'ē| n (also fig) laquais m.

lackluster, (Brit) **lacklustre** |lak'lustûr| a terne.

laconic |ləkân'ik| a laconique.

lacquer |lak'ûr| n laque f.

lacy |lā'sē| a comme de la dentelle, qui ressemble à de la dentelle.

lad |lad| n garçon m, gars m; (Brit: in stable etc) lad m.

ladder |lad'ûr| n échelle f; (Brit: in tights) maille filée ♦ vt, vi (Brit: tights) filer.

laden |lā'dən| a: **~ (with)** chargé(e) (de); **fully ~** (truck, ship) en pleine charge.

ladle |lā'dəl| n louche f.

lady |lā'dē| n dame f; **L~ Smith** lady Smith; **the ladies' (room)** les toilettes fpl des dames; **a ~ doctor** une doctoresse, une femme médecin.

ladybird |lā'dēbûrd| n (Brit) coccinelle f.

ladybug |lā'dēbug| n (US) coccinelle f.

lady finger n (US) boudoir m.

lady-in-waiting |lā'dēinwā'ting| n dame f

d'honneur.

ladykiller |lā'dēkilûr| n don Juan m.

ladylike |lā'dēlik| a distingué(e).

lag |lag| n = **time ~** ♦ vi (also: **~ behind**) rester en arrière, traîner ♦ vt (pipes) calorifuger.

lager |lâ'gûr| n bière blonde.

lagging |lag'ing| n enveloppe isolante, calorifuge m.

lagoon |ləgōōn'| n lagune f.

Lagos |lāg'ōs| n Lagos.

laid |lād| pt, pp of **lay**.

laid-back |lād'bak'| a (col) relaxe, décontracté(e).

lain |lān| pp of **lie**.

lair |lär| n tanière f, gîte m.

laissez-faire |lcs'āfär'| n libéralisme m.

laity |lā'itē| n laïques mpl.

lake |lāk| n lac m.

lamb |lam| n agneau m.

lamb chop n côtelette f d'agneau.

lambskin |lam'skin| n (peau f d')agneau m.

lambswool |lams'wōōl| n (Brit) laine f d'agneau.

lame |lām| a boiteux(euse); **~ duck** (fig) canard boiteux.

lamely |lām'lē| ad (fig) sans conviction.

lament |ləment'| n lamentation f ♦ vt pleurer, se lamenter sur.

lamentable |lam'əntəbəl| a déplorable, lamentable.

laminated |lam'ənātid| a laminé(e); (windshield) (en verre) feuilleté.

lamp |lamp| n lampe f.

lamplight |lamp'lit| n: **by ~** à la lumière de la (or d'une) lampe.

lampoon |lampōōn'| n pamphlet m.

lamppost |lamp'pōst| n réverbère m.

lampshade |lamp'shād| n abat-jour m inv.

lance |lans| n lance f ♦ vt (MED) inciser.

lance corporal n (Brit) ≈ (soldat m de) première classe m.

lancet |lan'sit| n (MED) bistouri m.

Lancs |langks| abbr (Brit) = Lancashire.

land |land| n (as opposed to sea) terre f (ferme); (country) pays m; (soil) terre; terrain m; (estate) terre(s), domaine(s) m(pl) ♦ vi (from ship) débarquer; (AVIAT) atterrir; (fig: fall) (re)tomber ♦ vt (passengers, goods) débarquer; (obtain) décrocher; **to go/travel by ~** se déplacer par voie de terre; **to own ~** être propriétaire foncier; **to ~ on one's feet** (also fig) retomber sur ses pieds.

land up vi atterrir, (finir par) se retrouver.

landing |lan'ding| n (from ship) débarquement m; (AVIAT) atterrissage m; (of staircase) palier m.

landing card n carte f de débarquement.

landing craft n péniche f de débarquement.

landing gear n train m d'atterrissage.

landing strip n piste f d'atterrissage.

landlady |land'lādē| n propriétaire f, logeuse f.

landlocked |land'läkt| a entouré(e) de terre(s), sans accès à la mer.

landlord |land'lôrd| n propriétaire m, logeur m; (of pub etc) patron m.

landlubber |land'lubûr| n terrien/ne.

landmark |land'mârk| n (point m de) repère

m; **to be a** ~ (*fig*) faire date *or* époque.
landowner [land'ōnûr] *n* propriétaire foncier *or* terrien.
landscape [land'skāp] *n* paysage *m*.
landscape architect, landscape gardener *n* paysagiste *m/f*.
landscape painting *n* (*ART*) paysage *m*.
landslide [land'slīd] *n* (*GEO*) glissement *m* (de terrain); (*fig: POL*) raz-de-marée (électoral).
lane [lān] *n* (*in country*) chemin *m*; (*in town*) ruelle *f*; (*AUT*) voie *f*; file *f*; (*in race*) couloir *m*; **shipping** ~ route *f* maritime *or* de navigation.
language [lang'gwij] *n* langue *f*; (*way one speaks*) langage *m*; **bad** ~ grossièretés *fpl*, langage grossier.
language laboratory *n* laboratoire *m* de langues.
languid [lang'gwid] *a* languissant(e); langoureux(euse).
languish [lang'gwish] *vi* languir.
lank [langk] *a* (*hair*) raide et terne.
lanky [lang'kē] *a* grand(e) et maigre, efflanqué(e).
lanolin(e) [lan'əlin] *n* lanoline *f*.
lantern [lan'tûrn] *n* lanterne *f*.
Laos [lā'ōs] *n* Laos *m*.
lap [lap] *n* (*of track*) tour *m* (de piste); (*of body*): **in** *or* **on one's** ~ sur les genoux ♦ *vt* (*also:* ~ **up**) laper ♦ *vi* (*waves*) clapoter.
lap up *vt* (*fig*) boire comme du petit-lait, se gargariser de; (*: lies etc*) gober.
La Paz [lä päs'] *n* La Paz.
lapdog [lap'dôg] *n* chien *m* d'appartement.
lapel [ləpel'] *n* revers *m*.
Lapland [lap'lənd] *n* Laponie *f*.
lapse [laps] *n* défaillance *f*; (*in behavior*) écart *m* (de conduite) ♦ *vi* (*LAW*) cesser d'être en vigueur; se périmer; **to** ~ **into bad habits** prendre de mauvaises habitudes; ~ **of time** laps *m* de temps, intervalle *m*; **a** ~ **of memory** un trou de mémoire.
laptop [lap'tâp] *n* (*also:* ~ **computer**) portatif *m*.
larceny [lâr'sənē] *n* vol *m*.
lard [lârd] *n* saindoux *m*.
larder [lâr'dûr] *n* garde-manger *m inv*.
large [lârj] *a* grand(e); (*person, animal*) gros(grosse); **to make** ~**r** agrandir; **a** ~ **number of people** beaucoup de gens; **by and** ~ en général; **on a** ~ **scale** sur une grande échelle; **at** ~ (*free*) en liberté; (*generally*) en général; pour la plupart.
largely [lârj'lē] *ad* en grande partie.
large-scale [lârj'skāl] *a* (*map, drawing etc*) à grande échelle; (*fig*) important(e).
lark [lârk] *n* (*bird*) alouette *f*; (*joke*) blague *f*, farce *f*.
lark about *vi* faire l'idiot, rigoler.
larva [lâr'və], *pl* **larvae** [lâr'vɔ, lâr'vā] *n* larve *f*.
laryngitis [larənjī'tis] *n* laryngite *f*.
larynx [lar'ingks] *n* larynx *m*.
lascivious [ləsiv'ēəs] *a* lascif(ive).
laser [lā'zûr] *n* laser *m*.
laser beam *n* rayon *m* laser.
laser printer *n* imprimante *f* laser.
lash [lash] *n* coup *m* de fouet; (*also:* **eye**~) cil *m* ♦ *vt* fouetter; (*tie*) attacher.
lash down *vt* attacher; amarrer; arrimer ♦

vi (*rain*) tomber avec violence.
lash out *vi*: **to** ~ **out (at** *or* **against sb/sth)** attaquer violemment (qn/qch); **to** ~ **out (on sth)** (*col: spend*) se fendre (de qch).
lass [las] *n* (jeune) fille *f*.
lasso [las'ō] *n* lasso *m* ♦ *vt* prendre au lasso.
last [last] *a* dernier(ière) ♦ *ad* en dernier ♦ *vi* durer; ~ **week** la semaine dernière; ~ **night** hier soir; la nuit dernière; **at** ~ enfin; **next to (the)** ~ avant-dernier(ière); **the** ~ **time** la dernière fois; **it** ~**s (for) 2 hours** ça dure 2 heures.
last-ditch [last'dich'] *a* ultime, désespéré(e).
lasting [las'ting] *a* durable.
lastly [last'lē] *ad* en dernier lieu, pour finir.
last-minute [last'min'it] *a* de dernière minute.
latch [lach] *n* loquet *m*.
latch on to *vt* (*cling to: person*) s'accrocher à; (*: idea*) trouver bon(ne).
latchkey [lach'kē] *n* clé *f* (de la porte d'entrée).
late [lāt] *a* (*not on time*) en retard; (*far on in day etc*) dernier(ière); tardif(ive); (*recent*) récent(e), dernier; (*former*) ancien(ne); (*dead*) défunt(e) ♦ *ad* tard; (*behind time, schedule*) en retard; **to be** ~ avoir du retard; **to be 10 minutes** ~ avoir 10 minutes de retard; **to work** ~ travailler tard; ~ **in life** sur le tard, à un âge avancé; **of** ~ dernièrement; **in** ~ **May** vers la fin (du mois) de mai, fin mai; **the** ~ **Mr X** feu M. X.
latecomer [lāt'kumûr] *n* retardataire *m/f*.
lately [lāt'lē] *ad* récemment.
lateness [lāt'nis] *n* (*of person*) retard *m*; (*of event*) heure tardive.
latent [lā'tənt] *a* latent(e); ~ **defect** vice caché.
later [lā'tûr] *a* (*date etc*) ultérieur(e); (*version etc*) plus récent(e) ♦ *ad* plus tard; ~ **on today** plus tard dans la journée.
lateral [lat'ûrəl] *a* latéral(e).
latest [lā'tist] *a* tout(e) dernier(ière); **the** ~ **news** les dernières nouvelles; **at the** ~ au plus tard.
latex [lā'teks] *n* latex *m*.
lath, *pl* ~**s** [lath, la**th**z] *n* latte *f*.
lathe [lā**th**] *n* tour *m*.
lather [la**th**'ûr] *n* mousse *f* (de savon) ♦ *vt* savonner ♦ *vi* mousser.
Latin [lat'in] *n* latin *m* ♦ *a* latin(e).
Latin America *n* Amérique latine.
Latin American *a* latino-américain(e), d'Amérique latine ♦ *n* Latino-Américain/e.
latitude [lat'ətōōd] *n* (*also fig*) latitude *f*.
latrine [lətrēn'] *n* latrines *fpl*.
latter [lat'ûr] *a* deuxième, dernier(ière) ♦ *n*: **the** ~ ce dernier, celui-ci.
latterly [lat'ûrlē] *ad* dernièrement, récemment.
lattice [lat'is] *n* treillis *m*; treillage *m*.
lattice window *n* fenêtre treillissée, fenêtre à croisillons.
Latvia [lat'vēə] *n* Lettonie *f*.
laudable [lôd'əbəl] *a* louable.
laudatory [lôd'ətôrē] *a* élogieux(euse).
laugh [laf] *n* rire *m* ♦ *vi* rire.
laugh at *vt fus* se moquer de; (*joke*) rire de.
laugh off *vt* écarter *or* rejeter par une plai-

santerie *or* par une boutade.

laughable [laf'əbəl] *a* risible, ridicule.

laughing [laf'ing] *a* rieur(euse); **this is no ~ matter** il n'y a pas de quoi rire, ça n'a rien d'amusant.

laughing gas *n* gaz hilarant.

laughing stock *n*: **the ~ of** la risée de.

laughter [laf'tûr] *n* rire *m*; (*people laughing*) rires *mpl*.

launch [lônch] *n* lancement *m*; (*boat*) chaloupe *f*; (*also:* **motor ~**) vedette *f* ♦ *vt* (*ship, rocket, plan*) lancer.
  launch out *vi*: **to ~ out (into)** se lancer (dans).

launching [lôn'ching] *n* lancement *m*.

launch(ing) pad *n* rampe *f* de lancement.

launder [lôn'dûr] *vt* blanchir.

launderette [lôndəret'] *n* (*Brit*) laverie *f* (automatique).

laundromat [lôn'drəmat] *n* (*US*) laverie *f* (automatique).

laundry [lôn'drē] *n* blanchisserie *f*; (*clothes*) linge *m*; **to do the ~** faire la lessive.

laureate [lôr'ēit] *a see* **poet laureate**.

laurel [lôr'əl] *n* laurier *m*; **to rest on one's ~s** se reposer sur ses lauriers.

lava [lâv'ə] *n* lave *f*.

lavatory [lav'ətôrē] *n* toilettes *fpl*.

lavender [lav'əndûr] *n* lavande *f*.

lavish [lav'ish] *a* copieux(euse); somptueux(euse); (*giving freely*): **~ with** prodigue de ♦ *vt*: **to ~ sth on sb** prodiguer qch à qn.

lavishly [lav'ishlē] *ad* (*give, spend*) sans compter; (*furnished*) luxueusement.

law [lô] *n* loi *f*; (*science*) droit *m*; **against the ~** contraire à la loi; **to study ~** faire du droit; **~ and order** *n* l'ordre public.

law-abiding [lô'əbīding] *a* respectueux(euse) des lois.

lawbreaker [lô'brīakûr] *n* personne *f* qui transgresse la loi.

law court *n* tribunal *m*, cour *f* de justice.

lawful [lô'fəl] *a* légal(e); permis(e).

lawfully [lô'fəlē] *ad* légalement.

lawless [lô'lis] *a* sans loi.

lawmaker [lô'mākûr] *n* législateur/trice.

lawn [lôn] *n* pelouse *f*.

lawnmower [lôn'mōûr] *n* tondeuse *f* à gazon.

lawn tennis *n* tennis *m*.

law school *n* faculté *f* de droit.

law student *n* étudiant/e en droit.

lawsuit [lô'sōōt] *n* procès *m*; **to bring a ~ against** engager des poursuites contre.

lawyer [lô'yûr] *n* (*consultant, with company*) juriste *m*; (*for sales, wills etc*) ≈ notaire *m*; (*partner, in court*) ≈ avocat *m*.

lax [laks] *a* relâché(e).

laxative [lak'sətiv] *n* laxatif *m*.

laxity [lak'sitē] *n* relâchement *m*.

lay [lā] *pt of* **lie** ♦ *a* laïque; profane ♦ *vt* (*pt, pp* **laid** [lād]) poser, mettre; (*eggs*) pondre; (*trap*) tendre; (*plans*) élaborer; **to ~ the table** (*Brit*) mettre la table; **to ~ the facts/one's proposals before sb** présenter les faits/ses propositions à qn; **to get laid** (*col!*) baiser (*!*); se faire baiser (*!*).

lay aside, lay by *vt* mettre de côté.

lay down *vt* poser; **to ~ down the law**

(*fig*) faire la loi.

lay in *vt* accumuler, s'approvisionner en.

lay into *vi* (*col: attack*) tomber sur; (*: scold*) passer une engueulade à.

lay off *vt* (*workers*) licencier.

lay on *vt* (*water, gas*) mettre, installer; (*provide: meal etc*) fournir; (*paint*) étaler.

lay out *vt* (*design*) dessiner, concevoir; (*display*) disposer; (*spend*) dépenser.

lay up *vt* (*to store*) amasser; (*car*) remiser; (*ship*) désarmer; (*subj: illness*) forcer à s'aliter.

layabout [lā'əbáut] *n* (*Brit*) fainéant/e.

lay-by [lā'bī] *n* (*Brit*) aire *f* de stationnement (sur le bas-côté).

lay days *npl* (*NAUT*) estarie *f*.

layer [lā'ûr] *n* couche *f*.

layette [lāet'] *n* layette *f*.

layman [lā'mən] *n* laïque *m*; profane *m*.

layoff [lā'ôf] *n* licenciement *m*.

layout [lā'áut] *n* disposition *f*, plan *m*, agencement *m*; (*PRESS*) mise *f* en page.

layover [lā'ōvûr] *n* (*US*) escale *f*.

laze [lāz] *vi* paresser.

laziness [lā'zēnis] *n* paresse *f*.

lazy [lā'zē] *a* paresseux(euse).

LB *abbr* (*Canada*) = Labrador.

lb. *abbr* (= *libra: pound*) unité de poids.

LC *n abbr* (*US*) = *Library of Congress*.

lc *abbr* (*TYP*: = *lower case*) b.d.c.

L/C *abbr* = **letter of credit**.

LCD *n abbr* = **liquid crystal display**.

LDS *n abbr* (= *Latter-day Saints*) *Église de Jésus-Christ des Saints du dernier jour*.

lead [lēd] *n* (*front position*) tête *f*; (*distance, time ahead*) avance *f*; (*clue*) piste *f*; (*to battery*) raccord *m*; (*ELEC*) fil *m*; (*for dog*) laisse *f*; (*THEATER*) rôle principal; [led] (*metal*) plomb *m*; (*in pencil*) mine *f* ♦ *vb* (*pt, pp* **led** [led]) *vt* mener, conduire; (*induce*) amener; (*be leader of*) être à la tête de; (*SPORT*) être en tête de; (*orchestra: US*) diriger; (*: Brit*) être le premier violon de ♦ *vi* mener, être en tête; **to ~ to** mener à; (*result in*) conduire à; aboutir à; **to ~ sb astray** détourner qn du droit chemin; **to be in the ~** (*SPORT*: *in race*) mener, être en tête; (*: match*) mener (à la marque); **to take the ~** (*SPORT*) passer en tête, prendre la tête; mener; (*fig*) prendre l'initiative; **to ~ sb to believe that ...** amener qn à croire que ...; **to ~ sb to do sth** amener qn à faire qch.

lead away *vt* emmener.

lead back *vt* ramener.

lead off *vi* (*in game etc*) commencer.

lead on *vt* (*tease*) faire marcher; **to ~ sb on to** (*induce*) amener qn à.

lead up to *vt* conduire à.

leaded [led'id] *a* (*gas*) avec plomb; (*windows*) à petits carreaux.

leaden [led'ən] *a* de *or* en plomb.

leader [lē'dûr] *n* (*of team*) chef *m*; (*of party etc*) dirigeant/e, leader *m*; (*of orchestra: US*) chef *m* d'orchestre; (*: Brit*) premier violon; (*Brit: in newspaper*) éditorial *m*; **they are ~s in their field** (*fig*) ils sont à la pointe du progrès dans leur domaine.

leadership [lē'dûrship] *n* direction *f*; **under the ~ of ...** sous la direction de ...; **qualities**

of ~ qualités *fpl* de chef *or* de meneur.
lead-free [lēdfrē'] *a* sans plomb.
leading [lē'ding] *a* de premier plan; (*main*) principal(e); **a** ~ **question** une question tendancieuse; ~ **role** rôle prépondérant *or* de premier plan.
leading lady *n* (*THEATER*) vedette (féminine).
leading light *n* (*person*) sommité *f*, personnalité *f* de premier plan.
leading man *n* (*THEATER*) vedette (masculine).
lead pencil *n* crayon noir *or* à papier.
lead poisoning *n* saturnisme *m*.
lead time *n* (*COMM*) délai *m* de livraison.
lead weight *n* plomb *m*.
leaf, *pl* **leaves** [lēf, lēvz] *n* feuille *f*; (*of table*) rallonge *f*; **to turn over a new** ~ (*fig*) changer de conduite *or* d'existence; **to take a** ~ **out of sb's book** (*fig*) prendre exemple sur qn.
leaf through *vt* (*book*) feuilleter.
leaflet [lēf'lit] *n* prospectus *m*, brochure *f*; (*POL*, *REL*) tract *m*.
leafy [lē'fē] *a* feuillu(e).
league [lēg] *n* ligue *f*; (*SOCCER*) championnat *m*; (*measure*) lieue *f*; **to be in** ~ **with** avoir partie liée avec, être de mèche avec.
leak [lēk] *n* (*out, also fig*) fuite *f*; (*in*) infiltration *f* ♦ *vi* (*pipe, liquid etc*) fuir; (*shoes*) prendre l'eau ♦ *vt* (*liquid*) répandre; (*information*) divulguer.
leak out *vi* fuir; (*information*) être divulgué(e).
leakage [lē'kij] *n* (*also fig*) fuite *f*.
leaky [lē'kē] *a* (*pipe, bucket*) qui fuit, percé(e); (*roof*) qui coule; (*shoe*) qui prend l'eau; (*boat*) qui fait eau.
lean [lēn] *a* maigre ♦ *n* (*of meat*) maigre *m* ♦ *vb* (*pt, pp* **leaned** *or* **leant** [lent]) *vt*: **to** ~ **sth on** appuyer qch sur ♦ *vi* (*slope*) pencher; (*rest*): **to** ~ **against** s'appuyer contre; être appuyé(e) contre; **to** ~ **on** s'appuyer sur.
lean back *vi* se pencher en arrière.
lean forward *vi* se pencher en avant.
lean out *vi*: **to** ~ **out (of)** se pencher au dehors (de).
lean over *vi* se pencher.
leaning [lē'ning] *a* penché(e) ♦ *n*: ~ **(towards)** penchant *m* (pour); **the** ~ **Tower of Pisa** la tour penchée de Pise.
leant [lent] *pt, pp of* **lean.**
lean-to [lēn'tōō] *n* appentis *m*.
leap [lēp] *n* bond *m*, saut *m* ♦ *vi* (*pt, pp* **leaped** *or* **leapt** [lept]) bondir, sauter; **to** ~ **at an offer** saisir une offre.
leap up *vi* (*person*) faire un bond; se lever d'un bond.
leapfrog [lēp'frâg] *n* jeu *m* de saute-mouton.
leapt [lept] *pt, pp of* **leap.**
leap year *n* année *f* bissextile.
learn, *pt, pp* **learned** *or* **learnt** [lûrn, -t] *vt, vi* apprendre; **to** ~ **how to do sth** apprendre à faire qch; **we were sorry to** ~ **that** ... nous apprenons avec regret que ...; **to** ~ **about sth** (*SCOL*) étudier qch; (*hear*) apprendre qch.
learned [lûr'nid] *a* érudit(e), savant(e).
learner [lûr'nûr] *n* débutant/e; (*Brit: also:* ~

driver) (conducteur/trice) débutant(e).
learning [lûr'ning] *n* savoir *m*.
lease [lēs] *n* bail *m* ♦ *vt* louer à bail; **on** ~ en location.
lease back *vt* (*Brit*) vendre en cession-bail.
leaseback [lēs'bak] *n* (*Brit*) cession-bail *f*.
leasehold [lēs'hōld] *n* (*contract*) bail *m* ♦ *a* loué(e) à bail.
leash [lēsh] *n* laisse *f*.
least [lēst] *a*: **the** ~ + *noun* le(la) plus petit(e), le(la) moindre; (*smallest amount of*) le moins de; **the** ~ + *adjective* le(la) moins; **the** ~ **money** le moins d'argent; **the** ~ **expensive** le moins cher; **at** ~ au moins; **not in the** ~ pas le moins du monde.
leather [leth'ûr] *n* cuir *m* ♦ *cpd* en *or* de cuir; ~ **goods** maroquinerie *f*.
leave [lēv] *vb* (*pt, pp* **left** [left]) *vt* laisser; (*go away from*) quitter ♦ *vi* partir, s'en aller ♦ *n* (*time off*) congé *m*; (*MIL, also: consent*) permission *f*; **to be left** rester; **there's some milk left over** il reste du lait; **to** ~ **school** quitter l'école, terminer sa scolarité; ~ **it to me!** laissez-moi faire!, je m'en occupe!; **on** ~ en permission; **to take one's** ~ **of** prendre congé de; ~ **of absence** *n* congé exceptionnel; (*MIL*) permission spéciale.
leave behind *vt* (*also fig*) laisser; (*opponent in race*) distancer; (*forget*) laisser, oublier.
leave off *vt* (*cover, lid, heating*) ne pas (re)mettre; (*light*) ne pas (r)allumer, laisser éteint(e).
leave on *vt* (*coat etc*) garder, ne pas enlever; (*lid*) laisser dessus; (*light, fire, stove*) laisser allumé(e).
leave out *vt* oublier, omettre.
leaves [lēvz] *npl of* **leaf.**
leavetaking [lēv'tāking] *n* adieux *mpl*.
Lebanese [lebənēz'] *a* libanais(e) ♦ *n* (*pl inv*) Libanais/e.
Lebanon [leb'ənən] *n* Liban *m*.
lecherous [lech'ûrəs] *a* lubrique.
lectern [lek'tûrn] *n* lutrin *m*, pupitre *m*.
lecture [lek'chûr] *n* conférence *f*; (*SCOL*) cours (magistral) ♦ *vi* donner des cours; enseigner ♦ *vt* (*reprove*) sermonner, réprimander; **to** ~ **on** faire un cours (*or* son cours) sur; **to give a** ~ **(on)** faire une conférence (sur); faire un cours (sur).
lecture hall *n* amphithéâtre *m*.
lecturer [lek'chûrûr] *n* (*speaker*) conférencier/ière; (*Brit: at university*) chargé/e de cours, ≈ maître assistant (*inv*).
LED *n abbr* (= *light-emitting diode*) LED *f*, diode électroluminescente.
led [led] *pt, pp of* **lead.**
ledge [lej] *n* (*of window, on wall*) rebord *m*; (*of mountain*) saillie *f*, corniche *f*.
ledger [lej'ûr] *n* registre *m*, grand livre.
lee [lē] *n* côté *m* sous le vent; **in the** ~ **of** à l'abri de.
leech [lēch] *n* sangsue *f*.
leek [lēk] *n* poireau *m*.
leer [lēr] *vi*: **to** ~ **at sb** regarder qn d'un air mauvais *or* concupiscent, lorgner qn.
leeward [lē'wûrd] *a, ad* sous le vent ♦ *n* côté *m* sous le vent; **to** ~ sous le vent.
leeway [lē'wā] *n* (*fig*): **to make up** ~ rattra-

per son retard; **to have some** ~ avoir une certaine liberté d'action.

left [left] *pt, pp of* **leave** ♦ *a* gauche ♦ *ad* à gauche ♦ *n* gauche *f*; **on the** ~, **to the** ~ à gauche; **the L**~ (*POL*) la gauche.

left-hand drive [left'hand' drīv] *n* conduite *f* à gauche.

left-handed [left'han'did] *a* gaucher(ère); (*scissors etc*) pour gauchers.

left-hand side [left'hand' sīd] *n* gauche *f*, côté *m* gauche.

leftist [lef'tist] *a* (*POL*) gauchiste, de gauche.

left-luggage (office) [leftlug'ij (ôf'is)] *n* (*Brit*) consigne *f*.

leftovers [left'ō'vûrz] *npl* restes *mpl*.

left wing *n* (*MIL, SPORT*) aile *f* gauche; (*POL*) gauche *f* ♦ *a*: **left-wing** (*POL*) de gauche.

left-winger [left'wing'ûr] *n* (*POL*) membre *m* de la gauche; (*SPORT*) ailier *m* gauche.

leg [leg] *n* jambe *f*; (*of animal*) patte *f*; (*of furniture*) pied *m*; (*CULIN*: *of chicken*) cuisse *f*; **lst/2nd** ~ (*SPORT*) match *m* aller/retour; (*of journey*) 1ère/2ème étape; ~ **of lamb** (*CULIN*) gigot *m* d'agneau; **to stretch one's** ~**s** se dégourdir les jambes.

legacy [leg'əsē] *n* (*also fig*) héritage *m*, legs *m*.

legal [lē'gəl] *a* légal(e); **to take** ~ **action** *or* **proceedings against sb** poursuivre qn en justice.

legal adviser *n* conseiller/ère juridique.

legal holiday *n* (*US*) jour férié.

legality [lēgal'itē] *n* légalité *f*.

legalize [lē'gəlīz] *vt* légaliser.

legally [lē'gəlē] *ad* légalement; ~ **binding** juridiquement contraignant(e).

legal tender *n* monnaie légale.

legation [ligā'shən] *n* légation *f*.

legend [lej'ənd] *n* légende *f*.

legendary [lej'əndärē] *a* légendaire.

-legged [leg'id] *suffix*: **two**~ à deux pattes (*or* jambes *or* pieds).

leggings [leg'ingz] *npl* jambières *fpl*, guêtres *fpl*.

legibility [lejəbil'ətē] *n* lisibilité *f*.

legible [lej'əbəl] *a* lisible.

legibly [lej'əblē] *ad* lisiblement.

legion [lē'jən] *n* légion *f*.

legionnaire [lējənär'] *n* légionnaire *m*; ~**'s disease** maladie *f* du légionnaire.

legislate [lej'islāt] *vi* légiférer.

legislation [lejislā'shən] *n* législation *f*; **a piece of** ~ un texte de loi.

legislative [lej'islātiv] *a* législatif(ive).

legislator [lej'islātûr] *n* législateur/trice.

legislature [lej'islāchûr] *n* corps législatif.

legitimacy [lijit'əməsē] *n* légitimité *f*.

legitimate [lijit'əmit] *a* légitime.

legitimize [lijit'əmīz] *vt* légitimer.

legroom [leg'rōōm] *n* place *f* pour les jambes.

leg warmers [leg' wôrm'ûrz] *npl* jambières *fpl*.

Leics *abbr* (*Brit*) = *Leicestershire.*

leisure [lē'zhûr] *n* (*time*) loisir *m*, temps *m*; (*free time*) temps libre, loisirs *mpl*; **at** ~ (tout) à loisir; à tête reposée.

leisurely [lē'zhûrlē] *a* tranquille; fait(e) sans se presser.

leisure suit *n* survêtement *m* (mode).

lemon [lem'ən] *n* citron *m*.

lemonade [lemənād'] *n* limonade *f*.

lemon cheese, lemon curd *n* crème *f* de citron.

lemon juice *n* jus *m* de citron.

lemon juicer [lem'ən jōō'sûr] *n* presse-citron *m inv*.

lemon tea *n* thé *m* au citron.

lend [lend] *pt, pp* **lent** [lend, lent] *vt*: **to** ~ **sth (to sb)** prêter qch (à qn); **to** ~ **a hand** donner un coup de main.

lender [len'dûr] *n* prêteur/euse.

lending library [len'ding lī'brärē] *n* bibliothèque *f* de prêt.

length [lengkth] *n* longueur *f*; (*section: of road, pipe etc*) morceau *m*, bout *m*; ~ **of time** durée *f*; **what** ~ **is it?** quelle longueur fait-il?; **it is 2 meters in** ~ cela fait 2 mètres de long; **to fall full** ~ tomber de tout son long; **at** ~ (*at last*) enfin, à la fin; (*lengthily*) longuement; **to go to any** ~**(s) to do sth** faire n'importe quoi pour faire qch, ne reculer devant rien pour faire qch.

lengthen [lengk'thən] *vt* allonger, prolonger ♦ *vi* s'allonger.

lengthwise [lengkth'wīz] *ad* dans le sens de la longueur, en long.

lengthy [lengk'thē] *a* (très) long(longue).

leniency [lē'nēənsē] *n* indulgence *f*, clémence *f*.

lenient [lē'nēənt] *a* indulgent(e), clément(e).

leniently [lē'nēəntlē] *ad* avec indulgence *or* clémence.

lens [lenz] *n* lentille *f*; (*of spectacles*) verre *m*; (*of camera*) objectif *m*.

Lent [lent] *n* Carême *m*.

lent [lent] *pt, pp of* **lend.**

lentil [len'təl] *n* lentille *f*.

Leo [lē'ō] *n* le Lion; **to be** ~ être du Lion.

leopard [lep'ûrd] *n* léopard *m*.

leotard [lē'ətârd] *n* maillot *m* (*de danseur etc*).

leper [lep'ûr] *n* lépreux/euse.

leper colony *n* léproserie *f*.

leprosy [lep'rəsē] *n* lèpre *f*.

lesbian [lez'bēən] *n* lesbienne *f* ♦ *a* lesbien(ne).

lesion [lē'zhən] *n* (*MED*) lésion *f*.

Lesotho [lisōō'tōō] *n* Lesotho *m*.

less [les] *a* moins de ♦ *pronoun, ad* moins; ~ **than that/you** moins que cela/vous; ~ **than half** moins de la moitié; ~ **than 1/a kilo/3 meters** moins de un/d'un kilo /de 3 mètres; ~ **and** ~ de moins en moins; **the** ~ **he works** ... moins il travaille ....

lessee [lesē'] *n* locataire *m/f* (à bail), preneur/euse du bail.

lessen [les'ən] *vi* diminuer, s'amoindrir, s'atténuer ♦ *vt* diminuer, réduire, atténuer.

lesser [les'ûr] *a* moindre; **to a** ~ **extent** *or* **degree** à un degré moindre.

lesson [les'ən] *n* leçon *f*; **a math** ~ une leçon *or* un cours de maths; **to give** ~**s** in donner des cours de; **it taught him a** ~ (*fig*) cela lui a servi de leçon.

lessor [les'ôr] *n* bailleur/eresse.

lest [lest] *cj* de peur de + *infinitive*, de peur que + *sub.*

let, *pt, pp* **let** [let] *vt* laisser; (*Brit*: *lease*) louer; **to ~ sb do sth** laisser qn faire qch; **to ~ sb know sth** faire savoir qch à qn, prévenir qn de qch; **he ~ me go** il m'a laissé partir; **~ the water boil and ...** faites bouillir l'eau et ...; **~'s go** allons-y; **~ him come** qu'il vienne; **"to ~"** (Brit) "à louer".

let down vt (lower) baisser; (dress) rallonger; (hair) défaire; (Brit: tire) dégonfler; (disappoint) décevoir.

let go vi lâcher prise ♦ vt lâcher.

let in vt laisser entrer; (visitor etc) faire entrer; **what have you ~ yourself in for?** à quoi t'es-tu engagé?

let off vt (allow to leave) laisser partir; (not punish) ne pas punir; (subj: taxi driver, bus driver) déposer; (firework etc) faire partir; (smell etc) dégager; **to ~ off steam** (fig: col) se défouler, décharger sa rate or bile.

let on vi (col): **to ~ on that ...** révéler que ..., dire que ....

let out vt laisser sortir; (dress) élargir; (scream) laisser échapper; (rent out) louer.

let up vi diminuer, s'arrêter.

letdown [let'dâun] n (disappointment) déception f.

lethal [lē'thəl] a mortel(le), fatal(e).

lethargic [ləthár'jik] a léthargique.

lethargy [leth'ûrjē] n léthargie f.

letter [let'ûr] n lettre f; **~s** npl (LITERATURE) lettres; **small/capital ~** minuscule f/ majuscule f; **~ of credit** lettre f de crédit.

letter bomb n lettre piégée.

letterbox [let'ûrbâks] n (Brit) boîte f aux or à lettres.

letterhead [let'ûrhed] n en-tête m.

lettering [let'ûring] n lettres fpl; caractères mpl.

letter opener n coupe-papier m.

letterpress [let'ûrpres] n (method) typographie f.

letter quality n qualité f "courrier".

letters patent npl brevet m d'invention.

lettuce [let'is] n laitue f, salade f.

letup [let'up] n répit m, détente f.

leukemia, (Brit) **leukaemia** [lookē'mēə] n leucémie f.

level [lev'əl] a plat(e), plan(e), uni(e); horizontal(e) ♦ n niveau m; (flat place) terrain plat; (also: **spirit ~**) niveau à bulle ♦ vt niveler, aplanir; (gun) pointer, braquer; (accusation): **to ~ (against)** lancer or porter (contre) ♦ vi (col): **to ~ with sb** être franc(franche) avec qn; **"A" ~s** npl (Brit) ≈ baccalauréat m; **"O" ~s** npl (Brit) ≈ B.E.P.C; **a ~ spoonful** (CULIN) une cuillerée à raser; **to be ~ with** être au même niveau que; **to draw ~ with** (team) arriver à égalité de points avec, égaliser avec; arriver au même classement que; (runner, car) arriver à la hauteur de, rattraper; **on the ~** à l'horizontale; (fig: honest) régulier(ière).

level off, level out vi (prices etc) se stabiliser ♦ vt (ground) aplanir, niveler.

level crossing n (Brit) passage m à niveau.

levelheaded [lev'əlhed'id] a équilibré(e).

leveling, (Brit) **levelling** [lev'əling] a (process, effect) de nivellement.

lever [le'vûr] n levier m ♦ vt: **to ~ up/out**

soulever/extraire au moyen d'un levier.

leverage [lev'ûrij] n: **~ (on or with)** prise f (sur).

levity [lev'itē] n manque m de sérieux, légèreté f.

levy [lev'ē] n taxe f, impôt m ♦ vt prélever, imposer; percevoir.

lewd [lood] a obscène, lubrique.

LF abbr (= low frequency) BF.

LI abbr (US) = Long Island.

liabilities [līəbil'ətēz] npl (COMM) obligations fpl, engagements mpl; (on balance sheet) passif m.

liability [līəbil'ətē] n responsabilité f; (handicap) handicap m.

liability insurance n (US) assurance f au tiers.

liable [lī'əbəl] a (subject): **~ to** sujet(te) à; passible de; (responsible): **~ (for)** responsable (de); (likely): **~ to do** susceptible de faire; **to be ~ to a fine** être passible d'une amende.

liaise [lēāz'] vi: **to ~ with** rester en liaison avec.

liaison [lēā'zân] n liaison f.

liar [lī'ûr] n menteur/euse.

libel [lī'bəl] n écrit m diffamatoire; diffamation f ♦ vt diffamer.

libelous, (Brit) **libellous** [lī'bələs] a diffamatoire.

liberal [lib'ûrəl] a libéral(e); (generous): **~ with** prodigue de, généreux(euse) avec ♦ n: **L~** (POL) libéral/e.

liberality [libəral'itē] n (generosity) générosité f, libéralité f.

liberalize [lib'ûrəlīz] vt libéraliser.

liberal-minded [lib'ûrəlmīn'did] a libéral(e), tolérant(e).

liberate [lib'ərāt] vt libérer.

liberation [libərā'shən] n libération f.

Liberia [lībē'rēə] n Libéria m, Liberia m.

Liberian [lībē'rēən] a libérien(ne) ♦ n Libérien/ne.

liberty [lib'ûrtē] n liberté f; **at ~ to do** libre de faire; **to take the ~ of** prendre la liberté de, se permettre de.

libido [libē'dō] n libido f.

Libra [lēb'rə] n la Balance; **to be ~** être de la Balance.

librarian [lībrär'ēən] n bibliothécaire m/f.

library [lī'brärē] n bibliothèque f.

library book n livre m de bibliothèque.

libretto [libret'ō] n livret m.

Libya [lib'ēə] n Libye f.

Libyan [lib'ēən] a libyen(ne), de Libye ♦ n Libyen/ne.

lice [līs] npl of **louse**.

licence [lī'səns] n (Brit) = **license**.

license [lī'səns] n (US) autorisation f, permis m; (COMM) licence f; (RADIO, TV) redevance f; (also: **driver's ~**, (Brit) **driving ~**) permis m (de conduire); (excessive freedom) licence; **import ~** licence d'importation; **produced under ~** fabriqué(e) sous licence ♦ vt donner une licence à; (car) acheter la vignette de; délivrer la vignette de.

licensed [lī'sənst] a (for alcohol) patenté(e) pour la vente des spiritueux, qui a une patente de débit de boissons.

license plate n (esp US AUT) plaque f minéralogique.

licentious [līsen'chəs] a licentieux(euse).

lichen [lī'kən] n lichen m.

lick [lik] vt lécher; (col: defeat) écraser, flanquer une piquette or raclée à ♦ n coup m de langue; **a ~ of paint** un petit coup de peinture.

licorice [lik'ûris] n (US) réglisse m.

lid [lid] n couvercle m; **to take the ~ off sth** (fig) exposer or étaler qch au grand jour.

lido [lē'dō] n piscine f en plein air; complexe m balnéaire.

lie [lī] n mensonge m ♦ vi mentir; (pt **lay**, pp **lain** [lā, 'lān]) (rest) être étendu(e) or allongé(e) or couché(e); (in grave) être enterré(e), reposer; (of object: be situated) se trouver, être; **to ~ low** (fig) se cacher, rester caché(e); **to tell ~s** mentir.
  lie around vi (things) traîner; (person) traînasser, flemmarder.
  lie back vi se renverser en arrière.
  lie down vi se coucher, s'étendre.
  lie up vi (hide) se cacher.

Liechtenstein [lēch'tenstīn] n Liechtenstein m.

lie detector n détecteur m de mensonges.

lieu [lōō]: **in ~ of** prep au lieu de, à la place de.

Lieut. abbr (= lieutenant) Lt.

lieutenant [lōōten'ənt] n lieutenant m.

lieutenant colonel n lieutenant-colonel m.

life, pl **lives** [līf, līvz] n vie f ♦ cpd de vie; de la vie; à vie; **true to ~** réaliste, fidèle à la réalité; **to paint from ~** peindre d'après nature; **to be sent to prison for ~** être condamné(e) (à la réclusion criminelle) à perpétuité; **country/city ~** la vie à la campagne/à la ville.

life annuity n pension f, rente viagère.

life belt n bouée f de sauvetage.

lifeblood [līf'blud] n (fig) élément moteur.

lifeboat [līf'bōt] n canot m or chaloupe f de sauvetage.

life buoy n bouée f de sauvetage.

life expectancy n espérance f de vie.

lifeguard [līf'gârd] n surveillant m de baignade.

life imprisonment n prison f à vie; (LAW) réclusion f à perpétuité.

life insurance n assurance-vie f.

life jacket n gilet m or ceinture f de sauvetage.

lifeless [līf'lis] a sans vie, inanimé(e); (dull) qui manque de vie or de vigueur.

lifelike [līf'līk] a qui semble vrai(e) or vivant(e); ressemblant(e).

lifeline [līf'līn] n corde f de sauvetage.

lifelong [līf'lông] a de toute une vie, de toujours.

life preserver [līf prēzûrv'ûr] n (US) gilet m or ceinture f de sauvetage.

life raft n radeau m de sauvetage.

lifesaver [līf'sāvûr] n surveillant m de baignade.

life sentence n condamnation f à vie or à perpétuité.

life-sized [līf'sīzd] a grandeur nature inv.

life span n (durée f de) vie f.

life style n style m de vie.

life support system n (MED) respirateur artificiel.

lifetime [līf'tīm] n: **in his ~** de son vivant; **the chance of a ~** la chance de ma (or sa etc) vie, une occasion unique.

lift [lift] vt soulever, lever; (steal) prendre, voler ♦ vi (fog) se lever ♦ n (Brit: elevator) ascenseur m; **to give sb a ~** (Brit) emmener or prendre qn en voiture.
  lift off vi (rocket, helicopter) décoller.
  lift out vt sortir; (troops, evacuees etc) évacuer par avion or hélicoptère.
  lift up vt soulever.

lift-off [lift'âf] n décollage m.

ligament [lig'əmənt] n ligament m.

light [līt] n lumière f; (daylight) lumière, jour m; (lamp) lampe f; (AUT: traffic ~, rear ~) feu m; (: headlamp) phare m; (for cigarette etc): **have you got a ~?** avez-vous du feu? ♦ vt (pt, pp **lighted** or **lit** [lit]) (candle, cigarette, fire) allumer; (room) éclairer ♦ a (room, color) clair(e); (not heavy, also fig) léger(ère) ♦ ad (travel) avec peu de bagages; **to turn the ~ on/off** allumer/éteindre; **to cast** or **shed** or **throw ~ on** éclaircir; **to come to ~** être dévoilé(e) or découvert(e); **in the ~ of** à la lumière de; étant donné; **to make ~ of sth** (fig) prendre qch à la légère, faire peu de cas de qch.
  light up vi s'allumer; (face) s'éclairer ♦ vt (illuminate) éclairer, illuminer.

light bulb n ampoule f.

lighten [lī'tən] vi s'éclairer ♦ vt (give light to) éclairer; (make lighter) éclaircir; (make less heavy) alléger.

lighter [lī'tûr] n (also: **cigarette ~**) briquet m; (: in car) allume-cigare m inv; (boat) péniche f.

lighter fluid n gaz m à briquet.

light-fingered [lit'finggûrd] a chapardeur(euse).

light-headed [lit'hed'id] a étourdi(e), écervelé(e).

lighthearted [lit'hâr'tid] a gai(e), joyeux(euse), enjoué(e).

lighthouse [lit'hâus] n phare m.

lighting [lī'ting] n (on road) éclairage m; (in theater) éclairages.

lightly [lit'lē] ad légèrement; **to get off ~** s'en tirer à bon compte.

light meter n (PHOT) photomètre m, posemètre m.

lightness [lit'nis] n clarté f; (in weight) légèreté f.

lightning [lit'ning] n éclair m, foudre f.

lightning conductor n (Brit) paratonnerre m.

lightning rod n (US) paratonnerre m.

lightning strike n (Brit) grève f surprise.

light pen n crayon m optique.

lightship [lit'ship] n bateau-phare m.

lightweight [lit'wāt] a (suit) léger(ère); (boxer) poids léger inv.

light-year [lit'yēr] n année-lumière f.

like [līk] vt aimer (bien) ♦ prep comme ♦ a semblable, pareil(le) ♦ n: **the ~** un(e) pareil(le) or semblable; le(la) pareil(le); (pej) (d')autres du même genre or acabit; **his ~s and dislikes** ses goûts mpl or préférences *fpl*; **I would ~, I'd ~** je voudrais, j'aimerais; **would you ~ a coffee?** voulez-vous du café?; **to be/look ~ sb/sth** ressembler à qn/qch; **what's he ~?** comment est-il?; **what's the weather ~?** quel temps fait-il?; **that's just ~ him** c'est bien de lui, ça lui ressemble; **something ~ that** quelque chose comme ça; **I feel ~ a drink** je boirais bien quelque chose; **if you ~** si vous voulez; **there's nothing ~ ...** il n'y a rien de tel que ....

likeable [lī'kəbəl] *a* sympathique, agréable.

likelihood [līk'lēhōōd] *n* probabilité *f*; **in all ~** selon toute vraisemblance.

likely [līk'lē] *a* (*result, outcome*) probable; (*excuse*) plausible; **he's ~ to leave** il va sûrement partir, il risque fort de partir; **not ~!** (*col*) pas de danger!

like-minded [līk'mīn'did] *a* de même opinion.

liken [lī'kən] *vt*: **to ~ sth to** comparer qch à.

likeness [līk'nis] *n* ressemblance *f*.

likewise [līk'wīz] *ad* de même, pareillement.

liking [lī'king] *n* affection *f*, penchant *m*; goût *m*; **to take a ~ to sb** se prendre d'amitié pour qn; **to be to sb's ~** être au goût de qn, plaire à qn.

lilac [lī'lək] *n* lilas *m* ♦ *a* lilas *inv*.

lilt [lilt] *n* rythme *m*, cadence *f*.

lilting [lil'ting] *a* aux cadences mélodieuses; chantant(e).

lily [lil'ē] *n* lis *m*; **~ of the valley** muguet *m*.

Lima [lē'mə] *n* Lima.

limb [lim] *n* membre *m*; **to be out on a ~** (*fig*) être isolé(e).

limber [lim'bûr]: **to ~ up** *vi* se dégourdir, se mettre en train.

limbo [lim'bō] *n*: **to be in ~** (*fig*) être tombé(e) dans l'oubli.

lime [līm] *n* (*tree*) tilleul *m*; (*fruit*) citron vert, lime *f*; (*GEO*) chaux *f*.

lime juice *n* jus *m* de citron vert.

limelight [līm'līt] *n*: **in the ~** (*fig*) en vedette, au premier plan.

limerick [lim'ûrik] *n* petit poème humoristique.

limestone [līm'stōn] *n* pierre *f* à chaux; (*GEO*) calcaire *m*.

limit [lim'it] *n* limite *f* ♦ *vt* limiter; **weight/speed ~** limite de poids/de vitesse.

limitation [limitā'shən] *n* limitation *f*, restriction *f*.

limited [lim'itid] *a* limité(e), restreint(e); **~ edition** édition *f* à tirage limité.

limited (liability) company (Ltd) *n* (*Brit*) ≈ société *f* anonyme (SA).

limitless [lim'itlis] *a* illimité(e).

limousine [lim'əzēn] *n* limousine *f*.

limp [limp] *n*: **to have a ~** boiter ♦ *vi* boiter ♦ *a* mou(molle).

limpet [lim'pit] *n* patelle *f*; **like a ~** (*fig*) comme une ventouse.

limpid [lim'pid] *a* limpide.

linchpin [linch'pin] *n* esse *f*; (*fig*) pivot *m*.

Lincs [lingks] *abbr* (*Brit*) = Lincolnshire.

line [līn] *n* (*gen*) ligne *f*; (*rope*) corde *f*; (*wire*) fil *m*; (*of poem*) vers *m*; (*row, series*) rangée *f*; file *f*, queue *f*; (*COMM: series of goods*) article(s) *m(pl)*, ligne de produits ♦ *vt* (*clothes*): **to ~ (with)** doubler (de); (*box*): **to ~ (with)** garnir *or* tapisser (de); (*subj:*

trees, crowd) border; **to cut in ~** (*US*) passer avant son tour; **in his ~ of business** dans sa partie, dans son rayon; **on the right ~s** sur la bonne voie; **a new ~ in cosmetics** une nouvelle ligne de produits de beauté; **hold the ~ please** (*Brit TEL*) ne quittez pas; **to be in ~ for sth** (*fig*) être en lice pour qch; **in ~ with** en accord avec, en conformité avec; **to bring sth into ~ with sth** aligner qch sur qch; **to draw the ~ at (doing) sth** (*fig*) se refuser à (faire) qch; ne pas tolérer *or* admettre (qu'on fasse) qch; **to take the ~ that ...** être d'avis *or* de l'opinion que ....

line up *vi* s'aligner, se mettre en rang(s) ♦ *vt* aligner; (*set up, have ready*) prévoir; trouver; **to have sb/sth ~d up** avoir qn/qch en vue *or* de prévu(e).

linear [lin'ēûr] *a* linéaire.

lined [līnd] *a* (*paper*) réglé(e); (*face*) marqué(e), ridé(e); (*clothes*) doublé(e).

line feed *n* (*COMPUT*) interligne *m*.

linen [lin'ən] *n* linge *m* (de corps *or* de maison); (*cloth*) lin *m*.

line printer *n* imprimante *f* (ligne par) ligne.

liner [lī'nûr] *n* paquebot *m* de ligne.

linesman [līnz'mən] *n* (*TENNIS*) juge *m* de ligne; (*SOCCER*) juge de touche.

lineup [līn'up] *n* file *f*; (*also:* **police ~**) parade *f* d'identification; (*SPORT*) (composition *f* de l')équipe *f*.

linger [ling'gûr] *vi* s'attarder; traîner; (*smell, tradition*) persister.

lingerie [län'jərā] *n* lingerie *f*.

lingering [ling'gûring] *a* persistant(e); qui subsiste; (*death*) lent(e).

lingo, ~es [ling'gō] *n* (*pej*) jargon *m*.

linguist [ling'gwist] *n* linguiste *m/f*; personne douée pour les langues.

linguistic [linggwis'tik] *a* linguistique.

linguistics [linggwis'tiks] *n* linguistique *f*.

lining [lī'ning] *n* doublure *f*; (*TECH*) revêtement *m*; (*: of brakes*) garniture *f*.

link [lingk] *n* (*of a chain*) maillon *m*; (*connection*) lien *m*, rapport *m* ♦ *vt* relier, lier, unir; rail ~ liaison *f* ferroviaire.

link up *vt* relier ♦ *vi* se rejoindre; s'associer.

links [lingks] *npl* (terrain *m* de) golf *m*.

linkup [lingk'up] *n* lien *m*, rapport *m*; (*of roads*) jonction *f*, raccordement *m*; (*of spaceships*) arrimage *m*; (*RADIO, TV*) liaison *f*; (*: program*) duplex *m*.

linoleum [linō'lēəm] *n* linoléum *m*.

linseed oil [lin'sēd oil] *n* huile *f* de lin.

lint [lint] *n* tissu ouaté (*pour pansements*).

lintel [lin'təl] *n* linteau *m*.

lion [lī'ən] *n* lion *m*.

lion cub *n* lionceau *m*.

lioness [lī'ənis] *n* lionne *f*.

lip [lip] *n* lèvre *f*; (*of cup etc*) rebord *m*; (*insolence*) insolences *fpl*.

lip-read [lip'rēd] *vi* lire sur les lèvres.

lip salve [lip sav] *n* pommade *f* des lèvres, pommade rosat.

lip service *n*: **to pay ~ to sth** ne reconnaître le mérite de qch que pour la forme *or* qu'en paroles.

lipstick [lip'stik] *n* rouge *m* à lèvres.

liquefy [lik'wəfī] *vt* liquéfier ♦ *vi* se liquéfier.

liqueur [likûr'] n liqueur f.
liquid [lik'wid] n liquide m ♦ a liquide.
liquid assets npl liquidités fpl, disponibilités fpl.
liquidate [lik'widāt] vt liquider.
liquidation [likwidā'shən] n liquidation f; **to go into** ~ déposer son bilan.
liquidation value n (US COMM) valeur f de liquidation.
liquidator [lik'widâtûr] n liquidateur m.
liquid crystal display (LCD) n affichage m à cristaux liquides.
liquidize [lik'widīz] vt (CULIN) passer au mixer.
liquidizer [lik'widīzûr] n (Brit CULIN) mixer m.
Liquid Paper n ® Tipp-Ex m ®.
liquor [lik'ûr] n spiritueux m, alcool m.
liquorice [lik'ûris] n (Brit) réglisse m.
liquor store n (US) débit m de vins et de spiritueux.
Lisbon [liz'bən] n Lisbonne.
lisp [lisp] n zézaiement m.
lissom [lis'əm] a souple, agile.
list [list] n liste f; (of ship) inclinaison f ♦ vt (write down) inscrire; faire la liste de; (enumerate) énumérer; (COMPUT) lister ♦ vi (ship) gîter, donner de la bande; **shopping** ~ liste des courses.
listed company [lis'tid kum'panē] n société cotée en bourse.
listen [lis'ən] vi écouter; **to** ~ **to** écouter.
listener [lis'ənûr] n auditeur/trice.
listing [lis'ting] n (COMPUT) listage m; (: hard copy) liste f, listing m.
listless [list'lis] a indolent(e), apathique.
listlessly [list'lislē] ad avec indolence or apathie.
list price n prix m de catalogue.
lit [lit] pt, pp of **light**.
litany [lit'ənē] n litanie f.
liter [lē'tûr] n (US) litre m.
literacy [lit'ûrəsē] n degré m d'alphabétisation, fait m de savoir lire et écrire.
literal [lit'ûrəl] a littéral(e).
literally [lit'ûrəlē] ad littéralement.
literary [lit'ərârē] a littéraire.
literate [lit'ûrit] a qui sait lire et écrire, instruit(e).
literature [lit'ûrəchûr] n littérature f; (brochures etc) copie f publicitaire, prospectus mpl.
lithe [līth] a agile, souple.
lithography [lithâg'rəfē] n lithographie f.
Lithuania [lithōōā'nēə] n Lituanie f.
litigate [lit'əgāt] vt mettre en litige ♦ vi plaider.
litigation [litəgā'shən] n litige m; contentieux m.
litmus [lit'məs] n: ~ **paper** papier m de tournesol.
litre [lē'tûr] n (Brit) litre m.
litter [lit'ûr] n (garbage) détritus mpl, ordures fpl; (young animals) portée f ♦ vt éparpiller; laisser des détritus dans; **~ed with** jonché(e) de, couvert(e) de.
litter bin n (Brit) boîte f à ordures, poubelle f.
litterbug [lit'ûrbug] n personne qui jette des détritus par terre.

little [lit'əl] a (small) petit(e); (not much): **it's** ~ **c'est** peu; ~ **milk** peu de lait ♦ ad peu; a ~ **un peu** (de); **a** ~ **milk** un peu de lait; **for a** ~ **while** pendant un petit moment; **with** ~ **difficulty** sans trop de difficulté; **as** ~ **as possible** le moins possible; ~ **by** ~ petit à petit, peu à peu; **to make** ~ **of** faire peu de cas de.
liturgy [lit'ûrjē] n liturgie f.
live vi [liv] vivre; (reside) vivre, habiter ♦ a [līv] (animal) vivant(e), en vie; (wire) sous tension; (broadcast) (transmis(e)) en direct; (issue) d'actualité, brûlant(e); (unexploded) non explosé(e); **to** ~ **in Chicago** habiter (à) Chicago; **to** ~ **together** vivre ensemble, cohabiter; ~ **ammunition** munitions fpl de combat.
live down vt faire oublier (avec le temps).
live in vi être logé(e) et nourri(e); être interne.
live off vt (land, fish etc) vivre de; (pej: parents etc) vivre aux crochets de.
live on vt fus (food) vivre de ♦ vi survivre; **to** ~ **on $150 a week** vivre avec 150 dollars par semaine.
live out vi (Brit: students) être externe ♦ vt: **to** ~ **out one's days** or **life** passer sa vie.
live up vt: **to** ~ **it up** (col) faire la fête; mener la grande vie.
live up to vt fus se montrer à la hauteur de.
livelihood [līv'lēhōōd] n moyens mpl d'existence.
liveliness [līv'lēnis] n vivacité f, entrain m.
lively [līv'lē] a vif(vive), plein(e) d'entrain.
liven up [lī'vən up] vt (room etc) égayer; (discussion, evening) animer.
liver [liv'ûr] n foie m.
liverish [liv'ûrish] a qui a mal au foie; (fig) grincheux(euse).
livery [liv'ûrē] n livrée f.
lives [līvz] npl of **life**.
livestock [līv'stâk] n cheptel m, bétail m.
livid [liv'id] a livide, blafard(e); (furious) furieux(euse), furibond(e).
living [liv'ing] a vivant(e), en vie ♦ n: **to earn** or **make a** ~ gagner sa vie; **cost of** ~ coût m de la vie; **within** ~ **memory** de mémoire d'homme.
living conditions npl conditions fpl de vie.
living expenses npl dépenses courantes.
living room n salle f de séjour.
living wage n salaire m permettant de vivre (décemment).
lizard [liz'ûrd] n lézard m.
llama [lâm'ə] n lama m.
LLB n abbr (= Bachelor of Laws) titre universitaire.
LLD n abbr (= Doctor of Laws) titre universitaire.
load [lōd] n (weight) poids m; (thing carried) chargement m, charge f; (ELEC, TECH) charge ♦ vt (truck, ship): **to** ~ (**with**) charger (de); (gun, camera): **to** ~ (**with**) charger (avec); (COMPUT) charger; **a** ~ **of**, ~**s of** (fig) un or des tas de, des masses de.
loaded [lō'did] a (dice) pipé(e); (question) insidieux(euse); (col: rich) bourré(e) de fric; (: drunk) bourré.

loading dock [lō'ding dåk] *n* (*US*) aire *f* de chargement.

loaf, *pl* **loaves** [lōf, lōvz] *n* pain *m*, miche *f* ♦ *vi* (*also*: ~ **about**, ~ **around**) fainéanter, traîner.

loafer [lō'fûr] *n* fainéant/e.

loam [lōm] *n* terreau *m*.

loan [lōn] *n* prêt *m* ♦ *vt* prêter; **on** ~ prêté(e), en prêt; **public** ~ emprunt public.

loan account *n* compte *m* de prêt.

loan capital *n* capital-obligations *m*.

loath [lōth] *a*: **to be** ~ **to do** répugner à faire.

loathe [lōth] *vt* détester, avoir en horreur.

loathing [lō'thing] *n* dégoût *m*, répugnance *f*.

loathsome [lōth'səm] *a* répugnant(e), détestable.

loaves [lōvz] *npl of* loaf.

lob [låb] *vt* (*ball*) lober.

lobby [låb'ē] *n* hall *m*, entrée *f*; (*POL*) groupe *m* de pression, lobby *m* ♦ *vt* faire pression sur.

lobbyist [låb'ēist] *n* membre *m/f* d'un groupe de pression.

lobe [lōb] *n* lobe *m*.

lobster [låb'stûr] *n* homard *m*.

lobster pot *n* casier *m* à homards.

local [lō'kəl] *a* local(e) ♦ *n* (*Brit*: *pub*) pub *m or* café *m* du coin; **the** ~**s** *npl* les gens *mpl* du pays *or* du coin.

local anesthetic *n* anesthésie locale.

local authority (*Brit*) *n* collectivité locale, municipalité *f*.

local call *n* (*TEL*) communication urbaine.

local government *n* administration locale *or* municipale.

locality [lōkal'itē] *n* région *f*, environs *mpl*; (*position*) lieu *m*.

localize [lō'kəliz] *vt* localiser.

locally [lō'kəlē] *ad* localement; dans les environs *or* la région.

locate [lō'kāt] *vt* (*find*) trouver, repérer; (*situate*) situer.

location [lōkā'shən] *n* emplacement *m*; **on** ~ (*CINEMA*) en extérieur.

loch [låkh] *n* lac *m*, loch *m*.

lock [låk] *n* (*of door, box*) serrure *f*; (*of canal*) écluse *f*; (*of hair*) mèche *f*, boucle *f* ♦ *vt* (*with key*) fermer à clé; (*immobilize*) bloquer ♦ *vi* (*door etc*) fermer à clé; (*wheels*) se bloquer; ~ **stock and barrel** (*fig*) en bloc.

lock away *vt* (*valuables*) mettre sous clé; (*criminal*) mettre sous les verrous, enfermer.

lock out *vt* enfermer dehors; (*on purpose*) mettre à la porte; (*: workers*) lock-outer.

lock up *vi* tout fermer (à clé).

locker [låk'ûr] *n* casier *m*.

locker room *n* (*US*) vestiaire *m*.

locket [låk'it] *n* médaillon *m*.

lockjaw [låk'jô] *n* tétanos *m*.

lockout [låk'out] *n* (*INDUSTRY*) lock-out *m*, grève patronale.

locksmith [låk'smith] *n* serrurier *m*.

lock-up [låk'up] *n* (*prison*) prison *f*; (*cell*) cellule *f* provisoire.

locomotive [lōkəmō'tiv] *n* locomotive *f*.

locum tenens [lō'kəm tē'nənz] *n* (*MED*) suppléant/e (de médecin).

locust [lō'kəst] *n* locuste *f*, sauterelle *f*.

lodge [låj] *n* pavillon *m* (de gardien); (*FREE-*

MASONRY) loge *f* ♦ *vi* (*person*): **to** ~ **with** être logé(e) chez, être en pension chez ♦ *vt* (*appeal etc*) présenter; déposer; **to** ~ **a complaint** porter plainte; **to** ~ **(itself) in/ between** se loger dans/entre.

lodger [låj'ûr] *n* locataire *m/f*; (*with room and meals*) pensionnaire *m/f*.

lodging [låj'ing] *n* logement *m*; *see also* **board.**

lodgings [låj'ingz] *n* chambre *f*, meublé *m*.

loft [lôft] *n* grenier *m*; (*US*) grenier aménagé (en appartement) (*gén dans ancien entrepôt ou fabrique*).

lofty [lôf'tē] *a* élevé(e); (*haughty*) hautain(e); (*sentiments, aims*) noble.

log [lôg] *n* (*of wood*) bûche *f*; (*book*) = **logbook** ♦ *n abbr* (= *logarithm*) log *m* ♦ *vt* enregistrer.

log in, **log on** *vi* (*COMPUT*) ouvrir une session, entrer dans le système.

log off, **log out** *vi* (*COMPUT*) clore une session, sortir du système.

logarithm [lôg'ərithəm] *n* logarithme *m*.

logbook [lôg'bŏŏk] *n* (*NAUT*) livre *m or* journal *m* de bord; (*AVIAT*) carnet *m* de vol; (*of truck-driver*) carnet de route; (*of events, movement of goods etc*) registre *m*; (*of car*) = carte grise.

log cabin *n* cabane *f* en rondins.

log fire *n* feu *m* de bois.

loggerheads [lôg'ûrhedz] *npl*: **at** ~ **(with)** à couteaux tirés (avec).

logic [låj'ik] *n* logique *f*.

logical [låj'ikəl] *a* logique.

logically [låj'iklē] *ad* logiquement.

logistics [lōjis'tiks] *n* logistique *f*.

logo [lō'gō] *n* logo *m*.

loin [loin] *n* (*CULIN*) filet *m*, longe *f*; ~**s** *npl* reins *mpl*.

loincloth [loin'klôth] *n* pagne *m*.

loiter [loi'tûr] *vi* s'attarder; **to** ~ **(about)** traîner, musarder; (*pej*) rôder.

loll [lål] *vi* (*also*: ~ **about**) se prélasser, fainéanter.

lollipop [lål'ēpåp] *n* sucette *f*.

London [lun'dən] *n* Londres *m*.

Londoner [lun'dənûr] *n* Londonien/ne.

lone [lōn] *a* solitaire.

loneliness [lōn'lēnis] *n* solitude *f*, isolement *m*.

lonely [lōn'lē] *a* seul(e); (*childhood etc*) solitaire; (*place*) solitaire, isolé(e); **to feel** ~ se sentir seul.

loner [lō'nûr] *n* solitaire *m/f*.

lonesome [lōn'səm] *a* seul(e); solitaire.

long [lông] *a* long(longue) ♦ *ad* longtemps ♦ *n*: **the** ~ **and the short of it is that** ... (*fig*) le fin mot de l'histoire c'est que ... ♦ *vi*: **to** ~ **for sth/to do** avoir très envie de qch/de faire; attendre qch avec impatience/impatience de faire; **he had** ~ **understood that** ... il avait compris depuis longtemps que ...; **how** ~ **is this river/course?** quelle est la longueur de ce fleuve/la durée de ce cours?; **6 meters** ~ (long) de 6 mètres; **6 months** ~ qui dure 6 mois, de 6 mois; **all night** ~ toute la nuit; **he no** ~**er comes** il ne vient plus; ~ **before** longtemps avant; **before** ~ (+ *future*) avant peu, dans peu de temps; (+ *past*) peu de temps après; ~ **ago** il y a longtemps; **don't be** ~! fais vite!, dépêche-toi!; **I won't be** ~ je n'en ai pas pour longtemps; **at** ~ **last** enfin; **in the** ~ **run** à la longue; finale- ment; **so** *or* **as** ~ **as** pourvu que.

long-distance [lông'dis'tɔns] *a* (*race*) de fond; (*call*) interurbain(e).

long-haired [lông'härd] *a* (*person*) aux che- veux longs; (*animal*) aux longs poils.

longhand [lông'hand] *n* écriture normale *or* courante.

longing [lông'ing] *n* désir *m*, envie *f*, nostalgie *f* ♦ *a* plein(e) d'envie *or* de nostalgie.

longingly [lông'inglē] *ad* avec désir *or* nostalgie.

longitude [lân'jɔtōōd] *n* longitude *f*.

long johns [lông jânz] *npl* caleçons longs.

long jump *n* saut *m* en longueur.

long-lost [lông'lóst] *a* perdu(e) depuis longtemps.

long-playing [lông'plā'ing] *a*: ~ **record (LP)** (disque *m*) 33 tours *m inv*.

long-range [lông'rānj'] *a* à longue portée; (*weather forecast*) à long terme.

longshoreman [lông'shôrmɔn] *n* (*US*) docker *m*, débardeur *m*.

longsighted [lông'sītid] *a* presbyte; (*fig*) pré- voyant(e).

long-standing [lông'standing] *a* de longue date.

long-suffering [lông'suf'ûring] *a* empreint(e) d'une patience résignée; extrêmement pa- tient(e).

long-term [lông'tûrm'] *a* à long terme.

long wave *n* (*RADIO*) grandes ondes, ondes longues.

long-winded [lông'win'did] *a* intarissable, interminable.

loo [lōō] *n* (*Brit col*) w.-c. *mpl*, petit coin.

loofah [lōō'fɔ] *n* (*Brit*) sorte d'éponge végéta- le.

look [lōōk] *vi* regarder; (*seem*) sembler, pa- raître, avoir l'air; (*building etc*): **to** ~ **south/on to the sea** donner au sud/sur la mer ♦ *n* regard *m*; (*appearance*) air *m*, allu- re *f*, aspect *m*; ~**s** *npl* physique *m*, beauté *f*; **to** ~ **like** ressembler à; **it** ~**s like him** on di- rait que c'est lui; **it** ~**s about 4 meters long** je dirais que ça fait 4 mètres de long, à vue de nez, ça fait 4 mètres de long; **it** ~**s all right to me** ça me paraît bien; **to have a** ~ **at sth** jeter un coup d'œil à qch; **to have a** ~ **for sth** chercher qch; **to** ~ **ahead** regarder devant soi; (*fig*) envisager l'avenir.

look after *vt fus* s'occuper de, prendre soin de; (*baggage etc: watch over*) garder, surveiller.

look around *vi* regarder autour de soi; (*turn*) regarder derrière soi, se retourner; **to** ~ **around for sth** chercher qch.

look at *vt fus* regarder.

look back *vi*: **to** ~ **back at sth/sb** se re- tourner pour regarder qch/qn; **to look back on** (*event, period*) évoquer, repenser à.

look down on *vt fus* (*fig*) regarder de haut, dédaigner.

look for *vt fus* chercher.

look forward to *vt fus* attendre avec impa- tience; **I'm not** ~**ing forward to it** cette

perspective ne me réjouit guère; ~**ing for- ward to hearing from you** (*in letter*) dans l'attente de vous lire.

look in *vi*: **to** ~ **in on sb** passer voir qn.

look into *vt fus* (*matter, possibility*) exami- ner, étudier.

look on *vi* regarder (en spectateur).

look out *vi* (*beware*): **to** ~ **out (for)** pren- dre garde (à), faire attention (à).

look out for *vt fus* être à la recherche de; guetter.

look over *vt* (*essay*) jeter un coup d'œil à; (*town, building*) visiter (rapidement); (*person*) jeter un coup d'œil à; examiner de la tête aux pieds.

look round *vi* (*Brit*) = **look around**.

look through *vt fus* (*papers, book*) exami- ner; (: *briefly*) parcourir; (*telescope*) re- garder à travers.

look to *vt fus* veiller à; (*rely on*) compter sur.

look up *vi* lever les yeux; (*improve*) s'amé- liorer ♦ *vt* (*word*) chercher; (*friend*) passer voir.

look up to *vt fus* avoir du respect pour.

lookout [lōōk'aut] *n* poste *m* de guet; guetteur *m*; **to be on the** ~ **(for)** guetter.

look-up table [lōōk'up tā'bɔl] *n* (*COMPUT*) ta- ble *f* à consulter.

LOOM *n abbr* (*US*: = *Loyal Order of Moose*) *association charitable*.

loom [lōōm] *n* métier *m* à tisser ♦ *vi* surgir; (*fig*) menacer, paraître imminent(e).

loony [lōō'nē] *a*, *n* (*col*) timbré(e), cinglé(e) (*m/f*).

loop [lōōp] *n* boucle *f*; (*contraceptive*) stérilet *m*.

loophole [lōōp'hōl] *n* porte *f* de sortie (*fig*); échappatoire *f*.

loose [lōōs] *a* (*knot, screw*) desserré(e); (*stone*) branlant(e); (*clothes*) vague, ample, lâche; (*animal*) en liberté, échappé(e); (*lifc*) dissolu(e); (*morals, discipline*) relâché(e); (*thinking*) peu rigoureux(euse), vague; (*translation*) approximatif(ive) ♦ *vt* (*free: animal*) lâcher; (: *prisoner*) relâcher, libé- rer; (*slacken*) détendre, relâcher; desserrer; défaire; donner du mou a; donner du ballant à; ~ **connection** (*ELEC*) mauvais contact; **to be at** ~ **ends** *or* (*Brit*) **at a** ~ **end** (*fig*) ne pas trop savoir quoi faire; **to tie up** ~ **ends** (*fig*) mettre au point *or* régler les derniers détails.

loose change *n* petite monnaie.

loose-fitting [lōōs'fit'ing] *a* (*clothes*) ample.

loose-leaf [lōōs'lēf] *a*: ~ **binder** *or* **folder** classeur *m* à feuilles *or* feuillets mobiles.

loosely [lōōs'lē] *ad* sans serrer; approximati- vement.

loosen [lōō'sɔn] *vt* desserrer, relâcher, dé- faire.

loosen up *vi* (*before game*) s'échauffer; (*col: relax*) se détendre, se laisser aller.

loot [lōōt] *n* butin *m* ♦ *vt* piller.

looter [lōō'tûr] *n* pillard *m*, casseur *m*.

looting [lōō'ting] *n* pillage *m*.

lop [lâp]: **to** ~ **off** *vt* couper, trancher.

lopsided [lâp'sīdid] *a* de travers, asymétrique.

lord [lôrd] *n* seigneur *m*; **L**~ **Smith** lord

Smith; **the L~** (*REL*) le Seigneur; **the (House of) L~s** (*Brit*) la Chambre des Lords.
lordly [lôrd'lē] *a* noble, majestueux(euse); (*arrogant*) hautain(e).
lore [lôr] *n* tradition(s) *f(pl)*.
lorry [lôr'ē] *n* (*Brit*) camion *m*.
lorry driver *n* (*Brit*) camionneur *m*, routier *m*.
lose, *pt, pp* **lost** [lōōz, lôst] *vt* perdre; (*opportunity*) manquer, perdre; (*pursuers*) distancer, semer ♦ *vi* perdre; **to ~ (time)** (*clock*) retarder; **to ~ no time (in doing sth)** ne pas perdre de temps (à faire qch); **to get lost** *vi* (*person*) se perdre; **my watch has got lost** ma montre est perdue.
loser [lōō'zûr] *n* perdant/e; **to be a good/bad ~** être beau/mauvais joueur.
loss [lôs] *n* perte *f*; **to cut one's ~es** limiter les dégâts; **to make a ~** enregistrer une perte; **to sell sth at a ~** vendre qch à perte; **to be at a ~** être perplexe *or* embarrassé(e); **to be at a ~ to do** se trouver incapable de faire.
loss adjuster *n* (*INSURANCE*) responsable *m/f* de l'évaluation des dommages.
loss leader *n* (*COMM*) article sacrifié.
lost [lôst] *pt, pp of* **lose** ♦ *a* perdu(e); **~ in thought** perdu dans ses pensées; **~ and found property** *n* (*US*) objets trouvés; **~ and found** *n* (*US*) bureau *m* des objets trouvés.
lost property *n* (*Brit*) objets trouvés; **~ office** *or* **department** *n* (*Brit*) (bureau *m* des) objets trouvés.
lot [lât] *n* (*at auctions*) lot *m*; (*destiny*) sort *m*, destinée *f*; (*US: plot of land*) lot *m* (de terrain), lotissement *m*; **the ~** le tout; tous *mpl*, toutes *fpl*; **a ~** beaucoup; **a ~ of** beaucoup de; **~s of** des tas de; **to draw ~s (for sth)** tirer (qch) au sort.
lotion [lō'shən] *n* lotion *f*.
lottery [lât'ûrē] *n* loterie *f*.
loud [loud] *a* bruyant(e), sonore, fort(e); (*gaudy*) voyant(e), tapageur(euse) ♦ *ad* (*speak etc*) fort; **out ~** tout haut.
loudly [loud'lē] *ad* fort, bruyamment.
loudspeaker [loud'spēkûr] *n* haut-parleur *m*.
lounge [lounj] *n* salon *m*; (*of airport*) salle *f* ♦ *vi* se prélasser, paresser.
lounge bar *n* (salle *f* de) bar *m*.
lounge suit *n* (*Brit*) complet *m*; (*: on invitation*) "tenue de ville".
louse, *pl* **lice** [lous, līs] *n* pou *m*.
louse up *vt* (*col*) gâcher.
lousy [lou'zē] *a* (*fig*) infect(e), moche.
lout [lout] *n* rustre *m*, butor *m*.
louver, (*Brit*) **louvre** [lōō'vûr] *a* (*door, window*) à claire-voie.
lovable [luv'əbəl] *a* très sympathique; adorable.
love [luv] *n* amour *m* ♦ *vt* aimer; aimer beaucoup; **to ~ to do** aimer beaucoup *or* adorer faire; **I'd ~ to come** cela me ferait très plaisir (de venir); **"15 ~"** (*TENNIS*) "15 à rien *or* zéro"; **to be/fall in ~ with** être/tomber amoureux(euse) de; **to make ~** faire l'amour; **~ at first sight** le coup de foudre; **to send one's ~ to sb** adresser ses amitiés à qn; **~ from Anne, ~, Anne** affectueusement, Anne.

love affair *n* liaison (amoureuse).
love letter *n* lettre *f* d'amour.
love life *n* vie sentimentale.
lovely [luv'lē] *a* (*house, garden*) ravissant(e); (*friend, wife*) charmant(e); (*vacation, surprise*) très agréable, merveilleux(euse); **we had a ~ time** c'était vraiment très bien, nous avons eu beaucoup de plaisir.
lover [luv'ûr] *n* amant *m*; (*amateur*): **a ~ of** un(e) ami(e) de, un(e) amoureux(euse) de.
lovesick [luv'sik] *a* qui se languit d'amour.
lovesong [luv'sông] *n* chanson *f* d'amour.
loving [luv'ing] *a* affectueux(euse), tendre, aimant(e).
low [lō] *a* bas(basse) ♦ *ad* bas ♦ *n* (*METEOROLOGY*) dépression *f* ♦ *vi* (*cow*) mugir; **to feel ~** se sentir déprimé(e); **he's very ~** (*ill*) il est bien bas *or* très affaibli; **to turn (down) ~** *vt* baisser; **to reach a new *or* an all-time ~** tomber au niveau le plus bas.
lowbrow [lō'brou] *a* sans prétentions intellectuelles.
low-calorie [lō'kal'ûrē] *a* hypocalorique.
low-cut [lō'kut'] *a* (*dress*) décolleté(e).
lowdown [lō'doun] *n* (*col*): **he gave me the ~ (on it)** il m'a mis au courant ♦ *a* (*mean*) méprisable.
lower [lō'ûr] *a, ad comparative of* **low** ♦ *vt* baisser; (*resistance*) diminuer; (*US AUT: lights*) mettre en code, baisser ♦ *vi* [lou'ûr] (*person*): **to ~ at sb** jeter un regard mauvais *or* noir à qn; (*sky, clouds*) être menaçant.
low-fat [lō'fat'] *a* maigre.
low-key [lō'kē'] *a* modéré(e); discret(ète).
lowland [lō'lənd] *n* plaine *f*.
low-level [lō'level] *a* bas(basse); (*flying*) à basse altitude.
lowly [lō'lē] *a* humble, modeste.
low-lying [lō'lī'ing] *a* à faible altitude.
low-paid [lō'pād'] *a* mal payé(e), aux salaires bas.
loyal [loi'əl] *a* loyal(e), fidèle.
loyalist [loi'əlist] *n* loyaliste *m/f*.
loyalty [loi'əltē] *n* loyauté *f*, fidélité *f*.
lozenge [lâz'inj] *n* (*MED*) pastille *f*; (*GEOM*) losange *m*.
LP *n abbr* = **long-playing record**.
L-plates [el'plāts] *npl* (*Brit*) plaques *fpl* (obligatoires) d'apprenti conducteur.
LPN *n abbr* (*US:* = *Licensed Practical Nurse*) infirmier/ière diplômé(e).
LSAT *n abbr* (*US*) = *Law School Admissions Test*.
LSD *n abbr* (= *lysergic acid diethylamide*) LSD *m*.
LSE *n abbr* = *London School of Economics*.
LST *abbr* (*US:* = *local standard time*) heure locale.
LT *abbr* (*ELEC:* = *low tension*) BT.
Lt. *abbr* (= *lieutenant*) Lt.
Ltd *abbr* (*Brit: COMM*) = **limited**.
lubricant [lōōb'rikənt] *n* lubrifiant *m*.
lubricate [lōōb'rikāt] *vt* lubrifier, graisser.
lucid [lōō'sid] *a* lucide.
lucidity [lōōsid'itē] *n* lucidité *f*.
luck [luk] *n* chance *f*; **bad ~** malchance *f*, malheur *m*; **to be in ~** avoir de la chance; **to be out of ~** ne pas avoir de chance; **good**

~! bonne chance!

luckily [luk'ilē] *ad* heureusement, par bonheur.

lucky [luk'ē] *a* (*person*) qui a de la chance; (*coincidence*) heureux(euse); (*number etc*) qui porte bonheur.

lucrative [lōōk'rətiv] *a* lucratif(ive), rentable, qui rapporte.

ludicrous [lōō'dəkrəs] *a* ridicule, absurde.

luffa [luf'ə] *n* (*US*) sorte d'éponge végétale.

lug [lug] *vt* traîner, tirer.

luggage [lug'ij] *n* bagages *mpl*.

luggage car *n* (*US RAIL*) fourgon *m* (à bagages).

luggage lockers *npl* consigne *f sg* automatique.

luggage rack *n* (*in train*) porte-bagages *m inv*; (*: made of string*) filet *m* à bagages; (*on car*) galerie *f*.

lugubrious [lōōgōō'brēəs] *a* lugubre.

lukewarm [lōōk'wôrm'] *a* tiède.

lull [lul] *n* accalmie *f* ♦ *vt* (*child*) bercer; (*person, fear*) apaiser, calmer.

lullaby [lul'əbī] *n* berceuse *f*.

lumbago [lumbā'gō] *n* lumbago *m*.

lumber [lum'bûr] *n* bric-à-brac *m inv*; (*wood*) bois *m* de charpente ♦ *vt* (*Brit col*): **to ~ sb with sth/sb** coller *or* refiler qch/qn à qn ♦ *vi* (*also*: ~ **about**, ~ **along**) marcher pesamment.

lumberjack [lum'bûrjak] *n* bûcheron *m*.

lumberyard [lum'bûryárd] *n* entrepôt *m* de bois.

luminous [lōō'minəs] *a* lumineux(euse).

lump [lump] *n* morceau *m*; (*in sauce*) grumeau *m*; (*swelling*) grosseur *f* ♦ *vt* (*also*: ~ **together**) réunir, mettre en tas.

lump sum *n* somme globale *or* forfaitaire.

lumpy [lum'pē] *a* (*sauce*) qui a des grumeaux.

lunacy [lōō'nəsē] *n* démence *f*, folie *f*.

lunar [lōō'nûr] *a* lunaire.

lunatic [lōō'nətik] *n* fou/folle, dément/e ♦ *a* fou(folle), dément(e); **the ~ fringe** les enragés *mpl*.

lunatic asylum *n* asile *m* d'aliénés.

lunch [lunch] *n* déjeuner *m* ♦ *vi* déjeuner; **it is his ~ hour** c'est l'heure où il déjeune; **to invite sb to** *or* **for ~** inviter qn à déjeuner.

luncheon [lun'chən] *n* déjeuner *m*.

luncheon meat *n* sorte de saucisson.

lunchtime [lunch'tīm] *n* l'heure *f* du déjeuner.

lung [lung] *n* poumon *m*.

lung cancer *n* cancer *m* du poumon.

lunge [lunj] *vi* (*also*: ~ **forward**) faire un mouvement brusque en avant; **to ~ at sb** envoyer *or* assener un coup à qn.

lupin [lōō'pin] *n* lupin *m*.

lurch [lûrch] *vi* vaciller, tituber ♦ *n* écart *m* brusque, embardée *f*; **to leave sb in the ~** laisser qn se débrouiller *or* se dépêtrer tout(e) seul(e).

lure [lōōr] *n* appât *m*, leurre *m* ♦ *vt* attirer *or* persuader par la ruse.

lurid [lōō'rid] *a* affreux(euse), atroce.

lurk [lûrk] *vi* se tapir, se cacher.

luscious [lush'əs] *a* succulent(e); appétissant(e).

lush [lush] *a* luxuriant(e).

lust [lust] *n* luxure *f*; lubricité *f*; désir *m*;

(*fig*): ~ **for** soif *f* de.

lust after *vt fus* convoiter, désirer.

luster [lus'tûr] *n* (*US*) lustre *m*, brillant *m*.

lustful [lust'fəl] *a* lascif(ive).

lustre [lus'tûr] *n* (*Brit*) = **luster**.

lusty [lus'tē] *a* vigoureux(euse), robuste.

lute [lōōt] *n* luth *m*.

Luxembourg [luk'səmbûrg] *n* Luxembourg *m*.

luxuriant [lōōgzhōō'rēənt] *a* luxuriant(e).

luxurious [lōōgzhōō'rēəs] *a* luxueux(euse).

luxury [luk'shûrē] *n* luxe *m* ♦ *cpd* de luxe.

LW *abbr* (*RADIO*: = *long wave*) GO.

lying [lī'ing] *n* mensonge(s) *m(pl)* ♦ *a* (*statement, story*) mensonger(ère), faux(fausse); (*person*) menteur(euse).

lynch [linch] *vt* lyncher.

lynx [lingks] *n* lynx *m inv*.

Lyons [lī'ənz] *n* Lyon.

lyre [lī'ûr] *n* lyre *f*.

lyric [lir'ik] *a* lyrique; ~**s** *npl* (*of song*) paroles *fpl*.

lyrical [lir'ikəl] *a* lyrique.

lyricism [lir'əsizəm] *n* lyrisme *m*.

M

M, m [em] *n* (*letter*) M, m *m*; **M for Mike** M comme Marcel.

M [em] *n abbr* (*Brit*: = *motorway*): **the M8** ≈ l'A8 ♦ *abbr* (– *medium*) M.

m [em] *abbr* (= *meter*) m; (= *million*) M; (= *mile*) mi.

MA *n abbr* (*SCOL*) = **Master of Arts**; (*US*) = *military academy*; (*US MAIL*) = *Massachusetts*.

mac [mak] *n* (*Brit*) imper(méable) *m*.

macabre [məkâ'brə] *a* macabre.

macaroni [makərō'nē] *n* macaronis *mpl*.

macaroon [makərōōn'] *n* macaron *m*.

mace [mās] *n* masse *f*; (*spice*) macis *m*.

machinations [makənā'shənz] *npl* machinations *fpl*, intrigues *fpl*.

machine [məshēn'] *n* machine *f* ♦ *vt* (*dress etc*) coudre à la machine; (*TECH*) usiner.

machine code *n* (*COMPUT*) code *m* machine.

machine gun *n* mitrailleuse *f*.

machine language *n* (*COMPUT*) langage *m* machine.

machine-readable [məshēn'rē'dəbəl] *a* (*COMPUT*) exploitable par une machine.

machinery [məshē'nûrē] *n* machinerie *f*, machines *fpl*; (*fig*) mécanisme(s) *m(pl)*.

machine shop *n* atelier *m* d'usinage.

machine tool *n* machine-outil *f*.

machine washable *a* (*garment*) lavable en machine.

machinist [məshē'nist] *n* machiniste *m/f*.

macho [mâch'ō] *a* macho *inv*.

mackerel [mak'ûrəl] *n* (*pl inv*) maquereau *m*.

mackintosh [mak'intâsh] *n* (*Brit*) imperméable *m*.

macro... [mak'rō] *prefix* macro....

macroeconomics [makrōēkənâm'iks] *n* macro-économie *f*.

mad [mad] *a* fou(folle); *(foolish)* insensé(e); *(angry)* furieux(euse); **to go ~** devenir fou; **to be ~ (keen) about** *or* **on sth** *(col)* être follement passionné de qch, être fou de qch.

madam [mad'əm] *n* madame *f*; **yes ~** oui Madame; **M~ Chairman** Madame la Présidente.

madden [mad'ən] *vt* exaspérer.

maddening [mad'əning] *a* exaspérant(e).

made [mād] *pt, pp of* **make.**

Madeira [mədē'rə] *n* (GEO) Madère *f*; *(wine)* madère *m*.

made-to-measure [mād'təmezh'ûr] *a* *(Brit)* fait(e) sur mesure.

made-to-order [mād'tōōôr'dûr] *a* *(US)* fait(e) sur mesure.

madly [mad'lē] *ad* follement.

madman [mad'man] *n* fou *m*, aliéné *m*.

madness [mad'nis] *n* folie *f*.

Madrid [mədrid'] *n* Madrid.

Mafia [mâf'eə] *n* maf(f)ia *f*.

magazine [magəzēn'] *n* (PRESS) magazine *m*, revue *f*; (MIL: *store*) dépôt *m*, arsenal *m*; *(of firearm)* magasin *m*.

maggot [mag'ət] *n* ver *m*, asticot *m*.

magic [maj'ik] *n* magie *f* ♦ *a* magique.

magical [maj'ikəl] *a* magique.

magician [məjish'ən] *n* magicien/ne.

magistrate [maj'istrāt] *n* magistrat *m*; juge *m*.

magnanimous [magnan'əməs] *a* magnanime.

magnate [mag'nāt] *n* magnat *m*.

magnesium [magnē'zēəm] *n* magnésium *m*.

magnet [mag'nit] *n* aimant *m*.

magnetic [magnet'ik] *a* magnétique.

magnetic disk *n* (COMPUT) disque *m* magnétique.

magnetic tape *n* bande *f* magnétique.

magnetism [mag'nitizəm] *n* magnétisme *m*.

magnification [magnəfəkā'shən] *n* grossissement *m*.

magnificence [magnif'isəns] *n* magnificence *f*.

magnificent [magnif'əsənt] *a* superbe, magnifique.

magnify [mag'nəfī] *vt* grossir; *(sound)* amplifier.

magnifying glass [mag'nəfīing glas] *n* loupe *f*.

magnitude [mag'nətōōd] *n* ampleur *f*.

magnolia [magnōl'yə] *n* magnolia *m*.

magpie [mag'pī] *n* pie *f*.

mahogany [məhâg'ənē] *n* acajou *m* ♦ *cpd* en (bois d')acajou.

maid [mād] *n* bonne *f*; **old ~** *(pej)* vieille fille.

maiden [mād'ən] *n* jeune fille *f* ♦ *a* *(aunt etc)* non mariée; *(speech, voyage)* inaugural(e).

maiden name *n* nom *m* de jeune fille.

mail [māl] *n* poste *f*; *(letters)* courrier *m* ♦ *vt* envoyer (par la poste); **by ~** par la poste.

mailbag [māl'bag] *n* sac postal; *(mailman's)* sacoche *f*.

mailbox [māl'bâks] *n* (US: *for letters etc*; COMPUT) boîte *f* aux lettres.

mailing [mā'ling] *n* publipostage *m*, mailing *m*.

mailing list [mā'ling list] *n* liste *f* d'adresses.

mailman [māl'man] *n* (US) facteur *m*.

mail order *n* vente *f* or achat *m* par correspondance ♦ *cpd*: **mail-order house** *or* *(Brit)* **firm** maison *f* de vente par correspondance.

mailshot [māl'shât] *n* *(Brit)* = **mailing.**

mail train *n* train postal.

mail truck *n* (US AUT) voiture *f* or fourgonnette *f* des postes.

mail van *n* *(Brit:* AUT) voiture *f* or fourgonnette *f* des postes; (· RAIL) wagonposte *m*.

maim [mām] *vt* mutiler.

main [mān] *a* principal(e) ♦ *n* *(pipe)* conduite principale, canalisation *f*; **the ~s** (ELEC) le secteur; **in the ~** dans l'ensemble.

main course *n* (CULIN) plat *m* de résistance.

mainframe [mān'frām] *n* *(also:* **~ computer)** (gros) ordinateur, unité centrale.

mainland [mān'lənd] *n* continent *m*.

mainline [mān'lin] *a* (RAIL) de grande ligne ♦ *vb* *(drugs slang)* *vt* se shooter à ♦ *vi* se shooter.

main line *n* (RAIL) grande ligne.

mainly [mān'lē] *ad* principalement, surtout.

main road *n* grand axe, route nationale.

mainstay [mān'stā] *n* *(fig)* pilier *m*.

mainstream [mān'strēm] *n* *(fig)* courant principal.

maintain [māntān'] *vt* entretenir; *(continue)* maintenir, préserver; *(affirm)* soutenir; **to ~ that ...** soutenir que ....

maintenance [mān'tənəns] *n* entretien *m*; (LAW: *alimony*) pension *f* alimentaire.

maintenance contract *n* contrat *m* d'entretien.

maintenance order *n* (LAW) obligation *f* alimentaire.

maisonette [māzənet'] *n* *(Brit)* appartement *m* en duplex.

maize [māz] *n* maïs *m*.

Maj. *abbr* (MIL) = **major.**

majestic [məjes'tik] *a* majestueux(euse).

majesty [maj'istē] *n* majesté *f*.

major [mā'jûr] *n* (MIL) commandant *m* ♦ *a* important(e), principal(e); *(MUS)* majeur(e) ♦ *vi* (US SCOL): **to ~ (in)** se spécialiser (en); **a ~ operation** (MED) une grosse opération.

Majorca [məyôr'kə] *n* Majorque *f*.

major general *n* (MIL) général *m* de division.

majority [məjôr'itē] *n* majorité *f* ♦ *cpd* *(verdict, holding)* majoritaire.

make [māk] *vt* *(pt, pp* **made** [mād]) faire; *(manufacture)* faire, fabriquer; *(cause to be)*: **to ~ sb sad** *etc* rendre qn triste *etc*; *(force)*: **to ~ sb do sth** obliger qn à faire qch, faire faire qch à qn; *(equal)*: **2 and 2 ~ 4** 2 et 2 font 4 ♦ *n* fabrication *f*; *(brand)* marque *f*; **to ~ it** *(in time etc)* y arriver; *(succeed)* réussir; **what time do you ~ it?** quelle heure avez-vous?; **to ~ good** *vi* *(succeed)* faire son chemin, réussir ♦ *vt* *(deficit)* combler; *(losses)* compenser; **to ~ do with** se contenter de; se débrouiller avec.

make for *vt fus* *(place)* se diriger vers.

make off *vi* filer.

make out *vt* *(write out)* écrire; *(understand)* comprendre; *(see)* distinguer; *(claim, imply)* prétendre, vouloir faire croire; **to ~ out a case for sth** présenter des arguments solides en faveur de qch.

make over *vt* *(assign)*: **to ~ over (to)** céder (à), transférer (au nom de).

make up *vt* (*invent*) inventer, imaginer; (*parcel*) faire ♦ *vi* se réconcilier; (*with cosmetics*) se maquiller, se farder; **to be made up of** se composer de.

make up for *vt fus* compenser; racheter.

make-believe [māk'bilēv] *n*: **a world of ~** un monde de chimères *or* d'illusions; **it's just ~** c'est de la fantaisie; c'est une illusion.

maker [mā'kûr] *n* fabricant *m*.

makeshift [māk'shift] *a* provisoire, improvisé(e).

make-up [māk'up] *n* maquillage *m*.

make-up bag *n* trousse *f* de maquillage.

make-up remover *n* démaquillant *m*.

making [mā'king] *n* (*fig*): **in the ~** en formation *or* gestation; **he has the ~s of an actor** il a l'étoffe d'un acteur.

maladjusted [malǝjus'tid] *a* inadapté(e).

malaise [malāz'] *n* malaise *m*.

malaria [mǝlär'ēǝ] *n* malaria *f*, paludisme *m*.

Malawi [mǝ'lâwē] *n* Malawi *m*.

Malay [mǝlā'] *a* malais(e) ♦ *n* (*person*) Malais/e; (*language*) malais *m*.

Malaya [mǝlā'yǝ] *n* Malaisie *f*.

Malayan [mǝlā'yǝn] *a*, *n* = **Malay.**

Malaysia [mǝlā'zhǝ] *n* Malaisie *f*.

Malaysian [mǝlā'zhǝn] *a* malaisien(ne) ♦ *n* Malaisien/ne.

Maldives [mal'dīvz] *npl*: **the ~** les Maldives *fpl*.

male [māl] *n* (*BIOL*, *ELEC*) mâle *m* ♦ *a* (*sex, attitude*) masculin(e); mâle; (*child etc*) du sexe masculin; **~ and female students** étudiants et étudiantes.

male chauvinist *n* phallocrate *m*.

male nurse *n* infirmier *m*.

malevolence [mǝlev'ǝlǝns] *n* malveillance *f*.

malevolent [mǝlev'ǝlǝnt] *a* malveillant(e).

malfunction [malfungk'shǝn] *n* fonctionnement défectueux.

malice [mal'is] *n* méchanceté *f*, malveillance *f*.

malicious [mǝlish'ǝs] *a* méchant(e), malveillant(e); (*LAW*) avec intention criminelle.

malign [mǝlīn'] *vt* diffamer, calomnier.

malignant [mǝlig'nǝnt] *a* (*MED*) malin(igne).

malingerer [mǝling'gûrûr] *n* simulateur/trice.

mall [môl] *n* (*also*: **shopping ~**) centre commercial.

malleable [mal'ēǝbǝl] *a* malléable.

mallet [mal'it] *n* maillet *m*.

malnutrition [malnōōtrish'ǝn] *n* malnutrition *f*.

malpractice [malprak'tis] *n* faute professionnelle; négligence *f*.

malt [môlt] *n* malt *m* ♦ *cpd* (*whisky*) pur malt.

Malta [môl'tǝ] *n* Malte *f*.

Maltese [môltēz'] *a* maltais(e) ♦ *n* (*pl inv*) Maltais/e; (*LING*) maltais *m*.

maltreat [maltrēt'] *vt* maltraiter.

mammal [mam'ǝl] *n* mammifère *m*.

mammoth [mam'ǝth] *n* mammouth *m* ♦ *a* géant(e), monstre.

Man. *abbr* (*Canada*) = *Manitoba*.

man, *pl* **men** [man, men] *n* homme *m*; (*CHESS*) pièce *f*; (*CHECKERS*) pion *m* ♦ *vt* garnir d'hommes; servir, assurer le fonctionnement de; être de service à; **an old ~** un vieillard; **~ and wife** mari et femme.

manacles [man'ǝkǝlz] *npl* menottes *fpl*.

manage [man'ij] *vi* se débrouiller; y arriver, réussir ♦ *vt* (*business*) gérer; (*team, operation*) diriger; (*device, things to do, carry etc*) arriver à se débrouiller avec, s'en tirer avec; **to ~ to do sth** se débrouiller pour faire; (*succeed*) réussir à faire.

manageable [man'ijǝbǝl] *a* maniable; (*task etc*) faisable.

management [man'ijmǝnt] *n* administration *f*, direction *f*; (*persons: of business, firm*) dirigeants *mpl*, cadres *mpl*; (: *of hotel, store, theater*) direction; **"under new ~"** "changement de gérant", "changement de propriétaire".

management accounting *n* comptabilité *f* de gestion.

management consultant *n* conseiller/ère de direction.

manager [man'ijûr] *n* (*of business*) directeur *m*; (*of institution etc*) administrateur *m*; (*of department, unit*) responsable *m/f*, chef *m*; (*of hotel etc*) gérant *m*; (*of artist*) impresario *m*; **sales ~** responsable *or* chef des ventes.

manageress [man'ijûris] *n* directrice *f*; (*of hotel etc*) gérante *f*.

managerial [manijē'rēǝl] *a* directorial(e); **~ staff** cadres *mpl*.

managing director (MD) [man'ijing dirǝk'tûr] *n* directeur général.

mandarin [man'dûrin] *n* (*also*: **~ orange**) mandarine *f*; (*person*) mandarin *m*.

mandate [man'dāt] *n* mandat *m*.

mandatory [man'dǝtôrē] *a* obligatoire; (*powers etc*) mandataire.

mandolin(e) [man'dǝlin] *n* mandoline *f*.

mane [mān] *n* crinière *f*.

maneuvrable [mǝnōō'vrǝbǝl] *a* facile à manoeuvrer.

maneuver [mǝnōō'vûr] (*US*) *vt*, *vi* manoeuvrer ♦ *n* manoeuvre *f*; **to ~ sb into doing sth** manipuler qn pour lui faire faire qch.

manfully [man'fǝlē] *ad* vaillamment.

manganese [mang'gǝnēz] *n* manganèse *m*.

mangle [mang'gǝl] *vt* déchiqueter; mutiler ♦ *n* essoreuse *f*; calandre *f*.

mango, **~es** [mang'gō] *n* mangue *f*.

mangrove [mang'grōv] *n* palétuvier *m*.

mangy [mān'jē] *a* galeux(euse).

manhandle [man'handǝl] *vt* (*mistreat*) maltraiter, malmener; (*move by hand*) manutentionner.

manhole [man'hōl] *n* trou *m* d'homme.

manhood [man'hōōd] *n* âge *m* d'homme; virilité *f*.

man-hour [man'ouûr] *n* heure-homme *f*, heure *f* de main-d'œuvre.

manhunt [man'hunt] *n* chasse *f* à l'homme.

mania [mā'nēǝ] *n* manie *f*.

maniac [mā'nēak] *n* maniaque *m/f*.

manic [man'ik] *a* maniaque.

manic-depressive [man'ikdipres'iv] *a*, *n* (*PSYCH*) maniaco-dépressif(ive).

manicure [man'ǝkyōōr] *n* manucure *f* ♦ *vt* (*person*) faire les mains à.

manicure set *n* trousse *f* à ongles.

manifest [man'ǝfest] *vt* manifester ♦ *a* manifeste, évident(e) ♦ *n* (*AVIAT*, *NAUT*) manifeste *m*.

manifestation [manəfestā'shən] *n* manifestation *f*.

manifesto [manəfes'tō] *n* manifeste *m* (*POL*).

manifold [man'əfōld] *a* multiple, varié(e) ♦ *n* (*AUT etc*): **exhaust** ~ collecteur *m* d'échappement.

Manila [mənil'ə] *n* Manille, Manila.

manila *a*: ~ **paper** papier *m* bulle.

manipulate [mənip'yəlāt] *vt* manipuler.

manipulation [mənipyəlā'shən] *n* manipulation *f*.

mankind [man'kīnd'] *n* humanité *f*, genre humain.

manliness [man'lēnis] *n* virilité *f*.

manly [man'lē] *a* viril(e); courageux(euse).

man-made [man'mād] *a* artificiel(le).

manna [man'ə] *n* manne *f*.

mannequin [man'əkin] *n* mannequin *m*.

manner [man'ûr] *n* manière *f*, façon *f*; **(good)** ~**s** (bonnes) manières; **bad** ~**s** mauvaises manières; **all** ~ **of** toutes sortes de.

mannerism [man'ərizəm] *n* particularité *f* de langage (*or* de comportement), tic *m*.

mannerly [man'ûrlē] *a* poli(e), courtois(e).

manoeuvre [mənōō'vûr] *etc* (*Brit*) = **maneuver.**

manor [man'ûr] *n* (*also*: ~ **house**) manoir *m*.

manpower [man'pouûr] *n* main-d'œuvre *f*.

Manpower Services Commission *n* (*Brit*) *agence nationale pour l'emploi.*

manservant, *pl* **menservants** [man'sûrvənt, men-] *n* domestique *m*.

mansion [man'chən] *n* château *m*, manoir *m*.

manslaughter [man'slôtûr] *n* homicide *m* involontaire.

mantelpiece [man'təlpēs] *n* cheminée *f*.

mantle [man'təl] *n* cape *f*; (*fig*) manteau *m*.

man-to-man [man'təman'] *a*, *ad* d'homme à homme.

manual [man'yōōəl] *a* manuel(le) ♦ *n* manuel *m*.

manual worker *n* travailleur manuel.

manufacture [manyəfak'chûr] *vt* fabriquer ♦ *n* fabrication *f*.

manufactured goods [manyəfak'chûrd gōōdz] *npl* produits manufacturés.

manufacturer [manyəfak'chûrûr] *n* fabricant *m*.

manufacturing industries [manyəfak'chûring in'dəstrēz] *npl* industries *fpl* de transformation.

manure [mənōōr'] *n* fumier *m*; (*artificial*) engrais *m*.

manuscript [man'yəskript] *n* manuscrit *m*.

many [men'ē] *a* beaucoup de, de nombreux(euses) ♦ *pronoun* beaucoup, un grand nombre; **how** ~? combien?; **a great** ~ un grand nombre (de); **too** ~ **difficulties** trop de difficultés; **twice as** ~ deux fois plus; ~ **a ...** bien des ..., plus d'un(e) ....

map [map] *n* carte *f* ♦ *vt* dresser la carte de.

map out *vt* tracer; (*fig: career, vacation*) organiser, préparer (à l'avance); (: *essay*) faire le plan de.

maple [mā'pəl] *n* érable *m*.

Mar. *abbr* = **March.**

mar [mâr] *vt* gâcher, gâter.

marathon [mar'əthán] *n* marathon *m* ♦ *a*: **a** ~ **session** une séance-marathon.

marathon runner *n* coureur/euse de marathon, marathonien/ne.

marauder [mərôd'ûr] *n* maraudeur/euse.

marble [mâr'bəl] *n* marbre *m*; (*toy*) bille *f*; ~**s** *n* (*game*) billes.

marble mason *n* (*US*) marbrier *m*.

March [mârch] *n* mars *m*; *for phrases see also* **July.**

march [mârch] *vi* marcher au pas; (*demonstrators*) défiler ♦ *n* marche *f*; (*demonstration*) rallye *m*; **to** ~ **out of/into** *etc* sortir de/entrer dans *etc* (*de manière décidée ou impulsive*).

marcher [mâr'chûr] *n* (*demonstrator*) manifestant/e, marcheur/euse.

marching [mâr'ching] *n*: **to give sb his** ~ **orders** (*fig*) renvoyer qn; envoyer promener qn.

march-past [mârch'past] *n* défilé *m*.

mare [mâr] *n* jument *f*.

marg. [mârj] *n abbr* (*col*) = **margarine.**

margarine [mâr'jûrin] *n* margarine *f*.

margin [mâr'jin] *n* marge *f*.

marginal [mâr'jinəl] *a* marginal(e); ~ **seat** (*POL*) siège disputé.

marginally [mâr'jinəlē] *ad* très légèrement, sensiblement.

marigold [mar'əgōld] *n* souci *m*.

marijuana [marəwä'nə] *n* marijuana *f*.

marina [mərē'nə] *n* marina *f*.

marinade [mar'ənād] *n* marinade *f* ♦ *vt* = **marinate.**

marinate [mar'ənāt] *vt* (faire) mariner.

marine [mərēn'] *a* marin(e) ♦ *n* fusilier marin; (*US*) marine *m*.

marine insurance *n* assurance *f* maritime.

marital [mar'itəl] *a* matrimonial(e); ~ **status** situation *f* de famille.

maritime [mar'itīm] *a* maritime.

maritime law *n* droit *m* maritime.

marjoram [mâr'jûrəm] *n* marjolaine *f*.

mark [mârk] *n* marque *f*; (*of skid etc*) trace *f*; (*Brit SCOL*) note *f*; (*SPORT*) cible *f*; (*currency*) mark *m*; (*Brit TECH*): **M~ 2/3** 2ème/3ème série *f or* version *f* ♦ *vt* (*also SPORT: player*) marquer; (*stain*) tacher; (*Brit SCOL*) noter; corriger; **punctuation** ~**s** signes *mpl* de ponctuation; **to** ~ **time** marquer le pas; **to be quick off the** ~ **(in doing)** (*fig*) ne pas perdre de temps (pour faire); **up to the** ~ (*in efficiency*) à la hauteur.

mark down *vt* (*prices, goods*) démarquer, réduire le prix de.

mark off *vt* (*tick off*) cocher, pointer.

mark out *vt* désigner.

mark up *vt* (*price*) majorer.

marked [mârkt] *a* marqué(e), net(te).

markedly [mâr'kidlē] *ad* visiblement, manifestement.

marker [mâr'kûr] *n* (*sign*) jalon *m*; (*bookmark*) signet *m*.

market [mâr'kit] *n* marché *m* ♦ *vt* (*COMM*) commercialiser; **to be on the** ~ être sur le marché; **on the open** ~ en vente libre; **to play the** ~ jouer à la *or* spéculer en Bourse.

marketable [mâr'kitəbəl] *a* commercialisable.

market analysis *n* analyse *f* de marché.

market day *n* jour *m* de marché.

market demand n besoins mpl du marché.
market forces npl tendances fpl du marché.
market garden n (Brit) jardin maraîcher.
marketing [mâr'kiting] n marketing m.
marketplace [mâr'kitplās] n place f du marché; (COMM) marché m.
market price n prix marchand.
market research n étude f de marché.
market value n valeur marchande; valeur du marché.
marking [mâr'king] n (on animal) marque f, tache f; (on road) signalisation f.
marksman [mârks'mən] n tireur m d'élite.
marksmanship [mârks'mənship] n adresse f au tir.
markup [mârk'up] n (COMM: margin) marge f (bénéficiaire); (: increase) majoration f.
marmalade [mâr'məlād] n confiture f d'oranges.
maroon [mərōōn'] vt (fig): **to be ~ed (in** or **at)** être bloqué(e) (à) ♦ a bordeaux inv.
marquee [mârkē'] n chapiteau m.
marquess, marquis [mâr'kwis] n marquis m.
Marrakech, Marrakesh [mâr'əkesh] n Marrakech.
marriage [mar'ij] n mariage m.
marriage bureau n agence matrimoniale.
marriage certificate n extrait m d'acte de mariage.
marriage counseling, (Brit) **marriage guidance** n conseils conjugaux.
married [mar'ēd] a marié(e); (life, love) conjugal(e).
marrow [mar'ō] n moelle f; (vegetable) courge f.
marrow squash n (US) courge f.
marry [mar'ē] vt épouser, se marier avec; (subj: father, priest etc) marier ♦ vi (also: **get married)** se marier.
Mars [mârz] n (planet) Mars f.
Marseilles [mârsā'] n Marseille.
marsh [mârsh] n marais m, marécage m.
marshal [mâr'shəl] n maréchal m; (US: fire, police) ≈ capitaine m ♦ vt rassembler.
marshalling yard [mâr'shəling yârd] n (Brit RAIL) gare f de triage.
marshmallow [mârsh'melō] n (BOT) guimauve f; (sweet) (pâte f de) guimauve.
marshy [mâr'shē] a marécageux(euse).
marsupial [mârsōō'pēəl] a marsupial(e) ♦ n marsupial m.
martial [mâr'shəl] a martial(e).
martial law n loi martiale.
Martian [mâr'shən] n Martien/ne.
martin [mâr'tən] n (also: **house ~)** martinet m.
martyr [mâr'tûr] n martyr/e ♦ vt martyriser.
martyrdom [mâr'tûrdəm] n martyre m.
marvel [mâr'vəl] n merveille f ♦ vi: **to ~ (at)** s'émerveiller (de).
marvelous, (Brit) **marvellous** [mâr'vələs] a merveilleux(euse).
Marxism [mârk'sizəm] n marxisme m.
Marxist [mârk'ksist] a, n marxiste (m/f).
marzipan [mâr'zəpan] n pâte f d'amandes.
mascara [maskar'ə] n mascara m.
mascot [mas'kət] n mascotte f.
masculine [mas'kyəlin] a masculin(e) ♦ n masculin m.

masculinity [maskyəlin'itē] n masculinité f.
MASH [mash] n abbr (US MIL) = mobile army surgical hospital.
mash [mash] vt (CULIN) faire une purée de.
mashed [masht] a: **~ potatoes** purée f de pommes de terre.
mask [mask] n masque m ♦ vt masquer.
masochism [mas'əkizəm] n masochisme m.
masochist [mas'əkist] n masochiste m/f.
mason [mā'sən] n (also: **stone~)** maçon m; (also: **free~)** franc-maçon m.
masonic [məsân'ik] a maçonnique.
masonry [mā'sənrē] n maçonnerie f.
masquerade [maskərād'] n bal masqué; (fig) mascarade f ♦ vi: **to ~ as** se faire passer pour.
Mass. abbr (US) = Massachusetts.
mass [mas] n multitude f, masse f; (PHYSICS) masse; (REL) messe f ♦ vi se masser; **the ~es** les masses; **to go to ~** aller à la messe.
massacre [mas'əkûr] n massacre m ♦ vt massacrer.
massage [məsâzh'] n massage m ♦ vt masser.
masseur [masûr'] n masseur m.
masseuse [məsōōs'] n masseuse f.
massive [mas'iv] a énorme, massif(ive).
mass market n marché m grand public.
mass media [mas mē'dēə] npl mass-media mpl.
mass meeting n rassemblement m de masse.
mass-produce [mas'prədōōs'] vt fabriquer en série.
mass production n fabrication f en série.
mast [mast] n mât m; (RADIO, TV) pylône m.
master [mas'tûr] n maître m; (Brit: in high school) professeur m; (title for boys): **M~ X** Monsieur X ♦ vt maîtriser; (learn) apprendre à fond; (understand) posséder parfaitement or à fond; **~ of ceremonies (MC)** n maître des cérémonies; **M~ of Arts/Science (MA/ MSc)** n ≈ titulaire m/f d'une maîtrise (en lettres/science); **M~ of Arts/Science degree (MA/MSc)** n ≈ maîtrise f; **M~'s degree** n ≈ maîtrise.
master disk n (COMPUT) disque original.
masterful [mas'tûrfəl] a autoritaire, impérieux(euse).
master key n passe-partout m inv.
masterly [mas'tûrlē] a magistral(e).
mastermind [mas'tûrmīnd] n esprit supérieur ♦ vt diriger, être le cerveau de.
masterpiece [mas'tûrpēs] n chef-d'œuvre m.
master plan n stratégie f d'ensemble.
masterstroke [mas'tûrstrōk] n coup m de maître.
mastery [mas'tûrē] n maîtrise f; connaissance parfaite.
mastiff [mas'tif] n mastiff m.
masturbate [mas'tûrbāt] vi se masturber.
masturbation [mastûrbā'shən] n masturbation f.
mat [mat] n petit tapis; (also: **door~)** paillasson m ♦ a = **matt.**
match [mach] n allumette f; (game) match m, partie f; (fig) égal/e; mariage m; parti m ♦ vt assortir; (go well with) aller bien avec, s'assortir à; (equal) égaler, valoir ♦ vi être assorti(e); **to be a good ~** être bien

assorti(e).
match up *vt* assortir.
matchbox [mach'báks] *n* boîte *f* d'allumettes.
matching [mach'ing] *a* assorti(e).
matchless [mach'lis] *a* sans égal.
mate [māt] *n* (*animal*) partenaire *m/f*, mâle/femelle; (*in merchant navy*) second *m*; (*Brit: colleague*) camarade *m/f* de travail; (: *col*) copain/copine ♦ *vi* s'accoupler ♦ *vt* accoupler.
material [mətē'rēəl] *n* (*substance*) matière *f*, matériau *m*; (*cloth*) tissu *m*, étoffe *f* ♦ *a* matériel(le); (*important*) essentiel(le); **~s** *npl* matériaux *mpl*; **reading** ~ de quoi lire, de la lecture.
materialistic [mətērēəlis'tik] *a* matérialiste.
materialize [mətēr'ēəlīz] *vi* se matérialiser, se réaliser.
materially [mətēr'ēəlē] *ad* matériellement; essentiellement.
maternal [mətûr'nəl] *a* maternel(le).
maternity [mətûr'nitē] *n* maternité *f* ♦ *cpd* de maternité, de grossesse.
maternity benefit *n* prestation *f* de maternité.
maternity hospital *n* maternité *f*.
math. [math] *n abbr* (*US*: = *mathematics*) maths *fpl*.
mathematical [mathəmat'ikəl] *a* mathématique.
mathematician [mathəmətish'ən] *n* mathématicien/ne.
mathematics [mathəmat'iks] *n* mathématiques *fpl*.
maths [maths] *n abbr* (*Brit*: = *mathematics*) maths *fpl*.
matinée [matənā'] *n* matinée *f*.
mating [mā'ting] *n* accouplement *m*.
mating call *n* appel *m* du mâle.
mating season *n* saison *f* des amours.
matriarchal [mātrēär'kəl] *a* matriarcal(e).
matrices [māt'risēz] *npl of* **matrix**.
matriculation [mətrikyəlā'shən] *n* inscription *f*.
matrimonial [matrəmō'nēəl] *a* matrimonial(e), conjugal(e).
matrimony [mat'rəmōnē] *n* mariage *m*.
matrix, pl matrices [mā'triks, māt'risēz] *n* matrice *f*.
matron [mā'trən] *n* (*in hospital*) infirmière-chef *f*; (*in school*) infirmière.
matronly [mā'trənlē] *a* de matrone, imposant(e).
matt [mat] *a* mat(e).
matted [mat'id] *a* emmêlé(e).
matter [mat'ûr] *n* question *f*; (*PHYSICS*) matière *f*, substance *f*; (*content*) contenu *m*, fond *m*; (*MED: pus*) pus *m* ♦ *vi* importer; **it doesn't** ~ cela n'a pas d'importance; (*I don't mind*) cela ne fait rien; **what's the** ~? qu'est-ce qu'il y a?, qu'est-ce qui ne va pas?; **no** ~ **what** quoiqu'il arrive; **that's another** ~ c'est une autre affaire; **as a** ~ **of course** tout naturellement; **as a** ~ **of fact** en fait; **it's a** ~ **of habit** c'est une question d'habitude; **printed** ~ imprimés *mpl*; **reading** ~ de quoi lire, de la lecture.
matter-of-fact [mat'ûrəvfakt'] *a* terre à terre, neutre.

matting [mat'ing] *n* natte *f*.
mattress [mat'ris] *n* matelas *m*.
mature [mətōōr'] *a* mûr(e); (*cheese*) fait(e) ♦ *vi* mûrir; se faire.
maturity [mətōō'ritē] *n* maturité *f*.
maudlin [môd'lin] *a* larmoyant(e).
maul [môl] *vt* lacérer.
Mauritania [môritā'nēə] *n* Mauritanie *f*.
Mauritius [môrish'ēəs] *n* l'île *f* Maurice.
mausoleum [môsəlē'əm] *n* mausolée *m*.
mauve [mōv] *a* mauve.
maverick [mav'ûrik] *n* (*fig*) franc-tireur *m*, non-conformiste *m/f*.
mawkish [môk'ish] *a* mièvre; fade.
max. *abbr* = **maximum.**
maxim [mak'sim] *n* maxime *f*.
maxima [mak'səmə] *npl of* **maximum.**
maximize [mak'səmīz] *vt* (*profits etc, chances*) maximiser.
maximum [mak'səməm] *a* maximum ♦ *n* (*pl* **maxima** [mak'səmə]) maximum *m*.
May [mā] *n* mai *m*; *for phrases see also* **July.**
may [mā] *vi* (*conditional*: **might**) (*indicating possibility*): **he** ~ **come** il se peut qu'il vienne; (*be allowed to*): ~ **I smoke?** puis-je fumer?; (*wishes*): ~ **God bless you!** (que) Dieu vous bénisse!; ~ **I sit here?** vous permettez que je m'assoie ici?; **he might be there** il pourrait bien y être, il se pourrait qu'il y soit; **I might as well go** je ferais aussi bien d'y aller, autant y aller; **you might like to try** vous pourriez (peut-être) essayer.
maybe [mā'bē] *ad* peut-être; ~ **he'll** ... peut-être qu'il ...; ~ **not** peut-être pas.
May Day *n* le Premier mai.
mayday [mā'dā] *n* S.O.S. *m*.
mayhem [mā'hem] *n* grabuge *m*.
mayonnaise [māənāz'] *n* mayonnaise *f*.
mayor [mā'ûr] *n* maire *m*.
mayoress [mā'ûris] *n* maire *m*; épouse *f* du maire.
maypole [mā'pōl] *n* mât enrubanné (*autour duquel on danse*).
maze [māz] *n* labyrinthe *m*, dédale *m*.
MB *abbr* (*COMPUT*) = **megabyte**; (*Canada*) = Manitoba.
MBA *n abbr* (= *Master of Business Administration*) *titre universitaire.*
MBBS, MBChB *n abbr* (*Brit*: = *Bachelor of Medicine and Surgery*) *titre universitaire.*
MC *n abbr* = **master of ceremonies.**
MCAT *n abbr* (*US*) = *Medical College Admissions Test.*
MCP *n abbr* (*Brit col*: = *male chauvinist pig*) phallocrate *m*.
MD *n abbr* (= *Doctor of Medicine*) *titre universitaire*; (*COMM*) = **managing director** ♦ *abbr* (*US MAIL*) = Maryland.
ME *abbr* (*US MAIL*) = Maine ♦ *n abbr* (*US MED*) = *medical examiner*; (*MED*: = *myalgic encephalomyelitis*)
me [mē] *pronoun* me, m' + *vowel*; (*stressed, after prep*) moi; **it's** ~ c'est moi; **it's for** ~ c'est pour moi.
meadow [med'ō] *n* prairie *f*, pré *m*.
meager, (*Brit*) **meagre** [mē'gûr] *a* maigre.
meal [mēl] *n* repas *m*; (*flour*) farine *f*; **to go out for a** ~ sortir manger.

meal ticket n (US) chèque-repas m, ticket-repas m.

mealtime [mēl'tīm] n heure f du repas.

mealy-mouthed [mē'lēmouthd] a mielleux(euse).

mean [mēn] a (with money) avare, radin(e); (unkind) mesquin(e), méchant(e); (US col: animal) méchant, vicieux(euse); (: person) vache; (average) moyen(ne) ♦ vt (pt, pp **meant** [ment]) (signify) signifier, vouloir dire; (intend): **to ~ to do** avoir l'intention de faire ♦ n moyenne f; **to be meant for** être destiné(e) à; **do you ~ it?** vous êtes sérieux?; **what do you ~?** que voulez-vous dire?

meander [mēan'dûr] vi faire des méandres; (fig) flâner.

meaning [mē'ning] n signification f, sens m.

meaningful [mē'ningfəl] a significatif(ive); (relationship) valable.

meaningless [mē'ninglis] a dénué(e) de sens.

meanness [mēn'nis] n avarice f; mesquinerie f.

means [mēnz] npl moyens mpl; **by ~ of** par l'intermédiaire de; au moyen de; **by all ~** je vous en prie.

means test n (ADMIN) contrôle m des conditions de ressources.

meant [ment] pt, pp of **mean**.

meantime [mēn'tīm] ad (also: **in the ~**) pendant ce temps.

meanwhile [mēn'wīl] ad pendant ce temps.

measles [mē'zəlz] n rougeole f.

measly [mēz'lē] a (col) minable.

measurable [mezh'ûrəbəl] a mesurable.

measure [mezh'ûr] vt, vi mesurer ♦ n mesure f; (ruler) règle (graduée); **a liter ~** un litre; **some ~ of success** un certain succès; **to take ~s to do sth** prendre des mesures pour faire qch.
  measure up vi: **to ~ up (to)** être à la hauteur (de).

measured [mezh'ûrd] a mesuré(e).

measurement [mezh'ûrmənt] n: **chest/hip ~** tour m de poitrine/hanches; **~s** npl mesures fpl; **to take sb's ~s** prendre les mesures de qn.

meat [mēt] n viande f; **cold ~s** (Brit) viandes froides; **crab ~** crabe f.

meatball [mēt'bôl] n boulette f de viande.

meat pie n pâté m en croûte.

meaty [mē'tē] a avec beaucoup de viande, plein(e) de viande; (fig) substantiel(le).

Mecca [mek'ə] n la Mecque; (fig): **a ~ (for)** la Mecque (de).

mechanic [məkan'ik] n mécanicien m.

mechanical [məkan'ikəl] a mécanique.

mechanical engineering n (science) mécanique f; (industry) construction f mécanique.

mechanical pencil n (US) porte-mine m inv.

mechanics [məkan'iks] n mécanique f ♦ npl mécanisme m.

mechanism [mek'ənizəm] n mécanisme m.

mechanization [mekənizā'shən] n mécanisation f.

MEd n abbr (= Master of Education) titre universitaire.

medal [med'əl] n médaille f.

medalist [med'əlist] n (US SPORT) médaillé/e.

medallion [mədal'yən] n médaillon m.

medallist [med'əlist] n (Brit) = **medalist**.

meddle [med'əl] vi: **to ~ in** se mêler de, s'occuper de; **to ~ with** toucher à.

meddlesome [med'əlsəm], **meddling** [med'ling] a indiscret(ète), qui se mêle de ce qui ne le (or la) regarde pas; touche-à-tout inv.

media [mē'dēə] npl media mpl.

mediaeval [mēdēē'vəl] a = **medieval**.

median [mē'dēən] n (US: also: **~ strip**) bande médiane.

media research n étude f de l'audience.

mediate [mē'dēāt] vi s'interposer; servir d'intermédiaire.

mediation [mēdēā'shən] n médiation f.

mediator [mē'dēātər] n médiateur/trice.

medical [med'ikəl] a médical(e) ♦ n (also: **~ examination**) visite médicale; examen médical.

medical certificate n certificat médical.

medical examiner n (US) médecin m légiste.

medical student n étudiant/e en médecine.

Medicare [med'əkär] n (US) régime d'assurance maladie.

medicated [med'ikātid] a traitant(e), médicamenteux(euse).

medication [medikā'shən] n (drugs etc) médication f.

medicinal [mədisin'ənəl] a médicinal(e).

medicine [med'isin] n médecine f; (drug) médicament m.

medicine chest n pharmacie f (murale ou portative).

medicine man n sorcier m.

medieval [mēdēē'vəl] a médiéval(e).

mediocre [mē'dēōkər] a médiocre.

mediocrity [mēdēāk'ritē] n médiocrité f.

meditate [med'ətāt] vi: **to ~ (on)** méditer (sur).

meditation [medətā'shən] n méditation f.

Mediterranean [meditərā'nēən] a méditerranéen(ne); **the ~ (Sea)** la (mer) Méditerranée.

medium [mē'dēəm] a moyen(ne) ♦ n (pl **media**) (means) moyen m; (pl **mediums**) (person) médium m; **the happy ~** le juste milieu.

medium-sized [mē'dēəmsīzd] a de taille moyenne.

medium wave n (RADIO) ondes moyennes, petites ondes.

medley [med'lē] n mélange m.

meek [mēk] a doux(douce), humble.

meet, pt, pp met [mēt, met] vt rencontrer; (by arrangement) retrouver, rejoindre; (for the first time) faire la connaissance de; (go and fetch): **I'll ~ you at the station** j'irai te chercher à la gare; (problem) faire face à; (requirements) satisfaire à, répondre à; (bill, expenses) régler, honorer ♦ vi se rencontrer; se retrouver; (in session) se réunir; (join: objects) se joindre ♦ n (US SPORT) rencontre f, meeting m; (Brit: HUNTING) rendez-vous m de chasse; **pleased to ~ you!** enchanté!
  meet up vi: **to ~ up with sb** rencontrer qn.
  meet with vt fus rencontrer.

meeting [mē'ting] *n* rencontre *f*; (*session: of club etc*) réunion *f*; (*formal*) assemblée *f*; (*SPORT: rally*) rencontre, meeting *m*; (*interview*) entrevue *f*; **she's at a** ~ (*COMM*) elle est en conférence; **to call a** ~ convoquer une réunion.

meeting place *n* lieu *m* de (la) réunion; (*for appointment*) lieu de rendez-vous.

megabyte [meg'əbīt] *n* (*COMPUT*) méga-octet *m*.

megalomaniac [megəlōmā'nēak] *n* mégalomane *m/f*.

megaphone [meg'əfōn] *n* porte-voix *m inv*.

melancholy [mel'ənkâlē] *n* mélancolie *f* ♦ *a* mélancolique.

mellow [mel'ō] *a* velouté(e); doux(douce); (*color*) riche et profond(e); (*fruit*) mûr(e) ♦ *vi* (*person*) s'adoucir.

melodious [məlō'dēəs] *a* mélodieux(euse).

melodrama [mel'ədrâmə] *n* mélodrame *m*.

melodramatic [melədrəmat'ik] *a* mélodramatique.

melody [mel'ədē] *n* mélodie *f*.

melon [mel'ən] *n* melon *m*.

melt [melt] *vi* fondre; (*become soft*) s'amollir; (*fig*) s'attendrir ♦ *vt* faire fondre; (*person*) attendrir.

melt away *vi* fondre complètement.

melt down *vt* fondre.

meltdown [melt'doun] *n* fusion *f* (du cœur d'un réacteur nucléaire).

melting point [melt'ing point] *n* point *m* de fusion.

melting pot [melt'ing pât] *n* (*fig*) creuset *m*; **to be in the** ~ être encore en discussion.

member [mem'bûr] *n* membre *m*; (*of club, political party*) membre, adhérent/e ♦ *cpd*: ~ **country/state** *n* pays *m*/état *m* membre; **M~ of Congress (MC)** *n* (*US*) membre du Congrès; **M~ of the House of Representatives (MHR)** *n* (*US*) membre de la Chambre des représentants; **M~ of Parliament (MP)** *n* (*Brit*) député *m*; **M~ of the European Parliament (MEP)** *n* Eurodéputé *m*.

membership [mem'bûrship] *n* (*becoming a member*) adhésion *f*; admission *f*; (*being a member*) qualité *f* de membre, fait *m* d'être membre; (*the members*) membres *mpl*, adhérents *mpl*; (*number of members*) nombre *m* des membres *or* adhérents.

membership card *n* carte *f* de membre.

membrane [mem'brān] *n* membrane *f*.

memento [məmen'tō] *n* souvenir *m*.

memo [mem'ō] *n* note *f* (de service).

memoir [mem'wâr] *n* mémoire *m*, étude *f*; ~**s** *npl* mémoires.

memo pad *n* bloc-notes *m*.

memorable [mem'ûrəbəl] *a* mémorable.

memorandum, *pl* **memoranda** [meməran'dəm, -də] *n* note *f* (de service); (*DIPLOMACY*) mémorandum *m*.

memorial [məmô'rēəl] *n* mémorial *m* ♦ *a* commémoratif(ive).

memorize [mem'ərīz] *vt* apprendre *or* retenir par cœur.

memory [mem'ûrē] *n* mémoire *f*; (*recollection*) souvenir *m*; **to have a good/bad** ~ avoir une bonne/mauvaise mémoire; **loss of** ~ perte *f* de mémoire; **in** ~ **of** à la mé-

moire de.

men [men] *npl of* **man.**

menace [men'is] *n* menace *f*; (*col: nuisance*) peste *f*, plaie *f* ♦ *vt* menacer; **a public** ~ un danger public.

menacing [men'ising] *a* menaçant(e).

menagerie [mənaj'ûrē] *n* ménagerie *f*.

mend [mend] *vt* réparer; (*darn*) raccommoder, repriser ♦ *n* reprise *f*; **on the** ~ en voie de guérison.

mending [mend'ing] *n* raccommodages *mpl*.

menial [mē'nēəl] *a* de domestique, inférieur(e); subalterne.

meningitis [meninji'tis] *n* méningite *f*.

menopause [men'əpôz] *n* ménopause *f*.

menservants [men'sûrvənts] *npl of* **manservant.**

menstruate [men'strōōāt] *vi* avoir ses règles.

menstruation [menstrōōā'shən] *n* menstruation *f*.

mental [men'təl] *a* mental(e); ~ **illness** maladie mentale.

mentality [mental'itē] *n* mentalité *f*.

mentally [men'təlē] *ad*: **to be** ~ **handicapped** être handicapé/e mental(e)

menthol [men'thôl] *n* menthol *m*.

mention [men'chən] *n* mention *f* ♦ *vt* mentionner, faire mention de; **don't** ~ **it!** je vous en prie, il n'y a pas de quoi!; **I need hardly** ~ **that** ... est-il besoin de rappeler que ...?; **not to** ~ ..., **without** ~**ing** ... sans parler de ..., sans compter ....

mentor [men'tûr] *n* mentor *m*.

menu [men'yōō] *n* (*in restaurant, COMPUT*) menu *m*; (*printed*) carte *f*.

menu-driven [men'yōōdriv'ən] *a* (*COMPUT*) piloté/e par menu.

meow [mēou'] *vi* miauler.

MEP *n abbr* = **Member of the European Parliament.**

mercantile [mûr'kəntil] *a* marchand(e); (*law*) commercial(e).

mercenary [mûr'sənerē] *a* mercantile ♦ *n* mercenaire *m*.

merchandise *n* [mûr'chəndīs] marchandises *fpl* ♦ *vt* [mûr'chəndīz] commercialiser.

merchandiser [mûr'chəndīzûr] *n* marchandiseur *m*.

merchant [mûr'chənt] *n* négociant *m*, marchand *m*; **timber/wine** ~ négociant en bois/vins, marchand de bois/vins.

merchant bank *n* (*Brit*) banque *f* d'affaires.

merchantman [mûr'chəntmən] *n* navire marchand.

merchant marine, (*Brit*) **merchant navy** *n* marine marchande.

merciful [mûr'sifəl] *a* miséricordieux(euse), clément(e).

mercifully [mûr'sifəlē] *ad* avec clémence; (*fortunately*) par bonheur, Dieu merci.

merciless [mûr'silis] *a* impitoyable, sans pitié.

mercurial [mûrkyōō'rēəl] *a* changeant(e); (*lively*) vif(vive).

mercury [mûrk'yûrē] *n* mercure *m*.

mercy [mûr'sē] *n* pitié *f*, merci *f*; (*REL*) miséricorde *f*; **to have** ~ **on sb** avoir pitié de qn; **at the** ~ **of** à la merci de.

mercy killing *n* euthanasie *f*.

mere [mēr] *a* simple.

merely |mēr'lē| *ad* simplement, purement.

merge |mûrj| *vt* unir; (*COMPUT*) fusionner, interclasser ♦ *vi* se fondre; (*COMM*) fusionner.

merger |mûr'jûr| *n* (*COMM*) fusion *f*.

meridian |mərid'ēən| *n* méridien *m*.

meringue |mərang'| *n* meringue *f*.

merit |mär'it| *n* mérite *m*, valeur *f* ♦ *vt* mériter.

meritocracy |märiták'rəsē| *n* méritocratie *f*.

mermaid |mûr'mād| *n* sirène *f*.

merrily |mär'ilē| *ad* joyeusement, gaiement.

merriment |mär'imənt| *n* gaieté *f*.

merry |mär'ē| *a* gai(e); **M~ Christmas!** joyeux Noël!

merry-go-round |mär'ēgōround| *n* manège *m*.

mesh |mesh| *n* maille *f*; filet *m* ♦ *vi* (*gears*) s'engrener; **wire ~** grillage *m* (métallique), treillis *m* (métallique).

mesmerize |mez'mərīz| *vt* hypnotiser; fasciner.

mess |mes| *n* désordre *m*, fouillis *m*, pagaille *f*; (*MIL*) mess *m*, cantine *f*; **to be (in) a ~** être en désordre; **to be/get o.s. in a ~** (*fig*) être/se mettre dans le pétrin.

mess about *vi* (*Brit*) = **mess around**.

mess around *vi* (*col*) faire l'imbécile; (: *waste time*) traînasser.

mess around with *vt fus* (*col*) chambarder, tripoter.

mess up *vt* salir; chambarder; gâcher.

message |mes'ij| *n* message *m*; **to get the ~** (*fig*: *col*) saisir, piger.

message switching *n* (*COMPUT*) commutation *f* de messages.

messenger |mes'injûr| *n* messager *m*.

Messiah |misī'ə| *n* Messie *m*.

Messrs, Messrs. |mes'ûrz| *abbr* (*on letters*: = *messieurs*) MM.

messy |mes'ē| *a* sale; en désordre.

Met |met| *n abbr* (*US*) = *Metropolitan Opera*.

met |met| *pt*, *pp of* **meet** ♦ *a abbr* (*Brit*: = *meteorological*) météo *inv*.

metabolism |mətab'əlizəm| *n* métabolisme *m*.

metal |met'əl| *n* métal *m* ♦ *vt* empierrer.

metallic |mital'ik| *a* métallique.

metallurgy |met'əlûrjē| *n* métallurgie *f*.

metalwork |met'əlwûrk| *n* (*craft*) ferronnerie *f*.

metamorphosis, *pl* **-phoses** |metəmôr'fəsis, -ēz| *n* métamorphose *f*.

metaphor |met'əfôr| *n* métaphore *f*.

metaphysics |metəfiz'iks| *n* métaphysique *f*.

mete |mēt| : **to ~ out** *vt fus* infliger.

meteor |mē'tēôr| *n* météore *m*.

meteoric |mētēôr'ik| *a* (*fig*) fulgurant(e).

meteorite |mē'tēərit| *n* météorite *m* or *f*.

meteorological |mētēûrəláj'ikəl| *a* météorologique.

meteorology |mētēərál'əjē| *n* météorologie *f*.

meter |mē'tûr| *n* (*instrument*) compteur *m*; (*also*: **parking ~**) parc(o)mètre *m*; (*US*: *measurement*) mètre *m*.

methane |meth'ān| *n* méthane *m*.

method |meth'əd| *n* méthode *f*; **~ of payment** mode *m* or modalité *f* de paiement.

methodical |məthád'ikəl| *a* méthodique.

Methodist |meth'ədist| *a*, *n* méthodiste (*m/f*).

methylated spirit(s) |meth'əlātid spir'its| *n*

(*Brit*: *also*: **meths**) alcool *m* à brûler.

meticulous |mətik'yələs| *a* méticuleux(euse).

metre |mē'tûr| *n* (*Brit*: *measurement*) mètre *m*.

metric |met'rik| *a* métrique; **to go ~** adopter le système métrique.

metrical |met'rikəl| *a* métrique.

metrication |metrikā'shən| *n* conversion *f* au système métrique.

metric system *n* système *m* métrique.

metric ton *n* tonne *f*.

metronome |met'rənōm| *n* métronome *m*.

metropolis |mitrảp'əlis| *n* métropole *f*.

metropolitan |metrəpál'itən| *a* métropolitain(e).

Metropolitan Police *n* (*Brit*): **the ~** la police londonienne.

mettle |met'əl| *n* courage *m*.

mew |myōō| *vi* (*cat*) miauler.

mews |myōōz| *n* (*Brit*): **~ cottage** *maisonnette aménagée dans une ancienne écurie ou remise.*

Mexican |mek'səkən| *a* mexicain(e) ♦ *n* Mexicain/e.

Mexico |mek'səkō| *n* Mexique *m*.

Mexico City *n* Mexico.

mezzanine |mez'ənēn| *n* mezzanine *f*; (*of shops, offices*) entresol *m*.

MFA *n abbr* (*US*: = *Master of Fine Arts*) titre universitaire.

mfr *abbr* = **manufacture, manufacturer.**

mg *abbr* (= *milligram*) mg.

Mgr *abbr* (= *Monseigneur, Monsignor*) Mgr; (= *manager*) dir.

MHR *n abbr* (*US*) = **Member of the House of Representatives.**

MHz *abbr* (= *megahertz*) MHz.

MI *abbr* (*US MAIL*) = *Michigan*.

MI5 *n abbr* (*Brit*: = *Military Intelligence 5*) ≈ DST *f*.

MI6 *n abbr* (*Brit*: = *Military Intelligence 6*) ≈ DGSE *f*.

MIA *abbr* (= *missing in action*) disparu au combat.

mice |mīs| *npl of* **mouse.**

Mich. *abbr* (*US*) = *Michigan*.

microbe |mī'krōb| *n* microbe *m*.

microbiology |mīkrōbīál'əjē| *n* microbiologie *f*.

microchip |mī'krəchip| *n* (*ELEC*) puce *f*.

micro(computer) |mīkrō(kəmpyōō'tûr)| *n* micro(-ordinateur) *m*.

microcosm |mī'krəkázəm| *n* microcosme *m*.

microeconomics |mīkrōēkənám'iks| *n* micro-économie *f*.

microfiche |mī'krōfēsh| *n* microfiche *f*.

microfilm |mī'krəfilm| *n* microfilm *m* ♦ *vt* microfilmer.

micrometer |mīkrám'itûr| *n* palmer *m*, micromètre *m*.

microphone |mī'krəfōn| *n* microphone *m*.

microprocessor |mīkrōprás'esûr| *n* microprocesseur *m*.

microscope |mī'krəskōp| *n* microscope *m*; **under the ~** au microscope.

microscopic |mī'krəskáp'ik| *a* microscopique.

microwave |mī'krōwāv| *n* (*also*: **~ oven**) four *m* à micro-ondes.

mid |mid| *a*: **~ May** la mi-mai; **~ afternoon**

le milieu de l'après-midi; **in ~ air** en plein ciel; **he's in his ~ thirties** il a dans les trente-cinq ans.

midday [mid'dā] *n* midi *m*.

middle [mid'əl] *n* milieu *m*; (*waist*) ceinture *f*, taille *f* ♦ *a* du milieu; **in the ~ of the night** au milieu de la nuit; **I'm in the ~ of reading it** je suis (justement) en train de le lire.

middle age *n* tranche d'âge aux limites floues, entre la quarantaine et le début du troisième âge.

middle-aged [mid'əlājd'] *a* (*people*) see *middle age*; d'un certain âge, ni vieux ni jeune; (*pej:* values, outlook) conventionnel(le), rassis(e).

Middle Ages *npl:* **the ~** le moyen âge.

middle class *n:* **the ~(es)** ≈ les classes moyennes ♦ *a* (*also:* **middle-class**) ≈ (petit(e)-)bourgeois(e).

Middle East *n:* **the ~** le Proche-Orient, le Moyen-Orient.

middleman [mid'əlman] *n* intermédiaire *m*.

middle management *n* cadres moyens.

middle name *n* second prénom.

middle-of-the-road [mid'əlʌvthərōd'] *a* (*policy*) modéré(e), du juste milieu; (*music etc*) plutôt classique, assez traditionnel(le).

middleweight [mid'əlwāt] *n* (*BOXING*) poids moyen.

middling [mid'ling] *a* moyen(ne).

Middx *abbr* (*Brit*) = *Middlesex*.

midge [mij] *n* moucheron *m*.

midget [mij'it] *n* nain/e ♦ *a* minuscule.

midnight [mid'nīt] *n* minuit *m*; **at ~** à minuit.

midriff [mid'rif] *n* estomac *m*, taille *f*.

midst [midst] *n:* **in the ~ of** au milieu de.

midsummer [mid'sum'ûr] *n* milieu *m* de l'été.

midway [mid'wā] *a, ad:* **~ (between)** à mi-chemin (entre).

midweek [mid'wēk] *n* milieu *m* de la semaine ♦ *ad* au milieu de la semaine, en pleine semaine.

midwife, midwives [mid'wif, -vz] *n* sage-femme *f*.

midwifery [mid'wīfûrē] *n* obstétrique *f*.

midwinter [mid'win'tûr] *n* milieu *m* de l'hiver.

might [mīt] *vb see* **may** ♦ *n* puissance *f*, force *f*.

mighty [mī'tē] *a* puissant(e) ♦ *ad* (*col*) rudement.

migraine [mī'grān] *n* migraine *f*.

migrant [mī'grənt] *n* (*bird, animal*) migrateur *m*; (*person*) migrant/e; nomade *m/f* ♦ *a* migrateur(trice); migrant(e); nomade; (*worker*) saisonnier(ière).

migrate [mī'grāt] *vi* émigrer.

migration [mīgrā'shən] *n* migration *f*.

mike [mīk] *n abbr* (= *microphone*) micro *m*.

Milan [milan'] *n* Milan.

mild [mīld] *a* doux(douce); (*reproach*) léger(ère); (*illness*) bénin(igne) ♦ *n* bière légère.

mildew [mil'dōō] *n* mildiou *m*.

mildly [mīld'lē] *ad* doucement; légèrement; **to put it ~** (*col*) c'est le moins qu'on puisse dire.

mildness [mīld'nis] *n* douceur *f*.

mile [mīl] *n* mil(l)e *m* (= *1609 m*); **to do 30 ~s per gallon** ≈ faire 9,4 litres aux cent.

mileage [mī'lij] *n* distance *f* en milles, ≈ kilométrage *m*.

mileage allowance *n* ≈ indemnité *f* kilométrique.

mileometer [mīlâm'itûr] *n* (*Brit*) = **milometer**.

milestone [mīl'stōn] *n* borne *f*; (*fig*) jalon *m*.

milieu [mēlyōō'] *n* milieu *m*.

militant [mil'ətənt] *a, n* militant(e).

militarism [mil'itərizəm] *n* militarisme *m*.

militaristic [militəris'tik] *a* militariste.

military [mil'itärē] *a* militaire ♦ *n:* **the ~** l'armée *f*, les militaires *mpl*.

militate [mil'ətāt] *vi:* **to ~ against** militer contre.

militia [milish'ə] *n* milice *f*.

milk [milk] *n* lait *m* ♦ *vt* (*cow*) traire; (*fig*) dépouiller, plumer.

milk chocolate *n* chocolat *m* au lait.

milk float *n* (*Brit*) = **milk truck**.

milking [mil'king] *n* traite *f*.

milkman [milk'man] *n* laitier *m*.

milk shake *n* milk-shake *m*.

milk tooth *n* dent *f* de lait.

milk truck *n* (*US*) voiture *f* or camionnette *f* du *or* de laitier.

milky [mil'kē] *a* lacté(e); (*color*) laiteux(euse).

Milky Way *n* Voie lactée.

mill [mil] *n* moulin *m*; (*factory*) usine *f*, fabrique *f*; (*spinning ~*) filature *f*; (*flour ~*) minoterie *f* ♦ *vt* moudre, broyer ♦ *vi* (*also:* **~ around**) grouiller.

millennium, pl ~s or millennia [milen'ēəm, -len'ēə] *n* millénaire *m*.

miller [mil'ûr] *n* meunier *m*.

millet [mil'it] *n* millet *m*.

milli... [mil'ə] *prefix* milli....

milligram(me) [mil'əgram] *n* milligramme *m*.

milliliter, (*Brit*) millilitre [mil'əlētûr] *n* millilitre *m*.

millimeter, (*Brit*) millimetre [mil'əmētûr] *n* millimètre *m*.

milliner [mil'inûr] *n* modiste *f*.

millinery [mil'ənärē] *n* modes *fpl*.

million [mil'yən] *n* million *m*.

millionaire [milyənär'] *n* millionnaire *m*.

millipede [mil'əpēd] *n* mille-pattes *m inv*.

millstone [mil'stōn] *n* meule *f*.

millwheel [mil'wēl] *n* roue *f* de moulin.

milometer [mī'lōmētûr] *n* (*Brit*) ≈ compteur *m* kilométrique.

mime [mīm] *n* mime *m* ♦ *vt, vi* mimer.

mimic [mim'ik] *n* imitateur/trice ♦ *vt, vi* imiter, contrefaire.

mimicry [mim'ikrē] *n* imitation *f*; (*ZOOL*) mimétisme *m*.

Min. *abbr* (*Brit POL*) = **ministry**.

min. *abbr* (= *minute*) mn.; (= *minimum*) min.

minaret [minəret'] *n* minaret *m*.

mince [mins] *vt* hacher ♦ *vi* (*in walking*) marcher à petits pas maniérés ♦ *n* (*Brit CULIN*) viande hachée, hachis *m*; **he does not ~ (his) words** il ne mâche pas ses mots.

mincemeat [mins'mēt] *n* hachis de fruits secs utilisés en pâtisserie.

mince pie *n* sorte de tarte aux fruits secs.

mincer [min'sûr] *n* hachoir *m*.

mincing [min'sing] *a* affecté(e).

mind [mīnd] *n* esprit *m* ♦ *vt* (*attend to, look after*) s'occuper de; (*be careful*) faire attention à; (*object to*): **I don't ~ the noise** je ne crains pas le bruit, le bruit ne me dérange pas; **do you ~ if ...?** est-ce que cela vous gêne si ...?; **I don't ~ cela ne me dérange pas; ~ you, ...** remarquez, ...; **never ~** peu importe, ça ne fait rien; **it is on my ~** cela me préoccupe; **to change one's ~** changer d'avis; **to be of two ~s about sth** être indécis(e) *or* irrésolu(e) en ce qui concerne qch; **to my ~** à mon avis, selon moi; **to be out of one's ~** ne plus avoir toute sa raison; **to keep sth in ~** ne pas oublier qch; **to bear sth in ~** tenir compte de qch; **to have sb/sth in ~** avoir qn/qch en tête; **it have in ~ to do** avoir l'intention de faire; **it went right out of my ~** ça m'est complètement sorti de la tête; **to bring** *or* **call sth to ~** se rappeler qch; **to make up one's ~** se décider.

-minded [mīn'did] *a*: **fair~** impartial(e); **an industrially~ nation** une nation orientée vers l'industrie.

minder [mīnd'ûr] *n* (*child ~*) gardienne *f*; (*bodyguard*) ange gardien (*fig*).

mindful [mīnd'fəl] *a*: **~ of** attentif(ive) à, soucieux(euse) de.

mindless [mīnd'lis] *a* irréfléchi(e); (*violence, crime*) insensé(e).

mine [mīn] *pronoun* le(la) mien(ne), les miens(miennes); **this book is ~** ce livre est à moi ♦ *n* mine *f* ♦ *vt* (*coal*) extraire; (*ship, beach*) miner.

mine detector *n* détecteur *m* de mines.

minefield [mīn'fēld] *n* champ *m* de mines.

miner [mīn'ûr] *n* mineur *m*.

mineral [min'ûrəl] *a* minéral(e) ♦ *n* minéral *m*; **~s** *npl* (*Brit*: *soft drinks*) boissons gazeuses (sucrées).

mineralogy [minərâl'əjē] *n* minéralogie *f*.

mineral water *n* eau minérale.

minesweeper [mīn'swēpûr] *n* dragueur *m* de mines.

mingle [ming'gəl] *vt* mêler, mélanger ♦ *vi*: **to ~ with** se mêler à.

mingy [min'jē] *a* (*col*) radin(e).

miniature [min'ēəchûr] *a* (en) miniature ♦ *n* miniature *f*.

miniature golf *n* golf-miniature *m*.

minibus [min'ēbus] *n* minibus *m*.

minicab [min'ēkab] *n* (*Brit*) minitaxi *m*.

minicomputer [min'ēkəmpyōōtûr] *n* mini-ordinateur *m*.

minim [min'əm] *n* (*MUS*) blanche *f*.

minima [min'əmə] *npl of* **minimum**.

minimal [min'əməl] *a* minimale(e).

minimize [min'əmīz] *vt* minimiser.

minimum [min'əməm] *n* (*pl*: **minima** [min'əmə]) minimum *m* ♦ *a* minimum; **to reduce to a ~** réduire au minimum.

minimum lending rate (MLR) *n* (*ECON*) taux *m* de crédit minimum.

mining [mī'ning] *n* exploitation minière ♦ *a* minier(ière); de mineurs.

minion [min'yən] *n* (*pej*) laquais *m*; favori/te.

miniskirt [min'ēskûrt] *n* mini-jupe *f*.

minister [min'istûr] *n* (*Brit POL*) ministre *m*;

(*REL*) pasteur *m* ♦ *vi*: **to ~ to sb** donner ses soins à qn; **to ~ to sb's needs** pourvoir aux besoins de qn.

ministerial [ministēr'ēəl] *a* (*Brit POL*) ministériel(le).

ministry [min'istrē] *n* (*Brit POL*) ministère *m*; (*REL*): **to go into the ~** devenir pasteur.

mink [mingk] *n* vison *m*.

mink coat *n* manteau *m* de vison.

Minn. *abbr* (*US*) = *Minnesota*.

minnow [min'ō] *n* vairon *m*.

minor [mī'nûr] *a* petit(e), de peu d'importance; (*MUS*) mineur(e) ♦ *n* (*LAW*) mineur/e; (*US SCOL*) matière *f* secondaire.

Minorca [minôr'kə] *n* Minorque *f*.

minority [minôr'itē] *n* minorité *f*; **to be in a ~** être en minorité.

minster [min'stûr] *n* église abbatiale.

minstrel [min'strəl] *n* trouvère *m*, ménestrel *m*.

mint [mint] *n* (*plant*) menthe *f*; (*candy*) bonbon *m* à la menthe ♦ *vt* (*coins*) battre; **the (US) M~,** (*Brit*) **the (Royal) M~** ≈ l'hôtel *m* de la Monnaie; **in ~ condition** à l'état de neuf.

mint sauce *n* sauce *f* à la menthe.

minuet [minyōōet'] *n* menuet *m*.

minus [mī'nəs] *n* (*also*: **~ sign**) signe *m* moins ♦ *prep* moins.

minute *a* [mīnōōt'] minuscule; (*detailed*) minutieux(euse) ♦ *n* [min'it] minute *f*; (*official record*) procès-verbal *m*, compte rendu; **~s** *npl* procès-verbal; **it is 5 ~s past 3** il est 3 heures 5; **wait a ~!** (attendez) un instant!; **at the last ~** à la dernière minute; **up to the ~** (*fashion*) dernier cri; (*news*) de dernière minute; (*machine, technology*) de pointe; **in ~ detail** par le menu.

minute book *n* registre *m* des procès-verbaux.

minute hand *n* aiguille *f* des minutes.

minutely [mīnōōt'lē] *ad* (*by a small amount*) de peu, de manière infime; (*in detail*) minutieusement, dans les moindres détails.

miracle [mir'əkəl] *n* miracle *m*.

miraculous [mirak'yələs] *a* miraculeux(euse).

mirage [mirâzh'] *n* mirage *m*.

mire [mī'ûr] *n* bourbe *f*, bouc *f*.

mirror [mir'ûr] *n* miroir *m*, glace *f* ♦ *vt* refléter.

mirror image *n* image inversée.

mirth [mûrth] *n* gaieté *f*.

misadventure [misədven'chûr] *n* mésaventure *f*; **death by ~** (*Brit*) décès accidentel.

misanthropist [misan'thrəpist] *n* misanthrope *m/f*.

misapply [misəplī'] *vt* mal employer.

misapprehension [misaprihen'chən] *n* malentendu *m*, méprise *f*.

misappropriate [misəprō'prēāt] *vt* détourner.

misappropriation [misəprōprēā'shən] *n* escroquerie *f*, détournement *m*.

misbehave [misbihāv'] *vi* se conduire mal.

misbehavior, (*Brit*) **misbehaviour** [misbihāv'yûr] *n* mauvaise conduite.

misc. *abbr* = **miscellaneous**.

miscalculate [miskal'kyəlāt] *vt* mal calculer.

miscalculation [miskalkyəlā'shən] *n* erreur *f* de calcul.

miscarriage [miskar'ij] *n* (*MED*) fausse couche; ~ **of justice** erreur *f* judiciaire.

miscarry [miskar'ē] *vi* (*MED*) faire une fausse couche; (*fail: plans*) échouer, mal tourner.

miscellaneous [misəlā'nēəs] *a* (*items, expenses*) divers(es); (*selection*) varié(e).

miscellany [mis'əlānē] *n* recueil *m*.

mischance [mischans'] *n* malchance *f*; **by (some)** ~ par malheur.

mischief [mis'chif] *n* (*naughtiness*) sottises *fpl*; (*harm*) mal *m*, dommage *m*; (*maliciousness*) méchanceté *f*.

mischievous [mis'chəvəs] *a* (*naughty*) coquin(e), espiègle; (*harmful*) méchant(e).

misconception [miskənsep'shən] *n* idée fausse.

misconduct [miskân'dukt] *n* inconduite *f*; **professional** ~ faute professionnelle.

misconstrue [miskənstrōō'] *vt* mal interpréter.

miscount [miskount'] *vt, vi* mal compter.

misdeed [misdēd'] *n* méfait *m*.

misdemeanor, (Brit) misdemeanour [misdimē'nûr] *n* écart *m* de conduite; infraction *f*.

misdirect [misdirekt'] *vt* (*person*) mal renseigner; (*letter*) mal adresser.

miser [mī'zûr] *n* avare *m/f*.

miserable [miz'ûrəbəl] *a* malheureux(euse); (*wretched*) misérable; **to feel** ~ avoir le cafard.

miserably [miz'ûrəblē] *ad* (*smile, answer*) tristement; (*live, pay*) misérablement; (*fail*) lamentablement.

miserly [mī'zûrlē] *a* avare.

misery [miz'ûrē] *n* (*unhappiness*) tristesse *f*; (*pain*) souffrances *fpl*; (*wretchedness*) misère *f*.

misfire [misfīr'] *vi* rater; (*car engine*) avoir des ratés.

misfit [mis'fit] *n* (*person*) inadapté/e.

misfortune [misfôr'chən] *n* malchance *f*, malheur *m*.

misgiving(s) [misgiv'ing(z)] *n(pl)* craintes *fpl*, soupçons *mpl*; **to have** ~**s about sth** avoir des doutes quant à qch.

misguided [misgī'did] *a* malavisé(e).

mishandle [mis·han'dəl] *vt* (*treat roughly*) malmener; (*mismanage*) mal s'y prendre pour faire *or* résoudre *etc*.

mishap [mis'hap] *n* mésaventure *f*.

mishear [mis·hiûr'] *vt, vi irg* mal entendre.

mishmash [mish'mash] *n* (*col*) fatras *m*, méli-mélo *m*.

misinform [misinfôrm'] *vt* mal renseigner.

misinterpret [misintûr'prit] *vt* mal interpréter.

misinterpretation [misintûrpritā'shən] *n* interprétation erronée, contresens *m*.

misjudge [misjuj'] *vt* méjuger, se méprendre sur le compte de.

mislay [mislā'] *vt irg* égarer.

mislead [mislēd'] *vt irg* induire en erreur.

misleading [mislē'ding] *a* trompeur(euse).

misled [misled'] *pt, pp of* **mislead**.

mismanage [misman'ij] *vt* mal gérer; mal s'y prendre pour faire *or* résoudre *etc*.

mismanagement [misman'ijmənt] *n* mauvaise gestion.

misnomer [misnō'mûr] *n* terme *or* qualificatif trompeur *or* peu approprié.

misogynist [misâj'ənist] *n* misogyne *m/f*.

misplace [misplās'] *vt* égarer; **to be** ~**d** (*trust etc*) être mal placé(e).

misprint [mis'print] *n* faute *f* d'impression.

mispronounce [misprənouns'] *vt* mal prononcer.

misquote [miskwōt'] *vt* citer erronément *or* inexactement.

misread [misrēd'] *vt irg* mal lire.

misrepresent [misreprizent'] *vt* présenter sous un faux jour.

Miss [mis] *n* Mademoiselle; **Dear** ~ **Smith** Chère Mademoiselle Smith.

miss [mis] *vt* (*fail to get*) manquer, rater; (*appointment, class*) manquer; (*escape, avoid*) échapper à, éviter; (*notice loss of: money etc*) s'apercevoir de l'absence de; (*regret the absence of*): **I** ~ **him/it** il/cela me manque ♦ *vi* manquer ♦ *n* (*shot*) coup manqué; **the bus just** ~**ed the wall** le bus a évité le mur de justesse; **you're** ~**ing the point** vous êtes à côté de la question.

miss out *vt* (*Brit*) oublier.

miss out on *vt fus* (*fun, party*) rater, manquer; (*chance, bargain*) laisser passer.

Miss. *abbr* (*US*) = Mississippi.

missal [mis'əl] *n* missel *m*.

misshapen [mis·shā'pən] *a* difforme.

missile [mis'əl] *n* (*AVIAT*) missile *m*; (*object thrown*) projectile *m*.

missile base *n* base *f* de missiles.

missile launcher *n* lance-missiles *m*.

missing [mis'ing] *a* manquant(e); (*after escape, disaster: person*) disparu(e); **to go** ~ disparaître; ~ **person** personne disparue, disparu/e.

mission [mish'ən] *n* mission *f*; **on a** ~ **to ob** en mission auprès de qn.

missionary [mish'ənärē] *n* missionnaire *m/f*.

missive [mis'iv] *n* missive *f*.

misspell [misspel'] *vt* (*irg: like* **spell**) mal orthographier.

misspent [misspent'] *a*: **his** ~ **youth** sa folle jeunesse.

mist [mist] *n* brume *f*, brouillard *m* ♦ *vi* (*also:* ~ **over,** ~ **up**) devenir brumeux(euse); (*Brit: windows*) s'embuer.

mistake [mistāk'] *n* erreur *f*, faute *f* ♦ *vt* (*irg: like* **take**) (*meaning*) mal comprendre; (*intentions*) se méprendre sur; **to** ~ **for** prendre pour; **by** ~ par erreur, par inadvertance; **to make a** ~ (*in writing*) faire une faute; (*in calculating etc*) faire une erreur; **to make a** ~ **about sb/sth** se tromper sur le compte de qn/sur qch.

mistaken [mistā'kən] *pp of* **mistake** ♦ *a* (*idea etc*) erroné(e); **to be** ~ faire erreur, se tromper.

mistaken identity *n* erreur *f* d'identité.

mistakenly [mistā'kənlē] *ad* par erreur, par mégarde.

mister [mis'tûr] *n* (*col*) Monsieur *m*; *see* **Mr.**

mistletoe [mis'əltō] *n* gui *m*.

mistook [mistōōk'] *pt of* **mistake**.

mistranslation [mistranzlā'shən] *n* erreur *f* de traduction, contresens *m*.

mistreat [mistrēt'] *vt* maltraiter.

mistress [mis'tris] *n* maîtresse *f*; (*Brit: in elementary school*) institutrice *f*; *see* **Mrs.**

mistrust [mistrust'] *vt* se méfier de ♦ *n*: ~ **(of)** méfiance *f* (à l'égard de).

mistrustful [mistrust'fəl] *a*: ~ **(of)** méfiant(e) (à l'égard de).

misty [mis'tē] *a* brumeux(euse).

misty-eyed [mis'tēīd'] *a* les yeux embués de larmes; (*fig*) sentimental(e).

misunderstand [misundûrstand'] *vt*, *vi irg* mal comprendre.

misunderstanding [misundûrstan'ding] *n* méprise *f*, malentendu *m*.

misunderstood [misundûrstŏŏd'] *pt*, *pp* of **misunderstand**.

misuse *n* [misyŏŏs'] mauvais emploi; (*of power*) abus *m* ♦ *vt* [misyŏŏz'] mal employer; abuser de.

MIT *n abbr* (*US*) = *Massachusetts Institute of Technology*.

mite [mīt] *n* (*small quantity*) grain *m*, miette *f*.

miter [mī'tûr] *n* (*US*) mitre *f*; (*CARPENTRY*) onglet *m*.

mitigate [mit'əgāt] *vt* atténuer; **mitigating circumstances** circonstances atténuantes.

mitigation [mitəgā'shən] *n* atténuation *f*.

mitre [mī'tûr] *n* (*Brit*) = **miter**.

mitt(en) [mit'(ən)] *n* mitaine *f*; moufle *f*.

mix [miks] *vt* mélanger ♦ *vi* se mélanger ♦ *n* mélange *m*; dosage *m*; **to ~ sth with sth** mélanger qch à qch; **to ~ business with pleasure** unir l'utile à l'agréable; **cake ~** préparation *f* pour gâteau.

mix in *vt* incorporer, mélanger.

mix up *vt* mélanger; (*confuse*) confondre; **to be ~ed up in sth** être mêlé(e) à qch *or* impliqué(e) dans qch.

mixed [mikst] *a* (*assorted*) assortis(ies); (*school etc*) mixte.

mixed doubles *npl* (*SPORT*) double *m* mixte.

mixed economy *n* économie *f* mixte.

mixed grill *n* (*Brit*) assortiment *m* de grillades.

mixed-up [mikst'up] *a* (*person*) désorienté(e) (*fig*).

mixer [mik'sûr] *n* (*for food*) batteur *m*, mixeur *m*; (*person*): **he is a good ~** il est très sociable.

mixture [miks'chûr] *n* assortiment *m*, mélange *m*; (*MED*) préparation *f*.

mix-up [miks'up] *n* confusion *f*.

MK *abbr* (*Brit TECH*) = **mark**.

mk *abbr* = **mark** (*currency*).

mkt *abbr* = **market**.

MLitt *n abbr* (= *Master of Literature, Master of Letters*) *titre universitaire*.

MLR *n abbr* (*Brit*) = **minimum lending rate**.

mm *abbr* (= *millimeter*) mm.

MN *abbr* (*Brit*) = **Merchant Navy**; (*US MAIL*) = *Minnesota*.

MO *n abbr* (*MED*) = *medical officer*; (*US col*: = *modus operandi*) méthode *f* ♦ *abbr* (*US MAIL*) = *Missouri*.

mo *abbr* = **month**.

m.o. *abbr* = **money order**.

moan [mōn] *n* gémissement *m* ♦ *vi* gémir; (*col*: *complain*): **to ~ (about)** se plaindre (de).

moaning [mō'ning] *n* gémissements *mpl*.

moat [mōt] *n* fossé *m*, douves *fpl*.

mob [mâb] *n* foule *f*; (*disorderly*) cohue *f*; (*pej*): **the ~** la populace ♦ *vt* assaillir.

mobile [mō'bəl] *a* mobile ♦ *n* (*ART*) mobile *m*.

mobile home *n* caravane *f*.

mobility [mōbil'ətē] *n* mobilité *f*.

mobilize [mō'bəlīz] *vt*, *vi* mobiliser.

moccasin [mâk'əsin] *n* mocassin *m*.

mock [mâk] *vt* ridiculiser, se moquer de ♦ *a* faux(fausse).

mockery [mâk'ûrē] *n* moquerie *f*, raillerie *f*; **to make a ~ of** ridiculiser, tourner en dérision.

mocking [mâk'ing] *a* moqueur(euse).

mockingbird [mâk'ingbûrd] *n* moqueur *m*.

mock-up [mâk'up] *n* maquette *f*.

MOD *n abbr* (*Brit*) = **Ministry of Defence**.

mod cons [mâd kânz] *npl abbr* (*Brit*) = **modern conveniences**.

mode [mōd] *n* mode *m*; (*of transport*) moyen *m*.

model [mâd'əl] *n* modèle *m*; (*person: for fashion*) mannequin *m*; (: *for artist*) modèle ♦ *vt* modeler ♦ *vi* travailler comme mannequin ♦ *a* (*railroad: toy*) modèle réduit *inv*; (*child, factory*) modèle; **to ~ clothes** présenter des vêtements; **to ~ sb/sth on** modeler qn/qch sur.

model apartment *n* (*US*) appartement-témoin.

modeler [mâd'əlûr] *n* (*US*) modeleur *m*; (*model maker*) maquettiste *m/f*; fabricant *m* de modèles réduits.

modeling clay [mâd'ling klā] *n* pâte *f* à modeler.

modeller [mâd'əlûr] *n* (*Brit*) = **modeler**.

modem [mō'dem] *n* modem *m*.

moderate *a*, *n* [mâd'ûrit] *a* modéré(e) ♦ *n* (*POL*) modéré(e) ♦ *vb* [mâd'ərāt] *vi* se modérer, se calmer ♦ *vt* modérer.

moderately [mâd'ûritlē] *ad* (*act*) avec modération *or* mesure; (*expensive*, *difficult*) moyennement; (*pleased*, *happy*) raisonnablement, assez; **~ priced** à un prix raisonnable.

moderation [mâdərā'shən] *n* modération *f*, mesure *f*; **in ~** à dose raisonnable, pris(e) *or* pratiqué(e) modérément.

modern [mâd'ûrn] *a* moderne; **~ languages** langues vivantes.

modernization [mâdûrnəzā'shən] *n* modernisation *f*.

modernize [mâd'ûrnīz] *vt* moderniser.

modest [mâd'ist] *a* modeste.

modesty [mâd'istē] *n* modestie *f*.

modicum [mâd'əkəm] *n*: **a ~ of** un minimum de.

modification [mâdəfəkā'shən] *n* modification *f*; **to make ~s** faire *or* apporter des modifications.

modify [mâd'əfī] *vt* modifier.

modular [mâj'əlûr] *a* (*filing, unit*) modulaire.

modulate [mâj'əlāt] *vt* moduler.

modulation [mâjəlā'shən] *n* modulation *f*.

module [mâj'ōōl] *n* module *m*.

mogul [mō'gəl] *n* (*fig*) nabab *m*; (*SKI*) bosse *f*.

mohair [mō'hâr] *n* mohair *m*.

Mohammed [mōham'id] *n* Mahomet *m*.

moist [moist] *a* humide, moite.

moisten [mois'ən] *vt* humecter, mouiller légèrement.

moisture |mois'chûr| *n* humidité *f*; (*on glass*) buée *f*.

moisturize |mois'chərīz| *vt* (*skin*) hydrater.

moisturizer |mois'chərīzûr| *n* produit hydratant.

molar |mō'lûr| *n* molaire *f*.

molasses |məlas'iz| *n* mélasse *f*.

mold |mōld| (*US*) *n* moule *m*; (*mildew*) moisissure *f* ♦ *vt* mouler, modeler; (*fig*) façonner.

molder |mōl'dûr| *vi* (*US: decay*) moisir.

molding |mōl'ding| *n* (*US ARCHIT*) moulure *f*.

moldy |mōl'dē| *a* (*US*) moisi(e).

mole |mōl| *n* (*animal*) taupe *f*; (*spot*) grain *m* de beauté.

molecule |mâl'əkyōōl| *n* molécule *f*.

molehill |mōl'hil| *n* taupinière *f*.

molest |məlest'| *vt* tracasser; molester.

mollusc |mâl'əsk| *n* mollusque *m*.

mollycoddle |mâl'ēkâdəl| *vt* chouchouter, couver.

molt |mōlt| *vi* (*US*) muer.

molten |mōl'tən| *a* fondu(e).

mom |mâm| *n* (*US*) maman *f*.

moment |mō'mənt| *n* moment *m*, instant *m*; (*importance*) importance *f*; **at the ~** en ce moment; **for the ~** pour l'instant; **in a ~** dans un instant; **"one ~ please"** (*TEL*) "ne quittez pas".

momentarily |mōməntār'ilē| *ad* momentanément; (*US: soon*) bientôt.

momentary |mō'məntārē| *a* momentané(e), passager(ère).

momentous |mōmen'təs| *a* important(e), capital(e).

momentum |mōmen'təm| *n* élan *m*, vitesse acquise, **to gather ~** prendre de la vitesse.

mommy |mâm'ē| *n* (*US*) maman *f*.

Mon. *abbr* (= *Monday*) l.

Monaco |mân'əkō| *n* Monaco *f*.

monarch |mân'ûrk| *n* monarque *m*.

monarchist |mân'ûrkist| *n* monarchiste *m/f*.

monarchy |mân'ûrkē| *n* monarchie *f*.

monastery |mân'əstārē| *n* monastère *m*.

monastic |mənas'tik| *a* monastique.

Monday |mun'dā| *n* lundi *m*; *for phrases see also* **Tuesday**.

monetarist |mân'itärist| *n* monétariste *m/f*.

monetary |mân'itärē| *a* monétaire.

money |mun'ē| *n* argent *m*; **to make ~** (*person*) gagner de l'argent; (*business*) rapporter; **I've got no ~ left** je n'ai plus d'argent, je n'ai plus un sou.

moneyed |mun'ēd| *a* riche.

moneylender |mun'ēlendûr| *n* prêteur/euse.

moneymaking |mun'ēmāking| *a* lucratif(ive), qui rapporte (de l'argent).

money market *n* marché financier.

money order *n* mandat *m*.

money-spinner |mun'ēspinûr| *n* (*col*) mine *f* d'or (*fig*).

money supply *n* masse *f* monétaire.

Mongol |mâng'gəl| *n* Mongol/e; (*LING*) mongol *m*.

mongol |mâng'gəl| *a, n* (*MED*) mongolien(ne).

Mongolia |mânggō'lēə| *n* Mongolie *f*.

Mongolian |mânggō'lēən| *a* mongol(e) ♦ *n* Mongol/e; (*LING*) mongol *m*.

mongoose |mâng'gōōs| *n* mangouste *f*.

mongrel |mung'grəl| *n* (*dog*) bâtard *m*.

monitor |mân'itûr| *n* (*US SCOL*) surveillant *m* (d'examen); (*Brit SCOL*) chef *m* de classe; (*TV, COMPUT*) écran *m*, moniteur *m* ♦ *vt* contrôler; (*foreign station*) être à l'écoute de.

monk |mungk| *n* moine *m*.

monkey |mung'kē| *n* singe *m*.

monkey nut *n* (*Brit*) cacahuète *f*.

monkey wrench *n* clé *f* à molette.

mono |mân'ō| *a* mono *inv*.

mono... |mân'ō| *prefix* mono....

monochrome |mân'əkrōm| *a* monochrome.

monocle |mân'əkəl| *n* monocle *m*.

monogram |mân'əgram| *n* monogramme *m*.

monolith |mân'əlith| *n* monolithe *m*.

monologue |mân'əlôg| *n* monologue *m*.

mononucleosis |mânōnōōklēō'sis| *n* (*US*) mononucléose infectieuse.

monoplane |mân'əplān| *n* monoplan *m*.

monopolize |mənâp'əlīz| *vt* monopoliser.

monopoly |mənâp'əlē| *n* monopole *m*; **Monopolies and Mergers Commission** (*Brit*) *Commission britannique d'enquête sur les monopoles.*

monorail |mân'ərāl| *n* monorail *m*.

monosodium glutamate (MSG) |mânəsō'dēəm glōō'təmāt| *n* glutamate *m* de sodium.

monosyllabic |mânəsilab'ik| *a* monosyllabique; (*person*) laconique.

monosyllable |mân'əsilabəl| *n* monosyllabe *m*.

monotone |mân'ətōn| *n* ton *m* (*or* voix *f*) monocorde; **to speak in a ~** parler sur un ton monocorde.

monotonous |mənât'ənəs| *a* monotone.

monotony |mənât'ənē| *n* monotonie *f*.

monoxide |mənâk'sīd| *n*: **carbon ~** oxyde *m* de carbone.

monsoon |mânsōōn'| *n* mousson *f*.

monster |mân'stûr| *n* monstre *m*.

monstrosity |mânstrâs'ətē| *n* monstruosité *f*, atrocité *f*.

monstrous |mân'strəs| *a* (*huge*) gigantesque; (*atrocious*) monstrueux(euse), atroce.

Mont. *abbr* (*US*) = *Montana*.

montage |mântâzh'| *n* montage *m*.

Mont Blanc |mânt blangk'| *n* Mont Blanc *m*.

month |munth| *n* mois *m*; **every ~** tous les mois; **$300 a ~** 300 dollars par mois.

monthly |munth'lē| *a* mensuel(le) ♦ *ad* mensuellement ♦ *n* (*magazine*) mensuel *m*, publication mensuelle; **twice ~** deux fois par mois.

Montreal |mântrēôl'| *n* Montréal.

monument |mân'yəmənt| *n* monument *m*.

monumental |mânyəmen'təl| *a* monumental(e).

moo |mōō| *vi* meugler, beugler.

mood |mōōd| *n* humeur *f*, disposition *f*; **to be in a good/bad ~** être de bonne/mauvaise humeur; **to be in the ~ for** être d'humeur à, avoir envie de.

moody |mōō'dē| *a* (*variable*) d'humeur changeante, lunatique; (*sullen*) morose, maussade.

moon |mōōn| *n* lune *f*.

moonbeam |mōōn'bēm| *n* rayon *m* de lune.

moon landing *n* alunissage *m*.

moonlight |mōōn'līt| *n* clair *m* de lune ♦ *vi*

travailler au noir.

moonlighting [mōōn'līting] *n* travail *m* au noir.

moonlit [mōōn'lit] *a* éclairé(e) par la lune; **a ~ night** une nuit de lune.

moonshot [mōōn'shât] *n* (*SPACE*) tir *m* lunaire.

moonstruck [mōōn'struk] *a* fou(folle), dérangé(e).

Moor [mōōr] *n* Maure/Mauresque.

moor [mōōr] *n* lande *f* ♦ *vt* (*ship*) amarrer ♦ *vi* mouiller.

moorings [mōōr'ingz] *npl* (*chains*) amarres *fpl*; (*place*) mouillage *m*.

Moorish [mōō'rish] *a* maure(mauresque).

moorland [mōōr'land] *n* lande *f*.

moose [mōōs] *n* (*pl inv*) élan *m*.

moot [mōōt] *vt* soulever ♦ *a*: **~ point** point *m* discutable.

mop [mâp] *n* balai *m* à laver ♦ *vt* éponger, essuyer; **~ of hair** tignasse *f*.
mop up *vt* éponger.

mope [mōp] *vi* avoir le cafard, se morfondre.
mope around *vi* broyer du noir, se morfondre.

moped [mō'ped] *n* cyclomoteur *m*.

moquette [mōket'] *n* moquette *f*.

moral [môr'əl] *a* moral(e) ♦ *n* morale *f*; **~s** *npl* moralité *f*.

morale [məral'] *n* moral *m*.

morality [məral'itē] *n* moralité *f*.

moralize [môr'əlīz] *vi*: **to ~ (about)** moraliser (sur).

morally [môr'əlē] *ad* moralement.

morass [məras'] *n* marais *m*, marécage *m*.

moratorium [môrətôr'ēəm] *n* moratoire *m*.

morbid [môr'bid] *a* morbide.

more [môr] *a* plus de, davantage de ♦ *ad* plus; **~ people** plus de gens; **I want ~** j'en veux plus *or* davantage; **is there any ~?** est-ce qu'il en reste?; **many/much ~** beaucoup plus; **~ and ~** de plus en plus; **once ~** encore une fois, une fois de plus; **no ~, not any ~** ne ... plus; **and what's ~ ...** et de plus ..., et qui plus est ...; **~ dangerous than** plus dangereux que; **~ or less** plus ou moins; **~ than ever** plus que jamais.

moreover [môrō'vûr] *ad* de plus.

morgue [môrg] *n* morgue *f*.

MORI [mō'rē] *n* *abbr* (*Brit*: = *Market & Opinion Research Institute*) institut de sondage.

moribund [môr'əbund] *a* moribond(e).

morning [môr'ning] *n* matin *m*; (*as duration*) matinée *f*; **in the ~** le matin; **7 o'clock in the ~** 7 heures du matin; **this ~** ce matin.
morning sickness *n* nausées matinales.

Moroccan [mərâk'ən] *a* marocain(e) ♦ *n* Marocain/e.

Morocco [mərâk'ō] *n* Maroc *m*.

moron [môr'ân] *n* idiot/e, minus *m/f*.

moronic [mərân'ik] *a* idiot(e), imbécile.

morose [mərōs'] *a* morose, maussade.

morphine [môr'fēn] *n* morphine *f*.

Morse [môrs] *n* (*also*: **~ code**) morse *m*.

morsel [môr'səl] *n* bouchée *f*.

mortal [môr'təl] *a*, *n* mortel(le).

mortality [môrtal'itē] *n* mortalité *f*.

mortality rate *n* (taux *m* de) mortalité *f*.

mortar [môr'tûr] *n* mortier *m*.

mortgage [môr'gij] *n* hypothèque *f*; (*loan*) prêt *m* (*or* crédit *m*) hypothécaire ♦ *vt* hypothéquer; **to take out a ~** prendre une hypothèque, faire un emprunt.

mortgage company *n* (*US*) société *f* de crédit immobilier.

mortgagee [môrgəjē'] *n* prêteur/euse (sur hypothèque).

mortgagor [môr'gəjûr] *n* emprunteur/euse (sur hypothèque).

mortician [môrtish'ən] *n* (*US*) entrepreneur *m* de pompes funèbres.

mortified [môr'təfīd] *a* mortifié(e).

mortise lock [môr'tis lâk] *n* serrure encastrée.

mortuary [môr'chōōārē] *n* dépôt *m* mortuaire; (*Brit*) morgue *f*.

mosaic [mōzā'ik] *n* mosaïque *f*.

Moscow [mâs'kou] *n* Moscou.

Moslem [mâz'ləm] *a*, *n* = **Muslim**.

mosque [mâsk] *n* mosquée *f*.

mosquito, ~es [məskē'tō] *n* moustique *m*.

mosquito net *n* moustiquaire *f*.

moss [môs] *n* mousse *f*.

mossy [môs'ē] *a* moussu(e).

most [mōst] *a* la plupart de; le plus de ♦ *pronoun* la plupart ♦ *ad* le plus; (*very*) très, extrêmement; **the ~** (*also: + adjective*) le plus; **~ fish** la plupart des poissons; **~ of** la plus grande partie de; **~ of them** la plupart d'entre eux; **at the (very) ~** au plus; **to make the ~ of** profiter au maximum de.

mostly [mōst'lē] *ad* surtout, principalement.

MOT *n* *abbr* (*Brit*: = *Ministry of Transport*): **the ~ (test)** visite technique (annuelle) obligatoire des véhicules à moteur.

motel [mōtel'] *n* motel *m*.

moth [môth] *n* papillon *m* de nuit; mite *f*.

mothball [môth'bôl] *n* boule *f* de naphtaline.

moth-eaten [môth'ētən] *a* mité(e).

mother [muth'ûr] *n* mère *f* ♦ *vt* (*care for*) dorloter.

mother board *n* (*COMPUT*) carte-mère *f*.

motherhood [muth'ûrhōōd] *n* maternité *f*.

mother-in-law [muth'ûrinlô] *n* belle-mère *f*.

motherly [muth'ûrlē] *a* maternel(le).

mother-of-pearl [muth'ûrəvpûrl'] *n* nacre *f*.

mother's help *n* aide *f* *or* auxiliaire *f* familiale.

mother-to-be [muth'ûrtəbē'] *n* future maman.

mother tongue *n* langue maternelle.

mothproof [môth'prōōf] *a* traité(e) à l'antimite.

motif [mōtēf'] *n* motif *m*.

motion [mō'shən] *n* mouvement *m*; (*gesture*) geste *m*; (*at meeting*) motion *f*; (*Brit*: *also*: **bowel ~**) selles *fpl* ♦ *vt*, *vi*: **to ~ (to) sb to do** faire signe à qn de faire; **to be in ~** (*vehicle*) être en marche; **to set in ~** mettre en marche; **to go through the ~s of doing sth** (*fig*) faire qch machinalement *or* sans conviction.

motionless [mō'shənlis] *a* immobile, sans mouvement.

motion picture *n* film *m*.

motivate [mō'təvāt] *vt* motiver.

motivated [mō'təvātid] *a* motivé(e).

motivation [mōtəvā'shən] *n* motivation *f*.

motive [mō'tiv] *n* motif *m*, mobile *m* ♦ *a* moteur(trice); **from the best (of)** ~s avec les meilleures intentions (du monde).

motley [mât'lē] *a* hétéroclite; bigarré(e), bariolé(e).

motor [mō'tûr] *n* moteur *m*; (*Brit col: vehicle*) auto *f* ♦ *a* moteur(trice).

motorbike [mō'tûrbīk] *n* moto *f*.

motorboat [mō'tûrbōt] *n* bateau *m* à moteur.

motorcar [mō'tûrkâr] *n* (*Brit*) automobile *f*.

motorcoach [mō'tûrkōch] *n* (*Brit*) car *m*.

motorcycle [mō'tûrsī'kəl] *n* vélomoteur *m*.

motorcyclist [mō'tûrsīklist] *n* motocycliste *m/f*.

motor home *n* (*US*) camping-car *m*, autocaravane *f*.

motoring [mō'tûring] (*Brit*) *n* tourisme *m* automobile ♦ *a* (*accident*) de voiture, de la route; ~ **holiday** (*Brit*) vacances *fpl* en voiture; ~ **offence** (*Brit*) infraction *f* au code de la route.

motorist [mō'tûrist] *n* automobiliste *m/f*.

motorize [mō'tərīz] *vt* motoriser.

motor oil *n* huile *f* de graissage.

motor racing *n* (*Brit*) course *f* automobile.

motor scooter *n* scooter *m*.

motor vehicle *n* véhicule *m* automobile.

motorway [mō'tûrwā] *n* (*Brit*) autoroute *f*.

mottled [mât'əld] *a* tacheté(e), marbré(e).

motto, ~es [mât'ō] *n* devise *f*.

mould [mōld] *etc* (*Brit*) = **mold**.

moult [mōlt] *vi* (*Brit*) = **molt**.

mound [mound] *n* monticule *m*, tertre *m*.

mount [mount] *n* mont *m*, montagne *f*; (*horse*) monture *f*; (*for jewel etc*) monture ♦ *vt* monter; (*exhibition*) organiser, monter; (*picture*) monter sur carton; (*stamp*) coller dans un album ♦ *vi* (*also:* ~ **up**) s'élever, monter.

mountain [moun'tən] *n* montagne *f* ♦ *cpd* de (la) montagne; **to make a ~ out of a mole-hill** (*fig*) se faire une montagne d'un rien.

mountaineer [mountənēr'] *n* alpiniste *m/f*.

mountaineering [mountənē'ring] *n* alpinisme *m*; **to go** ~ faire de l'alpinisme.

mountainous [moun'tənəs] *a* montagneux(euse).

mountain rescue team *n* colonne *f* de secours.

mountainside [moun'tənsīd] *n* flanc *m* or versant *m* de la montagne.

mounted [moun'tid] *a* monté(e).

Mount Everest [mount ev'ûrist] *n* le mont Everest.

mourn [môrn] *vt* pleurer ♦ *vi*: **to** ~ (**for**) se lamenter (sur).

mourner [môr'nûr] *n* parent/e or ami/e du défunt; personne *f* en deuil or venue rendre hommage au défunt.

mournful [môrn'fəl] *a* triste, lugubre.

mourning [môr'ning] *n* deuil *m* ♦ *cpd* (*dress*) de deuil; **in** ~ en deuil.

mouse, *pl* mice [mous, mīs] *n* (*also* COMPUT) souris *f*.

mousetrap [mous'trap] *n* souricière *f*.

mousse [mōōs] *n* mousse *f*.

moustache [məstash'] *n* (*Brit*) = **mustache**.

mousy [mou'sē] *a* (*person*) effacé(e); (*hair*) d'un châtain terne.

mouth, ~s [mouth, -*th*z] *n* bouche *f*; (*of dog,*

cat) gueule *f*; (*of river*) embouchure *f*; (*of bottle*) goulot *m*; (*opening*) orifice *m*.

mouthful [mouth'fōōl] *n* bouchée *f*.

mouth organ *n* harmonica *m*.

mouthpiece [mouth'pēs] *n* (*of musical instrument*) bec *m*, embouchure *f*; (*spokesman*) porte-parole *m inv*.

mouth-to-mouth [mouth'təmouth'] *a*: ~ **resuscitation** bouche à bouche *m*.

mouthwash [mouth'wôsh] *n* eau *f* dentifrice.

mouth-watering [mouth'wōtûring] *a* qui met l'eau à la bouche.

movable [mōō'vəbəl] *a* mobile.

move [mōōv] *n* (*movement*) mouvement *m*; (*in game*) coup *m*; (: *turn to play*) tour *m*; (*change of house*) déménagement *m* ♦ *vt* déplacer, bouger; (*emotionally*) émouvoir; (POL: *resolution etc*) proposer ♦ *vi* (*gen*) bouger, remuer; (*traffic*) circuler; (*also:* ~ **house**) déménager; **to** ~ **towards** se diriger vers; **to** ~ **sb to do sth** pousser or inciter qn à faire qch; **to get a** ~ **on** se dépêcher, se remuer.

move about *vi* (*Brit*) = **move around**.

move around *vi* (*fidget*) remuer; (*travel*) voyager, se déplacer.

move along *vi* se pousser.

move away *vi* s'en aller, s'éloigner.

move back *vi* revenir, retourner.

move forward *vi* avancer ♦ *vt* avancer; (*people*) faire avancer.

move in *vi* (*to a house*) emménager.

move off *vi* s'éloigner, s'en aller.

move on *vi* se remettre en route ♦ *vt* (*onlookers*) faire circuler.

move out *vi* (*of house*) déménager.

move over *vi* se pousser, se déplacer.

move up *vi* avancer; (*employee*) avoir de l'avancement.

movement [mōōv'mənt] *n* mouvement *m*; ~ (**of the bowels**) (MED) selles *fpl*.

mover [mōō'vûr] *n* auteur *m* d'une proposition; (*furniture* ~) déménageur *m*; (*firm*) entreprise *f* de déménagement.

movie [mōō'vē] *n* film *m*; **the** ~**s** le cinéma.

movie camera *n* caméra *f*.

moviegoer [mōō'vēgōûr] *n* cinéphile *m/f*.

movie projector *n* (*US*) projecteur *m* de cinéma.

movie theater *n* (*US*) cinéma *m*.

moving [mōō'ving] *a* en mouvement; (*touching*) émouvant(e) ♦ *n* (*US*) déménagement *m*.

moving van *n* (*US*) camion *m* de déménagement.

mow, pt mowed, pp mowed *or* **mown** [mō, -n] *vt* faucher; (*lawn*) tondre.

mow down *vt* faucher.

mower [mō'ûr] *n* (*also:* **lawn**~) tondeuse *f* à gazon.

Mozambique [mōzambēk'] *n* Mozambique *m*.

MP *n abbr* (= *Military Police*) PM; (*Brit*) = **Member of Parliament**; (*Canada*) = **Mounted Police**.

mpg *n abbr* = *miles per gallon* (30 *mpg* = 9,4 *l. aux* 100 *km*).

mph *abbr* = *miles per hour* (60 *mph* = 96 *km/ h*).

MPhil *n abbr* (*US*: = *Master of Philosophy*)

titre universitaire.

Mr, Mr. [mis'tûr] *n*: ~ X Monsieur X, M. X.

Mrs, Mrs. [mis'iz] *n*: ~ X Madame X, Mme X.

MS *n abbr* (= *manuscript*) ms; (= *multiple sclerosis*) SEP *f*; (*US*: = *Master of Science*) *titre universitaire* ♦ *abbr* (*US MAIL*) = *Mississippi.*

Ms, Ms. [miz] *n* (= *Miss or Mrs*): ~ X Madame X, Mme X.

MSA *n abbr* (*US*: = *Master of Science in Agriculture*) *titre universitaire.*

MSc *n abbr* = **Master of Science.**

MSG *n abbr* = **monosodium glutamate.**

MST *abbr* (*US*: = *Mountain Standard Time*) *heure d'hiver des Montagnes Rocheuses.*

MSW *n abbr* (*US*: = *Master of Social Work*) *titre universitaire.*

MT *n abbr* (= *machine translation*) TM ♦ *abbr* (*US MAIL*) = *Montana.*

Mt *abbr* (*GEO*: = *mount*) Mt.

much [much] *a* beaucoup de ♦ *ad, n or pronoun* beaucoup; ~ **milk** beaucoup de lait; **how ~ is it?** combien est-ce que ça coûte?; **it's not ~** ce n'est pas beaucoup; **too ~** trop (de); **so ~** tant (de); **I like it very/so ~** j'aime beaucoup/tellement ça; **thank you very ~** merci beaucoup; **~ to my amazement ...** à mon grand étonnement ....

muck [muk] *n* (*mud*) boue *f*; (*dirt*) ordures *fpl.*

   muck about *or* **around** *vi* (*Brit*) = **mess around.**

   muck in *vi* (*Brit col*) donner un coup de main.

   muck out *vt* (*stable*) nettoyer.

   muck up *vt* (*col: ruin*) gâcher, esquinter; (*: dirty*) salir.

muckraking [muk'rāk'ing] *n* (*fig: col*) déterrement *m* d'ordures.

mucky [muk'ē] *a* (*dirty*) boueux(euse), sale.

mucus [myōō'kəs] *n* mucus *m.*

mud [mud] *n* boue *f.*

muddle [mud'əl] *n* pagaille *f*; désordre *m*, fouillis *m* ♦ *vt* (*also:* ~ **up**) brouiller, embrouiller; **to be in a ~** (*person*) ne plus savoir ou l'on en est; **to get in a ~** (*while explaining etc*) s'embrouiller.

   muddle along *vi* aller son chemin tant bien que mal.

   muddle through *vi* se débrouiller.

muddle-headed [mud'əlhedid] *a* (*person*) à l'esprit embrouillé *or* confus, dans le brouillard.

muddy [mud'ē] *a* boueux(euse).

mud flats *npl* plage *f* de vase.

mudguard [mud'gârd] *n* garde-boue *m inv.*

mudpack [mud'pak] *n* masque *m* de beauté.

mudslinging [mud'slinging] *n* médisance *f*, dénigrement *m.*

muff [muf] *n* manchon *m* ♦ *vt* (*col: shot, catch etc*) rater, louper; **to ~ it** rater *or* louper son coup.

muffin [muf'in] *n* petit pain rond et plat.

muffle [muf'əl] *vt* (*sound*) assourdir, étouffer; (*against cold*) emmitoufler.

muffled [muf'əld] *a* étouffé(e), voilé(e).

muffler [muf'lûr] *n* (*scarf*) cache-nez *m inv*; (*US AUT*) silencieux *m.*

mufti [muf'tē] *n*: **in ~** en civil.

mug [mug] *n* (*cup*) tasse *f* (*sans soucoupe*); (: *for beer*) chope *f*; (*col: face*) bouille *f*; (: *fool*) poire *f* ♦ *vt* (*assault*) agresser.

   mug up *vt* (*Brit col: also:* ~ **up on**) bosser, bûcher.

mugger [mug'ûr] *n* agresseur *m.*

mugging [mug'ing] *n* agression *f.*

muggy [mug'ē] *a* lourd(e), moite.

mulatto, ~es [məlat'ō] *n* mulâtre/esse.

mulberry [mul'bärē] *n* (*fruit*) mûre *f*; (*tree*) mûrier *m.*

mule [myōōl] *n* mule *f.*

mull [mul]: **to ~ over** *vt* réfléchir à, ruminer.

mulled [muld] *a*: ~ **wine** vin chaud.

multi... [mul'tē] *prefix* multi....

multi-access [multēak'ses] *a* (*COMPUT*) à accès multiple.

multicolored, (*Brit*) **multicoloured** [mul'tikulûrd] *a* multicolore.

multifarious [multəfär'ēəs] *a* divers(es); varié(e).

multilateral [multilat'ûrəl] *a* (*POL*) multilatéral(e).

multilevel [multēlev'əl] *a* (*US: building*) à étages; (: *car park*) à étages *or* niveaux multiples.

multimillionaire [multēmilyənär'] *n* milliardaire *m/f.*

multinational [multənash'ənəl] *n* multinationale *f* ♦ *a* multinational(e).

multiple [mul'təpəl] *a* multiple ♦ *n* multiple *m*; (*Brit: also:* ~ **store**) magasin *m* à succursales (multiples).

multiple choice *a* à choix multiple.

multiple crash *n* carambolage *m.*

multiple sclerosis (MS) [mul'təpəl sklirō'sis] *n* sclérose *f* en plaques.

multiplication [multəpləkā'shən] *n* multiplication *f.*

multiplication table *n* table *f* de multiplication.

multiplicity [multəplis'ətē] *n* multiplicité *f.*

multiply [mul'təplī] *vt* multiplier ♦ *vi* se multiplier.

multiracial [multērā'shəl] *a* multiracial(e).

multistorey [multēstôr'ē] *a* (*Brit*) = **multilevel.**

multitude [mul'tətōōd] *n* multitude *f.*

mum [mum] (*Brit*) *n* maman *f* ♦ *a*: **to keep ~** ne pas souffler mot; **~'s the word!** motus et bouche cousue!

mumble [mum'bəl] *vt, vi* marmotter, marmonner.

mummify [mum'əfī] *vt* momifier.

mummy [mum'ē] *n* (*Brit: mother*) maman *f*; (*embalmed*) momie *f.*

mumps [mumps] *n* oreillons *mpl.*

munch [munch] *vt, vi* mâcher.

mundane [mundān'] *a* banal(e), terre à terre *inv.*

municipal [myōōnis'əpəl] *a* municipal(e).

municipality [myōōnisəpal'itē] *n* municipalité *f.*

munitions [myōōnish'ənz] *npl* munitions *fpl.*

mural [myōōr'əl] *n* peinture murale.

murder [mûr'dûr] *n* meurtre *m*, assassinat *m* ♦ *vt* assassiner; **to commit ~** commettre un meurtre.

murderer [mûr'dûrûr] *n* meurtrier *m*, assas-

sin *m*.
murderess [mûr'dûris] *n* meurtrière *f*.
murderous [mûr'dûrəs] *a* meurtrier(ière).
murk [mûrk] *n* obscurité *f*.
murky [mûr'kē] *a* sombre, ténébreux(euse).
murmur [mûr'mûr] *n* murmure *m* ♦ *vt, vi* murmurer; **heart** ~ (*MED*) souffle *m* au cœur.
MusB(ac) *n abbr* (= *Bachelor of Music*) titre universitaire.
muscle [mus'əl] *n* muscle *m*.
muscle in *vi* s'imposer, s'immiscer.
muscular [mus'kyəlûr] *a* musculaire; (*person, arm*) musclé(e).
MusD(oc) *n abbr* (= *Doctor of Music*) titre universitaire.
muse [myo͞oz] *vi* méditer, songer ♦ *n* muse *f*.
museum [myo͞ozē'əm] *n* musée *m*.
mush [mush] *n* bouillie *f*; (*pej*) sentimentalité *f* à l'eau de rose.
mushroom [mush'ro͞om] *n* champignon *m* ♦ *vi* (*fig*) pousser comme un (*or* des) champignon(s).
mushy [mush'ē] *a* en bouillie; (*pej*) à l'eau de rose.
music [myo͞o'zik] *n* musique *f*.
musical [myo͞o'zikəl] *a* musical(e); (*person*) musicien(ne) ♦ *n* (*show*) comédie musicale.
musical instrument *n* instrument *m* de musique.
music box *n* boîte *f* à musique.
music hall *n* music-hall *m*.
musician [myo͞ozish'ən] *n* musicien/ne.
music stand *n* pupitre *m* à musique.
musk [musk] *n* musc *m*.
musket [mus'kit] *n* mousquet *m*.
muskrat [musk'rat] *n* rat musqué.
muck rose *n* (*BOT*) rose *f* muscade.
Muslim [muz'lim] *a, n* musulman(e).
muslin [muz'lin] *n* mousseline *f*.
musquash [mus'kwâsh] *n* loutre *f*; (*fur*) rat *m* d'Amérique, ondatra *m*.
mussel [mus'əl] *n* moule *f*.
must [must] *auxiliary vb* (*obligation*): **I** ~ **do it** je dois le faire, il faut que je le fasse; (*probability*): **he** ~ **be there by now** il doit y être maintenant, il y est probablement maintenant; **I** ~ **have made a mistake** j'ai dû me tromper ♦ *n* nécessité *f*, impératif *m*; **it's a** ~ c'est indispensable.
mustache [məstash'] *n* (*US*) moustache(s) *f(pl)*.
mustard [mus'tûrd] *n* moutarde *f*.
mustard gas *n* ypérite *f*, gaz *m* moutarde.
muster [mus'tûr] *vt* rassembler; (*also*: ~ **up**: *strength, courage*) rassembler.
mustiness [mus'tēnis] *n* goût *m* de moisi; odeur *f* de moisi *or* de renfermé.
mustn't [mus'ənt] = **must not**.
musty [mus'tē] *a* qui sent le moisi *or* le renfermé.
mutant [myo͞o'tənt] *a* mutant(e) ♦ *n* mutant *m*.
mutate [myo͞o'tāt] *vi* subir une mutation.
mutation [myo͞otā'shən] *n* mutation *f*.
mute [myo͞ot] *a, n* muet(te).
muted [myo͞o'tid] *a* (*noise*) sourd(e), assourdi(e); (*criticism*) voilé(e); (*MUS*) en sourdine; (*: trumpet*) bouché(e).

mutilate [myo͞o'təlāt] *vt* mutiler.
mutilation [myo͞otəlā'shən] *n* mutilation *f*.
mutinous [myo͞o'tənəs] *a* (*troops*) mutiné(e); (*attitude*) rebelle.
mutiny [myo͞o'tənē] *n* mutinerie *f* ♦ *vi* se mutiner.
mutter [mut'ûr] *vt, vi* marmonner, marmotter.
mutton [mut'ən] *n* mouton *m*.
mutual [myo͞o'cho͞oəl] *a* mutuel(le), réciproque.
mutual fund *n* (*US*) fonds commun de placement, FCP *m*.
mutually [myo͞o'cho͞oəlē] *ad* mutuellement, réciproquement.
muzzle [muz'əl] *n* museau *m*; (*protective device*) muselière *f*; (*of gun*) gueule *f* ♦ *vt* museler.
MVP *n abbr* (*US SPORT*) = *most valuable player*.
MW *abbr* (= *medium wave*) PO.
my [mī] *a* mon(ma), mes *pl*.
myopic [mīâp'ik] *a* myope.
myriad [mir'ēəd] *n* myriade *f*.
myself [mīself'] *pronoun* (*reflexive*) me; (*emphatic*) moi-même; (*after prep*) moi.
mysterious [mistēr'ēəs] *a* mystérieux(euse).
mystery [mis'tûrē] *n* mystère *m*.
mystery story *n* roman *m* à suspense.
mystic [mis'tik] *n* mystique *m/f* ♦ *a* (*mysterious*) ésotérique.
mystical [mis'tikəl] *a* mystique.
mystify [mis'təfī] *vt* mystifier; (*puzzle*) ébahir.
mystique [mistēk'] *n* mystique *f*.
myth [mith] *n* mythe *m*
mythical [mith'ikəl] *a* mythique.
mythological [mithəláj'ikəl] *a* mythologique.
mythology [mithál'əjē] *n* mythologie *f*

N

N, n [en] *n* (*letter*) N, n *m*; **N for Nan** N comme Nicolas.
N [en] *abbr* (= *north*) N.
NA *n abbr* (*US*: = *Narcotics Anonymous*) association d'aide aux drogués; (*US*) = *National Academy*.
n/a *abbr* (= *not applicable*) n.a.; (*COMM etc*) = *no account*.
NAACP *n abbr* (*US*) = *National Association for the Advancement of Colored People*.
nab [nab] *vt* (*col*) pincer, attraper.
NACU *n abbr* (*US*) = *National Association of Colleges and Universities*.
nadir [nā'dûr] *n* (*ASTRONOMY*) nadir *m*; (*fig*) fond *m*, point *m* extrême.
nag [nag] *vt* (*person*) être toujours après, reprendre sans arrêt ♦ *n* (*pej*: *horse*) canasson *m*; (*person*): **she's an awful** ~ elle est constamment après lui (*or* eux *etc*), elle est terriblement casse-pieds.
nagging [nag'ing] *a* (*doubt, pain*) persistant(e) ♦ *n* remarques continuelles.

nail [nāl] *n* (*human*) ongle *m*; (*metal*) clou *m* ♦ *vt* clouer; **to ~ sb down to a date/price** contraindre qn à accepter *or* donner une date/un prix; **to pay cash on the ~** (*Brit*) payer rubis sur l'ongle.

nailbrush [nāl'brush] *n* brosse *f* à ongles.

nailfile [nāl'fīl] *n* lime *f* à ongles.

nail polish *n* vernis *m* à ongles.

nail polish remover *n* dissolvant *m*.

nail scissors *npl* ciseaux *mpl* à ongles.

nail varnish *n* (*Brit*) = **nail polish**.

Nairobi [nīrō'bē] *n* Nairobi.

naïve [nīēv'] *a* naïf(ïve).

naïveté, naïvety [nīēvtā'] *n* naïveté *f*.

naked [nā'kid] *a* nu(e); **with the ~ eye** à l'œil nu.

nakedness [nā'kidnis] *n* nudité *f*.

NAM *n abbr* (*US*) = *National Association of Manufacturers*.

name [nām] *n* nom *m*; (*reputation*) réputation *f* ♦ *vt* nommer; citer; (*price, date*) fixer, donner; **by ~** par son nom; de nom; **in the ~ of** au nom de; **what's your ~?** quel est votre nom?; **my ~ is Peter** je m'appelle Peter; **to take sb's ~ and address** relever l'identité de qn *or* les nom et adresse de qn; **to make a ~ for o.s.** se faire un nom; **to get (o.s.) a bad ~** se faire une mauvaise réputation; **to call sb ~s** traiter qn de tous les noms.

name dropping *n* mention *f* (*pour se faire valoir*) *du nom de personnalités qu'on connaît (ou prétend connaître)*.

nameless [nām'lis] *a* sans nom; (*witness, contributor*) anonyme.

namely [nām'lē] *ad* à savoir.

nameplate [nām'plāt] *n* (*on door etc*) plaque *f*.

namesake [nām'sāk] *n* homonyme *m*.

nanny [nan'ē] *n* bonne *f* d'enfants.

nanny goat *n* chèvre *f*.

nap [nap] *n* (*sleep*) (petit) somme ♦ *vi*: **to be caught ~ping** être pris(e) à l'improviste *or* en défaut.

NAPA *n abbr* (*US*: = *National Association of Performing Artists*) syndicat des gens du spectacle.

napalm [nā'pám] *n* napalm *m*.

nape [nāp] *n*: **~ of the neck** nuque *f*.

napkin [nap'kin] *n* serviette *f* (de table).

Naples [nā'pəlz] *n* Naples.

Napoleonic [nəpōlēən'ik] *a* napoléonien(ne).

nappy [nap'ē] *n* (*Brit*) couche *f* (*gen pl*).

narcissistic [nârsisis'tik] *a* narcissique.

narcissus, *pl* **narcissi** [nârsis'əs, -sī] *n* narcisse *m*.

narcotic [nârkât'ik] *n* (*MED*) narcotique *m*; **~s** *npl* (*drugs*) stupéfiants *mpl*.

narrate [nar'āt] *vt* raconter, narrer.

narration [narā'shən] *n* narration *f*.

narrative [nar'ətiv] *n* récit *m* ♦ *a* narratif(ive).

narrator [nar'ātûr] *n* narrateur/trice.

narrow [nar'ō] *a* étroit(e); (*fig*) restreint(e), limité(e) ♦ *vi* devenir plus étroit, se rétrécir; **to have a ~ escape** l'échapper belle; **to ~ sth down to** réduire qch à.

narrow gauge *a* (*RAIL*) à voie étroite.

narrowly [nar'ōlē] *ad*: **he ~ missed injury/the tree** il a failli se blesser/rentrer dans l'arbre; **he only ~ missed the target** il a manqué la cible de peu *or* de justesse.

narrow-minded [nar'ōmīn'did] *a* à l'esprit étroit, borné(e).

NAS *n abbr* (*US*) = *National Academy of Sciences*.

NASA [nas'ə] *n abbr* (*US*: = *National Aeronautics and Space Administration*) NASA *f*.

nasal [nā'zəl] *a* nasal(e).

Nassau [nas'ô] *n* (*in Bahamas*) Nassau.

nastily [nas'tilē] *ad* (*say, act*) méchamment.

nastiness [nas'tēnis] *n* (*of person, remark*) méchanceté *f*.

nasturtium [nəstûr'shəm] *n* capucine *f*.

nasty [nas'tē] *a* (*person*) méchant(e); très désagréable; (*smell*) dégoûtant(e); (*wound, situation*) mauvais(e), vilain(e); (*weather*) affreux(euse); **to turn ~** (*situation*) mal tourner; (*weather*) se gâter; (*person*) devenir méchant; **it's a ~ business** c'est une sale affaire.

nation [nā'shən] *n* nation *f*.

national [nash'ənəl] *a* national(e) ♦ *n* (*abroad*) ressortissant/e; (*when home*) national/e.

national anthem *n* hymne national.

national debt *n* dette publique.

national dress *n* costume national.

National Forest Service *n* (*US*) ≈ Office National des Forêts.

National Guard *n* (*US*) milice *f* (*de volontaires dans chaque Etat*).

National Health Service (NHS) *n* (*Brit*) service national de santé, ≈ Sécurité Sociale.

National Insurance *n* (*Brit*) ≈ Sécurité Sociale.

nationalism [nash'ənəlizəm] *n* nationalisme *m*.

nationalist [nash'nəlist] *a*, *n* nationaliste (*m/f*).

nationality [nashənal'ətē] *n* nationalité *f*.

nationalization [nashnələzā'shən] *n* nationalisation *f*.

nationalize [nash'nəlīz] *vt* nationaliser.

nationally [nash'nəlē] *ad* du point de vue national; dans le pays entier.

national park *n* parc national.

national press *n* presse nationale.

National Security Council *n* (*US*) conseil national de sécurité.

national service *n* (*MIL*) service *m* militaire.

National Weather Service *n* (*US*) ≈ météo *inv*.

nationwide [nā'shənwīd'] *a* s'étendant à l'ensemble du pays; (*problem*) à l'échelle du pays entier ♦ *ad* à travers *or* dans tout le pays.

native [nā'tiv] *n* habitant/e du pays, autochtone *m/f*; (*in colonies*) indigène *m/f* ♦ *a* du pays, indigène; (*country*) natal(e); (*language*) maternel(le); (*ability*) inné(e); **a ~ of Russia** une personne originaire de Russie; **a ~ speaker of French** une personne de langue maternelle française.

Nativity [nətiv'ətē] *n* (*REL*): **the ~** la Nativité.

NATO [nā'tō] *n abbr* (= *North Atlantic Treaty Organization*) OTAN *f*.

natter [nat'ûr] *vi* (*Brit*) bavarder.

natural [nach'ûrəl] *a* naturel(le); **to die of ~ causes** mourir d'une mort naturelle.

natural childbirth *n* accouchement *m* sans douleur.

natural gas *n* gaz naturel.

naturalist [nach'ûrəlist] *n* naturaliste *m/f*.

naturalization [nachûrələzā'shən] *n* naturalisation *f*; acclimatation *f*.

naturalize [nach'ûrəlīz] *vt* naturaliser; (*plant*) acclimater; **to become ~d** (*person*) se faire naturaliser.

naturally [nach'ûrəlē] *ad* naturellement.

naturalness [nach'ûrəlnis] *n* naturel *m*.

natural resources *npl* ressources naturelles.

natural wastage *n* (*INDUSTRY*) départs naturels et volontaires.

nature [nā'chûr] *n* nature *f*; **by ~** par tempérament, de nature; **documents of a confidential ~** documents à caractère confidentiel.

nature reserve *n* (*Brit*) réserve naturelle.

nature trail *n* sentier de découverte de la nature.

naturist [nā'chûrist] *n* naturiste *m/f*.

naught [nôt] *n* = **nought**.

naughtiness [nôt'ēnis] *n* (*of child*) désobéissance *f*; (*of story etc*) grivoiserie *f*.

naughty [nôt'ē] *a* (*child*) vilain(e), pas sage; (*story, film*) grivois(e).

nausea [nô'zēə] *n* nausée *f*.

nauseate [nô'zēāt] *vt* écœurer, donner la nausée à.

nauseating [nô'zēāting] *a* écœurant(e), dégoûtant(e).

nauseous [nô'shəs] *a* nauséabond(e), écœurant(e); (*feeling sick*): **to be ~** avoir des nausées.

nautical [nô'tikəl] *a* nautique.

nautical mile *n* mille marin (= 1853 m).

naval [nā'vəl] *a* naval(e).

naval officer *n* officier *m* de marine.

nave [nāv] *n* nef *f*.

navel [nā'vəl] *n* nombril *m*.

navigable [nav'əgəbəl] *a* navigable.

navigate [nav'əgāt] *vt* diriger, piloter ♦ *vi* naviguer; (*AUT*) indiquer la route à suivre.

navigation [navəgā'shən] *n* navigation *f*.

navigator [nav'əgātûr] *n* navigateur *m*.

navvy [nav'ē] *n* (*Brit*) terrassier *m*.

navy [nā'vē] *n* marine *f*; **Department of the N~** (*US*) ministère *m* de la Marine.

navy (blue) *a* bleu marine *inv*.

Nazareth [naz'ûrith] *n* Nazareth.

Nazi [nät'sē] *a* nazi(e) ♦ *n* Nazi/e.

NB *abbr* (= *nota bene*) NB; (*Canada*) = *New Brunswick*.

NBA *n abbr* (*US*) = *National Basketball Association, National Boxing Association*.

NBC *n abbr* (*US*: = *National Broadcasting Company*) chaîne de télévision.

NBS *n abbr* (*US*: = *National Bureau of Standards*) office de normalisation.

NC *abbr* (*COMM etc*) = *no charge*; (*US MAIL*) = *North Carolina*.

NCC *n abbr* (*US*) = *National Council of Churches*.

NCO *n abbr* = **non-commissioned officer**.

ND *abbr* (*US MAIL*) = *North Dakota*.

N. Dak. *abbr* (*US*) = *North Dakota*.

NE *abbr* (*US MAIL*) = *Nebraska, New England*.

NEA *n abbr* (*US*) = *National Education Association*.

neap [nēp] *n* (*also*: ~ **tide**) mortes-eaux *fpl*.

Neapolitan [nēəpâl'ətən] *a* napolitain(e) ♦ *n* Napolitain/e.

near [nēr] *a* proche ♦ *ad* près ♦ *prep* (*also*: ~ **to**) près de ♦ *vt* approcher de; **~ here/there** près d'ici/non loin de là; **in the ~ future** dans un proche avenir; **the building is ~ing completion** le bâtiment est presque terminé; **to come ~** *vi* s'approcher.

nearby [nēr'bī'] *a* proche ♦ *ad* tout près, à proximité.

Near East *n*: **the ~** le Proche-Orient.

nearer [nē'rûr] *a* plus proche ♦ *ad* plus près.

nearly [nēr'lē] *ad* presque; **I ~ fell** j'ai failli tomber; **it's not ~ big enough** ce n'est vraiment pas assez grand, c'est loin d'être assez grand.

near miss *n* collision évitée de justesse; (*when aiming*) coup manqué de peu *or* de justesse.

nearness [nēr'nis] *n* proximité *f*.

nearside [nēr'sīd] (*AUT*) *n* (*right-hand drive*) côté *m* gauche; (*left-hand drive*) côté droit ♦ *a* de gauche; de droite.

nearsighted [nēr'sītid] *a* myope.

neat [nēt] *a* (*person, work*) soigné(e); (*room etc*) bien tenu(e) *or* rangé(e); (*solution, plan*) habile; (*spirits*) pur(e); **I drink it ~** je le bois sec *or* sans eau.

neatly [nēt'lē] *ad* avec soin *or* ordre; habilement.

neatness [nēt'nis] *n* (*tidiness*) netteté *f*; (*skillfulness*) habileté *f*.

Nebr. *abbr* (*US*) = *Nebraska*.

nebulous [neb'yələs] *a* nébuleux(euse).

necessarily [nesəsär'ilē] *ad* nécessairement; **not ~** pas nécessairement *or* forcément.

necessary [nes'isârē] *a* nécessaire; **if ~** si besoin est, le cas échéant.

necessitate [nəses'ətāt] *vt* nécessiter.

necessity [nəses'itē] *n* nécessité *f*; chose nécessaire *or* essentielle; **in case of ~** en cas d'urgence.

neck [nek] *n* cou *m*; (*of horse, garment*) encolure *f*; (*of bottle*) goulot *m* ♦ *vi* (*col*) se peloter; **~ and ~** à égalité; **to stick one's ~ out** (*col*) se mouiller.

necklace [nek'lis] *n* collier *m*.

neckline [nek'līn] *n* encolure *f*.

necktie [nek'tī] *n* (*esp US*) cravate *f*.

nectar [nek'tûr] *n* nectar *m*.

nectarine [nektərēn'] *n* brugnon *m*, nectarine *f*.

née [nā] *a*: ~ **Scott** née Scott.

need [nēd] *n* besoin *m* ♦ *vt* avoir besoin de; **to ~ to do** devoir faire; avoir besoin de faire; **you don't ~ to go** vous n'avez pas besoin *or* vous n'êtes pas obligé de partir; **a signature is ~ed** il faut une signature; **to be in ~ of** *or* **have ~ of** avoir besoin de; **$10 will meet my immediate ~s** 10 dollars suffiront pour mes besoins immédiats; **in case of ~** en cas de besoin, au besoin; **there's no ~ to do ...** il n'y a pas lieu de faire ..., il n'est pas nécessaire de faire ...; **there's no ~ for that** ce n'est pas la peine, cela n'est pas nécessaire.

needle [nē'dəl] *n* aiguille *f*; (*on record player*) saphir *m* ♦ *vt* (*col*) asticoter, tourmenter.

needless [nēd'lis] *a* inutile; **~ to say, ...** inutile de dire que ....

needlessly [nēd'lislē] *ad* inutilement.

needlework [nĕd'əlwûrk] *n* (*activity*) travaux *mpl* d'aiguille; (*object*) ouvrage *m*.

needn't [nĕd'ənt] = **need not**.

needy [nē'dē] *a* nécessiteux(euse).

negation [nigā'shən] *n* négation *f*.

negative [nĕg'ətiv] *n* (*PHOT*, *ELEC*) négatif *m*; (*LING*) terme *m* de négation ♦ *a* négatif(ive); **to answer in the ~** répondre par la négative.

neglect [niglĕkt'] *vt* négliger ♦ *n* (*of person, duty, garden*) le fait de négliger; (**state of**) ~ abandon *m*; **to ~ to do sth** négliger *or* omettre de faire qch.

neglected [niglĕk'tid] *a* négligé(e), à l'abandon.

neglectful [niglĕkt'fəl] *a* (*gen*) négligent(e); **to be ~ of sb/sth** négliger qn/qch.

negligee [nĕg'ləzhā] *n* déshabillé *m*.

negligence [nĕg'lijəns] *n* négligence *f*.

negligent [nĕg'lijənt] *a* négligent(e).

negligently [nĕg'lijəntlē] *ad* par négligence; (*offhandedly*) négligemment.

negligible [nĕg'lijəbəl] *a* négligeable.

negotiable [nigō'shəbəl] *a* négociable; **not ~** (*check*) non négociable.

negotiate [nigō'shēāt] *vi* négocier ♦ *vt* (*COMM*) négocier; (*obstacle*) franchir, négocier; (*curve in road*) négocier; **to ~ with sb for sth** négocier avec qn en vue d'obtenir qch.

negotiation [nigōshēā'shən] *n* négociation *f*, pourparlers *mpl*; **to enter into ~s with sb** engager des négociations avec qn.

negotiator [nigō'shēātûr] *n* négociateur/trice.

Negress [nĕg'ris] *n* négresse *f*.

Negro [nĕg'rō] *a* (*gen*) noir(e); (*music*, *arts*) nègre, noir ♦ *n* (*pl*: **~es**) Noir/e.

neigh [nā] *vi* hennir.

neighbor [nā'bûr] *n* (*US*) voisin/e.

neighborhood [nā'bûrhŏŏd] *n* quartier *m*; voisinage *m*.

neighboring [nā'bûring] *a* voisin(e), avoisinant(e).

neighborly [nā'bûrlē] *a* obligeant(e); (*relations*) de bon voisinage.

neighbour [nā'bûr] *etc* (*Brit*) = **neighbor**.

neither [nē'thûr] *a*, *pronoun* aucun(e) (des deux), ni l'un(e) ni l'autre ♦ *cj*: **I didn't move and ~ did Claude** je n'ai pas bougé, (et) Claude non plus; **..., ~ did I refuse ...**, (et *or* mais) je n'ai pas non plus refusé ♦ *ad*: **~ good nor bad** ni bon ni mauvais.

neo... [nē'ō] *prefix* néo-.

neolithic [nēəlith'ik] *a* néolithique.

neologism [nēăl'əjizəm] *n* néologisme *m*.

neon [nē'án] *n* néon *m*.

neon light *n* lampe *f* au néon.

neon sign *n* enseigne (lumineuse) au néon.

Nepal [nəpôl'] *n* Népal *m*.

nephew [nef'yŏŏ] *n* neveu *m*.

nepotism [nep'ətizəm] *n* népotisme *m*.

nerve [nûrv] *n* nerf *m*; (*bravery*) sang-froid *m*, courage *m*; (*cheek*) aplomb *m*, toupet *m*; **he gets on my ~s** il m'énerve; **to have a fit of ~s** avoir le trac; **to lose one's ~** (*self-confidence*) perdre son sang-froid.

nerve center *n* (*ANAT*) centre nerveux; (*fig*) centre névralgique.

nerve gas *n* gaz *m* neuroplégique.

nerve-racking [nûrv'raking] *a* angoissant(e).

nervous [nûr'vəs] *a* nerveux(euse); (*apprehensive*) inquiet(ète), plein(e) d'appréhension.

nervous breakdown *n* dépression nerveuse.

nervously [nûr'vəslē] *ad* nerveusement.

nervousness [nûr'vəsnis] *n* nervosité *f*; inquiétude *f*, appréhension *f*.

nest [nest] *n* nid *m* ♦ *vi* (se) nicher, faire son nid; **~ of tables** table *f* gigogne.

nest egg *n* (*fig*) bas *m* de laine, magot *m*.

nestle [nes'əl] *vi* se blottir.

nestling [nest'ling] *n* oisillon *m*.

NET *abbr* (*US*) = *National Educational Television*.

net [net] *n* (*also fabric*) filet *m* ♦ *a* net(te) ♦ *vt* (*fish etc*) prendre au filet; (*money: subj: person*) toucher; (*: deal, sale*) rapporter; **~ of tax** net d'impôt; **he earns $10,000 ~ per year** il gagne 10 000 dollars net par an.

netball [net'bôl] *n* netball *m*.

net curtains *npl* (*Brit*) voilages *mpl*.

Netherlands [neth'ûrləndz] *npl*: **the ~** les Pays-Bas *mpl*.

net profit *n* bénéfice net.

nett [net] *a* = **net**.

netting [net'ing] *n* (*for fence etc*) treillis *m*, grillage *m*; (*fabric*) voile *m*.

nettle [net'əl] *n* ortie *f*.

network [net'wûrk] *n* réseau *m* ♦ *vt* (*RADIO*, *TV*) diffuser sur l'ensemble du réseau; (*computers*) interconnecter.

neuralgia [nŏŏral'jə] *n* névralgie *f*.

neurosis, *pl* **neuroses** [nŏŏrō'sis, -sēz] *n* névrose *f*.

neurotic [nŏŏrât'ik] *a*, *n* névrosé(e).

neuter [nŏŏ'tûr] *a*, *n* neutre (*m*) ♦ *vt* (*cat etc*) châtrer, couper.

neutral [nŏŏ'trəl] *a* neutre ♦ *n* (*AUT*) point mort.

neutrality [nŏŏtral'itē] *n* neutralité *f*.

neutralize [nŏŏ'trəlīz] *vt* neutraliser.

neutron bomb [nŏŏ'trän bám] *n* bombe *f* à neutrons.

Nev. *abbr* (*US*) = *Nevada*.

never [nev'ûr] *ad* (*ne ...*) jamais; **~ again** plus jamais; **~ in my life** jamais de ma vie; *see also* **mind**.

never-ending [nev'ûren'ding] *a* interminable.

nevertheless [nevûrthəles'] *ad* néanmoins, malgré tout.

new [nŏŏ] *a* nouveau(nouvelle); (*brand new*) neuf(neuve); **as good as ~** comme neuf.

newborn [nŏŏ'bôrn] *a* nouveau-né(e).

newcomer [nŏŏ'kumûr] *n* nouveau venu/nouvelle venue.

newfangled [nŏŏ'fang'gəld] *a* (*pej*) ultramoderne (et farfelu(e)).

newfound [nŏŏ'found] *a* de fraîche date; (*friend*) nouveau(nouvelle).

Newfoundland [nŏŏ'fəndland] *n* Terre-Neuve *f*.

New Guinea [nŏŏ gin'ē] *n* Nouvelle-Guinée *f*.

newly [nŏŏ'lē] *ad* nouvellement, récemment.

newlyweds [nŏŏ'lēwedz] *npl* jeunes mariés *mpl*.

new moon *n* nouvelle lune.

newness [nŏŏ'nis] *n* nouveauté *f*; (*of fabric, clothes etc*) état neuf.

New Orleans [nŏŏ ôr'lēənz] *n* la Nouvelle-

Orléans.

news [nōōz] *n* nouvelle(s) *f(pl)*; (*RADIO, TV*) informations *fpl*; **a piece of** ~ une nouvelle; **good/bad** ~ bonne/mauvaise nouvelle; **financial** ~ (*PRESS, RADIO, TV*) page financière.

news agency *n* agence *f* de presse.

newsagent [nōōz'ājənt] *n* (*Brit*) = **newsdealer**.

news bulletin *n* (*RADIO, TV*) bulletin *m* d'informations.

newscaster [nōōz'kastûr] *n* (*RADIO, TV*) présentateur/trice.

newsdealer [nōōz'dēlûr] *n* (*US*) marchand *m* de journaux.

news flash *n* flash *m* d'information.

newsletter [nōōz'letûr] *n* bulletin *m*.

newspaper [nōōz'pāpûr] *n* journal *m*; **daily** ~ quotidien *m*; **weekly** ~ hebdomadaire *m*.

newsprint [nōōz'print] *n* papier *m* (de) journal.

newsreader [nōōz'rēdûr] *n* (*Brit*) = **newscaster**.

newsreel [nōōz'rēl] *n* actualités (filmées).

newsroom [nōōz'rōōm] *n* (*PRESS*) salle *f* de rédaction; (*RADIO, TV*) studio *m*.

newsstand [nōōz'stand] *n* kiosque *m* à journaux.

newt [nōōt] *n* triton *m*.

New Year *n* Nouvel An; **Happy** ~! Bonne Année!; **to wish sb a happy** ~ souhaiter la Bonne Année à qn.

New Year's Day *n* le jour de l'An.

New Year's Eve *n* la Saint-Sylvestre.

New York [nōō yórk] *n* New York; (*also:* ~ **State**) New York *m*.

New Zealand [nōō zē'lənd] *n* Nouvelle-Zélande *f* ♦ *a* néo-zélandais(e).

New Zealander [nōō zē'ləndûr] *n* Néo-Zélandais/e.

next [nekst] *a* (*seat, room*) voisin(e), d'à côté; (*meeting, bus stop*) suivant(e); prochain(e) ♦ *ad* la fois suivante; la prochaine fois; (*afterwards*) ensuite; ~ **to** *prep* à côté de; ~ **to nothing** presque rien; ~ **time** *ad* la prochaine fois; **the** ~ **day** le lendemain, le jour suivant *or* d'après; ~ **week** la semaine prochaine; **the** ~ **week** la semaine suivante; ~ **year** l'année prochaine; **"turn to the** ~ **page"** "voir page suivante"; **who's** ~? c'est à qui?; **the week after** ~ dans deux semaines; **when do we meet** ~? quand nous revoyons-nous?

next door *ad* à côté.

next-of-kin [nekst'əvkin'] *n* parent *m* le plus proche.

NF *n abbr* (*Brit POL:* = *National Front*) ≈ FN ♦ *abbr* (*Canada*) = *Newfoundland*.

NFL *n abbr* (*US*) = *National Football League*.

Nfld. *abbr* (*Canada*) = *Newfoundland*.

NG *abbr* (*US*) = **National Guard**.

NGO *n abbr* (*US:* – *non-governmental organization*) ONG *f*.

NH *abbr* (*US MAIL*) = *New Hampshire*.

NHL *n abbr* (*US*) = *National Hockey League*.

NHS *n abbr* (*Brit*) = **National Health Service**.

NI *abbr* = *Northern Ireland*; (*Brit*) = **National Insurance**.

Niagara Falls [nīag'rə fôlz] *npl* chutes *fpl* du

Niagara.

nib [nib] *n* (*of pen*) (bec *m* de) plume *f*.

nibble [nib'əl] *vt* grignoter.

Nicaragua [nikərâg'wə] *n* Nicaragua *m*.

Nicaraguan [nikərâg'wən] *a* nicaraguayen(ne) ♦ *n* Nicaraguayen/ne.

nice [nīs] *a* (*vacation, trip, taste*) agréable; (*apartment, picture*) joli(e); (*person*) gentil(le); (*distinction, point*) subtil(e).

nice-looking [nīs'lōōk'ing] *a* joli(e).

nicely [nīs'lē] *ad* agréablement; joliment; gentiment; subtilement; **that will do** ~ ce sera parfait.

niceties [nī'sətēz] *npl* subtilités *fpl*.

niche [nich] *n* (*ARCHIT*) niche *f*.

nick [nik] *n* encoche *f* ♦ *vt* (*cut*): **to** ~ **o.s.** se couper; (*col: steal*) faucher, piquer; (*: Brit: arrest*) choper, pincer; **in the** ~ **of time** juste à temps.

nickel [nik'əl] *n* nickel *m*; (*US*) pièce *f* de 5 cents.

nickname [nik'nām] *n* surnom *m* ♦ *vt* surnommer.

Nicosia [nikōsē'ə] *n* Nicosie.

nicotine [nik'ətēn] *n* nicotine *f*.

niece [nēs] *n* nièce *f*.

nifty [nif'tē] *a* (*col: car, jacket*) qui a du chic or de la classe; (*: gadget, tool*) astucieux(euse).

Niger [nī'jûr] *n* (*country, river*) Niger *m*.

Nigeria [nījē'rēə] *n* Nigéria *m or f*.

Nigerian [nījē'rēən] *a* nigérien(ne) ♦ *n* Nigérien/ne.

niggardly [nig'ûrdlē] *a* (*person*) parcimonieux(euse), pingre; (*allowance, amount*) misérable.

nigger [nig'ûr] *n* (*col!: highly offensive*) nègre/négresse.

niggle [nig'əl] *vt* tracasser ♦ *vi* (*find fault*) trouver toujours à redire; (*fuss*) n'être jamais content(e).

niggling [nig'ling] *a* (*trifling*) à tatillon(ne); (*detail*) insignifiant(e); (*doubt, pain*) persistant(e).

night [nīt] *n* nuit *f*; (*evening*) soir *m*; **at** ~ la nuit; **by** ~ de nuit; **in the** ~, **during the** ~ pendant la nuit; **the** ~ **before last** avant-hier soir.

nightcap [nīt'kap] *n* boisson prise avant le coucher.

nightclub [nīt'klub] *n* boîte *f* de nuit.

nightdress [nīt'dres] *n* chemise *f* de nuit.

nightfall [nīt'fôl] *n* tombée *f* de la nuit.

nightgown [nīt'goun] *n* chemise *f* de nuit.

nightie [nīt'ē] *n* (*Brit*) chemise *f* de nuit.

nightingale [nī'təngāl] *n* rossignol *m*.

night life *n* vie *f* nocturne.

nightly [nīt'lē] *a* de chaque nuit *or* soir; (*by night*) nocturne ♦ *ad* chaque nuit *or* soir; nuitamment.

nightmare [nīt'mär] *n* cauchemar *m*.

night owl *n* (*fig*) couche-tard *m inv*, noctambule *m/f*.

night porter *n* gardien *m* de nuit, concierge *m* de service la nuit.

night safe *n* coffre *m* de nuit.

night school *n* cours *mpl* du soir.

nightshade [nīt'shād] *n*: **deadly** ~ (*BOT*) belladone *f*.

night shift *n* équipe *f* de nuit.

nightstick [nīt'stik] *n* (*US*) bâton *m* (d'agent de police).

night-time [nīt'tīm] *n* nuit *f*.

night watchman *n* veilleur *m* de nuit; poste *m* de nuit.

NIH *n abbr* (*US*) = *National Institutes of Health.*

nihilism [nē'əlizəm] *n* nihilisme *m*.

nil [nil] *n* rien *m*; zéro *m*.

Nile [nīl] *n*: **the** ~ le Nil.

nimble [nim'bəl] *a* agile.

nine [nīn] *num* neuf.

nineteen [nīn'tēn'] *num* dix-neuf.

ninety [nīn'tē] *num* quatre-vingt-dix.

ninth [nīnth] *num* neuvième.

nip [nip] *vt* pincer ♦ *vi* (*Brit col*): **to** ~ **out/down/up** sortir/descendre/monter en vitesse ♦ *n* pincement *m*; (*drink*) petit verre; **to** ~ **into a store** faire un saut dans un magasin.

nipple [nip'əl] *n* (*ANAT*) mamelon *m*, bout *m* du sein.

nippy [nip'ē] *a* (*Brit*: *person*) alerte, leste; (: *car*) nerveux(euse).

nit [nit] *n* (*in hair*) lente *f*.

nit-pick [nit'pik] *vi* (*col*) être tatillon(ne).

nitrogen [nī'trəjən] *n* azote *m*.

nitroglycerin(e) [nītrəglis'ûrin] *n* nitroglycérine *f*.

nitty-gritty [nit'ēgrit'ē] *n* (*fam*): **to get down to the** ~ en venir au fond du problème.

nitwit [nit'wit] *n* (*col*) nigaud/e.

NJ *abbr* (*US MAIL*) = *New Jersey.*

NLF *n abbr* (= *National Liberation Front*) FLN *m*.

NLQ *abbr* (= *near letter quality*) qualité *f* courrier.

NLRB *n abbr* (*US*: = *National Labor Relations Board*) organisme de protection des travailleurs.

NM *abbr* (*US MAIL*) = *New Mexico.*

N. Mex. *abbr* (*US*) = *New Mexico.*

no [nō] *a* pas de, aucun(e) + *sg* ♦ *ad*, *n* non *(m)*; **I have** ~ **more wine** je n'ai plus de vin; "~ **entry**" "défense d'entrer", "entrée interdite"; "~ **dogs**" "les chiens ne sont pas admis"; **I won't take** ~ **for an answer** il n'est pas question de refuser.

no. *abbr* (= *number*) nº.

nobble [nâb'əl] *vt* (*Brit col*: *bribe*: *person*) soudoyer, acheter; (: *person*: *to speak to*) mettre le grappin sur; (*RACING*: *horse*, *dog*) droguer (*pour l'empêcher de gagner*).

Nobel prize [nō'bel prīz'] *n* prix *m* Nobel.

nobility [nōbil'ətē] *n* noblesse *f*.

noble [nō'bəl] *a* noble.

nobleman [nō'bəlmən] *n* noble *m*.

nobly [nō'blē] *ad* noblement.

nobody [nō'bâdē] *pronoun* personne (*with negative*).

no-claims bonus [nō'klāmz bō'nəs] *n* (*Brit*) bonus *m*.

no-claims discount [nō'klāmz dis'kount] *n* (*US*) bonus *m*.

nocturnal [nâktûr'nəl] *a* nocturne.

nod [nâd] *vi* faire un signe de (la) tête (*affirmatif ou amical*); (*sleep*) somnoler ♦ *vt*: **to** ~ **one's head** faire un signe de (la) tête; (*in agreement*) faire signe que oui ♦ *n* signe *m* de (la) tête; **they** ~**ded their agree-**

ment ils ont acquiescé d'un signe de la tête.

nod off *vi* s'assoupir.

no fault agreement *n* (*US*) *convention entre compagnies d'assurance par laquelle chacune s'engage à dédommager son propre client.*

noise [noiz] *n* bruit *m*.

noiseless [noiz'lis] *a* silencieux(euse).

noisily [noi'zilē] *ad* bruyamment.

noisy [noi'zē] *a* bruyant(e).

nomad [nō'mad] *n* nomade *m/f*.

nomadic [nōmad'ik] *a* nomade.

no man's land *n* no man's land *m*.

nominal [nâm'ənəl] *a* (*rent*, *fee*) symbolique; (*value*) nominal(e).

nominate [nâm'ənāt] *vt* (*propose*) proposer; (*elect*) nommer.

nomination [nâmənā'shən] *n* nomination *f*.

nominee [nâmənē'] *n* candidat agréé; personne nommée.

non- [nân] *prefix* non-.

nonalcoholic [nânalkəhôl'ik] *a* non-alcoolisé(e).

nonbreakable [nânbrā'kəbəl] *a* incassable.

nonce word [nâns' wûrd] *n* mot créé pour l'occasion.

nonchalant [nânshəlant'] *a* nonchalant(e).

noncommissioned [nânkəmish'ənd] *a*: ~ **officer** sous-officier *m*.

noncommittal [nânkəmit'əl] *a* évasif(ive).

nonconformist [nânkənfôr'mist] *n* non-conformiste *m/f* ♦ *a* non-conformiste, dissident(e).

noncontributory [nânkəntrib'yətôrē] *a*: ~ **pension plan** *or* (*Brit*) **scheme** régime de retraite payée par l'employeur.

noncooperation [nânkōâpərā'shən] *n* refus *m* de coopérer, non-coopération *f*.

nondescript [nân'diskript] *a* quelconque, indéfinissable.

none [nun] *pronoun* aucun/e; ~ **of you** aucun d'entre vous, personne parmi vous; **I have** ~ je n'en ai pas; **I have** ~ **left** je n'en ai plus; ~ **at all** (*not one*) aucun(e); **how much milk?** — ~ **at all** combien de lait? — pas du tout; **he's** ~ **the worse for it** il ne s'en porte pas plus mal.

nonentity [nânen'titē] *n* personne insignifiante.

nonessential [nânəsen'chəl] *a* accessoire, superflu(e) ♦ *n*: ~**s** le superflu.

nonetheless [nun'thəles'] *ad* néanmoins.

nonexecutive [nânigzek'yətiv] *a*: ~ **director** administrateur/trice, conseiller/ère de direction.

nonexistent [nânigzis'tənt] *a* inexistant(e).

nonfiction [nânfik'shən] *n* littérature *f* non-romanesque.

nonflammable [nânflam'əbəl] *a* ininflammable.

nonintervention [nânintûrven'chən] *n* non-intervention *f*.

non obst. *abbr* (= *non obstante*: *notwithstanding*) nonobstant.

nonpayment [nânpā'mənt] *n* non-paiement *m*.

nonplussed [nânplust'] *a* perplexe.

nonprofit-making [nânpráf'itmāking] *a* à but non lucratif.

nonsense [nân'sens] *n* absurdités *fpl*, idioties *fpl*; ~! ne dites pas d'idioties!; **it is** ~ **to say that** ... il est absurde de dire que ....

nonskid [nânskid'] *a* antidérapant(e).

nonsmoker [nânsmō'kûr] *n* non-fumeur *m*.

nonstick [nânstik'] *a* qui n'attache pas.

nonstop [nân'stâp'] *a* direct(e), sans arrêt (*or* escale) ♦ *ad* sans arrêt.

nontaxable [nântak'səbəl] *a:* ~ **income** revenu *m* non imposable.

nonvolatile [nânvâl'ətəl] *a:* ~ **memory** (COMPUT) mémoire rémanente *or* non volatile.

nonvoting [nânvō'ting] *a:* ~ **shares** actions *fpl* sans droit de vote.

nonwhite [nânwīt'] *a* de couleur ♦ *n* personne *f* de couleur.

noodles [nōō'dəlz] *npl* nouilles *fpl*.

nook [nŏŏk] *n:* ~**s and crannies** recoins *mpl*.

noon [nōōn] *n* midi *m*.

no one [nō' wun] *pronoun* = **nobody**.

noose [nōōs] *n* nœud coulant; (*hangman's*) corde *f*.

nor [nôr] *cj* = **neither** ♦ *ad see* **neither**.

Norf *abbr* (*Brit*) = *Norfolk*.

norm [nôrm] *n* norme *f*.

normal [nôr'məl] *a* normal(e) ♦ *n:* **to return to** ~ redevenir normal(e).

normality [nôrmal'itē] *n* normalité *f*.

normally [nôr'məlē] *ad* normalement.

Normandy [nôr'məndē] *n* Normandie *f*.

north [nôrth] *n* nord *m* ♦ *a* au nord, nord *inv* ♦ *ad* au *or* vers le nord.

North Africa *n* Afrique *f* du Nord.

North African *a* nord-africain(e), d'Afrique du Nord ♦ *n* Nord-Africain/e.

North America *n* Amérique *f* du Nord.

North American *n* Nord-Américain/e ♦ *a* nord-américain(e), d'Amérique du Nord.

Northants [nôrthants'] *abbr* (*Brit*) = *Northamptonshire*.

northbound [nôrth'bound'] *a* (*traffic*) en direction du nord; (*lane*) nord *inv*.

Northd *abbr* (*Brit*) = *Northumberland*.

northeast [nôrthēst'] *n* nord-est *m*.

northerly [nôr'thûrlē] *a* (*wind, direction*) du nord.

northern [nôr'thûrn] *a* du nord, septentrional(e).

Northern Ireland *n* Irlande *f* du Nord.

North Pole *n:* **the** ~ le pôle Nord.

North Sea *n:* **the** ~ la mer du Nord.

North Sea oil *n* pétrole *m* de la mer du Nord.

northward(s) [nôrth'wûrd(z)] *ad* vers le nord.

northwest [nôrthwest'] *n* nord-ouest *m*.

Norway [nôr'wā] *n* Norvège *f*.

Norwegian [nôrwē'jən] *a* norvégien(ne) ♦ *n* Norvégien/ne; (LING) norvégien *m*.

nos. *abbr* (= *numbers*) n°.

nose [nōz] *n* nez *m*; (*fig*) flair *m* ♦ *vi* (*also:* ~ **one's way**) avancer précautionneusement; **to pay through the** ~ **(for sth)** (*col*) payer un prix excessif (pour qch).

nose around *vi* fouiner *or* fureter (partout).

nosebleed [nōz'blēd] *n* saignement *m* de nez.

nose dive *n* (descente *f* en) piqué *m*.

nose drops *npl* gouttes *fpl* pour le nez.

nosey [nō'zē] *a* curieux/euse (euse).

nostalgia [nəstal'jə] *n* nostalgie *f*.

nostalgic [nəstal'jik] *a* nostalgique.

nostril [nâs'trəl] *n* narine *f*; (*of horse*) naseau *m*.

nosy [nō'zē] *a* = **nosey**.

not [nât] *ad* (ne ...) pas; **I hope** ~ j'espère que non; ~ **at all** pas du tout; (*after thanks*) de rien; **you must** ~ *or* **mustn't do this** tu ne dois pas faire ça; **he isn't** ... il n'est pas ....

notable [nō'təbəl] *a* notable.

notably [nō'təblē] *ad* en particulier.

notary [nō'tûrē] *n* (*also:* ~ **public**) notaire *m*.

notation [nōtā'shən] *n* notation *f*.

notch [nâch] *n* encoche *f* ♦ *vt* (*score*) marquer; (*victory*) remporter.

note [nōt] *n* note *f*; (*letter*) mot *m*; (*banknote*) billet *m* ♦ *vt* (*also:* ~ **down**) noter; (*notice*) constater; **just a quick** ~ **to let you know** ... juste un mot pour vous dire ...; **to take** ~**s** prendre des notes; **to compare** ~**s** (*fig*) échanger des (*or* leurs *etc*) impressions; **to take** ~ **of** prendre note de; **a person of** ~ une personne éminente.

notebook [nōt'bŏŏk] *n* carnet *m*; (*for shorthand etc*) bloc-notes *m*.

note-case [nōt'kās] *n* (*Brit*) porte-feuille *m*.

noted [nō'tid] *a* réputé(e).

notepad [nōt'pad] *n* bloc-notes *m*.

notepaper [nōt'pāpûr] *n* papier *m* à lettres.

noteworthy [nōt'wûrthē] *a* remarquable.

nothing [nuth'ing] *n* rien *m*; **he does** ~ il ne fait rien; ~ **new** rien de nouveau; **for** ~ (*free*) pour rien, gratuitement; ~ **at all** rien du tout.

notice [nō'tis] *n* avis *m*; (*of leaving*) congé *m*; (*Brit:* *review: of play etc*) critique *f*, compte-rendu *m* ♦ *vt* remarquer, s'apercevoir de; **without** ~ sans préavis; **advance** ~ préavis *m*; **to give sb** ~ **of sth** notifier qn de qch; **at short** ~ dans un délai très court; **until further** ~ jusqu'à nouvel ordre; **to give** ~, **hand in one's** ~ (*subj: employee*) donner sa démission, démissionner; **to take** ~ **of** prêter attention à; **to bring sth to sb's** ~ porter qch à la connaissance de qn; **it has come to my** ~ **that** ... on m'a signalé que ...; **to escape** *or* **avoid** ~ (essayer de) passer inaperçu *or* ne pas se faire remarquer.

noticeable [nō'tisəbəl] *a* visible.

notice board *n* (*Brit*) panneau *m* d'affichage.

notification [nōtəfəkā'shən] *n* notification *f*.

notify [nō'təfī] *vt:* **to** ~ **sth to sb** notifier qch à qn; **to** ~ **sb of sth** avertir qn de qch.

notion [nō'shən] *n* idée *f*; (*concept*) notion *f*.

notions [nō'shənz] *npl* (*US*) mercerie *f*.

notoriety [nōtərī'ətē] *n* notoriété *f*.

notorious [nōtôr'ēəs] *a* notoire (*souvent en mal*).

notoriously [nōtôr'ēəslē] *ad* notoirement.

Notts [nâts] *abbr* (*Brit*) = *Nottinghamshire*.

notwithstanding [nâtwithstan'ding] *ad* néanmoins ♦ *prep* en dépit de.

nougat [nōō'gət] *n* nougat *m*.

nought [nôt] *n* zéro *m*.

noun [noun] *n* nom *m*.

nourish [nûr'ish] *vt* nourrir.

nourishing [nûr'ishing] *a* nourrissant(e).

nourishment [nûr'ishmənt] *n* nourriture *f*.

Nov. *abbr* (= *November*) nov.

Nova Scotia [nō'və skō'shə] *n* Nouvelle-Écosse *f*.

novel [nâv'əl] *n* roman *m* ♦ *a* nouveau(nouvelle), original(e).

novelist [nâv'əlist] *n* romancier *m*.

novelty [nâv'əltē] *n* nouveauté *f*.

November [nōvem'bûr] *n* novembre *m*; *for phrases see also* **July.**

novice [nâv'is] *n* novice *m/f*.

NOW [nou] *n abbr* (*US*) = *National Organization for Women.*

now [nou] *ad* maintenant ♦ *cj:* ~ **(that)** maintenant (que); **right** ~ tout de suite; **by** ~ à l'heure qu'il est; **I saw her right** ~ je viens de la voir, je l'ai vue à l'instant; **I'll read it right** ~ je vais le lire à l'instant *or* dès maintenant; ~ **and then,** ~ **and again** de temps en temps; **from** ~ **on** dorénavant; **in 3 days from** ~ dans *or* d'ici trois jours; **between** ~ **and Monday** d'ici (à) lundi; **that's all for** ~ c'est tout pour l'instant.

nowadays [nou'ədāz] *ad* de nos jours.

nowhere [nō'wär] *ad* nulle part; ~ **else** nulle part ailleurs.

noxious [nák'shəs] *a* toxique.

nozzle [nâz'əl] *n* (*of hose*) jet *m*, lance *f*.

NP *n abbr* = **notary public.**

NS *abbr* (*Canada*) = *Nova Scotia.*

NSC *n abbr* (*US*) = **National Security Council.**

NSF *n abbr* (*US*) = *National Science Foundation.*

NSW *abbr* (*Australia*) = *New South Wales.*

NT *n abbr* (= *New Testament*) NT *m* ♦ *abbr* (*Canada*) = *Northwest Territories.*

nth [enth] *a:* **for the** ~ **time** (*col*) pour la énième fois.

nuance [nōō'ânts] *n* nuance *f*.

nubile [nōō'bīl] *a* nubile; (*attractive*) jeune et désirable.

nuclear [nōō'klēur] *a* nucléaire.

nuclear disarmament *n* désarmement *m* nucléaire.

nucleus, *pl* **nuclei** [nōō'klēəs, nōō'klēī] *n* noyau *m*.

nude [nōōd] *a* nu(e) ♦ *n* (*ART*) nu *m*; **in the** ~ (tout(e)) nu(e).

nudge [nuj] *vt* donner un (petit) coup de coude à.

nudist [nōō'dist] *n* nudiste *m/f*.

nudist colony *n* colonie *f* de nudistes.

nudity [nōō'ditē] *n* nudité *f*.

nugget [nug'it] *n* pépite *f*.

nuisance [nōō'səns] *n:* **it's a** ~ c'est (très) ennuyeux *or* gênant; **he's a** ~ il est assommant *or* casse-pieds; **what a** ~! quelle barbe!

nuke [nōōk] *vt* (*attack*) lancer une attaque nucléaire contre; (*destroy*) détruire à l'arme nucléaire *or* atomique.

null [nul] *a:* ~ **and void** nul(le) et non avenu(e).

nullify [nul'əfī] *vt* invalider.

numb [num] *a* engourdi(e) ♦ *vt* engourdir; ~ **with cold** engourdi(e) par le froid, transi(e) (de froid); ~ **with fear** transi de peur, paralysé(e) par la peur.

number [num'bûr] *n* nombre *m*; (*numeral*) chiffre *m*; (*of house, car, telephone, newspaper*) numéro *m* ♦ *vt* numéroter; (*include*) compter; **a** ~ **of** un certain nombre de; **to be**

~**ed among** compter parmi; **the staff** ~**s 20** le nombre d'employés s'élève à *or* est de 20; **wrong** ~ (*TEL*) mauvais numéro.

numbered account [num'bûrd əkount'] *n* (*in bank*) compte numéroté.

number plate *n* (*Brit AUT*) plaque *f* minéralogique *or* d'immatriculation.

Number Ten *n* (*Brit:* = *10 Downing Street*) résidence du Premier ministre.

numbness [num'nis] *n* torpeur *f*; (*due to cold*) engourdissement *m*.

numeral [nōō'mûrəl] *n* chiffre *m*.

numerical [nōōmär'ikəl] *a* numérique.

numerous [nōō'mûrəs] *a* nombreux(euse).

nun [nun] *n* religieuse *f*, sœur *f*.

nuptial [nup'shəl] *a* nuptial(e).

nurse [nûrs] *n* infirmière *f*; (*also:* ~**maid**) bonne *f* d'enfants ♦ *vt* (*patient, cold*) soigner; (*baby: US*) allaiter, nourrir; (: *Brit*) bercer (dans ses bras); (*hope*) nourrir *m*.

nursery [nûr'sûrē] *n* (*room*) nursery *f*; (*institution*) pouponnière *f*; (*for plants*) pépinière *f*.

nursery rhyme *n* comptine *f*, chansonnette *f* pour enfants.

nursery school *n* école maternelle.

nursery slope *n* (*Brit SKI*) piste *f* pour débutants.

nursing [nûrs'ing] *n* (*profession*) profession *f* d'infirmière ♦ *a* (*mother*) qui allaite.

nursing home *n* clinique *f*; maison *f* de convalescence.

nurture [nûr'chûr] *vt* élever.

nut [nut] *n* (*of metal*) écrou *m*; (*fruit*) noix *f*, noisette *f*, cacahuète *f* (*terme générique en anglais*) ♦ *a* (*chocolate etc*) aux noisettes.

nutcase [nut'kās] *n* (*Brit col*) dingue *m/f*.

nutcracker [nut'krakûr] *n* casse-noix *m inv*, casse-noisette(s) *m*.

nutmeg [nut'meg] *n* (*noix f*) muscade *f*.

nutrient [nōō'trēənt] *a* nutritif(ive) ♦ *n* substance nutritive.

nutrition [nōōtrish'ən] *n* nutrition *f*, alimentation *f*.

nutritionist [nōōtrish'ənist] *n* nutritionniste *m/f*.

nutritious [nōōtrish'əs] *a* nutritif(ive), nourrissant(e).

nuts [nuts] *a* (*col*): **he's** ~ il est dingue ♦ *excl* zut!

nutshell [nut'shel] *n* coquille *f* de noix; **in a** ~ en un mot.

nuzzle [nuz'əl] *vi:* **to** ~ **up to** fourrer son nez contre.

NV *abbr* (*US MAIL*) = *Nevada.*

NWT *abbr* (*Canada*) = *Northwest Territories.*

NY *abbr* (*US MAIL*) = *New York.*

NYC *abbr* (*US MAIL*) = *New York City.*

nylon [nī'lán] *n* nylon *m* ♦ *a* de *or* en nylon; ~**s** *npl* bas *mpl* nylon.

nymph [nimf] *n* nymphe *f*.

nymphomaniac [nimfəmā'nēak] *a*, *n* nymphomane (*f*).

NYSE *n abbr* (*US*) = *New York Stock Exchange.*

NZ *abbr* = **New Zealand.**

O

O, o [ō] n (letter) O, o m; (US SCOL: = outstanding) tb (= très bien); **O for Oboe** O comme Oscar.

oaf [ōf] n balourd m.

oak [ōk] n chêne m ♦ cpd de or en (bois de) chêne.

OAP n abbr (Brit) = **old-age pensioner.**

oar [ōr] n aviron m, rame f; **to put** or **shove one's ~ in** (fig: col) mettre son grain de sel.

oarlock [ōr'lâk] n (US) dame f de nage, tolet m.

oarsman [ōrz'mən], **oarswoman** [ōrz'woomən] n rameur/euse.

OAS n abbr (= Organization of American States) OEA f (= Organisation des états américains).

oasis, pl **oases** [ōā'sis, ōā'sēz] n oasis f.

oath [ōth] n serment m; (swear word) juron m; **to take the ~** prêter serment; **under** or **on** (Brit) **~** sous serment; assermenté(e).

oatmeal [ōt'mēl] n flocons mpl d'avoine.

oats [ōts] n avoine f.

OAU n abbr (= Organization of African Unity) OUA f (= Organisation de l'unité africaine).

obdurate [âb'dyərit] a obstiné(e); impénitent(e); intraitable.

obedience [ōbē'dēəns] n obéissance f; **in ~ to** conformément a.

obedient [ōbē'dēənt] a obéissant(e); **to be ~ to sb/sth** obéir à qn/qch.

obelisk [âb'əlisk] n obélisque m.

obesity [ōbē'sitē] n obésité f.

obey [ōbā'] vt obéir à; (instructions, regulations) se conformer à ♦ vi obéir.

obituary [ōbich'ōōârē] n nécrologie f.

object n [âb'jikt] objet m; (purpose) but m, objet; (LING) complément m d'objet ♦ vi: [əbjekt'] **to ~ to** (attitude) désapprouver; (proposal) protester contre, élever une objection contre; **I ~!** je proteste!; **he ~ed that ...** il a fait valoir or a objecté que ...; **do you ~ to my smoking?** est-ce que cela vous gêne si je fume?; **what's the ~ of doing that?** quel est l'intérêt de faire cela?; **money is no ~** l'argent n'est pas un problème.

objection [əbjek'shən] n objection f; (drawback) inconvénient m; **if you have no ~** si vous n'y voyez pas d'inconvénient; **to make** or **raise an ~** élever une objection.

objectionable [əbjek'shənəbəl] a très désagréable; choquant(e).

objective [əbjek'tiv] n objectif m ♦ a objectif(ive).

objectivity [âbjektiv'ətē] n objectivité f.

object lesson n (fig) (bonne) illustration.

objector [əbjek'tûr] n opposant/e.

obligation [âbləgā'shən] n obligation f, devoir m; (debt) dette f (de reconnaissance); "**without ~**" "sans engagement".

obligatory [əblig'ətôrē] a obligatoire.

oblige [əblīj'] vt (force): **to ~ sb to do** obliger or forcer qn à faire; (do a favor) rendre service à, obliger; **to be ~d to sb for sth** être obligé(e) à qn de qch; **anything to ~!** (col) (toujours prêt à rendre) service!

obliging [əblī'jing] a obligeant(e), serviable.

oblique [əblēk'] a oblique; (allusion) indirect(e) ♦ n (Brit TYP): **~ (stroke)** barre f oblique.

obliterate [əblit'ərāt] vt effacer.

oblivion [əbliv'ēən] n oubli m.

oblivious [əbliv'ēəs] a: **~ of** oublieux(euse) de.

oblong [âb'lông] a oblong(ue) ♦ n rectangle m.

obnoxious [əbnâk'shəs] a odieux(euse); (smell) nauséabond(e).

o.b.o. abbr (US: = or best offer: in classified ads) ≈ à discuter.

oboe [ō'bō] n hautbois m.

obscene [əbsēn'] a obscène.

obscenity [əbsen'itē] n obscénité f.

obscure [əbskyōōr'] a obscur(e) ♦ vt obscurcir; (hide: sun) cacher.

obscurity [əbskyōōr'itē] n obscurité f.

obsequious [əbsē'kwēəs] a obséquieux(euse).

observable [əbzûr'vəbəl] a observable; (appreciable) notable.

observance [əbzûr'vəns] n observance f, observation f; **religious ~s** observances religieuses.

observant [əbzûr'vənt] a observateur(trice).

observation [âbzûrvā'shən] n observation f; (by police etc) surveillance f.

observation post n (MIL) poste m d'observation.

observatory [əbzûr'vətôrē] n observatoire m.

observe [əbzûrv'] vt observer; (remark) faire observer or remarquer.

observer [əbzûr'vûr] n observateur/trice.

obsess [əbses'] vt obséder; **to be ~ed by** or **with sb/sth** être obsédé(e) par qn/qch.

obsession [əbsesh'ən] n obsession f.

obsessive [əbses'iv] a obsédant(e).

obsolescence [âbsəles'əns] n vieillissement m; obsolescence f; **built-in** or **planned ~** (COMM) désuétude calculée.

obsolescent [âbsəles'ənt] a obsolescent(e), en voie d'être périmé(e).

obsolete [âbsəlēt'] a dépassé(e), périmé(e).

obstacle [âb'stəkəl] n obstacle m.

obstacle race n course f d'obstacles.

obstetrics [əbstet'riks] n obstétrique f.

obstinacy [âb'stənəsē] n obstination f.

obstinate [âb'stənit] a obstiné(e); (pain, cold) persistant(e).

obstreperous [əbstrep'ûrəs] a turbulent(e).

obstruct [əbstrukt'] vt (block) boucher, obstruer; (halt) arrêter; (hinder) entraver.

obstruction [əbstruk'shən] n obstruction f; obstacle m.

obstructive [əbstruk'tiv] a obstructionniste.

obtain [əbtān'] vt obtenir ♦ vi avoir cours.

obtainable [əbtān'əbəl] a qu'on peut obtenir.

obtrusive [əbtrōō'siv] a (person) importun(e); (smell) pénétrant(e); (building etc) trop en évidence.

obtuse [əbtōōs'] a obtus(e).

obverse [âb'vûrs] n (of medal, coin) côté m

face; (*fig*) contrepartie *f*.
obviate [âb'vēāt] *vt* parer à, obvier à.
obvious [âb'vēəs] *a* évident(e), manifeste.
obviously [âb'vēəslē] *ad* manifestement; (*of course*): ~, **he** ... *or* **he** ~ ... il est bien évident qu'il a ...; ~! bien sûr!; ~ **not!** évidemment pas!, bien sûr que non!
OCAS *n abbr* (= *Organization of Central American States*) ODEAC *f* (= *Organisation des États d'Amérique Centrale*).
occasion [əkā'zhən] *n* occasion *f*; (*event*) événement *m* ♦ *vt* occasionner, causer; **on that** ~ à cette occasion; **to rise to the** ~ se montrer à la hauteur de la situation.
occasional [əkā'zhənəl] *a* pris(e) (*or* fait(e) *etc*) de temps en temps; occasionnel(le).
occasionally [əkā'zhənəlē] *ad* de temps en temps; **very** ~ (assez) rarement.
occasional table *n* table décorative.
occult [əkult'] *a* occulte ♦ *n*: **the** ~ le surnaturel.
occupancy [âk'yəpənsē] *n* occupation *f*.
occupant [âk'yəpənt] *n* occupant *m*.
occupation [âkyəpā'shən] *n* occupation *f*; (*job*) métier *m*, profession *f*; **unfit for** ~ (*house*) impropre à l'habitation.
occupational [âkyəpā'shənəl] *a* (*accident, disease*) du travail; (*hazard*) du métier.
occupational pension *n* retraite professionnelle.
occupational therapy *n* ergothérapie *f*.
occupied [âk'yəpīd] *a* (*busy, in use*) occupé(e).
occupier [âk'yəpīûr] *n* occupant/e.
occupy [âk'yəpī] *vt* occuper; **to** ~ **o.s. with** *or* **by doing** s'occuper à faire; **to be occupied with sth** être occupé avec qch.
occur [əkûr'] *vi* se produire; (*difficulty, opportunity*) se présenter; (*phenomenon, error*) se rencontrer; **to** ~ **to sb** venir à l'esprit de qn.
occurrence [əkûr'əns] *n* présence *f*, existence *f*; cas *m*, fait *m*.
ocean [ō'shən] *n* océan *m*; ~**s of** (*col*) des masses de.
ocean bed *n* fond (sous-)marin.
ocean-going [ō'shəngōing] *a* de haute mer.
Oceania [ōshēan'ēə] *n* Océanie *f*.
ocean liner *n* paquebot *m*.
ocher, (*Brit*) **ochre** [ō'kûr] *a* ocre.
o'clock [əklâk'] *ad*: **it is 5** ~ il est 5 heures.
OCR *n abbr* = **optical character reader**, **optical character recognition**.
Oct. *abbr* (= *October*) oct.
octagonal [âktag'ənəl] *a* octogonal(e).
octane [âk'tān] *n* octane *m*; **high-**~ **gas** *or* (*Brit*) **petrol** essence *f* à indice d'octane élevé.
octave [âk'tiv] *n* octave *f*.
October [âktō'bûr] *n* octobre *m*; *for phrases see also* **July.**
octogenarian [âktəjənâr'ēən] *n* octogénaire *m/f*.
octopus [âk'təpəs] *n* pieuvre *f*.
odd [âd] *a* (*strange*) bizarre, curieux(euse); (*number*) impair(e); (*left over*) qui reste, en plus; (*not of a set*) dépareillé(e)(*f*): **60-**~ 60 et quelques; **at** ~ **times** de temps en temps; **the** ~ **one out** l'exception *f*.

oddball [âd'bôl] *n* (*col*) excentrique *m/f*.
oddity [âd'itē] *n* bizarrerie *f*; (*person*) excentrique *m/f*.
odd-job man [âdjâb' man] *n* homme *m* à tout faire.
odd jobs *npl* petits travaux divers.
oddly [âd'lē] *ad* bizarrement, curieusement.
oddments [âd'mənts] *npl* (*Brit* COMM) fins *fpl* de série.
odds [âdz] *npl* (*in betting*) cote *f*; **the** ~ **are against his coming** il y a peu de chances qu'il vienne; **it makes no** ~ cela n'a pas d'importance; **to succeed against all the** ~ réussir contre toute attente; ~ **and ends** de petites choses; **at** ~ en désaccord.
ode [ōd] *n* ode *f*.
odious [ō'dēəs] *a* odieux(euse), détestable.
odometer [ōdâm'itûr] *n* (*US*) ≈ compteur *m* kilométrique.
odor [ō'dûr] *n* (*US*) odeur *f*.
odorless [ō'dûrlis] *a* inodore.
odour [ō'dûr] *etc* (*Brit*) = **odor** *etc*.
OECD *n abbr* (= *Organization for Economic Cooperation and Development*) OCDE *f* (= *Organisation de coopération et de développement économique*).
oesophagus [isâf'əgəs] *n* (*Brit*) œsophage *m*.
oestrogen [es'trəjən] *n* (*Brit*) œstrogène *m*.
of [uv] *prep* de; **a friend** ~ **ours** un de nos amis; **3** ~ **them went** 3 d'entre eux y sont allés; **the 5th** ~ **July** le 5 juillet; **a boy** ~ **10** un garçon de 10 ans; **made** ~ **wood** (fait) en bois; **a kilo** ~ **flour** un kilo de farine; **that was very kind** ~ **you** c'était très gentil de votre part; **a quarter** ~ **4** (*US*) 4 heures moins le quart.
off [ôf] *a, ad* (*engine*) coupé(e); (*faucet*) fermé(e); (*Brit*: *food*) mauvais(e), avancé(e); (*: milk*) tourné(e); (*absent*) absent(e); (*cancelled*) annulé(e); (*removed*): **the lid was** ~ le couvercle était retiré *or* n'était pas mis ♦ *prep* de; sur; **to be** ~ (*to leave*) partir, s'en aller; **I must be** ~ il faut que je file; **to be** ~ **sick** être absent pour cause de maladie; **a day** ~ un jour de congé; **to have an** ~ **day** n'être pas en forme; **he had his coat** ~ il avait enlevé son manteau; **the hook is** ~ le crochet s'est détaché; **the** crochet n'est pas mis; **10%** ~ (*COMM*) 10% de rabais; **5 km** ~ **(the road)** à 5 km (de la route); ~ **the coast** au large de la côte; **a house** ~ **the main road** une maison à l'écart de la grand-route; **it's a long way** ~ c'est loin (d'ici); **I'm** ~ **meat** je ne mange plus de viande; je n'aime plus la viande; **on the** ~ **chance** à tout hasard; **to be well/badly** ~ être bien/mal loti; (*financially*) être aisé/dans la gêne; ~ **and on, on and** ~ de temps à autre; **to be** ~ **in one's calculations** s'être trompé dans ses calculs; **that's a bit** ~ (*fig*: *col*) c'est un peu fort.
offal [ôf'əl] *n* (*CULIN*) abats *mpl*.
offbeat [ôf'bēt'] *a* excentrique.
off-center [ôf'sen'tûr] *a* décentré(e), excentré(e).
off-colour [ôf'kul'ûr] *a* (*Brit*: *ill*) malade, mal fichu(e); **to feel** ~ être mal fichu.
offence [əfens'] *n* (*Brit*) = **offense.**
offend [əfend'] *vt* (*person*) offenser, blesser ♦

vi: **to ~ against** (*law, rule*) contrevenir à, enfreindre.

offender [əfen'dûr] *n* délinquant/e; (*against regulations*) contrevenant/e.

offense [əfens'] *n* (*US*) (*crime*) délit *m*, infraction *f*; **to give ~ to** blesser, offenser; **to take ~ at** se vexer de, s'offenser de; **to commit an ~** commettre une infraction.

offensive [əfen'siv] *a* offensant(e), choquant(e); (*smell etc*) très déplaisant(e); (*weapon*) offensif(ive) ♦ *n* (*MIL*) offensive *f*.

offer [ôf'ûr] *n* offre *f*, proposition *f* ♦ *vt* offrir, proposer; **to make an ~ for sth** faire une offre pour qch; **to ~ sth to sb, ~ sb sth** offrir qch à qn; **to ~ to do sth** proposer de faire qch; **"on ~"** (*Brit COMM*) "en promotion".

offering [ôf'ûring] *n* offrande *f*.

offhand [ôf'hand'] *a* désinvolte ♦ *ad* spontanément; **I can't tell you ~** je ne peux pas vous le dire comme ça.

office [ôf'is] *n* (*place*) bureau *m*; (*position*) charge *f*, fonction *f*; **doctor's ~** (*US*) cabinet (médical); **to take ~** entrer en fonctions; **through his good ~s** (*fig*) grâce à ses bons offices.

office automation *n* bureautique *f*.

office bearer *n* (*Brit*) = **office holder**.

office boy *n* garçon *m* de bureau.

office building, (*Brit*) **office block** *n* immeuble *m* de bureaux.

office holder *n* (*US*: *of club etc*) membre *m* du bureau.

office hours *npl* heures *fpl* de bureau; (*US MED*) heures de consultation.

office manager *n* responsable administratif(ive).

officer [ôf'isûr] *n* (*MIL etc*) officier *m*; (*of club*) membre *m* du bureau; (*of organization*) membre *m* du bureau directeur; (*also*: **police ~**) agent *m* (de police).

office work *n* travail *m* de bureau.

office worker *n* employé/e de bureau.

official [əfish'əl] *a* (*authorized*) officiel(le) ♦ *n* officiel *m*; (*civil servant*) fonctionnaire *m/f*; employé/e.

officialdom [əfish'əldəm] *n* bureaucratie *f*.

officially [əfish'əlē] *ad* officiellement.

officiate [əfish'ēāt] *vi* (*REL*) officier; **to ~ as Mayor** exercer les fonctions de maire; **to ~ at a marriage** célébrer un mariage.

officious [əfish'əs] *a* trop empressé(e).

offing [ôf'ing] *n*: **in the ~** (*fig*) en perspective.

off-key [ôfkē'] *a* faux(fausse) ♦ *ad* faux.

off-licence [ôf'līsəns] *n* (*Brit*: *store*) débit *m* de vins et de spiritueux.

off-limits [ôf'lim'its] *a* (*esp US*) dont l'accès est interdit.

off line *a* (*COMPUT*) (en mode) autonome; (: *switched off*) non connecté(e).

off-load [ôf'lōd'] *vt*: **to ~ sth (onto)** (*goods*) décharger qch (sur); (*job*) se décharger de qch (sur).

off-peak [ôf'pēk'] *a* aux heures creuses.

off-putting [ôf'pŏŏt'ing] *a* (*Brit*) rébarbatif(ive); rebutant(e), peu engageant(e).

off-ramp [ôf'ramp] *n* (*US AUT*) bretelle *f* d'accès.

off-season [ôf'sēzən] *a, ad* hors-saison (*inv*).

offset *vt irg* [ôfset'] (*counteract*) contrebalancer, compenser ♦ *n* [ôf'set] (*also*: **~ printing**) offset *m*.

offshoot [ôf'shōōt] *n* (*fig*) ramification *f*, antenne *f*; (: *of discussion etc*) conséquence *f*.

offshore [ôf'shôr'] *a* (*breeze*) de terre; (*island*) proche du littoral; (*fishing*) côtier(ière); **~ oilfield** gisement *m* pétrolifère en mer.

offside [ôf'sīd'] *n* (*AUT*: *with right-hand drive*) côté droit; (: *with left-hand drive*) côté gauche ♦ *a* (*AUT*) de droite; de gauche; (*SPORT*) hors jeu.

offspring [ôf'spring] *n* progéniture *f*.

offstage [ôf'stāj'] *ad* dans les coulisses.

off-the-cuff [ôf'thəkuf'] *ad* au pied levé; de chic.

off-the-job [ôf'thəjáb'] *a*: **~ training** formation professionnelle extérieure.

off-the-rack [ôf'thərak'], (*Brit*) **off-the-peg** [ôf'thəpeg'] *ad* en prêt-à-porter.

off-the-wall [ôf'thəwôl'] *a* (*col*) bizarre, dingue.

off-white [ôf'wīt] *a* blanc cassé *inv*.

off-year election [ôf'yēr ilek'shən] *n* (*US*) élection (législative) partielle.

often [ôf'ən] *ad* souvent; **how ~ do you go?** vous y allez tous les combien?; **how ~ have you gone there?** vous y êtes allé combien de fois?; **as ~ as not** la plupart du temps.

ogle [ō'gəl] *vt* lorgner.

ogre [ō'gûr] *n* ogre *m*.

OH *abbr* (*US MAIL*) = *Ohio.*

oh [ō] *excl* ô!, oh!, ah!

OHMS *abbr* (*Brit*) = *On His (or Her) Majesty's Service.*

oil [oil] *n* huile *f*; (*petroleum*) pétrole *m*; (*for central heating*) mazout *m* ♦ *vt* (*machine*) graisser.

oilcan [oil'kan] *n* burette *f* de graissage; (*for storing*) bidon *m* à huile.

oil change *n* vidange *f*.

oilfield [oil'fēld] *n* gisement *m* de pétrole.

oil filter *n* (*AUT*) filtre *m* à huile.

oil-fired [oil'fûrd] *a* au mazout.

oil gauge *n* jauge *f* de niveau d'huile.

oil industry *n* industrie pétrolière.

oil level *n* niveau *m* d'huile.

oil painting *n* peinture *f* à l'huile.

oil pan *n* (*US AUT*) carter *m*.

oil refinery *n* raffinerie *f* de pétrole.

oil rig *n* derrick *m*; (*at sea*) plate-forme pétrolière.

oilskins [oil'skinz] *npl* (*Brit*) ciré *m*.

oil slick *n* nappe *f* de mazout.

oil tanker *n* pétrolier *m*.

oil well *n* puits *m* de pétrole.

oily [oi'lē] *a* huileux(euse); (*food*) gras(se).

ointment [oint'mənt] *n* onguent *m*.

OJT *abbr* (*US*) = **on-the-job training.**

OK *abbr* (*US MAIL*) = *Oklahoma.*

O.K., okay [ōkā'] (*col*) *excl* d'accord! ♦ *vt* approuver, donner son accord ♦ *n*: **to give sth one's ~** donner son accord à qch ♦ *a* en règle; en bon état; sain et sauf; acceptable; **is it ~?, are you ~?** ça va?; **are you ~ for money?** ça va *or* ira question argent?; **it's ~ with** *or* **by me** ça me va, c'est d'accord en ce qui me concerne.

Okla. *abbr* (*US*) = *Oklahoma.*

old [ōld] *a* vieux(vieille); (*person*) vieux, âgé(e); (*former*) ancien(ne), vieux; **how ~ are you?** quel âge avez-vous?; **he's 10 years ~** il a 10 ans, il est âgé de 10 ans; **~er brother/sister** frère/sœur aîné(e); **any ~ thing will do** n'importe quoi fera l'affaire.

old age *n* vieillesse *f.*

old-age pensioner (OAP) [ōld'āj pen'chənûr] *n* (*Brit*) retraité/e.

old-fashioned [ōld'fash'ənd] *a* démodé(e); (*person*) vieux jeu *inv.*

old folk's home *n* maison *f* de retraite.

old maid *n* vieille fille.

old-time [ōld'tīm'] *a* du temps jadis, d'autrefois.

old-timer [ōld'tī'mûr] *n* ancien *m.*

old wives' tale *n* conte *m* de bonne femme.

olive [âl'iv] *n* (*fruit*) olive *f*; (*tree*) olivier *m* ♦ *a* (*also:* **~-green**) (vert) olive *inv.*

olive oil *n* huile *f* d'olive.

Olympic [ōlim'pik] *a* olympique; **the ~ Games, the ~s** les Jeux *mpl* olympiques.

O&M *n abbr* = *organization and method.*

Oman [ō'mân] *n* Oman *m.*

OMB *n abbr* (*US:* = *Office of Management and Budget*) *service conseillant le président en matière budgétaire.*

omelet(te) [âm'lit] *n* omelette *f*; **ham/cheese ~** omelette au jambon/fromage.

omen [ō'mən] *n* présage *m.*

ominous [âm'ənəs] *a* menaçant(e), inquiétant(e); (*event*) de mauvais augure.

omission [ōmish'ən] *n* omission *f.*

omit [ōmit'] *vt* omettre; **to ~ to do sth** négliger de faire qch.

omnivorous [âmniv'ûrəs] *a* omnivore.

ON *abbr* (*Canada*) = *Ontario.*

on [ân] *prep* sur ♦ *ad* (*machine*) en marche; (*light, radio*) allumé(e); (*tap*) ouvert(e); **is the meeting still ~?** est-ce que la réunion a bien lieu?; la réunion dure-t-elle encore?; **when is this film ~?** quand passe *or* passe-t-on ce film?; **~ the train** dans le train; **~ the wall** sur le *or* au mur; **~ television** à la télévision; **~ the Continent** sur le continent; **a book ~ physics** un livre de physique; **~ learning this** en apprenant cela; **~ arrival** à l'arrivée; **~ the left** à gauche; **~ Friday** vendredi; **~ Fridays** le vendredi; **~ vacation,** (*Brit*) **~ holiday** en vacances; **I haven't any money ~ me** je n'ai pas d'argent sur moi; **this round's ~ me** c'est ma tournée; **to have one's coat ~** avoir (mis) son manteau; **to walk** *etc* **~** continuer à marcher *etc*; **from that day ~** depuis ce jour; **that's not ~!** (*not acceptable*) cela ne se fait pas!; (*not possible*) pas question!; **~ and off** de temps à autre.

once [wuns] *ad* une fois; (*formerly*) autrefois ♦ *cj* une fois que; **~ he had left/it was done** une fois qu'il fut parti/que ce fut terminé; **at ~** tout de suite, immédiatement; (*simultaneously*) à la fois; **all at ~** *ad* tout d'un coup; **~ a week** une fois par semaine; **~ more** encore une fois; **I knew him ~** je l'ai connu autrefois; **~ and for all** une fois pour toutes; **~ upon a time** il y avait une fois, il était une fois.

oncoming [ân'kuming] *a* (*traffic*) venant en sens inverse.

one [wun] *a, num* un(e) ♦ *pronoun* un(e); (*impersonal*) on; **this ~** celui-ci/celle-ci; **that ~** celui-là/celle-là; **the ~ book which ...** l'unique livre que ...; **~ by ~** un(e) par un(e); **~ never knows** on ne sait jamais; **~ another** l'un(e) l'autre; **it's ~ (o'clock)** il est une heure; **which ~ do you want?** lequel voulez-vous?; **to be ~ up on sb** avoir l'avantage sur qn; **to be at ~ (with sb)** être d'accord (avec qn).

one-armed bandit [wun'ârmd ban'dit] *n* machine *f* à sous.

one-day excursion [wun'dā ikskûr'zhən] *n* (*US*) billet *m* d'aller-retour (valable pour la journée).

one-man [wun'man] *a* (*business*) dirigé(e) *etc* par un seul homme.

one-man band *n* homme-orchestre *m.*

one-off [wun'ôf] (*Brit col*) *n* exemplaire *m* unique ♦ *a* unique.

one-piece [wun'pēs] *a:* **~ bathing suit** maillot *m* une pièce.

onerous [ân'ûrəs] *a* (*task, duty*) pénible; (*responsibility*) lourd(e).

oneself [wunself'] *pronoun* se; (*after prep, also emphatic*) soi-même; **by ~** tout seul.

one-shot [wun'shât] *a* (*US col*) unique.

one-sided [wun'sîdid] *a* (*decision*) unilatéral(e); (*judgment, account*) partial(e); (*contest*) inégal(e).

one-time [wun'tîm] *a* d'autrefois.

one-to-one [wun'təwun'] *a* (*relationship*) univoque.

one-upmanship [wunup'mənship] *n:* **the art of ~** l'art de faire mieux que les autres.

one-way [wun'wā'] *a* (*street, traffic*) à sens unique.

one-way ticket *n* aller *m* (simple).

ongoing [ân'gōing] *a* en cours; suivi(e).

onion [un'yən] *n* oignon *m.*

on line *a* (*COMPUT*) en ligne; (: *switched on*) connecté(e).

onlooker [ân'lōōkûr] *n* spectateur/trice.

only [ōn'lē] *ad* seulement ♦ *a* seul(e), unique ♦ *cj* seulement, mais; **an ~ child** un enfant unique; **not ~** non seulement; **I ~ took one** j'en ai seulement pris un, je n'en ai pris qu'un; **I saw her ~ yesterday** je l'ai vue hier encore; **I'd be ~ too pleased to help** je ne serais que trop content de vous aider; **I would come, ~ I'm very busy** je viendrais bien mais j'ai beaucoup à faire.

ono *abbr* (*Brit:* = *or nearest offer:* in *classified ads*) ≈ à discuter.

on-ramp [ân'ramp] *n* (*US AUT*) bretelle *f* d'accès.

onset [ân'set] *n* début *m*; (*of winter, old age*) approche *f.*

onshore [ân'shôr'] *a* (*wind*) du large.

onslaught [ân'slôt] *n* attaque *f*, assaut *m.*

Ont. *abbr* (*Canada*) = *Ontario.*

on-the-job [ânthəjâb'] *a:* **~ training** formation *f* en cours d'emploi.

onto [ân'tōō] *prep* = **on to.**

onus [ō'nəs] *n* responsabilité *f*; **the ~ is upon him to prove it** c'est à lui de le prouver.

onward(s) [ân'wûrd(z)] *ad* (*move*) en avant.

onyx [ân'iks] *n* onyx *m.*
ooze [ōōz] *vi* suinter.
opacity [ōpas'itē] *n* opacité *f.*
opal [ō'pəl] *n* opale *f.*
opaque [ōpāk'] *a* opaque.
OPEC [ō'pek] *n* *abbr* (= *Organization of Petroleum-Exporting Countries*) OPEP *f* (= *Organisation des pays exportateurs de pétrole*).
open [ō'pən] *a* ouvert(e); (*car*) découvert(e); (*road, view*) dégagé(e); (*meeting*) public(ique); (*admiration*) manifeste; (*question*) non résolu(e); (*enemy*) déclaré(e) ♦ *vt* ouvrir ♦ *vi* (*flower, eyes, door, debate*) s'ouvrir; (*store, bank, museum*) ouvrir; (*book etc: commence*) commencer, débuter; **in the ~ (air)** en plein air; **the ~ sea** le large; **~ ground** (*among trees*) clairière *f*; (*waste ground*) terrain *m* vague; **to have an ~ mind (on sth)** avoir l'esprit ouvert (sur qch).
open on to *vt fus* (*subj: room, door*) donner sur.
open out *vt* ouvrir ♦ *vi* s'ouvrir.
open up *vt* ouvrir; (*blocked road*) dégager ♦ *vi* s'ouvrir.
open-air [ō'pənär'] *a* en plein air.
open-and-shut [ō'pənənshut'] *a*: **~ case** cas *m* limpide.
open day *n* (*Brit*) journée *f* portes ouvertes.
open-ended [ō'pənen'did] *a* (*fig*) non limité(e).
opener [ō'pənûr] *n* (*also*: **can ~, tin ~**) ouvre-boîtes *m.*
open-faced sandwich [ō'pənfāst' sand'wich] *n* (*US*) canapé *m.*
open-heart surgery [ō'pənhârt sûr'jûrē] *n* chirurgie *f* a cœur ouvert.
open house *n*: **to keep ~** tenir table ouverte.
opening [ō'pəning] *n* ouverture *f*; (*opportunity*) occasion *f*; débouché *m*; (*job*) poste vacant.
opening night *n* (*THEATER*) première *f.*
openly [ō'pənlē] *ad* ouvertement.
open-minded [ō'pənmīn'did] *a* à l'esprit ouvert.
open-necked [ō'pənnekt'] *a* à col ouvert.
openness [ō'pənnis] *n* (*frankness*) franchise *f.*
open-plan [ō'pənplan'] *a* sans cloisons.
open sandwich *n* (*Brit*) canapé *m.*
open shop *n* *entreprise qui admet les travailleurs non syndiqués.*
Open University *n* (*Brit*) *cours universitaires par correspondance.*
opera [âp'rə] *n* opéra *m.*
opera glasses *npl* jumelles *fpl* de théâtre.
opera house *n* opéra *m.*
opera singer *n* chanteur/euse d'opéra.
operate [âp'ərāt] *vt* (*machine*) faire marcher, faire fonctionner; (*system*) pratiquer ♦ *vi* fonctionner; (*drug*) faire effet; **to ~ on sb (for)** (*MED*) opérer qn (de).
operatic [âpərat'ik] *a* d'opéra.
operating [âp'ərāting] *a* (*COMM: costs, profit*) d'exploitation; (*MED*): **~ table** table *f* d'opération; **~ room** (*US*) *or* **theatre** (*Brit*) salle *f* d'opération.
operating system *n* (*COMPUT*) système *m*

d'exploitation.
operation [âpərā'shən] *n* opération *f*; (*of machine*) fonctionnement *m*; **to have an ~ (for)** se faire opérer (de); **to be in ~** (*machine*) être en service; (*system*) être en vigueur.
operational [âpərā'shənəl] *a* opérationnel(le); (*ready for use or action*) en état de marche; **when the service is fully ~** lorsque le service fonctionnera pleinement.
operative [âp'ûrətiv] *a* (*measure*) en vigueur ♦ *n* (*in factory*) ouvrier/ière; **the ~ word** le mot clef.
operator [âp'ərātûr] *n* (*of machine*) opérateur/trice; (*TEL*) téléphoniste *m/f.*
operetta [âpəret'ə] *n* opérette *f.*
ophthalmologist [âfthalmâl'əjist] *n* ophtalmologiste *m/f*, ophtalmologue *m/f.*
opinion [əpin'yən] *n* opinion *f*, avis *m*; **in my ~** à mon avis; **to seek a second ~** demander un deuxième avis.
opinionated [əpin'yənātid] *a* aux idées bien arrêtées.
opinion poll *n* sondage *m* d'opinion.
opium [ō'pēəm] *n* opium *m.*
opponent [əpō'nənt] *n* adversaire *m/f.*
opportune [âpûrtōōn'] *a* opportun(e).
opportunist [âpûrtōō'nist] *n* opportuniste *m/f.*
opportunity [âpûrtyōō'nitē] *n* occasion *f*; **to take the ~ to do** *or* **of doing** profiter de l'occasion pour faire.
oppose [əpōz'] *vt* s'opposer à; **~d to** *a* opposé(e) à; **as ~d to** par opposition à.
opposing [əpōz'ing] *a* (*side*) opposé(e).
opposite [âp'əzit] *a* opposé(e); (*house etc*) d'en face ♦ *ad* en face ♦ *prep* en face de ♦ *n* opposé *m*, contraire *m*; (*of word*) contraire; **"see ~ page"** "voir ci-contre".
opposite number *n* (*Brit*) homologue *m/f.*
opposite sex *n*: **the ~** l'autre sexe.
opposition [âpəzish'ən] *n* opposition *f.*
oppress [əpres'] *vt* opprimer.
oppression [əpresh'ən] *n* oppression *f.*
oppressive [əpres'iv] *a* oppressif(ive).
opprobrium [əprō'brēəm] *n* (*formal*) opprobre *m.*
opt [âpt] *vi*: **to ~ for** opter pour; **to ~ to do** choisir de faire; **to ~ out of** choisir de quitter.
optical [âp'tikəl] *a* optique; (*instrument*) d'optique.
optical character reader/recognition (OCR) *n* lecteur *m*/lecture *f* optique.
optical fiber *n* fibre *f* optique.
optician [âptish'ən] *n* opticien/ne.
optics [âp'tiks] *n* optique *f.*
optimism [âp'təmizəm] *n* optimisme *m.*
optimist [âp'təmist] *n* optimiste *m/f.*
optimistic [âptəmis'tik] *a* optimiste.
optimum [âp'təməm] *a* optimum.
option [âp'shən] *n* choix *m*, option *f*; (*SCOL*) matière *f* à option; (*COMM*) option; **~s** *npl* accessoires *mpl* en option, options; **to keep one's ~s open** (*fig*) ne pas s'engager; **I have no ~** je n'ai pas le choix.
optional [âp'shənəl] *a* facultatif(ive); (*COMM*) en option; **~ extras** (*Brit*) accessoires *mpl* en option, options *fpl.*
opulence [âp'yələns] *n* opulence *f*; abondance *f.*

opulent [áp'yələnt] *a* opulent(e); abondant(e).

OR *abbr* (*US MAIL*) = *Oregon*.

or [ôr] *cj* ou; (*with negative*): **he hasn't seen** ~ **heard anything** il n'a rien vu ni entendu; ~ **else** sinon; ou bien, ou alors.

oracle [ór'əkəl] *n* oracle *m*.

oral [ór'əl] *a* oral(e) ♦ *n* oral *m*.

orange [ór'inj] *n* (*fruit*) orange *f* ♦ *a* orange *inv*.

orangeade [órinjād'] *n* orangeade *f*.

orange juice *n* jus *m* d'orange.

oration [órā'shən] *n* discours solennel.

orator [ór'ətûr] *n* orateur/trice.

oratorio [órətór'ēō] *n* oratorio *m*.

orb [ôrb] *n* orbe *m*.

orbit [ór'bit] *n* orbite *f* ♦ *vt* décrire une *or* des orbite(s) autour de; **to be in/go into** ~ **(around)** être/entrer en orbite (autour de).

orchard [ór'chûrd] *n* verger *m*; **apple** ~ verger de pommiers.

orchestra [ór'kistrə] *n* orchestre *m*; (*US: THEATER*) (fauteuils *mpl* d')orchestre.

orchestral [órkes'trəl] *a* orchestral(e); (*concert*) symphonique.

orchestrate [ór'kistrāt] *vt* (*MUS, fig*) orchestrer.

orchid [ór'kid] *n* orchidée *f*.

ordain [órdān'] *vt* (*REL*) ordonner; (*decide*) décréter.

ordeal [órdēl'] *n* épreuve *f*.

order [ór'dûr] *n* ordre *m*; (*COMM*) commande *f* ♦ *vt* ordonner; (*COMM*) commander; **in** ~ en ordre; (*of document*) en règle; **out of** ~ hors service; (*telephone*) en dérangement; **a machine in working** ~ une machine en état de marche; **in** ~ **of size** par ordre de grandeur; **in** ~ **to do/that** pour faire/que + *sub*; **to** ~ **sb to do** ordonner à qn de faire; **to place an** ~ **for sth with sb** commander qch auprès de qn, passer commande de qch à qn; **to be on** ~ être en commande; **made to** ~ fait sur commande; **to be under** ~**s to do sth** avoir ordre de faire qch; **a point of** ~ un point de procédure; **to the** ~ **of** (*BANKING*) à l'ordre de.

order book *n* carnet *m* de commandes.

order form *n* bon *m* de commande.

orderly [ór'dûrlē] *n* (*MIL*) ordonnance *f* ♦ *a* (*room*) en ordre; (*mind*) méthodique; (*person*) qui a de l'ordre.

order number *n* numéro *m* de commande.

ordinal [ór'dənəl] *a* (*number*) ordinal(e).

ordinary [ór'dənārē] *a* ordinaire, normal(e); (*pej*) ordinaire, quelconque; **out of the** ~ exceptionnel(le).

ordinary seaman *n* (*Brit*) matelot *m*.

ordinary shares *npl* (*Brit*) actions *fpl* ordinaires.

ordination [órdənā'shən] *n* ordination *f*.

ordnance [órd'nəns] *n* (*MIL: unit*) service *m* du matériel.

Ore. *abbr* (*US*) = *Oregon*.

ore [ôr] *n* minerai *m*.

Oreg. *abbr* (*US*) = *Oregon*.

organ [ór'gən] *n* organe *m*; (*MUS*) orgue *m*, orgues *fpl*.

organic [órgan'ik] *a* organique; (*crops etc*) biologique, naturel(le).

organism [ór'gənizəm] *n* organisme *m*.

organist [ór'gənist] *n* organiste *m/f*.

organization [órgənəzā'shən] *n* organisation *f*.

organization chart *n* organigramme *m*.

organize [ór'gəniz] *vt* organiser; **to get** ~**d** s'organiser.

organized labor *n* main-d'œuvre syndiquée.

organizer [ór'gənizûr] *n* organisateur/trice.

orgasm [ór'gazəm] *n* orgasme *m*.

orgy [ór'jē] *n* orgie *f*.

Orient [ór'ēənt] *n*: **the** ~ l'Orient *m*.

oriental [órēen'təl] *a* oriental(e) ♦ *n* Oriental/e.

orientate [ór'ēəntāt] *vt* orienter.

orifice [ór'əfis] *n* orifice *m*.

origin [ór'ijin] *n* origine *f*; **country of** ~ pays *m* d'origine.

original [ərij'ənəl] *a* original(e); (*earliest*) originel(le) ♦ *n* original *m*.

originality [ərijənal'itē] *n* originalité *f*.

originally [ərij'ənəlē] *ad* (*at first*) à l'origine.

originate [ərij'ənāt] *vi*: **to** ~ **from** être originaire de; (*suggestion*) provenir de; **to** ~ **in** prendre naissance dans; avoir son origine dans.

originator [ərij'inātûr] *n* auteur *m*.

ornament [ór'nəmənt] *n* ornement *m*; (*trinket*) bibelot *m*.

ornamental [órnəmen'təl] *a* décoratif(ive); (*garden*) d'agrément.

ornamentation [órnəməntā'shən] *n* ornementation *f*.

ornate [órnāt'] *a* très orné(e).

ornithologist [órnəthál'əjist] *n* ornithologue *m/f*.

ornithology [órnəthál'əjē] *n* ornithologie *f*.

orphan [ór'fən] *n* orphelin/e ♦ *vt*: **to be** ~**ed** devenir orphelin.

orphanage [ór'fənij] *n* orphelinat *m*.

orthodox [ór'thədáks] *a* orthodoxe.

orthopedic, (*Brit*) **orthopaedic** [órthəpē'dik] *a* orthopédique.

O/S *abbr* = **out of stock.**

oscillate [ás'əlāt] *vi* osciller.

OSHA *n abbr* (*US:* = *Occupational Safety and Health Administration*) office de l'hygiène et de la sécurité au travail.

Oslo [áz'lō] *n* Oslo.

ostensible [âsten'səbəl] *a* prétendu(e); apparent(e).

ostensibly [âsten'səblē] *ad* en apparence.

ostentation [âstentā'shən] *n* ostentation *f*.

ostentatious [âstentā'shəs] *a* prétentieux(euse); ostentatoire.

osteopath [ás'tēəpath] *n* ostéopathe *m/f*.

ostracize [ás'trəsiz] *vt* frapper d'ostracisme.

ostrich [ós'trich] *n* autruche *f*.

OT *n abbr* (= *Old Testament*) AT *m*.

OTB *n abbr* (*US:* = *off-track betting*) paris *pris en dehors du champ de course*.

O.T.E. *abbr* (*Brit:* = *on-target earnings*) primes sur objectifs inclus.

other [uth'ûr] *a* autre ♦ *pronoun*: **the** ~ **(one)** l'autre; ~**s** (~ *people*) d'autres; **some** ~ **people have still to arrive** on attend encore quelques personnes; **the** ~ **day** l'autre jour; ~ **than** autrement que; à part; **some actor or** ~ (*Brit*) un certain acteur, je ne sais quel acteur; **somebody or** ~ quelqu'un; **the car was none** ~ **than John's** la voiture n'était autre que celle de John.

otherwise [ŭ$\backslash$'ûrwīz] *ad, cj* autrement; **an ~ good piece of work** par ailleurs, un beau travail.

OTT *abbr* (*col*) = **over the top**; *see* **top**.

otter [ât'ûr] *n* loutre *f*.

ouch [ouch] *excl* aïe!

ought, *pt* **ought** [ôt] *auxiliary vb*: **I ~ to do it** je devrais le faire, il faudrait que je le fasse; **this ~ to have been corrected** cela aurait dû être corrigé; **he ~ to win** il devrait gagner; **you ~ to go and see it** vous devriez aller le voir.

ounce [ouns] *n* once *f* (= *28.35g; 16 in a pound*).

our [ou'ûr] *a* notre, nos *pl*.

ours [ou'úrz] *pronoun* le(la) nôtre, les nôtres.

ourselves [ouûrselvz'] *pronoun pl* (*reflexive, after preposition*) nous; (*emphatic*) nous-mêmes; **we did it (all) by ~** nous avons fait ça tout seuls.

oust [oust] *vt* évincer.

out [out] *ad* dehors; (*published, not at home etc*) sorti(e); (*light, fire*) éteint(e); (*on strike*) en grève; **~ here** ici; **~ there** là-bas; **he's ~** (*absent*) il est sorti; (*unconscious*) il est sans connaissance; **to be ~ in one's calculations** (*Brit*) s'être trompé dans ses calculs; **to run/back** *etc* **~** sortir en courant/ en reculant *etc*; **to be ~ and around** *or* (*Brit*) **about again** être de nouveau sur pied; **before the week was ~** avant la fin de la semaine; **the journey ~** l'aller *m*; **the boat was 10 km ~** le bateau était à 10 km du rivage; **~ loud** *ad* à haute voix; **~ of** *prep* (*outside*) en dehors de; (*because of: anger etc*) par; (*from among*): **~ of 10** sur 10; (*without*): **~ of gas** sans essence, à court d'essence; **made ~ of wood** en *or* de bois; **~ of order** (*machine*) en panne; (*TEL: line*) en dérangement; **~ of stock** (*COMM: article*) épuisé(e); (: *store*) en rupture de stock.

outage [ou'tij] *n* (*esp US: power failure*) panne *f or* coupure *f* de courant.

out-and-out [out'əndout'] *a* véritable.

outback [out'bak] *n* campagne isolée; (*in Australia*) intérieur *m*.

outbid [outbid'] *vt* surenchérir.

outboard [out'bôrd] *n*: **~ (motor)** (moteur *m*) hors-bord *m*.

outbreak [out'brāk] *n* éruption *f*, explosion *f*; (*start*) déclenchement *m*.

outbuilding [out'bilding] *n* dépendance *f*.

outburst [out'bûrst] *n* explosion *f*, accès *m*.

outcast [out'kast] *n* exilé/e; (*socially*) paria *m*.

outclass [outklas'] *vt* surclasser.

outcome [out'kum] *n* issue *f*, résultat *m*.

outcrop [out'krâp] *n* affleurement *m*.

outcry [out'krī] *n* tollé (général).

outdated [outdā'tid] *a* démodé(e).

outdistance [outdis'təns] *vt* distancer.

outdo [outdoō'] *vt irg* surpasser; **to ~ o.s.** se surpasser.

outdoor [out'dôr] *a* de *or* en plein air.

outdoors [outdôrz'] *ad* dehors; au grand air.

outer [out'ûr] *a* extérieur(e); **~ suburbs** grande banlieue.

outer space *n* espace *m* cosmique.

outfit [out'fit] *n* équipement *m*; (*clothes*) tenue *f*; (: *col: COMM*) organisation *f*, boîte *f*.

outfitter [out'fitûr] *n*: **"~'s"** "confection pour hommes".

outgoing [out'gōing] *a* (*president, tenant*) sortant(e); (*character*) ouvert(e), extraverti(e).

outgoings [out'gōingz] *npl* (*Brit: expenses*) dépenses *fpl*.

outgrow [outgrō'] *vt irg* (*clothes*) devenir trop grand(e) pour.

outhouse [out'hous] *n* (*US*) cabinets extérieurs; (*Brit*) appentis *m*, remise *f*.

outing [ou'ting] *n* sortie *f*; excursion *f*.

outlandish [outlan'dish] *a* étrange.

outlast [outlast'] *vt* survivre à.

outlaw [out'lô] *n* hors-la-loi *m inv* ♦ *vt* (*person*) mettre hors la loi; (*practice*) proscrire.

outlay [out'lā] *n* dépenses *fpl*; (*investment*) mise *f* de fonds.

outlet [out'let] *n* (*for liquid etc*) issue *f*, sortie *f*; (*for emotion*) exutoire *m*; (*for goods*) débouché *m*; (*also*: **retail ~**) point *m* de vente; (*US ELEC*) prise *f* de courant.

outline [out'lin] *n* (*shape*) contour *m*; (*summary*) esquisse *f*, grandes lignes.

outlive [outliv'] *vt* survivre à.

outlook [out'loōk] *n* perspective *f*.

outlying [out'liing] *a* écarté(e).

outmaneuver, (*Brit*) **outmanoeuvre** [outmanoō'vûr] *vt* (*rival etc*) avoir au tournant.

outmoded [outmō'did] *a* démodé(e), dépassé(e).

outnumber [outnum'bûr] *vt* surpasser en nombre.

out-of-date [outəvdāt'] *a* (*passport, ticket*) périmé(e); (*theory, idea*) dépassé(e); (*custom*) désuet(ète); (*clothes*) démodé(e).

out-of-the-way [outəvthəwā'] *a* loin de tout; (*fig*) insolite.

outpatient [out'pāshənt] *n* malade *m/f* en consultation externe.

outpost [out'pōst] *n* avant-poste *m*.

output [out'poōt] *n* rendement *m*, production *f* ♦ *vt* (*COMPUT*) sortir.

outrage [out'rāj] *n* atrocité *f*, acte *m* de violence; scandale *m* ♦ *vt* outrager.

outrageous [outrā'jəs] *a* atroce; scandaleux(euse).

outrider [out'rīdûr] *n* (*on motorcycle*) motard *m*.

outright *ad* [outrīt'] complètement; catégoriquement; carrément; sur le coup ♦ *a* [out'rīt] complet(ète); catégorique.

outrun [outrun'] *vt irg* dépasser.

outset [out'set] *n* début *m*.

outshine [outshīn'] *vt irg* (*fig*) éclipser.

outside [out'sīd'] *n* extérieur *m* ♦ *a* extérieur(e); (*remote, unlikely*): **an ~ chance** une (très) faible chance ♦ *ad* (au) dehors, à l'extérieur ♦ *prep* hors de, à l'extérieur de; **at the ~** (*fig*) au plus *or* maximum; **~ left/ right** *n* (*SOCCER*) ailier gauche/droit.

outside broadcast *n* (*RADIO, TV*) reportage *m*.

outside line *n* (*TEL*) ligne extérieure.

outsider [outsī'dûr] *n* (*in race etc*) outsider *m*; (*stranger*) étranger/ère.

outsize [out'sīz] *a* (*Brit*) énorme; (*clothes*)

grande taille *inv*.

outskirts [out'skûrts] *npl* faubourgs *mpl*.

outsmart [outsmârt'] *vt* se montrer plus malin(igne) *or* futé(e) que.

outspoken [out'spō'kən] *a* très franc(franche).

outspread [out'spred] *a* (*wings*) déployé(e).

outstanding [outstan'ding] *a* remarquable, exceptionnel(le); (*unfinished*) en suspens; en souffrance; non réglé(e); **your account is still ~** vous n'avez pas encore tout remboursé.

outstretched [outstrecht'] *a* (*hand*) tendu(e); (*body*) étendu(e).

outstrip [outstrip'] *vt* (*also fig*) dépasser.

out-tray [out'trā] *n* courrier *m* 'départ'.

outvote [outvōt'] *vt*: **to ~ sb (by)** mettre qn en minorité (par); **to ~ sth (by)** rejeter qch (par).

outward [out'wûrd] *a* (*sign, appearances*) extérieur(e); (*journey*) (d')aller.

outwardly [out'wûrdlē] *ad* extérieurement; en apparence.

outweigh [outwā'] *vt* l'emporter sur.

outwit [outwit'] *vt* se montrer plus malin que.

oval [ō'vəl] *a*, *n* ovale *(m)*.

ovary [ō'vûrē] *n* ovaire *m*.

ovation [ōvā'shən] *n* ovation *f*.

oven [uv'ən] *n* four *m*.

ovenproof [uv'ənprōof] *a* allant au four.

oven-ready [uv'ənred'ē] *a* prêt(e) à cuire.

ovenware [uv'ənwâr] *n* plats *mpl* allant au four.

over [ō'vûr] *ad* (par-)dessus; (*excessively*) trop ♦ *a* (*or ad*) (*finished*) fini(e), terminé(e); (*too much*) en plus ♦ *prep* sur; par-dessus; (*above*) au-dessus de; (*on the other side of*) de l'autre côté de; (*more than*) plus de; (*during*) pendant; **~ here** ici; **~ there** là-bas; **all ~** (*everywhere*) partout; (*finished*) fini(e); **~ and ~ (again)** à plusieurs reprises; **~ and above** en plus de; **to ask sb ~** inviter qn (à passer); **to go ~ to sb's** passer chez qn; **the world ~** dans le monde entier.

over... [ō'vûr] *prefix*: **~abundant** surabondant(e).

overact [ōvûrakt'] *vi* (*THEATER*) outrer son rôle.

overall *a*, *n* [ō'vûrôl] *a* (*length*) total(e); (*study*) d'ensemble ♦ *n* (*Brit*) blouse *f* ♦ *ad* [ōvûrôl'] dans l'ensemble, en général; **~s** *npl* bleus *mpl* (de travail).

overanxious [ōvûrangk'shəs] *a* trop anxieux(euse).

overawe [ōvûrô'] *vt* impressionner.

overbalance [ōvûrbal'əns] *vi* basculer.

overbearing [ōvûrbär'ing] *a* impérieux(euse), autoritaire.

overboard [ō'vûrbôrd] *ad* (*NAUT*) par-dessus bord; **to go ~ for sth** (*fig*) s'emballer (pour qch).

overbook [ō'vûrbook'] *vi* faire du surbooking.

overcapitalize [ōvûrkap'itəlīz] *vt* surcapitaliser.

overcast [ō'vûrkast] *a* couvert(e).

overcharge [ōvûrchârj'] *vt*: **to ~ sb for sth** faire payer qch trop cher à qn.

overcoat [ō'vûrkōt] *n* pardessus *m*.

overcome [ōvûrkum'] *vt* *irg* triompher de;

surmonter ♦ *a* (*emotionally*) bouleversé(e); **~ with grief** accablé(e) de douleur.

overconfident [ōvûrkân'fidənt] *a* trop sûr(e) de soi.

overcrowded [ōvûrkrou'did] *a* bondé(e).

overcrowding [ōvûrkrou'ding] *n* surpeuplement *m*; (*in bus*) encombrement *m*.

overdo [ōvûrdoo'] *vt irg* exagérer; (*overcook*) trop cuire; **to ~ it, to ~ things** (*work too hard*) en faire trop, se surmener.

overdose [ō'vûrdōs] *n* dose excessive.

overdraft [ō'vûrdraft] *n* découvert *m*.

overdrawn [ōvûrdrôn'] *a* (*account*) à découvert.

overdrive [ō'vûrdrīv] *n* (*AUT*) (vitesse) surmultipliée *f*.

overdue [ōvûrdoo'] *a* en retard; (*bill*) impayé(e); (*recognition*) tardif(ive); **that change was long ~** ce changement n'avait que trop tardé.

overestimate [ōvûres'təmāt] *vt* surestimer.

overexcited [ōvûriksī'tid] *a* surexcité(e).

overexertion [ōvûrigzûr'shən] *n* surmenage *m* (physique).

overexpose [ōvûrikspōz'] *vt* (*PHOT*) surexposer.

overflow *vi* [ōvûrflō'] déborder ♦ *n* [ō'vûrflō] trop-plein *m*; (*also*: **~ pipe**) tuyau *m* d'écoulement, trop-plein *m*.

overfly [ōvûrflī'] *vt irg* survoler.

overgenerous [ōvûrjen'ûrəs] *a* (*person*) prodigue; (*offer*) excessif(ive).

overgrown [ōvûrgrōn'] *a* (*garden*) envahi(e) par la végétation; **he's just an ~ schoolboy** (*fig*) c'est un écolier attardé.

overhang [ōvûrhang'] *vt irg* surplomber ♦ *vi* faire saillie.

overhaul *vt* [ōvûrhôl'] réviser ♦ *n* [ō'vûrhôl] révision *f*.

overhead *ad* [ō'vûrhed'] au-dessus ♦ [ō'vûrhed] *a* aérien(ne); (*lighting*) vertical(e) ♦ *n* (*US*) frais généraux.

overheads [ō'vûrhedz] *npl* (*Brit*) frais généraux.

overhear [ōvûrhiûr'] *vt irg* entendre (par hasard).

overheat [ōvûrhēt'] *vi* devenir surchauffé(e); (*engine*) chauffer.

overjoyed [ōvûrjoid'] *a* ravi(e), enchanté(e).

overkill [ō'vûrkil] *n* (*fig*): **it would be ~** ce serait de trop.

overland [ō'vûrland] *a*, *ad* par voie de terre.

overlap *vi* [ōvûrlap'] se chevaucher ♦ *n* [ō'vûrlap] chevauchement *m*.

overleaf [ō'vûrlēf] *ad* au verso.

overload [ō'vûrlōd] *vt* surcharger.

overlook [ō'vûrlook] *vt* (*have view of*) donner sur; (*miss*) oublier, négliger; (*forgive*) fermer les yeux sur.

overlord [ō'vûrlôrd] *n* chef *m* suprême.

overmanning [ōvûrman'ing] *n* sureffectif *m*, main-d'œuvre *f* pléthorique.

overnight *ad* [ō'vûrnīt'] (*happen*) durant la nuit; (*fig*) soudain ♦ *a* [ō'vûrnīt] d'une (*or* de) nuit; soudain(e); **he stayed there ~** il y a passé la nuit; **if you travel ~ ...** si tu fais le voyage de nuit ...; **he'll be away ~** il ne rentrera pas ce soir.

overnight bag *n* sac *m* de voyage.

overpass [ō'vŭrpas] *n* pont autoroutier; (*US*) passerelle *f*, pont *m*.

overpay [ōvûrpā'] *vt*: **to ~ sb by $50** donner à qn 50 dollars de trop.

overpower [ōvûrpou'ûr] *vt* vaincre; (*fig*) accabler.

overpowering [ōvûrpou'ûring] *a* irrésistible; (*heat, stench*) suffocant(e).

overproduction [ōvûrprəduk'shən] *n* surproduction *f*.

overrate [ōvərrāt'] *vt* surestimer.

overreact [ōvərēakt'] *vi* réagir de façon excessive.

override [ōvərīd'] *vt* (*irg: like* ride) (*order, objection*) passer outre à; (*decision*) annuler.

overriding [ōvərīd'ing] *a* prépondérant(e).

overrule [ōvərōōl'] *vt* (*decision*) annuler; (*claim*) rejeter.

overrun [ō'vərun] *vt irg* (*MIL*: *country etc*) occuper; (*time limit etc*) dépasser ♦ *vi irg* dépasser le temps imparti; **the town is ~ with tourists** la ville est envahie de touristes.

overseas *ad* [ō'vûrsēz'] outre-mer; (*abroad*) à l'étranger ♦ *a* [ō'vûrsēz] (*trade*) extérieur(e); (*visitor*) étranger(ère).

overseas cap *n* (*US*) calot *m*.

overseer [ō'vûrsēûr] *n* (*in factory*) contremaître *m*.

overshadow [ōvûrshad'ō] *vt* (*fig*) éclipser.

overshoot [ōvûrshōōt'] *vt irg* dépasser.

oversight [ō'vûrsīt] *n* omission *f*, oubli *m*; **due to an ~** par suite d'une inadvertance.

oversimplify [ōvûrsim'pləfī] *vt* simplifier à l'excès.

oversize [ō'vûrsīz] *a* (*US*) énorme; (*clothes*) grande taille *inv*.

oversleep [ōvûrslēp'] *vi irg* se réveiller (trop) tard.

overspend [ōvûrspend'] *vi irg* dépenser de trop; **we have overspent by $5,000** nous avons dépassé notre budget de 5000 dollars, nous avons dépensé 5000 dollars de trop.

overspill [ō'vûrspil] *n* excédent *m* de population.

overstaffed [ō'vûrstaft] *a*: **to be ~** avoir trop de personnel, être en surnombre.

overstate [ōvûrstāt'] *vt* exagérer.

overstatement [ōvûrstāt'mənt] *n* exagération *f*.

overstay [ōvûrstā'] *vt*: **to ~ one's welcome** abuser de l'hospitalité de son hôte.

overstep [ōvûrstep'] *vt*: **to ~ the mark** dépasser la mesure.

overstock [ōvûrstäk'] *vt* stocker en surabondance.

overstrike [ō'vûrstrīk] *n* (*on printer*) superposition *f*, double frappe *f* ♦ *vt irg* surimprimer.

overt [ōvûrt'] *a* non dissimulé(e).

overtake [ōvûrtāk'] *vt irg* dépasser; (*Brit AUT*) dépasser, doubler.

overtaking [ōvûrtā'king] *n* (*Brit AUT*) dépassement *m*.

overtax [ōvûrtaks'] *vt* (*ECON*) surimposer; (*fig: strength, patience*) abuser de; **to ~ o.s.** se surmener.

overthrow [ōvûrthrō'] *vt irg* (*government*) renverser.

overtime [ō'vûrtim] *n* heures *fpl* supplémentai-

res; (*US SPORT*) prolongation *f*; **to do** *or* **work ~** faire des heures supplémentaires.

overtime ban *n* refus *m* de faire des heures supplémentaires.

overtone [ō'vûrtōn] *n* (*also*: **~s**) note *f*, sous-entendus *mpl*.

overture [ō'vûrchûr] *n* (*MUS, fig*) ouverture *f*.

overturn [ōvûrtûrn'] *vt* renverser ♦ *vi* se retourner.

overweight [ōvûrwāt'] *a* (*person*) trop gros(se); (*baggage*) trop lourd(e).

overwhelm [ōvûrwelm'] *vt* accabler; submerger; écraser.

overwhelming [ōvûrwel'ming] *a* (*victory, defeat*) écrasant(e); (*desire*) irrésistible; **one's ~ impression is of heat** on a une impression dominante de chaleur.

overwhelmingly [ōvûrwel'minglē] *ad* (*vote*) en masse; (*win*) d'une manière écrasante.

overwork [ōvûrwûrk'] *n* surmenage *m* ♦ *vt* surmener ♦ *vi* se surmener.

overwrite [ōvərīt'] *vt* (*COMPUT*) écraser.

overwrought [ō'vərōt'] *a* excédé(e).

ovulation [ävyəlā'shən] *n* ovulation *f*.

owe [ō] *vt* devoir; **to ~ sb sth, to ~ sth to sb** devoir qch à qn.

owing to [ō'ing tōō] *prep* à cause de, en raison de.

owl [oul] *n* hibou *m*.

own [ōn] *vt* posséder ♦ *vi* (*Brit*): **to ~ to sth** reconnaître *or* avouer qch; **to ~ to having done sth** avouer avoir fait qch ♦ *a* propre; **a room of my ~** une chambre à moi, ma propre chambre; **can I have it for my (very) ~?** puis-je l'avoir pour moi (tout) seul?; **on one's ~** tout(e) seul(e); **to come into one's ~** trouver sa voie; trouver sa justification.

own up *vi* avouer.

own brand *n* (*COMM*) marque *f* de distributeur.

owner [ō'nûr] *n* propriétaire *m/f*.

owner-occupier [ō'nûr âk'yəpīûr] *n* (*Brit*) propriétaire occupant.

ownership [ō'nûrship] *n* possession *f*; **it's under new ~** (*store etc*) il y a eu un changement de propriétaire.

ox, pl oxen [äks, äk'sən] *n* bœuf *m*.

Oxfam [äks'fam] *n abbr* (*Brit*: = *Oxford Committee for Famine Relief*) association humanitaire.

oxide [äk'sīd] *n* oxyde *m*.

oxtail [äks'tāl] *n*: **~ soup** soupe *f* à la queue de bœuf.

oxyacetylene [äksēəset'əlin] *a* oxyacétylénique; **~ burner, ~ lamp** chalumeau *m* oxyacétylénique.

oxygen [äk'sijən] *n* oxygène *m*.

oxygen mask *n* masque *m* à oxygène.

oxygen tent *n* tente *f* à oxygène.

oyster [ois'tûr] *n* huître *f*.

oz. *abbr* = **ounce**.

ozone [ō'zōn] *n* ozone *m*.

P

P, p [pē] *n* (*letter*) P, p *m*; **P for Peter** P comme Pierre.

P [pē] *abbr* = **president, prince.**

p [pē] *abbr* (= *page*) p; (*Brit*) = **penny, pence.**

PA *n abbr* = **personal assistant, public address system** ♦ *abbr* (*US MAIL*) = *Pennsylvania*.

pa [bä] *n* (*col*) papa *m*.

p.a. *abbr* = **per annum.**

PAC *n abbr* (*US*) = *political action committee*.

pace [pās] *n* pas *m*; (*speed*) allure *f*; vitesse *f* ♦ *vi*: **to ~ up and down** faire les cent pas; **to keep ~ with** aller à la même vitesse que; (*events*) se tenir au courant de; **to set the ~** (*running*) donner l'allure; (*fig*) donner le ton; **to put sb through his ~s** (*fig*) mettre qn à l'épreuve.

pacemaker [pās'mākûr] *n* (*MED*) stimulateur *m* cardiaque.

pacific [pəsif'ik] *a* pacifique ♦ *n*: **the P~ (Ocean)** le Pacifique, l'océan *m* Pacifique.

pacification [pasəfəkā'shən] *n* pacification *f*.

pacifier [pas'əfiûr] *n* (*US*) tétine *f*.

pacifist [pas'əfist] *n* pacifiste *m/f*.

pacify [pas'əfī] *vt* pacifier; (*soothe*) calmer.

pack [pak] *n* paquet *m*; ballot *m*; (*of hounds*) meute *f*; (*of thieves, wolves etc*) bande *f*; (*of cards*) jeu *m* ♦ *vt* (*goods*) empaqueter, emballer; (*in suitcase etc*) emballer; (*box*) remplir; (*cram*) entasser; (*press down*) tasser; (*COMPUT*) grouper, tasser ♦ *vi*: **to ~ (one's bags)** faire ses bagages; **to ~ into** (*room, stadium*) s'entasser dans; **to send sb ~ing** (*col*) envoyer promener qn.

pack in (*Brit col*) *vi* (*machine*) tomber en panne ♦ *vt* (*boyfriend*) plaquer.

pack off *vt* (*person*) envoyer (promener), expédier.

pack up *vt* (*belongings*) ranger; (*goods, presents*) empaqueter, emballer ♦ *vi* (*Brit col: machine*) tomber en panne; (*: person*) se tirer.

package [pak'ij] *n* paquet *m*; (*of goods*) emballage *m*, conditionnement *m*; (*also: ~ deal*) marché global; forfait *m*; (*COMPUT*) progiciel *m* ♦ *vt* empaqueter; (*COMM: goods*) conditionner.

package bomb *n* colis piégé.

package holiday *n* (*Brit*) vacances organisées.

package tour *n* voyage organisé.

packaging [pak'ijing] *n* conditionnement *m*.

packed [pakt] *a* (*crowded*) bondé(e); **~ lunch** (*Brit*) repas froid.

packer [pak'ûr] *n* (*person*) emballeur/euse; conditionneur/euse.

packet [pak'it] *n* paquet *m*.

packet switching *n* (*COMPUT*) commutation *f* de paquets.

pack ice [pak īs] *n* banquise *f*.

packing [pak'ing] *n* emballage *m*.

packing case *n* caisse *f* (d'emballage).

pact [pakt] *n* pacte *m*, traité *m*.

pad [pad] *n* bloc(-notes) *m*; (*for inking*) tampon encreur; (*col: apartment*) piaule *f* ♦ *vt* rembourrer ♦ *vi*: **to ~ in/around** *etc* entrer/aller et venir *etc* à pas feutrés.

padding [pad'ing] *n* rembourrage *m*; (*fig*) délayage *m*.

paddle [pad'əl] *n* (*oar*) pagaie *f*; (*US: for table tennis*) raquette *f* ♦ *vi* barboter, faire trempette ♦ *vt*: **to ~ a canoe** *etc* pagayer.

paddle steamer *n* bateau *m* à aubes.

paddling pool [pad'ling pōōl] *n* (*Brit*) petit bassin.

paddock [pad'ək] *n* enclos *m*; paddock *m*.

paddy [pad'ē] *n* (*also: US: rice ~*) rizière *f*.

padlock [pad'lâk] *n* cadenas *m* ♦ *vt* cadenasser.

paediatrics *etc* [pēdēat'riks] (*Brit*) = **pediatrics** *etc*.

pagan [pā'gən] *a*, *n* païen(ne).

page [pāj] *n* (*of book*) page *f*; (*also: ~ boy*) groom *m*, chasseur *m*; (*at wedding*) garçon *m* d'honneur ♦ *vt* (*in hotel etc*) (faire) appeler.

pageant [paj'ənt] *n* spectacle *m* historique; grande cérémonie.

pageantry [paj'əntrē] *n* apparat *m*, pompe *f*.

page break *n* fin *f* or saut *m* de page.

pager [pā'jûr] *n* système *m* de téléappel.

paginate [paj'ənāt] *vt* paginer.

pagination [pajənā'shən] *n* pagination *f*.

pagoda [pəgō'də] *n* pagode *f*.

paid [pād] *pt, pp of* **pay** ♦ *a* (*work, official*) rémunéré(e).

paid-up [pād'up] *a* (*member*) à jour de sa cotisation; (*shares*) libéré(e); **~ capital** capital versé.

pail [pāl] *n* seau *m*.

pain [pān] *n* douleur *f*; **to be in ~** souffrir, avoir mal; **to have a ~ in** avoir mal à *or* une douleur à *or* dans; **to take ~s to do se** donner du mal pour faire; **on ~ of death** sous peine de mort.

pained [pānd] *a* peiné(e), chagrin(e).

painful [pān'fəl] *a* douloureux(euse); (*difficult*) difficile, pénible.

painfully [pān'fəlē] *ad* (*fig: very*) terriblement.

painkiller [pān'kilûr] *n* calmant *m*.

painless [pān'lis] *a* indolore.

painstaking [pānz'tāking] *a* (*person*) soigneux(euse); (*work*) soigné(e).

paint [pānt] *n* peinture *f* ♦ *vt* peindre; (*fig*) dépeindre; **to ~ the door blue** peindre la porte en bleu; **to ~ in oils** faire de la peinture à l'huile.

paintbox [pānt'bâks] *n* boîte *f* de couleurs.

paintbrush [pānt'brush] *n* pinceau *m*.

painter [pān'tûr] *n* peintre *m*.

painting [pān'ting] *n* peinture *f*; (*picture*) tableau *m*.

paint stripper *n* décapant *m*.

paintwork [pānt'wûrk] *n* (*Brit*) peintures *fpl*; (*: of car*) peinture *f*.

pair [pär] *n* (*of shoes, gloves etc*) paire *f*; (*couple*) couple *m*; (*twosome*) duo *m*; **~ of**

scissors (paire de) ciseaux *mpl*; ~ **of pants** pantalon *m*.
pair off *vi* se mettre par deux.
pajamas [pəjám'əz] *npl* (*US*) pyjama *m*; **a pair of** ~ un pyjama.
Pakistan [pak'istan] *n* Pakistan *m*.
Pakistani [pak'əstan'ē] *a* pakistanais(e) ◆ *n* Pakistanais/e.
PAL [pal] *n abbr* (*TV*: *phase alternation line*) PAL *m*.
pal [pal] *n* (*col*) copain/copine.
palace [pal'is] *n* palais *m*.
palatable [pal'ətəbəl] *a* bon(bonne), agréable au goût.
palate [pal'it] *n* palais *m* (*ANAT*).
palatial [pəlā'shəl] *a* grandiose, magnifique.
palaver [pəlav'ûr] *n* palabres *fpl or mpl*; histoire(s) *f(pl)*.
pale [pāl] *a* pâle ◆ *vi* pâlir ◆ *n*: **to be beyond the** ~ être au ban de la société; **to grow** *or* **turn** ~ (*person*) pâlir; ~ **blue** *a* bleu pâle *inv*; **to** ~ **into insignificance (beside)** perdre beaucoup d'importance (par rapport à).
paleness [pāl'nis] *n* pâleur *f*.
Palestine [pal'istīn] *n* Palestine *f*.
Palestinian [palistin'ēən] *a* palestinien(ne) ◆ *n* Palestinien/ne.
palette [pal'it] *n* palette *f*.
paling [pā'ling] *n* (*stake*) palis *m*; (*fence*) palissade *f*.
palisade [palisād'] *n* palissade *f*.
pall [pôl] *n* (*of smoke*) voile *m* ◆ *vi*: **to** ~ **(on)** devenir lassant (pour).
pallet [pal'it] *n* (*for goods*) palette *f*.
pallid [pal'id] *a* blème.
pallor [pal'ûr] *n* pâleur *f*.
pally [pal'ē] *a* (*col*) copain(copine).
palm [pâm] *n* (*ANAT*) paume *f*; (*also*: ~ **tree**) palmier *m*; (*leaf*, *symbol*) palme *f* ◆ *vt*: **to** ~ **sth off on sb** (*col*) refiler qch à qn.
palmist [pâm'ist] *n* chiromancien/ne.
Palm Sunday *n* le dimanche des Rameaux.
palpable [pal'pəbəl] *a* évident(e), manifeste.
palpitation [palpitā'shən] *n* palpitation *f*.
paltry [pôl'trē] *a* dérisoire; piètre.
pamper [pam'pûr] *vt* gâter, dorloter.
pamphlet [pam'flit] *n* brochure *f*; (*political etc*) tract *m*.
pan [pan] *n* (*also*: **sauce**~) casserole *f*; (*also*: **frying** ~) poêle *f*; (*of lavatory*) cuvette *f* ◆ *vi* (*CINEMA*) faire un panoramique ◆ *vt* (*col*: *book*, *film*) éreinter; **to** ~ **for gold** laver du sable aurifère.
panacea [panəsē'ə] *n* panacée *f*.
Panama [pan'əmâ] *n* Panama *m*.
Panama canal *n* canal *m* de Panama.
pancake [pan'kāk] *n* crêpe *f*.
Pancake Day *n* (*Brit*) mardi gras.
pancreas [pan'krēəs] *n* pancréas *m*.
panda [pan'də] *n* panda *m*.
pandemonium [pandəmō'nēəm] *n* tohu-bohu *m*.
pander [pan'dûr] *vi*: **to** ~ **to** flatter bassement; obéir servilement à.
pane [pān] *n* carreau *m* (de fenêtre).
panel [pan'əl] *n* (*of wood*, *cloth etc*) panneau *m*; (*RADIO*, *TV*) panel *m*, invités *mpl*; (*of experts*) table ronde, comité *m*.
panel game *n* jeu *m* (radiophonique/télévisé).

paneling, (*Brit*) **panelling** [pan'əling] *n* boiseries *fpl*.
panelist, (*Brit*) **panellist** [pan'əlist] *n* invité/e (*d'un panel*), membre d'un panel.
pang [pang] *n*: ~**s of remorse** pincements *mpl* de remords; ~**s of hunger/conscience** tiraillements *mpl* d'estomac/de la conscience.
panic [pan'ik] *n* panique *f*, affolement *m* ◆ *vi* s'affoler, paniquer.
panicky [pan'ikē] *a* (*person*) qui panique *or* s'affole facilement.
panic-stricken [pan'ikstrikən] *a* affolé(e).
pannier [pan'yûr] *n* (*on animal*) bât *m*; (*on bicycle*) sacoche *f*.
panorama [panəram'ə] *n* panorama *m*.
panoramic [panəram'ik] *a* panoramique.
pansy [pan'zē] *n* (*BOT*) pensée *f*; (*col*) tapette *f*, pédé *m*.
pant [pant] *vi* haleter.
panther [pan'thûr] *n* panthère *f*.
panties [pan'tēz] *npl* slip *m*, culotte *f*.
pantomime [pan'təmīm] *n* (*Brit*) spectacle *m* de Noël.
pantry [pan'trē] *n* garde-manger *m inv*; (*room*) office *f or m*.
pants [pants] *n* (*trousers*) pantalon *m*; (*Brit*: *woman's*) culotte *f*, slip *m*; (: *man's*) slip, caleçon *m*.
pants press *n* (*US*) presse-pantalon *m inv*.
pantsuit [pant'sōōt] *n* (*US*) tailleur-pantalon *m*.
pantyhose [pan'tēhōz] *n* (*US*) collant *m*.
papacy [pā'pəsē] *n* papauté *f*.
papal [pā'pəl] *a* papal(e), pontifical(e).
paper [pā'pûr] *n* papier *m*; (*also*: **wall**~) papier peint; (*also*: **news**~) journal *m*; (*study*, *article*) article *m*; (*exam*) épreuve écrite ◆ *a* en *or* de papier ◆ *vt* tapisser (de papier peint); **a piece of** ~ (*odd bit*) un bout de papier; (*sheet*) une feuille de papier; **to put sth down on** ~ mettre qch par écrit.
paper advance *n* (*on printer*) avance *f* (du) papier.
paperback [pā'pûrbak] *n* livre *m* de poche; livre broché *or* non relié ◆ *a*: ~ **edition** édition brochée.
paper bag *n* sac *m* en papier.
paperboy [pā'pûrboi] *n* (*selling*) vendeur *m* de journaux; (*delivering*) livreur *m* de journaux.
paper clip *n* trombone *m*.
paper handkerchief *n* (*Brit*) mouchoir *m* en papier.
paper mill *n* papeterie *f*.
paper money *n* papier-monnaie *m*.
paper profit *n* profit *m* théorique.
papers [pā'pûrz] *npl* (*also*: **identity** ~) papiers *mpl* (d'identité).
paperweight [pā'pûrwāt] *n* presse-papiers *m inv*.
paperwork [pā'pûrwûrk] *n* paperasserie *f*.
papier-mâché [pā'pûrməshā'] *n* papier mâché.
paprika [paprē'kə] *n* paprika *m*.
par [pâr] *n* pair *m*; (*GOLF*) normale *f* du parcours; **on a** ~ **with** à égalité avec, au même niveau que; **at** ~ au pair; **above/below** ~ au-dessus/au-dessous du pair; **to feel below** *or* **under** *or* **not up to** ~ ne pas se sentir en forme.
parable [par'əbəl] *n* parabole *f* (*REL*).

parabola [pərab'ələ] *n* parabole *f* (*MATH*).
parachute [par'əshōōt] *n* parachute *m* ♦ *vi* sauter en parachute.
parachute jump *n* saut *m* en parachute.
parachutist [par'əshōōtist] *n* parachutiste *m*/*f*.
parade [pərād'] *n* défilé *m*; (*inspection*) revue *f*; (*street*) boulevard *m* ♦ *vt* (*fig*) faire étalage de ♦ *vi* défiler.
parade ground *n* terrain *m* de manœuvre.
paradise [par'ədīs] *n* paradis *m*.
paradox [par'ədâks] *n* paradoxe *m*.
paradoxical [parədâk'sikəl] *a* paradoxal(e).
paradoxically [parədâk'siklē] *ad* paradoxalement.
paraffin [par'əfin] *n* (*Brit*): ~ (**oil**) pétrole (lampant); **liquid** ~ huile *f* de paraffine.
paragon [par'əgân] *n* parangon *m*.
paragraph [par'əgraf] *n* paragraphe *m*; **to begin a new** ~ aller à la ligne.
Paraguay [par'əgwā] *n* Paraguay *m*.
Paraguayan [parəgwā'ən] *a* paraguayen(ne) ♦ *n* Paraguayen/ne.
parakeet [par'əkēt] *n* (*US*) perruche *f*.
parallel [par'əlel] *a*: ~ **(with** *or* **to)** parallèle (à); (*fig*) analogue (à) ♦ *n* (*line*) parallèle *f*; (*fig*, *GEO*) parallèle *m*.
paralysis, *pl* **paralyses** [pərəl'isis, -sēz] *n* paralysie *f*.
paralytic [parəlit'ik] *a* paralytique.
paralyze [par'əlīz] *vt* paralyser.
paramedic [parəmed'ik] *n* (*US*) ambulancier/ière; ~**s** *npl* (*US*) ≈ service *m* d'assistance médicale d'urgence (SAMU).
parameter [pəram'itûr] *n* paramètre *m*.
paramilitary [parəmil'itärē] *a* paramilitaire.
paramount [par'əmount] *a*: **of** ~ **importance** de la plus haute *or* grande importance.
paranoia [parənoi'ə] *n* paranoïa *f*.
paranoid [par'ənoid] *a* (*PSYCH*) paranoïaque; (*neurotic*) paranoïde.
paranormal [parənôr'məl] *a* paranormal(e).
paraphernalia [parəfûrnāl'yə] *n* attirail *m*, affaires *fpl*.
paraphrase [par'əfrāz] *vt* paraphraser.
paraplegic [parəplē'jik] *n* paraplégique *m*/*f*.
parapsychology [parəsīkâl'əjē] *n* parapsychologie *f*.
parasite [par'əsīt] *n* parasite *m*.
parasol [par'əsôl] *n* ombrelle *f*; (*at café etc*) parasol *m*.
paratrooper [par'ətrōōpûr] *n* parachutiste *m* (*soldat*).
parcel [pâr'səl] *n* paquet *m*, colis *m* ♦ *vt* empaqueter.
parcel out *vt* répartir.
parcel bomb *n* (*Brit*) colis piégé.
parcel post *n* service *m* de colis postaux.
parch [pârch] *vt* dessécher.
parched [pârcht] *a* (*person*) assoiffé(e).
parchment [pârch'mənt] *n* parchemin *m*.
pardon [pâr'dən] *n* pardon *m*; grâce *f* ♦ *vt* pardonner à; (*LAW*) gracier; ~! pardon!; ~ **me!** excusez-moi!; **I beg your** ~! pardon!, je suis désolé!; ~ **me?**, (*Brit*) (**I beg your**) ~? pardon?
pare [pär] *vt* (*Brit*: *nails*) couper; (*fruit etc*) peler; (*fig*: *costs etc*) réduire.
parent [pär'ənt] *n* père *m or* mère *f*; ~**s** *npl* parents *mpl*.

parentage [pär'əntij] *n* naissance *f*; **of unknown** ~ de parents inconnus.
parental [pəren'təl] *a* parental(e), des parents.
parent company *n* société *f* mère.
parenthesis, *pl* **parentheses** [pəren'thəsis, -sēz] *n* parenthèse *f*; **in parentheses** entre parenthèses.
parenthood [pär'ənt·hōōd] *n* paternité *f or* maternité *f*.
parenting [pär'ənting] *n* le métier de parent, le travail d'un parent.
Paris [par'is] *n* Paris.
parish [par'ish] *n* paroisse *f*; (*civil*) ≈ commune *f* ♦ *a* paroissial(e).
parish council *n* (*Brit*) ≈ conseil municipal.
parishioner [pərish'ənûr] *n* paroissien/ne.
Parisian [pərizh'ən] *a* parisien(ne) ♦ *n* Parisien/ne.
parity [par'itē] *n* parité *f*.
park [pârk] *n* parc *m*, jardin public ♦ *vt* garer ♦ *vi* se garer.
parka [pâr'kə] *n* parka *m*.
parking [pâr'king] *n* stationnement *m*; "**no** ~" "stationnement interdit".
parking lights *npl* feux *mpl* de stationnement.
parking lot *n* (*US*) parking *m*, parc *m* de stationnement.
parking meter *n* parcomètre *m*.
parking offence *n* (*Brit*) = **parking violation.**
parking place *n* place *f* de stationnement.
parking ticket *n* P.-V. *m*.
parking violation *n* (*US*) infraction *f* au stationnement.
parkway [pârk'wā] *n* (*US*) route *f* express (*en site vert ou aménagé*).
parlance [pâr'ləns] *n*: **in common/modern** ~ dans le langage courant/actuel.
parliament [pâr'ləmənt] *n* parlement *m*.
parliamentary [pârləmen'tûrē] *a* parlementaire.
parlor, (*Brit*) parlour [pâr'lûr] *n* salon *m*.
parlous [pâr'ləs] *a* (*formal*) précaire.
Parmesan [pâr'məzân] *n* (*also*: ~ **cheese**) Parmesan *m*.
parochial [pərō'kēəl] *a* paroissial(e); (*pej*) à l'esprit de clocher.
parody [par'ədē] *n* parodie *f*.
parole [pərōl'] *n*: **on** ~ en liberté conditionnelle.
paroxysm [par'əksizəm] *n* (*MED*, *of grief*) paroxysme *m*; (*of anger*) accès *m*.
parquet [pârkā'] *n*: ~ **floor(ing)** parquet *m*.
parrot [par'ət] *n* perroquet *m*.
parrot fashion *ad* comme un perroquet.
parry [par'ē] *vt* esquiver, parer à.
parsimonious [pârsəmō'nēəs] *a* parcimonieux(euse).
parsley [pârz'lē] *n* persil *m*.
parsnip [pârs'nip] *n* panais *m*.
parson [pâr'sən] *n* ecclésiastique *m*; (*Church of England*) pasteur *m*.
parsonage [pâr'sənij] *n* presbytère *m*.
part [pârt] *n* partie *f*; (*of machine*) pièce *f*; (*THEATER etc*) rôle *m*; (*MUS*) voix *f*; partie ♦ *a* partiel(le); (*US*: *in hair*) raie *f* ♦ *ad* = **partly** ♦ *vt* séparer ♦ *vi* (*people*) se séparer; (*roads*) se diviser; **to take** ~ **in** participer à,

prendre part à; **to take sb's** ~ prendre le parti de qn, prendre parti pour qn; **on his** ~ de sa part; **for my** ~ en ce qui me concerne; **for the most** ~ en grande partie; dans la plupart des cas; **for the better** ~ **of the day** pendant la plus grande partie de la journée; **to be** ~ **and parcel of** faire partie de; ~ **of speech** (LING) partie f du discours.
part with vt fus se séparer de; se défaire de.

partake [pârtāk'] vi irg (formal): **to** ~ **of sth** prendre part à qch, partager qch.
part exchange n (Brit): **in** ~ en reprise.
partial [pâr'shəl] a partiel(le); (unjust) partial(e); **to be** ~ **to** aimer, avoir un faible pour.
partially [pär'shəlē] ad en partie, partiellement; partialement.
participant [pârtis'əpənt] n: ~ **(in)** participant/e (à).
participate [pârtis'əpāt] vi: **to** ~ **(in)** participer (à), prendre part (à).
participation [pârtisəpā'shən] n participation f.
participle [pâr'tisipəl] n participe m.
particle [pâr'tikəl] n particule f.
particleboard [pâr'tikəlbôrd] n (US) aggloméré m.
particular [pûrtik'yəlûr] a (specific) particulier(ière); (special) particulier, spécial(e); (fussy) difficile, exigeant(e); méticuleux(euse); ~**s** npl détails mpl; (information) renseignements mpl; **in** ~ surtout, en particulier.
particularly [pûrtik'yəlûrlē] ad particulièrement; (in particular) en particulier.
parting [pâr'ting] n séparation f; (Brit: in hair) raie f ♦ a d'adieu; **his** ~ **shot was** ... il lança en partant ....
partisan [pâr'tizən] n partisan/e ♦ a partisan(e); de parti.
partition [pârtish'ən] n (POL) partition f, division f; (wall) cloison f.
partly [pârt'lē] ad en partie, partiellement.
partner [pârt'nûr] n (COMM) associé/e; (SPORT) partenaire m/f; (at dance) cavalier/ière ♦ vt être l'associé or le partenaire or le cavalier de.
partnership [pârt'nûrship] n association f; **to go into** ~ **(with), form a** ~ **(with)** s'associer (avec).
part payment n acompte m.
partridge [pâr'trij] n perdrix f.
part-time [pârt'tīm] a, ad à mi-temps, à temps partiel.
part-timer [pârttī'mûr] n (also: **part-time worker**) travailleur/euse à temps partiel.
party [pâr'tē] n (POL) parti m; (team) équipe f; groupe m; (LAW) partie f; (celebration) réception f; soirée f; réunion f, fête f; **dinner** ~ dîner m; **to give** or **throw a** ~ donner une réception; **we're having a** ~ **next Saturday** nous organisons une soirée or réunion entre amis samedi prochain; **it's for our son's birthday** ~ c'est pour la fête (or le goûter) d'anniversaire de notre garçon; **to be a** ~ **to a crime** être impliqué(e) dans un crime.
party line n (POL) ligne f politique; (TEL) ligne partagée.
par value n (of share, bond) valeur nominale.

pass [pas] vt (time, object) passer; (place) passer devant; (car, friend) croiser; (exam) être reçu(e) à, réussir; (candidate) admettre; (overtake, surpass) dépasser; (approve) approuver, accepter; (law) promulguer ♦ vi passer; (SCOL) être reçu(e) or admis(e), réussir ♦ n (permit) laissez-passer m inv; carte f d'accès or d'abonnement; (in mountains) col m; (SPORT) passe f; (SCOL): **to get a** ~ être reçu(e) (sans mention); **she could** ~ **for 25** on lui donnerait 25 ans; **to** ~ **sth through a ring** etc (faire) passer qch dans un anneau etc; **could you** ~ **the vegetables around?** pourriez-vous faire passer les légumes?; **to make a** ~ **at sb** (col) faire des avances à qn.
pass away vi mourir.
pass by vi passer ♦ vt négliger.
pass down vt (customs, inheritance) transmettre.
pass on vi (die) s'éteindre, décéder ♦ vt (hand on): **to** ~ **on (to)** transmettre (à); (: illness) passer (à); (: price rises) répercuter (sur).
pass out vi s'évanouir.
pass over vt (ignore) passer sous silence.
pass up vt (opportunity) laisser passer.
passable [pas'əbəl] a (road) praticable; (work) acceptable.
passage [pas'ij] n (also: ~**way**) couloir m; (gen, in book) passage m; (by boat) traversée f.
passbook [pas'book] n livret m.
passenger [pas'injûr] n passager/ère.
passer-by [pasûrbī'] n passant/e.
passing [pas'ing] a (fig) passager(ère); **in** ~ en passant.
passing place n (AUT) aire f de croisement.
passion [pash'ən] n passion f; **to have a** ~ **for sth** avoir la passion de qch.
passionate [pash'ənit] a passionné(e).
passive [pas'iv] a (also LING) passif(ive).
passkey [pas'kē] n passe m.
Passover [pas'ōvûr] n Pâque juive.
passport [pas'pôrt] n passeport m.
passport control n contrôle m des passeports.
password [pas'wûrd] n mot m de passe.
past [past] prep (further than) au delà de, plus loin que; après; (later than) après ♦ a passé(e); (president etc) ancien(ne) ♦ n passé m; **quarter/half** ~ **four** quatre heures et quart/demie; **ten/twenty** ~ **four** quatre heures dix/vingt; **he's** ~ **forty** il a dépassé la quarantaine, il a plus de or passé quarante ans; **it's** ~ **midnight** il est plus de minuit, il est passé minuit; **for the** ~ **few/3 days** depuis quelques/3 jours; ces derniers/3 derniers jours; **to run** ~ passer en courant; **he ran** ~ **me** il m'a dépassé en courant; il a passé devant moi en courant; **in the** ~ (gen) dans le temps, autrefois; (LING) au passé; **I'm** ~ **caring** je ne m'en fais plus; **to be** ~ **one's prime** avoir passé l'âge.
pasta [pâs'tə] n pâtes fpl.
paste [pāst] n (glue) colle f (de pâte); (jewelry) strass m; (CULIN) pâté m (à tartiner); pâte f ♦ vt coller; **tomato** ~ concentré m de tomate, purée f de tomate.

pastel |pastel'| *a* pastel *inv*.

pasteurized |pas'chərīzd| *a* pasteurisé(e).

pastille |pastēl'| *n* pastille *f*.

pastime |pas'tīm| *n* passe-temps *m inv*, distraction *f*.

pastor |pas'tûr| *n* pasteur *m*.

pastoral |pas'tûrəl| *a* pastoral(e).

pastry |pās'trē| *n* pâte *f*; (*cake*) pâtisserie *f*.

pastry shop *n* (*US*) pâtisserie *f*.

pasture |pas'chûr| *n* pâturage *m*.

pasty *a* |pās'tē| pâteux(euse); (*complexion*) terreux(euse) ♦ *n* |pas'tē| (*Brit*) petit pâté (en croûte).

pat |pat| *vt* donner une petite tape à ♦ *n*: **a ~ of butter** une noisette de beurre; **to give sb/o.s. a ~ on the back** (*fig*) congratuler qn/se congratuler; **he has it down ~** il sait cela sur le bout des doigts.

patch |pach| *n* (*of material*) pièce *f*; (*spot*) tache *f*; (*of land*) parcelle *f* ♦ *vt* (*clothes*) rapiécer.

  patch up *vt* réparer.

patchwork |pach'wûrk| *n* patchwork *m*.

patchy |pach'ē| *a* inégal(e).

pate |pāt| *n*: **a bald ~** un crâne chauve *or* dégarni.

pâté |pátā'| *n* pâté *m*, terrine *f*.

patent |pat'ənt| *n* brevet *m* (d'invention) ♦ *vt* faire breveter ♦ *a* patent(e), manifeste.

patent leather *n* cuir verni.

patently |pat'əntlē| *ad* manifestement.

patent medicine *n* spécialité *f* pharmaceutique.

patent office *n* bureau *m* des brevets.

paternal |pətûr'nəl| *a* paternel(le).

paternity |pətûr'nitē| *n* paternité *f*.

paternity suit *n* (*LAW*) action *f* en recherche de paternité.

path |path| *n* chemin *m*, sentier *m*; allée *f*; (*of planet*) course *f*; (*of missile*) trajectoire *f*.

pathetic |pəthet'ik| *a* (*pitiful*) pitoyable; (*very bad*) lamentable, minable; (*moving*) pathétique.

pathological |pathəlâj'ikəl| *a* pathologique.

pathologist |pəthâl'əjist| *n* pathologiste *m/f*.

pathology |pəthâl'əjē| *n* pathologie *f*.

pathos |pā'thâs| *n* pathétique *m*.

pathway |path'wā| *n* chemin *m*, sentier *m*.

patience |pā'shəns| *n* patience *f*; (*Brit CARDS*) réussite *f*; **to lose (one's) ~** perdre patience.

patient |pā'shənt| *n* patient/e; (*in hospital*) malade *m/f* ♦ *a* patient(e).

patiently |pā'shəntlē| *ad* patiemment.

patio |pat'ēō| *n* patio *m*.

patriot |pā'trēət| *n* patriote *m/f*.

patriotic |pātrēât'ik| *a* patriotique; (*person*) patriote.

patriotism |pā'trēətizəm| *n* patriotisme *m*.

patrol |pətrōl'| *n* patrouille *f* ♦ *vt* patrouiller dans; **to be on ~** être de patrouille.

patrol boat *n* patrouilleur *m*.

patrol car *n* voiture *f* de police.

patrolman |pətrōl'mən| *n* (*US*) agent *m* de police.

patron |pā'trən| *n* (*in shop*) client/e; (*of charity*) patron/ne; **~ of the arts** mécène *m*.

patronage |pā'trənij| *n* patronage *m*, appui *m*.

patronize |pā'trənīz| *vt* être (un) client *or* un habitué de; (*fig*) traiter avec condescen-

dance.

patronizing |pā'trənizing| *a* condescendant(e).

patron saint *n* saint(e) patron/ne.

patter |pat'ûr| *n* crépitement *m*, tapotement *m*; (*sales talk*) boniment *m* ♦ *vi* crépiter, tapoter.

pattern |pat'ûrn| *n* modèle *m*; (*SEWING*) patron *m*; (*design*) motif *m*; (*sample*) échantillon *m*; **behavior ~** mode *m* de comportement.

patterned |pat'ûrnd| *a* à motifs.

paucity |pô'sitē| *n* pénurie *f*, carence *f*.

paunch |pônch| *n* gros ventre, bedaine *f*.

pauper |pô'pûr| *n* indigent/e; **~'s grave** *n* fosse commune.

pause |pôz| *n* pause *f*, arrêt *m*; (*MUS*) silence *m* ♦ *vi* faire une pause, s'arrêter; **to ~ for breath** reprendre son souffle; (*fig*) faire une pause.

pave |pāv| *vt* paver, daller; **to ~ the way for** ouvrir la voie à.

pavement |pāv'mənt| *n* (*US*) chaussée *f*; (*Brit*) trottoir *m*.

pavilion |pəvil'yən| *n* pavillon *m*; tente *f*; (*SPORT*) stand *m*.

paving |pā'ving| *n* pavage *m*, dallage *m*.

paving stone *n* pavé *m*.

paw |pô| *n* patte *f* ♦ *vt* donner un coup de patte à; (*subj: person: pej*) tripoter.

pawn |pôn| *n* gage *m*; (*CHESS, also fig*) pion *m* ♦ *vt* mettre en gage.

pawnbroker |pôn'brōkûr| *n* prêteur *m* sur gages.

pawnshop |pôn'shâp| *n* mont-de-piété *m*.

pay |pā| *n* salaire *m*; (*of manual worker*) paie *f* ♦ *vb* (*pt, pp* **paid** |pād|) *vt* payer; (*be profitable: to: also fig*) rapporter à ♦ *vi* payer; (*be profitable*) être rentable; **how much did you ~ for it?** combien l'avez-vous payé?, vous l'avez payé combien?; **I paid $5 for that record** j'ai payé ce disque 5 dollars; **to ~ one's way** payer sa part; (*company*) couvrir ses frais; **to ~ dividends** (*fig*) porter ses fruits, s'avérer rentable; **it won't ~ you to do that** vous ne gagnerez rien à faire cela; **to ~ attention (to)** prêter attention (à).

pay back *vt* rembourser.

pay in *vt* verser.

pay off *vt* (*debts*) régler, acquitter; (*creditor, mortgage*) rembourser; (*workers*) licencier ♦ *vi* (*plan, patience*) se révéler payant(e); **to ~ sth off in installments** payer qch à tempérament.

pay out *vt* (*money*) payer, sortir de sa poche; (*rope*) laisser filer.

pay up *vt* (*debts*) régler; (*amount*) payer.

payable |pā'əbəl| *a* payable; **to make a check ~ to sb** établir un chèque à l'ordre de qn.

pay day *n* jour *m* de paie.

PAYE *n abbr* (*Brit*: = *pay as you earn*) système de retenue des impôts à la source.

payee |pāē'| *n* bénéficiaire *m/f*.

pay envelope *n* (*US*) (enveloppe *f* de) paie *f*.

paying |pā'ing| *a* payant(e); **~ guest** hôte payant.

payload |pā'lōd| *n* charge *f* utile.

payment |pā'mənt| *n* paiement *m*; (*of bill*) règlement *m*; (*of deposit, check*) versement *m*; **advance ~** (*part sum*) acompte *m*; (*total* *sum*) paiement anticipé; **deferred ~, ~ by installments** paiement par versements échelonnés; **monthly ~.** mensualité *f*; **in ~ for, in ~ of** en règlement de; **on ~ of $5** pour 5 dollars.

pay packet *n* (*Brit*) paie *f*.

pay phone *n* cabine *f* téléphonique, téléphone public.

payroll [pā'rōl] *n* registre *m* du personnel; **to be on a firm's ~** être employé par une entreprise.

pay slip *n* (*Brit*) bulletin *m* de paie, feuille *f* de paie.

pay station *n* (*US*) cabine *f* téléphonique.

PBS *n abbr* (*US*: = *Public Broadcasting Service*) *groupement d'aide à la réalisation d'émissions pour la TV publique*.

PBX *abbr* (= *private branch* (*telephone*) *exchange*) autocommutateur privé.

PC *n abbr* = **personal computer**; (*Brit*) = **police constable**.

pc *abbr* = **per cent, postcard**.

p/c *abbr* = **petty cash**.

PCB *n abbr* = **printed circuit board**.

PD *n abbr* (*US*) = **police department**.

pd *abbr* = **paid**.

PDT *abbr* (*US*: = *Pacific Daylight Time*) *heure d'été du Pacifique*.

PE *n abbr* (= *physical education*) EPS *f*.

pea [pē] *n* (*petit*) pois.

peace [pēs] *n* paix *f*; (*calm*) calme *m*, tranquillité *f*; **to be at ~ with sb/sth** être en paix avec qn/qch; **to keep the ~** (*subj: policeman*) assurer le maintien de l'ordre; (*: citizen*) ne pas troubler l'ordre.

peaceable [pē'səbəl] *a* paisible, pacifique.

Peace Corps *n* (*US*) ≈ coopération (civile).

peaceful [pēs'fəl] *a* paisible, calme.

peacekeeping [pēs'kēping] *n* maintien *m* de la paix.

peace offering *n* gage *m* de réconciliation; (*humorous*) gage de paix.

peach [pēch] *n* pêche *f*.

peacock [pē'kâk] *n* paon *m*.

peak [pēk] *n* (*mountain*) pic *m*, cime *f*; (*fig: highest level*) maximum *m*; (*: of career, fame*) apogée *m*.

peaked [pēkt] *a* (*US col*) fatigué(e).

peak-hour [pēk'ouàr] *a* (*traffic etc*) de pointe.

peak hours *npl* heures *fpl* d'affluence.

peak period *n* période *f* de pointe.

peaky [pē'kē] *a* (*Brit col*) = **peaked**.

peal [pēl] *n* (*of bells*) carillon *m*; **~s of laughter** éclats *mpl* de rire.

peanut [pē'nut] *n* arachide *f*, cacahuète *f*.

peanut butter *n* beurre *m* de cacahuète.

peanut oil *n* (*US*) huile *f* d'arachide.

pear [pär] *n* poire *f*.

pearl [pûrl] *n* perle *f*.

peasant [pez'ənt] *n* paysan/ne.

peat [pēt] *n* tourbe *f*.

pebble [peb'əl] *n* galet *m*, caillou *m*.

peck [pek] *vt* (*also: ~ at*) donner un coup de bec à; (*food*) picorer ♦ *n* coup *m* de bec; (*kiss*) bécot *m*.

pecking order [pek'ing ôrdûr] *n* ordre *m* hiérarchique.

peckish [pek'ish] *a* (*Brit col*): **I feel ~** je mangerais bien quelque chose, j'ai la dent.

peculiar [pikyōōl'yûr] *a* (*odd*) étrange, bizarre, curieux(euse); (*particular*) particulier(ière); **~ to** particulier à.

peculiarity [pikyōōlēar'itē] *n* bizarrerie *f*; particularité *f*.

pecuniary [pikyōō'nēàrē] *a* pécuniaire.

pedal [ped'əl] *n* pédale *f* ♦ *vi* pédaler.

pedal bin *n* (*Brit*) poubelle *f* à pédale.

pedantic [pədan'tik] *a* pédant(e).

peddle [ped'əl] *vt* colporter; (*drugs*) faire le trafic de.

peddler [ped'lûr] *n* colporteur *m*; camelot *m*.

pedestal [ped'istəl] *n* piédestal *m*.

pedestrian [pədes'trēən] *n* piéton *m* ♦ *a* piétonnier(ière); (*fig*) prosaïque, terre à terre *inv*.

pedestrian crossing *n* passage clouté.

pedestrian precinct *n* (*Brit*) zone piétonne.

pediatrician [pēdēatrish'ən] *n* (*US*) pédiatre *m/f*.

pediatrics [pēdēat'riks] *n* (*US*) pédiatrie *f*.

pedigree [ped'əgrē] *n* ascendance *f*; (*of animal*) pedigree *m* ♦ *cpd* (*animal*) de race.

pedlar [ped'lûr] *n* = **peddler**.

pee [pē] *vi* (*col*) faire pipi, pisser.

peek [pēk] *vi* jeter un coup d'œil (furtif).

peel [pēl] *n* pelure *f*, épluchure *f*; (*of orange, lemon*) écorce *f* ♦ *vt* peler, éplucher ♦ *vi* (*paint etc*) s'écailler; (*wallpaper*) se décoller.

peel back *vt* décoller.

peeler [pē'lûr] *n* (*potato etc ~*) éplucheur *m*.

peelings [pē'lingz] *npl* pelures *fpl*, épluchures *fpl*.

peep [pēp] *n* (*Brit: look*) coup d'œil furtif; (*sound*) pépiement *m* ♦ *vi* (*Brit*) jeter un coup d'œil (furtif).

peep out *vi* (*Brit*) se montrer (furtivement).

peephole [pēp'hōl] *n* judas *m*.

peer [pēr] *vi*: **to ~ at** regarder attentivement, scruter ♦ *n* (*noble*) pair *m*; (*equal*) pair, égal/e.

peerage [pē'rij] *n* pairie *f*.

peerless [pēr'lis] *a* incomparable, sans égal.

peeved [pēvd] *a* irrité(e), ennuyé(e).

peevish [pē'vish] *a* grincheux(euse), maussade.

peg [peg] *n* cheville *f*; (*for coat etc*) patère *f*; (*Brit: also:* **clothes ~**) pince *f* à linge ♦ *vt* (*clothes*) accrocher; (*fig: prices, wages*) contrôler, stabiliser.

PEI *abbr* (*Canada*) = *Prince Edward Island*.

pejorative [pijôr'ətiv] *a* péjoratif(ive).

Pekin [pē'kin] *n*, **Peking** [pēking'] *n* Pékin.

pekingese [pēkingēz'] *n* pékinois *m*.

pelican [pel'ikən] *n* pélican *m*.

pelican crossing *n* (*Brit AUT*) feu *m* à commande manuelle.

pellet [pel'it] *n* boulette *f*; (*of lead*) plomb *m*.

pell-mell [pel'mel'] *ad* pêle-mêle.

pelmet [pel'mit] *n* cantonnière *f*; lambrequin *m*.

pelt [pelt] *vt*: **to ~ sb (with)** bombarder qn (de) ♦ *vi* (*rain*) tomber à seaux ♦ *n* peau *f*.

pelvis [pel'vis] *n* bassin *m*.

pen [pen] *n* (*for writing*) stylo *m*; (*for sheep*) parc *m*; (*US col: prison*) taule *f*; **to put ~ to paper** prendre la plume.

penal [pē'nəl] *a* pénal(e).

penalize [pē'nəlīz] *vt* pénaliser; (*fig*) désavantager.

penal servitude [pē'nəl sûr'vətōōd] *n* travaux forcés.

penalty [pen'əltē] *n* pénalité *f*; sanction *f*; (*fine*) amende *f*; (*SPORT*) pénalisation *f*; (*SOCCER*: *also*: ~ **kick**) penalty *m*.

penalty clause *n* clause pénale.

penalty kick *n* (*SOCCER*) penalty *m*.

penance [pen'əns] *n* pénitence *f*.

pence [pens] *npl* (*Brit*) = **penny.**

penchant [pen'chənt] *n* penchant *m*.

pencil [pen'səl] *n* crayon *m* ♦ *vt*: **to** ~ **sth in** noter qch provisoirement.

pencil case *n* trousse *f* (d'écolier).

pencil sharpener *n* taille-crayon(s) *m inv*.

pendant [pen'dənt] *n* pendentif *m*.

pending [pen'ding] *prep* en attendant ♦ *a* en suspens.

pendulum [pen'jələm] *n* pendule *m*; (*of clock*) balancier *m*.

penetrate [pen'itrāt] *vt* pénétrer dans; pénétrer.

penetrating [pen'itrāting] *a* pénétrant(e).

penetration [penitrā'shən] *n* pénétration *f*.

pen friend *n* correspondant/e.

penguin [pen'gwin] *n* pingouin *m*.

penicillin [penisil'in] *n* pénicilline *f*.

peninsula [pənin'sələ] *n* péninsule *f*.

penis [pē'nis] *n* pénis *m*, verge *f*.

penitence [pen'itəns] *n* repentir *m*.

penitent [pen'itənt] *a* repentant(e).

penitentiary [peniten'chûrē] *n* (*US*) prison *f*.

penknife [pen'nīf] *n* canif *m*.

Penn., Penna. *abbr* (*US*) = *Pennsylvania.*

pen name [pen' nām] *n* nom *m* de plume, pseudonyme *m*.

pennant [pen'ənt] *n* flamme *f*, banderole *f*.

penniless [pen'ēlis] *a* sans le sou.

Pennines [pen'īnz] *npl* Pennines *fpl*.

penny, *pl* **pennies** *or* **pence** [pen'ē, pen'ēz, pens] *n* (*Brit*) penny *m* (*pl* pennies) *(new: 100 in a pound; old: 12 in a shilling; on tend à employer 'pennies' ou 'two-pence piece' etc pour les pièces, 'pence' pour la valeur)*; (*US*) = **cent.**

pen pal *n* correspondant/e.

pension [pen'chən] *n* retraite *f*; (*MIL*) pension *f*.

  pension off *vt* mettre à la retraite.

pensionable [pen'chənəbəl] *a* qui a droit à une retraite.

pensioner [pen'chənûr] *n* (*Brit*) retraité/e.

pension fund *n* caisse *f* de retraite.

pensive [pen'siv] *a* pensif(ive).

pentagon [pen'təgân] *n* pentagone *m*.

Pentecost [pen'təkôst] *n* Pentecôte *f*.

penthouse [pent'hous] *n* appartement *m* (de luxe) en attique.

pent-up [pent'up'] *a* (*feelings*) refoulé(e).

penultimate [pinul'təmit] *a* pénultième, avant-dernier(ière).

penury [pen'yûrē] *n* misère *f*.

people [pē'pəl] *npl* gens *mpl*; personnes *fpl*; (*citizens*) peuple *m* ♦ *n* (*nation, race*) peuple *m* ♦ *vt* peupler; **several** ~ **came** plusieurs personnes sont venues; **I know** ~ **who** ... je connais des gens qui ...; **the room was full of** ~ la salle était pleine de monde *or* de gens; ~ **say that** ... on dit *or* les gens disent que ...; **old** ~ les personnes âgées; **young** ~ les jeunes; **a man of the** ~ un homme du peuple.

pep [pep] *n* (*col*) entrain *m*, dynamisme *m*.

  pep up *vt* (*col*) remonter.

pepper [pep'ûr] *n* poivre *m*; (*vegetable*) poivron *m* ♦ *vt* poivrer.

pepper mill *n* moulin *m* à poivre.

peppermint [pep'ûrmint] *n* (*plant*) menthe poivrée; (*candy*) pastille *f* de menthe.

pepperpot [pep'ûrpât] *n* (*Brit*) poivrière *f*.

pepper shaker [pep'ûr shā'kûr] *n* (*US*) poivrière *f*.

pep talk *n* (*col*) (petit) discours d'encouragement.

per [pûr] *prep* par; ~ **hour** (*miles etc*) à l'heure; (*fee*) (de) l'heure; ~ **kilo** *etc* le kilo *etc*; ~ **day/person** par jour/personne; **as** ~ **your instructions** conformément à vos instructions.

per annum *ad* par an.

per capita *a, ad* par habitant, par personne.

perceive [pûrsēv'] *vt* percevoir; (*notice*) remarquer, s'apercevoir de.

percent [pûrsent'] *ad* pour cent; **a 20** ~ **discount** une réduction de 20 pour cent.

percentage [pûrsen'tij] *n* pourcentage *m*; **on a** ~ **basis** au pourcentage.

perceptible [pûrsep'təbəl] *a* perceptible.

perception [pûrsep'shən] *n* perception *f*; (*insight*) sensibilité *f*.

perceptive [pûrsep'tiv] *a* (*remark, person*) perspicace.

perch [pûrch] *n* (*fish*) perche *f*; (*for bird*) perchoir *m* ♦ *vi* (se) percher.

percolate [pûr'kəlāt] *vt, vi* passer.

percolator [pûr'kəlātûr] *n* percolateur *m*; cafetière *f* électrique.

percussion [pûrkush'ən] *n* percussion *f*.

peremptory [pəremp'tûrē] *a* péremptoire.

perennial [pəren'ēəl] *a* perpétuel(le); (*BOT*) vivace ♦ *n* plante *f* vivace.

perfect *a, n* [pûr'fikt] *a* parfait(e) ♦ *n* (*also*: ~ **tense**) parfait *m* ♦ *vt* [pərfekt'] parfaire; mettre au point; **he's a** ~ **stranger to me** il m'est totalement inconnu.

perfection [pûrfek'shən] *n* perfection *f*.

perfectionist [pûrfek'shənist] *n* perfectionniste *m/f*.

perfectly [pûr'fiktlē] *ad* parfaitement; **I'm** ~ **happy with the situation** cette situation me convient parfaitement; **you know** ~ **well** vous le savez très bien.

perforate [pûr'fûrāt] *vt* perforer, percer.

perforated ulcer *n* (*MED*) ulcère perforé.

perforation [pûrfərā'shən] *n* perforation *f*; (*line of holes*) pointillé *m*.

perform [pûrfôrm'] *vt* (*carry out*) exécuter, remplir; (*concert etc*) jouer, donner ♦ *vi* jouer.

performance [pûrfôr'məns] *n* représentation *f*, spectacle *m*; (*of an artist*) interprétation *f*; (*of player etc*) prestation *f*; (*of car, engine*) performance *f*.

performer [pûrfôr'mûr] *n* artiste *m/f*.

performing [pûrfôr'ming] *a* (*animal*) savant(e).

perfume [pûr'fyōōm] *n* parfum *m* ♦ *vt* parfumer.

perfunctory [pûrfungk'tûrē] *a* négligent(e), pour la forme.

perhaps [pûrhaps'] *ad* peut-être; ~ **he'll** ... peut-être qu'il ...; ~ **so/not** peut-être que oui/que non.

peril [pär'əl] *n* péril *m*.

perilous [pär'ələs] *a* périlleux(euse).

perilously [pär'ələslē] *ad*: **they came ~ close to being caught** ils ont été à deux doigts de se faire prendre.

perimeter [pərim'itûr] *n* périmètre *m*.

perimeter wall *n* mur *m* d'enceinte.

period [pēr'ēəd] *n* période *f*; (*HIST*) époque *f*; (*SCOL*) cours *m*; (*punctuation*) point *m*; (*MED*) règles *fpl* ♦ *a* (*costume, furniture*) d'époque; **for a ~ of three weeks** pour (une période de) trois semaines; **the vacation ~** la période des vacances.

periodic [pērēåd'ik] *a* périodique.

periodical [pērēåd'ikəl] *a* périodique ♦ *n* périodique *m*.

periodically [pērēåd'iklē] *ad* périodiquement.

peripatetic [päripətet'ik] *a* (*salesman*) ambulant; (*teacher*) qui travaille dans plusieurs établissements.

peripheral [pərif'ûrəl] *a* périphérique ♦ *n* (*COMPUT*) périphérique *m*.

periphery [pərif'ûrē] *n* périphérie *f*.

periscope [pär'iskōp] *n* périscope *m*.

perish [pär'ish] *vi* périr, mourir; (*decay*) se détériorer.

perishable [pär'ishəbəl] *a* périssable.

perishables [pär'ishəbəlz] *npl* denrées *fpl* périssables.

peritonitis [pär'itənī'tis] *n* péritonite *f*.

perjure [pûr'jûr] *vt*: **to ~ o.s.** se parjurer.

perjury [pûr'jûrē] *n* (*LAW: in court*) faux témoignage; (*breach of oath*) parjure *m*.

perk [pûrk] *n* (*col*) avantage *m*, à-côté *m*.

perk up *vi* (*col: cheer up*) se ragaillardir.

perky [pûr'kē] *a* (*cheerful*) guilleret(te), gai(e).

perm [pûrm] *n* (*for hair*) permanente *f* ♦ *vt*: **to have one's hair ~ed** se faire faire une permanente.

permanence [pûr'mənəns] *n* permanence *f*.

permanent [pûr'mənənt] *a* permanent(e); (*job, position*) permanent, fixe; (*dye, ink*) indélébile; **I'm not ~ here** je ne suis pas ici à titre définitif, ~ **address** adresse habituelle.

permanently [pûr'mənəntlē] *ad* de façon permanente.

permeable [pûr'mēəbəl] *a* perméable.

permeate [pûr'mēāt] *vi* s'infiltrer ♦ *vt* s'infiltrer dans; pénétrer.

permissible [pûrmis'əbəl] *a* permis(e), acceptable.

permission [pûrmish'ən] *n* permission *f*, autorisation *f*; **to give sb ~ to do sth** donner à qn la permission de faire qch.

permissive [pûrmis'iv] *a* tolérant(e); **the ~ society** la société de tolérance.

permit *n* [pûr'mit] permis *m*; (*entrance pass*) autorisation *f*, laisser-passer *m*; (*for goods*) licence *f* ♦ *vt* [pərmit'] permettre; **to ~ sb to do** autoriser qn à faire, permettre à qn de faire; **weather ~ting** si le temps le permet.

permutation [pûrmyətā'shən] *n* permutation *f*.

pernicious [pûrnish'əs] *a* pernicieux(euse), nocif(ive).

pernickety [pûrnik'ətē] *a* (*Brit*) = **persnickety**.

perpendicular [pûrpəndik'yəlûr] *a*, *n* perpendiculaire (*f*).

perpetrate [pûr'pitrāt] *vt* perpétrer, commettre.

perpetual [pûrpech'ōōəl] *a* perpétuel(le).

perpetuate [pûrpech'ōōāt] *vt* perpétuer.

perpetuity [pûrpətōō'itē] *n*: **in ~** à perpétuité.

perplex [pûrpleks'] *vt* rendre perplexe; (*complicate*) embrouiller.

perplexing [pûrplek'sing] *a* embarrassant(e).

perquisites [pûr'kwizits] *npl* (*also:* **perks**) avantages *mpl* annexes.

persecute [pûr'səkyōōt] *vt* persécuter.

persecution [pûrsəkyōō'shən] *n* persécution *f*.

perseverance [pûrsəvēr'əns] *n* persévérance *f*, ténacité *f*.

persevere [pûrsəvēr'] *vi* persévérer.

Persia [pûr'zhə] *n* Perse *f*.

Persian [pûr'zhən] *a* persan(e) ♦ *n* (*LING*) persan *m*; **the (~) Gulf** le golfe Persique.

persist [pûrsist'] *vi*: **to ~ (in doing)** persister (à faire), s'obstiner (à faire).

persistence [pûrsis'təns] *n* persistance *f*, obstination *f*; opiniâtreté *f*.

persistent [pûrsis'tənt] *a* persistant(e), tenace; (*lateness, rain*) persistant.

persnickety [pûrsnik'ətē] *a* (*US col*) pointilleux(euse), tatillon(ne); (*task*) minutieux(euse).

person [pûr'sən] *n* personne *f*; **in ~** en personne; **on** *or* **about one's ~** sur soi; ~ **to ~ call** (*TEL*) appel *m* avec préavis.

personable [pûr'sənəbəl] *a* de belle prestance, au physique attrayant.

personal [pûr'sənəl] *a* personnel(le); ~ **belongings**, ~ **effects** effets personnels; ~ **hygiene** hygiène *f* intime; **a ~ interview** un entretien.

personal allowance *n* (*TAX*) part *f* du revenu non imposable.

personal assistant (PA) *n* secrétaire personnel(le).

personal call *n* (*TEL*) communication *f* avec préavis.

personal column *n* annonces personnelles.

personal computer (PC) *n* ordinateur individuel, PC *m*.

personal details *npl* (*on form etc*) coordonnées *fpl*.

personality [pûrsənal'itē] *n* personnalité *f*.

personally [pûr'sənəlē] *ad* personnellement.

personal organizer *n* agenda *m* modulaire.

personal property *n* biens personnels.

personify [pûrsån'əfī] *vt* personnifier.

personnel [pûrsənel'] *n* personnel *m*.

personnel department *n* service *m* du personnel.

personnel manager *n* chef *m* du personnel.

perspective [pûrspek'tiv] *n* perspective *f*; **to get sth into ~** ramener qch à sa juste mesure.

Perspex [pûr'speks] *n* ® (*Brit*) matière plastique transparente, employée surtout comme verre de sécurité.

perspicacity [pûrspəka'sitē] *n* perspicacité *f*.

perspiration [pûrspərā'shən] *n* transpiration *f*.

perspire [pûrspīūr'] *vi* transpirer.

persuade [pûrswād'] *vt*: **to ~ sb to do sth** persuader qn de faire qch, amener *or* décider qn à faire qch; **to ~ sb of sth/that** persuader qn de qch/que.

persuasion [pûrswā'zhən] *n* persuasion *f*; (*creed*) conviction *f*.

persuasive [pûrswā'siv] *a* persuasif(ive).

pert [pûrt] *a* coquin(e), mutin(e).

pertaining [pûrtān'ing]: **~ to** *prep* relatif(ive) à.

pertinent [pûr'tənənt] *a* pertinent(e).

perturb [pûrtûrb'] *vt* troubler, inquiéter.

perturbing [pûrtûrb'ing] *a* troublant(e).

Peru [pərōō'] *n* Pérou *m*.

perusal [pərōō'zəl] *n* lecture (attentive).

Peruvian [pərōō'vēən] *a* péruvien(ne) ♦ *n* Péruvien/ne.

pervade [pûrvād'] *vt* se répandre dans, envahir.

pervasive [pûrvā'siv] *a* (*smell*) pénétrant(e); (*influence*) insidieux(euse); (*gloom, ideas*) diffus(e).

perverse [pûrvûrs'] *a* pervers(e); (*stubborn*) entêté(e), contrariant(e).

perversion [pûrvûr'zhən] *n* perversion *f*.

perversity [pûrvûr'sitē] *n* perversité *f*.

pervert *n* [pûr'vûrt] perverti/e ♦ *vt* [pûrvûrt'] pervertir.

pessimism [pes'əmizəm] *n* pessimisme *m*.

pessimist [pes'əmist] *n* pessimiste *m/f*.

pessimistic [pesəmis'tik] *a* pessimiste.

pest [pest] *n* animal *m* (*or* insecte *m*) nuisible; (*fig*) fléau *m*.

pest control *n* lutte *f* contre les nuisibles.

pester [pes'tûr] *vt* importuner, harceler.

pesticide [pes'tisīd] *n* pesticide *m*.

pestilent [pes'tələnt], **pestilential** [pestələn'shəl] *a* (*col: exasperating*) empoisonnant(e).

pestle [pes'əl] *n* pilon *m*.

pet [pet] *n* animal familier; (*favorite*) chouchou *m* ♦ *vt* choyer ♦ *vi* (*col*) se peloter; **~ lion** *etc* lion *etc* apprivoisé.

petal [pet'əl] *n* pétale *m*.

pet door *n* (*US*) chatière *f*.

peter [pē'tûr]: **to ~ out** *vi* s'épuiser; s'affaiblir.

petite [pətēt'] *a* menu(e).

petition [pətish'ən] *n* pétition *f* ♦ *vt* adresser une pétition à ♦ *vi*: **to ~ for divorce** demander le divorce.

pet name *n* (*Brit*) petit nom.

petrified [pet'rəfīd] *a* (*fig*) mort(e) de peur.

petrify [pet'rəfī] *vt* pétrifier.

petrochemical [petrōkem'ikəl] *a* pétrochimique.

petrodollars [petrōdâl'ûrz] *npl* pétrodollars *mpl*.

petrol [pet'rəl] *n* (*Brit*) essence *f*.

petrol can *n* (*Brit*) bidon *m* à essence.

petrol engine *n* (*Brit*) moteur *m* à essence.

petroleum [pətrō'lēəm] *n* pétrole *m*.

petroleum jelly *n* vaseline *f*.

petrol pump *n* (*Brit: in car, at garage*) pompe *f* à essence.

petrol station *n* (*Brit*) station-service *f*.

petrol tank *n* (*Brit*) réservoir *m* d'essence.

petticoat [pet'ēkōt] *n* jupon *m*.

pettifogging [pet'ēfâging] *a* chicanier(ière).

pettiness [pet'ēnis] *n* mesquinerie *f*.

petty [pet'ē] *a* (*mean*) mesquin(e); (*unimportant*) insignifiant(e), sans importance.

petty cash *n* caisse *f* des dépenses courantes, petite caisse.

petty officer *n* second-maître *m*.

petulant [pech'ələnt] *a* irritable.

pew [pyōō] *n* banc *m* (d'église).

pewter [pyōō'tûr] *n* étain *m*.

Pfc *abbr* (*US MIL*) = *private first class.*

PG *n abbr* (*CINEMA*: = *parental guidance*) *avis des parents recommandé.*

PGA *n abbr* = *Professional Golfers Association.*

PH *n abbr* (*US MIL*: = *Purple Heart*) *décoration accordée aux blessés de guerre.*

p&h *abbr* (*US*: = *postage and handling*) frais *mpl* de port.

PHA *n abbr* (*US*: = *Public Housing Administration*) *organisme d'aide à la construction.*

phallic [fal'ik] *a* phallique.

phantom [fan'təm] *n* fantôme *m*; (*vision*) fantasme *m*.

Pharaoh [fär'ō] *n* pharaon *m*.

pharmaceutical [fârməsōō'tikəl] *a* pharmaceutique ♦ *n*: **~s** produits *mpl* pharmaceutiques.

pharmacist [fâr'məsist] *n* pharmacien/ne.

pharmacy [fâr'məsē] *n* pharmacie *f*.

phase [fāz] *n* phase *f*, période *f* ♦ *vt*: **to ~ sth in/out** introduire/supprimer qch progressivement.

PhD *abbr* (= *Doctor of Philosophy*) *title* ≈ Docteur *m* en Droit *or* Lettres *etc* ♦ *n* ≈ doctorat *m*; titulaire *m* d'un doctorat.

pheasant [fez'ənt] *n* faisan *m*.

phenomenon, pl phenomena [finâm'ənân, -nə] *n* phénomène *m*.

phew [fyōō] *excl* ouf!

phial [fī'əl] *n* fiole *f*.

philanderer [filan'dûrûr] *n* don Juan *m*.

philanthropic [filənthrâp'ik] *a* philanthropique.

philanthropist [filan'thrəpist] *n* philanthrope *m/f*.

philatelist [filat'əlist] *n* philatéliste *m/f*.

philately [filat'əlē] *n* philatélie *f*.

Philippines [fil'ipēnz] *npl* (*also*: **Philippine Islands**): **the ~** les Philippines *fpl*.

philosopher [filâs'əfûr] *n* philosophe *m*.

philosophical [filəsâf'ikəl] *a* philosophique.

philosophy [filâs'əfē] *n* philosophie *f*.

phlegm [flem] *n* flegme *m*.

phlegmatic [flegmat'ik] *a* flegmatique.

phobia [fō'bēə] *n* phobie *f*.

phone [fōn] *n* téléphone *m* ♦ *vt* téléphoner à ♦ *vi* téléphoner; **to be on the ~** avoir le téléphone; (*be calling*) être au téléphone.

phone back *vt*, *vi* rappeler.

phone book *n* annuaire *m*.

phone booth, (*Brit*) **phone box** *n* cabine *f* téléphonique.

phone call *n* coup *m* de fil *or* de téléphone.

phone-in [fōn'in] *n* (*Brit RADIO*, *TV*) programme *m* à ligne ouverte.

phonetics [fənet'iks] *n* phonétique *f*.

phoney [fō'nē] *a* faux(fausse), factice ♦ *n* (*person*) charlatan *m*; fumiste *m/f*.

phonograph [fō'nəgraf] *n* (*US*) électro-

phone *m*.
phony [fō'nē] *a, n* = **phoney.**
phosphate [fâs'fāt] *n* phosphate *m*.
phosphorus [fâs'fûrəs] *n* phosphore *m*.
photo [fō'tō] *n* photo *f*.
photo... [fō'tō] *prefix* photo....
photocopier [fō'təkápēûr] *n* copieur *m*.
photocopy [fō'təkápē] *n* photocopie *f* ♦ *vt* photocopier.
photoelectric [fōtōilek'trik] *a* photoélectrique; ~ **cell** cellule *f* photoélectrique.
photogenic [fōtəjen'ik] *a* photogénique.
photograph [fō'təgraf] *n* photographie *f* ♦ *vt* photographier; **to take a** ~ **of sb** prendre qn en photo.
photographer [fətâg'rəfûr] *n* photographe *m/f*.
photographic [fōtəgraf'ik] *a* photographique.
photography [fətâg'rəfē] *n* photographie *f*.
photostat [fō'təstat] *n* photocopie *f*, photostat *m*.
photosynthesis [fōtəsin'thəsis] *n* photosynthèse *f*.
phrase [frāz] *n* expression *f*; (*LING*) locution *f* ♦ *vt* exprimer; (*letter*) rédiger.
phrase book *n* recueil *m* d'expressions (pour touristes).
physical [fiz'ikəl] *a* physique; ~ **examination** examen médical; ~ **education** éducation physique; ~ **exercises** gymnastique *f*.
physically [fiz'ikle] *ad* physiquement.
physician [fizish'ən] *n* médecin *m*.
physicist [fiz'əsist] *n* physicien/ne.
physics [fiz'iks] *n* physique *f*.
physiological [fizēəlâj'ikəl] *a* physiologique.
physiology [fizēâl'əjē] *n* physiologie *f*.
physiotherapist [fizēōthär'əpist] *n* kinésithérapeute *m/f*.
physiotherapy [fizēōthär'əpē] *n* kinésithérapie *f*.
physique [fizēk'] *n* (*appearance*) physique *m*; (*health etc*) constitution *f*.
pianist [pēan'ist] *n* pianiste *m/f*.
piano [pēan'ō] *n* piano *m*.
piano accordion *n* (*Brit*) accordéon *m* à touches.
Picardy [pik'ûrdē] *n* Picardie *f*.
piccolo [pik'əlō] *n* piccolo *m*.
pick [pik] *n* (*tool: also:* ~**ax**) pic *m*, pioche *f* ♦ *vt* choisir; (*gather*) cueillir; (*scab, spot*) gratter, écorcher; **take your** ~ faites votre choix; **the** ~ **of** le(la) meilleur(e) de; **to** ~ **a bone** ronger un os; **to** ~ **one's nose** se mettre le doigt dans le nez; **to** ~ **one's teeth** se curer les dents; **to** ~ **sb's brains** faire appel aux lumières de qn; **to** ~ **pockets** pratiquer le vol à la tire; **to** ~ **a fight with sb** chercher la bagarre avec qn.
pick off *vt* (*kill*) (viser soigneusement et) abattre.
pick on *vt fus* (*person*) harceler.
pick out *vt* choisir; (*distinguish*) distinguer.
pick up *vi* (*improve*) remonter, s'améliorer ♦ *vt* ramasser; (*telephone*) décrocher; (*collect*) passer prendre; (*AUT: give lift to*) prendre; (*learn*) apprendre; (*RADIO, TV, TEL*) capter; **to** ~ **up speed** prendre de la vitesse; **to** ~ **o.s. up** se relever; **to** ~ **up where one left off** reprendre là où l'on s'est arrêté.

pickax, (*Brit*) **pickaxe** [pik'aks] *n* pioche *f*.
picket [pik'it] *n* (*in strike*) gréviste *m/f* participant à un piquet de grève; piquet *m* de grève ♦ *vt* mettre un piquet de grève devant.
picket line *n* piquet *m* de grève.
pickings [pik'ingz] *npl*: **there are rich** ~ **to be had in** ... il y a gros à gagner dans ....
pickle [pik'əl] *n* (*also:* ~**s**: *as condiment*) pickles *mpl*; (*fig*): **in a** ~ dans le pétrin ♦ *vt* conserver dans du vinaigre *or* dans de la saumure.
pick-me-up [pik'mēup] *n* remontant *m*.
pickpocket [pik'pâkit] *n* pickpocket *m*.
pickup [pik'up] *n* (*also:* ~ **truck**) camionnette *f*; (*Brit: on record player*) bras *m* pick-up.
picnic [pik'nik] *n* pique-nique *m* ♦ *vi* pique-niquer.
picnicker [pik'nikûr] *n* pique-niqueur/euse.
pictorial [piktōr'ēəl] *a* illustré(e).
picture [pik'chûr] *n* (*also TV*) image *f*; (*painting*) peinture *f*, tableau *m*; (*photograph*) photo(graphie) *f*; (*drawing*) dessin *m*; (*film*) film *m* ♦ *vt* se représenter; (*describe*) dépeindre, représenter; **the** ~**s** (*Brit*) le cinéma; **to take a** ~ **of sb/sth** prendre qn/qch en photo; **the overall** ~ le tableau d'ensemble; **to put sb in the** ~ mettre qn au courant.
picture book *n* livre *m* d'images.
picturesque [pikchəresk'] *a* pittoresque.
picture window *n* baie vitrée, fenêtre *f* panoramique.
piddling [pid'ling] *a* (*col*) insignifiant(e).
pidgin [pij'in] *a*: ~ **English** pidgin *m*.
pie [pī] *n* tourte *f*; (*of meat*) pâté *m* en croûte.
piebald [pī'bôld] *a* pie *inv*.
piece [pēs] *n* morceau *m*; (*of land*) parcelle *f*; (*item*): **a** ~ **of furniture/advice** un meuble/conseil; (*CHECKERS etc*) pion *m* ♦ *vt*: **to** ~ **together** rassembler; **in** ~**s** (*broken*) en morceaux, en miettes; (*not yet assembled*) en pièces détachées; **to take to** ~**s** démonter; **in one** ~ (*object*) intact(e); **to get back all in one** ~ (*person*) rentrer sain et sauf; **a 10 cents** ~ une pièce de 10 cents; ~ **by** ~ morceau par morceau; **a six-** ~ **band** un orchestre de six musiciens; **to say one's** ~ réciter son morceau.
piecemeal [pēs'mēl] *ad* par bouts.
piece rate *n* taux *m or* tarif *m* à la pièce.
piecework [pēs'wûrk] *n* travail *m* aux pièces *or* à la pièce.
pie chart *n* graphique *m* à secteurs, camembert *m*.
pie crust pastry *n* (*US*) pâte brisée.
Piedmont [pēd'mânt] *n* Piémont *m*.
pier [pēr] *n* jetée *f*; (*of bridge etc*) pile *f*.
pierce [pērs] *vt* percer, transpercer; **to have one's ears** ~**d** se faire percer les oreilles.
piercing [pērs'ing] *a* (*cry*) perçant(e).
piety [pī'ətē] *n* piété *f*.
piffling [pif'ling] *a* insignifiant(e).
pig [pig] *n* cochon *m*, porc *m*.
pigeon [pij'ən] *n* pigeon *m*.
pigeonhole [pij'ənhōl] *n* casier *m*.
pigeon-toed [pij'əntōd] *a* marchant les pieds en dedans.
piggy bank [pig'ē bangk] *n* tirelire *f*.
pigheaded [pig'hedid] *a* entêté(e), têtu(e).

piglet [pig'lit] *n* petit cochon, porcelet *m*.
pigment [pig'mənt] *n* pigment *m*.
pigmentation [pigməntā'shən] *n* pigmentation *f*.
pigmy [pig'mē] *n* = **pygmy**.
pigskin [pig'skin] *n* (peau *f* de) porc *m*.
pigsty [pig'stī] *n* porcherie *f*.
pigtail [pig'tāl] *n* natte *f*, tresse *f*.
pike [pīk] *n* (*spear*) pique *f*; (*fish*) brochet *m*.
pilchard [pil'chûrd] *n* pilchard *m* (*sorte de sardine*).
pile [pīl] *n* (*pillar, of books*) pile *f*; (*heap*) tas *m*; (*of carpet*) épaisseur *f* ♦ *vb* (*also:* ~ **up**) *vt* empiler, entasser ♦ *vi* s'entasser; **in a ~** en tas.
   pile on *vt*: **to ~ it on** (*col*) exagérer.
piles [pīlz] *npl* hémorroïdes *fpl*.
pileup [pīl'up] *n* (*AUT*) télescopage *m*, collision *f* en série.
pilfer [pil'fûr] *vt* chaparder ♦ *vi* commettre des larcins.
pilfering [pil'fûring] *n* chapardage *m*.
pilgrim [pil'grim] *n* pèlerin *m*.
pilgrimage [pil'grəmij] *n* pèlerinage *m*.
pill [pil] *n* pilule *f*; **the ~** la pilule; **to be on the ~** prendre la pilule.
pillage [pil'ij] *vt* piller.
pillar [pil'ûr] *n* pilier *m*.
pillar box *n* (*Brit*) boîte *f* aux lettres.
pillion [pil'yən] *n* (*of motor cycle*) siège *m* arrière; **to ride ~** être derrière; (*on horse*) être en croupe.
pillory [pil'ûrē] *n* pilori *m* ♦ *vt* mettre au pilori.
pillow [pil'ō] *n* oreiller *m*.
pillowcase [pil'ōkās], **pillowslip** [pil'ōslip] *n* taie *f* d'oreiller.
pilot [pī'lət] *n* pilote *m* ♦ *cpd* (*plan etc*) pilote, expérimental(e) ♦ *vt* piloter.
pilot boat *n* bateau-pilote *m*.
pilot light *n* veilleuse *f*.
pimento [pimen'tō] *n* piment *m*.
pimp [pimp] *n* souteneur *m*, maquereau *m*.
pimple [pim'pəl] *n* bouton *m*.
pimply [pim'plē] *a* boutonneux(euse).
pin [pin] *n* épingle *f*; (*TECH*) cheville *f*; (*US: also:* **clothes ~**) pince *f* à linge; (*Brit: drawing ~*) punaise *f*; (*in grenade*) goupille *f*; (*Brit ELEC: of plug*) broche *f* ♦ *vt* épingler; **~s and needles** fourmis *fpl*; **to ~ sb against/to** clouer qn contre/à; **to ~ sth on sb** (*fig*) mettre qch sur le dos de qn.
   pin down *vt* (*fig*): **to ~ sb down** obliger qn à répondre; **there's something strange here but I can't quite ~ it down** il y a quelque chose d'étrange ici, mais je n'arrive pas exactement à savoir quoi.
pinafore [pin'əfôr] *n* tablier *m*.
pinafore dress *n* robe-chasuble *f*.
pinball [pin'bôl] *n* flipper *m*.
pincers [pin'sûrz] *npl* tenailles *fpl*.
pinch [pinch] *n* pincement *m*; (*of salt etc*) pincée *f* ♦ *vt* pincer; (*col: steal*) piquer, chiper ♦ *vi* (*shoe*) serrer; **at a ~** à la rigueur; **to feel the ~** (*fig*) se ressentir des restrictions (*or* de la récession *etc*).
pinched [pincht] *a* (*drawn*) tiré(e); **~ with cold** transi(e) de froid; **~ for** (*short of*): **~ for money** à court d'argent; **~ for space** à l'étroit.

pincushion [pin'kōōshən] *n* pelote *f* à épingles.
pine [pīn] *n* (*also:* ~ **tree**) pin *m* ♦ *vi*: **to ~ for** aspirer à, désirer ardemment.
   pine away *vi* dépérir.
pineapple [pīn'apəl] *n* ananas *m*.
pine nut, *n* pignon *m*.
ping [ping] *n* (*noise*) tintement *m*.
ping-pong [ping'pông] *n* ® ping-pong *m* ®.
pink [pingk] *a* rose ♦ *n* (*color*) rose *m*; (*BOT*) œillet *m*, mignardise *f*.
pinking shears [ping'king shirz], **pinking scissors** [ping'king siz'ûrz] *npl* ciseaux *mpl* à denteler.
pin money *n* argent *m* de poche.
pinnacle [pin'əkəl] *n* pinacle *m*.
pinpoint [pin'point] *vt* indiquer (avec précision).
pinstripe [pin'strīp] *n* rayure très fine.
pint [pīnt] *n* pinte *f* (*US = 0.47 l; Brit = 0.57 l*).
pinup [pin'up] *n* pin-up *f inv*.
pinwheel [pin'wēl] *n* (*US*) soleil *m* (*feu d'artifice*).
pioneer [pīənēr'] *n* explorateur/trice; (*early settler*) pionnier *m*; (*fig*) pionnier, précurseur *m* ♦ *vt* être un pionnier de.
pious [pī'əs] *a* pieux(euse).
pip [pip] *n* (*seed*) pépin *m*; (*Brit: time signal on radio*) top *m*.
pipe [pīp] *n* tuyau *m*, conduite *f*; (*for smoking*) pipe *f*; (*MUS*) pipeau *m* ♦ *vt* amener par tuyau; **~s** *npl* (*also:* **bag~s**) cornemuse *f*.
   pipe down *vi* (*col*) se taire.
pipe cleaner *n* cure-pipe *m*.
piped music [pīpt myōō'zik] *n* musique *f* de fond.
pipe dream *n* chimère *f*, utopie *f*.
pipeline [pīp'līn] *n* (*for gas*) gazoduc *m*, pipeline *m*; (*for oil*) oléoduc *m*, pipeline; **it is in the ~** (*fig*) c'est en route, ça va se faire.
piper [pī'pûr] *n* joueur/euse de pipeau (*or* de cornemuse).
pipe tobacco *n* tabac *m* pour la pipe.
piping [pī'ping] *ad*: **~ hot** très chaud(e).
piquant [pē'kənt] *a* piquant(e).
pique [pēk] *n* dépit *m*.
piracy [pī'rəsē] *n* piraterie *f*.
pirate [pī'rət] *n* pirate *m* ♦ *vt* (*record, video, book*) pirater.
pirate radio (station) *n* (station *f* de) radio *f* pirate.
pirouette [pirōōet'] *n* pirouette *f* ♦ *vi* faire une *or* des pirouette(s).
Pisces [pī'sēz] *n* les Poissons *mpl*; **to be ~** être des Poissons.
piss [pis] *vi* (*col!*) pisser (!); **~ off!** tire-toi! (!).
pissed [pist] *a* (*Brit col: drunk*) bourré(e).
pistol [pis'təl] *n* pistolet *m*.
piston [pis'tən] *n* piston *m*.
pit [pit] *n* trou *m*, fosse *f*; (*also:* **coal ~**) puits *m* de mine; (*also:* **orchestra ~**) fosse d'orchestre; (*US: of fruit*) noyau *m* ♦ *vt* (*US: fruit*) dénoyauter; **to ~ sb against sb** opposer qn à qn; **to ~ o.s. against** se mesurer à; **~s** *npl* (*in motor racing*) aire *f* de service.
pitapat [pit'əpat] *ad*: **to go ~** (*heart*) battre la chamade; (*rain*) tambouriner.
pitch [pich] *n* (*throw*) lancement *m*; (*MUS*) ton

m; (*of voice*) hauteur *f*; (*fig: degree*) degré *m*; (*also:* **sales** ~) baratin *m*, boniment *m*; (*Brit SPORT*) terrain *m*; (*NAUT*) tangage *m*; (*tar*) poix *f* ♦ *vt* (*throw*) lancer; (*tent*) dresser; (*set: price, message*) adapter, positionner ♦ *vi* (*NAUT*) tanguer; (*fall*): **to** ~ **into/off** tomber dans/de; **to be** ~**ed forward** être projeté(e) en avant; **at this** ~ à ce rythme.

pitch-black [pich'blak'] *a* noir(e) comme poix.
pitched battle [picht bat'əl] *n* bataille rangée.
pitcher [pich'ûr] *n* cruche *f*.
pitchfork [pich'fôrk] *n* fourche *f*.
piteous [pit'ēəs] *a* pitoyable.
pitfall [pit'fôl] *n* trappe *f*, piège *m*.
pith [pith] *n* (*of plant*) moellc *f*; (*of orange*) Intérieur *m* de l'écorce; (*fig*) essence *f*; vigueur *f*.
pithy [pith'ē] *a* piquant(e); vigoureux(euse).
pitiable [pit'ēəbəl] *a* pitoyable.
pitiful [pit'ifəl] *a* (*touching*) pitoyable; (*contemptible*) lamentable.
pitifully [pit'ifəlē] *ad* pitoyablement; lamentablement.
pitiless [pit'ilis] *a* impitoyable.
pittance [pit'əns] *n* salaire *m* de misère.
pitted [pit'id] *a*: ~ **with** (*chickenpox*) grêlé(e) par; (*rust*) piqué(e) de.
pity [pit'ē] *n* pitié *f* ♦ *vt* plaindre; **what a** ~! quel dommage!; **it is a** ~ **that you can't come** c'est dommage que vous ne puissiez venir; **to have** *or* **take** ~ **on sb** avoir pitié de qn.
pitying [pit'ēing] *a* compatissant(e).
pivot [piv'ət] *n* pivot *m* ♦ *vi* pivoter.
pixel [pik'səl] *n* (*COMPUT*) pixel *m*.
pixie [pik'sē] *n* lutin *m*.
pizza [pēt'sə] *n* pizza *f*.
P&L *abbr* = **profit and loss.**
placard [plak'ârd] *n* affiche *f*.
placate [plā'kāt] *vt* apaiser, calmer.
placatory [plā'kətôrē] *a* d'apaisement, léniflant(e).
place [plās] *n* endroit *m*, lieu *m*; (*proper position, rank, seat*) place *f*; (*house*) maison *f*, logement *m*; (*in street names*): **Laurel P**~ ≈ rue des Lauriers; (*home*): **at/to his** ~ chez lui ♦ *vt* (*position*) placer, mettre; (*identify*) situer; reconnaître; **to take** ~ avoir lieu; (*occur*) se produire; **from** ~ **to** ~ d'un endroit à l'autre; **all over the** ~ partout; **out of** ~ (*not suitable*) déplacé(e), inopportun(e); **I feel out of** ~ **here** je ne me sens pas à ma place ici; **in the first** ~ d'abord, en premier; **to put sb in his** ~ (*fig*) remettre qn à sa place; **he's going** ~**s** (*fig: col*) il fait son chemin; **it is not my** ~ **to do it** ce n'est pas à moi de le faire; **to** ~ **an order with sb (for)** (*COMM*) passer commande à qn (de); **to be** ~**d** (*in race, exam*) se placer; **how are you** ~**d next week?** comment ça se présente pour la semaine prochaine?
placebo [pləsē'bō] *n* placebo *m*.
place mat *n* set *m* de table; (*in linen etc*) napperon *m*.
placement [plās'mənt] *n* placement *m*; poste *m*.
place name *n* nom *m* de lieu.
placenta [pləsen'tə] *n* placenta *m*.

placid [plas'id] *a* placide.
placidity [pləsid'itē] *n* placidité *f*.
plagiarism [plā'jərizəm] *n* plagiat *m*.
plagiarist [plā'jûrist] *n* plagiaire *m/f*.
plagiarize [plā'jərīz] *vt* plagier.
plague [plāg] *n* fléau *m*; (*MED*) peste *f* ♦ *vt* (*fig*) tourmenter; **to** ~ **sb with questions** harceler qn de questions.
plaice [plās] *n* (*pl inv*) carrelet *m*.
plaid [plad] *n* tissu écossais.
plain [plān] *a* (*clear*) clair(e), évident(e); (*simple*) simple, ordinaire; (*frank*) franc(franche); (*not handsome*) quelconque, ordinaire; (*cigarette*) sans filtre; (*without seasoning etc*) nature *inv*; (*in one color*) uni(e) ♦ *ad* franchement, carrément ♦ *n* plaine *f*; **in** ~ **clothes** (*police*) en civil; **to make sth** ~ **to sb** faire clairement comprendre qch à qn.
plain chocolate *n* chocolat *m* à croquer.
plainly [plān'lē] *ad* clairement; (*frankly*) carrément, sans détours.
plainness [plān'nis] *n* simplicité *f*.
plaintiff [plān'tif] *n* plaignant/e.
plaintive [plān'tiv] *a* plaintif(ive).
plait [plat] *n* tresse *f*, natte *f* ♦ *vt* tresser, natter.
plan [plan] *n* plan *m*; (*scheme*) projet *m* ♦ *vt* (*think in advance*) projeter; (*prepare*) organiser ♦ *vi* faire des projets; **to** ~ **to do** projeter de faire; **how long do you** ~ **to stay?** combien de temps comptez-vous rester?
plane [plān] *n* (*AVIAT*) avion *m*; (*tree*) platane *m*; (*tool*) rabot *m*; (*ART, MATH etc*) plan *m* ♦ *a* plan(e), plat(e) ♦ *vt* (*with tool*) raboter.
planet [plan'it] *n* planète *f*.
planetarium [planitär'ēəm] *n* planétarium *m*.
plank [plangk] *n* planche *f*; (*POL*) point *m* d'un programme.
plankton [plangk'tən] *n* plancton *m*.
planner [plan'ûr] *n* planificateur/trice; (*chart*) planning *m*; **city** *or* (*Brit*) **town** ~ urbaniste *m/f*.
planning [plan'ing] *n* planification *f*; **family** ~ planning familial.
plant [plant] *n* plante *f*; (*machinery*) matériel *m*; (*factory*) usine *f* ♦ *vt* planter; (*bomb*) déposer, poser.
plantation [plantā'shən] *n* plantation *f*.
plant pot *n* (*Brit*) pot *m* de fleurs.
plaque [plak] *n* plaque *f*.
plasma [plaz'mə] *n* plasma *m*.
plaster [plas'tûr] *n* plâtre *m*; (*Brit: also:* **sticking** ~) pansement adhésif ♦ *vt* plâtrer; (*cover*): **to** ~ **with** couvrir de; **in** ~ (*Brit: leg etc*) dans le plâtre; ~ **of Paris** plâtre à mouler.
plaster cast *n* (*MED*) plâtre *m*; (*model, statue*) moule *m*.
plastered [plas'tûrd] *a* (*col*) soûl(e).
plasterer [plas'tərûr] *n* plâtrier *m*.
plastic [plas'tik] *n* plastique *m* ♦ *a* (*made of plastic*) en plastique; (*flexible*) plastique, malléable; (*art*) plastique.
plastic bag *n* sac *m* en plastique.
plastic surgery *n* chirurgie *f* esthétique.
plate [plāt] *n* (*dish*) assiette *f*; (*sheet of metal, on door, PHOT*) plaque *f*; (*TYP*) cliché *m*; (*in book*) gravure *f*; (*AUT: license* ~) plaque mi-

néralogique; **gold/silver** ~ (*dishes*) vaisselle *f* d'or/d'argent.

plateau, ~**s** *or* ~**x** [platō', -z] *n* plateau *m*.

plateful [plāt'fəl] *n* assiette *f*, assiettée *f*.

plate glass *n* verre *m* à vitre, vitre *f*.

platen [plat'ən] *n* (*on typewriter, printer*) rouleau *m*.

platform [plat'fôrm] *n* (*at meeting*) tribune *f*; (*Brit: of bus*) plate-forme *f*; (*stage*) estrade *f*; (*RAIL*) quai *m*; **the train leaves from** ~ **7** le train part de la voie 7.

platinum [plat'ənəm] *n* platine *m*.

platitude [plat'ətōōd] *n* platitude *f*, lieu commun.

platoon [plətōōn'] *n* peloton *m*.

platter [plat'ûr] *n* plat *m*.

plaudits [plô'dits] *npl* applaudissements *mpl*.

plausible [plô'zəbəl] *a* plausible; (*person*) convaincant(e).

play [plā] *n* jeu *m*; (*THEATER*) pièce *f* (de théâtre); ♦ *vt* (*game*) jouer à; (*team, opponent*) jouer contre; (*instrument*) jouer de; (*part, piece of music, note*) jouer ♦ *vi* jouer; **to bring** *or* **call into** ~ faire entrer en jeu; ~ **on words** jeu de mots; **to** ~ **a trick on sb** jouer un tour à qn; **they're** ~**ing at soldiers** ils jouent aux soldats; **to** ~ **for time** (*fig*) chercher à gagner du temps; **to** ~ **into sb's hands** (*fig*) faire le jeu de qn.

play around *vi* (*person*) s'amuser.

play along *vi* (*fig*): **to** ~ **along with** (*person*) entrer dans le jeu de.

play back *vt* repasser, réécouter.

play down *vt* minimiser.

play on *vt fus* (*sb's feelings, credulity*) jouer sur; **to** ~ **on sb's nerves** porter sur les nerfs de qn.

play up *vi* (*Brit: cause trouble*) faire des siennes.

playact [plā'akt] *vi* jouer la comédie.

playboy [plā'boi] *n* playboy *m*.

played-out [plād'out] *a* épuisé(e).

player [plā'ûr] *n* joueur/euse; (*THEATER*) acteur/trice; (*MUS*) musicien/ne.

playful [plā'fəl] *a* enjoué(e).

playgoer [plā'gōūr] *n* amateur/trice de théâtre, habitué/e des théâtres.

playground [plā'ground] *n* cour *f* de récréation.

playgroup [plā'grōōp] *n* garderie *f*.

playing card [plā'ing kârd] *n* carte *f* à jouer.

playing field *n* terrain *m* de sport.

playmate [plā'māt] *n* camarade *m/f*, copain/copine.

play-off [plā'ôf] *n* (*SPORT*) belle *f*.

playpen [plā'pen] *n* parc *m* (pour bébé).

playroom [plā'rōōm] *n* salle *f* de jeux.

plaything [plā'thing] *n* jouet *m*.

playtime [plā'tīm] *n* (*SCOL*) récréation *f*.

playwright [plā'rīt] *n* dramaturge *m*.

plc *abbr* (*Brit*) = **public limited company**.

plea [plē] *n* (*request*) appel *m*; (*excuse*) excuse *f*; (*LAW*) défense *f*.

plead [plēd] *vt* plaider; (*give as excuse*) invoquer ♦ *vi* (*LAW*) plaider; (*beg*): **to** ~ **with sb (for sth)** implorer qn (d'accorder qch); **to** ~ **for sth** implorer qch; **to** ~ **guilty/not guilty** plaider coupable/non coupable.

pleasant [plez'ənt] *a* agréable.

pleasantly [plez'əntlē] *ad* agréablement.

pleasantness [plez'əntnis] *n* (*of person*) amabilité *f*; (*of place*) agrément *m*.

pleasantry [plez'əntrē] *n* (*joke*) plaisanterie *f*; **pleasantries** *npl* (*polite remarks*) civilités *fpl*.

please [plēz] *vt* plaire à ♦ *vi* (*think fit*): **do as you** ~ faites comme il vous plaira; ~**!** s'il te (*or* vous) plaît; **my check,** ~ l'addition, s'il vous plaît; ~ **don't cry!** je t'en prie, ne pleure pas!; ~ **yourself!** (faites) comme vous voulez!

pleased [plēzd] *a*: ~ (**with**) content(e) (de); ~ **to meet you** enchanté (de faire votre connaissance); **we are** ~ **to inform you that** ... nous sommes heureux de vous annoncer que ....

pleasing [plē'zing] *a* plaisant(e), qui fait plaisir.

pleasurable [plezh'ûrəbəl] *a* très agréable.

pleasure [plezh'ûr] *n* plaisir *m*; **"it's a** ~**"** "je vous en prie"; **with** ~ avec plaisir; **is this trip for business or** ~**?** est-ce un voyage d'affaires ou d'agrément?

pleasure steamer *n* (*Brit*) vapeur *m* de plaisance.

pleat [plēt] *n* pli *m*.

plebiscite [pleb'isīt] *n* plébiscite *m*.

plebs [plebs] *npl* (*pej*) bas peuple.

plectrum [plek'trəm] *n* plectre *m*.

pledge [plej] *n* gage *m*; (*promise*) promesse *f* ♦ *vt* engager; promettre; **to** ~ **support for sb** s'engager à soutenir qn; **to** ~ **$500 per year to a charity** s'engager à verser $500 par an à une œuvre de bienfaisance; **to** ~ **sb to secrecy** faire promettre à qn de garder le secret.

plenary [plē'nûrē] *a*: **in** ~ **session** en séance plénière.

plentiful [plen'tifəl] *a* abondant(e), copieux(euse).

plenty [plen'tē] *n* abondance *f*; ~ **of** beaucoup de; (*sufficient*) (bien) assez de; **we've got** ~ **of time** nous avons largement le temps.

pleurisy [plōōr'isē] *n* pleurésie *f*.

Plexiglas [plek'səglas] *n* ® (*US*) Plexiglas *m* ®.

pliable [plī'əbəl] *a* flexible; (*person*) malléable.

pliers [plī'ûrz] *npl* pinces *fpl*.

plight [plīt] *n* situation *f* critique.

plimsolls [plim'səlz] *npl* (*Brit*) (chaussures *fpl*) tennis *fpl*.

plinth [plinth] *n* socle *m*.

PLO *n abbr* (= *Palestine Liberation Organization*) OLP *f*.

plod [plâd] *vi* avancer péniblement; (*fig*) peiner.

plodder [plâd'ûr] *n* bûcheur/euse.

plodding [plâd'ing] *a* pesant(e).

plonk [plângk] (*col*) *n* (*Brit: wine*) pinard *m*, piquette *f*.

plot [plât] *n* complot *m*, conspiration *f*; (*of story, play*) intrigue *f*; (*of land*) lot *m* de terrain, lopin *m* ♦ *vt* (*mark out*) pointer; relever; (*conspire*) comploter ♦ *vi* comploter.

plotter [plât'ûr] *n* conspirateur/trice; (*COMPUT*) traceur *m*.

plough [plou] *etc* (*Brit*) = **plow** *etc*.

plow [plou] (*US*) *n* charrue *f* ♦ *vt* (*earth*) labourer.

plow back *vt* (*COMM*) réinvestir.
plow through *vt fus* (*snow etc*) avancer péniblement dans.
plowing [plou'ing] *n* labourage *m*.
plowman [plou'mən] *n* laboureur *m*.
ploy [ploi] *n* stratagème *m*.
pluck [pluk] *vt* (*fruit*) cueillir; (*musical instrument*) pincer; (*bird*) plumer ♦ *n* courage *m*, cran *m*; **to ~ one's eyebrows** s'épiler les sourcils; **to ~ up courage** prendre son courage à deux mains.
plucky [pluk'ē] *a* courageux(euse).
plug [plug] *n* bouchon *m*, bonde *f*; (*ELEC*) prise *f* de courant; (*AUT: also:* **spark ~**) bougie *f* ♦ *vt* (*hole*) boucher; (*col: advertise*) faire du battage pour, matraquer; **to give sb/sth a ~** (*col*) faire de la pub pour qn/qch.
plug in (*ELEC*) *vt* brancher ♦ *vi* se brancher.
plughole [plug'hōl] *n* (*Brit*) trou *m* (d'écoulement).
plum [plum] *n* (*fruit*) prune *f* ♦ *a*: **~ job** (*col*) travail *m* en or.
plumage [plōo'mij] *n* plumage *m*.
plumb [plum] *a* vertical(e) ♦ *n* plomb *m* ♦ *ad* (*exactly*) en plein ♦ *vt* sonder.
plumb in *vt* (*washing machine*) faire le raccordement de.
plumber [plum'ûr] *n* plombier *m*.
plumbing [plum'ing] *n* (*trade*) plomberie *f*; (*piping*) tuyauterie *f*.
plumbline [plum'līn] *n* fil *m* à plomb.
plume [plōom] *n* plume *f*, plumet *m*.
plummet [plum'it] *vi* plonger, dégringoler.
plump [plump] *a* rondelet(te), dodu(e), bien en chair ♦ *vt*: **to ~ sth (down) on** laisser tomber qch lourdement sur.
plump up *vt* (*cushion*) battre (pour lui redonner forme).
plunder [plun'dûr] *n* pillage *m* ♦ *vt* piller.
plunge [plunj] *n* plongeon *m* ♦ *vt* plonger ♦ *vi* (*fall*) tomber, dégringoler; **to take the ~** se jeter à l'eau; **to ~ a room into darkness** plonger une pièce dans l'obscurité.
plunger [plun'jûr] *n* piston *m*; (*for blocked sink*) (débouchoir *m* à) ventouse *f*.
plunging [plun'jing] *a* (*neckline*) plongeant(e).
pluperfect [plōopûr'fikt] *n* plus-que-parfait *m*.
plural [plōor'əl] *a* pluriel(le) ♦ *n* pluriel *m*.
plus [plus] *n* (*also:* **~ sign**) signe *m* plus ♦ *prep* plus; **ten/twenty ~** plus de dix/vingt; **it's a ~** c'est un atout.
plus fours *npl* pantalon *m* (de) golf.
plush [plush] *a* somptueux(euse) ♦ *n* peluche *f*; **~ toy** (*US*) jouet *m* en peluche.
plutonium [plōotō'nēəm] *n* plutonium *m*.
ply [plī] *n* (*of wool*) fil *m*; (*of wood*) feuille *f*, épaisseur *f* ♦ *vt* (*tool*) manier; (*a trade*) exercer ♦ *vi* (*ship*) faire la navette; **three ~ (wool)** *n* laine *f* trois fils; **to ~ sb with drink** donner continuellement à boire à qn.
plywood [plī'wōod] *n* contre-plaqué *m*.
PM *n abbr* = **prime minister**.
p.m. *ad abbr* (= *post meridiem*) de l'après-midi.
pneumatic [nōomat'ik] *a* pneumatique; **~ drill** marteau-piqueur *m*.
pneumonia [nyōomōn'yə] *n* pneumonie *f*.
PO *n abbr* (= *Post Office*) PTT *fpl*; (*MIL*) =

petty officer.
po *abbr* (*Brit*) = **postal order**.
poach [pōch] *vt* (*cook*) pocher; (*steal*) pêcher (*or* chasser) sans permis ♦ *vi* braconner.
poached [pōcht] *a* (*egg*) poché(e).
poacher [pō'chûr] *n* braconnier *m*.
poaching [pō'ching] *n* braconnage *m*.
PO Box *n abbr* = **Post Office Box**.
pocket [påk'it] *n* poche *f* ♦ *vt* empocher.
pocketbook [påk'itbōok] *n* (*wallet*) portefeuille *m*; (*notebook*) carnet *m*; (*US: purse*) sac *m* à main.
pocket knife *n* canif *m*.
pocket money *n* argent *m* de poche.
pockmarked [påk'márkt] *a* (*face*) grêlé(e).
pod [påd] *n* cosse *f* ♦ *vt* écosser.
podgy [påj'ē] *a* rondelet(te).
podiatrist [pədī'ətrist] *n* (*US*) pédicure *m/f*.
podiatry [pədī'ətrē] *n* (*US*) pédicurie *f*.
podium [pō'dēəm] *n* podium *m*.
POE *n abbr* = *port of embarkation, port of entry*.
poem [pō'əm] *n* poème *m*.
poet [pō'it] *n* poète *m*.
poetic [pōet'ik] *a* poétique.
poet laureate [pō'it lô'rēit] *n* poète lauréat (*nommé et appointé par la Cour royale*).
poetry [pō'itrē] *n* poésie *f*.
poignant [poin'yənt] *a* poignant(e); (*sharp*) vif(vive).
point [point] *n* (*tip*) pointe *f*; (*in time*) moment *m*; (*in space*) endroit *m*; (*GEOM, SCOL, SPORT, on scale*) point *m*; (*subject, idea*) point, sujet *m*; (*also:* **decimal ~**): **2 ~ 3 (2.3)** 2 virgule 3 (2,3); (*Brit ELEC: also:* **power ~**) prise *f* (de courant) ♦ *vt* (*show*) indiquer; (*wall, window*) jointoyer; (*gun etc*): **to ~ sth at** braquer *or* diriger qch sur ♦ *vi* montrer du doigt; **to ~ to** montrer du doigt; (*fig*) signaler; **~s** *npl* (*AUT*) vis platinées; (*RAIL*) aiguillage *m*; **good ~s** qualités *fpl*; **the train stops at Boston and all ~s south** le train dessert Boston et toutes les gares vers le sud; **to make a ~** faire une remarque; **to make a ~ of doing sth** ne pas manquer de faire qch; **to make one's ~** se faire comprendre; **to get the ~** comprendre, saisir; **to come to the ~** en venir au fait; **when it comes to the ~** le moment venu; **there's no ~ (in doing)** cela ne sert à rien (de faire); **to be on the ~ of doing sth** être sur le point de faire qch; **that's the whole ~!** précisément!; **to be beside the ~** être à côté de la question; **you've got a ~ there!** (c'est) juste!; **in ~ of fact** en fait, en réalité; **~ of departure** (*also fig*) point de départ; **~ of order** point de procédure; **~ of sale** (*COMM*) point de vente; **~ of view** point de vue.
point out *vt* faire remarquer, souligner.
point-blank [point'blangk'] *ad* (*also:* **at ~ range**) à bout portant ♦ *a* (*fig*) catégorique.
pointed [poin'tid] *a* (*shape*) pointu(e); (*remark*) plein(e) de sous-entendus.
pointedly [poin'tidlē] *ad* d'une manière significative.
pointer [poin'tûr] *n* (*stick*) baguette *f*; (*needle*) aiguille *f*; (*dog*) chien *m* d'arrêt; (*clue*) indication *f*; (*advice*) tuyau *m*.

pointless [point'lis] *a* inutile, vain(e).
poise [poiz] *n* (*balance*) équilibre *m*; (*of head, body*) port *m*; (*calmness*) calme *m* ♦ *vt* placer en équilibre; **to be ~d for** (*fig*) être prêt à.
poison [poi'zən] *n* poison *m* ♦ *vt* empoisonner.
poisoning [poi'zəning] *n* empoisonnement *m*.
poisonous [poi'zənəs] *a* (*snake*) venimeux(euse); (*substance etc*) vénéneux(euse); (*fumes*) toxique; (*fig*) pernicieux(euse).
poke [pōk] *vt* (*fire*) tisonner; (*jab with finger, stick etc*) piquer; pousser du doigt; (*put*): **to ~ sth into** fourrer *or* enfoncer qch dans ♦ *n* (*jab*) (petit) coup; (*to fire*) coup *m* de tisonnier; **to ~ one's head out of the window** passer la tête par la fenêtre; **to ~ fun at sb** se moquer de qn.
poke around *vi* fureter.
poker [pō'kûr] *n* tisonnier *m*; (*CARDS*) poker *m*.
poker-faced [pō'kûrfāst'] *a* au visage impassible.
poky [pō'kē] *a* exigu(ë).
Poland [pō'lənd] *n* Pologne *f*.
polar [pō'lûr] *a* polaire.
polar bear *n* ours blanc.
polarize [pō'lərīz] *vt* polariser.
Pole [pōl] *n* Polonais/e.
pole [pōl] *n* (*of wood*) mât *m*, perche *f*; (*ELEC*) poteau *m*; (*GEO*) pôle *m*.
pole bean *n* (*US*) haricot *m* (à rames).
polecat [pōl'kat] *n* putois *m*; (*US*: *skunk*) mouffette *f*.
Pol. Econ. [pâl'ēkân] *n abbr* = *political economy*.
polemic [pəlem'ik] *n* polémique *f*.
polestar [pōl'stâr] *n* étoile *f* polaire.
pole vault *n* saut *m* à la perche.
police [pəlēs'] *npl* police *f* ♦ *vt* maintenir l'ordre dans; **a large number of ~ were hurt** de nombreux policiers ont été blessés.
police captain *n* (*US*) ≈ commissaire *m*.
police car *n* voiture *f* de police.
police constable *n* (*Brit*) agent *m* de police.
police department *n* (*US*) services *mpl* de police.
police force *n* police *f*, forces *fpl* de l'ordre.
policeman [pəlēs'mən] *n* agent *m* de police, policier *m*; (*US*: *also*: **traffic ~**) contractuel/le.
police officer *n* agent *m* de police.
police record *n* casier *m* judiciaire.
police state *n* état policier.
police station *n* commissariat *m* de police.
policewoman [pəlēs'wŏŏmən] *n* femme-agent *f*.
policy [pâl'isē] *n* politique *f*; (*also*: **insurance ~**) police *f* (d'assurance); (*of newspaper, company*) politique générale; **to take out a ~** (*INSURANCE*) souscrire une police d'assurance.
policy holder *n* assuré/e.
polio [pō'lēō] *n* polio *f*.
Polish [pō'lish] *a* polonais(e) ♦ *n* (*LING*) polonais *m*.
polish [pâl'ish] *n* (*for shoes*) cirage *m*; (*for floor*) cire *f*, encaustique *f*; (*for nails*) vernis *m*; (*shine*) éclat *m*, poli *m*; (*fig: refinement*)

raffinement *m* ♦ *vt* (*put polish on*: *shoes, wood*) cirer; (*make shiny*) astiquer, faire briller; (*fig: improve*) perfectionner.
polish off *vt* (*work*) expédier; (*food*) liquider.
polished [pâl'isht] *a* (*fig*) raffiné(e).
polite [pəlīt'] *a* poli(e); **it's not ~ to do that** ça ne se fait pas.
politely [pəlīt'lē] *ad* poliment.
politeness [pəlīt'nis] *n* politesse *f*.
politic [pâl'itik] *a* diplomatique.
political [pəlit'ikəl] *a* politique.
political asylum *n* asile *m* politique.
politically [pəlit'iklē] *ad* politiquement.
politician [pâlitish'ən] *n* homme/femme politique, politicien/ne.
politics [pâl'itiks] *npl* politique *f*.
polka [pōl'kə] *n* polka *f*.
polka dot *n* pois *m*.
poll [pōl] *n* scrutin *m*, vote *m*; (*also*: **opinion ~**) sondage *m* (d'opinion) ♦ *vt* obtenir; **to go to the ~s** (*voters*) aller aux urnes; (*government*) tenir des élections.
pollen [pâl'ən] *n* pollen *m*.
pollen count *n* taux *m* de pollen.
pollination [pâlənā'shən] *n* pollinisation *f*.
polling [pō'ling] *n* (*Brit POL*) élections *fpl*; (*TEL*) invitation *f* à émettre.
pollute [pəlōōt'] *vt* polluer.
pollution [pəlōō'shən] *n* pollution *f*.
polo [pō'lō] *n* polo *m*.
polo neck *n* col roulé ♦ *a* à col roulé.
poly [pâl'ē] *n abbr* (*Brit*) = **polytechnic**.
polyester [pâlēes'tûr] *n* polyester *m*.
polygamy [pəlig'əmē] *n* polygamie *f*.
Polynesia [pâlənē'zhə] *n* Polynésie *f*.
Polynesian [pâlənē'zhən] *a* polynésien(ne) ♦ *n* Polynésien/ne.
polyp [pâl'ip] *n* (*MED*) polype *m*.
polystyrene [pâlēstī'rēn] *n* polystyrène *m*.
polytechnic [pâlētek'nik] *n* (*college*) I.U.T. *m*, Institut *m* Universitaire de Technologie.
polythene [pâl'əthēn] *n* polyéthylène *m*.
polythene bag *n* sac *m* en plastique.
polyurethane [pâlēyōōr'əthān] *n* polyuréthane *m*.
pomegranate [pâm'əgranit] *n* grenade *f*.
pommel [pum'əl] *n* pommeau *m* ♦ *vt* = **pummel**.
pomp [pâmp] *n* pompe *f*, faste *f*, apparat *m*.
pompom [pâm'pâm], **pompon** [pâm'pân] *n* pompon *m*.
pompous [pâm'pəs] *a* pompeux(euse).
pond [pând] *n* étang *m*; (*stagnant*) mare *f*.
ponder [pân'dûr] *vi* réfléchir ♦ *vt* considérer, peser.
ponderous [pân'dûrəs] *a* pesant(e), lourd(e).
pong [pông] (*Brit col*) *n* puanteur *f* ♦ *vi* schlinguer.
pontiff [pân'tif] *n* pontife *m*.
pontificate [pântif'ikāt] *vi* (*fig*): **to ~ (about)** pontifier (sur).
pontoon [pântōōn'] *n* ponton *m*; (*Brit CARDS*) vingt-et-un *m*.
pony [pō'nē] *n* poney *m*.
ponytail [pō'nētāl] *n* queue *f* de cheval.
pony trekking [pō'nē trek'ing] *n* (*Brit*) randonnée *f* équestre *or* à cheval.
poodle [pōō'dəl] *n* caniche *m*.

pooh-pooh [pōōpōō'] *vt* dédaigner.

pool [pōōl] *n* (*of rain*) flaque *f*; (*pond*) mare *f*; (*artificial*) bassin *m*; (*also:* **swimming** ~) piscine *f*; (*sth shared*) fonds commun; (*money at cards*) cagnotte *f*; (*billiards*) poule *f*; (COMM: *consortium*) pool *m*; (US: *monopoly trust*) trust *m* ♦ *vt* mettre en commun; **secretary** ~, (*Brit*) **typing** ~ pool *m* dactylographique; **to do the (football)** ~s (*Brit*) ≈ jouer au loto sportif.

pooped [pōōpt] *a* (*US col*) crevé(e).

poor [pōōr] *a* pauvre; (*mediocre*) médiocre, faible, mauvais(e) ♦ *npl:* **the** ~ les pauvres *mpl.*

poorly [pōōr'lē] *ad* pauvrement; médiocrement ♦ *a* souffrant(e), malade.

pop [páp] *n* (*noise*) bruit sec; (MUS) musique *f* pop; (*col: drink*) soda *m*; (*US col: father*) papa *m* ♦ *vt* (*put*) fourrer, mettre (rapidement) ♦ *vi* éclater; (*cork*) sauter; **she** ~**ped her head out of the window** elle passa la tête par la fenêtre.

pop in *vi* entrer en passant.

pop out *vi* sortir.

pop up *vi* apparaître, surgir.

pop concert *n* concert *m* pop.

popcorn [páp'kôrn] *n* pop-corn *m*.

pope [pōp] *n* pape *m*.

poplar [páp'lûr] *n* peuplier *m*.

poplin [páp'lin] *n* popeline *f*.

poppy [páp'ē] *n* coquelicot *m*; pavot *m*.

poppycock [páp'ēkák] *n* (*col*) balivernes *fpl.*

Popsicle [páp'sikəl] *n* ® (*US*) ≈ esquimau *m* ® (*glace*).

populace [páp'yələs] *n* peuple *m*.

popular [páp'yəlûr] *a* populaire; (*fashionable*) à la mode; **to be** ~ **(with)** (*person*) avoir du succès (auprès de); (*decision*) être bien accueilli(e) (par).

popularity [páp'yələr'itē] *n* popularité *f.*

popularize [páp'yələrīz] *vt* populariser; (*science*) vulgariser.

populate [páp'yəlāt] *vt* peupler.

population [páp'yəlā'shən] *n* population *f.*

population explosion *n* explosion *f* démographique.

populous [páp'yələs] *a* populeux(euse).

porcelain [pôr'səlin] *n* porcelaine *f.*

porch [pôrch] *n* porche *m*.

porcupine [pôr'kyəpin] *n* porc-épic *m*.

pore [pôr] *n* pore *m* ♦ *vi:* **to** ~ **over** s'absorber dans, être plongé(e) dans.

pork [pôrk] *n* porc *m*.

pork chop *n* côte *f* de porc.

pornographic [pôrnəgraf'ik] *a* pornographique.

pornography [pôrná'grəfē] *n* pornographie *f.*

porous [pôr'əs] *a* poreux(euse).

porpoise [pôr'pəs] *n* marsouin *m*.

porridge [pôr'ij] *n* porridge *m*.

port [pôrt] *n* (*harbor*) port *m*; (*opening in ship*) sabord *m*; (NAUT: *left side*) bâbord *m*; (*wine*) porto *m*; (COMPUT) port *m*, accès *m* ♦ *cpd* portuaire, du port; **to** ~ (NAUT) à bâbord; ~ **of call** (port d')escale *f.*

portable [pôr'təbəl] *a* portatif(ive).

portal [pôr'təl] *n* portail *m*.

portcullis [pôrtkul'is] *n* herse *f.*

portend [pôrtend'] *vt* présager, annoncer.

portent [pôr'tent] *n* présage *m*.

porter [pôr'tûr] *n* (*for luggage*) porteur *m*; (*doorkeeper*) gardien/ne; portier *m*.

portfolio [pôrtfō'lēō] *n* portefeuille *m*; (*of artist*) portfolio *m*.

porthole [pôrt'hōl] *n* hublot *m*.

portico [pôr'tikō] *n* portique *m*.

portion [pôr'shən] *n* portion *f*, part *f.*

portly [pôrt'lē] *a* corpulent(e).

portrait [pôr'trit] *n* portrait *m*.

portray [pôrtrā'] *vt* faire le portrait de; (*in writing*) dépeindre, représenter.

portrayal [pôrtrā'əl] *n* portrait *m*, représentation *f.*

Portugal [pôr'chəgəl] *n* Portugal *m*.

Portuguese [pôrchəgēz'] *a* portugais(e) ♦ *n* (*pl inv*) Portugais/e; (LING) portugais *m*.

Portuguese man-of-war *n* (*jellyfish*) galère *f.*

pose [pōz] *n* pose *f*; (*pej*) affectation *f* ♦ *vi* poser; (*pretend*): **to** ~ **as** se poser en ♦ *vt* poser, créer; **to strike a** ~ poser (pour la galerie).

poser [pō'zûr] *n* question difficile *or* embarrassante; (*person*) = **poseur**.

poseur [pōzir'] *n* (*pej*) poseur/euse.

posh [pásh] *a* (*col*) chic *inv*; **to talk** ~ parler d'une manière affectée.

position [pəzish'ən] *n* position *f*; (*job*) situation *f* ♦ *vt* mettre en place *or* en position; **to be in a** ~ **to do sth** être en mesure de faire qch.

positive [páz'ətiv] *a* positif(ive); (*certain*) sûr(e), certain(e); (*definite*) formel(lc), catégorique; (*clear*) indéniable, réel(le).

posse [pás'ē] *n* (*US*) détachement *m*.

possess [pəzes'] *vt* posséder; **like one** ~**ed** comme un fou; **whatever can have** ~**ed you?** qu'est-ce qui vous a pris?

possession [pəzesh'ən] *n* possession *f*; **to take** ~ **of sth** prendre possession de qch.

possessive [pəzes'iv] *a* possessif(ive).

possessively [pəzes'ivlē] *ad* d'une façon possessive.

possessor [pəzes'ûr] *n* possesseur *m*.

possibility [pásəbil'ətē] *n* possibilité *f*; éventualité *f*; **he's a** ~ **for the part** c'est un candidat possible pour le rôle.

possible [pás'əbəl] *a* possible; (*solution*) envisageable, éventuel(le); **it is** ~ **to do it** il est possible de le faire; **as far as** ~ dans la mesure du possible, autant que possible; **if** ~ si possible; **as big as** ~ aussi gros que possible.

possibly [pás'əblē] *ad* (*perhaps*) peut-être; **if you** ~ **can** si cela vous est possible; **I cannot** ~ **come** il m'est impossible de venir.

post [pōst] *n* (*Brit: mail*) poste *f*; (: *collection*) levée *f*; (: *letters, delivery*) courrier *m*; (*job, situation*) poste *m*; (*pole*) poteau *m*; (*trading*) ~ comptoir (*commercial*) ♦ *vt* (*Brit: send by mail*, MIL) poster; (*Brit: appoint*): **to** ~ **to** affecter a; (*notice*) afficher; **by** ~ (*Brit*) par la poste; **by return of** ~ (*Brit*) par retour du courrier; **to keep sb** ~**ed** tenir qn au courant.

post... *prefix* post...; ~ **1990** *a* d'après 1990 ♦ *ad* après 1990.

postage [pōs'tij] *n* affranchissement *m*; ~ **paid** port payé; ~ **prepaid** (*US*) franco (de port).

postage meter *n* (*US*) machine *f* à affranchir.

postage stamp *n* timbre-poste *m*.

postal [pōs'təl] *a* postal(e).

postal order *n* (*Brit*) mandat(-poste) *m*.

postbag [pōst'bag] *n* (*Brit*) sac postal; (*mailman's*) sacoche *f*.

postbox [pōst'bâks] *n* (*Brit*) boîte *f* aux lettres.

postcard [pōst'kârd] *n* carte postale.

postcode [pōst'kōd] *n* (*Brit*) code postal.

postdate [pōst'dāt] *vt* (*check*) postdater.

poster [pōs'tûr] *n* affiche *f*.

posterior [pâstēr'ēûr] *n* (*col*) postérieur *m*, derrière *m*.

posterity [pâstär'itē] *n* postérité *f*.

poster paint *n* gouache *f*.

post exchange (PX) *n* (*US MIL*) magasin *m* de l'armée.

post-free [pōst'frē'] *a* (*Brit*) franco (de port).

postgraduate [pōstgraj'ōōit] *n* ≈ étudiant/e de troisième cycle.

posthumous [pâs'chəməs] *a* posthume.

posthumously [pâs'chəməslē] *ad* après la mort de l'auteur, à titre posthume.

postman [pōst'mən] *n* (*Brit*) facteur *m*.

postmark [pōst'mârk] *n* cachet *m* (de la poste).

postmaster [pōst'mastûr] *n* receveur *m* des postes.

Postmaster General *n* ≈ ministre *m* des Postes et Télécommunications.

postmistress [pōst'mistris] *n* receveuse *f* des postes.

post-mortem [pōstmôr'təm] *n* autopsie *f*.

postnatal [pōstnāt'əl] *a* post-natal(e).

post office *n* (*building*) poste *f*; (*organization*) postes *fpl*.

post office box (PO box) *n* boîte postale (B.P.).

post-paid [pōst'pād'] *a* port payé.

postpone [pōstpōn'] *vt* remettre (à plus tard), reculer.

postponement [pōstpōn'mənt] *n* ajournement *m*, renvoi *m*.

postscript [pōst'skript] *n* post-scriptum *m*.

postulate [pâs'chəlāt] *vt* postuler.

posture [pâs'chûr] *n* posture *f*, attitude *f* ♦ *vi* poser.

post-viral syndrome (PVS) [pōstvī'rəl sin'drōm] *n* syndrome *m* post-viral.

postwar [pōst'wôr'] *a* d'après-guerre.

posy [pō'zē] *n* petit bouquet.

pot [pât] *n* (*for cooking*) marmite *f*; casserole *f*; (*for plants, jam*) pot *m*; (*piece of pottery*) poterie *f*; (*col: marijuana*) herbe *f* ♦ *vt* (*plant*) mettre en pot; **to go to** ~ aller à vau-l'eau; **~s of** (*Brit col*) beaucoup de, plein de.

potash [pât'ash] *n* potasse *f*.

potassium [pətas'ēəm] *n* potassium *m*.

potato, ~es [pətā'tō] *n* pomme *f* de terre.

potato chips, (*Brit*) **potato crisps** *npl* chips *mpl*.

potato flour *n* fécule *f*.

potato peeler [pətā'tō pē'lûr] *n* épluche-légumes *m*.

potbellied [pât'belēd] *a* (*from overeating*) be-

donnant(e); (*from malnutrition*) au ventre ballonné.

potency [pōt'ənsē] *n* puissance *f*, force *f*; (*of drink*) degré *m* d'alcool.

potent [pōt'ənt] *a* puissant(e); (*drink*) fort(e), très alcoolisé(e).

potentate [pât'əntāt] *n* potentat *m*.

potential [pəten'chəl] *a* potentiel(le) ♦ *n* potentiel *m*; **to have** ~ être prometteur(euse); ouvrir des possibilités.

potentially [pəten'chəlē] *ad* potentiellement; **it's** ~ **dangerous** ça pourrait se révéler dangereux, il y a possibilité de danger.

pothole [pât'hōl] *n* (*in road*) nid *m* de poule; (*Brit: underground*) gouffre *m*, caverne *f*.

potholer [pât'hōlûr] *n* (*Brit*) spéléologue *m/f*.

potion [pō'shən] *n* potion *f*.

potluck [pât'luk] *n*: **to take** ~ tenter sa chance.

potpourri [pōpərē'] *n* pot-pourri *m*.

pot roast *n* rôti *m* à la cocotte.

potshot [pât'shât] *n*: **to take ~s at** canarder.

potted [pât'id] *a* (*food*) en conserve; (*plant*) en pot; (*fig: shortened*) abrégé(e).

potter [pât'ûr] *n* potier *m* ♦ *vi* (*Brit*): **to** ~ **around,** ~ **about** bricoler; **~'s wheel** tour *m* de potier.

pottery [pât'ûrē] *n* poterie *f*; **a piece of** ~ une poterie.

potty [pât'ē] *n* (*child's*) pot *m*.

potty training *n* apprentissage *m* de la propreté.

pouch [pouch] *n* (*ZOOL*) poche *f*; (*for tobacco*) blague *f*.

pouf(fe) [pōōf] *n* (*stool*) pouf *m*.

poultice [pōl'tis] *n* cataplasme *m*.

poultry [pōl'trē] *n* volaille *f*.

poultry farm *n* élevage *m* de volaille.

poultry farmer *n* aviculteur *m*.

pounce [pouns] *vi*: **to** ~ **(on)** bondir (sur), fondre (sur) ♦ *n* bond *m*, attaque *f*.

pound [pound] *n* livre *f* (*weight = 453g, 16 ounces; money = 100 pence*); (*for dogs, cars*) fourrière *f* ♦ *vt* (*beat*) bourrer de coups, marteler; (*crush*) piler, pulvériser; (*with guns*) pilonner ♦ *vi* (*beat*) battre violemment, taper; **half a** ~ **(of)** une demi-livre (de); **a five-~ note** un billet de cinq livres.

pounding [poun'ding] *n*: **to take a** ~ (*fig*) prendre une râclée.

pound sterling *n* livre *f* sterling.

pour [pôr] *vt* verser ♦ *vi* couler à flots; (*rain*) pleuvoir à verse; **to come ~ing in** (*water*) entrer à flots; (*letters*) arriver par milliers; (*cars, people*) affluer.

pour away, pour off *vt* vider.

pour in *vi* (*people*) affluer, se précipiter.

pour out *vi* (*people*) sortir en masse ♦ *vt* vider; déverser; (*serve: a drink*) verser.

pouring [pôr'ing] *a*: ~ **rain** pluie torrentielle.

pout [pout] *n* moue *f* ♦ *vi* faire la moue.

poverty [pâv'ûrtē] *n* pauvreté *f*, misère *f*.

poverty-stricken [pâv'ûrtēstrikən] *a* pauvre, déshérité(e).

POW *n* *abbr* = **prisoner of war**.

powder [pou'dûr] *n* poudre *f* ♦ *vt* poudrer; **to** ~ **one's nose** se poudrer; (*euphemism*) aller à la salle de bain; **~ed milk** lait *m* en poudre.

powder compact *n* poudrier *m*.
powdered sugar [pou'dûrd shoog'ûr] *n* (*US*) sucre *m* semoule.
powder puff *n* houppette *f*.
powder room *n* toilettes *fpl* (pour dames).
powdery [pou'dûrē] *a* poudreux(euse).
power [pou'ûr] *n* (*strength*) puissance *f*, force *f*; (*ability, POL*): *of party, leader*) pouvoir *m*; (*MATH*) puissance; (*of speech, thought*) faculté *f*; (*ELEC*) courant *m* ♦ *vt* faire marcher, actionner; **to do all in one's ~ to help sb** faire tout ce qui est en son pouvoir pour aider qn; **the world ~s** les grandes puissances; **to be in ~** être au pouvoir.
power cut *n* (*Brit*) coupure *f* de courant.
power-driven [pou'ûrdriv∂n] *a* à moteur; (*ELEC*) électrique.
powered [pou'ûrd] *a*: **~ by** actionné(e) par, fonctionnant à; **nuclear-~ submarine** sousmarin *m* (à propulsion) nucléaire.
power failure *n* panne *f* de courant.
powerful [pou'ûrf∂l] *a* puissant(e).
powerhouse [pou'ûrhous] *n* (*fig: person*) fonceur *m*; **a ~ of ideas** une mine d'idées.
powerless [pou'ûrlis] *a* impuissant(e).
power line *n* ligne *f* électrique.
power shovel *n* (*US*) pelle *f* mécanique.
power station *n* centrale *f* électrique.
power steering *n* direction assistée.
powwow [pou'wou] *n* conciliabule *m*.
pox [pâks] *n see* **chickenpox**.
pp *abbr* (= *per procurationem: by proxy*) p.p.
p&p *abbr* (*Brit*: = *postage and packing*) frais *mpl* de port.
PPS *n abbr* (= *post postscriptum*) PPS.
PQ *abbr* (*Canada*) = *Province of Quebec*.
PR *n abbr* = **proportional representation, public relations** ♦ *abbr* (*US MAIL*) = *Puerto Rico*.
Pr. *abbr* (= *prince*) Pce.
practicability [praktikəbil'∂tē] *n* possibilité *f* de réalisation.
practicable [prak'tikəbəl] *a* (*scheme*) réalisable.
practical [prak'tikəl] *a* pratique.
practicality [praktikal'itē] *n* (*of plan*) aspect *m* pratique; (*of person*) sens *m* pratique; **practicalities** *npl* détails *mpl* pratiques.
practical joke *n* farce *f*.
practically [prak'tiklē] *ad* (*almost*) pratiquement.
practice [prak'tis] *n* pratique *f*; (*of profession*) exercice *m*; (*at football etc*) entraînement *m*; (*business*) cabinet *m*; clientèle *f* ♦ *vt* (*US*) (*work at: piano, one's backhand etc*) s'exercer à, travailler; (*train for: skiing, running etc*) s'entraîner à; (*a sport, religion, method*) pratiquer; (*profession*) exercer ♦ *vi* (*US*) s'exercer, travailler; (*train*) s'entraîner; **in ~** (*in reality*) en pratique; **out of ~** rouillé(e); **2 hours' piano ~** 2 heures de travail *or* d'exercices au piano; **target ~** exercices de tir; **it's common ~** c'est courant, ça se fait couramment; **to put sth into ~** mettre qch en pratique; **to ~ for a match** s'entraîner pour un match.
practiced [prak'tist] *a* (*person*) expérimenté(e); (: *performance*) impeccable; (: *liar*) invétéré(e); **with a ~ eye** d'un œil exercé.
practice test *n* (*SCOL*) examen blanc.
practicing [prak'tising] *a* (*Christian etc*) pratiquant(e); (*lawyer*) en exercice; (*homosexual*) déclaré.
practise [prak'tis] *vt, vi* (*Brit*) = **practice**.
practitioner [praktish'∂nûr] *n* praticien/ne.
pragmatic [pragmat'ik] *a* pragmatique.
Prague [prâg] *n* Prague.
prairie [prär'ē] *n* savane *f*; (*US*): **the ~s** la Prairie.
praise [prāz] *n* éloge(s) *m(pl)*, louange(s) *f(pl)* ♦ *vt* louer, faire l'éloge de.
praiseworthy [prāz'wûrthē] *a* digne de louanges.
pram [pram] *n* (*Brit*) landau *m*, voiture *f* d'enfant.
prance [prans] *vi* (*horse*) caracoler.
prank [prangk] *n* farce *f*.
prattle [prat'∂l] *vi* jacasser.
prawn [prôn] *n* crevette *f* (rose).
pray [prā] *vi* prier.
prayer [prär] *n* prière *f*.
prayer book *n* livre *m* de prières.
pre... [prē] *prefix* pré...; **pre-1970** *a* d'avant 1970 ♦ *ad* avant 1970.
preach [prēch] *vt, vi* prêcher; **to ~ at sb** faire la morale à qn.
preacher [prē'chûr] *n* prédicateur *m*; (*clergyman*) pasteur *m*.
preamble [prē'ambəl] *n* préambule *m*.
prearranged [prēərānjd'] *a* organisé(e) *or* fixé(e) à l'avance.
precarious [prikär'ēəs] *a* précaire.
precaution [prikô'shən] *n* précaution *f*.
precautionary [prikô'shənärē] *a* (*measure*) de précaution.
precede [prisēd'] *vt, vi* précéder.
precedence [pres'idəns] *n* préséance *f*.
precedent [pres'idənt] *n* précédent *m*; **to establish** *or* **set a ~** créer un précédent.
preceding [prisē'ding] *a* qui précède (*or* précédait).
precept [prē'sept] *n* précepte *m*.
precinct [prē'singkt] *n* (*round cathedral*) pourtour *m*, enceinte *f*; (*US: district*) circonscription *f*, arrondissement *m*; **~s** *npl* (*neighborhood*) alentours *mpl*, environs *mpl*; **pedestrian ~** zone piétonne; **shopping ~** (*Brit*) centre commercial.
precious [presh'əs] *a* précieux(euse) ♦ *ad* (*col*): **~ little** *or* **few** fort peu.
precipice [pres'əpis] *n* précipice *m*.
precipitate *a* [prisip'itit] (*hasty*) précipité(e) ♦ *vt* [prisip'itāt] précipiter.
precipitation [prisipitā'shən] *n* précipitation *f*.
precipitous [prisip'itəs] *a* (*steep*) abrupt(e), à pic.
précis, *pl* **précis** [prā'sē] *n* résumé *m*.
precise [prisīs'] *a* précis(e).
precisely [prisīs'lē] *ad* précisément.
precision [prisizh'ən] *n* précision *f*.
preclude [priklood'] *vt* exclure, empêcher; **to ~ sb from doing** empêcher qn de faire.
precocious [prikō'shəs] *a* précoce.
preconceived [prēkənsēvd'] *a* (*idea*) préconçu(e).
preconception [prēkənsep'shən] *n* idée préconçue.

precondition [prēkəndish'ən] *n* condition *f* nécessaire.

precursor [prikûr'sûr] *n* précurseur *m*.

predate [prēdāt'] *vt* (*precede*) antidater.

predator [pred'ətûr] *n* prédateur *m*, rapace *m*.

predatory [pred'ətôrē] *a* rapace.

predecessor [pred'isesûr] *n* prédécesseur *m*.

predestination [prēdestinā'shən] *n* prédestination *f*.

predetermine [prēditûr'min] *vt* déterminer à l'avance.

predicament [pridik'əmənt] *n* situation *f* difficile.

predicate [pred'əkit] *n* (*LING*) prédicat *m*.

predict [pridikt'] *vt* prédire.

predictable [pridikt'əbəl] *a* prévisible.

predictably [pridikt'əblē] *ad* (*behave, react*) de façon prévisible; ~ **she didn't arrive** comme on pouvait s'y attendre, elle n'est pas venue.

prediction [pridik'shən] *n* prédiction *f*.

predispose [prēdispōz'] *vt* prédisposer.

predominance [pridâm'ənəns] *n* prédominance *f*.

predominant [pridâm'ənənt] *a* prédominant(e).

predominantly [pridâm'ənəntlē] *ad* en majeure partie; surtout.

predominate [pridâm'ənāt] *vi* prédominer.

preeminent [prēem'ənənt] *a* prééminent(e).

preempt [prēempt'] *vt* acquérir par droit de préemption; (*fig*) anticiper sur; **to ~ the issue** conclure avant même d'ouvrir les débats.

preemptive [prēemp'tiv] *a*: ~ **strike** attaque (*or* action) préventive.

preen [prēn] *vt*: **to ~ itself** (*bird*) se lisser les plumes; **to ~ o.s.** s'admirer.

prefab [prē'fab] *n* bâtiment préfabriqué.

prefabricated [prēfab'rikātid] *a* préfabriqué(e).

preface [pref'is] *n* préface *f*.

prefect [prē'fekt] *n* (*Brit: in school*) *élève chargé de certaines fonctions de discipline*; (*in France*) préfet *m*.

prefer [prifûr'] *vt* préférer; (*LAW*): **to ~ charges** procéder à une inculpation; **to ~ coffee to tea** préférer le café au thé.

preferable [pref'ûrəbəl] *a* préférable.

preferably [prifûr'əblē] *ad* de préférence.

preference [pref'ûrəns] *n* préférence *f*; **in ~ to sth** plutôt que qch, de préférence à qch.

preference shares *npl* (*Brit*) = **preferred stock**.

preferential [prefərən'chəl] *a* préférentiel(le); ~ **treatment** traitement *m* de faveur.

preferred stock [prifûrd' stâk] *npl* (*US*) actions privilégiées.

prefix [prē'fiks] *n* préfixe *m*.

pregnancy [preg'nənsē] *n* grossesse *f*.

pregnant [preg'nənt] *a* enceinte *af*; **3 months ~** enceinte de 3 mois.

prehistoric [prēhistôr'ik] *a* préhistorique.

prehistory [prēhis'tûrē] *n* préhistoire *f*.

prejudge [prējuj'] *vt* préjuger de.

prejudice [prej'ədis] *n* préjugé *m*; (*harm*) tort *m*, préjudice *m* ♦ *vt* porter préjudice à; (*bias*): **to ~ sb in favor of/against** prévenir qn en faveur de/contre.

prejudiced [prej'ədist] *a* (*person*) plein(e) de préjugés; (*view*) préconçu(e), partial(e); **to be ~ against sb/sth** avoir un parti-pris contre qn/qch.

prelate [prel'it] *n* prélat *m*.

preliminaries [prilim'ənärēz] *npl* préliminaires *mpl*.

preliminary [prilim'ənärē] *a* préliminaire.

prelude [prā'lōōd] *n* prélude *m*.

premarital [prēmar'itəl] *a* avant le mariage.

premature [prēməchōōr'] *a* prématuré(e); **to be ~ (in doing sth)** aller un peu (trop) vite (en faisant qch).

premeditated [primed'ətātid] *a* prémédité(e).

premeditation [primeditā'shən] *n* préméditation *f*.

premenstrual [prēmen'strōōəl] *a* prémenstruel(le).

premenstrual tension *n* irritabilité *f* avant les règles.

premier [primyēr'] *a* premier(ière), principal(e) ♦ *n* (*POL*) premier ministre.

première [primyēr'] *n* première *f*.

premise [prem'is] *n* prémisse *f*.

premises [prem'isiz] *npl* locaux *mpl*; **on the ~** sur les lieux; sur place; **business ~** locaux commerciaux.

premium [prē'mēəm] *n* prime *f*; **to be at a ~** (*fig: housing etc*) être très demandé(e), être rarissime; **to sell at a ~** (*shares*) vendre au-dessus du pair.

premium bond *n* (*Brit*) bon *m* à lots.

premium deal *n* (*COMM*) offre spéciale.

premium gas(oline) *n* (*US*) super *m*.

premonition [premənish'ən] *n* prémonition *f*.

prenatal [prēnāt'l] *a* (*US*) prénatal(e).

prenatal clinic *n* (*US*) service *m* de consultation prénatale.

preoccupation [prēâkyəpā'shən] *n* préoccupation *f*.

preoccupied [prēâk'yəpīd] *a* préoccupé(e).

prep [prep] *a* *abbr*: ~ **school** = **preparatory school**.

prepackaged [prēpak'ijd] *a* préempaqueté(e).

prepaid [prēpād'] *a* payé(e) d'avance.

preparation [prepərā'shən] *n* préparation *f*; ~**s** (*for trip, war*) préparatifs *mpl*; **in ~ for** en vue de.

preparatory [pripar'ətôrē] *a* préparatoire; ~ **to sth/to doing sth** en prévision de qch/avant de faire qch.

preparatory school *n* école primaire privée; (*US*) lycée privé.

prepare [pripâr'] *vt* préparer ♦ *vi*: **to ~ for** se préparer à.

prepared [pripârd'] *a*: ~ **for** préparé(e) à; ~ **to** prêt(e) à.

preponderance [pripân'dûrəns] *n* prépondérance *f*.

preposition [prepəzish'ən] *n* préposition *f*.

prepossessing [prēpəzes'ing] *a* avenant(e), engageant(e).

preposterous [pripâs'tûrəs] *a* absurde.

prep school *n* = **preparatory school**.

prerecord [prērikôrd'] *vt*: ~**ed broadcast** émission *f* en différé; ~**ed cassette** cassette enregistrée.

prerequisite [prirek'wizit] *n* condition *f* préalable.

prerogative [prərǎg'ətiv] n prérogative f.

presbyterian [prezbitēr'ēən] a, n presbytérien(ne).

presbytery [prez'bitārē] n presbytère m.

preschool [prē'skōōl'] a préscolaire; (child) d'âge préscolaire.

prescribe [priskrīb'] vt prescrire.

prescription [priskrip'shən] n prescription f; (MED) ordonnance f; **to fill a ~** faire une ordonnance.

prescriptive [priskrip'tiv] a normatif(ive).

presence [prez'əns] n présencè f; **~ of mind** présence d'esprit.

present [prez'ənt] a présent(e) ♦ n cadeau m; (also: **~ tense**) présent m ♦ vt [prizent'] présenter; (give): **to ~ sb with sth** offrir qch à qn; **to be ~ at** assister à; **those ~** les présents; **at ~** en ce moment; **to give sb a ~** offrir un cadeau à qn; **to ~ sb (to sb)** présenter qn (à qn).

presentable [prizen'təbəl] a présentable.

presentation [prezəntā'shən] n présentation f; (gift) cadeau m, présent m; (ceremony) remise f du cadeau; **on ~ of** (voucher etc) sur présentation de.

present-day [prez'əntdā'] a contemporain(e), actuel(le).

presenter [prizen'tûr] n (RADIO, TV) présentateur/trice.

presently [prez'əntlē] ad (soon) tout à l'heure, bientôt; (at present) en ce moment; (US: now) maintenant.

preservation [prezûrvā'shən] n préservation f, conservation f.

preservative [prizûr'vətiv] n agent m de conservation.

preserve [prizûrv'] vt (keep safe) préserver, protéger; (maintain) conserver, garder; (food) mettre en conserve ♦ n (for game, fish) réserve f; (often pl: jam) confiture f; (: fruit) fruits mpl en conserve.

preshrunk [prē'shrungk'] a irrétrécissable.

preside [prizīd'] vi présider.

presidency [prez'idənsē] n présidence f.

president [prez'idənt] n président/e; (US: of company) président-directeur général, PDG m.

presidential [prezidən'chəl] a présidentiel(le).

press [pres] n (tool, machine, newspapers) presse f; (for wine) pressoir m; (crowd) cohue f, foule f ♦ vt (push) appuyer sur; (squeeze) presser, serrer; (clothes: iron) repasser; (pursue) talonner; (insist): **to ~ sth on sb** presser qn d'accepter qch; (urge, entreat): **to ~ sb to do** or **into doing sth** pousser qn à faire qch ♦ vi appuyer, peser; se presser; **we are ~ed for time** le temps nous manque; **to ~ for sth** faire pression pour obtenir qch; **to ~ sb for an answer** presser qn de répondre; **to ~ charges against sb** (LAW) engager des poursuites contre qn; **to go to ~** (newspaper) aller à l'impression; **to be in the ~** (being printed) être sous presse; (in the newspapers) être dans le journal.

press on vi continuer.

press agency n agence f de presse.

press clipping n coupure f de presse.

press conference n conférence f de presse.

press cutting n (Brit) = **press clipping**.

press-gang [pres'gang] n recruteurs de la marine (jusqu'au 19ème siècle).

pressing [pres'ing] a urgent(e), pressant(e) ♦ n repassage m.

press release n communiqué m de presse.

press stud n (Brit) bouton-pression m.

press-up [pres'up] n (Brit) traction f.

pressure [presh'ûr] n pression f; (stress) tension f ♦ vt = **to put ~ on**; **to put ~ on sb (to do sth)** faire pression sur qn (pour qu'il fasse qch).

pressure cooker n cocotte-minute f.

pressure gauge n manomètre m.

pressure group n groupe m de pression.

pressurize [presh'ərīz] vt pressuriser; (Brit fig): **to ~ sb (into doing sth)** faire pression sur qn (pour qu'il fasse qch).

pressurized [presh'ərīzd] a pressurisé(e).

prestige [prestēzh'] n prestige m.

prestigious [prestij'əs] a prestigieux(euse).

presumably [prizōō'məblē] ad vraisemblablement; **~ he did it** c'est sans doute lui (qui a fait cela).

presume [prizōōm'] vt présumer, supposer; **to ~ to do** (dare) se permettre de faire.

presumption [prizump'shən] n supposition f, présomption f; (boldness) audace f.

presumptuous [prizump'chōōəs] a présomptueux(euse).

presuppose [prēsəpōz'] vt présupposer.

pretax [prē'taks] a avant impôt(s).

pretence [pritens'] n (Brit) = **pretense**.

pretend [pritend'] vt (feign) feindre, simuler ♦ vi (feign) faire semblant; (claim): **to ~ to sth** prétendre à qch; **to ~ to do** faire semblant de faire.

pretense [pritens'] n (US) (claim) prétention f; (pretext) prétexte m; **she is devoid of all ~** elle n'est pas du tout prétentieuse; **to make a ~ of doing** faire semblant de faire; **on** or **under the ~ of doing sth** sous prétexte de faire qch.

pretension [priten'chən] n (claim) prétention f; **to have no ~s to sth/to being sth** n'avoir aucune prétention à qch/à être qch.

pretentious [priten'chəs] a prétentieux(euse).

preterite [pret'ûrit] n prétérit m.

pretext [prē'tekst] n prétexte m; **on** or **under the ~ of doing sth** sous prétexte de faire qch.

pretty [prit'ē] a joli(e) ♦ ad assez.

prevail [privāl'] vi (win) l'emporter, prévaloir; (be usual) avoir cours; (persuade): **to ~ (up)on sb to do** persuader qn de faire.

prevailing [privā'ling] a dominant(e).

prevalent [prev'ələnt] a répandu(e), courant(e); (fashion) en vogue.

prevarication [privarikā'shən] n (usage m de) faux-fuyants mpl.

prevent [privent'] vt: **to ~ (from doing)** empêcher (de faire).

preventable [privent'əbəl] a évitable.

preventative [priven'tətiv] a préventif(ive).

prevention [priven'chən] n prévention f.

preventive [priven'tiv] a préventif(ive).

preview [prē'vyōō] n (of film) avant-première f; (fig) aperçu m.

previous [prē'vēəs] a (last) précédent(e);

(*earlier*) antérieur(e); (*question, experience*) préalable; **I have a ~ engagement** je suis déjà pris(e); **~ to doing** avant de faire.

previously [prē'vēəslē] *ad* précédemment, auparavant.

prewar [prē'wôr'] *a* d'avant-guerre.

prey [prā] *n* proie *f* ♦ *vi:* **to ~ on** s'attaquer à; **it was ~ing on his mind** ça le rongeait *or* minait.

price [prīs] *n* prix *m*; (*BETTING: odds*) cote *f* ♦ *vt* (*goods*) fixer le prix de; tarifer; **what is the ~ of ...?** combien coûte ...?, quel est le prix de ...?; **to go up** *or* **rise in ~** augmenter; **to put a ~ on sth** chiffrer qch; **to be ~d out of the market** (*article*) être trop cher pour soutenir la concurrence; (*producer, nation*) ne pas pouvoir soutenir la concurrence; **he regained his freedom, but at a ~** il a retrouvé sa liberté, mais cela lui a coûté cher.

price control *n* contrôle *m* des prix.

price-cutting [prīs'kuting] *n* réductions *fpl* de prix.

priceless [prīs'lis] *a* sans prix, inestimable; (*col: amusing*) impayable.

price list *n* tarif *m*.

price range *n* gamme *f* de prix; **it's within my ~** c'est dans mes prix.

price tag *n* étiquette *f*.

price war *n* guerre *f* des prix.

pricey [prī'sē] *a* (*col*) chérot *inv*.

prick [prik] *n* piqûre *f*; (*col!*) bitte *f* (*!*); connard *m* (*!*) ♦ *vt* piquer; **to ~ up one's ears** dresser *or* tendre l'oreille.

prickle [prik'əl] *n* (*of plant*) épine *f*; (*sensation*) picotement *m*.

prickly [prik'lē] *a* piquant(e), épineux(euse); (*fig: person*) irritable.

prickly heat *n* fièvre *f* miliaire.

prickly pear *n* figue *f* de Barbarie.

pride [prīd] *n* (*feeling proud*) fierté *f*; (: *pej*) orgueil *m*; (*self-esteem*) amour-propre *m* ♦ *vt:* **to ~ o.s. on** se flatter de; s'enorgueillir de; **to take (a) ~ in** être (très) fier(ère) de; **to take a ~ in doing** mettre sa fierté à faire.

priest [prēst] *n* prêtre *m*.

priestess [prēs'tis] *n* prêtresse *f*.

priesthood [prēst'hŏŏd] *n* prêtrise *f*, sacerdoce *m*.

prig [prig] *n* poseur/euse, fat *m*.

prim [prim] *a* collet monté *inv*, guindé(e).

prima facie [prē'mə fā'sē] *a:* **to have a ~ case** (*LAW*) avoir une affaire qui paraît fondée.

primarily [prīmār'ilē] *ad* principalement, essentiellement.

primary [prī'mārē] *a* primaire; (*first in importance*) premier(ière), primordial(e) ♦ *n* (*US: election*) (élection *f*) primaire.

primary color *n* couleur fondamentale.

primary products *npl* produits *mpl* de base.

primary school *n* (*Brit*) école primaire *f*.

primate *n* (*REL*) [prī'mit] primat *m*; (*ZOOL*) [prī'māt] primate *m*.

prime [prīm] *a* primordial(e), fondamental(e); (*excellent*) excellent(e) ♦ *vt* (*gun, pump*) amorcer; (*fig*) mettre au courant; **in the ~ of life** dans la fleur de l'âge.

prime minister *n* premier ministre.

primer [prī'mûr] *n* (*book*) premier livre, manuel *m* élémentaire; (*paint*) apprêt *m*; (*of gun*) amorce *f*.

prime time *n* (*RADIO. TV*) heure(s) *f(pl)* de grande écoute.

primeval [prīmē'vəl] *a* primitif(ive).

primitive [prim'ətiv] *a* primitif(ive).

primrose [prim'rōz] *n* primevère *f*.

primus (stove) [prī'məs (stōv)] *n* ® (*Brit*) réchaud *m* de camping.

prince [prins] *n* prince *m*.

princess [prin'sis] *n* princesse *f*.

principal [prin'səpəl] *a* principal(e) ♦ *n* (*headmaster*) directeur *m*, principal *m*; (*in play*) rôle principal; (*money*) principal *m*.

principality [prinsəpal'itē] *n* principauté *f*.

principally [prin'səpəlē] *ad* principalement.

principle [prin'səpəl] *n* principe *m*; **in ~** en principe; **on ~** par principe.

print [print] *n* (*mark*) empreinte *f*; (*letters*) caractères *mpl*; (*fabric*) imprimé *m*; (*ART*) gravure *f*, estampe *f*; (*PHOT*) épreuve *f* ♦ *vt* imprimer; (*publish*) publier; (*write in capitals*) écrire en majuscules; **out of ~** épuisé(e).

print out *vt* (*COMPUT*) imprimer.

printed circuit board (PCB) *n* carte *f* à circuit imprimé.

printed matter *n* imprimés *mpl*.

printer [prin'tûr] *n* imprimeur *m*; (*machine*) imprimante *f*.

printhead [print'hed] *n* tête *f* d'impression.

printing [prin'ting] *n* impression *f*.

printing press *n* presse *f* typographique.

print-out [print'out] *n* listing *m*.

print shop *n* imprimerie *f*.

print wheel *n* marguerite *f*.

prior [prī'ûr] *a* antérieur(e), précédent(e) ♦ *n* (*REL*) prieur *m*; **~ to doing** avant de faire; **without ~ notice** sans préavis; **to have a ~ claim to sth** avoir priorité pour qch.

priority [prīôr'itē] *n* priorité *f*; **to have** *or* **take ~ over sth/sb** avoir la priorité sur qch/qn.

priory [prī'ərē] *n* prieuré *m*.

prise [prīz] *vt* (*Brit*): **to ~ open** forcer.

prism [priz'əm] *n* prisme *m*.

prison [priz'ən] *n* prison *f*.

prison camp *n* camp *m* de prisonniers.

prisoner [priz'ənûr] *n* prisonnier/ière; **the ~ at the bar** l'accusé/e; **to take sb ~** faire qn prisonnier; **~ of war** prisonnier de guerre.

prison warden *n* (*US*) directeur/trice de prison.

prissy [pris'ē] *a* bégueule.

pristine [pris'tēn] *a* virginal(e).

privacy [prī'vəsē] *n* intimité *f*, solitude *f*.

private [prī'vit] *a* (*not public*) privé(e); (*personal*) personnel(le); (*house, car, lesson*) particulier(ière) ♦ *n* (*US MIL*) soldat *m* de deuxième classe; **"~"** (*on envelope*) "personnelle"; **in ~** en privé; **in (his) ~ life** dans sa vie privée; **he is a very ~ person** il est très secret; **to be in ~ practice** être médecin *or* dentiste *etc*) non conventionné; **~ hearing** (*LAW*) audience *f* à huis-clos.

private enterprise *n* entreprise privée.

private eye *n* détective privé.

private limited company *n* (*Brit*) société *f* à participation restreinte (*non cotée en*

Bourse).

privately [prī'vitlē] *ad* en privé; (*within one-self*) intérieurement.

private parts *npl* parties (génitales).

private property *n* propriété privée.

private school *n* école privée.

privation [prīvā'shən] *n* privation *f*.

privatize [prī'vətiz] *vt* privatiser.

privet [priv'it] *n* troène *m*.

privilege [priv'əlij] *n* privilège *m*.

privileged [priv'əlijd] *a* privilégié(e); **to be ~ to do sth** avoir le privilège de faire qch.

privy [priv'ē] *a*: **to be ~ to** être au courant de.

privy council *n* conseil privé.

prize [prīz] *n* prix *m* ♦ *a* (*example, idiot*) parfait(e); (*bull, novel*) primé(e) ♦ *vt* priser, faire grand cas de; (*US*): **to ~ open** forcer.

prize fight *n* combat professionnel.

prize giving *n* distribution *f* des prix.

prize money *n* argent *m* du prix.

prizewinner [prīz'winûr] *n* gagnant/e.

prizewinning [prīz'wining] *a* gagnant(e); (*novel, essay etc*) primé(e).

PRO *n abbr* = **public relations officer.**

pro [prō] *n* (*SPORT*) professionnel/le; **the ~s and cons** le pour et le contre.

pro- [prō] *prefix* (*in favor of*) pro-.

probability [prâbəbil'ətē] *n* probabilité *f*; **in all ~** très probablement.

probable [prâb'əbəl] *a* probable; **it is ~/ hardly ~ that ...** il est probable/peu probable que ....

probably [prâb'əblē] *ad* probablement.

probate [prō'bāt] *n* (*LAW*) validation *f*, homologation *f*.

probation [prəbā'shən] *n* (*in employment*) (période *f* d')essai *m*; (*LAW*) liberté surveillée; (*REL*) noviciat *m*, probation *f*; **on ~** (*employee*) à l'essai; (*LAW*) en liberté surveillée.

probationary [prəbā'shənârē] *a* (*period*) d'essai.

probe [prōb] *n* (*MED, SPACE*) sonde *f*; (*enquiry*) enquête *f*, investigation *f* ♦ *vt* sonder, explorer.

probity [prō'bitē] *n* probité *f*.

problem [prâb'ləm] *n* problème *m*; **to have ~s with the car** avoir des ennuis avec la voiture; **what's the ~?** qu'y a-t-il?, quel est le problème?; **I had no ~ in finding her** je n'ai pas eu de mal à la trouver; **no ~!** pas de problème!

problematic [prâbləmat'ik] *a* problématique.

procedure [prəsē'jûr] *n* (*ADMIN, LAW*) procédure *f*; (*method*) marche *f* à suivre, façon *f* de procéder.

proceed [prəsēd'] *vi* (*go forward*) avancer; (*go about it*) procéder; (*continue*): **to ~ (with)** continuer, poursuivre; **to ~ to** aller à; passer à; **to ~ to do** se mettre à faire; **I am not sure how to ~** je ne sais pas exactement comment m'y prendre; **to ~ against sb** (*LAW*) intenter des poursuites contre qn.

proceeding [prəsē'ding] *n* procédé *m*, façon *f* d'agir.

proceedings [prəsē'dingz] *npl* mesures *fpl*; (*LAW*) poursuites *fpl*; (*meeting*) réunion *f*, séance *f*; (*records*) compte rendu; actes *mpl*.

proceeds [prō'sēds] *npl* produit *m*, recette *f*.

process *n* [prâs'es] processus *m*; (*method*)

procédé *m* ♦ *vt* traiter ♦ *vi* [prases'] (*Brit formal: go in procession*) défiler; **in ~** en cours; **we are in the ~ of doing** nous sommes en train de faire.

process(ed) cheese [prâs'es(t) chēz] *n* ≈ fromage fondu.

processing [prâs'esing] *n* traitement *m*.

procession [prəsesh'ən] *n* défilé *m*, cortège *m*; **funeral ~** cortège funèbre, convoi *m* mortuaire.

proclaim [prəklām'] *vt* déclarer, proclamer.

proclamation [prâkləmā'shən] *n* proclamation *f*.

proclivity [prōkliv'ətē] *n* inclination *f*.

procrastination [prōkrastənā'shən] *n* procrastination *f*.

procreation [prōkrēā'shən] *n* procréation *f*.

proctor [prâk'tûr] *n* (*US*) surveillant *m* d'examen.

procure [prəkyōōr'] *vt* (*for o.s.*) se procurer; (*for sb*) procurer.

procurement [prəkyōōr'mənt] *n* achat *m*, approvisionnement *m*.

prod [prâd] *vt* pousser ♦ *n* (*push, jab*) petit coup, poussée *f*.

prodigal [prâd'əgəl] *a* prodigue.

prodigious [prədij'əs] *a* prodigieux(euse).

prodigy [prâd'əjē] *n* prodige *m*.

produce *n* [prō'dōōs] (*AGR*) produits *mpl* ♦ *vt* [prədōōs'] produire; (*to show*) présenter; (*cause*) provoquer, causer; (*THEATER*) monter, mettre en scène.

producer [prədōō'sûr] *n* (*THEATER*) metteur *m* en scène; (*AGR, CINEMA*) producteur *m*.

product [prâd'əkt] *n* produit *m*.

production [prəduk'shən] *n* production *f*; (*THEATER*) mise *f* en scène; **to put into ~** (*goods*) entreprendre la fabrication de.

production agreement *n* (*US*) accord *m* de productivité.

production control *n* contrôle *m* de production.

production line *n* chaîne *f* (de fabrication).

production manager *n* directeur/trice de la production.

productive [prəduk'tiv] *a* productif(ive).

productivity [prâdəktiv'ətē] *n* productivité *f*.

productivity agreement *n* (*Brit*) = **production agreement.**

productivity bonus *n* prime *f* de rendement.

Prof. [prâf] *abbr* (= *professor*) Prof.

profane [prəfān'] *a* sacrilège; (*lay*) profane.

profess [prəfes'] *vt* professer; **I do not ~ to be an expert** je ne prétends pas être spécialiste.

professed [prəfest'] *a* (*self-declared*) déclaré(e).

profession [prəfesh'ən] *n* profession *f*; **the ~s** les professions libérales.

professional [prəfesh'ənəl] *n* (*SPORT*) professionnel/le ♦ *a* professionnel(le); (*work*) de professionnel; **he's a ~ man** il exerce une profession libérale; **to seek ~ advice** consulter un spécialiste.

professionalism [prəfesh'ənəlizəm] *n* professionnalisme *m*.

professionally [prəfesh'ənəlē] *ad* professionnellement; (*SPORT: play*) en professionnel; **I only know him ~** je n'ai avec lui que des relations de travail.

professor [prəfes'ûr] *n* professeur *m* (*titulaire d'une chaire*); (*US: teacher*) professeur *m*.

professorship [prəfes'ûrship] *n* chaire *f*.

proffer [prâf'ûr] *vt* (*hand*) tendre; (*remark*) faire; (*apologies*) présenter.

proficiency [prəfish'ənsē] *n* compétence *f*, aptitude *f*.

proficient [prəfish'ənt] *a* compétent(e), capable.

profile [prō'fil] *n* profil *m*; **to keep a high/low** ~ (*fig*) rester *or* être très en évidence/discret(ète).

profit [prâf'it] *n* (*from trading*) bénéfice *m*; (*advantage*) profit *m* ♦ *vi*: **to** ~ (**by** *or* **from**) profiter (de); ~ **and loss statement** compte *m* de profits et pertes; **to make a** ~ faire un *or* des bénéfice(s); **to sell sth at a** ~ vendre qch à profit.

profitability [prâfitəbil'ətē] *n* rentabilité *f*.

profitable [prâf'itəbəl] *a* lucratif(ive), rentable; (*fig: beneficial*) avantageux(euse); (: *meeting*) fructueux(euse).

profit center *n* centre *m* de profit.

profiteering [prâfitēr'ing] *n* (*pej*) mercantilisme *m*.

profit-making [prâf'itmāking] *a* à but lucratif.

profit margin *n* marge *f* bénéficiaire.

profit sharing [prâf'it shä'ring] *n* intéressement *m* aux bénéfices.

profligate [prâf'ləgit] *a* (*behavior, act*) dissolu(e); (*person*) débauché(e); (*extravagant*): ~ (**with**) prodigue (de).

pro forma [prō fôr'mə] *a*: ~ **invoice** facture *f* pro-forma.

profound [prəfound'] *a* profond(e).

profuse [prəfyōōs'] *a* abondant(e).

profusely [prəfyōōs'lē] *ad* abondamment; (*thank etc*) avec effusion.

profusion [prəfyōō'zhən] *n* profusion *f*, abondance *f*.

progeny [prâj'ənē] *n* progéniture *f*; descendants *mpl*.

program (*US*) *n* [prō'grəm] programme *m*; (*RADIO, TV*) émission *f* ♦ *vt* [prō'gram] (*also: Brit: COMPUT*) programmer.

program(m)er [prō'gramûr] *n* programmeur/euse.

program(m)ing [prō'graming] *n* programmation *f*.

program(m)ing language *n* langage *m* de programmation.

programme [prō'gram] *etc* (*Brit*) = **program** *etc*.

progress [prâg'res] *n* progrès *m* ♦ *vi* [prəgres'] progresser, avancer; **in** ~ en cours; **to make** ~ progresser, faire des progrès, être en progrès; **as the match** ~**ed** au fur et à mesure que la partie avançait.

progression [prəgresh'ən] *n* progression *f*.

progressive [prəgres'iv] *a* progressif(ive); (*person*) progressiste.

progressively [prəgres'ivlē] *ad* progressivement.

progress report *n* (*MED*) bulletin *m* de santé; (*ADMIN*) rapport *m* d'activité; rapport sur l'état (d'avancement) des travaux.

prohibit [prōhib'it] *vt* interdire, défendre; **to** ~ **sb from doing sth** défendre *or* interdire à

qn de faire qch; **"smoking** ~**ed"** "défense de fumer".

prohibition [prōəbish'ən] *n* prohibition *f*.

prohibitive [prōhib'ətiv] *a* (*price etc*) prohibitif(ive).

project *n* [prâj'ekt] (*plan*) projet *m*, plan *m*; (*venture*) opération *f*, entreprise *f*; (*gen SCOL: research*) étude *f*, dossier *m* ♦ *vb* [prəjekt'] *vt* projeter ♦ *vi* (*stick out*) faire saillie, s'avancer.

projectile [prəjek'təl] *n* projectile *m*.

projection [prəjek'shən] *n* projection *f*; (*overhang*) saillie *f*.

projectionist [prəjek'shənist] *n* (*CINEMA*) projectionniste *m/f*.

projection room *n* (*CINEMA*) cabine *f* de projection.

projector [prəjek'tûr] *n* (*CINEMA etc*) projecteur *m*.

proletarian [prōlitär'ēən] *a* prolétarien(ne) ♦ *n* prolétaire *m/f*.

proletariat [prōlitär'ēət] *n* prolétariat *m*.

proliferate [prōlif'ərāt] *vi* proliférer.

proliferation [prōlifərā'shən] *n* prolifération *f*.

prolific [prōlif'ik] *a* prolifique.

prolog(ue) [prō'lôg] *n* prologue *m*.

prolong [prəlông'] *vt* prolonger.

prom [prâm] *n abbr* = **promenade**; (*Brit*) **promenade concert**; (*US: ball*) bal *m* d'étudiants.

promenade [prâmənād'] *n* (*by sea*) esplanade *f*, promenade *f*.

promenade concert *n* (*Brit*) concert *m* (de musique classique).

promenade deck *n* (*NAUT*) pont *m* promenade.

prominence [prâm'ənəns] *n* proéminence *f*; importance *f*.

prominent [prâm'ənənt] *a* (*standing out*) proéminent(e); (*important*) important(e); **he is** ~ **in the field of** ... il est très connu dans le domaine de ....

prominently [prâm'ənəntlē] *ad* (*display, set*) bien en évidence; **he figured** ~ **in the case** il a joué un rôle important dans l'affaire.

promiscuity [prâmiskyōō'itē] *n* (*sexual*) légèreté *f* de mœurs.

promiscuous [prəmis'kyōōəs] *a* (*sexually*) de mœurs légères.

promise [prâm'is] *n* promesse *f* ♦ *vt, vi* promettre; **to make sb a** ~ faire une promesse à qn; **to** ~ (**sb**) **to do sth** promettre (à qn) de faire qch; **a young man of** ~ un jeune homme plein d'avenir; **to** ~ **well** *vi* prometttre.

promising [prâm'ising] *a* prometteur(euse).

promissory note [prâm'isôrē nōt] *n* billet *m* à ordre.

promontory [prâm'əntôrē] *n* promontoire *m*.

promote [prəmōt'] *vt* promouvoir; (*venture, event*) organiser, mettre sur pied; (*new product*) lancer; **the team was** ~**d to the second division** (*Brit SOCCER*) l'équipe est montée en 2e division.

promoter [prəmō'tûr] *n* (*of event*) organisateur/trice; (*of cause etc*) partisan/e, défenseur *m*.

promotion [prəmō'shən] *n* promotion *f*.

prompt [prâmpt] *a* rapide ♦ *n* (*COMPUT*)

message *m* (de guidage) ♦ *vt* inciter; (*cause*) entraîner, provoquer; (*THEATER*) souffler (son rôle *or* ses répliques) à; **they're very ~** (*punctual*) ils sont ponctuels; **at 8 o'clock ~** à 8 heures précises; **he was ~ to accept** il a tout de suite accepté; **to ~ sb to do** inciter *or* pousser qn à faire.

prompter [prámp'tûr] *n* (*THEATER*) souffleur *m*.

promptly [prámpt'lē] *ad* rapidement, sans délai; ponctuellement.

promptness [prámpt'nis] *n* rapidité *f*; promptitude *f*; ponctualité *f*.

promulgate [prám'əlgāt] *vt* promulguer.

prone [prōn] *a* (*lying*) couché(e) (face contre terre); (*liable*): **~ to** enclin(e) à; **to be ~ to illness** être facilement malade; **to be ~ to an illness** être sujet à une maladie; **she is ~ to burst into tears if** ... elle a tendance à tomber en larmes si ....

prong [prông] *n* pointe *f*; (*of fork*) dent *f*.

pronoun [prō'noun] *n* pronom *m*.

pronounce [prənouns'] *vt* prononcer ♦ *vi*: **to ~ (up)on** se prononcer sur; **they ~d him unfit to drive** ils l'ont déclaré inapte à la conduite.

pronounced [prənounst'] *a* (*marked*) prononcé(e).

pronouncement [prənouns'mənt] *n* déclaration *f*.

pronunciation [prənunsēā'shən] *n* prononciation *f*.

proof [proot] *n* preuve *f*; (*test, of book*, *PHOT*) épreuve *f*; (*of alcohol*) degré *m* ♦ *a*: **~ against** à l'épreuve de; **to be 35% ~** ≈ titrer 40 degrés.

proofreader [proof'rēdûr] *n* correcteur/trice (d'épreuves).

prop [präp] *n* support *m*, étai *m* ♦ *vt* (*also*: **~ up**) étayer, soutenir; (*lean*): **to ~ sth against** appuyer qch contre *or* à.

Prop. *abbr* (*COMM*) = **proprietor**.

propaganda [präpəgan'də] *n* propagande *f*.

propagation [präpəgā'shən] *n* propagation *f*.

propel [prəpel'] *vt* propulser, faire avancer.

propeller [prəpel'ûr] *n* hélice *f*.

propelling pencil [prəpel'ing pen'səl] *n* (*Brit*) porte-mine *m inv*.

propensity [prəpen'sitē] *n* propension *f*.

proper [präp'ûr] *a* (*suited, right*) approprié(e), bon(bonne); (*seemly*) correct(e), convenable; (*authentic*) vrai(e), véritable; (*col: real*) *n* + fini(e), vrai(e); **to go through the ~ channels** (*ADMIN*) passer par la voie officielle.

properly [präp'ûrlē] *ad* correctement, convenablement; (*really*) bel et bien.

proper noun *n* nom *m* propre.

property [präp'ûrtē] *n* (*possessions*) biens *mpl*; (*house etc*) propriété *f*; (*land*) terres *fpl*, domaine *m*; (*CHEMISTRY etc: quality*) propriété *f*; **it's their ~** cela leur appartient, c'est leur propriété.

property developer *n* (*Brit*) promoteur immobilier.

property owner *n* propriétaire *m*.

property tax *n* impôt foncier.

prophecy [präf'isē] *n* prophétie *f*.

prophesy [präf'isī] *vt* prédire ♦ *vi* prophétiser.

prophet [präf'it] *n* prophète *m*.

prophetic [prəfet'ik] *a* prophétique.

prophylactic [prōfəlak'tik] *n* préservatif *m*.

proportion [prəpôr'shən] *n* proportion *f*; (*share*) part *f*; partie *f* ♦ *vt* proportionner; **to be in/out of ~ to** *or* **with sth** être à la mesure de/hors de proportion avec qch; **to see sth in ~** (*fig*) ramener qch à de justes proportions.

proportional [prəpôr'shənəl] *a* proportionnel(le).

proportional representation (PR) *n* (*POL*) représentation proportionnelle.

proportionate [prəpôr'shənit] *a* proportionnel(le).

proposal [prəpō'zəl] *n* proposition *f*, offre *f*; (*plan*) projet *m*; (*of marriage*) demande *f* en mariage.

propose [prəpōz'] *vt* proposer, suggérer; (*have in mind*): **to ~ sth/to do** *or* **doing sth** envisager qch/de faire qch ♦ *vi* faire sa demande en mariage; **to ~ to do** avoir l'intention de faire.

proposer [prəpō'zûr] *n* (*of motion etc*) auteur *m*.

proposition [präpəzish'ən] *n* proposition *f*; **to make sb a ~** faire une proposition à qn.

propound [prəpound'] *vt* proposer, soumettre.

proprietary [prəprī'itārē] *a* de marque déposée; **~ article** article *m* *or* produit *m* de marque; **~ brand** marque déposée.

proprietor [prəprī'ətûr] *n* propriétaire *m/f*.

propriety [prəprī'ətē] *n* (*seemliness*) bienséance *f*, convenance *f*.

propulsion [prəpul'shən] *n* propulsion *f*.

pro rata [prō ra'tə] *ad* au prorata.

prosaic [prōzā'ik] *a* prosaïque.

Pros. Atty. *abbr* (*US*) = **prosecuting attorney.**

proscribe [prōskrīb'] *vt* proscrire.

prose [prōz] *n* prose *f*; (*Brit SCOL: translation*) thème *m*.

prosecute [präs'əkyōōt] *vt* poursuivre.

prosecuting attorney (Pros. Atty.) *n* (*US*) procureur *m*.

prosecution [präsəkyōō'shən] *n* poursuites *fpl* judiciaires; (*accusing side*) accusation *f*.

prosecutor [präs'əkyōōtûr] *n* procureur *m*; (*also*: **public ~**) ministère public.

prospect [präs'pekt] *n* perspective *f*; (*hope*) espoir *m*, chances *fpl* ♦ *vt*, *vi* prospecter; **we are faced with the ~ of leaving** nous risquons de devoir partir; **there is every ~ of an early victory** tout laisse prévoir une victoire rapide.

prospecting [präs'pekting] *n* prospection *f*.

prospective [präspek'tiv] *a* (*possible*) éventuel(le); (*future*) futur(e).

prospector [präs'pektûr] *n* prospecteur *m*; **gold ~** chercheur *m* d'or.

prospects [präs'pekts] *npl* (*for work etc*) possibilités *fpl* d'avenir, débouchés *mpl*.

prospectus [präspek'təs] *n* prospectus *m*.

prosper [präs'pûr] *vi* prospérer.

prosperity [präspär'itē] *n* prospérité *f*.

prosperous [präs'pûrəs] *a* prospère.

prostate [präs'tāt] *n* (*also*: **~ gland**) prostate *f*.

prostitute [präs'titōōt] *n* prostituée *f*; **male ~**

prostitué *m*.
prostitution [prâstitōō'shən] *n* prostitution *f*.
prostrate [prás'trāt] *a* prosterné(e); (*fig*) prostré(e) ♦ *vt*: **to ~ o.s. (before sb)** se prosterner (devant qn).
protagonist [prōtag'ənist] *n* protagoniste *m*.
protect [prətekt'] *vt* protéger.
protection [prətek'shən] *n* protection *f*; **to be under sb's ~** être sous la protection de qn.
protectionism [prətek'shənizəm] *n* protectionnisme *m*.
protection racket *n* racket *m*.
protective [prətek'tiv] *a* protecteur(trice); **~ custody** (*LAW*) détention préventive.
protector [prətek'tûr] *n* protecteur/trice.
protégé [prō'təzhā] *n* protégé *m*.
protégée [prō'təzhā] *n* protégée *f*.
protein [prō'tēn] *n* protéine *f*.
pro tem [prō tem] *ad abbr* (= *pro tempore: for the time being*) provisoirement.
protest *n* [prō'test] protestation *f* ♦ *vb* [prōtest'] *vi*: **to ~ against/about** protester contre/à propos de ♦ *vt* protester de.
Protestant [prât'istənt] *a*, *n* protestant(e).
protester, protestor [prətes'tûr] *n* (*in demonstration*) manifestant/e.
protest march *n* manifestation *f*.
protocol [prō'təkôl] *n* protocole *m*.
prototype [prō'tətip] *n* prototype *m*.
protracted [prōtrak'tid] *a* prolongé(e).
protractor [prōtrak'tûr] *n* (*GEOM*) rapporteur *m*.
protrude [prōtrōōd'] *vi* avancer, dépasser.
protuberance [prōtōō'bûrəns] *n* protubérance *f*.
proud [proud] *a* fier(ère); (*pej*) orgueilleux(euse); **to be ~ to do sth** être fier de faire qch; **to do sb ~** (*col*) faire honneur à qn; **to do o.s. ~** (*col*) ne se priver de rien.
proudly [proud'lē] *ad* fièrement.
prove [prōōv] *vt* prouver, démontrer ♦ *vi*: **to ~ correct** *etc* s'avérer juste *etc*; **to ~ o.s.** montrer ce dont on est capable; **to ~ o.s./itself (to be) useful** *etc* se montrer *or* se révéler utile *etc*; **he was ~d right in the end** il s'est avéré qu'il avait raison.
proverb [prâv'ûrb] *n* proverbe *m*.
proverbial [prəvûr'bēəl] *a* proverbial(e).
provide [prəvīd'] *vt* fournir; **to ~ sb with sth** fournir qch à qn; **to be ~d with** (*person*) disposer de; (*thing*) être équipé(e) *or* muni(e) de.
provide for *vt fus* (*person*) subvenir aux besoins de; (*emergency*) prévoir.
provided [prəvī'did] *cj*: **~ (that)** à condition que + *sub*.
Providence [prâv'idəns] *n* la Providence.
providing [prəvī'ding] *cj* à condition que + *sub*.
province [prâv'ins] *n* province *f*.
provincial [prəvin'chəl] *a* provincial(e).
provision [prəvizh'ən] *n* (*supply*) provision *f*; (*supplying*) fourniture *f*; approvisionnement *m*; (*stipulation*) disposition *f*; **~s** *npl* (*food*) provisions *fpl*; **to make ~ for** (*one's future*) assurer; (*one's family*) assurer l'avenir de; **there's no ~ for this in the contract** le contrat ne prévoit pas cela.

provisional [prəvizh'ənəl] *a* provisoire ♦ *n*: **P~** (*Irish POL*) Provisional *m* (*membre de la tendance activiste de l'IRA*).
provisional licence *n* (*Brit AUT*) permis *m* provisoire.
provisionally [prəvizh'ənəlē] *ad* provisoirement.
proviso [prəvī'zō] *n* condition *f*; **with the ~ that** à la condition (expresse) que.
Provo [prō'vō] *n abbr* (*Irish POL*) = **Provisional**.
provocation [prâvəkā'shən] *n* provocation *f*.
provocative [prəvâk'ətiv] *a* provocateur(trice), provocant(e).
provoke [prəvōk'] *vt* provoquer; **to ~ sb to sth/to do** *or* **into doing sth** pousser qn à qch/à faire qch.
provoking [prəvōk'ing] *a* énervant(e), exaspérant(e).
provost [prâv'əst] *n* (*of university*) principal *m*; (*Scottish*) maire *m*.
prow [prou] *n* proue *f*.
prowess [prou'is] *n* prouesse *f*.
prowl [proul] *vi* (*also*: **~ around**) rôder ♦ *n*: **to be on the ~** rôder.
prowler [prou'lûr] *n* rôdeur/euse.
proximity [prâksim'itē] *n* proximité *f*.
proxy [prâk'sē] *n* procuration *f*; **by ~** par procuration.
prude [prōōd] *n* prude *f*.
prudence [prōō'dəns] *n* prudence *f*.
prudent [prōō'dənt] *a* prudent(e).
prudish [prōō'dish] *a* prude, pudibond(e).
prune [prōōn] *n* pruneau *m* ♦ *vt* élaguer.
pruning shears [prōōn'ing shirz] *npl* sécateur *m*.
pry [prī] *vi*: **to ~ into** fourrer son nez dans; **to ~ open** (*US*) forcer.
PS *n abbr* (= *postscript*) PS *m*.
psalm [sâm] *n* psaume *m*.
PSAT *n abbr* (*US*) = *Preliminary Scholastic Aptitude Test.*
pseudo- [sōō'dō] *prefix* pseudo-.
pseudonym [sōō'dənim] *n* pseudonyme *m*.
PST *abbr* (*US*: = *Pacific Standard Time*) *heure d'hiver du Pacifique.*
psyche [sī'kē] *n* psychisme *m*.
psychiatric [sīkēat'rik] *a* psychiatrique.
psychiatrist [siki'ətrist] *n* psychiatre *m/f*.
psychiatry [siki'ətrē] *n* psychiatrie *f*.
psychic [sī'kik] *a* (*also*: **~al**) (méta-) psychique; (*person*) doué(e) de télépathie *or* d'un sixième sens.
psychoanalyze, (*Brit*) **psychoanalyse** [sīkōan'əliz] *vt* psychanalyser.
psychoanalysis, *pl* **-lyses** [sīkōanal'isis, -sēz] *n* psychanalyse *f*.
psychoanalyst [sīkōan'əlist] *n* psychanalyste *m/f*.
psychological [sīkələj'ikəl] *a* psychologique.
psychologist [sīkâl'əjist] *n* psychologue *m/f*.
psychology [sīkâl'əjē] *n* psychologie *f*.
psychopath [sī'kəpath] *n* psychopathe *m/f*.
psychosis, *pl* **psychoses** [sīkō'sis, -sēz] *n* psychose *f.*
psychosomatic [sīkōsōmat'ik] *a* psychosomatique.
psychotherapy [sīkōthär'əpē] *n* psychothérapie *f*.

psychotic [sīkât'ik] *a*, *n* psychotique *(m/f)*.
PT *n abbr (Brit: = physical training)* EPS *f*.
pt *abbr* = **pint, point.**
PTA *n abbr = Parent-Teacher Association.*
PTO *abbr (= please turn over)* TSVP (= *tournez s'il vous plaît)*.
PTV *n abbr (US) = pay television, public television.*
pub [pub] *n (Brit)* pub *m*.
puberty [pyōō'bûrtē] *n* puberté *f*.
pubic [pyōō'bik] *a* pubien(ne), du pubis.
public [pub'lik] *a* public(ique), ♦ *n* public *m*; **in ~** en public; **the general ~** le grand public; **to be ~ knowledge** être de notoriété publique; **to go ~** *(COMM)* être coté(e) en Bourse.
public address system (PA) *n* (système *m* de) sonorisation *f*, sono *f (col)*.
publican [pub'likən] *n* patron *m* or gérant *m* de pub.
publication [publikā'shən] *n* publication *f*.
public company *n* société *f* anonyme *(cotée en Bourse)*.
public convenience *n (Brit)* toilettes *fpl*.
public holiday *n (Brit)* jour férié.
public house *n (Brit)* pub *m*.
public housing unit *n (US)* habitation *f* à loyer modéré.
publicity [publis'ətē] *n* publicité *f*.
publicize [pub'ləsīz] *vt* faire connaître, rendre public.
public limited company (plc) *n (Brit)* ≈ société anonyme (SA) *(cotée en Bourse)*.
publicly [pub'liklē] *ad* publiquement, en public.
public opinion *n* opinion publique.
public ownership *n*: **to be taken into ~** être nationalisé(e), devenir propriété de l'État.
public relations (PR) *n or npl* relations publiques (RP).
public relations officer (PRO) *n* responsable *m/f* des relations publiques.
public school *n (US)* école publique; *(Brit)* école privée.
public sector *n* secteur public.
public service vehicle (PSV) *n (Brit)* véhicule affecté au transport de personnes.
public-spirited [pub'likspir'itid] *a* qui fait preuve de civisme.
public transportation, *(Brit)* **public transport** *n* transports *mpl* en commun.
public utility *n* service public.
public works *npl* travaux publics.
publish [pub'lish] *vt* publier.
publisher [pub'lishûr] *n* éditeur *m*.
publishing [pub'lishing] *n (industry)* édition *f*; *(of a book)* publication *f*.
publishing company *n* maison *f* d'édition.
puce [pyōōs] *a* puce.
puck [puk] *n (elf)* lutin *m*; *(ICE HOCKEY)* palet *m*.
pucker [puk'ûr] *vt* plisser.
pudding [pŏŏd'ing] *n (dessert)* dessert *m*, entremets *m*; **rice ~** ≈ riz *m* au lait.
puddle [pud'əl] *n* flaque *f* d'eau.
pudgy [puj'ē] *a (US)* rondelet(te).
puerile [pyōō'ûrəl] *a* puéril(e).
Puerto Rico [pwär'tō rē'kō] *n* Porto Rico *f*.
puff [puf] *n* bouffée *f* ♦ *vt*: **to ~ one's pipe** ti-

rer sur sa pipe; *(also: ~ out: sails, cheeks)* gonfler ♦ *vi* sortir par bouffées; *(pant)* haleter; **to ~ out smoke** envoyer des bouffées de fumée.
puffed [puft] *a (col: out of breath)* tout(e) essouflé(e).
puffin [puf'in] *n* macareux *m*.
puff paste, *(Brit)* **puff pastry** *n* pâte feuilletée.
puffy [puf'ē] *a* bouffi(e), boursouflé(e).
pugnacious [pugnā'shəs] *a* pugnace, batailleur(euse).
pull [pŏŏl] *n (tug)*: **to give sth a ~** tirer sur qch; *(of moon, magnet, the sea etc)* attraction *f*; *(fig)* influence *f* ♦ *vt* tirer; *(strain: muscle, tendon)* se claquer ♦ *vi* tirer; **to ~ to pieces** mettre en morceaux; **to ~ one's punches** *(also fig)* ménager son adversaire; **to ~ one's weight** y mettre du sien; **to ~ o.s. together** se ressaisir; **to ~ sb's leg** *(fig)* faire marcher qn; **to ~ strings (for sb)** intervenir (en faveur de qn).
pull apart *vt* séparer; *(break)* mettre en pièces, démantibuler.
pull around *vt (handle roughly: object)* maltraiter; *(: person)* malmener.
pull down *vt* baisser, abaisser; *(house)* démolir; *(tree)* abattre.
pull in *vi (AUT)* se ranger; *(RAIL)* entrer en gare.
pull off *vt* enlever, ôter; *(deal etc)* conclure.
pull out *vi* démarrer, partir; *(withdraw)* se retirer; *(AUT: come out of line)* déboîter ♦ *vt* sortir; arracher; *(withdraw)* retirer.
pull over *vi (AUT)* se ranger.
pull through *vi* s'en sortir.
pull up *vi (stop)* s'arrêter ♦ *vt* remonter; *(uproot)* déraciner, arracher; *(stop)* arrêter.
pulley [pŏŏl'ē] *n* poulie *f*.
Pullman [pŏŏl'mən] *n (US)* wagon-lits *m*, voiture-lits *f*.
pull-out [pŏŏl'out] *n (of forces etc)* retrait *m* ♦ *cpd (magazine, pages)* détachable.
pullover [pŏŏl'ōvûr] *n* pull-over *m*, tricot *m*.
pulp [pulp] *n (of fruit)* pulpe *f*; *(for paper)* pâte *f* à papier; *(pej: also: ~ magazines etc)* presse *f* à sensation or de bas étage; **to reduce sth to (a) ~** réduire qch en purée.
pulpit [pŏŏl'pit] *n* chaire *f*.
pulsate [pul'sāt] *vi* battre, palpiter; *(music)* vibrer.
pulse [puls] *n (of blood)* pouls *m*; *(of heart)* battement *m*; *(of music, engine)* vibrations *fpl*; **to feel or take sb's ~** prendre le pouls à qn.
pulses [pul'siz] *npl (CULIN)* légumineuses *fpl*.
pulverize [pul'vərīz] *vt* pulvériser.
puma [pyōō'mə] *n* puma *m*.
pumice [pum'is] *n (also: ~ stone)* pierre *f* ponce.
pummel [pum'əl] *vt* rouer de coups.
pump [pump] *n* pompe *f*; *(shoe)* escarpin *m* ♦ *vt* pomper; *(fig: col)* faire parler; **to ~ sb for information** essayer de soutirer des renseignements à qn.
pump up *vt* gonfler.
pumpkin [pump'kin] *n* potiron *m*, citrouille *f*.
pun [pun] *n* jeu *m* de mots, calembour *m*.

punch [punch] *n* (*blow*) coup *m* de poing; (*fig: force*) vivacité *f*, mordant *m*; (*tool*) poinçon *m*; (*drink*) punch *m* ♦ *vt* (*hit*): **to ~ sb/sth** donner un coup de poing à qn/sur qch; (*make a hole*) poinçonner, perforer; **to ~ a hole (in)** faire un trou (dans).
punch in *vi* (*US*) pointer (en arrivant).
punch out *vi* (*US*) pointer (en partant).
punch-drunk [punch'drungk] *a* (*Brit*) sonné(e).
punch(ed) card [punch(t) kârd] *n* carte perforée.
punch line *n* (*of joke*) conclusion *f*.
punch-up [punch'up] *n* (*Brit col*) bagarre *f*.
punctual [pungk'chōōəl] *a* ponctuel(le).
punctuality [pungkchōōal'itē] *n* ponctualité *f*.
punctually [pungk'chōōəlē] *ad* ponctuellement; **it will start ~ at 6** cela commencera à 6 heures précises.
punctuate [pungk'chōōāt] *vt* ponctuer.
punctuation [pungkchōōā'shən] *n* ponctuation *f*.
punctuation mark *n* signe *m* de ponctuation.
puncture [pungk'chûr] *n* (*Brit*) crevaison *f* ♦ *vt* crever; **I have a ~** (*AUT*) j'ai (un pneu) crevé.
pundit [pun'dit] *n* individu *m* qui pontifie, pontife *m*.
pungent [pun'jənt] *a* piquant(e); (*fig*) mordant(e), caustique.
punish [pun'ish] *vt* punir; **to ~ sb for sth/for doing sth** punir qn de/d'avoir fait qch.
punishable [pun'ishəbəl] *a* punissable.
punishing [pun'ishing] *a* (*fig: exhausting*) épuisant(e) ♦ *n* punition *f*.
punishment [pun'ishmənt] *n* punition *f*, châtiment *m*; (*fig: col*): **to take a lot of ~** (*boxer*) encaisser; (*car, person etc*) être mis(e) à dure épreuve.
punk [pungk] *n* (*person: also:* **~ rocker**) punk *m/f*; (*music: also:* **~ rock**) le punk; (*US col: hoodlum*) voyou *m*.
punt [punt] *n* (*boat*) bachot *m*.
puny [pyōō'nē] *a* chétif(ive).
pup [pup] *n* chiot *m*.
pupil [pyōō'pəl] *n* élève *m/f*.
puppet [pup'it] *n* marionnette *f*, pantin *m*.
puppet government *n* gouvernement *m* fantoche.
puppy [pup'ē] *n* chiot *m*, petit chien.
purchase [pûr'chis] *n* achat *m*; (*grip*) prise *f* ♦ *vt* acheter; **to get a ~ on** trouver appui sur.
purchase order *n* ordre *m* d'achat.
purchase price *n* prix *m* d'achat.
purchaser [pûr'chisûr] *n* acheteur/euse.
purchasing power [pûr'chising pouûr] *n* pouvoir *m* d'achat.
pure [pyōōr] *a* pur(e); **a ~ wool sweater** un pull en pure laine; **~ and simple** pur(e) et simple.
purebred [pyōōr'bred'] *a* de race.
purée [pyōōrā'] *n* purée *f*.
purely [pyōōr'lē] *ad* purement.
purge [pûrj] *n* (*MED*) purge *f*; (*POL*) épuration *f*, purge ♦ *vt* purger; (*fig*) épurer, purger.
purification [pyōōrəfəkā'shən] *n* purification *f*.
purify [pyōōr'əfī] *vt* purifier, épurer.
purist [pyōōr'ist] *n* puriste *m/f*.
puritan [pyōōr'itən] *n* puritain/e.

puritanical [pyōōritan'ikəl] *a* puritain(e).
purity [pyōōr'itē] *n* pureté *f*.
purl [pûrl] *n* maille *f* à l'envers ♦ *vt* tricoter à l'envers.
purloin [pûrloin'] *vt* dérober.
purple [pûr'pəl] *a* violet(te); cramoisi(e).
purport [pərpôrt'] *vi*: **to ~ to be/do** prétendre être/faire.
purpose [pûr'pəs] *n* intention *f*, but *m*; **on ~** exprès; **for illustrative ~s** à titre d'illustration; **for teaching ~s** dans un but pédagogique; **for the ~s of this meeting** pour cette réunion; **to no ~** en pure perte.
purpose-built [pûr'pəsbilt'] *a* (*Brit*) fait(e) sur mesure.
purposeful [pûr'pəsfəl] *a* déterminé(e), résolu(e).
purposely [pûr'pəslē] *ad* exprès.
purr [pûr] *n* ronronnement *m* ♦ *vi* ronronner.
purse [pûrs] *n* (*US*) sac *m* (à main); (*Brit*) porte-monnaie *m inv*, bourse *f* ♦ *vt* serrer, pincer.
purser [pûr'sûr] *n* (*NAUT*) commissaire *m* du bord.
purse snatcher [pûrs' snach'ûr] *n* (*US*) voleur *m* à l'arraché.
pursue [pûrsōō'] *vt* poursuivre; (*pleasures*) rechercher; (*inquiry, matter*) approfondir.
pursuer [pûrsōō'ûr] *n* poursuivant/e.
pursuit [pûrsōōt'] *n* poursuite *f*; (*occupation*) occupation *f*, activité *f*; **scientific ~s** recherches *fpl* scientifiques; **in (the) ~ of sth** à la recherche de qch.
purveyor [pûrvā'ûr] *n* fournisseur *m*.
pus [pus] *n* pus *m*.
push [pōōsh] *n* poussée *f*; (*effort*) gros effort; (*drive*) énergie *f* ♦ *vt* pousser; (*button*) appuyer sur; (*thrust*): **to ~ sth (into)** enfoncer qch (dans); (*fig*) mettre en avant, faire de la publicité pour ♦ *vi* pousser; appuyer; **to ~ a door open/shut** pousser une porte (pour l'ouvrir/pour la fermer); "~" (*on door*) "pousser"; (*on bell*) "appuyer"; **to ~ for** (*better pay, conditions*) réclamer; **to be ~ed for time/money** être à court de temps/d'argent; **she is ~ing fifty** (*col*) elle frise la cinquantaine; **at a ~** (*Brit col*) à la limite, à la rigueur.
push aside *vt* écarter.
push in *vi* s'introduire de force.
push off *vi* (*col*) filer, ficher le camp.
push on *vi* (*continue*) continuer.
push over *vt* renverser.
push through *vt* (*measure*) faire voter.
push up *vt* (*total, prices*) faire monter.
push button *n* bouton(-poussoir) *m*.
pushchair [pōōsh'chär] *n* (*Brit*) poussette *f*.
pusher [pōōsh'ûr] *n* (*also:* **drug ~**) revendeur/euse (de drogue), ravitailleur/euse (en drogue).
pushing [pōōsh'ing] *a* dynamique.
pushover [pōōsh'ōvûr] *n* (*col*): **it's a ~** c'est un jeu d'enfant.
push-up [pōōsh'up] *n* traction *f*.
pushy [pōōsh'ē] *a* (*pej*) arriviste.
pussycat [pōōs'ēkat] *n* minet *m*.
put, *pt, pp* **put** [pōōt] *vt* mettre; (*place*) poser, placer; (*say*) dire, exprimer; (*a question*) poser; (*estimate*) estimer; **to ~ sb in a good/**

bad mood mettre qn de bonne/mauvaise humeur; **to ~ sb to bed** mettre qn au lit, coucher qn; **to ~ sb to a lot of trouble** déranger qn; **how shall I ~ it?** comment dirais-je?, comment dire?; **to ~ a lot of time into sth** passer beaucoup de temps à qch; **to ~ money on a horse** miser sur un cheval; **to stay ~** ne pas bouger.

put about *vi* (*NAUT*) virer de bord ♦ *vt* (*rumor*) faire courir.

put across *vt* (*ideas etc*) communiquer; faire comprendre.

put aside *vt* mettre de côté.

put away *vt* (*store*) ranger.

put back *vt* (*replace*) remettre, replacer; (*postpone*) remettre; (*delay, also: watch, clock*) retarder; **this will ~ us back 10 years** cela nous ramènera dix ans en arrière.

put down *vt* (*parcel etc*) poser, déposer; (*pay*) verser; (*in writing*) mettre par écrit, inscrire; (*suppress: revolt etc*) réprimer, faire cesser; (*attribute*) attribuer.

put forward *vt* (*ideas*) avancer, proposer; (*date, watch, clock*) avancer.

put in *vt* (*gas, electricity*) installer; (*application, complaint*) soumettre.

put in for *vt fus* (*job*) poser sa candidature pour; (*promotion*) solliciter.

put off *vt* (*light etc*) éteindre; (*postpone*) remettre à plus tard, ajourner; (*discourage*) dissuader.

put on *vt* (*clothes, lipstick etc*) mettre; (*light etc*) allumer; (*play etc*) monter; (*bus, train etc*) mettre en service; (*food, meal*) servir; (*weight*) prendre; (*assume: accent, manner*) prendre; (*: airs*) se donner, prendre; (*brake*) mettre; (*col; tease*): **to ~ sb on** faire marcher qn; (*inform, indicate*): **to ~ sb on to sb/sth** indiquer qn/qch à qn.

put out *vt* mettre dehors; (*one's hand*) tendre; (*news, rumor*) faire courir, répandre; (*light etc*) éteindre; (*person: inconvenience*) déranger, gêner; (*Brit: dislocate*) se démettre ♦ *vi* (*NAUT*): **to ~ out to sea** prendre le large; **to ~ out from New York** quitter New York.

put through *vt* (*caller*) mettre en communication; (*call*) passer; **~ me through to Miss Blair** passez-moi Miss Blair.

put together *vt* mettre ensemble; (*assemble: furniture, toy etc*) monter, assembler; (*meal*) préparer.

put up *vt* (*raise*) lever, relever, remonter; (*pin up*) afficher; (*hang*) accrocher; (*build*) construire, ériger; (*a tent*) monter; (*increase*) augmenter; (*accommodate*) loger; (*incite*): **to ~ sb up to doing sth** pousser qn à faire qch; **to ~ sth up for sale** mettre qch en vente.

put upon *vt fus*: **to be ~ upon** (*imposed on*) se laisser faire.

put up with *vt fus* supporter.

putrid [pyōō'trid] *a* putride.

putt [put] *vt* poter (la balle) ♦ *n* coup roulé.

putter [put'ûr] *n* (*GOLF*) putter *m* ♦ *vi* (*US*): **to ~ around** bricoler.

putting green [put'ing grēn] *n* green *m*.

putty [put'ē] *n* mastic *m*.

put-up [pŏŏt'up] *a*: **~ job** affaire montée.

puzzle [puz'əl] *n* énigme *f*, mystère *m*; (*jigsaw*) puzzle *m*; (*also*: **crossword ~**) problème *m* de mots croisés ♦ *vt* intriguer, rendre perplexe ♦ *vi* se creuser la tête; **to ~ over** chercher à comprendre; **to be ~d about sth** être perplexe au sujet de qch.

puzzling [puz'ling] *a* déconcertant(e), inexplicable.

PVC *n abbr* (= *polyvinyl chloride*) PVC *m*, polyvinyle *m*.

PVS *n abbr* = **post-viral syndrome**.

Pvt. *abbr* (*US MIL*) = **private**.

pw *abbr* (= *per week*) p.sem.

PX *n abbr* (*US MIL*) = **post exchange**.

pygmy [pig'mē] *n* pygmée *m/f*.

pyjamas [pəjâm'əz] *npl* (*Brit*) = **pajamas**.

pylon [pī'lân] *n* pylône *m*.

pyramid [pir'əmid] *n* pyramide *f*.

Pyrenean [pirənē'ən] *a* pyrénéen(ne), des Pyrénées.

Pyrenees [pir'ənēz] *npl*: **the ~** les Pyrénées *fpl*.

python [pī'thân] *n* python *m*.

Q

Q, q [kyōō] *n* (*letter*) Q, q *m*; **Q for Queen** Q comme Quintal.

Qatar [kətâr'] *n* Qatar *m*, Katar *m*.

QC *n abbr* (= *Queen's Counsel*) titre donné à certains avocats.

QED *abbr* (= *quod erat demonstrandum*) CQFD.

QM *n abbr* = **quartermaster**.

q.t. *n abbr* (*col*: = *quiet*): **on the ~** discrètement.

qty *abbr* (= *quantity*) qté.

quack [kwak] *n* (*of duck*) coin-coin *m inv*; (*pej: doctor*) charlatan *m* ♦ *vi* faire coin-coin.

quad [kwâd] *n abbr* = **quadruple, quadruplet, quadrangle**.

quadrangle [kwâd'ranggəl] *n* (*MATH*) quadrilatère *m*; (*courtyard*: *abbr*: **quad**) cour *f*.

quadruped [kwâd'rōōped] *n* quadrupède *m*.

quadruple [kwâdrōō'pəl] *a, n* quadruple (*m*) ♦ *vt, vi* quadrupler.

quadruplet [kwâdru'plit] *n* quadruplé/e.

quagmire [kwag'mīûr] *n* bourbier *m*.

quail [kwāl] *n* (*ZOOL*) caille *f* ♦ *vi*: **to ~ at** *or* **before** se décourager devant.

quaint [kwānt] *a* bizarre; (*old-fashioned*) désuet(ète); au charme vieillot, pittoresque.

quake [kwāk] *vi* trembler ♦ *n abbr* = **earthquake**.

Quaker [kwā'kûr] *n* quaker/esse.

qualification [kwâləfəkā'shən] *n* (*degree etc*) diplôme *m*; (*ability*) compétence *f*, qualification *f*; (*limitation*) réserve *f*, restriction *f*; **what are your ~s?** qu'avez-vous comme diplômes?; quelles sont vos qualifications?

qualified [kwâl'əfīd] *a* diplômé(e); (*able*) compétent(e), qualifié(e); (*limited*) conditionnel(le); **it was a ~ success** ce fut un succès mitigé; ~ **for/to do** qui a les diplômes requis pour/pour faire; qualifié pour/pour faire.

qualify [kwâl'əfī] *vt* qualifier;. (*limit: statement*) apporter des réserves à ♦ *vi*: **to ~ (as)** obtenir son diplôme (de); **to ~ (for)** remplir les conditions requises (pour); (*SPORT*) se qualifier (pour).

qualifying [kwâl'əfīing] *a*: ~ **exam** examen *m* d'entrée; ~ **round** éliminatoires *fpl*.

qualitative [kwâl'itātiv] *a* qualitatif(ive).

quality [kwâl'itē] *n* qualité *f* ♦ *cpd* de qualité; **of good/poor** ~ de bonne/mauvaise qualité.

quality control *n* contrôle *m* de qualité.

qualm [kwâm] *n* doute *m*; scrupule *m*; **to have ~s about sth** avoir des doutes sur qch; éprouver des scrupules à propos de qch.

quandary [kwân'drē] *n*: **in a ~** devant un dilemme, dans l'embarras.

quantitative [kwân'titātiv] *a* quantitatif(ive).

quantity [kwân'titē] *n* quantité *f*; **in ~** en grande quantité.

quarantine [kwôr'əntēn] *n* quarantaine *f*.

quarrel [kwôr'əl] *n* querelle *f*, dispute *f* ♦ *vi* se disputer, se quereller; **to have a ~ with sb** se quereller avec qn; **I've no ~ with him** je n'ai rien contre lui; **I can't ~ with that** je ne vois rien à redire à cela.

quarrelsome [kwôr'əlsəm] *a* querelleur(euse).

quarry [kwôr'ē] *n* (*for stone*) carrière *f*; (*animal*) proie *f*, gibier *m* ♦ *vt* (*marble etc*) extraire.

quart [kwôrt] *n* ≈ litre *m*.

quarter [kwôr'tûr] *n* quart *m*; (*of year*) trimestre *m*; (*district*) quartier *m*; (*US, Canada: 25 cents*) (pièce *f* de) vingt-cinq cents *mpl* ♦ *vt* partager en quartiers *or* en quatre; (*MIL*) caserner, cantonner; **~s** *npl* logement *m*; (*MIL*) quartiers *mpl*, cantonnement *m*; **a ~ of an hour** un quart d'heure; **it's a ~ of 3**, (*Brit*) **it's a ~ to 3** il est 3 heures moins le quart; **it's a ~ after 3**, (*Brit*) **it's a ~ past 3** il est 3 heures et quart; **from all ~s** de tous côtés; **at close ~s** tout près.

quarter-deck [kwôr'tûrdek] *n* (*NAUT*) plage *f* arrière.

quarter final *n* quart *m* de finale.

quarterly [kwôr'tûrlē] *a* trimestriel(le) ♦ *ad* tous les trois mois ♦ *n* (*PRESS*) revue trimestrielle.

quartermaster [kwôr'tûrmastûr] *n* (*MIL*) intendant *m* militaire de troisième classe; (*NAUT*) maître *m* de manœuvre.

quarter note *n* (*US*) noire *f*.

quartet(te) [kwôrtet'] *n* quatuor *m*; (*jazz players*) quartette *m*.

quarto [kwôr'tō] *a*, *n* in-quarto *(m) inv*.

quartz [kwôrts] *n* quartz *m* ♦ *cpd* de *or* en quartz; (*watch, clock*) à quartz.

quash [kwâsh] *vt* (*verdict*) annuler, casser.

quasi- [kwā'zī] *prefix* quasi- + *noun*; quasi, presque + *adjective*.

quaver [kwā'vûr] *n* (*Brit MUS*) croche *f* ♦ *vi* trembler.

quay [kē] *n* (*also*: **~side**) quai *m*.

Que. *abbr* (*Canada*) = *Quebec*.

queasy [kwē'zē] *a* (*stomach*) délicat(e); **to feel ~** avoir mal au cœur.

Quebec [kwibek'] *n* Québec *m*.

queen [kwēn] *n* (*gen*) reine *f*; (*CARDS etc*) dame *f*.

queen mother *n* reine mère *f*.

queer [kwēr] *a* étrange, curieux(euse); (*suspicious*) louche; (*sick*): **I feel ~** je ne me sens pas bien ♦ *n* (*col*) homosexuel *m*.

quell [kwel] *vt* réprimer, étouffer.

quench [kwench] *vt* (*flames*) éteindre; **to ~ one's thirst** se désaltérer.

querulous [kwär'ələs] *a* (*person*) récriminateur(trice); (*voice*) plaintif(ive).

query [kwiûr'ē] *n* question *f*; (*doubt*) doute *m*; (*question mark*) point *m* d'interrogation ♦ *vt* (*disagree with, dispute*) mettre en doute, questionner.

quest [kwest] *n* recherche *f*, quête *f*.

question [kwes'chən] *n* question *f* ♦ *vt* (*person*) interroger; (*plan, idea*) mettre en question *or* en doute; **to ask sb a ~, to put a ~ to sb** poser une question à qn; **to bring** *or* **call sth into ~** remettre qch en question; **the ~ is ...** la question est de savoir ...; **it's a ~ of doing** il s'agit de faire; **there's some ~ of doing** il est question de faire; **beyond ~** sans aucun doute; **out of the ~** hors de question.

questionable [kwes'chənəbəl] *a* discutable.

questioner [kwes'chənûr] *n* personne *f* qui pose une question (*or* qui a posé la question *etc*).

questioning [kwes'chəning] *a* interrogateur(trice) ♦ *n* interrogatoire *m*.

question mark *n* point *m* d'interrogation.

questionnaire [kweschənär'] *n* questionnaire *m*.

queue [kyōō] (*Brit*) *n* queue *f*, file *f* ♦ *vi* faire la queue; **to jump the ~** passer avant son tour.

quibble [kwib'əl] *vi* ergoter, chicaner.

quick [kwik] *a* rapide; (*reply*) prompt(e), rapide; (*mind*) vif(vive) ♦ *ad* vite, rapidement ♦ *n*: **cut to the ~** (*fig*) touché(e) au vif; **be ~!** dépêche-toi!; **to be ~ to act** agir tout de suite.

quicken [kwik'ən] *vt* accélérer, presser; (*rouse*) stimuler ♦ *vi* s'accélérer, devenir plus rapide.

quicklime [kwik'līm] *n* chaux vive.

quickly [kwik'lē] *ad* (*fast*) vite, rapidement; (*immediately*) tout de suite.

quickness [kwik'nis] *n* rapidité *f*, promptitude *f*; (*of mind*) vivacité *f*.

quicksand [kwik'sand] *n* sables mouvants.

quickstep [kwik'step] *n* fox-trot *m*.

quick-tempered [kwik'tempûrd] *a* emporté(e).

quick-witted [kwik'wit'id] *a* à l'esprit vif.

quid [kwid] *n* (*pl inv*) (*Brit col*) livre *f*.

quid pro quo [kwid' prō' kwō] *n* contrepartie *f*.

quiet [kwī'it] *a* tranquille, calme; (*not noisy: engine*) silencieux(euse); (*reserved*) réservé(e); (*not busy: day, business*) calme; (*ceremony, color*) discret(ète) ♦ *n* tranquillité *f*, calme *m* ♦ *vb* (*US: also*: **~ down**) *vi* se calmer, s'apaiser ♦ *vt* calmer, apaiser; **keep ~!** taisez-vous!; **on the ~** en secret, discrètement; **I'll have a ~ word with him** je lui en parlerai discrètement.

quieten [kwī'itən] (*Brit*: *also*: **~ down**) *vi, vt*

= **quiet.**
quietly [kwī'itlē] *ad* tranquillement, calmement; discrètement.
quietness [kwī'itnis] *n* tranquillité *f*, calme *m*; silence *m*.
quill [kwil] *n* plume *f* (d'oie).
quilt [kwilt] *n* édredon *m*; (*continental* ~) couette *f*.
quilting [kwil'ting] *n* ouatine *f*; molletonnage *m*.
quin [kwin] *n abbr* = **quintuplet.**
quince [kwins] *n* coing *m*; (*tree*) cognassier *m*.
quinine [kwī'nīn] *n* quinine *f*.
quintet(te) [kwintet'] *n* quintette *m*.
quintuplet [kwintu'plit] *n* quintuplé/e.
quip [kwip] *n* remarque piquante *or* spirituelle, pointe *f* ♦ *vt*: ... **he ~ped** ... lança-t-il.
quire [kwīûr] *n* ≈ main *f* (*de papier*).
quirk [kwûrk] *n* bizarrerie *f*; **by some ~ of fate** par un caprice du hasard.
quit, *pt*, *pp* quit *or* **quitted** [kwit] *vt* quitter ♦ *vi* (*give up*) abandonner, renoncer; (*resign*) démissionner; **to ~ doing** arrêter de faire; **~ stalling!** (*US col*) arrête de te dérober!; **notice to ~** (*Brit*) congé *m* (*signifié au locataire*).
quite [kwīt] *ad* (*rather*) assez, plutôt; (*entirely*) complètement, tout à fait; **~ new** plutôt neuf; tout à fait neuf; **she's ~ pretty** elle est plutôt jolie; **I ~ understand** je comprends très bien; **~ a few of them** un assez grand nombre d'entre eux; **that's not ~ right** ce n'est pas tout à fait juste; **not ~ as many as last time** pas tout à fait autant que la dernière fois; **~ (so)!** exactement!
Quito [kē'tō] *n* Quito.
quits [kwits] *a*: **~ (with)** quitte (envers); **let's call it ~** restons-en là.
quiver [kwiv'ûr] *vi* trembler, frémir ♦ *n* (*for arrows*) carquois *m*.
quiz [kwiz] *n* (*on TV*) jeu-concours *m* (télévisé); (*in magazine etc*) test *m* de connaissances ♦ *vt* interroger.
quizzical [kwiz'ikəl] *a* narquois(e).
quoits [kwoits] *npl* jeu *m* du palet.
quorum [kwôr'əm] *n* quorum *m*.
quota [kwō'tə] *n* quota *m*.
quotation [kwōtā'shən] *n* citation *f*; (*Brit*: *estimate*) devis *m*.
quotation marks *npl* guillemets *mpl*.
quote [kwōt] *n* citation *f*; (*estimate*) devis *m* ♦ *vt* (*sentence, author*) citer; (*price*) donner, soumettre; (*shares*) coter ♦ *vi*: **to ~ from** citer; **to ~ for a job** établir un devis pour des travaux; **~s** *npl* (*col*) = **quotation marks**; **in ~s** entre guillemets; **~ ... unquote** (*in dictation*) ouvrez les guillemets; **...** fermez les guillemets.
quotient [kwō'shənt] *n* quotient *m*.
qv *abbr* (= *quod vide: which see*) voir.
qwerty keyboard [kwûr'tē kē'bôrd] *n* (*Brit*) clavier *m* QWERTY.

R

R, r [âr] *n* (*letter*) R, r *m*; **R for Roger** R comme Raoul.
R [âr] *abbr* (= *right*) dr; (= *river*) riv., fl.; (= *Réaumur* (*scale*)) R; (*US CINEMA*: = *restricted*) interdit aux moins de 17 ans; (*US POL*) = **republican**; (*Brit*) = *Rex*, *Regina*.
RA *abbr* = **rear admiral.**
RAAF *n abbr* = *Royal Australian Air Force*.
Rabat [râbât'] *n* Rabat.
rabbi [rab'ī] *n* rabbin *m*.
rabbit [rab'it] *n* lapin *m*.
rabbit hole *n* terrier *m* (de lapin).
rabbit hutch *n* clapier *m*.
rabble [rab'əl] *n* (*pej*) populace *f*.
rabid [rab'id] *a* enragé(e).
rabies [rā'bēz] *n* rage *f*.
RAC *n abbr* (*Brit*: = *Royal Automobile Club*) ≈ ACF *m*.
raccoon [rakōōn'] *n* raton *m* laveur.
race [rās] *n* race *f*; (*competition, rush*) course *f* ♦ *vt* (*person*) faire la course avec; (*horse*) faire courir; (*engine*) emballer ♦ *vi* courir; (*engine*) s'emballer; **the human ~** la race humaine; **to ~ in/out** *etc* entrer/sortir *etc* à toute vitesse.
race car *n* (*US*) voiture de course.
race car driver *n* (*US*) pilote de course.
racecourse [rās'kôrs] *n* champ *m* de courses.
racehorse [rās'hôrs] *n* cheval *m* de course.
race relations *npl* rapports *mpl* entre les races.
racetrack [rās'trak] *n* piste *f*.
racial [rā'shəl] *a* racial(e).
racialism [rā'shəlizəm] *n* racisme *m*.
racialist [rā'shəlist] *a, n* raciste (*m/f*).
racing [rā'sing] *n* courses *fpl*.
racing car *n* (*Brit*) = **race car.**
racing driver *n* (*Brit*) = **race car driver.**
racism [rā'sizəm] *n* racisme *m*.
racist [rā'sist] *a, n* (*pej*) raciste (*m/f*).
rack [rak] *n* (*also*: **luggage ~**) filet *m* à bagages; (*also*: **roof ~**) galerie *f* ♦ *vt* tourmenter; **magazine ~** porte-revues *m inv*; **shoe ~** étagère *f* à chaussures; **toast ~** porte-toast *m*; **to ~ one's brains** se creuser la cervelle; **to go to ~ and ruin** (*building*) tomber en ruine; (*business*) péricliter.
rack up *vt* accumuler.
rack-and-pinion [rak'əndpin'yən] *n* (*TECH*) crémaillère *f*.
racket [rak'it] *n* (*for tennis*) raquette *f*; (*noise*) tapage *m*, vacarme *m*; (*swindle*) escroquerie *f*; (*organized crime*) racket *m*.
racketeer [rakitēr'] *n* (*esp US*) racketteur *m*.
racoon [rakōōn'] *n* = **raccoon.**
racquet [rak'it] *n* raquette *f*.
racy [rā'sē] *a* plein(e) de verve; osé(e).
radar [rā'dâr] *n* radar *m* ♦ *cpd* radar *inv*.
radar trap *n* contrôle *m* radar.

radial [rā'dēəl] *a* (*also:* ~-ply) à carcasse radiale.

radiance [rā'dēəns] *n* éclat *m*, rayonnement *m*.

radiant [rā'dēənt] *a* rayonnant(e); (*PHYSICS*) radiant(e).

radiate [rā'dēāt] *vt* (*heat*) émettre, dégager ♦ *vi* (*lines*) rayonner.

radiation [rādēā'shən] *n* rayonnement *m*; (*radioactive*) radiation *f*.

radiation sickness *n* mal *m* des rayons.

radiator [rā'dēātûr] *n* radiateur *m*.

radiator cap *n* bouchon *m* de radiateur.

radiator grill *n* (*AUT*) calandre *f*.

radical [rad'ikəl] *a* radical(e).

radii [rā'dēī] *npl of* **radius.**

radio [rā'dēō] *n* radio *f* ♦ *vi:* **to ~ to sb** envoyer un message radio à qn ♦ *vt* (*information*) transmettre par radio; (*one's position*) signaler par radio; (*person*) appeler par radio; **on the ~** à la radio.

radioactive [rādēōak'tiv] *a* radioactif(ive).

radioactivity [rādēōaktiv'ətē] *n* radioactivité *f*.

radio announcer *n* annonceur *m*.

radio-controlled [rā'dēōkəntrōld'] *a* radioguidé(e).

radiographer [rādēág'rəfûr] *n* radiologue *m/f* (*technicien*).

radiography [rādēág'rəfē] *n* radiographie *f*.

radiologist [rādēál'əjist] *n* radiologue *m/f* (*médecin*).

radiology [rādēál'əjē] *n* radiologie *f*.

radio station *n* station *f* de radio.

radio taxi *n* radio-taxi *m*.

radiotelephone [rādēōtel'əfōn] *n* radiotéléphone *m*.

radiotherapist [rādēōthär'əpist] *n* radiothérapeute *m/f*.

radiotherapy [rādēōthär'əpē] *n* radiothérapie *f*.

radish [rad'ish] *n* radis *m*.

radium [rā'dēəm] *n* radium *m*.

radius, *pl* **radii** [rā'dēəs, -ēī] *n* rayon *m*; (*ANAT*) radius *m*; **within a ~ of 50 miles** dans un rayon de 50 milles.

RAF *n abbr* (*Brit*) = **Royal Air Force.**

raffia [raf'ēə] *n* raphia *m*.

raffish [raf'ish] *a* dissolu(e); canaille.

raffle [raf'əl] *n* tombola *f* ♦ *vt* mettre comme lot dans une tombola.

raft [raft] *n* (*craft; also:* **life** ~) radeau *m*; (*logs*) train *m* de flottage.

rafter [raf'tûr] *n* chevron *m*.

rag [rag] *n* chiffon *m*; (*pej: newspaper*) feuille *f*, torchon *m*; (*for charity*) attractions organisées par les étudiants au profit d'œuvres de charité; ~**s** *npl* haillons *mpl*; **in** ~**s** (*person*) en haillons; (*clothes*) en lambeaux.

rag-and-bone man [ragənbōn' man] *n* (*Brit*) = **ragman.**

ragbag [rag'bag] *n* (*fig*) ramassis *m*.

rag doll *n* poupée *f* de chiffon.

rage [rāj] *n* (*fury*) rage *f*, fureur *f* ♦ *vi* (*person*) être fou(folle) de rage; (*storm*) faire rage, être déchaîné(e); **to fly into a ~** se mettre en rage; **it's all the ~** cela fait fureur.

ragged [rag'id] *a* (*edge*) inégal(e), qui accroche; (*cuff*) effiloché(e); (*appearance*) déguenillé(e).

raging [rā'jing] *a* (*sea, storm*) en furie; (*fever, pain*) violent(e); ~ **toothache** rage *f* de dents; **in a ~ temper** dans une rage folle.

ragman [rag'man] *n* chiffonnier *m*.

rag trade *n* (*col*): **the ~** la confection.

raid [rād] *n* (*MIL*) raid *m*; (*criminal*) hold-up *m inv*; (*by police*) descente *f*, rafle *f* ♦ *vt* faire un raid sur *or* un hold-up dans *or* une descente dans.

raider [rā'dûr] *n* malfaiteur *m*.

rail [rāl] *n* (*on stair*) rampe *f*; (*on bridge, balcony*) balustrade *f*; (*of ship*) bastingage *m*; (*for train*) rail *m*; ~**s** *npl* rails *mpl*, voie ferrée; **by ~** par chemin de fer, par le train.

railing(s) [rā'ling(z)] *n(pl)* grille *f*.

railroad [rāl'rōd] *n* (*US*) chemin *m* de fer.

railroader [rāl'rōdûr] *n* (*US*) cheminot *m*.

railroad line *n* ligne *f* de chemin de fer.

railroad station *n* gare *f*.

railway [rāl'wā] *etc* (*Brit*) = **railroad** *etc*.

railway engine *n* (*Brit*) locomotive *f*.

railwayman [rāl'wāmən] *n* (*Brit*) = **railroader.**

rain [rān] *n* pluie *f* ♦ *vi* pleuvoir; **in the ~** sous la pluie; **it's** ~**ing** il pleut; **it's** ~**ing cats and dogs** il pleut à torrents.

rainbow [rān'bō] *n* arc-en-ciel *m*.

raincoat [rān'kōt] *n* imperméable *m*.

raindrop [rān'dráp] *n* goutte *f* de pluie.

rainfall [rān'fól] *n* chute *f* de pluie; (*measurement*) hauteur *f* des précipitations.

rainforest [rān'fór'ist] *n* forêt tropicale.

rainproof [rān'prōōf] *a* imperméable.

rainstorm [rān'stôrm] *n* pluie torrentielle.

rainwater [rān'wôtûr] *n* eau *f* de pluie.

rainy [rā'nē] *a* pluvieux(euse).

raise [rāz] *n* augmentation *f* ♦ *vt* (*lift*) lever; hausser; (*end: siege, embargo*) lever; (*build*) ériger; (*increase*) augmenter; (*a protest, doubt*) provoquer, causer; (*a question*) soulever; (*cattle, family*) élever; (*crop*) faire pousser; (*army, funds*) rassembler; (*loan*) obtenir; **to ~ one's glass to sb/sth** porter un toast en l'honneur de qn/qch; **to ~ one's voice** élever la voix; **to ~ sb's hopes** donner de l'espoir à qn; **to ~ a laugh/a smile** faire rire/sourire.

raisin [rā'zin] *n* raisin sec.

Raj [ráj] *n*: **the ~** l'empire *m* (*aux Indes*).

rajah [rá'jə] *n* radja(h) *m*.

rake [rāk] *n* (*tool*) râteau *m*; (*person*) débauché *m* ♦ *vt* (*garden*) ratisser; (*fire*) tisonner; (*with machine gun*) balayer ♦ *vi:* **to ~ through** (*fig: search*) fouiller (dans).

rake-off [rāk'ôf] *n* (*col*) pourcentage *m*.

rakish [rā'kish] *a* dissolu(e); cavalier(ière).

rally [ral'ē] *n* (*POL etc*) meeting *m*, rassemblement *m*; (*AUT*) rallye *m*; (*TENNIS*) échange *m* ♦ *vt* rassembler, rallier ♦ *vi* se rallier; (*sick person*) aller mieux; (*Stock Exchange*) reprendre.

rally around *vi* venir en aide ♦ *vt fus* se rallier à; venir en aide à.

rallying point [ral'ēing point] *n* (*MIL*) point *m* de ralliement.

RAM [ram] *n abbr* (*COMPUT*) = **random access memory.**

ram [ram] *n* bélier *m* ♦ *vt* enfoncer; (*soil*) tasser; (*crash into*) emboutir; percuter; éperonner.

ramble [ram'bəl] *n* randonnée *f* ♦ *vi* (*pej*: *also*: ~ **on**) discourir, pérorer.
rambler [ram'blûr] *n* promeneur/euse, randonneur/euse; (*BOT*) rosier grimpant.
rambling [ram'bling] *a* (*speech*) décousu(e); (*house*) plein(e) de coins et de recoins; (*BOT*) grimpant(e).
rambunctious [rambungk'shəs] *a* (*US*: *person*) exubérante(e).
ramification [raməfəkā'shən] *n* ramification *f*.
ramp [ramp] *n* (*incline*) rampe *f*; dénivellation *f*; (*in garage*) pont *m*.
rampage [ram'pāj] *n*: **to be on the** ~ se déchaîner ♦ *vi*: **they went rampaging through the town** ils ont envahi les rues et ont tout saccagé sur leur passage.
rampant [ram'pənt] *a* (*disease etc*) qui sévit.
rampart [ram'pârt] *n* rempart *m*.
ramshackle [ram'shakəl] *a* (*house*) délabré(e); (*car etc*) déglingué(e).
ran [ran] *pt of* **run**.
ranch [ranch] *n* ranch *m*.
rancher [ran'chûr] *n* (*owner*) propriétaire *m* de ranch; (*ranch hand*) cowboy *m*.
rancid [ran'sid] *a* rance.
rancor, (*Brit*) **rancour** [rang'kûr] *n* rancune *f*, rancœur *f*.
random [ran'dəm] *a* fait(e) *or* établi(e) au hasard; (*COMPUT, MATH*) aléatoire ♦ *n*: **at** ~ au hasard.
random access memory (RAM) *n* (*COMPUT*) mémoire vive, RAM *f*.
randy [ran'dē] *a* (*Brit col*) excité(e); lubrique.
rang [rang] *pt of* **ring**.
range [rānj] *n* (*of mountains*) chaîne *f*; (*of missile, voice*) portée *f*; (*of products*) choix *m*, gamme *f*; (*also*: **shooting** ~) champ *m* de tir; (: *indoor*) stand *m* de tir; (*also*: **kitchen** ~) fourneau *m* (de cuisine) ♦ *vt* (*place*) mettre en rang, placer; (*roam*) parcourir ♦ *vi*: **to** ~ **over** couvrir; **to** ~ **from ... to** aller de ... à; **price** ~ éventail *m* des prix; **do you have anything else in this price** ~? avez-vous autre chose dans ces prix?; **within (firing)** ~ à portée (de tir); ~**d left/right** (*text*) justifié à gauche/à droite.
ranger [rān'jûr] *n* garde *m* forestier.
Rangoon [ranggōōn'] *n* Rangoon.
rank [rangk] *n* rang *m*; (*MIL*) grade *m*; (*Brit*: *also*: **taxi** ~) station *f* de taxis ♦ *vi*: **to** ~ **among** compter *or* se classer parmi ♦ *vt*: **to** ~ **him sixth** je le place sixième ♦ *a* (*smell*) nauséabond(e); (*hypocrisy, injustice etc*) flagrant(e); **the** ~**s** (*MIL*) la troupe; **the** ~ **and file** (*fig*) la masse, la base; **to close** ~**s** (*MIL, fig*) serrer les rangs.
rankle [rang'kəl] *vi* (*insult*) rester sur le cœur.
ransack [ran'sak] *vt* fouiller (à fond); (*plunder*) piller.
ransom [ran'səm] *n* rançon *f*; **to hold sb to** ~ (*fig*) exercer un chantage sur qn.
rant [rant] *vi* fulminer.
ranting [ran'ting] *n* invectives *fpl*.
rap [rap] *n* petit coup sec; tape *f* ♦ *vt* frapper sur *or* à; taper sur.
rape [rāp] *n* viol *m*; (*BOT*) colza *m* ♦ *vt* violer.
rape(seed) oil [rāp'(sēd) oil] *n* huile *f* de colza.
rapid [rap'id] *a* rapide.

rapidity [rəpid'itē] *n* rapidité *f*.
rapidly [rap'idlē] *ad* rapidement.
rapids [rap'idz] *npl* (*GEO*) rapides *mpl*.
rapist [rā'pist] *n* auteur *m* d'un viol.
rapport [rapôr'] *n* entente *f*.
rapt [rapt] *a* (*attention*) extrême; **to be** ~ **in contemplation** être perdu(e) dans la contemplation.
rapture [rap'chûr] *n* extase *f*, ravissement *m*; **to go into** ~**s over** s'extasier sur.
rapturous [rap'chûrəs] *a* extasié(e); frénétique.
rare [rär] *a* rare; (*CULIN*: *steak*) saignant(e).
rarebit [rär'bit] *n see* **Welsh rarebit**.
rarefied [rär'əfīd] *a* (*air, atmosphere*) raréfié(e).
rarely [reûr'lē] *ad* rarement.
raring [rär'ing] *a*: **to be** ~ **to go** (*col*) être très impatient(e) de commencer.
rarity [rär'itē] *n* rareté *f*.
rascal [ras'kəl] *n* vaurien *m*.
rash [rash] *a* imprudent(e), irréfléchi(e) ♦ *n* (*MED*) rougeur *f*, éruption *f*; **to come out in a** ~ avoir une éruption.
rasher [rash'ûr] *n* fine tranche (de lard).
rasp [rasp] *n* (*tool*) lime *f* ♦ *vt* (*speak*: *also*: ~ **out**) dire d'une voix grinçante.
raspberry [raz'bärē] *n* framboise *f*.
raspberry bush *n* framboisier *m*.
rasping [ras'ping] *a*: ~ **noise** grincement *m*.
rat [rat] *n* rat *m*.
ratchet [rach'it] *n*: ~ **wheel** roue *f* à rochet.
rate [rāt] *n* (*ratio*) taux *m*, pourcentage *m*; (*speed*) vitesse *f*, rythme *m*; (*price*) tarif *m* ♦ *vt* classer; évaluer; **to** ~ **sb/sth as** considérer qn/qch comme; **to** ~ **sb/sth among** classer qn/qch parmi; **to** ~ **sb/sth highly** avoir une haute opinion de qn/qch; **at a** ~ **of 60 kph** à une vitesse de 60 km/h; ~ **of exchange** taux *or* cours *m* du change; ~ **of flow** débit *m*; ~ **of return** (taux de) rendement *m*; **pulse** ~ fréquence *f* des pulsations.
rates [rāts] *npl* (*Brit*) impôts locaux.
rather [rath'ûr] *ad* (*somewhat*) assez, plutôt; (*to some extent*) un peu; **it's** ~ **expensive** c'est assez cher; (*too much*) c'est un peu cher; **there's** ~ **a lot** (*Brit*) il y en a beaucoup; **I would** *or* **I'd** ~ **go** j'aimerais mieux *or* je préférerais partir; **I had** ~ **go** il vaudrait mieux que je parte; **I'd** ~ **not leave** j'aimerais mieux ne pas partir; **or** ~ (*more accurately*) ou plutôt.
ratification [ratəfəkā'shən] *n* ratification *f*.
ratify [rat'əfī] *vt* ratifier.
rating [rā'ting] *n* classement *m*; cote *f*; (*NAUT*: *category*) classe *f*; (: *sailor*: *Brit*) matelot *m*; ~**s** *npl* (*RADIO, TV*) indice(s) *m(pl)* d'écoute.
ratio [rā'shō] *n* proportion *f*; **in the** ~ **of 100 to 1** dans la proportion de 100 contre 1.
ration [rash'ən] *n* (*gen pl*) ration(s) *f(pl)* ♦ *vt* rationner.
rational [rash'ənəl] *a* raisonnable, sensé(e); (*solution, reasoning*) logique; (*MED*) lucide.
rationale [rashənal'] *n* raisonnement *m*; justification *f*.
rationalization [rashənələzā'shən] *n* rationalisation *f*.
rationalize [rash'ənəlīz] *vt* rationaliser;

rationally [rash'ənəlē] *ad* raisonnablement; logiquement.
rationing [rash'əning] *n* rationnement *m*.
rat poison *n* mort-aux-rats *f inv*.
rat race *n* foire *f* d'empoigne.
rattan [ratan'] *n* rotin *m*.
rattle [rat'əl] *n* cliquetis *m*; (*louder*) bruit *m* de ferraille; (*object: of baby*) hochet *m*; (*: of sports fan*) crécelle *f* ♦ *vi* cliqueter; faire un bruit de ferraille *or* du bruit ♦ *vt* agiter (bruyamment); (*col: disconcert*) décontenancer; (*: annoy*) embêter.
rattlesnake [rat'əlsnāk] *n* serpent *m* à sonnettes.
ratty [rat'ē] *a* (*col: US: shabby*) miteux(euse); (*: Brit: annoyed*) en rogne.
raucous [rô'kəs] *a* rauque.
raucously [rô'kəslē] *ad* d'une voix rauque.
ravage [rav'ij] *vt* ravager.
ravages [rav'ijiz] *npl* ravages *mpl*.
rave [rāv] *vi* (*in anger*) s'emporter; (*with enthusiasm*) s'extasier; (*MED*) délirer ♦ *cpd*: ~ **review** (*col*) critique *f* dithyrambique.
raven [rā'vən] *n* grand corbeau.
ravenous [rav'ənəs] *a* affamé(e).
ravine [rəvēn'] *n* ravin *m*.
raving [rā'ving] *a*: ~ **lunatic** *n* fou furieux/folle furieuse.
ravings [rā'vingz] *npl* divagations *fpl*.
ravioli [ravēō'lē] *n* ravioli *mpl*.
ravish [rav'ish] *vt* ravir.
ravishing [rav'ishing] *a* enchanteur(eresse).
raw [rô] *a* (*uncooked*) cru(e); (*not processed*) brut(e); (*sore*) à vif, irrité(e); (*inexperienced*) inexpérimenté(e); ~ **deal** (*col: bad bargain*) sale coup *m*; (*: unfair treatment*): **to get a** ~ **deal** être traité(e) injustement.
Rawalpindi [râwəlpin'dē] *n* Rawalpindi.
raw material *n* matière première.
ray [rā] *n* rayon *m*; ~ **of hope** lueur *f* d'espoir.
rayon [rā'ân] *n* rayonne *f*.
raze [rāz] *vt* (*also*: ~ **to the ground**) raser.
razor [rā'zûr] *n* rasoir *m*.
razor blade *n* lame *f* de rasoir.
razzmatazz [raz'mətaz] *n* (*col*) tralala *m*, tapage *m*.
R&B *n abbr* = *rhythm and blues*.
RC *abbr* = **Roman Catholic**.
RCAF *n abbr* = *Royal Canadian Air Force*.
RCMP *n abbr* = *Royal Canadian Mounted Police*.
RCN *n abbr* = *Royal Canadian Navy*.
RD *abbr* (*US MAIL*) = *rural delivery*.
Rd *abbr* = **road**.
R&D *n abbr* (= *research and development*) R-D *f*.
R&R *n abbr* (*US MIL*) = *rest and recuperation*.
re [rā] *prep* concernant.
reach [rēch] *n* portée *f*, atteinte *f*; (*of river etc*) étendue *f* ♦ *vt* atteindre, arriver à ♦ *vi* s'étendre; (*stretch out hand*): **to** ~ **up/down/out** *etc* (*for sth*) lever/baisser/allonger *etc* le bras (pour prendre qch); **to** ~ **sb by phone** joindre qn par téléphone; **out of/within** ~ (*object*) hors de/à portée; **within easy** ~ **(of)** (*place*) à proximité (de), proche (de).
react [rēakt'] *vi* réagir.

reaction [rēak'shən] *n* réaction *f*.
reactionary [rēak'shənārē] *a*, *n* réactionnaire (*m/f*).
reactor [rēak'tûr] *n* réacteur *m*.
read, *pt*, *pp* **read** [rēd, rēd, red] *vi* lire ♦ *vt* lire; (*understand*) comprendre, interpréter; (*study*) étudier; (*subj: instrument etc*) indiquer, marquer; **to take sth as read** (*fig*) considérer qch comme accepté; **do you** ~ **me?** (*TEL*) est-ce que vous me recevez?
read out *vt* lire à haute voix.
read over *vt* relire.
read through *vt* (*quickly*) parcourir; (*thoroughly*) lire jusqu'au bout.
read up *vt*, **read up on** *vt fus* étudier.
readable [rē'dəbəl] *a* facile *or* agréable à lire.
reader [rē'dûr] *n* lecteur/trice; (*book*) livre *m* de lecture.
readership [rē'dûrship] *n* (*of paper etc*) (nombre *m* de) lecteurs *mpl*.
readily [red'əlē] *ad* volontiers, avec empressement; (*easily*) facilement.
readiness [red'ēnis] *n* empressement *m*; **in** ~ (*prepared*) prêt(e).
reading [rēd'ing] *n* lecture *f*; (*understanding*) interprétation *f*; (*on instrument*) indications *fpl*.
reading lamp *n* lampe *f* de bureau.
reading room *n* salle *f* de lecture.
readjust [rēəjust'] *vt* rajuster; (*instrument*) régler de nouveau ♦ *vi* (*person*): **to** ~ **(to)** se réadapter (à).
ready [red'ē] *a* prêt(e); (*willing*) prêt, disposé(e); (*quick*) prompt(e); (*available*) disponible ♦ *n*: **at the** ~ (*MIL*) prêt à faire feu; (*fig*) tout(e) prêt(e); ~ **for use** prêt à l'emploi; **to be** ~ **to do sth** être prêt à faire qch; **to get** ~ *vi* se préparer ♦ *vt* préparer.
ready cash *n* (argent *m*) liquide *m*.
ready-made [red'ēmād'] *a* tout(e) fait(e).
ready-mix [red'ēmiks] *n* (*for cakes etc*) préparation *f* en sachet.
ready-to-wear [red'ētəwär'] *a* (en) prêt-à-porter.
reagent [rēā'jənt] *n* réactif *m*.
real [rēl] *a* réel(le); (*genuine*) véritable; (*proper*) vrai(e) ♦ *ad* (*US col: very*) vraiment; **in** ~ **life** dans la vie réelle.
real estate *n* biens fonciers *or* immobiliers.
real estate agency *n* agence immobilière.
real estate agent *n* agent immobilier.
realism [rē'əlizəm] *n* réalisme *m*.
realist [rē'əlist] *n* réaliste *m/f*.
realistic [rēəlis'tik] *a* réaliste.
reality [rēal'itē] *n* réalité *f*; **in** ~ en réalité, en fait.
realization [rēələzā'shən] *n* prise *f* de conscience; réalisation *f*.
realize [rē'əlīz] *vt* (*understand*) se rendre compte de, prendre conscience de; (*a project, COMM: asset*) réaliser.
really [rē'əlē] *ad* vraiment.
realm [relm] *n* royaume *m*.
real-time [rēltīm'] *a* (*COMPUT*) en temps réel.
realtor [rē'əltûr] *n* (*US*) agent immobilier.
ream [rēm] *n* rame *f* (*de papier*); ~**s** (*fig: col*) des pages et des pages.
reap [rēp] *vt* moissonner; (*fig*) récolter.
reaper [rē'pûr] *n* (*machine*) moissonneuse *f*.

reappear [rēəpi'ûr] *vi* réapparaître, reparaître.
reappearance [rēəpēr'əns] *n* réapparition *f*.
reapply [rēəpli'] *vi*: **to ~ for** faire une nouvelle demande d'emploi concernant; reposer sa candidature à.
reappraisal [rēəprā'zəl] *n* réévaluation *f*.
rear [rēr] *a* de derrière, arrière *inv*; (AUT: *wheel etc*) arrière ♦ *n* arrière *m*, derrière *m* ♦ *vt* (*cattle, family*) élever ♦ *vi* (*also*: **~ up**: *animal*) se cabrer.
rear admiral (RA) *n* vice-amiral *m*.
rear-engined [rēr'en'jənd] *a* (AUT) avec moteur à l'arrière.
rearguard [rēr'gârd] *n* arrière-garde *f*.
rearm [rēärm'] *vt, vi* réarmer.
rearmament [rēärm'əmənt] *n* réarmement *m*.
rearrange [rēərānj'] *vt* réarranger.
rear-view [rēr'vyōō']: **~ mirror** *n* (AUT) rétroviseur *m*.
reason [rē'zən] *n* raison *f* ♦ *vi*: **to ~ with sb** raisonner qn, faire entendre raison à qn; **the ~ for/why** la raison de/pour laquelle; **to have ~ to think** avoir lieu de penser; **it stands to ~ that** il va sans dire que; **she claims with good ~ that** ... elle affirme à juste titre que ...; **all the more ~ why** raison de plus *pour* + *infinitive or* pour que + *sub*.
reasonable [rē'zənəbəl] *a* raisonnable; (*not bad*) acceptable.
reasonably [rē'zənəblē] *ad* (*to behave*) raisonnablement; (*fairly*) assez; **one can ~ assume that** ... on est fondé à *or* il est permis de supposer que ....
reasoned [rē'zənd] *a* (*argument*) raisonné(e).
reasoning [rē'zəning] *n* raisonnement *m*.
reassemble [rēəsem'bəl] *vt* rassembler; (*machine*) remonter.
reassert [rēəsûrt'] *vt* réaffirmer.
reassurance [rēəshoōr'əns] *n* assurance *f*, garantie *f*; (*comfort*) réconfort *m*.
reassure [rēəshoōr'] *vt* rassurer; **to ~ sb of** donner à qn l'assurance répétée de.
reassuring [rēəshoōr'ing] *a* rassurant(e).
reawakening [rēəwā'kəning] *n* réveil *m*.
rebate [rē'hāt] *n* (*on product*) rabais *m*; (*on tax etc*) dégrèvement *m*; (*repayment*) remboursement *m*.
rebel *n* [reb'əl] rebelle *m/f* ♦ *vi* [ribel'] se rebeller, se révolter.
rebellion [ribel'yən] *n* rébellion *f*, révolte *f*.
rebellious [ribel'yəs] *a* rebelle.
rebirth [rēbûrth'] *n* renaissance *f*.
rebound *vi* [ribound'] (*ball*) rebondir ♦ *n* [rē'bound] rebond *m*.
rebuff [ribuf'] *n* rebuffade *f* ♦ *vt* repousser.
rebuild [rēbild'] *vt irg* reconstruire.
rebuke [ribyōōk'] *n* réprimande *f*, reproche *m* ♦ *vt* réprimander.
rebut [ribut'] *vt* réfuter.
rebuttal [ribut'əl] *n* réfutation *f*.
recalcitrant [rikal'sitrənt] *a* récalcitrant(e).
recall [rikôl'] *vt* rappeler; (*remember*) se rappeler, se souvenir de ♦ *n* rappel *m*; **beyond ~** a irrévocable.
recant [rikant'] *vi* se rétracter; (REL) abjurer.
recap [rē'kap] *n* récapitulation *f* ♦ *vt, vi* récapituler.
recapture [rēkap'chûr] *vt* reprendre; (*atmosphere*) recréer.

recd. *abbr* = **received.**
recede [risēd'] *vi* s'éloigner; reculer; redescendre.
receding [risē'ding] *a* (*forehead, chin*) fuyant(e); **~ hairline** front dégarni.
receipt [risēt'] *n* (*document*) reçu *m*; (*for parcel etc*) accusé *m* de réception; (*act of receiving*) réception *f*; **~s** *npl* (COMM) recettes *fpl*; **to acknowledge ~ of** accuser réception de; **we are in ~ of** ... nous avons reçu ....
receivable [risē'vəbəl] *a* (COMM) recevable; (: *owing*) à recevoir.
receive [risēv'] *vt* recevoir; (*guest*) recevoir, accueillir; **"~d with thanks"** (COMM) "pour acquit".
receiver [risē'vûr] *n* (TEL) récepteur *m*, combiné *m*; (RADIO) récepteur; (*of stolen goods*) receleur *m*; (COMM) administrateur *m* judiciaire.
recent [rē'sənt] *a* récent(e); **in ~ years** au cours de ces dernières années.
recently [rē'səntlē] *ad* récemment; **as ~ as** pas plus tard que; **until ~** jusqu'à il y a peu de temps encore.
receptacle [risep'takəl] *n* récipient *m*.
reception [risep'shən] *n* réception *f*; (*welcome*) accueil *m*, réception.
reception center *n* centre *m* d'accueil.
reception desk *n* réception *f*.
receptionist [risep'shənist] *n* réceptionniste *m/ f*.
receptive [risep'tiv] *a* réceptif(ive).
recess [rē'ses] *n* (*in room*) renfoncement *m*; (*for bed*) alcôve *f*; (*secret place*) recoin *m*; (POL *etc*: *vacation*) vacances *fpl*; (US LAW: *short break*) suspension *f* d'audience; (SCOL. *esp US*) récréation *f*.
recession [risesh'ən] *n* (ECON) récession *f*.
recharge [rēchârj'] *vt* (*battery*) recharger.
rechargeable [rēchâr'jəbəl] *a* rechargeable.
recipe [res'əpē] *n* recette *f*.
recipient [risip'ēənt] *n* bénéficiaire *m/f*; (*of letter*) destinataire *m/f*.
reciprocal [risip'rəkəl] *a* réciproque.
reciprocate [risip'rəkāt] *vt* retourner, offrir en retour ♦ *vi* en faire autant.
recital [risīt'əl] *n* récital *m*.
recite [risīt'] *vt* (*poem*) réciter; (*complaints etc*) énumérer.
reckless [rek'lis] *a* (*driver etc*) imprudent(e); (*spender etc*) insouciant(e).
recklessly [rek'lislē] *ad* imprudemment; avec insouciance.
reckon [rek'ən] *vt* (*count*) calculer, compter; (*consider*) considérer, estimer; (*think*): **I ~ (that)** ... je pense (que) ..., j'estime (que) ... ♦ *vi*: **he is somebody to be ~ed with** il ne faut pas le sous-estimer; **to ~ without sb/ sth** ne pas tenir compte de qn/qch.
reckon on *vt fus* compter sur, s'attendre à.
reckoning [rek'əning] *n* compte *m*, calcul *m*; estimation *f*; **the day of ~** le jour du Jugement.
reclaim [riklām'] *vt* (*land*) amender; (: *from sea*) assécher; (: *from forest*) défricher; (*demand back*) réclamer (le remboursement *or* la restitution de).
reclamation [rekləmā'shən] *n* (*of land*) amendement *m*; assèchement *m*; défriche-

ment *m*.
recline [riklīn'] *vi* être allongé(e) *or* étendu(e).
reclining [riklīn'ing] *a* (*seat*) à dossier réglable.
recluse [rɛk'lōōs] *n* reclus/e, ermite *m*.
recognition [rɛkəgnish'ən] *n* reconnaissance *f*; **in ~ of** en reconnaissance de; **to gain ~** être reconnu(e); **transformed beyond ~** méconnaissable.
recognizable [rɛkəgnī'zəbəl] *a*: **~ (by)** reconnaissable (à).
recognize [rɛk'əgnīz] *vt*: **to ~ (by/as)** reconnaître (à/comme étant).
recoil [rikoil'] *vi* (*person*): **to ~ (from)** reculer (devant) ♦ *n* (*of gun*) recul *m*.
recollect [rɛkəlɛkt'] *vt* se rappeler, se souvenir de.
recollection [rɛkəlɛk'shən] *n* souvenir *m*; **to the best of my ~** autant que je m'en souvienne.
recommend [rɛkəmɛnd'] *vt* recommander; **she has a lot to ~ her** elle a beaucoup de choses en sa faveur.
recommendation [rɛkəmɛndā'shən] *n* recommandation *f*.
recommended retail price (RRP) *n* (*Brit*) prix conseillé.
recompense [rɛk'əmpɛns] *vt* récompenser; (*compensate*) dédommager ♦ *n* récompense *f*; dédommagement *m*.
reconcilable [rɛk'ənsīləbəl] *a* (*ideas*) conciliable.
reconcile [rɛk'ənsīl] *vt* (*two people*) réconcilier; (*two facts*) concilier, accorder; **to ~ o.s. to** se résigner à.
reconciliation [rɛkənsīlēā'shən] *n* réconciliation *f*; conciliation *f*.
recondite [rɛk'əndīt] *a* abstrus(e), obscur(e).
recondition [rɛkəndi'shən] *vt* remettre à neuf; réviser entièrement.
reconnaissance [rikân'isəns] *n* (*MIL*) reconnaissance *f*.
reconnoiter, (*Brit*) reconnoitre [rɛkənoi'tûr] (*MIL*) *vt* reconnaître ♦ *vi* faire une reconnaissance.
reconsider [rēkənsid'ûr] *vt* reconsidérer.
reconstitute [rēkān'stitōōt] *vt* reconstituer.
reconstruct [rēkənstrukt'] *vt* (*building*) reconstruire; (*crime*) reconstituer.
reconstruction [rēkənstruk'shən] *n* reconstruction *f*; reconstitution *f*.
record *n* [rɛk'ûrd] rapport *m*, récit *m*; (*of meeting etc*) procès-verbal *m*; (*register*) registre *m*; (*file*) dossier *m*; (*COMPUT*) article *m*; (*also*: **police ~**) casier *m* judiciaire; (*MUS*: *disc*) disque *m*; (*SPORT*) record *m* ♦ *vt* [rikôrd'] (*set down*) noter; (*relate*) rapporter; (*MUS*: *song etc*) enregistrer; **in ~ time** dans un temps record *inv*; **public ~s** archives *fpl*; **to keep a ~ of** noter; **to keep the ~ straight** (*fig*) mettre les choses au point; **he is on ~ as saying that** ... il a déclaré en public que ...; **Italy's excellent ~** les excellents résultats obtenus par l'Italie; **off the ~** *a* officieux(euse) ♦ *ad* officieusement.
record card *n* (*in file*) fiche *f*.
recorded delivery letter *n* (*Brit MAIL*) ≈ lettre recommandée.
recorder [rikôr'dûr] *n* (*MUS*) flûte *f* à bec.

record holder *n* (*SPORT*) détenteur/trice du record.
recording [rikôr'ding] *n* (*MUS*) enregistrement *m*.
recording studio *n* studio *m* d'enregistrement.
record library *n* discothèque *f*.
record player *n* électrophone *m*.
recount [rikount'] *vt* raconter.
re-count *n* [rē'kount] (*POL*: *of votes*) nouveau décompte (des suffrages) ♦ *vt* [rēkount'] recompter.
recoup [rikōōp'] *vt*: **to ~ one's losses** récupérer ce qu'on a perdu, se refaire.
recourse [rē'kôrs] *n* recours *m*; expédient *m*; **to have ~ to** recourir à, avoir recours à.
recover [rikuv'ûr] *vt* récupérer ♦ *vi* (*from illness*) se rétablir; (*from shock*) se remettre; (*country*) se redresser.
re-cover [rēkuv'ûr] *vt* (*chair etc*) recouvrir.
recovery [rikuv'ûrē] *n* récupération *f*; rétablissement *m*; redressement *m*.
re-create [rēkrēāt'] *vt* recréer.
recreation [rɛkrēā'shən] *n* récréation *f*, détente *f*.
recreation center *n* centre *m* de loisirs.
recreational [rɛkrēā'shənəl] *a* pour la détente, récréatif(ive).
recreational vehicle (RV) *n* (*US*) camping-car *m*.
recrimination [rikrimənā'shən] *n* récrimination *f*.
recruit [rikrōōt'] *n* recrue *f* ♦ *vt* recruter.
recruiting office [rikrōōt'ing ôf'is] *n* bureau *m* de recrutement.
recruitment [rikrōōt'mənt] *n* recrutement *m*.
rectangle [rɛk'tanggəl] *n* rectangle *m*.
rectangular [rɛktang'gyəlûr] *a* rectangulaire.
rectify [rɛk'təfī] *vt* (*error*) rectifier, corriger; (*omission*) réparer.
rector [rɛk'tûr] *n* (*REL*) pasteur *m*; (*in Scottish universities*) personnalité élue par les étudiants pour les représenter.
rectory [rɛk'tûrē] *n* presbytère *m*.
rectum [rɛk'təm] *n* (*ANAT*) rectum *m*.
recuperate [rikōō'pərāt] *vi* (*from illness*) se rétablir.
recur [rikûr'] *vi* se reproduire; (*idea, opportunity*) se retrouver; (*symptoms*) réapparaître.
recurrence [rikûr'əns] *n* répétition *f*; réapparition *f*.
recurrent [rikûr'ənt] *a* périodique, fréquent(e).
recurring [rikûr'ing] *a* (*MATH*) périodique.
recycle [rēsi'kəl] *vt* recycler.
red [rɛd] *n* rouge *m*; (*POL*: *pej*) rouge *m/f* ♦ *a* rouge; **in the ~** (*account*) à découvert; (*business*) en déficit.
red carpet treatment *n* réception *f* en grande pompe.
Red Cross *n* Croix-Rouge *f*.
redcurrant [rɛd'kur'ənt] *n* groseille *f* (rouge).
redden [rɛd'ən] *vt*, *vi* rougir.
reddish [rɛd'ish] *a* rougeâtre; (*hair*) plutôt roux(rousse).
redecorate [rēdɛk'ərāt] *vt* refaire à neuf, repeindre et retapisser.
redecoration [rēdɛkərā'shən] *n* remise *f* à neuf.
redeem [ridēm'] *vt* (*debt*) rembourser; (*sth in pawn*) dégager; (*fig, also REL*) racheter.

redeemable [ridē'məbəl] *a* rachetable; remboursable, amortissable.

redeeming [ridē'ming] *a* (*feature*) qui sauve, qui rachète (le reste).

redeploy [rēdiploi'] *vt* (*MIL*) redéployer; (*staff, resources*) reconvertir.

redeployment [rēdiploi'mənt] *n* redéploiement *m*; reconversion *f*.

redevelop [rēdivel'əp] *vt* rénover.

redevelopment [rēdivel'əpmənt] *n* rénovation *f*.

red-haired [red'härd] *a* roux(rousse).

red-handed [red'han'did] *a*: **to be caught ~** être pris(e) en flagrant délit *or* la main dans le sac.

redhead [red'hed] *n* roux/rousse.

red herring *n* (*fig*) diversion *f*, fausse piste.

red-hot [red'hât'] *a* chauffé(e) au rouge, brûlant(e).

redirect [rēdərekt'] *vt* (*mail*) faire suivre.

redistribute [rēdistrib'yōōt] *vt* redistribuer.

red-letter day [red'let'ûr dā] *n* grand jour, jour mémorable.

red light *n*: **to go through a ~** (*AUT*) brûler un feu rouge.

red-light district *n* quartier réservé.

redness [red'nis] *n* rougeur *f*; (*of hair*) rousseur *f*.

redo [rēdōō'] *vt irg* refaire.

redolent [red'ələnt] *a*: **~ of** qui sent; (*fig*) qui évoque.

redouble [rēdub'əl] *vt*: **to ~ one's efforts** redoubler d'efforts.

redraft [rēdraft'] *vt* remanier.

redress [ridres'] *n* réparation *f* ♦ *vt* redresser; **to ~ the balance** rétablir l'équilibre.

Red Sea *n*: **the ~** la mer Rouge.

redskin [red'skin] *n* Peau-Rouge *m/f*.

red tape *n* (*fig*) paperasserie (administrative).

reduce [ridōōs'] *vt* réduire; (*lower*) abaisser; **to ~ sth by/to** réduire qch de/à; **to ~ sb to tears** faire pleurer qn.

reduced [ridōōst'] *a* réduit(e); **"greatly ~ prices"** "gros rabais"; **at a ~ price** (*goods*) au rabais; (*ticket etc*) à prix réduit.

reduction [riduk'shən] *n* réduction *f*; (*of price*) baisse *f*; (*discount*) rabais *m*; réduction.

redundancy [ridun'dənsē] *n* (*Brit*) licenciement *m*, mise *f* au chômage; **compulsory ~** licenciement; **voluntary ~** départ *m* volontaire.

redundancy payment *n* (*Brit*) indemnité *f* de licenciement.

redundant [ridun'dənt] *a* (*Brit: worker*) licencié(e), mis(e) au chômage; (*detail, object*) superflu(e); **to be made ~** (*worker*) être licencié, être mis au chômage.

reed [rēd] *n* (*BOT*) roseau *m*; (*MUS: of clarinet etc*) anche *f*.

reedy [rē'dē] *a* (*voice, instrument*) ténu(e).

reef [rēf] *n* (*at sea*) récif *m*, écueil *m*.

reek [rēk] *vi*: **to ~ (of)** puer, empester.

reel [rēl] *n* bobine *f*; (*TECH*) dévidoir *m*; (*FISHING*) moulinet *m*; (*CINEMA*) bande *f* ♦ *vt* (*TECH*) bobiner; (*also*: **~ up**) enrouler ♦ *vi* (*sway*) chanceler; **my head is ~ing** j'ai la tête qui tourne.

reel off *vt* (*say*) énumérer, débiter.

re-election [rēilek'shən] *n* réélection *f*.

re-enter [rēen'tûr] *vt* (*also SPACE*) rentrer dans.

re-entry [rēen'trē] *n* (*also SPACE*) rentrée *f*.

re-export *vt* [rēekspôrt'] réexporter ♦ *n* [rēeks'pôrt] marchandise réexportée; (*act*) réexportation *f*.

ref [ref] *n abbr* (*col*: = *referee*) arbitre *m*.

ref. *abbr* (*COMM*: = *with reference to*) réf.

refectory [rifek'tûrē] *n* réfectoire *m*.

refer [rifûr'] *vt*: **to ~ sth to** (*dispute, decision*) soumettre qch à; **to ~ sb to** (*inquirer: for information*) adresser *or* envoyer qn à; (*reader: to text*) renvoyer qn à; **he ~red me to the manager** il m'a dit de m'adresser au directeur.

refer to *vt fus* (*allude to*) parler de, faire allusion à; (*apply to*) s'appliquer à; (*consult*) se reporter à; **~ring to your letter** (*COMM*) en réponse à votre lettre.

referee [refərē'] *n* arbitre *m*; (*TENNIS*) juge-arbitre *m*; (*Brit: for job application*) répondant/e ♦ *vt* arbitrer.

reference [ref'ûrəns] *n* référence *f*, renvoi *m*; (*mention*) allusion *f*, mention *f*; (*for job application: letter*) références; lettre *f* de recommandation; (*: person*) répondant/e; **with ~ to** en ce qui concerne; (*COMM: in letter*) me référant à; **"please quote this ~"** (*COMM*) "prière de rappeler cette référence".

reference book *n* ouvrage *m* de référence.

reference number *n* (*COMM*) numéro *m* de référence.

reference table *n* (*COMPUT*) table *f* à consulter.

referendum, pl referenda [retərən'dəm, -də] *n* référendum *m*.

refill *vt* [rēfil'] remplir à nouveau; (*pen, lighter etc*) recharger ♦ *n* [rē'fil] (*for pen etc*) recharge *f*.

refine [rifīn'] *vt* (*sugar, oil*) raffiner; (*taste*) affiner.

refined [rifīnd'] *a* (*person, taste*) raffiné(e).

refinement [rifīn'mənt] *n* (*of person*) raffinement *m*.

refinery [rifī'nûrē] *n* raffinerie *f*.

refit *n* [rē'fit] (*NAUT*) remise *f* en état ♦ *vt* [rēfit'] remettre en état.

reflate [riflāt'] *vt* (*economy*) relancer.

reflation [riflā'shən] *n* relance *f*.

reflationary [riflā'shənärē] *a* de relance.

reflect [riflekt'] *vt* (*light, image*) réfléchir, refléter; (*fig*) refléter ♦ *vi* (*think*) réfléchir, méditer.

reflect on *vt fus* (*discredit*) porter atteinte à, faire tort à.

reflection [riflek'shən] *n* réflexion *f*; (*image*) reflet *m*; (*criticism*): **~ on** critique *f* de; atteinte *f* à; **on ~** réflexion faite.

reflector [riflek'tûr] *n* (*also AUT*) réflecteur *m*.

reflex [rē'fleks] *a, n* réflexe (*m*).

reflexive [riflek'siv] *a* (*LING*) réfléchi(e).

reforestation [rēfôrista'shən] *n* reboisement *m*.

reform [rifôrm'] *n* réforme *f* ♦ *vt* réformer.

reformat [rēfôr'mat] *vt* (*COMPUT*) reformater.

Reformation [refûrmā'shən] *n*: **the ~** la Réforme.

reformatory [rifôr'mətôrē] *n* centre *m* d'éducation surveillée.

reformed [rifôrmd'] *a* amendé(e), assagi(e).
reformer [rifôr'mûr'] *n* réformateur/trice.
refrain [rifrān'] *vi*: **to ~ from doing** s'abstenir de faire ♦ *n* refrain *m*.
refresh [rifresh'] *vt* rafraîchir; *(subj: food, sleep etc)* redonner des forces à.
refresher course [rifresh'ûr kôrs] *n* cours *m* de recyclage.
refreshing [rifresh'ing] *a* rafraîchissant(e); *(sleep)* réparateur(trice); *(fact, idea etc)* qui réjouit par son originalité *or* sa rareté.
refreshment [rifresh'mənt] *n*: **for some ~** *(eating)* pour se restaurer *or* sustenter; **in need of ~** *(resting etc)* ayant besoin de refaire ses forces; **~(s)** rafraîchissement(s) *m(pl)*.
refreshment stand *n* buvette *f*.
refrigeration [rifrijərā'shən] *n* réfrigération *f*.
refrigerator [rifrij'ərātûr] *n* réfrigérateur *m*, frigidaire *m*.
refuel [rēfyoo'əl] *vt* ravitailler en carburant ♦ *vi* se ravitailler en carburant.
refuge [ref'yooj] *n* refuge *m*; **to take ~ in** se réfugier dans.
refugee [refyoojē'] *n* réfugié/e.
refugee camp *n* camp *m* de réfugiés.
refund *n* [rē'fund] remboursement *m* ♦ *vt* [rifund'] rembourser.
refurbish [rēfûr'bish] *vt* remettre à neuf.
refurnish [rēfûr'nish] *vt* remeubler.
refusal [rifyoo'zəl] *n* refus *m*; **to have first ~ on sth** avoir droit de préemption sur qch.
refuse *n* [ref'yoos] ordures *fpl*, détritus *mpl* ♦ *vt, vi* [rifyooz'] refuser; **to ~ to do sth** refuser de faire qch.
refuse collection *n (Brit)* ramassage *m* d'ordures.
refuse collector *n (Brit)* éboueur *m*.
refuse disposal *n (Brit)* élimination *f* des ordures.
refute [rifyoot'] *vt* réfuter.
regain [rigān'] *vt* regagner; retrouver.
regal [rē'gəl] *a* royal(e).
regale [rigāl'] *vt*: **to ~ sb with sth** régaler qn de qch.
regalia [rigā'lēə] *n* insignes *mpl* de la royauté.
regard [rigârd'] *n* respect *m*, estime *f*, considération *f* ♦ *vt* considérer; **to give one's ~s to** faire ses amities à; **"with kindest ~s"** "bien amicalement"; **as ~s, with ~ to** en ce qui concerne.
regarding [rigâr'ding] *prep* en ce qui concerne.
regardless [rigârd'lis] *ad* quand même; **~ of** sans se soucier de.
regatta [rigât'ə] *n* régate *f*.
regency [rē'jənsē] *n* régence *f*.
regenerate [rējen'ûrāt] *vt* régénérer ♦ *vi* se régénérer.
regent [rē'jənt] *n* régent/e.
régime [rāzhēm'] *n* régime *m*.
regiment *n* [rej'əmənt] régiment *m* ♦ *vt* [rej'əment] imposer une discipline trop stricte à.
regimental [rejəmen'təl] *a* d'un *or* du régiment.
regimentation [rejəməntā'shən] *n* réglementation excessive.
region [rē'jən] *n* région *f*; **in the ~ of** *(fig)* aux alentours de.

regional [rē'jənəl] *a* régional(e).
regional development *n* aménagement *m* du territoire.
register [rej'istûr] *n* registre *m*; *(also: **electoral ~**)* liste électorale ♦ *vt* enregistrer, inscrire; *(birth)* déclarer; *(vehicle)* immatriculer; *(luggage)* enregistrer; *(letter)* envoyer en recommandé; *(subj: instrument)* marquer ♦ *vi* se faire inscrire; *(at hotel)* signer le registre; *(make impression)* être (bien) compris(e); **to ~ for a course** s'inscrire à un cours; **to ~ a protest** protester.
registered [rej'istûrd] *a* *(design)* déposé(e); *(Brit: letter)* recommandé(e); *(student, voter)* inscrit(e).
registered company *n* société immatriculée.
registered nurse *n (US)* infirmier/ière diplômé(e) d'Etat.
registered office *n (Brit)* siège social.
registered trademark *n* marque déposée.
registrar [rej'istrâr] *n* officier *m* de l'état civil; secrétaire (général).
registration [rejistrā'shən] *n (act)* enregistrement *m*; inscription *f*; *(Brit AUT: also: **~ number**)* numéro *m* d'immatriculation.
registry [rej'istrē] *n* bureau *m* de l'enregistrement.
registry office [rej'istrē ôfis] *n (Brit)* bureau *m* de l'état civil; **to get married in a ~** ≈ se marier à la mairie.
regret [rigret'] *n* regret *m* ♦ *vt* regretter; **to ~ that** regretter que + *sub*; **we ~ to inform you that ...** nous sommes au regret de vous informer que ....
regretfully [rigret'fəlē] *ad* à *or* avec regret.
regrettable [rigret'əbəl] *a* regrettable, fâcheux(euse).
regrettably [rigret'əblē] *ad* *(drunk, late)* fâcheusement; **~, he ...** malheureusement, il ....
regroup [rēgroop'] *vt* regrouper ♦ *vi* se regrouper.
regt *abbr* = **regiment**.
regular [reg'yəlûr] *a* régulier(ière); *(usual)* habituel(le), normal(e); *(listener, reader)* fidèle; *(soldier)* de métier; *(COMM: size)* ordinaire ♦ *n* *(client etc)* habitué/e; **~ (gas)** *(US)* essence *f* ordinaire.
regularity [regyəlar'itē] *n* régularité *f*.
regularly [reg'yəlûrlē] *ad* régulièrement.
regulate [reg'yəlāt] *vt* régler.
regulation [regyəlā'shən] *n (rule)* règlement *m*; *(adjustment)* réglage *m* ♦ *cpd* réglementaire.
rehabilitation [rēhəbilətā'shən] *n (of offender)* réhabilitation *f*; *(of disabled)* rééducation *f*, réadaptation *f*.
rehash [rēhash'] *vt (col)* remanier.
rehearsal [rihûr'səl] *n* répétition *f*; **dress ~** (répétition) générale.
rehearse [rihûrs'] *vt* répéter.
rehouse [rēhouz'] *vt* reloger.
reign [rān] *n* règne *m* ♦ *vi* régner.
reigning [rā'ning] *a* *(monarch)* régnant(e); *(champion)* actuel(le).
reimburse [rēimbûrs'] *vt* rembourser.
rein [rān] *n (for horse)* rêne *f*; **to give sb free ~** *(fig)* donner carte blanche à qn.
reincarnation [rēinkârnā'shən] *n* réincar-

nation *f*.

reindeer [rān'dēr] *n* (*pl inv*) renne *m*.

reinforce [rēinfôrs'] *vt* renforcer.

reinforced concrete [rēinfôrst' kân'krēt] *n* béton armé.

reinforcement [rēinfôrs'mənt] *n* (*action*) renforcement *m*; **~s** *npl* (*MIL*) renfort(s) *m(pl)*.

reinstate [rēinstāt'] *vt* rétablir, réintégrer.

reinstatement [rēinstāt'mənt] *n* réintégration *f*.

reissue [rēish'ōō] *vt* (*book*) rééditer; (*film*) ressortir.

reiterate [rēit'ərāt] *vt* réitérer, répéter.

reject *n* [rē'jekt] (*COMM*) article *m* de rebut ♦ *vt* [rijekt'] refuser; (*COMM: goods*) mettre au rebut; (*idea*) rejeter.

rejection [rijek'shən] *n* rejet *m*, refus *m*.

rejoice [rijois'] *vi*: **to ~** (**at** *or* **over**) se réjouir (de).

rejoinder [rijoin'dûr] *n* (*retort*) réplique *f*.

rejuvenate [rijōō'vənāt] *vt* rajeunir.

rekindle [rēkin'dəl] *vt* rallumer; (*fig*) raviver.

relapse [rilaps'] *n* (*MED*) rechute *f*.

relate [rilāt'] *vt* (*tell*) raconter; (*connect*) établir un rapport entre ♦ *vi*: **to ~ to** (*connect*) se rapporter à; (*interact*) établir un rapport *or* une entente avec.

related [rilā'tid] *a* apparenté(e).

relating [rilā'ting] : **~ to** *prep* concernant.

relation [rilā'shən] *n* (*person*) parent/e; (*link*) rapport *m*, lien *m*; **diplomatic/international ~s** relations diplomatiques/internationales; **in ~ to** en ce qui concerne; par rapport à; **to bear no ~ to** être sans rapport avec.

relationship [rilā'shənship] *n* rapport *m*, lien *m*; (*personal ties*) relations *fpl*, rapports, (*also:* **family ~**) lien de parenté; (*affair*) liaison *f*; **they have a good ~** ils s'entendent bien.

relative [rel'ətiv] *n* parent/e ♦ *a* relatif(ive); (*respective*) respectif(ive); **all her ~s** toute sa famille.

relatively [rel'ətivlē] *ad* relativement.

relax [rilaks'] *vi* se relâcher; (*person: unwind*) se détendre; (*calm down*) se calmer ♦ *vt* relâcher; (*mind, person*) détendre.

relaxation [rēlaksā'shən] *n* relâchement *m*; détente *f*; (*entertainment*) distraction *f*.

relaxed [rilakst'] *a* relâché(e); détendu(e).

relaxing [rilaks'ing] *a* délassant(e).

relay *n* [rē'lā] (*SPORT*) course *f* de relais ♦ *vt* [rēlā'] (*message*) retransmettre, relayer.

release [rilēs'] *n* (*from prison, obligation*) libération *f*; (*of gas etc*) émission *f*; (*of film etc*) sortie *f*; (*record*) disque *m*; (*device*) déclencheur *m* ♦ *vt* (*prisoner*) libérer; (*book, film*) sortir; (*report, news*) rendre public, publier; (*gas etc*) émettre, dégager; (*free: from wreckage etc*) dégager; (*TECH: catch, spring etc*) déclencher; (*let go*) relâcher; lâcher; desserrer; **to ~ one's grip** *or* **hold** lâcher prise; **to ~ the clutch** (*AUT*) débrayer.

relegate [rel'əgāt] *vt* reléguer; (*SPORT*): **to be ~d** descendre dans une division inférieure.

relent [rilent'] *vi* se laisser fléchir.

relentless [rilent'lis] *a* implacable.

relevance [rel'əvəns] *n* pertinence *f*; **~ of sth to sth** rapport *m* entre qch et qch.

relevant [rel'əvənt] *a* approprié(e); (*fact*) significatif(ive); (*information*) utile, pertinent(e); **~ to** ayant rapport à, approprié à.

reliability [rilīəbil'ətē] *n* sérieux *m*; fiabilité *f*.

reliable [rilī'əbəl] *a* (*person, firm*) sérieux(euse), fiable; (*method, machine*) fiable.

reliably [rilī'əblē] *ad*: **to be ~ informed** savoir de source sûre.

reliance [rilī'əns] *n*: **~ (on)** (*trust*) confiance *f* (en); (*dependence*) besoin *m* (de), dépendance *f* (de).

reliant [rilī'ənt] *a*: **to be ~ on sth/sb** dépendre de qch/qn.

relic [rel'ik] *n* (*REL*) relique *f*; (*of the past*) vestige *m*.

relief [rilēf'] *n* (*from pain, anxiety*) soulagement *m*; (*help, supplies*) secours *m(pl)*; (*of guard*) relève *f*; (*ART, GEO*) relief *m*; **by way of light ~** pour faire diversion.

relief map *n* carte *f* en relief.

relief road *n* (*Brit*) route *f* de délestage.

relieve [rilēv'] *vt* (*pain, patient*) soulager; (*bring help*) secourir; (*take over from: gen*) relayer; (*: guard*) relever; **to ~ sb of sth** débarrasser qn de qch; **to ~ sb of his command** (*MIL*) relever qn de ses fonctions; **to ~ o.s.** (*euphemism*) se soulager, faire ses besoins.

religion [rilij'ən] *n* religion *f*.

religious [rilij'əs] *a* religieux(euse); (*book*) de piété.

reline [rēlīn'] *vt* (*brakes*) refaire la garniture de.

relinquish [riling'kwish] *vt* abandonner; (*plan, habit*) renoncer à.

relish [rel'ish] *n* (*CULIN*) condiment *m*; (*enjoyment*) délectation *f* ♦ *vt* (*food etc*) savourer; **to ~ doing** se délecter à faire.

relive [rēliv'] *vt* revivre.

reload [rēlōd'] *vt* recharger.

relocate [rēlō'kāt] *vt* (*business*) transférer ♦ *vi* se transférer, s'installer *or* s'établir ailleurs; **to ~ in** (*déménager et*) s'installer *or* s'établir à, se transférer à.

reluctance [riluk'təns] *n* répugnance *f*.

reluctant [riluk'tənt] *a* peu disposé(e), qui hésite; **to be ~ to do sth** hésiter à faire qch.

reluctantly [riluk'təntlē] *ad* à contrecœur, sans enthousiasme.

rely [rilī'] : **to ~ on** *vt fus* compter sur; (*be dependent*) dépendre de.

remain [rimān'] *vi* rester; **to ~ silent** garder le silence.

remainder [rimān'dûr] *n* reste *m*; (*COMM*) fin *f* de série.

remaining [rimā'ning] *a* qui reste.

remains [rimānz'] *npl* restes *mpl*.

remand [rimand'] *n*: **on ~** en détention préventive ♦ *vt*: **to ~ in custody** écrouer; renvoyer en détention provisoire.

remark [rimârk'] *n* remarque *f*, observation *f* ♦ *vt* (faire) remarquer, dire; (*notice*) remarquer; **to ~ on sth** faire une *or* des remarque(s) sur qch.

remarkable [rimâr'kəbəl] *a* remarquable.

remarry [rēmar'ē] *vi* se remarier.

remedial [rimē'dēəl] *a* (*tuition, classes*) de rattrapage.

remedy [rem'idē] *n*: **~ (for)** remède *m* (contre

or à). ♦ *vt* remédier à.

remember [rimem'bûr] *vt* se rappeler, sc souvenir de; **I ~ seeing it, I ~ having seen it** je me rappelle l'avoir vu *or* que je l'ai vu; **she ~ed to do it** elle a pensé à le faire; **~ me to your wife** rappelez-moi au bon souvenir de votre femme.

remembrance [rimem'brəns] *n* souvenir *m*; mémoire *f*.

remind [rimīnd'] *vt*: **to ~ sb of sth** rappeler qch à qn; **to ~ sb to do** faire penser à qn à faire, rappeler à qn qu'il doit faire; **that ~s me!** j'y pense!

reminder [rimīnd'ûr] *n* rappel *m*; (*note etc*) pense-bête *m*.

reminisce [remənis'] *vi*: **to ~ (about)** évoquer ses souvenirs (de).

reminiscences [remənis'ənsiz] *npl* réminiscences *fpl*, souvenirs *mpl*.

reminiscent [remənis'ənt] *a*: **~ of** qui rappelle, qui fait penser à.

remiss [rimis'] *a* négligent(e); **it was ~ of me** c'était une négligence de ma part.

remission [rimish'ən] *n* rémission *f*; (*of debt, sentence*) remise *f*; (*of fee*) exemption *f*.

remit [rimit'] *vt* (*send: money*) envoyer.

remittance [rimit'əns] *n* envoi *m*, paiement *m*.

remnant [rem'nənt] *n* reste *m*, restant *m*; **~s** *npl* (*COMM*) coupons *mpl*; fins *fpl* de série.

remonstrate [rimən'strāt] *vi*: **to ~ (with sb about sth)** se plaindre (à qn de qch).

remorse [rimôrs'] *n* remords *m*.

remorseful [rimôrs'fəl] *a* plein(e) de remords.

remorseless [rimôrs'lis] *a* (*fig*) impitoyable.

remote [rimōt'] *a* éloigné(e), lointain(e); (*person*) distant(e); **there is a ~ possibility that** ... il est tout juste possible que ....

remote control *n* télécommande *f*.

remote-controlled [rimōt'kəntrōld'] *a* téléguidé(e).

remotely [rimōt'lē] *ad* au loin; (*slightly*) très vaguement.

remoteness [rimōt'nis] *n* éloignement *m*.

remould [rē'mōld] *n* (*Brit: tire*) pneu rechapé.

removable [rimoo'vəbəl] *a* (*detachable*) amovible.

removal [rimoo'vəl] *n* (*taking away*) enlèvement *m*; suppression *f*; (*Brit: from house*) déménagement *m*; (*from office: dismissal*) renvoi *m*; (*MED*) ablation *f*.

removal man *n* (*Brit*) déménageur *m*.

removal van *n* (*Brit*) camion *m* de déménagement.

remove [rimoov'] *vt* enlever, retirer; (*employee*) renvoyer; (*stain*) faire partir; (*doubt, abuse*) supprimer; **first cousin once ~d** cousin/e au deuxième degré.

remover [rimoo'vûr] *n* (*for paint*) décapant *m*; (*for varnish*) dissolvant *m*; **make-up ~** démaquillant *m*; **~s** *npl* (*Brit: company*) entreprise *f* de déménagement.

remunerate [rimyoo'nərāt] *vt* rémunérer.

remuneration [rimyoonərā'shən] *n* rémunération *f*.

rename [rēnām'] *vt* rebaptiser.

rend, *pt, pp* **rent** [rend, rent] *vt* déchirer.

render [ren'dûr] *vt* rendre; (*CULIN: fat*) clarifier.

rendering [ren'dûring] *n* (*MUS etc*) interpréta-

tion *f*.

rendezvous [rân'dāvoo] *n* rendez-vous *m inv* ♦ *vi* opérer une jonction, se rejoindre; (*spaceship*) effectuer une rendez-vous (dans l'espace); **to ~ with sb** rejoindre qn.

renegade [ren'əgād] *n* rénégat/e.

renew [rinoo'] *vt* renouveler; (*negotiations*) reprendre; (*acquaintance*) renouer.

renewable [rinoo'əbəl] *a* renouvelable.

renewal [rinoo'əl] *n* renouvellement *m*; reprise *f*.

renounce [rinouns'] *vt* renoncer à; (*disown*) renier.

renovate [ren'əvāt] *vt* rénover; (*work of art*) restaurer.

renovation [renəvā'shən] *n* rénovation *f*; restauration *f*.

renown [rinoun'] *n* renommée *f*.

renowned [rinound'] *a* renommé(e).

rent [rent] *pt, pp of* **rend** ♦ *n* loyer *m* ♦ *vt* louer; (*car, TV*) louer, prendre en location; (*also: ~ out: car, TV*) louer, donner en location; **"for rent"** "a louer".

rental [ren'təl] *n* (*for television, car*) (prix *m* de) location *f*.

rental car *n* (*US*) voiture louée.

renunciation [rinunsēā'shən] *n* renonciation *f*; (*self-denial*) renoncement *m*.

reopen [rēō'pən] *vt* rouvrir.

reopening [rēō'pəning] *n* réouverture *f*.

reorder [rēôr'dûr] *vt* commander de nouveau; (*rearrange*) réorganiser.

reorganize [rēôr'gənīz] *vt* réorganiser.

rep [rep] *n abbr* (*COMM*) = **representative;** (*THEATER*) = **repertory.**

Rep. *abbr* (*US POL*) = **representative, republican.**

repair [ripär'] *n* réparation *f* ♦ *vt* réparer; **in good/bad ~** en bon/mauvais état; **under ~** en réparation.

repair kit *n* trousse *f* de réparations.

repair man *n* réparateur *m*.

repair shop *n* (*AUT etc*) atelier *m* de réparations.

repartee [repûrtē'] *n* repartie *f*.

repast [ripast'] *n* (*formal*) repas *m*.

repatriate [rēpā'trēāt] *vt* rapatrier.

repay [ripā'] *vt* (*money, creditor*) rembourser; (*sb's efforts*) récompenser.

repayment [ripā'mənt] *n* remboursement *m*; récompense *f*.

repeal [ripēl'] *n* (*of law*) abrogation *f*; (*of sentence*) annulation *f* ♦ *vt* abroger; annuler.

repeat [ripēt'] *n* (*RADIO, TV*) reprise *f* ♦ *vt* répéter; (*pattern*) reproduire; (*promise, attack, also COMM: order*) renouveler; (*SCOL: a class*) redoubler ♦ *vi* répéter.

repeatedly [ripēt'idlē] *ad* souvent, à plusieurs reprises.

repel [ripel'] *vt* repousser.

repellent [ripel'ənt] *a* repoussant(e) ♦ *n*: **insect ~** insectifuge *m*; **moth ~** produit *m* antimite(s).

repent [ripent'] *vi*: **to ~ (of)** se repentir (de).

repentance [ripen'təns] *n* repentir *m*.

repercussion [rēpûrkush'ən] *n* (*consequence*) répercussion *f*.

repertoire [rep'ûrtwâr] *n* répertoire *m*.

repertory [rep'ûrtōrē] *n* (*also:* **~ theater**)

théâtre *m* de répertoire.
repertory company *n* troupe théâtrale permanente.
repetition [rɛpitish'ən] *n* répétition *f*.
repetitious [rɛpitish'əs] *a* (*speech*) plein(e) de redites.
repetitive [ripɛt'ətiv] *a* (*movement, work*) répétitif(ive); (*speech*) plein(e) de redites.
replace [riplās'] *vt* (*put back*) remettre, replacer; (*take the place of*) remplacer; (*TEL*): "~ **the receiver**" "raccrochez".
replacement [riplās'mənt] *n* replacement *m*; remplacement *m*; (*person*) remplaçant/e.
replacement part *n* pièce *f* de rechange.
replay [rēplā'] *n* (*of match*) match rejoué; (*of tape, film*) répétition *f*.
replenish [riplen'ish] *vt* (*glass*) remplir (de nouveau); (*stock etc*) réapprovisionner.
replete [riplēt'] *a* rempli(e); (*well-fed*): ~ (**with**) rassasié(e) (de).
replica [rep'ləkə] *n* réplique *f*, copie exacte.
reply [ripli'] *n* réponse *f* ♦ *vi* répondre; **in** ~ (**to**) en réponse (à).
report [ripórt'] *n* rapport *m*; (*PRESS etc*) reportage *m*; (*Brit: also:* **school** ~) bulletin *m* (scolaire); (*of gun*) détonation *f* ♦ *vt* rapporter, faire un compte rendu de; (*PRESS etc*) faire un reportage sur; (*bring to notice: occurrence*) signaler; (*: person*) dénoncer ♦ *vi* (*make a report*): **to** ~ (**on**) faire un rapport (sur); (*for newspaper*) faire un reportage (sur); (*present o.s.*): **to** ~ (**to sb**) se présenter (chez qn); **it is** ~**ed that** on dit *or* annonce que; **it is** ~**ed from Berlin that** on nous apprend de Berlin que.
report card *n* (*US, Scottish*) bulletin *m* (scolaire).
reportedly [ripór'tidlē] *ad*: **she is** ~ **living in Spain** elle habiterait en Espagne; **he** ~ **ordered them to** ... il leur aurait ordonné de ....
reporter [ripór'túr] *n* reporter *m*.
repose [ripōz'] *n*: **in** ~ en *or* au repos.
repossess [rēpəzes'] *vt* saisir.
reprehensible [reprihen'səbəl] *a* répréhensible.
represent [reprizent'] *vt* représenter; (*explain*): **to** ~ **to sb that** expliquer à qn que.
representation [reprizentā'shən] *n* représentation *f*; ~**s** *npl* (*protest*) démarche *f*.
representative [reprizen'tətiv] *n* représentant/e; (*COMM*) représentant/e (de commerce); (*US POL*) député *m* ♦ *a*: ~ (**of**) représentatif(ive) (de), caractéristique (de).
repress [ripres'] *vt* réprimer.
repression [ripresh'ən] *n* répression *f*.
repressive [ipres'iv] *a* répressif(ive).
reprieve [riprēv'] *n* (*LAW*) grâce *f*; (*fig*) sursis *m*, délai *m* ♦ *vt* gracier; accorder un sursis *or* un délai à.
reprimand [rep'rəmand] *n* réprimande *f* ♦ *vt* réprimander.
reprint *n* [rē'print] réimpression *f* ♦ *vt* [rēprint'] réimprimer.
reprisal [riprī'zəl] *n* représailles *fpl*; **to take** ~**s** user de représailles.
reproach [riprōch'] *n* reproche *m* ♦ *vt*: **to** ~ **sb with sth** reprocher qch à qn; **beyond** ~ irréprochable.

reproachful [riprōch'fəl] *a* de reproche.
reproduce [rēprədōōs'] *vt* reproduire ♦ *vi* se reproduire.
reproduction [rēprəduk'shən] *n* reproduction *f*.
reproductive [rēprəduk'tiv] *a* reproducteur(trice).
reproof [riprōōf'] *n* reproche *m*.
reprove [riprōōv'] *vt* (*action*) réprouver; (*person*): **to** ~ (**for**) blâmer (de).
reproving [riprōō'ving] *a* réprobateur(trice).
reptile [rep'tīl] *n* reptile *m*.
Repub. *abbr* (*US POL*) = **republican**.
republic [ripub'lik] *n* république *f*.
republican [ripub'likən] *a*, *n* républicain(e).
repudiate [ripyōō'dēāt] *vt* (*ally, behavior*) désavouer; (*accusation*) rejeter; (*wife*) répudier.
repugnant [ripug'nənt] *a* répugnant(e).
repulse [ripuls'] *vt* repousser.
repulsion [ripul'shən] *n* répulsion *f*.
repulsive [ripul'siv] *a* repoussant(e), répulsif(ive).
reputable [rep'yətəbəl] *a* de bonne réputation; (*occupation*) honorable.
reputation [repyətā'shən] *n* réputation *f*; **to have a** ~ **for** être réputé(e) pour; **he has a** ~ **for being awkward** il a la réputation de ne pas être commode.
repute [ripyōōt'] *n* (*bonne*) réputation.
reputed [ripyōō'tid] *a* réputé(e); **he is** ~ **to be rich/intelligent** *etc* on dit qu'il est riche/ intelligent *etc*.
reputedly [ripyōō'tidlē] *ad* d'après ce qu'on dit.
request [rikwest'] *n* demande *f*; (*formal*) requête *f* ♦ *vt*: **to** ~ (**of** *or* **from sb**) demander (à qn); **at the** ~ **of** à la demande de.
request stop *n* (*Brit: for bus*) arrêt facultatif.
requiem [rek'wēəm] *n* requiem *m*.
require [rikwīūr'] *vt* (*need: subj: person*) avoir besoin de; (*: thing, situation*) nécessiter, demander; (*demand*) exiger, requérir; (*order*): **to** ~ **sb to do sth/sth of sb** exiger que qn fasse qch/qch de qn; **if** ~**d** s'il le faut; **what qualifications are** ~**d?** quelles sont les qualifications requises?; ~**d by law** requis par la loi.
required [rikwīūrd'] *a* requis(e), voulu(e).
requirement [rikwīūr'mənt] *n* exigence *f*; besoin *m*; condition *f* (requise).
requisite [rek'wizit] *n* chose *f* nécessaire ♦ *a* requis(e), nécessaire; **toilet** ~**s** accessoires *mpl* de toilette.
requisition [rekwizish'ən] *n*: ~ (**for**) demande *f* (de) ♦ *vt* (*MIL*) réquisitionner.
reroute [rērout'] *vt* (*train etc*) dérouter.
resale [rē'sāl] *n* revente *f*.
resale price maintenance [rē'sāl prīs mān'tənəns] *n* vente au détail à prix imposé.
rescind [risind'] *vt* annuler; (*law*) abroger; (*judgment*) rescinder.
rescue [res'kyōō] *n* sauvetage *m*; (*help*) secours *mpl* ♦ *vt* sauver; **to come to sb's** ~ venir au secours de qn.
rescue party *n* équipe *f* de sauvetage.
rescuer [res'kyōōúr] *n* sauveteur *m*.
research [risúrch'] *n* recherche(s) *f(pl)* ♦ *vt*

faire des recherches sur ♦ *vi*: **to ~ (into sth)**
faire des recherches (sur qch); **a piece of ~**
un travail de recherche; **~ and development
(R & D)** recherche-développement (R-D).
researcher [risûr'chûr] *n* chercheur/euse.
research work *n* recherches *fpl*.
resell [rēsel'] *vt irg* revendre.
resemblance [rizem'bləns] *n* ressemblance *f*;
to bear a strong ~ to ressembler beaucoup
à.
resemble [rizem'bəl] *vt* ressembler à.
resent [rizent'] *vt* éprouver du ressentiment
de, être contrarié(e) par.
resentful [rizent'fəl] *a* irrité(e), plein(e) de
ressentiment.
resentment [rizent'mənt] *n* ressentiment *m*.
reservation [rezûrvā'shən] *n* (*booking*) réservation *f*; (*doubt*) réserve *f*; (*protected
area*) réserve; (*Brit AUT*: also: **central ~**)
bande médiane; **to make a ~ (in an hotel/a
restaurant/on a plane)** réserver *or* retenir
une chambre/une table/une place; **with ~s**
(*doubts*) avec certaines réserves.
reservation desk *n* (*US*: *in hotel*) réception
f.
reserve [rizûrv'] *n* réserve *f*; (*SPORT*)
remplaçant/e ♦ *vt* (*seats etc*) réserver, retenir; **~s** *npl* (*MIL*) réservistes *mpl*; **in ~** en
réserve.
reserve currency *n* monnaie *f* de réserve.
reserved [rizûrvd'] *a* réservé(e).
reserve price *n* (*Brit*) mise *f* à prix, prix *m*
de départ.
reservist [rizûr'vist] *n* (*MIL*) réserviste *m*.
reservoir [rez'ûrvwâr] *n* réservoir *m*.
reset [rēset'] *vt irg* remettre; (*clock, watch*)
mettre à l'heure; (*COMPUT*) remettre à zéro.
reshape [rēshāp'] *vt* (*policy*) réorganiser.
reshuffle [rēshuf'əl] *n*: **Cabinet ~** (*POL*) remaniement ministériel.
reside [rizīd'] *vi* résider.
residence [rez'idəns] *n* résidence *f*; **to take up
~** s'installer; **in ~** (*queen etc*) en résidence;
(*doctor*) résidant(e).
resident [rez'idənt] *n* résident/e ♦ *a* rési-
dant(e).
residential [reziden'chəl] *a* de résidence;
(*area*) résidentiel(le).
residue [rez'idōō] *n* reste *m*; (*CHEMISTRY,
PHYSICS*) résidu *m*.
resign [rizīn'] *vt* (*one's post*) se démettre de ♦
vi: **to ~ (from)** démissionner (de); **to ~ o.s.
to** (*endure*) se résigner à.
resignation [rezignā'shən] *n* demission *f*; résignation *f*; **to tender one's ~** donner sa démission.
resigned [rizīnd'] *a* résigné(e).
resilience [rizil'yəns] *n* (*of material*) élasticité
f; (*of person*) ressort *m*.
resilient [rizil'yənt] *a* (*person*) qui réagit, qui a
du ressort.
resin [rez'in] *n* résine *f*.
resist [rizist'] *vt* résister à.
resistance [rizis'təns] *n* résistance *f*.
resistant [rizis'tənt] *a*: **~ (to)** résistant(e) (à).
resolute [rez'əlōōt] *a* résolu(e).
resolution [rezəlōō'shən] *n* résolution *f*; **to
make a ~** prendre une résolution.
resolve [rizâlv'] *n* résolution *f* ♦ *vt* (*decide*): **to**

~ to do résoudre *or* décider de faire; (*problem*) résoudre.
resolved [rizâlvd'] *a* résolu(e).
resonance [rez'ənəns] *n* résonance *f*.
resonant [rez'ənənt] *a* résonnant(e).
resort [rizôrt'] *n* (*town*) station *f* (de vacances); (*recourse*) recours *m* ♦ *vi*: **to ~ to**
avoir recours à; **seaside/winter sports ~**
station balnéaire/de sports d'hiver; **in the
last ~** en dernier ressort.
resound [rizound'] *vi*: **to ~ (with)** retentir
(de).
resounding [rizoun'ding] *a* retentissant(e).
resource [rē'sôrs] *n* ressource *f*; **~s** *npl*
ressources; **natural ~s** ressources naturelles;
to leave sb to his (*or* **her**) **own ~s** (*fig*) livrer qn à lui-même (*or* elle-même).
resourceful [risôrs'fəl] *a* plein(e) de ressource,
débrouillard(e).
resourcefulness [risôrs'fəlnis] *n* ressource *f*.
respect [rispekt'] *n* respect *m*; (*point, detail*):
in some ~s à certains égards ♦ *vt* respecter;
~s *npl* respects, hommages *mpl*; **to have** *or*
show ~ for sb/sth respecter qn/qch; **out of
~ for** par respect pour; **with ~ to** en ce qui
concerne; **in ~ of** sous le rapport de, quant
à; **in this ~** sous ce rapport, à cet égard;
with due ~ I ... malgré le respect que je
vous dois, je ....
respectability [rispektəbil'ətē] *n* respectabilité
f.
respectable [rispek'təbəl] *a* respectable;
(*quite good: result etc*) honorable; (*player*)
assez bon(bonne).
respectful [rispekt'fəl] *a* respectueux(euse).
respective [rispek'tiv] *a* respectif(ive).
respectively [rispek'tivlē] *ad* respectivement.
respiration [respərā'shən] *n* respiration *f*.
respirator [res'pərātûr] *n* respirateur *m*.
respiratory [res'pûrətôrē] *a* respiratoire.
respite [res'pit] *n* répit *m*.
resplendent [risplen'dənt] *a* resplendissant(e).
respond [rispând'] *vi* répondre; (*to treatment*)
réagir.
respondent [rispân'dənt] *n* (*LAW*) défendeur/
deresse.
response [rispâns'] *n* réponse *f*; (*to treatment*)
réaction *f*; **in ~ to** en réponse à.
responsibility [rispânsəbil'ətē] *n* responsabilité
f; **to take ~ for sth/sb** accepter la responsabilité de qch/d'être responsable de qn.
responsible [rispân'səbəl] *a* (*liable*): **~ (for)**
responsable (de); (*person*) digne de
confiance; (*job*) qui comporte des responsabilités; **to be ~ to sb (for sth)** être responsable devant qn (de qch).
responsibly [rispân'səblē] *ad* avec sérieux.
responsive [rispân'siv] *a* qui n'est pas ré-
servé(e) *or* indifférent(e).
rest [rest] *n* repos *m*; (*stop*) arrêt *m*, pause *f*;
(*MUS*) silence *m*; (*support*) support *m*, appui
m; (*remainder*) reste *m*, restant *m* ♦ *vi* se
reposer; (*be supported*): **to ~ on** appuyer *or*
reposer sur; (*remain*) rester ♦ *vt* (*lean*): **to
~ sth on/against** appuyer qch sur/contre;
the ~ of them les autres; **to set sb's mind
at ~** tranquilliser qn; **it ~s with him to**
c'est à lui de; **~ assured that ...** soyez assuré que ....

rest area n (US AUT) aire f de stationnement (sur le bas-côté).

restart [rēstârt'] vt (engine) remettre en marche; (work) reprendre.

restaurant [res'tûrənt] n restaurant m.

restaurant car n (Brit) wagon-restaurant m.

rest cure n cure f de repos.

restful [rest'fəl] a reposant(e).

rest home n maison f de repos.

restitution [restitoo'shən] n (act) restitution f; (reparation) réparation f.

restive [res'tiv] a agité(e), impatient(e); (horse) rétif(ive).

restless [rest'lis] a agité(e); **to get** ~ s'impatienter.

restlessly [rest'lislē] ad avec agitation.

restock [rēstâk'] vt réapprovisionner.

restoration [restərā'shən] n restauration f; restitution f.

restorative [restôr'ətiv] reconstituant(e) ♦ n reconstituant m.

restore [ristôr'] vt (building) restaurer; (sth stolen) restituer; (peace, health) rétablir.

restorer [ristôr'ûr] n (ART etc) restaurateur/trice (d'œuvres d'art).

restrain [ristrān'] vt (feeling) contenir; (person): **to** ~ **(from doing)** retenir (de faire).

restrained [ristrānd'] a (style) sobre; (manner) mesuré(e).

restraint [ristrānt'] n (restriction) contrainte f; (moderation) retenue f; (of style) sobriété f; **wage** ~ limitations salariales.

restrict [ristrikt'] vt restreindre, limiter.

restricted area n (AUT) zone f à vitesse limitée.

restriction [ristrik'shən] n restriction f, limitation f.

restrictive [ristrik'tiv] a restrictif(ive).

restrictive practices npl (INDUSTRY) pratiques fpl entravant la libre concurrence.

rest room n (US) toilettes fpl.

rest stop n (US AUT) aire f de stationnement (sur le bas-côté).

restructure [rēstruk'chûr] vt restructurer.

result [rizult'] n résultat m ♦ vi: **to** ~ **(from)** résulter (de); **to** ~ **in** aboutir à, se terminer par; **as a** ~ **it** is too expensive il en résulte que c'est trop cher; **as a** ~ **of** à la suite de.

resultant [rizul'tənt] a résultant(e).

resume [rēzoom'] vt (work, journey) reprendre; (sum up) résumer ♦ vi (work etc) reprendre.

résumé [rez'oomā'] n (summary) résumé m; (US: curriculum vitae) curriculum vitae m inv.

resumption [rizump'shən] n reprise f.

resurgence [risûr'jəns] n réapparition f.

resurrection [rezərek'shən] n résurrection f.

resuscitate [risus'ətāt] vt (MED) réanimer.

resuscitation [risusətā'shən] n réanimation f.

retail [rē'tāl] n (vente f au) détail m ♦ cpd de or au détail ♦ vt vendre au détail ♦ vi: **to** ~ **at 10 francs** se vendre au détail à 10 F.

retailer [rē'tālûr] n détaillant/e.

retail outlet n point m de vente.

retail price n prix m de détail.

retail price index n ≈ indice m des prix.

retain [ritān'] vt (keep) garder, conserver;

(employ) engager.

retainer [ritā'nûr] n (servant) serviteur m; (fee) acompte m, provision f.

retaliate [rital'ēāt] vi: **to** ~ **(against)** se venger (de); **to** ~ **(on sb)** rendre la pareille (à qn).

retaliation [ritalēā'shən] n représailles fpl, vengeance f; **in** ~ **for** par représailles pour.

retaliatory [rital'ēətôrē] a de représailles.

retarded [ritâr'did] a retardé(e).

retch [rech] vi avoir des haut-le-cœur.

retentive [riten'tiv] a: ~ **memory** excellente mémoire.

rethink [rēthingk'] vt repenser.

reticence [ret'isəns] n réticence f.

reticent [ret'isənt] a réticent(e).

retina [ret'ənə] n rétine f.

retinue [ret'ənoo] n suite f, cortège m.

retire [ritīûr'] vi (give up work) prendre sa retraite; (withdraw) se retirer, partir; (go to bed) (aller) se coucher.

retired [ritīûrd'] a (person) retraité(e).

retirement [ritīûr'mənt] n retraite f.

retirement age n âge m de la retraite.

retiring [ritīûr'ing] a (person) réservé(e); (chairman etc) sortant(e).

retort [ritôrt'] n (reply) riposte f; (container) cornue f ♦ vi riposter.

retrace [rētrās'] vt reconstituer; **to** ~ **one's steps** revenir sur ses pas.

retract [ritrakt'] vt (statement, claws) rétracter; (undercarriage, aerial) rentrer, escamoter ♦ vi se rétracter; rentrer.

retractable [ritrakt'əbəl] a escamotable.

retrain [rētrān'] vt recycler ♦ vi se recycler.

retraining [rētrā'ning] n recyclage m.

retread vt [rētred'] (AUT: tire) rechaper ♦ n [re'tred] pneu rechapé.

retreat [ritrēt'] n retraite f ♦ vi battre en retraite; (flood) reculer; **to beat a hasty** ~ (fig) partir avec précipitation.

retrial [rētril'] n nouveau procès.

retribution [retrəbyoo'shən] n châtiment m.

retrieval [ritrē'vəl] n récupération f; réparation f, recherche f et extraction f.

retrieve [ritrēv'] vt (sth lost) récupérer; (situation, honor) sauver; (error, loss) réparer; (COMPUT) rechercher.

retriever [ritrē'vûr] n chien m d'arrêt.

retroactive [retrōak'tiv] a rétroactif(ive).

retrograde [ret'rəgrād] a rétrograde.

retrospect [ret'rəspekt] n: **in** ~ rétrospectivement, après coup.

retrospective [retrəspek'tiv] a (law) rétroactif(ive) ♦ n (ART) rétrospective f.

return [ritûrn'] n (going or coming back) retour m; (of sth stolen etc) restitution f; (recompense) récompense f; (FINANCE: from land, shares) rapport m; (report) relevé m, rapport ♦ cpd (journey) de retour; (Brit: ticket) aller et retour; (match) retour ♦ vi (person etc: come back) revenir; (: go back) retourner ♦ vt rendre; (bring back) rapporter; (send back) renvoyer; (put back) remettre; (POL: candidate) élire; ~**s** npl (COMM) recettes fpl; bénéfices mpl; (: ~ed goods) marchandises renvoyées; **many happy** ~**s (of the day)!** bon anniversaire!; **by** ~ **mail** par retour (du courrier); **in** ~ **(for)** en

échange (de).
returnable [ritûr'nəbəl] *a* (*bottle etc*) consigné(e).
return key *n* (*COMPUT*) touche *f* de retour.
return on investment (ROI) *n* (*US*) rentabilité *f* de l'investissement.
reunion [rēyŌŌn'yən] *n* réunion *f*.
reunite [rēyŌŌnīt'] *vt* réunir.
rev [rev] *n abbr* (= *revolution*: *AUT*) tour *m* ♦ *vb* (*also*: ~ **up**) *vt* emballer ♦ *vi* s'emballer.
revaluation [rēval'yŌŌāshən] *n* réévaluation *f*.
revamp [rēvamp'] *vt* (*house*) retaper; (*firm*) réorganiser.
Rev(d). *abbr* = **reverend**.
reveal [rivēl'] *vt* (*make known*) révéler; (*display*) laisser voir.
revealing [rivē'ling] *a* révélateur(trice); (*dress*) au décolleté généreux *or* suggestif.
reveille [rev'əlē] *n* (*MIL*) réveil *m*.
revel [rev'əl] *vi*: **to ~ in** sth/in doing se délecter de qch/à faire.
revelation [revəlā'shən] *n* révélation *f*.
reveler, (*Brit*) **reveller** [rev'əlûr] *n* fêtard *m*.
revelry [rev'əlrē] *n* festivités *fpl*.
revenge [rivenj'] *n* vengeance *f*; (*in game etc*) revanche *f* ♦ *vt* venger; **to take ~** se venger.
revengeful [rivenj'fəl] *a* vengeur(eresse); vindicatif(ive).
revenue [rev'ənŌŌ] *n* revenu *m*.
reverberate [rivûr'bərāt] *vi* (*sound*) retentir, se répercuter; (*light*) se réverbérer.
reverberation [rivûrbərā'shən] *n* répercussion *f*; réverbération *f*.
revere [rivēr'] *vt* vénérer, révérer.
reverence [rev'ûrəns] *n* vénération *f*, révérence *f*.
reverend [rev'ûrənd] *a* vénérable; **the R~ John Smith** (*Anglican*) le révérend John Smith; (*Catholic*) l'abbé John Smith; (*Protestant*) le pasteur John Smith.
reverent [rev'ûrənt] *a* respectueux(euse).
reverie [rev'ûrē] *n* rêverie *f*.
reversal [rivûr'səl] *n* (*of opinion*) revirement *m*.
reverse [rivûrs'] *n* contraire *m*, opposé *m*; (*back*) dos *m*, envers *m*; (*AUT*: *also*: ~ **gear**) marche *f* arrière ♦ *a* (*order*, *direction*) opposé(e), inverse ♦ *vt* (*turn*) renverser, retourner; (*change*) renverser, changer complètement; (*LAW*: *judgment*) réformer ♦ *vi* (*Brit AUT*) faire marche arrière; **to go into ~** faire marche arrière; **in ~ order** en ordre inverse.
reversed charge call *n* (*Brit TEL*) communication *f* en PCV.
reverse video *n* vidéo *m* inverse.
reversible [rivûr'səbəl] *a* (*garment*) réversible; (*procedure*) révocable.
reversing lights [rivûr'sing līts] *npl* (*Brit AUT*) feux *mpl* de marche arrière *or* de recul.
reversion [rivûr'zhən] *n* retour *m*.
revert [rivûrt'] *vi*: **to ~ to** revenir à, retourner à.
review [rivyŌŌ'] *n* revue *f*; (*of book*, *film*) critique *f* ♦ *vt* passer en revue; faire la critique de; (*US SCOL*) réviser; **to come under ~** être révisé(e).
reviewer [rivyŌŌ'ûr] *n* critique *m*.
revile [rivīl'] *vt* injurier.

revise [rivīz'] *vt* (*manuscript*) revoir, corriger; (*opinion*) réviser, modifier; (*study: subject*, *notes*) réviser; ~**d edition** édition revue et corrigée.
revision [rivizh'ən] *n* révision *f*; (*revised version*) version corrigée.
revitalize [rēvī'təlīz] *vt* revitaliser.
revival [rivī'vəl] *n* reprise *f*; rétablissement *m*; (*of faith*) renouveau *m*.
revive [rivīv'] *vt* (*person*) ranimer; (*custom*) rétablir; (*hope*, *courage*) redonner; (*play*, *fashion*) reprendre ♦ *vi* (*person*) reprendre connaissance; (*hope*) renaître; (*activity*) reprendre.
revoke [rivōk'] *vt* révoquer; (*promise*, *decision*) revenir sur.
revolt [rivōlt'] *n* révolte *f* ♦ *vi* se révolter, se rebeller.
revolting [rivōl'ting] *a* dégoûtant(e).
revolution [revəlŌŌ'shən] *n* révolution *f*; (*of wheel etc*) tour *m*, révolution.
revolutionary [revəlŌŌ'shənärē] *a*, *n* révolutionnaire (*m/f*).
revolutionize [revəlŌŌ'shənīz] *vt* révolutionner.
revolve [rivâlv'] *vi* tourner.
revolver [rivâl'vûr] *n* revolver *m*.
revolving [rivâl'ving] *a* (*chair*) pivotant(e); (*light*) tournant(e).
revolving credit [rivâl'ving kred'it] *n* crédit *m* à renouvellement automatique.
revolving door *n* (porte *f* à) tambour *m*.
revue [rivyŌŌ'] *n* (*THEATER*) revue *f*.
revulsion [rivul'shən] *n* dégoût *m*, répugnance *f*.
reward [riwôrd'] *n* récompense *f* ♦ *vt*: **to ~** (**for**) récompenser (de).
rewarding [riwôrd'ing] *a* (*fig*) qui (en) vaut la peine, gratifiant(e); **financially ~** financièrement intéressant(e).
rewind [rēwīnd'] *vt irg* (*watch*) remonter; (*ribbon etc*) réembobiner.
rewire [rēwīûr'] *vt* (*house*) refaire l'installation électrique de.
reword [rēwûrd'] *vt* formuler *or* exprimer différemment.
rewrite [rērīt'] *vt irg* récrire.
Reykjavik [rā'kyəvik] *n* Reykjavik.
RFD *abbr* (*US MAIL*) = *rural free delivery*.
Rh *abbr* (= *rhesus*) Rh.
rhapsody [rap'sədē] *n* (*MUS*) rhapsodie *f*; (*fig*) éloge délirant.
Rh factor *n* (*MED*) facteur *m* rhésus.
rhetoric [ret'ûrik] *n* rhétorique *f*.
rhetorical [ritôr'ikəl] *a* rhétorique.
rheumatic [rŌŌmat'ik] *a* rhumatismal(e).
rheumatism [rŌŌ'mətizəm] *n* rhumatisme *m*.
rheumatoid arthritis [rŌŌ'mətoid ârthrī'tis] *n* polyarthrite *f* chronique.
Rhine [rīn] *n*: **the ~** le Rhin.
rhinestone [rīn'stōn] *n* faux diamant.
rhinoceros [rīnâs'ûrəs] *n* rhinocéros *m*.
Rhodes [rōdz] *n* Rhodes *f*.
Rhodesia [rōdē'zhə] *n* Rhodésie *f*.
Rhodesian [rōdē'zhən] *a* rhodésien(ne) ♦ *n* Rhodésien/ne.
rhododendron [rōdəden'drən] *n* rhododendron *m*.
Rhone [rōn] *n*: **the ~** le Rhône.

rhubarb [rōō'bárb] *n* rhubarbe *f*.

rhyme [rīm] *n* rime *f*; (*verse*) vers *mpl* ♦ *vi*: **to ~ (with)** rimer (avec); **without ~ or reason** sans rime ni raison.

rhythm [ritʰ'əm] *n* rythme *m*.

rhythmic(al) [ritʰ'mik(əl)] *a* rythmique.

rhythmically [ritʰ'miklē] *ad* avec rythme.

RI *abbr* (*US MAIL*) = *Rhode Island*.

rib [rib] *n* (*ANAT*) côte *f* ♦ *vt* (*mock*) taquiner.

ribald [rib'əld] *a* paillard(e).

ribbed [ribd] *a* (*knitting*) à côtes; (*shell*) strié(e).

ribbon [rib'ən] *n* ruban *m*; **in ~s** (*torn*) en lambeaux.

rice [rīs] *n* riz *m*.

ricefield [rīs'fēld] *n* rizière *f*.

rich [rich] *a* riche; (*gift*, *clothes*) somptueux(euse); **the ~** *npl* les riches *mpl*; **~es** *npl* richesses *fpl*; **to be ~ in sth** être riche en qch.

richly [rich'lē] *ad* richement; (*deserved*, *earned*) largement, grandement.

richness [rich'nis] *n* richesse *f*.

rickets [rik'its] *n* rachitisme *m*.

rickety [rik'ətē] *a* branlant(e).

rickshaw [rik'shó] *n* pousse(-pousse) *m inv*.

ricochet [rikəshā'] *n* ricochet *m* ♦ *vi* ricocher.

rid, *pt*, *pp* **rid** [rid] *vt*: **to ~ sb of** débarrasser qn de; **to get ~ of** se débarrasser de.

riddance [rid'əns] *n*: **good ~!** bon débarras!

ridden [rid'ən] *pp of* **ride**.

riddle [rid'əl] *n* (*puzzle*) énigme *f* ♦ *vt*: **to be ~d with** être criblé(e) de.

ride [rīd] *n* promenade *f*, tour *m*; (*distance covered*) trajet *m* ♦ *vb* (*pt* **rode**, *pp* **ridden** [rōd, rid'ən]) *vi* (*as sport*) monter à (cheval), faire du cheval; (*go somewhere: on horse, bicycle*) aller (à cheval *or* bicyclette *etc*); **to give sb a ~** (*to work etc*) emmener *or* prendre qn en voiture; (*journey: on bicycle, motor cycle, bus*) rouler ♦ *vt* (*a certain horse*); (*distance*) parcourir, faire; **we rode all day/all the way** nous sommes restés toute la journée en selle/avons fait tout le chemin en selle *or* à cheval; **to ~ a horse/bicycle/camel** monter à cheval/à bicyclette/à dos de chameau; **can you ~ a bike?** est-ce que tu sais monter à bicyclette?; **to ~ at anchor** (*NAUT*) être à l'ancre; **horse/car ~** promenade *or* tour à cheval/en voiture; **to go for a ~** faire une promenade (en voiture *or* à bicyclette *etc*); **to give sb a ~** (*to work etc*) emmener *or* prendre qn en voiture; **to take sb for a ~** (*fig*) faire marcher qn; rouler qn.

  ride out *vt*: **to ~ out the storm** (*fig*) surmonter les difficultés.

rider [rī'dûr] *n* cavalier/ière; (*in race*) jockey *m*; (*on bicycle*) cycliste *m/f*; (*on motorcycle*) motocycliste *m/f*; (*in document*) annexe *f*, clause additionnelle.

ridge [rij] *n* (*of hill*) faîte *m*; (*of roof, mountain*) arête *f*; (*on object*) strie *f*.

ridicule [rid'əkyōōl] *n* ridicule *m*; dérision *f* ♦ *vt* ridiculiser, tourner en dérision; **to hold sb/sth up to ~** tourner qn/qch en ridicule.

ridiculous [ridik'yələs] *a* ridicule.

riding [rī'ding] *n* équitation *f*.

riding school *n* manège *m*, école *f* d'équita-tion.

rife [rīf] *a* répandu(e); **~ with** abondant(e) en.

riffraff [rif'raf] *n* racaille *f*.

rifle [rī'fəl] *n* fusil *m* (à canon rayé) ♦ *vt* vider, dévaliser.

  rifle through *vt fus* fouiller dans.

rifle range *n* champ *m* de tir; (*indoor*) stand *m* de tir.

rift [rift] *n* fente *f*, fissure *f*; (*fig: disagreement*) désaccord *m*.

rig [rig] *n* (*also*: **oil ~:** *on land*) derrick *m*; (: *at sea*) plate-forme pétrolière ♦ *vt* (*election etc*) truquer.

  rig up *vt* arranger, faire avec des moyens de fortune.

rigging [rig'ing] *n* (*NAUT*) gréement *m*.

right [rīt] *a* (*true*) juste, exact(e); (*correctly chosen: answer, road etc*) bon(bonne); (*suitable*) approprié(e), convenable; (*just*) juste, équitable; (*morally good*) bien *inv*; (*not left*) droit(e) ♦ *n* (*title, claim*) droit *m*; (*not left*) droite *f* ♦ *ad* (*answer*) correctement; (*not on the left*) à droite ♦ *vt* redresser ♦ *excl* bon!; **the ~ time** (*precise*) l'heure exacte; (*not wrong*) la bonne heure; **to be ~** (*person*) avoir raison; (*answer*) être juste *or* correct(e); **to get sth ~** ne pas se tromper sur qch; **let's get it ~ this time!** essayons de ne pas nous tromper cette fois-ci!; **you did the ~ thing** vous avez bien fait; **~ now** en ce moment même; tout de suite; **~ before/after** juste avant/après; **~ off** sans hesiter; (*at once*) tout de suite; **~ against the wall** tout contre le mur; **~ ahead** tout droit; droit devant; **~ in the middle** en plein milieu; **~ away** immédiatement; **to go ~ to the end of sth** aller jusqu'au bout de qch; **by ~s** en toute justice; **on the ~** à droite; **~ and wrong** le bien et le mal; **to be in the ~** avoir raison; **film ~s** droits d'adaptation cinématographique; **~ of way** droit *m* de passage; (*AUT*) priorité *f*.

right angle *n* angle droit.

righteous [rī'chəs] *a* droit(e), vertueux(euse); (*anger*) justifié(e).

righteousness [rī'chəsnis] *n* droiture *f*, vertu *f*.

rightful [rīt'fəl] *a* (*heir*) légitime.

rightfully [rīt'fəlē] *ad* à juste titre, légitimement.

right-handed [rīt'handid] *a* (*person*) droitier(ière).

right-hand man [rīt'hand' man] *n* bras droit (*fig*).

right-hand side [rīt'hand' sīd] *n* côté droit.

rightly [rīt'lē] *ad* bien, correctement; (*with reason*) à juste titre; **if I remember ~** (*Brit*) si je me souviens bien.

right-minded [rīt'mīndid] *a* sensé(e), sain(e) d'esprit.

rights issue *n* (*STOCK EXCHANGE*) émission préférentielle *or* de droit de souscription.

right wing *n* (*MIL*, *SPORT*) aile droite; (*POL*) droite *f* ♦ *a*: **right-wing** (*POL*) de droite.

right-winger [rīt'wing'ûr] *n* (*POL*) membre *m* de la droite; (*SPORT*) ailier droit.

rigid [rij'id] *a* rigide; (*principle*) strict(e).

rigidity [rijid'itē] *n* rigidité *f*.

rigidly [rij'idlē] *ad* rigidement; (*behave*)

inflexiblement.

rigmarole |rig'mərōl| *n* galimatias *m*, comédie *f*.

rigor |rig'ûr| *n* (*US*) rigueur *f*.

rigor mortis |rig'ûr môr'tis| *n* rigidité *f* cadavérique.

rigorous |rig'ûrəs| *a* rigoureux(euse).

rigorously |rig'ûrəslē| *ad* rigoureusement.

rigour |rig'ûr| *n* (*Brit*) = **rigor**.

rig-out |rig'out| *n* (*Brit col*) tenue *f*.

rile |rīl| *vt* agacer.

rim |rim| *n* bord *m*; (*of spectacles*) monture *f*; (*of wheel*) jante *f*.

rimless |rim'lis| *a* (*spectacles*) à monture invisible.

rind |rīnd| *n* (*of bacon*) couenne *f*; (*of lemon etc*) écorce *f*.

ring |ring| *n* anneau *m*; (*on finger*) bague *f*; (*also:* **wedding** ~) alliance *f*; (*for napkin*) rond *m*; (*of people, objects*) cercle *m*; (*of spies*) réseau *m*; (*of smoke etc*) rond; (*arena*) piste *f*, arène *f*; (*for boxing*) ring *m*; (*sound of bell, US TEL: tone*) sonnerie *f*; (*telephone call*) coup *m* de téléphone ♦ *vb* (*pt* **rang**, *pp* **rung** |rang, rung|) *vi* (*person, bell*) sonner; (*also:* ~ **out**: *voice, words*) retentir; (*TEL*) téléphoner ♦ *vt* (*Brit TEL: also:* ~ **up**) téléphoner à; **to** ~ **the bell** sonner; **to give sb a** ~ (*TEL*) passer un coup de téléphone *or* de fil à qn; **that has the** ~ **of truth about it** cela sonne vrai; **the name doesn't** ~ **a bell (with me)** ce nom ne me dit rien.

ring back *vt, vi* (*Brit TEL*) rappeler.

ring off *vi* (*Brit TEL*) raccrocher.

ring binder *n* classeur *m* à anneaux.

ring finger *n* annulaire *m*.

ringing |ring'ing| *n* (*of bell*) tintement *m*; (*louder, also of telephone*) sonnerie *f*; (*in ears*) bourdonnement *m*.

ringing tone *n* (*TEL*) sonnerie *f*.

ringleader |ring'lēdûr| *n* (*of gang*) chef *m*, meneur *m*.

ringlets |ring'lits| *npl* anglaises *fpl*.

ring road *n* (*Brit*) route *f* de ceinture.

rink |ringk| *n* (*also:* **ice** ~) patinoire *f*; (*for roller-skating*) skating *m*.

rinse |rins| *n* rinçage *m* ♦ *vt* rincer.

Rio (de Janeiro) |rē'ō (dē zhənər'ō)| *n* Rio de Janeiro.

riot |rī'ət| *n* émeute *f*, bagarres *fpl* ♦ *vi* manifester avec violence; **a** ~ **of colors** une débauche *or* orgie de couleurs; **to run** ~ se déchaîner.

rioter |rī'ətûr| *n* émeutier/ière, manifestant/e.

riotous |rī'ətəs| *a* tapageur(euse); tordant(e).

riotously |rī'ətəslē| *ad*: ~ **funny** tordant(e).

riot police *n* forces *fpl* de police intervenant en cas d'émeute; **hundreds of** ~ des centaines de policiers casqués et armés.

RIP *abbr* (= *rest in peace*) RIP.

rip |rip| *n* déchirure *f* ♦ *vt* déchirer ♦ *vi* se déchirer.

rip up *vt* déchirer.

ripcord |rip'kôrd| *n* poignée *f* d'ouverture.

ripe |rīp| *a* (*fruit*) mûr(e); (*cheese*) fait(e).

ripen |rī'pən| *vt* mûrir ♦ *vi* mûrir; se faire.

ripeness |rīp'nis| *n* maturité *f*.

rip-off |rip'ôf| *n* (*col*): **it's a** ~! c'est du vol manifeste!

riposte |ripōst'| *n* riposte *f*.

ripple |rip'əl| *n* ride *f*, ondulation *f*; égrènement *m*, cascade *f* ♦ *vi* se rider, onduler ♦ *vt* rider, faire onduler.

rise |rīz| *n* (*slope*) côte *f*, pente *f*; (*hill*) élévation *f*; (*increase: in prices, temperature*) hausse *f*, augmentation; (: *in wages :* Brit) augmentation *f*; (*fig*) ascension *f* ♦ *vi* (*pt* **rose**, *pp* **risen** |rōs, riz'ən|) s'élever, monter; (*prices*) augmenter, monter; (*waters, river*) monter; (*sun, wind, person: from chair, bed*) se lever; (*also:* ~ **up**: *rebel*) se révolter; se rebeller; ~ **to power** montée *f* au pouvoir; **to give** ~ **to** donner lieu à; **to** ~ **to the occasion** se montrer à la hauteur.

rising |rī'zing| *a* (*increasing: number, prices*) en hausse; (*tide*) montant(e); (*sun, moon*) levant(e) ♦ *n* (*uprising*) soulèvement *m*, insurrection *f*.

rising damp *n* (*Brit*) humidité *f* (montant des fondations).

risk |risk| *n* risque *m*, danger *m*; (*deliberate*) risque ♦ *vt* risquer; **to take** *or* **run the** ~ **of doing** courir le risque de faire; **at** ~ en danger; **at one's own** ~ à ses risques et périls; **it's a fire/health** ~ cela présente un risque d'incendie/pour la santé; **I'll** ~ **it** je vais risquer le coup.

risk capital *n* capital-risques *m*.

risky |ris'kē| *a* risqué(e).

risqué |riskā'| *a* (*joke*) risqué(e).

rissole |ris'ōl| *n* croquette *f*.

rite |rīt| *n* rite *m*; **the last** ~s les derniers sacrements.

ritual |rich'ōōəl| *a* rituel(le) ♦ *n* rituel *m*.

rival |rī'vəl| *n* rival/e; (*in business*) concurrent/e ♦ *a* rival(e); qui fait concurrence ♦ *vt* être en concurrence avec; **to** ~ **sb/sth in** rivaliser avec qn/qch de.

rivalry |rī'vəlrē| *n* rivalité *f*; concurrence *f*.

river |riv'ûr| *n* rivière *f*; (*major, also fig*) fleuve *m* ♦ *cpd* (*port, traffic*) fluvial(e); **up/down** ~ en amont/aval.

riverbank |riv'ûrbangk| *n* rive *f*, berge *f*.

riverbed |riv'ûrbed| *n* lit *m* (de rivière *or* de fleuve).

riverside |riv'ûrsīd| *n* bord *m* de la rivière *or* du fleuve.

rivet |riv'it| *n* rivet *m* ♦ *vt* riveter; (*fig*) river, fixer.

riveting |riv'iting| *a* (*fig*) fascinant(e).

Riviera |rivēâr'ə| *n*: **the (French)** ~ la Côte d'Azur; **the Italian** ~ la Riviera (italienne).

Riyadh |rēyâd'| *n* Riyad.

RN *n abbr* (*US*) = **registered nurse**; (*Brit*) = **Royal Navy**.

RNA *n abbr* (= *ribonucleic acid*) ARN *m*.

road |rōd| *n* route *f*; (*in town*) rue *f*; (*fig*) chemin, voie *f*; **main** ~ grande route; **major** ~ route principale *or* à priorité; **minor** ~ voie secondaire; **it takes four hours by** ~ il y a quatre heures de route.

roadblock |rōd'blâk| *n* barrage routier.

road haulage *n* transports routiers.

road hog *n* chauffard *m*.

road map *n* carte routière.

road safety *n* sécurité routière.

roadside |rōd'sīd| *n* bord *m* de la route, bascôté *m* ♦ *cpd* (*situé etc*) au bord de la rou-

te; **by the** ~ au bord de la route.
road sign n panneau m de signalisation.
roadsweeper [rōd'swēpûr] n (Brit: person) balayeur/euse.
road transport n transports routiers.
road user n usager m de la route.
roadway [rōd'wā] n chaussée f.
roadworthy [rōd'wûrᵗħē] a en bon état de marche.
roam [rōm] vi errer, vagabonder ♦ vt parcourir, errer par.
roar [rôr] n rugissement m; (of crowd) hurlements mpl; (of vehicle, thunder, storm) grondement m ♦ vi rugir; hurler; gronder; **to** ~ **with laughter** éclater de rire.
roaring [rôr'ing] a: **a** ~ **fire** une belle flambée; **a** ~ **success** un succès fou; **to do a** ~ **trade** faire des affaires d'or.
roast [rōst] n rôti m ♦ vt (meat) (faire) rôtir.
roast beef n rôti m de bœuf, rosbif m.
rob [râb] vt (person) voler; (bank) dévaliser; **to** ~ **sb of sth** voler or dérober qch à qn; (fig: deprive) priver qn de qch.
robber [râb'ûr] n bandit m, voleur m.
robbery [râb'ûrē] n vol m.
robe [rōb] n (for ceremony etc) robe f; (also: **bath**~) peignoir m ♦ vt revêtir (d'une robe).
robin [râb'in] n rouge-gorge m.
robot [rō'bət] n robot m.
robotics [rōbât'iks] n robotique m.
robust [rōbust'] a robuste; (material, appetite) solide.
rock [râk] n (substance) roche f, roc m; (boulder) rocher m; roche; (Brit: candy) ~ sucre m d'orge ♦ vt (swing gently: cradle) balancer; (: child) bercer; (shake) ébranler, secouer ♦ vi (se) balancer; être ébranlé(e) or secoué(e); **on the** ~**s** (drink) avec des glaçons; (ship) sur les écueils; (marriage etc) en train de craquer; **to** ~ **the boat** (fig) jouer les trouble-fête.
rock and roll n rock (and roll) m, rock'n'roll m.
rock-bottom [râk'bāt'əm] n (fig) niveau le plus bas ♦ a (fig: prices) sacrifié(e); **to reach** or **touch** ~ (price, person) tomber au plus bas.
rock climber n varappeur/euse.
rock climbing n varappe f.
rocket [râk'it] n fusée f; (MIL) fusée, roquette f ♦ vi (prices) monter en flèche.
rocket launcher [râk'it lônch'ûr] n lance-roquettes m inv.
rock face n paroi rocheuse.
rock fall n chute f de pierres.
rock garden n (jardin m de) rocaille f.
rocking chair [râk'ing chär] n fauteuil m à bascule.
rocking horse [râk'ing hôrs] n cheval m à bascule.
rocky [râk'ē] a (hill) rocheux(euse); (path) rocailleux(euse); (unsteady: table) branlant(e).
Rocky Mountains npl: **the** ~ les (montagnes fpl) Rocheuses fpl.
rod [râd] n (metallic) tringle f; (TECH) tige f; (wooden) baguette f; (also: **fishing** ~) canne f à pêche.
rode [rōd] pt of **ride**.
rodent [rō'dənt] n rongeur m.

rodeo [rō'dēō] n rodéo m.
roe [rō] n (species: also: ~ **deer**) chevreuil m; (of fish: also: **hard** ~) œufs mpl de poisson; **soft** ~ laitance f.
roe deer n chevreuil m; chevreuil femelle.
rogue [rōg] n coquin/e.
roguish [rō'gish] a coquin(e).
ROI n abbr (US) = **return on investment**.
role [rōl] n rôle m.
roll [rōl] n rouleau m; (of banknotes) liasse f; (also: **bread** ~) petit pain; (register) liste f; (sound: of drums etc) roulement m; (movement: of ship) roulis m ♦ vt rouler; (also: ~ **up**: string) enrouler; (also: ~ **out**: pastry) étendre au rouleau ♦ vi rouler; (wheel) tourner; **cheese** ~ ≈ sandwich m au fromage (dans un petit pain).
roll about, roll around vi rouler çà et là; (person) se rouler par terre.
roll by vi (time) s'écouler, passer.
roll in vi (mail, cash) affluer.
roll over vi se retourner.
roll up vi (col: arrive) arriver, s'amener ♦ vt (carpet, cloth, map) rouler; (sleeves) retrousser; **to** ~ **o.s. up into a ball** se rouler en boule.
roll call n appel m.
roller [rō'lûr] n rouleau m; (wheel) roulette f.
roller coaster n montagnes fpl russes.
roller skates npl patins mpl à roulettes.
rollicking [râl'iking] a bruyant(e) et joyeux(euse); (play) bouffon(ne); **to have a** ~ **time** s'amuser follement.
rolling [rō'ling] a (landscape) onduleux(euse).
rolling mill n laminoir m.
rolling pin n rouleau m à pâtisserie.
rolling stock n (RAIL) matériel roulant.
ROM [râm] n abbr (COMPUT: = read-only memory) mémoire morte, ROM f.
romaine (lettuce) [rōmān' (let'is)] n (US) (laitue f) romaine f.
Roman [rō'mən] a romain(e) ♦ n Romain/e.
Roman Catholic a, n catholique (m/f).
romance [rōmans'] n histoire f (or film m or aventure f) romanesque; (charm) poésie f; (love affair) idylle f.
Romanesque [rōmənesk'] a roman(e).
Romania [rōmā'nēə] n Roumanie f.
Romanian [rəmā'nēən] a roumain(e) ♦ n Roumain/e; (LING) roumain m.
Roman numeral n chiffre romain.
romantic [rōman'tik] a romantique; (play, attachment) sentimental(e).
romanticism [rōman'tisizəm] n romantisme m.
Romany [rōm'ənē] a de bohémien ♦ n bohémien/ne; (LING) romani m.
Rome [rōm] n Rome.
romp [râmp] n jeux bruyants ♦ vi (also: ~ **about**) s'ébattre, jouer bruyamment; **to** ~ **home** (horse) arriver bon premier.
rompers [râm'pûrz] npl barboteuse f.
rondo [rân'dō] n (MUS) rondeau m.
roof [rōof] n toit m; (of tunnel, cave) plafond m ♦ vt couvrir (d'un toit); **the** ~ **of the mouth** la voûte du palais.
roof garden n toit-terrasse m.
roofing [rōō'fing] n toiture f.
roof rack n (AUT) galerie f.
rook [rōok] n (bird) freux m; (CHESS) tour f ♦

vt (col: cheat) rouler, escroquer.

room [rōōm] *n (in house)* pièce *f*; *(also:* **bed~)** chambre *f* (à coucher); *(in school etc)* salle *f*; *(space)* place *f*; **~s** *npl (lodging)* meublé *m*; "**~s for rent**", *(Brit)* "**~s to let**" "chambres à louer"; **is there ~ for this?** est-ce qu'il y a de la place pour ceci?; **to make ~ for sb** faire de la place à qn; **there is ~ for improvement** on peut faire mieux.

rooming house [rōō'ming hous] *n (US)* maison *f* de rapport.

roommate [rōōm'māt] *n* camarade *m/f* de chambre.

room service *n* service *m* des chambres *(dans un hôtel).*

room temperature *n* température ambiante; "**serve at ~**" *(wine)* "servir chambré".

roomy [rōō'mē] *a* spacieux(euse); *(garment)* ample.

roost [rōōst] *n* juchoir *m* ♦ *vi* se jucher.

rooster [rōōs'tûr] *n* coq *m*.

root [rōōt] *n (BOT, MATH)* racine *f*; *(fig: of problem)* origine *f*, fond *m* ♦ *vi (plant)* s'enraciner; **to take ~** *(plant, idea)* prendre racine.

   root around, *(Brit)* **root about** *vi (fig)* fouiller.

   root for *vt fus (col)* applaudir.

   root out *vt* extirper.

rope [rōp] *n* corde *f*; *(NAUT)* cordage *m* ♦ *vt (box)* corder; *(climbers)* encorder; **to jump** *or* **skip ~** *(US)* sauter à la corde; **to ~ sb in** *(fig)* embringuer qn; **to know the ~s** *(fig)* être au courant, connaître les ficelles; **at the end of one's ~** à bout (de patience).

rope ladder *n* échelle *f* de corde.

rosary [rō'zûrē] *n* chapelet *m*.

rose [rōz] *pt of* **rise** ♦ *n* rose *f*; *(also:* **~bush)** rosier *m*; *(on watering can)* pomme *f* ♦ *a* rose.

rosé [rōzā'] *n* rosé *m*.

rosebed [rōz'bed] *n* massif *m* de rosiers.

rosebud [rōz'bud] *n* bouton *m* de rose.

rosebush [rōz'bōōsh] *n* rosier *m*.

rosemary [rōz'märē] *n* romarin *m*.

rosette [rōzet'] *n* rosette *f*; *(larger)* cocarde *f*.

roster [rás'tûr] *n*: **duty ~** tableau *m* de service.

rostrum [rás'trəm] *n* tribune *f* *(pour un orateur etc)*.

rosy [rō'zē] *a* rose; **a ~ future** un bel avenir.

rot [rât] *n (decay)* pourriture *f*; *(fig: pej)* idioties *fpl*, balivernes *fpl* ♦ *vt, vi* pourrir; **to stop the ~** *(Brit fig)* rétablir la situation; **dry ~** pourriture sèche *(du bois)*; **wet ~** pourriture (du bois).

rota [rō'tə] *n* liste *f*, tableau *m* de service; **on a ~ basis** par roulement.

rotary [rō'tûrē] *a* rotatif(ive).

rotate [rō'tāt] *vt (revolve)* faire tourner; *(change round: crops)* alterner; *(: jobs)* faire à tour de rôle ♦ *vi (revolve)* tourner.

rotating [rō'tāting] *a (movement)* tournant(e).

rotation [rōtā'shən] *n* rotation *f*; **in ~** à tour de rôle.

rote [rōt] *n*: **by ~** machinalement, par cœur.

rotor [rō'tûr] *n* rotor *m*.

rotten [rât'ən] *a (decayed)* pourri(e); *(dishonest)* corrompu(e); *(col: bad)* mauvais(e),

moche; **to feel ~** *(ill)* être mal fichu(e).

rotting [rât'ing] *a* pourrissant(e).

rotund [rōtund'] *a* rondelet(te); arrondi(e).

rouge [rōōzh] *n* rouge *m* (à joues).

rough [ruf] *a (cloth, skin)* rêche, rugueux(euse); *(terrain)* accidenté(e); *(path)* rocailleux(euse); *(voice)* rauque, rude; *(person, manner: coarse)* rude, fruste; *(: violent)* brutal(e); *(district, weather)* mauvais(e); *(plan)* ébauché(e); *(guess)* approximatif(ive) ♦ *n (GOLF)* rough *m*; **the sea is ~ today** la mer est agitée aujourd'hui; **to have a ~ time (of it)** en voir de dures; **~ estimate** approximation *f*; **to ~ it** vivre à la dure; **to play ~** jouer avec brutalité.

rough out *vt (draft)* ébaucher.

roughage [ruf'ij] *n* fibres *fpl* diététiques.

rough-and-ready [ruf'ənred'ē] *a (accommodation, method)* rudimentaire.

rough-and-tumble [ruf'əntum'bəl] *n* agitation *f*.

roughcast [ruf'kast] *n* crépi *m*.

rough copy, rough draft *n* brouillon *m*.

roughen [ruf'ən] *vt (a surface)* rendre rude *or* rugueux(euse).

roughly [ruf'lē] *ad (handle)* rudement, brutalement; *(make)* grossièrement; *(approximately)* à peu près, en gros; **~ speaking** en gros.

roughness [ruf'nis] *n (of cloth, skin)* rugosité *f*; *(of person)* rudesse *f*; brutalité *f*.

roughshod [ruf'shâd'] *ad*: **to ride ~ over** ne tenir aucun compte de.

rough work *n (Brit: at school etc)* brouillon *m*.

roulette [rōōlet'] *n* roulette *f*.

Roumania [rōōmā'nēə] *etc* = **Romania** *etc*.

round [round] *a* rond(e) ♦ *n* rond *m*, cercle *m*; *(Brit: of toast)* tranche *f*; *(duty: of policeman, milkman etc)* tournée *f*; *(: of doctor)* visites *fpl*; *(game: of cards, in competition)* partie *f*; *(BOXING)* round *m*; *(of talks)* série *f* ♦ *vt (corner)* tourner; *(bend)* prendre; *(cape)* doubler ♦ *prep* autour de ♦ *ad*: **right ~** tout autour; **all the year ~** toute l'année; **in ~ figures** en chiffres ronds; **she arrived ~ (about) noon** *(Brit)* elle est arrivée vers midi; **to go the ~s** *(disease, story)* circuler; **the daily ~** *(fig)* la routine quotidienne; **~ of ammunition** cartouche *f*; **~ of applause** ban *m*, applaudissements *mpl*; **~ of drinks** tournée *f*; **~ of sandwiches** *(Brit)* sandwich *m*; *see also* **around**.

round off *vt (speech etc)* terminer.

round up *vt* rassembler; *(criminals)* effectuer une rafle de; *(prices)* arrondir (au chiffre supérieur).

roundabout [round'əbout] *n (Brit AUT)* rond-point *m* (à sens giratoire); *(at fair)* manège *m* (de chevaux de bois) ♦ *a (route, means)* détourné(e).

rounded [roun'did] *a* arrondi(e); *(style)* harmonieux(euse).

rounders [roun'dûrz] *npl (game)* ≈ balle *f* au camp.

roundly [round'lē] *ad (fig)* tout net, carrément.

round-shouldered [round'shōldûrd] *a* au dos rond.

round trip *n* (voyage *m*) aller et retour *m*.

round trip ticket n (US) (billet m d')aller et retour m.

roundup [round'up] n rassemblement m; (of criminals) rafle f; **a ~ of the latest news** un rappel des derniers événements.

rouse [rouz] vt (wake up) réveiller; (stir up) susciter; provoquer; éveiller.

rousing [rou'zing] a (welcome) enthousiaste.

rout [rout] n (MIL) déroute f ♦ vt mettre en déroute.

route [rōōt] n itinéraire m; (of bus) parcours m; (of trade, shipping) route f; **"all ~s"** (AUT) "toutes directions"; **the best ~ to Chicago** le meilleur itinéraire pour aller à Chicago; **en ~ for** en route pour.

routine [rōōtēn'] a (work) ordinaire, courant(e); (procedure) d'usage ♦ n routine f; (THEATER) numéro m; **daily ~** occupations journalières.

roving [ro'ving] a (life) vagabond(e).

roving reporter n reporter volant.

row [rō] n (line) rangée f; (of people, seats, KNITTING) rang m; (behind one another: of cars, people) file f; [rou] (noise) vacarme m; (dispute) dispute f, querelle f; (scolding) réprimande f, savon m ♦ vi (in boat) ramer; (as sport) faire de l'aviron; [rou] se disputer, se quereller ♦ vt (boat) faire aller à la rame or à l'aviron; **in a ~** (fig) d'affilée; **to have a ~** se disputer, se quereller.

rowboat [rō'bōt] n (US) canot m (à rames).

rowdiness [rou'dēnis] n tapage m, chahut m; (fighting) bagarre f.

rowdy [rou'dē] a chahuteur(euse); bagarreur(euse) ♦ n voyou m.

rowdyism [rou'dēizəm] n tendances fpl à la violence; actes mpl de violence.

rowing [rō'ing] n canotage m; (as sport) aviron m.

rowing boat n (Brit) = **rowboat**.

rowlock [rō'lâk] n (Brit) dame f de nage, tolet m.

royal [roi'əl] a royal(e).

Royal Air Force (RAF) n (Brit) armée de l'air britannique.

royal blue a bleu roi inv.

royalist [roi'əlist] a, n royaliste (m/f).

Royal Navy (RN) n (Brit) marine de guerre britannique.

royalty [roi'əltē] n (royal persons) (membres mpl de la) famille royale; (payment: to author) droits mpl d'auteur; (: to inventor) royalties fpl.

RP n abbr (Brit: = received pronunciation) prononciation f standard.

rpm abbr (= revolutions per minute) t/mn (= tours/minute).

RR abbr (US) = **railroad**.

R&R n abbr (US MIL) = rest and recreation.

RSVP abbr (= répondez s'il vous plaît) RSVP.

Rt Hon. abbr (Brit: = Right Honourable) titre donné aux députés de la Chambre des communes.

Rt Rev. abbr (= Right Reverend) très révérend.

rub [rub] n (with cloth) coup m de chiffon or de torchon; (on person) friction f ♦ vt frotter; frictionner; **to ~ sb** or (Brit) **~ sb up the wrong way** prendre qn à rebrousse-poil.

rub down vt (body) frictionner; (horse) bouchonner.

rub in vt (ointment) faire pénétrer.

rub off vi partir; **to ~ off on** déteindre sur.

rub out vt effacer ♦ vi s'effacer.

rubber [rub'ûr] n caoutchouc m; (US col) préservatif m; (Brit: eraser) gomme f (à effacer).

rubber band n élastique m.

rubber plant n caoutchouc m (plante verte).

rubber stamp n tampon m.

rubber-stamp [rubûrstamp'] vt (fig) approuver sans discussion.

rubbery [rub'ûrē] a caoutchouteux(euse).

rubbing alcohol [rub'ing al'kəhól] n (US) alcool m à 90°.

rubbish [rub'ish] n (fig: pej) choses fpl sans valeur; camelote f; (nonsense) bêtises fpl, idioties fpl; (Brit: from household) ordures fpl ♦ vt (Brit col) dénigrer, rabaisser; **what you've just said is ~** tu viens de dire une bêtise.

rubbish bin n (Brit) boîte f à ordures, poubelle f.

rubbish dump n (Brit: in town) décharge publique, dépotoir m.

rubbishy [rub'ishē] a (Brit col) qui ne vaut rien, moche.

rubble [rub'əl] n décombres mpl; (smaller) gravats mpl.

ruble [rōō'bəl] n rouble m.

ruby [rōō'bē] n rubis m.

RUC n abbr (Brit) = Royal Ulster Constabulary.

rucksack [ruk'sak] n sac m à dos.

rudder [rud'ûr] n gouvernail m.

ruddy [rud'ē] a (face) coloré(e).

rude [rōōd] a (impolite: person) impoli(e); (: word, manners) grossier(ière); (shocking) indécent(e), inconvenant(e); **to be ~ to sb** être grossier envers qn.

rudely [rōōd'lē] ad impoliment; grossièrement.

rudeness [rōōd'nis] n impolitesse f; grossièreté f.

rudiment [rōō'dəmənt] n rudiment m.

rudimentary [rōōdəmen'tûrē] a rudimentaire.

rueful [rōō'fəl] a triste.

ruff [ruf] n fraise f, collerette f.

ruffian [ruf'ēən] n brute f, voyou m.

ruffle [ruf'əl] vt (hair) ébouriffer; (clothes) chiffonner; (water) agiter; (fig: person) émouvoir, faire perdre son flegme à.

rug [rug] n petit tapis.

rugby [rug'bē] n (also: ~ football) rugby m.

rugged [rug'id] a (landscape) accidenté(e); (features, kindness, character) rude; (determination) farouche.

ruin [rōō'in] n ruine f ♦ vt ruiner; (spoil: clothes) abîmer; **~s** npl ruine(s); **in ~s** en ruine.

ruination [rōōinā'shən] n ruine f.

ruinous [rōō'inəs] a ruineux(euse).

rule [rōōl] n règle f; (regulation) règlement m; (government) autorité f, gouvernement m; (dominion etc): **under British ~** sous l'autorité britannique ♦ vt (country) gouverner; (person) dominer; (decide) décider ♦ vi commander; décider; (LAW): **to ~ against/ in favor of/on** statuer contre/en faveur de/

sur; **to ~ that** (*umpire, judge etc*) décider que; **it's against the ~s** c'est contraire au règlement; **the ~s of the road** le code de la route; **by ~ of thumb** à vue de nez; **as a ~** normalement, en règle générale.

rule out *vt* exclure; **murder cannot be ~d out** l'hypothèse d'un meurtre ne peut être exclue.

ruled [rōōld] *a* (*paper*) réglé(e).

ruler [rōō'lûr] *n* (*sovereign*) souverain/e; (*leader*) chef *m* (d'État); (*for measuring*) règle *f*.

ruling [rōō'ling] *a* (*party*) au pouvoir; (*class*) dirigeant(e) ♦ *n* (*LAW*) décision *f*.

rum [rum] *n* rhum *m*.

Rumania [rōōmā'nēə] *etc* = **Romania** *etc*.

rumble [rum'bəl] *n* grondement *m*; gargouillement *m* ♦ *vi* gronder; (*stomach, pipe*) gargouiller.

rumbustious [rumbus'chəs] *a* (*person*) exubérant(e).

rummage [rum'ij] *vi* fouiller.

rummage sale *n* vente *f* de charité.

rumor, (*Brit*) **rumour** [rōō'mûr] *n* rumeur *f*, bruit *m* (qui court) ♦ *vt:* **it is ~ed that** le bruit court que.

rump [rump] *n* (*of animal*) croupe *f*; (*also:* **~ steak**) romsteck *m*.

rumple [rum'pəl] *vt* (*hair*) ébouriffer; (*clothes*) chiffonner, friper.

rumpus [rum'pəs] *n* (*col*) tapage *m*, chahut *m*; (*quarrel*) prise *f* de bec; **to kick up a ~** faire toute une histoire.

run [run] *n* (*race*) course *f*; (*trip*) tour *m* or promenade *f* (en voiture); (*journey*) parcours *m*, trajet *m*; (*series*) suite *f*, série *f*; (*THEATER*) série de représentations; (*SKI*) piste *f*; (*in tights, stockings*) maille filée, échelle *f* ♦ *vb* (*pt* **ran**, *pp* **run** [ran, run]) *vt* (*business*) diriger; (*competition, course*) organiser; (*hotel, house*) tenir; (*COMPUT: program*) exécuter; (*force through: rope, pipe*): **to ~ sth through** faire passer qch à travers; (*to pass: hand, finger*): **to ~ sth over** promener or passer qch sur; (*water, bath*) faire couler ♦ *vi* courir; (*pass: road etc*) passer; (*work: machine, factory*) marcher; (*bus, train*) circuler; (*continue: play*) se jouer, être à l'affiche; (*: contract*) être valide or en vigueur; (*slide: drawer etc*) glisser; (*flow: river, bath*) couler; (*colors, washing*) déteindre; (*in election*) être candidat, se présenter; **to go for a ~** aller courir or faire un peu de course à pied; (*in car*) faire un tour or une promenade (en voiture); **to break into a ~** se mettre à courir; **a ~ of luck** une série de coups de chance; **to have the ~ of sb's house** avoir la maison de qn à sa disposition; **there was a ~ on** (*meat, tickets*) les gens se sont rués sur; **in the long ~** à longue échéance; à la longue; en fin de compte; **in the short ~** à brève échéance, à court terme; **on the ~** en fuite; **to make a ~ for it** s'enfuir; **I'll ~ you to the station** je vais vous emmener or conduire à la gare; **to ~ a stoplight** (*US*) griller un feu rouge; **to ~ errands** faire des commissions; **the train ~s between New York and Boston** le train assure le service entre New York et Boston; **the bus ~s every 20 minutes** il y a un auto-

bus toutes les 20 minutes; **it's very cheap to ~** (*car, machine*) c'est très économique; **to ~ on gas** or (*Brit*) **petrol/on diesel/off batteries** marcher à l'essence/au diesel/sur piles; **to ~ for president** être candidat à la présidence; **their losses ran into millions** leurs pertes se sont élevées à plusieurs millions.

run about *vi* (*Brit*) = **run around**.

run across *vt fus* (*find*) trouver par hasard.

run around *vi* (*children*) courir çà et là.

run away *vi* s'enfuir.

run down *vi* (*clock*) s'arrêter (faute d'avoir été remonté) ♦ *vt* (*AUT*) renverser; (*Brit: reduce: production*) réduire progressivement; (*: factory/shop*) réduire progressivement la production/l'activité de; (*criticize*) critiquer, dénigrer; **to be ~ down** être fatigué(e) or à plat.

run in *vt* (*Brit: car*) roder.

run into *vt fus* (*meet: person*) rencontrer par hasard; (*: trouble*) se heurter à; (*collide with*) heurter; **to ~ into debt** contracter des dettes.

run off *vi* s'enfuir ♦ *vt* (*water*) laisser s'écouler.

run out *vi* (*person*) sortir en courant; (*liquid*) couler; (*lease*) expirer; (*money*) être épuisé(e).

run out of *vt fus* se trouver à court de; **I've ~ out of gas** or (*Brit*) **petrol** je suis en panne d'essence.

run over *vt* (*AUT*) écraser ♦ *vt fus* (*revise*) revoir, reprendre.

run through *vt fus* (*instructions*) reprendre, revoir.

run up *vt* (*debt*) laisser accumuler; **to ~ up against** (*difficulties*) se heurter à.

runaway [run'əwā] *a* (*horse*) emballé(e); (*truck*) fou(folle); (*inflation*) galopant(e).

rundown [run'doun] *n* (*Brit: of industry etc*) réduction progressive.

rung [rung] *pp of* **ring** ♦ *n* (*of ladder*) barreau *m*.

run-in [run'in] *n* (*col*) accrochage *m*, prise *f* de bec.

runner [run'ûr] *n* (*in race: person*) coureur/euse; (*: horse*) partant *m*; (*on sleigh*) patin *m*; (*for drawer etc*) coulisseau *m*; (*carpet: in hall etc*) chemin *m*.

runner bean *n* (*Brit*) haricot *m* (à rames).

runner-up [runûrup'] *n* second/e.

running [run'ing] *n* (*in race etc*) course *f*; (*of business*) direction *f*; (*of event*) organisation *f*; (*of machine etc*) marche *f*, fonctionnement *m* ♦ *a* (*water*) courant(e); (*commentary*) suivi(e); **6 days ~** 6 jours de suite; **to be in/out of the ~ for sth** être/ne pas être sur les rangs pour qch.

running costs *npl* (*of business*) frais *mpl* de gestion; (*of car*): **the ~ are high** elle revient cher.

running head *n* (*TYP etc*) titre courant.

running mate *n* (*US POL*) candidat à la vice-présidence.

runny [run'ē] *a* qui coule.

run-off [run'ôf] *n* (*in contest, election*) deuxième tour *m*; (*extra race etc*) épreuve *f* supplémentaire.

run-of-the-mill [runəv'thəmil'] *a* ordinaire, banal(e).

runt [runt] *n* (*also pej*) avorton *m*.

run-through [run'thrōō] *n* répétition *f*, essai *m*.

run-up [run'up] *n* (*Brit*): ~ **to sth** période *f* précédant qch.

runway [run'wā] *n* (*AVIAT*) piste *f* (d'envol *or* d'atterrissage).

rupee [rōō'pē] *n* roupie *f*.

rupture [rup'chûr] *n* (*MED*) hernie *f* ♦ *vt*: **to ~ o.s.** se donner une hernie.

rural [rōōr'əl] *a* rural(e).

ruse [rōōz] *n* ruse *f*.

rush [rush] *n* course précipitée; (*of crowd*) ruée *f*, bousculade *f*; (*hurry*) hâte *f*, bousculade; (*current*) flot *m*; (*BOT*) jonc *m*; (*for chair*) paille *f* ♦ *vt* transporter *or* envoyer d'urgence; (*attack: town etc*) prendre d'assaut ♦ *vi* se précipiter; **don't ~ me!** laissez-moi le temps de souffler!; **to ~ sth off** (*do quickly*) faire qch à la hâte; (*send*) envoyer d'urgence; **is there any ~ for this?** est-ce urgent?; **we've had a ~ of orders** nous avons reçu une avalanche de commandes; **I'm in a ~ (to do)** je suis vraiment pressé (de faire); **gold ~** ruée vers l'or.

rush through *vt fus* (*work*) exécuter à la hâte ♦ *vt* (*COMM: order*) exécuter d'urgence.

rush hour *n* heures *fpl* de pointe *or* d'affluence.

rush job *n* travail urgent.

rush matting [rush mat'ing] *n* natte *f* de paille.

rusk [rusk] *n* biscotte *f*.

Russia [rush'ə] *n* Russie *f*.

Russian [rush'ən] *a* russe ♦ *n* Russe *m/f*; (*LING*) russe *m*.

rust [rust] *n* rouille *f* ♦ *vi* rouiller.

rustic [rus'tik] *a* rustique ♦ *n* (*pej*) rustaud/e.

rustle [rus'əl] *vi* bruire, produire un bruissement ♦ *vt* (*paper*) froisser; (*US: cattle*) voler.

rustproof [rust'prōōf] *a* inoxydable.

rustproofing [rust'prōōfing] *n* traitement *m* antirouille.

rusty [rus'tē] *a* rouillé(e).

rut [rut] *n* ornière *f*; (*ZOOL*) rut *m*; **to be in a ~** (*fig*) suivre l'ornière, s'encroûter.

rutabaga [rōōtəbā'gə] *n* (*US*) rutabaga *m*.

ruthless [rōōth'lis] *a* sans pitié, impitoyable.

ruthlessness [rōōth'lisnis] *n* dureté *f*, cruauté *f*.

RV *abbr* (= *revised version*) traduction anglaise de la Bible de 1885 ♦ *n abbr* (*US*) = **recreational vehicle**.

rye [rī] *n* seigle *m*.

rye bread *n* pain *m* de seigle.

S

S, s [es] *n* (*letter*) S, s *m*; (*US SCOL*: = sat-

isfactory) ≈ assez bien; **S for Sugar** S comme Suzanne.

S [es] *abbr* (= *south, small*) S; (= *saint*) St.

SA *n abbr* = **South Africa, South America**.

Sabbath [sab'əth] *n* (*Jewish*) sabbat *m*; (*Christian*) dimanche *m*.

sabbatical [səbat'ikəl] *a*: ~ **year** année *f* sabbatique.

sabotage [sab'ətâzh] *n* sabotage *m* ♦ *vt* saboter.

saccharin(e) [sak'ûrin] *n* saccharine *f*.

sachet [sashā'] *n* sachet *m*.

sack [sak] *n* (*bag*) sac *m* ♦ *vt* (*dismiss*) renvoyer, mettre à la porte; (*plunder*) piller, mettre à sac; **to get the ~** être renvoyé(e) *or* mis(e) à la porte.

sackful [sak'fəl] *n*: **a ~ of** un (plein) sac de.

sacking [sak'ing] *n* toile *f* à sac; (*dismissal*) renvoi *m*.

sacrament [sak'rəmənt] *n* sacrement *m*.

sacred [sā'krid] *a* sacré(e).

sacrifice [sak'rəfīs] *n* sacrifice *m* ♦ *vt* sacrifier; **to make ~s (for sb)** se sacrifier *or* faire des sacrifices (pour qn).

sacrilege [sak'rəlij] *n* sacrilège *m*.

sacrosanct [sak'rōsangkt] *a* sacro-saint(e).

sad [sad] *a* (*unhappy*) triste; (*deplorable*) triste, fâcheux(euse).

sadden [sad'ən] *vt* attrister, affliger.

saddle [sad'əl] *n* selle *f* ♦ *vt* (*horse*) seller; **to be ~d with sth** (*col*) avoir qch sur les bras.

saddlebag [sad'əlbag] *n* sacoche *f*.

sadism [sā'dizəm] *n* sadisme *m*.

sadist [sā'dist] *n* sadique *m/f*.

sadistic [sədis'tik] *a* sadique.

sadly [sad'lē] *ad* tristement; (*regrettably*) malheureusement.

sadness [sad'nis] *n* tristesse *f*.

sae *abbr* (*Brit*: = *stamped addressed envelope*) enveloppe affranchie pour la réponse.

safari [səfâ'rē] *n* safari *m*.

safari park *n* réserve *f*.

safe [sāf] *a* (*out of danger*) hors de danger, en sécurité; (*not dangerous*) sans danger; (*cautious*) prudent(e); (*sure: bet etc*) assuré(e) ♦ *n* coffre-fort *m*; ~ **from** à l'abri de; ~ **and sound** sain(e) et sauf(sauve); (**just**) **to be on the ~ side** pour plus de sûreté, par précaution; **to play ~** ne prendre aucun risque; **it is ~ to say that** ... on peut dire sans crainte que ...; ~ **journey!** bon voyage!

safe-breaker [sāf'brākûr] *n* (*Brit*) = **safe-cracker**.

safe-conduct [sāf'kân'dukt] *n* sauf-conduit *m*.

safe-cracker [sāf'krakûr] *n* perceur *m* de coffre-fort.

safe-deposit [sāf'dipâzit] *n* (*vault*) dépôt *m* de coffres-forts; (*box*) coffre-fort *m*.

safeguard [sāf'gârd] *n* sauvegarde *f*, protection *f* ♦ *vt* sauvegarder, protéger.

safekeeping [sāfkē'ping] *n* bonne garde.

safely [sāf'lē] *ad* sans danger, sans risque; (*without mishap*) sans accident; **I can ~ say** ... je peux dire à coup sûr ....

safety [sāf'tē] *n* sécurité *f*; ~ **first!** la sécurité d'abord!

safety belt *n* ceinture *f* de sécurité.

safety curtain *n* rideau *m* de fer.

safety net *n* filet *m* de sécurité.
safety pin *n* épingle *f* de sûreté *or* de nourrice.
safety valve *n* soupape *f* de sûreté.
saffron [saf'rən] *n* safran *m*.
sag [sag] *vi* s'affaisser, fléchir; pendre.
saga [sâ'gə] *n* saga *f*; (*fig*) épopée *f*.
sage [sāj] *n* (*herb*) sauge *f*; (*man*) sage *m*.
Sagittarius [sajitär'ēəs] *n* le Sagittaire; **to be ~** être du Sagittaire.
sago [sā'gō] *n* sagou *m*.
Sahara [səhär'ə] *n*: **the ~ (Desert)** le (désert du) Sahara *m*.
Sahel [sâhel] *n* Sahel *m*.
said [sed] *pt*, *pp of* **say**.
Saigon [sīgän'] *n* Saigon.
sail [sāl] *n* (*on boat*) voile *f*; (*trip*): **to go for a ~** faire un tour en bateau ♦ *vt* (*boat*) manœuvrer, piloter ♦ *vi* (*travel: ship*) avancer, naviguer; (*: passenger*) aller *or* se rendre (en bateau); (*set off*) partir, prendre la mer; (*SPORT*) faire de la voile; **they ~ed into Le Havre** ils sont entrés dans le port du Havre.
sail through *vi*, *vt fus* (*fig*) réussir haut la main.
sailboard [sāl'bôrd] *n* planche *f* à voile.
sailboat [sāl'bōt] *n* (*US*) bateau *m* à voiles, voilier *m*.
sailing [sā'ling] *n* (*SPORT*) voile *f*; **to go ~** faire de la voile.
sailing boat *n* (*Brit*) = **sailboat**.
sailing ship *n* grand voilier.
sailor [sā'lûr] *n* marin *m*, matelot *m*.
saint [sānt] *n* saint/e.
saintly [sānt'lē] *a* saint(e), plein(e) de bonté.
sake [sāk] *n*: **for the ~ of** (*out of concern for*) pour, dans l'intérêt de; (*out of consideration for*) par égard pour; (*in order to achieve*) pour plus de, par souci de; **arguing for arguing's ~** discuter pour (le plaisir de) discuter; **for the ~ of argument** à titre d'exemple; **for heaven's ~!** pour l'amour du ciel!
salad [sal'əd] *n* salade *f*; **tomato ~** salade de tomates.
salad bowl *n* saladier *m*.
salad cream *n* (*Brit*) (sorte *f* de) mayonnaise *f*.
salad dressing *n* vinaigrette *f*.
salad oil *n* huile *f* de table.
salami [səlâ'mē] *n* salami *m*.
salaried [sal'ûrēd] *a* (*staff*) salarié(e), qui touche un traitement.
salary [sal'ûrē] *n* salaire *m*, traitement *m*.
salary scale *n* échelle *f* des traitements.
sale [sāl] *n* vente *f*; (*at reduced prices*) soldes *mpl*; **"for ~"** "à vendre"; **on ~** en vente; **on ~ or return** vendu(e) avec faculté de retour; **liquidation ~** liquidation *f* (*avant fermeture*); **~ and lease back** *n* cession-bail *f*.
saleroom [sāl'rōōm] *n* (*Brit*) = **salesroom**.
sales assistant *n* (*Brit*) = **sales clerk**.
sales clerk *n* (*US*) vendeur/euse.
sales conference *n* réunion *f* de vente.
sales drive *n* campagne commerciale, animation *f* des ventes.
sales force *n* (ensemble *m* du) service des ventes.
salesman [sālz'mən] *n* vendeur *m*; (*representative*) représentant *m* de commerce.

sales manager *n* directeur commercial.
salesmanship [sālz'mənship] *n* art *m* de la vente.
salesroom [sālz'rōōm] *n* (*US*) salle *f* des ventes.
sales slip *n* ticket *m* de caisse.
sales tax *n* (*US*) taxe *f* à l'achat.
saleswoman [sālz'wōōmən] *n* vendeuse *f*.
salient [sā'lēənt] *a* saillant(e).
saline [sā'lēn] *a* salin(e).
saliva [səlī'və] *n* salive *f*.
sallow [sal'ō] *a* cireux(euse).
salmon [sam'ən] *n* (*pl inv*) saumon *m*.
salmon trout *n* truite saumonée.
saloon [səlōōn'] *n* (*US*) bar *m*; (*Brit AUT*) berline *f*; (*ship's lounge*) salon *m*.
Salop [sal'əp] *n abbr* (*Brit*) = Shropshire.
SALT [sôlt] *n abbr* (= *Strategic Arms Limitation Talks/Treaty*) SALT *m*.
salt [sôlt] *n* sel *m* ♦ *vt* saler ♦ *cpd* de sel; (*CULIN*) salé(e); **an old ~** un vieux loup de mer.
salt away *vt* mettre de côté.
saltcellar [sôlt'sclûr] *n* (*Brit*) salière *f*.
salt-free [sôlt'frē'] *a* sans sel.
salt shaker [sôlt shā'kûr] *n* (*US*) salière *f*.
saltwater [sôlt'wôtûr] *a* (*fish etc*) (d'eau) de mer.
salty [sôl'tē] *a* salé(e).
salubrious [səlōō'brēəs] *a* salubre.
salutary [sal'yətärē] *a* salutaire.
salute [səlōōt'] *n* salut *m* ♦ *vt* saluer.
salvage [sal'vij] *n* (*saving*) sauvetage *m*; (*things saved*) biens sauvés *or* récupérés ♦ *vt* sauver, récupérer.
salvage vessel *n* bateau *m* de sauvetage.
salvation [salvā'shən] *n* salut *m*.
Salvation Army *n* Armée *f* du Salut.
salver [sal'vûr] *n* plateau *m* de métal.
salvo [sal'vō] *n* salve *f*.
same [sām] *a* même ♦ *pronoun*: **the ~** le(la) même, les mêmes; **the ~ book as** le même livre que; **on the ~ day** le même jour; **at the ~ time** en même temps; **all** *or* **just the ~** tout de même, quand même; **they're one and the ~** (*person/thing*) c'est une seule et même personne/chose; **to do the ~** faire de même, en faire autant; **to do the ~ as sb** faire comme qn; **and the ~ to you!** et à vous de même!; (*after insult*) toi-même!; **here!** moi aussi!; **the ~ again!** (*in bar etc*) la même chose!
sample [sam'pəl] *n* échantillon *m*; (*MED*) prélèvement *m* ♦ *vt* (*food, wine*) goûter; **to take a ~** prélever un échantillon; **free ~** échantillon gratuit.
sanatorium, *pl* **sanatoria** [sanətôr'ēəm, -tôr'ēə] *n* (*Brit*) = **sanitarium**.
sanctify [sangk'təfī] *vt* sanctifier.
sanctimonious [sangktəmō'nēəs] *a* moralisateur(trice).
sanction [sangk'shən] *n* sanction *f* ♦ *vt* cautionner, sanctionner; **to impose economic ~s on** *or* **against** prendre des sanctions économiques contre.
sanctity [sangk'titē] *n* sainteté *f*, caractère sacré.
sanctuary [sangk'chōōärē] *n* (*holy place*) sanctuaire *m*; (*refuge*) asile *m*; (*for wild*

life) réserve _f_.
sand [sand] _n_ sable _m_ ♦ _vt_ sabler; (_also:_ ~
down: _wood etc_) poncer.
sandal [san'dəl] _n_ sandale _f_.
sandbag [sand'bag] _n_ sac _m_ de sable.
sandblast [sand'blast] _vt_ décaper à la sableuse.
sandbox [sand'báks] _n_ (_US:_ _for children_) tas
_m_ de sable.
sand castle _n_ château _m_ de sable.
sand dune _n_ dune _f_ de sable.
sandpaper [sand'pāpûr] _n_ papier _m_ de verre.
sand pie _n_ pâté _m_ (de sable).
sandpit [sand'pit] _n_ (_Brit_) = **sandbox**.
sands [sandz] _npl_ plage _f_ (de sable).
sandstone [sand'stōn] _n_ grès _m_.
sandstorm [sand'stôrm] _n_ tempête _f_ de sable.
sandwich [sand'wich] _n_ sandwich _m_ ♦ _vt_
(_also:_ ~ **in**) intercaler; **~ed between** pris en
sandwich entre; **cheese/ham** ~ sandwich au
fromage/jambon.
sandwich board _n_ panneau _m_ publicitaire
(porté par un homme-sandwich).
sandy [san'dē] _a_ sablonneux(euse); couvert(e)
de sable; (_color_) sable _inv_, blond roux _inv_.
sane [sān] _a_ (_person_) sain(e) d'esprit;
(_outlook_) sensé(e), sain(e).
sang [sang] _pt of_ **sing**.
sanguine [sang'gwin] _a_ optimiste.
sanitarium, _pl_ **sanitaria** [sanitär'cəm, -tär'cə] _n_
sanatorium _m_.
sanitary [san'itärē] _a_ (_system, arrangements_)
sanitaire; (_clean_) hygiénique.
sanitary napkin _n_ serviette _f_ hygiénique.
sanitation [sanitā'shən] _n_ (_in house_) installations _fpl_ sanitaires; (_in town_) système _m_ sanitaire.
sanitation department _n_ (_US_) service _m_ de
voirie.
sanity [san'itē] _n_ santé mentale; (_common
sense_) bon sens.
sank [sangk] _pt of_ **sink**.
San Marino [san mərē'nō] _n_ Saint-Marin _m_.
Santa Claus [san'tə klôz] _n_ le Père Noël.
Santiago [santēã'gō] _n_ (_also:_ ~ **de Chile**)
Santiago (du Chili).
sap [sap] _n_ (_of plants_) sève _f_ ♦ _vt_ (_strength_)
saper, miner.
sapling [sap'ling] _n_ jeune arbre _m_.
sapphire [saf'iûr] _n_ saphir _m_.
sarcasm [sâr'kazəm] _n_ sarcasme _m_, raillerie _f_.
sarcastic [sârkas'tik] _a_ sarcastique.
sarcophagus, _pl_ **sarcophagi** [sârkâf'əgəs, -gī]
_n_ sarcophage _m_.
sardine [sârdēn'] _n_ sardine _f_.
Sardinia [sârdin'ēə] _n_ Sardaigne _f_.
Sardinian [sârdin'ēən] _a_ sarde ♦ _n_ Sarde _m/f_;
(_LING_) sarde _m_.
sardonic [sârdân'ik] _a_ sardonique.
sari [sâ'rē] _n_ sari _m_.
sartorial [sârtôr'ēəl] _a_ vestimentaire.
SAS _n abbr_ (_Brit MIL:_ = _Special Air Service_)
≈ GIGN _m_.
SASE _n abbr_ (_US:_ = _self-addressed stamped
envelope_) enveloppe affranchie pour la réponse.
sash [sash] _n_ écharpe _f_.
sash window _n_ fenêtre _f_ à guillotine.
Sask. _abbr_ (_Canada_) = _Saskatchewan_.
sassy [sas'ē] _a_ (_US_) effronté(e), culotté(e).

SAT _n abbr_ (_US_) = _Scholastic Aptitude Test_.
Sat. _abbr_ (= _Saturday_) sa.
sat [sat] _pt, pp of_ **sit**.
Satan [sā'tən] _n_ Satan _m_.
satanic [sətan'ik] _a_ satanique, démoniaque.
satchel [sach'əl] _n_ cartable _m_.
sated [sā'tid] _a_ repu(e); blasé(e).
satellite [sat'əlīt] _a_, _n_ satellite _(m)_.
satellite dish _n_ antenne _f_ parabolique.
satiate [sā'shēāt] _vt_ rassasier.
satin [sat'ən] _n_ satin _m_ ♦ _a_ en _or_ de satin, sati-
né(e); **with a** ~ **finish** satiné(e).
satire [sat'iûr] _n_ satire _f_.
satirical [sətir'ikəl] _a_ satirique.
satirist [sat'ûrist] _n_ (_writer_) auteur _m_ satirique; (_cartoonist_) caricaturiste _m/f_.
satirize [sat'əriz] _vt_ faire la satire de, satiriser.
satisfaction [satisfak'shən] _n_ satisfaction _f_.
satisfactory [satisfak'tûrē] _a_ satisfaisant(e).
satisfy [sat'isfī] _vt_ satisfaire, contenter;
(_convince_) convaincre, persuader; **to** ~ **the
requirements** remplir les conditions; **to** ~ **sb
(that)** convaincre qn (que); **to** ~ **o.s. of sth**
vérifier qch, s'assurer de qch.
satisfying [sat'isfīing] _a_ satisfaisant(e).
saturate [sach'ûrāt] _vt:_ **to** ~ **(with)** saturer
(de).
saturation [sachərā'shən] _n_ saturation _f_.
Saturday [sat'ûrdā] _n_ samedi _m_; _for phrases
see also_ **Tuesday.**
sauce [sôs] _n_ sauce _f_.
saucepan [sôs'pan] _n_ casserole _f_.
saucer [sô'sûr] _n_ soucoupe _f_.
saucy [sô'sē] _a_ impertinent(e).
Saudi Arabia [sou'dē ərā'bēə] _n_ Arabie _f_
Saoudite _or_ Séoudite.
Saudi (Arabian) [sou'dē (ərā'bēən)] _a_ saou-
dien(ne) ♦ _n_ Saoudien/ne.
sauna [sô'nə] _n_ sauna _m_.
saunter [sôn'tûr] _vi:_ **to** ~ **to** aller en flânant
_or_ se balader jusqu'à.
sausage [sô'sij] _n_ saucisse _f_; (_salami etc_) saucisson _m_.
sausage roll _n_ friand _m_.
sauté [sôtā'] _a_ (_CULIN:_ _potatoes_) sauté(e); (:
onions) revenu(e) ♦ _vt_ faire sauter; faire revenir.
savage [sav'ij] _a_ (_cruel, fierce_) brutal(e), féroce; (_primitive_) primitif(ive), sauvage ♦ _n_
sauvage _m/f_ ♦ _vt_ attaquer férocement.
savagery [sav'ijrē] _n_ sauvagerie _f_, brutalité _f_,
férocité _f_.
save [sāv] _vt_ (_person, belongings_) sauver;
(_money_) mettre de côté, économiser; (_time_)
(faire) gagner; (_food_) garder; (_COMPUT_)
sauvegarder; (_avoid: trouble_) éviter ♦ _vi_
(_also:_ ~ **up**) mettre de l'argent de côté ♦ _n_
(_SPORT_) arrêt _m_ (du ballon) ♦ _prep_ sauf, à
l'exception de; **it will** ~ **me an hour** ça me
fera gagner une heure; **to** ~ **face** sauver la
face; **God** ~ **the Queen!** vive la Reine!
saving [sā'ving] _n_ économie _f_ ♦ _a:_ **the** ~ **grace
of** ce qui rachète; **~s** _npl_ économies _fpl_; **to
make** ~**s** faire des économies.
savings account _n_ compte _m_ d'épargne.
savings and loan association _n_ (_US_) société _f_ de crédit immobilier.
savings bank _n_ caisse _f_ d'épargne.
savior, (_Brit_) **saviour** [sāv'yûr] _n_ sauveur _m_.

savor [sā'vûr] (*US*) *n* saveur *f*, goût *m* ♦ *vt* savourer.

savory [sā'vûrē] *a* savoureux(euse); (*dish: not sweet*) salé(e).

savour [sā'vûr] *etc* (*Brit*) = **savor** *etc*.

savvy [sav'ē] *n* (*col*) jugeote *f*.

saw [sô] *pt of* **see** ♦ *n* (*tool*) scie *f* ♦ *vt* (*pt sawed*, *pp* **sawed** *or* (*Brit*) **sawn** [sôn]) scier; **to** ~ **sth up** débiter qch à la scie.

sawdust [sô'dust] *n* sciure *f*.

sawed-off [sôd'ôf] *a* (*US*): ~ **shotgun** carabine *f* à canon scié.

sawmill [sô'mil] *n* scierie *f*.

sawn-off [sôn'ôf] *a* (*Brit*) = **sawed-off.**

saxophone [sak'səfōn] *n* saxophone *m*.

say [sā] *n*: **to have one's** ~ dire ce qu'on a à dire; **to have a** ~ avoir voix au chapitre ♦ *vt* (*pt, pp* **said** [sed]) dire; **could you** ~ **that again?** pourriez-vous répéter ceci?; **to** ~ **yes/no** dire oui/non; **she said (that) I was to give you this** elle m'a chargé de vous remettre ceci; **my watch** ~**s 3 o'clock** ma montre indique 3 heures, il est 3 heures à ma montre; **shall we** ~ **Tuesday?** disons mardi?; **that doesn't** ~ **much for him** ce n'est pas vraiment à son honneur; **when all is said and done** en fin de compte, en définitive; **there is something** *or* **a lot to be said for it** cela a des avantages; **that is to** ~ c'est-à-dire; **to** ~ **nothing of** sans compter; ~ **that** ... mettons *or* disons que ...; **that goes without** ~**ing** cela va sans dire, cela va de soi.

saying [sā'ing] *n* dicton *m*, proverbe *m*.

SBA *n abbr* (*US*: = *Small Business Administration*) *organisme d'aide aux PME.*

SC *n abbr* (*US*) = **supreme court** ♦ *abbr* (*US MAIL*) = *South Carolina.*

s/c *abbr* = **self-contained.**

scab [skab] *n* croûte *f*; (*pej*) jaune *m*.

scabby [skab'ē] *a* croûteux(euse).

scaffold [skaf'əld] *n* échafaud *m*.

scaffolding [skaf'əlding] *n* échafaudage *m*.

scald [skôld] *n* brûlure *f* ♦ *vt* ébouillanter.

scalding [skôl'ding] *a* (*also:* ~ **hot**) brûlant(e), bouillant(e).

scale [skāl] *n* (*of fish*) écaille *f*; (*MUS*) gamme *f*; (*of ruler, thermometer etc*) graduation *f*, échelle (graduée); (*of salaries, fees etc*) barème *m*; (*of map, also size, extent*) échelle ♦ *vt* (*mountain*) escalader; (*fish*) écailler; **pay** ~ échelle des salaires; ~ **of charges** tarif *m* (des consultations *or* prestations *etc*); **on a large** ~ sur une grande échelle, en grand; **to draw sth to** ~ dessiner qch à l'échelle; **small-**~ **model** modèle réduit. **scale down** *vt* réduire.

scale drawing *n* dessin *m* à l'échelle.

scale model *n* modèle réduit.

scales [skālz] *npl* balance *f*; (*larger*) bascule *f*.

scallion [skal'yən] *n* oignon *m*; (*US: shallot*) échalote *f*; (: *leek*) poireau *m*.

scallop [skâl'əp] *n* coquille *f* Saint-Jacques.

scalp [skalp] *n* cuir chevelu ♦ *vt* scalper.

scalpel [skal'pəl] *n* scalpel *m*.

scalper [skal'pûr] *n* (*US col: of tickets*) revendeur *m* de billets.

scamp [skamp] *vt* bâcler.

scamper [skam'pûr] *vi*: **to** ~ **away,** ~ **off** détaler.

scampi [skam'pē] *npl* langoustines (frites), scampi *mpl*.

scan [skan] *vt* scruter, examiner; (*glance at quickly*) parcourir; (*poetry*) scander; (*TV, RADAR*) balayer ♦ *n* (*MED*) scanographie *f*.

scandal [skan'dəl] *n* scandale *m*; (*gossip*) ragots *mpl*.

scandalize [skan'dəlīz] *vt* scandaliser, indigner.

scandalous [skan'dələs] *a* scandaleux(euse).

Scandinavia [skandənā'vēə] *n* Scandinavie *f*.

Scandinavian [skandənā'vēən] *a* scandinave ♦ *n* Scandinave *m/f*.

scanner [skan'ûr] *n* (*RADAR, MED*) scanner *m*, scanographe *m*.

scant [skant] *a* insuffisant(e).

scantily [skan'tilē] *ad*: ~ **clad** *or* **dressed** vêtu(e) du strict minimum.

scanty [skan'tē] *a* peu abondant(e), insuffisant(e), maigre.

scapegoat [skāp'gōt] *n* bouc *m* émissaire.

scar [skär] *n* cicatrice *f* ♦ *vt* laisser une cicatrice *or* une marque à.

scarce [skärs] *a* rare, peu abondant(e).

scarcely [skärs'lē] *ad* à peine, presque pas; ~ **anybody** pratiquement personne; **I can** ~ **believe it** j'ai du mal à le croire.

scarcity [skär'sitē] *n* rareté *f*, manque *m*, pénurie *f*.

scarcity value *n* valeur *f* de rareté.

scare [skär] *n* peur *f*, panique *f* ♦ *vt* effrayer, faire peur à; **to** ~ **sb stiff** faire une peur bleue à qn; **bomb** ~ alerte *f* à la bombe. **scare away, scare off** *vt* faire fuir.

scarecrow [skär'krō] *n* épouvantail *m*.

scared [skärd] *a*: **to be** ~ avoir peur.

scaremonger [skär'munggûr] *n* alarmiste *m/f*.

scarf, *pl* **scarves** [skärf, skärvz] *n* (*long*) écharpe *f*; (*square*) foulard *m*.

scarlet [skär'lit] *a* écarlate.

scarlet fever *n* scarlatine *f*.

scarves [skärvz] *npl of* **scarf.**

scary [skär'ē] *a* (*col*) qui fiche la frousse.

scathing [skā'thing] *a* cinglant(e), acerbe; **to be** ~ **about sth** être très critique vis-à-vis de qch.

scatter [skat'ûr] *vt* éparpiller, répandre; (*crowd*) disperser ♦ *vi* se disperser.

scatterbrained [skat'ûrbrānd] *a* écervelé(e), étourdi(e).

scattered [skat'ûrd] *a* épars(e), dispersé(e).

scatty [skat'ē] *a* (*Brit col*) loufoque.

scavenge [skav'inj] *vi* (*person*): **to** ~ (**for**) faire les poubelles (pour trouver); **to** ~ **for food** (*hyenas etc*) se nourrir de charognes.

scavenger [skav'injûr] *n* éboueur *m*.

scenario [sinär'ēō] *n* scénario *m*.

scene [sēn] *n* (*THEATER, fig etc*) scène *f*; (*of crime, accident*) lieu(x) *m(pl)*, endroit *m*; (*sight, view*) spectacle *m*, vue *f*; **behind the** ~**s** (*also fig*) dans les coulisses; **to make a** ~ (*col: fuss*) faire une scène *or* toute une histoire; **to appear on the** ~ (*also fig*) faire son apparition, arriver; **the political** ~ la situation politique.

scenery [sē'nûrē] *n* (*THEATER*) décor(s) *m(pl)*; (*landscape*) paysage *m*.

scenic [sē'nik] *a* scénique; offrant de beaux paysages *or* panoramas.

scent [sent] *n* parfum *m*, odeur *f*; (*fig: track*) piste *f*; (*sense of smell*) odorat *m* ♦ *vt* parfumer; (*smell, also fig*) flairer; **to put or throw sb off the** ~ (*fig*) mettre *or* lancer qn sur une mauvaise piste.

scepter [sep'tûr] *n* (*US*) sceptre *m*.

sceptic [skep'tik] *etc* (*Brit*) = **skeptic** *etc*.

sceptre [sep'tûr] *n* (*Brit*) = **scepter**.

schedule [skej'ōōl, (*Brit*) shed'yōōl] *n* programme *m*, plan *m*; (*of trains*) horaire *m*; (*of prices etc*) barème *m*, tarif *m* ♦ *vt* prévoir; **as ~d** comme prévu; **on** ~ à l'heure (prévue); à la date prévue; **to be ahead of/ behind** ~ avoir de l'avance/du retard; **we are working to a very tight** ~ notre programme de travail est très serré *or* intense; **everything went according to** ~ tout s'est passé comme prévu.

scheduled [skej'ōōld, (*Brit*) shed'yōōld] *a* (*date, time*) prévu(e), indiqué(e); (*visit, event*) programmé(e), prévu; (*train, bus, stop, flight*) régulier(ière).

schematic [skēmat'ik] *a* schématique.

scheme [skēm] *n* plan *m*, projet *m*; (*method*) procédé *m*; (*dishonest plan, plot*) complot *m*, combine *f*; (*arrangement*) arrangement *m*, classification *f* ♦ *vt*, *vi* comploter, manigancer; **color** ~ combinaison *f* de(s) couleurs.

scheming [skēm'ing] *a* rusé(e), intrigant(e) ♦ *n* manigances *fpl*, intrigues *fpl*.

schism [skiz'əm] *n* schisme *m*.

schizophrenia [skitsəfrē'nēə] *n* schizophrénie *f*.

schizophrenic [skitsəfren'ik] *a* schizophrène.

scholar [skâl'ûr] *n* érudit/e.

scholarly [skâl'ûrlē] *a* érudit(e), savant(e).

scholarship [skâl'ûrship] *n* érudition *f*; (*grant*) bourse *f* (d'études).

school [skōōl] *n* (*gen*) école *f*; (*in university*) faculté *f*; (*high school*) collège *m*, lycée *m*; (*of fish*) banc *m* ♦ *cpd* scolaire ♦ *vt* (*animal*) dresser.

school age *n* âge *m* scolaire.

school bag *n* cartable *m*.

schoolbook [skōōl'bōōk] *n* livre *m* scolaire *or* de classe.

schoolboy [skōōl'boi] *n* écolier *m*; collégien *m*, lycéen *m*.

schoolchild, *pl* **-children** [skōōl'chīld, -childrən] *n* écolier/ière, collégien/ne, lycéen/ ne.

schooldays [skōōl'dāz] *npl* années *fpl* de scolarité.

schoolgirl [skōōl'gûrl] *n* écolière *f*; collégienne *f*, lycéenne *f*.

schooling [skōō'ling] *n* instruction *f*, études *fpl*.

school-leaving age [skōōl'lēving āj] *n* âge *m* de fin de scolarité.

schoolmaster [skōōl'mastûr] *n* (*elementary*) instituteur *m*; (*high*) professeur *m*.

schoolmistress [skōōl'mistris] *n* (*elementary*) institutrice *f*; (*high*) professeur *m*.

schoolroom [skōōl'rōōm] *n* (salle *f* de) classe *f*.

schoolteacher [skōōl'tēchûr] *n* (*elementary*) instituteur/trice; (*high*) professeur *m*.

schoolyard [skōōl'yârd] *n* cour *f* de récréation.

schooner [skōō'nûr] *n* (*ship*) schooner *m*, goélette *f*; (*glass*) grand verre (à xérès).

sciatica [sīat'ikə] *n* sciatique *f*.

science [sī'əns] *n* science *f*; **the ~s** les sciences; (*SCOL*) les matières *fpl* scientifiques.

science fiction *n* science-fiction *f*.

scientific [sīəntif'ik] *a* scientifique.

scientist [sī'əntist] *n* scientifique *m/f*; (*eminent*) savant *m*.

sci-fi [sī'fī'] *n abbr* (*col*: = *science fiction*) SF *f*.

scintillating [sin'təlāting] *a* scintillant(e), étincelant(e); (*wit etc*) brillant(e).

scissors [siz'ûrz] *npl* ciseaux *mpl*; **a pair of** ~ une paire de ciseaux.

sclerosis [sklirō'sis] *n* sclérose *f*.

scoff [skâf] *vi*: **to** ~ **(at)** (*mock*) se moquer (de).

scold [skōld] *vt* gronder, attraper, réprimander.

scolding [skōld'ing] *n* réprimande *f*.

scone [skōn] *n* sorte de petit pain rond au lait.

scoop [skōōp] *n* pelle *f* (à main); (*for ice cream*) boule *f* à glace; (*PRESS*) reportage exclusif *or* à sensation.

scoop out *vt* évider, creuser.

scoop up *vt* ramasser.

scooter [skōō'tûr] *n* (*motorcycle*) scooter *m*; (*toy*) trottinette *f*.

scope [skōp] *n* (*capacity: of plan, undertaking*) portée *f*, envergure *f*; (: *of person*) compétence *f*, capacités *fpl*; (*opportunity*) possibilités *fpl*; **within the** ~ **of** dans les limites de; **there is plenty of** ~ **for improvement** (*Brit*) cela pourrait être beaucoup mieux.

scorch [skôrch] *vt* (*clothes*) brûler (légèrement), roussir; (*earth, grass*) dessécher, brûler.

scorched earth policy *n* politique *f* de la terre brûlée.

scorcher [skôr'chûr] *n* (*col: hot day*) journée *f* torride.

scorching [skôrch'ing] *a* torride, brûlant(e).

score [skôr] *n* score *m*, décompte *m* des points; (*MUS*) partition *f*; (*twenty*) vingt ♦ *vt* (*goal, point*) marquer; (*success*) remporter; (*cut: leather, wood, card*) entailler, inciser ♦ *vi* marquer des points; (*SOCCER*) marquer un but; (*keep* ~) compter les points; **on that** ~ sur ce chapitre, à cet égard; **to have an old** ~ **to settle with sb** (*fig*) avoir un (vieux) compte à régler avec qn; **~s of** (*fig*) des tas de; **to** ~ **well/6 out of 10** obtenir un bon résultat/6 sur 10.

score out *vt* rayer, barrer, biffer.

scoreboard [skôr'bôrd] *n* tableau *m*.

scorecard [skôr'kârd] *n* (*SPORT*) carton *m*, feuille *f* de marque.

scorer [skôr'ûr] *n* (*SOCCER*) auteur *m* du but; buteur *m*; (*keeping score*) marqueur *m*.

scorn [skôrn] *n* mépris *m*, dédain *m* ♦ *vt* mépriser, dédaigner.

scornful [skôrn'fəl] *a* méprisant(e), dédaigneux(euse).

Scorpio [skôr'pēō] *n* le Scorpion; **to be** ~ être du Scorpion.

scorpion [skôr'pēən] *n* scorpion *m*.

Scot [skât] *n* Écossais/e.
Scotch [skâch] *n* whisky *m*, scotch *m*.
scotch [skâch] *vt* faire échouer; enrayer; étouffer.
Scotch tape *n* ® (*US*) scotch *m* ®, ruban adhésif.
scot-free [skât'frē'] *a*: **to get off** ~ s'en tirer sans être puni(e) (*or* sans payer); s'en sortir indemne.
Scotland [skât'lənd] *n* Écosse *f*.
Scots [skâts] *a* écossais(e).
Scotsman [skâts'mən] *n* Ecossais *m*.
Scotswoman [skâts'woomən] *n* Écossaise *f*.
Scottish [skât'ish] *a* écossais(e).
scoundrel [skoun'drəl] *n* vaurien *m*.
scour [skour] *vt* (*clean*) récurer; frotter; décaper; (*search*) battre, parcourir.
scourer [skour'ûr] *n* (*powder*) poudre *f* à récurer; (*Brit*) = **scouring pad**.
scourge [skûrj] *n* fléau *m*.
scouring pad [skour'ing pad] *n* tampon abrasif *or* à récurer.
scout [skout] *n* (*MIL*) éclaireur *m*; (*also*: **boy** ~) scout *m*.
scout around *vi* chercher.
scowl [skoul] *vi* se renfrogner, avoir l'air maussade; **to** ~ **at** regarder de travers.
scrabble [skrab'əl] *vi* (*claw*): **to** ~ (**at**) gratter; **to** ~ **about** *or* **around for sth** chercher qch à tâtons ♦ *n*: **S**~ ® Scrabble *m* ®.
scraggy [skrag'ē] *a* décharné(e), efflanqué(e), famélique.
scram [skram] *vi* (*col*) ficher le camp.
scramble [skram'bəl] *n* bousculade *f*, ruée *f* ♦ *vi* avancer tant bien que mal (à quatre pattes *or* en grimpant); **to** ~ **for** se bousculer *or* se disputer pour (avoir); **to go scrambling** (*SPORT*) faire du trial.
scrambled eggs [skram'bəld egz] *npl* œufs brouillés.
scrap [skrap] *n* bout *m*, morceau *m*; (*fight*) bagarre *f*; (*also*: ~ **iron**) ferraille *f* ♦ *vt* jeter, mettre au rebut; (*fig*) abandonner, laisser tomber; ~**s** *npl* (*waste*) déchets *mpl*; **to sell sth for** ~ vendre qch à la casse *or* à la ferraille.
scrapbook [skrap'book] *n* album *m*.
scrap dealer *n* marchand *m* de ferraille.
scrape [skrāp] *vt*, *vi* gratter, racler ♦ *n*: **to get into a** ~ s'attirer des ennuis.
scrape through *vi* (*in exam etc*) réussir de justesse.
scraper [skrā'pûr] *n* grattoir *m*, racloir *m*.
scrapheap [skrap'hēp] *n* tas *m* de ferraille; (*fig*): **on the** ~ au rancart *or* rebut.
scrap metal *n* ferraille *f*.
scrap paper *n* papier *m* brouillon.
scrappy [skrap'ē] *a* fragmentaire, décousu(e).
scrap yard *n* (*Brit*) parc *m* à ferrailles; (: *for cars*) cimetière *m* de voitures.
scratch [skrach] *n* égratignure *f*, rayure *f*; éraflure *f*; (*from claw*) coup *m* de griffe ♦ *vt* (*record*) rayer; (*paint etc*) érafler; (*with claw, nail*) griffer ♦ *vi* (se) gratter; **to start from** ~ partir de zéro; **to be up to** ~ être à la hauteur.
scrawl [skrôl] *n* gribouillage *m* ♦ *vi* gribouiller.
scrawny [skrô'nē] *a* décharné(e).
scream [skrēm] *n* cri perçant, hurlement *m* ♦

vi crier, hurler; **to be a** ~ (*col*) être impayable; **to** ~ **at sb to do sth** crier *or* hurler à qn de faire qch.
scree [skrē] *n* éboulis *m*.
screech [skrēch] *n* cri strident, hurlement *m*; (*of tires, brakes*) crissement *m*, grincement *m* ♦ *vi* hurler; crisser, grincer.
screen [skrēn] *n* écran *m*, paravent *m*; (*CINEMA, TV*) écran; (*fig*) écran, rideau *m* ♦ *vt* masquer, cacher; (*from the wind etc*) abriter, protéger; (*film*) projeter; (*candidates etc*) filtrer; (*for illness*): **to** ~ **sb for sth** faire subir un test de dépistage de qch à qn.
screen editing *n* (*COMPUT*) édition *f* or correction *f* sur écran.
screening [skrē'ning] *n* (*of film*) projection *f*; (*MED*) test *m* (*or* tests) de dépistage; (*for security*) filtrage *m*.
screen memory *n* (*COMPUT*) mémoire *f* écran.
screenplay [skrēn'plā] *n* scénario *m*.
screen test *n* bout *m* d'essai.
screw [skroo] *n* vis *f*; (*propeller*) hélice *f* ♦ *vt* visser; (*col!: woman*) baiser (!); **to** ~ **sth to the wall** visser qch au mur; **to have one's head** ~**ed on** (*fig*) avoir la tête sur les épaules.
screw up *vt* (*paper, material*) froisser; (*col: ruin*) bousiller; **to** ~ **up one's face** faire la grimace.
screwball [skroo'bôl] *n* (*col*) cinglé/e, tordu/e.
screwdriver [skroo'drīvûr] *n* tournevis *m*.
screwy [skroo'ē] *a* (*col*) dingue, cinglé(e).
scribble [skrib'əl] *n* gribouillage *m* ♦ *vt* gribouiller, griffonner; **to** ~ **sth down** griffonner qch.
scribe [skrīb] *n* scribe *m*.
script [skript] *n* (*CINEMA etc*) scénario *m*, texte *m*; (*in exam*) copie *f*; (*writing*) (écriture *f*) script *m*.
scripted [skrip'tid] *a* (*RADIO, TV*) préparé(e) à l'avance.
Scripture [skrip'chûr] *n* Écriture Sainte.
scriptwriter [skript'rītûr] *n* scénariste *m/f*, dialoguiste *m/f*.
scroll [skrōl] *n* rouleau *m* ♦ *vt* (*COMPUT*) faire défiler (sur l'écran).
scrotum [skrō'təm] *n* scrotum *m*.
scrounge [skrounj] (*col*) *vt*: **to** ~ **sth** (**off** *or* **from sb**) se faire payer qch (par qn), emprunter qch (à qn) ♦ *vi*: **to** ~ **on sb** vivre aux crochets de qn.
scrounger [skrounj'ûr] *n* parasite *m*.
scrub [skrub] *n* (*clean*) nettoyage *m* (à la brosse); (*land*) broussailles *fpl* ♦ *vt* (*floor*) nettoyer à la brosse; (*pan*) récurer; (*washing*) frotter; (*reject*) annuler.
scrub brush *n* brosse dure.
scrubbing brush [skrub'ing brush] *n* (*Brit*) = **scrub brush**.
scruff [skruf] *n*: **by the** ~ **of the neck** par la peau du cou.
scruffy [skruf'ē] *a* débraillé(e).
scrum(mage) [skrum'(ij)] *n* (*RUGBY*) mêlée *f*.
scruple [skroo'pəl] *n* scrupule *m*; **to have no** ~**s about doing sth** n'avoir aucun scrupule à faire qch.
scrupulous [skroo'pyələs] *a* scrupuleux(euse).
scrupulously [skroo'pyələslē] *ad* scrupuleuse-

ment; **to be ~ honest** être d'une honnêteté scrupuleuse.
scrutinize [skrōō'tənīz] vt scruter, examiner minutieusement.
scrutiny [skrōō'tənē] n examen minutieux; **under the ~ of sb** sous la surveillance de qn.
scuba [skōō'bə] n scaphandre m (autonome).
scuba diving n plongée sous-marine (autonome).
scuff [skuf] vt érafler.
scuffle [skuf'əl] n échauffourée f, rixe f.
scull [skul] n aviron m.
scullery [skul'ûrē] n arrière-cuisine f.
sculptor [skulp'tûr] n sculpteur m.
sculpture [skulp'chûr] n sculpture f.
scum [skum] n écume f, mousse f; (pej: people) rebut m, lie f.
scurrilous [skûr'ələs] a haineux(euse), virulent(e); calomnieux(euse).
scurry [skûr'ē] vi filer à toute allure; **to ~ off** détaler, se sauver.
scurvy [skûr'vē] n scorbut m.
scuttle [skut'əl] n (NAUT) écoutille f; (also: **coal ~**) seau m (à charbon) ♦ vt (ship) saborder ♦ vi (scamper): **to ~ away, ~ off** détaler.
scythe [sīth] n faux f.
SD abbr (US MAIL) = South Dakota.
S.Dak. abbr (US) = South Dakota.
SDI n abbr (= Strategic Defense Initiative) IDS f.
SDLP n abbr (Brit POL) = Social Democratic and Labour Party.
SDP n abbr (Brit POL) = Social Democratic Party.
sea [sē] n mer f ♦ cpd marin(e), de (la) mer, maritime; **on the ~** (boat) en mer; (town) au bord de la mer; **by or beside the ~** (vacation) au bord de la mer; (village) près de la mer; **by ~** par mer, en bateau; **out to ~** au large; **(out) at ~** en mer; **heavy or rough ~(s)** grosse mer, mer agitée; **a ~ of faces** (fig) une multitude de visages.
sea bed n fond m de la mer.
sea bird n oiseau m de mer.
seaboard [sē'bôrd] n côte f.
sea breeze n brise f de mer.
seafarer [sē'fârûr] n marin m.
seafaring [sē'fâring] a (life) de marin; **~ people** les gens mpl de mer.
seafood [sē'fōōd] n fruits mpl de mer.
sea front n bord m de mer.
seagoing [sē'gōing] a (ship) de haute mer.
seagull [sē'gul] n mouette f.
seal [sēl] n (animal) phoque m; (stamp) sceau m, cachet m; (impression) cachet m, estampille f ♦ vt sceller; (envelope) coller; (: with seal) cacheter; (decide: sb's fate) décider (de); (: bargain) conclure; **~ of approval** approbation f.
seal off vt (close) condamner; (forbid entry to) interdire l'accès de.
sea level n niveau m de la mer.
sealing wax [sē'ling waks] n cire f à cacheter.
sea lion n lion m de mer.
sealskin [sēl'skin] n peau f de phoque.
seam [sēm] n couture f; (of coal) veine f, filon m; **the hall was bursting at the ~s** la salle était pleine à craquer.

seaman [sē'mən] n marin m.
seamanship [sē'mənship] n qualités fpl de marin.
seamless [sēm'lis] a sans couture(s).
seamy [sē'mē] a louche, mal famé(e).
seance [sā'âns] n séance f de spiritisme.
seaplane [sē'plān] n hydravion m.
seaport [sē'pôrt] n port m de mer.
search [sûrch] n (for person, thing) recherche(s) f(pl); (of drawer, pockets) fouille f; (LAW: at sb's home) perquisition f ♦ vt fouiller; (examine) examiner minutieusement; scruter ♦ vi: **to ~ for** chercher; **in ~ of** à la recherche de; **"~ and replace"** (COMPUT) "rechercher et remplacer".
search through vt fus fouiller.
searcher [sûr'chûr] n chercheur/euse.
searching [sûr'ching] a (look, question) pénétrant(e); (examination) minutieux(euse).
searchlight [sûrch'līt] n projecteur m.
search party n expédition f de secours.
search warrant n mandat m de perquisition.
searing [sē'ring] a (heat) brûlant(e); (pain) aigu(ë).
seashore [sē'shôr] n rivage m, plage f, bord m de (la) mer; **on the ~** sur le rivage.
seasick [sē'sik] a: **to be ~** avoir le mal de mer.
seaside [sē'sīd] n bord m de la mer.
seaside resort n station f balnéaire.
season [sē'zən] n saison f ♦ vt assaisonner, relever; **to be in/out of ~** être/ne pas être de saison; **the busy ~** (for shops) la période de pointe; (for hotels etc) la pleine saison; **the open ~** (HUNTING) saison f de la chasse.
seasonal [sē'zənəl] a saisonnier(ière).
seasoned [sē'zənd] a (wood) séché(e); (fig: worker, actor, troops) expérimenté(e); **a ~ campaigner** un vieux militant, un vétéran.
seasoning [sē'zəning] n assaisonnement m.
season ticket n carte f d'abonnement.
seat [sēt] n siège m; (in bus, train: place) place f; (PARLIAMENT) siège; (buttocks) postérieur m; (of pants) fond m ♦ vt faire asseoir, placer; (have room for) avoir des places assises pour, pouvoir accueillir; **are there any ~s left?** est-ce qu'il reste des places?; **to take one's ~** prendre place; **to be ~ed** être assis; **please be ~ed** veuillez vous asseoir.
seat belt n ceinture f de sécurité.
seating capacity [sē'ting kəpas'itē] n nombre m de places assises.
seating room [sē'ting rōōm] n places assises.
SEATO [sē'tō] n abbr (= Southeast Asia Treaty Organization) OTASE f (= Organisation du traité de l'Asie du Sud-Est).
sea water n eau f de mer.
seaweed [sē'wēd] n algues fpl.
seaworthy [sē'wûrthē] a en état de naviguer.
SEC n abbr (US: = Securities and Exchange Commission) ≈ COB f (= Commission des opérations de Bourse).
sec. abbr (= second) sec.
secateurs [sek'ətûrz] npl (Brit) sécateur m.
secede [sisēd'] vi faire sécession.
secluded [siklōō'did] a retiré(e), à l'écart.
seclusion [siklōō'zhən] n solitude f.
second [sek'ənd] num deuxième, second(e) ♦ ad (in race etc) en seconde position ♦ n (unit

of time) seconde *f*; (*in series, position*) deuxième *m/f*, second/e; (*Brit SCOL*) ≈ licence *f* avec mention bien *or* assez bien; (*AUT*: *also*: ~ **gear**) seconde *f*; (*COMM*: *imperfect*) article *m* de second choix ♦ *vt* (*motion*) appuyer; [sikând'] (*employee*) détacher, mettre en détachement; **Charles the S**~ Charles II; **just a** ~! une seconde!, un instant!; (*stopping sb*) pas si vite!; ~ **floor** (*US*) premier (étage) *m*; (*Brit*) deuxième (étage) *m*; **to ask for a** ~ **opinion** (*MED*) demander l'avis d'un autre médecin; **to have** ~ **thoughts (about doing sth)** changer d'avis (à propos de faire qch); **on** ~ **thought** *or* (*Brit*) **thoughts** à la réflexion.

secondary [sɛk'əndärē] *a* secondaire.

secondary picket *n* piquet *m* (de grève) secondaire.

secondary school *n* (*Brit*) collège *m*, lycée *m*.

second-best [sɛk'əndbɛst'] *n* deuxième choix *m*; **as a** ~ faute de mieux.

second-class [sɛk'əndklas'] *a* de deuxième classe ♦ *ad*: **to send sth** ~ envoyer qch à tarif réduit; **to travel** ~ voyager en seconde; ~ **citizen** citoyen/ne de deuxième classe.

second cousin *n* cousin/e issu(e) de germains.

seconder [sɛk'əndûr] *n* personne *f* qui appuie une motion.

secondhand [sɛk'əndhand'] *a* d'occasion; ♦ *ad* (*buy*) d'occasion; **to hear sth** ~ apprendre qch indirectement.

second hand *n* (*on clock*) trotteuse *f*.

second-in-command [sɛk'əndinkəmand'] *n* (*MIL*) commandant *m* en second; (*ADMIN*) adjoint/e, sous-chef *m*.

secondly [sɛk'əndlē] *ad* deuxièmement.

second-rate [sɛk'əndrrāt'] *a* de deuxième ordre, de qualité inférieure.

secrecy [sē'krisē] *n* secret *m*; **in** ~ en secret, dans le secret.

secret [sē'krit] *a* secret(ète) ♦ *n* secret *m*; **in** ~ *ad* en secret, secrètement, en cachette; **to keep sth** ~ **from sb** cacher qch à qn, ne pas révéler qch à qn; **keep it** ~ n'en parle à personne; **to make no** ~ **of sth** ne pas cacher qch.

secret agent *n* agent secret.

secretarial [sɛkritär'ēəl] *a* de secrétaire, de secrétariat.

secretariat [sɛkritär'ēət] *n* secrétariat *m*.

secretary [sɛk'ritärē] *n* secrétaire *m/f*; (*COMM*) secrétaire général; **S**~ **of State** (*US POL*) ≈ ministre *m* des Affaires étrangères; (*Brit POL*): **S**~ **of State (for)** ministre *m* (de).

secrete [sikrēt'] *vt* (*ANAT, BIOL, MED*) sécréter; (*hide*) cacher.

secretion [sikrē'shən] *n* sécrétion *f*.

secretive [sē'kritiv] *a* réservé(e); (*pej*) cachottier(ière), dissimulé(e).

secretly [sē'kritlē] *ad* en secret, secrètement, en cachette.

sect [sɛkt] *n* secte *f*.

sectarian [sɛktär'ēən] *a* sectaire.

section [sɛk'shən] *n* coupe *f*, section *f*; (*department*) section; (*COMM*) rayon *m*; (*of document*) section, article *m*, paragraphe *m* ♦ *vt* sectionner; **the business** *etc* ~ (*PRESS*)

la page des affaires *etc*.

sectional [sɛk'shənəl] *a* (*drawing*) en coupe.

sector [sɛk'tûr] *n* secteur *m*.

secular [sɛk'yələr] *a* profane; laïque; séculier(ière).

secure [sikyōōr'] *a* (*free from anxiety*) sans inquiétude, sécurisé(e); (*firmly fixed*) solide, bien attaché(e) (*or* fermé(e) *etc*); (*in safe place*) en lieu sûr, en sûreté *f* ♦ *vt* (*fix*) fixer, attacher; (*get*) obtenir, se procurer; (*COMM*: *loan*) garantir; **to make sth** ~ bien fixer *or* attacher qch; **to** ~ **sth for sb** obtenir qch pour qn, procurer qch à qn.

secured creditor [sikyōōrd' kred'itûr] *n* créancier/ière privilégié(e).

security [sikyōōr'itē] *n* sécurité *f*, mesures *fpl* de sécurité; (*for loan*) caution *f*, garantie *f*; **securities** *npl* (*STOCK EXCHANGE*) valeurs *fpl*, titres *mpl*; **to increase** *or* **tighten** ~ renforcer les mesures de sécurité; ~ **of tenure** stabilité *f* d'un emploi, titularisation *f*.

security forces *npl* forces *fpl* de sécurité.

security guard *n* garde chargé de la sécurité; (*transporting money*) convoyeur *m* de fonds.

security risk *n* menace *f* pour la sécurité de l'état (*or* d'une entreprise *etc*).

secy *abbr* (= *secretary*) secr.

sedan [sidan'] *n* (*US AUT*) berline *f*.

sedate [sidāt'] *a* calme; posé(e) ♦ *vt* donner des sédatifs à.

sedation [sidā'shən] *n* (*MED*) sédation *f*; **to be under** ~ être sous calmants.

sedative [sed'ətiv] *n* calmant *m*, sédatif *m*.

sedentary [sed'əntärē] *a* sédentaire.

sediment [sed'əmənt] *n* sédiment *m*, dépôt *m*.

sedition [sidish'ən] *n* sédition *f*.

seduce [sidōōs'] *vt* séduire.

seduction [siduk'shən] *n* séduction *f*.

seductive [siduk'tiv] *a* séduisant(e), séducteur(trice).

see [sē] *vb* (*pt* **saw**, *pp* **seen** [sô, sēn] *vt* (*gen*) voir; (*accompany*): **to** ~ **sb to the door** reconduire *or* raccompagner qn jusqu'à la porte ♦ *vi* voir ♦ *n* évêché *m*; **to** ~ **that** (*ensure*) veiller à ce que + *sub*, faire en sorte que + *sub*, s'assurer que; **there was nobody to be** ~**n** il n'y avait pas un chat; **let me** ~ (*show me*) fais(-moi) voir; (*let me think*) voyons (un peu); **to go and** ~ **sb** aller voir qn; ~ **for yourself** voyez vous-même; **I don't know what she** ~**s in him** je ne sais pas ce qu'elle lui trouve; **as far as I can** ~ pour autant que je puisse en juger; ~ **you!** au revoir!, à bientôt!; ~ **you soon/later/tomorrow!** à bientôt/plus tard/demain!

see about *vt fus* (*deal with*) s'occuper de.

see off *vt* accompagner (à la gare *or* à l'aéroport *etc*).

see through *vt* mener à bonne fin ♦ *vt fus* voir clair dans.

see to *vt fus* s'occuper de, se charger de.

seed [sēd] *n* graine *f*; (*fig*) germe *m*; (*TENNIS*) tête *f* de série; **to go to** ~ monter en graine; (*fig*) se laisser aller.

seedless [sēd'lis] *a* sans pépins.

seedling [sēd'ling] *n* jeune plant *m*, semis *m*.

seedy [sē'dē] *a* (*shabby*) minable, miteux(euse).

seeing [sē'ing] *cj*: ~ **(that)** vu que, étant donné que.

seek, *pt*, *pp* **sought** [sēk, sôt] *vt* chercher, rechercher; **to ~ advice/help from sb** demander conseil/de l'aide à qn.

seek out *vt* (*person*) chercher.

seem [sēm] *vi* sembler, paraître; **there ~s to be** ... il semble qu'il y a ..., on dirait qu'il y a ...; **it ~s (that)** ... il semble que ...; **what ~s to be the trouble?** qu'est-ce qui ne va pas?

seemingly [sē'minglē] *ad* apparemment.

seen [sēn] *pp of* **see**.

seep [sēp] *vi* suinter, filtrer.

seer [sēr] *n* prophète/prophétesse, voyant/e.

seersucker [sēr'sukûr] *n* cloqué *m*, étoffe cloquée.

seesaw [sē'sô] *n* (jeu *m* de) bascule *f*.

seethe [sēth] *vi* être en effervescence; **to ~ with anger** bouillir de colère.

see-through [sē'thrōō] *a* transparent(e).

segment [seg'mənt] *n* segment *m*.

segregate [seg'rəgāt] *vt* séparer, isoler.

segregation [segrəgā'shən] *n* ségrégation *f*.

Seine [sān] *n*: **the ~** la Seine.

seismic [sīz'mik] *a* sismique.

seize [sēz] *vt* (*grasp*) saisir, attraper; (*take possession of*) s'emparer de; (*LAW*) saisir.

seize up *vi* (*TECH*) se gripper.

seize (up)on *vt fus* saisir, sauter sur.

seizure [sē'zhûr] *n* (*MED*) crise *f*, attaque *f*; (*LAW*) saisie *f*.

seldom [sel'dəm] *ad* rarement.

select [silekt'] *a* choisi(e), d'élite; (*hotel, restaurant, club*) chic *inv*, sélect *inv* ♦ *vt* sélectionner, choisir; **a ~ few** quelques privilégiés.

selection [silek'shən] *n* sélection *f*, choix *m*.

selection committee *n* comité *m* de sélection.

selective [silek'tiv] *a* sélectif(ive); (*school*) à recrutement sélectif.

selector [silek'tûr] *n* (*person*) sélectionneur/euse; (*TECH*) sélecteur *m*.

self [self] *n* (*pl* **selves** [selvz]): **the ~** le moi *inv* ♦ *prefix* auto-.

self-addressed [self'ədrest'] *a*: **~ envelope** enveloppe *f* à mon (*or* votre *etc*) nom; **~ stamped envelope (SASE)** (*US*) enveloppe affranchie pour la réponse.

self-adhesive [self'adhē'siv] *a* autocollant(e).

self-assertive [self'əsûr'tiv] *a* autoritaire.

self-assurance [self'əshōōr'əns] *n* assurance *f*.

self-assured [self'əshōōrd'] *a* sûr(e) de soi, plein(e) d'assurance.

self-catering [self'kā'tûring] *a* (*Brit: apartment*) avec cuisine, où l'on peut faire sa cuisine; (: *holiday*) en appartement (*or* chalet *etc*) loué.

self-centered [self'sen'tûrd] *a* égocentrique.

self-cleaning [self'klē'ning] *a* auto-nettoyant(e).

self-colored [self'kul'ûrd] *a* uni(e).

self-confessed [self'kənfest'] *a* (*alcoholic etc*) déclaré(e), qui ne s'en cache pas.

self-confidence [self'kân'fidəns] *n* confiance *f* en soi.

self-conscious [self'kân'chəs] *a* timide, qui manque d'assurance.

self-contained [self'kəntānd'] *a* (*Brit:*

apartment) avec entrée particulière, indépendant(e).

self-control [self'kəntrōl'] *n* maîtrise *f* de soi.

self-defeating [self'difē'ting] *a* qui a un effet contraire à l'effet recherché.

self-defense [self'difens'] *n* légitime défense *f*.

self-discipline [self'dis'əplin] *n* discipline personnelle.

self-employed [self'imploid'] *a* qui travaille à son compte.

self-esteem [self'əstēm'] *n* amour-propre *m*.

self-evident [self'ev'idənt] *a* évident(e), qui va de soi.

self-explanatory [self'iksplan'ətôrē] *a* qui se passe d'explication.

self-governing [self'guv'ûrning] *a* autonome.

self-help [self'help'] *n* initiative personnelle, efforts personnels.

self-importance [self'impôr'təns] *n* suffisance *f*.

self-indulgent [self'indul'jənt] *a* qui ne se refuse rien.

self-inflicted [self'inflik'tid] *a* volontaire.

self-interest [self'in'trist] *n* intérêt personnel.

selfish [sel'fish] *a* égoïste.

selfishness [sel'fishnis] *n* égoïsme *m*.

selfless [self'lis] *a* désintéressé(e).

selflessly [self'lislē] *ad* sans penser à soi.

self-made man [self'mād' man'] *n* self-made man *m*.

self-pity [self'pit'ē] *n* apitoiement *m* sur soi-même.

self-portrait [self'pôr'trit] *n* autoportrait *m*.

self-possessed [self'pəzest'] *a* assuré(e).

self-preservation [self'prezûrvā'shən] *n* instinct *m* de conservation.

self-raising [self'rā'zing] *a* (*Brit*) = **self-rising**.

self-reliant [self'rili'ənt] *a* indépendant(e).

self-respect [self'rispekt'] *n* respect *m* de soi, amour-propre *m*.

self-respecting [self'rispekt'ing] *a* qui se respecte.

self-righteous [self'rī'chəs] *a* satisfait(e) de soi, pharisaïque.

self-rising [self'rī'zing] *a* (*US*): **~ flour** farine *f* pour gâteaux (*avec levure incorporée*).

self-sacrifice [self'sak'rəfīs] *n* abnégation *f*.

self-same [self'sām] *a* même.

self-satisfied [self'sat'isfīd] *a* content(e) de soi, suffisant(e).

self-sealing [self'sēl'ing] *a* (*envelope*) auto-collant(e).

self-service [self'sûr'vis] *a*, *n* libre-service (*m*), self-service (*m*).

self-styled [self'stīld'] *a* soi-disant *inv*.

self-sufficient [self'səfish'ənt] *a* indépendant(e).

self-supporting [self'səpôrt'ing] *a* financièrement indépendant(e).

self-taught [self'tôt'] *a* autodidacte.

self-test [self'test'] *n* (*COMPUT*) test *m* automatique.

sell, *pt*, *pp* **sold** [sel, sōld] *vt* vendre ♦ *vi* se vendre; **to ~ at** *or* **for 10 F** se vendre 10 F; **to ~ sb an idea** (*fig*) faire accepter une idée à qn.

sell off *vt* liquider.

sell out *vi*: **to ~ out (to)** (*COMM*) vendre son fonds *or* son affaire (à) ♦ *vt* vendre tout son stock de; **the tickets are all sold out** il ne reste plus de billets.

sell-by date [sel'bī dāt] n date f limite de vente.

seller [sel'ûr] n vendeur/euse, marchand/e; ~'s **market** marché m à la hausse.

selling price [sel'ing prīs] n prix m de vente.

sellotape [sel'ətāp] n ® (Brit) papier collant, scotch m ®.

sellout [sel'out] n trahison f, capitulation f; (of tickets): **it was a** ~ tous les billets ont été vendus.

selves [selvz] npl of **self**.

semantic [siman'tik] a sémantique.

semantics [siman'tiks] n sémantique f.

semaphore [sem'əfôr] n signaux mpl à bras; (RAIL) sémaphore m.

semblance [sem'bləns] n semblant m.

semen [sē'mən] n sperme m.

semester [simes'tûr] n semestre m.

semi... [sem'ē] prefix semi-, demi-; à demi, à moitié ♦ n (Brit): **semi** = **semidetached (house)**.

semiannual [sem'ēan'yōōəl] a (US) semestriel(le).

semiannually [sem'ēan'yōōəlē] ad (US) deux fois par an.

semibreve [sem'ēbrēv] n (Brit) = **whole note**.

semicircle [sem'ēsûrkəl] n demi-cercle m.

semicircular [semēsûr'kyəlûr] a en demi-cercle, semi-circulaire.

semicolon [sem'ēkōlən] n point-virgule m.

semiconductor [semēkənduk'tûr] n semi-conducteur m.

semiconscious [semēkân'chəs] a à demi conscient(e).

semidetached (house) [semēditacht' (hous')] n (Brit) maison jumelée or jumelle.

semifinal [semēfī'nəl] n demi-finale f.

seminar [sem'ənâr] n séminaire m.

seminary [sem'ənärē] n (REL: for priests) séminaire m.

semiprecious [semēpresh'əs] a semi-précieux(euse).

semiquaver [sem'ēkwāvûr] n (Brit) = sixteenth note.

semiskilled [semēskild'] a: ~ **worker** n ouvrier/ière spécialisé(e).

semitone [sem'ētōn] n (MUS) demi-ton m.

semi(trailer) [sem'ē(trā'lûr)] n (US) (camion m) semi-remorque m.

semolina [seməlē'nə] n semoule f.

Sen., sen. abbr = **senator, senior**.

senate [sen'it] n sénat m.

senator [sen'ətûr] n sénateur m.

send, pt, pp **sent** [send, sent] vt envoyer; **to** ~ **by mail** envoyer or expédier par la poste; **to** ~ **sb for sth** envoyer qn chercher qch; **to** ~ **word that** ... faire dire que ...; **she** ~**s (you) her love** elle vous adresse ses amitiés; **to** ~ **sb to sleep** endormir qn; **to** ~ **sb into fits of laughter** faire rire qn aux éclats; **to** ~ **sth flying** envoyer valser qch.

send (a)round vt (letter, document etc) faire circuler.

send away vt (letter, goods) envoyer, expédier.

send away for vt fus commander par correspondance, se faire envoyer.

send back vt renvoyer.

send for vt fus envoyer chercher; faire venir; (by mail) se faire envoyer, commander par correspondance.

send in vt (report, application, resignation) remettre.

send off vt (goods) envoyer, expédier.

send on vt (letter) faire suivre; (luggage etc: in advance) (faire) expédier à l'avance.

send out vt (invitation) envoyer (par la poste); (emit: light, heat, signals) émettre.

send up vt (person, price) faire monter.

sender [send'ûr] n expéditeur/trice.

send-off [send'ôf] n: **a good** ~ des adieux chaleureux.

Senegal [sen'əgâl] n Sénégal m.

Senegalese [senəgəlēz'] a sénégalais(e) ♦ n (pl inv) Sénégalais/e.

senile [sē'nīl] a sénile.

senility [sinil'ətē] n sénilité f.

senior [sēn'yûr] a (older) aîné(e), plus âgé(e); (of higher rank) supérieur(e) ♦ n aîné/e; (in service) personne f qui a plus d'ancienneté; **P. Jones** ~ **P. Jones** père.

senior citizen n personne âgée.

senior high school n (US) ≈ lycée m.

seniority [sēnyôr'itē] n priorité f d'âge, ancienneté f; (in rank) supériorité f (hiérarchique).

sensation [sensā'shən] n sensation f; **to create a** ~ faire sensation.

sensational [sensā'shənəl] a qui fait sensation; (marvellous) sensationnel(le).

sense [sens] n sens m; (feeling) sentiment m; (meaning) signification f; (wisdom) bon sens ♦ vt sentir, pressentir; ~**s** npl raison f; **it makes** ~ c'est logique; ~ **of humor** sens de l'humour; **there is no** ~ **in (doing) that** cela n'a pas de sens; **to come to one's** ~**s** (regain consciousness) reprendre conscience; (become reasonable) revenir à la raison; **to take leave of one's** ~**s** perdre la tête.

senseless [sens'lis] a insensé(e), stupide; (unconscious) sans connaissance.

sensibility [sensəbil'ətē] n sensibilité f; **sensibilities** npl susceptibilité f.

sensible [sen'səbəl] a sensé(e), raisonnable; (shoes etc) pratique.

sensitive [sen'sətiv] a: ~ **(to)** sensible (à); **he is very** ~ **about** it c'est un point très sensible (chez lui).

sensitivity [sensətiv'ətē] n sensibilité f.

sensual [sen'shōōəl] a sensuel(le).

sensuous [sen'shōōəs] a voluptueux(euse), sensuel(le).

sent [sent] pt, pp of **send**.

sentence [sen'təns] n (LING) phrase f; (LAW: judgment) condamnation f, sentence f; (: punishment) peine f ♦ vt: **to** ~ **sb to death/ to 5 years** condamner qn à mort/à 5 ans; **to pass** ~ **on sb** prononcer une peine contre qn.

sentiment [sen'təmənt] n sentiment m; (opinion) opinion f, avis m.

sentimental [sentəmen'təl] a sentimental(e).

sentimentality [sentəmental'itē] n sentimentalité f, sensiblerie f.

sentry [sen'trē] n sentinelle f, factionnaire m.

sentry duty n: **to be on** ~ être de faction.

Seoul [sōl] n Séoul.

separable [sep'ûrəbəl] a séparable.

separate a [sep'rit] séparé(e), indépendant(e), différent(e) ♦ vb [sep'erāt] vt séparer ♦ vi se séparer; ~ **from** distinct(e) de; **under** ~ **cover** (COMM) sous pli séparé; **to** ~ **into** diviser en.

separately [sep'ritlē] ad séparément.

separates [sep'rits] npl (clothes) coordonnés mpl.

separation [sepərā'shən] n séparation f.

Sept. abbr (= September) sept.

September [septem'bûr] n septembre m; for phrases see also **July**.

septic [sep'tik] a septique; (wound) infecté(e); **to go** ~ s'infecter.

septicemia, (Brit) **septicaemia** [septisē'mēə] n septicémie f.

septic tank n fosse f septique.

sequel [sē'kwəl] n conséquence f; séquelles fpl; (of story) suite f.

sequence [sē'kwins] n ordre m, suite f; **in** ~ par ordre, dans l'ordre, les uns après les autres; ~ **of tenses** concordance f des temps.

sequential [sikwen'chəl] a: ~ **access** (COMPUT) accès séquentiel.

sequin [sē'kwin] n paillette f.

Serbo-Croat [sûr'bōkrōat] n (LING) serbo-croate m.

serenade [särənād'] n sérénade f ♦ vt donner une sérénade à.

serene [sərēn'] a serein(e), calme, paisible.

serenity [sərən'itē] n sérénité f, calme m.

sergeant [sär'jənt] n sergent m; (POLICE) brigadier m.

sergeant major n sergent-major m.

serial [sēr'ēəl] n feuilleton m ♦ a (COMPUT: interface, printer) série inv; (: access) séquentiel(le).

serialize [sēr'ēəliz] vt publier (or adapter) en feuilleton.

serial number n numéro m de série.

series [sēr'ēz] n série f; (PUBLISHING) collection f.

serious [sēr'ēəs] a sérieux(euse); (accident etc) grave; **are you** ~ **(about it?)** parlez-vous sérieusement?

seriously [sē'rēəslē] ad sérieusement, gravement; **to take sth/sb** ~ prendre qch/qn au sérieux.

seriousness [sē'rēəsnis] n sérieux m, gravité f.

sermon [sûr'mən] n sermon m.

serrated [särā'tid] a en dents de scie.

serum [sēr'əm] n sérum m.

servant [sûr'vənt] n domestique m/f; (fig) serviteur/servante.

serve [sûrv] vt (employer etc) servir, être au service de; (purpose) servir à; (customer, food, meal) servir; (apprenticeship) faire, accomplir; (prison term) faire; purger ♦ vi (also TENNIS) servir; (be useful): **to** ~ **as/for/to do** servir de/à/à faire ♦ n (TENNIS) service m; **are you being** ~**d?** (Brit) est-ce qu'on s'occupe de vous?; **to** ~ **on a committee/jury** faire partie d'un comité/jury; **it** ~**s him right** c'est bien fait pour lui; **it** ~**s my purpose** cela fait mon affaire.

serve up vt (food) servir.

service [sûr'vis] n (gen) service m; (AUT: maintenance) révision f; (REL) office m ♦ vt

(car, washing machine) réviser; **the Armed S**~**s** npl les forces armées; **to be of** ~ **to sb**, **to do sb a** ~ rendre service à qn; **to put one's car in for a** ~ donner sa voiture à réviser; **dinner** ~ service de table.

serviceable [sûr'visəbəl] a pratique, commode.

service area n (on motorway) aire f de services.

service charge n (Brit) service m.

service industries npl les industries fpl de service, les services mpl.

serviceman [sûr'visman] n militaire m.

service station n station-service f.

serviette [sûrvēet'] n (Brit) serviette f (de table).

servile [sûr'vil] a servile.

serving cart [sûr'ving kärt] n (US) table roulante.

session [sesh'ən] n (sitting) séance f; (SCOL) année f scolaire (or universitaire); **to be in** ~ siéger, être en session or en séance.

set [set] n série f, assortiment m; (of tools etc) jeu m; (RADIO, TV) poste m; (TENNIS) set m; (group of people) cercle m, milieu m; (CINEMA) plateau m; (THEATER: stage) scène f; (: scenery) décor m; (MATH) ensemble m; (HAIRDRESSING) mise f en plis ♦ a (fixed) fixe, déterminé(e); (ready) prêt(e) ♦ vb (pt, pp **set**) vt (place) mettre, poser, placer; (table) mettre; (fix, establish) fixer; (: record) établir; (assign: task, homework) donner; (adjust) régler; (decide: rules etc) fixer, choisir; (TYP) composer ♦ vi (sun) se coucher; (jam, jelly, concrete) prendre, **to be** ~ **on doing** être résolu(e) à faire; **to be all** ~ **to do** être (fin) prêt(e) pour faire, **to be (dead)** ~ **against** être (totalement) opposé à; **he's** ~ **in his ways** il n'est pas très souple, il tient à ses habitudes; **to** ~ **to music** mettre en musique; **to** ~ **fire** mettre le feu à; **to** ~ **free** libérer; **to** ~ **sth going** déclencher qch; **to** ~ **sail** partir, prendre la mer; **a** ~ **phrase** une expression toute faite, une locution; **a** ~ **of false teeth** un dentier; **a** ~ **of dining-room furniture** une salle à manger.

set about vt fus (task) entreprendre, se mettre à; **to** ~ **about doing sth** se mettre à faire qch.

set aside vt mettre de côté.

set back vt (in time): **to** ~ **back (by)** retarder (de); (place): **a house** ~ **back from the road** une maison située en retrait de la route.

set in vi (infection, bad weather) s'installer; (complications) survenir, surgir; **the rain has** ~ **in for the day** c'est parti pour qu'il pleuve toute la journée.

set off vi se mettre en route, partir ♦ vt (bomb) faire exploser; (cause to start) déclencher; (show up well) mettre en valeur, faire valoir.

set out vi: **to** ~ **out to do** entreprendre de faire; avoir pour but or intention de faire ♦ vt (arrange) disposer; (state) présenter, exposer; **to** ~ **out (from)** partir (de).

set up vt (organization) fonder, constituer; (monument) ériger; **to** ~ **up shop** (fig) s'établir, s'installer.

setback [set'bak] n (hitch) revers m, contretemps m; (in health) rechute f.

set menu n menu m.

set square n (Brit) équerre f.

settee [setē'] n canapé m.

setting [set'ing] n cadre m; (of jewel) monture f.

settle [set'əl] vt (argument, matter, account) régler; (problem) résoudre; (MED: calm) calmer; (colonize: land) coloniser ♦ vi (bird, dust etc) se poser; (sediment) se déposer; (also: ~ **down**) s'installer, se fixer; (: become calmer) se calmer; se ranger; **to ~ to sth** se mettre sérieusement à qch; **to ~ for sth** accepter qch, se contenter de qch; **to ~ on sth** opter or se décider pour qch; **that's ~d then** alors, c'est d'accord!; **to ~ one's stomach** calmer les maux d'estomac.

settle in vi s'installer.

settle up vi: **to ~ up with sb** régler (ce que l'on doit à) qn.

settlement [set'əlmənt] n (payment) règlement m; (agreement) accord m; (colony) colonie f; (village etc) établissement m; hameau m; **in ~ of our account** (COMM) en règlement de notre compte.

settler [set'lûr] n colon m.

setup [set'up] n (arrangement) manière f dont les choses sont organisées; (situation) situation f, allure f des choses.

seven [sev'ən] num sept.

seventeen [sev'əntēn'] num dix-sept.

seventh [sev'ənth] num septième; **to be in ~ heaven** être au septième ciel.

seventy [sev'əntē] num soixante-dix.

sever [sev'ûr] vt couper, trancher; (relations) rompre.

several [sev'ûrəl] a, pronoun plusieurs (m/fpl); **~ of us** plusieurs d'entre nous; **~ times** plusieurs fois.

severance [sev'ûrəns] n (of relations) rupture f.

severance pay n indemnité f de licenciement.

severe [sivēr'] a sévère, strict(e); (serious) grave, sérieux(euse); (hard) rigoureux(euse), dur(e); (plain) sévère, austère.

severely [sivēr'lē] ad sévèrement; (wounded, ill) gravement.

severity [sivâr'itē] n sévérité f; gravité f; rigueur f.

sew [sō] pt **sewed**, pp **sewn** [sō, sōd, sōn] vt, vi coudre.

sew up vt (re)coudre; **it is all sewn up** (fig) c'est dans le sac or dans la poche.

sewage [sōō'ij] n vidange(s) f(pl).

sewer [sōō'ûr] n égout m.

sewing [sō'ing] n couture f.

sewing machine n machine f à coudre.

sewn [sōn] pp of **sew**.

sex [seks] n sexe m; **to have ~ with** avoir des rapports (sexuels) avec.

sex act n acte sexuel.

sexism [sek'sizəm] n sexisme m.

sexist [seks'ist] a sexiste.

sextet [sekstet'] n sextuor m.

sexual [sek'shōōəl] a sexuel(le); **~ assault** attentat m à la pudeur; **~ intercourse** rapports sexuels.

sexy [sek'sē] a sexy inv.

Seychelles [sāshel'] npl: **the ~** les Seychelles fpl.

SF n abbr (= science fiction) SF f.

SG n abbr (US) = **Surgeon General**.

Sgt abbr (= sergeant) Sgt.

shabbiness [shab'ēnis] n aspect miteux; mesquinerie f.

shabby [shab'ē] a miteux(euse); (behavior) mesquin(e), méprisable.

shack [shak] n cabane f, hutte f.

shackles [shak'əlz] npl chaînes fpl, entraves fpl.

shade [shād] n ombre f; (for lamp) abat-jour m inv; (of color) nuance f, ton m; (US: window ~) store m; (small quantity): **a ~ of** un soupçon de ♦ vt abriter du soleil, ombrager; **~s** npl (sunglasses) lunettes fpl de soleil; **in the ~** à l'ombre; **a ~ smaller** un tout petit peu plus petit.

shadow [shad'ō] n ombre f ♦ vt (follow) filer; **without** or **beyond a ~ of doubt** sans l'ombre d'un doute.

shadow cabinet n (Brit POL) cabinet parallèle formé par le parti qui n'est pas au pouvoir.

shadowy [shad'ōē] a ombragé(e); (dim) vague, indistinct(e).

shady [shā'dē] a ombragé(e); (fig: dishonest) louche, véreux(euse).

shaft [shaft] n (of arrow, spear) hampe f; (AUT, TECH) arbre m; (of mine) puits m; (of elevator) cage f; (of light) rayon m, trait m; **ventilator ~** conduit m d'aération or de ventilation.

shaggy [shag'ē] a hirsute; en broussaille.

shake [shāk] vb (pt **shook**, pp **shaken** [shōōk, shā'kən]) vt secouer; (bottle, cocktail) agiter; (house, confidence) ébranler ♦ vi trembler ♦ n secousse f; **to ~ one's head** (in refusal etc) dire or faire non de la tête; (in dismay) secouer la tête; **to ~ hands with sb** serrer la main à qn.

shake off vt secouer; (fig) se débarrasser de.

shake up vt secouer.

shake-up [shāk'up] n grand remaniement.

shakily [shā'kilē] ad (reply) d'une voix tremblante; (walk) d'un pas mal assuré; (write) d'une main tremblante.

shaky [shā'kē] a (hand, voice) tremblant(e); (building) branlant(e), peu solide; (memory) chancelant(e); (knowledge) incertain(e).

shale [shāl] n schiste argileux.

shall [shal] auxiliary vb: **I ~ go** j'irai.

shallot [shəlât'] n échalote f.

shallow [shal'ō] a peu profond(e); (fig) superficiel(le), qui manque de profondeur.

sham [sham] n frime f; (jewelry, furniture) imitation f ♦ a feint(e), simulé(e) ♦ vt feindre, simuler.

shambles [sham'bəlz] n confusion f, pagaïe f, fouillis m; **the economy is (in) a complete ~** l'économie est dans la confusion la plus totale.

shame [shām] n honte f ♦ vt faire honte à; **it is a ~ (that/to do)** c'est dommage (que + sub/de faire); **what a ~!** quel dommage!; **to put sb/sth to ~** (fig) faire honte à qn/qch.

shamefaced [shām'fāst] a honteux(euse), penaud(e).

shameful [shām'fəl] a honteux(euse), scandaleux(euse).

shameless [shām'lis] *a* éhonté(e), effronté(e); (*immodest*) impudique.

shampoo [shampōō'] *n* shampooing *m* ♦ *vt* faire un shampooing à; ~ **and set** shampooing et mise *f* en plis.

shamrock [sham'rák] *n* trèfle *m* (*emblème national de l'Irlande*).

shandy [shan'dē] *n* bière panachée.

shan't [shant] = **shall not**.

shanty town [shan'tē toun] *n* bidonville *m*.

SHAPE [shāp] *n abbr* (= *Supreme Headquarters Allied Powers, Europe*) quartier général des forces alliées en Europe.

shape [shāp] *n* forme *f* ♦ *vt* façonner, modeler; (*clay, stone*) donner forme à; (*statement*) formuler; (*sb's ideas, character*) former; (*sb's life*) déterminer; (*course of events*) influer sur le cours de ♦ *vi* (*also:* ~ **up:** *events*) prendre tournure; (: *person*) faire des progrès, s'en sortir; **to take** ~ prendre forme *or* tournure; **in the** ~ **of a heart** en forme de cœur; **I can't bear gardening in any** ~ **or form** je déteste le jardinage sous quelque forme que ce soit; **to get o.s. into** ~ (re)trouver la forme.

-shaped [shāpt] *suffix:* **heart**~ en forme de cœur.

shapeless [shāp'lis] *a* informe, sans forme.

shapely [shāp'lē] *a* bien proportionné(e), beau(belle).

share [shär] *n* (*thing received, contribution*) part *f*; (*COMM*) action *f* ♦ *vt* partager; (*have in common*) avoir en commun; **to** ~ **out** (**among** *or* **between**) partager (entre); **to** ~ **in** (*joy, sorrow*) prendre part à; (*profits*) participer à, avoir part à; (*work*) partager.

share capital *n* capital social.

share certificate *n* certificat *m or* titre *m* d'action.

shareholder [shär'hōldûr] *n* actionnaire *m/f*.

share index *n* indice *m* de la Bourse.

shark [shárk] *n* requin *m*.

sharp [shárp] *a* (*razor, knife*) tranchant(e), bien aiguisé(e); (*point*) aigu(ë); (*nose, chin*) pointu(e); (*outline*) net(te); (*curve, bend*) brusque; (*cold, pain*) vif(vive); (*MUS*) dièse; (*voice*) coupant(e); (*person: quick-witted*) vif(vive), éveillé(e); (: *unscrupulous*) malhonnête ♦ *n* (*MUS*) dièse *m* ♦ *ad:* **at 2 o'clock** ~ à 2 heures pile *or* tapantes; **turn** ~ **left** tournez immédiatement à gauche; **to be** ~ **with sb** être brusque avec qn; **look** ~! dépêche-toi!

sharpen [shár'pən] *vt* aiguiser; (*pencil*) tailler; (*fig*) aviver.

sharpener [shár'pənûr] *n* (*also:* **pencil** ~) taille-crayon(s) *m inv*; (*also:* **knife** ~) aiguisoir *m*.

sharp-eyed [shárp'īd] *a* à qui rien n'échappe.

sharply [shárp'lē] *ad* (*abruptly*) brusquement; (*clearly*) nettement; (*harshly*) sèchement, vertement.

sharp-tempered [shárp'tempûrd] *a* prompt(e) à se mettre en colère.

sharp-witted [shárp'wit'id] *a* à l'esprit vif, malin(igne).

shatter [shat'ûr] *vt* fracasser, briser, faire voler en éclats; (*fig: upset*) bouleverser; (:

ruin) briser, ruiner ♦ *vi* voler en éclats, se briser, se fracasser.

shattered [shat'ûrd] *a* (*overwhelmed, grief-stricken*) bouleversé(e); (*col: exhausted*) éreinté(e).

shatterproof [shat'ûrprōōf] *a* incassable.

shave [shāv] *vt* raser ♦ *vi* se raser ♦ *n:* **to have a** ~ se raser.

shaven [shā'vən] *a* (*head*) rasé(e).

shaver [shā'vûr] *n* (*also:* **electric** ~) rasoir *m* électrique.

shaving [shā'ving] *n* (*action*) rasage *m*; ~**s** *npl* (*of wood etc*) copeaux *mpl*.

shaving brush *n* blaireau *m*.

shaving cream *n* crème *f* à raser.

shaving soap *n* savon *m* à barbe.

shawl [shôl] *n* châle *m*.

she [shē] *pronoun* elle; **there** ~ **is** la voilà; ~ **elephant** *etc* éléphant *etc* femelle; *NB: for ships, countries follow the gender of your translation.*

sheaf, *pl* **sheaves** [shēf, shēvz] *n* gerbe *f*.

shear [shē'ûr] *vt* (*pt* ~**ed**, *pp* ~**ed** *or* **shorn** [shôrn]) (*sheep*) tondre.

shear off *vt* tondre; (*branch*) élaguer.

shears [shē'ûrz] *npl* (*for hedge*) cisaille(s) *f(pl)*.

sheath [shēth] *n* gaine *f*, fourreau *m*, étui *m*; (*contraceptive*) préservatif *m*.

sheathe [shēth] *vt* gainer; (*sword*) rengainer.

sheath knife *n* couteau *m* à gaine.

sheaves [shēvz] *npl of* **sheaf**.

shed [shed] *n* remise *f*, resserre *f*; (*INDUSTRY, RAIL*) hangar *m* ♦ *vt* (*pt, pp* **shed**) (*leaves, fur etc*) perdre; (*tears*) verser, répandre; **to** ~ **light on** (*problem, mystery*) faire la lumière sur.

she'd [shēd] = **she had, she would**.

sheen [shēn] *n* lustre *m*.

sheep [shēp] *n* (*pl inv*) mouton *m*.

sheepdog [shēp'dôg] *n* chien *m* de berger.

sheep farmer *n* éleveur *m* de moutons.

sheepish [shē'pish] *a* penaud(e), timide.

sheepskin [shēp'skin] *n* peau *f* de mouton.

sheepskin jacket *n* canadienne *f*.

sheer [shēr] *a* (*utter*) pur(e), pur et simple; (*steep*) à pic, abrupt(e); (*almost transparent*) extrêmement fin(e) ♦ *ad* à pic, abruptement; **by** ~ **chance** par pur hasard.

sheer curtains *npl* (*US*) voilages *mpl*.

sheet [shēt] *n* (*on bed*) drap *m*; (*of paper*) feuille *f*; (*of glass, metal*) feuille, plaque *f*.

sheet feed *n* (*on printer*) alimentation *f* en papier (feuille à feuille).

sheet lightning *n* éclair *m* en nappe(s).

sheet metal *n* tôle *f*.

sheet music *n* partition(s) *f(pl)*.

sheik(h) [shēk] *n* cheik *m*.

shelf, *pl* **shelves** [shelf, shelvz] *n* étagère *f*, rayon *m*; **set of shelves** rayonnage *m*.

shelf life *n* (*COMM*) durée *f* de conservation (avant la vente).

shell [shel] *n* (*on beach*) coquillage *m*; (*of egg, nut etc*) coquille *f*; (*explosive*) obus *m*; (*of building*) carcasse *f* ♦ *vt* (*crab, prawn etc*) décortiquer; (*peas*) écosser; (*MIL*) bombarder (d'obus).

shell out *vi* (*col*): **to** ~ **out** (**for**) casquer (pour).

she'll [shēl] = **she will, she shall.**
shellfish [shel'fish] *n* (*pl inv*) (*crab etc*) crustacé *m*; (*scallop etc*) coquillage *m*; (*pl: as food*) crustacés; coquillages.
shelter [shcl'tûr] *n* abri *m*, refuge *m* ♦ *vt* abriter, protéger; (*give lodging to*) donner asile à ♦ *vi* s'abriter, se mettre à l'abri; **to take ~ (from)** s'abriter (de).
sheltered [shel'tûrd] *a* (*life*) retiré(e), à l'abri des soucis; (*spot*) abrité(e).
shelve [shelv] *vt* (*fig*) mettre en suspens *or* en sommeil.
shelves [shelvz] *npl of* **shelf.**
shelving [shel'ving] *n* (*shelves*) rayonnage(s) *m(pl)*.
shepherd [shep'ûrd] *n* berger *m* ♦ *vt* (*guide*) guider, escorter.
shepherdess [shep'ûrdis] *n* bergère *f*.
shepherd's pie *n* ≈ hachis *m* Parmentier.
sherbet [shûr'bit] *n* (*US: dessert*) sorbet *m*; (*Brit: powder*) poudre acidulée.
sheriff [shär'if] *n* shérif *m*.
sherry [shär'ē] *n* xérès *m*, sherry *m*.
she's [shēz] = **she is, she has.**
Shetland [shet'lənd] *n* (*also:* **the ~s, the ~ Isles** *or* **Islands**) les îles *fpl* Shetland.
shield [shēld] *n* bouclier *m* ♦ *vt:* **to ~ (from)** protéger (de *or* contre).
shift [shift] *n* (*change*) changement *m*; (*of workers*) équipe *f*, poste *m* ♦ *vt* déplacer, changer de place; (*remove*) enlever ♦ *vi* changer de place, bouger; **the wind has ~ed to the south** le vent a tourné au sud; **a ~ in demand** (*COMM*) un déplacement de la demande.
shift key *n* (*on typewriter*) touche *f* de majuscule.
shiftless [shift'lis] *a* fainéant(e).
shift work *n* travail *m* par roulement; **to do ~** travailler par roulement.
shifty [shif'tē] *a* sournois(e); (*eyes*) fuyant(e).
shilling [shil'ing] *n* (*Brit*) shilling *m* (= *12 old pence; 20 in a pound*).
shilly-shally [shil'ēshalē] *vi* tergiverser, atermoyer.
shimmer [shim'ûr] *n* miroitement *m*, chatoiement *m* ♦ *vi* miroiter, chatoyer.
shin [shin] *n* tibia *m* ♦ *vi:* **to ~ up/down a tree** grimper dans un/descendre d'un arbre.
shindig [shin'dig] *n* (*col*) bamboula *f*.
shine [shīn] *n* éclat *m*, brillant *m* ♦ *vb* (*pt, pp* **shone** [shōn]) *vi* briller ♦ *vt* faire briller *or* reluire; (*flashlight*): **to ~ on** braquer sur.
shingle [shing'gəl] *n* (*on beach*) galets *mpl*; (*on roof*) bardeau *m*.
shingles [shing'gəlz] *n* (*MED*) zona *m*.
shining [shī'ning] *a* brillant(e).
shiny [shī'nē] *a* brillant(e).
ship [ship] *n* bateau *m*; (*large*) navire *m* ♦ *vt* transporter (par mer); (*send*) expédier (par mer); (*load*) charger, embarquer; **on board ~** à bord.
shipbuilder [ship'bildûr] *n* constructeur *m* de navires.
shipbuilding [ship'bilding] *n* construction navale.
ship canal *n* canal *m* maritime *or* de navigation.
ship chandler [ship chan'dlûr] *n* fournisseur

m maritime, shipchandler *m*.
shipment [ship'mənt] *n* cargaison *f*.
shipowner [ship'ōnûr] *n* armateur *m*.
shipper [ship'ûr] *n* affréteur *m*, expéditeur *m*.
shipping [ship'ing] *n* (*ships*) navires *mpl*; (*traffic*) navigation *f*.
shipping agent *n* agent *m* maritime.
shipping company *n* compagnie *f* de navigation.
shipping lane *n* couloir *m* de navigation.
shipping line *n* = **shipping company.**
shipshape [ship'shāp] *a* en ordre impeccable.
shipwreck [ship'rek] *n* épave *f*; (*event*) naufrage *m* ♦ *vt:* **to be ~ed** faire naufrage.
shipyard [ship'yârd] *n* chantier naval.
shirk [shûrk] *vt* esquiver, se dérober à.
shirt [shûrt] *n* chemise *f*; **in ~ sleeves** en bras de chemise.
shit [shit] *excl* (*col!*) merde (*!*).
shiver [shiv'ûr] *n* frisson *m* ♦ *vi* frissonner.
shoal [shōl] *n* (*Brit: of fish*) banc *m*.
shock [shâk] *n* (*impact*) choc *m*, heurt *m*; (*ELEC*) secousse *f*, décharge *f*; (*emotional*) choc; (*MED*) commotion *f*, choc ♦ *vt* (*scandalize*) choquer, scandaliser; (*upset*) bouleverser; **suffering from ~** (*MED*) commotionné(e); **it gave us a ~** ça nous a fait un choc; **it came as a ~ to hear that ...** nous avons appris avec stupeur que ....
shock absorber [shâk' absôrb'ûr] *n* amortisseur *m*.
shocking [shâk'ing] *a* choquant(e), scandaleux(euse); (*weather, handwriting*) épouvantable.
shockproof [shâk'prōōf] *a* anti-choc *inv*.
shock therapy, shock treatment *n* (*MED*) (traitement *m* par) électrochoc(s) *m(pl)*.
shod [shâd] *pt, pp of* **shoe; well-~** bien chaussé(e).
shoddy [shâd'ē] *a* de mauvaise qualité, mal fait(e).
shoe [shōō] *n* chaussure *f*, soulier *m*; (*also:* **horse~**) fer *m* à cheval; (*also:* **brake ~**) mâchoire *f* de frein ♦ *vt* (*pt, pp* **shod** [shâd]) (*horse*) ferrer.
shoe brush *n* brosse *f* à chaussures.
shoehorn [shōō'hôrn] *n* chausse-pied *m*.
shoelace [shōō'lâs] *n* lacet *m* (de soulier).
shoemaker [shōō'mâkûr] *n* cordonnier *m*, fabricant *m* de chaussures.
shoe polish *n* cirage *m*.
shoe shop *n* magasin *m* de chaussures.
shoestring [shōō'string] *n:* **on a ~** (*fig*) avec un budget dérisoire; avec des moyens très restreints.
shoetree [shōō'trē] *n* embauchoir *m*.
shone [shōn] *pt, pp of* **shine.**
shoo [shōō] *excl* (allez,) ouste! ♦ *vt* (*also:* **~ away, ~ off**) chasser.
shook [shōōk] *pt of* **shake.**
shoot [shōōt] *n* (*on branch, seedling*) pousse *f*; (*shooting party*) partie *f* de chasse ♦ *vb* (*pt, pp* **shot** [shât]) *vt* (*game: Brit*) chasser; tirer; abattre; (*person*) blesser (*or* tuer) d'un coup de fusil (*or* de revolver); (*execute*) fusiller; (*CINEMA*) tourner ♦ *vi* (*with gun, bow*): **to ~ (at)** tirer (sur); (*SOCCER*) shooter, tirer; **to ~ past sb** passer en flèche devant qn; **to ~ in/out** entrer/sortir comme

une flèche.
shoot down vt (plane) abattre.
shoot up vi (fig) monter en flèche.
shooting [shoo'ting] n (shots) coups mpl de feu; (attack) fusillade f; (: murder) homicide m (à l'aide d'une arme à feu); (HUNTING) chasse f; (CINEMA) tournage m.
shooting range n stand m de tir.
shooting star n étoile filante.
shop [shâp] n magasin m; (workshop) atelier m ♦ vi (also: **go ~ping**) faire ses courses or ses achats; **repair** ~ atelier de réparations; **to talk** ~ (fig) parler boutique.
shop around vi faire le tour des magasins (pour comparer les prix); (fig) se renseigner avant de choisir or decider.
shop assistant n (Brit) vendeur/euse.
shop floor n (fig) ouvriers mpl.
shopkeeper [shâp'kēpûr] n marchand/e, commerçant/e.
shoplift [shâp'lift] vi voler à l'étalage.
shoplifter [shâp'liftûr] n voleur/euse à l'étalage.
shoplifting [shâp'lifting] n vol m à l'étalage.
shopper [shâp'ûr] n personne f qui fait ses courses, acheteur/euse.
shopping [shâp'ing] n (goods) achats mpl, provisions fpl.
shopping bag n sac m (à provisions).
shopping cart n (US) caddie m.
shopping center n centre commercial.
shopping mall n centre commercial.
shop-soiled [shâp'soild] a (Brit) = **shopworn**.
shop steward n (INDUSTRY) délégué/e syndical(e).
shop window n vitrine f.
shopworn [shâp'wôrn] a (US) défraichi(e), qui a fait la vitrine.
shore [shôr] n (of sea, lake) rivage m, rive f ♦ vt: **to** ~ **(up)** étayer; **on** ~ à terre.
shore leave n (NAUT) permission f à terre.
shorn [shôrn] pp of **shear**; ~ **of** dépouillé(e) de.
short [shôrt] a (not long) court(e); (soon finished) court, bref(brève); (person, step) petit(e); (curt) brusque, sec(sèche); (insufficient) insuffisant(e) ♦ n (also: ~ **film**) court métrage; **to be** ~ **of sth** être à court de or manquer de qch; **to be in** ~ **supply** manquer, être difficile à trouver; **I'm 3** ~ il m'en manque 3; **in** ~ bref; en bref; ~ **of doing** à moins de faire; **everything** ~ **of** tout sauf; **it is** ~ **for** c'est l'abréviation or le diminutif de; **a** ~ **time ago** il y a peu de temps; **in the** ~ **term** à court terme; **to cut** ~ (speech, visit) abréger, écourter; (person) couper la parole à; **to fall** ~ **of** sth être à la hauteur de; **to stop** ~ s'arrêter net; **to stop** ~ **of** ne pas aller jusqu'à.
shortage [shôr'tij] n manque m, pénurie f.
shortbread [shôrt'bred] n ≈ sablé m.
shortchange [shôrt'chânj] vt: **to** ~ **sb** ne pas rendre assez à qn.
short circuit n court-circuit m.
short-circuit [shôrtsûr'kit] vt court-circuiter ♦ vi se mettre en court-circuit.
shortcoming [shôrt'kuming] n défaut m.
short(crust) pastry [shôrt'(krust) pâs'trē] n (Brit) pâte brisée.

shortcut [shôrt'kut] n raccourci m.
shorten [shôr'tən] vt raccourcir; (text, visit) abréger.
shortening [shôr'təning] n (CULIN) matière grasse.
shortfall [shôrt'fôl] n déficit m.
shorthand [shôrt'hand] n sténo(graphie) f; **to take sth down in** ~ prendre qch en sténo.
shorthand notebook n bloc m sténo.
shorthand typist n (Brit) sténodactylo m/f.
short list n (for job) liste f des candidats sélectionnés.
short-lived [shôrt'livd'] a de courte durée.
shortly [shôrt'lē] ad bientôt, sous peu.
shortness [shôrt'nis] n brièveté f.
shorts [shôrts] npl (also: **a pair of** ~) un short.
shortsighted [shôrt'sī'tid] a myope; (fig) qui manque de clairvoyance.
short-staffed [shôrt'staft'] a à court de personnel.
short story n nouvelle f.
short-tempered [shôrt'tempûrd] a qui s'emporte facilement.
short-term [shôrt'tûrm'] a (effect) à court terme.
short time n: **to work** ~, **to be on** ~ (INDUSTRY) être en chômage partiel, travailler à horaire réduit.
short wave n (RADIO) ondes courtes.
shot [shât] pt, pp of **shoot** ♦ n coup m (de feu); (shotgun pellets) plombs mpl; (person) tireur m; (try) coup, essai m; (MED) piqûre f; (PHOT) photo f; **to fire a** ~ **at sb/sth** tirer sur qn/qch; **to have a** ~ **at (doing)** sth essayer de faire qch; **like a** ~ comme une flèche; (very readily) sans hésiter; **to get** ~ **of sb/sth** (col) se débarrasser de qn/qch; **a big** ~ (col) un gros bonnet.
shotgun [shât'gun] n fusil m de chasse.
should [shood] auxiliary vb: **I** ~ **go now** je devrais partir maintenant; **he** ~ **be there now** il devrait être arrivé maintenant; ~ **he phone** ... si jamais il téléphone ....
shoulder [shol'dûr] n épaule f; (Brit: of road): **hard** ~ accotement m ♦ vt (fig) endosser, se charger de; **to look over one's** ~ regarder derrière soi (en tournant la tête); **to rub** ~s **with sb** (fig) côtoyer qn; **to give sb the cold** ~ (fig) battre froid à qn.
shoulder bag n sac m à bandoulière.
shoulder blade n omoplate f.
shoulder strap n bretelle f.
shouldn't [shood'ənt] = **should not**.
shout [shout] n cri m ♦ vt crier ♦ vi crier, pousser des cris; **to give sb a** ~ appeler qn.
shout down vt huer.
shouting [shout'ing] n cris mpl.
shove [shuv] vt pousser; (col: put): **to** ~ **sth in** fourrer or ficher qch dans ♦ n poussée f; **he** ~**d me out of the way** il m'a écarté en me poussant.
shove off vi (NAUT) pousser au large; (fig: col) ficher le camp.
shovel [shuv'əl] n pelle f ♦ vt pelleter, enlever (or enfourner) à la pelle.
show [sho] n (of emotion) manifestation f, démonstration f; (semblance) semblant m, apparence f; (exhibition) exposition f, salon

m; (*THEATER*) spectacle *m*, représentation *f*; (*CINEMA*) séance *f* ♦ *vb* (*pt* ~**ed**, *pp* **shown** [shŏd, shŏn]) *vt* montrer; (*courage etc*) faire preuve de, manifester; (*exhibit*) exposer ♦ *vi* se voir, être visible; **to ~ sb to his seat/to the door** accompagner qn jusqu'à sa place/la porte; **to ~ a profit/loss** (*COMM*) indiquer un bénéfice/une perte; **it just goes to ~ that** ... ça prouve bien que ...; **to ask for a ~ of hands** demander que l'on vote à main levée; **to be on ~** être exposé(e); **it's just for ~** c'est juste pour l'effet; **who's running the ~ here?** (*col*) qui est-ce qui commande ici? **show in** *vt* faire entrer.

show off *vi* (*pej*) crâner ♦ *vt* (*display*) faire valoir; (*pej*) faire étalage de.

show out *vt* reconduire à la porte.

show up *vi* (*stand out*) ressortir; (*col: turn up*) se montrer ♦ *vt* démontrer; (*unmask*) démasquer, dénoncer.

show business *n* le monde du spectacle.

showcase [shŏ'kās] *n* vitrine *f*.

showdown [shŏ'doun] *n* épreuve *f* de force.

shower [shou'ûr] *n* (*also*: ~ **bath**) douche *f*; (*rain*) averse *f*; (*of stones etc*) pluie *f*, grêle *f*; (*US: party*) réunion organisée pour la remise de cadeaux ♦ *vi* prendre une douche, se doucher ♦ *vt*: **to ~ sb with** (*gifts etc*) combler qn de; (*abuse etc*) accabler qn de; (*missiles*) bombarder qn de; **to have** *or* **take a ~** prendre une douche, se doucher.

shower cap *n* bonnet *m* de douche.

showerproof [shou'ûrprŏof] *a* imperméable.

showery [shou'ûrē] *a* (*weather*) pluvieux(euse).

showground [shŏ'ground] *n* (*Brit*) champ *m* de foire.

showing [shŏ'ing] *n* (*of film*) projection *f*.

show jumping [shŏ' jum'ping] *n* concours *m* hippique.

showman [shŏ'mən] *n* (*at fair, circus*) forain *m*; (*fig*) comédien *m*.

showmanship [shŏ'mənship] *n* art *m* de la mise en scène.

shown [shŏn] *pp of* **show**.

show-off [shŏ'ôf] *n* (*col: person*) crâneur/euse, m'as-tu-vu/e.

showpiece [shŏ'pēs] *n* (*of exhibition etc*) joyau *m*, clou *m*; **that hospital is a ~** cet hôpital est un modèle du genre.

showroom [shŏ'rŏom] *n* magasin *m or* salle *f* d'exposition.

showy [shŏ'ē] *a* tapageur(euse).

shrank [shrangk] *pt of* **shrink**.

shrapnel [shrap'nəl] *n* éclats *mpl* d'obus.

shred [shred] *n* (*gen pl*) lambeau *m*, petit morceau; (*fig: of truth, evidence*) parcelle *f* ♦ *vt* mettre en lambeaux, déchirer; (*documents*) détruire; (*CULIN*) râper; couper en lanières.

shredder [shred'ûr] *n* (*for vegetables*) râpeur *m*; (*for documents, papers*) déchiqueteuse *f*.

shrewd [shrŏod] *a* astucieux(euse), perspicace.

shrewdness [shrŏod'nis] *n* perspicacité *f*.

shriek [shrēk] *n* cri perçant *or* aigu, hurlement *m* ♦ *vt, vi* hurler, crier.

shrift [shrift] *n*: **to give sb short ~** expédier qn sans ménagements.

shrill [shril] *a* perçant(e), aigu(ë), strident(e).

shrimp [shrimp] *n* crevette grise.

shrine [shrīn] *n* châsse *f*; (*place*) lieu *m* de pèlerinage.

shrink [shringk], *pt* **shrank**, *pp* **shrunk** [shringk, shrangk, shrungk] *vi* rétrécir; (*fig*) se réduire; se contracter ♦ *vt* (*wool*) (faire) rétrécir ♦ *n* (*col: pej*) psychanalyste *m/f*; **to ~ from (doing) sth** reculer devant (la pensée de faire) qch.

shrinkage [shringk'ij] *n* (*of clothes*) rétrécissement *m*.

shrink-wrap [shringk'rap] *vt* emballer sous film plastique.

shrivel [shriv'əl] (*also*: ~ **up**) *vt* ratatiner, flétrir ♦ *vi* se ratatiner, se flétrir.

shroud [shroud] *n* linceul *m* ♦ *vt*: ~**ed in mystery** enveloppé(e) de mystère.

Shrove Tuesday [shrŏv tŏoz'dā] *n* (le) Mardi gras.

shrub [shrub] *n* arbuste *m*.

shrubbery [shrub'ûrē] *n* massif *m* d'arbustes.

shrug [shrug] *n* haussement *m* d'épaules ♦ *vt, vi*: **to ~ (one's shoulders)** hausser les épaules.

shrug off *vt* faire fi de; (*cold, illness*) se débarrasser de.

shrunk [shrungk] *pp of* **shrink**.

shrunken [shrungk'ən] *a* ratatiné(e).

shudder [shud'ûr] *n* frisson *m*, frémissement *m* ♦ *vi* frissonner, frémir.

shuffle [shuf'əl] *vt* (*cards*) battre; **to ~ (one's feet)** traîner les pieds.

shun [shun] *vt* éviter, fuir.

shunt [shunt] *vt* (*RAIL: direct*) aiguiller; (: *divert*) détourner ♦ *vi*: **to ~ (to and fro)** faire la navette.

shunting [shun'ting] *n* (*RAIL*) triage *m*.

shush [shush] *excl* chut!

shut, *pt, pp* **shut** [shut] *vt* fermer ♦ *vi* (se) fermer.

shut down *vt* fermer définitivement; (*machine*) arrêter ♦ *vi* fermer définitivement.

shut off *vt* couper, arrêter.

shut out *vt* (*person, cold*) empêcher d'entrer; (*noise*) éviter d'entendre; (*block: view*) boucher; (: *memory of sth*) chasser de son esprit.

shut up *vi* (*col: keep quiet*) se taire ♦ *vt* (*close*) fermer; (*silence*) faire taire.

shutdown [shut'doun] *n* fermeture *f*.

shutter [shut'ûr] *n* volet *m*; (*PHOT*) obturateur *m*.

shuttle [shut'əl] *n* navette *f*; (*also*: ~ **service**) (service *m* de) navette *f* ♦ *vi* (*vehicle, person*) faire la navette ♦ *vt* (*passengers*) transporter par un système de navette.

shuttlecock [shut'əlkâk] *n* volant *m* (*de badminton*).

shy [shī] *a* timide; **to fight ~ of** se dérober devant; **to be ~ of doing sth** hésiter à faire qch, ne pas oser faire qch ♦ *vi*: **to ~ away from doing sth** (*fig*) craindre de faire qch.

shyness [shī'nis] *n* timidité *f*.

Siam [sīam'] *n* Siam *m*.

Siamese [sīəmēz'] *a*: ~ **cat** chat siamois; ~ **twins** (frères *mpl*) siamois, (sœurs *fpl*) siamoises.

Siberia [sībē'rēə] *n* Sibérie *f*.

siblings [sib'lingz] *npl* (*formal*) enfants *mpl* d'un même couple.
Sicilian [sisil'yən] *a* sicilien(ne) ♦ *n* Sicilien/ne.
Sicily [sis'ilē] *n* Sicile *f*.
sick [sik] *a* (*ill*) malade; (*vomiting*): **to be ~** vomir; (*humor*) noir(e), macabre; **to feel ~ to one's stomach** avoir envie de vomir, avoir mal au cœur; **to fall ~** tomber malade; **to be (off) ~** être absent(e) pour cause de maladie; **a ~ person** un(e) malade; **to be ~ of** (*fig*) en avoir assez de.
sick bay *n* infirmerie *f*.
sick benefit *n* (*US*) (prestations *fpl* de l')assurance-maladie *f*.
sicken [sik'ən] *vt* écœurer.
sickening [sik'əning] *a* (*fig*) écœurant(e), révoltant(e), répugnant(e).
sickle [sik'əl] *n* faucille *f*.
sick leave *n* congé *m* de maladie.
sickly [sik'lē] *a* maladif(ive), souffreteux(euse); (*causing nausea*) écœurant(e).
sickness [sik'nis] *n* maladie *f*; (*vomiting*) vomissement(s) *m(pl)*.
sickness benefit *n* (Brit) = **sick benefit**.
sick pay *n* indemnité *f* de maladie.
sickroom [sik'rōōm] *n* infirmerie *f*.
side [sīd] *n* côté *m*; (*of animal*) flanc *m*; (*of lake, road*) bord *m*; (*of mountain*) versant *m*; (*fig: aspect*) côté, aspect *m*; (*team: SPORT*) équipe *f* ♦ *cpd* (*door, entrance*) latéral(e) ♦ *vi*: **to ~ with sb** prendre le parti de qn, se ranger du côté de qn; **by the ~ of** au bord de; **~ by ~** côte à côte; **the right/wrong ~** le bon/mauvais côté, l'endroit/l'envers *m*; **they are on our ~** ils sont avec nous; **from all ~s** de tous côtés; **to take ~s (with)** prendre parti (pour); **a ~ of beef** ≈ un quartier de bœuf.
sideboard [sīd'bôrd] *n* buffet *m*.
sideburns [sīd'bûrnz] *npl* (*whiskers*) pattes *fpl*.
sidecar [sīd'kâr] *n* side-car *m*.
side dish *n* (plat *m* d')accompagnement *m*.
side drum *n* (*MUS*) tambour plat, caisse claire.
side effect *n* (*MED*) effet *m* secondaire.
sidekick [sīd'kik] *n* (*col*) sous-fifre *m*.
sidelight [sīd'līt] *n* (*AUT*) veilleuse *f*.
sideline [sīd'līn] *n* (*SPORT*) (ligne *f* de) touche *f*; (*fig*) activité *f* secondaire.
sidelong [sīd'lông] *a*: **to give sb a ~ glance** regarder qn du coin de l'œil.
side plate *n* petite assiette.
side road *n* petite route, route transversale.
sidesaddle [sīd'sadəl] *ad* en amazone.
sideshow [sīd'shō] *n* attraction *f*.
sidestep [sīd'step] *vt* (*question*) éluder; (*problem*) éviter ♦ *vi* (*BOXING etc*) esquiver.
side street *n* rue transversale.
sidetrack [sīd'trak] *vt* (*fig*) faire dévier de son sujet.
sidewalk [sīd'wôk] *n* (*US*) trottoir *m*.
sideways [sīd'wāz] *ad* de côté.
siding [sī'ding] *n* (*RAIL*) voie *f* de garage.
sidle [sī'dəl] *vi*: **to ~ up (to)** s'approcher furtivement (de).
siege [sēj] *n* siège *m*; **to lay ~ to** assiéger.
siege economy *n* économie *f* de (temps de) siège.

Sierra Leone [sēăr'ə lēōn'] *n* Sierra Leone *f*.
sieve [siv] *n* tamis *m*, passoire *f* ♦ *vt* tamiser, passer (au tamis).
sift [sift] *vt* passer au tamis *or* au crible; (*fig*) passer au crible ♦ *vi* (*fig*): **to ~ through** passer en revue.
sigh [sī] *n* soupir *m* ♦ *vi* soupirer, pousser un soupir.
sight [sīt] *n* (*faculty*) vue *f*; (*spectacle*) spectacle *m*; (*on gun*) mire *f* ♦ *vt* apercevoir; **in ~** visible; (*fig*) en vue; **out of ~** hors de vue; **on ~** (*COMM*) à vue; **at first ~** à première vue, au premier abord; **I know her by ~** je la connais de vue; **to catch ~ of sb/sth** apercevoir qn/qch; **to lose ~ of sb/ sth** perdre qn/qch de vue; **to set one's ~s on sth** jeter son dévolu sur qch.
sighted [sī'tid] *a* qui voit; **partially ~** qui a un certain degré de vision.
sightseeing [sīt'sēing] *n* tourisme *m*; **to go ~** faire du tourisme.
sightseer [sīt'sēr] *n* touriste *m/f*.
sign [sīn] *n* (*gen*) signe *m*; (*with hand etc*) signe, geste *m*; (*notice*) panneau *m*, écriteau *m*; (*also: road ~*) panneau de signalisation ♦ *vt* signer; **as a ~ of** en signe de; **it's a good/bad ~** c'est bon/mauvais signe; **plus/ minus ~** signe plus/moins; **there's no ~ of a change of mind** rien ne laisse présager un revirement; **he was showing ~s of improvement** il commençait visiblement à faire des progrès; **to ~ one's name** signer.
sign away *vt* (*rights etc*) renoncer officiellement à.
sign in *vi* signer le registre (en arrivant).
sign off *vi* (*RADIO, TV*) terminer l'émission.
sign on *vi* (*as unemployed*) s'inscrire au chômage; (*enrol*): **to ~ on for a course** s'inscrire pour un cours ♦ *vt* (*MIL*) engager; (*employee*) embaucher.
sign out *vi* signer le registre (en partant).
sign over *vt*: **to ~ sth over to sb** céder qch par écrit à qn.
sign up (*MIL*) *vt* engager ♦ *vi* s'engager.
signal [sig'nəl] *n* signal *m* ♦ *vi* (*AUT*) mettre son clignotant ♦ *vt* (*person*) faire signe à; (*message*) communiquer par signaux; **to ~ a left/right turn** (*AUT*) indiquer *or* signaler que l'on tourne à gauche/droite; **to ~ to sb (to do sth)** faire signe à qn (de faire qch).
signal box *n* (Brit *RAIL*) poste *m* d'aiguillage.
signalman [sig'nəlmən] *n* (*RAIL*) aiguilleur *m*.
signatory [sig'nətôrē] *n* signataire *m/f*.
signature [sig'nəchûr] *n* signature *f*.
signature tune *n* indicatif musical.
signet ring [sig'nit ring] *n* chevalière *f*.
significance [signif'əkəns] *n* signification *f*; importance *f*; **that is of no ~** ceci n'a pas d'importance.
significant [signif'ikənt] *a* significatif(ive); (*important*) important(e), considérable.
significantly [signif'ikəntlē] *ad* (*improve, increase*) sensiblement; (*smile*) d'un air entendu, éloquemment; **~, ...** fait significatif, ...
signify [sig'nəfī] *vt* signifier.
sign language *n* langage *m* par signes.
signpost [sīn'pōst] *n* poteau indicateur.
silage [sī'lij] *n* (*fodder*) fourrage vert; (*meth-*

od) ensilage *m*.

silence [sī'ləns] *n* silence *m* ♦ *vt* faire taire, réduire au silence.

silencer [sī'lənsûr] *n* (*on gun*, *Brit* AUT) silencieux *m*.

silent [sī'lənt] *a* silencieux(euse); (*film*) muet(te); **to keep** *or* **remain** ~ garder le silence, ne rien dire.

silently [sī'ləntlē] *ad* silencieusement.

silent partner *n* (*US* COMM) bailleur *m* de fonds, commanditaire *m*.

silhouette [silōōet'] *n* silhouette *f* ♦ *vt*: ~d **against** se profilant sur, se découpant contre.

silicon [sil'ikən] *n* silicium *m*.

silicon chip [sil'ikən chip'] *n* puce *f* électronique.

silicone [sil'əkōn] *n* silicone *f*.

silk [silk] *n* soie *f* ♦ *cpd* de *or* en soie.

silky [sil'kē] *a* soyeux(euse).

sill [sil] *n* (*also*: **window**~) rebord *m* (de la fenêtre); (*of door*) seuil *m*; (AUT) bas *m* de marche.

silly [sil'ē] *a* stupide, sot(te), bête; **to do something** ~ faire une bêtise.

silo [sī'lō] *n* silo *m*.

silt [silt] *n* vase *f*; limon *m*.

silver [sil'vûr] *n* argent *m*; (*money*) monnaie *f* (en pièces d'argent); (*also*: ~**ware**) argenterie *f* ♦ *cpd* d'argent, en argent.

silver foil *n* papier *m* d'argent *or* d'étain.

silver-plated [sil'vûrplā'tid] *a* plaqué(e) argent.

silversmith [sil'vûrsmith] *n* orfèvre *m/f*.

silverware [sil'vûrwär] *n* argenterie *f*.

silver wedding (anniversary) *n* noces *fpl* d'argent.

silvery [sil'vûrē] *a* argenté(e).

similar [sim'əlûr] *a*: ~ **(to)** semblable (à).

similarity [siməlar'itē] *n* ressemblance *f*, similarité *f*.

similarly [sim'əlûrlē] *ad* de la même façon, de même.

simile [sim'əlē] *n* comparaison *f*.

simmer [sim'ûr] *vi* cuire à feu doux, mijoter.

simmer down *vi* (*fig*: *col*) se calmer.

simper [sim'pûr] *vi* minauder.

simpering [sim'pûring] *a* stupide.

simple [sim'pəl] *a* simple; **the** ~ **truth** la vérité pure et simple.

simple interest *n* (MATH, COMM) intérêts *mpl* simples.

simple-minded [sim'pəlmīn'did] *a* simplet(te), simple d'esprit.

simpleton [sim'pəltən] *n* nigaud/e, niais/e.

simplicity [simplis'ətē] *n* simplicité *f*.

simplification [simpləfəkā'shən] *n* simplification *f*.

simplify [sim'pləfī] *vt* simplifier.

simply [sim'plē] *ad* simplement; (*without fuss*) avec simplicité.

simulate [sim'yəlāt] *vt* simuler, feindre.

simulation [simyəlā'shən] *n* simulation *f*.

simultaneous [sīməltā'nēəs] *a* simultané(e).

simultaneously [sīməltā'nēəslē] *ad* simultanément.

sin [sin] *n* péché *m* ♦ *vi* pécher.

Sinai [sī'nī] *n* Sinaï *m*.

since [sins] *ad*, *prep* depuis ♦ *cj* (*time*) depuis que; (*because*) puisque, étant donné que,

comme; ~ **then** depuis ce moment-là; ~ **Monday** depuis lundi; **(ever)** ~ **I arrived** depuis mon arrivée, depuis que je suis arrivé.

sincere [sinsēr'] *a* sincère.

sincerely [sinsēr'lē] *ad* sincèrement; ~ **yours**, (*Brit*) **yours** ~ (*at end of letter*) veuillez agréer, Monsieur (*or* Madame), l'expression de mes sentiments distingués *or* les meilleurs.

sincerity [sinsär'itē] *n* sincérité *f*.

sine [sīn] *n* (MATH) sinus *m*.

sinew [sin'yōō] *n* tendon *m*; ~**s** *npl* muscles *mpl*.

sinful [sin'fəl] *a* coupable.

sing [sing], *pt* **sang**, *pp* **sung** [sing, sang, sung] *vt*, *vi* chanter.

Singapore [sing'gəpôr] *n* Singapour *m*.

singe [sinj] *vt* brûler légèrement; (*clothes*) roussir.

singer [sing'ûr] *n* chanteur/euse.

Singhalese [singəlēz'] *a* = **Sinhalese**.

singing [sing'ing] *n* (*of person*, *bird*) chant *m*; façon *f* de chanter; (*of kettle*, *bullet*, *in ears*) sifflement *m*.

single [sing'gəl] *a* seul(e), unique; (*unmarried*) célibataire; (*not double*) simple ♦ *n* (*Brit*: *also*: ~ **ticket**) aller *m* (simple); (*record*) 45 tours *m*; **not a** ~ **one was left** il n'en est pas resté un(e) seul(e); **every** ~ **day** chaque jour sans exception.

single out *vt* choisir; distinguer.

single bed *n* lit à une place.

single-breasted [sing'gəlbres'tid] *a* droit(e).

single file *n*: **in** ~ en file indienne.

single-handed [sing'gəlhan'did] *ad* tout(e) seul(e), sans (aucune) aide.

single-minded [sing'gəlmīn'did] *a* résolu(e), tenace.

single parent *n* parent unique (*or* célibataire).

single room *n* chambre *f* à un lit *or* pour une personne.

singles [sing'gəlz] *npl* (TENNIS) simple *m*; (*US*: *single people*) célibataires *m/fpl*.

singly [sing'glē] *ad* séparément.

singsong [sing'sông] *a* (*tone*) chantant(e).

singular [sing'gyəlûr] *a* singulier(ière); (*odd*) singulier, étrange; (LING) (au) singulier, du singulier ♦ *n* (LING) singulier *m*; **in the feminine** ~ au féminin singulier.

singularly [sing'gyəlûrlē] *ad* singulièrement; étrangement.

Sinhalese [sinhəlēz'] *a* cingalais(e).

sinister [sin'istûr] *a* sinistre.

sink [singk] *n* évier *m* ♦ *vb* (*pt* **sank**, *pp* **sunk** [sangk, sungk]) *vt* (*ship*) (faire) couler, faire sombrer; (*foundations*) creuser; (*piles etc*): **to** ~ **sth into** enfoncer qch dans ♦ *vi* couler, sombrer; (*ground etc*) s'affaisser; **he sank into a chair/the mud** il s'est enfoncé dans un fauteuil/la boue; **a** ~**ing feeling** un serrement de cœur.

sink in *vi* s'enfoncer, pénétrer; (*explanation*): **it took a long time to** ~ **in** il a fallu longtemps pour que ça rentre.

sinking fund [sing'king fund] *n* fonds *mpl* d'amortissement.

sink unit *n* bloc-évier *m*.

sinner [sin'ûr] *n* pécheur/eresse.

Sino- [sī'nō] *prefix* sino-.
sinuous [sin'yŏŏəs] *a* sinueux(euse).
sinus [sī'nəs] *n* (*ANAT*) sinus *m inv*.
sip [sip] *n* petite gorgée ♦ *vt* boire à petites gorgées.
siphon [sī'fən] *n* siphon *m* ♦ *vt* (*also*: ~ **off**) siphonner; (: *fig: funds*) transférer; (: *illegally*) détourner.
sir [sûr] *n* monsieur *m*; **S~ John Smith** sir John Smith; **yes ~** oui Monsieur; **Dear S~** (*in letter*) Monsieur.
siren [sī'rən] *n* sirène *f*.
sirloin [sûr'loin] *n* aloyau *m*.
sirloin steak [sûr'loin stāk'] *n* bifteck *m* dans l'aloyau.
sirocco [sərâk'ō] *n* sirocco *m*.
sisal [sī'səl] *n* sisal *m*.
sissy [sis'ē] *n* (*col: coward*) poule mouillée.
sister [sis'tûr] *n* sœur *f*; (*nun*) religieuse *f*, (bonne) sœur; (*Brit: nurse*) infirmière *f* en chef ♦ *cpd*: ~ **organization** organisation *f* sœur; ~ **ship** sister(-)ship *m*.
sister-in-law [sis'tûrinlô] *n* belle-sœur *f*.
sit, *pt*, *pp* **sat** [sit, sat] *vi* s'asseoir; (*assembly*) être en séance, siéger; (*for painter*) poser; (*dress etc*) tomber ♦ *vt* (*exam*) passer, se présenter à; **to ~ on a committee** faire partie d'un comité; **to ~ tight** ne pas bouger.
sit about *vi* (*Brit*) = **sit around**.
sit around *vi* être assis(e) *or* rester à ne rien faire.
sit back *vi* (*in seat*) bien s'installer, se carrer.
sit down *vi* s'asseoir; **to be ~ting down** être assis(e).
sit in *vi*: **to ~ in on a discussion** assister à une discussion.
sit up *vi* s'asseoir; (*not go to bed*) rester debout, ne pas se coucher.
sitcom [sit'kâm] *n abbr* (*TV*: = *situation comedy*) série *f* comique.
sit-down [sit'doun] *a*: **a ~ strike** une grève sur le tas; **a ~ meal** un repas assis.
site [sīt] *n* emplacement *m*, site *m*; (*also*: **building ~**) chantier *m* ♦ *vt* placer.
sit-in [sit'in] *n* (*demonstration*) sit-in *m inv*, occupation *f* de locaux.
siting [sī'ting] *n* (*location*) emplacement *m*.
sitter [sit'ûr] *n* (*also*: **baby~**) baby-sitter *m/f*.
sitting [sit'ing] *n* (*of assembly etc*) séance *f*; (*in canteen*) service *m*.
sitting member *n* (*POL*) parlementaire *m/f* en exercice.
sitting room *n* salon *m*.
situate [sich'ŏŏāt] *vt* situer.
situated [sich'ŏŏātid] *a* situé(e).
situation [sichŏŏā'shən] *n* situation *f*.
situation comedy *n* (*THEATER*) comédie *f* de situation.
six [siks] *num* six.
sixteen [siks'tēn'] *num* seize.
sixteenth note [siks'tēnth' nōt] *n* (*US*) double croche *f*.
sixth [siksth] *a* sixième; **the upper/lower ~** (*Brit SCOL*) la terminale/la première.
sixty [siks'tē] *num* soixante.
size [sīz] *n* dimensions *fpl*; (*of person*) taille *f*; (*of estate, area*) étendue *f*; (*of problem*) ampleur *f*; (*of company*) importance *f*; (*of*

clothing) taille; (*of shoes*) pointure *f*; (*glue*) colle *f*; **I take ~ 14** (*of dress etc*) ≈ je prends du 42 *or* la taille 42; **the small/large ~** (*of soap powder etc*) le petit/grand modèle; **it's the ~ of ...** c'est de la taille (*or* grosseur) de ..., c'est grand (*or* gros) comme ...; **cut to ~** découpé(e) aux dimensions voulues.
size up *vt* juger, jauger.
sizeable [sī'zəbəl] *a* assez grand(e) *or* gros(se); assez important(e).
sizzle [siz'əl] *vi* grésiller.
SK *abbr* (*Canada*) = Saskatchewan.
skate [skāt] *n* patin *m*; (*fish: pl inv*) raie *f* ♦ *vi* patiner.
skate over, skate around *vt* (*problem, issue*) éluder.
skateboard [skāt'bôrd] *n* skateboard *m*, planche *f* à roulettes.
skater [skā'tûr] *n* patineur/euse.
skating [skā'ting] *n* patinage *m*.
skating rink *n* patinoire *f*.
skeleton [skel'itən] *n* squelette *m*; (*outline*) schéma *m*.
skeleton key *n* passe-partout *m*.
skeleton staff *n* effectifs réduits.
skeptic [skep'tik] *n* (*US*) sceptique *m/f*.
skeptical [skep'tikəl] *a* sceptique.
skepticism [skep'tisizəm] *n* scepticisme *m*.
sketch [skech] *n* (*drawing*) croquis *m*, esquisse *f*; (*THEATER*) sketch *m*, saynète *f* ♦ *vt* esquisser, faire un croquis *or* une esquisse de.
sketch book *n* carnet *m* à dessin.
sketch pad *n* bloc *m* à dessin.
sketchy [skech'ē] *a* incomplet(ète), fragmentaire.
skew [skyōō] *n* (*Brit*): **on the ~** de travers, en biais.
skewer [skyōō'ûr] *n* brochette *f*.
ski [skē] *n* ski *m* ♦ *vi* skier, faire du ski.
ski boot *n* chaussure *f* de ski.
skid [skid] *n* dérapage *m* ♦ *vi* déraper; **to go into a ~** déraper.
skid mark *n* trace *f* de dérapage.
skier [skē'ûr] *n* skieur/euse.
skiing [skē'ing] *n* ski *m*; **to go ~** (aller) faire du ski.
ski instructor *n* moniteur/trice de ski.
ski jump *n* (*ramp*) tremplin *m*; (*event*) saut *m* à skis.
skilful [skil'fəl] *etc* = **skillful** *etc*.
ski lift *n* remonte-pente *m inv*.
skill [skil] *n* (*ability*) habileté *f*, adresse *f*, talent *m*; (*art, craft*) technique(s) *f(pl)*, compétences *fpl*.
skilled [skild] *a* habile, adroit(e); (*worker*) qualifié(e).
skillet [skil'it] *n* poêlon *m*.
skillful [skil'fəl] *a* (*US*) habile, adroit(e).
skillfully [skil'fəlē] *ad* habilement, adroitement.
skim [skim] *vt* (*milk*) écrémer; (*soup*) écumer; (*glide over*) raser, effleurer ♦ *vi*: **to ~ through** (*fig*) parcourir.
skimmed milk [skimd milk] *n* lait écrémé *m*.
skimp [skimp] *vt* (*work*) bâcler, faire à la vavite; (*cloth etc*) lésiner sur.
skimpy [skim'pē] *a* étriqué(e); maigre.
skin [skin] *n* peau *f* ♦ *vt* (*fru̇i*) (*animal*) écorcher; ·

trempé(e) jusqu'aux os.

skin-deep [skin'dēp'] a superficiel(le).

skin diver n plongeur/euse sous-marin(e).

skin diving n plongée sous-marine.

skinflint [skin'flint] n grippe-sou m.

skin graft n greffe f de peau.

skinny [skin'ē] a maigre, maigrichon(ne).

skin test n cuti(-réaction) f.

skintight [skin'tīt] a (dress etc) collant(e), ajusté(c).

skip [skip] n petit bond or saut; (Brit: container) benne f ♦ vi gambader, sautiller; (with rope) sauter à la corde ♦ vt (pass over) sauter; **to ~ school** (esp US) faire l'école buissonnière.

ski pants npl pantalon m de ski.

ski pole n bâton m de ski.

skipper [skip'ûr] n (NAUT, SPORT) capitaine m ♦ vt (boat) commander; (team) être le chef de.

skipping rope [skip'ing rōp] n (Brit) corde f à sauter.

ski resort n station f de sports d'hiver.

skirmish [skûr'mish] n escarmouche f, accrochage m.

skirt [skûrt] n jupe f ♦ vt longer, contourner.

skirting board [skûr'ting bōrd] n (Brit) plinthe f.

ski run n piste f de ski.

ski suit n combinaison f de ski.

skit [skit] n sketch m satirique.

ski tow n = **ski lift.**

skittle [skit'əl] n quille f; **~s** (game) (jeu m de) quilles fpl.

skive [skīv] vi (Brit col) tirer au flanc.

skulk [skulk] vi rôder furtivement.

skull [skul] n crâne m.

skullcap [skul'kap] n calotte f.

skunk [skungk] n mouffette f; (fur) sconse m.

sky [skī] n ciel m; **to praise sb to the skies** porter qn aux nues.

sky-blue [skī'blōō'] a bleu ciel inv.

sky-high [skī'hī'] ad très haut ♦ a: **prices are ~** les prix sont exorbitants.

skylark [skī'lârk] n (bird) alouette f (des champs).

skylight [skī'līt] n lucarne f.

skyline [skī'līn] n (horizon) (ligne f d')horizon m; (of city) ligne des toits.

skyscraper [skī'skrāpûr] n gratte-ciel m inv.

slab [slab] n plaque f; dalle f; (of wood) bloc m; (of meat, cheese) tranche épaisse.

slack [slak] a (loose) lâche, desserré(e); (slow) stagnant(e); (careless) négligent(e), peu sérieux(euse) or consciencieux(euse); (COMM: market) peu actif(ive); (: demand) faible; (period) creux(euse) ♦ n (in rope etc) mou m; **business is ~** les affaires vont mal.

slacken [slak'ən] (also: **~ off**) vi ralentir, di-
ʾnuer ♦ vt relâcher.
‑ʾaks] npl pantalon m.
‑‑cories fpl.
‑‑sier m.

‑‑ʾ étancher.

‑‑r; (throw)
‑‑iticize)

slander [slan'dûr] n calomnie f; (LAW) diffamation f ♦ vt calomnier; diffamer.

slanderous [slan'dûrəs] a calomnieux(euse); diffamatoire.

slang [slang] n argot m.

slant [slant] n inclinaison f; (fig) angle m, point m de vue.

slanted [slan'tid] a tendancieux(euse).

slanting [slan'ting] a en pente, incliné(e); couché(e).

slap [slap] n claque f, gifle f; (on the back) tape f ♦ vt donner une claque or une gifle (or une tape) à ♦ ad (directly) tout droit, en plein.

slapdash [slap'dash] a (work) fait(e) sans soin or à la va-vite; (person) insouciant(e), négligent(e).

slapstick [slap'stik] n (comedy) grosse farce, style m tarte à la crème.

slash [slash] vt entailler, taillader; (fig: prices) casser.

slat [slat] n (of wood) latte f, lame f.

slate [slāt] n ardoise f ♦ vt (fig: criticize) éreinter, démolir.

slaughter [slô'tûr] n carnage m, massacre m; (of animals) abattage m ♦ vt (animal) abattre; (people) massacrer.

slaughterhouse [slô'tûrhous] n abattoir m.

Slav [slâv] a slave.

slave [slāv] n esclave m/f ♦ vi (also: **~ away**) trimer, travailler comme un forçat; **to ~ (away) at sth/at doing sth** se tuer à qch/à faire qch.

slave labor n travail m d'esclave; **it's just ~** (fig) c'est de l'esclavage.

slaver [slā'vûr] vi (dribble) baver.

slavery [slā'vûrē] n esclavage m.

Slavic [slâv'ik] a slave.

slavish [slā'vish] a servile.

Slavonic [sləvân'ik] a slave.

slay, pt **slew,** pp **slain** [slā, slōō, slān] vt (literary) tuer.

SLD n abbr (Brit POL) = Social and Liberal Democratic Party.

sleazy [slē'zē] a miteux(euse), minable.

sled [sled] n (US) luge f.

sledge [slej] n (Brit) = **sled.**

sledgehammer [slej'hamûr] n marteau m de forgeron.

sleek [slēk] a (hair, fur) brillant(e), luisant(e); (car, boat) aux lignes pures or élégantes.

sleep [slēp] n sommeil m ♦ vi (pt, pp **slept** [slept]) dormir; (spend night) dormir, coucher ♦ vt: **we can ~ 4** on peut coucher or loger 4 personnes; **to go to ~** s'endormir; **to have a good night's ~** passer une bonne nuit; **to put to ~** (patient) endormir; (animal: euphemism: kill) piquer; **to ~ lightly** avoir le sommeil léger; **to ~ with sb** (euphemism) coucher avec qn.

sleep in vi (lie late) faire la grasse matinée; (oversleep) se réveiller trop tard.

sleeper [slē'pûr] n (person) dormeur/euse f; (US: for baby) grenouillère f; (Brit RAIL: on track) traverse f; (: train) train m de voitures-lits; (: carriage) wagon-lits m, voiture-lits f; (: berth) couchette f.

sleepily [slēp'ilē] ad d'un air endormi.

sleeping [slē'ping] *a* qui dort, endormi(e).

sleeping bag [slē'ping bag] *n* sac *m* de couchage.

sleeping car *n* wagon-lits *m*, voiture-lits *f*.

sleeping partner *n* (*Brit COMM*) = **silent partner**.

sleeping pill *n* somnifère *m*.

sleepless [slēp'lis] *a*: **a ~ night** une nuit blanche.

sleeplessness [slēp'lisnis] *n* insomnie *f*.

sleepwalker [slēp'wôkûr] *n* somnambule *m/f*.

sleepy [slē'pē] *a* qui a envie de dormir; (*fig*) endormi(e); **to be** *or* **feel ~** avoir sommeil, avoir envie de dormir.

sleet [slēt] *n* neige fondue.

sleeve [slēv] *n* manche *f*; (*of record*) pochette *f*.

sleeveless [slēv'lis] *a* (*garment*) sans manches.

sleigh [slā] *n* traîneau *m*.

sleight [slīt] *n*: **~ of hand** tour *m* de passe-passe.

slender [slen'dûr] *a* svelte, mince; (*fig*) faible, ténu(e).

slept [slept] *pt, pp of* **sleep.**

sleuth [slooth] *n* (*col*) détective (privé).

slew [sloo] *vi* (*Brit*) = **slue** ♦ *pt of* **slay.**

slice [slīs] *n* tranche *f*; (*round*) rondelle *f* ♦ *vt* couper en tranches (*or* en rondelles); **~d bread** pain *m* en tranches.

slick [slik] *a* brillant(e) en apparence; mielleux(euse) ♦ *n* (*also*: **oil ~**) nappe *f* de pétrole, marée noire.

slid [slid] *pt, pp of* **slide.**

slide [slīd] *n* (*in playground*) toboggan *m*; (*PHOT*) diapositive *f*; (*Brit: also:* **hair ~**) barrette *f*; (*microscope ~*) (lame *f*) porte-objet *m*; (*in prices*) chute *f*, baisse *f* ♦ *vb* (*pt, pp* **slid** [slid]) *vt* (faire) glisser ♦ *vi* glisser; **to let things ~** (*fig*) laisser les choses aller à la dérive.

slide projector *n* (*PHOT*) projecteur *m* de diapositives.

slide rule *n* règle *f* à calcul.

sliding [slī'ding] *a* (*door*) coulissant(e); **~ roof** (*AUT*) toit ouvrant.

sliding scale *n* échelle *f* mobile.

slight [slīt] *a* (*slim*) mince, menu(e); (*frail*) frêle; (*trivial*) faible, insignifiant(e); (*small*) petit(e), léger(ère) (*before n*) ♦ *n* offense *f*, affront *m* ♦ *vt* (*offend*) blesser, offenser; **the ~est** le (*or* la) moindre; **not in the ~est** pas le moins du monde, pas du tout.

slightly [slīt'lē] *ad* légèrement, un peu; **~ built** fluet(te).

slim [slim] *a* mince ♦ *vi* maigrir, suivre un régime amaigrissant.

slime [slīm] *n* vase *f*; substance visqueuse.

slimming [slim'ing] *n* amaigrissement *m* ♦ *a* (*diet, pills*) amaigrissant(e), pour maigrir.

slimy [slī'mē] *a* visqueux(euse), gluant(e); (*covered with mud*) vaseux(euse).

sling [sling] *n* (*MED*) écharpe *f* ♦ *vt* (*pt, pp* **slung** [slung]) lancer, jeter; **to have one's arm in a ~** avoir le bras en écharpe.

slingshot [sling'shât] *n* (*US*) lance-pierres *m inv*, fronde *f*.

slink [slingk], *pt, pp* **slunk** [slingk, slungk] *vi*: **to ~ away** *or* **off** s'en aller furtivement.

slip [slip] *n* faux pas; (*mistake*) erreur *f*, bévue *f*; (*underskirt*) combinaison *f*; (*of paper*) petite feuille, fiche *f* ♦ *vt* (*slide*) glisser ♦ *vi* (*slide*) glisser; (*move smoothly*): **to ~ into/out of** se glisser *or* se faufiler dans/hors de; (*decline*) baisser; **to let go ~ by** laisser passer une occasion; **to ~ sth on/off** enfiler/enlever qch; **it ~ped from her hand** cela lui a glissé des mains; **to give sb the ~** fausser compagnie à qn; **a ~ of the tongue** un lapsus.

slip away *vi* s'esquiver.

slip in *vt* glisser.

slip out *vi* sortir.

slip-on [slip'ân] *a* facile à enfiler; **~ shoes** mocassins *mpl*.

slipped disc [slipt disk] *n* déplacement *m* de vertèbres.

slipper [slip'ûr] *n* pantoufle *f*.

slippery [slip'ûrē] *a* glissant(e); (*fig: person*) insaisissable.

slip road *n* (*Brit: to freeway*) bretelle *f* d'accès.

slipshod [slip'shâd] *a* négligé(e), peu soigné(e).

slip-up [slip'up] *n* bévue *f*.

slipway [slip'wā] *n* cale *f* (de construction *or* de lancement).

slit [slit] *n* fente *f*; (*cut*) incision *f*; (*tear*) déchirure *f* ♦ *vt* (*pt, pp* **slit**) fendre; couper; inciser; déchirer; **to ~ sb's throat** trancher la gorge à qn.

slither [slith'ûr] *vi* glisser, déraper.

sliver [sliv'ûr] *n* (*of glass, wood*) éclat *m*; (*of cheese, sausage*) petit morceau.

slob [slâb] *n* (*col*) rustaud(e).

slog [slâg] *n* (*Brit*) gros effort; tâche fastidieuse ♦ *vi* travailler très dur.

slogan [slō'gən] *n* slogan *m*.

slop [slâp] *vi* (*also*: **~ over**) se renverser; déborder ♦ *vt* répandre; renverser.

slope [slōp] *n* pente *f*; (*side of mountain*) versant *m*; (*slant*) inclinaison *f* ♦ *vi*: **to ~ down** être *or* descendre en pente; **to ~ up** monter.

sloping [slō'ping] *a* en pente, incliné(e); (*handwriting*) penché(e).

sloppy [slâp'ē] *a* (*work*) peu soigné(e), bâclé(e); (*appearance*) négligé(e), débraillé(e); (*film etc*) sentimental(e).

slosh [slâsh] *vi* (*col*): **to ~ around** (*children*) patauger; (*liquid*) clapoter.

sloshed [slâsht] *a* (*col: drunk*) bourré(e).

slot [slât] *n* fente *f*; (*fig: in timetable, RADIO, TV*) créneau *m*, plage *f* ♦ *vt*: **to ~ into** encastrer *or* insérer dans ♦ *vi*: **to ~ into** s'encastrer *or* s'insérer dans.

sloth [slôth] *n* (*vice*) paresse *f*; (*ZOOL*) paresseux *m*.

slot machine *n* (*for gambling*) appareil *m* or machine *f* à sous; (*Brit: vending machine*) distributeur *m* (automatique), machine à sous.

slouch [slouch] *vi* avoir le dos rond, être voûté(e).

slouch about, slouch around *vi* traîner à ne rien faire.

slovenly [sluv'ənlē] *a* sale, débraillé(e), négligé(e).

slow [slō] *a* lent(e); (*watch*): **to be** ~ retarder ♦ *ad* lentement ♦ *vt, vi* (*also:* ~ **down,** ~ **up**) ralentir; **at a** ~ **speed** à petite vitesse; **to be** ~ **to act/decide** être lent à agir/décider; **my watch is 20 minutes** ~ ma montre retarde de 20 minutes; **business is** ~ les affaires marchent au ralenti; **to go** ~ (*driver*) rouler lentement; (*in industrial dispute*) faire la grève perlée.
slow-acting [slō'ak'ting] *a* qui agit lentement, à action lente.
slowdown [slō'doun] *n* grève perlée.
slowly [slō'lē] *ad* lentement.
slow motion *n*: **in** ~ au ralenti.
slowness [slō'nis] *n* lenteur *f*.
slowpoke [slō'pōk] *n* (*US*) tortue *f*.
sludge [sluj] *n* boue *f*.
slue [slōō] *vi* (*US*) (*also:* ~ **around**) virer, pivoter.
slug [slug] *n* limace *f*; (*bullet*) balle *f*.
sluggish [slug'ish] *a* mou(molle), lent(e); (*business, sales*) stagnant(e).
sluice [slōōs] *n* écluse *f*; (*also:* ~ **gate**) vanne *f* ♦ *vt*: **to** ~ **down** *or* **out** laver à grande eau.
slum [slum] *n* taudis *m*.
slumber [slum'bûr] *n* sommeil *m*.
slump [slump] *n* baisse soudaine, effondrement *m*; crise *f* ♦ *vi* s'effondrer, s'affaisser.
slung [slung] *pt, pp of* **sling**.
slunk [slungk] *pt, pp of* **slink**.
slur [slûr] *n* bredouillement *m*; (*smear*): ~ **(on)** atteinte *f* (à); insinuation *f* (contre) ♦ *vt* mal articuler; **to be a** ~ **on** porter atteinte à.
slurred [slûrd] *a* (*pronunciation*) inarticulé(e), indistinct(e).
slush [slush] *n* neige fondue.
slush fund *n* caisse noire, fonds secrets.
slushy [slush'ē] *a* (*snow*) fondu(e); (*street*) couvert(e) de neige fondue; (*Brit fig*) à l'eau de rose.
slut [slut] *n* souillon *f*.
sly [slī] *a* rusé(e); sournois(e); **on the** ~ en cachette.
smack [smak] *n* (*slap*) tape *f*; (*on face*) gifle *f* ♦ *vt* donner une tape à; gifler; (*child*) donner la fessée à ♦ *vi*: **to** ~ **of** avoir des relents de, sentir ♦ *ad* (*col*): **it fell** ~ **in the middle** c'est tombé en plein milieu *or* en plein dedans; **to** ~ **one's lips** se lécher les babines.
smacker [smak'ûr] *n* (*col: kiss*) bisou *m or* bise *f* sonore; (*: US: dollar bill*) dollar *m*; (*: Brit: pound note*) livre *f*.
small [smôl] *a* petit(e); (*letter*) minuscule ♦ *n*: **the** ~ **of the back** le creux des reins; **to get** *or* **grow** ~**er** diminuer; **to make** ~**er** (*amount, income*) diminuer; (*object, garment*) rapetisser; **a** ~ **storekeeper** un petit commerçant.
small ads *npl* (*Brit*) petites annonces.
small change *n* petite *or* menue monnaie.
smallholding [smôl'hōlding] *n* (*Brit*) petite ferme.
small hours *npl*: **in the** ~ au petit matin.
smallish [smô'lish] *a* plutôt *or* assez petit(e).
small-minded [smôl'mīn'did] *a* mesquin(e).
smallpox [smôl'pâks] *n* variole *f*.
small print *n* (*in contract etc*) clause(s) imprimée(s) en petits caractères.

small-scale [smôl'skāl] *a* (*map, model*) à échelle réduite, à petite échelle; (*business, farming*) peu important(e), modeste.
small talk *n* menus propos.
small-time [smôl'tīm'] *a* (*farmer etc*) petit(e); **a** ~ **thief** un voleur à la petite semaine.
smart [smârt] *a* élégant(e), chic *inv*; (*clever*) intelligent(e); (*pej*) futé(e); (*quick*) vif(vive), prompt(e) ♦ *vi* faire mal, brûler; **the** ~ **set** le beau monde; **to look** ~ être élégant(e); **my eyes are** ~**ing** j'ai les yeux irrités *or* qui me piquent.
smart-ass [smârt'as] *n* (*US col*) je-sais-tout *m/f*.
smarten up [smâr'tən up] *vi* devenir plus élégant(e), se faire beau(belle) ♦ *vt* rendre plus élégant(e).
smash [smash] *n* (*also:* ~-**up**) collision *f*, accident *m*; (*sound*) fracas *m* ♦ *vt* casser, briser, fracasser; (*opponent*) écraser; (*hopes*) ruiner, détruire; (*SPORT: record*) pulvériser ♦ *vi* se briser, se fracasser; s'écraser.
smash up *vt* (*car*) bousiller; (*room*) tout casser dans.
smash hit *n* (grand) succès.
smattering [smat'ûring] *n*: **a** ~ **of** quelques notions de.
smear [smē'ûr] *n* tache *f*, salissure *f*; trace *f*; (*MED*) frottis *m*; (*insult*) calomnie *f* ♦ *vt* enduire; (*fig*) porter atteinte à; **his hands were** ~**ed with oil/ink** il avait les mains maculées de cambouis/d'encre.
smear campaign *n* campagne *f* de dénigrement.
smell [smel] *n* odeur *f*; (*sense*) odorat *m* ♦ *vb* (*pt, pp* ~**ed** *or* **smelt** [smeld, smelt]) *vt* sentir ♦ *vi* (*food etc*): **to** ~ **(of)** sentir; (*pej*) sentir mauvais; **it** ~**s good** ça sent bon.
smelly [smel'ē] *a* qui sent mauvais, malodorant(e).
smelt [smelt] *pt, pp of* **smell** ♦ *vt* (*ore*) fondre.
smile [smīl] *n* sourire *m* ♦ *vi* sourire.
smiling [smī'ling] *a* souriant(e).
smirk [smûrk] *n* petit sourire suffisant *or* affecté.
smith [smith] *n* maréchal-ferrant *m*; forgeron *m*.
smithy [smith'ē] *n* forge *f*.
smitten [smit'ən] *a*: ~ **with** pris(e) de; frappé(e) de.
smock [smâk] *n* blouse *f*, sarrau *m*.
smog [smâg] *n* brouillard mêlé de fumée.
smoke [smōk] *n* fumée *f* ♦ *vt, vi* fumer; **to have a** ~ fumer une cigarette; **do you** ~? est-ce que vous fumez?; **to go up in** ~ (*house etc*) brûler; (*fig*) partir en fumée.
smoked [smōkt] *a* (*bacon, glass*) fumé(e).
smokeless fuel [smōk'lis fyōō'əl] *n* combustible non polluant.
smoker [smō'kûr] *n* (*person*) fumeur/euse; (*RAIL*) wagon *m* fumeurs.
smoke screen *n* rideau *m or* écran *m* de fumée; (*fig*) paravent *m*.
smoking [smō'king] *n*: "**no** ~" (*sign*) "défense de fumer"; **he's given up** ~ il a arrêté de fumer.
smoking car *n* wagon *m* fumeurs.
smoking room *n* fumoir *m*.
smoky [smō'kē] *a* enfumé(e).

smolder [smōl'dûr] *vi* (*US*) couver.

smooth [smōōth̩] *a* lisse; (*sauce*) onctueux(euse); (*flavor, whiskey*) moelleux(euse); (*cigarette*) doux(douce); (*movement*) régulier(ière), sans à-coups *or* heurts; (*landing, take-off*) en douceur; (*flight*) sans secousses; (*person*) doucereux(euse), mielleux(euse) ♦ *vt* lisser, défroisser; (*also*: ~ **out**: *creases, difficulties*) faire disparaître.
  smooth over *vt*: **to** ~ **things over** (*fig*) arranger les choses.

smoothly [smōōth̩'lē] *ad* (*easily*) facilement, sans difficulté(s); **everything went** ~ **tout** s'est bien passé.

smother [smuth̩'ûr] *vt* étouffer.

smoulder [smōl'dûr] *vi* (*Brit*) = **smolder**.

smudge [smuj] *n* tache *f*, bavure *f* ♦ *vt* salir, maculer.

smug [smug] *a* suffisant(e), content(e) de soi.

smuggle [smug'əl] *vt* passer en contrebande *or* en fraude; **to** ~ **in/out** (*goods etc*) faire entrer/sortir clandestinement *or* en fraude.

smuggler [smug'lûr] *n* contrebandier/ière.

smuggling [smug'ling] *n* contrebande *f*.

smut [smut] *n* (*grain of soot*) grain *m* de suie; (*mark*) tache *f* de suie; (*in conversation etc*) obscénités *fpl*.

smutty [smut'ē] *a* (*fig*) grossier(ière), obscène.

snack [snak] *n* casse-croûte *m inv*; **to have a** ~ prendre un en-cas, manger quelque chose (de léger).

snack bar *n* snack(-bar) *m*.

snag [snag] *n* inconvénient *m*, difficulté *f*.

snail [snāl] *n* escargot *m*.

snake [snāk] *n* serpent *m*.

snap [snap] *n* (*sound*) claquement *m*, bruit sec; (*photograph*) photo *f*, instantané *m*; (*game*) sorte de jeu de bataille ♦ *a* subit(e); fait(e) sans réfléchir ♦ *vt* faire claquer; (*break*) casser net ♦ *vi* se casser net *or* avec un bruit sec; (*fig: person*) craquer; **to** ~ **at sb** (*subj: person*) parler d'un ton brusque à qn; (*: dog*) essayer de mordre qn; **to** ~ **open/shut** s'ouvrir/se refermer brusquement; **to** ~ **one's fingers at** (*fig*) se moquer de; **a cold** ~ (*of weather*) un refroidissement soudain de la température.

snap off *vt* (*break*) casser net.

snap up *vt* sauter sur, saisir.

snap fastener *n* bouton-pression *m*.

snappy [snap'ē] *a* prompt(e); (*slogan*) qui a du punch; **make it** ~! (*col: hurry up*) grouille-toi!, magne-toi!

snapshot [snap'shät] *n* photo *f*, instantané *m*.

snare [snär] *n* piège *m* ♦ *vt* attraper, prendre au piège.

snarl [snârl] *n* grondement *m or* grognement *m* féroce ♦ *vi* gronder ♦ *vt*: **to get** ~**ed up** (*wool, plans*) s'emmêler; (*traffic*) se bloquer.

snatch [snach] *n* (*fig*) vol *m*; (*small amount*): ~**es** *of* des fragments *mpl or* bribes *fpl* de ♦ *vt* saisir (*d'un geste vif*); (*steal*) voler.

snatch up *vt* sauter sur, s'emparer de.

sneak [snēk] *vi*: **to** ~ **in/out** entrer/sortir furtivement *or* à la dérobée ♦ *vt*: **to** ~ **a look at sth** regarder furtivement qn.

sneakers [snē'kûrz] *npl* chaussures *fpl* de tennis *or* basket.

sneaking [snē'king] *a*: **to have a** ~ **feeling or**

suspicion that ... avoir la vague impression que ....

sneaky [snē'kē] *a* sournois(e).

sneer [snēr] *n* ricanement *m* ♦ *vi* ricaner, sourire d'un air sarcastique; **to** ~ **at sb/sth** se moquer de qn/qch avec mépris.

sneeze [snēz] *n* éternuement *m* ♦ *vi* éternuer.

snicker [snik'ûr] *n* ricanement *m*; rire moquer ♦ *vi* ricaner; pouffer de rire.

snide [snīd] *a* sarcastique, narquois(e).

sniff [snif] *n* reniflement *m* ♦ *vi* renifler ♦ *vt* renifler, flairer; (*glue, drug*) sniffer, respirer.
  sniff at *vt fus*: **it's not to be** ~**ed at** il ne faut pas cracher dessus, ce n'est pas à dédaigner.

snigger [snig'ûr] *n*, *vi* = **snicker**.

snip [snip] *n* petit bout; (*bargain*) (bonne) occasion *or* affaire ♦ *vt* couper.

sniper [snī'pûr] *n* (*marksman*) tireur embusqué.

snippet [snip'it] *n* bribes *fpl*.

snivel(l)ing [sniv'əling] *a* larmoyant(e), pleurnicheur(euse).

snob [snäb] *n* snob *m/f*.

snobbery [snäb'ûrē] *n* snobisme *m*.

snobbish [snäb'ish] *a* snob *inv*.

snooker [snŏŏk'ûr] *n* sorte de jeu de billard.

snoop [snōōp] *vi*: **to** ~ **on sb** espionner qn; **to** ~ **around somewhere** fourrer son nez quelque part.

snooper [snōō'pûr] *n* fureteur/euse.

snooty [snōō'tē] *a* snob *inv*, prétentieux(euse).

snooze [snōōz] *n* petit somme ♦ *vi* faire un petit somme.

snore [snôr] *vi* ronfler ♦ *n* ronflement *m*.

snoring [snôr'ing] *n* ronflement(s) *m(pl)*.

snorkel [snôr'kəl] *n* (*of swimmer*) tuba *m*.

snort [snôrt] *n* grognement *m* ♦ *vi* grogner; (*horse*) renâcler ♦ *vt* (*col: drugs*) sniffer.

snotty [snät'ē] *a* morveux(euse).

snout [snout] *n* museau *m*.

snow [snō] *n* neige *f* ♦ *vi* neiger ♦ *vt*: **to be** ~**ed under with work** être débordé(e) de travail.

snowball [snō'bôl] *n* boule *f* de neige.

snowbound [snō'bound] *a* enneigé(e), bloqué(e) par la neige.

snowcapped [snō'kapt] *a* (*peak, mountain*) couvert(e) de neige.

snowdrift [snō'drift] *n* congère *f*.

snowdrop [snō'dräp] *n* perce-neige *m*.

snowfall [snō'fôl] *n* chute *f* de neige.

snowflake [snō'flāk] *n* flocon *m* de neige.

snowman [snō'man] *n* bonhomme *m* de neige.

snowmobile [snō'mōbēl] *n* motoneige *f*.

snowplow, (*Brit*) **snowplough** [snō'plou] *n* chasse-neige *m inv*.

snowshoe [snō'shōō] *n* raquette *f* (*pour la neige*).

snowstorm [snō'stôrm] *n* tempête *f* de neige.

snowy [snō'ē] *a* neigeux(euse); (*covered with snow*) enneigé(e).

SNP *n abbr* (*Brit POL*) = *Scottish National Party*.

snub [snub] *vt* repousser, snober ♦ *n* rebuffade *f*.

snub-nosed [snub'nōzd] *a* au nez retroussé.

snuff [snuf] *n* tabac *m* à priser ♦ *vt* (*also*: ~ **out**: *candle*) moucher.

snug [snug] *a* douillet(te), confortable; **it's a ~ fit** c'est bien ajusté(e).

snuggle [snug'əl] *vi*: **to ~ down in bed/up to sb** se pelotonner dans son lit/contre qn.

SO *abbr* (*BANKING*) = **standing order.**

so [sō] *ad* (*degree*) si, tellement; (*manner: thus*) ainsi, de cette façon ♦ *cj* donc, par conséquent; **~ as to do** afin de *or* pour faire; **~ that** (*purpose*) afin de + *infinitive*, pour que *or* afin que + *sub*; (*result*) si bien que, de (telle) sorte que; **~ that's the reason!** c'est donc (pour) ça!; **~ do I, ~ am I** *etc* moi *etc* aussi; **~ it is!, ~ it does!** c'est vrai!; **if ~** si oui; **I hope ~** je l'espère; **10 or ~** 10 à peu près *or* environ; **quite ~!** exactement!, c'est bien ça!; **even ~** quand même, tout de même; **~ far** jusqu'ici, jusqu'à maintenant; (*in past*) jusque-là; **~ long!** à bientôt!, au revoir!; **~ many** tant de; **~ much** *ad* tant ♦ *a* tant de; **~ to speak** pour ainsi dire; **~ (what)?** (*col*) (bon) et alors?, et après?

soak [sōk] *vt* faire *or* laisser tremper ♦ *vi* tremper; **to be ~ed through** être trempé jusqu'aux os.

soak in *vi* pénétrer, être absorbé(e).

soak up *vt* absorber.

soaking [sō'king] *a* (*also*: **~ wet**) trempé(e).

so and so *n* un tel/une telle.

soap [sōp] *n* savon *m*.

soapflakes [sōp'flāks] *npl* paillettes *fpl* de savon.

soap opera *n* feuilleton télévisé (*quotidienneté réaliste ou embellie*).

soap powder *n* lessive *f*, détergent *m*.

soapsuds [sōp'sudz] *npl* mousse *f* de savon.

soapy [sō'pē] *a* savonneux(euse).

soar [sōr] *vi* monter (en flèche), s'élancer; **~ing prices** prix qui grimpent.

sob [sâb] *n* sanglot *m* ♦ *vi* sangloter.

s.o.b. *n abbr* (*US col!*): = *son of a bitch*) salaud *m* (!).

sober [sō'bûr] *a* qui n'est pas (*or* plus) ivre; (*sedate*) sérieux(euse), sensé(e); (*moderate*) mesuré(e); (*color, style*) sobre, discret(ète).

sober up *vt* dégriser ♦ *vi* se dégriser.

sobriety [səbrī'ətē] *n* (*not being drunk*) sobriété *f*; (*seriousness, sedateness*) sérieux *m*.

Soc. *abbr* (= *society*) Soc.

so-called [sō'kōld'] *a* soi-disant *inv*.

soccer [sâk'ûr] *n* football *m*.

soccer player *n* footballeur *m*.

sociable [sō'shəbəl] *a* sociable.

social [sō'shəl] *a* social(e) ♦ *n* (petite) fête.

social climber *n* arriviste *m/f*.

social club *n* amicale *f*, foyer *m*.

Social Democrat *n* social-démocrate *m/f*.

socialism [sō'shəlizəm] *n* socialisme *m*.

socialist [sō'shəlist] *a*, *n* socialiste (*m/f*).

socialite [sō'shəlīt] *n* personnalité mondaine.

socialize [sō'shəlīz] *vi* voir *or* rencontrer des gens, se faire des amis; **to ~ with** fréquenter; lier connaissance *or* parler avec.

socially [sō'shəlē] *ad* socialement, en société.

social science *n* sciences humaines.

social security *n* aide sociale; **Department of S~ S~** (*Brit*) *ministère de la Sécurité Sociale.*

social welfare *n* sécurité sociale.

social work *n* assistance sociale.

social worker *n* assistant/e social(e).

society [səsī'ətē] *n* société *f*; (*club*) société, association *f*; (*also*: **high ~**) (haute) société, grand monde ♦ *cpd* (*party*) mondain(e).

socioeconomic [sōshēōēkənâm'ik] *a* socio-économique.

sociological [sōsēəlâj'ikəl] *a* sociologique.

sociologist [sōsēâl'əjist] *n* sociologue *m/f*.

sociology [sōsēâl'əjē] *n* sociologie *f*.

sock [sâk] *n* chaussette *f* ♦ *vt* (*col: hit*) flanquer un coup à; **to pull one's ~s up** (*fig*) se secouer (les puces).

socket [sâk'it] *n* cavité *f*; (*ELEC*: *also*: **wall ~**) prise *f* de courant; (: *for light bulb*) douille *f*.

sod [sâd] *n* (*of earth*) motte *f*; (*Brit col!*) con *m* (!); salaud *m* (!).

soda [sō'də] *n* (*CHEMISTRY*) soude *f*; (*also*: **~ water**) eau *f* de Seltz; (*US: also*: **~ pop**) soda *m*.

sodden [sâd'ən] *a* trempé(e); détrempé(e).

sodium [sō'dēəm] *n* sodium *m*.

sodium chloride *n* chlorure *m* de sodium.

sofa [sō'fə] *n* sofa *m*, canapé *m*.

Sofia [sō'fēə] *n* Sofia.

soft [sôft] *a* (*not rough*) doux(douce); (*not hard*) doux; mou(molle); (*not loud*) doux, léger(ère); (*kind*) doux, gentil(le); (*weak*) indulgent(e); (*stupid*) stupide, débile.

soft-boiled [sôft'boild'] *a* (*egg*) à la coque.

soft drink *n* boisson non alcoolisée.

soft drugs *npl* drogues douces.

soften [sôf'ən] *vt* (r)amollir; adoucir; atténuer ♦ *vi* se ramollir; s'adoucir; s'atténuer.

softener [sôf'ənûr] *n* (*water ~*) adoucisseur *m*; (*fabric ~*) produit assouplissant.

softhearted [sôft'hâr'tid] *a* au cœur tendre.

softly [sôft'lē] *ad* doucement; légèrement; gentiment.

softness [sôft'nis] *n* douceur *f*.

soft sell *n* promotion *f* de vente discrète.

soft toy *n* jouet *m* en peluche.

software [sôft'wâr] *n* logiciel *m*, software *m*.

software package *n* progiciel *m*.

soggy [sâg'ē] *a* trempé(e); détrempé(e).

soil [soil] *n* (*earth*) sol *m*, terre *f* ♦ *vt* salir; (*fig*) souiller.

soiled [soild] *a* sale; (*COMM*) défraîchi(e).

sojourn [sō'jûrn] *n* (*formal*) séjour *m*.

solace [sâl'is] *n* consolation *f*, réconfort *m*.

solar [sō'lûr] *a* solaire.

solarium [sōlär'ēəm, -lâr'ēə] *n* pl **solaria** solarium *m*.

solar plexus [sō'lûr plek'səs] *n* (*ANAT*) plexus *m* solaire.

sold [sōld] *pt*, *pp* of **sell.**

solder [sâd'ûr] *vt* souder (*au fil à souder*) ♦ *n* soudure *f*.

soldier [sōl'jûr] *n* soldat *m*, militaire *m*; **toy ~** petit soldat.

sold out *a* (*COMM*) épuisé(e).

sole [sōl] *n* (*of foot*) plante *f*; (*of shoe*) semelle *f*; (*fish: pl inv*) sole *f* ♦ *a* seul(e), unique; **the ~ reason** la seule et unique raison.

solely [sōl'lē] *ad* seulement, uniquement; **I will hold you ~ responsible** je vous en tiendrai pour seul responsable.

solemn [sâl'əm] *a* solennel(le); sérieux(euse), grave.

sole trader *n* (COMM) chef *m* d'entreprise individuelle.
solicit [səlis'it] *vt* (*request*) solliciter ♦ *vi* (*prostitute*) racoler.
solicitor [səlis'itûr] *n* (*Brit: for wills etc*) ≈ notaire *m*; (: *in court*) ≈ avocat *m*.
solid [sâl'id] *a* (*not hollow*) plein(e), compact(e), massif(ive); (*strong, sound, reliable, not liquid*) solide; (*meal*) consistant(e), substantiel(le); (*vote*) unanime ♦ *n* solide *m*; **to be on ~ ground** être sur la terre ferme; (*fig*) être en terrain sûr; **we waited 2 ~ hours** nous avons attendu deux heures entières.
solidarity [sâlidar'itē] *n* solidarité *f*.
solidify [səlid'əfī] *vi* se solidifier ♦ *vt* solidifier.
solidity [səlid'itē] *n* solidité *f*.
solid-state [sâl'idstāt'] *a* (ELEC) à circuits intégrés.
soliloquy [səlil'əkwē] *n* monologue *m*.
solitaire [sâl'itär] *n* (*US: card game*) réussite *f*; (*gem, Brit: game*) solitaire *m*.
solitary [sâl'itärē] *a* solitaire.
solitary confinement *n* (LAW) isolement *m* (cellulaire).
solitude [sâl'ətood] *n* solitude *f*.
solo [sō'lō] *n* solo *m*.
soloist [sō'lōist] *n* soliste *m/f*.
Solomon Islands [sâl'əmən i'ləndz] *npl*: **the ~** les (îles *fpl*) Salomon *fpl*.
solstice [sâl'stis] *n* solstice *m*.
soluble [sâl'yəbəl] *a* soluble.
solution [səlōō'shən] *n* solution *f*.
solve [sâlv] *vt* résoudre.
solvency [sâl'vənsē] *n* (COMM) solvabilité *f*.
solvent [sâl'vənt] *a* (COMM) solvable ♦ *n* (CHEMISTRY) (dis)solvant *m*.
solvent abuse *n* usage *m* de solvants hallucinogènes.
Som. *abbr* (*Brit*) = *Somerset*.
Somali [sōmâ'lē] *a* somali(e), somalien(ne) ♦ *n* Somali/e, Somalien/ne.
Somalia [sōmâl'ēə] *n* (République *f* de) Somalie *f*.
somber, (*Brit*) **sombre** [sâm'bûr] *a* sombre, morne.
some [sum] *a* (*a few*) quelques; (*certain*) certains(certaines); (*a certain number or amount*) *see phrases below*; (*unspecified*) un(e) ... (quelconque) ♦ *pronoun* quelques uns(unes); un peu ♦ *ad*: **~ 10 people** quelque 10 personnes, 10 personnes environ; **~ children came** des enfants sont venus; **~ people say that ...** certains disent que ...; **have ~ tea/ice-cream/water** prends du thé/ de la glace/de l'eau; **there's ~ milk in the fridge** il y a du lait *or* un peu de lait dans le frigo; **~ (of it) was left** il en est resté un peu; **could I have ~ of that cheese?** pourriez-vous me donner un peu de ce fromage?; **I've got ~** (*i.e. books etc*) j'en ai (quelques uns); (*i.e. milk, money etc*) j'en ai (un peu); **would you like ~?** est-ce que vous en voulez?, en voulez-vous?; **after ~ time** après un certain temps; **at ~ length** assez longuement; **in ~ form or other** sous une forme ou une autre, sous une forme quelconque.
somebody [sum'bädē] *pronoun* quelqu'un; **~**

or other quelqu'un, je ne sais qui.
someday [sum'dā] *ad* un de ces jours, un jour ou l'autre.
somehow [sum'hou] *ad* d'une façon ou d'une autre; (*for some reason*) pour une raison ou une autre.
someone [sum'wun] *pronoun* = **somebody**.
someplace [sum'plās] *ad* (US) = **somewhere**.
somersault [sum'ûrsôlt] *n* culbute *f*, saut périlleux ♦ *vi* faire la culbute *or* un saut périlleux; (*car*) faire un tonneau.
something [sum'thing] *pronoun* quelque chose *m*; **~ interesting** quelque chose d'intéressant; **~ to do** quelque chose à faire; **he's ~ like me** il est un peu comme moi; **it's ~ of a problem** il y a là un problème.
sometime [sum'tīm] *ad* (*in future*) un de ces jours, un jour ou l'autre; (*in past*): **~ last month** au cours du mois dernier.
sometimes [sum'tīmz] *ad* quelquefois, parfois.
somewhat [sum'wut] *ad* quelque peu, un peu.
somewhere [sum'wär] *ad* quelque part; **~ else** ailleurs, autre part.
son [sun] *n* fils *m*.
sonar [sō'når] *n* sonar *m*.
sonata [sənât'ə] *n* sonate *f*.
song [sông] *n* chanson *f*.
songbook [sông'book] *n* chansonnier *m*.
songwriter [sông'rī'tûr] *n* auteur-compositeur *m*.
sonic [sân'ik] *a* (*boom*) supersonique.
son-in-law [sun'inlô] *n* gendre *m*, beau-fils *m*.
sonnet [sân'it] *n* sonnet *m*.
sonny [sun'ē] *n* (*col*) fiston *m*.
soon [sōōn] *ad* bientôt; (*early*) tôt; **~ afterwards** peu après; **quite ~** sous peu; **how ~ can you do it?** combien de temps vous faut-il pour le faire, au plus pressé?; **how ~ can you come back?** quand *or* dans combien de temps pouvez-vous revenir, au plus tôt; **see you ~!** à bientôt!; *see also* **as**.
sooner [sōō'nûr] *ad* (*time*) plus tôt; (*preference*): **I would ~ do** j'aimerais autant *or* je préférerais faire; **~ or later** tôt ou tard; **no ~ said than done** sitôt dit, sitôt fait; **the ~ the better** le plus tôt sera le mieux; **no ~ had we left than ...** à peine étions-nous partis que ....
soot [soot] *n* suie *f*.
soothe [sōōth] *vt* calmer, apaiser.
soothing [sōō'thing] *a* (*ointment etc*) lénitif(ive), lénifiant(e); (*tone, words etc*) apaisant(e); (*drink, bath*) relaxant(e).
SOP *n abbr* = *standard operating procedure*.
sop [sâp] *n*: **that's only a ~** c'est pour nous (*or* les *etc*) amadouer.
sophisticated [səfis'tikātid] *a* raffiné(e), sophistiqué(e); (*system etc*) très perfectionné(e), sophistiqué.
sophistication [səfis'tikā'shən] *n* raffinement *m*; (niveau *m* de) perfectionnement *m*.
sophomore [sâf'əmôr] *n* (US) étudiant/e de seconde année.
soporific [sâpərif'ik] *a* soporifique ♦ *n* somnifère *m*.
sopping [sâp'ing] *a* (*also*: **~ wet**) tout(e) trempé(e).
soprano [səpran'ō] *n* (*voice*) soprano *m*; (*singer*) soprano *m/f*.

sorbet [sôrbā'] *n* sorbet *m*.
sorcerer [sôr'sərûr] *n* sorcier *m*.
sordid [sôr'did] *a* sordide.
sore [sôr] *a (painful)* douloureux(euse), sensible; *(offended)* contrarié(e), vexé(e) ♦ *n* plaie *f*; **to have a ~ throat** avoir mal à la gorge; **it's a ~ point** *(fig)* c'est un point délicat.
sorely [sôr'lē] *ad (tempted)* fortement.
sorrel [sôr'əl] *n* oseille *f*.
sorrow [sâr'ō] *n* peine *f*, chagrin *m*.
sorrowful [sâr'ōfəl] *a* triste.
sorry [sâr'ē] *a* désolé(e); *(condition, excuse, tale)* triste, déplorable; *(sight)* désolant(e); **~!** pardon!, excusez-moi!; **to feel ~ for sb** plaindre qn; **I'm ~ to hear that ...** je suis désolé(e) *or* navré(e) d'apprendre que ...; **to be ~ about sth** regretter qch.
sort [sôrt] *n* genre *m*, espèce *f*, sorte *f*; *(make: of coffee, car etc)* marque *f* ♦ *vt (also: ~ out: papers)* trier; classer; ranger; *(: letters etc)* trier; *(: problems)* résoudre, régler; *(COMPUT)* trier; **what ~ do you want?** quelle sorte *or* quel genre voulez-vous?; **what ~ of car?** quelle marque de voiture?; **I'll do nothing of the ~!** je ne ferai rien de tel!; **it's ~ of awkward** *(col)* c'est plutôt gênant.
sortie [sôr'tē] *n* sortie *f*.
sorting office [sôr'ting ô'fis] *n (MAIL)* bureau *m* de tri.
SOS [es'ō'es'] *n abbr* (= *save our souls*) SOS *m*.
so-so [sō'sō'] *ad* comme ci comme ça.
soufflé [sōōflā'] *n* soufflé *m*.
sought [sôt] *pt, pp of* **seek**.
sought-after [sôt'af'tûr] *a* recherché(e).
soul [sōl] *n* âme *f*; **the poor ~ had nowhere to sleep** le pauvre n'avait nulle part où dormir; **I didn't see a ~** je n'ai vu (absolument) personne.
soul-destroying [sōl'distroiing] *a* démoralisant(e).
soulful [sōl'fəl] *a* plein(e) de sentiment.
soulless [sōl'lis] *a* sans cœur, inhumain(e).
soul mate *n* âme *f* sœur.
soul-searching [sōl'sûrching] *n*: **after much ~, I decided ...** j'ai longuement réfléchi avant de décider ....
sound [sound] *a (healthy)* en bonne santé, sain(e); *(safe, not damaged)* solide, en bon état; *(reliable, not superficial)* sérieux(euse), solide; *(sensible)* sensé(e); ♦ *ad*: **~ asleep** dormant d'un profond sommeil ♦ *n (noise)* son *m*; bruit *m*; *(GEO)* détroit *m*, bras *m* de mer ♦ *vt (alarm)* sonner; *(also: ~ out: opinions)* sonder ♦ *vi* sonner, retentir; *(fig: seem)* sembler (être); **to be of ~ mind** être sain(e) d'esprit; **I don't like the ~ of it** ça ne me dit rien qui vaille; **to ~ one's horn** *(AUT)* klaxonner, actionner son avertisseur; **to ~ like** ressembler à; **it ~s as if ...** il semblerait que ..., j'ai l'impression que ....
  sound off *vi (col)*: **to ~ off (about)** la ramener (sur).
sound barrier *n* mur *m* du son.
sound effects *npl* bruitage *m*.
sound engineer *n* ingénieur *m* du son.
sounding [soun'ding] *n (NAUT etc)* sondage *m*.
sounding board *n (MUS)* table *f* d'harmonie;

(fig): **to use sb as a ~ for one's ideas** essayer ses idées sur qn.
soundly [sound'lē] *ad (sleep)* profondément; *(beat)* complètement, à plate couture.
soundproof [sound'prōōf] *vt* insonoriser ♦ *a* insonorisé(e).
sound track *n (of film)* bande *f* sonore.
sound wave *n (PHYSICS)* onde *f* sonore.
soup [sōōp] *n* soupe *f*, potage *m*; **in the ~** *(fig)* dans le pétrin.
soup course *n* potage *m*.
soup kitchen *n* soupe *f* populaire.
soup plate *n* assiette creuse *or* à soupe.
soupspoon [sōōp'spōōn] *n* cuiller *f* à soupe.
sour [sou'ûr] *a* aigre, acide; *(milk)* tourné(e), aigre; *(fig)* acerbe, aigre; revêche; **to go** *or* **turn ~** *(milk, wine)* tourner; *(fig: relationship, plans)* mal tourner; **it's ~ grapes** c'est du dépit.
source [sôrs] *n* source *f*; **I have it from a reliable ~ that** je sais de source sûre que.
south [south] *n* sud *m* ♦ *a* sud *inv*, du sud ♦ *ad* au sud, vers le sud; **(to the) ~ of** au sud de; **to travel ~** aller en direction du sud; **the S~ of France** le Sud de la France, le Midi.
South Africa *n* Afrique *f* du Sud.
South African *a* sud-africain(e) ♦ *n* Sud-Africain/e.
South America *n* Amérique *f* du Sud.
South American *a* sud-américain(e) ♦ *n* Sud-Américain/e.
southbound [south'bound'] *a* en direction du sud; *(carriageway)* sud *inv*.
southeast [southēst'] *n* sud-est *m*.
Southeast Asia *n* le Sud-Est asiatique.
southerly [suth'ûrlē] *a* du sud; au sud.
southern [suth'ûrn] *a (du)* sud; méridional(e); **with a ~ aspect** orienté(e) *or* exposé(e) au sud; **the ~ hemisphere** l'hémisphère sud *or* austral.
South Pole *n* Pôle *m* Sud.
South Sea Islands *npl*: **the ~** l'Océanie *f*.
South Seas *npl*: **the ~** les mers *fpl* du Sud.
southward(s) [south'wûrd(z)] *ad* vers le sud.
southwest [southwest'] *n* sud-ouest *m*.
souvenir [sōōvənēr'] *n* souvenir *m (objet)*.
sovereign [sâv'rin] *a, n* souverain(e).
sovereignty [sâv'rəntē] *n* souveraineté *f*.
soviet [sō'vēit] *a* soviétique.
Soviet Union *n*: **the ~** l'Union *f* soviétique.
sow *n* [sou] truie *f* ♦ *vt* [sō] *(pt* **~ed**, *pp* **sown** [sōn])* semer.
soy [soi] *n* soja *m*.
soya [soi'ə] *n (Brit)* = **soy.**
soybean [soi'bēn] *n* graine *f* de soja.
soy sauce *n* sauce *f* au soja.
spa [spā] *n (town)* station thermale; *(US: also: health ~)* établissement *m* de cure de rajeunissement.
space [spās] *n (gen)* espace *m*; *(room)* place *f*; espace; *(length of time)* laps *m* de temps ♦ *cpd* spatial(e) ♦ *vt (also: ~ out)* espacer; **to clear a ~ for sth** faire de la place pour qch; **in a confined ~** dans un espace réduit *or* restreint; **in a short ~ of time** dans peu de temps; **(with)in the ~ of an hour** en l'espace d'une heure.
space bar *n (on typewriter)* barre *f* d'espacement.

spacecraft [spās'kraft] *n* engin spatial.

spaceman [spās'man] *n* astronaute *m*, cosmonaute *m*.

spaceship [spās'ship] *n* engin *or* vaisseau spatial.

space shuttle *n* navette spatiale.

spacesuit [spās'sōōt] *n* combinaison spatiale.

spacewoman [spās'wōōmən] *n* astronaute *f*, cosmonaute *f*.

spacing [spā'sing] *n* espacement *m*; **single/double** ~ (*TYP etc*) interligne *m* simple/double.

spacious [spā'shəs] *a* spacieux(euse), grand(e).

spade [spād] *n* (*tool*) bêche *f*, pelle *f*; (*child's*) pelle; ~**s** *npl* (*CARDS*) pique *m*.

spadework [spād'wûrk] *n* (*fig*) gros *m* du travail.

spaghetti [spəget'ē] *n* spaghetti *mpl*.

Spain [spān] *n* Espagne *f*.

span [span] *pt of* **spin** ♦ *n* (*of bird, plane*) envergure *f*; (*of arch*) portée *f*; (*in time*) espace *m* de temps, durée *f* ♦ *vt* enjamber, franchir; (*fig*) couvrir, embrasser.

Spaniard [span'yûrd] *n* Espagnol/e.

spaniel [span'yəl] *n* épagneul *m*.

Spanish [span'ish] *a* espagnol(e), d'Espagne ♦ *n* (*LING*) espagnol *m*; **the** ~ *npl* les Espagnols; ~ **omelette** omelette *f* à l'espagnole.

spank [spangk] *vt* donner une fessée à.

spanner [span'ûr] *n* (*Brit*) clé *f* (de mécanicien).

spar [spär] *n* espar *m* ♦ *vi* (*BOXING*) s'entraîner.

spare [spär] *a* de réserve, de rechange; (*surplus*) de *or* en trop, de reste ♦ *n* (*part*) pièce *f* de rechange, pièce détachée ♦ *vt* (*do without*) se passer de; (*afford to give*) donner, accorder, passer; (*refrain from hurting*) épargner; (*refrain from using*) ménager; **to** ~ (*surplus*) en surplus, de trop; **to** ~ **no expense** ne pas reculer devant la dépense; **can you** ~ **the time?** est-ce que vous avez le temps?; **there is no time to** ~ il n'y a pas de temps à perdre; **I've a few minutes to** ~ je dispose de quelques minutes.

spare part *n* pièce *f* de rechange, pièce détachée.

spare room *n* chambre *f* d'ami.

spare time *n* moments *mpl* de loisir.

spare tire, (*Brit*) **spare tyre** *n* (*AUT*) pneu *m* de rechange.

spare wheel *n* (*AUT*) roue *f* de secours.

sparing [spär'ing] *a*: **to be** ~ **with** ménager.

sparingly [spär'inglē] *ad* avec modération.

spark [spärk] *n* étincelle *f*; (*fig*) étincelle, lueur *f*.

spark plug [spärk' plug] *n* bougie *f*.

sparkle [spär'kəl] *n* scintillement *m*, étincellement *m*, éclat *m* ♦ *vi* étinceler, scintiller; (*bubble*) pétiller.

sparkling [spär'kling] *a* étincelant(e), scintillant(e); (*wine*) mousseux(euse), pétillant(e).

sparrow [spar'ō] *n* moineau *m*.

sparse [spärs] *a* clairsemé(e).

spartan [spär'tən] *a* (*fig*) spartiate.

spasm [spaz'əm] *n* (*MED*) spasme *m*; (*fig*) accès *m*.

spasmodic [spazmâd'ik] *a* (*fig*) intermittent(e).

spastic [spas'tik] *n* handicapé/e moteur.

spat [spat] *pt, pp of* **spit** ♦ *n* (*US*) prise *f* de bec.

spate [spāt] *n* (*fig*): ~ **of** avalanche *f or* torrent *m* de; **in** ~ (*river*) en crue.

spatial [spā'shəl] *a* spatial(e).

spatter [spat'ûr] *n* éclaboussure(s) *f(pl)* ♦ *vt* éclabousser ♦ *vi* gicler.

spatula [spach'ələ] *n* spatule *f*.

spawn [spôn] *vt* pondre; (*pej*) engendrer ♦ *vi* frayer ♦ *n* frai *m*.

SPCA *n abbr* (*US*: = *Society for the Prevention of Cruelty to Animals*) ≈ SPA *f*.

SPCC *n abbr* (*US*) = *Society for the Prevention of Cruelty to Children*.

speak, *pt* **spoke,** *pp* **spoken** [spēk, spōk, spō'kən] *vt* (*language*) parler; (*truth*) dire ♦ *vi* parler; (*make a speech*) prendre la parole; **to** ~ **to sb/of** *or* **about sth** parler à qn/de qch; ~**ing!** (*on telephone*) c'est moi-même!; **to** ~ **one's mind** dire ce que l'on pense; **it** ~**s for itself** c'est évident; ~ **up!** parle plus fort!; **he has no money to** ~ **of** il n'a pas d'argent.

speak for *vt fus*: **to** ~ **for sb** parler pour qn; **that picture is already spoken for** (*in shop*) ce tableau est déjà réservé.

speaker [spē'kûr] *n* (*in public*) orateur *m*; (*also*: **loud**~) haut-parleur *m*; (*POL*): **the S**~ *le président de la Chambre des représentants* (*US*) *or des communes* (*Brit*); **are you a Welsh** ~? parlez-vous gallois?

speaking [spē'king] *a* parlant(e); **French-**~ **people** les francophones; **to be on** ~ **terms** se parler.

spear [spi'ûr] *n* lance *f* ♦ *vt* transpercer.

spearhead [spēr'hed] *n* fer *m* de lance; (*MIL*) colonne *f* d'attaque ♦ *vt* (*attack etc*) mener.

spearmint [spēr'mint] *n* (*BOT etc*) menthe verte.

special [spesh'əl] *a* spécial(e) ♦ *n* (*train*) train spécial; **take** ~ **care** soyez particulièrement prudents; **nothing** ~ rien de spécial; **"on special"** (*US COMM*) en promotion; **today's** ~ (*at restaurant*) le plat du jour.

special agent *n* agent secret.

special correspondent *n* envoyé spécial.

special delivery *n* (*MAIL*): **by** ~ en exprès.

specialist [spesh'əlist] *n* spécialiste *m/f*; **heart** ~ cardiologue *m/f*.

speciality [speshēal'ətē] *n* (*Brit*) = **specialty**.

specialize [spesh'əlīz] *vi*: **to** ~ **(in)** se spécialiser (dans).

specially [spesh'əlē] *ad* spécialement, particulièrement.

special offer *n* (*COMM*) réclame *f*.

specialty [spesh'əltē] *n* (*US*) spécialité *f*.

species [spē'shēz] *n* (*pl inv*) espèce *f*.

specific [spisif'ik] *a* (*not vague*) précis(e), explicite; (*particular*) particulier(ière); (*BOT, CHEMISTRY etc*) spécifique; **to be** ~ **to** être particulier à, être le *or* un caractère (*or les caractères*) spécifique(s) de.

specifically [spisif'iklē] *ad* explicitement, précisément; (*intend, ask, design*) expressément, spécialement; (*exclusively*) exclusivement, spécifiquement.

specification [spesəfəkā'shən] *n* spécification *f*; stipulation *f*; **~s** *npl* (*of car, building etc*) spécification.

specify [spes'əfī] *vt* spécifier, préciser; **unless otherwise specified** sauf indication contraire.

specimen [spes'əmən] *n* spécimen *m*, échantillon *m*; (*MED*) prélèvement *m*.

specimen copy *n* spécimen *m*.

specimen signature *n* spécimen *m* de signature.

speck [spek] *n* petite tache, petit point; (*particle*) grain *m*; **to have a ~ in one's eye** (*US*) avoir une poussière *or* une saleté dans l'œil.

speckled [spek'əld] *a* tacheté(e), moucheté(e).

specs [speks] *npl* (*col*) lunettes *fpl*.

spectacle [spek'təkəl] *n* spectacle *m*.

spectacles [spek'təkəlz] *npl* (*Brit*) lunettes *fpl*.

spectacular [spektak'yəlûr] *a* spectaculaire ♦ *n* (*CINEMA etc*) superproduction *f*.

spectator [spek'tātûr] *n* spectateur/trice.

specter, (*Brit*) **spectre** [spek'tûr] *n* spectre *m*, fantôme *m*.

spectrum, *pl* **spectra** [spek'trəm, -rə] *n* spectre *m*; (*fig*) gamme *f*.

speculate [spek'yəlāt] *vi* spéculer; (*try to guess*): **to ~ about** s'interroger sur.

speculation [spekyəlā'shən] *n* spéculation *f*; conjectures *fpl*.

speculative [spek'yəlātiv] *a* spéculatif(ive).

speculator [spek'yəlātûr] *n* spéculateur/trice.

speech [spēch] *n* (*faculty*) parole *f*; (*talk*) discours *m*, allocution *f*; (*manner of speaking*) façon *f* de parler, langage *m*; (*language*) langage *m*; (*enunciation*) élocution *f*.

speech day *n* (*Brit SCOL*) distribution *f* des prix.

speech impediment *n* défaut *m* d'élocution.

speechless [spēch'lis] *a* muet(te).

speech therapy *n* orthophonie *f*.

speed [spēd] *n* vitesse *f*; (*promptness*) rapidité *f* ♦ *vi* (*pt, pp* **sped** [sped]): **to ~ along/by** *etc* aller/passer *etc* à toute vitesse; (*AUT*: *exceed ~ limit*) faire un excès de vitesse; **at full** *or* **top ~** à toute vitesse *or* allure; **at a ~ of 70 km/h** à une vitesse de 70 km/h; **shorthand/typing ~s** nombre *m* de mots à la minute en sténographie/dactylographie; **five-~ transmission** boîte cinq vitesses.

speed up, *pt, pp* **~ed up** *vi* aller plus vite, accélérer ♦ *vt* accélérer.

speedboat [spēd'bōt] *n* vedette *f*, hors-bord *m* *inv*.

speedily [spē'dilē] *ad* rapidement, promptement.

speeding [spē'ding] *n* (*AUT*) excès *m* de vitesse.

speed limit *n* limitation *f* de vitesse, vitesse maximale permise.

speedometer [spēdâm'itûr] *n* compteur *m* (de vitesse).

speed trap *n* (*AUT*) piège *m* de police pour contrôle de vitesse.

speedway [spēd'wā] *n* (*SPORT*) piste *f* de vitesse pour motos; (: *also*: **~ racing**) épreuve(s) *f(pl)* de vitesse de motos.

speedy [spē'dē] *a* rapide, prompt(e).

speleologist [spēlēâl'əjist] *n* spéléologue *m/f*.

spell [spel] *n* (*also*: **magic ~**) sortilège *m*,

charme *m*; (*period of time*) (courte) période *f* ♦ *vt* (*pt, pp* **~ed** *or* **spelt** [speld, spelt]) (*in writing*) écrire, orthographier; (*aloud*) épeler; (*fig*) signifier; **to cast a ~ on sb** jeter un sort à qn; **he can't ~** il fait des fautes d'orthographe; **how do you ~ your name?** comment écrivez-vous votre nom?; **can you ~ it for me?** pouvez-vous me l'épeler?

spellbound [spel'bound] *a* envoûté(e), subjugué(e).

spelling [spel'ing] *n* orthographe *f*.

spelt [spelt] *pt, pp of* **spell**.

spelunker [spēlung'kûr] *n* (*US*) spéléologue *mf*.

spend, *pt, pp* **spent** [spend, spent] *vt* (*money*) dépenser; (*time, life*) passer; (*devote*): **to ~ time/money/effort on sth** consacrer du temps/de l'argent/de l'énergie à qch.

spending [spen'ding] *n* dépenses *fpl*; **government ~** les dépenses publiques.

spending money *n* argent *m* de poche.

spending power *n* pouvoir *m* d'achat.

spendthrift [spend'thrift] *n* dépensier/ière.

spent [spent] *pt, pp of* **spend** ♦ *a* (*patience*) épuisé(e), à bout; (*cartridge, bullets*) vide.

sperm [spûrm] *n* spermatozoïde *m*; (*semen*) sperme *m*.

sperm whale *n* cachalot *m*.

spew [spyōō] *vt* vomir.

sphere [sfēr] *n* sphère *f*; (*fig*) sphère, domaine *m*.

spherical [sfär'ikəl] *a* sphérique.

sphinx [sfingks] *n* sphinx *m*.

spice [spīs] *n* épice *f* ♦ *vt* épicer.

spick-and-span [spik'ənspan'] *a* impeccable.

spicy [spī'sē] *a* épicé(e), relevé(e); (*fig*) piquant(e).

spider [spī'dûr] *n* araignée *f*; **~'s web** toile *f* d'araignée.

spiel [spēl] *n* laïus *m inv*.

spike [spīk] *n* pointe *f*; (*ELEC*) pointe de tension; **~s** *npl* (*SPORT*) chaussures *fpl* à pointes.

spike heel *n* (*US*) talon *m* aiguille.

spiky [spī'kē] *a* (*bush, branch*) épineux(euse); (*animal*) plein(e) de piquants.

spill, *pt, pp* **~ed** *or* **spilt** [spil, -d, -t] *vt* renverser; répandre ♦ *vi* se répandre; **to ~ the beans** (*col*) vendre la mèche; (: *confess*) lâcher le morceau.

spill out *vi* sortir à flots, se répandre.

spill over *vi* déborder.

spin [spin] *n* (*revolution of wheel*) tour *m*; (*AVIAT*) (chute *f* en) vrille *f*; (*trip in car*) petit tour, balade *f* ♦ *vb* (*pt* **spun, span**, *pp* **spun** [spun, span]) *vt* (*wool etc*) filer; (*wheel*) faire tourner; (*Brit*: *clothes*) essorer ♦ *vi* tourner, tournoyer; **to ~ a yarn** débiter une longue histoire.

spin out *vt* faire durer.

spinach [spin'ich] *n* épinard *m*; (*as food*) épinards.

spinal [spī'nəl] *a* vertébral(e), spinal(e).

spinal column *n* colonne vertébrale.

spinal cord *n* moelle épinière.

spindly [spind'lē] *a* grêle, filiforme.

spin-dry [spindrī'] *vt* essorer.

spin-dryer [spindrī'ûr] *n* (*Brit*) essoreuse *f*.

spine [spīn] *n* colonne vertébrale); (*thorn*)

épine *f*, piquant *m*.

spine-chilling [spīn'chiling] *a* terrifiant(e).

spineless [spīn'lis] *a* invertébré(e); (*fig*) mou(molle), sans caractère.

spinner [spin'ûr] *n* (*of thread*) fileur/euse.

spinning [spin'ing] *n* (*of thread*) filage *m*; (*by machine*) filature *f*.

spinning top *n* toupie *f*.

spinning wheel *n* rouet *m*.

spin-off [spin'óf] *n* sous-produit *m*; avantage inattendu.

spinster [spin'stûr] *n* célibataire *f*; vieille fille.

spiral [spī'rəl] *n* spirale *f* ♦ *a* en spirale ♦ *vi* (*fig: prices etc*) monter en flèche; **the inflationary ~** la spirale inflationniste.

spiral staircase *n* escalier *m* en colimaçon.

spire [spī'ûr] *n* flèche *f*, aiguille *f*.

spirit [spir'it] *n* (*soul*) esprit *m*, âme *f*; (*ghost*) esprit, revenant *m*; (*mood*) esprit, état *m* d'esprit; (*courage*) courage *m*, énergie *f*; **~s** *npl* (*drink*) spiritueux *mpl*, alcool *m*; **in good ~s** de bonne humeur; **in low ~s** démoralisé(e); **community ~** solidarité *f*; **public ~** civisme *m*.

spirit duplicator *n* duplicateur *m* à alcool.

spirited [spir'itid] *a* vif(vive), fougueux(euse), plein(e) d'allant.

spirit level *n* niveau *m* à bulle.

spiritual [spir'ichōōəl] *a* spirituel(le); religieux(euse) ♦ *n* (*also:* **Negro ~**) spiritual *m*.

spiritualism [spir'ichōōəlizəm] *n* spiritisme *m*.

spit [spit] *n* (*for roasting*) broche *f*; (*spittle*) crachat *m*; (*saliva*) salive *f* ♦ *vi* (*pt, pp* spat [spat]) cracher; (*sound*) crépiter.

spite [spīt] *n* rancune *f*, dépit *m* ♦ *vt* contrarier, vexer; **in ~ of** en dépit de, malgré.

spiteful [spīt'fəl] *a* malveillant(e), rancunier(ière).

spitroast [spit'rōst] *vt* faire rôtir à la broche.

spitting [spit'ing] *n*: **"~ prohibited"** "défense de cracher" ♦ *a*: **to be the ~ image of sb** être le portrait tout craché de qn.

spittle [spit'əl] *n* salive *f*; bave *f*; crachat *m*.

splash [splash] *n* éclaboussement *m*; (*of color*) tache *f* ♦ *excl* (*sound*) plouf! ♦ *vt* éclabousser ♦ *vi* (*also:* **~ about**) barboter, patauger.

splashdown [splash'doun] *n* amerrissage *m*.

splay [splā] *a*: **~footed** marchant les pieds en dehors.

spleen [splēn] *n* (*ANAT*) rate *f*.

splendid [splen'did] *a* splendide, superbe, magnifique.

splendor, (*Brit*) **splendour** [splen'dûr] *n* splendeur *f*, magnificence *f*.

splice [splīs] *vt* épisser.

splint [splint] *n* attelle *f*, éclisse *f*.

splinter [splin'tûr] *n* (*wood*) écharde *f*; (*metal*) éclat *m* ♦ *vi* se fragmenter.

splinter group *n* groupe dissident.

split [split] *n* fente *f*, déchirure *f*; (*fig: POL*) scission *f* ♦ *vb* (*pt, pp* split) *vt* fendre, déchirer; (*party*) diviser; (*work, profits*) partager, répartir ♦ *vi* (*break*) se fendre, se briser; (*divide*) se diviser; **let's ~ the difference** coupons la poire en deux; **to do the ~s** faire le grand écart.

  split up *vi* (*couple*) se séparer, rompre; (*meeting*) se disperser.

split-level [split'lev'əl] *a* (*house*) à deux *or* plu-

sieurs niveaux.

split peas *npl* pois cassés.

split personality *n* double personnalité *f*.

split second *n* fraction *f* de seconde.

splitting [split'ing] *a*: **a ~ headache** un mal de tête atroce.

splutter [splut'ûr] *vi* = **sputter.**

spoil [spoil], *pt, pp* **~ed** *or* **spoilt** [spoil, -d, -t] *vt* (*damage*) abîmer; (*mar*) gâcher; (*child*) gâter; (*ballot paper*) rendre nul ♦ *vi*: **to be ~ing for a fight** chercher la bagarre.

spoiler [spoi'lûr] *n* spoiler *m*.

spoils [spoilz] *npl* butin *m*.

spoilsport [spoil'spórt] *n* trouble-fête *m/f inv*, rabat-joie *m inv*.

spoilt [spoilt] *pt, pp of* **spoil.**

spoke [spōk] *pt of* **speak** ♦ *n* rayon *m*.

spoken [spō'kən] *pp of* **speak.**

spokesman [spōks'mən] *n* porte-parole *m inv.*

sponge [spunj] *n* éponge *f*; (*CULIN: also:* **~ cake**) ≈ biscuit *m* de Savoie ♦ *vt* éponger ♦ *vi*: **to ~ off sb** vivre aux crochets de qn.

sponge bag *n* (*Brit*) trousse *f* de toilette.

sponge cake *n* ≈ biscuit *m* de Savoie.

sponger [spun'jûr] *n* (*pej*) parasite *m.*

spongy [spun'jē] *a* spongieux(euse).

sponsor [spán'sûr] *n* sponsor *m*, personne *f* (*ou* organisme *m*) qui assure le parrainage; (*of new member*) parrain *m*/marraine *f* ♦ *vt* (*program, competition etc*) parrainer, patronner, sponsoriser; (*POL: bill*) présenter; (*new member*) parrainer; **I ~ed him at 25¢ a mile** (*in fund-raising race*) je me suis engagé à lui donner 25 cents par mile.

sponsorship [spán'sûrship] *n* patronage *m*, parrainage *m.*

spontaneity [spántəne'itē] *n* spontanéité *f.*

spontaneous [spántā'nēəs] *a* spontané(e).

spooky [spōō'kē] *a* qui donne la chair de poule.

spool [spōōl] *n* bobine *f.*

spoon [spōōn] *n* cuiller *f.*

spoon-feed [spōōn'fēd] *vt* nourrir à la cuiller; (*fig*) mâcher le travail à.

spoonful [spōōn'fōōl] *n* cuillerée *f.*

sporadic [spôrad'ik] *a* sporadique.

sport [spórt] *n* sport *m*; (*amusement*) divertissement *m*; (*person*) chic type/chic fille ♦ *vt* arborer; **indoor/outdoor ~s** sports en salle/de plein air; **to say sth in ~** dire qch pour rire.

sporting [spôr'ting] *a* sportif(ive); **to give sb a ~ chance** donner sa chance à qn.

sports car [spôrts kâr] *n* voiture *f* de sport.

sport(s) coat *n* (*US*) veste *f* de sport.

sports field *n* terrain *m* de sport.

sports jacket *n* (*Brit*) = **sport(s) coat.**

sportsman [spôrts'mən] *n* sportif *m.*

sportsmanship [spôrts'mənship] *n* esprit sportif, esprit *f* de jeu.

sports page *n* page *f* des sports.

sportswear [spôrts'weûr] *n* vêtements *mpl* de sport.

sportswoman [spôrts'wōōmən] *n* sportive *f.*

sporty [spôr'tē] *a* sportif(ive).

spot [spât] *n* tache *f*; (*dot: on pattern*) pois *m*; (*pimple*) bouton *m*; (*place*) endroit *m*, coin *m*; (*also:* **~ advertisement**) message *m* publicitaire; (*small amount*): **a ~ of** un peu de

♦ *vt* (*notice*) apercevoir, repérer; **on the ~** sur place, sur les lieux; (*immediately*) sur le champ; **to pay cash on the ~** (*US*) payer rubis sur l'ongle; **to put sb on the ~** (*fig*) mettre qn dans l'embarras; **to come out in ~s** se couvrir de boutons, avoir une éruption de boutons.

spot check *n* contrôle intermittent.

spotless [spât'lis] *a* immaculé(e).

spotlight [spât'līt] *n* projecteur *m*; (*AUT*) phare *m* auxiliaire.

spot price *n* prix *m* sur place.

spotted [spât'id] *a* tacheté(e), moucheté(e); à pois; **~ with** tacheté(e) de.

spotty [spât'ē] *a* (*face*) boutonneux(euse).

spouse [spous] *n* époux/épouse.

spout [spout] *n* (*of jug*) bec *m*; (*of liquid*) jet *m* ♦ *vi* jaillir.

sprain [sprān] *n* entorse *f*, foulure *f* ♦ *vt*: **to ~ one's ankle** se fouler *or* se tordre la cheville.

sprang [sprang] *pt of* **spring**.

sprawl [sprôl] *vi* s'étaler ♦ *n*: **urban ~** expansion urbaine; **to send sb ~ing** envoyer qn rouler par terre.

spray [sprā] *n* jet *m* (en fines gouttelettes); (*container*) vaporisateur *m*, bombe *f*; (*of flowers*) petit bouquet ♦ *vt* vaporiser, pulvériser; (*crops*) traiter ♦ *cpd* (*deodorant etc*) en bombe *or* atomiseur.

spread [spred] *n* (*distribution*) répartition *f*; (*CULIN*) pâte *f* à tartiner; (*PRESS, TYP*: *two pages*) double page *f* ♦ *vb* (*pt, pp* **spread**) *vt* (*paste, contents*) étendre, étaler; (*rumor, disease*) répandre, propager; (*repayments*) échelonner, étaler; (*wealth*) répartir ♦ *vi* s'étendre; se répandre; se propager; **middle-age ~** embonpoint *m* (pris avec l'âge).

spread-eagled [spred'ēgəld] *a*: **to be** *or* **lie ~** être étendu(e) bras et jambes écartés.

spreadsheet [spred'shēt] *n* (*COMPUT*) tableur *m*.

spree [sprē] *n*: **to go on a ~** faire la fête.

sprig [sprig] *n* rameau *m*.

sprightly [sprīt'lē] *a* alerte.

spring [spring] *n* (*leap*) bond *m*, saut *m*; (*coiled metal*) ressort *m*; (*bounciness*) élasticité *f*; (*season*) printemps *m*; (*of water*) source *f* ♦ *vb* (*pt* **sprang**, *pp* **sprung** [sprang, sprung]) *vi* bondir, sauter ♦ *vt*: **to ~ a leak** (*pipe etc*) se mettre à fuir; **he sprang the news on me** il m'a annoncé la nouvelle de but en blanc; **in ~, in the ~** au printemps; **to ~ from** provenir de; **to ~ into action** passer à l'action; **to walk with a ~ in one's step** marcher d'un pas souple.

spring up *vi* (*problem*) se présenter, surgir.

springboard [spring'bôrd] *n* tremplin *m*.

spring-clean [spring'klēn'] *n* (*also:* **~ing**) grand nettoyage de printemps.

spring onion *n* (*Brit*) ciboule *f*, cive *f*.

springtime [spring'tīm] *n* printemps *m*.

springy [spring'ē] *a* élastique, souple.

sprinkle [spring'kəl] *vt* (*pour*) répandre; verser; **to ~ water** *etc* **on, ~ with water** *etc* asperger d'eau *etc*; **to ~ sugar** *etc* **on, ~ with sugar** *etc* saupoudrer de sucre *etc*; **~d with** (*fig*) parsemé(e) de.

sprinkler [spring'klûr] *n* (*for lawn etc*) arro-

seur *m*; (*to put out fire*) diffuseur *m* d'extincteur automatique d'incendie.

sprinkling [spring'kling] *n* (*of water*) quelques gouttes *fpl*; (*of salt*) pincée *f*; (*of sugar*) légère couche.

sprint [sprint] *n* sprint *m* ♦ *vi* sprinter.

sprinter [sprin'tûr] *n* sprinteur/euse.

sprite [sprīt] *n* lutin *m*.

sprocket [sprâk'it] *n* (*on printer etc*) picot *m*.

sprout [sprout] *vi* germer, pousser.

sprouts [sprouts] *npl* (*also:* **Brussels ~**) choux *mpl* de Bruxelles.

spruce [sproōs] *n* épicéa *m* ♦ *a* net(te), pimpant(e).

spruce up *vt* (*smarten up: room etc*) apprêter; **to ~ o.s. up** se faire beau(belle).

sprung [sprung] *pp of* **spring**.

spry [sprī] *a* alerte, vif(vive).

SPUC *n* *abbr* = *Society for the Protection of Unborn Children*.

spud [spud] *n* (*col: potato*) patate *f*.

spun [spun] *pt, pp of* **spin**.

spur [spûr] *n* éperon *m*; (*fig*) aiguillon *m* ♦ *vt* (*also:* **~ on**) éperonner; aiguillonner; **on the ~ of the moment** sous l'impulsion du moment.

spurious [spyoōr'ēəs] *a* faux(fausse).

spurn [spûrn] *vt* repousser avec mépris.

spurt [spûrt] *n* jet *m*; (*of energy*) sursaut *m* ♦ *vi* jaillir, gicler; **to put in** *or* **on a ~** (*runner*) piquer un sprint; (*fig: in work etc*) donner un coup de collier.

sputter [sput'ûr] *vi* bafouiller; postillonner.

spy [spī] *n* espion/ne ♦ *vi*: **to ~ on** espionner, épier ♦ *vt* (*see*) apercevoir ♦ *cpd* (*film, story*) d'espionnage.

spying [spī'ing] *n* espionnage *m*.

Sq. *abbr* (*in address*) = **square**.

sq. *abbr* (*MATH etc*) = **square**.

squabble [skwâb'əl] *n* querelle *f*, chamaillerie *f* ♦ *vi* se chamailler.

squad [skwâd] *n* (*MIL, POLICE*) escouade *f*, groupe *m*; (*SOCCER*) contingent *m*.

squad car *n* (*POLICE*) voiture *f* de police.

squadron [skwâd'rən] *n* (*MIL*) escadron *m*; (*AVIAT, NAUT*) escadrille *f*.

squalid [skwâl'id] *a* sordide, ignoble.

squall [skwôl] *n* rafale *f*, bourrasque *f*.

squalor [skwâl'ûr] *n* conditions *fpl* sordides.

squander [skwân'dûr] *vt* gaspiller, dilapider.

square [skwär] *n* carré *m*; (*in town*) place *f*; (*US: block*) îlot *m*, pâté *m* de maisons; (*instrument*) équerre *f* ♦ *a* carré(e); (*honest*) honnête, régulier(ière); (*col: ideas, tastes*) vieux jeu *inv*, qui retarde ♦ *vt* (*arrange*) régler; arranger; (*MATH*) élever au carré; (*reconcile*) concilier ♦ *vi* (*agree*) cadrer, s'accorder; **all ~** quitte; à égalité; **a ~ meal** un repas convenable; **2 meters ~** (de) 2 mètres sur 2; **1 ~ meter** 1 mètre carré; **we're back to ~ one** (*fig*) on se retrouve à la case départ.

square bracket *n* (*TYP*) crochet *m*.

squarely [skwär'lē] *ad* carrément; (*honestly, fairly*) honnêtement, équitablement.

square root *n* racine carrée.

squash [skwâsh] *n* (*SPORT*) squash *m*; (*vegetable*) courge *f*; (*Brit: drink*): **lemon/orange ~** citronnade/orangeade *f* ♦ *vt* écraser.

squat [skwât] *a* petit(e) et épais(se), ramassé(e) ♦ *vi* s'accroupir; (*on property*) squatter, squattériser.
squatter [skwât'ûr] *n* squatter *m*.
squawk [skwôk] *vi* pousser un *or* des gloussement(s).
squeak [skwēk] *n* (*of hinge, wheel etc*) grincement *m*; (*of shoes*) craquement *m*; (*of mouse etc*) petit cri aigu ♦ *vi* grincer, crier.
squeal [skwēl] *vi* pousser un *or* des cri(s) aigu(s) *or* perçant(s).
squeamish [skwē'mish] *a* facilement dégoûté(e); facilement scandalisé(e).
squeeze [skwēz] *n* pression *f*; (*also:* **credit** ~) encadrement *m* du crédit, restrictions *fpl* de crédit ♦ *vt* presser; (*hand, arm*) serrer ♦ *vi*: **to ~ past/under sth** se glisser avec (beaucoup de) difficulté devant/sous qch; **a ~ of lemon** quelques gouttes de citron.
  squeeze out *vt* exprimer; (*fig*) soutirer.
squelch [skwelch] *vi* faire un bruit de succion; patauger.
squib [skwib] *n* pétard *m*.
squid [skwid] *n* calmar *m*.
squiggle [skwig'əl] *n* gribouillis *m*.
squint [skwint] *vt* loucher ♦ *n*: **he has a ~** il louche, il souffre de strabisme; **to ~ at sth** regarder qch du coin de l'œil; (*quickly*) jeter un coup d'œil à qch.
squirm [skwûrm] *vi* se tortiller.
squirrel [skwûr'əl] *n* écureuil *m*.
squirt [skwûrt] *n* jet *m* ♦ *vi* jaillir, gicler.
Sr *abbr* = **senior, sister** (*REL*).
Sri Lanka [srē lángk'ə] *n* Sri Lanka *m or f*.
SRO *abbr* (*US*) = *standing room only*.
SS *abbr* (= *steamship*) S/S.
SSA *n abbr* (*US:* = *Social Security Administration*) organisme de sécurité sociale.
SST *n abbr* (*US*) = *supersonic transport*.
St *abbr* (= *saint*) St; (= *street*) R.
stab [stab] *n* (*with knife etc*) coup *m* (de couteau *etc*); (*col: try*): **to have a ~** (at (doing) sth s'essayer à (faire) qch ♦ *vt* poignarder; **to ~ sb to death** tuer qn à coups de couteau.
stabbing [stab'ing] *n*: **there's been a ~** quelqu'un a été attaqué à coups de couteau ♦ *a* (*pain, ache*) lancinant(e).
stability [stəbil'ətē] *n* stabilité *f*.
stabilization [stābiləzā'shən] *n* stabilisation *f*.
stabilize [stā'bəlīz] *vt* stabiliser ♦ *vi* se stabiliser.
stabilizer [stā'bəlīzûr] *n* stabilisateur *m*.
stable [stā'bəl] *n* écurie *f* ♦ *a* stable; **riding ~s** centre *m* d'équitation.
stableboy [stā'bəlboi] *n* garçon *m* d'écurie.
staccato [stəkâ'tō] *ad* staccato ♦ *a* (*MUS*) piqué(e); (*noise, voice*) saccadé(e).
stack [stak] *n* tas *m*, pile *f* ♦ *vt* empiler, entasser.
stadium [stā'dēəm] *n* stade *m*.
staff [staf] *n* (*work force*) personnel *m*; (*Brit SCOL: also:* **teaching ~**) professeurs *mpl*, enseignants *mpl*, personnel enseignant; (*servants*) domestiques *mpl*; (*MIL*) état-major *m*; (*stick*) perche *f*, bâton *m* ♦ *vt* pourvoir en personnel.
Staffs *abbr* (*Brit*) = *Staffordshire*.
stag [stag] *n* cerf *m*; (*Brit STOCK EXCHANGE*) loup *m*.

stage [stāj] *n* scène *f*; (*profession*): **the ~** le théâtre; (*point*) étape *f*, stade *m*; (*platform*) estrade *f* ♦ *vt* (*play*) monter, mettre en scène; (*demonstration*) organiser; (*fig: recovery etc*) effectuer; **in ~s** par étapes, par degrés; **to go through a difficult ~** traverser une période difficile; **in the early ~s** au début; **in the final ~s** à la fin.
stagecoach [stāj'kōch] *n* diligence *f*.
stage door *n* entrée *f* des artistes.
stage fright *n* trac *m*.
stagehand [stāj'hand] *n* machiniste *m*.
stage-manage [stāj'man'ij] *vt* (*fig*) orchestrer.
stage manager *n* régisseur *m*.
stagger [stag'ûr] *vi* chanceler, tituber ♦ *vt* (*person*) stupéfier; bouleverser; (*hours, vacation*) étaler, échelonner.
staggering [stag'ûring] *a* (*amazing*) stupéfiant(e), renversant(e).
stagnant [stag'nənt] *a* stagnant(e).
stagnate [stag'nāt] *vi* stagner, croupir.
stagnation [stagnā'shən] *n* stagnation *f*.
stag party *n* enterrement *m* de vie de garçon.
staid [stād] *a* posé(e), rassis(e).
stain [stān] *n* tache *f*; (*coloring*) colorant *m* ♦ *vt* tacher; (*wood*) teindre.
stained glass window [stānd' glas win'dō] *n* vitrail *m*.
stainless [stān'lis] *a* (*steel*) inoxydable.
stain remover *n* détachant *m*.
stair [stär] *n* (*step*) marche *f*; **~s** *npl* escalier *m*; **on the ~s** dans l'escalier.
staircase [stär'kās], **stairway** [stär'wā] *n* escalier *m*.
stairwell [stär'wel] *n* cage *f* d'escalier.
stake [stāk] *n* pieu *m*, poteau *m*; (*BETTING*) enjeu *m* ♦ *vt* risquer, jouer; (*also:* **~ out:** *area*) marquer, délimiter; **to be at ~** être en jeu; **to have a ~ in sth** avoir des intérêts (en jeu) dans qch; **to ~ a claim (to sth)** revendiquer (qch).
stalactite [stəlak'tīt] *n* stalactite *f*.
stalagmite [stəlag'mīt] *n* stalagmite *f*.
stale [stāl] *a* (*bread*) rassis(e); (*beer*) éventé(e); (*smell*) de renfermé.
stalemate [stāl'māt] *n* pat *m*; (*fig*) impasse *f*.
stalk [stôk] *n* tige *f* ♦ *vt* traquer ♦ *vi*: **to ~ in/out** *etc* entrer/sortir *etc* avec raideur.
stall [stôl] *n* (*in stable*) stalle *f*; (*Brit: in street, market etc*) éventaire *m*, étal *m* ♦ *vt* (*AUT*) caler ♦ *vi* (*AUT*) caler; (*fig*) essayer de gagner du temps; **~s** *npl* (*Brit: in cinema, theater*) orchestre *m*; **a newspaper/flower ~** un kiosque à journaux/de fleuriste.
stallholder [stôl'hōldûr] *n* (*Brit*) marchand/e en plein air.
stallion [stal'yən] *n* étalon *m* (*cheval*).
stalwart [stôl'wûrt] *n* partisan *m* fidèle.
stamen [stā'mən] *n* étamine *f*.
stamina [stam'inə] *n* vigueur *f*, endurance *f*.
stammer [stam'ûr] *n* bégaiement *m* ♦ *vi* bégayer.
stamp [stamp] *n* timbre *m*; (*mark, also fig*) empreinte *f*; (*on document*) cachet *m* ♦ *vi* (*also:* **~ one's foot**) taper du pied ♦ *vt* tamponner, estamper; (*letter*) timbrer; **~ed addressed envelope (sae)** (*Brit*) *enveloppe affranchie pour la réponse.*
  stamp out *vt* (*fire*) piétiner; (*crime*) éradi-

quer; (opposition) éliminer.
stamp album n album m de timbres(-poste).
stamp collecting n philatélie f.
stampede [stampēd'] n ruée f; (of cattle) débandade f.
stamp machine n distributeur m de timbres-poste.
stance [stans] n position f.
stand [stand] n (position) position f; (MIL) résistance f; (structure) guéridon m; support m; (COMM) étalage m, stand m; (SPORT) tribune f; (also: **music** ~) pupitre m ♦ vb (pt, pp **stood** [stŏŏd]) vi être or se tenir (debout); (rise) se lever, se mettre debout; (be placed) se trouver ♦ vt (place) mettre, poser; (tolerate, withstand) supporter; **to make a** ~ prendre position; **to take a** ~ **on an issue** prendre position sur un problème; **to** ~ **for parliament** (Brit) se présenter aux élections (comme candidat à la députation); **to** ~ **guard** or **watch** (MIL) monter la garde; **it** ~**s to reason** c'est logique; cela va de soi; **as things** ~ dans l'état actuel des choses; **to** ~ **sb a drink/meal** payer à boire/à manger à qn; **I can't** ~ **him** je ne peux pas le voir.
stand aside vi s'écarter.
stand by vi (be ready) se tenir prêt(e) ♦ vt fus (opinion) s'en tenir à.
stand down vi (withdraw) se retirer; (LAW) renoncer à ses droits.
stand for vt fus (signify) représenter, signifier; (tolerate) supporter, tolérer.
stand in for vt fus remplacer.
stand out vi (be prominent) ressortir.
stand up vi (rise) se lever, se mettre debout.
stand up for vt fus défendre.
stand up to vt fus tenir tête à, résister à.
stand-alone [stand'əlōn'] a (COMPUT) autonome.
standard [stan'dûrd] n (reference) norme f; (level) niveau m; (flag) étendard m ♦ a (size etc) ordinaire, normal(e); (model, feature) standard inv; (practice) courant(e); (text) de base ~**s** npl (morals) morale f, principes mpl; **to be** or **come up to** ~ être du niveau voulu or à la hauteur; **to apply a double** ~ avoir or appliquer deux poids deux mesures; ~ **of living** niveau de vie.
standardization [standûrdəzā'shən] n standardisation f.
standardize [stan'dûrdīz] vt standardiser.
standard lamp n (Brit) lampadaire m.
standard time n heure légale.
standby [stand'bī] n remplaçant/e ♦ a (provisions) de réserve; (generator) de secours; (ticket, passenger) sans garantie; **to be on** ~ se tenir prêt(e) (à intervenir); (doctor) être de garde.
stand-in [stand'in] n remplaçant/e; (CINEMA) doublure f.
standing [stan'ding] a debout inv; (permanent: rule) immuable; (army) de métier; (grievance) constant(e), de longue date ♦ n réputation f, rang m, standing m; (duration): **of 6 months'** ~ qui dure depuis 6 mois; **of many years'** ~ qui dure or existe depuis longtemps; **he was given a** ~ **ovation** on s'est levé pour l'acclamer; **it's a** ~ **joke** c'est

un vieux sujet de plaisanterie; **a man of some** ~ un homme estimé; **"no** ~**"** (US AUT) "stationnement interdit".
standing committee n commission permanente.
standing order n (Brit: at bank) virement permanent; ~**s** npl (MIL) règlement m.
standing room n places fpl debout.
standoffish [standôf'ish] a distant(e), froid(e).
standpat [stand'pat] a (US) inflexible, rigide.
standpipe [stand'pīp] n colonne f d'alimentation.
standpoint [stand'point] n point m de vue.
standstill [stand'stil] n: **at a** ~ à l'arrêt; (fig) au point mort; **to come to a** ~ s'immobiliser, s'arrêter.
stank [stangk] pt of **stink**.
stanza [stan'zə] n strophe f; couplet m.
staple [stā'pəl] n (for papers) agrafe f; (chief product) produit m de base ♦ a (food, crop, industry etc) de base, principal(e) ♦ vt agrafer.
stapler [stā'plûr] n agrafeuse f.
star [stâr] n étoile f; (celebrity) vedette f ♦ vi: **to** ~ **(in)** être la vedette (de) ♦ vt (CINEMA) avoir pour vedette; **4-**~ **hotel** hôtel m 4 étoiles; **4-**~ **petrol** (Brit) super m.
star attraction n grande attraction.
starboard [stâr'bûrd] n tribord m; **to** ~ à tribord.
starch [stârch] n amidon m.
starched [stârcht] a (collar) amidonné(e), empesé(e).
starchy [stâr'chē] a riche en féculents; (person) guindé(e).
stardom [stâr'dəm] n célébrité f.
stare [stär] n regard m fixe ♦ vi: **to** ~ **at** regarder fixement.
starfish [stâr'fish] n étoile f de mer.
stark [stârk] a (bleak) désolé(e), morne; (simplicity, color) austère; (reality, poverty) nu(e) ♦ ad: ~ **naked** complètement nu(e).
starlet [stâr'lit] n (CINEMA) starlette f.
starlight [stâr'līt] n: **by** ~ à la lumière des étoiles.
starling [stâr'ling] n étourneau m.
starlit [stâr'lit] a étoilé(e); illuminé(e) par les étoiles.
starry [stâr'ē] a étoilé(e).
starry-eyed [stâr'ēīd] a (innocent) ingénu(e).
star-studded [stâr'studid] a: **a** ~ **cast** une distribution prestigieuse.
start [stârt] n commencement m, début m; (of race) départ m; (sudden movement) sursaut m; (advantage) avance f ♦ vt commencer; (found: business, newspaper) lancer, créer ♦ vi partir, se mettre en route; (jump) sursauter; **to** ~ **doing sth** se mettre à faire qch; **at the** ~ au début; **for a** ~ d'abord, pour commencer; **to make an early** ~ partir or commencer de bonne heure; **to** ~ **(off) with** ... (firstly) d'abord ...; (at the beginning) au commencement ....
start off vi commencer; (leave) partir.
start over vi (US) recommencer.
start up vi commencer; (car) démarrer ♦ vt déclencher; (car) mettre en marche.
starter [stâr'tûr] n (AUT) démarreur m; (SPORT: official) starter m; (: runner, horse)

partant *m*; (*Brit* CULIN) entrée *f*; **for** ~**s** d'abord, pour commencer.

starting point [stâr'ting point] *n* point *m* de départ.

starting price [stâr'ting prīs] *n* prix initial.

startle [stâr'təl] *vt* faire sursauter; donner un choc à.

startling [stârt'ling] *a* surprenant(e), saisissant(e).

starvation [stârvā'shən] *n* faim *f*, famine *f*; **to die of** ~ mourir de faim *or* d'inanition.

starve [stârv] *vi* mourir de faim; être affamé(e) ♦ *vt* affamer; **I'm starving** je meurs de faim.

state [stāt] *n* état *m*; (*pomp*): **in** ~ en grande pompe ♦ *vt* (*declare*) déclarer, affirmer; (*specify*) indiquer, spécifier; **to be in a** ~ être dans ses états; ~ **of emergency** état d'urgence; ~ **of mind** état d'esprit; **the** ~ **of the art** l'état actuel de la technologie (*or* des connaissances).

state control *n* contrôle *m* de l'État.

stated [stā'tid] *a* fixé(e), prescrit(e).

State Department *n* (US) Département *m* d'État, ≈ ministère *m* des Affaires étrangères.

state highway *n* (US AUT) route nationale.

stateless [stāt'lis] *a* apatride.

stately [stāt'lē] *a* majestueux(euse), imposant(e).

statement [stāt'mənt] *n* déclaration *f*; (LAW) déposition *f*; (ECON) relevé *m*; **official** ~ communiqué officiel; ~ **of account, bank** ~ relevé de compte.

state-owned [stāt'ōnd'] *a* étatisé(e).

States [stāts] *npl*: **the** ~ les États-Unis *mpl*.

state secret *n* secret *m* d'État.

statesman [stāts'mən] *n* homme *m* d'État.

statesmanship [stāts'mənship] *n* qualités *fpl* d'homme d'état.

static [stat'ik] *n* (RADIO) parasites *mpl*; (*also*: ~ **electricity**) électricité *f* statique ♦ *a* statique.

station [stā'shən] *n* gare *f*; (MIL, POLICE) poste *m* (militaire *or* de police *etc*); (*rank*) condition *f*, rang *m* ♦ *vt* placer, poster; **action** ~**s** postes de combat; **to be** ~**ed in** (MIL) être en garnison à.

stationary [stā'shənārē] *a* à l'arrêt, immobile.

stationer [stā'shənûr] *n* papetier/ière; ~**'s (shop)** papeterie *f*.

stationery [stā'shənārē] *n* papier *m* à lettres, petit matériel de bureau.

station master *n* (RAIL) chef *m* de gare.

station wagon *n* (US) break *m*.

statistic [stətis'tik] *n* statistique *f*.

statistical [stətis'tikəl] *a* statistique.

statistics [stətis'tiks] *n* (*science*) statistique *f*.

statue [stach'ōō] *n* statue *f*.

statuesque [stachōōesk'] *a* sculptural(e).

statuette [stachōōet'] *n* statuette *f*.

stature [stach'ûr] *n* stature *f*; (*fig*) envergure *f*.

status [stā'təs] *n* position *f*, situation *f*; (*prestige*) prestige *m*; (ADMIN, *official position*) statut *m*.

status quo [stā'təs kwō] *n*: **the** ~ le statu quo.

status symbol *n* marque *f* de standing, signe

extérieur de richesse.

statute [stach'ōōt] *n* loi *f*; ~**s** *npl* (*of club etc*) statuts *mpl*.

statute book *n* ≈ code *m*, textes *mpl* de loi.

statutory [stach'ōōtôrē] *a* statutaire, prévu(e) par un article de loi; ~ **meeting** assemblée constitutive *or* statutaire.

staunch [stônch] *a* sûr(e), loyal(e) ♦ *vt* étancher.

stave [stāv] *n* (MUS) portée *f* ♦ *vt*: **to** ~ **off** (*attack*) parer; (*threat*) conjurer.

stay [stā] *n* (*period of time*) séjour *m*; (LAW): ~ **of execution** sursis *m* à statuer ♦ *vi* rester; (*reside*) loger; (*spend some time*) séjourner; **to** ~ **put** ne pas bouger; **to** ~ **with friends** loger chez des amis; **to** ~ **the night** passer la nuit.

stay behind *vi* rester en arrière.

stay in *vi* (*at home*) rester à la maison.

stay on *vi* rester.

stay out *vi* (*of house*) ne pas rentrer; (*strikers*) rester en grève.

stay up *vi* (*at night*) ne pas se coucher.

staying power [stā'ing pou'ûr] *n* endurance *f*.

STD *n abbr* (*Brit*: – *subscriber trunk dialling*) l'automatique *m*; (= *sexually transmitted disease*) MST *f*.

stead [sted] *n*: **in sb's** ~ à la place de qn.

steadfast [sted'fast] *a* ferme, résolu(e).

steadily [sted'ilē] *ad* régulièrement; fermement; d'une voix *etc* ferme.

steady [sted'ē] *a* stable, solide, ferme; (*regular*) constant(e), régulier(ière); (*person*) calme, pondéré(e) ♦ *vt* assurer, stabiliser; (*voice*) assurer; **to** ~ **oneself** reprendre son aplomb.

steak [stāk] *n* (*meat*) bifteck *m*, steak *m*; (*fish*) tranche *f*.

steakhouse [stāk'hous] *n* ≈ grill-room *m*.

steal, *pt* **stole**, *pp* **stolen** [stēl, stōl, stō'lən] *vt*, *vi* voler.

steal away, steal off *vi* s'esquiver.

stealth [stelth] *n*: **by** ~ furtivement.

stealthy [stel'thē] *a* furtif(ive).

steam [stēm] *n* vapeur *f* ♦ *vt* passer à la vapeur; (CULIN) cuire à la vapeur ♦ *vi* fumer; (*ship*): **to** ~ **along** filer; **under one's own** ~ (*fig*) par ses propres moyens; **to run out of** ~ (*fig*: *person*) caler; être à bout; **to let off** ~ (*fig*: *col*) se défouler.

steam up *vi* (*window*) se couvrir de buée; **to get** ~**ed up about sth** (*fig*: *col*) s'exciter à propos de qch.

steam engine *n* locomotive *f* à vapeur.

steamer [stē'mûr] *n* (bateau *m* à) vapeur *m*; (CULIN) ≈ couscoussier *m*.

steam iron *n* fer *m* à repasser à vapeur.

steamroller [stēm'rōlûr] *n* rouleau compresseur.

steamy [stē'mē] *a* embué(e), humide.

steed [stēd] *n* (*literary*) coursier *m*.

steel [stēl] *n* acier *m* ♦ *cpd* d'acier.

steel band *n* steel band *m*.

steel industry *n* sidérurgie *f*.

steel mill *n* aciérie *f*, usine *f* sidérurgique.

steelworks [stēl'wûrks] *n* aciérie *f*.

steely [stē'lē] *a* (*determination*) inflexible; (*eyes, gaze*) d'acier.

steep [stēp] *a* raide, escarpé(e); (*price*) très

élevé(e), excessif(ive) ♦ *vt* (faire) tremper.
steeple [stē'pəl] *n* clocher *m*.
steeplechase [stē'pəlchās] *n* steeple(-chase) *m*.
steeplejack [stē'pəljak] *n* réparateur *m* de clochers et de hautes cheminées.
steeply [stēp'lē] *ad* en pente raide.
steer [stēr] *n* bœuf *m* ♦ *vt* diriger, gouverner; (*lead*) guider ♦ *vi* tenir le gouvernail; **to ~ clear of sb/sth** (*fig*) éviter qn/qch.
steering [stēr'ing] *n* (*AUT*) conduite *f*.
steering column *n* (*AUT*) colonne *f* de direction.
steering committee *n* comité *m* d'organisation.
steering wheel *n* volant *m*.
stellar [stel'ûr] *a* stellaire.
stem [stem] *n* (*of plant*) tige *f*; (*of leaf, fruit*) queue *f*; (*of glass*) pied *m* ♦ *vt* contenir, endiguer, juguler.
stem from *vt fus* provenir de, découler de.
stench [stench] *n* puanteur *f*.
stencil [sten'səl] *n* stencil *m*; pochoir *m* ♦ *vt* polycopier.
stenographer [stənâg'rəfûr] *n* (*US*) sténographe *m/f*.
stenography [stənâg'rəfē] *n* (*US*) sténo(graphie) *f*.
step [step] *n* pas *m*; (*stair*) marche *f*; (*action*) mesure *f*, disposition *f* ♦ *vi*: **to ~ forward** faire un pas en avant, avancer; **~ by ~** à pas; (*fig*) petit à petit; **to be in ~ (with)** (*fig*) être déphasé(e) (par rapport à).
step down *vi* (*fig*) se retirer, se désister.
step in *vi* (*fig*) intervenir.
step off *vt fus* descendre de.
step over *vt fus* enjamber.
step up *vt* augmenter; intensifier.
stepbrother [step'bruthûr] *n* demi-frère *m*.
stepchild [step'chīld] *n* beau-fils/belle-fille.
stepdaughter [step'dôtûr] *n* belle-fille *f*.
stepfather [step'fâthûr] *n* beau-père *m*.
stepladder [step'ladûr] *n* escabeau *m*.
stepmother [step'muthûr] *n* belle-mère *f*.
stepping stone [step'ing stōn] *n* pierre *f* de gué; (*fig*) tremplin *m*.
stepsister [step'sistûr] *n* demi-sœur *f*.
stepson [step'sun] *n* beau-fils *m*.
stereo [stär'ēō] *n* (*system*) stéréo *f*; (*record player*) chaîne *f* stéréo ♦ *a* (*also*: **~phonic**) stéréophonique; **in ~** en stéréo.
stereotype [stär'ēətīp] *n* stéréotype *m* ♦ *vt* stéréotyper.
sterile [stär'əl] *a* stérile.
sterility [stəril'ətē] *n* stérilité *f*.
sterilization [stärəlzā'shən] *n* stérilisation *f*.
sterilize [stär'əlīz] *vt* stériliser.
sterling [stûr'ling] *a* sterling *inv*; (*silver*) de bon aloi, fin(e); (*fig*) à toute épreuve, excellent(e) ♦ *n* (*currency*) livre *f* sterling *inv*; **a pound ~** une livre sterling.
sterling area *n* zone *f* sterling *inv*.
stern [stûrn] *a* sévère ♦ *n* (*NAUT*) arrière *m*, poupe *f*.
sternum [stûr'nəm] *n* sternum *m*.
steroid [stär'oid] *n* stéroïde *m*.
stethoscope [steth'əskōp] *n* stéthoscope *m*.
stew [stoō] *n* ragoût *m* ♦ *vt*, *vi* cuire à la

casserole; **~ed tea** thé trop infusé; **~ed fruit** fruits cuits *or* en compote.
steward [stoō'ûrd] *n* (*AVIAT, NAUT, RAIL*) steward *m*; (*in club etc*) intendant *m*; (*also*: **shop ~**) délégué syndical.
stewardess [stoō'ûrdis] *n* hôtesse *f*.
stew meat, (*Brit*) **stewing steak** [stoō'ing stāk] *n* bœuf *m* à braiser.
stewpan [stoō'pan] *n* fait-tout *m inv*, faitout *m*.
St. Ex. *abbr* = **stock exchange**.
stg *abbr* = **sterling**.
stick [stik] *n* bâton *m*; (*of chalk etc*) morceau *m* ♦ *vb* (*pt, pp* **stuck** [stuk]) *vt* (*glue*) coller; (*thrust*): **to ~ sth into** piquer *or* planter *or* enfoncer qch dans; (*col: put*) mettre, fourrer; (: *tolerate*) supporter ♦ *vi* (*adhere*) coller; (*remain*) rester; (*get jammed: door, elevator*) se bloquer; **to ~ to** (*one's word, promise*) s'en tenir à; (*principles*) rester fidèle à.
stick around *vi* (*col*) rester (dans les parages).
stick out *vi* dépasser, sortir ♦ *vt*: **to ~ it out** (*col*) tenir le coup.
stick up *vi* dépasser, sortir.
stick up for *vt fus* défendre.
sticker [stik'ûr] *n* auto-collant *m*.
sticking plaster [stik'ing plas'tûr] *n* sparadrap *m*, pansement adhésif.
stickleback [stik'əlbak] *n* épinoche *f*.
stickler [stik'lûr] *n*: **to be a ~ for** être pointilleux(euse) sur.
stick-up [stik'up] *n* (*col*) braquage *m*, hold-up *m*.
sticky [stik'ē] *a* poisseux(euse); (*label*) adhésif(ive).
stiff [stif] *a* (*gen*) raide, rigide; (*door, brush*) dur(e); (*difficult*) difficile, ardu(e); (*cold*) froid(e), distant(e); (*strong, high*) fort(e), élevé(e); **to be** *or* **feel ~** (*person*) avoir des courbatures; **to have a ~ back** avoir mal au dos; **~ neck** torticolis *m*.
stiffen [stif'ən] *vt* raidir, renforcer ♦ *vi* se raidir; se durcir.
stiffness [stif'nis] *n* raideur *f*.
stifle [stī'fəl] *vt* étouffer, réprimer.
stifling [stīf'ling] *a* (*heat*) suffocant(e).
stigma, *pl* (*BOT, MED, REL*) **~ta**, (*fig*) **~s** [stigmə, stigmâ'tə] *n* stigmate *m*.
stile [stīl] *n* échalier *m*.
stiletto [stilet'ō] *n* (*Brit: also*: **~ heel**) talon *m* aiguille.
still [stil] *a* (*motionless*) immobile; (*calm*) calme, tranquille; (*Brit: orange drink etc*) non gazeux(euse) ♦ *ad* (*up to this time*) encore, toujours; (*even*) encore; (*nonetheless*) quand même, tout de même ♦ *n* (*CINEMA*) photo *f*; **to stand ~** rester immobile, ne pas bouger; **keep ~!** ne bouge pas!; **he ~ hasn't arrived** il n'est pas encore arrivé, il n'est toujours pas arrivé.
stillborn [stil'bôrn] *a* mort-né(e).
still life *n* nature morte.
stilt [stilt] *n* échasse *f*; (*pile*) pilotis *m*.
stilted [stil'tid] *a* guindé(e), emprunté(e).
stimulant [stim'yələnt] *n* stimulant *m*.
stimulate [stim'yəlāt] *vt* stimuler.
stimulating [stim'yəlāting] *a* stimulant(e).

stimulation [stimyəlā'shən] *n* stimulation *f*.
stimulus, *pl* **stimuli** [stim'yələs, stim'yəlī] *n* stimulant *m*; (*BIOL, PSYCH*) stimulus *m*.
sting [sting] *n* piqûre *f*; (*organ*) dard *m*; (*col: confidence trick*) arnaque *m* ♦ *vt* (*pt, pp* **stung** [stung]) piquer ♦ *vi* piquer; **my eyes are ~ing** j'ai les yeux qui piquent.
stingy [stin'jē] *a* avare, pingre, chiche.
stink [stingk] *n* puanteur *f* ♦ *vi* (*pt* **stank,** *pp* **stunk** [stangk, stungk]) puer, empester.
stinker [stingk'ûr] *n* (*col: problem, exam*) vacherie *f*; (: *person*) dégueulasse *m/f*.
stinking [sting'king] *a* (*fig: col*) infect(e); ~ **rich** bourré(e) de pognon.
stint [stint] *n* part *f* de travail ♦ *vi*: **to ~ on** lésiner sur, être chiche de.
stipend [stī'pend] *n* (*of vicar etc*) traitement *m*.
stipendiary [stīpen'dēārē] *a*: **~ magistrate** juge *m* de tribunal d'instance.
stipulate [stip'yəlāt] *vt* stipuler.
stipulation [stipyəlā'shən] *n* stipulation *f*, condition *f*.
stir [stûr] *n* agitation *f*, sensation *f* ♦ *vt* remuer ♦ *vi* remuer, bouger; **to give sth a ~** remuer qch; **to cause a ~** faire sensation.
stir up *vt* exciter.
stirring [stûr'ing] *a* excitant(e); émouvant(e).
stirrup [stûr'əp] *n* étrier *m*.
stitch [stich] *n* (*SEWING*) point *m*; (*KNITTING*) maille *f*; (*MED*) point de suture; (*pain*) point de côté ♦ *vt* coudre, piquer; suturer.
stoat [stōt] *n* hermine *f* (*avec son pelage d'été*).
stock [stâk] *n* réserve *f*, provision *f*; (*COMM*) stock *m*; (*AGR*) cheptel *m*, bétail *m*; (*CULIN*) bouillon *m*; (*FINANCE*) valeurs *fpl*, titres *mpl*; (*RAIL: also:* **rolling ~**) matériel roulant; (*descent, origin*) souche *f* ♦ *a* (*fig: reply etc*) courant(e); classique ♦ *vt* (*have in stock*) avoir, vendre; **well-~ed** bien approvisionné(e) *or* fourni(e); **in ~** en stock, en magasin; **out of ~** épuisé(e); **to take ~** (*fig*) faire le point; **~s and shares** valeurs (mobilières), titres; **government ~** fonds *mpl* publics.
stock up *vi*: **to ~ up (with)** s'approvisionner (en).
stockade [stâkād'] *n* palissade *f*.
stockbroker [stâk'brōkûr] *n* agent *m* de change.
stock control *n* (*COMM*) gestion *f* des stocks.
stock cube *n* (*Brit CULIN*) bouillon-cube *m*.
stock exchange *n* Bourse *f* (des valeurs).
stockholder [stâk'hōldûr] *n* actionnaire *m/f*.
Stockholm [stâk'hōm] *n* Stockholm.
stocking [stâk'ing] *n* bas *m*.
stock-in-trade [stâk'intrād'] *n* (*fig*): **it's his ~** c'est sa spécialité.
stockist [stâk'ist] *n* (*Brit*) stockiste *m*.
stock market *n* Bourse *f*, marché financier.
stock phrase *n* cliché *m*.
stockpile [stâk'pīl] *n* stock *m*, réserve *f* ♦ *vt* stocker, accumuler.
stockroom [stâk'rōōm] *n* réserve *f*, magasin *m*.
stocktaking [stâk'tāking] *n* (*Brit COMM*) inventaire *m*.
stocky [stâk'ē] *a* trapu(e), râblé(e).

stodgy [stâj'ē] *a* bourratif(ive), lourd(e).
stoic [stō'ik] *n* stoïque *m/f*.
stoical [stō'ikəl] *a* stoïque.
stoke [stōk] *vt* garnir, entretenir; chauffer.
stoker [stō'kûr] *n* (*RAIL, NAUT etc*) chauffeur *m*.
stole [stōl] *pt of* **steal** ♦ *n* étole *f*.
stolen [stō'lən] *pp of* **steal**.
stolid [stâl'id] *a* impassible, flegmatique.
stomach [stum'ək] *n* estomac *m*; (*abdomen*) ventre *m* ♦ *vt* supporter, digérer; **to have no ~ for heights** être sujet(te) au vertige.
stomachache [stum'əkāk] *n* mal *m* à l'estomac *or* au ventre.
stomach pump *n* pompe stomacale.
stomach ulcer *n* ulcère *m* à l'estomac.
stomp [stâmp] *vi*: **to ~ in/out** entrer/sortir d'un pas bruyant.
stone [stōn] *n* pierre *f*; (*pebble*) caillou *m*, galet *m*; (*in fruit*) noyau *m*; (*MED*) calcul *m*; (*Brit: weight*) = *6.348 kg; 14 pounds* ♦ *cpd* de *or* en pierre ♦ *vt* dénoyauter; **within a ~'s throw of the station** à deux pas de la gare.
Stone Age *n*: **the ~** l'âge *m* de pierre.
stone-cold [stōn'kōld'] *a* complètement froid(e).
stoned [stōnd] *a* (*col: drunk*) bourré(e); (: *on drugs*) défoncé(e).
stone-deaf [stōn'def'] *a* sourd(e) comme un pot.
stonemason [stōn'māsən] *n* tailleur *m* de pierre(s).
stonework [stōn'wûrk] *n* maçonnerie *f*.
stony [stō'nē] *a* pierreux(euse), rocailleux(euse).
stood [stōōd] *pt, pp of* **stand**.
stool [stōōl] *n* tabouret *m*.
stoop [stōōp] *vi* (*also:* **have a ~**) être voûté(e); (*bend*) se baisser, se courber; (*fig*): **to ~ to sth/doing sth** s'abaisser jusqu'à qch/jusqu'à faire qch.
stop [stâp] *n* arrêt *m*; (*short stay*) halte *f*; (*in punctuation*) point *m* ♦ *vt* arrêter; (*break off*) interrompre; (*also:* **put a ~ to**) mettre fin à; (*prevent*) empêcher ♦ *vi* s'arrêter; (*rain, noise etc*) cesser, s'arrêter; **to ~ doing sth** cesser *or* arrêter de faire qch; **to ~ sb (from) doing sth** empêcher qn de faire qch; **to ~ dead** *vi* s'arrêter net; **~ it!** arrête!
stop by *vi* s'arrêter (au passage).
stop off *vi* faire une courte halte.
stop up *vt* (*hole*) boucher.
stopcock [stâp'kâk] *n* robinet *m* d'arrêt.
stopgap [stâp'gap] *n* (*person*) bouche-trou *m*; (*also:* ~ **measure**) mesure *f* intérimaire.
stoplights [stâp'līts] *npl* (*AUT*) signaux *mpl* de stop, feux *mpl* arrière.
stopover [stâp'ōvûr] *n* halte *f*; (*AVIAT*) escale *f*.
stoppage [stâp'ij] *n* arrêt *m*; (*of pay*) retenue *f*; (*strike*) arrêt de travail.
stopper [stâp'ûr] *n* bouchon *m*.
stop press *n* (*Brit*) nouvelles *fpl* de dernière heure.
stopwatch [stâp'wâch] *n* chronomètre *m*.
storage [stôr'ij] *n* emmagasinage *m*; (*of nuclear waste etc*) stockage *m*; (*in house*) rangement *m*; (*COMPUT*) mise *f* en mémoire

or réserve.

storage heater *n* (*Brit*) radiateur *m* électrique par accumulation.

storage room *n* (*US*) débarras *m*.

store [stôr] *n* provision *f*, réserve *f*; (*depot*) entrepôt *m*; magasin *m*; (*Brit: large shop*) grand magasin ♦ *vt* emmagasiner; (*nuclear waste etc*) stocker; (*in filing system*) classer, ranger; (*COMPUT*) mettre en mémoire; **~s** *npl* provisions; **who knows what is in ~ for us?** qui sait ce que l'avenir nous réserve *or* ce qui nous attend?; **to set great/little ~ by sth** faire grand cas/peu de cas de qch.

store up *vt* mettre en réserve, emmagasiner.

storehouse [stôr'hous] *n* entrepôt *m*.

storekeeper [stôr'kēpûr] *n* commerçant/e.

storeroom [stôr'rōōm] *n* réserve *f*, magasin *m*.

storey [stôr'ē] *n* (*Brit*) étage *m*.

stork [stôrk] *n* cigogne *f*.

storm [stôrm] *n* tempête *f*; (*also:* **electric ~**) orage *m* ♦ *vi* (*fig*) fulminer ♦ *vt* prendre d'assaut.

storm cloud *n* nuage *m* d'orage.

storm door *n* double-porte (extérieure).

stormy [stôr'mē] *a* orageux(euse).

story [stôr'ē] *n* histoire *f*; récit *m*; (*PRESS: article*) article *m*; (: *subject*) affaire *f*; (*US: floor*) étage *m*.

storybook [stôr'ēbōōk] *n* livre *m* d'histoires *or* de contes.

storyteller [stôr'ētelûr] *n* conteur/euse.

stout [stout] *a* solide; (*brave*) intrépide; (*fat*) gros(se), corpulent(e) ♦ *n* bière brune.

stove [stōv] *n* (*for cooking*) fourneau *m*; (: *small*) réchaud *m*; (*for heating*) poêle *m*; **gas/electric ~** (*cooker*) cuisinière *f* à gaz/électrique.

stow [stō] *vt* ranger; cacher.

stowaway [stō'əwā] *n* passager/ère clandestin(e).

straddle [strad'əl] *vt* enjamber, être à cheval sur.

strafe [strāf] *vt* mitrailler.

straggle [strag'əl] *vi* être (*or* marcher) en désordre; **~d along the coast** disséminé(e) tout au long de la côte.

straggler [strag'lûr] *n* traînard/e.

straggling [strag'ling], **straggly** [strag'lē] *a* (*hair*) en désordre.

straight [strāt] *a* droit(e); (*frank*) honnête, franc(franche); (*plain, uncomplicated*) simple; (*THEATER: part, play*) sérieux(euse); (*col: not bent*) normal(e); réglo *inv* ♦ *ad* (*tout*) droit; (*drink*) sec, sans eau ♦ *n:* **the ~** (*SPORT*) la ligne droite; **to put** *or* **get ~** mettre en ordre, mettre de l'ordre dans; **let's get this ~** mettons les choses au point; **10 ~ wins** 10 victoires d'affilée; **to go ~ home** rentrer directement à la maison; **~ away, ~ off** (*at once*) tout de suite.

straighten [strā'tən] *vt* (*also:* **~ out**) redresser; **to ~ things out** arranger les choses.

straight-faced [strāt'fāst] *a* impassible ♦ *ad* en gardant son sérieux.

straightforward [strātfôr'wûrd] *a* simple; (*frank*) honnête, direct(e).

strain [strān] *n* (*TECH*) tension *f*; pression *f*; (*physical*) effort *m*; (*mental*) tension (nerveuse); (*MED*) entorse *f*; (*streak, trace*) tendance *f*; élément *m*; (*breed*) variété *f*; (*of virus*) souche *f*; **~s** *npl* (*of music*) accents *mpl*, accords *mpl* ♦ *vt* tendre fortement; mettre à l'épreuve; (*filter*) passer, filtrer ♦ *vi* peiner, fournir un gros effort; **he's been under a lot of ~** il a traversé des moments très difficiles, il est très éprouvé nerveusement.

strained [strānd] *a* (*laugh etc*) forcé(e), contraint(e); (*relations*) tendu(e).

strainer [strā'nûr] *n* passoire *f*.

strait [strāt] *n* (*GEO*) détroit *m*; **to be in dire ~s** (*fig*) être dans une situation désespérée.

straitjacket [strāt'jakit] *n* camisole *f* de force.

strait-laced [strāt'lāst] *a* collet monté *inv*.

strand [strand] *n* (*of thread*) fil *m*, brin *m* ♦ *vt* (*boat*) échouer.

stranded [stran'did] *a* en rade, en plan.

strange [strānj] *a* (*not known*) inconnu(e); (*odd*) étrange, bizarre.

strangely [strānj'lē] *ad* étrangement, bizarrement.

stranger [strān'jûr] *n* (*unknown*) inconnu/e; (*from somewhere else*) étranger/ère; **I'm a ~ here** je ne suis pas d'ici.

strangle [strang'gəl] *vt* étrangler.

stranglehold [strang'gəlhōld] *n* (*fig*) emprise totale, mainmise *f*.

strangulation [stranggyəlā'shən] *n* strangulation *f*.

strap [strap] *n* lanière *f*, courroie *f*, sangle *f*; (*of slip, dress*) bretelle *f* ♦ *vt* attacher (avec une courroie *etc*).

straphanging [strap'hanging] *n* (fait *m* de) voyager debout (dans le métro *etc*).

strapless [strap'lis] *a* (*bra, dress*) sans bretelles.

strapping [strap'ing] *a* bien découplé(e), costaud(e).

Strasbourg [stras'bûrg] *n* Strasbourg.

strata [strā'tə] *npl of* **stratum**.

stratagem [strat'əjəm] *n* stratagème *m*.

strategic [strətē'jik] *a* stratégique.

strategist [strat'ijist] *n* stratège *m*.

strategy [strat'ijē] *n* stratégie *f*.

stratosphere [strat'əsfēr] *n* stratosphère *f*.

stratum, *pl* **strata** [strā'təm, strā'tə] *n* strate *f*, couche *f*.

straw [strô] *n* paille *f*; **that's the last ~!** ça c'est le comble!

strawberry [strô'barē] *n* fraise *f*; (*plant*) fraisier *m*.

stray [strā] *a* (*animal*) perdu(e), errant(e) ♦ *vi* s'égarer; **~ bullet** balle perdue.

streak [strēk] *n* raie *f*, bande *f*, filet *m*; (*fig: of madness etc*): **a ~ of** une *or* des tendance(s) à ♦ *vt* zébrer, strier ♦ *vi:* **to ~ past** passer à toute allure; **to have ~s in one's hair** s'être fait faire des mèches; **a winning/losing ~** une bonne/mauvaise série *or* période.

streaky [strē'kē] *a* zébré(e), strié(e).

streaky bacon *n* (*Brit*) ≈ lard *m* (maigre).

stream [strēm] *n* (*brook*) ruisseau *m*; (*current*) courant *m*, flot *m*; (*of people*) défilé ininterrompu, flot ♦ *vt* (*SCOL*) répartir par niveau ♦ *vi* ruisseler; **to ~ in/out** entrer/sortir

à flots; **against the** ~ à contre courant.
streamer [strē'mûr] *n* serpentin *m*, banderole
f.
streamline [strēm'līn] *vt* donner un profil aérodynamique à; *(fig)* rationaliser.
streamlined [strēm'līnd] *a (AVIAT)* fuselé(e),
profilé(e); *(AUT)* aérodynamique; *(fig)* ratio-
nalisé(e).
street [strēt] *n* rue *f*; **the back** ~s les
quartiers pauvres; **to walk the** ~s *(homeless)* être à la rue *or* sans abri; *(as prostitute)* faire le trottoir.
streetcar [strēt'kâr] *n (US)* tramway *m*.
streetlight [strēt'līt] *n* réverbère *m*.
street lighting *n* éclairage public.
street map, street plan *n* plan *m* des rues.
street market *n* marché *m* à ciel ouvert.
streetsweeper [strēt'swēp'ûr] *n (US: person)*
balayeur/euse.
streetwise [strēt'wīz] *a (col)* futé(e), réaliste.
strength [strengkth] *n* force *f*; *(of girder, knot
etc)* solidité *f*; *(of chemical solution)* titre *m*;
(of wine) degré *m* d'alcool; **on the** ~ **of** en
vertu de; **at full** ~ au grand complet; **below**
~ à effectifs réduits.
strengthen [strengk'thən] *vt* renforcer; *(muscle)* fortifier.
strenuous [stren'yōōəs] *a* vigoureux(euse),
énergique; *(tiring)* ardu(e), fatigant(e).
stress [stres] *n (force, pressure)* pression *f*;
(mental strain) tension (nerveuse); *(accent)*
accent *m*; *(emphasis)* insistance *f* ♦ *vt*
insister sur, souligner; **to lay great** ~ **on sth**
insister beaucoup sur qch; **to be under** ~
être stressé(e).
stressful [stres'fəl] *a (job)* stressant(e).
stretch [strech] *n (of sand etc)* étendue *f*; *(of
time)* période *f* ♦ *vi* s'étirer; *(extend)*: **to** ~
to *or* **as far as** s'étendre jusqu'à; *(be
enough: money, food)*: **to** ~ **to** aller pour ♦
vt tendre, étirer; *(spread)* étendre; *(fig)*
pousser (au maximum); **at a** ~ sans discontinuer, sans interruption; **to** ~ **a muscle** se
distendre un muscle; **to** ~ **one's legs** se dégourdir les jambes.
stretch out *vi* s'étendre ♦ *vt (arm etc)*
allonger, tendre; *(to spread)* étendre; **to** ~
out for sth allonger la main pour prendre
qch.
stretcher [strech'ûr] *n* brancard *m*, civière *f*.
stretcher-bearer [strech'ûrbârûr] *n*
brancardier *m*.
stretch marks *npl (on skin)* vergetures *fpl*.
strewn [strōōn] *a*: ~ **with** jonché(e) de.
stricken [strik'ən] *a* très éprouvé(e); dé-
vasté(e); ~ **with** frappé(e) *or* atteint(e) de.
strict [strikt] *a* strict(e); **in** ~ **confidence** tout
à fait confidentiellement.
strictly [strikt'lē] *ad* strictement; ~ **confidential** strictement confidentiel(le); ~
speaking à strictement parler.
strictness [strikt'nis] *n* sévérité *f*.
stride [strīd] *n* grand pas, enjambée *f* ♦ *vi (pt
strode, pp stridden* [strōd, strid'ən]*)* marcher
à grands pas; **to take in one's** ~ *(fig:
changes etc)* accepter sans sourciller.
strident [strīd'ənt] *a* strident(e).
strife [strīf] *n* conflit *m*, dissensions *fpl*.
strike [strīk] *n* grève *f*; *(of oil etc)* découverte

f; *(attack)* raid *m* ♦ *vb (pt, pp* **struck** [struk]*)*
vt frapper; *(oil etc)* trouver, découvrir;
(make: agreement, deal) conclure ♦ *vi* faire
grève; *(attack)* attaquer; *(clock)* sonner; **to
go on** *or* **come out on** ~ se mettre en grève,
faire grève; **to** ~ **a match** frotter une allumette; **to** ~ **a balance** *(fig)* trouver un juste
milieu.
strike back *vi (MIL, fig)* contre-attaquer.
strike down *vt (fig)* terrasser.
strike off *vt (from list)* rayer; *(: doctor
etc)* radier.
strike out *vt* rayer.
strike up *vt (MUS)* se mettre à jouer; **to** ~
up a friendship with se lier d'amitié avec.
strikebreaker [strīk'brākûr] *n* briseur *m* de
grève.
striker [strī'kûr] *n* gréviste *m/f*; *(SPORT)* buteur *m*.
striking [strī'king] *a* frappant(e), saisissant(e).
string [string] *n* ficelle *f*, fil *m*; *(row: of beads)*
rang *m*; *(: of onions, excuses)* chapelet *m*; *(:
of people, cars)* file *f*; *(MUS)* corde *f*;
(COMPUT) châine *f* ♦ *vt (pt, pp* **strung**
[strung]*)*: **to** ~ **out** échelonner; **to** ~ **together** enchaîner; **to** ~ **sb along** faire marcher qn; **the** ~s *(MUS)* les instruments *mpl* à
cordes; **to get a job by pulling** ~s obtenir
un emploi en faisant jouer le piston; **with no**
~s attached *(fig)* sans conditions.
string bean *n* haricot vert.
string(ed) instrument [string(d)' in'strəmənt]
n (MUS) instrument *m* à cordes.
stringent [strin'jənt] *a* rigoureux(euse); *(need)*
impérieux(euse).
string quartet *n* quatuor *m* à cordes.
strip [strip] *n* bande *f* ♦ *vt* déshabiller; *(fig)* dégarnir, dépouiller; *(also:* ~ **down:** *machine)*
démonter ♦ *vi* se déshabiller.
stripe [strīp] *n* raie *f*, rayure *f*.
striped [strīpt] *a* rayé(e), à rayures.
strip light *n (Brit)* (tube *m* au) néon *m*.
stripper [strip'ûr] *n* strip-teaseuse *f*.
striptease [strip'tēz] *n* strip-tease *m*.
strive [strīv], *pt* **strove**, *pp* **striven** [strīv,
strōv, striv'ən] *vi*: **to** ~ **to do** s'efforcer de faire.
strode [strōd] *pt of* **stride.**
stroke [strōk] *n* coup *m*; *(MED)* attaque *f*; *(caress)* caresse *f*; *(SWIMMING: style)* (sorte *f*
de) nage *f*; *(of piston)* course *f* ♦ *vt* caresser;
at a ~ d'un (seul) coup; **on the** ~ **of 5** à 5
heures sonnantes; **a** ~ **of luck** un coup de
chance; **a 2-~ engine** un moteur à 2 temps.
stroll [strōl] *n* petite promenade ♦ *vi* flâner, se
promener nonchalamment; **to go for a** ~
aller se promener ou faire un tour.
stroller [strō'lûr] *n (US)* poussette *f*.
strong [strông] *a (gen)* fort(e); *(healthy)* vi-
goureux(euse); *(object, material)* solide;
(distaste, desire) vif(vive); *(drugs, chemicals)* puissant(e) ♦ *ad*: **to be going** ~
(company) marcher bien; *(person)* être toujours solide; **they are 50** ~ ils sont au nombre de 50.
strong-arm [strông'ârm] *a (tactics, methods)*
musclé(e).
strongbox [strông'bâks] *n* coffre-fort *m*.
strong drink *n* boisson alcoolisée.
stronghold [strông'hōld] *n* bastion *m*.

strong language n grossièretés fpl.

strongly [strông'lē] ad fortement, avec force; vigoureusement; solidement; **I feel ~ about it** c'est une question qui me tient particulièrement à cœur; (negatively) j'y suis profondément opposé(e).

strongman [strông'man] n hercule m, colosse m; (fig) homme m à poigne.

strongroom [strông'rōōm] n chambre forte.

strove [strōv] pt of **strive**.

struck [struk] pt, pp of **strike**.

structural [struk'chûrəl] a structural(e); (CONSTR) de construction; affectant les parties portantes.

structurally [struk'chûrəlē] ad du point de vue de la construction.

structure [struk'chûr] n structure f; (building) construction f.

struggle [strug'əl] n lutte f ♦ vi lutter, se battre; **to have a ~ to do sth** avoir beaucoup de mal à faire qch.

strum [strum] vt (guitar) gratter de.

strung [strung] pt, pp of **string**.

strut [strut] n étai m, support m ♦ vi se pavaner.

strychnine [strik'nīn] n strychnine f.

stub [stub] n bout m; (of ticket etc) talon m, souche f ♦ vt: **to ~ one's toe (on sth)** se heurter le doigt de pied (contre qch).

stub out vt écraser.

stubble [stub'əl] n chaume m; (on chin) barbe f de plusieurs jours.

stubborn [stub'ûrn] a têtu(e), obstiné(e), opiniâtre.

stubby [stub'ē] a trapu(e); gros(se) et court(e).

stucco [stuk'ō] n stuc m.

stuck [stuk] pt, pp of **stick** ♦ a (jammed) bloqué(e), coincé(e); **to get ~** se bloquer or coincer.

stuck-up [stuk'up'] a prétentieux(euse).

stud [stud] n clou m (à grosse tête); (collar ~) bouton m de col; (of horses) écurie f, haras m; (also: ~ **horse**) étalon m ♦ vt (fig): **~ded with** parsemé(e) or criblé(e) de.

student [stōō'dənt] n étudiant/e; (US: at school) élève m/f ♦ cpd estudiantin(e); universitaire; d'étudiant; **law/medical ~** étudiant en droit/médecine.

student driver n (US) (conducteur/trice) débutant(e).

student teacher n professeur m stagiaire.

studied [stud'ēd] a étudié(e), calculé(e).

studio [stōō'dēō] n studio m, atelier m.

studio apartment n studio m.

studious [stōō'dēəs] a studieux(euse), appliqué(e); (studied) étudié(e).

studiously [stōō'dēəslē] ad (carefully) soigneusement.

study [stud'ē] n étude f; (room) bureau m ♦ vt étudier ♦ vi étudier, faire ses études; **to make a ~ of sth** étudier qch, faire une étude de qch; **to ~ for an exam** préparer un examen.

stuff [stuf] n (gen) chose(s) f(pl), truc m; (belongings) affaires fpl, trucs m; (substance) substance f ♦ vt rembourrer; (CULIN) farcir; (animal: for exhibition) empailler; **my nose is ~ed up** j'ai le nez bouché; **get ~ed!** (col!)

va te faire foutre! (!); **~ed toy** jouet m en peluche.

stuffing [stuf'ing] n bourre f, rembourrage m; (CULIN) farce f.

stuffy [stuf'ē] a (room) mal ventilé(e) or aéré(e); (ideas) vieux jeu inv.

stumble [stum'bəl] vi trébucher.

stumble across vt fus (fig) tomber sur.

stumbling block [stum'bling blâk] n pierre f d'achoppement.

stump [stump] n souche f; (of limb) moignon m ♦ vt: **to be ~ed** sécher, ne pas savoir que répondre.

stun [stun] vt (subj: blow) étourdir; (: news) abasourdir, stupéfier.

stung [stung] pt, pp of **sting**.

stunk [stungk] pp of **stink**.

stunning [stun'ing] a étourdissant(e); (fabulous) stupéfiant(e), sensationnel(le).

stunt [stunt] n tour m de force; truc m publicitaire; (AVIAT) acrobatie f ♦ vt retarder, arrêter.

stunted [stun'tid] a rabougri(e).

stuntman [stunt'mən] n cascadeur m.

stupefaction [stōōpəfak'shən] n stupéfaction f, stupeur f.

stupefy [stōō'pəfī] vt étourdir; abrutir; (fig) stupéfier.

stupendous [stōōpen'dəs] a prodigieux(euse), fantastique.

stupid [stōō'pid] a stupide, bête.

stupidity [stōōpid'itē] n stupidité f, bêtise f.

stupidly [stōō'pidlē] ad stupidement, bêtement.

stupor [stōō'pûr] n stupeur f.

sturdy [stûr'dē] a robuste, vigoureux(euse); solide.

sturgeon [stûr'jən] n esturgeon m.

stutter [stut'ûr] n bégaiement m ♦ vi bégayer.

sty [stī] n (of pigs) porcherie f.

stye [stī] n (MED) orgelet m.

style [stīl] n style m; (of dress etc) genre m; (distinction) allure f, cachet m, style; **in the latest ~** à la dernière mode; **hair ~** coiffure f.

stylish [stī'lish] a élégant(e), chic inv.

stylist [stī'list] n (hair ~) coiffeur/euse; (literary ~) styliste m/f.

stylized [stī'līzd] a stylisé(e).

stylus, pl **styli** or **styluses** [stī'ləs, -lī] n (of record player) pointe f de lecture.

suave [swâv] a doucereux(euse), onctueux(euse).

sub [sub] n abbr = **submarine, subscription**.

sub... [sub] prefix sub..., sous-.

subcommittee [sub'kəmitē] n sous-comité m.

subconscious [subkân'chəs] a subconscient(e) ♦ n subconscient m.

subcontinent [subkân'tənənt] n: **the (Indian) ~** le sous-continent indien.

subcontract n [subkân'trakt] contrat m de sous-traitance ♦ vt [subkəntrakt'] sous-traiter.

subcontractor [subkân'traktûr] n sous-traitant m.

subdivide [subdivīd'] vt subdiviser.

subdivision [sub'divizhən] n subdivision f.

subdue [səbdōō'] vt subjuguer, soumettre.

subdued [səbdōōd'] a contenu(e), atténué(e); (light) tamisé(e); (person) qui a perdu de son entrain.

subject n [sub'jikt] sujet m; (SCOL) matière f ♦ vt [səbjekt']: **to ~ to** soumettre à; exposer à; **to be ~ to** (law) être soumis(e) à; (disease) être sujet(te) à; **~ to confirmation in writing** sous réserve de confirmation écrite; **to change the ~** changer de conversation.
subjection [səbjek'shən] n soumission f, sujétion f.
subjective [səbjek'tiv] a subjectif(ive).
subject matter n sujet m; contenu m.
sub judice [sub jōō'disē] a (LAW) devant les tribunaux.
subjugate [sub'jəgāt] vt subjuguer.
subjunctive [səbjungk'tiv] a subjonctif(ive) ♦ n subjonctif m.
sublease [sublēs'] (US) vt vendre en cession-bail ♦ n cession-bail f.
sublet [sublet'] vt sous-louer.
sublime [səblīm'] a sublime.
subliminal [sublim'ənəl] a subliminal(e).
submachine gun [subməshēn' gun] n fusil-mitrailleur m.
submarine [sub'mərēn] n sous-marin m.
submerge [səbmûrj'] vt submerger; immerger ♦ vi plonger.
submersion [səbmûr'zhən] n submersion f; immersion f.
submission [səbmish'ən] n soumission f; (to committee etc) présentation f.
submissive [səbmis'iv] a soumis(e).
submit [səbmit'] vt soumettre ♦ vi se soumettre.
subnormal [subnôr'məl] a au-dessous de la normale; (person) arriéré(e).
subordinate [səbôr'dənit] a, n subordonné(e).
subpoena [səpē'nə] (LAW) n citation f, assignation f ♦ vt citer or assigner (à comparaître).
subroutine [subrōōtēn'] n (COMPUT) sous-programme m.
subscribe [səbskrīb'] vi cotiser; **to ~ to** (opinion, fund) souscrire à; (newspaper) s'abonner à; être abonné(e) à.
subscriber [səbskrīb'ûr] n (to periodical, telephone) abonné/e.
subscript [sub'skript] n (TYP) indice inférieur.
subscription [səbskrip'shən] n (to fund) souscription f; (to magazine etc) abonnement m; (membership dues) cotisation f; **to take out a ~ to** s'abonner à.
subsequent [sub'səkwənt] a ultérieur(e), suivant(e); **~ to** prep à la suite de.
subsequently [sub'səkwəntlē] ad par la suite.
subservient [səbsûr'vēənt] a obséquieux(euse).
subside [səbsīd'] vi s'affaisser; (flood) baisser; (wind) tomber.
subsidence [səbsīd'əns] n affaissement m.
subsidiary [səbsid'ēârē] a subsidiaire; accessoire; (Brit SCOL: subject) complémentaire ♦ n filiale f.
subsidize [sub'sidīz] vt subventionner.
subsidy [sub'sidē] n subvention f.
subsist [səbsist'] vi: **to ~ on sth** (arriver à) vivre avec ou subsister avec qch.
subsistence [səbsis'təns] n existence f, subsistance f.
subsistence allowance n indemnité f de séjour.
subsistence level n niveau m de vie minimum.

substance [sub'stəns] n substance f; (fig) essentiel m; **a man of ~** un homme jouissant d'une certaine fortune; **to lack ~** être plutôt mince (fig).
substandard [substan'dûrd] a (goods) de qualité inférieure, qui laisse à désirer; (housing) inférieur(e) aux normes requises.
substantial [səbstan'chəl] a substantiel(le); (fig) important(e).
substantially [səbstan'chəlē] ad considérablement; en grande partie.
substantiate [səbstan'chēāt] vt étayer, fournir des preuves à l'appui de.
substitute [sub'stitōōt] n (person) remplaçant/e; (thing) succédané m ♦ vt: **to ~ sth/sb for** substituer qch/qn à, remplacer par qch/qn.
substitute teacher n (US) suppléant/e.
substitution [substitōō'shən] n substitution f.
subterfuge [sub'tûrfyōōj] n subterfuge m.
subterranean [subtərā'nēən] a souterrain(e).
subtitle [sub'tītəl] n (CINEMA) sous-titre m.
subtle [sut'əl] a subtil(e).
subtlety [sut'əltē] n subtilité f.
subtly [sut'lē] ad subtilement.
subtotal [subtō'təl] n total partiel.
subtract [səbtrakt'] vt soustraire, retrancher.
subtraction [səbtrak'shən] n soustraction f.
subtropical [subtráp'ikəl] a subtropical(e).
suburb [sub'ûrb] n faubourg m; **the ~s** la banlieue.
suburban [səbûr'bən] a de banlieue, suburbain(e).
suburbia [səbûr'bēə] n la banlieue.
subvention [səbven'chən] n (subsidy) subvention f.
subversion [səbvûr'zhən] n subversion f.
subversive [səbvûr'siv] a subversif(ive).
subway [sub'wā] n (US) métro m; (Brit) passage souterrain.
subway station n (US) station f de métro.
sub-zero [sub'zē'rō] a au-dessous de zéro.
succeed [səksēd'] vi réussir ♦ vt succéder à; **to ~ in doing** réussir à faire.
succeeding [səksē'ding] a suivant(e), qui suit (or suivent or suivront etc).
success [səkses'] n succès m; réussite f.
successful [səkses'fəl] a qui a du succès; (candidate) choisi(e), agréé(e); (business) prospère, qui réussit; (attempt) couronné(e) de succès; **to be ~ (in doing)** réussir (à faire).
successfully [səkses'fəlē] ad avec succès.
succession [səksesh'ən] n succession f; **in ~** successivement; **3 years in ~** 3 ans de suite.
successive [səkses'iv] a successif(ive); **on 3 ~ days** 3 jours de suite ou consécutifs.
successor [səkses'ûr] n successeur m.
succinct [səksingkt'] a succinct(e), bref(brève).
succulent [suk'yələnt] a succulent(e) ♦ n (BOT): **~s** plantes grasses.
succumb [səkum'] vi succomber.
such [such] a tel(telle); (of that kind): **~ a book** un livre de ce genre or pareil, un tel livre; **~ books** des livres de ce genre or pareils, de tels livres; (so much): **~ courage** un tel courage ♦ ad si; **~ a long trip** un si

long voyage; ~ **good books** de si bons livres; ~ **a long trip that** un voyage si or tellement long que; ~ **a lot of** tellement or tant de; **making** ~ **a noise that** faisant un tel bruit que or tellement de bruit que; ~ **a long time ago** il y a si or tellement longtemps; ~ **as** (like) tel(telle) que, comme; **a noise** ~ **as to** un bruit de nature à; ~ **books as I have** les quelques livres que j'ai; **as** ~ **ad** en tant que tel(telle), à proprement parler.

such-and-such [such'ənsuch] a tel(telle) ou tel(telle).

suchlike [such'līk] pronoun (col): **and** ~ et le reste.

suck [suk] vt sucer; (breast, bottle) téter; (subj: pump, machine) aspirer.

sucker [suk'ûr] n (BOT, ZOOL, TECH) ventouse f; (col) naïf/ïve, poire f.

suckle [suk'əl] vt allaiter.

suction [suk'shən] n succion f.

suction pump n pompe aspirante.

Sudan [sōōdan'] n Soudan m.

Sudanese [sōōdənēz'] a soudanais(e) ♦ n Soudanais/e.

sudden [sud'ən] a soudain(e), subit(e); **all of a** ~ soudain, tout à coup.

suddenly [sud'ənlē] ad brusquement, tout à coup, soudain.

suds [sudz] npl eau savonneuse.

sue [sōō] vt poursuivre en justice, intenter un procès à ♦ vi: **to** ~ **(for)** intenter un procès (pour); **to** ~ **for divorce** engager une procédure de divorce; **to** ~ **sb for damages** poursuivre qn en dommages-intérêts.

suede [swād] n daim m, cuir suédé ♦ cpd de daim.

suet [sōō'it] n graisse f de rognon or de bœuf.

Suez Canal [sōōez' kənal'] n canal m de Suez.

Suff. abbr (Brit) = Suffolk.

suffer [suf'ûr] vt souffrir, subir; (bear) tolérer, supporter, subir ♦ vi souffrir; **to** ~ **from** (illness) souffrir de, avoir; **to** ~ **from the effects of alcohol/a fall** se ressentir des effets de l'alcool/des conséquences d'une chute.

sufferance [suf'ûrəns] n: **he was only there on** ~ sa présence était seulement tolérée.

sufferer [suf'ûrûr] n malade m/f; victime m/f.

suffering [suf'ûring] n souffrance(s) f(pl).

suffice [səfīs'] vi suffire.

sufficient [səfish'ənt] a suffisant(e); ~ **money** suffisamment d'argent.

sufficiently [səfish'əntlē] ad suffisamment, assez.

suffix [suf'iks] n suffixe m.

suffocate [suf'əkāt] vi suffoquer; étouffer.

suffocation [sufəkā'shən] n suffocation f; (MED) asphyxie f.

suffrage [suf'rij] n suffrage m; droit m de suffrage or de vote.

suffuse [səfyōōz'] vt baigner, imprégner; **the room was** ~**d with light** la pièce baignait dans la lumière or était imprégnée de lumière.

sugar [shōōg'ûr] n sucre m ♦ vt sucrer.

sugar beet n betterave sucrière.

sugar bowl n sucrier m.

sugar cane n canne f à sucre.

sugar-coated [shōōg'ûrkō'tid] a dragéifié(e).

sugar lump n morceau m de sucre.

sugar refinery n raffinerie f de sucre.

sugary [shōōg'ûrē] a sucré(e).

suggest [səgjest'] vt suggérer, proposer; (indicate) laisser supposer, suggérer; **what do you** ~ **I do?** que vous me suggérez de faire?

suggestion [səgjes'chən] n suggestion f.

suggestive [səgjes'tiv] a suggestif(ive).

suicidal [sōōisīd'əl] a suicidaire.

suicide [sōō'isīd] n suicide m; **to commit** ~ se suicider.

suicide attempt, suicide bid n tentative f de suicide.

suit [sōōt] n (man's) costume m, complet m; (woman's) tailleur m, ensemble m; (CARDS) couleur f; (law~) procès m ♦ vt aller à; convenir à; (adapt): **to** ~ **sth to** adapter or approprier qch à; **to be** ~**ed to sth** (suitable for) être adapté(e) or approprié(e) à qch; **well** ~**ed** (couple) faits l'un pour l'autre, très bien assortis; **to bring a** ~ **against sb** intenter un procès contre qn; **to follow** ~ (fig) faire de même.

suitable [sōō'təbəl] a qui convient; approprié(e), adéquat(e); **would tomorrow be** ~**?** est-ce que demain vous conviendrait?; **we found somebody** ~ nous avons trouvé la personne qui'il nous faut.

suitably [sōō'təblē] ad comme il se doit (or se devait etc), convenablement.

suitcase [sōōt'kās] n valise f.

suite [swēt] n (of rooms, also MUS) suite f; (furniture): **bedroom/dining room** ~ (ensemble m de) chambre f à coucher/salle f à manger; **a three-piece** ~ un salon (canapé et deux fauteuils).

suitor [sōō'tûr] n soupirant m, prétendant m.

sulfate [sul'fāt] n (US) sulfate m; **copper** ~ sulfate de cuivre.

sulfur [sul'fûr] n (US) soufre m.

sulfuric [sulfyōōr'ik] a: ~ **acid** acide m sulfurique.

sulk [sulk] vi bouder.

sulky [sul'kē] a bouderu(euse), maussade.

sullen [sul'ən] a renfrogné(e), maussade; morne.

sulphate [sul'fāt] n (Brit) = **sulfate**.

sulphur [sul'fûr] etc (Brit) = **sulfur** etc.

sultan [sul'tən] n sultan m.

sultana [sultan'ə] n (fruit) raisin (sec) de Smyrne.

sultry [sul'trē] a étouffant(e).

sum [sum] n somme f; (SCOL etc) calcul m. **sum up** vt résumer; (evaluate rapidly) récapituler ♦ vi résumer.

Sumatra [sōōmât'rə] n Sumatra.

summarize [sum'ərīz] vt résumer.

summary [sum'ûrē] n résumé m ♦ a (justice) sommaire.

summer [sum'ûr] n été m ♦ cpd d'été, estival(e); **in (the)** ~ en été, pendant l'été.

summer camp n (US) colonie f de vacances.

summerhouse [sum'ûrhous] n (in garden) pavillon m.

summertime [sum'ûrtīm] n (season) été m.

summer time n (by clock) heure f d'été.

summery [sum'ûrē] a estival(e); d'été.

summing-up [sum'ingup'] n résumé m, réca-

pitulation *f*.
summit [sum'it] *n* sommet *m*; (*also*: ~ **conference**) (conférence *f* au) sommet *m*.
summon [sum'ən] *vt* appeler, convoquer; **to ~ a witness** citer *or* assigner un témoin.
summon up *vt* rassembler, faire appel à.
summons [sum'ənz] *n* citation *f*, assignation *f* ♦ *vt* citer, assigner; **to serve a ~ on sb** remettre une assignation à qn.
sump [sump] *n* (*Brit AUT*) carter *m*.
sumptuous [sump'chōōəs] *a* somptueux(euse).
Sun. *abbr* (= *Sunday*) dim.
sun [sun] *n* soleil *m*; **in the ~** au soleil; **to catch the ~** prendre le soleil; **everything under the ~** absolument tout.
sunbathe [sun'bāth] *vi* prendre un bain de soleil.
sunbeam [sun'bēm] *n* rayon *m* de soleil.
sunbed [sun'bed] *n* (*Brit*) lit pliant; (: *with sun lamp*) lit à ultra-violets.
sunburn [sun'bûrn] *n* coup *m* de soleil.
sunburnt [sun'bûrnt], **sunburned** [sun'bûrnd] *a* bronzé(e), hâlé(e); (*painfully*) brûlé(e) par le soleil.
sundae [sun'dē] *n* sundae *m*, coupe glacée.
Sunday [sun'dā] *n* dimanche *m*; *for phrases see also* **Tuesday**.
Sunday school *n* ≈ catéchisme *m*.
sundial [sun'dīl] *n* cadran *m* solaire.
sundown [sun'doun] *n* coucher *m* du soleil.
sundries [sun'drēz] *npl* articles divers.
sundry [sun'drē] *a* divers(e), différent(e); **all and ~** tout le monde, n'importe qui.
sunflower [sun'flouûr] *n* tournesol *m*.
sung [sung] *pp of* **sing**.
sunglasses [sun'glasiz] *npl* lunettes *fpl* de soleil.
sunk [sungk] *pp of* **sink**.
sunken [sung'kən] *a* (*rock, ship*) submergé(e); (*eyes, cheeks*) creux(euse); (*bath*) encastré(e).
sunlamp [sun'lamp] *n* lampe *f* à rayons ultra-violets.
sunlight [sun'līt] *n* (lumière *f* du) soleil *m*.
sunlit [sun'lit] *a* ensoleillé(e).
sunny [sun'ē] *a* ensoleillé(e); (*fig*) épanoui(e), radieux(euse); **it is ~** il fait (du) soleil, il y a du soleil.
sunrise [sun'rīz] *n* lever *m* du soleil.
sun roof *n* (*AUT*) toit ouvrant.
sunset [sun'set] *n* coucher *m* du soleil.
sunshade [sun'shād] *n* (*lady's*) ombrelle *f*; (*over table*) parasol *m*.
sunshine [sun'shīn] *n* (lumière *f* du) soleil *m*.
sunspot [sun'spät] *n* tache *f* solaire.
sunstroke [sun'strōk] *n* insolation *f*, coup *m* de soleil.
suntan [sun'tan] *n* bronzage *m*.
suntan lotion *n* lotion *f* or lait *m* solaire.
suntanned [sun'tand] *a* bronzé(e).
suntan oil *n* huile *f* solaire.
super [sōō'pûr] *a* (*col*) formidable.
superannuation [sōōpûranyōōā'shən] *n* cotisations *fpl* pour la pension.
superb [sōōpûrb'] *a* superbe, magnifique.
supercilious [sōōpûrsil'ēəs] *a* hautain(e), dédaigneux(euse).
superficial [sōōpûrfish'əl] *a* superficiel(le).
superficially [sōōpûrfish'əlē] *ad* superficielle-

ment.
superfluous [sōōpûr'flōōəs] *a* superflu(e).
superhuman [sōōpûrhyōō'mən] *a* surhumain(e).
superimpose [sōōpûrimpōz'] *vt* superposer.
superintend [sōōpûrintend'] *vt* surveiller.
superintendent [sōōpûrinten'dənt] *n* directeur/trice; (*Brit POLICE*) ≈ commissaire *m*.
superior [səpēr'ēûr] *a* supérieur(e); (*COMM: goods, quality*) de qualité supérieure; (*smug*) condescendant(e), méprisant(e) ♦ *n* supérieur/e; **Mother S~** (*REL*) Mère supérieure.
superiority [səpērēôr'itē] *n* supériorité *f*.
superlative [səpûr'lətiv] *a* sans pareil(le), suprême ♦ *n* (*LING*) superlatif *m*.
superman [sōō'pûrman] *n* surhomme *m*.
supermarket [sōō'pûrmârkit] *n* supermarché *m*.
supernatural [sōōpûrnach'ûrəl] *a* surnaturel(le).
superpower [sōō'pûrpou'ûr] *n* (*POL*) superpuissance *f*.
supersede [sōōpûrsēd'] *vt* remplacer, supplanter.
supersonic [sōōpûrsän'ik] *a* supersonique.
superstition [sōōpûrstish'ən] *n* superstition *f*.
superstitious [sōōpûrstish'əs] *a* superstitieux(euse).
superstore [sōō'pûrstôr] *n* (*Brit*) hypermarché *m*, grand surface.
supertanker [sōō'pûrtangkûr] *n* pétrolier géant, superpétrolier *m*.
supertax [sōō'pûrtaks] *n* tranche supérieure de l'impôt.
supervise [sōō'pûrvīz] *vt* (*children etc*) surveiller; (*organization, work*) diriger.
supervision [sōōpûrvizh'ən] *n* surveillance *f*; direction *f*; **under medical ~** sous contrôle du médecin.
supervisor [sōō'pûrvīzûr] *n* surveillant/e; (*in shop*) chef *m* de rayon; (*SCOL*) directeur/trice de thèse.
supervisory [sōōpûrvī'zûrē] *a* de surveillance.
supine [sōō'pīn] *a* couché(e) or étendu(e) sur le dos.
supper [sup'ûr] *n* dîner *m*; (*late*) souper *m*; **to have ~** dîner; souper.
supplant [səplant'] *vt* supplanter.
supple [sup'əl] *a* souple.
supplement *n* [sup'ləmənt] supplément *m* ♦ *vt* [sup'ləmənt] ajouter à, compléter.
supplementary [supləmən'tûrē] *a* supplémentaire.
supplementary benefit *n* (*Brit*) allocation *f* supplémentaire d'aide sociale.
supplier [səplī'ûr] *n* fournisseur *m*.
supply [səplī'] *vt* (*goods*): **to ~ sth** (**to sb**) fournir qch (à qn); (*people, organization*): **to ~ sb** (**with sth**) approvisionner *or* ravitailler qn (en qch); fournir qn (en qch), fournir qch à qn; (*system, machine*): **to ~ sth** (**with sth**) alimenter qch (en qch); (*a need*) répondre à ♦ *n* provision *f*, réserve *f*; (*supplying*) approvisionnement *m*; (*TECH*) alimentation; **supplies** *npl* (*food*) vivres *mpl*; (*MIL*) subsistances *fpl*; **office supplies** fournitures *fpl* de bureau; **to be in short ~** être rare,

manquer; **the electricity/water/gas** ~ l'alimentation en électricité/eau/gaz; ~ **and demand** l'offre *f* et la demande; **it comes supplied with an adaptor** il (*or* elle) est pourvu(e) d'un adaptateur.

supply teacher *n* (*Brit*) suppléant/e.

support [səpôrt'] *n* (*moral, financial etc*) soutien *m*, appui *m*; (*TECH*) support *m*, soutien ◆ *vt* soutenir, supporter; (*financially*) subvenir aux besoins de; (*uphold*) être pour, être partisan de, appuyer; (*SPORT: team*) être pour; **to** ~ **o.s.** (*financially*) gagner sa vie.

supporter [səpôr'tûr] *n* (*POL etc*) partisan/e; (*SPORT*) supporter *m*.

supporting [səpôr'ting] *a* (*THEATER etc: role*) secondaire; (: *actor*) qui a un rôle secondaire.

suppose [səpōz'] *vt, vi* supposer; imaginer; **to be** ~**d to do/be** être censé(e) faire/être; **I don't** ~ **she'll come** je suppose qu'elle ne viendra pas, cela m'étonnerait qu'elle vienne.

supposedly [səpō'zidlē] *ad* soi-disant.

supposing [səpō'zing] *cj* si, à supposer que + *sub.*

supposition [supəzish'ən] *n* supposition *f*, hypothèse *f*.

suppository [səpâz'itôrē] *n* suppositoire *m*.

suppress [səpres'] *vt* (*revolt, feeling*) réprimer; (*publication*) supprimer; (*scandal*) étouffer.

suppression [səpresh'ən] *n* suppression *f*, répression *f*.

suppressor [səpres'ûr] *n* (*ELEC etc*) dispositif *m* antiparasite.

supremacy [səprem'əsē] *n* suprématie *f*.

supreme [səprēm'] *a* suprême.

Supreme Court *n* (*US*) Cour *f* suprême.

Supt. *abbr* (*POLICE*) = **superintendent.**

surcharge [sûr'chârj] *n* surcharge *f*; (*extra tax*) surtaxe *f*.

sure [shōōr] *a* (*gen*) sûr(e); (*definite, convinced*) sûr, certain(e) ◆ *ad* (*col: esp US*): **that** ~ **is pretty, that's** ~ **pretty** c'est drôlement joli(e); ~! (*of course*) bien sûr!; ~ **enough** effectivement; **I'm not** ~ **how/ why/when** je ne sais pas très bien comment/ pourquoi/quand; **to be** ~ **of o.s.** être sûr de soi; **to make** ~ **of** s'assurer de; vérifier.

sure-footed [shōōr'fōōt'id] *a* au pied sûr.

surely [shōōr'lē] *ad* sûrement; certainement; ~ **you don't mean that!** vous ne parlez pas sérieusement!

surety [shōōr'ətē] *n* caution *f*; **to go** *or* **stand** ~ **for sb** se porter caution pour qn.

surf [sûrf] *n* ressac *m*.

surface [sûr'fis] *n* surface *f* ◆ *vt* (*road*) poser le revêtement de ◆ *vi* remonter à la surface; faire surface; **on the** ~ (*fig*) au premier abord.

surface area *n* superficie *f*, aire *f*.

surface mail *n* courrier *m* par voie de terre (*or* maritime).

surfboard [sûrf'bôrd] *n* planche *f* de surf.

surfeit [sûr'fit] *n*: **a** ~ **of** un excès de; une indigestion de.

surfer [sûrf'ûr] *n* surfiste *m/f*.

surfing [sûrf'ing] *n* surf *m*.

surge [sûrj] *n* vague *f*, montée *f*; (*ELEC*) pointe *f* de courant ◆ *vi* déferler; **to** ~ **for-**

ward se précipiter (en avant).

surgeon [sûr'jən] *n* chirurgien *m*.

Surgeon General *n* (*US*) chef *m* du service fédéral de la santé publique.

surgery [sûr'jûrē] *n* chirurgie *f*; (*Brit: room*) cabinet *m* (de consultation); (: *session*) consultation *f*; (: *of MP etc*) permanence *f* (*où le député etc reçoit les électeurs etc*); **to undergo** ~ être opéré(e).

surgery hours *npl* (*Brit*) heures *fpl* de consultation.

surgical [sûr'jikəl] *a* chirurgical(e).

surgical spirit *n* (*Brit*) alcool *m* à 90°.

surly [sûr'lē] *a* revêche, maussade.

surmise [sûrmīz'] *vt* présumer, conjecturer.

surmount [sûrmount'] *vt* surmonter.

surname [sûr'nām] *n* nom *m* de famille.

surpass [sûrpas'] *vt* surpasser, dépasser.

surplus [sûr'pləs] *n* surplus *m*, excédent *m* ◆ *a* en surplus, de trop; **it is** ~ **to our requirements** cela dépasse nos besoins; ~ **stock** surplus *m*.

surprise [sûrprīz'] *n* (*gen*) surprise *f*; (*astonishment*) étonnement *m* ◆ *vt* surprendre; étonner; **to take by** ~ (*person*) prendre au dépourvu; (*MIL: town, fort*) prendre par surprise.

surprising [sûrprī'zing] *a* surprenant(e), étonnant(e).

surprisingly [sûrprī'zinglē] *ad* (*easy, helpful*) étonnamment, étrangement; (**somewhat**) ~, **he agreed** curieusement, il a accepté.

surrealism [sərē'əlizəm] *n* surréalisme *m*.

surrealist [sərē'əlist] *a, n* surréaliste (*m/f*).

surrender [səren'dûr] *n* reddition *f*, capitulation *f* ◆ *vi* se rendre, capituler ◆ *vt* (*claim, right*) renoncer à.

surrender value *n* valeur *f* de rachat.

surreptitious [sûrəptish'əs] *a* subreptice, furtif(ive).

surrogate [sûr'əgit] *n* (*substitute*) substitut *m* ◆ *a* de substitution, de remplacement; **a food** ~ un succédané alimentaire; ~ **coffee** (*Brit*) ersatz *m or* succédané *m* de café.

surrogate mother *n* mère porteuse *or* de substitution.

surround [səround'] *vt* entourer; (*MIL etc*) encercler.

surrounding [səroun'ding] *a* environnant(e).

surroundings [səroun'dingz] *npl* environs *mpl*, alentours *mpl*.

surtax [sûr'taks] *n* surtaxe *f*.

surveillance [sûrvā'ləns] *n* surveillance *f*.

survey *n* [sûr'vā] enquête *f*, étude *f*; (*Brit: in house buying etc*) inspection *f*, (rapport *m* d')expertise *f*; (*of land*) levé *m*; (*comprehensive view: of situation etc*) vue *f* d'ensemble ◆ *vt* [sərvā'] passer en revue; enquêter sur; inspecter; (*building*) expertiser; (*land*) faire le levé de.

surveying [sûrvā'ing] *n* arpentage *m*.

surveyor [sûrvā'ûr] *n* (*of building*) expert *m*; (*of land*) (arpenteur *m*) géomètre *m*.

survival [sûrvī'vəl] *n* survie *f*; (*relic*) vestige *m* ◆ *cpd* (*course, kit*) de survie.

survive [sûrvīv'] *vi* survivre; (*custom etc*) subsister ◆ *vt* survivre à, réchapper de; (*person*) survivre à.

survivor [sûrvī'vûr] *n* survivant/e.

susceptible [səsep'təbəl] *a*: ~ **(to)** sensible (à); (*disease*) prédisposé(e) (à).

suspect *a*, *n* [sus'pekt] suspect(e) ♦ *vt* [səspekt'] soupçonner, suspecter.

suspend [səspend'] *vt* suspendre.

suspended sentence [səspen'did sen'təns] *n* condamnation *f* avec sursis.

suspender belt [səspen'dûr belt] *n* (*Brit*) porte-jarretelles *m inv*.

suspenders [səspen'dûrz] *npl* (*US*) bretelles *fpl*.

suspense [səspens'] *n* attente *f*; (*in film etc*) suspense *m*.

suspense account *n* compte *m* d'attente.

suspension [səspen'chən] *n* (*gen*, *AUT*) suspension *f*; (*of driver's license*) retrait *m* provisoire.

suspension bridge *n* pont suspendu.

suspicion [səspish'ən] *n* soupçon(s) *m(pl)*; **to be under** ~ être considéré(e) comme suspect(e), être suspecté(e); **arrested on** ~ **of murder** arrêté sur présomption de meurtre.

suspicious [səspish'əs] *a* (*suspecting*) soupçonneux(euse), méfiant(e); (*causing suspicion*) suspect(e); **to be** ~ **of** *or* **about sb/sth** avoir des doutes à propos de qn/sur qch, trouver qn/qch suspect(e).

suss out [sus out] *vt* (*Brit col*: *discover*) supputer; (: *understand*) piger.

sustain [səstān'] *vt* supporter; soutenir; corroborer; (*suffer*) subir; recevoir.

sustained [səstānd'] *a* (*effort*) soutenu(e), prolongé(e).

sustenance [sus'tənəns] *n* nourriture *f*; moyens *mpl* de subsistance.

suture [sōō'chûr] *n* suture *f*.

SW *abbr* (= *short wave*) OC.

swab [swâb] *n* (*MED*) tampon *m*; prélèvement *m* ♦ *vt* (*NAUT*: also: ~ **down**) nettoyer.

swagger [swag'ûr] *vi* plastronner, parader.

swallow [swâl'ō] *n* (*bird*) hirondelle *f*; (*of food etc*) gorgée *f* ♦ *vt* avaler; (*fig*) gober.

swallow up *vt* engloutir.

swam [swam] *pt of* **swim**.

swamp [swâmp] *n* marais *m*, marécage *m* ♦ *vt* submerger.

swampy [swâmp'ē] *a* marécageux(euse).

swan [swân] *n* cygne *m*.

swank [swangk] *vi* (*col*) faire de l'épate.

swan song *n* (*fig*) chant *m* du cygne.

swap [swâp] *n* échange *m*, troc *m* ♦ *vt*: **to** ~ **(for)** échanger (contre), troquer (contre).

swarm [swôrm] *n* essaim *m* ♦ *vi* essaimer; fourmiller, grouiller.

swarthy [swôr'thē] *a* basané(e), bistré(e).

swashbuckling [swâsh'bukling] *a* (*film*) de cape et d'épée.

swastika [swâs'tikə] *n* croix gammée.

swathe [swâth] *vt*: **to** ~ **in** (*bandages, blankets*) emboîturer de.

swatter [swât'ûr] *n* (*also*: **fly** ~) tapette *f*.

sway [swā] *vi* se balancer, osciller; tanguer ♦ *vt* (*influence*) influencer ♦ *n* (*rule, power*): ~ **(over)** emprise *f* (sur); **to hold** ~ **over sb** avoir de l'emprise sur qn.

Swaziland [swâ'zēland] *n* Swaziland *m*.

swear, *pt* **swore,** *pp* **sworn** [swe'ûr, swôr, swôrn] *vi* jurer; **to** ~ **to sth** jurer de qch; **to**

~ **an oath** prêter serment.

swear in *vt* assermenter.

swearword [swâr'wûrd] *n* gros mot, juron *m*.

sweat [swet] *n* sueur *f*, transpiration *f* ♦ *vi* suer; **in a** ~ en sueur.

sweatband [swet'band] *n* (*SPORT*) bandeau *m*.

sweater [swet'ûr] *n* tricot *m*, pull *m*.

sweatshirt [swet'shûrt] *n* sweat-shirt *m*.

sweatshop [swet'shâp] *n* atelier *m* où les ouvriers sont exploités.

sweat suit *n* survêtement *m*.

sweaty [swet'ē] *a* en sueur, moite *or* mouillé(e) de sueur.

Swede [swēd] *n* Suédois/e.

swede [swēd] *n* (*Brit*) rutabaga *m*.

Sweden [swēd'ən] *n* Suède *f*.

Swedish [swē'dish] *a* suédois(e) ♦ *n* (*LING*) suédois *m*.

sweep [swēp] *n* coup *m* de balai; (*curve*) grande courbe; (*range*) champ *m*; (*also:* **chimney** ~) ramoneur *m* ♦ *vb* (*pt, pp* **swept** [swept]) *vt* balayer; (*fashion, craze*) se répandre dans ♦ *vi* avancer majestueusement *or* rapidement; s'élancer; s'étendre.

sweep away *vt* balayer; entraîner, emporter.

sweep past *vi* passer majestueusement *or* rapidement.

sweep up *vt*, *vi* balayer.

sweeping [swē'ping] *a* (*gesture*) large; circulaire; (*changes, reforms*) radical(e); a ~ **statement** une généralisation hâtive.

sweepstake [swēp'stāk] *n* sweepstake *m*.

sweet [swet] *n* (*Brit*) dessert *m*; (*candy*) bonbon *m* ♦ *a* doux(douce); (*not savory*) sucré(e); (*fresh*) frais(fraîche), pur(e); (*kind*) gentil(le); (*cute*) mignon(ne) ♦ *ud*: **to smell** ~ sentir bon; **to taste** ~ avoir un goût sucré; ~ **and sour** *a* aigre-doux(douce).

sweetbread [swet'bred] *n* ris *m* de veau.

sweetcorn [swet'kôrn] *n* maïs doux.

sweeten [swet'ən] *vt* sucrer; (*fig*) adoucir.

sweetener [swet'ənûr] *n* (*CULIN*) édulcorant *m*.

sweetheart [swet'hârt] *n* amoureux/euse.

sweetly [swet'lē] *ad* (*smile*) gentiment; (*sing, play*) mélodieusement.

sweetness [swet'nis] *n* douceur *f*; (*of taste*) goût sucré.

sweet pea *n* pois *m* de senteur.

sweet potato *n* patate douce.

sweetshop [swet'shâp] *n* (*Brit*) confiserie *f*.

sweet tooth *n*: **to have a** ~ aimer les sucreries.

swell [swel] *n* (*of sea*) houle *f* ♦ *a* (*col*: *excellent*) chouette ♦ *vb* (*pt* ~**ed**, *pp* **swollen** *or* ~**ed** [swō'lən]) *vt* augmenter; grossir ♦ *vi* grossir, augmenter; (*sound*) s'enfler; (*MED*) enfler.

swelling [swel'ing] *n* (*MED*) enflure *f*; grosseur *f*.

sweltering [swel'tûring] *a* étouffant(e), oppressant(e).

swept [swept] *pt*, *pp of* **sweep**.

swerve [swûrv] *vi* faire une embardée *or* un écart; dévier.

swift [swift] *n* (*bird*) martinet *m* ♦ *a* rapide, prompt(e).

swiftly [swift'lē] *ad* rapidement, vite.

swiftness [swift'nis] *n* rapidité *f*.
swig [swig] *n* (*col*: *drink*) lampée *f*.
swill [swil] *n* pâtée *f* ♦ *vt* (*also*: ~ **out**, ~ **down**) laver à grande eau.
swim [swim] *n*: **to go for a** ~ aller nager *or* se baigner ♦ *vb* (*pt* **swam**, *pp* **swum** [swam, swum]) *vi* nager; (*SPORT*) faire de la natation; (*fig*: *head, room*) tourner ♦ *vt* traverser (à la nage); (*distance*) faire (à la nage); **to** ~ **a length** nager une longueur; **to go** ~**ming** aller nager.
swimmer [swim'ûr] *n* nageur/euse.
swimming [swim'ing] *n* nage *f*, natation *f*.
swimming baths *npl* (*Brit*) piscine *f*.
swimming cap *n* bonnet *m* de bain.
swimming costume *n* (*Brit*) maillot *m* (de bain).
swimming pool *n* piscine *f*.
swimming trunks *npl* maillot *m* de bain.
swimsuit [swim'sōōt] *n* maillot *m* (de bain).
swindle [swin'dəl] *n* escroquerie *f* ♦ *vt* escroquer.
swindler [swind'lûr] *n* escroc *m*.
swine [swīn] *n* (*pl inv*) pourceau *m*, porc *m*; (*col!*) salaud *m* (*!*).
swing [swing] *n* balançoire *f*; (*movement*) balancement *m*, oscillations *fpl*; (*MUS*) swing *m*; rythme *m* ♦ *vb* (*pt, pp* **swung** [swung]) *vt* balancer, faire osciller; (*also*: ~ **around**) tourner, faire virer ♦ *vi* se balancer, osciller; (*also*: ~ **around**) virer, tourner; **a** ~ **to the left** (*POL*) un revirement en faveur de la gauche; **to be in full** ~ battre son plein; **to get into the** ~ **of things** se mettre dans le bain; **the road** ~**s south** la route prend la direction sud.
swing bridge *n* pont tournant.
swing door *n* (*Brit*) porte battante.
swingeing [swin'jing] *a* (*Brit*) écrasant(e); considérable.
swinging [swing'ing] *a* rythmé(e); entraînant(e); (*col*) dans le vent.
swinging door *n* (*US*) porte battante.
swipe [swīp] *n* grand coup; gifle *f* ♦ *vt* (*hit*) frapper à toute volée; gifler; (*col*: *steal*) piquer.
swirl [swûrl] *n* tourbillon *m* ♦ *vi* tourbillonner, tournoyer.
swish [swish] *vi* (*whip*) siffler; (*skirt, long grass*) bruire.
Swiss [swis] *a* suisse ♦ *n* (*pl inv*) Suisse/esse.
Swiss French *a* suisse romand(e).
Swiss German *a* suisse-allemand(e).
Swiss roll *n* gâteau roulé.
switch [swich] *n* (*for light, radio etc*) bouton *m*; (*change*) changement *m*, revirement *m* ♦ *vt* (*change*) changer; (*exchange*) intervertir; (*invert*): **to** ~ (**around** *or* **over**) changer de place.
switch off *vt* éteindre; (*engine*) arrêter.
switch on *vt* allumer; (*engine, machine*) mettre en marche.
switchback [swich'bak] *n* (*Brit*) montagnes *fpl* russes.
switchblade [swich'blād] *n* (*also*: ~ **knife**) couteau *m* à cran d'arrêt.
switchboard [swich'bôrd] *n* (*TEL*) standard *m*.
switchboard operator *n* (*TEL*) standardiste

m/f.
switchtower [swich'touûr] *n* (*US*) poste *m* d'aiguillage.
switchyard [swich'yârd] *n* (*US*) voies *fpl* de garage *or* de triage.
Switzerland [swit'sûrlənd] *n* Suisse *f*.
swivel [swiv'əl] *vi* (*also*: ~ **around**) pivoter, tourner.
swollen [swō'lən] *pp of* **swell** ♦ *a* (*ankle etc*) enflé(e).
swoon [swōōn] *vi* se pâmer.
swoop [swōōp] *n* (*by police etc*) rafle *f*, descente *f*; (*of bird etc*) descente *f* en piqué ♦ *vi* (*also*: ~ **down**) descendre en piqué, piquer.
swop [swâp] *n*, *vt* = **swap**.
sword [sôrd] *n* épée *f*; **to be at** ~**s' points with sb** (*US*) être à couteaux tirés avec qn.
swordfish [sôrd'fish] *n* espadon *m*.
swore [swôr] *pt of* **swear**.
sworn [swôrn] *pp of* **swear**.
swot [swât] *vt, vi* bûcher, potasser.
swum [swum] *pp of* **swim**.
swung [swung] *pt, pp of* **swing**.
sycamore [sik'əmôr] *n* sycomore *m*.
sycophant [sik'əfənt] *n* flagorneur/euse.
sycophantic [sikəfan'tik] *a* flagorneur(euse).
Sydney [sid'nē] *n* Sydney.
syllable [sil'əbəl] *n* syllabe *f*.
syllabus [sil'əbəs] *n* programme *m*; **on the** ~ au programme.
symbol [sim'bəl] *n* symbole *m*.
symbolic(al) [simbâl'ik(əl)] *a* symbolique.
symbolism [sim'bəlizəm] *n* symbolisme *m*.
symbolize [sim'bəlīz] *vt* symboliser.
symmetrical [simet'rikəl] *a* symétrique.
symmetry [sim'itrē] *n* symétrie *f*.
sympathetic [simpəthet'ik] *a* (*showing pity*) compatissant(e); (*understanding*) bienveillant(e), compréhensif(ive); ~ **towards** bien disposé(e) envers.
sympathetically [simpəthet'iklē] *ad* avec compassion (*or* bienveillance).
sympathize [sim'pəthīz] *vi*: **to** ~ **with sb** (*in grief*) être de tout cœur avec qn, compatir à la douleur de qn; (*in predicament*) partager les sentiments de qn; **to** ~ **with** (*sb's feelings*) comprendre.
sympathizer [sim'pəthīzûr] *n* (*POL*) sympathisant/e.
sympathy [sim'pəthē] *n* compassion *f*; **in** ~ **with** en accord avec; (*strike*) en or par solidarité avec; **with our deepest** ~ en vous priant d'accepter nos sincères condoléances.
symphonic [simfân'ik] *a* symphonique.
symphony [sim'fənē] *n* symphonie *f*.
symphony orchestra *n* orchestre *m* symphonique.
symposium [simpō'zēəm] *n* symposium *m*.
symptom [simp'təm] *n* symptôme *m*; indice *m*.
symptomatic [simptəmat'ik] *a* symptomatique.
synagogue [sin'əgâg] *n* synagogue *f*.
synchromesh [sing'krəmesh] *n* (*AUT*) synchronisation *f*.
synchronize [sing'krənīz] *vt* synchroniser ♦ *vi*: **to** ~ **with** se produire en même temps que.
syncopated [sing'kəpātid] *a* syncopé(e).
syndicate [sin'dəkit] *n* syndicat *m*, coopérative

f; (*PRESS*) agence *f* de presse.
syndrome [sin'drōm] *n* syndrome *m*.
synonym [sin'ənim] *n* synonyme *m*.
synonymous [sinân'əməs] *a*: ~ **(with)** synonyme (de).
synopsis, *pl* **synopses** [sinâp'sis, -sēz] *n* résumé *m*, synopsis *m or f*.
syntax [sin'taks] *n* syntaxe *f*.
synthesis, *pl* **syntheses** [sin'thəsis, -sēz] *n* synthèse *f*.
synthesizer [sin'thisīzûr] *n* (*MUS*) synthétiseur *m*.
synthetic [sinthet'ik] *a* synthétique ♦ *n* matière *f* synthétique; ~**s** *npl* textiles artificiels.
syphilis [sif'əlis] *n* syphilis *f*.
syphon [sī'fən] *n, vb* = **siphon**.
Syrla [sēr'ēə] *n* Syrie *f*.
Syrian [sēr'ēən] *a* syrien(ne) ♦ *n* Syrien/ne.
syringe [sərinj'] *n* seringue *f*.
syrup [sir'əp] *n* sirop *m*; (*Brit: also*: **golden** ~) mélasse raffinée.
syrupy [sir'əpē] *a* sirupeux(euse).
system [sis'təm] *n* système *m*; (*order*) méthode *f*; (*ANAT*) organisme *m*.
systematic [sistəmat'ik] *a* systématique; méthodique.
system disk *n* (*COMPUT*) disque *m* système.
systems analyst [sis'təmz an'əlist] *n* analyste-programmeur *m/f*.

T

T, t [tē] *n* (*letter*) T, t *m*; **T for Tommy** T comme Thérèse.
ta [tâ] *excl* (*Brit col*) merci!
tab [tab] *n abbr* = **tabulator** ♦ *n* (*loop on coat etc*) attache *f*; (*label*) étiquette *f*; **to keep** ~**s on** (*fig*) surveiller.
tabby [tab'ē] *n* (*also*: ~ **cat**) chat/te tigré(e).
tabernacle [tab'ûrnakəl] *n* tabernacle *m*.
table [tā'bəl] *n* table *f*; **to lay** *or* **set the** ~ mettre le couvert *or* la table; **to clear the** ~ débarrasser la table; ~ **of contents** table des matières.
tablecloth [tā'bəlklôth] *n* nappe *f*.
table d'hôte [tab'əl dōt'] *a* (*meal*) à prix fixe.
table lamp *n* lampe décorative.
tableland [tā'bəlland] *n* plateau *m*.
tablemat [tā'bəlmat] *n* (*Brit: for plate*) napperon *m*, set *m*; (: *for hot dish*) dessous-de-plat *m inv*.
table salt *n* sel fin *or* de table.
tablespoon [tā'bəlspōon] *n* cuiller *f* de service; (*also*: ~**ful**: *as measurement*) cuillerée *f* à soupe.
tablet [tab'lit] *n* (*MED*) comprimé *m*; (: *for sucking*) pastille *f*; (*for writing*) bloc *m*; (*of stone*) plaque *f*.
table tennis *n* ping-pong *m*, tennis *m* de table.
table wine *n* vin *m* de table.
tabloid [tab'loid] *n* (*newspaper*) tabloïde *m*;

the ~**s** les journaux *mpl* populaires.
taboo [taboo'] *a, n* tabou (*m*).
tabulate [tab'yəlāt] *vt* (*data, figures*) mettre sous forme de table(s).
tabulator [tab'yəlātûr] *n* tabulateur *m*.
tachograph [tak'əgraf] *n* tachygraphe *m*.
tachometer [təkâm'ətûr] *n* tachymètre *m*.
tacit [tas'it] *a* tacite.
taciturn [tas'itûrn] *a* taciturne.
tack [tak] *n* (*nail*) petit clou; (*stitch*) point *m* de bâti; (*NAUT*) bord *m*, bordée *f* ♦ *vt* clouer; bâtir ♦ *vi* tirer un *or* des bord(s); **to change** ~ virer de bord; **on the wrong** ~ (*fig*) sur la mauvaise voie; **to** ~ **sth on to (the end of) sth** (*of letter, book*) rajouter qch à la fin de qch.
tackle [tak'əl] *n* matériel *m*, équipement *m*; (*for lifting*) appareil *m* de levage; (*FOOTBALL, SOCCER, RUGBY*) plaquage *m* ♦ *vt* (*difficulty*) s'attaquer à; (*SOCCER, RUGBY*) plaquer.
tacky [tak'ē] *a* collant(e); pas sec(sèche); (*col: shabby*) moche.
tact [takt] *n* tact *m*.
tactful [takt'fəl] *a* plein(e) de tact.
tactfully [takt'fəlē] *ad* avec tact.
tactical [tak'tikəl] *a* tactique; ~ **error** erreur *f* de tactique.
tactics [tak'tiks] *n, npl* tactique *f*.
tactless [takt'lis] *a* qui manque de tact.
tactlessly [takt'lislē] *ad* sans tact.
tadpole [tad'pōl] *n* têtard *m*.
taffy [taf'ē] *n* (*US*) (bonbon *m* au) caramel *m*.
tag [tag] *n* étiquette *f*; **price/name** ~ étiquette (portant le prix/le nom).
tag along *vi* suivre.
Tahiti [təhē'tē] *n* Tahiti *m*.
tail [tāl] *n* queue *f*; (*of shirt*) pan *m* ♦ *vt* (*follow*) suivre, filer; **to turn** ~ se sauver à toutes jambes; *see also* **head**.
tail away, tail off *vi* (*in size, quality etc*) baisser peu à peu.
tailback [tāl'bak] *n* (*Brit*) bouchon *m*.
tail coat *n* habit *m*.
tail end *n* bout *m*, fin *f*.
tailgate [tāl'gāt] *n* (*AUT*) hayon *m* arrière.
taillight [tāl'līt] *n* (*AUT*) feu *m* arrière.
tailor [tā'lûr] *n* tailleur *m* (*artisan*) ♦ *vt*: **to** ~ **sth (to)** adapter qch exactement (à); ~**'s (shop)** (boutique *f* de) tailleur *m*.
tailoring [tā'lûring] *n* (*cut*) coupe *f*.
tailor-made [tā'lûrmād] *a* fait(e) sur mesure; (*fig*) conçu(e) spécialement.
tailwind [tāl'wind] *n* vent *m* arrière *inv*.
taint [tānt] *vt* (*meat, food*) gâter; (*fig: reputation*) salir.
tainted [tānt'id] *a* (*food*) gâté(e); (*water, air*) infecté(e); (*fig*) souillé(e).
Taiwan [tī'wân'] *n* Taiwan (*no article*).
take [tāk] *vb* (*pt* **took**, *pp* **taken** [tōōk, tā'kən]) *vt* prendre; (*gain: prize*) remporter; (*require: effort, courage*) demander; (*tolerate*) accepter, supporter; (*hold: passengers etc*) contenir; (*accompany*) emmener, accompagner; (*bring, carry*) apporter, emporter; (*exam*) passer, se présenter à; (*conduct: meeting*) présider ♦ *vi* (*dye, fire etc*) prendre ♦ *n* (*CINEMA*) prise *f* de vues; **to** ~ **sth from** (*drawer etc*) prendre qch dans; (*person*)

prendre qch à; **I ~ it that** je suppose que; **I took him for a doctor** je l'ai pris pour un docteur; **to ~ sb's hand** prendre qn par la main; **to ~ for a walk** (*child, dog*) emmener promener; **to be taken ill** tomber malade; **to ~ it upon o.s.** to do sth prendre sur soi de faire qch; **~ the first (street) on the left** prenez la première à gauche; **it won't ~ long** ça ne prendra pas longtemps; **I was quite taken with her/it** elle/cela m'a beaucoup plu.
take after *vt fus* ressembler à.
take apart *vt* démonter.
take away *vt* emporter; (*remove*) enlever; (*subtract*) soustraire ♦ *vi*: **to ~ away from** diminuer.
take back *vt* (*return*) rendre, rapporter; (*one's words*) retirer.
take down *vt* (*building*) démolir; (*dismantle: scaffolding*) démonter; (*letter etc*) prendre, écrire.
take in *vt* (*deceive*) tromper, rouler; (*understand*) comprendre, saisir; (*include*) couvrir, inclure; (*lodger*) prendre; (*orphan, stray dog*) recueillir; (*dress, waistband*) reprendre.
take off *vi* (*AVIAT*) décoller; (*leave*) décamper ♦ *vt* (*remove*) enlever; (*imitate*) imiter, pasticher.
take on *vt* (*work*) accepter, se charger de; (*employee*) prendre, embaucher; (*opponent*) accepter de se battre contre.
take out *vt* sortir; (*remove*) enlever; (*license*) prendre, se procurer; **to ~ sth out of** enlever qch de; prendre qch dans; **don't ~ it out on me!** ne t'en prends pas à moi!
take over *vt* (*business*) reprendre ♦ *vi*: **to ~ over from sb** prendre la relève de qn.
take to *vt fus* (*person*) se prendre d'amitié pour; (*activity*) prendre goût à; **to ~ to doing sth** prendre l'habitude de faire qch.
take up *vt* (*one's story, a dress*) reprendre; (*occupy: time, space*) prendre, occuper; (*engage in: hobby etc*) se mettre à; (*accept: offer, challenge*) accepter; (*absorb: liquids*) absorber ♦ *vi*: **to ~ up with sb** se lier d'amitié avec qn.
takeaway [tā'kəwā] *a* (*Brit*) = **takeout.**
take-home pay [tāk'hōm pā] *n* salaire net.
taken [tā'kən] *pp of* **take.**
takeoff [tāk'ôf] *n* (*AVIAT*) décollage *m*.
takeout [tāk'out] *a* (*US: food*) à emporter.
takeover [tāk'ōvûr] *n* (*COMM*) rachat *m*.
takeover bid *n* offre publique d'achat, OPA *f*.
takings [tā'kingz] *npl* (*COMM*) recette *f*.
talc [talk] *n* (*also:* **~um powder**) talc *m*.
tale [tāl] *n* (*story*) conte *m*, histoire *f*; (*account*) récit *m*; (*pej*) histoire; **to tell ~s** (*fig*) rapporter.
talent [tal'ənt] *n* talent *m*, don *m*.
talented [tal'əntid] *a* doué(e), plein(e) de talent.
talent scout *n* découvreur *m* de vedettes (*or* joueurs *etc*).
talk [tôk] *n* propos *mpl*; (*gossip*) racontars *mpl* (*pej*); (*conversation*) discussion *f*; (*interview*) entretien *m*; (*a speech*) causerie *f*, exposé *m* ♦ *vi* (*chatter*) bavarder; **~s** *npl* (*POL etc*) entretiens *mpl*; conférence *f*; **to give a ~** faire un exposé; **to ~ about** parler

de; (*converse*) s'entretenir *or* parler de; **~ing of films, have you seen ...?** à propos de films, avez-vous vu ...?; **to ~ sb out of/into doing** persuader qn de ne pas faire/de faire; **to ~ shop** parler métier *or* affaires.
talk over *vt* discuter (de).
talkative [tô'kətiv] *a* bavard(e).
talker [tô'kûr] *n* causeur/euse; (*pej*) bavard/e.
talking point [tô'king point] *n* sujet *m* de conversation.
talking-to [tô'kingtōō] *n*: **to give sb a good ~** passer un savon à qn.
talk show *n* (*TV, RADIO*) causerie (télévisée *or* radiodiffusée).
tall [tôl] *a* (*person*) grand(e); (*building, tree*) haut(e); **to be 6 feet ~** ≈ mesurer 1 mètre 80; **how ~ are you?** combien mesurez-vous?
tallboy [tôl'boi] *n* (*Brit*) grande commode.
tallness [tôl'nis] *n* grande taille; hauteur *f*.
tall story *n* histoire *f* invraisemblable.
tally [tal'ē] *n* compte *m* ♦ *vi*: **to ~ (with)** correspondre (à); **to keep a ~ of sth** tenir le compte de qch.
talon [tal'ən] *n* griffe *f*; (*of eagle*) serre *f*.
tambourine [tam'bərēn] *n* tambourin *m*.
tame [tām] *a* apprivoisé(e); (*fig: story, style*) insipide.
tamper [tam'pûr] *vi*: **to ~ with** toucher à (*en cachette ou sans permission*).
tampon [tam'pân] *n* tampon *m* hygiénique *or* périodique.
tan [tan] *n* (*also:* **sun~**) bronzage *m* ♦ *vt*, *vi* bronzer, brunir ♦ *a* (*color*) brun roux *inv*; **to get a ~** bronzer.
tandem [tan'dəm] *n* tandem *m*.
tang [tang] *n* odeur (*or* saveur) piquante.
tangent [tan'jənt] *n* (*MATH*) tangente *f*; **to go off at a ~** (*fig*) changer complètement de direction.
tangerine [tanjərēn'] *n* mandarine *f*.
tangible [tan'jəbəl] *a* tangible; **~ assets** biens réels.
Tangier [tanjiûr'] *n* Tanger *m*.
tangle [tang'gəl] *n* enchevêtrement *m* ♦ *vt* enchevêtrer; **to get in(to) a ~** s'emmêler.
tango [tang'gō] *n* tango *m*.
tank [tangk] *n* réservoir *m*; (*for processing*) cuve *f*; (*for fish*) aquarium *m*; (*MIL*) char *m* d'assaut, tank *m*.
tankard [tangk'ûrd] *n* chope *f*.
tanker [tangk'ûr] *n* (*ship*) pétrolier *m*, tanker *m*; (*truck*) camion-citerne *m*; (*RAIL*) wagon-citerne *m*.
tanned [tand] *a* bronzé(e).
tannin [tan'in] *n* tanin *m*.
tanning [tan'ing] *n* (*of leather*) tannage *m*.
tantalizing [tan'təlīzing] *a* (*a smell*) extrêmement appétissant(e); (*offer*) terriblement tentant(e).
tantamount [tan'təmount] *a*: **~ to** qui équivaut à.
tantrum [tan'trəm] *n* accès *m* de colère; **to throw a ~** piquer une colère.
Tanzania [tanzənē'ə] *n* Tanzanie *f*.
Tanzanian [tanzənē'ən] *a* tanzanien(ne) ♦ *n* Tanzanien/ne.
tap [tap] *n* (*on sink etc*) robinet *m*; (*gentle blow*) petite tape ♦ *vt* frapper *or* taper légèrement; (*resources*) exploiter, utiliser; (*tele-*

phone) mettre sur écoute; **on** ~ (*beer*) en tonneau; (*fig: resources*) disponible.

tap-dancing [tap'dansing] *n* claquettes *fpl*.

tape [tāp] *n* ruban *m*; (*also:* **magnetic** ~) bande *f* (magnétique) ♦ *vt* (*record*) enregistrer (au magnétophone *or* sur bande); **on** ~ (*song etc*) enregistré(e).

tape deck *n* platine *f* d'enregistrement.

tape measure *n* mètre *m* à ruban.

taper [tā'pûr] *n* cierge *m* ♦ *vi* s'effiler.

tape-record [tāp'rikôrd] *vt* enregistrer (au magnétophone *or* sur bande).

tape recorder *n* magnétophone *m*.

tape recording *n* enregistrement *m* (au magnétophone).

tapered [tā'pûrd], **tapering** [tā'pûring] *a* fuselé(e), effilé(e).

tapestry [tap'istrē] *n* tapisserie *f*.

tapeworm [tāp'wûrm'] *n* ver *m* solitaire, ténia *m*.

tapioca [tapēō'kə] *n* tapioca *m*.

tappet [tap'it] *n* (*AUT*) poussoir *m* (de soupape).

tar [târ] *n* goudron *m*; **low-/middle-**~ **cigarettes** cigarettes *fpl* à faible/moyenne teneur en goudron.

tarantula [tәran'chәlә] *n* tarentule *f*.

tardy [târ'dē] *a* tardif(ive).

target [târ'git] *n* cible *f*; (*fig: objective*) objectif *m*; **to be on** ~ (*project*) progresser comme prévu.

target practice *n* exercices *mpl* de tir (à la cible).

tariff [tar'if] *n* (*COMM*) tarif *m*; (*taxes*) tarif douanier.

tariff barrier *n* barrière douanière.

tarmac [târ'mak] *n* (*AVIAT*) aire *f* d'envol; (*Brit: on road*) macadam *m*.

tarnish [târ'nish] *vt* ternir.

tarpaulin [târpô'lin] *n* bâche goudronnée.

tarragon [tar'әgәn] *n* estragon *m*.

tart [târt] *n* (*CULIN*) tarte *f*; (*Brit col: pej: woman*) poule *f* ♦ *a* (*flavor*) âpre, aigrelet(te).

tart up *vt* (*col*): **to** ~ **o.s. up** se faire beau(belle); (: *pej*) s'attifer.

tartan [târ'tәn] *n* tartan *m* ♦ *a* écossais(e).

tartar [târ'tûr] *n* (*on teeth*) tartre *m*.

tartar sauce *n* sauce *f* tartare.

task [task] *n* tâche *f*; **to take to** ~ prendre à partie.

task force *n* (*MIL, POLICE*) détachement spécial.

taskmaster [task'mastûr] *n*: **he's a hard** ~ il est très exigeant dans le travail.

Tasmania [tazmā'nēә] *n* Tasmanie *f*.

tassel [tas'әl] *n* gland *m*; pompon *m*.

taste [tāst] *n* goût *m*; (*fig: glimpse, idea*) idée *f*, aperçu *m* ♦ *vt* goûter ♦ *vi*: **to** ~ **of** (*fish etc*) avoir le *or* un goût de; **it** ~**s like fish** ça a un *or* le goût de poisson, on dirait du poisson; **what does it** ~ **like?** quel goût ça a?; **you can** ~ **the garlic (in it)** on sent bien l'ail; **can I have a** ~ **of this wine?** puis-je goûter un peu de ce vin?; **to have a** ~ **of sth** goûter (à) qch; **to have a** ~ **for sth** aimer qch, avoir un penchant pour qch; **to be in good/bad** *or* **poor** ~ être de bon/mauvais goût.

taste bud *n* papille *f*.

tasteful [tāst'fәl] *a* de bon goût.

tastefully [tāst'fәlē] *ad* avec goût.

tasteless [tāst'lis] *a* (*food*) qui n'a aucun goût; (*remark*) de mauvais goût.

tasty [tās'tē] *a* savoureux(euse), délicieux(euse).

tattered [tat'ûrd] *a see* **tatters**.

tatters [tat'ûrz] *npl*: **in** ~ (*also:* **tattered**) en lambeaux.

tattoo [tatōō'] *n* tatouage *m*; (*spectacle*) parade *f* militaire ♦ *vt* tatouer.

tatty [tat'ē] *a* (*Brit col*) défraîchi(e), en piteux état.

taught [tôt] *pt, pp of* **teach**.

taunt [tônt] *n* raillerie *f* ♦ *vt* railler.

Taurus [tôr'әs] *n* le Taureau; **to be** ~ être du Taureau.

taut [tôt] *a* tendu(e).

tavern [tav'ûrn] *n* taverne *f*.

tawdry [tô'drē] *a* (d'un mauvais goût) criard.

tawny [tô'nē] *a* fauve (*couleur*).

tax [taks] *n* (*on goods etc*) taxe *f*; (*on income*) impôts *mpl*, contributions *fpl* ♦ *vt* taxer; imposer; (*fig: strain: patience etc*) mettre à l'épreuve; **before/after** ~ avant/après l'impôt; **free of** ~ exonéré(e) d'impôt.

taxable [tak'sәbәl] *a* (*income*) imposable.

tax allowance *n* part *f* du revenu non imposable, abattement *m* à la base.

taxation [taksā'shәn] *n* taxation *f*; impôts *mpl*, contributions *fpl*; **system of** ~ système fiscal.

tax avoidance *n* évasion fiscale.

tax collector *n* percepteur *m*.

tax disc *n* (*Brit AUT*) vignette *f* (automobile).

tax evasion *n* fraude fiscale.

tax exemption *n* exonération fiscale, exemption *f* d'impôts.

tax exile *n* personne qui s'expatrie pour fuir une fiscalité excessive.

tax-free [taks'frē'] *a* exempt(e) d'impôts.

tax haven *n* paradis fiscal.

taxi [tak'sē] *n* taxi *m* ♦ *vi* (*AVIAT*) rouler (lentement) au sol.

taxidermist [tak'sidûrmist] *n* empailleur/euse (*d'animaux*).

taxi driver *n* chauffeur *m* de taxi.

taximeter [tak'simētûr] *n* taximètre *m*.

tax inspector *n* (*Brit*) percepteur *m*.

taxi stand, (*Brit*) **taxi rank** *n* station *f* de taxis.

tax payer *n* contribuable *m/f*.

tax rebate *n* ristourne *f* d'impôt.

tax relief *n* dégrèvement *or* allègement fiscal, réduction *f* d'impôt.

tax return *n* déclaration *f* d'impôts *or* de revenus.

tax year *n* année fiscale.

TB *n abbr* = **tuberculosis**.

TD *n abbr* (*US*) = **Treasury Department**; (: *FOOTBALL*) = **touchdown**.

tea [tē] *n* thé *m*; (*Brit: snack: for children*) goûter *m*; **high** ~ (*Brit*) collation combinant goûter et dîner.

tea bag *n* sachet *m* de thé.

tea break *n* (*Brit*) pause-thé *f*.

teach, *pt, pp* **taught** [tēch, tôt] *vt*: **to** ~ **sb sth**, ~ **sth to sb** apprendre qch à qn; (*in* *school etc*) enseigner qch à qn ♦ *vi* enseigner; **it taught him a lesson** *(fig)* ça lui a servi de leçon.

teacher [tē'chûr] *n (in high school)* professeur *m*; *(in elementary school)* instituteur/trice; **French ~** professeur de français.

teacher training college *n (for elementary schools)* ≈ école normale d'instituteurs; *(for high schools)* collège *m* de formation pédagogique *(pour l'enseignement secondaire)*.

teaching [tē'ching] *n* enseignement *m*.

teaching aids *npl* supports *mpl* pédagogiques.

teaching hospital *n* C.H.U. *m*, centre *m* hospitalo-universitaire.

tea cosy *n* couvre-théière *m*.

teacup [tē'kup] *n* tasse *f* à thé.

teak [tēk] *n* teck *m* ♦ *a* en *or* de teck.

tea leaves *npl* feuilles *fpl* de thé.

team [tēm] *n* équipe *f*; *(of animals)* attelage *m*.

   team up *vi*: **to ~ up (with)** faire équipe (avec).

team games *npl* jeux *mpl* d'équipe.

teamwork [tēm'wûrk] *n* travail *m* d'équipe.

tea party *n* thé *m (réception)*.

teapot [tē'pât] *n* théière *f*.

tear *n* [tär] déchirure *f*; [tēr] larme *f* ♦ *vb* [tär] *(pt* **tore,** *pp* **torn** [tôr, tôrn]) *vt* déchirer ♦ *vi* se déchirer; **in ~s** en larmes; **to burst into ~s** fondre en larmes; **to ~ to pieces** *or* **to bits** *or* **to shreds** mettre en pièces; *(fig)* démolir.

   tear along *vi (rush)* aller à toute vitesse.

   tear apart *vt (also fig)* déchirer.

   tear away *vt*: **to ~ o.s. away (from sth)** *(fig)* s'arracher (de qch).

   tear out *vt (sheet of paper, check)* arracher.

   tear up *vt (sheet of paper etc)* déchirer, mettre en morceaux *or* pièces.

tearaway [tär'əwā] *n (Brit: col)* casse-cou *m inv*.

teardrop [tēr'drâp] *n* larme *f*.

tearful [tēr'fəl] *a* larmoyant(e).

tear gas *n* gaz *m* lacrymogène.

tearoom [tē'rōōm] *n* salon *m* de thé.

tease [tēz] *n* taquin/e ♦ *vt* taquiner; *(unkindly)* tourmenter; *(hair)* crêper.

tea set *n* service *m* à thé.

teashop [tē'shâp] *n (Brit)* pâtisserie-salon de thé *f*.

teaspoon [tē'spōōn] *n* petite cuiller; *(also:* **~ful:** *as measurement)* ≈ cuillerée *f* à café.

tea strainer *n* passoire *f* (à thé).

teat [tēt] *n* tétine *f*.

teatime [tē'tīm] *n* l'heure *f* du thé.

tea towel *n (Brit)* torchon *m* (à vaisselle).

tea urn *n* fontaine *f* à thé.

tech [tek] *n abbr (col)* = **technology, technical college.**

technical [tek'nikəl] *a* technique.

technical college *n* C.E.T. *m*, collège *m* d'enseignement technique.

technicality [teknikal'itē] *n* technicité *f*; *(detail)* détail *m* technique; **on a legal ~** à cause de (*or* grâce à) l'application à la lettre d'une subtilité juridique; pour vice de forme.

technically [tek'niklē] *ad* techniquement.

technician [teknish'ən] *n* technicien/ne.

technique [teknēk'] *n* technique *f*.

technocrat [tek'nəkrat] *n* technocrate *m/f*.

technological [teknəlâj'ikəl] *a* technologique.

technologist [teknâl'əjist] *n* technologue *m/f*.

technology [teknâl'əjē] *n* technologie *f*.

teddy (bear) [ted'ē bär] *n* ours *m* (en peluche).

tedious [tē'dēəs] *a* fastidieux(euse).

tedium [tē'dēəm] *n* ennui *m*.

tee [tē] *n (GOLF)* tee *m*.

teem [tēm] *vi*: **to ~ (with)** grouiller (de).

teenage [tēn'āj] *a (fashions etc)* pour jeunes, pour adolescents.

teenager [tēn'ājûr] *n* jeune *m/f*, adolescent/e.

teens [tēnz] *npl*: **to be in one's ~** être adolescent(e).

tee shirt *n* = **T-shirt.**

teeter [tē'tûr] *vi* chanceler, vaciller.

teeth [tēth] *npl of* **tooth.**

teethe [tēth] *vi* percer ses dents.

teething ring [tē'thing ring] *n* anneau *m (pour bébé qui perce ses dents)*.

teething troubles [tē'thing trub'əlz] *npl (fig)* difficultés initiales.

teetotal [tētōt'əl] *a (person)* qui ne boit jamais d'alcool.

teetotaler, *(Brit)* **teetotaller** [tētōt'əlûr] *n* personne *f* qui ne boit jamais d'alcool.

TEFL [tef'əl] *n abbr = Teaching of English as a Foreign Language.*

Teheran [teərân'] *n* Téhéran.

tel. *abbr (= telephone)* tél.

Tel Aviv [tel'əvēv'] *n* Tel Aviv.

telecast [tel'əkast] *vt* télédiffuser, téléviser.

telecommunications [teləkəmyōōnikā'shənz] *n* télécommunications *fpl*.

telegram [tel'əgram] *n* télégramme *m*.

telegraph [tel'əgraf] *n* télégraphe *m*.

telegraphic [teləgraf'ik] *a* télégraphique.

telegraph pole *n* poteau *m* télégraphique.

telegraph wire *n* fil *m* télégraphique.

telepathic [teləpath'ik] *a* télépathique.

telepathy [təlep'əthē] *n* télépathie *f*.

telephone [tel'əfōn] *n* téléphone *m* ♦ *vt (person)* téléphoner à; *(message)* téléphoner; **to have a ~** *(subscriber)* être abonné(e) au téléphone; **to be on the ~** *(be speaking)* être au téléphone.

telephone booth, *(Brit)* **telephone box** *n* cabine *f* téléphonique.

telephone call *n* appel *m* téléphonique, communication *f* téléphonique.

telephone directory *n* annuaire *m* (du téléphone).

telephone exchange *n* central *m* (téléphonique).

telephone kiosk *n (Brit)* cabine *f* téléphonique.

telephone number *n* numéro *m* de téléphone.

telephone operator *n* téléphoniste *m/f*, standardiste *m/f*.

telephone tapping [tel'əfōn ta'ping] *n* mise *f* sur écoute.

telephonist [tel'əfōnist] *n (Brit)* téléphoniste *m/f*.

telephoto [teləfō'tō] *a*: **~ lens** téléobjectif *m*.

teleprinter [tel'əprintûr] *n* téléscripteur *m*.

telescope [tel'əskōp] *n* télescope *m* ♦ *vi* se télescoper ♦ *vt* télescoper.

telescopic [teliskáp'ik] *a* télescopique; *(umbrella)* à manche télescopique.

teletext [tel'ətekst] *n* télétexte *m*.

telethon [tel'əthân] *n* téléthon *m*.

televiewer [tel'əvyōōûr] *n* téléspectateur/trice.

televise [tel'əvīz] *vt* téléviser.

television [tel'əvizhən] *n* télévision *f*.

television licence *n (Brit)* redevance *f* (de l'audio-visuel).

television program *n* émission *f* de télévision.

television set *n* poste *m* de télévision, téléviseur *m*.

telex [tel'eks] *n* télex *m* ♦ *vt (message)* envoyer par télex; *(person)* envoyer un télex à ♦ *vi* envoyer un télex.

tell, *pt, pp* **told** [tel, tōld] *vt* dire; *(relate: story)* raconter; *(distinguish):* **to ~ sth from** distinguer qch de ♦ *vi (talk):* **to ~ (of)** parler (de); *(have effect)* se faire sentir, se voir; **to ~ sb to do** dire à qn de faire; **to ~ sb about sth** *(place, object etc)* parler de qch à qn; *(what happened etc)* raconter qch à qn; **to ~ the time** *(know how to)* savoir lire l'heure; **can you ~ me the time?** pourriez-vous me dire l'heure?; **(I) ~ you what ...** écoute, ...; **I can't ~ them apart** je n'arrive pas à les distinguer.

tell off *vt* réprimander, gronder.

tell on *vt fus (inform against)* dénoncer, rapporter contre.

teller [tel'ûr] *n (in bank)* caissier/ière.

telling [tel'ing] *a (remark, detail)* révélateur(trice).

telltale [tel'tāl] *a (sign)* éloquent(e), révélateur(trice).

telly [tel'ē] *n abbr (Brit col: = television)* télé *f*.

temerity [təmär'itē] *n* témérité *f*.

temp [temp] *abbr (Brit col: = temporary) n* intérimaire *m/f* ♦ *vi* travailler comme intérimaire.

temper [tem'pûr] *n (nature)* caractère *m*; *(mood)* humeur *f*; *(fit of anger)* colère *f* ♦ *vt (moderate)* tempérer, adoucir; **to be in a ~** être en colère; **to lose one's ~** se mettre en colère; **to keep one's ~** rester calme.

temperament [tem'pûrəmənt] *n (nature)* tempérament *m*.

temperamental [tempûrəmen'təl] *a* capricieux(euse).

temperance [tem'pûrəns] *n* modération *f*; *(in drinking)* tempérance *f*.

temperate [tem'pûrit] *a* modéré(e); *(climate)* tempéré(e).

temperature [tem'pûrəchûr] *n* température *f*; **to have** *or* **run a ~** avoir de la fièvre.

temperature chart *n (MED)* feuille *f* de température.

tempered [tem'pûrd] *a (steel)* trempé(e).

tempest [tem'pist] *n* tempête *f*.

tempestuous [tempes'chōōəs] *a (fig)* orageux(euse); *(: person)* passionné(e).

tempi [tem'pē] *npl of* **tempo**.

template [tem'plit] *n* patron *m*.

temple [tem'pəl] *n (building)* temple *m*; *(ANAT)* tempe *f*.

templet [tem'plit] *n* = **template**.

tempo, ~s *or* **tempi** [tem'pō, tem'pē] *n* tempo *m*; *(fig: of life etc)* rythme *m*.

temporal [tem'pûrəl] *a* temporel(le).

temporarily [tempərär'ilē] *ad* temporairement; provisoirement.

temporary [tem'pərärē] *a* temporaire, provisoire; *(job, worker)* temporaire; **~ license** *(US AUT)* permis *m* provisoire; **~ secretary** (secrétaire *f*) intérimaire *f*; **a ~ teacher** un professeur remplaçant *or* suppléant.

temporize [tem'pərīz] *vi* atermoyer; transiger.

tempt [tempt] *vt* tenter; **to ~ sb into doing** induire qn à faire; **to be ~ed to do sth** être tenté(e) de faire qch.

temptation [temptā'shən] *n* tentation *f*.

tempting [temp'ting] *a* tentant(e).

ten [ten] *num* dix ♦ *n:* **~s of thousands** des dizaines *fpl* de milliers.

tenable [ten'əbəl] *a* défendable.

tenacious [tənā'shəs] *a* tenace.

tenacity [tənas'itē] *n* ténacité *f*.

tenancy [ten'ənsē] *n* location *f*; état *m* de locataire.

tenant [ten'ənt] *n* locataire *m/f*.

tend [tend] *vt* s'occuper de; *(sick etc)* soigner ♦ *vi:* **to ~ to do** avoir tendance à faire; *(color):* **to ~ to** tirer sur.

tendency [ten'dənsē] *n* tendance *f*.

tender [ten'dûr] *a* tendre; *(delicate)* délicat(e); *(sore)* sensible; *(affectionate)* tendre, doux(douce) ♦ *n (COMM: offer)* soumission *f*; *(money):* **legal ~** cours légal ♦ *vt* offrir; **to ~ one's resignation** donner *or* remettre sa démission; **to put in a ~ (for)** faire une soumission (pour).

tenderize [ten'dərīz] *vt (CULIN)* attendrir.

tenderly [ten'dûrlē] *ad* tendrement.

tenderness [ten'dûrnis] *n* tendresse *f*; *(of meat)* tendreté *f*.

tendon [ten'dən] *n* tendon *m*.

tenement [ten'əmənt] *n* immeuble *m* (de rapport).

Tenerife [tenərēf'] *n* Ténérife *f*.

tenet [ten'it] *n* principe *m*.

Tenn. *abbr (US)* = **Tennessee.**

tenner [ten'ûr] *n (col: US)* billet *m* de dix dollars; *(: Brit)* billet *m* de dix livres.

tennis [ten'is] *n* tennis *m* ♦ *cpd (club, match, racket, player)* de tennis.

tennis ball *n* balle *f* de tennis.

tennis court *n* (court *m* de) tennis *m*.

tennis elbow *n (MED)* synovite *f* du coude.

tennis shoes *npl* (chaussures *fpl* de) tennis *mpl*.

tenor [ten'ûr] *n (MUS)* ténor *m*; *(of speech etc)* sens général.

tenpin bowling [ten'pin bō'ling] *n (Brit)* = **tenpins.**

tenpins [ten'pinz] *n (US)* bowling *m* (à 10 quilles).

tense [tens] *a* tendu(e); *(person)* tendu, crispé(e) ♦ *n (LING)* temps *m* ♦ *vt (tighten: muscles)* tendre.

tenseness [tens'nis] *n* tension *f*.

tension [ten'chən] *n* tension *f*.

tent [tent] *n* tente *f*.

tentacle [ten'təkəl] *n* tentacule *m*.

tentative [ten'tətiv] *a* timide, hésitant(e);

(*conclusion*) provisoire.

tenterhooks [tɛn'tûrhŏŏks] *npl*: **on ~** sur des charbons ardents.

tenth [tɛnth] *num* dixième.

tent peg *n* piquet *m* de tente.

tent pole *n* montant *m* de tente.

tenuous [tɛn'yŏŏəs] *a* ténu(e).

tenure [tɛn'yûr] *n* (*of property*) bail *m*; (*of job*) période *f* de jouissance; statut *m* de titulaire.

tepid [tɛp'id] *a* tiède.

term [tûrm] *n* (*limit*) terme *m*; (*word*) terme, mot *m*; (*SCOL*) trimestre *m*; (*LAW*) session *f* ♦ *vt* appeler; **~s** *npl* (*conditions*) conditions *fpl*; (*COMM*) tarif *m*; **~ of imprisonment** peine *f* de prison; **his ~ of office** la période où il était en fonction; **in the short/long ~** à court/long terme; **"easy ~s"** (*COMM*) "facilités de paiement"; **to come to ~s with** (*problem*) faire face à; **to be on good ~s with** bien s'entendre avec, être en bons termes avec.

terminal [tûr'mənəl] *a* terminal(e); (*disease*) dans sa phase terminale ♦ *n* (*ELEC*) borne *f*; (*for oil, ore etc, also COMPUT*) terminal *m*; (*also*: **air ~**) aérogare *f*; (*Brit: also*: **coach ~**) gare routière.

terminate [tûr'mənāt] *vt* mettre fin à ♦ *vi*: **to ~ in** finir en *or* par.

termination [tûrmənā'shən] *n* fin *f*; cessation *f*; (*of contract*) résiliation *f*; **~ of pregnancy** (*MED*) interruption *f* de grossesse.

termini [tûr'mənē] *npl of* **terminus.**

terminology [tûrmənâl'əjē] *n* terminologie *f*.

terminus, *pl* **termini** [tûr'mənəs, tûr'mənē] *n* terminus *m inv*.

termite [tûr'mīt] *n* termite *m*.

Ter(r). *abbr* = **terrace.**

terrace [tär'əs] *n* terrasse *f*; (*Brit: row of houses*) rangée *f* de maisons (*attenantes les unes aux autres*); **the ~s** (*Brit SPORT*) les gradins *mpl*.

terraced [tär'əst] *a* (*garden*) en terrasses; (*in a row: house, cottage etc*) attenant(e) aux maisons voisines.

terracotta [tärəkât'ə] *n* terre cuite.

terrain [tərān'] *n* terrain *m* (*sol*).

terrible [tär'əbəl] *a* terrible, atroce; (*weather, work*) affreux(euse), épouvantable.

terribly [tär'əblē] *ad* terriblement; (*very badly*) affreusement mal.

terrier [tär'ēûr] *n* terrier *m* (*chien*).

terrific [tərif'ik] *a* fantastique, incroyable, terrible; (*wonderful*) formidable, sensationnel(le).

terrify [tär'əfī] *vt* terrifier.

territorial [täritôr'ēəl] *a* territorial(e).

territorial waters *npl* eaux territoriales.

territory [tär'itôrē] *n* territoire *m*.

terror [tär'ûr] *n* terreur *f*.

terrorism [tär'ərizəm] *n* terrorisme *m*.

terrorist [tär'ûrist] *n* terroriste *m/f*.

terrorize [tär'ərīz] *vt* terroriser.

terse [tûrs] *a* (*style*) concis(e); (*reply*) laconique.

tertiary [tûr'shēârē] *a* tertiaire.

Terylene [tär'əlēn] *n* ® (*Brit*) tergal *m* ®.

TESL [tɛs'əl] *n abbr* = *Teaching of English as a Second Language*.

test [tɛst] *n* (*trial, check*) essai *m*; (: *of goods in factory*) contrôle *m*; (*of courage etc*) épreuve *f*; (*MED*) examens *mpl*; (*CHEM*) analyses *fpl*; (*exam: of intelligence etc*) test *m* (d'aptitude); (: *in school*) interrogation *f* de contrôle; (*also*: **driving ~**) (examen du) permis *m* de conduire ♦ *vt* essayer; contrôler; mettre à l'épreuve; examiner; analyser; tester; faire subir une interrogation (de contrôle) à; **to put sth to the ~** mettre qch à l'épreuve.

testament [tɛs'təmənt] *n* testament *m*; **the Old/New T~** l'Ancien/le Nouveau Testament.

test ban *n* (*also*: **nuclear ~**) interdiction *f* des essais nucléaires.

test case *n* (*LAW, fig*) affaire-test *f*.

test flight *n* vol *m* d'essai.

testicle [tɛs'tikəl] *n* testicule *m*.

testify [tɛs'təfī] *vi* (*LAW*) témoigner, déposer; **to ~ to sth** (*LAW*) attester qch; (*gen*) témoigner de qch.

testimonial [tɛstimō'nēəl] *n* (*gift*) témoignage *m* d'estime; (*Brit: reference*) recommandation *f*.

testimony [tɛs'təmōnē] *n* (*LAW*) témoignage *m*, déposition *f*.

testing [tɛs'ting] *a* (*situation, period*) difficile.

testing ground *n* banc *m* d'essai.

test match *n* (*CRICKET, RUGBY*) match international.

test paper *n* (*SCOL*) interrogation écrite.

test pilot *n* pilote *m* d'essai.

test tube *n* éprouvette *f*.

test-tube baby [tɛst'tŏŏb bā'bē] *n* bébé-éprouvette *m*.

testy [tɛs'tē] *a* irritable.

tetanus [tɛt'ənəs] *n* tétanos *m*.

tetchy [tɛch'ē] *a* hargneux(euse).

tether [tɛth'ûr] *vt* attacher ♦ *n*: **at the end of one's ~** (*Brit*) à bout (de patience).

Tex. *abbr* (*US*) = *Texas*.

text [tɛkst] *n* texte *m*.

textbook [tɛkst'bŏŏk] *n* manuel *m*.

textile [tɛks'təl] *n* textile *m*.

texture [tɛks'chûr] *n* texture *f*; (*of skin, paper etc*) grain *m*.

TGIF *abbr* (*col*) = *thank God it's Friday*.

Thai [tī] *a* thaïlandais(e) ♦ *n* Thaïlandais/e; (*LING*) thaï *m*.

Thailand [tī'lənd] *n* Thaïlande *f*.

thalidomide [thəlid'əmīd] *n* ® thalidomide *f* ®.

Thames [tɛmz] *n*: **the ~** la Tamise.

than [than, thɛn] *cj* que; (*with numerals*): **more ~ 10/once** plus de 10/d'une fois; **I have more/less ~ you** j'en ai plus/moins que toi; **she has more apples ~ pears** elle a plus de pommes que de poires; **it is better to phone ~ to write** il vaut mieux téléphoner (plutôt) qu'écrire; **no sooner did he leave ~ the phone rang** il venait de partir quand le téléphone a sonné.

thank [thangk] *vt* remercier, dire merci à; **~ you (very much)** merci (beaucoup); **~ heavens, ~ God** Dieu merci.

thankful [thangk'fəl] *a*: **~ (for)** reconnaissant(e) (de); **~ for/that** (*relieved*) soulagé(e) de/que.

thankfully [thangk'fəlē] *ad* avec re-

connaissance; avec soulagement; ~ **there were few victims** il y eut fort heureusement peu de victimes.
thankless [thangk'lis] *a* ingrat(e).
thanks [thangks] *npl* remerciements *mpl* ♦ *excl* merci!; ~ **to** *prep* grâce à.
Thanksgiving (Day) [thangksgiv'ing (dā)] *n* jour *m* d'action de grâce.

that [that, thət] *cj* que ♦ *a* (*pl* **those**) ce(cet + *vowel or h mute*), *f* cette; (*not "this"*): ~ **book** ce livre-là ♦ *pronoun* (*pl* **those**) ce; (*not "this one"*) cela, ça; (*the one*) celui(celle); (*relative: subject*) qui; (*: object*) que, *prep* + lequel(laquelle); (*with time*): **on the day** ~ **he came** le jour où il est venu ♦ *ad*: ~ **high** aussi haut; si haut; **it's about** ~ **high** c'est à peu près de cette hauteur; ~ **one** celui-là(celle-là); ~ **one over there** celui-là (*or* celle-là) là-bas; **what's** ~**?** qu'est-ce que c'est?; **who's** ~**?** qui est-ce?; **is** ~ **you?** c'est toi?; ~**'s what he said** c'est *or* voilà ce qu'il a dit; ~ **is** ... c'est-à-dire ..., à savoir ...; **all** ~ tout cela, tout ça; **I can't work** ~ **much** je ne peux pas travailler autant que cela; **at** *or* **with** ~, **she** ... là-dessus, elle ...; **do it like** ~ fais-le comme ça; **not** ~ **I know of** pas à ma connaissance.
thatched [thacht] *a* (*roof*) de chaume; ~ **cottage** chaumière *f*.
thaw [thô] *n* dégel *m* ♦ *vi* (*ice*) fondre; (*food*) dégeler ♦ *vt* (*food*) (faire) dégeler; **it's** ~**ing** (*weather*) il dégèle.
the [thə, thē] *definite article* le, *f* la, (l' + *vowel or h mute*), *pl* les (NB: à + *le*(ε) = au(x); *de* + *le* = du; *de* + *les* = des); (*in titles*): **Richard** ~ **Second** Richard Deux ♦ *ad*: ~ **more he works** ~ **more he earns** plus il travaille, plus il gagne d'argent; ~ **sooner** ~ **better** le plus tôt sera le mieux; ~ **rich and** ~ **poor** les riches et les pauvres.
theater, (*Brit*) **theatre** [thē'ətûr] *n* théâtre *m*.
theatergoer [thē'ətûrgōûr] *n* habitué/e du théâtre.
theatrical [thēat'rikəl] *a* théâtral(e); ~ **company** troupe *f* de théâtre.
theft [theft] *n* vol *m* (*larcin*).
their [thär] *a* leur, *pl* leurs.
theirs [thärz] *pronoun* le(la) leur, les leurs; **it is** ~ c'est à eux; **a friend of** ~ un de leurs amis.
them [them, thəm] *pronoun* (*direct*) les; (*indirect*) leur; (*stressed, after prep*) eux(elles); **I see** ~ je les vois; **give** ~ **the book** donne-leur le livre; **give me a few of** ~ donnez m'en quelques uns (*or* quelques unes).
theme [thēm] *n* thème *m*.
theme song *n* chanson principale.
themselves [thəmselvz'] *pl pronoun* (*reflexive*) se; (*emphatic*) eux-mêmes(elles-mêmes); **between** ~ entre eux(elles).
then [then] *ad* (*at that time*) alors, à ce moment-là; (*next*) puis, ensuite; (*and also*) et puis ♦ *cj* (*therefore*) alors, dans ce cas ♦ *a*: **the** ~ **president** le président d'alors *or* de l'époque; **by** ~ (*past*) à ce moment-là; (*future*) d'ici là; **from** ~ **on** dès lors; **before** ~ avant; **until** ~ jusqu'à ce moment-là, jusque-là; **and** ~ **what?** et puis après?; **what do you want me to do** ~**?** (*afterwards*) que

veux-tu que je fasse ensuite?; (*in that case*) bon alors, qu'est-ce que je fais?
theologian [thēəlō'jən] *n* théologien/ne.
theological [thēəlâj'ikəl] *a* théologique.
theology [thēäl'əjē] *n* théologie *f*.
theorem [thēr'əm] *n* théorème *m*.
theoretical [thēəret'ikəl] *a* théorique.
theorize [thē'ərīz] *vi* élaborer une théorie; (*pej*) faire des théories.
theory [thiûr'ē] *n* théorie *f*.
therapeutic(al) [thärəpyōōtik(əl)] *a* thérapeutique.
therapist [thär'əpist] *n* thérapeute *m/f*.
therapy [thär'əpē] *n* thérapie *f*.
there [thär] *ad* là, là-bas; ~, ~! allons, allons!; **it's** ~ c'est là; **he went** ~ il y est allé; ~ **is**, ~ **are** il y a; ~ **he is** le voilà; ~ **has been** il y a eu; **on/in** ~ là-dessus/-dedans; **back** ~ là-bas; **down** ~ là-bas en bas; **over** ~ là-bas; **through** ~ par là; **to go** ~ **and back** faire l'aller et retour.
thereabouts [thär'əbouts] *ad* (*place*) par là, près de là; (*amount*) environ, à peu près.
thereafter [thäraf'tûr] *ad* par la suite.
thereby [thärbī'] *ad* ainsi.
therefore [thär'fôr] *ad* donc, par conséquent.
there's [thärz] = **there is, there has**.
thereupon [thärəpän'] *ad* (*at that point*) sur ce; (*formal: on that subject*) à ce sujet.
thermal [thûr'məl] *a* thermique; ~ **paper/printer** papier *m*/imprimante *f* thermique.
thermodynamics [thûrmōdīnam'iks] *n* thermodynamique *f*.
thermometer [thûrmäm'itûr] *n* thermomètre *m*.
thermonuclear [thûrmōnōō'klēûr] *a* thermonucléaire.
Thermos [thûr'məs] *n* ® thermos *m or f inv* ®.
thermostat [thûr'məstat] *n* thermostat *m*.
thesaurus [thisôr'əs] *n* dictionnaire *m* synonymique.
these [thēz] *pl pronoun* ceux-ci(celles-ci) ♦ *pl a* ces; (*not "those"*): ~ **books** ces livres-ci.
thesis, *pl* **theses** [thē'sis, -sēz] *n* thèse *f*.
they [thā] *pl pronoun* ils(elles); (*stressed*) eux(elles); ~ **say that** ... (*it is said that*) on dit que ....
they'd [thād] = **they had, they would**.
they'll [thāl] = **they shall, they will**.
they're [thär] = **they are.**
they've [thāv] = **they have.**
thick [thik] *a* épais(se); (*crowd*) dense; (*stupid*) bête, borné(e) ♦ *n*: **in the** ~ **of** au beau milieu de, en plein cœur de; **it's 20 cm** ~ ça a 20 cm d'épaisseur.
thicken [thik'ən] *vi* s'épaissir ♦ *vt* (*sauce etc*) épaissir.
thicket [thik'it] *n* fourré *m*, hallier *m*.
thickly [thik'lē] *ad* (*spread*) en couche épaisse; (*cut*) en tranches épaisses; ~ **populated** à forte densité de population.
thickness [thik'nis] *n* épaisseur *f*.
thickset [thik'set'] *a* trapu(e), costaud(e).
thickskinned [thik'skind] *a* (*fig*) peu sensible.
thief, *pl* **thieves** [thēf, thēvz] *n* voleur/euse.
thieving [thē'ving] *n* vol *m* (*larcin*).
thigh [thī] *n* cuisse *f*.
thighbone [thī'bōn] *n* fémur *m*.

thimble [thim'bəl] *n* dé *m* (à coudre).

thin [thin] *a* mince; *(person)* maigre; *(soup)* peu épais(se); *(hair, crowd)* clairsemé(e); *(fog)* léger(ère) ♦ *vt (hair)* éclaircir; *(also:* ~ **down:** *sauce, paint)* délayer ♦ *vi (fog)* s'éclaircir; *(also:* ~ **out:** *crowd)* se disperser; **his hair is** ~**ning** il se dégarnit.

thing [thing] *n* chose *f*; *(object)* objet *m*; *(contraption)* truc *m*; ~**s** *npl (belongings)* affaires *fpl*; **first** ~ **(in the morning)** à la première heure, tout de suite (le matin); **last** ~ **(at night), he** ... juste avant de se coucher, il ...; **the** ~ **is** ... c'est que ...; **for one** ~ d'abord; **the best** ~ **would be to** le mieux serait de; **how are** ~**s?** comment ça va?; **she's got a** ~ **about** ... elle déteste ...; **poor** ~**!** le (*or* la) pauvre!

think, *pt, pp* **thought** [thingk, thôt] *vi* penser, réfléchir ♦ *vt* penser, croire; *(imagine)* s'imaginer; **to** ~ **of** penser à; **what do you** ~ **of it?** qu'en pensez-vous?; **what did you** ~ **of them?** qu'avez-vous pensé d'eux?; **to** ~ **about sth/sb** penser à qch/qn; **I'll** ~ **about it** je vais y réfléchir; **to** ~ **of doing** avoir l'idée de faire; **I** ~ **so/not** je crois *or* pense que oui/non; **to** ~ **well of** avoir une haute opinion de; ~ **again!** attention, réfléchis bien!; **to** ~ **aloud** penser tout haut.

think out *vt (plan)* bien réfléchir à; *(solution)* trouver.

think over *vt* bien réfléchir à; **I'd like to** ~ **things over** *(offer, suggestion)* j'aimerais bien y réfléchir un peu.

think through *vt* étudier dans tous les détails.

think up *vt* inventer, trouver.

thinking [thingk'ing] *n*: **to my (way of)** ~ selon moi.

think tank *n* groupe *m* de réflexion.

thinly [thin'lē] *ad (cut)* en tranches fines; *(spread)* en couche mince.

thinness [thin'is] *n* minceur *f*; maigreur *f*.

third [thûrd] *num* troisième ♦ *n* troisième *m/f*; *(fraction)* tiers *m*; **a** ~ **of** le tiers de.

third-degree burns [thûrd'digrē bûrnz] *npl* brûlures *fpl* au troisième degré.

thirdly [thûrd'lē] *ad* troisièmement.

third party insurance *n (Brit)* assurance *f* au tiers.

third-rate [thûrd'rāt'] *a* de qualité médiocre.

Third World *n*: **the** ~ le Tiers-Monde.

thirst [thûrst] *n* soif *f*.

thirsty [thûrs'tē] *a* qui a soif, assoiffé(e); **to be** ~ avoir soif.

thirteen [thûr'tēn'] *num* treize.

thirtieth [thûr'tēith] *num* trentième.

thirty [thûr'tē] *num* trente.

this [this] *a (pl* **these)** ce(cet + *vowel or h mute)*, *f* cette; *(not "that")*: ~ **book** ce livre-ci ♦ *pronoun (pl* **these)** ce; ceci; *(not "that one")* celui-ci(celle-ci) ♦ *ad*: ~ **high** aussi haut; si haut; **it's about** ~ **high** c'est à peu près de cette hauteur; **who is** ~**?** qui est-ce?; **what is** ~**?** qu'est-ce que c'est?; ~ **is Mr Brown** *(in photo)* voici M. Brown; *(in introduction)* je vous présente M. Brown; *(on telephone)* (c'est) M. Brown à l'appareil; ~ **is what he said** voici ce qu'il a dit; ~ **time** cette fois-ci; ~ **time last year** l'année dernière à la même époque; ~ **way** *(in this direction)* par ici; *(in this fashion)* de cette façon, ainsi; **they were talking of** ~ **and that** ils parlaient de choses et d'autres.

thistle [this'əl] *n* chardon *m*.

thong [thông] *n* lanière *f*.

thorn [thôrn] *n* épine *f*.

thorny [thôr'nē] *a* épineux(euse).

thorough [thûr'ō] *a (search)* minutieux(euse); *(knowledge, research)* approfondi(e); *(work)* consciencieux(euse); *(cleaning)* à fond.

thoroughbred [thûr'ōbred] *n (horse)* pur-sang *m inv.*

thoroughfare [thûr'ōfär] *n* rue *f*.

thoroughly [thûr'ōlē] *ad* minutieusement; en profondeur; à fond; **he** ~ **agreed** il était tout à fait d'accord.

thoroughness [thûr'ōnis] *n* soin (méticuleux).

those [thōz] *pl pronoun* ceux-là(celles-là) ♦ *pl a* ces; *(not "these")*: ~ **books** ces livres-là.

though [thō] *cj* bien que + *sub*, quoique + *sub* ♦ *ad* pourtant; **even** ~ quand bien même + *conditional*; **it's not easy,** ~ pourtant, ce n'est pas facile.

thought [thôt] *pt, pp* of **think** ♦ *n* pensée *f*; *(opinion)* avis *m*; *(intention)* intention *f*; **after much** ~ après mûre réflexion; **I've just had a** ~ je viens de penser à quelque chose; **to give sth some** ~ réfléchir à qch.

thoughtful [thôt'fəl] *a* pensif(ive); *(considerate)* prévenant(e).

thoughtfully [thôt'fəlē] *ad* pensivement; avec prévenance.

thoughtless [thôt'lis] *a* étourdi(e); qui manque de considération.

thoughtlessly [thôt'lislē] *ad* inconsidérément.

thousand [thou'zənd] *num* mille; **one** ~ mille; ~**s of** des milliers de.

thousandth [thou'zəndth] *num* millième.

thrash [thrash] *vt* rouer de coups; donner une correction à; *(defeat)* battre à plate(s) couture(s).

thrash about *vi* se débattre.

thrash out *vt* débattre de.

thrashing [thrash'ing] *n*: **to give sb a** ~ = **to thrash sb.**

thread [thred] *n* fil *m*; *(of screw)* pas *m*, filetage *m* ♦ *vt (needle)* enfiler; **to** ~ **one's way between** se faufiler entre.

threadbare [thred'bär] *a* râpé(e), élimé(e).

threat [thret] *n* menace *f*; **to be under** ~ **of** être menacé(e) de.

threaten [thret'ən] *vi (storm)* menacer ♦ *vt*: **to** ~ **sb with sth/to do** menacer qn de qch/ de faire.

threatening [thret'əning] *a* menaçant(e).

three [thrē] *num* trois.

three-dimensional [thrē'dimen'chənəl] *a* à trois dimensions; *(film)* en relief.

threefold [thrē'fōld] *ad*: **to increase** ~ tripler.

three-piece [thrē'pēs] : ~ **suit** *n* complet *m* (avec gilet); ~ **suite** *n* salon *m* comprenant un canapé et deux fauteuils assortis.

three-ply [thrē'plī] *a (wood)* à trois épaisseurs; *(wool)* trois fils *inv.*

three-quarters [thrē'kwôr'tûrz] *npl* trois-quarts *mpl*; ~ **full** aux trois-quarts plein.

thresh [thresh] *vt (AGR)* battre.

threshing machine [thresh'ing məshēn'] *n*

batteuse *f*.
threshold [thresh'ōld] *n* seuil *m*; **to be on the ~ of** (*fig*) être au seuil de.
threshold agreement *n* (*ECON*) accord *m* d'indexation des salaires.
threw [thrōō] *pt of* **throw**.
thrift [thrift] *n* économie *f*.
thrifty [thrif'tē] *a* économe.
thrill [thril] *n* frisson *m*, émotion *f* ♦ *vi* tressaillir, frissonner ♦ *vt* (*audience*) électriser; **to be ~ed** (*with gift etc*) être ravi(e).
thriller [thril'ûr] *n* film *m* (*or* roman *m or* pièce *f*) à suspense.
thrilling [thril'ing] *a* (*book, play etc*) saisissant(e); (*news, discovery*) excitant(e).
thrive, *pt* **thrived, throve**, *pp* **thrived, thriven** [thrīv, thrōv, thriv'ən] *vi* pousser *or* se développer bien; (*business*) prospérer; **he ~s on it** cela lui réussit.
thriving [thriv'ing] *a* vigoureux(euse); (*industry etc*) prospère.
throat [thrōt] *n* gorge *f*; **to have a sore ~** avoir mal à la gorge.
throb [thrâb] *n* (*of heart*) pulsation *f*; (*of engine*) vibration *f*; (*of pain*) élancement *m* ♦ *vi* (*heart*) palpiter; (*engine*) vibrer; (*pain*) lanciner; (*wound*) causer des élancements; **my head is ~bing** j'ai des élancements dans la tête.
throes [thrōz] *npl*: **in the ~ of** au beau milieu de; en proie à; **in the ~ of death** à l'agonie.
thrombosis [thrâmbō'sis] *n* thrombose *f*.
throne [thrōn] *n* trône *m*.
throng [thrông] *n* foule *f* ♦ *vt* se presser dans.
throttle [thrât'əl] *n* (*AUT*) accélérateur *m* ♦ *vt* étrangler.
through [thrōō] *prep* à travers; (*time*) pendant, durant; (*by means of*) par, par l'intermédiaire de; (*owing to*) à cause de ♦ *a* (*ticket, train, passage*) direct(e) ♦ *ad* à travers; **(from) Monday ~ Friday** (*US*) de lundi à vendredi; **to let sb ~** laisser passer qn; **to put sb ~ to sb** (*TEL*) passer qn à qn; **to be ~** (*TEL*) avoir la communication; (*have finished*) avoir fini; **"no ~ traffic"** (*US*) "passage interdit"; **"no ~ road"** "impasse".
throughout [thrōōout'] *prep* (*place*) partout dans; (*time*) durant tout(e) le(la) ♦ *ad* partout.
throughput [thrōō'pŏŏt] *n* (*of goods, materials*) quantité de matières premières utilisée; (*COMPUT*) débit *m*.
throve [thrōv] *pt of* **thrive**.
throw [thrō] *n* jet *m*; (*SPORT*) lancer *m* ♦ *vt* (*pt* **threw**, *pp* **thrown** [thrōō, thrōn]) lancer, jeter; (*SPORT*) lancer; (*rider*) désarçonner; (*fig*) décontenancer; (*pottery*) tourner; **to ~ a party** donner une réception.
throw about *vt* (*Brit*) = **throw around**.
throw around *vt* (*litter etc*) éparpiller.
throw away *vt* jeter.
throw off *vt* se débarrasser de.
throw out *vt* jeter dehors; (*reject*) rejeter.
throw together *vt* (*clothes, meal etc*) assembler à la hâte; (*essay*) bâcler.
throw up *vi* vomir.
throwaway [thrō'əwā] *a* à jeter.
throwback [thrō'bak] *n*: **it's a ~ to** ça nous

etc ramène à.
throw-in [thrō'in] *n* (*SPORT*) remise *f* en jeu.
thru [thrōō] *prep, a, ad* (*US*) = **through**.
thrush [thrush] *n* (*ZOOL*) grive *f*; (*MED: esp in children*) muguet *m*; (: *Brit: in women*) muguet vaginal.
thrust [thrust] *n* (*TECH*) poussée *f* ♦ *vt* (*pt, pp* **thrust**) pousser brusquement; (*push in*) enfoncer.
thrusting [thrust'ing] *a* dynamique; qui se met trop en avant.
thud [thud] *n* bruit sourd.
thug [thug] *n* voyou *m*.
thumb [thum] *n* (*ANAT*) pouce *m* ♦ *vt* (*book*) feuilleter; **to ~ a lift** faire de l'auto-stop, arrêter une voiture; **to give sb/sth the ~s up** (*approve*) donner le feu vert à qn/qch.
thumb index *n* répertoire *m* (à onglets).
thumbnail [thum'nāl] *n* ongle *m* du pouce.
thumbnail sketch *n* croquis *m*.
thumbtack [thum'tak] *n* (*US*) punaise *f* (*clou*).
thump [thump] *n* grand coup *m*; (*sound*) bruit sourd *m* ♦ *vt* cogner sur ♦ *vi* cogner, frapper.
thunder [thun'dûr] *n* tonnerre *m* ♦ *vi* tonner; (*train etc*) · **to ~ past** passer dans un grondement *or* un bruit de tonnerre.
thunderbolt [thun'dûrbōlt] *n* foudre *f*.
thunderclap [thun'dûrklap] *n* coup *m* de tonnerre.
thunderous [thun'dûrəs] *a* étourdissant(e).
thunderstorm [thun'dûrstôrm] *n* orage *m*.
thunderstruck [thun'dûrstruk] *a* (*fig*) abasourdi(e).
thundery [thun'dûrē] *a* orageux(euse).
Thur(s). *abbr* (= *Thursday*) jeu.
Thursday [thûrz'dā] *n* jeudi *m*; *for phrases see also* **Tuesday.**
thus [thus] *ad* ainsi.
thwart [thwôrt] *vt* contrecarrer.
thyme [tīm] *n* thym *m*.
thyroid [thī'roid] *n* thyroïde *f*.
tiara [tēar'ə] *n* (*woman's*) diadème *m*.
Tibet [tibet'] *n* Tibet *m*.
Tibetan [tibet'ən] *a* tibétain(e) ♦ *n* Tibétain/e; (*LING*) tibétain *m*.
tibia [tib'ēə] *n* tibia *m*.
tic [tik] *n* tic (nerveux).
tick [tik] *n* (*sound: of clock*) tic-tac *m*; (*mark*) coche *f*; (*ZOOL*) tique *f* ♦ *vi* faire tic-tac ♦ *vt* cocher; **to put a ~ against sth** cocher qch.
tick off *vt* cocher; (*person*) réprimander, attraper.
tick over *vi* (*Brit: engine*) tourner au ralenti; (: *fig*) aller *or* marcher doucettement.
ticker tape [tik'ûr tāp] *n* bande *f* de téléscripteur; (*US: in celebrations*) ≈ serpentin *m*.
ticket [tik'it] *n* billet *m*; (*for bus, subway*) ticket *m*; (*in store: on goods*) étiquette *f*; (: *from cash register*) reçu *m*, ticket; (*US POL*) liste électorale (*soutenue par un parti*); **to get a (parking) ~** (*AUT*) attraper une contravention (pour stationnement illégal).
ticket agency *n* (*THEATER*) agence *f* de spectacles.
ticket collector *n* contrôleur/euse.
ticket holder *n* personne munie d'un billet.
ticket inspector *n* (*Brit*) contrôleur/euse.
ticket office *n* guichet *m*, bureau *m* de vente

des billets.
tickle [tik'əl] *n* chatouillement *m* ♦ *vt* chatouiller; (*fig*) plaire à; faire rire.
ticklish [tik'lish] *a* (*person*) chatouilleux(euse); (*which tickles: blanket*) qui chatouille; (: *cough*) qui irrite.
tidal [tīd'əl] *a* à marée.
tidal wave *n* raz-de-marée *m inv*.
tidbit [tid'bit] *n* (*US: food*) friandise *f*; (: *before meal*) amuse-gueule *m inv*; (: *news*) po tin *m*.
tiddlywinks [tid'lēwingks] *n* jeu *m* de puce.
tide [tīd] *n* marée *f*; (*fig: of events*) cours *m* ♦ *vt*: **to ~ sb over** dépanner qn; **high/low ~** marée haute/basse.
tidily [tī'dilē] *ad* avec soin, soigneusement.
tidiness [tī'dēnis] *n* bon ordre; goût *m* de l'ordre.
tidy [tī'dē] *a* (*room*) bien rangé(e); (*dress, work*) net(nette), soigné(e); (*person*) ordonné(e), qui a de l'ordre; (: *in character*) soigneux(euse); (*mind*) méthodique ♦ *vt* (*also*: ~ **up**) ranger; **to ~ o.s. up** s'arranger.
tie [tī] *n* (*string etc*) cordon *m*; (*US RAIL*) traverse *f*; (*Brit: also*: **neck~**) cravate *f*; (*fig: link*) lien *m*; (*SPORT: draw*) égalité *f* de points; match nul; (: *match*) rencontre *f* ♦ *vt* (*parcel*) attacher; (*ribbon*) nouer ♦ *vi* (*SPORT*) faire match nul; finir à égalité de points; **"black/white ~"** "smoking/habit de rigueur"; **family ~s** liens de famille; **to ~ sth in a bow** faire un nœud à *or* avec qch; **to ~ a knot in sth** faire un nœud à qch.
tie down *vt* attacher; (*fig*): **to ~ sb down to** contraindre qn à accepter.
tie in *vi*: **to ~ in (with)** (*correspond*) correspondre (à).
tie on *vt* (*Brit: label etc*) attacher (avec une ficelle).
tie up *vt* (*parcel*) ficeler; (*dog, boat*) attacher; (*arrangements*) conclure; **to be ~d up** (*busy*) être pris or occupé.
tie-break(er) [tī'brāk(ûr)] *n* (*TENNIS*) tie-break *m*; (*in quiz*) question *f* subsidiaire.
tie-on [tī'ân] *a* (*Brit: label*) qui s'attache.
tiepin [tī'pin] *n* (*Brit*) épingle *f* de cravate.
tier [tēr] *n* gradin *m*; (*of cake*) étage *m*.
Tierra del Fuego [tēär'ə del fwā'gō] *n* Terre *f* de Feu.
tie tack *n* (*US*) épingle *f* de cravate.
tiff [tif] *n* petite querelle.
tiger [tī'gûr] *n* tigre *m*.
tight [tīt] *a* (*rope*) tendu(e), raide; (*clothes*) étroit(e), très juste; (*budget, schedule, curve*) serré(e); (*control*) strict(e), sévère; (*col: drunk*) ivre, rond(e) ♦ *ad* (*squeeze*) très fort; (*shut*) à bloc, hermétiquement; **to be packed ~** (*suitcase*) être bourré(e); (*people*) être serré(e); **everybody hold ~!** accrochez-vous bien!
tighten [tīt'ən] *vt* (*rope*) tendre; (*screw*) resserrer; (*control*) renforcer ♦ *vi* se tendre; se resserrer.
tightfisted [tīt'fis'tid] *a* avare.
tightly [tīt'lē] *ad* (*grasp*) bien, très fort.
tightrope [tīt'rōp] *n* corde *f* raide.
tightrope walker *n* funambule *m/f*.
tights [tīts] *npl* (*Brit*) collant *m*.

tigress [tī'gris] *n* tigresse *f*.
tilde [til'də] *n* tilde *m*.
tile [tīl] *n* (*on roof*) tuile *f*; (*on wall or floor*) carreau *m* ♦ *vt* (*floor, bathroom etc*) carreler.
tiled [tīld] *a* en tuiles; carrelé(e).
till [til] *n* caisse (enregistreuse) ♦ *vt* (*land*) cultiver ♦ *prep, cj* = **until.**
tiller [til'ûr] *n* (*NAUT*) barre *f* (du gouvernail).
tilt [tilt] *vt* pencher, incliner ♦ *vi* pencher, être incliné(e) ♦ *n* (*slope*) inclinaison *f*; **to wear one's hat at a ~** porter son chapeau incliné sur le côté; **(at) full ~** à toute vitesse.
timber [tim'bûr] *n* (*material*) bois *m* de construction; (*trees*) arbres *mpl*.
time [tīm] *n* temps *m*; (*epoch: often pl*) époque *f*, temps; (*by clock*) heure *f*; (*moment*) moment *m*; (*occasion, also MATH*) fois *f*; (*MUS*) mesure *f* ♦ *vt* (*race*) chronométrer; (*program*) minuter; (*remark etc*) choisir le moment de; **a long ~** un long moment, longtemps; **for the ~ being** pour le moment; **from ~ to ~** de temps en temps; **~ after ~,** **~ and again** bien des fois; **in ~** (*soon enough*) à temps; (*after some time*) avec le temps, à la longue; (*MUS*) en mesure; **in a week's ~** dans une semaine; **in no ~** en un rien de temps; **on ~** à l'heure; **to be 30 minutes behind/ahead of ~** avoir 30 minutes de retard/d'avance; **by the ~ he arrived** quand il est arrivé, le temps qu'il arrive (*sub*); **5 ~s 5** 5 fois 5; **what ~ is it?** quelle heure est-il?; **to have a good ~** bien s'amuser; **we (or they etc) had a hard ~** ça a été difficile *or* pénible; **~'s up!** c'est l'heure!; **I've no ~ for it** (*fig*) cela m'agace; **he'll do it in his own ~** (*without being hurried*) il le fera quand il en aura le temps; **he'll do it on** *or* (*Brit*) **in his own ~** (*out of working hours*) il le fera à ses heures perdues; **to be behind the ~s** retarder (*sur* son temps).
time-and-motion study [tīm'ənmōshən stu'dē] *n* étude *f* des cadences.
time bomb *n* bombe *f* à retardement.
time clock *n* horloge pointeuse.
time-consuming [tim'kənsōōming] *a* qui prend beaucoup de temps.
time difference *n* décalage *m* horaire.
time-honored [tīm'ânûrd] *a* consacré(e).
timekeeper [tīm'kēpûr] *n* (*SPORT*) chrono-mètre *m*.
time lag *n* (*Brit*) décalage *m*; (: *in travel*) décalage horaire.
timeless [tīm'lis] *a* éternel(le).
time limit *n* limite *f* de temps, délai *m*.
timely [tīm'lē] *a* opportun(e).
time off *n* temps *m* libre.
timeout [tīm'out'] *n* (*US*) temps mort.
timer [tī'mûr] *n* (*in kitchen*) compte-minutes *m inv*; (*TECH*) minuteur *m*.
timesaving [tīm'sāving] *a* qui fait gagner du temps.
time scale *n* délais *mpl*.
time sharing [tīm' shä'ring] *n* (*COMPUT*) temps partagé.
time sheet *n* feuille *f* de présence.
time signal *n* signal *m* horaire.
time switch *n* (*Brit*) minuteur *m*; (: *for*

lighting) minuterie *f.*

timetable [tïm'tābəl] *n* (*RAIL*) (indicateur *m*) horaire *m*; (*SCOL*) emploi *m* du temps; (*program of events etc*) programme *m.*

time zone *n* fuseau *m* horaire.

timid [tim'id] *a* timide; (*easily scared*) peureux(euse).

timidity [timid'itē] *n* timidité *f.*

timing [tï'ming] *n* minutage *m*; chronométrage *m*; **the ~ of his resignation** le moment choisi pour sa démission.

timing device *n* (*on bomb*) mécanisme *m* de retardement.

timpani [tim'pənē] *npl* timbales *fpl.*

tin [tin] *n* étain *m*; (*also:* **~ plate**) fer-blanc *m*; (*Brit: can*) boîte *f* (de conserve); (*: for baking*) moule *m* (à gâteau); **a ~ of paint** un pot de peinture.

tin foil *n* papier *m* d'étain.

tinge [tinj] *n* nuance *f* ♦ *vt*: ~d **with** teinté(e) de.

tingle [ting'gəl] *n* picotement *m*; frisson *m* ♦ *vi* picoter.

tinker [tingk'ûr] *n* rétameur ambulant; (*gipsy*) romanichel *m.*

tinker with *vt fus* bricoler, rafistoler.

tinkle [ting'kəl] *vi* tinter ♦ *n* (*col*): **to give sb a ~** passer un coup de fil à qn.

tin mine *n* mine *f* d'étain.

tinned [tind] *a* (*Brit: food*) en boîte, en conserve.

tinny [tin'ē] *a* métallique.

tin opener [tin' ōpənûr] *n* (*Brit*) ouvre-boîte(s) *m.*

tinsel [tin'səl] *n* guirlandes *fpl* de Noël (*argentées*).

tint [tint] *n* teinte *f*; (*for hair*) shampooing colorant ♦ *vt* (*hair*) faire un shampooing colorant à.

tinted [tin'tid] *a* (*hair*) teint(e); (*glass*) teinté(e).

T-intersection [tē'intərsek'shən] *n* (*US*) croisement *m* en T.

tiny [tï'nē] *a* minuscule.

tip [tip] *n* (*end*) bout *m*; (*protective: on umbrella etc*) embout *m*; (*gratuity*) pourboire *m*; (*Brit: for garbage*) décharge *f*; (*advice*) tuyau *m* ♦ *vt* (*waiter*) donner un pourboire à; (*tilt*) incliner; (*overturn: also:* ~ **over**) renverser; (*empty: also:* ~ **out**) déverser; (*predict: winner etc*) pronostiquer.

tip off *vt* prévenir, avertir.

tip-off [tip'ôf] *n* (*hint*) tuyau *m.*

tipped [tipt] *a* (*Brit: cigarette*) (à bout) filtre *inv*; **steel-~** à bout métallique, à embout de métal.

Tipp-Ex [tip'eks] *n* ® (*Brit*) Tipp-Ex *m* ®.

tipple [tip'əl] (*Brit*) *vi* picoler ♦ *n*: **to have a ~** boire un petit coup.

tippy-toe [tip'ētō] *n* (*US*): **on ~** sur la pointe des pieds.

tipsy [tip'sē] *a* un peu ivre, éméché(e).

tiptoe [tip'tō] *n* = **tippy-toe.**

tiptop [tip'tâp] *a*: **in ~ condition** en excellent état.

tire [tïûr'] *n* pneu *m* ♦ *vt* fatiguer ♦ *vi* se fatiguer.

tire out *vt* épuiser.

tired [tïûrd] *a* fatigué(e); **to be/feel/look ~**

être/se sentir/avoir l'air fatigué; **to be ~ of** en avoir assez de, être las(lasse) de.

tiredness [tïûrd'nis] *n* fatigue *f.*

tireless [tïûr'lis] *a* infatigable, inlassable.

tire pressure *n* (*US*) pression *f* de gonflage.

tiresome [tïûr'səm] *a* ennuyeux(euse).

tiring [tïûr'ing] *a* fatigant(e).

tissue [tish'ōō] *n* tissu *m*; (*paper handkerchief*) mouchoir *m* en papier, kleenex *m* ®.

tissue paper *n* papier *m* de soie.

tit [tit] *n* (*bird*) mésange *f*; (*col: breast*) nichon *m*; **to give ~ for tat** rendre coup pour coup.

titanium [tïtā'nēəm] *n* titane *m.*

titbit [tit'bit] *n* (*Brit*) = **tidbit.**

titillate [tit'əlāt] *vt* titiller, exciter.

titivate [tit'əvāt] *vt* pomponner.

title [tit'əl] *n* titre *m*; (*LAW: right*): ~ **(to)** droit *m* (à).

title deed *n* (*LAW*) titre (constitutif) de propriété.

title page *n* page *f* de titre.

title role *n* rôle principal.

titter [tit'ûr] *vi* rire (bêtement).

tittle-tattle [tit'əltatəl] *n* bavardages *mpl.*

titular [tich'ələr] *a* (*in name only*) nominal(e).

tizzy [tiz'ē] *n*: **to be in a ~** être dans tous ses états.

T-junction [tējung'kshən] *n* (*Brit*) = **T-intersection.**

TM *n abbr* = **trademark, transcendental meditation.**

TN *abbr* (*US MAIL*) = *Tennessee.*

TNT *n abbr* (= *trinitrotoluene*) TNT *m.*

to [tōō, tōō] *prep* à; (*towards*) vers; envers ♦ *with vb* (*simple infinitive*): ~ **go/eat** aller/manger; (*following another vb*): **to want/try ~ do** vouloir faire/essayer de faire; (*purpose, result*) pour, afin de; **to give sth ~ sb** donner qch à qn; **give it ~ me** donne-le-moi; **the key ~ the front door** la clé de la porte d'entrée; **it belongs ~ him** cela lui appartient, c'est à lui; **the main thing is ~** ... l'important est de ...; **to go ~ France/Portugal** aller en France/au Portugal; **the road ~ Philadelphia** la route de Philadelphie; **I went ~ Claude's** je suis allé chez Claude; **to go ~ town/school** aller en ville/à l'école; **8 apples ~ the kilo** 8 pommes le kilo; **it's 25 ~ 3** il est 3 heures moins 25; **pull/push the door ~** tirez/poussez la porte; **to go ~ and fro** aller et venir; **he did it ~ help you** il l'a fait pour t'aider; **I don't want ~** je ne veux pas; **I have things ~ do** j'ai des choses à faire; **ready ~ go** prêt à partir.

toad [tōd] *n* crapaud *m.*

toadstool [tōd'stōōl] *n* champignon (vénéneux).

toady [tō'dē] *vi* flatter bassement.

toast [tōst] *n* (*CULIN*) pain grillé, toast *m*; (*drink, speech*) toast ♦ *vt* (*CULIN*) faire griller; (*drink to*) porter un toast à; **a piece or slice of ~** un toast.

toaster [tōs'tûr] *n* grille-pain *m inv.*

toastmaster [tōst'mastûr] *n* animateur *m* pour réceptions.

toast rack *n* porte-toast *m inv.*

tobacco [təbak'ō] *n* tabac *m*; **pipe ~** tabac à pipe.

tobacconist [təbak'ənist] *n* marchand/e de tabac; ~'s **(shop)** (bureau *m* de) tabac *m*.

Tobago [tōbā'gō] *n see* **Trinidad and Tobago.**

toboggan [təbág'ən] *n* toboggan *m*; (*child's*) luge *f*.

today [tədā'] *ad, n* (*also fig*) aujourd'hui *(m)*; **what day is it** ~**?** quel jour sommes-nous aujourd'hui?; **what date is it** ~**?** quelle est la date aujourd'hui?; ~ **is the 4th of March** aujourd'hui nous sommes le 4 mars; **a week ago** ~ il y a huit jours aujourd'hui.

toddler [tád'lúr] *n* enfant *m/f* qui commence à marcher, bambin *m*.

toddy [tád'ē] *n* grog *m*.

to-do [tədōō'] *n* (*fuss*) histoire *f*, affaire *f*.

toe [tō] *n* doigt *m* de pied, orteil *m*; (*of shoe*) bout *m* ♦ *vt*: **to** ~ **the line** (*fig*) obéir, se conformer; **big** ~ gros orteil; **little** ~ petit orteil.

toehold [tō'hōld] *n* prise *f*.

toenail [tō'nāl] *n* ongle *m* de l'orteil.

toffee [tóf'ē] *n* caramel *m*.

tofu [tō'fōō] *n* tofou *m*.

toga [tō'gə] *n* toge *f*.

together [tōōgeth'úr] *ad* ensemble; (*at same time*) en même temps; ~ **with** *prep* avec.

togetherness [tōōgeth'úrnis] *n* camaraderie *f*, intimité *f*.

toggle switch [tåg'əl swich] *n* (*COMPUT*) interrupteur *m* à bascule.

Togo [tō'gō] *n* Togo *m*.

togs [tágz] *npl* (*col: clothes*) fringues *fpl*.

toil [toil] *n* dur travail, labeur *m* ♦ *vi* travailler dur; peiner.

toilet [toi'lit] *n* (*Brit: lavatory*) toilettes *fpl*, cabinets *mpl* ♦ *cpd* (*bag, soap etc*) de toilette; **to go to the** ~ aller aux toilettes.

toilet bag *n* (*Brit*) nécessaire *m* de toilette.

toilet bowl *n* cuvette *f* des W.-C.

toilet paper *n* papier *m* hygiénique.

toiletries [toi'litrēz] *npl* articles *mpl* de toilette.

toilet roll *n* rouleau *m* de papier hygiénique.

toilet water *n* eau *f* de toilette.

token [tō'kən] *n* (*sign*) marque *f*, témoignage *m*; (*voucher*) bon *m*, coupon *m* ♦ *cpd* (*fee, strike*) symbolique; **by the same** ~ (*fig*) de même.

Tokyo [tō'kēyō] *n* Tokyo.

told [tōld] *pt, pp of* **tell.**

tolerable [tål'úrəbəl] *a* (*bearable*) tolérable; (*fairly good*) passable.

tolerably [tål'úrəblē] *ad*: ~ **good** tolérable.

tolerance [tål'úrəns] *n* (*also TECH*) tolérance *f*.

tolerant [tål'úrənt] *a*: ~ **(of)** tolérant(e) (à l'égard de).

tolerate [tål'ərāt] *vt* supporter; (*MED, TECH*) tolérer.

toleration [tålərā'shən] *n* tolérance *f*.

toll [tōl] *n* (*tax, charge*) péage *m* ♦ *vi* (*bell*) sonner; **the accident** ~ **on the roads** le nombre des victimes de la route.

tollbridge [tōl'brij] *n* pont *m* à péage.

toll-free [tōl'frē'] *a* (*US TEL*): ~ **number**) numéro vert.

tomato, ~**es** [təmā'tō] *n* tomate *f*.

tomb [tōōm] *n* tombe *f*.

tomboy [tâm'boi] *n* garçon manqué.

tombstone [tōōm'stōn] *n* pierre tombale.

tomcat [tâm'kat] *n* matou *m*.

tomorrow [təmôr'ō] *ad, n* (*also fig*) demain *(m)*; **the day after** ~ après-demain; **a week** ~ demain en huit; ~ **morning** demain matin.

ton [tun] *n* tonne *f* (*US: also:* **short** ~ = *907 kg*; *Brit:* = *1016 kg*; *metric* = *1000 kg*); (*NAUT: also:* **register** ~) tonneau *m* (= *2.83 cu.m*).

tonal [tō'nəl] *a* tonal(e).

tone [tōn] *n* ton *m*; (*of radio, Brit TEL*) tonalité *f* ♦ *vi* s'harmoniser.

tone down *vt* (*color, criticism*) adoucir; (*sound*) baisser.

tone up *vt* (*muscles*) tonifier.

tone-deaf [tōn'def] *a* qui n'a pas d'oreille.

toner [tō'nûr] *n* (*for photocopier*) encre *f*.

Tonga [tång'gə] *n* îles *fpl* Tonga.

tongs [tôngz] *npl* pinces *fpl*; (*for coal*) pincettes *fpl*; (*for hair*) fer *m* à friser.

tongue [tung] *n* langue *f*; ~ **in cheek** *ad* ironiquement.

tongue-tied [tung'tīd] *a* (*fig*) muet(te).

tongue twister [tung' twistûr] *n* phrase *f* très difficile à prononcer.

tonic [tân'ik] *n* (*MED*) tonique *m*; (*MUS*) tonique *f*; (*also:* ~ **water**) tonic *m*.

tonight [tənīt'] *ad, n* cette nuit; (*this evening*) ce soir; **(I'll) see you** ~! à ce soir!

tonnage [tun'ij] *n* (*NAUT*) tonnage *m*.

tonsil [tân'səl] *n* amygdale *f*; **to have one's** ~**s out** se faire opérer des amygdales.

tonsillitis [tânsəlī'tis] *n* amygdalite *f*; **to have** ~ avoir une angine or une amygdalite.

too [tōō] *ad* (*excessively*) trop; (*also*) aussi; **it's** ~ **sweet** c'est trop sucré; **I went** ~ moi aussi, j'y suis allé; ~ **much** *ad* trop ♦ *a* trop de; ~ **many** a trop de; ~ **bad!** tant pis!

took [tōōk] *pt of* **take.**

tool [tōōl] *n* outil *m*; (*fig*) instrument *m* ♦ *vt* travailler, ouvrager.

tool box *n* boîte *f* à outils.

tool kit *n* trousse *f* à outils.

toot [tōōt] *n* coup *m* de sifflet (*or* de klaxon) ♦ *vi* siffler; (*with car-horn*) klaxonner.

tooth, *pl* **teeth** [tōōth, tēth] *n* (*ANAT, TECH*) dent *f*; **to have a** ~ **pulled** *or* (*Brit*) **out** se faire arracher une dent; **to brush one's teeth** se laver les dents; **by the skin of one's teeth** (*fig*) de justesse.

toothache [tōōth'āk] *n* mal *m* de dents; **to have** ~ avoir mal aux dents.

toothbrush [tōōth'brush] *n* brosse *f* à dents.

toothpaste [tōōth'pāst] *n* (pâte *f*) dentifrice *m*.

toothpick [tōōth'pik] *n* cure-dent *m*.

tooth powder *n* poudre *f* dentifrice.

top [tâp] *n* (*of mountain, head*) sommet *m*; (*of page, ladder*) haut *m*; (*of list, line*) commencement *m*; (*of box, cupboard, table*) dessus *m*; (*lid: of box, jar*) couvercle *m*; (: *of bottle*) bouchon *m*; (*US AUT*) capote *f*; (*toy*) toupie *f*; (*DRESS: blouse etc*) haut *m*; (*of pajamas*) veste *f* ♦ *a* du haut; (*in rank*) premier(ière); (*best*) meilleur(e) ♦ *vt* (*exceed*) dépasser; (*be first in*) être en tête de; **at the** ~ **of the stairs/page/street** en haut de l'escalier/de la page/de la rue; **on** ~ **of** sur; (*in addition to*) en plus de; **at the** ~ **of the list** en tête de liste; **at the** ~ **of one's voice**

à tue-tête; **at ~ speed** à toute vitesse; **over the ~** (col: behavior etc) qui dépasse les limites.
top off, (Brit) **top up** vt remplir.
topaz [tō'paz] n topaze f.
topcoat [tåp'kōt] n pardessus m.
topflight [tåp'flīt'] a excellent(e).
top floor n dernier étage.
top hat n haut-de-forme m.
top-heavy [tåp'hevē] a (object) trop lourd(e) du haut.
topic [tåp'ik] n sujet m, thème m.
topical [tåp'ikəl] a d'actualité.
topless [tåp'lis] a (bather etc) aux seins nus; **~ swimsuit** monokini m.
top-level [tåp'lev'əl] a (talks) à l'échelon le plus élevé.
topmost [tåp'mōst] a le(la) plus haut(e).
topography [təpåg'rəfē] n topographie f.
topping [tåp'ing] n (CULIN) couche f de crème, fromage etc qui recouvre un plat.
topple [tåp'əl] vt renverser, faire tomber ♦ vi basculer; tomber.
top-ranking [tåp'rang'king] a très haut placé(e).
top-secret [tåp'sē'krit] a ultra-secret(ète).
topsy-turvy [tåp'sētûr'vē] a, ad sens dessus dessous.
top-up [tåp'up] n (Brit): **would you like a ~?** je vous en remets or rajoute?
torch [tôrch] n torche f; (Brit: electric) lampe f de poche.
tore [tôr] pt of tear.
torment n [tôr'ment] tourment m ♦ vt [tôrment'] tourmenter; (fig: annoy) agacer.
torn [tôrn] pp of tear ♦ a: **~ between** (fig) tiraillé(e) entre.
tornado, **~es** [tôrnā'dō] n tornade f.
torpedo, **~es** [tôrpē'dō] n torpille f.
torpedo boat n torpilleur m.
torpor [tôr'pûr] n torpeur f.
torque [tôrk] n couple m de torsion.
torrent [tôr'ənt] n torrent m.
torrential [tôren'chəl] a torrentiel(le).
torrid [tôr'id] a torride; (fig) ardent(e).
torso [tôr'sō] n torse m.
tortoise [tôr'təs] n tortue f.
tortoiseshell [tor'təs-shel] a en écaille.
tortuous [tôr'chōōəs] a tortueux(euse).
torture [tôr'chûr] n torture f ♦ vt torturer.
torturer [tôr'chûrûr] n tortionnaire m.
Tory [tôr'ē] a (Brit POL) tory (pl tories), conservateur(trice) ♦ n tory m/f, conservateur/trice.
toss [tôs] vt lancer, jeter; (head) rejeter en arrière ♦ n (movement: of head etc) mouvement soudain; (of coin) tirage m à pile ou face; **to ~ a coin** jouer à pile ou face; **to ~ and turn** (in bed) se tourner et se retourner; **to win/lose the ~** gagner/perdre à pile ou face; (SPORT) gagner/perdre le tirage au sort.
tot [tåt] n (Brit: drink) petit verre; (child) bambin m.
total [tōt'əl] a total(e) ♦ n total m ♦ vt (add up) faire le total de, totaliser; (amount to) s'élever à; **in ~** au total.
totalitarian [tōtalitär'ēən] a totalitaire.
totality [tōtal'itē] n totalité f.

totally [tō'təlē] ad totalement.
tote bag [tōt' bag] n fourre-tout m inv.
totem pole [tō'təm pōl] n mât m totémique.
totter [tât'ûr] vi chanceler; (object, government) être chancelant(e).
touch [tuch] n contact m, toucher m; (sense, also skill: of pianist etc) toucher; (fig: note, also SOCCER) touche f ♦ vt (gen) toucher; (tamper with) toucher à; **the personal ~** la petite note personnelle; **to put the finishing ~es to sth** mettre la dernière main à qch; **a ~ of** (fig) un petit peu de; une touche de; **in ~ with** en contact or rapport avec; **to get in ~ with** prendre contact avec; **I'll be in ~** je resterai en contact; **to lose ~** (friends) se perdre de vue; **to be out of ~ with events** ne pas être au courant de ce qui se passe.
touch on vt fus (topic) effleurer, toucher.
touch up vt (paint) retoucher.
touch-and-go [tuch'əngō'] a incertain(e); **it was ~ whether we did it** nous avons failli ne pas le faire.
touchdown [tuch'doun] n atterrissage m; (on sea) amerrissage m; (US FOOTBALL) touché-en-but m.
touched [tucht] a touché(e); (col) cinglé(e).
touching [tuch'ing] a touchant(e), attendrissant(e).
touchline [tuch'līn] n (SPORT) (ligne f de) touche f.
touch-type [tuch'tīp] vi taper au toucher.
touchy [tuch'ē] a (person) susceptible.
tough [tuf] a dur(e); (resistant) résistant(e), solide; (meat) dur, coriace; (journey) pénible; (task, problem, situation) difficile; (rough) dur ♦ n (gangster etc) dur m; **~ luck!** pas de chance!; tant pis!
toughen [tuf'ən] vt rendre plus dur(e) (or plus résistant(e) or plus solide).
toughness [tuf'nis] n dureté f; résistance f; solidité f.
toupee [tōōpā'] n postiche m.
tour [tōōr] n voyage m; (also: **package ~**) voyage organisé; (of town, museum) tour m, visite f; (by artist) tournée f ♦ vt visiter; **to go on a ~ of** (museum, region) visiter; **to go on ~** partir en tournée.
touring [tōō'ring] n voyages mpl touristiques, tourisme m.
tourism [tōōr'izəm] n tourisme m.
tourist [tōōr'ist] n touriste m/f ♦ ad (travel) en classe touriste ♦ cpd touristique; **the ~ trade** le tourisme.
tourist office n syndicat m d'initiative.
tournament [tōōr'nəmənt] n tournoi m.
tourniquet [tûr'nikit] n (MED) garrot m.
tour operator [tōōr' åp'ərātûr] n (Brit) organisateur m de voyages, tour-opérateur m.
tousled [tou'zəld] a (hair) ébouriffé(e).
tout [tout] vi: **to ~ for** essayer de raccrocher, racoler ♦ n (Brit: ticket ~) revendeur m de billets.
tow [tō] n: **to give sb a ~** (AUT) remorquer qn ♦ vt remorquer; **"in ~"**, (Brit) **"on ~"** (AUT) "véhicule en remorque".
toward(s) [tôrd(z)] prep vers; (of attitude) envers, à l'égard de; (of purpose) pour; **~ noon/the end of the year** vers midi/la fin de l'année; **to feel friendly ~ sb** être bien dispo-

sé envers qn.

towel [tou'əl] n serviette f (de toilette); **to throw in the ~** (fig) jeter l'éponge.

towelling [tou'əling] n (fabric) tissu-éponge m.

towel rack, (Brit) **towel rail** n porte-serviettes m inv.

tower [tou'ûr] n tour f ♦ vi (building, mountain) se dresser (majestueusement); **to ~ above** or **over sb/sth** dominer qn/qch.

tower block n (Brit) tour f (d'habitation).

towering [tou'ûring] a très haut(e), imposant(e).

towline [tō'līn] n (câble m de) remorque f.

town [toun] n ville f; **to go to ~** aller en ville; (fig) y mettre le paquet; **in the ~** dans la ville, en ville; **to be out of ~** (person) être en déplacement.

town center n centre m de la ville, centre-ville m.

town clerk n ≈ secrétaire m/f de mairie.

town council n conseil municipal.

town hall n ≈ mairie f.

town house n maison f en ville; (US: in a complex) maison mitoyenne.

town planner n (Brit) urbaniste m/f.

town planning n (Brit) urbanisme m.

townspeople [tounz'pēpəl] npl citadins mpl.

towpath [tō'path] n (chemin m de) halage m.

towrope [tō'rōp] n (câble m de) remorque f.

tow truck n (US) dépanneuse f.

toxic [tâk'sik] a toxique.

toxin [tâk'sin] n toxine f.

toy [toi] n jouet m.

toy with vt fus jouer avec; (idea) caresser.

toyshop [toi'shâp] m magasin m de jouets.

trace [trās] n trace f ♦ vt (draw) tracer, dessiner; (follow) suivre la trace de; (locate) retrouver; **without ~** (disappear) sans laisser de traces; **there was no ~ of it** il n'y en avait pas trace.

trace element n oligo-élément m.

trachea [trā'kēə] n (ANAT) trachée f.

tracing paper [trā'sing pā'pûr] n papier-calque m.

track [trak] n (mark) trace f; (path: gen) chemin m, piste f; (: of bullet etc) trajectoire f; (: of suspect, animal) piste; (RAIL) voie ferrée, rails mpl; (on tape, COMPUT, SPORT) piste; (on record) plage f ♦ vt suivre la trace or la piste de; **to keep ~ of** suivre; **to be on the right ~** (fig) être sur la bonne voie.

track down vt (prey) trouver et capturer; (sth lost) finir par retrouver.

tracked [trakt] a (AUT) à chenille.

track events npl (SPORT) épreuves fpl sur piste.

tracking station [trak'ing stā'shən] n (SPACE) centre m d'observation de satellites.

track record n: **to have a good ~** (fig) avoir fait ses preuves.

tracksuit [trak'sōōt] n survêtement m.

tract [trakt] n (GEO) étendue f, zone f; (pamphlet) tract m; **respiratory ~** (ANAT) système m respiratoire.

traction [trak'shən] n traction f.

tractor [trak'tûr] n tracteur m.

tractor feed n (on printer) entraînement m par ergots.

trade [trād] n commerce m; (skill, job) métier m ♦ vi faire du commerce; **to ~ with/in** faire du commerce avec/le commerce de; **foreign ~** commerce extérieur; **Department of T~ and Industry (DTI)** (Brit) ministère m du Commerce et de l'Industrie.

trade in vt (old car etc) faire reprendre.

trade barrier n barrière commerciale.

trade deficit n déficit extérieur.

trade discount n remise f au détaillant.

trade fair n foire(-exposition) commerciale.

trade-in [trād'in] n reprise f.

trade-in price n prix m à la reprise.

trademark [trād'mârk] n marque f de fabrique.

trade mission n mission commerciale.

trade name n marque déposée.

trader [trā'dûr] n commerçant/e, négociant/e.

trade secret n secret m de fabrication.

tradesman [trādz'mən] n (storekeeper) commerçant.

trade union n syndicat m.

trade unionist [trād yōōn'yənist] n syndicaliste m/f.

trade wind n alizé m.

trading [trā'ding] n affaires fpl, commerce m.

trading estate n (Brit) zone industrielle.

trading stamp n timbre-prime m.

tradition [trədish'ən] n tradition f; **~s** npl coutumes fpl, traditions.

traditional [trədish'ənəl] a traditionnel(le).

traffic [traf'ik] n trafic m; (cars) circulation f ♦ vi: **to ~ in** (pej: liquor, drugs) faire le trafic de.

traffic circle n (US) rond-point m.

traffic island n refuge m (pour piétons).

traffic jam n embouteillage m.

trafficker [traf'ikûr] n trafiquant/e.

traffic lights npl feux mpl (de signalisation).

traffic offence n (Brit) = **traffic violation.**

traffic sign n panneau m de signalisation.

traffic violation n (US) infraction f au code de la route.

traffic warden n contractuel/le.

tragedy [traj'idē] n tragédie f.

tragic [traj'ik] a tragique.

trail [trāl] n (tracks) trace f, piste f; (path) chemin m, piste; (of smoke etc) traînée f ♦ vt traîner, tirer; (follow) suivre ♦ vi traîner; **to be on sb's ~** être sur la piste de qn.

trail away, trail off vi (sound, voice) s'évanouir; (interest) disparaître.

trail behind vi traîner, être à la traîne.

trailer [trā'lûr] n (AUT) remorque f; (US) caravane f; (CINEMA) bande-annonce f.

trailer park n (US) camping m pour caravanes.

trailer truck n (US) (camion m) semi-remorque m.

train [trān] n train m; (in subway) rame f; (of dress) traîne f; (Brit: series): **~ of events** série f d'événements ♦ vt (apprentice, doctor etc) former; (sportsman) entraîner; (dog) dresser; (memory) exercer; (point: gun etc): **to ~ sth on** braquer qch sur ♦ vi recevoir sa formation; s'entraîner; **one's ~ of thought** le fil de sa pensée; **to go by ~** voyager par le train or en train; **to ~ sb to do sth** apprendre à qn à faire qch; (employee) former qn à faire qch.

train attendant *n* (*US*) employé/e des wagons-lits.

trained [trānd] *a* qualifié(e), qui a reçu une formation; dressé(e).

trainee [trānē'] *n* stagiaire *m/f*; (*in trade*) apprenti/e.

trainer [trā'nûr] *n* (*SPORT*) entraîneur/euse; (*of dogs etc*) dresseur/euse; **~s** *npl* (*shoes*) chaussures *fpl* de sport.

training [trā'ning] *n* formation *f*; entraînement *m*; dressage *m*; **in ~** (*SPORT*) à l'entraînement; (*fit*) en forme.

training college *n* école professionnelle; (*for teachers*) ≈ école normale.

training course *n* cours *m* de formation professionnelle.

training shoes *npl* chaussures *fpl* de sport.

train station *n* gare *f*.

traipse [trāps] *vi* (se) traîner, déambuler.

trait [trāt] *n* trait *m* (de caractère).

traitor [trā'tûr] *n* traître *m*.

trajectory [trəjek'tûrē] *n* trajectoire *f*.

tram [tram] *n* (*Brit: also:* **~car**) tram(way) *m*.

tramline [tram'līn] *n* ligne *f* de tram(way).

tramp [tramp] *n* (*person*) vagabond/e, clochard/e; (*col: pej: woman*): **to be a ~** être coureuse ♦ *vi* marcher d'un pas lourd ♦ *vt* (*walk through: town, streets*) parcourir à pied.

trample [tram'pəl] *vt*: **to ~ (underfoot)** piétiner; (*fig*) bafouer.

trampoline [trampəlēn'] *n* trampolino *m*.

trance [trans] *n* transe *f*; (*MED*) catalepsie *f*; **to go into a ~** entrer en transe.

tranquil [trang'kwil] *a* tranquille.

tranquil(l)ity [trangkwil'itē] *n* tranquillité *f*.

tranquil(l)izer [trang'kwəlīzûr] *n* (*MED*) tranquillisant *m*.

transact [transakt'] *vt* (*business*) traiter.

transaction [transak'shən] *n* transaction *f*; **~s** *npl* (*minutes*) actes *mpl*; **cash ~** transaction au comptant.

transatlantic [transətlan'tik] *a* transatlantique.

transcend [transend'] *vt* transcender; (*excel over*) surpasser.

transcendental [transenden'təl] *a*: **~ meditation** méditation transcendantale.

transcribe [transkrīb'] *vt* transcrire.

transcript [tran'skript] *n* transcription *f* (*texte*).

transcription [transkrip'shən] *n* transcription *f*.

transcriptionist [transkrip'shənist] *n* (*US*) audiotypiste *m/f*.

transept [tran'sept] *n* transept *m*.

transfer *n* [trans'fûr] (*gen, also SPORT*) transfert *m*; (*POL: of power*) passation *f*; (*of money*) virement *m*; (*picture, design*) décalcomanie *f* ♦ *vt* [transfûr'] transférer; passer; virer; décalquer; **by bank ~** par virement bancaire.

transferable [transfûr'əbəl] *a* transmissible, transférable; **"not ~"** "personnel".

transfix [transfiks'] *vt* transpercer; (*fig*): **~ed with fear** paralysé(e) par la peur.

transform [transfôrm'] *vt* transformer.

transformation [transfûrmā'shən] *n*

transformation *f*.

transformer [transfôr'mûr] *n* (*ELEC*) transformateur *m*.

transfusion [transfyōō'zhən] *n* transfusion *f*.

transgress [transgres'] *vt* transgresser.

transient [tran'shənt] *a* transitoire, éphémère.

transistor [tranzis'tûr] *n* (*ELEC*; *also*: **~ radio**) transistor *m*.

transit [tran'sit] *n*: **in ~** en transit.

transit camp *n* camp *m* de transit.

transition [tranzish'ən] *n* transition *f*.

transitional [tranzish'ənəl] *a* transitoire.

transitive [tran'sətiv] *a* (*LING*) transitif(ive).

transit lounge *n* (*AVIAT*) salle *f* de transit.

transitory [tran'sitôrē] *a* transitoire.

translate [tranz'lāt] *vt*: **to ~ (from/into)** traduire (du/en).

translation [tranzlā'shən] *n* traduction *f*; (*SCOL: as opposed to prose*) version *f*.

translator [translā'tûr] *n* traducteur/trice.

translucent [translōō'sənt] *a* translucide.

transmission [transmish'ən] *n* transmission *f*.

transmit [transmit'] *vt* transmettre; (*RADIO, TV*) émettre.

transmitter [transmit'ûr] *n* émetteur *m*.

transom [tran'səm] *n* (*US*) vasistas *m*.

transparency [transpär'ənsē] *n* (*PHOT*) diapositive *f*.

transparent [transpär'ənt] *a* transparent(e).

transpire [transpīûr'] *vi* (*become known*): **it finally ~d that** ... on a finalement appris que ...; (*happen*) arriver.

transplant *vt* [tranzplant'] transplanter; (*seedlings*) repiquer ♦ *n* [tranz'plant] (*MED*) transplantation *f*; **to have a heart ~** subir une greffe du cœur.

transport *n* [trans'pôrt] transport *m* ♦ *vt* [transpôrt'] transporter; **Department of T~** (*Brit*) ministère *m* des Transports.

transportation [transpûrtā'shən] *n* (*moyen m de*) transport *m*; (*of prisoners*) transportation *f*; **public ~** transports en commun; **Department of T~** (*US*) ministère *m* des Transports.

transport café *n* (*Brit*) ≈ relais *m* routier.

transpose [tranzpōz'] *vt* transposer.

transship [transship'] *vt* transborder.

transverse [transvûrs'] *a* transversal(e).

transvestite [transves'tīt] *n* travesti/e.

trap [trap] *n* (*snare, trick*) piège *m*; (*carriage*) cabriolet *m* ♦ *vt* prendre au piège; (*immobilize*) bloquer; (*jam*) coincer; **to set** or **lay a ~ (for sb)** tendre un piège (à qn); **to shut one's ~** (*col*) la fermer.

trap door *n* trappe *f*.

trapeze [trapēz'] *n* trapèze *m*.

trapper [trap'ûr] *n* trappeur *m*.

trappings [trap'ingz] *npl* ornements *mpl*; attributs *mpl*.

trash [trash] *n* (*pej: goods*) camelote *f*; (: *nonsense*) sottises *fpl*; (*garbage*) ordures *fpl*; *vt* (*US col*): **to ~ sb** dénigrer qn.

trash can *n* (*US*) boîte *f* à ordures.

trauma [trou'mə] *n* traumatisme *m*.

traumatic [trômat'ik] *a* traumatisant(e).

travel [trav'əl] *n* voyage(s) *m(pl)* ♦ *vi* voyager; (*move*) aller, se déplacer ♦ *vt* (*distance*) parcourir; **this wine doesn't ~ well** ce vin voyage mal.

travel agency *n* agence *f* de voyages.

travel agent *n* agent *m* de voyages.

travel brochure *n* brochure *f* touristique.

traveler, (*Brit*) **traveller** [trav'əlûr] *n* voyageur/euse; (*COMM*) représentant *m* de commerce.

traveler's check, (*Brit*) **traveller's cheque** *n* chèque *m* de voyage.

traveling [trav'əling] (*US*) *n* voyage(s) *m(pl)* ♦ *a* (*circus, exhibition*) ambulant(e) ♦ *cpd* (*bag, clock*) de voyage; (*expenses*) de déplacement.

traveling salesman *n* voyageur *m* de commerce.

travelling *etc* [trav'əling] (*Brit*) = **traveling** *etc*.

travelog(ue) [trav'əlôg] *n* (*book, talk*) récit *m* de voyage; (*film*) documentaire *m* de voyage.

travel sickness *n* mal *m* de la route (*or* de mer *or* de l'air).

traverse [trav'ûrs] *vt* traverser.

travesty [trav'istē] *n* parodie *f*.

trawler [trô'lûr] *n* chalutier *m*.

tray [trā] *n* (*for carrying*) plateau *m*; (*on desk*) corbeille *f*.

treacherous [trech'ûrəs] *a* traître(sse); **road conditions are ~** l'état des routes est dangereux.

treachery [trech'ûrē] *n* traîtrise *f*.

treacle [trē'kəl] *n* (*Brit*) mélasse *f*.

tread [tred] *n* pas *m*; (*sound*) bruit *m* de pas; (*of tire*) chape *f*, bande *f* de roulement ♦ *vi* (*pt* **trod**, *pp* **trodden** [tråd, tråd'ən]) marcher.
tread on *vt fus* marcher sur.

treadle [tred'əl] *n* pédale *f* (*de machine*).

treas. *abbr* = **treasurer**.

treason [trē'zən] *n* trahison *f*.

treasure [trezh'ûr] *n* trésor *m* ♦ *vt* (*value*) tenir beaucoup à; (*store*) conserver précieusement.

treasure hunt *n* chasse *f* au trésor.

treasurer [trezh'ûrûr] *n* trésorier/ière; (*US*) économe *m/f*.

treasury [trezh'ûrē] *n* trésorerie *f*; (*US*) economat *m*; **the T~ Department,** (*Brit*) **the T~** ≈ le ministère des Finances.

treasury bill *n* bon *m* du Trésor.

treat [trēt] *n* petit cadeau, petite surprise ♦ *vt* traiter; **it was a ~** ça m'a (*or* nous a *etc*) vraiment fait plaisir; **to ~ sb to sth** offrir qch à qn; **to ~ sth as a joke** prendre qch à la plaisanterie.

treatise [trē'tis] *n* traité *m* (*ouvrage*).

treatment [trēt'mənt] *n* traitement *m*; **to have ~ for sth** (*MED*) suivre un traitement pour qch.

treaty [trē'tē] *n* traité *m*.

treble [treb'əl] *a* triple ♦ *n* (*MUS*) soprano *m* ♦ *vt, vi* tripler.

treble clef *n* clé *f* de sol.

tree [trē] *n* arbre *m*.

tree-lined [trē'līnd] *a* bordé(e) d'arbres.

treetop [trē'tâp] *n* cime *f* d'un arbre.

tree trunk *n* tronc *m* d'arbre.

trek [trek] *n* voyage *m*; randonnée *f*; (*tiring walk*) tirée *f* ♦ *vi* (*as vacation*) faire de la randonnée.

trellis [trel'is] *n* treillis *m*, treillage *m*.

tremble [trem'bəl] *vi* trembler.

trembling [trem'bling] *n* tremblement *m* ♦ *a* tremblant(e).

tremendous [trimen'dəs] *a* énorme, formidable; (*excellent*) fantastique, formidable.

tremendously [trimen'dəslē] *ad* énormément, extrêmement + *adjective*; formidablement.

tremor [trem'ûr] *n* tremblement *m*; (*also:* **earth ~**) secousse *f* sismique.

trench [trench] *n* tranchée *f*.

trench coat *n* trench-coat *m*.

trench warfare *n* guerre *f* de tranchées.

trend [trend] *n* (*tendency*) tendance *f*; (*of events*) cours *m*; (*fashion*) mode *f*; **~ towards/away from doing** tendance à faire/à ne pas faire; **to set the ~** donner le ton; **to set a ~** lancer une mode.

trendy [tren'dē] *a* (*idea*) dans le vent; (*clothes*) dernier cri *inv*.

trepidation [trepidā'shən] *n* vive agitation.

trespass [tres'pas] *vi*: **to ~ on** s'introduire sans permission dans; (*fig*) empiéter sur; **"no ~ing"** "propriété privée", "défense d'entrer".

trespasser [tres'pasûr] *n* intrus/e; **"~s will be prosecuted"** "interdiction d'entrer sous peine de poursuites".

tress [tres] *n* boucle *f* de cheveux.

trestle [tres'əl] *n* tréteau *m*.

trestle table *n* table *f* à tréteaux.

trial [trīl] *n* (*LAW*) procès *m*, jugement *m*; (*test: of machine etc*) essai *m*; (*hardship*) épreuve *f*; (*worry*) souci *m*; **~s** *npl* (*SPORT*) épreuves éliminatoires; **horse ~s** concours *m* hippique; **~ by jury** jugement par jury; **to be sent for ~** être traduit(e) en justice; **to be on ~** passer en jugement; **by ~ and error** par tâtonnements.

trial balance *n* (*COMM*) balance *f* de vérification.

trial basis *n*: **on a ~** pour une période d'essai.

trial run *n* essai *m*.

triangle [trī'anggəl] *n* (*MATH, MUS*) triangle *m*; (*US*) équerre *f*.

triangular [trīang'gyəlûr] *a* triangulaire.

tribal [trī'bəl] *a* tribal(e).

tribe [trīb] *n* tribu *f*.

tribesman [trībz'mən] *n* membre *m* de la tribu.

tribulation [tribyəlā'shən] *n* tribulation *f*, malheur *m*.

tribunal [trībyōō'nəl] *n* tribunal *m*.

tributary [trib'yətärē] *n* (*river*) affluent *m*.

tribute [trib'yōōt] *n* tribut *m*, hommage *m*; **to pay ~** to rendre hommage à.

trice [trīs] *n*: **in a ~** en un clin d'œil.

trick [trik] *n* ruse *f*; (*clever act*) astuce *f*; (*prank*) tour *m*; (*CARDS*) levée *f* ♦ *vt* attraper, rouler; **to play a ~ on sb** jouer un tour à qn; **to ~ sb into doing sth** persuader qn par la ruse de faire qch; **to ~ sb out of sth** obtenir qch de qn par la ruse; **it's a ~ of the light** c'est une illusion d'optique causée par la lumière; **that should do the ~** (*col*) ça devrait faire l'affaire.

trickery [trik'ûrē] *n* ruse *f*.

trickle [trik'əl] *n* (*of water etc*) filet *m* ♦ *vi* couler en un filet *or* goutte à goutte; **to ~ in/out** (*people*) entrer/sortir par petits groupes.

trick question n question-piège f.

trickster [trik'stûr] n arnaqueur/euse, filou m.

tricky [trik'ē] a difficile, délicat(e).

tricycle [trī'sikəl] n tricycle m.

trifle [trī'fəl] n bagatelle f; (CULIN) ≈ diplomate m ♦ ad: **a ~ long** un peu long ♦ vi: **to ~ with** traiter à la légère.

trifling [trīf'ling] a insignifiant(e).

trigger [trig'ûr] n (of gun) gâchette f.
  trigger off vt déclencher.

trigonometry [trigənâm'ətrē] n trigonométrie f.

trilby [tril'bē] n (Brit: also: **~ hat**) chapeau mou, feutre m.

trill [tril] n (of bird, MUS) trille m.

trillion [tril'yən] n (US) billion m.

trilogy [tril'əjē] n trilogie f.

trim [trim] a net(te); (house, garden) bien tenu(e); (figure) svelte ♦ n (haircut etc) légère coupe; (embellishment) finitions fpl; (on car) garnitures fpl ♦ vt couper légèrement; (decorate): **to ~ (with)** décorer (de); (NAUT: a sail) gréer; **to keep in (good) ~** maintenir en (bon) état.

trimmings [trim'ingz] npl décorations fpl; (extras: gen CULIN) garniture f.

Trinidad and Tobago [trin'idad and tōbā'gō] n Trinité et Tobago f.

Trinity [trin'itē] n: **the ~** la Trinité.

trinket [tring'kit] n bibelot m; (piece of jewelry) colifichet m.

trio [trē'ō] n trio m.

trip [trip] n voyage m; (excursion) excursion f; (stumble) faux pas ♦ vi faire un faux pas, trébucher; (go lightly) marcher d'un pas léger; **on a ~** en voyage.
  trip up vi trébucher ♦ vt faire un croc-en-jambe à.

tripartite [trīpâr'tīt] a triparti(e).

tripe [trīp] n (CULIN) tripes fpl; (pej: rubbish) idioties fpl.

triple [trip'əl] a triple ♦ ad: **~ the distance/the speed** trois fois la distance/la vitesse.

triplets [trip'lits] npl triplés/ées.

triplicate [trip'ləkit] n: **in ~** en trois exemplaires.

tripod [trī'pâd] n trépied m.

Tripoli [trip'əlē] n Tripoli.

tripwire [trip'wīûr] n fil m de déclenchement.

trite [trīt] a banal(e).

triumph [trī'əmf] n triomphe m ♦ vi: **to ~ (over)** triompher (de).

triumphal [trīum'fəl] a triomphal(e).

triumphant [trīum'fənt] a triomphant(e).

trivia [triv'ēə] npl futilités fpl.

trivial [triv'ēəl] a insignifiant(e); (commonplace) banal(e).

triviality [trivēal'ətē] n caractère insignifiant; banalité f.

trivialize [triv'ēəlīz] vt rendre banal(e).

trod [trâd] pt of **tread**.

trodden [trâd'ən] pp of **tread**.

trolley [trâl'ē] n (Brit) chariot m.

trolley bus n trolleybus m.

trollop [trâl'əp] n prostituée f.

trombone [trâmbōn'] n trombone m.

troop [trōōp] n bande f, groupe m ♦ vi: **to ~ in/out** entrer/sortir en groupe.

troop carrier n (plane) avion m de transport de troupes; (NAUT: also: **troopship**) transport m (navire).

trooper [trōō'pûr] n (MIL) soldat m de cavalerie; (US: policeman) ≈ gendarme m.

troops [trōōps] npl (MIL) troupes fpl; (: men) hommes mpl, soldats mpl.

troopship [trōōp'ship] n transport m (navire).

trophy [trō'fē] n trophée m.

tropic [trâp'ik] n tropique m; **in the ~s** sous les tropiques; **T~ of Cancer/Capricorn** tropique du Cancer/Capricorne.

tropical [trâp'ikəl] a tropical(e).

trot [trât] n trot m ♦ vi trotter; **on the ~** (Brit: fig) d'affilée.
  trot out vt (excuse, reason) débiter; (names, facts) réciter les uns après les autres.

trouble [trub'əl] n difficulté(s) f(pl), problème(s) m(pl); (worry) ennuis mpl, soucis mpl; (bother, effort) peine f; (POL) conflit(s) m(pl), troubles mpl; (MED): **stomach** etc **~** troubles gastriques etc ♦ vt déranger, gêner; (worry) inquiéter ♦ vi: **to ~ to do** prendre la peine de faire; **~s** npl (POL etc) troubles mpl; **to be in ~** avoir des ennuis; (ship, climber etc) être en difficulté; **to have ~ doing sth** avoir du mal à faire qch; **to go to the ~ of doing** se donner le mal de faire; **it's no ~!** je vous en prie!; **please don't ~ yourself** je vous en prie, ne vous dérangez pas!; **the ~ is ...** le problème, c'est que ...; **what's the ~?** qu'est-ce qui ne va pas?

troubled [trub'əld] a (person) inquiet(ète); (epoch, life) agité(e).

trouble-free [trub'əlfrē] a sans problèmes or ennuis.

troublemaker [trub'əlmākûr] n élément perturbateur, fauteur m de troubles.

troubleshooter [trub'əlshōōtûr] n (in conflict) conciliateur m.

troublesome [trub'əlsəm] a ennuyeux(euse), gênant(e).

trouble spot n point chaud (fig).

trough [trôf] n (also: **drinking ~**) abreuvoir m; (also: **feeding ~**) auge f; (channel) chenal m; **~ of low pressure** (METEOROLOGY) dépression f.

trounce [trouns] vt (defeat) battre à plates coutures.

troupe [trōōp] n troupe f.

trouser press n (Brit) presse-pantalon m inv.

trousers [trou'zûrz] npl pantalon m; **short ~** (Brit) culottes courtes.

trouser suit n (Brit) tailleur-pantalon m.

trousseau, pl **~x** or **~s** [trōō'sō, z] n trousseau m.

trout [trout] n (pl inv) truite f.

trowel [trou'əl] n truelle f.

truant [trōō'ənt] n: **to be** or (Brit) **play ~** faire l'école buissonnière.

truce [trōōs] n trêve f.

truck [truk] n camion m; (RAIL) wagon m à plate-forme; (for luggage) chariot m (à bagages).

truck driver n camionneur m.

trucker [truk'ûr] n (esp US) camionneur m.

truck farm n (US) jardin maraîcher.

trucking [truk'ing] n (esp US) transport routier.

trucking company n (*US*) entreprise f de transport (routier).

truck stop n (*US*) relais m routier.

truculent [truk'yələnt] a agressif(ive).

trudge [truj] vi marcher lourdement, se traîner.

true [trōō] a vrai(e); (*accurate*) exact(e); (*genuine*) vrai, véritable; (*faithful*) fidèle; (*wall*) d'aplomb; (*beam*) droit(e); (*wheel*) dans l'axe; **to come** ~ se réaliser; ~ **to life** réaliste.

truffle [truf'əl] n truffe f.

truly [trōō'lē] ad vraiment, réellement; (*truthfully*) sans mentir; (*faithfully*) fidèlement; **yours** ~ (*in letter*) je vous prie d'agréer, Monsieur (*or* Madame *etc*), l'expression de mes sentiments respectueux.

trump [trump] n atout m; **to turn up** ~s (*fig*) faire des miracles.

trump card n atout m; (*fig*) carte maîtresse f.

trumped-up [trumpt'up'] a inventé(e) (de toutes pièces).

trumpet [trum'pit] n trompette f.

truncated [trung'kātid] a tronqué(e).

truncheon [trun'chən] n bâton m (d'agent de police); matraque f.

trundle [trun'dəl] vt, vi: **to** ~ **along** rouler bruyamment.

trunk [trungk] n (*of tree, person*) tronc m; (*of elephant*) trompe f; (*case*) malle f; (*US AUT*) coffre m.

trunk road n (*Brit*) ≈ (route) nationale.

trunks [trungks] npl (*also:* **swimming** ~) maillot m *or* slip m de bain.

truss [trus] n (*MED*) bandage m herniaire ♦ vt: **to** ~ **(up)** (*CULIN*) brider.

trust [trust] n confiance f; (*LAW*) fidéicommis m; (*COMM*) trust m ♦ vt (*rely on*) avoir confiance en; (*entrust*): **to** ~ **sth to sb** confier qch à qn; (*hope*): **to** ~ **(that)** espérer (que); **to take sth on** ~ accepter qch sans garanties (*or* sans preuves); **in** ~ (*LAW*) par fidéicommis.

trust company n société f fiduciaire.

trusted [trus'tid] a en qui l'on a confiance.

trustee [trustē'] n (*LAW*) fidéicommissaire m/ f; (*of school etc*) administrateur/trice.

trustful [trust'fəl] a confiant(e).

trust fund n fonds m en fidéicommis.

trusting [trus'ting] a confiant(e).

trustworthy [trust'wûrᵺē] a digne de confiance.

trusty [trus'tē] a fidèle.

truth, ~s [trōōth, trōōᵺz] n vérité f.

truthful [trōōth'fəl] a (*person*) qui dit la vérité; (*description*) exact(e), vrai(e).

truthfully [trōōth'fəlē] ad sincèrement, sans mentir.

truthfulness [trōōth'fəlnis] n véracité f.

try [trī] n essai m, tentative f; (*RUGBY*) essai ♦ vt (*LAW*) juger; (*test: sth new*) essayer, tester; (*strain*) éprouver ♦ vi essayer; **to** ~ **to do** essayer de faire; (*seek*) chercher à faire; **to** ~ **one's (very) best** *or* **one's (very) hardest** faire de son mieux; **to give sth a** ~ essayer qch.

try on vt (*clothes*) essayer; **to** ~ **it on** (*fig*)

tenter le coup, bluffer.

try out vt essayer, mettre à l'essai.

trying [trī'ing] a pénible.

tsar [zâr] n tsar m.

T-shirt [tē'shûrt] n tee-shirt m.

T-square [tē'skwär] n équerre f en T.

TT abbr (*US MAIL*) = *Trust Territory* ♦ a abbr (*Brit col*) = **teetotal**.

tub [tub] n cuve f; baquet m; (*bath*) baignoire f.

tuba [tōō'bə] n tuba m.

tubby [tub'ē] a rondelet(te).

tube [tōōb] n tube m; (*for tire*) chambre f à air; (*col: television*): **the** ~ la télé; (*Brit: subway*) métro m; **down the** ~s (*col*) fichu(e), foutu(e) (!).

tubeless [tōōb'lis] a (*tire*) sans chambre à air.

tuber [tōō'bûr] n (*BOT*) tubercule m.

tuberculosis [tōōbûrkyəlō'sis] n tuberculose f.

tube station [tōōb' stā'shən] n (*Brit*) station f de métro.

tubing [tōō'bing] n tubes mpl; **a piece of** ~ un tube.

tubular [tōō'byələr] a tubulaire.

TUC n abbr (*Brit*: = *Trades Union Congress*) confédération f des syndicats britanniques.

tuck [tuk] n (*SEWING*) pli m, rempli m ♦ vt (*put*) mettre.

tuck away vt cacher, ranger.

tuck in vt rentrer; (*child*) border ♦ vi (*eat*) manger de bon appétit; attaquer le repas.

tuck up vt (*child*) border.

Tue(s). abbr (= *Tuesday*) ma.

Tuesday [tōōz'dā] n mardi m; **(the date) today is** ~ **23rd March** nous sommes aujourd'hui le mardi 23 mars; **on** ~ mardi; **on** ~s le mardi; **every** ~ tous les mardis, chaque mardi; **every other** ~ un mardi sur deux; **last/next** ~ mardi dernier/prochain; ~ **next** mardi qui vient; **the following** ~ le mardi suivant; **a week on** ~, ~ **week** mardi en huit; **the** ~ **before last** l'autre mardi; **the** ~ **after next** mardi en huit; **the** ~ **morning/ lunchtime/afternoon/evening** mardi matin/ midi/après-midi/soir; ~ **night** mardi soir; (*overnight*) la nuit de mardi (à mercredi); ~'s **newspaper** le journal de mardi.

tuft [tuft] n touffe f.

tug [tug] n (*ship*) remorqueur m ♦ vt tirer (sur).

tug-of-war [tug'əvwôr'] n lutte f à la corde.

tuition [tōōish'ən] n (*US: fees*) frais mpl de scolarité; (*Brit: lessons*) leçons fpl.

tulip [tōō'lip] n tulipe f.

tumble [tum'bəl] n (*fall*) chute f, culbute f ♦ vi tomber, dégringoler; (*somersault*) faire une *or* des culbute(s) ♦ vt renverser, faire tomber; **to** ~ **to sth** (*col*) réaliser qch.

tumbledown [tum'bəldoun] a délabré(e).

tumble dryer n (*Brit*) séchoir m (à linge) à air chaud.

tumbler [tum'blûr] n verre (droit), gobelet m.

tummy [tum'ē] n (*col*) ventre m.

tumor, (*Brit*) **tumour** [tōō'mûr] n tumeur f.

tumult [tōō'məlt] n tumulte m.

tumultuous [tōōmul'chōōəs] a tumultueux(euse).

tuna [tōō'nə] n (*pl inv*) (*also:* ~ **fish**) thon m.

tune [tōōn] n (*melody*) air m ♦ vt (*MUS*)

accorder; (*RADIO*, *TV*, *AUT*) régler, mettre au point; **to be in/out of** ~ (*instrument*) être accordé/désaccordé; (*singer*) chanter juste/faux; **to be in/out of** ~ **with** (*fig*) être en accord/désaccord avec; **she was robbed to the** ~ **of $10,000** (*fig*) on lui a volé la jolie somme de 10 000 dollars.

tune in *vi* (*RADIO*, *TV*): **to** ~ **in (to)** se mettre à l'écoute (de).

tune up *vi* (*musician*) accorder son instrument.

tuneful [tōōn'fəl] *a* mélodieux(euse).

tuner [tōō'nûr] *n* (*radio set*) radio-préamplificateur *m*; **piano** ~ accordeur *m* de pianos.

tuner amplifier *n* radio-ampli *m*.

tungsten [tung'stən] *n* tungstène *m*.

tunic [tōō'nik] *n* tunique *f*.

tuning [tōō'ning] *n* réglage *m*.

tuning fork *n* diapason *m*.

Tunis [tōō'nis] *n* Tunis.

Tunisia [tōōnē'zhə] *n* Tunisie *f*.

Tunisian [tōōnē'zhən] *a* tunisien(ne) ♦ *n* Tunisien/ne.

tunnel [tun'əl] *n* tunnel *m*; (*in mine*) galerie *f* ♦ *vi* creuser un tunnel (*or* une galerie).

tunny [tun'ē] *n* thon *m*.

turban [tûr'bən] *n* turban *m*.

turbid [tûr'bid] *a* boueux(euse).

turbine [tûr'bin] *n* turbine *f*.

turbojet [tûr'bōjet] *n* turboréacteur *m*.

turboprop [tûr'bōpråp] *n* (*engine*) turbopropulseur *m*.

turbot [tûr'bət] *n* (*pl inv*) turbot *m*.

turbulence [tûr'byələns] *n* (*AVIAT*) turbulence *f*.

turbulent [tûr'byələnt] *a* turbulent(e); (*sea*) agité(e).

tureen [tərēn'] *n* soupière *f*.

turf [tûrf] *n* gazon *m*; (*clod*) motte *f* (de gazon) ♦ *vt* gazonner; **the T**~ le turf, les courses *fpl*.

turf out *vt* (*col*) jeter; jeter dehors.

turgid [tûr'jid] *a* (*speech*) pompeux(euse).

Turin [tōō'rin] *n* Turin.

Turk [tûrk] *n* Turc/Turque.

Turkey [tûr'kē] *n* Turquie *f*.

turkey [tûr'kē] *n* dindon *m*, dinde *f*.

Turkish [tûr'kish] *a* turc(turque) ♦ *n* (*LING*) turc *m*.

Turkish bath *n* bain turc.

Turkish delight *n* loukoum *m*.

turmeric [tûr'mûrik] *n* curcuma *m*.

turmoil [tûr'moil] *n* trouble *m*, bouleversement *m*.

turn [tûrn] *n* tour *m*; (*in road*) tournant *m*; (*tendency: of mind, events*) tournure *f*; (*performance*) numéro *m*; (*MED*) crise *f*, attaque *f* ♦ *vt* tourner; (*collar, steak*) retourner; (*milk*) faire tourner; (*change*): **to** ~ **sth into** changer qch en; (*shape: wood, metal*) tourner ♦ *vi* tourner; (*person: look back*) se (re)tourner; (*reverse direction*) faire demi-tour; (*change*) changer; (*become*) devenir; **to** ~ **into** se changer en, se transformer en; **a good** ~ un service; **a bad** ~ un mauvais tour; **it gave me quite a** ~ ça m'a fait un coup; **"no left ~"** (*AUT*) "défense de tourner à gauche"; **the first** ~ **on**

the right (*US*) la première (rue *or* route) à droite; **it's your** ~ c'est (à) votre tour; **in** ~ à son tour; **à tour de rôle; to take** ~**s** se relayer; **to take** ~**s at** faire à tour de rôle; **at the** ~ **of the year/century** à la fin de l'année/du siècle; **to take a** ~ **for the worse** (*situation, events*) empirer; **his health** *or* **he has taken a** ~ **for the worse** son état s'est aggravé.

turn around *vi* faire demi-tour; (*rotate*) tourner.

turn away *vi* se détourner, tourner la tête ♦ *vt* (*reject: person*) renvoyer; (: *business*) refuser.

turn back *vi* revenir, faire demi-tour.

turn down *vt* (*refuse*) rejeter, refuser; (*reduce*) baisser; (*fold*) rabattre.

turn in *vi* (*col: go to bed*) aller se coucher ♦ *vt* (*fold*) rentrer.

turn off *vi* (*from road*) tourner ♦ *vt* (*light, radio etc*) éteindre; (*engine*) arrêter.

turn on *vt* (*light, radio etc*) allumer; (*engine*) mettre en marche.

turn out *vt* (*light, gas*) éteindre; (*produce: goods, novel, good pupils*) produire ♦ *vi* (*appear, attend: troops, doctor etc*) être présent(e); **to** ~ **out to be** ... s'avérer ..., se révéler ....

turn over *vi* (*person*) se retourner ♦ *vt* (*object*) retourner; (*page*) tourner.

turn round *vi* (*Brit*) = **turn around**.

turn up *vi* (*person*) arriver, se pointer; (*lost object*) être retrouvé(e) ♦ *vt* (*collar*) remonter; (*increase: sound, volume etc*) mettre plus fort.

turnabout [tûr'nəbout], **turnaround** [tûr'nəround] *n* volte-face *f inv*.

turncoat [tûrn'kōt] *n* rénégat/e.

turned-up [tûrnd'up] *a* (*nose*) retroussé(e).

turning [tûr'ning] *n* (*in road*) tournant *m*; **the first** ~ **on the right** (*Brit*) la première (rue *or* route) à droite.

turning circle *n* (*Brit*) = **turning radius**.

turning point *n* (*fig*) tournant *m*, moment décisif.

turning radius *n* (*US*) rayon *m* de braquage.

turnip [tûr'nip] *n* navet *m*.

turnout [tûrn'out] *n* (nombre *m* de personnes dans l')assistance *f*.

turnover [tûrn'ōvûr] *n* (*COMM: amount of money*) chiffre *m* d'affaires; (: *of goods*) roulement *m*; (*CULIN*) sorte de chausson; **there is a rapid** ~ **in staff** le personnel change souvent.

turnpike [tûrn'pīk] *n* (*US*) autoroute *f* à péage.

turn signal *n* (*US AUT*) clignotant *m*.

turnstile [tûrn'stīl] *n* tourniquet *m* (d'entrée).

turntable [tûrn'tābəl] *n* (*on record player*) platine *f*.

turn-up [tûrn'up] *n* (*Brit: on pants*) revers *m*.

turpentine [tûr'pəntīn] *n* (*also:* **turps**) (essence *f* de) térébenthine *f*.

turquoise [tûr'koiz] *n* (*stone*) turquoise *f* ♦ *a* turquoise *inv*.

turret [tûr'it] *n* tourelle *f*.

turtle [tûr'təl] *n* tortue marine.

turtleneck (sweater) [tûr'təlnek (swêt'ûr)] *n* pullover *m* à col montant.

Tuscany [tus'kənē] *n* Toscane *f*.

tusk [tusk] *n* défense *f* (*d'éléphant*).
tussle [tus'əl] *n* bagarre *f*, mêlée *f*.
tutor [tōō'tûr] *n* (*private teacher*) précepteur/trice; (*Brit SCOL*) directeur/trice d'études.
tutorial [tōōtôr'ēəl] *n* (*SCOL*) (séance *f* de) travaux *mpl* pratiques.
tuxedo [tuksē'dō] *n* smoking *m*.
TV [tēvē] *n abbr* (= *television*) télé *f*, TV *f*.
TV dinner *n* plateau-repas *m*.
TVP *n abbr* (= *texturized vegetable protein*) protéine végétale texturisée.
twaddle [twâd'əl] *n* balivernes *fpl*.
twang [twang] *n* (*of instrument*) son vibrant; (*of voice*) ton nasillard ♦ *vi* vibrer ♦ *vt* (*guitar*) pincer les cordes de.
tweak [twēk] *vt* (*nose*) tordre; (*ear, hair*) tirer.
tweed [twēd] *n* tweed *m*.
tweezers [twē'zûrz] *npl* pince *f* à épiler.
twelfth [twelfth] *num* douzième.
Twelfth Night *n* la fête des Rois.
twelve [twelv] *num* douze; **at ~ (o'clock)** à midi; (*midnight*) à minuit.
twentieth [twen'tēith] *num* vingtième.
twenty [twen'tē] *num* vingt.
twerp [twûrp] *n* (*col*) imbécile *m/f*.
twice [twīs] *ad* deux fois; **~ as much** deux fois plus; **~ a week** deux fois par semaine; **she is ~ your age** elle a deux fois ton âge.
twiddle [twid'əl] *vt, vi:* **to ~ (with) sth** tripoter qch; **to ~ one's thumbs** (*fig*) se tourner les pouces.
twig [twig] *n* brindille *f* ♦ *vt, vi* (*col*) piger.
twilight [twī'līt] *n* crépuscule *m*; (*morning*) aube *f*; **in the ~** dans la pénombre.
twill [twil] *n* sergé *m*.
twin [twin] *a, n* jumeau(elle) ♦ *vt* jumeler.
twin beds *npl* lits *mpl* jumeaux.
twin-carburetor [twinkâr'bərātûr] *a* à double carburateur.
twine [twīn] *n* ficelle *f* ♦ *vi* (*plant*) s'enrouler.
twin-engined [twin'enjənd] *a* bimoteur; **~ aircraft** bimoteur *m*.
twinge [twinj] *n* (*of pain*) élancement *m*; (*of conscience*) remords *m*.
twinkle [twing'kəl] *n* scintillement *m*; pétillement *m* ♦ *vi* scintiller; (*eyes*) pétiller.
twin town *n* ville jumelée.
twirl [twûrl] *n* tournoiement *m* ♦ *vt* faire tournoyer ♦ *vi* tournoyer.
twist [twist] *n* torsion *f*, tour *m*; (*in wire, cord*) tortillon *m*; (*bend: in road*) tournant *m*; (*in story*) coup *m* de théâtre ♦ *vt* tordre; (*weave*) entortiller; (*roll around*) enrouler; (*fig*) déformer ♦ *vi* s'entortiller; s'enrouler; (*road*) serpenter; **to ~ one's ankle/wrist** (*MED*) se tordre la cheville/le poignet.
twisted [twis'tid] *a* (*wire, rope*) entortillé(e); (*ankle, wrist*) tordu(e), foulé(e); (*fig: logic, mind*) tordu.
twit [twit] *n* (*col*) crétin/e.
twitch [twich] *n* saccade *f*; (*nervous*) tic *m* ♦ *vi* se convulser; avoir un tic.
two [tōō] *num* deux; **~ by ~, in ~s** par deux; **to put ~ and ~ together** (*fig*) faire le rapport.
two-door [tōō'dôr] *a* (*AUT*) à deux portes.
two-faced [tōō'fāst] *a* (*pej: person*) faux(fausse).

twofold [tōō'fōld] *ad:* **to increase ~** doubler ♦ *a* (*increase*) de cent pour cent; (*reply*) en deux parties.
two-piece [tōō'pēs] *n* (*also:* **~ suit**) (costume *m*) deux-pièces *m inv*; (*also:* **~ swimsuit**) (maillot *m* de bain) deux-pièces.
two-seater [tōō'sē'tûr] *n* (*plane*) (avion *m*) biplace *m*; (*car*) voiture *f* à deux places.
twosome [tōō'səm] *n* (*people*) couple *m*.
two-stroke [tōō'strōk'] *n* (*also:* **~ engine**) moteur *m* à deux temps ♦ *a* à deux temps.
two-tone [tōō'tōn'] *a* (*in color*) à deux tons.
two-way [tōō'wā'] *a* (*traffic*) dans les deux sens; **~ radio** émetteur-récepteur *m*.
TX *abbr* (*US MAIL*) = *Texas*.
tycoon [tīkōōn'] *n:* **(business) ~** gros homme d'affaires.
type [tīp] *n* (*category*) genre *m*, espèce *f*; (*model*) modèle *m*; (*example*) type *m*; (*TYP*) type, caractère *m* ♦ *vt* (*letter etc*) taper (à la machine); **what ~ do you want?** quel genre voulez-vous?; **in bold/italic ~** en caractères gras/en italiques.
typecast [tīp'kast] *a* condamné(e) à toujours jouer le même rôle.
typeface [tīp'fās] *n* police *f* (de caractères).
typescript [tīp'skript] *n* texte dactylographié.
typeset [tīp'set] *vt* composer (*en imprimerie*).
typesetter [tīp'setûr] *n* compositeur *m*.
typewriter [tīp'rītûr] *n* machine *f* à écrire.
typewritten [tīp'ritən] *a* dactylographié(e).
typhoid [tī'foid] *n* typhoïde *f*.
typhoon [tīfōōn'] *n* typhon *m*.
typhus [tī'fəs] *n* typhus *m*.
typical [tip'ikəl] *a* typique, caractéristique.
typify [tip'əfī] *vt* être caractéristique de.
typing [tī'ping] *n* dactylo(graphie) *f*.
typing error *n* faute *f* de frappe.
typing pool *n* pool *m* de dactylos.
typist [tī'pist] *n* dactylo *m/f*.
typo [tī'pō] *n abbr* (*col:* = *typographical error*) coquille *f*.
typography [tīpâg'rəfē] *n* typographie *f*.
tyranny [tēr'ənē] *n* tyrannie *f*.
tyrant [tī'rənt] *n* tyran *m*.
tyre [tīûr'] *n* (*Brit*) pneu *m*.
tyre pressure *n* (*Brit*) pression *f* (de gonflage).
Tyrol [tirōl'] *n* Tyrol *m*.
Tyrolean [tīrō'lēən], **Tyrolese** [tirəlēz'] *a* tyrolien(ne) ♦ *n* Tyrolien/ne.
Tyrrhenian Sea [tīrē'nēən sē'] *n:* **the ~** la mer Tyrrhénienne.
tzar [zár] *n* = **tsar**.

U, u [yōō] *n* (*letter*) U, u *m*; **U for Uncle** U comme Ursule.
U [yōō] *n abbr* (*Brit CINEMA:* = *universal*) ≈ tous publics.
UAW *n abbr* (*US:* = *United Automobile*

Workers) syndicat des ouvriers de l'automobile.

U-bend [yōō'bend] n (Brit AUT) coude m, virage m en épingle à cheveux; (in pipe) coude.

ubiquitous [yōōbik'witəs] a doué(e) d'ubiquité, omniprésent(e).

UDA n abbr (Brit) = Ulster Defence Association.

udder [ud'ûr] n pis m, mamelle f.

UDI n abbr (Brit POL) = unilateral declaration of independence.

UDR n abbr (Brit) = Ulster Defence Regiment.

UEFA [yōōā'fa] n abbr (= Union of European Football Associations) UEFA f.

UFO [yōōefō'] n abbr (= unidentified flying object) ovni m (= objet volant non identifié).

Uganda [yōōgan'də] n Ouganda m.

Ugandan [yōōgan'dən] a ougandais(e) ♦ n Ougandais/e.

ugh [u] excl pouah!

ugliness [ug'lēnis] n laideur f.

ugly [ug'lē] a laid(e), vilain(e); (fig) répugnant(e).

UHF abbr (= ultra-high frequency) UHF.

UHT a abbr (= ultra-heat treated): ~ milk n lait UHT or longue conservation.

UK n abbr = United Kingdom.

ulcer [ul'sûr] n ulcère m; mouth ~ aphte f.

Ulster [ul'stûr] n Ulster m.

ulterior [ultēr'ēûr] a ultérieur(e); ~ motive arrière-pensée f.

ultimate [ul'təmit] a ultime, final(e); (authority) suprême ♦ n: the ~ in luxury le summum du luxe.

ultimately [ul'təmitlē] ad (in the end) en fin de compte; (at last) finalement; (eventually) par la suite.

ultimatum, pl ~s or **ultimata** [ultimā'təm, -tə] n ultimatum m.

ultralight [ultrəlīt'] n (US) ULM m (= ultra léger motorisé).

ultrasonic [ultrəsân'ik] a ultrasonique.

ultrasound [ul'trəsound] n (MED) ultrason m.

ultraviolet [ultrəvī'əlit] a ultraviolet(te).

umbilical [umbil'ikəl] a: ~ cord cordon ombilical.

umbrage [um'brij] n: to take ~ prendre ombrage, se froisser.

umbrella [umbrel'ə] n parapluie m; (fig): under the ~ of sous les auspices de; chapeauté(e) par.

umpire [um'pīûr] n arbitre m; (TENNIS) juge m de chaise ♦ vt arbitrer.

umpteen [ump'tēn'] a je ne sais combien de; for the ~th time pour la nième fois.

UMW n abbr (= United Mineworkers of America) syndicat des mineurs.

UN n abbr = United Nations.

unabashed [unəbasht'] a nullement intimidé(e).

unabated [unəbā'tid] a non diminué(e).

unable [unā'bəl] a: to be ~ to ne (pas) pouvoir, être dans l'impossibilité de; (not capable) être incapable de.

unabridged [unəbrijd'] a complet(ète), intégral(e).

unacceptable [unaksep'təbəl] a (behavior)

inadmissible; (price, proposal) inacceptable.

unaccompanied [unəkum'pənēd] a (child, lady) non accompagné(e); (singing, song) sans accompagnement.

unaccountably [unəkount'əblē] ad inexplicablement.

unaccounted [unəkoun'tid] a: two passengers are ~ for on est sans nouvelles de deux passagers.

unaccustomed [unəkus'təmd] a inaccoutumé(e), inhabituel(le); to be ~ to sth ne pas avoir l'habitude de qch.

unacquainted [unəkwān'tid] a: to be ~ with ne pas connaître.

unadulterated [unədul'tərātid] a pur(e), naturel(le).

unaffected [unəfek'tid] a (person, behavior) naturel(le); (emotionally): to be ~ by ne pas être touché(e) par.

unafraid [unəfrād'] a: to be ~ ne pas avoir peur.

unaided [unā'did] a sans aide, tout(e) seul(e).

unanimity [yōōnənim'itē] n unanimité f.

unanimous [yōōnan'əməs] a unanime.

unanimously [yōōnan'əməslē] ad à l'unanimité.

unanswered [unan'sûrd] a (question, letter) sans réponse.

unappetizing [unap'itīzing] a peu appétissant(e).

unappreciative [unəprē'shēətiv] a indifférent(e).

unarmed [unârmd'] a (person) non armé(e); (combat) sans armes.

unashamed [unəshāmd'] a sans honte; impudent(e).

unassisted [unəsis'tid] a non assisté(e) ♦ ad sans aide, tout(e) seul(e).

unassuming [unəsōō'ming] a modeste, sans prétentions.

unattached [unətacht'] a libre, sans attaches.

unattended [unəten'did] a (car, child, luggage) sans surveillance.

unattractive [unətrak'tiv] a peu attrayant(e).

unauthorized [unôth'ərīzd] a non autorisé(e), sans autorisation.

unavailable [unəvā'ləbəl] a (article, room, book) (qui n'est) pas disponible; (person) (qui n'est) pas libre.

unavoidable [unəvoi'dəbəl] a inévitable.

unavoidably [unəvoi'dəblē] ad inévitablement.

unaware [unəwär'] a: to be ~ of ignorer, ne pas savoir, être inconscient(e) de.

unawares [unəwärz'] ad à l'improviste, au dépourvu.

unbalanced [unbal'ənst] a déséquilibré(e).

unbearable [unbär'əbəl] a insupportable.

unbeatable [unbē'təbəl] a imbattable.

unbeaten [unbēt'ən] a invaincu(e); (record) non battu(e).

unbecoming [unbikum'ing] a (unseemly: language, behavior) malséant(e), inconvenant(e); (unflattering: garment) peu seyant(e).

unbeknown(st) [unbinōn(st)'] ad: ~ to à l'insu de.

unbelief [unbilēf'] n incrédulité f.

unbelievable [unbilē'vəbəl] a incroyable.

unbelievingly [unbilē'vinglē] ad avec incrédu-

lité.
unbend [unbend'] *vb (irg) vi* se détendre ♦ *vt (wire)* redresser, détordre.
unbending [unben'ding] *a (fig)* inflexible.
unbias(s)ed [unbī'əst] *a* impartial(e).
unblemished [unblem'isht] *a* impeccable.
unblock [unblák'] *vt (pipe)* déboucher; *(road)* dégager.
unborn [unbôrn'] *a* à naître.
unbounded [unboun'did] *a* sans bornes, illimité(e).
unbreakable [unbrā'kəbəl] *a* incassable.
unbridled [unbrī'dəld] *a* débridé(e), déchaîné(e).
unbroken [unbrō'kən] *a* intact(e); *(line)* continu(e); *(record)* non battu(e).
unbuckle [unbuk'əl] *vt* déboucler.
unburden [unbûr'dən] *vt*: **to ~ o.s.** s'épancher, se livrer.
unbutton [unbut'ən] *vt* déboutonner.
uncalled-for [unkôld'fôr] *a* déplacé(e), injustifié(e).
uncanny [unkan'ē] *a* étrange, troublant(e).
unceasing [unsē'sing] *a* incessant(e), continu(e).
unceremonious [unsärəmō'nēəs] *a (abrupt, rude)* brusque.
uncertain [unsûr'tən] *a* incertain(e); **we were ~ whether ...** nous ne savions pas vraiment si ...; **in no ~ terms** sans équivoque possible.
uncertainty [unsûr'təntē] *n* incertitude *f*, doutes *mpl*.
unchallenged [unchal'injd] *a (gen)* incontesté(e); *(information)* non contesté(e); **to go ~** ne pas être contesté.
unchanged [unchānjd'] *a* inchangé(e).
uncharitable [unchar'itəbəl] *a* peu charitable.
uncharted [unchâr'tid] *a* inexploré(e).
unchecked [unchekt'] *a* non réprimé(e).
uncivilized [unsiv'ilīzd] *a* non civilisé(e); *(fig)* barbare.
uncle [ung'kəl] *n* oncle *m*.
unclear [unkliûr'] *a* (qui n'est) pas clair(e) *or* évident(e); **I'm still ~ about what I'm supposed to do** je ne sais pas encore exactement ce que je dois faire.
uncoil [unkoil'] *vt* dérouler ♦ *vi* se dérouler.
uncomfortable [unkumf'tabəl] *a* inconfortable; *(uneasy)* mal à l'aise, gêné(e); *(situation)* désagréable.
uncomfortably [unkumf'təblē] *ad* inconfortablement; d'un ton *etc* gêné *or* embarrassé; désagréablement.
uncommitted [unkəmit'id] *a (attitude, country)* non engagé(e).
uncommon [unkâm'ən] *a* rare, singulier(ière), peu commun(e).
uncommunicative [unkəmyōō'nikətiv] *a* réservé(e).
uncomplicated [unkâm'plikātid] *a* simple, peu compliqué(e).
uncompromising [unkâm'prəmīzing] *a* intransigeant(e), inflexible.
unconcerned [unkənsûrnd'] *a (unworried)*: **to be ~ (about)** ne pas s'inquiéter (de).
unconditional [unkəndish'ənəl] *a* sans conditions.
uncongenial [unkənjēn'yəl] *a* peu agréable.
unconnected [unkənek'tid] *a (unrelated)*: **~**

(with) sans rapport (avec).
unconscious [unkân'chəs] *a* sans connaissance, évanoui(e); *(unaware)* inconscient(e) ♦ *n*: **the ~** l'inconscient *m*; **to knock sb ~** assommer qn.
unconsciously [unkân'chəslē] *ad* inconsciemment.
unconstitutional [unkânstitōō'shənəl] *a* anticonstitutionnel(le).
uncontested [unkəntes'tid] *a (champion)* incontesté(e); *(POL: seat)* non disputé(e).
uncontrollable [unkəntrō'ləbəl] *a (child, dog)* indiscipliné(e); *(emotion)* irrépressible.
uncontrolled [unkəntrōld'] *a (laughter, price rises)* incontrôlé(e).
unconventional [unkənven'chənəl] *a* non conventionnel(le).
unconvinced [unkənvinst'] *a*: **to be ~** ne pas être convaincu(e).
unconvincing [unkənvin'sing] *a* peu convaincant(e).
uncork [unkôrk'] *vt* déboucher.
uncorroborated [unkəráb'ərátid] *a* non confirmé(e).
uncouth [unkōōth'] *a* grossier(ière), fruste.
uncover [unkuv'ûr] *vt* découvrir.
uncovered [unkuv'ûrd] *a (US: check)* sans provision.
unctuous [ungk'chōōəs] *a* onctueux(euse), mielleux(euse).
undamaged [undam'ijd] *a (goods)* intact(e), en bon état; *(fig: reputation)* intact.
undaunted [undôn'tid] *a* non intimidé(e), inébranlable.
undecided [undisī'did] *a* indécis(e), irrésolu(e).
undelivered [undiliv'ûrd] *a* non remis(e), non livré(e).
undeniable [undinī'əbəl] *a* indéniable, incontestable.
under [un'dûr] *prep* sous; *(less than)* (de) moins de; au-dessous de; *(according to)* selon, en vertu de ♦ *ad* au-dessous; en dessous; **from ~ sth** de dessous *or* de sous qch; **~ there** là-dessous; **in ~ 2 hours** en moins de 2 heures; **~ anesthetic** sous anesthésie; **~ discussion** en discussion; **~ the circumstances** étant donné les circonstances; **~ repair** en (cours de) réparation.
under... *prefix* sous-.
underage [undûrāj'] *a* qui n'a pas l'âge réglementaire.
underarm [un'dûrârm] *ad* par en-dessous ♦ *a (throw)* par en-dessous; *(deodorant)* pour les aisselles.
undercapitalized [undûrkap'itəlīzd] *a* sous-capitalisé(e).
undercarriage [un'dûrkarij] *n (Brit AVIAT)* train *m* d'atterrissage.
undercharge [undûrchârj'] *vt* ne pas faire payer assez à.
underclothes [un'dûrklōz] *npl* sous-vêtements *mpl*; *(women's only)* dessous *mpl*.
undercoat [un'dûrkōt] *n (paint)* couche *f* de fond ♦ *vt (US AUT)* traiter contre la rouille.
undercover [undûrkuv'ûr] *a* secret(ète), clandestin(e).
undercurrent [un'dûrkûrənt] *n* courant sous-jacent.

undercut [undûrkut'] *vt irg* vendre moins cher que.

underdeveloped [un'dûrdivel'əpt] *a* sous-développé(e).

underdog [un'dûrdôg] *n* opprimé *m.*

underdone [un'dûrdun'] *a* (*food*) pas assez cuit(e).

underemployment [undûremploi'mənt] *n* sous-emploi *m.*

underestimate [undûres'təmāt] *vt* sous-estimer, mésestimer.

underexposed [undûrikspōzd'] *a* (*PHOT*) sous-exposé(e).

underfed [undûrfed'] *a* sous-alimenté(e).

underfoot [undûrfŏot'] *ad* sous les pieds.

undergo [undûrgō'] *vt irg* subir; (*treatment*) suivre; **the car is ~ing repairs** la voiture est en réparation.

undergraduate [undûrgraj'ōŏit] *n* étudiant/e (qui prépare la licence) ♦ *cpd*: **~ courses** cours *mpl* préparant à la licence.

underground [un'dûrground] *a* souterrain(e); (*fig*) clandestin(e) ♦ *n* (*Brit*) métro *m*; (*POL*) clandestinité *f.*

undergrowth [un'dûrgrōth] *n* broussailles *fpl,* sous-bois *m.*

underhand(ed) [un'dûrhand(id)] *a* (*fig*) sournois(e), en dessous.

underinsured [undûrinshŏord'] *a* sous-assuré(e).

underlie [undûrlī'] *vt irg* être à la base de; **the underlying cause** la cause sous-jacente.

underline [undûrlīn'] *vt* souligner.

underling [un'dûrling] *n* (*pej*) sous-fifre *m,* subalterne *m.*

undermanning [un'dûrman'ing] *n* pénurie *f* de main-d'œuvre.

undermentioned [un'dûrmenchənd] *a* mentionné(e) ci-dessous.

undermine [undûrmīn'] *vt* saper, miner.

underneath [undûrnēth'] *ad* (en) dessous ♦ *prep* sous, au-dessous de.

undernourished [undûrnûr'isht] *a* sous-alimenté(e).

underpaid [undûrpād'] *a* sous-payé(e).

underpants [un'dûrpants] *npl* caleçon *m,* slip *m.*

underpass [un'dûrpas] *n* passage souterrain; (*Brit: on freeway*) passage inférieur.

underpin [undûrpin'] *vt* (*argument, case*) étayer.

underplay [undûrplā'] *vt* minimiser.

underpopulated [un'dûrpâp'yəlātid] *a* sous-peuplé(e).

underprice [undûrprīs'] *vt* vendre à un prix trop bas.

underprivileged [undûrpriv'əlijd] *a* défavorisé(e), déshérité(e).

underrate [undərāt'] *vt* sous-estimer, mésestimer.

underscore [undûrskôr'] *vt* souligner.

underseal [un'dûrsēl] *vt* (*Brit*) traiter contre la rouille.

undersecretary [un'dûrsek'ritārē] *n* sous-secrétaire *m.*

undersell [undûrsel'] *vt* (*competitors*) vendre moins cher que.

undershirt [un'dûrshûrt] *n* (*US*) tricot *m* de corps.

undershorts [un'dûrshôrts] *npl* (*US*) caleçon *m,* slip *m.*

underside [un'dûrsīd] *n* dessous *m.*

undersigned [un'dûrsīnd'] *a, n* soussigné(e) (*m/f*).

underskirt [un'dûrskûrt] *n* jupon *m.*

understaffed [undûrstaft'] *a* qui manque de personnel.

understand [undûrstand'] *vb* (*irg: like* **stand**) *vt, vi* comprendre; **I ~ that** ... je me suis laissé dire que ...; je crois comprendre que ...; **to make o.s. understood** se faire comprendre.

understandable [undûrstan'dəbəl] *a* compréhensible.

understanding [undûrstan'ding] *a* compréhensif(ive) ♦ *n* compréhension *f*; (*agreement*) accord *m*; **to come to an ~ with sb** s'entendre avec qn; **on the ~ that** ... à condition que ....

understate [undûrstāt'] *vt* minimiser.

understatement [undûrstāt'mənt] *n*: **that's an ~** c'est (bien) peu dire, le terme est faible.

understood [undûrstŏod'] *pt, pp of* **understand** ♦ *a* entendu(e); (*implied*) sous-entendu(e).

understudy [un'dûrstudē] *n* doublure *f.*

undertake [undûrtāk'] *vt irg* (*job, task*) entreprendre; (*duty*) se charger de; **to ~ to do sth** s'engager à faire qch.

undertaker [un'dûrtākûr] *n* entrepreneur *m* des pompes funèbres, croque-mort *m.*

undertaking [un'dûrtāking] *n* entreprise *f*; (*promise*) promesse *f.*

undertone [un'dûrtōn] *n* (*low voice*): **in an ~** à mi-voix; (*of criticism etc*) nuance cachée.

undervalue [undûrval'yōō] *vt* sous-estimer.

underwater [un'dûrwôt'ûr] *ad* sous l'eau ♦ *a* sous-marin(e).

underwear [un'dûrwär] *n* sous-vêtements *mpl*; (*women's only*) dessous *mpl.*

underweight [un'dûrwāt] *a* d'un poids insuffisant; (*person*) (trop) maigre.

underworld [un'dûrwûrld] *n* (*of crime*) milieu *m,* pègre *f.*

underwrite [un'dərit] *vt* (*FINANCE*) garantir; (*INSURANCE*) souscrire.

underwriter [un'dərītûr] *n* (*INSURANCE*) sous-cripteur *m.*

undeserving [undizûr'ving] *a*: **to be ~ of** ne pas mériter.

undesirable [undizīûr'əbəl] *a* peu souhaitable, indésirable.

undeveloped [undivel'əpt] *a* (*land, resources*) non exploité(e).

undies [un'dēz] *npl* (*col*) dessous *mpl,* lingerie *f.*

undiluted [undilŏo'tid] *a* pur(e), non dilué(e).

undiplomatic [undipləmat'ik] *a* peu diplomatique, maladroit(e).

undischarged [undischârjd'] *a*: **~ bankrupt** failli/e non réhabilité(e).

undisciplined [undis'əplind] *a* indiscipliné(e).

undisguised [undisgīzd'] *a* (*dislike, amusement etc*) franc(franche).

undisputed [undispyōō'tid] *a* incontesté(e).

undistinguished [undisting'gwisht] *a* médiocre, quelconque.

undisturbed [undistûrbd'] *a* (*sleep*) tranquille,

paisible; **to leave** ~ ne pas déranger.

undivided [undivī'did] *a*: **can I have your ~ attention?** puis-je avoir toute votre attention?

undo [undōō'] *vt irg* défaire.

undoing [undōō'ing] *n* ruine *f*, perte *f*.

undone [undun'] *pp of* **undo**; **to come ~** se défaire.

undoubted [undou'tid] *a* indubitable, certain(e).

undoubtedly [undou'tidlē] *ad* sans aucun doute.

undress [undres'] *vi* se déshabiller ♦ *vt* déshabiller.

undrinkable [undringk'əbəl] *a* (*unpalatable*) imbuvable; (*poisonous*) non potable.

undue [undōō'] *a* indu(e), excessif(ive).

undulating [un'jəlāting] *a* ondoyant(e), onduleux(euse).

unduly [undōō'lē] *ad* trop, excessivement.

undying [undī'ing] *a* éternel(le).

unearned [unûrnd'] *a* (*praise, respect*) immérité(e); **~ income** rentes *fpl*.

unearth [unûrth'] *vt* déterrer; (*fig*) dénicher.

unearthly [unûrth'lē] *a* surnaturel(le); (*hour*) indu(e), impossible.

uneasy [unē'zē] *a* mal à l'aise, gêné(e); (*worried*) inquiet(ète); **to feel ~ about doing sth** se sentir mal à l'aise à l'idée de faire qch.

uneconomic(al) [unēkənâm'ik(əl)] *a* peu économique; peu rentable.

uneducated [unej'ōōkātid] *a* sans éducation.

unemployed [unemploid'] *a* sans travail, au chômage ♦ *n*: **the ~** les chômeurs *mpl*.

unemployment [unemploi'mənt] *n* chômage *m*.

unemployment compensation, (*Brit*) **unemployment benefit** *n* allocation *f* de chômage.

unending [unen'ding] *a* interminable.

unenviable [unen'vēəbəl] *a* peu enviable.

unequal [unēk'wəl] *a* inégal(e).

unequaled, (*Brit*) **unequalled** [unēk'wəld] *a* inégalé(e).

unequivocal [unikwiv'əkəl] *a* (*answer*) sans équivoque; (*person*) catégorique.

unerring [unûr'ing] *a* infaillible, sûr(e).

UNESCO [yōōnes'kō] *n abbr* (= *United Nations Educational, Scientific and Cultural Organization*) UNESCO *f*.

unethical [uneth'ikəl] *a* (*methods*) immoral(e); (*doctor's behavior*) qui ne respecte pas l'éthique.

uneven [unē'vən] *a* inégal(e); irrégulier(ière).

uneventful [univent'fəl] *a* tranquille, sans histoires.

unexceptional [uniksep'shənəl] *a* banal(e), quelconque.

unexciting [uniksī'ting] *a* pas passionnant(e).

unexpected [unikspek'tid] *a* inattendu(e), imprévu(e).

unexpectedly [unikspek'tidlē] *ad* contre toute attente; (*arrive*) à l'improviste.

unexplained [uniksplānd'] *a* inexpliqué(e).

unexploded [uniksplō'did] *a* non explosé(e) *or* éclaté(e).

unfailing [unfā'ling] *a* inépuisable; infaillible.

unfair [unfär'] *a*: **~ (to)** injuste (envers); **it's**

~ **that** ... il n'est pas juste que ....

unfair dismissal *n* licenciement abusif.

unfairly [unfär'lē] *ad* injustement.

unfaithful [unfāth'fəl] *a* infidèle.

unfamiliar [unfəmil'yûr] *a* étrange, inconnu(e); **to be ~ with sth** mal connaître qch. ,

unfashionable [unfash'ənəbəl] *a* (*clothes*) démodé(e); (*district*) déshérité(e), pas à la mode.

unfasten [unfas'ən] *vt* défaire; détacher.

unfathomable [unfath'əməbəl] *a* insondable.

unfavorable [unfā'vûrəbəl] *a* (*US*) défavorable.

unfavorably [unfā'vûrəblē] *ad*: **to look ~ upon** ne pas être favorable à.

unfavourable [unfā'vûrəbəl] *etc* (*Brit*) = **unfavorable** *etc*.

unfeeling [unfē'ling] *a* insensible, dur(e).

unfinished [unfin'isht] *a* inachevé(e).

unfit [unfit'] *a* (*physically*) pas en forme; (*incompetent*): **~ (for)** impropre (à); (*work, service*) inapte (à).

unflagging [unflag'ing] *a* infatigable, inlassable.

unflappable [unflap'əbəl] *a* imperturbable.

unflattering [unflat'ûring] *a* (*dress, hairstyle*) qui n'avantage pas; (*remark*) peu flatteur(euse).

unflinching [unflin'ching] *a* stoïque.

unfold [unfōld'] *vt* déplier; (*fig*) révéler, exposer ♦ *vi* se dérouler.

unforeseeable [unfôrsē'əbəl] *a* imprévisible.

unforeseen [unfôrsēn'] *a* imprévu(e).

unforgettable [unfûrget'əbəl] *a* inoubliable.

unforgivable [unfûrgiv'əbəl] *a* impardonnable.

unformatted [unfôr'matid] *a* (*disk, text*) non formaté(e).

unfortunate [unfôr'chənit] *a* malheureux(euse); (*event, remark*) malencontreux(euse).

unfortunately [unfôr'chənitlē] *ad* malheureusement.

unfounded [unfoun'did] *a* sans fondement.

unfriendly [unfrend'lē] *a* froid(e), inamical(e).

unfulfilled [unfōōlfild'] *a* (*ambition, prophecy*) non réalisé(e); (*desire*) insatisfait(e); (*promise*) non tenu(e); (*terms of contract*) non rempli(e); (*person*) qui n'a pas su se réaliser.

unfurl [unfûrl'] *vt* déployer.

unfurnished [unfûr'nisht] *a* non meublé(e).

ungainly [ungān'lē] *a* gauche, dégingandé(e).

ungodly [ungâd'lē] *a* impie; **at an ~ hour** à une heure indue.

ungrateful [ungrāt'fəl] *a* qui manque de reconnaissance, ingrat(e).

unguarded [ungâr'did] *a*: **~ moment** moment *m* d'inattention.

unhappily [unhap'ilē] *ad* tristement; (*unfortunately*) malheureusement.

unhappiness [unhap'ēnis] *n* tristesse *f*, peine *f*.

unhappy [unhap'ē] *a* triste, malheureux(euse); (*unfortunate: remark etc*) malheureux(euse); (*not pleased*): **~ with** mécontent(e) de, peu satisfait(e) de.

unharmed [unhârmd'] *a* indemne, sain(e) et sauf(sauve).

unhealthy [unhel'thē] *a* (*gen*) malsain(e); (*person*) maladif(ive).

unheard-of [unhûrd'əv] *a* inouï(e), sans précédent.

unhelpful [unhelp'fəl] *a* (*person*) peu serviable; (*advice*) peu utile.

unhesitating [unhez'itāting] *a* (*loyalty*) spontané(e); (*reply, offer*) immédiat(e).

unhook [unhŏŏk'] *vt* décrocher; dégrafer.

unhurt [unhûrt'] *a* indemne, sain(e) et sauf(sauve).

unhygienic [unhījēen'ik] *a* antihygiénique.

UNICEF [yŏŏ'nisef] *n abbr* (= *United Nations International Children's Emergency Fund*) UNICEF *m*, FISE *m*.

unicolor, (*Brit*) **unicolour** [yŏŏnəkul'ûr] *a* uni(e).

unicorn [yŏŏ'nəkôrn] *n* licorne *f*.

unidentified [unīden'təfīd] *a* non identifié(e).

uniform [yŏŏ'nəfôrm] *n* uniforme *m* ♦ *a* uniforme.

uniformity [yŏŏnəfôr'mitē] *n* uniformité *f*.

unify [yŏŏ'nəfī] *vt* unifier.

unilateral [yŏŏnəlat'ûrəl] *a* unilatéral(e).

unimaginable [unimaj'ənəbəl] *a* inimaginable, inconcevable.

unimaginative [unimaj'ənətiv] *a* sans imagination.

unimpaired [unimpärd'] *a* intact(e).

unimportant [unimpôr'tənt] *a* sans importance.

unimpressed [unimprest'] *a* pas impressionné(e).

uninhabited [uninhab'itid] *a* inhabité(e).

uninhibited [uninhib'itid] *a* sans inhibitions; sans retenue.

uninjured [unin'jûrd] *a* indemne.

unintelligent [unintel'ijənt] *a* inintelligent(e).

unintentional [uninten'chənəl] *a* involontaire.

unintentionally [uninten'chənəlē] *ad* sans le vouloir.

uninvited [uninvī'tid] *a* (*guest*) qui n'a pas été invité(e).

uninviting [uninvī'ting] *a* (*place*) peu attirant(e); (*food*) peu appétissant(e).

union [yŏŏn'yən] *n* union *f*; (*also*: **trade** ~) syndicat *m* ♦ *cpd* du syndicat, syndical(e).

unionize [yŏŏn'yənīz] *vt* syndiquer.

Union Jack *n* drapeau du *Royaume-Uni*.

Union of Soviet Socialist Republics (USSR) *n* Union *f* des républiques socialistes soviétiques (URSS).

union shop *n* entreprise où tous les travailleurs doivent être syndiqués.

unique [yŏŏnēk'] *a* unique.

unisex [yŏŏ'niseks] *a* unisexe.

unison [yŏŏ'nisən] *n*: **in** ~ à l'unisson, en chœur.

unit [yŏŏ'nit] *n* unité *f*; (*section: of furniture etc*) élément *m*, bloc *m*; (*team, squad*) groupe *m*, service *m*; **production** ~ atelier *m* de fabrication; **sink** ~ bloc-évier *m*.

unit cost *n* coût *m* unitaire.

unite [yŏŏnīt'] *vt* unir ♦ *vi* s'unir.

united [yŏŏnī'tid] *a* uni(e); unifié(e); (*efforts*) conjugué(e).

United Arab Emirates *npl* Émirats Arabes Unis.

United Kingdom (UK) *n* Royaume-Uni *m* (R.U.).

United Nations (Organization) (UN, UNO) *n* (Organisation *f* des) Nations unies (ONU).

United States (of America) (US, USA) *n* États-Unis *mpl*.

unit price *n* prix *m* unitaire.

unit trust *n* (*Brit COMM*) fonds commun de placement, FCP *m*.

unity [yŏŏ'nitē] *n* unité *f*.

Univ. *abbr* = **university**.

universal [yŏŏnəvûr'səl] *a* universel(le).

universe [yŏŏ'nəvûrs] *n* univers *m*.

university [yŏŏnəvûr'sitē] *n* université *f* ♦ *cpd* (*student, professor*) d'université; (*education, year, degree*) universitaire.

unjust [unjust'] *a* injuste.

unjustifiable [unjus'tifīəbəl] *a* injustifiable.

unjustified [unjus'təfīd] *a* injustifié(e); (*text*) non justifié(e).

unkempt [unkempt'] *a* mal tenu(e), débraillé(e); mal peigné(e).

unkind [unkīnd'] *a* peu gentil(le), méchant(e).

unkindly [unkīnd'lē] *ad* (*treat, speak*) avec méchanceté.

unknown [unnōn'] *a* inconnu(e); ~ **to me** sans que je le sache; ~ **quantity** (*MATH, fig*) inconnue *f*.

unladen [unlā'dən] *a* (*ship, weight*) à vide.

unlawful [unlô'fəl] *a* illégal(e).

unleaded [unled'id] *a* sans plomb.

unleash [unlēsh'] *vt* détacher; (*fig*) déchaîner, déclencher.

unleavened [unlev'ənd] *a* sans levain.

unless [unles'] *cj*: ~ **he leaves** à moins qu'il (ne) parte; ~ **we leave** à moins de partir, à moins que nous (ne) partions; ~ **otherwise stated** sauf indication contraire; ~ **I am mistaken** si je ne me trompe.

unlicensed [unlī'sənst] *a* (*Brit*) non patenté(e) pour la vente des spiritueux.

unlike [unlīk'] *a* dissemblable, différent(e) ♦ *prep* à la différence de, contrairement à.

unlikelihood [unlīk'lēhŏŏd] *a* improbabilité *f*.

unlikely [unlīk'lē] *a* (*result, event*) improbable; (*explanation*) invraisemblable.

unlimited [unlim'itid] *a* illimité(e).

unlisted [unlis'tid] *a* (*US TEL*) sur la liste rouge; (*STOCK EXCHANGE*) non coté(e) en bourse.

unlit [unlit'] *a* (*room*) non éclairé(e).

unload [unlōd'] *vt* décharger.

unlock [unlâk'] *vt* ouvrir.

unlucky [unluk'ē] *a* malchanceux(euse); (*object, number*) qui porte malheur; **to be** ~ (*person*) ne pas avoir de chance.

unmanageable [unman'ijəbəl] *a* (*unwieldy: tool, vehicle*) peu maniable; (: *situation*) inextricable.

unmanned [unmand'] *a* sans équipage.

unmannerly [unman'ûrlē] *a* mal élevé(e), impoli(e).

unmarked [unmârkt'] *a* (*unstained*) sans marque; ~ **police car** voiture de police banalisée.

unmarried [unmar'ēd] *a* célibataire.

unmask [unmask'] *vt* démasquer.

unmatched [unmacht'] *a* sans égal(e).

unmentionable [unmen'chənəbəl] *a* (*topic*)

dont on ne parle pas; (word) qui ne se dit pas.

unmerciful [unmûr'sifəl] a sans pitié.

unmistakable [unmistā'kəbəl] a indubitable; qu'on ne peut pas ne pas reconnaître.

unmitigated [unmit'əgātid] a non mitigé(e), absolu(e), pur(e).

unnamed [unnāmd'] a (nameless) sans nom; (anonymous) anonyme.

unnatural [unnach'ûrəl] a non naturel(le); contre nature.

unnecessary [unnes'isārē] a inutile, superflu(e).

unnerve [unnûrv'] vt faire perdre son sang-froid à.

unnoticed [unnō'tist] a inaperçu(e).

UNO [ōō'nō] n abbr = United Nations Organization.

unobservant [unəbzûr'vənt] a pas observateur(trice).

unobtainable [unəbtā'nəbəl] a (TEL) impossible à obtenir.

unobtrusive [unəbtrōō'siv] a discret(ète).

unoccupied [unák'yəpīd] a (seat, table, also MIL) libre; (house) inoccupé(e).

unofficial [unəfish'əl] a non officiel(le); (strike) ≈ non sanctionné(e) par la centrale.

unopposed [unəpōzd'] a sans opposition.

unorthodox [unôr'thədáks] a peu orthodoxe.

unpack [unpak'] vi défaire sa valise, déballer ses affaires.

unpaid [unpād'] a (bill) impayé(e); (vacation) non-payé(e), sans salaire; (work) non rétribué(e); (worker) bénévole.

unpalatable [unpal'ətəbəl] a (truth) désagréable (à entendre).

unparalleled [unpar'əleld] a incomparable, sans égal.

unpatriotic [unpātrēāt'ik] a (person) manquant de patriotisme; (speech, attitude) antipatriotique.

unplanned [unpland'] a (visit) imprévu(e); (baby) non prévu(e).

unpleasant [unplez'ənt] a déplaisant(e), désagréable.

unplug [unplug'] vt débrancher.

unpolluted [unpəlōō'tid] a non pollué(e).

unpopular [unpáp'yəlûr] a impopulaire; **to make o.s. ~ (with)** se rendre impopulaire (auprès de).

unprecedented [unpres'identid] a sans précédent.

unpredictable [unpridik'təbəl] a imprévisible.

unprejudiced [unprej'ədist] a (not biased) impartial(e); (having no prejudices) qui n'a pas de préjugés.

unprepared [unpripärd'] a (person) qui n'est pas suffisamment préparé(e); (speech) improvisé(e).

unprepossessing [unprēpəzes'ing] a peu avenant(e).

unpretentious [unpriten'chəs] a sans prétention(s).

unprincipled [unprin'səpəld] a sans principes.

unproductive [unprəduk'tiv] a improductif(ive); (discussion) stérile.

unprofessional [unprəfesh'ənəl] a (conduct) contraire à la déontologie.

unprofitable [unpráf'itəbəl] a non rentable.

unprovoked [unprəvōkt'] a (attack) sans provocation.

unpunished [unpun'isht] a impuni(e).

unqualified [unkwâl'əfid] a (teacher) non diplômé(e), sans titres; (success) sans réserve, total(e).

unquestionably [unkwes'chənəblē] ad incontestablement.

unquestioning [unkwes'chəning] a (obedience, acceptance) inconditionnel(le).

unravel [unrav'əl] vt démêler.

unreal [unrēl'] a irréel(le).

unrealistic [unrēəlis'tik] a (idea) irréaliste; (estimate) peu réaliste.

unreasonable [unrē'zənəbəl] a qui n'est pas raisonnable; **to make ~ demands on sb** exiger trop de qn.

unrecognizable [unrek'əgnīzəbəl] a pas reconnaissable.

unrecognized [unrek'əgnīzd] a (talent, genius) méconnu(e).

unrecorded [unrikôr'did] a non enregistré(e).

unrefined [unrifīnd'] a (sugar, petroleum) non raffiné(e).

unrehearsed [unrihûrst'] a (THEATER etc) qui n'a pas été répété(e); (spontaneous) spontané(e).

unrelated [unrilā'tid] a sans rapport; sans lien de parenté.

unrelenting [unrilen'ting] a implacable; acharné(e).

unreliable [unrilī'əbəl] a sur qui (or quoi) on ne peut pas compter, peu fiable.

unrelieved [unrilēvd'] a (monotony) constant(e), uniforme.

unremitting [unrimit'ing] a inlassable, infatigable, acharné(e).

unrepeatable [unripē'təbəl] a (offer) unique, exceptionnel(le).

unrepentant [unripen'tənt] a impénitent(e).

unrepresentative [unreprizen'tətiv] a: **~ (of)** peu représentatif(ive) (de).

unreserved [unrizûrvd'] a (seat) non réservé(e); (approval, admiration) sans réserve.

unresponsive [unrispân'siv] a insensible.

unrest [unrest'] n agitation f, troubles mpl.

unrestricted [unristrik'tid] a illimité(e); **to have ~ access to** avoir librement accès or accès en tout temps à.

unrewarded [unriwôr'did] a pas récompensé(e).

unripe [unrīp'] a pas mûr(e).

unrivaled, (Brit) **unrivalled** [unrī'vəld] a sans égal, incomparable.

unroll [unrōl'] vt dérouler.

unruffled [unruf'əld] a (person) imperturbable; (hair) qui n'est pas ébouriffé(e).

unruly [unrōō'lē] a indiscipliné(e).

unsafe [unsāf'] a (machine, wiring) dangereux(euse); (method) hasardeux(euse); **~ to drink/eat** non potable/comestible.

unsaid [unsed'] a: **to leave sth ~** passer qch sous silence.

unsalable, (Brit) **unsaleable** [unsā'ləbəl] a invendable.

unsatisfactory [unsatisfak'tûrē] a qui laisse à désirer.

unsavory, (Brit) **unsavoury** [unsā'vûrē] a (fig)

peu recommandable, répugnant(e).
unscathed [unskāt͟hd'] *a* indemne.
unscientific [unsīəntif'ik] *a* non scientifique.
unscrew [unskrōō'] *vt* dévisser.
unscrupulous [unskrōō'pyələs] *a* sans scrupules.
unsecured [unsikyōōrd'] *a:* ~ **creditor** créancier/ière sans garantie.
unseemly [unsēm'lē] *a* inconvenant(e).
unseen [unsēn'] *a* (*person*) invisible; (*danger*) imprévu(e).
unselfish [unsel'fish] *a* désintéressé(e).
unsettled [unset'əld] *a* (*restless*) perturbé(e); (*unpredictable*) instable; incertain(e); (*not finalized*) non résolu(e).
unsettling [unset'ling] *a* qui a un effet perturbateur.
unshak(e)able [unshā'kəbəl] *a* inébranlable.
unshaven [unshā'vən] *a* non *or* mal rasé(e).
unsightly [unsīt'lē] *a* disgracieux(euse), laid(e).
unskilled [unskild'] *a:* ~ **worker** manœuvre *m.*
unsociable [unsō'shəbəl] *a* (*person*) peu sociable; (*behavior*) qui manque de sociabilité.
unsocial [unsō'shəl] *a* (*hours*) en dehors de l'horaire normal.
unsold [unsōld'] *a* invendu(e), non vendu(e).
unsolicited [unsəlis'itid] *a* non sollicité(e).
unsophisticated [unsəfis'tikātid] *a* simple, naturel(le).
unsound [unsound'] *a* (*health*) chancelant(e); (*floor, foundations*) peu solide; (*policy, advice*) peu judicieux(euse).
unspeakable [unspē'kəbəl] *a* indicible; (*awful*) innommable.
unspoken [unspō'kən] *a* (*word*) qui n'est pas prononcé(e); (*agreement, approval*) tacite.
unsteady [unsted'ē] *a* mal assuré(e), chancelant(e), instable.
unstinting [unstin'ting] *a* (*support*) total(e), sans réserve; (*generosity*) sans limites.
unstuck [unstuk'] *a:* **to come** ~ se décoller; (*fig*) faire fiasco.
unsubstantiated [unsəbstan'chēātid] *a* (*rumor*) qui n'est pas confirmé(e); (*accusation*) sans preuve.
unsuccessful [unsəkses'fəl] *a* (*attempt*) infructueux(euse); (*writer, proposal*) qui n'a pas de succès; (*marriage*) malheureux(euse), qui ne réussit pas; **to be** ~ (*in attempting sth*) ne pas réussir; ne pas avoir de succès; (*application*) ne pas être retenu(e).
unsuccessfully [unsəkses'fəlē] *ad* en vain.
unsuitable [unsōō'təbəl] *a* qui ne convient pas, peu approprié(e); inopportun(e).
unsuited [unsōō'tid] *a:* **to be** ~ **for** *or* **to** être inapte *or* impropre à.
unsupported [unsəpôr'tid] *a* (*claim*) non soutenu(e); (*theory*) qui n'est pas corroboré(e).
unsure [unshōōr'] *a* pas sûr(e); **to be** ~ **of o.s.** ne pas être sûr de soi, manquer de confiance en soi.
unsuspecting [unsəspek'ting] *a* qui ne se méfie pas.
unsweetened [unswēt'ənd] *a* non sucré(e).
unswerving [unswûr'ving] *a* inébranlable.
unsympathetic [unsimpəthet'ik] *a* hostile; (*unpleasant*) antipathique; ~ **to** indiffé-

rent(e) à.
untangle [untang'gəl] *vt* démêler, débrouiller.
untapped [untapt'] *a* (*resources*) inexploité(e).
untaxed [untakst'] *a* (*goods*) non taxé(e); (*income*) non imposé(e).
unthinkable [unthingk'əbəl] *a* impensable, inconcevable.
untidy [untī'dē] *a* (*room*) en désordre; (*appearance*) désordonné(e), débraillé(e); (*person*) sans ordre, désordonné; débraillé; (*work*) peu soigné(e).
untie [untī'] *vt* (*knot, parcel*) défaire; (*prisoner, dog*) détacher.
until [until'] *prep* jusqu'à; (*after negative*) avant ♦ *cj* jusqu'à ce que + *sub*, en attendant que + *sub*; (*in past, after negative*) avant que + *sub*; ~ **now** jusqu'à présent, jusqu'ici; ~ **then** jusque-là; **from morning** ~ **night** du matin au soir *or* jusqu'au soir.
untimely [untīm'lē] *a* inopportun(e); (*death*) prématuré(e).
untold [untōld'] *a* incalculable; indescriptible.
untouched [untucht'] *a* (*not used etc*) tel(le) quel(le), intact(e); (*safe: person*) indemne; (*unaffected*): ~ **by** indifférent(e) à.
untoward [untôrd'] *a* fâcheux(euse), malencontreux(euse).
untrammeled, (*Brit*) **untrammelled** [untram'əld] *a* sans entraves.
untranslatable [untranz'lātəbəl] *a* intraduisible.
untrue [untrōō'] *a* (*statement*) faux(fausse).
untrustworthy [untrust'wûrt͟hē] *a* (*person*) pas digne de confiance, peu sûr(e).
unusable [unyōō'zəbəl] *a* inutilisable.
unused [unyōōzd'] *a* (*new*) neuf(neuve); [unyōōst'] : **to be** ~ **to sth/to doing sth** ne pas avoir l'habitude de qch/de faire qch.
unusual [unyōō'zhōōəl] *a* insolite, exceptionnel(le), rare.
unusually [unyōō'zhōōəlē] *ad* exceptionnellement, particulièrement.
unveil [unvāl'] *vt* dévoiler.
unwanted [unwôn'tid] *a* non désiré(e).
unwarranted [unwôr'əntid] *a* injustifié(e).
unwary [unwâr'ē] *a* imprudent(e).
unwavering [unwā'vûring] *a* inébranlable.
unwelcome [unwel'kəm] *a* importun(e); **to feel** ~ se sentir de trop.
unwell [unwel'] *a* indisposé(e), souffrant(e); **to feel** ~ ne pas se sentir bien.
unwieldy [unwēl'dē] *a* difficile à manier.
unwilling [unwil'ing] *a:* **to be** ~ **to do** ne pas vouloir faire.
unwillingly [unwil'inglē] *ad* à contrecœur, contre son gré.
unwind [unwīnd'] *vb* (*irg*) *vt* dérouler ♦ *vi* (*relax*) se détendre.
unwise [unwīz'] *a* imprudent(e), peu judicieux(euse).
unwitting [unwit'ing] *a* involontaire.
unworkable [unwûr'kəbəl] *a* (*plan etc*) inexploitable.
unworthy [unwûr't͟hē] *a* indigne.
unwrap [unrap'] *vt* défaire; ouvrir.
unwritten [unrit'ən] *a* (*agreement*) tacite.
unzip [unzip'] *vt* ouvrir (la fermeture éclair de).

up [up] *prep*: **to go/be ~ sth** monter/être sur qch ♦ *ad* en haut; en l'air ♦ *vi* (*col*): **she ~ped and left** elle a fichu le camp sans plus attendre ♦ *vt* (*col: price etc*) augmenter; **~ there** là-haut; **~ above** au-dessus; **~ to** jusqu'à; **"this side ~"** "haut"; **to be ~** (*out of bed*) être levé(e), être debout *inv*; **to be ~ (by)** (*of price, value*) avoir augmenté (de); **when the year was ~** (*finished*) à la fin de l'année; **time's ~** c'est l'heure; **it is ~ to you** c'est à vous de décider, ça ne tient qu'à vous; **what is he ~ to?** qu'est-ce qu'il peut bien faire?; **he is not ~ to it** il n'en est pas capable; **what's ~?** (*col*) qu'est-ce qui ne va pas?; **what's ~ with him?** (*col*) qu'est-ce qui lui arrive?; **~s and downs** *npl* (*fig*) hauts et bas *mpl*.

up-and-coming [upənkum'ing] *a* plein(e) d'avenir *or* de promesses.

upbeat [up'bēt] *n* (*MUS*) levé *m*; (*in economy, prosperity*) amélioration *f* ♦ *a* (*optimistic*) optimiste.

upbraid [upbrād'] *vt* morigéner.

upbringing [up'bringing] *n* éducation *f*.

update [updāt'] *vt* mettre à jour.

upend [upend'] *vt* mettre debout.

upgrade [upgrād'] *vt* (*person*) promouvoir; (*job*) revaloriser; (*property, equipment*) moderniser.

upheaval [uphē'vəl] *n* bouleversement *m*; branle-bas *m*; crise *f*.

uphill *a* [up'hil'] qui monte; (*fig: task*) difficile, pénible ♦ *ad* [uphil'] (*face, look*) en amont, vers l'amont; (*go, move*) vers le haut, en haut; **to go ~** monter.

uphold [uphōld'] *vt irg* maintenir; soutenir.

upholstery [uphōl'stŭrē] *n* rembourrage *m*; (*of car*) garniture *f*.

UPI *abbr* = *United Press International*.

upkeep [up'kēp] *n* entretien *m*.

up-market [up'mâr'kit] *a* (*product*) haut de gamme *inv*.

upon [əpän'] *prep* sur.

upper [up'ûr] *a* supérieur(e); du dessus ♦ *n* (*of shoe*) empeigne *f*.

upper class *n*: **the ~ ≈** la haute bourgeoisie ♦ *a*: **upper-class** (*district*) élégant(e), huppé(e); (*accent, attitude*) caractéristique des classes supérieures.

upper hand *n*: **to have the ~** avoir le dessus.

uppermost [up'ûrmōst] *a* le(la) plus haut(e); en dessus; **it was ~ in my mind** j'y pensais avant tout autre chose.

Upper Volta [up'ûr vōl'tə] *n* Haute Volta.

upright [up'rīt] *a* droit(e); vertical(e); (*fig*) droit, honnête ♦ *n* montant *m*.

uprising [up'rīzing] *n* soulèvement *m*, insurrection *f*.

uproar [up'rôr] *n* tumulte *m*, vacarme *m*.

uproot [uprōōt'] *vt* déraciner.

upset *n* [up'set] dérangement *m* ♦ *vt* [upset'] (*irg: like* **set**) (*glass etc*) renverser; (*plan*) déranger; (*person: offend*) contrarier; (*: grieve*) faire de la peine à; bouleverser ♦ *a* [upset'] contrarié(e); peiné(e); (*stomach*) détraqué(e), dérangé(e); **to get ~** (*sad*) devenir triste; (*offended*) se vexer; **to have a stomach ~** (*Brit*) avoir une indigestion.

upset price *n* (*US, Scottish*) mise *f* à prix, prix *m* de départ.

upsetting [upset'ing] *a* (*offending*) vexant(e); (*annoying*) ennuyeux(euse).

upshot [up'shât] *n* résultat *m*; **the ~ of it all was that ...** il a résulté de tout cela que ....

upside down [up'sid doun'] *ad* à l'envers.

upstairs [up'stärz] *ad* en haut ♦ *a* (*room*) du dessus, d'en haut ♦ *n*: **there's no ~** il n'y a pas d'étage.

upstart [up'stârt] *n* parvenu/e.

upstream [up'strēm] *ad* en amont.

upsurge [up'sûrj] *n* (*of enthusiasm etc*) vague *f*.

uptake [up'tāk] *n*: **he is quick/slow on the ~** il comprend vite/est lent à comprendre.

uptight [up'tīt'] *a* (*col*) très tendu(e), crispé(e).

up-to-date [up'tədāt'] *a* moderne; très récent(e).

upturn [up'tûrn] *n* (*in economy*) reprise *f*.

upturned [upturnd'] *a* (*nose*) retroussé(e).

upward [up'wûrd] *a* ascendant(e); vers le haut.

upward(s) [up'wûrd(z)] *ad* vers le haut; **and ~** et plus, et au-dessus.

URA *n abbr* (*US*) = *Urban Renewal Administration*.

Ural Mountains [yōōr'əl moun'tənz] *npl*: **the ~** (*also*: **the Urals**) les monts *mpl* Oural, l'Oural *m*.

uranium [yōōrā'nēəm] *n* uranium *m*.

Uranus [yōōr'ānəs] *n* Uranus *f*.

urban [ûr'bən] *a* urbain(e).

urbane [ûrbān'] *a* urbain(e), courtois(e).

urbanization [ûrbənəzā'shən] *n* urbanisation *f*.

urchin [û'chin] *n* gosse *m*, garnement *m*; **sea ~** oursin *m*.

urge [ûrj] *n* besoin (impératif), envie (pressante) ♦ *vt* (*caution etc*) recommander avec insistance; (*person*): **to ~ sb to do** presser qn de faire, recommander avec insistance à qn de faire.

urge on *vt* pousser, presser.

urgency [ûr'jənsē] *n* urgence *f*; (*of tone*) insistance *f*.

urgent [ûr'jənt] *a* urgent(e); (*plea, tone*) pressant(e).

urgently [ûr'jəntlē] *ad* d'urgence, de toute urgence; (*need*) sans délai.

urinal [yōōr'ənəl] *n* (*Brit*) urinoir *m*.

urinate [yōōr'ənāt] *vi* uriner.

urine [yōōr'in] *n* urine *f*.

urn [ûrn] *n* urne *f*; (*also*: **tea ~**) fontaine *f* à thé.

Uruguay [yōō'rəgwā] *n* Uruguay *m*.

Uruguayan [yōōrəgwā'ən] *a* uruguayen(ne) ♦ *n* Uruguayen/ne.

US *n abbr* = **United States**.

us [us] *pronoun* nous.

USA *n abbr* = **United States of America**; (*MIL*) = *United States Army*.

usable [yōō'zəbəl] *a* utilisable.

USAF *n abbr* = *United States Air Force*.

usage [yōō'sij] *n* usage *m*.

USCG *n abbr* = *United States Coast Guard*.

USDA *n abbr* = *United States Department of Agriculture*.

USDI *n abbr* = *United States Department of*

the Interior.

use *n* [yo͞os] emploi *m*, utilisation *f*; usage *m* ♦ *vt* [yo͞oz] se servir de, utiliser, employer; **she ~d to do it** elle le faisait (autrefois), elle avait coutume de le faire; **in ~** en usage; **out of ~** hors d'usage; **to be of ~** servir, être utile; **to make ~ of sth** utiliser qch; **ready for ~** prêt à l'emploi; **to be of ~** être utile; **it's no ~** ça ne sert à rien; **to have the ~ of** avoir l'usage de; **what's this ~d for?** à quoi est-ce que ça sert?; [yo͞ost']: **to be ~d to** avoir l'habitude de, être habitué(e) à; **to get ~d to** s'habituer à.

use up [yo͞oz up] *vt* finir, épuiser; *(food)* consommer.

used [yo͞ozd] *a* *(car)* d'occasion; *(match)* vieux(vieille).

useful [yo͞os'fəl] *a* utile; **to come in ~** être utile.

usefulness [yo͞os'fəlnis] *n* utilité *f*.

useless [yo͞os'lis] *a* inutile.

user [yo͞o'zûr] *n* utilisateur/trice, usager *m*.

user-friendly [yo͞o'zûrfrend'lē] *a* convivial(e), facile d'emploi.

USES *n abbr* = *United States Employment Service*.

usher [ush'ûr] *n* placeur *m* ♦ *vt*: **to ~ sb in** faire entrer qn.

usherette [ushəret'] *n* *(in cinema)* ouvreuse *f*.

USIA *n abbr* = *United States Information Agency*.

USM *n abbr* = *United States Mail, United States Mint*.

USN *n abbr* = *United States Navy*.

USPHS *n abbr* = *United States Public Health Service*.

USPS *n abbr* = *United States Postal Service*.

USS *abbr* = *United States Ship*.

USSR *n abbr* = **Union of Soviet Socialist Republics**.

usu. *abbr* = **usually**.

usual [yo͞o'zho͞oəl] *a* habituel(le); **as ~** comme d'habitude.

usually [yo͞o'zho͞oəlē] *ad* d'habitude, d'ordinaire.

usurer [yo͞o'zhûrûr] *n* usurier/ière.

usurp [yo͞osûrp'] *vt* usurper.

UT *abbr* *(US MAIL)* = *Utah*.

utensil [yo͞oten'səl] *n* ustensile *m*; **kitchen ~s** batterie *f* de cuisine.

uterus [yo͞o'tûrəs] *n* utérus *m*.

utilitarian [yo͞otilitär'ēən] *a* utilitaire.

utility [yo͞otil'itē] *n* utilité *f*; *(also:* **public ~)** service public.

utility room *n* buanderie *f*.

utilization [yo͞otəlizā'shən] *n* utilisation *f*.

utilize [yo͞o'təliz] *vt* utiliser; exploiter.

utmost [ut'mōst] *a* extrême, le(la) plus grand(e) ♦ *n*: **to do one's ~** faire tout son possible; **of the ~ importance** d'une importance capitale, de la plus haute importance.

utter [ut'ûr] *a* total(e), complet(ète) ♦ *vt* prononcer, proférer; émettre.

utterance [ut'ûrəns] *n* paroles *fpl*.

utterly [ut'ûrlē] *ad* complètement, totalement.

U-turn [yo͞o'tûrn] *n* demi-tour *m*; *(fig)* volte-face *f inv*.

V

V, v [vē] *n* *(letter)* V, v *m*; **V for Victor** V comme Victor.

v [vē] *abbr* (= *verse*, = *vide: see*) v.; (= *versus*) c.; (= *volt*) V.

VA *abbr* *(US MAIL)* = *Virginia*.

vac [vak] *n abbr* *(Brit col)* = **vacation**.

vacancy [vā'kənsē] *n* *(room)* chambre *f* disponible; *(Brit: job)* poste vacant; **"no vacancies"** "complet".

vacant [vā'kənt] *a* *(post)* vacant(e); *(seat etc)* libre, disponible; *(expression)* distrait(e).

vacant lot *n* terrain inoccupé; *(for sale)* terrain à vendre.

vacate [vā'kāt] *vt* quitter.

vacation [vākā'shən] *n* *(esp US)* vacances *fpl*; **to take a ~** prendre des vacances; **on ~** en vacances.

vacation course *n* cours *mpl* de vacances.

vacationer [vākā'shənûr] *n* *(US)* vacancier/ère.

vacation pay *n* *(US)* paie *f* des vacances.

vacation season *n* *(US)* période *f* des vacances.

vaccinate [vak'sənāt] *vt* vacciner.

vaccination [vak'sənā'shən] *n* vaccination *f*.

vaccine [vaksēn'] *n* vaccin *m*.

vacuum [vak'yo͞om] *n* vide *m*; *(also:* **cleaner)** aspirateur *m* ♦ *vt* passer l'aspirateur.

vacuum bottle *n* *(US)* bouteille *f* thermos ®.

vacuum flask *n* *(Brit)* = **vacuum bottle**.

vacuum-packed [vak'yo͞ompakt'] *a* emballé(e) sous vide.

vagabond [vag'əbând] *n* vagabond/e; *(tramp)* chemineau *m*, clochard/e.

vagary [vā'gûrē] *n* caprice *m*.

vagina [vəji'nə] *n* vagin *m*.

vagrancy [vā'grənsē] *n* vagabondage *m*.

vagrant [vā'grənt] *n* vagabond/e, mendiant/e.

vague [vāg] *a* vague, imprécis(e); *(blurred: photo, memory)* flou(e); **I haven't the ~st idea** je n'en ai pas la moindre idée.

vaguely [vāg'lē] *ad* vaguement.

vain [vān] *a* *(useless)* vain(e); *(conceited)* vaniteux(euse); **in ~** en vain.

valance [val'əns] *n* *(of bed)* tour *m* de lit.

valedictory [validik'tûrē] *a* d'adieu.

valentine [val'əntīn] *n* *(also:* **~ card)** carte *f* de la Saint-Valentin.

valet [valā'] *n* valet *m* de chambre.

valet parking *n* parcage *m* par les soins du personnel (de l'hôtel *etc*).

valet service *n* *(for clothes)* pressing *m*; *(for car)* nettoyage complet.

valiant [val'yənt] *a* vaillant(e), courageux(euse).

valid [val'id] *a* valide, valable; *(excuse)* valable.

validate [val'idāt] *vt* *(contract, document)* valider; *(argument, claim)* prouver la justesse

de, confirmer.
validity [vəlid'itē] *n* validité *f*.
valise [vəlēs'] *n* sac *m* de voyage.
valley [val'ē] *n* vallée *f*.
valor, (*Brit*) **valour** [val'ûr] *n* courage *m*.
valuable [val'yōōəbəl] *a* (*jewel*) de grande valeur; (*time*) précieux(euse); **~s** *npl* objets *mpl* de valeur.
valuation [valyōōā'shən] *n* évaluation *f*, expertise *f*.
value [val'yōō] *n* valeur *f* ♦ *vt* (*fix price*) évaluer, expertiser; (*cherish*) tenir à; **you get good ~ (for money) in that store** vous en avez pour votre argent dans ce magasin; **to lose (in) ~** (*currency*) baisser; (*property*) se déprécier; **to gain (in) ~** (*currency*) monter; (*property*) prendre de la valeur; **to be of great ~ to sb** (*fig*) être très utile à qn.
value added tax (VAT) *n* taxe *f* à la valeur ajoutée (TVA).
valued [val'yōōd] *a* (*appreciated*) estimé(e).
valuer [val'yōōûr] *n* expert *m* (en estimations).
valve [valv] *n* (*in machine*) soupape *f*; (*on tire*) valve *f*; (*in radio*) lampe *f*.
vampire [vam'pīûr] *n* vampire *m*.
van [van] *n* (*AUT*) camionnette *f*; (*Brit RAIL*) fourgon *m*.
vandal [van'dəl] *n* vandale *m/f*.
vandalism [van'dəlizəm] *n* vandalisme *m*.
vandalize [van'dəlīz] *vt* saccager.
vanguard [van'gârd] *n* avant-garde *m*.
vanilla [vənil'ə] *n* vanille *f* ♦ *cpd* (*ice cream*) à la vanille.
vanish [van'ish] *vi* disparaître.
vanity [van'itē] *n* vanité *f*.
vanity case *n* sac *m* de toilette.
vantage [van'tij] *n*: **~ point** bonne position.
vaporize [vā'pərīz] *vt* vaporiser ♦ *vi* se vaporiser.
vapor [vā'pûr] *n* (*US*) vapeur *f*; (*on window*) buée *f*.
vapor trail *n* (*AVIAT*) traînée *f* de condensation.
vapour [vā'pûr] *etc* (*Brit*) = **vapor** *etc*.
variable [vär'ēəbəl] *a* variable; (*mood*) changeant(e) ♦ *n* variable *f*.
variance [vär'ēəns] *n*: **to be at ~ (with)** être en désaccord (avec); (*facts*) être en contradiction (avec).
variant [vär'ēənt] *n* variante *f*.
variation [värēā'shən] *n* variation *f*; (*in opinion*) changement *m*.
varicose [var'əkōs] *a*: **~ veins** varices *fpl*.
varied [vär'ēd] *a* varié(e), divers(e).
variety [vərī'ətē] *n* variété *f*; (*quantity*): **a wide ~ of ...** une quantité *or* un grand nombre de ... (différent(e)s *or* divers(es)); **for a ~ of reasons** pour diverses raisons.
variety show *n* (spectacle *m* de) variétés *fpl*.
various [vär'ēəs] *a* divers(e), différent(e); (*several*) divers, plusieurs; **at ~ times** (*different*) en diverses occasions; (*several*) à plusieurs reprises.
varnish [vär'nish] *n* vernis *m*; (*for nails*) vernis (à ongles) ♦ *vt* vernir; **to ~ one's nails** se vernir les ongles.
vary [vär'ē] *vt*, *vi* varier, changer; **to ~ with** *or* **according to** varier selon.
varying [vär'ēing] *a* variable.

vase [vās] *n* vase *m*.
vasectomy [vasek'təmē] *n* vasectomie *f*.
vaseline [vas'əlēn] *n* ® vaseline *f*.
vast [vast] *a* vaste, immense; (*amount, success*) énorme.
vastly [vast'lē] *ad* infiniment, extrêmement.
vastness [vast'nis] *n* immensité *f*.
VAT [vat] *n abbr* = **value added tax.**
vat [vat] *n* cuve *f*.
Vatican [vat'ikən] *n*: **the ~** le Vatican.
vault [vôlt] *n* (*of roof*) voûte *f*; (*tomb*) caveau *m*; (*in bank*) salle *f* des coffres; chambre forte; (*jump*) saut *m* ♦ *vt* (*also*: **~ over**) sauter (d'un bond).
vaunted [vôn'tid] *a*: **much-~** tant célébré(e).
VC *n abbr* = **vice-chairman.**
VCR *n abbr* = **video cassette recorder.**
VD *n abbr* = **venereal disease.**
VDU *n abbr* = **visual display unit.**
veal [vēl] *n* veau *m*.
veer [vēr] *vi* tourner; virer.
vegan [vē'gən] *n* végétalien/ne.
vegetable [vej'təbəl] *n* légume *m* ♦ *a* végétal(e).
vegetable garden *n* (jardin *m*) potager *m*.
vegetarian [vejitär'ēən] *a*, *n* végétarien(ne).
vegetate [vej'itāt] *vi* végéter.
vegetation [vejitā'shən] *n* végétation *f*.
vehemence [vē'əməns] *n* véhémence *f*, violence *f*.
vehement [vē'əmənt] *a* violent(e), impétueux(euse); (*impassioned*) ardent(e).
vehicle [vē'ikəl] *n* véhicule *m*.
vehicular [vēhik'yəlûr] *a*: **"no ~ traffic"** "interdit à tout véhicule".
veil [vāl] *n* voile *m* ♦ *vt* voiler; **under a ~ of secrecy** (*fig*) dans le plus grand secret.
veiled [vāld] *a* voilé(e).
vein [vān] *n* veine *f*; (*on leaf*) nervure *f*; (*fig: mood*) esprit *m*.
vellum [vel'əm] *n* (*writing paper*) vélin *m*.
velocity [vəlâs'itē] *n* vitesse *f*, velocité *f*.
velvet [vel'vit] *n* velours *m*.
vending machine [ven'ding məshēn'] *n* distributeur *m* automatique.
vendor [ven'dûr] *n* vendeur/euse; **street ~** marchand ambulant.
veneer [vənēr'] *n* placage *m* de bois; (*fig*) vernis *m*.
venerable [ven'ûrəbəl] *a* vénérable.
venereal [vənēr'ēəl] *a*: **~ disease (VD)** maladie vénérienne.
Venetian [vənē'shən] *a*: **~ blind** store vénitien.
Venezuela [venizwā'lə] *n* Venezuela *m*.
Venezuelan [venizwā'lən] *a* vénézuélien(ne) ♦ *n* Vénézuélien/ne.
vengeance [ven'jəns] *n* vengeance *f*; **with a ~** (*fig*) vraiment, pour de bon.
vengeful [venj'fəl] *a* vengeur(geresse).
Venice [ven'is] *n* Venise.
venison [ven'isən] *n* venaison *f*.
venom [ven'əm] *n* venin *m*.
venomous [ven'əməs] *a* venimeux(euse).
vent [vent] *n* conduit *m* d'aération; (*in dress, jacket*) fente *f* ♦ *vt* (*fig: one's feelings*) donner libre cours à.
ventilate [ven'təlāt] *vt* (*room*) ventiler, aérer.
ventilation [ventəlā'shən] *n* ventilation *f*, aéra-

tion *f*.
ventilation shaft *n* conduit *m* de ventilation *or* d'aération.
ventilator [ven'təlātûr] *n* ventilateur *m*.
ventriloquist [ventril'əkwist] *n* ventriloque *m/ f*.
venture [ven'chûr] *n* entreprise *f* ♦ *vt* risquer, hasarder ♦ *vi* s'aventurer, se risquer; **a business** ~ une entreprise commerciale; **to** ~ **to do sth** se risquer à faire qch.
venture capital *n* capital-risques *m*.
venue [ven'yōō] *n* (*of conference etc*) lieu *m* de la réunion (*or* manifestation *etc*); (*of game*) lieu de la rencontre.
Venus [vē'nəs] *n* (*planet*) Vénus *f*.
veracity [vəras'itē] *n* véracité *f*.
veranda(h) [vərandə] *n* véranda *f*.
verb [vûrb] *n* verbe *m*.
verbal [vûr'bəl] *a* verbal(e); (*translation*) littéral(e).
verbally [vûr'bəlē] *ad* verbalement.
verbatim [vûrbā'tim] *a*, *ad* mot pour mot.
verbose [vûrbōs'] *a* verbeux(euse).
verdict [vûr'dikt] *n* verdict *m*; ~ **of guilty/not guilty** verdict de culpabilité/de non-culpabilité.
verge [vûrj] *n* bord *m*; **on the** ~ **of doing** sur le point de faire.
  verge on *vt fus* approcher de.
verger [vûr'jûr] *n* (*REL*) bedeau *m*.
verification [värəfəkā'shən] *n* vérification *f*.
verify [vär'əfī] *vt* vérifier.
veritable [vär'itəbəl] *a* véritable.
vermin [vûr'min] *npl* animaux *mpl* nuisibles; (*insects*) vermine *f*.
vermouth [vûrmōōth'] *n* vermouth *m*.
vernacular [vûrnak'yəlûr] *n* langue *f* vernaculaire, dialecte *m*.
versatile [vûr'sətəl] *a* polyvalent(e).
verse [vûrs] *n* vers *mpl*; (*stanza*) strophe *f*; (*in bible*) verset *m*; **in** ~ en vers.
versed [vûrst] *a*: (**well-**)~ **in** versé(e) dans.
version [vûr'zhən] *n* version *f*.
versus [vûr'səs] *prep* contre.
vertebra, *pl* ~**e** [vûr'təbrə, brē] *n* vertèbre *f*.
vertebrate [vûr'təbrāt] *n* vertébré *m*.
vertical [vûr'tikəl] *a* vertical(e) ♦ *n* verticale *f*.
vertically [vûr'tiklē] *ad* verticalement.
vertigo [vûr'təgō] *n* vertige *m*; **to suffer from** ~ avoir des vertiges.
verve [vûrv] *n* brio *m*; enthousiasme *m*.
very [vär'ē] *ad* très ♦ *a*: **the** ~ **book which** le livre même que; **the** ~ **thought (of it)** ... rien que d'y penser ...; **at the** ~ **end** tout à la fin; **the** ~ **last** le tout dernier; **at the** ~ **least** au moins; ~ **well** très bien; ~ **little** très peu; ~ **much** beaucoup.
vespers [ves'pûrz] *npl* vêpres *fpl*.
vessel [ves'əl] *n* (*ANAT, NAUT*) vaisseau *m*; (*container*) récipient *m*.
vest [vest] *n* (*US*) gilet *m*; (*Brit*) tricot *m* de corps ♦ *vt*: **to** ~ **sb with sth, to** ~ **sth in sb** investir qn de qch.
vested interest [ves'tid in'trist] *n*: **to have a** ~ **in doing** avoir tout intérêt à faire; ~**s** *npl* (*COMM*) droits acquis.
vestibule [ves'təbyōōl] *n* vestibule *m*.
vestige [ves'tij] *n* vestige *m*.
vestry [ves'trē] *n* sacristie *f*.

Vesuvius [vəsōō'vēəs] *n* Vésuve *m*.
vet [vet] *n abbr* (= *veterinary surgeon*) vétérinaire *m/f* ♦ *vt* examiner minutieusement; (*text*) revoir; (*candidate*) se renseigner soigneusement sur, soumettre à une enquête approfondie.
veteran [vet'ûrən] *n* vétéran *m*; (*also*: **war** ~) ancien combattant ♦ *a*: **she's a** ~ **campaigner for** ... cela fait très longtemps qu'elle lutte pour ....
veteran car *n* voiture *f* d'époque.
veterinarian [vetûrənär'ēən] *n* (*US*) vétérinaire *m/f*.
veterinary [vet'ûrənärē] *a* vétérinaire.
veterinary surgeon *n* (*Brit*) = **veterinarian**.
veto [vē'tō] *n* (*pl* ~**es**) veto *m* ♦ *vt* opposer son veto à; **to put a** ~ **on** mettre (*or* opposer) son veto à.
vex [veks] *vt* fâcher, contrarier.
vexed [vekst] *a* (*question*) controversé(e).
VFD *n abbr* (*US*) = *voluntary fire department*.
VHF *abbr* (= *very high frequency*) VHF.
VI *abbr* (*US MAIL*) = *Virgin Islands*.
via [vī'ə] *prep* par, via.
viability [vīəbil'ətē] *n* viabilité *f*.
viable [vī'əbəl] *a* viable.
viaduct [vī'ədukt] *n* viaduc *m*.
vibrant [vī'brənt] *a* (*sound, color*) vibrant(e).
vibrate [vī'brāt] *vi*: **to** ~ (**with**) vibrer (de); (*resound*) retentir (de).
vibration [vībrā'shən] *n* vibration *f*.
vicar [vik'ûr] *n* pasteur *m* (*de l'Église anglicane*).
vicarage [vik'ûrij] *n* presbytère *m*.
vicarious [vīkār'ēəs] *a* (*pleasure, experience*) indirect(e).
vice [vīs] *n* (*evil*) vice *m*; (*TECH*) étau *m*.
vice- *prefix* vice-.
vice-chairman [vīs'chär'mən] *n* ♦ vice-président/ e.
vice-chancellor [vīs'chan'səlûr] *n* (*Brit*) ≈ président/e d'université.
vice-president [vīs'prez'idənt] *n* vice-président/e.
vice-principal [vīs'prin'səpəl] *n* (*SCOL*) censeur *m*.
vice squad *n* ≈ brigade mondaine.
vice versa [vīs'vûr'sə] *ad* vice versa.
vicinity [visin'ətē] *n* environs *mpl*, alentours *mpl*.
vicious [vish'əs] *a* (*remark*) cruel(le), méchant(e); (*blow*) brutal(e); **a** ~ **circle** un cercle vicieux.
viciousness [vish'əsnis] *n* méchanceté *f*, cruauté *f*; brutalité *f*.
vicissitudes [visis'ətōōdz] *npl* vicissitudes *fpl*.
victim [vik'tim] *n* victime *f*; **to be the** ~ **of** être victime de.
victimization [viktiməzā'shən] *n* brimades *fpl*; représailles *fpl*.
victimize [vik'təmīz] *vt* brimer; exercer des représailles sur.
victor [vik'tûr] *n* vainqueur *m*.
Victorian [viktōr'ēən] *a* victorien(ne).
victorious [viktōr'ēəs] *a* victorieux(euse).
victory [vik'tûrē] *n* victoire *f*; **to win a** ~ **over sb** remporter une victoire sur qn.
video [vid'ēō] *n* (~ *film*) vidéo *f*; (*also*: ~ **cassette**) vidéocassette *f*; (*also*: ~ **cassette**

recorder) magnétoscope *m* ♦ *cpd* vidéo *inv*.
video cassette *n* vidéocassette *f*.
video cassette recorder (VCR) *n* magnétoscope *m*.
video recording *n* enregistrement *m* (en) vidéo.
video tape *n* bande *f* vidéo *inv*; (*cassette*) vidéocassette *f*.
video tape recorder (VTR) magnétoscope *m* (à bande).
videotex [vid'ēōteks] *n* télétexte *m*.
vie [vī] *vi*: **to ~ with** lutter avec, rivaliser avec.
Vienna [vēen'ə] *n* Vienne.
Vietnam, Viet Nam [vēetnâm'] *n* Viet-Nam *or* Vietnam *m*.
Vietnamese [vēetnâmēz'] *a* vietnamien(ne) ♦ *n* (*pl inv*) Vietnamien/ne; (*LING*) vietnamien *m*.
view [vyōō] *n* vue *f*; (*opinion*) avis *m*, vue ♦ *vt* (*situation*) considérer; (*house*) visiter; **on ~** (*in museum etc*) exposé(e); **in full ~ of sb** sous les yeux de qn; **to be within ~ (of sth)** être à portée de vue (de qch); **an overall ~ of the situation** une vue d'ensemble de la situation; **in my ~** à mon avis; **in ~ of the fact that** étant donné que; **with a ~ to doing sth** dans l'intention de faire qch.
viewdata [vyōō'dātə] *n* (*Brit*) télétexte *m* (*version téléphonique*).
viewer [vyōō'ûr] *n* (*viewfinder*) viseur *m*; (*small projector*) visionneuse *f*; (*TV*) téléspectateur/trice.
viewfinder [vyōō'fîndûr] *n* viseur *m*.
viewpoint [vyōō'point] *n* point *m* de vue.
vigil [vij'əl] *n* veille *f*; **to keep ~** veiller.
vigilance [vij'ələns] *n* vigilance *f*.
vigilance committee *n* comité *m* d'autodéfense.
vigilant [vij'ələnt] *a* vigilant(e).
vigor [vig'ûr] *n* (*US*) vigueur *f*.
vigorous [vig'ûrəs] *a* vigoureux(euse).
vigour [vig'ûr] *n* (*Brit*) = **vigor**.
vile [vīl] *a* (*action*) vil(e); (*smell*) abominable; (*temper*) massacrant(e).
vilify [vil'əfī] *vt* calomnier, vilipender.
villa [vil'ə] *n* villa *f*.
village [vil'ij] *n* village *m*.
villager [vil'ijûr] *n* villageois/e.
villain [vil'in] *n* (*scoundrel*) scélérat *m*; (*criminal*) bandit *m*; (*in novel etc*) traître *m*.
VIN *n abbr* (*US*) = *vehicle identification number*.
vindicate [vin'dikāt] *vt* défendre avec succès; justifier.
vindication [vindikā'shən] *n*: **in ~ of** pour justifier.
vindictive [vindik'tiv] *a* vindicatif(ive), rancunier(ière).
vine [vīn] *n* vigne *f*; (*climbing plant*) plante grimpante.
vinegar [vin'əgûr] *n* vinaigre *m*.
vine grower *n* viticulteur *m*.
vine-growing [vīn'grōing] *a* viticole ♦ *n* viticulture *f*.
vineyard [vin'yûrd] *n* vignoble *m*.
vintage [vin'tij] *n* (*year*) année *f*, millésime *m*; **the 1970 ~** le millésime 1970.
vintage car *n* voiture ancienne.

vintage wine *n* vin *m* de grand cru.
vinyl [vī'nil] *n* vinyle *m*.
viola [vēō'lə] *n* alto *m*.
violate [vī'əlāt] *vt* violer.
violation [vīəlā'shən] *n* violation *f*; **in ~ of** (*rule, law*) en infraction à, en violation de.
violence [vī'ələns] *n* violence *f*; (*POL etc*) incidents violents.
violent [vī'ələnt] *a* violent(e); **a ~ dislike of sb/sth** une aversion profonde pour qn/qch.
violently [vī'ələntlē] *ad* violemment; (*ill, angry*) terriblement.
violet [vī'əlit] *a* (*color*) violet(te) ♦ *n* (*plant*) violette *f*.
violin [vīəlin'] *n* violon *m*.
violinist [vīəlin'ist] *n* violoniste *m/f*.
VIP *n abbr* (= *very important person*) VIP *m*.
viper [vī'pûr] *n* vipère *f*.
virgin [vûr'jin] *n* vierge *f* ♦ *a* vierge; **she is a ~** elle est vierge; **the Blessed V~** la Sainte Vierge.
virginity [vûrjin'ətē] *n* virginité *f*.
Virgo [vûr'gō] *n* la Vierge; **to be ~** être de la Vierge.
virile [vir'əl] *a* viril(e).
virility [vəril'ətē] *n* virilité *f*.
virtual [vûr'chōōəl] *a* (*COMPUT, PHYSICS*) virtuel(le); (*in effect*): **it's a ~ impossibility** c'est pratiquement impossible; **the ~ leader** le chef dans la pratique.
virtually [vûr'chōōəlē] *ad* (*almost*) pratiquement; **it is ~ impossible** c'est quasiment impossible.
virtue [vûr'chōō] *n* vertu *f*; (*advantage*) mérite *m*, avantage *m*; **by ~ of** par le fait de.
virtuoso [vûrchōō'sō] *n* virtuose *m/f*.
virtuous [vûr'chōōəs] *a* vertueux(euse).
virulent [vir'yələnt] *a* virulent(e).
virus [vī'rəs] *n* (*also COMPUT*) virus *m*.
visa [vē'zə] *n* visa *m*.
vis-à-vis [vēzâvē'] *prep* vis-à-vis de.
viscount [vī'kount] *n* vicomte *m*.
viscous [vis'kəs] *a* visqueux(euse), gluant(e).
vise [vīs] *n* (*US TECH*) étau *m*.
visibility [vizəbil'ətē] *n* visibilité *f*.
visible [viz'əbəl] *a* visible; **~ exports/imports** exportations/importations *fpl* visibles.
visibly [viz'əblē] *ad* visiblement.
vision [vizh'ən] *n* (*sight*) vue *f*, vision *f*; (*foresight, in dream*) vision.
visionary [vizh'ənärē] *n* visionnaire *m/f*.
visit [viz'it] *n* visite *f*; (*stay*) séjour *m* ♦ *vt* (*person*) rendre visite à; (*place*) visiter; **on a private/official ~** en visite privée/officielle.
visiting [viz'iting] *a* (*speaker, team*) invité(e), de l'extérieur.
visiting card *n* carte *f* de visite.
visiting hours *npl* heures *fpl* de visite.
visiting professor *n* ≈ professeur associé.
visitor [viz'itûr] *n* visiteur/euse; (*in hotel*) client/e.
visitors' book *n* livre *m* d'or; (*in hotel*) registre *m*.
visor [vī'zûr] *n* visière *f*.
VISTA [vis'tə] *n abbr* (= *Volunteers in Service to America*) programme d'assistance bénévole aux régions pauvres.
vista [vis'tə] *n* vue *f*, perspective *f*.
visual [vizh'ōōəl] *a* visuel(le).

visual aid *n* support visuel (pour l'enseignement).

visual display unit (VDU) *n* console *f* de visualisation, visuel *m*.

visualize [vizh'ōōəlīz] *vt* se représenter; *(foresee)* prévoir.

visually [vizh'ōōəlē] *ad* visuellement; ~ **handicapped** handicapé(e) visuel(le).

vital [vit'əl] *a* vital(e); **of** ~ **importance (to sb/sth)** d'une importance capitale (pour qn/qch).

vitality [vītal'itē] *n* vitalité *f*.

vitally [vi'təlē] *ad* extrêmement.

vital statistics *npl* (*of population*) statistiques *fpl* démographiques; (*col: woman's*) mensurations *fpl*.

vitamin [vī'təmin] *n* vitamine *f*.

vitiate [vish'ēāt] *vt* vicier.

vitreous [vit'rēəs] *a* (*china*) vitreux(euse); (*enamel*) vitrifié(e).

vitriolic [vitrēāl'ik] *a* (*fig*) venimeux(euse).

viva [vē'və] *n* (*also:* ~ **voce**) (examen) oral.

vivacious [vivā'shəs] *a* animé(e), qui a de la vivacité.

vivacity [vivas'itē] *n* vivacité *f*.

vivid [viv'id] *a* (*account*) frappant(e); (*light, imagination*) vif(vive).

vividly [viv'idlē] *ad* (*describe*) d'une manière vivante; (*remember*) de façon précise.

vivisection [vivisek'shən] *n* vivisection *f*.

vixen [vik'sən] *n* renarde *f*; (*pej: woman*) mégère *f*.

viz *abbr* (= *videlicet: namely*) à savoir, c. à d.

VLF *abbr* = *very low frequency*.

V-neck [vē'nek] *n* décolleté *m* en V.

VOA *n abbr* (= *Voice of America*) voix *f* de l'Amérique (*émissions de radio à destination de l'étranger*).

vocabulary [vōkab'yəlärē] *n* vocabulaire *m*.

vocal [vō'kəl] *a* vocal(e); (*articulate*) qui n'hésite pas à s'exprimer, qui sait faire entendre ses opinions; ~**s** *npl* voix *fpl*.

vocal cords *npl* cordes vocales.

vocalist [vō'kəlist] *n* chanteur/euse.

vocation [vōkā'shən] *n* vocation *f*.

vocational [vōkā'shənəl] *a* professionnel(le); ~ **guidance/training** orientation/formation professionnelle; ~ **guidance counselor** (*US*) conseiller/ère d'orientation (professionnelle).

vociferous [vōsif'ūrəs] *a* bruyant(e).

vodka [vâd'kə] *n* vodka *f*.

vogue [vōg] *n* mode *f*; (*popularity*) vogue *f*; **to be in** ~ être en vogue *or* à la mode.

voice [vois] *n* voix *f*; (*opinion*) avis *m* ♦ *vt* (*opinion*) exprimer, formuler; **in a loud/soft** ~ à voix haute/basse; **to give** ~ **to** exprimer.

void [void] *n* vide *m* ♦ *a* (*invalid*) nul(le); (*empty*): ~ **of** vide de, dépourvu(e) de.

voile [voil] *n* voile *m* (*tissu*).

vol. *abbr* (= *volume*) vol.

volatile [vâl'ətəl] *a* volatil(e); (*fig*) versatile.

volcanic [vâlkan'ik] *a* volcanique.

volcano, ~**es** [vâlkā'nō] *n* volcan *m*.

volition [vōlish'ən] *n*: **of one's own** ~ de son propre gré.

volley [vâl'ē] *n* (*of gunfire*) salve *f*; (*of stones etc*) pluie *f*, volée *f*; (*TENNIS etc*) volée *f*.

volleyball [vâl'ēbôl] *n* volley(-ball) *m*.

volt [vōlt] *n* volt *m*.

voltage [vōl'tij] *n* tension *f*, voltage *m*; **high/low** ~ haute/basse tension.

voluble [vâl'yəbəl] *a* volubile.

volume [vâl'yōōm] *n* volume *m*; (*of tank*) capacité *f*; ~ **one/two** (*of book*) tome un/deux; **his expression spoke** ~**s** son expression en disait long.

volume control *n* (*RADIO, TV*) bouton *m* de réglage du volume.

volume discount *n* (*COMM*) remise *f* sur la quantité.

voluminous [vəlōō'minəs] *a* volumineux(euse).

voluntarily [vâləntär'ilē] *ad* volontairement; bénévolement.

voluntary [vâl'əntärē] *a* volontaire; (*unpaid*) bénévole.

voluntary liquidation *n* (*COMM*) dépôt *m* de bilan.

voluntary redundancy *n* (*Brit*) départ *m* volontaire (*en cas de licenciements*).

volunteer [vâləntēr'] *n* volontaire *m/f* ♦ *vi* (*MIL*) s'engager comme volontaire; **to** ~ **to do** se proposer pour faire.

voluptuous [vəlup'chōōəs] *a* voluptueux(euse).

vomit [vâm'it] *n* vomissure *f* ♦ *vt, vi* vomir.

vote [vōt] *n* vote *m*, suffrage *m*; (*cast*) voix *f*, vote; (*franchise*) droit *m* de vote ♦ *vt* (*bill*) voter; (*chairman*) élire ♦ *vi* voter; **to put sth to the** ~, **to take a** ~ **on sth** mettre qch aux voix, procéder à un vote sur qch; ~ **for** *or* **in favor of/against** vote pour/contre; **to** ~ **to do sth** voter en faveur de faire qch; ~ **of censure** motion *f* de censure; ~ **of thanks** discours *m* de remerciement.

voter [vō'tûr] *n* électeur/trice.

voting [vō'ting] *n* scrutin *m*.

voting right *n* droit *m* de vote.

vouch [vouch]: **to** ~ **for** *vt fus* se porter garant de.

voucher [vou'chûr] *n* (*for meal, gasoline*) bon *m*; (*receipt*) reçu *m*; **travel** ~ bon *m* de transport.

vow [vou] *n* vœu *m*, serment *m* ♦ *vi* jurer; **to take** *or* **make a** ~ **to do sth** faire le vœu de faire qch.

vowel [vou'əl] *n* voyelle *f*.

voyage [voi'ij] *n* voyage *m* par mer, traversée *f*.

VP *n abbr* = **vice-president**.

vs *abbr* (= *versus*) c.

VSO *n abbr* (*Brit*): = *Voluntary Service Overseas*) ≈ coopération civile.

VT *abbr* (*US MAIL*) = *Vermont*.

VTR *n abbr* = **video tape recorder**.

vulgar [vul'gûr] *a* vulgaire.

vulgarity [vulgar'itē] *n* vulgarité *f*.

vulnerability [vulnûrəbil'ətē] *n* vulnérabilité *f*.

vulnerable [vul'nûrəbəl] *a* vulnérable.

vulture [vul'chûr] *n* vautour *m*.

W

W, w [dub'əlyōō] *n* (*letter*) W, w *m*; **W for William** W comme William.

W [dub'əlyōō] *abbr* (= *west*) O; (*ELEC*: = *watt*) W.

WA *abbr* (*US MAIL*) = Washington.

wad [wâd] *n* (*of absorbent cotton, paper*) tampon *m*; (*of banknotes etc*) liasse *f*.

wadding [wâd'ing] *n* rembourrage *m*.

waddle [wâd'əl] *vi* se dandiner.

wade [wād] *vi*: **to ~ through** marcher dans, patauger dans ♦ *vt* passer à gué.

wading pool [wād'ing pōōl] *n* (*US*) petit bassin.

wafer [wā'fûr] *n* (*CULIN*) gaufrette *f*; (*REL*) pain *m* d'hostie; (*COMPUT*) tranche *f* (de silicium).

wafer-thin [wā'fûrthin'] *a* ultra-mince, mince comme du papier à cigarette.

waffle [wâf'əl] *n* (*CULIN*) gaufre *f*; (*col*) rabâchage *m*; remplissage *m* ♦ *vi* parler pour ne rien dire; faire du remplissage.

waffle iron *n* gaufrier *m*.

waft [waft] *vt* porter ♦ *vi* flotter.

wag [wag] *vt* agiter, remuer ♦ *vi* remuer; **the dog ~ged its tail** le chien a remué la queue.

wage [wāj] *n* (*also*: **~s**) salaire *m*, paye *f* ♦ *vt*: **to ~ war** faire la guerre; **a day's ~s** un jour de salaire.

wage claim *n* demande *f* d'augmentation de salaire.

wage differential *n* éventail *m* des salaires.

wage earner *n* salarié/e; (*breadwinner*) soutien *m* de famille.

wage freeze *n* blocage *m* des salaires.

wage packet *n* (*Brit*) (enveloppe *f* de) paye *f*.

wager [wā'jûr] *n* pari *m* ♦ *vt* parier.

waggle [wag'əl] *vt*, *vi* remuer.

wagon, (*Brit*) **waggon** [wag'ən] *n* (*horse-drawn*) chariot *m*; (*Brit RAIL*) wagon *m* (de marchandises).

wail [wāl] *n* gémissement *m*; (*of siren*) hurlement *m* ♦ *vi* gémir; hurler.

waist [wāst] *n* taille *f*, ceinture *f*.

waistcoat [wāst'kōt] *n* (*Brit*) gilet *m*.

waistline [wāst'lin] *n* (tour *m* de) taille *f*.

wait [wāt] *n* attente *f* ♦ *vi* attendre; **to ~ for sb/sth** attendre qn/qch; **to keep sb ~ing** faire attendre qn; **~ a minute!** un instant!; **"repairs while you ~"** "réparations minute"; **I can't ~ to ...** (*fig*) je meurs d'envie de ...; **to lie in ~ for** guetter.

wait behind *vi* rester (à attendre).

wait on *vt fus* servir.

wait up *vi* attendre, ne pas se coucher; **don't ~ up for me** ne m'attendez pas pour aller vous coucher.

waiter [wā'tûr] *n* garçon *m* (de café), serveur *m*.

waiting list [wāt'ing list] *n* liste *f* d'attente.

waiting room *n* salle *f* d'attente.

waitress [wā'tris] *n* serveuse *f*.

waive [wāv] *vt* renoncer à, abandonner.

waiver [wā'vûr] *n* dispense *f*.

wake [wāk] *vb* (*pt* **woke, ~d**, *pp* **woken, ~d** [wōk, wō'kən]) *vt* (*also*: ~ **up**) réveiller ♦ *vi* (*also*: ~ **up**) se réveiller ♦ *n* (*for dead person*) veillée *f* mortuaire; (*NAUT*) sillage *m*; **to ~ up to sth** (*fig*) se rendre compte de qch; **in the ~ of** (*fig*) à la suite de; **to follow in sb's ~** (*fig*) marcher sur les traces de qn.

waken [wā'kən] *vt*, *vi* = **wake**.

Wales [wālz] *n* pays *m* de Galles.

walk [wôk] *n* promenade *f*; (*short*) petit tour; (*gait*) démarche *f*; (*pace*): **at a quick ~** d'un pas rapide; (*path*) chemin *m*; (*in park etc*) allée *f* ♦ *vi* marcher; (*for pleasure, exercise*) se promener ♦ *vt* (*distance*) faire à pied; (*dog*) promener; **10 minutes' ~ from** à 10 minutes de marche de; **to go for a ~** se promener; faire un tour; **I'll ~ you home** je vais vous raccompagner chez vous; **from all ~s of life** de toutes conditions sociales.

walk out *vi* (*go out*) sortir; (*as protest*) partir (en signe de protestation); (*strike*) se mettre en grève; **to ~ out on sb** quitter qn.

walker [wôk'ûr] *n* (*person*) marcheur/euse.

walkie-talkie [wô'kētô'kē] *n* talkie-walkie *m*.

walking [wô'king] *n* marche *f* à pied; **it's within ~ distance** on peut y aller à pied.

walking shoes *npl* chaussures *fpl* de marche.

walking stick *n* canne *f*.

walk-on [wôk'ân] *a* (*THEATER*: *part*) de figurant/e.

walkout [wôk'out] *n* (*of workers*) grève-surprise *f*.

walkover [wôk'ōvûr] *n* (*col*) victoire *f* or examen *m* etc facile.

walkway [wôk'wā] *n* promenade *f*, cheminement piéton.

wall [wôl] *n* mur *m*; (*of tunnel, cave*) paroi *f*; **to go to the ~** (*fig: firm etc*) faire faillite.

wall in *vt* (*garden etc*) entourer d'un mur.

wall cupboard *n* placard mural.

walled [wôld] *a* (*city*) fortifié(e).

wallet [wâl'it] *n* portefeuille *m*.

wallflower [wôl'flouûr] *n* giroflée *f*; **to be a ~** (*fig*) faire tapisserie.

wall hanging *n* tenture (murale), tapisserie *f*.

wallop [wâl'əp] *vt* (*col*) taper sur, cogner.

wallow [wâl'ō] *vi* se vautrer; **to ~ in one's grief** se complaire à sa douleur.

wallpaper [wôl'pāpûr] *n* papier peint.

wall-to-wall [wôl'təwôl'] *a*: ~ **carpeting** moquette *f*.

wally [wâ'lē] *n* (*Brit col*) imbécile *m/f*.

walnut [wôl'nut] *n* noix *f*; (*tree*) noyer *m*.

walrus, *pl* ~ *or* **~es** [wôl'rəs] *n* morse *m*.

waltz [wôlts] *n* valse *f* ♦ *vi* valser.

wan [wân] *a* pâle; triste.

wand [wând] *n* (*also*: **magic ~**) baguette *f* (magique).

wander [wân'dûr] *vi* (*person*) errer, aller sans but; (*thoughts*) vagabonder; (*river*) serpenter ♦ *vt* errer dans.

wanderer [wân'dûrûr] *n* vagabond/e.

wandering [wân'dûring] *a* (*tribe*) nomade;

(*minstrel, actor*) ambulant(e).
wane [wān] *vi* (*moon*) décroître; (*reputation*)
décliner.
wangle [wang'gəl] (*col*) *vt* se débrouiller pour
avoir; carotter ♦ *n* combine *f*, magouille *f*.
want [wônt] *vt* vouloir; (*need*) avoir besoin
de; (*lack*) manquer de ♦ *n* (*poverty*) pauvreté *f*, besoin *m*; ~**s** *npl* (*needs*) besoins *mpl*;
for ~ **of** par manque de, faute de; **to** ~ **to
do** vouloir faire; **to** ~ **sb to do** vouloir que
qn fasse; **you're** ~**ed on the phone** on vous
demande au téléphone; **"cook** ~**ed"** "on demande un cuisinier".
want ads *npl* (*US*) petites annonces.
wanting [wôn'ting] *a*: **to be** ~ (**in**) manquer
(de); **to be found** ~ ne pas être à la hauteur.
wanton [wân'tən] *a* capricieux(euse); dé-
vergondé(e).
war [wôr] *n* guerre *f*; **to go to** ~ se mettre en
guerre.
warble [wôr'bəl] *n* (*of bird*) gazouillis *m* ♦ *vi*
gazouiller.
war cry *n* cri *m* de guerre.
ward [wôrd] *n* (*in hospital*) salle *f*; (*LAW*:
child) pupille *m/f*.
ward off *vt* parer, éviter.
warden [wôr'dən] *n* (*US: of prison*) directeur/
trice; (*of park, game reserve*) gardien/ne;
(*Brit: of institution*) directeur/trice; (*also:*
traffic ~) contractuel/le.
warder [wôr'dûr] *n* (*Brit*) gardien *m* de prison.
wardrobe [wôrd'rōb] *n* (*closet*) armoire *f*;
(*clothes*) garde-robe *f*; (*THEATER*) costumes
mpl.
warehouse [wär'hous] *n* entrepôt *m*.
wares [wärz] *npl* marchandises *fpl*.
warfare [wôr'fär] *n* guerre *f*.
war game *n* jeu *m* de stratégie militaire.
warhead [wôr'hed] *n* (*MIL*) ogive *f*.
warily [wär'ilē] *ad* avec prudence, avec précaution.
warlike [wôr'līk] *a* guerrier(ière).
warm [wôrm] *a* chaud(e); (*person, greeting,
welcome, applause*) chaleureux(euse);
(*supporter*) ardent(e), enthousiaste; **it's** ~ il
fait chaud; **I'm** ~ j'ai chaud; **to keep sth** ~
tenir qch au chaud; **with my** ~**est thanks/
congratulations** avec mes remerciements/
mes félicitations les plus sincères.
warm up *vi* (*person, room*) se réchauffer;
(*water*) chauffer; (*athlete, discussion*)
s'échauffer ♦ *vt* réchauffer; chauffer; (*engine*) faire chauffer.
warm-blooded [wôrm'blud'id] *a* (*ZOOL*) à
sang chaud.
war memorial *n* monument *m* aux morts.
warm-hearted [wôrm'hâr'tid] *a*
affectueux(euse).
warmly [wôrm'lē] *ad* chaudement; chaleureusement.
warmonger [wôr'munggûr] *n* belliciste *m/f*.
warmongering [wôr'munggûring] *n* propagande *f* belliciste, bellicisme *m*.
warmth [wôrmth] *n* chaleur *f*.
warm-up [wôrm'up] *n* (*SPORT*) période *f*
d'échauffement.
warn [wôrn] *vt* avertir, prévenir; **to** ~ **sb not
to do sth** *or* **against doing sth** prévenir qn

de ne pas faire qch.
warning [wôr'ning] *n* avertissement *m*; (*notice*) avis *m*; **without (any)** ~ (*suddenly*)
inopinément; (*without notifying*) sans prévenir; **gale** ~ (*METEOROLOGY*) avis de grand
vent.
warning light *n* avertisseur lumineux.
warning triangle *n* (*AUT*) triangle *m* de pré-
signalisation.
warp [wôrp] *n* (*TEXTILES*) chaîne *f* ♦ *vi* (*wood*)
travailler, se voiler *or* gauchir ♦ *vt* voiler;
(*fig*) pervertir.
warpath [wôr'path] *n*: **to be on the** ~ (*fig*)
être sur le sentier de la guerre.
warped [wôrpt] *a* (*wood*) gauchi(e); (*fig*)
perverti(e).
warrant [wôr'ənt] *n* (*guarantee*) garantie *f*;
(*LAW: to arrest*) mandat *m* d'arrêt; (: *to
search*) mandat de perquisition ♦ *vt* (*justify,
merit*) justifier.
warrant officer *n* (*MIL*) adjudant *m*; (*NAUT*)
premier-maître *m*.
warranty [wôr'əntē] *n* garantie *f*; **under** ~
(*COMM*) sous garantie.
warren [wôr'ən] *n* (*of rabbits*) terriers *mpl*,
garenne *f*.
warring [wô'ring] *a* (*nations*) en guerre;
(*interests etc*) contradictoire, opposé(e).
warrior [wôr'ēûr] *n* guerrier/ière.
Warsaw [wôr'sô] *n* Varsovie.
warship [wôr'ship] *n* navire *m* de guerre.
wart [wôrt] *n* verrue *f*.
wartime [wôr'tīm] *n*: **in** ~ en temps de
guerre.
wary [wär'ē] *a* prudent(e); **to be** ~ **about** *or*
of doing sth hésiter beaucoup à faire qch.
was [wuz] *pt of* **be**.
wash [wâsh] *vt* laver; (*sweep, carry: sea etc*)
emporter, entraîner; (: *ashore*) rejeter ♦ *vi*
se laver ♦ *n* (*paint*) badigeon *m*; (*washing
program*) lavage *m*; (*of ship*) sillage *m*; **to
give sth a** ~ laver qch; **to have a** ~ se laver, faire sa toilette; **he was** ~**ed overboard**
il a été emporté par une vague.
wash away *vt* (*stain*) enlever au lavage;
(*subj: river etc*) emporter.
wash down *vt* laver; laver à grande eau.
wash off *vi* partir au lavage.
wash up *vi* faire la vaisselle; (*US: have a
wash*) se débarbouiller.
Wash. *abbr* (*US*) = *Washington*.
washable [wâsh'əbəl] *a* lavable.
washbag [wâsh'bag] *n* trousse *f* de toilette.
washbasin [wâsh'bāsin] *n* lavabo *m*.
washcloth [wâsh'klôth] *n* (*US*) gant *m* de toilette.
washer [wâsh'ûr] *n* (*TECH*) rondelle *f*, joint *m*.
washing [wâsh'ing] *n* (*Brit: linen etc*) lessive
f.
washing line *n* (*Brit*) corde *f* à linge.
washing machine *n* machine *f* à laver.
washing powder *n* (*Brit*) lessive *f* (en poudre).
Washington [wâsh'ingtən] *n* (*city, state*)
Washington *m*.
washing-up [wâsh'ingup'] *n* (*Brit*) vaisselle *f*.
washing-up liquid *n* (*Brit*) produit *m* pour
la vaisselle.
wash-out [wâsh'out] *n* (*col*) désastre *m*.

washroom [wâsh'rōōm] *n* toilettes *fpl*.
wasn't [wuz'ənt] = **was not**.
Wasp, WASP [wâsp] *n abbr* (*US col:* = *White Anglo-Saxon Protestant*) surnom, *souvent péjoratif, donné à l'américain de souche anglo-saxonne, aisé et de tendance conservatrice.*
wasp [wâsp] *n* guêpe *f*.
waspish [wâs'pish] *a* irritable.
wastage [wãs'tij] *n* gaspillage *m*; (*in manufacturing, transport etc*) déchet *m*.
waste [wãst] *n* gaspillage *m*; (*of time*) perte *f*; (*garbage*) déchets *mpl*; (*also:* **household ~**) ordures *fpl* ♦ *a* (*material*) de rebut; (*energy, heat*) perdu(e); (*food*) inutilisé(e); (*land, ground: in city*) à l'abandon; (*: in country*) inculte, en friche ♦ *vt* gaspiller; (*time, opportunity*) perdre; **~s** *npl* étendue *f* désertique; **it's a ~ of money** c'est de l'argent jeté en l'air; **to go to ~** être gaspillé(e); **to lay ~** (*destroy*) dévaster.
  waste away *vi* dépérir.
wastebin [wãst'bin] *n* (*Brit*) corbeille *f* à papier; (*in kitchen*) boîte *f* à ordures.
wasteful [wãst'fəl] *a* gaspilleur(euse); (*process*) peu économique.
waste ground *n* (*Brit*) terrain *m* vague.
wasteland [wãst'land] *n* terres *fpl* à l'abandon; (*in town*) terrain(s) *m*(*pl*) vague(s).
wastepaper basket [wãst'pāpûr bas'kit] *n* corbeille *f* à papier.
waste products *n* (*INDUSTRY*) déchets *mpl* (de fabrication).
watch [wâch] *n* montre *f*; (*act of watching*) surveillance *f*; guet *m*; (*guard: MIL*) sentinelle *f*; (*: NAUT*) homme *m* de quart; (*NAUT: spell of duty*) quart *m* ♦ *vt* (*look at*) observer; (*: match, program*) regarder; (*spy on, guard*) surveiller; (*be careful of*) faire attention à ♦ *vi* regarder; (*keep guard*) monter la garde; **to keep a close ~ on sb/sth** surveiller qn/qch de près; **~ what you're doing** fais attention à ce que tu fais.
  watch out *vi* faire attention.
watchband [wâch'band] *n* (*US*) bracelet *m* de montre.
watchdog [wâch'dôg] *n* chien *m* de garde; (*fig*) gardien/ne.
watchful [wâch'fəl] *a* attentif(ive), vigilant(e).
watchmaker [wâch'mākûr] *n* horloger/ère.
watchman [wâch'mən] *n* gardien *m*; (*also:* **night ~**) veilleur *m* de nuit.
watch stem *n* (*US*) remontoir *m*.
watch strap *n* bracelet *m* de montre.
watchword [wâch'wûrd] *n* mot *m* de passe.
water [wô'tûr] *n* eau *f* ♦ *vt* (*plant*) arroser ♦ *vi* (*eyes*) larmoyer; **a drink of ~** un verre d'eau; **in British ~s** dans les eaux territoriales Britanniques; **to pass ~** uriner; **to make sb's mouth ~** mettre l'eau à la bouche de qn.
  water down *vt* (*milk*) couper d'eau; (*fig: story*) édulcorer.
water closet *n* (*Brit*) w.-c. *mpl*, waters *mpl*.
watercolor, (*Brit*) **watercolour** [wô'tûrkulûr] *n* aquarelle *f*; **~s** *npl* couleurs *fpl* pour aquarelle.
water-cooled [wô'tûrkōōld] *a* à refroidissement par eau.

watercress [wô'tûrkres] *n* cresson *m* (de fontaine).
waterfall [wô'tûrfôl] *n* chute *f* d'eau.
waterfront [wô'tûrfrunt] *n* (*seafront*) front *m* de mer; (*at docks*) quais *mpl*.
water heater *n* chauffe-eau *m*.
water hole *n* mare *f*.
watering can [wô'tûring kan] *n* arrosoir *m*.
water level *n* niveau *m* de l'eau; (*of flood*) niveau des eaux.
water lily *n* nénuphar *m*.
waterline [wô'tûrlīn] *n* (*NAUT*) ligne *f* de flottaison.
waterlogged [wô'tûrlôgd] *a* détrempé(e); imbibé(e) d'eau.
water main *n* canalisation *f* d'eau.
watermark [wô'tûrmârk] *n* (*on paper*) filigrane *m*.
watermelon [wô'tûrmelən] *n* pastèque *f*.
water polo *n* water-polo *m*.
waterproof [wô'tûrprōōf] *a* imperméable.
water-repellent [wô'təripel'ənt] *a* hydrofuge.
watershed [wô'tûrshed] *n* (*GEO*) ligne *f* de partage des eaux; (*fig*) moment *m* critique, point décisif.
water-skiing [wô'tûrskēing] *n* ski *m* nautique.
water softener *n* adoucisseur *m* d'eau.
water tank *n* réservoir *m* d'eau.
watertight [wô'tûrtīt] *a* étanche.
water vapor *n* vapeur *f* d'eau.
waterway [wô'tûrwā] *n* cours *m* d'eau navigable.
waterworks [wô'tûrwûrks] *npl* station *f* hydraulique.
watery [wô'tûrē] *a* (*color*) délavé(e); (*coffee*) trop faible.
WATS *abbr* (*US:* = *Wide Area Telecommunications Service*) service téléphonique longue distance à tarif forfaitaire.
watt [wât] *n* watt *m*.
wattage [wât'ij] *n* puissance *f* or consommation *f* en watts.
wattle [wât'əl] *n* clayonnage *m*.
wave [wāv] *n* vague *f*; (*of hand*) geste *m*, signe *m*; (*RADIO*) onde *f*; (*in hair*) ondulation *f*; (*fig: of enthusiasm, strikes etc*) vague ♦ *vi* faire signe de la main; (*flag*) flotter au vent ♦ *vt* (*handkerchief*) agiter; (*stick*) brandir; (*hair*) onduler; **to ~ goodbye to sb** dire au revoir de la main à qn; **short/medium ~** (*RADIO*) ondes courtes/moyennes; **long ~** (*RADIO*) grandes ondes; **the new ~** (*CINEMA, MUS*) la nouvelle vague.
wave aside, wave away *vt* (*person*): **to ~ sb aside** faire signe à qn de s'écarter; (*fig: suggestion, objection*) rejeter, repousser; (*: doubts*) chasser.
waveband [wāv'band] *n* bande *f* de fréquences.
wavelength [wāv'lengkth] *n* longueur *f* d'ondes.
waver [wā'vûr] *vi* vaciller; (*voice*) trembler; (*person*) hésiter.
wavy [wā'vē] *a* ondulé(e); onduleux(euse).
wax [waks] *n* cire *f*; (*for skis*) fart *m* ♦ *vt* cirer; (*car*) lustrer ♦ *vi* (*moon*) croître.
waxen [wak'sən] *a* cireux(euse).
wax paper *n* papier sulfurisé.
waxworks [waks'wûrks] *npl* personnages *mpl*

de cire; musée *m* de cire.

way [wā] *n* chemin *m*, voie *f*; (*path, access*) passage *m*; (*distance*) distance *f*; (*direction*) chemin, direction *f*; (*manner*) façon *f*, manière *f*; (*habit*) habitude *f*, façon; (*condition*) état *m*; **which ~?** — **this ~** par où *or* de quel côté? — par ici; **to crawl one's ~ to ...** ramper jusqu'à ...; **to lie one's ~ out of it** s'en sortir par un mensonge; **to lose one's ~** perdre son chemin; **on the ~ (to)** en route (pour); **to be on one's ~** être en route; **to be in the ~** bloquer le passage; (*fig*) gêner; **to keep out of sb's ~** éviter qn; **it's a long ~ away** c'est loin d'ici; **the village is rather out of the ~** le village est plutôt à l'écart *or* isolé; **to go out of one's ~ to do** (*fig*) se donner beaucoup de mal pour faire; **to be under ~** (*work, project*) être en cours; **to make ~ (for sb/sth)** faire place (à qn/qch), s'écarter pour laisser passer (qn/qch); **to get one's own ~** arriver à ses fins; **put it the right ~ up** (*Brit*) mettez-le dans le bon sens; **to be the wrong ~ around** être à l'envers, ne pas être dans le bon sens; **he's in a bad ~** il va mal; **in a ~ d'un côté; in some ~s** à certains égards; d'un côté; **in the ~ of** en fait de, comme; **by ~ of** (*through*) en passant par, via; (*as a sort of*) en guise de; **~ in** entrée *f*; **~ out** sortie *f*; **the ~ back** le chemin du retour; **this ~ and that** par-ci par-là; **"give ~"** (*Brit AUT*) "cédez la priorité"; **no ~!** (*col*) pas question!

waybill [wā'bil] *n* (*COMM*) récépissé *m*.

waylay [wālā'] *vt irg* attaquer; (*fig*): **I got waylaid** quelqu'un m'a accroché.

wayside [wā'sīd] *n* bord *m* de la route; **to fall by the ~** (*fig*) abandonner; (*morally*) quitter le droit chemin.

way station *n* (*US: RAIL*) petite gare; (*: fig*) étape *f*.

wayward [wā'wûrd] *a* capricieux(euse), entêté(e).

WC *n abbr* (*Brit:* = *water closet*) w.-c. *mpl*, waters *mpl*.

WCC *n abbr* (= *World Council of Churches*) COE *m* (= *Conseil œcuménique des Églises*).

we [wē] *pl pronoun* nous.

weak [wēk] *a* faible; (*health*) fragile; (*beam etc*) peu solide; (*tea, coffee*) léger(ère); **to grow ~(er)** s'affaiblir, faiblir.

weaken [wē'kən] *vi* faiblir ♦ *vt* affaiblir.

weak-kneed [wēk'nēd] *a* (*fig*) lâche, faible.

weakling [wēk'ling] *n* gringalet *m*; faible *m/f*.

weakly [wēk'lē] *a* chétif(ive) ♦ *ad* faiblement.

weakness [wēk'nis] *n* faiblesse *f*; (*fault*) point *m* faible.

wealth [welth] *n* (*money, resources*) richesse(s) *f(pl)*; (*of details*) profusion *f*.

wealth tax *n* impôt *m* sur la fortune.

wealthy [wel'thē] *a* riche.

wean [wēn] *vt* sevrer.

weapon [wep'ən] *n* arme *f*.

wear [wār] *n* (*use*) usage *m*; (*deterioration through use*) usure *f*; (*clothing*): **sports/baby~** vêtements *mpl* de sport/pour bébés; **evening ~** tenue *f* de soirée ♦ *vb* (*pt* **wore**, *pp* **worn** [wôr, wôrn]) *vt* (*clothes*) porter; (*beard etc*) avoir; (*damage: through use*) user ♦ *vi* (*last*) faire de l'usage; (*rub etc*

through) s'user; **~ and tear** usure *f*; **to ~ a hole in sth** faire (à la longue) un trou dans qch.

wear away *vt* user, ronger ♦ *vi* s'user, être rongé(e).

wear down *vt* user; (*strength*) épuiser.

wear off *vi* disparaître.

wear on *vi* se poursuivre; passer.

wear out *vt* user; (*person, strength*) épuiser.

wearable [wār'əbəl] *a* mettable.

wearily [wē'rilē] *ad* avec lassitude.

weariness [wē'rēnis] *n* épuisement *m*, lassitude *f*.

wearisome [wē'rēsəm] *a* (*tiring*) fatigant(e); (*boring*) ennuyeux(euse).

wear resistant *a* (*US*) solide.

weary [wēr'ē] *a* (*tired*) épuisé(e); (*dispirited*) las(lasse); abattu(e) ♦ *vt* lasser ♦ *vi:* **to ~ of** se lasser de.

weasel [wē'zəl] *n* (*ZOOL*) belette *f*.

weather [weth'ûr] *n* temps *m* ♦ *vt* (*wood*) faire mûrir; (*tempest, crisis*) essuyer, être pris(e) dans; survivre à, tenir le coup durant; **what's the ~ like?** quel temps fait il?; **under the ~** (*fig: ill*) mal fichu(e).

weather-beaten [weth'ûrbētən] *a* (*person*) hâlé(e); (*building*) dégradé(e) par les intempéries.

weather cock *n* girouette *f*.

weather forecast *n* prévisions *fpl* météorologiques, météo *f*.

weatherman [weth'ûrman] *n* météorologue *m*.

weatherproof [weth'ûrproof] *a* (*garment*) imperméable; (*building*) étanche.

weather report *n* bulletin *m* météo, météo *f*.

weather strip(ping) [weth'ûr strip('ing)] *n* bourrelet *m*.

weather vane *n* = **weather cock**.

weave [wēv] *pt* **wove**, *pp* **woven** [wēv, wōv, wō'vən] *vt* (*cloth*) tisser; (*basket*) tresser ♦ *vi* (*fig: pt, pp* **~d:** *move in and out*) se faufiler.

weaver [wē'vûr] *n* tisserand/e.

weaving [wē'ving] *n* tissage *m*.

web [web] *n* (*of spider*) toile *f*; (*on foot*) palmure *f*; (*fabric, also fig*) tissu *m*.

webbed [webd] *a* (*foot*) palmé(e).

webbing [web'ing] *n* (*on chair*) sangles *fpl*.

wed [wed] *vt* (*pt, pp* **wedded**) épouser ♦ *n:* **the newly~s** les jeunes mariés.

Wed. *abbr* (= **Wednesday**) me.

we'd [wēd] = **we had**, **we would**.

wedded [wed'id] *pt, pp of* **wed**.

wedding [wed'ing] *n* mariage *m*.

wedding anniversary *n* anniversaire *m* de mariage; **silver/golden ~** noces *fpl* d'argent/d'or.

wedding day *n* jour *m* du mariage.

wedding dress *n* robe *f* de mariage.

wedding present *n* cadeau *m* de mariage.

wedding ring *n* alliance *f*.

wedge [wej] *n* (*of wood etc*) coin *m*; (*under door etc*) cale *f*; (*of cake*) part *f* ♦ *vt* (*fix*) caler; (*push*) enfoncer, coincer.

wedge-heeled shoes [wej'hēld shooz'] *npl* chaussures *fpl* à semelles compensées.

wedlock [wed'lâk] *n* (union *f* du) mariage *m*.

Wednesday [wenz'dā] *n* mercredi *m*; *for*

phrases see also **Tuesday.**

wee [wē] *a* (*Scottish*) petit(e); tout(e) petit(e).

weed [wēd] *n* mauvaise herbe ♦ *vt* désherber.

weedkiller [wēd'kilûr] *n* désherbant *m*.

weedy [wē'dē] *a* (*man*) gringalet.

week [wēk] *n* semaine *f*; **once/twice a** ~ une fois/deux fois par semaine; **in two** ~s' **time** dans quinze jours; **Tuesday** ~, **a** ~ **from Tuesday** mardi en huit.

weekday [wēk'dā] *n* jour *m* de semaine; (*COMM*) jour ouvrable; **on** ~s en semaine.

weekend [wēk'end] *n* week-end *m*.

weekend case *n* sac *m* de voyage.

weekly [wēk'lē] *ad* une fois par semaine, chaque semaine ♦ *a*, *n* hebdomadaire (*m*).

weep, *pt*, *pp* **wept** [wēp, wept] *vi* (*person*) pleurer; (*MED*: *wound etc*) suinter.

weeping willow [wē'ping wil'ō] *n* saule pleureur.

weft [weft] *n* (*TEXTILES*) trame *f*.

weigh [wā] *vt*, *vi* peser; **to** ~ **anchor** lever l'ancre; **to** ~ **the pros and cons** peser le pour et le contre.

weigh down *vt* (*branch*) faire plier; (*fig*: *with worry*) accabler.

weigh out *vt* (*goods*) peser.

weigh up *vt* examiner.

weighing machine [wā'ing məshēn'] *n* balance *f*, bascule *f*.

weight [wāt] *n* poids *m* ♦ *vt* alourdir; (*fig*: *factor*) pondérer; **sold by** ~ vendu au poids; **to put on/lose** ~ grossir/maigrir; ~s **and measures** poids et mesures.

weighting [wā'ting] *n*: ~ **allowance** indemnité *f* de résidence.

weightlessness [wāt'lisnis] *n* apesanteur *f*.

weight lifter [wāt' liftûr] *n* haltérophile *m*.

weighty [wā'tē] *a* lourd(e).

weir [wēr] *n* barrage *m*.

weird [wērd] *a* bizarre; (*eerie*) surnaturel(le).

welcome [wel'kəm] *a* bienvenu(e) ♦ *n* accueil *m* ♦ *vt* accueillir; (*also*: **bid** ~) souhaiter la bienvenue à; (*be glad of*) se réjouir de; **to be** ~ être le(la) bienvenu(e); **to make sb** ~ faire bon accueil à qn; **you're** ~ **to try** vous pouvez essayer si vous voulez; **you're** ~! (*after thanks*) de rien, il n'y a pas de quoi.

welcoming [wel'kəming] *a* accueillant(e); (*speech*) d'accueil.

weld [weld] *n* soudure *f* ♦ *vt* souder.

welder [weld'ûr] *n* (*person*) soudeur *m*.

welding [weld'ing] *n* soudure *f* (autogène).

welfare [wel'fär] *n* bien-être *m*; **to be on** ~ (*US*) recevoir l'aide sociale.

welfare state *n* État-providence *m*.

welfare work *n* travail social.

well [wel] *n* puits *m* ♦ *ad* bien ♦ *a*: **to be** ~ aller bien ♦ *excl* eh bien!; bon!; enfin!; ~ **done!** bravo!; **I don't feel** ~ je ne me sens pas bien; **get** ~ **soon!** remets-toi vite!; **to do** ~ **in sth** bien réussir en *or* dans qch; **to think** ~ **of sb** penser du bien de qn; **as** ~ (*in addition*) aussi, également; **you might as** ~ **tell me** tu ferais aussi bien de me le dire; **as** ~ **as** aussi bien que *or* de; en plus de; ~, **as I was saying** ... donc, comme je disais ....

well up *vi* (*tears, emotions*) monter.

we'll [wēl] = **we will, we shall.**

well-behaved [welbihāvd'] *a* sage,

obéissant(e).

well-being [wel'bē'ing] *n* bien-être *m*.

well-bred [wel'bred'] *a* bien élevé(e).

well-built [wel'bilt'] *a* (*house*) bien construit(e); (*person*) bien bâti(e).

well-chosen [wel'chō'zən] *a* (*remarks, words*) bien choisi(e), pertinent(e).

well-developed [wel'divel'əpt] *a* (*girl*) bien fait(e).

well-disposed [wel'dispōzd'] *a*: ~ **to(wards)** bien disposé(e) envers.

well-dressed [wel'drest'] *a* bien habillé(e), bien vêtu(e).

well-earned [wel'ûrnd'] *a* (*rest*) bien mérité(e).

well-groomed [wel'grōomd] *a* très soigné(e) de sa personne.

well-heeled [wel'hēld'] *a* (*col*: *wealthy*) fortuné(e), riche.

well-informed [wel'infôrmd'] *a* (*having knowledge of sth*) bien renseigné(e); (*having general knowledge*) cultivé(e).

Wellington [wel'ingtən] *n* Wellington.

wellingtons [wel'ingtənz] *npl* (*also*: **wellington boots**) bottes *fpl* de caoutchouc.

well-kept [wel'kept'] *a* (*house, grounds*) bien tenu(e), bien entretenu(e); (*secret*) bien gardé(e); (*hair, hands*) soigné(e).

well-known [wel'nōn'] *a* (*person*) bien connu(e).

well-mannered [wel'man'ûrd] *a* bien élevé(e).

well-meaning [wel'mē'ning] *a* bien intentionné(e).

well-nigh [wel'nī'] *ad*: ~ **impossible** pratiquement impossible.

well-off [wel'ôf'] *a* aisé(e), assez riche.

well-read [wel'red'] *a* cultivé(e).

well-spoken [wel'spō'kən] *a* (*person*) qui parle bien; (*words*) bien choisi(e).

well-stocked [wel'stâkt'] *a* bien approvisionné(e).

well-timed [wel'tīmd'] *a* opportun(e).

well-to-do [wel'tədōō'] *a* aisé(e), assez riche.

well-wisher [wel'wishûr] *n* ami/e, admirateur/trice; **scores of** ~s **had gathered** de nombreux amis et admirateurs s'étaient rassemblés; **letters from** ~s des lettres d'encouragement.

Welsh [welsh] *a* gallois(e) ♦ *n* (*LING*) gallois *m*; **the** ~ *npl* les Gallois.

Welshman, **Welshwoman** [welsh'mən, -wōomən] *n* Gallois/e.

Welsh rarebit [welsh rär'bit] *n* croûte *f* au fromage.

welter [wel'tûr] *n* fatras *m*.

went [went] *pt of* **go.**

wept [wept] *pt*, *pp of* **weep.**

were [wûr] *pt of* **be.**

we're [wēr] = **we are.**

weren't [wûr'ənt] = **were not.**

werewolf, *pl* **-wolves** [wär'wōōlf, -wōōlvz] *n* loup-garou *m*.

west [west] *n* ouest *m* ♦ *a* ouest *inv*, de *or* à l'ouest ♦ *ad* à *or* vers l'ouest; **the W**~ l'Occident *m*, l'Ouest.

westbound [west'bound] *a* (*traffic*) en direction de l'ouest; (*lane*) ouest *inv*.

West Country *n*: **the** ~ le sud-ouest de l'Angleterre.

westerly [wes'tûrlē] *a* (*situation*) à l'ouest; (*wind*) d'ouest.

western [wes'tûrn] *a* occidental(e), de *or* à l'ouest ♦ *n* (*CINEMA*) western *m*.

westernized [wes'tûrnīzd] *a* occidentalisé(e).

West German *a* ouest-allemand(e) ♦ *n* Allemand/e de l'Ouest.

West Germany *n* Allemagne *f* de l'Ouest.

West Indian *a* antillais(e) ♦ *n* Antillais/e.

West Indies [west in'dēz] *npl*: **the** ~ les Antilles *fpl*.

westward(s) [west'wûrd(z)] *ad* vers l'ouest.

wet [wet] *a* (*damp*) humide; (*soaked*) trempé(e); (*rainy*) pluvieux(euse) ♦ *vt*: **to** ~ **one's pants** *or* **o.s.** mouiller sa culotte, faire pipi dans sa culotte; **to get** ~ se mouiller; "~ **paint**" "attention peinture fraîche".

wet blanket *n* (*fig*) rabat-joie *m inv*.

wetness [wet'nis] *n* humidité *f*.

wet suit *n* combinaison *f* de plongée.

we've [wēv] = **we have.**

whack [wak] *vt* donner un grand coup à.

whale [wāl] *n* (*ZOOL*) baleine *f*.

whaler [wā'lûr] *n* (*ship*) balcinier *m*.

wharf, *pl* **wharves** [wôrf, wôrvz] *n* quai *m*.

what [wut] *excl* quoi!, comment! ♦ *a* quel(le) ♦ *pronoun* (*interrogative*) que, prep + quoi; (*relative, indirect: object*) ce que; (: *subject*) ce qui; ~ **are you doing?** que fais-tu?, qu'est-ce que tu fais?; ~ **has happened?** que s'est-il passé?, qu'est-ce qui s'est passé?; ~'**s in there?** qu'y a-t-il là-dedans?, qu'est-ce qu'il y a là-dedans?; **for** ~ **reason?** pour quelle raison?; **I saw** ~ **you did/is on the table** j'ai vu ce que vous avez fait/ce qui est sur la table; **I don't know** ~ **to do** je ne sais pas que *or* quoi faire; ~ **a mess!** quel désordre!; ~ **is his address?** quelle est son adresse?; ~ **will it cost?** combien est-ce que ça coûtera?; ~ **is it called?** comment est-ce que ça s'appelle?; ~ **I want is a cup of tea** ce que je veux, c'est une tasse de thé; ~ **about doing ...?** et si on faisait ...?; ~ **about me?** et moi?

whatever [wutev'ûr] *a*: ~ **book** quel que soit le livre que (*or* qui) + *sub*; n'importe quel livre ♦ *pronoun*: **do** ~ **is necessary** faites (tout) ce qui est nécessaire; ~ **happens** quoi qu'il arrive; **no reason** ~ *or* **whatsoever** pas la moindre raison; **nothing** ~ *or* **whatsoever** rien du tout.

wheat [wēt] *n* blé *m*, froment *m*.

wheat germ *n* germe *m* de blé.

wheatmeal [wēt'mēl] *n* farine bise.

wheedle [wēd'əl] *vt*: **to** ~ **sb into doing sth** cajoler *or* enjôler qn pour qu'il fasse qch; **to** ~ **sth out of sb** obtenir qch de qn par des cajoleries.

wheel [wēl] *n* roue *f*; (*AUT*: *also*: **steering** ~) volant *m*; (*NAUT*) gouvernail *m* ♦ *vt* pousser, rouler ♦ *vi* (*also*: ~ **around**) tourner.

wheelbarrow [wēl'barō] *n* brouette *f*.

wheelbase [wēl'bās] *n* empattement *m*.

wheelchair [wēl'chär] *n* fauteuil roulant.

wheel clamp *n* (*Brit AUT*) sabot *m* (de Denver).

wheeler-dealer [wē'lûrdē'lûr] *n* (*pej*) combinard/e, affairiste *m/f*.

wheeling [wē'ling] *n*: ~ **and dealing** (*pej*) manigances *fpl*, magouilles *fpl*.

wheeze [wēz] *n* respiration bruyante (*d'asthmatique*) ♦ *vi* respirer bruyamment.

when [wen] *ad* quand ♦ *cj* quand, lorsque; (*whereas*) alors que; **on the day** ~ **I met him** le jour où je l'ai rencontré.

whenever [wenev'ûr] *ad* quand donc ♦ *cj* quand; (*every time that*) chaque fois que; **I go** ~ **I can** j'y vais quand *or* chaque fois que je le peux.

where [wär] *ad, cj* où; **this is** ~ c'est là que; ~ **are you from?** d'où venez vous?

whereabouts [wär'əbouts] *ad* où donc ♦ *n*: **sb's** ~ l'endroit où se trouve qn.

whereas [wäraz'] *cj* alors que.

whereby [wärbī'] *ad* (*formal*) par lequel (*or* laquelle *etc*).

whereupon [wärəpân'] *ad* sur quoi, et sur ce.

wherever [wärev'ûr] *ad* où donc ♦ *cj* où que + *sub*; **sit** ~ **you like** asseyez-vous (là) où vous voulez.

wherewithal [wär'withôl] *n*: **the** ~ (**to do sth**) les moyens *mpl* (de faire qch).

whet [wet] *vt* aiguiser.

whether [weth'ûr] *cj* si; **I don't know** ~ **to accept or not** je ne sais pas si je dois accepter ou non; **it's doubtful** ~ il est peu probable que; ~ **you go or not** que vous y alliez ou non.

whey [wā] *n* petit-lait *m*.

which [wich] *a* (*interrogative*) quel(le), *pl* quels(quelles); ~ **one of you?** lequel(laquelle) d'entre vous?; **tell me** ~ **one you want** dis-moi lequel tu veux *or* celui que tu veux ♦ *pronoun* (*interrogative*) lequel(laquelle), *pl* lesquels(lesquelles); (*indirect*) celui(celle) qui (*or* que); (*relative: subject*) qui; (: *object*) que, *prep* + lequel(laquelle) (NB: à + *lequel* = auquel; *de* + *lequel* = duquel); ~ **do you want?** lequel *or* laquelle *etc* veux-tu?; **I don't mind** ~ peu importe lequel; **the apple** ~ **you ate/**~ **is on the table** la pomme que vous avez mangée/qui est sur la table; **the chair on** ~ la chaise sur laquelle; **the book of** ~ le livre dont *or* duquel; **he said he knew,** ~ **is true/I feared** il a dit qu'il le savait, ce qui est vrai/ce que je craignais; **after** ~ après quoi; **in** ~ **case** auquel cas; **by** ~ **time ...** heure (*or* moment) à laquelle(auquel) ..., et à ce moment-là ....

whichever [wichev'ûr] *a*: **take** ~ **book you prefer** prenez le livre que vous préférez, peu importe lequel; ~ **book you take** quel que soit le livre que vous preniez; ~ **way you** de quelque façon que vous + *sub*.

whiff [wif] *n* bouffée *f*; **to catch a** ~ **of sth** sentir l'odeur de qch.

while [wīl] *n* moment *m* ♦ *cj* pendant que; (*as long as*) tant que; (*as, whereas*) alors que; (*though*) quoique + *sub*; **for a** ~ pendant quelque temps; **in a** ~ dans un moment; **all the** ~ pendant tout ce temps-là; **we'll make it worth your** ~ nous vous récompenserons de votre peine.

while away *vt* (*time*) (faire) passer.

whilst [wīlst] *cj* = **while.**

whim [wim] *n* caprice *m*.

whimper [wim'pûr] *n* geignement *m* ♦ *vi*

geindre.

whimsical [wim'zikəl] a (person) capricieux(euse); (look) étrange.

whine [wīn] n gémissement m ◆ vi gémir, geindre; pleurnicher.

whip [wip] n fouet m; (for riding) cravache f; (POL: person) chef m de file (assurant la discipline dans son groupe parlementaire) ◆ vt fouetter; (snatch) enlever (or sortir) brusquement.

whip up vt (cream) fouetter; (col: meal) préparer en vitesse; (stir up: support) stimuler; (: feeling) attiser, aviver.

whiplash [wip'lash] n (MED: also: ~ injury) coup m du lapin.

whipped cream [wipt krēm] n crème fouettée.

whipping boy [wip'ing boi] n (fig) bouc m émissaire.

whip-round [wip'round] n (Brit) collecte f.

whirl [wûrl] n tourbillon m ◆ vt faire tourbillonner; faire tournoyer ◆ vi tourbillonner.

whirlpool [wûrl'pool] n tourbillon m.

whirlwind [wûrl'wind] n tornade f.

whirr [wär] vi bruire; ronronner; vrombir.

whisk [wisk] n (CULIN) fouet m ◆ vt fouetter, battre; **to ~ sb away** or **off** emmener qn rapidement.

whiskers [wis'kûrz] npl (of animal) moustaches fpl; (of man) favoris mpl.

whiskey (US, Ireland), **whisky** (Brit) [wis'kē] n whisky m.

whisper [wis'pûr] n chuchotement m; (fig: of leaves) bruissement m; (rumor) rumeur f ◆ vt, vi chuchoter; **to ~ sth to sb** chuchoter qch à (l'oreille de) qn.

whispering [wis'pûring] n chuchotement(s) m(pl).

whist [wist] n (Brit) whist m.

whistle [wis'əl] n (sound) sifflement m; (object) sifflet m ◆ vi siffler ◆ vt siffler, siffloter.

whistle-stop [wis'əlstâp] a: **to make a ~ tour of** (POL) faire la tournée électorale des petits patelins de.

Whit [wit] n la Pentecôte.

white [wit] a blanc(blanche); (with fear) blême ◆ n blanc m; (person) blanc/blanche; **to turn** or **go ~** (person) pâlir, blêmir; (hair) blanchir; **the ~s** (washing) le linge blanc; **tennis ~s** tenue f de tennis.

whitebait [wit'bāt] n blanchaille f.

white coffee n (Brit) café m au lait, (café) crème m.

white-collar worker [wit'kâl'ûr wûr'kûr] n employé/e de bureau.

white elephant n (fig) objet dispendieux et superflu.

white goods npl (appliances) (gros) électroménager m; (linen etc) linge m de maison.

white-hot [wit'hât'] a (metal) incandescent(e).

white lie n pieux mensonge.

whiteness [wit'nis] n blancheur f.

white noise n son m blanc.

whiteout [wit'out] n jour blanc.

white paper n (POL) livre blanc.

whitewash [wit'wâsh] n (paint) lait m de

chaux ◆ vt blanchir à la chaux; (fig) blanchir.

whiting [wī'ting] n (pl inv) (fish) merlan m.

Whit Monday n le lundi de Pentecôte.

Whitsun [wit'sən] n la Pentecôte.

whittle [wit'əl] vt: **to ~ away**, **~ down** (costs) réduire, rogner.

whizz [wiz] vi aller (or passer) à toute vitesse.

whizz kid n (col) petit prodige.

WHO n abbr (= World Health Organization) OMS f (= Organisation mondiale de la Santé).

who [hoo] pronoun qui.

whodunit [hoodun'it] n (col) roman policier.

whoever [hooev'ûr] pronoun: **~ finds it** celui(celle) qui le trouve (, qui que ce soit), quiconque le trouve; **ask ~ you like** demandez à qui vous voulez; **~ he marries** qui que ce soit or quelle que soit la personne qu'il épouse; **~ told you that?** qui a bien pu vous dire ça?, qui donc vous a dit ça?

whole [hōl] a (complete) entier(ière), tout(e); (not broken) intact(e), complet(ète) ◆ n (total) totalité f; (sth not broken) tout m; **the ~ lot (of it)** tout; **the ~ lot (of them)** tous (sans exception); **the ~ of the time** tout le temps; **the ~ of the town** la ville tout entière; **~ villages were destroyed** des villages entiers ont été détruits; **on the ~**, **as a ~** dans l'ensemble.

wholefoods [hōl'foodz] npl aliments naturels.

wholehearted [hōl'hâr'tid] a sans réserve(s), sincère.

wholemeal [hōl'mēl] a (Brit) = **wholewheat**.

whole milk n (US) lait entier.

whole note n (US) ronde f.

wholesale [hōl'sāl] n (vente f en) gros m ◆ a de gros; (destruction) systématique.

wholesaler [hōl'sālûr] n grossiste m/f.

wholesome [hōl'səm] a sain(e); (advice) salutaire.

wholewheat [hōl'wēt'] a (US: flour, bread) complet(ète).

wholly [hō'lē] ad entièrement, tout à fait.

whom [hoom] pronoun que, prep + qui (check syntax of French verb used); (interrogative) qui; **those to ~ I spoke** ceux à qui j'ai parlé.

whooping cough [woo'ping kôf] n coqueluche f.

whoosh [woosh] n, vi: **the skiers ~ed past**, **the skiers came by with a ~** les skieurs passèrent dans un glissement rapide.

whopper [wâp'ûr] n (col: lie) gros bobard; (: large thing) monstre m, phénomène m.

whopping [wâp'ing] a (col: big) énorme.

whore [hôr] n (col: pej) putain f.

whose [hooz] a: **~ book is this?** à qui est ce livre?; **~ pencil have you taken?** à qui est le crayon que vous avez pris?, c'est le crayon de qui que vous avez pris?; **the man ~ son you rescued** l'homme dont or de qui vous avez sauvé le fils; **the girl ~ sister you were speaking to** la fille à la sœur de qui or laquelle vous parliez ◆ pronoun: **~ is this?** à qui est ceci?; **I know ~ it is** je sais à qui c'est.

Who's Who [hooz' hoo'] n ≈ Bottin Mondain.

why [wī] ad pourquoi ◆ excl eh bien!, tiens!; **the reason ~** la raison pour laquelle; **~ is**

he late? pourquoi est-il en retard?

whyever [wī'evûr] *ad* pourquoi donc, mais pourquoi.

WI *abbr* (*GEO*) = **West Indies**; (*US MAIL*) = *Wisconsin*.

wick [wik] *n* mèche *f* (*de bougie*).

wicked [wik'id] *a* foncièrement mauvais(e), inique; (*mischievous*: *grin*, *look*) espiègle, malicieux(euse); (*terrible*: *prices*, *weather*) épouvantable.

wicker [wik'ûr] *n* osier *m*; (*also*: ~**work**) vannerie *f*.

wicket [wik'it] *n* (*CRICKET*) guichet *m*; espace compris entre les deux guichets.

wide [wīd] *a* large; (*region*, *knowledge*) vaste, très étendu(e); (*choice*) grand(e) ♦ *ad*: **to open** ~ ouvrir tout grand; **to shoot** ~ tirer à côté; **it is 3 meters** ~ cela fait 3 mètres de large.

wide-angle lens [wīd'ang'gəl lenz] *n* objectif *m* grand-angulaire.

wide-awake [wīd'əwāk'] *a* bien éveillé(e).

wide-eyed [wīd'īd] *a* aux yeux écarquillés; (*fig*) naïf(ïve), crédule.

widely [wīd'lē] *ad* (*different*) radicalement; (*spaced*) sur une grande étendue; (*believed*) généralement; **to be** ~ **read** (*author*) être beaucoup lu(e); (*reader*) avoir beaucoup lu, être cultivé(e).

widen [wīd'ən] *vt* élargir.

wideness [wīd'nis] *n* largeur *f*.

wide open *a* grand(e) ouvert(e).

wide-ranging [wīd'rān'jing] *a* (*survey*, *report*) vaste; (*interests*) divers(e).

widespread [wīdspred'] *a* (*belief etc*) très répandu(e).

widow [wid'ō] *n* veuve *f*.

widowed [wid'ōd] *a* (qui est devenu(e)) veuf(veuve).

widower [wid'ōûr] *n* veuf *m*.

width [width] *n* largeur *f*; **it's 7 meters in** ~ cela fait 7 mètres de large.

widthwise [width'wīz] *ad* en largeur.

wield [wēld] *vt* (*sword*) manier; (*power*) exercer.

wife, *pl* **wives** [wīf, wīvz] *n* femme (mariée), épouse *f*.

wig [wig] *n* perruque *f*.

wiggle [wig'əl] *vt* agiter, remuer ♦ *vi* (*loose screw etc*) branler; (*worm*) se tortiller.

wiggly [wig'lē] *a* (*line*) ondulé(e).

wild [wīld] *a* sauvage; (*sea*) déchaîné(e); (*idea*, *life*) fou(folle); extravagant(e); (*col*: *angry*) hors de soi, furieux(euse); (: *enthusiastic*): **to be** ~ **about** être fou(folle) *or* dingue de ♦ *n*: **the** ~ la nature; ~**s** *npl* régions *fpl* sauvages.

wild card *n* (*COMPUT*) caractère *m* de remplacement.

wildcat [wīld'kat] *n* chat *m* sauvage.

wildcat strike *n* grève *f* sauvage.

wilderness [wil'dûrnis] *n* désert *m*, région *f* sauvage.

wildfire [wīld'fīûr] *n*: **to spread like** ~ se répandre comme une traînée de poudre.

wild game reserve *n* (*US*) réserve *f*.

wild-goose chase [wīld'gōōs' chās] *n* (*fig*) fausse piste.

wildlife [wīld'līf] *n* faune *f* (et flore *f*) sau-

vage(s).

wildly [wīld'lē] *ad* (*applaud*) frénétiquement; (*hit*, *guess*) au hasard; (*happy*) follement.

wiles [wīlz] *npl* ruses *fpl*, artifices *mpl*.

wilful [wil'fəl] *a* (*Brit*) = **willful**.

will [wil] *auxiliary vb*: **he** ~ **come** il viendra; **you won't lose it,** ~ **you?** vous ne le perdrez pas, n'est-ce pas?; **that** ~ **be the mailman** c'est probablement *or* ça doit être le facteur; ~ **you sit down** voulez-vous vous asseoir; **the car won't start** la voiture ne veut pas démarrer ♦ *vt* (*pt*, *pp* ~**ed**) exhorter par la pensée; **he** ~**ed himself to go on** par un suprême effort de volonté, il continua ♦ *n* volonté *f*; (*LAW*) testament *m*; **to do sth of one's own free** ~ faire qch de son propre gré; **against one's** ~ à contre-cœur.

willful [wil'fəl] *a* (*US*) (*person*) obstiné(e); (*action*) délibéré(e); (*crime*) prémédité(e).

willing [wil'ing] *a* de bonne volonté, serviable ♦ *n*: **to show** ~ faire preuve de bonne volonté; **he's** ~ **to do it** il est disposé à le faire, il veut bien le faire.

willingly [wil'inglē] *ad* volontiers.

willingness [wil'ingnis] *n* bonne volonté.

will-o'-the wisp [wil'ōthə wisp'] *n* (*also fig*) feu follet *m*.

willow [wil'ō] *n* saule *m*.

will power *n* volonté *f*.

willy-nilly [wil'ēnil'ē] *ad* bon gré mal gré.

wilt [wilt] *vi* dépérir.

Wilts [wilts] *abbr* (*Brit*) = **Wiltshire**.

wily [wī'lē] *a* rusé(e).

wimp [wimp] *n* (*col*) mauviette *f*.

win [win] *n* (*in sports etc*) victoire *f* ♦ *vb* (*pt*, *pp* **won** [wun]) *vt* (*battle*, *money*) gagner; (*prize*, *contract*) remporter; (*popularity*) acquérir ♦ *vi* gagner.

win over, (*Brit*) **win round** *vt* gagner, convaincre.

wince [wins] *n* tressaillement *m* ♦ *vi* tressaillir.

winch [winch] *n* treuil *m*.

Winchester disk [win'chestûr disk] *n* (*COMPUT*) disque *m* Winchester.

wind *n* [wind] (*also MED*) vent *m* ♦ *vb* [wīnd] (*pt*, *pp* **wound** [wound]) *vt* enrouler; (*wrap*) envelopper; (*clock*, *toy*) remonter; (*take breath away*: [wind]) couper le souffle à ♦ *vi* (*road*, *river*) serpenter; **the** ~**(s)** (*MUS*) les instruments *mpl* à vent; **into** *or* **against the** ~ contre le vent; **to get** ~ **of sth** (*fig*) avoir vent de qch; **to break** ~ avoir des gaz.

wind down [wīnd doun] *vt* (*car window*) baisser; (*fig*: *production*, *business*) réduire progressivement.

wind up [wīnd up] *vt* (*clock*) remonter; (*debate*) terminer, clôturer.

windbreak [wind'brāk] *n* brise-vent *m inv*.

windbreaker [wind'brākûr] *n* (*US*) anorak *m*.

windfall [wind'fôl] *n* coup *m* de chance.

winding [wīn'ding] *a* (*road*) sinueux(euse); (*staircase*) tournant(e).

wind instrument [wind in'strəmənt] *n* (*MUS*) instrument *m* à vent.

windmill [wind'mil] *n* moulin *m* à vent.

window [win'dō] *n* fenêtre *f*; (*in car*, *train*, *also*: ~**pane**) vitre *f*; (*in store etc*) vitrine *f*.

window box *n* jardinière *f*.

window cleaner *n* (*person*) laveur/euse de vitres.
window dressing *n* arrangement *m* de la vitrine.
window envelope *n* enveloppe *f* à fenêtre.
window frame *n* châssis *m* de fenêtre.
window ledge *n* rebord *m* de la fenêtre.
window pane *n* vitre *f*, carreau *m*.
window-shopping [win'dōshâping] *n*: **to go ~** faire du lèche-vitrines.
windowsill [win'dōsil] *n* (*inside*) appui *m* de la fenêtre; (*outside*) rebord *m* de la fenêtre.
windpipe [wind'pīp] *n* gosier *m*.
windscreen [wind'skrēn] *n* (*Brit*) = **windshield**.
windshield [wind'shēld] *n* (*US*) pare-brise *m* *inv*.
windshield washer *n* lave-glace *m* *inv*.
windshield wiper *n* essuie-glace *m* *inv*.
windsurfing [wind'sûrfing] *n* planche *f* à voile.
windswept [wind'swept] *a* balayé(e) par le vent.
wind tunnel *n* soufflerie *f*.
windy [win'dē] *a* venté(e), venteux(euse); **it's ~** il y a du vent.
wine [wīn] *n* vin *m* ♦ *vt*: **to ~ and dine sb** offrir un dîner bien arrosé à qn.
wine cellar *n* cave *f* à vins.
wineglass [wīn'glas] *n* verre *m* à vin.
wine list *n* carte *f* des vins.
wine merchant *n* marchand/e de vins.
wine tasting *n* dégustation *f* (de vins).
wine waiter *n* sommelier *m*.
wing [wing] *n* aile *f*; (*in air force*) groupe *m* d'escadrilles; (*SPORT*) ailier *m*; **~s** *npl* (*THEATER*) coulisses *fpl*.
winger [wing'ûr] *n* (*Brit SPORT*) ailier *m*.
wing mirror *n* (*Brit*) rétroviseur latéral.
wing nut *n* papillon *m*, écrou *m* à ailettes.
wingspan [wing'span] *n*, **wingspread** [wing'spred] *n* envergure *f*.
wink [wingk] *n* clin *m* d'œil ♦ *vi* faire un clin d'œil; (*blink*) cligner des yeux.
winkle [win'kəl] *n* bigorneau *m*.
winner [win'ûr] *n* gagnant/e.
winning [win'ing] *a* (*team*) gagnant(e); (*goal*) décisif(ive); (*charming*) charmeur(euse).
winning post *n* poteau *m* d'arrivée.
winnings [win'ingz] *npl* gains *mpl*.
winsome [win'səm] *a* avenant(e), engageant(e).
winter [win'tûr] *n* hiver *m* ♦ *vi* hiverner.
winter sports *npl* sports *mpl* d'hiver.
wintry [win'trē] *a* hivernal(e).
wipe [wīp] *n* coup *m* de torchon (*or* de chiffon *or* d'éponge) ♦ *vt* essuyer; **to give sth a ~** donner un coup de torchon à qch; **to ~ one's nose** se moucher.
  wipe off *vt* essuyer.
  wipe out *vt* (*debt*) régler; (*memory*) oublier; (*destroy*) anéantir.
  wipe up *vt* essuyer.
wire [wī'ûr] *n* fil *m* (de fer); (*ELEC*) fil électrique; (*TEL*) télégramme *m* ♦ *vt* (*fence*) grillager; (*house*) faire l'installation électrique de; (*also*: **~ up**) brancher.
wire brush *n* brosse *f* métallique.
wire cutters *npl* cisaille *f*.
wire netting *n* treillis *m* métallique,

grillage *m*.
wiretapping [wī'ûrtaping] *n* écoute *f* téléphonique.
wiring [wīûr'ing] *n* (*ELEC*) installation *f* électrique.
wiry [wiûr'ē] *a* noueux(euse), nerveux(euse).
Wis., Wisc. *abbr* (*US*) = *Wisconsin*.
wisdom [wiz'dəm] *n* sagesse *f*; (*of action*) prudence *f*.
wisdom tooth *n* dent *f* de sagesse.
wise [wīz] *a* sage, prudent(e), judicieux(euse); **I'm none the ~r** je ne suis pas plus avancé(e) pour autant.
  wise up *vi* (*col*): **to ~ up to** commencer à se rendre compte de.
wisecrack [wīz'krak] *n* sarcasme *m*.
wish [wish] *n* (*desire*) désir *m*; (*specific desire*) souhait *m*, vœu *m* ♦ *vt* souhaiter, désirer, vouloir; **best ~es** (*on birthday etc*) meilleurs vœux; **with best ~es** (*in letter*) bien amicalement; **give her my best ~es** faites-lui mes amitiés; **to ~ sb goodbye** dire au revoir à qn; **he ~ed me well** il me souhaitait de réussir; **to ~ to do/sb to do** désirer *or* vouloir faire/que qn fasse; **to ~ for** souhaiter; **to ~ sth on sb** souhaiter qch à qn.
wishful [wish'fəl] *a*: **it's ~ thinking** c'est prendre ses désirs pour des réalités.
wishy-washy [wish'ēwâshē] *a* (*col*: *person*) qui manque de caractère, falot(e); (: *ideas, thinking*) faiblard(e).
wisp [wisp] *n* fine mèche (de *cheveux*); (*of smoke*) mince volute *f*; **a ~ of straw** un fétu de paille.
wistful [wist'fəl] *a* mélancolique.
wit [wit] *n* (*gen pl*: *intelligence*) intelligence *f*, esprit *m*; (*presence of mind*) présence *f* d'esprit; (*wittiness*) esprit; (*person*) homme/femme d'esprit; **to be at one's ~s' end** (*fig*) ne plus savoir que faire; **to have one's ~s about one** avoir toute sa présence d'esprit, ne pas perdre la tête; **to ~ ad** à savoir.
witch [wich] *n* sorcière *f*.
witchcraft [wich'kraft] *n* sorcellerie *f*.
witch doctor *n* sorcier *m*.
witch-hunt [wich'hunt] *n* chasse *f* aux sorcières.
with [with, with] *prep* avec; **red ~ anger** rouge de colère; **to shake ~ fear** trembler de peur; **the man ~ the gray hat** l'homme au chapeau gris; **to stay overnight ~ friends** passer la nuit chez des amis; **to be ~ it** (*fig*) être dans le vent; **I am ~ you** (*I understand*) je vous suis.
withdraw [withdrô'] *vb* (*irg*) *vt* retirer ♦ *vi* se retirer; (*go back on promise*) se rétracter; **to ~ into o.s.** se replier sur soi-même.
withdrawal [withdrô'əl] *n* retrait *m*; (*MED*) état *m* de manque.
withdrawal symptoms *npl*: **to have ~** être en état de manque, présenter les symptômes *mpl* de sevrage.
withdrawn [withdrôn'] *pp of* **withdraw** ♦ *a* (*person*) renfermé(e).
wither [with'ûr] *vi* se faner.
withered [with'ûrd] *a* fané(e), flétri(e); (*limb*) atrophié(e).
withhold [withhōld'] *vt* *irg* (*money*) retenir;

(*decision*) remettre; (*permission*): **to** ~
(from) refuser (à); (*information*): **to** ~
(from) cacher (à).

within [wɪˈθɪn'] *prep* à l'intérieur de ♦ *ad* à
l'intérieur; ~ **sight of** en vue de; ~ **a mile
of** à moins d'un mille de; ~ **the week** avant
la fin de la semaine; ~ **an hour from now**
d'ici une heure; **to be** ~ **the law** être lé-
gal(e) *or* dans les limites de la légalité.

without [wɪˈθaʊt'] *prep* sans; ~ **anybody
knowing** sans que personne le sache; **to go**
or **do** ~ **sth** se passer de qch.

withstand [wɪθˈstænd'] *vt irg* résister à.

witness [wɪtˈnɪs] *n* (*person*) témoin *m*; (*evidence*) témoignage *m* ♦ *vt* (*event*) être témoin de; (*document*) attester l'authenticité
de; **to bear** ~ **to sth** témoigner de qch; ~
for the prosecution/defense témoin à
charge/à décharge; **to** ~ **to sth/having seen
sth** témoigner de qch/d'avoir vu qch.

witness stand, (*Brit*) **witness box** *n* barre *f*
des témoins.

witticism [wɪtˈəsɪzəm] *n* mot *m* d'esprit.

witty [wɪtˈē] *a* spirituel(le), plein(e) d'esprit.

wives [wīvz] *npl of* **wife**.

wizard [wɪzˈûrd] *n* magicien *m*.

wizened [wɪzˈənd] *a* ratatiné(e).

wk *abbr* = **week**.

Wm. *abbr* = **William**.

WO *n abbr* = **warrant officer.**

wobble [wâbˈəl] *vi* trembler; (*chair*) branler.

wobbly [wâbˈlē] *a* tremblant(e); branlant(e).

woe [wō] *n* malheur *m*.

woke [wōk] *pt of* **wake**.

woken [wōˈkən] *pp of* **wake**.

wolf, *pl* **wolves** [wŏŏlf, wŏŏlvz] *n* loup *m*.

woman, *pl* **women** [wŏŏmˈən, wɪmˈən] *n*
femme *f* ♦ *cpd*: ~ **doctor** femme *f* médecin;
~ **friend** amie *f*; ~ **teacher** professeur *m*
femme; **young** ~ jeune femme; **women's
page** (*PRESS*) page *f* des lectrices.

womanize [wŏŏmˈənīz] *vi* jouer les sé-
ducteurs.

womanly [wŏŏmˈənlē] *a* féminin(e).

womb [wŏŏm] *n* (*ANAT*) utérus *m*.

women [wɪmˈən] *npl of* **woman**.

Women's (Liberation) Movement *n* (*also:*
women's lib) mouvement *m* de libération de
la femme, MLF *m*.

won [wʌn] *pt, pp of* **win**.

wonder [wʌnˈdûr] *n* merveille *f*, miracle *m*;
(*feeling*) émerveillement *m* ♦ *vi:* **to** ~
whether se demander si; **to** ~ **at** s'étonner
de; s'émerveiller de; **to** ~ **about** songer à;
it's no ~ **that** il n'est pas étonnant que +
sub.

wonderful [wʌnˈdûrfəl] *a* merveilleux(euse).

wonderfully [wʌnˈdûrfəlē] *ad* (+ *adjective*)
merveilleusement; (+ *vb*) à merveille.

wonky [wângˈkē] *a* (*Brit col*) qui ne va *or* ne
marche pas très bien.

won't [wōnt] = **will not**.

woo [wŏŏ] *vt* (*woman*) faire la cour à.

wood [wŏŏd] *n* (*timber, forest*) bois *m* ♦ *cpd*
de bois, en bois.

wood alcohol *n* (*US*) alcool *m* à brûler.

wood carving *n* sculpture *f* en *or* sur bois.

wooded [wŏŏdˈid] *a* boisé(e).

wooden [wŏŏdˈən] *a* en bois; (*fig*) raide; inex-

pressif(ive).

woodland [wŏŏdˈlənd] *n* forêt *f*, région boisée.

woodpecker [wŏŏdˈpekûr] *n* pic *m* (*oiseau*).

wood pigeon *n* ramier *m*.

woodwind [wŏŏdˈwɪnd] *n* (*MUS*) bois *m*; **the**
~ (*MUS*) les bois.

woodwork [wŏŏdˈwûrk] *n* menuiserie *f*.

woodworm [wŏŏdˈwûrm] *n* ver *m* du bois.

woof [wŏŏf] *n* (*of dog*) aboiement *m* ♦ *vi*
aboyer; ~, ~! oua, oua!

wool [wŏŏl] *n* laine *f*; **to pull the** ~ **over sb's
eyes** (*fig*) en faire accroire à qn.

woolen, (*Brit*) **woollen** [wŏŏlˈən] *a* de laine;
(*industry*) lainier(ière) ♦ *n:* ~**s** lainages *mpl*.

wooly, (*Brit*) **woolly** [wŏŏlˈē] *a* laineux(euse);
(*fig: ideas*) confus(e).

word [wûrd] *n* mot *m*; (*spoken*) mot, parole *f*;
(*promise*) parole; (*news*) nouvelles *fpl* ♦ *vt*
rédiger, formuler; ~ **for** ~ (*repeat*) mot pour
mot; (*translate*) mot à mot; **what's the** ~
for "pen" in French? comment dit-on "pen"
en français?; **to put sth into** ~**s** exprimer
qch; **in other** ~**s** en d'autres termes; **to
have a** ~ **with sb** toucher un mot à qn; **to
have** ~**s with sb** (*quarrel with*) avoir des
mots avec qn; **to break/keep one's** ~
manquer à/tenir sa parole; **I'll take your** ~
for it je vous crois sur parole; **to send** ~ **of**
prévenir de; **to leave** ~ **(with sb/for sb) that**
... laisser un mot (à qn/pour qn) disant que
....

wording [wûrˈdɪng] *n* termes *mpl*, langage *m*;
libellé *m*.

word-perfect [wûrdˈpûrfɪkt] *a:* **he was** ~ **(in
his speech** *etc*), **his speech** *etc* **was** ~ il savait son discours *etc* sur le bout du doigt.

word processing *n* traitement *m* de texte.

word processor *n* machine *f* de traitement
de texte.

wordwrap [wûrdˈrap] *n* (*COMPUT*) retour *m*
(automatique) à la ligne.

wordy [wûrˈdē] *a* verbeux(euse).

wore [wôr] *pt of* **wear**.

work [wûrk] *n* travail *m*; (*ART, LITERATURE*)
œuvre *f* ♦ *vi* travailler; (*mechanism*) marcher, fonctionner; (*plan etc*) marcher; (*medicine*) agir ♦ *vt* (*clay, wood etc*) travailler;
(*mine etc*) exploiter; (*machine*) faire marcher *or* fonctionner ♦ *cpd* (*day, tools etc,
conditions*) de travail; **to go to** ~ aller travailler; **to set to** ~, **to start** ~ se mettre à
l'œuvre; **to be at** ~ **(on sth)** travailler (sur
qch); **to be out of** ~ être au chômage; **"~
wanted"** (*US*) "demandes *fpl* d'emploi"; **to**
~ **hard** travailler dur; **to** ~ **loose** se défaire,
se desserrer.

work on *vt fus* travailler à; (*principle*) se
baser sur.

work out *vi* (*plans etc*) marcher; (*SPORT*)
s'entraîner ♦ *vt* (*problem*) résoudre; (*plan*)
élaborer; **it** ~**s out at $100** ça fait 100
dollars.

workable [wûrˈkəbəl] *a* (*solution*) réalisable.

workaholic [wûrkəhâlˈik] *n* bourreau *m* de travail.

workbench [wûrkˈbench] *n* établi *m*.

workbook [wûrkˈbŏŏk] *n* cahier *m* d'exercices.

work council *n* comité *m* d'entreprise.

worked up [wûrkt up] *a*: **to get** ~ se mettre dans tous ses états.
worker [wûr'kûr] *n* travailleur/euse, ouvrier/ière; **office** ~ employé/e de bureau.
work force *n* main-d'œuvre *f*.
work-in [wûrk'in] *n* (*Brit*) occupation *f* d'usine etc (*sans arrêt de la production*).
working [wûr'king] *a* (*Brit*: *day, tools etc, conditions*) de travail; (*wife*) qui travaille; (*partner, population*) actif(ive); **in** ~ **order** en état de marche; **a** ~ **knowledge of English** une connaissance toute pratique de l'anglais.
working capital *n* (*COMM*) fonds *mpl* de roulement.
working class *n* classe ouvrière ♦ *a*: **working-class** ouvrier(ière), de la classe ouvrière.
working man *n* travailleur *m*.
working model *n* modèle opérationnel.
working week *n* (*Brit*) semaine *f* de travail.
work-in-progress [wûrkinprâg'res] *n* (*COMM*) en-cours *m inv*; (: *value*) valeur *f* des encours.
workload [wûrk'lōd] *n* charge *f* de travail.
workman [wûrk'mən] *n* ouvrier *m*.
workmanship [wûrk'mənship] *n* métier *m*, habileté *f*; facture *f*.
workmate [wûrk'māt] *n* collègue *m/f*.
workout [wûrk'out] *n* (*SPORT*) séance *f* d'entraînement.
work party *n* groupe *m* de travail.
work permit *n* permis *m* de travail.
works [wûrks] *n* (*Brit*: *factory*) usine *f* ♦ *npl* (*of clock, machine*) mécanisme *m*; **road** ~ travaux *mpl* (d'entretien des routes).
work sheet *n* (*COMPUT*) feuille *f* de programmation.
workshop [wûrk'shâp] *n* atelier *m*.
work station *n* poste *m* de travail.
work study *n* étude *f* du travail.
work-to-rule [wûrk'tərōōl'] *n* (*Brit*) grève *f* du zèle.
work week *n* (*US*) semaine *f* de travail.
world [wûrld] *n* monde *m* ♦ *cpd* (*champion*) du monde; (*power, war*) mondial(e); **all over the** ~ dans le monde entier, partout dans le monde; **to think the** ~ **of sb** (*fig*) ne jurer que par qn; **what in the** ~ **is he doing?** qu'est-ce qu'il peut bien être en train de faire?; **to do sb a** ~ **of good** faire le plus grand bien à qn; **W**~ **War One/Two** la Première/Deuxième guerre mondiale; **out of this** ~ a extraordinaire.
World Cup *n*: **the** ~ (*SOCCER*) la Coupe du monde.
world-famous [wûrldfā'məs] *a* de renommée mondiale.
worldly [wûrld'lē] *a* de ce monde.
worldwide [wûrld'wīd'] *a* universel(le) ♦ *ad* dans le monde entier.
worm [wûrm] *n* ver *m*.
worn [wôrn] *pp* of **wear** ♦ *a* usé(e).
worn-out [wôrn'out'] *a* (*object*) complètement usé(e); (*person*) épuisé(e).
worried [wûr'ēd] *a* inquiet(ète); **to be** ~ **about sth** être inquiet au sujet de qch.
worrier [wûr'ēûr] *n* inquiet/ète.
worrisome [wûr'ēsəm] *a* inquiétant(e).

worry [wûr'ē] *n* souci *m* ♦ *vt* inquiéter ♦ *vi* s'inquiéter, se faire du souci; **to** ~ **about** or **over sth/sb** se faire du souci pour or à propos de qch/qn.
worrying [wûr'ēing] *a* inquiétant(e).
worse [wûrs] *a* pire, plus mauvais(e) ♦ *ad* plus mal ♦ *n* pire *m*; **to get** ~ (*condition, situation*) empirer, se dégrader; **a change for the** ~ une détérioration; **he is none the** ~ **for it** il ne s'en porte pas plus mal; **so much the** ~ **for you!** tant pis pour vous!
worsen [wûr'sən] *vt, vi* empirer.
worse off *a* moins à l'aise financièrement; (*fig*): **you'll be** ~ **this way** ça ira moins bien de cette façon; **he is now** ~ **than before** il se retrouve dans une situation pire qu'auparavant.
worship [wûr'ship] *n* culte *m* ♦ *vt* (*God*) rendre un culte à; (*person*) adorer; **Your W**~ (*Brit*: *to mayor*) Monsieur le Maire; (: *to judge*) Monsieur le Juge.
worship(p)er [wûr'shipûr] *n* adorateur/trice; (*in church*) fidèle *m/f*.
worst [wûrst] *a* le(la) pire, le(la) plus mauvais(e) ♦ *ad* le plus mal ♦ *n* pire *m*; **at** ~ au pis aller; **if** ~ **comes to** ~, (*Brit*) **if the** ~ **comes to the** ~ si le pire doit arriver.
worsted [wōōs'tid] *n*: (**wool**) ~ laine peignée.
worth [wûrth] *n* valeur *f* ♦ *a*: **to be** ~ valoir; **how much is it** ~? ça vaut combien?; **it's** ~ **it** cela en vaut la peine; **$2** ~ **of apples** (pour) 2 dollars de pommes.
worthless [wûrth'lis] *a* qui ne vaut rien.
worthwhile [wûrth'wīl'] *a* (*activity*) qui en vaut la peine; (*cause*) louable; **a** ~ **book** un livre qui vaut la peine d'être lu.
worthy [wûr'thē] *a* (*person*) digne; (*motive*) louable; ~ **of** digne de.
would [wōōd] *auxiliary vb*: **she** ~ **come** elle viendrait; **he** ~ **have come** il serait venu; ~ **you like a cookie?** voulez-vous or voudriez-vous un biscuit?; ~ **you close the door, please?** voulez-vous fermer la porte, s'il vous plaît; **he** ~ **go there on Mondays** il y allait le lundi; **you WOULD say that,** ~**n't you!** bien évidemment tu dis ça!; c'est bien de toi de dire ça!; **she** ~**n't leave** elle a refusé de partir.
would-be [wōōd'bē'] *a* (*pej*) soi-disant.
wound *vb* [wound] *pt, pp* of **wind** ♦ *n, vt* [wōōnd] *n* blessure *f* ♦ *vt* blesser; ~**ed in the** **leg** blessé à la jambe.
wove [wōv] *pt* of **weave**.
woven [wō'vən] *pp* of **weave**.
WP *n* *abbr* = **word processing, word processor**.
WPC *n* *abbr* (*Brit*) = *woman police constable*.
wpm *abbr* (= *words per minute*) mots/minute.
wrangle [rang'gəl] *n* dispute *f* ♦ *vi* se disputer.
wrap [rap] *n* (*stole*) écharpe *f*; (*cape*) pèlerine *f* ♦ *vt* (*also*: ~ **up**) envelopper; **under** ~**s** (*fig*: *plan, scheme*) secret(ète).
wrapper [rap'ûr] *n* (*on chocolate etc*) papier *m*.
wrapping paper [rap'ing pā'pûr] *n* papier *m* d'emballage; (*for gift*) papier cadeau.
wrath [rath] *n* courroux *m*.
wreak [rēk] *vt* (*destruction*) entraîner; **to** ~

havoc faire des ravages; **to ~ vengeance on** se venger de, exercer sa vengeance sur.
wreath, ~s [rēth, rēthz] *n* couronne *f*.
wreck [rek] *n* (*sea disaster*) naufrage *m*; (*ship*) épave *f*; (*pej: person*) loque (humaine) ♦ *vt* démolir; (*ship*) provoquer le naufrage de; (*fig*) briser, ruiner.
wreckage [rek'ij] *n* débris *mpl*; (*of building*) décombres *mpl*; (*of ship*) naufrage *m*.
wrecker [rek'ûr] *n* (*US*) dépanneuse *f*.
wren [ren] *n* (*ZOOL*) roitelet *m*.
wrench [rench] *n* (*TECH*) clé *f* (à écrous); (*tug*) violent mouvement de torsion; (*fig*) arrachement *m* ♦ *vt* tirer violemment sur, tordre; **to ~ sth from** arracher qch (violemment) à *or* de.
wrest [rest] *vt*: **to ~ sth from sb** arracher *or* ravir qch à qn.
wrestle [res'əl] *vi*: **to ~ (with sb)** lutter (avec qn); **to ~ with** (*fig*) se débattre avec, lutter contre.
wrestler [res'lûr] *n* lutteur/euse.
wrestling [res'ling] *n* lutte *f*.
wrestling match *n* rencontre *f* de lutte (*or* de catch).
wretch [rech] *n* pauvre malheureux/euse; **little ~!** (*often humorous*) petit(e) misérable!
wretched [rech'id] *a* misérable; (*col*) maudit(e).
wriggle [rig'əl] *n* tortillement *m* ♦ *vi* se tortiller.
wring, *pt, pp* **wrung** [ring, rung] *vt* tordre; (*wet clothes*) essorer; (*fig*): **to ~ sth out of** arracher qch à.
wringer [ring'ûr] *n* essoreuse *f*.
wringing [ring'ing] *a* (*also*: **~ wet**) tout mouillé(e), trempé(e).
wrinkle [ring'kəl] *n* (*on skin*) ride *f*; (*on paper etc*) pli *m* ♦ *vt* rider, plisser ♦ *vi* se plisser.
wrinkled [ring'kəld], **wrinkly** [rng'klē] *a* (*fabric, paper*) froissé(e), plissé(e); (*surface*) plissé; (*skin*) ridé(e), plissé.
wrist [rist] *n* poignet *m*.
wristwatch [rist'wâch] *n* montre-bracelet *f*.
writ [rit] *n* acte *m* judiciaire; **to issue a ~ against sb, serve a ~ on sb** assigner qn en justice.
write, *pt* **wrote,** *pp* **written** [rīt, rōt, rit'ən] *vt, vi* écrire; **to ~ sb a letter** écrire une lettre à qn.
write away *vi*: **to ~ away for** (*information*) (écrire pour) demander; (*goods*) (écrire pour) commander.
write down *vt* noter; (*put in writing*) mettre par écrit.
write off *vt* (*debt*) passer aux profits et pertes; (*depreciate*) amortir; (*smash up: car etc*) démolir complètement.
write out *vt* écrire; (*copy*) recopier.
write up *vt* rédiger.
write-off [rīt'ôf] *n* perte totale; **the car is a ~** (*Brit*) la voiture est bonne pour la casse.
write-protect [rīt'prətekt'] *vt* (*COMPUT*) protéger contre l'écriture.
writer [rī'tûr] *n* auteur *m*, écrivain *m*.
write-up [rīt'up] *n* (*review*) critique *f*.
writhe [rīth] *vi* se tordre.
writing [rī'ting] *n* écriture *f*; (*of author*) œuvres *fpl*; **in ~** par écrit; **in my own ~**

écrit(e) de ma main.
writing case *n* nécessaire *m* de correspondance.
writing desk *n* secrétaire *m*.
writing paper *n* papier *m* à lettres.
written [rit'ən] *pp of* **write**.
wrong [rông] *a* faux(fausse); (*incorrectly chosen: number, road etc*) mauvais(e); (*not suitable*) qui ne convient pas; (*wicked*) mal; (*unfair*) injuste ♦ *ad* faux ♦ *n* tort *m* ♦ *vt* faire du tort à, léser; **to be ~** (*answer*) être faux(fausse); (*in doing/saying*) avoir tort (de dire/faire); **you are ~ to do it** tu as tort de le faire; **it's ~ to steal, stealing is ~** c'est mal de voler; **you are ~ about that, you've got it ~** tu te trompes; **to be in the ~** avoir tort; **what's ~?** qu'est-ce qui ne va pas?; **there's nothing ~** tout va bien; **what's ~ with the car?** qu'est-ce qu'elle a, la voiture?; **to go ~** (*person*) se tromper; (*plan*) mal tourner; (*machine*) se détraquer.
wrongful [rông'fəl] *a* injustifié(e); **~ dismissal** (*INDUSTRY*) licenciement abusif.
wrongly [rông'lē] *ad* à tort; (*answer, do, count*) mal, incorrectement; (*treat*) injustement.
wrong number *n* (*TEL*): **you have the ~** vous vous êtes trompé de numéro.
wrong side *n* (*of cloth*) envers *m*.
wrote [rōt] *pt of* **write**.
wrought [rôt] *a*: **~ iron** fer forgé.
wrung [rung] *pt, pp of* **wring**.
wry [rī] *a* désabusé(e).
wt. *abbr* (= *weight*) pds.
WV *abbr* (*US MAIL*) = *West Virginia*.
W.Va. *abbr* (*US*) = *West Virginia*.
WY *abbr* (*US MAIL*) = *Wyoming*.
Wyo. *abbr* (*US*) = *Wyoming*.
WYSIWYG [wiz'ēwig] *abbr* (*COMPUT*: = *what you see is what you get*) ce que vous voyez est ce que vous aurez.

X

X, x [eks] *n* (*letter*) X, x *m*; **X for Xmas** X comme Xavier.
Xerox [zē'râks] ® *n* (*also*: **~ machine**) photocopieuse *f*; (*photocopy*) photocopie *f* ♦ *vt* photocopier.
XL *abbr* (= *extra large*) XL.
Xmas [eks'mis] *n abbr* = **Christmas**.
X-rated [eks'rātid] *a* (*US: film*) interdit(e) aux moins de 18 ans.
X-ray [eks'rā] *n* rayon *m* X; (*photograph*) radio(graphie) *f* ♦ *vt* radiographier.
xylophone [zī'ləfōn] *n* xylophone *m*.

Y

Y, y [wī] *n* (*letter*) Y, y *m*; **Y for Yoke** Y comme Yvonne.

yacht [yât] *n* voilier *m*; (*motor, luxury* ~) yacht *m*.

yachting [yât'ing] *n* yachting *m*, navigation *f* de plaisance.

yachtsman [yâts'mən] *n* yacht(s)man *m*.

yam [yam] *n* igname *f*.

Yank [yangk], **Yankee** [yang'kē] *n* (*pej*) Amerloque *m/f*, Ricain/e.

yank [yangk] *vt* tirer d'un coup sec.

yap [yap] *vi* (*dog*) japper.

yard [yârd] *n* (*of house etc*) cour *f*; (*US: garden*) jardin *m*; (*measure*) yard *m* (= *914 mm; 3 feet*); **builder's** ~ chantier *m*.

yardstick [yârd'stik] *n* (*fig*) mesure *f*, critère *m*.

yarn [yârn] *n* fil *m*; (*tale*) longue histoire.

yawn [yôn] *n* bâillement *m* ♦ *vi* bâiller.

yawning [yôn'ing] *a* (*gap*) béant(e).

yd *abbr* = **yard.**

yeah [ye] *ad* (*col*) ouais.

year [yēr] *n* an *m*, année *f*; (*Brit SCOL etc*) année; **every** ~ tous les ans, chaque année; **this** ~ cette année; **a** *or* **per** ~ par an; ~ **in**, ~ **out** année après année; **to be 8** ~**s** old avoir 8 ans; **an eight-**~**-old child** un enfant de huit ans.

yearbook [yēr'book] *n* annuaire *m*.

yearly [yēr'lē] *a* annuel(le) ♦ *ad* annuellement; **twice** ~ deux fois par an.

yearn [yûrn] *vi*: **to** ~ **for sth/to do** aspirer à qch/à faire, languir après qch.

yearning [yûr'ning] *n* désir ardent, envie *f*.

yeast [yēst] *n* levure *f*.

yell [yel] *n* hurlement *m*, cri *m* ♦ *vi* hurler.

yellow [yel'ō] *a, n* jaune (*m*); **(at)** ~ (*US AUT*) à l'orange.

yellow fever *n* fièvre *f* jaune.

yellowish [yel'ōish] *a* qui tire sur le jaune, jaunâtre (*péj*).

Yellow Sea *n*: **the** ~ la mer Jaune.

yelp [yelp] *n* jappement *m*; glapissement *m* ♦ *vi* japper; glapir.

Yemen [yem'ən] *n* Yémen *m*.

yen [yen] *n* (*currency*) yen *m*; (*craving*): ~ **for/to do** grand(e) envie *f* *or* désir *m* de/de faire.

yeoman [yō'mən] *n*: **Y**~ **of the Guard** hallebardier *m* de la garde royale.

yes [yes] *ad* oui; (*answering negative question*) si ♦ *n* oui *m*; **to say** ~ **(to)** dire oui (à).

yes man *n* béni-oui-oui *m inv*.

yesterday [yes'tûrdā] *ad, n* hier (*m*); ~ **morning/evening** hier matin/soir; **the day before** ~ avant-hier; **all day** ~ toute la journée d'hier.

yet [yet] *ad* encore; déjà ♦ *cj* pourtant, néanmoins; **it is not finished** ~ ce n'est pas

encore fini *or* toujours pas fini; **the best** ~ le meilleur jusqu'ici *or* jusque-là; **as** ~ jusqu'ici, encore; **a few days** ~ encore quelques jours; ~ **again** une fois de plus.

yew [yōo] *n* if *m*.

YHA *n abbr* (*Brit*) = *Youth Hostels Association.*

Yiddish [yid'ish] *n* yiddish *m*.

yield [yēld] *n* production *f*, rendement *m*; (*FINANCE*) rapport *m* ♦ *vt* produire, rendre, rapporter; (*surrender*) céder ♦ *vi* céder; (*US AUT*) céder la priorité; **a** ~ **of 5%** un rendement de 5%.

YMCA *n abbr* (= *Young Men's Christian Association*) ≈ union chrétienne de jeunes gens (UCJG).

yodel [yōd'əl] *vi* faire des tyroliennes, jodler.

yoga [yō'gə] *n* yoga *m*.

yog(h)ourt, yog(h)urt [yō'gûrt] *n* yaourt *m*.

yoke [yōk] *n* joug *m* ♦ *vt* (*also*: ~ **together**: *oxen*) accoupler.

yolk [yōk] *n* jaune *m* (d'œuf).

yonder [yân'dûr] *ad* là(-bas).

Yorks [] *abbr* (*Brit*) = *Yorkshire.*

you [yōo] *pronoun* tu; (*polite form*) vous; (*pl*) vous; (*complement*) te, t' + *vowel*; vous; (*stressed*) toi; vous; (*impersonal: one*) on; **if I was** *or* **were** ~ si j'étais vous, à votre place; **fresh air does** ~ **good** l'air frais (vous) fait du bien; ~ **never know** on ne sait jamais.

you'd [yōod] = **you had, you would.**

you'll [yōol] = **you will, you shall.**

young [yung] *a* jeune ♦ *npl* (*of animal*) petits *mpl*; (*people*): **the** ~ les jeunes, la jeunesse; **a** ~ **man** un jeune homme; **a** ~ **lady** (*unmarried*) une jeune fille, une demoiselle; (*married*) une jeune femme *or* dame; **my** ~**er brother** mon frère cadet; **the** ~**er generation** la jeune génération.

youngish [yung'ish] *a* assez jeune.

youngster [yung'stûr] *n* jeune *m/f*; (*child*) enfant *m/f*.

your [yōor] *a* ton(ta), tes *pl*; (*polite form, pl*) votre, vos *pl*.

you're [yōor] = **you are.**

yours [yōorz] *pronoun* le(la) tien(ne), les tiens(tiennes); (*polite form, pl*) le(la) vôtre, les vôtres; **is it** ~**?** c'est à toi (*or* à vous)?; **a friend of** ~ un(e) de tes (*or* de vos) amis.

yourself [yōorself'] *pronoun* (*reflexive*) te; (*: polite form*) vous; (*after prep*) toi; vous; (*emphatic*) toi-même; vous-même; **you** ~ **told me** c'est vous qui me l'avez dit, vous me l'avez dit vous-même.

yourselves [yōorselvz'] *pl pronoun* vous; (*emphatic*) vous-mêmes.

youth [yōoth] *n* jeunesse *f*; (*young man*) (*pl* ~**s** [yōothz]) jeune homme *m*; **in my** ~ dans ma jeunesse, quand j'étais jeune.

youth club *n* centre *m* de jeunes.

youthful [yōoth'fəl] *a* jeune; (*enthusiasm etc*) juvénile; (*misdemeanor*) de jeunesse.

youthfulness [yōoth'fəlnis] *n* jeunesse *f*.

youth hostel *n* auberge *f* de jeunesse.

youth movement *n* mouvement *m* de jeunes.

you've [yōov] = **you have.**

yowl [youl] *n* hurlement *m*; miaulement *m* ♦

vi hurler; miauler.

YT *abbr* (*Canada*) = *Yukon Territory*.

yuck [yuk] *excl* (*col*) beurk!

Yugoslav [yōō'gōslâv] *a* yougoslave ♦ *n* Yougoslave *m/f*.

Yugoslavia [yōōgōslâ'vēə] *n* Yougoslavie *f*.

Yugoslavian [yōō'gōslâ'vēən] *a* yougoslave.

Yule [yōōl]: ~ **log** *n* bûche *f* de Noël.

yuppie [yup'ē] *n* yuppie *m/f*.

YWCA *n abbr* (= *Young Women's Christian Association*) union chrétienne féminine.

Z

Z, z [zē, (*Brit*) zed] *n* (*letter*) Z, z *m*; **Z for Zebra** Z comme Zoé.

Zaire [zâēr'] *n* Zaïre *m*.

Zambia [zam'bēə] *n* Zambie *f*.

Zambian [zam'bēən] *a* zambien(ne) ♦ *n* Zambien/ne.

zany [zā'nē] *a* farfelu(e), loufoque.

zap [zap] *vt* (*COMPUT*) effacer.

zeal [zēl] *n* (*revolutionary etc*) ferveur *f*; (*keenness*) ardeur *f*, zèle *m*.

zealot [zel'ət] *n* fanatique *m/f*.

zealous [zel'əs] *a* fervent(e); ardent(e), zélé(e).

zebra [zēb'rə] *n* zèbre *m*.

zebra crossing *n* (*Brit*) passage *m* pour piétons.

zenith [zē'nith] *n* (*ASTRONOMY*) zénith *m*; (*fig*) zénith, apogée *m*.

zero [zē'rō] *n* zéro *m* ♦ *vi*: **to ~ in on** (*target*) se diriger droit sur; **5° below** ~ 5 degrés au-dessous de zéro.

zero hour *n* l'heure *f* H.

zero-rated [zē'rōrā'tid] *a* (*Brit*) exonéré(e) de TVA.

zest [zest] *n* entrain *m*, élan *m*; (*of lemon etc*) zeste *m*.

zigzag [zig'zag] *n* zigzag *m* ♦ *vi* zigzaguer, faire des zigzags.

Zimbabwe [zimbâ'bwā] *n* Zimbabwe *m*.

Zimbabwean [zimbâ'bwāən] *a* zimbabwéen(ne) ♦ *n* Zimbabwéen/ne.

zinc [zingk] *n* zinc *m*.

Zionism [zī'ənizəm] *n* sionisme *m*.

Zionist [zī'ənist] *a* sioniste ♦ *n* Sioniste *m/f*.

zip [zip] *n* (*also*: **~per**) fermeture *f* éclair ® *or* à glissière; (*energy*) entrain *m* ♦ *vt* (*also*: **~ up**) fermer (avec une fermeture éclair ®).

zip code *n* (*US*) code postal.

zither [zith'ûr] *n* cithare *f*.

zodiac [zō'dēak] *n* zodiaque *m*.

zombie [zâm'bē] *n* (*fig*): **like a** ~ avec l'air d'un zombie, comme un automate.

zone [zōn] *n* zone *f*.

zoo [zōō] *n* zoo *m*.

zoological [zōōlâj'ikəl] *a* zoologique.

zoologist [zōâl'əjist] *n* zoologiste *m/f*.

zoology [zōâl'əjē] *n* zoologie *f*.

zoom [zōōm] *vi*: **to ~ past** passer en trombe; **to ~ in (on sb/sth)** (*PHOT, CINEMA*) zoomer (sur qn/qch).

zoom lens *n* zoom *m*, objectif *m* à focale variable.

zucchini [zōōkē'nē] *n(pl)* (*US*) courgette(s) *f(pl)*.

Zulu [zōō'lōō] *a* zoulou ♦ *n* Zoulou *m/f*.

Zurich [zûr'ik] *n* Zurich *m*.